D0115696

The New College

FRENCH & ENGLISH
Dictionary

The New College

FRENCH & ENGLISH
Dictionary

ROGER J. STEINER
University of Delaware

Dedicated to serving

our nation's youth

AMSCO SCHOOL PUBLICATIONS, INC.
315 HUDSON STREET / NEW YORK, N.Y. 10013

THE NEW COLLEGE FRENCH & ENGLISH DICTIONARY

ISBN 0-87720-463-2

The photogɪaph of Place Vendôme, Paris, on the cover has been provided by the French Government Tourist Office.

Printed in the United States of America

Tenth Printing

11   12   13   14   15   16   17   18   19   20

Roger J. Steiner, A.B., A.M., Ph.D., author of *The New College French & English Dictionary,* has done extensive linguistic research in France, where he has traveled widely and taught for two years at the University of Bordeaux. Now a member of the French faculty at the University of Delaware, he is the author of a book dealing with the origin and development of bilingual dictionaries, *Two Centuries of Spanish and English Lexicography* (The Hague and Paris, 1970), and has contributed articles and reviews to learned journals.

Edwin B. Williams, A.B., A.M., Ph.D., LL.D., L.H.D., Doctor of the University of Montpellier (France), under whose editorship *The New College French & English Dictionary* has been prepared, is the author of *The New College Spanish & English Dictionary* and the General Editor of The New College Dictionary Series. Dr. Williams has been Chairman of the Department of Romance Languages, Dean of the Graduate School, and Provost of the University of Pennsylvania. He is the author of many other works on the Spanish, French, and Portuguese languages.

The New College French & English Dictionary is the most modern, authoritative, and usefully organized French and English dictionary in print, and the most extensive one in a paperback edition. There are 70,000 entries, based on spoken and written sources, and organized to achieve the utmost clarity, precision, and convenience.

Important features:

1. Shows which of two or more words is appropriate   ⟶

file [faɪl] *s* (*tool*) lime *f*; (*for papers*) classeur *m*; (*for cards*) fichier *m*; (*personal record*) dossier *m*; (*line*) file *f* . . .

bache‧lier [baʃəlje] **‑lière** [ljɛr] *mf* bachelor (*holder of degree*) ‖ *m* (hist) bachelor (*young knight*)

2. Transitive verbs translated strictly by transitive verbs and expressions   ⟶

boucler [bukle] *tr* to buckle; to curl (*the hair*); to lock up (*prisoners*) . . .

3. Centered period shows where endings are to be added   ⟶

car‧ry ['kæri] *v* (*pret & pp* **‑ried**) *tr* . . .
habi‧tant [abitɑ̃] **‑tante** [tɑ̃t] *mf* . . .

4. Shows the position of the French adjective according to change of meaning   ⟶

der‧nier [dɛrnje] **‑nière** [njɛr] *adj* . . .; last (*just elapsed*), e.g., **la semaine dernière** last week ‖ (when standing before noun) *adj* last (*in a series*), e.g., **la dernière semaine de la guerre** the last week of the war

5. Reference numbers show where to find grammatical information   ⟶

it'self' *pron pers* soi §85; lui‑même §86; se §87

le [lə] *art* §77 ‖ *pron* §87

déplacer [deplase] §51 *tr* . . .

Contents

To the Student

You are studying French. You may know very little French. Or you may know a great deal. You are constantly finding words whose meaning you do not know. You are constantly wondering what the word for something is in French, how to say something in French. You need a dictionary—this Dictionary. It is indispensable in starting to learn French, it is indispensable in improving and perfecting your knowledge of French. It will give you the words and the meanings you need.

If you see a French word, you want to know how it is pronounced. If you hear a French word, you want to know how it is spelled. And you may want to know how it is used in a sentence or you may want to use it yourself in a sentence.

This book is really two dictionaries, a dictionary of French words with their translations in English and a dictionary of English words with their translations in French. And all the words in each of these dictionaries are listed in strict alphabetical order. The order of the letters in the French alphabet is the same as in the English alphabet.

Now, look up in the first of the two dictionaries the French word whose meaning you do not know or about which you wish to know more. It is printed in boldface type. You will immediately learn its spelling, its pronunciation, its part of speech, its many forms if it changes, its gender if it is a noun, its function (transitive, intransitive, etc.) if it is a verb, its meaning or meanings in English, and how to use it in a sentence. Take what you need from this vast amount of information, take it all if you need it.

You have an English word in mind. You want to know what the French word for it is. Look up the English word in the second of the two dictionaries. It is printed in boldface type. You will immediately learn the French word or words that may be used to translate it. If the English word has two or more meanings, the French translations representing these meanings will be separated by semicolons. And there will be an explanation in English showing which of these words has the meaning you want. Then, if you wish to find out more about this French word, look it up in the first of the two dictionaries.

In the first of the two dictionaries you move from French to

English and get the meanings of the French words you need in order to read and understand French. In the second of the two dictionaries you move from English to French and get the French words you need in order to write and speak French. And you may wish to go back to the first of the two dictionaries to get more information on the French words you have found. Thus this book provides what the English-speaking person needs in order to read, understand, write, and speak French.

Preface

A. Inasmuch as the basic function of a bilingual dictionary is to provide semantic equivalences, syntactical constructions are shown in both the source and target languages on both sides of the Dictionary. In performing this function, a bilingual dictionary must fulfill six purposes. For example, a French and English bilingual dictionary must provide (1) French words which an English-speaking person wishes to use in speaking and writing (by means of the English-French part), (2) English meanings of French words which an English-speaking person encounters in listening and reading (by means of the French-English part), (3) the spelling, pronunciation, and inflection of French words and the gender of French nouns which an English-speaking person needs in order to use French words correctly (by means of the French-English part), (4) English words which a French-speaking person wishes to use in speaking and writing (by means of the French-English part), (5) French meanings of English words which a French-speaking person encounters in listening and reading (by means of the English-French part), and (6) the spelling, pronunciation, and inflection of English words which a French-speaking person needs in order to use English words correctly (by means of the English-French part).

It may seem logical to provide the pronunciation and inflection of English words and the pronunciation and inflection of French words and the gender of French nouns where these words appear as target words inasmuch as target words, according to (1) and (4) above, are sought for the purpose of speaking and writing. Thus the user would find not only the words he seeks but all the information he needs about them at one and the same place. But this technique is impractical because target words are not alphabetized and could, therefore, be found only by the roundabout and uncertain way of seeking them through their translations in the other part of the dictionary. And this would be particularly inconvenient for persons using the dictionary for purposes (2) and (5) above. It is much more convenient to provide immediate alphabetized access to pronunciation and inflection where the words appear as source words. Showing the gender of nouns takes so little space that this information is provided with both source and target words.

B. Prepositional phrases and expressions containing a verb and a noun are listed under the noun, e.g.,

> **channel** ['tʃænɔl] *s* . . . ; **through channels** par la voie hiérarchique
>
> **sky** [skaɪ] *s* (*pl* **skies**) ciel *m*; **to praise to the skies** porter aux nues
>
> **scrutin** [skrytɛ̃] *m* . . . ; **dépouiller le scrutin** to count the votes

C. All subentries are listed alphabetically, e.g.,

> **avis** [avi] *m* . . . ; **à mon avis** . . . ; **avis au lecteur** . . . ; **changer d'avis** . . .

D. French expressions consisting of a noun and an adjective or a noun and an adjective phrase are listed under the noun, e.g.,

> **scaphandre** [skafɑ̃dr] *m* diving suit; spacesuit; **scaphandre autonome** aqualung
>
> **portrait** [pɔrtrɛ] *m* . . . ; **portrait à mi-corps** half-length portrait

E. All solid, hyphenated, and spaced compound English words are listed as separate entries, e.g.,

> **mail′man′** *s* (*pl* **-men′**) facteur *m*
>
> **point′-blank′** *adj & adv* . . . à bout portant
>
> **tape′ record′er** *s* magnétophone *m*

F. All words are treated in a fixed order according to the parts of speech and the functions of verbs, as follows: article, adjective, substantive, pronoun, adverb, preposition, conjunction, transitive verb, intransitive verb, impersonal verb, auxiliary verb, reflexive verb, impersonal reflexive verb, interjection.

G. Meanings with subject and usage labels come after more general meanings. Subject and usage labels (printed in roman and in parentheses) refer to the preceding entry or phrase (printed in boldface). However, when labels come immediately, i.e., without any intervening punctuation mark, after a target word, they refer to that target word and the preceding word or words separated from it only by commas, e.g.,

> **optometrist** [ɑp'tɑmɪtrɪst] *s* opticien *m*; optométriste *mf* (Canad)

H. English adjectives are always translated by the French masculine form regardless of whether the translation of the exemplary noun modified would be masculine or feminine, e.g.,

close [klos] *adj* . . . ; (*friendship*) étroit; (*room*) renfermé

I. In order to facilitate the finding of the meaning and use sought for, changes within a vocabulary entry in part of speech and function of verb, in irregular inflection, in the gender of French nouns, and in the pronunciation of French and English words are marked with paral lels: ||, instead of the usual semicolons.

J. Since vocabulary entries are not determined on the basis of etymology, homographs are included in a single entry. When the pronunciation of a homograph changes, this is shown in the proper place after parallels.

Note, however, that plurals and words spelled with capitals are shown as run-on entries. They must be preceded by parallels only when there is a change in part of speech, in pronunciation, or in inflection.

K. Peculiarities in the pronunciation of the plural of French nouns and run-on entries are generally shown, e.g.,

guet-apens [gɛtapɑ̃] *m* (*pl* **guets-apens** [gɛtapɑ̃])
œil [œj] *m* . . . ; **entre quatre yeux** [ɑ̃trəkatzjø]

L. Periods are omitted after labels and grammatical abbreviations and at the end of vocabulary entries.

M. Proper nouns and abbreviations are listed in their alphabetical position in the main body of the Dictionary. Thus **Algérie** and **algérien** or **Suède** and **suédois** do not have to be looked up in two different parts of the book. And all subentries are listed in strictly alphabetical order.

N. The feminine form of a French adjective used as a noun (or a French feminine noun having identical spelling with the feminine form of an adjective) which falls alphabetically in a separate position from the adjective is treated in that position and is listed again as a cross reference under the adjective, e.g.,

cher chère [ʃɛr] *adj* . . . || *f* see **chère** || . . .
chère [ʃɛr] *f* fare, food and drink; . . .

O. The centered period is used in vocabulary entries of inflected words to mark off, according to standard orthographic principles in the two languages, the final syllable that has to be detached before the syllable showing the inflection is added, e.g.,

habi·tant [abitɑ̃] **-tante** [tɑ̃t] *mf*
satis·fy ['sætɪsˌfaɪ] *v* (*pret & pp* **-fied**) *tr*

P. Since the orthographic break coming in French words (a) between the two l's of liquid **l**, (b) between **s** and **c** followed by **e**, **i**, or **y**, and (c) between the two elements of any double consonant pronounced as a single consonant does not correspond to the phonetic break, the centered period is used as usual but the full form of the inflected variant is shown, also with the centered period, and the full phonetic transcription of both forms is shown without a break, e.g.,

(a) **merveil·leux** [mɛrvɛjø] **merveil·leuse** [mɛrvɛjøz]
(b) **évanes·cent** [evanesɑ̃] **évanes·cente** [evanesɑ̃t]
(c) **éton·nant** [etɔnɑ̃] **éton·nante** [etɔnɑ̃t]
    miel·leux [mjɛlø] **miel·leuse** [mjɛløz]

Where the orthographic break, according to some authorities,* is not permitted, for example, between a **y** and a following vowel, the centered period is not used, e.g.,

croyant [krwajɑ̃] **croyante** [krwajɑ̃t]
métayer [metɛje] **métayère** [metɛjɛr]

Q. If the two components of an English solid compound are not separated by an accent mark, a centered period is used to mark off the division between them, e.g., **la'dy·bird'**.

R. Numbers referring to the model tables of French verbs (p. 7 ff.) are placed before the abbreviation indicating the part of speech. Numbers referring to the model tables of other French parts of speech (p. 21 ff.) are placed after the French word on both sides of the Dictionary.

S. Many French verbs which take an indirect object have as their equivalent English verbs which take a direct object. This is shown on both sides of this Dictionary by the insertion of (with *dat*) after the French verb, e.g.,

obéir [ɔbeir] *intr* . . . ; (with *dat*) to obey
obey [ə'be] *tr* obéir (with *dat*)

T. There are some French transitive verbs which, when used reflexively, take the reflexive pronoun in the dative. As reflexive verbs they may still take a direct object and may, accordingly, be translated by English transitive verbs. And they may in turn be used to translate English transitive verbs. This equation is shown on the French-English side after the abbreviation *ref* by the insertion of (with *dat* of

---

* V. Maurice Grevisse, *Le Bon Usage*, 8th ed., 1964, §89, p. 52.

reflex pron). It is not shown on the English-French side, as the abbreviation *tr* indicates unmistakably the syntactical relationship, e.g.,

laver [lave] *tr* . . . || *ref* . . . ; (with *dat* of *reflex pron*) to wash (*e.g., one's hands*)

The author wishes to express his gratitude to many persons who helped him in the production of this book and particularly to Dr. Edwin B. Williams, whose efforts were unstinting in the attempt to make this a useful dictionary, to his dear wife Kathryn, whose patience carried through the ten years of research and compilation, and to René Coulet du Gard and to Claud J. Pujolle for their constant help, as well as to the following: Jean Béranger, Brigitte Callay, Paul Dumestre, Maurice Jonas, Marc and Philomena Lampe, Daniel Pralus, Wayne and Paule Ready, and André Vincent.

Labels and Grammatical Abbreviations
Rubriques et abréviations grammaticales

abbr abbreviation—abréviation
(acronym) word formed from the initial letters or syllables of a series of words—mot formé de la suite des lettres initiales ou des syllabes initiales d'une série de mots
adj adjective—adjectif
adv adverb—adverbe
(aer) aeronautics—aéronautique
(agr) agriculture—agriculture
(alg) algebra—algèbre
(anat) anatomy—anatomie
(archaic) archaïque
(archeol) archeology—archéologie
(archit) architecture—architecture
(arith) arithmetic—arithmétique
art article—article
(arti) artillery—artillerie
(astr) astronomy—astronomie
(astrol) astrology—astrologie
(aut) automobile—automobile
aux auxiliary verb—verbe auxiliaire
(bact) bacteriology—bactériologie
(baseball) base-ball
(bb) bookbinding—reliure
(Bib) Biblical—biblique
(billiards) billard
(biochem) biochemistry—biochimie
(biol) biology—biologie
(bk) bookkeeping—comptabilité
(bot) botany—botanique
(bowling) jeu de quilles, jeu de boules
(boxing) boxe
(Brit) British—britannique
(Canad) Canadian—canadien
(*cap*) capital—majuscule
(cards) cartes
(carpentry) charpenterie
(checkers) jeu de dames
(chem) chemistry—chimie
(chess) échecs
(coll) colloquial—familier
(com) commercial—commercial
comp comparative—comparatif
(comp) computers—ordinateurs
(complimentary close) formule de politesse
cond conditional—conditionnel
conj conjunction—conjonction; conjunctive—atone
(culin) cooking—cuisine
dat dative—datif
def definite—défini
dem demonstrative—démonstratif
(dentistry) art dentaire
(dial) dialectal—dialectal

(dipl) diplomacy—diplomatie
disj disjunctive—tonique
(eccl) ecclesiastical—ecclésiastique
(econ) economics—économique
(educ) education—éducation, pédagogie
e.g. par ex.
(elec) electricity—électricité
(electron) electronics—électronique
(embryol) embryology—embryologie
(eng) engineering—profession de l'ingénieur, génie
(ent) entomology—entomologie
(equit) horseback riding—équitation
(escr) fencing—escrime
f feminine noun—nom féminin
(fa) fine arts—beaux-arts
fem feminine—féminin
(feudal) feudalism—féodalité
(fig) figurative—figuré
(fishing) pêche
fpl feminine noun plural—nom féminin pluriel
fut future—futur
(game) jeu
(geog) geography—géographie
(geol) geology—géologie
(geom) geometry—géométrie
ger gerund—gérondif
(govt) government—gouvernement
(gram) grammar—grammaire
(gymnastics) gymnastique
(heral) heraldry—héraldique, blason
(hist) history—histoire
(hort) horticulture—horticulture
(hum) humorous—humoristique
(hunting) chasse
(ichth) ichthyology—ichtyologie
i.e. c.-à-d.
imperf imperfect—imparfait
impers impersonal verb—verbe impersonnel
impv imperative—impératif
ind indicative—indicatif
indef indefinite—indéfini
inf infinitive—infinitif
(ins) insurance—assurance
interj interjection—interjection
interr interrogative—interrogatif
intr intransitive—intransitif
invar invariable—invariable
(ironical) ironique
(jewelry) bijouterie
(journ) journalism—journalisme
(Lat) Latin—latin
(law) droit
(*l.c.*) lower case—bas de casse

xiii

(letterword) word in the form of an abbreviation which is pronounced by sounding the names of its letters in succession and which functions as a part of speech—mot en forme d'abréviation qu'on prononce en faisant sonner le nom de chaque lettre consécutivement et qui fonctionne comme partie du discours
(lit) literary—littéraire
(logic) logique
m masculine noun—nom masculin
(mach) machinery—machinerie
(mas) masonry—maçonnerie
masc masculine—masculin
(Masonry) franc-maçonnerie
(math) mathematics—mathématiques
(mech) mechanics—mécanique
(med) medicine—médecine
(metallurgy) métallurgie
(meteo) meteorology—météorologie
mf masculine or feminine noun according to sex—nom masculin ou nom féminin selon le sexe
[for *m* & *f* see abbreviation following (mythol)]
(mil) military—militaire
(min) mining—travail des mines
(mineral) mineralogy—minéralogie
(mountaineering) alpinisme
(mov) moving pictures—cinéma
mpl masculine noun plural—nom masculin pluriel
(mus) music—musique
(mythol) mythology—mythologie
m & *f* masculine and feminine noun without regard to sex—nom masculin et féminin sans distinction de sexe
(naut) nautical—nautique
(nav) naval—naval
neut neuter—neutre
(nucl) nuclear physics—physique nucléaire
(obs) obsolete—vieilli, vieux
(obstet) obstetrics—obstétrique
(opt) optics—optique
(orn) ornithology—ornithologie
(painting) peinture
(parl) parliamentary procedure—usages parlementaires
(pathol) pathology—pathologie
(pej) pejorative—péjoratif
perf perfect—parfait
pers personal—personnel; person—personne
(pharm) pharmacy—pharmacie
(phila) philately—philatélie
(philos) philosophy—philosophie
(phonet) phonetics—phonétique
(phot) photography—photographie
(phys) physics—physique
(physiol) physiology—physiologie
pl plural—pluriel
(poetic) poetical—poétique

(pol) politics—politique
poss possessive—possessif
pp past participle—participe passé
prep preposition—préposition
pres present—présent
pret preterit—prétérit, passé simple
pron pronoun—pronom
(pros) prosody—métrique, prosodie
(psychoanal) psychoanalytic—psychanalytique
(psychol) psychology—psychologie
(psychopathol) psychopathology—psychopathologie
(public sign) affiche, écriteau
q.ch. or *q.ch.* quelque chose—something
qn or *qn* quelqu'un—someone
(rad) radio—radio
ref reflexive verb—verbe pronominal, réfléchi ou réciproque
reflex reflexive—réfléchi
(rel) relative—relatif
(rel) religion—religion
(rhet) rhetoric—rhétorique
(rok) rocketry—fusées
(rowing) canotage
(rr) railroad—chemin de fer
s substantive—substantif
(sculp) sculpture—sculpture
(seismol) seismology—sismologie
(sewing) couture
sg singular—singulier
(slang) populaire, argotique
s.o. or *s.o.* someone—quelqu'un
spl substantive plural—substantif pluriel
(sports) sports
s.th. or *s.th.* something—quelque chose
subj subjunctive—subjonctif
super superlative—superlatif
(surg) surgery—chirurgie
(surv) surveying—topographie
(swimming) nage
(taur) bullfighting—tauromachie
(telg) telegraphy—télégraphie
(telp) telephony—téléphonie
(telv) television—télévision
(tennis) tennis
(tex) textile—textile
(theat) theater—théâtre
(theol) theology—théologie
tr transitive verb—verbe transitif
(trademark) marque déposée
(turf) horse racing—courses de chevaux
(typ) printing—imprimerie
(U.S.A.) U.S.A., E.-U.A.
v verb—verbe
var variant—variante
(vet) veterinary medicine—médecine vétérinaire
(vulg) vulgar—grossier
(wrestling) lutte, catch
(zool) zoology—zoologie

Part One

FRENCH-ENGLISH

FRENCH PRONUNCIATION

The following phonetic symbols represent all the sounds of the French language.

VOWELS

SYMBOL	SOUND	EXAMPLE
[a]	A little more open than the a in English hat.	patte [pat]
[α]	Like a in English father.	pâte [pαt] phase [fαz]
[ε]	Like e in English met.	sec [sεk] fer [fεr] fête [fεt] aile [εl] parallèle [paralεl]
[e]	Like a in English fate, but without the glide the English sound sometimes has.	été [ete] fée [fe] et [e] créer [kree]
[ə]	Like a in English comma or like e in English pardon.	le [lə] petit [pəti]
[i]	Like i in English machine or like e in English she.	si [si]
[ɔ]	A little more open and rounded than aw in English law.	donne [dɔn] joli [jɔli]
[o]	Like o in English note but without the glide the English sound sometimes has.	mot [mo] eau [o] faute [fot]
[u]	Like u in English rude.	sou [su] four [fur]
[y]	The lips are rounded for [u] and held without moving while the sound [i] is pronounced.	su [sy] sûr [syr]
[ø]	The lips are rounded for [o] and held without moving while the sound [e] is pronounced.	peu [pø] eux [ø] feutre [føtr]
[œ]	The lips are rounded for [ɔ] and held without moving while the sound [ε] is pronounced.	peur [pœr] seul [sœl]

NASAL VOWELS

To produce the nasal vowels, sound is emitted through both nose and mouth by means of a lowering of the velum. The orthographic **m** or **n** has no consonantal value.

SYMBOL	SOUND	EXAMPLE
[ã]	Like a in English father and nasalized.	en [ã] tant [tã] temps [tã] paon [pã]
[ɔ̃]	More close than aw in English law and nasalized.	on [ɔ̃] pont [pɔ̃] comte [kɔ̃t]
[ɛ̃]	Like e in English met and nasalized.	pin [pɛ̃] pain [pɛ̃] faim [fɛ̃] teint [tɛ̃]
[œ̃]	Like [œ] of French bœuf and nasalized. There has been a tendency in this century to assimilate the nasal sound [œ̃] to the nasal sound [ɛ̃], making **brun** [brœ̃] and **brin** [brɛ̃] sound much the same.	un [œ̃] parfum [parfœ̃]

3

DIPHTHONGS

The sounds [j], [ɥ], and [w] are used to form diphthongs.

SYMBOL	SOUND	EXAMPLE
[j]	Like y in English year or like y in English toy.	hier [jɛr] ail [aj]
[ɥ]	Like the letter u [y] pronounced with consonantal value preceding a vowel.	lui [lɥi] situation [sitɥɑsjɔ̃] nuage [nɥaʒ] écuelle [ekɥɛl]
[w]	Like w in English water.	oie [wa] jouer [ʒwe] jouir [ʒwir]

CONSONANTS

The speaker of French characteristically keeps the tip of his tongue down behind his lower teeth and arches the back of the tongue at the same time. Thus, sounds such as [t], [d], [n], [s], [z], [l], and [r] must in French be articulated with the tongue tip and blade in the proximity of the back surface of the teeth.

SYMBOL	SOUND	EXAMPLE
[b]	Like b in English baby.	basse [bɑs]
[d]	Like d in English dead.	doux [du]
[f]	Like f in English face.	fou [fu]
[g]	Like g in English go.	gare [gar]
[k]	Like k in English kill, but without the aspiration which normally accompanies k in English.	cas [kɑ] kiosque [kjɔsk]
[l]	Like l in English like or in English slip—pronounced toward the front of the mouth. Not like l in old.	lit [li] houle [ul]
[m]	Like m in English more.	masse [mas]
[n]	Like n in English nest.	nous [nu]
[ɲ]	Like ny in English canyon or like ni in English onion.	signe [siɲ] agneau [aɲo]
[ŋ]	Like ng in English parking.	parking [parkiŋ]
[p]	Like p in English pen, but without the aspiration which normally accompanies p in English.	passe [pɑs]
[r]	Sometimes the uvular r but for some decades now usually a friction r with the point of articulation between the rounded back of the tongue and the hard palate. It resembles the Spanish aspirate in jota, the German aspirate in ach, and the g in the modern Greek gamma more than it resembles the modern American retroflex r. The tip of the tongue must point down near the back of the lower teeth and must not move during the utterance of the French [r].	rire [rir] caractère [karaktɛr] roi [rwa] roue [ru]
[s]	Like s in English send.	sot [so] leçon [ləsɔ̃] place [plas] lassitude [lɑsityd] attention [atɑ̃sjɔ̃]
[ʃ]	Like sh in English shall or ch in English machine.	cheval [ʃval] mèche [mɛʃ]
[t]	Like t in English ten, but without the aspiration which normally accompanies t in English.	toux [tu] thé [te]

4

SYMBOL	SOUND	EXAMPLE
[v]	Like **v** in English **vest**.	**verre** [vɛr]
[z]	Like **z** in English **zeal**.	**zèle** [zel]
		oser [oze]
[ʒ]	Like **s** in English **pleasure**.	**joue** [ʒu]
		rouge [ruʒ]
		mangeur [mãʒœr]

FRENCH STRESS

Stress is not shown on French words in this Dictionary because stress is not a fixed characteristic of the pronunciation of French words. It depends on the position of the word in the sentence and it falls on the last syllable of the word that terminates a rhythmic or sense grouping unless the vowel of that syllable is a mute **e** [ə], in which case it falls on the immediately preceding syllable.

VOWEL LENGTH

Vowel length is not shown in the phonetic transcription of French words in this Dictionary because it, like stress, is not a fixed characteristic of the pronunciation of French words. The following vowel sounds in the positions indicated are long when stressed: 1) all when followed by [r], [z], [v], [ʒ], or [vr]; 2) all spelled with a circumflex accent and followed by a consonant sound; and 3) [ã], [õ], [ɛ̃], [œ̃], [ɑ], [o], and [ø] followed by a consonant sound. When these conditions are not fulfilled, all vowel sounds are normal in length (or sometimes they may be short in length, even when stressed, if followed by [k], [p], [t], [kt], [rk], [rp], or [rt]).

ELISION AND LIAISON

Elision and liaison are usually made with words beginning with a vowel or a mute **h**. Elision and liaison are made with some words beginning with **y**, such as: **yèbe, yeuse, yeux, Yonne,** and **York**.

However, there are words which begin with a vowel or an **h** with which elision and liaison are not made. Most of these words begin with **h**, called aspirate **h**, although it has not been pronounced for centuries. In this Dictionary these words are indicated by an asterisk placed before the opening bracket of the phonetic symbols, e.g., **hameau** *[amo], **onze** *[ɔ̃z], **a** *[ɑ], **s** *[ɛs].

TABLE OF FRENCH REGULAR VERBS

The letters standing before the names of the tenses in this table correspond to the designation of the tenses shown on the following page. The forms printed in boldface correspond to the key forms described likewise on the following page.

TENSE	FIRST CONJUGATION	SECOND CONJUGATION	THIRD CONJUGATION
inf	**DONNER**	**FINIR**	**VENDRE**
ger	donnant	finissant	vendant
pp	donné	fini	vendu
a) *impv*	donne donnons donnez	finis finissons finissez	vends vendons vendez
b) *pres ind*	**donne** donnes donne **donnons** donnez **donnent**	**finis** finis finit **finissons** finissez **finissent**	**vends** vends vend **vendons** vendez **vendent**
c) *pres subj*	donne donnes donne donnions donniez donnent	finisse finisses finisse finissions finissiez finissent	vende vendes vende vendions vendiez vendent
d) *imperf ind*	donnais donnais donnait donnions donniez donnaient	finissais finissais finissait finissions finissiez finissaient	vendais vendais vendait vendions vendiez vendaient
e) *fut ind*	**donnerai** donneras donnera donnerons donnerez donneront	**finirai** finiras finira finirons finirez finiront	**vendrai** vendras vendra vendrons vendrez vendront
pres cond	donnerais donnerais donnerait donnerions donneriez donneraient	finirais finirais finirait finirions finiriez finiraient	vendrais vendrais vendrait vendrions vendriez vendraient
f) *pret ind*	**donnai** donnas donna donnâmes donnâtes donnèrent	**finis** finis finit finîmes finîtes finirent	**vendis** vendis vendit vendîmes vendîtes vendirent
imperf subj	donnasse donnasses donnât donnassions donnassiez donnassent	finisse finisses finît finissions finissiez finissent	vendisse vendisses vendît vendissions vendissiez vendissent

MODEL VERBS

ORDER OF TENSES

(a) imperative
(b) present indicative
(c) present subjunctive

(d) imperfect indicative
(e) future indicative
(f) preterit indicative

In addition to the infinitive, gerund, and past participle, all simple tenses are shown in these tables if they contain one irregular form or more, except the conditional (which can always be derived from the stem of the future indicative) and the imperfect subjunctive (which can always be derived from the preterit indicative). Those forms are considered irregular which deviate morphologically and/or orthographically in root, stem, or ending from the paradigms of regular verbs which appear on page **6**. The infinitive is printed in boldface capital letters. And the following forms are printed in boldface: (1) key forms (that is, irregular forms from which other irregular forms can be derived, but not the derived forms), e.g., **buvons**, (2) individual irregular forms which occupy the place of key forms but cannot function as key forms because other irregular forms cannot be derived from them, e.g., **sommes**, and (3) individual irregular forms which cannot be derived from key forms, e.g., **dites**. The names of the key forms and the forms derived from each of them are listed below.

KEY FORM	DERIVED FORMS
1st sg pres ind	*2d & 3d sg pres ind & 2d sg impv* *
1st pl pres ind	*2d pl pres ind, 1st & 2d pl pres subj,* whole *imperf ind, 1st & 2d pl impv, &* *ger*
3d pl pres ind	whole *sg & 3d pl pres subj*
1st sg fut ind	rest of *fut ind* & whole *conditional*
1st sg pret ind	rest of *pret ind* & whole *imperf subj*

* Some irregular verbs of the third conjugation which end in s, not preceded by d, in the *1st sg pres ind*, end in s also in the *2d sg pres ind* and the *2d sg impv*, and in t in the *3d sg pres ind*, e.g., **crains, crains, craint** and **bois, bois, boit.** And three verbs, namely, **pouvoir, valoir,** and **vouloir,** which end in x in the *1st sg pres ind*, end in x also in the *2d sg pres ind* and the *2d sg impv*, and in t in the *3d sg pres ind*, e.g., **veux, veux, veut.**

7

1st sg pres subj of **faire,**   rest of *pres subj*
      pouvoir, & savoir
1st sg pres subj of **aller,**   *2d & 3d sg & 3d pl pres subj*
      valoir, & vouloir

§1 **ABRÉGER**—abrégeant—abrégé   Combination of §10 and §38
   (a) abrège, abrégeons, abrégez
   (b) **abrège,** abrèges, abrège, **abrégeons,** abrégez, **abrègent**
   (c) abrège, abrèges, abrège, abrégions, abrégiez, abrègent
   (d) abrégeais, abrégeais, abrégeait, abrégions, abrégiez, abré-
       geaient
   (f) **abrégeai,** abrégeas, abrégea, abrégeâmes, abrégeâtes, abré-
       gèrent

§2 **ACHETER**—achetant—acheté
   (a) achète, achetons, achetez
   (b) **achète,** achètes, achète, achetons, achetez, **achètent**
   (c) achète, achètes, achète, achetions, achetiez, achètent
   (e) **achèterai,** achèteras, achètera, achèterons, achèterez, achè-
       teront

§3 **ACQUÉRIR**—acquérant—**acquis**
   (a) acquiers, acquérons, acquérez
   (b) **acquiers,** acquiers, acquiert, **acquérons,** acquérez, **acquiè-
       rent**
   (c) acquière, acquières, acquière, acquérions, acquériez,
       acquièrent
   (d) acquérais, acquérais, acquérait, acquérions, acquériez,
       acquéraient
   (e) **acquerrai,** acquerras, acquerra, acquerrons, acquerrez,
       acquerront
   (f) **acquis,** acquis, acquit, acquîmes, acquîtes, acquirent

§4 **ALLER**—allant—allé
   (a) **va,** allons, allez
   (b) **vais** [ve], **vas, va,** allons, allez, **vont**
   (c) **aille** [aj], ailles, aille, allions, alliez, aillent
   (e) **irai,** iras, ira, irons, irez, iront

§5A **ASSEOIR**—asseyant—**assis**
   (a) assieds, asseyons, asseyez
   (b) **assieds,** assieds, assied, **asseyons,** asseyez, **asseyent**
   (c) asseye, asseyes, asseye, asseyions, asseyiez, asseyent
   (d) asseyais, asseyais, asseyait, asseyions, asseyiez, asseyaient
   (e) **assiérai,** assiéras, assiéra, assiérons, assiérez, assiéront
   (f) **assis,** assis, assit, assîmes, assîtes, assirent

§5B ASSEOIR—assoyant—**assis**
  (a) assois, assoyons, assoyez
  (b) **assois**, assois, assoit, **assoyons**, assoyez, **assoient**
  (c) assoie, assoies, assoie, assoyions, assoyiez, assoient
  (d) assoyais, assoyais, assoyait, assoyions, assoyiez, assoyaient
  (e) **assoirai**, assoiras, assoira, assoirons, assoirez, assoiront
  (f) **assis**, assis, assit, assîmes, assîtes, assirent

§6 AVOIR—ayant—**eu** [y]
  (a) **aie** [e], **ayons, ayez**
  (b) **ai** [e], **as, a, avons**, avez, **ont**
  (c) **aie, aies, ait, ayons, ayez, aient**
  (d) avais, avais, avait, avions, aviez, avaient
  (e) **aurai**, auras, aura, aurons, aurez, auront
  (f) **eus** [y], eus, eut, eûmes, eûtes, eurent

§7 BATTRE—battant—battu
  (a) bats, battons, battez
  (b) **bats**, bats, bat, battons, battez, battent

§8 BOIRE—buvant—**bu**
  (a) bois, buvons, buvez
  (b) bois, bois, boit, **buvons**, buvez, **boivent**
  (c) boive, boives, boive, buvions, buviez, boivent
  (d) buvais, buvais, buvait, buvions, buviez, buvaient
  (f) **bus**, bus, but, bûmes, bûtes, burent

§9 BOUILLIR—bouillant—bouilli
  (a) bous, bouillons, bouillez
  (b) **bous**, bous, bout, **bouillons**, bouillez, **bouillent**
  (c) bouille, bouilles, bouille, bouillions, bouilliez, bouillent
  (d) bouillais, bouillais, bouillait, bouillions, bouilliez, bouil-
      laient

§10 CÉDER—cédant—cédé
  (a) cède, cédons, cédez
  (b) **cède**, cèdes, cède, cédons, cédez, **cèdent**
  (c) cède, cèdes, cède, cédions, cédiez, cèdent

§11 CONCLURE—concluant—**conclu**
  (f) **conclus**, conclus, conclut, conclûmes, conclûtes, conclurent

§12 CONNAÎTRE—connaissant—**connu**
  (a) connais, connaissons, connaissez
  (b) **connais**, connais, connaît, **connaissons**, connaissez, **con-
      naissent**
  (c) connaisse, connaisses, connaisse, connaissions, connaissiez,
      connaissent

(d) connaissais, connaissais, connaissait, connaissions, connaissiez, connaissaient
(f) **connus**, connus, connut, connûmes, connûtes, connurent

§13 COUDRE—cousant—**cousu**
(a) couds, cousons, cousez
(b) couds, couds, coud, **cousons**, cousez, **cousent**
(c) couse, couses, couse, cousions, cousiez, cousent
(d) cousais, cousais, cousait, cousions, cousiez, cousaient
(f) **cousis**, cousis, cousit, cousîmes, cousîtes, cousirent

§14 COURIR—courant—**couru**
(a) cours, courons, courez
(b) **cours**, cours, court, **courons**, courez, **courent**
(c) coure, coures, coure, courions, couriez, courent
(d) courais, courais, courait, courions, couriez, couraient
(e) **courrai**, courras, courra, courrons, courrez, courront
(f) **courus**, courus, courut, courûmes, courûtes, coururent

§15 CRAINDRE—craignant—**craint**
(a) crains, craignons, craignez
(b) **crains**, crains, craint, **craignons**, craignez, **craignent**
(c) craigne, craignes, craigne, craignions, craigniez, craignent
(d) craignais, craignais, craignait, craignions, craigniez, craignaient
(f) **craignis**, craignis, craignit, cragnîmes, craignîtes, craignirent

§16 CROIRE—croyant—**cru**
(a) crois, croyons, croyez
(b) crois, crois, croit, **croyons**, croyez, croient
(c) croie, croies, croie, croyions, croyiez, croient
(d) croyais, croyais, croyait, croyions, croyiez, croyaient
(f) **crus**, crus, crut, crûmes, crûtes, crurent

§17 CROÎTRE—croissant—**crû, crue**
(a) croîs, croissons, croissez
(b) **croîs**, croîs, croît, **croissons**, croissez, **croissent**
(c) croisse, croisses, croisse, croissions, croissiez, croissent
(d) croissais, croissais, croissait, croissions, croissiez, croissaient
(f) **crûs**, crûs, crût, crûmes, crûtes, crûrent

§18 CUEILLIR—cueillant—cueilli
(a) cueille, cueillons, cueillez
(b) **cueille**, cueilles, cueille, **cueillons**, cueillez, **cueillent**
(c) cueille, cueilles, cueille, cueillions, cueilliez, cueillent

  (d) cueillais, cueillais, cueillait, cueillions, cueilliez, cueillaient
  (e) **cueillerai**, cueilleras, cueillera, cueillerons, cueillerez,
    cueilleront

§19 CUIRE—cuisant—**cuit**
  (a) cuis, cuisons, cuisez
  (b) cuis, cuis, cuit, **cuisons**, cuisez, **cuisent**
  (c) cuise, cuises, cuise, cuisions, cuisiez, cuisent
  (d) cuisais, cuisais, cuisait, cuisions, cuisiez, cuisaient
  (f) **cuisis**, cuisis, cuisit, cuisîmes, cuisîtes, cuisirent

§20 DÉPECER—dépeçant—dépecé Combination of §2 and §51
  (a) dépèce, dépeçons, dépecez
  (b) **dépèce**, dépèces, dépèce, **dépeçons**, dépecez, **dépècent**
  (c) dépèce, dépèces, dépèce, dépecions, dépeciez, dépècent
  (d) dépeçais, dépeçais, dépeçait, dépecions, dépeciez, dépe-
    çaient
  (e) **dépècerai**, dépèceras, dépècera, dépècerons, dépècerez,
    dépèceront
  (f) **dépeçai**, dépeças, dépeça, dépeçâmes, dépeçâtes, dépecè-
    rent

§21 DEVOIR—devant—**dû, due**
  (a) missing
  (b) **dois**, dois, doit, **devons**, devez, **doivent**
  (c) doive, doives, doive, devions, deviez, doivent
  (d) devais, devais, devait, devions, deviez, devaient
  (e) **devrai**, devras, devra, devrons, devrez, devront
  (f) **dus**, dus, dut, dûmes, dûtes, durent

§22 DIRE—disant—**dit**
  (a) dis, disons, **dites**
  (b) dis, dis, dit, **disons, dites**, disent
  (c) dise, dises, dise, disions, disiez, disent
  (d) disais, disais, disait, disions, disiez, disaient
  (f) **dis**, dis, dit, dîmes, dîtes, dirent

§23 DORMIR—dormant—dormi
  (a) dors, dormons, dormez
  (b) **dors**, dors, dort, **dormons**, dormez, **dorment**
  (c) dorme, dormes, dorme, dormions, dormiez, dorment
  (d) dormais, dormais, dormait, dormions, dormiez, dormaient

§24 ÉCLORE—éclosant—**éclos**
  (a) éclos
  (b) éclos, éclos, **éclôt, éclosent**
  (c) éclose, écloses, éclose, **éclosions, éclosiez**, éclosent
  (d) missing
  (f) missing

§25 ÉCRIRE—écrivant—écrit
- (a) écris, écrivons, écrivez
- (b) écris, écris, écrit, **écrivons**, écrivez, **écrivent**
- (c) écrive, écrives, écrive, écrivions, écriviez, écrivent
- (d) écrivais, écrivais, écrivait, écrivions, écriviez, écrivaient
- (f) **écrivis**, écrivis, écrivit, écrivîmes, écrivîtes, écrivirent

§26 ENVOYER—envoyant—envoyé
- (a) envoie, envoyons, envoyez
- (b) **envoie**, envoies, envoie, envoyons, envoyez, **envoient**
- (c) envoie, envoies, envoie, envoyions, envoyiez, envoient
- (e) **enverrai**, enverras, enverra, enverrons, enverrez, enverront

§27 ESSUYER—essuyant—essuyé
- (a) essuie, essuyons, essuyez
- (b) **essuie**, essuies, essuie, essuyons, essuyez, **essuient**
- (c) essuie, essuies, essuie, essuyions, essuyiez, essuient
- (e) **essuierai**, essuieras, essuiera, essuierons, essuierez, essuieront

§28 ÊTRE—étant—été
- (a) **sois, soyons, soyez**
- (b) **suis, es, est, sommes, êtes, sont**
- (c) **sois, sois, soit, soyons, soyez, soient**
- (d) **étais, étais, était, étions, étiez, étaient**
- (e) **serai**, seras, sera, serons, serez, seront
- (f) **fus**, fus, fut, fûmes, fûtes, furent

§29 FAIRE—faisant—fait
- (a) fais, faisons, **faites**
- (b) fais, fais, fait, **faisons, faites, font**
- (c) **fasse**, fasses, fasse, fassions, fassiez, fassent
- (d) faisais, faisais, faisait, faisions, faisiez, faisaient
- (e) **ferai**, feras, fera, ferons, ferez, feront
- (f) **fis**, fis, fit, fîmes, fîtes, firent

§30 FALLOIR—missing—fallu
- (a) missing
- (b) **faut**
- (c) **faille**
- (d) **fallait**
- (e) **faudra**
- (f) **fallut**

§31 FUIR—fuyant—fui
- (a) fuis, fuyons, fuyez
- (b) fuis, fuis, fuit, **fuyons**, fuyez, **fuient**

12

(c) fuie, fuies, fuie, fuyions, fuyiez, fuient
(d) fuyais, fuyais, fuyait, fuyions, fuyiez, fuyaient

§32 **GRASSEYER**—grasseyant—grasseyé
(regular, unlike other verbs with stem ending in **y**)

§33 **HAÏR**—haïssant—**haï**
(a) hais [ɛ], haïssons, haïssez
(b) **hais** [ɛ], hais, hait, **haïssons**, haïssez, **haïssent**
(c) haïsse, haïsses, haïsse, haïssions, haïssiez, haïssent
(d) haïssais, haïssais, haïssait, haïssions, haïssiez, haïssaient
(f) haïs, haïs, haït, **haïmes**, **haïtes**, haïrent

§34 **JETER**—jetant—jeté
(a) jette, jetons, jetez
(b) **jette**, jettes, jette, jetons, jetez, **jettent**
(c) jette, jettes, jette, jetions, jetiez, jettent
(e) **jetterai**, jetteras, jettera, jetterons, jetterez, jetteront

§35 **JOINDRE**—joignant—**joint**
(a) joins, joignons, joignez
(b) **joins**, joins, joint, **joignons**, joignez, **joignent**
(c) joigne, joignes, joigne, joignions, joigniez, joignent
(d) joignais, joignais, joignait, joignions, joigniez, joignaient
(f) **joignis**, joignis, joignit, joignîmes, joignîtes, joignirent

§36 **LIRE**—lisant—**lu**
(a) lis, lisons, lisez
(b) lis, lis, lit, **lisons**, lisez, **lisent**
(c) lise, lises, lise, lisions, lisiez, lisent
(d) lisais, lisais, lisait, lisions, lisiez, lisaient
(f) **lus**, lus, lut, lûmes, lûtes, lurent

§37 **LUIRE**—luisant—**lui**
(a) luis, luisons, luisez
(b) luis, luis, luit, **luisons**, luisez, **luisent**
(c) luise, luises, luise, luisions, luisiez, luisent
(d) luisais, luisais, luisait, luisions, luisiez, luisaient
(f) archaic

§38 **MANGER**—mangeant—mangé
(a) mange, mangeons, mangez
(b) mange, manges, mange, **mangeons**, mangez, mangent
(d) mangeais, mangeais, mangeait, mangions, mangiez, mangeaient
(f) **mangeai,** mangeas, mangea, mangeâmes, mangeâtes, mangèrent

13

§39 MAUDIRE—maudissant—**maudit**
- (a) maudis, maudissons, maudissez
- (b) maudis, maudis, maudit, **maudissons**, maudissez, **maudissent**
- (c) maudisse, maudisses, maudisse, maudissions, maudissiez, maudissent
- (d) maudissais, maudissais, maudissait, maudissions, maudissiez, maudissaient
- (f) **maudis**, maudis, maudit, maudîmes, maudîtes, maudirent

§40 MÉDIRE—médisant—**médit**
- (a) médis, médisons, médisez
- (b) médis, médis, médit, **médisons**, médisez, **médisent**
- (c) médise, médises, médise, médisions, médisiez, médisent
- (d) médisais, médisais, médisait, médisions, médisiez, médisaient
- (f) **médis**, médis, médit, médîmes, médîtes, médirent

§41 MENTIR—mentant—**menti**
- (a) mens, mentons, mentez
- (b) **mens**, mens, ment, **mentons**, mentez, **mentent**
- (c) mente, mentes, mente, mentions, mentiez, mentent
- (d) mentais, mentais, mentait, mentions, mentiez, mentaient

§42 METTRE—mettant—**mis**
- (a) mets, mettons, mettez
- (b) **mets**, mets, met, mettons, mettez, mettent
- (f) **mis**, mis, mit, mîmes, mîtes, mirent

§43 MOUDRE—moulant—**moulu**
- (a) mouds, moulons, moulez
- (b) mouds, mouds, moud, **moulons**, moulez, **moulent**
- (c) moule, moules, moule, moulions, mouliez, moulent
- (d) moulais, moulais, moulait, moulions, mouliez, moulaient
- (f) **moulus**, moulus, moulut, moulûmes, moulûtes, moulurent

§44 MOURIR—mourant—**mort**
- (a) meurs, mourons, mourez
- (b) **meurs**, meurs, meurt, **mourons**, mourez, **meurent**
- (c) meure, meures, meure, mourions, mouriez, meurent
- (d) mourais, mourais, mourait, mourions, mouriez, mouraient
- (e) **mourrai**, mourras, mourra, mourrons, mourrez, mourront
- (f) **mourus**, mourus, mourut, mourûmes, mourûtes, moururent

§45 MOUVOIR—mouvant—**mû, mue, mus, mues**
- (a) meus, mouvons, mouvez
- (b) **meus**, meus, meut, **mouvons**, mouvez, **meuvent**

(c) meuve, meuves, meuve, mouvions, mouviez, meuvent
(d) mouvais, mouvais, mouvait, mouvions, mouviez, mouvaient
(e) **mouvrai**, mouvras, mouvra, mouvrons, mouvrez, mouvront
(f) **mus**, mus, mut, mûmes, mûtes, murent

§46 NAÎTRE—naissant—né
(a) nais, naissons, naissez
(b) **nais**, nais, naît, **naissons**, naissez, **naissent**
(c) naisse, naisses, naisse, naissions, naissiez, naissent
(d) naissais, naissais, naissait, naissions, naissiez, naissaient
(f) **naquis**, naquis, naquit, naquîmes, naquîtes, naquirent

§47 NETTOYER—nettoyant—nettoyé
(a) nettoie, nettoyons, nettoyez
(b) **nettoie**, nettoies, nettoie, nettoyons, nettoyez, **nettoient**
(c) nettoie, nettoies, nettoie, nettoyions, nettoyiez, nettoient
(e) **nettoierai**, nettoieras, nettoiera, nettoierons, nettoierez, nettoieront

§48 PAÎTRE—paissant—pu
(a) pais, paissez
(b) **pais**, pais, paît, **paissons**, paissez, **paissent**
(c) paisse, paisses, paisse, paissions, paissiez, paissent
(d) paissais, paissais, paissait, paissions, paissiez, paissaient
(f) missing

§49 PAYER—payant—payé
(a) paie or paye, payons, payez
(b) **paie**, paies, paie, payons, payez, **paient** or
paye, payes, paye, payons, payez, payent
(c) paie, paies, paie, payions, payiez, paient or
paye, payes, paye, payions, payiez, payent
(e) **paierai**, paieras, paiera, paierons, paierez, paieront or
payerai, payeras, payera, payerons, payerez, payeront

§50 PEINDRE—peignant—peint
(a) peins, peignons, peignez
(b) **peins**, peins, peint, **peignons**, peignez, **peignent**
(c) peigne, peignes, peigne, peignions, peigniez, peignent
(d) peignais, peignais, peignait, peignions, peigniez, peignaient
(f) **peignis**, peignis, peignit, peignîmes, peignîtes, peignirent

§51 PLACER—plaçant—placé
(a) place, plaçons, placez
(b) place, places, place, **plaçons**, placez, placent
(d) plaçais, plaçais, plaçait, placions, placiez, plaçaient
(f) **plaçai**, plaças, plaça, plaçâmes, plaçâtes, placèrent

§52 PLAIRE—plaisant—plu
- (a) plais, plaisons, plaisez
- (b) plais, plais, **plaît**, **plaisons**, plaisez, **plaisent**
- (c) plaise, plaises, plaise, plaisions, plaisiez, plaisent
- (d) plaisais, plaisais, plaisait, plaisions, plaisiez, plaisaient
- (f) **plus**, plus, plut, plûmes, plûtes, plurent

§53 PLEUVOIR—pleuvant—plu
- (a) **pleus, pleuvons, pleuvez** (fig & rare)
- (b) **pleut, pleuvent**
- (c) pleuve, pleuvent
- (d) **pleuvait, pleuvaient**
- (e) **pleuvra, pleuvront**
- (f) **plut, plurent**

§54 POURVOIR—pourvoyant—**pourvu**
- (a) pourvois, pouvoyons, pourvoyez
- (b) **pourvois**, pourvois, pourvoit, **pourvoyons**, pourvoyez, **pourvoient**
- (c) pourvoie, pourvoies, pourvoie, pourvoyions, pourvoyiez, pourvoient
- (d) pourvoyais, pourvoyais, pourvoyait, pourvoyions, pourvoyiez, pourvoyaient
- (f) **pourvus**, pourvus, pourvut, pourvûmes, pourvûtes, pourvurent

§55 POUVOIR—pouvant—**pu**
- (a) missing
- (b) **peux** or **puis**, peux, peut, **pouvons**, pouvez, **peuvent**
- (c) **puisse**, puisses, puisse, puissions, puissiez, puissent
- (d) pouvais, pouvais, pouvait, pouvions, pouviez, pouvaient
- (e) **pourrai**, pourras, pourra, pourrons, pourrez, pourront
- (f) **pus**, pus, put, pûmes, pûtes, purent

§56 PRENDRE—prenant—**pris**
- (a) prends, prenons, prenez
- (b) prends, prends, prend, **prenons**, prenez, **prennent**
- (c) prenne, prennes, prenne, prenions, preniez, prennent
- (d) prenais, prenais, prenait, prenions, preniez, prenaient
- (f) **pris**, pris, prit, prîmes, prîtes, prirent

§57 PRÉVOIR—prévoyant—**prévu**
- (a) prévois, prévoyons, prévoyez
- (b) **prévois**, prévois, prévoit, **prévoyons**, prévoyez, **prévoient**
- (c) prévoie, prévoies, prévoie, prévoyions, prévoyiez, prévoient
- (d) prévoyais, prévoyais, prévoyait, prévoyions, prévoyiez, prévoyaient
- (f) **prévis**, prévis, prévit, prévîmes, prévîtes, prévirent

§58 RAPIÉCER—rapiéçant—rapiécé Combination of §10 and §51
(a) rapièce, rapiéçons, rapiécez
(b) **rapièce**, rapièces, rapièce, **rapiéçons**, rapiécez, **rapiècent**
(c) rapièce, rapièces, rapièce, rapiécions, rapiéciez, rapiècent
(d) rapiéçais, rapiéçais, rapiéçait, rapiécions, rapiéciez, rapiéçaient
(f) **rapiéçai**, rapiéças, rapiéça, rapiéçâmes, rapiéçâtes, rapiécèrent

§59 RECEVOIR—recevant—**reçu**
(a) reçois, recevons, recevez
(b) **reçois**, reçois, reçoit, **recevons**, recevez, **reçoivent**
(c) reçoive, reçoives, reçoive, recevions, receviez, reçoivent
(d) recevais, recevais, recevait, recevions, receviez, recevaient
(e) **recevrai**, recevras, recevra, recevrons, recevrez, recevront
(f) **reçus**, reçus, reçut, reçûmes, reçûtes, reçurent

§60 RÉSOUDRE—résolvant—**résolu; résout** (invar)
(a) résous, résolvons, résolvez
(b) **résous**, résous, résout, **résolvons**, résolvez, **résolvent**
(c) résolve, résolves, résolve, résolvions, résolviez, résolvent
(d) résolvais, résolvais, résolvait, résolvions, résolviez, résolvaient
(f) **résolus**, résolus, résolut, résolûmes, résolûtes, résolurent

§61 RIRE—riant—**ri**
(f) **ris**, ris, rit, rîmes, rîtes, rirent

§62 SAVOIR—sachant—**su**
(a) **sache, sachons, sachez**
(b) **sais**, sais, sait, **savons**, savez, **savent**
(c) **sache**, saches, sache, sachions, sachiez, sachent
(d) savais, savais, savait, savions, saviez, savaient
(e) **saurai**, sauras, saura, saurons, saurez, sauront
(f) **sus**, sus, sut, sûmes, sûtes, surent

§63 SERVIR—servant—servi
(a) sers, servons, servez
(b) **sers**, sers, sert, **servons**, servez, **servent**
(c) serve, serves, serve, servions, serviez, servent
(d) servais, servais, servait, servions, serviez, servaient

§64 SORTIR—sortant—sorti
(a) sors, sortons, sortez
(b) **sors**, sors, sort, **sortons**, sortez, **sortent**
(c) sorte, sortes, sorte, sortions, sortiez, sortent
(d) sortais, sortais, sortait, sortions, sortiez, sortaient

§65 SOUFFRIR—souffrant—**souffert**
(a) souffre, souffrons, souffrez
(b) **souffre**, souffres, souffre, **souffrons**, souffrez, **souffrent**
(c) souffre, souffres, souffre, souffrions, souffriez, souffrent
(d) souffrais, souffrais, souffrait, souffrions, souffriez, souffraient

§66 SUFFIRE—suffisant—**suffi**
(a) suffis, suffisons, suffisez
(b) suffis, suffis, suffit, **suffisons**, suffisez, **suffisent**
(c) suffise, suffises, suffise, suffisions, suffisiez, suffisent
(d) suffisais, suffisais, suffisait, suffisions, suffisiez, suffisaient
(f) **suffis**, suffis, suffit, suffîmes, suffîtes, suffirent

§67 SUIVRE—suivant—**suivi**
(a) suis, suivons, suivez
(b) **suis**, suis, suit, suivons, suivez, suivent

§68 TRAIRE—trayant—**trait**
(a) trais, trayons, trayez
(b) trais, trais, trait, **trayons**, trayez, traient
(c) traie, traies, traie, trayions, trayiez, traient
(d) trayais, trayais, trayait, trayions, trayiez, trayaient
(f) missing

§69 TRESSAILLIR—tressaillant—tressailli
(a) tressaille, tressaillons, tressaillez
(b) **tressaille**, tressailles, tressaille, **tressaillons**, tressaillez, **tressaillent**
(c) tressaille, tressailles, tressaille, tressaillions, tressailliez, tressaillent
(d) tressaillais, tressaillais, tressaillait, tressaillions, tressailliez, tressaillaient
(e) **tressaillirai**, tressailliras, tressaillira, tressaillirons, tressaillirez, tressailliront, or **tressaillerai**, tressailleras, tressaillera, tressaillerons, tressaillerez, tressailleront

§70 VAINCRE—vainquant—vaincu
(a) vaincs [vɛ̃], vainquons, vainquez
(b) vaincs, vaincs, vainc, **vainquons**, vainquez, **vainquent**
(c) vainque, vainques, vainque, vainquions, vainquiez, vainquent
(d) vainquais, vainquais, vainquait, vainquions, vainquiez, vainquaient
(f) **vainquis**, vainquis, vainquit, vainquîmes, vainquîtes, vainquirent

§71 VALOIR—valant—**valu**
(a) vaux, valons, valez
(b) **vaux**, vaux, vaut, **valons**, valez, **valent**

18

   (c) **vaille** [vaj], vailles, vaille, valions, valiez, vaillent
   (d) valais, valais, valait, valions, valiez, valaient
   (e) **vaudrai**, vaudras, vaudra, vaudrons, vaudrez, vaudront
   (f) **valus**, valus, valut, valûmes, valûtes, valurent

§72 **VENIR**—venant—**venu**
   (a) viens, venons, venez
   (b) **viens**, viens, vient, **venons**, venez, **viennent**
   (c) vienne, viennes, vienne, venions, veniez, viennent
   (e) **viendrai**, viendras, viendra, viendrons, viendrez, viendront
   (f) **vins**, vins, vint, vînmes [vɛ̃m], vîntes [vɛ̃t], vinrent [vɛ̃r]

§73 **VÊTIR**—vêtant—**vêtu**
   (a) vêts, vêtons, vêtez
   (b) **vêts**, vêts, vêt, **vêtons**, vêtez, **vêtent**
   (c) vête, vêtes, vête, vêtions, vêtiez, vêtent
   (d) vêtais, vêtais, vêtait, vêtions, vêtiez, vêtaient

§74 **VIVRE**—vivant—**vécu**
   (a) vis, vivons, vivez
   (b) **vis**, vis, vit, vivons, vivez, vivent
   (f) **vécus**, vécus, vécut, vécûmes, vécûtes, vécurent

§75 **VOIR**—voyant—**vu**
   (a) vois, voyons, voyez
   (b) **vois**, vois, voit, **voyons**, voyez, **voient**
   (c) voie, voies, voie, voyions, voyiez, voient
   (d) voyais, voyais, voyait, voyions, voyiez, voyaient
   (e) **verrai**, verras, verra, verrons, verrez, verront
   (f) **vis**, vis, vit, vîmes, vîtes, virent

§76 **VOULOIR**—voulant—**voulu**
   (a) veux, voulons, voulez
   (b) **veux**, veux, veut, **voulons**, voulez, **veulent**
   (c) **veuille**, veuilles, veuille, voulions, vouliez, veuillent
   (d) voulais, voulais, voulait, voulions, vouliez, voulaient
   (e) **voudrai**, voudras, voudra, voudrons, voudrez, voudront
   (f) **voulus**, voulus, voulut, voulûmes, voulûtes, voulurent

GRAMMATICAL TABLES

§77 le *art def* the. The following table shows the forms of the definite article, the combination of **le** with **à** and **de**, and the combinations of **les** with **à, de,** and **en.**

		masc	*fem*
	sg	**le; l'** before a vowel or mute **h**	**la; l'** before a vowel or mute **h**
	pl	**les**	**les**
with **à**	*sg*	**au; à l'** before a vowel or mute **h**	**à la; à l'** before a vowel or mute **h**
with **à**	*pl*	**aux**	**aux**
with **de**	*sg*	**du; de l'** before a vowel or mute **h**	**de la; de l'** before a vowel or mute **h**
with **de**	*pl*	**des**	**des**
with **en**	*pl*	**ès,** e.g., **maître ès arts**	**ès,** e.g., **docteur ès lettres**

§78 lequel *pron rel* who, whom; which ‖ *pron interr* which, which one. The following table shows all the forms of the word **lequel** and their combinations with the prepositions **à** and **de.**

		masc	*fem*
	sg	**lequel**	**laquelle**
	pl	**lesquels**	**lesquelles**
with **à**	*sg*	**auquel**	**à laquelle**
with **à**	*pl*	**auxquels**	**auxquelles**
with **de**	*sg*	**duquel**	**de laquelle**
with **de**	*pl*	**desquels**	**desquelles**

The forms combined with **de** and used as relative pronouns sometimes mean: whose, e.g., **l'étudiant avec la sœur duquel j'ai dansé** the student with whose sister I danced

§79 dont *rel pron* of whom; of which; from which; with which; on which; at which; which; whose. The relative pronoun **dont** may be: a) the complement of the subject of the dependent verb, e.g., **cette malheureuse dont la jambe droite était brisée** that wretched woman whose right leg was broken; b) the complement of the object of the dependent verb, e.g., **sa grande chambre dont on avait fermé les volets** his large bedroom the shutters of which they had closed;

c) the complement of the verb itself, e.g., **les termes dont il se servait** the expressions which he used.

If the antecedent is one of point of origin, **d'où** is used, e.g., **la porte d'où il est sorti** the door from which he went out, unless the point of origin is one of ancestry or extraction having to do with a person, e.g., **la famille distinguée dont il sortait** the distinguished family from which he came.

The relative pronoun **dont** cannot be the complement of a noun which is the object of a preposition but must be replaced by a form of **lequel** combined with **de** (see §78), or by **de qui**, e.g., **l'étudiante avec le frère de laquelle** (or **de qui**) **j'ai dansé** the student with whose brother I danced.

§80 quel *adj* what; what sort of; which; what a, e.g., **quelle belle ville!** what a beautiful city!; **n'importe quel** any ‖ *adj interr* what, e.g., **quel est le but de la vie?** what is the purpose of life?; who, e.g., **quel est cet homme?** who is that man? ‖ *adj indef*—**quel que** whoever, e.g., **quel que soit l'homme** whoever the man may be; whatever, e.g., **quelles que soient les difficultés** whatever difficulties there may be; whichever, e.g., **quel que soit le pied sur lequel il s'appuie** whichever foot he leans on. The following table shows all the forms of the word **quel.**

	masc	*fem*
sg	quel	quelle
pl	quels	quelles

§81 quelqu'un *pron indef* someone, somebody; anyone, anybody; **quelques-uns** some; any, a few. The following table shows all the forms of the word **quelqu'un.**

	masc	*fem*
sg	quelqu'un	quelqu'une
pl	quelques-uns	quelques-unes

§82A ce *adj dem* this; that; **ces** these; those. The following table shows all the forms of this word.

	masc	*fem*
sg	ce; cet before a vowel or mute **h**	cette
pl	ces	ces

This word has two meanings as exemplified by the following example:

cet homme this man; that man

However, the particles **-ci** and **-là** are attached to the noun modified by the forms of **ce** to distinguish what is near the person speaking (i.e., the first person) from what is near the person spoken to (i.e., the second person) or what is remote from both (i.e., the third person), for example:

cet homme-ci this man (*not that man*)
cet homme-là that man (*not this man*)
cet homme-là that man (*yonder*)

§82B ce *pron dem*
  it, e.g., **c'est un bon livre** it is a good book;
  he, e.g., **c'est un bon professeur** he is a good professor;
  she, e.g., **c'est une belle femme** she is a beautiful woman;
  they, e.g., **ce sont des élèves** they are students

§83 **celui** *pron dem* this one; that one. The following table shows all the forms of the demonstrative pronoun with their translations into English.

	masc	*fem*
sg	**celui** this one; that one; he	**celle** this one; that one; she
pl	**ceux** these; those	**celles** these; those

This word in all its forms is generally used with a following **de** or the relative pronouns **que** and **qui**:

celui de
celle de
ceux de
celles de } 's, e.g., **celui de Marie** Mary's

celui que	he whom; the one that; the one which	} whomever; whichever
celle que	she whom; the one that; the one which	
ceux que	those whom; the ones whom; the ones which	
celles que	those whom; the ones whom; the ones which	

celui qui	he who; the one that; the one which	} whoever; whichever
celle qui	she who; the one that; the one which	
ceux qui	those who; the ones who; the ones which	
celles qui	those who; the ones who; the ones which	

§84 **celui-ci** *pron dem* this one; he; the latter. The particles -ci and -là are attached to the forms of **celui** to distinguish what is near the person speaking (i.e., the first person) from what is near the person spoken to (i.e., the second person) or remote from both (i.e., the third person). The following table shows all the forms of this word with particles attached and with their translations into English.

	masc	*fem*
sg	**celui-ci** this one	**celle-ci** this one
	celui-là that one	**celle-là** that one
pl	**ceux-ci** these	**celles-ci** these
	ceux-là those	**celles-là** those

The forms of **celui-ci** also mean the latter; and the forms of **celui-là**, the former, e.g., **Henri était roi et Catherine était reine. Celle-ci était espagnole et celui-là anglais.** Henry was a king and Catherine was a queen. The former was English and the latter Spanish. (The English word order requires the inversion.)

§85 Disjunctive personal and reflexive pronouns.
This table shows all the forms of the disjunctive personal and reflexive pronouns with their translations into English.

moi	me; myself; I	**nous**	we, us; ourselves
toi	you, thee; yourself	**vous**	you; yourselves
lui	he, him, it; himself	**eux**	they, them *masc*; themselves *masc*
elle	she, her, it; herself	**elles**	they, them *fem*; themselves *fem*
soi	oneself; himself, herself, itself	**soi**	themselves

A) The disjunctive personal pronouns are used:
1) as the object of a preposition, e.g., **Jean a été invité chez elle** John was invited to her house; e.g., **il est très content de lui** he is very satisfied with himself
Disjunctive pronouns especially as objects of prepositions rarely stand for things. Prepositional phrases which would include them are generally expressed by **y** (see §87), e.g., **je m'y suis avancé** I walked up to it, as contrasted with **je me suis avancé vers lui** I walked up to him; or are expressed by one of the adverbs **là-dessus, là-dessous, là-dedans,** etc., e.g., **voilà mon nom; écrivez le vôtre là-dessous** there is my name; write yours under it, as contrasted with **il n'a pas d'argent sur lui** he has no money with him.
2) after the preposition **à** in phrases which are used to clarify or to stress the meaning of a conjunctive personal pronoun, e.g., **il lui a parlé, à elle** he spoke to her (or, he spoke to *her*)
3) after the preposition **à** in phrases which are used to clarify the meaning of a preceding possessive adjective, e.g., **son chapeau à elle** her hat
4) as predicate pronouns after the verb **être**, especially after **c'est** and **ce sont:**

c'est moi	it is I	**c'est nous**	it is we
c'est toi	it is you, it is thee	**c'est vous**	it is you
c'est lui	it is he	**ce sont eux**	it is they *masc*
c'est elle	it is she	**ce sont elles**	it is they *fem*

5) after **que** (than, as) in comparisons, e.g., **nous y allons plus souvent qu'eux** we go there more often than they; e.g., **nous y allons aussi souvent que vous** we go there as often as you
6) when the verb is not expressed, e.g., **qui a fait cela? Lui** who did that? He did

7) to stress the subject or object of the sentence, e.g., **lui, il a raison** he is right
8) in compound subjects and objects, e.g., **lui et moi, nous sommes médecins** he and I are doctors
9) when an adverb separates the subject pronoun from the verb, e.g., **lui toujours arrive en retard** he always arrives late
10) after **être + à** to contrast ownership, e.g., **ce stylo est à lui mais ce papier est à elle** this pen is his but this paper is hers.

B) The disjunctive indefinite reflexive pronoun **soi** corresponds to **on** and is used mainly as the object of a preposition, that is, according to **A**, 1 above, e.g., **on doit parler rarement de soi** one should seldom talk about oneself. But it may also be used in the predicate after the verb **être**, according to **A**, 4 above, e.g., **on a plus confiance quand c'est soi qui conduit** one has more confidence when it is oneself who drives.

§86 The following table shows all the forms of the intensive personal pronouns. They are made by combining the disjunctive personal pronouns with the forms of **même**.

moi-même	myself; I myself	**nous-mêmes**	ourselves; we ourselves
toi-même	yourself, thyself; you yourself	**vous-même**	yourself; you yourself
lui-même	himself; he himself; itself	**vous-mêmes**	yourselves; you yourselves
elle-même	herself; she herself; itself	**eux-mêmes**	themselves; they themselves
soi-même	oneself; itself	**elles-mêmes**	themselves; they themselves

§87 Conjunctive personal and reflexive pronouns.

person	1 subject	2 negative	3 direct & indirect object	4 direct object	5 indirect object
1	je (j')—I		me (m')—me, to me; myself, to myself	le (l')—him; it la (l')—her; it	lui—to him; to her
2	tu—you, thou		te (t')—you, to you; thee, to thee; thyself, to thyself		
3	il—he; it elle—she; it on—one, they	ne (n')—not §90B	se (s')—himself, herself, itself, oneself; to himself, to herself, to itself, to oneself		
4	nous—we		nous—us, to us; ourselves, to ourselves	les—them	leur—to them
5	vous—you		vous—you, to you; yourself, to yourself; yourselves, to yourselves		
6	ils—they elles—they		se (s')—themselves; to themselves		

This table shows all the forms of the conjunctive personal and reflexive pronouns with their translations into English and their positions (reading horizontally, not vertically) with respect to each other and with respect to the verb; and in negative declarative sentences, with respect to **ne** and **pas** and **personne**. All of the elements in this table except the verb and **pas** and **personne** (and the other negative words listed in §90) are unstressed.

In affirmative and negative interrogative sentences, the subject pronouns in column 1 are placed after the verb or auxiliary in column 8 and attached to it with a hyphen. A **t**, preceded and followed by hyphens, is intercalated between third-singular forms ending in a vowel and the subject pronoun. The interrogative forms of the first singular present indicative whose final sound is a nasal vowel or a consonant are not used, while those whose final sound is an oral vowel are, e.g., **où vais-je?** where am I going?; e.g., **que dirai-je?** what shall I say? And the ending **-e** of the first singular

person	6	7	8	9	10	11
				negative		*negative*
	y—there; to it; to them	*en*—some; of it; of them	VERB or AUX-ILIARY	*pas*—not **§90B**	past participle	**personne**—no one **§90B**
1						
2						
3						
4						
5						
6						

present indicative of verbs of the first conjugation is changed to **-é**, e.g., **donné-je?** do I give?, but these forms are not in current use in prose. All the forms not used are replaced by the affirmative forms introduced by **est-ce que** in affirmative interrogative sentences and by **n'est-ce pas que** in negative interrogative sentences. And **est-ce que** and **n'est-ce pas que** may be thus used in any person of any tense of the indicative. The ending **-e** of the first singular imperfect subjunctive of some verbs is likewise changed to **-é** in conditional clauses without **si** in literary usage, e.g., **dussé-je** if I should.

In affirmative imperative sentences, the subject pronouns are not expressed and the pronouns in columns 3, 4, 5, 6, and 7 are placed after the verb and attached to it and to each other with hyphens except where elision occurs, and the pronouns in column 4 precede those in column 3. And unless followed by **en** or **y**, **me** is replaced by **moi** and **te** is replaced by **toi**; and **moi** and **toi** are stressed.

In negative imperative sentences, the subject pronouns are not expressed either and columns 2, 3, 4, 5, 6, 7, 8, and 9 have the same order as in negative declarative sentences.

A pronoun of column 5 cannot be used with a pronoun of column 3 but is replaced by a disjunctive pronoun preceded by the preposition **à**.

27

§88 The following table shows all the forms of possessive adjectives with their translations into English.

masc sg	fem sg	masc & fem pl	
mon	ma*	mes	my
ton	ta*	tes	your, thy, thine
son	sa*	ses	his, her, its
notre	notre	nos	our
votre	votre	vos	your
leur	leur	leurs	their

* The forms **mon, ton,** and **son** are used instead of **ma, ta,** and **sa** respectively before feminine nouns and adjectives beginning with a vowel or mute **h,** e.g., **Marie a fait un cadeau à son aïeule** Mary gave a present to her grandmother; e.g., **elle y est venue avec son aimable tante** she came with her nice aunt.

The possessive adjectives:
1) agree in gender and number with the thing possessed rather than with the possessor, e.g., **Marie lit son livre** Mary is reading her book
2) must be repeated before each noun in a series, e.g., **Marie apporte son stylo et son crayon** Mary is bringing her pen and pencil

§89 The following table shows all the forms of possessive pronouns with their translations into English.

	sg	pl	
masc	le mien	les miens	mine
fem	la mienne	les miennes	
masc	le tien	les tiens	yours, thine
fem	la tienne	les tiennes	
masc	le sien	les siens	his, hers, its
fem	la sienne	les siennes	
masc	le nôtre	les nôtres	ours
fem	la nôtre		
masc	le vôtre	les vôtres	yours
fem	la vôtre		
masc	le leur	les leurs	theirs
fem	la leur		

The possessive pronouns:
1) agree in gender and number with the thing possessed rather than with the possessor, e.g., **donnez votre livre à Marie, elle a perdu le sien** give your book to Mary; she has lost hers
2) are preceded by a definite article, e.g., **tu dois obéir à son ordre et au mien** you must obey his order and mine
3) are sometimes used without antecedent: a) **le mien** mine, my own (*i.e., property*); **le sien** his, his own (*i.e., property*); hers, her own (*i.e., property*); etc.; b) **les miens** my folks, my family;

28

my friends; my men; **les siens** his folks, his family; his friends; his men; her folks, etc.; c) **faire des siennes** (coll) to be up to one's (his, etc.) old tricks.

§90 The adverb **ne** is a conjunctive particle, that is, it always precedes a verb and, like conjunctive pronouns, is unstressed. Because of its weakness, it is generally accompanied by another word, which follows the verb (or auxiliary) in most cases, is stressed, and gives force or added meaning to the negation, e.g., **il n'est pas ici** he is not here.

A) The following table shows **ne** with the various words with which it is associated. (For more detail, see each expression under the second word in the body of the Dictionary, e.g., s.v. **aucun**; e.g., s.v. **aucunement**; etc.)

ne . . . aucun	no, none; no one, nobody	**ne . . . ni . . . ni**	neither . . . nor
		ne . . . nul	no, none
ne . . . aucunement	by no means	**ne . . . nullement**	not at all
ne . . . brin (archaic)	not a bit, not a single	**ne . . . pas**	not, no
		ne . . . pas un	not one
ne . . . davantage	no more	**ne . . . personne**	no one, nobody
ne . . . goutte (archaic)	not a drop, nothing	**ne . . . plus**	no more, no longer
ne . . . guère	hardly, scarcely; hardly ever	**ne . . . plus jamais**	never any more
		ne . . . plus que	now only
ne . . . jamais	never	**ne . . . point**	not, no, not at all
ne . . . mie (archaic)	not a crumb, not	**ne . . . que**	only, but
ne . . . mot (archaic)	not a word, nothing	**ne . . . rien**	nothing

B) The position of **ne** in the sentence is that of column 2 of §87. The position of **pas** and all the other like words, with the exception of **aucun, ni . . . ni, nul, personne,** and **que** is that of column 9. The position of **aucun, nul, personne,** and **que** is that of column 11. And the position of the first **ni** of **ni . . . ni** is that of column 11 unless the past participle is one of the correlatives, in which case its position is that of column 9.

Aucun, nul, pas un, personne, and rien may be used as subjects of the verb; they then precede **ne** and the verb, e.g., **personne n'est ici** no one is here. And **aucun, nul,** and **pas un** may be used as adjectives in the same position, e.g., **nul péril ne l'arrête** no danger stops him.

Usually when an infinitive is in the negative, **pas** immediately follows **ne**, e.g., **il m'a dit de ne pas y aller** he told me not to go there; e.g., **il regrette de ne pas me l'avoir dit** he regrets not having told me it.

C) The adverb **ne** is often used without **pas** or a similar word with the verbs **bouger, cesser, oser, pouvoir,** and **savoir,** e.g., **je ne saurais vous le dire** I can't tell you. And it is not translated (1) with a compound tense after **il y a . . . que, voilà . . . que,** and **depuis que,** e.g., **il y a trois jours que je ne l'ai vu** it is three days since I saw him or

(2) with the verb of a clause introduced by a) **à moins que, avant que, empêcher . . . que,** and éviter **. . . que,** e.g., **à moins que je ne sois retenu** unless I am detained; b) **si** meaning unless, e.g., **si je ne me trompe** unless I am mistaken; c) a comparative + **que,** e.g., **vous étiez plus occupé qu'il ne l'était** you were busier than he was; d) a verb or expression of fear such as **avoir peur que, craindre que, redouter que,** e.g., **je crains qu'il ne soit malade** I am afraid that he is sick; e) a negative verb or expression of doubt, denial, despair such as **ne pas désespérer que, ne pas disconvenir que, ne pas douter que, ne pas nier que,** e.g., **je ne doute pas qu'il ne vienne** I do not doubt that he will come.

§91 *adj & adv comp & super* The comparative of superiority of adjectives and adverbs is formed by placing **plus** before the positive, e.g., **heureux** happy, **plus heureux** happier. The superlative of superiority of adjectives and adverbs is the same as the comparative, e.g., **heureux** happy, **plus heureux** happier and happiest. It is to be observed that the superlative is generally used in both French and English with the definite article or the possessive pronoun, e.g., **le plus heureux** the happiest, **son plus heureux** his happiest.

Some adjectives and adverbs have irregular comparatives and superlatives.

ADJECTIVES		ADVERBS	
positive	*comp and super*	*positive*	*comp and super*
bon good	**meilleur** better; best	**beaucoup** much	**plus** more; most
mauvais bad	**pire** worse; worst	**bien** well	**mieux** better; best
petit small	**moindre** lesser, less; least	**mal** badly	**pis** worse; worst
		peu little	**moins** less; least

FRENCH–ENGLISH

A

A, a [α], *[α] *m invar* first letter of the French alphabet
à [a] *prep* to, into; at; by, e.g., **à l'année** by the year; from, e.g., **arracher à** to snatch from; in, e.g., **à l'italienne** in the Italian manner; on, e.g., **à temps** on time; with, e.g., **la jeune fille aux yeux bleus** the girl with the blue eyes
abaisse-langue [abɛslɑ̃g] *m invar* tongue depressor
abaissement [abɛsmɑ̃] *m* lowering; drop; humbling
abaisser [abɛse] *tr* to lower; to humble || *ref* to go down; to humble oneself; to condescend
abandon [abɑ̃dɔ̃] *m* abandon; abandonment; desertion; neglect
abandonner [abɑ̃dɔne] *tr* to abandon; to forsake; to give up || *ref* to neglect oneself, become slovenly; **s'abandonner à** to give way to
abasourdir [abazurdir] *tr* to dumfound, flabbergast; to deafen
abasourdis•sant [abazurdisɑ̃] **abasourdis•sante** [abazurdisɑ̃t] *adj* astounding
abâtardir [abɑtardir] *tr* to debase || *ref* to deteriorate, to degenerate
abâtardissement [abɑtardismɑ̃] *m* debasement; deterioration, degeneration
abat-jour [abaʒur] *m invar* lampshade; eyeshade, sun visor; skylight
abats [aba] *mpl* giblets
abattage [abataʒ] *m* slaughtering (*of animals*); felling (*of trees*); demolition (*of a building*); bag, bagging (*of game*)
abattant [abatɑ̃] *m* drop leaf
abattement [abatmɑ̃] *m* dejection, despondency; prostration; tax deduction
abatteur [abatœr] *m* slaughterer; woodcutter; **abatteur de besogne** hard worker
abattis [abati] *m* felling (*of trees*); clearing (*of woods*); (mil) abatis; **abattis** *mpl* giblets; (slang) arms and legs
abattoir [abatwar] *m* slaughterhouse
abattre [abatr] §7 *tr* to pull down, to demolish; to fell; to slaughter; to overthrow; to discourage; to shoot down, to bring down (*a bird, airplane, etc.*); to lay (*dust*); (cards) to lay down (*one's hand*) || *ref* to abate, subside; to be dejected; to swoop down; to pounce; to crash (*said of airplane*)
abat•tu -tue [abaty] *adj* dejected, downcast

abat-vent [abavɑ̃] *m invar* chimney pot
abbaye [abei] *f* abbey
abbé [abe] *m* abbot; abbé, father
abbesse [abɛs] *f* abbess
a b c [abese] *m* (letterword) ABC's; speller
abcès [apsɛ] *m* abscess
abdiquer [abdike] *tr & intr* to abdicate
abdomen [abdɔmɛn] *m* abdomen
abécédaire [abesedɛr] *m* speller
abeille [abɛj] *f* bee
abêtir [abɛtir] *tr* to make stupid || *intr & ref* to become stupid
abhorrer [abɔre] *tr* to abhor
abîme [abim] *m* abyss; depth
abîmer [abime] *tr* to spoil; to damage || *ref* to sink; to be sunk; to get spoiled
ab•ject -jecte [abʒɛkt] *adj* abject
abjurer [abʒyre] *tr* to abjure
abla•tif [ablatif] **-tive** [tiv] *adj & m* ablative
aboiement [abwamɑ̃] *m* barking; yelp, cry, outcry
abois [abwa] *mpl* desperate straits; **aux abois** at bay; hard pressed
abolir [abɔlir] *tr* to abolish; to annul
abomination [abɔminɑsjɔ̃] *f* abomination
abondamment [abɔ̃damɑ̃] *adv* abundantly
abondance [abɔ̃dɑ̃s] *f* abundance, plenty; wealth; flow (*of words*); **parler d'abondance** to ad-lib
abon•dant [abɔ̃dɑ̃] **-dante** [dɑ̃t] *adj* abundant, plentiful; wordy
abon•né -née [abɔne] *mf* subscriber; season-ticket holder; consumer (*of gas, electricity, etc.*); commuter (*on railroad*)
abonnement [abɔnmɑ̃] *m* subscription
abonner [abɔne] *tr* to take out a subscription for (*s.o.*) || *ref* to subscribe, take out a subscription
abord [abɔr] *m* approach; **abords** outskirts, surroundings; **d'abord** at first; **d'un abord facile** easy to approach; **tout d'abord** first of all
abordable [abɔrdabl] *adj* approachable, accessible; reasonable (*price*)
abordage [abɔrdaʒ] *m* (naut) boarding; (naut) collision
aborder [abɔrde] *tr* to approach, to accost; to board; to collide with, run afoul of || *intr* to land, to go ashore
aborigène [abɔriʒɛn] *adj & m* native, aboriginal
abor•tif [abɔrtif] **-tive** [tiv] *adj* abortive
aboucher [abuʃe] *tr* to join; to bring together || *ref* to have an interview

aboutir [abutir] *intr* to end; to come to an end

aboutissement [abutismã] *m* outcome, result

aboyer [abwaje] §47 *intr* to bark; to bay

abracada·brant [abrakadabrã] **-brante** [brãt] *adj* amazing, breath-taking

abra·sif [abrazif] **-sive** [ziv] *adj & m* abrasive

abrégé [abreʒe] *m* abridgment, summary

abrégement [abreʒmã] *m* abridgment

abréger [abreʒe] §1 *tr* to abridge; to shorten, curtail

abreuvage [abrœvaʒ] *m* watering

abreuver [abrœve] *tr* to water; to soak; to overwhelm, to shower || *ref* to drink

abreuvoir [abrœvwar] *m* drinking trough, watering trough, horsepond

abréviation [abrevjɑsjɔ̃] *f* abbreviation; abridgment, curtailment

abri [abri] *m* shelter, refuge, cover; air-raid shelter; **à l'abri de** protected from

abricot [abriko] *m* apricot

abricotier [abrikɔtje] *m* apricot tree

abri-promenade [abriprɔmnad] *m* hurricane deck, shelter deck

abriter [abrite] *tr* to shelter, protect, shield, screen || *ref* to take shelter

abroger [abrɔʒe] §38 *tr* to abrogate, repeal

a·brupt -brupte [abrypt] *adj* abrupt, steep; rough, crude; blunt

abru·ti -tie [abryti] *adj* sottish

abrutir [abrytir] *tr* to brutalize; to besot; to overwhelm

abrutis·sant [abrytisã] **abrutis·sante** [abrytisãt] *adj* stupefying; deadening

absence [apsãs] *f* absence

ab·sent [apsã] **-sente** [sãt] *adj* absent; absent-minded || *mf* absentee

absenter [apsãte] *ref* to absent oneself, be absent, stay away

abside [apsid] *f* apse

absinthe [apsɛ̃t] *f* absinthe, wormwood; absinthe (*liqueur*)

abso·lu -lue [apsɔly] *adj* absolute

absolument [apsɔlymã] *adv* absolutely

absor·bant [apsɔrbã] **-bante** [bãt] *adj* absorbent; absorbing || *m* absorbent

absorber [apsɔrbe] *tr* to absorb, to soak up; to eat up; to drink || *ref* to become absorbed, be deeply interested

absoudre [apsudr] §60 (*pp* **absous, absoute**; no *pret* or *imperf subj*) *tr* to absolve; to forgive; to acquit

abstenir [apstənir] §72 *ref* to abstain, refrain

absti·nent [apstinã] **-nente** [nãt] *adj* abstinent; abstemious || *mf* moderate eater or drinker

abstraction [apstraksjɔ̃] *f* abstraction; **faire abstraction de** to leave out, to disregard

abstraire [apstrɛr] §68 (no *pret* or *imperf subj*) *tr* to abstract || *ref* to become engrossed

abs·trait [apstrɛ] **-traite** [trɛt] *adj* abstract

abs·trus [apstry] **-truse** [tryz] *adj* abstruse

absurde [apsyrd] *adj* absurd

absurdité [apsyrdite] *f* absurdity

abus [aby] *m* abuse

abuser [abyze] *tr* to deceive || *intr* to exaggerate; **abuser de** to take advantage of, to impose upon; to indulge unwisely in || *ref* to be mistaken

abu·sif [abyzif] **-sive** [ziv] *adj* abusive, wrong

acacia [akasja] *m* locust tree; **faux acacia** black locust tree

académicien [akademisjɛ̃] *m* academician

académie [akademi] *f* academy

académique [akademik] *adj* academic

acagnarder [akaɲarde] *tr* to make lazy || *ref* to grow lazy; to lounge

acajou [akaʒu] *m* mahogany; mahogany tree; **acajou à pommes** (bot) cashew

acariâtre [akarjɑtr] *adj* grumpy

acca·blant [akɑblã] **-blante** [blɑ̃t] *adj* overwhelming

accabler [akɑble] *tr* to overwhelm; to weigh down

accalmie [akalmi] *f* lull, standstill

accaparer [akapare] *tr* to corner (*the market*); to monopolize

accéder [aksede] §10 *intr* to accede; to acquiesce; to have access

accéléra·teur [akseleratœr] **-trice** [tris] *adj* accelerating || *m* accelerator

accélérer [akselere] §10 *tr, intr, & ref* to accelerate

accent [aksã] *m* accent; **accent de hauteur** pitch accent; **accent d'insistance** emphasis; **accent d'intensité** stress accent; **accent tonique** tonic accent

accentuer [aksãtɥe] *tr* to accent || *ref* to become more marked

acceptable [aksɛptabl] *adj* acceptable

acceptation [aksɛptasjɔ̃] *f* acceptance

accepter [aksɛpte] *tr* to accept || *intr—* **accepter de** to agree to

acception [aksɛpsjɔ̃] *f* sense, meaning; preference, partiality

accès [aksɛ] *m* access; outburst; (pathol) attack, bout; **accès aux quais** (public sign) to the docks

accessible [aksɛsibl] *adj* accessible; susceptible

accession [aksɛsjɔ̃] *f* accession

accessit [aksesit] *m* honorable mention

accessoire [aksɛswar] *adj* accessory || **accessoires** *mpl* accessories; (theat) properties

accident [aksidã] *m* accident; unevenness (*of ground*); (mus) accidental

acciden·té -tée [aksidãte] *adj* rough, uneven; bumpy (*road*); eventful (*life*); (coll) wrecked (*car*) || *mf* (coll) casualty, victim

acciden·tel -telle [aksidãtɛl] *adj* accidental

accidenter [aksidãte] *tr* to make uneven; to vary; to injure

accise [aksiz] *f* excise tax

acclamer [aklame] *tr* to acclaim

acclimater [aklimate] *tr* to acclimate || *ref* to become acclimated

accolade [akɔlad] *f* embrace; accolade; (mus, typ) brace

accoler [akɔle] *tr* to hug; to join side by side; to couple (*names*); (typ) to brace

accommo·dant [akɔmɔdɑ̃] -**dante** [dɑ̃t] *adj* accommodating, obliging

accommodation [akɔmɔdɑsjɔ̃] *f* accommodation

accommodement [akɔmɔdmɑ̃] *m* settlement, compromise; arrangement

accommoder [akɔmɔde] *tr* to accommodate; to conciliate; to arrange (*furniture*); to prepare (*food*)

accompagna·teur [akɔ̃paɲatœr] -**trice** [tris] *mf* accompanist

accompagnement [akɔ̃paɲmɑ̃] *m* accompaniment

accompagner [akɔ̃paɲe] *tr* to accompany

accom·pli -plie [akɔ̃pli] *adj* completed; polished; accomplished

accomplir [akɔ̃plir] *tr* to accomplish; to complete; to fulfill (*a promise*) ‖ *ref* to come to pass

accomplissement [akɔ̃plismɑ̃] *m* accomplishment, performance

accord [akɔr] *m* accord, agreement, consent; harmony; settlement, bargain; (mus) chord; (mus) tuning; **d'accord** in accord; **d'accord!** O.K.!, check!; **d'un commun accord** by common consent

accordage [akɔrdaʒ] *m* tuning

accordéon [akɔrdeɔ̃] *m* accordion; **en accordéon** squashed; accordion-pleated

accorder [akɔrde] *tr* to grant; to reconcile; (mus, rad) to tune ‖ *intr*— **accorder à qn de** to allow s.o. to ‖ *ref* to harmonize; to tally; to agree

ac·cort [akɔr] **ac·corte** [akɔrt] *adj* sprightly, engaging (e.g., *young lady*)

accoster [akɔste] *tr* to approach ‖ *intr* to dock, to berth

accotement [akɔtmɑ̃] *m* shoulder (*of a road*)

accoter [akɔte] *tr* to shore up ‖ *ref* to lean

accouchement [akuʃmɑ̃] *m* childbirth

accoucher [akuʃe] *tr* to deliver ‖ *intr* (*aux:* ÊTRE) to be confined, to be delivered ‖ *intr* (*aux:* AVOIR)—**accoucher de** to give birth to

accou·cheur [akuʃœr] -**cheuse** [ʃøz] *mf* obstetrician

accouder [akude] *ref* to lean on one's elbows

accoudoir [akudwar] *m* armrest

accouple [akupl] *f* leash

accouplement [akupləmɑ̃] *m* coupling; **accouplement consanguin** inbreeding

accoupler [akuple] *tr* to couple; to yoke; to bring together for breeding; to link; (elec) to hook up ‖ *ref* to mate

accourir [akurir] §14 *intr* (*aux:* AVOIR or ÊTRE) to run up

accoutrement [akutrəmɑ̃] *m* togs, get-up

accoutrer [akutre] *tr* to rig out ‖ *ref* to dress ridiculously

accoutu·mé -mée [akutyme] *adj* accustomed; **à l'accoutumée** as usual ‖ *mf* regular customer; frequent visitor

accoutumer [akutyme] *tr* to accustom ‖ *ref* to become accustomed

accouvage [akuvaʒ] *m* artificial incubation

accouver [akuve] *tr* to set (*a hen*) ‖ *intr* to set (*said of a hen*) ‖ *ref* to begin to set

accréditer [akredite] *tr* to accredit; to win a hearing for; **accrédité auprès de** accredited to ‖ *ref* to gain credence or favor

accréditeur [akreditœr] *m* bondsman

accroc [akro] *m* tear (*in a dress*); (fig) snag, hitch

accrochage [akrɔʃaʒ] *m* hanging; hooking; clinch (*in boxing*); collision; (mil) encounter; (rad) receiving; (coll) squabble

accroche [akrɔʃ] *m* hanger

accrocher [akrɔʃe] *tr* to hang, to hang up; to hook; to catch; (mil) to come to grips with; (rad) to pick up; (coll) to buttonhole ‖ *ref* (coll) to come to blows; to cling; to catch; to get caught

accroire [akrwar] (used only in *inf* after **faire**) *tr*—**faire accroire** (with *dat*) to make (s.o.) believe ‖ *ref*— **s'en faire accroire** to get a swelled head

accroissement [akrwasmɑ̃] *m* growth; accumulation (*of capital*); increment

accroître [akrwatr] §17 (*pp* **accru**; *pres ind* **accrois**; *pret* **accrus**, etc.) *tr* & *ref* to increase

accroupir [akrupir] *ref* to squat, to crouch

accu [aky] *m* storage battery

accueil [akœj] *m* reception, welcome

accueil·lant [akœjɑ̃] **accueil·lante** [akœjɑ̃t] *adj* hospitable, gracious

accueillir [akœjir] §18 *tr* to welcome; to honor (*a bill*)

acculer [akyle] *tr* to corner

accumulateur [akymylatœr] *m* storage battery

accumuler [akymyle] *tr, intr,* & *ref* to accumulate

accusa·teur [akyzatœr] -**trice** [tris] *adj* incriminating ‖ *mf* accuser

accusatif [akyzatif] *m* accusative

accusation [akyzasjɔ̃] *f* accusation; charge

accu·sé -sée [akyze] *adj* marked; prominent (*features*) ‖ *mf* defendant ‖ *m* acknowledgment (*of receipt*)

accuser [akyze] *tr* to accuse; to acknowledge (*receipt*)

acerbe [asɛrb] *adj* sour; sharp; caustic (*remark*)

acé·ré -rée [asere] *adj* keen (*edge*); sharp (*tongue*)

acétate [asetat] *m* acetate

acétique [asetik] *adj* acetic

acétone [asetɔn] *f* acetone

achalander [aʃalɑ̃de] *tr* to attract customers to ‖ *ref* to get customers

achar·né -née [aʃarne] *adj* fierce; relentless (*pursuit*); inveterate (*gambler*); bitter (*enemy*); **acharné à** bent on, set on

acharnement [aʃarnəmã] *m* fierceness, fury; stubbornness; eagerness
acharner [aʃarne] *tr* to set, to sic (*dogs*); to bait (*a trap*) ‖ *ref* to fight bitterly; s'acharner à to work away at; to be bent on, to persist in; s'acharner contre to attack fiercely; s'acharner sur to light into; to swoop down upon; to bear down on; to be dead set against
achat [aʃa] *m* purchase; achat à terme installment buying; aller aux achats to go shopping
ache [aʃ] *f* wild celery
acheminement [aʃminmã] *m* forwarding; progress
acheminer [aʃmine] *tr* to direct ‖ *ref* to proceed
acheter [aʃte] §2 *tr* to buy; acheter à to buy from; to buy for; acheter de to buy from; acheter pour to buy for
achèvement [aʃɛvmã] *m* completion
achever [aʃve] §2 *tr* to complete; to finish off, kill ‖ *intr* to end; to be just finishing ‖ *ref* to come to an end
Achille [aʃil] *m* Achilles
achoppement [aʃɔpmã] *m* obstacle; impact
achopper [aʃɔpe] *intr & ref* to stumble
achromatique [akrɔmatik] *adj* achromatic
acide [asid] *adj & m* acid; acide phénique carbolic acid
acidité [asidite] *f* acidity
acidu·lé -lée [asidyle] *adj* acid; fruit-flavored
aciduler [asidyle] *tr* to acidulate
acier [asje] *m* steel; (fig) sword; acier inoxydable stainless steel
aciérie [asjeri] *f* steelworks, steel mill
acmé [akme] *f* acme; (pathol) crisis
acolyte [akɔlit] *m* acolyte; accomplice
acompte [akɔ̃t] *m* installment; deposit, down payment; acompte provisionnel payment on estimated income tax
Açores [asɔr] *fpl* Azores
à-côté [akote] *m* (*pl* -côtés) sidelight; path (*beside road*); kickback
à-coup [aku] *m* (*pl* -coups) jerk; par à-coups by fits and starts
acoustique [akustik] *adj* acoustic, acoustical ‖ *f* acoustics
acquéreur [akerœr] *m* buyer
acquérir [akerir] §3 *tr* to acquire, to get
acquiescement [akjɛsmã] *m* acquiescence
acquiescer [akjese] §51 *intr* to acquiesce
ac·quis [aki] -quise [kiz] *adj* established ‖ *m* know-how
acquisition [akizisjɔ̃] *f* acquisition
acquit [aki] *m* receipt; pour acquit paid in full
acquit-à-caution [akitakosjɔ̃] *m* (*pl* acquits-à-caution) permit to transport in bond
acquittement [akitmã] *m* acquittal
acquitter [akite] *tr* to acquit; to receipt (*a bill*); to pay, discharge ‖ *ref* to pay one's debts; s'acquitter de to fulfill, to perform
âcre [akr] *adj* acrid

acrimo·nieux [akrimɔnjø] -nieuse [njøz] *adj* acrimonious
acrobate [akrɔbat] *mf* acrobat
acrobatie [akrɔbasi] *f* acrobatics
acropole [akrɔpɔl] *f* acropolis
acrostiche [akrɔstiʃ] *m* acrostic
acte [akt] *m* action; bill; act; certificate, deed; acte de présence personal appearance; acte de vente bill of sale; actes minutes; faire acte to make a declaration; prendre acte to take minutes
acteur [aktœr] *m* actor
ac·tif [aktif] -tive [tiv] *adj* active; full (*citizen*) ‖ *m* credit side (*of an account*); assets; (gram) active voice
action [aksjɔ̃] *f* action; share (*of stock*); action de grâces thanksgiving
actionnaire [aksjɔnɛr] *mf* stockholder
actionner [aksjɔne] *tr* to actuate; to drive; to sue
activer [aktive] *tr* to activate; to hasten ‖ *ref* to hasten
activité [aktivite] *f* activity; active service; en pleine activité in full swing
actrice [aktris] *f* actress
actuaire [aktɥɛr] *mf* actuary
actualisation [aktɥalizɑsjɔ̃] *f* modernization
actualiser [aktɥalize] *tr* to modernize, to bring up to date
actualité [aktɥalite] *f* present condition; actualités current events; newsreel; d'actualité newsworthy
ac·tuel -tuelle [aktɥɛl] *adj* present, present-day, current
actuellement [aktɥɛlmã] *adv* now, at the present time
acuité [akɥite] *f* acuity
adage [adaʒ] *m* adage
Adam [adɑ̃] *m* Adam
adapta·teur [adaptatœr] -trice [tris] *mf* adapter ‖ *m* (mov) adapter
adaptation [adaptɑsjɔ̃] *f* adaptation
adapter [adapte] *tr & ref* to adapt
addenda [adɛ̃da] *m invar* addendum
addi·tif [aditif] -tive [tiv] *adj & m* additive
addition [adisjɔ̃] *f* addition; check (*for a restaurant meal*)
additionner [adisjɔne] *tr* to add up; to add; to dilute, mix
adénoïde [adenɔid] *adj* adenoid
adent [adɑ̃] *m* dovetail
adepte [adɛpt] *mf* adept
adé·quat [adekwa] -quate [kwat] *adj* adequate
adhérence [aderɑ̃s] *f* adherence; traction; (pathol) adhesion
adhé·rent [adeɑ̃] -rente [rɑ̃t] *adj & mf* adherent
adhérer [adere] §10 *intr* to adhere; to stick; adhérer à la route to hold the road
adhé·sif [adezif] -sive [ziv] *adj & m* adhesive
adhésion [adezjɔ̃] *f* adhesion
adieu [adjø] *m* (*pl* adieux) farewell ‖ *interj* adieu!, bon voyage!; good riddance!; sans adieu! see you later!
adja·cent [adʒasɑ̃] -cente [sɑ̃t] *adj* adjacent

adjec·tif [adʒɛktif] -**tive** [tiv] *adj* & *m* adjective
adjoindre [adʒwɛ̃dr] §35 *tr* & *ref* to join
ad·joint [adʒwɛ̃] -**jointe** [ʒwɛ̃t] *adj* & *mf* assistant, stand-by
adjudant [adʒydɑ̃] *m* warrant officer; sergeant major; (pej) martinet
adjudication [adʒydikɑsjɔ̃] *f* auction; awarding (*of a contract*)
adjuger [adʒyʒe] §38 *tr* to adjudge, award; to knock down (*at auction*)
admettre [admɛtr] §42 *tr* to admit
administra·teur [administratœr] -**trice** [tris] *mf* administrator, director
administration [administrɑsjɔ̃] *f* administration; **administration des ponts et chaussées** highway department
administrer [administre] *tr* to administer
admira·teur [admiratœr] -**trice** [tris] *mf* admirer
admira·tif [admiratif] -**tive** [tiv] *adj* admiring; amazed
admiration [admirɑsjɔ̃] *f* admiration; wonder
admirer [admire] *tr* to admire; to wonder at
admissible [admisibl] *adj* admissible; eligible
admission [admisjɔ̃] *f* admission; (aut) intake
admonester [admɔnɛste] *tr* to admonish
adolescence [adɔlesɑ̃s] *f* adolescence
adoles·cent [adɔlesɑ̃] **adoles·cente** [adɔlesɑ̃t] *adj* & *mf* adolescent
adonner [adɔne] *ref* to devote oneself; **s'adonner à** to give oneself up to
adopter [adɔpte] *tr* to adopt
adop·tif [adɔptif] -**tive** [tiv] *adj* adopted; adoptive
adoption [adɔpsjɔ̃] *f* adoption
adorable [adɔrabl] *adj* adorable
adora·teur [adɔratœr] -**trice** [tris] *mf* adorer; worshiper
adoration [adɔrɑsjɔ̃] *f* adoration
adorer [adɔre] *tr* to adore, worship
adosser [adɔse] *tr*—**adosser q.ch. à** to turn the back of s.th. against || *ref*—**s'adosser à** to lean back against
adouber [adube] *tr* to dub
adoucir [adusir] *tr* to soften || *ref* to soften; to grow milder
adrénaline [adrenalin] *f* adrenalin
adresse [adrɛs] *f* address; skill, dexterity; neatness; expertness, expertise; **adresse particulière** home address
adresser [adrɛse] *tr* to address || *ref* to apply
Adriatique [adriatik] *adj* & *f* Adriatic
a·droit [adrwa] -**droite** [drwat] *adj* adroit, clever; neat
aduler [adyle] *tr* to adulate
adulte [adylt] *adj* & *mf* adult
adultère [adyltɛr] *adj* adulterous || *m* adultery; adulterer || *f* adulteress
adultérer [adyltere] §10 *tr* to adulterate; to falsify (*a text*)
adulté·rin [adylterɛ̃] -**rine** [rin] *adj* born in adultery
advenir [advənir] §72 (used only in *inf*; *pp*; 3d *pers sg* & *pl*) *intr* (*aux*: ÊTRE)

to come to pass; **advienne que pourra** come what may
adventice [advɑ̃tis] *adj* adventitious
adverbe [advɛrb] *m* adverb
adversaire [advɛrsɛr] *mf* adversary
adverse [advɛrs] *adj* adverse; opposite (*side*)
adversité [advɛrsite] *f* adversity
aérer [aere] §10 *tr* to aerate; to ventilate; to air
aé·rien [aɛrjɛ̃] -**rienne** [rjɛn] *adj* aerial || *m* elevated railway
aéro [aero] *m* airplane
aérodynamique [aerɔdinamik] *adj* aerodynamic; streamlined || *f* aerodynamics
aérogare [aerɔgar] *f* air terminal
aéroglisseur [aerɔglisœr] *m* hydrofoil
aérogramme [aerɔgram] *m* air letter
aérolite or **aérolithe** [aerɔlit] *m* meteorite, aerolite
aéronef [aerɔnɛf] *m* aircraft
aérophare [aerɔfar] *m* air beacon
aéroport [aerɔpɔr] *m* airport
aéropor·té -**tée** [aerɔpɔrte] *adj* airborne
aéropos·tal -**tale** [aerɔpɔstal] *adj* (*pl* -**taux** [to]) air-mail
aérosol [aerɔsɔl] *m* aerosol
aérospa·tial -**tiale** [aerɔspasjal] *adj* (*pl* -**tiaux** [sjo]) aerospace
A.F. *abbr* (**allocations familiales**) family (social security) allotments
affable [afabl] *adj* affable
affadir [afadir] *tr* & *ref* to stale
affaiblir [afɛblir] *tr* & *ref* to weaken
affaire [afɛr] *f* affair; job; business; trouble; (law) case; (coll) belongings; **affaire à saisir** bargain; **affaire d'or** (fig) gold mine; **affaire en instance** unfinished business; **affaires** business; **bonne affaire** bargain; **cela fait mon affaire** that is just what I want
affai·ré -**rée** [afere] *adj* busy, bustling
affairiste [aferist] *m* slicker, operator
affaissement [afɛsmɑ̃] *m* sagging; cave-in, collapse
affaisser [afɛse] *tr* to weigh down; to depress || *ref* to sag; to cave in, to collapse
affaler [afale] *tr* to haul down || *ref* to drop, sink, flop
affa·mé -**mée** [afame] *adj* famished, starved
affamer [afame] *tr* to starve
affectable [afɛktabl] *adj* impressionable; mortgageable
affectation [afɛktɑsjɔ̃] *f* affectation; assignment; allotment
affec·té -**tée** [afɛkte] *adj* affected; assigned
affecter [afɛkte] *tr* to affect; to assign; to assume (*various shapes or manners*) || *ref* to grieve
affec·tif [afɛktif] -**tive** [tiv] *adj* affective, emotional
affection [afɛksjɔ̃] *f* affection; mental state; disease, affection
affection·né -**née** [afɛksjɔne] *adj* loving, fond, devoted

affectionner [afɛksjɔne] *tr* to be fond of || *ref* to become attached
affectueusement [afɛktɥøzmɑ̃] *adv* affectionately
affec·tueux [afɛktɥø] -tueuse [tɥøz] *adj* affectionate
affé·rent [aferɑ̃] -rente [rɑ̃t] *adj* due, accruing
affermer [afɛrme] *tr* to lease, to rent
affermir [afɛrmir] *tr* to strengthen, harden || *ref* to become stronger, sounder
affichage [afiʃaʒ] *m* billposting
affiche [afiʃ] *f* poster, bill; (theat) playbill
afficher [afiʃe] *tr* to post, to post up; to display; (theat) to bill || *ref* to seek the limelight; **s'afficher avec** to hang around with
afficheur [afiʃœr] *m* billposter
affi·lé -lée [afile] *adj* sharpened; sharp *(tongue)* || *adv*—**d'affilée** in a row
affiler [afile] *tr* to sharpen, to whet; to hone, to strop; to set *(a saw)*
affi·lié -liée [afilje] *adj* & *mf* affiliate
affilier [afilje] *tr* & *ref* to affiliate
affiloir [afilwar] *m* sharpener; whetstone; hone, strop
affiner [afine] *tr* to improve; to refine; to sift || *ref* to improve; to mature, ripen
affinité [afinite] *f* affinity; in-law relationship
affirma·tif [afirmatif] -tive [tiv] *adj* & *f* affirmative
affirmer [afirme] *tr* to affirm || *ref* to assert oneself; **s'affirmer comme** to take one's place as
affixe [afiks] *m* affix
affleurer [aflœre] *tr* to level; to come up to the level of || *intr* to come to the surface
affliction [afliksjɔ̃] *f* affliction
affli·gé -gée [afliʒe] *adj* sorrowful
affli·geant [afliʒɑ̃] -geante [ʒɑ̃t] *adj* sorrowful *(news)*
affliger [afliʒe] §38 *tr* to afflict || *ref* to grieve, to sorrow; **s'affliger de** to sorrow for
affluence [aflyɑ̃s] *f* crowd
af·fluent [aflyɑ̃] af·fluente [aflyɑ̃t] *adj* & *m* tributary
affluer [aflye] *intr* to flow; to throng, crowd, flock
afflux [afly] *m* afflux, flow; rush
affo·lé -lée [afɔle] *adj* panic-stricken
affolement [afɔlmɑ̃] *m* distraction, panic; infatuation; unsteadiness *(of a compass)*
affoler [afɔle] *tr* to distract, to panic; to infatuate; to disturb *(compass)* || *ref* to be distracted; to stampede; to become infatuated; to spin *(as a compass)*
affran·chi -chie [afrɑ̃ʃi] *adj* emancipated; postpaid || *mf* freethinker
affranchir [afrɑ̃ʃir] *tr* to emancipate, free; to pay the postage for
affranchissement [afrɑ̃ʃismɑ̃] *m* emancipation; payment of postage; cancellation *(of mail)*; **affranchissement insuffisant** postage due
affres [afr] *fpl* pangs

affrètement [afrɛtmɑ̃] *m* chartering *(of a boat)*
affréter [afrete] §10 *tr* to charter *(a boat)*
af·freux [afrø] af·freuse [afrøz] *adj* frightful
affront [afrɔ̃] *m* affront
affronter [afrɔ̃te] *tr* to confront; to face
affût [afy] *m* hunting blind; mount *(for cannon)*; **être à l'affût de** to lie in wait for
affûter [afyte] *tr* to sharpen
afin [afɛ̃] *adv*—**afin de** in order to; **afin que** in order that, so that
afri·cain [afrikɛ̃] -caine [kɛn] *adj* African || *(cap)* *mf* African
Afrique [afrik] *f* Africa; **l'Afrique** Africa
agacement [agasmɑ̃] *m* irritation, annoyance
agacer [agase] §51 *tr* to irritate, annoy; to tease; to set on edge
agape [agap] *f* agape; **agapes** banquet
âge [aʒ] *m* age; **d'un certain âge** middle-aged; **quel âge avez-vous?** how old are you?
â·gé -gée [aʒe] *adj* old, aged; old, e.g., **âgé de seize ans** sixteen years old
agence [aʒɑ̃s] *f* agency, office, service, bureau; **agence de location** rental service; real-estate office; **agence de voyages** travel bureau; **agence immobilière** real-estate office
agencement [aʒɑ̃smɑ̃] *m* arrangement; furnishing *(of a house)*; construction *(of a sentence)*; **agencements** fixtures
agencer [aʒɑ̃se] §51 *tr* to arrange
agenda [aʒɛ̃da] *m* engagement book
agenouiller [aʒnuje] *ref* to kneel
agent [aʒɑ̃] *m* agent; policeman; **agent comptable** accountant; **agent de change** stockbroker; **agent de location** realtor
agglomération [aglɔmerasjɔ̃] *f* agglomeration; metropolitan area; built-up area
agglomé·ré -rée [aglɔmere] *adj* compressed || *m* briquette; adobe
agglomérer [aglɔmere] §10 *tr* & *ref* to agglomerate
aggraver [agrave] *tr* to aggravate || *ref* to become more serious
agile [aʒil] *adj* agile, nimble
agilité [aʒilite] *f* agility
agio·teur [aʒjɔtœr] -teuse [tøz] *mf* speculator
agir [aʒir] *intr* to act; to take action || *ref*—**il s'agit de** it is a question of
agis·sant [aʒisɑ̃] agis·sante [aʒisɑ̃t] *adj* active
agissements [aʒismɑ̃] *mpl* machinations
agita·teur [aʒitatœr] -trice [tris] *mf* agitator *(person)* || *m* stirrer
agi·té -tée [aʒite] *adj* restless; rough *(sea)*
agiter [aʒite] *tr* to agitate; to stir; to wave; to discuss || *ref* to move about
a·gneau [aɲo] *m* *(pl* -gneaux) lamb
agnostique [agnɔstik] *adj* & *mf* agnostic
agonie [agɔni] *f* agony, death throes

agrafe [agraf] *f* clasp, pin; paper clip; staple (*for papers*); belt buckle; snap, hook; (med) clamp

agrafer [agrafe] *tr* to clasp, pin; to buckle; to snap; to hook; to fasten, to clip; to staple; (med) to clamp

agrafeuse [agraføz] *f* stapler

agraire [agrɛr] *adj* agrarian

agrandir [agrɑ̃dir] *tr* to enlarge ‖ *ref* to grow, become larger

agrandissement [agrɑ̃dismɑ̃] *m* enlargement

agréable [agreabl] *adj* agreeable, pleasant; neighborly

agréé agréée [agree] *adj* approved ‖ *m* attorney

agréer [agree] *tr* to accept, approve; **veuillez agréer l'expression de mes sentiments distingués** (complimentary close) sincerely yours ‖ *intr* (with *dat*) to agree with, to please

agrégat [agrega] *m* aggregate

agrégation [agregɑsjɔ̃] *f* aggregation; admittance (*as a member of an organization*); competitive teacher's examination

agré·gé -gée [agreʒe] *adj* aggregate ‖ *mf* one who has passed his *agrégation*

agréger [agreʒe] §1 *tr* to attach, to add ‖ *ref*—**s'agréger (à)** to join

agrément [agremɑ̃] *m* approval; pleasantness; pleasure, pastime; **agréments** adornments

agrès [agrɛ] *mpl* rigging; gym equipment

agresseur [agrɛsœr] *adj* & *m* aggressor

agres·sif [agresif] **agres·sive** [agresiv] *adj* aggressive

agression [agresjɔ̃] *f* aggression; (law) assault

agreste [agrɛst] *adj* rustic, rural

agricole [agrikɔl] *adj* agricultural

agriculture [agrikyltyr] *f* agriculture

agrumes [agrym] *mpl* citrus fruit

aguerrir [agɛrir] *tr* to season, inure ‖ *ref* to become seasoned, inured

aguets [agɛ] *mpl* watch, look-out; **être aux aguets** to be on the look-out

agui·chant [agi/ɑ̃] **-chante** [/ɑ̃t] *adj* alluring ‖ *adj fem* sexy

ah [a] *interj* ah!; now then!; **ah çà!** now then!

ahu·ri -rie [ayri] *adj* dumfounded

ahurir [ayrir] *tr* to dumfound

ahurissement [ayrismɑ̃] *m* stupefaction

aide [ɛd] *mf* aid, assistant, helper ‖ *f* aid, assistance, help; **aide sociale** welfare department

aider [ede] *tr* to aid, help; **aider** + *inf* to help to + *inf* ‖ *intr* to help ‖ *ref* —**s'aider de** to use

aïe [aj] *interj* ouch!

aïeul aïeule [ajœl] *mf* grandparent ‖ *m* grandfather ‖ *m* (*pl* **aïeux** [ajø]) ancestor ‖ *f* grandmother

aigle [ɛgl] *mf* eagle; **aigle de mer** eagle ray; **aigle pêcheur, grand aigle de mer** osprey, fish hawk; **grand aigle** spread eagle

aiglefin [ɛgləfɛ̃] *m* haddock

ai·glon [ɛglɔ̃] **-glonne** [glɔn] *mf* eaglet

aigre [ɛgr] *adj* sour, tart, bitter; harsh (*voice*)

aigre-doux [ɛgrədu] **-douce** [dus] *adj* bittersweet

aigrefin [ɛgrəfɛ̃] *m* crook

aigre·let [ɛgrəlɛ] **-lette** [lɛt] *adj* tart

aigrir [egrir] *tr* to turn (*s.th.*) sour ‖ *intr* & *ref* to turn sour

ai·gu -guë [egy] *adj* sharp; acute; shrill, high-pitched ‖ *m* (mus) treble

aigue-marine [ɛgmarin] *f* (*pl* **aigues-marines**) aquamarine

aiguille [egɥij] *f* needle; peak; spire (*of steeple*); hand (*of clock*); (rr) switch

aiguiller [egɥije] *tr* to switch, shunt ‖ *ref* to be switched, shunted

aiguilleur [egɥijœr] *m* (aer, rr) towerman

aiguillon [egɥijɔ̃] *m* goad; sting

aiguiser [egɥize] *tr* to sharpen; to whet (*appetite*)

ail [aj] *m* (*pl* **ails** or **aulx** [o]) garlic

aile [ɛl] *f* wing; flank (*of army*); fender (*of auto*); brim (*of hat*); blade (*of propeller*); vane, arm (*of windmill*); **aile en flèche** (aer) backswept wing

aileron [ɛlrɔ̃] *m* aileron

aílleurs [ajœr] *adv* elsewhere; **d'ailleurs** moreover, besides; from somewhere else; **par ailleurs** furthermore

aimable [emabl] *adj* kind, likeable; **voulez-vous être assez aimable de** will you be good enough to

aimant [emɑ̃] *m* magnet

aimanter [emɑ̃te] *tr* to magnetize

aimer [eme], [ɛme] *tr* to love; to like; to like to; **aimer à** to like to; **aimer bien** to like, to be fond of; to like to; **aimer mieux** to prefer; to prefer to

aine [ɛn] *f* groin

aî·né -née [ene] *adj* & *mf* elder, eldest; oldest; senior

aînesse [enɛs] *f* seniority

ainsi [ɛ̃si] *adv* thus; **ainsi de suite** and so forth; **ainsi nommé** so-called; **ainsi que** as well as; **ainsi soit-il** amen

air [ɛr] *m* air; look, appearance; **air de famille** family resemblance; **avoir l'air de** to seem to; **en l'air** empty, idle (*threats, talk*)

airain [ɛrɛ̃] *m* brass; bronze

aire [ɛr] *f* area; threshing floor; eyrie; **aire de lancement** launching pad

airelle [ɛrɛl] *f* huckleberry; blueberry

aisance [ɛzɑ̃s] *f* ease, comfort

aise [ɛz] *adj*—**bien aise** glad, content ‖ *f* ease; **aises** comforts; **à son aise** well-to-do

ai·sé -sée [eze] *adj* easy; natural; well-to-do

aisément [ezemɑ̃] *adv* easily

aisselle [ɛsɛl] *f* armpit

ajonc [aʒɔ̃] *m* furze

ajou·ré -rée [aʒure] *adj* openwork, perforated

ajourer [aʒure] *tr* to cut openings in

ajournement [aʒurnəmɑ̃] *m* adjournment, postponement; subpoenaing; rejection (*of a candidate*)

ajourner [aʒurne] *tr* to postpone; to subpoena; to reject (*a candidate in an examination*)

ajouter [aʒute] *tr & intr* to add || *ref* to be added

ajus·té **-tée** [aʒyste] *adj* tight-fitting

ajuster [aʒyste] *tr* to adjust; to arrange; to fit; to aim at

ajusteur [aʒystœr] *m* fitter

alacrité [alakrite] *f* gaiety, vivacity

alambic [alɑ̃bik] *m* still

alambi·qué **-quée** [alɑ̃bike] *adj* finespun, far-fetched

alanguir [alɑ̃gir] *tr* to weaken || *ref* to languish

alar·mant [alarmɑ̃] **-mante** [mɑ̃t] *adj* alarming

alarme [alarm] *f* alarm

alarmer [alarme] *tr* to alarm || *ref* to be alarmed

alba·nais [albanɛ] **-naise** [nɛz] *adj* Albanian || *m* Albanian (*language*) || (*cap*) *mf* Albanian (*person*)

albâtre [albɑtr] *m* alabaster

albatros [albatros] *m* albatross

albi·geois [albiʒwa] **-geoise** [ʒwaz] *adj* Albigensian || (*cap*) *mf* Albigensian

albinos [albinos] *adj & m* albino

album [albɔm] *m* album; scrapbook

albumen [albymɛn] *m* albumen

alcali [alkali] *m* alkali

alca·lin [alkalɛ̃] **-line** [lin] *adj* alkaline

alchimie [alʃimi] *f* alchemy

alcool [alkɔl] *m* alcohol; **alcool à friction** rubbing alcohol; **alcool dénaturé** denatured alcohol

alcoolique [alkɔɔlik], [alkɔlik] *adj & mf* alcoholic

alcôve [alkov] *f* alcove; **d'alcôve** amatory, gallant

ale [ɛl] *f* ale

aléa [alea] *m* risk

aléatoire [aleatwar] *adj* risky; aleatory

alène [alɛn] *f* awl

alentour [alɑ̃tur] *adv* round about || **alentours** *mpl* neighborhood

alerte [alɛrt] *adj & f* alert; **alerte aérienne** air-raid alarm

alerter [alɛrte] *tr* to alert

alésage [alezaʒ] *m* bore (*of cylinder*)

aléser [aleze] §10 *tr* to ream; to bore

ale·zan [alzɑ̃] **-zane** [zan] *adj* chestnut (*colored*)

algarade [algarad] *f* altercation

algèbre [alʒɛbr] *f* algebra

Alger [alʒe] *m* Algiers

Algérie [alʒeri] *f* Algeria

algé·rien [alʒerjɛ̃] **-rienne** [rjɛn] *adj* Algerian || (*cap*) *mf* Algerian

algé·rois [alʒerwa] **-roise** [rwaz] *adj* of Algiers; Algerian || (*cap*) *mf* native of Algiers; Algerian

algues [alg] *fpl* algae

alias [aljɑs] *adv* alias

alibi [alibi] *m* (*law*) alibi

alié·né **-née** [aljene] *adj* alienated; insane || *mf* insane person

aliéner [aljene] §10 *tr* to transfer, alienate || *ref* (with *dat* of *reflex pron*) to alienate (*s.o.*); (with *dat* of *reflex pron*) to lose (*e.g., s.o.'s sympathy*)

alignement [aliɲmɑ̃] *m* alignment

aligner [aliɲe] *tr* to align; **aligner ses phrases** to choose one's words with care || *ref* to line up

aliment [alimɑ̃] *m* aliment, food; **aliments** (law) necessities

alimentaire [alimɑ̃tɛr] *adj* alimentary; subsistence, e.g., **pension alimentaire** subsistence allowance

alimentation [alimɑ̃tasjɔ̃] *f* nourishment; supplying; feeding (*a fire, a machine*)

alimenter [alimɑ̃te] *tr* to nourish; to supply; to feed (*a fire, a machine*)

alinéa [alinea] *m* indentation (*of the first line of a paragraph*); paragraph

aliter [alite] *tr* to keep in bed || *ref* to be confined to bed

alizés [alize] *mpl* trade winds

allaiter [alɛte] *tr* to nurse

al·lant [alɑ̃] **al·lante** [alɑ̃t] *adj* active || *m*—**allants et venants** passers-by; **beaucoup d'allant** (coll) a lot of pep

allé·chant [aleʃɑ̃] **-chante** [ʃɑ̃t] *adj* enticing, tempting

allécher [aleʃe] §10 *tr* to allure

allée [ale] *f* walk, path; going; city street, boulevard; aisle (*of theater*)

allégeance [aleʒɑ̃s] *f* allegiance; lightening (*of care*); handicapping (*of a race*)

alléger [aleʒe] §1 *tr* to lighten; to alleviate, mitigate, relieve

allégorie [allegɔri] *f* allegory

allègre [allegr] *adj* lively, cheerful

alléguer [alege] §10 *tr* to allege as an excuse; to cite (*an authority*)

Allemagne [almaɲ] *f* Germany; **l'Allemagne** Germany

alle·mand [almɑ̃] **-mande** [mɑ̃d] *adj* German || *m* German (*language*) || (*cap*) *mf* German (*person*)

aller [ale] *m* going; go; **aller (et) retour** round trip; round-trip ticket; **au pis aller** at the worst || §4 *intr* (*aux:* ÊTRE) to go; to work, function; (with *dat*) to suit, fit, become, e.g., **la robe lui va bien** the dress becomes her; **aller** + *inf* to be going to + *inf*, e.g., **je vais au magasin acheter des souliers** I am going to the store to buy some shoes; **allez!, allons!,** allons donc! well!, come on!, all right!; **allez-y doucement!** take it easy!; **ça va?, comment allez-vous?** how are you? || *ref*—**s'en aller** to go away || *aux*—**aller** + *inf* to be going to + *inf* (to express futurity), e.g., **il va se marier** he is going to get married

allergie [alɛrʒi] *f* allergy

aller-retour [alerətur] *m*—**faire l'aller-retour** to go and come back

alliage [aljaʒ] *m* alloy

alliance [aljɑ̃s] *f* alliance; marriage; wedding ring; **ancienne alliance** Old Covenant; **nouvelle alliance** New Covenant

al·lié **-liée** [alje] *adj* allied (*by treaty*); united (*in marriage*) || *mf* ally; kin, in-law

allier [alje] *tr* to ally; to alloy || *ref* to become allied, to ally oneself

alligator [alligatɔr] *m* alligator

allô [alo] *interj* hello!

allocation [alɔkɑsjɔ̃] f allocation, allotment; allocations familiales family (social security) allotments

allocution [alɔkysjɔ̃] f short speech

allonger [alɔ̃ʒe] §38 tr, intr, & ref to lengthen

allouer [alwe] tr to allow, allocate

allumage [alymaʒ] m lighting; switching on (of a light); kindling (of a fire); ignition

allume-feu [alymfø] m invar kindling

allumer [alyme] tr to ignite; to light (a cigarette); to light up (a room); to put on, switch on (a light; a radio; a heater); to provoke (anger) || ref to go on (said of a light); to light up (said of eyes); to catch fire

allumette [alymɛt] f match; allumette de sûreté safety match

allumette-gaz [alymɛtgɑz] m pilot light

allumeur [alymœr] m ignition system; allumeur de réverbères lamplighter

allumeuse [alymøz] f (coll) vamp

allure [alyr] f speed, pace; gait, bearing, aspect; à l'allure de l'escargot at a snail's pace; à toute allure at top speed

allusion [allyzjɔ̃] f allusion

almanach [almana] m almanac; yearbook

aloès [alɔɛs] m aloe

aloi [alwa] m legal alloy; quality; de bon aloi genuine

alors [alɔr] adv then; alors même que even though; alors que whereas

alose [aloz] f shad

alouette [alwɛt] f lark, skylark; alouette sans tête rolled veal

alourdir [alurdir] tr to weigh down, to make heavy || ref to become heavy

aloyau [alwajo] m (pl aloyaux) sirloin

Alpes [alp] fpl—les Alpes the Alps

alphabet [alfabɛ] m alphabet

alpinisme [alpinism] m mountain climbing

alpiniste [alpinist] mf mountain climber

alpiste [alpist] m birdseed

alsa•cien [alzasjɛ̃] -cienne [sjɛn] adj Alsatian || m Alsatian (dialect) || (cap) mf Alsatian (person)

alté•rant [alterɑ̃] -rante [rɑ̃t] adj thirst-provoking

altération [alterɑsjɔ̃] f alteration, falsification; deterioration; heavy thirst; (mus) accidental

altérer [altere] §10 tr to alter, falsify; to ruin (one's health); to weaken, impair; to make thirsty || ref to undergo a change for the worse; to become thirsty

alternance [alternɑ̃s] f alternation; (agr) rotation

alterna•tif [alternatif] -tive [tiv] adj alternative; alternating; alternate || f alternative, dilemma; alternation

alterne [altern] adj alternate (angles)

alterner [alterne] tr to rotate (crops) || intr to alternate

al•tier [altje] -tière [tjɛr] adj haughty

altitude [altityd] f altitude

alto [alto] m alto; viola

altruiste [altrɥist] adj & mf altruist

aluminium [alyminjɔm] m aluminum

alun [alœ̃] m alum

alunir [alynir] intr to land on the moon

alunissage [alynisaʒ] m landing on the moon

alvéole [alveɔl] m & f alveolus; cavity; cell (of honeycomb); socket (of tooth)

amadou [amadu] m punk, tinder

amadouer [amadwe] tr to wheedle

amaigrir [amɛgrir] tr to emaciate; to make thin || ref to grow thin

amalgame [amalgam] m amalgam

amalgamer [amalgame] tr & ref to amalgamate

aman [amɑ̃] m—demander l'aman to give in

amande [amɑ̃d] f almond; kernel; amande de Malaga Jordan almond

amandier [amɑ̃dje] m almond tree

a•mant [amɑ̃] -mante [mɑ̃t] mf lover

amareyeur [amarɛjœr] m oysterman

amariner [amarine] tr to season (a crew); to impress (a ship)

amarre [amar] f hawser

amarrer [amare] tr & ref to moor

amas [ama] m mass; heap; cluster (of stars); amas de neige snowdrift

amasser [amase] tr to amass; to gather || intr to hoard || ref to pile up, to crowd

amateur [amatœr] adj amateur || m amateur; (coll) prospective buyer

amatir [amatir] tr to mat, dull (metal or glass)

amazone [amazon] f amazon; horse-woman; riding habit; monter en amazone to ride sidesaddle || (cap) f Amazon

ambages [ɑ̃baʒ] fpl circumlocutions; sans ambages without beating around the bush

ambassade [ɑ̃basad] f embassy

ambassadeur [ɑ̃basadœr] m ambassador

ambassadrice [ɑ̃basadris] f ambassadress; wife of ambassador; emissary

ambiance [ɑ̃bjɑ̃s] f environment, milieu; atmosphere, tone

ambidextre [ɑ̃bidɛkstrə] adj ambidextrous || mf ambidextrous person

ambi•gu -guë [ɑ̃bigy] adj ambiguous || m ambiguousness; buffet lunch; odd mixture

ambiguïté [ɑ̃biguite] f ambiguity

ambi•tieux [ɑ̃bisjø] -tieuse [sjøz] adj ambitious

ambition [ɑ̃bisjɔ̃] f ambition

amble [ɑ̃bl] m amble

ambler [ɑ̃ble] intr (equit) to amble

ambre [ɑ̃br] m—ambre gris ambergris; ambre (jaune or succin) amber

ambulance [ɑ̃bylɑ̃s] f ambulance

ambulan•cier [ɑ̃bylɑsje] -cière [sjɛr] mf ambulance driver or attendant

ambu•lant [ɑ̃bylɑ̃] -lante [lɑ̃t] adj ambulant || m railway mail clerk

ambulatoire [ɑ̃bylatwar] adj ambulatory; itinerant

âme [ɑm] f soul; spirit, heart, mind;

core (*of cable*); bore (*of cannon*); web (*of rail*); sound post (*of violin*); **âme damnée** evil genius; **rendre l'âme** to give up the ghost

améliorer [ameljɔre] *tr* & *ref* to ameliorate, to improve

amen [amɛn] *m invar* Amen

aménagement [amenaʒmɑ̃] *m* arrangement, equipping; preparation, development (*of land*); adjustment (*of taxes*); **aménagements** furnishings

aménager [amenaʒe] §38 *tr* to arrange, equip; to remodel; to parcel out; to grade (*a roadbed*); to feed (*a machine*); to harness (*a waterfall*)

amende [ɑmɑ̃d] *f* fine; forfeit (*in a game*); **faire amende honorable** (coll) to apologize

amendement [amɑ̃dmɑ̃] *m* amendment; fertilizer

amender [amɑ̃de] *tr* to amend; to manure ‖ *ref* to mend one's ways, to amend

amène [amɛn] *adj* pleasant

amener [amne] §2 *tr* to bring; to lead; to bring on; to furnish (*proof*); (naut) to lower; **amener pavillon** to surrender ‖ *ref* (coll) to arrive; **amenez-vous!** (slang) get a move on!

aménité [amenite] *f* amenity; **aménités** cutting remarks

amenuiser [amənɥize] *tr* to whittle ‖ *ref* to be whittled down

a·mer -mère [amɛr] *adj* bitter ‖ *m* bitters; seamark; gall (*of animal*)

améri·cain [amerikɛ̃] **-caine** [kɛn] *adj* American ‖ *m* American English ‖ *f* phaeton; bicycle relay ‖ (*cap*) *mf* American (*person*)

américanisme [amerikanism] *m* Americanism; American studies

Amérique [amerik] *f* America; **l'Amérique** America

amerrir [amerir] *intr* to land, alight on water

amerrissage [amerisaʒ] *m* landing (on water); (rok) splashdown; **amerrissage forcé** ditching; **faire un amerrissage forcé** to ditch

amertume [amɛrtym] *f* bitterness

améthyste [ametist] *f* amethyst

ameublement [amœbləmɑ̃] *m* furnishings; furniture, suite

ameublir [amœblir] *tr* (agr) to soften, to mellow (*soil*)

ameuter [amøte] *tr* to rouse (*the pack*) ‖ *ref* to riot

a·mi -mie [ami] *adj* friendly ‖ *mf* friend ‖ *f* mistress

amiable [amjabl] *adj* amicable; **à l'amiable** privately, out of court

amiante [amjɑ̃t] *m* asbestos

amibe [amib] *f* amoeba

ami·bien [amibjɛ̃] **-bienne** [bjɛn] *adj* amoebic

ami·cal -cale [amikal] *adj* (*pl* -caux [ko]) amicable ‖ *f* professional club

amidon [amidɔ̃] *m* starch

amidonner [amidɔne] *tr* to starch

amincir [amɛ̃sir] *tr* to make more slender, to attenuate ‖ *ref* to grow thinner

ami·ral [amiral] *m* (*pl* -raux [ro]) admiral

amirale [amiral] *f* admiral's wife

amirauté [amirote] *f* admiralty

amitié [amitje] *f* friendship; **amitiés** (complimentary close) cordially yours; **faites mes amitiés à** give my regards to; **faites-moi l'amitié de** do me the favor of

ammo·niac -niaque [amɔnjak] *adj* ammoniacal ‖ *m* ammonia (*gas*) ‖ *f* ammonia (*gas dissolved in water*)

amnésie [amnezi] *f* amnesia

amnistie [amnisti] *f* amnesty

amnistier [amnistje] *tr* to amnesty

amoindrir [amwɛ̃drir] *tr* to lessen ‖ *ref* to diminish

amollir [amɔlir] *tr* & *ref* to soften

amollissement [amɔlismɑ̃] *m* softening

amonceler [amɔ̃sle] §34 *tr* to pile up, to gather ‖ *ref* to pile up, to gather; to drift (*said of snow*)

amont [amɔ̃] *m* upper waters; **en amont** upstream; **en amont de** above

amorçage [amɔrsaʒ] *m* baiting; priming

amorce [amɔrs] *f* bait, lure; fuse, percussion cap; beginning; leader (*of strip of film*); (mov) preview

amorcer [amɔrse] §51 *tr* to bait; to prime; to entice; to begin

amorphe [amɔrf] *adj* amorphous

amortir [amɔrtir] *tr* to absorb (*shock*); to subdue (*color; pain; passions*); to damp (*waves*); to amortize

amortissement [amɔrtismɑ̃] *m* absorption (*of shock, sound, etc.*); amortization

amortisseur [amɔrtisœr] *m* shock absorber

amour [amur] *m* love; love affair; **premières amours** puppy love ‖ (*cap*) *m* Cupid

amou·reux [amurø] **-reuse** [røz] *adj* amorous; loving; fond, devoted; **amoureux de** in love with ‖ *m* lover ‖ *f* sweetheart

amour-propre [amurprɔpr] *m* (*pl* amours-propres) self-esteem; vanity

amovible [amɔvibl] *adj* removable; detachable; (jur) revocable

ampère [ɑ̃per] *m* ampere

ampèremètre [ɑ̃permɛtr] *m* ammeter

amphibie [ɑ̃fibi] *adj* amphibious, amphibian ‖ *m* amphibian

amphibien [ɑ̃fibjɛ̃] *m* amphibian

amphithéâtre [ɑ̃fiteatr] *m* amphitheater; auditorium (*with raised seats*)

amphitryon [ɑ̃fitrijɔ̃] *m* host at dinner ‖ (*cap*) *m* Amphitryon

ample [ɑ̃pl] *adj* ample; long (*speech*); liberal (*reward*)

amplifica·teur [ɑ̃plifikatœr] **-trice** [tris] *adj* amplifying ‖ *mf* exaggerator ‖ *m* amplifier; (phot) enlarger

amplifier [ɑ̃plifje] *tr* to amplify, to enlarge

amplitude [ɑ̃plityd] *f* amplitude

ampoule [ɑ̃pul] *f* ampule; (elec) bulb; (pathol) blister

ampu·té -tée [ɑ̃pyte] *mf* amputee

amputer [ãpyte] *tr* to amputate; to cut (*an article, speech*)
amuïr [amµir] *ref* to become silent
amuïssement [amµismã] *m* (phonet) silencing
amulette [amylɛt] *f* amulet
amure [amyr] *f* tack (*of sail*)
amuse-gueule [amyzgœl] *m* (*pl* -**gueule** or -**gueules**) (coll) appetizer, snack
amusement [amyzmã] *m* amusement
amuser [amyze] *tr* to amuse; to mislead || *ref* to have a good time; to sow one's wild oats; **s'amuser à** to pass the time by; **s'amuser de** to play with; to make fun of
amygdale [amigdal] *f* tonsil
an [ã] *m* year; **l'an de grâce** the year of Our Lord
anacarde [anakard] *m* cashew nut
anachronisme [anakrɔnism] *m* anachronism
analogie [analɔʒi] *f* analogy
analogue [analɔg] *adj* analogous; similar
analphabète [analfabɛt] *adj* & *mf* illiterate
analphabétisme [analfabetism] *m* illiteracy
analyse [analiz] *f* analysis; **analyse des renseignements** data processing
analyser [analize] *tr* to analyze
analyseur [analizœr] *m* analyzer, tester
analyste [analist] *mf* analyst
analytique [analitik] *adj* analytic(al)
ananas [anana] *m* pineapple
anarchie [anarʃi] *f* anarchy
anarchiste [anarʃist] *mf* anarchist
anathème [anatɛm] *m* anathema
anatife [anatif] *m* barnacle
anatomie [anatɔmi] *f* anatomy
anatomique [anatɔmik] *adj* anatomic(al)
ances·tral -**trale** [ãsɛstral] *adj* (*pl* -**traux** [tro]) ancestral
ancêtre [ãsɛtr] *m* ancestor
anche [ãʃ] *f* (mus) reed
anchois [ãʃwa] *m* anchovy
an·cien [ãsjɛ̃] -**cienne** [sjɛn] *adj* ancient, old, long-standing; antiquated; antique || (when standing before noun) *adj* former, previous, old; retired (*businessman*); ancient (*Greece, Rome*) || *mf* senior (*in rank*); oldster; **les Anciens** the Ancients
anciennement [ãsjɛnmã] *adv* formerly
ancienneté [ãsjɛnte] *f* antiquity; seniority (*in rank*)
ancre [ãkr] *f* anchor; **ancres levées** anchors aweigh
ancrer [ãkre] *tr* & *intr* to anchor || *ref* to become established
andain [ãdɛ̃] *m* swath; row of shocks
andouille [ãduj] *f* (coll) fool, sap
andouiller [ãduje] *m* antler
âne [ɑn] *m* ass, donkey
anéantir [aneãtir] *tr* to annihilate; to prostrate || *ref* to disappear; to humble oneself (*before God*)
anéantissement [aneãtismã] *m* annihilation; prostration
anecdote [anɛgdɔt] *f* anecdote
anémie [anemi] *f* anemia
ânesse [ɑnɛs] *f* she-ass

anesthésie [anɛstezi] *f* anesthesia
anesthésier [anɛstezje] *tr* to anesthetize
anesthésique [anɛstezik] *adj* & *m* anesthetic
anesthésiste [anɛstezist] *mf* anesthetist
anévrisme [anevrism] *m* aneurysm
anfractuosité [ãfraktµozite] *f* roughness outline (*of coast*); ruggedness, cragginess
ange [ãʒ] *m* angel; **ange gardien, ange tutélaire** guardian angel; **être aux anges** to walk on air
angélique [ãʒelik] *adj* angelic(al)
angélus [ãʒelys] *m* Angelus
angine [ãʒin] *f* tonsillitis, quinsy; **angine de poitrine** angina pectoris
an·glais [ãglɛ] -**glaise** [glɛz] *adj* English; **à l'anglaise** in the English manner; **filer à l'anglaise** to take French leave || *m* English (*language*) || (*cap*) *m* Englishman; **les Anglais** the English || *f* Englishwoman
angle [ãgl] *m* angle; corner
Angleterre [ãglətɛr] *f* England; **l'Angleterre** England
angois·sant [ãgwasã] **angois·sante** [ãgwasãt] *adj* agonizing
angoisse [ãgwas] *f* anguish
anguille [ãgij] *f* eel; **anguille de mer** conger eel
angulaire [ãgylɛr] *adj* angular
angu·leux [ãgylø] -**leuse** [løz] *adj* angular, sharp
anicroche [anikrɔʃ] *f* (coll) hitch, snag
ani·mal -**male** [animal] (*pl* -**maux** [mo]) *adj* animal || *m* animal, brute, beast; (coll) blockhead
anima·teur [animatœr] -**trice** [tris] *adj* animating || *mf* animator, moving spirit; master of ceremonies; **animateur de théâtre** theatrical producer
animation [animasjɔ̃] *f* animation
animer [anime] *tr* to animate; to encourage || *ref* to become alive, liven up
animosité [animozite] *f* animosity
anion [anjɔ̃] *m* anion
anis [ani] *m* anise
annales [anal] *fpl* annals
an·neau [ano] *m* (*pl* -**neaux**) ring
année [ane] *f* year; **année bissextile** leap year; **année de lumière** light-year; **bonne année** Happy New Year
année-lumière [anelymjɛr] *f* (*pl* **années-lumière**) light-year
annexe [anɛks] *adj* annexed || *f* annex
annexer [anɛkse] *tr* to annex
annexion [anɛksjɔ̃] *f* annexation
annihiler [aniile] *tr* to annihilate
anniversaire [anivɛrsɛr] *adj* & *m* anniversary; **anniversaire de naissance** birthday
annonce [anɔ̃s] *f* announcement; advertisement; (cards) bid; **petites annonces** classified ads
annoncer [anɔ̃se] §51 *tr* to announce; to advertise || *ref* to augur; to promise to be
annonceur [anɔ̃sœr] *m* advertiser
annoncia·teur [anɔ̃sjatœr] -**trice** [tris] *adj* betokening, foreboding || *m* harbinger

annoter [anɔte] *tr* to annotate
annuaire [anɥɛr] *m* annual, yearbook, directory; catalog, bulletin (*e.g., of a school*)
an·nuel -nuelle [anɥɛl] *adj* annual
annuité [anɥite] *f* annuity
annuler [anyle] *tr* to annul
ano·din [anɔdɛ̃] -dine [din] *adj & m* anodyne
ânon [anɔ̃] *m* foal of an ass
anonner [anɔne] *tr* to recite in a stumbling manner
anonymat [anɔnima] *m* anonymity
anonyme [anɔnim] *adj* anonymous; incorporated; (fig) colorless, drab || *mf* unidentified person
anor·mal -male [anɔrmal] (*pl* -maux [mo]) *adj* abnormal || *mf* abnormal person
anse [ɑ̃s] *f* handle; faire danser l'anse du panier to pad the bill
antagonisme [ɑ̃tagɔnism] *m* antagonism
antan [ɑ̃tɑ̃] *m* yesteryear
Antarctique [ɑ̃tarktik] *adj & m* Antarctic || *f* Antarctic (*region*); l'Antarctique Antarctica
antécé·dent [ɑ̃tesedɑ̃] -dente [dɑ̃t] *adj & m* antecedent
antenne [ɑ̃tɛn] *f* antenna (*feeler; aerial*); outpost; (naut) lateen yard; porter à l'antenne to put on the air
antépénultième [ɑ̃tepenyltjɛm] *adj* antepenultimate || *f* antepenult
anté·rieur -rieure [ɑ̃terjœr] *adj* anterior; former; previous, preceding; earlier; front
antériorité [ɑ̃terjɔrite] *f* priority
anthologie [ɑ̃tɔlɔʒi] *f* anthology
anthropoïde [ɑ̃trɔpɔid] *adj & m* anthropoid
anthropophage [ɑ̃trɔpɔfaʒ] *adj & mf* cannibal
antiaé·rien [ɑ̃tiɑerjɛ̃] -rienne [rjɛn] *adj* antiaircraft
antialcoolique [ɑ̃tialkɔɔlik] *adj* antialcoholic || *mf* teetotaler; temperance worker
antibiotique [ɑ̃tibjɔtik] *adj & m* antibiotic
antichambre [ɑ̃tiʃɑ̃br] *f* antechamber, anteroom
antichar [ɑ̃tiʃar] *adj* antitank
anticipation [ɑ̃tisipasjɔ̃] *f* anticipation; anticipations prophecies (*of science fiction*); d'anticipation science fiction (*stories, films, etc.*); par anticipation in advance
antici·pé -pée [ɑ̃tisipe] *adj* anticipated, advanced, ahead of time; premature (*e.g., death*)
anticiper [ɑ̃tisipe] *tr* to anticipate; to advance || *intr* to act ahead of time; anticiper sur to encroach on; to pay ahead of time; to spend ahead of time
anticléri·cal -cale [ɑ̃tiklerikal] *adj* (*pl* -caux [ko]) anticlerical
anticonception·nel -nelle [ɑ̃tikɔ̃sɛpsjɔnɛl] *adj* contraceptive
anticorps [ɑ̃tikɔr] *m* antibody
antidéra·pant [ɑ̃tiderapɑ̃] -pante [pɑ̃t] *adj* nonskid || *m* nonskid tire

antidéto·nant [ɑ̃tidetɔnɑ̃] -nante [nɑ̃t] *adj & m* antiknock
antidote [ɑ̃tidɔt] *m* antidote
antienne [ɑ̃tjɛn] *f* antiphon, anthem; chanter toujours la même antienne to harp on the same subject
antigel [ɑ̃tiʒɛl] *m* antifreeze
antigi·vrant [ɑ̃tiʒivrɑ̃] -vrante [vrɑ̃t] *adj* deicing, defrosting || *m* deicer
antigivre [ɑ̃tiʒivr] *m* deicer, defroster
Antilles [ɑ̃tij] *fpl* West Indies
antilope [ɑ̃tilɔp] *f* antelope
antimite [ɑ̃timit] *adj* mothproof || *m* moth killer
antimoine [ɑ̃timwan] *m* antimony
antiparasite [ɑ̃tiparazit] *adj* (rad) static-eliminating || *m* (rad) static eliminator; insecticide
antipathie [ɑ̃tipati] *f* antipathy
antiquaire [ɑ̃tikɛr] *m* antique dealer
antique [ɑ̃tik] *adj* antique, classic; old-fashioned || *m* antique
antiquité [ɑ̃tikite] *f* antiquity; antiquités antiques
antisémite [ɑ̃tisemit] *adj* anti-Semitic || *mf* anti-Semite
antisémitique [ɑ̃tisemitik] *adj* anti-Semitic
antiseptique [ɑ̃tisɛptik] *adj & m* antiseptic
antiso·cial -ciale [ɑ̃tisɔsjal] *adj* (*pl* -ciaux [sjo]) antisocial
antispor·tif [ɑ̃tispɔrtif] -tive [tiv] *adj* unsportsmanlike
antithèse [ɑ̃titɛz] *f* antithesis
antitoxine [ɑ̃titɔksin] *f* antitoxin
antitranspirant [ɑ̃titrɑ̃spirɑ̃] *m* antiperspirant
antonyme [ɑ̃tɔnim] *m* antonym
antre [ɑ̃tr] *m* den, lair; cave
anxiété [ɑ̃ksjete] *f* anxiety
anxieux [ɑ̃ksjø] anxieuse [ɑ̃ksjøz] *adj* anxious, worried
aorte [aɔrt] *f* aorta
août [u], [ut] *m* August
A.P. *abbr* (assistance publique) welfare department
apache [apaʃ] *m* apache, hoodlum
apaisement [apɛzmɑ̃] *m* appeasement
apaiser [apɛze] *tr* to appease || *ref* to quiet down
apanage [apanaʒ] *m* attribute
aparté [aparte] *m* stage whisper, aside; en aparté privately
apathie [apati] *f* apathy
apathique [apatik] *adj* apathetic
apatride [apatrid] *adj* stateless || *mf* stateless person
apercevoir [apersəvwar] §59 *tr* to perceive || *ref* to notice; to realize; s'apercevoir de to notice, realize, be aware of
aperçu [apersy] *m* glimpse; view, look; outline
apéri·tif [aperitif] -tive [tiv] *adj* appetizing || *m* appetizer
aperture [apɛrtyr] *f* (phonet) aperture
apesanteur [apezɑ̃tœr] *f* weightlessness
à-peu-près [apøprɛ] *m invar* approximation, rough estimate
apeu·ré -rée [apœre] *adj* frightened
aphorisme [afɔrism] *m* aphorism

aphrodisiaque [afrɔdizjak] adj & m aphrodisiac

aphte [aft] m mouth canker, cold sore

apiculteur [apikyltœr] m beekeeper

apiculture [apikyltyr] f beekeeping

apitoiement [apitwamɑ̃] m compassion

apitoyant [apitwajɑ̃] apitoyante [apitwajɑ̃t] adj piteous, pitiful

apitoyer [apitwaje] §47 tr to move (s.o.) to pity || ref—s'apitoyer sur to feel compassion for

ap. J.-C. abbr (après Jésus-Christ) A.D.

aplanir [aplanir] tr to even off; to iron out (difficulties)

aplatir [aplatir] tr to flatten || ref to go flat; to grovel

aplomb [aplɔ̃] m aplomb; hang (of gown); (coll) cheek, rudeness; aplombs stand (of horse); d'aplomb plumb; steadily

apocalyptique [apɔkaliptik] adj apocalyptic

apocryphe [apɔkrif] adj apocryphal || Apocryphes mpl Apocrypha

apogée [apɔʒe] m apogee

Apollon [apɔllɔ̃] m Apollo

apologie [apɔlɔʒi] f apology

apophonie [apɔfɔni] f ablaut

apoplectique [apɔplɛktik] adj & mf apoplectic

apoplexie [apɔplɛksi] f apoplexy

apostille [apɔstij] f endorsement

apostiller [apɔstije] tr to endorse

apostolat [apɔstɔla] m apostleship

apostrophe [apɔstrɔf] f apostrophe; sharp reprimand

apostropher [apɔstrɔfe] tr to apostrophize; to reprimand sharply

apothicaire [apɔtikɛr] m apothecary

apôtre [apotr] m apostle; faire le bon apôtre to play the hypocrite

apparaître [aparɛtr] §12 intr (aux: AVOIR or ÊTRE) to appear, come into view; to become evident

apparat [apara] m pomp, ostentation

apparaux [aparo] mpl rigging

appareil [aparɛj] m apparatus, machine, appliance; apparel; radio set; airplane; pomp, show, display; camera; telephone; (archit) bond; à l'appareil! speaking!; appareil à sous slot machine; appareil plâtré plaster cast

appareiller [apareje] tr to prepare; to bond (stones); to pair, match; (naut) to rig || intr to set sail

apparemment [aparamɑ̃] adv apparently

apparence [aparɑ̃s] f appearance

appa·rent [aparɑ̃] -rente [rɑ̃t] adj apparent

apparenter [aparɑ̃te] tr to relate by marriage || ref to become related

apparier [aparje] tr to pair off, to match

apparition [aparisjɔ̃] f apparition; appearance

apparoir [aparwar] (used only in: inf; 3d sg pres ind appert) impers—il appert de it follows from; il appert que it is evident that

appartement [apartəmɑ̃] m apartment

appartenance [apartənɑ̃s] f appurtenance

appartenir [apartənir] §72 intr—appartenir à to belong to; to pertain to || impers—il appartient à qn de it behooves s.o. to || ref to be one's own master

appas [apɑ] mpl charms; bosom

appât [apɑ] m bait

appâter [apɑte] tr to lure; to fatten up (fowl)

appauvrir [apovrir] tr to impoverish || ref to become impoverished

ap·peau [apo] m (pl -peaux) decoy; bird call

appel [apɛl] m call; appeal; summons; roll call; ring (on telephone); (mil) draft; appel interurbain long-distance call; appel nominal roll call; faire l'appel to call the roll

appe·lant [aplɑ̃] -lante [lɑ̃t] adj appellant || mf appellant || m decoy

appelé [aple] m draftee

appeler [aple] §34 tr to call; to name; to summon; to subpoena; to require; to call up, to draft || intr to call; to appeal (in court); en appeler à to appeal to || ref to be named, e.g., elle s'appelle Marie she is named Mary, her name is Mary

appendice [apɛ̃dis] m appendix

appendicectomie [apɛ̃disektɔmi] f appendectomy

appendicite [apɛ̃disit] f appendicitis

appentis [apɑ̃ti] m lean-to

appesantir [apzɑ̃tir] tr to weigh down; to slow down (e.g., bodily activity); to make (a burden) heavier || ref to be weighed down; s'appesantir sur to dwell on, to expatiate on

appétis·sant [apetisɑ̃] appétis·sante [apetisɑ̃t] adj appetizing, tempting

appétit [apeti] m appetite

applaudir [aplodir] tr to applaud; applaudir qn de to commend, applaud s.o. for || intr to applaud; applaudir à to approve, commend, applaud || ref—s'applaudir de to congratulate oneself on, to pat oneself on the back for

applaudissement [aplodismɑ̃] m round of applause; applaudissements applause

applicable [aplikabl] adj applicable

application [aplikasjɔ̃] f application

applique [aplik] f appliqué; sconce

appli·qué -quée [aplike] adj industrious, studious; applied (science)

appliquer [aplike] tr to apply || ref to apply; to apply oneself

appoint [apwɛ̃] m addition; balance; aid, help; faire l'appoint to have the right change

appointements [apwɛ̃tmɑ̃] mpl salary

appointer [apwɛte] tr to point, sharpen; to pay a salary to

appontage [apɔ̃taʒ] m deck-landing

appontement [apɔ̃tmɑ̃] m jetty (landing pier)

apponter [apɔ̃te] intr to deck-land

apport [apɔr] m contribution

apporter [apɔrte] tr to bring

apposer [apoze] *tr* to affix; to insert (*a clause in a contract*)
appréciable [apresjabl] *adj* appreciable
appréciation [apresjɑsjɔ̃] *f* appreciation, appraisal
apprécier [apresje] *tr* to appreciate
appréhender [apreɑde] *tr* to apprehend; to be apprehensive about
appréhension [apreɑsjɔ̃] *f* apprehension
apprendre [aprɑ̃dr] §56 *tr* to learn; **apprendre à vivre à qn** to teach s.o. manners; **apprendre q.ch. à qn** to inform s.o. of s.th.; **to teach s.o. s.th.** ‖ *intr* to learn
appren·ti -tie [aprɑ̃ti] *mf* apprentice; beginner, learner
apprentissage [aprɑ̃tisaʒ] *m* apprenticeship
apprêt [aprɛ] *m* preparation, finishing touches; **sans apprêt** unaffectedly
apprêter [aprɛte] *tr* & *ref* to prepare
apprivoi·sé -sée [aprivwaze] *adj* tame, domesticated
apprivoiser [aprivwaze] *tr* to tame; to contain (*sorrow*) ‖ *ref* to become tame; to become sociable
approba·teur [aprɔbatœr] **-trice** [tris] *adj* approving ‖ *m* (slang) yes man
approbation [aprɔbɑsjɔ̃] *f* approbation, approval, consent
appro·chant [aprɔʃɑ̃] **-chante** [ʃɑ̃t] *adj* similar ‖ **approchant** *adv* thereabouts
approche [aprɔʃ] *f* approach
approcher [aprɔʃe] *tr* to approach; to draw up (*e.g., a chair*) ‖ *intr* to approach; **approcher de** to approach, approximate ‖ *ref* to approach, to come near; **s'approcher de** to approach, to come near to, to go up to
approfon·di -die [aprɔfɔ̃di] *adj* thorough, deep
approfondir [aprɔfɔ̃dir] *tr* to deepen; to go deep into, get to the bottom of
appropriation [aprɔprijɑsjɔ̃] *m* appropriation; adaptation
appro·prié -priée [aprɔprije] *adj* appropriate
approprier [aprɔprije] *tr* to fit, adapt ‖ *ref* to appropriate, preempt
approuver [apruve] *tr* to approve, to approve of
approvisionnement [aprɔvizjɔnmɑ̃] *m* provisioning, stocking; **approvisionnements** supplies
approvisionner [aprɔvizjɔne] *tr* to provision, to stock ‖ *ref* to lay in supplies
approxima·tif [aprɔksimatif] **-tive** [tiv] *adj* approximate
appui [apɥi] *m* support; endorsement
appui-bras [apɥibra] *m* (*pl* **appuis-bras**) armrest
appui-livres [apɥilivr] *m* (*pl* **appuis-livres**) book end
appui-main [apɥimɛ̃] *m* (*pl* **appuis-main**) maulstick
appui-tête [apɥitɛt] *m* (*pl* **appuis-tête**) headrest
appuyer [apɥije] §27 *tr* to support; to prop; to rest, lean; to endorse (*a candidate*); **appuyer le doigt sur** to push (*a button, a lever, a switch*) with the

finger ‖ *intr*—**appuyer sur** to lean on; to press (*a button*); to move (*a lever*); to pull (*a trigger*); to bear down on (*a pen or pencil*); to stress (*a syllable*) ‖ *ref*—**s'appuyer sur** to lean on; to be based on; to rely on; (slang) to put up with
âpre [ɑpr] *adj* harsh, rough; bitter; greedy (*for gain*)
après [aprɛ] *adv* after, afterward; behind; **après que** after ‖ *prep* after; behind; **après Jésus-Christ** (ap. J.-C.) after Christ (A.D.); **d'après** after, from; by, according to
après-demain [apredəmɛ̃] *adv* & *m* the day after tomorrow
après-guerre [apreger] *m* & *f* (*pl* **-guerres**) postwar period
après-midi [apremidi] *m* & *f* invar afternoon
âpreté [aprəte] *f* harshness; bitterness
à-propos [aprɔpo] *m* opportuneness, aptness
apte [apt] *adj* apt; **apte à** suitable for
aptitude [aptityd] *f* aptitude; proficiency
apurement [apyrmɑ̃] *m* audit, check
apurer [apyre] *tr* to audit, to check
apyre [apir] *adj* fireproof
aquafortiste [akwafɔrtist] *mf* etcher
aquaplane [akwaplan] *m* aquaplane
aquarelle [akwarɛl] *f* watercolor
aquarium [akwarjɔm] *m* aquarium
aquatique [akwatik] *adj* aquatic
aqueduc [akdyk] *m* aqueduct
aquilin [akilɛ̃] *adj* masc aquiline
aquilon [akilɔ̃] *m* north wind
ara [ara] *m* (orn) macaw
arabe [arab] *adj* Arabian, Arab ‖ *m* Arabic; Arab (*horse*) ‖ (*cap*) *mf* Arabian, Arab
arachide [araʃid] *f* peanut
araignée [arɛɲe] *f* spider; grapnel; **araignée de mer** spider crab; **avoir une araignée dans le plafond** (coll) to have bats in the belfry
aratoire [aratwar] *adj* agricultural
arbitrage [arbitraʒ] *m* arbitration
arbitraire [arbitrɛr] *adj* arbitrary ‖ *m* arbitrariness, despotism
arbitre [arbitr] *m* arbiter; arbitrator; umpire, judge; **libre arbitre** free will
arbitrer [arbitre] *tr* & *intr* to arbitrate; to umpire
arborer [arbɔre] *tr* to hoist (*a flag*); to show off (*new clothes*)
arbouse [arbuz] *f* arbutus berry
arbousier [arbuzje] *m* arbutus
arbre [arbr] *m* tree; (mach) arbor, shaft; **arbre de Noël** Christmas tree; **arbre généalogique** family tree
arbris·seau [arbriso] *m* (*pl* **-seaux**) bushy tree
arbuste [arbyst] *m* shrub
arc [ark] *m* bow; arch; (elec, geom) arc
arcade [arkad] *f* arcade, archway
arcanes [arkan] *mpl* mysteries, secrets
arcanson [arkɑ̃sɔ̃] *m* rosin
arc-boutant [arkbutɑ̃] *m* (*pl* **arcs-boutants**) flying buttress
arc-en-ciel [arkɑ̃sjɛl] *m* (*pl* **arcs-en-ciel** [arkɑ̃sjɛl]) rainbow

archaïque [arkaik] *adj* archaic

archaïsme [arkaism] *m* archaism

archange [arkɑ̃ʒ] *m* archangel

arche [arʃ] *f* arch (*of bridge*); Ark

archéologie [arkeɔlɔʒi] *f* archaeology

archéologue [arkeɔlɔg] *mf* archaeologist

archer [arʃe] *m* archer, bowman

archet [arʃɛ] *m* bow

archétype [arketip] *m* archetype

archevêque [arʃəvɛk] *m* archbishop

archiduc [arʃidyk] *m* archduke

archipel [arʃipɛl] *m* archipelago

archiprêtre [arʃipretr] *m* archpriest

architecte [arʃitɛkt] *m* architect

architecture [arʃitɛktyr] *f* architecture

archives [arʃiv] *fpl* archives

arçon [arsɔ̃] *m* saddletree

Arctique [arktik] *adj* & *m* Arctic || *f* Arctic (*region*)

ardemment [ardamɑ̃] *adv* ardently

ar·dent [ardɑ̃] **-dente** [dɑ̃t] *adj* ardent; burning; bright-red (*hair*)

ardeur [ardœr] *f* ardor; intense heat

ardoise [ardwaz] *f* slate

ardoi·sier [ardwazje] **-sière** [zjɛr] *adj* slate || *m* slate-quarry worker || *f* slate quarry

ar·du -due [ardy] *adj* steep; arduous

arène [arɛn] *f* arena; sand; (fig) arena; **arènes** arena, coliseum, amphitheater

arête [arɛt] *f* fishbone; beard (*of wheat*); angle, ridge

argent [arʒɑ̃] *m* silver; money; **argent comptant** cash

argenter [arʒɑ̃te] *tr* to silver || *ref* to turn silvery (*i.e., gray*)

argenterie [arʒɑ̃tri] *f* silver plate, silverware

argentier [arʒɑ̃tje] *m* silverware cabinet; (hist) Treasurer

argen·tin [arʒɑ̃tɛ̃] **-tine** [tin] *adj* silvery (*voice*); Argentinian || (*cap*) *mf* Argentinian (*person*) || **l'Argentine** *f* Argentina

argile [arʒil] *f* clay

argot [argo] *m* slang; jargon, cant

argotique [argɔtik] *adj* slangy

arguer [argɥe] (many authorities write: **j'arguë, tu arguës,** etc.) *tr* to argue, imply; **arguer de faux** to doubt the authenticity of (*a document*) || *intr* to draw a conclusion; **arguer de** to use as a pretext

argument [argymɑ̃] *m* argument

argumentation [argymɑ̃tasjɔ̃] *f* argument

argumenter [argymɑ̃te] *intr* to argue

argus [argys] *m* look-out, spy; price list, book (*e.g., for used cars*); **argus de la presse** clipping service

aria [arja] *m* (coll) fuss, bother || *f* aria

aride [arid] *adj* arid; (*subject, speaker, etc.*) dry

aridité [aridite] *f* aridity; (fig) dryness, dullness

aristocrate [aristɔkrat] *adj* aristocratic || *mf* aristocrat

aristocratie [aristɔkrasi] *f* aristocracy

Aristote [aristɔt] *m* Aristotle

arithméti·cien [aritmetisjɛ̃] **-cienne** [sjɛn] *mf* arithmetician

arithmétique [aritmetik] *f* arithmetic

arlequin [arləkɛ̃] *m* goulash; wrench || (*cap*) *m* Harlequin

armateur [armatœr] *m* ship outfitter; shipowner

armature [armatyr] *f* framework; keeper (*of a horseshoe magnet*); (mus) key signature

arme [arm] *f* arm; weapon; **arme blanche** cold steel; steel blade; **armes portatives** small arms; **faire ses premières armes** to make one's début

armée [arme] *f* army

armement [armamɑ̃] *m* armament; fire power; (naut) outfitting

armé·nien [armenjɛ̃] **-nienne** [njɛn] *adj* Armenian || *m* Armenian (*language*) || (*cap*) *mf* Armenian (*person*)

armer [arme] *tr* to arm; to cock (*a gun*); to reinforce (*concrete*); **armer chevalier** to knight || *ref* to arm oneself, to arm

armistice [armistis] *m* armistice

armoire [armwar] *f* wardrobe, closet; **armoire à pharmacie** medicine cabinet; **armoire frigorifique** freezer

armoiries [armwari] *fpl* arms, coat of arms

armoise [armwaz] *f* sagebrush

armorier [armɔrje] *tr* to emblazon

armure [armyr] *f* armor; (tex) weave

aromatique [arɔmatik] *adj* aromatic

arôme [arom] *m* aroma

aronde [arɔ̃d] *f* swallow

arpège [arpeʒ] *m* arpeggio

arpent [arpɑ̃] *m* acre

arpentage [arpɑ̃taʒ] *m* surveying

arpenter [arpɑ̃te] *tr* to survey; (coll) to pace (*the floor*)

arpenteur [arpɑ̃tœr] *m* surveyor

ar·qué -quée [arke] *adj* arched, bowed; cambered (*beam*); hooked (*nose*)

arquer [arke] *tr* to arch, to bow || *ref* to arch, to be bowed

arraché [araʃe] *m* (sports) lift

arrache-clou [araʃklu] *m* (*pl* **-clous**) claw hammer

arrache-pied [araʃpje] *adv*—**d'arrache-pied** at a stretch, without stopping

arracher [araʃe] *tr* to dig up, uproot, tear out, pull out; to wheedle (*money; a confession*); **arracher q.ch. à qn** to take away, snatch, or pry s.th. from s.o.; **arracher q.ch. de q.ch.** to pull s.th. off, from, or out of s.th.; to strip s.th. of s.th.; **arracher qn à** to deliver s.o. from (*evil; temptation; death*); **arracher qn de** to make s.o. get out of (*e.g., bed*) || *ref* to tear oneself away

arra·cheur [araʃœr] **-cheuse** [ʃøz] *mf* puller || *f* (mach) picker

arraisonnement [arɛzɔnmɑ̃] *m* port inspection

arraisonner [arɛzɔne] *tr* to inspect (*a ship*)

arrangement [arɑ̃ʒmɑ̃] *m* arrangement

arranger [arɑ̃ʒe] §38 *tr* to arrange; to settle (*a difficulty*); to fix (*to repair; to punish*) || *ref* to be arranged; to get ready; to agree

arrérages [areraʒ] *mpl* arrears

arrestation [arɛstasjɔ̃] *f* arrest

arrêt [arɛ] *m* stop; stopping; arrest; decree; **arrêt complet** standstill; **arrêt facultatif** whistle stop; **mettre aux arrêts** to keep in, to confine to quarters

arrê·té -tée [arɛte] *adj* stopped, standing; decided, fixed || *m* decree; authorization; (com) closing out (*of an account*); **arrêté de police** police ordinance; **prendre un arrêté** to pass a decree

arrêter [arɛte] *tr* to stop; to arrest; to fix (*one's gaze*); to settle, decide upon; to hire, engage; to point (*game, as hunting dog does*) || *intr* to stop; to point (*said of hunting dog*) || *ref* to stop; **s'arrêter à** to decide on; **s'arrêter de** + *inf* to stop + *ger*

arrhes [ar] *fpl* deposit, down payment

arriération [arjerɑsjɔ̃] *f* retardation

arrière [arjɛr] *adj invar* back, rear; tail (*wind*) || *m* back, rear; stern; **à l'arrière** in back; astern; **en arrière** backward; **en arrière de** behind || *adv* back

arrié·ré -rée [arjere] *adj* backward; delinquent (*in payment*); back (*pay, taxes, etc.*); old-fashioned || *mf* backward child || *m* arrears; back pay; back payment; backlog

arrière-boutique [arjɛrbutik] *f* (*pl* **-boutiques**) back room (*of a shop*)

arrière-cour [arjɛrkur] *f* (*pl* **-cours**) backyard

arrière-garde [arjɛrgard] *f* (*pl* **-gardes**) rear guard

arrière-goût [arjɛrgu] *m* (*pl* **-goûts**) aftertaste

arrière-grand-mère [arjɛrgrɑ̃mɛr] *f* (*pl* **-grand-mères**) great-grandmother

arrière-grand-père [arjɛrgrɑ̃pɛr] *m* (*pl* **-grands-pères**) great-grandfather

arrière-pays [arjɛrpei] *m invar* back country

arrière-pensée [arjɛrpɑ̃se] *f* (*pl* **-pensées**) mental reservation, ulterior motive

arrière-plan [arjɛrplɑ̃] *m* (*pl* **-plans**) background

arriérer [arjere] §10 *tr* to delay || *ref* to fall behind (*in payment*)

arrière-train [arjɛrtrɛ̃] *m* (*pl* **-trains**) rear (*of a vehicle*); hindquarters

arrimage [arimaʒ] *m* stowage; docking (*of space vehicle*)

arrimer [arime] *tr* to stow

arrimeur [arimœr] *m* stevedore

arrivage [arivaʒ] *m* arrival (*of goods or ships*)

arrivée [arive] *f* arrival; intake; (sports) finish, goal; **arrivée en douceur** (rok) soft landing

arriver [arive] *intr* (*aux:* ÊTRE) to arrive; to succeed; to happen; **arriver à** to attain, reach; **en arriver à** + *inf* to be reduced to + *ger*

arriviste [arivist] *mf* upstart, parvenu

arrogance [arɔgɑ̃s] *f* arrogance

arro·gant [arɔgɑ̃] **-gante** [gɑ̃t] *adj* arrogant

arroger [arɔʒe] §38 *ref* to arrogate to oneself

arrondir [arɔ̃dir] *tr* to round, round off, round out || *ref* to become round

arrondissement [arɔ̃dismɑ̃] *m* district

arrosage [arozaʒ] *m* sprinkling; irrigation; (mil) heavy bombing

arroser [aroze] *tr* to sprinkle, to water; to irrigate; to flow through (*e.g., a city*); to wash down (*a meal*); (coll) to bribe; (coll) to drink to (*a success*)

arro·seur [arozœr] **-seuse** [zøz] *mf* sprinkler (*person*) || *f* street sprinkler

arrosoir [arozwar] *m* sprinkling can

arse·nal [arsənal] *m* (*pl* **-naux** [no]) shipyard, navy yard; (fig) storehouse; (archaic) arsenal, armory

arsenic [arsənik] *m* arsenic

art [ar] *m* art; **arts d'agréments** music, drawing, dancing, etc.; **arts ménagers** home economics; **le huitième art** television; **les arts du spectacle** the performing arts; **le septième art** the cinema

artère [artɛr] *f* artery

arté·riel -rielle [arterjɛl] *adj* arterial

artériosclé·reux [arterjosklerø] **-reuse** [røz] *adj & mf* arteriosclerotic

arté·sien [artezjɛ̃] **-sienne** [zjɛn] *adj* of Artois; artesian (*well*)

arthrite [artrit] *f* arthritis

artichaut [arti∫o] *m* artichoke

article [artikl] *m* article; entry (*in a dictionary*); **à l'article de la mort** on the point of death; **article de fond** leader; editorial; **article de tête** front-page story; **articles divers** sundries

articuler [artikyle] *tr & ref* to articulate

artifice [artifis] *m* artifice; craftsmanship

artifi·ciel -cielle [artifisjɛl] *adj* artificial

artificier [artifisje] *m* fireworks maker; soldier in charge of ammunition supply

artifi·cieux [artifisjø] **-cieuse** [sjøz] *adj* artful, cunning

artillerie [artijəri] *f* artillery

artilleur [artijœr] *m* artilleryman

arti·san [artizɑ̃] **-sane** [zan] *mf* artisan, artificer || *m* craftsman

artiste [artist] *adj* artistic; artist, of art, artistic; **le monde artiste** the world of art || *mf* artist; actor

artistique [artistik] *adj* artistic

ar·yen [arjɛ̃] **-yenne** [jɛn] *adj* Aryan || (*cap*) *mf* Aryan (*person*)

as [as] *m* ace; **as du volant** speed king

A.S. *abbr* (**assurances sociales**) social security

a/s *abbr* (**aux bons soins de**) c/o

asbeste [asbɛst] *m* asbestos

ascendance [asɑ̃dɑ̃s] *f* lineal ancestry; rising (*of air; of star*)

ascenseur [asɑ̃sœr] *m* elevator

ascension [asɑ̃sjɔ̃] *f* ascension; **Ascension** *f* Ascension Day

ascèse [asɛz] *f* asceticism

ascète [asɛt] *mf* ascetic

ascétique [asetik] *adj* ascetic

ascétisme [asetism] *m* asceticism

aseptique [asɛptik] *adj* aseptic

Asie [azi] *f* Asia; **Asie Mineure** Asia Minor; **l'Asie** Asia; **l'Asie Mineure** Asia Minor

asile [azil] *m* asylum, shelter, home
aspect [aspɛ], [aspɛk] *m* aspect
asperge [aspɛrʒ] *f* asparagus; **des asperges** asparagus (*stalks and tips used as food*)
asperger [aspɛrʒe] §38 *tr* to sprinkle
aspérité [asperite] *f* roughness; harshness; gruffness
aspersion [aspɛrsjɔ̃] *f* sprinkling
asphalte [asfalt] *m* asphalt
asphyxier [asfiksje] *tr* to asphyxiate || *ref* to be asphyxiated
aspic [aspik] *m* asp
aspi•rant [aspirɑ̃] **-rante** [rɑ̃t] *adj* aspirant, aspiring; suction (*pump*) || *mf* candidate (*for a degree*) || *m* midshipman
aspirateur [aspiratœr] *m* vacuum cleaner; **aspirateur de buée** kitchen fan
aspi•ré -rée [aspire] *adj & m* (phonet) aspirate
aspirer [aspire] *tr* to inhale; to suck in || *intr*—**aspirer à** to aspire to
aspirine [aspirin] *f* aspirin
assagir [asaʒir] *tr* to make wiser || *ref* to become wiser
assail•lant [asajɑ̃] **assail-lante** [asajɑ̃t] *adj* attacking || *mf* assailant
assaillir [asajir] §69 *tr* to assail, to assault
assainir [asɛnir] *tr* to purify, to clean up; to drain (*a swamp*)
assainissement [asɛnismɑ̃] *m* purification; draining
assaisonnement [asɛzɔnmɑ̃] *m* seasoning
assaisonner [asɛzɔne] *tr* to season, to flavor
assas•sin [asasɛ̃] **assas•sine** [asasin] *adj* murderous || *m* assassin
assassinat [asasina] *m* assassination
assassiner [asasine] *tr* to assassinate; (coll) to bore to death
assaut [aso] *m* assault
assèchement [asɛʃmɑ̃] *m* drainage, drying; dryness
assécher [aseʃe] §10 *tr* to drain, to dry up
assemblage [asɑ̃blaʒ] *m* assemblage; assembling (*e.g., of printed pages*); (woodworking) joint, joining
assemblée [asɑ̃ble] *f* assembly, meeting
assembler [asɑ̃ble] *tr* to assemble || *ref* to assemble, convene, meet
assener [asne] §2 *tr* to land (*a blow*)
assentiment [asɑ̃timɑ̃] *m* assent, consent
asseoir [aswar] §5 *tr* to seat, sit, place; to base (*an opinion*) || *ref* to sit down
assermen•té -tée [asɛrmɑ̃te] *adj* under oath
assertion [asɛrsjɔ̃] *f* assertion
asser•vi -vie [asɛrvi] *adj* subservient
asservir [asɛrvir] *tr* to enslave; to subdue (*e.g., passions*) || *ref* to submit (*to convention; to tyranny*)
asservissement [asɛrvismɑ̃] *m* enslavement; subservience
assesseur [asɛsœr] *adj & m* assistant; associate (*judge*)
assez [ase] *adv* enough; fairly, rather; **assez de** enough; **en voilà assez!**

that's enough!, cut it out! || *interj* enough!, stop!
assi•du -due [asidy] *adj* assiduous; attentive
assidûment [asidymɑ̃] *adv* assiduously
assié•geant [asjeʒɑ̃] **-geante** [ʒɑ̃t] *adj* besieging || *mf* besieger
assiéger [asjeʒe] §1 *tr* to besiege
assiette [asjɛt] *f* plate, dish; plateful; seat (*of a rider on horseback*); position, condition; **assiette anglaise, assiette de viandes froides** cold cuts; **assiette au beurre** (fig) gravy train; **assiette creuse** soup plate
assignation [asiɲasjɔ̃] *f* assignation; subpoena, summons
assi•gné -gnée [asiɲe] *mf* appointee; **assigné à résidence** permanent appointee; **assigné intérim** temporary appointee
assigner [asiɲe] *tr* to assign, allot; to fix (*a date*); to subpoena, summon
assimilable [asimilabl] *adj* assimilable; comparable
assimilation [asimilasjɔ̃] *f* assimilation
assimiler [asimile] *tr* to assimilate; to compare; to identify with || *ref* to assimilate
as•sis [asi] **as•sise** [asiz] *adj* seated, sitting; firmly established || *f* foundation; stratum; **assises** assizes
assistance [asistɑ̃s] *f* assistance; audience, persons present; presence; **assistance judiciaire** public defender; **assistance publique** welfare department; **assistance sociale** social service
assis•tant [asistɑ̃] **-tante** [tɑ̃t] *adj* assistant || *mf* assistant; bystander, spectator; **assistante sociale** public health nurse
assister [asiste] *tr* to assist, help || *intr*—**assister à** to attend, be present at
association [asɔsjasjɔ̃] *f* association; (sports) soccer; **association des spectateurs** theater club
asso•cié -ciée [asɔsje] *adj & mf* associate
associer [asɔsje] *tr* to associate || *ref* to go into partnership
assoif•fé -fée [aswafe] *adj* thirsty
assolement [asɔlmɑ̃] *m* rotation (*of crops*)
assombrir [asɔ̃brir] *tr & ref* to darken
assom•mant [asɔmɑ̃] **assom•mante** [asɔmɑ̃t] *adj* (coll) boring, fatiguing
assommer [asɔme] *tr* to kill with a heavy blow; to beat up; to stun; (coll) to heckle; (coll) to bore
assommoir [asɔmwar] *m* bludgeon; (coll) gin mill, dive, clip joint
Assomption [asɔ̃psjɔ̃] *f* Assumption
assonance [asɔnɑ̃s] *f* assonance
assor•ti -tie [asɔrti] *adj* assorted (*e.g., cakes*); well-matched (*couple*); stocked, supplied (*store*); to match, e.g., **une cravate assortie** a necktie to match
assortiment [asɔrtimɑ̃] *m* assortment; matching (*of colors*); set (*of dishes*); platter (*of cold cuts*)
assortir [asɔrtir] *tr* to assort, match;

to stock || *ref* to match, harmonize; **s'assortir de** to be accompanied with
assoupir [asupir] *tr* to make drowsy, to lull; to deaden (*pain*) || *ref* to doze off; to lessen (*with time*)
assoupissement [asupismã] *m* drowsiness; lethargy
assouplir [asuplir] *tr* to make supple, flexible; to break in (*a horse*) || *ref* to become supple, manageable
assouplissement [asuplismã] *m* suppleness, flexibility; limbering up; relaxation (*of a rule*)
assourdir [asurdir] *tr* to deafen; to tone down, muffle
assouvir [asuvir] *tr* to assuage, appease, satiate; to satisfy (*e.g., a thirst for vengeance*)
assouvissement [asuvismã] *m* assuagement, appeasement, satisfying
assujet·ti -tie [asyʒɛti] *adj* fastened; subject, liable || *mf* taxpayer; contributor (*e.g., to social security*)
assujettir [asyʒetir] *tr* to subjugate; to subject; to fasten, secure || *ref* to submit
assujettis·sant [asyʒetisã] **assujettis·sante** [asyʒetisãt] *adj* demanding
assujettissement [asyʒetismã] *m* subjugation, subduing; submission (*to a stronger force*); fastening, securing
assumer [asyme] *tr* to assume, take upon oneself
assurance [asyrãs] *f* assurance; insurance; **assurances sociales** social security
assu·ré -rée [asyre] *adj* assured, satisfied; insured || *mf* insured
assurément [asyremã] *adv* assuredly
assurer [asyre] *tr* to assure; to secure; to insure || *ref* to be assured; to make sure; to be insured
astate [astat] *m* astatine
aster [astɛr] *m* (bot) aster
astérie [asteri] *f* starfish
astérisque [asterisk] *m* asterisk
asthénie [asteni] *f* debility
asthme [asm] *m* asthma
asticot [astiko] *m* maggot
astiquer [astike] *tr* to polish
as·tral -trale [astral] *adj* (*pl* **-traux** [tro]) astral
astre [astrə] *m* star, heavenly body; leading light; **astre de la nuit** moon; **astre du jour** sun
astreindre [astrɛ̃dr] §50 *tr* to force, compel, subject || *ref* to force oneself; to be subjected
astrologie [astrɔlɔʒi] *f* astrology
astrologue [astrɔlɔg] *m* astrologer
astronaute [astrɔnot] *mf* astronaut
astronautique [astrɔnotik] *f* astronautics
astronef [astrɔnɛf] *m* spaceship
astronome [astrɔnɔm] *mf* astronomer
astronomie [astrɔnɔmi] *f* astronomy
astronomique [astrɔnɔmik] *adj* astronomical
astuce [astys] *f* slyness, guile; tricks (*of a trade*)
astu·cieux [astysjø] **-cieuse** [sjøz] *adj* astute, crafty.
atelier [atəlje] *m* studio; workshop

atermoiement [atɛrmwamã] *m* procrastination; extension of a loan
athée [ate] *adj* atheistic || *mf* atheist
athéisme [ateism] *m* atheism
Athènes [atɛn] *f* Athens
athlète [atlɛt] *mf* athlete
athlétique [atletik] *adj* athletic
athlétisme [atletism] *m* athletics
Atlantique [atlãtik] *adj & m* Atlantic
atlas [atlɑs] *m* atlas || (*cap*) *m* Atlas
atmosphère [atmɔsfɛr] *f* atmosphere
atome [atom] *m* atom
atomique [atɔmik] *adj* atomic
atomi·sé -sée [atɔmize] *adj* afflicted with radiation sickness
atomiser [atɔmize] *tr* to atomize
atone [atɔn] *adj* dull, expressionless; drab (*life*); (phonet) unaccented
atours [atur] *mpl* finery
atout [atu] *m* trump; **sans atout** no-trump
atrabilaire [atrabilɛr] *adj & mf* hypochondriac
âtre [ɑtr] *m* hearth
atroce [atrɔs] *adj* atrocious
atrocité [atrɔsite] *f* atrocity
atrophie [atrɔfi] *f* atrophy
atrophier [atrɔfje] *tr & ref* to atrophy
atta·chant [ataʃã] **-chante** [ʃãt] *adj* appealing, attractive
attache [ataʃ] *f* attachment, tie; paper clip; (anat) joint; **attache parisienne** paper clip
attachement [ataʃmã] *m* attachment
attacher [ataʃe] *tr* to attach; to tie up || *intr* (culin) to stick || *ref* to be fastened, tied; **s'attacher à** to stick to; to become devoted to
attaque [atak] *f* attack; (pathol) stroke; **attaque brusque** or **attaque brusquée** surprise attack; **attaque de nerfs** case of nerves
attaquer [atake] *tr & intr* to attack || *ref*—**s'attaquer à** to attack
attar·dé -dée [atarde] *adj* retarded; behind the times; belated, delayed || *mf* mentally retarded person; lover of the past
attarder [atarde] *tr* to delay, retard || *ref* to be delayed; to stay, remain
atteindre [atɛ̃dr] §50 *tr* to attain; to reach || *intr*—**atteindre à** to attain; to reach; to attain to
at·teint [atɛ̃] **at·teinte** [atɛ̃t] *adj* stricken || *f* reaching; injury; **hors d'atteinte** out of reach; **porter atteinte à** to endanger; **premières atteintes** first signs (*of illness*)
attelage [atlaʒ] *m* harnessing; coupling
atteler [atle] §34 *tr* to harness; to hitch; to couple (*cars on a railroad*) || *ref*—**s'atteler à** (coll) to buckle down to
attelle [atɛl] *m* splint; **attelles** hames
atte·nant [atənã] **-nante** [nãt] *adj* adjoining
attendre [atãdr] *tr* to wait for, await; to expect || *intr* to wait || *ref*—**s'attendre à** to expect; to rely on; **s'attendre à** + *inf* to expect to + *inf*; **s'attendre à ce que** + *subj* to expect (*s.o.*) to + *inf*, e.g., **il s'attend à ce que je lui raconte toute l'affaire** he

expects me to tell him the whole story; **s'y attendre** to expect it or them

attendrir [atɑ̃drir] *tr* to tenderize; to soften ‖ *ref* to become tender; to be deeply touched or moved

attendrissement [atɑ̃drismɑ̃] *m* softening; compassion

atten·du -due [atɑ̃dy] *adj* expected ‖ **attendus** *mpl* (law) grounds ‖ *adv*— **attendu que** whereas, inasmuch as ‖ **attendu** *prep* in view of

attentat [atɑ̃ta] *m* attempt, assault; outrage (*to decency*); offense (*against the state*)

attente [atɑ̃t] *f* wait; expectation

attenter [atɑ̃te] *intr*—**attenter à** to attempt (*e.g., s.o.'s life*); **attenter à ses jours** to attempt suicide

atten·tif [atɑ̃tif] **-tive** [tiv] *adj* attentive

attention [atɑ̃sjɔ̃] *f* attention; **attentions** attention, care, consideration ‖ *interj* attention!, be careful!

attention·né -née [atɑ̃sjɔne] *adj* considerate

atténuation [atenɥasjɔ̃] *f* attenuation

atténuer [atenɥe] *tr* to subdue, soften (*color; pain; passions*); to attenuate (*words; bacteria*); to extenuate (*a fault*) ‖ *ref* to soften; to lessen

atterrer [atere] *tr* to dismay

atterrir [aterir] *intr* (*aux:* AVOIR or ÊTRE) to land

atterrissage [aterisaʒ] *m* landing; **atterrissage forcé** forced landing; **atterrissage sur le ventre** pancake landing

attestation [atestasjɔ̃] *f* attestation; **attestation d'études** transcript

attester [ateste] *tr* to attest, to attest to; **attester qn de q.ch.** to call s.o. to witness to s.th.

attiédir [atjedir] *tr & ref* to cool off; to warm up

attifer [atife] *tr & ref* to spruce up

attirail [atiraj] *m* gear, tackle, outfit; (coll) paraphernalia

attirance [atirɑ̃s] *f* attraction, lure, attractiveness

atti·rant [atirɑ̃] **-rante** [rɑ̃t] *adj* appealing, attractive

attirer [atire] *tr* to attract ‖ *ref* to be attracted; to attract each other; to call forth (*criticism*)

attiser [atize] *tr* to stir, stir up, to poke

atti·tré -trée [atitre] *adj* appointed; regular (*dealer*)

attitude [atityd] *f* attitude

attrac·tif [atraktif] **-tive** [tiv] *adj* attractive (*force*)

attraction [atraksjɔ̃] *f* attraction; **les attractions** vaudeville

attrait [atre] *m* attraction, attractiveness, appeal; **attraits** charms

attrape [atrap] *f* trap; (coll) trick, joke

attrape-mouche [atrapmuʃ] *m* (*pl* **-mouche** or **-mouches**) flypaper; Venus's-flytrap

attrape-nigaud [atrapnigo] *m* (*pl* **-nigauds**) booby trap

attraper [atrape] *tr* to catch; to snare,

trap; to trick ‖ *ref* to trick each other; to hang on

attrayant [atrejɑ̃] **attrayante** [atrejɑ̃t] *adj* attractive

attribuer [atribɥe] *tr* to ascribe, attribute; to assign (*a share*) ‖ *ref* to claim, assume

attribut [atriby] *m* attribute; predicate

attribu·tif [atribytif] **-tive** [tiv] *adj* (gram) predicative

attribution [atribysjɔ̃] *f* attribution; assignment, assignation

attris·té -tée [atriste] *adj* sorrowful

attrister [atriste] *tr* to sadden ‖ *ref* to become sad

attrition [atrisjɔ̃] *f* attrition

attroupement [atrupmɑ̃] *m* mob

attrouper [atrupe] *tr* to bring together in a mob ‖ *ref* to flock together in a mob

au [o] §77

aubaine [obɛn] *f* windfall, godsend, bonanza

aube [ob] *f* dawn

aubépine [obepin] *f* hawthorn

auberge [obɛrʒ] *f* inn; **auberge de la jeunesse** youth hostel

aubergine [obɛrʒin] *f* eggplant

auburn [obœrn] *adj invar* auburn

au·cun [okœ̃] **-cune** [kyn] *adj*—**aucun . . . ne** or **ne . . . aucun** §90 no, none, not any ‖ *pron indef*—**aucun ne** §90B no one, nobody; **d'aucuns** some, some people

aucunement [okynmɑ̃] §90 *adv*—**ne . . . aucunement** not at all, by no means

audace [odas] *f* audacity

auda·cieux [odasjø] **-cieuse** [sjøz] *adj* audacious

au-deçà [odəsa] *adv* (obs) on this side; **au-deçà de** (obs) on this side of

au-dedans [odədɑ̃] *adv* inside; **au-dedans de** inside, inside of

au-dehors [odəɔr] *adv* outside; **au-dehors de** outside, outside of

au-delà [odəla] *m*—**l'au-delà** the beyond ‖ *adv* beyond; **au-delà de** beyond

au-dessous [odəsu] *adv* below; **au-dessous de** under

au-dessus [odəsy] *adv* above; **au-dessus de** above

au-devant [odəvɑ̃] *adv*—**aller au-devant de** to go to meet; to anticipate (*s.o.'s wishes*); to court (*defeat*)

audience [odjɑ̃s] *f* audience

audio-fréquence [odjofrekɑ̃s] *f* audio frequency

audiomètre [odjɔmɛtr] *m* audiometer

audi·teur [oditœr] **-trice** [tris] *mf* listener; auditor (*in class*); **auditeur libre** auditor (*in class*)

audi·tif [oditif] **-tive** [tiv] *adj* auditory

audition [odisjɔ̃] *f* audition; public hearing; musical recital

auditionner [odisjɔne] *tr & intr* to audition

auditoire [oditwar] *m* audience; courtroom

auditorium [oditɔrjɔm] *m* auditorium; concert hall; projection room

auge [oʒ] *f* trough

augmentation 50 autopsier

augmentation [ɔgmɑ̄tɑsjɔ̄] *f* augmentation; raise (*in salary*)
augmenter [ɔgmɑ̄te] *tr* to augment; to increase or supplement (*income*); to raise (*prices*); to raise the salary of (*an employee*) ‖ *intr* to augment, increase; augmenter de to increase by (*a stated amount*)
augure [ɔgyr] *m* augur; augury
augurer [ɔgyre] *tr & intr* to augur
auguste [ɔgyst] *adj* august
aujourd'hui [oʒurdɥi], [oʒordɥi] *m & adv* today; d'aujourd'hui en huit a week from today; d'aujourd'hui en quinze two weeks from today
aumône [omon] *f* alms; faire l'aumône to give alms; faire l'aumône de (fig) to hand out
aumônier [omonje] *m* chaplain
aune [on] *m* alder ‖ *f* ell
auparavant [oparavɑ̄] *adv* before, previously
auprès [oprɛ] *adv* close by, in the neighborhood; auprès de near, close to; at the side of; to, at the side of; to (*a king, a government*); with; compared with
auquel [okɛl] (*pl* auxquels) §78
auréole [ɔreɔl] *f* aureole, halo
auréomycine [ɔreɔmisin] *f* aureomycin
auriculaire [ɔrikylɛr] *adj* firsthand (*witness*); auricular (*confession*) ‖ *m* little finger
auricule [ɔrikyl] *f* auricle
aurifier [ɔrifje] *tr* to fill (*a tooth*) with gold
aurore [ɔrɔr] *f* aurora, dawn
ausculter [ɔskylte] *tr* to auscultate
auspice [ospis] *m* omen; sous les auspices de under the auspices of
aussi [osi] *adv* also, too; therefore, and so; so; aussi . . . que as . . . as
aussitôt [osito] *adv* right away, immediately; aussitôt dit, aussitôt fait no sooner said than done; aussitôt que as soon as
austère [ɔstɛr] *adj* austere
Australie [ɔstrali] *f* Australia; l'Australie Australia
austra·lien [ɔstraljɛ̃] -lienne [ljɛn] *adj* Australian ‖ (*cap*) *mf* Australian
autant [otɑ̄] *adv* as much, as many; as far, as long; autant de so many; autant que as much as, as far as; d'autant by so much; d'autant plus all the more; d'autant plus (or moins) . . . que . . . plus (or moins) all the more (*or* less) . . . as (*or* in proportion as) . . . more (*or* less); d'autant que inasmuch as
autel [otɛl], [otɛl] *m* altar
auteur [otœr] *adj*—une femme auteur an authoress ‖ *m* author
authentifier [ɔtɑ̄tifje] *tr* to authenticate
authentique [otɑ̄tik] *adj* authentic; genuine (*antique*); notarized
authentiquer [ɔtɑ̄tike] *tr* to notarize
auto [ɔto], [oto] *f* auto
auto-allumage [ɔtoalymaʒ] *m* preignition
autobiographie [ɔtobjɔgrafi] *f* autobiography

auto-buffet [ɔtobyfɛ] *m* drive-in; curb service
autobus [ɔtobys] *m* bus, city bus
autocar [ɔtokar] *m* interurban bus
autochenille [ɔtoʃənij] *f* caterpillar (*tractor*)
autochtone [ɔtoktɔn] *adj & mf* native
autoclave [ɔtoklav] *m* pressure cooker; autoclave, sterilizer
autocopie [ɔtokɔpi] *f* duplicating, multicopying; duplicated copy
autocopier [ɔtokɔpje] *tr* to run off, to duplicate, to ditto
auto-couchette [ɔtokuʃɛt] *f*—en auto-couchette piggyback
autocrate [ɔtokrat] *mf* autocrat
autocratique [ɔtokratik] *adj* autocratic
autocritique [ɔtokritik] *f* self-criticism
autocuiseur [ɔtokɥizœr] *m* pressure cooker
autodétermination [ɔtodetɛrminasjɔ̄] *f* self-determination
autodidacte [ɔtodidakt] *adj* self-taught ‖ *mf* self-taught person
autodrome [ɔtodrom] *m* race track; test strip
auto-école [ɔtoekɔl] *f* (*pl* -écoles) driving school
autogare [ɔtogar] *f* bus station
autographe [ɔtograf] *adj & m* autograph
autographie [ɔtografi] *f* multicopying
autographier [ɔtografje] *tr* to duplicate
autogreffe [ɔtogrɛf] *f* skin grafting
auto-grue [ɔtogry] *f* (*pl* -grues) tow truck
autoguidage [ɔtogidaʒ] *m* automatic piloting
auto-intoxication [ɔtoɛ̃toksikasjɔ̄] *f* autointoxication
automate [ɔtomat] *m* automaton
automation [ɔtomasjɔ̄] *f* automation
automatique [ɔtomatik] *adj* automatic ‖ *m* dial telephone
automatisation [ɔtomatizasjɔ̄] *f* automation
automatiser [ɔtomatize] *tr* to automate
automitrailleuse [ɔtomitrajøz] *f* armored car mounting machine guns
autom·nal -nale [ɔtomnal] *adj* (*pl* -naux [no]) autumnal
automne [ɔton], [otɔn] *m* fall, autumn; à l'automne, en automne in the fall
automobile [ɔtomɔbil), [otomɔbil] *adj* automotive ‖ *f* automobile
automobilisme [ɔtomɔbilism] *m* driving, motoring
automobiliste [ɔtomɔbilist] *mf* motorist
automo·teur [ɔtomɔtœr] -trice [tris] *adj* self-propelling, automatic ‖ *m* self-propelled river barge ‖ *f* rail car
autonome [ɔtonɔm] *adj* autonomous, independent
autonomie [ɔtonɔmi] *f* autonomy; cruising radius, range (*of ship, plane, or tank*)
autoplastie [ɔtoplasti] *f* plastic surgery
autoportrait [ɔtopɔrtrɛ] *m* self-portrait
auto-propul·sé -sée [ɔtoprɔpylse] *adj* self-propelled
autopsie [ɔtopsi] *f* autopsy
autopsier [ɔtopsje] *tr* to perform an autopsy on

autorail [ɔtɔrɑj] *m* rail car
autorisation [ɔtɔrizɑsjɔ̃] *f* authorization
autoriser [ɔtɔrize] *tr* to authorize ‖ *ref*
—s'autoriser de to take as authority,
to base one's opinion on
autoritaire [ɔtɔritɛr] *adj* authoritarian,
bossy
autorité [ɔtɔrite] *f* authority
autoroute [ɔtɔrut] *f* superhighway
auto-stop [ɔtɔstɔp] *m* hitchhiking; faire
de l'auto-stop to hitchhike
auto-stop·peur [ɔtɔstɔpœr] -stop·peuse
[stɔpøz] *mf* (*pl* -stop·peurs -stop·
peuses) hitchhiker
autostrade [ɔtɔstrad] *f* superhighway
autour [otur] *m* goshawk ‖ *adv* around;
autour de around; about
autre [otr] *adj indef* other; autre chose
(coll) something else; nous autres we,
e.g., nous autres Américains we
Americans; vous autres you ‖ *pron
indef* other; d'autres others; j'en ai
vu bien d'autres I have seen worse
than that; un autre another
autrefois [otrəfwa] *adv* formerly, of
old; d'autrefois of yore
autrement [otrəmɑ̃] *adv* otherwise
Autriche [otriʃ] *f* Austria; l'Autriche
Austria
autri·chien [otriʃjɛ̃] -chienne [ʃjen]
adj Austrian ‖ (*cap*) *mf* Austrian
autruche [otryʃ] *f* ostrich
autrui [otrɥi] *pron indef* others
auvent [ovɑ̃] *m* canopy (*over door*);
flap (*of tent*)
aux [o] §77
auxiliaire [oksiljer] *adj* auxiliary, stand-
by; ancillary ‖ *m* (gram) auxiliary ‖
f noncombatant unit
aux·quels -quelles [okɛl] §78
aval [aval] *m* lower waters; en aval
downstream; en aval de below ‖ *m*
(*pl* avals) endorsement
avalanche [avalɑ̃ʃ] *f* avalanche
avaler [avale] *tr* to swallow ‖ *intr* to
go downstream
ava·leur [avalœr] -leuse [løz] *mf* swal-
lower; avaleur de sabres sword swal-
lower
avaliser [avalize] *tr* to endorse
avance [avɑ̃s] *f* advance; en avance
fast (*clock*)
avan·cé -cée [avɑ̃se] *adj* advanced;
overripe; tainted (*meat*)
avancement [avɑ̃smɑ̃] *m* advancement
avancer [avɑ̃se] §51 *tr, intr, & ref* to
advance
avanie [avani] *f* snub, insult; essuyer
une avanie to swallow an affront
avant [avɑ̃] *adj invar* front ‖ *m* front;
(aer) nose; (naut) bow; d'avant previous; en avant forward; en avant de
in front of, ahead of ‖ *adv* before;
avant de (with *inf*) before; avant que
before; bien (or très) avant dans late
into; far into; deep into; plus avant
farther on ‖ *prep* before; avant Jésus-
Christ (av. J.-C.) before Christ
(B.C.)
avantage [avɑ̃taʒ] *m* advantage; (tennis) add; avantages en nature payment in kind
avanta·geux [avɑ̃taʒø] -geuse [ʒøz] *adj*

advantageous; bargain (*price*); becoming (*e.g.*, hairdo); conceited
(*manner*)
avant-bras [avɑ̃bra] *m invar* forearm
avant-cour [avɑ̃kur] *f* (*pl* -cours) front
yard
avant-coureur [avɑ̃kurœr] (*pl* -cou-
reurs) *adj masc* presaging (*signs*) ‖ *m*
forerunner, precursor, harbinger
avant-goût [avɑ̃gu] *m* (*pl* -goûts) fore-
taste
avant-guerre [avɑ̃gɛr] *m & f* (*pl* -guer-
res) prewar period
avant-hier [avɑ̃tjɛr], [avɑ̃jɛr] *adv & m*
the day before yesterday
avant-port [avɑ̃pɔr] *m* (*pl* -ports) outer
harbor
avant-poste [avɑ̃pɔst] *m* (*pl* -postes)
outpost; avant-postes front lines
avant-première [avɑ̃prəmjɛr] *f* (*pl* -pre-
mières) review (*of a play*); premiere
(*for the drama critics*); preview
avant-projet [avɑ̃prɔʒe] *m* (*pl* -projets)
rough draft; draft (*of a law*)
avant-propos [avɑ̃prɔpo] *m invar* foreword
avant-scène [avɑ̃sɛn] *f* (*pl* -scènes)
forestage, proscenium
avant-toit [avɑ̃twa] *m* (*pl* -toits) eave
avant-train [avɑ̃trɛ̃] *m* (*pl* -trains) front
end, front assembly (*of vehicle*)
avant-veille [avɑ̃vɛj] *f* (*pl* -veilles) two
days before
avare [avar] *adj* avaricious, miserly;
saving, economical ‖ *mf* miser
avarice [avaris] *f* avarice
avari·cieux [avarisjø] -cieuse [sjøz] *adj*
avaricious
avarie [avari] *f* damage; breakdown;
spoilage; (naut) average
avarier [avarje] *tr* to damage; to spoil
‖ *ref* to spoil
avatar [avatar] *m* avatar; avatars
vicissitudes
avec [avɛk] *adv* (coll) with it; (coll)
along, with me, etc. ‖ *prep* with
aveline [avlin] *f* filbert
ave·nant [avnɑ̃] -nante [nɑ̃t] *adj* gracious, charming; à l'avenant in keeping, to match; à l'avenant de in accord with ‖ *m* (ins) endorsement
avènement [avɛnmɑ̃] *m* Advent; accession (*to the throne*)
avenir [avnir] *m* future; à l'avenir in
the future
Avent [avɑ̃] *m* Advent
aventure [avɑ̃tyr] *f* adventure; à l'aventure at random; aimlessly; d'aventure
by chance; la bonne aventure fortunetelling; par aventure by chance
aventurer [avɑ̃tyre] *tr* to venture ‖ *ref*
to take a chance; s'aventurer à to
venture to
aventu·reux [avɑ̃tyrø] -reuse [røz] *adj*
adventurous
aventurier [avɑ̃tyrje] *m* adventurer
aventurière [avɑ̃tyrjer] *f* adventuress
avenue [avny] *f* avenue
avé·ré -rée [avere] *adj* established,
authenticated
avérer [avere] §10 *tr* to aver ‖ *ref* to
prove to be (*e.g.*, difficult)

avers [aver] *m* heads (*of coin*), face (*of medal*)
averse [avers] *f* shower
aversion [aversjɔ̃] *f* aversion
avertir [avertir] *tr* to warn; avertir qn de + *inf* to warn s.o. to + *inf*
avertissement [avertismã] *m* warning; notification; foreword
avertisseur [avertisœr] *adj masc* warning || *m* alarm; (aut) horn; (theat) callboy; avertisseur d'incendie fire alarm
a•veu [avø] *m* (*pl* -veux) avowal, confession; consent; sans aveu unscrupulous
aveu•glant [avœglã] -glante [glãt] *adj* blinding
aveugle [avœgl] *adj* blind || *mf* blind person; en aveugle without thinking
aveuglement [avœgləmã] *m* (fig) blindness
aveuglément [avœglemã] *adv* blindly
aveugler [avœgle] *tr* to blind; to dazzle; to stop up, to plug; to board up (*a window*) || *ref*—s'aveugler sur to shut one's eyes to
aveuglette [avœglɛt] *adv*—à l'aveuglette blindly
aveulir [avølir] *tr* to enervate, deaden || *ref* to become limp, enervated
aveulissement [avølismã] *m* enervation
aviateur [avjatœr] *m* aviator
aviation [avjasjɔ̃] *f* aviation
aviatrice [avjatris] *f* aviatrix
avide [avid] *adj* avid, eager; greedy; voracious; avide de avid for
avidité [avidite] *f* avidity, eagerness; greed; voracity
avilir [avilir] *tr* to debase, dishonor; (com) to lower the price of || *ref* to debase oneself; (com) to deteriorate
avilis•sant [avilisã] avilis•sante [avilisãt] *adj* debasing
avilissement [avilismã] *m* debasement; (com) depreciation
avi•né -née [avine] *adj* drunk
aviner [avine] *tr* to soak (*a new barrel*) with wine || *ref* (coll) to booze
avion [avjɔ̃] *m* airplane; avion à réaction jet; avion de chasse fighter plane; avion long-courrier long-range plane; en avion by plane; par avion air mail
avion-cargo [avjɔ̃kargo] *m* (*pl* avions-cargos) cargo liner, freighter
avion-taxi [avjɔ̃taksi] *m* (*pl* avions-taxis) taxiplane
aviron [avirɔ̃] *m* oar; aviron de couple scull
avis [avi] *m* opinion; advice; notice, warning; decision; à mon avis in my opinion; avis au lecteur note to the reader; changer d'avis to change one's mind
avi•sé -sée [avize] *adj* prudent, shrewd; bien avisé well-advised

aviser [avize] *tr* to glimpse, descry; to advise, inform, warn || *intr* to decide; aviser à to think of, look into; to deal with || *ref*—s'aviser de to contrive, to think up; to be on the look-out for; s'aviser de + *inf* to take it into one's head to + *inf*
aviso [avizo] *m* dispatch boat, sloop
avivage [avivaʒ] *m* brightening; polishing
aviver [avive] *tr* to revive, to stir up (*fire; passions*); to brighten (*colors*); (med & fig) to open (*a wound*)
av. J.-C. *abbr* (avant Jésus-Christ) B.C.
avo•cat [avɔka] -cate [kat] *mf* lawyer; advocate; barrister (Brit); avocat du diable devil's advocate || *m* avocado
avoine [avwan] *f* oats
avoir [avwar] *m* wealth; credit side (*of ledger*) || §6 *tr* to have; to get; avoir . . . ans to be . . . years old, e.g., mon fils a dix ans my son is ten years old; avoir beau + *inf* to be useless for (s.o.) to + *inf*, e.g., j'ai beau travailler it is useless for me to work; for expressions like avoir froid to be cold, avoir raison to be right, see the noun || *intr*—avoir à to have to; en avoir à or contre to be angry with || *impers*—il y a there is, there are, e.g., il n'y a pas d'espoir there is no hope || *aux* to have, e.g., j'ai couru trop vite I have run too fast
avoisiner [avwazine] *tr* to neighbor, to be near
avortement [avɔrtəmã] *m* abortion; miscarriage
avorter [avɔrte] *intr* to abort; to miscarry
avorton [avɔrtɔ̃] *m* runt; (biol) stunt
avoué [avwe] *m* lawyer (*doing notarial work*); solicitor (Brit)
avouer [avwe] *tr* to avow, to admit; to claim, to acknowledge authorship of || *ref* to be admitted; s'avouer vaincu to admit defeat
avril [avril] *m* April
axe [aks] *m* axis
axer [akse] *tr* to set on an axis; to orient
axiomatique [aksjɔmatik] *adj* axiomatic
axiome [aksjom] *m* axiom
axonge [aksɔ̃ʒ] *f* lard
ayant-droit [ejãdrwa] *m* (*pl* ayants-droit) claimant; beneficiary
azalée [azale] *f* azalea
azimut or azimuth [azimyt] *m* azimuth
azote [azɔt] *m* nitrogen
azo•té -tée [azɔte] *adj* nitrogenous
Aztèques [aztɛk] *mpl* Aztecs
azur [azyr] *adj* & *m* azure
azyme [azim] *adj* unleavened || *m* unleavened bread

B, b [be] *m invar* second letter of the French alphabet
baba [baba] *adj* (coll) flabbergasted, wide-eyed ‖ *m* baba
babeurre [babœr] *m* buttermilk
babil [babil], [babi] *m* babble, chatter; **babil enfantin** baby talk
babillage [babijaʒ] *m* babbling
babil·lard [babijar] **babil·larde** [babijard] *adj* babbling ‖ *mf* babbler ‖ *f* (slang) letter
babiller [babije] *intr* to babble, to chatter
babine [babin] *f* chop (*mouth*); **s'essuyer** or **se lécher les babines** to lick one's chops
babiole [babjɔl] *f* (coll) bauble
bâbord [babɔr] *m* (naut) port, portside; **à bâbord** port; **bâbord armures** port sail
babouche [babuʃ] *f* babouche, slipper
babouin [babwɛ̃] *m* baboon; pimple on the lips; brat
bac [bak] *m* ferryboat; tub, vat; box, bin; tray (*for ice cubes*); drawer (*of refrigerator*); case (*of battery*); (slang) baccalaureate
baccalauréat [bakalɔrea] *m* baccalaureate, bachelor's degree
bacchanale [bakanal] *f* bacchanal
bâche [baʃ] *f* tarpaulin; hot-water tank
bache·lier [baʃəlje] **-lière** [ljɛr] *mf* bachelor (*holder of degree*) ‖ *m* (hist) bachelor (*young knight*)
bâcher [baʃe] *tr* to cover with a tarpaulin
bachique [baʃik] *adj* bacchanalian, bacchic; drinking (*song*)
bachot [baʃo] *m* dinghy, punt; (coll) baccalaureate
bachotage [baʃɔtaʒ] *m* (coll) cramming (*for an exam*)
bachoter [baʃɔte] *intr* (coll) to cram
bacille [basil] *m* bacillus
bâclage [baklaʒ] *m* blocking up (*of harbor*); (slang) botching (*of work*)
bâcle [bakl] *f* bolt (*of door*)
bâcler [bakle] *tr* to bolt (*a door*); to close up (*a harbor*); (coll) to botch, to hurry through carelessly
bâ·cleur [baklœr] **-cleuse** [klØz] *mf* (coll) botcher
bacon [bakɔ̃] *m* bacon
bactéricide [bakterisid] *adj* bactericidal ‖ *m* bactericide
bactérie [bakteri] *f* bacterium; **bactéries** bacteria
bactériologie [bakterjɔlɔʒi] *f* bacteriology
ba·daud [bado] **-daude** [dod] *mf* rubberneck, gawk, idler
badauder [badode] *intr* to stand and stare
badigeon [badiʒɔ̃] *m* whitewash
badigeonner [badiʒɔne] *tr* to whitewash; (med) to paint (*e.g., the throat*)
ba·din [badɛ̃] **-dine** [din] *adj* sprightly, playful, teasing ‖ *mf* tease ‖ *m* (aer) air-speed indicator ‖ *f* cane, switch

badinage [badinaʒ] *m* banter; **badinage amoureux** necking
badiner [badine] *intr* to joke, to tease; to trifle, to be flippant
badinerie [badinri] *f* teasing; childishness
bafouer [bafwe] *tr* to heckle, to humiliate
bafouiller [bafuje] *intr* (coll) to stammer, mumble, babble
bâfrer [bafre] *tr* & *intr* (slang) to guzzle
bagage [bagaʒ] *m* baggage; **bagages** baggage, luggage; **bagages non accompagnés** baggage sent on ahead; **menus bagages** hand luggage; **plier bagage** to pack one's bags; (coll) to scram; (coll) to kick the bucket
bagarre [bagar] *f* brawl, row, riot; **chercher la bagarre** (coll) to be looking for a fight
bagarrer [bagare] *intr* & *ref* to riot; (coll) to brawl, scrap, scuffle
bagar·reur [bagarœr] **bagar·reuse** [bagarØz] *mf* (coll) rioter, brawler
bagatelle [bagatɛl] *f* trifle, bagatelle; frivolity ‖ *interj* nonsense!
bagnard [baɲar] *m* convict
bagne [baɲ] *m* penitentiary, penal colony; (nav) prison ship; (slang) sweatshop
bagnole [baɲɔl] *f* (slang) jalopy
bagou [bagu] *m* (coll) gift of gab
bague [bag] *f* ring; cigar band; (mach) collar, sleeve; **bague de fiançailles** engagement ring
baguenauder [bagnode] *intr* to waste time, to fool around ‖ *ref* (coll) to wander about
baguer [bage] *tr* to band (*a tree*); to baste (*cloth*)
baguette [bagɛt] *f* stick, switch, rod; baton; long thin loaf of bread; chopstick; **baguette de fée** fairy wand; **baguettes de tambour** drumsticks; **mener qn à la baguette** (coll) to lead s.o. by the nose; **passer par les baguettes** to run the gauntlet
baguier [bagje] *m* jewel box
bahut [bay] *m* trunk, chest; cupboard; (slang) high school
bai baie [bɛ] *adj* bay (*horse*) ‖ *f* bay; berry; bayberry; bay window
baignade [beɲad] *f* bathing, swimming; swimming hole, bathing spot
baigner [beɲe] *tr* to bathe; to wash (*the coast*) ‖ *intr* to be immersed, to soak ‖ *ref* to bathe; to go bathing
bai·gneur [beɲœr] **-gneuse** [ɲØz] *mf* bather; vacationist at a spa or seaside resort; bathhouse attendant ‖ *m* doll
baignoire [beɲwar] *f* bathtub; (theat) orchestra box
bail [baj] *m* (*pl* **baux** [bo]) lease; **passer un bail** to sign a lease; **prendre à bail** to lease
bâillement [bajmɑ̃] *m* yawn
bailler [baje] *tr*—**vous me la baillez belle** (coll) you're pulling my leg

bâiller [bɑje] *intr* to yawn; to be ajar, to be half open

bail·leur [bajœr] bail·leresse [bajərɛs] *mf* lessor; bailleur de fonds lender

bailli [baji] *m* bailiff

bailliage [bajaʒ] *m* bailiwick

bâillon [bɑjɔ̃] *m* gag, muzzle

bâillonner [bɑjɔne] *tr* to gag; (fig) to muzzle

bain [bɛ̃] *m* bath; bain de soleil sun bath; bains watering place, spa; bathing establishment; être dans le bain (coll) to be in hot water

baïonnette [bajɔnɛt] *f* bayonet

baiser [beze], [bɛze] *m* kiss || *tr* (vulgar) to have sex with; (archaic) to kiss

baisoter [bɛzɔte] *tr* (coll) to keep on kissing || *ref* (coll) to bill and coo

baisse [bɛs] *f* fall; jouer à la baisse (com) to bear the market

baissement [bɛsmɑ̃] *m* lowering

baisser [bese] *m* lowering; baisser du rideau curtain fall || *tr* to lower; to take in (*sail*) || *intr* to fall, drop, sink || *ref* to bend, stoop

baissier [bɛsje] *m* bear (*on the stock exchange*)

bajoue [baʒu] *f* jowl

bal [bal] *m* (*pl* bals) ball, dance; bal travesti fancy-dress ball

balade [balad] *f* stroll; balade en auto joy ride

balader [balade] *ref* to go for a stroll; se balader en auto to go joy-riding

bala·deur [baladœr] -deuse [døz] *adj* strolling || *mf* stroller || *m* gear || *f* cart (*of street vendor*); lamp with long cord

baladin [baladɛ̃] *m* mountebank, showman; oaf

balafre [balɑfr] *f* gash, scar

balafrer [balafre] *tr* to gash, to scar

balai [balɛ] *m* broom; balai à laver mop; balai de sorcière witches'-broom; balai électrique vacuum cleaner; balai mécanique carpet sweeper; donner un coup de balai à to make a clean sweep of (*s.th.*); to kick (*s.o.*) out

balai-éponge [balɛepɔ̃ʒ] *m* (*pl* balais-éponges) mop

balance [balɑ̃s] *f* balance; scales; faire la balance de (bk) to balance

balancement [balɑ̃smɑ̃] *m* swaying, teetering; (fig) indecision, wavering; (fig) harmony (*of phrase*)

balancer [balɑ̃se] §51 *tr* to balance; to move (*arms or legs*) in order to balance; to balance (*an account*); to weigh (*the pros and cons*); to swing, rock; (coll) to fire (*s.o.*) || *intr* to swing, rock; to hesitate, waver || *ref* to swing or to seesaw; to sway, rock; to ride (*at anchor*)

balancier [balɑ̃sje] *m* pendulum; balance wheel; pole (*of tightrope walker*)

balançoire [balɑ̃swar] *f* swing; seesaw, teeter-totter; (slang) nonsense

balayage [balɛjaʒ] *m* sweeping; (telv) scanning

balayer [balɛje], [baleje] §49 *tr* to sweep, to sweep up; to sweep out; to scour (*the sea*); (telv) to scan

balayeur [balɛjœr] balayeuse [balɛjøz] *mf* sweeper, scavenger || *f* street-cleaning truck

balayures [balɛjyr] *fpl* sweepings

balbutiement [balbysimɑ̃] *m* stammering, mumbling; initial effort

balbutier [balbysje] *tr* to stammer out || *intr* to stammer, to mumble

balbuzard [balbyzar] *m* osprey, bald buzzard, sea eagle

balcon [balkɔ̃] *m* balcony; (theat) dress circle

baldaquin [baldakɛ̃] *m* canopy, tester

Baléares [balear] *fpl* Balearic Islands

baleine [balɛn] *f* right whale, whale-bone whale; whalebone; rib (*of umbrella*); stay (*of a corset*)

baleinier [balɛnje] *m* whaling vessel

baleinière [balɛnjer] *f* whaleboat; life-boat

balisage [balizaʒ] *m* (aer) ground lights; (naut) buoys

balise [baliz] *f* buoy, marker; ground light, beacon; landing signal

baliser [balize] *tr* to furnish with markers, buoys, landing lights, beacons, or radio signals

balistique [balistik] *adj* ballistic || *f* ballistics

baliverne [balivɛrn] *f* nonsense, humbug

balkanique [balkanik] *adj* Balkan

ballade [balad] *f* ballade

bal·lant [balɑ̃] bal·lante [balɑ̃t] *adj* waving, swinging, dangling || *m* oscillation, shaking

balle [bal] *f* ball; bullet; hull, chaff; bale; (tennis) match point; balle traçante tracer bullet; prendre or saisir la balle au bond to seize time by the forelock

ballerine [balrin] *f* ballerina

ballet [balɛ] *m* ballet

ballon [balɔ̃] *m* balloon; ball; football; soccer ball; round-bottom flask; rounded mountaintop; ballon d'essai trial balloon

ballonner [balɔne] *tr, intr, & ref* to balloon

ballot [balo] *m* pack; bundle; (slang) blockhead, chump

ballottage [balɔtaʒ] *m* tossing, shaking; second ballot

ballotter [balɔte] *tr & intr* to toss about

balnéaire [balneer] *adj* seaside

ba·lourd [balur] -lourde [lurd] *adj* awkward, lumpish || *mf* blockhead, bumpkin || *m* wobble

balte [balt] *adj* Baltic || (*cap*) *mf* Balt

Baltique [baltik] *f* Baltic (*sea*)

balustrade [balystrad] *f* balustrade, banisters

balustre [balystr] *m* baluster, banister

bal·zan [balzɑ̃] -zane [zan] *adj* white-footed (*horse*) || *f* white spot (*on horse's foot*)

bam·bin [bɑ̃bɛ̃] -bine [bin] *mf* (coll) babe

bambo·chard [bɑ̃bɔʃar] -charde [ʃard] *adj* (coll) carousing || *mf* (coll) carouser

bamboche [bãbɔʃ] f (slang) jag, bender
bambocher [bãbɔʃe] intr (coll) to carouse, to go on a spree
bambo·cheur [bãbɔʃœr] -cheuse [ʃøz] adj (coll) carousing || mf (coll) carouser
bambou [bãbu] m bamboo
ban [bã] m ban; cadenced applause; ban de mariage banns; convoquer le ban et l'arrière-ban to invite everyone and his brother; mettre au ban to banish, to ban
ba·nal -nale [banal] adj (pl -nals -nales) banal, trite, commonplace || adj (pl -naux [no] -nales) (archaic) common, public, in common
banaliser [banalize] tr to vulgarize, to make commonplace
banalité [banalite] f banality; triteness
banane [banan] f banana
bananier [bananje] m banana tree
banc [bã] m bench; shoal; school (of fish); pew (reserved for church officials); (hist) privy council; être sur les bancs to go to high school
bancaire [bãker] adj banking, of banks
ban·cal -cale [bãkal] adj (pl -cals -cales) bowlegged, bandy-legged
bandage [bãdaʒ] m bandage; bandaging; truss; tire (of metal or rubber)
bande [bãd] f band; movie film; recording tape; cushion (in billiards); wrapper (of a newspaper); bande magnétique recording tape; tape recording; bande sonore or parlante sound track; donner de la bande to heel, to list; faire bande à part to keep to oneself
ban·deau [bãdo] m (pl -deaux) blindfold; headband; bending (of a bow); bandeau royal diadem; bandeaux hair parted in the middle
bander [bãde] tr to band, to put a band on; to bandage; to blindfold; to bend (a bow); to put a tire on; to draw taut || ref to band together; to put up resistance
banderole [bãdrɔl] f pennant, streamer; strap (of gun)
bandière [bãdjer] f battle, e.g., front de bandière battle front
bandit [bãdi] m bandit
bandoulière [bãduljer] f shoulder strap, sling; en bandoulière slung over the shoulder
banlieue [bãljø] f suburbs; de banlieue suburban
banlieu·sard [bãljøzar] -sarde [zard] mf suburbanite (especially of a Parisian suburb)
banne [ban] f awning (of store)
ban·ni -nie [bani] adj banished, exiled || mf exile
bannière [banjer] f banner, flag
bannir [banir] tr to banish
bannissement [banismã] m banishment
banque [bãk] f bank; banque des yeux eye bank; banque du sang blood bank; faire sauter la banque to break the bank
banqueroute [bãkrut] f bankruptcy (with blame for negligence or fraud)

banquerou·tier [bãkrutje] -tière [tjer] adj & mf bankrupt (with culpability)
banquet [bãke] m banquet
banqueter [bãkte] §34 intr to banquet
banquette [bãket] f seat (in a train, bus, automobile); bank (of earth or sand); bunker (in a golf course); banquette arrière back seat; banquette de tir (mil) emplacement for shooting; jouer devant les banquettes to play to an empty house
ban·quier [bãkje] -quière [kjer] mf banker
banquise [bãkiz] f pack ice
banquiste [bãkist] m charlatan, quack
baptême [batem] m baptism; christening; baptême de la ligne, baptême des tropiques or du tropique polliwog initiation
baptiser [batize] tr to baptize; to christen; (slang) to dilute (wine) with water
baptis·mal -male [batismal] adj (pl -maux [mo]) baptismal
baptistaire [batister] adj baptismal (certificate)
baptiste [batist] mf Baptist
baptistère [batister] m baptistery
baquet [bake] m wooden tub, bucket; (aut) bucket seat
bar [bar] m bar; (ichth) bass, perch
baragouin [baragwẽ] m (slang) gibberish
baragouiner [baragwine] tr (coll) to murder (a language); (coll) to stumble through (a speech) || intr (coll) to jabber
baraque [barak] f booth, stall; shanty, hovel
baraterie [baratri] f barratry
baratin [baratẽ] m (slang) blah-blah, hokum
baratte [barat] f churn
baratter [barate] tr to churn
Barbade [barbad] f Barbados; la Barbade Barbados
barbare [barbar] adj barbarous, barbaric, savage || mf barbarian
barbaresque [barbaresk] adj of Barbary
barbarie [barbari] f barbarity, barbarism || (cap) f Barbary
barbarisme [barbarism] m barbarism (in speech or writing)
barbe [barb] f beard; bristle; whiskers (of an animal); barbel; barbes vane (of a feather); deckle edge; faire q.ch. à la barbe de qn to do s.th. right under the nose of s.o.; rire dans sa barbe to laugh up one's sleeve; se faire la barbe to shave || interj—la barbe! shut up!
bar·beau [barbo] m (pl -beaux) cornflower; (ichth) barbel; (slang) pimp
barbe·lé -lée [barbəle] adj barbed || barbelés mpl barbed wire
bar·bet [barbe] -bette [bet] mf water spaniel
barbiche [barbiʃ] f goatee
barbier [barbje] m barber
barbillon [barbijɔ̃] m barb
barbiturique [barbityrik] m barbiturate
barbon [barbɔ̃] m (pej) old fogy

barboter [barbɔte] *intr* to paddle (*like ducks*); to wallow (*like pigs*); to bubble (*like carbonated water*); (coll) to splutter; (slang) to steal
barbo·teur [barbɔtœr] **-teuse** [tøz] *mf* (slang) muddler ‖ *m* duck; wash bottle ‖ *f* rompers
barbouiller [barbuje] *tr* to smear, blur; to daub; (coll) to scribble; **barbouiller le cœur à** to nauseate
barbouil·leur [barbujœr] **barbouil·leuse** [barbujøz] *mf* dauber; messy person; scribbler
bar·bu -bue [barby] *adj* bearded
bard [bar] *m* handbarrow
bardane [bardan] *f* burdock
barde [bard] *m* bard ‖ *f* blanket of bacon
bar·deau [bardo] *m* (*pl* **-deaux**) shingle; lath
barder [barde] *tr* to carry with a handbarrow; to armor (*a horse*); to blanket (*a roast*)
bardot [bardo] *m* hinny
barème [barɛm] *m* schedule (*of rates, taxes. etc.*)
baréter [barete] §10 *intr* to trumpet (*like an elephant*)
barge [barʒ] *f* barge; haystack; godwit, black-tailed godwit
barguigner [bargiɲe] *intr* to shilly-shally, to have trouble deciding
bargui·gneur [bargiɲœr] **-gneuse** [ɲøz] *mf* shilly-shallyer, procrastinator
baricaut [bariko] *m* small cask, keg
baril [baril], [bari] *m* small barrel, cask, keg
barillet [barije] *m* small barrel; revolver cylinder; spring case
bariolage [barjɔlaʒ] *m* (coll) motley, mixture of colors
bario·lé -lée [barjɔle] *adj* speckled, multicolored, variegated
barioler [barjɔle] *tr* to variegate
bariolure [barjɔlyr] *f* clashing colors, motley
bar·man [barman] *m* (*pl* **-men** [mɛn] or **-mans**) bartender
baromètre [barɔmetr] *m* barometer
barométrique [barɔmetrik] *adj* barometric
baron [barɔ̃] *m* baron
baronne [barɔn] *f* baroness
baroque [barɔk] *adj* & *m* baroque
barque [bark] *f* boat
barrage [baraʒ] *m* dam; barrage, cordon (*of police*); tollgate; barricade, roadblock, checkpoint; (sports) play-off
barre [bar], [bar] *f* bar; crossbar (*of a t*); tiller, helm; bore (*tidal flood*); **barre de justice** rod to hold shackles; **barre du gouvernail** helm; **barres** (typ) parallels; **jouer aux barres** to play prisoner's base
bar·reau [baro] *m* (*pl* **-reaux**) bar, crossbar, rail; rung (*of ladder or chair*); (law) bar
barrer [bare] *tr* to cross out, strike out, cancel; to cross (*a t; a check in a British bank*); to bar (*the door; the way*); to block off (*a street*); to dam (*a stream*); to steer (*a boat*)

barrette [barɛt], [barɛt] *f* biretta; bar; slide; pin
barreur [barœr] *m* helmsman
barricade [barikad] *f* barricade
barricader [barikade] *tr* to barricade
barrière [barjer] *f* barrier; gate (*of a town; of a grade crossing*); tollgate; neighborhood shopping district
barrique [barik] *f* cask; hogshead, large barrel
barrir [barir] *intr* to trumpet (*like an elephant*)
barrot [baro] *m* beam (*of a ship*)
baryton [baritɔ̃] *m* baritone; alto (*saxhorn*)
baryum [barjɔm] *m* barium
bas [ba] **basse** [bas] *adj* low; base, vile; cloudy (*weather*) ‖ (when standing before noun) *adj* low; base, vile; early (*age*) ‖ *m* stocking; lower part, bottom; **à bas . . . !** down with . . . !; **bas de casse** (typ) lower case; **bas de laine** nest egg, savings; **en bas** at the bottom; downstairs ‖ *f* see **basse** ‖ **bas** *adv* softly; down, low
ba·sal -sale [bazal] *adj* (*pl* **-saux** [zo]) basic; basal (*metabolism*)
basalte [bazalt] *m* basalt
basa·né -née [bazane] *adj* tanned, sunburned
basaner [bazane] *tr* to tan, to sunburn
bas-bleu [bablø] *m* (*pl* **-bleus**) bluestocking
bas-côté [bakote] *m* (*pl* **-côtés**) aisle (*of a church*); footpath (*beside a road*)
bascule [baskyl] *f* scale; rocker; seesaw
basculement [baskylmɑ̃] *m* rocking, seesawing, tipping; dimming
basculer [baskyle] *tr* to tip over ‖ *intr* to tip over; to seesaw, rock, swing; **faire basculer** to dim (*the headlights*)
bas-dessus [badəsy] *m* mezzo-soprano
base [baz] *f* base; basis; **à la base** at heart, to the core; **de base** basic
base-ball [bɛzbol] *m* baseball
baser [baze] *tr* to base; to ground, found (*an opinion*) ‖ *ref* to be based
bas-fond [bafɔ̃] *m* (*pl* **-fonds**) lowland; shallows; **bas-fonds** dregs, underworld; slums
basilic [bazilik] *m* basil
basilique [bazilik] *f* basilica
basin [bazɛ̃] *m* dimity
basique [bazik] *adj* basic, alkaline
basket [baskɛt] *m* basketball
basoche [bazɔʃ] *f* law, legal profession
basque [bask] *adj* Basque ‖ *m* Basque (*language*) ‖ *f* coattail ‖ (*cap*) *mf* Basque (*person*)
basse [bas] *f* shoal; tuba; (mus) bass; **basse chiffrée** (mus) figured bass
basse-contre [baskɔ̃tr] *f* (*pl* **basses-contre**) basso profundo
basse-cour [baskur] *f* (*pl* **basses-cours**) barnyard, farmyard; barnyard animals; poultry yard
bassesse [basɛs] *f* baseness; base act
basset [basɛ] *m* basset hound
bassin [basɛ̃] *m* basin; dock; artificial lake; collection plate; pelvis; **bassin**

de lit bedpan; **bassin de radoub** dry dock; **bassin hygiénique** bedpan
bassine [basin] *f* dishpan
bassinoire [basinwar] *f* bedwarmer
basson [basɔ̃] *m* bassoon
baste [bast] *m* ace of clubs; saddle basket || *interj* enough!
bastille [bastij] *f* small fortress
bastion [bastjɔ̃] *m* bastion
bastonnade [bastɔnad] *f* beating
bas-ventre [bavɑ̃tr] *m* abdomen, lower part of the belly
bât [bɑ] *m* packsaddle
bataclan [bataklɑ̃] *m*—**tout le bataclan** (slang) the whole caboodle
bataille [batɑj], [bataj] *f* battle, fight
batailler [batɑje], [bataje] *intr* to battle, to fight
batail•leur [batajœr] **batail•leuse** [batajøz] *adj* belligerent || *mf* fighter
bataillon [batajɔ̃] *m* battalion
bâ•tard [bɑtar] **-tarde** [tard] *adj & mf* mongrel; bastard || *m* one-pound loaf of short-length type of bread || *f* cursive handwriting
bâtar•deau [bɑtardo] *m* (*pl* **-deaux**) cofferdam, caisson
ba•teau [bato] *m* (*pl* **-teaux**) boat; **bateau automobile** motorboat, motor launch; **bateau à vapeur** steamboat; **bateau à voiles** sailboat; **bateau de guerre** warship; **bateau de pêche** fishing boat; **bateau de sauvetage** lifeboat; **monter un bateau à qn** (slang) to pull s.o.'s leg; **par (le) bateau** by boat
bateau-citerne [batositɛrn] *m* (*pl* **bateaux-citernes**) tanker
bateau-feu [batofø] *m* (*pl* **bateaux-feux**) lightship
bateau-maison [batomezɔ̃] *m* (*pl* **bateaux-maisons**) houseboat
bateau-mouche [batomuʃ] *m* (*pl* **bateaux-mouches**) excursion boat
bateau-pompe [batopɔ̃p] *m* (*pl* **bateaux-pompes**) fireboat
batelage [batlaʒ] *m* lighterage; juggling; tumbling
batelée [batle] *f* boatload
bateler [batle] §34 *tr* to lighter || *intr* to juggle; to tumble
bateleur [batlœr] **-leuse** [løz] *mf* juggler; tumbler
bate•lier [batlje] **-lière** [ljɛr] *mf* skipper || *m* boatman; ferryman
batellerie [batɛlri] *f* lighterage
bâter [bɑte] *tr* to packsaddle
bath [bat] *adj* (slang) A-one, swell
bâ•ti **-tie** [bɑti] *adj* built; **bien bâti** well-built (*person*) || *m* frame; basting (*thread*); basted garment
batifoler [batifɔle] *intr* (coll) to frolic
bâtiment [bɑtimɑ̃] *m* building; ship
bâtir [bɑtir] *tr* to build; to baste, to tack || *ref* to be built
bâtisse [bɑtis] *f* masonry, construction; building, edifice; ramshackle house
bâtis•seur [bɑtisœr] **bâtis•seuse** [bɑtisøz] *mf* builder
bâton [bɑtɔ̃] *m* stick; baton; staff, cane; rung (*of a chair*); stroke (*of a pen*); stick (*of gum*); **à bâtons rompus** by fits and starts; impromptu;

(archit) with zigzag molding; **bâton de reprise** (mus) repeat bar; **bâton de rouge à lèvres** lipstick; **bâton de vieillesse** helper or nurse for the aged; **mettre des bâtons dans les roues** to throw a monkey wrench into the works
bâtonner [bɑtɔne] *tr* to cudgel; to cross out
bâtonnet [bɑtɔnɛ] *m* rod (*in the retina*); chopstick
battage [bataʒ] *m* beating; threshing; churning; (slang) ballyhoo
bat•tant [batɑ̃] **bat•tante** [batɑ̃t] *adj* beating; pelting, driving; swinging (*door*) || *m* flap; clapper (*of bell*); **à deux battants** double (*door*)
batte [bat] *f* mallet, beater; dasher, plunger; bench for beating clothes; wooden sword (*for slapstick comedy*); (sports) bat; **batte de l'or** goldbeating
battement [batmɑ̃] *m* beating, beat; throbbing, pulsing; clapping (*of hands*); dance step; wait (*e.g., between trains*)
batterie [batri] *f* (elec, mil, mus) battery; train service (*in one direction*); ruse, scheming; **batterie de cuisine** kitchen utensils
batteur [batœr] *m* beater; thresher; (sports) batter; **batteur de grève** beachcomber; **batteur de pieux** piledriver; **batteur électrique** electric mixer
batteuse [batøz] *f* threshing machine
battoir [batwar] *m* bat, beetle (*for washing clothes*); tennis racket
battre [batr] §7 *tr* to beat; to clap (*one's hands*); to flap, flutter; to wink; to bang; to pound (*the sidewalk*); to search; to shuffle (*the cards*); **battre la mesure** to beat time; **battre monnaie** to mint money || *intr* to beat || *ref* to fight
bau [bo] *m* (*pl* **baux**) beam (*of a ship*)
baudet [bodɛ] *m* ass, donkey; stallion ass; sawhorse; (slang) jackass, idiot
baudrier [bodrije] *m* shoulder belt
bauge [boʒ] *f* lair, den; clay and straw mortar; (coll) pigsty
baume [bom] *m* balsam; (*consolation*) balm
ba•vard [bavar] **-varde** [vard] *adj* talkative, loquacious; tattletale || *mf* chatterer; tattletale; gossip
bavardage [bavardaʒ] *m* chattering; gossiping
bavarder [bavarde] *intr* to chatter; to gossip
bava•rois [bavarwa] **-roise** [rwaz] *adj* Bavarian || (*cap*) *mf* Bavarian (*person*)
bave [bav] *f* dribble, froth, spittle; (fig) slander
baver [bave] *intr* to dribble, to drool; to run (*like a pen*); **baver sur** to besmirch
bavette [bavɛt] *f* bib
ba•veux [bavø] **-veuse** [vøz] *adj* drooling; tendentious, wordy; undercooked

Bavière [bavjɛr] *f* Bavaria; **la Bavière** Bavaria

bavocher [bavɔʃe] *intr* to smear

bavochure [bavɔʃyr] *f* smear

bavure [bavyr] *f* bur (*of metal*); smear

bayer [baje] §49 *intr*—**bayer aux corneilles** to gawk, to stargaze

bazar [bazar] *m* bazaar; five-and-ten; **tout le bazar** (slang) the whole shebang

béant [beɑ̃] **béante** [beɑ̃t] *adj* gaping, wide-open

béat [bea] **béate** [beat] *adj* smug, complacent, sanctimonious

béatifier [beatifje] *tr* to beatify

béatitude [beatityd] *f* beatitude

beau [bo] (or **bel** [bɛl] before vowel or mute **h**) **belle** [bɛl] (*pl* **beaux belles**) *adj* beautiful; handsome; **bel et bien** truly, for sure; **de plus belle** more than ever; **il fait beau** it is nice out, we are having fair weather; **tout beau!** steady!, easy does it! ‖ (when standing before noun) *adj* beautiful; handsome; fine, good; considerable, large, long; fair (*weather*); odd-numbered or recto (*page*) ‖ *mf* fair one; **faire le beau, faire la belle** to strut, swagger; to sit up and beg (*said of a dog*); **la belle** the deciding match; **la Belle au bois dormant** Sleeping Beauty ‖ **beau** *adv*—**il a beau parler** it is no use for him to speak ‖ **belle** *adv*—**la bailler belle** (slang) to tell a whopper; **l'échapper belle** to have a narrow escape

beaucoup [boku] §91 *adv* much, many; **beaucoup de** much, many; **de beaucoup** by far

beau-fils [bofis] *m* (*pl* **beaux-fils**) son-in-law; stepson

beau-frère [bofrɛr] *m* (*pl* **beaux-frères**) brother-in-law

beau-père [bopɛr] *m* (*pl* **beaux-pères**) father-in-law; stepfather

beau-petit-fils [bopətifis] *m* (*pl* **beaux-petits-fils**) son of a stepson or of a stepdaughter

beaupré [bopre] *m* bowsprit

beauté [bote] *f* beauty; **beauté du diable** (coll) bloom of youth; **se faire une beauté** (coll) to doll up

beaux-arts [bozar] *mpl* fine arts

beaux-parents [boparɑ̃] *mpl* in-laws

bébé [bebe] *m* baby

bec [bɛk] *m* beak; nozzle, jet, burner; point (*of a pen*); (mus) mouthpiece; (slang) beak, face, mouth; **avoir bon bec** to be gossipy; **claquer du bec** (coll) to be hungry; **clore, clouer le bec à qn** (coll) to shut s.o. up; **tomber sur un bec** (coll) to encounter an unforeseen obstacle

bécane [bekan] *f* (coll) bike, bicycle

bécarre [bekar] *m* (mus) natural

bécasse [bekas] *f* woodcock; (slang) stupid woman

bécas·seau [bekaso] *m* (*pl* **bécas·seaux**) sandpiper

bec-de-cane [bɛkdəkan] *m* (*pl* **becs-de-cane**) door handle; flat-nosed pliers

bec-de-corbeau [bɛkdəkɔrbo] *m* (*pl* **becs-de-corbeau**) wire cutters

bec-de-corbin [bɛkdəkɔrbɛ̃] *m* (*pl* **becs-de-corbin**) crowbar

bec-de-lièvre [bɛkdəljɛvr] *m* (*pl* **becs-de-lièvre**) harelip

bêche [bɛʃ] *f* spade

bêcher [bɛʃe] *tr* to dig; (slang) to run (*s.th.*) down, to give (*s.o.*) a dig

bê·cheur [bɛʃœr] **-cheuse** [ʃøz] *mf* (coll) detractor, critic; (slang) stuffed shirt

bêchoir [bɛʃwar] *m* hoe

bécoter [bekɔte] *tr* to give (*s.o.*) a peck or little kiss on the cheek

becqueter [bɛkte] §34 *tr* to peck at; (coll) to eat ‖ *ref* to bill and coo

bedaine [bədɛn] *f* paunch, beer belly

bédane [bedan] *m* cold chisel

be·deau [bədo] *m* (*pl* **-deaux**) beadle

bé·douin [bedwɛ̃] **-douine** [dwin] *adj* Bedouin ‖ (*cap*) *mf* Bedouin (*person*)

bée [be] *adj*—**bouche bée** mouth agape, flabbergasted ‖ *f* penstock

beffroi [befrwa] *m* belfry

bégaiement [begɛmɑ̃] *m* stammering, stuttering

bégayer [begeje] §49 *tr* & *intr* to stammer, stutter

bègue [bɛg] *adj* stammering, stuttering ‖ *mf* stammerer

bégueter [begte] §2 *intr* to bleat

bégueule [begœl] *adj* (coll) prudish ‖ *f* (coll) prudish woman

béguin [begɛ̃] *m* hood, cap; sweetheart; (coll) infatuation

béguine [begin] *f* Beguine; sanctimonious woman

beige [bɛʒ] *adj* & *m* beige

beignet [bɛɲe] *m* fritter

béjaune [beʒon] *m* nestling; greenhorn, novice, ninny

bêlement [bɛlmɑ̃] *m* bleat, bleating

bêler [bɛle] *intr* to bleat

belette [bəlɛt] *f* weasel

belge [bɛlʒ] *adj* Belgian ‖ (*cap*) *mf* Belgian (*person*)

Belgique [bɛlʒik] *f* Belgium; **la Belgique** Belgium

bélier [belje] *m* ram; battering ram

bélière [beljɛr] *f* sheepbell

bélinogramme [belinɔgram] *m* Wirephoto (*trademark*)

bélinographe [belinɔgraf] *m* Wirephoto transmitter

bélître [belitr] *m* scoundrel

belladone [beladɔn] *f* belladonna

bellâtre [belɑtr] *adj* foppish ‖ *m* fop

belle-dame [beldam] *f* belladonna

belle-de-jour [beldəʒur] *f* (*pl* **belles-de-jour**) morning glory

belle-de-nuit [beldənɥi] *f* (*pl* **belles-de-nuit**) marvel-of-Peru

belle-d'un-jour [beldœ̃ʒur] *f* (*pl* **belles-d'un-jour**) day lily

belle-fille [belfij] *f* (*pl* **belles-filles**) daughter-in-law; stepdaughter

belle-mère [belmɛr] *f* (*pl* **belles-mères**) mother-in-law; stepmother

belle-petite-fille [belpətitfij] *f* (*pl* **belles-petites-filles**) daughter of a stepson or of a stepdaughter

belles-lettres [belletr] *fpl* belles-lettres, literature

belle-sœur [bɛlsœr] *f* (*pl* **belles-sœurs**) sister-in-law

belliciste [bɛlisist] *mf* warmonger

belligé·rant [bɛliʒerɑ̃] **-rante** [rɑ̃t] *adj* & *m* belligerent

belli·queux [bɛlikø] **-queuse** [køz] *adj* bellicose, warlike

bel·lot [bɛlo] **bel·lote** [bɛlɔt] *adj* pretty, cute; dapper

bémol [bemɔl] *adj invar* & *m* (mus) flat

bémoliser [bemɔlize] *tr* to flat (*a note*); to provide (*a key signature*) with flats

ben [bɛ̃] *interj* (slang) well!

bénédicité [benedisite] *m* grace (*before a meal*)

bénédic·tin [benediktɛ̃] **-tine** [tin] *adj* & *m* Benedictine ‖ (*cap*) *f* Benedictine (*liqueur*)

bénédiction [benediksjɔ̃] *f* benediction; manna from heaven

bénéfice [benefis] *m* profit; benefit; benefice; parsonage, rectory; **à bénéfice** benefit (*performance*); **sous bénéfice d'inventaire** with grave reservations

bénéficiaire [benefisjɛr] *adj* profit, e.g., **marge bénéficiaire** profit margin ‖ *mf* beneficiary

bénéficier [benefisje] *intr* to profit, benefit

benêt [bənɛ] *adj masc* simple-minded ‖ *m* simpleton, numskull

bé·nin [benɛ̃] **-nigne** [niɲ] *adj* benign; mild, slight; benignant, accommodating

béni-oui-oui [beniwiwi] *mpl* yes men

bénir [benir] *tr* to bless, to consecrate

bé·nit [beni] **-nite** [nit] *adj* consecrated (*bread*); holy (*water*)

bénitier [benitje] *m* font (*for holy water*)

benja·min [bɛ̃ʒamɛ̃] **-mine** [min] *mf* baby (*the youngest child*) ‖ (*cap*) *m* Benjamin

benne [bɛn] *f* bucket, bin, hopper; dumper; cage (*in mine*); **benne preneuse** (mach) scoop, jaws (*of crane*)

be·noît [bənwa] **-noîte** [nwat] *adj* indulgent; sanctimonious ‖ (*cap*) *m* Benedict

benzène [bɛ̃zɛn] *m* (chem) benzene

benzine [bɛ̃zin] *f* benzine

béquille [bekij] *f* crutch

béquiller [bekije] *intr* to walk with a crutch or crutches

bercail [bɛrkaj] *m* fold, bosom (*of church or family*)

ber·ceau [bɛrso] *m* (*pl* **-ceaux**) cradle; bower; **berceau de verdure** or **de chèvrefeuille** arbor

bercelonnette [bɛrsəlɔnɛt] *f* bassinet

bercer [bɛrse] §51 *tr* to cradle, rock; to beguile; to assuage (*grief, pain*) ‖ *ref* to rock, swing; to delude oneself (*with vain hopes*)

ber·ceur [bɛrsœr] **-ceuse** [søz] *adj* rocking, cradling ‖ *f* rocking chair; cradle song, lullaby

berge [bɛrʒ] *f* bank, steep bank

berger [bɛrʒe] *m* shepherd; shepherd dog

bergère [bɛrʒɛr] *f* shepherdess; wing chair

bergerie [bɛrʒəri] *f* sheepfold; pastoral poem

berle [bɛrl] *f* water parsnip

Berlin [bɛrlɛ̃] *m* Berlin; **Berlin-Est** East Berlin; **Berlin-Ouest** West Berlin

berline [bɛrlin] *f* sedan (*automobile*); berlin (*carriage*)

berlingot [bɛrlɛ̃go] *m* caramel candy; milk carton

berli·nois [bɛrlinwa] **-noise** [nwaz] *adj* Berlin ‖ *mf* Berliner (*person*)

berlue [bɛrly] *f*—**avoir la berlue** (coll) to be blind to what is going on

Bermudes [bɛrmyd] *fpl*—**les Bermudes** Bermuda

bernacle [bɛrnakl] *f* (orn) anatid; (zool) barnacle

berne [bɛrn] *f* hazing; **en berne** at half-mast

berner [bɛrne] *tr* to toss in a blanket; to ridicule; to fool

bernique [bɛrnik] *interj* (coll) shucks!, heck!, what a shame!

berthe [bɛrt] *f* corsage; cape

béryllium [beriljɔm] *m* beryllium

besace [bəzas] *f* beggar's bag; mendicancy

besicles [bəzikl] *fpl* (archaic) spectacles; **prenez donc vos besicles!** (coll) put your specs on!

besogne [bəzɔɲ] *f* work, task; **abattre de la besogne** to accomplish a great deal of work; **aller vite en besogne** to work too hastily

besogner [bəzɔɲe] *intr* to drudge, slave

beso·gneux [bəzɔɲø] **-gneuse** [ɲøz] *adj* needy ‖ *mf* needy person

besoin [bəzwɛ̃] *m* need; poverty, distress; **au besoin** if necessary; **avoir besoin de** to need; **si besoin est** if need be

bes·son [besɔ̃] **bes·sonne** [besɔn] *mf* (dial) twin

bestiaire [bɛstjɛr] *m* bestiary

bes·tial -tiale [bɛstjal] (*pl* **-tiaux** [tjo]) *adj* bestial ‖ *mpl* see **bestiaux**

bestialité [bɛstjalite] *f* bestiality

bestiaux [bɛstjo] *mpl* livestock, cattle and horses

bestiole [bɛstjɔl] *f* bug, vermin

bê·ta [beta] **-tasse** [tɑs] *adj* (coll) silly ‖ *mf* (coll) sap, dolt

bétail [betaj] *m invar* grazing animals (*on a farm*); **gros bétail** cattle and horses; **menu bétail** or **petit bétail** sheep, goats, pigs, etc.

bête [bɛt] *adj* stupid, foolish ‖ *f* animal; beast; **bête à bon Dieu** (ent) ladybird; **bête de charge, bête de somme** pack animal; **bonne bête** harmless fool

bêtifier [betifje], [betifje] *tr* to make stupid ‖ *intr* to play the fool, to talk foolishly

bêtise [betiz], [betiz] *f* foolishness, stupidity, nonsense; trifle; **faire des bêtises** to blunder, do stupid things; to throw money around

béton [betɔ̃] *m* concrete; **béton armé** reinforced concrete
bétonner [betɔne] *tr* to make of concrete
bétonnière [betɔnjɛr] *f* cement mixer
bette [bɛt] *f* Swiss chard; **bette à carde** Swiss chard
betterave [bɛtrav] *f* beet; **betterave sucrière** sugar beet
beuglement [bøgləmɑ̃] *m* bellow, bellowing, lowing
beugler [bøgle], [bœgle] *tr* (slang) to bawl out (*a song*) ‖ *intr* to bellow (*like a bull*); to low (*like cattle*)
beurre [bœr] *m* butter; **faire son beurre** (coll) to feather one's nest
beurrée [bœre] *f* slice of bread and butter
beurrer [bœre] *tr* to butter
beur·rier [bœrje] **beur·rière** [bœrjɛr] *adj* butter ‖ *m* butter dish
beuverie [bœvri] *f* drinking party
bévue [bevy] *f* blunder, slip, boner
biais [bjɛ] **biaise** [bjɛz] *adj* bias, oblique, slanting; skew (*arch*) ‖ *m* bias, slant; skew (*of an arch*); **de biais** or **en biais** aslant, askew
biaiser [bjɛze] *intr* to slant; (fig) to be evasive
bibelot [biblo] *m* curio, trinket, knick-knack
bibeloter [biblɔte] *intr* to buy or collect curios
bibe·ron [bibrɔ̃] **-ronne** [rɔn] *adj* addicted to the bottle ‖ *mf* heavy drinker ‖ *m* nursing bottle
Bible [bibl] *f* Bible
bibliobus [biblɔbys] *m* bookmobile
bibliographe [bibliɔgraf] *m* bibliographer
bibliographie [bibliɔgrafi] *f* bibliography
bibliomane [bibliɔman] *mf* book collector
bibliothécaire [bibliɔtekɛr] *mf* librarian
bibliothèque [bibliɔtɛk] *f* library; bookstand; **bibliothèque vivante** walking encyclopedia
biblique [biblik] *adj* Biblical
biceps [bisɛps] *m* biceps
biche [biʃ] *f* hind; doe; **ma biche** (coll) my darling
bicher [biʃe] *intr*—**ça biche!** (slang) fine!, it's fine!
bichlamar [biʃlamar] *m* pidgin
bichof [biʃɔf] *m* spiced wine
bi·chon [biʃɔ̃] **-chonne** [ʃɔn] *mf* lap dog
bichonner [biʃɔne] *tr* to curl (*one's hair*); to doll up ‖ *ref* to doll up
bicoque [bikɔk] *f* shack, ramshackle house
bicorne [bikɔrn] *adj* two-cornered ‖ *m* cocked hat
bicot [biko] *m* (coll) kid (*goat*); (pej) North African, Arab
bicyclette [bisiklɛt] *f* bicycle
bident [bidɑ̃] *m* two-pronged fork
bidet [bidɛ] *m* bidet; nag (*horse*)
bidon [bidɔ̃] *m* drum (*for liquids*); canteen, water bottle
bidonville [bidɔ̃vil] *m* shantytown
bidule [bidyl] *m* (slang) gadget

bief [bjɛf] *m* millrace; reach, level (*of a stream or canal*)
bielle [bjɛl] *f* connecting rod, tie rod
bien [bjɛ̃] *m* good; welfare; estate, fortune; **biens** property, possessions; **biens consomptibles** consumer goods; **biens immeubles** real estate; **biens meubles** personal property ‖ *adv* §91 well; rightly, properly, quite; indeed, certainly; fine, e.g., **je vais bien** I'm fine; **bien de** + *art* much, e.g., **bien de l'eau** much water; many, e.g., **bien des gens** many people; **bien entendu** of course; **bien que** although; **eh bien!** so!; **si bien que** so that; **tant bien que mal** so-so, as well as possible ‖ *interj* good!; all right!; that's enough!
bien-ai·mé -mée [bjɛ̃neme] *adj & mf* beloved, darling
bien-dire [bjɛ̃dir] *m* gracious speech, eloquent delivery; **être sur son bien-dire** to be on one's best behavior
bien-di·sant [bjɛ̃dizɑ̃] **-sante** [zɑ̃t] *adj* smooth-spoken, smooth-tongued
bien-être [bjɛ̃nɛtr] *m* well-being, welfare
bienfaisance [bjɛ̃fəzɑ̃s] *f* charity, beneficence
bienfai·sant [bjɛ̃fəzɑ̃] **-sante** [zɑ̃t] *adj* charitable, beneficent
bienfait [bjɛ̃fɛ] *m* good turn, good deed, favor; **bienfaits** benefits
bienfai·teur [bjɛ̃fɛtœr] **-trice** [tris] *mf* benefactor ‖ *f* benefactress
bien-fondé [bjɛ̃fɔ̃de] *m* cogency
bien-fonds [bjɛ̃fɔ̃] *m* (*pl* **biens-fonds**) real estate
bienheu·reux [bjɛ̃nœrø] **-reuse** [røz] *adj & mf* blessed
bien·nal -nale [bjɛnnal] *adj* (*pl* **-naux** [no]) biennial ‖ *f* biennial exposition
bienséance [bjɛ̃seɑ̃s] *f* propriety
bienséant [bjɛ̃seɑ̃] **bienséante** [bjɛ̃seɑ̃t] *adj* fitting, proper, appropriate
bientôt [bjɛ̃to] *adv* soon; **à bientôt!** so long!
bienveillance [bjɛ̃vɛjɑ̃s] *f* benevolence, kindness
bienveil·lant [bjɛ̃vɛjɑ̃] **bienveil·lante** [bjɛ̃vɛjɑ̃t] *adj* benevolent, kindly, kind
bienvenir [bjɛ̃vnir] *intr*—**se faire bienvenir** to make oneself welcome
bienve·nu -nue [bjɛ̃vny] *adj* welcome ‖ *m*—**soyez le bienvenu!** welcome! ‖ *f* welcome; **souhaiter la bienvenue à** to welcome
bière [bjɛr] *f* beer; coffin; **bière à la pression** draft beer
biffer [bife] *tr* to cross out, to cancel, to erase; (slang) to cut (*class*)
biffin [bifɛ̃] *m* (slang) ragman; (slang) doughboy, G.I. Joe
bifo·cal -cale [bifɔkal] *adj* (*pl* **-caux** [ko]) bifocal
bifteck [biftɛk] *m* beefsteak
bifurquer [bifyrke] *tr* to bifurcate, divide into two branches ‖ *intr & ref* to bifurcate, fork; to branch off
bigame [bigam] *adj* bigamous ‖ *mf* bigamist
bigamie [bigami] *f* bigamy

bigar·ré -rée [bigare] *adj* mottled, variegated; motley (*crowd*)
bigar·reau [bigaro] *m* (*pl* **-reaux**) white-heart cherry
bigarrer [bigare] *tr* to mottle, to variegate, to streak
bigarrure [bigaryr] *f* variegation, medley, mixture
bigle [bigl] *adj* cross-eyed
bigler [bigle] *intr* to squint; to be cross-eyed
bigorne [bigɔrn] *f* two-horn anvil
bigorner [bigɔrne] *tr* to form on the anvil; (slang) to smash
bi·got [bigo] **-gote** [gɔt] *adj* sanctimonious ǁ *mf* religious bigot
bigoterie [bigɔtri] *f* religious bigotry
bigoudi [bigudi] *m* hair curler, roller
bihebdomadaire [biɛbdɔmadɛr] *adj* semiweekly
bi·jou [biʒu] *m* (*pl* **-joux**) jewel
bijouterie [biʒutri] *f* jewelry; jewelry shop; jewelry business
bijou·tier [biʒutje] **-tière** [tjɛr] *mf* jeweler
bilan [bilɑ̃] *m* balance sheet; balance; petition of bankruptcy; **faire le bilan** to tabulate the results
bilboquet [bilbɔkɛ] *m* job printing
bile [bil] *f* bile; **se faire de la bile** (coll) to worry, fret
bi·lieux [biljø] **-lieuse** [ljøz] *adj* bilious; irascible, grouchy
bilingue [bilɛ̃g] *adj* bilingual
billard [bijar] *m* billiards; billiard table; billiard room
bille [bij] *f* ball; ball bearing; billiard ball; marble; log; **à bille** ball-point (*pen*)
billet [bijɛ] *m* note; ticket; bill (*currency*); **billet à ordre** promissory note; **billet d'abonnement** season ticket; **billet d'aller et retour** round-trip ticket; **billet de banque** bank note; **billet de correspondance** transfer; **billet de faire-part** announcement, notification (*of birth, wedding, death*); **billet de logement** billet; **billet doux** love letter; **billet simple** one-way ticket
billette [bijɛt] *f* billet
billevesée [bijvəze], [bilvəze] *f* nonsense
billion [biljɔ̃] *m* trillion (U.S.A.); billion (Brit)
billot [bijo] *m* block, chopping block; executioner's block
biloquer [bilɔke] *tr* to plow deeply
bimen·suel -suelle [bimɑ̃sɥɛl] *adj* semimonthly
bimes·triel -trielle [bimɛstriɛl] *adj* bimonthly (*every two months*)
bimoteur [bimɔtœr] *adj* twin-motor ǁ *m* twin-motor plane
binaire [binɛr] *adj* binary
biner [bine] *tr* to hoe; to cultivate, to work over (*the soil*) ǁ *intr* to say two masses the same day
binette [binɛt] *f* hoe; (hist) wig; (slang) phiz
bineur [binœr] *m* or **bineuse** [binøz] *f* cultivator (*implement*)
binocle [binɔkl] *m* lorgnette

binoculaire [binɔkylɛr] *adj* & *f* binocular
binôme [binom] *adj* & *m* binomial
biochimie [bjɔʃimi] *f* biochemistry
biographe [bjɔgraf] *mf* biographer
biographie [bjɔgrafi] *f* biography
biographique [bjɔgrafik] *adj* biographical
biologie [bjɔlɔʒi] *f* biology
biologiste [bjɔlɔʒist] *mf* biologist
biophysique [bjɔfizik] *f* biophysics
biopsie [bjɔpsi] *f* biopsy
bioxyde [biɔksid] *m* dioxide
bipar·ti -tie [biparti] *adj* bipartite
bipartisme [bipartism] *m* bipartisanship
bipartite [bipartit] *adj* bipartite; bipartisan
bipède [bipɛd] *adj* & *mf* biped ǁ *m* pair of legs of a horse
biplan [biplɑ̃] *m* biplane
bique [bik] *f* nanny goat
bir·man [birmɑ̃] **-mane** [man] *adj* Burmese ǁ (*cap*) *mf* Burmese (*person*)
Birmanie [birmani] *f* Burma; **la Birmanie** Burma
bis [bi] **bise** [biz] *adj* gray-brown ǁ [bis] *m*—**un bis** an encore ǁ *f* see **bise** ǁ *bis* [bis] *adv* twice; (mus) repeat; **sept bis** seven A, seven and a half ǁ *bis* [bis] *interj* encore!
bisaïeul bisaïeule [bizajœl] *mf* great-grand-parent ǁ *m* great-grandfather ǁ *f* great-grandmother
bisan·nuel -nuelle [bizanɥɛl] *adj* biennial
bisbille [bisbij] *f* (coll) squabble
biscaïen [biskajɛ̃] **biscaïenne** [biskajɛn] *adj* Biscayan ǁ (*cap*) *mf* Biscayan (*person*)
biscor·nu -nue [biskɔrny] *adj* misshapen, distorted
biscotin [biskɔtɛ̃] *m* hardtack
biscotte [biskɔt] *f* zwieback
biscuit [biskɥi] *m* hardtack; cracker; cookie; unglazed porcelain; **biscuit soda** soda cracker
bise [biz] *f* north wind; (fig) winter; (slang) kiss
bi·seau [bizo] *m* (*pl* **-seaux**) bevel, chamfer; **en biseau** beveled, chamfered
biseauter [bizote] *tr* to bevel, chamfer; to mark (*cards*)
biser [bize] *tr* to redye ǁ *intr* to blacken
bi·son [bizɔ̃] **-sonne** [zɔn] *mf* bison, buffalo
bisque [bisk] *f* bisque
bisquer [biske] *intr* (coll) to be resentful
bissac [bisak] *m* bag, sack
bisser [bise] *tr* to encore; to repeat
bissextile [bisɛkstil] *adj* bissextile, leap, e.g., **année bissextile** leap year
bissexué bissexuée [bisɛksɥe] *adj* bisexual
bissexuel bissexuelle [bisɛksɥɛl] *adj* bisexual
bistouri [bisturi] *m* scalpel
bistournage [bisturnaʒ] *m* castration
bistre [bistr] *adj invar* soot-brown ǁ *m* bister, soot-brown
bis·tré -trée [bistre] *adj* swarthy

bisulfate [bisylfat] *m* bisulfate
bisulfite [bisylfit] *m* bisulfite
bitter [biter] *m* bitters
bitume [bitym] *m* bitumen
bitumer [bityme] *tr* to asphalt
bitumi·neux [bityminø] **-neuse** [nøz] *adj* bituminous
bivouac [bivwak] *m* bivouac
bivouaquer [bivwake] *intr* to bivouac
bizarre [bizar] *adj* bizarre, strange
bizutage [bizyta3] *m* (slang) initiation, hazing
bizuth [bizyt] *m* (slang) freshman
blackbouler [blakbule] *tr* to blackball; (coll) to flunk
bla·fard [blafar] **-farde** [fard] *adj* pallid, pale, wan; lambent (*flame*)
blague [blag] *f* tobacco pouch; (coll) yarn, tall story, blarney; **blague à part** (coll) all joking aside; **faire une blague** (coll) to play a trick; **sale blague** (coll) dirty trick; **sans blague!** (coll) no kidding!
blaguer [blage] *tr* (coll) to kid; **blaguer qn** (coll) to pull s.o.'s leg || *intr* (coll) to kid, to tell tall stories
bla·gueur [blagœr] **-gueuse** [gøz] *adj* (coll) kidding, tongue-in-cheek || *mf* (coll) kidder, joker
blai·reau [blɛro] *m* (*pl* **-reaux**) badger; shaving brush
blâmable [blɑmabl] *adj* blameworthy
blâme [blɑm] *m* blame; **s'attirer un blâme** to receive a reprimand
blâmer [blɑme] *tr* to blame; to disapprove of
blanc [blɑ̃] **blanche** [blɑ̃ʃ] *adj* white; blank; clean; sleepless (*night*); expressionless (*voice*); **blanc comme un linge** white as a sheet || *m* white; blank; white meat; white man; white goods; chalk; bull's-eye; **à blanc** with blank cartridges; **blanc de baleine** spermaceti; **blanc de chaux** whitewash; **en blanc** blank; **en blanc et noir** in black and white
blanc-bec [blɑ̃bɛk] *m* (*pl* **blancs-becs**) (coll) greenhorn, callow youth
blanchâtre [blɑ̃ʃɑtr] *adj* whitish
blanchir [blɑ̃ʃir] *tr* to whiten; to wash or bleach; to whitewash; to blanch (*almonds*) || *intr* to blanch, whiten; to grow old
blanchissage [blɑ̃ʃisa3] *m* laundering; sugar refining
blanchisserie [blɑ̃ʃisri] *f* laundry
blanchis·seur [blɑ̃ʃisœr] **blanchis-seuse** [blɑ̃ʃisøz] *mf* launderer || *m* laundryman || *f* laundress, washerwoman
blanc-manger [blɑ̃mɑ̃3e] *m* (*pl* **blancs-manger**) blancmange
blanc-seing [blɑ̃sɛ̃] *m* (*pl* **blancs-seings**) carte blanche
bla·sé -sée [blaze] *adj* blasé, jaded
blaser [blaze] *tr* to cloy, to blunt
blason [blazɔ̃] *m* (heral) blazon
blasonner [blazɔne] *tr* (heral) to blazon
blasphéma·teur [blasfematœr] **-teuse** [tøz] *adj* blasphemous, blaspheming || *mf* blasphemer
blasphématoire [blasfematwar] *adj* blasphemous
blasphème [blasfɛm] *m* blasphemy

blasphémer [blasfeme] §10 *tr* & *intr* to blaspheme
blatte [blat] *f* cockroach
blé [ble] *m* wheat; **blé à moudre** grist; **blé de Turquie** corn; **blé froment** wheat; **blé noir** buckwheat; **manger son blé en herbe** to spend one's money before one has it
bled [blɛd] *m* (coll) backwoods, hinterland
blême [blɛm] *adj* pale; livid, sallow, wan; ghastly
blêmir [blemir] *intr* to turn pale or livid, to blanch; to grow dim
blennorragie [blɛnɔra3i] *f* gonorrhea
blèse [blɛz] *adj* lisping || *mf* lisper
blésement [blɛzmɑ̃] *m* lisping
bléser [bleze] §10 *intr* to lisp
bles·sé -sée [blese] *adj* wounded || *mf* injured person; victim; casualty
blesser [blese], [blese] *tr* to wound; to injure
blessure [blesyr] *f* wound; injury
blet blette [blɛt] *adj* overripe || *f* chard
blettir [blɛtir] *intr* to overripen
bleu bleue [blø] (*pl* **bleus bleues**) *adj* blue; fairy (*stories*); violent (*anger*); rare (*meat*) || *m* blue; bluing; bruise; sauce for cooking fish; telegram or pneumatic letter; (coll) raw recruit, greenhorn; **bleu barbeau** light blue; **bleu marine** navy blue; **bleus** coveralls, dungarees; **passer au bleu** to avoid, elude (*a question*); **petit bleu** bad wine
bleuâtre [bløɑtr] *adj* bluish
bleuet [bløɛ] *m* bachelor's-button
bleuir [bløir] *tr* & *intr* to turn blue
bleu·té -tée [bløte] *adj* bluish
blindage [blɛ̃da3] *m* armor plate; armor plating; (elec) shield
blin·dé -dée [blɛ̃de] *adj* armored; armor-plated; (elec) shielded || *m* (mil) tank
blinder [blɛ̃de] *tr* to armor-plate; (elec) to shield
bloc [blɔk] *m* block; blocking; tablet, pad (*of paper*); (elec, mach) unit; **à bloc** tight; **en bloc** all together, in a lump; **envoyer** or **mettre au bloc** (slang) to throw (*s.o.*) in the jug; **serrer le frein à bloc** to jam on the brakes
blocage [blɔka3] *m* blockage, blocking; lumping together; rubble; freezing (*of prices; of wages*); application (*of brakes*)
blocaille [blɔkɑj] *f* rubble
bloc-diagramme [blɔkdjagram] *m* (*pl* **blocs-diagrammes**) cross section
bloc-moteur [blɔkmɔtœr] *m* (aut) motor and transmission system
bloc-notes [blɔknɔt] *m* (*pl* **blocs-notes**) scratch pad, note pad
blocus [blɔkys] *m* blockade
blond [blɔ̃] **blonde** [blɔ̃d] *adj* blond || *m* blond || *f* see **blonde**
blondasse [blɔ̃das] *adj* washed-out blond
blonde [blɔ̃d] *f* blonde; blond lace; **blonde platinée** platinum blonde
blon·din [blɔ̃dɛ̃] **-dine** [din] *adj* fair-

haired ‖ *mf* blond ‖ *m* cableway; hopper for concrete; (obs) fop
blondir [blɔ̃dir] *tr* to bleach ‖ *intr* to turn yellow, become blond
bloquer [blɔke] *tr* to blockade; to block up; to fill with rubble; to jam on (*the brakes*); to stop (*a car*) by jamming on the brakes; to pocket (*a billiard ball*); to run on (*two paragraphs*); to tighten (*a nut or bolt*) as much as possible; to freeze (*wages*)
blottir [blɔtir] *ref* to cower; to curl up
blouse [bluz] *f* smock; billiard pocket
blouser [bluze] *tr* to deceive, take in ‖ *intr* to pucker around the waist ‖ *ref* to be mistaken
blouson [bluzɔ̃] *m* jacket
blouson-noir [bluzɔ̃nwar] *m* (*pl* **blousons-noirs**) juvenile delinquent
blue-jean [bludʒin] *m* blue jeans
bluet [blyɛ] *m* bachelor's-button; (Canad) blueberry
bluette [blyɛt] *f* piece of light fiction; spark, flash
bluffer [blyfe] *tr & intr* to bluff
bluf·feur [blyfœr] **bluf·feuse** [blyføz] *mf* bluffer
blutage [blytaʒ] *m* bolting, sifting; boltings, siftings
bluter [blyte] *tr* to bolt, to sift
blutoir [blytwar] *m* bolter, sifter
B.N. *abbr* (**Bibliothèque Nationale**) National Library
boa [bɔa] *m* boa
bobard [bɔbar] *m* (coll) fish story, tall tale
bobèche [bɔbɛʃ] *f* bobeche (*disk to catch drippings of candle*)
bobine [bɔbin] *f* bobbin; spool, reel; (elec) coil; **bobine d'allumage** (aut) ignition coil
bobiner [bɔbine] *tr* to spool, wind
bocage [bɔkaʒ] *m* grove
boca·ger [bɔkaʒe] **-gère** [ʒer] *adj* wooded
bo·cal [bɔkal] *m* (*pl* **-caux** [ko]) jar, bottle, globe; fishbowl
boche [bɔʃ] *adj & mf* (slang & pej) German
bock [bɔk] *m* beer glass (*half pint*); glass of beer; enema; douche
boëte [bwɛt] *f* fish bait
bœuf [bœf] *m* (*pl* **bœufs** [bø]) beef; head of beef; steer; ox; **bœuf en conserve** corned beef
boggie [bɔʒi] *m* (rr) truck
bogue [bɔgi] *f* chestnut bur
Bohême [bɔɛm] *f* Bohemia; **la Bohême** Bohemia
bohème [bɔɛm] *adj & mf* Bohemian (*artist*) ‖ *f*—**la bohème** Bohemia (*of the artistic world*)
bohé·mien [bɔemjɛ̃] **-mienne** [mjɛn] *adj* Bohemian; gypsy ‖ (*cap*) *mf* Bohemian; gypsy
boire [bwar] *m* drink; drinking; **le boire et le manger** food and drink ‖ §8 *tr* to drink; to swallow (*an affront*) ‖ *intr* to drink; **boire à la santé** de to drink to the health of; **boire à (même)** to drink out of (*a bottle*); **boire comme un trou** to

drink like a fish; **boire dans** to drink out of (*a glass*)
bois [bwɑ], [bwa] *m* wood; woods; horns, antlers; **bois de chauffage** firewood; **bois de lit** bedstead; **bois flotté** driftwood; **bois fondu** plastic wood; **les bois** (mus) the woodwinds
boisage [bwazaʒ] *m* timbering
boi·sé **-sée** [bwaze] *adj* wooded; paneled
boiser [bwaze] *tr* to panel, to wainscot; to timber (*a mine*); to reforest
boiserie [bwazri] *f* woodwork, paneling, wainscoting
bois·seau [bwaso] *m* (*pl* **bois·seaux**) bushel
boisson [bwasɔ̃] *f* drink, beverage; **boissons hygiéniques** light wines, beer, and soft drinks
boîte [bwat] *f* box; can; canister; (slang) joint, dump; **boîte aux lettres** mailbox; **boîte de nuit** night club; **boîte d'essieu** (mach) journal box; **boîte de vitesses** transmission-gear box; **boîte postale** post-office box; **en boîte** boxed; canned; **ferme ta boîte!** (slang) shut up!, **mettre en boîte** to box; to can; (slang) to make fun of
boiter [bwate] *intr* to limp
boi·teux [bwatø] **-teuse** [tøz] *adj* lame, limping; unsteady, wobbly (*chair*) ‖ *mf* lame person
boî·tier [bwatje] **-tière** [tjer] *mf* box-maker; mail collector (*from mail-boxes*) ‖ *m* box, case; kit; medicine kit; (mach) housing; **boîtier de montre** watchcase
boitte [bwat] *f* fish bait
bol [bɔl] *m* bowl, basin; cud; bolus, pellet
bolchevique [bɔlʃəvik] *adj* Bolshevik ‖ (*cap*) *mf* Bolshevik
bolcheviste [bɔlʃəvist] *adj* Bolshevik ‖ (*cap*) *mf* Bolshevik
bolduc [bɔldyk] *m* colored ribbon
bolée [bɔle] *f* bowlful
bolide [bɔlid] *m* meteorite, fireball; racing car
bombance [bɔ̃bɑ̃s] *f* (coll) feast; **faire bombance** (coll) to have a blowout
bombardement [bɔ̃bardəmɑ̃] *m* bombing; bombardment
bombarder [bɔ̃barde] *tr* to bomb; to bombard; (coll) to appoint at the last minute
bombardier [bɔ̃bardje] *m* bomber; bombardier
bombe [bɔ̃b] *f* bomb; **bombe à hydrogène** hydrogen bomb; **bombe atomique** atomic bomb; **bombe glacée** molded ice cream; **bombe volante** buzz bomb; **faire la bombe** (slang) to go on a spree
bom·bé **-bée** [bɔ̃be] *adj* convex, bulging
bomber [bɔ̃be] *tr* to bend, to arch; to stick out (*one's chest*); **bomber le torse** (fig) to stick one's nose up ‖ *intr & ref* to bulge
bon [bɔ̃] **bonne** [bɔn] *adj* §91 good; **à quoi bon?** what's the use?; **sentir bon** to smell good; **tenir bon** to hold fast

‖ (when standing before noun) *adj*
§91 good; fast (*color*) ‖ *m* coupon;
bon de commande order blank; **pour
de bon** or **pour tout de bon** for good,
really ‖ *f* see **bonne** ‖ **bon** *interj*
good!; what!

bonace [bɔnas] *f* calm (*of the sea*)

bonasse [bɔnas] *adj* simple, naïve

bon-bec [bɔbɛk] *m* (*pl* **bons-becs**) fast
talker

bonbon [bɔ̃bɔ̃] *m* bonbon, piece of
candy

bonbonne [bɔ̃bɔn] *f* demijohn

bonbonnière [bɔ̃bɔnjɛr] *f* candy dish;
candy box

bond [bɔ̃] *m* bound, bounce; leap,
jump; **faire faux bond** to miss an appointment; **faux bond** misstep

bonde [bɔ̃d] *f* plug; bunghole; sluice
gate

bon·dé -dée [bɔ̃de] *adj* crammed

bondir [bɔ̃dir] *intr* to bound, to bounce;
to leap, to jump; **faire bondir** to
make (*s.o.*) hit the ceiling

bondissement [bɔ̃dismɑ̃] *m* bouncing,
leaping

bondon [bɔ̃dɔ̃] *m* bung

bonheur [bɔnœr] *m* happiness; good
luck; **au petit bonheur** by chance, at
random; **par bonheur** luckily

bonheur-du-jour [bɔnœrdyʒur] *m* (*pl*
bonheurs-du-jour) escritoire

bonhomie [bɔnɔmi] *f* good nature; cre-
dulity

bonhomme [bɔnɔm] *adj* good-natured,
simple-minded ‖ *m* (*pl* **bonshommes**
[bɔ̃zɔm]) fellow, guy; old fellow;
bonhomme de neige snowman; **Bonhomme Hiver** Jack Frost; **faux bonhomme** humbug; **petit bonhomme**
little man (*child*)

boni [bɔni] *m* bonus; discount coupon;
surplus (*over estimated expenses*)

bonification [bɔnifikasjɔ̃] *f* improvement; discount; bonus; advantage

bonifier [bɔnifje] *tr* to improve; to give
a discount to

boniment [bɔnimɑ̃] *m* sales talk,
smooth talk

bonimenteur [bɔnimɑ̃tœr] *m* huckster,
charlatan

bonjour [bɔ̃ʒur] *m* good day, good
morning, good afternoon, hello

bonne [bɔn] *f* maid; **bonne à tout faire**
maid of all work

bonne-maman [bɔnmamɑ̃] *f* (*pl* **bon-
nes-mamans**) grandma

bonnement [bɔnmɑ̃] *adv* honestly,
plainly

bonnet [bɔnɛ] *m* bonnet; stocking cap;
cup (*of a brassiere*); (mil) undress
hat; **bonnet d'âne** dunce cap; **bonnet
de nuit** nightcap; **gros bonnet** (coll)
VIP

bonneterie [bɔnɛtri] *f* hosiery; knit-
wear

bon-papa [bɔ̃papa] *m* (*pl* **bons-papas**)
grandpa

bonsoir [bɔ̃swar] *m* good evening;
(coll) good night

bonté [bɔ̃te] *f* goodness; kindness

booster [bustœr] *m* (rok) booster

borborygme [bɔrbɔrigm] *m* rumbling
(*in the stomach*)

bord [bɔr] *m* edge, border; rim, brim;
side (*of a ship*); **à bord** on board; **à
pleins bords** overflowing; without
hindrance; **à ras bords** full to the
brim; **être du (même) bord de** to be
of the same mind as; **faux bord** list
(*of ship*); **jeter par-dessus bord** to
throw overboard

bordage [bɔrdaʒ] *m* edging (*of dress*);
planking (*of ship*)

bordé [bɔrde] *m* border, edging

bordée [bɔrde] *f* broadside, volley;
(naut) tack; **bordée de bâbord** port
watch; **bordée de tribord** starboard
watch; **courir une bordée** to go sky-
larking on shore leave; **tirer une bordée** to jump ship

bordel [bɔrdɛl] *m* (vulgar) brothel

borde·lais [bɔrdəlɛ] **-laise** [lɛz] *adj* of
Bordeaux ‖ *f* Bordeaux cask ‖ (*cap*)
mf native or inhabitant of Bordeaux

border [bɔrde] *tr* to border; to hem;
to sail along (*the coast*); **border un
lit** to make a bed

borde·reau [bɔrdəro] *m* (*pl* **-reaux**)
itemized account, memorandum

bordure [bɔrdyr] *f* border

bore [bɔr] *m* boron

boréal boréale [bɔreal] *adj* (*pl* **boréaux**
[bɔreo] or **boréals**) boreal; northern

borgne [bɔrɲ] *adj* one-eyed; blind in
one eye; disreputable (*bar, house,
etc.*) ‖ *mf* one-eyed person

borne [bɔrn] *f* landmark; boundary
stone; milestone; (elec) binding post,
terminal; (slang) kilometer; **bornes**
bounds, limits

bor·né -née [bɔrne] *adj* limited, narrow; dull (*mind*)

borner [bɔrne] *tr* to mark out the
boundary of; to set limits to ‖ *ref* to
restrain oneself

bosquet [bɔskɛ] *m* grove

bosse [bɔs] *f* hump; bump; (coll) flair

bosseler [bɔsle] §34 *tr* to emboss; to
dent

bossoir [bɔswar] *m* davit; bow (*of
ship*)

bos·su -sue [bɔsy] *adj* hunchbacked ‖
mf hunchback; **rire comme un bossu**
to split one's sides laughing

botanique [bɔtanik] *adj* botanical ‖ *f*
botany

botte [bɔt] *f* boot; bunch (*e.g., of
radishes*); sword thrust; **lécher les
bottes à qn** (coll) to lick s.o.'s boots

botteler [bɔtle] §34 *tr* to tie in bunches

botter [bɔte] *tr* to boot, to boot out;
cela me botte that suits me ‖ *ref* to
put on one's boots

bottier [bɔtje] *m* custom shoemaker

Bottin [bɔtɛ̃] *m* business directory

bottine [bɔtin] *f* high button shoe

boubouler [bubule] *intr* to hoot like an
owl

bouc [buk] *m* billy goat; goatee; **bouc
émissaire** scapegoat

boucan [bukɑ̃] *m* smokehouse; (coll)
uproar

boucaner [bukane] *tr* to smoke (*meat*)

boucanier [bukanje] *m* buccaneer

boucharde [buʃard] ƒ bushhammer
bouche [buʃ] ƒ mouth; muzzle (of gun); door (of oven); entrance (to subway); **bouche close!** mum's the word!; **bouche d'incendie** fire hydrant; **bouches** mouth (of river); **faire la petite bouche à** to turn up one's nose at
bouchée [buʃe] ƒ mouthful; patty; chocolate cream (candy)
boucher [buʃe] m butcher || tr to stop up, to plug; to wall up; to cut off (the view); to bung (a barrel); to cork (a bottle); **bouché à l'émeri** (coll) completely dumb || ref to be stopped up
boucherie [buʃri] ƒ butcher shop; **boucherie chevaline** horsemeat butcher shop
bouche-trou [buʃtru] m (pl -trous) stopgap
bouchon [buʃɔ̃] m cork, stopper; bob (on a fishline); **bouchon de circulation** traffic jam
bouclage [buklaʒ] m closing of circuit; (mil) encirclement
boucle [bukl] ƒ buckle; earring; curl; (aer) loop; **boucler la boucle** to loop the loop
boucler [bukle] tr to buckle; to curl (the hair); to lock up (prisoners); to put a nose ring on (a bull); **boucler son budget** (coll) to make ends meet; **la boucler** (slang) to shut up, to button one's lip || intr to curl
bouclier [buklije] m shield; **bouclier antithermique** heat shield
bouddhisme [budism] m Buddhism
bouddhiste [budist] adj & mƒ Buddhist
bouder [bude] tr to be distant toward || intr to pout, sulk
bou·deur [budœr] **-deuse** [døz] adj pouting || mƒ sullen person
boudin [budɛ̃] m blood sausage; **à boudin** spiral
boudiner [budine] tr to twist
boue [bu] ƒ mud
bouée [bwe] ƒ buoy; **bouée de sauvetage** life preserver
boueur [bwœr] m garbage collector; scavenger
boueux [bwø] **boueuse** [bwøz] adj muddy; grimy; (typ) smeary
bouf·fant [bufɑ̃] **bouf·fante** [bufɑ̃t] adj puffed (sleeves); baggy (trousers)
bouffe [buf] adj comic (opera) || ƒ (slang) grub
bouffée [bufe] ƒ puff, gust
bouffer [bufe] tr (slang) to gobble up || intr to puff out
bouf·fi -fie [bufi] adj puffed up or out
bouffir [bufir] tr & intr to puff up
bouffissure [bufisyr] ƒ swelling
bouf·fon [bufɔ̃] **bouf·fonne** [bufɔn] adj & m buffoon, comic
bouffonnerie [bufɔnri] ƒ buffoonery
bouge [buʒ] m bulge; hovel, dive
bougeoir [buʒwar] m flat candlestick
bougeotte [buʒɔt] ƒ (coll) wanderlust
bouger [buʒe] §38 tr—**ne bougez rien!** (coll) don't move a thing! || intr to budge, stir

bougie [buʒi] ƒ candle; candlepower; spark plug
bou·gon [bugɔ̃] **-gonne** [gɔn] adj grumbling || mƒ grumbler
bougran [bugrɑ̃] m buckram
bou·gre [bugr] **-gresse** [grɛs] mƒ (slang) customer; **bougre d'âne** (slang) perfect ass || m (slang) guy; **bon bougre** (slang) swell guy || ƒ (slang) wench
bougrement [bugrəmɑ̃] adv (slang) awfully, darned
bouillabaisse [bujabɛs] ƒ bouillabaisse, fish stew, chowder
bouil·lant [bujɑ̃] **bouil·lante** [bujɑ̃t] adj boiling; fiery, impetuous
bouilleur [bujœr] m distiller (of brandy); boiler tube; small nuclear reactor
bouilli [buji] m beef stew
bouillir [bujir] §9 tr & intr to boil; **faire bouillir la marmite** (coll) to bring home the bacon
bouilloire [bujwar] ƒ kettle
bouillon [bujɔ̃] m broth, bouillon; bubble; bubbling; cheap restaurant; **à gros bouillons** gushing; **boire un bouillon** (coll) to gulp water; (coll) to suffer business losses; **bouillon de culture** (bact) broth; **bouillon d'onze heures** poisoned drink; **bouillons** unsold copies, remainders
bouillonnement [bujɔnmɑ̃] m boiling; effervescence
bouillonner [bujɔne] tr to put puffs in (a dress) || intr to boil up; to have copies left over
bouillotte [bujɔt] ƒ hot-water bottle
boulanger [bulɑ̃ʒe] m baker || §38 intr to bake bread
boulangerie [bulɑ̃ʒri] ƒ bakery
boule [bul] ƒ ball; (slang) nut, head; **boule d'eau chaude** hot-water bottle; **boule de neige** snowball; **boule noire** blackball; **boules** bowling; **en boule** (fig) tied in a knot, on edge; **perdre la boule** (slang) to go off one's rocker; **se mettre en boule** (coll) to get mad
bou·leau [bulo] m (pl -leaux) birch
boule-de-neige [buldənɛʒ] ƒ (pl boules-de-neige) guelder-rose; meadow mushroom
bouledogue [buldɔg] m bulldog
bouler [bule] tr to pad (a bull's horn) || intr to roll like a ball; **envoyer bouler** (slang) to send (s.o.) packing
boulet [bulɛ] m cannonball; (coll) cross to bear
boulette [bulɛt] ƒ ball, pellet
boulevard [bulvar] m boulevard; **boulevard périphérique** belt road
boulevar·dier [bulvardje] **-dière** [djɛr] adj fashionable || m boulevardier, man about town
bouleversement [bulvɛrsmɑ̃] m upset
bouleverser [bulvɛrse] tr to upset; to overthrow
boulier [bulje] m abacus (for scoring billiards)
bouline [bulin] ƒ (naut) bowline
boulingrin [bulɛ̃grɛ̃] m bowling green
bouliste [bulist] mƒ bowler

boulodrome [bulɔdrɔm] *m* bowling alley

boulon [bulɔ̃] *m* bolt; **boulon à œil** eyebolt

boulonner [bulɔne] *tr* to bolt ‖ *intr* (slang) to work

bou·lot [bulo] **-lotte** [lɔt] *adj* (coll) dumpy, squat ‖ *m* (slang) cylindrical loaf of bread; (slang) work

boulotter [bulɔte] *tr* (slang) to eat

boum [bum] *interj* boom!

bouquet [bukɛ] *m* bouquet; clump (*of trees*); prawn; jack rabbit; **c'est le bouquet** (coll) it's tops; (coll) that's the last straw

bouquetière [buktjɛr] *f* flower girl

bouquin [bukɛ̃] *m* (coll) book; (coll) old book

bouquiner [bukine] *intr* to shop around for old books; (coll) to read

bouquinerie [bukinri] *f* secondhand books; secondhand bookstore

bouqui·neur [bukinœr] **-neuse** [nøz] *mf* collector of old books; browser in bookstores

bouquiniste [bukinist] *mf* secondhand bookdealer

bourbe [burb] *f* mire

bour·beux [burbø] **-beuse** [bøz] *adj* miry, muddy

bourbier [burbje] *m* quagmire

bourbillon [burbijɔ̃] *m* core (*of boil*)

bourde [burd] *f* (coll) boner

bourdon [burdɔ̃] *m* bumblebee; big bell; (mus) bourdon; **avoir le bourdon** (slang) to have the blues; **faux bourdon** drone

bourdonnement [burdɔnmã] *m* buzzing

bourdonner [burdɔne] *tr* (coll) to hum (*a tune*) ‖ *intr* to buzz

bourg [bur] *m* market town

bourgade [burgad] *f* small town

bour·geois [burʒwa] **-geoise** [ʒwaz] *adj* bourgeois, middle-class ‖ *mf* commoner, middle-class person; Philistine; **gros bourgeois** solid citizen ‖ *m* businessman; **en bourgeois** in civies ‖ *f* (slang) old woman (*wife*)

bourgeoisie [burʒwazi] *f* middle class; **haute bourgeoisie** upper middle class; **petite bourgeoisie** lower middle class

bourgeon [burʒɔ̃] *m* bud; pimple

bourgeonnement [burʒɔnmã] *m* budding

bourgeonner [burʒɔne] *intr* to bud; to break out in pimples

bourgeron [burʒərɔ̃] *m* jumper, overalls; sweat shirt

bourgogne [burgɔɲ] *m* Burgundy (*wine*) ‖ (*cap*) *f* Burgundy (*province*); **la Bourgogne** Burgundy

bourgui·gnon [burgiɲɔ̃] **-gnonne** [ɲɔn] *adj* Burgundian ‖ *m* Burgundian (*dialect*) ‖ (*cap*) *mf* Burgundian

bourlinguer [burlɛ̃ge] *intr* to labor (*in high seas*); (coll) to travel, to venture forth

bourrade [burad] *f* sharp blow; poke

bourrage [buraʒ] *m* cramming; **bourrage de crâne** (coll) ballyhoo

bourre [bur] *f* stuffing, animal hair

bour·reau [buro] *m* (*pl* **-reaux**) executioner; torturer; **bourreau des cœurs** lady-killer; **bourreau de travail** glutton for work

bourrée [bure] *f* fagot of twigs

bourreler [burle] §34 *tr* to torment

bourrelet [burlɛ] *m* weather stripping; roll (*of fat*); contour pillow

bourrer [bure] *tr* to stuff, cram; **bourrer de coups** to pummel, slug; **bourrer le crâne à** (coll) to hand (*s.o.*) a line, to take (*s.o.*) in ‖ *ref* to stuff

bourriche [buriʃ] *f* hamper

bourrique [burik] *f* she-ass; (coll) ass

bour·ru -rue [bury] *adj* rough; grumpy; unfermented (*wine*)

bourse [burs] *f* purse; scholarship, fellowship; stock exchange, bourse; **bourse du travail** labor union hall; **bourses** scrotum

bourse-à-pasteur [bursapastœr] *f* (*pl* **bourses-à-pasteur** [bursapastœr]) (bot) shepherd's-purse

boursicaut or **boursicot** [bursiko] *m* little purse; nest egg

boursicoter [bursikɔte] *intr* to dabble in the stock market

bour·sier [bursje] **-sière** [sjɛr] *adj* scholarship (*student*); stock-market (*operation*) ‖ *mf* scholar (*holder of scholarship*); speculator

boursoufler [bursufle] *tr* to puff up

bousculer [buskyle] *tr* to jostle

bouse [buz] *f*—**bouse de vache** cow dung

bouseux [buzø] *m* (slang) peasant

bousillage [buzijaʒ] *m* cob (*mixture of clay and straw*); (coll) botched job

bousiller [buzije] *tr* (coll) to bungle; (slang) to smash up ‖ *intr* to build with cob

boussole [busɔl] *f* compass; **perdre la boussole** (coll) to go off one's rocker

boustifaille [bustifaj] *f* (slang) feasting; (slang) good food

bout [bu] *m* end; piece, scrap, bit; **à bout** exhausted; **à bout de bras** at arm's length; **à bout portant** point-blank; **à tout bout de champ** at every turn, repeatedly; **au bout du compte** after all; **bout de fil** (telp) (coll) ring, call; **bout de l'an** watch night; **bout d'essai** screen test; **bout d'homme** wisp of a man; **bout filtre** filter tip; **de bout en bout** from start to finish; **montrer le bout de l'oreille** to show one's true colors; **rire du bout des dents** to force a laugh; **sur le bout du doigt** at one's fingertips; **venir à bout de** to succeed in, to triumph over

boutade [butad] *f* sally, quip; whim

bout-dehors [budɔɔr] *m* (*pl* **bouts-dehors**) (naut) boom

boute-en-train [butɑ̃trɛ̃] *m invar* life of the party

boute-feu [butfø] *m* (*pl* **-feux**) firebrand

bouteille [butɛj] *f* bottle; **bouteille isolante** vacuum bottle

bouteiller [butɛje] *m* (hist) cupbearer

bouterolle [butrɔl] *f* ward (*of lock*); rivet snap

boute-selle [butsɛl] *m* boots and saddles (*trumpet call*)
boutique [butik] *f* shop; stock, goods; workshop; set of tools; **boutique cadeaux, boutique de souvenirs** gift shop; **boutique de modiste** millinery shop; **quelle boutique!** (coll) what a hellhole!, what an awful place!
boutiquier [butikje] *m* shopkeeper
bouton [butɔ̃] *m* button; pimple; doorknob; bud; **bouton de puissance** volume control
bouton-d'argent [butɔ̃darʒɑ̃] *m* (*pl* **boutons-d'argent**) sneezewort
bouton-d'or [butɔ̃dɔr] *m* (*pl* **boutons-d'or**) buttercup
boutonner [butɔne] *tr* to button ǁ *intr* to bud
bouton·neux [butɔnø] **bouton-neuse** [butɔnøz] *adj* pimply
boutonnière [butɔnjɛr] *f* buttonhole
bouton-pression [butɔ̃prɛsjɔ̃] *m* (*pl* **boutons-pression**) snap fastener
bouture [butyr] *f* cutting (*from a plant*)
bouturer [butyre] *tr* to propagate (*plants*) by cuttings ǁ *intr* to shoot suckers
bouverie [buvri] *f* cowshed
bou·vier [buvje] **-vière** [vjɛr] *mf* cowherd
bouvillon [buvijɔ̃] *m* steer, young bullock
bouvreuil [buvrœj] *m* bullfinch; **bouvreuil cramoisi** scarlet grosbeak
box [bɔks] *m* (*pl* **boxes**) stall
boxe [bɔks] *f* boxing
boxer [bɔksœr] *m* boxer (*dog*) ǁ [bɔkse] *tr* & *intr* to box
boxeur [bɔksœr] *m* (sports) boxer
boy [bɔj] *m* houseboy; chorus boy
boyau [bwajo] *m* (*pl* **boyaux**) intestine, gut; inner tube; (mil) communication trench
boycottage [bɔjkɔtaʒ] *m* boycott
boycotter [bɔjkɔte] *tr* to boycott
boy-scout [bɔjskut] *m* (*pl* **-scouts**) boy scout
b. p. f. *abbr* (**bon pour francs**) value in francs
bracelet [braslɛ] *m* bracelet; wristband; **bracelet de caoutchouc** rubber band; **bracelet de cheville** anklet
bracelet-montre [braslɛmɔ̃tr] *m* (*pl* **bracelets-montres**) wrist watch
braconnage [brakɔnaʒ] *m* poaching
braconner [brakɔne] *intr* to poach
bracon·nier [brakɔnje] **bracon·nière** [brakɔnjɛr] *mf* poacher
brader [brade] *tr* to sell off
braderie [bradəri] *f* clearance sale
braguette [bragɛt] *f* fly (*of trousers*)
brahmane [braman] *m* Brahman
brai [brɛ] *m* resin, pitch
braille [braj] *m* braille
brailler [braje] *tr* & *intr* to bawl
brail·leur [brajœr] **brail·leuse** [brajøz] *adj* loudmouthed ǁ *mf* loudmouth
braiment [brɛmɑ̃] *m* bray
braire [brɛr] §68 (usually used in: *inf*; *ger*; *pp*; 3d *sg* & *pl*) *intr* to bray
braise [brɛz] *f* embers, coals
braiser [brɛze] *tr* to braise
braisière [brɛzjɛr] *f* braising pan

bramer [brame] *intr* to bell
bran [brɑ̃] *m* bran; (slang) dung; **bran de scie** sawdust
brancard [brɑ̃kar] *m* stretcher; shaft (*of carriage*)
brancardier [brɑ̃kardje] *m* stretcher-bearer
branche [brɑ̃ʃ] *f* branch
brancher [brɑ̃ʃe] *tr* to branch, fork; to hook up, connect; (elec) to plug in ǁ *intr* to perch
brande [brɑ̃d] *f* heather; heath
brandir [brɑ̃dir] *tr* to brandish
brandon [brɑ̃dɔ̃] *m* torch; firebrand; **brandon de discorde** mischief-maker
bran·lant [brɑ̃lɑ̃] **-lante** [lɑ̃t] *adj* shaky, tottering, unsteady
branle [brɑ̃l] *m* oscillation; impetus; **mener le branle** to lead the dance; **mettre en branle** to set in motion
branle-bas [brɑ̃ləba] *m invar* call to battle stations; bustle, commotion
branler [brɑ̃le] *tr* to shake (*the head*) ǁ *intr* to shake; to oscillate; to be loose (*said of tooth*); **branler dans le manche** to be about to fall
braque [brak] *adj* (coll) featherbrained ǁ *mf* (coll) featherbrain ǁ *m* pointer (*dog*)
braquer [brake] *tr* to aim, point; to fix (*the eyes*); to turn (*a steering wheel*); **braquer contre** to turn (*e.g., an audience*) against ǁ *intr* to steer
bras [bra] *m* arm; handle; shaft; **à bras raccourcis** violently; **bras de mer** sound (*passage of water*); **bras de pick-up** pickup arm, tone arm; **bras dessus bras dessous** arm in arm; **en bras de chemise** in shirt sleeves; **manquer de bras** to be short-handed
braser [braze] *tr* to braze
brasero [brazero] *m* brazier
brasier [brazje] *m* glowing coals; blaze
bras-le-corps [bralkɔr] *m*—**à bras-le-corps** around the waist
brassage [brasaʒ] *m* brewing
brasse [bras], [bras] *f* fathom; breast stroke
brassée [brase] *f* armful; stroke (*in swimming*)
brasser [brase] *tr* to brew
brasserie [brasri] *f* brewery; restaurant, lunchroom
bras·seur [brasœr] **bras·seuse** [brasøz] *mf* brewer; swimmer doing the breast stroke; **brasseur d'affaires** person with many irons in the fire
brassière [brasjɛr] *f* sleeved shirt (*for an infant*); shoulder strap; **brassière de sauvetage** life preserver
bravache [bravaʃ] *adj* & *m* braggart
bravade [bravad] *f* bravado
brave [brav] *adj* brave ǁ (when standing before noun) *adj* worthy, honest ǁ *m* brave man
braver [brave] *tr* to brave
bravoure [bravur] *f* bravery, gallantry
break [brɛk] *m* station wagon
brebis [brəbi] *f* ewe; sheep, lamb; **brebis galeuse** black sheep
brèche [brɛʃ] *f* breach (*in a wall*); gap (*between mountains*); nick (*e.g., on china*); (fig) dent (*in a fortune*);

battre en brèche to batter; (fig) to disparage; **mourir sur la brèche** to go down fighting

bredouille [brəduj]—**rentrer** or **revenir bredouille** to return empty-handed

bredouiller [brəduje] *tr* to stammer out (*an excuse*) ‖ *intr* to mumble

bref [brɛf] **brève** [brɛv] *adj* brief, short; curt ‖ *m* papal brief ‖ *f* short syllable; **brèves et longues** dots and dashes ‖ **bref** *adv* briefly, in short

brelan [brəlɑ̃] *m* (cards) three of a kind

breloque [brələk] *f* trinket, charm; **battre la breloque** to sound the all clear; to keep irregular time; (coll) to have a screw loose somewhere

brème [brɛm] *f* (ichth) bream

Brésil [brezil] *m*—**le Brésil** Brazil

brési·lien [breziljɛ̃] **-lienne** [ljɛn] *adj* Brazilian ‖ (*cap*) *mf* Brazilian

Bretagne [brətaɲ] *f* Brittany; **la Bretagne** Brittany

bretelle [brətɛl] *f* strap, sling; access route; **bretelles** suspenders

bre·ton [brətɔ̃] **-tonne** [tɔn] *adj* Breton ‖ *m* Breton (*language*) ‖ (*cap*) *mf* Breton (*person*)

bretteur [brɛtœr] *m* swashbuckler

bretzel [brɛtzɛl] *m* pretzel

breuvage [brœvaʒ] *m* beverage, drink

brevet [brəvɛ] *m* diploma; license; (mil) commission; **brevet d'invention** patent

breve·té -tée [brəvte] *adj* commissioned; patented; **non breveté** noncommissioned ‖ *m* commissioned officer

breveter [brəvte] §34 *tr* to patent

bréviaire [brevjɛr] *m* (eccl) breviary

bribe [brib] *f* hunk of bread; **bribes** scraps, leavings, fragments

bric [brik] *m*—**de bric et de broc** with odds and ends; somehow

bric-à-brac [brikabrak] *m invar* secondhand merchandise; junk shop

brick [brik] *m* brig (*kind of ship*)

bricolage [brikɔlaʒ] *m* do-it-yourself

bricoler [brikɔle] *intr* to do odd jobs; to putter around

brico·leur [brikɔlœr] **-leuse** [løz] *mf* jack-of-all-trades ‖ *m* handyman

bride [brid] *f* bridle; strap; clamp; **à toute bride** or **à bride abattue** full speed ahead

bridge [bridʒ] *m* (cards, dentistry) bridge

bridger [bridʒe] *intr* to play bridge

brid·geur [bridʒœr] **-geuse** [ʒøz] *mf* bridge player

briefing [brifiŋ] *m* briefing

brièvement [brijɛvmɑ̃] *adv* briefly

brièveté [brijɛvte] *f* brevity

brigade [brigad] *f* brigade

brigadier [brigadje] *m* corporal; police sergeant; noncom

brigand [brigɑ̃] *m* brigand

brigantin [brigɑ̃tɛ̃] *m* brigantine

brigue [brig] *f* intrigue, lobbying

briguer [brige] *tr* to influence underhandedly; to lobby for (*s.th.*); to court (*favor, votes*)

brigueur [brigœr] *m* schemer

bril·lant [brijɑ̃] **bril·lante** [brijɑ̃t] *adj* brilliant, bright ‖ *m* brilliancy, luster; fingernail polish

briller [brije] *intr* to shine; to sparkle; **faire briller** to show (*s.o.*) off

brimade [brimad] *f* hazing

brimborion [brɛ̃bɔrjɔ̃] *m* mere trifle

brimer [brime] *tr* to haze

brin [brɛ̃] *m* blade; sprig, shoot; staple (*of hemp, linen*); strand (*of rope*); belt (*of pulley*); (coll) (little) bit, e.g., **un brin d'air** a (little) bit of air; **ne . . . brin** §90 (archaic) not a bit, not a single; **un beau brin de fille** (coll) a fine figure of a girl

brinde [brɛ̃d] *f* (archaic) toast

brindille [brɛ̃dij] *f* twig, sprig

brioche [brijɔʃ] *f* brioche, breakfast roll

brique [brik] *f* brick

briquer [brike] *tr* (coll) to polish up, scour

briquet [brikɛ] *m* lighter

briquetage [briktaʒ] *m* brickwork

briqueter [brikte] §34 *tr* to brick (up)

briqueterie [brikətri] *f* brickyard

briqueteur [briktœr] *m* bricklayer

brisant [brizɑ̃] *m* breakers; **brisants** surf

brise [briz] *f* breeze

bri·sé -sée [brize] *adj* broken; folding (*door*) ‖ *fpl* see **brisées**

brise-bise [brizbiz] *m invar* weather stripping; café curtain

brisées [brize] *fpl* track, footsteps

brise-glace [brizglas] *m invar* (naut) icebreaker

brise-jet [brizʒɛ] *m invar* (anti)splash attachment (*for water faucet*), spray filter

brise-lames [brizlam] *m invar* breakwater

brisement [brizmɑ̃] *m* breaking

briser [brize] *tr, intr, & ref* to break

brise-tout [briztu] *m invar* (coll) butterfingers, clumsy person

bri·seur [brizœr] **-seuse** [zøz] *mf* breaker (*person*); **briseur de grève** strikebreaker

brise-vent [brizvɑ̃] *m invar* windbreak

brisque [brisk] *f* service stripe

bristol [bristɔl] *m* Bristol board, pasteboard; visiting card

brisure [brizyr] *f* break; joint

britannique [britanik] *adj* British ‖ (*cap*) *mf* Briton

broc [bro] *m* pitcher, jug

brocanter [brɔkɑ̃te] *tr* to buy, sell, or trade (*secondhand articles*) ‖ *intr* to deal in secondhand articles

brocan·teur [brɔkɑ̃tœr] **-teuse** [tøz] *mf* secondhand dealer

brocard [brɔkar] *m* lampoon, brickbat; (zool) brocket; **lancer des brocards** to make sarcastic remarks, to gibe

brocart [brɔkar] *m* brocade

broche [brɔʃ] *f* brooch; pin; (culin) spit, skewer

bro·ché -chée [brɔʃe] *adj* paperback, paperbound

brocher [brɔʃe] *tr* to brocade; to sew (*book bindings*); (coll) to hurry through

brochet [brɔʃɛ] *m* (ichth) pike

brochette [brɔʃɛt] *f* skewer; skewerful; string (*of decorations*)

bro·cheur [brɔʃœr] **-cheuse** [ʃøz] *mf* bookbinder ‖ *f* stapler

brochure [brɔʃyr] *f* brochure, pamphlet

brocoli [brɔkɔli] *m* broccoli

brodequin [brɔdkɛ̃] *m* buskin

broder [brɔde] *tr & intr* to embroider

broderie [brɔdri] *f* embroidery

brome [brom] *m* (chem) bromine

bromure [brɔmyr] *m* bromide

bronche [brɔ̃ʃ] *f* bronchial tube

broncher [brɔ̃ʃe] *intr* to stumble; to flinch; to grumble

bronchique [brɔ̃ʃik] *adj* bronchial

bronchite [brɔ̃ʃit] *f* bronchitis

bronze [brɔ̃z] *m* bronze

bron·zé -zée [brɔ̃ze] *adj* bronze; suntanned

bronzer [brɔ̃ze] *tr & ref* to bronze; to sun-tan

brook [bruk] *m* (turf) water jump

broquette [brɔkɛt] *f* brad, tack

brossage [brɔsaʒ] *m* brushing

brosse [brɔs] *f* brush; **brosse à cheveux** hairbrush; **brosse à dents** toothbrush; **brosse à habits** clothesbrush; **brosse de chiendent** scrubbing brush; **brosses** shrubs, bushes

brosser [brɔse] *tr* to brush; to paint the broad outlines of (*a picture*); (fig) to sketch; (slang) to beat, conquer ‖ *ref* to brush one's clothes; (coll) to skimp, to scrimp

brouet [bruɛ] *m* gruel, broth

brouette [bruɛt] *f* wheelbarrow

brouetter [bruɛte] *tr* to carry in a wheelbarrow

brouhaha [bruaa] *m* (coll) babel, hubbub

brouillage [brujaʒ] *m* (rad) jamming

brouillamini [brujamini] *m* (coll) mess

brouillard [brujar] *adj masc* blotting (*paper*) ‖ *m* fog, mist; (com) daybook

brouillasse [brujas] *f* (coll) drizzle

brouillasser [brujase] *intr* (coll) to drizzle

brouille [bruj] *f* discord, misunderstanding

brouiller [bruje] *tr* to mix up; to jam (*a broadcast*); to scramble (*eggs*); **brouiller mes** (**ses, etc.**) **pistes** to cover my (his, etc.) tracks ‖ *ref* to quarrel; to cloud over

brouil·lon [brujɔ̃] **brouil·lonne** [brujɔn] *adj* crackpot; blundering; at loose ends ‖ *mf* crackpot ‖ *m* scratch pad; draft; outline

broussailles [brusaj] *fpl* underbrush, brushwood; **en broussailles** disheveled

broussail·leux [brusajø] **broussail·leuse** [brusajøz] *adj* bushy

broussard [brusar] *m* (coll) bushman, colonist

brousse [brus] *f* veldt, bush

broutage [brutaʒ] *m* grazing (*of animal*); ratatat (*of a machine*)

brouter [brute] *intr* to browze, graze; to jerk, to grab (*said of clutch, cutting tool, brake*)

broutille [brutij] *f* twig; trifle, bauble

broyage [brwajaʒ] *m* grinding, crushing

broyer [brwaje] §47 *tr* to grind, crush; **broyer du noir** (coll) to be down in the dumps

broyeur [brwajœr] **broyeuse** [brwajøz] *adj* grinding, crushing ‖ *mf* grinder, crusher ‖ *f* (mach) grinder

bru [bry] *f* daughter-in-law

bruant [bryɑ̃] *m* (orn) bunting; **bruant jaune** yellowhammer

brucelles [brysɛl] *fpl* tweezers

brugnon [bryɲɔ̃] *m* nectarine

bruine [brɥin] *f* drizzle

bruiner [brɥine] *intr* to drizzle

bruire [brɥir] (usually used in: *inf*; 3d *sg pres* ind **bruit**; 3d *sg & pl imperf* ind **bruyait** or **bruissait, bruyaient** or **bruissaient**) *intr* to rustle; to hum, buzz; to splash

bruissement [brɥismɑ̃] *m* rustling

bruit [brɥi] *m* noise; stir, fuss; **le bruit court que** it is rumored that

bruitage [brɥitaʒ] *m* sound effects

brû·lant [brylɑ̃] **-lante** [lɑ̃t] *adj* burning; ardent; ticklish (*question*)

brû·lé -lée [bryle] *adj* burned ‖ *m* smell of burning; burned taste ‖ *f* (slang) beating

brûle-gueule [brylgœl] *m invar* (slang) short pipe (*for smoking*)

brûle-parfum [brylparfœ̃] *m invar* incense burner

brûle-pourpoint [brylpurpwɛ̃]—**à brûlepourpoint** point-blank

brûler [bryle] *tr* to burn; to burn out (*a fuse*); to go through (*a red light*); to pass (*another car*); to roast (*coffee*); to distill (*liquor*); **brûler la cervelle à qn** to blow s.o.'s brains out ‖ *intr* to burn, burn up ‖ *ref* to burn up, to be burned

brû·leur [brylœr] **-leuse** [løz] *mf* arsonist; distiller ‖ *m* (mach) burner; **brûleur à café** coffee roaster

brûloir [brylwar] *m* roaster

brûlure [brylyr] *f* burn

brume [brym] *f* fog, mist

brumer [bryme] *intr* to be foggy

bru·meux [brymø] **-meuse** [møz] *adj* foggy, misty

brun [brœ̃] **brune** [bryn] *adj* darkbrown; dark ‖ *m* brunet; dark brown ‖ *f* see **brune**

brunâtre [brynɑtr] *adj* brownish

brune [bryn] *f* brunette; twilight

bru·net [brynɛ] **-nette** [nɛt] *adj* blackhaired ‖ *m* dark-haired man, brunet ‖ *f* brunette

bru·ni -nie [bryni] *adj* burnished, polished ‖ *m* burnishment, polish

brunir [brynir] *tr* to brown; to burnish, polish ‖ *intr* to turn brown

brunissoir [bryniswar] *m* (mach) buffer

brusque [brysk] *adj* brusque; sudden; surprise (*attack*); quick (*movements; decision*)

brusquer [bryske] *tr* to hurry, rush through; to be blunt with

brusquerie [bryskri] *f* brusqueness; suddenness

brut [bryt] **brute** [bryt] *adj* crude, un-

polished, unrefined, uncivilized; uncut (*diamond*); raw (*material*); dry (*champagne*); brown (*sugar*); gross (*weight*) ‖ *f* see **brute** ‖ **brut** *adv*— **peser brut** to have a gross weight of
bru·tal -tale [brytal] (*pl* **-taux** [to]) *adj* brutal, rough; outspoken; coarse, beastly ‖ *mf* brute, bully
brutaliser [brytalize] *tr* to bully; to mistreat
brutalité [brytalite] *f* brutality; **brutalité policière** police brutality
brute *f* brute
Bruxelles [brysɛl] *f* Brussels
bruxel·lois [brysɛlwa] **bruxel·loise** [brysɛlwaz] *adj* of Brussels ‖ (*cap*) *mf* native or inhabitant of Brussels
bruyamment [brɥijamã] *adv* noisily
bruyant [brɥijã] **bruyante** [brɥijãt] *adj* noisy
bruyère [brɥijɛr] *f* heather; heath
buanderie [bɥãdəri] *f* laundry room
buan·dier [bɥãdje] **-dière** [djɛr] *mf* laundry worker ‖ *f* laundress
bubonique [bybɔnik] *adj* bubonic
bûche [byʃ] *f* log; (slang) dunce; **bûche de Noël** yule log; cake decorated as a yule log; **ramasser une bûche** (slang) to take a tumble
bûcher [byʃe] *m* woodshed; pyre; stake (*e.g., for burning witches*) ‖ *tr* to rough-hew; (slang) to bone up on ‖ *intr* (slang) to keep on working; to slave away ‖ *ref* (slang) to fight
bûche·ron [byʃrɔ̃] **-ronne** [rɔn] *mf* woodcutter ‖ *m* lumberjack
bûchette [byʃɛt] *f* stick of wood
bû·cheur [byʃœr] **-cheuse** [ʃøz] *mf* (coll) eager beaver
budget [bydʒɛ] *m* budget; **boucler son budget** (coll) to make ends meet
budgétaire [bydʒetɛr] *adj* budgetary
buée [bɥe] *f* steam; mist
buffet [byfɛ] *m* buffet; snack bar; station restaurant; **danser devant le buffet** to miss a meal
buf·fle [byfl] **buf·flonne** [byflɔn] *mf* water buffalo; Cape buffalo
bugle [bygl] *m* (mus) saxhorn; bugle ‖ *f* (bot) bugle
building [bildiŋ] *m* large office building, skyscraper
buire [bɥir] *f* ewer
buis [bɥi] *m* boxwood
buisson [bɥisɔ̃] *m* bush
buisson·neux [bɥisɔnø] **buisson·neuse** [bɥisɔnøz] *adj* bushy
buisson·nier [bɥisɔnje] **buisson·nière** [bɥisɔnjɛr] *adj*—**faire l'école buissonnière** (coll) to play hooky
bulbe [bylb] *m* bulb
bul·beux [bylbø] **-beuse** [bøz] *adj* bulbous
bulgare [bylgar] *adj* Bulgarian ‖ *m* Bulgarian (*language*) ‖ (*cap*) *mf* Bulgarian (*person*)
Bulgarie [bylgari] *f* Bulgaria; **la Bulgarie** Bulgaria
bulle [byl] *m* wrapping paper ‖ *f* bubble; blister; (eccl) bull
bulletin [byltɛ̃] *m* bulletin; ballot; **bulletin de bagages** baggage check; **bulletin de commande** order blank;

bulletin de naissance birth certificate; **bulletin scolaire** report card
bul·leux [bylø] **bul·leuse** [byløz] *adj* blistery
bure [byr] *m* mine shaft ‖ *f* drugget, sackcloth
bu·reau [byro] *m* (*pl* **-reaux**) desk; office; **bureau à cylindre** roll-top desk; **bureau ambulant** post-office car; **bureau d'aide sociale** welfare department; **Bureau de l'état civil** Bureau of Vital Statistics; **bureau de location** box office; **bureau de placement** employment agency; **bureau de poste** post office; **bureau des objets trouvés** lost-and-found department; **bureau de tabac** tobacco shop; **bureau directoire** cabinet, committee; **deuxième bureau** intelligence division
bureaucrate [byrokrat] *mf* bureaucrat
bureaucratie [byrokrasi] *f* bureaucracy
bureaucratique [byrokratik] *adj* bureaucratic
burette [byrɛt] *f* cruet; oilcan
burin [byrɛ̃] *m* engraving; burin (*tool*)
burlesque [byrlɛsk] *adj* & *m* burlesque
busard [byzar] *m* harrier, marsh hawk
busc [bysk] *m* whalebone
buse [byz] *f* buzzard
business [biznɛs] *m* (slang) work; (slang) complicated business
bus·qué -quée [byske] *adj* arched
buste [byst] *m* bust
but [by], [byt] *m* mark, goal, target; aim, end, purpose; point (*scored in game*); **aller droit au but** to come straight to the point; **de but en blanc** point-blank
bu·té -tée [byte] *adj* obstinate, headstrong ‖ *f* abutment
buter [byte] *tr* to prop up; (slang) to bump off, kill ‖ *intr*—**buter contre** to bump into, to stumble on ‖ *ref*—**se buter à** to butt up against; (fig) to be dead set on
buteur [bytœr] *m* scorer
butin [bytɛ̃] *m* booty; profits, savings
butiner [bytine] *tr* to pillage; to gather honey from ‖ *intr* to pillage; to gather honey (*said of bees*); **butiner dans** to browse among (*books*)
butoir [bytwar] *m* buffer, stop, catch
bu·tor [bytɔr] **-torde** [tɔrd] *mf* (slang) lout, good-for-nothing
butte [byt] *f* butte, knoll; **butte de tir** butt, mound (*for target practice*); **être en butte à** to be exposed to
butter [byte] *tr* to hill (*plants*)
buttoir [bytwar] *m* (agr) hiller
buty·reux [bytirø] **-reuse** [røz] *adj* buttery
buvable [byvabl] *adj* drinkable; (pharm) to be taken by mouth
buvard [byvar] *adj* blotting (*paper*) ‖ *m* blotter
buvette [byvɛt] *f* bar, fountain
buvette-buffet [byvɛtbyfɛ] *f* (coll) snack bar
bu·veur [byvœr] **-veuse** [vøz] *mf* drinker; **buveur d'eau** abstainer; vacationist at a spa
byzan·tin [bizãtɛ̃] **-tine** [tin] *adj* Byzantine

C

C, c [se] *m invar* third letter of the French alphabet
C/ *abbr* (**compte**) account
ça [sa] *pron indef* (coll) that; **ah ça non!** no indeed!; **avec ça!** tell me another!; **ça y est** that's that; that's it, that's right; **comment ça!** how so?; **et avec ça?** what else?; **où ça,** where? **çà** [sa] *adv*—ah çà! now then! **çà et là** here and there
cabale [kabal] *f* cabal, intrigue
cabaler [kabale] *intr* to cabal, intrigue
caban [kabã] *m* (naut) peacoat
cabane [kaban] *f* cabin, hut
cabanon [kabanɔ̃] *m* hut; padded cell
cabaret [kabarɛ] *m* tavern; cabaret, night club; liquor closet
cabas [kaba] *m* basket
cabestan [kabɛstã] *m* capstan
cabillaud [kabijo] *m* haddock; (coll) fresh cod
cabine [kabin] *f* cabin (*of ship or airplane*); bathhouse; car (*of elevator*); cab (*of locomotive or truck*); **cabine téléphonique** telephone booth
cabinet [kabinɛ] *m* (*ministry*) cabinet; study (*of scholar*); office (*of professional man*); clientele; staff (*of a cabinet officer*); toilet; storeroom closet; **cabinet d'aisance** rest room; **cabinet de débarras** storeroom closet; **cabinet de toilette** powder room; **cabinets** rest rooms
câble [kabl] *m* cable
câbler [kable] *tr & intr* to cable
câblier [kablije] *m* cable ship
câblogramme [kablɔgram] *m* cablegram
cabo-chard [kabɔʃar] **-charde** [ʃard] *adj* obstinate, pigheaded
caboche [kabɔʃ] *f* hobnail; (coll) noodle (*head*)
cabochon [kabɔʃɔ̃] *m* uncut gem; stud, upholstery nail
cabot [kabo] *m* (ichth) miller's-thumb, bullhead; (coll) ham (actor)
cabotage [kabɔtaʒ] *m* coastal navigation, coasting trade
cabo-tin [kabɔtɛ̃] **-tine** [tin] *mf* barnstormer; (coll) ham actor; **cabotin de la politique** (coll) corny politician, political orator given to histrionics
cabotinage [kabɔtinaʒ] *m* barnstorming; (coll) ham acting
cabotiner [kabɔtine] *intr* to barnstorm; (coll) to play to the grandstand
cabrer [kabre] *tr* to make (*a horse*) rear; to nose up (*a plane*) ‖ *ref* to rear; to kick over the traces; (aer) to nose up
cabri [kabri] *m* (zool) kid
cabriole [kabrijɔl] *f* caper
cabrioler [kabrijɔle] *intr* to caper
cacahouète [kakawɛt] or **cacahuète** [kakaɥɛt] *f* peanut
cacao [kakao] *m* cocoa; cocoa bean
cacaotier [kakaɔtje] *m* (bot) cacao
cacaoyer [kakaɔje] *m* (bot) cacao
cacarder [kakarde] *intr* to cackle

cacatoès [kakatɔɛs] or **cacatois** [kakatwa] *m* cockatoo
cachalot [kaʃalo] *m* sperm whale
cache [kaʃ] *m* masking tape ‖ *f* hiding place
cache-cache [kaʃkaʃ] *m invar* hide-and-seek
cache-col [kaʃkɔl] *m invar* scarf
cachemire [kaʃmir] *m* cashmere
cache-nez [kaʃne] *m invar* muffler
cache-poussière [kaʃpusjɛr] *m invar* duster (*overgarment*)
cacher [kaʃe] *tr* to hide; **cacher q.ch. à qn** to hide s.th. from s.o. ‖ *ref* to hide; **se cacher à** to hide from; **se cacher de q.ch.** to make a secret of s.th.
cache-radiateur [kaʃradjatœr] *m invar* radiator cover
cache-sexe [kaʃsɛks] *m invar* G-string
cachet [kaʃɛ] *m* seal; postmark; fee; price of a lesson; meal ticket; (pharm, phila) cachet; (fig) seal; stylishness; **payer au cachet** to pay a set fee
cacheter [kaʃte] §34 *tr* to seal, to seal up; to seal with wax
cachette [kaʃɛt] *f* hiding place; **en cachette** secretly
cachot [kaʃo] *m* dungeon; prison
cacophonie [kakɔfɔni] *f* cacophony
cactier [kaktje] or **cactus** [kaktys] *m* cactus
c.-à-d. *abbr* (**c'est-à-dire**) that is
cadastre [kadastr] *m* land-survey register
cadavre [kadavr] *m* corpse, cadaver; (slang) dead soldier (*bottle*)
ca-deau [kado] *m* (*pl* **-deaux**) gift
cadenas [kadna] *m* padlock
cadenasser [kadnase] *tr* to padlock
cadence [kadãs] *f* cadence, rhythm, time; output (*of worker, of factory, etc.*); **cadence de tir** rate of firing
cadencer [kadãse] §51 *tr* to cadence ‖ *intr* to call out cadence
ca-det [kadɛ] **-dette** [dɛt] *adj* younger ‖ *mf* youngest; junior; (sports) player fifteen to eighteen years old; **le cadet de mes soucis** (coll) the least of my worries ‖ *m* caddy; (mil) cadet; younger brother; younger son ‖ *f* younger sister; younger daughter
cadmium [kadmjɔm] *m* cadmium
cadrage [kadraʒ] *m* (mov, telv) framing; (phot) centering
cadran [kadrã] *m* dial; **cadran d'appel** telephone dial; **cadran solaire** sundial; **faire le tour du cadran** to sleep around the clock
cadre [kadr] *m* frame; framework; setting; outline, framework (*of a literary work*); limits, scope (*of activities or duties*); (mil) cadre; (naut) cot; **cadres** officials; (mil) regulars; **cadres sociaux** memorable dates or events
cadrer [kadre] *tr* to frame (*film*) ‖ *intr* to conform, tally
ca-duc -duque [kadyk] *adj* decrepit,

frail; outlived (*custom*); deciduous (*leaves*); lapsed (*insurance policy*); (law) null and void
caducée [kadyse] *m* caduceus
C.A.F. *abbr* (**coût, assurance, fret**)
C.I.F. (*cost, insurance, and freight*)
ca·fard [kafar] **-farde** [fard] *adj* sanctimonious ‖ *mf* hypocrite; (coll) squealer ‖ *m* (coll) cockroach; (coll) blues
café [kafe] *adj invar* tan ‖ *m* coffee; café; coffeehouse; **café chantant** music hall (*with tables*); **café complet** coffee, hot milk, rolls, butter, and jam; **café nature, café noir** black coffee
café-concert [kafekɔ̃ser] *m* (*pl* **cafés-concerts**) music hall (*with tables*), cabaret
caféier [kafeje] *m* coffee plant
caféière [kafejer] *f* coffee plantation
caféine [kafein] *f* caffeine
cafe·tier [kaftje] **-tière** [tjer] *mf* café owner ‖ *f* coffeepot
cafouiller [kafuje] *intr* (slang) to miss (*said of engine*); (slang) to flounder around
cage [kaʒ] *f* cage; **cage d'un ascenseur** elevator shaft; **cage d'un escalier** stairwell; **cage thoracique** thoracic cavity; **en cage** (coll) in the clink, in the pen
cageot [kaʒo] *m* crate
ca·gnard [kaɲar] **-gnarde** [ɲard] *adj* indolent, lazy ‖ *m* (coll) sunny spot
ca·gneux [kaɲø] **-gneuse** [ɲøz] *adj* knock-kneed; pigeon-toed
cagnotte [kaɲɔt] *f* kitty, pool
ca·got [kago] **-gotte** [gɔt] *adj* hypocritical ‖ *mf* hypocrite
cagoule [kagul] *f* cowl; hood (*with eye-holes*)
cahier [kaje] *m* notebook; **cahier à feuilles mobiles** loose-leaf notebook; **cahier des charges** (com) specifications
cahin-caha [kaɛ̃kaa] *adv* (coll) so-so
cahot [kao] *m* jolt, bump
cahoter [kaɔte] *tr & intr* to jolt
caho·teux [kaɔtø] **-teuse** [tøz] *adj* bumpy (*road*)
cahute [kayt] *f* hut, shack
caille [kɑj] *f* quail
cail·lé -lée [kaje] *adj* curdled ‖ *m* curd
caillebotis [kajbɔti] *m* boardwalk; (mil) duckboard; (naut) grating
caillebotte [kajbɔt] *f* curds
caillebotter [kajbɔte] *tr & intr* to curdle
cailler [kaje] *tr & ref* to clot, curdle, curd
caillot [kajo] *m* clot; blood clot
cail·lou [kaju] *m* (*pl* **-loux**) pebble; (coll) bald head; **caillou du Rhin** rhinestone
caillou·teux [kajutø] **-teuse** [tøz] *adj* stony (*road*); pebbly (*beach*)
cailloutis [kajuti] *m* crushed stone, gravel
Caïn [kaɛ̃] *m* Cain
Caire [ker] *m*—**Le Caire** Cairo
caisse [kes] *f* chest, box; case (*for packing; of a clock or piano*); chest-

ful, boxful; till, cash register, coffer, safe; cashier, cashier's window; desk (*in a hotel*); **caisse à eau** water tank; **caisse claire** snare drum; **caisse d'épargne** savings bank; **caisse des écoles** scholarship fund; **grosse caisse** bass drum; bass drummer; **petite caisse** petty cash
caisson [kesɔ̃] *m* caisson
cajoler [kaʒɔle] *tr* to cajole, wheedle
cajolerie [kaʒɔlri] *f* cajolery
cajou [kaʒu] *m* cashew nut
cake [kek] *m* fruit cake
cal [kal] *m* (*pl* **cals**) callus, callosity; **cal vicieux** badly knitted bone
calage [kalaʒ] *m* wedging, chocking; stalling (*of motor*)
calamité [kalamite] *f* calamity
calami·teux [kalamitø] **-teuse** [tøz] *adj* calamitous
calandre [kalɑ̃dr] *f* mangle (*for clothes*); calender (*for paper*); grill (*for car radiator*); (ent) weevil; (orn) lark
calandrer [kalɑ̃dre] *tr* to calender
calcaire [kalker] *adj* calcareous; chalky; hard (*water*) ‖ *m* limestone
calcifier [kalsifje] *tr & ref* to calcify
calciner [kalsine] *tr & ref* to burn to a cinder
calcium [kalsjɔm] *m* calcium
calcul [kalkyl] *m* calculation; (math, pathol) calculus; **calcul biliaire** gallstone; **calcul mental** mental arithmetic; **calcul rénal** kidney stone
calcula·teur [kalkylatœr] **-trice** [tris] *adj* calculating ‖ *mf* calculator (*person*) ‖ *m* (mach) calculator ‖ *f* (mach) computer
calculer [kalkyle] *tr & intr* to calculate
cale [kal] *f* wedge, chock; hold (*of ship*); **cale de construction** stocks; **cale sèche** dry dock
ca·lé -lée [kale] *adj* stalled; (coll) well-informed; (slang) involved, difficult; **calé en** (coll) strong in, up on
calebasse [kalbɑs] *f* calabash
calèche [kaleʃ] *f* open carriage
caleçon [kalsɔ̃] *m* drawers, shorts; **caleçon de bain** swimming trunks
calembour [kalɑ̃bur] *m* pun
calendes [kalɑ̃d] *fpl* calends; **aux calendes grecques** (coll) when pigs fly
calendrier [kalɑ̃drije] *m* calendar
calepin [kalpɛ̃] *m* notebook
caler [kale] *tr* to wedge, to chock; to jam; to stall; to lower (*sail*); (naut) to draw ‖ *intr* to stall (*said of motor*); (coll) to give in ‖ *ref* to stall; to get nicely settled
calfater [kalfate] *tr* to caulk
calfeutrer [kalføtre] *tr* to stop up ‖ *ref* to shut oneself up
calibre [kalibr] *m* caliber
calibrer [kalibre] *tr* to calibrate
calice [kalis] *m* chalice; (bot) calyx
calicot [kaliko] *m* calico; sign, banner; (slang) sales clerk
califat [kalifa] *m* caliphate
calife [kalif] *m* caliph
Californie [kalifɔrni] *f* California; **la basse Californie** Lower California; **la Californie** California

califourchon [kalifurʃɔ̃]—**à califourchon** astride, astraddle; **s'asseoir à califourchon** to straddle
câ·lin [kɑlɛ̃] **-line** [lin] *adj* coaxing; caressing
câliner [kaline] *tr* to coax; to caress
cal·leux [kalø] **cal·leuse** [kaløz] *adj* callous, calloused
callisthénie [kalisteni] *f* calisthenics
cal·mant [kalmɑ̃] **-mante** [mɑ̃t] *adj* calming || *m* sedative
calmar [kalmar] *m* squid
calme [kalm] *adj* & *m* calm
calmement [kalməmɑ̃] *adv* calmly
calmer [kalme] *tr* to calm || *ref* to become calm, to calm down
calmir [kalmir] *intr* to abate
calomnie [kalɔmni] *f* calumny, slander
calomnier [kalɔmnje] *tr* to calumniate
calorie [kalɔri] *f* calory
calorifère [kalɔrifɛr] *adj* heating, heat-conducting || *m* heater; **calorifère à air chaud** hot-air heater; **calorifère à eau chaude** hot-water heater
calorifuge [kalɔrifyʒ] *adj* insulating || *m* insulator
calorifuger [kalɔrifyʒe] §38 *tr* to insulate
calorique [kalɔrik] *adj* caloric
calot [kalo] *m* policeman's hat, kepi
calotte [kalɔt] *f* skullcap; dome; (coll) box on the ear; (coll) clergy; **calotte des cieux** vault of heaven; **flanquer une calotte à** (coll) to box on the ear
calotter [kalɔte] *tr* (coll) to box on the ear, to cuff; (slang) to snitch
calque [kalk] *m* tracing; decal; word-for-word correspondence (*between two languages*); slavish imitation; spitting image
calquer [kalke] *tr* to trace; to imitate slavishly
calumet [kalymɛ] *m* calumet; **calumet de paix** peace pipe
calvados [kalvados] *m* applejack
calvaire [kalvɛr] *m* calvary
calviniste [kalvinist] *adj* & *mf* Calvinist
calvitie [kalvisi] *f* baldness
camarade [kamarad] *mf* comrade; **camarade de chambre** roommate; **camarade de travail** fellow worker; **camarade d'étude** schoolmate
camaraderie [kamaradri] *f* comradeship; camaraderie, fellowship
ca·mard [kamar] **-marde** [mard] *adj* snub-nosed
cambouis [kɑ̃bwi] *m* axle grease
cambrer [kɑ̃bre] *tr* to curve, arch
cambrioler [kɑ̃brijɔle] *tr* to break into, to burglarize
cambrio·leur [kɑ̃brijɔlœr] **-leuse** [løz] *mf* burglar
cambrure [kɑ̃bryr] *f* curve, arch
cambuse [kɑ̃byz] *f* (naut) storeroom between decks
came [kam] *f* cam
camée [kame] *m* cameo
caméléon [kamele ɔ̃] *m* chameleon
camélia [kamelja] *m* camellia
camelot [kamlo] *m* cheap woolen cloth; huckster; newsboy
camelote [kamlɔt] *f* shoddy merchandise, rubbish, junk

caméra [kamera] *f* (mov, telv) camera
camion [kamjɔ̃] *m* truck; paint bucket; **camion à remorque** trailer (truck); **camion à semi-remorque** semitrailer; **camion d'enregistrement** (mov) sound truck
camion-benne [kamjɔ̃bɛn] *m* (*pl* **camions-bennes**) dump truck
camion-citerne [kamjɔ̃sitɛrn] *m* (*pl* **camions-citernes**) tank truck
camion-grue [kamjɔ̃gry] *m* (*pl* **camions-grues**) tow truck
camionnage [kamjɔnaʒ] *m* trucking
camionner [kamjɔne] *tr* to truck
camionnette [kamjɔnɛt] *f* van; **camionnette de police** police wagon; **camionnette sanitaire** mobile health unit
camionneur [kamjɔnœr] *m* trucker; truckdriver, teamster
camisole [kamizɔl] *f* camisole; **camisole de force** strait jacket
camouflage [kamuflaʒ] *m* camouflage
camoufler [kamufle] *tr* to camouflage
camp [kɑ̃] *m* camp
campa·gnard [kɑ̃paɲar] **-gnarde** [ɲard] *adj* & *mf* rustic
campagne [kɑ̃paɲ] *f* campaign; country
cam·pé **-pée** [kɑ̃pe] *adj* encamped; **bien campé** well-built (*man*); clearly presented (*story*); firmly fixed
campement [kɑ̃pmɑ̃] *m* encampment; camping
camper [kɑ̃pe] *tr* to camp; (coll) to clap (*e.g., one's hat on one's head*); **camper là qn** (coll) to run out on s.o. || *intr* & *ref* to camp
cam·peur [kɑ̃pœr] **-peuse** [pøz] *mf* camper
camphre [kɑ̃fr] *m* camphor
camping [kɑ̃piŋ] *m* campground; trailer; camping
campos [kɑ̃po] *m* (coll) vacation, day off
campus [kɑ̃pys] *m* campus
ca·mus [kamy] **-muse** [myz] *adj* snub-nosed, pug-nosed, flat-nosed
Canada [kanada] *m*—**le Canada** Canada
cana·dien [kanadjɛ̃] **-dienne** [djɛn] *adj* Canadian || *f* sheepskin jacket; station wagon || (*cap*) *mf* Canadian
canaille [kanɑj] *adj* vulgar, coarse || *f* rabble, riffraff; scoundrel
ca·nal [kanal] *m* (*pl* **-naux** [no]) canal; tube, pipe; ditch, drain; (rad, telv) channel; **canal de Panama** Panama Canal; **canal de Suez** [sɥɛz] Suez Canal; **par le canal de** through the good offices of
canapé [kanape] *m* sofa, davenport; (culin) canapé; **canapé à deux places** settee
canapé-lit [kanapeli] *m* (*pl* **canapés-lits**) sofa bed, day bed
canard [kanar] *m* duck; sugar soaked in coffee, brandy, etc.; (mus) false note; (coll) hoax; (coll) rag, paper; **canard mâle** drake; **canard publicitaire** publicity stunt; **canard sauvage** wild duck

canarder [kanarde] *tr* to snipe at ǁ *intr* to snipe
canari [kanari] *m* canary
cancan [kãkã] *m* cancan (*dance*); (coll) gossip
cancaner [kãkane] *intr* to quack; (coll) to gossip
canca·nier [kãkanje] **-nière** [njɛr] *adj* (coll) catty ǁ *mf* (coll) gossip
cancer [kãsɛr] *m* cancer
cancé·reux [kãserø] **-reuse** [røz] *adj* cancerous
cancre [kãkr] *m* (coll) dunce, lazy student; (coll) tightwad; (zool) crab
candélabre [kãdelɑbr] *m* candelabrum; espaliered fruit tree; cactus; lamppost
candeur [kãdœr] *f* naïveté
candi [kãdi] *adj* candied (*fruit*) ǁ *m* rock candy
candi·dat [kãdida] **-date** [dat] *mf* candidate; nominee
candidature [kãdidatyr] *f* candidacy
candide [kãdid] *adj* naïve
candir [kãdir] *intr*—**faire candir** to candy, to crystallize (*sugar*) ǁ *ref* to candy, to crystallize
cane [kan] *f* duck, female duck
caner [kane] *intr* (slang) to chicken out
caneton [kantɔ̃] *m* duckling
canette [kanɛt] *f* female duckling; beer bottle; **canette de bière** can of beer
canevas [kanva] *m* canvas (*cloth*); outline (*of novel, story, etc.*); embroidery netting; (in *artillery*, in *cartography*) triangulation
canezou [kanzu] *m* sleeveless lace blouse
caniche [kaniʃ] *m* poodle
canicule [kanikyl] *f* dog days
canif [kanif] *m* penknife, pocketknife
ca·nin [kanɛ̃] **-nine** [nin] *adj* canine ǁ *f* canine (*tooth*)
canitie [kanisi] *f* grayness (*of hair*)
cani·veau [kanivo] *m* (*pl* **-veaux**) gutter; (elec) conduit
cannaie [kanɛ] *f* sugar plantation
canne [kan] *f* cane; reed; cane, walking stick; **canne à pêche** fishing rod; **canne à sucre** sugar cane
canneberge [kanbɛrʒ] *f* cranberry
canneler [kanle] §34 *tr* to groove; to corrugate; to flute (*a column*)
cannelle [kanɛl] *f* cinnamon; spout
cannelure [kanlyr] *f* groove, channel; corrugation; fluting (*of column*)
canner [kane] *tr* to cane (*a chair*)
cannibale [kanibal] *adj* & *mf* cannibal
canoë [kanɔe] *m* canoe
canoéiste [kanɔeist] *mf* canoeist
canon [kanɔ̃] *m* canon; cannon; gun barrel; tube; nozzle, spout; **canon à électrons** electron gun
cañon [kaɲɔ̃] *m* canyon
cano·nial **-niale** [kanɔnjal] *adj* (*pl* **-niaux** [njo]) canonical
canonique [kanɔnik] *adj* canonical
canoniser [kanɔnize] *tr* to canonize
cannonnade [kanɔnad] *f* cannonade
canonner [kanɔne] *tr* to cannonade
canonnier [kanɔnje] *m* cannoneer

canonnière [kanɔnjɛr] *f* gunboat; popgun
canot [kano] *m* rowboat, launch; **canot automobile** speedboat, motorboat; **canot de sauvetage** lifeboat
canotage [kanɔtaʒ] *m* boating
canoter [kanɔte] *intr* to go boating
canotier [kanɔtje] *m* rower; skimmer
cant [kã] *m* cant
cantaloup [kãtalu] *m* cantaloupe
cantate [kãtat] *f* cantata
cantatrice [kãtatris] *f* singer
cantilever [kãtilevœr] *adj* & *m* cantilever
cantine [kãtin] *f* canteen (*restaurant*); **cantine d'officier** officer's kit
cantique [kãtik] *m* canticle, ode; **cantique de Noël** (eccl) Christmas carol; **Cantique des Cantiques** (Bib) Song of Songs
canton [kãtɔ̃] *m* canton, district; **Cantons de l'Est** Eastern Townships (*in Canada*)
cantonade [kãtɔnad] *f* (theat) wings; **à la cantonade** (theat) offstage; **crier à la cantonade** to yell out (*s.th.*); **parler à la cantonade** to seem to be talking to oneself; (theat) to speak toward the wings
cantonnement [kãtɔnmã] *m* billeting
cantonner [kãtɔne] *tr* to billet
cantonnier [kãtɔnje] *m* road laborer; (rr) section hand
canular [kanylar] *m* (coll) practical joke, hoax, canard
canule [kanyl] *f* nozzle (*of syringe or injection needle*)
canuler [kanyle] *tr* (slang) to bother
caoutchouc [kautʃu] *m* rubber; **caoutchouc mousse** foam rubber; **caoutchoucs** rubbers, overshoes
caoutchouter [kautʃute] *tr* to rubberize
caoutchou·teux [kautʃutø] **-teuse** [tøz] *adj* rubbery
cap [kap] *m* cape, headland; bow, head (*of ship*); **Cap de Bonne Espérance** Cape of Good Hope; **mettre le cap sur** (coll) to set a course for
capable [kapabl] *adj* capable
capacité [kapasite] *f* capacity; ability
cape [kap] *f* cape; hood; derby; outer leaf, wrapper (*of cigar*); **à la cape** (naut) hove to; **de cape et d'épée** cloak-and-dagger (*novel, movie, etc.*); **rire sous cape** to laugh up one's sleeve; **vendre sous cape** (coll) to sell under the counter
C.A.P.E.S. [kapɛs] *m* (acronym) (**certificat d'aptitude au professorat de l'enseignement du second degré**) secondary-school teachers certificate
capillaire [kapilɛr] *adj* capillary ǁ *m* (bot) maidenhair (*fern*)
capitaine [kapitɛn] *m* captain
capi·tal **-tale** [kapital] (*pl* **-taux** [to] **-tales**) *adj* capital, principal, essential; capital (*city; punishment; crime; letter*); death (*sentence*); deadly (*sins*) ǁ *m* capital, assets; principal (*main sum*); **avec de minces capitaux** on a shoestring; **capitaux** capital ǁ *f* capital (*city; letter*)

capitalisation [kapitalizɑsjɔ̃] ƒ capitalization; hoarding (of money)
capitaliser [kapitalize] tr to capitalize (an income); to compound (interest) || intr to hoard
capitalisme [kapitalism] m capitalism
capitaliste [kapitalist] adj capitalist || mƒ capitalist; investor
capi·teux [kapitø] -teuse [tøz] adj heady (wine, champagne, etc.)
Capitole [kapitɔl] m Capitol
capitonner [kapitɔne] tr to upholster
capituler [kapityle] intr to capitulate; to parley
ca·pon [kapɔ̃] -ponne [pɔn] adj cowardly || mƒ coward; sneak; tattletale
capo·ral [kapɔral] m (pl -raux [ro]) corporal; shag, caporal (tobacco); Caporal a dit ... Simon says ...
caporalisme [kapɔralism] m militarism; dictatorial government
capot [kapo] adj invar speechless, confused; (cards) trickless || m cover; hood (of automobile); (naut) hatch
capotage [kapɔtaʒ] m overturning
capote [kapɔt] ƒ coat with a hood; hood (of baby carriage); capote rebattable (aut) folding top
capoter [kapɔte] intr to capsize; to overturn, upset
câpre [kɑpr] ƒ (bot) caper
caprice [kapris] m caprice, whim
capri·cieux [kaprisjø] -cieuse [sjøz] adj capricious, whimsical
capsule [kapsyl] ƒ capsule; bottle cap; percussion cap; (bot) capsule, pod; (rok) capsule; capsules surrénales adrenal glands
capsuler [kapsyle] tr to cap
capter [kapte] tr to win over; to harness (a river); to tap (electric current; a water supply); (rad, telv) to receive, pick up
cap·tieux [kapsjø] -tieuse [sjøz] adj captious, insidious; specious
cap·tif [kaptif] -tive [tiv] adj & mƒ captive
captiver [kaptive] tr to captivate
captivité [kaptivite] ƒ captivity
capture [kaptyr] ƒ capture
capturer [kaptyre] tr to capture
capuce [kapys] m (eccl) pointed hood
capuchon [kapyʃɔ̃] m hood (of coat); cap (of pen); (aut) valve cap; (eccl) cowl
capucine [kapysin] ƒ nasturtium
caque [kak] ƒ keg, barrel
caquet [kakɛ] m cackle
caqueter [kakte] §34 intr to cackle; to gossip
car [kar] m bus, sightseeing bus, interurban; car de police patrol wagon; car sonore loudspeaker truck || conj for, because
carabe [karab] m ground beetle
carabine [karabin] ƒ carbine
carabi·né -née [karabine] adj (coll) violent (wind, cold, criticism)
caraco [karako] m loose blouse
caractère [karaktɛr] m character; caractères gras (typ) boldface
caractériser [karakterize] tr to characterize

caractéristique [karakteristik] adj & ƒ characteristic
carafe [karaf] ƒ carafe; rester en carafe (slang) to be left out in the cold
carafon [karafɔ̃] m small carafe
caraïbe [karaib] adj Caribbean, Carib || (cap) mƒ Carib (person)
carambolage [karɑ̃bɔlaʒ] m jostling; (coll) bumping (e.g., of autos)
caramboler [karɑ̃bɔle] tr (coll) to strike, bump into || intr (billiards) to carom
caramel [karamɛl] m caramel
carapace [karapas] ƒ turtle shell, carapace
carapater [karapate] ref (slang) to beat it
carat [kara] m carat
caravane [karavan] ƒ caravan; house trailer; group (of tourists)
caravaning [karavaniŋ] m trailer camping
caravansérail [karavɑ̃seraj] m caravansary; (fig) world crossroads
caravelle [karavɛl] ƒ caravel
carbonade [karbɔnad] ƒ see carbonnade
carbone [karbɔn] m carbon
carbonique [karbɔnik] adj carbonic
carboniser [karbɔnize] tr to carbonize, char
carbonnade [karbɔnad] ƒ charcoal-grilled steak (ham, etc.); beef and onion stew (in northern France); à la carbonnade charcoal-grilled
carburant [karbyrɑ̃] m motor fuel
carburateur [karbyratœr] m carburetor
carbure [karbyr] m carbide
carburéacteur [karbyreaktœr] m jet fuel
carcan [karkɑ̃] m pillory
carcasse [karkas] ƒ skeleton; framework; (coll) carcass
cardan [kardɑ̃] m (mach) universal joint
carde [kard] ƒ card; leaf rib; teasel head
carder [karde] tr to card
cardiaque [kardjak] adj & mƒ cardiac
cardi·nal -nale [kardinal] adj & m (pl -naux [no]) cardinal
cardiogramme [kardjɔgram] m cardiogram
carême [karɛm] m Lent; de carême Lenten
carême-prenant [karɛmprənɑ̃] m (pl carêmes-prenants) Shrovetide
carence [karɑ̃s] ƒ lack, deficiency; failure
carène [karɛn] ƒ hull
caréner [karene] §10 tr to streamline; (naut) to careen
caren·tiel -tielle [karɑ̃sjɛl] adj deficiency (disease)
cares·sant [karɛsɑ̃] cares·sante [karɛsɑ̃t] adj caressing; lovable; nice to pet; soothing (e.g., voice)
caresse [karɛs] ƒ caress; endearment
caresser [karɛse] tr to caress; to pet; to nourish (a hope)
cargaison [kargɛzɔ̃] ƒ cargo
cargo [kargo] m freighter; cargo mixte freighter carrying passengers

cari [kari] *m* curry
caricature [karikatyr] *f* caricature; cartoon
caricaturer [karikatyre] *tr* to caricature
caricaturiste [karikatyrist] *mf* caricaturist; cartoonist
carie [kari] *f* caries; carie sèche dry rot
carillon [karijõ] *m* carillon
carillonner [karijɔne] *tr* & *intr* to carillon, to chime
carlingue [karlẽg] *f* (aer) cockpit
carmin [karmẽ] *adj* & *m* carmine
carnage [karnaʒ] *m* carnage
carnas·sier [karnasje] carnas·sière [karnasjer] *adj* carnivorous || *m* carnivore || *f* game bag
carnation [karnɑsjõ] *f* flesh tint
carna·val [karnaval] *m* (*pl* -vals) carnival; parade dummy
car·né -née [karne] *adj* flesh-colored; meat (*diet*)
carnet [karne] *m* notebook, address book; memo pad; book (*of tickets, checks, stamps, etc.*); carnet à feuilles mobiles loose-leaf notebook
carnier [karnje] *m* hunting bag
carotte [karɔt] *f* carrot; (min) core sample; tirer une carotte à (coll) to cheat
carotter [karɔte] *tr* (coll) to cheat
carpe [karp] *m* (anat) wrist bones || *f* carp; être muet comme une carpe to be still as a mouse
carpette [karpɛt] *f* rug, mat
carquois [karkwa] *m* quiver
carre [kar] *f* thickness (*of board*); crown (*of hat*); edge (*of ice skate*); square toe (*of shoe*); d'une bonne carre broad-shouldered (*man*)
car·ré -rée [kare] *adj* square; forthright || *m* square; landing (*of staircase*); patch (*in garden*); (cards) four of a kind; (naut) wardroom || *f* (slang) room, pad
car·reau [karo] *m* (*pl* -reaux) tile, flagstone; windowpane; stall (*in market*); pithead (*of mine*); goose (*of tailor*); quarrel (*square-headed arrow*); (cards) diamond; (cards) diamonds; à carreaux checked (*design*); rester sur le carreaux (coll) to be left out of the running; se garder à carreau (coll) to be on one's guard
carrefour [karfur] *m* crossroads; square (*in a city*)
carrelage [karlaʒ] *m* tiling
carreler [karle] §34 *tr* to tile
carrément [karemã] *adv* squarely; frankly
carrer [kare] *tr* to square || *ref* (coll) to plunk oneself down; (coll) to strut
carrier [karje] *m* quarryman
carrière [karjer] *f* career; course (*e.g., of the sun*); quarry; donner carrière à to give free rein to
carriole [karjɔl] *f* light cart, trap; (coll) jalopy
carrossable [karɔsabl] *adj* passable
carrosse [karɔs] *m* carriage, coach
carrosserie [karɔsri] *f* (aut) body
carrossier [karɔsje] *m* coachmaker
carrousel [karuzel] *m* carrousel; parade ground; tiltyard

carrure [karyr] *f* width (*of shoulders, garment, etc.*); d'une belle carrure broad-shouldered (*man*)
cartable [kartabl] *m* briefcase
cartayer [karteje] §49 *intr* to avoid the ruts
carte [kart] *f* card; map, chart; bill (*to pay*); bill of fare, menu; carte d'abonnement commutation ticket; season ticket; carte d'entrée pass, ticket of admission; carte des vins wine list; carte grise automobile registration; carte postale post card; cartes truquées marked cards, stacked deck; tirer les cartes à qn to tell s.o.'s fortunes with cards
cartel [kartɛl] *m* cartel; wall clock; challenge (*to a duel*)
carte-lettre [kartəletr] *f* (*pl* cartes-lettres) gummed letter-envelope
carter [karter] *m* housing; bicycle chain guard; (aut) crankcase
cartilage [kartilaʒ] *m* cartilage, gristle
cartographe [kartɔgraf] *m* cartographer
cartomancie [kartɔmãsi] *f* fortunetelling with cards
carton [kartõ] *m* pasteboard, cardboard; cardboard box, carton; carton (*of cigarettes*); cartoon (*preliminary sketch*); (typ) cancel; carton à chapeau hatbox; carton à dessin portfolio for drawings and plans
carton-pâte [kartõpɑt] *m* papier-mâché
cartouche [kartuʃ] *m* (archit) cartouche, tablet || *f* cartridge; carton (*of cigarettes*); canister (*of gas mask*); refill (*of pen*); cartouche à blanc blank cartridge
cartouchière [kartuʃjer] *f* cartridge belt, cartridge case
carvi [karvi] *m* caraway
cas [kɑ] *m* case; cas urgent emergency; en cas de in the event of, in a time of; en cas d'imprévu in case of emergency; en cas que, au cas que, au cas où, dans le cas où in the event that; faire cas de to esteem, to make much of; le cas échéant should the occasion arise, if necessary; selon le cas as the case may be
casa·nier [kazanje] -nière [njer] *adj* home-loving || *mf* homebody
casaque [kazak] *f* jockey coat; blouse; tourner casaque to be a turncoat
cascade [kaskad] *f* cascade; jerk; spree; prendre à la cascade to ad-lib
cascader [kaskade] *intr* to cascade; (slang) to lead a wild life
casca·deur [kaskadœr] -deuse [døz] *mf* (mov) double || *m* stunt man || *f* stunt girl
case [kɑz] *f* compartment; pigeonhole; square (*e.g., of checkerboard or ledger*); box (*to be filled out on a form*); hut, cabin; case postale post-office box
caséine [kazein] *f* casein
caser [kaze] *tr* to put away (*e.g., in a drawer*); to arrange (*e.g., a counter display in a store*); (coll) to place, to find a job for || *ref* (coll) to get settled

caserne [kazɛrn] *f* barracks; **de caserne** off-color (*jokes*); regimented
caserner [kazɛrne] *tr* & *intr* to barrack
ca·sher **-shère** [kaʃer] *adj* kosher
casier [kasje] *m* rack (*for papers, magazines, letters, bottles*); cabinet; **casier à homards** lobster pot; **casier à tiroirs** music cabinet; **casier judiciaire** police record
casque [kask] *m* helmet; earphones, headset; comb (*of rooster*); **casque à mèche** nightcap; **casque à pointe** spiked helmet; **casque blindé** crash helmet
casquer [kaske] *intr* to fall into a trap; (slang) to shell out
casquette [kaskɛt] *f* cap
cas·sant [kasɑ̃] **cas·sante** [kasɑ̃t] *adj* brittle; abrupt, curt
casse [kas] *m* (slang) burglarizing ‖ *f* breakage ‖ [kas], [kɑs] *f* ladle, scoop; crucible; (bot) cassia; (pharm) senna; (typ) case; (coll) scrap heap, junk
cas·sé **-sée** [kase] *adj* broken-down; shaky, weak (*voice*)
casse-cou [kasku] *m invar* (coll) daredevil; (coll) stunt man; (coll) danger spot ‖ *interj* look out!
casse-croûte [kaskrut] *m invar* snack
casse-gueule [kasgœl] *adj invar* (slang) risky ‖ *m invar* (coll) risky business
casse-noisettes [kasnwazɛt] *m invar* nutcracker
casse-noix [kasnwa], [kasnwa] *m invar* nutcracker
casse-pieds [kaspje] *m invar* (coll) pain in the neck
casser [kase] *tr* to break; to crack, to shatter; (law) to break (*a will*); (mil) to break, to bust; (coll) to split (*one's eardrums*); **casser sa pipe** (coll) to kick the bucket ‖ *ref* to break; (coll) to rack (*one's brains*); **se casser le nez** (coll) to fail
casserole [kasrɔl] *f* saucepan
casse-tête [kastɛt] *m invar* truncheon; din; brain teaser, puzzler; **casse-tête chinois** jigsaw puzzle
cassette [kasɛt], [kasɛt] *f* strongbox, coffer; casket (*for jewels*)
cassis [kasi], [kasis] *m* black currant; cassis (*liqueur*); gutter
cassolette [kasɔlɛt] *f* incense burner
cassonade [kasɔnad] *f* brown sugar
cassoulet [kasulɛ] *m* pork and beans
cassure [kasyr] *f* break; crease; rift
castagnettes [kastaɲɛt] *fpl* castanets
caste [kast] *f* caste; **hors caste** outcaste
castil·lan [kastijɑ̃] **castil·lane** [kastijan] *adj* Castilian ‖ *m* Castilian (*language*) ‖ (*cap*) *mf* Castilian (*person*)
Castille [kastij] *f* Castile; **la Castille** Castile
castor [kastɔr] *m* beaver
castrat [kastra] *m* castrato
castrer [kastre] *tr* to castrate
ca·suel **-suelle** [kazɥɛl] *adj* casual; (coll) brittle ‖ *m* perquisites
cataclysme [kataklism] *m* cataclysm
catacombes [katakɔ̃b] *fpl* catacombs
catafalque [katafalk] *m* catafalque
cataire [katɛr] *f* catnip

Catalogne [katalɔɲ] *f* Catalonia; **la Catalogne** Catalonia
catalogue [katalɔg] *m* catalogue
cataloguer [katalɔge] *tr* to catalogue
catalyseur [katalizœr] *m* catalyst
cataplasme [kataplasm] *m* poultice
catapulte [katapylt] *f* catapult
catapulter [katapylte] *tr* to catapult
cataracte [katarakt] *f* cataract
catarrhe [katar] *m* catarrh; bad cold
catastrophe [katastrɔf] *f* catastrophe
catch [katʃ] *m* wrestling
catcheur [katʃœr] *m* wrestler
catéchiser [kateʃize] *tr* to catechize; to reason with
catéchisme [kateʃism] *m* catechism
catégorie [kategɔri] *f* category
catégorique [kategɔrik] *adj* categorical
catgut [katgyt] *m* (surg) catgut
cathédrale [katedral] *f* cathedral
cathéter [katetɛr] *m* (med) catheter
cathode [katɔd] *f* cathode
catholicisme [katɔlisism] *m* Catholicism
catholicité [katɔlisite] *f* catholicity; Catholicism; Catholics
catholique [katɔlik] *adj* catholic; Catholic; orthodox; **pas très catholique** (coll) questionable ‖ *mf* Catholic
cati [kati] *m* glaze, gloss
catimini [katimini]—**en catimini** (coll) on the sly
catir [katir] *tr* to glaze
cauca·sien [kɔkazjɛ̃] **-sienne** [zjɛn] *adj* Caucasian ‖ (*cap*) *mf* Caucasian
caucasique [kɔkazik] *adj* Caucasian
cauchemar [koʃmar] *m* nightmare
cause [koz] *f* cause; (law) case; **à cause de** because of, on account of, for the sake of; **et pour cause** with good reason; **hors de cause** irrelevant, beside the point; **mettre q.ch. en cause** to question s.th.; **mettre qn en cause** to implicate s.o.
causer [koze] *tr* to cause ‖ *intr* to chat
causerie [kozri] *f* chat; informal lecture
causette [kozɛt] *f*—**faire la causette** (coll) to chat
cau·seur [kozœr] **-seuse** [zøz] *adj* talkative, chatty ‖ *mf* speaker, conversationalist ‖ *f* love seat
caustique [kostik] *adj* caustic
caute·leux [kotlø] **-leuse** [løz] *adj* crafty, wily; cunning (*mind*)
cautériser [koterize] *tr* to cauterize
caution [kosjɔ̃] *f* security, collateral; guarantor, bondsman; **mettre en liberté sous caution** to let out on bail; **se porter caution pour qn** to put up bail for s.o.; **sujet à caution** unreliable; **verser une caution** to make a deposit
cautionnement [kosjɔnmɑ̃] *m* surety bond, guaranty; bail; deposit
cautionner [kosjɔne] *tr* to bail out; to guarantee
cavalcade [kavalkad] *f* cavalcade
cavalerie [kavalri] *f* cavalry
cava·lier [kavalje] **-lière** [ljɛr] *adj* cavalier; bridle (*path*) ‖ *mf* horseback rider; dance partner ‖ *m* cava-

lier, horseman; escort; (chess) knight
|| *f* horsewoman
cave [kav] *adj* hollow (*cheeks*) || *f*
cellar; liquor cabinet; liquor store;
night club; bank (*in game of chance*);
stake (*in gambling*); **cave à vin** wine
cellar
ca·veau [kavo] *m* (*pl* **-veaux**) small
cellar; vault, crypt; rathskeller
caver [kave] *tr* to hollow out || *intr* to
ante || *ref* to become hollow (*said of
eyes*); to wager
caverne [kavɛrn] *f* cave, cavern;
(pathol) cavity (*e.g., in lung*)
caver·neux [kavɛrnø] **-neuse** [nøz] *adj*
cavernous; hollow (*voice*)
caviar [kavjar] *m* caviar
caviarder [kavjarde] *tr* to censor
cavité [kavite] *f* cavity, hollow
caw·cher -chère [kaʃɛr] *adj* kosher
Cayes [kaj] *fpl*—**Cayes de la Floride**
Florida Keys
C.C.P. *abbr* (**Compte chèques postaux**)
postal banking account
ce [sə] (or **cet** [sɛt] before vowel or
mute **h**) **cette** [sɛt] *adj dem* (*pl* **ces**
[se]) §82A || **ce** *pron* §82B, §85A4
C.E.A. *abbr* (**Commissariat à l'Énergie
atomique**) Atomic Energy Commission
céans [seɑ̃] *adv* herein
ceci [sesi] *pron dem indef* this, this
thing, this matter
cécité [sesite] *f* blindness
céder [sede] §10 *tr* to cede, transfer;
to yield, give up; **ne le céder à per-
sonne** to be second to none || *intr* to
yield, succumb, give way
cédille [sedij] *f* cedilla
cédrat [sedra] *m* citron
cèdre [sɛdr] *m* cedar
cédule [sedyl] *f* rate, schedule; (law)
notification
C.E.E. *abbr* (**Communauté économique européenne**) Common Market
cégétiste [seʒetist] *mf* unionist
ceindre [sɛ̃dr] §50 *tr* to buckle on, to
gird; to encircle; to wreathe (*one's
head*); **ceindre la couronne** to assume
the crown || *ref*—**se ceindre de** to
gird on
ceinture [sɛ̃tyr] *f* belt; waist, waistline;
sash, waistband; girdle; **ceinture de
sauvetage** life belt; **ceinture de sécurité** safety belt; **se mettre la ceinture**
or **se serrer la ceinture** to tighten
one's belt
ceinturer [sɛ̃tyre] *tr* to girdle, to belt;
to encircle, to belt; (wrestling) to
grip around the waist
cela [səla] *pron dem indef* that, that
thing; that matter; **à cela près** with
that one exception; **et avec cela?** what
else?
célébrant [selebrɑ̃] *m* (eccl) celebrant
célébration [selebrɑsjɔ̃] *f* celebration
célèbre [selɛbr] *adj* famous
célébrer [selebre] §10 *tr* to celebrate
célébrité [selebrite] *f* celebrity
celer [səle] §2 *tr* to hide, conceal
céleri [selri], [sɛlri] *m* celery
céleste [selɛst] *adj* celestial
célibat [seliba] *m* celibacy

célibataire [selibatɛr] *adj* single || *mf*
celibate || *m* bachelor || *f* spinster
celle [sɛl] §83
celle-ci [sɛlsi] §84
celle-là [sɛlla] §84
cellier [selje] *m* wine cellar; fruit cellar
cellophane [seləfan] *f* cellophane
cellule [selyl], [sɛlyl] *f* cell
celluloïd [selyləid] *m* celluloid
celte [sɛlt] *adj* Celtic || (*cap*) *mf* Celt
celtique [sɛltik] *adj* & *m* Celtic
celui [səlɥi] **celle** [sɛl] (*pl* **ceux** [sø]
celles) §83
celui-ci [səlɥisi] **celle-ci** [sɛlsi] (*pl
ceux-ci [søsi] **celles-ci**) §84
celui-là [səlɥila] **celle-là** [sɛlla] (*pl
ceux-là [søla] **celles-là**) §84
cémentation [semɑ̃tɑsjɔ̃] *f* casehard80en-
ing
cendre [sɑ̃dr] *f* cinder; **cendres** ashes
cendrée [sɑ̃dre] *f* shot; buckshot;
(sports) cinder track
cendrer [sɑ̃dre] *tr* to cinder
cendrier [sɑ̃drije] *m* ashtray
Cendrillon [sɑ̃drijɔ̃] *f* Cinderella
cène [sɛn] *f* (eccl) Holy Communion ||
(*cap*) *f* (eccl) Last Supper
cens [sɑ̃s] *m* census; poll tax
cen·sé -sée [sɑ̃se] *adj* supposed to, e.g.,
je ne suis pas censé le savoir I am
not supposed to know it; reputed to
be, e.g., **il est censé juge infaillible**
he is reputed to be an infallible judge
censément [sɑ̃semɑ̃] *adv* supposedly,
apparently, allegedly
censeur [sɑ̃sœr] *m* censor; census taker;
critic; auditor; proctor
censure [sɑ̃syr] *f* censure; censorship;
(psychoanal) censor
censurer [sɑ̃syre] *tr* to censure; to
censor
cent [sɑ̃] *adj* & *pron* (*pl* **cents** in multiples when standing before modified
noun, e.g., **trois cents œufs** three
hundred eggs) one hundred, a hundred; hundred; **cent pour cent** one
hundred percent; **cent un** [sɑ̃œ̃] one
hundred and one, a hundred and
one, hundred and one; **l'an dix-neuf
cent** the year nineteen hundred; **page
deux cent** page two hundred || *m*
hundred, one hundred || [sɛnt] *m*
cent
centaine [sɑ̃tɛn] *f* hundred; **par centaines** by the hundreds; **une centaine
de** about a hundred
centaure [sɑ̃tɔr] *m* centaur
centenaire [sɑ̃tnɛr] *adj* centenary || *mf*
centenarian || *m* centennial
centen·nal -nale [sɑ̃tennal] *adj* (*pl
-naux [no]) centennial
centième [sɑ̃tjɛm] *adj, pron* (*masc,
fem*), & *m* hundredth || *f* hundredth
performance
centigrade [sɑ̃tigrad] *adj* & *m* centigrade
centime [sɑ̃tim] *m* centime
centimètre [sɑ̃timɛtr] *m* centimeter;
tape measure
centrage [sɑ̃traʒ] *m* centering
cen·tral -trale [sɑ̃tral] *adj* (*pl* **-traux**
[tro]) central; main (*office*) || *m*
(telp) central || *f* powerhouse; labor

union; **centrale atomique** or **nucléaire** atomic generator

centralisation [sɑ̃tralizɑsjɔ̃] *f* centralization

centraliser [sɑ̃tralize] *tr & ref* to centralize

centre [sɑ̃tr] *m* center; **centre commercial** shopping district; **centre de dépression** storm center; **centre de triage** (rr) switchyard; **centre d'études** college; **centre de villégiature** resort; **centre social des étudiants** student center, student union

centrer [sɑ̃tre] *tr* to center

centrifuge [sɑ̃trifyʒ] *adj* centrifugal

centuple [sɑ̃typl] *adj & m* hundredfold; **au centuple** hundredfold

cep [sɛp] *m* vine stock

cépage [sepaʒ] *m* (bot) vine

cèpe [sɛp] *f* cepe mushroom

cependant [səpɑ̃dɑ̃] *adv* meanwhile; however, but, still; **cependant que** while, whereas; **et cependant** and yet

céramique [seramik] *adj* ceramic ‖ *f* (art of) ceramics; ceramic piece; **céramiques** ceramics (*objects*)

cerbère [sɛrbɛr] *m* (coll) watchdog ‖ (*cap*) *m* Cerberus

cer·ceau [sɛrso] *m* (*pl* **-ceaux**) hoop; **cerceaux** pinfeathers

cercle [sɛrkl] *m* circle; circle, club, society; clubhouse; hoop; **en cercle** in the cask

cercler [sɛrkle] *tr* to ring, encircle; to hoop

cercueil [sɛrkœj] *m* coffin

céréale [sereal] *adj & f* cereal

céré·bral -brale [serebral] *adj* (*pl* **-braux** [bro]) cerebral

cérémo·nial -niale [seremɔnjal] *adj & m* ceremonial

cérémonie [seremɔni] *f* ceremony; **faire des cérémonies** to stand on ceremony

cérémo·niel -nielle [seremɔnjɛl] *adj* ceremonial

cérémo·nieux [seremɔnjø] **-nieuse** [njøz] *adj* ceremonious, formal, stiff

cerf [sɛr] *m* deer, red deer; stag, buck

cerf-volant [sɛrvɔlɑ̃] *m* (*pl* **cerfs-volants**) kite

cerisaie [sərize] *f* cherry orchard

cerise [səriz] *f* cherry

cerisier [sərizje] *m* cherry tree

cerne [sɛrn] *m* annual ring (*of tree*); ring (*around moon, black eye, wound*)

cer·neau [sɛrno] *m* (*pl* **-neaux**) unripe nutmeat

cerner [sɛrne] *tr* to ring, encircle; to hem in, besiege; to shell (*nuts*)

cer·tain [sɛrtɛ̃] **-taine** [tɛn] *adj* certain, sure ‖ (when standing before noun) *adj* certain, some; **certain auteur** a certain author; **depuis un certain temps** for some time; **d'un certain âge** middle-aged ‖ **certains** *pron indef pl* certain people

certainement [sɛrtɛnmɑ̃] *adv* certainly

certes [sɛrt] *adv* indeed, certainly

certificat [sɛrtifika] *m* certificate

certifier [sɛrtifje] *tr* to certify

certitude [sɛrtityd] *f* certainty

cérumen [serymɛn] *m* earwax

céruse [seryz] *f* white lead

cer·veau [sɛrvo] *m* (*pl* **-veaux**) brain; mind; **cerveau brûlé** (coll) hothead

cervelas [sɛrvəla] *m* salami

cervelet [sɛrvəle] *m* cerebellum

cervelle [sɛrvɛl] *f* brains; **brûler la cervelle à qn** (coll) to shoot s.o.'s brains out

ces [se] §82A

césa·rien [sezarjɛ̃] **-rienne** [rjɛn] *adj* Caesarean ‖ *f* Caesarean section

cesse [sɛs] *f* cessation, ceasing; **sans cesse** unceasingly, incessantly

cesser [sese] *tr* to stop, to cease, to leave off (*e.g., work*) ‖ *intr* to cease, stop; **cesser de** + *inf* to stop, cease, quit + *ger*

cessez-le-feu [sesɛlfø] *m invar* ceasefire

cession [sesjɔ̃] *f* ceding, surrender; (law) transfer

c'est-à-dire [sɛtadir] *conj* that is, namely

césure [sezyr] *f* caesura

cet [sɛt] §82A

cette [sɛt] §82A

ceux [sø] §83

ceux-ci [søsi] §84

ceux-là [søla] §84

Ceylan [sɛlɑ̃] *m* Ceylon

C.G.T. [seʒete] *f* (letterword) (**confédération générale du travail**) national labor union ‖ *abbr* (**Cie Générale transatlantique**) French Line

cha·cal [ʃakal] *m* (*pl* **-cals**) jackal

cha·cun [ʃakœ̃] **-cune** [kyn] *pron indef* each, each one, every one; everybody, everyone; **chacun pour soi** every man for himself; **chacun son goût** every man to his own taste; **tout chacun** (coll) every Tom, Dick, and Harry

chadburn [tʃadbœrn] *m* (naut) public-address system

chadouf [ʃaduf] *m* well sweep

cha·grin [ʃagrɛ̃] **-grine** [grin] *adj* sad, downcast ‖ *m* grief, sorrow

chagriner [ʃagrine] *tr* to grieve, distress; to make into shagreen leather ‖ *intr* to grieve, worry

chah [ʃa] *m* shah

chahut [ʃay] *m* (coll) horseplay, row

chahuter [ʃayte] *tr* (coll) to upset; (coll) to boo, heckle ‖ *intr* (coll) to create a disturbance

chai [ʃe] *m* wine cellar

chaîne [ʃɛn] *f* chain; warp (*of fabric*); necklace; (archit) pier; (archit) tie; (naut) cable; (rad, telv) network; (telv) channel; **chaîne de fabrication** or **chaîne de montage** assembly line; **faire la chaîne** to form a bucket brigade

chaînon [ʃɛnɔ̃] *m* link

chair [ʃɛr] *f* flesh; pulp (*of fruits*); meat (*of animals*); **chair de poule** gooseflesh; **chair de sa chair** one's flesh and blood; **chairs** (painting, sculpture) nude parts; **en chair et en os** in the flesh; **ni chair ni poisson** neither fish nor fowl

chaire [ʃɛr] *f* pulpit; lectern; chair (*held by university professor*)

chaise [ʃɛz] *f* chair; bowline knot; (mach) bracket; **chaise à bascule** rocking chair; **chaise à porteurs** sedan chair; **chaise berceuse** rocking chair; **chaise brisée** folding chair; **chaise d'enfant** high chair; **chaise électrique** electric chair; **chaise percée** commode, toilet; **chaise pliante** folding chair

cha·land [ʃalɑ̃] **-lande** [lɑ̃d] *mf* customer ‖ *m* barge; **chaland de débarquement** (mil) landing craft

châle [ʃɑl] *m* shawl

chalet [ʃalɛ] *m* chalet, cottage, summer home; **chalet de nécessité** public rest room

chaleur [ʃalœr] *f* heat; warmth; **les grandes chaleurs de l'été** the hot weather of summer

chaleu·reux [ʃalœrø] **-reuse** [røz] *adj* warm, heated

châlit [ʃali] *m* bedstead

chaloupe [ʃalup] *f* launch

chalu·meau [ʃalymo] *m* (*pl* **-meaux**) reed; blowtorch; (mus) pipe; **chalumeau oxhydrique** or **chalumeau oxyacétylénique** acetylene torch

chalut [ʃaly] *m* trawl

chalutier [ʃalytje] *m* trawler

chamade [ʃamad] *f*—**battre la chamade** to beat wildly (*said of the heart*)

chamailler [ʃamaje] *ref* to squabble

chamarrer [ʃamare] *tr* to decorate, to ornament; to bedizen, to bedeck; (slang) to cover (*s.o.*) with ridicule

chambarder [ʃɑ̃barde] *tr* (slang) to upset, to turn upside down

chambellan [ʃɑ̃bellɑ̃] *m* chamberlain

chambouler [ʃɑ̃bule] *tr* (slang) to upset, to turn topsy-turvy

chambranle [ʃɑ̃brɑ̃l] *m* frame (*of a door or window*); mantelpiece

chambre [ʃɑ̃br] *f* chamber; room; **chambre à air** inner tube; **chambre à coucher** bedroom; **chambre d'ami** guest room; **chambre de compensation** clearing house; **chambre noire** darkroom

chambrée [ʃɑ̃bre] *f* dormitory, barracks; bunkmates

chambrer [ʃɑ̃bre] *tr* to keep under lock and key; to keep (*wine*) at room temperature

cha·meau [ʃamo] **-melle** [mɛl] *mf* (*pl* **-meaux**) camel ‖ *m* (slang) bitch (*person*)

chamois [ʃamwa] *adj & m* chamois

champ [ʃɑ̃] *m* field; **aux champs** salute (*played on trumpet or drum*); **champ clos** lists, dueling field; **champ de courses** race track; **champ de repos** cemetery; **champ de tir** firing range; **champ libre** clear field; **champs Élysées** Elysian Fields; **Champs-Élysées** Champs Elysées (*street*)

champagne [ʃɑ̃paɲ] *m* champagne; **champagne brut** extra dry champagne; **champagne d'origine** vintage champagne ‖ (*cap*) *f* Champagne; **la Champagne** Champagne

champe·nois [ʃɑ̃pənwa] **-noise** [nwaz] *adj* Champagne ‖ *m* Champagne

dialect ‖ (*cap*) *mf* inhabitant of Champagne

champêtre [ʃɑ̃pɛtr] *adj* rustic, rural

champignon [ʃɑ̃piɲɔ̃] *m* mushroom; fungus; (slang) accelerator pedal; **champignon de couche** cultivated mushroom; **champignon vénéneux** toadstool

champignonner [ʃɑ̃piɲɔne] *intr* to mushroom

cham·pion [ʃɑ̃pjɔ̃] **-pionne** [pjɔn] *mf* champion ‖ *f* championess

championnat [ʃɑ̃pjɔna] *m* championship

champlever [ʃɑ̃lve] §2 *tr* to chase out, to gouge out

chan·çard [ʃɑ̃sar] **-çarde** [sard] *adj* (slang) in luck ‖ *mf* (slang) lucky person

chance [ʃɑ̃s] *f* luck; good luck; **avoir de la chance** to be lucky; **bonne chance** good luck; **chance moyenne** off chance; **chances** chances, risks, probability, possibility

chance·lant [ʃɑ̃slɑ̃] **-lante** [lɑ̃t] *adj* shaky, unsteady, tottering; delicate (*health, constitution*)

chanceler [ʃɑ̃sle] §34 *intr* to stagger, to totter, to teeter; to waver

chancelier [ʃɑ̃səlje] *m* chancellor

chancellerie [ʃɑ̃sɛlri] *f* chancellery

chan·ceux [ʃɑ̃sø] **-ceuse** [søz] *adj* lucky; risky

chanci [ʃɑ̃si] *m* manure pile for mushroom growing

chancir [ʃɑ̃sir] *intr* to grow moldy

chancre [ʃɑ̃kr] *m* chancre; ulcer, canker

chandail [ʃɑ̃daj] *m* sweater; **chandail à col roulé** turtleneck sweater

chandeleur [ʃɑ̃dlœr] *f*—**la chandeleur** Candlemas

chandelier [ʃɑ̃dəlje] *m* candlestick; chandler

chandelle [ʃɑ̃dɛl] *f* tallow candle; prop, stay (*used in construction*); **chandelle de glace** icicle; **en chandelle** vertically; **voir trente-six chandelles** to see stars (*on account of a blow*)

chanfrein [ʃɑ̃frɛ̃] *m* forehead (*of a horse*); chamfer, beveled edge

chanfreiner [ʃɑ̃frene] *tr* to chamfer, to bevel

change [ʃɑ̃ʒ] *m* exchange; rate of exchange; **de change** in reserve, extra; **donner le change à** to throw off the trail; **prendre le change** to let one self be duped; **rendre le change à qn** to give s.o. a taste of his own medicine

changeable [ʃɑ̃ʒabl] *adj* changeable

chan·geant [ʃɑ̃ʒɑ̃] **-geante** [ʒɑ̃t] *adj* changeable, changing, fickle; iridescent

changement [ʃɑ̃ʒmɑ̃] *m* change; shift, shifting; **changement de propriétaire** under new ownership; **changement de vitesse** gearshift

changer [ʃɑ̃ʒe] §38 *tr* to change; **changer contre** to exchange for ‖ *intr* to change; **changer d'avis** to change one's mind; **changer de place** to change one's seat; **changer de ton**

(coll) to change one's tune; **changer de visage** to blush; to change color ‖ *ref* to change, change clothes
chanoine [ʃanwan] *m* (eccl) canon
chanson [ʃɑ̃sɔ̃] *f* song; **chanson bachique** drinking song; **chanson de geste** medieval epic; **chanson de Noël** Christmas carol; **chanson du terroir** folk song; **chanson sentimentale** torch song
chansonner [ʃɑ̃sɔne] *tr* to lampoon in a satirical song
chansonneur [ʃɑ̃sɔnœr] *m* lampooner (*who writes satirical songs*)
chanson·nier [ʃɑ̃sɔnje] **chanson·nière** [ʃɑ̃sɔnjer] *mf* songwriter ‖ *m* chansonnier; song book
chant [ʃɑ̃] *m* singing; song, chant; canto; crowing (*of rooster*); side (*e.g., of a brick*); **chant du cygne** swan song; **chant de Noël** Christmas carol; **chant national** national anthem; **chants** poetry; **de chant** on end, edgewise
chantage [ʃɑ̃taʒ] *m* blackmail
chan·tant [ʃɑ̃tɑ̃] **-tante** [tɑ̃t] *adj* singable, melodious; singsong (*accent*); musical (*evening*)
chan·teau [ʃɑ̃to] *m* (*pl* **-teaux**) chunk (*of bread*); remnant
chantepleure [ʃɑ̃tplœr] *f* wine funnel; tap (*of cask*); sprinkler; weep hole
chanter [ʃɑ̃te] *tr* to sing ‖ *intr* to sing; to crow (*as a rooster*); to pay blackmail; **chanter faux** to sing out of tune; **chanter juste** to sing in tune; **faire chanter** to blackmail
chanterelle [ʃɑ̃trɛl] *f* first string (*of violin*); decoy bird; mushroom; **appuyer sur la chanterelle** (coll) to rub it in
chan·teur [ʃɑ̃tœr] **-teuse** [tøz] *adj* singing; song (*bird*) ‖ *mf* singer; **chanteur de charme** crooner; **chanteur de rythme** jazz singer
chantier [ʃɑ̃tje] *m* shipyard; stocks, slip; workshop, yard; gantry, stand (*for barrels*); (public sign) men at work; **chantier de démolition** junkyard, scrap heap; **mettre en** or **sur le chantier** to start work on
chantilly [ʃɑ̃tiji] *m* whipped cream
chantonner [ʃɑ̃tɔne] *tr & intr* to hum
chantoung [ʃɑ̃tuŋ] *m* shantung
chantourner [ʃɑ̃turne] *tr* to jigsaw
chantre [ʃɑ̃tr] *m* cantor, chanter; precentor; songster; bard, poet
chanvre [ʃɑ̃vr] *m* hemp; **en chanvre** hempen; flaxen (*color*)
chan·vrier [ʃɑ̃vrije] **-vrière** [vrijer] *adj* hemp (*industry*) ‖ *mf* dealer in hemp; hemp dresser
chaos [kao] *m* chaos
chaotique [kaɔtik] *adj* chaotic
chaparder [ʃaparde] *tr* (coll) to pilfer, to filch
chape [ʃap] *f* cover, covering; tread (*of tire*); coping (*of bridge*); frame, shell (*of pulley block*); (eccl) cope
cha·peau [ʃapo] *m* (*pl* **-peaux**) hat; head (*of mushroom*); lead (*of magazine or newspaper article*); cap (*of fountain pen; of valve*); cowl (*of

chimney*); **chapeau à cornes** cocked hat; **chapeau bas** hat in hand; **chapeau bas!** hats off!; **chapeau chinois** Chinese bells; **chapeau de roue** hubcap; **chapeau haut de forme** top hat; **chapeau melon** derby; **chapeau mou** fedora
chapeau-cloche [ʃapoklɔʃ] *m* (*pl* **chapeaux-cloches**) cloche (hat)
chapeauter [ʃapote] *tr* (coll) to put a hat on (*e.g., a child*)
chapelain [ʃaplɛ̃] *m* chaplain (*of a private chapel*)
chapeler [ʃaple] §34 *tr* to scrape the crust off of (*bread*)
chapelet [ʃaple] *m* chaplet, rosary; string (*of onions; of islands; of insults*); chain (*of events; of mountains*); series (*e.g., of attacks*); (mil) stick (*of bombs*); **chapelet hydraulique** bucket conveyor; **défiler son chapelet** (coll) to speak one's mind; **dire son chapelet** to tell one's beads; **en chapelet** (elec) in series
chape·lier [ʃaplje] **-lière** [ljer] *mf* hatter ‖ *f* Saratoga trunk
chapelle [ʃapɛl] *f* chapel; clique, coterie; **chapelle ardente** mortuary chamber lighted by candles; hearse
chapellerie [ʃapɛlri] *f* hatmaking; millinery; hat shop; millinery shop
chapelure [ʃaplyr] *f* bread crumbs
chaperon [ʃaprɔ̃] *m* chaperon; hood; cape with a hood; coping (*of wall*); **le Petit Chaperon rouge** Little Red Ridinghood
chaperonner [ʃaprɔne] *tr* to chaperon
chapi·teau [ʃapito] *m* (*pl* **-teaux**) capital (*of column*); circus tent
chapitre [ʃapitr] *m* chapter; **commencer un nouveau chapitre** to turn over a new leaf
chapon [ʃapɔ̃] *m* capon; (culin) crust rubbed with garlic
chaque [ʃak] *adj indef* each, every ‖ *pron indef* (coll) each, each one
char [ʃar] *m* chariot; float (*in parade*); (mil) tank; **char d'assaut** or **char de combat** (mil) tank; **char funèbre** hearse
charabia [ʃarabja] *m* gibberish
charançon [ʃarɑ̃sɔ̃] *m* weevil
charbon [ʃarbɔ̃] *m* coal; soft coal; charcoal; carbon (*of an electric cell or arc*); cinder (*in the eye*); **charbon ardent** live coal; **charbon de bois** charcoal; **charbon de terre** coal; **être sur les charbons ardents** to be on pins and needles
charbonnage [ʃarbɔnaʒ] *m* coal mining; coal mine
charbonner [ʃarbɔne] *tr* to char; to draw (*a picture*) with charcoal ‖ *intr & ref* to char, to carbonize
charbon·neux [ʃarbɔnø] **charbon·neuse** [ʃarbɔnøz] *adj* sooty; anthrax-carrying
charbon·nier [ʃarbɔnje] **charbon·nière** [ʃarbɔnjer] *adj* coal (*e.g., industry*) ‖ *mf* coal dealer ‖ *m* charcoal burner; coaler ‖ *f* coal scuttle; charcoal kiln; (orn) coal titmouse

charcuter [ʃarkyte] *tr* to butcher, mangle

charcuterie [ʃarkytri] *f* delicatessen; pork butcher shop

charcu·tier [ʃarkytje] -**tière** [tjɛr] *mf* pork butcher; (coll) sawbones

chardon [ʃardɔ̃] *m* thistle

chardonneret [ʃardɔnrɛ] *m* (orn) goldfinch

charge [ʃarʒ] *f* charge; load, burden; caricature; public office; **à charge de** on condition of, with the proviso of; **à charge de revanche** on condition of getting the same thing in return; **charges de famille** dependents; **être à charge à** to be dependent upon; **être à la charge de** to be supported by; **faire la charge de** to do a takeoff of

char·gé -**gée** [ʃarʒe] *adj* loaded; full; overcast (*sky*); registered (*letter*) ‖ *m* assistant, deputy, envoy; **chargé de cours** assistant professor

chargement [ʃarʒəmɑ̃] *m* charging; loading; cargo

charger [ʃarʒe] §38 *tr* to charge; to drive, to take (*s.o. in one's car*) ‖ *intr* (mil) to charge; (naut) to load ‖ *ref* to be loaded; **se charger de** to take charge of; to take up (*a question*)

chargeur [ʃarʒœr] *m* loader; stoker; shipper; clip (*of gun*); (elec) charger

chariot [ʃarjo] *m* wagon, cart; typewriter carriage; **chariot d'enfant** walker; **chariot élévateur** fork-lift truck; **Grand Chariot, Chariot de David** Big Dipper; **Petit Chariot** Little Dipper

charitable [ʃaritabl] *adj* charitable

charité [ʃarite] *f* charity; **faire la charité** to give alms; **faites la charité de** or **ayez la charité de** have the goodness to; **par charité** for charity's sake

charlatan [ʃarlatɑ̃] *m* charlatan

charlemagne [ʃarləmaɲ] *m* (cards) king of hearts; **faire charlemagne** to quit while winning

char·mant [ʃarmɑ̃] -**mante** [mɑ̃t] *adj* charming

charme [ʃarm] *m* charm; (*Carpinus betulus*) hornbeam; **se porter comme un charme** to be fit as a fiddle

charmer [ʃarme] *tr* to charm

char·meur [ʃarmœr] -**meuse** [møz] *adj* charming ‖ *mf* charmer

charmille [ʃarmij] *f* bower, arbor

char·nel -**nelle** [ʃarnɛl] *adj* carnal

charnière [ʃarnjɛr] *f* hinge

char·nu -**nue** [ʃarny] *adj* fleshy; plump; pulpy

charogne [ʃarɔɲ] *f* carrion

charpentage [ʃarpɑ̃taʒ] *m* carpentry

charpente [ʃarpɑ̃t] *f* framework; scaffolding; frame, build (*of body*)

charpenter [ʃarpɑ̃te] *tr* to square (*timber*); to outline, map out, plan (*a novel, speech, etc.*); **être solidement charpenté** to be well built or well constructed ‖ *intr* to carpenter

charpenterie [ʃarpɑ̃tri] *f* carpentry; structure (*of building*)

charpentier [ʃarpɑ̃tje] *m* carpenter

charpie [ʃarpi] *f* lint; **en charpie in shreds**

charrée [ʃare] *f* lye

charre·tier [ʃartje] -**tière** [tjɛr] *mf* teamster; **jurer comme un charretier** to swear like a trooper

charrette [ʃarɛt] *f* cart

charriage [ʃarjaʒ] *m* cartage; drifting (*of ice*); (slang) exaggeration

charrier [ʃarje] *tr* to cart, to transport; to carry away (*sand, as the river does*); (slang) to poke fun at ‖ *intr* to be full of ice (*said of river*); (slang) to exaggerate

charroi [ʃarwa], [ʃarwa] *m* cartage

charron [ʃarɔ̃], [ʃarɔ̃] *m* wheelwright, cartwright

charroyer [ʃarwaje] §47 *tr* to cart

charrue [ʃary] *f* plow; **mettre la charrue devant les bœufs** to put the cart before the horse

charte [ʃart] *f* charter; title deed; fundamental principle

chas [ʃa] *m* eye (*of needle*)

chasse [ʃas] *f* hunt, hunting; hunting song; chase; bag (*game caught*); **aller à la chasse** to go hunting; **chasse à courre** riding to the hounds; **chasse aux appartements** house hunting; **chasse aux fauves** big-game hunting; **chasse d'eau** flush; **chasse gardée** game preserve; **chasse réservée** (public sign) no shooting; **tirer la chasse** to pull the toilet chain

châsse [ʃas] *f* reliquary; frame (*e.g., for eyeglasses*) ‖ **châsses** *mpl* (slang) blinkers, eyes

chasse-bestiaux [ʃasbɛstjo] *m invar* cowcatcher

chasse-clou [ʃasklu] *m* (*pl* -**clous**) punch, nail set

chassé-croisé [ʃasekrwaze] *m* (*pl* **chassés-croisées**) futile efforts

chasselas [ʃasla] *m* white table grape

chasse-mouches [ʃasmuʃ] *m invar* fly swatter; fly net

chasse-neige [ʃasnɛʒ] *m invar* snowplow

chasse-pierres [ʃaspjɛr] *m invar* (rr) cowcatcher

chasser [ʃase] *tr* to hunt; to chase; to chase away, to put to flight; to drive (*e.g., a herd of cattle*); (coll) to fire (*e.g., a servant*) ‖ *intr* to hunt; to skid; to come, e.g., **le vent chasse du nord** the wind is coming from the north; **chasser de race** (coll) to be a chip off the old block

chasseresse [ʃasrɛs] *f* huntress

chas·seur [ʃasœr] **chas·seuse** [ʃasøz] *mf* hunter; bellhop ‖ *m* chasseur; fighter pilot; **chasseur à réaction** jet fighter; **chasseur d'assaut** fighter plane; **chasseur de chars** antitank tank; **chasseur de sous-marins** submarine chaser

chasseur-bombardier [ʃasœrbɔ̃bardje] *m* fighter-bomber

chassie [ʃasi] *f* gum (*on eyelids*)

chas·sieux [ʃasjø] **chas·sieuse** [ʃasjøz] *adj* gummy (*eyelids*)

châssis [ʃasi] *m* chassis; window frame; chase (*for printing*); **châssis à**

demeure or dormant sealed window frame; **châssis couche** (hort) hotbed; **châssis mobile** movable sash
châssis-presse [ʃɑsipres] *m* (*pl* -**presses**) printing frame
chaste [ʃast] *adj* chaste
chasteté [ʃastəte] *f* chastity
chat [ʃa] **chatte** [ʃat] *mf* cat || *m* tomcat; **à bon chat bon rat** tit for tat; **acheter chat en poche** (coll) to buy a pig in a poke; **appeler un chat un chat** (coll) to call a spade a spade; **chat à neuf queues** cat-o'-nine-tails; **chat dans la gorge** (coll) frog in the throat; **chat de gouttière** alley cat; **chat sauvage** wildcat; **d'autres chats à fouetter** (coll) other fish to fry; **il ne faut pas réveiller le chat qui dort** let sleeping dogs lie; **le Chat botté** Puss in Boots; **mon petit chat!** darling!; **pas un chat** (coll) not a soul || *f* see **chatte**
châtaigne [ʃatɛɲ] *f* chestnut
châtaignier [ʃatɛɲe] *m* chestnut tree
chataire [ʃater] *f* catnip
châ•teau [ʃato] *m* (*pl* -**teaux**) chateau; palace; estate, manor; **château d'eau** water tower; **château de cartes** house of cards; **château fort** castle, fort, citadel; **châteaux en Espagne** castles in the air; **mener une vie de château** to live like a prince
châteaubriand or **châteaubriant** [ʃatobriɑ̃] *m* grilled beefsteak
châte•lain [ʃatlɛ̃] -**laine** [lɛn] *mf* proprietor of a country estate || *f* wife of the lord of the manor; bracelet
châtelet [ʃatlɛ] *m* small chateau
chat-huant [ʃaɥɑ̃] *m* (*pl* **chats-huants** [ʃaɥɑ̃]) screech owl
châtier [ʃatje] *tr* to chasten, chastise; to correct; to purify (*style*)
chatière [ʃatjer] *f* ventilation hole; cathole
châtiment [ʃatimɑ̃] *m* punishment
chatoiement [ʃatwamɑ̃] *m* glisten, sparkle; sheen, shimmer; play of colors
chaton [ʃatɔ̃] *m* kitten; setting (*of ring*); (bot) catkin
chatonner [ʃatɔne] *tr* to set (*a gem*) || *intr* to have kittens
chatouillement [ʃatujmɑ̃] *m* tickle; tickling sensation
chatouiller [ʃatuje] *tr* to tickle; (fig) to excite, arouse || *intr* to tickle
chatouil•leux [ʃatujø] **chatouil•leuse** [ʃatujøz] *adj* ticklish; touchy
chatoyer [ʃatwaje] §47 *intr* to glisten, to sparkle; to shimmer
chat-pard [ʃapar] *m* (*pl* **chats-pards**) ocelot
châtrer [ʃatre] *tr* to castrate
chatte [ʃat] *adj fem* kittenish || *f* cat, female cat
chatterie [ʃatri] *f* cajoling; sweets
chatterton [ʃatertɔn] *m* friction tape
chaud [ʃo] **chaude** [ʃod] *adj* hot, warm; last-minute (*news flash*); **il fait chaud** it is warm (weather); **pleurer à chaudes larmes** to cry one's eyes out || *m* heat, warmth; **à chaud** emergency (*operation*); (med) in the

acute stage; **avoir chaud** to be warm, to be hot (*said of person*); **il a eu chaud** (coll) he had a narrow escape || *adv*—**coûter chaud** (coll) to cost a pretty penny; **servir chaud** to serve (*s.th.*) piping hot
chaudière [ʃodjer] *f* boiler
chaudron [ʃodrɔ̃] *m* cauldron
chaudron•nier [ʃodrɔnje] **chaudron•nière** [ʃodrɔnjer] *mf* coppersmith; boilermaker
chauffage [ʃofaʒ] *m* heating; stoking; (coll) coaching
chauffard [ʃofar] *m* road hog, Sunday driver
chauffe [ʃof] *f* stoking; furnace
chauffe-assiettes [ʃofasjet] *m invar* hot plate
chauffe-bain [ʃofbɛ̃] *m* (*pl* -**bains**) bathroom water heater
chauffe-eau [ʃofo] *m invar* water heater
chauffe-lit [ʃofli] *m* (*pl* -**lits**) bedwarmer
chauffe-pieds [ʃofpje] *m invar* foot warmer
chauffe-plats [ʃofpla] *m invar* chafing dish
chauffer [ʃofe] *tr* to heat; to warm up; to limber up; (coll) to coach; (slang) to snitch, filch || *intr* to heat up; to get up steam; to overheat; **ça va chauffer!** (coll) watch the fur fly! || *ref* to warm oneself; to heat up
chaufferette [ʃofret] *f* foot warmer; space heater; car heater
chauffeur [ʃofœr] *m* driver; chauffeur; (rr) stoker, fireman
chauffeuse [ʃoføz] *f* fireside chair
chaume [ʃom] *m* stubble; thatch
chaumière [ʃomjer] *f* thatched cottage
chaussée [ʃose] *f* pavement, road; causeway
chausse-pied [ʃospje] *m* (*pl* -**pieds**) shoehorn
chausser [ʃose] *tr* to put on (*shoes, skis, glasses, tires, etc.*); to shoe; to fit || *intr* to fit (*said of shoe*); **chausser de** to wear (*a certain size shoe*) || *ref* to put one's shoes on
chausses [ʃos] *fpl* hose (*in medieval dress*); **aux chausses de** on the heels of; **c'est elle qui porte les chausses** (coll) she wears the pants
chausse-trape [ʃostrap] *f* (*pl* -**trapes**) trap
chaussette [ʃoset] *f* sock
chausseur [ʃosœr] *m* shoe salesman
chausson [ʃosɔ̃] *m* pump, slipper, savate; **chausson aux pommes** apple turnover
chaussure [ʃosyr] *f* footwear, shoes; shoe; **trouver chaussure à son pied** to find what one needs
chauve [ʃov] *adj* bald
chauve-souris [ʃovsuri] *f* (*pl* **chauves-souris**) (zool) bat
chau•vin [ʃovɛ̃] -**vine** [vin] *adj* chauvinistic || *mf* chauvinist
chauvir [ʃovir] *intr*—**chauvir de l'oreille** or **chauvir des oreilles** to prick up the ears (*said of horse, mule, donkey*)
chaux [ʃo] *f* lime

chavirement [ʃavirmɑ̃] *m* capsizing, overturning
chavirer [ʃavire] *tr & intr* to tip over, to capsize
chef [ʃɛf] *m* head, chief, leader; boss; scoutmaster; **chef de bande** ringleader, gang leader; **chef de cuisine** chef; **chef de file** leader, standard-bearer; **chef de gare** stationmaster; **chef de l'exécutif** chief executive; **chef de musique** bandmaster; **chef de rayon** floorwalker; **chef de tribu** chieftain; **chef d'orchestre** conductor; bandleader; **de son propre chef** by one's own authority, on one's own
chef-d'œuvre [ʃɛdœvr] *m* (*pl* **chefs-d'œuvre**) masterpiece
chef-lieu [ʃɛfljø] *m* (*pl* **chefs-lieux**) county seat, capital city
cheftaine [ʃɛftɛn] *f* Girl Scout unit leader
cheik [ʃɛk] *m* sheik
chelem [ʃlɛm] *m* slam (*at bridge*); **être chelem** (*cards*) to be shut out
chemin [ʃmɛ̃] *m* way; road; **chemin battu** beaten path; **chemin de la Croix** (eccl) Way of the Cross; **chemin de fer** railroad; **chemin des écoliers** (coll) long way around; **chemin de table** table runner; **chemin de traverse** side road; shortcut; **chemin de velours** primrose path; **n'y pas aller par quatre chemins** (coll) to come straight to the point
chemi·neau [ʃmino] *m* (*pl* **-neaux**) hobo, tramp; deadbeat
cheminée [ʃmine] *f* chimney, stack, smokestack; fireplace; (naut) funnel
cheminer [ʃmine] *intr* to trudge, tramp; to make headway
cheminot [ʃmino] *m* railroader
chemise [ʃmiz] *f* shirt; dust jacket (*of book*); folder, file; jacket, shell, metal casing; **chemise de mailles** coat of mail; **chemise de nuit** nightgown
chemiser [ʃmize] *tr* (mach) to case, to jacket
chemiserie [ʃmizri] *f* haberdashery
chemisette [ʃmizɛt] *f* short-sleeved shirt
chemi·sier [ʃmizje] **-sière** [zjɛr] *mf* haberdasher || *m* shirtwaist
che·nal [ʃnal] *m* (*pl* **-naux** [no]) channel; millrace
chenapan [ʃnapɑ̃] *m* rogue, scoundrel
chêne [ʃɛn] *m* oak
ché·neau [ʃeno] *m* (*pl* **-neaux**) rain spout
chêne-liège [ʃɛnljɛʒ] *m* (*pl* **chênes-lièges**) cork oak
chenet [ʃnɛ] *m* andiron
chènevis [ʃɛnvi] *m* hempseed, birdseed
chenil [ʃni] *m* kennel
chenille [ʃnij] *f* caterpillar; chenille; caterpillar tread
chenil·lé -lée [ʃnije] *adj* with a caterpillar tread
che·nu -nue [ʃny] *adj* hoary
cheptel [ʃɛptɛl], [ʃɛtɛl] *m* livestock; **cheptel mort** implements and buildings
chèque [ʃɛk] *m* check; **chèque de voyage** traveler's check; **chèque**

prescrit lapsed check; **chèque sans provision** worthless check
chéquier [ʃekje] *m* checkbook
cher chère [ʃɛr] *adj* expensive, dear || (when standing before noun) *adj* dear, beloved || *f* see **chère** || **cher** *adv* dear(ly); **coûter cher** to cost a great deal
chercher [ʃɛrʃe] *tr* to look for, search for, seek, hunt; to try to get; **aller chercher** to go and get; **envoyer chercher** to send for || *intr* to search; **chercher à** to try to, to endeavor to || *ref* to look for each other; to feel one's way
cher·cheur [ʃɛrʃœr] **-cheuse** [ʃøz] *adj* inquiring (*mind*); homing (*device*) || *mf* seeker; researcher, scholar; investigator; prospector (*for gold, uranium, etc.*)
chère [ʃɛr] *f* fare, food and drink; **faire bonne chère** to live high
ché·ri -rie [ʃeri] *adj & mf* darling
chérir [ʃerir] *tr* to cherish
cherry [ʃeri] *m* cherry cordial
cherté [ʃerte] *f* high price; **cherté de la vie** high cost of living
chérubin [ʃerybɛ̃] *m* cherub
ché·tif [ʃetif] **-tive** [tiv] *adj* puny, sickly; poor, wretched
che·val [ʃəval] *m* (*pl* **-vaux** [vo]) horse; metric or French horsepower (*735 watts*); **à cheval** on horseback; **à cheval sur** astride; insistent upon; **cheval de bois** or **cheval d'arçons** horse (*for vaulting*); **cheval de course** race horse; **cheval de race** thoroughbred; **cheval de retour** (coll) jailbird; **cheval entier** stallion; **monter sur ses grands chevaux** (fig) to get up on one's high horse
chevalement [ʃəvalmɑ̃] *m* support, shoring; (min) headframe
chevaler [ʃəvale] *tr* to shore up
chevaleresque [ʃəvalrɛsk] *adj* knightly, chivalrous
chevalerie [ʃəvalri] *f* chivalry
chevalet [ʃəvalɛ] *m* easel; sawhorse; stand, frame; bridge (*of violin*)
chevalier [ʃəvalje] *m* knight; (orn) sandpiper; **chevalier d'industrie** manipulator, swindler; **chevalier errant** knight-errant; **Chevaliers du taste-vin** wine-tasting club
chevalière [ʃəvaljɛr] *f* signet ring
cheva·lin [ʃəvalɛ̃] **-line** [lin] *adj* equine
cheval-vapeur [ʃəvalvapœr] *m* (*pl* **chevaux-vapeur**) metric or French horsepower (*735 watts*)
chevauchée [ʃəvoʃe] *f* ride
chevaucher [ʃəvoʃe] *tr* to straddle || *intr* to ride horseback; to overlap
cheve·lu -lue [ʃəvly] *adj* hairy; long-haired
chevelure [ʃəvlyr] *f* hair, head of hair; tail (*of a comet*)
chevet [ʃəvɛ] *m* headboard; bolster; **de chevet** bedside (*lamp, table, book*)
che·veu [ʃəvø] *m* (*pl* **-veux**) hair; **avoir mal aux cheveux** (coll) to have a hangover; **cheveux** hair (*of the head*); hairs; **cheveux en brosse** crew cut; **couper les cheveux en quatre** (coll)

to split hairs; **en cheveux** hatless; **faire dresser les cheveux** (coll) to make one's hair stand on end; **ne tenir qu'à un cheveu** (coll) to hang by a thread; **saisir l'occasion aux cheveux** (coll) to take time by the forelock; **se faire des cheveux** (coll) to worry oneself gray; **tiré par les cheveux** (coll) far-fetched

chevillard [ʃəvijar] m wholesale cattle dealer or jobber

cheville [ʃəvij] f peg; pin; bolt; padding (*of verse*); ankle; **cheville ouvrière** (mach) kingbolt; (fig) mainspring (*of an enterprise*); **être en cheville avec** (coll) to be in cahoots with; **ne pas arriver à la cheville de qn** (coll) not to hold a candle to s.o.

chèvre [ʃevr] f goat; nanny goat

che·vreau [ʃəvro] m (pl **-vreaux**) kid

chèvrefeuille [ʃevrəfœj] m honeysuckle

chevrette [ʃəvrɛt] f kid; doe (*roe deer*); shrimp; tripod

chevreuil [ʃəvrœj] m roe deer; roebuck

chevron [ʃəvrɔ̃] m rafter; chevron, hash mark; **en chevron** in a herringbone pattern

chevron·né -née [ʃəvrɔne] adj wearing chevrons; experienced, oldest

chevronner [ʃəvrɔne] tr to put rafters on; to give chevrons to

chevroter [ʃəvrɔte] intr to bleat; to sing or speak in a quavering voice

chewing-gum [ʃwiŋgɔm], [tʃuwiŋgɔm] m chewing gum

chez [ʃe] prep at the house, home, office, etc., of, e.g., **chez mes amis** at my friends' house; e.g., **chez le boulanger** at the baker's; in the country of, among, e.g., **chez les Français** among the French; in the time of, e.g., **chez les anciens Grecs** in the time of the ancient Greeks; in the work of, e.g., **chez Homère** in Homer's works; with, e.g., **c'est chez lui une habitude** it's a habit with him

chez-soi [ʃeswa] m invar home

chialer [ʃjale] intr (slang) to cry

chiasse [ʃjas] f flyspecks; (metallurgy) dross; (coll) loose bowels

chic [ʃik] adj invar stylish, chic; **un chic type** (coll) a good egg ‖ m style; skill, knack; (coll) smartness, elegance; (slang) ovation; **de chic** from memory ‖ interj (coll) fine!, grand!

chicane [ʃikan] f chicanery; shady lawsuit; baffle, baffle plate; **chercher chicane à** to engage in a petty quarrel with; **en chicane** staggered, zigzag; curved (*tube*)

chicaner [ʃikane] tr to pick a fight with; **chicaner q.ch. à qn** to quibble over s.th. with s.o. ‖ intr to quibble

chicanerie [ʃikanri] f chicanery

chiche [ʃiʃ] adj stingy; small, dwarf ‖ interj (coll) I dare you!

chicon [ʃikɔ̃] m (coll) romaine

chicorée [ʃikɔre] f chicory; **chicorée frisée** endive

chicot [ʃiko] m stump (*of tree*); (coll) stump, stub (*of tooth*)

chien [ʃjɛ̃] **chienne** [ʃjɛn] mf dog ‖ m hammer (*of gun*); glamour; **à la chien** (coll) with bangs; **chien couchant** setter; (slang) apple polisher; **chien d'arrêt** pointer; **chien d'aveugle** Seeing Eye dog; **chien de** or **chienne de** (coll) dickens of a; **chien de garde** watchdog; **chien du jardinier** (coll) dog in the manger; **chien savant** performing dog; **de chien** (coll) miserable (*weather, life, etc.*); **en chien de fusil** (coll) curled up (*e.g., to sleep*); **entre chien et loup** (coll) at dusk; **les chiens écrasés** (slang) the accident page (*of newspaper*); **petit chien** pup; **se regarder en chiens de faïence** (coll) to glare at one another ‖ f see **chienne**

chiendent [ʃjɛ̃dɑ̃] m couch grass; (coll) trouble

chienlit [ʃjɑ̃li] mf (vulgar) person who soils his bed ‖ m carnival mask; masquerade, fantastic costume

chien-loup [ʃjɛ̃lu] m (pl **chiens-loups**) wolfhound

chienne [ʃjɛn] f bitch

chienner [ʃjɛne] intr to whelp

chiennerie [ʃjɛnri] f stinginess, meanness

chiffe [ʃif] f rag; (coll) weakling

chiffon [ʃifɔ̃] m rag; scrap of paper; **chiffons** (coll) fashions

chiffonnade [ʃifɔnad] f salad greens

chiffonner [ʃifɔne] tr to rumple, crumple; to make (*a dress*); (coll) to ruffle (*tempers*), to bother ‖ intr to make dresses

chiffon·nier [ʃifɔnje] **chiffon·nière** [ʃifɔnjɛr] mf scavenger, ragpicker ‖ m chiffonier

chiffre [ʃifr] m figure, number; cipher, code; sum total; combination (*of lock*); monogram; **chiffre d'affaires** turnover; **chiffres romains** roman numerals

chiffrer [ʃifre] tr to number; to monogram; to figure the cost of; to cipher, code ‖ intr to calculate; to mount up; to cipher, code ‖ ref—**se chiffrer par** to amount to

chignole [ʃiɲɔl] f breast drill, hand drill; (coll) jalopy

chignon [ʃiɲɔ̃] m chignon, bun, knot

Chili [ʃili] m—**le Chili** Chile

chimère [ʃimɛr] f chimera; **se forger des chimères** to indulge in wishful thinking

chimie [ʃimi] f chemistry

chimique [ʃimik] adj chemical

chimiste [ʃimist] mf chemist

chimpanzé [ʃɛ̃pɑ̃ze] m chimpanzee

Chine [ʃin] f China; **la Chine** China

chi·né -née [ʃine] adj mottled, figured

chiner [ʃine] tr to mottle (*cloth*); (coll) to make fun of

chi·nois [ʃinwa] **-noise** [nwaz] adj Chinese ‖ m Chinese (*language*) ‖ (*cap*) mf Chinese (*person*)

chinoiserie [ʃinwazri] f Chinese curio; **chinoiseries administratives** (coll) red tape

chiot [ʃjo] m puppy

chiourme [ʃjurm] f chain gang

chiper [ʃipe] tr (slang) to swipe

chipie [ʃipi] f (coll) shrew

chipoter [ʃipɔte] *intr* to haggle
chips [ʃips] *mpl* potato chips
chique [ʃik] *f* chew, quid (*of tobacco*); (ent) chigger
chiqué [ʃike] *m* (slang) sham, bluff
chiquenaude [ʃiknod] *f* fillip, flick
chiquer [ʃike] *tr* to chew (*tobacco*) ‖ *intr* to chew tobacco
chiromancie [kirɔmɑ̃si] *f* palmistry
chiroman·cien [kirɔmɑ̃sjɛ̃] **-cienne** [sjɛn] *mf* palm reader
chiropracteur [kirɔpraktœr] *m* chiropractor
chirurgi·cal -cale [ʃiryrʒikal] *adj* (*pl* **-caux** [ko]) surgical
chirurgie [ʃiryrʒi] *f* surgery
chirur·gien [ʃiryrʒjɛ̃] **-gienne** [ʒjɛn] *mf* surgeon
chirurgien-dentiste [ʃiryrʒjɛ̃dɑ̃tist] *m* (*pl* **chirurgiens-dentistes**) dental surgeon
chiure [ʃjyr] *f* flyspeck
chlore [klɔr] *m* chlorine
chlo·ré -rée [klɔre] *adj* chlorinated
chlorhydrique [klɔridrik] *adj* hydrochloric
chloroforme [klɔrɔfɔrm] *m* chloroform
chloroformer [klɔrɔfɔrme] *tr* to chloroform
chlorophylle [klɔrɔfil] *f* chlorophyll
chlorure [klɔryr] *m* chloride; **chlorure de soude** sodium chloride
choc [ʃɔk] *m* shock; clash; bump; clink (*of glasses*)
chocolat [ʃɔkɔla] *adj invar* & *m* chocolate
chocolaterie [ʃɔkɔlatri] *f* chocolate factory
chœur [kœr] *m* choir, chorus
choir [ʃwar] (usually used only in *inf* and *pp* **chu**; sometimes used in *pres ind* **chois**, etc.; *pret* **chus**, etc.; *fut* **choirai**, etc.) *intr* (*aux:* ÊTRE or AVOIR) to fall; **se laisser choir** to drop, to flop
choi·si -sie [ʃwazi] *adj* choice, select; chosen; selected (*works*)
choisir [ʃwazir] *tr* & *intr* to choose
choix [ʃwa] *m* choice; **au choix** at one's discretion; **de choix** choice
choléra [kɔlera] *m* cholera
cholérique [kɔlerik] *mf* cholera victim
cholestérol [kɔlesterɔl] *m* cholesterol
chômage [ʃomaʒ] *m* unemployment; **en chômage** unemployed
chô·mé -mée [ʃome] *adj* closed for business, off, e.g., **jour chômé** day off
chômer [ʃome] *tr* to take (*a day*) off; to observe (*a holiday*) ‖ *intr* to take off (*from work*); to be unemployed
chô·meur [ʃomœr] **-meuse** [møz] *mf* unemployed worker
chope [ʃɔp] *f* stein, beer mug
chopine [ʃɔpin] *f* half-liter measure; (slang) bottle
chopper [ʃɔpe] *intr* to stumble; to blunder
choquer [ʃɔke] *tr* to shock; to bump; to clink (*glasses*); (elec) to shock ‖ *ref* to collide; to take offense
cho·ral -rale [kɔral] *adj* (*pl* **-raux** [ro]) choral ‖ *m* (*pl* **-rals**) chorale ‖ *f* choral society, glee club

chorégraphie [kɔregrafi] *f* choreography
choriste [kɔrist] *mf* chorister
chorus [kɔrys] *m*—**faire chorus** to repeat in unison; to chime in; to approve unanimously
chose [ʃoz] *adj invar* (coll) odd; **être tout chose** (coll) to feel funny ‖ *m* thingamajig; **Monsieur Chose** (coll) Mr. what's-his-name ‖ *f* thing ‖ *pron indef masc*—**autre chose** something else; **quelque chose** something
chou [ʃu] **choute** [ʃut] *mf*—**ma choute, mon chou** (coll) sweetheart ‖ *m* (*pl* **choux**) cabbage; **chou à la crème** cream puff; **chou de Bruxelles** Brussels sprouts; **de chou** (coll) of little value; **faire chou blanc** (coll) to draw a blank; **finir dans le chou** (coll) to come in last
choucas [ʃuka] *m* jackdaw
choucroute [ʃukrut] *f* sauerkraut; **choucroute garnie** sauerkraut with ham or sausage
chouette [ʃwet] *adj* (coll) swell; **chouette alors!** (coll) oh boy! ‖ *f* owl; (coll) radio; **chouette épervière** hawk owl
chou-fleur [ʃuflœr] *m* (*pl* **choux-fleurs**) cauliflower
chou-rave [ʃurav] *m* (*pl* **choux-raves**) kohlrabi
chow-chow [ʃuʃu] *m* (*pl* **-chows**) chow (*dog*)
choyer [ʃwaje] §47 *tr* to pamper, coddle; to cherish (*a hope*); to entertain (*an idea*)
chrestomatie [krestɔmati], [krestɔmasi] *f* chrestomathy
chré·tien [kretjɛ̃] **-tienne** [tjɛn] *adj* & *mf* Christian
chrétiennement [kretjɛnmɑ̃] *adv* in the faith
chrétienté [kretjɛ̃te] *f* Christendom
christ [krist] *m* crucifix ‖ (*cap*) *m* Christ; **le Christ** Christ
christianiser [kristjanize] *tr* to Christianize
christianisme [kristjanism] *m* Christianity
chromatique [krɔmatik] *adj* chromatic
chrome [krom] *m* chrome, chromium
chromer [krome] *tr* to chrome
chromosome [krɔmozom] *m* chromosome
chronique [krɔnik] *adj* chronic ‖ *f* chronicle; column (*in newspaper*); **chronique financière** financial page; **chronique mondaine** society news; **chronique théâtrale** theater page
chroniqueur [krɔnikœr] *m* chronicler; columnist; **chroniqueur dramatique** drama critic
chrono [krono] *m*—**faire du 60 chrono** (coll) to do 60 by the clock
chronologie [krɔnɔlɔʒi] *f* chronology
chronologique [krɔnɔlɔʒik] *adj* chronological
chronomètre [krɔnɔmɛtr] *m* chronometer; stopwatch
chronométrer [krɔnɔmetre] §10 *tr* to clock, to time

chronométreur [krɔnɔmetrœr] *m* time-keeper
chrysalide [krizalid] *f* chrysalis
chrysanthème [krizãtɛm] *m* chrysanthemum
chuchotement [ʃyʃɔtmã] *m* whisper, whispering
chuchoter [ʃyʃɔte] *tr & intr* to whisper
chuinter [ʃɥɛ̃te] *intr* to hoot (*said of owl*); to make a swishing sound, to hiss (*said of escaping gas*); to pronounce [ʃ] instead of [s] and [ʒ] instead of [z]
chut [ʃyt] *interj* sh!
chute [ʃyt] *f* fall; downfall; drop (*in prices, voltage, etc.*); **chute d'eau** waterfall
chuter [ʃyte] *tr* to hush; to hiss (*an actor*) ‖ *intr* (coll) to fall; (cards) to be down
Chypre [ʃipr] *f* Cyprus
ci [si] *pron indef*—**comme ci comme ça** so-so ‖ *adv*—**entre ci et là** between now and then
-ci [si] §82, §84
ci-après [siaprɛ] *adv* hereafter, below, further on
ci-bas [siba] *adv* below
cible [sibl] *f* target
ciboule [sibul] *f* scallion
ciboulette [sibulɛt] *f* chive, chives
cicatrice [sikatris] *f* scar
cicatriser [sikatrize] *tr* to heal; to scar ‖ *ref* to heal
Cicéron [siserɔ̃] *m* Cicero
cicérone [siserɔn] *m* guide
ci-contre [sikɔ̃tr] *adv* opposite, on the opposite page; in the margin
ci-dessous [sidəsu] *adv* further on, below, hereunder
ci-dessus [sidəsy] *adv* above
ci-devant [sidəvã] *mf invar* (hist) aristocrat; (coll) back number ‖ *adv* previously, formerly
cidre [sidr] *m* cider
Cie *abbr* (**Compagnie**) Co.
ciel [sjɛl] *m* (*pl* **cieux** [sjø]) sky, heavens (*firmament*); heaven (*state of great happiness*) ‖ *m* (*pl* **ciels**) heaven (*abode of the blessed*); sky (*upper atmosphere, especially with reference to meteorological conditions; representation of sky in a painting*); canopy (*of a bed*) ‖ *m* (*pl* **cieux** or **ciels**) clime, sky
cierge [sjɛrʒ] *m* wax candle; cactus; **droit comme un cierge** straight as a ramrod; **en cierge** straight up
cigale [sigal] *f* cicada, grasshopper
cigare [sigar] *m* cigar
cigarette [sigarɛt] *f* cigarette
ci-gît [siʒi] see **gésir**
cigogne [sigɔɲ] *f* stork
ciguë [sigy] *f* hemlock (*herb and poison*)
ci-in·clus [siɛ̃kly] **-cluse** [klyz] *adj* enclosed ‖ **ci-inclus** *adv* enclosed
ci-joint [siʒwɛ̃] **-jointe** [jwɛ̃t] *adj* enclosed ‖ **ci-joint** *adv* enclosed
cil [sil] *m* eyelash; **cils** eyelash (*fringe of hair*)
cilice [silis] *m* hair shirt
ciller [sije] *tr & intr* to blink

cime [sim] *f* summit, top
ciment [simã] *m* cement; **ciment armé** reinforced concrete
cimentation [simãtasjɔ̃] *f* cementing
cimenter [simãte] *tr* to cement
cimeterre [simter] *m* scimitar
cimetière [simtjer] *m* cemetery
cinéaste [sineast] *mf* film producer; movie director; scenarist; movie technician
cinégraphiste [sinegrafist] *mf* scenarist
cinéma [sinema] *m* movies; moving-picture theater; cinema; **cinéma auto** drive-in movie; **cinéma d'essai** preview theater; **cinéma muet** silent movie
cinémathèque [sinematɛk] *f* film library
cinématographique [sinematɔgrafik] *adj* motion-picture, film
cinéphile [sinefil] *mf* movie fan
cinéprojecteur [sineprɔʒɛktœr] *m* motion-picture projector
ciné-roman [sinerɔmã] *m* (*pl* **-romans**) published story (*of a film*)
cinétique [sinetik] *adj* kinetic ‖ *f* kinetics
cin·glant [sɛ̃glã] **-glante** [glãt] *adj* scathing
cin·glé -glée [sɛ̃gle] *adj* (slang) screwy ‖ *mf* (slang) screwball
cingler [sɛ̃gle] *tr* to whip; to cut to the quick ‖ *intr* to go full sail
cinq [sɛ̃(k)] *adj & pron* five; the Fifth, e.g., **Jean cinq** John the Fifth; **cinq heures** five o'clock ‖ *m* five; fifth (*in dates*); **il était moins cinq** (coll) it was a close shave
cinquantaine [sɛ̃kãtɛn] *f* about fifty; age of fifty, fifty mark, fifties
cinquante [sɛ̃kãt] *adj, pron, & m* fifty; **cinquante et un** fifty-one; **cinquante et unième** fifty-first
cinquantième [sɛ̃kãtjɛm] *adj, pron* (*masc, fem*), & *m* fiftieth
cinquième [sɛ̃kjɛm] *adj, pron* (*masc, fem*), & *m* fifth
cintre [sɛ̃tr] *m* arch; coat hanger; bend; **plein cintre** semicircular arch
cin·tré -trée [sɛ̃tre] *adj* (slang) crazy
cintrer [sɛ̃tre] *tr* to arch, to bend
cirage [siraʒ] *m* waxing; shoe polish; **dans le cirage** (coll) in the dark
circoncire [sirkɔ̃sir] §66 (*pp* **circoncis**) *tr* to circumcise
circoncision [sirkɔ̃sizjɔ̃] *f* circumcision
circonférence [sirkɔ̃ferãs] *f* circumference
circonflexe [sirkɔ̃flɛks] *adj & m* circumflex
circonscription [sirkɔ̃skripsjɔ̃] *f* circumscription; ward, district
circonscrire [sirkɔ̃skrir] §25 *tr* to circumscribe
circons·pect [sirkɔ̃spɛ], [sirkɔ̃spɛk(t)] **-pecte** [pɛkt] *adj* circumspect
circonstance [sirkɔ̃stãs] *f* circumstance; **circonstances et dépendances** appurtenances; **de circonstance** proper for the occasion, topical; emergency (*measure*); guest, e.g., **orateur de circonstance** guest speaker

circonstan•cié -ciée [sirkɔ̃stɑ̃sje] adj circumstantial, in detail
circonstan•ciel -cielle [sirkɔ̃stɑ̃sjɛl] adj (gram) adverbial
circonvenir [sirkɔ̃vnir] §72 tr to circumvent
circonvoi•sin [sirkɔ̃vwazɛ̃] -sine [zin] adj nearby, neighboring
circuit [sirkɥi] m circuit; circumference; detour; tour
circulaire [sirkylɛr] adj & f circular
circulation [sirkylɑsjɔ̃] f circulation; traffic; circulation interdite (public sign) no thoroughfare
circuler [sirkyle] intr to circulate
cire [sir] f wax; cire à cacheter sealing wax; cire molle (fig) wax in one's hands
ci•ré -rée [sire] adj waxed ‖ m waterproof garment; raincoat
cirer [sire] tr to wax; to polish
ci•reur [sirœr] -reuse [røz] mf waxer, polisher (person); shoeblack, bootblack ‖ f floor waxer (machine)
ci•reux [sirø] -reuse [røz] adj waxy
ciron [sirɔ̃] m mite
cirque [sirk] m circus; amphitheater
cirrhose [siroz] f cirrhosis
cisaille [sizaj] f metal clippings, scissel; cisailles clippers, shears; wire cutter
cisailler [sizaje] tr to shear
ci•seau [sizo] m (pl -seaux) chisel; ciseau à froid cold chisel; ciseaux scissors; ciseaux à ongles nail scissors; ciseaux à raisin pruning shears; ciseaux à tondre sheep shears
ciseler [sizle] §2 tr to chisel; to chase; to cut, shear; to prune
ciseleur [sizlœr] m chaser, tooler
citadelle [sitadɛl] f citadel
cita•din [sitadɛ̃] -dine [din] adj urban ‖ mf city dweller
citation [sitɑsjɔ̃] f citation, quotation; citation, summons
cité [site] f housing development; (hist) fortified city, citadel; cité ouvrière low-cost housing development; cité sainte Holy City; cité universitaire university dormitory complex; la Cité the City (district within ancient boundaries)
citer [site] tr to cite, quote; to summon, subpoena
citerne [sitɛrn] f cistern; tank; citerne flottante tanker
cithare [sitar] f cither, zither
citoyen [sitwajɛ̃] citoyenne [sitwajɛn] mf citizen; (coll) individual, person; citoyens citizenry
citoyenneté [sitwajɛnte] f citizenship; citizenry
citrique [sitrik] adj citric
citron [sitrɔ̃] adj & m lemon
citronnade [sitrɔnad] f lemonade
citron•né -née [sitrɔne] adj lemon-flavored
citronnelle [sitrɔnɛl] f citronella
citronner [sitrɔne] tr to flavor with lemon
citronnier [sitrɔnje] m lemon tree
citrouille [sitruj] f pumpkin, gourd
cive [siv] f scallion
civet [sivɛ] m stew

civette [sivɛt] f civet; civet cat; chive, chives
civière [sivjɛr] f stretcher, litter
ci•vil -vile [sivil] adj civil; civilian; secular ‖ m civilian; layman; en civil plain-clothes (man); in civies
civilisation [sivilizɑsjɔ̃] f civilization
civiliser [sivilize] tr to civilize ‖ ref to become civilized
civilité [sivilite] f civility; civilités kind regards; amenities
civique [sivik] adj civic; civil (rights); national (guard)
civisme [sivism] m good citizenship
clabauder [klabode] intr to clamor
claie [klɛ] f wickerwork; trellis
clair claire [klɛr] adj clear, bright; evident, plain; light, pale ‖ m light, brightness; clair de lune moonlight; clairs highlights ‖ f oyster bed
clai•ret [klɛrɛ] -rette [rɛt] adj light-red; thin, high-pitched (voice) ‖ m light, red wine ‖ f light sparkling wine
claire-voie [klɛrvwa] f (pl claires-voies) latticework, slats; clerestory; à claire-voie with open spaces
clairière [klɛrjɛr] f clearing, glade
clairon [klɛrɔ̃] m bugle; bugler
claironner [klɛrɔne] tr to announce ‖ intr to sound the bugle
clairse•mé -mée [klɛrsəme] adj scattered, sparse; thin, thinned out
clairvoyance [klɛrvwajɑ̃s] f clair-sightedness, clairvoyance
clairvoyant [klɛrvwajɑ̃] clairvoyante [klɛrvwajɑ̃t] adj clear-sighted, clairvoyant
clamer [klame] tr & intr to cry out
clameur [klamœr] f clamor, outcry
clamp [klɑ̃] m (med) clamp
clampin [klɑ̃pɛ̃] m (mil) straggler
clan [klɑ̃] m clan, clique
clandes•tin [klɑ̃dɛstɛ̃] -tine [tin] adj clandestine
clapet [klapɛ] m valve; ferme ton clapet! (slang) shut your trap!
clapier [klapje] m rabbit hutch
clapoter [klapɔte] intr to splash; to be choppy
claque [klak] m opera hat ‖ f slap, smack; claque, paid applauders
cla•qué -quée [klake] adj dog-tired; sprained
claquement [klakmɑ̃] m clapping; slam (of a door); chattering (of teeth)
claquemurer [klakmyre] tr to shut in ‖ ref to shut oneself up at home
claquer [klake] tr to slap; to clap; to smack (the lips); to slam (the door); to crack (the whip); to click (the heels); to snap (the fingers); (coll) to tire out; (coll) to waste ‖ intr to clap, slap, slam; to crack; (slang) to fail; (slang) to die ‖ ref (with dat of reflex pron) to sprain; (slang) to work oneself to death
claquettes [klakɛt] fpl tap-dancing
claqueur [klakœr] m applauder, member of a claque
clarifier [klarifje] tr to clarify ‖ ref to become clear
clarine [klarin] f cowbell

clarinette [klarinɛt] *f* clarinet
clarté [klarte] *f* clarity; brightness; **clarté du soleil** sunshine
classe [klɑs] *f* class; classroom; **classe de rattrapage** refresher course (*for backward children*); **classe de travaux pratiques** lab class
clas·sé -sée [klɑse] *adj* pigeonholed, tabled; standard (*literary work*); listed; **non classé** (sports) also-ran
classer [klɑse] *tr* to class; to sort out, to file; to pigeonhole, to table
classeur [klɑsœr] *m* file (*for letters, documents*); filing cabinet
classicisme [klasisism] *m* classicism
classification [klasifikɑsjɔ̃] *f* classification
classifier [klasifje] *tr* to classify; to sort out
classique [klasik] *adj* classic, classical; standard (*author, work*) ‖ *mf* classicist ‖ *m* classic; standard work
claudication [klodikɑsjɔ̃] *f* limping
clause [kloz] *f* clause, stipulation, provision; **clause additionnelle** rider; **clause ambiguë** joker clause; **clause de style** unwritten provision
claustration [klostrɑsjɔ̃] *f* confinement; cloistering
clavecin [klavsɛ̃] *m* harpsichord
claveciniste [klavsinist] *mf* harpsichordist
clavette [klavɛt] *f* pin, cotter pin; key
clavicule [klavikyl] *f* collarbone
clavier [klavje] *m* keyboard; key ring; range (*e.g., of the voice*); **clavier universel** standard keyboard
clayère [klɛjɛr] *f* oyster bed
clé [kle] *f* see **clef**
clef [kle] *adj invar* key ‖ *f* key; wrench; (wrestling) lock; **clef anglaise** monkey wrench; **clef à tube** socket wrench; **clef crocodile** alligator wrench; **clef des champs** vacation; **clef de voûte** keystone; **sous clef** under lock and key
clémence [klemɑ̃s] *f* clemency
clé·ment -mente [klemɑ̃] *adj* mild, clement
clenche [klɑ̃ʃ] *f* latch
cleptomane [kleptɔman] *mf* kleptomaniac
clerc [klɛr] *m* cleric, clergyman; scholar; clerk
clergé [klɛrʒe] *m* clergy
clergie [klɛrʒi] *f* learning, scholarship; clergy
cléri·cal -cale [klerikal] *adj & mf* (*pl* **-caux** [ko]) clerical
cliché [kliʃe] *m* cliché; (phot) negative; (typ) plate, stereotype; **prendre un cliché** (phot) to make an exposure
clicher [kliʃe] *tr* (typ) to stereotype
client [klijɑ̃] **cliente** [kljɑ̃t] *mf* client; patient; customer; guest (*of a hotel*)
clientèle [klijɑ̃tɛl] *f* clientele; adherents
cligner [kliɲe] *tr* to squint (*one's eyes*) ‖ *intr* to squint, to blink; **cligner de l'œil à** to wink at
cligno·tant [kliɲɔtɑ̃] **-tante** [tɑ̃t] *adj* blinking ‖ *m* (aut) directional signal
clignotement [kliɲɔtmɑ̃] *m* blinking; twinkling; flickering

clignoter [kliɲɔte] *intr* to blink; to twinkle; to flicker
clignoteur [kliɲɔtœr] *m* (aut) directional signal
climat [klima], [klima] *m* climate
climatisation [klimatizɑsjɔ̃] *f* air conditioning
climati·sé -sée [klimatize] *adj* air-conditioned
climatiseur [klimatizœr] *m* air conditioner
clin [klɛ̃] *m*—à **clin** (carpentry) overlapping, covering; **clin d'œil** wink; **en un clin d'œil** in the twinkling of an eye
clinicien [klinisjɛ̃] *adj masc* clinical ‖ *m* clinician
clinique [klinik] *adj* clinical ‖ *f* clinic; private hospital
clinquant [klɛ̃kɑ̃] *m* foil, tinsel; flashiness, tawdriness
clip [klip] *m* clip, brooch
clique [klik] *f* drum and bugle corps; (coll) gang; **cliques** wooden shoes
cliquet [klikɛ] *m* (mach) pawl, catch
cliqueter [klikte] §34 *intr* to click, to clink, to clank, to jangle
cliquetis [klikti] *m* click, clink, clank, jangle
cliquette [klikɛt] *f* castanets; (fishing) sinker
clisse [klis] *f* draining rack, wicker bottleholder
clivage [klivaʒ] *m* cleavage
cliver [klive] *tr* to cleave; to cut
cloaque [klɔak] *m* cesspool
clo·chard [klɔʃar] **-charde** [ʃard] *mf* beggar, tramp
cloche [klɔʃ] *adj* bell (*skirt*) ‖ *f* bell; bell glass; blister (*on skin*); **cloche à plongeurs** diving bell; **cloche de sauvetage** escape hatch (*on submarine*); **déménager à la cloche de bois** (coll) to skip out without paying; **la cloche** (slang) beggars
clochement [klɔʃmɑ̃] *m* limp, limping
cloche-pied [klɔʃpje]—à **cloche-pied** on one foot, hopping
clocher [klɔʃe] *m* steeple; belfry; parish, home town; **de clocher** local (*politics*) ‖ *intr* to limp; **quelque chose cloche** something jars, is not right
clocheton [klɔʃtɔ̃] *m* little steeple
clochette [klɔʃɛt] *f* little bell; (bot) bellflower
cloison [klwazɔ̃] *f* partition; division, barrier (*e.g., between classes*); (anat, bot) septum, dividing membrane; (naut) bulkhead; **cloison étanche** (naut) watertight compartment
cloisonner [klwazɔne] *tr* to partition
cloître [klwatr] *m* cloister
cloîtrer [klwatre] *tr* to cloister; to confine
clopin-clopant [klɔpɛ̃klɔpɑ̃] *adv* (coll) so-so; **aller clopin-clopant** (coll) to go hobbling along
clopiner [klɔpine] *intr* to hobble
cloque [klɔk] *f* blister
cloquer [klɔke] *tr & intr* to blister
clore [klɔr] §24 *tr & intr* to close

clos [klo] **close** [kloz] *adj* closed ‖ *m* enclosure; **clos de vigne** vineyard

clôture [klotyr] *f* fence; wall; cloistered life; closing of an account

clôturer [klotyre] *tr* to enclose, to wall in; to close out (*an account*); to conclude (*a discussion*)

clou [klu] *m* nail; (coll) boil; (coll) jalopy; (coll) feature attraction; (slang) pawnshop; **clou de girofle** clove; **clous** pedestrian crossing; **des clous!** (slang) nothing at all!

clouer [klue] *tr* to nail; to immobilize, rivet; **clouer le bec à qn** (coll) to shut s.o.'s mouth

clouter [klute] *tr* to stud; to trim or border with studs, e.g., **passage clouté** pedestrian crossing (bordered with studs)

clown [klun] *m* clown; **faire le clown** to clown (around)

clownerie [klunri] *f* high jinks, clowning

club [klyb] *m* (literary) society; (political) association ‖ [klœb] *m* club (*for social and athletic purposes, etc.*); clubhouse; (golf) club; armchair

clubiste [klybist] *mf* (coll) club member; (coll) joiner

clubman [klœbman] *m* club member

coaccu·sé -sée [kɔakyze] *mf* codefendant

coaguler [koagyle] *tr* & *ref* to coagulate

coaliser [koalize] *tr* to form into a coalition ‖ *ref* to form a coalition

coalition [koalisjɔ̃] *f* coalition

coassement [kɔasmɑ̃] *m* croak, croaking

coasser [kɔase] *intr* to croak

coasso·cié -ciée [kɔasɔsje] *mf* copartner

coauteur [kɔotœr] *m* coauthor

cobalt [kɔbalt] *m* cobalt

cobaye [kɔbaj] *m* guinea pig

cocaïne [kɔkain] *f* cocaine

cocarde [kɔkard] *f* cockade; rosette of ribbons; **avoir sa cocarde** (coll) to be tipsy; **prendre la cocarde** (coll) to enlist

cocasse [kɔkas] *adj* (coll) funny, ridiculous

coccinelle [kɔksinɛl] *f* ladybug

coche [kɔʃ] *m* coach, stagecoach; two-door sedan; barge ‖ *f* notch, score; (zool) sow

cocher [kɔʃe] *m* coachman, driver ‖ *tr* to notch, to score; to check off

cochère [kɔʃɛr] *adj* carriage (*entrance*)

co·chon [kɔʃɔ̃] **-chonne** [ʃɔn] *mf* (coll) skunk, slob ‖ *m* pig, hog; **cochon de lait** suckling pig; **cochon de mer** porpoise; **cochon d'Inde** guinea pig

cochonnerie [kɔʃɔnri] *f* (slang) dirty trick; (slang) filthy speech, smut

cocker [kɔkɛr] *m* cocker spaniel

cockpit [kɔkpit] *m* (aer) cockpit

cocktail [kɔktɛl] *m* cocktail; cocktail party

coco [kɔko], [koko] *m* coconut; licorice water; **mon coco** (coll) my darling; **un joli coco** (coll) a stinker ‖ *f* (slang) cocaine

cocon [kɔkɔ̃] *m* cocoon

cocorico [kɔkɔriko] *m* cockcrow ‖ *interj* cock-a-doodle-doo!

cocotier [kɔkɔtje] *m* coconut tree

cocotte [kɔkɔt] *f* saucepan; cocotte, floozy; **ma cocotte** (coll) my little chick, my baby doll

co·cu -cue [kɔky] *adj* & *m* cuckold

cocufier [kɔkyfje] *tr* (slang) to cuckold

code [kɔd] *m* code; **code de la route** traffic regulations; **code pénal** criminal code; **codes** (slang) dimmers; **se mettre en code** to dip one's headlights

codex [kɔdɛks] *m* pharmacopoeia

codicille [kɔdisil] *m* codicil

codifier [kɔdifje] *tr* to codify

coéducation [kɔedykɑsjɔ̃] *f* coeducation

coefficient [koefisjɑ̃] *m* coefficient

coéqui·pier [kɔekipje] **-pière** [pjɛr] *mf* teammate

coercition [kɔɛrsisjɔ̃] *f* coercion

cœur [kœr] *m* heart; core; courage; spirit; bosom, breast; depth (*of winter*); (cards) heart; (cards) hearts; **à cœur joie** to one's heart's content; **avoir du cœur** to be kind-hearted; **avoir du cœur au ventre** (coll) to have guts; **avoir le cœur sur la main** (coll) to be open-handed; **avoir le cœur sur les lèvres** to wear one's heart on one's sleeve; **cœur de bronze** heart of stone; **de bon cœur** willingly, heartily; **de mauvais cœur** reluctantly; **en avoir le cœur net** to get to the bottom of it; **épancher son cœur à** to open one's heart to; **fendre le cœur à** to break the heart of; **le cœur gros** with a heavy heart; **mal au cœur** or **mal de cœur** stomach ache; nausea; **par cœur** by heart; **prendre à cœur** to take to heart; **se ronger le cœur** to eat one's heart out; **soulever le cœur** to turn the stomach

coexistence [koegzistɑ̃s] *f* coexistence

coexister [koegziste] *intr* to coexist

coffre [kɔfr] *m* chest; coffer, bin; safe-deposit box; trunk (*of car*); buoy (*for mooring*); cofferdam

coffre-fort [kɔfrəfɔr] *m* (pl **coffres-forts**) safe, strongbox, vault

coffret [kɔfrɛ] *m* gift box

cognac [kɔɲak] *m* cognac

cognat [kɔɲa] *m* blood kin

cognée [kɔɲe] *f* ax, hatchet

cogner [kɔɲe] *tr, intr,* & *ref* to knock, bump

cohabiter [kɔabite] *intr* to cohabit

cohé·rent [kɔerɑ̃] **-rente** [rɑ̃t] *adj* coherent

cohériter [kɔerite] *intr* to inherit jointly

cohéri·tier [kɔeritje] **-tière** [tjɛr] *mf* coheir

cohésion [kɔesjɔ̃] *f* cohesion

cohorte [kɔɔrt] *f* cohort

cohue [kɔy] *f* crowd, throng, mob

coi [kwa] **coite** [kwat] *adj* quiet; **demeurer** or **se tenir coi** to keep still

coiffe [kwaf] *f* cap; headdress; caul

coif·fé -fée [kwafe] *adj*—**coiffé de** wearing (*a hat*); (fig) crazy about (*a person*); **être coiffé** to be wearing a

hairdo; **être né coiffé** (fig) to be lucky
coiffer [kwafe] *tr* to put a hat or cap on (*s.o.*); to dress or do the hair of; (mil) to reach (*an objective*) ‖ *intr*— **coiffer de** to wear (*a certain size hat*) ‖ *ref* to do one's hair; **se coiffer de** (coll) to set one's cap for
coif·feur [kwafœr] **coif·feuse** [kwaføz] *mf* hairdresser; barber; **coiffeur pour dames** coiffeur ‖ *f* dresser, dressing table
coiffure [kwafyr] *f* coiffure; headdress; **coiffure en brosse** crew cut
coin [kwɛ̃] *m* corner; angle; nook; wedge, coin; stamp, die (*for coining money*); (typ) quoin; **le petit coin** (coll) the powder room
coinçage [kwɛ̃saʒ] *m* wedging
coincer [kwɛ̃se] §51 *tr* to wedge, jam; (coll) to pinch, arrest ‖ *ref* to jam
coïncidence [kɔɛ̃sidɑ̃s] *f* coincidence
coïncider [kɔɛ̃side] *intr* to coincide
coin-coin [kwɛ̃kwɛ̃] *m invar* quack (*of duck*); toot (*of horn*)
coing [kwɛ̃] *m* quince
coït [kɔit] *m* coition
coke [kɔk] *m* coke
cokéfier [kɔkefje] *tr & ref* to coke
col [kɔl] *m* neck (*of bottle; of womb*); collar (*of dress*); mountain pass; (coll) head (*on beer*); **col de fourrure** neckpiece; **col roulé** turtleneck; **faux col** detachable collar
colback [kɔlbak] *m* busby
colère [kɔlɛr] *f* anger; **en colère** angry; **se mettre en colère** to become angry
colé·reux [kɔlerø] **-reuse** [røz] *adj* irascible, choleric
colérique [kɔlerik] *adj* choleric
colibri [kɔlibri] *m* hummingbird
colimaçon [kɔlimasɔ̃] *m* snail; **en colimaçon** spiral
colin [kɔlɛ̃] *m* hake·
colin-maillard [kɔlɛ̃majar] *m* blindman's buff
colique [kɔlik] *f* colic
colis [kɔli] *m* piece of baggage, package, parcel; **colis postal** parcel post
colisée [kɔlize] *m* coliseum
collabora·teur [kɔlabɔratœr] **-trice** [tris] *mf* collaborator; contributor
collaborationniste [kɔlabɔrasjɔnist] *mf* collaborationist
collaborer [kɔlabɔre] *intr* to collaborate; **collaborer à** to contribute to
collage [kɔlaʒ] *m* pasting, mounting; collage; sizing; clarifying (*of wine*); (coll) common-law marriage
col·lant [kɔlɑ̃] **col·lante** [kɔlɑ̃t] *adj* sticky; tight, close-fitting ‖ *m* tights
collapsus [kɔllapsys] *m* (pathol) collapse
collaté·ral -rale [kɔllateral] (*pl* **-raux** [ro]) *adj* collateral; parallel; intermediate (*points of the compass*) ‖ *mf* collateral (relative) ‖ *m* side aisle of a church
collation [kɔllasjɔ̃] *f* conferring (*of titles, degrees, etc.*); collation (*of texts*) ‖ [kɔlasjɔ̃] *f* snack
collationner [kɔllasjɔne] *tr* to collate,

to compare; **faire collationner un télégramme** to request a copy of a telegram ‖ *intr* to have a snack
colle [kɔl] *f* paste, glue; (coll) brainteaser, stickler; (slang) detention; (slang) oral exam; (slang) flunking; **colle forte** glue; **poser une colle** (slang) to ask a hard one
collecte [kɔlɛkt] *f* collection (*for charitable cause*); (eccl) collect
collecteur [kɔlɛktœr] *adj* main, e.g., **égout collecteur** main sewer ‖ *m* collector; commutator (*of motor or dynamo*); (aut) manifold; **collecteur d'ondes** aerial
collec·tif [kɔlɛktif] **-tive** [tiv] *adj* collective
collection [kɔlɛksjɔ̃] *f* collection
collectionner [kɔlɛksjɔne] *tr* to collect
collection·neur [kɔlɛksjɔnœr] **collection·neuse** [kɔlɛksjɔnøz] *mf* collector
collège [kɔlɛʒ] *m* high school; preparatory school; college (*of cardinals, electors, etc.*); **collège universitaire** junior college
collé·gial -giale [kɔleʒjal] (*pl* **-giaux** [ʒjo]) *adj* collegiate ‖ *f* collegiate church
collé·gien [kɔleʒjɛ̃] **-gienne** [ʒjɛn] *adj* high-school ‖ *m* schoolboy ‖ *f* schoolgirl; coed
collègue [kɔllɛg] *mf* colleague
coller [kɔle] *tr* to paste, stick, glue; to clarify (*wine*); to mat (*e.g., with blood*); (coll) to floor, to stump; (coll) to punish (*a pupil*); (coll) to flunk; (coll) to sock (*e.g., on the jaw*) ‖· *intr* to cling, to fit tightly (*said of dress*); (coll) to stick close; **ça colle!** (slang) O.K.! ‖ *ref* (slang) to have a common-law marriage; **se coller contre** to stand close to; to cling to
collet [kɔle] *m* collar; neck (*of person; of tooth*); neck, scrag (*e.g., of mutton*); cape; snare; stalk and roots; lasso, noose; **collet monté** (coll) stuffed shirt
colleter [kɔlte] §34 *tr* to collar ‖ *ref* to fight, scuffle
collier [kɔlje] *m* necklace; collar; dog collar; horse collar; **à collier** ringnecked; **reprendre le collier** (coll) to get back into harness
colliger [kɔlliʒe] §38 *tr* to make a collection of
colline [kɔlin] *f* hill
collision [kɔllizjɔ̃] *f* collision
colloï·dal -dale [kɔllɔidal] *adj* (*pl* **-daux** [do]) colloid, colloidal
colloïde [kɔllɔid] *m* colloid
colloque [kɔllɔk] *m* colloquy, symposium
colloquer [kɔllɔke] *tr* to classify (*creditors' claims*); **colloquer q.ch. à qn** (coll) to palm off s.th. on s.o.
collusion [kɔllyzjɔ̃] *f* collusion
collyre [kɔllir] *m* (med) eyewash
Cologne [kɔlɔɲ] *f* Cologne
Colomb [kɔlɔ̃] *m* Columbus
colombe [kɔlɔ̃b] *f* dove
Colombie [kɔlɔ̃bi] *f* Colombia; **la Colombie** Colombia

colombier [kɔlɔ̃bje] m dovecote; large-size paper
colom·bin [kɔlɔ̃bɛ̃] -bine [bin] adj columbine || m stock dove; lead ore || f bird droppings; (bot) columbine
colon [kɔlɔ̃] m colonist; tenant farmer; summer camper
côlon [kolɔ̃] m (anat) colon
colonel [kɔlɔnɛl] m colonel
colonelle [kɔlɔnɛl] f colonel's wife; (theat) performance for the press
colonie [kɔlɔni] f colony; colonie de déportation penal settlement; colonie de vacances summer camp
coloniser [kɔlɔnize] tr to colonize
colonnade [kɔlɔnad] f colonnade
colonne [kɔlɔn] f column; pillar; cinquième colonne fifth column; colonne vertébrale spinal column
colophane [kɔlɔfan] f rosin
colophon [kɔlɔfɔ̃] m colophon
colo·rant [kɔlɔrɑ̃] -rante [rɑ̃t] adj coloring || m dye, stain
colorer [kɔlɔre] tr & ref to color
colorier [kɔlɔrje] tr to paint, color
coloris [kɔlɔri] m hue; brilliance
colos·sal -sale [kɔlɔsal] adj (pl colos·saux [kɔlɔso]) colossal
colosse [kɔlɔs] m colossus
colporter [kɔlpɔrte] tr to peddle
colporteur [kɔlpɔrtœr] m peddler
coltiner [kɔltine] tr to lug on one's back or on one's head
coma [kɔma] m (pathol) coma
coma·teux [kɔmatø] -teuse [tøz] adj comatose || mf person in a coma
combat [kɔ̃ba] m combat; combat tournoyant (aer) dogfight; hors de combat disabled
comba·tif [kɔ̃batif] -tive [tiv] adj combative
combat·tant [kɔ̃batɑ̃] combat·tante [kɔ̃batɑ̃t] adj & mf combatant; anciens combattants veterans
combattre [kɔ̃batr] §7 tr & intr to combat
combien [kɔ̃bjɛ̃] adv how much, how many; how far; how long; how, e.g., combien il était brave! how brave he was! || m invar—du combien chaussez-vous? what size shoes do you wear?; du combien coiffez-vous? what size hat do you wear?; le combien? which one (in a series)?; le combien êtes-vous? (coll) what rank do you have?; le combien sommes-nous? (coll) what day of the month is it?; tous les combien? how often?
combinaison [kɔ̃binɛzɔ̃] f combination; coveralls; slip, undergarment
combi·né -née [kɔ̃bine] adj combined || m French telephone, handset; radio phonograph
combiner [kɔ̃bine] tr to combine; to arrange, group; to concoct (a scheme) || ref (chem) to combine
comble [kɔ̃bl] adj full, packed || m summit; roof, coping; au comble de at the height of; c'est le comble!, c'est un comble! (coll) that's the limit!, that takes the cake!; sous les combles in the attic
combler [kɔ̃ble] tr to heap up; to fill

to the brim; to overwhelm; combler d'honneurs to shower honors upon
combustible [kɔ̃bystibl] adj & m combustible, fuel
combustion [kɔ̃bystjɔ̃] f combustion
comédie [kɔmedi] f comedy; play; sham
comé·dien [kɔmedjɛ̃] -dienne [djɛn] mf comedian; actor; hypocrite; comédien ambulant strolling player || f comedienne; actress
comédon [kɔmedɔ̃] m blackhead
comestible [kɔmɛstibl] adj edible || comestibles mpl foodstuffs
comète [kɔmɛt] f comet
comique [kɔmik] adj & m comic
comité [kɔmite] m committee
commandant [kɔmɑ̃dɑ̃] m commandant, commander; major
commande [kɔmɑ̃d] f order (for goods or services); control, command; à la commande (paid) down; commande postale mail order; de commande operating; (fait) sur commande (made) to order
commandement [kɔmɑ̃dəmɑ̃] m command, order; commandment
commander [kɔmɑ̃de] tr to order (goods or services); to command, order || intr (mil) to command; commander à to control, to have command over; commander à qn de + inf to order s.o. to + inf || ref to control oneself
commanditaire [kɔmɑ̃diter] adj sponsoring || mf (com) sponsor, backer
commandite [kɔmɑ̃dit] f joint-stock company
commanditer [kɔmɑ̃dite] tr to back, to finance; (rad, telv) to sponsor
comme [kɔm] adv as; how; comme ci comme ça so-so || prep as, like || conj as; since
commémorer [kɔmmemɔre] tr to commemorate
commen·çant [kɔmɑ̃sɑ̃] -çante [sɑ̃t] mf beginner
commencement [kɔmɑ̃smɑ̃] m beginning
commencer [kɔmɑ̃se] §51 tr & intr to begin; commencer à to begin to
comment [kɔmɑ̃] m invar how; wherefore || adv how; why; mais comment donc! by all means!; n'importe comment any way || interj what!; indeed!
commentaire [kɔmɑ̃ter] m commentary; unfriendly comment
commenta·teur [kɔmɑ̃tatœr] -trice [tris] mf commentator
commenter [kɔmɑ̃te] tr to comment on; to make a commentary on; to criticize
commérage [kɔmeraʒ] m (coll) gossip
commer·çant [kɔmɛrsɑ̃] -çante [sɑ̃t] adj commercial, business || mf merchant, dealer
commerce [kɔmɛrs] m commerce, trade
commercer [kɔmɛrse] §51 intr to trade
commer·cial -ciale [kɔmɛrsjal] adj (pl -ciaux [sjo] -ciales) commercial || f station wagon

commercialisation [kɔmɛrsjalizɑsjɔ̃] *f* marketing
commercialiser [kɔmɛrsjalize] *tr* to commercialize
commère [kɔmɛr] *f* (coll) busybody, gossip
commettre [kɔmɛtr] §42 *tr* to commit; **to compromise** || *ref* to compromise oneself
commis [kɔmi] *m* clerk; **commis voyageur** traveling salesman
commisération [kɔmizerɑsjɔ̃] *f* commiseration
commissaire [kɔmisɛr] *m* commissioner; commissary
commissaire-priseur [kɔmisɛrprizœr] *m* (*pl* **commissaires-priseurs**) appraiser; auctioneer
commissariat [kɔmisarja] *m* commissariat; **commissariat de police** police station
commission [kɔmisjɔ̃] *f* commission; errand; committee
commissionnaire [kɔmisjɔnɛr] *m* agent, broker; messenger
commissionner [kɔmisjɔne] *tr* to commission
commissure [kɔmisyr] *f* corner (*of lips*)
commode [kɔmɔd] *adj* convenient; comfortable; easygoing || *f* chest of drawers, bureau
commodité [kɔmɔdite] *f* comfort, accommodation; **à votre commodité** at your convenience; **commodités** comfort station
commotion [kɔmosjɔ̃] *f* commotion; concussion; shock
commotionner [kɔmɔsjɔne] *tr* to shake up, injure, shock
commuer [kɔmɥe] *tr* (law) to commute
com·mun [kɔmœ̃] **com·mune** [kɔmyn] *adj* common || *m* common run || *f* see **commune**
commu·nal -nale [kɔmynal] (*pl* **-naux** [no]) *adj* communal, common || *mpl* common property, commons
communautaire [kɔmynotɛr] *adj* communal
communauté [kɔmynote] *f* community; **Communauté économique européenne** Common Market
commune [kɔmyn] *f* commune; **communes** Commons
commu·niant [kɔmynjɑ̃] **-niante** [njɑ̃t] *mf* communicant
communicable [kɔmynikabl] *adj* communicable
communi·cant [kɔmynikɑ̃] **-cante** [kɑ̃t] *adj* communicating
communica·teur [kɔmynikatœr] **-trice** [tris] *adj* connecting (*wire*)
communica·tif [kɔmynikatif] **-tive** [tiv] *adj* communicative; infectious (*laughter*)
communication [kɔmynikɑsjɔ̃] *f* communication; telephone call; (telp) connection; **communication avec avis d'appel** (telp) messenger call; **communication avec préavis** person-to-person call; **communication payable à l'arrivée, communication P.C.V.** collect call; **en communication** in touch; **fausse communication** (telp)

wrong number; **vous avez la communication!** (telp) go ahead!
communier [kɔmynje] *intr* to take communion; to have a common bond of sympathy, to be in accord
communion [kɔmynjɔ̃] *f* communion
communiqué [kɔmynike] *m* communiqué
communiquer [kɔmynike] *tr* & *intr* to communicate
communi·sant [kɔmynizɑ̃] **-sante** [zɑ̃t] *adj* fellow-traveling || *mf* fellow traveler
communisme [kɔmynism] *m* communism
communiste [kɔmynist] *adj* & *mf* communist
commutateur [kɔmytatœr] *m* (elec) changeover switch, two-way switch
commutation [kɔmytɑsjɔ̃] *f* commutation
commutatrice [kɔmytatris] *f* (elec) rotary converter
com·pact -pacte [kɔ̃pakt] *adj* compact
compagne [kɔ̃paɲ] *f* companion; helpmate
compagnie [kɔ̃paɲi] *f* company; **de compagnie** or **en compagnie** together; **fausser compagnie à** to give (*s.o.*) the slip; **tenir compagnie à** to keep (*s.o.*) company
compagnon [kɔ̃paɲɔ̃] *m* companion; **compagnon d'armes** comrade in arms; **compagnon de jeu** playmate; **compagnon de route** fellow traveler; **compagnon d'infortune** fellow sufferer; **joyeux compagnon** good fellow
comparaison [kɔ̃parezɔ̃] *f* comparison; **en comparaison de** compared to; **par comparaison** in comparison; **sans comparaison** beyond comparison
comparaître [kɔ̃parɛtr] §12 *intr* (law) to appear (in court)
compara·tif [kɔ̃paratif] **-tive** [tiv] *adj* & *m* comparative
compa·ré -rée [kɔ̃pare] *adj* comparative
comparer [kɔ̃pare] *tr* to compare
comparoir [kɔ̃parwar] (used only in: *inf*; *ger* **comparant**) *intr* (law) to appear in court
comparse [kɔ̃pars] *mf* (theat) walk-on; (fig) nobody, unimportant person
compartiment [kɔ̃partimɑ̃] *m* compartment
comparution [kɔ̃parysjɔ̃] *f* appearance in court
compas [kɔ̃pa] *m* compasses (*for drawing circles*); calipers; (naut) compass; **avoir le compas dans l'œil** to have a sharp eye
compas·sé -sée [kɔ̃pase] *adj* stiff, studied
compasser [kɔ̃pase] *tr* to measure out, to lay off; **compasser ses discours** to speak like a book
compassion [kɔ̃pasjɔ̃] *f* compassion
compatibilité [kɔ̃patibilite] *f* compatibility
compatir [kɔ̃patir] *intr*—**compatir à** to take pity on, to feel for; to be indulgent toward; to share in (*s.o.'s*

bereavement); **ne pouvoir compatir** to be unable to agree

compatis·sant [kɔ̃patisɑ̃] **compatis·sante** [kɔ̃patisɑ̃t] *adj* compassionate, sympathetic, indulgent

compatriote [kɔ̃patriɔt] *mf* compatriot

compensa·teur [kɔ̃pɑ̃satœr] **-trice** [tris] *adj* compensating, equalizing

compensation [kɔ̃pɑ̃sasjɔ̃] *f* compensation

compenser [kɔ̃pɑ̃se] *tr* to compensate; to compensate for ‖ *ref* to balance each other

compérage [kɔ̃peraʒ] *m* complicity

compère [kɔ̃per] *m* accomplice; comrade; stooge (*for a clown*)

compétence [kɔ̃petɑ̃s] *f* competence, proficiency; (law) jurisdiction

compé·tent [kɔ̃petɑ̃] **-tente** [tɑ̃t] *adj* competent, proficient; (law) having jurisdiction, expert

compéter [kɔ̃pete] §10 *intr*—**compéter à** to belong to by right; to be within the competency of (*a court*)

compéti·teur [kɔ̃petitœr] **-trice** [tris] *mf* rival, competitor

compétition [kɔ̃petisjɔ̃] *f* competition

compilation [kɔ̃pilɑsjɔ̃] *f* compilation

compiler [kɔ̃pile] *tr* to compile

complainte [kɔ̃plɛ̃t] *f* sad ballad; (law) complaint

complaire [kɔ̃plɛr] §52 *intr* (with *dat*) to please, gratify ‖ *ref*—**se complaire à** to take pleasure in

complaisance [kɔ̃plɛzɑ̃s] *f* compliance; courtesy; complacency; **auriez-vous la complaisance de . . . ?** would you be so kind as to . . . ?; **de complaisance** out of kindness

complai·sant [kɔ̃plɛzɑ̃] **-sante** [zɑ̃t] *adj* complaisant, obliging; complacent

complément [kɔ̃plemɑ̃] *m* complement; (gram) object; **complément d'attribution** (gram) indirect object

com·plet [kɔ̃plɛ] **-plète** [plɛt] *adj* complete, full; **c'est complet!** that's the last straw! ‖ *m* suit (*of clothes*); **au complet** full (*house*); **au grand complet** at full strength

compléter [kɔ̃plete] §10 *tr* to complete ‖ *ref* to be completed; to complement one another

complet-veston [kɔ̃plɛvɛstɔ̃] *m* (*pl* **complets-veston**) man's suit

complexe [kɔ̃plɛks] *adj & m* complex; **complexe de culpabilité** guilt complex

complexé complexée [kɔ̃plɛkse] *adj* (coll) timid, withdrawn ‖ *mf* person with complexes

complexion [kɔ̃plɛksjɔ̃] *f* constitution, disposition

complication [kɔ̃plikɑsjɔ̃] *f* complication

complice [kɔ̃plis] *adj* accessory, abetting ‖ *mf* accomplice; **complice d'adultère** corespondent

complicité [kɔ̃plisite] *f* complicity

compliment [kɔ̃plimɑ̃] *m* compliment

complimenter [kɔ̃plimɑ̃te] *tr* to compliment; to congratulate

complimen·teur [kɔ̃plimɑ̃tœr] **-teuse** [tøz] *adj* complimentary ‖ *mf* flatterer, yes man

compli·qué -quée [kɔ̃plike] *adj* complicated

compliquer [kɔ̃plike] *tr* to complicate ‖ *ref* to become complicated; to have complications

complot [kɔ̃plo] *m* plot, conspiracy

comploter [kɔ̃plɔte] *tr & intr* to plot, conspire

comploteur [kɔ̃plɔtœr] *m* conspirator

comportement [kɔ̃pɔrtəmɑ̃] *m* behavior

comporter [kɔ̃pɔrte] *tr* to permit; to include ‖ *ref* to behave

compo·sant [kɔ̃pozɑ̃] **-sante** [zɑ̃t] *adj* constituent ‖ *m* (chem) component ‖ *f* (mech) component

compo·sé -sée [kɔ̃poze] *adj & m* compound

composer [kɔ̃poze] *tr* to compose; to compound; to dial (*a telephone number*) ‖ *intr* to take an exam; to come to terms ‖ *ref*—**se composer de** to be composed of

composi·teur [kɔ̃pozitœr] **-trice** [tris] *mf* composer; compositor; **amiable compositeur** (law) arbitrator

composition [kɔ̃pozisjɔ̃] *f* composition; compound; dialing (*of telephone number*); term paper; **de bonne composition** easygoing, reasonable; **entrer en composition** to reach an agreement

composteur [kɔ̃pɔstœr] *m* composing stick; dating and numbering machine, dating stamp

compote [kɔ̃pɔt] *f* compote; **compote de pommes** applesauce

compotier [kɔ̃pɔtje] *m* compote (*dish*)

compréhensible [kɔ̃preɑ̃sibl] *adj* comprehensible

compréhen·sif [kɔ̃preɑ̃sif] **-sive** [siv] *adj* understanding; comprehensive

compréhension [kɔ̃preɑ̃sjɔ̃] *f* comprehension, understanding

comprendre [kɔ̃prɑ̃dr] §56 *tr* to understand; to comprehend, to include, to comprise ‖ *intr* to understand ‖ *ref* to be understood; to be included

compresse [kɔ̃prɛs] *f* (med) compress

compresseur [kɔ̃prɛsœr] *m* compressor

compression [kɔ̃prɛsjɔ̃] *f* compression; repression; reduction

compri·mé -mée [kɔ̃prime] *adj* compressed ‖ *m* (pharm) tablet, lozenge

comprimer [kɔ̃prime] *tr* to compress; to repress

com·pris [kɔ̃pri] **-prise** [priz] *adj* understood; included, including, e.g., **la ferme comprise** or **y compris la ferme** the farm included, including the farm

compromet·tant [kɔ̃prɔmetɑ̃] **compromet·tante** [kɔ̃prɔmetɑ̃t] *adj* compromising, incriminating

compromettre [kɔ̃prɔmetr] §42 *tr* to compromise ‖ *intr* to submit to arbitration ‖ *ref* to compromise oneself

compromis [kɔ̃prɔmi] *m* compromise

comptabiliser [kɔ̃tabilize] *tr* (com) to enter into the books

comptabilité [kɔ̃tabilite] *f* bookkeeping, accounting; accounting department, accounts; **comptabilité à partie double** double-entry bookkeeping; **comptabilité simple** single-entry bookkeeping; **tenir la comptabilité** to keep the books
comptable [kɔ̃tabl] *adj* accountable, responsible; accounting (*machine*) ‖ *mf* bookkeeper; **comptable agréé** or expert comptable certified public accountant; **comptable contrôleur** auditor
comp•tant [kɔ̃tɑ̃] -tante [tɑ̃t] *adj* spot (*cash*); down, e.g., **argent comptant cash down** ‖ *m*—**au comptant** cash, for cash ‖ **comptant** *adv* cash (down), e.g., **payer comptant** to pay cash
compte [kɔ̃t] *m* account; accounting; (sports) count; **à bon compte** cheap; **à ce compte** in that case; **à compte** on account; **au bout du compte** or **en fin de compte** when all is said and done; **compte à rebours** countdown; **compte courant** current account; charge account; **compte de dépôt** checking account; **compte de profits et pertes** profit and loss statement; **compte en banque** bank account; **compte rendu** report, review; **compte rond** round numbers; **donner son compte à** to give the final paycheck to, to discharge; **être en compte à demi** to go fifty-fifty; **loin de compte** wide of the mark; **rendre compte de** to review; **se rendre compte de** to realize, to be aware of; **tenir compte de** to bear in mind
compte-fils [kɔ̃tfil] *m invar* cloth prover
compte-gouttes [kɔ̃tgut] *m invar* dropper; **au compte-gouttes** in driblets
compter [kɔ̃te] *tr* to count; to number, have; **compter + inf** to count on + *ger*; **sans compter** not to mention ‖ *intr* to count; **à compter de** starting from; **compter avec** to reckon with; **compter sur** to count on
compte-tours [kɔ̃tətur] *m invar* tachometer, r.p.m. counter
comp•teur [kɔ̃tœr] -teuse [tøz] *mf* counter, checker (*person*) ‖ *m* meter; counter; speedometer; **compteur de gaz** gas meter; **compteur de Geiger** Geiger counter; **compteur de stationnement** parking meter; **relever le compteur** to read the meter
compteur-indicateur [kɔ̃tœrɛ̃dikatœr] *m* (*pl* compteurs-indicateurs) speedometer
comptine [kɔ̃tin] *f* counting-out rhyme
comptoir [kɔ̃twar] *m* counter; branch bank; bank; **comptoir postal** mail-order house
compulser [kɔ̃pylse] *tr* to go through, examine (*books, papers, etc.*)
computer [kɔ̃pyte] *tr* to compute
comte [kɔ̃t] *m* count
comté [kɔ̃te] *m* county
comtesse [kɔ̃tɛs] *f* countess
concasser [kɔ̃kase] *tr* to crush, pound

concasseur [kɔ̃kasœr] *adj masc* crushing ‖ *m* (mach) crusher
concave [kɔ̃kav] *adj* concave
concéder [kɔ̃sede] §10 *tr & intr* to concede
concen•tré -trée [kɔ̃sɑ̃tre] *adj* concentrated; condensed (*milk*); reserved (*person*)
concentrer [kɔ̃sɑ̃tre] *tr* to concentrate; to repress, hold back
concentrique [kɔ̃sɑ̃trik] *adj* concentric
concept [kɔ̃sɛpt] *m* concept
conception [kɔ̃sɛpsjɔ̃] *f* conception
concerner [kɔ̃sɛrne] *tr* to concern; **en ce qui concerne** concerning
concert [kɔ̃sɛr] *m* concert; **de concert** together, in concert
concer•tant [kɔ̃sɛrtɑ̃] -tante [tɑ̃t] *adj* performing together ‖ *mf* (mus) performer
concerter [kɔ̃sɛrte] *tr & ref* to concert, to plan
concertiste [kɔ̃sɛrtist] *mf* concert performer
concession [kɔ̃sɛsjɔ̃] *f* concession
concessionnaire [kɔ̃sɛsjɔner] *mf* grantee, licensee; dealer (*in automobiles*); agent (*for insurance*)
concetti [kɔ̃t/eti] *mpl* conceits
concevable [kɔ̃səvabl] *adj* conceivable
concevoir [kɔ̃səvwar] §59 *tr* to conceive; to compose (*a letter, telegram*)
concierge [kɔ̃sjɛrʒ] *mf* concierge, building superintendent
concile [kɔ̃sil] *m* (eccl) council
concilia•teur [kɔ̃siljatœr] -trice [tris] *adj* conciliating ‖ *mf* conciliator
conciliatoire [kɔ̃siljatwar] *adj* conciliatory
concilier [kɔ̃silje] *tr* to reconcile (*two parties, two ideas, etc.*); to win (*e.g., favor*) ‖ *ref* to win over, gain (*e.g., esteem*); to agree
con•cis [kɔ̃si] -cise [siz] *adj* concise
concitoyen [kɔ̃sitwajɛ̃] concitoyenne [kɔ̃sitwajen] *mf* fellow citizen
concluant [kɔ̃klyɑ̃] concluante [kɔ̃klyɑ̃t] *adj* conclusive
conclure [kɔ̃klyr] §11 *tr* to conclude ‖ *intr* to conclude; **conclure à** to decide on, to decide in favor of
conclusion [kɔ̃klyzjɔ̃] *f* conclusion
concombre [kɔ̃kɔ̃br] *m* cucumber
concomi•tant [kɔ̃kɔmitɑ̃] -tante [tɑ̃t] *adj* concomitant
concordance [kɔ̃kɔrdɑ̃s] *f* agreement; concordance (*of Bible*)
concorde [kɔ̃kɔrd] *f* concord
concorder [kɔ̃kɔrde] *intr* to agree
concourir [kɔ̃kurir] §14 *intr* to compete; to cooperate; to converge, concur
concours [kɔ̃kur] *m* crowd; cooperation; contest, competition, meet; competitive examination; **concours de beauté** beauty contest; **concours de créanciers** meeting of creditors; **concours hippique** horse show; **hors concours** not competing; in a class by itself
con•cret [kɔ̃krɛ] -crète [krɛt] *adj & m* concrete

concrétiser [kɔ̃kretize] *tr* to put in concrete form
concubine [kɔ̃kybin] *f* concubine
concurrence [kɔ̃kyrɑ̃s] *f* competition; competitors; **jusqu'à concurrence de** to the amount of; **libre concurrence** free enterprise
concurrencer [kɔ̃kyrɑ̃se] §51 *tr* to rival, to compete with
concur·rent [kɔ̃kyrɑ̃] **concur·rente** [kɔ̃-kyrɑ̃t] *adj* competitive || *mf* competitor; contestant
concurren·tiel -tielle [kɔ̃kyrɑ̃sjɛl] *adj* competitive
concussion [kɔ̃kysjɔ̃] *f* extortion; embezzlement
condamnable [kɔ̃danabl] *adj* blameworthy
condamnation [kɔ̃danasjɔ̃] *f* condemnation
condamner [kɔ̃dane] *tr* to condemn; to give up (*an incurable patient*); to forbid the use of; to board up (*a window*); to batten down (*the hatches*)
condensateur [kɔ̃dɑ̃satœr] *m* (elec) condenser
condenser [kɔ̃dɑ̃se] *tr* & *ref* to condense
condenseur [kɔ̃dɑ̃sœr] *m* condenser
condescendance [kɔ̃desɑ̃dɑ̃s] *f* condescension
condescen·dant [kɔ̃desɑ̃dɑ̃] **-dante** [dɑ̃t] *adj* condescending
condescendre [kɔ̃desɑ̃dr] *intr* to condescend; to yield, comply
condiment [kɔ̃dimɑ̃] *m* condiment
condisciple [kɔ̃disipl] *mf* classmate
condition [kɔ̃disjɔ̃] *f* condition; **à condition, sous condition** conditionally; on approval; **à condition que** on condition that; **dans de bonnes conditions** in good condition; **sans conditions** unconditional
condition·nel -nelle [kɔ̃disjɔnɛl] *adj* & *m* conditional
conditionner [kɔ̃disjɔne] *tr* to condition; (com) to package
condoléances [kɔ̃dɔleɑ̃s] *fpl* condolence
conduc·teur [kɔ̃dyktœr] **-trice** [tris] *adj* conducting; driving; (elec) power (*line*); (elec) lead (*wire*) || *adj masc* (elec, phys) (in predicate after être, it may be translated by a noun) conductor, e.g., **les métaux sont bons conducteurs de l'électricité** metals are good conductors of electricity || *mf* guide; leader; driver || *m* motorman; foreman; pressman; (elec, phys) conductor
conduire [kɔ̃dɥir] §19 *tr* to conduct; to lead; to drive; to see (*s.o. to the door*) || *intr* to drive || *ref* to conduct oneself
conduit [kɔ̃dɥi] *m* conduit; **conduit auditif** auditory canal; **conduits lacrymaux** tear ducts
conduite [kɔ̃dɥit] *f* conduct, behavior; management, command; driving (*of a car; of cattle*); pipe line; duct, flue; **avoir de la conduite** to be well behaved; **conduite d'eau** water main; **conduite intérieure** closed car; **faire la conduite à** to escort; **faire une**

conduite de Grenoble à qn (coll) to kick s.o. out
cône [kon] *m* cone
confection [kɔ̃fɛksjɔ̃] *f* manufacture; construction (*e.g., of a machine*); ready-made clothes; **de confection** ready-made (*suit, dress, etc.*)
confectionner [kɔ̃fɛksjɔne] *tr* to manufacture; to prepare (*a dish*)
confection·neur [kɔ̃fɛksjɔnœr] **confection·neuse** [kɔ̃fɛksjɔnøz] *mf* manufacturer (*esp. of ready-made clothes*)
confédération [kɔ̃federasjɔ̃] *f* confederation, confederacy
confédérer [kɔ̃federe] §10 *tr* & *ref* to confederate
conférence [kɔ̃ferɑ̃s] *f* conference; lecture, speech; **conférence au sommet** summit conference; **conférence de presse** press conference
conféren·cier [kɔ̃ferɑ̃sje] **-cière** [sjɛr] *mf* lecturer, speaker
conférer [kɔ̃fere] §10 *tr* to confer, award; to administer (*a sacrament*); to collate, compare || *intr* to confer
confesse [kɔ̃fɛs] *f*—**à confesse** to confession; **de confesse** from confession
confesser [kɔ̃fɛse] *tr* to confess; (coll) to pump (*s.o.*) || *ref* to confess
confesseur [kɔ̃fɛsœr] *m* confessor
confession [kɔ̃fɛsjɔ̃] *f* confession; (eccl) denomination
confessionnal [kɔ̃fɛsjɔnal] *m* confessional
confession·nel -nelle [kɔ̃fɛsjɔnɛl] *adj* denominational
confiance [kɔ̃fjɑ̃s] *f* confidence; **confiance en soi** self-confidence; **de confiance** reliable; confidently; **en confiance** with confidence
con·fiant [kɔ̃fjɑ̃] **-fiante** [fjɑ̃t] *adj* confident; confiding, trusting
confidence [kɔ̃fidɑ̃s] *f* confidence, secret
confi·dent [kɔ̃fidɑ̃] **-dente** [dɑ̃t] *mf* confident
confiden·tiel -tielle [kɔ̃fidɑ̃sjɛl] *adj* confidential
confier [kɔ̃fje] *tr* to entrust; to confide, disclose; to commit (*to memory*); to consign; **confier à** to put (*seed*) in (*the ground*) || *ref*—**se confier à** to confide in, to trust; **se confier en** to put one's trust in
confinement [kɔ̃finmɑ̃] *m* imprisonment
confiner [kɔ̃fine] *tr* to confine || *intr*—**confiner à** to border on, to verge on || *ref* to confine oneself; **se confiner dans** to confine oneself to
confins [kɔ̃fɛ̃] *mpl* confines
confire [kɔ̃fir] §66 (*pp* confit) *tr* to preserve; to pickle; to candy; to can (*goose, chicken, etc.*); to dip (*skins*) || *ref* to become immersed (*in work, prayer, etc.*)
confirmer [kɔ̃firme] *tr* to confirm
confiserie [kɔ̃fizri] *f* confectionery
confi·seur [kɔ̃fizœr] **-seuse** [zøz] *mf* confectioner, candymaker
confisquer [kɔ̃fiske] *tr* to confiscate
con·fit [kɔ̃fi] **-fite** [fit] *adj* preserved; pickled; candied; steeped (*e.g., in*

piety); incrusted (*in bigotry*) ‖ *m* canned chicken, goose, etc.

confiture [kɔ̃fityr] *f* preserves, jam
confitu·rier [kɔ̃fityrje] **-rière** [rjɛr] *mf* manufacturer of jams ‖ *m* jelly glass, jam jar
conflagration [kɔ̃flagrɑsjɔ̃] *f* conflagration, turmoil
conflit [kɔ̃fli] *m* conflict
confluer [kɔ̃flye] *intr* to meet, come together (*said of two rivers*)
confondre [kɔ̃fɔ̃dr] *tr* to confuse, mix up, mingle; to confound ‖ *ref* to become bewildered, mixed up; **se confondre en excuses** to fall all over oneself apologizing
conforme [kɔ̃fɔrm] *adj* corresponding; certified, e.g., **pour copie conforme** certified copy; **conforme à** conformable to, consistent with; **conforme à l'échantillon** identical with sample; **conforme aux normes** according to specifications; **conforme aux règles** in order
confor·mé -mée [kɔ̃fɔrme] *adj* shaped, built; **bien conformé** well-built; **mal conformé** misshapen
conformément [kɔ̃fɔrmemɑ̃] *adv*—**conformément à** in compliance with
conformer [kɔ̃fɔrme] *tr* & *ref* to conform
conformiste [kɔ̃fɔrmist] *mf* conformist
conformité [kɔ̃fɔrmite] *f* conformity, conformance
confort [kɔ̃fɔr] *m* comfort; convenience; **pneu confort** balloon tire
confortable [kɔ̃fɔrtabl] *adj* comfortable ‖ *m* comfort; easy chair
confrère [kɔ̃frɛr] *m* confrere, colleague
confrérie [kɔ̃freri] *f* brotherhood
confronter [kɔ̃frɔ̃te] *tr* to confront; to compare, collate
con·fus [kɔ̃fy] **-fuse** [fyz] *adj* confused; vague, blurred; embarrassed
confusion [kɔ̃fyzjɔ̃] *f* confusion
congé [kɔ̃ʒe] *m* leave; vacation; dismissal; **congé libérable** military discharge; **congé payé** vacation with pay; **donner congé à** to lay off; **donner son congé à** to give notice to; **prendre congé de** to take leave of
congédiement [kɔ̃ʒedimɑ̃] *m* dismissal, discharge; paying off (*of crew*)
congédier [kɔ̃ʒedje] *tr* to dismiss
congélateur [kɔ̃ʒelatœr] *m* freezer (*for frozen foods*)
congélation [kɔ̃ʒelɑsjɔ̃] *f* freezing
congeler [kɔ̃ʒəle] §2 *tr* & *ref* to freeze; to congeal; **congeler à basse température** to deep-freeze
congéni·tal -tale [kɔ̃ʒenital] *adj* (*pl* -taux [to]) congenital
congère [kɔ̃ʒɛr] *f* snowdrift
congestion [kɔ̃ʒɛstjɔ̃] *f* congestion; **congestion cérébrale** stroke; **congestion pulmonaire** pneumonia
congestionner [kɔ̃ʒɛstjɔne] *tr* & *ref* to congest
conglomération [kɔ̃glɔmerɑsjɔ̃] *f* conglomeration
conglomérer [kɔ̃glɔmere] §10 *tr* & *ref* to conglomerate

congratulation [kɔ̃gratylɑsjɔ̃] *f* congratulation
congratuler [kɔ̃gratyle] *tr* to congratulate
congre [kɔ̃gr] *m* conger eel
congréer [kɔ̃gree] *tr* to worm (*rope*)
congrégation [kɔ̃gregɑsjɔ̃] *f* (eccl) congregation
congrès [kɔ̃grɛ] *m* congress, convention
congressiste [kɔ̃grɛsist] *mf* delegate ‖ *m* congressman ‖ *f* congresswoman
con·gru -grue [kɔ̃gry] *adj* precise, suitable; scanty; (math) congruent
conifère [kɔnifɛr] *adj* coniferous ‖ *m* conifer
conique [kɔnik] *adj* conical ‖ *f* conic section
conjecture [kɔ̃ʒɛktyr] *f* conjecture
conjecturer [kɔ̃ʒɛktyre] *tr* & *intr* to conjecture, to surmise
conjoindre [kɔ̃ʒwɛ̃dr] §35 *tr* to join in marriage
con·joint [kɔ̃ʒwɛ̃] **-jointe** [ʒwɛ̃t] *adj* united, joint ‖ *mf* spouse, consort
conjoncteur [kɔ̃ʒɔ̃ktœr] *m* automatic switch
conjonction [kɔ̃ʒɔ̃ksjɔ̃] *f* conjunction
conjugaison [kɔ̃ʒygɛzɔ̃] *f* conjugation
conju·gal -gale [kɔ̃ʒygal] *adj* (*pl* -gaux [go]) conjugal, connubial
conjuguer [kɔ̃ʒyge] *tr* to combine (*e.g., forces*); to conjugate
conjuration [kɔ̃ʒyrɑsjɔ̃] *f* conjuration; conspiracy; **conjurations** entreaties
conju·ré -rée [kɔ̃ʒyre] *mf* conspirator
conjurer [kɔ̃ʒyre] *tr* to conjure; to conjure away; to conjure up; to conspire for, to plot; **conjurer qn de** + *inf* to entreat s.o. to + *inf* ‖ *intr* to hatch a plot ‖ *ref* to plot together, conspire
connaissance [kɔnɛsɑ̃s] *f* knowledge; acquaintance; consciousness; attention; **connaissance des temps** nautical almanac; **connaissances** knowledge; **en connaissance de** with full knowledge of; **faire connaissance avec** to become acquainted with; **faire la connaissance de** to meet; **parler en connaissance de cause** to know what one is talking about; **perdre connaissance** to lose consciousness; **sans connaissance** unconscious
connaissement [kɔnɛsmɑ̃] *m* bill of lading
connais·seur [kɔnɛsœr] **connais·seuse** [kɔnɛsøz] *mf* connoisseur; expert
connaître [kɔnɛtr] §12 *tr* to know; to be acquainted with ‖ *intr*—**connaître de** (law) to have jurisdiction over ‖ *ref* to be acquainted; to become acquainted; **se connaître à** or **en** to know a lot about; **s'y connaître** to know what one is talking about; **s'y connaître en** to know a lot about
connecter [kɔnɛkte] *tr* to connect
connétable [kɔnetabl] *m* constable
connexe [kɔnɛks] *adj* connected
connexion [kɔnɛksjɔ̃] *f* connection
connexité [kɔnɛksite] *f* connection
con·nu -nue [kɔny] *adj* well-known ‖ *m*—**le connu** the known

conque [kɔ̃k] *f* conch

conqué·rant [kɔ̃kerɑ̃] **-rante** [rɑ̃t] *adj* (coll) swaggering || *mf* conqueror

conquérir [kɔ̃kerir] §3 *tr* to conquer

conquête [kɔ̃kɛt] *f* conquest

consa·cré -crée [kɔ̃sakre] *adj* accepted, time-honored, stock

consacrer [kɔ̃sakre] *tr* to consecrate; to devote, dedicate (*time, energy, effort*); to give, to spare (*e.g., time*); to sanction, confirm || *ref*—**se consacrer à** to devote or dedicate oneself to

consan·guin [kɔ̃sɑ̃gɛ̃] **-guine** [gin] *adj* consanguineous; on the father's side || *mf* blood relation

consciemment [kɔ̃sjamɑ̃] *adv* consciously

conscience [kɔ̃sjɑ̃s] *f* conscience; conscientiousness; consciousness; **avoir la conscience large** to be broadminded; **en conscience** conscientiously

conscien·cieux [kɔ̃sjɑ̃sjø] **-cieuse** [sjøz] *adj* conscientious

cons·cient [kɔ̃sjɑ̃] **cons·ciente** [kɔ̃sjɑ̃t] *adj* conscious, aware, knowing

conscription [kɔ̃skripsjɔ̃] *f* draft, conscription

conscrit [kɔ̃skri] *m* draftee, conscript

consécration [kɔ̃sekrasjɔ̃] *f* consecration; confirmation

consécu·tif [kɔ̃sekytif] **-tive** [tiv] *adj* consecutive; dependent (*clause*); **consécutif à** resulting from

conseil [kɔ̃sɛj] *m* advice, counsel; counselor; council, board, committee; **conseil d'administration** board of directors; **conseil de guerre** court-martial; staff meeting of top brass; **conseil de prud'hommes** arbitration board; **conseil de révision** draft board; **conseils** advice; **un conseil** a piece of advice

conseil·ler [kɔ̃seje] **conseil·lère** [kɔ̃sejɛr] *mf* councilor; counselor, adviser || *f* councilor's wife; counselor's wife || **conseiller** *tr* to advise, to counsel (*s.o. or s.th.*); **conseiller q.ch. à qn** to recommend s.th. to s.o. || *intr* to advise, to counsel; **conseiller à qn de** + *inf* to advise s.o. to + *inf*

conseil·leur [kɔ̃sejœr] **conseil·leuse** [kɔ̃sejøz] *mf* adviser; know-it-all

consensus [kɔ̃sɛ̃sys] *m* consensus

consentement [kɔ̃sɑ̃tmɑ̃] *m* consent

consentir [kɔ̃sɑ̃tir] §41 *tr* to grant, allow; to accept, recognize; **consentir que** + *subj* to permit (*s.o.*) to + *inf* || *intr* to consent; **consentir à** to consent to, to agree to, to approve of

conséquemment [kɔ̃sekamɑ̃] *adv* consequently; consistently

conséquence [kɔ̃sekɑ̃s] *f* consequence; consistency; **en conséquence** accordingly

consé·quent [kɔ̃sekɑ̃] **-quente** [kɑ̃t] *adj* consequent; consistent; important || *m* (logic, math) consequent; **par conséquent** consequently

conserva·teur [kɔ̃sɛrvatœr] **-trice** [tris] *adj* conservative || *mf* conservative;

curator, keeper; warden, ranger; registrar

conservation [kɔ̃sɛrvɑsjɔ̃] *f* conservation, preservation; curatorship; curator's office

conservatisme [kɔ̃sɛrvatism] *m* conservatism

conservatoire [kɔ̃sɛrvatwar] *m* conservatory (*of music*); museum, academy

conserve [kɔ̃sɛrv] *f* canned food, preserves; escort, convoy; **conserves** dark glasses; **conserves au vinaigre** pickles; **mettre en conserve** to can; **voler de conserve avec** to fly alongside of

conserver [kɔ̃sɛrve] *tr* to conserve; to preserve; to keep (*one's health; one's equanimity; a secret*); to escort, to convoy (*a ship*) || *ref* to stay in good shape; to take care of oneself

conserverie [kɔ̃sɛrvəri] *f* canning factory; canning

considérable [kɔ̃siderabl] *adj* considerable; important; large, great

considérant [kɔ̃siderɑ̃] *m* motive, grounds; **considérant que** whereas

considération [kɔ̃siderɑsjɔ̃] *f* consideration

considérer [kɔ̃sidere] §10 *tr* to consider, examine; to esteem, consider

consignataire [kɔ̃siɲatɛr] *m* consignee, trustee

consignation [kɔ̃siɲɑsjɔ̃] *f* consignment; **en consignation** on consignment

consigne [kɔ̃siɲ] *f* password; baggage room, checkroom; checking fee; confinement to barracks, detention; deposit; (mil) orders, instructions; **en consigne à la douane** held up in customs; **être de consigne** to be on duty; **manquer à la consigne** to disobey orders

consigner [kɔ̃siɲe] *tr* to consign; to check (*baggage*); to put down in writing, to enter in the record; to confine to barracks, to keep (*a student*) in; to put out of bounds (*e.g., for military personnel*); to close (*a port*); **consigner sa** (or **la**) **porte** to be at home to no one

consistance [kɔ̃sistɑ̃s] *f* consistency; stability (*of character*); credit, reality, standing; **en consistance de** consisting of

consis·tant [kɔ̃sistɑ̃] **-tante** [tɑ̃t] *adj* consistent; stable (*character*); **consistant en** consisting of

consister [kɔ̃siste] *intr*—**consister à** + *inf* to consist in + *ger*; **consister dans** or **en** to consist in; to consist of

consistoire [kɔ̃sistwar] *m* consistory

consola·teur [kɔ̃sɔlatœr] **-trice** [tris] *adj* consoling || *mf* comforter

consolation [kɔ̃sɔlɑsjɔ̃] *f* consolation

console [kɔ̃sɔl] *f* console; console table; bracket

consoler [kɔ̃sɔle] *tr* to console

consolider [kɔ̃sɔlide] *tr* to consolidate; to fund (*a debt*)

consomma·teur [kɔ̃sɔmatœr] **-trice**

[tris] *mf* consumer; customer (*in a restaurant or bar*)
consommation [kɔ̃sɔmɑsjɔ̃] *f* consummation (*e.g., of a marriage*); perpetration (*e.g., of a crime*); consumption, use; drink (*e.g., in a café*)
consom·mé -mée [kɔ̃sɔme] *adj* consummate; skilled (*e.g., technician*); consumed, used up || *m* consommé
consommer [kɔ̃sɔme] *tr* to consummate, complete; to perpetrate (*e.g., a crime*); to consume
consomp·tif [kɔ̃sɔ̃ptif] **-tive** [tiv] *adj* wasting away
consomption [kɔ̃sɔ̃psjɔ̃] *f* wasting away, decline
conso·nant [kɔ̃sɔnɑ̃] **-nante** [nɑ̃t] *adj* consonant, harmonious
consonne [kɔ̃sɔn] *f* consonant
consorts [kɔ̃sɔr] *mpl* partners, associates; (pej) confederates
conspira·teur [kɔ̃spiratœr] **-trice** [tris] *mf* conspirator
conspiration [kɔ̃spirɑsjɔ̃] *f* conspiracy
conspirer [kɔ̃spire] *tr & intr* to conspire
conspuer [kɔ̃spɥe] *tr* to boo, hiss
constamment [kɔ̃stamɑ̃] *adv* constantly
constance [kɔ̃stɑ̃s] *f* constancy
cons·tant [kɔ̃stɑ̃] **-tante** [tɑ̃t] *adj* constant; true; established, evident || *f* constant
constat [kɔ̃sta] *m* affidavit
constatation [kɔ̃statɑsjɔ̃] *f* authentication; declaration, claim
constater [kɔ̃state] *tr* to certify; to find out; to prove, establish
constellation [kɔ̃stɛllɑsjɔ̃] *f* constellation
consteller [kɔ̃stɛlle] *tr* to spangle
consterner [kɔ̃sterne] *tr* to dismay
constipation [kɔ̃stipɑsjɔ̃] *f* constipation
constiper [kɔ̃stipe] *tr* to constipate
consti·tuant [kɔ̃stitɥɑ̃] **-tuante** [tɥɑ̃t] *adj & m* constituent
constituer [kɔ̃stitɥe] *tr* to constitute; to settle (*a dowry*); to form (*a cabinet; a corporation*); to empanel (*a jury*); to appoint (*a lawyer*) || *ref* to be formed; **se constituer prisonnier** to give oneself up
constitu·tif [kɔ̃stitytif] **-tive** [tiv] *adj* constituent
constitution [kɔ̃stitysjɔ̃] *f* constitution; settlement (*of a dowry*); **constitution en société** incorporation
construc·teur [kɔ̃stryktœr] **-trice** [tris] *adj* constructive, building || *mf* constructor, builder
construc·tif [kɔ̃stryktif] **-tive** [tiv] *adj* constructive
construction [kɔ̃stryksjɔ̃] *f* construction; **construction mécanique** mechanical engineering
construire [kɔ̃strɥir] §19 *tr* to construct, to build; to draw (*e.g., a triangle*); (gram) to construe
consul [kɔ̃syl] *m* consul
consulaire [kɔ̃sylɛr] *adj* consular
consulat [kɔ̃syla] *m* consulate
consul·tant [kɔ̃syltɑ̃] **-tante** [tɑ̃t] *adj* consulting || *mf* consultant

consulta·tif [kɔ̃syltatif] **-tive** [tiv] *adj* advisory
consultation [kɔ̃syltɑsjɔ̃] *f* consultation; **consultation externe** outpatient clinic; **consultation populaire** poll, referendum
consulte [kɔ̃sylt] *f* (eccl, law) consultation
consulter [kɔ̃sylte] *tr* to consult || *intr* to consult, to give consultations || *ref* to deliberate
consumer [kɔ̃syme] *tr* to consume, use up, destroy || *ref* to burn out; to waste away; to fail
contact [kɔ̃takt] *m* contact; **mettre en contact** to put in touch, to connect; **prendre contact** to make contact
contacter [kɔ̃takte] *tr* (coll) to contact
conta·gieux [kɔ̃taʒjø] **-gieuse** [ʒjøz] *adj* contagious
contagion [kɔ̃taʒjɔ̃] *f* contagion
contamination [kɔ̃taminɑsjɔ̃] *f* contamination
contaminer [kɔ̃tamine] *tr* to contaminate
conte [kɔ̃t] *m* tale, story; **conte à dormir debout** cock-and-bull story, baloney; **conte de fées** fairy tale
contemplation [kɔ̃tɑ̃plɑsjɔ̃] *f* contemplation
contempler [kɔ̃tɑ̃ple] *tr* to contemplate
contempo·rain [kɔ̃tɑ̃pɔrɛ̃] **-raine** [ren] *adj & m* contemporary
contemp·teur [kɔ̃tɑ̃ptœr] **-trice** [tris] *mf* scoffer
contenance [kɔ̃tnɑ̃s] *f* capacity; area; countenance; **faire bonne contenance** to put up a bold front
conte·nant [kɔ̃tnɑ̃] **-nante** [nɑ̃t] *adj* containing || *m* container
contenir [kɔ̃tnir] §72 *tr* to contain; to restrain || *ref* to contain oneself, to hold oneself back
con·tent [kɔ̃tɑ̃] **-tente** [tɑ̃t] *adj* content; happy, glad, pleased; **content de** satisfied with || *m* fill, e.g., **avoir son content** to have one's fill
contentement [kɔ̃tɑ̃tmɑ̃] *m* contentment
contenter [kɔ̃tɑ̃te] *tr* to content, satisfy || *ref* to satisfy one's desires; **se contenter de** to be content or satisfied with
conten·tieux [kɔ̃tɑ̃sjø] **-tieuse** [sjøz] *adj* contentious || *m* contention, litigation; claims department
contention [kɔ̃tɑ̃sjɔ̃] *f* application, intentness
conte·nu -nue [kɔ̃tny] *adj* contained, restrained, stifled || *m* contents
conter [kɔ̃te] *tr* to relate, tell; **en conter à** (coll) to take (*s.o.*) in; **en conter (de belles)** (coll) to tell tall tales || *intr* to narrate, to tell a story
contestation [kɔ̃tɛstɑsjɔ̃] *f* argument, dispute; **sans contestation** without opposition
conteste [kɔ̃tɛst] *f*—**sans conteste** incontestably, unquestionably
contester [kɔ̃tɛste] *tr & intr* to contest
con·teur [kɔ̃tœr] **-teuse** [tøz] *mf* storyteller
contexte [kɔ̃tɛkst] *m* context

conti·gu -guë [kɔ̃tigy] *adj* contiguous; contigu à adjoining
continence [kɔ̃tinãs] *f* continence
conti·nent [kɔ̃tinã] -nente [nãt] *adj* & *m* continent
continen·tal -tale [kɔ̃tinãtal] *adj* (*pl* -taux [to]) continental
contingence [kɔ̃tẽʒãs] *f* contingency
contin·gent [kɔ̃tẽʒã] -gente [ʒãt] *adj* contingent || *m* contingent; quota
conti·nu -nue [kɔ̃tiny] *adj* continuous; direct (*current*) || *m* continuum
continuation [kɔ̃tinɥasjɔ̃] *f* continuation
conti·nuel -nuelle [kɔ̃tinɥɛl] *adj* continual
continuité [kɔ̃tinɥite] *f* continuity
continûment [kɔ̃tinymã] *adv* continuously
contorsion [kɔ̃tɔrsjɔ̃] *f* contortion
contour [kɔ̃tur] *m* contour
contourner [kɔ̃turne] *tr* to contour; to go around, to skirt; to get around (*the law*); to twist, distort
contrac·tant [kɔ̃traktã] -tante [tãt] *adj* contracting (*parties*) || *mf* contracting party
contracter [kɔ̃trakte] *tr* to contract; to float (*a loan*) || *ref* to contract; to be contracted
contraction [kɔ̃traksjɔ̃] *f* contraction
contradiction [kɔ̃tradiksjɔ̃] *f* contradiction
contradictoire [kɔ̃tradiktwar] *adj* contradictory
contraindre [kɔ̃trẽdr] §15 *tr* to compel, force, constrain; to restrain, to curb || *ref* to restrain oneself
con·traint [kɔ̃trẽ] -trainte [trẽt] *adj* constrained, forced; stiff (*person*) || *f* constraint; restraint; exigencies (*e.g., of the rhyme*)
contraire [kɔ̃trɛr] *adj* contrary; opposite (*e.g., direction*); injurious (*e.g., to health*) || *m* contrary, opposite; antonym; au contraire on the contrary
contrairement [kɔ̃trɛrmã] *adv* contrary
contrarier [kɔ̃trarje] *tr* to thwart; to vex, annoy; to contrast (*e.g., colors*)
contrariété [kɔ̃trarjete] *f* vexation, annoyance; clashing (*e.g., of colors*)
contraste [kɔ̃trast] *m* contrast
contraster [kɔ̃traste] *tr* & *intr* to contrast
contrat [kɔ̃tra] *m* contract
contravention [kɔ̃travãsjɔ̃] *f* infraction; dresser une contravention to write out a (traffic) ticket; recevoir une contravention to get a ticket
contre [kɔ̃tr] *m* opposite, con; (cards) double; par contre on the contrary || *adv* against; nearby; contre à contre alongside || *prep* against; contrary to; to, e.g., dix contre un ten to one; for, e.g., échanger contre to exchange for; e.g., remède contre la toux remedy for a cough; (sports) versus; contre remboursement (com) collect on delivery
contre-allée [kɔ̃trale] *f* (*pl* -allées) parallel walk

contre-amiral [kɔ̃tramiral] *m* (*pl* -amiraux [amiro]) rear admiral
contre-appel [kɔ̃trapɛl] *m* (*pl* -appels) second roll call; double-check
contre-attaque [kɔ̃tratak] *f* (*pl* -attaques) counterattack
contre-attaquer [kɔ̃tratake] *tr* to counterattack
contrebalancer [kɔ̃trəbalãse] §51 *tr* to counterbalance
contrebande [kɔ̃trəbãd] *f* contraband; smuggling; faire la contrebande to smuggle
contreban·dier [kɔ̃trəbãdje] -dière [djɛr] *adj* smuggled, contraband || *mf* smuggler
contrebas [kɔ̃trəba]—en contrebas downwards
contrebasse [kɔ̃trəbas] *f* contrabass
contre-biais [kɔ̃trəbjɛ]—à contre-biais the wrong way, against the grain
contre-boutant [kɔ̃trəbutã] *m* (*pl* -boutants) shore
contrecarrer [kɔ̃trəkare] *tr* to stymie, to thwart
contre-chant [kɔ̃trəʃã] *m* (*pl* -chants) counter melody
contrecœur [kɔ̃trəkœr] *m* smoke shelf; à contrecœur unwillingly
contrecoup [kɔ̃trəku] *m* rebound, recoil, backlash; repercussion
contre-courant [kɔ̃trəkurã] *m* (*pl* -courants) countercurrent; à contre-courant upstream; behind the times
contredire [kɔ̃trədir] §40 *tr* to contradict || *ref* to contradict oneself
contrée [kɔ̃tre] *f* region, countryside
contre-écrou [kɔ̃trekru] *m* (*pl* -écrous) lock nut
contre-espion [kɔ̃trɛspjɔ̃] *m* (*pl* -espions) counterspy
contre-espionnage [kɔ̃trɛspjɔnaʒ] *m* (*pl* -espionnages) counterespionage
contrefaçon [kɔ̃trəfasɔ̃] *f* infringement (*of patent or copyright*); forgery; counterfeit; plagiarism
contrefacteur [kɔ̃trəfaktœr] *m* forger; counterfeiter; plagiarist
contrefaction [kɔ̃trəfaksjɔ̃] *f* forgery; counterfeiting
contrefaire [kɔ̃trəfɛr] §29 *tr* to forge; to counterfeit; to imitate, to mimic; to disguise
contre·fait [kɔ̃trəfɛ] -faite [fɛt] *adj* counterfeit; deformed
contre-fenêtre [kɔ̃trəfnɛtr] *f* (*pl* -fenêtres) inner sash; storm window
contre-feu [kɔ̃trəfø] *m* (*pl* -feux) backfire (*in fire fighting*)
contreficher [kɔ̃trəfiʃe] *ref* (slang) to not give a rap
contre-fil [kɔ̃trəfil] *m* (*pl* -fils) opposite direction, wrong way; à contre-fil upstream; against the grain
contre-filet [kɔ̃trəfilɛ] *m* short loin (*club and porterhouse steaks*)
contrefort [kɔ̃trəfɔr] *m* buttress, abutment; foothills
contre-haut [kɔ̃trəo]—en contre-haut on a higher level; from top to bottom
contre-interrogatoire [kɔ̃trẽtɛrɔgatwar] *m* cross-examination

contre-interroger [kɔ̃trɛ̃tɛrɔʒe] §38 *tr* to cross-examine
contre-jour [kɔ̃traʒur] *m invar* backlighting; **à contre-jour** against the light
contremaî·tre [kɔ̃trəmɛtr] **-tresse** [trɛs] *mf* overseer ‖ *m* foreman; (naut) (hist) boatswain's mate; (nav) petty officer ‖ *f* forewoman
contremander [kɔ̃trəmɑ̃de] *tr* to countermand; to call off
contremarche [kɔ̃trəmarʃ] *f* countermarch; riser (*of stair step*)
contremarque [kɔ̃trəmark] *f* countersign; pass-out check
contremarquer [kɔ̃trəmarke] *tr* to countersign
contre-mesure [kɔ̃trəmzyr] *f* (*pl* **-mesures**) countermeasure
contre-offensive [kɔ̃trɔfɑ̃siv] *f* (*pl* **-offensives**) counteroffensive
contrepartie [kɔ̃trəparti] *f* counterpart; (bk) duplicate entry; **en contrepartie** as against this
contre-pas [kɔ̃trəpɑ] *m invar* half step (*taken in order to get in step*)
contre-pente [kɔ̃trəpɑ̃t] *f* (*pl* **-pentes**) reverse slope
contre-performance [kɔ̃trəpɛrfɔrmɑ̃s] *f* (*pl* **-performances**) unexpected defeat
contrepèterie [kɔ̃trəpɛtri] *f* spoonerism
contre-pied [kɔ̃trəpje] *m* (*pl* **-pieds**) backtrack; opposite opinion; **à contre-pied** off balance
contre-plaqué [kɔ̃trəplake] *m* (*pl* **-plaqués**) plywood
contre-plaquer [kɔ̃trəplake] *tr* to laminate
contrepoids [kɔ̃trəpwa] *m invar* counterweight, counterbalance
contre-poil [kɔ̃trəpwal] *m* wrong way (*e.g., of fur*); **à contre-poil** the wrong way; at the wrong end
contrepoint [kɔ̃trəpwɛ̃] *m* counterpoint
contre-pointe [kɔ̃trəpwɛ̃t] *f* (*pl* **-pointes**) false edge (*of sword*); tailstock (*of lathe*)
contre-pointer [kɔ̃trəpwɛ̃te] *tr* to quilt
contrepoison [kɔ̃trəpwazɔ̃] *m* antidote
contrer [kɔ̃tre] *tr & intr* (cards) to double; (coll) to counter
contreseing [kɔ̃trəsɛ̃] *m* countersignature
contresens [kɔ̃trəsɑ̃s] *m invar* misinterpretation; mistranslation; wrong way; **à contresens** in the wrong sense; in the wrong direction
contresigner [kɔ̃trəsiɲe] *tr* to countersign
contretemps [kɔ̃trətɑ̃] *m*—**à contretemps** at the wrong moment; syncopated
contre-torpilleur [kɔ̃trətɔrpijœr] *m* (*pl* **-torpilleurs**) (nav) torpedo-boat destroyer
contreve·nant [kɔ̃trəvnɑ̃] **-nante** [nɑ̃t] *mf* lawbreaker, delinquent
contrevenir [kɔ̃trəvnir] §72 *intr* (with *dat*) to contravene, to break (*a law*)
contrevent [kɔ̃trəvɑ̃] *m* shutter, window shutter
contre-voie [kɔ̃trəvwa] *f* (*pl* **-voies**)

parallel route; **à contre-voie** in reverse (*of the usual direction*); on the side opposite the platform
contribuable [kɔ̃tribɥabl] *adj* taxpaying ‖ *mf* taxpayer
contribuer [kɔ̃tribɥe] *intr* to contribute
contribution [kɔ̃tribysjɔ̃] *f* contribution; tax
contrister [kɔ̃triste] *tr* to sadden
con·trit [kɔ̃tri] **-trite** [trit] *adj* contrite
contrôlable [kɔ̃trolabl] *adj* verifiable
contrôle [kɔ̃trol] *m* inspection, verification, check; supervision, observation; auditing; inspection booth; ticket window; (mil) muster roll; **contrôle des naissances** birth control; **contrôle de soi** self-control; **contrôle par sondage** spot check
contrôler [kɔ̃trole] *tr* to inspect, verify, check; to supervise, to put under observation; to audit; to criticize ‖ *ref* to control oneself
contrô·leur [kɔ̃trolœr] **-leuse** [løz] *mf* inspector, checker; supervisor, observer; auditor, comptroller; conductor, ticket collector ‖ *m* gauge; **contrôleur de vitesse** speedometer; **contrôleur de vol** flight indicator
controversable [kɔ̃trɔvɛrsabl] *adj* controversial
controverse [kɔ̃trɔvɛrs] *f* controversy
controverser [kɔ̃trɔvɛrse] *tr* to controvert
contumace [kɔ̃tymas] *f* contempt of court
con·tus [kɔ̃ty] **-tuse** [tyz] *adj* bruised
contusion [kɔ̃tyzjɔ̃] *f* contusion, bruise
contusionner [kɔ̃tyzjɔne] *tr* to bruise
convain·cant [kɔ̃vɛ̃kɑ̃] **-cante** [kɑ̃t] *adj* convincing
convaincre [kɔ̃vɛ̃kr] §70 *tr* to convince; to convict ‖ *ref* to be satisfied
convain·cu **-cue** [kɔ̃vɛ̃ky] *adj* convinced, dyed-in-the-wool; convicted
convalescence [kɔ̃valesɑ̃s] *f* convalescence
convales·cent [kɔ̃valesɑ̃] **convales·cente** [kɔ̃valesɑ̃t] *adj & mf* convalescent
convenable [kɔ̃vnabl] *adj* suitable, proper; opportune (*moment*)
convenance [kɔ̃vnɑ̃s] *f* suitability, propriety; conformity; **convenances** conventions
convenir [kɔ̃vnir] §72 *intr* to agree; (with *dat*) to fit, suit; **convenir de** to admit, to admit to, to admit the truth of; to agree on ‖ *ref* to be satisfied with one another ‖ *impers*—**il convient** it is fitting, it is appropriate
convention [kɔ̃vɑ̃sjɔ̃] *f* convention
convention·nel **-nelle** [kɔ̃vɑ̃sjɔnɛl] *adj* conventional
conve·nu **-nue** [kɔ̃vny] *adj* settled; stipulated (*price*); appointed (*time, place*); trite, stereotyped (*language*)
converger [kɔ̃vɛrʒe] §38 *intr* to converge
conversation [kɔ̃vɛrsasjɔ̃] *f* conversation
converser [kɔ̃vɛrse] *intr* to converse
conversion [kɔ̃vɛrsjɔ̃] *f* conversion; turning

conver·ti -tie [kɔ̃vɛrti] *adj* converted || *mf* convert
convertible [kɔ̃vɛrtibl] *adj* convertible
convertir [kɔ̃vɛrtir] *tr* to convert || *ref* to convert, to be converted; to change one's mind
convertissable [kɔ̃vɛrtisabl] *adj* convertible
convertisseur [kɔ̃vɛrtisœr] *m* converter; (elec) converter
convexe [kɔ̃vɛks] *adj* convex
conviction [kɔ̃viksjɔ̃] *f* conviction
convier [kɔ̃vje] *tr* to invite
convive [kɔ̃viv] *mf* dinner guest; table companion
convocation [kɔ̃vɔkasjɔ̃] *f* convocation; summoning
convoi [kɔ̃vwa] *m* convoy; funeral pro cession
convoiter [kɔ̃vwate] *tr* to covet
convoi·teur [kɔ̃vwatœr] **-teuse** [tøz] *adj* covetous || *mf* covetous person
convoitise [kɔ̃vwatiz] *f* covetousness, cupidity
convoquer [kɔ̃vɔke] *tr* to convoke; to summon
convoyer [kɔ̃vwaje] §47 *tr* to convoy
convoyeur [kɔ̃vwajœr] *adj* convoying || *m* (mach) conveyor; (nav) escort
convulser [kɔ̃vylse] *tr* to convulse
convulsion [kɔ̃vylsjɔ̃] *f* convulsion
convulsionner [kɔ̃vylsjɔne] *tr* to convulse
coordon·né -née [kɔɔrdɔne] *adj & f* coordinate
coordonner [kɔɔrdɔne] *tr* to coordinate
co·pain [kɔpɛ̃] **-pine** [pin] *mf* (coll) pal, chum
co·peau [kɔpo] *m* (pl **-peaux**) chip, shaving
copie [kɔpi] *f* copy; exercise, composition (*at school*); **pour copie conforme** true copy
copier [kɔpje] *tr & intr* to copy
co·pieux [kɔpjø] **-pieuse** [pjøz] *adj* copious
copilote [kɔpilɔt] *m* copilot
copiste [kɔpist] *mf* copyist; copier
coposséder [kɔpɔsede] §10 *tr* to own jointly
copropriété [kɔprɔprijete] *f* joint ownership
copula·tif [kɔpylatif] **-tive** [tiv] *adj* (gram) coordinating
copulation [kɔpylɑsjɔ̃] *f* copulation
copule [kɔpyl] *f* (gram) copula
coq [kɔk] *adj* bantam || *m* cock rooster; (naut) cook
coq-à-l'âne [kɔkalɑn] *m invar* cock-and-bull story
coque [kɔk] *f* shell; cocoon; hull; **coque de noix** coconut
coquelicot [kɔkliko] *m* poppy
coqueluche [kɔklyʃ] *f* whooping cough; (coll) rage, vogue
coquemar [kɔkmar] *m* teakettle
coquerie [kɔkri] *f* (naut) galley
coqueriquer [kɔkrike] *intr* to crow
co·quet [kɔkɛ] **-quette** [kɛt] *adj* coquettish; stylish; considerable (*sum*)
coqueter [kɔkte] §34 *intr* to flirt
coquetier [kɔkətje] *m* eggcup; egg man
coquetterie [kɔkɛtri] *f* coquetry

coquillage [kɔkijaʒ] *m* shellfish; shell
coquille [kɔkij] *f* shell; typographical error (*of transposed letters*); pat (*of butter*); **coquille de noix** nutshell; **coquille Saint-Jacques** scallop
co·quin [kɔkɛ̃] **-quine** [kin] *adj* deceitful; roguish || *mf* scoundrel; rogue
cor [kɔr] *m* horn; corn (*on foot*); prong (*of antler*); horn player; **à cor et à cri** with hue and cry; **cor anglais** English horn; **cor de chasse** hunting horn; **cor d'harmonie** French horn
co·rail [kɔraj] *m* (pl **-raux** [ro]) coral
cor·beau [kɔrbo] *m* (pl **-beaux**) crow, raven
corbeille [kɔrbɛj] *f* basket; flower bed; (theat) dress circle; **corbeille à papier** wastebasket; **corbeille de mariage** wedding present
corbillard [kɔrbijar] *m* hearse
corbillon [kɔrbijɔ̃] *m* small basket; word game
cordage [kɔrdaʒ] *m* cordage, rope; (naut) rigging
corde [kɔrd] *f* rope, cord; tightrope; inside track; (geom) chord; **corde à** or **de boyau** catgut (*for, e.g., violin*); **corde à linge** wash line; **corde à nœuds** knotted rope; **cordes vocales** vocal cords; **être sur la corde raide** to be out on a limb; **les cordes** (mus) the strings; **toucher la corde sensible** to touch a sympathetic chord; **usé jusqu'à la corde** threadbare
cor·dé -dée [kɔrde] *adj* heart-shaped || *f* cord (*of wood*); roped party (*of mountain climbers*)
cor·deau [kɔrdo] *m* (pl **-deaux**) tracing line; tracing thread; mine fuse; **tiré au cordeau** in a straight line
cordelier [kɔrdəlje] *m* Franciscan friar
corder [kɔrde] *tr* to twist; to string (*a tennis racket*)
cor·dial -diale [kɔrdjal] *adj & m* (pl **-diaux** [djo]) cordial
cordialité [kɔrdjalite] *f* cordiality
cordier [kɔrdje] *m* ropemaker; tailpiece (*of violin*)
cordon [kɔrdɔ̃] *m* cordon; cord; latchstring; **cordon de sonnette** bellpull; **cordon de soulier** shoestring
cordon-bleu [kɔrdɔ̃blø] *m* (pl **cordons-bleus**) cordon bleu
cordonnerie [kɔrdɔnri] *f* shoemaking; shoe repairing; shoe store; shoemaker's
cordon·nier [kɔrdɔnje] **cordon·nière** [kɔrdɔnjer] *mf* shoemaker
Corée [kɔre] *f* Korea; **la Corée** Korea
coréen [kɔreɛ̃] **coréenne** [kɔreɛn] *adj* Korean || *m* Korean (*language*) || (*cap*) *mf* Korean (*person*)
coriace [kɔrjas] *adj* tough, leathery; (coll) stubborn
coricide [kɔrisid] *m* corn remover
cormoran [kɔrmɔrɑ̃] *m* cormorant
cornac [kɔrnak] *m* mahout
cor·nard [kɔrnar] **-narde** [nard] *adj* horned; (slang) cuckold; (*of horse*) wheezing || *m* (slang) cuckold
corne [kɔrn] *f* horn; dog-ear (*of page*); hoof; shoehorn; **corne d'abondance**

horn of plenty; **faire les cornes à** (coll) to make a face at

cor·né ·née [kɔrne] *adj* horny ‖ *f* cornea

corneille [kɔrnɛj] *f* crow, rook; **corneille d'église** jackdaw

cornemuse [kɔrnəmyz] *f* bagpipe

cornemuseur [kɔrnəmyzœr] *m* bagpiper

corner [kɔrne] *tr* to dog-ear; to give (*s.o.*) the horn; (coll) to trumpet (*news*) about ‖ *intr* to blow the horn, to honk; to ring (*said of ears*); (mus) to blow a horn; **cornez!** sound your horn!

cornet [kɔrnɛ] *m* cornet; horn; dicebox; cornetist; mouthpiece (*of microphone*); receiver (*of telephone*); **cornet acoustique** ear trumpet; **cornet à pistons** cornet; **cornet de glace** ice-cream cone

cornette [kɔrnɛt] *m* (mil) cornet ‖ *f* (*headdress*) cornet

cornettiste [kɔrnetist] *mf* cornetist

corniche [kɔrniʃ] *f* cornice

cornichon [kɔrniʃɔ̃] *m* pickle, gherkin; (*fool*) (coll) dope, drip

cor·nier [kɔrnje] **-nière** [njɛr] *adj* corner ‖ *f* valley (*joining roofs*); angle iron

corniste [kɔrnist] *mf* horn player

Cornouailles [kɔrnwaj] *f* Cornwall

cornouiller [kɔrnuje] *m* dogwood

cor·nu -nue [kɔrny] *adj* horned; preposterous (*ideas*) ‖ *f* (chem) retort

corollaire [kɔrɔllɛr] *m* corollary

coronaire [kɔrɔnɛr] *adj* coronary

coroner [kɔrɔnœr] *m* coroner

corporation [kɔrpɔrasjɔ̃] *f* association, guild

corpo·rel -relle [kɔrpɔrɛl] *adj* corporal, bodily

corps [kɔr] *m* body; corps; **à corps perdu** without thinking; **à mon** (**ton,** etc.) **corps défendant** in self-defense; reluctantly; **corps à corps** hand-to-hand; in a clinch; **corps céleste** heavenly body; **corps composé** (chem) compound; **corps de garde** guardhouse, guardroom; **corps de logis** main part of the building; **corps du délit** corpus delicti; **corps enseignant** faculty; **corps simple** (chem) simple substance; **prendre corps** to take shape; **saisir au corps** (law) to arrest

corps-à-corps [kɔrakɔr] *m* hand-to-hand combat; (boxing) infighting

corpulence [kɔrpylɑ̃s] *f* corpulence

corpuscule [kɔrpyskyl] *m* (phys) corpuscle

corral [kɔral] *m* corral

cor·rect -recte [kɔrrɛkt] *adj* correct

correc·teur [kɔrrɛktœr] **-trice** [tris] *mf* corrector; proofreader

correc·tif [kɔrrɛktif] **-tive** [tiv] *adj* & *m* corrective

correction [kɔrrɛksjɔ̃] *f* correction; correctness; proofreading

corrélation [kɔrrelasjɔ̃] *f* correlation

correspondance [kɔrɛspɔ̃dɑ̃s] *f* correspondence; transfer, connection

correspon·dant [kɔrɛspɔ̃dɑ̃] **-dante** [dɑ̃t] *adj* corresponding, correspondent ‖ *mf* correspondent; party (*per-*

son who gets a telephone call)

correspondre [kɔrɛspɔ̃dr] *intr* to correspond; **correspondre à** to correspond to, to correlate with; **correspondre avec** to correspond with (*a letter writer*); to connect with (*e.g., a train*)

corridor [kɔridɔr] *m* corridor

corriger [kɔriʒe] §38 *tr* to correct; to proofread

corroborer [kɔrrɔbɔre] *tr* to corroborate

corroder [kɔrrɔde] *tr* & *ref* to corrode; to erode

corrompre [kɔrɔ̃pr] (3d *sg pres ind* **corrompt**) *tr* to corrupt; to rot; to bribe; to seduce; to spoil

corro·sif [kɔrrozif] **-sive** [ziv] *adj* & *m* corrosive

corrosion [kɔrrosjɔ̃] *f* corrosion; erosion

corroyer [kɔrwaje] §47 *tr* to weld; to plane (*wood*); to prepare (*leather*)

corruption [kɔrrypsjɔ̃] *f* corruption; bribery; seduction

corsage [kɔrsaʒ] *m* blouse, corsage

corsaire [kɔrsɛr] *m* corsair; **corsaire de finance** ruthless businessman, robber baron

corse [kɔrs] *adj* Corsican ‖ *m* Corsican (*language*) ‖ (*cap*) *f* Corsica; **la Corse** Corsica ‖ (*cap*) *mf* Corsican (*person*)

cor·sé -sée [kɔrse] *adj* full-bodied, heavy; spicy, racy

corser [kɔrse] *tr* to spike, to give body to (*wine*); to spice up (*a story*) ‖ *ref* to become serious; **ça se corse** the plot thickens

corset [kɔrsɛ] *m* corset

cortège [kɔrtɛʒ] *m* cortege; parade; **cortège funèbre** funeral procession

cortisone [kɔrtizɔn] *f* cortisone

corvée [kɔrve] *f* chore; forced labor; work party

coryphée [kɔrife] *m* coryphée; (fig) leader

cosaque [kɔzak] *adj* Cossack ‖ (*cap*) *mf* Cossack

cosmétique [kɔsmetik] *adj* cosmetic ‖ *m* cosmetic; hair set, hair spray ‖ *f* beauty culture

cosmique [kɔsmik] *adj* cosmic

cosmonaute [kɔsmɔnot] *mf* cosmonaut

cosmopolite [kɔsmɔpɔlit] *adj* & *mf* cosmopolitan

cosmos [kɔsmos], [kɔsmɔs] *m* cosmos; outer space

cosse [kɔs] *f* pod; **avoir la cosse** (slang) to be lazy

cos·su -sue [kɔsy] *adj* rich; well-to-do

cos·taud [kɔsto] **-taude** [tod] *adj* (slang) husky, strapping ‖ *m* (slang) muscleman

costume [kɔstym] *m* costume; suit; **costume sur mesure** custom-made or tailor-made suit; **costume tailleur** lady's tailor-made suit

costumer [kɔstyme] *tr* & *ref* to dress up (*for a fancy-dress ball*); **se costumer en** to come dressed as a

costu·mier [kɔstymje] **-mière** [mjɛr] *mf* costumer

cote [kɔt] *f* assessment, quota; identification mark, letter, or number; call number (*of book*); altitude (*above sea level*); bench mark; book value (*of, e.g., used cars*); racing odds; (telv) rating; **avoir la cote** (coll) to be highly thought of; **cote d'alerte** danger point; **cote d'amour** moral qualifications; **cote de la Bourse** stock-market quotations; **cote mal taillée** rough compromise

côte [kot] *f* rib; chop; coast; slope; **à côtes** ribbed, corded; **aller or se mettre à la côte, faire côte** to run aground; **avoir les côtes en long** (coll) to feel lazy; **côte à côte** side by side; **côte d'Azur** French Riviera; **côtes découvertes, plates côtes** spareribs; **en côte** uphill; **être à la côte** to be broke; **faire côte** to run aground

co·té -tée [kɔte] *adj* listed (*on the stock market*); (fig) esteemed

côté [kote] *m* side; **à côté** in the next room; near; **à côté de** beside; **côté cour** (theat) stage right; **côté jardin** (theat) stage left; **d'à côté** next-door; **de côté** sideways; sidelong; aside; **de mon côté** for my part; **donner, passer,** or **toucher à côté** to miss the mark; **du côté de** in the direction of, toward; on the side of; **d'un côté . . . de l'autre côté** or **d'un autre côté** on the one hand . . . on the other hand; **répondre à côté** to miss the point

co·teau [kɔto] *m* (*pl* **-teaux**) knoll; slope

Côte-de-l'Or [kotdəlɔr] *f* Gold Coast

côte·lé -lée [kotle] *adj* ribbed, corded

côtelette [kotlɛt] *f* cutlet, chop; **côtelettes découvertes** spareribs

coter [kɔte] *tr* to assess; to mark; to number; to esteem; (com) to quote, to give a quotation on; (geog) to mark the elevations on

coterie [kɔtri] *f* coterie, clique

cothurne [kɔtyrn] *m* buskin

cô·tier [kotje] **-tière** [tjɛr] *adj* coastal

cotir [kɔtir] *tr* to bruise (*fruit*)

cotisation [kɔtizɑsjɔ̃] *f* dues; assessment

cotiser [kɔtize] *tr* to assess (*each member of a group*) ‖ *intr* to pay one's dues ‖ *ref* to club together

coton [kɔtɔ̃] *m* cotton; **c'est coton** (slang) it's difficult; **coton de verre** glass wool; **coton hydrophile** absorbent cotton; cotton batting; **élever dans le coton** to coddle; **filer un mauvais coton** (coll) to be in a bad way

cotonnade [kɔtɔnad] *f* cotton cloth

cotonner [kɔtɔne] *tr* to pad or stuff with cotton ‖ *ref* to become fluffy; to become spongy or mealy

cotonnerie [kɔtɔnri] *f* cotton field; cotton mill

coton·neux [kɔtɔnø] **coton·neuse** [kɔtɔnøz] *adj* cottony; spongy, mealy

coton·nier [kɔtɔnje] **-nière** [njɛr] *adj* cotton ‖ *mf* cotton picker ‖ *m* cotton plant

côtoyer [kotwaje] §47 *tr* to skirt (*the*

edge); to hug (*the shore*); to border on (*the truth, the ridiculous, etc.*)

cotre [kɔtr] *m* (naut) cutter

cotte [kɔt] *f* petticoat; peasant skirt; overalls; **cotte de mailles** coat of mail

cou [ku] *m* neck; **sauter au cou de** to throw one's arms around

couard [kwar] **couarde** [kward] *adj* *mf* coward

couardise [kwardiz] *f* cowardice

couchage [kuʃaʒ] *m* bedding; bed for the night

cou·chant [kuʃɑ̃] **-chante** [ʃɑ̃t] *adj* setting ‖ *m* west; decline, old age

couche [kuʃ] *f* layer, stratum; coat (*of paint*); diaper, (hort) hotbed; **couche de fond** primer, prime coat; **couches** strata; childbirth, e.g., **une femme en couches** a woman in childbirth; **fausse couche** miscarriage

coucher [kuʃe] *m* setting (*of sun*); going to bed; **coucher du soleil** sunset; **le coucher et la nourriture** room and board ‖ *tr* to put to bed; to put down, lay down; to bend down, flatten; to mention (*in one's will*); **coucher en joue** to aim at; **coucher par écrit** to set down in writing ‖ *intr* to spend the night; (naut) to heel over ‖ *ref* to go to bed, to lie down; to set (*said of sun*); to bend; **allez vous coucher!** (coll) go to blazes!

couchette [kuʃɛt] *f* berth; crib

couci-couça [kusikusa] or **couci-couci** [kusikusi] *adv* so-so

coucou [kuku] *m* cuckoo; cuckoo clock; (coll) marsh marigold

coude [kud] *m* elbow; angle, bend, turn; **coude à coude** shoulder to shoulder; **jouer des coudes à travers** to elbow one's way through (*a crowd*)

coudée [kude] *f* cubit; **avoir ses coudées franches** to have a free hand; to have elbowroom

cou-de-pied [kudpje] *m* (*pl* **cous-de-pied**) instep

couder [kude] *tr* to bend like an elbow

coudoiement [kudwamɑ̃] *m* elbowing

coudoyer [kudwaje] §47 *tr* to elbow, to jostle; to rub shoulders with

coudraie [kudrɛ] *f* hazel grove

coudre [kudr] §13 *tr & intr* to sew

coudrier [kudrije] *m* hazel tree

couenne [kwan] *f* pigskin; rind, crackling; mole, birthmark

couette [kwɛt] *f* feather bed; (little) tail; (mach) bearing; **couette de lapin** scut; **couettes** (naut) slip

cougouar or **couguar** [kugwar] *m* cougar

couiner [kwine] *intr* to send Morse code; (coll) to squeak (*said of animal*)

coulage [kulaʒ] *m* flow; leakage; casting (*of metal*); pouring (*of concrete*); (naut) scuttling; (coll) wasting

cou·lant [kulɑ̃] **-lante** [lɑ̃t] *adj* flowing, running; accommodating (*person*) ‖ *m* sliding ring; (bot) runner

coule [kul] *f* cowl; **être à la coule** (slang) to know the ropes

cou·lé -lée [kule] *adj* cast; sunken;

(coll) sunk ‖ *m* (mus) slur ‖ *f* casting; run (*of wild beasts*); **coulée volcanique** outflow of lava

couler [kule] *tr* to pour; to cast (*e.g., a statue*); to scuttle; to pass (*e.g., many happy hours*); (mus) to slur ‖ *intr* to flow; to run; to leak; to sink; to slip (away) ‖ *ref* to slip, slide; (coll) to be done for, to be sunk; **se la couler douce** (coll) to take it easy

couleur [kulœr] *f* color; policy (*of newspaper*); (cards) suit; **de couleur** colored; **les trois couleurs** the tricolor; **sous couleur de** with the pretext of, with a show of

couleuvre [kulœvr] *f* snake; **avaler des couleuvres** (coll) to swallow insults; (coll) to be gullible; **couleuvre à collier** grass snake

coulis [kuli] *m*—**coulis de tomates** tomato sauce

coulisse [kulis] *f* groove; slide (*of trombone*); (com) curb exchange; (pol) lobby; **à coulisse** sliding; **coulisses** (theat) wings; (theat) backstage; **dans les coulisses** behind the scenes, out of sight; **travailler dans les coulisses** to pull strings

coulis-seau [kuliso] *m* (*pl* -**seaux**) slide, runner

couloir [kulwar] *m* corridor; hallway; lobby

couloire [kulwar] *f* strainer

coup [ku] *m* blow; stroke; blast (*of whistle*); jolt; **à coup de** with the aid of; **à coup sûr** certainly; **après coup** when it is too late; **à tout coup** each time; **boire à petits coups** to sip; **coup de bélier** water hammer (*in pipe*); **coup de coude** nudge; **coup de dés** throw of the dice; risky business; **coup de fer** pressing, ironing; **coup de feu, coup de fusil** shot, gunshot; **coup de fion** (slang) finishing touch; **coup de foudre** thunderbolt; love at first sight; bolt from the blue; **coup de fouet** whiplash; stimulus; **coup de froid** cold snap; **coup de grâce** last straw; deathblow; **coup de Jarnac** [ʒarnak] stab in the back; **coup de patte** expert stroke (*e.g., of the brush*); (coll) dig, insult; **coup de pied** kick; **coup d'épingle** pinprick; **coup de poing** punch; **coup de sang** (pathol) stroke; **coup de semonce** warning shot; **coup de sifflet** whistle, toot; **coup de soleil** sunburn; (coll) sunstroke; **coup de téléphone** telephone call; **coup de tête** butt; sudden impulse; **coup de théâtre** dramatic turn of events; **coup de tonnerre** thunderclap; **coup d'œil** glance, look; **coup manqué, coup raté** miss; **coup monté** put-up job, frame-up; **coups et blessures** assault and battery; **coup sur coup** one right after the other; **donner un coup de main (à)** to lend a helping hand (to); **encore un coup** once again; **en venir aux coups** to come to blows; **être dans le coup** (coll) to be in on it; **faire coup double** to kill two birds with one stone; **faire les quatre coups** (coll) to

live it up, to dissipate; **faire un coup de main** to go on a raid; **manquer son coup** to miss one's chance; **se faire donner un coup de piston** (coll) to pull wires, to use influence; **sous le coup de** under the (immediate) influence of; **sur le coup** on the spot, outright; **tout à coup** suddenly; **tout d'un coup** at one shot, at once

coupable [kupabl] *adj* guilty ‖ *mf* culprit

cou·pant [kupã] -**pante** [pãt] *adj* cutting, sharp ‖ *m* (cutting) edge

coup-de-poing [kudpwɛ̃] *m* (*pl* **coups-de-poing**) brass knuckles

coupe [kup] *f* champagne glass; loving cup, trophy; cup competition; cutting; cross section; wood acreage to be cut; cut (*of cloth; of clothes; of playing cards*); division (*of verse*); **coupe claire** cutover forest; **coupe de cheveux** haircut; **coupe sombre** harvested forest; **être sous la coupe de qn** (coll) to be under s.o.'s thumb; **il y a loin de la coupe aux lèvres** there is many a slip between the cup and the lip; **mettre en coupe réglée** (coll) to fleece

cou·pé -pée [kupe] *adj* cut, cut off; interrupted (*sleep*); diluted (*wine*) ‖ *m* coupé ‖ *f* gangway

coupe-circuit [kupsirkɥi] *m invar* (elec) fuse

coupe-coupe [kupkup] *m invar* machete

coupe-feu [kupfø] *m invar* firebreak

coupe-fil [kupfil] *m invar* wire cutter

coupe-fil [kupfil] *m invar* police pass (*for emergency vehicles*)

coupe-gorge [kupgɔrʒ] *m invar* deathtrap, dangerous territory

coupe-jarret [kupʒarɛ] *m* (*pl* -**jarrets**) cutthroat

coupe-ongles [kupɔ̃gl] *m invar* nail clippers

coupe-papier [kuppapje] *m invar* paper knife, letter opener

couper [kupe] *tr* to cut; to cut off; to cut out; to break off, interrupt; to cut, water down; to turn off; to trump; to castrate, geld; **ça te la coupe!** (coll) top that!; **couper la file** (aut) to leave one's lane; **couper la parole à** to interrupt; **couper menu** to mince ‖ *intr* to cut; **couper court à** to cut (*s.o. or s.th.*) short ‖ *ref* to cut oneself; to intersect; (coll) to contradict oneself; (coll) to give oneself away

couperet [kuprɛ] *m* cleaver; guillotine blade

couperose [kuproz] *f* (pathol) acne

cou·peur [kupœr] -**peuse** [pøz] *mf* cutter; **coupeur de bourses** (coll) purse snatcher; **coupeur d'oreilles** (coll) hatchet man, hired thug

couplage [kuplaʒ] *m* (mach) coupling

couple [kupl] *m* couple (*e.g., of friends, cronies, thieves, etc.; man and wife*); pair (*e.g., of pigeons*); (mech) couple, torque; **couple thermo-électrique** thermoelectric couple;

maître couple (naut) midship frame ‖ *f* yoke (*of oxen*); couple; leash

coupler [kuple] *tr* to couple; to pair

coupleur [kuplœr] *m* (mach) coupler

coupole [kupɔl] *f* cupola

coupon [kupɔ̃] *m* coupon; remnant (*of cloth*); theater ticket

coupon-réponse [kupɔ̃repɔ̃s] *m*—**coupon-réponse international** international (postal) reply coupon; **coupon-réponse postal** return-reply post card or letter

coupure [kupyr] *f* cut, incision, slit; cut, deletion; newspaper clipping; small note; interruption, break; drain (*e.g., through a marsh*)

cour [kur] *f* court; courtyard; courtship; **bien en cour** in favor; **cour anglaise** courtyard or court (*of apartment building*); **cour d'appel** appellate court; **cour d'assises** criminal court; **cour de cassation** supreme court of appeals; **cour d'école** school playground; **faire la cour à** to court; **mal en cour** out of favor

courage [kuraʒ] *m* courage;. **reprendre courage** to take heart; **travailler avec courage** to work hard ‖ *interj* buck up!, cheer up!

coura·geux [kuraʒø] **-geuse** [ʒøz] *adj* courageous; hard-working

courailler [kuraje] *intr* to gallivant

couramment [kuramã] *adv* currently; fluently, easily

cou·rant [kurã] **-rante** [rãt] *adj* current; running (*water*); present-day (*language, customs, etc.*) ‖ *m* current; flow; shift (*of opinion, population, etc.*); **courant alternatif** alternating current; **courant continu** direct current; **courant d'air** draft; **Courant du Golfe** Gulf Stream; **dans le courant du mois (de la semaine, etc.)** in the course of the month (of the week, etc.); **être au courant de** to be informed about

courba·tu -tue [kurbaty] *adj* stiff in the joints, aching all over

courbature [kurbatyr] *f* stiffness, aching

courbaturer [kɔrbatyre] *tr* to make stiff; to exhaust (*the body*)

courbe [kurb] *adj* curved ‖ *f* curve; **courbe de niveau** contour line

cour·bé -bée [kurbe] *adj* curved, bent, crooked

courber [kurbe] *tr* to bend, curve ‖ *intr & ref* to bend, curve; to give in

courbure [kurbyr] *f* curve, curvature; **double courbure** S-curve

courette [kuret] *f* small courtyard

cou·reur [kurœr] **-reuse** [røz] *mf* runner; **coureur cycliste** bicycle racer; **coureur de cotillons** (coll) wolf; **coureur de dot** fortune hunter; **coureur de filles** Casanova, Don Juan; **coureur de girls** stage-door Johnny; **coureur de spectacles** playgoer; **coureur de vitesse** sprinter

courge [kurʒ] *f* gourd, squash

courir [kurir] §14 *tr* to run; to run after; to roam; to frequent ‖ *intr* to run; **le bruit court que** rumor has it

that; **par le temps qui court** at the present time

courlis [kurli] *m* curlew

couronne [kurɔn] *f* crown; wreath; coronet; rim (*of atomic structures*)

couronnement [kurɔnmã] *m* crowning; coronation; coping

couronner [kurɔne] *tr* to crown; to top, cap; to reward ‖ *ref* to be crowned; to be covered (*with flowers*)

courrier [kurje] *m* courier; mail; **courrier du cœur** advice to the lovelorn; **courrier mondain** gossip column; **courrier théâtral** theater section

courriériste [kurjerist] *mf* columnist

courroie [kurwa] *f* strap; belt

courroucer [kuruse] §51 *tr* (lit) to anger

courroux [kuru] *m* (lit) wrath, anger

cours [kur] *m* course; current (*of river*); tree-lined walk; rate (*of exchange*); market quotation; style, vogue; **au cours de** in the course of; **avoir cours** to be in circulation; to be legal tender; to have classes; **cours d'eau** stream, river; **cours d'été** or **cours de vacances** summer school; **cours du soir** night school; **de cours** in length (*said of a river*); **de long cours** long-range; **suivre un cours** to take a course (*in school*)

course [kurs] *f* running; race; errand; trip; ride (*e.g., in a taxi*); course, path; privateering; stroke (*of a piston*); **course à pied** foot race; **course attelée** harness race; **course au trot** trotting race; **course aux armements** arms race; **course de chevaux** horse race; **course de côte** hill climb; **course de taureaux** bullfight; **course de vitesse** sprint; **course d'obstacles** steeplechase; **courses sur route** road racing; **de course** at a run; racing (*car; track; crowd*); (mil) on the double; **en pleine course** in full swing; **faire des courses** to go shopping

cour·sier [kursje] **-sière** [sjɛr] *mf* messenger ‖ *m* errand boy; steed

coursive [kursiv] *f* (naut) alleyway, gangway (*connecting staterooms*)

court [kur] **courte** [kurt] *adj* short; brief; concise; choppy (*sea*); thick (*sauce, gravy*); **à court** short; **de court** by surprise; **prendre le plus court** to take a shortcut; **tenir de court** to hold on a short leash ‖ (when standing before noun) *adj* short, brief (*interval, time, life*) ‖ *m* court (*for tennis*) ‖ *court adv* short; **demeurer court** to forget what one wanted to say; **tourner court** to turn sharp; to stop short, to change the subject; **tout court** simply, merely; plain

courtage [kurtaʒ] *m* brokerage; broker's commission

cour·taud [kurto] **-taude** [tod] *adj* stocky, short and stocky

court-circuit [kursirkɥi] *m* (*pl* **courts-circuits**) short circuit

court-circuiter [kursirkɥite] *tr* to short-circuit

courtepointe [kurtəpwɛ̃t] *f* counterpane

cour·tier [kurtje] -**tière** [tjer] *mf* broker; agent; **courtier électoral** canvasser

courtisan [kurtizɑ̃] *m* courtier

courtisane [kurtizan] *f* courtesan

courtiser [kurtize] *tr* to court

cour·tois [kurtwa] -**toise** [twaz] *adj* courteous; courtly

courtoisie [kurtwazi] *f* courtesy

court-vê·tu -**tue** [kurvɛty] *adj* shortskirted

cou·ru -**rue** [kuru] *adj* sought after, popular; **c'est couru** (coll) it's a sure thing

cou·seur [kuzœr] -**seuse** [zøz] *mf* sewer ‖ *f* seamstress; (mach) stitcher

cou·sin [kuzɛ̃] -**sine** [zin] *mf* cousin; **cousin germain** first cousin; **cousins issus de germains** first cousins once removed ‖ *m* mosquito

cousinage [kuzinaʒ] *m* cousinship; (coll) relatives

coussin [kusɛ̃] *m* cushion

coussinet [kusinɛ] *m* little cushion; (mach) bearing

coût [ku] *m* cost; **coût de la vie** cost of living

cou·teau [kuto] *m* (*pl* -**teaux**) knife; **couteau à cran d'arrêt** clasp knife with safety catch; switchblade knife; **couteau à découper** carving knife; **couteau à ressort** switchblade knife; **couteau pliant, couteau de poche** jackknife

coutelas [kutlɑ] *m* cutlass; butcher knife

coutellerie [kutɛlri] *f* cutlery

coûter [kute] *tr* to cost; **coûte que coûte** cost what it may; **il m'en coûte de** + *inf* it's hard for me to + *inf*

coû·teux [kutø] -**teuse** [tøz] *adj* costly, expensive

coutil [kuti] *m* duck (*cloth*); mattress ticking

coutume [kutym] *f* custom; habit; common law; **de coutume** ordinarily

coutu·mier [kutymje] -**mière** [mjɛr] *adj* customary; common (*law*); accustomed ‖ *m* book of common law

couture [kutyr] *f* needlework; sewing; seam; suture; scar; **battre qn à plate couture** (coll) to beat s.o. hollow; **examiner sur toutes les coutures** to examine inside and out or from every angle; **haute couture** fashion designing, haute couture; **sans couture** seamless

couturer [kutyre] *tr* to scar

coutu·rier [kutyrje] -**rière** [rjɛr] *mf* dressmaker ‖ *m* dress designer ‖ *f* seamstress

couvaison [kuvɛzɔ̃] *f* incubation period

couvée [kuve] *f* brood

couvent [kuvɑ̃] *m* convent; monastery; convent school

couver [kuve] *tr* to brood, hatch ‖ *intr* to brood; to smolder

couvercle [kuvɛrkl] *m* cover, lid

cou·vert [kuver] -**verte** [vert] *adj* covered; dressed, clothed; cloudy (*weather*); wooded (*countryside*) ‖ *m* cover; setting (*of table*); service (*fork and spoon*); cover charge; room, lodging;

authority (*given by a superior*); à **couvert** sheltered; **mettre le couvert** to set the table; **sous le couvert de** under cover of; **sous les couverts** under cover (*of trees*) ‖ *f* glaze

couverture [kuvɛrtyr] *f* cover; coverage; covering; wrapper; blanket, bedspread

couveuse [kuvøz] *f* brood hen; incubator

couvre-chef [kuvrəʃɛf] *m* (*pl* -**chefs**) (coll) headgear

couvre-feu [kuvrəfø] *m* (*pl* -**feux**) curfew

couvre-lit [kuvrəli] *m* (*pl* -**lits**) bedspread

couvre-livre [kuvrəlivr] *m* (*pl* -**livres**) dust jacket

couvre-pieds [kuvrəpje] *m invar* bedspread; quilt

couvre-plat [kuvrəpla] *m* (*pl* -**plats**) dish cover

couvre-théière [kuvrətejer] *m* (*pl* -**théières**) tea cozy

couvreur [kuvrœr] *m* roofer

couvrir [kuvrir] §65 *tr* to cover ‖ *ref* to cover; to cover oneself; to get cloudy; to put one's hat on

cow-boy [kaubɔj], [kɔbɔj] *m* (*pl* -**boys**) cowboy

C.P. *abbr* (**case postale**) post-office box

C.R. [seer] *adv* (letterword) (**contre remboursement**) C.O.D.; **envoyez-le-moi C.R.** send it to me C.O.D.

crabe [krɑb], [krab] *m* crab; caterpillar (tractor)

crachat [kraʃa] *m* sputum, spit

cra·ché -**chée** [kraʃe] *adj* (coll) spitting (*image*)

cracher [kraʃe] *tr & intr* to spit

crachin [kraʃɛ̃] *m* light drizzle

crachoir [kraʃwar] *m* spittoon; **tenir le crachoir** (slang) to have the floor, to speak

crachoter [kraʃɔte] *intr* to keep on spitting; to sputter

crack [krak] *m* favorite (*the horse favored to win*); (coll) champion, ace; (coll) crackerjack

cracking [krakiŋ] *m* cracking (*of oil*)

craie [krɛ] *f* chalk; piece of chalk

crailler [kraje] *intr* to caw

craindre [krɛ̃dr] §15 *tr* to fear, to be afraid of, to dread; to respect ‖ *intr* to be afraid

crainte [krɛ̃t] *f* fear, dread; **dans la crainte que** or **de crainte que** for fear that

crain·tif [krɛ̃tif] -**tive** [tiv] *adj* fearful; timid

cramoi·si -**sie** [kramwazi] *adj & m* crimson

crampe [krɑ̃p] *f* cramp (*in a muscle*)

crampon [krɑ̃pɔ̃] *m* clamp; cleat (*on a shoe*); (coll) pest, bore

cramponner [krɑ̃pɔne] *tr* to clamp together; (coll) to pester ‖ *ref* to hold fast, hang on, cling

cran [krɑ̃] *m* notch; cog, catch, tooth; **avoir du cran** (coll) to be game (*for anything*); **baisser un cran** to come down a peg; **être à cran** (coll) to be exasperated, cross

crâne [krɑn] *adj* bold, daring ‖ *m* skull, cranium; **bourrer le crâne à qn** (coll) to hand s.o. a line

crâner [krɑne] *intr* (coll) to swagger

cra·neur [krɑnœr] **-neuse** [nøz] *adj* & *mf* (coll) braggart

crapaud [krapo] *m* toad; baby grand; flaw (*in diamond*); low armchair; (coll) brat; **avaler un crapaud** (coll) to put up with a lot

crapule [krapyl] *f* underworld, scum; bum, punk; **vivre dans la crapule** to live in debauchery

crapu·leux [krapylø] **-leuse** [løz] *adj* debauched, lewd, filthy

craquage [krakaʒ] *m* cracking (*of petroleum*)

craquement [krakmɑ̃] *m* crack, crackle

craquer [krake] *intr* to crack; to burst; (coll) to crash, fail

craqueter [krakte] §34 *intr* to crackle

crash [kraʃ] *m* crash landing

crasse [kras] *adj* gross; crass (*ignorance*) ‖ *f* filth, squalor; avarice; dross; **faire une crasse à qn** (slang) to play a dirty trick on s.o.

cras·seux [krasø] **cras·seuse** [krasøz] *adj* filthy, squalid; (coll) stingy

crassier [krasje] *m* slag heap

cratère [krater] *m* crater; ewer

cravache [kravaʃ] *f* riding whip, horsewhip

cravacher [kravaʃe] *tr* to horsewhip

cravate [kravat] *f* necktie, cravat; scarf; sling (*for unloading goods*); **cravate de chanvre** (coll) noose; **cravate de drapeau** pennant

cravater [kravate] *tr* to tie a necktie on (*s.o.*) ‖ *intr* (slang) to tell a fish story

crawl [krol] *m* crawl (*in swimming*)

crayeux [krejø] **crayeuse** [krejøz] *adj* chalky

crayon [krejɔ̃] *m* pencil; **crayon de pastel** wax crayon; **crayon de rouge à lèvres** lipstick

crayonner [krejɔne] *tr* to crayon, to pencil, to sketch

créance [kreɑ̃s] *f* belief, credence; **créances gelées** frozen assets; **créances véreuses** bad debts

créan·cier [kreɑ̃sje] **-cière** [sjer] *mf* creditor; **créancier hypothécaire** mortgage holder

créa·teur [kreatœr] **-trice** [tris] *adj* creative ‖ *mf* creator; originator

création [kreasjɔ̃] *f* creation

créature [kreatyr] *f* creature

crécelle [kresɛl] *f* rattle; chatterbox; **de crécelle** rasping

crèche [krɛʃ] *f* manger; crèche; day nursery

crédence [kredɑ̃s] *f* buffet, sideboard, credenza

crédibilité [kredibilite] *f* credibility

crédit [kredi] *m* credit; (govt) appropriation

créditer [kredite] *tr* (com) to credit

crédi·teur [kreditœr] **-trice** [tris] *adj* credit (*side, account*) ‖ *mf* creditor

credo [kredo] *m invar* credo, creed

crédule [kredyl] *adj* credulous

créer [kree] *tr* to create

crémaillère [kremajer] *f* pothook; rack; rack rail; **crémaillère et pignon** rack and pinion; **pendre la crémaillère** to have a housewarming

crémation [kremasjɔ̃] *f* cremation

crématoire [krematwar] *adj* & *m* crematory

crème [krɛm] *f* cream; **crème chantilly** whipped cream; **crème de démaquillage** cleansing cream; **crème fouettée** whipped cream; **crème glacée** ice cream

crémer [kreme] §10 *intr* to cream

crémerie [kremri] *f* dairy; milkhouse (*on a farm*); dairy luncheonette

cré·meux [kremø] **-meuse** [møz] *adj* creamy

crémier [kremje] *m* dairyman

crémière [kremjer] *f* dairymaid; cream pitcher

crémone [kremɔn] *f* casement bolt

cré·neau [kreno] *m* (*pl* **-neaux**) crenel; loophole; **créneaux** battlements

créneler [krenle] §34 *tr* to crenelate; to tooth (*a wheel*); to mill (*a coin*)

créole [kreɔl] *adj* Creole ‖ *m* Creole (*language*) ‖ *mf* Creole (*person*)

crêpe [krep] *m* crepe ‖ *f* pancake

crépitation [krepitasjɔ̃] *f* crackle

crépitement [krepitmɑ̃] *m* crackling

crépiter [krepite] *intr* to crackle

cré·pu **-pue** [krepy] *adj* crimped, frizzly, crinkled

crépuscule [krepyskyl] *m* twilight

cresson [kresɔ̃] *m* cress; **cresson de fontaine** watercress

crête [kret] *f* crest; **crête de coq** cockscomb

Crète [kret] *f* Crete; **la Crète** Crete

crête-de-coq [kretdəkɔk] *f* (*pl* **crêtes-de-coq**) (bot) cockscomb

cré·tin [kretɛ̃] **-tine** [tin] *mf* cretin; (coll) jackass, fathead

cré·tois [kretwa] **-toise** [twaz] *adj* Cretan ‖ (*cap*) *mf* Cretan

creuser [krøze] *tr* to dig, excavate; to hollow out; to furrow; to go into thoroughly ‖ *ref*—**se creuser la tête** (coll) to rack one's brains

creuset [krøze] *m* crucible

creux [krø] **creuse** [krøz] *adj* hollow; concave; sunken, deep-set; empty (*stomach*); deep (*voice*); off-peak (*hours*); **songer creux** to dream idle dreams; **sonner creux** to sound hollow ‖ *m* hollow (*of hand*); hole (*in ground*); pit (*of stomach*); trough (*of wave*); **creux de l'aisselle** armpit; **creux des reins** small of the back

crevaison [krəvezɔ̃] *f* blowout

crevasse [krəvas] *f* crevice; crack (*in skin*); rift (*in clouds*); flaw (*in metal*)

crevasser [krəvase] *tr* to chap ‖ *intr* & *ref* to crack, to chap

crève-cœur [krevkœr] *m invar* heartbreak, keen disappointment

crever [krəve] §2 *tr* to burst; to work to death (*e.g., a horse*) ‖ *intr* to burst; to split; to burst, go flat (*said of a tire*); (slang) to die, kick the bucket ‖ *ref* to work oneself to death

crevette [krəvɛt] *f* shrimp; **crevette**

grise shrimp; **crevette rose, crevette bouquet** prawn

C.-R.F. *abbr* (**Croix-Rouge française**) French Red Cross

cri [kri] *m* cry; shout; whine, squeal; **dernier cri** last word, latest thing

criailler [kriɑje] *intr* to honk (*said of goose*); (coll) to whine, complain, grouse; **criailler après, criailler contre** (coll) to nag at

criaillerie [kriɑjri] *f* (coll) shouting; (coll) whining, complaining; (coll) nagging

criant [krijɑ̃] **criante** [krijɑ̃t] *adj* crying (*shame*); obvious (*truth*); flagrant (*injustice*)

criard [krijar] **criarde** [krijard] *adj* complaining; shrill (*voice*); loud (*color*); pressing (*debts*) || *mf* complainer || *f* scold, shrew

crible [kribl] *m* sieve; **crible à gravier** gravel screen; **crible à minerai** jig; **passer au crible** to sift or screen

cri·blé -blée [krible] *adj* riddled (*with, e.g., debts*); pitted (*by, e.g., smallpox*)

cribler [krible] *tr* to sift, screen; to riddle; **cribler de ridicule** to cover with ridicule

cric [krik] *m* (aut) jack || *interj* crack!, snap!

cricket [krikɛt] *m* (sports) cricket

cricri [krikri] *m* (ent) cricket

crier [krije] *tr* to cry; to cry out; to shout; to cry for (*revenge*); **crier misère** to complain of being poor; to cry poverty (*said of clothing, furniture, etc.*) || *intr* to cry; to cry out; to shout; to creak, to squeak; to squeal; **crier à** to cry out against (*scandal, injustice, etc.*); to cry for (*help*); **crier après** to yell at, to bawl out; **crier contre** to cry out against; to rail at

crieur [krijœr] **crieuse** [krijøz] *mf* crier; hawker, peddler; **crieur public** town crier

crime [krim] *m* crime; felony

crimi·nel -nelle [kriminɛl] *adj & mf* criminal

crin [krɛ̃] *m* horsehair (*on mane and tail*); **à tous crins** out-and-out, hardcore (*e.g., revolutionist*)

crinière [krinjɛr] *f* mane

crique [krik] *f* cove

criquet [krikɛ] *m* locust; weak wine; (coll) shrimp (*person*)

crise [kriz] *f* crisis; **crise d'appendicite** appendicitis attack; **crise de foi** shaken faith; **crise de main-d'œuvre** labor shortage; **crise de nerfs** fit of hysterics; **crise du foie** liver upset; **crise du logement** housing shortage; **crise économique** (com) depression

cris·pant [krispɑ̃] **-pante** [pɑ̃t] *adj* irritating, annoying

crispation [krispɑsjɔ̃] *f* contraction, shriveling up; (coll) fidgeting

crisper [krispe] *tr* to contract, clench; (coll) to make fidgety || *ref* to contract, to curl up

crisser [krise] *tr* to grind or grit (*one's teeth*) || *intr* to grate, crunch

cris·tal [kristal] *m* (*pl* -**taux** [to]) crystal; **cristal de roche** rock crystal; **cristal taillé** cut glass; **cristaux** glassware; **cristaux de soude** washing soda

cristal·lin [kristalɛ̃] **cristal·line** [kristalin] *adj* crystalline || *m* crystalline lens (*of the eye*)

cristalliser [kristalize] *tr, intr, & ref* to crystallize

critère [kriter] *m* criterion

critérium [kriterjɔm] *m* championship game

critiquable [kritikabl] *adj* open to criticism, questionable

critique [kritik] *adj* critical || *mf* critic || *f* criticism; critics; **critiques** censure

critiquer [kritike] *tr* to criticize, find fault with || *intr* to find fault

critiqueur [kritikœr] *m* critic, faultfinder

croassement [krɔasmɑ̃] *m* croak, caw, croaking (*of raven*)

croasser [krɔase] *intr* to croak, to caw

croate [krɔat] *adj* Croatian || *m* Croat, Croatian (*language*) || (*cap*) *mf* Croatian (*person*)

croc [kro] *m* hook; fang (*of dog*); tusk (*of walrus*)

croc-en-jambe [krɔkɑ̃jɑ̃b] *m* (*pl* **crocs-en-jambes** [krɔkɑ̃jɑ̃b])—**faire un croc-en-jambe à qn** to trip s.o. up

croche [krɔʃ] *f* (mus) quaver

crochet [krɔʃɛ] *m* hook; fang (*of snake*); crochet work; crochet needle; picklock; **crochet radiophonique** talent show; **crochets** (typ) brackets; **faire un crochet** to swerve; **vivre aux crochets de** to live on or at the expense of

crocheter [krɔʃte] §2 *tr* to pick (*a lock*)

crocheteur [krɔʃtœr] *m* picklock; porter

cro·chu -chue [krɔʃy] *adj* hooked (*e.g., nose*); crooked; **avoir les mains crochues** to be light-fingered

crocodile [krɔkɔdil] *m* crocodile

crocus [krɔkys] *m* crocus

croire [krwar] §16 *tr* to believe; **croire** + *inf* to think that + *ind*; **croire qn** + *adj* to believe s.o. to be + *adj*; **croire que non** to think not; **croire que oui** to think so; **je crois bien** or **je le crois bien** I should say so || *intr* to believe; **croire à** to believe in; **croire en Dieu** to believe in God; **j'y crois** I believe in it || *ref* to believe oneself to be

croisade [krwazad] *f* crusade

croi·sé -sée [krwaze] *adj* crossed; twilled (*cloth*); double-breasted (*suit*); alternate (*rhymes*) || *m* Crusader || *f* crossing, crossroads

croisement [krwazmɑ̃] *m* crossing; intersection; meeting, passing (*of two vehicles*); cross-breeding; **croisement en trèfle** cloverleaf, cloverleaf intersection

croiser [krwaze] *tr* to cross; to fold over; to meet, to pass || *intr* to fold over, to lap; to cruise || *ref* to cross, intersect; to go on a crusade

croiseur [krwazœr] *m* cruiser; **croiseur de bataille** battle cruiser

croisière [krwazjɛr] *f* cruise; **en croisière** cruising

croissance [krwasɑ̃s] *f* growth

crois·sant [krwasɑ̃] **crois·sante** [krwasɑ̃t] *adj* growing, increasing, rising ‖ *m* crescent; crescent roll; billhook

croître [krwatr] §17 *intr* to grow; to increase, to rise

croix [krwa] *f* cross; (typ) dagger; **croix gammée** swastika; **en croix** crossed, crosswise

Croix-Rouge [krwaruʒ] *f* Red Cross

cro·quant [krɔkɑ̃] **-quante** [kɑ̃t] *adj* crisp, crunchy ‖ *m* wretch

croque-mitaine [krɔkmitɛn] *m* (*pl* -**mitaines**) bugaboo, bogeyman

croque-monsieur [krɔkməsjø] *m invar* grilled ham-and-cheese sandwich

croque-mort [krɔkmɔr] *m* (*pl* -**morts**) (coll) funeral attendant

croquer [krɔke] *tr* to munch; to sketch; to dissipate (*a fortune*) ‖ *intr* to crunch

croquet [krɔkɛ] *m* croquet; almond cookie

croquis [krɔki] *m* sketch; draft, outline; **croquis coté** diagram, sketch

crosse [krɔs] *f* crosier; butt (*of gun*); hockey stick; lacrosse stick; golf club; **chercher des crosses à** (slang) to pick a fight with; **mettre la crosse en l'air** to show the white flag, to surrender

crotale [krɔtal] *m* rattlesnake

crotte [krɔt] *f* dung; mud; **crotte de chocolat** chocolate cream (candy)

crotter [krɔte] *tr* to dirty ‖ *ref* to get dirty; to commit a nuisance (*said of dog*)

crottin [krɔtɛ̃] *m* horse manure

crouler [krule] *intr* to collapse

croup [krup] *m* (pathol) croup

croupe [krup] *f* croup, rump: ridge, brow; **en croupe** behind the rider

croupetons [kruptɔ̃]—**à croupetons** squatting

crou·pi -pie [krupi] *adj* stagnant

croupier [krupje] *m* croupier; financial partner

croupière [krupjɛr] *f* crupper; **tailler des croupières à** (coll) to make it hard for

croupion [krupjɔ̃] *m* rump

croupir [krupir] *intr* to stagnate; to wallow (*in vice, filth*); to remain (*e.g., in ignorance*)

croustil·lant [krustijɑ̃] **croustil·lante** [krustijɑ̃t] *adj* crisp, crunchy; spicy (*story*)

croustille [krustij] *f* piece of crust; snack; **croustilles** potato chips

croustiller [krustije] *intr* to munch, to nibble

croustil·leux [krustijø] **croustil·leuse** [krustijøz] *adj* spicy (*story*)

croûte [krut] *f* crust; pastry shell (*of meat pie*); scab (*of wound*); (coll) daub, worthless painting; **casser la croûte** (coll) to have a snack

croû·teux [krutø] **-teuse** [tøz] *adj* scabby

croûton [krutɔ̃] *m* crouton; heel (*of bread*); **vieux croûton** (coll) old dodo

croyable [krwajabl], [krwajabl] *adj* believable

croyance [krwajɑ̃s] *f* belief

croyant [krwajɑ̃] **croyante** [krwajɑ̃t] *adj* believing ‖ *mf* believer

C.R.S. [seɛrɛs] *fpl* (letterword) (**Compagnies républicaines de sécurité**) state troopers

cru crue [kry] *adj* raw, uncooked; indigestible; crude (*language; art*); glaring, harsh (*light*); hard (*water*); plain (*terms*); **à cru** directly; bareback ‖ *m* region (*in which s.th. is grown*); vineyard; vintage; **de son cru** of his own invention; **du cru** local, at the vineyard ‖ *see* **crue**

cruauté [kryote] *f* cruelty

cruche [kry/] *f* pitcher, jug

cruchon [kry/ɔ̃] *m* small pitcher or jug

cru·cial -ciale [krysjal] *adj* (*pl* -**ciaux** [sjo]) crucial; cross-shaped

crucifiement [krysifimɑ̃] *m* crucifixion

crucifier [krysifje] *tr* to crucify

crucifix [krysifi] *m* crucifix

crucifixion [krysifiksjɔ̃] *f* crucifixion

crudité [krydite] *f* crudity; indigestibility; rawness (*of food*); harshness (*of light*); hardness (*of water*); **crudités** raw fruits and vegetables; off-color remarks

crue [kry] *f* overflow (*of river*); growth

cruel cruelle [kryɛl] *adj* cruel

cruellement [kryɛlmɑ̃] *adv* cruelly; sorely

crû·ment [krymɑ̃] *adv* crudely; roughly

crustacé [krystase] *m* crustacean

crypte [kript] *f* crypt

CᵗᵉCᵗ *abbr* (**compte courant**) current account

cubage [kybaʒ] *m* volume

cu·bain [kybɛ̃] **-baine** [bɛn] *adj* Cuban ‖ (*cap*) *mf* Cuban

cube [kyb] *adj* cubic ‖ *m* cube

cuber [kybe] *tr* to cube

cubique [kybik] *adj* cubic

cueillaison [kœjɛzɔ̃] *f* picking, gathering; harvest time

cueil·leur [kœjœr] **cueil·leuse** [kœjøz] *mf* picker; fruit picker

cueillir [kœjir] §18 *tr* to pick; to pluck; to gather; to win (*laurels*); to steal (*a kiss*); (coll) to nab (*a thief*); (coll) to pick up (*a friend*)

cuiller or **cuillère** [kɥijɛr] *f* spoon; ladle (*for molten metal*); scoop (*of a dredger*); **cuiller à bouche** tablespoon; **cuiller à café** teaspoon; **cuiller à pot** ladle; **cuiller à soupe** soupspoon; **cuiller et fourchette** fork and spoon

cuillerée [kɥijre] *f* spoonful

cuilleron [kɥijrɔ̃] *m* bowl (*of spoon*)

cuir [kɥir] *m* leather; hide; **cuir chevelu** scalp; **cuir verni** patent leather; **cuir vert** rawhide; **faire des cuirs** to make mistakes in liaison

cuirasse [kɥiras] *f* cuirass, breastplate; armor

cuiras·sé -sée [kɥirase] *adj* armored ‖ *m* battleship

cuirasser [kɥirase] *tr* to armor ‖ *ref* to steel oneself

cuire [kɥir] §19 *tr* to cook; to ripen ‖ *intr* to cook; to sting, smart; **faire cuire** to cook; **il vous en cuira** you'll suffer for it

cui·sant [kɥizã] **-sante** [zãt] *adj* stinging, smarting

cuisine [kɥizin] *f* kitchen; cooking; cuisine; (coll) skulduggery; **cuisine roulante** chuck wagon, field kitchen; **faire la cuisine** to cook

cuisiner [kɥizine] *tr* to cook; (coll) to grill (*a suspect*); (coll) to fix (*an election*) ‖ *intr* to cook

cuisi·nier [kɥizinje] **-nière** [njɛr] *mf* cook ‖ *f* kitchen stove, cookstove

cuisse [kɥis] *f* thigh; (culin) drumstick; **cuisses de grenouille** frogs' legs; **il se croit sorti de la cuisse de Jupiter** (coll) he thinks he is the Lord God Almighty

cuis·seau [kɥiso] *m* (*pl* **-seaux**) leg of veal

cuisson [kɥisɔ̃] *f* baking, cooking; (fig) burning sensation, smarting; **en cuisson** on the stove, on the grill, in the oven

cuissot [kɥiso] *m* leg (*of game*)

cuistre [kɥistr] *m* pedant, prig

cuit [kɥi] **cuite** [kɥit] *adj* cooked; **nous sommes cuits** (coll) our goose is cooked ‖ *f* firing (*in a kiln*); **prendre une cuite** (slang) to get soused

cuivre [kɥivr] *m* copper; **cuivre jaune** brass; **les cuivres** (mus) the brasses

cui·vré **-vrée** [kɥivre] *adj* coppercolored, bronzed; brassy, metallic (*sound or voice*)

cuivrer [kɥivre] *tr* to copper; to bronze, tan; to make (*a sound or one's voice*) brassy or metallic ‖ *ref* to become copper-colored

cui·vreux [kɥivrø] **-vreuse** [vrøz] *adj* (chem) cuprous

cul [ky] *m* bottom (*of bottle, bag*); (slang) ass, hind end, rump; **faire cul sec** (slang) to chug-a-lug

culasse [kylas] *f* breechblock; (mach) cylinder head

cul-blanc [kyblã] *m* (*pl* **culs-blancs**) wheatear, whitetail

culbute [kylbyt] *f* somersault; tumble, bad fall; (coll) failure; (coll) fall (*of a cabinet*); **faire la culbute** to sell at double the purchase price

culbuter [kylbyte] *tr* to overthrow; to overwhelm (*the enemy*) ‖ *intr* to tumble, to fall backwards; to somersault

culbuteur [kylbytœr] *m* (mach) rocker arm

cul-de-basse-fosse [kydbasfos] *m* (*pl* **culs-de-basse-fosse**) dungeon

cul-de-jatte [kydəʒat] *mf* (*pl* **culs-de-jatte**) legless person

cul-de-sac [kydəsak] *m* (*pl* **culs-de-sac**) dead end; (public sign) no outlet

culée [kyle] *f* abutment

culer [kyle] *intr* to back water

culinaire [kyliner] *adj* culinary

culmi·nant [kylminã] **-nante** [nãt] *adj* culminating; highest (*point*)

culmination [kylminasjɔ̃] *f* (astr) culmination

culminer [kylmine] *intr* to rise high, to tower; (astr) to culminate

culot [kylo] *m* base, bottom; (coll) baby of the family; **avoir du culot** (slang) to have a lot of nerve

culotte [kylɔt] *f* breeches, pants; forked legs; panties (*feminine undergarment*); (culin) rump; **culotte de golf** plus fours; **culotte de peau** (slang) old soldier; **culotte de sport** shorts; **porter la culotte** (coll) to wear the pants; **prendre une culotte** (slang) to lose one's shirt; (slang) to have a jag on

culot·té -tée [kylɔte] *adj* (coll) nervy, fresh

culotter [kylɔte] *tr* to cure (*a pipe*) ‖ *ref* to put one's pants on

culte [kylt] *m* worship; cult; divine service, ritual; religion, creed; **avoir un culte pour** to worship (*e.g., one's parents*)

cul-terreux [kyterø] *m* (*pl* **culs-terreux**) (coll) clodhopper, hayseed

cultivable [kyltivabl] *adj* arable, tillable

cultiva·teur [kyltivatœr] **-trice** [tris] *adj* farming ‖ *mf* farmer ‖ *m* (mach) cultivator

cultiver [kyltive] *tr* to cultivate; to culture

cultu·ral -rale [kyltyral] *adj* (*pl* **-raux** [ro]) agricultural

culture [kyltyr] *f* culture; cultivation

cultu·rel -relle [kyltyrɛl] *adj* cultural

cumula·tif [kymylatif] **-tive** [tiv] *adj* cumulative

cunéiforme [kyneiform] *adj* cuneiform

cupide [kypid] *adj* greedy

cupidité [kypidite] *f* cupidity

Cupidon [kypidɔ̃] *m* Cupid

curage [kyraʒ] *m* cleansing, cleaning out; unstopping (*of a drain*)

curatelle [kyratɛl] *f* guardianship, trusteeship

cura·teur [kyratœr] **-trice** [tris] *mf* guardian, trustee

cura·tif [kyratif] **-tive** [tiv] *adj* curative

cure [kyr] *f* treatment, cure; vicarage, rectory; parish; sun porch; **n'avoir cure de rien** or **n'en avoir cure** not to care

curé [kyre] *m* parish priest

cure-dent [kyrdã] *m* (*pl* **-dents**) toothpick

curée [kyre] *f* quarry (*given to the hounds*); scramble, mad race (*for gold, power, recognition, etc.*)

cure-oreille [kyrɔrɛj] *m* (*pl* **-oreilles**) earpick

cure-pipe [kyrpip] *m* (*pl* **-pipes**) pipe cleaner

curer [kyre] *tr* to clean out; to dredge ‖ *ref* (with *dat* of *reflex pron*) to pick (*one's nails, one's teeth, etc.*)

cu·rieux [kyrjø] **-rieuse** [rjøz] *adj* curious

curiosité [kyrjozite] *f* curiosity; curio; connoisseurs, e.g., **le langage de la curiosité** the jargon of connoisseurs;

curiosités sights; **visiter les curiosités** to go sightseeing
curseur [kyrsœr] *m* slide, runner
cur•sif [kyrsif] **-sive** [siv] *adj* cursory; cursive (*handwriting*) || *f* cursive
cuta•né -née [kytane] *adj* cutaneous
cuticule [kytikyl] *f* cuticle
cuve [kyv] *f* vat, tub, tank
cu•veau [kyvo] *m* (*pl* **-veaux**) small vat or tank
cuver [kyve] *tr* to leave to ferment; **cuver son vin** (coll) to sleep it off || *intr* to ferment in a wine vat
cuvette [kyvɛt] *f* basin, pan; bulb (*of a thermometer*); (chem, phot) tray
cuvier [kyvje] *m* washtub
C.V. [seve] *m* (letterword) (**cheval-vapeur**) hp, horsepower
cyanamide [sjanamid] *f* cyanamide
cyanose [sjanoz] *f* cyanosis
cyanure [sjanyr] *m* cyanide
cyclable [siklabl] *adj* reserved for bicycles
cycle [sikl] *m* cycle
cyclique [siklik] *adj* cyclic(al)

cycliste [siklist] *mf* cyclist
cyclomoteur [siklɔmɔtœr] *m* motorbike
cyclone [siklon] *m* cyclone
cyclope [siklɔp] *m* cyclops
cyclotron [siklɔtrɔ̃] *m* cyclotron
cygne [siɲ] *m* swan
cylindrage [silɛ̃draʒ] *m* rolling (*of roads, gardens, etc.*); calendering, mangling
cylindre [silɛ̃dr] *m* cylinder; roller (*e.g., of rolling mill*); steam roller
cylindrée [silɛ̃dre] *f* piston displacement
cylindrer [silɛ̃dre] *tr* to roll (*a road, garden, etc.*); to calender, to mangle
cylindrique [silɛ̃drik] *adj* cylindrical
cymbale [sɛ̃bal] *f* cymbal
cynique [sinik] *adj & m* cynic
cynisme [sinism] *m* cynicism
cyprès [siprɛ] *m* cypress
cyrillique [sirilik] *adj* Cyrillic
cytoplasme [sitɔplasm] *m* cytoplasm
czar [ksar] *m* czar
czarine [ksarin] *f* czarina

D

D, d [de] *m invar* fourth letter of the French alphabet
d' = **de** before vowel or mute **h**
d'abord [dabɔr] see **abord**
dactylo [daktilo] *mf* (coll) typist
dactylographe [daktilɔgraf] *mf* typist
dactylographier [daktilɔgrafje] *tr* to type
dactyloscopie [daktilɔskɔpi] *f* fingerprinting
dada [dada] *m* hobby-horse; hobby, fad, pet subject; **enfourcher son dada** to ride one's hobby
dague [dag] *f* dagger; first antler; tusk
dahlia [dalja] *m* dahlia
daigner [deɲe] *intr*—**daigner** + *inf* to deign to, to condescend to + *inf*; **daignez** please
d'ailleurs [dajœr] see **ailleurs**
daim [dɛ̃] *m* fallow deer; suede
daine [dɛn] *f* doe
dais [dɛ] *m* canopy
dalle [dal] *f* flagstone, slab, paving block; **se rincer la dalle** (slang) to wet one's whistle
daller [dale] *tr* to pave with flagstones
dalto•nien [daltɔnjɛ̃] **-nienne** [njɛn] *adj* color-blind || *mf* color-blind person
dam [dɑ̃] *m*—**au dam de** to the detriment of
damas [damɑ] *m* damask || (*cap*) [damɑs] *f* Damascus
damasquiner [damaskine] *tr* to damascene
damas•sé -sée [damase] *adj & m* damask
dame [dam] *f* dame; lady; tamp, tamper; rowlock; (cards, chess) queen; (checkers) king; **aller à dame** (checkers) to crown a man king; (chess) to

queen a pawn; **dames** (public sign) ladies || *interj* for heaven's sake!
damer [dame] *tr* to tamp (*the earth*); (checkers) to crown (*a checker*); (chess) to queen (*a pawn*); **damer le pion à qn** to outwit s.o.
damier [damje] *m* checkerboard
damnation [dɑnasjɔ̃] *f* damnation
dam•né -née [dɑne] *adj & mf* damned
damner [dɑne] *tr* to damn
damoi•seau [damwazo] **-selle** [zɛl] *mf* (*pl* **-seaux**) (archaic) young member of the nobility || *m* lady's man || *f* (archaic) damsel
dancing [dɑ̃siŋ] *m* dance hall
dandiner [dɑ̃dine] *tr* to dandle || *ref* to waddle along
dandy [dɑ̃di] *m* dandy
Danemark [danmark] *m*—**le Danemark** Denmark
danger [dɑ̃ʒe] *m* danger
dange•reux [dɑ̃ʒrø] **-reuse** [røz] *adj* dangerous
da•nois [danwa] **-noise** [nwaz] *adj* Danish || *m* Danish (*language*) || (*cap*) *mf* Dane
dans [dɑ̃] *prep* in; into; **boire dans un verre** to drink out of a glass; **dans la suite** later
danse [dɑ̃s] *f* dance; **danse guerrière** war dance
danser [dɑ̃se] *tr & intr* to dance; **faire danser** to mistreat
dan•seur [dɑ̃sœr] **-seuse** [søz] *mf* dancer; **danseur de corde** tightrope walker; **en danseuse** in a standing position (*taken by cyclist*)
Danube [danyb] *m* Danube
d'après [daprɛ] see **après**
dard [dar] *m* dart; sting; snake's tongue; harpoon

darder [darde] *tr* to dart, to hurl
dare-dare [dardar] *adv* (coll) on the double
darse [dars] *f* wet dock
date [dat] *f* date; **de fraîche date** recent; **de longue date** of long standing; **en date de** from; **faire date** to mark an epoch; **prendre date** to make an appointment
dater [date] *tr* & *intr* to date; **à dater de** dating from
datif [datif] *m* dative
datte [dat] *f* date
dattier [datje] *m* date palm
daube [dob] *f* braised meat; **en daube** braised
dauber [dobe] *tr* to braise; to heckle; to slander; (coll) to pummel ‖ *intr*—**dauber sur qn** to heckle s.o., to slander s.o.
dau·beur [dobœr] **-beuse** [bøz] *mf* heckler
dauphin [dofɛ̃] *m* dolphin; dauphin
dauphine [dofin] *f* dauphiness
dauphinelle [dofinɛl] *f* delphinium
davantage [davɑ̃taʒ] §90 *adv* more; any more; any longer; **ne . . . davantage** no more; **pas davantage** no longer
de [də] §77, §78, §79 *prep* of, from; with, e.g., **frapper d'une épée** to strike with a sword; (to indicate the agent with the passive voice) by, e.g., **ils sont aimés de tous** they are loved by all; (to indicate the point of departure) from, e.g., **de Paris à Madrid** from Paris to Madrid; (to indicate the point of arrival) for, e.g., **le train de Paris** the train for Paris; (with a following infinitive after certain verbs) to, e.g., **il essaie d'écrire la lettre** he is trying to write the letter; (with a following infinitive after an adjective used with the impersonal expression **il est**) to, e.g., **il est facile de chanter cette chanson** it is easy to sing that song; (after **changer, se souvenir, avoir besoin,** etc.), e.g., **changer de vêtements** to change clothes; (after a comparative and before a numeral) than, e.g., **plus de quarante** more than forty; (to express the indefinite plural or partitive idea), e.g., **de l'eau** water, some water; (to form prepositional phrases with some adverbs), e.g., **auprès de vous** near you; (with the historical infinitive), e.g., **et chacun de pleurer** and everyone cried
dé [de] *m* die (*singular of dice*); thimble; domino; golf tee; **dés** dice
déambuler [deɑ̃byle] *intr* to stroll
débâcle [debɑkl] *f* debacle; breakup (*of ice*)
débâcler [debɑkle] *intr* to break up (*said of ice in a river*)
déballage [debalaʒ] *m* unpacking; cut-rate merchandise (*sold by street vendor*)
déballer [debale] *tr* to unpack (*merchandise*); to display (*merchandise*)
débandade [debɑ̃dad] *f* rout, stampede; **à la débandade** in confusion, helter-skelter

débander [debɑ̃de] *tr* to rout, to stampede; to slacken (*s.th. under tension*); to unwind; **débander les yeux à qn** to take the blindfold from s.o.'s eyes ‖ *intr* to flee, to stampede
débaptiser [debatize] *tr* to change the name of, to rename
débarbouiller [debarbuje] *tr* to wash the face of
débarcadère [debarkadɛr] *m* wharf, dock, landing platform
débarder [debarde] *tr* to unload
débardeur [debardœr] *m* stevedore, longshoreman
débar·qué -quée [debarke] *adj* disembarking ‖ *mf* new arrival ‖ *m* disembarkment; **au débarqué** on arrival
débarquement [debarkmɑ̃] *m* disembarkation
débarquer [debarke] *m*—**au débarquer de qn** at the moment of s.o.'s arrival ‖ *tr* to unload; to lower (*a lifeboat, seaplane, etc.*); (coll) to sack (*s.o.*) ‖ *intr* to disembark, get off
débarras [debara] *m* catchall
débarrasser [debarase] *tr* to disencumber, to disentangle; to clear (*the table*); to rid ‖ *ref*—**se débarrasser de** to get rid of
débarrer [debare] *tr* to unbar
débat [deba] *m* debate; dispute; **débats** discussion (*in a meeting*); proceedings (*in a court*)
débâter [debɑte] *tr* to unsaddle
débattre [debatr] §7 *tr* to debate, argue, discuss; to haggle over (*a price*); to question (*items in an account*) ‖ *ref* to struggle; to be debated
débauche [deboʃ] *f* debauch, debauchery; riot (*e.g., of colors*); overeating; striking, quitting work
débaucher [deboʃe] *tr* to debauch; to induce (*a worker*) to strike; to lay off (*workers*); to steal (*a worker*) from another employer ‖ *ref* to become debauched
débile [debil] *adj* weak ‖ *mf* mental defective
débilité [debilite] *f* debility
débiliter [debilite] *tr* to debilitate
débiner [debine] *tr* (slang) to run (*s.o.*) down ‖ *ref* (slang) to fly the coop
débit [debi] *m* debit; retail sale; shop; cutting up (*of wood*); output; way of speaking
débiter [debite] *tr* to debit; to cut up in pieces; to retail; to produce; to speak (*one's part*); to repeat thoughtlessly
débi·teur [debitœr] **-trice** [tris] *adj* debit (*account, balance*); delivery (*spool*) ‖ *mf* debtor ‖ **-teur** [tœr] **-teuse** [tøz] *mf* gossip, talebearer; salesclerk
déblai [deblɛ] *m* excavation; **déblais** rubble, fill
déblaiement [deblɛmɑ̃] *m* clearing away
déblatérer [deblatere] §10 *tr* to bluster or fling (*threats, abuse*) ‖ *intr*—**déblatérer contre** to rail at

déblayer [debleje] §49 *tr* to clear, to clear away

débloquer [deblɔke] *tr* to unblock; to unfreeze (*funds, credits, etc.*)

déboire [debwar] *m* unpleasant aftertaste; disappointment

déboisement [debwɑzmɑ̃] *m* deforestation

déboîter [debwate] *tr* to disconnect (*pipe*); to dislocate (*a shoulder*) ‖ *intr* to move into another lane (*said of automobile*); (naut) to haul (*out of a line*)

débonder [debɔ̃de] *tr* to unbung

débonnaire [debɔnɛr] *adj* good-natured, easygoing; (Bib) meek

débor·dant [debɔrdɑ̃] **-dante** [dɑ̃t] *adj* overflowing

débor·dé -dée [debɔrde] *adj* overwhelmed

déborder [debɔrde] *tr* to extend beyond, to jut out over; to trim the border from; to overwhelm; to untuck (*a bed*); (mil) to outflank ‖ *intr* to overflow; (naut) to shove off

débotté [debɔte] *m*—**au débotté** immediately upon arrival, at once

débouché [debuʃe] *m* outlet; opening (*for trade; of an attack*)

déboucher [debuʃe] *tr* to free from obstruction; to uncork ‖ *intr*—**déboucher dans** to empty into (*said of river*); **déboucher sur** to open onto, to emerge into

déboucler [debukle] *tr* to unbuckle; to take the curls out of

débouler [debule] *tr* to fly down (*e.g., a stairway*) ‖ *intr* to run suddenly out of cover (*said of rabbits*); to dash; **débouler dans** to roll down (*a stairway*)

déboulonner [debulɔne] *tr* to unbolt; (coll) to ruin, have fired; (coll) to debunk

débourber [deburbe] *tr* to clear of mud, to clean

débourrer [debure] *tr* to unhair (*a hide*); to remove the stuffing from (*a chair*); to knock (*a pipe*) clean

débours [debur] *m* disbursement; **rentrer dans ses débours** to recover one's investment

déboursement [debursmɑ̃] *m* disbursing

débourser [deburse] *tr* to disburse

debout [dəbu] *adv* upright, on end; standing; up (*out of bed*)

déboutonner [debutɔne] *tr* to unbutton; **à ventre déboutonné** immoderately ‖ *ref* (coll) to get something off one's chest

débrail·lé -lée [debrɑje] *adj* untidy, mussed up, unkempt; loose (*morals*); vulgar (*speech*) ‖ *m* untidiness

débrancher [debrɑ̃ʃe] *tr* to switch (*railroad cars*) to a siding; (elec) to disconnect

débrayage [debrɛjaʒ] *m* (aut) clutch release; (coll) walkout

débrayer [debrɛje] §49 *tr* to disengage, throw out (*the clutch*) ‖ *intr* to throw out the clutch; (coll) to walk out (*said of strikers*)

débri·dé -dée [debride] *adj* unbridled

débris [debri] *mpl* debris; remains

débrouil·lard [debrujar] **débrouil·larde** [debrujard] *adj* (coll) resourceful ‖ *mf* (coll) smart customer

débrouiller [debruje] *tr* to disentangle, to unravel; to clear up (*a mystery*); to make out (*e.g., a signature*); (coll) to teach (*s.o.*) to be resourceful ‖ *ref* to clear (*said of sky*); (coll) to manage to get along, to take care of oneself; (coll) to extricate oneself (*from a difficult situation*)

débucher [debyʃe] *tr* to flush out (*game*) ‖ *intr* to run out of cover (*said of game*)

débusquer [debyske] *tr* to flush out (*game; the enemy*)

début [deby] *m* debut; beginning, commencement; opening play

débu·tant [debytɑ̃] **-tante** [tɑ̃t] *adj* beginning ‖ *mf* beginner; newcomer (*e.g., to stage or screen*) ‖ *f* debutante

débuter [debyte] *intr* to make one's debut, to begin; to start up a business; to make the opening play

deçà [dəsa] *adv*—**deçà delà** here and there; **en deçà de** on this side of

décacheter [deka/te] §34 *tr* to unseal

décade [dekad] *f* period of ten days; (hist, lit) decade

décadence [dekadɑ̃s] *f* decadence

déca·dent [dekadɑ̃] **-dente** [dɑ̃t] *adj* & *mf* decadent

décaféi·né -née [dekafeine] *adj* decaffeinated, caffeine-free

décagénaires [dekaʒenɛr] *mfpl* teenagers

décaisser [dekɛse] *tr* to uncrate; to disburse, pay out

décalage [dekalaʒ] *m* unkeying; shift; slippage; (aer) stagger

décalcomanie [dekalkɔmani] *f* decal

décaler [dekale] *tr* to unkey; to shift

décalquage [dekalkaʒ] or **décalque** [dekalk] *m* decal

décalquer [dekalke] *tr* to transfer (*a decal*) onto paper, canvas, metal, etc.; **décalquer sur** to transfer (*a decal*) onto (*e.g., paper*)

décamper [dekɑ̃pe] *intr* to decamp

décanat [dekana] *m* deanship

décanter [dekɑ̃te] *tr* to decant

décapant [dekapɑ̃] *m* scouring agent

décaper [dekape] *tr* to scour, scale

décapiter [dekapite] *tr* to behead, to decapitate; to top (*a tree*)

décapotable [dekapɔtabl] *adj* & *f* (aut) convertible

déca·ti -tie [dekati] *adj* haggard, worn-out, faded

décatir [dekatir] *tr* to steam (*cloth*)

décaver [dekave] *tr* (coll) to fleece

décéder [desede] §10 *intr* (aux: ÊTRE) to die (*said of human being*)

décèlement [desɛlmɑ̃] *m* disclosure

déceler [desle] §2 *tr* to uncover, detect; to betray (*confusion*)

décélération [deselerasjɔ̃] *f* deceleration

décembre [desɑ̃br] *m* December

décennie [deseni] *f* decade

dé·cent [desã] -cente [sãt] adj decent
décentraliser [desãtralize] tr to decentralize
déception [desεpsjɔ̃] f disappointment
décernement [desεrnəmã] m awarding
décerner [desεrne] tr to award (a prize); to confer (an honor); to issue (a writ)
décès [desε] m decease, demise
déce·vant [desvã] -vante [vãt] adj disappointing; deceptive
décevoir [desvwar] §59 tr to disappoint; to deceive
déchaînement [deʃεnmã] m unchaining, unleashing; outburst, wave
déchaîner [deʃεne] tr to unchain, let loose || ref to fly into a rage; to break out (said of storm)
déchanter [deʃãte] intr (coll) to sing a different tune
décharge [deʃarʒ] f discharge; drain; rubbish heap; storeroom, shed; à décharge for the defense
déchargement [deʃarʒəmã] m unloading
décharger [deʃarʒe] §38 tr to discharge; to unload; to unburden; to exculpate (a defendant) || ref to vent one's anger; to go off (said of gun); to run down (said of battery); se décharger de q.ch. sur qn to shift the responsibility for s.th. on s.o.
déchargeur [deʃarʒœr] m porter (e.g., in a market); dock hand
déchar·né -née [deʃarne] adj emaciated, skinny, bony
décharner [deʃarne] tr to strip the flesh from; to emaciate || ref to waste away
déchaus·sé -sée [deʃose] adj barefoot
déchausser [deʃose] tr to take the shoes off of (s.o.); to expose the roots of (a tree, a tooth) || ref to take off one's shoes; to shrink (said of gums)
déchéance [deʃeãs] f downfall; lapse, forfeiture (of a right); expiration, term (of a note or loan)
déchet [deʃε] m loss, decrease; déchet de route loss in transit; déchets waste products
décheveler [deʃəvle] §34 tr to dishevel, to muss (s.o.'s hair)
déchiffonner [deʃifɔne] tr to iron (wrinkled material)
déchiffrable [deʃifrabl] adj legible; decipherable
déchiffrement [deʃifrəmã] m deciphering, decoding; sight-reading
déchiffrer [deʃifre] tr to decipher; to sight-read (music)
déchif·freur [deʃifrœr] déchif·freuse [deʃifrøz] mf decipherer, decoder; sight-reader
déchique·té -tée [deʃikte] adj jagged, torn
déchiqueter [deʃikte] §34 tr to cut into strips; to shred; to slash
déchi·rant [deʃirã] -rante [rãt] adj heartrending
déchi·ré -rée [deʃire] adj torn; sorry
déchirer [deʃire] tr to tear, to tear up; to split (a country; one's eardrums);

to pick (s.o.'s character) to pieces || ref (with dat of reflex pron) to skin (e.g., one's knee)
déchirure [deʃirur] f tear, rent; sprain
déchoir [deʃwar] (usually used only in: inf; pp déchu; sometimes used in: pres ind déchois, etc.; fut déchoirai, etc.; cond déchoirais, etc.) intr (aux: AVOIR or ÊTRE) to fall (from high estate); to decline, to fail
dé·chu -chue [deʃy] adj fallen; deprived (of rights); expired (insurance policy)
décider [deside] tr to decide, to decide on; décider qn à + inf to persuade s.o. to + inf || intr to decide; décider de to decide, determine the outcome of, e.g., le coup a décidé de la partie the trick decided the (outcome of the) game; décider de + inf to decide to + inf || ref to decide, to make up one's mind, to resolve; se décider à + inf to decide to + inf
déci·mal -male [desimal] adj (pl -maux [mo]) decimal || f decimal
décimer [desime] tr to decimate
déci·sif [desizif] -sive [ziv] adj decisive
décision [desizjɔ̃] f decision; decisiveness
déclama·teur [deklamatœr] -trice [tris] adj bombastic || mf declaimer
déclamatoire [deklamatwar] adj declamatory
déclamer [deklame] tr to declaim || intr to rant; déclamer contre to inveigh against
déclara·tif [deklaratif] -tive [tiv] adj declarative
déclaration [deklarasjɔ̃] f declaration; déclaration de revenus income-tax return
déclarer [deklare] tr & intr to declare || ref to declare oneself; to arise, break out, occur
déclassement [deklasmã] m disarrangement; drop in social status; transfer to another class (on ship, train, etc.); dismantling; demoting
déclasser [deklase] tr to disarrange; to dismantle; to demote
déclenchement [deklãʃmã] m releasing; launching (of an attack)
déclencher [deklãʃe] tr to unlatch, disengage; to release (the shutter); to open (fire); to launch (an attack)
déclencheur [deklãʃœr] m (mach, phot) release
déclic [deklik] m pawl, catch; hair trigger
déclin [deklε̃] m decline
déclinaison [deklinεzɔ̃] f (astr) declination; (gram) declension
décliner [dekline] tr & intr to decline
déclive [dekliv] adj sloping || f slope
déclivité [deklivite] f declivity
dé·clos [deklo] -close [kloz] adj in bloom
décocher [dekɔʃe] tr to let fly; to flash (a smile)
décoder [dekɔde] tr to decode
décoiffer [dekwafe] tr to loosen or muss the hair of; to uncap (a bottle)

|| *ref* to muss one's hair; to take one's hair down

décoincer [dekwɛ̃se] §51 *tr* to unwedge, to loosen (*a jammed part*)

décolérer [dekɔlere] §10 *intr* to calm down

décollage [dekɔlaʒ] *m* unsticking, ungluing; takeoff (*of airplane*)

décoller [dekɔle] *tr* to unstick, detach || *intr* (aer) to take off

décolletage [dekɔltaʒ] *m* low-cut neck; screw cutting; topping

décolle·té -tée [dekɔlte] *adj* décolleté || *m* low-cut neckline; bare neck and shoulders

décolleter [dekɔlte] §34 *tr* to cut the neck of (*a dress*) low; to bare the neck and shoulders of || *ref* to wear a low-necked dress

décoloration [dekɔlɔrasjɔ̃] *f* discoloration

décolorer [dekɔlɔre] *tr & ref* to bleach; to fade

décombres [dekɔ̃br] *mpl* debris, ruins

décommander [dekɔ̃mɑ̃de] *tr* to cancel an order for; to call off (*a dinner*); to cancel the invitation to (*a guest*) || *ref* to cancel a meeting

décompléter [dekɔ̃plete] §10 *tr* to break up (*a set*)

décomposer [dekɔ̃poze] *tr & ref* to decompose

décomposition [dekɔ̃pozisjɔ̃] *f* decomposition

décompression [dekɔ̃presjɔ̃] *f* decompression

décomprimer [dekɔ̃prime] *tr* to decompress

décompte [dekɔ̃t] *m* itemized statement; discount (*to be deducted from total*); disappointment

décompter [dekɔ̃te] *tr* to deduct (*a sum from an account*) || *intr* to strike the wrong hour

déconcerter [dekɔ̃sɛrte] *tr* to disconcert

décon·fit [dekɔ̃fi] -**fite** [fit] *adj* discomfited, baffled, confused

déconfiture [dekɔ̃fityr] *f* discomfiture; downfall, rout; business failure

décongeler [dekɔ̃ʒle] §2 *tr* to thaw; to defrost

décongestionner [dekɔ̃ʒɛstjɔne] *tr* to relieve congestion

déconseiller [dekɔ̃seje] *tr* to dissuade; **déconseiller q.ch. à qn** to advise s.o. against s.th. || *intr*—**déconseiller à qn de** + *inf* to advise s.o. against + *ger*

déconsidération [dekɔ̃siderasjɔ̃] *f* disrepute

déconsidérer [dekɔ̃sidere] §10 *tr* to bring into disrepute, to discredit

déconsigner [dekɔ̃siɲe] *tr* to take (*one's baggage*) out of the checkroom; to free (*soldiers*) from detention

décontenancer [dekɔ̃tnɑ̃se] §51 *tr* to discountenance, abash || *ref* to lose one's self-assurance

décontrac·té -tée [dekɔ̃trakte] *adj* relaxed, at ease; indifferent

décontracter [dekɔ̃trakte] *tr* to loosen

up (*one's muscles*) || *intr* to stretch one's muscles; to relax

déconvenue [dekɔ̃vny] *f* disappointment, mortification

décor [dekɔr] *m* décor, decoration; (theat) setting; **décor découpé** cutout; **décors** (theat) set, stage setting

décora·teur [dekɔratœr] -**trice** [tris] *mf* interior decorator; stage designer

décora·tif [dekɔratif] -**tive** [tiv] *adj* decorative, ornamental

décoration [dekɔrasjɔ̃] *f* decoration

décorum [dekɔrɔm] *m invar* decorum

découcher [dekuʃe] *intr* to sleep away from home

découdre [dekudr] §13 *tr* to unstitch, to rip up; to gore || *intr*—**en découdre** to cross swords || *ref* to come unsewn, to rip at the seam

découler [dekule] *intr* to trickle; to proceed, arise, be derived

découpage [dekupaʒ] *m* shooting script

découper [dekupe] *tr* to carve (*e.g., a turkey*); to cut out (*a design*); to indent (*the coast*) || *ref*—**se découper sur** to stand out against (*the horizon*)

décou·plé -plée [dekuple] *adj* wellbuilt, brawny

découpler [dekuple] *tr* to unleash

découpure [dekupyr] *f* cutting out; ornamental cutout; indentation (*in coast*)

découragement [dekuraʒmɑ̃] *m* discouragement

décourager [dekuraʒe] §38 *tr* to discourage || *ref* to become discouraged

décours [dekur] *m* wane

décou·su -sue [dekuzy] *adj* unsewn; disjointed, unsystematic; incoherent (*words*); desultory (*remarks*)

décou·vert [dekuvɛr] -**verte** [vɛrt] *adj* uncovered, open, exposed || *m* deficit; overdraft || *f* uncovering; discovery

décou·vreur [dekuvrœr] -**vreuse** [vrøz] *mf* discoverer

découvrir [dekuvrir] §65 *tr* to discover; to discern (*in the distance*); to pick out (*with a searchlight*); to uncover || *intr* to become visible (*said of rocks at low tide*) || *ref* to take off one's hat; to lower one's guard; to clear up (*said of the sky*); to say what one is thinking; to come to light, to be revealed

décrasser [dekrase] *tr* to clean; to polish up

décré·pit [dekrepi] -**pite** [pit] *adj* decrepit

décret [dekrɛ] *m* decree

décrier [dekrije] *tr* to decry, disparage, run down

décrire [dekrir] §25 *tr* to describe

décrocher [dekrɔʃe] *tr* to unhook, take down; (coll) to wangle; **décrocher la timbale** (coll) to hit the jackpot || *intr* to withdraw

décrochez-moi-ça [dekrɔʃemwasa] *m invar* (coll) secondhand clothing store

décroît [dekrwa] *m* last quarter (*of moon*)

décroître [dekrwatr] §17 (*pp* **décru**; *pres ind* **décrois**, etc.; *pret* **décrus**,

etc.) *intr* to decrease; to shorten (*said of days*); to fall (*said of river*)
décrotter [dekrɔte] *tr* to remove mud from; (coll) to teach how to behave
décrotteur [dekrɔtœr] *m* shoeshine boy
décrottoir [dekrɔtwar] *m* doormat; scraper (*for shoes*)
décrue [dekry] *f* fall, drop, subsiding
décrypter [dekripte] *tr* to decipher
déculotter [dekylɔte] *tr* to take the pants off of || *ref* to take off one's pants
décuple [dekypl] *adj* & *m* tenfold
décupler [dekyple] *tr* & *intr* to increase tenfold
dédaigner [dedɛɲe] *tr* to disdain; to reject (*e.g., an offer*); **dédaigner de** + *inf* not to condescend to + *inf*
dédai·gneux [dedɛɲø] **-gneuse** [ɲøz] *adj* disdainful
dédain [dedɛ̃] *m* disdain
dedans [dədɑ̃] *m* inside; **en dedans** inside || *adv* inside, within; **mettre dedans** (coll) to take in, to fool
dédicace [dedikas] *f* dedication
dédicacer [dedikase] §51 *tr* to dedicate, to autograph
dédicatoire [dedikatwar] *adj* dedicatory
dédier [dedje] *tr* to dedicate; to offer (*e.g., a collection to a museum*)
dédire [dedir] §40 *tr*—**dédire qn** to disavow s.o.'s words or actions || *ref* to make a retraction, to back down; **se dédire de** to go back on, to fail to keep
dédit [dedi] *m* penalty (*for breaking a contract*); breach of contract
dédommagement [dedɔmaʒmɑ̃] *m* compensation, damages, indemnity
dédommager [dedɔmaʒe] §38 *tr* to compensate for a loss, to indemnify
dédouaner [dedwane] *tr* to clear through customs; to rehabilitate (*a politician, statesman, etc.*)
dédoublement [dedubləmɑ̃] *m* splitting; subdivision; unfolding
dédoubler [deduble] *tr* to divide or split in two; to remove the lining from; to unfold; to put on another section of (*a train*)
déduction [dedyksjɔ̃] *f* deduction
déduire [dedɥir] §19 *tr* to deduce; to infer; (com) to deduct
déesse [deɛs] *f* goddess
défaillance [defajɑ̃s] *f* failure, failing; faint; lapse (*of memory*); nonappearance (*of witness*); **défaillance cardiaque** heart failure; **sans défaillance** unflinching
défail·lant [defajɑ̃] **défail·lante** [defajɑ̃t] *adj* failing, faltering
défaillir [defajir] §69 *intr* to fail; to falter, weaken, flag; to faint
défaire [defɛr] §29 *tr* to undo; to untie, unwrap, unpack; to rearrange; to let down (*one's hair*); to rid; to defeat, to rout (*s.o.*) down, to tire (*s.o.*) out || *ref* to come undone; **se défaire de** to get rid of
dé·fait -faite [defɛ] [fɛt] *adj* undone, untied; loose; disheveled; drawn

(*countenance*) || *f* defeat; disposal, turnover; (fig) loophole
défaitisme [defɛtism] *m* defeatism
défaitiste [defɛtist] *mf* defeatist
défalcation [defalkasjɔ̃] *f* deduction
défalquer [defalke] *tr* to deduct
défaufiler [defofile] *tr* to untack
défausser [defose] *tr* to straighten || *ref*—**se défausser (de)** to discard
défaut [defo] *m* defect, fault; lack (*of knowledge, memory, etc.*); flaw; chink (*in armor*); **à défaut de** in default of, lacking; **faire défaut à** to abandon, fail (*e.g., one's friends*); (law) to default; **mettre en défaut** to foil
défaveur [defavœr] *f* disfavor
défavorable [defavɔrabl] *adj* unfavorable
défavoriser [defavɔrize] *tr* to handicap, to put at a disadvantage
défécation [defekasjɔ̃] *f* defecation
défec·tif [defɛktif] **-tive** [tiv] *adj* (gram) defective
défection [defɛksjɔ̃] *f* defection; **faire défection** to defect
défec·tueux [defɛktɥø] **-tueuse** [tɥøz] *adj* defective, faulty
défectuosité [defɛktɥozite] *f* imperfection
défen·deur [defɑ̃dœr] **-deresse** [drɛs] *mf* defendant
défendre [defɑ̃dr] *tr* to defend; to protect (*e.g., against the cold*); **à son corps défendant** in self-defense; against one's will; **défendre q ch. à qn** to forbid s.o. s.th. || *intr*—**défendre à qn de** + *inf* to forbid s.o. to + *inf* || *ref* to defend oneself; (coll) to hold one's own, **se défendre de** to deny (*e.g., having said s.th.*); to refrain from, to keep from
défen·du -due [defɑ̃dy] *adj* forbidden
défense [defɑ̃s] *f* defense; tusk; **défense passive** civil defense (*against air raids*); (public signs): **défense d'afficher** post no bills; **défense de dépasser** no passing; **défense de déposer des ordures** no dumping, no littering; **défense de doubler** no passing; **défense de faire des ordures** commit no nuisance; **défense de fumer** no smoking; **défense d'entrer** private, keep out, no admittance
défenseur [defɑ̃sœr] *m* defender; lawyer for the defense; stand-by
défen·sif [defɑ̃sif] **-sive** [siv] *adj* & *f* defensive
déférence [deferɑ̃s] *f* deference
défé·rent [deferɑ̃] **-rente** [rɑ̃t] *adj* deferential
déférer [defere] §10 *tr* to confer, award; to refer (*a case to a court*); **déférer en justice** to haul into court || *intr* to comply; **déférer à** to defer to, to comply with
déferler [deferle] *tr* to unfurl; to set (*the sails of a ship*) || *intr* to spread out (*said of a crowd*); to break (*said of waves*)
défeuiller [defœje] *tr* to defoliate || *ref* to lose its leaves
défi [defi] *m* challenge, dare; **défi à**

l'autorité defiance of authority; **porter un défi à** to defy; **relever un défi** to take a dare
défiance [defjɑ̃s] *f* distrust
dé·fiant [defjɑ̃] **-fiante** [fjɑ̃t] *adj* distrustful
déficeler [defisle] §34 *tr* to untie
déficience [defisjɑ̃s] *f* deficiency
défi·cient [defisjɑ̃] **-ciente** [sjɑ̃t] *adj* deficient
déficit [defisit] *m* deficit
déficitaire [defisiter] *adj* deficit; meager (*crop*); lean (*year*)
défier [defje] *tr* to˙challenge; to defy (*death, time, etc.*); **défier qn de** to dare s.o. to || *ref*—**se défier de** to mistrust
défiger [defiʒe] §38 *tr* to liquefy
défiguration [defigyrasjɔ̃] *f* disfigurement; defacement
défigurer [defigyre] *tr* to disfigure; to deface; to distort
défilé [defile] *m* defile (*in mountains*); parade, procession, line of march
défilement [defilmɑ̃] *m* (mil) defilade, cover
défiler [defile] *tr* to unstring; (mil) to put under cover || *intr* to march by, to parade, to defile || *ref* to come unstrung; to take cover; (coll) to gold-brick
défi·ni -nie [defini] *adj* definite; defined
définir [definir] *tr* to define || *ref* to be defined
définissable [definisabl] *adj* definable
défini·tif [definitif] **-tive** [tiv] *adj* definitive; standard (*edition*); **en définitive** in short, all things considered
définition [definisjɔ̃] *f* definition
définitivement [definitivmɑ̃] *adv* definitively, for good, permanently
déflation [deflɑsjɔ̃] *f* deflation (*of currency*); sudden drop (*in wind*)
défleurir [deflœrir] *tr* to deflower, to strip of flowers || *intr & ref* to lose its flowers
déflexion [deflɛksjɔ̃] *f* deflection
défloraison [deflɔrɛzɔ̃] *f* dropping of petals
déflorer [deflɔre] *tr* to deflower
défon·cé -cée [defɔ̃se] *adj* battered, smashed, crumpled; bumpy
défoncer [defɔ̃se] §51 *tr* to batter in; to stave in (*a cask*); to remove the seat of (*a chair*); to break up (*ground; a road*) || *ref* to be broken up (*said of road*)
déformation [defɔrmɑsjɔ̃] *f* deformation, distortion; **déformation professionnelle** narrow professionalism
défor·mé -mée [defɔrme] *adj* out of shape; rough (*road*)
déformer [defɔrme] *tr* to deform, distort || *ref* to become deformed
défoulement [defulmɑ̃] *m* (psychoanal) insight, recall; (coll) relief
défrai·chi -chie [defrɛ/i] *adj* dingy, faded
défraîchir [defrɛ/ir] *tr* to make stale, to fade
défrayer [defrɛje] §49 *tr* to defray the

expenses of (*s.o.*); **défrayer la conversation** to be the subject of the conversation
défricher [defri/e] *tr* to reclaim; to clear up (*a puzzler*)
défricheur [defri/œr] *m* pioneer, explorer
défriser [defrize] *tr & ref* to uncurl
défroncer [defrɔ̃se] §51 *tr* to remove the wrinkles from
défroque [defrɔk] *f* piece of discarded clothing
défroquer [defrɔke] *tr* to unfrock || *ref* to give up the frock
dé·funt [defœ̃] **-funte** [fœ̃t] *adj & mf* deceased
déga·gé -gée [degaʒe] *adj* breezy, jaunty, nonchalant; free, detached
dégagement [degaʒmɑ̃] *m* disengagement; clearing, relieving of congestion; liberation (*e.g., of heat*); exit; retraction (*of promise*); redemption, taking out of hock
dégager [degaʒe] §38 *tr* to disengage; to free, clear, release; to draw, extract (*the moral or essential points*); to give off, liberate; to take back (*one's word*); to redeem, ·to take out of hock
dégaine [degen] *f* (coll) awkward bearing; ridiculous posture
dégainer [degene] *tr* to unsheathe || *intr* to take up a sword
dégar·ni -nie [degarni] *adj* empty, depleted, stripped
dégarnir [degarnir] *tr* to clear (*a table*); to withdraw soldiers from (*a sector*); to prune || *ref* to thin out
dégât [degɑ] *m* damage, havoc
dégauchir [dego/ir] *tr* to smooth out the rough edges of (*stone, wood; an inexperienced person*)
dégel [deʒɛl] *m* thaw
dégeler [deʒle] §2 *tr* to thaw, to defrost; to loosen up, relax || *intr* to thaw out; **il dégèle** it is thawing
dégéné·ré -rée [deʒenere] *adj & mf* degenerate
dégénérer [deʒenere] §10 *intr* to degenerate
dégénérescence [deʒeneresɑ̃s] *f* degeneration
dégingan·dé -dée [deʒɛ̃gɑ̃de] *adj* gangling, ungainly
dégivrage [deʒivraʒ] *m* defrosting
dégivrer [deʒivre] *tr* to defrost, to de-ice
dégivreur [deʒivrœr] *m* defroster, de-icer
déglacer [deglase] §51 *tr* to deice; to remove the glaze from (*paper*)
dégommer [degome] *tr* to ungum; (coll) to fire (*s.o.*)
dégon·flé -flée [degɔ̃fle] *adj* flat (*tire*)
dégonflement [degɔ̃fləmɑ̃] *m* deflation
dégonfler [degɔ̃fle] *tr* to deflate || *ref* to go flat; to go down, to subside (*said of swelling*); (slang) to lose one's nerve
dégorger [degɔrʒe] §38 *tr* to disgorge; to unstop, open (*a pipe*); to scour (*e.g., wool*) || *intr* to discharge, to overflow

dégour·di -die [degurdi] *adj* limbered up, lively, sharp, adroit || *mf* smart aleck
dégourdir [degurdir] *tr* to remove stiffness or numbness from (*e.g., legs*); to stretch (*one's limbs*); to take the chill off; to teach (*s.o.*) the ropes, to polish (*s.o.*) || *ref* to limber up
dégoût [degu] *m* distaste, dislike
dégoû·tant [degutã] **-tante** [tãt] *adj* disgusting, distasteful
dégoû·té -tée [degute] *adj* fastidious, hard to please || *mf* finicky person
dégoûter [degute] *tr* to disgust; **dégoûter qn de** to make s.o. dislike || *ref* to become fed up
dégoutter [degute] *intr* to drip, trickle
dégradation [degradasjɔ̃] *f* degradation; defacement; shading off, graduation; worsening (*of a situation*); (mil) demotion; **dégradation civique** loss of civil rights
dégrader [degrade] *tr* to degrade, to bring down; to deface; to shade off, to graduate; (mil) to demote, to break || *ref* to debase oneself; to become dilapidated
dégrafer [degrafe] *tr* to unhook, to unclasp
dégraissage [degresaʒ] *m* dry cleaning
dégraisser [degrese] *tr* to remove grease from; to dry-clean
dégrais·seur [degrescer] **dégrais·seuse** [degresøz] *mf* dry cleaner, cleaner and dyer
degré [dəgre] *m* degree; step (*of stairs*); **monter d'un degré** to take a step up (*on the ladder of success*)
dégringolade [degrɛ̃gɔlad] *f* (coll) tumble; (coll) comedown, collapse, downfall
dégringoler [degrɛ̃gɔle] *tr* to bring down (*a government*) || *intr* (coll) to tumble, to tumble down
dégriser [degrize] *tr & ref* to sober up
dégrossir [degrosir] *tr* to rough-hew; to make the preliminary sketches of; to refine or polish (*a hick*)
déguenil·lé -lée [degənije] *adj* ragged, in tatters || *mf* ragamuffin
déguerpir [degɛrpir] *intr* (coll) to clear out, to beat it; **faire déguerpir** to evict
déguisement [degizmã] *m* disguise
déguiser [degize] *tr* to disguise
dégusta·teur [degystatœr] **-trice** [tris] *mf* winetaster
dégustation [degystasjɔ̃] *f* tasting, art of tasting; consumption (*of beverages*)
déguster [degyste] *tr* to taste discriminatingly; to sip, drink; to consume
déhancher [deɑ̃ʃe] *tr* to dislocate the hip of || *intr* to swing one's hips
déharnacher [dearnaʃe] *tr* to unsaddle, unharness || *ref* (coll) to throw off one's heavy clothing
dehors [dəɔr] *m* outside; **dehors** *mpl* outward appearance; **du dehors** from without, foreign, external; **en dehors** outside; **en dehors de** outside of; beyond || *adv* outside, out; out-of-doors

déification [deifikɑsjɔ̃] *f* deification
déifier [deifje] *tr* to deify
déiste [deist] *adj & mf* deist
déité [deite] *f* deity
déjà [deʒa] *adv* already
déjanter [deʒɑ̃te] *tr* to take (*a tire*) off the rim || *ref* to come off
déjection [deʒɛksjɔ̃] *f* excretion; volcanic debris
déjeter [deʒte] §34 *tr & ref* to warp, to spring
déjeuner [deʒœne] *m* lunch; breakfast; breakfast set; **petit déjeuner** breakfast || *intr* to have lunch; to have breakfast
déjouer [deʒwe] *tr* to foil, thwart
déjucher [deʒyʃe] *tr* to unroost || *intr* to come off the roost (*said of fowl*)
déjuger [deʒyʒe] §38 *ref* to change one's mind
delà [dəla] *adv*—**au delà de** beyond; **par delà** beyond
délabrement [delabrəmã] *m* decay, dilapidation; impairment (*of health*)
délabrer [delabre] *tr* to ruin, wreck || *ref* to become dilapidated
délacer [delase] §51 *tr* to unlace
délai [delɛ] *m* term, duration, period (*of time*); postponement, extension; **à bref délai** at short notice; **dans le plus bref délai** in the shortest possible time; **dans un délai de** within; **dans un délai record** in record time; **dernier délai** deadline; **sans délai** without delay
délais·sé -sée [delɛse] *adj* forsaken, forlorn, neglected
délaissement [delɛsmã] *m* abandonment
delaisser [delɛse] *tr* to abandon, desert; to relinquish (*a right*)
délassement [delasmã] *m* relaxation
délasser [delase] *tr* to rest, refresh, relax || *ref* to rest up
déla·teur [delatœr] **-trice** [tris] *mf* informer
délation [delasjɔ̃] *f* paid informing
déla·vé -vée [delave] *adj* washed-out, weak
délayer [deleje] §49 *tr* to add water to, to dilute; **délayer un discours** to stretch out a speech
deleatur [deleatyr] *m* dele
délébile [delebil] *adj* erasable
délectable [delɛktabl] *adj* delectable
délectation [delɛktɑsjɔ̃] *f* pleasure
délecter [delɛkte] *ref*—**se délecter à** to find pleasure in
délégation [delegɑsjɔ̃] *f* delegation
délé·gué -guée [delege] *adj* delegated || *mf* delegate, spokesman
déléguer [delege] §10 *tr* to delegate
délester [delɛste] *tr* to unballast; to unburden, relieve
délétère [deletɛr] *adj* deleterious
délibération [deliberɑsjɔ̃] *f* deliberation
délibé·ré -rée [delibere] *adj* deliberate, firm, decided
délibérer [delibere] §10 *tr & intr* to deliberate
déli·cat [delika] **-cate** [kat] *adj* delicate; fine, sensitive (*ear, mind, taste*); touchy; tactful; scrupulous, honest

délicatesse [delikatɛs] *f* delicacy; refinement, fineness; fastidiousness; fragility, weakness
délice [delis] *m* great pleasure || **délices** *fpl* delights, pleasures
déli·cieux [delisjø] **-cieuse** [sjøz] *adj* delicious; delightful, charming
dé·lié -liée [delje] *adj* slender (*figure*); nimble (*mind*); fine (*handwriting*); glib (*tongue*) || *m* upstroke, thin stroke
délier [delje] *tr* to untie, to loosen, to release || *ref* to come loose
délinéament [delineamã] *m* delineation
délinéer [delinee] *tr* to delineate
délinquance [delɛ̃kãs] *f* delinquency; **délinquance juvénile** juvenile delinquency
délin·quant [delɛ̃kã] **-quante** [kãt] *adj & mf* delinquent; **délinquant primaire** first offender
déli·rant [delirã] **-rante** [rãt] *adj* delirious, raving
délire [delir] *m* delirium; **en délire** delirious, in a frenzy
délirer [delire] *intr* to be delirious, to rave
délit [deli] *m* offense, wrong, crime; **en flagrant délit** in the act
délivrance [delivrãs] *f* delivrance; delivery
délivre [delivr] *m* afterbirth, placenta
délivrer [delivre] *tr* to deliver
déloger [delɔʒe] §38 *tr* to dislodge; (coll) to oust, to evict || *intr* to move out (*of a house*)
déloyal déloyale [delwajal] *adj* (*pl* **déloyaux** [delwajo]) disloyal; unfair, dishonest
déloyauté [delwajote] *f* disloyalty; disloyal act; dishonesty
delta [dɛlta] *m* delta
déluge [delyʒ] *m* deluge, flood
délu·ré -rée [delyre] *adj* smart, clever; smart-alecky, forward
délurer [delyre] *tr & ref* to wise up
délustrer [delystre] *tr* to take the gloss off of
démagnétiser [demaɲetize] *tr* to demagnetize
démagogie [demagɔʒi] *f* demagogy
démagogique [demagɔʒik] *adj* demagogic
démagogue [demagɔg] *adj* demagogic || *mf* demagogue
démaigrir [demɛgrir] *tr* to thin down
démailler [demaje] *tr* to unshackle (*a chain*); to unravel (*e.g., a knitted sweater*); to make a run in (*a stocking*) || *ref* to run (*said of stocking*)
démailloter [demajote] *tr* to take the diaper off of
demain [dəmɛ̃] *adv & m* tomorrow; **à demain** until tomorrow; so long; **de demain en huit** a week from tomorrow; **de demain en quinze** two weeks from tomorrow; **demain matin** tomorrow morning
démancher [demãʃe] *tr* to remove the handle of; (coll) to dislocate
demande [dəmãd] *f* request; application (*for a position*); inquiry; demand (*by buyers for goods*)

demander [dəmãde] *tr* to ask (*a favor; one's way*); to ask for (*a package; a porter*); to require, to need (*attention*); **demander q.ch. à qn** to ask s.o. for s.th. || *intr*—**demander à or de** + *inf* to ask permission to + *inf*; to insist upon + *ger*; **demander après** to ask about, ask for (*s.o.*); **demander à qn de** + *inf* to ask s.o. to + *inf*; **je ne demande pas mieux** I wish I could || *ref* to be needed; to wonder
deman·deur [dəmãdœr] **-deuse** [døz] *mf* asker; buyer || **-deur** [dœr] **-deresse** [drɛs] *mf* plaintiff
démangeaison [demãʒɛzɔ̃] *f* itch
démanger [demãʒe] §38 *tr & intr* to itch || *intr* (with *dat*) to itch; **la langue lui démange** he is itching to speak
démanteler [demãtle] §2 *tr* to dismantle (*a fort or town*); to uncover (*a spy ring*)
démaquillage [demakijaʒ] *m* removal of paint or make-up
démaquillant [demakijã] *m* cleansing cream, make-up remover
démaquiller [demakije] *tr & ref* to take the paint or make-up off
démarcation [demarkasjɔ̃] *f* demarcation
démarche [demarʃ] *f* gait, step, bearing; method; step, move, action
démarier [demarje] *tr* to thin out (*plants*)
démarque [demark] *f* (com) markdown
démarquer [demarke] *tr* to remove the identification marks from; to plagiarize; to mark down
démarrage [demaraʒ] *m* start
démarrer [demare] *tr* to unmoor || *intr* to cast off (*said of ship*); to start (*said of train or car*); to spurt (*said of racing contestant; said of economy*); **démarrer trop tôt** to jump the gun; **faire démarrer** to start (*a car*); **ne démarrez pas!** don't stir!
démarreur [demarœr] *m* starter (*of car*)
démasquer [demaske] *tr & ref* to unmask
démâter [demate] *tr* to dismast || *intr* to lose her masts (*said of ship*)
démêlé [demɛle] *m* quarrel, dispute; **avoir des démêlés avec** to be at odds with, to run afoul of
démêler [demɛle] *tr* to disentangle, unravel; to bring to light, uncover (*a plot*); to make out, discern
démembrement [demãbrəmã] *m* dismemberment
déménagement [demenaʒmã] *m* moving
déménager [demenaʒe] §38 *tr* to move (*household effects*) to another residence; to move the furniture from (*a house*) || *intr* to move, to change one's residence; (coll) to become childish; **tu déménages!** (coll) you're out of your mind!
déménageur [demenaʒœr] *m* mover

démence [demãs] *f* madness, insanity; en démence demented

démener [demne] §2 *ref* to struggle, to be agitated; to take great pains

dé·ment [demã] -mente [mãt] *adj & mf* lunatic

démenti [demãti] *m* contradiction, denial; proof to the contrary; (coll) shame (*on account of a failure*)

démentir [demãtir] §41 *tr* to contradict, to deny; to give the lie to, to belie || *intr* to go back on one's word; to be inconsistent

démériter [demerite] *intr* to lose esteem, to become unworthy

démesure [deməzyr] *f* lack of moderation, excess

démesu·ré -rée [deməzyre] *adj* measureless, immense; immoderate, excessive

démettre [demɛtr] §42 *tr* to dismiss (*from a job or position*); to dislocate (*an arm*) || *ref* to resign, retire

démeubler [demœble] *tr* to remove the furniture from

demeurant [demœrã]—au demeurant all things considered, after all

demeure [demœr] *f* home, abode, dwelling; à demeure permanently; dernière demeure final resting place; en demeure in arrears; mettre qn en demeure de to oblige s.o. to; sans plus longue demeure without further delay

demeurer [demœre] *intr* to live, dwell || *intr* (aux: ÊTRE) to stay, remain; en demeurer to leave off; en demeurer là to stop, rest there; to leave it at that

demi [demi] *m* half; (sports) center; (sports) halfback; à demi half; et demi and a half, e.g., un centimètre et demi a centimeter and a half; (after midi or minuit) half past, e.g., midi et demi half past twelve

demi-bas [demibɑ] *m* half hose

demi-botte [demibɔt] *f* (*pl* -bottes) half boot

demi-cercle [demisɛrk̦l] *m* (*pl* -cercles) semicircle

demi-clef [demikle] *f* (*pl* -clefs) half hitch; demi-clef à capeler clove hitch; deux demi-clefs two half hitches

demi-congé [demikɔ̃ʒe] *m* (*pl* -congés) half-holiday

demi-deuil [demidœj] *m* (*pl* -deuils) half mourning

demi-dieu [demidjø] *m* (*pl* -dieux) demigod

demie [demi] *f* half hour; et demie half past, e.g., deux heures et demie half past two

demi-finale [demifinal] *f* (*pl* -finales) semifinal

demi-frère [demifrɛr] *m* (*pl* -frères) half brother; stepbrother

demi-heure [demiœr] *f* (*pl* -heures) half-hour; toutes les demi-heures à la demi-heure juste every half-hour on the half-hour

demi-jour [demiʒur] *m* invar twilight, half-light

demi-journée [demiʒurne] *f* (*pl* -journées) half-day; à demi-journée half-time

démilitariser [demilitarize] *tr* to demilitarize

demi-longueur [demilɔ̃gœr] *f* half-length

demi-lune [demilyn] *f* (*pl* -lunes) half-moon

demi-mondaine [demimɔ̃dɛn] *f* (*pl* -mondaines) demimondaine

demi-monde [demimɔ̃d] *m* demimonde

demi-mot [demimo] *m* (*pl* -mots) understatement, euphemism; comprendre à demi-mot to get the drift of; to take the hint

déminer [demine] *tr* to clear of mines

demi-pause [demipoz] *f* (*pl* -pauses) (mus) half rest

demi-pension [demipãsjɔ̃] *f* (*pl* -pensions) breakfast and one meal

demi-place [demiplas] *f* (*pl* -places) half fare; half-price seat

demi-reliure [demirəljyr] *f* (*pl* -reliures) quarter binding; demi-reliure à petits coins half binding

demi-saison [demisɛzɔ̃] *f* in-between season; de demi-saison spring-and-fall (coat)

demi-sang [demisã] *m* invar half-bred horse

demi-sœur [demisœr] *f* (*pl* -sœurs) half sister; stepsister

demi-solde [demisɔld] *m* invar pensioned officer || *f* (*pl* -soldes) army pension, half pay

demi-soupir [demisupir] *m* (*pl* -soupirs) (mus) eighth rest

démission [demisjɔ̃] *f* resignation

démissionnaire [demisjɔnɛr] *adj* outgoing || *mf* former incumbent

démissionner [demisjɔne] *tr* (coll) to fire || *intr* to resign

demi-tasse [demitɑs] *f* (*pl* -tasses) halfcup; small cup, demitasse

demi-teinte [demitɛ̃t] *f* (*pl* -teintes) halftone

demi-ton [demitɔ̃] *m* (*pl* -tons) (mus) half tone

demi-tour [demitur] *m* (*pl* -tours) about-face; half turn; demi-tour, (à) droite! about face!; demi-tour, à terre! to the rear!; faire demi-tour to do an about-face; to turn back

démobiliser [demɔbilize] *tr* to demobilize

démocrate [demɔkrat] *mf* democrat

démocratie [demɔkrasi] *f* democracy

démocratique [demɔkratik] *adj* democratic

démo·dé -dée [demɔde] *adj* oldfashioned, out-of-date, outmoded

démoder [demɔde] *ref* to be outmoded

demoiselle [dəmwazɛl] *f* single girl, young lady, miss; dragonfly; (slang) girl; demoiselle de magasin salesgirl; demoiselle d'honneur maid of honor, bridesmaid; lady-in-waiting

démolir [demɔlir] *tr* to demolish; to overturn (a cabinet or government)

démolition [demɔlisjɔ̃] *f* demolition; démolitions scrap, rubble

démon [demɔ̃] *m* demon

démoniaque [demɔnjak] *adj* demonic, demoniac(al) || *mf* demoniac
démonstra·teur [demɔ̃nstratœr] **-trice** [tris] *mf* demonstrator
démonstra·tif [demɔ̃stratif] **-tive** [tiv] *adj* & *m* demonstrative
démontable [demɔ̃tabl] *adj* collapsible, detachable; knockdown
démonte-pneu [demɔ̃tpnø] *m* (*pl* **-pneus**) tire iron
démonter [demɔ̃te] *tr* to dismount; to dismantle || *ref* to come apart; to go to pieces (*while taking an exam*)
démontrable [demɔ̃trabl] *adj* demonstrable
démontrer [demɔ̃tre] *tr* to demonstrate
démoraliser [demɔralize] *tr* to demoralize
démouler [demule] *tr* to remove from a mold
dému·ni -nie [demyni] *adj* out of money; **démuni de** out of; devoid of
démunir [demynir] *tr* to strip, deprive; to deplete (*a garrison*) || *ref* to deprive oneself
démystifier [demistifje] *tr* to debunk
dénationaliser [denasjɔnalize] *tr* to denationalize
dénaturaliser [denatyralize] *tr* to denaturalize
dénatu·ré -rée [denatyre] *adj* denatured; unnatural, perverse
dénaturer [denatyre] *tr* to denature; to pervert; to distort
dénégation [denegɑsjɔ̃] *f* denial
déni [deni] *m* refusal; (law) denial
dénicher [denife] *tr* to dislodge; to take out of the nest; to make (*s.o.*) move; to search out || *intr* to leave the nest
déni·cheur [denifœr] **-cheuse** [føz] *mf* hunter (*of rare books, antiques, etc.*); **dénicheur de vedettes** talent scout
denier [dənje] *m* (fig) penny, farthing; **denier à Dieu** gratuity; **deniers** money, funds; **de ses deniers** with his own money
dénier [denje] *tr* to deny, refuse
dénigrer [denigre] *tr* to disparage
déniveler [denivle] §34 *tr* to make uneven, to change the level of
dénivellation [denivɛllɑsjɔ̃] *f* or **dénivellement** [denivɛlmɑ̃] *m* unevenness; depression, settling
dénombrement [denɔ̃brəmɑ̃] *m* census, enumeration
dénombrer [denɔ̃bre] *tr* to take a census of, to enumerate
dénomination [denɔminɑsjɔ̃] *f* denomination, appellation, designation
dénommer [denɔme] *tr* to denominate, to name
dénoncer [denɔ̃se] §51 *tr* to renounce; to indicate, reveal || *ref* to give oneself up
dénonciation [denɔ̃sjɑsjɔ̃] *f* denunciation; declaration
dénoter [denɔte] *tr* to denote
dénouement [denumɑ̃] *m* outcome, denouement; untying
dénouer [denwe] *tr* to untie; to unravel

dénoyer [denwaje] §47 *tr* to pump out
denrée [dɑre] *f* commodity; **denrées** provisions, products
dense [dɑs] *adj* dense
densité [dɑsite] *f* density
dent [dɑ̃] *f* tooth; cog; scallop (*of an edge*); **dent d'éléphant** tusk; **dents de lait** baby teeth; **dents de sagesse** wisdom teeth; **sur les dents** on one's toes
dentaire [dɑter] *adj* dental
den·tal -tale [dɑtal] *adj* & *f* (*pl* **-taux** [to] **-tales**) dental
dent-de-chien [dɑ̃dəʃjɛ̃] *f* (*pl* **dents-de-chien**) dogtooth violet
dent-de-lion [dɑ̃dəljɔ̃] *f* (*pl* **dents-de-lion**) dandelion
denteler [dɑtle] §34 *tr* to notch, to indent
dentelle [dɑtɛl] *f* lace; lacework
dentelure [dɑtlyr] *f* notching; serration; scalloping; (phila) perforation
denter [dɑte] *tr* to furnish with cogs or teeth
dentier [dɑtje] *m* false teeth, denture
dentifrice [dɑtifris] *m* dentifrice
dentiste [dɑtist] *mf* dentist
denture [dɑtyr] *f* denture; **denture artificielle** false teeth
dénuder [denyde] *tr* to strip, denude
dénuement [denymɑ̃] *m* destitution
dénuer [denɥe] *tr* to deprive, strip
déontologie [deɔ̃tɔlɔʒi] *f* study of ethics; **déontologie médicale** (med) code of medical ethics
dépannage [depanaʒ] *m* emergency service, repairs
dépanner [depane] *tr* to give emergency service to; (coll) to get (*s.o.*) out of a scrape
dépan·neur [depanœr] **dépan·neuse** [depanøz] *adj* repairing || *m* serviceman, repairman || *f* tow truck, wrecker
dépaqueter [depakte] §34 *tr* to unpack, unwrap
dépareil·lé -lée [depareje] *adj* incomplete, broken (*set*); odd (*sock*)
dépareiller [depareje] *tr* to break (*a set*)
déparer [depare] *tr* to mar, to spoil the beauty of; to strip of ornaments
déparier [deparje] *tr* to break, split up the pair of
départ [depar] *m* departure; beginning; division; sorting out; **départ usine** F.O.B.; **faux départ** false start
département [departəmɑ̃] *m* (govt) department
départir [departir] §64 (or sometimes like **finir**) *tr* to divide up, to distribute || *ref*—**se départir de** to give up; to depart from
dépassement [depasmɑ̃] *m* passing
dépasser [depase] *tr* to pass, overtake; to go beyond; to overshoot (*the mark*); to exceed; to extend beyond; to be longer than; (coll) to surprise || *intr* to pass; to stick out, to overlap, to show
dépayser [depeize] *tr* to take out of one's familiar surroundings; to bewilder || *ref* to leave one's country

dépecer [depǝse] §20 *tr* to carve, to cut up

dépêche [depɛʃ] *f* dispatch; telegram

dépêcher [depɛʃe] *tr* to dispatch ‖ *ref* to hurry

dépeigner [depɛɲe] *tr* to tousle, to muss up (*the hair*)

dépeindre [depɛ̃dr] §50 *tr* to depict

dépendance [depɑ̃dɑ̃s] *f* dependence; **dépendances** outbuildings, annex; dependencies, possessions

dépen·dant [depɑ̃dɑ̃] **-dante** [dɑ̃t] *adj* dependent

dépendre [depɑ̃dr] *tr* to take down ‖ *intr* to depend; **dépendre de** to depend on; to belong to; **il dépend de vous de** it is for you to

dépens [depɑ̃] *mpl* expenses, costs; **aux dépens de** at the expense of

dépense [depɑ̃s] *f* expense; pantry; dispensary (*of hospital*); flow (*of water*); consumption (*of fuel*)

dépenser [depɑ̃se] *tr* to spend, expend ‖ *ref* to exert oneself, to spend one's energy

dépen·sier [depɑ̃sje] **-sière** [sjɛr] *adj* & *mf* spendthrift

dépérir [deperir] *intr* to waste away, decline

dépêtrer [depɛtre] *tr* to get (*s.o.*) out of a jam

dépeupler [depœple] *tr* to depopulate; to unstock (*a pond*)

dépha·sé -sée [defaze] *adj* out of phase

dépiauter [depjote] *tr* to skin

dépiécer [depjese] §58 *tr* to dismember

dépiler [depile] *tr* to remove the hair from

dépister [depiste] *tr* to track down

dépit [depi] *m* spite, resentment; **en dépit de** in spite of

dépiter [depite] *tr* to spite, to vex ‖ *ref* to take offense

dépla·cé -cée [deplase] *adj* displaced (*person*); misplaced, out of place

déplacement [deplasmɑ̃] *m* displacement; movement; travel; transfer (*of an official*); shift (*in votes*); change (*in schedule*); (naut) displacement

déplacer [deplase] §51 *tr* to displace; to move; **déplacer la question** to stray from the subject ‖ *ref* to move

déplaire [deplɛr] §52 *intr* (with *dat*) to displease; (with *dat*) to dislike, e.g., **le lait lui déplaît** he dislikes milk; **ne vous en déplaise** if you have no objection, by your leave ‖ *ref* to be displeased, e.g., **ils se sont déplu** they were displeased; **se déplaire à** not to like it in, e.g., **je me déplais à la campagne** I don't like it in the country

déplai·sant [deplɛzɑ̃] **-sante** [zɑ̃t] *adj* unpleasant, disagreeable

déplaisir [deplɛzir] *m* displeasure

déplanter [deplɑ̃te] *tr* to dig up for transplanting

déplantoir [deplɑ̃twar] *m* garden trowel

dépliant [deplijɑ̃] *m* folder, brochure

déplier [deplie] *tr* & *ref* to unfold

déplisser [deplise] *tr* to unpleat

déploiement [deplwamɑ̃] *m* unfolding, unfurling; display, array; (mil) deployment

déplorable [deplɔrabl] *adj* deplorable

déplorer [deplɔre] *tr* to deplore; to grieve over

déployer [deplwaje] §47 *tr* to unfold, to unfurl; to display; (mil) to deploy ‖ *ref* (mil) to deploy

déplumer [deplyme] *tr* to pluck (*a chicken*) ‖ *ref* (coll) to lose one's hair

dépolariser [depɔlarize] *tr* to depolarize

dépo·li -lie [depɔli] *adj* ground (*glass*)

dépolir [depɔlir] *tr* to remove the polish from; to frost (*glass*)

déport [depɔr] *m* disqualifying of oneself; (com) commission; **sans déport** without delay

déportation [depɔrtasjɔ̃] *f* deportation; internment in a concentration camp

dépor·té -tée [depɔrte] *mf* deported criminal, convict; prisoner in a concentration camp

déportement [depɔrtǝmɑ̃] *m* swerve; **déportements** misconduct, immoral conduct, bad habits

déporter [depɔrte] *tr* to deport; to send to a concentration camp; to make (*an automobile*) swerve; to deflect (*an airplane*) from its course ‖ *intr* to swerve

dépo·sant [depɔzɑ̃] **-sante** [zɑ̃t] *adj* testifying; depositing ‖ *mf* deponent, witness; depositor

dépose [depoz] *f* removal

déposer [depoze] *tr* to deposit; to depose; to drop, leave off; to register (*a trademark*); to lodge (*a complaint*); to file (*a petition*) ‖ *intr* & *ref* to depose; to settle, to form a deposit

dépositaire [depozitɛr] *mf* trustee, holder; dealer

déposséder [depɔsede] §10 *tr* to dispossess

dépôt [depo] *m* deposit; depository, depot; warehouse; delivery, handing in; **dépôt d'autobus** carbarn; **dépôt de locomotives** roundhouse; **dépôt de mendicité** poorhouse; **dépôt des bagages** baggage room; **dépôt d'essence** filling station; **dépôt de vivres** commissary; **dépôt d'ordures** dump

dépouille [depuj] *f* castoff skin; hide (*taken from animal*); **dépouille mortelle** mortal remains; **dépouilles** spoils (*of war*)

dépouillement [depujmɑ̃] *m* gathering, selection, sifting; despoilment; counting (*of votes*); **dépouillement volontaire** relinquishing

dépouiller [depuje] *tr* to skin; to strip; to gather, select, sift; to count (*votes*) ‖ *ref* to shed one's skin (*said of insects and reptiles*); to strip oneself, to divest oneself

dépour·vu -vue [depurvy] *adj* destitute; **au dépourvu** unaware; **dépourvu de** devoid of, lacking in

dépoussiérer [depusjere] §10 *tr* to vacuum

dépravation [depravɑsjɔ̃] *f* depravity
dépraver [deprave] *tr* to deprave
déprécation [deprekɑsjɔ̃] *f* supplication
dépréciation [depresjɑsjɔ̃] *f* depreciation
déprécier [depresje] *tr & ref* to depreciate
déprédation [depredɑsjɔ̃] *f* depredation; embezzlement, misappropriation
déprendre [deprɑ̃dr] §56 *ref* to detach oneself; to come loose; to melt
dépres•sif [depresif] dépres-sive [depresiv] *adj* depressive
dépression [depresjɔ̃] *f* depression
déprimer [deprime] *tr* to depress, to lower || *ref* to be depressed
dépriser [deprize] *tr* to undervalue
depuis [dəpɥi] *adv* since; depuis que since || *prep* since, for, e.g., je suis à Paris depuis trois jours I have been in Paris for three days; depuis . . . jusqu'à from . . . to
dépurer [depyre] *tr* to purify
députation [depytɑsjɔ̃] *f* deputation
député [depyte] *m* deputy
députer [depyte] *tr* to deputize
der [der] *f*—la der des der (coll) the war to end all wars
déraci•né -née [derasine] *adj* uprooted || *mf* uprooted person, wanderer
déraciner [derasine] *tr* to uproot, to root out; to eradicate
déraillement [derajmɑ̃] *m* derailment
dérailler [deraje] *intr* to jump the track; (coll) to get off the track
déraison [derezɔ̃] *f* unreasonableness, irrationality
déraisonnable [derezɔnabl] *adj* unreasonable
déraisonner [derezɔne] *intr* to talk nonsense
dérangement [derɑ̃ʒmɑ̃] *m* derangement; breakdown; disturbance, bother
déranger [derɑ̃ʒe] §38 *tr* to derange, to put out of order; to disturb, trouble || *ref* to move, to change jobs; to become disordered, upset; ne vous dérangez pas! don't get up!; don't bother!
déraper [derape] *intr* to skid, to sideslip; to weigh anchor
dératé [derate] *m*—courir comme un dératé to run like a jack rabbit
dératiser [deratize] *tr* to derat
derby [derbi] *m* derby (*race*)
derechef [dərəʃef] *adv* (lit) once again
déré•glé -glée [deregle] *adj* out of order; irregular (*pulse*); disorderly, excessive
dérégler [deregle] §10 *tr* to put out of order, upset || *ref* to get out of order; to run wild
dérider [deride] *tr* to smooth, unwrinkle; to cheer up || *ref* to cheer up
dérision [derizjɔ̃] *f* derision
dérisoire [derizwar] *adj* derisive
dérivation [derivɑsjɔ̃] *f* derivation; drift; by-pass; diversion (*of river, stream, etc.*); en dérivation shunted (*circuit*)

dérive [deriv] *f* drift; (aer) fin; (naut) centerboard; à la dérive adrift
déri•vé -vée [derive] *adj* drifting; shunted (*current*) || *m* derivative
dériver [derive] *tr* to derive; to divert (*e.g., a river*); to unrivet || *intr* to derive; to be derived; to result; to drift
dermatologie [dermatɔlɔʒi] *f* dermatology
der•nier [dernje] -nière [njer] *adj* last; latest; latter; final; last (*just elapsed*), e.g., la semaine dernière last week || (when standing before noun) *adj* last (*in a series*), e.g., la dernière semaine de la guerre the last week of the war
dernièrement [dernjermɑ̃] *adv* lately
dernier-né [dernjene] dernière-née [dernjerne] *mf* (*pl* -nés -nées) lastborn child
déro•bé -bée [derɔbe] *adj* secret; à la dérobée stealthily, on the sly
dérober [derɔbe] *tr* to steal; to hide; dérober à to steal from; to rescue from (*e.g., death*) || *ref* to steal away, disappear; to hide; to shy away, balk; to shirk; to give way (*said of knees or one's footing*); se dérober à to slip away from, to escape from
dérogation [derɔgɑsjɔ̃] *f*—dérogation à departure from (*custom*); waiving of (*principle*); deviation from (*instructions*); par dérogation à notwithstanding
déroger [derɔʒe] §38 *intr*—déroger à to depart from (*custom*); to waive (*a principle*); to derogate from (*dignity; one's rank*)
dérouiller [deruje] *tr* to remove the rust from; to polish (*s.o.*); (coll) to limber up; (coll) to brush up on || *ref* to lose its rust; to brush up; to limber up
dérouler [derule] *tr & ref* to unroll, unfold
dérou•tant [derutɑ̃] -tante [tɑ̃t] *adj* baffling, misleading
déroute [derut] *f* rout, downfall
dérouter [derute] *tr* to steer off the course; to reroute; to disconcert, baffle || *ref* to go astray; to become confused
derrick [derik] *m* oil derrick
derrière [derjer] *m* rear, backside || *adv & prep* behind
derviche [dervij] *m* dervish
des [de] §77
dès [de] *prep* by (*a certain time*); from (*a certain place*); as early as, as far back as; from, beginning with; dès lors from that time, ever since; dès lors que since, inasmuch as; dès que as soon as
désabonner [dezabɔne] *tr* to cancel the subscription of || *ref* to cancel one's subscription
désabu•sé -sée [dezabyze] *adj* disillusioned
désabuser [dezabyze] *tr* to disabuse, disillusion || *ref* to have one's eyes opened

désaccord [dezakɔr] *m* disagreement, discord

désaccorder [dezakɔrde] *tr* to put (*an instrument*) out of tune || *ref* to get out of tune

désaccoupler [dezakuple] *tr* to unpair; to uncouple

désaccoutumer [dezakutyme] *tr* to break (*s.o.*) of a habit || *ref* to break oneself of a habit

désaffecter [dezafɛkte] *tr* to turn from its intended use

désagréable [dezagreabl] *adj* disagreeable; unpleasant

désagréger [dezagreʒe] §1 *tr* to break up, to dissolve, to disintegrate

désagrément [dezagremã] *m* unpleasantness, annoyance

désaimanter [dezɛmãte] *tr* to demagnetize

desalté·rant [dezalterã] **-rante** [rãt] *adj* thirst-quenching, refreshing

désaltérer [dezaltere] §10 *tr* to quench the thirst of; to refresh with a drink || *ref* to quench one's thirst

désamorcer [dezamɔrse] §51 *tr* to deactivate, to disconnect the fuse of; to unprime

désappointement [dezapwɛ̃tmã] *m* disappointment

désappointer [dezapwɛ̃te] *tr* to disappoint; to break the point of, to blunt

désapprendre [dezaprãdr] §56 *tr* to unlearn, to forget

désapproba·teur [dezaprɔbatœr] **-trice** [tris] *adj* disapproving || *mf* critic

désapprouver [dezapruve] *tr* to disapprove of, to disapprove

désarçonner [dezarsɔne] *tr* to unhorse, buck off; (coll) to dumfound

désarmement [dezarməmã] *m* disarmament; disarming; dismantling (*of ship*)

désarmer [dezarme] *tr* to disarm; to deactivate; to dismantle; to appease || *intr* to disarm; to slacken, let up (*said of hostility*)

désarroi [dezarwa] *m* disorder, disarray, confusion

désarticulation [dezartikylɑsjɔ̃] *f* dislocation

désassembler [dezasãble] *tr* to disassemble

désastre [dezastr] *m* disaster

désas·treux [dezastrø] **-treuse** [trøz] *adj* disastrous

désavantage [dezavãtaʒ] *m* disadvantage

désavantager [dezavãtaʒe] §38 *tr* to put at a disadvantage, to handicap

désavanta·geux [dezavãtaʒø] **-geuse** [ʒøz] *adj* disadvantageous

désa·veu [dezavø] *m* (*pl* **-veux**) disavowal, denial, repudiation

désavouer [dezavwe] *tr* to disavow, to deny, to repudiate, to disown

désaxé désaxée [dezakse] *adj* unbalanced, out of joint

desceller [desɛle] *tr* to unseal

descendance [desãdãs] *f* descent

descendeur [desãdœr] *m* ski jumper

descendre [desãdr], [dɛsãdr] *tr* to descend, to go down (*a hill, street,*

stairway); to take down, to lower (*a picture*); (coll) to bring down (*an airplane; luggage*); (coll) to drop off, let off at the door || *intr* (*aux:* ÊTRE) to descend; to go down, to go downstairs; to stay, to stop (*at a hotel*); **descendre** + *inf* to go down to + *inf*; to stop off to + *inf*; **descendre court** to undershoot (*said of airplane*); **descendre de** to come down from (*a mountain, ladder, tree*); to be descended from

descente [desãt] *f* descent; invasion; raid; stay (*at a hotel*); stop (*en route*); **descente à terre** (nav) shore leave; **descente de lit** bedside rug

descriptible [dɛskriptibl] *adj* describable

descrip·tif [dɛskriptif] **-tive** [tiv] *adj* descriptive

description [dɛskripsjɔ̃] *f* description

déségrégation [desegregɑsjɔ̃] *f* desegregation

désempa·ré -rée [dezãpare] *adj* disconcerted; disabled (*ship*)

désemparer [dezãpare] *tr* to disable (*a ship*) || *intr*—**sans désemparer** continuously, without intermission

désemplir [dezãplir] *intr*—**ne pas désemplir** to be always full

désenchaîner [dezãʃɛne] *tr* to unchain

désenchantement [dezãʃãtmã] *m* disenchantment

désenchanter [dezãʃãte] *tr* to disenchant

désencombrer [dezãkɔ̃bre] *tr* to disencumber, to clear, to free

désengager [dezãgaʒe] §38 *tr* to release from a promise

désengorger [dezãgɔrʒe] §38 *tr* to unstop

désengrener [dezãgrəne] §2 *tr* to disengage, to throw out of gear

désenivrer [dezãnivre] *tr & intr* to sober up

désenlacer [dezãlase] §51 *tr* to unbind

désennuyer [dezãnɥije] §27 *tr* to divert, cheer up || *ref* to find relief from boredom

désensabler [dezãsable] *tr* to free (*a ship*) from the sand; to dredge the sand from (*a canal*)

désensibiliser [desãsibilize] *tr* to desensitize

désensorceler [dezãsɔrsəle] §34 *tr* to remove the spell from

désentortiller [dezãtɔrtije] *tr* to straighten out

désenvelopper [dezãvlɔpe] *tr* to unwrap

déséquilibre [dezekilibr] *m* mental instability

déséquili·bré -brée [dezekilibre] *adj* mentally unbalanced || *mf* unbalanced person

déséquilibrer [dezekilibre] *tr* to unbalance

dé·sert [dezɛr] **-serte** [zɛrt] *adj & m* desert

déserter [dezɛrte] *tr & intr* to desert

déserteur [dezɛrtœr] *m* deserter

désertion [dezɛrsjɔ̃] *f* desertion

désespérance [dezɛsperãs] *f* despair

désespé·ré -rée [dezɛspere] *adj* desperate, hopeless || *mf* desperate person
désespérer [dezɛspere] §10 *tr* to be the despair of || *ref* to lose hope
désespoir [dezɛspwar] *m* despair; **en désespoir de cause** as a last resort
déshabillage [dezabijaʒ] *m* striptease
déshabillé [dezabije] *m* morning wrap
déshabiller [dezabije] *tr* & *ref* to undress; **déshabiller saint Pierre pour habiller saint Paul** to rob Peter to pay Paul
déshabituer [dezabitɥe] *tr* to break (*s.o.*) of a habit
déshéri·té -tée [dezerite] *adj* underprivileged; **les déshérités** the underprivileged
déshériter [dezerite] *tr* to disinherit; to disadvantage
déshonnête [dezɔnɛt] *adj* improper, immodest
déshonnêteté [dezɔnɛtəte] *f* impropriety, immodesty, indecency
déshonneur [dezɔnœr] *m* dishonor
déshono·rant [dezɔnɔrɑ̃] **-rante** [rɑ̃t] *adj* dishonorable, discreditable
déshonorer [dezɔnɔre] *tr* to dishonor
déshydratation [dezidratɑsjɔ̃] *f* dehydration
déshydrater [dezidrate] *tr* to dehydrate
désignation [deziɲɑsjɔ̃] *f* designation; appointment, nomination
dési·gné -gnée [desiɲe] *mf* nominee
désigner [desiɲe] *tr* to designate; to indicate, point out; to appoint, nominate; to signify, mean; to set (*the hour of an appointment*) || *ref*—**se désigner à l'attention de** to bring oneself to the attention of
désillusion [dezillyzjɔ̃] *f* disillusion; disappointment
désillusionner [dezillyzjɔne] *tr* to disillusion; to disappoint
désinence [dezinɑ̃s] *f* (gram) ending
désinfecter [dezɛ̃fɛkte] *tr* to disinfect
désintégration [dezɛ̃tegrɑsjɔ̃] *f* disintegration
désintégrer [dezɛ̃tegre] §10 *tr* & *ref* to disintegrate
désintéres·sé -sée [dezɛ̃terese] *adj* disinterested, impartial; unselfish
désintéressement [dezɛ̃teresmɑ̃] *m* disinterestedness, impartiality; payment, satisfaction (*of a debt*); paying off (*of a creditor*)
désintéresser [dezɛ̃terese] *tr* to pay off; to buy out || *ref*—**se désintéresser de** to lose interest in
désintoxication [dezɛ̃tɔksikɑsjɔ̃] *f* treatment for alcoholism, drug addiction, or poisoning; disintoxification
désinvolte [dezɛ̃vɔlt] *adj* free and easy, casual; offhanded, impertinent
désinvolture [dezɛ̃vɔltyr] *f* free and easy manner, offhandedness; impertinence
désir [dezir] *m* desire
désirable [dezirabl] *adj* desirable
désirer [dezire] *tr* to desire, wish
dési·reux [dezirø] **-reuse** [røz] *adj* desirous
désister [deziste] *ref* to desist; to withdraw from a runoff election; **se dé-**

sister de to waive (*a claim*); to drop (*a lawsuit*)
désobéir [dezɔbeir] *intr* to disobey; (with *dat*) to disobey; **être désobéi** to be disobeyed
désobli·geant [dezɔbliʒɑ̃] **-geante** [ʒɑ̃t] *adj* disagreeable, ungracious
désobliger [dezɔbliʒe] §38 *tr* to offend, displease, disoblige
désodori·sant [dezɔdɔrizɑ̃] **-sante** [zɑ̃t] *adj* & *m* deodorant
désodoriser [dezɔdɔrize] *tr* to deodorize
désœu·vré -vrée [dezœvre] *adj* idle, unoccupied, out of work; **les désœuvrés** the unemployed
désœuvrement [dezœvrəmɑ̃] *m* idleness, unemployment
déso·lant [dezɔlɑ̃] **-lante** [lɑ̃t] *adj* distressing, sad
désolation [dezɔlɑsjɔ̃] *f* desolation; grief, distress
déso·lé -lée [dezɔle] *adj* desolate; distressed
désoler [dezɔle] *tr* to desolate, destroy; to distress || *ref* to be distressed
désopi·lant [dezɔpilɑ̃] **-lante** [lɑ̃t] *adj* hilarious, sidesplitting
désordon·né -née [dezɔrdɔne] *adj* disordered; untidy; disorderly
désordonner [dezɔrdɔne] *tr* to upset, confuse
désordre [dezɔrdr] *m* disorder, confusion; moral laxity
désorganisa·teur [dezɔrganizatœr] **-trice** [tris] *adj* disorganizing || *mf* troublemaker
désorganisation [dezɔrganizɑsjɔ̃] *f* disorganization
désorganiser [dezɔrganize] *tr* to disorganize
désorien·té -tée [dezɔrjɑ̃te] *adj* disoriented, bewildered
désorienter [dezɔrjɑ̃te] *tr* to disorient; to mislead; to disconcert || *ref* to become confused; to lose one's bearings
désormais [dezɔrme] *adv* henceforth
désosser [dezɔse] *tr* to bone
despote [dɛspɔt] *m* despot
despotique [dɛspɔtik] *adj* despotic
despotisme [dɛspɔtism] *m* despotism
des·quels -quelles [dekɛl] §78
dessaisir [desɛzir] *tr* to dispossess; to let go, to release || *ref*—**se dessaisir de** to relinquish
dessalement [desalmɑ̃] *m* desalinization
dessaler [desale] *tr* to desalt, to desalinate || *ref* (coll) to wise up
dessécher [deseʃe] §10 *tr* to dry up, wither; to drain (*a pond*); to dehydrate (*the body*); to sear (*the heart*) || *ref* to dry up; to waste away
dessein [desɛ̃] *m* design, plan, intent; **à dessein** on purpose
desseller [desɛle] *tr* to unsaddle
desserrer [desɛre] *tr* to loosen; **ne pas desserrer les dents** to keep mum
dessert [desɛr] *m* dessert, last course
desserte [desɛrt] *f* buffet, sideboard; branch (*of railroad or bus line*); ministry (*of a substituting clergyman*)

dessertir [desɛrtir] *tr* to remove (*a gem*) from its setting
desservant [desɛrvã] *m* parish priest
desservir [desɛrvir] §63 *tr* to clear (*the table*); to be of disservice to, to harm; (aer, aut, rr) to stop at (*a town or station*); (aer, aut, eccl, rr) to serve (*a locality*); (elec) to supply (*a region*)
dessiller [desije] *tr*—**dessiller les yeux à qn** or **de qn** to open s.o.'s eyes, to undeceive s.o.
dessin [desɛ̃] *m* drawing, sketch, design; profile (*of face*); **dessins animés** (mov) animated cartoons
dessina·teur [desinatœr] **-trice** [tris] *mf* designer; cartoonist
dessiner [desine] *tr* to draw, sketch, design; to delineate, outline || *ref* to stand out, to be outlined
dessoûler or **dessouler** [desule] *tr* & *intr* to sober up
dessous [dəsu] *m* underpart; reverse side, wrong side; coaster (*underneath a glass*); seamy side, machinations behind the scenes; **au dessous de** below; **avoir le dessous** to get the short end of the deal; **du dessous** below; **en dessous** underneath; **les dessous** lingerie, undergarments || *adv* & *prep* under, underneath, below
dessous-de-bouteille [dəsudəbutɛj] *m invar* coaster
dessous-de-bras [dəsudəbra] *m invar* underarm pad
dessous-de-carafe [dəsudəkaraf] *m invar* coaster
dessous-de-plat [dəsudəpla] *m invar* hot pad
dessous-de-table [dəsudətabl] *m invar* under-the-counter money
dessus [dəsy] *m* upper part; back (*of the hand*); right side (*of material*); (mus) treble part; **au dessus de** beyond, above; **avoir le dessus** to have the upper hand; **le dessus du panier** the cream of the crop || *adv* above || *prep* on, above, over
dessus-de-cheminée [dəsydəʃmine] *m invar* mantelpiece
dessus-de-lit [dəsydəli] *m invar* bedspread
dessus-de-porte [dəsydəpɔrt] *m invar* overdoor
dessus-de-table [dəsydətabl] *m invar* table cover
destin [destɛ̃] *m* destiny, fate
destinataire [destinatɛr] *mf* addressee; payee; **destinataire inconnu** or **absent** (formula stamped on envelope) not at this address
destination [destinasjɔ̃] *f* destination; **à destination de** to, bound for
destinée [destine] *f* destiny
destiner [destine] *tr* to destine; to set aside, to reserve; **destiner q.ch. à qn** to mean or intend s.th. for s.o.
destituer [destitɥe] *tr* to remove from office
destitution [destitysjɔ̃] *f* dismissal, removal from office
destrier [destrije] *m* (hist) steed, charger

destroyer [destrɔjœr] *m* (nav) destroyer
destruc·teur [destryktœr] **-trice** [tris] *adj* destroying, destructive || *mf* destroyer
destruc·tif [destryktif] **-tive** [tiv] *adj* destructive
destruction [destryksjɔ̃] *f* destruction
dé·suet [dezɥɛ] **-suète** [zɥɛt] *adj* obsolete, antiquated, out-of-date
désuétude [dezɥetyd] *f* desuetude, disuse
désu·ni -nie [dezyni] *adj* at odds, divided against itself; uncoordinated
désunion [dezynjɔ̃] *f* dissension
désunir [dezynir] *tr* to disunite, divide; to estrange
déta·ché -chée [detaʃe] *adj* detached; clean; spare (*parts*); acting, temporary (*official*); staccato (*note*)
détachement [detaʃmã] *m* detachment; (mil) detail
détacher [detaʃe] *tr* to detach; to let loose; to clean; to make (*s.th.*) stand out in relief || *ref* to come loose; to break loose; to stand out in relief
détacheur [detaʃœr] *m* spot remover
détail [detaj] *m* detail; retail; item (*of an account*); **au détail** at retail; **en détail** detailed
détail·lant [detajã] **détail·lante** [detajãt] *adj* retail || *mf* retailer
détailler [detaje] *tr* to detail; to cut up into pieces; to retail; to itemize (*an account*)
détartrer [detartre] *tr* to remove the scale from (*a boiler*); to remove the tartar from (*teeth*)
détaxation [detaksasjɔ̃] *f* lowering or removal of taxes
détaxer [detakse] *tr* to lower or remove the tax from
détecter [detɛkte] *tr* to detect
détecteur [detɛktœr] *m* detector; **détecteur de mines** mine detector
détection [detɛksjɔ̃] *f* detection
détective [detɛktiv] *m* detective, private detective; box camera
déteindre [detɛ̃dr] §50 *tr* to fade, bleach || *intr* to fade, run
dételer [detle] §34 *tr* to unharness || *intr* to let up; to settle down
détendre [detãdr] *tr* to relax; to stretch out (*one's legs*); to lower (*the gas*) || *ref* to relax, to enjoy oneself
détenir [detnir] §72 *tr* to detain (*in prison*); to hold, withhold; to own
détente [detãt] *f* trigger; relaxation, easing (*of tension*); relaxation of tension (*in international affairs*)
déten·teur [detãtœr] **-trice** [tris] *mf* holder (*of stock; of a record*); keeper (*of a secret*)
détention [detãsjɔ̃] *f* detention, custody; possession; **détention préventive** pretrial imprisonment, custody
déte·nu -nue [detny] *adj* detained, imprisoned || *mf* prisoner
déterger [detɛrʒe] §38 *tr* to clean
détérioration [deterjɔrasjɔ̃] *f* deterioration
détériorer [deterjɔre] *tr* to damage || *intr* to deteriorate

détermination [detɛrminɑsjɔ̃] ƒ determination

déterminer [detɛrmine] *tr* to determine ‖ *ref* to decide

déter·ré -rée [detɛre] *adj* disinterred ‖ *mf* (fig) corpse, ghost

déterrer [detɛre] *tr* to dig up; to exhume

déter·sif [detɛrsif] **-sive** [siv] *adj* & *m* detergent

détester [detɛste] *tr* to detest, to hate

déto·nant [detɔnɑ̃] **-nante** [nɑ̃t] *adj* & *m* explosive

détoner [detɔne] *intr* to detonate, to explode

détonner [detɔne] *intr* to sing or play off key; to clash (*said of colors*)

détordre [detɔrdr] *tr* to untwist

détortiller [detɔrtije] *tr* to untangle

détour [detur] *m* turn, curve, bend; roundabout way, detour; **sans détour** frankly, honestly

détour·né -née [deturne] *adj* off the beaten track, isolated; indirect, roundabout; twisted (*meaning*)

détourner [deturne] *tr* to divert; to deter; to embezzle; to lead astray; to distort, twist

détrac·teur [detraktœr] **-trice** [tris] *adj* disparaging ‖ *mf* detractor

détra·qué -quée [detrake] *adj* out of order; broken (*in health*); unhinged, deranged ‖ *mf* nervous wreck

détraquer [detrake] *tr* to put out of commission; (coll) to upset, unhinge ‖ *ref* to break down

détrempe [detrɑ̃p] ƒ distemper (*painting*); annealing (*of steel*)

détremper [detrɑ̃pe] *tr* to soak; to dilute; to anneal (*steel*)

détresse [detrɛs] ƒ distress

détriment [detrimɑ̃] *m* detriment

détritus [detritys] *m* debris, rubbish, refuse

détroit [detrwa] *m* strait, sound

détromper [detrɔ̃pe] *tr* to undeceive, to enlighten

détrôner [detrone] *tr* to dethrone

détrousser [detruse] *tr* to let down (*e.g., one's sleeves*); to hold up (*s.o.*) in the street ‖ *ref* to let down a garment

détrousseur [detrusœr] *m* highwayman

détruire [detrɥir] §19 *tr* to destroy; to put an end to ‖ *ref* (coll) to commit suicide

dette [dɛt] ƒ debt; **dette active** asset; **dette passive** liability

deuil [dœj] *m* mourning; grief, sorrow; bereavement; funeral procession; **deuil de veuve** widow's weeds; **faire son deuil de** (coll) to say good-by to

deux [dø] *adj* & *pron* two; the Second, e.g., **Charles deux** Charles the Second; **deux heures** two o'clock ‖ *m* two; second (*in dates*)

deuxième [døzjɛm] *adj* & *m* second

deux-pièces [døpjɛs] *m invar* two-piece suit

deux-points [døpwɛ̃] *m invar* colon

deux-ponts [døpɔ̃] *m invar* (aer, naut) double-decker

dévaler [devale] *tr* to descend (*a slope*) ‖ *intr* to descend quickly

dévaluation [devalɥasjɔ̃] ƒ devaluation

dévaluer [devalɥe] *tr* to devaluate

devant [dəvɑ̃] *m* front; **par devant** in front; **prendre les devants** to make the first move; to get ahead; to take precautions ‖ *adv* before, in front ‖ *prep* before, in front of

devanture [dəvɑ̃tyr] ƒ show window; display; storefront

dévasta·teur [devastatœr] **-trice** [tris] *adj* devastating

dévastation [devastɑsjɔ̃] ƒ devastation

dévaster [devaste] *tr* to devastate

déveine [devɛn] ƒ bad luck

développé [devlɔpe] *m* press (*in weight lifting*)

développement [devlɔpmɑ̃] *m* development; unwrapping (*of package*); expansion

développer [devlɔpe] *tr* to develop; to unwrap (*a package*); to reveal, show (*e.g., a card*); to spread out, open out; to expand (*an algebraic expression*) ‖ *ref* to develop

devenir [dəvnir] §72 *intr* (aux: ÊTRE) to become; **qu'est devenu Robert?** what has become of Robert?

dévergondage [devɛrgɔ̃daʒ] *m* profligacy

dévergon·dé -dée [devɛrgɔ̃de] *adj* & *mf* profligate

dévergonder [devɛrgɔ̃de] *ref* to become dissolute

dévernir [devɛrnir] *tr* to remove the varnish from

déverrouiller [devɛruje] *tr* to unbolt

dé·vers [devɛr] **-verse** [vɛrs] *adj* warped; out of alignment ‖ *m* inclination, slope; banking

déverser [devɛrse] *tr* to pour out; to slope, bank ‖ *intr* to pour out; to lean, to become lopsided ‖ *ref* to empty, flow (*said of river*)

dévêtir [devɛtir] §73 *tr* & *ref* to undress

déviation [devjɑsjɔ̃] ƒ deviation; detour

dévider [devide] *tr* to unwind, to reel off

dévier [devje] *tr* to deflect, to by-pass ‖ *intr* to deviate, to swerve

de·vin [dəvɛ̃] **-vineresse** [vinrɛs] *mf* fortuneteller

deviner [dəvine] *tr* to guess

devinette [dəvinɛt] ƒ riddle

dévirer [devire] *tr* to turn back; to bend back; to feather (*an oar*)

devis [dəvi] *m* estimate

dévisager [devisaʒe] §38 *tr* to stare at, to stare down

devise [dəviz] ƒ motto, slogan; heraldic device; name of a ship; currency; **devise forte** strong currency

deviser [dəvize] *intr* to chat

dévisser [devise] *tr* to unscrew

dévitaliser [devitalize] *tr* to kill the nerve of (*a tooth*)

dévoiler [devwale] *tr* to unveil; to straighten (*e.g., a bent wheel*) ‖ *ref* to unveil; to come to light

devoir [dəvwar] *m* duty; exercise,

homework; **devoirs** respects; homework || §21 *tr* to owe || *aux* used to express 1) necessity, e.g., **il doit s'en aller** he must go away; **il devra s'en aller** he will have to go away; **il a dû s'en aller** he had to go away; 2) obligation, e.g., **il devrait s'en aller** he ought to go away, he should go away; **il aurait dû s'en aller** he ought to have gone away, he should have gone away; 3) conjecture, e.g., **il doit être malade** he must be ill; **il a dû être malade** he must have been ill; 4) what is expected or scheduled, e.g., **que dois-je faire maintenant?** what am I to do now?; **le train devait arriver à six heures** the train was to arrive at six o'clock

dévo·lu -lue [devɔly] *adj*—**dévolu à** devolving upon, vested in || *m*—**jeter son dévolu sur** to fix one's choice upon

dévora·teur [devɔratœr] **-trice** [tris] *adj* devouring

dévorer [devɔre] *tr* to devour, eat up

dévo·reur [devɔrœr] **-reuse** [røz] *mf* devourer; (fig) glutton

dé·vot [devo] **-vote** [vɔt] *adj* devout, pious || *mf* devout, pious person; **dev**otee; **faux dévot** hypocrite

dévotion [devosjɔ̃] *f* devotion, devoutness; **à votre dévotion** at your service, at your disposal; **être à la dévotion de qn** to be at s.o.'s beck and call

dé·voué -vouée [devwe] *adj* devoted; **dévoué à vos ordres** (complimentary close) at your service; **votre dévoué** (complimentary close) yours truly

dévouement [devumɑ̃] *m* devotion

dévouer [devwe] *tr* to dedicate, sacrifice || *ref* to devote oneself

dévoyé dévoyée [devwaje] *adj* delinquent (*young person*) || *mf* delinquent

dévoyer [devwaje] §47 *tr* to lead astray

dextérité [dɛksterite] *f* dexterity

dextrose [dɛkstroz] *m* dextrose

diabète [djabɛt] *m* diabetes

diabétique [djabetik] *adj* & *mf* diabetic

diable [djɑbl] *m* devil; hand truck, dolly; (coll) fellow; **à la diable** haphazardly; **c'est là le diable** (coll) there's the rub; **diable à ressort** jack-in-the-box; **du diable** extreme; **en diable** extremely; **faire le diable à quatre** (coll) to raise Cain; **tirer le diable par la queue** (coll) to be hard up

diablerie [djɑbləri] *f* deviltry

diabolique [djabɔlik] *adj* diabolic(al)

diaconesse [djakɔnɛs] *f* deaconess

diacre [djakr] *m* deacon

diacritique [djakritik] *adj* diacritical

diadème [djadɛm] *m* diadem; (*woman's headdress*) tiara, coronet

diagnose [djagnoz] *f* diagnostics, diagnosis

diagnostic [djagnɔstik] *m* diagnosis

diagnostiquer [djagnɔstike] *tr* to diagnose

diago·nal -nale [djagɔnal] *adj* & *f* (*pl* **-naux** [no] **-nales**) diagonal

diagonalement [djagɔnalmɑ̃] *adv* diagonally, cater-cornered

diagramme [djagram] *m* diagram

dialecte [djalɛkt] *m* dialect

dialogue [djalɔg] *m* dialogue

diamant [djamɑ̃] *m* diamond

diamantaire [djamɑ̃tɛr] *adj* diamond-bright || *m* dealer in diamonds

diamé·tral -trale [djametral] *adj* (*pl* **-traux** [tro]) diametric(al)

diamètre [djametr] *m* diameter

diane [djan] *f* reveille

diantre [djɑ̃tr] *interj* the dickens!

diapason [djapazɔ̃] *m* range (*of voice or instrument*); pitch, standard pitch; tuning fork

diaphane [djafan] *adj* diaphanous

diaphragme [djafragm] *m* diaphragm

diapo [djapo] *f* (coll) slide

diapositive [diapozitiv] *f* (phot) transparency, slide

diaprer [djapre] *tr* to variegate

diarrhée [djare] *f* diarrhea

diastole [djastɔl] *f* diastole

diathermie [djatermi] *f* diathermy

diatribe [djatrib] *f* diatribe

dichotomie [dikɔtɔmi] *f* dichotomy; split fee (*between physicians*)

dictaphone [diktafɔn] *m* dictaphone

dictateur [diktatœr] *m* dictator

dictature [diktatyr] *f* dictatorship

dictée [dikte] *f* dictation; **écrire sous la dictée de** to take dictation from

dicter [dikte] *tr* & *intr* to dictate

diction [diksjɔ̃] *f* diction

dictionnaire [diksjɔnɛr] *m* dictionary; **dictionnaire vivant** (coll) walking encyclopedia

dicton [diktɔ̃] *m* saying, proverb

didactique [didaktik] *adj* didactic(al)

dièdre [djɛdr] *adj* & *m* dihedral

diérèse [djerɛz] *f* diaeresis

dièse [djɛz] *adj* & *m* (mus) sharp

diesel [dizɛl] *m* Diesel motor

diéser [djeze] §10 *tr* (mus) to sharp

diète [djɛt] *f* diet

diététi·cien [djetetisjɛ̃] **-cienne** [sjɛn] *mf* dietitian

diététique [djetetik] *adj* dietetic || *f* dietetics

dieu [djø] *m* (*pl* **dieux**) god || (*cap*) *m* God; **Dieu merci!** thank heavens!; **mon Dieu!** good gracious!

diffamation [difamasjɔ̃] *f* defamation

diffamer [difame] *tr* to defame

diffé·ré -rée [difere] *adj* deferred; delayed (*action*) || *m* (rad, telv) prerecording; **en différé** (rad, telv) prerecorded

différemment [diferamɑ̃] *adv* differently

différence [diferɑ̃s] *f* difference; **à la différence de** unlike, contrary to

différencier [diferɑ̃sje] *tr* & *ref* to differentiate

différend [diferɑ̃] *m* dispute, disagreement, difference; **partager le différend** to split the difference

diffé·rent [diferɑ̃] **-rente** [rɑ̃t] *adj* different

différen·tiel -tielle [diferɑ̃sjɛl] *adj* dif-

ferential ‖ *m* (mach) differential ‖ *f* (math) differential
différer [difere] §10 *tr* to defer, to put off ‖ *intr* to differ; to disagree
difficile [difisil] *adj* difficult, hard; hard to please, crotchety; **faire le difficile** to be hard to please
difficulté [difikylte] *f* difficulty
difforme [difɔrm] *adj* deformed
difformité [difɔrmite] *f* deformity
dif·fus [dify] **dif·fuse** [difyz] *adj* diffuse; verbose, windy
diffuser [difyze] *tr* to broadcast ‖ *ref* to diffuse
diffuseur [difyzœr] *m* spreader (*of news*); loudspeaker; nozzle
digérer [diʒere] §10 *tr & intr* to digest ‖ *ref* to be digested
digeste [diʒɛst] *adj* (coll) easy to digest ‖ *m* (law) digest
digestible [diʒɛstibl] *adj* digestible
diges·tif [diʒɛstif] **-tive** [tiv] *adj* digestive
digestion [diʒɛstjɔ̃] *f* digestion
digi·tal -tale [diʒital] *adj* (*pl* **-taux** [to]) digital ‖ *f* digitalis, foxglove
digitaline [diʒitalin] *f* (pharm) digitalis
digne [diɲ] *adj* worthy; dignified; haughty, uppish
dignitaire [diɲiter] *mf* dignitary
dignité [diɲite] *f* dignity
digression [digrɛsjɔ̃] *f* digression
digue [dig] *f* dike; breakwater; (fig) barrier
dilacérer [dilasere] §10 *tr* to lacerate
dilapider [dilapide] *tr* to squander; to embezzle
dilater [dilate] *tr & ref* to dilate
dilatoire [dilatwar] *adj* dilatory
dilemme [dilɛm] *m* dilemma
dilettante [diletãt] *mf* dilettante
diligemment [diliʒamã] *adv* diligently
diligence [diliʒãs] *f* diligence; **à la diligence de** at the request of
dili·gent [diliʒã] **-gente** [ʒãt] *adj* diligent
diluer [dilɥe] *tr* to dilute
dilution [dilysjɔ̃] *f* dilution
dimanche [dimã/] *m* Sunday; **du dimanche** (coll) Sunday (*driver*); (coll) amateur (*painter*); **le dimanche des Rameaux** Palm Sunday
dîme [dim] *f* tithe
dimension [dimãsjɔ̃] *f* dimension
diminuer [diminɥe] *tr & intr* to diminish
diminu·tif [diminytif] **-tive** [tiv] *adj & m* diminutive
dinde [dɛ̃d] *f* turkey; (culin) turkey; (coll) silly girl
dindon [dɛ̃dɔ̃] *m* turkey
dindonner [dɛ̃dɔne] *tr* to dupe, take in
dîner [dine] *m* dinner; **dîner de garçons** stag dinner; **dîner prié** formal dinner ‖ *intr* to dine
dînette [dinɛt] *f* family meal; children's playtime meal
dî·neur [dinœr] **-neuse** [nøz] *mf* diner, dinner guest
dinosaure [dinɔzɔr] *m* dinosaur
diocèse [djɔsɛz] *m* diocese
diode [djɔd] *f* diode

dionée [djɔne] *f* Venus's-flytrap
diphtérie [difteri] *f* diphtheria
diphtongue [diftɔ̃g] *f* diphthong
diplomate [diplɔmat] *adj* diplomatic ‖ *mf* diplomat
diplomatie [diplɔmasi] *f* diplomacy
diplomatique [diplɔmatik] *adj* diplomatic
diplôme [diplom] *m* diploma
dire [dir] *m* statement; **au dire de** according to ‖ §22 *tr* to say, tell, relate; **à l'heure dite** at the appointed time; **à qui le dites-vous?** (coll) you're telling me!; **autrement dit** in other words; **dire que . . .** to think that; **dites-lui bien des choses de ma part** say hello for me; **tu l'as dit!** (coll) you said it! ‖ *intr* to say; **à vrai dire** to tell the truth; **cela va sans dire** it goes without saying; **c'est beaucoup dire** (coll) that's going rather far; **c'est pas peu dire** (slang) that's saying a lot; **comme on dit** as the saying goes; **dites donc!** hey!, say!; **il n'y a pas à dire** make no mistake about it ‖ *ref* to be said; to say to oneself or to each other; to claim to be, to call oneself
di·rect -recte [dirɛkt] *adj* direct ‖ *m* (boxing) solid punch; **en direct** (rad, telv) live
direc·teur [dirɛktœr] **-trice** [tris] *adj* directing, guiding; principal; driving (*rod, wheel*) ‖ *mf* director ‖ *f* directress
direction [dirɛksjɔ̃] *f* direction; administration, management, board; head office; (aut) steering
direction·nel -nelle [dirɛksjɔnɛl] *adj* directional
directorat [dirɛktɔra] *m* directorship
dirigeable [diriʒabl] *adj & m* dirigible
diri·geant [diriʒã] **-geante** [ʒãt] *adj* governing, ruling ‖ *mf* ruler, leader, head, executive
diriger [diriʒe] §38 *tr* to direct, control, manage; to steer ‖ *ref* to go; **se diriger vers** to head for
dirigisme [diriʒism] *m* government economic planning and control
discernable [disɛrnabl] *adj* discernible
discernement [disɛrnamã] *m* discernment, perception
discerner [disɛrne] *tr* to discern
disciple [disipl] *m* disciple
disciplinaire [disipliner] *adj* disciplinary ‖ *m* military policeman
discipline [disiplin] *f* discipline; scourge
discipliner [disipline] *tr* to discipline
disconti·nu -nue [diskɔ̃tiny] *adj* discontinuous
discontinuer [diskɔ̃tinɥe] *tr* to discontinue
disconvenir [diskɔ̃vnir] §72 *tr* to deny ‖ *intr* (with *dat*) to not suit, displease ‖ *intr* (*aux:* ÊTRE)—**ne pas disconvenir de** to admit, not deny
discophile [diskɔfil] *mf* record collector
discord [diskɔr] *adj masc* out of tune ‖ *m* instrument out of tune
discordance [diskɔrdãs] *f* discordance
discor·dant [diskɔrdã] **-dante** [dãt] *adj* discordant

discorde [diskɔrd] *f* discord
discorder [diskɔrde] *intr* to be discordant, to jar
discothèque [diskɔtɛk] *f* record cabinet; record library; discotheque
discourir [diskurir] §14 *intr* to discourse
discours [diskur] *m* discourse; speech
discour·tois [diskurtwa] **-toise** [twaz] *adj* discourteous
discourtoisie [diskurtwazi] *f* discourtesy
discrédit [diskredi] *m* discredit
discréditer [diskredite] *tr* to discredit
dis·cret [diskrɛ] **-crète** [krɛt] *adj* discreet; discrete
discrétion [diskresjɔ̃] *f* discretion; **à discrétion** as much as one wants
discrimination [diskriminɑsjɔ̃] *f* discrimination
discriminatoire [diskriminatwar] *adj* discriminatory
discriminer [diskrimine] *tr* to discriminate
disculper [diskylpe] *tr* to clear, exonerate || *ref* to clear oneself
discur·sif [diskyrsif] **-sive** [siv] *adj* discursive
discussion [diskysjɔ̃] *f* discussion
discuter [diskyte] *tr* & *intr* to discuss; to question, debate
di·sert [dizɛr] **-serte** [zɛrt] *adj* eloquent, fluent
disertement [dizɛrtəmɑ̃] *adv* eloquently, fluently
disette [dizɛt] *f* shortage, scarcity; famine
di·seur [dizœr] **-seuse** [zøz] *mf* talker, speaker; monologuist; **diseuse de bonne aventure** fortuneteller
disgrâce [disgrɑs] *f* disfavor; misfortune; surliness, gruffness
disgra·cié **-ciée** [disgrɑsje] *adj* out of favor; ill-favored, homely; unfortunate
disgracier [disgrɑsje] *tr* to deprive of favor
disgra·cieux [disgrɑsjø] **-cieuse** [sjøz] *adj* awkward; homely, ugly; disagreeable
disjoindre [disʒwɛ̃dr] §35 *tr* to sever, to separate
disjoncteur [disʒɔ̃ktœr] *m* circuit breaker
dislocation [dislɔkɑsjɔ̃] *f* dislocation; separation; dismemberment
disloquer [dislɔke] *tr* to dislocate; to disperse; to dismember || *ref* to break up, disperse
disparaître [disparɛtr] §12 *intr* to disappear
disparate [disparat] *adj* incongruous || *f* incongruity; clash (*of colors*)
disparité [disparite] *f* disparity
disparition [disparisjɔ̃] *f* disappearance
dispa·ru **-rue** [dispary] *adj* disappeared; missing (*in battle*) || *mf* missing person; **le disparu** the deceased
dispen·dieux [dispɑ̃djø] **-dieuse** [djøz] *adj* expensive
dispensaire [dispɑ̃ser] *m* dispensary, outpatient clinic

dispensa·teur [dispɑ̃satœr] **-trice** [tris] *mf* dispenser
dispense [dispɑ̃s] *f* dispensation, exemption
dispenser [dispɑ̃se] *tr* to dispense; **dispensé du timbrage** (label on envelope) mailing permit
disperser [dispɛrse] *tr* & *ref* to disperse
dispersion [dispɛrsjɔ̃] *f* dispersion, dissipation
disponibilité [dispɔnibilite] *f* availability; **disponibilités** liquid assets; **en disponibilité** in the reserves
disponible [dispɔnibl] *adj* available; vacant (*seat*); (govt, mil) subject to call
dis·pos [dispo] **-pose** [poz] *adj* alert, fit, in good condition
dispo·sé **-sée** [dispoze] *adj* disposed; arranged; **disposé d'avance** predisposed; **peu disposé** reluctant
disposer [dispoze] *tr* to dispose || *intr* to dispose; **disposer de** to dispose of, to have at one's disposal; to have at hand; to make use of; **disposer pour** to provide for (*e.g., the future*); **vous pouvez disposer** you may leave || *ref* —**se disposer à** to be disposed to; to plan on
dispositif [dispozitif] *m* apparatus, device; (mil) disposition
disposition [dispozisjɔ̃] *f* disposition; disposal; **dispositions** arrangements; aptitude; provisions (*of a legal document*)
disproportion·né **-née** [disprɔpɔrsjɔne] *adj* disproportionate, incompatible
dispute [dispyt] *f* dispute
disputer [dispyte] *tr* to dispute; (coll) to bawl out || *ref* to dispute
disquaire [disker] *m* record dealer
disqualification [diskalifikɑsjɔ̃] *f* disqualification
disqualifier [diskalifje] *tr* & *ref* to disqualify
disque [disk] *m* disk; record, disk; (sports) discus; **changer de disque** (coll) to change the subject; **disque de longue durée** long-playing record
dissection [disɛksjɔ̃] *f* dissection
dissemblable [disɑ̃blabl] *adj* dissimilar
dissemblance [disɑ̃blɑ̃s] *f* dissimilarity
disséminer [disemine] *tr* to disseminate
dissension [disɑ̃sjɔ̃] *f* dissension
dissentiment [disɑ̃timɑ̃] *m* dissent
disséquer [diseke] §10 *tr* to dissect
dissertation [disɛrtɑsjɔ̃] *f* dissertation; (*in school*) essay, term paper
dissidence [disidɑ̃s] *f* dissent
dissi·dent [disidɑ̃] **-dente** [dɑ̃t] *adj* dissenting || *mf* dissenter, dissident
dissimiler [disimile] *tr* (phonet) to dissimilate
dissimulation [disimylɑsjɔ̃] *f* dissemblance
dissimuler [disimyle] *tr* & *intr* to dissemble; **dissimuler q.ch. à qn** to conceal s.th. from s.o. || *ref* to hide, skulk
dissipation [disipɑsjɔ̃] *f* dissipation
dissi·pé **-pée** [disipe] *adj* dissipated; pleasure-seeking; unruly (*schoolboy*)
dissiper [disipe] *tr* & *ref* to dissipate

dissocier [disɔsje] *tr & ref* to dissociate
disso·lu -lue [disɔly] *adj* dissolute ‖ *mf* profligate
dissolution [disɔlysjɔ̃] *f* dissolution; dissoluteness; rubber cement
dissol·vant [disɔlvɑ̃] -vante [vɑ̃t] *adj & m* solvent
dissonance [disɔnɑ̃s] *f* dissonance
dissoudre [disudr] §60 (*pp* dissous, dissoute; no *pret* or *imperf subj*) *tr & ref* to dissolve
dissuader [disɥade] *tr* to dissuade
distance [distɑ̃s] *f* distance; à distance at a distance
distancer [distɑ̃se] §51 *tr* to outdistance; to distance (*a race horse*)
dis·tant [distɑ̃] -tante [tɑ̃t] *adj* distant
distendre [distɑ̃dr] *tr & ref* to distend; to strain (*a muscle*)
distillation [distilɑsjɔ̃] *f* distillation
distiller [distile] *tr* to distill
distillerie [distilri] *f* distillery; distilling industry
dis·tinct [distɛ̃], [distɛ̃kt] -tincte [tɛ̃kt] *adj* distinct
distinc·tif [distɛ̃ktif] -tive [tiv] *adj* distinctive
distinction [distɛ̃ksjɔ̃] *f* distinction
distin·gué -guée [distɛ̃ge] *adj* distinguished; famous; sincere, e.g., veuillez accepter nos sentiments distingués (complimentary close) please accept our sincere regards
distinguer [distɛ̃ge] *tr* to distinguish ‖ *ref* to be distinguished; to distinguish oneself
distordre [distɔrdr] *tr* to twist, to sprain
dis·tors [distɔr] -torse [tɔrs] *adj* twisted
distorsion [distɔrsjɔ̃] *f* sprain; convulsive twist; (electron, opt) distorsion
distraction [distraksjɔ̃] *f* distraction; heedlessness, lapse; embezzlement; appropriation (*of a sum of money*)
distraire [distrɛr] §68 *tr* to distract, amuse; to separate, set aside (*e.g., part of one's savings*) ‖ *ref* to amuse oneself
dis·trait [distrɛ] -traite [trɛt] *adj* absent-minded
distribuer [distribɥe] *tr* to distribute; to arrange the furnishings of (*an apartment*)
distribu·teur [distribytœr] -trice [tris] *mf* distributor (*person*) ‖ *m* (mach) distributor; distributeur automatique vending machine; distributeur de musique jukebox
distribution [distribysjɔ̃] *f* distribution; mail delivery; supply system (*of gas, water, or electricity*); valve gear (*of steam engine*); timing gears (*of internal-combustion engine*); (theat) cast
district [distrik], [distrikt] *m* district
dit [di] dite [dit] *adj* agreed upon, stated ‖ *m* saying
dito [dito] *adv* ditto
diva [diva] *f* diva
divaguer [divage] *intr* to ramble
divan [divɑ̃] *m* divan

diverger [divɛrʒe] §38 *intr* to diverge
di·vers [divɛr] -verse [vɛrs] *adj* changing, varied ‖ di·vers -verses *adj pl* diverse, different, several
diversifier [divɛrsifje] *tr & ref* to diversify
diversion [divɛrsjɔ̃] *f* diversion
diversité [divɛrsite] *f* diversity
divertir [divɛrtir] *tr* to divert, amuse ‖ *ref* to be diverted, amused
dividende [dividɑ̃d] *m* dividend
di·vin [divɛ̃] -vine [vin] *adj* divine
divination [divinɑsjɔ̃] *f* divination
divinité [divinite] *f* divinity
diviser [divize] *tr & ref* to divide
diviseur [divizœr] *m* (math) divisor; (fig) troublemaker
divisible [divizibl] *adj* divisible
division [divizjɔ̃] *f* division
divisionnaire [divizjɔnɛr] *adj* divisional ‖ *m* division head
divorce [divɔrs] *m* divorce
divor·cé -cée [divɔrse] *mf* divorced person ‖ *f* divorcee
divorcer [divɔrse] §51 *tr* to divorce (*a married couple*) ‖ *intr* to divorce, to get a divorce; divorcer avec to withdraw from (*the world*); divorcer d'avec to get a divorce from, to be divorced from, to divorce (*husband or wife*); to withdraw from (*the world*)
divulguer [divylge] *tr* to divulge
dix [di(s)] *adj & pron* ten; the Tenth, e.g., Jean dix John the Tenth; dix heures ten o'clock ‖ *m* ten; tenth (*in dates*)
dix-huit [dizɥi], [dizɥit] *adj & pron* eighteen; the Eighteenth, e.g., Jean dix-huit John the Eighteenth ‖ *m* eighteen; eighteenth (*in dates*)
dix-huitième [dizɥitjɛm] *adj & m* eighteenth
dixième [dizjɛm] *adj, pron* (*masc, fem*), *& m* tenth
dix-neuf [diznœf] *adj & pron* nineteen; the Nineteenth, e.g., Jean dix-neuf John the Nineteenth ‖ *m* nineteen; nineteenth (*in dates*)
dix-neuvième [diznœvjɛm] *adj & m* nineteenth
dix-sept [disɛt] *adj & pron* seventeen; the Seventeenth, e.g., Jean dix-sept John the Seventeenth ‖ *m* seventeen; seventeenth (*in dates*)
dix-septième [disɛtjɛm] *adj & m* seventeenth
djinn [dʒin] *m* jinn
d° *abbr* (dito) do. (ditto)
docile [dɔsil] *adj* docile
dock [dɔk] *m* dock; warehouse; dock flottant floating dry dock
docker [dɔkɛr] *m* dock worker
docte [dɔkt] *adj* learned, scholarly ‖ *mf* scholar ‖ *m* learned man
doc·teur [dɔktœr] -toresse [tɔrɛs] *mf* doctor
docto·ral -rale [dɔktɔral] *adj* (*pl* -raux [ro]) doctoral
doctorat [dɔktɔra] *m* doctorate
doctrine [dɔktrin] *f* doctrine
document [dɔkymɑ̃] *m* document

documentaire [dɔkymãtɛr] *adj & m* documentary
documentation [dɔkymãtasjɔ̃] *f* documentation; literature (*about a region, business, etc.*)
documenter [dɔkymãte] *tr* to document || *ref* to gather documentary evidence
dodeliner [dɔdline] *tr & intr* to sway, rock
dodo [dodo] *m* (orn) dodo; **aller au dodo** (*baby talk*) to go to bed; **faire dodo** to sleep
do·du -due [dɔdy] *adj* (coll) plump
dogmatique [dɔgmatik] *adj* dogmatic || *mf* dogmatic person || *f* dogmatics
dogmatiser [dɔgmatize] *intr* to dogmatize
dogme [dɔgm] *m* dogma
dogue [dɔg] *m* bulldog
doigt [dwa] *m* finger; **à deux doigts de** a hairbreadth away from; **doigt annulaire** ring finger; **doigt de Dieu** hand of God; **doigt du pied** toe; **mettre le doigt dessus** to hit the nail on the head; **mon petit doigt m'a dit** (coll) a little bird told me; **montrer du doigt** to single out (*for ridicule*); to point at; **petit doigt** little finger; **se mettre le doigt dans l'œil** (coll) to put one's foot in one's mouth; **se mordre les doigts** to be sorry
doigté [dwate] *m* touch; adroitness, skillfulness; fingering
doigter [dwate] *m* fingering || *tr & intr* to finger
doigtier [dwatje] *m* fingerstall
doit [dwa] *m* debit
doléances [dɔleɑ̃s] *fpl* grievances
do·lent -lente [dɔlɑ̃ -lɑ̃t] *adj* doleful
dollar [dɔlar] *m* dollar
domaine [dɔmɛn] *m* domain
dôme [dom] *m* dome; cathedral
domestication [dɔmɛstikasjɔ̃] *f* domestication
domesticité [dɔmɛstisite] *f* domestication; staff of servants
domestique [dɔmɛstik] *adj & mf* domestic
domestiquer [dɔmɛstike] *tr* to domesticate
domicile [dɔmisil] *m* residence
domicilier [dɔmisilje] *tr* to domicile || *ref* to take up residence
dominance [dɔminɑ̃s] *f* (genetics) dominance
domi·nant [dɔminɑ̃] **-nante** [nɑ̃t] *adj* dominant || *f* dominating trait; (mus) dominant
domina·teur [dɔminatœr] **-trice** [tris] *adj* domineering, overbearing || *mf* ruler, conqueror
domination [dɔminasjɔ̃] *f* domination
dominer [dɔmine] *tr & intr* to dominate || *ref* to control oneself
domini·cal -cale [dɔminikal] *adj* (*pl* -caux [ko]) Sunday; dominical
domino [dɔmino] *m* domino
dommage [dɔmaʒ] *m* loss; injury; **c'est dommage!** that's too bad! **dommages et intérêts** (law) damages; **quel dommage!** what a pity!
dommageable [dɔmaʒabl] *adj* injurious

dommages-intérêts [dɔmaʒɛterɛ] *mpl* (law) damages
dompter [dɔ̃te] *tr* to tame; to train (*animals*); to subdue
domp·teur [dɔ̃tœr] **-teuse** [tøz] *mf* tamer, trainer; conquerer
don [dɔ̃] *m* gift; don (*Spanish title*)
donataire [dɔnatɛr] *mf* legatee
dona·teur [dɔnatœr] **-trice** [tris] *mf* (law) donor, legator
donation [dɔnasjɔ̃] *f* donation, gift, grant
donc [dɔ̃k], [dɔ̃] *adv* therefore, then; thus; now, of course; (often used for emphasis), e.g., **entrez donc!** do come in!
donjon [dɔ̃ʒɔ̃] *m* keep, donjon; (nav) turret
don·nant [dɔnɑ̃] **don·nante** [dɔnɑ̃t] *adj* generous, open-handed; **donnant donnant** tit for tat; cash down; **peu donnant** closefisted
donne [dɔn] *f* (cards) deal; doña (*Spanish title*); **fausse donne** misdeal
don·né -née [dɔne] *adj* given; **étant donné que** whereas, since || *f* datum; **données** data, facts
donner [dɔne] *tr* to give; (cards) to deal || *intr* to give; **donner sur** to open onto, to look out on; **donner sur les doigts** to rap one's knuckles
don·neur [dɔnœr] **don·neuse** [dɔnøz] *mf* donor; **donneur universel** type-O blood donor || *m* (cards) dealer
dont [dɔ̃] §79
donzelle [dɔ̃zɛl] *f* woman of easy virtue
doper [dɔpe] *tr* to dope
doping [dɔpiŋ] *m* dope, pep pill
dorade [dɔrad] *f* gilthead
dorénavant [dɔrenavɑ̃] *adv* henceforth
dorer [dɔre] *tr* to gild; (fig) to sugarcoat
d'ores [dɔr] see **ores**
dorlotement [dɔrlɔtmɑ̃] *m* coddling
dorloter [dɔrlɔte] *tr* to coddle
dor·mant [dɔrmɑ̃] **-mante** [mɑ̃t] *adj* stagnant, immovable || *m* doorframe
dor·meur [dɔrmœr] **-meuse** [møz] *adj* sleeping || *mf* sleeper || *f* earring
dormir [dɔrmir] §23 *intr* to sleep; to lie dormant; **à dormir debout** boring, dull; **dormir debout** to sleep standing up; **dormir sur les deux oreilles** to feel secure
dortoir [dɔrtwar] *m* dormitory
dorure [dɔryr] *f* gilding; gilt; icing
dos [do] *m* back; bridge (*of nose*); **dans le dos de** behind the back of; **en dos d'âne** saddle-backed, hog-backed; **se mettre qn à dos** to make an enemy of s.o.; **voir au dos** see other side
dosage [dozaʒ] *m* dosage
dose [doz] *f* dose
doser [doze] *tr* to dose out; to measure out, to proportion
dossier [dosje] *m* chair back; dossier
dotation [dɔtasjɔ̃] *f* endowment
doter [dɔte] *tr* to endow; to dower; to give a dowry to
douaire [dwɛr] *m* dower
douairière [dwɛrjɛr] *f* dowager

douane [dwan] *f* customs, duty; customhouse

doua·nier [dwanjε] **-nière** [njεr] *adj* customs || *m* customs officer

doublage [dublaʒ] *m* doubling; metal plating of a ship; lining (*act of lining*); dubbing (*on tape or film*)

double [dubl] *adj & adv* double; **à double face** two-faced || *m* double; duplicate, copy; **au double** twice; **double au carbone** carbon copy; **en double** in duplicate

doublement [dubləmɑ̃] *m* doubling || *adv* doubly

doubler [duble] *tr* to double; to parallel, to run alongside; to pass (*s.o., s.th. going in the same direction*); to line (*a coat*); to dub (*a film*); to copy, dub (*a sound tape*); to replace (*an actor*); to gain one lap on (*another contestant*); (coll) to cheat || *intr* to double; to pass (*on highway*)

doublure [dublyr] *f* lining; (theat) understudy, replacement

douce-amère [dusamεr] *f* (*pl* **douces-amères**) (bot) bittersweet

douceâtre [dusɑtr] *adj* sweetish; mawkish

doucement [dusmɑ̃] *adv* softly; slowly || *interj* easy now!, just a minute!

douce·reux [dusrø] **-reuse** [røz] *adj* unpleasantly sweet, cloying; mealymouthed

douceur [dusœr] *f* sweetness; softness, gentleness; **douceurs** sweets

douche [duʃ] *f* shower bath; douche; (coll) dressing down; (coll) shock, disappointment

doucher [duʃe] *tr* to give a shower bath to; (coll) to reprimand; (coll) to disappoint || *ref* to take a shower bath

doucir [dusir] *tr* to polish, rub

doué douée [dwe] *adj* gifted, endowed

douer [dwe] *tr* to endow; **douer de** to endow or gift (*s.o.*) with

douille [duj] *f* cartridge case; sconce (*of candlestick*); bushing; (elec) socket

douil·let [dujε] **douil·lette** [dujεt] *adj* soft, delicate; oversensitive || *f* child's padded coat

douleur [dulœr] *f* pain; sorrow; soreness

doulou·reux [dulurø] **-reuse** [røz] *adj* painful; sad; sore

doute [dut] *m* doubt; **sans doute** no doubt

douter [dute] *tr* to doubt, e.g., **je doute qu'il vienne** I doubt that he will come || *intr* to doubt; **à n'en pas douter** beyond a doubt; **douter de** to doubt; to distrust || *ref*—**se douter de** to suspect; **se douter que** to suspect that

dou·teur [dutœr] **-teuse** [tøz] *adj* doubting || *mf* doubter

dou·teux [dutø] **-teuse** [tøz] *adj* doubtful; dubious

Douvres [duvr] Dover

doux [du] **douce** [dus] *adj* sweet; soft; pleasing, suave; quiet; new (*wine*); fresh (*water*); gentle (*slope*); mild

(*weather, climate*); **en douce** on the sly, on the q.t. || **doux** *interj*—**tout doux!** easy there!

douzain [duzɛ̃] *m* twelve-line verse

douzaine [duzεn] *f* dozen; **à la douzaine** by the dozen; **une douzaine de** a dozen

douze [duz] *adj & pron* twelve; the Twelfth, e.g., **Jean douze** John the Twelfth || *m* twelve; twelfth (*in dates*)

douzième [duzjεm] *adj, pron* (*masc, fem*), *& m* twelfth

doyen [dwajɛ̃] **doyenne** [dwajεn] *mf* dean; **doyen d'âge** oldest member

doyenneté [dwajεnte] *f* seniority

Dʳ *abbr* (**Docteur**) Dr.

drachme [drakm] *m* drachma; dram

dragage [dragaʒ] *m* dredging

dragée [draʒe] *f* sugar-coated almond; (pharm) pill; (coll) bitter pill; **tenir la dragée haute à qn** to make s.o. pay through the nose; to be high-handed with s.o.

drageon [draʒɔ̃] *m* (bot) sucker

dragon [dragɔ̃] *m* dragon; dragoon; shrew; **dragon de vertu** prude

dragonne [dragɔn] *f* tassel, sword knot

drague [drag] *f* dredge; minesweeping apparatus

draguer [drage] *tr* to dredge, drag; to sweep for mines

dragueur [dragœr] *adj* minesweeping || *m* dredger; **dragueur de mines** minesweeper

drain [drɛ̃] *m* drainpipe; (med) drain

drainage [drεnaʒ] *m* drainage

drainer [drεne], [drene] *tr* to drain

draisine [drεzin] *f* (rr) handcar

dramatique [dramatik] *adj* dramatic

dramatiser [dramatize] *tr* to dramatize

dramaturge [dramatyrʒ] *mf* playwright

dramaturgie [dramatyrʒi] *f* dramatics

drame [dram] *m* drama; tragic event

drap [dra] *m* cloth; sheet; **être dans de beaux draps** to be in a pretty pickle

dra·peau [drapo] *m* (*pl* **-peaux**) flag; **au drapeau!** colors (*bugle call*)!; **drapeau parlementaire** flag of truce; **être sous les drapeaux** to be a serviceman

draper [drape] *tr* to drape || *ref* to drape oneself

draperie [drapəri] *f* drapery; drygoods business; textile industry

dra·pier [drapje] **-pière** [pjεr] *mf* draper; textile manufacturer

drastique [drastik] *adj* (med) drastic

drêche [drεʃ] *f* draff, residue of malt

drège [drεʒ] *f* dragnet

drelin [drəlɛ̃] *m* ting-a-ling

dressage [drεsaʒ] *m* training (*of animals*); erection

dresser [drεse] *tr* to raise, to hold erect; to train; to put up, to erect; to set (*the table; a trap*); to draw up, to draft; to plane, smooth; **dresser l'oreille** to prick up one's ears || *ref* to stand or sit up straight; **se dresser contre** to be dead set against

dressoir [drεswar] *m* sideboard, buffet, dish closet

dribble [dribl] *m* (sports) dribble

dribbler [drible] *tr* & *intr* (sports) to dribble
drille [drij] *m*—**joyeux drille** gay blade ‖ *f* jeweler's drill brace; **drilles** rags (*for papermaking*)
drisse [dris] *f* halyard, rope
drogue [drɔg] *f* drug; chemical; nostrum, concoction; narcotic; (coll) trash, rubbish
droguer [drɔge] *tr* to drug or dope (*with too much medicine*) ‖ *intr* (coll) to cool one's heels ‖ *ref* to drug or dope oneself
droguerie [drɔgri] *f* drysaltery (Brit)
droguiste [drɔgist] *mf* drysalter (Brit)
droit [drwɑ], [drwa] **droite** [drwat], [drwat] *adj* right; honest, sincere; fair, just ‖ *m* law; right, justice; tax; right angle; **à bon droit** with reason; **de (plein) droit** rightfully, by rights, incontestably; **droit coutumier** common law; **droit de cité** key to the city; acceptability; **droits** duties, customs; rights; **droits civils** rights to manage property; **droits civiques, droits politiques** civil rights; **droits d'auteur** royalty; **droits de reproduction réservés** copyrighted; **tous droits réservés** all rights reserved, copyrighted ‖ *f* right, right-hand side; right hand; straight line; **à droite** to or on the right ‖ **droit** *adv* —**droit au but** straight to the point; **tout droit** straight ahead
droi·tier [drwɑtje], [drwatje] **-tière** [tjɛr] *adj* right-handed ‖ *mf* right-handed person; rightist
droiture [drwatyr], [drwatyr] *f* integrity
drolatique [drɔlatik] *adj* droll, comic
drôle [drol] *adj* droll, funny, strange; **drôle de** funny, e.g., **une drôle d'idée** a funny idea; **drôle de guerre** phony war; **drôle d'homme, de corps, de pistolet,** or **de pierrot** (coll) queer duck ‖ *mf* (coll) queer duck, strange person
drôlerie [drolri] *f* drollery
drôlesse [droles] *f* wench, hussy
dromadaire [drɔmadɛr] *m* dromedary
dronte [drɔ̃t] *m* (orn) dodo
droppage [drɔpaʒ] *m* airdrop
drosser [drose] *tr* to drive, carry (*as the wind drives a ship ashore*)
dru drue [dry] *adj* thick, dense; fine (*rain*) ‖ **dru** *adv* thickly, heavily
druide [drɥid] *m* druid
du [dy] §77
dû due [dy] *adj* & *m* due
duc [dyk] *m* duke; horned owl

ducat [dyka] *m* ducat
duché [dyʃe] *m* duchy, dukedom
duchesse [dyʃɛs] *f* duchess
duègne [dɥɛɲ] *f* duenna
duel [dɥɛl] *m* duel; dual number; **duel oratoire** verbal battle
duelliste [dɥɛlist] *m* duelist
dulcifier [dylsifje] *tr* to sweeten
dûment [dymɑ̃] *adv* duly
dune [dyn] *f* dune
dunette [dynɛt] *f* (naut) poop
Dunkerque [dœ̃kɛrk] *f* Dunkirk
duo [dɥo] *m* duet; duo; **duo d'injures** exchange of words, insults
duodénum [dɥɔdenɔm] *m* duodenum
dupe [dyp] *f* dupe
duper [dype] *tr* to dupe
duperie [dypri] *f* deception, trickery
duplicata [dyplikata] *m* duplicate
duplicateur [dyplikatœr] *m* duplicating machine
duplication [dyplikasjɔ̃] *f* duplication
duplicité [dyplisite] *f* duplicity
duquel [dykɛl] §78
dur dure [dyr] *adj* hard; tough; difficult; **coucher sur la dure** to sleep on the bare ground or floor; **dur à la détente** tight-fisted; **dur d'oreille** hard of hearing; **élever un enfant à la dure** to give a child a strict upbringing ‖ *mf* (coll) tough customer ‖ *m* hard material, concrete ‖ **dur** *adv* hard, e.g., **travailler dur** to work hard
durable [dyrabl] *adj* durable
durant [dyrɑ̃] *prep* during; (sometimes stands after noun), e.g., **sa vie durant** during his life
durcir [dyrsir] *tr, intr* & *ref* to harden
durcissement [dyrsismɑ̃] *m* hardening
durée [dyre] *f* duration; wear
durer [dyre] *intr* to last, endure
dureté [dyrte] *f* hardness; cruelty
durillon [dyrijɔ̃] *m* callus, corn
duvet [dyvɛ] *m* down, fuzz; nap (*of cloth*)
duve·té -tée [dyvte] *adj* downy
duve·teux [dyvtø] **-teuse** [tøz] *adj* fuzzy
dynamique [dinamik] *adj* dynamic ‖ *f* dynamics
dynamite [dinamit] *f* dynamite
dynamiter [dinamite] *tr* to dynamite
dynamo [dinamo] *f* dynamo
dynaste [dinast] *m* dynast
dynastie [dinasti] *f* dynasty
dysenterie [disɑ̃tri] *f* dysentery
dyspepsie [dispɛpsi] *f* dyspepsia

E

E, e [ə], ***[ə] *m invar* fifth letter of the French alphabet
eau [o] *f* (*pl* **eaux**) water; wake (*of ship*); **à l'eau de rose** maudlin; **de la plus belle eau** of the first water; **eau**

calcaire hard water; **eau de cale** bilge water; **eau de Javel** bleach; **eau dentifrice** mouthwash; **eau douce** soft water; fresh water; **eau dure** hard water; **eau lourde** heavy water;

eau oxygénée hydrogen peroxide; **eau vive** running water; **eaux waters**; waterworks; **eaux juvéniles** mineral waters; **eaux thermales** hot springs; **eaux usées, eaux résiduelles** polluted water; **eaux vives** swift current; **être en eau** to sweat; **faire de l'eau** to take in water; **faire eau** to leak; **grandes eaux** fountains; **nager entre deux eaux** to float under the surface; to play both sides of the street; **pêcher en eau trouble** to fish in troubled waters; **porter de l'eau à la rivière** or **à la mer** to carry coals to Newcastle; **tomber à l'eau** to fizzle out

eau-de-vie [odvi] *f* (*pl* **eaux-de-vie**) brandy; spirits

eau-forte [ofɔrt] *f* (*pl* **eaux-fortes**) aqua fortis; etching

éba·hi -hie [ebai] *adj* dumfounded

ébattre [ebatr] §7 *ref* to frolic, to gambol

ébauche [eboʃ] *f* rough sketch or draft; suspicion (*of a smile*)

ébaucher [eboʃe] *tr* to sketch, to make a rough draft of

ébène [ebɛn] *f* ebony

ébénier [ebenje] *m* ebony (*tree*)

ébéniste [ebenist] *m* cabinetmaker

ébénisterie [ebenistri] *f* cabinetmaking

éberluer [ebɛrlɥe] *tr* to astonish

éblouir [ebluir] *tr* to dazzle, blind

éblouissement [ebluismɑ̃] *m* dazzle; glare; (*pathol*) dizziness

éboueur [ebwœr] *m* street cleaner, trash man; garbage collector

ébouillanter [ebujɑ̃te] *tr* to scald

éboulement [ebulmɑ̃] *m* cave-in, landslide

ébouler [ebule] *tr* & *ref* to cave in

ébourif·fant [eburifɑ̃] **ébourif·fante** [eburifɑ̃t] *adj* (coll) astounding

ébouriffer [eburife] *tr* to ruffle; (coll) to astound

ébouter [ebute] *tr* to cut off the end of

ébranchage [ebrɑ̃ʃaʒ] *m* pruning

ébrancher [ebrɑ̃ʃe] *tr* to prune

ébranlement [ebrɑ̃lmɑ̃] *m* shaking; shock

ébranler [ebrɑ̃le] *tr* to shake, jar || *ref* to start out; to be shaken

ébrécher [ebreʃe] §10 *tr* to nick, chip; to make a dent in (*e.g., a fortune*) || *ref* to be nicked, chipped; (with *dat* of *reflex pron*) to break off (*a tooth*)

ébriété [ebrijete] *f* inebriation

ébrouer [ebrue] *ref* to snort (*said of horse*); to splash about; to shake the water off oneself

ébruiter [ebrɥite] *tr* to noise about, to blab || *ref* to get around (*said of news*); to leak out (*said of secret*)

ébullition [ebylisjɔ̃] *f* boiling; ebullience, ferment

ébur·né -née [ebyrne] *adj* ivory

écaille [ekɑj] *f* scale (*of fish, snake*); shell; tortoise shell

écail·ler [ekɑje] **écail·lère** [ekɑjɛr] *mf* oyster opener || *m* oysterman || *f* oysterwoman || **écailler** *tr* & *ref* to scale

écale [ekal] *f* shell, husk, hull

écaler [ekale] *tr* to shell, husk, hull

écarlate [ekarlat] *adj* & *f* scarlet

écarquiller [ekarkije] *tr* (coll) to open wide, to spread apart

écart [ekar] *m* swerve, side step; digression, flight (*of imagination*); difference, gap, spread; error (*in range*); lapse (*in good conduct*); (cards) discard; **à l'écart** aside; aloof; **à l'écart de** far from; **faire le grand écart** to do the splits; **faire un écart** to shy (*said of horse*); to swerve (*said of car*); to step aside (*said of person*)

écar·té -tée [ekarte] *adj* lonely, secluded; wide-apart

écartèlement [ekartɛlmɑ̃] *m* quartering

écarteler [ekartəle] §2 *tr* to quarter

écartement [ekartəmɑ̃] *m* removal, separation; spreading; space between; spark gap; gauge (*of rails*)

écarter [ekarte] *tr* to put aside; to keep away; to ward off; to draw aside; to spread; (cards) to discard || *ref* to turn away; to stray

ecchymose [ɛkimoz] *f* black-and-blue mark

ecclésiastique [eklezjastik] *adj* & *m* ecclesiastic

écervel·lé -lée [esɛrvəle] *adj* scatterbrained || *mf* scatterbrain

échafaud [eʃafo] *m* scaffold

échafaudage [eʃafodaʒ] *m* scaffolding

échafauder [eʃafode] *tr* to pile up; to lay the groundwork for || *intr* to erect a scaffolding

échalasser [eʃalase] *tr* to stake

échalote [eʃalɔt] *f* shallot

échancrer [eʃɑ̃kre] *tr* to make a V-shaped cut in (*the neck of a dress*); to cut (*a dress*) low in the neck; to indent; to hollow out

échange [eʃɑ̃ʒ] *m* exchange

échanger [eʃɑ̃ʒe] §38 *tr* to exchange; **échanger pour** or **contre** to exchange (*s.th.*) for

échangeur [eʃɑ̃ʒœr] *m* interchange

échanson [eʃɑ̃sɔ̃] *m* cupbearer

échantillon [eʃɑ̃tijɔ̃] *m* sample; **comparer à l'échantillon** to spot-check

échantillonnage [eʃɑ̃tijɔnaʒ] *m* sampling; spot check

échantillonner [eʃɑ̃tijɔne] *tr* to cut samples of; to spot-check; to select (*a sampling to be polled*)

échappatoire [eʃapatwar] *f* loophole, way out

échap·pé -pée [eʃape] *mf* escapee || *f* escape; short period; glimpse; (sports) spurt; **à l'échappée** stealthily

échappement [eʃapmɑ̃] *m* escape, leak; exhaust; escapement (*of watch*); **échappement libre** cutout

échapper [eʃape] *tr*—**l'échapper belle** to have a narrow escape || *intr* to escape; **échapper à** to escape from; **échapper de** to slip out of || *ref* to escape

écharde [eʃard] *f* splinter

écharpe [eʃarp] *f* scarf; sash; sling; **en écharpe** diagonally, crosswise; in a sling; across the shoulder

écharper [eʃarpe] *tr* to slash, cut up

échasse [eʃɑs] *f* stilt

échauder [eʃode] *tr* to scald; to whitewash; to gouge (*a customer*)

échauffement [eʃofmɑ̃] *m* heating; overexcitement

échauffer [eʃofe] *tr* to heat; to warm; **échauffer les oreilles à qn** to get s.o.'s dander up || *ref* to heat up; to become excited

échauffourée [eʃofure] *f* skirmish; rash undertaking

èche [ɛʃ] *f* bait

échéance [eʃeɑ̃s] *f* due date, expiration

échec [eʃɛk] *m* check; chessman; failure; **échec et mat** checkmate; **échecs** [eʃe] chess; chess set; **être échec** to be in check; **jouer aux échecs** to play chess

échelle [eʃɛl] *f* ladder; scale; **échelle de sauvetage** fire escape; **échelle mobile** sliding scale; **échelle pliante** stepladder; **monter à l'échelle** (coll) to bite, be fooled

échelon [eʃlɔ̃] *m* echelon; rung (*of ladder*)

échelonner [eʃlɔne] *tr* to spread out, to space out

écheniller [eʃnije] *tr* to remove caterpillars from; to exterminate (*pests*); to eradicate (*corruption*)

éche·veau [eʃvo] *m* (*pl* **-veaux**) skein

écheve·lé -lée [eʃəvle] *adj* disheveled; wild (*dance, race*)

écheveler [eʃəvle] §34 *tr* to dishevel

échevin [eʃvɛ̃] *m* (hist) alderman

échine [eʃin] *f* spine, backbone; **avoir l'échine souple** (coll) to be a yes man

échiner [eʃine] *tr* to break the back of; to beat, kill || *ref* to tire oneself out

échiquier [eʃikje] *m* chessboard; exchequer

écho [eko] *m* echo; piece of gossip; **échos** gossip column; **faire écho to** echo

échoir [eʃwar] (usually used only in: *inf; ger* **échéant**; *pp* **échu**; 3d *sg: pres ind* **échoit**; *pret* **échut**; *fut* **échoira**; *cond* **échoirait**) *intr* (*aux*: AVOIR or ÊTRE) to fall, devolve; to fall due

échoppe [eʃɔp] *f* burin; (com) stand, booth; workshop

échopper [eʃɔpe] *tr* to scoop out

échotier [ekɔtje] *m* gossip columnist, society editor

échouer [eʃwe] *tr* to ground, to beach || *intr* to sink; to run aground; to fail || *ref* to run aground

é·chu -chue [eʃy] *adj* due, payable

écimer [esime] *tr* to top

éclaboussement [eklabusmɑ̃] *m* splash

éclabousser [eklabuse] *tr* to splash

éclair [eklɛr] *adj* lightning (*e.g., speed*); flash (*bulb*) || *m* flash (*of light, of lightning, of the eyes, of wit*); (culin) éclair; **éclairs** lightning; **éclairs de chaleur** heat lightning; **éclairs en nappe** sheet lightning; **il fait des éclairs** it is lightening; **passer comme un éclair** to flash by

éclairage [eklɛraʒ] *m* lighting; **sous cet éclairage** (fig) in this light

éclaircie [eklɛrsi] *f* break, clearing; spell of good weather

éclaircissement [eklɛrsismɑ̃] *m* explanation, clearing up

éclairement [eklɛrmɑ̃] *m* illumination

éclairer [eklɛre] *tr* to light; to enlighten; **éclairer sa lanterne** (fig) to ring a bell for s.o. || *intr* to light up, to glitter; **il éclaire** it is lightening || *ref* to be lighted

éclai·reur [eklɛrœr] **-reuse** [røz] *mf* scout || *m* boy scout || *f* girl scout

éclat [ekla] *m* splinter; ray (*of sunshine*); peal (*of thunder*); burst (*of laughter*); brightness, splendor

éclatement [eklatmɑ̃] *m* explosion; blowout (*of tire*); (fig) split

éclater [eklate] *intr* to splinter; to sparkle, glitter; to burst; to break out; to blow up

éclateur [eklatœr] *m* spark gap (*of induction coil*)

éclectique [eklɛktik] *adj* eclectic

éclipse [eklips] *f* eclipse; **à éclipses** flashing, blinking

éclipser [eklipse] *tr* to eclipse || *ref* to be eclipsed; (coll) to vanish; (coll) to sneak off

éclisse [eklis] *f* splinter; (med) splint; (rr) fishplate

éclisser [eklise] *tr* to splint

éclo·pé -pée [eklɔpe] *adj* lame || *mf* cripple

éclore [eklɔr] §24 *intr* (*aux*: ÊTRE) to hatch; to blossom out

éclosion [eklozjɔ̃] *f* hatching; blooming

écluse [eklyz] *f* lock (*of canal, river, etc.*); floodgate

écluser [eklyze] *tr* to close (*a canal*) by a lock; to pass (*a boat*) through a lock

écœurer [ekœre] *tr* to sicken; to dishearten

école [ekɔl] *f* school; **école à tir** artillery practice; **école d'application** model school; **école d'arts et métiers** trade school; **école dominicale, école du dimanche** Sunday School; **école libre** private school; **école maternelle** nursery school; **école mixte** coeducational school; **être à bonne école** to be in good hands; **faire école** to set a fashion; to form a school (*to set up a doctrine, gain adherents*); **faire l'école buissonnière** (coll) to play hooky

éco·lier [ekɔlje] **-lière** [ljɛr] *adj* schoolboy || *mf* pupil, scholar; novice || *m* schoolboy || *f* schoolgirl

écologie [ekɔlɔʒi] *f* ecology

éconduire [ekɔ̃dɥir] §19 *tr* to show out

économat [ekɔnɔma] *m* comptroller's office; commissary, company or co-op store; **économats** chain stores

économe [ekɔnɔm] *adj* economical || *mf* treasurer; housekeeper || *m* bursar

économie [ekɔnɔmi] *f* economy; **économie de marché** free enterprise; **économies** savings

économique [ekɔnɔmik] *adj* economic; economical || *f* economics

économiser [ekɔnɔmize] *tr & intr* to economize, save

écope [ekɔp] *f* scoop (*for bailing*)
écoper [ekɔpe] *tr* to bail out ‖ *intr* (coll) to get a bawling out
écorce [ekɔrs] *f* bark (*of tree*); peel, rind; crust (*of earth*)
écorcer [ekɔrse] §51 *tr* to peel, to strip off
écorcher [ekɔrʃe] *tr* to peel; to chafe; to fleece, overcharge; to grate on (*the ears*); to burn (*the throat*); to murder (*a language*) ‖ *ref* (with *dat* of *reflex pron*) to skin (*e.g.*, *one's arm*)
écor·cheur [ekɔrʃœr] **-cheuse** [ʃøz] *mf* skinner; fleecer, swindler
écorchure [ekɔrʃyr] *f* scratch, abrasion
écorner [ekɔrne] *tr* to poll, break the horns of; to dog-ear; to make a hole in (*e.g.*, *a fortune*)
écornifler [ekɔrnifle] *tr* to cadge; **écornifler un dîner à qn** to bum a dinner off s.o.
écorni·fleur [ekɔrniflœr] **-fleuse** [fløz] *mf* sponger, moocher
écos·sais [ekɔsɛ] **écos·saise** [ekɔsɛz] *adj* Scotch, Scottish ‖ *m* Scotch, Scottish (*language*); Scotch plaid ‖ (*cap*) *mf* Scot; **les Écossais** the Scotch ‖ *m* Scotchman
Écosse [ekɔs] *f* Scotland; **l'Écosse** Scotland
écosser [ekɔse] *tr* to shell, hull, husk
écot [eko] *m* share; tree stump; **payer son écot** to pay one's share
écoulement [ekulmɑ̃] *m* flow; (com) sale, turnover; (pathol) discharge; **écoulement d'eau** drainage
écouler [ekule] *tr* to sell, dispose of ‖ *ref* to run (*said, e.g., of water*); to flow; to drain; to leak; to elapse, go by
écourter [ekurte] *tr* to shorten (*a dress, coat, etc.*); to crop (*the tail, ears, etc.*); to cut short, curtail
écoute [ekut] *f* listening post; monitoring; (naut) sheet; **écoutes** wild boar's ears; **être aux écoutes** to eavesdrop, to keep one's ears to the ground; **se mettre à l'écoute** to listen to the radio
écouter [ekute] *tr* to listen to; **écouter parler** to listen to (*s.o.*) speaking ‖ *intr* to listen; **écouter aux portes** to eavesdrop ‖ *ref* to coddle oneself; **s'écouter parler** to be pleased with the sound of one's own voice
écou·teur [ekutœr] **-teuse** [tøz] *mf* listener; **écouteur aux portes** eavesdropper ‖ *m* telephone receiver; earphone
écoutille [ekutij] *f* hatchway
écouvillon [ekuvijɔ̃] *m* swab, mop
écrabouiller [ekrabuje] *tr* (coll) to squash
écran [ekrɑ̃] *m* screen; (phot) filter; **écran de cheminée** fire screen; **écran de protection aérienne** air umbrella; **le petit écran** television screen; **porter à l'écran** to put on the screen
écra·sant [ekrazɑ̃] **-sante** [zɑ̃t] *adj* crushing
écraser [ekraze] *tr* to crush; to overwhelm; to run over ‖ *ref* to be crushed; to crash

écrémer [ekreme] §10 *tr* to skim; (fig) to skim the cream off
écrémeuse [ekremøz] *f* cream separator
écrevisse [ekrəvis] *f* crayfish
écrier [ekrije] *ref* to cry out, exclaim
écrin [ekrɛ̃] *m* jewel case
écrire [ekrir] §25 *tr* to write; to spell ‖ *intr* to write ‖ *ref* to write to each other; to be written; to be spelled
é·crit [ekri] **-crite** [krit] *adj* written; **c'était écrit** it was fate ‖ *m* writing, written word; written examination; **écrits** writings, works; **par écrit** in writing
écri·teau [ekrito] *m* (*pl* -teaux) sign, placard
écritoire [ekritwar] *f* desk set
écriture [ekrityr] *f* handwriting; writing (*style of writing*); **écriture de chat** scrawl; **écritures** accounts; **Écritures** Scriptures; **écritures publiques** government documents
écrivailleur [ekrivɑ̃jœr] *m* (coll) scribbler, hack writer
écrivain [ekrivɛ̃] *adj*—**femme écrivain** woman writer ‖ *m* writer; **écrivain public** public letter writer
écrivasser [ekrivase] *intr* (coll) to scribble
écrou [ekru] *m* nut (*with internal thread*); register (*on police blotter*); **écrou à oreille** thumb nut
écrouer [ekrue] *tr* to jail, to book
écrouler [ekrule] *ref* to collapse; to crumble; to flop (*in a chair*)
é·cru -crue [ekry] *adj* raw; unbleached
écu [eky] *m* shield; crown (*money*); **écus** money
écubier [ekybje] *m* (naut) hawsehole
écueil [ekœj] *m* reef, sandbank; stumbling block
écuelle [ekɥɛl] *f* bowl
éculer [ekyle] *tr* to wear down at the heel
écu·mant [ekymɑ̃] **-mante** [mɑ̃t] *adj* foaming; fuming (*with rage*)
écume [ekym] *f* foam; froth; lather; dross; scum (*on liquids; on metal; of society*); **écume de mer** meerschaum
écumer [ekyme] *tr* to skim, scum; to pick up (*e.g., gossip*); to scour (*the seas*) ‖ *intr* to foam; to scum; to fume (*with anger*)
écu·meur [ekymœr] **-meuse** [møz] *mf* drifter; **écumeur de marmite** hanger-on; **écumeur de mer** pirate
écu·meux [ekymø] **-meuse** [møz] *adj* foamy, frothy
écumoire [ekymwar] *f* skimmer
écurage [ekyraʒ] *m* scouring; cleaning out
écurer [ekyre] *tr* to scour; to clean out
écureuil [ekyrœj] *m* squirrel
écurie [ekyri] *f* stable (*for horses, mules, etc.*); string of horses
écusson [ekysɔ̃] *m* escutcheon; bud (*for grafting*); (mil) identification tag
écuyer [ekɥije] **écuyère** [ekɥijɛr] *mf* horseback rider ‖ *m* horseman; squire; riding master ‖ *f* horsewoman
eczéma [ɛkzema], [ɛgzema] *m* eczema

edelweiss [edəlvɑjs], [edɛlvɛs] *m* edelweiss
éden [edɛn] *m* Eden || (*cap*) *m* Garden of Eden
éden·té -tée [edɑ̃te] *adj* toothless
E.D.F. *abbr* (**Électricité de France**) French national electric company
édicter [edikte] *tr* to decree, to promulgate
édicule [edikyl] *m* kiosk; street urinal
édi·fiant [edifjɑ̃] **-fiante** [fjɑ̃t] *adj* edifying
édification [edifikɑsjɔ̃] *f* edification; construction, building
édifice [edifis] *m* edifice, building
édifier [edifje] *tr* to edify; to inform, enlighten; to construct, to build; to found
édit [edi] *m* edict
éditer [edite] *tr* to publish; to edit (*a manuscript*)
édi·teur [editœr] **-trice** [tris] *mf* publisher; editor (*of a manuscript*)
édition [edisjɔ̃] *f* edition; publishing
édito·rial -riale [editɔrjal] *adj & m* (*pl* **-riaux** [rjo]) editorial
édredon [edrədɔ̃] *m* eiderdown
éduca·teur [edykatœr] **-trice** [tris] *adj* educational || *mf* educator
éduca·tif [edykatif] **-tive** [tiv] *adj* educational
éducation [edykɑsjɔ̃] *f* education, bringing-up, nurture
éduquer [edyke] *tr* to bring up (*children*); to educate, train
éfaufiler [efofile] *tr* to unravel
effacement [efasmɑ̃] *m* effacement, erasing; self-effacement
effacer [efase] §51 *tr* to efface; to erase || *ref* to efface oneself; to stand aside
effarement [efarmɑ̃] *m* fright, scare
effaroucher [efaruʃe] *tr* to frighten, scare off
effec·tif [efɛktif] **-tive** [tiv] *adj* actual, real || *m* personnel, manpower; strength (*of military unit*); complement (*of ship*); size (*of class*)
effectivement [efɛktivmɑ̃] *adv* actually, really, sure enough
effectuer [efɛktɥe] *tr* to effect
effémi·né -née [efemine] *adj* effeminate
efféminer [efemine] *tr* to make a sissy of; to unman || *ref* to become effeminate
effervescence [efɛrvesɑ̃s] *f* effervescence; excitement, ferment
efferves·cent [efɛrvesɑ̃] **efferves·cente** [efɛrvesɑ̃t] *adj* effervescent
effet [efɛ] *m* effect; (billiards) english; **à cet effet** for that purpose; **en effet** indeed, actually, sure enough; **effet de commerce** bill of exchange; **effets publics** government bonds; **faire de l'effet** to be striking; **faire l'effet de** to give the impression of
effeuillage [efœjaʒ] *m* thinning of leaves
effeuillaison [efœjɛzɔ̃] *f* fall of leaves
effeuiller [efœje] *tr* to thin out the leaves of, to pluck off the petals of || *ref* to shed its leaves

effeuilleuse [efœjøz] *f* (coll) strip-teaser
efficace [efikas] *adj* effective
efficacement [efikasmɑ̃] *adv* effectively
efficacité [efikasite] *f* efficacy, efficiency
efficience [efisjɑ̃s] *f* efficiency
effi·cient [efisjɑ̃] **-ciente** [sjɑ̃t] *adj* efficient
effigie [efiʒi] *f* effigy
effiler [efile] *tr* to unravel; to taper
effilocher [efilɔʃe] *tr* to unravel
efflan·qué -quée [eflɑ̃ke] *adj* skinny
effleurer [eflœre] *tr* to graze; to touch on
effluve [eflyv] *m* effluvium, emanation
effondrement [efɔ̃drəmɑ̃] *m* collapse
effondrer [efɔ̃dre] *tr* to break open; to break (*ground*) || *ref* to collapse, cave in; to sink
efforcer [efɔrse] §51 *ref*—**s'efforcer à** or **de** to try hard to, to strive to
effort [efɔr] *m* effort; (med) hernia, rupture; **effort de rupture** breaking stress; **effort de tension** torque; **faire effort sur soi-même** to get a hold of oneself
effraction [efraksjɔ̃] *f* housebreaking
effraie [efrɛ] *f* screech owl
effranger [efrɑ̃ʒe] §38 *tr & ref* to fray
effrayant [efrɛjɑ̃] **effrayante** [efrɛjɑ̃t] *adj* frightful, dreadful
effrayer [efrɛje] §49 *tr* to frighten || *ref* to be frightened
effré·né -née [efrene] *adj* unbridled
effritement [efritmɑ̃] *m* crumbling
effriter [efrite] *tr & ref* to crumble
effroi [efrwa], [efrwa] *m* fright
effron·té -tée [efrɔ̃te] *adj* impudent; shameless; (slang) saucy, sassy
effronterie [efrɔ̃tri] *f* effrontery
effroyable [efrwajabl] *adj* frightful
effusion [efyzjɔ̃] *f* effusion; shedding (*of blood*); (fig) gushing
égailler [egaje] *ref* to scatter
é·gal -gale [egal] *adj* (*pl* **-gaux** [go]) equal; level; (coll) indifferent; **ça m'est égal** (coll) it's all the same to me, it's all right || *mf* equal; **à l'égal de** as much as, no less than
également [egalmɑ̃] *adv* equally, likewise, also
égaler [egale] *tr* to equal, match
égaliser [egalize] *tr* to equalize; to equate
égalitaire [egaliter] *adj & mf* equalitarian
égalité [egalite] *f* equality; evenness; **être à égalité** to be tied
égard [egar] *m* respect; **à l'égard de** with regard to; **à tous (les) égards** in all respects; **eu égard à** in consideration of
éga·ré -rée [egare] *adj* stray, lost
égarement [egarmɑ̃] *m* wandering (*of mind, senses, etc.*); frenzy (*of sorrow, anger, etc.*)
égarer [egare] *tr* to mislead; to misplace; to bewilder || *ref* to get lost, to stray; to be on the wrong track
égayer [egeje] §49 *tr & ref* to cheer up; to brighten

égide [eʒid] *f* aegis
églefin [egləfɛ̃] *m* haddock
église [egliz] *f* church
églogue [eglɔg] *f* eclogue
égoïne [egɔin] *f* handsaw
égoïsme [egɔism] *m* egoism
égoïste [egɔist] *adj* selfish || *mf* egoist
égorgement [egɔrʒəmɑ̃] *m* slaughter
égorger [egɔrʒe] §38 *tr* to cut the throat of; (coll) to overcharge
égosiller [egozije] *ref* to shout oneself hoarse
égotisme [egɔtism] *m* egotism
égotiste [egɔtist] *adj* egotistical || *mf* egotist
égout [egu] *m* drainage; sewer; sink, cesspool (*e.g., of iniquity*)
égoutier [egutje] *m* sewer worker
égoutter [egute] *tr* to drain; to let drip || *ref* to drip
égouttoir [egutwar] *m* drainboard
égrapper [egrape] *tr* to pick off from the cluster
égratigner [egratiɲe] *tr* to scratch; to take a dig at, to tease
égratignure [egratiɲyr] *f* scratch; gibe, dig
égrener [egrəne] §2 *tr* to shell (*e.g., peas*); to gin (*cotton*); to pick off (*grapes*); to unstring (*pearls*); to tell (*beads*) || *ref* to drop one by one; to be strung out
égril·lard [egrijar] **égril·larde** [egrijard] *adj* spicy, lewd || *mf* shameless, unblushing person
égrugeoir [egryʒwar] *m* mortar (*for pounding or grinding*)
égruger [egryʒe] §38 *tr* to pound (*in a mortar*)
égueuler [egœle] *tr* to break the neck of (*e.g., a bottle*)
Égypte [eʒipt] *f* Egypt; **l'Égypte** Egypt
égyp·tien [eʒipsjɛ̃] **-tienne** [sjɛn] *adj* Egyptian || (*cap*) *mf* Egyptian
éhon·té -tée [eɔ̃te] *adj* shameless
eider [ɛjdɛr] *m* eider duck
éjaculation [eʒakylɑsjɔ̃] *f* ejaculation; (eccl) short, fervent prayer
éjaculer [eʒakyle] *tr & intr* to ejaculate
éjecter [eʒɛkte] *tr* to eject; (coll) to oust
éjection [eʒɛksjɔ̃] *f* ejection
élabo·ré -rée [elabɔre] *adj* elaborated; prepared, elaborate
élaborer [elabɔre] *tr* to elaborate; to work out, develop
élaguer [elage] *tr* to prune
élan [elɑ̃] *m* dash; impulse, outburst; spirit, glow; (zool) elk, moose; **avec élan** with enthusiasm
élan·cé -cée [elɑ̃se] *adj* slender, slim
élancement [elɑ̃smɑ̃] *m* throbbing, twinge; yearning (*e.g., for God*)
élancer [elɑ̃se] §51 *intr* to throb, to twinge || *ref* to rush, spring, dash; to spurt out
élargir [elarʒir] *tr* to widen; to broaden; to release (*a prisoner*) || *ref* to widen; to become more lax
élasticité [elastisite] *f* elasticity
élastique [elastik] *adj* elastic || *m* elastic; rubber band

élec·teur [elɛktœr] **-trice** [tris] *adj* voting || *mf* voter, constituent; (hist) elector; **électeurs** electorate
élec·tif [elɛktif] **-tive** [tiv] *adj* elective
élection [elɛksjɔ̃] *f* election; choice
électorat [elɛktɔra] *m* right to vote; (hist) electorate
électri·cien [elɛktrisjɛ̃] **-cienne** [sjɛn] *adj* electrical (*worker*) || *mf* electrician
électricité [elɛktrisite] *f* electricity
électrifier [elɛktrifje] *tr* to electrify
électrique [elɛktrik] *adj* electric(al)
électriser [elɛktrize] *tr* to electrify
électro [elɛktro] *m* electromagnet
électro-aimant [elɛktrɔɛmɑ̃] *m* (*pl* -aimants*) electromagnet
électrochoc [elɛktrɔʃɔk] *m* (med) electric shock treatment
électro-culinaire [elɛktrɔkylinɛr] *adj* electric kitchen (*appliances*)
électrocuter [elɛktrɔkyte] *tr* to electrocute
électrode [elɛktrɔd] *f* electrode
électrolyse [elɛktrɔliz] *f* electrolysis
électrolyte [elɛktrɔlit] *m* electrolyte
électromagnétique [elɛktrɔmaɲetik] *adj* electromagnetic
électroména·ger [elɛktrɔmenaʒe] **-gère** [ʒɛr] *adj* household-electric
électromo·teur [elɛktrɔmɔtœr] **-trice** [tris] *adj* electromotive || *m* electric motor
électron [elɛktrɔ̃] *m* electron
électronique [elɛktrɔnik] *adj* electronic || *f* electronics
électron-volt [elɛktrɔvɔlt] *m* (*pl* électrons-volts) electron-volt
électrophone [elɛktrɔfɔn] *m* electric phonograph
électrotype [elɛktrɔtip] *m* electrotype
électrotyper [elɛktrɔtipe] *tr* to electrotype
élégance [elegɑ̃s] *f* elegance
élé·gant [elegɑ̃] **-gante** [gɑ̃t] *adj* elegant
élégiaque [eleʒjak] *adj* elegiac || *mf* elegist
élégie [eleʒi] *f* elegy
élément [elemɑ̃] *m* element; (*of an electric battery*) cell, element; (elec, mach) unit; **élément standard** standard part
élémentaire [elemɑ̃tɛr] *adj* elementary
éléphant [elefɑ̃] *m* elephant
éléphantesque [elefɑ̃tɛsk] *adj* (coll) gigantic, elephantine
élevage [elvaʒ], [ɛlvaʒ] *m* rearing, raising, breeding; ranch
éléva·teur [elevatœr] **-trice** [tris] *adj* lifting || *m* elevator; hoist
élévation [elevɑsjɔ̃] *f* elevation; promotion; increase; (rok) lift-off
élève [elɛv] *mf* pupil, student; **ancien élève** alumnus; **élève externe** day student; **élève interne** boarding student || *f* breeder (*animal*); (hort) seedling
éle·vé -vée [elve] *adj* high, elevated; lofty, noble; **bien élevé** well-bred; **mal élevé** ill-bred
élever [elve] §2 *tr* to raise; to raise,

bring up, nurture; to erect ‖ *ref* to rise; to arise; to be built, to stand

éle·veur [ɛlvœr] **-veuse** [vøz] *mf* breeder, rancher

elfe [ɛlf] *m* elf

élider [elide] *tr* to elide

éligible [eliʒibl] *adj* eligible

élimer [elime] *tr & ref* to wear threadbare

éliminatoire [eliminatwar] *adj* (sports) preliminary ‖ *f* (sports) preliminaries

éliminer [elimine] *tr* to eliminate

élire [elir] §36 *tr* to elect

élision [elizjɔ̃] *f* elision

élite [elit] *f* elite

elle [ɛl] *pron disj* §85 ‖ *pron conj* §87

elle-même [ɛlmɛm] §86

ellipse [elips] *f* (gram) ellipsis; (math) ellipse

elliptique [eliptik] *adj* elliptic(al)

élocution [elɔkysjɔ̃] *f* elocution; choice and arrangement of words

éloge [elɔʒ] *m* eulogy; praise

élo·gieux [elɔʒjø] **-gieuse** [ʒjøz] *adj* full of praise

éloi·gné -gnée [elwaɲe] *adj* distant

éloignement [elwaɲəmɑ̃] *m* remoteness; aversion; postponement

éloigner [elwaɲe] *tr* to move away; to remove; to drive away; to postpone ‖ *ref* to move away; to digress, deviate; to become estranged

élongation [elɔ̃gasjɔ̃] *f* stretching

élonger [elɔ̃ʒe] §38 *tr* to lay (*e.g., a cable*); **élonger la terre** to skirt the coast

éloquence [elɔkɑ̃s] *f* eloquence

élo·quent [elɔkɑ̃] **-quente** [kɑ̃t] *adj* eloquent

é·lu -lue [ely] *adj* elected ‖ *mf* chosen one; **les élus** the elect

élucider [elyside] *tr* to elucidate

éluder [elyde] *tr* to elude, avoid

éma·cié -ciée [emasje] *adj* emaciated

émacier [emasje] *ref* to become emaciated

é·mail [emaj] *m* (*pl* **-maux** [mo]) enamel ‖ *m* (*pl* **-mails**) nail polish; car or bicycle paint

émaillage [emajaʒ] *m* enameling

émailler [emaje] *tr* to enamel; to sprinkle (*e.g., with quotations, metaphors, etc.*); to dot (*e.g., the fields, as flowers do*)

émanation [emanɑsjɔ̃] *f* emanation; manifestation (*e.g., of authority*)

émanciper [emɑ̃sipe] *tr* to emancipate ‖ *ref* to be emancipated; (coll) to get out of hand

émaner [emane] *intr* to emanate

émarger [emarʒe] §38 *tr* to trim (*e.g., a book*); to initial (*a document*) ‖ *intr* to get paid; **émarger à** to be paid from

émasculer [emaskyle] *tr* to emasculate

embâcle [ɑ̃bɑkl] *m* pack ice, ice floe

emballage [ɑ̃balaʒ] *m* packing, wrapping

emballer [ɑ̃bale] *tr* to wrap up, to pack; to race (*a motor*); (coll) to thrill; (coll) to bawl out ‖ *ref* to bolt, to run away; (mach) to race; (coll) to get worked up

embal·leur [ɑ̃balœr] **embal·leuse** [ɑ̃baløz] *mf* packer

embarbouiller [ɑ̃barbuje] *tr* to besmear; (coll) to muddle, confuse ‖ *ref* (coll) to get tangled up

embarcadère [ɑ̃barkadɛr] *m* wharf; (rr) platform

embarcation [ɑ̃barkɑsjɔ̃] *f* small boat

embardée [ɑ̃barde] *f* lurch; (aut) swerve; (aer, naut) yaw

embarder [ɑ̃barde] *intr* (aut) to swerve; (aer, naut) to yaw

embargo [ɑ̃bargo] *m* embargo

embarquement [ɑ̃barkəmɑ̃] *m* embarkation; shipping; loading

embarquer [ɑ̃barke] *tr* to embark; to ship (*a sea*); to load (*in car, plane, etc.*); (coll) to put in the clink ‖ *ref* to embark; to board; to get into a car

embarras [ɑ̃bara] *m* embarrassment; trouble, inconvenience; encumbrance, obstruction; perplexity; financial difficulties; **embarras de voitures** traffic jam; **embarras du choix** too much to choose from; **faire des embarras** (coll) to put on airs

embarrasser [ɑ̃barase] *tr* to embarrass; to hamper, to obstruct; to stump, to perplex ‖ *ref*—**s'embarrasser de** to take an interest in; to bother with

embaucher [ɑ̃boʃe] *tr* to hire, to sign on; (coll) to entice (*soldiers*) to desert ‖ *intr* to hire; **on n'embauche pas** (public sign) no help wanted

embauchoir [ɑ̃boʃwar] *m* shoetree

embaumement [ɑ̃boməmɑ̃] *m* embalming; perfuming

embaumer [ɑ̃bome] *tr* to embalm; to perfume ‖ *intr* to smell good

embaumeur [ɑ̃bomœr] *m* embalmer

embellir [ɑ̃belir] *tr* to embellish ‖ *intr* to clear up (*said of weather*); to improve in looks ‖ *ref* to grow more beautiful

embellissement [ɑ̃belismɑ̃] *m* embellishment

embêtement [ɑ̃bɛtmɑ̃] *m* (coll) annoyance

embêter [ɑ̃bɛte], [ɑ̃bete] *tr* (coll) to annoy

emblave [ɑ̃blav] *f* grainfield

emblaver [ɑ̃blave] *tr* to sow

emblée [ɑ̃ble]—**d'emblée** then and there, right off; without difficulty

emblématique [ɑ̃blematik] *adj* emblematic(al)

emblème [ɑ̃blɛm] *m* emblem

embobeliner [ɑ̃bɔbline] *tr* (coll) to bamboozle

embobiner [ɑ̃bɔbine] *tr* to wind up (*e.g., on a reel*); (coll) to bamboozle

emboîter [ɑ̃bwate] *tr* to encase; to nest (*boxes, boats, etc.*); (mach) to interlock, joint; **emboîter le pas to** fall into step

embolie [ɑ̃bɔli] *f* (pathol) embolism

embonpoint [ɑ̃bɔ̃pwɛ̃] *m* portliness; **prendre de l'embonpoint** to put on flesh

embouche [ɑ̃buʃ] *f* pasture

embou·ché -chée [ãbuʃe] *adj—mal embouché* foul-mouthed
emboucher [ãbuʃe] *tr* to blow, sound
embouchoir [ãbuʃwar] *m* mouthpiece
embouchure [ãbuʃyr] *f* mouth (*of a river*); mouthpiece
embourber [ãburbe] *tr* to stick in the mud; to vilify, to implicate
embout [ãbu] *m* tip, ferrule; rubber tip (*for chair*)
embouteillage [ãbutejaʒ] *m* bottling; bottleneck, traffic jam
emboutir [ãbutir] *tr* to stamp, emboss; to smash (*e.g., a fender*) ‖ *ref* to bump
embranchement [ãbrãʃmã] *m* branching (off); branch; branch line; junction (*of roads, track, etc.*)
embrasement [ãbrɑzmã] *m* conflagration; illumination, glow
embraser [ãbrɑze] *tr* to set aflame or aglow ‖ *ref* to flame up; to glow
embrassade [ãbrasad] *f* embrace; kissing
embrasse [ãbrɑs] *f* curtain tieback
embrassement [ãbrasmã] *m* embrace
embrasser [ãbrase] *tr* to embrace; to kiss; to join; to undertake; to take in (*at a glance*); to take (*the opportunity*) ‖ *ref* to embrace; to neck
embras·seur [ãbrasœr] **embras·seuse** [ãbrasøz] *mf* smoocher
embrasure [ãbrazyr] *f* embrasure, loophole; opening (*for door or window*)
embrayage [ãbrejaʒ] *m* coupling, engagement; (aut) clutch
embrayer [ãbreje], [ãbreje] §49 *tr* to engage, connect; to throw into gear ‖ *intr* to throw the clutch in
embrocher [ãbrɔʃe] *tr* to put on a spit
embrouiller [ãbruje] *tr* to embroil ‖ *ref* to become embroiled
embroussail·lé -lée [ãbrusaje] *adj* bushy; tangled; complicated, complex
embru·mé -mée [ãbryme] *adj* foggy, misty
embruns [ãbrœ̃] *mpl* spray
embryologie [ãbrijɔlɔʒi] *f* embryology
embryon [ãbrijɔ̃] *m* embryo
embryonnaire [ãbrijɔnɛr] *adj* embryonic
em·bu -bue [ãby] *adj* lifeless, dull ‖ *m* dull tone (*of a painting*)
embûche [ãbyʃ] *f* snare, trap
embuer [ãbɥe] *tr* to cloud with steam; *embué de larmes* dimmed with tears
embuscade [ãbyskad] *f* ambush
embus·qué -quée [ãbyske] *adj* in ambush; *se tenir embusqué* to lie in ambush ‖ *m* (mil) goldbricker, shirker
embusquer [ãbyske] *tr* to ambush, trap ‖ *ref* to lie in ambush; (mil) to get a safe assignment
émé·ché -chée [emeʃe] *adj* (coll) tipsy, high
émender [emãde] *tr* to amend (*a sentence, decree, etc.*)
émeraude [ɛmrod] *f* emerald
émergence [emɛrʒãs] *f* emergence
émerger [emɛrʒe] §38 *intr* to emerge
émeri [ɛmri] *m* emery

émerillon [ɛmrijɔ̃] *m* swivel; (orn) merlin
émerillon·né -née [ɛmrijɔne] *adj* lively, gay
émérite [emerit] *adj* experienced; distinguished, remarkable; confirmed (*smoker*); (obs) retired, emeritus
émersion [emɛrsjɔ̃] *f* emersion
émerveillement [emɛrvɛjmã] *m* wonderment
émerveiller [emɛrveje] *tr* to astonish, amaze
émétique [emetik] *adj & m* emetic
émet·teur [emetœr] **émet·trice** [emetris] *adj* issuing; transmitting ‖ *mf* maker (*of check, draft*); issuer ‖ *m* broadcasting station; (rad) transmitter
émetteur-récepteur [emɛtœrresɛptœr] *m* (*pl* **émetteurs-récepteurs**) (rad) walkie-talkie
émettre [emɛtr] §42 *tr* to emit; to express (*an opinion*); to issue (*stamps, bank notes, etc.*); to transmit (*a radio signal*) ‖ *intr* to transmit, broadcast
é·meu [emø] *m* (*pl* **-meus**) (zool) emu
émeute [emøt] *f* riot
émeutier [emøtje] *m* rioter
émietter [emjete] *tr* to crumble; to break up (*an estate*)
émi·grant [emigrã] **-grante** [grãt] *adj & mf* emigrant; migrant
émi·gré -grée [emigre] *adj* emigrating ‖ *mf* emigrant; émigré
émigrer [emigre] *intr* to emigrate; to migrate
émincer [emɛ̃se] §51 *tr* to cut in thin slices
éminemment [eminamã] *adv* eminently
éminence [eminãs] *f* eminence
émi·nent -nente [eminã] **-nente** [nãt] *adj* eminent
émissaire [emisɛr] *m* emissary; outlet (*of lake, basin, etc.*)
émission [emisjɔ̃] *f* emission; utterance; issue (*of stamps, bank notes, etc.*); (rad) transmission, broadcast
emmagasiner [ãmagazine] *tr* to put in storage; to store up; to stockpile
emmailloter [ãmajəte] *tr* to swathe; to bandage
emmancher [ãmãʃe] *tr* to put a handle on ‖ *ref* (coll) to begin; *s'emmancher bien* (coll) to get off to a good start; *s'emmancher mal* (coll) to get off to a bad start
emmêler [ãmɛle], [ãmele] *tr* to tangle up; to mix up
emménagement [ãmenaʒmã] *m* moving in; installation
emménager [ãmenaʒe] §38 *tr & intr* to move in
emmener [ãmne] §2 *tr* to take or lead away; to take out (*e.g., to dinner*); to take (*on a visit*)
emmenthal [emɛtal], [emɑ̃tal] *m* Swiss cheese
emmiel·lé -lée [ãmjɛle], [ãmjele] *adj* honeyed (*e.g., words*)
emmitoufler [ãmitufle] *tr & ref* to bundle up (*in warm clothing*)
emmurer [ãmyre] *tr* to wall in, immure

émoi [emwa] *m* agitation, alarm

émolument [emɔlymã] *m* share; émoluments emolument, fee, salary

émonder [emɔ̃de] *tr* to prune, trim

émo·tif [emɔtif] -tive [tiv] *adj* emotional || *mf* emotional person

émotion [emosjɔ̃] *f* emotion; commotion

émotionnable [emosjɔnabl] *adj* emotional

émotion·nant [emosjɔnã] émotion·nante [emosjɔnãt] *adj* stirring, moving

émotionner [emosjɔne] *tr* to move deeply, thrill, affect || *ref* to get excited, flustered

émoucher [emuʃe] *tr* to chase flies away from

émouchet [emuʃɛ] *m* sparrow hawk

émouchoir [emuʃwar] *m* whisk, fly swatter

émoudre [emudr] §43 *tr* to grind, sharpen

émoulage [emulaʒ] *m* grinding, sharpening

émou·lu -lue [emuly] *adj*—frais émoulu de (fig) fresh from, just back from

émous·sé -sée [emuse] *adj* blunt

émousser [emuse] *tr* to dull, blunt

émoustiller [emustije] *tr* (coll) to exhilarate, to rouse

émouvoir [emuvwar] §45 (*pp* ému) *tr* to move; to excite || *ref* to be moved; to be excited

empailler [ãpaje] *tr* to stuff (*animals*); to cane (*a chair*)

empail·leur [ãpajœr] empail·leuse [ãpajøz] *mf* taxidermist; caner

empaler [ãpale] *tr* to impale

empan [ãpã] *m* span (*of hand*)

empanacher [ãpanaʃe] *tr* to plume

empaquetage [ãpaktaʒ] *m* packaging; package

empaqueter [ãpakte] §34 *tr* to package

emparer [ãpare] *ref*—s'emparer de to seize, take hold of

empâter [ãpate] *tr* to make sticky; to fatten up (*chickens, turkeys, etc.*); to coat (*the tongue*); (typ) to overink || *ref* to put on weight; to become coated (*said of tongue*); to become husky (*said of voice*)

empattement [ãpatmã] *m* foundation, footing; (aut) wheelbase

empaumer [ãpome] *tr* to catch in the hand; to hit with a racket; to palm (*a card*); (coll) to hoodwink

empêchement [ãpɛʃmã] *m* impediment, bar; hindrance, obstacle

empêcher [ãpɛʃe] *tr* to hinder; empêcher qn de + *inf* to prevent or keep s.o. from + *ger*; n'empêche que all the same, e.g., n'empêche qu'il est très poli he's very polite all the same || *ref*—ne pouvoir s'empêcher de + *inf* not to be able to help + *ger*, e.g., je n'ai pu m'empêcher de rire I could not help laughing

empê·cheur [ãpɛʃœr] -cheuse [ʃøz] *mf*—empêcheur de danser en rond (coll) wet blanket

empeigne [ãpɛɲ] *f* upper (*of shoe*)

empennage [ãpɛnnaʒ] *m* feathers (*of arrow*); fins, vanes; (aer) empennage

empereur [ãprœr] *m* emperor

emperler [ãpɛrle] *tr* to ornament with pearls; to cover with drops; la sueur emperlait son front his forehead was covered with beads of perspiration

empe·sé -sée [ãpəze] *adj* starched, stiff, wooden (*style*)

empeser [ãpəze] §2 *tr* to starch

empes·té -tée [ãpeste] *adj* pestilential; stinking, reeking; depraved

empester [ãpeste] *tr* to stink; to corrupt || *intr* to stink

empêtrer [ãpɛtre] *tr* to hamper; to involve, entangle || *ref* to become involved, entangled

emphase [ãfaz] *f* overemphasis; bombast, pretentiousness

emphatique [ãfatik] *adj* overemphasized; bombastic, pretentious

emphysème [ãfizɛm] *m* emphysema

empiècement [ãpjɛsmã] *m* yoke (*of shirt, blouse, etc.*)

empierrer [ãpjere] *tr* to pave with stones; (rr) to ballast

empiétement [ãpjetmã] *m* encroachment, incursion

empiéter [ãpjete] §10 *intr* to encroach

empiffrer [ãpifre] *tr* (coll) to stuff, fatten || *ref* (coll) to stuff oneself, to guzzle

empiler [ãpile] *tr* to pile up, stack; (slang) to dupe || *ref* to pile up; se faire empiler (slang) to be had

empire [ãpir] *m* empire; control, supremacy

empirer [ãpire] *tr* to make worse, to aggravate || *intr* (*aux:* AVOIR or ÊTRE) to grow worse

empirique [ãpirik] *adj* empiric(al) || *m* empiricist; charlatan, quack

emplacement [ãplasmã] *m* emplacement; location, site

emplâtre [ãplɑtr] *m* patch (*on tire*); (med) plaster; (coll) boob

emplette [ãplɛt] *f* purchase; aller faire des emplettes to go shopping

emplir [ãplir] *tr* & *ref* to fill up

emploi [ãplwa] *m* employment, job; employment, use; (theat) type (*of role*); double emploi useless duplication; emploi du temps schedule

employé·e [ãplwaje] *mf* employee; clerk

employer [ãplwaje] §47 *tr* to employ; to use || *ref* to be employed; s'employer à to try to, to do one's best to

employeur [ãplwajœr] employeuse [ãplwajøz] *mf* employer

empocher [ãpɔʃe] *tr* (coll) to pocket

empoi·gnant [ãpwaɲã] -gnante [ɲãt] *adj* exciting, arresting, thrilling

empoigner [ãpwaɲe] *tr* to grasp; to collar (*a crook*); to grip, move (*an audience*)

empois [ãpwa] *m* starch

empoisonnement [ãpwazɔnmã] *m* poisoning; avoir des empoisonnements (coll) to be annoyed

empoisonner [ãpwazɔne] *tr* to poison; to infect (*the air*); to corrupt; (coll) to bother || *intr* to reek || *ref* to be poisoned

empoison·neur [ɑ̃pwazɔnœr] **empoison·neuse** [ɑ̃pwazɔnǿz] *adj* poisoning || *mf* poisoner; corrupter

empoissonner [ɑ̃pwasɔne] *tr* to stock with fish

empor·té -tée [ɑ̃pɔrte] *adj* quick-tempered, impetuous

emportement [ɑ̃pɔrtəmɑ̃] *m* anger, temper

emporte-pièce [ɑ̃pɔrtəpjɛs] *m* (*pl* **-pièces**) punch; **à l'emporte-pièce** trenchant, cutting, biting (*style, words, etc.*)

emporter [ɑ̃pɔrte] *tr* to take away; to carry off; to remove; **à emporter** to take out, to go (*e.g., said of food to take out of the restaurant*); **l'emporter sur** to have the upper hand over || *ref* to be carried away; to lose one's temper; to run away

empo·té -tée [ɑ̃pɔte] *adj* (coll) clumsy || *mf* (coll) butterfingers

empoter [ɑ̃pɔte] *tr* to pot (*a plant*)

empourprer [ɑ̃purpre] *tr* to set aglow || *ref* to turn crimson; to flush

empoussiérer [ɑ̃pusjere] §10 *tr* to cover with dust

empreindre [ɑ̃prɛ̃dr] §50 *tr* to imprint, stamp

empreinte [ɑ̃prɛ̃t] *f* imprint, stamp; **empreinte des roues** wheel tracks; **empreinte digitale** fingerprint; **empreinte du pied** or **empreinte de pas** footprint

empres·sé -sée [ɑ̃prɛse] *adj* eager

empressement [ɑ̃prɛsmɑ̃] *m* haste, alacrity; eagerness, readiness

empresser [ɑ̃prɛse] *ref* to hasten; **s'empresser à** to be anxious to; **s'empresser auprès de** to be attentive to, make a fuss over; to press around; **s'empresser de** to hasten to

emprise [ɑ̃priz] *f* expropriation; control, ascendancy

emprisonnement [ɑ̃prizɔnmɑ̃] *m* imprisonment

emprisonner [ɑ̃prizɔne] *tr* to imprison

emprunt [ɑ̃prœ̃] *m* loan; loan word; **d'emprunt** feigned, assumed

emprunter [ɑ̃prœ̃te] *tr* to borrow; to take (*a road, a route*); to take on (*false appearances*); **emprunter q.ch. à** to borrow s.th. from; to get s.th. from

empuantir [ɑ̃pɥɑ̃tir] *tr* to stink up

empyème [ɑ̃pjɛm] *m* empyema

empyrée [ɑ̃pire] *m* empyrean

é·mu -mue [emy] *adj* moved, touched; tender (*memory*); **ému de** alarmed by

émulation [emylɑsjɔ̃] *f* emulation, rivalry

émule [emyl] *mf* emulator, rival

émulsion [emylsjɔ̃] *f* emulsion

émulsionner [emylsjɔne] *tr* to emulsify

en [ɑ̃] *pron indef & adv* §87 || *prep* in; into; to, e.g., **aller en France** to go to France; e.g., **de mal en pis** from bad to worse; at, e.g., **en mer** at sea; e.g., **en guerre** at war; on, e.g., **en congé** on leave; by, e.g., **en chemin**

de fer by rail; of, made of, e.g., **en bois** (made) of wood

enamourer [ɑ̃namure] *ref* to become enamored, to fall in love

encabaner [ɑ̃kabane] *ref* (Canad) to hole up, to dig in (*e.g., for the winter*)

encablure [ɑ̃kablyr] *f* cable's length (*unit of measure*)

encadrement [ɑ̃kadrəmɑ̃] *m* framing; frame: framework; window frame; doorframe; border, edge; staffing; officering (*furnishing with officers*)

encadrer [ɑ̃kadre] *tr* to frame; to staff (*an organization*); to officer (*troops*); to incorporate (*recruits*) into a unit

encadreur [ɑ̃kadrœr] *m* framer (*person*)

encager [ɑ̃kaʒe] §38 *tr* to cage

encaisse [ɑ̃kɛs] *f* cash on hand, cash balance; **encaisse métallique** bullion

encais·sé -sée [ɑ̃kese] *adj* deeply embanked, sunken

encaissement [ɑ̃kɛsmɑ̃] *m* cashing (*e.g., of check*); boxing, crating; embankment

encaisser [ɑ̃kɛse], [ɑ̃kese] *tr* to cash; to box, to crate; to receive (*a blow*); to embank (*a river*); (coll) to put up with || *ref* to be steeply embanked

encaisseur [ɑ̃kɛsœr] *m* collector; payee; cashier

encan [ɑ̃kɑ̃] *m* auction

encanailler [ɑ̃kanaje] *tr* to debase || *ref* to acquire bad habits; to keep low company

encapuchonner [ɑ̃kapyʃɔne] *tr* to hood

encaquer [ɑ̃kake] *tr* to barrel; to pack (*sardines*); (coll) to pack in like sardines

encart [ɑ̃kar] *m* inset, insert

encarter [ɑ̃karte] *tr* to card (*buttons, pins, etc.*); (bb) to tip in

en-cas [ɑ̃ka] *m invar* snack; reserve, emergency supply

encasernement [ɑ̃kazɛrnəmɑ̃] *m—encasernement de conscience* thought control, regimentation

encaserner [ɑ̃kazɛrne] *tr* to quarter, to barrack (*troops*)

encastrement [ɑ̃kastrəmɑ̃] *m* groove; fitting

encastrer [ɑ̃kastre] *tr & ref* to fit

encaustique [ɑ̃kɔstik] *f* furniture polish; floor wax; encaustic painting

encaustiquer [ɑ̃kɔstike] *tr* to wax

encaver [ɑ̃kave] *tr* to cellar (*wine*)

enceindre [ɑ̃sɛ̃dr] §50 *tr* to enclose, to encircle

enceinte [ɑ̃sɛ̃t] *adj fem* pregnant || *f* enclosure; walls, ramparts; precinct, compass; (boxing) ring

encens [ɑ̃sɑ̃] *m* incense; flattery

encenser [ɑ̃sɑ̃se] *tr* to incense, perfume with incense; to flatter

encensoir [ɑ̃sɑ̃swar] *m* censer

encéphalite [ɑ̃sefalit] *f* encephalitis

encercler [ɑ̃sɛrkle] *tr* to encircle

enchaînement [ɑ̃ʃɛnmɑ̃] *m* chaining up; chain, sequence

enchaîner [ɑ̃ʃɛne], [ɑ̃ʃene], *tr* to chain; to connect || *intr* to go on speaking || *ref* to be connected

enchan·té -tée [ãʃāte] *adj* delighted, pleased

enchantement [ãʃātmā] *m* enchantment

enchanter [ãʃāte] *tr* to enchant

enchan·teur [ãʃātœr] **-teresse** [trɛs] *adj* enchanting, bewitching || *m* enchanter, magician || *f* enchantress

enchâsser [ãʃɑse] *tr* to enshrine; to insert; to set, chase (*a gem*)

enchère [ãʃɛr] *f* bid, bidding; **folle enchère** bid that cannot be made good; folly

enchérir [ãʃerir] *tr* to bid on; to raise the price of || *intr* to bid; to rise in price; **enchérir sur** to improve on; to outbid

enchérisseur [ãʃerisœr] *m* bidder; **dernier enchérisseur** highest bidder

enchevêtrement [ãʃvɛtrəmā] *m* entanglement; network; jumble

enchevêtrer [ãʃvɛtre] *tr* to tangle up; to halter (*a horse*) || *ref* to become complicated or confused

enchifre·né -née [ãʃifrəne] *adj* stuffed-up (*with a cold*)

enclave [ãklav] *f* enclave

enclaver [ãklave] *tr* to enclose; to dovetail

enclencher [ãklãʃe] *tr* & *ref* to interlock

en·clin [ãklɛ̃] **-cline** [klin] *adj* inclined, prone

encliquetage [ãkliktaʒ] *m* ratchet

encliqueter [ãklikte] §34 *tr* to cog, to mesh

enclitique [ãklitik] *adj* & *m* & *f* enclitic

enclore [ãklɔr] §24 (has also 1st & 2d *pl pres ind* **enclosons, enclosez**) *tr* to close in, to wall in

enclos [ãklo] *m* enclosure, close

enclume [ãklym] *f* anvil; **se trouver entre l'enclume et le marteau** (coll) to be between the devil and the deep blue sea

encoche [ãkɔʃ] *f* notch, nick; slot; thumb index

encocher [ãkɔʃe] *tr* to notch, to nick; to slot

encoignure [ãkɔɲyr] *f* corner; corner piece; corner cabinet

encollage [ãkɔlaʒ] *m* gluing; sizing

encoller [ãkɔle] *tr* to glue; to size

encolure [ãkɔlyr] *f* collar size; neck line; neck and withers (*of horse*); **gagner par une encolure** to win by a neck

encombre [ãkɔ̃br] *m*—**sans encombre** without a hitch, without hindrance

encombrement [ãkɔ̃brəmā] *m* encumbrance, congestion

encombrer [ãkɔ̃bre] *tr* to encumber; to crowd, congest; to block up, to jam; to litter, to load down || *ref*—**s'encombrer de** (coll) to be saddled with

encontre [ãkɔ̃tr]—**à l'encontre de** counter to, against; contrary to

encore [ãkɔr] *adv* still, e.g., **il est encore ici** he is still here; yet, e.g., **encore mieux** better yet; e.g., **pas encore** not yet; only, e.g., **si encore vous m'en aviez parlé!** if only you had told me!; **encore que** although;

encore une fois once more, once again; **en voulez-vous encore?** do you want some more? || *interj* again!, oh no, not again! (*expressing impatience or astonishment*)

encorner [ãkɔrne] *tr* to gore, to toss

encouragement [ãkuraʒmā] *m* encouragement

encourager [ãkuraʒe] §38 *tr* to encourage

encourir [ãkurir] §14 *tr* to incur

encrasser [ãkrase] *tr* to soil, to dirty; to soot (*a chimney*); to foul (*a gun*) || *ref* to get dirty; to stop up, clog; to soot up

encre [ãkr] *f* ink; **encre de Chine** India ink; **encre sympathique** invisible ink

encrer [ãkre] *tr* to ink

encreur [ãkrœr] *adj* inking (*ribbon, roller*) || *m* ink roller

encrier [ãkrije] *m* inkwell

encroûter [ãkrute] *tr* to encrust; to plaster (*walls*) || *ref* to become encrusted; to get rusty; to become hidebound, prejudiced

encyclique [ãsiklik] *adj* & *f* encyclical

encyclopédie [ãsiklɔpedi] *f* encyclopedia

encyclopédique [ãsiklɔpedik] *adj* encyclopedic

endauber [ãdobe] *tr* to braise

endémie [ãdemi] *f* endemic

endémique [ãdemik] *adj* endemic

endenter [ãdāte] *tr* to tooth, to cog; to mesh (*gears*); **bien endenté** (coll) with plenty of teeth; (coll) with a hearty appetite

endetter [ãdete] *tr* & *ref* to run into debt

endêver [ãdeve] *intr*—**faire endêver** to bedevil, to drive wild

endia·blé -blée [ãdjable] *adj* devilish, reckless; full of pep

endiguement [ãdigmā] *m* damming up; embankment

endiguer [ãdige] *tr* to dam up

endimancher [ãdimãʃe] *tr* & *ref* to put on Sunday clothes, to dress up

endive [ãdiv] *f* endive

endocrine [ãdɔkrin] *adj* endocrine

endoctriner [ãdɔktrine] *tr* to indoctrinate; to win over

endolo·ri -rie [ãdɔlɔri] *adj* painful, sore

endommagement [ãdɔmaʒmā] *m* damage

endommager [ãdɔmaʒe] §38 *tr* to damage || *ref* to suffer damage

endor·mi -mie [ãdɔrmi] *adj* asleep, sleeping; sluggish, apathetic; dormant; numb (*arm or leg*)

endormir [ãdɔrmir] §23 *tr* to put to sleep; to lull, to put off guard || *ref* to go to sleep; to slack off; to let down one's guard

endos [ãdo] *m* endorsement

endosse [ãdos] *f* responsibility

endossement [ãdosmā] *m* endorsement

endosser [ãdose] *tr* to endorse; to take on the responsibility of

endosseur [ãdosœr] *m* endorser

endroit [ãdrwa], [ãdrwɑ] *m* place, spot; right side (*of cloth*); **à l'endroit**

right side out; **à l'endroit de** with regard to; **le petit endroit** (coll) the toilet; **mettre à l'endroit** to put on right side out
enduire [ãdҷir] §19 *tr* to coat, smear
enduit [ãdҷi] *m* coat, coating
endurance [ãdyrãs] *f* endurance
endu·rant [ãdyrã] **-rante** [rãt] *adj* untiring; meek, patient
endur·ci -cie [ãdyrsi] *adj* hardened; tough, calloused; inveterate
endurcir [ãdyrsir] *tr* to harden; to inure, to toughen ‖ *ref* to harden; **s'endurcir à** to become accustomed to, to become inured to
endurcissement [ãdyrsismã] *m* hardening
endurer [ãdyre] *tr* to endure
énergétique [enerʒetik] *adj* energy, power
énergie [enerʒi] *f* energy
énergique [enerʒik] *adj* energetic
énergumène [energymen] *mf* ranter, wild person, maniac
éner·vant [enervã] **-vante** [vãt] *adj* annoying, nerve-racking
énerver [enerve] *tr* to enervate; to unnerve ‖ *ref* to get nervous; to be exasperated
enfance [ãfãs] *f* childhood; infancy; dotage, second childhood; **c'est l'enfance de l'art** (coll) it's child's play; **enfance délinquante** juvenile delinquents; **première enfance** infancy
enfant [ãfã] *adj invar* childish, childlike; **bon enfant** good-natured ‖ *mf* child; **enfant de chœur** altar boy; **enfant de la balle** child who follows in his father's footsteps; **enfant en bas âge** infant; **enfant terrible** (fig) stormy petrel; **enfant trouvé** foundling; **mon enfant!** my boy!; **petit enfant** infant
enfantement [ãfãtmã] *m* childbirth
enfanter [ãfãte] *tr* to give birth to
enfantillage [ãfãtijaʒ] *m* childishness
enfan·tin [ãfãtɛ̃] **-tine** [tin] *adj* childish, infantile
enfari·né -née [ãfarine] *adj* smeared with flour
enfer [ãfɛr] *m* hell
enfermer [ãfɛrme] *tr* to enclose; to shut up, to lock up ‖ *ref* to shut oneself in; to closet oneself
enferrer [ãfɛre] *tr* to pierce, to run through ‖ *ref* to run oneself through with a sword; to bite (*said of fish*); (fig) to be caught in one's own trap
enfiévrer [ãfjevre] §10 *tr* to inflame, to make feverish
enfilade [ãfilad] *f* row, string, series; (mil) enfilade; **en enfilade** connecting, e.g., **chambres en enfilade** connecting rooms
enfile-aiguille [ãfilegҷij] *m invar* threader, needle threader
enfiler [ãfile] *tr* to pierce; to thread (*a needle*); to string (*beads*); to start down (*a street*); (coll) to put on (*clothes*)
enfin [ãfɛ̃] *adv* finally, at last; in short; after all, anyway

enflam·mé -mée [ãflame], [ãflame] *adj* flaming; bright red; inflamed
enflammer [ãflame], [ãflame] *tr* to inflame ‖ *ref* to be inflamed; to flare up
enfler [ãfle] *tr* to swell; to puff up or out; to exaggerate ‖ *intr & ref* to swell, to puff up
enflure [ãflyr] *f* swelling; (fig) exaggeration
enfon·cé -cée [ãfɔ̃se] *adj* sunken, deep; deep-set; broken (*ribs*); (coll) taken, had (*bested*)
enfoncement [ãfɔ̃smã] *m* driving in; breaking open; hollow, recess
enfoncer [ãfɔ̃se] §51 *tr* to drive in; to push in, break open; (coll) to get the better of ‖ *intr* to sink to the bottom ‖ *ref* to sink, plunge; to give way; to disappear; to penetrate (*said of root, bullet, etc.*)
enforcir [ãfɔrsir] *tr* to reinforce ‖ *intr & ref* to become stronger; to grow
enfouir [ãfwir] *tr* to bury; to hide ‖ *ref* to burrow; to bury oneself (*e.g., in an out-of-the-way locality*)
enfourcher [ãfurʃe] *tr* to stick a pitchfork into; to mount, straddle
enfourchure [ãfurʃyr] *f* crotch
enfourner [ãfurne] *tr* to put in the oven; (coll) to gobble down
enfreindre [ãfrɛ̃dr] §50 *tr* to violate, break (*e.g., a law*)
enfuir [ãfҷir] §31 *ref* to run away; to escape; to elope
enfu·mé -mée [ãfyme] *adj* blackened; smoky (*color*)
enfumer [ãfyme] *tr* to smoke up, blacken; to smoke out
enfutailler [ãfytaje] *tr* to cask, to barrel
enga·gé -gée [ãgaʒe] *adj* committed; hocked ‖ *m* (mil) enlisted man
engagement [ãgaʒmã] *m* engagement; hocking; obligation; promise; (mil) enlistment; (mil) engagement
engager [ãgaʒe] §38 *tr* to engage; to hock; to enlist, urge, involve; to open, to begin (*negotiations, the conversation, etc.*) ‖ *ref* to commit oneself; to promise, to pledge; to enter a contest; to become engaged to be married; (mil) to enlist; **s'engager dans** to begin (*battle; a conversation*); to plunge into; to fit into
engainer [ãgene], [ãgene] *tr* to sheathe, to envelop
engazonner [ãgazɔne] *tr* to sod
engeance [ãʒãs] *f* (pej) breed, brood
engelure [ãʒlyr] *f* chilblain
engendrer [ãʒãdre] *tr* to engender
engin [ãʒɛ̃] *m* device; **engin balistique** ballistic missile; **engin guidé** or **engin spécial** guided missile; **engins de pêche** fishing tackle
englober [ãglɔbe] *tr* to put together, to unite; to embrace, to comprise
engloutir [ãglutir] *tr* to gobble down; to swallow up, to engulf
engluer [ãglye] *tr* to lime (*a trap*); to catch; to take in, hoodwink ‖ *ref* to be caught; to fall into a trap, to be taken in

engommer [ãgɔme] *tr* to gum

engon·cé -cée [ãgõse] *adj* awkward, stiff (*air*)

engoncer [ãgõse] §51 *tr* to bundle up; to cramp

engorgement [ãgɔrʒəmã] *m* obstruction, blocking

engorger [ãgɔrʒe] §38 *tr* to obstruct, block

engouement [ãgumã] *m* infatuation; (pathol) obstruction

engouer [ãgwe] *tr* to obstruct || *ref*—**s'engouer de** (coll) to be infatuated with, to be wild about

engouffrer [ãgufre] *tr* to engulf; to gobble up; to eat up (*e.g., a fortune*) || *ref* to be swallowed up; to dash; to surge

engour·di -die [ãgurdi] *adj* numb

engourdir [ãgurdir] *tr* to numb; to dull || *ref* to grow numb

engourdissement [ãgurdismã] *m* numbness; dullness, torpidity

engrais [ãgrɛ] *m* fertilizer; manure; fodder; **mettre à l'engrais** to fatten

engraisser [ãgrese], [ãgrese] *tr* to fatten; to fertilize; to enrich || *intr* (*aux*: AVOIR or ÊTRE) to fatten up, to get fat || *ref* to become fat; to become rich

engranger [ãgrãʒe] §38 *tr* to garner; to get in, to put in the barn

engraver [ãgrave] *tr, intr,* & *ref* to silt up; (naut) to run aground

engrenage [ãgrənaʒ] *m* gear; gearing; (coll) mesh, toils; **engrenage à vis sans fin** worm gear; **engrenages de distribution** timing gears

engrener [ãgrəne] §2 *tr* to feed (*a hopper, a thresher; a fowl*); to put into gear, to mesh || *intr* & *ref* (mach) to mesh, engage

engrenure [ãgrənyr] *f* engaging (*of toothed wheels*)

engrumeler [ãgrymle] §34 *tr* & *ref* to clot, to curdle

engueuler [ãgœle] *tr* (slang) to bawl out

enguirlander [ãgirlãde] *tr* to garland; to adorn; (coll) to bawl out

enhardir [ãardir] *tr* to embolden || *ref*—**s'enhardir à** to be so bold as to

énième [ɛnjɛm] *adj* nth

énigmatique [enigmatik] *adj* enigmatic(al), puzzling

énigme [enigm] *f* enigma, riddle, puzzle

enivrement [ãnivrəmã] *m* intoxication

enivrer [ãnivre] *tr* to intoxicate; to elate || *ref* to get drunk

enjambée [ãʒãbe] *f* stride

enjambement [ãʒãbmã] *m* enjambment

enjamber [ãʒãbe] *tr* to stride over, to span || *intr* to stride along; to run on (*said of line of poetry*); **enjamber sur** to project over; to encroach on

en·jeu [ãʒø] *m* (*pl* -jeux) stake, bet

enjoindre [ãʒwɛ̃dr] §35 *tr* to enjoin

enjôler [ãʒole] *tr* (coll) to cajole

enjô·leur [ãʒolœr] **-leuse** [løz] *adj* cajoling || *mf* cajoler, wheedler

enjoliver [ãʒɔlive] *tr* to embellish

enjoli·veur [ãʒɔlivœr] **-veuse** [vøz] *mf* embellisher || *m* hubcap

en·joué -jouée [ãʒwe] *adj* sprightly

enjouement [ãʒumã] *m* playfulness

enlacement [ãlasmã] *m* embrace, hug; lacing, interweaving

enlacer [ãlase] §51 *tr* & *ref* to enlace, to entwine; to embrace

enlaidir [ãledir], [ãledir] *tr* to disfigure || *intr* to grow ugly || *ref* to disfigure oneself

enlèvement [ãlɛvmã] *m* removal; kidnaping, abduction

enlever [ãlve] §2 *tr* to take away, take off, remove; to carry off; to lift, lift up; to send up (*a balloon*); (fig) to carry away (*an audience*); **enlever le couvert** to clear the table; **enlever q.ch. à** to take s.th. from, remove s.th. from || *ref* to come off, wear off; to rise; to boil over; (fig) to flare up

enliasser [ãljase] *tr* to tie up in bundles

enliser [ãlize] *ref* to get stuck

enluminer [ãlymine] *tr* to illuminate; to make colorful

enluminure [ãlyminyr] *f* illuminated drawing; (painting) illumination

enneiger [ãneʒe], [ãneʒe] §38 *tr* to cover with snow

enne·mi -mie [ɛnmi] *adj* hostile, inimical; enemy, e.g., **en pays ennemi** in enemy country || *mf* enemy

ennoblir [ãnɔblir] *tr* to ennoble

ennui [ãnɥi] *m* ennui, boredom; nuisance, bother; worry, trouble

ennuyer [ãnɥije] §27 *tr* to bore; to bother || *ref* to be bored

énon·cé -cée [enõse] *m* statement; wording (*of a document*); terms (*of a theorem*)

énoncer [enõse] §51 *tr* to state, enunciate; to utter

enorgueillir [ãnɔrgœjir] *tr* to make proud or boastful || *ref*—**s'enorgueillir de** to pride oneself on, to boast of, to glory in

énorme [enɔrm] *adj* enormous; (coll) shocking; (coll) outrageous

énormément [enɔrmemã] *adv* enormously, tremendously; (coll) awfully; **énormément de** lots of

énormité [enɔrmite] *f* enormity; (coll) nonsense; (coll) blunder

enquérir [ãkerir] §3 *ref*—**s'enquérir de** to ask or inquire about

enquête [ãkɛt] *f* investigation, inquiry; inquest; **enquête par sondage** public-opinion poll

enquêter [ãkete] *intr* to conduct an investigation

enraciner [ãrasine] *tr* to root; to instill || *ref* to take root

enra·gé -gée [ãraʒe] *adj* enraged, hotheaded; mad (*dog*); rabid (*communist*); out-and-out (*socialist*); inveterate (*gambler*); enthusiastic (*sportsman*) || *mf* enthusiast, fan; fanatic, fiend

enrager [ãraʒe] §38 *intr* to be mad; **faire enrager** to enrage

enrayer [ãreje], [ãreje] §49 *tr* to put

spokes to; to jam, lock; to stem, halt || *ref* to jam
enrayure [ãrɛjyr] *f* (mach) skid, shoe
enrégimenter [ãreʒimãte] *tr* to regiment
enregistrement [ãrəʒistrəmã] *m* recording; registration; transcription; checking (*of baggage*); **enregistrement sur bande** or **sur ruban** tape recording
enregistrer [ãrəʒistre] *tr* to record; to register; to transcribe; to check (*baggage*)
enregis•treur [ãrəʒistrœr] **-treuse** [trøz] *adj* recording || *mf* recorder
enrhumer [ãryme] *tr* to give a cold to || *ref* to catch cold
enrichir [ãri/ir] *tr* to enrich || *ref* to become rich
enrichissement [ãri/ismã] *m* enrichment
enrober [ãrɔbe] *tr* to coat; to wrap
enrôlement [ãrolmã] *m* enrollment; enlistment
enrôler [ãrole] *tr* & *ref* to enroll, enlist
enrouement [ãrumã] *m* hoarseness, huskiness
enrouer [ãrwe] *tr* to make hoarse || *ref* to become hoarse
enrouiller [ãruje] *tr* & *ref* to rust
enroulement [ãrulmã] *m* coil; (archit) volute; (elec) winding
enrouler [ãrule] *tr* & *ref* to wind, coil; to roll up
ensabler [ãsable] *tr* & *ref* to run aground on the sand
ensacher [ãsa/e] *tr* to bag
ensanglanter [ãsãglãte] *tr* to stain with blood; to steep in blood
ensei•gnant [ãsɛɲã] **-gnante** [ɲãt] *adj* teaching || *mf* teacher
enseigne [ãsɛɲ] *m* (nav) ensign || *f* flag, ensign; sign (*on tavern, store*)
enseignement [ãsɛɲəmã] *m* teaching, instruction, education; **enseignement confessionnel** parochial school education; **enseignement libre** or **privé** private-school education; **enseignement supérieur** higher education
enseigner [ãsɛɲe] *tr* to teach; to show; **enseigner q.ch. à qn** to teach s.o. s.th. || *intr* to teach; **enseigner à qn à + *inf*** to teach s.o. to + *inf*
ensemble [ãsãbl] *m* ensemble; **avec ensemble** in harmony, with one mind; **dans son ensemble** as a whole; **d'ensemble** general, comprehensive, overall; **grand ensemble** housing development || *adv* together
ensemencement [ãsmãsmã] *m* sowing
ensemencer [ãsmãse] §51 *tr* to seed, sow; to culture (*microorganisms*)
enserrer [ãsɛre] *tr* to enclose; to squeeze, clasp
ensevelir [ãsəvlir] *tr* to bury; to shroud
ensevelissement [ãsəvlismã] *m* burial; shrouding
ensilage [ãsilaʒ] *m* storing in a pit or silo
ensiler [ãsile] *tr* to ensilage
ensoleiller [ãsɔleje] *tr* to make sunny, to brighten

ensommeil•lé -lée [ãsɔmeje], [ãsɔmeje] *adj* drowsy
ensorceler [ãsɔrsəle] §34 *tr* to bewitch, to enchant
ensorce•leur [ãsɔrsəlœr] **-leuse** [løz] *adj* bewitching, enchanting || *m* sorcerer, wizard; charmer || *f* witch; enchantress
ensorcellement [ãsɔrsɛlmã] *m* sorcery, enchantment; spell, charm
ensuite [ãsɥit] *adv* then, next; afterwards, after; **ensuite?** what then?, what next?; anything else?
ensuivre [ãsɥivr] §67 (used only in 3d *sg* & *pl*) *ref* to ensue; **il s'ensuit que** . . . it follows that . . .
entacher [ãta/e] *tr* to blemish; **entaché de nullité** null and void
entaille [ãtaj] *f* notch, nick; gash
entailler [ãtaje] *tr* to notch, to nick; to gash
entame [ãtam] *f* top slice, first slice, end slice
entamer [ãtame] *tr* to cut the first slice of; to begin; to engage in, to start (*a conversation*); to make a break in (*the skin; a battle line*); to cast a slur upon; to open (*a bottle; negotiations; a card suit*); (coll) to make a dent in (*e.g., one's savings*)
entartrer [ãtartre] *tr* & *ref* to scale, fur
entassement [ãtasmã] *m* piling up
entasser [ãtase] *tr* & *ref* to pile up, to accumulate; to crowd
ente [ãt] *f* paintbrush handle; (hort) graft, scion
entendement [ãtãdmã] *m* understanding; consciousness
entendre [ãtãdr] *tr* to hear; to understand; to mean; **entendre chanter** to hear (*s.o.*) singing, to hear (*s.o.*) sing; to hear (*s.th.*) sung; **entendre dire que** to hear that; **entendre parler de** to hear of or about; **entendre raison** to listen to reason; **il entend que je le fasse** he expects me to do it, he insists that I do it || *intr* to hear || *ref* to understand one another; to get along; **s'entendre à to** be skilled in, to know
enten•du -due [ãtãdy] *adj* agreed; **bien entendu** of course; **c'est entendu!** all right!
enténébrer [ãtenebre] §10 *tr* to plunge into darkness
entente [ãtãt] *f* understanding; agreement, pact; **à double entente** with a double meaning, e.g., **expression à double entente** expression with a double meaning, double entendre; **entente industrielle** (com) combine
enter [ãte] *tr* to graft; to splice (*pieces of wood*)
entérinement [ãterinmã] *m* ratification
entériner [ãterine] *tr* to ratify
enterrement [ãtɛrmã] *m* burial, interment; funeral procession; funeral; funeral expenses; pigeonholing
enterrer [ãtɛre] *tr* to bury, inter; to pigeonhole, sidetrack; (coll) to attend the funeral services of; **enterrer sa vie de garçon** (coll) to give a fare-

well stag party ‖ *ref* to bury oneself; (mil) to dig oneself in

en-tête [ɑ̄tɛt] *m* (*pl* **-têtes**) headline; chapter heading; letterhead

entê·té -tée [ɑ̄tete] *adj* obstinate, stubborn

entêtement [ɑ̄tɛtmɑ̄] *m* obstinacy, stubbornness

entêter [ɑ̄tete] *tr* to give a headache to; to make giddy ‖ *intr* to go to one's head ‖ *ref* to persist

enthousiasme [ɑ̄tuzjasm] *m* enthusiasm

enthousiasmer [ɑ̄tuzjasme] *tr & ref* to enthuse

enthousiaste [ɑ̄tuzjast] *adj* enthusiastic ‖ *mf* enthusiast, fan, buff

entichement [ɑ̄tiʃmɑ̄] *m* infatuation

enticher [ɑ̄tiʃe] *tr* to infatuate ‖ *ref* to become infatuated

en·tier [ɑ̄tje] **-tière** [tjɛr] *adj* entire, whole, full; obstinate ‖ *m* whole, entirety; **en entier** in full

entièrement [ɑ̄tjɛrmɑ̄] *adv* entirely

entité [ɑ̄tite] *f* entity, being

entoiler [ɑ̄twale] *tr* to put a backing on; to mount

entomologie [ɑ̄tɔmɔlɔʒi] *f* entomology

entonner [ɑ̄tɔne] *tr* to barrel; to intone, start off (*a song*); to sing (*s.o.'s praises*) ‖ *ref* to rush up and down (*said of wind*)

entonnoir [ɑ̄tɔnwar] *m* funnel; shell hole

entorse [ɑ̄tɔrs] *f* sprain; infringement (*of a rule*); stretching (*of the truth*)

entortiller [ɑ̄tɔrtije] *tr & ref* to twist

entour [ɑ̄tur] *m*—à l'entour in the vicinity; **à l'entour de** around; **entours** surroundings

entourage [ɑ̄turaʒ] *m* setting, surroundings; entourage; (mach) casing

entourer [ɑ̄ture] *tr* to surround

entourloupette [ɑ̄turlupɛt] *f* (coll) double cross; **faire une entourloupette à** (coll) to double-cross

entournure [ɑ̄turnyr] *f* armhole; **gêné dans les entournures** ill at ease

entraccuser [ɑ̄trakyze] *ref* to accuse one another

entracte [ɑ̄trakt] *m* intermission

entraide [ɑ̄trɛd] *f* mutual assistance

entrailles [ɑ̄traj] *fpl* entrails; tenderness, pity; bowels (*of the earth*); **sans entrailles** (fig) heartless

entr'aimer [ɑ̄trɛme], [ɑ̄treme] *ref* to love each other

entrain [ɑ̄trɛ̄] *m* spirit, gusto, pep

entraînement [ɑ̄trɛnmɑ̄] *m* training; enthusiasm

entraîner [ɑ̄trene] *tr* to carry along or away, to entrain; to involve, entail; to pull (*railroad cars*); to work (*a pump*); to train (*an athlete*) ‖ *ref* (sports) to train

entraîneur [ɑ̄trɛnœr] *m* trainer, coach

entraîneuse [ɑ̄trɛnøz] *f* B-girl

entr'apercevoir [ɑ̄trapɛrsəvwar] §59 *tr* to catch a glimpse of

entrave [ɑ̄trav] *f* shackle; hindrance

entra·vé -vée [ɑ̄trave] *adj* impeded, hampered; checked (*vowel*)

entraver [ɑ̄trave] *tr* to shackle; to hinder, impede

entre [ɑ̄tr] *prep* between; among; in or into, e.g., **entre les mains de** in or into the hands of; **d'entre** among; from among, out of; of, e.g., **l'un d'entre eux** one of them; **entre deux eaux** under the surface of the water

entrebâillement [ɑ̄trəbajmɑ̄] *m* chink, slit, crack

entrebâiller [ɑ̄trəbaje] *tr* to leave ajar

entrechat [ɑ̄trəʃa] *m* caper; entrechat

entrechoquer [ɑ̄trəʃɔke] *tr* to bump together ‖ *ref* to clash

entrecôte [ɑ̄trəkot] *f* sirloin steak, loin of beef; top chuck roast

entrecouper [ɑ̄trəkupe] *tr* to interrupt; to intersect ‖ *ref* to intersect

entrecroiser [ɑ̄trəkrwaze] *tr & ref* to interlace; to intersect

entre-deux [ɑ̄trədø] *m invar* space between; interval; partition; (sports) jump ball

entre-deux-guerres [ɑ̄trədøgɛr] *m & f invar* period between the wars (*the First and Second World War*)

entrée [ɑ̄tre] *f* entrance, entry; admission, admittance; beginning; customs duty; (culin) entree; **avoir ses entrées à, chez,** or **dans** to have the entree into; **d'entrée** at the start, right off; **entrée de serrure** keyhole; **entrée d'un chapeau** hat size; **entrée interdite** (public sign) keep out, no admittance

entrefaites [ɑ̄trəfɛt] *fpl*—**sur ces entrefaites** meanwhile

entrefer [ɑ̄trəfɛr] *m* (elec) air gap

entrefermer [ɑ̄trəfɛrme] *tr* to close part way

entrefilet [ɑ̄trəfile] *m* short feature, special item

entregent [ɑ̄trəʒɑ̄] *m* tact, diplomacy, savoir-faire; **avoir de l'entregent** to be a good mixer

entrejambe [ɑ̄trəʒɑ̄b] *m* crotch

entrelacer [ɑ̄trəlase] §51 *tr & ref* to interlace, to entwine, intertwine

entrelarder [ɑ̄trəlarde] *tr* to lard; to interlard

entre-ligne [ɑ̄trəliɲ] *m* (*pl* **-lignes**) space (*between the lines*); insertion (*written between the lines*); **à l'entre-ligne** double-spaced

entremêler [ɑ̄trəmele] *tr* to mix, mingle; to intersperse

entremets [ɑ̄trəme] *m* side dish; dessert

entremet·teur [ɑ̄trəmɛtœr] **entremet·teuse** [ɑ̄trəmɛtøz] *mf* go-between ‖ *m* (pej) pimp

entremettre [ɑ̄trəmɛtr] §42 *ref* to intervene, to intercede

entremise [ɑ̄trəmiz] *f* intervention; **par l'entremise de** through the medium of

entre-nuire [ɑ̄trənɥir] §19 (*pp* **nui**) *ref* (with *dat* of *reflex pron*) to hurt each other

entrepont [ɑ̄trəpɔ̄] *m* (naut) between-decks

entreposer [ɑ̄trəpoze] *tr* to place in a warehouse, to store; to bond

entrepôt [ɑ̄trəpo] *m* warehouse; **en entrepôt** in bond

entrepre·nant [ɑ̄trəprənɑ̄] **-nante** [nɑ̄t]

adj enterprising; bold, audacious; gallant

entreprendre [ãtrəprãdr] §56 *tr* to undertake; to contract for; to enter upon; (coll) to try to win over ‖ *intr*—**entreprendre sur** to encroach upon

entrepre·neur [ãtrəprənœr] -**neuse** [nøz] *mf* contractor; entrepreneur; **entrepreneur de camionnage** trucker; **entrepreneur de pompes funèbres** undertaker

entreprise [ãtrəpriz] *f* undertaking; business, firm; contract

entrer [ãtre] *tr* to introduce, bring in ‖ *intr* (*aux*: ÊTRE) to enter; to go in, to come in; **entrer à, dans,** or **en** to enter; to enter into; to begin; **entrer pour** to enter into, to be an ingredient of

entre-rail [ãtrərɑj] *m* (rr) gauge

entre-regarder [ãtrərəgarde] *ref* to exchange glances

entresol [ãtrəsɔl] *m* mezzanine

entre-temps [ãtrətã] *m invar* interval; **dans l'entre-temps** in the meantime ‖ *adv* meanwhile

entreteneur [ãtrətnœr] *m* keeper of a mistress

entretenir [ãtrətnir] §72 *tr* to maintain, keep up; to carry on (*a conversation*); to keep (*a mistress*); to entertain, harbor ‖ *ref* to converse, talk

entrete·nu -nue [ãtrətny] *adj* kept (*woman*); continuous, undamped (*waves*)

entretien [ãtrətjē] *m* maintenance, upkeep; support (*of family, army, etc.*); interview

entretoise [ãtrətwaz] *f* strut, brace, crosspiece

entre-tuer [ãtrətɥe] *ref* to kill each other, to fight to the death

entre-voie [ãtrəvwa] *f* (rr) gauge

entrevoir [ãtrəvwar] §75 *tr* to glimpse; to foresee

entre·vu -vue [ãtrəvy] *adj* half-seen; vaguely foreseen ‖ *f* interview

entrouvrir [ãtruvrir] §65 *tr* & *ref* to open part way

enture [ãtyr] *f* splice (*of pieces of wood*)

énumérer [enymere] §10 *tr* to enumerate

envahir [ãvair] *tr* to invade

envahissement [ãvaismã] *m* invasion

envaser [ãvaze] *tr* to fill with mud; to stick in the mud

enveloppe [ãvlɔp] *f* envelope; **enveloppe à fenêtre** window envelope

envelopper [ãvlɔpe] *tr* to envelop; to wrap up

envenimer [ãvnime] *tr* to inflame, make sore; (fig) to envenom, embitter

envergure [ãvergyr] *f* span; wingspread; spread of sail; span, scope

envers [ãver] *m* wrong side, reverse, back; **à l'envers** inside out; upside down; back to front; topsy-turvy; **mettre à l'envers** to put on backwards ‖ *prep* towards; with regard to; **envers et contre tous** in spite of everyone else

envi [ãvi]—**à l'envi** vying with each other; **à l'envi de** vying with

enviable [ãvjabl] *adj* enviable

envie [ãvi] *f* desire, longing; envy; birthmark; hangnail; **avoir envie de** to feel like, to have a notion to

envier [ãvje] *tr* to envy; to desire; **envier q.ch. à qn** to begrudge s.o. s.th.

en·vieux [ãvjø] -**vieuse** [vjøz] *adj* envious ‖ *mf* envious person

environ [ãvirɔ̃] *m* outlying section; **aux environs de** in the vicinity of; around, about; **environs** surroundings ‖ *adv* about, approximately

environnement [ãvirɔnmã] *m* environment

environner [ãvirɔne] *tr* to surround

envisager [ãvizaʒe] §38 *tr* to envisage ‖ *intr*—**envisager de** + *inf* to plan to + *inf*. to expect to + *inf*

envoi [ãvwa] *m* consignment; remittance; envoy (*of ballad*)

envol [ãvɔl] *m* flight; (aer) takeoff

envolée [ãvɔle] *f* flight; (aer) takeoff

envoler [ãvɔle] *ref* to fly (*said of time*); (aer) to take off

envoûtement [ãvutmã] *m* spell, voodoo

envoûter [ãvute] *tr* to cast a spell on

envoyé envoyée [ãvwaje] *mf* envoy; messenger; **envoyé spécial** special correspondent (*of newspaper*)

envoyer [ãvwaje] §26 *tr* to send; to send out; to throw (*e.g., a stone*); to give (*a kick*); **envoyer promener** to send (*s.o.*) about his business; **envoyer qn** + *inf* to send s.o. to + *inf*; **envoyer qn chercher q.ch.** or **qn** to send s.o. for s.th. or s.o. ‖ *intr*—**envoyer chercher** to send for (*s.o.* or *s.th.*) ‖ *ref* (coll) to gulp down

enzyme [ãzim] *m* & *f* enzyme

épa·gneul -gneule [epaɲœl] *mf* spaniel

épais [epɛ] **épaisse** [ɛpɛs] *adj* thick ‖ **épais** *adv* thickly

épaisseur [epɛsœr] *f* thickness

épaissir [epɛsir] *tr, intr,* & *ref* to thicken

épanchement [epãʃmã] *m* outpouring, effusion; (pathol) discharge

épancher [epãʃe] *tr* to pour out; to unburden (*e.g., one's feelings*) ‖ *ref* to pour out; **s'épancher auprès de** to unbosom oneself to; **s'épancher de q.ch.** to get s.th. off one's chest

épandre [epãdr] *tr* & *ref* to spread; to scatter

épanouir [epanwir] *tr* to make (*flowers*) bloom; to light up (*the face*) ‖ *ref* to bloom; to beam (*said of face*)

épanouissement [epanwismã] *m* blossoming; brightening up (*of a face*)

épar·gnant -gnante [eparɲã] *adj* thrifty ‖ *mf* depositor

épargne [eparɲ] *f* saving, thrift; **épargnes** savings

épargner [eparɲe] *tr* to save; to spare; to husband

éparpillement [eparpijmã] *m* scattering

éparpiller [eparpije] *tr* to scatter; to dissipate (*e.g., one's efforts*)

épars [epar] **éparse** [epars] *adj* scattered, sparse; in disorder

épa·tant [epatɑ̃] **-tante** [tɑ̃t] *adj* (coll) wonderful, terrific

épate [epat] *f*—**faire de l'épate** (slang) to make a big show, to splurge

épa·té -tée [epate] *adj* flattened; (slang) flabbergasted

épater [epate] *tr* (coll) to shock, amaze

épaulard [epolar] *m* killer whale

épaule [epol] *f* shoulder; **donner un coup d'épaule à qn** (coll) to give s.o. a hand; **par-dessus l'épaule** (fig) contemptuously

épaulé-jeté [epoleʒte] *m* clean and jerk (*in weight lifting*)

épaulement [epolmɑ̃] *m* breastworks

épauler [epole] *tr* to back, support ‖ *intr* to take aim

épaulette [epolɛt] *f* epaulet

épave [epav] *f* wreck; derelict, stray; **épaves** wreckage

épée [epe] *f* sword

épéiste [epeist] *m* swordsman

épeler [eple] §34 *tr* to spell, to spell out; to read letter by letter

épellation [epellɑsjɔ̃] *f* spelling

éper·du -due [epɛrdy] *adj* bewildered; desperate (*resistance*); mad (*with pain*); wild (*with joy*)

éperdument [epɛrdymɑ̃] *adv* desperately, madly, wildly

éperlan [epɛrlɑ̃] *m* smelt

éperon [eprɔ̃] *m* spur

éperonner [eprɔne] *tr* to spur

épervier [epɛrvje] *m* sparrow hawk; fish net

éphémère [efemɛr] *adj* ephemeral ‖ *m* mayfly

épi [epi] *m* ear, cob, spike; cowlick

épice [epis] *f* spice

épicéa [episea] *m* Norway spruce

épicer [epise] §51 *tr* to spice

épicerie [episri] *f* grocery store; canned goods

épi·cier [episje] **-cière** [sjɛr] *mf* grocer

épidémie [epidemi] *f* epidemic

épidémiologie [epidemjɔlɔʒi] *f* epidemiology

épidémique [epidemik] *adj* epidemic; contagious (*e.g., laughter*)

épiderme [epidɛrm] *m* epidermis

épier [epje] *tr* to spy upon; to be on the lookout for ‖ *intr* to ear, to head

épieu [epjø] *m* (*pl* **épieux**) pike

épiglotte [epiglɔt] *f* epiglottis

épigramme [epigram] *f* epigram

épigraphe [epigraf] *f* epigraph

épilepsie [epilɛpsi] *f* epilepsy

épileptique [epilɛptik] *adj* & *mf* epileptic

épiler [epile] *tr* to pluck (*one's eyebrows*); to remove hair from

épilogue [epilɔg] *m* epilogue

épiloguer [epilɔge] *intr* to split hairs; **épiloguer sur** to carp at

épinard [epinar] *m* spinach; **des épinards** spinach (*leaves used as food*)

épine [epin] *f* thorn; **épine dorsale** backbone; **épine noire** blackthorn; **être sur les épines** to be on pins and needles

épinette [epinɛt] *f* spinet; hencoop

épi·neux [epinø] **-neuse** [nøz] *adj* thorny; ticklish (*question*)

épingle [epɛ̃gl] *f* pin; **épingle à chapeau** hatpin; **épingle à cheveux** hairpin; **épingle à linge** clothespin; **épingle anglaise** safety pin; **épingle dans une meule de foin** needle in a haystack; **épingle de cravate** stickpin; **épingle de sûreté** safety pin; **monter en épingle** (coll) to make much of; **tiré à quatre épingles** (coll) spic-and-span; (coll) all dolled up; **tirer son épingle du jeu** (coll) to get out by the skin of one's teeth

épingler [epɛ̃gle] *tr* to pin; (coll) to pin down (*s.o.*)

épinière [epinjɛr] *adj fem* spinal (*cord*)

Épiphanie [epifani] *f* Epiphany, Twelfth-night

épique [epik] *adj* epic

épisco·pal -pale [episkɔpal] (*pl* **-paux** [po]) *adj* episcopal; Episcopalian ‖ *mf* Episcopalian

épisode [epizɔd] *m* episode

épisodique [epizɔdik] *adj* episodic

épisser [epise] *tr* to splice

épissure [episyr] *f* splice

épistémologie [epistemɔlɔʒi] *f* epistemology

épitaphe [epitaf] *f* epitaph

épithète [epitɛt] *f* epithet

épitoge [epitɔʒ] *f* shoulder band (*worn by French lawyers and holders of French degrees*)

épitomé [epitɔme] *m* epitome

épitre [epitr] *f* epistle

éplo·ré -rée [eplɔre] *adj* in tears

épluchage [eplyʃaʒ] *m* peeling; examination

éplucher [eplyʃe] *tr* to peel, pare; to clean, pick; (fig) to find fault with, to pick holes in

éplu·cheur [eplyʃœr] **-cheuse** [ʃøz] *mf* (coll) faultfinder ‖ *m* potato peeler, orange peeler, peeling knife ‖ *f*—**éplucheuse électrique** electric peeler

épluchure [eplyʃyr] *f* peelings; **épluchure de maïs** cornhusks

épointer [epwɛ̃te] *tr* to dull the point of

éponge [epɔ̃ʒ] *f* sponge

éponger [epɔ̃ʒe] §38 *tr* to sponge off, to mop up

épopée [epɔpe] *f* epic

époque [epɔk] *f* epoch; time; period; **à l'époque** at the time of; **d'époque** a real antique; **faire époque** to be epoch-making

épouiller [epuje] *tr* to delouse

époumoner [epumɔne] *ref* to shout oneself out of breath

épousailles [epuzaj] *fpl* wedding

épouser [epuze] *tr* to marry; to espouse; **épouser la forme de** to take the exact shape of

époussetage [epustaʒ] *m* dusting

épousseter [epuste] §34 *tr* to dust

époussette [epusɛt] *f* duster

épouvantable [epuvɑ̃tabl] *adj* frightful, terrible

épouvantail [epuvɑ̃taj] *m* scarecrow

épouvante [epuvɑ̃t] *f* fright, terror

épouvanter [epuvãte] *tr* to frighten, terrify

époux [epu] **épouse** [epuz] *mf* spouse || *m* husband; **les époux** husband and wife || *f* wife

éprendre [eprãdr] §56 *ref*—**s'éprendre de** to fall in love with; to hold fast to (*liberty, justice, etc.*)

épreuve [eprœv] *f* proof, test, trial; ordeal; examination; (phot, typ) proof

épris [epri] **éprise** [epriz] *adj* infatuated; **épris de** in love with

éprouver [epruve] *tr* to prove, test, try; to experience, to feel; to put to the test

éprouvette [epruvɛt] *f* test tube; specimen; (med) probe

epsomite [ɛpsɔmit] *f* Epsom salts

épucer [epyse] §51 *tr* to clean of fleas, to delouse

épui·sé -sée [epɥize] *adj* exhausted, tired out; sold out

épuisement [epɥizmã] *m* exhaustion; diminution, draining off

épuiser [epɥize] *tr* to exhaust, use up; to wear out; to tire out || *ref* to run out; to wear out

épuration [epyrɑsjɔ̃] *f* purification; refining (*e.g., of petroleum*); (pol) purge

épure [epyr] *f* working drawing

épurement [epyrmã] *m* expurgation

épurer [epyre] *tr* to purify; to expurgate; to weed out, to purge

équanimité [ekwanimite] *f* equanimity

équarrir [ekarir] *tr* to cut up, quarter (*an animal*); to square off

équateur [ekwatœr] *m* equator; **l'Équateur** Ecuador

équation [ekwɑsjɔ̃] *f* equation

équato·rial -riale [ekwatɔrjal] *adj* (*pl* -riaux [rjo]) equatorial

équerrage [ekɛraʒ] *m* bevel; beveling

équerre [ekɛr] *f* square (*L- or T-shaped instrument*); **d'équerre** square, true; **mettre d'équerre** to square, to true

équerrer [ekɛre] *tr* to bevel

équestre [ekɛstr] *adj* equestrian

équilaté·ral -rale [ekɥilateral] *adj* (*pl* -raux [ro]) equilateral

équilibre [ekilibr] *m* equilibrium, balance; equipoise

équilibrer [ekilibre] *tr & ref* to balance

équilibriste [ekilibrist] *mf* balancer, ropedancer

équinoxe [ekinɔks] *m* equinox

équipage [ekipaʒ] *m* crew; retinue, suite; attire

équipe [ekip] *f* team; crew; gang, work party; (naut) train of boats; **équipe de jour** day shift; **équipe de nuit** night shift; **équipe de secours** rescue squad

équipée [ekipe] *f* escapade, lark; crazy project

équipement [ekipmã] *m* equipment

équiper [ekipe] *tr* to equip

équi·pier [ekipje] **-pière** [pjɛr] *mf* teammate; crew member

équitable [ekitabl] *adj* equitable

équitation [ekitɑsjɔ̃] *f* horseback riding

équité [ekite] *f* equity

équiva·lent [ekivalã] **-lente** [lãt] *adj & m* equivalent

équivaloir [ekivalwar] §71 *intr*—**équivaloir à** to be equivalent to; to be tantamount to

équivoque [ekivɔk] *adj* equivocal; questionable (*e.g., reputation*) || *f* double entendre; uncertainty; **sans équivoque** without equivocation

équivoquer [ekivɔke] *intr* to equivocate, quibble; to pun

érable [erabl] *m* maple; **érable à sucre** sugar maple

érafler [erɑfle] *tr* to graze, scratch

éraflure [erɑflyr] *f* graze, scratch

érail·lé -lée [erɑje] *adj* bloodshot (*eyes*); hoarse (*voice*)

érailler [erɑje] *tr* to fray

ère [ɛr] *f* era

érection [erɛksjɔ̃] *f* erection

érein·té -tée [erẽte] *adj* all in, worn out, tired out

éreinter [erẽte] *tr* to exhaust, tire out; (coll) to criticize unmercifully, to run down (*an author, play, etc.*) || *ref* to wear oneself out; to drudge

erg [ɛrg] *m* erg

ergot [ɛrgo] *m* spur (*of rooster*); **monter** or **se dresser sur ses ergots** (fig) to get up on a high horse

ergotage [ɛrgotaʒ] *m* (coll) quibbling

ergoter [ɛrgote] *tr* (coll) to quibble

ériger [eriʒe] §38 *tr* to erect || *ref*—**s'ériger en** to set oneself up as

ermitage [ɛrmitaʒ] *m* hermitage

ermite [ɛrmit] *m* hermit

éroder [erɔde] *tr* to erode

érosion [erozjɔ̃] *f* erosion

érotique [erɔtik] *adj* erotic

érotisme [erɔtism] *m* eroticism

er·rant [erã] **er·rante** [erãt] *adj* wandering, stray; errant

erratique [eratik] *adj* intermittent, irregular, erratic

erre [ɛr] *f* (naut) headway; **erres** track (*e.g., of deer*)

errements [ermã] *mpl* ways, methods; (pej) erring ways, bad habits

errer [ɛre] *intr* to wander; to err; to play (*said of smile*)

erreur [ɛrœr] *f* error, mistake; **erreur de frappe** typing error

erro·né -née [erɔne] *adj* erroneous

éructation [eryktɑsjɔ̃] *f* belch

éructer [erykte] *tr* (fig) to belch forth || *intr* to belch

éru·dit -dite [erydi] [dit] *adj* erudite, learned || *mf* scholar, erudite

érudition [erydisjɔ̃] *f* erudition

éruption [erypsjɔ̃] *f* eruption

ès [ɛs] *prep* §77

esc. *abbr* (**escompte**) discount

esca·beau [ɛskabo] *m* (*pl* -**beaux**) stool; stepladder

escadre [ɛskadr] *f* squadron; fleet

escadron [ɛskadrɔ̃] *m* (mil) squadron

escalade [ɛskalad] *f* scaling, climbing

escalader [ɛskalade] *tr* to scale, to climb; to clamber over or up

escalator [ɛskalatɔr] *m* escalator

escale [ɛskal] *f* port of call, stop; **faire escale** to make a stop; **sans escale** nonstop escalier [ɛskalje] m stairway; escalier à vis circular stairway; escalier de sauvetage fire escape; escalier en colimaçon spiral staircase; escalier mécanique or roulant escalator

escalope [ɛskalɔp] f scallop

escamotable [ɛskamɔtabl] adj retractable (e.g., landing gear); concealable (piece of furniture)

escamotage [ɛskamɔtaʒ] m sleight of hand; side-stepping, avoiding; theft

escamoter [ɛskamɔte] tr to palm (a card); to pick (a wallet); to dodge (a question); to slur (a word); to hush up (a scandal); (aer) to retract (landing gear)

escamo•teur [ɛskamɔtœr] -teuse [tøz] mf prestidigitator; pickpocket

escapade [ɛskapad] f escapade, escape

escarbille [ɛskarbij] f cinder, clinker

escarbot [ɛskarbo] m beetle

escarboucle [ɛskarbukl] f (mineral) carbuncle

escargot [ɛskargo] m snail

escarmouche [ɛskarmuʃ] f skirmish

escarmoucher [ɛskarmuʃe] intr to skirmish

escarpe [ɛskarp] m ruffian, bandit || f escarpment (of a fort)

escar•pé -pée [ɛskarpe] adj steep

escarpement [ɛskarpəmɑ̃] m escarpment

escarpin [ɛskarpɛ̃] m pump, dancing shoe

escarpolette [ɛskarpɔlɛt] f swing

escarre [ɛskar] f scab

escarrifier [ɛskarifje] tr to form a scab on

esche [ɛʃ] f bait

Eschyle [ɛʃil], [eʃil] m Aeschylus

escient [ɛsjɑ̃]—à bon escient knowingly, wittingly; à mon (ton, etc.) escient to my (your, etc.) certain knowledge

esclaffer [ɛsklafe] ref to burst out laughing

esclandre [ɛsklɑ̃dr] m scandal

esclavage [ɛsklavaʒ] m slavery

esclavagiste [ɛsklavaʒist] adj pro-slavery || mf advocate of slavery

esclave [ɛsklav] adj & mf slave

escompte [ɛskɔ̃t] m discount, rebate; escompte de caisse cash discount; escompte en dehors bank discount; prendre à l'escompte to discount

escompter [ɛskɔ̃te] tr to discount (a premature note); to anticipate

escompteur [ɛskɔ̃tœr] adj discounting (banker) || m discount broker

escopette [ɛskɔpɛt] f blunderbuss

escorte [ɛskɔrt] f escort

escorter [ɛskɔrte] tr to escort

escouade [ɛskwad] f infantry section; gang (of laborers)

escrime [ɛskrim] f fencing

escrimer [ɛskrime] intr & ref to fence; s'escrimer à to work with might and main at; s'escrimer contre to fence with

escri•meur [ɛskrimœr] -meuse [møz] mf fencer

escroc [ɛskro] m crook, swindler

escroquer [ɛskrɔke] tr to swindle

escroquerie [ɛskrɔkri] f swindling, cheating; racket, swindle

ésotérique [ezɔterik] adj esoteric

espace [ɛspɑs] m space; room; espace cosmique outer space || f (typ) space

espacement [ɛspɑsmɑ̃] m spacing

espacer [ɛspɑse] §51 tr to space

espadon [ɛspadɔ̃] m swordfish

espadrille [ɛspadrij] f tennis shoe; beach sandal; esparto sandal

Espagne [ɛspaɲ] f Spain; l'Espagne Spain

espa•gnol -gnole [ɛspaɲɔl] adj Spanish || m Spanish (language) || (cap) mf Spaniard (person); les Espagnols the Spanish

espagnolette [ɛspaɲɔlɛt] f espagnolette (door fastener for French casement window)

espalier [ɛspalje] m espalier

espèce [ɛspɛs] f species; sort, kind; en espèces in specie; en l'espèce in the matter; espèces sonnantes hard cash; sale espèce cad, bounder || mf— espèce de (coll) damn, e.g., cet espèce d'idiot that damn fool

espérance [ɛsperɑ̃s] f hope; espérances expectations; prospects

espérer [ɛspere] §10 tr to hope, to hope for; (coll) to wait for; espérer + inf to hope to + inf || intr to trust; (coll) to wait

espiègle [ɛspjɛgl] adj mischievous || mf rogue

espièglerie [ɛspjɛgləri] f mischievousness; prank

es•pion [ɛspjɔ̃] -pionne [pjɔn] mf spy || m concealed microphone; busybody (mirror)

espionnage [ɛspjɔnaʒ] m espionage

espionner [ɛspjɔne] tr to spy on

espoir [ɛspwar] m hope; promise

esprit [ɛspri] m spirit; mind; intelligence; wit; spirits (of wine); à l'esprit clair clearheaded; avoir l'esprit de l'escalier to think of what to say too late; bel esprit man of letters; esprit d'équipe teamwork; esprit de système love of order; (pej) pigheadedness; esprit fort freethinker; rendre l'esprit to give up the ghost

esquif [ɛskif] m skiff

esqui•mau [ɛskimo] -maude [mod] (pl -maux) adj Eskimo || m husky, Eskimo dog; Eskimo (language) || (cap) mf Eskimo (person)

esquinter [ɛskɛ̃te] tr (coll) to tire out; (coll) to wear out; (coll) to run down, knock, criticize

esquisse [ɛskis] f sketch; outline, draft; beginning (e.g., of a smile)

esquisser [ɛskise] tr to sketch; to outline, draft; to begin

esquiver [ɛskive] tr to dodge, to sidestep; esquiver de la tête to duck || ref to sneak away

essai [ɛsɛ] m essay; trial, test; à l'essai on trial; essais first attempts (of artist, writer, etc.); faire l'essai de to try out

essaim [ɛsɛ̃] m swarm

essaimer [ɛseme] intr to swarm

essarter [ɛsarte] tr to clear (brush)

essarts [esar] *mpl* clearings

essayage [esɛjaʒ] *m* fitting, trying on

essayer [esɛje], [eseje] §49 *tr* to try on or try out; to assay (*ore*) ‖ *intr* to try; **essayer de** to try to ‖ *ref*—**s'essayer à** to try one's skill at

essayeur [esɛjœr] **essayeuse** [esɛjøz] *mf* assayer

essayiste [esɛjist] *mf* essayist

esse [ɛs] *f* S-hook; sound hole (*of violin*)

essence [esɑ̃s] *f* essence; gasoline; kind, species; **par essence** by definition

essen·tiel -tielle [esɑ̃sjɛl] *adj* & *m* essential

esseu·lé -lée [esœle] *adj* abandoned

es·sieu [esjø] *m* (*pl* -**sieux**) axle

essor [esɔr] *m* flight; development; boom (*in business*); **donner libre essor à** to give vent to; to give full scope to; **prendre son essor** to take wing

essorer [esɔre] *tr* to spin-dry; to wring; to centrifuge

essoreuse [esɔrøz] *f* spin-drier; wringer; centrifuge

essouf·flé -flée [esufle] *adj* breathless, out of breath

essuie-glace [esɥiglas] *m* (*pl* -**glaces**) windshield wiper

essuie-mains [esɥimɛ̃] *m invar* towel

essuie-plume [esɥiplym] *m* (*pl* -**plumes**) penwiper

essuyer [esɥije], [esɥije] §27 *tr* to wipe; to wipe off; to wipe away; to suffer, endure; to undergo; to weather (*a storm*); **essuyer les plâtres** (coll) to be the first to occupy a house

est [ɛst] *adj invar* & *m* east

estacade [ɛstakad] *f* breakwater; pier; boom (*barrier of floating logs*); railway trestle

estafette [ɛstafɛt] *f* messenger

estaminet [ɛstaminɛ] *m* bar, café

estampe [ɛstɑ̃p] *f* print, engraving; (*tool*) stamp

estamper [ɛstɑ̃pe] *tr* to stamp (*with a design*); to engrave; to overcharge, to fleece

estampille [ɛstɑ̃pij] *f* identification mark; trademark; hallmark

ester [ɛstɛr] *m* ester ‖ [ɛste] *intr*—**ester en justice** to go to law, to sue

esthète [ɛstɛt] *mf* aesthete

esthéti·cien [ɛstetisjɛ̃] -**cienne** [sjɛn] *mf* aesthetician ‖ *f* beautician

esthétique [ɛstetik] *adj* aesthetic ‖ *f* aesthetics

estimable [ɛstimabl] *adj* estimable

estimateur [ɛstimatœr] *m* estimator, appraiser

estimation [ɛstimasjɔ̃] *f* estimation, appraisal

estime [ɛstim] *f* esteem; **à l'estime** by guesswork; (naut) by dead reckoning

estimer [ɛstime] *tr* to esteem; to estimate, to assess; **estimer** + *inf* to think that + *ind*, e.g., **j'estime avoir fait mon devoir** I think that I did my duty

esti·val -vale [ɛstival] *adj* (*pl* -**vaux** [vo]) summer

esti·vant [ɛstivɑ̃] -**vante** [vɑ̃t] *mf* summer vacationist, summer resident

estiver [ɛstive] *intr* to summer

estocade [ɛstɔkad] *f* thrust (*in fencing*); unexpected attack

estomac [ɛstɔma] *m* stomach

estomaquer [ɛstɔmake] *tr* (coll) to astound ‖ *ref* (coll) to be angered

estomper [ɛstɔ̃pe] *tr* to shade off, to rub away (*a drawing*); to blur ‖ *ref* to be blurred

Estonie [ɛstɔni] *f* Estonia; **l'Estonie** Estonia

estrade [ɛstrad] *f* platform

estragon [ɛstragɔ̃] *m* tarragon

estro·pié -piée [ɛstrɔpje] *adj* crippled ‖ *mf* cripple

estuaire [ɛstɥɛr] *m* estuary

estudian·tin [ɛstydjɑ̃tɛ̃] -**tine** [tin] *adj* student

esturgeon [ɛstyrʒɔ̃] *m* sturgeon

et [e] *conj* and; **et . . . et** both . . . and

Établ. *abbr* (**Établissement**) company, establishment

étable [etabl] *f* stable, cowshed

établer [etable] *tr* to stable

établi [etabli] *m* workbench

établir [etablir] *tr* to establish ‖ *ref* to settle down; to set up headquarters

établissement [etablismɑ̃] *m* establishment

étage [etaʒ] *m* floor, story; tier; level; rank, social level; (rok) stage; **de bas étage** lower-class; **dernier étage** top floor; **premier étage** first floor above ground floor

étager [etaʒe] §38 *tr* to arrange in tiers; to stagger; to perform in stages

étagère [etaʒɛr] *f* rack, shelf

étai [etɛ] *m* prop, stay

étain [etɛ̃] *m* tin; pewter

étal [etal] *m* (*pl* **étals** or **étaux** [eto]) stall, stand; butcher's block

étalage [etalaʒ] *m* display

étalager [etalaʒe] §38 *tr* to display

étalagiste [etalaʒist] *mf* window dresser, display artist; demonstrator

étaler [etale] *tr* to display; to spread out ‖ *ref* (coll) to sprawl

étalon [etalɔ̃] *m* stallion; monetary standard

étalonner [etalɔne] *tr* to verify, control; to standardize; to graduate, calibrate

étalon-or [etalɔ̃ɔr] *m* gold standard

étambot [etɑ̃bo] *m* (naut) sternpost

étamer [etame] *tr* to tin-plate; to silver (*a mirror*)

étamine [etamin] *f* stamen; sieve; cheesecloth

étampe [etɑ̃p] *f* stamp, die, punch

étamper [etɑ̃pe] *tr* to stamp, punch

étanche [etɑ̃ʃ] *adj* watertight, airtight

étancher [etɑ̃ʃe] *tr* to check, stanch the flow of; to quench (*one's thirst*); to make watertight or airtight

étang [etɑ̃] *m* pond

étape [etap] *f* stage; stop, halt; day's march; (sports) lap; **brûler les étapes** to go straight through

état [eta] *m* state; statement, record; trade, occupation; government; (hist) estate; **en tout état de cause** at all costs; in any case; **état civil** marital status; **état tampon** buffer state; **être dans tous ses états** to stew; **être en état de** to be in a position to; **faire état de** to take into account; to expect to; **hors d'état** out of order, unfit; **tenir en état** to keep in shape, to repair

étatisation [etatizɑsjɔ̃] *f* nationalization

étatiser [etatize] *tr* to nationalize

étatisme [etatism] *m* statism

état-major [etamaʒɔr] *m* (*pl* **états-majors**) headquarters, staff

état-providence [etaprɔvidɑ̃s] *m* welfare state

États-Unis [etazyni] *mpl* United States

étau [eto] *m* (*pl* **étaux**) vise

étayer [eteje] §49 *tr* to prop, stay

et Cie *abbr* (**et Compagnie**) & Co.

été [ete] *m* summer

éteignoir [etɛɲwar] *m* candle snuffer; (coll) kill-joy, wet blanket

éteindre [etɛ̃dr] §50 *tr* to extinguish, put out; to turn off; to wipe out; to appease (*e.g., one's thirst*); to dull (*a color*) || *intr* to put out the light || *ref* to go out; (fig) to die, pass away

éteint [etɛ̃] **éteinte** [etɛ̃t] *adj* extinguished; extinct; dull, dim

étendard [etɑ̃dar] *m* flag, banner

étendoir [etɑ̃dwar] *m* clothesline; drying rack

étendre [etɑ̃dr] *tr* to extend, spread out || *ref* to stretch out; to spread

éten·du -due [etɑ̃dy] *adj* outspread; extensive; vast; diluted, adulterated || *f* stretch; range, scope

éter·nel -nelle [etɛrnɛl] *adj* eternal

éterniser [etɛrnize] *tr* to perpetuate (*a name*); to drag out || *ref* (coll) to drag on; **s'éterniser chez qn** (coll) to overstay an invitation

éternité [etɛrnite] *f* eternity

éternuement [etɛrnymɑ̃] *m* sneeze; sneezing

éternuer [etɛrnɥe] *intr* to sneeze

étêter [etete] *tr* to top (*a tree*); to take the head off (*a fish, nail, etc.*)

éteule [etœl] *f* stubble

éther [etɛr] *m* ether

éthé·ré -rée [etere] *adj* ethereal

Éthiopie [etjɔpi] *f* Ethiopia; **l'Éthiopie** Ethiopia

éthio·pien [etjɔpjɛ̃] **-pienne** [pjɛn] *adj* Ethiopian || *m* Ethiopian (*language*) || (*cap*) *mf* Ethiopian (*person*)

éthique [etik] *adj* ethical || *f* ethics

ethnique [ɛtnik] *adj* ethnic(al)

ethnographie [ɛtnɔgrafi] *f* ethnography

ethnologie [ɛtnɔlɔʒi] *f* ethnology

éthyle [etil] *m* ethyl

éthylène [etilɛn] *m* ethylene

étiage [etjaʒ] *m* low-water mark

étince·lant [etɛ̃slɑ̃] **-lante** [lɑ̃t] *adj* sparkling, glittering

étinceler [etɛ̃sle] §34 *intr* to sparkle, glitter

étincelle [etɛ̃sɛl] *f* spark; (fig) flash

étiolement [etjɔlmɑ̃] *m* wilting

étioler [etjɔle] *tr & ref* to wilt

étique [etik] *adj* lean, emaciated

étiqueter [etikte] §34 *tr* to label

étiquette [etikɛt] *f* etiquette; label; **étiquette gommée** sticker

étirer [etire] *tr* to stretch, lengthen, elongate || *ref* (coll) to stretch one's limbs

étoffe [etɔf] *f* stuff; material, fabric; quality, worth

étoile [etwal] *f* star; traffic circle; **à la belle étoile** out of doors; **étoile de mer** starfish; **étoile filante** shooting or falling star; **étoile polaire** polestar

étoi·lé -lée [etwale] *adj* star-spangled, starry

étole [etɔl] *f* stole

éton·nant [etɔnɑ̃] **éton·nante** [etɔnɑ̃t] *adj* astonishing

étonnement [etɔnmɑ̃] *m* surprise, astonishment; fissure, crack

étonner [etɔne] *tr* to surprise, astonish; to shake or crack (*masonry*) || *ref* to be surprised

étouf·fant [etufɑ̃] **étouf·fante** [etufɑ̃t] *adj* suffocating; sweltering

étouffée [etufe] *f* braising; **cuire à l'étouffée** to braise

étouffer [etufe] *tr, intr, & ref* to suffocate; to stifle; to choke

étoupe [etup] *f* oakum, tow

étourderie [eturdri] *f* thoughtlessness

étour·di -die [eturdi] *adj* scatterbrained || *mf* scatterbrain

étourdir [eturdir] *tr* to stun, daze; to numb; to deafen (*with loud noise*) || *ref* to try to forget, get in a daze

étourdissement [eturdismɑ̃] *m* dizziness; numbing

étour·neau [eturno] *m* (*pl* **-neaux**) starling

étrange [etrɑ̃ʒ] *adj* strange

étran·ger [etrɑ̃ʒe] **-gère** [ʒɛr] *adj* foreign; irrelevant; unknown, strange; **être étranger à** to be unacquainted with || *mf* foreigner; stranger; **à l'étranger** abroad, in a foreign country

étrangeté [etrɑ̃ʒte] *f* strangeness

étrangler [etrɑ̃gle] *tr & intr* to strangle || *ref* to choke; to narrow (*said of passageway, valley, etc.*)

étran·gleur [etrɑ̃glœr] **-gleuse** [glØz] *mf* strangler

étrave [etrav] *f* (naut) stempost; **de l'étrave à l'étambot** from stem to stern

être [etr] *m* being || §28 *intr* to be; **en être pour sa peine** to have nothing for one's trouble; **être à** + *pron disj* to be + *pron poss, e.g.*, **le livre est à moi** the book is mine; **n'est-ce pas** see **ne** || *aux* (used with some intransitive verbs and reflexive verbs) to have, e.g., **elles sont arrivées** they have arrived; (used to form the passive voice) to be, e.g., **il est aimé de tout le monde** he is loved by everybody

étrécir [etresir] *tr & ref* to shrink

étreindre [etrɛ̃dr] §50 *tr* to embrace; to grip, seize

étreinte [etrɛ̃t] *f* embrace; hold, grasp

étrenne [etrɛn] *f* first sale of the day;

avoir l'étrenne de to have the first use of; étrennes New-Year gifts
étrenner [etrɛne] tr to put on for the first time; to be the first to wear || intr (coll) to be the first to catch it
étrier [etrije] m stirrup
étrille [etrij] f currycomb
étriller [etrije] tr to curry; (coll) to thrash, to tan the hide of; (coll) to overcharge, to fleece
étriper [etripe] tr to gut, disembowel
étri·qué -quée [etrike] adj skimpy, tight; narrow, cramped
étriquer [etrike] tr to make too tight; to shorten (e.g., a speech)
étroit [etrwa] étroite [etrwat] adj narrow; strict; tight; close; à l'étroit confined, cramped
étroitesse [etrwatɛs] f narrowness; étroitesse d'esprit narrow-mindedness
étude [etyd] f study; law office; law practice; spadework, planning; à 'l'étude under consideration; mettre à l'étude to study; terminer ses études to finish one's courses
étu·diant [etydjɑ̃] -diante [djɑ̃t] mf student
étu·dié -diée [etydje] adj studied; set (speech); artificial, affected
étudier [etydje] tr to study; to practice, rehearse; to learn by heart; to design || intr to study || ref to be overly introspective; s'étudier à to take pains to, to make a point of
étui [etɥi] m case, box
étuve [etyv] f steam bath or room; drying room; steam sterilizer; incubator (for breeding cultures)
étuver [etyve] tr to stew; to steam; to dry
étymologie [etimɔlɔʒi] f etymology
étymon [etimɔ̃] m etymon
eucalyptus [økaliptys] m eucalyptus
Eucharistie [økaristi] f Eucharist
eunuque [ønyk] m eunuch
euphémique [øfemik] adj euphemistic
euphémisme [øfemism] m euphemism
euphonie [øfɔni] f euphony
euphonique [øfɔnik] adj euphonic
euphorie [øfɔri] f euphoria
Europe [ørɔp] f Europe; l'Europe Europe
européen [ørɔpeɛ̃] européenne [ørɔpeɛn] adj European || (cap) mf European
eux [ø] §85
eux-mêmes [ømɛm] §86
évacuer [evakɥe] tr & ref to evacuate
éva·dé -dée [evade] mf escapee
évader [evade] ref to escape, evade
évaluer [evalɥe] tr to evaluate, appraise; to estimate
évanes·cent [evanesɑ̃] évanes·cente [evanesɑ̃t] adj evanescent
évangélique [evɑ̃ʒelik] adj evangelic(al)
évangéliste [evɑ̃ʒelist] m evangelist
évangile [evɑ̃ʒil] m gospel
évanouir [evanwir] ref to faint; to lose consciousness; to vanish; (rad) to fade
évanouissement [evanwismɑ̃] m fainting; disappearance
évapo·ré -rée [evapɔre] adj flighty, fickle, giddy

évaporer [evapɔre] tr & ref to evaporate
évaser [evɑze] tr & ref to widen
éva·sif [evɑzif] -sive [ziv] adj evasive
évasion [evɑzjɔ̃] f evasion; escape; d'évasion escapist (literature)
Ève [ɛv] f Eve; je ne le connais ni d'Ève ni d'Adam (coll) I don't know him from Adam
évêché [eveʃe] m bishopric
éveil [evɛj] m awakening; alarm, warning
éveil·lé -lée [eveje] adj alert, lively; sharp, intelligent
éveiller [eveje] tr & ref to wake up
événement [evenəmɑ̃], [evɛnmɑ̃] m event; outcome, development; faire événement to cause quite a stir
évent [evɑ̃] m vent; staleness
éventail [evɑ̃taj] m fan; range, spread; screen
éventaire [evɑ̃tɛr] m tray (carried by flower girl, cigarette girl, etc.); sidewalk display
éventer [evɑ̃te] tr to fan; to ventilate; to get wind of (a secret); éventer la mèche (coll) to let the cat out of the bag || ref to fan oneself; to fade away (said of odor); to go stale or flat
éventrer [evɑ̃tre] tr to disembowel; to smash open
éventualité [evɑ̃tɥalite] f eventuality; possibility
éven·tuel -tuelle [evɑ̃tɥɛl] adj eventual; possible, contingent; forthcoming || m eventuality; possibility; possibilities (e.g., of a job)
éventuellement [evɑ̃tɥɛlmɑ̃] adv eventually; possibly; if need be
évêque [evɛk] m bishop
évertuer [evɛrtɥe] ref—s'évertuer à or pour + inf to strive to + inf
éviction [eviksjɔ̃] f eviction, removal; éviction scolaire quarantine
évidement [evidmɑ̃] m hollowing out
évidemment [evidamɑ̃] adv evidently
évidence [evidɑ̃s] f evidence, obviousness; conspicuousness; de toute évidence by all appearances; se mettre en évidence to come to the fore
évi·dent [evidɑ̃] -dente [dɑ̃t] adj evident
évider [evide] tr to hollow out
évier [evje] m sink
évincer [evɛ̃se] §51 tr to evict, to oust; to discriminate against
éviter [evite] tr to avoid, escape
évoca·teur [evɔkatœr] -trice [tris] adj evocative, suggestive
évocation [evɔkasjɔ̃] f evocation
évoluer [evɔlɥe] intr to evolve; to change one's mind
évolution [evɔlysjɔ̃] f evolution
évoquer [evɔke] tr to evoke; to recall, to call to mind
exact [ɛgza], [ɛgzakt] exacte [ɛgzakt] adj exact
exactitude [ɛgzaktityd] f exactness; punctuality
exagérer [ɛgzaʒere] §10 tr to exaggerate; to overdo
exal·té -tée [ɛgzalte] adj impassioned;

high-strung, wrought-up ‖ *mf* hot-head, fanatic
exalter [εgzalte] *tr* to exalt; to excite (*e.g., the imagination*) ‖ *ref* to get excited
examen [εgzamɛ̃] *m* examination; **à l'examen** under consideration; on approval; **examen de fin d'études** or **examen de fin de classe** final examination; **examen probatoire** placement exam; **libre examen** free inquiry; **se présenter à, passer,** or **subir un examen** to take an examination
examina·teur [εgzaminatœr] **-trice** [tris] *mf* examiner
examiner [εgzamine] *tr* to examine
exaspération [εgzasperɑsjɔ̃] *f* exasperation; crisis, aggravation
exaspérer [εgzaspere] §10 *tr* to exasperate; to make worse
exaucer [εgzose] §51 *tr* to answer the prayer of; to fulfill (*a wish*)
excava·teur [εkskavatœr] **-trice** [tris] *m & f* excavator, steam shovel
excaver [εkskave] *tr* to excavate
excé·dant [εksedɑ̃] **-dante** [dɑ̃t] *adj* excess; tiresome
excédent [εksedɑ̃] *m* excess, surplus
excédentaire [εksedɑ̃tεr] *adj* excess
excéder [εksede] §10 *tr* to exceed; to tire out; to overtax
excellence [εksεlɑ̃s] *f* excellence; **Votre Excellence** Your Excellency
exceller [εksεle] *intr* to excel
excentricité [εksɑ̃trisite] *f* eccentricity
excentrique [εksɑ̃trik] *adj* eccentric; remote, outlying ‖ *mf* eccentric ‖ *m* (mach) eccentric
excep·té -tée [εksεpte] *adj* excepted ‖ **excepté** *adv*—**excepté que** except that ‖ **excepté** *prep* except, except for
exception [εksεpsjɔ̃] *f* exception; **à l'exception de** with the exception of
exception·nel -nelle [εksεpsjɔnεl] *adj* exceptional
excès [εksε] *m* excess; **excès de pose** (phot) overexposure; **excès de vitesse** speeding
exces·sif [εksεsif] **exces·sive** [εksεsiv] *adj* excessive
exciper [εksipe] *intr*—**exciper de** (law) to offer a plea of, to allege
excitable [εksitabl] *adj* excitable
exci·tant [εksitɑ̃] **-tante** [tɑ̃t] *adj* stimulating ‖ *m* stimulant
exciter [εksite] *tr* to excite, stimulate; to stir, incite; to provoke (*e.g., laughter*)
exclamation [εksklamɑsjɔ̃] *f* exclamation
exclamer [εksklame] *ref* to exclaim
exclure [εksklyr] §11 *tr* to exclude
exclu·sif [εksklyzif] **-sive** [ziv] *adj* exclusive
exclusion [εksklyzjɔ̃] *f* exclusion; **à l'exclusion de** exclusive of, excluding
exclusivité [εksklyzivite] *f* exclusiveness; exclusive rights; newsbeat; **en exclusivité** (public sign in front of a theater) exclusive showing

excommunication [εkskɔmynikɑsjɔ̃] *f* excommunication
excommunier [εkskɔmynje] *tr* to excommunicate
excorier [εkskɔrje] *tr* to scratch, skin
excrément [εkskremɑ̃] *m* excrement
excroissance [εkskrwasɑ̃s] *f* growth, tumor
excursion [εkskyrsjɔ̃] *f* excursion; tour, trip; outing
excursionner [εkskyrsjɔne] *intr* to go on an excursion
excusable [εkskyzabl] *adj* excusable
excuse [εkskyz] *f* excuse; **des excuses** apologies
excuser [εkskyze] *tr* to excuse ‖ *ref* to excuse oneself, to apologize; **je m'excuse!** (coll) excuse me!
exécrer [εgzekre] §10 *tr* to execrate
exécu·tant [εgzekytɑ̃] **-tante** [tɑ̃t] *mf* performer
exécuter [εgzekyte] *tr* to execute; to perform; to make (*copies*) ‖ *ref* to comply
exécuteur [εgzekytœr] *m*—**exécuteur testamentaire** executor; **exécuteur des hautes œuvres** hangman
exécu·tif [εgzekytif] **-tive** [tiv] *adj & m* executive
exécution [εgzekysjɔ̃] *f* execution; performance; fulfillment; **mettre à exécution** to carry out
exécutrice [εgzekytris] *f* executrix
exemplaire [εgzɑ̃plεr] *adj* exemplary ‖ *m* exemplar, model; sample, specimen; copy (*e.g., of book*); **en double exemplaire** with carbon copy; **exemplaire dédicacé** autographed copy; **exemplaires de passe** extra copies
exemple [εgzɑ̃pl] *m* example; **à l'exemple de** after the example of; **par exemple** for example; **par exemple!** the idea!, well I never!; **prêcher d'exemple** to practice what one preaches; **sans exemple** unprecedented
exempt [εgzɑ̃] **exempte** [εgzɑ̃t] *adj* exempt ‖ *m* (hist) police officer
exempter [εgzɑ̃te] *tr* to exempt
exemption [εgzɑ̃psjɔ̃] *f* exemption
exer·cé -cée [εgzεrse] *adj* practiced, experienced
exercer [εgzεrse] §51 *tr* to exercise; to exert; to practice (*e.g., medicine*) ‖ *ref* to exercise; to practice, to drill
exercice [εgzεrsis] *m* exercise; drill; practice; **exercice budgétaire** fiscal year
exhalaison [εgzalεzɔ̃] *f* exhalation (*of gas, vapors, etc.*)
exhalation [εgzalɑsjɔ̃] *f* exhalation (*of air from lungs*)
exhaler [εgzale] *tr, intr, & ref* to exhale
exhaure [εgzɔr] *f* pumping out (*of a mine*); drain pumps
exhaussement [εgzosmɑ̃] *m* raising; rise
exhausser [εgzose] *tr* to raise, to increase the height of ‖ *ref* to rise
exhaus·tif [εgzostif] **-tive** [tiv] *adj* exhaustive

exhiber [εgzibe] *tr* to exhibit; to show (*a ticket, passport, etc.*) || *ref* to make an exhibition of oneself

exhibition [εgzibisjɔ̃] *f* exhibition

exhorter [εgzɔrte] *tr* to exhort

exhumer [εgzyme] *tr* to exhume

exi·geant [εgziʒɑ̃] **-geante** [ʒɑ̃t] *adj* exigent, exacting; unreasonable

exigence [εgziʒɑ̃s] *f* demand, claim; requirement; unreasonableness; **exigences** exigencies

exiger [εgziʒe] §38 *tr* to demand, require, exact

exigible [εgziʒibl] *adj* required; due, on demand

exi·gu -guë [εgzigy] *adj* tiny; insufficient

exiguïté [εgzigɥite] *f* smallness; insufficiency

exil [εgzil] *m* exile

exi·lé -lée [εgzile] *adj* & *mf* exile

exiler [εgzile] *tr* to exile

existence [εgzistɑ̃s] *f* existence

exister [εgziste] *intr* to exist

exode [εgzɔd] *m* exodus; flight (*of capital; of emigrants, refugees, etc.*)

exonération [εgzɔnerasjɔ̃] *f* exemption, exoneration

exonérer [εgzɔnere] §10 *tr* to exempt, exonerate || *ref* to pay up a debt

exorbi·tant [εgzɔrbitɑ̃] **-tante** [tɑ̃t] *adj* exorbitant

exorciser [εgzorsize] *tr* to exorcise

exotique [εgzɔtik] *adj* exotic

expan·sif [εkspɑ̃sif] **-sive** [siv] *adj* expansive

expansion [εkspɑ̃sjɔ̃] *f* expansion; expansiveness; spread (*of a belief*)

expa·trié -triée [εkspatrije] *adj* & *mf* expatriate

expatrier [εkspatrije] *tr* to expatriate

expectorer [εkspεktɔre] *tr* & *intr* to expectorate

expé·dient [εkspedjɑ̃] **-diente** [djɑ̃t] *adj* expedient || *m* expedient; (coll) makeshift; **expédient provisoire** emergency measure; **vivre d'expédients** to live by one's wits

expédier [εkspedje] *tr* to expedite; to ship; to make a certified copy of; (coll) to dash off, do hurriedly

expédi·teur [εkspeditœr] **-trice** [tris] *adj* forwarding (*station, agency, etc.*) || *mf* sender, shipper

expédi·tif [εkspeditif] **-tive** [tiv] *adj* expeditious

expédition [εkspedisjɔ̃] *f* expedition; shipping; shipment; certified copy

expéditionnaire [εkspedisjɔnεr] *adj* expeditionary || *mf* sender; clerk

expérience [εksperjɑ̃s] *f* experience; experiment

expérimen·té -tée [εksperimɑ̃te] *adj* experienced

expérimenter [εksperimɑ̃te] *tr* to try out, to test || *intr* to conduct experiments

ex·pert [εkspεr] **-perte** [pεrt] *adj* expert || *m* expert; connoisseur; appraiser

expert-comptable [εkspεrkɔ̃tabl] *m* (*pl* **experts-comptables**) certified public accountant

expertise [εkspεrtiz] *f* expert appraisal

expertiser [εkspεrtize] *tr* to appraise

expier [εkspje] *tr* to expiate, to atone for

expirer [εkspire] *tr* & *intr* to expire; to exhale

explicable [εksplikabl] *adj* explicable, explainable

explica·tif [εksplikatif] **-tive** [tiv] *adj* explanatory

explication [εksplikɑsjɔ̃] *f* explanation; interpretation (*of a text*); **avoir une explication avec qn** to have it out with s.o.

explicite [εksplisit] *adj* explicit

expliciter [εksplisite] *tr* to make explicit

expliquer [εksplike] *tr* to explain; to give an interpretation of || *ref* to explain oneself; to understand

exploit [εksplwa] *m* exploit; **exploit d'ajournement** subpoena; **signifier un exploit** to serve a summons

exploi·tant [εksplwatɑ̃] **-tante** [tɑ̃t] *adj* operating, working || *mf* operator (*of enterprise*); developer; cultivator; (mov) exhibitor

exploitation [εksplwatɑsjɔ̃] *f* exploitation; management, development, cultivation; land under cultivation

exploiter [εksplwate] *tr* to exploit; to manage, develop, cultivate || *intr* to serve summonses

explora·teur [εksplɔratœr] **-trice** [tris] *mf* explorer

exploration [εksplɔrɑsjɔ̃] *f* exploration

explorer [εksplɔre] *tr* to explore; (telv) to scan

exploser [εksplɔze] *intr* to explode

explosible [εksplɔzibl] *adj* explosive

explo·sif [εksplɔzif] **-sive** [ziv] *adj* & *m* explosive

explosion [εksplɔzjɔ̃] *f* explosion; **à explosion** internal-combustion (*engine*)

exporta·teur [εkspɔrtatœr] **-trice** [tris] *adj* exporting || *mf* exporter

exportation [εkspɔrtɑsjɔ̃] *f* export; exportation

exporter [εkspɔrte] *tr* & *intr* to export

expo·sant [εkspozɑ̃] **-sante** [zɑ̃t] *mf* exhibitor; petitioner || *m* (math) exponent

exposé [εkspoze] *m* exposition, account, statement; report (*given by a student in class*)

exposer [εkspoze] *tr* to expose; to explain, expound; to exhibit, display

exposition [εkspozisjɔ̃] *f* exposition; exposure (*to one of the points of the compass*); introduction (*of a book*); lying in state; **exposition canine** dog show; **exposition d'horticulture** flower show; **exposition hippique** horse show

ex·près [εksprε] **-presse** [prεs] *adj* express || **exprès** *adj invar* special-delivery (*letter, package, etc.*) || *m* express; **par exprès** by special delivery || **exprès** *adv* expressly, on purpose

express [εksprεs] *adj* & *m* express (*train*)

expressément [ɛkspresemɑ̃] adv expressly
expres·sif [ɛkspresif] expres·sive [ɛkspresiv] adj expressive
expression [ɛksprɛsjɔ̃] f expression; d'expression française native Frenchspeaking
exprimer [ɛksprime] tr to express; to squeeze out
exproprier [ɛksprɔprije] tr to expropriate
expul·sé -sée [ɛkspylse] adj deported ‖ mf deportee
expulser [ɛkspylse] tr to expel; to evict; to throw out
expulsion [ɛkspylsjɔ̃] f expulsion
expurger [ɛkspyrʒe] §38 tr to expurgate
ex·quis [ɛkski] -quise [kiz] adj exquisite; sharp (pain)
exsangue [ɛksɑ̃g] adj bloodless, anemic
exsuder [ɛksyde] tr & intr to exude
extase [ɛkstɑz] f ecstasy
exta·sié -siée [ɛkstɑzje] adj enraptured, ecstatic, in ecstasy
extasier [ɛkstɑzje] ref to be enraptured
extatique [ɛkstatik] adj & mf ecstatic
extempora·né -née [ɛkstɑ̃pɔrane] adj (law) unpremeditated; (pharm) ready for use
exten·sif [ɛkstɑ̃sif] -sive [siv] adj wide (meaning); (mech) tensile
extension [ɛkstɑ̃sjɔ̃] f extension
exténuer [ɛkstenɥe] tr to exhaust, tire out ‖ ref to tire oneself out
exté·rieur -rieure [ɛksterjœr] adj exterior; external; outer, outside; foreign (policy) ‖ m exterior; outside; (mov) location shot; (mov) location; abroad; en extérieur (mov) on location
extérieurement [ɛksterjœrmɑ̃] adv externally; superficially; on the outside
extérioriser [ɛksterjɔrize] tr to reveal, to show ‖ ref to open one's heart
exterminer [ɛkstɛrmine] tr to exterminate
externat [ɛkstɛrna] m day school
externe [ɛkstɛrn] adj external ‖ m day student; outpatient; (med) nonresident intern
extinc·teur [ɛkstɛ̃ktœr] -trice [tris] adj extinguishing ‖ m fire extinguisher
extinction [ɛkstɛ̃ksjɔ̃] f extinction; extinguishing; loss (of voice); l'extinction des feux (mil) lights out, taps
extirper [ɛkstirpe] tr to extirpate

extorquer [ɛkstɔrke] tr to extort
extor·queur [ɛkstɔrkœr] -queuse [køz] mf extortionist
extorsion [ɛkstɔrsjɔ̃] f extortion
extra [ɛkstra] adj invar (coll) extraspecial, extra ‖ m invar extra
extraction [ɛkstraksjɔ̃] f extraction
extrader [ɛkstrade] tr to extradite
extradition [ɛkstradisjɔ̃] f extradition
extra-fin [ɛkstrafɛ̃] -fine [fin] adj high-quality
extraire [ɛkstrɛr] §68 tr to extract; to excerpt; to get out ‖ ref to extricate oneself
extrait [ɛkstrɛ] m extract; excerpt; abstract; certified copy; extrait de baptême baptismal certificate; extrait de naissance birth certificate; extraits selections (e.g., in an anthology)
extra-muros [ɛkstramyros] adj invar extramural; suburban ‖ adv outside the town
extraordinaire [ɛkstraɔrdinɛr], [ɛkstrɔrdinɛr] adj extraordinary
extrapoler [ɛkstrapɔle] tr to extrapolate
extra-sensoriel -sensorielle [ɛkstrasɑ̃sɔrjɛl] adj extrasensory
extravagance [ɛkstravagɑ̃s] f extravagance; excess; absurdity, wildness
extrava·gant [ɛkstravagɑ̃] -gante [gɑ̃t] adj excessive, extravagant; absurd, wild, eccentric ‖ mf eccentric, screwball
extraver·ti -tie [ɛkstravɛrti] adj & mf extrovert
extrême [ɛkstrɛm] adj & m extreme
extrêmement [ɛkstrɛmǝmɑ̃] adv extremely
extrême-onction [ɛkstrɛmɔ̃ksjɔ̃] f extreme unction
Extrême-Orient [ɛkstrɛmɔrjɑ̃] m Far East
extrémiste [ɛkstremist] adj & mf extremist
extrémité [ɛkstremite] f extremity; en venir à des extrémités to resort to violence; être à toute extrémité to be at death's door
extrinsèque [ɛkstrɛ̃sɛk] adj extrinsic
exubé·rant [ɛgzyberɑ̃] -rante [rɑ̃t] adj exuberant
exulter [ɛgzylte] intr to exult
ex-voto [ɛksvɔto] m invar votive inscription or tablet

F

F, f [ɛf], *[ef] m invar sixth letter of the French alphabet
F abbr (franc) franc
fable [fɑbl] f fable; laughingstock
fabri·cant [fabrikɑ̃] -cante [kɑ̃t] mf manufacturer

fabrica·teur [fabrikatœr] -trice [tris] mf fabricator (e.g., of lies); forger; counterfeiter
fabrication [fabrikɑsjɔ̃] f manufacture; forging; counterfeiting
fabrique [fabrik] f factory; factory

workers; mill hands; (obs) church trustees; (obs) church revenue; **fabrique de papier** paper mill
fabriquer [fabrike] *tr* to manufacture; to fabricate; to forge; to counterfeit
fabu·leux [fabylø] **-leuse** [løz] *adj* fabulous
façade [fasad] *f* façade; frontage; **en façade sur** facing, overlooking
face [fas] *f* face; side (*of a diamond; of a phonograph record*); surface; heads (*of coin*); **de face** full-faced (*portrait*); **en face (de)** opposite, facing; **faire face à** to face; to face up to; **to meet** (*an obligation*); **perdre la face** to lose face; **sauver la face** to save face
face-à-main [fasamɛ̃] *m* (*pl* **faces-à-main**) lorgnette
facétie [fasesi] *f* off-color joke; practical joke
facé·tieux [fasesjø] **-tieuse** [sjøz] *adj* droll, funny ‖ *mf* wag
facette [faset] *f* facet
fâ·ché -chée [faʃe] *adj* angry; sorry; **fâché avec** at odds with; **fâché contre** angry with (*a person*); **fâché de** angry at (*a thing*); sorry for
fâcher [faʃe] *tr* to anger ‖ *ref* to get angry; to be sorry
fâ·cheux [faʃø] **-cheuse** [ʃøz] *adj* annoying, tiresome; unfortunate ‖ *mf* nuisance, bore
fa·cial -ciale [fasjal] *adj* (*pl* **-ciaux** [sjo]) facial; face (*value*)
facile [fasil] *adj* easy; easygoing; facile, glib
facilité [fasilite] *f* facility; opportunity (*e.g., to meet s.o.*); **facilités de paiement** installments; easy terms
faciliter [fasilite] *tr* to facilitate
façon [fasɔ̃] *f* fashion; fashioning; way, manner; fit (*of clothes*); **à façon** job (*work; workman*); **à la façon de** like; **de façon à** so as to; **de façon que or de telle façon que** so that, e.g., **parlez de telle façon qu'on vous comprenne** speak so that you can be understood; **de toute façon** in any event; **façons** manners; **faire des façons** to stand on ceremony; **sans façon** informal
faconde [fakɔ̃d] *f* glibness, gift of gab
façonner [fasɔne] *tr* to fashion, shape; to work (*the land*); to accustom
façon·nier [fasɔnje] **façon·nière** [fasɔnjɛr] *adj* jobbing; fussy ‖ *mf* pieceworker; stuffed shirt
fac-similé [faksimile] *m* (*pl* **-similés**) facsimile
factage [faktaʒ] *m* delivery service; home delivery
facteur [faktœr] *m* factor; mailman; expressman; auctioneer (*at a market*); maker (*of musical instruments*)
factice [faktis] *adj* imitation, artificial
fac·tieux [faksjø] **-tieuse** [sjøz] *adj* factious, seditious ‖ *mf* troublemaker, agitator
faction [faksjɔ̃] *f* faction; **être de faction** to be on sentry duty
factionnaire [faksjɔnɛr] *m* sentry
factorerie [faktɔrəri] *f* trading post

factotum [faktɔtɔm] *m* factotum; meddler; jack-of-all-trades
factum [faktɔm] *m* political pamphlet; (law) brief
facturation [faktyrasjɔ̃] *f* billing, invoicing
facture [faktyr] *f* invoice; bill; workmanship; **établir une facture** to make out an invoice; **suivant facture** as per invoice
facturer [faktyre] *tr* to bill
factu·rier [faktyrje] **-rière** [rjer] *mf* billing clerk ‖ *m* invoice book
faculta·tif [fakyltatif] **-tive** [tiv] *adj* optional
faculté [fakylte] *f* faculty; school, college (*of law, medicine, etc.*); **la Faculté** medical men
fadaise [fadɛz] *f* piece of nonsense; **fadaises** drivel
fade [fad] *adj* tasteless, flat; insipid, namby-pamby
fader [fade] *tr* (coll) to beat; (coll) to share the swag with; **il est fadé** (coll) he's done for
fadeur [fadœr] *f* insipidity; pointlessness; **fadeurs** platitudes
fagot [fago] *m* faggot; **fagot d'épines** ill-tempered person; **sentir le fagot** to smell of heresy
fagoter [fagote] *tr* to tie up in bundles, to faggot; (coll) to dress like a scarecrow
faible [fɛbl] *adj* feeble, weak; low (*figure; moan*); poor (*harvest*); slight (*difference*) ‖ *mf* weakling ‖ *m* weakness; foible, weak spot; **faible d'esprit** feeble-minded person
faiblesse [fɛblɛs] *f* feebleness, weakness, frailty
faiblir [fɛblir] *intr* to weaken; to diminish
faïence [fajɑ̃s] *f* earthenware, pottery
faille [faj] *f* (geol) fault; (tex) faille; (fig) defect; (fig) rift
fail-li -lie [faji] *adj* & *mf* bankrupt
faillible [fajibl] *adj* fallible
faillir [fajir] *intr* to fail, to go bankrupt ‖ (used only in: *inf; ger* **faillant**; *pp* & compound tenses: *pret; fut; cond*) *intr* to fail; to give way; (with *dat*) to fail, let (*s.o.*) down; **faillir à** to fail in (*a duty*); to fail to keep (*a promise*); **faillir à + inf** to fail to + *inf*; **sans faillir** without fail ‖ (used only in *pret* and *past indef*) *intr*—nearly, almost, e.g., **il a failli être écrasé** he was nearly run over
faillite [fajit] *f* bankruptcy; **faire faillite** to go bankrupt
faim [fɛ̃] *f* hunger; **avoir faim** to be hungry; **avoir une faim de loup** to be hungry as a bear; **manger à sa faim** to eat one's fill
fainéant [feneɑ̃] **fainéante** [feneɑ̃t] *adj* lazy ‖ *mf* loafer, do-nothing
fainéanter [feneɑ̃te] *intr* (coll) to loaf
faire [fer] *m* making, doing ‖ §29 *tr* to make; to do; to give (*an order; a lecture; alms, a gift; thanks*); to take (*a walk; a step*); to pack (*a trunk*); to clean (*the room, the shoes, etc.*); to follow (*a trade*); to keep (*silence*);

to perform (*a play; a miracle*); to play the part of; to charge for, e.g., **combien faites-vous ces souliers?** how much do you charge for these shoes?; to say, e.g., **oui, fit-il** yes, said he; (coll) to estimate the cost of; for expressions like **il fait chaud** it is warm, see the noun; **cela ne fait rien** it doesn't matter; **faire** + *inf* to have + *inf*, e.g., **je le ferai aller** I shall have him go; **faire** + *inf* to make + *inf*, e.g., **je le ferai parler** I will make him talk; **faire** + *inf* to have + *pp*, e.g., **je vais faire faire un complet** I am going to have a suit made; **il n'en fait pas d'autres** that's just like him; **ne faire que** + *inf* to keep on + *ger*, e.g., **il ne fait que crier** he keeps on yelling ‖ *intr* to go, e.g., **la cravate fait bien avec la chemise** the tie goes well with the shirt; to act; **comment faire?** what shall I do?; **faire dans** to make a mess in; **ne faire que de** + *inf* to have just + *pp*, e.g., **il ne fait que d'arriver** he has just arrived ‖ *ref* to become (*a doctor, lawyer, etc.*); to grow (*e.g., old*); to improve; to happen; to pretend to be; **faire à** to get accustomed to, to adjust to; **s'en faire** to worry, e.g., **ne vous en faites pas!** don't worry!

faire-part [fɛrpar] *m invar* announcement (*of birth, marriage, death*)

faire-valoir [fɛrvalwar] *m invar* turning to account; **faire-valoir direct** farming by the owner

faisable [fəzabl] *adj* feasible

fai·san [fəzɑ̃] **-sane** [zan] *or* **-sande** [zɑ̃d] *mf* pheasant

faisander [fəzɑ̃de] *tr* to jerk (*game*) ‖ *intr* to become gamy, to get high

fais·ceau [fɛso] *m* (*pl* **-ceaux**) bundle, cluster; beam (*of light*); pencil (*of rays*); **faisceaux** fasces; **faisceaux de preuves** cumulative evidence; **former les faisceaux** to stack or pile arms

fai·seur [fəzœr] **-seuse** [zøz] *mf*—**bon faiseur** first-rate workman; **faiseur de mariages** matchmaker; **faiseur de vers** versifier, poetaster ‖ *m* bluffer; schemer

fait [fɛ] **faite** [fɛt] *adj* well-built, shapely; full-grown; made-up (*with cosmetics*); **fait à la main** hand-made; **tout fait** ready-made ‖ *m* deed, act; fact; **dire son fait à qn** (coll) to give s.o. a piece of one's mind; **prendre fait et cause pour** to take up the cudgels for; **si fait** yes, indeed; **sur le fait** redhanded, in the act; **tout à fait** entirely ‖ [fɛt] *m*—**au fait** to the point; after all; **de fait** de facto; **du fait que** owing to the fact that; **en fait** as a matter of fact

faîtage [fɛtaʒ] *m* ridgepole; roofs; roofing

fait-divers [fɛdivɛr] *m* (*pl* **faits-divers**) news item

faîte [fɛt] *m* peak; top (*of tree*); ridge (*of roof*)

faîtière [fɛtjɛr] *adj fem* ridge ‖ *f* ridge tile; skylight

fait-tout [fɛtu] *m invar* stewpan, casserole

faix [fɛ] *m* load, burden; (archit) settling; (physiol) fetus and placenta

falaise [falɛz] *f* cliff, bluff

falla·cieux [falasjø] **-cieuse** [sjøz] *adj* fallacious

falloir [falwar] §30 *impers* to be necessary; **c'est plus qu'il n'en faut** that's more than enough; **comme il faut** proper; properly; the right kind of, e.g., **un chapeau comme il faut** the right kind of hat; **il fallait le dire!** why didn't you say so!; **il faut** + *inf* it is necessary to + *inf*, one must + *inf*; **il faut qu'il** + *subj* it is necessary that he + *subj*, it is necessary for him to + *inf*; he must + *inf* (expressing conjecture), e.g., **il n'est pas venu, il faut qu'il soit malade** he did not come, he must be sick; **il faut qu'il ne** + *subj* + **pas** he must not + *inf*, e.g., **il faut qu'il ne vienne pas** he must not come; **il faut une connaissance des affaires à ce travail** the work requires business experience; **il faut une heure** it takes an hour; **il leur a fallu trois jours** it took them three days; **il leur faut** + *inf* they have to + *inf*, they must + *inf*; **il leur faut du repos** they need rest; **il leur faut sept dollars** they need seven dollars; **il ne faut pas** + *inf* one must or· should not + *inf*, e.g., **il ne faut pas se fier à ce garçon** one must not trust that boy; **il ne faut pas qu'il** + *subj* he must not + *inf*; **que leur faut-il?** what do they need?; **qu'il ne fallait pas** what do they require?; **qu'il ne fallait pas** wrong, e.g., **la police a arrêté l'homme qu'il ne fallait pas** the police arrested the wrong man ‖ *ref*— **il s'en faut de beaucoup** not by a long shot, far from it, not by any means; **il s'en faut de dix dollars** there is a shortage of ten dollars; **peu m'en est fallu que . . .** it very nearly happened that . . . ; **peu s'en faut** very nearly; **tant s'en faut que** far from, e.g., **tant s'en faut qu'il soit artiste** he is far from being an artist

fa·lot [falo] **-lotte** [lɔt] *adj* wan, colorless; quaint, droll ‖ *m* lantern

falsification [falsifikɑsjɔ̃] *f* falsification; adulteration; debasement (*of coin*)

falsifier [falsifje] *tr* to falsify; to adulterate; to debase (*coin*)

fa·mé -mée [fame] *adj*—**mal famé** disreputable

famélique [famelik] *adj* famished

fa·meux [famø] **-meuse** [møz] *adj* famous ‖ (when standing before noun) *adj* (coll) notorious; well-known

fami·lial -liale [familjal] *adj* (*pl* **-liaux** [ljo]) family, domestic ‖ *f* station wagon

familiariser [familjarize] *tr* to familiarize ‖ *ref* to become familiar

familiarité [familjarite] *f* familiarity

fami·lier [familje] **-lière** [ljɛr] *adj*

familiar, intimate; household (*gods*); pet (*animal*) || *mf* familiar, intimate; pet animal

famille [famij] *f* family; **en famille** in the family circle, at home; (Canad) pregnant

famine [famin] *f* famine

fa·nal [fanal] *m* (*pl* **-naux** [no]) lantern; (naut) running light

fanatique [fanatik] *adj* fanatic(al) || *mf* fanatic; enthusiast, fan

fanatisme [fanatism] *m* fanaticism

faner [fane] *tr* & *ref* to fade

fanfare [fɑ̃far] *f* fanfare; brass band

fanfa·ron [fɑ̃farɔ̃] **-ronne** [rɔn] *adj* bragging || *mf* braggart

fanfaronner [fɑ̃farɔne] *intr* to brag

fange [fɑ̃ʒ] *f* mire, mud; (fig) mire, gutter

fan·geux [fɑ̃ʒø] **-geuse** [ʒøz] *adj* muddy; (fig) dirty, soiled

fanion [fanjɔ̃] *m* pennant, flag

fanon [fanɔ̃] *m* dewlap (*of ox*); whalebone; fetlock; wattle

fantaisie [fɑ̃tezi] *f* imagination; fantasy; fancy, whim; **de fantaisie** fanciful; fancy, e.g., **pain de fantaisie** fancy bread

fantaisiste [fɑ̃tezist] *adj* fantastic, whimsical || *mf* whimsical person; singing comedian

fantasque [fɑ̃task] *adj* fantastic; whimsical, temperamental

fantassin [fɑ̃tasɛ̃] *m* foot soldier

fantastique [fɑ̃tastik] *adj* fantastic

fantoche [fɑ̃tɔʃ] *m* puppet

fantôme [fɑ̃tom] *adj* shadow (*government*) || *m* phantom, ghost

fanum [fanɔm] *m* hallowed ground

faon [fɑ̃] *m* fawn

faonner [fane] *intr* to bring forth young (*said especially of deer*)

faquin [fakɛ̃] *m* rascal

fa·raud [faro] **-raude** [rod] *adj* (coll) swanky || *mf* (coll) fop, bumpkin; **faire le faraud** (coll) to show off

farce [fars] *f* farce; trick, joke; (culin) stuffing

far·ceur [farsœr] **-ceuse** [søz] *mf* practical joker; phony

farcir [farsir] *tr* to stuff

fard [far] *m* make-up; **parler sans fard** to speak plainly, to tell the unvarnished truth; **piquer un fard** (coll) to blush

far·deau [fardo] *m* (*pl* **-deaux**) load, burden; weight (*of years*)

farder [farde] *tr* to make up (*an actor*); to disguise (*the truth*) || *ref* to weigh heavily; (archit) to sink; (theat) to make up

fardier [fardje] *m* dray, cart

farfe·lu -lue [farfəly] *adj* (coll) harebrained, cockeyed, bizarre

farfouiller [farfuje] *tr* (coll) to rummage about in || *intr* (coll) to rummage about; **farfouiller dans** (coll) to rummage about in

farine [farin] *f* flour, meal; **farine de froment** whole-wheat flour; **farine de riz** ground rice; **farine lactée** malted milk

fariner [farine] *tr* (culin) to flour

fari·neux [farinø] **-neuse** [nøz] *adj* white with flour; mealy; starchy

farouche [faruʃ] *adj* wild, savage; unsociable; shy; stubborn (*resistance*); fierce (*look*)

fascicule [fasikyl] *m* fascicle; **fascicule de mobilisation** marching orders

fascina·teur [fasinatœr] **-trice** [tris] *adj* fascinating || *mf* spellbinder

fasciner [fasine] *tr* to fascinate; to spellbind

fascisme [faʃism] *m* fascism

fasciste [faʃist] *adj* & *mf* fascist

faste [fast] *adj* auspicious; feast (*day*) || *m* pomp; **fastes** annals

fasti·dieux [fastidjø] **-dieuse** [djøz] *adj* tedious, wearisome

fas·tueux [fastyø] **-tueuse** [tyøz] *adj* pompous, ostentatious

fat [fat] *adj masc* conceited, foppish || *m* fop

fa·tal -tale [fatal] *adj* (*pl* **-tals**) fatal; fateful; inevitable

fatalisme [fatalism] *m* fatalism

fataliste [fatalist] *adj* fatalistic || *mf* fatalist

fatalité [fatalite] *f* fatality; fatalism; fate; curse, misfortune

fatidique [fatidik] *adj* fateful; prophetic

fati·gant [fatigɑ̃] **-gante** [gɑ̃t] *adj* fatiguing; tiresome (*person*)

fatigue [fatig] *f* fatigue

fati·gué -guée [fatige] *adj* fatigued; worn-out (*clothing*); well-thumbed (*book*)

fatiguer [fatige] *tr* to fatigue; to wear out; to weary || *intr* to strain, labor; to pull (*said of engine*); to bear a heavy strain (*said of beam*) || *ref* to get tired

fatras [fatra] *m* jumble, hodgepodge

fatuité [fatчite] *f* conceit; foppishness

faubert [fobɛr] *m* (naut) swab

faubourg [fobur] *m* suburb; outskirts; quarter, district (*especially of Paris*)

faubou·rien [foburjɛ̃] **-rienne** [rjɛn] *adj* working-class, vulgar || *mf* resident of the outskirts of a city; local inhabitant

fau·ché -chée [foʃe] *adj* (coll) broke (*without money*)

faucher [foʃe] *tr* to mow, reap; (coll) to swipe

fau·cheur [foʃœr] **-cheuse** [ʃøz] *mf* reaper || *m* (ent) daddy-longlegs || *f* (mach) reaper, mower

faucheux [foʃø] *m* (ent) daddy-longlegs

faucille [fosij] *f* sickle

faucon [fokɔ̃] *m* falcon

fauconnier [fokɔnje] *m* falconer

faufil [fofil] *m* basting thread

faufiler [fofile] *tr* to baste || *ref* to thread one's way, to worm one's way

faune [fon] *m* faun || *f* fauna

faunesse [fonɛs] *f* female faun

faussaire [fosɛr] *mf* forger

fausser [fose] *tr* to falsify, distort; to bend, twist; to warp (*the judgment*); to force (*a lock*); to strain (*the voice*); **fausser compagnie à qn** (coll) to give s.o. the slip || *intr* to sing or play out of tune ‖ *ref* to bend, buckle; to crack (*said of voice*)

fausset [fosɛ] *m* falsetto; plug (*for wine barrel*)

fausseté [foste] *f* falsity; double-dealing

faute [fot] *f* fault; mistake; blame; lack, need, want; (sports) foul; (sports) error; **faire faute** to be lacking; **faute de** for want of; **faute de copiste** clerical error; **faute de frappe** typing error; **faute d'impression** misprint; **sans faute** without fail

fauter [fote] *intr* (coll) to go wrong (*said of a woman*)

fauteuil [fotœj] *m* armchair, easy chair; seat (*of member of an academy*); chair (*of presiding officer; presiding officer himself*); **fauteuil à bascule** or **à balançoire** rocking chair; **fauteuil à oreilles** wing chair; **fauteuil d'orchestre** orchestra seat; **fauteuil pliant** folding chair; **fauteuil roulant pour malade** wheelchair; **siéger au fauteuil présidentiel** to preside

fau·teur [fotœr] **-trice** [tris] *mf* instigator, agitator

fau·tif [fotif] **-tive** [tiv] *adj* faulty

fauve [fov] *adj* fawn (*color*); musky (*odor*); wild (*beast*) ‖ *m* fawn color; wild beast; **fauves** big game

fauvette [fovɛt] *f* warbler

faux [fo] **fausse** [fos] *adj* false; counterfeit; wrong, e.g., **fausse date** wrong date; e.g., **fausse note** wrong note ‖ *m* imitation; forgery; **à faux** wrongly ‖ **faux** *f* scythe ‖ **faux** *adv* out of tune, off key

faux-bourdon [foburdɔ̃] *m* (*pl* **-bourdons**) *m* (ent) drone

faux-col [fokɔl] *m* (*pl* **-cols**) collar, detachable collar

faux-filet [fofilɛ] *m* (*pl* **-filets**) sirloin

faux-fuyant [fofɥijɑ̃] *m* (*pl* **-fuyants**) subterfuge, pretext

faux-jour [foʒur] *m* (*pl* **-jours**) halflight

faux-monnayeur [fomɔnɛjœr] *m* (*pl* **-monnayeurs**) counterfeiter

faux-pas [fopɑ] *m invar* faux pas, slip, blunder

faux-semblant [fosɑ̃blɑ̃] *m* (*pl* **-semblants**) false pretense

faveur [favœr] *f* favor; **à la faveur de** under cover of; **en faveur de** in favor of; on behalf of

favorable [favɔrabl] *adj* favorable

favo·ri [favɔri] **-rite** [rit] *adj* & *mf* favorite ‖ **favoris** *mpl* sideburns ‖ *f* mistress

favoriser [favɔrize] *tr* to favor; to encourage, promote

Fco or **fco** *abbr* (**franco**) postpaid

fébrile [febril] *adj* feverish

fèces [fɛs] *fpl* feces

fé·cond [fekɔ̃] **-conde** [kɔ̃d] *adj* fecund, fertile

féconder [fekɔ̃de] *tr* to impregnate

fécondité [fekɔ̃dite] *f* fecundity, fertility

fécule [fekyl] *f* starch; **fécule de maïs** cornstarch

fécu·lent [fekylɑ̃] **-lente** [lɑ̃t] *adj* starchy ‖ *m* starchy food

fédé·ral **-rale** [federal] *adj* & *m* (*pl* **-raux** [ro]) federal

fédéra·tif [federatif] **-tive** [tiv] *adj* federated, federative

fédération [federɑsjɔ̃] *f* federation

fédérer [federe] §10 *tr* & *ref* to federate

fée [fe] *f* fairy; **de fée** fairy; meticulous (*work*); **vieille fée** old hag

féerie [feri] *f* fairyland; fantasy

féerique [ferik] *adj* fairy, magic(al)

feindre [fɛ̃dr] §50 *tr* to feign ‖ *intr* to feign; to limp (*said of horse*)

feinte [fɛ̃t] *f* feint

feinter [fɛ̃te] *tr* (coll) to trick ‖ *intr* to feint

feldspath [fɛldspat], [fɛlspat] *m* feldspar

fê·lé **-lée** [fele] *adj* (coll) cracked, crazy

fêler [fele] *tr* to crack

félicitations [felisitɑsjɔ̃] *fpl* congratulations

féliciter [felisite] *tr* to congratulate; **féliciter qn de** + *inf* to congratulate s.o. for + *ger;* **féliciter qn de** or **pour** to congratulate s.o. for ‖ *ref—se* **féliciter de** to congratulate oneself on, to be pleased with oneself because of

fé·lon [felɔ̃] **-lonne** [lɔn] *adj* disloyal, treasonable

félonie [feloni] *f* disloyalty, treason

fêlure [felyr] *f* crack, chink

femelle [fəmɛl] *adj* & *f* female

fémi·nin [feminɛ̃] **-nine** [nin] *adj* & *m* feminine

féminisme [feminism] *m* feminism

femme [fam] *f* woman; wife; bride; **bonne femme** (coll) simple, good-natured woman; **femme agent** (*pl* **femmes agents**) policewoman; **femme auteur** (*pl* **femmes auteurs**) authoress; **femme de chambre** chambermaid; **femme de charge** housekeeper; **femme de journée** cleaning woman; **femme de ménage** cleaning woman; **femme d'intérieur** homebody; **femme docteur** woman doctor (*e.g., with Ph.D. degree*); **femme juge** woman judge; **femme médecin** woman doctor (*physician*); **femme pasteur** woman preacher

fendiller [fɑ̃dije] *tr* & *ref* to crack

fendoir [fɑ̃dwar] *m* cleaver, chopper

fendre [fɑ̃dr] *tr* to crack; to split (*e.g., wood*); to cleave (*e.g., the air*); to break (*one's heart*); to elbow one's way through (*a crowd*) ‖ *ref* to crack; (escr) to lunge

fenêtre [fənɛtr] *f* window; **fenêtre à battants** casement window, French window; **fenêtre à guillotine** sash window; **fenêtre en saillie** bay window

fenil [fənil], [fəni] *m* hayloft

fenouil [fənuj] *m* fennel; **fenouil bâtard** dill

fente [fɑ̃t] *f* crack, split, fissure; notch; slot (*e.g., in a coin telephone*); (escr) lunge

féo·dal **-dale** [feɔdal] *adj* (*pl* **-daux** [do]) feudal

féodalisme [feɔdalism] *m* feudalism

fer [fɛr] *m* iron; head (*of tool*); point (*of weapon*); **croiser le fer avec** to cross swords with; **fer à cheval** horseshoe; **fer à friser** curling iron; **fer à marquer** or **flétrir** branding iron; **fer à repasser** iron, flatiron; **fer à souder** soldering iron; **fer de fonte** cast iron; **fer forgé** wrought iron; **fers** irons, chains, fetters; **marquer au fer** to brand; **remuer le fer dans la plaie** (coll) to rub it in

ferblanterie [fɛrblɑ̃tri] *f* tinware; tinwork, sheet-metal work; tinsmith's shop

ferblantier [fɛrblɑ̃tje] *m* tinsmith

fé·rié **-riée** [ferje] *adj* feast (*day*)

férir [ferir] *tr*—**sans coup férir** without striking a blow

ferler [fɛrle] *tr* (naut) to furl

fermage [fɛrmaʒ] *m* tenant farming; rent

ferme [fɛrm] *adj* firm || *f* farm, tenant farm; farmhouse || *adv* firmly, fast

fer·mé **-mée** [fɛrme] *adj* exclusive, restricted; inscrutable (*countenance*)

ferment [fɛrmɑ̃] *m* ferment

fermenter [fɛrmɑ̃te] *intr* to ferment

fermer [fɛrme] *tr* to close, to shut; to turn off; **fermer à clef** to lock; **fermer au verrou** to bolt; **la ferme!** (slang) shut up!, shut your trap! || *intr & ref* to close, to shut

fermeté [fɛrməte] *f* firmness

fermeture [fɛrmətyr] *f* closing; fastening; **fermeture éclair** zipper

fer·mier [fɛrmje] **-mière** [mjɛr] *adj* farming || *m* farmer; tenant farmer; lessee || *f* farmer's wife

fermoir [fɛrmwar] *m* snap, clasp

féroce [ferɔs] *adj* ferocious

férocité [ferɔsite] *f* ferocity

ferraille [fɛrɑj] *f* scrap iron; (coll) small change; **mettre à la ferraille** to junk

ferrailleur [fɛrɑjœr] *m* dealer in scrap iron; sword rattler

fer·ré **-rée** [fɛre] *adj* ironclad; hobnailed (*shoe*); paved (*road*); **ferré sur** well versed in

ferrer [fɛre] *tr* to shoe (*a horse*)

ferret [fɛre] *m* tag (*of shoelace*); (geol) hard core

ferronnerie [fɛrɔnri] *f* ironwork; hardware

ferron·nier [fɛrɔnje] **ferron·nière** [fɛrɔnjɛr] *mf* ironworker; hardware dealer

ferrotypie [fɛrɔtipi] *f* tintype

ferroviaire [fɛrɔvjɛr] *adj* railway

ferrure [fɛryr] *f* horseshoeing; **ferrures** hardware; metal trim

ferry-boat [feribot] *m* (*pl* **-boats**) train ferry

fertile [fɛrtil] *adj* fertile

fertiliser [fɛrtilize] *tr* to fertilize

fertilité [fɛrtilite] *f* fertility

fé·ru **-rue** [fery] *adj*—**féru de** wrapped up in (*an idea, an interest*)

fer·vent [fɛrvɑ̃] **-vente** [vɑ̃t] *adj* fervent || *mf* devotee

ferveur [fɛrvœr] *f* fervor

fesse [fɛs] *f* buttock

fessée [fɛse] *f* spanking

fesse-mathieu [fɛsmatjø] *m* (*pl* **-mathieux**) usurer; skinflint

fesser [fɛse] *tr* to spank

fes·su **-sue** [fɛsy] *adj* broad-bottomed

festin [fɛstɛ̃] *m* feast, banquet

festi·val [fɛstival] *m* (*pl* **-vals**) music festival

festivité [fɛstivite] *f* festivity

feston [fɛstɔ̃] *m* festoon

festonner [fɛstɔne] *tr* to festoon; to scallop

festoyer [fɛstwaye] §47 *tr* to fete, regale || *intr* to feast

fê·tard [fɛtar] **-tarde** [tard] *mf* merrymaker

fête [fɛt] *f* festival; feast day, holiday; name day; party, festivity; **être à la fête** (coll) to be very pleased or gratified; **faire fête à** to receive with open arms; **faire la fête** (coll) to carouse; **fête foraine** carnival; **fête légale** or **fête nationale** legal holiday; **la fête des Mères** Mother's Day; **la fête des Morts** All Souls' Day; **la fête des Rois** Twelfth-night; **se faire une fête de** to look forward with pleasure to; **souhaiter une bonne fête à qn** to wish s.o. many happy returns

Fête-Dieu [fɛtdjø] *f* (*pl* **Fêtes-Dieu**)—**la Fête-Dieu** Corpus Christi

fêter [fɛte] *tr* to fete; to celebrate (*a special event*)

fétiche [fetiʃ] *m* fetish

fétu [fety] *m* straw; trifle

feu **feue** [fø] *adj* (*pl* **feus**) (standing before noun) late, deceased, e.g., **la feue reine** the late queen || **feu** *adj invar* (standing before article and noun) late, deceased, e.g., **la reine** the late queen || *m* (*pl* **feux**) fire; flame; traffic light; burner (*of stove*); **à petit feu** by inches; **du feu** a light (*to ignite a cigar, etc.*); **être sous les feux de la rampe** to be in the limelight; **faire du feu** to light a fire; **faire long feu** to hang fire; to fail; (arti) to miss; **feu d'artifice** fireworks; **feu de joie** bonfire; **feu de paille** (fig) flash in the pan; **feu follet** will-o'-the-wisp; **feux de position**, **feux de stationnement** parking lights; **mettre le feu à** to set on fire; **prendre feu** to catch fire || **feu** *interj* fire! (*command to fire*); **au feu!** fire! (*warning*)

feuillage [fœjaʒ] *m* foliage; **feuillages** fallen branches

feuille [fœj] *f* leaf; sheet; form (*to be filled out*); **feuille de chou** (coll) rag (*newspaper of little value*); **feuille de présence** time sheet; **feuille d'étain** tin foil; **feuille de température** temperature chart; **feuille d'imposition** income-tax blank

feuil·lé **feuil·lée** [fœje] *adj* leafy, foliaged || *f* bower; **feuillées** (mil) camp latrine

feuiller [fœje] *intr* to leaf

feuille·té -tée [fœjte] *adj* foliated; in flaky layers

feuilleter [fœjte] §34 *tr* to leaf through; to foliate; (culin) to roll into thin layers

feuilleton [fœjtɔ̃] *m* newspaper serial (*printed at bottom of page*); (rad, telv) serial

feuil·lu feuil·lue [fœjy] *adj* leafy || *m* foliage

feuillure [fœjyr] *f* groove

feuler [føle] *intr* to growl (*said of cat*)

feutre [føtr] *m* felt

feu·tré -trée [føtre] *adj* velvetlike; muffled (*steps*)

feutrer [føtre] *tr* to felt

fève [fɛv] *f* bean; fève des Rois bean or figurine baked in the Twelfth-night cake; fèves au lard pork and beans

février [fevrie] *m* February

fi [fi] *interj* fie!; faire fi de to scorn

fiacre [fjakr] *m* horse-drawn cab

fiançailles [fjɑ̃sɑj] *fpl* engagement, betrothal

fian·cé -cée [fjɑ̃se] *mf* betrothed || *m* fiancé || *f* fiancée

fiancer [fjɑ̃se] §51 *tr* to betroth || *ref* to become engaged

fiasco [fjasko] *m* (coll) fiasco, failure; faire fiasco to flop, fail

fibre [fibr] *f* fiber; (fig) feeling, sensibility; avoir la fibre sensible to be easily moved

fi·breux [fibrø] -breuse [brøz] *adj* fibrous

ficeler [fisle] §34 *tr* to tie up

ficelle [fisɛl] *adj* (coll) knowing || *f* string; connaître les ficelles (fig) to know the ropes; tenir or tirer les ficelles (fig) to pull strings; vieille ficelle (coll) old hand

fiche [fiʃ] *f* peg; slip, form, blank; filing card, index card; membership card; (cards) chip, counter; (elec) plug; fiche de consolation booby prize; fiche femelle (elec) jack; fiche perforée punch card; fiche scolaire report card

ficher [fiʃe] *tr* to drive in (*a stake*); to take down (*information on a form*); to fasten, fix, stick; ficher qn à la porte (coll) to kick s.o. out; ficher une gifle à qn (coll) to box s.o. on the ear; fichez-moi le camp! (slang) beat it! || *ref*—se ficher de (slang) to make fun of

fichier [fiʃje] *m* card catalogue; cabinet, file (*for cards or papers*)

fichtre [fiʃtrə] *interj* (coll) gosh!

fi·chu -chue [fiʃy] *adj* (coll) wretched, ugly; fichu de capable of || *m* scarf, shawl

fic·tif [fiktif] -tive [tiv] *adj* fictitious

fiction [fiksjɔ̃] *f* fiction

fidéicommis [fideikɔmi] *m* (law) trust

fidèle [fidɛl] *adj* faithful || *mf* supporter; les fidèles (eccl) the congregation, the faithful

fidélité [fidelite] *f* fidelity, faithfulness; haute fidélité high fidelity

fief·fé fief·fée [fjɛfe] *adj* (coll) downright, real, regular (*liar, coward, etc.*)

fiel [fjɛl] *m* bile; gall

fiel·leux [fjɛlø] fiel·leuse [fjɛløz] *adj* galling

fiente [fjɑ̃t] *f* droppings

fier fière [fjɛr] *adj* proud; haughty || fier [fje] *tr* (archaic) to entrust || *ref*—se fier à or en to trust, to have confidence in, to rely upon; se fier à qn de to entrust s.o. with; s'y fier to trust it

fier-à-bras [fjɛrabra] *m* (*pl* fier-à-bras or fiers-à-bras [fjɛrabra]) braggart

fierté [fjɛrte] *f* pride

fièvre [fjɛvr] *f* fever; fièvre aphteuse foot-and-mouth disease

fifre [fifr] *m* fife; fife player

fi·gé -gée [fiʒe] *adj* curdled; fixed, set; frozen (*smile*); figé sur place rooted to the spot

figement [fiʒmɑ̃] *m* clotting, coagulation

figer [fiʒe] §38 *tr* to curdle; to stop dead || *ref* to curdle; to set, to freeze (*said, e.g., of smile*)

fignoler [fiɲɔle] *tr* to work carefully at || *intr* to be finicky

figue [fig] *f* fig; figue de Barbarie prickly pear

figuier [figje] *m* fig tree

figu·rant [figyrɑ̃] -rante [rɑ̃t] *mf* (theat) supernumerary, extra

figura·tif [figyratif] -tive [tiv] *adj* figurative, emblematic

figure [figyr] *f* figure; face (*of a person*); face card; faire figure to cut a figure; figure de proue (naut) figurehead; prendre figure to take shape

figu·ré -rée [figyre] *adj* figurative; figured || *m* figurative sense

figurer [figyre] *tr* to figure || *intr* to figure, take part; (theat) to walk on || *ref* to imagine, believe

fil [fil] *m* thread; wire; edge (*e.g., of knife*); grain (*of wood*); au fil de l'eau with the stream; droit fil with the grain; elle lui a donné du fil à retordre (fig) she gave him more than he bargained for; fil à plomb plumb line; fil de fer barbelé barbed wire; fil de lin yarn; fil d'or spun gold; fils de la vierge gossamer; passer au fil de l'épée to put to the sword; plein de fils stringy; sans fil wireless

filament [filamɑ̃] *m* filament

filamen·teux [filamɑ̃tø] -teuse [tøz] *adj* stringy

filan·dreux [filɑ̃drø] -dreuse [drøz] *adj* stringy (*meat*); long, drawn-out

fi·lant [filɑ̃] -lante [lɑ̃t] *adj* ropy (*liquid*); shooting (*star*)

filasse [filas] *f* tow, oakum

filature [filatyr] *f* manufacture of thread; spinning mill; shadowing (*of a suspect*)

fil-de-fériste [fildəferist] *mf* tightwire walker

file [fil] *f* file, row, lane; à la file one after another, in a row; file d'attente waiting line; marcher en file indienne to walk Indian file

filer [file] *tr* to spin; to pay out (*rope, cable*); to prolong; to shadow (*a suspect*) || *intr* to ooze; to smoke (*said of lamp*); (coll) to go fast; filer à

l'anglaise (coll) to take French leave; **filer doux** (coll) to back down, to give in; **filez!** (coll) get out!
filet [filɛ] *m* net; trickle (*of water*); streak (*of light*); thread (*of screw or nut*); (culin) fillet; (typ) rule; **faux filet** sirloin; **filet à bagage** baggage rack; **filet à cheveux** hair net; **filet à provisions** string bag, mesh bag
fileter [filte] §2 *tr* to thread (*a screw*); to draw (*wire*)
fi·leur [filœr] **-leuse** [løz] *mf* spinner
fi·lial -liale [filjal] *adj* (*pl* -liaux [ljo]) filial ‖ *f* (com) branch, subsidiary
filiation [filjɑsjɔ̃] *f* filiation
filière [filjɛr] *f* (mach) die; (mach) drawplate; **filière administrative** official channels; **passer par la filière** (coll) to go through channels; (coll) to work one's way up
filigrane [filigran] *m* filigree; watermark (*in paper*)
filigraner [filigrane] *tr* to filigree
filin [filɛ̃] *m* (naut) rope
fille [fij] *f* daughter; unmarried girl; servant; (pej) tart; **fille de joie, des rues, or de vie, fille publique** prostitute; **fille de salle** nurse's aid; **fille d'honneur** bridesmaid; **jeune fille** girl; **vieille fille** old maid
fillette [fijet] *f* young girl, little lass
fil·leul fil·leule [fijœl] *mf* godchild ‖ *m* godson ‖ *f* goddaughter
film [film] *m* film; (fig) train (*of events*); **film sonore** sound film
filmage [filmaʒ] *m* filming
filmer [filme] *tr* to film
filmique [filmik] *adj* film
filon [filɔ̃] *m* vein, lode; (coll) soft job; (coll) bonanza, strike; **filon guide** leader vein
filoselle [filɔzɛl] *f* floss silk
filou [filu] *m* sneak thief; cheat, sharper
filouter [filute] *tr* (coll) to swindle, cheat; **filouter q.ch. à qn** (coll) to do s.o. out of s.th. ‖ *intr* to cheat at cards
fils [fis] *m* son; (when following proper name) junior; **fils à papa** (coll) rich man's son, playboy; **fils de ses œuvres** (fig) self-made man
filtrage [filtraʒ] *m* filtering; surveillance (*by the police*)
fil·trant [filtrɑ̃] **-trante** [trɑ̃t] *adj* filterable; filter, e.g., **papier filtrant** filter paper
filtre [filtrə] *m* filter
filtrer [filtre] *tr & intr* to filter
fin [fɛ̃] **fine** [fin] *adj* fine ‖ (when standing before noun) *adj* clever, sly, smart; secret, hidden ‖ *m* fine linen; smart person; **le fin du fin** the finest of the fine ‖ **fin** *f* end; **à la fin** at last; **à seule fin de** for the sole purpose of; **à toutes fins utiles** for your information; **c'est la fin des haricots** (slang) that takes the cake; **en fin de compte** in the end; to get to the point; **fin d'interdiction de dépasser** (public sign) end of no passing; **mot de la fin** clincher; **sans**

fin endless ‖ **fin** *adv* absolutely; finely (*ground*); small, e.g., **écrire fin** to write small
fi·nal -nale [final] (*pl* -nals or -naux [no]) *adj* final ‖ *m* finale ‖ *f* last syllable or letter; (mus) keynote; (sports) finals
finalement [finalmɑ̃] *adv* finally
finaliste [finalist] *mf* finalist
financement [finɑ̃smɑ̃] *m* financing
financer [finɑ̃se] §51 *tr* to finance
finan·cier [finɑ̃sje] **-cière** [sjɛr] *adj* financial; spicy (*sauce for vol-au-vent*) ‖ *m* financier
finasser [finase] *intr* (coll) to use finesse, to finagle
finasserie [finasri] *f* shrewdness
fi·naud [fino] **-naude** [nod] *adj* wily, sly ‖ *mf* sly fox; smart aleck
finesse [fines] *f* finesse; fineness; **savoir les finesses** to know the fine points or niceties
fi·ni -nie [fini] *adj* finished; finite; ruined (*in health, financially, etc.*); arrant (*rogue*) ‖ *m* finish; finite
finir [finir] *tr & intr* to finish; **en finir avec** to have done with; **finir de** + *inf* to finish + *ger;* **finir par** + *inf* to finish by + *inf*
finissage [finisaʒ] *m* finishing touch, final step
finition [finisjɔ̃] *f* finish; **finitions** finishing touches
finlan·dais [fɛ̃lɑ̃dɛ] **-daise** [dɛz] *adj* Finnish ‖ *m* Finnish (*language*) ‖ (*cap*) *mf* Finn
Finlande [fɛ̃lɑ̃d] *f* Finland; **la Finlande** Finland
fin·nois [finwa] **fin·noise** [finwaz] *adj* Finnish ‖ *m* Finnish (*language;* Finnic (*branch of Uralic*) ‖ (*cap*) *mf* Finn
fiole [fjɔl] *f* phial
fioriture [fjɔrityr] *f* flourish, curlicue
firmament [firmamɑ̃] *m* firmament
firme [firm] *f* firm, house, company
fisc [fisk] *m* bureau of internal revenue, tax-collection agency
fis·cal -cale [fiskal] *adj* (*pl* -caux [ko]) fiscal; revenue, taxation
fiscaliser [fiskalize] *tr* to subject to tax
fiscalité [fiskalite] *f* tax collections; fiscal policy
fissile [fisil] *adj* fissionable
fission [fisjɔ̃] *f* fission
fissure [fisyr] *f* fissure, crack
fissurer [fisyre] *tr & ref* to fissure
fiston [fistɔ̃] *m* (slang) sonny
fixation [fiksɑsjɔ̃] *f* fixation; fixing
fixe [fiks] *adj* fixed; permanent (*ink*); glassy (*stare*); regular (*time*); set (*price*); standing (*rule*) ‖ *m* fixed income ‖ *interj* (mil) eyes front!
fixe-chaussette [fiksəʃoset] *m* (*pl* -chaussettes) garter (*for men's socks*)
fixement [fiksəmɑ̃] *adv* fixedly
fixer [fikse] *tr* to fix; to appoint; (coll) to stare at; **fixer son choix sur** to fix on; **pour fixer les idées** for the sake of argument ‖ *ref* to be fastened; to establish residence; to make up one's mind
flacon [flakɔ̃] *m* small bottle; flask

flageller [flaʒɛlle] *tr* to flagellate
flageoler [flaʒɔle] *intr* to quiver
flageolet [flaʒɔlɛ] *m* flageolet; kidney bean
flagorner [flagɔrne] *tr* to flatter
fla·grant [flagrɑ̃] -grante [grɑ̃t] *adj* flagrant, glaring, obvious
flair [flɛr] *m* scent, sense of smell; (*discernment*) flair, keen nose
flairer [flɛre] *tr* to smell, to sniff; to scent, to smell out
fla·mand [flamɑ̃] -mande [mɑ̃d] *adj* Flemish ‖ *m* Flemish (*language*) ‖ (*cap*) *mf* Fleming (*person*)
flamant [flamɑ̃] *m* flamingo
flam·bant [flɑ̃bɑ̃] -bante [bɑ̃t] *adj* flaming; flambant neuf (coll) brand-new
flam·beau [flɑ̃bo] *m* (*pl* -beaux) torch; candlestick; large wax candle; (fig) light
flambée [flɑ̃be] *f* blaze
flamber [flɑ̃be] *tr* to singe; to sterilize; être flambé (coll) to be all washed up, ruined ‖ *intr* to flame
flamberge [flɑ̃bɛrʒ] *f* (archaic) sword, blade; mettre flamberge au vent to unsheathe the sword
flamboiement [flɑ̃bwamɑ̃] *m* glow, flare
flamboyant [flɑ̃bwajɑ̃] flamboyante [flɑ̃bwajɑ̃t] *adj* flaming, blazing; (archit) flamboyant
flamboyer [flɑ̃bwaje] §47 *intr* to flame
flamme [flɑm], [flam] *f* flame; pennant
flammèche [flamɛʃ] *f* ember, large spark
flan [flɑ̃] *m* custard; blank (*coin, medal, record*); à la flan (slang) happy-go-lucky; botched (*job*); c'est du flan (slang) it's ridiculous
flanc [flɑ̃] *m* flank; side (*of ship, mountain, etc.*); battre du flanc to pant; être sur le flanc (coll) to be laid up; flancs (archaic) womb; bosom; prêter le flanc à to lay oneself open to; se battre les flancs to go to a lot of trouble for nothing; tirer au flanc (coll) to gold-brick, to malinger
flancher [flɑ̃ʃe] *intr* (coll) to give in; (coll) to weaken, give way
flanchet [flɑ̃ʃɛ] *m* flank (*of beef*)
Flandre [flɑ̃dr] *f* Flanders; la Flandre Flanders
flanelle [flanɛl] *f* flannel
flâner [flɑne] *intr* to stroll, saunter; to loaf
flânerie [flɑnri] *f* strolling; loafing
flâ·neur [flɑnœr] -neuse [nøz] *mf* stroller; loafer
flanquer [flɑ̃ke] *tr* to flank; (coll) to throw, fling; flanquer à la porte (coll) to kick out; flanquer un coup à (coll) to take a swing at
fla·pi -pie [flapi] *adj* (coll) tired out, fagged out
flaque [flak] *f* puddle, pool
flash [flaʃ] *m* (*pl* flashes) news flash; (phot) flash attachment; (phot) flash bulb

flasque [flask] *adj* flabby ‖ *m* metal trim ‖ *f* flask; powder horn
flatter [flate] *tr* to flatter; to stroke; to delight; to cater to; to delude ‖ *intr* to flatter ‖ *ref—se* flatter de to flatter oneself on
flatterie [flatri] *f* flattery
flat·teur [flatœr] flat·teuse [flatøz] *adj* flattering ‖ *mf* flatterer
flatulence [flatylɑ̃s] *f* (pathol) flatulence
flatuosité [flatɥozite] *f* (pathol) flatulence
fléau [fleo] *m* (*pl* fléaux) flail; beam (*of balance*); (fig) scourge, plague
flèche [flɛʃ] *f* arrow; spire (*of church*); boom (*of crane*); flitch (*of bacon*); en flèche like an arrow; in tandem; faire flèche de tout bois to leave no stone unturned; flèche d'eau (bot) arrowhead
fléchette [fleʃɛt] *f* dart (*used in game*)
fléchir [fleʃir] *tr* to bend; to move (*e.g., to pity*) ‖ *intr* to bend, give way; to weaken, to flag; to go down, to sag (*said of prices*)
flegmatique [flɛgmatik] *adj* phlegmatic, stolid
flegme [flɛgm] *m* phlegm
flemme [flɛm] *f* (slang) sluggishness; tirer sa flemme (slang) to not lift a finger
flet [flɛ] *m* flounder
flétan [fletɑ̃] *m* halibut
flétrir [fletrir] *tr* & *ref* to fade, wither; to weaken
flétrissure [fletrisyr] *f* fading, withering; branding (*of criminals*); blot, stigma
fleur [flœr] *f* flower; blossom; à fleur de level with, even with; on the surface of; à fleur de peau skin-deep; à fleur de tête bulging (*eyes*); en fleur in bloom; en fleurs in bloom (*said of group of different varieties*); fleur de farine fine white flour; fleur de l'âge prime of life; fleur de lis [flœrdəlis] fleur-de-lis; fleur des pois (coll) pick of the lot; fleurs mold (*on wine, cider, etc.*)
fleurer [flœre] *intr* to exhale or give off an odor; fleurer bon to smell good
fleuret [flœrɛ] *m* fencing foil
fleurette [flœrɛt] *f* little flower; conter fleurette to flirt
fleu·ri -rie [flœri] *adj* in bloom; flowery; florid (*complexion; style*)
fleurir [flœrir] *tr* to decorate with flowers ‖ *intr* to flower, bloom ‖ *intr* (*ger* florissant; *imperf* florissais, etc.) to flourish
fleuriste [flœrist] *mf* florist; floral gardener; maker or seller of artificial flowers
fleuron [flœrɔ̃] *m* floret; (archit) finial; fleuron à sa couronne feather in his cap
fleuve [flœv] *m* river (*flowing directly to the sea*); (fig) river (*of tears, blood, etc.*)
flexible [flɛksibl] *adj* flexible; (fig) pliant

flexion [flɛksjɔ̃] *f* bending, flexion; (gram) inflection
flibuster [flibyste] *tr* to rob, to snitch ‖ *intr* to filibuster
flibustier [flibystje] *m* filibuster (*pirate*)
flic [flik] *m* (slang) copper, fuzz
flirt [flœrt] *m* flirt; flirtation
flirter [flœrte] *intr* to flirt
flir·teur [flœrtœr] -**teuse** [tøz] *adj* flirtatious ‖ *mf* flirt
flocon [flɔkɔ̃] *m* flake; snowflake; tuft (*e.g.*, *of wool*); **flocons d'avoine** oatmeal; **flocons de maïs** cornflakes; **flocons de neige** snowflakes
floconner [flɔkɔne] *intr* to form flakes; to become fleecy
flocon·neux [flɔkɔnø] **flocon·neuse** [flɔkɔnøz] *adj* flaky; fleecy
floraison [flɔrɛzɔ̃] *f* flowering, blooming
flo·ral -**rale** [flɔral] *adj* (*pl* -**raux** [ro]) floral
floralies [flɔrali] *fpl* flower show
flore [flɔr] *f* flora
floren·tin [flɔrɑ̃tɛ̃] -**tine** [tin] *adj* Florentine; **à la florentine** with spinach ‖ (*cap*) *mf* Florentine (*native or inhabitant of Florence*)
Floride [flɔriʔ] *f* Florida; **la Floride** Florida
florilège [flɔrilɛʒ] *m* anthology
floris·sant [flɔrisɑ̃] **floris·sante** [flɔrisɑ̃t] *adj* flourishing
floss [flɔs] *m* (coll) dental floss
flot [flo] *m* wave; tide; flood, multitude; **à flot** afloat; **à flots** in torrents, abundantly; **flots** waters (*of a lake, the sea, etc.*); **flots de** lots of
flottabilité [flɔtabilite] *f* buoyancy
flottable [flɔtabl] *adj* buoyant; navigable (*for rafts*)
flottage [flɔtaʒ] *m* log driving
flottaison [flɔtɛzɔ̃] *f* water line
flot·tant [flɔtɑ̃] **flot·tante** [flɔtɑ̃t] *adj* floating; vacillating, undecided
flotte [flɔt] *f* fleet; buoy; float (*on fishline*); (slang) water, rain
flottement [flɔtmɑ̃] *m* floating; hesitation, vacillation; undulation
flotter [flɔte] *intr* to float; to waver, hesitate; to fly (*said of flag*); **il flotte** (slang) it is raining
flotteur [flɔtœr] *m* log driver; float (*of fishline, carburetor, etc.*); pontoon, float (*of seaplane*)
flottille [flɔtij] *f* flotilla; **flottille de pêche** fishing fleet
flou floue [flu] *adj* blurred, hazy; fluffy (*hair*); loose-fitting (*dress*); light and soft (*tones, lines in a painting*) ‖ *m* blur, fuzziness; dressmaking
fluctuation [flyktɥɑsjɔ̃] *f* fluctuation
fluctuer [flyktɥe] *intr* to fluctuate
fluet [flyɛ] **fluette** [flyɛt] *adj* thin, slender
fluide [flɥid] *adj & m* fluid
fluidifier [flɥidifje] *tr* to liquefy
fluor [flyɔr] *m* fluorine
fluores·cent [flyɔresɑ̃] **fluores·cente** [flyɔresɑ̃t] *adj* fluorescent
fluoridation [flyɔridɑsjɔ̃] *f* fluoridation
fluorider [flyɔride] *tr & intr* to fluoridate

fluorure [flyɔryr] *m* fluoride
flûte [flyt] *f* flute; long thin loaf of French bread; tall champagne glass; **flûte à bec** recorder; **flûte de Pan** Pan's pipes; **flûtes** (slang) legs; **grande flûte** concert flute; **jouer or se tirer des flûtes** (slang) to run for it; **petite flûte** piccolo ‖ *interj* shucks!, rats!
flûtiste [flytist] *mf* flutist
flux [fly] *m* flow; flood tide; (cards) flush; (chem, elec, med, metallurgy) flux; **flux de sang** flush, blush; dysentery; **flux de ventre** diarrhea; **flux et reflux** ebb and flow
fluxion [flyksjɔ̃] *f* inflammation
foc [fɔk] *m* (naut) jib
fo·cal -**cale** [fɔkal] *adj* (*pl* -**caux** [ko]) focal
fœtus [fetys] *m* fetus
foi [fwa] *f* faith; word (*of a gentleman*); **ajouter foi à** to give credence to; **bonne foi** good faith, sincerity; **de bonne foi** sincere; sincerely; **de mauvaise foi** dishonest; dishonestly; **en foi de quoi** in witness whereof; **faire foi de** to be evidence of; **ma foi!** upon my word; **manquer de foi** à to break faith with; **mauvaise foi** bad faith, insincerity; **sur la foi de** on the strength of
foie [fwa] *m* liver; **avoir les foies** (slang) to be scared stiff; **foie gras** goose liver
foin [fwɛ̃] *m* hay; **avoir du foin dans ses bottes** (coll) to be well heeled; **faire du foin** (slang) to kick up a fuss
foire [fwar] *f* fair; market; (coll) chaos, mess; **foire d'empoigne** free-for-all
foirer [fware] *intr* (slang) to flop, fail; (slang) to hang fire; (slang) to be stripped (*said of screw, nut, etc.*)
fois [fwa] *f* time, e.g., **visiter trois fois par semaine** to visit three times a week; times, e.g., **deux fois deux font quatre** two times two is four; **à la fois** at the same time, together; **deux fois** twice; twofold; **encore une fois** once more, again; **il y avait une fois** once upon a time there was; **maintes et maintes fois** time and time again; **une fois** one time, once; **une fois pour toutes** or **une bonne fois** once and for all
foison [fwazɔ̃] *f*—**à foison** in abundance
foison·nant [fwazɔnɑ̃] **foison·nante** [fwazɔnɑ̃t] *adj* abundant, plentiful
foisonner [fwazɔne] *intr* to abound
folâtre [fɔlɑtr] *adj* frisky, playful
folâtrer [fɔlɑtre] *intr* to frolic, romp
folie [fɔli] *f* madness, insanity; folly, piece of folly; country lodge, hideaway (*for romantic trysts*); **à la folie** madly, passionately; **faire une folie** to do something crazy; **folie de la persécution** persecution complex
folio [fɔljo] *m* folio
folioter [fɔljɔte] *tr* to folio
folle [fɔl] *f* crazy woman
follement [fɔlmɑ̃] *adv* madly

fol·let [fɔlɛ] **fol·lette** [fɔlɛt] *adj* merry, playful; elfish

follicule [fɔlikyl] *m* follicle

fomenta·teur [fɔmɑ̃tatœr] **-trice** [tris] *mf* agitator, troublemaker

fomenter [fɔmɑ̃te] *tr* to foment

fon·cé -cée [fɔ̃se] *adj* dark; deep

foncer [fɔ̃se] §51 *tr* to darken; to dig (*a well*); to fit a bottom to (*a cask*) || *intr* to charge, to rush

fon·cier [fɔ̃sje] **-cière** [sjɛr] *adj* landed (*property*); property (*tax*); fundamental, natural || *m* real-estate tax

foncièrement [fɔ̃sjɛrmɑ̃] *adv* fundamentally, naturally

fonction [fɔ̃ksjɔ̃] *f* function; duty; **faire fonction de** to function as

fonctionnaire [fɔ̃ksjɔnɛr] *mf* civil servant; officeholder

fonctionnarisme [fɔ̃ksjɔnarism] *m* bureaucracy

fonction·nel -nelle [fɔ̃ksjɔnɛl] *adj* functional

fonctionner [fɔ̃ksjɔne] *intr* to function, to work

fond [fɔ̃] *m* bottom; back, far end; background; foundation; dregs; core, inner meaning, main issue; **à fond** thoroughly; **à fond de train** at full speed; **au fond, dans le fond,** or **par le fond** actually, really, basically; **de fond** fundamental, main; **de fond en comble** from top to bottom; **faire fond sur** to rely on; **fond sonore** background noise; **râcler les fonds du tiroir** to scrape the bottom of the barrel; **sans fond** bottomless; **y aller au fond** to go the whole way || see **fonds**

fondamen·tal -tale [fɔ̃damɑ̃tal] *adj* (*pl* **-taux** [to]) fundamental, basic

fon·dant [fɔ̃dɑ̃] **-dante** [dɑ̃t] *adj* melting; juicy, luscious || *m* fondant (*candy*); (metallurgy) flux

fonda·teur [fɔ̃datœr] **-trice** [tris] *mf* founder

fondation [fɔ̃dɑsjɔ̃] *f* foundation; founding; endowment

fon·dé -dée [fɔ̃de] *adj* founded; justified; authorized; **bien fondé** well-founded || *m*—**fondé de pouvoir** proxy, authorized agent

fondement [fɔ̃dmɑ̃] *m* foundation, basis; (coll) behind; **sans fondement** unfounded

fonder [fɔ̃de] *tr* to found

fonderie [fɔ̃dri] *f* foundry; smelting

fondeur [fɔ̃dœr] *m* founder, smelter

fondre [fɔ̃dr] *tr* to melt, dissolve; to smelt; to cast (*metal*); to blend (*colors*); to merge (*companies*) || *intr* to melt; (coll) to lose weight; **fondre en larmes** to burst into tears; **fondre sur** to pounce on

fondrière [fɔ̃drijɛr] *f* quagmire; mudhole, rut, pothole

fonds [fɔ̃] *m* land (*of an estate*); business, good will; fund; **bon fonds** good nature; **fonds** *mpl* capital; **fonds de commerce** business house; **fonds de prévoyance** reserve fund; **fonds d'État** *mpl* government bonds

fon·du -due [fɔ̃dy] *adj* melted; molten

|| *m* blending (*of colors*); (mov, telv) dissolve, fade-out

fontaine [fɔ̃tɛn] *f* fountain; spring; well; cistern; **fontaine de Jouvence** Fountain of Youth

fonte [fɔ̃t] *f* melting; casting; cast iron; holster; (typ) font; **venir de fonte avec** to be cast in one piece with

fonts [fɔ̃] *mpl*—**fonts baptismaux** baptismal font

football [futbol] *m* soccer

footing [futiŋ] *m* walking

for [fɔr] *m*—**dans son for intérieur** in his heart of hearts; **for intérieur** conscience

forage [fɔraʒ] *m* drilling

fo·rain [fɔrɛ̃] **-raine** [rɛn] *adj* traveling, itinerant || **forains** *mpl* carnival people

forban [fɔrbɑ̃] *m* pirate

forçage [fɔrsaʒ] *m* (agr) forcing

forçat [fɔrsa] *m* convict; (hist) galley slave; (fig) drudge

force [fɔrs] *f* force; strength; **à force de** by dint of, as a result of; **à toute force** at all costs; **de première force** foremost (*musician, artist, scientist, etc.*); **de toutes ses forces** with all one's might; **force de frappe** striking force; **force m'est de . . .** (lit) I am obliged to . . . ; **force majeure** (law) act of God; **forces** sheep shears; **force vive** (phys) kinetic energy; **la force de l'âge** the prime of life || *adj invar* (archaic) many

forcément [fɔrsemɑ̃] *adv* inevitably, necessarily

force·né -née [fɔrsəne] *adj* frenzied, frantic || *m* madman || *f* crazy woman

forceps [fɔrsɛps] *m* (obstet) forceps

forcer [fɔrse] §51 *tr* to force; to do violence to; to bring to bay; to increase (*the dose*); to strain (*a muscle*); to mark up (*a receipt*); **forcer la main à qn** to force s.o.'s hand; **forcer la note** (coll) to overdo it; **forcer le respect de qn** to compel respect from s.o.; **forcer qn à** or **de** + *inf* to force s.o. to + *inf* || *ref* to overdo; to do violence to one's feelings

forclore [fɔrklɔr] (used only in *inf* and *pp* **forclos**) *tr* to foreclose

forclusion [fɔrklyzjɔ̃] *f* foreclosure

forer [fɔre] *tr* to drill, to bore

fores·tier [fɔrɛstje] **-tière** [tjɛr] *adj* forest || *m* forester

foret [fɔrɛ] *m* drill

forêt [fɔrɛ] *f* forest

fo·reur [fɔrœr] **-reuse** [røz] *adj* drilling || *mf* driller || *f* drill, machine drill

forfaire [fɔrfɛr] §29 (used only in *inf*; 1st, 2d, & 3d *sg pres ind*; compound tenses) *intr*—**forfaire à** to forfeit (*one's honor*); to fail in (*a duty*)

forfait [fɔrfɛ] *m* heinous crime; contract; package deal; (turf) forfeit; **à forfait** for a lump sum

forfaitaire [fɔrfɛter] *adj* contractual

forfaiture [fɔrfɛtyr] *f* malfeasance

forfanterie [fɔrfɑ̃tri] *f* bragging

forge [fɔrʒ] *f* forge; steel mill
forger [fɔrʒe] §38 *tr* to forge
forgeron [fɔrʒərɔ̃] *m* blacksmith
forgeur [fɔrʒœr] *m* forger, smith; coiner (*e.g., of new expressions*); fabricator (*of false stories*)
formaliser [fɔrmalize] *ref* to take offense
formaliste [fɔrmalist] *adj* formalistic, conventional || *mf* formalist
formalité [fɔrmalite] *f* formality, convention
format [fɔrma] *m* size, format
formation [fɔrmasjɔ̃] *f* formation; education, training
forme [fɔrm] *f* form; **en forme** fit, in shape; **en forme, en bonne forme,** or **en bonne et due forme** in order, in due form; **pour la forme** for appearances
for·mel -melle [fɔrmɛl] *adj* explicit; strict; formal, superficial
formellement [fɔrmɛlmɑ̃] *adv* absolutely, strictly
former [fɔrme] *tr & ref* to form
formidable [fɔrmidabl] *adj* formidable; (coll) tremendous, terrific
formulaire [fɔrmylɛr] *m* formulary; form (*with spaces for answers*)
formule [fɔrmyl] *f* formula; form, blank; format; **formule de politesse** complimentary close
formuler [fɔrmyle] *tr* to formulate; to draw up
fort [fɔr] **forte** [fɔrt] *adj* strong; fortified (*city*); **c'est fort!** it's hard to believe! || (when standing before noun) *adj* high (*fever*); large (*sum*); hard (*task*) || *m* fort; strong man; forte; height (*of summer*) || **fort** *adv* exceedingly; loud; hard
forteresse [fɔrtərɛs] *f* fortress, fort
forti·fiant [fɔrtifjɑ̃] **-fiante** [fjɑ̃t] *adj & m* tonic
fortification [fɔrtifikasjɔ̃] *f* fortification
fortifier [fɔrtifje] *tr* to fortify; to confirm (*one's opinions*)
fortin [fɔrtɛ̃] *m* small fort
for·tuit [fɔrtɥi] **-tuite** [tɥit] *adj* fortuitous, accidental
fortune [fɔrtyn] *f* fortune; **faire fortune** to make a fortune
fortu·né -née [fɔrtyne] *adj* fortunate; rich
fosse [fos] *f* pit; grave; **fosse aux lions** lions' den; **fosse commune** pauper's grave; **fosse d'aisances** cesspool; **fosse septique** septic tank
fossé [fose] *m* ditch, trench; moat; **sauter le fossé** to take the plunge
fossette [fosɛt] *f* dimple
fossile [fosil] *adj & m* fossil || *mf* fossil (*person*)
fossoyeur [foswajœr] *m* gravedigger
fou [fu] or **fol** [fɔl] **folle** [fɔl] (*pl* **fous folles**) *adj* mad, insane; foolish; extravagant; unsteady; loose (*pulley*); (coll) tremendous (*success*); **être fou à lier** to be raving mad; **être fou de** to be wild about; to be wild with (*joy, pain, etc.*) || **fou** *m* madman; fool; jester; (cards) joker; (chess) bishop || *f* see **folle**

foucade [fukad] *f* whim, impulse
foudre [fudr] *m* thunderbolt (*of Zeus*); large cask; **foudre de guerre** great captain; **foudre d'éloquence** powerful orator || *f* lightning; **foudres** displeasure (*e.g., of a prince*); **foudres de l'Église** excommunication
foudroyant [fudrwajɑ̃] **foudroyante** [fudrwajɑ̃t] *adj* lightning-like; crushing, overwhelming
foudroyer [fudrwaje] §47 *tr* to strike with lightning; to strike suddenly; to dumfound; **foudroyer d'un regard** to cast a withering glance at || *intr* to hurl thunderbolts
fouet [fwɛ] *m* whip; (culin) beater
fouetter [fwɛte] *tr & intr* to whip
fougère [fuʒɛr] *f* fern
fougue [fug] *f* spirit, ardor
fou·gueux [fugø] **-gueuse** [gøz] *adj* spirited, fiery, impetuous
fouille [fuj] *f* excavation; search
fouiller [fuje] *tr* to excavate; to search, comb, inspect
fouillis [fuji] *m* jumble, disorder
fouine [fwin] *f* beech marten; pitchfork; harpoon
fouiner [fwine] *intr* (coll) to pry, meddle
fouir [fwir] *tr* to dig, burrow
foulard [fular] *m* scarf, neckerchief
foule [ful] *f* crowd, mob; **en foule** in great numbers
fouler [fule] *tr* to tread on, to press; to sprain || *ref* (with *dat* of *reflex pron*) to sprain; (slang) to put oneself out, to tire oneself out
foulque [fulk] *f* (zool) coot
foulure [fulyr] *f* sprain
four [fur] *m* oven; kiln, furnace; (coll) flop, turkey; **faire cuire au four** to bake; to roast; **faire four** (coll) to flop; **four à briques** brickkiln; **four à chaux** limekiln; **petit four** teacake
fourbe [furb] *adj* deceiving, cheating || *mf* deceiver, cheat
fourberie [furbəri] *f* deceit, cheating
fourbir [furbir] *tr* to furbish, polish
fourbissage [furbisaʒ] *m* furbishing, polishing
four·bu -bue [furby] *adj* broken-down (*horse*); (coll) dead tired, all in
fourche [furʃ] *f* fork; pitchfork; **fourche avant** front fork (*of bicycle*); **fourches patibulaires** (hist) gallows
fourcher [furʃe] *tr & intr* to fork; **la langue lui a fourché** (coll) he made a slip of the tongue
fourchette [furʃɛt] *f* fork; wishbone
four·chu -chue [furʃy] *adj* forked; cloven
fourgon [furgɔ̃] *m* truck; poker; (rr) baggage car; (rr) boxcar; **fourgon bancaire** armored car; **fourgon de queue** caboose; **fourgon funèbre** hearse
fourmi [furmi] *f* ant; **fourmi blanche** white ant, termite
fourmilier [furmilje] *m* anteater
fourmilière [furmiljɛr] *f* ant hill
fourmiller [furmije] *intr* to swarm; to tingle (*said, e.g., of foot*); **fourmiller de** to teem with

fournaise [furnɛz] *f* furnace; (fig) oven
four·neau [furno] *m* (*pl* -neaux) furnace; cooking stove; **haut fourneau** blast furnace
fournée [furne] *f* batch
four·ni -nie [furni] *adj* bushy, thick; **bien fourni** well-stocked
fourniment [furnimɑ̃] *m* (mil) kit
fournir [furnir] *tr* to furnish, to supply, to provide; to follow (*a suit in cards*) ‖ *intr* (with *dat*) to supply (*s.o.'s needs*); (with *dat*) to defray (*expenses*); (with *dat*) (cards) to follow (*suit*) ‖ *ref* to grow thick; to be a customer
fournissement [furnismɑ̃] *m* contribution, holdings (*of each shareholder*); statement of holdings
fournisseur [furnisœr] *m* supplier, dealer
fourniture [furnityr] *f* furnishing, supplying; (culin) seasoning; **fournitures** supplies
fourrage [furaʒ] *m* fodder
fourrager [furaʒe] §38 *tr* to forage; to rummage, to rummage through ‖ *intr* to rummage (about), to forage
fourragère [furaʒɛr] *f* lanyard; tailboard
four·ré -rée [fure] *adj* lined with fur; furred (*tongue*); stuffed (*dates*); filled (*candies*); sham, hollow (*peace*) ‖ *m* thicket
four·reau [furo] *m* (*pl* -reaux) sheath; scabbard; tight skirt; **coucher dans son fourreau** (coll) to sleep in one's clothes
fourrer [fure] *tr* to line with fur; (coll) to cram, stuff; (coll) to shut up (*in prison*); (coll) to stick, poke ‖ *ref* (coll) to turn, go; (coll) to curl up (*in bed*); **se fourrer dans** (coll) to stick one's nose in
fourre-tout [furtu] *m invar* catchall; duffel bag
fourreur [furœr] *m* furrier
fourrier [furje] *m* quartermaster
fourrière [furjɛr] *f* pound (*for automobiles; for stray dogs*)
fourrure [furyr] *f* fur
fourvoyer [furvwaje] §47 *tr* to lead astray
fox [fɔks] *m* fox terrier
fox-terrier [fɔksterje] *m* fox terrier
fox-trot [fɔkstrɔt] *m invar* fox trot
foyer [fwaje] *m* foyer, lobby; hearth, fireside; firebox; focus; home; greenroom; center (*of learning; of infection*); **à double foyer** bifocal; **foyer des étudiants** student center; **foyer du soldat** service club; **foyers** native land
frac [frak] *m* cutaway coat
fracas [fraka] *m* crash; roar (*of waves*); peal (*of thunder*)
fracasser [frakase] *tr* & *ref* to break; to shatter, break to pieces
fraction [fraksjɔ̃] *f* fraction; breaking (*e.g., of bread*)
fractionnaire [fraksjɔnɛr] *adj* fractional
fractionnement [fraksjɔnmɑ̃] *m* cracking (*of petroleum*)
fractionner [fraksjɔne] *tr* to divide into fractions
fracture [fraktyr] *f* fracture; breaking open
fracturer [fraktyre] *tr* to fracture; to break open
fragile [fraʒil] *adj* fragile
fragment [fragmɑ̃] *m* fragment
fragmenter [fragmɑ̃te] *tr* to fragment
frai [frɛ] *m* spawning; spawn, roe
fraîche [frɛʃ] *f* cool of the day
fraîchement [frɛʃmɑ̃] *adv* in the open air; recently; (coll) cordially
fraîcheur [frɛʃœr] *f* coolness; freshness; newness
fraîchir [frɛʃir] *intr* to become cooler; to freshen (*said of wind*)
frais [frɛ] **fraîche** [frɛʃ] *adj* cool; fresh; wet (*paint*); **il fait frais** it is cool out ‖ (when standing before noun) *adj* recent (*date*) ‖ *m* cool place; fresh air; **aux frais de** at the expense of; **de frais** just, freshly; **faire les frais de la conversation** (coll) to take the lead in the conversation; to be the subject of the conversation; **frais** *mpl* expenses; **se mettre en frais** (coll) to go to a great deal of expense or trouble ‖ *f* see **fraîche** ‖ **frais** *adv*—**boire frais** to have a cool drink ‖ **frais fraîche** *adv* (agrees with following *pp*) just, freshly, e.g., **garçon frais arrivé de l'école** boy just arrived from school; e.g., **roses fraîches cueillies** freshly gathered roses
fraise [frɛz] *f* strawberry; wattle (*of turkey*); (mach) countersink
fraiser [treze] *tr* (mach) to countersink
fraisier [frɛzje] *m* strawberry plant
framboise [frɑ̃bwaz] *f* raspberry
framboisier [frɑ̃bwazje] *m* raspberry bush
franc [frɑ̃] **franche** [frɑ̃ʃ] *adj* free; frank, sincere; complete ‖ (when standing before noun) *adj* arrant (*knave*); downright (*fool*) ‖ **franc franque** [frɑ̃k] *adj* Frankish ‖ *m* franc (*unit of currency*) ‖ (*cap*) *m* Frank (*medieval German*) ‖ **franc** *adv* frankly
fran·çais [frɑ̃sɛ] -çaise [sɛz] *adj* French ‖ *m* French (*language*); **en bon français** in correct French ‖ (*cap*) *m* Frenchman; **les Français** the French ‖ *f* Frenchwoman
franc-alleu [frɑ̃kalø] *m* (*pl* **francs-alleux** [frɑ̃kalø]) (hist) freehold
France [frɑ̃s] *f* France; **la France** France
franchement [frɑ̃ʃmɑ̃] *adv* frankly, sincerely; without hesitation
franchir [frɑ̃ʃir] *tr* to cross, to go over or through; to jump over; to overcome (*an obstacle*)
franchise [frɑ̃ʃiz] *f* exemption; frankness; freedom; **franchise postale** frank
francique [frɑ̃sik] *m* Frankish
franciser [frɑ̃size] *tr* to make French
franc-maçon [frɑ̃mɑsɔ̃] *m* (*pl* **francs-maçons**) Freemason

franc-maçonnerie [frãmasɔnri] *f* Freemasonry

franco [frãko] *adv* free, without shipping costs; franco de bord free on board; franco de port postpaid

franco-cana·dien [frãkɔkanadjẽ] -dienne [djɛn] *adj* French-Canadian || Franco-Cana·dien -dienne *mf* French Canadian

francophone [frãkɔfɔn] *adj* French-speaking || *mf* French speaker

franc-parler [frãparle] *m*—avoir son franc-parler to be free-spoken

franc-tireur [frãtirœr] *m* (*pl* francs-tireurs) free lance; sniper

frange [frãʒ] *f* fringe; à frange fringed

franger [frãʒe] §38 *tr* to fringe

franquette [frãkɛt] *f*—à la bonne franquette (coll) simply, without fuss

frap·pant [frapã] frap·pante [frapãt] *adj* striking, surprising

frappe [frap] *f* minting, striking; stamp (*on coins, medals, etc.*); touch (*in typing*)

frap·pé frap·pée [frape] *adj* struck; iced; (slang) crazy || *m* (mus) downbeat

frapper [frape] *tr* to strike, hit, knock; to mint (*coin*); to stamp (*cloth*); to ice (*e.g., champagne*) || *intr* to strike, hit, knock || *ref* (coll) to become panic-stricken

frasque [frask] *f* escapade

frater·nel -nelle [fratɛrnɛl] *adj* fraternal, brotherly

fraterniser [fratɛrnize] *intr* to fraternize

fraternité [fratɛrnite] *f* fraternity, brotherhood

fraude [frod] *f* fraud; smuggling; en fraude fraudulently; faire la fraude to smuggle; fraude fiscale tax evasion

fraudu·leux [frodylø] -leuse [løz] *adj* fraudulent

frayer [frɛje], [freje] §49 *tr* to mark out (*a path*) || *intr* to spawn; frayer avec to associate with

frayeur [frɛjœr] *f* fright, scare

fredaine [frədɛn] *f* (coll) escapade, prank, spree

fredon [frədɔ̃] *m* (cards) three of a kind

fredonnement [frədɔnmã] *m* hum, humming

fredonner [frədɔne] *tr & intr* to hum

frégate [fregat] *f* frigate

frein [frɛ̃] *m* bit (*of bridle*); brake (*of car*); frein à main hand brake; frein à pied foot brake; mettre le frein to put the brake on; mettre un frein à to curb, check; ronger son frein to champ at the bit

freiner [frɛne] *tr & intr* to brake

frelater [frəlate] *tr* to adulterate

frêle [frɛl] *adj* frail

frelon [frəlɔ̃] *m* hornet

frémir [fremir] *intr* to shudder

frémissement [fremismã] *m* shudder

frêne [frɛn] *m* ash tree

frénésie [frenezi] *f* frenzy

frénétique [frenetik] *adj* frenzied

fréquemment [frekamã] *adv* frequently

fréquence [frekãs] *f* frequency; basse fréquence low frequency; fréquence du pouls pulse rate; haute fréquence high frequency

fré·quent [frekã] -quente [kãt] *adj* frequent; rapid (*pulse*)

fréquenter [frekãte] *tr* to frequent; to associate with; (coll) to go steady with (*a boy or girl*)

frère [frɛr] *m* brother; frère consanguin half brother (*by the father*); frère convers (eccl) lay brother; frère de lait foster brother; frère germain whole brother; frère jumeau twin brother; frères siamois Siamese twins; frère utérin half brother (*by the mother*)

fresque [frɛsk] *f* fresco

fret [frɛ] *m* freight; chartering; cargo

fréter [frete] §10 *tr* to charter (*a ship*); to rent (*a car*)

fréteur [fretœr] *m* shipowner

frétiller [fretije] *intr* to wriggle; to quiver; frétiller de to wag (*its tail*)

fretin [frətẽ] *m*—le menu fretin small fry

frette [frɛt] *f* hoop, iron ring

freudisme [frødism] *m* Freudianism

freux [frø] *m* rook, crow

friand [frijã] friande [frijãd] *adj* tasty; fond (*of food, praise, etc.*) || *m* sausage roll

friandise [frijãdiz] *f* candy, sweet; delicacy, tidbit

fric [frik] *m* (slang) jack, money

fricasser [frikase] *tr* to fricassee; to squander

friche [friʃ] *f* fallow land; en friche fallow

friction [friksjɔ̃] *f* friction; massage

frictionner [friksjɔne] *tr* to rub, massage

frigide [friʒid] *adj* frigid

frigidité [friʒidite] *f* frigidity

frigorifier [frigɔrifje] *tr* to refrigerate

frigorifique [frigɔrifik] *adj* refrigerating || *m* cold-storage plant

fri·leux [frilø] -leuse [løz] *adj* chilly, shivery

frimas [frima] *m* icy mist, rime

frime [frim] *f* (coll) sham, fake, hoax

frimousse [frimus] *f* (coll) little face, cute face

fringale [frẽgal] *f* (coll) mad hunger

frin·gant [frẽgã] -gante [gãt] *adj* dashing, spirited

fringuer [frẽge] *tr* (slang) to dress || *intr* (obs) to frisk about

fringues [frẽg] *fpl* (slang) duds

fri·pé -pée [fripe] *adj* rumpled, mussed; worn, tired (*face*)

friper [fripe] *tr* to wrinkle, rumple

friperie [fripri] *f* secondhand clothes; secondhand furniture

fri·pier [fripje] -pière [pjɛr] *mf* old-clothes dealer; junk dealer

fri·pon [fripɔ̃] -ponne [pɔn] *adj* roguish || *mf* rogue, rascal

friponnerie [fripɔnri] *f* rascality, cheating

fripouille [fripuj] *f* (slang) scoundrel

frire [frir] §22 (used in *inf; pp;* 1st, 2d, 3d *sg pres ind; sg imperv;* rarely used

in *fut; cond*) *tr* to fry; to deep-fry; être frit (coll) to be done for ‖ *intr* to fry
frise [friz] *f* frieze
friselis [frizli] *m* soft rustling; gentle lapping (*of water*)
friser [frize] *tr* to curl; to border on; to graze ‖ *intr* to curl
frisoir [frizwar] *m* curling iron
fri·son [frizõ] -sonne [zɔn] *adj* Frisian ‖ *m* wave, curl; Frisian (*language*) ‖ (*cap*) *mf* Frisian
fris·quet [friskɛ] -quette [kɛt] *adj* (coll) chilly
frisson [frisõ] *m* shiver; shudder, thrill; frissons shivering
frissonner [frisɔne] *intr* to shiver
frisure [frizyr] *f* curling; curls
frites [frit] *fpl* French fries
frittage [fritaʒ] *m* (metallurgy) sintering
friture [frityr] *f* frying; deep fat; fried fish; (rad, telv) static
frivole [frivɔl] *adj* frivolous, trifling
froc [frɔk] *m* (eccl) frock
froid [frwɑ] froide [frwad] *adj* cold; chilly (*manner*) ‖ *m* cold; coolness (*between persons*); avoir froid to be cold; il fait froid it is cold; jeter un froid sur (fig) to put a damper on
froideur [frwadœr] *f* coldness; coolness
froissement [frwɑsmɑ̃] *m* bruising; rumpling, crumpling; clash (*of interests*); ruffling (*of feelings*)
froisser [frwɑse] *tr* to bruise; to rumple, crumple ‖ *ref* to take offense
frôlement [frolmɑ̃] *m* grazing; rustle
frôler [frole] *tr* to graze, to brush against; (coll) to have a narrow escape from
fromage [frɔmaʒ] *m* cheese; (coll) soft job; fromage blanc cream cheese; fromage de tête headcheese
froma·ger [frɔmaʒe] -gère [ʒɛr] *adj* cheese (*industry*) ‖ *m* cheesemaker; (bot) silk-cotton tree
fromagerie [frɔmaʒri] *f* cheese factory; cheese store
froment [frɔmɑ̃] *m* wheat
fronce [frõs] *f* crease, fold; à fronces shirred
froncement [frõsmɑ̃] *m* puckering; froncement de sourcils frown
froncer [frõse] §51 *tr* to pucker; froncer les sourcils to frown, to wrinkle one's brow
frondaison [frõdɛzõ] *f* foliation; foliage
fronde [frõd] *f* slingshot
fronder [frõde] *tr* to scoff at
fron·deur [frõdœr] -deuse [døz] *adj* bantering, irreverent ‖ *mf* scoffer
front [frõ] *m* forehead; impudence; brow (*of hill*); (geog, mil, pol) front; de front abreast; frontal; at the same time; faire front à to face up to
fronta·lier [frõtalje] -lière [ljɛr] *adj* frontier ‖ *m* frontiersman ‖ *f* frontier woman
frontière [frõtjɛr] *adj* & *f* frontier
frontispice [frõtispis] *m* frontispiece; title page

frottement [frɔtmɑ̃] *m* rubbing, friction
frotter [frɔte] *tr* to rub; to polish; to strike (*a match*); frotter les oreilles à qn (coll) to box s.o.'s ears ‖ *ref*— se frotter à (coll) to attack, to challenge; (coll) to rub shoulders with
froufrou [frufru] *m* rustle, swish
frousse [frus] *f* (slang) jitters
fructifier [fryktifje] *intr* to bear fruit
fruc·tueux [fryktɥø] -tueuse [tɥøz] *adj* fruitful, profitable
fru·gal -gale [frygal] *adj* (*pl* -gaux [go]) temperate; frugal (*meal*)
fruit [frɥi] *m* fruit; des fruits fruit; fruits civils income (*from rent, interest, etc.*); fruits de mer seafood; fruit sec (fig) flop, failure
fruiterie [frɥitri] *f* fruit store
frui·tier [frɥitje] -tière [tjɛr] *adj* fruit; fruit-bearing ‖ *mf* fruit vendor
fruste [fryst] *adj* worn; rough, uncouth
frustrer [frystre] *tr* to frustrate, disappoint; to cheat, defraud
fugace [fygas] *adj* fleeting, evanescent
fugi·tif [fyʒitif] -tive [tiv] *adj* & *mf* fugitive
fugue [fyg] *f* sudden disappearance; (mus) fugue
fuir [fɥir] §31 *tr* to flee, to run away from ‖ *intr* to flee; to leak; to recede (*said of forehead*)
fuite [fɥit] *f* flight; leak
fulgu·rant [fylgyrɑ̃] -rante [rɑ̃t] *adj* flashing; vivid; stabbing (*pain*)
fulguration [fylgyrasjõ] *f* sheet lightning
fulgurer [fylgyre] *intr* to flash
fuligi·neux [fyliʒinø] -neuse [nøz] *adj* sooty
fumage [fymaʒ] *m* smoking (*of meat*); manuring (*of fields*)
fume-cigare [fymsigar] *m invar* cigar holder
fume-cigarette [fymsigarɛt] *m invar* cigarette holder
fumée [fyme] *f* smoke; steam; fumées fumes
fumer [fyme] *tr* & *intr* to smoke; to fume; to manure
fumerie [fymri] *f* opium den; smoking room
fumet [fymɛ] *m* aroma; bouquet (*of wine*)
fu·meur [fymœr] -meuse [møz] *mf* smoker; fumeur à la file chain smoker
fu·meux [fymø] -meuse [møz] *adj* smoky; foggy, hazy (*ideas*)
fumier [fymje] *m* manure; dunghill; (slang) skunk, scoundrel
fumiger [fymiʒe] §38 *tr* to fumigate
fumiste [fymist] *m* heater man; (coll) practical joker
fumisterie [fymistri] *f* heater work; heater shop; (coll) hooey
fumoir [fymwar] *m* smoking room; smokehouse
funambule [fynɑ̃byl] *mf* tightrope walker
funèbre [fynɛbr] *adj* funereal; funeral (*march, procession, service*)
funérailles [fyneraj] *fpl* funeral
funéraire [fynerɛr] *adj* funeral
funeste [fynɛst] *adj* baleful, fatal

funiculaire [fynikylɛr] *adj & m* funicular
fur [fyr] *m*—**au fur et à mesure** progressively, gradually; **au fur et à mesure de** in proportion to; **au fur et à mesure que** as, in proportion as
furet [fyrɛ] *m* ferret; snoop; ring-in-the-circle (*parlor game*)
fureter [fyrte] §2 *intr* to ferret
fureur [fyrœr] *f* fury; **à la fureur** passionately; **faire fureur** to be the rage
furi·bond [fyribɔ̃] **-bonde** [bɔ̃d] *adj* furious; withering (*look*) ‖ *mf* irascible individual
furie [fyri] *f* fury; termagant
fu·rieux [fyrjø] **-rieuse** [rjøz] *adj* furious; angry (*wind*)
furoncle [fyrɔ̃kl] *m* boil
fur·tif [fyrtif] **-tive** [tiv] *adj* furtive, stealthy
fusain [fyzɛ̃] *m* charcoal; charcoal drawing; spindle tree
fu·seau [fuzo] *m* (*pl* **-seaux**) spindle; **à fuseau** tapering; **fuseau horaire** time zone (*between two meridians*)
fusée [fyze] *f* rocket; spindleful; spindle (*of axle*); (coll) ripple, burst (*of laughter*); **fusée à retard** delayed-action fuse; **fusée d'artifice** or **fusée volante** skyrocket; **fusée éclairante** flare; **fusée engin** rocket engine; **fusée fusante** time fuse; **fusée percutante** percussion fuse
fuselage [fyzlaʒ] *m* fuselage
fuse·lé -lée [fyzle] *adj* spindle-shaped; tapering, slender (*fingers*); streamlined

fuseler [fyzle] §34 *tr* to taper; to streamline
fuser [fyze] *intr* to melt; to run (*said of colors*); to fizz, to spurt; to stream in or out (*said of light*)
fusible [fyzibl] *adj* fusible ‖ *m* fuse
fusil [fyzi] *m* gun, rifle; whetstone; rifleman; **fusil à deux coups** double-barreled gun; **fusil de chasse** shotgun; **fusil mitrailleur** light machine gun; **un bon fusil** a good shot (*person*)
fusillade [fyzijad] *f* fusillade
fusiller [fyzije] *tr* to shoot, to execute by a firing squad
fusion [fyzjɔ̃] *f* fusion
fusionner [fyzjɔne] *tr & intr* to blend, to fuse; (com) to merge
fustiger [fystiʒe] §38 *tr* to thrash, flog; to castigate
fût [fy] *m* cask, keg; barrel (*of drum*); stock (*of gun*); trunk (*of tree*); shaft (*of column*); stem (*of candelabrum*)
futaie [fyte] *f* stand of timber; **de haute futaie** full-grown
futaille [fytɑj] *f* cask, barrel
futaine [fyten] *f* fustian
fu·té -tée [fyte] *adj* (coll) cunning, shrewd ‖ *f* mastic, filler
futile [fytil] *adj* futile
futilité [fytilite] *f* futility; **futilités** trifles
fu·tur -ture [fytyr] *adj* future ‖ *m* future; husband-to-be ‖ *f* future wife
fuyant [fɥijɑ̃] **fuyante** [fɥijɑ̃t] *adj* fleeting; receding (*forehead*)
fuyard [fɥijar] **fuyarde** [fɥijard] *adj & mf* runaway

G

G, g [ʒe] *m invar* seventh letter of the French alphabet
gabardine [gabardin] *f* gabardine
gabare [gabar] *f* barge
gabarit [gabari] *m* templet; (rr) maximum structure; (coll) size
gabelle [gabɛl] *f* (hist) salt tax
gâche [gɑʃ] *f* catch (*at a door*); trowel; wooden spatula
gâcher [gɑʃe] *tr* to mix (*cement*); to spoil, bungle; to squander
gâchette [gɑʃɛt] *f* trigger; pawl, spring catch
gâ·cheur [gɑʃœr] **-cheuse** [ʃøz] *adj* bungling ‖ *mf* bungler
gâchis [gɑʃi] *m* wet cement; mud, slush; (coll) mess, muddle
gaélique [gaelik] *adj & m* Gaelic
gaffe [gaf] *f* gaff; (coll) social blunder, faux pas
gaffer [gafe] *tr* to hook with a gaff ‖ *intr* (coll) to make a blunder
gaga [gaga] *adj* (coll) doddering ‖ *mf* (coll) dotard
gage [gaʒ] *m* pledge, pawn; forfeit (*in a game*); **gages** wage, wages; **prêter sur gages** to pawn
gager [gaʒe] §38 *tr* to wager, to bet; to pay wages to
ga·geur [gaʒœr] **-geuse** [ʒøz] *mf* bettor
gageure [gaʒyr] *f* wager, bet
gagiste [gaʒist] *mf* pledger; wage earner; (theat) extra
ga·gnant [gɑɲɑ̃] **-gnante** [ɲɑ̃t] *adj* winning ‖ *mf* winner
gagne-pain [gaɲpɛ̃] *m invar* bread-winner; livelihood, bread and butter
gagne-petit [gaɲpəti] *m invar* cheapjack, low-salaried worker
gagner [gaɲe] *tr* to gain; to win; to earn; to reach; to save (*time*) ‖ *intr* to improve; to gain; to spread ‖ *ref* to be catching (*said of disease*)
ga·gneur [gaɲœr] **-gneuse** [ɲøz] *mf* winner; earner
gai gaie [ge] *adj* gay; (coll) tipsy
gaiement [gemɑ̃] *adv* gaily
gaieté [gete] *f* gaiety; **de gaieté de cœur** of one's own free will
gail·lard [gajar] **gail·larde** [gajard] *adj*

healthy, hearty; merry; ribald, spicy || *m* sturdy fellow; tricky fellow; **gaillard d'arrière** quarter-deck; **gaillard d'avant** forecastle || *f* bold young lady; husky young woman
gaillardise [gajardiz] *f* cheerfulness; **gaillardises** spicy stories
gain [gɛ̃] *m* gain; earnings; winning (e.g., *of bet*); **avoir gain de cause** to win one's case
gaine [gɛn] *f* sheath; case, covering; girdle (*corset*); **gaine d'aération** ventilation shaft
gainer [gɛne] *tr* to sheath, to encase
gaîté [gete] *f* gaiety
gala [gala] *m* gala; state dinner
galamment [galamɑ̃] *adv* gallantly
ga·lant [galɑ̃] **-lante** [lɑ̃t] *adj* gallant; amorous; kept (*woman*) || *m* gallant; **vert gallant** gay old blade
galanterie [galɑ̃tri] *f* gallantry; libertinism
galaxie [galaksi] *f* galaxy
galbe [galb] *m* curve, sweep, graceful outline
gale [gal] *f* mange; (coll) backbiter, cad
galée [gale] *f* (typ) galley
galéjade [galeʒad] *f* joke, far-fetched story
galère [galɛr] *f* galley; drudgery; mason's hand truck
galerie [galri] *f* gallery; cornice, rim; baggage rack; **galerie marchande** shopping center
galérien [galerjɛ̃] *m* galley slave
galet [galɛ] *m* pebble; (mach) roller
galetas [galta] *m* hovel
galette [galɛt] *f* cake; buckwheat pancake; hardtack; (slang) dough, money; **galette des Rois** twelfth-cake (*eaten at Epiphany*)
ga·leux [galø] **-leuse** [løz] *adj* mangy
galimatias [galimatja] *m* nonsense, gibberish
galion [galjɔ̃] *m* galleon
Galles [gal]—**le pays de Galles** Wales; **prince de Galles** Prince of Wales
gal·lois [galwa] **gal·loise** [galwaz] *adj* Welsh || *m* Welsh (*language*) || (*cap*) *m* Welshman; **les Gallois** the Welsh || (*cap*) *f* Welshwoman
gallon [galɔ̃] *m* gallon (*imperial or American*)
galoche [galɔʃ] *f* clog (*shoe*); **de** or **en galoche** pointed (*chin*)
galon [galɔ̃] *m* galloon, braid; (mil) stripe, chevron; **prendre du galon** to move up
galonner [galɔne] *tr* to trim with braid
galop [galo] *m* gallop; **petit galop** canter
galoper [galɔpe] *tr & intr* to gallop
galopin [galɔpɛ̃] *m* (coll) urchin
galvaniser [galvanize] *tr* to galvanize
galvauder [galvode] *tr* (coll) to botch; (coll) to waste (*e.g., one's talent*); (coll) to sully (*a name*) || *intr* (slang) to walk the streets || *ref* (slang) to go bad
gambade [gɑ̃bad] *f* gambol
gambader [gɑ̃bade] *intr* to gambol
gambit [gɑ̃bi] *m* gambit

gamelle [gamɛl] *f* mess kit
ga·min [gamɛ̃] **-mine** [min] *mf* street urchin; youngster
gaminerie [gaminri] *f* mischievousness
gamme [gam] *f* gamut, range; set (*of tools*); (mus) scale, gamut
Gand [gɑ̃] *m* Ghent
ganglion [gɑ̃glijɔ̃] *m* ganglion
gangrène [gɑ̃grɛn] *f* gangrene
gangrener [gɑ̃grəne] §2 *tr & ref* to gangrene
ganse [gɑ̃s] *f* braid, piping
gant [gɑ̃] *m* glove; **jeter le gant** to throw down the gauntlet; **prendre des gants pour** to put on kid gloves to; **relever le gant** to take up the gauntlet; **se donner des gants** to take all the credit
gantelet [gɑ̃tlɛ] *m* protective glove
ganter [gɑ̃te] *tr* to put gloves on (*s.o.*); to fit, to become (*s.o.; said of gloves*); **cela me gante** (coll) that suits me || *intr*—**ganter de** to wear, to take (*a certain size of glove*) || *ref* to put on one's gloves
garage [garaʒ] *m* garage; turnout
garagiste [garaʒist] *m* garageman, mechanic
ga·rant [garɑ̃] **-rante** [rɑ̃t] *adj* guaranteeing || *mf* guarantor, warrantor; **se porter garant de** to guarantee || *m* guarantee, warranty
garantie [garɑ̃ti] *f* guarantee
garantir [garɑ̃tir] *tr* to guarantee; to vouch for; to shelter, protect
garce [gars] *f* (coll) wench; (coll) bitch
garçon [garsɔ̃] *m* boy; young man; bachelor; apprentice; waiter; **garçon de courses** errand boy; **garçon de recette** bank messenger; **garçon de salle** orderly; **garçon d'honneur** best man; **garçon manqué** tomboy; **vieux garçon** old bachelor
garçonne [garsɔn] *f* bachelor girl
garçonnet [garsɔnɛ] *m* little boy
garçon·nier [garsɔnje] **garçon·nière** [garsɔnjɛr] *adj* bachelor; tomboyish || *f* bachelor apartment; tomboy
garde [gard] *m* guard, guardsman; keeper, custodian; **garde champêtre** constable; **garde de nuit** night watchman; **garde forestier** ranger || *f* guard; custody; nurse; flyleaf; **de garde** on duty; **garde à vous!** (mil) attention!; **garde civique** national guard; **monter la garde** to go on guard duty; **prendre garde à** to look out for, to take notice of; **prendre garde de** to take care not to; to be careful to; **prendre garde que** to notice that; **prendre garde que ...** **ne** + *subj* to be careful lest, to be careful that ... not; **sur ses gardes** on one's guard
garde-à-vous [gardavu] *m invar* (military position) attention
garde-à-vue [gardavy] *f* custody, imprisonment
garde-barrière [gardəbarjɛr] *mf* (*pl* **gardes-barrière** or **gardes-barrières**) crossing guard
garde-bébé [gardəbebe] *mf* (*pl* **-bébés**) baby-sitter

garde-boue [gardəbu] *m invar* mudguard

garde-chasse [gardəʃas] *m* (*pl* **gardeschasse** or **gardes-chasses**) gamekeeper

garde-corps [gardəkɔr] *m invar* guardrail; (naut) life line

garde-côte [gardəkot] *m* (*pl* **-côtes**) coast-guard cutter || *m* (*pl* **gardescôtes**) (obs) coastguardsman; (obs) coast guard

garde-feu [gardəfø] *m invar* fire screen

garde-fou [gardəfu] *m* (*pl* **-fous**) guardrail

garde-frein [gardəfrɛ̃] *m* (*pl* **gardesfrein** or **gardes-freins**) brakeman

garde-magasin [gardəmagazɛ̃] *m* (*pl* **gardes-magasin** or **gardes-magasins**) warehouseman

garde-malade [gardəmalad] *mf* (*pl* **gardes-malades**) nurse

garde-manger [gardəmɑ̃ʒe] *m invar* icebox; larder ˎ

garde-meuble [gardəmœbl] *m* (*pl* **-meuble** or **meubles**) furniture warehouse

garde-nappe [gardənap] *m* (*pl* **-nappe** or **nappes**) table mat, place mat

garde-pêche [gardəpɛʃ] *m* (*pl* **gardespêche**) fish warden || *m invar* fishery service boat

garder [garde] *tr* to guard; to keep; **garder à vue** to hold in custody; **garder jusqu'à l'arrivée** (formula on envelope) hold for arrival; **garder la chambre** to stay in one's room; **garder la ligne** to keep one's figure || *ref* to keep (*to stay free of deterioration*); **se garder de** to protect oneself from; to watch out for; to take care not to

garde-rats [gardəra] *m invar* rat guard

garderie [gardəri] *f* nursery; forest reserve

garde-robe [gardərɔb] *f* (*pl* **-robes**) wardrobe

gar·deur [gardœr] **-deuse** [døz] *mf* keeper, herder

garde-voie [gardəvwa] *m* (*pl* **gardesvoie** or **gardes-voies**) trackwalker

garde-vue [gardəvy] *m invar* eyeshade, visor

gar·dien [gardjɛ̃] **-dienne** [djɛn] *adj* guardian (*angel*) || *mf* guard, guardian; keeper; caretaker; attendant (*at a garage*); **gardien de but** goalkeeper; **gardien de la paix** policeman

gare [gar], [gar] *f* station; **gare aérienne** airport; **gare de triage** switchyard; **gare maritime** port, dock; **gare routière** or **gare d'autobus** bus station || [gar] *interj* look out!

garer [gare] *tr* to park; to put in the garage; (naut) to dock; (rr) to shunt; (coll) to secure (*e.g., a fortune*) || *ref* to get out of the way; to park, park one's car; **se garer de** to look out for

gargariser [gargarize] *ref* to gargle

gargarisme [gargarism] *m* gargle

gargote [gargɔt] *f* (coll) hash house, beanery

gargouille [garguj] *f* gargoyle

gargouillement [gargujmɑ̃] *m* gurgling; rumbling (*in stomach*)

gargouiller [garguje] *intr* to gurgle

garnement [garnəmɑ̃] *m* scamp, bad boy

gar·ni **-nie** [garni] *adj* furnished (*room*) || *m* furnished room; furnished house

garnir [garnir] *tr* to garnish, adorn; to furnish; to strengthen; to line (*a brake*) || *ref* to fill up (*said of crowded room, theater seats, etc.*)

garnison [garnizɔ̃] *f* garrison

garniture [garnityr] *f* garniture, decoration; fittings; accessories; complete set; (culin) garnish; **garniture de feu** fire irons; **garniture de lit** bedding

garrot [garo] *m* garrote (*instrument of torture*); (med) tourniquet; (zool) withers

garrotte [garɔt] *f* garrote (*torture*)

garrotter [garɔte] *tr* to garrote; to pinion

gars [gɑ] *m* (coll) lad

Gascogne [gaskɔɲ] *f* Gascony; **la Gascogne** Gascony

gasconnade [gaskɔnad] *f* gasconade; insincere invitation

gas-oil [gazwal] *m* diesel oil

Gaspésie [gaspezi] *f* Gaspé Peninsula

gaspiller [gaspije] *tr* to waste, squander

gastrique [gastrik] *adj* gastric

gastronomie [gastrɔnɔmi] *f* gastronomy

gâ·teau [gato] *adj invar* (coll) fond (*papa*); (coll) fairy (*godmother*) || *m* (*pl* **-teaux**) cake; (coll) booty, loot; **gâteau de miel** honeycomb; **gâteau des Rois** twelfth-cake

gâte-métier [gatmetje] *m invar* undercutter

gâte-papier [gatpapje] *m invar* hack writer

gâter [gate] *tr* & *ref* to spoil

gâte-sauce [gatsos] *m invar* poor cook; kitchen boy

gâ·teux [gatø] **-teuse** [tøz] *adj* (coll) senile || *mf* (coll) dotard

gâtisme [gatism] *m* senility

gauche [goʃ] *adj* left; left-hand; crooked; awkward || *f* left hand; left side; (pol) left wing; **à gauche** to the left; **à gauche, gauche!** (mil) left, face!

gau·cher [goʃe] **-chère** [ʃɛr] *adj* left-handed || *mf* left-hander

gauchir [goʃir] *tr* & *intr* to warp

gauchiste [goʃist] *adj* & *mf* leftist

gaudriole [godrijɔl] *f* broad joke

gaufre [gofr] *f* waffle; **gaufre de miel** honeycomb

gaufrer [gofre] *tr* to emboss, figure; to flute; to corrugate

gaufrette [gofrɛt] *f* wafer

gaufrier [gofrije] *m* waffle iron

gaule [gol] *f* pole; **la Gaule** Gaul

gauler [gole] *tr* to bring down (*e.g., fruit*) with a pole

gau·lois [golwa] **-loise** [lwaz] *adj* Gaulish, Gallic; broad (*humor*) || *m* Gaulish (*language*) || (*cap*) *mf* Gaul || (*cap*) *f* gauloise (*cigarette*)

gauloiserie [golwazri] *f* racy joking

gaulthérie [goteri] *f* (bot) wintergreen

gausser [gose] *ref*—**se gausser de** (coll) to poke fun at

gaver [gave] *tr & ref* to cram

gavroche [gavrɔʃ] *mf* street urchin

gaz [gɑz] *m* gas; gaslight; gas company; **gaz d'échappement** exhaust; **gaz d'éclairage** illuminating gas; **gaz de combat** poison gas; **gaz en cylindre** bottled gas; **gaz hilarant** laughing gas; **gaz lacrimogène** tear gas; **mettre les gaz** (aut) to step on the gas

gaze [gɑz] *f* gauze; cheesecloth

ga·zé -zée [gɑze] *adj* gassed ‖ *mf* gas casualty

gazéifier [gɑzeifje] *tr* to gasify; to carbonate, charge

gazelle [gazɛl] *f* gazelle

gazer [gɑze] *tr* to gas; to cover with gauze; to tone down ‖ *intr* (coll) to go full steam ahead; **ça gaze?** (coll) how goes it?

ga·zeux [gɑzø] **-zeuse** [zøz] *adj* gaseous; carbonated

ga·zier [gɑzje] **-zière** [zjɛr] *adj* gas ‖ *m* gasman; gas fitter

gazoduc [gɑzɔdyk] *m* gas pipe line

gazogène [gɑzɔʒɛn] *m* gas producer

gazoline [gɑzɔlin] *f* petroleum ether

gazomètre [gɑzɔmɛtr] *m* gasholder, gas tank

gazon [gɑzɔ̃] *m* lawn; turf, sod

gazonner [gɑzɔne] *tr* to sod

gazouiller [gazuje] *intr* to chirp, twitter; to warble; to babble

gazouillis [gazuji] *m* chirping; warbling; babbling

geai [ʒɛ] *m* jay

géant [ʒeɑ̃] **géante** [ʒeɑ̃t] *adj* gigantic ‖ *m* giant ‖ *f* giantess

Gédéon [ʒedeɔ̃] *m* (Bib) Gideon

gei·gnard [ʒɛɲar] **-gnard** [ɲard] *adj* (coll) whining ‖ *mf* (coll) whiner

geignement [ʒɛɲmɑ̃] *m* whining, whimper

geindre [ʒɛ̃dr] §50 *intr* to whine, whimper; (coll) to complain

gel [ʒɛl] *m* frost, freezing; (chem) gel

gélatine [ʒelatin] *f* gelatin

gelée [ʒəle] *f* frost; (culin) jelly; **gelée blanche** hoarfrost

geler [ʒəle] §2 *tr, intr & ref* to freeze; to congeal

gelure [ʒəlyr] *f* frostbite

gémi·né -née [ʒemine] *adj* twin; coeducational (*school*)

gémir [ʒemir] *intr* to groan, moan

gémissement [ʒemismɑ̃] *m* groaning, moaning

gemme [ʒɛm] *f* gem; bud; pine resin

gemmer [ʒɛmme] *tr* to tap for resin ‖ *intr* to bud

gê·nant [ʒɛnɑ̃] **-nante** [nɑ̃t] *adj* troublesome, embarrassing

gencive [ʒɑ̃siv] *f* (anat) gum

gendarme [ʒɑ̃darm] *m* policeman; rock pinnacle; flaw (*of gem*); (coll) virago; (slang) red herring

gendarmerie [ʒɑ̃darmri] *f* police headquarters

gendre [ʒɑ̃dr] *m* son-in-law

gêne [ʒɛn] *f* discomfort, embarrassment; **être dans la gêne** to be hard

up; **être sans gêne** (coll) to be rude, casual

gène [ʒɛn] *m* (biol) gene

généalogie [ʒenealɔʒi] *f* genealogy

gêner [ʒɛne] *tr* to embarrass; to inconvenience; to hinder; to embarrass financially; to pinch (*the feet*)

géné·ral -rale [ʒeneral] *adj & m* (*pl* **-raux** [ro]) general; **en général** in general; **général de brigade** brigadier general; **général de corps d'armée** lieutenant general; **général de division** major general ‖ *f* general's wife; (theat) opening night; **battre la générale** (mil) to sound the alarm

généralat [ʒenerala] *m* generalship

généraliser [ʒeneralize] *tr & intr* to generalize

généralissime [ʒeneralisim] *m* generalissimo

généralité [ʒeneralite] *f* generality; **la généralité de** the general run of

généra·teur [ʒeneratœr] **-trice** [tris] *adj* generating ‖ *m* boiler ‖ *f* generator

génération [ʒenerasjɔ̃] *f* generation

générer [ʒenere] §10 *tr* to generate

géné·reux [ʒenerø] **-reuse** [røz] *adj* generous; full (*bosom*); rich, full (*wine*)

générique [ʒenerik] *adj* generic ‖ *m* (mov) credit line

générosité [ʒenerozite] *f* generosity; **générosités** acts of generosity

Gênes [ʒɛn] *f* Genoa

genèse [ʒɑ̃ɛz] *f* genesis

genet [ʒɑ̃ɛ] *m* jennet (*horse*)

genêt [ʒɑ̃ɛ] *m* (bot) broom; **genêt épineux** furze

génétique [ʒenetik] *adj* genetic ‖ *f* genetics

gê·neur [ʒɛnœr] **-neuse** [nøz] *mf* intruder, spoilsport

Genève [ʒɑ̃ɛv] *f* Geneva

gene·vois [ʒɑ̃nvwa], [ʒɛnvwa] **-voise** [vwaz] *adj* Genevan ‖ (*cap*) *mf* Genevan (*person*)

genévrier [ʒɑ̃nevrije] *m* juniper

gé·nial -niale [ʒenjal] *adj* (*pl* **-niaux** [njo]) brilliant, ingenious; geniuslike, of genius

génie [ʒeni] *m* genius; bent, inclination; genie; engineer corps; **génie civil** civil engineering; **génie industriel** industrial engineering; **génie maritime** naval construction

genièvre [ʒɑ̃njɛvr] *m* juniper; juniper berry; gin

génisse [ʒenis] *f* heifer

géni·tal -tale [ʒenital] *adj* (*pl* **-taux** [to]) genital

géni·teur [ʒenitœr] **-trice** [tris] *adj* engendering ‖ *m* sire ‖ *f* genetrix

géni·tif [ʒenitif] **-tive** [tiv] *adj & m* genitive

génocide [ʒenɔsid] *m* genocide

gé·nois [ʒenwa] **-noise** [nwaz] *adj* Genoese ‖ (*cap*) *mf* Genoese

ge·nou [ʒənu] *m* (*pl* **-noux**) knee; (mach) joint

genouillère [ʒənujɛr] *f* kneecap; kneepad

genre [ʒɑ̃r] *m* genre; genus; kind, sort;

manner, way; fashion, taste; (gram) gender; **de genre** (fa) genre; **faire du genre** (coll) to put on airs; **genre humain** humankind

gens [ʒɑ̃] *mpl* (an immediately preceding adjective that varies in its feminine form is put in that form, and so are **certain, quel, tel,** and **tout** that precede that preceding adjective, but the noun remains masculine for pronouns that stand for it, for past participles that agree with it, and for adjectives in all other positions, e.g., **toutes ces vieilles gens sont intéressants** all these old people are interesting) people; nations, e.g., **droit des gens** law of nations; men, e.g., **gens de lettres** men of letters; **gens d'affaires** businessmen; **gens d'Église** clergy; **gens de la presse** newsmen; **gens de mer** seamen; **gens de robe** bar; **jeunes gens** young people (*men and women*); young men

gent [ʒɑ̃] *f* (obs) nation, race
gentiane [ʒɑ̃sjan] *f* gentian
gen·til [ʒɑ̃ti] **-tille** [tij] *adj* nice, kind || (*cap*) *m* pagan, gentile
gentilhomme [ʒɑ̃tijɔm] *m* (*pl* **gentils-hommes** [ʒɑ̃tizɔm]) nobleman
gentillesse [ʒɑ̃tijɛs] *f* niceness, kindness; **gentillesses** nice things, kind words
gentil·let [ʒɑ̃tijɛ] **gentil·lette** [ʒɑ̃tijɛt] *adj* rather nice
gentiment [ʒɑ̃timɑ̃] *adv* nicely; gracefully
géographie [ʒeɔgrafi] *f* geography
geôle [ʒol] *f* jail
geô·lier [ʒolje] **-lière** [ljɛr] *mf* jailer
géologie [ʒeɔlɔʒi] *f* geology
géologique [ʒeɔlɔʒik] *adj* geologic(al)
géomé·tral -trale [ʒeɔmetral] *adj* (*pl* **-traux** [tro]) flat (*projection*)
géométrie [ʒeɔmetri] *f* geometry
géométrique [ʒeɔmetrik] *adj* geometric(al)
géophysique [ʒeɔfizik] *f* geophysics
géopolitique [ʒeɔpɔlitik] *f* geopolitics
Georges [ʒɔrʒ] *m* George
gérance [ʒerɑ̃s] *f* management; board of directors
géranium [ʒeranjɔm] *m* geranium
gé·rant [ʒerɑ̃] **-rante** [rɑ̃t] *mf* manager; **gérant d'une publication** managing editor
gerbe [ʒɛrb] *f* sheaf; spray (*of flowers; of water; of bullets*); shower (*of sparks*)
gerbée [ʒɛrbe] *f* straw
gerber [ʒɛrbe] *tr* to sheave; to stack
gerce [ʒɛrs] *f* crack, split; clothes moth
gercer [ʒɛrse] §51 *tr, intr, & ref* to crack, to chap
gerçure [ʒɛrsyr] *f* crack, chap
gérer [ʒere] §10 *tr* to manage, to run
gériatrie [ʒerjatri] *f* geriatrics
ger·main [ʒɛrmɛ̃] **-maine** [mɛn] *adj* german, first (*cousin*)
germe [ʒɛrm] *m* germ
germer [ʒɛrme] *intr* to germinate
germicide [ʒɛrmisid] *adj* germicidal || *m* germicide
gérondif [ʒerɔ̃dif] *m* gerund

gérontologie [ʒerɔ̃tɔlɔʒi] *f* gerontology
gésier [ʒesje] *m* gizzard
gésir [ʒezir] (used only in *inf*; *ger* **gisant**; 3d *sg pres ind* **gît**; 1st, 2d, 3d *pl pres ind* **gisons, gisez, gisent**; *imperf ind* **gisais, gisait, gisions, gisiez, gisaient**) *intr* to lie; **ci-gît** here lies (*buried*)
gesse [ʒɛs] *f* vetch; **gesse odorante** sweet pea
gestation [ʒɛstɑsjɔ̃] *f* gestation
geste [ʒɛst] *m* gesture || *f* medieval epic poem
gesticuler [ʒɛstikyle] *intr* to gesticulate
gestion [ʒɛstjɔ̃] *f* management, administration
gestionnaire [ʒɛstjɔnɛr] *adj* managing || *mf* manager, administrator
geyser [ʒezɛr], [ʒejzɛr] *m* geyser
ghetto [geto], [gɛtto] *m* ghetto
gib·beux [ʒibØ] **gib·beuse** [ʒibØz] *adj* humped, hunchbacked
gibecière [ʒibsjɛr] *f* game bag; sack (*for papers, books, etc.*)
gibelotte [ʒiblɔt] *f* rabbit stew
gibet [ʒibɛ] *m* gibbet, gallows
gibier [ʒibje] *m* game; **gibier à plume** feathered game; **gibier de potence** gallows bird
giboulée [ʒibule] *f* shower; hailstorm
giboyeux [ʒibwajØ] **giboyeuse** [ʒibwajØz] *adj* full of game
gibus [ʒibys] *m* opera hat
giclée [ʒikle] *f* spurt
gicler [ʒikle] *intr* to spurt
gicleur [ʒiklœr] *m* atomizer; (aut) spray nozzle (*of carburetor*)
gifle [ʒifl] *f* slap in the face
gifler [ʒifle] *tr* to slap in the face
gigantesque [ʒigɑ̃tɛsk] *adj* gigantic
gigogne [ʒigɔɲ] *adj*—**table gigogne** nest of tables || (*cap*) *f*—**la mère Gigogne** the old woman who lived in a shoe
gigolo [ʒigɔlo] *m* (coll) gigolo
gigot [ʒigo] *m* leg of lamb, leg of mutton; **à gigot** leg-of-mutton (*sleeve*)
gigue [ʒig] *f* jig; haunch (*of venison*); (coll) leg; (slang) long-legged gawky girl
gilet [ʒilɛ] *m* vest; **gilet de sauvetage** life jacket; **gilet pare-balles** bulletproof vest; **pleurer dans le gilet de qn** (coll) to cry on s.o.'s shoulder
gingembre [ʒɛ̃ʒɑ̃br] *m* ginger
girafe [ʒiraf] *f* giraffe
giration [ʒirɑsjɔ̃] *f* gyration
girl [gœrl] *f* chorus girl
girofle [ʒirɔfl] *m* clove
giroflée [ʒirɔfle] *f* gillyflower
giron [ʒirɔ̃] *m* lap; bosom (*of the Church*)
girouette [ʒirwɛt] *f* weather vane
gisement [ʒizmɑ̃] *m* deposit; lode, seam; (naut) bearing; **gisement de pétrole** oil field
gi·tan [ʒitɑ̃] **-tane** [tan] *adj & mf* gypsy
gîte [ʒit] *m* lodging; lair, cover; deposit (*of ore*); **gîte à la noix** round steak || *f* (naut) list; **donner de la gîte** to heel
gîter [ʒite] *intr* to lodge; to lie, couch;

to perch; (naut) to list, heel ‖ *ref* to find shelter
givre [ʒivr] *m* rime, hoarfrost
givrer [ʒivre] *tr* to frost
glabre [glɑbr] *adj* beardless
glaçage [glasaʒ] *m* icing (*on cake*)
glace [glas] *f* ice; ice cream; mirror; plate glass; car window; glaze, icing; flaw (*of gem*); **être de glace** (fig) to be hard as stone; **glace au sirop** sundae; **glace panachée** Neapolitan ice cream; **rompre la glace** (fig) to break the ice
gla·cé -cée [glase] *adj* frozen; iced, chilled; icy, frosty; glazed, glossy
glacer [glase] §51 *tr* to freeze; to chill; to glaze; to ice (*a cake*)
glacerie [glasri] *f* glass factory
glaciaire [glasjɛr] *adj* glacial
gla·cial -ciale [glasjal] *adj* (*pl* **-cials**) glacial
glacier [glasje] *m* glacier; ice-cream man
glacière [glasjɛr] *f* icehouse; icebox; freezer
glacis [glasi] *m* slope; ramp; (mil) glacis; (painting) glaze
glaçon [glasɔ̃] *m* icicle; ice cube; ice floe; (fig) cold fish, iceberg
glaçure [glasyr] *f* (ceramics) glaze
gladiateur [gladjatœr] *m* gladiator
glaïeul [glajœl] *m* gladiola
glaire [glɛr] *f* white of egg; mucus
glaise [glɛz] *f* clay, loam
glaisière [glɛzjɛr] *f* clay pit
glaive [glɛv] *m* (lit) sword
gland [glɑ̃] *m* acorn; tassel
glande [glɑ̃d] *f* gland
glane [glan] *f* gleaning; cluster
glaner [glane] *tr* to glean
glanure [glanyr] *f* gleaning
glapir [glapir] *intr* to yelp, yap
glas [glɑ] *m* knell, tolling
glauque [glok] *adj* & *m* blue-green
glèbe [glɛb] *f* clod (*sod*); soil (*land*)
glène [glɛn] *f* (anat) socket; (naut) coil of rope
glissade [glisad] *f* slip; sliding; (dancing) glide; **glissade de terre** landslide; **glissade sur l'aile** (aer) sideslip; **glissade sur la queue** (aer) tail dive
glis·sant [glisɑ̃] **glis·sante** [glisɑ̃t] *adj* slippery
glissement [glismɑ̃] *m* sliding; gliding
glisser [glise] *tr* to slip; to drop (*a word into s.o.'s ear*) ‖ *intr* to slip; to slide; to skid; to glide ‖ *ref* to slip
glissière [glisjɛr] *f* slide, groove; **à glissière** sliding; zippered
glissoire [gliswar] *f* slide (*on ice or snow*)
glo·bal -bale [glɔbal] *adj* (*pl* **-baux** [bo]) global; lump (*sum*)
globe [glɔb] *m* globe; **globe de feu** fireball; **globe de l'œil** eyeball
globule [glɔbyl] *m* globule; (physiol) corpuscle
gloire [glwar] *f* glory; pride; halo; **pour la gloire** for fun, for nothing; **se faire gloire de** to glory in
gloriette [glɔrjet] *f* arbor, summerhouse
glo·rieux [glɔrjø] **-rieuse** [rjøz] *adj* glorious; blessed; vain

glorifier [glɔrifje] *tr* to glorify ‖ *ref*—**se glorifier de** to glory in
gloriole [glɔrjɔl] *f* vainglory
glose [gloz] *f* gloss; (coll) gossip
gloser [gloze] *intr* (coll) to gossip
glossaire [glɔser] *m* glossary
glotte [glɔt] *f* glottis
glouglou [gluglu] *m* gurgle, glug; gobble-gobble; coo (*of dove*)
glouglouter [gluglute] *intr* to gurgle; to gobble (*said of turkey*)
glousser [gluse] *intr* to cluck; to chuckle
glou·ton [glutɔ̃] **-tonne** [tɔn] *adj* gluttonous ‖ *mf* glutton ‖ *m* (zool) glutton, wolverine
gloutonnerie [glutɔnri] *f* gluttony
glu [gly] *f* birdlime; (coll) trap
gluant [glyɑ̃] **gluante** [glyɑ̃t] *adj* sticky, gummy; (fig) tenacious
glucose [glykoz] *m* glucose
glycérine [gliserin] *f* glycerine
gnognote [ɲɔɲɔt] *f* (coll) junk
gnome [gnom] *m* gnome
gnomon [gnɔmɔ̃] *m* sundial
gnon [ɲɔ̃] *m* (slang) blow, punch
go [go]—**tout de go** (coll) straight off, at once
goal [gol] *m* goalkeeper
gobelet [gɔblɛ] *m* cup, tumbler, mug; **gobelets utilisés** (public sign) used paper drinking cups
gobe-mouches [gɔbmuʃ] *m invar* (zool) flycatcher; (fig) sucker, gull
gober [gɔbe] *tr* to gulp down, to gobble; to suck (*an egg*); (coll) to swallow, to be a sucker for
goberger [gɔbɛrʒe] §38 *ref* (coll) to guzzle; (coll) to live in comfort
gobeter [gɔbte] §34 *tr* to plaster, to fill in the cracks of
go·beur [gɔbœr] **-beuse** [bøz] *mf* (coll) sucker, gullible person
godet [gɔde] *m* cup; basin; bucket (*of water wheel*); (bot) calyx; **à godets** flared
godille [gɔdij] *f* scull, oar
godiller [gɔdije] *intr* to scull
godillot [gɔdijo] *m* (slang) clodhopper (*shoe*)
goéland [gɔelɑ̃] *m* sea gull
goélette [gɔelet] *f* (naut) schooner
goémon [gɔemɔ̃] *m* seaweed
gogo [gɔgo] *m* (coll) sucker, gull; **à gogo** (coll) galore
gogue·nard [gɔgnar] **-narde** [nard] *adj* jeering, mocking
goguenarder [gɔgnarde] *intr* to jeer
goguette [gɔget] *f*—**en goguette** (coll) tipsy
goinfre [gwɛ̃fr] *m* glutton, guzzler
goitre [gwatr] *m* goiter
golf [gɔlf] *m* golf
golfe [gɔlf] *m* gulf
gomme [gɔm] *f* gum; eraser; **gomme à mâcher** chewing gum; **gomme d'épinette** spruce gum; **gomme de sapin** balsam; **gomme élastique** India rubber; **mettre la gomme** (slang) to speed it up
gomme-laque [gɔmlak] *f* (*pl* **gommes-laques**) shellac
gommelaquer [gɔmlake] *tr* to shellac

gommer [gɔme] *tr* to gum; to erase ‖ *intr* to stick, to gum up
gond [gɔ̃] *m* hinge; **sortir de ses gonds** (coll) to fly off the handle
gondole [gɔ̃dɔl] *f* gondola
gondoler [gɔ̃dɔle] *intr* & *ref* to buckle up
gondolier [gɔ̃dɔlje] *m* gondolier
gonfalon [gɔ̃falɔ̃] *m* pennant
gonflement [gɔ̃fləmɑ̃] *m* swelling
gonfler [gɔ̃fle] *tr* to swell, inflate ‖ *intr* to swell up, puff up ‖ *ref* to become inflated; (coll) to swell up with pride
gonfleur [gɔ̃flœr] *m* tire pump
gong [gɔ̃g] *m* gong
goret [gɔrɛ] *m* piglet; (coll) slob
gorge [gɔrʒ] *f* throat; bust, breasts (*of woman*); gorge; **à pleine gorge** or **à gorge déployée** at the top of one's voice; **avoir la gorge serrée** to have a lump in one's throat; **faire des gorges chaudes de** (coll) to scoff at; to gloat over; **rendre gorge** to make restitution
gorger [gɔrʒe] §38 *tr* & *ref* to gorge, stuff
gorille [gɔrij] *m* gorilla; (slang) strongarm man, bodyguard; (slang) bouncer (*in a night club*)
gosier [gozje] *m* throat, gullet; **à plein gosier** loudly, lustily; **gosier serré** with one's heart in one's mouth; **s'humecter** or **se rincer le gosier** (slang) to wet one's whistle
gosse [gɔs] *mf* (coll) kid, youngster
gothique [gɔtik] *adj* Gothic ‖ *m* Gothic (*language*); Gothic art ‖ *f* black letter, Old English
gouailler [gwaje] *tr* to jeer at ‖ *intr* to jeer
gouape [gwap] *f* (slang) hoodlum, blackguard
gouaper [gwape] *intr* (slang) to lead a disreputable life
goudron [gudrɔ̃] *m* tar
goudronner [gudrɔne] *tr* to tar
gouffre [gufr] *m* gulf, abyss; whirlpool
gouge [guʒ] *f* gouge; harlot
gouger [guʒe] §38 *tr* to gouge
goujat [guʒa] *m* boor, cad
goujon [guʒɔ̃] *m* gudgeon, pin; pintle (*of hinge*); dowel; (ichth) gudgeon; **taquiner le goujon** to go fishing
goulasch [gulaʃ] *m* & *f* goulash
goule [gul] *f* ghoul
goulet [gulɛ] *m* narrows, sound; **goulet d'étranglement** bottleneck
goulot [gulo] *m* neck (*of bottle*); **boire au goulot** to drink right out of the bottle
gou·lu -lue [guly] *adj* gluttonous
goupil [gupi] *m* (obs) fox
goupille [gupij] *f* pin; **goupille fendue** cotter pin
goupiller [gupije] *tr* to cotter; (slang) to contrive, wangle
goupillon [gupijɔ̃] *m* bottle brush; sprinkler (*for holy water*); **goupillon nettoie-pipes** pipe cleaner
gourd [gur] **gourde** [gurd] *adj* numb (*with cold*) ‖ *adj fem* (coll) dumb ‖

f gourd; canteen, metal flask; (coll) dumbbell
gourdin [gurdɛ̃] *m* cudgel
gourgandine [gurgɑ̃din] *f* (hist) low-necked bodice; (coll) trollop
gour·mand [gurmɑ̃] **-mande** [mɑ̃d] *adj* & *mf* gourmand, gourmet
gourmander [gurmɑ̃de] *tr* to bawl out
gourmandise [gurmɑ̃diz] *f* gluttony; love of good food; **gourmandises** delicacies
gourme [gurm] *f* impetigo; **jeter sa gourme** (coll) to sow one's wild oats
gour·mé -mée [gurme] *adj* stiff, stuckup
gourmet [gurmɛ] *m* gourmet
gourmette [gurmɛt] *f* curb (*of harness*);.curb watch chain
gousse [gus] *f* pod; clove (*of garlic*)
gousset [guse] *m* vest pocket; fob, watch pocket (*in trousers*)
goût [gu] *m* taste; flavor; sense of taste; **au goût du jour** up to date
goûter [gute] *m* afternoon snack ‖ *tr* to taste; to sample; to relish, enjoy ‖ *intr* to have a bite to eat; **goûter à** to sample, try; **goûter de** (coll) to try out (*e.g., a trade*)
goutte [gut] *f* drop, drip; (pathol) gout; **boire la goutte** (coll) to take a nip of brandy; **la goutte d'eau qui a fait déborder le vase** the straw which broke the camel's back; **ne . . . goutte** §90 (used only with **comprendre, connaître, entendre,** and **voir**) (archaic & hum) not at all, e.g., **je n'y vois goutte** I don't see at all; **tomber goutte à goutte** to drip
goutte-à-goutte [gutagut] *m invar* (med) dropping bottle (*for intravenous drip*)
gouttelette [gutlɛt] *f* droplet
goutter [gute] *intr* to drip
gouttière [gutjɛr] *f* eavestrough, gutter; (med) splint
gouvernail [guvɛrnaj] *m* rudder, helm; **gouvernail de profondeur** (aer) elevator
gouver·nant [guvɛrnɑ̃] **-nante** [nɑ̃t] *adj* governing ‖ **gouvernants** *mpl* powers that be, rulers ‖ *f* governess; housekeeper
gouverne [guvɛrn] *f* guidance; **gouvernes** (aer) controls; **pour votre gouverne** for your guidance
gouvernement [guvɛrnəmɑ̃] *m* government; **gouvernement fantoche** puppet government
gouvernemen·tal -tale [guvɛrnəmɑ̃tal] *adj* (*pl* **-taux** [to]) governmental
gouverner [guvɛrne] *tr* to govern, to control; to steer; to manage with care ‖ *intr* to govern; (naut) to answer to the helm
gouverneur [guvɛrnœr] *m* governor; tutor; director (*e.g., of a bank*)
goyave [gɔjav] *f* guava
goyavier [gɔjavje] *m* guava tree
Graal [gral] *m* Grail
grabat [graba] *m* pallet, straw bed
grâce [grɑs] *f* grace; **de bonne grâce** willingly; **de grâce** for mercy's sake; **de mauvaise grâce** unwillingly; **faire**

grâce à to pardon; to spare; **faites-moi la grâce de** be kind enough to; **grâce!** mercy!; **grâce à** thanks to
gracier [grasje] *tr* to reprieve
gra·cieux [grasjø] **-cieuse** [sjøz] *adj* gracious; graceful
gracile [grasil] *adj* slender, slim
gradation [gradɑsjɔ̃] *f* gradation
grade [grad] *m* grade; rank; degree (*in school*); **en prendre pour son grade** (coll) to get called down
gra·dé **-dée** [grade] *adj* noncommissioned ‖ *mf* noncommissioned officer
gradient [gradjɑ̃] *m* gradient
gradin [gradɛ̃] *m* tier
graduation [gradɥɑsjɔ̃] *f* graduation
gra·dué **-duée** [gradɥe] *adj* graduated (*scale*); graded (*lessons*) ‖ *mf* graduate
gra·duel **-duelle** [gradɥɛl] *adj & m* gradual
graduer [gradɥe] *tr* to graduate
grailler [grɑje] *intr* to speak hoarsely; to sound the horn to recall the dogs
grain [grɛ̃] *m* grain; particle, speck; bean; squall; **grain de beauté** beauty spot, mole; **grain de raisin** grape; **grains** grain, cereals; **veiller au grain** (fig) to be on one's guard
graine [grɛn] *f* seed; **graine d'anis** aniseed; **mauvaise graine** (coll) shady character; **monter en graine** to run to seed; to soon be on the shelf (*said of young girl*); (coll) to grow; **prendre de la graine de** (coll) to follow the example of
graissage [grɛsaʒ] *m* (aut) lubrication
graisse [grɛs] *f* grease; fat; mother (*of wine*)
graisser [grɛse], [grese] *tr* to grease; to lubricate; to get grease stains on; **graisser la patte à qn** (coll) to grease s.o.'s palm
grais·seux [grɛsø] **grais·seuse** [grɛsøz] *adj* greasy
grammaire [gramɛr] *f* grammar
grammai·rien [gramɛrjɛ̃] **-rienne** [rjɛn] *mf* grammarian
grammati·cal **-cale** [gramatikal] *adj* (*pl* **-caux** [ko]) grammatical
gramme [gram] *m* gram
grand [grɑ̃] **grande** [grɑ̃d] *adj* tall ‖ (when standing before noun) *adj* large; great; important; high (*priest; mass; society; explosive*); vain, empty (*words*); broad (*daylight*); grand (*dignitary; officer; lady*); main (*road*); (fig) big (*heart*) ‖ *m* adult, grownup, grandee, noble; **en grand** life-size; on a grand scale; enlarged (*copy*); wide (*open*); **grands et petits** young and old ‖ **grand** *adv*—**voir grand** to see big, to envisage great projects
grand-chose [grɑ̃ʃoz] *mf* invar—**pas grand-chose** (coll) nobody, person of no importance ‖ *adv*—**pas grand-chose** not much
grand-duc [grɑ̃dyk] *m* (*pl* **grands-ducs**) grand duke
grand-duché [grɑ̃dyʃe] *m* (*pl* **grands-duchés**) grand duchy

Grande-Bretagne [grɑ̃dbrətaɲ] *f* Great Britain; **la Grande-Bretagne** Great Britain
grande-duchesse [grɑ̃dədyʃɛs] *f* (*pl* **grandes-duchesses**) grand duchess
grande·let [grɑ̃dle] **-lette** [lɛt] *adj* tall for his or her age
grandement [grɑ̃dmɑ̃] *adv* highly; handsomely; **se tromper grandement** to be very mistaken
grand-erre [grɑ̃tɛr] *adv* at full speed
gran·det [grɑ̃de] **-dette** [dɛt] *adj* rather big; rather tall
grandeur [grɑ̃dœr] *f* size; height; greatness; (astr) magnitude
grandiose [grɑ̃djoz] *adj* grandiose
grandir [grɑ̃dir] *tr* to enlarge; to increase ‖ *intr* to grow; to grow up
grandissement [grɑ̃dismɑ̃] *m* magnification, enlargement; growth
grand-livre [grɑ̃livr] *m* (*pl* **grands-livres**) ledger
grand-maman [grɑ̃mamɑ̃] *f* (*pl* **-mamans**) grandma
grand-mère [grɑ̃mɛr] *f* (*pl* **-mères** or **grands-mères**) grandmother; (coll) old lady
grand-messe [grɑ̃mɛs] *f* (*pl* **-messes**) high mass
grand-oncle [grɑ̃tɔ̃kl] *m* (*pl* **grands-oncles**) granduncle
Grand-Orient [grɑ̃tɔrjɑ̃] *m* grand lodge
grand-papa [grɑ̃papa] *m* (*pl* **grands-papas**) grandpa
grand-peine [grɑ̃pɛn]—**à grand-peine** with great difficulty
grand-père [grɑ̃pɛr] *m* (*pl* **grands-pères**) grandfather
grand-route [grɑ̃rut] *f* (*pl* **-routes**) highway
grand-rue [grɑ̃ry] *f* (*pl* **-rues**) main street
Grands Lacs [grɑ̃lak] *mpl* Great Lakes
grands-parents [grɑ̃parɑ̃] *mpl* grandparents
grand-tante [grɑ̃tɑ̃t] *f* (*pl* **-tantes**) grandaunt
grange [grɑ̃ʒ] *f* barn
granit [grani], [granit] *m* granite
granite [granit] *m* granite
granulaire [granylɛr] *adj* granular
granule [granyl] *m* granule
granu·lé **-lée** [granyle] *adj* granulated ‖ *m* little pill; medicine in granulated form
granuler [granyle] *tr & ref* to granulate
graphie [grafi] *f* spelling
graphique [grafik] *adj* graphic(al) ‖ *m* graph
graphite [grafit] *m* graphite
grappe [grap] *f* bunch, cluster; string (*of onions*); **une grappe humaine** a bunch of people
grappillage [grapijaʒ] *m* gleaning; (coll) graft
grappiller [grapije] *tr & intr* (in vineyard) to glean; (coll) to pilfer
grappillon [grapijɔ̃] *m* little bunch
grappin [grapɛ̃] *m* grapnel; **jeter or mettre le grappin sur qn** (coll) to get one's hooks into s.o.
gras [grɑ] **grasse** [grɑs] *adj* fat; greasy; rich (*soil*); carnival (*days*); smutty

(*stories*); (typ) bold-faced || *m* fatty part; calf (*of leg*); foggy weather; **au gras** with meat sauce; **faire gras** to eat meat || **gras** *adv*—**parler gras** to speak with uvular r; to tell smutty stories

gras-double [grɑdubl] *m* (*pl* -**doubles**) tripe

grassement [grɑsmɑ̃] *adv* comfortably; generously

grasseyer [grɑseje] §32 *tr* to make (*one's r's*) uvular || *intr* to speak with uvular r

grassouil·let [grɑsujɛ] **grassouil·lette** [grɑsujɛt] *adj* (coll) plump, chubby

gratification [gratifikɑsjɔ̃] *f* tip, gratuity

gratifier [gratifje] *tr* to favor, reward; **gratifier qn de q.ch.** to bestow s.th. upon s.o.

gratin [gratɛ̃] *m* (culin) crust; (coll) upper crust; **au gratin** breaded

gratiner [gratine] *tr* to cook au gratin || *intr* to brown, to crisp

gratis [gratis] *adv* gratis

gratitude [gratityd] *f* gratitude

gratte [grat] *f* scraper; (coll) graft

gratte-ciel [gratsjɛl] *m invar* skyscraper

gratte-cul [gratky] *m invar* (bot) hip

gratte-dos [gratdo] *m invar* back scratcher

gratte-papier [gratpapje] *m invar* (coll) pencil pusher, office drudge

gratte-pieds [gratpje] *m invar* shoescraper

gratter [grate] *tr* to scratch; to scratch out; to scrape up, scrape together; to itch; (coll) to pocket || *intr* to knock gently || *ref* to scratch; (with *dat* of *reflex pron*) to scratch (*e.g., one's arm*)

grattoir [gratwar] *m* scraper; knife eraser

gra·tuit [gratɥi] -**tuite** [tɥit] *adj* free of charge; gratuitous; unfounded

gratuité [gratɥite] *f* gratuity

grave [grav], [grɑv] *adj* grave; low (*frequency*); (mus) bass; (mus) flat

grave·leux [gravlø] -**leuse** [løz] *adj* gravelly, gritty; smutty, licentious

gravelle [gravɛl] *f* (pathol) gravel

graver [grave] *tr* to engrave; to cut (*a phonograph record*)

graveur [gravœr] *m* engraver; etcher

gravier [gravje] *m* gravel

gravir [gravir] *tr* to climb, climb up

gravitation [gravitɑsjɔ̃] *f* gravitation

gravité [gravite] *f* gravity

graviter [gravite] *intr* to gravitate

gravure [gravyr] *f* engraving; etching; cutting (*of phonograph record*)

gré [gre] *m* will; **à son gré** to one's liking; **bon gré mal gré** willy-nilly; **de bon gré** willingly; **de gré à gré** by mutual consent; **de gré ou de force** willy-nilly; **savoir (bon) gré de** to be grateful for; **savoir mauvais gré de** to be displeased with

grec grecque [grɛk] *adj* Greek; classic (*profile*) || *m* Greek (*language*) || *f* Greek fret || (cap) *mf* Greek

Grèce [grɛs] *f* Greece; **la Grèce** Greece

gre·din [grədɛ̃] -**dine** [din] *mf* scoundrel

gréement [gremɑ̃] *m* (naut) rigging

gréer [gree] *tr* (naut) to rig

greffe [grɛf] *m* (jur) office of the court clerk || *f* grafting; (hort, med) graft; **greffe du cœur** heart transplant

greffer [grefe] *tr* to graft; to add || *ref* to be added

greffier [grefje] *m* clerk of court, recorder; court reporter

greffon [grefɔ̃] *m* (hort) graft; (surg) transplant

grégaire [greger] *adj* gregarious

grège [grɛʒ] *adj* raw (*silk*) || *f* raw silk

grégo·rien [gregɔrjɛ̃] -**rienne** [rjɛn] *adj* Gregorian

grêle [grɛl] *adj* slender, slim; thin, high-pitched || *f* hail; (fig) shower

grê·lé -lée [grɛle] *adj* pockmarked

grêler [grɛle] *tr* to damage by hail; to pockmark || *intr* (fig) to rain down thick; **il grêle** it is hailing

grêlon [grɛlɔ̃] *m* hailstone

grelot [grəlo] *m* sleigh bell

grelottement [grələtmɑ̃] *m* shivering, trembling; jingle, jingling

grelotter [grələte] *intr* to shiver, tremble; to jingle

grenade [grənad] *f* grenade; (bot) pomegranate; **grenade à main** hand grenade; **grenade éclairante** flare; **grenade lacrymogène** tear bomb; **grenade sous-marine** depth charge

grenadier [grənadje] *m* pomegranate tree; (mil) grenadier

grenadine [grənadin] *f* grenadine

grenaille [grənɑj] *f* shot; **grenaille de plomb** buckshot

grenailler [grənaje] *tr* to granulate

grenat [grəna] *adj invar* & *m* garnet

grenier [grənje] *m* attic, loft; granary

grenouille [grənuj] *f* frog; **grenouille mugissante** or **taureau** bullfrog; **manger la grenouille** (coll) to make off with the money, to abscond

grenouillère [grənujer] *f* marsh

gre·nu -nue [grəny] *adj* full of grain; grainy (*leather*); granular (*marble*) || *m* graininess; granularity

grès [grɛ] *m* gritstone, sandstone; stoneware; terra cotta (*for drainpipes*)

grésil [grezil] *m* sleet

grésillement [grezijmɑ̃] *m* sizzling; chirping (*of cricket*)

grésiller [grezije] *tr* to scorch, to shrivel up || *intr* to sizzle, to sputter; **il grésille** it is sleeting

grève [grɛv] *f* beach; strike; (armor) greave; **faire (la) grève** to strike; **faire la grève de la faim** to go on a hunger strike; **grève de solidarité** sympathy strike; **grève du zèle** slowdown (*caused by rigid application of rules*); **grève improvisée, grève inattendue, grève surprise** walkout; **grève perlée** slowdown; **grève sauvage, grève spontanée** wildcat strike; **grève sur le tas** sitdown strike; **grève tournante** strike in one industry at a time or for several hours at a time; **se mettre en grève** to go on strike

grever [grəve] §2 *tr* to burden; to assess (*property*); **grever de** to burden with

gréviste [grevist] *mf* striker

gribouillage [gribujaʒ] *m* (coll) scribble, scrawl; (coll) daub (*in painting*)

gribouiller [gribuje] *tr* (coll) to scribble off (*a note*) || *intr* (coll) to scribble, scrawl; (coll) to daub

grief [grijɛf] *m* grievance, complaint; **faire grief de q.ch. à qn** to complain to s.o. about s.th.

grièvement [grijɛvmɑ̃] *adv* seriously, badly

griffe [grif] *f* claw, talon; signature stamp; (bot) tendril; (mach) hook, grip; **faire ses griffes** to sharpen its claws (*said of cat*); **griffe à papiers** paper clip; **porter la griffe de** to carry the stamp of; **tomber sous la griffe de** (coll) to fall into the clutches of

griffer [grife] *tr* to claw, scratch

griffon [grifɔ̃] *m* griffin

griffonner [grifɔne] *tr* to scrawl; (coll) to scribble off (*a letter*)

grignoter [grinote] *tr* to nibble on or at; to wear down (*e.g., the enemy*) || *intr* (coll) to make a little profit, to get a cut

gril [gril] *m* gridiron, grid, grill; (theat) upper flies; **être sur le gril** (coll) to be on tenterhooks

grillade [grijad] *f* grilled meat; broiling

grillage [grijaʒ] *m* grating, latticework, trellis; broiling; roasting; toasting; burning out (*of a light bulb*); (tex) singeing

grille [grij] *f* grille; grate, grating; bars; railing; gate; squares (*of crossword puzzle*); grid (*of storage battery and vacuum tube*); **grille des salaires** salary schedule

grille-pain [grijpɛ̃] *m invar* toaster

griller [grije] *tr* to grill, broil; to put a grill on; to roast (*coffee*); to toast (*bread*); to burn out (*a fuse, lamp, electric iron, etc.*); to singe, scorch; to nip (*a bud, as the frost does*) || *intr* to grill; to toast; to burn out; **griller de** to long to

grilloir [grijwar] *m* roaster; (culin) broiler

grillon [grijɔ̃] *m* cricket

grimace [grimas] *f* grimace; **faire des grimaces** to make faces; to smirk, simper; to be full of wrinkles

grimacer [grimase] §51 *intr* to grimace; to make wrong creases

grime [grim] *m* dotard, old fogey

grimer [grime] *tr* to make up (*an actor*) || *ref* to make up

grimper [grɛ̃pe] *tr* to climb || *intr* to climb; **grimper à** or **sur** to climb up on

grimpe·reau [grɛ̃pro] *m* (*pl* -**reaux**) (orn) tree creeper

grim·peur [grɛ̃pœr] -**peuse** [pøz] *adj* climbing || *m* climber

grincement [grɛ̃smɑ̃] *m* grating

grincer [grɛ̃se] §51 *tr* to gnash, grit (*the teeth*) || *intr* to grate, grind, creak; to scratch (*said of pen*)

grin·cheux [grɛ̃ʃ/ø] -**cheuse** [ʃøz] *adj* grumpy || *mf* grumbler, sorehead

gringa·let [grɛ̃galɛ] -**lette** [lɛt] *adj* weak, puny || *m* (coll) weakling, shrimp

griot [grijo] **griotte** [grijɔt] *mf* witch doctor || *m* seconds (*in milling grain*) || *f* sour cherry

grippe [grip] *f* grippe; **prendre en grippe** to take a dislike to

grippeminaud [gripmino] *m* (coll) smoothy, hypocrite

gripper [gripe] *tr* to snatch; (slang) to steal || *intr* (mach) to jam || *ref* to get stuck

grippe-sou [gripsu] *m* (*pl* -**sou** or -**sous**) (coll) tightwad, skinflint

gris [gri] **grise** [griz] *adj* gray; cloudy; brown (*paper*); (coll) tipsy

grisailler [grizaje] *tr* to paint gray || *intr* to turn gray

grisâtre [grizɑtr] *adj* grayish

griser [grize] *tr* to paint gray; (coll) to intoxicate; **les succès l'ont grisé** (coll) success has gone to his head || *ref* to get tipsy; **se griser de** (coll) to revel in

griserie [grizri] *f* intoxication

grisette [grizɛt] *f* gay working girl

gris-gris [grigri] *m* lucky charm

grisonner [grizɔne] *intr* to turn gray

grisotte [grizɔt] *f* clock (*in stocking*)

grisou [grizu] *m* firedamp

grive [griv] *f* thrush; **grive mauvis** song thrush; **grive migratoire** (*Turdus migratorius*) robin

grive·lé -**lée** [grivle] *adj* speckled

grivèlerie [grivɛlri] *f* sneaking out without paying the check

gri·vois [grivwa] -**voise** [vwaz] *adj* spicy, off-color

grizzly [grizli] *m* grizzly bear

Groënland [grɔɛnlɑ̃d] *m*—**le Groënland** Greenland

grog [grɔg] *m* grog

gro·gnard [grɔɲar] -**gnarde** [ɲard] *adj* grumbling || *mf* grumbler

grogner [grɔɲe] *intr* to grunt, to growl; to grumble, to grouch

gro·gnon [grɔɲɔ̃] -**gnonne** [ɲɔn] *adj* grouchy, grumbling || *mf* grouch, grumbler

grognonner [grɔɲɔne] *intr* to grunt; to be a complainer, to whine

groin [grwɛ̃] *m* snout; (coll) ugly mug

grommeler [grɔmle] §34 *tr* & *intr* to mutter, grumble; to growl

grondement [grɔ̃dmɑ̃] *m* growl; rumble

gronder [grɔ̃de] *tr* to scold || *intr* to scold; to growl; to rumble

gron·deur [grɔ̃dœr] -**deuse** [døz] *adj* scolding; grumbling || *mf* grumbler

groom [grum] *m* bellhop, pageboy

gros [gro] **grosse** [gros] *adj* big (*with child*); heavy (*heart*) || (when standing before noun) *adj* big, large, bulky; coarse; plain (*common sense*); main (*walls*); high (*stakes*); rich (*merchant*); booming (*voice*); bad (*weather*); heavy, rough (*sea*); swear (*words*) || *m* bulk, main part; **en gros**

wholesale; roughly, without going into detail; **faire le gros et le détail** to deal in wholesale and retail ‖ *f* see **grosse** ‖ **gros** *adv* much, a great deal; (fig) probably

gros-bec [grobɛk] *m* (*pl* **-becs**) grosbeak

groseille [grozɛj] *f* currant; **groseille à maquereau** gooseberry

groseillier [grozɛje] *m* currant bush

Gros-Jean [groʒɑ̃] *m*—**être Gros-Jean comme devant** to be in the same fix again

grosse [gros] *f* fat woman; (com) gross; (law) engrossed copy

grosserie [grosri] *f* silver dishes

grossesse [grosɛs] *f* pregnancy

grosseur [grosœr] *f* size; swelling, tumor

gros·sier [grosje] **gros·sière** [grosjɛr] *adj* coarse; crude, rude; vulgar, ribald; glaring (*error*)

grossièrement [grosjɛrmɑ̃] *adv* grossly

grossièreté [grosjɛrte] *f* coarseness, grossness, vulgarity

grossir [grosir] *tr* to enlarge; to increase ‖ *intr* to grow larger; to put on weight

grossis·sant [grosisɑ̃] **grossis·sante** [grosisɑ̃t] *adj* swelling; magnifying (*glasses*)

grossiste [grosist] *m* wholesaler, jobber

grotesque [grotɛsk] *adj* grotesque ‖ *mf* grotesque person ‖ *m* grotesque ‖ *f* grotesque (*ornament*)

grotte [grot] *f* grotto

grouillement [grujmɑ̃] *m* swarming; rumbling

grouiller [gruje] *intr* to swarm; **grouiller de** to teem with ‖ *ref* (slang) to get a move on

groupe [grup] *m* group; (mach & mil) unit; **groupe franc** (mil) commando; **groupe sanguin** blood type

groupement [grupmɑ̃] *m* grouping; organization

grouper [grupe] *tr* & *ref* to group

gruau [gryo] *m* (*pl* **gruaux**) groats; (culin) gruel; (orn) small crane

grue [gry] *f* crane; (orn) crane; (coll) tart

gruger [gryʒe] §38 *tr* to sponge on, exploit; to crunch

grume [grym] *f* bark; **en grume** rough (*timber*)

gru·meau [grymo] *m* (*pl* **-meaux**) gob; curd

grumeler [grymle] §34 *intr* to curdle, clot

gruyère [gryjɛr] *m* Gruyère cheese

guatémaltèque [gwatemaltɛk] *adj* Guatemalan ‖ (*cap*) *mf* Guatemalan

gué [ge] *m* ford, crossing; **sonder le gué** (coll) to see how the land lies ‖ *interj* hurrah!

guéable [geabl] *adj* fordable

guéer [gee] *tr* to ford; to water (*a horse*)

guelte [gɛlt] *f* commission, percentage

guenille [gənij] *f* ragged garment; **en guenilles** in tatters

guenon [gənɔ̃] *f* female monkey; long-tailed monkey; (coll) hag, old bag

guépard [gepar] *m* cheetah

guêpe [gɛp] *f* wasp

guère [gɛr] §90 *adv* hardly ever; **ne . . . guère** hardly, scarcely; hardly ever; not very; **ne . . . guère de** hardly any; **ne . . . guère que** hardly any but; hardly anyone but; **ne . . . plus guère** hardly ever any more; not much longer

guères [gɛr] *adv* (poetic) var of **guère**

guéret [gere] *m* fallow land

guéridon [geridɔ̃] *m* pedestal table

guérilla [gerija] *f* guerrilla warfare

guérillero [gerijero] *m* guerrilla

guérir [gerir] *tr* to cure ‖ *intr* to get well; to get better; to heal ‖ *ref* to cure oneself; to recover

guérison [gerizɔ̃] *f* cure, healing; recovery

guérissable [gerisabl] *adj* curable

guéris·seur [gerisœr] **guéris·seuse** [gerisøz] *mf* healer; quack

guérite [gerit] *f* sentry box; (rr) signal box; **guérite téléphonique** call box

guerre [gɛr] *f* war; **de guerre lasse** for the sake of peace and quiet; **être de bonne guerre** to be fair, to be cricket; **guerre à outrance** all-out war; **Guerre de Troie** Trojan War; **guerre d'usure** war of attrition; **guerre éclair** blitzkrieg; **guerre froide** cold war; **guerre presse-bouton** push-button war

guer·rier [gɛrje] **guer·rière** [gɛrjɛr] *adj* warlike, martial ‖ *m* warrior ‖ *f* amazon

guerroyant [gɛrwajɑ̃] **guerroyante** [gɛrwajɑ̃t] *adj* warlike, bellicose

guerroyer [gɛrwaje] §47 *intr* to make war

guerroyeur [gɛrwajœr] **guerroyeuse** [gɛrwajøz] *adj* fighting (*spirit*) ‖ *mf* fighter

guet [gɛ] *m* watch, lookout

guet-apens [gɛtapɑ̃] *m* (*pl* **guets-apens** [gɛtapɑ̃]) ambush, trap

guêtre [gɛtr] *f* gaiter, legging

guêtrer [gɛtre] *tr* & *ref* to put gaiters on

guetter [gete] *tr* to watch; to watch for; (coll) to lie in wait for

guetteur [getœr] *m* lookout, sentinel

gueu·lard [gœlar] **-larde** [lard] *adj* (slang) loud-mouthed; (slang) fond of good eating ‖ *mf* gourmet; (slang) loud-mouth ‖ *m* mouth (*of blast furnace; of cannon*); (naut) megaphone

gueule [gœl] *f* mouth (*of animal; of furnace, cannon, etc.*); (slang) mouth, mug (*of person*); **avoir de la gueule** (coll) to have a certain air; **avoir la gueule de bois** (coll) to have a hangover; **fine gueule** (coll) gourmet; **gueule cassée** (coll) disabled veteran; **gueule noire** (coll) miner; **ta gueule!** (slang) shut up!

gueule-de-loup [gœldəlu] *f* (*pl* **gueules-de-loup**) (bot) snapdragon

gueuler [gœle] *tr* & *intr* (slang) to bellow

gueuleton [gœltɔ̃] *m* (slang) big feed

gueux [gø] **gueuse** [gøz] *adj* beggarly, wretched ‖ *mf* beggar; scamp ‖ *f*

pig iron; pig (*mold*); woolen jacket; (coll) whore; **courir la gueuse** (coll) to go whoring
gugusse [gygys] *m* clown
gui [gi] *m* mistletoe; (naut) boom
guichet [giʃe] *m* window (*in post office, bank, box office, etc.*); counter (*e.g., in bank*); wicket
guidage [gidaʒ] *m* (rok) guidance
guide [gid] *m* guide; guidebook ‖ *f* rein; **mener la vie à grandes guides** to live extravagantly
guide-âne [gidɑn] *m* (*pl* -**âne** or -**ânes**) manual, guide
guider [gide] *tr* to guide
guidon [gidɔ̃] *m* handlebars; sight, bead (*of gun*); (naut) pennant
guigne [giɲ] *f* heart cherry; (coll) jinx
guigner [giɲe] *tr* to steal a glance at; (coll) to covet ‖ *intr* to peep
guignol [giɲɔl] *m* Punch (*puppet*); Punch and Judy show; (aer) king post
guignolet [giɲɔlɛ] *m* cherry brandy
guillaume [gijom] *m* rabbet plane; **Guillaume** William
guilledou [gijdu] *m*—**courir le guilledou** (coll) to make the rounds
guillemet [gijmɛ] *m* quotation mark; **fermer les guillemets** to close quotes; **ouvrir les guillemets** to quote
guillemeter [gijməte] §34 *tr* to put in quotes
guiller [gije] *intr* to ferment
guille·ret [gijrɛ] -**rette** [rɛt] *adj* chipper, lively, gay
guillotine [gijɔtin] *f* guillotine; **à guillotine** sliding; sash (*window*)
guillotiner [gijɔtine] *tr* to guillotine

guimauve [gimov] *f* (bot) marshmallow
guimbarde [gɛ̃bard] *f* (mus) jew's-harp; (coll) jalopy
guimpe [gɛ̃p] *f* wimple
guin·dé -**dée** [gɛ̃de] *adj* affected, stiff
guin·deau [gɛ̃do] *m* (*pl* -**deaux**) windlass
guinder [gɛ̃de] *tr* to hoist ‖ *ref* to put on airs
guinée [gine] *f* guinea (*coin*); **Guinée** Guinea; **la Guinée** Guinea
guingan [gɛ̃gɑ̃] *m* gingham
guingois [gɛ̃gwa] *m*—**de guingois** askew; lopsidedly
guinguette [gɛ̃gɛt] *f* roadside inn, roadside park
guipage [gipaʒ] *m* wrapping, lapping
guiper [gipe] *tr* to wind; to cover (*a wire*)
guipure [gipyr] *f* pillow lace
guirlande [girlɑ̃d] *f* garland, wreath
guirlander [girlɑ̃de] *tr* to garland
guise [giz] *f* manner; **à sa guise** as one pleases; **en guise de** by way of
guitare [gitar] *f* guitar
guitariste [gitarist] *mf* guitarist
guppy [gypi] *m* guppy
gustation [gystasjɔ̃] *f* tasting; drinking
guttu·ral -**rale** [gytyral] (*pl* -**raux** [ro] -**rales**) *adj & f* guttural
Guyane [gɥijan] *f* Guiana; **la Guyane** Guiana
gymnase [ʒimnɑz] *m* gymnasium
gymnaste [ʒimnast] *mf* gymnast
gymnote [ʒimnɔt] *m* electric eel
gynécologie [ʒinekɔlɔʒi] *f* gynecology
gypse [ʒips] *m* gypsum
gyrocompas [ʒirɔkɔ̃pa] *m* gyrocompass
gyroscope [ʒirɔskɔp] *m* gyroscope

H

H, h [aʃ], *[aʃ] *m invar* eighth letter of the French alphabet
habile [abil] *adj* skillful; clever
habileté [abilte] *f* skill; cleverness
habiliter [abilite] *tr* to qualify, entitle
habillement [abijmɑ̃] *m* clothing; clothes
habiller [abije] *tr* to dress; to clothe; to put together ‖ *intr* to be becoming, e.g., **robe qui habille** bien becoming dress ‖ *ref* to dress; to get dressed; **s'habiller chez** to buy one's clothes at or from
habit [abi] *m* dress suit; habit, frock; **habit de cérémonie** or **soirée, habit à queue de pie, habit à queue de morue** tails; **habits** clothes
habitacle [abitakl] *m* (aer) cockpit; (naut) binnacle; (poetic) dwelling
habi·tant [abitɑ̃] -**tante** [tɑ̃t] *mf* inhabitant
habitat [abita] *m* habitat; living conditions, housing
habitation [abitasjɔ̃] *f* habitation;

dwelling; residence; **habitation à bon marché** or **à loyer modéré** low-rent apartment
habi·té -**tée** [abite] *adj* inhabited; (rok) manned
habiter [abite] *tr* to live in, to inhabit ‖ *intr* to live, reside
habitude [abityd] *f* habit, custom; **comme d'habitude** as usual; **d'habitude** usually
habi·tuel -**tuelle** [abitɥɛl] *adj* habitual
habituer [abitɥe] *tr* to accustom
hâbler *[able] *intr* to brag, to boast
hâblerie *[ablǝri] *f* bragging
hâ·bleur *[ablœr] -**bleuse** [bløz] *adj* boastful ‖ *mf* braggart, boaster
hache *[aʃ] *f* ax, hatchet
ha·ché -**chée** *[aʃe] *adj* ground, chopped; hachured; choppy (*sea*); jerky (*style*); dotted (*line*)
hacher *[aʃe] *tr* to hack; to grind, chop up; **hacher menu** to mince
hache·reau *[aʃro] *m* (*pl* -**reaux**) hatchet

hachette *[aʃɛt] f hatchet
hachis *[aʃi] m hash, forcemeat
hachisch *[aʃiʃ] m hashish
hachoir *[aʃwar] m cleaver; chopping board
hachure *[aʃyr] f shading
hachurer *[aʃyre] tr to shade, hatch
haddock *[adɔk] m finnan haddie
ha·gard *[agar] -garde [gard] adj haggard
haie *[ɛ] f hedge; hurdle; line, row
haïe *[aj] interj giddap!
haillon *[ɑjɔ̃] m old piece of clothing; en haillons in rags and tatters
haillon·neux *[ɑjɔnø] haillon·neuse *[ɑjɔnøz] adj ragged, tattered
haine *[ɛn] f hate
hai·neux *[ɛnø] -neuse [nøz] adj full of hate, spiteful, malevolent
haïr *[air] §33 tr to hate, to detest || intr—haïr de to hate to
haire *[ɛr] f hair shirt
haïssable *[aisabl] adj hateful
Haïti [aiti] f Haiti
haï·tien [aisjɛ̃] -tienne [sjɛn] adj Haitian || (cap) mf Haitian
halcyon [alsjɔ̃] m (orn) kingfisher
hâle *[ɑl] m sun tan
haleine [alɛn] f breath; avoir l'haleine courte to be short-winded; (fig) to have little inspiration; de longue haleine hard, arduous (work); en haleine in good form; hors d'haleine out of breath; perdre haleine to get out of breath; reprendre haleine to catch one's breath; tenir en haleine to hold (e.g., an audience) breathless
halenée [alne] f whiff; strong breath
haler *[ale] tr to haul, to tow
hâler *[ɑle] tr to tan
hale·tant *[altɑ̃] -tante [tɑ̃t] adj breathless, panting
haleter *[alte] §2 intr to pant, puff
hall *[ol] m lobby; hall, auditorium
halle *[al] f market, marketplace; exchange
hallebarde *[albard] f halberd; il pleut des hallebardes (coll) it's raining cats and dogs
hallier *[alje] m thicket
hallucination [allysinɑsjɔ̃] f hallucination
halo *[alo] m halo
halogène [alɔʒen] m halogen
halte *[alt] f halt; stop; (rr) flag stop, way station; faire faire halte à to halt || interj halt!
halte-là *[altla] interj (mil) halt!
haltère [alter] m dumbbell
haltérophile [alterɔfil] m weight lifter
haltérophilie [alterɔfili] f weight lifting
hamac [amak] m hammock
ha·meau *[amo] m (pl -meaux) hamlet
hameçon [amsɔ̃] m hook, fishhook; (fig) bait
hammam *[ammam] m Turkish bath
hampe *[ɑ̃p] f staff, pole; shaft; downstroke; (culin) flank
hamster *[amster] m hamster
han *[ɑ̃], [hɑ̃] m grunt
hanap *[anap] m hanap, goblet
hanche *[ɑ̃ʃ] f hip; haunch

hancher *[ɑ̃ʃe] intr to lean on one leg || ref (mil) to stand at ease
handball *[ɑ̃bol] m handball
handicap *[ɑ̃dikap] m handicap
handicaper *[ɑ̃dikape] tr to handicap
hangar *[ɑ̃gar] m hangar; shed
hanneton *[antɔ̃] m June bug, chafer
hanter *[ɑ̃te] tr to haunt
hantise *[ɑ̃tiz] f obsession
happe *[ap] f crucible tongs; (carp) cramp, staple
happer *[ape] tr to snap up; (coll) to nab || intr to stick
haquenée *[akne] f palfrey
haquet *[akɛ] m dray; haquet à main pushcart
harangue *[arɑ̃g] f harangue
haranguer *[arɑ̃ge] tr & intr to harangue
haras *[arɑ] m stud farm
harasser *[arase] tr to tire out
harceler *[arsəle] §2 or §34 tr to harass, to harry; to pester; to dun
harde *[ard] f herd; leash; set (of dogs); hardes old clothes
har·di -die *[ardi] adj bold || hardi interj up and at them!
hardiesse *[ardjɛs] f boldness
harem *[arɛm] m harem
hareng *[arɑ̃] m herring; hareng fumé kipper; hareng saur red herring; sec comme un hareng (coll) long and thin; serrés comme des harengs (coll) packed like sardines
harengère *[arɑ̃ʒer] f fishwife; (coll) shrew
harenguet *[arɑ̃gɛ] m sprat
hargne *[arɲ] f bad temper
har·gneux *[arɲø] -gneuse [ɲøz] adj bad-tempered, peevish, surly
haricot *[ariko] m bean; haricot beurre lima bean, butter bean; haricot de Lima lima bean; haricot de mouton haricot (stew); haricot de Soissons kidney bean; haricot vert string bean
harmonica [armɔnika] m mouth organ
harmonie [armɔni] f harmony; (mus) band
harmo·nieux [armɔnjø] -nieuse [njøz] adj harmonious
harmonique [armɔnik] adj harmonic
harmoniser [armɔnize] tr & ref to harmonize
harnachement *[arnaʃmɑ̃] m harness; harnessing
harnacher *[arnaʃe] tr to harness; to rig out
harnais *[arnɛ] m harness
haro *[aro] m—crier haro sur (coll) to make a hue and cry against
harpagon [arpagɔ̃] m scrooge
harpe *[arp] f harp
harpie *[arpi] f harpy
harpiste *[arpist] mf harpist
harpon *[arpɔ̃] m harpoon
harponner *[arpɔne] tr to harpoon; (coll) to nab (e.g., a thief)
hart *[ar] f noose
hasard *[azar] m hazard, chance; à tout hasard just in case, come what may; au hasard at random; par hasard by chance

hasar·dé -dée *[azarde] *adj* hazardous
hasar·deux *[azardø] -deuse [døz] *adj*
risky, uncertain
hase *[az] *f* doe hare
hâte *[ɑt] *f* haste; **à la hâte** hastily;
avoir hâte de to be eager to; **en hâte**,
en toute hâte posthaste
hâter *[ɑte] *tr & ref* to hasten
hâ·tif *[ɑtif] -tive [tiv] *adj* premature;
(*hort*) early
hauban *[obɑ̃] *m* (naut) shroud; (naut)
guy
haubert *[obɛr] *m* coat of mail
hausse *[os] *f* rise, increase; block,
wedge, prop; (mil) elevation, range;
jouer à la hausse to bull the market
haussement *[osmɑ̃] *m* shrug
hausser *[ose] *tr* to raise, to lift; to
shrug (*one's shoulders*) || *intr* to rise
haussier *[osje] *m* bull (*on the stock
exchange*)
haussière *[osjɛr] *f* (naut) hawser
haut *[o] **haute** *[ot] *adj* high; loud;
high and mighty || (when standing
before noun) *adj* high; loud; upper,
higher; extra (*pay*); early (*antiquity,
Middle Ages, etc.*) || *m* top; height;
de haut en bas from top to bottom;
en haut up; upstairs; **haut de casse**
(*typ*) upper case; **haut des côtes**
sparerib; **le prendre de haut** to get
on one's high horse; **traiter de haut
en bas** to high-hat || *f* see **haute** ||
haut *adv* high; up high; loudly; **haut
les bras!** start working!; **haut les
cœurs!** lift up your hearts!; **haut les
mains!** hands up!
hau·tain *[otɛ̃] -taine [tɛn] *adj*
haughty
hautbois *[obwa] *m* oboe
haut-de-chausses *[odəʃos] *m* (*pl*
hauts-de-chausses) trunk hose,
breeches
haut-de-forme *[odəfɔrm] *m* (*pl* **hauts-
de-forme**) top hat
haute *[ot] *f* high society
hautement *[otmɑ̃] *adv* loudly; openly,
clearly; highly (*qualified*); proudly
hauteur *[otœr] *f* height; hill, upland;
altitude; nobility; haughtiness; (phys)
pitch (*of sound*); **à la hauteur de**
equal to, up to; (naut) off
haut-fond *[ofɔ̃] *m* (*pl* **hauts-fonds**)
shoal, shallows
haut-le-cœur *[oləkœr] *m invar* nausea
haut-le-corps *[oləkɔr] *m invar* jump,
sudden start
haut-parleur *[oparlœr] *m* (*pl* **haut-
parleurs**) loudspeaker
hautu·rier *[otyrje] -rière [rjɛr] *adj*
deep-sea
havage *[avaʒ] *m* (min) cutting
havane *[avan] *adj invar* tan, brown
|| *m* Havana cigar || (*cap*) *f*—**La
Havane** Havana
hâve *[av] *adj* haggard, peaked
havir *[avir] *tr* (culin) to sear
havre *[avr] *m* haven, harbor
havresac *[avrəsak] *m* haversack,
knapsack; tool bag
hawaïen or **hawaiien** [awajɛ̃], [avajɛ̃]
hawaïenne or **hawaiienne** [awajɛn],

[avajɛn] *adj* Hawaiian || (*cap*) *mf*
Hawaiian
Haye *[ɛ] *f*—**La Haye** The Hague
H.B.M. [aʃbeɛm] *f* (letterword) (habitation à bon marché) low-rent
apartment
he *[e], [he] *interj* hey!
heaume *[om] *m* helmet
hebdomadaire [ɛbdɔmadɛr] *adj & m*
weekly
héberger [ebɛrʒe] §38 *tr* to lodge
hébé·té -tée [ebete] *adj* dazed
hébéter [ebete] §10 *tr* to daze, stupefy
hébraïque [ebraik] *adj* Hebrew
hébraï·sant [ebraizɑ̃] -sante [zɑ̃t] *mf*
Hebraist
hébraïser [ebraize] *tr & intr* to He-
braize
hé·breu [ebrø] (*pl* **-breux**) *adj masc*
Hebrew || *m* Hebrew (*language*);
c'est de l'hébreu pour moi it's Greek
to me || (*cap*) *m* Hebrew (*man*)
hécatombe [ekatɔ̃b] *f* hecatomb
hein *[ɛ̃] *interj* (coll) eh!, what!
hélas [elɑs] *interj* alas!
Hélène [elɛn] *f* Helen
héler *[ele] §10 *tr* to hail, to call
hélice [elis] *f* (aer) propeller; (math)
helix, spiral; (naut) screw
hélicoptère [elikɔptɛr] *m* helicopter
héliport [elipɔr] *m* heliport
hélium [eljɔm] *m* helium
hélix [eliks] *m* helix
hellène [elɛn] *adj* Hellenic || (*cap*) *mf*
Hellene
helvétique [ɛlvetik] *adj* Swiss
hématie [emati] *f* red blood corpuscle
hémisphère [emisfɛr] *m* hemisphere
hémistiche [emisti/] *m* hemistich
hémoglobine [emɔglɔbin] *f* hemoglobin
hémophilie [emɔfili] *f* hemophilia
hémorragie [emɔraʒi] *f* hemorrhage
hémorroïdes [emɔrɔid] *fpl* hemorrhoids
hémostatique [emɔstatik] *adj* hemo-
static || *m* hemostatic, hemostat
henné *[ɛnne] *m* henna
hennir *[enir] *intr* to neigh, whinny
hennissement *[enismɑ̃] *m* neigh,
whinny
Henri [ɑ̃ri], *[ɑ̃ri] *m* Henry
héraldique [eraldik] *adj* heraldic
héraut *[ero] *m* herald
herbe [ɛrb] *f* grass; lawn; herb; **couper
l'herbe sous le pied de qn** (coll) to
pull the rug from under s.o.'s feet;
en herbe unripe; budding; **fines
herbes** herbs for seasoning; **herbe à
la puce** (*Canad*) poison ivy; **herbe
aux chats** catnip; **herbes médicinales**
or **officinales** (pharm) herbs; **herbes
potagères** potherbs; **mauvaise herbe**
weed
her·beux [ɛrbø] -beuse [bøz] *adj* grassy
herboristerie [ɛrbɔristri] *f* herb shop
her·bu -bue [ɛrby] *adj* grassy
herculéen [ɛrkyleɛ̃] **herculéenne** [ɛrky-
leɛn] *adj* herculean
hère *[ɛr] *m* wretch
héréditaire [erediter] *adj* hereditary
hérédité [eredite] *f* heredity
hérésie [erezi] *f* heresy
hérétique [eretik] *adj & mf* heretic

héris·sé héris·sée *[erise] *adj* bristly; shaggy; prickly; surly
hérisser *[erise] *tr* & *intr* to bristle
hérisson *[eris5] *m* hedgehog
héritage [erita3] *m* heritage; inheritance
hériter [erite] *tr* to inherit || *intr* to inherit; hériter de to become the heir of; to inherit, to come into
héri·tier [eritje] -tière [tjɛr] *mf* heir || *f* heiress
hermétique [ɛrmetik] *adj* hermetic(al), airtight; (fig) obscure
hermine [ɛrmin] *f* ermine
herminette [ɛrminɛt] *f* adze
hernie *[ɛrni] *f* hernia
her·nieux *[ɛrnjø] -nieuse [njøz] *adj* ruptured
héroïne [erɔin] *f* heroine; (*drug*) heroin
héroïque [erɔik] *adj* heroic
héroïsme [erɔism] *m* heroism
héron *[er5] *m* heron
héros *[ero] *m* hero
herse *[ɛrs] *f* harrow; portcullis; les herses (theat) stage lights
herser *[ɛrse] *tr* to harrow
hési·tant [ezitɑ̃] -tante [tɑ̃t] *adj* hesitant
hésitation [ezitɑsj5] *f* hesitation
hésiter [ezite] *intr* to hesitate
hétéroclite [eterɔklit] *adj* unusual, odd
hétérodoxe [eterɔdɔks] *adj* heterodox
hétérodyne [eterɔdin] *adj* heterodyne
hétérogène [eterɔʒɛn] *adj* heterogeneous
hêtre *[ɛtr] *m* beech, beech tree
heur [œr] *m* pleasure; heur et malheur joys and sorrows
heure [œr] *f* hour; time (*of day*); o'clock; à la bonne heure! fine!; à l'heure on time; by the hour, per hour; à l'heure juste, à l'heure sonnante on the hour; à tout à l'heure! see you later!; à toute heure at any time; de bonne heure early; heure d'été daylight-saving time; heure H zero hour; heure légale twelve-month daylight time (standard time); heure militaire sharp, e.g., huit heures, heure militaire eight sharp; heures d'affluence rush hours; heures de consultation office hours; heures de pointe rush hours; heures d'ouverture business hours; heures supplémentaires overtime; l'heure du déjeuner lunch hour; tout à l'heure in a little while; a little while ago
heu·reux [œrø], [ørø] -reuse [røz] *adj* happy, pleased; lucky, fortunate
heurt *[œr] *m* knock, bump; clash; bruise; sans heurt without a hitch
heur·té -tée *[œrte] *adj* clashing (*colors*); abrupt (*style*)
heurter *[œrte] *tr* to knock against, to bump into; to antagonize || *intr*— heurter contre to bump into || *ref* to clash, to collide; se heurter à to come up against
heurtoir *[œrtwar] *m* door knocker; (rr) buffer
hi *[i] *m* *invar*—hi hi hi! ho ho ho!;

pousser des hi et des ha to sputter in amazement
hiatus [jatys], *[jatys] *m* hiatus
hiberner [ibɛrne] *intr* to hibernate
hibiscus [ibiskys] *m* hibiscus
hi·bou *[ibu] *m* (*pl* -boux) owl
hic *[ik] *m*—voilà le hic! (coll) there's the rub!
hi·deux *[idø] -deuse [døz] *adj* hideous
hie *[i] *f* pile driver
hièble [jɛbl] *f* (bot) elder
hié·mal -male [jemal] *adj* (*pl* -maux [mo]) winter
hier [jɛr] *adv* & *m* yesterday; hier soir last evening, last night
hiérarchie *[jerarʃi] *f* hierarchy
hiéroglyphe [jerɔglif] *m* hieroglyphic
hiéroglyphique [jerɔglifik] *adj* hieroglyphic
hila·rant [ilarɑ̃] -rante [rɑ̃t] *adj* hilarious; laughing (*gas*)
hilare [ilar] *adj* hilarious
hin·dou -doue [ɛ̃du] *adj* Hindu || (*cap*) *mf* Hindu
hippique [ipik] *adj* horse (*race, show*)
hippisme [ipism] *m* horse racing
hippodrome [ipɔdrom] *m* hippodrome, race track
hippopotame [ipɔpɔtam] *m* hippopotamus
hirondelle [ir5dɛl] *f* (orn) swallow; (coll) bicycle cop
hispanique [ispanik] *adj* Hispanic
hispani·sant [ispanizɑ̃] -sante [zɑ̃t] *mf* Hispanist
hisser *[ise] *tr* to hoist, to raise
histoire [istwar] *f* history; story; faire des histoires à (coll) to make trouble for; histoire à dormir debout (coll) tall tale; histoire de rire (coll) just for fun; histoire de s'informer (coll) out of curiosity; pas d'histoires (coll) no fuss
histologie [istɔlɔʒi] *f* histology
histo·rien [istɔrjɛ̃] -rienne [rjɛn] *mf* historian
historier [istɔrje] *tr* to illustrate, adorn
historique [istɔrik] *adj* historic(al) || *m* historical account
histrion [istrij5] *m* ham actor
hiver [ivɛr] *m* winter
hiver·nal -nale [ivɛrnal] *adj* (*pl* -naux [no]) winter
hiverner [ivɛrne] *intr* to winter
H.L.M. [aʃɛlɛm] *m* (letterword) (habitation à loyer modéré) low-rent apartment
ho *[o], [ho] *interj* hey there!; what!
hobe·reau *[ɔbro] *m* (*pl* -reaux) (orn) hobby; (coll) squire
hoche [ɔʃ] *f* nick on a blade
hochement *[ɔʃmɑ̃] *m* shake, toss
hochepot *[ɔʃpo] *m* (culin) hotchpotch
hochequeue *[ɔʃkø] *m* (orn) wagtail
hocher *[ɔʃe] *tr* to shake; to nod
hochet *[ɔʃɛ] *m* rattle (*toy*); bauble
hockey *[ɔkɛ] *m* hockey; hockey sur glace ice hockey
hoirie [wari] *f* legacy
holà *[ɔla], [hɔla] *m* *invar*—mettre le

holà à (coll) to put a stop to || *interj* hey!; stop!

holding *[ɔldiŋ] *m* holding company

hold-up *[ɔldœp] *m invar* holdup

hollan·dais *[ɔlɑ̃dɛ] **-daise** [dɛz] *adj* Dutch || *m* Dutch (*language*) || (*cap*) *mf* Hollander (*person*)

hollande *[ɔlɑ̃d] *m* Edam cheese || *f* Holland (*linen*) || (*cap*) *f* Holland; **la Hollande** Holland

holocauste [ɔlɔkost] *m* holocaust

homard *[ɔmar] *m* lobster

home *[om] *m* home

homélie [ɔmeli] *f* homily

homéopathie [ɔmeɔpati] *f* homeopathy

homicide [ɔmisid] *adj* homicidal || *mf* homicide (*person*) || *m* homicide (*act*)

hommage [ɔmaʒ] *m* homage; **hommage de l'auteur** (formula in presenting complimentary copies) with the compliments of the author; **hommages** respects, compliments

hommasse [ɔmas] *adj* mannish (*woman*)

homme [ɔm] *m* man; **brave homme** fine man, honest man; **être homme à** to be the man to, to be capable of; **homme à tout faire** jack-of-all-trades, handyman; **homme d'affaires** businessman; **homme d'armes** man-at-arms; **homme de droite** rightist; **homme de gauche** leftist; **homme d'église** churchman; **homme de guerre** or **d'épée** military man; **homme de la rue** man in the street, first comer; **homme de l'espace** spaceman; **homme de lettres** man of letters; **homme de paille** figurehead, stooge; **homme de peine** working-man; **homme des bois** orang-utan; **homme d'État** statesman; **homme de troupe** (*pl* **hommes des troupes**) (mil) enlisted man, private; **homme d'expédition** go-getter; **homme d'intérieur** homebody; **homme du monde** man of the world; **homme galant** ladies' man; **hommes de bien** men of good will; **honnête homme** upright man; man of culture, gentleman; **jeune homme** young man; teen-age boy; **le vieil homme** (Bib) the old Adam; **un homme à la mer!** man overboard!

homme-grenouille [ɔmgrənuj] *m* (*pl* **hommes-grenouilles**) frogman

homme-sandwich [ɔmsɑ̃dwitʃ], [ɔmsɑ̃dwiʃ] *m* (*pl* **hommes-sandwichs**) sandwich man

homogène [ɔmɔʒɛn] *adj* homogeneous

homogénéiser [ɔmɔʒeneize] *tr* to homogenize

homologation [ɔmɔlɔgasjɔ̃] *f* validation

homologue [ɔmɔlɔg] *adj* homologous || *mf* (fig) opposite number

homologuer [ɔmɔlɔge] *tr* to confirm, endorse; to probate (*e.g., a will*)

homonyme [ɔmɔnim] *adj* homonymous || *m* homonym; namesake

homosexuel homosexuelle [ɔmɔsɛksɥɛl] *adj & mf* homosexual

hongre *[ɔ̃gr] *adj* gelded || *m* gelding

hongrer *[ɔ̃gre] *tr* to geld

Hongrie *[ɔ̃gri] *f* Hungary; **la Hongrie** Hungary

hon·grois *[ɔ̃grwa] **-groise** [grwaz] *adj* Hungarian || *m* Hungarian (*language*) || (*cap*) *mf* Hungarian (*person*)

honnête [ɔnɛt] *adj* honest, honorable

honnêteté [ɔnɛtəte] *f* honesty, uprightness

honneur [ɔnœr] *m* honor; **faire honneur à sa parole** to keep one's word

honnir *[ɔnir] *tr* to shame

honorabilité [ɔnɔrabilite] *f* respectability

honorable [ɔnɔrabl] *adj* honorable

honoraire [ɔnɔrɛr] *adj* honorary, emeritus || **honoraires** *mpl* honorarium, fee

honorer [ɔnɔre] *tr* to honor || *ref*— **s'honorer de** to pride oneself on

honorifique [ɔnɔrifik] *adj* honorific

honte *[ɔ̃t] *f* shame; **avoir honte** to be ashamed; **faire honte à qn** to make s.o. ashamed; **faire honte à ses parents** to be a disgrace to one's parents; **fausse honte** bashfulness; **sans honte** unashamedly

hon·teux *[ɔ̃tø] **-teuse** [tøz] *adj* ashamed; shameful

hop *[ɔp] *interj* go!, off with you!

hôpi·tal [ɔpital] *m* (*pl* **-taux** [to]) hospital; charity hospital

hoquet *[ɔkɛ] *m* hiccough

hoqueter *[ɔkte] §34 *intr* to hiccough

horaire [ɔrɛr] *adj* hourly, by hour || *m* timetable; schedule

horde *[ɔrd] *f* horde

horion *[ɔrjɔ̃] *m* punch, clout

horizon [ɔrizɔ̃] *m* horizon

horizon·tal -tale [ɔrizɔ̃tal] (*pl* **-taux** [to] **-tales**) *adj & f* horizontal

horloge [ɔrlɔʒ] *f* clock

horlo·ger [ɔrlɔʒe] **-gère** [ʒɛr] *adj* clockmaking, watchmaking || *mf* clockmaker, watchmaker

horlogerie [ɔrlɔʒri] *f* clockmaking, watchmaking; **d'horlogerie** clockwork

hormis *[ɔrmi] *prep* (lit) except for

hormone [ɔrmon] *f* hormone

horoscope [ɔrɔskɔp] *m* horoscope; **tirer l'horoscope de qn** to cast s.o.'s horoscope

horreur [ɔrœr] *f* horror; **avoir horreur de** to have a horror of; **commettre des horreurs** to commit atrocities; **dire des horreurs** to say obscene things; **dire des horreurs de** to say shocking things about

horrible [ɔribl] *adj* horrible

horrifier [ɔrifje] *tr* to horrify

horripi·lant [ɔrripilɑ̃] **-lante** [lɑ̃t] (coll) *adj* hair-raising

horripilation [ɔrripilasjɔ̃] *f* gooseflesh, (coll) exasperation

horripiler [ɔrripile] *tr* to give gooseflesh to; (coll) to exasperate

hors *[ɔr] *prep* out, beyond, outside; except, except for, save; **hors de** out of, outside of; **hors de soi** beside oneself, frantic; **hors d'ici!** get out!; **hors tout** overall

hors-bord *[ɔrbɔr] *m invar* outboard (*motor or motorboat*)

hors-caste *[ɔrkast] *mf invar* outcaste

hors-concours *[ɔrkɔ̃kur] *adj invar* excluded from competition || *m invar* contestant excluded from competition

hors-d'œuvre *[ɔrdœvr] *m invar* hors-d'oeuvre

hors-jeu *[ɔrjø] *m invar* offside position

hors-la-loi *[ɔrlalwa] *m invar* outlaw

hors-ligne *[ɔrliɲ] *adj invar* (coll) exceptional || *m invar* roadside

hors-texte *[ɔrtɛks] *m invar* (bb) insert

hortensia [ɔrtɑ̃sja] *m* hydrangea

horticole [ɔrtikɔl] *adj* horticultural

horticulture [ɔrtikyltyr] *f* horticulture

hospice [ɔspis] *m* hospice; home (*for the old, infirm, orphaned, etc.*)

hospita·lier [ɔspitalje] **-lière** [ljɛr] *adj* hospitable; hospital || *mf* hospital employee

hospitaliser [ɔspitalize] *tr* to hospitalize

hospitalité [ɔspitalite] *f* hospitality

hostie [ɔsti] *f* (eccl) Host

hostile [ɔstil] *adj* hostile

hostilité [ɔstilite] *f* hostility

hôte [ot] *m* host; guest

hôtel [otɛl], [ɔtɛl] *m* hotel; mansion; **hôtel des Monnaies** mint; **hôtel des Postes** main post office; **hôtel de ville** city hall; **hôtel meublé** rooming house, residential hotel

hôtel-Dieu [otɛldjø], [ɔtɛldjø] *m* (*pl* **hôtels-Dieu**) city hospital

hôte·lier [otəlje], [ɔtəlje] **-lière** [ljɛr] *adj* hotel (*business*) || *mf* hotel manager

hôtellerie [otɛlri], [ɔtɛlri] *f* hotel business; fine restaurant; hostelry, hostel

hôtesse [otɛs] *f* hostess; **hôtesse de l'air** air hostess, stewardess

hotte *[ɔt] *f* basket (*carried on back*); hod (*of mason*); hood (*of chimney*)

hou *[u] *interj* oh no!

houache *[waʃ] *f* wake (*of ship*)

houblon *[ublɔ̃] *m* hop (*vine*); hops (*dried flowers*)

houe *[u] *f* hoe

houer *[we] *tr* to hoe

houille *[uj] *f* coal; **houille blanche** water power; **houille bleue** tide power; **houille d'or** energy from the sun; **houille grasse** or **collante** soft coal; **houille incolore** wind power; **houille maigre** or **éclatante** hard coal; **houille rouge** energy from the heat of the earth

houil·ler *[uje] **houil·lère** *[ujɛr] *adj* coal-bearing, carboniferous; coal (*industry*) || *f* coal mine

houilleur *[ujœr] *m* coal miner

houle *[ul] *f* swell

houlette *[ulɛt] *f* crook (*of shepherd*); (hort) trowel

hou·leux *[ulø] **-leuse** [løz] *adj* swelling (*sea*); (fig) stormy, turbulent

houp *[up], [hup] *interj* go to it!

houppe *[up] *f* tuft; crest; tassel; **houppe à poudre** powder puff

houppelande *[uplɑ̃d] *f* greatcoat

houppette *[upɛt] *f* tuft; powder puff

hourra *[ura], [hura] *m*—**pousser trois hourras** to give three cheers || *interj* hurrah!

hourvari *[urvari] *m* call to the hounds; (coll) uproar

houspiller *[uspije] *tr* to jostle, knock around; to rake over the coals, to tell off

housse *[us] *f* slipcover; cover (*e.g., for typewriter*); garment bag; housing, horsecloth; (aut) seat cover

housser *[use] *tr* to dust (*with feather duster*)

houssine *[usin] *f* rug beater; switch

houssoir *[uswar] *m* feather duster; whisk broom

houx *[u] *m* holly

hoyau *[wajo] *m* (*pl* **hoyaux**) mattock; pickax

hublot *[yblo] *m* porthole

huche *[yʃ] *f* hutch; bin

hucher *[yʃe] *tr* to call, to shout to

hue *[y] *interj* gee!; gee up! **tirer à hue et à dia** (fig) to pull in opposite directions

huée *[ɥe] *f* hoot, boo

huer *[ɥe] *tr & intr* to hoot, to boo

hugue·not *[ygno] **-note** [nɔt] *adj* Huguenot || *f* pipkin || (*cap*) *mf* Huguenot (*person*)

huile [ɥil] *f* oil; big shot; **d'huile** calm, e.g., **mer d'huile** calm sea; **huile de coude** elbow grease; **huile de foie de morue** cod-liver oil; **huile de freins** brake fluid; **huile de ricin** castor oil; **huile lourde** diesel fuel; **huile solaire** suntan oil; **les huiles** (coll) the VIP's; **sentir l'huile** (fig) to smell of midnight oil; **verser de l'huile sur le feu** (fig) to add fuel to the fire

huiler [ɥile] *tr* to oil; to grease

hui·leux [ɥilø] **-leuse** [løz] *adj* oily; greasy

huis [ɥi] *m* (archaic) door; **à huis clos** behind closed doors; (law) in camera; **à huis ouvert** spectators admitted || *[ɥi] *m*—**demander le huis clos** to request a closed-door session

huisserie [ɥisri] *f* doorframe

huissier [ɥisje] *m* doorman; usher (*before a person of rank*); **huissier audiencier** bailiff; **huissier exploitant** process server

huit *[ɥi(t)] *adj & pron* eight; the Eighth, e.g., **Jean huit** John the Eighth; **huit heures** eight o'clock || *m* eight; eighth (*in dates*); **faire des huit** to cut figures of eight (*in figure skating*)

huitain *[ɥitɛ̃] *m* eight-line verse

huitaine *[ɥitɛn] *f* (grouping of) eight; week; **à huitaine** the same day next week; **une huitaine de** about eight

huitième *[ɥitjɛm] *adj, pron* (*masc, fem*), & *m* eighth

huître [ɥitr] *f* oyster

huit-reflets *[ɥirəflɛ] *m invar* top hat

huî·trier [ɥitrije] **-trière** [trijɛr] *adj* oyster (*industry*) || *m* (orn) oyster-catcher || *f* oyster bed

hulotte *[ylɔt] *f* hoot owl
hululer *[ylyle] *intr* to hoot
hum *[œm], [hœm] *interj* hum!
hu·main [ymɛ̃] **-maine** [mɛn] *adj* human; humane
humaniste [ymanist] *adj & m* humanist
humanitaire [ymanitɛr] *adj & mf* humanitarian
humanité [ymanite] *f* humanity; **humanités (classiques)** humanities (*Greek & Latin classics*); **humanités modernes** humanities, belles-lettres; **humanités scientifiques** liberal studies (*concerned with the observation and classification of facts*)
humble [œ̃bl] *adj* humble
humecter [ymɛkte] *tr* to moisten ‖ *ref* to become damp; **s'humecter le gosier** (slang) to wet one's whistle
humer *[yme] *tr* to suck, to suck up; to sip; to inhale, to breathe in
humérus [ymerys] *m* humerus
humeur [ymœr] *f* humor, body fluid; humor, mood, spirits; **avec humeur** testily; **avoir de l'humeur** to be in a bad mood; **être de bonne humeur** to be in a good humor
humide [ymid] *adj* humid, damp; wet
humidifier [ymidifje] *tr* to humidify
humidité [ymidite] *f* humidity
humi·liant [ymiljɑ̃] **-liante** [ljɑ̃t] *adj* humiliating
humiliation [ymiljɑsjɔ̃] *f* humiliation
humilier [ymilje] *tr* to humiliate, to humble ‖ *ref* to humble oneself
humilité [ymilite] *f* humility
humoriste [ymɔrist] *adj* humorous (*writer*) ‖ *mf* humorist
humoristique [ymɔristik] *adj* humorous
humour [ymur] *m* humor; **humour noir** macabre humor, sick humor
humus [ymys] *m* humus
hune *[yn] *f* (naut) top; **hune de vigie** (naut) crow's-nest
huppe *[yp] *f* tuft, crest (*of bird*); (orn) hoopoe
hup·pé -pée *[ype] *adj* tufted, crested; (coll) smart, stylish
hure *[yr] *f* head (*of boar, salmon, etc.*); (culin) headcheese
hurlement *[yrlmɑ̃] *m* howl, roar; howling, roaring (*e.g., of wind*)
hurler *[yrle] *tr* to cry out, yell ‖ *intr* to howl, to roar
hur·leur *[yrlœr] **-leuse** [løz] *adj* howling ‖ *mf* howler ‖ *m* (zool) howler
hurluberlu [yrlybɛrly] *m* (coll) scatterbrain
hu·ron *[yrɔ̃] **-ronne** [rɔn] *adj* (coll) boorish, uncouth ‖ *mf* (coll) boor
hurricane *[urikan], *[œrikɛn] *m* hurricane
hutte *[yt] *f* hut, cabin
hyacinthe [jasɛ̃t] *f* hyacinth (*stone*)
hya·lin [jalɛ̃] **-line** [lin] *adj* glassy
hybride [ibrid] *adj & m* hybrid
hydrate [idrat] *m* hydrate
hydrater [idrate] *tr & ref* to hydrate

hydraulique [idrolik] *adj* hydraulic ‖ *f* hydraulics
hydravion [idravjɔ̃] *m* hydroplane
hydre [idr] *f* hydra
hydrocarbure [idrɔkarbyr] *m* hydrocarbon
hydro-électrique [idrɔelɛktrik] *adj* hydroelectric
hydrofoil [idrɔfɔjl] *m* hydrofoil
hydrofuge [idrɔfyʒ] *adj* waterproof
hydrofuger [idrɔfyʒe] §38 *tr* to waterproof
hydrogène [idrɔʒen] *m* hydrogen
hydroglisseur [idrɔglisœr] *m* speedboat
hydromètre [idrɔmetr] *m* hydrometer ‖ *f* (ent) water spider
hydrophile [idrɔfil] *adj* absorbent ‖ *m* —**hydrophile brun** (ent) water devil
hydrophobie [idrɔfɔbi] *f* hydrophobia
hydropisie [idrɔpizi] *f* dropsy
hydroscope [idrɔskɔp] *m* dowser
hydroxyde [idrɔksid] *m* hydroxide
hyène [jen] *f* hyena
hygiène [iʒjen] *f* hygiene
hygiénique [iʒjenik] *adj* hygienic
hymnaire [imnɛr] *m* hymnal
hymne [imnə], [im] *m* hymn, ode, anthem; **hymne national** national anthem ‖ *f* (eccl) hymn, canticle
hyperacidité [iperasidite] *f* hyperacidity
hyperbole [iperbɔl] *f* (math) hyperbola; (rhet) hyperbole
hypersensible [ipersɑ̃sibl] *adj* hypersensitive, supersensitive
hypersensi·tif [ipersɑ̃sitif] **-tive** [tiv] *adj* hypersensitive, supersensitive
hypertension [ipertɑ̃sjɔ̃] *f* high blood pressure, hypertension
hypnose [ipnoz] *f* hypnosis
hypnotique [ipnɔtik] *adj & m* hypnotic
hypnotiser [ipnɔtize] *tr* to hypnotize ‖ *ref* —**s'hypnotiser sur** (fig) to be hypnotized by
hypnoti·seur [ipnɔtizœr] **-seuse** [zøz] *mf* hypnotist
hypnotisme [ipnɔtism] *m* hypnotism
hypocondriaque [ipɔkɔ̃drijak] *adj & mf* hypochondriac
hypocrisie [ipɔkrizi] *f* hypocrisy
hypocrite [ipɔkrit] *adj* hypocritical ‖ *mf* hypocrite
hypodermique [ipɔdermik] *adj* hypodermic
hyposulfite [ipɔsylfit] *m* hyposulfite
hypotension [ipɔtɑ̃sjɔ̃] *f* low blood pressure
hypoténuse [ipɔtenyz] *f* hypotenuse
hypothèque [ipɔtek] *f* mortgage; **prendre une hypothèque sur** to put a mortgage on; **purger une hypothèque** to pay off a mortgage
hypothéquer [ipɔteke] §10 *tr* to mortgage
hypothèse [ipɔtez] *f* hypothesis
hypothétique [ipɔtetik] *adj* hypothetic(al)
hystérie [isteri] *f* hysteria
hystérique [isterik] *adj* hysteric(al)

I

I, i [i], *[i] *m invar* ninth letter of the French alphabet
ïambique [jãbik] *adj* iambic
ibé·rien [iberjɛ̃] **-rienne** [rjɛn] *adj* Iberian || (*cap*) *mf* Iberian
ibérique [iberik] *adj* Iberian
iceberg [isbɛrg] *m* iceberg
ichtyologie [iktjɔlɔʒi] *f* ichthyology
ici [isi] *adv* here; this is, e.g., **ici Paris** (rad, telv) this is Paris; e.g., **ici Robert** (telp) this is Robert; **d'ici** hereabouts; from today; **d'ici demain** before tomorrow; **d'ici là** between now and then, in the meantime; **d'ici peu** before long; **jusqu'ici** up to now, hitherto; **par ici** this way, through here
ici-bas [isiba] *adv* here below, on earth
icône [ikon] *f* icon
iconoclaste [ikɔnɔklast] *adj* iconoclastic || *mf* iconoclast
iconographie [ikɔnɔgrafi] *f* iconography; pictures, pictorial material
iconoscope [ikɔnɔskɔp] *m* iconoscope
ictère [iktɛr] *m* jaundice
ictérique [ikterik] *adj* jaundiced
idéal idéale [ideal] *adj & m* (*pl* **idéaux** [ideo] or **idéals**) ideal
idéaliser [idealize] *tr* to idealize
idéaliste [idealist] *adj & mf* idealist
idée [ide] *f* idea; mind, head; opinion, esteem; (coll) shade, touch; **changer d'idée** to change one's mind
identification [idãtifikɑsjɔ̃] *f* identification
identifier [idãtifje] *tr* to identify
identique [idãtik] *adj* identic(al)
identité [idãtite] *f* identity
idéologie [ideɔlɔʒi] *f* ideology; (pej) utopianism
idéologique [ideɔlɔʒik] *adj* ideologic(al); conceptual
ides [id] *fpl* ides
idiomatique [idjɔmatik] *adj* idiomatic
idiome [idjom] *m* idiom, language
idiosyncrasie [idjɔsɛ̃krazi] *f* idiosyncrasy
i·diot [idjo] **-diote** [djɔt] *adj* idiotic || *mf* idiot
idiotie [idjɔsi] *f* idiocy
idiotisme [idjɔtism] *m* idiom, idiomatic expression
idolâtrer [idɔlɑtre] *tr* to idolize
idolâtrie [idɔlɑtri] *f* idolatry
idole [idɔl] *f* idol
idylle [idil] *f* idyll; romance, love affair
idyllique [idilik] *adj* idyllic
if [if] *m* yew
IGAME [igam] *m* (acronym) (**Inspecteur Général de l'Administration en Mission Extraordinaire**) head prefect
igname [iɲam], [ignam] *f* yam
ignare [iɲar] *adj* ignorant
ig·né -née [igne] *adj* igneous
ignifuge [ignifyʒ] *adj* fireproof || *m* fireproofing
ignifuger [ignifyʒe] §38 *tr* to fireproof

ignition [ignisjɔ̃] *f* ignition; red heat (*of metal*)
ignoble [iɲɔbl] *adj* ignoble; disgusting
ignomi·nieux [iɲɔminjø] **-nieuse** [njøz] *adj* ignominious
ignorance [iɲɔrãs] *f* ignorance
igno·rant [iɲɔrã] **-rante** [rãt] *adj* ignorant || *mf* ignoramus
ignorer [iɲɔre] *tr* not to know, to be ignorant of; to be unacquainted with
il [il] §87
île [il] *f* island, isle; **les îles Normandes** the Channel Islands
illé·gal -gale [illegal] *adj* (*pl* **-gaux** [go]) illegal
illégitime [illeʒitim] *adj* illegitimate; unjustified
illet·tré -trée [illɛtre] *adj & mf* illiterate
illicite [illisit] *adj* illicit; foul (*blow*)
illimi·té -tée [illimite] *adj* unlimited
illisible [illizibl] *adj* illegible; unreadable (*book*)
illogique [illɔʒik] *adj* illogical
illumination [illyminɑsjɔ̃] *f* illumination
illumi·né -née [illymine] *adj & mf* fanatic, visionary
illuminer [illymine] *tr* to illuminate
illusion [illyzjɔ̃] *f* illusion; **illusion de la vue** optical illusion; **se faire des illusions** to indulge in wishful thinking
illusionner [illyzjɔne] *tr* to delude || *ref* to delude oneself
illusionniste [illyzjɔnist] *mf* magician
illusoire [illyzwar] *adj* illusory, illusive
illustra·teur [illystratœr] *m* illustrator
illustration [illystrɑsjɔ̃] *f* illustration; glorification; glory; celebrity
illustre [illystr] *adj* illustrious, renowned
illus·tré -trée [illystre] *adj* illustrated || *m* illustrated magazine
illustrer [illystre] *tr* to illustrate || *ref* to distinguish oneself
îlot [ilo] *m* small island, isle; block (*of houses*)
ils [il] §87
image [imaʒ] *f* image; picture; **images** imagery
imager [imaʒe] §38 *tr* to embellish with metaphors, to color
imagerie [imaʒri] *f*—**imagerie d'Épinal** cardboard cutouts
imaginaire [imaʒinɛr] *adj* imaginary
imagination [imaʒinɑsjɔ̃] *f* imagination
imaginer [imaʒine] *tr* to imagine; to invent || *intr* to imagine; **imaginer de** + *inf* to have the idea of + *ger* || *ref* to imagine oneself; (with *dat* of *reflex pron*) to imagine
imbattable [ɛ̃batabl] *adj* unbeatable
imbat·tu -tue [ɛ̃baty] *adj* unbeaten
imbécile [ɛ̃besil] *adj & mf* imbecile
imbécillité [ɛ̃besilite] *f* imbecility
imberbe [ɛ̃bɛrb] *adj* beardless
imbiber [ɛ̃bibe] *tr & ref* to soak; **s'imbiber de** to soak up; to be imbued with

imbri·qué -quée [ɛ̃brike] *adj* overlapping
imbrisable [ɛ̃brizabl] *adj* unbreakable
imbrûlable [ɛ̃brylabl] *adj* fireproof
im·bu -bue [ɛ̃by] *adj*—imbu de imbued with, steeped in
imita·teur [imitatœr] -trice [tris] *mf* imitator
imitation [imitɑsjɔ̃] *f* imitation
imiter [imite] *tr* to imitate
immacu·lé -lée [immakyle] *adj* immaculate
immangeable [ɛ̃mɑ̃ʒabl] *adj* inedible
immanquable [ɛ̃mɑ̃kabl] *adj* infallible; inevitable
immaté·riel -rielle [immaterjɛl] *adj* immaterial
immatriculation [immatrikylɑsjɔ̃] *f* registration; enrollment
immatriculer [immatrikyle] *tr* to register
immature [immatyr] *adj* unmatured
immé·diat [immedja] -diàte [djat] *adj* immediate
immédiatement [immedjatmɑ̃] *adv* immediately
immémo·rial -riale [immemɔrjal] *adj* (*pl* -riaux [rjo]) immemorial
immense [immɑ̃s] *adj* immense
immensurable [immɑ̃syrabl] *adj* immeasurable, immensurable
immerger [immɛrʒe] §38 *tr* to immerse, to dip; to throw overboard; to lay (*a cable*)
imméri·té -tée [immerite] *adj* undeserved
immersion [immɛrsjɔ̃] *f* immersion
immettable [ɛ̃mɛtabl] *adj* unwearable
immeuble [immœbl] *adj* real, e.g., biens immeubles real estate ‖ *m* building, apartment building
immi·grant [immigrɑ̃] -grante [grɑ̃t] *adj & mf* immigrant
immigration [immigrɑsjɔ̃] *f* immigration
immi·gré -grée [immigre] *adj & mf* immigrant
immigrer [immigre] *intr* to immigrate
immi·nent [imminɑ̃] -nente [nɑ̃t] *adj* imminent, impending
immiscer [immise] §51 *ref*—s'immiscer dans to interfere with, to meddle with
immixtion [immiksjɔ̃] *f* interference
immobile [immɔbil] *adj* motionless; immobile (*resolute*); dead (*typewriter key*)
immobi·lier [immɔbilje] -lière [ljɛr] *adj* real-estate, property; real, e.g., biens immobiliers real estate
immobiliser [immɔbilize] *tr* to immobilize; to tie up ‖ *ref* to come to a stop
immodé·ré -rée [immɔdere] *adj* immoderate
immonde [immɔ̃d] *adj* foul, filthy; (eccl) unclean
immondices [immɔ̃dis] *fpl* garbage, refuse
immo·ral -rale [immɔral] *adj* (*pl* -raux [ro]) immoral
immortaliser [immɔrtalize] *tr* to immortalize

immor·tel -telle [immɔrtɛl] *adj & mf* immortal ‖ *f* (bot) everlasting
immoti·vé -vée [immɔtive] *adj* groundless
immuable [immɥabl] *adj* changeless
immuniser [immynize] *tr* to immunize
immunité [immynite] *f* immunity
im·pair -paire [ɛ̃pɛr] *adj* odd, uneven ‖ *m* (coll) blunder
impardonnable [ɛ̃pardɔnabl] *adj* unpardonable
impar·fait [ɛ̃parfɛ] -faite [fɛt] *adj & m* imperfect
imparité [ɛ̃parite] *f* inequality, disparity
impar·tial -tiale [ɛ̃parsjal] *adj* (*pl* -tiaux [sjo]) impartial
impartir [ɛ̃partir] *tr* to grant
impasse [ɛ̃pɑs] *f* blind alley, dead-end street; impasse, deadlock; (cards) finesse; faire l'impasse à (cards) to finesse
impassible [ɛ̃pasibl] *adj* impassible; impassive (*look, face, etc.*)
impatience [ɛ̃pasjɑ̃s] *f* impatience; impatiences (coll) attack of nerves
impa·tient [ɛ̃pasjɑ̃] -tiente [sjɑ̃t] *adj* impatient
impatienter [ɛ̃pasjɑ̃te] *tr* to make impatient ‖ *ref* to lose patience
impatroniser [ɛ̃patrɔnize] *ref* to take charge; to take hold
impavide [ɛ̃pavid] *adj* fearless
impayable [ɛ̃pɛjabl] *adj* (coll) priceless, very funny
impayé impayée [ɛ̃peje] *adj* unpaid
impeccable [ɛ̃pɛkabl] *adj* impeccable
impénétrable [ɛ̃penetrabl] *adj* impenetrable
impéni·tent [ɛ̃penitɑ̃] -tente [tɑ̃t] *adj* impenitent, obdurate, inveterate
impensable [ɛ̃pɑ̃sabl] *adj* unthinkable
imper [ɛ̃pɛr] *m* (coll) raincoat
impéra·tif [ɛ̃peratif] -tive [tiv] *adj & m* imperative
impératrice [ɛ̃peratris] *f* empress
imperceptible [ɛ̃pɛrsɛptibl] *adj* imperceptible; negligible
imperdable [ɛ̃pɛrdabl] *adj* unlosable
imperfection [ɛ̃pɛrfɛksjɔ̃] *f* imperfection, defect
impé·rial -riale [ɛ̃perjal] *adj* (*pl* -riaux [rjo]) imperial ‖ *f* goatee; upper deck (*of bus, coach, etc.*)
impérialiste [ɛ̃perjalist] *adj & mf* imperialist
impé·rieux [ɛ̃perjø] -rieuse [rjøz] *adj* imperious, haughty; imperative, urgent
impérissable [ɛ̃perisabl] *adj* imperishable
impéritie [ɛ̃perisi] *f* incompetence
imperméabiliser [ɛ̃pɛrmeabilize] *tr* to waterproof
imperméable [ɛ̃pɛrmeabl] *adj* waterproof; impervious ‖ *m* raincoat
imperson·nel -nelle [ɛ̃pɛrsɔnɛl] *adj* impersonal; commonplace; ordinary
imperti·nent [ɛ̃pɛrtinɑ̃] -nente [nɑ̃t] *adj* impertinent ‖ *mf* impertinent person
impé·trant [ɛ̃petrɑ̃] -trante [trɑ̃t] *mf* holder (*of a title or degree*)

impé·tueux [ɛ̃petɥø] **-tueuse** [tɥøz] *adj* impetuous

impie [ɛ̃pi] *adj* impious, ungodly; blasphemous ‖ *mf* unbeliever; blasphemer

impiété [ɛ̃pjete] *f* impiety; disrespect

impitoyable [ɛ̃pitwajabl] *adj* unmerciful

implanter [ɛ̃plɑ̃te] *tr* to implant; to introduce ‖ *ref* to take root; **s'implanter chez** (coll) to thrust oneself upon

implication [ɛ̃plikɑsjɔ̃] *f* implication

implicite [ɛ̃plisit] *adj* implicit

impliquer [ɛ̃plike] *tr* to implicate; to imply

implorer [ɛ̃plɔre] *tr* to implore

imployable [ɛ̃plwajabl] *adj* pitiless; inflexible

impo·li -lie [ɛ̃pɔli] *adj* impolite

impolitique [ɛ̃pɔlitik] *adj* ill-advised

impondérable [ɛ̃pɔ̃derabl] *adj & m* imponderable

impopulaire [ɛ̃pɔpylɛr] *adj* unpopular

impopularité [ɛ̃pɔpylarite] *f* unpopularity

importance [ɛ̃pɔrtɑ̃s] *f* importance; size; **d'importance** large, of consequence; thoroughly, very hard

impor·tant [ɛ̃pɔrtɑ̃] **-tante** [tɑ̃t] *adj* important; large, considerable ‖ *m* main thing; **faire l'important** (coll) to act big

importa·teur [ɛ̃pɔrtatœr] **-trice** [tris] *mf* importer

importer [ɛ̃pɔrte] *tr* to import ‖ *intr* to matter; to be important; **n'importe** no matter, never mind; **n'importe comment** any way; **n'importe où** anywhere; **n'importe quand** anytime; **n'importe quel . . .** any **. . .** ; **n'importe qui** anybody; **n'importe quoi** anything; **peu m'importe** it doesn't matter to me; **qu'importe?** what does it matter?

impor·tun [ɛ̃pɔrtœ̃] **-tune** [tyn] *adj* bothersome ‖ *mf* pest, nuisance

importuner [ɛ̃pɔrtyne] *tr* to importune

imposable [ɛ̃pozabl] *adj* taxable

impo·sant [ɛ̃pozɑ̃] **-sante** [zɑ̃t] *adj* imposing

impo·sé -sée [ɛ̃poze] *adj* taxed; fixed (*price*) ‖ *mf* taxpayer

imposer [ɛ̃poze] *tr* to impose; to levy a tax on ‖ *intr*—**en imposer à** to make an impression on; to impose on ‖ *ref* to assert oneself; to be indispensable; **s'imposer à** to force itself upon; **s'imposer chez** to foist oneself upon

imposition [ɛ̃pozisjɔ̃] *f* imposition; taxation; laying on, levying

impossible [ɛ̃pɔsibl] *adj* impossible

imposte [ɛ̃pɔst] *f* transom; (archit) impost

imposteur [ɛ̃pɔstœr] *m* impostor

imposture [ɛ̃pɔstyr] *f* imposture

impôt [ɛ̃po] *m* tax; **impôt du sang** military duty; **impôt foncier** property tax; **impôt indirecte** sales tax; **impôt retenu à la source** withholding tax; **impôt sur le revenu** income tax

impotence [ɛ̃pɔtɑ̃s] *f* lameness, infirmity

impo·tent [ɛ̃pɔtɑ̃] **-tente** [tɑ̃t] *adj* crippled; bedridden ‖ *mf* cripple

impraticable [ɛ̃pratikabl] *adj* impracticable; impassable (*e.g., road*)

impré·cis [ɛ̃presi] **-cise** [siz] *adj* vague, hazy

imprégner [ɛ̃preɲe] §10 *tr* to impregnate

imprenable [ɛ̃prənabl] *adj* impregnable

impréparation [ɛ̃preparɑsjɔ̃] *f* unpreparedness

imprésario [ɛ̃presarjo] *m* impresario

impression [ɛ̃prɛsjɔ̃] *f* impression; printing

impression·nant [ɛ̃prɛsjɔnɑ̃] **impression·nante** [ɛ̃prɛsjɔnɑ̃t] *adj* impressive

impressionner [ɛ̃prɛsjɔne] *tr* to impress, to affect; (phot) to expose

imprévisible [ɛ̃previzibl] *adj* unforeseeable

imprévision [ɛ̃previzjɔ̃] *f* lack of foresight

imprévoyant [ɛ̃prevwajɑ̃] **imprévoyante** [ɛ̃prevwajɑ̃t] *adj* improvident, shortsighted

impré·vu -vue [ɛ̃prevy] *adj & m* unforeseen, unexpected; **sauf imprévu** unless something unforeseen happens

impri·mé -mée [ɛ̃prime] *adj* printed ‖ *m* print, calico; printed work, book; printing (*as opposed to script*); **imprimés** printed matter

imprimer [ɛ̃prime] *tr* to print; to imprint; to impress; to impart (*e.g., movement*)

imprimerie [ɛ̃primri] *f* printing; printing office, print shop

imprimeur [ɛ̃primœr] *m* printer

imprimeur-éditeur [ɛ̃primœreditœr] *m* (*pl* **imprimeurs-éditeurs**) printer and publisher

imprimeur-libraire [ɛ̃primœrlibrɛr] *m* (*pl* **imprimeurs-libraires**) printer and publisher

imprimeuse [ɛ̃primøz] *f* printing press

improbable [ɛ̃prɔbabl] *adj* improbable

improba·tif [ɛ̃prɔbatif] **-tive** [tiv] *adj* disapproving

improbité [ɛ̃prɔbite] *f* dishonesty

improduc·tif [ɛ̃prɔdyktif] **-tive** [tiv] *adj* unproductive

impromp·tu -tue [ɛ̃prɔ̃pty] *adj* impromptu ‖ *m* impromptu play; (mus) impromptu ‖ **impromptu** *adv* impromptu

impropre [ɛ̃prɔpr] *adj* improper (*not right*); **impropre à** unfit for

impropriété [ɛ̃prɔprijete] *f* incorrectness

improviser [ɛ̃prɔvize] *tr & intr* to improvise

improviste [ɛ̃prɔvist]—**à l'improviste** unexpectedly, impromptu; **prendre à l'improviste** to catch napping

impru·dent [ɛ̃prydɑ̃] **-dente** [dɑ̃t] *adj* imprudent

impubère [ɛ̃pybɛr] *adj* under the age of puberty

impubliable [ɛ̃pybljabl] *adj* unpublishable, not fit to print

impu·dent [ɛ̃pydɑ̃] **-dente** [dɑ̃t] *adj* impudent

impudeur [ɛ̃pydœr] *f* immodesty

impudicité [ɛ̃pydisite] *f* indecency

impudique [ɛ̃pydik] *adj* immodest

impuissance [ɛ̃pЧisɑ̃s] *f* impotence; **être dans l'impuissance de faire q.ch.** to be powerless to do s.th.

impuis·sant [ɛ̃pЧisɑ̃] **impuis·sante** [ɛ̃pЧisɑ̃t] *adj* impotent, powerless, helpless; (pathol) impotent

impul·sif [ɛ̃pylsif] **-sive** [siv] *adj* impulsive || *mf* impulsive person

impulsion [ɛ̃pylsjɔ̃] *f* impulse; **donner l'impulsion à** to give an impetus to; **sous l'impulsion du moment** on the spur of the moment

impunément [ɛ̃pynemɑ̃] *adv* with impunity

impu·ni -nie [ɛ̃pyni] *adj* unpunished

impunité [ɛ̃pynite] *f* impunity

im·pur -pure [ɛ̃pyr] *adj* impure

impureté [ɛ̃pyrte] *f* impurity

imputation [ɛ̃pytɑsjɔ̃] *f* imputation; (com) charge; (com) deduction

imputer [ɛ̃pyte] *tr* to impute, ascribe; (com) **imputer q.ch. à** to charge s.th. to

inaccessible [inaksesibl] *adj* inaccessible

inac·tif [inaktif] **-tive** [tiv] *adj* inactive

inaction [inaksjɔ̃] *f* inaction

inactivité [inaktivite] *f* inactivity

inadaptation [inadaptɑsjɔ̃] *f* maladjustment

inadap·té -tée [inadapte] *adj* maladjusted || *mf* misfit

inadvertance [inadvɛrtɑ̃s] *f*—**par inadvertance** inadvertently

inalté·ré -rée [inaltere] *adj* unspoiled

inani·mé -mée [inanime] *adj* inanimate

inappréciable [inapresjabl] *adj* inappreciable, imperceptible; invaluable

inapprivoisable [inaprivwazabl] *adj* untamable

inapte [inapt] *adj* inept; **inapte à** unfit for, unsuitable for || *mf* dropout, washout; **les inaptes** the unfit; the unemployable

inaptitude [inaptityd] *f* unfitness

inarticu·lé -lée [inartikyle] *adj* inarticulate

inassou·vi -vie [inasuvi] *adj* unsatisfied

inattaquable [inatakabl] *adj* unquestionable; unassailable; **inattaquable par** unaffected by, resistant to

inatten·du -due [inatɑ̃dy] *adj* unexpected

inatten·tif [inatɑ̃tif] **-tive** [tiv] *adj* inattentive; careless

inattention [inatɑ̃sjɔ̃] *f* inattentiveness, carelessness

inaudible [inodibl] *adj* inaudible

inaugu·ral -rale [inogyral] *adj* (*pl* **-raux** [ro]) inaugural

inauguration [inogyrɑsjɔ̃] *f* inauguration

inaugurer [inogyre] *tr* to inaugurate; to unveil (*a statue*)

inauthentique [inotɑ̃tik] *adj* unauthentic

inavouable [inavuabl] *adj* shameful

ina·voué -vouée [inavwe] *adj* unacknowledged

inca [ɛ̃ka] *adj invar* Inca || (*cap*) *m* Inca

incandes·cent [ɛ̃kɑ̃desɑ̃] **incandes·cente** [ɛ̃kɑ̃desɑ̃t] *adj* incandescent; wild, stirred up (*crowd*)

incapable [ɛ̃kapabl] *adj* incapable; (law) incompetent || *mf* (law) incompetent person

incapacité [ɛ̃kapasite] *f* incapacity; disability

incarcérer [ɛ̃karsere] §10 *tr* to incarcerate

incar·nat [ɛ̃karna] **-nate** [nat] *adj* flesh-colored; rosy || *m* flesh color

incarnation [ɛ̃karnɑsjɔ̃] *f* incarnation

incar·né -née [ɛ̃karne] *adj* incarnate; ingrowing (*nail*)

incarner [ɛ̃karne] *tr* to incarnate, to embody || *ref* to become incarnate; (pathol) to become ingrown; **s'incarner dans** to become the embodiment of

incartade [ɛ̃kartad] *f* indiscretion; prank

incassable [ɛ̃kasabl] *adj* unbreakable

incendiaire [ɛ̃sɑ̃djɛr] *adj & mf* incendiary

incendie [ɛ̃sɑ̃di] *m* fire, conflagration; **incendie volontaire** arson

incen·dié -diée [ɛ̃sɑ̃dje] *adj* burnt down || *mf* fire victim

incendier [ɛ̃sɑ̃dje] *tr* to set on fire; to burn down; (fig) to fire, inflame; (slang) to give a tongue-lashing to

incer·tain [ɛ̃sɛrtɛ̃] **-taine** [tɛn] *adj* uncertain; indistinct; unsettled (*weather*)

incertitude [ɛ̃sɛrtityd] *f* incertitude, uncertainty; **dans l'incertitude** in doubt

incessamment [ɛ̃sesamɑ̃] *adv* incessantly; without delay, at any moment

inces·sant [ɛ̃sesɑ̃] **inces·sante** [ɛ̃sesɑ̃t] *adj* incessant

inceste [ɛ̃sɛst] *m* incest

inces·tueux [ɛ̃sɛstЧø] **-tueuse** [tЧøz] *adj* incestuous

inchan·gé -gée [ɛ̃ʃɑ̃ʒe] *adj* unchanged

incidemment [ɛ̃sidamɑ̃] *adv* incidentally

incidence [ɛ̃sidɑ̃s] *f* incidence

inci·dent [ɛ̃sidɑ̃] **-dente** [dɑ̃t] *adj & m* incident

incinérer [ɛ̃sinere] §10 *tr* to incinerate; to cremate

incirconcis [ɛ̃sirkɔ̃si] *adj masc* uncircumcised

inciser [ɛ̃size] *tr* to make an incision in; to tap (*a tree*); (med) to lance

inci·sif [ɛ̃sizif] **-sive** [ziv] *adj* incisive || *f* incisor

incision [ɛ̃sizjɔ̃] *f* incision

incitation [ɛ̃sitɑsjɔ̃] *f* incitement

inciter [ɛ̃site] *tr* to incite

inci·vil -vile [ɛ̃sivil] *adj* uncivil

incivili·sé -sée [ɛ̃sivilize] *adj* uncivilized

inclassable [ɛ̃klasabl] *adj* unclassifiable

inclé·ment -mente [ɛ̃klemɑ̃] **-mente** [mɑ̃t] *adj* inclement

inclinaison [ɛ̃klinɛzɔ̃] *f* inclination; slope

inclination [ɛ̃klinɑsjɔ̃] *f* inclination; bow; love, affection

incliner [ɛ̃kline] *tr & ref* to incline; to bend; to bow

inclure [ɛklyr] §11 (*pp* **inclus**) *tr* to include; to enclose
in·clus [ɛkly] **-cluse** [klyz] *adj* including, e.g., **jusqu'à la page dix incluse** up to and including page ten; inclusive, e.g., **de mercredi à samedi inclus** from Wednesday to Saturday inclusive
inclu·sif [ɛklyzif] **-sive** [ziv] *adj* inclusive
inclusivement [ɛklyzivmɑ̃] *adv* inclusively, inclusive
incognito [ɛkɔɲito] *m* & *adv* incognito
incohé·rent [ɛkɔerɑ̃] **-rente** [rɑ̃t] *adj* incoherent; inconsistent, illogical
incolore [ɛkɔlɔr] *adj* colorless
incomber [ɛkɔ̃be] *intr*—**incomber à** to devolve on, to fall upon; **il incombe à qn de** it behooves s.o. to
incombustible [ɛkɔ̃bystibl] *adj* incombustible; fireproof
incommode [ɛkɔmɔd] *adj* inconvenient; unwieldy
incommoder [ɛkɔmɔde] *tr* to inconvenience
incommodité [ɛkɔmɔdite] *f* inconvenience
incomparable [ɛkɔ̃parabl] *adj* incomparable
incompatible [ɛkɔ̃patibl] *adj* incompatible; conflicting
incompétence [ɛkɔ̃petɑ̃s] *f* incompetence; lack of jurisdiction
incompé·tent [ɛkɔ̃petɑ̃] **-tente** [tɑ̃t] *adj* incompetent; lacking jurisdiction
incom·plet [ɛkɔ̃plɛ] **-plète** [plɛt] *adj* incomplete
incompréhensible [ɛkɔ̃preɑ̃sibl] *adj* incomprehensible
incom·pris [ɛkɔ̃pri] **-prise** [priz] *adj* misunderstood
inconcevable [ɛkɔ̃svabl] *adj* inconceivable
inconciliable [ɛkɔ̃siljabl] *adj* irreconcilable
incondition·nel -nelle [ɛkɔ̃disjɔnɛl] *adj* unconditional
inconduite [ɛkɔ̃dɥit] *f* misconduct
inconfort [ɛkɔ̃fɔr] *m* discomfort
incon·gru -grue [ɛkɔ̃gry] *adj* incongruous
incon·nu -nue [ɛkɔny] *adj* unknown; **inconnu à cette adresse** address unknown || *mf* unknown (*person*) || *m* unknown (*what is not known*) || *f* (math) unknown
inconsciemment [ɛkɔ̃sjamɑ̃] *adv* subconsciously; unconsciously
inconscience [ɛkɔ̃sjɑ̃s] *f* unconsciousness; unawareness
incons·cient [ɛkɔ̃sjɑ̃] **incons·ciente** [ɛkɔ̃sjɑ̃t] *adj* unconscious, unaware, oblivious; thoughtless; subconscious || *mf* dazed person || *m* unconscious
inconséquence [ɛkɔ̃sekɑ̃s] *f* inconsistency; thoughtlessness, inconsiderateness
inconsé·quent [ɛkɔ̃sekɑ̃] **-quente** [kɑ̃t] *adj* inconsistent; thoughtless, inconsiderate
inconsidé·ré -rée [ɛkɔ̃sidere] *adj* inconsiderate

inconsistance [ɛkɔ̃sistɑ̃s] *f* inconsistency; flimsiness, instability
inconsis·tant [ɛkɔ̃sistɑ̃] **-tante** [tɑ̃t] *adj* inconsistent; flimsy, unstable
inconsolable [ɛkɔ̃sɔlabl] *adj* inconsolable
incons·tant [ɛkɔ̃stɑ̃] **-tante** [tɑ̃t] *adj* inconstant
inconstitution·nel -nelle [ɛkɔ̃stitysjɔnɛl] *adj* unconstitutional
inconti·nent [ɛkɔ̃tinɑ̃] **-nente** [nɑ̃t] *adj* incontinent || **incontinent** *adv* at once, forthwith
incontrôlable [ɛkɔ̃trolabl] *adj* unverifiable
incontrô·lé -lée [ɛkɔ̃trole] *adj* unverified; unchecked, uncontrollable
inconvenance [ɛkɔ̃vnɑ̃s] *f* impropriety
inconve·nant [ɛkɔ̃vnɑ̃] **-nante** [nɑ̃t] *adj* improper, indecent
inconvénient [ɛkɔ̃venjɑ̃] *m* inconvenience, disadvantage; **voir un inconvénient à** to have an objection to
incorporation [ɛkɔrpɔrɑsjɔ̃] *f* incorporation; (mil) induction
incorpo·ré -rée [ɛkɔrpɔre] *adj* built-in
incorpo·rel -relle [ɛkɔrpɔrɛl] *adj* incorporeal; intangible (*property*)
incorporer [ɛkɔrpɔre] *tr* to incorporate; (mil) to induct || *ref* to incorporate
incor·rect -recte [ɛkɔrɛkt] *adj* incorrect; unfair
incrédule [ɛkredyl] *adj* incredulous; unbelieving || *mf* unbeliever, freethinker
incrédulité [ɛkredylite] *f* incredulity; disbelief
increvable [ɛkrəvabl] *adj* punctureproof; (slang) untiring
incriminer [ɛkrimine] *tr* to incriminate
incrochetable [ɛkrɔʃtabl] *adj* burglarproof (*lock*)
incroyable [ɛkrwajabl] *adj* unbelievable
incroyant [ɛkrwajɑ̃] **incroyante** [ɛkrwajɑ̃t] *adj* unbelieving || *mf* unbeliever
incrustation [ɛkrystɑsjɔ̃] *f* incrustation; inlay; (sewing) insert
incruster [ɛkryste] *tr* to incrust; to inlay || *ref* to take root, to become ingrained
incubateur [ɛkybatœr] *m* incubator
incuber [ɛkybe] *tr* to incubate
inculpation [ɛkylpɑsjɔ̃] *f* indictment; **sous l'inculpation de** on a charge of
incul·pé -pée [ɛkylpe] *adj* indicted; **inculpé de** charged with, accused of || *mf* accused, defendant
inculper [ɛkylpe] *tr* to indict, to charge
inculquer [ɛkylke] *tr* to inculcate
inculte [ɛkylt] *adj* uncultivated; uncouth
incunables [ɛkynabl] *mpl* incunabula
incurable [ɛkyrabl] *adj* & *mf* incurable
incurie [ɛkyri] *f* carelessness
incursion [ɛkyrsjɔ̃] *f* incursion, foray
Inde [ɛd] *f* India; **Indes Occidentales** West Indies; **Indes Orientales Néerlandaises** Dutch East Indies; **l'Inde** India
indébrouillable [ɛdebrujabl] *adj* inextricable, hopelessly involved

indécence [ɛ̃desɑ̃s] f indecency
indé·cent [ɛ̃desɑ̃] -cente [sɑ̃t] adj indecent
indéchiffrable [ɛ̃deʃifrabl] adj undecipherable; incomprehensible; illegible
indé·cis [ɛ̃desi] -cise [siz] adj indecisive; uncertain, undecided; blurred
indéclinable [ɛ̃deklinabl] adj indeclinable
indécrottable [ɛ̃dekrɔtabl] adj (coll) incorrigible, hopeless
indéfectible [ɛ̃defɛktibl] adj everlasting; unfailing
indéfendable [ɛ̃defɑ̃dabl] adj indefensible
indéfi·ni -nie [ɛ̃defini] adj indefinite
indéfinissable [ɛ̃definisabl] adj indefinable
indéfrisable [ɛ̃defrizabl] adj permanent (wave) || f permanent wave
indélébile [ɛ̃delebil] adj indelible
indéli·cat [ɛ̃delika] -cate [kat] adj indelicate; dishonest
indémaillable [ɛ̃demɑjabl] adj runproof
indemne [ɛ̃dɛmn] adj undamaged, unharmed
indemnisation [ɛ̃dɛmnizɑsjɔ̃] f indemnification, compensation
indemniser [ɛ̃dɛmnize] tr to compensate
indemnité [ɛ̃dɛmnite] f indemnity; allowance, grant; compensation; indemnité journalière workmen's compensation; indemnité parlementaire salary of members (of parliamentary body)
indéniable [ɛ̃denjabl] adj undeniable
indépendance [ɛ̃depɑ̃dɑ̃s] f independence
indépen·dant [ɛ̃depɑ̃dɑ̃] -dante [dɑ̃t] adj & mf independent
indéréglable [ɛ̃dereglabl] adj foolproof
indescriptible [ɛ̃dɛskriptibl] adj indescribable
indésirable [ɛ̃dezirabl] adj undesirable
indestructible [ɛ̃dɛstryktibl] adj indestructible
indétermi·né -née [ɛ̃detɛrmine] adj indeterminate
indétraquable [ɛ̃detrakabl] adj foolproof
index [ɛ̃dɛks] m index; forefinger; index number; Index (eccl) Index
indica·teur [ɛ̃dikatœr] -trice [tris] adj indicating || mf informer || m gauge; indicator, pointer; timetable; road sign; guidebook; street guide
indica·tif [ɛ̃dikatif] -tive [tiv] adj indicative, suggestive || m (gram) indicative; (rad) station identification; indicatif d'appel (rad, telg) call letters or number
indication [ɛ̃dikɑsjɔ̃] f indication; fausse indication wrong piece of information; indications directions; sauf indication contraire unless otherwise directed; sur l'indication de at the suggestion of
indice [ɛ̃dis] m indication, sign; clue; indice des prix price index; indice d'octane octane number; indice du coût de la vie cost-of-living index

indicible [ɛ̃disibl] adj inexpressible
in·dien [ɛ̃djɛ̃] -dienne [djɛn] adj Indian || f calico, chintz || (cap) mf Indian
indifféremment [ɛ̃diferamɑ̃] adv indiscriminately
indiffé·rent [ɛ̃diferɑ̃] -rente [rɑ̃t] adj indifferent; unimportant; cela m'est indifférent it's all the same to me
indigence [ɛ̃diʒɑ̃s] f indigence, poverty
indigène [ɛ̃diʒɛn] adj indigenous, native || mf native
indi·gent [ɛ̃diʒɑ̃] -gente [ʒɑ̃t] adj indigent || mf pauper; les indigents the poor
indigeste [ɛ̃diʒɛst] adj indigestible; heavy, stodgy; undigested, mixed up
indigestion [ɛ̃diʒɛstjɔ̃] f indigestion
indignation [ɛ̃diɲɑsjɔ̃] f indignation
indigne [ɛ̃diɲ] adj unworthy; shameful
indi·gné -gnée [ɛ̃diɲe] adj indignant
indigner [ɛ̃diɲe] tr to outrage || ref to be indignant
indignité [ɛ̃diɲite] f unworthiness; indignity, outrage
indigo [ɛ̃digo] adj invar & m indigo
indi·qué -quée [ɛ̃dike] adj advisable, appropriate; être tout indiqué pour to be just the thing for; to be just the man for
indiquer [ɛ̃dike] tr to indicate; to name; indiquer du doigt to point to, to point out
indi·rect -recte [ɛ̃dirɛkt] adj indirect
indisciplinable [ɛ̃disiplinabl] adj unruly
indiscipline [ɛ̃disiplin] f lack of discipline, disobedience
indiscipli·né -née [ɛ̃disipline] adj undisciplined
indis·cret [ɛ̃diskrɛ] -crète [krɛt] adj indiscreet
indiscrétion [ɛ̃diskresjɔ̃] f indiscretion; sans indiscrétion ... if I may ask ...
indiscutable [ɛ̃diskytabl] adj unquestionable
indiscu·té -tée [ɛ̃diskyte] adj unquestioned
indispensable [ɛ̃dispɑ̃sabl] adj & m indispensable, essential
indisponible [ɛ̃dispɔnibl] adj unavailable; out of commission (said of car, machine, etc.)
indispo·sé -sée [ɛ̃dispoze] adj indisposed (slightly ill); ill-disposed
indisposer [ɛ̃dispoze] tr to indispose
indissoluble [ɛ̃disɔlybl] adj indissoluble
indis·tinct [ɛ̃distɛ̃] -tincte [ɛ̃distɛ̃kt] adj indistinct
indistinctement [ɛ̃distɛ̃ktəmɑ̃] adv indistinctly; indiscriminately
individu [ɛ̃dividy] m individual; (coll) fellow, guy
individualiser [ɛ̃dividɥalize] tr to individualize
individualité [ɛ̃dividɥalite] f individuality
indivi·duel -duelle [ɛ̃dividɥɛl] adj individual; separate
indi·vis [ɛ̃divi] -vise [viz] adj joint; par indivis jointly
indivisible [ɛ̃divizibl] adj indivisible
Indochine [ɛ̃dɔʃin] f Indochina; l'Indochine Indochina

indocile [ɛ̃dɔsil] *adj* rebellious, unruly
indo-européen [ɛ̃dɔørɔpeɛ̃] **-européen-
ne** [ørɔpɛɛn] *adj* Indo-European ‖ *m*
Indo-European (*language*) ‖ (*cap*)
mf Indo-European
indo·lent [ɛ̃dɔlɑ̃] **-lente** [lɑ̃t] *adj* indolent; apathetic; painless (*e.g.*, *tumor*) ‖ *mf* idler
indolore [ɛ̃dɔlɔr] *adj* painless
indomptable [ɛ̃dɔ̃tabl] *adj* indomitable
indomp·té -tée [ɛ̃dɔ̃te] *adj* untamed
Indonésie [ɛ̃dɔnezi] *f* Indonesia; **l'Indonésie** Indonesia
indoné·sien [ɛ̃dɔnezjɛ̃] **-sienne** [zjɛn]
adj Indonesian ‖ *m* Indonesian (*language*) ‖ (*cap*) *mf* Indonesian (*person*)
in-douze [ɛ̃duz] *adj invar* & *m invar*
duodecimo
in·du -due [ɛ̃dy] *adj* unseemly (*e.g.*,
hour); undue (*haste*); unwarranted
(*remark*) ‖ *m* something not due
inducteur [ɛ̃dyktœr] *m* (elec) field
induction [ɛ̃dyksjɔ̃] *f* (elec, logic) induction
induire [ɛ̃dɥir] §19 *tr* to induce; **induire en** to lead into (*temptation*, *error*, *etc.*)
in·duit [ɛ̃dɥi] **-duite** [dɥit] *adj* induced
‖ *m* (elec) armature
indulgence [ɛ̃dylʒɑ̃s] *f* indulgence
indul·gent [ɛ̃dylʒɑ̃] **-gente** [ʒɑ̃t] *adj* indulgent
indûment [ɛ̃dymɑ̃] *adv* unduly
indurer [ɛ̃dyre] *tr* & *ref* to harden
industrialiser [ɛ̃dystrijalize] *tr* to industrialize ‖ *ref* to become indus-
trialized
industrie [ɛ̃dystri] *f* industry; trickery;
(obs) occupation, trade; **l'industrie
du spectacle** show business
industrie-clef [ɛ̃dystrikle] *f* (*pl* **indus-
tries-clefs**) key industry
indus·triel -trielle [ɛ̃dystrijɛl] *adj* industrial ‖ *m* industrialist
indus·trieux [ɛ̃dystrijø] **-trieuse** [trijøz]
adj industrious; skilled
inébranlable [inebrɑ̃labl] *adj* unshak-
able
inéchangeable [ineʃɑ̃ʒabl] *adj* unex-
changeable
iné·dit [inedi] **-dite** [dit] *adj* unpublished; new, novel
inéducable [inedykabl] *adj* unteach-
able
ineffable [inɛfabl] *adj* ineffable
ineffaçable [inɛfasabl] *adj* indelible
inefficace [inɛfikas] *adj* ineffective, inefficient
iné·gal -gale [inegal] *adj* (*pl* **-gaux**
[go]) unequal; uneven
inégalité [inegalite] *f* inequality; unevenness
inéligible [ineliʒibl] *adj* ineligible
inéluctable [inelyktabl] *adj* unavoidable
inénarrable [inenarabl] *adj* beyond
words, too funny for words
inepte [inɛpt] *adj* inept, inane
ineptie [inɛpsi] *f* ineptitude, inanity;
inane remark
inépuisable [inepɥizabl] *adj* inexhaustible

inerme [inɛrm] *adj* thornless
inertie [inɛrsi] *f* inertia
inescomptable [inɛskɔ̃tabl] *adj* not
subject to discount
inespé·ré -rée [inɛspere] *adj* unhoped-
for, unexpected
inévitable [inevitabl] *adj* inevitable
inexact inexacte [inɛgzakt] *adj* inexact,
inaccurate; unpunctual
inexactitude [inɛgzaktityd] *f* inexact-
ness, inaccuracy; unpunctuality
inexau·cé -cée [inɛgzose] *adj* unfulfilled, unanswered
inexcitable [inɛksitabl] *adj* unexcitable
inexcusable [inɛkskyzabl] *adj* inexcusable
inexécutable [inɛgzekytabl] *adj* impracticable
inexécution [inɛgzekysjɔ̃] *f* nonfulfillment
inexer·cé -cée [inɛgzɛrse] *adj* untried;
untrained
inexhaustible [inɛgzostibl] *adj* inexhaustible
inexigible [inɛgziʒibl] *adj* uncollectable
inexis·tant [inɛksistɑ̃] **-tante** [tɑ̃t] *adj*
nonexistent
inexorable [inɛgzɔrabl] *adj* inexorable
inexpérience [inɛksperjɑ̃s] *f* inexperience
inexpérimen·té -tée [inɛksperimɑ̃te]
adj inexperienced; untried
inex·pié -piée [inɛkspje] *adj* unexpiated
inexplicable [inɛksplikabl] *adj* inexplicable, unexplainable
inexpli·qué -quée [inɛksplike] *adj* unexplained
inexploi·té -tée [inɛksplwate] *adj* un-
tapped
inexplo·ré -rée [inɛksplɔre] *adj* unexplored
inexpres·sif [inɛksprɛsif] **inexpres·sive**
[inɛkspresiv] *adj* expressionless
inexprimable [inɛksprimabl] *adj* inexpressible
inexpri·mé -mée [inɛksprime] *adj* un-
expressed
inexpugnable [inɛkspygnabl] *adj* impregnable
inextinguible [inɛkstɛ̃gibl], [inɛkstɛ̃-
gɥibl] *adj* inextinguishable; uncontrollable; unquenchable
infaillible [ɛ̃fajibl] *adj* infallible
infaisable [ɛ̃fəzabl] *adj* unfeasible
infa·mant [ɛ̃famɑ̃] **-mante** [mɑ̃t] *adj*
opprobrious
infâme [ɛ̃fɑm] *adj* infamous; squalid
infamie [ɛ̃fami] *f* infamy; **dire des
infamies à** to hurl insults at; **noter
d'infamie** to brand as infamous
infant [ɛ̃fɑ̃] *m* infante
infante [ɛ̃fɑ̃t] *f* infanta
infanterie [ɛ̃fɑ̃tri] *f* infantry; **infanterie
de l'air**, **infanterie aéroportée** parachute troops; **infanterie de marine**
overseas troops; **infanterie portée**,
infanterie motorisée motorized troops
infantile [ɛ̃fɑ̃til] *adj* infantile
infatigable [ɛ̃fatigabl] *adj* indefatigable
infatuation [ɛ̃fatɥasjɔ̃] *f* conceit, false
pride
infa·tué -tuée [ɛ̃fatɥe] *adj* infatuated
with oneself, conceited

infé·cond [ɛ̃fekɔ̃] **-conde** [kɔ̃d] *adj* sterile, barren

in·fect -fecte [ɛ̃fɛkt] *adj* stinking; foul, vile

infecter [ɛ̃fɛkte] *tr* to infect; to pollute; to stink up

infec·tieux [ɛ̃fɛksjø] **-tieuse** [sjøz] *adj* infectious

infection [ɛ̃fɛksjɔ̃] *f* infection; stench

inférer [ɛ̃fere] §10 *tr* to infer, conclude

infé·rieur -rieure [ɛ̃ferjœr] *adj* lower; inferior; **inférieur à** below; less than ‖ *mf* subordinate, inferior

infériorité [ɛ̃ferjɔrite] *f* inferiority

infer·nal -nale [ɛ̃fɛrnal] *adj* (*pl* **-naux** [no]) infernal

infester [ɛ̃fɛste] *tr* to infest

infidèle [ɛ̃fidɛl] *adj* infidel; unfaithful ‖ *mf* infidel ‖ *m* unfaithful husband ‖ *f* unfaithful wife

infidélité [ɛ̃fidelite] *f* infidelity; inaccuracy, unfaithfulness

infiltration [ɛ̃filtrɑsjɔ̃] *f* infiltration

infiltrer [ɛ̃filtre] *ref* to infiltrate; to seep, percolate; **s'infiltrer à travers** or **dans** to infiltrate

infime [ɛ̃fim] *adj* very small, infinitesimal; very low; trifling, negligible

infi·ni -nie [ɛ̃fini] *adj* infinite ‖ *m* infinite; (math) infinity; **à l'infini** infinitely

infiniment [ɛ̃finimɑ̃] *adv* infinitely; (coll) greatly, deeply, terribly

infinité [ɛ̃finite] *f* infinity

infini·tif -tive [tiv] *adj & m* infinitive

infirme [ɛ̃firm] *adj* infirm, crippled, disabled ‖ *mf* invalid, cripple

infirmer [ɛ̃firme] *tr* (law) to invalidate

infirmerie [ɛ̃firməri] *f* infirmary; (nav) sick bay

infir·mier [ɛ̃firmje] **-mière** [mjɛr] *mf* nurse; **infirmière bénévole** volunteer nurse; **infirmière diplômée** registered nurse ‖ *m* male nurse; orderly, attendant

infirmière-major [ɛ̃firmjɛrmaʒɔr] *f* head nurse

infirmité [ɛ̃firmite] *f* infirmity

infixe [ɛ̃fiks] *m* infix

inflammable [ɛ̃flamabl] *adj* inflammable

inflammation [ɛ̃flamɑsjɔ̃] *f* inflammation

inflammatoire [ɛ̃flamatwar] *adj* inflammatory

inflation [ɛ̃flɑsjɔ̃] *f* inflation

inflationniste [ɛ̃flɑsjɔnist] *adj* inflationary

infléchir [ɛ̃fleʃir] *tr* to inflect, bend ‖ *ref* to bend, curve

inflexible [ɛ̃flɛksibl] *adj* inflexible

inflexion [ɛ̃flɛksjɔ̃] *f* inflection; change; bend, curve; metaphony

infliger [ɛ̃fliʒe] §38 *tr* to inflict; **infliger q.ch. à** to inflict s.th. on

influence [ɛ̃flyɑ̃s] *f* influence

influencer [ɛ̃flyɑ̃se] §51 *tr* to influence

influent [ɛ̃flyɑ̃] **influente** [ɛ̃flyɑ̃t] *adj* influential

influenza [ɛ̃flyɑ̃za] *f* influenza

influer [ɛ̃flye] *intr*—**influer sur** to influence

in-folio [ɛ̃fɔljo] *adj & m* (*pl* **-folio** or **-folios**) folio

informa·teur [ɛ̃fɔrmatœr] **-trice** [tris] *mf* informant

information [ɛ̃fɔrmɑsjɔ̃] *f* information; piece of information; (law) investigation; **aller aux informations** to make inquiries; **information génétique** genetic characteristics; **informations** news; information; **informations de presse** press reports

informatique [ɛ̃fɔrmatik] *adj* informational ‖ *f* information storage

informe [ɛ̃fɔrm] *adj* formless, shapeless

informer [ɛ̃fɔrme] *tr* to inform, advise ‖ *intr*—**informer contre** to inform on ‖ *ref* to inquire, to keep oneself informed

infortune [ɛ̃fɔrtyn] *f* misfortune

infortu·né -née [ɛ̃fɔrtyne] *adj* unfortunate

infraction [ɛ̃fraksjɔ̃] *f* infraction

infranchissable [ɛ̃frɑ̃ʃisabl] *adj* insuperable; impassable (*e.g., mountain*)

infrarouge [ɛ̃fraruʒ] *adj & m* infrared

infrason [ɛ̃frasɔ̃] *m* infrasonic vibration

infrastructure [ɛ̃frastryktyr] *f* infrastructure; (rr) roadbed

infroissable [ɛ̃frwasabl] *adj* creaseless, wrinkleproof

infruc·tueux [ɛ̃fryktɥø] **-tueuse** [tɥøz] *adj* unfruitful, fruitless

in·fus [ɛ̃fy] **-fuse** [fyz] *adj* inborn, innate, intuitive

infuser [ɛ̃fyze] *tr* to infuse; to brew; **infuser un sang nouveau à** to put new blood or life into ‖ *intr* to steep

infusion [ɛ̃fyzjɔ̃] *f* steeping; brew

ingambe [ɛ̃gɑ̃b] *adj* spry, nimble, alert

ingénier [ɛ̃ʒenje] *ref* to strive hard

ingénierie [ɛ̃ʒeniri] or **ingéniérie** [ɛ̃ʒenjeri] *f* engineering

ingénieur [ɛ̃ʒenjœr] *m* engineer; **ingénieur des ponts et chaussées** civil engineer

ingé·nieux [ɛ̃ʒenjø] **-nieuse** [njøz] *adj* ingenious

ingéniosité [ɛ̃ʒenjozite] *f* ingenuity

ingé·nu -nue [ɛ̃ʒeny] *adj* ingenuous, artless ‖ *mf* naïve person ‖ *f* ingénue

ingénuité [ɛ̃ʒenɥite] *f* ingenuousness

ingérer [ɛ̃ʒere] §10 *tr* to ingest ‖ *ref* to meddle

ingouvernable [ɛ̃guvɛrnabl] *adj* unruly, unmanageable

in·grat [ɛ̃gra] **-grate** [grat] *adj* ungrateful; disagreeable; thankless (*task*); unprofitable (*work*); barren (*soil*); awkward (*age*) ‖ *mf* ingrate

ingratitude [ɛ̃gratityd] *f* ingratitude

ingrédient [ɛ̃gredjɑ̃] *m* ingredient

inguérissable [ɛ̃gerisabl] *adj & mf* incurable

ingurgiter [ɛ̃gyrʒite] *tr* to swallow; to gulp down

inhabile [inabil] *adj* unskilled; unfitted, unqualified

inhabileté [inabilte] *f* inability; clumsiness; unfitness

inhabitable [inabitabl] *adj* uninhabitable

inhabi·té -tée [inabite] *adj* uninhabited

inhabi·tuel -tuelle [inabityɛl] *adj* unusual
inhé·rent [inerɑ̃] -rente [rɑ̃t] *adj* inherent
inhiber [inibe] *tr* to inhibit
inhibition [inibisjɔ̃] *f* inhibition
inhospita·lier [inɔspitalje] -lière [ljɛr] *adj* inhospitable
inhu·main [inymɛ̃] -maine [mɛn] *adj* inhuman
inhumanité [inymanite] *f* inhumanity
inhumation [inymɑsjɔ̃] *f* burial
inhumer [inyme] *tr* to bury, to inter
inimitié [inimitje] *f* enmity
inintelli·gent [inɛ̃teliʒɑ̃] -gente [ʒɑ̃t] *adj* unintelligent
inintéres·sant [inɛ̃terɛsɑ̃] inintéres·sante [inɛ̃terɛsɑ̃t] *adj* uninteresting
ininterrom·pu -pue [inɛ̃terɔ̃py] *adj* uninterrupted
inique [inik] *adj* iniquitous, unjust
iniquité [inikite] *f* iniquity
ini·tial -tiale [inisjal] (*pl* -tiaux [sjo] -tiales) *adj* & *f* initial
initia·teur [inisjatœr] -trice [tris] *adj* initiating ǁ *mf* initiator
initiation [inisjɑsjɔ̃] *f* initiation
initiative [inisjativ] *f* initiative
initier [inisje] *tr* to initiate; to introduce ǁ *ref* to become initiated
injecter [ɛ̃ʒɛkte] *tr* to inject; to impregnate ǁ *ref* to become bloodshot
injec·teur [ɛ̃ʒɛktœr] -trice [tris] *adj* injecting ǁ *m* injector; nozzle (*in motor*)
injection [ɛ̃ʒɛksjɔ̃] *f* injection; impregnation; redness (*of eyes*); (geog) intrusion
injonction [ɛ̃ʒɔ̃ksjɔ̃] *f* injunction, order
injouable [ɛ̃ʒwabl] *adj* unplayable
injure [ɛ̃ʒyr] *f* insult; wrong; l'injure des ans the ravages of time
injurier [ɛ̃ʒyrje] *tr* to insult, to abuse
inju·rieux [ɛ̃ʒyrjø] -rieuse [rjøz] *adj* insulting, abusive; harmful, offensive
injuste [ɛ̃ʒyst] *adj* unjust
injustice [ɛ̃ʒystis] *f* injustice
injusti·fié -fiée [ɛ̃ʒystifje] *adj* unjustified
inlassable [ɛ̃lɑsabl] *adj* untiring
in·né -née [inne] *adj* innate, inborn
innocence [inɔsɑ̃s] *f* innocence
inno·cent [inɔsɑ̃] -cente [sɑ̃t] *adj* & *mf* innocent
innocenter [inɔsɑ̃te] *tr* to exonerate
innocuité [inɔkɥite] *f* innocuousness
innombrable [inɔ̃brabl] *adj* innumerable
innova·teur [inɔvatœr] -trice [tris] *adj* innovating ǁ *mf* innovator
innovation [inɔvɑsjɔ̃] *f* innovation
innover [inɔve] *tr* & *intr* to innovate
inoccu·pé -pée [inɔkype] *adj* unoccupied; unemployed, idle ǁ *mf* idler
in-octavo [inɔktavo] *adj* & *m* (*pl* -octavo or -octavos) octavo
inoculation [inɔkylɑsjɔ̃] *f* inoculation
inoculer [inɔkyle] *tr* to inoculate
inodore [inɔdɔr] *adj* odorless
inoffen·sif [inɔfɑ̃sif] -sive [siv] *adj* inoffensive
inondation [inɔ̃dɑsjɔ̃] *f* flood
inonder [inɔ̃de] *tr* to flood

inopi·né -née [inɔpine] *adj* unexpected
inoppor·tun [inɔpɔrtœ̃] -tune [tyn] *adj* untimely, inconvenient
inopportunité [inɔpɔrtynite] *f* untimeliness
inorganique [inɔrganik] *adj* inorganic
inorgani·sé -sée [inɔrganize] *adj* unorganized (*workers*), nonunion
inoubliable [inublijabl] *adj* unforgettable
inouï inouïe [inwi] *adj* unheard-of
inoxydable [inɔksidabl] *adj* inoxidizable, stainless, rustproof
inqualifiable [ɛ̃kalifjabl] *adj* unspeakable
in·quiet [ɛ̃kjɛ] -quiète [kjɛt] *adj* anxious, worried, uneasy; restless
inquié·tant [ɛ̃kjetɑ̃] -tante [tɑ̃t] *adj* disquieting, worrisome
inquiéter [ɛ̃kjete] §10 *tr* & *intr* to worry
inquiétude [ɛ̃kjetyd] *f* uneasiness, worry
inquisi·teur [ɛ̃kizitœr] -trice [tris] *adj* inquisitorial; searching (*e.g., look*) ǁ *m* inquisitor
inquisition [ɛ̃kizisjɔ̃] *f* inquisition; investigation
inracontable [ɛ̃rakɔ̃tabl] *adj* untellable
insaisissable [ɛ̃sezisabl] *adj* hard to catch; elusive
insalubre [ɛ̃salybr] *adj* unhealthy
insane [ɛ̃san] *adj* insane, crazy
insanité [ɛ̃sanite] *f* insanity; piece of folly
insatiable [ɛ̃sasjabl] *adj* insatiable
insatisfaction [ɛ̃satisfaksjɔ̃] *f* dissatisfaction
inscription [ɛ̃skripsjɔ̃] *f* inscription; registration, enrollment; inscription de or en faux (law) plea of forgery; prendre ses inscriptions to register at a university
inscrire [ɛ̃skrir] §25 *tr* to inscribe; to register; to record ǁ *ref* to register, enroll; s'inscrire à to join; s'inscrire en faux contre to deny; s'inscrire pour to sign up for
ins·crit [ɛ̃skri] -crite [krit] *adj* inscribed; registered, enrolled ǁ *mf* registered student; (sports) entry; inscrit maritime naval recruit
insecte [ɛ̃sɛkt] *m* insect, bug
insecticide [ɛ̃sɛktisid] *adj* insecticidal ǁ *m* insecticide
insen·sé -sée [ɛ̃sɑ̃se] *adj* senseless, insane, crazy ǁ *m* madman ǁ *f* madwoman
insensible [ɛ̃sɑ̃sibl] *adj* insensitive; imperceptible
inséparable [ɛ̃separabl] *adj* inseparable ǁ *m* lovebird
insérer [ɛ̃sere] §10 *tr* to insert
insertion [ɛ̃sersjɔ̃] *f* insertion
insi·dieux [ɛ̃sidjø] -dieuse [djøz] *adj* insidious
insigne [ɛ̃siɲ] *adj* signal, noteworthy; notorious ǁ *m* badge, mark; insignes insignia
insigni·fiant [ɛ̃siɲifjɑ̃] -fiante [fjɑ̃t] *adj* insignificant
insincère [ɛ̃sɛ̃sɛr] *adj* insincere
insinuation [ɛ̃sinɥɑsjɔ̃] *f* insinuation
insinuer [ɛ̃sinɥe] *tr* to insinuate; to

hint, hint at; to work in, introduce ‖ *ref*—s'insinuer dans to worm one's way into
insipide [ɛ̃sipid] *adj* insipid, tasteless; insipid, dull
insister [ɛ̃siste] *intr* to insist; (coll) to continue, persevere; insister pour to insist on; insister sur to stress
insociable [ɛ̃sɔsjabl] *adj* unsociable
insolation [ɛ̃sɔlɑsjɔ̃] *f* exposure to the sun; sunstroke
insolence [ɛ̃sɔlɑ̃s] *f* insolence
inso•lent [ɛ̃sɔlɑ̃] -lente [lɑ̃t] *adj* insolent; extraordinary, unexpected
insolite [ɛ̃sɔlit] *adj* bizarre
insoluble [ɛ̃sɔlybl] *adj* insoluble
insolvabilité [ɛ̃sɔlvabilite] *f* insolvency
insolvable [ɛ̃sɔlvabl] *adj* insolvent
insomnie [ɛ̃sɔmni] *f* insomnia
insondable [ɛ̃sɔ̃dabl] *adj* unfathomable
insonore [ɛ̃sɔnɔr] *adj* soundproof; noiseless
insonoriser [ɛ̃sɔnɔrize] *tr* to soundproof
insouciance [ɛ̃susjɑ̃s] *f* carefreeness; indifference, carelessness
insou•ciant [ɛ̃susjɑ̃] -ciante [sjɑ̃t] *adj* carefree, unconcerned
insou•cieux [ɛ̃susjø] -cieuse [sjøz] *adj* carefree, unmindful
insou•mis [ɛ̃sumi] -mise [miz] *adj* unruly; unsubjugated ‖ *mf* rebel ‖ *m* (mil) A.W.O.L.
insoumission [ɛ̃sumisjɔ̃] *f* insubordination, rebellion; (mil) absence without leave
insoupçonnable [ɛ̃supsɔnabl] *adj* above suspicion
insoupçon•né -née [ɛ̃supsɔne] *adj* unsuspected
insoutenable [ɛ̃sutnabl] *adj* untenable; unbearable
inspecter [ɛ̃spɛkte] *tr* to inspect
inspec•teur [ɛ̃spɛktœr] -trice [tris] *mf* inspector
inspection [ɛ̃spɛksjɔ̃] *f* inspection; inspectorship
inspiration [ɛ̃spirɑsjɔ̃] *f* inspiration
inspirer [ɛ̃spire] *tr* to inspire; to breathe in; inspirer à qn de to inspire s.o. to; inspirer q.ch. à qn to inspire s.o. with s.th. ‖ *ref*—s'inspirer de to be inspired by
instable [ɛ̃stabl] *adj* unstable
installateur [ɛ̃stalatœr] *m* heater man; fitter, plumber
installation [ɛ̃stalɑsjɔ̃] *f* installation; equipment, outfit; appointments, fittings
installer [ɛ̃stale] *tr* to install; to equip, furnish; être bien installé to be comfortably settled ‖ *ref* to settle down, to set up shop; s'installer chez to foist oneself on
instamment [ɛ̃stamɑ̃] *adv* urgently, earnestly
instance [ɛ̃stɑ̃s] *f* insistence; avec instance earnestly; en instance pending; en instance de on the point of; en seconde instance on appeal; instances entreaties; introduire une instance to start proceedings
ins•tant [ɛ̃stɑ̃] -tante [tɑ̃t] *adj* urgent, pressing ‖ *m* instant, moment; à cha-

que instant, à tout instant continually; à l'instant at once, right away; just now; at the moment; par instants from time to time
instanta•né -née [ɛ̃stɑ̃tane] *adj* instantaneous ‖ *m* snapshot
instantanément [ɛ̃stɑ̃tanemɑ̃] *adv* instantaneously; instantly
instar [ɛ̃star]—à l'instar de in the manner of
instauration [ɛ̃stɔrɑsjɔ̃] *f* establishment
instaurer [ɛ̃stɔre] *tr* to establish
instigation [ɛ̃stigɑsjɔ̃] *f* instigation
instiller [ɛ̃stile] *tr* to instill
instinct [ɛ̃stɛ̃] *m* instinct; d'instinct, par instinct by instinct
instinc•tif [ɛ̃stɛ̃ktif] -tive [tiv] *adj* instinctive
instituer [ɛ̃stitɥe] *tr* to found; to institute (*e.g., proceedings*)
institut [ɛ̃stity] *m* institute; institut de beauté beauty parlor; institut de coupe tonsorial parlor; institut dentaire dental school
institu•teur [ɛ̃stitytœr] -trice [tris] *mf* schoolteacher; founder
institution [ɛ̃stitysjɔ̃] *f* institution
instructeur [ɛ̃stryktœr] *m* instructor
instruc•tif [ɛ̃stryktif] -tive [tiv] *adj* instructive
instruction [ɛ̃stryksjɔ̃] *f* instruction; education; instruction judiciaire (law) preliminary investigation; instructions permanentes standing orders
instruire [ɛ̃strɥir] §19 *tr* to instruct; instruire qn de to inform s.o. of ‖ *ref* to improve one's mind
instrument [ɛ̃strymɑ̃] *m* instrument; instrument à anche reed instrument; instrument à cordes stringed instrument; instrument à vent wind instrument; instrument en bois woodwind; instrument en cuivre brass
instrumen•tal -tale [ɛ̃strymɑ̃tal] *adj* (*pl* -taux [to]) instrumental
instrumenter [ɛ̃strymɑ̃te] *tr* to instrument
instrumentiste [ɛ̃strymɑ̃tist] *mf* instrumentalist
insu [ɛ̃sy] *m*—à l'insu de unknown to; à mon insu unknown to me
insubmersible [ɛ̃sybmɛrsibl] *adj* unsinkable
insubordon•né -née [ɛ̃sybɔrdɔne] *adj* insubordinate
insuccès [ɛ̃syksɛ] *m* failure
insuffi•sant [ɛ̃syfizɑ̃] -sante [zɑ̃t] *adj* insufficient
insulaire [ɛ̃sylɛr] *adj* insular ‖ *mf* islander
insuline [ɛ̃sylin] *f* insulin
insulte [ɛ̃sylt] *f* insult
insulter [ɛ̃sylte] *tr* to insult ‖ *intr* (with *dat*) to offend, outrage
insupportable [ɛ̃sypɔrtabl] *adj* unbearable
insur•gé -gée [ɛ̃syrʒe] *adj* & *mf* insurgent
insurger [ɛ̃syrʒe] §38 *ref* to revolt, rebel
insurmontable [ɛ̃syrmɔ̃tabl] *adj* insurmountable

insurrection [ɛ̃syrɛksjɔ̃] *f* insurrection
in·tact -tacte [ɛ̃takt] *adj* intact, untouched
intangible [ɛ̃tɑ̃ʒibl] *adj* intangible
intarissable [ɛ̃tarisabl] *adj* inexhaustible
inté·gral -grale [ɛ̃tegral] *adj (pl -graux* [gro]) integral; complete (e.g., edition); full (e.g., payment) ‖ *f* complete works; (math) integral
inté·grant [ɛ̃tegrɑ̃] **-grante** [grɑ̃t] *adj* integral
intégration [ɛ̃tegrɑsjɔ̃] *f* integration
intègre [ɛ̃tɛgr] *adj* honest, upright
intégrer [ɛ̃tegre] §10 *tr* to integrate ‖ *ref* to form an integral part; (slang) to be accepted *(at an exclusive school)*
intégrité [ɛ̃tegrite] *f* integrity
intellect [ɛ̃telɛkt] *m* intellect
intellec·tuel -tuelle [ɛ̃telɛktɥɛl] *adj & mf* intellectual
intelligence [ɛ̃teliʒɑ̃s] *f* intelligence; intellect *(person)*; **en bonne intelligence avec** on good terms with; **être d'intelligence** to be in collusion
intelli·gent [ɛ̃teliʒɑ̃] **-gente** [ʒɑ̃t] *adj* intelligent
intelligible [ɛ̃teliʒibl] *adj* intelligible
intempé·rant [ɛ̃tɑ̃perɑ̃] **-rante** [rɑ̃t] *adj* intemperate
intempéries [ɛ̃tɑ̃peri] *fpl* bad weather
intempes·tif [ɛ̃tɑ̃pɛstif] **-tive** [tiv] *adj* untimely
intenable [ɛ̃tnabl] *adj* untenable
intendance [ɛ̃tɑ̃dɑ̃s] *f* stewardship; controllership, office of bursar; **Intendance** (mil) Quartermaster Corps
inten·dant [ɛ̃tɑ̃dɑ̃] **-dante** [dɑ̃t] *mf* steward, superintendent; controller, bursar; **intendant militaire** quartermaster
intense [ɛ̃tɑ̃s] *adj* intense
inten·sif [ɛ̃tɑ̃sif] **-sive** [siv] *adj* intensive
intensifier [ɛ̃tɑ̃sifje] *tr & ref* to intensify
intensité [ɛ̃tɑ̃site] *f* intensity
intenter [ɛ̃tɑ̃te] *tr* to start *(a suit)*; to bring *(an action)*
intention [ɛ̃tɑ̃sjɔ̃] *f* intention, intent; **à l'intention de** for (the sake of)
intention·né -née [ɛ̃tɑ̃sjɔne] *adj* motivated; **bien intentionné** well-meaning; **mal intentionné** ill-disposed
intention·nel -nelle [ɛ̃tɑ̃sjɔnɛl] *adj* intentional
inter [ɛ̃tɛr] *m* (coll) long distance
interaction [ɛ̃tɛraksjɔ̃] *f* interaction, interplay
intercaler [ɛ̃tɛrkale] *tr* to intercalate; to insert, to sandwich
intercéder [ɛ̃tɛrsede] §10 *intr* to intercede
intercepter [ɛ̃tɛrsɛpte] *tr* to intercept
intercepteur [ɛ̃tɛrsɛptœr] *m* interceptor
interchangeable [ɛ̃tɛrʃɑ̃ʒabl] *adj* interchangeable
interclasse [ɛ̃tɛrklɑs] *m* (educ) break between classes
intercourse [ɛ̃tɛrkurs] *f* (naut) free entry

interdépen·dant [ɛ̃tɛrdepɑ̃dɑ̃] **-dante** [dɑ̃t] *adj* interdependent
interdiction [ɛ̃tɛrdiksjɔ̃] *f* interdiction; suspension; **interdiction de séjour** forbidden entry
interdire [ɛ̃tɛrdir] §40 *tr* to prohibit, to forbid; to confound, to abash; to interdict; to suspend; **interdire q.ch. à qn** to forbid s.o. s.th.
inter·dit [ɛ̃tɛrdi] **-dite** [dit] *adj* prohibited, forbidden; dumfounded, abashed; deprived of rights; (mil) off limits ‖ *m* interdict
intéres·sant [ɛ̃teresɑ̃] **intéres·sante** [ɛ̃teresɑ̃t] *adj* interesting; attractive *(offer)*
intéres·sé -sée [ɛ̃terese] *adj* interested; self-seeking ‖ *mf* interested party
intéresser [ɛ̃terese] *tr* to interest; to involve ‖ *ref*—**s'intéresser à** or **dans** to be interested in
intérêt [ɛ̃terɛ] *m* interest; **intérêts composés** compound interest
interférence [ɛ̃tɛrferɑ̃s] *f* interference
interférer [ɛ̃tɛrfere] §10 *intr* (phys) to interfere ‖ *ref* to interfere with each other
inté·rieur -rieure [ɛ̃terjœr] *adj* interior; inner, inside ‖ *m* interior; inside; house, home
intérieurement [ɛ̃terjœrmɑ̃] *adv* inwardly, internally; to oneself
intérim [ɛ̃terim] *m invar* interim; **dans l'intérim** in the meantime; **par intérim** acting, pro tem, interim
intérimaire [ɛ̃terimɛr] *adj* temporary, acting
interjection [ɛ̃tɛrʒɛksjɔ̃] *f* interjection
interligne [ɛ̃tɛrliɲ] *m* space between the lines; writing in the space between the lines; **à double interligne** double-spaced ‖ *f* lead
interligner [ɛ̃tɛrliɲe] *tr* to interline; (typ) to lead out
interlocu·teur [ɛ̃tɛrlɔkytœr] **-trice** [tris] *mf* interlocutor; intermediary; party *(with whom one is conversing)*
interlope [ɛ̃tɛrlɔp] *adj* illegal, shady ‖ *m* (naut) smuggling vessel
interloquer [ɛ̃tɛrlɔke] *tr* to disconcert
interlude [ɛ̃tɛrlyd] *m* interlude
intermède [ɛ̃tɛrmɛd] *m* (theat & fig) interlude
intermédiaire [ɛ̃tɛrmedjɛr] *adj* intermediate, intermediary ‖ *mf* intermediary ‖ *m* (com) middleman; **par l'intermédiaire de** by means of, by the medium of
interminable [ɛ̃tɛrminabl] *adj* interminable
intermit·tent [ɛ̃tɛrmitɑ̃] **intermit·tente** [ɛ̃tɛrmitɑ̃t] *adj* intermittent
internat [ɛ̃tɛrna] *m* boarding school; boarding-school life; (med) internship
internatio·nal -nale [ɛ̃tɛrnasjɔnal] *adj (pl -naux* [no]) international
interne [ɛ̃tɛrn] *adj* inner; (math) interior ‖ *mf* boarder *(at a school)*; (med) intern
inter·né -née [ɛ̃tɛrne] *mf* internee
internement [ɛ̃tɛrnəmɑ̃] *m* internment; confinement *(of a mental patient)*

interner [ɛterne] *tr* to intern
interpeller [ɛterpele] *tr* to question, to interrogate; to yell at; to heckle
interphone [ɛterfɔn] *m* intercom
interplanétaire [ɛterplaneter] *adj* interplanetary
interpoler [ɛterpɔle] *tr* to interpolate
interposer [ɛterpoze] *tr* to interpose
interprétation [ɛterpretasjɔ̃] *f* interpretation
interprète [ɛterpret] *mf* interpreter
interpréter [ɛterprete] §10 *tr* to interpret; **mal interpréter** to misinterpret
interrogation [ɛterɔgasjɔ̃] *f* interrogation
interroger [ɛterɔʒe] §38 *tr* to interrogate, to question
interrompre [ɛterɔ̃pr] (3d *sg pres ind* **interrompt** [ɛterɔ̃]) *tr* to interrupt; to heckle || *ref* to break off, to be interrupted
interrup•teur [ɛteryptœr] **-trice** [tris] *adj* interrupting; circuit-breaking || *m* switch; **interrupteur à couteau** knife switch; **interrupteur à culbuteur** or **à bascule** toggle switch; **interrupteur d'escalier** two-way switch; **interrupteur encastré** flush switch; **interrupteur olive** pear switch
interruption [ɛterypsjɔ̃] *f* interruption
intersection [ɛterseksjɔ̃] *f* intersection
intersigne [ɛtersiɲ] *m* omen, portent
interstellaire [ɛtersteler] *adj* interstellar
interstice [ɛterstis] *m* interstice
interur•bain [ɛteryrbɛ̃] **-baine** [bɛn] *adj* interurban; (telp) long-distance || *m* (telp) long distance
intervalle [ɛterval] *m* interval
intervenir [ɛtervnir] §72 (*aux:* ÊTRE) *intr* to intervene; to take place, happen; (med) to operate; **faire intervenir** to call in
intervention [ɛtervɑ̃sjɔ̃] *f* intervention; (med) operation
intervertir [ɛtervertir] *tr* to invert, to transpose
interview [ɛtervju] *f* (journ) interview
interviewer [ɛtervjuvœr] *m* interviewer || [ɛtervjuve] *tr* to interview
intestat [ɛtesta] *adj & mf invar* intestate
intes•tin [ɛtestɛ̃] **-tine** [tin] *adj* intestine, internal || *m* intestine; **gros intestin** large intestine; **intestin grêle** small intestine
intimation [ɛtimasjɔ̃] *f* (law) summons
intime [ɛtim] *adj & mf* intimate
inti•mé -mée [ɛtime] *mf* (law) defendant
intimer [ɛtime] *tr* to notify; to give (*an order*)
intimider [ɛtimide] *tr* to intimidate
intimité [ɛtimite] *f* intimacy; privacy; depths (*of one's being*)
intituler [ɛtityle] *tr* to entitle
intolérable [ɛtɔlerabl] *adj* intolerable
intolé•rant [ɛtɔlerɑ̃] **-rante** [rɑ̃t] *adj* intolerant
intonation [ɛtɔnasjɔ̃] *f* intonation
intouchable [ɛtuʃabl] *adj & mf* untouchable
intoxication [ɛtɔksikasjɔ̃] *f* poisoning
intoxiquer [ɛtɔksike] *tr* to poison

intraitable [ɛtretabl] *adj* intractable
intransi•geant [ɛtrɑ̃ziʒɑ̃] **-geante** [ʒɑ̃t] *adj* intransigent || *mf* diehard, standpatter
intransi•tif [ɛtrɑ̃zitif] **-tive** [tiv] *adj* intransitive
intravei•neux [ɛtravɛnø] **-neuse** [nøz] *adj* intravenous
intrépide [ɛtrepid] *adj* intrepid; persistent
intri•gant [ɛtrigɑ̃] **-gante** [gɑ̃t] *adj* intriguing || *mf* plotter, schemer
intrigue [ɛtrig] *f* intrigue, plot; love affair; **intrigues de couloir** lobbying
intriguer [ɛtrige] *tr & intr* to intrigue
intrinsèque [ɛtrɛ̃sek] *adj* intrinsic
introduction [ɛtrɔdyksjɔ̃] *f* introduction; admission
introduire [ɛtrɔdɥir] §19 *tr* to introduce, to bring in; to show in; to interject (*e.g., a remark*) || *ref* to be introduced; **s'introduire dans** to slip in
intronisation [ɛtrɔnizasjɔ̃] *f* investiture, inauguration
introniser [ɛtrɔnize] *tr* to enthrone
introspec•tif [ɛtrɔspektif] **-tive** [tiv] *adj* introspective
introuvable [ɛtruvabl] *adj* unfindable
introver•ti -tie [ɛtrɔverti] *adj & mf* introvert
in•trus [ɛtry] **-truse** [tryz] *adj* intruding || *mf* intruder
intrusion [ɛtryzjɔ̃] *f* intrusion
intuition [ɛtɥisjɔ̃] *f* intuition
inusable [inyzabl] *adj* durable, wearproof
inusi•té -tée [inyzite] *adj* obsolete
inutile [inytil] *adj* useless, unnecessary
inutilement [inytilmɑ̃] *adv* in vain, uselessly; unnecessarily
inutilité [inytilite] *f* uselessness
invain•cu -cue [ɛ̃vɛ̃ky] *adj* unconquered
invalide [ɛ̃valid] *adj* invalid || *mf* invalid, cripple; **invalide de guerre** disabled veteran
invalider [ɛ̃valide] *tr* to invalidate
invalidité [ɛ̃validite] *f* invalidity; disability
invariable [ɛ̃varjabl] *adj* invariable
invasion [ɛ̃vazjɔ̃] *f* invasion
invective [ɛ̃vektiv] *f* invective
invectiver [ɛ̃vektive] *tr* to rail at || *intr* to inveigh
invendable [ɛ̃vɑ̃dabl] *adj* unsalable
inven•du -due [ɛ̃vɑ̃dy] *adj* unsold || *m* —les invendus the unsold copies; the unsold articles
inventaire [ɛ̃vɑ̃ter] *m* inventory
inventer [ɛ̃vɑ̃te] *tr* to invent
inven•teur [ɛ̃vɑ̃tœr] **-trice** [tris] *mf* inventor; (law) finder
inven•tif [ɛ̃vɑ̃tif] **-tive** [tiv] *adj* inventive
invention [ɛ̃vɑ̃sjɔ̃] *f* invention
inventorier [ɛ̃vɑ̃tɔrje] *tr* to inventory
inversable [ɛ̃versabl] *adj* untippable, uncapsizable
inverse [ɛ̃vers] *adj & m* inverse; **faire l'inverse de** to do the opposite of
inverser [ɛ̃verse] *tr* to invert, to reverse || *intr* (elec) to reverse

inverseur [ɛ̃vɛrsœr] *m* reversing device; **inverseur des phares** (aut) dimmer
inversion [ɛ̃vɛrsjɔ̃] *f* inversion
inverté·bré -brée [ɛ̃vɛrtebre] *adj* & *m* invertebrate
inver·ti -tie [ɛ̃vɛrti] *mf* invert
invertir [ɛ̃vɛrtir] *tr* to invert, reverse
investiga·teur [ɛ̃vɛstigatœr] **-trice** [tris] *adj* investigative; searching || *mf* investigator
investigation [ɛ̃vɛstigasjɔ̃] *f* investigation
investir [ɛ̃vɛstir] *tr* to invest; to vest; **investir qn de sa confiance** to place one's confidence in s.o.
investissement [ɛ̃vɛstismɑ̃] *m* investment
investiture [ɛ̃vɛstityr] *f* investiture; nomination (*as a candidate for election*)
invété·ré -rée [ɛ̃vetere] *adj* inveterate
invétérer [ɛ̃vetere] *ref* to become inveterate
invincible [ɛ̃vɛ̃sibl] *adj* invincible
invisible [ɛ̃vizibl] *adj* invisible; (coll) hiding, keeping out of sight
invitation [ɛ̃vitasjɔ̃] *f* invitation
invite [ɛ̃vit] *f* invitation, inducement; **répondre à l'invite de qn** (cards) to return s.o.'s lead; (fig) to respond to s.o.'s advances
invi·té -tée [ɛ̃vite] *adj* invited || *mf* guest
inviter [ɛ̃vite] *tr* to invite
involontaire [ɛ̃vɔlɔ̃tɛr] *adj* involuntary
invoquer [ɛ̃vɔke] *tr* to invoke
invraisemblable [ɛ̃vrɛsɑ̃blabl] *adj* improbable, unlikely, hard to believe; (coll) strange, weird
invraisemblance [ɛ̃vrɛsɑ̃blɑ̃s] *f* improbability, unlikelihood; (coll) queerness
invulnérable [ɛ̃vylnerabl] *adj* invulnerable
iode [jɔd] *m* iodine
iodure [jɔdyr] *m* iodide
ion [jɔ̃] *m* ion
ioniser [jɔnize] *tr* to ionize
iota [jɔta] *m* iota
Irak [irak] *m*—**l'Irak** Iraq
ira·kien [irakjɛ̃] **-kienne** [kjɛn] *adj* Iraqi || (*cap*) *mf* Iraqi
Iran [irɑ̃] *m*—**l'Iran** Iran
ira·nien [iranjɛ̃] **-nienne** [njɛn] *adj* Iranian || *m* Iranian (*language*) || (*cap*) *mf* Iranian (*person*)
iris [iris] *m* iris
irlan·dais [irlɑ̃dɛ] **-daise** [dɛz] *adj* Irish || *m* Irish (*language*) || (*cap*) *m* Irishman; **les Irlandais** the Irish || (*cap*) *f* Irishwoman
Irlande [irlɑ̃d] *f* Ireland; **l'Irlande** Ireland
ironie [irɔni] *f* irony
ironique [irɔnik] *adj* ironic(al)
ironiser [irɔnize] *tr* to say ironically || *intr* to speak ironically, to jeer
irradier [iradje] *tr* & *ref* to irradiate
irraison·né -née [irɛzɔne] *adj* unreasoning
irration·nel -nelle [irasjɔnɛl] *adj* irrational
irréalisable [irealizabl] *adj* impractical, unattainable

irréalité [irealite] *f* unreality
irrécouvrable [irekuvrabl] *adj* uncollectible
irrécupérable [irekyperabl] *adj* irretrievable
irrécusable [irekyzabl] *adj* unimpeachable, incontestable, indisputable
irréel irréelle [ireel] *adj* unreal
irréflé·chi -chie [irefleʃi] *adj* rash, thoughtless
irréfutable [irefytabl] *adj* irrefutable
irrégu·lier [iregylje] **-lière** [ljɛr] *adj* & *m* irregular
irréli·gieux [irelizjø] **-gieuse** [zjøz] *adj* irreligious
irrémédiable [iremedjabl] *adj* irremediable
irremplaçable [irɑ̃plasabl] *adj* irreplaceable
irréparable [ireparabl] *adj* irreparable; irretrievable (*loss, mistake, etc.*)
irrépressible [irepresibl] *adj* irrepressible
irréprochable [ireprɔʃabl] *adj* irreproachable
irrésistible [irezistibl] *adj* irresistible
irréso·lu -lue [irezɔly] *adj* irresolute
irrespect [irɛspɛ] *m* disrespect
irrespec·tueux [irɛspɛktɥø] **-tueuse** [tɥøz] *adj* disrespectful
irrespirable [irɛspirabl] *adj* unbreathable
irresponsable [irɛspɔ̃sabl] *adj* irresponsible
irrétrécissable [iretresisabl] *adj* preshrunk, unshrinkable
irrévéren·cieux [ireverɑ̃sjø] **-cieuse** [sjøz] *adj* irreverent
irréversible [ireversibl] *adj* irreversible
irrévocable [irevɔkabl] *adj* irrevocable
irrigation [irigasjɔ̃] *f* irrigation
irriguer [irige] *tr* to irrigate
irri·tant [iritɑ̃] **-tante** [tɑ̃t] *adj* irritating || *m* irritant
irritation [iritasjɔ̃] *f* irritation
irriter [irite] *tr* to irritate || *ref* to become irritated
irruption [irypsjɔ̃] *f* irruption; invasion; **faire irruption** to burst in
isabelle [izabɛl] *m* dun or light-bay horse || (*cap*) *f* Isabel
Isaïe [izai] *m* Isaiah
Islam [islam] *m*—**l'Islam** Islam
islan·dais [islɑ̃dɛ] **-daise** [dɛz] *adj* Icelandic || *m* Icelandic (*language*) || (*cap*) *mf* Icelander
Islande [islɑ̃d] *f* Iceland; **l'Islande** Iceland
isocèle [izɔsɛl] *adj* isosceles
iso·lant [izɔlɑ̃] **-lante** [lɑ̃t] *adj* insulating || *m* insulator
isolateur [izɔlatœr] *m* insulator
isolation [izɔlasjɔ̃] *f* insulation; **isolation phonique** soundproofing
isolationniste [izɔlasjɔnist] *adj* & *mf* isolationist
iso·lé -lée [izɔle] *adj* isolated; independent; insulated
isolement [izɔlmɑ̃] *m* isolation; insulation
isolément [izɔlemɑ̃] *adv* separately, independently

isoler [izɔle] *tr* to isolate; to insulate ‖ *ref* to cut oneself off
isoloir [izɔlwar] *m* polling booth
isotope [izɔtɔp] *m* isotope
Israël [israɛl] *m*—**Israël** Israel
israé·lien [israeljɛ̃] **-lienne** [ljɛn] *adj* Israeli ‖ (*cap*) *mf* Israeli
israélite [israelit] *adj* Israelite ‖ (*cap*) *mf* Israelite
is·su is·sue [isy] *adj*—**issu de** descended from, born of ‖ *f* exit, way out; outlet; outcome, issue; **à l'issue de** on the way out from; at the end of; **issues** sharps, middlings (*in milling flour*); offal (*in butchering*); **sans issue** without exit; without any way out
isthme [ism] *m* isthmus
Italie [itali] *f* Italy; **l'Italie** Italy
ita·lien [italjɛ̃] **-lienne** [ljɛn] *adj* Italian ‖ *m* Italian (*language*) ‖ (*cap*) *mf* Italian (*person*)
italique [italik] *adj* Italic; (typ) italic ‖ *m* (typ) italics
item [itɛm] *m* question (*in a test*) ‖ *adv* ditto
itinéraire [itinerɛr] *adj & m* itinerary
itiné·rant [itinerɑ̃] **-rante** [rɑ̃t] *adj & mf* itinerant
itou [itu] *adv* (slang) also, likewise
ivoire [ivwar] *m* ivory
ivraie [ivrɛ] *f* darnel, cockle; (Bib) tares
ivre [ivr] *adj* drunk, intoxicated
ivresse [ivrɛs] *f* drunkenness; ecstasy, rapture
ivrogne [ivrɔɲ] *adj* hard-drinking ‖ *m* drunkard
ivrognerie [ivrɔɲri] *f* drunkenness
ivrognesse [ivrɔɲɛs] *f* drinking woman

J

J, j [ʒi] *m invar* tenth letter of the French alphabet
jabot [ʒabo] *m* jabot; crop (*of bird*)
jabotage [ʒabɔtaʒ] *m* jabbering
jaboter [ʒabɔte] *tr & intr* to jabber
jacasse [ʒakas] *f* magpie; chatterbox
jacasser [ʒakase] *intr* to chatter, to jabber
jacasserie [ʒakasri] *f* chatter, jabber
jachère [ʒaʃɛr] *f* fallow ground
jacinthe [ʒasɛ̃t] *f* hyacinth; **jacinthe des bois** bluebell
Jacques [ʒak] *m* James, Jacob; **Jacques Bonhomme** the typical Frenchman
jactance [ʒaktɑ̃s] *f* bragging
jade [ʒad] *m* jade
jadis [ʒadis] *adv* formerly, of yore
jaguar [ʒagwar] *m* jaguar
jaillir [ʒajir] *intr* to gush, to burst forth
jaillissement [ʒajismɑ̃] *m* gush
jais [ʒɛ] *m* jet
jalon [ʒalɔ̃] *m* stake; landmark; surveying staff
jalonner [ʒalɔne] *tr* to stake out; to mark (*a way, a channel*)
jalousie [ʒaluzi] *f* jealousy; awning; Venetian blind
ja·loux [ʒalu] **-louse** [luz] *adj* jealous
jamais [ʒamɛ] *adv* ever; never; **jamais de la vie!** not on your life!; **jamais plus** never again; **ne . . . jamais** §90 never; **pour jamais** forever
jambe [ʒɑ̃b] *f* leg; **à toutes jambes** as fast as possible; **prendre ses jambes à son cou** to take to one's heels
jambon [ʒɑ̃bɔ̃] *m* ham; **jambon d'York** boiled ham
jambon·neau [ʒɑ̃bɔno] *m* (*pl* **-neaux**) ham knuckle
jamboree [ʒɑ̃bɔre], [dʒɑmbɔri] *m* jamboree
jante [ʒɑ̃t] *f* felloe; rim (*of auto wheel*)
janvier [ʒɑ̃vje] *m* January
Japon [ʒapɔ̃] *m*—**le Japon** Japan
japo·nais [ʒapɔnɛ] **-naise** [nɛz] *adj* Japanese ‖ *m* Japanese (*language*) ‖ (*cap*) *mf* Japanese (*person*)
japper [ʒape] *intr* to yap, to yelp
jaquemart [ʒakmar] *m* jack (*figurine striking the time on a bell*)
jaquette [ʒakɛt] *f* coat, jacket; cutaway coat, morning coat; book jacket
jardin [ʒardɛ̃] *m* garden; **jardin d'acclimatation** zoo; **jardin d'enfants** kindergarten; **jardin d'hiver** greenhouse
jardiner [ʒardine] *tr* to clear out, to trim ‖ *intr* to garden
jardi·nier [ʒardinje] **-nière** [njɛr] *adj* garden ‖ *mf* gardener ‖ *m* flower stand; mixed vegetables; spring wagon ‖ *f* kindergartner (*teacher*)
jargon [ʒargɔ̃] *m* jargon
jarre [ʒar] *f* earthenware jar
jarret [ʒarɛ] *m* hock, gambrel; shin (*of beef or veal*); back of the knee
jarretelle [ʒartɛl] *f* garter
jarretière [ʒartjɛr] *f* garter
jars [ʒar] *m* gander
jaser [ʒaze] *intr* to babble, prattle; to blab, gossip
jasmin [ʒasmɛ̃] *m* jasmine
jaspe [ʒasp] *m* jasper; (bb) marbling
jasper [ʒaspe] *tr* to marble, speckle
jatte [ʒat] *f* bowl
jauge [ʒoʒ] *f* gauge; dipstick; (agr) trench; (naut) tonnage
jauger [ʒoʒe] §38 *tr* to gauge, measure; (naut) to draw
jaunâtre [ʒonɑtr] *adj* yellowish; sallow
jaune [ʒon] *adj* yellow ‖ *mf* yellow

person (*Oriental*) ‖ *m* yellow; yolk (*of egg*); scab, strikebreaker
jaunir [ʒonir] *tr* & *intr* to yellow
jaunisse [ʒonis] *f* jaundice
Javel [ʒavɛl] *f*—**eau de Javel** bleach
javelle [ʒavɛl] *f* swath (*of grain*); bunch (*of twigs*)
javelliser [ʒavɛlize] *tr* to chlorinate (*water*)
javelot [ʒavlo] *m* javelin
jazz [dʒaz] *m* jazz
je [ʒə] §87
Jean [ʒɑ̃] *m* John
Jeanne [ʒɑn] *f* Jane, Jean, Joan
jeannette [ʒanɛt] *f* gold cross (*ornament*); sleeveboard
Jeannot [ʒano] *m* (coll) Johnny, Jack
jeep [dʒip] *f* jeep
Jéhovah [ʒeɔva] *m* Jehovah
je-m'en-fichisme [ʒmɑ̃fiʃism] *m* (slang) what-the-hell attitude
je-ne-sais-quoi [ʒənsekwa] *m invar* what-you-call-it
Jérôme [ʒerom] *m* Jerome
jerrycan [dʒerikan] *m* gasoline can
jersey [ʒɛrsɛ] *m* jersey, sweater
Jérusalem [ʒeryzalɛm] *f* Jerusalem
Jésuite [ʒezɥit] *m* Jesuit
Jésus [ʒezy] *m* Jesus
Jésus-Christ [ʒezykri] *m* Jesus Christ
jet [ʒɛ] *m* throw, cast; jet; spurt, gush; flash (*of light*); **du premier jet** at the first try; **jet à la mer** jettison; **jet d'eau** fountain; **jet de pierre** stone's throw
jetée [ʒəte] *f* breakwater, jetty
jeter [ʒəte] §34 *tr* to throw; to throw away; to throw down; to hurl, fling; to toss; to cast (*a glance*); to shed (*the skin*); to pour forth; to utter; to drop (*anchor*); to lay (*the foundations*) ‖ *intr* to sprout ‖ *ref* to throw oneself; to rush; to empty (*said of a river*)
jeton [ʒətɔ̃] *m* token, counter; slug
jeu [ʒø] *m* (*pl* jeux) play; game, sport; gambling; pack, deck (*of cards*); set (*of chessmen; of tools*); playing; acting; execution, performance; **en jeu** in gear; at stake; **franc jeu** fair play; **gros jeu** high stakes; **jeu d'eau** dancing waters; **jeu de dames** checkers; **jeu de hasard** game of chance; **jeu de massacre** hit-the-baby (*game at fair*); **jeu de mots** pun, play on words; **jeu d'enfant** child's play; **jeu de patience** jigsaw puzzle; **jeu de puce** tiddly-winks; **jeu de société** parlor game; **jeu d'orgue** organ stop; **jouer un jeu d'enfer** to play for high stakes; **vieux jeu** old hat
jeudi [ʒødi] *m* Thursday; **jeudi saint** Maundy Thursday
jeun [ʒœ̃]—**à jeun** fasting; on an empty stomach
jeune [ʒœn] *adj* young; youthful; junior, younger ‖ *m* young man; **jeunes délinquants** juvenile delinquents; **les jeunes** young people; the young (*of an animal*)
jeûne [ʒøn] *m* fast, fasting

jeûner [ʒøne] *intr* to fast; to abstain; to eat sparingly
jeunesse [ʒœnɛs] *f* youth; youthfulness; boyhood, girlhood; **jeunesse dorée** young people of wealth and fashion
jeu·net [ʒœnɛ] -**nette** [nɛt] *adj* youngish
jeû·neur [ʒønœr] -**neuse** [nøz] *mf* faster
joaillerie [ʒɔɑjri] *f* jewelry; jewelry business; jewelry shop
joail·lier [ʒɔɑje] **joail·lière** [ʒɔɑjer] *mf* jeweler
jobard [ʒɔbar] *m* (coll) dupe
jobarderie [ʒɔbardri] *f* gullibility
jockey [ʒɔkɛ] *m* jockey
jodler [ʒɔdle] *tr* & *intr* to yodel
joie [ʒwa] *f* joy; **joies** pleasures
joindre [ʒwɛ̃dr] §35 *tr* to join; to add; to adjoin; to catch up with; **joindre les deux bouts** to make both ends meet ‖ *intr* to join ‖ *ref* to join, unite; to be adjacent, to come together
joint [ʒwɛ̃] **jointe** [ʒwɛ̃t] *adj* joined; joint (*effort*); **joint à** added to ‖ *m* joint; **joint de cardan** (mach) universal joint; **joint de culasse** (aut) gasket (*of cylinder head*); **joint de dilatation thermique** expansion joint; **trouver le joint** (coll) to hit on the solution
jointure [ʒwɛ̃tyr] *f* knuckle; joint
joker [ʒɔkɛr] *m* joker
jo·li -lie [ʒɔli] *adj* pretty; tidy (*income*)
joliment [ʒɔlimɑ̃] *adv* nicely; (coll) extremely, awfully
Jonas [ʒɔnɑs], [ʒɔnɑ] *m* Jonah
jonc [ʒɔ̃] *m* rush; **jonc d'Inde** rattan
jonchée [ʒɔ̃ʃe] *f* litter (*things strewn about*); cottage cheese
joncher [ʒɔ̃ʃe] *tr* to strew; to litter
jonction [ʒɔ̃ksjɔ̃] *f* junction
jongler [ʒɔ̃gle] *intr* to juggle
jonglerie [ʒɔ̃gləri] *f* jugglery
jongleur [ʒɔ̃glœr] *m* juggler; jongleur
jonque [ʒɔ̃k] *f* (naut) junk
jonquille [ʒɔ̃kij] *adj invar* pale-yellow ‖ *m* pale yellow ‖ *f* jonquil
Jordanie [ʒɔrdani] *f* Jordan; **la Jordanie** Jordan
joue [ʒu] *f* cheek; **se caler les joues** (slang) to stuff oneself
jouer [ʒwe] *tr* to play; to gamble away; to feign; to act (*a part*) ‖ *intr* to play; to gamble; to feign; **faire jouer** to spring (*a lock*); **jouer à** to play (*a game*); **jouer à la baisse** to bear the market; **jouer à la hausse** to bull the market; **jouer de** to play (*a musical instrument*) ‖ *ref* to frolic; **se jouer de** to make fun of; to be independent of; to make light of
jouet [ʒwɛ] *m* toy, plaything
joueur [ʒwœr] **joueuse** [ʒwøz] *mf* player (*of games; of musical instruments*); gambler; **beau joueur** good sport; **joueur à la baisse** bear; **joueur à la hausse** bull; **mauvais joueur** poor sport
jouf·flu -flue [ʒufly] *adj* chubby
joug [ʒu] *m* yoke

jouir [ʒwir] *intr* to enjoy oneself, enjoy life; **jouir de** to enjoy

jouissance [ʒwisɑ̃s] *f* enjoyment; use, possession

jouis·seur [ʒwisœr] **jouis·seuse** [ʒwisøz] *adj* pleasure-loving ‖ *mf* pleasure lover

jou·jou [ʒuʒu] *m* (*pl* **-joux**) toy, plaything

jour [ʒur] *m* day; daylight; light, window, opening; **à jour** openwork; **up to date**; **de nos jours** nowadays; **grand jour** broad daylight; **huit jours** a week; **il fait jour** it is getting light; **jour chômé** day off; **jour de ma fête** my birthday; **jour férié** legal holiday; **jour ouvrable** workday; **le jour de l'An** New Year's day; **le jour J** D-Day; **quinze jours** two weeks; **sous un faux jour** in a false light; **vivre au jour le jour** to live from hand to mouth

Jourdain [ʒurdɛ̃] *m* Jordan (*river*)

jour·nal [ʒurnal] *m* (*pl* **-naux** [no]) newspaper; journal; diary; (naut) logbook, journal; **journal parlé** newscast; **journal télévisé** telecast

journa·lier [ʒurnalje] **-lière** [ljer] *adj* daily ‖ *m* day laborer

journalisme [ʒurnalism] *m* journalism

journaliste [ʒurnalist] *mf* journalist

journée [ʒurne] *f* day; day's journey; day's pay; day's work; **journée d'accueil** open house; **toute la journée** all day long

journellement [ʒurnɛlmɑ̃] *adv* daily

joute [ʒut] *f* joust

jouter [ʒute] *intr* to joust

ju·vial -vlale [ʒɔvjal] *adj* (*pl* **-vlals** or **-viaux** [vjo] **-viales**) jovial, jocose

joyau [ʒwajo] *m* (*pl* **joyaux**) jewel

joyeux [ʒwajø] **joyeuse** [ʒwajøz] *adj* joyful, cheerful; jocose

jubi·lant [ʒybilɑ̃] **-lante** [lɑ̃t] *adj* jubilant

jubilé [ʒybile] *m* jubilee; golden-wedding anniversary

jucher [ʒyʃe] *tr & intr* to perch ‖ *ref* to go to roost

judaïque [ʒydaik] *adj* Jewish

judaïsme [ʒydaism] *m* Judaism

judas [ʒyda] *m* peephole ‖ (*cap*) *m* Judas

judicature [ʒydikatyr] *f* judiciary

judiciaire [ʒydisjer] *adj* legal, judicial

judi·cieux [ʒydisjø] **-cieuse** [sjøz] *adj* judicious, judicial

juge [ʒyʒ] *m* judge; umpire; **juge assesseur** associate judge

jugement [ʒyʒmɑ̃] *m* judgment

juger [ʒyʒe] §38 *tr & intr* to judge

jugulaire [ʒygyler] *adj* jugular ‖ *f* chin strap

juif [ʒɥif] **juive** [ʒɥiv] *adj* Jewish ‖ (*cap*) *mf* Jew

juillet [ʒɥije] *m* July

juin [ʒɥɛ̃] *m* June

Jules [ʒyl] *m* Julius; (coll) Mack; (slang) pimp; (slang) chamber pot

ju·lien [ʒyljɛ̃] **-lienne** [ljen] *adj* Julian ‖ *f* (*soup*) julienne; (bot) rocket

ju·meau [ʒymo] **-melle** [mel] (*pl* **-meaux -melles**) *adj & mf* twin ‖ *f* see **jumelles**

jumelage [ʒymlaʒ] *m* twinning

jume·lé -lée [ʒymle] *adj* double; twin (*cities*); semidetached (*house*); bilingual (*text*)

jumeler [ʒymle] §34 *tr* to couple, to join; to pair

jumelles [ʒymel] *fpl* opera glasses; field glasses; **jumelles de manchettes** cuff links

jument [ʒymɑ̃] *f* mare

jungle [ʒɔ̃gl] *f* jungle

jupe [ʒyp] *f* skirt

jupon [ʒypɔ̃] *m* petticoat

juré [ʒyre] *m* juror; member of an examining board

jurer [ʒyre] *tr* to swear ‖ *intr* to swear; to clash

juridiction [ʒyridiksjɔ̃] *f* jurisdiction

juridique [ʒyridik] *adj* legal, judicial

juriste [ʒyrist] *m* writer on legal matters

juron [ʒyrɔ̃] *m* oath

jury [ʒyri] *m* jury; examining board

jus [ʒy] *m* juice; gravy; (slang) drink (*body of water*)

jusqu'au-boutiste [ʒyskobutist] *mf* (coll) bitterender, diehard

jusque [ʒysk(ə)] *adv* even; **jusqu'à** as far as, down to, up to; until; even; **jusqu'à ce que** until; **jusqu'après** until after; **jusqu'à quand** how long ‖ *prep* as far as; until; **jusques et y compris** [ʒyskəzeikɔ̃pri] up to and including; **jusqu'ici** this far; until now; **jusqu'où** how far

jusque-là [ʒyskəla] *adv* that far; until then

jusquiame [ʒyskjam] *f* henbane

juste [ʒyst] *adj* just, righteous; accurate; just enough; sharp, e.g., **à six heures justes** at six o'clock sharp; (mus) in tune, on key ‖ *adv* justly; correctly, exactly

justement [ʒystəmɑ̃] *adv* just; justly; exactly; as it happens

juste-milieu [ʒystəmiljø] *m* happy medium, golden mean

justesse [ʒystes] *f* justness; precision, accuracy; **de justesse** barely

justice [ʒystis] *f* justice; **faire justice de** to mete out just punishment to; to make short work of

justiciable [ʒystisjabl] *adj*—**justiciable de** accountable to; subject to

justifier [ʒystifje] *tr* to justify ‖ *intr*—**justifier de** to account for, to prove ‖ *ref* to clear oneself

jute [ʒyt] *m* jute

ju·teux [ʒytø] **-teuse** [tøz] *adj* juicy

juvénile [ʒyvenil] *adj* juvenile, youthful

juxtaposer [ʒykstapoze] *tr* to juxtapose

K

K, k [ka] *m invar* eleventh letter of the French alphabet
kaki [kaki] *adj invar* & *m* khaki
kaléidoscope [kaleidɔskɔp] *m* kaleidoscope
kangourou [kãguru] *m* kangaroo
keepsake [kipsɛk] *m* giftbook, keepsake
képi [kepi] *m* kepi
kermesse [kɛrmɛs] *f* charity bazaar
kérosène [kerozɛn] *m* kerosene
ketchup [kɛtʃœp] *m* ketchup
khan [kã] *m* khan
kidnapper [kidnape] *tr* to kidnap
kidnap·peur [kidnapœr] **kidnap·peuse** [kidnapøz] *mf* kidnaper
kif [kif] *m* (coll) pot, marijuana
kif-kif [kifkif] *adj invar* (coll) all the same; **c'est kif-kif** (coll) it's fifty-fifty
kilo [kilo] *m* kilo, kilogram
kilocycle [kilɔsikl] *m* kilocycle
kilogramme [kilɔgram] *m* kilogram
kilomètre [kilɔmɛtr] *m* kilometer, kilo
kilowatt [kilɔwat] *m* kilowatt
kilowatt-heure [kilɔwatœr] *m* (*pl* **kilowatts-heures**) kilowatt-hour

kilt [kilt] *m* kilt
kimono [kimɔno] *m* kimono
kinescope [kinɛskɔp] *m* kinescope
kiosque [kjɔsk] *m* newsstand; bandstand; summerhouse
kipper [kipœr], [kipɛr] *m* kipper
klaxon [klaksɔn] *m* (aut) horn
klaxonner [klaksɔne] *intr* to sound the horn
kleptomane [klɛptɔman] *adj* & *mf* kleptomaniac
km/h *abbr* (**kilomètres-heure, kilomètres à l'heure**) kilometers per hour
knock-out [nɔkaut], [knɔkut] *adj invar* (boxing) knocked out, groggy ‖ *m* (boxing) knockout
k.o. [kao] (letterword) (**knock-out**) *adj* k.o., knocked out; **mettre k.o.** to knock out ‖ *m* k.o., knockout
krach [krak] *m* crash (*e.g., on the stock market*)
kraft [kraft] *m* strong wrapping paper
krak [krak] *m* medieval castle
kyrielle [kirjɛl] *f* rigmarole, string
kyste [kist] *m* cyst

L

L, l [ɛl], *[ɛl] m invar* twelfth letter of the French alphabet
la [la] *art* §77 ‖ *m* (mus) la ‖ *pron* §87
là [la] *adv* there; here, e.g., **je suis là** I am here; in, e.g., **est-il là?** is he in?; **il n'était pas là** he was out; **là, là! there, there!** (*it's not as bad as that!*)
-là [la] §82, §84
là-bas [laba] *adv* yonder, over there
label [labɛl] *m* union label
labeur [labœr] *m* labor, toil
la·bial -biale [labjal] (*pl* **-biaux** [bjo] **-biales**) *adj* & *f* labial
laboran·tin [labɔrãtɛ̃] **-tine** [tin] *mf* laboratory assistant
laboratoire [labɔratwar] *m* laboratory
labo·rieux [labɔrjø] **-rieuse** [rjøz] *adj* laborious; arduous; industrious; working (*classes*); **c'est laborieux!** (coll) it's endless!
labour [labur] *m* tilling, plowing
labourable [laburabl] *adj* arable, tillable
labourer [labure] *tr* to till, to plow; to furrow (*the brow*); to scratch
laboureur [laburœr] *m* farm hand, plowman
Labrador [labradɔr] *m*—**le Labrador** Labrador
labyrinthe [labirɛ̃t] *m* labyrinth, maze
lac [lak] *m* lake; **Grands Lacs** Great Lakes
lacer [lase] §51 *tr* to lace; to tie (*one's shoes*)

lacération [laserasjɔ̃] *f* tearing
lacérer [lasere] §10 *tr* to lacerate; to tear up
lacet [lasɛ] *m* lace; snare, noose; bowstring (*for strangling*); hairpin curve; **en lacet** winding (*road*); **lacet de soulier** shoelace
lâche [laʃ] *adj* slack, loose; lax, careless; cowardly ‖ *mf* coward
lâcher [laʃe] *tr* to loosen; to let go, to release; to turn loose; to blurt out (*a word*); to fire (*a shot*); (coll) to drop (*one's friends*); **lâcher pied** to give ground; **lâcher prise** to let go
lâcheté [laʃte] *f* cowardice
là·cheur [laʃœr] **-cheuse** [ʃøz] *mf* fickle friend, turncoat
lacis [lasi] *m* network (*of threads, nerves*)
laconique [lakɔnik] *adj* laconic
lacrymogène [lakrimɔʒɛn] *adj* tear (*gas*)
lacs [la] *m* noose, snare; **lacs d'amour** love knot
lac·té -tée [lakte] *adj* milky; milk (*diet*)
lacune [lakyn] *f* lacuna, gap, blank
lad [lad] *m* stableboy
là-dedans [ladədã] §85A *adv* in it, within, in that, in there
là-dessous [ladəsu] §85A *adv* under it, under that, under there
là-dessus [ladəsy] §85A *adv* on it, on that; thereupon

ladre [lɑdr] *adj* stingy, niggardly || *mf* miser
ladrerie [lɑdrəri] *f* miserliness
lagon [lagɔ̃] *m* lagoon
lagune [lagyn] *f* lagoon
lai laie [lɛ] *adj* lay || *m* lay (*poem*) || *f* see **laie**
laïc laïque [laik] *adj* lay, secular || *mf* layman || *f* laywoman
laiche [lɛʃ] *f* (bot) sedge, reed grass
laïcisation [laisizɑsjɔ̃] *f* secularization
laïciser [laisize] *tr* to secularize
laid [lɛ] **laide** [lɛd] *adj* ugly; plain, homely; mean, low-down
laide·ron [lɛdrɔ̃] **-ronne** [rɔn] *adj* homely, ugly || **laideron** *m* or *f* ugly wench
laideur [lɛdœr] *f* ugliness; meanness
laie [lɛ] *f* (zool) wild sow
lainage [lɛnaʒ] *m* woolens
laine [lɛn] *f* wool; **laine d'acier** steel wool; **manger** or **tondre la laine sur le dos à** (fig) to fleece
lainer [lɛne] *tr* to teasel, to nap
lai·neux [lɛnø] **-neuse** [nøz] *adj* wooly; downy
lai·nier [lɛnje] **-nière** [njɛr] *adj* wool (*industry*) || *mf* dealer in wool; worker in wool
laïque [laik] *adj* lay, secular || *mf* layman || *f* laywoman
laisse [lɛs] *f* leash; foreshore; laisse
laissé-pour-compte laissée-pour-compte [lesepurkɔ̃t] *adj* returned (*merchandise*) || *m* (*pl* **laissés-pour-compte**) reject; leftover merchandise
laisser [lese], [lese] *tr* to leave, to quit; to let, to allow; to let go (*at a low price*); to let have, e.g., **il me l'a laissé pour trois dollars** he let me have it for three dollars; **laisser** + *inf* + **qn** to let s.o. + *inf*, e.g., **il a laissé Marie aller au théâtre** he let Mary go to the theater; e.g., **il me l'a laissé peindre** or **il m'a laissé le peindre** he let me paint it || *intr*—**ne pas laisser de** to not fail to, to not stop || *ref* to let oneself, e.g., **se laisser aller** to let oneself go; **se laisser aller à** to give way to
laisser-aller [leseale] *m* abandon, easygoingness; slovenliness, negligence
laisser-passer [lesepase] *m invar* permit, pass
lait [lɛ] *m* milk; **lait de chaux** whitewash; **lait de poule** eggnog; **lait écrémé** skim milk; **se mettre au lait** to go on a milk diet
laitage [lɛtaʒ] *m* dairy products
laitance [lɛtɑ̃s] *f* milt
laiterie [lɛtri] *f* dairy, creamery; dairy farming
lai·tier [lɛtje] **-tière** [tjɛr] *adj* dairy; milch (*cow*) || *m* milkman; (metallurgy) slag, dross || *f* dairymaid; milch cow
laiton [lɛtɔ̃] *m* brass
laitonner [lɛtɔne] *tr* to plate with brass
laitue [lɛty] *f* lettuce; **laitue romaine** romaine
laïus [lajys] *m* (coll) speech, impromptu remarks; (coll) hot air

laïus·seur [lajysœr] **laïus·seuse** [lajysøz] *mf* (coll) windbag
laize [lɛz] *f* width (*of cloth*)
lamanage [lamanaʒ] *m* harborage
lamaneur [lamanœr] *m* harbor pilot
lam·beau [lɑ̃bo] *m* (*pl* **-beaux**) scrap, bit; rag; **en lambeaux** in tatters, in shreds
lam·bin [lɑ̃bɛ̃] **-bine** [bin] *adj* (coll) slow || *mf* (coll) slowpoke
lambiner [lɑ̃bine] *intr* (coll) to dawdle
lambris [lɑ̃bri] *m* paneling, wainscoting; plaster (*of ceiling*); **lambris dorés** (fig) palatial home
lambrisser [lɑ̃brise] *tr* to panel, to wainscot; to plaster
lame [lam] *f* blade; slat (*of blinds*); runner (*of skate*); wave: lamina, thin plate; sword; (fig) swordsman; **lame de fond** ground swell
la·mé -mée [lame] *adj* gold-trimmed, silver-trimmed, spangled || *m*—**de lamé**, e.g., **une robe de lamé** a spangled dress
lamelle [lamɛl] *f* lamella, thin strip; slide (*of microscope*)
lamentable [lamɑ̃tabl] *adj* lamentable
lamentation [lamɑ̃tasjɔ̃] *f* lamentation, lament
lamenter [lamɑ̃te] *intr & ref* to lament
laminer [lamine] *tr* to laminate; to roll (*a metal*)
laminoir [laminwar] *m* rolling mill; calender
lampadaire [lɑ̃padɛr] *m* lamppost; floor lamp
lampe [lɑ̃p] *f* lamp; (electron) tube; **lampe à pétrole** kerosene lamp; **lampe à rayons ultraviolets** sun lamp; **lampe à souder** blowtorch; **lampe au néon** neon light; **lampe de chevet** bedlamp; **lampe de poche** flashlight; **lampe survoltée** photoflood bulb; **s'en mettre plein la lampe** (slang) to fill one's belly
lampée [lɑ̃pe] *f* (coll) gulp, swig
lamper [lɑ̃pe] *tr* (coll) to gulp down, to guzzle
lampe-tempête [lɑ̃ptɛpɛt] *f* (*pl* **lampes-tempête**) hurricane lamp
lampion [lɑ̃pjɔ̃] *m* Chinese lantern
lampiste [lɑ̃pist] *m* lightman; (coll) scapegoat; (coll) underling
lamproie [lɑ̃prwa] *f* lamprey
lampyre [lɑ̃pir] *m* glowworm
lance [lɑ̃s] *f* lance; nozzle (*of hose*); **rompre une lance avec** to cross swords with
lan·cé -cée [lɑ̃se] *adj* flying (*start*); in the swim
lance-bombes [lɑ̃sbɔ̃b] *m invar* trench mortar; (aer) bomb release
lancée [lɑ̃se] *f* impetus
lance-flammes [lɑ̃sflam] *m invar* flamethrower
lance-fusées [lɑ̃sfyze] *m invar* rocket launcher
lancement [lɑ̃smɑ̃] *m* launching, throwing; (*of ship; of new product on the market*) launching; (aer) airdrop; (aer) release; (baseball) pitching
lance-mines [lɑ̃smin] *m invar* minelayer

lance-pierres [lɑ̃spjɛr] *m invar* slingshot
lancer [lɑ̃se] §51 *tr* to throw, fling, cast; to launch (*e.g., a ship, a new product*); to issue (*e.g., an appeal*); (baseball) to pitch || *ref* to rush, dash; **se lancer dans** to launch out into, to take up
lance-roquettes [lɑ̃srɔkɛt] *m invar* (arti) bazooka
lance-torpilles [lɑ̃stɔrpij] *m invar* torpedo tube
lancette [lɑ̃sɛt] *f* (surg) lancet
lan·ceur [lɑ̃sœr] **-ceuse** [søz] *mf* promoter; (baseball) pitcher; (sports) hurler, thrower || *m* (rok) booster
lanci·nant [lɑ̃sinɑ̃] **-nante** [nɑ̃t] *adj* shooting, throbbing (*pain*); gnawing (*regret*)
lanciner [lɑ̃sine] *tr* to torment || *intr* to shoot; to throb
lan·dau [lɑ̃do] *m* (*pl* **-daus**) landau; baby carriage
lande [lɑ̃d] *f* moor, heath
landier [lɑ̃dje] *m* kitchen firedog with pothangers
langage [lɑ̃gaʒ] *m* language, speech
lange [lɑ̃ʒ] *m* diaper
langer [lɑ̃ʒe] §38 *tr* to swaddle, diaper
langou·reux [lɑ̃gurø] **-reuse** [røz] *adj* languorous
langouste [lɑ̃gust] *f* spiny lobster, crayfish
langous·tier [lɑ̃gustje] **-tière** [tjɛr] *m & f* lobster net || *m* lobster boat
langoustine [lɑ̃gustin] *f* prawn
langue [lɑ̃g] *f* tongue; language, speech; **avoir la langue bien pendue** (coll) to have the gift of gab; **donner sa langue au chat** (coll) to give up; **langue cible** target language; **langue source** source language; **langues vivantes** modern languages; **langue verte** slang; **mauvaise langue** backbiter, gossip; **prendre langue avec** to open up a conversation with; **tirer la langue à** to stick out one's tongue at
langue-de-chat [lɑ̃gdəʃa] *f* (*pl* **langues-de-chat**) (culin) ladyfinger
languette [lɑ̃gɛt] *f* tongue (*e.g., of shoe*); pointer (*of scale*); flap, strip
langueur [lɑ̃gœr] *f* languor
languir [lɑ̃gir] *intr* to languish; to pine away
languis·sant [lɑ̃gisɑ̃] **languis·sante** [lɑ̃gisɑ̃t] *adj* languid; languishing; long-drawn-out, tiresome
lanière [lanjɛr] *f* strap, strip, thong
lanoline [lanɔlin] *f* lanolin
lanterne [lɑ̃tɛrn] *f* lantern; (aut) parking light; (obs) street lamp; **conter des lanternes** (coll) to talk nonsense; **lanterne d'agrandissement** (phot) enlarger; **lanterne de projection, lanterne à projections** slide projector, filmstrip projector; **lanterne rouge** (slang) tail end, last to arrive; **lanterne sourde** dark lantern; **lanterne vénitienne** Japanese lantern; **oublier d'éclairer** or **d'allumer sa lanterne** (coll) to leave out the most important point

lanterner [lɑ̃tɛrne] *tr* (coll) to string along, to put off || *intr* to loaf around, to dawdle; **faire lanterner** qn to keep s.o. waiting
lapider [lapide] *tr* to stone; to vilify
la·pin [lapɛ̃] **-pine** [pin] *mf* rabbit; **lapin de garenne** wild rabbit; **lapin russe** albino rabbit; **poser un lapin à** qn (coll) to stand s.o. up
la·pon [lapɔ̃] **-pone** [pɔn] *adj* Lappish || *m* Lapp, Lappish (*language*) || (*cap*) *mf* Lapp, Laplander (*person*)
Laponie [lapɔni] *f* Lapland; **la Laponie** Lapland
lapsus [lapsys] *m* slip (*of tongue, pen, etc.*)
laquais [lakɛ] *m* lackey, footman
laque [lak] *m & f* lacquer || *m* lacquer ware || *f* lac; shellac; hair spray
laquelle [lakɛl] §78
laquer [lake] *tr* to shellac; to lacquer
larcin [larsɛ̃] *m* petty larceny; plagiarism
lard [lar] *m* bacon, side pork; (coll) fat (*of a person*); (slang) fat slob; **se faire du lard** (coll) to get fat
larder [larde] *tr* to lard; to pierce, riddle
large [larʒ] *adj* wide, broad; generous; ample; large, e.g., **pour une large part** to a large extent || *m* width, breadth; open sea; room, e.g., **donner du large à** qn to give s.o. room; **au large** in the offing; **au large de** off, e.g., **au large du Havre** off Le Havre; **prendre le large** (coll) to shove off || *adv* boldly; **calculer large** to figure roughly; **habiller large** to dress in loose-fitting clothes; **il n'en mène pas large** (fig) he gets rattled in a tight spot; **voir large** (fig) to think big
largement [larʒəmɑ̃] *adv* widely; abundantly; fully; plenty, e.g., **vous avez largement le temps** you have plenty of time
largesse [larʒɛs] *f* largess
largeur [larʒœr] *f* width, breadth; (naut) beam
larguer [large] *tr* to let go, to release
larme [larm] *f* tear; (coll) drop; **fondre en larmes** to burst into tears; **pleurer à chaudes larmes** to shed bitter tears
larmoyant [larmwajɑ̃] **larmoyante** [larmwajɑ̃t] *adj* tearful; watery (*eyes*)
larmoyer [larmwaje] §47 *intr* to water (*said of eyes*); to snivel, to blubber
lar·ron [larɔ̃] **lar·ronnesse** [larɔnɛs] *mf* thief; **s'entendre comme larrons en foire** to be as thick as thieves
larve [larv] *f* larva
laryn·gé -gée [larɛ̃ʒe] *adj* laryngeal
laryn·gien [larɛ̃ʒjɛ̃] **-gienne** [ʒjɛn] *adj* laryngeal
laryngite [larɛ̃ʒit] *f* laryngitis
laryngoscope [larɛ̃gɔskɔp] *m* laryngoscope
larynx [larɛ̃ks] *m* larynx
las [lɑ] **lasse** [lɑs] *adj* weary || **las** [lɑs], [la] *interj* alas!
las·cif [lasif] **las·cive** [lasiv] *adj* lascivious
lasciveté [lasivte] *f* lasciviousness

laser [lazɛr] *m* laser
las•sant [lɑsɑ̃] las•sante [lɑsɑ̃t] *adj* tiring, tedious
lasser [lɑse] *tr* to tire, to weary; to wear out (*s.o.'s patience*) || *ref*— sans se lasser unceasingly; se lasser de + *inf* to tire of + *ger*; to tire oneself out + *ger*
lassitude [lɑsityd] *f* lassitude, weariness
lasso [lɑso] *m* lasso
latence [latɑ̃s] *f* latency
la•tent [latɑ̃] -tente [tɑ̃t] *adj* latent
laté•ral -rale [lateral] *adj* (*pl* -raux) lateral
la•tin [latɛ̃] -tine [tin] *adj* Latin || *m* Latin (*language*) || (*cap*) *mf* Latin (*person*)
latino-améri•cain [latinoamerikɛ̃] -caine [kɛn] (*pl* -américains) *adj* Latin-American || (*cap*) *mf* Latin American
latitude [latityd] *f* latitude
latrines [latrin] *fpl* latrine
latte [lat] *f* lath; broadsword
latter [late] *tr* to lath
lattis [lati] *m* lathing, laths
laudanum [lodanɔm] *m* laudanum
lauda•tif [lodatif] -tive [tiv] *adj* laudatory
lauréat [lɔrea] lauréate [lɔreat] *adj* laureate || *mf* winner, laureate
laurier [lɔrje] *m* laurel, sweet bay; laurier rose rosebay; s'endormir sur ses lauriers to rest on one's laurels
lavable [lavabl] *adj* washable
lavabo [lavabo] *m* washbowl; washroom; lavabos toilet, lavatory
lavage [lavaʒ] *m* washing; lavage de cerveau (coll) brainwashing; lavage des titres wash sale; lavage de tête (coll) dressing down
lavallière [lavaljer] *f* loosely tied bow
lavande [lavɑ̃d] *f* lavender
lavandière [lavɑ̃djer] *f* washerwoman
lave [lav] *f* lava
lave-glace [lavglas] *m* (*pl* -glaces) (aut) windshield washer
lavement [lavmɑ̃] *m* enema
laver [lave] *tr* to wash; laver le cerveau à (coll) to brainwash || *intr* to wash || *ref* to wash oneself, wash; (with *dat* of *reflex pron*) to wash (*e.g., one's hands*)
laverie [lavri] *f* (min) washery; laverie automatique, laverie libre-service self-service laundry
lavette [lavɛt] *f* dishcloth
la•veur [lavœr] -veuse [vøz] *mf* washer; laveur de vaisselle dishwasher (*person*); laveur de vitres window washer (*person*) || *f* washerwoman; washing machine
lavoir [lavwar] *m* place for washing clothes
lavure [lavyr] *f* dishwater; (coll) swill, hogwash
laxa•tif [laksatif] -tive [tiv] *adj* & *m* laxative
layer [leje] §49 *tr* to blaze a trail through; to blaze (*trees to mark a trail*)
layette [lejɛt] *f* layette; packing case

lazzi [lazi] *mpl* jeers
le [lə] *art* §77 || *pron* §87
leader [lidœr] *m* leader
lèche [lɛʃ] *f* (coll) thin slice (*e.g., of bread*); faire de la lèche à qn (slang) to lick s.o.'s boots
lèche-carreaux [lɛʃkaro] *m invar* (slang) window-shopping
lèchefrite [lɛʃfrit] *f* dripping pan
lécher [lɛʃe] §10 *tr* to lick; to over-polish (*one's style*)
lé•cheur [lɛʃœr] -cheuse [ʃøz] *mf* (coll) bootlicker, flatterer
lèche-vitrines [lɛʃvitrin] *m invar* window-shopping; faire du lèche-vitrines to go window-shopping
leçon [ləsɔ̃] *f* lesson; reading (*of manuscript*); faire la leçon à to lecture, sermonize; to prime on what to say
lec•teur [lɛktœr] -trice [tris] *mf* reader; lecturer (*of university rank*) || *m* playback
lecture [lɛktyr] *f* reading; playback; lecture sur les lèvres lip reading
ledit [lədi] ladite [ladit] *adj* (*pl* lesdits [ledi] lesdites [ledit]) the aforesaid
lé•gal -gale [legal] *adj* (*pl* -gaux [go]) legal; statutory
légaliser [legalize] *tr* to legalize
légalité [legalite] *f* legality
légat [lega] *m* papal legate
légataire [legater] *mf* legatee; légataire universel residual heir
légation [legasjɔ̃] *f* legation
légendaire [leʒɑ̃der] *adj* legendary
légende [leʒɑ̃d] *f* legend; caption
lé•ger [leʒe] -gère [ʒer] *adj* light; slight (*accent, difference, pain, mistake, etc.*); faint (*sound, tint, etc.*); delicate (*odor, perfume, etc.*); mild, weak (*drink*); scanty (*dress*); graceful (*figure*); empty (*stomach*); agile, active; frivolous, carefree; à la légère lightly; without due consideration
légèreté [leʒerte] *f* lightness; gracefulness; frivolity; fickleness
leggings [legiŋs] *mpl* & *fpl* leggings
leghorn [legɔrn] *f* leghorn (*chicken*)
légiférer [leʒifere] §10 *intr* to legislate
légion [leʒjɔ̃] *f* legion
législa•teur [leʒislatœr] -trice [tris] *mf* legislator
législa•tif [leʒislatif] -tive [tiv] *adj* legislative
législation [leʒislasjɔ̃] *f* legislation
législature [leʒislatyr] *f* legislative session; legislature
légiste [leʒist] *m* jurist
légitime [leʒitim] *adj* legitimate || *f* (slang) lawful spouse; ma légitime (slang) my better half
légitimer [leʒitime] *tr* to legitimate; to justify
légitimité [leʒitimite] *f* legitimacy
legs [lɛ] *m* legacy
léguer [lege] §10 *tr* to bequeath
légume [legym] *m* vegetable; legume (*pod*) || *f*—grosse légume (slang) bigwig, big wheel
légu•mier [legymje] -mière [mjer] *adj* vegetable (*garden, farming, etc.*) || *m* vegetable dish
lendemain [lɑ̃dmɛ̃] *m* next day; results,

outcome, e.g., **avoir d'heureux lendemains** to have happy results or a happy outcome; **au lendemain de** the day after; **le lendemain matin** the next morning; **sans lendemain** short-lived

lénifier [lenifje] *tr* (med) to soothe

lent [lã] **lente** [lãt] *adj* slow || *f* nit

lentement [lãtmã] *adv* slowly; deliberately

lenteur [lãtœr] *f* slowness, sluggishness; **lenteurs** delays, dilatoriness

lentille [lãtij] *f* lens; (bot) lentil; **lentilles** freckles

léopard [leɔpar] *m* leopard

lèpre [lɛpr] *f* leprosy

lé·preux [leprø] **-preuse** [prøz] *adj* leprous || *mf* leper

lequel [ləkɛl] §78

les [le] *art* §77 || *pron* §87 || *prep* near (*in place names*)

les·bien [lɛsbjɛ̃] **-bienne** [bjɛn] *adj* Lesbian || *f* lesbian || (*cap*) *mf* Lesbian

lèse-majesté [lɛzmaʒɛste] *f*—**crime de lèse-majesté** lese majesty, high treason

léser [leze] §10 *tr* to injure

lésine [lezin] *f* stinginess

lésiner [lezine] *intr* to haggle, to be stingy

lésion [lezjɔ̃] *f* lesion; wrong, damage

les·quels -quelles [lekɛl] §78

lessivage [lesivaʒ] *m* washing; **lessivage de crâne** (coll) brainwashing

lessive [lesiv] *f* washing (*of clothes*); wash; washing soda, lye; **faire la lessive** to do the wash

lessiver [lesive] *tr* to wash; to scrub (*with a cleaning agent*); (slang) to clean out (*e.g., another poker player*); **être lessivé** (slang) to be exhausted

lessiveuse [lesivøz] *f* washing machine

lest [lɛst] *m* ballast

leste [lɛst] *adj* nimble, quick; suggestive, broad; flippant

lestement [lɛstəmã] *adv* nimbly, deftly

lester [lɛste] *tr* to ballast; (coll) to fill (*one's stomach, pockets, etc.*) || *ref* (coll) to stuff oneself

léthargie [letarʒi] *f* lethargy

léthargique [letarʒik] *adj* lethargic || *mf* lethargic person

Lettonie [lɛtɔni] *f* Latvia; **la Lettonie** Latvia

lettrage [letraʒ] *m* lettering

lettre [letr] *f* letter; **à la lettre, au pied de la lettre** to the letter; **avant la lettre** before complete development; **en toutes lettres** in full; in so many words; **lettre de change** bill of exchange; **lettre de faire-part** announcement; **lettre de voiture** bill of lading; **lettre d'imprimerie** printed letter; **lettre majuscule** capital letter; **lettres numérales** roman numerals; **mettre une lettre à la poste** to mail a letter

let·tré -trée [letre] *adj* lettered, literate || *mf* learned person

lettre-morte [letrəmɔrt] *f* letter returned to sender

lettrine [letrin] *f* catchword; initial letter

leu [lø] *m*—**à la queue leu leu** in single file

leucémie [løsemi] *f* leukemia

leucorrhée [løkɔre] *f* leucorrhea

leur [lœr] *adj poss* §88 || *pron poss* §89 || *pron pers* §87

leurre [lœr] *m* lure; delusion

leurrer [lœre] *tr* to lure; to trick, delude || *ref* to be deceived

levain [ləvɛ̃] *m* leaven

levant [ləvã] *adj masc* rising (*sun*) || *m* east || (*cap*) *m* Levant

levan·tin [ləvãtɛ̃] **-tine** [tin] *adj* Levantine || (*cap*) *mf* Levantine

le·vé -vée [ləve] *adj* rising (*sun*); raised (*e.g., hand*); up, e.g., **le soleil est levé** the sun is up || *m* (mus) upbeat; (surv) survey || *f* levee, embankment; collection (*of mail*); levying (*of troops, taxes, etc.*); raising (*of siege*); lifting (*of embargo*); striking (*of camp*); breaking (*of seals*); upstroke (*of piston*); **faire une levée** (cards) to take a trick; **levée de boucliers** public protest, outcry; **levée d'écrou** discharge (*from prison*); **levée de séance** adjournment; **levée du corps** removal of the body; funeral service (*in front of the coffin*); **levées manquantes** (cards) undertricks

lever [ləve] *m* rising; (surv) survey; **lever du rideau** rise of the curtain; curtain raiser; **lever du soleil** sunrise || §2 *tr* to lift; to raise; to collect, to pick up (*the mail*); to levy (*troops, taxes, etc.*); to strike (*camp*); to adjourn (*a meeting*); to weigh (*anchor*); to relieve (*a guard*); to remit (*a punishment*); to flush (*e.g., a partridge*); to effect (*a survey*); to break (*the seals*) || *intr* to come up (*said of plants*); to rise (*said of dough*) || *ref* to get up; to stand up; to rise; to heave (*said of sea*); to clear up (*said of weather*)

léviathan [levjatã] *m* leviathan

levier [ləvje] *m* lever; crowbar; **être aux leviers de commande** (aer) to be at the controls; (fig) to be in control; **levier de changement de vitesse** gearshift lever

lévitation [levitasjɔ̃] *f* levitation

levraut [ləvro] *m* young hare, leveret

lèvre [levr] *f* lip; rim; **du bout des lèvres** half-heartedly, guardedly; **embrasser sur les lèvres** to kiss; **serrer les lèvres** to purse one's lips

lévrier [levrije] *m* greyhound

levure [ləvyr] *f* yeast; **levure anglaise** or **chimique** baking powder; **levure de bière** brewer's yeast

lexi·cal -cale [lɛksikal] *adj* (*pl* **-caux** [ko]) lexical

lexicographe [lɛksikɔgraf] *mf* lexicographer

lexicographie [lɛksikɔgrafi] *f* lexicography

lexicographique [lɛksikɔgrafik] *adj* lexicographic(al)

lexicologie [lɛksikɔlɔʒi] *f* lexicology

lexique [lɛksik] *m* lexicon, vocabulary; abridged dictionary
lez [le] *prep* near (*in place names*)
lézard [lezar] *m* lizard; **faire le lézard** (coll) to sun oneself, to loaf
lézarde [lezard] *f* crack, split, crevice; gimp (*of furniture*); braid; (mil) gold braid
lézarder [lezarde] *tr & ref* to crack, to split || *intr* (coll) to bask in the sun
liaison [ljezɔ̃] *f* liaison
liant [ljɑ̃] **liante** [ljɑ̃t] *adj* flexible, supple; sociable, affable || *m* flexibility; sociability; binder, binding material; **avoir du liant** to be a good mixer
liard [ljar] *m* (fig) farthing
liasse [ljas] *f* packet, bundle (*e.g., of letters*); wad (*of bank notes*)
Liban [libɑ̃] *m*—**le Liban** Lebanon
liba·nais [libanɛ] **-naise** [nɛz] *adj* Lebanese || (*cap*) *mf* Lebanese
libation [libasjɔ̃] *f* libation
libelle [libɛl] *m* lampoon
libellé [libɛlle] *m* wording
libeller [libele], [libɛlle] *tr* to word; to draw up (*e.g., a contract*); to make out (*a check*)
libellule [libɛllyl] *f* dragonfly
libé·ral -rale [liberal] *adj & mf* (*pl* **-raux** [ro]) liberal
libéralisme [liberalism] *m* liberalism
libéralité [liberalite] *f* liberality
libéra·teur [liberatœr] **-trice** [tris] *adj* liberating || *mf* liberator
libération [liberasjɔ̃] *f* liberation
libérer [libere] §10 *tr* to liberate || *ref* to free oneself; to pay up
liberté [libɛrte] *f* liberty, freedom; **liberté d'association** or **liberté de réunion** right of assembly; **liberté de langage** freedom of speech; **liberté de la presse** freedom of the press; **liberté de la propriété** right to own private property; **liberté du commerce et de l'industrie** free enterprise; **liberté du culte** freedom of worship
liber·tin [libɛrtɛ̃] **-tine** [tin] *adj* libertine; (archaic) freethinking || *mf* libertine; (archaic) freethinker
libidi·neux [libidinø] **-neuse** [nøz] *adj* libidinous
libido [libido] *f* libido
libraire [librɛr] *mf* bookseller; publisher
libraire-éditeur [librɛreditœr] *m* (*pl* **libraires-éditeurs**) publisher and bookseller
librairie [librɛri] *f* bookstore; book trade; publishing house
libre [libr] *adj* free; **je suis libre de mon temps** my time is my own; **libre arbitre** free will; **libre de** free to, at liberty to
libre-échange [librefɑ̃ʒ] *m* free trade
libre-échangiste [librefɑ̃ʒist] *m* (*pl* **-échangistes**) free trader
libre-pen·seur [librǝpɑ̃sœr] **-seuse** [søz] *mf* (*pl* **libres-penseurs**) freethinker
libre-service [librǝsɛrvis] *m* (*pl* **libres-services**) self-service; self-service store

lice [lis] *f* enclosure or fence (*of race track, fairground, tiltyard, etc.*); (zool) hound bitch; **de basse lice** (tex) low-warp; **de haute lice** (tex) high-warp; **entrer en lice** to enter the lists
licence [lisɑ̃s] *f* license; **licence ès lettres** advanced liberal-arts degree, master of arts; **prendre des licences avec** to take liberties with
licen·cié -ciée [lisɑ̃sje] *mf* holder of a master's degree
licenciement [lisɑ̃simɑ̃] *m* discharge, layoff
licencier [lisɑ̃sje] *tr* to discharge, lay off
licen·cieux [lisɑ̃sjø] **-cieuse** [sjøz] *adj* licentious
lichen [likɛn] *m* lichen
licher [liʃe] *tr* (slang) to gulp down
licite [lisit] *adj* lawful, licit
licorne [likɔrn] *f* unicorn
licou [liku] *m* halter
lie [li] *f* dregs, lees; (fig) dregs, scum
lie-de-vin [lidvɛ̃] *adj invar* maroon
liège [ljeʒ] *m* cork
lien [ljɛ̃] *m* tie, bond, link
lier [lje] *tr* to tie, to bind, to link || *ref* to bind together; to make friends; **lier conversation avec** to fall into conversation with; **se lier d'amitié avec** to become friends with
lierre [ljɛr] *m* ivy
liesse [ljes] *f*—**en liesse** in festive mood, gay
lieu [ljø] *m* (*pl* **lieux**) place; **au lieu de** instead of, in lieu of; **avoir lieu** to take place; **avoir lieu de** to have reason to; **donner lieu à** to give rise to; **en aucun lieu** nowhere; **en dernier lieu** finally; **en haut lieu** high up, in responsible circles; **en premier lieu** first of all; **en quelque lieu que** wherever; **en tous lieux** everywhere; **il y a lieu à** there is room for; **lieu commun** commonplace; platitude; **lieu de villégiature** resort; **lieu géométrique** locus; **lieux** premises; **lieux d'aisances** rest rooms; **lieux payants** comfort station, public lavatory; **sur les lieux** on the spot; on the premises; **tenir lieu** to take place; **tenir lieu de** to take the place of
lieu-dit [ljødi] *m* (*pl* **lieux-dits**)—**le lieu-dit . . .** the place called . . .
lieue [ljø] *f* league
lieur [ljœr] **lieuse** [ljøz] *mf* binder || *f* (mach) binder
lieutenant [ljøtnɑ̃] *m* lieutenant; (merchant marine) mate; **lieutenant de port** harbor master; **lieutenant de vaisseau** (nav) lieutenant commander
lieutenant-colonel [ljøtnɑ̃kɔlɔnɛl] *m* (*pl* **lieutenants-colonels**) lieutenant colonel
lièvre [ljɛvr] *m* hare; **c'est là que gît le lièvre** there's the rub; **lever un lièvre** (fig) to raise an embarrassing question; **prendre le lièvre au gîte** (fig) to catch s.o. napping
ligament [ligamɑ̃] *m* ligament
ligature [ligatyr] *f* ligature
ligaturer [ligatyre] *tr* to tie up

ligne [liɲ] *f* line; figure, waistline; (*of an automobile*) lines; **aller à la ligne** to begin a new paragraph; **avoir de la ligne** to have a good figure; **en première ligne** of the first importance; on the firing line; **garder sa ligne** to keep one's figure; **grande ligne** (rr) main line; **grandes lignes** broad outline; **hors ligne** unrivaled, outstanding; **ligne à postes groupés** (telp) party line; **ligne de changement de date** international date line; **ligne de flottaison** water line; **ligne de mire** (arti) line of sight; **ligne de partage des eaux** watershed; **ligne partagée** (telp) party line; **ligne pointillée** or **hachée** dotted line

lignée [liɲe] *f* lineage, offspring

li·gneux [liɲø] **-gneuse** [ɲøz] *adj* woody

lignifier [liɲifje] *tr* & *ref* to turn into wood

ligot [ligo] *m* firewood (*in tied bundle*)

ligoter [ligɔte] *tr* to tie up, to bind

ligue [lig] *f* league

liguer [lige] *tr* & *ref* to league

lilas [lila] *adj invar* & *m* lilac

li·lial -liale [liljal] *adj* (*pl* **-liaux** [ljo]) lily-white, lily-like

lillipu·tien [lilipysjɛ̃] **-tienne** [sjɛn] *adj* & *mf* Lilliputian

limace [limas] *f* (zool) slug; (coll) slowpoke; (slang) shirt

limaçon [limasɔ̃] *m* snail; **en limaçon** spiral

limaille [limɑj] *f* filings

limbe [lɛ̃b] *m* (astr, bot) limb; **limbes** limbo

lime [lim] *f* file; (*Citrus limetta*) sweet lime; **dernier coup de lime** finishing touches; **enlever à la lime** to file off; **lime à ongles** nail file; **lime émeri** emery board

limer [lime] *tr* to file; to fray; (fig) to polish

limette [limɛt] *f* (*Citrus limetta*) sweet lime

limier [limje] *m* bloodhound; (coll) sleuth

liminaire [liminɛr] *adj* preliminary

limitation [limitɑsjɔ̃] *f* limitation

limite [limit] *f* limit; maximum, e.g., **vitesse limite** maximum speed; **dernière limite** deadline

limiter [limite] *tr* to limit || *ref* to be limited; to limit oneself

limitrophe [limitrɔf] *adj* frontier; **limitrophe de** adjacent to

limogeage [limɔʒaʒ] *m* (coll) removal from office

limoger [limɔʒe] §38 *tr* (coll) to remove from office, to relieve of a command

limon [limɔ̃] *m* silt; clay; mud; shaft (*of wagon*)

limonade [limɔnad] *f* lemon soda

limona·dier [limɔnadje] **-dière** [djɛr] *mf* soft-drink manufacturer; café manager

limo·neux [limɔnø] **-neuse** [nøz] *adj* silty; muddy

limousine [limuzin] *f* heavy cloak; (aut) limousine

limpide [lɛ̃pid] *adj* limpid

lin [lɛ̃] *m* flax; linen

linceul [lɛ̃sœl] *m* shroud; cover (*of snow*)

linéament [lineamɑ̃] *m* lineament

linge [lɛ̃ʒ] *m* linen (*sheets, tablecloths, underclothes, etc.*); piece of linen; **laver le linge** to do the wash; **linge de corps** underclothes

lingère [lɛ̃ʒɛr] *f* linen maid; linen closet

lingerie [lɛ̃ʒri] *f* linen (*sheets, tablecloths, underclothes, etc.*); linen closet; **lingerie de dame** lingerie; **lingerie d'homme** men's underwear

lingot [lɛ̃go] *m* ingot

lin·gual -guale [lɛ̃gwal] (*pl* **-guaux** [gwo] **-guales**) *adj* & *f* lingual

linguiste [lɛ̃gɥist] *mf* linguist

linguistique [lɛ̃gɥistik] *adj* linguistic || *f* linguistics

liniment [linimɑ̃] *m* liniment

linoléum [linɔleɔm] *m* linoleum

linon [linɔ̃] *m* lawn (*sheer linen*)

linotte [linɔt] *f* (orn) linnet

linotype [linɔtip] *f* linotype

linotypiste [linɔtipist] *mf* linotype operator

lin·teau [lɛ̃to] *m* (*pl* **-teaux**) lintel

lion [ljɔ̃] **lionne** [ljɔn] *mf* lion || *f* lioness

lion·ceau [ljɔso] *m* (*pl* **-ceaux**) lion cub

lippe [lip] *f* thick lower lip, blubber lip

lip·pu -pue [lipy] *adj* thick-lipped

liquéfier [likefje] *tr* to liquefy

liqueur [likœr] *f* liqueur; liquid; (chem, pharm) liquor

liquidation [likidɑsjɔ̃] *f* liquidation; settlement; clearance sale

liquide [likid] *adj* & *m* liquid || *f* liquid (*consonant*)

liquider [likide] *tr* to liquidate; to settle (*a score*); to wind up (*a piece of business*); (coll) to get rid of; to put an end to

liquidité [likidite] *f* liquidity

liquo·reux [likɔrø] **-reuse** [røz] *adj* sweet

lire [lir] §36 *tr* & *intr* to read; **lire à haute voix** to read aloud; **lire à vue** to sight-read; **lire sur les lèvres** to lip-read || *ref* to read; to show, e.g., **la surprise se lit sur votre visage** your face shows surprise

lis [lis] *m* lily; **lis blanc** lily; **lis jaune** day lily

Lisbonne [lizbɔn] *f* Lisbon

liseré [lizre] or **liséré** [lizere] *m* braid, border, strip

li·seur [lizœr] **-seuse** [zøz] *mf* reader || *f* bookmark; reading lamp; book jacket; bed jacket

lisibilité [lizibilie] *f* legibility

lisible [lizibl] *adj* legible; readable

lisière [lisjɛr] *f* edge, border; list, selvage; **tenir en lisières** to keep in leading strings

lisse [lis] *adj* smooth, polished, sleek || *f* (naut) handrail

lisser [lise] *tr* to smooth, to polish, to

sleek; to glaze (*paper*) ‖ *ref* to become smooth; **se lisser les plumes** to preen its feathers
liste [list] *f* list
lit [li] *m* bed; layer; stratum; **dans le lit de la marée** in the tideway; **dans le lit du vent** in the wind's eye; **du premier lit** by or of the first marriage; **lit de mort** deathbed; **lit d'époque** period bed; **lit de sangle, lit de camp** folding cot, camp bed; **lit en portefeuille** apple-pie bed; **lit pliant, lit escamotable, lit à rabattement** foldaway bed; **lits jumeaux** twin beds
litanie [litani] *f* litany; tale of woe
lit-cage [likaʒ] *m* (*pl* **lits-cages**) foldaway bed
litée [lite] *f* litter (*of animals*)
literie [litri] *f* bedding, bedclothes
lithine [litin] *f* lithia
lithium [litjɔm] *m* lithium
lithographe [litɔgraf] *mf* lithographer
lithographie [litɔgrafi] *f* lithography; lithograph
lithographier [litɔgrafje] *tr* to lithograph
litière [litjɛr] *f* litter (*bedding for animals*); **faire litière de** to trample
litige [litiʒ] *m* litigation
liti·gieux [litiʒjø] **-gieuse** [ʒjøz] *adj* litigious
litre [litr] *m* liter
littéraire [literɛr] *adj* literary ‖ *mf* teacher of literature; belletrist
litté·ral -rale [literal] *adj* (*pl* **-raux** [ro]) literal; literary, written
littérature [literatyr] *f* literature
litto·ral -rale [litɔral] (*pl* **-raux** [ro]) *adj* littoral, coastal ‖ *m* coast, coastline
Lituanie [litɥani] *f* Lithuania; **la Lituanie** Lithuania
litua·nien [litɥanjɛ̃] **-nienne** [njɛn] *adj* Lithuanian ‖ *m* Lithuanian (*language*) ‖ (*cap*) *mf* Lithuanian (*person*)
liturgie [lityrʒi] *f* liturgy
liturgique [lityrʒik] *adj* liturgic(al)
livide [livid] *adj* livid
Livourne [livurn] *f* Leghorn
livrable [livrabl] *adj* ready for delivery
livraison [livrɛzɔ̃] *f* delivery; installment; **livraison contre remboursement** cash on delivery
livre [livr] *m* book; **à livre ouvert** at sight; **faire un livre** to write a book; (*racing*) to make book; **feuilleter un livre** to glance through a book; **grand livre** (*bk*) ledger; **livre de bord** (aer, naut) logbook; **livre de classe** textbook; **livre de cuisine, livre de recettes** cookbook; **livre d'or** blue book; testimonial volume; **livre jaune** white book; **petit livre** (*bk*) journal, day book; **porter au grand livre** (*bk*) to post ‖ *f* pound (*weight; currency*)
livrée [livre] *f* livery; appearances; coat (*of horse, deer, etc.*)
livrer [livre] *tr* to deliver; to surrender; to betray ‖ *ref*—**se livrer à** to sur-

render oneself to; to give way to; to indulge in
livresque [livrɛsk] *adj* bookish
livret [livrɛ] *m* booklet; (mus) libretto; **livret de caisse d'épargne** bankbook; **livret de famille** marriage certificate; **livret militaire** military record; **livret scolaire** transcript (*of grades*)
li·vreur [livrœr] **-vreuse** [vrøz] *mf* deliverer (*of parcels, packages, etc.*) ‖ *m* deliveryman ‖ *f* woman who makes deliveries; delivery truck
lobe [lɔb] *m* lobe
lo·cal -cale [lɔkal] (*pl* **-caux** [ko]) *adj* local ‖ *m* place, premises, quarters; headquarters; **locaux** (sports) home team; **locaux commerciaux** office space
localiser [lɔkalize] *tr* to locate; to localize
localité [lɔkalite] *f* locality
locataire [lɔkatɛr] *mf* tenant, renter
location [lɔkɑsjɔ̃] *f* rental; reservation
loch [lɔk] *m* (naut) log (*to determine speed*)
locomotive [lɔkɔmɔtiv] *f* locomotive; (fig) mover
locuste [lɔkyst] *f* (ent) locust
locu·teur [lɔkytœr] **-trice** [tris] *mf* speaker
locution [lɔkysjɔ̃] *f* locution; phrase
lof [lɔf] *m* windward side; **aller** or **venir au lof** to sail into the wind
logarithme [lɔgaritm] *m* logarithm
loge [lɔʒ] *f* lodge; circus cage; concierge's room; chamber, cell; (theat) dressing room; (theat) box
logeabilité [lɔʒabilite] *f* spaciousness
logeable [lɔʒabl] *adj* livable, inhabitable
logement [lɔʒmã] *m* lodging, lodgings
loger [lɔʒe] §38 *tr, intr, & ref* to lodge
lo·geur [lɔʒœr] **-geuse** [ʒøz] *mf* proprietor of a boardinghouse ‖ *m* landlord ‖ *f* landlady
logi·cien [lɔʒisjɛ̃] **-cienne** [sjɛn] *mf* logician
logique [lɔʒik] *adj* logical ‖ *f* logic
logis [lɔʒi] *m* abode
logistique [lɔʒistik] *adj* logistic(al) ‖ *f* logistics
loi [lwa] *f* law; **faire des lois** to legislate; **faire la loi** to lay down the law; **loi exceptionnelle** emergency leglislation
loin [lwɛ̃] *adv* far; far away, far off; **au loin** in the distance; **d'aussi loin que, du plus loin que** as soon as; as far back as; **de loin** from afar; far from; far be it from (*e.g., me*); **de loin en loin** now and then; **il y a loin de** it is a far cry from
loin·tain [lwɛ̃tɛ̃] **-taine** [tɛn] *adj* faraway, distant, remote; early (*e.g., memories*) ‖ *m* distance, background; **le lointain** (theat) upstage
loir [lwar] *m* dormouse; **dormir comme un loir** to sleep like a log
loisible [lwazibl] *adj*—**il m'est (lui est, etc.) loisible de** I am (he is, etc.) free to or entitled to, it is open for me (him, etc.) to

loisir [lwazir] *m* leisure, spare time; loisirs diversions
lolo [lolo] *m* (coll) milk (*in baby talk*)
lombes [lɔ̃b] *mpl* loins
londo·nien [lɔ̃dɔnjɛ̃] -nienne [njɛn] *adj* London || (*cap*) *mf* Londoner
Londres [lɔ̃dr] *m* London
londrès [lɔ̃drɛs] *m* Havana cigar
long [lɔ̃] longue [lɔ̃g] *adj* long; lengthy (*speech*); long (*syllable, vowel*); thin, weak (*sauce, gravy*); slow (*to understand, to decide*) || (when standing before noun) *adj* long; de longue main of long standing || *m* length; extent; au long at length; de long lengthwise; de long en large up and down, back and forth; le long de along || *f* see longue || long *adv* much; en dire long to talk a long time; to speak volumes; en savoir long sur to know a great deal about; en savoir plus long to know more about it
longanimité [lɔ̃ganimite] *f* long-suffering
long·courrier [lɔ̃kurje] (*pl* -courriers) *adj* long-range || *m* airliner; liner, ocean liner
longe [lɔ̃ʒ] *f* tether, leash; (culin) loin
longer [lɔ̃ʒe] §38 *tr* to walk along, to go beside; to extend along, to skirt
longeron [lɔ̃ʒrɔ̃] *m* crossbeam, girder
longévité [lɔ̃ʒevite] *f* longevity
longitude [lɔ̃ʒityd] *f* longitude
longtemps [lɔ̃tɑ̃] *m* a long time; avant longtemps before long; depuis longtemps for a long time; long since; ne . . . plus longtemps no . . . longer || *adv* long; for a long time
longue [lɔ̃g] *f* long syllable; long vowel; long suit (*in cards*); à la longue in the long run
longuement [lɔ̃gmɑ̃] *adv* at length, a long time
lon·guet [lɔ̃gɛ] -guette [gɛt] *adj* (coll) longish, rather long
longueur [lɔ̃gœr] *f* length; lengthiness; de longueur, dans la longueur lengthwise; d'une longueur by a length, by a head; longueur d'onde wavelength
longue-vue [lɔ̃gvy] *f* (*pl* longues-vues) telescope, spyglass
looping [lupiŋ] *m* loop-the-loop
lopin [lɔpɛ̃] *m* patch of ground, plot
loquace [lɔkwas], [lɔkas] *adj* loquacious
loque [lɔk] *f* rag; être comme une loque to feel like a dishrag; être en loques to be in tatters
loquet [lɔkɛ] *m* latch
loque·teux [lɔktø] -teuse [tøz] *adj* in tatters || *mf* tatterdemalion
lorgner [lɔrɲe] *tr* to cast a sidelong glance at; to ogle; to have one's eyes on (*a job, an inheritance, etc.*)
lorgnette [lɔrɲɛt] *f* opera glasses
lorgnon [lɔrɲɔ̃] *m* pince-nez; lorgnette
loriot [lɔrjo] *m* golden oriole
lorry [lɔri] *m* lorry, small flatcar
lors [lɔr] *adv*—lors de at the time of; lors même que even if
lorsque [lɔrsk] *conj* when

losange [lɔzɑ̃ʒ] *m* (geom) lozenge; en losange diamond-shaped; oval-shaped
lot [lo] *m* lot; prize (*e.g., in lottery*); gagner le gros lot to hit the jackpot
loterie [lɔtri] *f* lottery
lo·ti -tie [lɔti] *adj*—bien loti well off; mal loti badly off
lotion [losjɔ̃] *f* lotion; lotion capillaire hair tonic
lotionner [losjɔne] *tr* to bathe (*a wound*)
lotir [lɔtir] *tr* to parcel out; lotir qn de q.ch. to allot s.th. to s.o.
lotissement [lɔtismɑ̃] *m* allotment, apportionment; building lot
louable [lwabl] *adj* praiseworthy; for hire
louage [lwaʒ] *m* hire
louange [lwɑ̃ʒ] *f* praise; à la louange de in praise of
louanger [lwɑ̃ʒe] §38 *tr* to praise, extol
louan·geur [lwɑ̃ʒœr] -geuse [ʒøz] *adj* laudatory, flattering
louche [luʃ] *adj* ambiguous; suspicious, shady; cross-eyed; cloudy (*e.g., wine*) || *f* ladle; basting spoon
loucher [luʃe] *intr* to be cross-eyed, to squint; faire loucher qn de jalousie (coll) to turn s.o. green with envy; loucher sur (coll) to cast longing eyes at
louchet [luʃɛ] *m* spade (*for digging*)
louer [lwe] *tr* to rent, hire; to reserve (*a seat*); to praise || *ref* to be rented; to hire oneself out; se louer de to be satisfied with
loueur [lwœr] loueuse [lwøz] *mf* operator of a rental service; flatterer
loufoque [lufɔk] *adj* (slang) cracked || *m* (slang) crackpot
lougre [lugr] *m* (naut) lugger
Louisiane [lwizjan] *f* Louisiana; la Louisiane Louisiana
lou·lou [lulu] -loute [lut] *mf* (coll) darling, pet || *m*—loulou de Poméranie Pomeranian, spitz
loup [lu] *m* wolf; mask; flaw; avoir vu le loup to have lost one's innocence; crier au loup to cry wolf; loup de mer (ichth) wolf eel; (coll) old salt; mon petit loup (coll) my pet
loup-cervier [lusɛrvje] *m* (*pl* loups-cerviers) lynx
loupe [lup] *f* magnifying glass; gnarl (*on tree*); (pathol) wen
lou·pé -pée [lupe] *adj* bungled; defective || *m* defect
louper [lupe] *tr* (coll) to goof up, to muff; (coll) to miss (*e.g., one's train*) || *intr* (coll) to fail, to goof
loup-garou [lugaru] *m* (*pl* loups-garous) werewolf
lou·piot [lupjo] -piotte [pjɔt] *mf* (coll) kid, child; loupiots (coll) small fry
lourd [lur] lourde [lurd] *adj* heavy; hefty; clumsy; sultry (*weather*); off-color (*joke*); dull (*mind*); (agr) hard to cultivate || (when standing before noun) *adj* heavy; grave; clumsy (*e.g., compliments*); off-color (*joke*) || lourd *adv* heavy, heavily

lour·daud [lurdo] **-daude** [dod] *adj* clumsy, loutish, dull ‖ *mf* lout, oaf
lourdement [lurdəmã] *adv* heavily; clumsily; **avancer** or **rouler lourdement** to lumber along
lourdeur [lurdœr] *f* heaviness; clumsiness; sultriness; dullness
loustic [lustik] *m* wag, clown; (coll) screwball, character
loutre [lutr] *f* otter
louve [luv] *f* she-wolf
louve·teau [luvto] *m* (*pl* **-teaux**) wolf cub; cub scout
louvoyer [luvwaje] §47 *intr* to be evasive; (naut) to tack
lovelace [lɔvlas] *m* seducer, Don Juan
lover [lɔve] *tr & ref* to coil
loyal loyale [lwajal] *adj* (*pl* **loyaux** [lwajo]) loyal; honest; fair, just
loyaliste [lwajalist] *mf* loyalist
loyauté [lwajote] *f* loyalty; honesty; fairness
loyer [lwaje] *m* rent
lubie [lybi] *f* whim
lubricité [lybrisite] *f* lubricity, lewdness
lubri·fiant [lybrifjã] **-fiante** [fjãt] *adj* & *m* lubricant
lubrifier [lybrifje] *tr* to lubricate
lucarne [lykarn] *f* dormer window; skylight
lucide [lysid] *adj* lucid
luciole [lysjɔl] *f* firefly
lucra·tif [lykratif] **-tive** [tiv] *adj* lucrative
lucre [lykr] *m* lucre
luette [lɥɛt] *f* uvula
lueur [lɥœr] *f* glimmer, gleam; flash, blink
luge [lyʒ] *f* sled
lugubre [lygybr] *adj* gloomy
lui [lɥi] *pron disj* §85 ‖ *pron conj* §87
lui-même [lɥimɛm] §86
luire [lɥir] §37 *intr* to shine; to gleam, glow, glisten; to dawn
lui·sant [lɥizã] **-sante** [zãt] *adj* shining
lulu [lyly] *m* (orn) tree pipit
lumbago [lɔ̃bago] *m* lumbago
lumière [lymjɛr] *f* light; aperture; (person) luminary; **avoir des lumières de** to have knowledge of
lumignon [lymiɲɔ̃] *m* feeble light
luminaire [lyminɛr] *m* luminary
lumines·cent [lyminesã] **lumines·cente** [lyminesãt] *adj* luminescent
lumi·neux [lyminø] **-neuse** [nøz] *adj* luminous; light (*e.g., spot*); bright (*idea*)
lunaire [lynɛr] *adj* lunar ‖ *f* (bot) honesty
lunatique [lynatik] *adj* whimsical, eccentric ‖ *mf* whimsical person, eccentric
lunch [lœntʃ], [lœ̃ʃ] *m* buffet lunch
lundi [lœ̃di] m Monday
lune [lyn] *f* moon; **être dans la lune** to be daydreaming; **lune de miel** honeymoon; **lune des moissons** harvest moon; **vieilles lunes** good old days, bygone days
lu·né -née [lyne] *adj* moon-shaped;

bien luné in a good mood; **mal luné** in a bad mood
lune·tier [lyntje] **-tière** [tjɛr] *mf* optician
lunette [lynɛt] *f* telescope, spyglass; toilet seat; hole (*in toilet seat*); wishbone (*of turkey, chicken*); (archit) lunette; (aut) rear window; **lunettes** eyeglasses, spectacles; goggles; **lunettes de lecture, lunettes pour lire** reading glasses; **lunettes de soleil** sunglasses; **lunettes noires** dark glasses
lurette [lyrɛt] *f—il y a belle lurette* (coll) ages ago
luron [lyrɔ̃] *m* (coll) playboy
luronne [lyrɔn] *f* (coll) hussy
lustre [lystr] *m* luster; five-year period; chandelier
lus·tré -trée [lystre] *adj* lustrous, glossy
lustrine [lystrin] *f* cotton satin
lut [lyt] *m* (chem) lute
luth [lyt] *m* (mus) lute
lutherie [lytri] *f* violin making
luthé·rien [lyterjɛ̃] **-rienne** [rjɛn] *adj* Lutheran ‖ (*cap*) *mf* Lutheran
luthier [lytje] *m* violin maker
lu·tin [lytɛ̃] **-tine** [tin] *adj* impish ‖ *m* imp
lutiner [lytine] *tr* to tease
lutrin [lytrɛ̃] *m* lectern
lutte [lyt] *f* struggle, fight; wrestling; **de bonne lutte** aboveboard; **de haute lutte** by force; in open competition; hard-won; **lutte à la corde de traction** tug of war; **lutte libre** catch-as-catch-can
lutter [lyte] *intr* to fight, to struggle; to wrestle
lut·teur [lytœr] **lut·teuse** [lytøz] *mf* wrestler; (fig) fighter
luxation [lyksasjɔ̃] *f* dislocation
luxe [lyks] *m* luxury
Luxembourg [lyksãbur] *m—le Luxembourg** Luxembourg
luxer [lykse] *tr* to dislocate
luxueux [lyksɥø] **luxueuse** [lyksɥøz] *adj* luxurious
luxure [lyksyr] *f* lechery, lust
luxu·riant [lyksyrjã] **-riante** [rjãt] *adj* luxuriant
luxu·rieux [lyksyrjø] **-rieuse** [rjøz] *adj* lecherous, lustful
luzerne [lyzɛrn] *f* alfalfa
lycée [lise] *m* high school; lyceum
lycéen [liseɛ̃] **lycéenne** [liseɛn] *mf* high-school student
lymphatique [lɛ̃fatik] *adj* lymphatic
lymphe [lɛ̃f] *f* lymph
lynchage [lɛ̃ʃaʒ] *m* lynching
lyncher [lɛ̃ʃe] *tr* to lynch
lynx [lɛ̃ks] *m* lynx
Lyon [ljɔ̃] *m* Lyons
lyon·nais [ljonɛ] **lyon·naise** [ljonɛz] *adj* Lyonese; **à la lyonnaise** lyonnaise
lyre [lir] *f* lyre
lyrique [lirik] *adj* lyric(al) ‖ *m* lyric poet ‖ *f* lyric poetry
lyrisme [lirism] *m* lyricism
lys [lis] *m* lily; **lys blanc** lily; **lys jaune** day lily
lysimaque [lizimak] *f* loosestrife

M

M, m [εm], *[εm] *m invar* thirteenth letter of the French alphabet
M. *abbr* (**Monsieur**) Mr.
ma [ma] §88
ma·boul -boule [mabul] *adj* (slang) nuts, balmy ‖ *mf* (slang) nut
macabre [makɑbr] *adj* macabre
macadam [makadam] *m* macadam
macadamiser [makadamize] *tr* to macadamize
macaron [makarɔ̃] *m* macaroon
macchabée [makabe] *m* (slang) stiff (*corpse*)
macédoine [masedwan] *f* macédoine, medley; **macédoine de fruits** fruit salad; **macédoine de légumes** mixed vegetables
macérer [masere] §10 *tr* to macerate; to mortify (*the flesh*); to soak, to steep ‖ *intr* to soak, to steep
mâchefer [mɑʃfεr] *m* clinker
mâcher [mɑʃe] *tr* to chew; **mâcher la besogne à qn** to do all one's work for one; **ne pas mâcher ses mots** to not mince words
machin [maʃε̃] *m* (coll) what-do-you-call-it; (coll) what's-his-name, so-and-so
machi·nal -nale [maʃinal] *adj* (*pl* **-naux** [no]) mechanical
machination [maʃinɑsjɔ̃] *f* machination
machine [maʃin] *f* machine; engine; **faire machine arrière** to go into reverse; **machine à calculer** adding machine; **machine à coudre** sewing machine; **machine à écrire** typewriter; **machine à laver** washing machine; **machine à laver la vaisselle** dishwasher; **machine à vapeur** steam engine; **machines** machinery
machine-outil [maʃinuti] *f* (*pl* **machines-outils**) machine tool
machinerie [maʃinri] *f* machinery; engine room
machiniste [maʃinist] *m* (theat) stage-hand
mâchoire [mɑʃwar] *f* jaw; jawbone; lower jaw
mâchonner [mɑʃɔne] *tr* to chew, munch; to mumble (*e.g., the end of a sentence*)
mâchurer [mɑʃyre] *tr* to crush; to smudge
maçon [masɔ̃] *m* mason
maçonner [masɔne] *tr* to mason, to wall up
maçonnerie [masɔnri] *f* masonry
macule [makyl] *f* spot, blotch; inkblot; birthmark
maculer [makyle] *tr* to soil, spot; (typ) to smear
madame [madam] *f* (*pl* **mesdames** [medam]) madam; Mrs.; (not translated), e.g., **madame votre femme** your wife
Madeleine [madlεn] *f* Madeleine, Magdalen; sponge cake; **pleurer comme une Madeleine** to weep bitterly
mademoiselle [madmwazεl] *f* (*pl* **mesdemoiselles** [medmwazεl]) Miss;

eldest daughter; (not translated), e.g., **mademoiselle votre fille** your daughter
Madone [madɔn] *f* Madonna
ma·dré -drée [madre] *adj* sly, cagey ‖ *mf* sly one
madrier [madrije] *m* beam
maf·flu -flue [mafly] *adj* heavy-jowled
magasin [magazε̃] *m* store; warehouse; magazine (*of gun or camera; for munitions or powder*); **avoir en magasin** to have in stock; **grands magasins** department store; **magasin à libre service** self-service store; **magasin à succursales multiples** chain store; **magasin d'antiquités** antique shop; **magasin de modes** dress shop
magasinage [magazinaʒ] *m* storage, warehousing; storage charges; (Canad) shopping
magasinier [magazinje] *m* warehouse-man
magazine [magazin] *m* magazine; (mov, telv) hour, program, e.g., **magazine féminin** woman's hour
mages [maʒ] *mpl* Magi
magi·cien [maʒisjε̃] **-cienne** [sjεn] *mf* magician
magie [maʒi] *f* magic
magique [maʒik] *adj* magic
magis·tral -trale [maʒistral] *adj* (*pl* **-traux** [tro]) masterful, masterly; magisterial; (pharm) magistral
magistrat [maʒistra] *m* magistrate
magnanime [maɲanim] *adj* magnanimous
magnat [magna] *m* magnate
magnésium [maɲezjɔm] *m* magnesium
magnétique [maɲetik] *adj* magnetic; hypnotic
magnétiser [maɲetize] *tr* to magnetize; to hypnotize; to spellbind
magnétisme [maɲetism] *m* magnetism
magnéto [maɲeto] *f* magneto
magnétophone [maɲetɔfɔn] *m* tape recorder
magnétoscope [maɲetɔskɔp] *m* video tape recorder; video tape recording
magnifier [magnifje] *tr* to extol, glorify
magnifique [maɲifik] *adj* magnificent; lavishly generous
magnitude [magnityd] *f* (astr) magnitude
magot [mago] *m* Barbary ape; figurine; (coll) hoard, pile (*of money*)
Mahomet [maɔmε] *m* Mahomet
mahomé·tan [maɔmetɑ̃] **-tane** [tan] *adj & m* Mohammedan
mai [mε] *m* May; Maypole
maie [mε] *f* bread bin; kneading trough
maigre [mεgr] *adj* lean; thin; meager; meatless (*day*); **faire maigre** to abstain from meat
maigreur [mεgrœr] *f* leanness; meagerness
maigri·chon [megriʃɔ̃] **-chonne** [ʃɔn] *adj* (coll) skinny

maigrir [megrir] *tr* to slim; to make (*s.o.*) look thinner ‖ *intr* to lose weight
mail [maj] *m* mall
maille [mɑj] *f* link; stitch; mesh, loop; **avoir maille à partir avec qn** to have a bone to pick with s.o.; **mailles** mail
maillet [majɛ] *m* mallet
maillon [mɑjɔ̃] *m* link (*of a chain*)
maillot [majo] *m* swimming suit; jersey; **maillot de bain** swimming suit; **maillot de corps** undershirt; **maillot de danseur** tights; **maillot des acrobates** tights
main [mɛ̃] *f* hand; quire; **à la main** by hand; **à main levée** in one stroke; **avoir la haute main sur** to control; **avoir la main, être la main** (cards) to be the dealer; **battre des mains** to applaud; **de la main à la main** privately; **de longue main** carefully; for a long time; **de main à main** from one person to another; **de première main** firsthand; **donner les mains à** q.ch. to be in favor of s.th.; **en venir aux mains** to come to blows; **faire main basse sur** to grab, to steal; **haut les mains!** hands up!; **passer la main dans le dos à qn** to soft-soap s.o.; **serrer la main à** to shake hands with; **sous main** secretly; **tout main** handmade
main-d'œuvre [mɛ̃dœvr] *f* (*pl* **mains-d'œuvre**) labor; laborers; manpower
maint [mɛ̃] **mainte** [mɛ̃t] *adj* many a; **à maintes reprises** time and again
maintenant [mɛ̃tənɑ̃] *adv* now
maintenir [mɛ̃tnir] §72 *intr* to maintain; to hold up ‖ *ref* to keep on; to keep up
maintien [mɛ̃tjɛ̃] *m* maintenance; bearing
maire [mɛr] *m* mayor
mairesse [mɛrɛs] *f* (coll) mayor's wife
mairie [meri] *f* town hall, city hall
mais [mɛ] *m* but ‖ *adv* why, well; **mais non** certainly not ‖ *conj* but
maïs [mais] *m* corn, maize
maison [mɛzɔ̃] *f* house; home; household, family; house, firm, business; **à la maison** at home, home; **fait à la maison** homemade; **maison centrale** state or federal prison; **maison close, borgne, publique, mal famée, de débauche, de passe, de rendezvous, de tolérance** house of ill fame; **maison d'accouchement** lying-in hospital; **maison d'antiquités, de meubles d'époque,** or **d'originaux** antique shop; **maison de commerce** firm; **maison de confiance** (com) trustworthy firm; **maison de correction** reform school; **maison de couture** dressmaking establishment; **maison de fous** madhouse; **maison de jeux** gambling house; **maison de plaisance** or **de campagne** cottage, summer home; **maison de rapport** apartment house; **maison de repos** rest home; **maison de retraite** old-people's home; **maison de santé** nursing home; **maison jumelée** semi-detached house; **maison mère** head office; **maison**

mortuaire home of the deceased; **maison religieuse** convent
maisonnée [mɛzɔne] *f* household
maisonnette [mɛzɔnɛt] *f* little house, cottage
maî•tre [mɛtr] *adj* expert, capable; basic, key; main (*beam, girder*); utter (*fool*); arrant (*knave*); high (*card*) ‖ *m* master; Mr. (*when addressing a lawyer*); (naut) mate; (naut) petty officer; **être passé maître en** to be a past master of or in; **maître chanteur** blackmailer; **maître d'armes** fencing master; **maître de chapelle** choirmaster; **maître d'école** schoolmaster; **maître de conférences** associate professor; **maître de forges** ironmaster; **maître de maison** man of the house, householder; **maître d'équipage** boatswain; **maître d'études** monitor, supervisor; **maître d'hôtel** headwaiter; butler; **maître d'œuvre** foreman; **maître Jacques** jack-of-all-trades; **maître mécanicien** chief engineer; **maître mineur** mine foreman; **maître queue** chef; **passer maître** to know one's trade § *f* see **maîtresse**
maître-autel [mɛtrotɛl] *m* (*pl* **maîtres-autels**) high altar
maîtresse [mɛtrɛs] *f* mistress; **maîtresse d'école** schoolmistress; **maîtresse de maison** lady of the house
maîtrise [mɛtriz] *f* mastery, command; master's degree; **maîtrise de soi** self-control
maîtriser [mɛtrize] *tr* to master, control; to subdue
maj. *abbr* (**majuscule**) cap.
majesté [maʒɛste] *f* majesty
majes•tueux [maʒɛstɥø] **-tueuse** [tɥøz] *adj* majestic
ma•jeur -jeure [maʒœr] *adj* & *m* major
major [maʒɔr] *m* regimental quartermaster; army doctor; **être le major de sa promotion** to be at the head of one's class
majordome [maʒɔrdɔm] *m* major-domo
majorer [maʒɔre] *tr* to increase the price of; to overprice; to raise (*the price*)
majoritaire [maʒɔritɛr] *adj* majority
majorité [maʒɔrite] *f* majority
Majorque [maʒɔrk] *f* Majorca
major•quin [maʒɔrkɛ̃] **-quine** [kin] *adj* Majorcan ‖ (*cap*) *mf* Majorcan
majuscule [maʒyskyl] *adj* capital (*letter*) ‖ *f* capital letter
mal [mal] *adj*—**de mal** bad, e.g., **dire q.ch. de mal** to say s.th. bad; **pas mal** not bad, quite good-looking ‖ *m* (*pl* **maux** [mo]) evil; trouble; hurt; pain; wrong; **avoir du mal à + inf** to have a hard time + *ger*; to have difficulty in + *ger*; **avoir mal à la tête** to have a headache; **avoir mal au cœur** to be nauseated; **avoir mal aux dents** to have a toothache; **avoir mal de gorge** to have a sore throat; **dire du mal de qn** to speak ill of s.o.; **faire mal à, faire du mal à** to hurt, to harm; **le Mal** Evil; **mal aux reins**

backache; **mal blanc** whitlow; **mal de l'air** airsickness; **mal de la route** carsickness; **mal de mer** seasickness; **mal des rayons** radiation sickness; **mal du pays** homesickness; **mal du siècle** Weltschmerz, romantic melancholy; **se donner du mal** to take pains || *adv* §91 badly, bad; **de mal en pis** from bad to worse; **être mal avec qn** to be on bad terms with s.o.; **pas mal** not bad; **pas mal de a** lot of, quite a few

malade [malad] *adj* sick, ill || *mf* patient, sick person

maladie [maladi] *f* disease, sickness; distemper; **elle va en faire une maladie** (coll) she'll be terribly upset over it; **maladie de carence** or **par carence** deficiency disease; **maladie de cœur** heart trouble; **maladie des caissons** bends; **maladie diplomatique** malingering; **revenir de maladie** to convalesce

mala·dif [maladif] **-dive** [div] *adj* sickly; morbid

maladresse [maladrɛs] *f* awkwardness; blunder

mala·droit [maladrwa] **-droite** [drwat] *adj* clumsy, awkward

ma·lais [malɛ] **-laise** [lɛz] *adj* Malay || *m* Malay (*language*) || see **malaise** *m* || (*cap*) *mf* Malay (*person*)

malaise [malɛz] *m* malaise, discomfort

malai·sé -sée [maleze] *adj* difficult

malap·pris [malapri] **malap·prise** [malapriz] *adj* uncouth, ill-bred || *mf* ill-bred person

malard [malar] *m* (orn) mallard

malaria [malarja] *f* malaria

malavi·sé -sée [malavize] *adj* ill-advised, indiscreet

malaxer [malakse] *tr* to knead; to churn (*butter*); to massage

malaxeur [malaksœr] *m* churn; (mach) mixer

malchance [malʃɑ̃s] *f* bad luck; **par malchance** unluckily; **une malchance** a piece of bad luck

malchan·ceux [malʃɑ̃sø] **-ceuse** [søz] *adj* unlucky

malcommode [malkɔmɔd] *adj* inconvenient; unsuitable, impracticable

maldonne [maldɔn] *f* misdeal

mâle [mɑl] *adj* male; energetic, virile || *m* male

malédiction [malediksjɔ̃] *f* curse

maléfice [malefis] *m* evil spell

maléfique [malefik] *adj* baleful

malencon·treux [malɑ̃kɔ̃trø] **-treuse** [trøz] *adj* untimely, unfortunate

malentendu [malɑ̃tɑ̃dy] *m* misunderstanding

malfaçon [malfasɔ̃] *f* defect

malfai·sant [malfəzɑ̃] **-sante** [zɑ̃t] *adj* mischievous, harmful

malfaiteur [malfɛtœr] *m* malefactor

malfa·mé -mée [malfame] *adj* ill-famed

malgra·cieux [malgrasjø] **-cieuse** [sjøz] *adj* ungracious

malgré [malgre] *prep* in spite of; **malgré que** in spite of the fact that, although

malhabile [malabil] *adj* inexperienced, clumsy

malheur [malœr] *m* misfortune; unhappiness; bad luck; **faire un malheur** to commit an act of violence; **jouer de malheur** to be unlucky

malheu·reux [malœrø] **-reuse** [røz] *adj* unfortunate; unhappy; unlucky; paltry || *m* poor man, wretch; **les malheureux** the unfortunate || *f* poor woman, wretch

malhonnête [malɔnɛt] *adj* dishonest; (slang) rude, uncivil

malhonnêteté [malɔnɛtte] *f* dishonesty

malice [malis] *f* mischievousness

mali·cieux [malisjø] **-cieuse** [sjøz] *adj* malicious, mischievous

malignité [maliɲite] *f* malignancy

ma·lin [malɛ̃] **-ligne** [liɲ] *adj* cunning, sly, smart; mischievous; malignant (*e.g., tumor*); **ce n'est pas malin** (coll) it's easy || *mf* sly one; **Le Malin** the Evil One

malingre [malɛ̃gr] *adj* weakly, puny

malintention·né -née [malɛ̃tɑ̃sjɔne] *adj* evil-minded, ill-disposed

mal-jugé [malʒyʒe] *m* miscarriage (*of justice*)

malle [mal] *f* trunk; mailboat; **faire ses malles** to pack

malléable [maleabl] *adj* malleable; compliant, pliable

mallette [malɛt] *f* valise; case

malmener [malməne] §2 *tr* to rough up

malodo·rant [malɔdɔrɑ̃] **-rante** [rɑ̃t] *adj* malodorous; bad (*breath*)

malo·tru -true [malɔtry] *adj* coarse, uncouth || *mf* ill-bred person, oaf

malpropre [malprɔpr] *adj* dirty; improper; crude, clumsy (*workmanship*)

mal·sain [malsɛ̃] **-saine** [sɛn] *adj* unhealthy

malséant [malseɑ̃] **malséante** [malseɑ̃t] *adj* improper

malson·nant [malsɔnɑ̃] **malson·nante** [malsɔnɑ̃t] *adj* offensive, objectionable

malt [malt] *m* malt

maltraiter [maltrete] *tr* to mistreat

malveil·lant [malvejɑ̃] **malveil·lante** [malvejɑ̃t] *adj* malevolent

malve·nu -nue [malvəny] *adj* ill-advised, out of place; poorly developed

malversation [malvɛrsasjɔ̃] *f* embezzlement

maman [mamɑ̃] *f* mamma

mamelle [mamɛl] *f* breast; udder

mamelon [mamlɔ̃] *m* nipple, teat; knoll

mamie [mami] *f* (coll) my dear

mammifère [mamifɛr] *adj* mammalian || *m* mammal

mammouth [mamut] *m* mammoth

mamours [mamur] *mpl* (coll) caresses

mam'selle or **mam'zelle** [mamzɛl] *f* (coll) Miss

manant [manɑ̃] *m* hick, yokel

manche [mɑ̃ʃ] *m* handle; stick, stock; neck (*of violin*); (culin) knuckle; **branler au manche** or **dans le manche** to be shaky; **manche à balai** broomstick; (aer) joy stick; **manche à gigot** holder (*for carving*) || *f* sleeve; hose; channel; game, heat, round; shaft, chute; (baseball) inning; (bridge) game; (tennis) set; **en manches de chemise** in shirt sleeves; **la Manche** the English Channel; **manche à air** windsock; **manche à manche** neck and neck, even up; **manches à gigot** leg-of-mutton sleeves

manchette [mɑ̃ʃɛt] ƒ cuff; (journ) headline

manchon [mɑ̃ʃɔ̃] m muff; (of gaslight) mantle; (mach) casing, sleeve

man·chot [mɑ̃ʃo] **-chote** [ʃɔt] adj one-armed; one-handed; (coll) clumsy ‖ mƒ one-armed person; one-handed person ‖ m (orn) penguin

mandarine [mɑ̃darin] ƒ mandarin orange

mandat [mɑ̃da] m mandate; term of office; money order; power of attorney; proxy; **mandat d'arrêt** warrant; **mandat de perquisition** search warrant

mandataire [mɑ̃datɛr] mƒ representative; proxy; defender

mandat-carte [mɑ̃dakart] m (pl **mandats-carte**) postal-card money order

mandat-poste [mɑ̃dapɔst] m (pl **mandats-poste**) postal money order

Mandchourie [mɑ̃tʃuri] ƒ Manchuria; **la Mandchourie** Manchuria

mander [mɑ̃de] tr to summon

mandoline [mɑ̃dɔlin] ƒ mandolin

mandragore [mɑ̃dragɔr] ƒ mandrake

mandrin [mɑ̃drɛ̃] m (mach) punch; (mach) chuck

manécanterie [manekɑ̃tri] ƒ choir school

manège [manɛʒ] m horsemanship; riding school; trick, little game; **manège de chevaux de bois** merry-go-round

mânes [mɑn] mpl shades, spirits (of ancestors)

maneton [mantɔ̃] m crank handle; pin (of crankshaft)

manette [manɛt] ƒ lever, switch

manganèse [mɑ̃ganɛz] m manganese

mangeable [mɑ̃ʒabl] adj edible; barely fit to eat

mangeaille [mɑ̃ʒɑj] ƒ swill; (coll) grub, chow

mangeotter [mɑ̃ʒɔte] tr to pick at (one's food)

manger [mɑ̃ʒe] m food, e.g., **le boire et le manger** food and drink; (slang) meal ‖ §38 tr to eat; to eat up; to mumble (one's words); **manger du bout des lèvres** to nibble at ‖ intr to eat

mangerie [mɑ̃ʒri] ƒ (coll) big meal

mange-tout [mɑ̃ʒtu] m invar sugar pea

man·geur [mɑ̃ʒœr] **-geuse** [ʒøz] mƒ eater; wastrel, spendthrift; **mangeur d'hommes** man-eater

mangouste [mɑ̃gust] ƒ mongoose

maniable [manjabl] adj maneuverable, easy to handle, supple

maniaque [manjak] adj & mƒ maniac

manie [mani] ƒ mania

maniement [manimɑ̃] m handling

manier [manje] tr to handle ‖ reƒ (coll) to get a move on

manière [manjɛr] ƒ manner; **à la ma-**

nière de in the manner of; **de manière à** so as to; **de manière que** so that; **de toute manière** in any case; **d'une manière ou d'une autre** one way or another; **en aucune manière** by no means; **faire des manières** to pretend to be indifferent, to want to be coaxed; **manière de voir** point of view; **manières** manners

manié·ré -rée [manjere] adj mannered, affected

maniérisme [manjerism] m mannerism

ma·nieur [manjœr] **-nieuse** [njøz] mƒ handler; **grand manieur d'argent** tycoon

manifes·tant [manifɛstɑ̃] **-tante** [tɑ̃t] mƒ demonstrator

manifestation [manifɛstasjɔ̃] ƒ demonstration, manifestation

manifeste [manifɛst] adj manifest ‖ m manifesto; (naut) manifest

manifester [manifɛste] tr to manifest ‖ intr to demonstrate ‖ reƒ to reveal oneself

manigance [manigɑ̃s] ƒ trick, intrigue

manipuler [manipyle] tr to manipulate; to handle (e.g., packages); to arrange (equipment) for an experiment

manitou [manitu] m manitou; (coll) bigwig

manivelle [manivɛl] ƒ crank

manne [man] ƒ manna

mannequin [mankɛ̃] m mannequin; scarecrow

manœuvre [manœvr] m hand, laborer ‖ ƒ maneuver; (naut) handling, maneuvering; (rr) shifting; **fausse manœuvre** wrong move; **manœuvres** rigging

manœuvrer [manœvre] tr & intr to maneuver; (rr) to shift

manoir [manwar] m manor, manor house

man·quant [mɑ̃kɑ̃] **-quante** [kɑ̃t] adj missing ‖ mƒ absentee ‖ m missing article; **manquants** shortages

manque [mɑ̃k] m lack; shortage; insufficiency; **manque à gagner** lost opportunity; **manque de parole** breach of faith; **par manque de** for lack of ‖ ƒ—**à la manque** (coll) rotten, poor, dud

man·qué -quée [mɑ̃ke] adj missed, unsuccessful; broken (engagement); (with abilities which were not professionally developed), e.g., **le docteur est un cuisinier manqué** the doctor could have been a cook by profession

manquement [mɑ̃kmɑ̃] m breach, lapse

manquer [mɑ̃ke] tr to miss; to flunk ‖ intr to misfire; to be missing, e.g., **il en manque trois** three are missing; to be missed, e.g., **vous lui manquez beaucoup** you are very much missed by him, he misses you very much; to be short, e.g., **il lui manque cinq francs** he is five francs short; **manquer à** to break (one's word); to disobey (an order); to fail to observe (a rule); to fail, e.g., **le cœur lui a manqué** his heart failed him; **manquer de** to lack, to be short of, to

run out of; **manquer de** + *inf* to nearly + *inf*, e.g., **il a manqué de se noyer** he nearly drowned; **sans manquer** without fail ‖ *ref* to miss each other; to fail
mansarde [mãsard] *f* mansard roof; mansard
manse [mãs] *m & f* (hist) small manor
mante [mãt] *f* mantle; **mante religieuse** (ent) praying mantis
man·teau [mãto] *m* (*pl* -**teaux**) overcoat; mantle, cloak; mantelpiece; **sous le manteau** sub rosa
mantille [mãtij] *f* mantilla
manucure [manykyr] *mf* manicurist
ma·nuel -**nuelle** [manɥɛl] *adj* manual ‖ *mf* laborer, blue-collar worker ‖ *m* manual, handbook
manufacture [manyfaktyr] *f* factory, plant
manufacturer [manyfaktyre] *tr* to manufacture
manus·crit [manyskri] -**crite** [krit] *adj & m* manuscript
manutention [manytãsjɔ̃] *f* handling (*of merchandise*)
manutentionner [manytãsjɔne] *tr* to handle (*merchandise*)
mappemonde [mapmɔ̃d] *f* world map; **mappemonde céleste** map of the heavens
maque·reau [makro] -**relle** [rɛl] (*pl* -**reaux** -**relles**) *mf* (slang) procurer ‖ *m* mackerel; (slang) pimp ‖ *f* (slang) madam (*of a brothel*)
maquette [makɛt] *f* maquette, model; dummy (*of book*); rough sketch
maquignon [makiɲɔ̃] *m* horse trader; wholesale cattle dealer; (coll) go-between
maquignonnage [makiɲɔnaʒ] *m* horse trading
maquignonner [makiɲɔne] *intr* to horse-trade
maquillage [makijaʒ] *m* make-up; fakery
maquiller [makije] *tr* to make up; to fake, to distort ‖ *ref* to make up
maquil·leur [makijœr] **maquil·leuse** [makijøz] *mf* make-up artist ‖ *m* make-up man
maquis [maki] *m* bush; maquis; **prendre le maquis** to go underground
maraî·cher [mareʃe] -**chère** [ʃɛr] *adj* truck-farming ‖ *mf* truck farmer
marais [marɛ] *m* marsh; truck farm; **marais salant** saltern
marasme [marasm] *m* depression; doldrums, standstill
marathon [maratɔ̃] *m* marathon
marâtre [marɑtr] *f* stepmother; cruel mother
maraude [marod] *f* marauding; **en maraude** cruising (*taxi*)
marauder [marode] *intr* to maraud; to cruise (*said of taxi*)
marau·deur [marodœr] -**deuse** [døz] *adj* marauding ‖ *mf* marauder
marbre [marbr] *m* marble; (typ) stone
marbrer [marbre] *tr* to marble; to mottle, vein; to bruise, blotch
marc [mar] *m* mark (*old coin*); marc, pulp; **marc de café** coffee grounds;

marc de thé tea leaves ‖ [mark] (*cap*) *m* Mark
marcassin [markasɛ̃] *m* young wild boar
mar·chand [marʃɑ̃] -**chande** [ʃɑ̃d] *adj* marketable; sale (*value*); trading (*center*); wholesale (*price*); merchant (*marine*) ‖ *mf* merchant; **marchand ambulant** peddler; **marchand de canons** munitions maker; **marchand de couleurs** paint dealer, dealer in household articles; **marchand de ferraille** junk dealer; **marchand de journaux** newsdealer; **marchand des quatre-saisons** fruit vendor; **marchand en gros** wholesaler; **marchand forain** hawker ‖ *f*—**marchande d'amour** or **de plaisir** prostitute
marchandage [marʃɑ̃daʒ] *m* bargaining; haggling; deal, underhanded arrangement
marchander [marʃɑ̃de] *tr* to bargain over; to haggle over; to be stingy with (*e.g., one's compliments*) ‖ *intr* to haggle
marchan·deur [marʃɑ̃dœr] -**deuse** [døz] *mf* bargainer; haggler
marchandise [marʃɑ̃diz] *f* merchandise; **marchandises** goods
mar·chant [marʃɑ̃] -**chante** [ʃɑ̃t] *adj* marching; militant (*wing of political party*); (mil) wheeling (*flank*)
marche [marʃ] *f* march; step (*of stairway*); walking; movement; progress, course; (aut) gear; **à dix minutes de marche** ten minutes walk from here; **attention à la marche!** watch your step!; **en marche** in motion, running, operating; **faire marche arrière** to back up, to reverse; **fermer la marche** to bring up the rear; **marche funèbre** funeral march; **ouvrir la marche** to lead off the procession
marché [marʃe] *m* market; marketing; shopping; deal, bargain; **à bon marché** cheap, cheaply; **à meilleur marché** cheaper, more cheaply; **bon marché** cheapness; cheap; cheaply; **faire bon marché de** to set little store by; **faire son marché** to do the marketing; **lancer, mettre,** or **vendre sur le marché** to market; **marché noir** black market; **par-dessus le marché** into the bargain
marchepied [marʃəpje] *m* footstool; little stepladder; running board; (fig) stepping stone
marcher [marʃe] *intr* to walk; to run, operate; to march; **marcher à grands pas** to stride; **marcher au pas** to walk in step; **marcher dans l'espace** to take a space walk; **marcher sur** to tread on, to walk on; **marchez au pas** (public sign) drive slowly
mar·cheur [marʃœr] -**cheuse** [ʃøz] *mf* walker
mardi [mardi] *m* Tuesday; **mardi gras** Shrove Tuesday; Mardi gras
mare [mar] *f* pool, pond
marécage [marekaʒ] *m* marsh, swamp
maréca·geux [marekaʒø] -**geuse** [ʒøz] *adj* marshy, swampy
maré·chal [mareʃal] *m* (*pl* -**chaux**

[ʃo]) marshal; blacksmith; **maréchal des logis** artillery or cavalry sergeant
maréchale [mareʃal] *f* marshal's wife
maréchal-ferrant [mareʃalferɑ̃] *m* (*pl* **maréchaux-ferrants**) blacksmith, farrier
marée [mare] *f* tide; fresh seafood; **marée descendante** ebb tide; **marée montante** flood tide
marelle [marɛl] *f* hopscotch
marémo·teur [maremɔtœr] **-trice** [tris] *adj* tide-driven
margarine [margarin] *f* margarine
marge [marʒ] *f* margin; border, edge; leeway, room; **en marge de** on the fringe of; a footnote to; **marge bénéficiaire** margin of profit; **marge de sécurité** margin of safety
margelle [marʒɛl] *f* curb, edge (*of well, fountain, etc.*)
margeur [marʒœr] *m* margin stop
margi·nal -nale [marʒinal] *adj* (*pl* **-naux** [no]) marginal
margot [margo] *f* (coll) magpie; (coll) chatterbox; **Margot** (coll) Maggie
margotin [margɔtɛ̃] *m* kindling
margouillis [marguji] *m* (coll) rotten stinking mess
margou·lin [margulɛ̃] **-line** [lin] *mf* sharpster, shyster
marguerite [margərit] *f* daisy; **Marguerite** Margaret
marguillier [margije] *m* churchwarden
mari [mari] *m* husband
mariable [marjabl] *adj* marriageable
mariage [marjaʒ] *m* marriage; wedding; blend, combination
Marianne [marjan] *f* Marian; Marianne (*symbol of the French Republic*)
ma·rié -riée [marje] *adj* married ‖ *m* bridegroom; **jeunes mariés** newlyweds; **les mariés** the bride and groom ‖ *f* bride
marier [marje] *tr* to marry, join in wedlock; to marry off; to blend, harmonize ‖ *ref* to get married; **se marier avec** to marry
marie-salope [marisalɔp] *f* (*pl* **maries-salopes**) dredger; (slang) slut
ma·rieur [marjœr] **-rieuse** [rjøz] *mf* (coll) matchmaker
marihuana [mariꞯana] or **marijuana** [mariʒꞯana] *f* marijuana
ma·rin [marɛ̃] **-rine** [rin] *adj* marine; seagoing; sea, e.g., **brise marine** sea breeze ‖ *m* sailor, seaman; sailor suit ‖ *f* navy; seascape; **marine marchande** merchant marine
mariner [marine] *tr & intr* to marinate
mari·nier [marinje] **-nière** [njɛr] *adj* naval; petty (*officer*); **à la marinière** cooked in gravy with onions ‖ *m* waterman ‖ *f* blouse; (swimming) sidestroke
marionnette [marjɔnɛt] *f* marionette; (fig) puppet
mari·tal -tale [marital] *adj* (*pl* **-taux** [to]) of the husband
maritime [maritim] *adj* maritime
maritorne [maritɔrn] *f* slut
marivaudage [marivodaʒ] *m* playful flirting; sophisticated conversation
marjolaine [marʒɔlɛn] *f* marjoram

marlou [marlu] *m* (slang) pimp
marmaille [marmɑj] *f* (coll) brats
marmelade [marməlad] *f* marmalade; (coll) mess
marmite [marmit] *f* pot, pan; (geol) pothole; (mil) shell, heavy shell; **marmite autoclave, marmite sous pression** pressure cooker; **marmite norvégienne** double boiler
marmiton [marmitɔ̃] *m* cook's helper
marmonner [marmɔne] *tr & intr* to mumble
marmot [marmo] *m* (coll) lad; (coll) grotesque figurine (*on knocker*); **croquer le marmot** (coll) to cool one's heels; **marmots** (coll) urchins, kids
marmotte [marmɔt] *f* woodchuck; **dormir comme une marmotte** to sleep like a log; **marmotte d'Amérique** groundhog; **marmotte de commis voyageur** traveling salesman's sample case
marmouset [marmuzɛ] *m* grotesque figurine; little man
marner [marne] *tr* to marl
marner [marne] *tr* to marl
Maroc [marɔk] *m*—**le Maroc** Morocco
maro·cain [marɔkɛ̃] **-caine** [kɛn] *adj* Moroccan ‖ (*cap*) *mf* Moroccan
maronner [marɔne] *intr* (coll) to grumble
maroquin [marɔkɛ̃] *m* morocco leather
maroquinerie [marɔkinri] *f* leather goods
marotte [marɔt] *f* fad; whim; dummy head (*of milliner*); jester's staff
mar·quant [markɑ̃] **-quante** [kɑ̃t] *adj* remarkable, outstanding; purple (*passages*)
marque [mark] *f* mark; brand, make; hallmark; token, sign; **de marque** distinguished; **marque déposée** trademark
marquer [marke] *tr* to mark; to brand; to score; to indicate, show ‖ *intr* to make a mark, to leave an impression
marqueterie [markətri], [markɛtri] *f* marquetry, inlay
mar·queur [markœr] **-queuse** [køz] *mf* marker ‖ *m* scorekeeper; scorer ‖ *f* (mach) stenciler
marquis [marki] *m* marquis
marquise [markiz] *f* marchioness, marquise; marquee, awning; (rr) roof (*over platform*)
marraine [marɛn] *f* godmother, sponsor; christener; **marraine de guerre** war mother
mar·rant [marɑ̃] **mar·rante** [marɑ̃t] *adj* (slang) sidesplitting; (slang) funny, queer
marre [mar] *adv*—**en avoir marre** (coll) to be fed up
marrer [mare] *ref* (slang) to have a good laugh
mar·ron [marɔ̃] **mar·ronne** [marɔn] *adj* quack (*doctor*); shyster (*lawyer*) ‖ **marron** *adj invar* reddish-brown, chestnut ‖ *m* chestnut; **marron d'Inde** horse chestnut
marronnier [marɔnje] *m* chestnut tree; **marronnier d'Inde** horse-chestnut tree

mars [mars] *m* March; **Mars** Mars
Marseille [marsɛj] *f* Marseilles
marsouin [marswɛ̃] *m* porpoise
marte [mart] *f* (zool) marten
mar·teau [marto] (*pl* -teaux) *adj* (coll)
cracked; balmy || *m* hammer; (ichth)
hammerhead; **marteau de porte**
knocker
marteau-pilon [martopilɔ̃] *m* (*pl* **mar-
teaux-pilons**) drop hammer
marteler [martəle] §2 *tr* to hammer; to
hammer at; to hammer out
Marthe [mart] *f* Martha
mar·tial -tiale [marsjal] *adj* (*pl* -tiaux
[sjo]) martial
martinet [martinɛ] *m* triphammer;
scourge, cat-o'-nine-tails; (orn) martin, swift
martin-pêcheur [martɛ̃peʃœr] *m* (*pl*
martins-pêcheurs) (orn) kingfisher
martre [martr] *f* (zool) marten
mar·tyr -tyre [martir] *adj & mf* martyr
|| **martyre** *m* martyrdom
martyriser [martirize] *tr* to martyr
marxiste [marksist] *adj & mf* Marxist
maryland [marilɑ̃] *m* choice tobacco ||
(*cap*) *m*—**le Maryland** Maryland
mas [ma], [mas] *m* farmhouse or farm
(*in Provence*)
mascarade [maskarad] *f* masquerade
mascaret [maskarɛ] *m* bore
mascaron [maskarɔ̃] *m* mask, mascaron
mascotte [maskɔt] *f* mascot
mascu·lin [maskylɛ̃] -**line** [lin] *adj &
m* masculine
masque [mask] *m* mask; **masque à
gaz** gas mask; **masque mortuaire**
death mask
masquer [maske] *tr & ref* to mask
massacre [masakr] *m* massacre;
botched job
massacrer [masakre] *tr* to massacre;
to botch
massage [masaʒ] *m* massage
masse [mas] *f* mass; sledge hammer;
mace; pool, common fund; (elec)
ground (*e.g., of an automobile*);
masse d'air froid cold front; **mettre
à la masse** (elec) to ground; **une
masse de** (coll) a lot of
massepain [maspɛ̃] *m* marzipan
masser [mase] *tr* to mass; to massage
|| *ref* to mass; to massage oneself
massette [masɛt] *f* sledge hammer (*of
stonemason*); (bot) bulrush
mas·seur [masœr] **mas·seuse** [masøz]
mf masseur || *m* massager (*instru-
ment*)
mas·sif [masif] **mas·sive** [masiv] *adj*
massive; heavyset; solid (*e.g., gold*)
|| *m* massif, high plateau; clump (*of
flowers, trees, etc.*)
massue [masy] *f* club, bludgeon
mastic [mastik] *m* putty
mastiquer [mastike] *tr* to masticate; to
putty
mastoc [mastɔk] *adj invar* heavy, massive
masturber [mastyrbe] *tr & ref* to masturbate
m'as-tu-vu -vue [matyvy] (*pl* -vu -vue)
adj (coll) stuck-up || *mf* (coll) show-

off, smart aleck; (coll) bragging
actor
masure [mazyr] *f* hovel, shack, shanty
mat mate [mat] *adj* dull, flat || **mat** *adj
invar* checkmated || *m* checkmate ||
mat *adv* dull
mât [mɑ] *m* mast; pole
matamore [matamɔr] *m* braggart
match [matʃ] *m* match, contest, game
matelas [matla] *m* mattress; (coll) roll
(*of bills*)
matelasser [matlase] *tr* to pad, to cushion
matelot [matlo] *m* sailor, seaman
matelote [matlɔt] *f* fish stew in wine
mater [mate] *tr* to dull; to checkmate;
to subdue
matérialiser [materjalize] *ref* to materialize
matérialiste [materjalist] *adj* mate-
rialistic || *mf* materialist
maté·riau [materjo] *m* (*pl* -riaux) material
maté·riel -rielle [materjɛl] *adj* ma-
terial; materialistic || *m* material;
equipment; (mil) matériel; **matériel
roulant** (rr) rolling stock || *f* (slang)
living
mater·nel -nelle [matɛrnɛl] *adj* mater-
nal || *f* nursery school
maternité [matɛrnite] *f* maternity;
maternity hospital
math or **maths** [mat] *fpl* (coll) math
mathémati·cien [matematisjɛ̃] -**cienne**
[sjɛn] *mf* mathematician
mathématique [matematik] *adj* mathe-
matical || **mathématiques** *fpl* mathe-
matics
matière [matjɛr] *f* matter; subject matter; material; **matière première** raw
material
matin [matɛ̃] *m* morning; early part of
the morning; **au petit matin** in the
wee hours of the morning; **de bon
matin, de grand matin** very early;
du matin in the morning, A.M., e.g.,
onze heures du matin eleven o'clock
in the morning, eleven A.M. || *adv*
early
mâ·tin [matɛ̃] -**tine** [tin] *mf* (coll) sly
one || *m* (zool) mastiff || **mâtin** *adv*
indeed!, well I'll be!
mati·nal -nale [matinal] *adj* (*pl* -naux
[no]) morning; early-rising
mâti·né -née [matine] *adj* crossbred;
mâtiné de mixed with, crossbred with
matinée [matine] *f* morning; matinée;
faire la grasse matinée to sleep late
mâtiner [matine] *tr* to crossbreed
matines [matin] *fpl* matins
matité [matite] *f* dullness
ma·tois [matwa] -**toise** [twaz] *adj* sly,
cunning || *mf* sly dog
matou [matu] *m* tomcat
matraque [matrak] *f* bludgeon; club,
billy
matraquer [matrake] *tr* to club, bludgeon
matriarcat [matrijarka] *m* matriarchy
matrice [matris] *f* matrix
matricide [matrisid] *mf* matricide (*per-
son*) || *m* matricide (*action*)
matricule [matrikyl] *adj* serial (*num-*

ber) ‖ *m* serial number ‖ *f* roll, register

matrimo·nial -niale [matrimɔnjal] *adj* (*pl* **-niaux** [njo]) matrimonial, marital

matrone [matrɔn] *f* matron; matriarch; old hag; midwife; abortionist

mâture [matyr] *f* masts (*of ship*)

maudire [modir] §39 *tr* to curse, to damn

mau·dit [modi] **-dite** [dit] *adj* cursed

maugréer [mogree] *intr* to grumble, gripe

maure [mɔr] *adj* Moorish ‖ (*cap*) *m* Moor

mauresque [mɔrɛsk] *adj* Moorish ‖ (*cap*) *f* Moorish woman

mausolée [mozɔle] *m* mausoleum

maussade [mosad] *adj* sullen, gloomy

mau·vais [mɔvɛ], [movɛ] **-vaise** [vɛz] *adj* §91 bad; evil; wrong; **il fait mauvais** the weather is bad; **sentir mauvais** to smell bad ‖ *mf* wicked person; **le Mauvais** the Evil One ‖ *m* evil

mauve [mov] *adj* mauve ‖ *f* (bot) mallow

mauviette [movjɛt] *f* (orn) lark; (coll) milquetoast

mauvis [movi] *m* (orn) redwing

maxillaire [maksilɛr] *m* jawbone

maxime [maksim] *f* maxim

maximum [maksimɔm] *adj & m* maximum

mayonnaise [majɔnɛz] *f* mayonnaise

mazette [mazɛt] *f* duffer ‖ *interj* gosh!

mazout [mazut] *m* fuel oil

mazouter [mazute] *intr* to fuel up

Me *abbr* (**Maître**) Mr.

me [mə] §87

méandre [meɑ̃dr] *m* meander

mec [mɛk] *m* (slang) guy; (slang) tough egg

mécanicien [mekanisjɛ̃] *m* mechanic; machinist; engineer (*of locomotive*)

mécanicienne [mekanisjɛn] *f* sewing-machine operator

mécanique [mekanik] *adj* mechanical ‖ *f* mechanism; mechanics

mécaniser [mekanize] *tr* to mechanize

mécanisme [mekanism] *m* mechanism

mécano [mekano] *m* (coll) mechanic

mécène [mesen] *m* patron, Maecenas

méchanceté [meʃɑ̃ste] *f* malice, wickedness; nastiness

mé·chant [meʃɑ̃] **-chante** [ʃɑ̃t] *adj* malicious, wicked; nasty; naughty (*child*) ‖ *mf* mean person; **faire le méchant** to threaten; (coll) to strike back; **les méchants** the wicked; **méchant!** naughty boy!

mèche [mɛʃ] *f* wick; fuse; lock (*of hair*); bit (*of drill*); **être de mèche avec** (coll) to be in cahoots with; **éventer** or **découvrir la mèche** to discover the plot; **il n'y a pas mèche** (coll) it's no go, nothing doing; **vendre la mèche** (coll) to let the cat out of the bag

mécompte [mekɔ̃t] *m* miscalculation; disappointment

méconnaissable [mekɔnɛsabl] *adj* unrecognizable

méconnaître [mekɔnɛtr] §12 *tr* to ignore; to underestimate

mécon·nu -nue [mekɔny] *adj* underestimated, misunderstood

mécon·tent [mekɔ̃tɑ̃] **-tente** [tɑ̃t] *adj* dissatisfied, displeased ‖ *mf* grumbler

mécontentement [mekɔ̃tɑ̃tmɑ̃] *m* dissatisfaction, displeasure

mécontenter [mekɔ̃tɑ̃te] *tr* to displease

Mecque [mɛk] *f*—**La Mecque** Mecca

mécréant [mekreɑ̃] **mécréante** [mekreɑ̃t] *adj* unbelieving ‖ *mf* unbeliever

médaille [medaj] *f* medal

médaillon [medajɔ̃] *m* medallion; locket; thin round slice (*e.g., of meat*); pat (*of butter*)

médecin [mɛdsɛ̃], [mɛtsɛ̃] *m* doctor; **femme médecin** woman doctor

médecine [mɛdsin], [metsin] *f* medicine (*science and art*)

mé·dian [medjɑ̃] **-diane** [djan] *adj & f* median

média·teur [medjatœr] **-trice** [tris] *mf* mediator

médiation [medjɑsjɔ̃] *f* mediation

médi·cal -cale [medikal] *adj* (*pl* **-caux** [ko]) medical

médicament [medikamɑ̃] *m* (pharm) medicine

médicamenter [medikamɑ̃te] *tr* to dose

médicamen·teux [medikamɑ̃tø] **-teuse** [tøz] *adj* medicinal

médici·nal -nale [medisinal] *adj* (*pl* **-naux** [no]) medicinal

médié·val -vale [medjeval] *adj* (*pl* **-vaux** [vo]) medieval

médiéviste [medjevist] *mf* medievalist

médiocre [medjɔkr] *adj* mediocre, poor; average

médiocrité [medjɔkrite] *f* mediocrity

médire [medir] §40 *intr* to backbite; **médire de** to run down, to disparage

médisance [medizɑ̃s] *f* disparagement, backbiting

médi·sant [medizɑ̃] **-sante** [zɑ̃t] *adj* disparaging, backbiting ‖ *mf* slanderer

méditation [meditɑsjɔ̃] *f* meditation

méditer [medite] *tr & intr* to meditate

méditerra·né -née [mediterane] *adj* Mediterranean; inland ‖ (*cap*) *f* Mediterranean (Sea)

méditerranéen [mediteraneɛ̃] **méditerranéenne** [mediteraneen] *adj* Mediterranean

médium [medjɔm] *m* medium (*in spiritualism*); range (*of voice*)

médiumnique [medjɔmnik] *adj* psychic

médius [medjys] *m* middle finger

méduse [medyz] *f* jellyfish, medusa ‖ (*cap*) *f* Medusa

méduser [medyze] *tr* to petrify (*with terror*)

meeting [mitiŋ] *m* rally, meet, meeting

méfait [mefɛ] *m* misdeed; **méfaits** ravages

méfiance [mefjɑ̃s] *f* mistrust

mé·fiant [mefjɑ̃] **-fiante** [fjɑ̃t] *adj* mistrustful

méfier [mefje] *ref* to beware; **se méfier de** to guard against, to mistrust

mégacycle [megasikl] *m* megacycle

mégaphone [megafɔn] *m* megaphone
mégarde [megard] *f*—**par mégarde** inadvertently
mégère [meʒɛr] *f* shrew
mégohm [megom] *m* megohm
mégot [mego] *m* butt (*of cigarette or cigar*)
meil·leur -leure [mɛjœr] §91 *adj comp* & *super* better; best; **meilleur marché** cheaper
mélancolie [melãkɔli] *f* melancholy, melancholia
mélancolique [melãkɔlik] *adj* melancholy
mélange [melãʒ] *m* mixing, blending; mixture, blend
mélanger [melãʒe] §38 *tr* to mix, to blend
mélan·geur [melãʒœr] **-geuse** [ʒøz] *m* & *f* mixer
mélasse [melas] *f* molasses; **dans la mélasse** (coll) in the soup
mê·lé -lée [mele] *adj* mixed ‖ *f* melee
mêler [mele] *tr* to mix; to tangle; to shuffle (*the cards*) ‖ *ref* to mix; **se mêler à** to mingle with; to join in; **se mêler de** to meddle with, to interfere with
mélèze [melɛz] *m* (bot) larch
mélodie [melɔdi] *f* melody
mélo·dieux [melɔdjø] **-dieuse** [djøz] *adj* melodious
mélodique [melɔdik] *adj* melodic
mélodramatique [melɔdramatik] *adj* melodramatic
mélomane [melɔman] *adj* music-loving ‖ *mf* music lover
melon [məlɔ̃] *m* melon; derby; **melon d'eau** watermelon
mélopée [melɔpe] *f* singsong, chant
membrane [mãbran] *f* membrane; **membrane vibrante** (elec) diaphragm
membre [mãbr] *m* member; limb, member; **membre de phrase** clause
membrure [mãbryr] *f* frame, limbs
même [mɛm] *adj indef* very, e.g., **le jour même** on that very day ‖ (when standing before noun) *adj indef* same, e.g., **en même temps** at the same time ‖ *pron indef* same, same one; **à même de** + *inf* up to + *ger*, in a position to + *inf*; **à même le** (**la**, etc.) straight out of the (*e.g., bottle*); flush with the (*e.g., pavement*); next to one's (*e.g., skin*); on the bare (*ground, sand, etc.*); **cela revient au même** that amounts to the same thing; **de même likewise; de même que** in the same way as; **tout de même** nevertheless ‖ *adv* even; **même quand** even when; **même si** even if
-même [mɛm] §86
mémento [memɛto] *m* memento; memo book
mémère [memɛr] *f* (coll) granny; (coll) blowsy dame
mémoire [memwar] *m* memorandum; statement, account; term paper; treatise; petition; **mémoires** memoirs ‖ *f* memory; **de mémoire** from memory; **de mémoire d'homme** within memory; **pour mémoire** for the record

mémorandum [memɔrãdɔm] *m* memorandum; **mémorandum de combat** battle orders
mémo·rial [memɔrjal] *m* (*pl* **-riaux** [rjo]) memorial; (dipl) memorandum; memoirs
menace [mənas] *f* menace, threat
menacer [mənase] §51 *tr* & *intr* to menace, to threaten
ménage [menaʒ] *m* household; family; married couple; furniture; **de ménage** homemade; **faire bon ménage** to get along well; **faire des ménages** to do housework (*for hire*); **faire le ménage** to do the housework; **se mettre en ménage** to set up housekeeping; (coll) to live together (*without being married*)
ménagement [menaʒmã] *m* discretion; consideration
ména·ger [menaʒe] **-gère** [ʒɛr] *adj* household; **ménager de** thrifty with ‖ *f* housewife, homemaker; silverware; silverware case ‖ **ménager** §38 *tr* to be careful with, to spare; to save (*money; one's strength*); to husband (*one's resources, one's strength*); to be considerate of, to handle with kid gloves; to arrange, to bring about; to install, to provide; to make (*e.g., a hole*) ‖ *intr* to save ‖ *ref* to take good care of oneself
ménagerie [menaʒri] *f* menagerie
men·diant [mãdjã] **-diante** [djãt] *adj* & *mf* beggar; **des mendiants** dessert (*of dried fruits and nuts*)
mendier [mãdje] *tr* & *intr* to beg
menées [məne] *fpl* intrigues, schemes
mener [məne] §2 *tr* to lead; to take; to manage; to draw (*e.g., a line*) ‖ *intr* to lead
ménestrel [menɛstrɛl] *m* wandering minstrel
ménétrier [menetrije] *m* fiddler
me·neur [mənœr] **-neuse** [nøz] *mf* leader; ringleader; **meneur de jeu** master of ceremonies; narrator; moving spirit
menotte [mənɔt] *f* tiny hand; **menottes** handcuffs; **mettre** or **passer les menottes à** to handcuff
mensonge [mãsɔ̃ʒ] *m* lie; **pieux mensonge** white lie
menson·ger [mãsɔ̃ʒe] **-gère** [ʒɛr] *adj* lying, false; illusory, deceptive
menstrues [mãstry] *fpl* menses
mensualité [mãsɥalite] *f* monthly installment; monthly salary
men·suel -suelle [mãsɥɛl] *adj* monthly
men·tal -tale [mãtal] *adj* (*pl* **-taux** [to]) mental
mentalité [mãtalite] *f* mentality
men·teur [mãtœr] **-teuse** [tøz] *adj* lying ‖ *mf* liar
menthe [mãt] *f* mint; **menthe poivrée** peppermint; **menthe verte** spearmint
mention [mãsjɔ̃] *f* mention; **avec mention** with honors; **biffer les mentions inutiles** to cross out the questions which do not apply; **être reçu sans mention** to receive just a passing grade
mentionner [mãsjɔne] *tr* to mention

mentir [mɑ̃tir] §41 *intr* to lie
menton [mɑ̃tɔ̃] *m* chin
mentonnière [mɑ̃tɔnjɛr] *f* chin rest; chin strap
me·nu -nue [məny] *adj* small, little; tiny, fine ‖ *m* menu; minute detail
menuet [mənɥɛ] *m* minuet
menuiserie [mənɥizri] *f* carpentry; woodwork
menuisier [mənɥizje] *m* carpenter
méprendre [meprɑ̃dr] §56 *ref* to be mistaken; **à s'y méprendre** enough to take one for the other; **il n'y a pas à s'y méprendre** there's no mistake about it
mépris [mepri] *m* contempt, scorn
méprisable [meprizabl] *adj* contemptible, despicable
mépri·sant [meprizɑ̃] **-sante** [zɑ̃t] *adj* contemptuous, scornful
méprise [mepriz] *f* mistake
mépriser [meprize] *tr* to despise, scorn
mer [mɛr] *f* sea; **basse mer** low tide; **de haute mer** seagoing; **haute mer, pleine mer** high seas; high tide; **mer des Indes** Indian Ocean; **sur mer** afloat
mercanti [mɛrkɑ̃ti] *m* profiteer
mercantile [mɛrkɑ̃til] *adj* profiteering, mercenary
mercenaire [mɛrsənɛr] *adj & mf* mercenary
mercerie [mɛrsəri] *f* notions
merci [mɛrsi] *m* thanks, thank you; **merci de** + *inf* thank you for + *ger;* **merci de** or **pour** thank you for ‖ *f*— **à la merci de** at the mercy of; **Dieu merci!** thank heavens! ‖ *interj* thanks!, thank you!; no thanks!, no thank you!
mercredi [mɛrkrədi] *m* Wednesday; **mercredi des Cendres** Ash Wednesday
mercure [mɛrkyr] *m* mercury
mercuriale [mɛrkyrjal] *f* reprimand; market quotations; mercury (*weed*)
merde [mɛrd] *f* excrement; **merde alors!** (coll) well I'll be!
mère [mɛr] *f* mother; **la mère Gigogne** the old woman who lived in a shoe
méri·dien [meridjɛ̃] **-dienne** [djɛn] *adj & m* meridian ‖ *f* meridian line; couch, sofa; siesta
méridio·nal -nale [meridjɔnal] (*pl* **-naux** [no]) *adj* meridional, southern ‖ (*cap*) *mf* inhabitant of the Midi
meringue [mərɛ̃g] *f* meringue
merise [məriz] *f* wild cherry
merisier [mərizje] *m* wild cherry (tree)
méri·tant [meritɑ̃] **-tante** [tɑ̃t] *adj* deserving, worthy
mérite [merit] *m* merit
mériter [merite] *tr* to merit, to deserve; to win, earn ‖ *intr*—**mériter bien de** to deserve the gratitude of
méritoire [meritwar] *adj* deserving, meritorious
merlan [mɛrlɑ̃] *m* (ichth) whiting
merle [mɛrl] *m* (orn) blackbird; **merle blanc** (fig) rara avis; **vilain merle** (fig) dirty dog
merlin [mɛrlɛ̃] *m* ax; poleax; (naut) marline

merluche [mɛrlyʃ] *f* (ichth) hake, cod
merveille [mɛrvɛj] *f* marvel, wonder; **à merveille** marvelously, wonderfully
merveil·leux [mɛrvɛjø] **merveil·leuse** [mɛrvɛjøz] *adj* marvelous, wonderful
mes [me] §88
mésalliance [mezaljɑ̃s] *f* misalliance, mismatch
mésallier [mezalje] *tr* to misally ‖ *ref* to marry beneath one's station
mésange [mezɑ̃ʒ] *f* (orn) chickadee, titmouse
mésaventure [mezavɑ̃tyr] *f* misadventure
mésentente [mezɑ̃tɑ̃t] *f* misunderstanding
mésestimer [mezɛstime] *tr* to underestimate
mésintelligence [mezɛ̃teliʒɑ̃s] *f* misunderstanding, discord
mes·quin [mɛskɛ̃] **-quine** [kin] *adj* mean; stingy; petty
mess [mɛs] *m* officer's mess
message [mesaʒ] *m* message
messa·ger [mesaʒe] **-gère** [ʒɛr] *mf* messenger
messagerie [mesaʒri] *f* express; **messageries** express company
messe [mɛs] *f* (eccl) Mass; **dire** or **faire des messes basses** (coll) to speak in an undertone; **messe basse, petite messe** Low Mass; **première messe, messe du début** early Mass
Messie [mesi] *m* Messiah
messieurs-dames [mesjødam] *interj* ladies and gentlemen!
mesure [məzyr] *f* measure; measurement; (mus, poetic) measure; **à mesure** successively, one by one; **à mesure que** as; according as, proportionately as; **battre la mesure** to keep time; **dans la mesure de** insofar as; **dans une certaine mesure** to a certain extent; **être en mesure de** to be in a position to; **faire sur mesure** to make (*clothing*) to order; (fig) to tailor-make; **mesure de circonstance** emergency measure; **mesure en ruban** tape measure; **prendre des mesures de** to take measures to; **prendre la mesure de** to size up; **prendre les mesures de** to measure
mesurer [məzyre] *tr* to measure; to measure off or out ‖ *ref* to measure; **se mesurer avec** to measure swords with
métairie [meteri] *f* farm (*of a sharecropper*)
mé·tal [metal] *m* (*pl* **-taux** [to]) metal
métallique [metalik] *adj* metallic
métalloïde [metalɔid] *m* nonmetal
métallurgie [metalyrʒi] *f* metallurgy
métamorphose [metamɔrfoz] *f* metamorphosis
métaphore [metafɔr] *f* metaphor
métaphorique [metafɔrik] *adj* metaphorical
métathèse [metatez] *f* metathesis
métayage [metejaʒ] *m* sharecropping, tenant farming
métayer [meteje] **métayère** [metejɛr] *mf* sharecropper

méteil [metɛj] *m* wheat and rye
météo [meteo] *adj invar* meteorological || *m* weatherman || *f* meteorology; weather bureau; weather report
météore [meteɔr] *m* meteor (*atmospheric phenomenon*)
météorite [meteɔrit] *m & f* meteorite
météorologie [meteɔrɔlɔʒi] *f* meteorology; weather bureau; weather report
météque [metɛk] *m* (pej) foreigner
méthane [metan] *m* methane
méthode [metɔd] *f* method
méthodique [metɔdik] *adj* methodic(al)
méthodiste [metɔdist] *adj & mf* Methodist
méticu·leux [metikylø] **-leuse** [løz] *adj* meticulous
métier [metje] *m* trade, craft; loom; **faites votre métier!** mind your own business!; **sur le métier** on the stocks
mé·tis **-tisse** [metis] *adj & mf* halfbreed
métisser [metise] *tr* to crossbreed
métrage [metraʒ] *m* length in meters; length (*of remnant, film, etc.*); (mov) length of film in meters (*in English: footage, i.e., length of film in feet*); **court métrage** (mov) short subject, short; **long métrage** (mov) full-length movie, feature
mètre [mɛtr] *m* meter; **mètre à ruban** tape measure; **mètre pliant** folding rule
métrer [metre] §10 *tr* to measure out by the meter
métrique [metrik] *adj* metric(al) || *f* metrics
métro [metro] *m* subway
métronome [metrɔnɔm] *m* metronome
métropole [metrɔpɔl] *f* metropolis; mother country
métropoli·tain [metrɔpɔlitɛ̃] **-taine** [tɛn] *adj* metropolitan || *m* subway; (eccl) metropolitan
mets [mɛ] *m* dish, food
mettable [mɛtabl] *adj* wearable
met·teur [mɛtœr] **met·teuse** [mɛtøz] *mf*—**metteur au point** mechanic; **metteur en œuvre** setter; (fig) promoter; **metteur en ondes** (rad) director, producer; **metteur en pages** (typ) make-up man; **metteur en scène** (mov, theat) director, producer
mettre [mɛtr] §42 *tr* to put, lay, place; to put on (*clothes*); to set (*the table*); to take (*time*); **mettre à feu** (rok) to fire; **mettre au point** to carry out, complete; to tune up, adjust; (opt) to focus; (rad) to tune; **mettre au rancart** to pigeonhole; **mettre en accusation** to indict; **mettre en marche** to start; **mettre en œuvre** to put into action; **mettre en valeur** to develop, improve; to set off, enhance; **mettre en vigueur** to enforce; **mettre feu à** to set fire to; **mettre que** (coll) to suppose that || *intr*—**mettre bas** (zool) to litter || *ref* to sit or stand; to go; **se mettre à** to begin to; **se mettre à table** to sit down to eat; (slang) to confess; **se mettre en colère** to get angry; **se**

mettre en route to set out; **se mettre mal avec** to quarrel with
meuble [mœbl] *adj* uncemented; loose (*ground*); personal (*property*) || *m* piece of furniture; **meubles** furniture; **meubles d'occasion** secondhand furniture
meubler [mœble] *tr* to furnish
meuglement [møgləmɑ̃] *m* lowing (*of cow*)
meugler [møgle] *intr* to low
meule [møl] *f* millstone; grindstone; stack (*e.g., of hay*)
meuler [møle] *tr* to grind
meu·nier [mønje] **-nière** [njɛr] *adj* milling (*e.g., industry*) || *m* miller || *f* miller's wife; **à la meunière** sautéed in butter
meurt-de-faim [mœrdəfɛ̃] *mf invar* starveling; **de meurt-de-faim** starvation (*wages*)
meurtre [mœrtr] *m* manslaughter; (fig) shame, crime; **meurtre commis avec préméditation** murder
meur·trier [mœrtrije] **-trière** [trijɛr] *adj* murderous, deadly || *m* murderer || *f* murderess; gun slit, loophole
meurtrir [mœrtrir] *tr* to bruise
meute [møt] *f* pack, band
mévente [mevɑ̃t] *f* slump (*in sales*)
mexi·cain [mɛksikɛ̃] **-caine** [kɛn] *adj* Mexican || (*cap*) *mf* Mexican
Mexico [mɛksiko] Mexico City
Mexique [mɛksik] *m—le* **Mexique** Mexico
mezzanine [mɛdzanin] *m & f* (theat) mezzanine || *f* mezzanine; mezzanine window
miaou [mjau] *m* meow
miaulement [mjolmɑ̃] *m* meow; caterwauling; catcall
miauler [mjole] *intr* to meow
mi-bas [miba] *m invar* half hose
mica [mika] *m* mica
miche [miʃ] *f* round loaf of bread
mi-chemin [miʃmɛ̃] *m—à* **mi-chemin** halfway
mi-clos [miklo] **-close** [kloz] *adj* (*pl* **-clos** **-closes**) half-shut
micmac [mikmak] *m* (coll) underhand dealing
mi-corps [mikɔr]—**à mi-corps** to the waist
mi-côte [mikot]—**à mi-côte** halfway up the hill
microbe [mikrɔb] *m* microbe
microbicide [mikrɔbisid] *adj & m* germicide
microbiologie [mikrɔbjɔlɔʒi] *f* microbiology
microfilm [mikrɔfilm] *m* microfilm
microfilmer [mikrɔfilme] *tr* to microfilm
micro-onde [mikrɔɔ̃d] *f* (*pl* **-ondes**) microwave
microphone [mikrɔfɔn] *m* microphone
microscope [mikrɔskɔp] *m* microscope
microscopique [mikrɔskɔpik] *adj* microscopic
microsillon [mikrɔsijɔ̃] *adj & m* microgroove
midi [midi] *m* noon; south; twelve, e.g., **midi dix** ten minutes after

twelve; **chercher midi à quatorze heures** (fig) to look for difficulties where there are none; **Midi** south of France
midinette [midinɛt] *f* dressmaker's assistant; working girl
mie [mi] *f* soft part, crumb; female friend; **ne . . . mie** §90 (archaic) not a crumb, not, e.g., **je n'en veux mie** I don't want any
miel [mjɛl] *m* honey
miel·leux [mjɛlø] **miel·leuse** [mjɛløz] *adj* honeyed, unctuous
mien [mjɛ̃] **mienne** [mjɛn] §89
miette [mjɛt] *f* crumb
mieux [mjø] §91 *adv comp & super* better; **aimer mieux** to prefer; **à qui mieux mieux** trying to outdo each other; **de mieux en mieux** better and better; **être mieux, aller mieux** to feel better; **tant mieux** so much the better; **valoir mieux** to be better
mieux-être [mjøzɛtr] *m* improved well-being
mièvre [mjɛvr] *adj* dainty, affected
mi-figue [mifig] *f*—**mi-figue mi-raisin** half one way half the other; half in jest half in earnest
mi·gnard [miɲar] **-gnarde** [ɲard] *adj* affected, mincing
mi·gnon [miɲɔ̃] **-gnonne** [ɲɔn] *adj* cute, darling || *mf* darling
mignon·net [miɲɔnɛ] **mignon·nette** [miɲɔnɛt] *adj* dainty || *f* fine lace; pepper; (bot) pink
mignoter [miɲɔte] *tr* (coll) to pet (*a child*)
migraine [migrɛn] *f* migraine, headache
migratoire [migratwar] *adj* migratory
mi-jambe [miʒɑ̃b] *f*—**à mi-jambe** up to one's knee
mijoter [miʒɔte] *tr* to simmer; (coll) to cook up, to brew || *intr* to simmer
mil [mil] *adj* one thousand, e.g., **l'an mil neuf cent soixante-six** the year one thousand nine hundred and sixty-six || *m* Indian club; millet
milan [milɑ̃] *m* (orn) kite
milice [milis] *f* militia
mi·lieu [miljø] *m* (*pl* **-lieux**) middle; milieu; **milieu de table** centerpiece
militaire [militɛr] *adj* military || *m* soldier; **le militaire** the military
mili·tant [militɑ̃] **-tante** [tɑ̃t] *adj & mf* militant
militariser [militarize] *tr* to militarize
militarisme [militarism] *m* militarism
militer [milite] *intr* to militate
mille [mil] *adj & pron* thousand || *m* thousand; mile; **mettre dans le mille** to hit the bull's-eye; **mille marin** international nautical mile
millefeuille [milfœj] *m* napoleon (*pastry*)
mille-feuille [milfœj] *f* (*pl* **-feuilles**) (bot) yarrow
millénaire [milenɛr] *adj* millennial || *m* millennium
mille-pattes [milpat] *m invar* centipede
millésime [milezim] *m* date, vintage
millet [mijɛ] *m* millet; birdseed
milliard [miljar] *m* billion

milliardaire [miljardɛr] *mf* billionaire
millième [miljɛm] *adj, pron* (*masc, fem*) thousandth || *m* thousandth; mill (*thousandth part of a dollar*)
millier [milje] *m* thousand; about a thousand; **par milliers** by the thousands; **un millier de** a thousand
milligramme [miligram] *m* milligram
millimètre [milimɛtr] *m* millimeter
million [miljɔ̃] *m* million; **un million de** a million
millionième [miljɔnjɛm] *adj, pron* (*masc, fem*), & *m* millionth
millionnaire [miljɔnɛr] *adj & m* millionaire
mime [mim] *mf* mime; mimic
mimer [mime] *tr & intr* to mime; to mimic
mimique [mimik] *adj* sign (*language*) || *f* mimicry
minable [minabl] *adj* wretched, shabby; (coll) pitiful (*performance, existence, etc.*) || *mf* unfortunate
minaret [minarɛ] *m* minaret
minauder [minode] *intr* to simper, smirk
minau·dier [minodje] **-dière** [djɛr] *adj* mincing
mince [mɛ̃s] *adj* thin, slim, slight; **mince!** or **mince alors!** golly!
mine [min] *f* mine; lead (*of pencil*); look, face; looks; (fig) mine (*of information*); **avoir bonne mine** to look well; **avoir la mine d'être** to look to be; **avoir mauvaise mine** to look badly; **faire bonne mine à** to be nice to; **faire des mines** to simper; **faire la mine à** to pout at; **faire mauvaise mine à** to be unpleasant to; **faire mine de** to make as if to
miner [mine] *tr* to mine; to undermine; to wear away
minerai [minrɛ] *m* ore
miné·ral -rale [mineral] (*pl* **-raux** [ro]) *adj & m* mineral
minéralogie [mineralɔʒi] *f* mineralogy
mi·net [minɛ] **-nette** [nɛt] *mf* (coll) kitty, pussy; (coll) darling
mi·neur -neure [minœr] *adj & mf* minor || *m* miner
miniature [minjatyr] *f* miniature
miniaturisation [minjatyrizɑsjɔ̃] *f* miniaturization
miniaturiser [minjatyrize] *tr* to miniaturize
minijupe [miniʒyp] *f* miniskirt
mini·mal -male [minimal] *adj* (*pl* **-maux** [mo]) minimum (*temperature*)
minime [minim] *adj* tiny; derisory (*salary*)
minimiser [minimize] *tr* to minimize
minimum [minimɔm] *adj & m* minimum; **minimum vital** minimum wage
ministère [ministɛr] *m* ministry; **ministère des Affaires étrangères** Department of State
ministé·riel -rielle [ministerjɛl] *adj* ministerial
ministre [ministr] *m* minister; **ministre des Affaires étrangères** secretary of state; **premier ministre** premier, prime minister

minium [minjɔm] *m* red lead
minois [minwa] *m* (coll) pretty little
face
minoritaire [minɔritɛr] *adj* minority
minorité [minɔrite] *f* minority
Minorque [minɔrk] *f* Minorca
minoterie [minɔtri] *f* flour mill; flour
industry
minotier [minɔtje] *m* miller
minuit [minɥi] *m* midnight; twelve,
e.g., minuit et demi twelve thirty
minuscule [minyskyl] *adj* tiny; small
(*letter*) ‖ *f* small letter
minus habens [minysabɛ̃s] *mf invar*
(coll) moron, idiot
minutage [minytaʒ] *m* timing
minute [minyt] *f* minute; moment, instant; à la minute that very moment
‖ *interj* (coll) just a minute!
minuter [minyte] *tr* to itemize; to time
minuterie [minytri] *f* delayed-action
switch; (mach) timing mechanism
minutie [minysi] *f* minute detail; great
care; minuties minutiae
minu·tieux [minysjø] -tieuse [sjøz]
adj meticulous, thorough
mioche [mjɔʃ] *mf* (coll) brat
mi-pente [mipãt]—à mi-pente halfway
up or halfway down
mirabilis [mirabilis] *m* (bot) marvel-
of-Peru
miracle [mirakl] *m* miracle; wonder,
marvel; miracle play; crier au miracle
to go into ecstasies
miracu·leux [mirakylø] -leuse [løz]
adj miraculous; wonderful, marvelous
mirador [miradɔr] *m* watchtower
mirage [miraʒ] *m* mirage
mire [mir] *f* sight (*of gun*); surveyor's
pole; (telv) test pattern
mire-œufs [mirø] *m invar* candler
mirer [mire] *tr* to candle (*eggs*) ‖ *ref*
to look at oneself; to be reflected
mirifique [mirifik] *adj* (coll) marvelous
mirobo·lant [mirɔbɔlã] -lante [lãt] *adj*
(coll) astounding
miroir [mirwar] *m* mirror; miroir à
alouettes decoy
miroiter [mirwate] *intr* to sparkle,
gleam; faire miroiter q.ch. à qn to
lure s.o. with s.th.
miroton [mirɔtɔ̃] *m* Irish stew
misaine [mizɛn] *f* foresail
misanthrope [mizãtrɔp] *mf* misanthrope
miscellanées [miselane], [misɛllane]
fpl miscellany
mise [miz] *f* placing, putting; dress, attire; (cards) stake, ante; de mise acceptable, proper; mise à feu firing
(*e.g., of missile*); mise à l'eau launching; mise à prix opening bid; mise
au point carrying out, completion;
tuning up, adjustment; (opt) focus-
ing; (rad) tuning; mise au rancart
pigeonholing; mise bas delivery (*of
litter*); mise de fonds investment;
mise en accusation indictment; mise
en demeure (law) injunction; mise en
marche starting; mise en œuvre putting into action; mise en scène (theat)
direction; (theat & fig) staging; mise

en valeur development, improvement;
mise en vigueur enforcement
miser [mize] *tr & intr* to ante; to stake,
bet; to bid (*e.g., at auction*)
misérable [mizerabl] *adj* miserable ‖
mf wretch
misère [mizɛr] *f* misery, wretchedness;
poverty; worry; (coll) trifle; crier
misère to make a poor mouth; to
look forsaken; faire des misères à
to pester
misé·reux [mizerø] -reuse [røz] *adj*
destitute, wretched ‖ *mf* pauper
miséricorde [mizerikɔrd] *f* mercy
miséricor·dieux [mizerikɔrdjø] -dieuse
[djøz] *adj* merciful
missel [misɛl] *m* missal
missile [misil] *m* guided missile
mission [misjɔ̃] *f* mission
missionnaire [misjɔnɛr] *adj & m* mis-
sionary
missive [misiv] *adj & f* missive
mitaine [mitɛn] *f* mitt
mite [mit] *f* (ent) mite; (ent) clothes
moth
mi·té -tée [mite] *adj* moth-eaten; (coll)
shabby
mi-temps [mitã] *f invar* (sports) half
time; à mi-temps half time
miter [mite] *ref* to become moth-eaten
mi·teux [mitø] -teuse [tøz] *adj* shabby
‖ *mf* (coll) shabby-looking person
mitiger [mitiʒe] §38 *tr* to mitigate
mitonner [mitɔne] *tr* to simmer; to
pamper; (coll) to contrive, devise ‖
intr to simmer
mitoyen [mitwajɛ̃] mitoyenne [mi-
twajɛn] *adj* midway, intermediate,
dividing; jointly owned, common
mitraille [mitraj] *f* scrap iron; grape-
shot; artillery fire
mitrailler [mitraje] *tr* to machine-gun;
to pepper (*with gunfire, flash bulbs,
etc.*)
mitraillette [mitrajɛt] *f* submachine
gun, Tommy gun
mitrail·leur [mitrajœr] mitrail·leuse
[mitrajøz] *adj* repeating, automatic
(*firearm*) ‖ *m* machine gunner ‖ *f*
machine gun
mitre [mitr] *f* miter; chimney pot
mitron [mitrɔ̃] *m* baker's boy
mi-voix [mivwa]—à mi-voix in a low
voice, under one's breath
mixte [mikst] *adj* mixed; coeducational; composite; joint (*e.g., commission*); (rr) freight-and-passenger
mixtion [mikstjɔ̃] *f* mixing; mixture
mixture [mikstyr] *f* mixture
Mlle *abbr* (Mademoiselle) Miss
MM. *abbr* (Messieurs) Messrs.
Mme *abbr* (Madame) Mrs.; Mme.
mobile [mɔbil] *adj* mobile ‖ *m* motive;
(fa) mobile
mobi·lier [mɔbilje] -lière [ljɛr] *adj*
personal ‖ *m* furniture
mobilisable [mɔbilizabl] *adj* (mil) subject to call
mobilisation [mɔbilizɑsjɔ̃] *f* mobilization
mobiliser [mɔbilize] *tr & intr* to mobilize
mobilité [mɔbilite] *f* mobility

moche [mɔʃ] *adj* (coll) ugly; (coll) lousy

modalité [mɔdalite] *f* modality, manner, method; **modalités** terms

mode [mɔd] *m* kind, method, mode; (gram) mood; (mus) mode; **mode d'emploi** directions for use ‖ *f* fashion; **à la mode** in style, fashionable; **à la mode de** in the manner of; **modes** fashions; millinery

modèle [mɔdɛl] *adj* & *m* model

modeler [mɔdle] §2 *tr* to model; to shape, mold ‖ *ref*—**se modeler sur** to take as a model

modéliste [mɔdelist] *mf* model-airplane designer, etc.; dress designer

modéra•teur [mɔderatœr] **-trice** [tris] *adj* moderating ‖ *mf* moderator; regulator; moderator (*for slowing down neutrons*); **modérateur de son** volume control

modé•ré -rée [mɔdere] *adj* moderate

modérer [mɔdere] §10 *tr* & *ref* to moderate

moderne [mɔdɛrn] *adj* modern

moderniser [mɔdɛrnize] *tr* to modernize

modeste [mɔdɛst] *adj* modest

modestie [mɔdɛsti] *f* modesty

modicité [mɔdisite] *f* paucity (*of resources*); lowness (*of price*)

modifica•teur [mɔdifikatœr] **-trice** [tris] *adj* modifying ‖ *m* modifier

modifier [mɔdifje] *tr* to modify

modique [mɔdik] *adj* moderate, reasonable

modiste [mɔdist] *f* milliner

modulation [mɔdylɑsjɔ̃] *f* modulation; **modulation d'amplitude** amplitude modulation; **modulation de fréquence** frequency modulation

module [mɔdyl] *m* module; **module lunaire** (rok) lunar module

moduler [mɔdyle] *tr* & *intr* to modulate

moelle [mwal] *f* marrow; (bot) pith; **moelle épinière** spinal cord

moel•leux [mwalø] **moel•leuse** [mwaløz] *adj* soft; mellow; flowing (*brush stroke*)

moellon [mwalɔ̃] *m* building stone

mœurs [mœr], [mœrs] *fpl* customs, habits; morals

mohair [mɔɛr] *m* mohair

moi [mwa] §85, §87

moignon [mwaɲɔ̃] *m* stump

moi-même [mwamɛm] §86

moindre [mwɛ̃dr] §91 *adj comp* & *super* less; lesser; least, slightest

moine [mwan] *m* monk

moi•neau [mwano] *m* (*pl* **-neaux**) sparrow

moins [mwɛ̃] *m* less; minus; **au moins** or **du moins** at least; (le) **moins** (the) least; **moins de** fewer ‖ *adv comp* & *super* §91 less; fewer; **à moins de** + *inf* without + *ger*, unless + *ind*; **à moins que** unless; **de moins en moins** less and less; **en moins de rien** in no time at all; **moins de** (followed by numeral) less than; **moins que** less than; **rien moins que** anything but ‖

prep minus; to, e.g., **dix heures moins le quart** a quarter to ten

moire [mwar] *f* moire; **moire de soie** watered silk

moi•ré -rée [mware] *adj* watered (*silk*) ‖ *m* wavy sheen

mois [mwa] *m* month

Moïse [mɔiz] *m* Moses

moi•si -sie [mwazi] *adj* moldy ‖ *m* mold; **sentir le moisi** to have a musty smell

moisir [mwazir] *tr* to mold ‖ *intr* to become moldy, to mold; (fig) to vegetate ‖ *ref* to mold

moisissure [mwazisyr] *f* mold

moisson [mwasɔ̃] *f* harvest

moissonner [mwasɔne] *tr* to harvest, reap

moisson•neur [mwasɔnœr] **moisson• neuse** [mwasɔnøz] *mf* reaper ‖ *f* (mach) reaper

moite [mwat] *adj* moist, damp; clammy

moiteur [mwatœr] *f* moistness, dampness; **moiteur froide** clamminess

moitié [mwatje] *f* half; (coll) better half (*wife*); **à moitié, la moitié** half; **à moitié chemin** halfway; **à moitié prix** at half price; **de moitié** by half ‖ *adv* half

moka [mɔka] *m* mocha coffee; mocha cake

molaire [mɔler] *adj* & *f* molar

môle [mol] *m* mole, breakwater ‖ *f* (ichth) sunfish

molécule [mɔlekyl] *f* molecule

moleskine [mɔleskin] *f* (*fabric*) moleskin; imitation leather

molester [mɔlɛste] *tr* to molest

moleter [mɔlte] §34 *tr* to knurl, to mill

mollas•son [mɔlasɔ̃] **mollas•sonne** [mɔlasɔn] *mf* (coll) softy

mollement [mɔlmɑ̃] *adv* flabbily; listlessly

mollesse [mɔles] *f* flabbiness; apathy; softness (*of contour*); mildness (*of climate*)

mol•let [mɔle] **mol•lette** [mɔlet] *adj* soft, downy; soft-boiled (*egg*) ‖ *m* (anat) calf

molletière [mɔltjer] *f* puttee, legging

molleton [mɔltɔ̃] *m* flannel

mollir [mɔlir] *intr* to weaken

mollusque [mɔlysk] *m* mollusk

molosse [mɔlɔs] *m* watchdog

molybdène [mɔlibdɛn] *m* molybdenum

môme [mom] *adj* (slang) little ‖ *mf* (coll) kid ‖ *f* (slang) babe

moment [mɔmɑ̃] *m* moment; **à aucun moment** at no time; **à ce moment-là** then, at that time; **à tout moment, à tous moments** continually; **au moment où** just when; **c'est le moment** now is the time; **d'un moment à l'autre** at any moment; **en ce moment** now; at this moment; **par•moments** now and then; **sur le moment** at the very moment; **un petit moment** a little while

momenta•né -née [mɔmɑ̃tane] *adj* momentary

momerie [mɔmri] *f* mummery

momie [mɔmi] *f* mummy

mon [mɔ̃] §88

M^{on} abbr (**Maison**) (com) House
mona·cal -cale [mɔnakal] adj (pl **-caux** [ko]) monastic, monkish
monachisme [mɔnaʃism], [mɔnakism] m monasticism
monarchique [mɔnarʃik] adj monarchic
monarque [mɔnark] m monarch
monastère [mɔnaster] m monastery
monastique [mɔnastik] adj monastic
mon·ceau [mɔ̃so] m (pl **-ceaux**) heap, pile
mon·dain [mɔ̃dɛ̃] **-daine** [dɛn] adj worldly; social (life, functions, etc.); sophisticated || mf worldly-minded person; socialite
mondanité [mɔ̃danite] f worldliness; **mondanités** social events; (journ) social news
monde [mɔ̃d] m world; people; **avoir du monde chez soi** to have company; **il y a du monde, il y a un monde fou** there is a big crowd; **le beau monde, le grand monde** high society, fashionable society; **mettre au monde** to give birth to; **tout le monde** everybody, everyone
monder [mɔ̃de] tr to hull; to blanch; to stone
mon·dial -diale [mɔ̃djal] adj (pl **-diaux** [djo]) world; world-wide
monétaire [mɔnetɛr] adj monetary
mon·gol -gole [mɔ̃gɔl] adj Mongol || m Mongol (language) || (cap) mf Mongol (person)
moni·teur [mɔnitœr] **-trice** [tris] mf coach, trainer, instructor; monitor (at school)
monnaie [mɔnɛ] f change, small change; money (legal tender of a country); **fausse monnaie** counterfeit money; **la Monnaie** the Mint; **monnaie forte** hard currency; **payer en monnaie de singe** to give lip service to
monnayer [mɔneje] §49 tr to mint, to coin; to convert into cash; to cash in on
monnayeur [mɔnɛjœr] m—**faux monnayeur** counterfeiter
monocle [mɔnɔkl] m monocle
monogamie [mɔnɔgami] f monogamy
monogramme [mɔnɔgram] m monogram
monographie [mɔnɔgrafi] f monograph
monolithique [mɔnɔlitik] adj monolithic
monologue [mɔnɔlɔg] m monologue
monologuer [mɔnɔlɔge] tr to soliloquize
monomanie [mɔnɔmani] f monomania
monôme [mɔnom] m single file (of students); (math) monomial
monoplan [mɔnɔplɑ̃] m monoplane
monopole [mɔnɔpɔl] m monopoly
monopoliser [mɔnɔpɔlize] tr to monopolize
monorail [mɔnɔraj] m monorail
monosyllabe [mɔnɔsilab] m monosyllable
monothéiste [mɔnɔteist] adj & mf monotheist
monotone [mɔnɔtɔn] adj monotonous
monotonie [mɔnɔtɔni] f monotony
monotype [mɔnɔtip] adj monotypic ||

m monotype || f Monotype (machine to set type)
monseigneur [mɔ̃sɛɲœr] m (pl **messeigneurs** [mesɛɲœr]) monseigneur
monsieur [məsjø] m (pl **messieurs** [mesjø]) gentleman; sir; mister; Mr.
monstre [mɔ̃str] adj huge, monster || m monster; freak; **monstres sacrés** (fig) sacred cows, idols
mons·trueux [mɔ̃stryø] **-trueuse** [tryøz] adj monstrous
mont [mɔ̃] m mount; mountain; **par monts et par vaux** over hill and dale; **passer les monts** to cross the Alps
montage [mɔ̃taʒ] m hoisting; setting up (of a machine); (elec) hookup; (mov) cutting, editing
monta·gnard [mɔ̃taɲar] **-gnarde** [ɲard] adj mountain || mf mountaineer
montagne [mɔ̃taɲ] f mountain; **montagnes russes** roller coaster
monta·gneux [mɔ̃taɲø] **-gneuse** [ɲøz] adj mountainous
mon·tant [mɔ̃tɑ̃] **-tante** [tɑ̃t] adj rising, ascending; uphill; vertical; high-necked (dress) || m upright, riser; gatepost; total (sum); allure; (culin) tang; **montants** goal posts; (slang) pair of trousers
mont-de-piété [mɔ̃dpjete] m (pl **monts-de-piété**) pawnshop
mon·té -tée [mɔ̃te] adj mounted; organized; equipped, well-provided; worked-up, angry || f climb; slope
monte-charge [mɔ̃tʃarʒ] m invar freight elevator
monte-plats [mɔ̃tpla] m invar dumbwaiter
monter [mɔ̃te] tr to go up, to climb; to mount; to set up; to carry up, take up, bring up || intr (aux: ÊTRE) to go up, to come up; to come upstairs; to rise; to come in (said of tide); **monter** + inf to go up to + inf; **monter à** or **en** to go up, to climb, to ascend, to mount; **monter sur** to mount (the throne); to go on (the stage) || ref—**se monter à** to amount to; **se monter en** to lay in a supply of; **se monter la tête** to get excited
montre [mɔ̃tr] f show, display; watch; **en montre** in the window, on display; **faire montre de** to show off, to parade; **montre à remontoir** stemwinder; **montre à répétition** repeater
montre-bracelet [mɔ̃trəbraslɛ] f (pl **montres-bracelets**) wrist watch
montrer [mɔ̃tre] tr to show; **montrer du doigt** to point out or at || ref to appear; to show oneself to be (e.g., patient)
mon·treur [mɔ̃trœr] **-treuse** [trøz] mf showman, exhibitor
mon·tueux [mɔ̃tɥø] **-tueuse** [tɥøz] adj rolling, hilly
monture [mɔ̃tyr] f mounting; assembling; mount (e.g., horse)
monument [mɔnymɑ̃] m monument; **monument aux morts** memorial monument
moquer [mɔke] tr & ref to mock; **se moquer de** to make fun of, to laugh at

moquerie [mɔkri] *f* mockery
moquette [mɔkɛt] *f* pile carpet
mo·ral -rale [mɔral] (*pl* **-raux** [ro])
  adj moral || *m* morale || *f* ethics;
  moral (*of a fable*); **faire la morale**
  à qn to lecture s.o.
moralité [mɔralite] *f* morality; moral
  (*e.g., of a fable*)
morasse [mɔras] *f* final proof (*of newspaper*)
moratoire [mɔratwar] *m* moratorium
moratorium [mɔratɔrjɔm] *m* moratorium
morbide [mɔrbid] *adj* morbid
morbleu [mɔrblø] *interj* (obs) zounds!
mor·ceau [mɔrso] *m* (*pl* **-ceaux**) piece,
  bit; morsel; **bas morceaux** (culin)
  cheap cuts; **en morceaux** in cubes
  (*of sugar*); **morceaux choisis** selected
  passages
morceler [mɔrsəle] §34 *tr* to parcel out
morcellement [mɔrsɛlmɑ̃] *m* parceling
  out, division
mordancer [mɔrdɑ̃se] §51 *tr* to size
mor·dant [mɔrdɑ̃] **-dante** [dɑ̃t] *adj*
  mordant, caustic || *m* mordant; cut-
  ting edge; fighting spirit; (mus)
  mordent
mordicus [mɔrdikys] *adv* (coll) stoutly,
  tenaciously
mordiller [mɔrdije] *tr & intr* to nibble;
  to nip
mordo·ré -rée [mɔrdɔre] *adj* golden-
  brown, bronze-colored
mordre [mɔrdr] *tr* to bite || *intr* to bite;
  mordre à to bite on; to take to, to
  find easy; **mordre dans** to bite into;
  mordre sur to encroach upon || *ref*
  to bite
mor·du -due [mɔrdy] *adj* bitten;
  smitten || *mf* (coll) fan (*person*)
morelle [mɔrɛl] *f* nightshade
morfondre [mɔrfɔ̃dr] *tr* to chill to the
  bone || *ref* to be bored waiting
morgue [mɔrg] *f* morgue; haughtiness
mori·caud [mɔriko] **-caude** [kod] *adj*
  (coll) dark-skinned, dusky
morigéner [mɔriʒene] §10 *tr* to scold
morillon [mɔrijɔ̃] *m* rough emerald;
  duck; **morillon à dos blanc** canvas-
  back
mor·mon [mɔrmɔ̃] **-mone** [mɔn] *adj*
  & *mf* Mormon
morne [mɔrn] *adj* dismal, gloomy || *m*
  hillock, knoll
mornifle [mɔrnifl] *f* (coll) slap
morose [mɔroz] *adj* morose
morphine [mɔrfin] *f* morphine
morphologie [mɔrfɔlɔʒi] *f* morphology
morpion [mɔrpjɔ̃] *m* tick-tack-toe;
  (*youngster*) (slang) squirt; (*Phthirius
  pubis*) (slang) crab louse
mors [mɔr] *m* bit; jaw (*of vise*)
morse [mɔrs] *m* Morse code; walrus
morsure [mɔrsyr] *f* bite
mort [mɔr] **morte** [mɔrt] *adj* dead;
  spent (*bullet*); (aut) neutral || *mf*
  dead person, corpse || *m* (bridge)
  dummy; **faire le mort** to play dead
  || **mort** *f* death; **attraper la mort** to
  catch one's death of cold
mortadelle [mɔrtadɛl] *f* bologna

mortaise [mɔrtɛz] *f* mortise
mortaiser [mɔrteze] *tr* to mortise
mortalité [mɔrtalite] *f* mortality
mort-aux-rats [mɔrtora], [mɔrora] *f*
  invar rat poison
mort-bois [mɔrbwa] *m* deadwood
morte-eau [mɔrto] *f* (*pl* **mortes-eaux**
  [mɔrtazo]) low tide
mor·tel -telle [mɔrtɛl] *adj & mf* mortal
morte-saison [mɔrtəsɛzɔ̃] *f* (*pl* **mortes-
  saisons**) off-season
mortier [mɔrtje] *m* mortar; round
  judicial cap
mortifier [mɔrtifje] *tr* to mortify; to
  tenderize (*meat*)
mort-né -née [mɔrne] (*pl* **-nés**) *adj* still-
  born || *mf* stillborn child
mortuaire [mɔrtɥɛr] *adj* mortuary;
  funeral (*e.g., service*); death (*notice*)
morue [mɔry] *f* cod
morve [mɔrv] *f* snot
mor·veux [mɔrvø] **-veuse** [vøz] *adj*
  snotty || *mf* (coll) young snot, brat,
  whippersnapper
mosaïque [mɔzaik] *adj* mosaic; Mosaic
  || *f* mosaic
Moscou [mɔsku] *m* Moscow
mosquée [mɔske] *f* mosque
mot [mo] *m* word; answer (*to riddle*);
  à mots couverts guardedly; **au bas
  mot** at least; **avoir toujours le mot
  pour rire** to be always cracking
  jokes; **bon mot** witticism; **gros mots**
  foul words; **le mot à mot** the word-
  for-word translation; **mot à double
  sens** double entendre; **mot de passe**
  password; **mot d'ordre** slogan; **mot
  pour mot** word for word; **mots croisés**
  crossword puzzle; **ne . . . mot** §90
  (archaic) not a word, nothing; **placer
  un mot** to put in a word; **prendre qn
  au mot** to take s.o. at his word; **sans
  mot dire** without a word
motard [mɔtar] *m* (coll) motorcyclist;
  (coll) motorcycle cop
mot-clé [mɔkle] *m* (*pl* **mots-clés**) key
  word
motel [mɔtɛl] *m* motel
mo·teur [mɔtœr] **-trice** [tris] *adj* driving (*wheel*); drive (*shaft*); motive
  (*power*); power (*brake*); motor
  (*nerve*) || *m* motor, engine; prime
  mover; instigator; **moteur à deux
  temps** two-cycle engine; **moteur à
  explosion** internal-combustion engine; **moteur à quatre temps** four-
  cycle engine; **moteur à réaction** jet
  engine; **moteur hors bord** outboard
  motor
moteur-fusée *m* (*pl* **moteurs-fusées**)
  rocket engine
motif [mɔtif] *m* motive; (fa, mus)
  motif
motion [mosjɔ̃] *f* (parl) motion
motiver [mɔtive] *tr* to motivate
moto [mɔto] *f* motorcycle
motoriser [mɔtɔrize] *tr* to motorize
mot-outil [mɔuti] *m* (*pl* **mots-outils**)
  link word
mot-piège [mɔpjɛʒ] *m* (*pl* **mots-pièges**)
  tricky word

mots-croisés [mokrwaze] *mpl* crossword puzzle

mot-souche [mosuʃ] *m* (*pl* **mots-souches**) entry word; (typ) catchword

motte [mɔt] *f* clod, lump; slab (*of butter*); **motte de gazon** turf

motus [mɔtys] *interj* mum's the word!

mou [mu] (or **mol** [mɔl] before vowel or mute h) **molle** [mɔl] (*pl* **mous molles**) *adj* soft; limp, flabby, slack; spineless, listless ‖ *m* slack; lights, lungs; (coll) softy

mou·chard [muʃar] **-charde** [ʃard] *mf* (coll) stool pigeon, squealer

moucharder [muʃarde] *tr* (coll) to spy on; (coll) to squeal on ‖ *intr* (coll) to squeal

mouche [muʃ] *f* fly; beauty spot; **faire d'une mouche un éléphant** to make a mountain out of a molehill; **faire la mouche** to fly into a rage; **faire mouche** to hit the bull's-eye; **mouche à miel** honeybee; **mouche d'Espagne** (pharm) Spanish fly; **mouche du coche** busybody

moucher [muʃe] *tr* to blow (*one's nose*); to snuff, to trim; (coll) to scold ‖ *ref* to blow one's nose

moucherolle [muʃrɔl] *f* (orn) flycatcher

moucheron [muʃrɔ̃] *m* gnat; snuff (*of candle*)

moucheter [muʃte] §34 *tr* to speckle

mouchoir [muʃwar] *m* handkerchief

moudre [mudr] §43 *tr* to grind

moue [mu] *f* wry face; **faire la moue** to pout

mouette [mwet] *f* gull, sea gull; **mouette rieuse** black-headed gull

mouffette [mufɛt] *f* skunk

moufle [mufl] *m* & *f* pulley block ‖ *f* mitten

mouillage [muja3] *m* anchorage; wetting; watering, diluting

mouil·lé -lée [muje] *adj* wet; at anchor; palatalized; liquid (*l*)

mouiller [muje] *tr* to wet; to water, dilute; to palatalize; to drop (*anchor*) ‖ *intr* to drop anchor ‖ *ref* to get wet; to water; (coll) to become involved

moulage [mula3] *m* molding, casting; mold, cast; grinding, milling

moule [mul] *m* mold, form ‖ *f* mussel; (slang) fleabrain; (slang) jellyfish

mouler [mule] *tr* to mold; to outline, e.g., **corsage qui moule le buste** blouse which outlines the bosom

moulin [mulɛ̃] *m* mill; **moulin à café** coffee grinder; **moulin à paroles** (coll) windbag; **moulin à vent** windmill

moulinet [mulinɛ] *m* winch; reel (*of casting rod*); turnstile; pinwheel (*child's toy*); **faire le moulinet avec** to twirl

moult [mult] *adv* (obs) much, many

mou·lu -lue [muly] *adj* ground; (coll) done in

moulure [mulyr] *f* molding

mou·rant [murɑ̃] **-rante** [rɑ̃t] *adj* dying ‖ *mf* dying person

mourir [murir] §44 *intr* (*aux:* ÊTRE) to die ‖ *ref* to be dying

mouron [murɔ̃] *m* (bot) starwort, stitchwort; (bot) pimpernel

mousquetaire [muskətɛr] *m* musketeer

mousse [mus] *adj* dull ‖ *m* cabin boy ‖ *f* moss; froth, foam; lather, suds; whipped cream

mousseline [muslin] *f* muslin; **mousseline de soie** chiffon

mousser [muse] *intr* to froth, to foam; to lather; **faire mousser** (coll) to crack up, to build up; (slang) to enrage

mous·seux [musø] **mous·seuse** [musøz] *adj* mossy; frothy, foamy; sudsy, sparkling (*wine*)

mousson [musɔ̃] *f* monsoon

moustache [mustaʃ] *f* moustache; **moustaches** whiskers (*of, e.g., cat*); **moustaches en croc** handle-bar mustache

moustiquaire [mustikɛr] *f* mosquito net

moustique [mustik] *m* mosquito

moût [mu] *m* must; wort

moutard [mutar] *m* (slang) kid

moutarde [mutard] *f* mustard

moutier [mutje] *m* (obs) monastery

mouton [mutɔ̃] *m* sheep; mutton; (slang) stool pigeon; **doux comme un mouton** gentle as a lamb; **moutons** whitecaps; **moutons de Panurge** (fig) chameleons, yes men; **revenons à nos moutons** let's get back to our subject

mouton·né -née [mutɔne] *adj* fleecy; frothy (*sea*); mackerel (*sky*)

moutonner [mutɔne] *tr* to curl ‖ *intr* to break into whitecaps

mouton·neux [mutɔnø] **mouton·neuse** [mutɔnøz] *adj* frothy; fleecy (*e.g., cloud*)

mouture [mutyr] *f* grinding; mixture of wheat, rye, and barley; (fig) reworking

mouvement [muvmɑ̃] *m* movement; motion; **mouvement d'horlogerie** clockwork; **mouvement d'humeur** of bad temper; **mouvement ondulatoire** wave motion

mouvemen·té -tée [muvmɑ̃te] *adj* lively; eventful; hilly, broken (*terrain*)

mouvementer [muvmɑ̃te] *tr* to enliven

mouvoir [muvwar] §45 *tr* to move; to set in motion, to drive ‖ *ref* to move, stir

moyen [mwajɛ̃] **moyenne** [mwajɛn] *adj* average; ordinary; middle, intermediate; medium ‖ *m* way, manner; **au moyen de** by means of; **moyens** means ‖ *f* average; mean; passing mark; **en moyenne** on an average

moyen-âge [mwajɛnaʒ] *m* Middle Ages

moyen-courrier [mwajɛ̃kurje] *m* (*pl* **moyens-courriers**) medium-range plane

moyennant [mwajɛnɑ̃] *prep* in exchange for ‖ *conj* provided that

Moyen-Orient [mwajɛnɔrjɑ̃] *m* Middle East

moyeu [mwajǿ] *m* (*pl* **moyeux**) hub
mû mue [my] *adj* driven, propelled ‖ *f*
see **mue**
mucosité [mykozite] *f* mucus
mucus [mykys] *m* mucus
mue [my] *f* molt, shedding
muer [mɥe] *intr* to molt; to shed;
(*said of voice*) to break, change
muet [mɥɛ] **muette** [mɥɛt] *adj* mute;
silent; non-speaking (*rôle*); blank;
dead (*key*) ‖ *mf* mute ‖ *m* silent
movie
mufle [myfl] *m* muzzle, snout; (coll)
cad, skunk
mugir [myʒir] *intr* to bellow
mugissement [myʒismã] *m* bellow
muguet [mygɛ] *m* lily of the valley
mulâ·tre [mylɑtr] **-tresse** [trɛs] *mf*
mulatto
mule [myl] *f* mule
mulet [mylɛ] *m* mule; (ichth) mullet
mule·tier [myltje] **-tière** [tjer] *adj* mule
(*e.g., trail*) ‖ *mf* muleteer
mulette [mylɛt] *f* fresh-water clam
mulot [mylo] *m* field mouse
multilaté·ral -rale [myltilateral] *adj* (*pl*
-raux [ro]) multilateral
multiple [myltipl] *adj* & *m* multiple
multiplicité [myltiplisite] *f* multiplicity
multiplier [myltiplije] *tr* & *ref* to multiply
multitude [myltityd] *f* multitude
munici·pal -pale [mynisipal] *adj* (*pl*
-paux [po]) municipal
municipalité [mynisipalite] *f* municipality; city officials; city hall
munifi·cent [mynifisã] **-cente** [sãt] *adj*
munificent
munir [mynir] *tr* to provide, equip ‖
ref—**se munir de** to provide oneself
with
munitions [mynisjɔ̃] *fpl* munitions
mu·queux [mykǿ] **-queuse** [køz] *adj*
mucous ‖ *f* mucous membrane
mur [myr] *m* wall; **mettre au pied du
mur** to corner; **mur de soutènement**
retaining wall; **mur sonique, mur du
son** sound barrier
mûr mûre [myr] *adj* ripe, mature ‖ *f*
see **mûre**
muraille [myrɑj] *f* wall, rampart
mu·ral -rale [myral] *adj* (*pl* **-raux**
[ro]) mural
mûre [myr] *f* mulberry; blackberry
murer [myre] *tr* to wall up or in ‖ *ref*
to shut oneself up
mûrier [myrje] *m* mulberry tree
mûrir [myrir] *tr* & *intr* to ripen, mature
murmure [myrmyr] *m* murmur
murmurer [myrmyre] *tr* & *intr* to murmur
musaraigne [myzarɛɲ] *f* (zool) shrew
musarder [myzarde] *intr* to dawdle
musc [mysk] *m* musk
muscade [myskad] *f* nutmeg; **passez
muscade!** presto!
muscardin [myskardɛ̃] *m* dormouse
muscat [myska] *m* muscatel
muscle [myskl] *m* muscle

mus·clé -clée [myskle] *adj* muscular;
(coll) powerful (*e.g., drama*); (slang)
difficult
musculaire [myskylɛr] *adj* muscular
muscu·leux [myskylǿ] **-leuse** [lǿz] *adj*
muscular
muse [myz] *f* muse; **les Muses** the
Muses
mu·seau [myzo] *m* (*pl* **-seaux**) snout;
(coll) mug, face
musée [myze] *m* museum
museler [myzle] §34 *tr* to muzzle
muselière [myzəljer] *f* muzzle
muser [myze] *intr* to dawdle
musette [myzɛt] *f* feed bag; kit bag;
haversack
muséum [myzeɔm] *m* museum of natural history
musi·cal -cale [myzikal] *adj* (*pl* **-caux**
[ko]) musical
music-hall [myzikol] *m* (*pl* **-halls**)
vaudeville; vaudeville house; music
hall (Brit)
musi·cien [myzisjɛ̃] **-cienne** [sjɛn] *mf*
musician
musicologie [myzikɔlɔʒi] *f* musicology
musique [myzik] *f* music; band; **toujours la même musique** (coll) the
same old song
mus·qué -quée [myske] *adj* muskscented
musul·man [myzylmã] **-mane** [man]
adj & *mf* Mussulman
mutation [mytɑsjɔ̃] *f* mutation; transfer; (biol) mutation, sport
muter [myte] *tr* to transfer
muti·lé -lée [mytile] *mf* disabled veteran
mutiler [mytile] *tr* to mutilate; to deface; to disable; to garble (*e.g., the
truth*)
mu·tin [mytɛ̃] **-tine** [tin] *adj* roguish ‖
mf mutineer
muti·né -née [mytine] *adj* mutinous ‖
mf mutineer
mutiner [mytine] *ref* to mutiny
mutualité [mytɥalite] *f* mutual insurance
mu·tuel -tuelle [mytɥɛl] *adj* mutual ‖
f mutual benefit association
myope [mjɔp] *adj* near-sighted ‖ *mf*
near-sighted person
myriade [mirjad] *f* myriad
myrrhe [mir] *f* myrrh
myrte [mirt] *m* myrtle
myrtille [mirtij] *f* blueberry
mystère [mistɛr] *m* mystery
mysté·rieux [misterjǿ] **-rieuse** [rjǿz]
adj mysterious
mysticisme [mistisism] *m* mysticism
mystification [mistifikɑsjɔ̃] *f* mystification; hoax
mystifier [mistifje] *tr* to mystify; to
hoax
mystique [mistik] *adj* & *mf* mystic
mythe [mit] *m* myth
mythique [mitik] *adj* mythical
mythologie [mitɔlɔʒi] *f* mythology
mythologique [mitɔlɔʒik] *adj* mythological

N

N, n [εn], *[εn] *m invar* fourteenth letter of the French alphabet
na·bot [nabo] **-bote** [bɔt] *adj* dwarfish ‖ *mf* dwarf, midget
nacelle [nasεl] *f* (aer) nacelle; (naut) wherry, skiff; (fig) boat
nacre [nakr] *f* mother-of-pearl
na·cré -crée [nacre] *adj* pearly
nage [naʒ] *f* swimming; rowing, paddling; **être (tout) en nage** to be wet with sweat; **nage à la pagaie** paddling; **nage de côté** sidestroke; **nage en couple** sculling; **nage en grenouille** breaststroke
nagée [naʒe] *f* swimming stroke
nageoire [naʒwar] *f* fin; flipper (*of seal*); float (*for swimmers*)
nager [naʒe] §38 *intr* to swim; to float; to row; **nager à culer** (naut) to back water; **nager debout** to tread water; to, row standing up; **nager entre deux eaux** to swim under water; (fig) to carry water on both shoulders
na·geur [naʒœr] **-geuse** [ʒøz] *adj* swimming; floating ‖ *mf* swimmer; rower
naguère or **naguères** [nagεr] *adv* lately, just now
naïf [naif] **naïve** [naiv] *adj* naïve ‖ *mf* simple-minded person
nain [nε̃] **naine** [nεn] *adj* & *mf* dwarf
naissain [nεsε̃] *m* seed oysters
naissance [nεsɑ̃s] *f* birth; lineage; descent; beginning; (archit) springing line; **de basse naissance** lowborn; **de haute naissance** highborn; **de naissance** by birth; **donner naissance à** to give birth to; to give rise to; **naissance de la gorge** bosom, throat; **naissance des cheveux** hairline; **naissance du jour** daybreak; **prendre naissance** to arise, originate
nais·sant [nεsɑ̃] **nais·sante** [nεsɑ̃t] *adj* nascent, rising, budding
naître [nεtr] §46 *intr* (*aux:* ÊTRE) to be born; to bud; to arise, originate; to dawn; **faire naître** to give birth to; to give rise to
naïveté [naivte] *f* naïveté; artlessness
nanan [nɑ̃nɑ̃], [nɑ̃nɑ̃] *m* (coll) goody; **du nanan** (coll) nice
nantir [nɑ̃tir] *tr* to give security or a pledge to; **nantir de** to provide with ‖ *intr* to stock up; to feather one's nest ‖ *ref*—**se nantir de** to provide oneself with
nantissement [nɑ̃tismɑ̃] *m* security
napée [nape] *f* wood nymph
napel [napεl] *m* monkshood, wolfsbane
naphte [naft] *m* naphtha
napoléo·nien [napɔleɔnjε̃] **-nienne** [njεn] *adj* Napoleonic
nappage [napaʒ] *m* table linen
nappe [nap] *f* tablecloth; sheet (*of water, flame*); net (*for fishing; for bird catching*); **mettre la nappe** to set the table; **nappe d'autel** altar cloth; **ôter la nappe** to clear the table
napperon [naprɔ̃] *m* tablecloth cover; **petit napperon** doily

narcisse [narsis] *m* narcissus; **narcisse des bois** daffodil; **Narcisse** Narcissus
narcotique [narkɔtik] *adj* & *m* narcotic
narcotiser [narkɔtize] *tr* to dope
nargue [narg] *f* scorn, contempt; **faire nargue de** to defy; **nargue de . . .!** fie on . . .!
narguer [narge] *tr* to flout, to snap one's fingers at
narguilé [nargile] *m* hookah
narine [narin] *f* nostril
nar·quois [narkwa] **-quoise** [kwaz] *adj* sly, cunning; sneering
narra·teur [naratœr] **-trice** [tris] *mf* narrator, storyteller
narra·tif [naratif] **-tive** [tiv] *adj* narrative
narration [narɑsjɔ̃] *f* narration; narrative
narrer [nare] *tr* to narrate, relate
na·sal -sale [nazal] *adj* (*pl* **-saux** [zo]) nasal ‖ *f* nasal (*vowel*)
nasaliser [nazalize] *tr* & *intr* to nasalize
nasarde [nazard] *f* fillip on one's nose (*in contempt*); snub, insult
na·seau [nazo] *m* (*pl* **-seaux**) nostril (*of horse, etc.*); **naseaux** (coll) snout
nasil·lard [nazijar] **nasil·larde** [nazijard] *adj* nasal
nasiller [nazije] *intr* to talk through one's nose; to squawk, quack
nasse [nas] *f* fish trap; (sports) basket
na·tal -tale [natal] *adj* (*pl* **-tals**) natal, of birth, native
natalité [natalite] *f* birth rate
natation [natɑsjɔ̃] *f* swimming
na·tif [natif] **-tive** [tiv] *adj* & *mf* native
nation [nɑsjɔ̃] *f* nation; **Nations Unies** United Nations
natio·nal -nale [nɑsjɔnal] *adj* & *mf* (*pl* **-naux** [no] **-nales**) national
nationaliser [nɑsjɔnalize] *tr* to nationalize
nationalité [nɑsjɔnalite] *f* nationality
nativité [nativite] *f* nativity; nativity scene; **Nativité** Nativity
natte [nat] *f* mat, matting; braid
natter [nate] *tr* to weave; to braid
naturalisation [natyralizɑsjɔ̃] *f* naturalization
naturaliser [natyralize] *tr* to naturalize
naturalisme [natyralism] *m* naturalism
naturaliste [natyralist] *adj* & *mf* naturalist
nature [natyr] *adj invar* raw; black (*coffee*) ‖ *f* nature; **nature morte** (painting) still life
natu·rel -relle [natyrεl] *adj* natural; native ‖ *m* naturalness; native, citizen
naturellement [natyrεlmɑ̃] *adv* naturally; of course
naufrage [nofraʒ] *m* shipwreck
naufra·gé -gée [nofraʒe] *adj* shipwrecked ‖ *mf* shipwrecked person
nauséa·bond [nozeabɔ̃] **-bonde** [bɔ̃d] *adj* nauseating
nausée [noze] *f* nausea

nauséeux [nozeǿ] **nauséeuse** [nozeǿz] *adj* nauseous
nautique [notik] *adj* nautical
nautisme [notism] *m* yachting
nauto·nier [notɔnje] **-nière** [njɛr] *mf* pilot
na·val -vale [naval] *adj* (*pl* **-vals**) naval; nautical, maritime
navel [navɛl] *f* navel orange
navet [navɛ] *m* turnip
navette [navɛt] *f* shuttle; shuttle train; **faire la navette** to shuttle, to ply back and forth
navigable [navigabl] *adj* navigable (*river*); seaworthy (*ship*)
naviga·teur [navigatœr] **-trice** [tris] *adj* seafaring || *m* navigator
navigation [navigɑsjɔ̃] *f* navigation; sailing; **navigation de plaisance** (sports) sailing
naviguer [navige] *intr* to navigate, sail; **naviguer sur** to navigate, sail (*the sea*)
navire [navir] *m* ship; **navire de débarquement** landing craft; **navire marchand** merchantman
navire-citerne [navirsitɛrn] *m* (*pl* **navires-citernes**) tanker
navire-école [navirekɔl] *m* (*pl* **navires-écoles**) training ship
navire-jumeau [navirʒymo] *m* (*pl* **navires-jumeaux**) sister ship
na·vrant [navrɑ̃] **-vrante** [vrɑ̃t] *adj* distressing, heartrending
na·vré -vrée [navre] *adj* sorry, grieved
navrer [navre] *tr* to distress, grieve
nazaréen [nazareɛ̃] **nazaréenne** [nazareɛn] *adj* Nazarene || (*cap*) *mf* Nazarene
N.-D. *abbr* (**Notre-Dame**) Our Lady
ne [nə] §87, §90; **n'est-ce pas?** isn't that so? La traduction précédente est généralement remplacée par diverses locutions. Si l'énoncé est négatif, la question qui équivaut à **n'est-ce pas?** sera affirmative, par ex., **Vous ne travaillez pas. N'est-ce pas?** You are not working. Are you? Si l'énoncé est affirmatif, la question sera négative, par ex., **Vous travaillez. N'est-ce pas?** You are working. Are you not? ou Aren't you? Si l'énoncé contient un auxiliaire, la question contiendra cet auxiliaire moins l'infinitif ou moins le participe passé, par ex., **Il arrivera demain. N'est-ce pas?** He will arrive tomorrow. Won't he?; par ex., **Paul est déjà arrivé. N'est-ce pas?** Paul has already arrived. Hasn't he? Si l'énoncé ne contient ni auxiliaire ni forme de la copule "to be," la question contiendra l'auxiliaire "do" ou "did" moins l'infinitif, par ex., **Marie parle anglais. N'est-ce pas?** Mary speaks English. Doesn't she?
né née [ne] *adj* born; by birth; **bien né** highborn; **né pour** cut out for
néanmoins [neɑ̃mwɛ̃] *adv* nevertheless
néant [neɑ̃] *m* nothing, nothingness; worthlessness; obscurity; none (*as a response on the appropriate blank of an official form*)

nébu·leux [nebylǿ] **-leuse** [lǿz] *adj* nebulous; gloomy (*facial expression*); worried (*brow*) || *f* nebula
nécessaire [nesesɛr] *adj* necessary, needful; **nécessaire à required for** || *m* necessities; kit, dressing case
nécessairement [nesesɛrmɑ̃] *adv* necessarily
nécessité [nesesite] *f* necessity; need; **nécessité préalable** prerequisite
nécessiter [nesesite] *tr* to necessitate
nécessi·teux [nesesitǿ] **-teuse** [tǿz] *adj* needy || *mf* needy person; **les nécessiteux** the needy
nécrologie [nekrɔlɔʒi] *f* necrology, obituary
nectar [nɛktar] *m* nectar
néerlan·dais [neɛrlɑ̃dɛ] **-daise** [dɛz] *adj* Dutch || *m* Dutch (*language*) || (*cap*) *mf* Netherlander
nef [nɛf] *f* nave; (archaic) ship; **nef latérale** aisle
néfaste [nefast] *adj* ill-starred, unlucky
nèfle [nɛfl] *f* medlar
néflier [neflije] *m* medlar tree
néga·teur [negatœr] **-trice** [tris] *adj* negative
néga·tif [negatif] **-tive** [tiv] *adj* negative || *m* (phot) negative || *f* negative (*side of a question*)
négation [negɑsjɔ̃] *f* negation; (gram) negative
négli·gé -gée [negliʒe] *adj* careless; unadorned, unstudied || *m* carelessness; negligee, dressing gown
négligeable [negliʒabl] *adj* negligible
négligence [negliʒɑ̃s] *f* negligence; **avec négligence** slovenly
négli·gent [negliʒɑ̃] **-gente** [ʒɑ̃t] *adj* negligent || *mf* careless person
négliger [negliʒe] §38 *tr* to neglect || *ref* to neglect oneself
négoce [negɔs] *m* trade, commerce; (com) company
négociable [negɔsjabl] *adj* negotiable
négo·ciant [negɔsjɑ̃] **-ciante** [sjɑ̃t] *mf* wholesaler, dealer
négocia·teur [negɔsjatœr] **-trice** [tris] *mf* negotiator
négociation [negɔsjɑsjɔ̃] *f* negotiation
négocier [negɔsje] *tr* to negotiate || *intr* to negotiate; to deal
nègre [nɛgr] *adj* Negro; dark brown || *m* Negro; ghost writer; **petit nègre** pidgin, Creole
négrerie [negrəri] *f* slave quarters
négrier [negrije] *adj masc* slave || *m* slave driver; slave ship
neige [nɛʒ] *f* snow
neiger [neʒe] §38 *intr* to snow
Némésis [nemezis] *f* Nemesis
nenni [nani], [neni], [nɛni] *adv* (archaic) no, not
nénuphar [nenyfar] *m* water lily
néologisme [neɔlɔʒism] *m* neologism
néon [neɔ̃] *m* neon
néophyte [neɔfit] *mf* neophyte, convert
neptunium [nɛptynjɔm] *m* neptunium
nerf [nɛr] *m* nerve; tendon, sinew; (archit, bb) rib; (fig) backbone, sinew; **avoir du nerf** to have nerves of steel; **avoir les nerfs à fleur de peau** to be on edge; **nerf de bœuf**

scourge; **porter sur les nerfs à qn** to get on s.o.'s nerves

Néron [nerɔ̃] *m* Nero

ner·veux [nɛrvø] **-veuse** [vøz] *adj* nervous; nerve; jittery; sinewy, muscular; forceful (*style*)

nervure [nɛrvyr] *f* rib

net nette [nɛt] *adj* clean; clear, sharp, distinct; net; **net d'impôt** tax-exempt || *m*—**mettre au net** to make a fair copy of || **net** *adv* flatly, point-blank, outright

netteté [nɛtəte] *f* neatness; clearness, sharpness

nettoiement [nɛtwamɑ̃] *m* cleaning

nettoyage [nɛtwajaʒ] *m* cleaning; **nettoyage à sec** dry cleaning

nettoyer [nɛtwaje] §47 *tr* to clean; to wash up or out; **nettoyer à sec** to dryclean || *ref* to wash up, to clean oneself

nettoyeur [nɛtwajœr] **nettoyeuse** [nɛtwajøz] *mf* cleaner

neuf [nœf] **neuve** [nœv] *adj* new; **flambant neuf, tout neuf** brand-new || **neuf** *adj & pron* nine; the Ninth, e.g., **Jean neuf** John the Ninth; **neuf heures** nine o'clock || *m* nine; ninth (*in dates*)

neutraliser [nøtralize] *tr* to neutralize

neutralité [nøtralite] *f* neutrality

neutre [nøtr] *adj & m* neuter; neutral

neuvième [nœvjɛm] *adj, pron* (*masc, fem*), *& m* ninth

ne·veu [nəvø] *m* (*pl* **-veux**) nephew; **nos neveux** our posterity

névralgie [nevralʒi] *f* neuralgia

névrose [nevroz] *f* neurosis

névro·sé -sée [nevroze] *adj & mf* neurotic

New York [nujɔrk], [nœjɔrk] *m* New York

newyor·kais [nœjɔrkɛ] **-kaise** [kɛz] *adj* New York || (*cap*) *mf* New Yorker

nez [ne] *m* nose; cape, headland; **nez à nez** face to face

ni [ni] §90 *conj*—**ne . . . ni . . . ni** neither . . . nor, e.g., **elle n'a ni papier ni stylo** she has neither paper nor pen; **ni . . . ni** neither . . . nor; **ni . . . non plus** nor . . . either

niable [njabl] *adj* deniable

niais [njɛ] **niaise** [njɛz] *adj* foolish, silly, simple-minded || *mf* fool, simpleton

niaiserie [njɛzəri] *f* foolishness, silliness, simpleness

niche [niʃ] *f* niche; alcove; prank; **niche à chien** doghouse

nichée [niʃe] *f* brood

nicher [niʃe] *tr* to niche, to lodge || *intr* to nestle; to nest; to hide || *ref* to nest

nickeler [nikle] §34 *tr* to nickel-plate

nickelure [niklyr] *f* nickel plate

nicotine [nikɔtin] *f* nicotine

nid [ni] *m* nest; **en nid d'abeilles** honeycombed; **nid de pie** crow's-nest

nièce [njɛs] *f* niece

nième [njɛm] *adj* nth

nier [nje] *tr* to deny || *intr* to plead not guilty

ni·gaud [nigo] **-gaude** [god] *adj* silly || *mf* nincompoop

nigauderie [nigodri] *f* silliness

nihilisme [niilism] *m* nihilism

Nil [nil] *m* Nile

nimbe [nɛ̃b] *m* halo, nimbus

nimber [nɛ̃be] *tr* to halo

nimbus [nɛ̃bys] *m* (meteo) nimbus

nipper [nipe] *tr* (coll) to tog || *ref* (coll) to tog oneself out

nippes [nip] *fpl* (coll) worn-out clothes; (slang) duds

nique [nik] *f*—**faire la nique à** to turn up one's nose at

nitrate [nitrat] *m* nitrate

nitre [nitr] *m* niter, nitrate

ni·treux [nitrø] **-treuse** [trøz] *adj* nitrous

nitrière [nitrijɛr] *f* saltpeter bed

nitrique [nitrik] *adj* nitric

nitrogène [nitrɔʒɛn] *m* nitrogen

nitroglycérine [nitrɔgliserin] *f* nitroglycerin

ni·veau [nivo] *m* (*pl* **-veaux**) level; **au niveau de** on a par with; **niveau à bulle d'air** spirit level; **niveau à lunettes** surveyor's level; **niveau d'essence** gasoline gauge; **niveau de vie** standard of living; **niveau d'huile** oil gauge; **niveau mental I.Q.**

niveler [nivle] §34 *tr* to level; to survey

nive·leur [nivlœr] **-leuse** [løz] *mf* leveler || *m* harrow || *f* (agr) leveler

nivellement [nivɛlmɑ̃] *m* leveling; surveying

N°, n° *abbr* (**numéro**) no.

noble [nɔbl] *adj & mf* noble

noblesse [nɔbles] *f* nobility; nobleness

noce [nɔs] *f* wedding; wedding party; **faire la noce** to go on a spree; **ne pas être à la noce** to be in trouble; **noces** wedding

no·ceur [nɔsœr] **-ceuse** [søz] *adj* (coll) bacchanalian, reveling || *mf* (coll) reveler, debauchee

no·cif [nɔsif] **-cive** [siv] *adj* noxious

noctambule [nɔktɑ̃byl] *mf* nighthawk; sleepwalker

nocturne [nɔktyrn] *adj* nocturnal; night; nightly || *m* (mus) nocturne || *f* open night (*of store*)

nodosité [nɔdozite] *f* nodule (*of root*); node, wart

Noé [nɔe] *m* Noah

noël [nɔɛl] *m* Christmas carol; (coll) Christmas present; **Noël** Christmas

nœud [nø] *m* knot; rosette; finger joint; Adam's apple; tie, alliance; crux (*of question, plot, crisis*); node; (naut) knot; **nœud de vache** granny knot; **nœud plat** square knot; **nœuds** coils (*of snake*); **nœud vital** nerve center

noir noire [nwar] *adj* black; **noir comme poix** pitch-black || *mf* Negro || *m* black; bruise; **broyer du noir** to be blue, down in the dumps; **noir de fumée** lampblack || *f* (mus) quarter note

noirâtre [nwarɑtr] *adj* blackish

noi·raud [nwaro] **-raude** [rod] *adj* swarthy

noirceur [nwarsœr] *f* blackness; black spot

noircir [nwarsir] *tr* to blacken ‖ *intr* & *ref* to burn black; to turn dark

noircissure [nwarsisyr] *f* black spot, smudge

noise [nwaz] *f* squabble; **chercher noise à** to pick a quarrel with

noisetier [nwaztje] *m* hazelnut tree

noisette [nwazet] *adj invar* reddish-brown ‖ *f* hazelnut

noix [nwa], [nwa] *f* walnut; nut; **à la noix** (slang) trifling; **noix d'acajou**, **noix de cajou** cashew nut; **noix du Brésil** Brazil nut; **noix de coco** coconut; **noix de galle** nutgall; **noix de muscade** nutmeg; **noix de veau** round of veal

nolis [nɔli] *m* freight

noliser [nɔlize] *tr* to charter (*a ship*)

nom [nɔ̃] *m* name; noun; **de nom** by name; **nom à rallonges, nom à tiroirs** (coll) word made up of several parts; **nom commercial** trade name; **nom de baptême** baptismal name, Christian name; **nom de demoiselle** maiden name; **nom de famille** surname; **nom de guerre** fictitious name, assumed name; **nom de jeune fille** maiden name; **nom d'emprunt** assumed name; **nom de théâtre** stage name; **nom marchand** trade name; **petit nom** first name; **petit nom d'amitié** pet name; **sans nom** nameless; **sous le nom de** by the name of

nomade [nɔmad] *adj* & *mf* nomad

nombre [nɔ̃br] *m* number, quantity

nombrer [nɔ̃bre] *tr* to number

nom·breux [nɔ̃brø] **-breuse** [brøz] *adj* numerous; rhythmic, harmonious (*e.g., prose*)

nombril [nɔ̃bri] *m* navel

nomenclature [nɔmɑ̃klatyr] *f* nomenclature; vocabulary; body (*of dictionary*)

nomi·nal **-nale** [nɔminal] *adj* (*pl* **-naux** [no]) nominal; **appel nominal** roll call

nomina·tif [nɔminatif] **-tive** [tiv] *adj* nominative; registered (*stocks, bonds, etc.*) ‖ *m* nominative

nomination [nɔminasjɔ̃] *f* appointment

nom·mé **-mée** [nɔme] *adj* named; appointed; called ‖ *m*—**le nommé . . .** the man called . . .

nommément [nɔmemɑ̃] *adv* namely, particularly

nommer [nɔme] *tr* to name, call; to appoint ‖ *ref* to be named, e.g., **je me nomme . . .** my name is . . .

non [nɔ̃] *m invar* no ‖ *adv* no, not; **non pas** not so; **non plus** neither, not, nor . . . either, e.g., **moi non plus** nor I either; **non point!** by no means!; **que non!** no indeed!

non-belligé·rant [nɔ̃bɛliiʒerɑ̃] **-rante** [rɑ̃t] *adj* & *mf* nonbelligerent

nonce [nɔ̃s] *m* nuncio

noncha·lant [nɔ̃ʃalɑ̃] **-lante** [lɑ̃t] *adj* nonchalant

non-combat·tant [nɔ̃kɔ̃batɑ̃] **non-combat·tante** [nɔ̃kɔ̃batɑ̃t] *adj* & *mf* noncombatant

non-conformiste [nɔ̃kɔ̃fɔrmist] *adj* & *mf* nonconformist

non-enga·gé **-gée** [nɔ̃ɑ̃gaʒe] *adj* unaligned, uncommitted

nonnain [nɔnɛ̃] *f* (pej) nun

nonne [nɔn] *f* nun

nonobstant [nɔnɔpstɑ̃] *adv* notwithstanding; **nonobstant que** although ‖ *prep* in spite of

non-pesanteur [nɔ̃pəzɑ̃tœr] *f* weightlessness

non-rési·dent [nɔ̃rezidɑ̃] **-dente** [dɑ̃t] *adj* & *mf* nonresident

non-réussite [nɔ̃reysit] *f* failure

non-sens [nɔ̃sɑ̃s] *m* absurdity, nonsense

non-usage [nɔnyzaʒ] *m* disuse

non-violence [nɔ̃vjɔlɑ̃s] *f* nonviolence

nord [nɔr] *adj invar* north, northern ‖ *m* north; **du nord** northern; **faire le nord** to steer northward; **vers le nord** northward

nord-est [nɔrest] *adj invar* & *m* northeast

nord-ouest [nɔrwest] *adj invar* & *m* northwest

nor·mal **-male** [nɔrmal] *adj* (*pl* **-maux** [mo]) normal; regular, standard; perpendicular ‖ *f* normal; perpendicular

norma·lien [nɔrmaljɛ̃] **-lienne** [ljɛn] *mf* student at a teachers college

nor·mand [nɔrmɑ̃] **-mande** [mɑ̃d] *adj* Norman ‖ *m* Norman (*dialect*) ‖ (*cap*) *mf* Norman (*person*)

Normandie [nɔrmɑ̃di] *f* Normandy; **la Normandie** Normandy

norme [nɔrm] *f* norm; specifications

nor·rois [nɔrwa] **nor·roise** [nɔrwaz] *adj* Norse ‖ *m* Norse (*language*) ‖ (*cap*) *m* Norseman

Norvège [nɔrveʒ] *f* Norway; **la Norvège** Norway

norvé·gien [nɔrveʒjɛ̃] **-gienne** [ʒjɛn] *adj* Norwegian ‖ *m* Norwegian (*language*) ‖ *f* round-stemmed rowboat ‖ (*cap*) *mf* Norwegian (*person*)

nos [no] §88

nostalgie [nɔstalʒi] *f* nostalgia, homesickness

nostalgique [nɔstalʒik] *adj* nostalgic, homesick

notable [nɔtabl] *adj* notable, noteworthy ‖ *m* notable

notaire [nɔter] *m* notary; lawyer

notamment [nɔtamɑ̃] *adv* especially

notation [nɔtasjɔ̃] *f* notation

note [nɔt] *f* note; bill (*to be paid*); grade, mark (*in school*); footnote; **être dans la note** to be in the swing of things; **note de rappel** reminder; **prendre note de** to note down

noter [nɔte] *tr* to note; to note down; to notice; to mark (*a student*); to write down (*a tune*)

notice [nɔtis] *f* notice (*review, sketch*)

notification [nɔtifikasjɔ̃] *f* notification, notice

notifier [nɔtifje] *tr* to report on; to serve (*a summons*)

notion [nosjɔ̃] *f* notion

notoire [nɔtwar] *adj* well-known

notoriété [nɔtɔrjete] *f* fame

notre [nɔtr] §88
nôtre [notr] §89; **serez-vous des nô-tres?** will you join us?
noue [nu] *f* pasture land; roof gutter
noué nouée [nwe] *adj* afflicted with rickets
nouer [nwe] *tr* to knot; to tie; to form; to cook up (*a plot*) ǁ *ref* to form knots; to be tied; (hort) to set
noueux [nwø] **noueuse** [nwøz] *adj* knotty, gnarled
nouille [nuj] *f* noodle
nounou [nunu] *f* nanny
nour•ri -rie [nuri] *adj* heavy, sustained; rich (*style*)
nourrice [nuris] *f* wet nurse; can; (aut) reserve tank
nourricerie [nurisri] *f* baby farm; stock farm; silkworm farm
nourri•cier [nurisje] **-cière** [sjɛr] *adj* nutritive; nourishing; foster
nourrir [nurir] *tr* to nourish; to suckle; to feed (*a fire*); to nurse (*plants; hopes*) ǁ *intr* to be nourishing ǁ *ref* to feed; to thrive
nourrisseur [nurisœr] *m* stock raiser, dairyman
nourrisson [nurisɔ̃] *m* nursling, suckling; foster child
nourriture [nurityr] *f* nourishment, food; nourishing; nursing; breast-feeding; **nourriture du feu** firewood
nous [nu] §85, §87; **nous autres Américains** we Americans
nous-mêmes [numɛm] §86
nou•veau [nuvo] (or **-vel** [vɛl] before vowel or mute h) **-velle** [vɛl] (*pl* **-veaux -velles**) *adj* new (*recent*) ǁ (when standing before noun) *adj* new (*other, additional, different*) ǁ *m* freshman; **à nouveau** anew; **de nouveau** again; **du nouveau** something new; **le nouveau** the new ǁ *f* see **nouvelle**
nouveau-né -née [nuvone] *adj* & *mf* (*pl* **-nés**) newborn
nouveauté [nuvote] *f* newness, novelty
nouvelle [nuvɛl] *f* piece of news; novelette, short story; **donnez-moi de vos nouvelles** let me hear from you; **nouvelles** news
Nouvelle-Angleterre [nuvɛlɑ̃glətɛr] *f* New England; **la Nouvelle-Angleterre** New England
Nouvelle-Écosse [nuvɛlekɔs] *f* Nova Scotia; **la Nouvelle-Écosse** Nova Scotia
Nouvelle-Orléans [nuvɛlɔrleɑ̃] *f*—**la Nouvelle-Orléans** New Orleans
nouvelliste [nuvɛlist] *mf* short-story writer
nova•teur [nɔvatœr] **-trice** [tris] *adj* innovating ǁ *mf* innovator
novembre [nɔvɑ̃br] *m* November
novice [nɔvis] *adj* inexperienced, new ǁ *mf* novice, neophyte
noviciat [nɔvisja] *m* novitiate
novocaïne [nɔvɔkain] *f* novocaine
noyade [nwajad] *f* drowning
noyau [nwajo] *m* (*pl* **noyaux**) nucleus; stone, kernel; pit (*of fruit*); core (*of electromagnet*); newel; hub; (fig) cell (*of conspirators*); (fig) bunch (*of*

card players); **noyau d'atome** atomic nucleus
noyautage [nwajota3] *m* infiltration (*e.g., of communists*)
noyer [nwaje] *m* walnut tree; **en noyer** in walnut (*wood*) ǁ §47 *tr* & *ref* to drown
nu nue [ny] *adj* naked, nude; bare; barren; uncarpeted; unharnassed, unsaddled (*horse*); (aut) stripped ǁ *m* nude; **à nu** exposed; bareback ǁ *f* see **nue**
nuage [nɥa3] *m* cloud
nua•geux [nɥa3ø] **-geuse** [3øz] *adj* cloudy
nuance [nɥɑ̃s] *f* hue, shade, tone, nuance
nucléaire [nykleɛr] *adj* nuclear
nucléole [nykleɔl] *m* nucleolus
nucléon [nykleɔ̃] *m* nucleon
nudiste [nydist] *adj* & *mf* nudist
nudité [nydite] *f* nakedness; nudity; plainness (*of style*); nude
nue [ny] *f* clouds; sky; **mettre** or **porter aux nues** to praise to the skies
nuée [nɥe] *f* cloud, storm cloud; flock
nuire [nɥir] §19 (*pp* **nui**) *intr* (with *dat*) to harm, to injure
nuisible [nɥizibl] *adj* harmful
nuit [nɥi] *f* night; **à la nuit close** after dark; **bonne nuit** good night; **cette nuit** last night; **nuit blanche** sleepless night
nuitamment [nɥitamɑ̃] *adv* at night
nu-jambes [nyʒɑ̃b] *adj invar* barelegged
nul nulle [nyl] *adj indef* no; **ne . . . nul** or **nul . . . ne** §90 no; **nul et non avenu, nulle et non avenue** [nylenɔnavny] null and void ǁ *f* dummy word or letter ǁ **nul** *pron indef*—**nul ne** §90B no one, nobody
nullement [nylmɑ̃] §90 *adv* not at all
nullité [nyllite] *f* nonentity, nobody
nûment [nymɑ̃] *adv* candidly, frankly
numé•ral -rale [nymeral] *adj* & *m* (*pl* **-raux** [ro]) numeral
numération [nymerasjɔ̃] *f* numeration; **numération globulaire** blood count
numérique [nymerik] *adj* numerical
numéro [nymero] *m* numeral; number; issue, number (*of a periodical*), e.g., **dernier numéro** current issue; e.g., **numéro ancien** back number; (slang) queer duck; **faire un numéro** to dial; **numéro de vestiaire** check (*of checkroom*); **numéro d'ordre** serial number
numéroter [nymerɔte] *tr* to number
numismatique [nymismatik] *adj* numismatic ǁ *f* numismatics
nu-pieds [nypje] *adj invar* barefooted
nup•tial -tiale [nypsjal] *adj* (*pl* **-tiaux** [sjo]) nuptial
nuque [nyk] *f* nape, scruff
nurse [nœrs] *f* children's nurse
nu-tête [nytɛt] *adj invar* bareheaded
nutri•tif [nytritif] **-tive** [tiv] *adj* nutritive; nutritious
nutrition [nytrisjɔ̃] *f* nutrition
nylon [nilɔ̃] *m* nylon
nymphe [nɛ̃f] *f* nymph

O

O, o [o], *[o] *m invar* fifteenth letter of the French alphabet
oasis [ɔazis] *f* oasis
obéir [ɔbeir] *intr* to obey; (with *dat*) to obey, yield to; (with *dat*) to be subject to; **être obéi** to be obeyed; **obéir au doigt et à l'œil** to obey blindly
obéissance [ɔbeisɑ̃s] *f* obedience
obéis•sant [ɔbeisɑ̃] **obéis•sante** [ɔbeisɑ̃t] *adj* obedient
obélisque [ɔbelisk] *m* obelisk
obérer [ɔbere] §10 *tr* to burden with debt ‖ *ref* to run into debt
obèse [ɔbez] *adj* obese
obésité [ɔbezite] *f* obesity
objecter [ɔbʒɛkte] *tr* to object, e.g., **objecter que . . .** to object that . . . ; to bring up, e.g., **objecter q.ch. à qn** to bring up s.th. against s.o.; to put forward (*in opposition*), e.g., **objecter de bonnes raisons à** or **contre un argument** to put forward good reasons against an argument
objecteur [ɔbʒɛktœr] *m*—**objecteur de conscience** conscientious objector
objec•tif [ɔbʒɛktif] **-tive** [tiv] *adj* objective ‖ *m* objective; object lens; (mil) target
objection [ɔbʒɛksjɔ̃] *f* objection; **faire des objections** to object
objectivité [ɔbʒɛktivite] *f* objectivity
objet [ɔbʒɛ] *m* object; **menus objets** notions; **objet d'art** work of art; **objet de risée** laughingstock; **objets de première nécessité** articles of everyday use; **remplir son object** to attain one's end
obligation [ɔbligasjɔ̃] *f* obligation; (com) bond, debenture; **être dans l'obligation de** to be obliged to
obligatoire [ɔbligatwar] *adj* required, obligatory; (coll) inevitable
obli•gé -gée [ɔbliʒe] *adj* obliged, compelled; necessary, indispensable; **bien obligé** much obliged; **c'est obligé** (coll) it has to be; **être obligé de** to be obliged to
obli•geant [ɔbliʒɑ̃] **-geante** [ʒɑ̃t] *adj* obliging
obliger [ɔbliʒe] §38 *tr* to oblige ‖ *ref*—**s'obliger à** + *inf* to undertake to + *inf*; **s'obliger pour qn** to stand surety for s.o.
oblique [ɔblik] *adj* oblique
oblitération [ɔbliterasjɔ̃] *f* obliteration; cancellation (*of postage stamp*); (pathol) occlusion
oblitérer [ɔblitere] §10 *tr* to obliterate; to cancel (*a postage stamp*); to obstruct (*e.g., a vein*)
o•blong [ɔblɔ̃] **-blongue** [blɔ̃g] *adj* oblong
obnubiler [ɔbnybile] *tr* to cloud, befog
obole [ɔbɔl] *f* widow's mite
obscène [ɔpsɛn] *adj* obscene
obscénité [ɔpsenite] *f* obscenity
obs•cur -cure [ɔpskyr] *adj* obscure
obscurcir [ɔpskyrsir] *tr* to obscure; to dim ‖ *ref* to grow dark; to grow dim

obscurité [ɔpskyrite] *f* obscurity
obséder [ɔpsede] §10 *tr* to obsess; to importune, to harass
obsèques [ɔpsɛk] *fpl* obsequies, funeral rites
obsé•quieux [ɔpsekjø] **-quieuse** [kjøz] *adj* obsequious
observance [ɔpsɛrvɑ̃s] *f* observance
observa•teur [ɔpsɛrvatœr] **-trice** [tris] *adj* observant ‖ *mf* observer
observation [ɔpsɛrvasjɔ̃] *f* observation
observatoire [ɔpsɛrvatwar] *m* observatory
observer [ɔpsɛrve] *tr* to observe ‖ *ref* to watch oneself; to watch each other
obsession [ɔpsesjɔ̃] *f* obsession
obsolète [ɔpsɔlɛt] *adj* obsolete
obstacle [ɔpstakl] *m* obstacle
obstétrique [ɔpstetrik] *adj* obstetrical ‖ *f* obstetrics
obstination [ɔpstinasjɔ̃] *f* obstinacy
obsti•né -née [ɔpstine] *adj* obstinate
obstruction [ɔpstryksjɔ̃] *f* obstruction; (sports) blocking; **faire de l'obstruction** (pol) to filibuster; **obstruction systématique** filibustering
obstruer [ɔpstrye] *tr* to obstruct
obtempérer [ɔptɑ̃pere] §10 *intr* (with *dat*) to comply with, to obey
obtenir [ɔptənir] §72 *tr* to obtain, get
obtention [ɔptɑ̃sjɔ̃] *f* obtaining
obtura•teur [ɔptyratœr] **-trice** [tris] *adj* stopping, closing ‖ *m* (mach) stopcock;·(phot) shutter
obturation [ɔptyrasjɔ̃] *f* stopping up; filling (*of tooth*); **obturation des lumières** blackout
obturer [ɔptyre] *tr* to stop up; to fill (*a tooth*)
ob•tus [ɔpty] **-tuse** [tyz] *adj* obtuse
obus [ɔby] *m* (mil) shell; plunger (*of tire valve*); **obus à balles** shrapnel; **obus à mitraille** shrapnel; **obus de rupture** armor-piercing shell
obvier [ɔbvje] *intr* (with *dat*) to obviate, to prevent
oc [ɔk] *adv* (Old Provençal) yes
occasion [ɔkazjɔ̃], [ɔkazjɔ̃] *f* occasion; opportunity; bargain; **à l'occasion** on occasion; **à l'occasion de** for (*e.g., s.o.'s birthday*); **d'occasion** secondhand (*clothing*); used (*car*)
occasion•nel -nelle [ɔkazjɔnɛl] *adj* occasional; chance (*meeting*); determining (*cause*)
occasionnellement [ɔkazjɔnɛlmɑ̃] *adv* occasionally; by chance, accidentally
occasionner [ɔkazjɔne] *tr* to occasion
occident [ɔksidɑ̃] *m* occident, west
occiden•tal -tale [ɔksidɑ̃tal] *adj* & *mf* (*pl* **-taux** [to]) occidental
occlu•sif [ɔklyzif] **-sive** [ziv] *adj* & *f* occlusive
occlusion [ɔklyzjɔ̃] *f* occlusion
occulte [ɔkylt] *adj* occult
occu•pant [ɔkypɑ̃] **-pante** [pɑ̃t] *adj* occupying ‖ *mf* occupant
occupation [ɔkypasjɔ̃] *f* occupation
occu•pé -pée [ɔkype] *adj* occupied; **occupé** (public sign) in use

occuper [ɔkype] *tr* to occupy ‖ *ref* to find something to do; s'occuper de to be occupied with, to be busy with; to take care of, to handle

occurrence [ɔkyrɑ̃s] *f* occurrence; en l'occurrence under the circumstances; être en occurrence to occur; selon l'occurrence as the case may be

océan [ɔseɑ̃] *m* ocean; océan glacial arctique Arctic Ocean; océan Indien Indian Ocean

océanique [ɔseanik] *adj* oceanic

ocre [ɔkr] *f* ochre

octane [ɔktan] *m* octane

octave [ɔktav] *f* octave

octa·von [ɔktavɔ̃] -vonne [vɔn] *mf* octoroon

octobre [ɔktɔbr] *m* October

octroi [ɔktrwa] *m* granting (*of a favor*); tax on provisions being brought into town

octroyer [ɔktrwaje] §47 *tr* to grant, concede; to bestow

oculaire [ɔkylɛr] *adj* ocular, eye ‖ *m* ocular, eyepiece

oculariste [ɔkylarist] *mf* optician (*who specializes in glass eyes*)

oculiste [ɔkylist] *mf* oculist

ode [ɔd] *f* ode

odeur [ɔdœr] *f* odor, scent

o·dieux [ɔdjø] -dieuse [djøz] *adj* odious ‖ *m* odium, odiousness

odo·rant [ɔdɔrɑ̃] -rante [rɑ̃t] *adj* fragrant

odorat [ɔdɔra] *m* (sense of) smell

Odyssée [ɔdise] *f* Odyssey

œcuménique [ekymenik] *adj* ecumenical

œdème [edɛm] *m* (pathol) edema

Œdipe [edip] *m* Oedipus

œil [œj] *m* (*pl* yeux [jø]) les yeux [lezjø]) eye; typeface, font; bud; avoir l'œil (américain) (coll) to be observant; coûter les yeux de la tête (coll) to cost a fortune; donner de l'œil à to give a better appearance to; entre quatre yeux [ɑ̃trəkatzjø] (coll) between you and me; faire les gros yeux à (coll) to glare at; faire les yeux doux à to make eyes at; ne pas avoir les yeux dans la poche (coll) to keep one's eyes peeled; (coll) to be no shrinking violet; œil au beurre noir (coll) black eye; œil de pie (naut) eyelet; œil de verre glass eye; œil électrique electric eye; pocher un œil à qn to give s.o. a black eye; sale œil disapproving or dirty look; sauter aux yeux, crever les yeux to be obvious; se mettre le doigt dans l'œil (coll) to put one's foot in one's mouth; se rincer l'œil (slang) to get an eyeful; taper dans l'œil à or de qn (coll) to take s.o.'s fancy; voir d'un mauvais œil to take a dim view of

œil-de-bœuf [œjdəbœf] *m* (*pl* œils-de-bœuf) bull's-eye, small oval window

œil-de-chat [œjdəʃa] *m* (*pl* œils-de-chat) cat's-eye (*gem*)

œil-de-perdrix [œjdəpɛrdri] *m* (*pl* œils-de-perdrix) (pathol) soft corn

œillade [œjad] *f* glance, leer, wink;

lancer, jeter, or décocher une œillade à to ogle

œillère [œjer] *f* eyecup; blinker; avoir des œillères to be biased

œillet [œjɛ] *m* eyelet; eyelet hole; carnation, clove pink; œillet d'Inde (*Tagetes*) marigold

œilleton [œjtɔ̃] *m* eye, bud; eyepiece; sight (*of rifle, camera, etc.*)

œillette [œjɛt] *f* opium poppy

œnologie [enɔlɔʒi] *f* science of viniculture, oenology

œsophage [ezɔfaʒ] *m* esophagus

œstres [ɛstr] *mpl* botflies, nose flies

œuf [œf] *m* (*pl* œufs [ø]) egg; marcher sur des œufs to walk on thin ice; œuf à la coque soft-boiled egg; œuf à repriser darning egg; œuf de Colomb ingenious, though obvious, solution to a problem; œuf de Pâques or œuf rouge Easter egg; œuf dur hard-boiled egg; œuf mollet soft-boiled egg; œuf poché poached egg; œufs spawn, roe; œufs au lait custard; œufs au miroir fried eggs; œufs brouillés scrambled eggs; œuf sur le plat fried egg; plein comme un œuf chock-full; tondre un œuf to squeeze blood out of a turnip; tuer, écraser, or étouffer dans l'œuf to nip in the bud

œuvre [œvr] *m* works (*of a painter*); dans œuvre inside (*measurements*); hors d'œuvre out of alignment; le grand œuvre the philosopher's stone; le gros œuvre (archit) the foundation, walls, and roof ‖ *f* work; piece of work; bonnes œuvres good works; mettre en œuvre to implement, to use; mettre qn à l'œuvre to set s.o. to work; mettre tout en œuvre to leave no stone unturned; œuvres complètes collected works; œuvres mortes (naut) topsides; œuvre pie good deed, good work; œuvres vives (naut) hull below water line; se mettre à l'œuvre to get to work

offen·sant [ɔfɑ̃sɑ̃] -sante [sɑ̃t] *adj* offensive

offense [ɔfɑ̃s] *f* offense; faire offense à qn to offend s.o.; soit dit sans offense with all due respect

offenser [ɔfɑ̃se] *tr* to offend ‖ *ref* to be offended

offen·sif [ɔfɑ̃sif] -sive [siv] *adj* & *f* offensive

office [ɔfis] *m* office; (eccl) office, service; d'office ex officio; faire l'office de to act as; office d'ami friendly turn; remplir son office (fig) to do its job ‖ *f* pantry

offi·ciel -cielle [ɔfisjɛl] *adj* & *mf* official

officier [ɔfisje] *m* officer; (naut) mate; officier de service (mil) officer of the day; officier ministériel notary public; officier supérieur (mil) field officer ‖ *intr* to officiate

offi·cieux [ɔfisjø] -cieuse [sjøz] *adj* unofficial, off-the-cuff; zealous; well-meant (*lie*); faire l'officieux to be officious

offrant [ɔfrã] *m*—**le plus offrant** the highest bidder

offre [ɔfr] *f* offer; **l'offre et la demande** supply and demand; **offres d'emploi** (formula in want ads) help wanted

offrir [ɔfrir] §65 *tr* to offer ‖ *ref* to offer oneself; to offer itself, to occur

offset [ɔfsɛt] *m invar* offset

offusquer [ɔfyske] *tr* to obfuscate, obscure; to irritate, displease ‖ *ref*—**s'offusquer de** to take offense at

ogive [ɔʒiv] *f* ogive; (rok) nose cone

ogre [ɔgr] **ogresse** [ɔgrɛs] *mf* ogre; **manger comme un ogre** (coll) to eat like a horse

ohé [ɔe] *interj* hey!; **ohé du navire!** ship ahoy!

ohm [om] *m* ohm

oie [wa] *f* goose; simpleton; **oie blanche** simple little goose (*naïve girl*); **oie sauvage** wild goose

oignon [ɔɲɔ̃] *m* onion; (hort) bulb; (pathol) bunion; (coll) turnip, pocket watch; **aux petits oignons** (coll) perfect; **occupe-toi de tes oignons** (coll) mind your own business

oïl [ɔil], [ɔj] *adv* (Old French) yes

oindre [wɛ̃dr] §35 *tr* to anoint

oi·seau [wazo] *m* (*pl* -seaux) bird; hod (*of mason*); (coll) character; **être comme l'oiseau sur la branche** to be here today and gone tomorrow; **oiseau de paradis, oiseau des îles** bird of paradise; **oiseau des tempêtes** stormy petrel; **oiseaux domestiques, oiseaux de basse-cour** poultry

oiseau-mouche [wazomuʃ] *m* (*pl* -mouches) hummingbird

oiseler [wazle] §34 *tr* to train (*hawks*) ‖ *intr* to trap birds

oiselet [wazlɛ] *m* little bird

oiseleur [wazlœr] *m* fowler

oise·lier [wazəlje] -**lière** [ljɛr] *mf* bird fancier

oi·seux [wazø] -**seuse** [zøz] *adj* useless

oi·sif [wazif] -**sive** [ziv] *adj* idle ‖ *mf* idler

oisillon [wazijɔ̃] *m* fledgling

oisiveté [wazivte] *f* idleness

oison [wazɔ̃] *m* gosling; (coll) ninny

O.K. [oke] *interj* (letterword) O.K.!

oléagi·neux [ɔleaʒinø] -**neuse** [nøz] *adj* oily

olfac·tif [ɔlfaktif] -**tive** [tiv] *adj* olfactory

olibrius [ɔlibrijys] *m* pedant; pest; braggart (*in medieval plays*)

oligarchie [ɔligarʃi] *f* oligarchy

olivaie [ɔlivɛ] *f* olive grove

olivâtre [ɔlivɑtr] *adj* olive (*complexion*)

olive [ɔliv] *adj invar & f* olive

olivette [ɔlivɛt] *f* olive grove

olivier [ɔlivje] *m* olive tree; olive wood; **Olivier** Oliver

olympiade [ɔlɛ̃pjad] *f* olympiad

olym·pien [ɔlɛ̃pjɛ̃] -**pienne** [pjɛn] *adj* Olympian

olympique [ɔlɛ̃pik] *adj* Olympic

ombilic [ɔ̃bilik] *m* umbilicus

ombili·cal -**cale** [ɔ̃bilikal] *adj* (*pl* -**caux** [ko]) umbilical

ombrage [ɔ̃braʒ] *m* shade; **porter om-**

brage à to offend; **prendre ombrage (de)** to take offense (at)

ombrager [ɔ̃braʒe] §38 *tr* to shade

ombra·geux [ɔ̃braʒø] -**geuse** [ʒøz] *adj* shy, skittish; touchy; distrustful

ombre [ɔ̃br] *f* shadow; shade; **ombres (chinoises)** shadow play, shadowgraph; **une ombre au tableau** (coll) a fly in the ointment

ombrelle [ɔ̃brɛl] *f* parasol; (aer) umbrella

ombrer [ɔ̃bre] *tr* to shade; to apply eye shadow to

om·breux [ɔ̃brø] -**breuse** [brøz] *adj* shady

omelette [ɔmlɛt] *f* omelet

omettre [ɔmɛtr] §42 *tr* to omit

omission [ɔmisjɔ̃] *f* omission

omnibus [ɔmnibys] *adj* omnibus; local (*train*) ‖ *m* omnibus; local (train)

omnipo·tent [ɔmnipɔtɑ̃] -**tente** [tɑ̃t] *adj* omnipotent

omnis·cient [ɔmnisjɑ̃] **omnis·ciente** [ɔmnisjɑ̃t] *adj* omniscient

omnium [ɔmnjɔm] *m* (com) holding company, general trading company; (sports) open race

omnivore [ɔmnivɔr] *adj* omnivorous

omoplate [ɔmɔplat] *f* shoulder blade

on [ɔ̃] §87 *pron indef* one, they, people; (coll) we, e.g., **y va-t-on?** are we going there?; (coll) I, e.g., **on est fatigué** I am tired; (often translated by passive forms), e.g., **on sait que** it is generally known that

once [ɔ̃s] *f* ounce

oncle [ɔ̃kl] *m* uncle

onction [ɔ̃ksjɔ̃] *f* unction; eloquence

onc·tueux [ɔ̃ktɥø] -**tueuse** [tɥøz] *adj* unctuous; greasy; bland

onde [ɔ̃d] *f* wave; watering (*of silk*); (poetic) water; **les petites ondes** (rad) shortwave; **mettre en ondes** to put on the air; **onde de choc** (aer) shock wave; **onde porteuse** (rad) carrier wave; **ondes amorties** (rad) damped waves; **ondes entretenues** (rad) continuous waves; **ondes radiophoniques** airwaves; **onde sonore** sound wave

ondée [ɔ̃de] *f* shower

on-dit [ɔ̃di] *m invar* gossip, scuttlebutt

ondoyant [ɔ̃dwajɑ̃] **ondoyante** [ɔ̃dwajɑ̃t] *adj* undulating, wavy; wavering (*person*)

ondoyer [ɔ̃dwaje] §47 *tr* to baptize in an emergency ‖ *intr* to undulate, wave

ondulation [ɔ̃dylɑsjɔ̃] *f* undulation, waving; flowing (*e.g., of drapery*); wave (*of hair*); **à ondulations** rolling (*ground*); **ondulation permanente** permanent wave

ondu·lé -**lée** [ɔ̃dyle] *adj* wavy; corrugated

onduler [ɔ̃dyle] *tr* to wave (*hair*) ‖ *intr* to wave, to undulate

oné·reux [ɔnerø] -**reuse** [røz] *adj* onerous

ongle [ɔ̃gl] *m* nail, fingernail; **jusqu'au bout des ongles** to or at one's fingertips; **ongle des pieds** toenail

onglée [ɔ̃gle] *f* numbness in the fingertips

onglet [ɔ̃glɛ] *m* nail hole, groove (*in blade*); thimble; **à onglets** thumb-indexed; **monter sur onglet** (bb) to insert (*a page*)
onguent [ɔ̃gɑ̃] *m* ointment, salve
O.N.U. [ɔny] (acronym) or [ɔɛny] (letterword) (**Organisation des Nations Unies**) *f* UN
onyx [ɔniks] *m* onyx
onzain *[ɔ̃zɛ̃] m* eleven-line verse
onze *[ɔ̃z] adj & pron* eleven; the Eleventh, e.g., **Jean onze** John the Eleventh; **onze heures** eleven o'clock || *m* eleven; eleventh (*in dates*), e.g., **le onze mai** the eleventh of May
onzième *[ɔ̃zjɛm] adj, pron (masc, fem), & m* eleventh
opale [ɔpal] *f* opal
opaque [ɔpak] *adj* opaque
opéra [ɔpera] *m* opera; opera house; **grand opéra, opéra sérieux** grand opera; **opéra bouffe** comic opera, opéra bouffe
opéra-comique [ɔperakɔmik] *m* (*pl* opéras-comiques) light opera
opéra·teur [ɔperatœr] **-trice** [tris] *mf* operator || *m* cameraman
opération [ɔperasjɔ̃] *f* operation
opé·ré -rée [ɔpere] *mf* surgical patient
opérer [ɔpere] §10 *tr* to operate on; **opérer à chaud** to perform an emergency operation on (*s.o.*); **opérer qn de q.ch.** (med) to operate on s.o. for s.th. || *intr* to operate; to work || *ref* to occur, take place
opérette [ɔperet] *f* operetta, musical comedy
opia·cé -cée [ɔpjase] *adj* opiate
opiner [ɔpine] *intr* to opine; **opiner du bonnet** (coll) to be a yes man
opiniâtre [ɔpinjɑtr] *adj* stubborn
opiniâtreté [ɔpinjɑtrəte] *f* stubbornness
opinion [ɔpinjɔ̃] *f* opinion; public opinion; **avoir bonne opinion de** to think highly of; **avoir une piètre opinion de** to take a dim view of
opium [ɔpjɔm] *m* opium
oponce [ɔpɔ̃s] *m* prickly pear
opossum [ɔpɔsɔm] *m* opossum
oppor·tun [ɔpɔrtœ̃] **-tune** [tyn] *adj* opportune, timely, expedient
opportuniste [ɔpɔrtynist] *adj* opportunistic || *mf* opportunist
opportunité [ɔpɔrtynite] *f* opportuneness
oppo·sant [ɔpozɑ̃] **-sante** [zɑ̃t] *adj* opposing || *mf* opponent
oppo·sé -sée [ɔpoze] *adj & m* opposite, contrary; **à l'opposé de** contrary to
opposer [ɔpoze] *tr* to raise (*an objection*); **opposer q.ch. à** to set up s.th. against; to place s.th. opposite; to contrast s.th. with || *ref*—**s'opposer à** to oppose, object to
opposite [ɔpozit] *m*—**à l'opposite (de)** opposite
opposition [ɔpozisjɔ̃] *f* opposition; contrast
oppresser [ɔprese] *tr* to oppress; to impede (*respiration*); to weigh upon (*one's heart*)
oppresseur [ɔprescœr] *m* oppressor

oppres·sif [ɔpresif] **oppres·sive** [ɔpresiv] *adj* oppressive
oppression [ɔpresjɔ̃] *f* oppression; difficulty in breathing
opprimer [ɔprime] *tr* to oppress
opprobre [ɔprɔbr] *m* opprobrium, shame
opter [ɔpte] *intr* to opt, to choose
opticien [ɔptisjɛ̃] *m* optician
optimisme [ɔptimism] *m* optimism
optimiste [ɔptimist] *adj* optimistic || *mf* optimist
option [ɔpsjɔ̃] *f* option
optique [ɔptik] *adj* optic(al) || *f* optics; perspective; **sous cette optique** from that point of view
opu·lent [ɔpylɑ̃] **-lente** [lɑ̃t] *adj* opulent
opuscule [ɔpyskyl] *m* opuscule, treatise; brochure, pamphlet
or [ɔr] *m* gold; **rouler sur l'or** to be rolling in money || *adv* now; therefore
oracle [ɔrakl] *m* oracle
orage [ɔraʒ] *m* storm
ora·geux [ɔraʒø] **-geuse** [ʒøz] *adj* stormy
oraison [ɔrɛzɔ̃] *f* prayer; **oraison dominicale** Lord's Prayer; **oraison funèbre** funeral oration; **prononcer l'oraison funèbre de** (coll) to write off (*a custom, institution, etc.*)
o·ral -rale [ɔral] *adj* (*pl* -raux [ro]) oral
orange [ɔrɑ̃ʒ] *adj invar* orange (*color*) || *m* orange (*color*) || *f* orange (*fruit*)
oran·gé -gée [ɔrɑ̃ʒe] *adj & m* orange (*color*)
orangeade [ɔrɑ̃ʒad] *f* orangeade
oranger [ɔrɑ̃ʒe] *m* orange tree
orangeraie [ɔrɑ̃ʒrɛ] *f* orange grove
orangerie [ɔrɑ̃ʒri] *f* orangery; orange grove
orang-outan [ɔrɑ̃utɑ̃] *m* (*pl* orangs-outans) orang-outang
ora·teur [ɔratœr] **-trice** [tris] *mf* orator; speaker
oratoire [ɔratwar] *adj* oratorical || *m* (eccl) oratory
oratorio [ɔratɔrjo] *m* oratorio
orbite [ɔrbit] *f* orbit; socket (*of eye*); **placer sur son orbite, mettre en orbite** to orbit; **sur orbite** in orbit
orchestre [ɔrkɛstr] *m* orchestra; band; **orchestre de typique** rumba band
orchestrer [ɔrkɛstre] *tr* to orchestrate
orchidée [ɔrkide] *f* orchid
ordalie [ɔrdali] *f* (hist) ordeal
ordinaire [ɔrdinɛr] *adj* ordinary || *m* ordinary; regular bill of fare; (mil) mess; **d'ordinaire, à l'ordinaire** ordinarily
ordi·nal -nale [ɔrdinal] *adj & m* (*pl* -naux [no]) ordinal
ordinateur [ɔrdinatœr] *m* (electron) computer
ordination [ɔrdinasjɔ̃] *f* ordination
ordonnance [ɔrdɔnɑ̃s] *f* ordinance; order, arrangement; (pharm) prescription
ordonna·teur [ɔrdɔnatœr] **-trice** [tris]

mf organizer; marshal; **ordonnateur des pompes funèbres** funeral director
ordon·né -née [ɔrdɔne] *adj* orderly
ordonner [ɔrdɔne] *tr* to arrange, put in order; to order; to prescribe (*e.g., medicine*); (eccl) to ordain; **ordonner à qn de + inf** to order s.o. to + *inf*; **ordonner q.ch. à qn** to order s.o. to do s.th.
ordre [ɔrdr] *m* order; **avoir de l'ordre** to be neat, orderly; **à vos ordres** at your service; **dans l'ordre d'entrée en scène** (theat) in order of appearance; **en ordre** in order; **jusqu'à nouvel ordre** until further notice; as things stand; **les ordres** (eccl) orders; **ordre du jour** (mil) order of the day; (parl) agenda; **ordre public** law and order; **payez à l'ordre de** (com) pay to the order of; **sous les ordres de** under the command of
ordure [ɔrdyr] *f* rubbish, filth; **ordures ménagères** garbage
ordu·rier [ɔrdyrje] **-rière** [rjɛr] *adj* lewd, filthy
orée [ɔre] *f* edge (*of a forest*)
oreille [ɔrɛj] *f* ear; **avoir l'oreille basse** to be humiliated; **dormir sur les deux oreilles** to sleep soundly; **dresser** or **tendre l'oreille** to prick up one's ears; **échauffer les oreilles à qn** to rile s.o. up; **faire la sourde oreille** to turn a deaf ear; **rompre les oreilles à qn** (coll) to talk s.o.'s head off; **se faire tirer l'oreille** (coll) to play hard to get
oreiller [ɔreje] *m* pillow
oreillette [ɔrɛjɛt] *f* earflap (*of cap*); (anat) auricle
oreillons [ɔrɛjɔ̃] *mpl* mumps
ores [ɔr] *adv*—**d'ores et déjà** [dɔrzedeʒa] from now on
Orfée [ɔrfe] *m* Orpheus
orfèvre [ɔrfɛvr] *m* goldsmith; silversmith; **être orfèvre en la matière** (coll) to know one's onions
orfèvrerie [ɔrfɛvrəri] *f* goldsmith's shop; goldsmith's trade; gold plate; gold or silver jewelry
orfraie [ɔrfrɛ] *f* osprey, fish hawk
organdi [ɔrgɑ̃di] *m* organdy
organe [ɔrgan] *m* organ; part (*of a machine*)
organique [ɔrganik] *adj* organic
organisa·teur [ɔrganizatœr] **-trice** [tris] *adj* organizing ‖ *mf* organizer
organisation [ɔrganizɑsjɔ̃] *f* organization
organiser [ɔrganize] *tr* to organize
organisme [ɔrganism] *m* organism; organization
organiste [ɔrganist] *mf* organist
orgasme [ɔrgasm] *m* orgasm
orge [ɔrʒ] *f* barley
orgelet [ɔrʒəlɛ] *m* (pathol) sty
orgie [ɔrʒi] *f* orgy
orgue [ɔrg] *m* organ; **orgue de Barbarie** hand organ; **orgue de cinéma** theater organ ‖ *f*—**les grandes orgues** the pipe organ
orgueil [ɔrgœj] *m* pride, conceit; **avoir l'orgueil de** to take pride in

orgueil·leux [ɔrgœjø] **orgueil·leuse** [ɔrgœjøz] *adj* proud, haughty
orient [ɔrjɑ̃] *m* orient; east; **Orient** Orient, East
orien·tal -tale [ɔrjɑ̃tal] (*pl* **-taux** [to]) *adj* oriental; eastern, east ‖ (*cap*) *mf* Oriental (*person*)
orientation [ɔrjɑ̃tɑsjɔ̃] *f* orientation; **orientation professionnelle** vocational guidance
orienter [ɔrjɑ̃te] *tr* to orient; to guide ‖ *ref* to take one's bearings
orien·teur [ɔrjɑ̃tœr] **-teuse** [tøz] *mf* guidance counselor
orifice [ɔrifis] *m* orifice, hole, opening
origan [ɔrigɑ̃] *m* marjoram
originaire [ɔriʒinɛr] *adj* native; original, first
origi·nal -nale [ɔriʒinal] *adj* (*pl* **-naux** [no]) original; eccentric, peculiar ‖ *m* antique (*piece of furniture*); eccentric, card (*person*); (typ) copy, original
originalité [ɔriʒinalite] *f* originality; eccentricity
origine [ɔriʒin] *f* origin
origi·nel -nelle [ɔriʒinɛl] *adj* original (*sin; meaning*); primitive, early
ori·gnal [ɔriɲal] *m* (*pl* **-gnaux** [ɲo]) moose, elk
orillon [ɔrijɔ̃] *m* ear, handle; (archit) projection
ori·peau [ɔripo] *m* (*pl* **-peaux**) tinsel; **oripeaux** cheap finery
Orléans [ɔrleɑ̃] *f* Orléans; **la Nouvelle Orléans** New Orleans
orme [ɔrm] *m* elm; **attendez-moi sous l'orme** (coll) I won't be there
or·né -née [ɔrne] *adj* ornate
ornement [ɔrnəmɑ̃] *m* ornament
ornemen·tal -tale [ɔrnəmɑ̃tal] *adj* (*pl* **-taux** [to]) ornamental
orner [ɔrne] *tr* to ornament, to adorn
ornière [ɔrnjɛr] *f* rut, groove
ornithologie [ɔrnitɔlɔʒi] *f* ornithology
orphe·lin [ɔrfəlɛ̃] **-line** [lin] *adj & mf* orphan
orphelinat [ɔrfəlina] *m* orphanage (*asylum*)
orphéon [ɔrfeɔ̃] *m* male choir, glee club; brass band
orteil [ɔrtɛj] *m* toe; big toe; **gros orteil** big toe
O.R.T.F. [ɔɛrteɛf] *m* (letterword) (**office de radio-télévision française**) French radio and television system
orthodoxe [ɔrtɔdɔks] *adj* orthodox
orthographe [ɔrtɔgraf] *f* spelling, orthography
orthographier [ɔrtɔgrafje] *tr* to spell
ortie [ɔrti] *f* nettle
orviétan [ɔrvjetɑ̃] *m* nostrum
os [ɔs] *m* (*pl* **os** [o]) bone; **à gros os** big-boned; **os à moelle** marrowbone; **trempé jusqu'aux os** soaked to the skin
osciller [ɔsile] *intr* to oscillate; to waver, hesitate
o·sé -sée [oze] *adj* daring, bold; risqué, off-color
oseille [ozɛj] *f* sorrel; (slang) dough
oser [oze] *tr & intr* to dare
osier [ozje] *m* osier; **d'osier** wicker

osmose [ɔsmoz] *f* osmosis
ossature [ɔsatyr] *f* bone structure; framework, skeleton
ossements [ɔsmɑ̃] *mpl* bones, remains
os•seux [ɔsǿ] **os•seuse** [ɔsǿz] *adj* bony
ossifier [ɔsifje] *tr & ref* to ossify
os•su -sue [ɔsy] *adj* bony; big-boned
ostensible [ɔstɑ̃sibl] *adj* conspicuous, ostensible; ostentatious
ostensoir [ɔstɑ̃swar] *m* monstrance
ostentatoire [ɔstɑ̃tatwar] *adj* ostentatious
ostracisme [ɔstrasism] *m* ostracism
otage [ɔtaʒ] *m* hostage
otalgie [ɔtalʒi] *f* earache
O.T.A.N. or **OTAN** [ɔtan], [otan], [otɑ̃] *f* (acronym) (**Organisation du traité de l'Atlantique Nord**)— **l'O.T.A.N.** NATO
otarie [ɔtari] *f* sea lion
OTASE [ɔtaz] *f* (acronym) (**Organisation du traité de l'Asie du Sud-Est**) —**l'OTASE** SEATO
ôter [ote] *tr* to remove, to take away; to take off; to tip (*one's hat*); **ôter q.ch. à qn** to remove or take away s.th. from s.o.; **ôter q.ch. de q.ch.** to take s.th. away from s.th. || *ref* to withdraw, to get out of the way
otto•man [ɔtɔmɑ̃] **-mane** [man] *adj* Ottoman || *m* ottoman (*corded fabric*) || *f* ottoman (*divan*) || (*cap*) *mf* Ottoman (*person*)
ou [u] *conj* or; **ou . . . ou** either . . . or
où [u] *adv* where; **d'où** from where, whence; **où que** wherever; **par où** which way || *conj* where; when; **d'où** from where, whence; **par où** through which; **partout où** wherever
ouailles [waj] *fpl* (eccl) flock
ouais [wɛ] *interj* (coll) oh yeah!
ouate *[wat] *f* cotton batting, wadding
ouater *[wate] *tr* to pad, to wad
oubli [ubli] *m* forgetfulness; omission, oversight; **tomber dans l'oubli** to fall into oblivion
oublier [ublije] *tr & intr* to forget || *ref* to forget oneself; to be forgotten
oubliettes [ublijɛt] *fpl* dungeon of oblivion
ou•blieux [ublijǿ] **-blieuse** [blijǿz] *adj* forgetful, oblivious, unmindful
ouche [uʃ] *f* orchard; vegetable garden
ouest [wɛst] *adj invar & m* west
ouest-alle•mand [wɛstalmɑ̃] **-mande** [mɑ̃d] *adj* West German || (*cap*) *mf* West German
ouf *[uf] *interj* whew!
oui *[wi] *m invar* yes; **les oui l'emportent** the ayes have it || *adv* yes; **je crois que oui** I think so; **oui madame** yes ma'am; **oui monsieur** yes sir; **oui mon capitaine (mon général, etc.)** yes sir
ouï-dire [widir] *m invar* hearsay; **simples ouï-dire** (law) hearsay evidence
ouïe [wi] *f* hearing; **être tout ouïe** [tutwi] to be all ears; **ouïes** gills; sound holes (*of violin*) || *interj* oh my!
ouïr [wir] (used only in: *inf*, compound tenses with *pp* **ouï**, and 2d *pl impv*

oyez) *tr* to hear; **oyez . . . !** hear ye . . . !
ouragan [uragɑ̃] *m* hurricane
ourdir [urdir] *tr* to warp (*cloth before weaving*); to hatch (*e.g., a plot*)
ourler [urle] *tr* to hem; **ourler à jour** to hemstitch
ourlet [urlɛ] *m* hem; **ourlet de la jupe** hemline
ours [urs] *m* bear; (fig) lone wolf; **ours en peluche** teddy bear; **ours mal léché** unmannerly boor; **ours marin** (zool) seal; **vendre la peau de l'ours avant de l'avoir tué** to count one's chickens before they are hatched
ourse [urs] *f* she-bear; **la Grande Ourse** the Big Dipper, the Great Bear; **la Petite Ourse** the Little Dipper, the Little Bear
oursin [ursɛ̃] *m* sea urchin
ourson [ursɔ̃] *m* bear cub
ouste [ust] *interj* (coll) out!, out you go!
outarde [utard] *f* (orn) bustard
outil [uti] *m* tool, implement
outillage [utijaʒ] *m* tools; equipment
outil•lé -lée [utije] *adj* equipped with tools; tooled-up (*factory*)
outiller [utije] *tr* to equip with tools; to tool up (*a factory*) || *ref* to supply oneself with equipment; to tool up
outilleur [utijœr] *m* toolmaker
outrage [utraʒ] *m* outrage, affront; ravages (*of time*); contempt of court; **faire outrage à qn** to outrage s.o.; **outrage aux bonnes mœurs** traffic in pornography; **outrage public à la pudeur** indecent exposure
outrager [utraʒe] §38 *tr* to outrage, to affront
outra•geux [utraʒǿ] **-geuse** [ʒǿz] *adj* outrageous, insulting
outrance [utrɑ̃s] *f* excess; exaggeration; **à outrance** to the limit
outran•cier [utrɑ̃sje] **-cière** [sjɛr] *adj* extreme, excessive, out-and-out || *mf* extremist, out-and-outer
outre [utr] *f* goatskin canteen || *adv* further; **d'outre en d'outre** right through; **en outre** besides, moreover; **passer outre à** to ignore (*e.g., an order*) || *prep* in addition to, apart from; beyond
ou•tré -trée [utre] *adj* overdone, exaggerated; exasperated
outrecui•dant [utrəkɥidɑ̃] **-dante** [dɑ̃t] *adj* self-satisfied; insolent, presumptuous
outre-Manche [utrəmɑ̃ʃ] *adv* across the Channel
outremer [utrəmɛr] *m* ultramarine, lapis lazuli (*color*)
outre-mer [utrəmɛr] *adv* overseas
outre-monts [utrəmɔ̃] *adv* over the mountains (*i.e., the Alps*)
outrepasser [utrəpase] *tr* to go beyond, to exceed
outrer [utre] *tr* to overdo, to exaggerate; to exasperate
outre-tombe [utrətɔ̃b] *adv*—**d'outre-tombe** posthumous
ou•vert [uvɛr] **-verte** [vɛrt] *adj* open;

exposed; frank, candid; on (said of
meter, gas, etc.)
ouverture [uvɛrtyr] *f* opening; hole,
gap; (mus) overture; (phot) aperture
ouvrable [uvrabl] *adj* working, e.g.,
jour ouvrable working day
ouvrage [uvraʒ] *m* work, handiwork;
piece of work; work, treatise
ouvrager [uvraʒe] §38 *tr* to work (e.g.,
iron); to turn (wood)
ou·vré -vrée [uvre] *adj* worked,
wrought; finished (product)
ouvre-boîtes [uvrəbwat] *m invar* can
opener
ouvre-bouteilles [uvrəbutɛj] *m invar*
bottle opener
ouvreur [uvrœr] *m* opener (in poker)
ouvreuse [uvrøz] *f* usher
ou·vrier [uvrije] **-vrière** [vrijɛr] *adj*
working, worker; worker's, working-
man's || *mf* worker || *m* workman,
laborer; workingman || *f* working-
woman

ouvrir [uvrir] §65 *tr* to open; to turn
on (the light; the radio or television;
the gas); **ouvrir boutique** to set up
shop || *intr* to be open; to open (said
of store, school, etc.; said of card
player) || *ref* to open; to be opened;
s'ouvrir à to open up to, confide in
ouvroir [uvrwar] *m* workroom
ovaire [ɔvɛr] *m* ovary
ovale [ɔval] *adj* & *m* oval
ovation [ɔvasjɔ̃] *f* ovation
ovationner [ɔvasjɔne] *tr* to give an ovation to
Ovide [ɔvid] *m* Ovid
oxford [ɔksfɔr] *m* oxford cloth
oxyde [ɔksid] *m* oxide
oxyder [ɔkside] *tr* & *ref* to oxidize
oxygène [ɔksiʒɛn] *m* oxygen
oxygéner [ɔksiʒene] §10 *tr* to oxygen-
ate; to bleach (hair) || *ref*—**s'oxygé-
ner les poumons** (coll) to fill one's
lungs full of ozone
oxyton [ɔksitɔ̃] *adj* & *m* oxytone
ozone [ozɔn] *m* ozone

P

P, p [pe] *m invar* sixteenth letter of
the French alphabet
pacage [pakaʒ] *m* pasture
pacifica·teur [pasifikatœr] **-trice** [tris]
mf pacifier
pacifier [pasifje] *tr* to pacify
pacifique [pasifik] *adj* pacific || **Paci-
fique** *adj* & *m* Pacific
pacifisme [pasifism] *m* pacifism
pacifiste [pasifist] *mf* pacifist
pacotille [pakɔtij] *f* junk; **de pacotille**
shoddy; junky
pacte [pakt] *m* pact, covenant
pactiser [paktize] *intr* to compromise;
to traffic (with the enemy)
paf [paf] *adj* (slang) tipsy, tight ||
interj bang!
pagaie [pagɛ] *f* paddle
pagaïe or **pagaille** [pagaj] *f* disorder;
en pagaïe (coll) in great quantity;
(coll) in a mess
paganisme [paganism] *m* paganism
pagayer [pageje] §49 *tr* & *intr* to paddle
page [paʒ] *m* page || *f* page (of a
book); **être à la page** to be up to date
paginer [paʒine] *tr* to page
pagne [paɲ] *m* loincloth
paie [pɛ] *f* pay, wages
paiement [pemɑ̃] *m* payment
païen [pajɛ̃] **païenne** [pajɛn] *adj* & *mf*
pagan
pail·lard [pajar] **pail·larde** [pajard]
adj ribald || *mf* debauchee
paillasse [pajas] *m* buffoon || *f* straw
mattress; (slang) whore
paillasson [pajasɔ̃] *m* doormat
paille [paj] *f* straw; flaw; (Bib) mote;
paille de fer iron shavings
pail·lé -lée [paje] *adj* rush-bottomed
(chair)

pailler [paje] *m* straw stack || *tr* to
bottom (a chair) with straw; to
mulch
pailleter [pajte] §34 *tr* to spangle
paillette [pajɛt] *f* spangle; flake (of
mica; of soap); grain (of gold); flaw
(in a diamond)
pain [pɛ̃] *m* bread; loaf (of bread, of
sugar); cake (of soap); pat (of butter); **avoir du pain sur la planche**
(coll) to have a lot to do; **pain à
cacheter** sealing wafer; **pain aux
raisins** raisin roll; **pain bis** brown
bread; **pain complet** whole-wheat
bread; **pain de fantaisie** bread sold
by the loaf (instead of by weight);
pain de mie sandwich bread; **pain
d'épice** gingerbread; **pain grillé** toast;
pain perdu French toast; **petit pain**
roll; **se vendre comme des petits
pains** (coll) to sell like hot cakes
pair paire [pɛr] *adj* even (number) ||
m peer; equal; (com) par; **hors de
pair,** **hors pair** unrivaled; **marcher
de pair avec** to keep abreast of; **travailler au pair** (coll) to work for
one's keep; **au pair** at par || *f* pair;
couple; brace (of dogs, pistols, etc.);
yoke (of oxen)
pairesse [pɛrɛs] *f* peeress
pairie [peri], [peri] *f* peerage
paisible [pezibl] *adj* peaceful
paître [pɛtr] §48 *tr* & *intr* to graze;
envoyer paître (coll) to send packing
paix [pe] *f* peace
Pakistan [pakistɑ̃] *m*—**le Pakistan**
Pakistan
pakista·nais [pakistanɛ] **-naise** [nɛz]
adj Pakistani || (cap) *mf* Pakistani

pal [pal] *m* (*pl* **paux** [po] or **pals**) pale, stake
palabre [palabr] *m & f* palaver
palace [palas] *m* luxury hotel
palais [palɛ] *m* palace; palate; courthouse, law courts
palan [palɑ̃] *m* block and tackle
palanque [palɑ̃k] *f* stockade
pala·tal -**tale** [palatal] (*pl* -**taux** [to] -**tales**) *adj & f* palatal
pale [pal] *f* blade (*of, e.g., oar*); stake; sluice gate; (eccl) pall
pâle [pɑl] *adj* pale
palefrenier [palfrənje] *m* groom; (coll) hick, oaf
palefroi [palfrwa] *m* palfrey
paleron [palrɔ̃] *m* bottom chuck roast
palet [palɛ] *m* disk, flat stone; puck
paletot [palto] *m* topcoat
palette [palɛt] *f* palette; paddle
pâleur [pɑlœr] *f* pallor; paleness
palier [palje] *m* landing (*of stairs*); plateau (*of curve of a graph*); (mach) bearing; **en palier** on the level; **palier à billes** ball bearing; **par paliers** graduated (*e.g., tax*)
pâlir [pɑlir] *tr & intr* to pale, turn pale
palis [pali] *m* picket fence
palissade [palisad] *f* palisade; fence
palissandre [palisɑ̃dr] *m* rosewood
pallier [palje] *tr* to palliate; to mitigate || *intr* (with *dat*) to mitigate
palmarès [palmarɛs] *m* list of winners
palme [palm] *f* (bot) palm
palmeraie [palmərɛ] *f* palm grove
palmier [palmje] *m* palm tree
palmipède [palmipɛd] *adj* webfooted || *m* webfoot
palombe [palɔ̃b] *f* ringdove
palourde [palurd] *f* clam
palpable [palpabl] *adj* palpable; plain, obvious
palper [palpe] *tr* to feel; to palpate; (coll) to pocket (*money*)
palpiter [palpite] *intr* to palpitate
palsambleu [palsɑ̃blø] *interj* zounds!
paltoquet [paltɔkɛ] *m* nonentity
palu·déen [palydeɛ̃] -**déenne** [deɛn] *adj* marsh (*plant*); swamp (*fever*)
paludisme [palydism] *m* malaria
pâmer [pame] *ref* to swoon
pâmoison [pamwazɔ̃] *f* swoon
pamphlet [pɑ̃flɛ] *m* lampoon
pamplemousse [pɑ̃pləmus] *m & f* grapefruit
pan [pɑ̃] *m* tail (*of shirt or coat*); section; side, face; patch (*of sky*); **Pan** Pan || *interj* bang!
panacée [panase] *f* panacea
panachage [panaʃaʒ] *m* mixing; **faire du panachage** to split one's vote
panache [panaʃ] *m* plume; wreath (*of smoke*); **aimer le panache** to be fond of show; **avoir son panache** (coll) to be tipsy; **faire panache** to somersault, to turn over
pana·ché -**chée** [panaʃe] *adj* variegated; mixed (*salad*); motley (*crowd*)
panacher [panaʃe] *tr* to variegate; to plume; to split (*one's vote*) || *ref* to become variegated
panais [panɛ] *m* parsnip
panama [panama] *m* panama hat; **le**

Panama Panama; **Panama** Panama City
panaris [panari] *m* (pathol) whitlow, felon
pancarte [pɑ̃kart] *f* placard; poster, sign
panchromatique [pɑ̃krɔmatik] *adj* panchromatic
pancréas [pɑ̃kreɑs] *m* pancreas
pandémonium [pɑ̃demɔnjɔm] *m* den of iniquity; pandemonium
pa·né -**née** [pane] *adj* breaded
panetière [pantjɛr] *f* breadbox
panier [panje] *m* basket; hoop (*of skirt*); creel (*trap*); **être dans le même panier** to be in the same boat; **panier à ouvrage** work basket; **panier à papier** wastepaper basket; **panier à provisions** shopping basket; **panier à salade** wire salad washer; (coll) paddy wagon; **panier percé** spendthrift
panier-repas [panjerəpa] *m* (*pl* **paniers-repas**) box lunch
panique [panik] *adj & f* panic
panne [pan] *f* breakdown, trouble; plush; fat (*of pig*); peen (*of hammer*); tip (*of soldering iron*); bank (*of clouds*); purlin (*of roof*); daub; (theat) small part; (en) **panne sèche** (public sign) out of gas; **être dans la panne** (coll) to be hard up; **être en panne** (coll) to be unable to continue; **être en panne de** (coll) to be deprived of; **laisser en panne** to leave in the lurch; **mettre en panne** (naut) to heave to; **panne fendue** claw (*of hammer*); **rester en panne** to come to a standstill; **tomber en panne** to have a breakdown
pan·né -**née** [pane] *adj* (slang) hard up
pan·neau [pano] *m* (*pl* -**neaux**) panel; snare, net; (naut) to batten down the hatches; **donner dans le panneau** to walk into the trap; **panneau d'affichage** billboard; **panneau de tête** headboard (*of bed*); **panneaux** paneling; **panneaux de signalisation** traffic signs; **tomber** or **donner dans le panneau** to be taken in, to fall into a trap
panoplie [panɔpli] *f* panoply
panorama [panɔrama] *m* panorama
panoramiquer [panɔramike] *intr* (mov, telv) to pan
panse [pɑ̃s] *f* belly; rumen, first stomach
pansement [pɑ̃smɑ̃] *m* (surg) dressing
panser [pɑ̃se] *tr* to dress, bandage; to groom (*an animal*)
pan·su -**sue** [pɑ̃sy] *adj* potbellied
pantalon [pɑ̃talɔ̃] *m* trousers, pair of trousers; panties; slacks; **pantalon à pattes d'éléphant** bell-bottomed trousers; **pantalon corsaire** pedal pushers; **pantalon de coutil** ducks; blue jeans; **pantalon de golf** knickers; **pantalon de ski** ski pants
pante [pɑ̃t] *m* (slang) guy
panteler [pɑ̃tle] §34 *intr* to pant
panthéisme [pɑ̃teism] *m* pantheism
panthéon [pɑ̃teɔ̃] *m* pantheon
panthère [pɑ̃tɛr] *f* panther

pantin [pɑ̃tɛ̃] *m* puppet; jumping jack; **pantin articulé** string puppet
pantomime [pɑ̃tɔmim] *f* pantomime
pantou·flard [pɑ̃tuflar] -**flarde** [flard] *mf* (coll) homebody
pantoufle [pɑ̃tufl] *f* slipper
pantoufler [pɑ̃tufle] *intr* to leave government service
paon [pɑ̃] *m* peacock, peafowl; peacock butterfly
paonne [pan] *f* peahen
papa [papa] *m* papa; **à la papa** (coll) cautiously; **de papa** (coll) outmoded; **papa gâteau** (coll) sugar daddy
papas [papɑs] *m* pope (*in Orthodox Church*)
papauté [papote] *f* papacy
pape [pap] *m* pope
pape·lard [paplar] -**larde** [lard] *adj* hypocritical ‖ *mf* hypocrite ‖ *m* scrap of paper
paperasse [papras] *f* old paper
paperasserie [paprasri] *f* red tape
paperas·sier [paprasje] **paperas·sière** [paprasjɛr] *adj* fond of red tape ‖ *mf* bureaucrat
papeterie [paptri] *f* paper mill; stationery store
pape·tier [paptje] -**tière** [tjɛr] *mf* stationer
papier [papje] *m* paper; newspaper article; document; piece of paper; **être dans les petits papiers de** (coll) to be in the good graces of; **gratter du papier** to scribble; **papier à calquer**, **papier végétal** tracing paper; **papier à en-tête** letterhead; **papier à lettres** writing paper; **papier à machine** typewriter paper; **papier à musique** staff paper; **papier bible**, **indien**, or **pelure** Bible paper, onionskin; **papier buvard** blotting paper; **papier carbone** carbon paper; **papier collant** Scotch tape; **papier d'emballage** wrapping paper; **papier de soie** tissue paper; **papier d'étain** tin foil; **papier de verre** sandpaper; **papier hygiénique** toilet paper; **papier journal** newsprint; **papier kraft** cardboard (*for packing*); **papier mâché** papier-maché; **papier ministre** foolscap; **papier paraffiné** wax paper; **papier peint** wallpaper; **papier rayé** lined paper; **papier sensible** photographic paper; **papier tue-mouches** flypaper; **rayez cela de vos papiers!** (coll) don't count on it!
papier-filtre [papjefiltrə] *m* filter paper
papier-monnaie [papjemɔnɛ] *m* paper money
papier-pierre [papjepjɛr] *m* (*pl* **papiers-pierre**) papier-mâché
papille [papij], [papil] *f* papilla; **papille gustative** taste bud
papillon [papijɔ̃] *m* butterfly; flier; handbill; inset; form, application; thumbscrew, wing nut; butterfly valve; rider (*to document*); (coll) parking ticket; **papillon de nuit** moth; **papillons noirs** gloomy thoughts
papillonner [papijɔne] *intr* to flit about

papillote [papijɔt] *f* curlpaper; (culin) paper wrapper
papilloter [papijɔte] *intr* to blink; to flicker
papoter [papɔte] *intr* to chitchat
paprika [paprika] *m* paprika
papyrus [papirys] *m* papyrus
pâque [pɑk] *f* Passover; **la pâque russe** Russian Easter; **Pâque** Passover
paquebot [pakbo] *m* liner
pâquerette [pɑkrɛt] *f* white daisy
Pâques [pɑk] *m* Easter ‖ *fpl* Easter; **faire ses pâques** or **Pâques** to take Easter Communion; **Pâques fleuries** Palm Sunday
paquet [pakɛ] *m* packet, bundle; package; parcel; pack (*of cigarettes*); dressing down; **être un paquet d'os** [dɔs] to be nothing but skin and bones; **faire son paquet** (coll) to pack up; **mettre le paquet** (coll) to shoot the works; **paquet de mer** heavy sea; **petit paquet** parcel (*under a kilogram*); **petits paquets** parcel post; **un paquet de** a lot of
par [par] *prep* by; through; out of, e.g., **par la fenêtre** out of the window; per, a, e.g., **huit dollars par jour** eight dollars per day, eight dollars a day; on, e.g., **par une belle matinée** on a beautiful morning; in, e.g., **par temps de brume** in foggy weather; **de par la loi** in the name of the law; **par avion** (formula on envelope) air mail; **par delà** beyond; **par derrière** at the back, the back way; **par devant** in front, before; **par exemple** for example; **par ici** this way; **par là** that way; **par où?** which way?
para [para] *m* (coll) paratrooper
parabole [parabɔl] *f* parable; (*curve*) parabola
parachever [paraʃve] §2 *tr* to finish off
parachutage [paraʃytaʒ] *m* airdrop, airdropping
parachute [paraʃyt] *m* parachute
parachuter [paraʃyte] *tr* to airdrop; (coll) to appoint in haste
parachutisme [paraʃytism] *m* parachuting; (sports) skydiving
parachutiste [paraʃytist] *mf* parachutist; (sports) skydiver ‖ *m* paratrooper
parade [parad] *f* show; parry; sudden stop (*of horse*); come-on (*in front of sideshow*); (mil) inspection, parade; **à la parade** on parade; **faire parade de** to show off, to display
parader [parade] *intr* to show off
paradis [paradi] *m* paradise; (theat) peanut gallery
paradoxal paradoxale [paradɔksal] *adj* (*pl* **paradoxaux** [paradɔkso]) paradoxical
paradoxe [paradɔks] *m* paradox
parafe [paraf] *m* flourish; initials
parafer [parafe] *tr* to initial
paraffine [parafin] *f* paraffin
paraffiner [parafine] *tr* to paraffin
parages [paraʒ] *mpl* region, vicinity; **dans ces parages** in these parts
paragraphe [paragraf] *m* paragraph

Paraguay [parage] *m*—le Paraguay Paraguay
paraguayen [paragejē] paraguayenne [paragejen] *adj* Paraguayan ‖ (*cap*) *mf* Paraguayan
paraître [paretr] §12 *intr* to appear; to seem; to come out; to show off; à ce qu'il paraît from all appearances; faire paraître to publish; vient de paraître just out
parallèle [paralɛl] *adj* parallel ‖ *m* parallel, comparison; (geog) parallel ‖ *f* (geom) parallel
paralyser [paralize] *tr* to paralyze
paralysie [paralizi] *f* paralysis
paralytique [paralitik] *adj* & *mf* paralytic
parangon [parɑ̃gɔ̃] *m* paragon
paranoïaque [paranɔjak] *adj* & *mf* paranoiac
parapet [parapɛ] *m* railing, parapet; (mil) parapet
paraphe [paraf] *m* flourish; initials
parapher [parafe] *tr* to initial
paraphrase [parafrɑz] *f* circumlocution, paraphrase; commentary
paraphraser [parafrɑze] *tr* to paraphrase
parapluie [paraplɥi] *m* umbrella
parasite [parazit] *adj* parasitic(al) ‖ *m* parasite; parasites (rad) static
parasiter [parazite] *tr* to live as a parasite on or in (*a host*); (fig) to sponge on
parasol [parasɔl] *m* parasol; beach umbrella
paratonnerre [paratɔner] *m* lightning rod
parâtre [parɑtr] *m* stepfather; cruel father
paravent [paravɑ̃] *m* folding screen
parbleu [parblø] *interj* rather!, by Jove!, you bet!
parc [park] *m* park; sheepfold; corral, pen; playpen; grounds, property; (mil) supply depot; (rr) rolling stock; parc à huîtres oyster bed; parc automobile motor pool; parc de stationnement (payant) parking lot
parcage [parkaʒ] *m* parking
parcelle [parsɛl] *f* particle; plot
parce que [pars(ə)kə] *conj* because
parchemin [parʃəmē] *m* parchment; (coll) sheepskin (*diploma*)
parchemi·né -née [parʃəmine] *adj* wrinkled
parcheminer [parʃəmine] *tr* to parchmentize ‖ *ref* to shrivel up
par-ci [parsi] *adv*—par-ci par-là here and there
parcimo·nieux [parsimɔnjø] -nieuse [njøz] *adj* parsimonious
parcomètre [parkɔmetr] *m* parking meter
parcourir [parkurir] §14 *tr* to travel through, to tour; to wander about; to cover (*a distance*); to scour (*the country*); to glance through
parcours [parkur] *m* run, trip; route, distance covered; round (*e.g., of golf*); stroke (*of piston*)
par-delà [pardəla] *adv* & *prep* beyond

par-derrière [parderjer] *adv* & *prep* behind
par-dessous [pardəsu] *adv* & *prep* underneath
pardessus [pardəsy] *m* overcoat
par-dessus [pardəsy] *adv* on top, over ‖ *prep* on top of, over
par-devant [pardəvɑ̃] *adv* in front ‖ *prep* in front of, before
par-devers [pardəver] *prep* in the presence of; par-devers soi in one's own possession
pardi [pardi] *interj* (coll) of course!
pardon [pardɔ̃] *m* pardon; Breton pilgrimage ‖ *adv* (to contradict a negative statement or question) yes, e.g., Vous ne parlez pas français, n'est-ce pas? Pardon, je le parle très bien You don't speak French, do you? Yes, I speak it very well ‖ *interj* pardon me!; (slang) oh boy!
pardonnable [pardɔnabl] *adj* pardonable
pardonner [pardɔne] *tr* to pardon; pardonner q.ch. à qn to pardon s.o. for s.th. ‖ *intr* (with *dat*) to pardon, to forgive; ne pas pardonner to be fatal (*said of illness, mistake, etc.*)
pare-balles [parbal] *adj invar* bulletproof
pare-boue [parbu] *m invar* mudguard
pare-brise [parbriz] *m invar* windshield
pare-chocs [parʃɔk] *m invar* (aut) bumper
pare-étincelles [paretēsɛl] *m invar* fire screen
pa·reil -reille [parej] *adj* identical, the same; such, such a ‖ *mf* equal, match; sans pareil, sans pareille without parallel, unequaled ‖ *m*—c'est du pareil au même (coll) it's six of one and half dozen of the other ‖ *f* same (thing); rendre la pareille à qn to pay s.o. back in his own coin
pareillement [parejmɑ̃] *adv* likewise
parement [parmɑ̃] *m* cuff; facing; trimming; (eccl) parament
pa·rent [parɑ̃] -rente [rɑ̃t] *adj* like ‖ *mf* relative; parents parents; relatives; ancestors; plus proche parent next of kin
parenté [parɑ̃te] *f* relationship; relations
parenthèse [parɑ̃tez] *f* parenthesis; entre parenthèses in parentheses
parer [pare] *tr* an adorn; to parry; to prepare ‖ *intr*—parer à to provide for ‖ *ref* to show off
pare-soleil [parsɔlej] *m invar* sun visor
paresse [pares] *f* laziness
paresser [parese] *intr* (coll) to loaf
pares·seux [paresø] pares·seuse [paresøz] *adj* lazy ‖ *mf* lazy person, lazybones; malingerer ‖ *m* (zool) sloth
par ex. *abbr* (par exemple) e.g.
parfaire [parfer] §29 *tr* to perfect; to make up (*e.g., a sum of money*)
par·fait [parfɛ] -faite [fɛt] *adj* & *m* perfect ‖ parfait *interj* fine!, excellent!
parfaitement [parfetmɑ̃] *adv* perfectly; completely; certainly, of course
parfois [parfwa] *adv* sometimes

parfum [parfœ̃] *m* perfume; aroma; bouquet (*of wines*); flavor (*of ice cream*)
parfumer [parfyme] *tr* to perfume; to flavor || *ref* to use perfume
pari [pari] *m* bet, wager
paria [parja] *m* pariah
parier [parje] *tr & intr* to bet, wager
Paris [pari] *m* Paris
pari·sien [parizjɛ̃] **-sienne** [zjɛn] *adj* Parisian || (*cap*) *mf* Parisian
parité [parite] *f* parity; likeness; evenness (*of numbers*)
parjure [parȝyr] *adj* perjured || *mf* perjurer || *m* perjury
parking [parkiŋ] *m* parking lot
par·lant [parlɑ̃] **-lante** [lɑ̃t] *adj* speaking; talking (*e.g., picture*); eloquent, expressive
parlement [parləmɑ̃] *m* parliament
parlementaire [parləmɑ̃tɛr] *adj* parliamentary || *mf* peace envoy; member of a parliament, legislator
parlementer [parləmɑ̃te] *intr* to parley
parler [parle] *m* speech, way of speaking; dialect || *tr & intr* to speak, to talk
par·leur [parlœr] **-leuse** [løz] *mf*—**beau parleur** good talker; windbag
parloir [parlwar] *m* reception room
parlote [parlɔt] *f* (coll) talk, gossip, rumor
parmi [parmi] *prep* among
Parnasse [parnɑs] *m*—**le Parnasse** Parnassus (*poetry*); Mount Parnassus
parodie [parɔdi] *f* parody, travesty
parodier [parɔdje] *tr* to parody, to travesty
paroi [parwa] *f* partition, wall; inner side; (anat) wall
paroisse [parwas] *f* parish
parois·sial -siale [parwasjal] *adj* (*pl* **parois·siaux** [parwasjo]) parochial, parish
parois·sien [parwasjɛ̃] **parois·sienne** [parwasjɛn] *mf* parishioner || *m* prayer book; (coll) fellow
parole [parɔl] *f* word; speech; word, promise; **avoir la parole** to have the floor; **donner la parole à** to recognize, to give the floor to; **sur parole** on one's word
paro·lier [parɔlje] **-lière** [ljɛr] *mf* lyricist; librettist
parpaing [parpɛ̃] *m* concrete block; building block
parquer [parke] *tr* to park; to pen in || *intr* to be penned in || *ref* to park
Parques [park] *fpl* Fates
parquet [parkɛ] *m* parquet, floor; floor (*of stock exchange*); public prosecutor's office
parqueter [parkəte] §34 *tr* to parquet, to floor
parrain [parɛ̃] *m* godfather; sponsor
parricide [parisid] *mf* parricide, patricide (*person*) || *m* parricide, patricide (*act*)
parsemer [parsəme] §2 *tr* to sprinkle; to spangle
part [par] *m* newborn child; dropping (*of young by animal in labor*) || *f* part, share; **aller quelque part** (coll)

to go to the toilet; **à part** aside; aside from; **à part entière** with full privileges; **autre part** elsewhere; **avoir part au gâteau** (coll) to have a slice in the pie; **d'autre part** besides; **de la part de** on the part of, from; **de part en part** through and through; **de toutes parts** on all sides; **d'une part** . . . **d'autre part**; on the one hand . . . on the other hand; **faire la part de** to make allowance for; **faire part de** to announce; **faire part de q.ch. à qn** to inform s.o. of s.th.; **nulle part** nowhere; **nulle part ailleurs** nowhere else; **pour ma part** as for me, for my part; **prendre en bonne part** to take good-naturedly; **prendre en mauvaise part** to take offense at; **prendre part à** to take part in; **quelque part** somewhere
partage [partaȝ] *m* division, partition; sharing; share; tie vote; **échoir en partage à qn** to fall to s.o.'s lot
partager [partaȝe] §38 *tr* to share; to divide
partance [partɑ̃s] *f* departure; **en partance** leaving; **en partance pour** bound for
partant [partɑ̃] *m* (sports) starter; **partants** departing guests, departing travelers, etc. || *adv* (lit) consequently
partenaire [partənɛr] *mf* partner; sparring partner
parterre [partɛr] *m* orchestra circle; flower bed
parti [parti] *m* party; side; match, good catch; **faire un mauvais parti à** to rough up, to mistreat; **parti pris** fixed opinion; prejudice; **prendre le parti de** to decide to; **prendre le parti de qn** to take s.o.'s side; **prendre parti** to take sides; **prendre son parti** to make up one's mind; **prendre son parti de** to resign oneself to; **tirer parti de** to take advantage of
par·tial -tiale [parsjal] *adj* (*pl* **-tiaux** [sjo]) partial, biased
partici·pant [partisipɑ̃] **-pante** [pɑ̃t] *adj & mf* participant
participation [partisipɑsjɔ̃] *f* participation
participe [partisip] *m* participle
participer [partisipe] *intr*—**participer à** to participate in; **participer de** to partake of
particulariser [partikylarize] *tr* to specify || *ref* to make oneself conspicuous
particularité [partikylarite] *f* peculiarity; detail
particule [partikyl] *f* particle
particu·lier [partikylje] **-lière** [ljɛr] *adj* particular; special; private || *mf* private citizen; (coll) odd person || *m* particular
partie [parti] *f* part; line, specialty; game, winning score; contest; party (*diversion*); (law) party; **avoir partie liée avec** to be in league with; **faire partie de** to belong to; **faire partie intégrante de** to be part and parcel of; **partie civile** plaintiff; **partie de chasse** hunting party; **partie de plai-**

sir outing, picnic; **partie nulle** tie game; **prendre à partie** to take to task

par•tiel -tielle [parsjɛl] *adj* partial

partir [partir] (used only in *inf*) *tr*— **avoir maille à partir** to have a bone to pick ‖ §64 *intr* (*aux*: ÊTRE) to leave; to go off (*said of firearm*); to begin; **à partir de** from; from . . . on, e.g., **à partir de maintenant** from now on; **faire partir** to send off; to remove (*a spot*); to set off (*an explosive*); to fire (*a gun*); **partir +** *inf* to leave in order to + *inf*; **partir de** to come from; to start with; **partir pour** or **à** to leave for

parti•san [partizɑ̃] **-sane** [zan] *adj* & *mf* partisan

partition [partisjɔ̃] *f* (mus) score

partout [partu] *adv* everywhere; **partout ailleurs** anywhere else; everywhere else; **partout où** wherever; everywhere

parure [paryr] *f* ornament; set; finery; necklace

parution [parysjɔ̃] *f* appearance, publication

parvenir [parvənir] §72 *intr* (*aux*: ÊTRE) **—parvenir à** to reach; **parvenir à +** *inf* to succeed in + *ger*

parve•nu -nue [parvəny] *adj* & *mf* upstart

parvis [parvi] *m* square (*in front of a church*)

pas [pɑ] *m* step; pace; footprint; footfall; pass; straits; pitch (*of screw*); **allonger le pas** to quicken one's pace; to put one's best foot forward; **à pas comptés** with measured tread; **à pas de loup, à pas feutrés** stealthily; **à pas de tortue** at a snail's pace; **à quatre pas** nearby; **au pas** at a walk; **céder le pas (à)** to stand aside (for); to keep clear (*in front of a driveway*); **de ce pas** at once; **être au pas** to be in step; **faire le premier pas** to make the first move; **faire les cent pas** to come and go; **faux pas** misstep; blunder; **marcher sur les pas de** to follow in the footsteps of; **marquer le pas** to mark time; **mauvais pas** tight squeeze, fix; **pas à pas** little by little, cautiously; **pas d'armes** passage at arms; **Pas de Calais** Straits of Dover; **pas de cheval** hoofbeat; **pas de clerc** blunder; **pas de deux** two-step; **pas de la porte** doorstep; **pas de l'oie** goosestep; **pas de porte** (com) price paid for good will; **prendre le pas sur** to get ahead of ‖ *adv*—**ne . . . pas** §90 not, e.g., **je ne sais pas** I do not know; e.g., **ne pas signer** not to sign; (used with **non**), e.g., **non pas** no; (used without **ne**) (slang) not, e.g., **je fais pas de politique** I don't meddle in politics; **n'est-ce pas?** see **ne**; **pas?** (coll) not so?; **pas de** no; **pas du tout** not at all; **pas encore** not yet

pas•cal -cale [paskal] *adj* (*pl* **-caux** [ko]) Passover; Easter

passable [pasabl] *adj* passable, fair; mediocre, so-so

passade [pasad] *f* passing fancy

passage [pasaʒ] *m* passage; crossing; pass; **barrer le passage** to block the way; **livrer passage à** to let through; **passage à niveau** grade crossing; **passage au-dessous de la voie, passage souterrain** underpass; **passage au-dessus de la voie** overpass; **passage clouté, passage zébré** pedestrian crossing; **passage de vitesses** gear shifting; **passage interdit** (public sign) do not enter; (public sign) no thoroughfare; **passage protégé** arterial crossing (*vehicles intersecting highway must stop*)

passa•ger [pasaʒe] **-gère** [ʒer] *adj* passing, fleeting; migratory; busy (*road*) ‖ *mf* passenger; **passager clandestin, passager de cale** stowaway; **passager d'entrepont** steerage passenger

pas•sant [pasɑ̃] **pas•sante** [pasɑ̃t] *adj* busy (*street*) ‖ *mf* passer-by

passation [pasasjɔ̃] *f* handing over

passavant [pasavɑ̃] *m* permit; (naut) gangway

passe [pas] *m* master key ‖ *f* pass; channel; **être en bonne passe de** to be in a fair way to; **être en passe de** to be about to; **mauvaise passe** tight spot

pas•sé -sée [pase] *adj* past; faded; overripe; last (*week*) ‖ *m* past; past tense ‖ **passé** *prep* past, beyond, after

passe-bouillon [pasbujɔ̃] *m invar* soup strainer

passe-droit [pasdrwa] *m* (*pl* **-droits**) illegal favor; injustice

passe-lacet [paslasɛ] *m* (*pl* **-lacets**) bodkin

passe-lait [paslɛ] *m invar* milk strainer

passe-lettres [pasletr] *m* (*pl* **-lettres**) letter drop

passement [pasmɑ̃] *m* braid, trimming

passementer [pasmɑ̃te] *tr* to trim

passementerie [pasmɑ̃tri] *f* trimmings

passe-montagne [pasmɔ̃taɲ] *m* (*pl* **-montagnes**) storm hood, ski mask

passe-partout [paspartu] *m invar* master key; slip mount

passe-passe [paspas] *m invar* legerdemain

passepoil [paspwal] *m* piping, braid

passeport [paspɔr] *m* passport

passer [pase] *tr* to pass; to ferry; to get across (*e.g., a river*); to spend, to pass (*e.g., the evening*); to take (*an exam*); to slip on (*e.g., a dressing gown*); to show (*a film*); to make (*a telephone call*); to go on (*one's way*); **passer q.ch. à qn** to hand or lend s.o. s.th.; to forgive s.o. s.th. ‖ *intr* (*aux*: AVOIR or ÊTRE) to pass; to pass away; to become; **en passer par là** to knuckle under; **faire passer** to get (*e.g., a message*) through; to while away (*the time*); **passer à** to pass over to; **passer chez** or **passer voir** to drop in on; **passer outre à** to override; **passer par** to pass through, to go through; **passer pour** to pass for or as; **passons!** let's skip it! ‖ *ref* to happen, to take place; **se passer de** to do without

passe·reau [pɑsro] *m* (*pl* **-reaux**) sparrow

passerelle [pɑsrɛl] *f* footbridge; gangplank; (naut) bridge

passe-temps [pɑstɑ̃] *m invar* pastime, hobby

passe-thé [pɑste] *m invar* tea strainer

pas·seur [pɑsœr] **pas·seuse** [pɑsøz] *mf* smuggler ‖ *m* ferryman

passible [pɑsibl] *adj*—**passible de** liable for, subject to

pas·sif [pɑsif] **pas·sive** [pɑsiv] *adj* passive ‖ *m* passive; debts, liabilities

passiflore [pɑsiflɔr] *f* passionflower

passion [pɑsjɔ̃], [pɑsjɔ̃] *f* passion

passion·nant [pɑsjɔnɑ̃] **passion·nante** [pɑsjɔnɑ̃t] *adj* thrilling, fascinating

passion·né -née [pɑsjɔne] *adj* passionate; impassioned; **passionné de** or **pour** passionately fond of ‖ *mf* enthusiast, fan

passion·nel -nelle [pɑsjɔnɛl] *adj* of passion, of jealousy

passionner [pɑsjɔne] *tr* to excite the interest of, to arouse ‖ *ref*—**se passionner pour** or **à** to be passionately fond of

passoire [pɑswar] *f* colander; strainer; (fig) sieve

pastel [pɑstɛl] *m* pastel; (bot) woad

pastèque [pɑstɛk] *f* watermelon

pasteur [pɑstœr] *m* pastor, minister; shepherd

pasteuriser [pɑstœrize] *tr* to pasteurize

pastiche [pɑstiʃ] *m* pastiche; parody

pastille [pɑstij] *f* lozenge, drop; tire patch; polka dot; **pastille pectorale** cough drop

pasto·ral -rale [pɑstɔral] (*pl* **-raux** [ro] **-rales**) *adj & f* pastoral

pastorat [pɑstɔra] *m* pastorate

pat [pat] *adj invar* (chess) in stalemate; **faire pat** to stalemate ‖ *m* (chess) stalemate

patache [pataʃ] *f* police boat; (coll) rattletrap

patachon [pataʃɔ̃] *m*—**mener une vie de patachon** to lead a wild life

patapouf [patapuf] *m* (coll) roly-poly ‖ *interj* flop!

pataquès [patakɛs] *m* faulty liaison; blooper, goof

patate [patat] *f* sweet potato; (coll) spud

patati [patati]—**et patati et patata!** (coll) and so on and on!

patatras [patatra] *interj* bang!, crash!

pa·taud [pato] **-taude** [tod] *adj* clumsy, loutish ‖ *mf* lout

patauger [patoʒe] §38 *intr* to splash; (coll) to flounder

pâte [pat] *f* paste; dough, batter; **en pâte** (typ) pied; **mettre la main à la pâte** to put one's shoulder to the wheel; **pâte à papier** wood pulp; **pâte brisée**, **pâte feuilletée** puff paste; **pâte dentifrice** toothpaste; **pâte molle** spineless person; **pâtes alimentaires** pastas (*macaroni, noodles, spaghetti, etc.*); **peindre à la pâte** to paint with a full brush; **une bonne pâte d'homme** (coll) a good sort

pâté [pate] *m* blot, splotch; (typ) pi; **pâté de foie gras** minced goose livers; **pâté de maisons** block of houses; **pâté en croûte** meat or fish pie; **pâté maison** chef's-special pâté

pâtée [pate] *f* dog food, cat food; chicken feed

pate·lin [patlɛ̃] **-line** [lin] *adj* fawning, wheedling ‖ *m* wheedler; (coll) native village

patenôtre [patnotr] *f* prayer; (archaic) mumbo jumbo

pa·tent [patɑ̃] **-tente** [tɑ̃t] *adj* patent ‖ *f* license; tax; **patente (de santé)** (naut) bill of health

paten·té -tée [patɑ̃te] *adj* licensed ‖ *mf* licensed dealer

patenter [patɑ̃te] *tr* to license

Pater [pater] *m invar* Lord's Prayer

patère [pater] *f* clothes hook; curtain hook

paterne [patern] *adj* mawkish, mealy-mouthed

pater·nel -nelle [paternɛl] *adj* paternal; fatherly ‖ *m* (slang) pop, dad

paternité [paternite] *f* paternity; fatherhood; authorship

pâ·teux [patø] **-teuse** [tøz] *adj* pasty; thick; coated (*tongue*)

pathétique [patetik] *adj* pathetic ‖ *m* pathos

pathologie [patɔlɔʒi] *f* pathology

pathos [patos] *m* bathos

patibulaire [patibyler] *adj* hangdog (*look*)

patience [pasjɑ̃s] *f* patience

pa·tient [pasjɑ̃] **-tiente** [sjɑ̃t] *adj & mf* patient

patienter [pasjɑ̃te] *intr* to be patient

patin [patɛ̃] *m* skate; runner; sill, sleeper, (sole) patten; (aer) skid; (rr) base, flange (*of rails*); **patin à glace** ice skate; **patin à roulettes** roller skate; **patin de frein** brake shoe

patiner [patine] *intr* to skate; to slide; to skid

patinette [patinet] *f* scooter

pati·neur [patinœr] **-neuse** [nøz] *mf* skater

patinoire [patinwar] *f* skating rink

patio [patjo], [pasjo] *m* patio

pâtir [patir] *intr*—**pâtir de** to suffer from

pâtisserie [patisri] *f* pastry; pastry shop; pastry making

pâtis·sier [patisje] **pâtis·sière** [patisjer] *mf* pastry cook; proprietor of a pastry shop

patoche [patɔʃ] *f* (coll) hand, paw

patois [patwa] *m* patois; jargon, lingo

patouiller [patuje] *tr* (coll) to paw, maul ‖ *intr* (coll) to splash

patraque [patrak] *adj* in bad shape ‖ *f* (coll) turnip (*old watch*)

pâtre [patr] *m* herdsman

patriarche [patrijarʃ] *m* patriarch

patrice [patris] *m* patrician; **Patrice** Patrick

patri·cien [patrisjɛ̃] **-cienne** [sjɛn] *adj & mf* patrician

patrie [patri] *f* native land, fatherland

patrimoine [patrimwan] *m* patrimony

patrio·tard [patrijɔtar] **-tarde** [tard] *adj* flag-waving, chauvinistic

patriote [patrijɔt] *adj* patriotic ‖ *mf* patriot

patriotique [patrijɔtik] *adj* patriotic

patriotisme [patrijɔtism] *m* patriotism

pa·tron [patrɔ̃] **-tronne** [trɔn] *mf* patron saint; proprietor; boss; sponsor ‖ *m* pattern, model; captain, skipper; coxswain; master, lord; medium size; **grand patron** large size; **patron à jours** stencil; **patron de thèse** thesis sponsor ‖ *f* mistress of the house; (slang) better half

patronage [patrɔnaʒ] *m* patronage, protection; sponsorship; (eccl) social center

patronat [patrɔna] *m* management

patronner [patrɔne] *tr* to patronize, to protect; to sponsor; to stencil

patrouille [patruj] *f* patrol

patrouiller [patruje] *intr* to patrol

patte [pat] *f* paw; foot (*of bird*); leg (*of insect*); flap, tab; hook; (coll) hand, foot, or leg (*of person*); **à pattes d'éléphant** bell-bottom (*trousers*); **à quatre pattes** on all fours; **faire patte de velours** (coll) to pull in one's claws; **graisser la patte à** (coll) to grease the palm of; **patte d'épaule** shoulder strap; **pattes de mouche** (coll) scrawl

patte-d'oie [patdwa] *f* (*pl* **pattes-d'oie**) crow's-foot; crossroads; (bot) goose-foot

pattemouille [patmuj] *f* damp cloth

pâturage [pɑtyraʒ] *m* pasture; pasturage; pasture rights

pâture [pɑtyr] *f* fodder; pasture; (fig) food

paume [pom] *f* palm; (archaic) tennis

pau·mé -mée [pome] *adj* (coll) lost

paupière [popjɛr] *f* eyelid

pause [poz] *f* pause; (mus) full rest; **pause café** coffee break

pauvre [povr] *adj* poor; **pauvre de moi!** woe is me!; **pauvre d'esprit** (coll) dim-witted ‖ (when standing before noun) *adj* poor, wretched; late (*deceased*) ‖ *mf* pauper; **les pauvres** the poor

pauvreté [povrəte] *f* poverty

P.A.V. [peave] *adj* (letterword) (**payable avec préavis**) person-to-person (*telephone call*)

pavaner [pavane] *ref* to strut

pavé [pave] *m* pavement, street; paving stone; paving block; (culin) slab; **sur le pavé** pounding the streets, out of work

pavement [pavmɑ̃] *m* paving (*act*); mosaic or marble flooring

paver [pave] *tr* to pave

pavillon [pavijɔ̃] *m* pavilion, tent, canopy; lodge, one-story house; wing, pavilion; flag; bell (*of trumpet*); **amener son pavillon** to strike one's colors; **baisser pavillon** to knuckle under

pavois [pavwa] *m* shield; **élever sur le pavois** to extol

pavoiser [pavwaze] *tr* to deck out with bunting, to decorate

pavot [pavo] *m* poppy

payable [pɛjabl] *adj* payable

payant [pɛjɑ̃] **payante** [pɛjɑ̃t] *adj* paying

paye [pɛj] *f* pay, wages

payement [pɛjmɑ̃] *m* payment

payer [peje] §49 *tr* to pay; to pay for; **payer comptant** to pay cash for; **payer de retour** to pay back; **payer q.ch. à qn** to pay s.o. for s.th.; to pay for s.th. for s.o.; **payer qn de q.ch.** to pay s.o. for s.th.; **payer rubis sur l'ongle** to pay down on the nail ‖ *intr* to pay ‖ *ref* to treat oneself to; to take what is due; **pouvoir se** (*dat*) **payer** to be able to afford; **se payer de** to be satisfied with

pays [pei] *m* country; region; town; (coll) fellow countryman; **du pays** local; **le pays de** the land of; **pays de cocagne** land of milk and honey

paysage [peizaʒ] *m* landscape, scenery; (painting) landscape

paysagiste [peizaʒist] *m* landscape painter

pay·san [peizɑ̃] **-sane** [zan] *adj* & *mf* peasant

Pays-Bas [peibɑ], [pɛibɑ] *mpl*—**les Pays-Bas** The Netherlands

payse [peiz] *f* countrywoman

P.C. [pese] *m* (letterword) (**parti communiste**) Communist party; (**poste de commandement**) command post

P.c.c. *abbr* (**pour copie conforme**) certified copy

p.c.v. or **P.C.V.** [peseve] *m* (letterword) (**payable chez vous**) or (**à percevoir**)—**téléphoner en p.c.v.** to telephone collect

péage [peaʒ] *m* toll

peau [po] *f* (*pl* **peaux**) skin; pelt; hide; film (*on milk*); (slang) bag, whore; **entrer dans la peau d'un personnage** (theat) to get right inside a part; **faire peau neuve** to turn over a new leaf; **la peau!** (slang) nothing doing!; **peau d'âne** (coll) sheepskin; **peau de tambour** drumhead; **vendre la peau de l'ours avant de l'avoir tué** to count one's chickens before they are hatched

peau-rouge [poruʒ] *mf* (*pl* **peaux-rouges**) redskin

pêche [pɛʃ] *f* peach; fishing; **pêche à la mouche noyée** fly casting; **pêche au coup** fishing with hook, line, and pole; **pêche au lancer** casting; **pêche sous-marine** deep-sea fishing; **pêche sportive** fishing with a fly rod or casting rod

péché [peʃe] *m* sin

pécher [peʃe] §10 *intr* to sin

pêcher [peʃe] *m* peach tree ‖ *tr* to fish, fish for; (coll) to get ‖ *intr* to fish; **pêcher à la mouche** to fly-fish

pêcherie [pɛʃri] *f* fishery

pé·cheur [peʃœr] **-cheresse** [ʃrɛs] *mf* sinner

pê·cheur [pɛʃœr] **-cheuse** [ʃøz] *mf* fisher; **pêcheur de perles** pearl diver ‖ *m* fisherman

pécore [pekɔr] *f* (coll) silly goose

pecque [pɛk] *f* (coll) silly affected woman

péculat [pekyla] *m* embezzlement

pécule [pekyl] *m* nest egg
pédagogie [pedagɔʒi] *f* pedagogy, education
pédagogue [pedagɔg] *adj* pedagogical || *mf* pedagogue; teacher
pédale [pedal] *f* pedal; treadle; (vulg) pederast; **pédale d'embrayage** (aut) clutch pedal
pédaler [pedale] *intr* to pedal
pédalier [pedalje] *m* pedal keyboard; pedal and sprocket-wheel assembly
pédalo [pedalo] *m* water bicycle
pé·dant [pedɑ̃] -**dante** [dɑ̃t] *adj* pedantic || *mf* pedant
pédanterie [pedɑ̃tri] *f* pedantry
pédantesque [pedɑ̃tɛsk] *adj* pedantic
pédestre [pedɛstr] *adj* on foot
pédiatrie [pedjatri] *f* pediatrics
pédicure [pedikyr] *mf* chiropodist
pedigree [pedigri] *m* pedigree
Pégase [pegɑz] *m* Pegasus
pègre [pɛgr] *f* underworld
peigne [pɛɲ] *m* comb; card (*for wool*); reed (*of loom*); (zool) scallop
peigner [peɲe] *tr* to comb; to card || *ref* to comb one's hair
peignoir [peɲwar] *m* bathrobe; dressing gown, peignoir
peindre [pɛ̃dr] §50 *tr & intr* to paint
peine [pɛn] *f* pain; trouble; difficulty; penalty; **à peine** hardly, scarcely; **en être pour sa peine** to have nothing to show for one's trouble; **faire (de la) peine à** to grieve; **faire peine à voir** to be pathetic; **peine capitale** capital punishment; **peine de cœur** heartache; **peine de mort** death penalty; **peine pécuniaire** financial distress; **purger sa peine** to serve one's sentence; **valoir la peine** to be worth while; **veuillez vous donner la peine de** please be so kind as to
peiner [pene] *tr* to pain, grieve; to fatigue || *intr* to labor
peintre [pɛ̃tr] *m* painter
peinture [pɛ̃tyr] *f* paint; painting; **attention à la peinture** (public sign) wet paint; **je ne peux pas le voir en peinture** (coll) I can't stand him
peinturer [pɛ̃tyre] *tr* to lay a coat of paint on; to daub
peinturlurer [pɛ̃tyrlyre] *tr* (coll) to paint in all the colors of the rainbow
péjora·tif [peʒɔratif] -**tive** [tiv] *adj & m* pejorative
pékin [pekɛ̃] *m* pekin; **en pékin** (slang) in civies; **Pékin** Peking
péki·nois [pekinwa] -**noise** [nwaz] *adj* Pekingese || *m* Pekingese (*language; dog*) || (cap) *mf* Pekingese (*inhabitant*)
pelage [pəlaʒ] *m* coat (*of animal*)
pe·lé -**lée** [pəle] *adj* bald; bare
pêle-mêle [pɛlmɛl] *m invar* jumble || *adv* pell-mell
peler [pəle] §2 *tr, intr, & ref* to peel, to peel off
pèle·rin [pɛlrɛ̃] -**rine** [rin] *mf* pilgrim || *m* peregrine falcon; basking shark || *f* see pèlerine
pèlerinage [pɛlrinaʒ] *m* pilgrimage
pèlerine [pɛlrin] *f* pelerine, cape; hooded cape

péliade [peljad] *f* adder
pélican [pelikɑ̃] *m* pelican
pellagre [pelagr] *f* pellagra
pelle [pɛl] *f* shovel; scoop; **pelle à poussière** dustpan; **pelle à vapeur** steam shovel; **pelle mécanique** power shovel; **ramasser à la pelle** to shovel, to shovel up
pelletée [pɛlte] *f* shovelful
pelleter [pɛlte] §34 *tr* to shovel
pelleterie [pɛltri] *f* fur trade; skin, pelt
pelleteuse [pɛltøz] *f* power shovel
pellicule [pelikyl], [pɛllikyl] *f* film; pellicle; speck of dandruff; (phot) film; **pellicules** dandruff
pelote [plɔt] *f* ball (*of string, of snow, etc.*); **faire sa pelote** (coll) to make one's pile; **pelote basque** pelota; **pelote d'épingles** pincushion
peloter [plɔte] *tr* to wind into a ball; (fig) to flatter; (slang) to feel up, to paw || *intr* to bat the ball back and forth
pelo·teur [plɔtœr] -**teuse** [tøz] *adj* flattering, ingratiating; (coll) fresh, amorous, spoony || *mf* (coll) masher, spooner
peloton [plɔtɔ̃] *m* little ball (*e.g., of wool*); group (*of racers*); (mil) platoon, troop, detachment; **peloton d'exécution** firing squad
pelotonner [plɔtone] *tr* to wind into a ball || *ref* to curl up, to snuggle
pelouse [pluz] *f* lawn; (golf) green
peluche [plyʃ] *f* plush
pelure [plyr] *f* peel, peeling, skin; rind; (coll) coat
pénaliser [penalize] *tr* to penalize
pénalité [penalite] *f* penalty
pe·naud [pəno] -**naude** [nod] *adj* bashful, shy; shamefaced; crestfallen
penchant [pɑ̃ʃɑ̃] *m* penchant, bent
pen·ché -**chée** [pɑ̃ʃe] *adj* leaning; stooping, bent over
pencher [pɑ̃ʃe] *tr, intr, & ref* to lean, to bend, to incline; **se pencher sur** to make a close study of
pendable [pɑ̃dabl] *adj* outrageous; (archaic) hangable
pendaison [pɑ̃dɛzɔ̃] *f* hanging
pen·dant [pɑ̃dɑ̃] -**dante** [dɑ̃t] *adj* hanging; pending || *m* pendant; counterpart; **pendant d'oreille** eardrop; **se faire pendant** to make a pair || **pendant** *adv*—**pendant que** while || **pendant** *prep* during
pendeloque [pɑ̃dlɔk] *f* pendant; jewel (*of eardrop*)
pendentif [pɑ̃dɑ̃tif] *m* pendant; eardrop; lavaliere
penderie [pɑ̃dri] *f* clothes closet
pendoir [pɑ̃dwar] *m* meat hook
pendre [pɑ̃dr] *tr* to hang; to hang up; **être pendu à** to hang on (*e.g., the telephone*) || *intr* to hang; to hang down; to sag; **ça lui pend au nez** he's got it coming to him || *ref* to hang oneself; **se pendre à** to hang on to
pen·du -**due** [pɑ̃dy] *adj* hanging; hanged || *mf* hanged person
pendule [pɑ̃dyl] *m* pendulum || *f* clock; **pendule à pile** battery clock

pêne [pɛn] *m* bolt; latch
pénétration [penetrɑsjɔ̃] *f* penetration; permeation
pénétrer [penetre] §10 *tr* to penetrate, to permeate || *intr* to penetrate; to enter || *ref* to mix; se pénétrer de to become imbued with
pénible [penibl] *adj* hard, painful
péniche [peni∫] *f* barge; houseboat; péniche de débarquement landing craft
pénicilline [penisilin] *f* penicillin
péninsulaire [penɛ̃sylɛr] *adj* peninsular
péninsule [penɛ̃syl] *f* large peninsula
pénitence [penitɑ̃s] *f* penitence; penalty (*in games*); punishment; en pénitence in disgrace; faire pénitence to do penance
pénitencier [penitɑ̃sje] *m* penitentiary; penal colony
péni•tent [penitɑ̃] -tente [tɑ̃t] *adj & mf* penitent
penne [pɛn] *f* quill, feather
Pennsylvanie [pɛnsilvani] *f* Pennsylvania; la Pennsylvanie Pennsylvania
pénombre [penɔ̃br] *f* penumbra; half-light; dans la pénombre out∙ of the limelight
pense-bête [pɑ̃sbɛt] *m* (*pl* -bêtes) (coll) reminder
pensée [pɑ̃se] *f* thought; thinking; (bot) pansy
penser [pɑ̃se] *tr* to think; penser de to think of (*to have as an opinion of*); penser + *inf* to intend to + *inf* || *intr* to think; penser à to think of (*to direct one's thoughts toward*); y penser to think of it, e.g., pendant que j'y pense while I think of it
penseur [pɑ̃sœr] *m* thinker
pen•sif [pɑ̃sif] -sive [siv] *adj* pensive; absent-minded
pension [pɑ̃sjɔ̃] *f* pension (*annuity; room and board; boardinghouse*); avec pension complète with three meals; pension de famille residential hotel; pension de retraite, pension viagère annuity; prendre pension to board; sans pension without meals
pensionnaire [pɑ̃sjɔnɛr] *mf* boarder; guest (*in hotel*); resident student || *f* naïve girl
pensionnat [pɑ̃sjɔna] *m* boarding school
pension•né -née [pɑ̃sjɔne] *adj* pensioned || *mf* pensioner
pensionner [pɑ̃sjɔne] *tr* to pension
pensum [pɛ̃sɔm] *m* thankless task
Pentagone [pɛ̃tagɔn] *m* Pentagon
pente [pɑ̃t] *f* slope; inclination, bent; fall (*of river*); en pente sloping
Pentecôte [pɑ̃tkot] *f*—la Pentecôte Pentecost, Whitsunday
pénultième [penyltjɛm] *adj* next to the last || *f* penult
pénurie [penyri] *f* lack, shortage
pépé [pepe] *m* (slang) grandpa
pépée [pepe] *f* doll; (slang) doll
pépère [pepɛr] *adj* (coll) easygoing || *m* grandpa; (coll) old duffer; (coll) overgrown boy
pépètes [pepɛt] *fpl* (slang) dough

pépie [pepi] *f* (vet) pip; avoir la pépie (coll) to be thirsty
pépiement [pepimɑ̃] *m* chirp
pépier [pepje] *intr* to chirp
pépin [pepɛ̃] *m* pip, seed; (coll) umbrella; avoir un pépin (coll) to strike a snag
pépinière [pepinjɛr] *f* (hort) nursery; (fig) training school; (fig) hotbed
pépiniériste [pepinjerist] *m* nurseryman
pépite [pepit] *f* nugget
péque•naud [pɛkno] -naude [nod] *adj & mf* (slang) peasant
péquenot [pɛkno] *m* (slang) peasant
perçage [pɛrsaʒ] *m* drilling, boring
per•çant [pɛrsɑ̃] -çante [sɑ̃t] *adj* piercing, penetrating
perce [pɛrs] *f* drill, bore; en perce on tap
perce-neige [pɛrsənɛʒ] *m invar* (bot) snowdrop
percepteur [pɛrsɛptœr] *m* tax collector
perception [pɛrsɛpsjɔ̃] *f* perception; tax collection; tax; tax department; bureau of internal revenue
percer [pɛrse] §51 *tr* to pierce; to drill; to tap (*a barrel*); to break through || *intr* to come through or out; to burst (*said, e.g., of abscess*); to make a name for oneself
perceuse [pɛrsøz] *f* drill; machine drill
percevoir [pɛrsəvwar] §59 *tr* to perceive; to collect
perche [pɛr∫] *f* pole; (ichth) perch; (coll) beanpole; perche à sauter vaulting pole; perche à son microphone stand; tendre la perche à to lend a helping hand to
percher [pɛr∫e] *tr* to perch || *intr* to perch, to roost
perchoir [pɛr∫war] *m* perch
per•clus [pɛrkly] -cluse [klyz] *adj* crippled, paralyzed
percolateur [pɛrkɔlatœr] *m* large coffee maker
percuter [pɛrkyte] *tr* to strike; to crash into; to percuss || *intr* to crash
percuteur [pɛrkytœr] *m* firing pin
per•dant [pɛrdɑ̃] -dante [dɑ̃t] *adj* losing || *mf* loser
perdition [pɛrdisjɔ̃] *f* perdition; en perdition (naut) in distress
perdre [pɛrdrə] *tr* to lose; to ruin || *intr* to lose; to leak; to deteriorate || *ref* to get lost; to disappear
per•dreau [pɛrdro] *m* (*pl* -dreaux) young partridge
perdrix [pɛrdri] *f* partridge
per•du -due [pɛrdy] *adj* lost; spare (*time*); stray (*bullet*); remote (*locality*); advance (*sentry*)
père [pɛr] *m* father; senior, e.g., M. Martin père Mr. Martin, senior; père de famille head of the household; père spirituel father confessor
péréquation [perekwasjɔ̃] *f* equalizing
perfection [pɛrfɛksjɔ̃] *f* perfection
perfectionner [pɛrfɛksjɔne] *tr* to perfect || *ref* to improve
perfide [pɛrfid] *adj* perfidious || *mf* treacherous person
perfidie [pɛrfidi] *f* perfidy

perforation [pɛrfɔrɑsjɔ̃] *f* perforation
perforatrice [pɛrfɔratris] *f* pneumatic drill; perforator; keypunch (machine)
perforer [pɛrfɔre] *tr* to perforate; to drill, bore; to punch (*a card*)
performance [pɛrfɔrmɑ̃s] *f* (sports) performance
péricliter [periklite] *intr* to fail
péril [peril] *m* peril
péril·leux [perijø] **péril·leuse** [perijøz] *adj* perilous
péri·mé -mée [perime] *adj* expired, elapsed; out-of-date
périmer [perime] *intr* & *ref* to lapse
période [perjɔd] *f* period; (phys) cycle
périodique [perjɔdik] *adj* periodic(al)
péripétie [peripesi] *f* vicissitude
périphérie [periferi] *f* periphery
périphérique [periferik] *adj* peripheral
périple [peripl] *m* journey
périr [perir] *intr* to perish
périscope [periskɔp] *m* periscope
périssable [perisabl] *adj* perishable
perle [pɛrl] *f* pearl; bead
perler [pɛrle] *tr* to pearl; to do to perfection || *intr* to form beads
permanence [pɛrmanɑ̃s] *f* permanence; headquarters, station; **en permanence** at all hours
perma·nent [pɛrmanɑ̃] **-nente** [nɑ̃t] *adj* permanent; standing; continuous, nonstop || *f* permanent
perme [pɛrm] *f* (coll) furlough
permettre [pɛrmɛtr] §42 *tr* to permit; **permettre q.ch. à qn** to allow s.o. s.th. || *intr*—**permettez!** excuse me!; **permettre à qn de + *inf*** to permit s.o. to or let s.o. + *inf*; **vous permettez?** may I? || *ref*—**se permettre de** to take the liberty of
permis [pɛrmi] *m* permit, license; **permis de conduire** driver's license
permission [pɛrmisjɔ̃] *f* permission; (mil) furlough, leave
permissionnaire [pɛrmisjɔnɛr] *m* soldier on leave
permutation [pɛrmytɑsjɔ̃] *f* permutation; exchange of posts; transposition
permuter [pɛrmyte] *tr* to permute; to exchange || *intr* to change places
perni·cieux [pɛrnisjø] **-cieuse** [sjøz] *adj* pernicious
péroné [perɔne] *m* (anat) fibula
pérorer [perɔre] *intr* to hold forth
Pérou [peru] *m*—**le Pérou** Peru
peroxyde [perɔksid] *m* peroxide
perpendiculaire [pɛrpɑ̃dikylɛr] *adj* & *f* perpendicular
perpète [pɛrpɛt]—**à perpète** (slang) forever
perpétrer [perpetre] §10 *tr* to perpetrate
perpé·tuel -tuelle [pɛrpetɥɛl] *adj* perpetual; life (*imprisonment*); constant, continual
perpétuer [pɛrpetɥe] *tr* to perpetuate || *ref* to be perpetuated
perpétuité [pɛrpetɥite] *f* perpetuity; **à perpétuité** forever; for life

perplexe [pɛrplɛks] *adj* perplexed; **rendre perplexe** to perplex
perplexité [pɛrplɛksite] *f* perplexity
perquisition [pɛrkizisjɔ̃] *f* search
perquisitionner [pɛrkizisjɔne] *intr* to make a search
perron [pɛrɔ̃] *m* front-entrance stone steps
perroquet [pɛrɔkɛ] *m* parrot
perruche [peryʃ] *f* parakeet; hen parrot
perruque [peryk] *f* wig; **vieille perruque** (coll) old fogey
per·san [pɛrsɑ̃] **-sane** [san] *adj* Persian || *m* Persian (*language*) || (*cap*) *mf* Persian (*person*)
perse [pɛrs] *adj* Persian || (*cap*) *mf* Persian || (*cap*) *f* Persia; **la Perse** Persia
persécuter [pɛrsekyte] *tr* to persecute
persécution [pɛrsekysjɔ̃] *f* persecution
persévérer [pɛrsevere] §10 *intr* to persevere
persienne [pɛrsjɛn] *f* Persian blind, slatted shutter
persil [pɛrsi] *m* parsley
persis·tant [pɛrsistɑ̃] **-tante** [tɑ̃t] *adj* persistent
persister [pɛrsiste] *intr* to persist; **persister à** to persist in
personnage [pɛrsɔnaʒ] *m* personage; (theat) character
personnalité [pɛrsɔnalite] *f* personality
personne [pɛrsɔn] *f* person; self; appearance; lady, e.g., **belle personne** beautiful lady; e.g., **jolie personne** pretty lady; **grande personne** grownup; **par personne** per person; **payer de sa personne** to not spare one's efforts; **s'assurer de la personne de** to arrest; **une tierce personne** a third party || *pron indef* no one, nobody; **personne ne** or **ne . . . personne** §90B no one, nobody, not anyone
person·nel -nelle [pɛrsɔnɛl] *adj* personal || *m* personnel
personnifier [pɛrsɔnifje] *tr* to personify
perspective [pɛrspɛktiv] *f* perspective; outlook; **en perspective** in view
perspicace [pɛrspikas] *adj* perspicacious
persuader [pɛrsɥade] *tr* to persuade; **persuader q.ch. à qn** or **persuader qn de q.ch.** to persuade s.o. of s.th. || *intr* **persuader à qn de** to persuade s.o. to || *ref* to be convinced
persuasion [pɛrsɥazjɔ̃] *f* persuasion
perte [pɛrt] *f* loss; ruin, downfall; **à perte de vue** as far as the eye can see; **en pure perte** uselessly
perti·nent [pɛrtinɑ̃] **-nente** [nɑ̃t] *adj* pertinent
perturba·teur [pɛrtyrbatœr] **-trice** [tris] *adj* disturbing || *mf* troublemaker
perturber [pɛrtyrbe] *tr* to perturb
péru·vien [peryvjɛ̃] **-vienne** [vjɛn] *adj* Peruvian || (*cap*) *mf* Peruvian
pervenche [pɛrvɑ̃ʃ] *f* periwinkle
per·vers [pɛrvɛr] **-verse** [vɛrs] *adj* perverted || *mf* pervert
perversion [pɛrvɛrsjɔ̃] *f* perversion

perversité [pɛrvɛrsite] *f* perversity, depravity
pervertir [pɛrvɛrtir] *tr* to pervert
pesage [pəzaʒ] *m* weigh-in; paddock
pe·sant [pəzɑ̃] **-sante** [zɑ̃t] *adj* heavy
‖ *m*—**valoir son pesant d'or** to be worth one's weight in gold
pesanteur [pəzɑ̃tœr] *f* heaviness; weight; (phys) gravity
pèse-bébé [pɛzbebe] *m* (*pl* **-bébés**) baby scale
pesée [pəze] *f* weighing; leverage
pèse-lettre [pɛzlɛtr] *m* (*pl* **-lettres**) letter scale
pèse-personne [pɛzpɛrsɔn] *m* (*pl* **-personnes**) bathroom scale
peser [pəze] §2 *tr* to weigh ‖ *intr* to weigh; **peser à** to hang heavy on; **peser sur** to bear down on; to lie down on; to lie heavy on; to stress ‖ *ref* to weigh oneself; to weigh in
peson [pəzɔ̃] *m* spring scale
pessimisme [pesimism] *m* pessimism
pessimiste [pesimist) *adj* pessimistic ‖ *mf* pessimist
peste [pɛst] *f* plague; pest, nuisance ‖ *interj* gosh!
pester [pɛste] *intr* to grouse; **pester contre** to rail at
pestifé·ré -rée [pɛstifere] *adj* plague-ridden ‖ *mf* victim of the plague
pestilence [pɛstilɑ̃s] *f* pestilence
pet [pɛ] *m* (slang) scandal; (vulgar) wind; **ça ne vaut pas un pet (de lapin)** (coll) it's not worth a wooden nickel ‖ *interj* (coll) look out!
pétale [petal] *m* petal
pétarade [petarad] *f* series of explosions; backfire
pétard [petar] *m* firecracker; blast; (slang) gat, revolver; (slang) backside; **faire du pétard** (coll) to kick up a fuss; **lancer un pétard** (coll) to drop a bombshell
pet-de-loup [pɛdlu] *m* (*pl* **pets-de-loup**) absent-minded professor
pet-de-nonne [pɛdnɔn] *m* (*pl* **pets-de-nonne**) fritter
pet-en-l'air [pɛtɑ̃lɛr] *m invar* short jacket
péter [pete] §10 *tr*—**péter du feu** (coll) to be a live wire ‖ *intr* (coll) to go bang; (vulg) to break wind
pètesec [pɛtsɛk] *adj invar* (coll) bossy, despotic ‖ *m invar* (coll) martinet, bossy fellow
pétil·lant [petijɑ̃] **pétil·lante** [petijɑ̃t] *adj* crackling; sparkling
pétiller [petije] *intr* to crackle; to sparkle
pe·tiot [pətjo] **-tiote** [tjɔt] *adj* (coll) tiny, wee ‖ *mf* (coll) tot
pe·tit [pəti] **-tite** [tit] *adj* §91 small, little; short; minor, lower; **en petit** shortened; miniature; **petit à petit** little by little, bit by bit ‖ *mf* youngster; young (*of an animal*); poor little thing ‖ *m* little boy ‖ *f* little girl
petit-beurre [pətibœr] *m* (*pl* **petits-beurre**) cookie
petit-cou·sin [pətikuzɛ̃] **-sine** [zin] *mf* (*pl* **petits-cousins**) second cousin

petite-fille [pətitfij] *f* (*pl* **petites-filles**) granddaughter
petite-nièce [pətitnjɛs] *f* (*pl* **petites-nièces**) great-niece
petitesse [pətites] *f* smallness
petit-fils [pətifis] *m* (*pl* **petits-fils**) grandson; grandchild
petit-gris [pətigri] *m* (*pl* **petits-gris**) miniver; snail
pétition [petisjɔ̃] *f* petition; **faire une pétition de principe** to beg the question
petit-lait [pətilɛ] *m* (*pl* **petits-laits**) whey
petit-neveu [pətinvø] *m* (*pl* **petits-neveux**) great-nephew
petits-enfants [pətizɑ̃fɑ̃] *mpl* grandchildren
petit-suisse [pətisɥis] *m* (*pl* **petits-suisses**) cream cheese
peton [pətɔ̃] *m* (coll) tiny foot
pétoncle [petɔ̃kl] *m* scallop
Pétrarque [petrark] *m* Petrarch
pétrifier [petrifje] *tr & ref* to petrify
pétrin [petrɛ̃] *m* kneading trough; (coll) mess, jam
pétrir [petrir] *tr* to knead; to mold
pétrole [petrɔl] *m* petroleum; **à pétrole** kerosene (*lamp*); **pétrole brut** crude oil; **pétrole lampant** kerosene
pétro·lier [petrɔlje] **-lière** [ljɛr] *adj* oil ‖ *m* tanker; oil baron
P et T [peete] *fpl* (letterword) (**Postes et télécommunications**) post office, telephone, and telegraph
pétu·lant [petylɑ̃] **-lante** [lɑ̃t] *adj* lively, frisky
peu [pø] *m* bit, little; **peu de** few; not much; not many; **peu de chose** not much ‖ *adv* §91 little; not very; **à peu près** about, practically; **depuis peu** of late; **peu ou prou** more or less; **peu probable** improbable; **peu s'en faut** very nearly; **pour peu que**, **si peu que** however little; **quelque peu** somewhat; **sous peu** before long; **tant soit peu** ever so little
peuplade [pœplad] *f* tribe
peuple [pœpl] *adj* plebeian, common ‖ *m* people
peuplement [pœpləmɑ̃] *m* populating; planting; stocking (*e.g., with fish*)
peupler [pœple] *tr* to people; to plant; to stock ‖ *intr* to multiply, to breed
peuplier [pøplje] *m* poplar
peur [pœr] *f* fear; **avoir peur (de)** to be afraid (of); **de peur que** lest, for fear that; **une peur bleue** (coll) an awful fright
peu·reux [pœrø] **-reuse** [røz] *adj* fearful, timid
peut-être [pøtɛtr] *adv* perhaps; **peut-être que non** perhaps not
p. ex. *abbr* (**par exemple**) e.g.
phalange [falɑ̃ʒ] *f* phalanx
phalène [falɛn] *m & f* moth
Pharaon [faraɔ̃] *m* Pharaoh
phare [far] *m* lighthouse; beacon; (aut) headlight; **phares code** dimmers
phari·sien [farizjɛ̃] **-sienne** [zjɛn] *adj* pharisaic ‖ *mf* pharisee

pharmaceutique [farmasøtik] adj pharmaceutical ‖ f pharmaceutics
pharmacie [farmasi] f drugstore, pharmacy; medicine chest; drugs
pharma·cien [farmasjẽ] -cienne [sjɛn] mf pharmacist
pharynx [farɛ̃ks] m pharynx
phase [faz] f phase
Phébé [febe] f Phoebe
Phénicie [fenisi] f Phoenicia; la Phénicie Phoenicia
phéni·cien [fenisjẽ] -cienne [sjɛn] adj Phoenician ‖ (cap) mf Phoenician
phénix [feniks] m phoenix
phénomé·nal -nale [fenɔmenal] adj (pl -naux [no]) phenomenal
phénomène [fenɔmɛn] m phenomenon; (coll) monster, freak
philanthrope [filãtrɔp] mf philanthropist
philanthropie [filantrɔpi] f philanthropy
philatélie [filateli] f philately
philatéliste [filatelist] mf philatelist
philip·pin [filipẽ] -pine [pin] adj Philippine ‖ (cap) mf Filipino
Philippines [filipin] fpl Philippines
philistin [filistẽ] adj masc & m Philistine
philologie [filɔlɔʒi] f philology
philologue [filɔlɔg] mf philologist
philosophe [filɔzɔf] adj philosophic ‖ mf philosopher
philosophie [filɔzɔfi] f philosophy
philosophique [filɔzɔfik] adj philosophic(al)
philtre [filtr] m philter
phlébite [flebit] f phlebitis
phobie [fɔbi] f phobia
phonétique [fɔnetik] adj phonetic ‖ f phonetics
phoniatrie [fɔnjatri] f speech therapy
phono [fɔno] m (coll) phonograph
phonographe [fɔnɔgraf] m phonograph
phonologie [fɔnɔlɔʒi] f phonology
phonothèque [fɔnɔtɛk] f record library
phoque [fɔk] m seal
phosphate [fɔsfat] m phosphate
phosphore [fɔsfɔr] m phosphorus
phosphores·cent [fɔsfɔresã] phosphores·cente [fɔsfɔresãt] adj phosphorescent
photo [fɔtɔ] f photo, snapshot
photocopier [fɔtɔkɔpje] tr to photocopy, to photostat
photogénique [fɔtɔʒenik] adj photogenic
photographe [fɔtɔgraf] mf photographer
photographie [fɔtɔgrafi] f photography; photograph
photographier [fɔtɔgrafje] tr to photograph
photogravure [fɔtɔgravyr] f photoengraving
photostat [fɔtɔsta] m photostat
phrase [fraz] f sentence; (mus) phrase; phrase de choc punch line
phrénologie [frenɔlɔʒi] f phrenology
physi·cien [fizisjẽ] -cienne [sjɛn] mf physicist
physiologie [fizjɔlɔʒi] f physiology

physiologique [fizjɔlɔʒik] adj physiological
physionomie [fizjɔnɔmi] f physiognomy
physique [fizik] adj physical; material ‖ m physique; appearance ‖ f physics
piaffer [pjafe] intr to paw the ground; to fidget, fume
piailler [pjaje] intr (coll) to cheep; (coll) to squeal
pianiste [pjanist] mf pianist
piano [pjano] m piano; piano à queue grand piano; piano droit upright piano ‖ adv (coll) quietly
pianoter [pjanɔte] intr to strum; to drum, to thrum; to rattle away
piastre [pjastr] f (Canad) dollar
piauler [pjole] intr to peep; to screech (said of pulley); (coll) to whine
pic [pik] m peak; (tool) pick; (orn) woodpecker; à pic sheer, steep; (coll) in the nick of time; couler à pic to sink like a stone
picaillons [pikajɔ̃] mpl (slang) dough
picaresque [pikarɛsk] adj picaresque
piccolo [pikɔlo] m piccolo
pichet [piʃɛ] m pitcher, jug
pick-up [pikœp] m invar pickup; record player; pickup truck
picoler [pikɔle] intr (slang) to get pickled
picorer [pikɔre] tr & intr to peck
picoter [pikɔte] tr to prick; to peck at; to sting
picotin [pikɔtẽ] m peck (measure)
pictu·ral -rale [piktyral] adj (pl -raux [ro]) pictorial
pie [pi] adj invar piebald ‖ f magpie
pièce [pjɛs] f piece; patch; room; play; document; coin; wine barrel; à la pièce separately; donner la pièce to tip; faire pièce à to play a trick on; to put a check on; inventé de toutes pièces made up out of the whole cloth; la pièce apiece; pièce à conviction (law) exhibit; pièce comptable voucher; pièce d'eau ornamental pond; pièce de rechange, pièce détachée spare part; pièce de résistance pièce de résistance; (culin) entree; tout d'une pièce in one piece; (coll) rigid; (coll) stiffly ‖ adv apiece
pied [pje] m foot; foothold; à pied on foot; au pied de la lettre literally; au pied levé offhand; de pied en cap from head to toe; faire le pied de grue (coll) to cool one's heels, to stand around waiting; faire les pieds à (coll) to give what's coming to; faire un pied de nez (coll) to thumb one's nose; lever le pied to abscond; mettre à pied to dismiss, fire; mettre les pieds dans le plat (coll) to put one's foot in one's mouth; mettre pied à terre to dismount; pied équin clubfoot; travailler comme un pied (coll) to botch one's work
pied-à-terre [pjetater] m invar hangout, temporary base
pied-bot [pjebo] m (pl pieds-bots) clubfooted person

pied-d'alouette [pjedalwɛt] *m* (*pl* **pieds-d'alouette**) delphinium
pied-droit [pjedrwa] *m* (*pl* **pieds-droits**) (archit) pier
piédes·tal -tale [pjedɛstal] *m* (*pl* **-taux** [to]) pedestal
pied-noir [pjenwar] *m* (*pl* **pieds-noirs**) Algerian of European descent
piège [pjɛʒ] *m* trap, snare
piéger [pjeʒe] §1 *tr* to trap, to snare; to booby-trap
pie-grièche [pigrijɛʃ] *f* (*pl* **pies-grièches**) shrike; shrew
pierraille [pjɛraj] *f* rubble
pierre [pjɛr] *f* stone; **faire d'une pierre deux coups** to kill two birds with one stone; **Pierre** Peter; **pierre à aiguiser** whetstone; **pierre à briquet** flint; **pierre à chaux, pierre à plâtre** gypsum; **pierre à feu, pierre à fusil** gunflint; **pierre angulaire** cornerstone; **pierre à rasoir** hone; **pierre calcaire** limestone; **pierre d'achoppement** stumbling block; **pierre de gué** stepping stone; **pierre de touche** touchstone; **pierre tombale** tombstone
pierreries [pjɛrri] *fpl* precious stones
pier·reux [pjɛrø] **pier-reuse** [pjɛrøz] *adj* stony ‖ *f* (coll) streetwalker
pierrot [pjɛro] *m* clown; sparrow; (coll) oddball; (coll) greenhorn
piété [pjete] *f* piety; devotion
piéter [pjete] §10 *intr* to toe the line ‖ *ref* to stand firm
piétiner [pjetine] *tr* to trample on ‖ *intr* to stamp; to mark time
piéton [pjetɔ̃] *m* pedestrian
piètre [pjɛtr] *adj* poor, wretched
pieu [pjø] *m* (*pl* **pieux**) post, stake; (archit) pile
pieuvre [pjœvr] *f* octopus; (coll) leech
pieux [pjø] **pieuse** [pjøz] *adj* pious; dutiful; white (*lie*)
pif [pif] *m* (slang) snout (*nose*) ‖ *interj* bang!
pige [piʒ] *f* (slang) year; **à la pige** (journ) so much a line; **faire la pige à** (slang) to outdo
pigeon [piʒɔ̃] *m* pigeon; **pigeon voyageur** homing pigeon
pigeonner [piʒɔne] *tr* (coll) to dupe
pigeonnier [piʒɔnje] *m* dovecote
piger [piʒe] §38 *tr* (slang) to look at; (slang) to get ‖ *intr*—**tu piges?** (slang) do you get it?
pigment [pigmɑ̃] *m* pigment
pignocher [piɲɔʃe] *intr* to pick at one's food
pignon [piɲɔ̃] *m* gable; (mach) pinion; **avoir pignon sur rue** (coll) to have a home of one's own; (coll) to be well off; **pignon de chaîne** sprocket wheel
pile [pil] *f* stack, pile; pier; (elec) battery (*primary cell*); (coll) thrashing; **pile atomique** atomic pile; **pile ou face** heads or tails; **pile sèche** dry cell ‖ *adv* (coll) short; (coll) exactly
piler [pile] *tr* to grind, to crush
pilier [pilje] *m* pillar; **pilier de cabaret** barfly

pillage [pijaʒ] *m* looting
pil·lard [pijar] **pil·larde** [pijard] *adj* looting ‖ *mf* looter
piller [pije] *tr & intr* to loot; to plagiarize
pil·leur [pijœr] **pil·leuse** [pijøz] *mf* pillager
pilon [pilɔ̃] *m* pestle; (coll) drumstick (*of chicken*); (coll) wooden leg; **pilon à vapeur** steam hammer
pilonnage [pilɔnaʒ] *m* crushing; **pilonnage aérien** saturation bombing
pilonner [pilɔne] *tr* to crush; to bomb
pilori [pilɔri] *m* pillory
pilot [pilo] *m* pile (*in piling*); rags (*for paper*)
pilotage [pilɔtaʒ] *m* piloting; **pilotage sans visibilité** blind flying
pilote [pilɔt] *m* pilot; **pilote de ligne** airline pilot; **pilote d'essai** test pilot
piloter [pilɔte] *tr* to pilot; to guide; to drive piles into ‖ *intr* to pilot; to be a guide
pilotis [pilɔti] *m* piles
pilule [pilyl] *f* pill; (coll) bitter pill; **dorer la pilule** to gild the lily
piment [pimɑ̃] *m* allspice (*berry*); (fig) spice; **piment doux** sweet pepper; **piment rouge** red or hot pepper
pimenter [pimɑ̃te] *tr* to season with red pepper; (fig) to spice
pim·pant [pɛ̃pɑ̃] **-pante** [pɑ̃t] *adj* smart, spruce
pin [pɛ̃] *m* pine; **pin de Weymouth** (*Pinus strobus*) white pine; **pin sylvestre** (*Pinus sylvestris*) Scotch pine
pinacle [pinakl] *m* pinnacle
pince [pɛ̃s] *f* tongs; pliers; forceps; crowbar; gripper; grip; pleat; claw (*of crab*); **aller à pinces** (slang) to hoof it; **petites pinces, pince à épiler** tweezers; **pince à linge** clothespin; **pince à sucre** sugar tongs; **pince hémostatique** hemostat; **pinces** tongs; pincers, pliers; **pinces de cycliste** bicycle clips; **serrer la pince à** (slang) to shake hands with
pin·cé -cée [pɛ̃se] *adj* prim, tight-lipped; thin, pinched ‖ *f* see **pincée**
pin·ceau [pɛ̃so] *m* (*pl* **-ceaux**) paintbrush; pencil (*of light*)
pincée [pɛ̃se] *f* pinch
pincement [pɛ̃smɑ̃] *m* pinching; plucking
pince-monseigneur [pɛ̃smɔ̃sɛɲœr] *f* (*pl* **pinces-monseigneur**) jimmy
pince-nez [pɛ̃sne] *m invar* nose glasses
pincer [pɛ̃se] §51 *tr* to pinch; to grip; to nip off; to pluck; to top (*plants*); to purse (*the lips*); to pleat; (coll) to nab, to catch ‖ *intr* to bite (*said of cold*); **en pincer pour** (slang) to have a crush on; **pincer de** (mus) to strum on
pince-sans-rire [pɛ̃ssɑ̃rir] *adj invar* deadpan ‖ *mf invar* deadpan comic
pincette [pɛ̃sɛt] *f* tweezers; **pincettes** tweezers; fire tongs
pinçon [pɛ̃sɔ̃] *m* bruise (*from pinch*)
pinède [pinɛd] *f* pine grove
pingouin [pɛ̃gwɛ̃] *m* (*family*: Alcidae) auk

pingre [pɛ̃gr] *adj* (coll) stingy ‖ *mf* (coll) tightwad
pinson [pɛ̃sɔ̃] *m* (orn) finch
pintade [pɛ̃tad] *f* guinea fowl
pin up [pinœp] *f invar* (coll) pinup girl
pioche [pjɔʃ] *f* pickax
piocher [pjɔʃe] *tr & intr* to dig, to pick; (coll) to cram
pio·cheur [pjɔʃœr] -cheuse [ʃøz] *mf* digger; (coll) grind ‖ *f* (mach) cultivator
piolet [pjɔlɛ] *m* ice ax
pion [pjɔ̃] *m* (checkers) man; (chess & fig) pawn; (slang) proctor; damer le pion à (coll) to get the better of
pionnier [pjɔnje] *m* pioneer
pipe [pip] *f* pipe; casser sa pipe (slang) to kick the bucket
pi·peau [pipo] *m* (*pl* -peaux) bird call; shepherd's pipe; lime twig
piper [pipe] *tr* to snare, to catch; to load (*the dice*); to mark (*the cards*) ‖ *intr*—ne pipe pas! (coll) not a peep out of you!
pi·quant [pikɑ̃] -quante [kɑ̃t] *adj* piquant, intriguing; racy, spicy ‖ *m* sting; prickle; quill (*of porcupine*); piquancy, pungency; point (*of story*); (fig) bite
pique [pik] *m* (cards) spade; (cards) spades ‖ *f* pike; pique
pi·qué -quée [pike] *adj* stung; sour; (mus) staccato; (coll) batty; piqué de studded with ‖ *m* quilt; descendre en piqué to nose-dive
pique-assiette [pikasjɛt] *mf* (*pl* -assiettes) (coll) sponger
pique-feu [pikfø] *m invar* poker
pique-nique [piknik] *m* (*pl* -niques) picnic
pique-niquer [piknike] *intr* to picnic
piquer [pike] *tr* to sting; to prick; to pique; to stimulate; to quilt; to spur; to give a shot to; (mus) to play staccato; (slang) to filch; (slang) to pinch, to nab ‖ *intr* to turn sour; (aer) to nose-dive ‖ *ref* to be piqued; to spot; to give oneself a shot; se piquer de to take pride in; se piquer pour to take a fancy to
piquet [pikɛ] *m* peg, stake; picket; piquet de grève picket line
piqueter [pikte] §34 *tr* to stake out; to spot, dot
piquette [pikɛt] *f* poor wine; (coll) crushing defeat
pi·queur [pikœr] -queuse [køz] *mf* stitcher ‖ *m* huntsman; outrider
piqûre [pikyr] *f* sting, bite; prick; injection, shot; stitching; puncture; piqûre de ver moth hole
pirate [pirat] *m* pirate; pirate de l'air hijacker
pirater [pirate] *intr* to pirate
piraterie [piratri] *f* piracy; piraterie aérienne hijacking
pire [pir] §91 *adj comp & super* worse; worst ‖ *m* (the) worst
pirouette [pirwɛt] *f* pirouette
pirouetter [pirwete] *intr* to pirouette
pis [pi] *adj comp & super* worse; worst ‖ *m* udder; au pis aller at worst; de pis en pis worse and worse; (le) pis (the) worst; qui pis est what's worse; tant pis so much the worse ‖ *adv comp & super* §91 worse; worst
pis-aller [pizale] *m invar* makeshift
piscine [pisin] *f* swimming pool
pissenlit [pisɑ̃li] *m* dandelion
pisser [pise] *tr* (coll) to spout (*water*); (coll) to leak; (slang) to pass (e.g., *blood*); pisser de la copie (slang) to be a hack writer ‖ *intr* (slang) to urinate
pisse-vinaigre [pisvinɛgr] *m invar* (coll) skinflint
pissoir [piswar] *m* (coll) urinal
pissotière [pisɔtjɛr] *f* (coll) street urinal
pistache [pistaʃ] *f* pistachio
piste [pist] *f* track; trail; ring (*of, e.g., circus*); rink; lane (*of highway*); à double piste four-lane (*highway*); piste cavalière bridle path; piste cyclable bicycle path; piste d'atterrissage landing strip; piste de danse dance floor; piste d'envol runway; piste pour skieurs ski run; piste sonore sound track
pister [piste] *tr* to track, trail
pistolet [pistɔlɛ] *m* pistol; spray gun; (coll) card; pistolet à bouchon popgun; pistolet d'arçon horse pistol; pistolet mitrailleur submachine gun
piston [pistɔ̃] *m* piston; (coll) pull
pistonner [pistɔne] *tr* (coll) to push, to back
pitance [pitɑ̃s] *f* ration; food
pi·teux [pitø] -teuse [tøz] *adj* pitiful, sorry, sad
pitié [pitje] *f* pity; à faire pitié (coll) very badly; par pitié! for pity's sake!; quelle pitié! how awful!
piton [pitɔ̃] *m* screw eye; peak
pitou [pitu] *m* (Canad) dog; (Canad) tyke
pitoyable [pitwajabl] *adj* pitiful
pitre [pitr] *m* clown
pittoresque [pitɔrɛsk] *adj* picturesque
pivoine [pivwan] *f* peony
pivot [pivo] *m* pivot
pivoter [pivɔte] *intr* to pivot
P.J. [peʒi] *f* (letterword) (police judiciaire) (coll) police (*dealing with criminal cases*)
placage [plakaʒ] *m* veneering; plating
placard [plakar] *m* cupboard; closet; placard, poster; (typ) galley
placarder [plakarde] *tr* to placard; (typ) to print in galleys
place [plas] *f* place; city square; room; seat; job, position; fare; sur place on the spot
placement [plasmɑ̃] *m* placement; investment; de placement employment (*agency*)
placer [plase] §51 *tr* to place; to invest; to slip in ‖ *ref* to seat oneself; to rank; to get a job; to take place
pla·ceur [plasœr] -ceuse [søz] *mf* employment agent ‖ *m* usher
placide [plasid] *adj* placid

pla·cier [plasje] **-cière** [sjer] *mf* agent, representative
plafond [plafɔ̃] *m* ceiling
plafonner [plafɔne] *intr*—**plafonner (à)** to hit the top (at)
plafonnier [plafɔnje] *m* ceiling light; (aut) dome light
plage [plaʒ] *f* beach; band (*of record*); (poetic) clime
plagiaire [plaʒjɛr] *mf* plagiarist
plagiat [plaʒja] *m* plagiarism
plagier [plaʒje] *tr & intr* to plagiarize
plagiste [plaʒist] *mf* beach concessionaire
plaider [plede] *tr* to argue (*a case*); to plead (*e.g., ignorance*) ‖ *intr* to plead; to go to law
plai·deur [plɛdœr] **-deuse** [døz] *mf* litigant
plaidoirie [plɛdwari] *f* pleading
plaidoyer [plɛdwaje] *m* appeal (*of lawyer to judge or jury*)
plaie [plɛ] *f* wound, sore; plague; **plaie en séton** flesh wound
plai·gnant [plɛɲɑ̃] **-gnante** [ɲɑ̃t] *mf* plaintiff
plain [plɛ̃] *m* high tide
plaindre [plɛ̃dr] §15 *tr* to pity ‖ *ref* to complain
plaine [plɛn] *f* plain
plain-pied [plɛ̃pje] *m*—**de plain-pied** on the same floor; (fig) on an equal footing
plainte [plɛ̃t] *f* complaint; moan
plain·tif [plɛ̃tif] **-tive** [tiv] *adj* plaintive
plaire [plɛr] §52 *intr* (with *dat*) to please; (with *dat*) to like, e.g., **le lait lui plaît** he likes milk; **s'il vous plaît** please ‖ *ref* to be pleased; to enjoy oneself; to like one another; **se plaire à** to like it in, e.g., **je me plais à la campagne** I like it in the country
plaisance [plɛzɑ̃s] *f*—**de plaisance** pleasure (*e.g., boat*)
plai·sant [plɛzɑ̃] **-sante** [zɑ̃t] *adj* pleasant; funny ‖ *m*—**mauvais plaisant** practical joker
plaisanter [plɛzɑ̃te] *tr* to poke fun at ‖ *intr* to joke
plaisanterie [plɛzɑ̃tri] *f* joke; joking
plaisantin [plɛzɑ̃tɛ̃] *adj masc* roguish, waggish ‖ *m* wag
plaisir [plezir] *m* pleasure; **à plaisir** without cause; at one's pleasure; **au plaisir (de vous revoir)** good-by; **faire plaisir à** to please, give pleasure to
plan [plɑ̃] **plane** [plan] *adj* even, flat; **plane** (*angle*) ‖ *m* plan; design; (geom) plane; **au deuxième plan** in the background; **au premier plan** in the foreground; downstage; **au troisième plan** far in the background; **gros plan** (mov) close-up; **laisser en plan** (coll) to leave stranded; (coll) to put off, delay; **lever un plan** to survey; **plan de travail** work schedule; **rester en plan** (coll) to remain in suspense; **sur le plan de** from the point of view of ‖ *f* see **plane**

planche [plɑ̃ʃ] *f* board; plank; (hort) bed; (typ) plate; (slang) blackboard; **faire la planche** to float on one's back; **planche de bord** instrument panel; **planche de débarquement** gangplank; **planche de salut** sheet anchor
planchéier [plɑ̃ʃeje] *tr* to floor; to board
plancher [plɑ̃ʃe] *m* floor; **le plancher des vaches** (coll) terra firma
plane [plan] *f* drawknife
planer [plane] *tr* to plane ‖ *intr* to hover; to glide; to float; **planer sur** to overlook, to sweep (*e.g., a landscape with one's eyes*); (fig) to hover over
planète [planɛt] *f* planet
planeur [planœr] *m* glider
planeuse [planøz] *f* planing machine
planification [planifikɑsjɔ̃] *f* planning
planifier [planifje] *tr* to plan
planning [planiŋ] *m* detailed plan; **planning familial** birth control
plan-plan [plɑ̃plɑ̃] *adv* (coll) quietly, without hurrying
planque [plɑ̃k] *f* (coll) soft job; (slang) hideout
planquer [plɑ̃ke] *tr* to hide ‖ *ref* (mil) to take cover; (slang) to hide out
plant [plɑ̃] *m* planting; bed, patch; seedling, sapling
plantation [plɑ̃tɑsjɔ̃] *f* planting; plantation; **plantation de cheveux** hairline; head of hair
plante [plɑ̃t] *f* plant; sole
plan·té-tée [plɑ̃te] *adj* set, situated
planter [plɑ̃te] *tr* to plant; to set; **planter là** to give the slip to ‖ *ref* to stand
planteur [plɑ̃tœr] *m* planter
plantoir [plɑ̃twar] *m* (hort) dibble
planton [plɑ̃tɔ̃] *m* (mil) orderly
plantu·reux [plɑ̃tyrø] **-reuse** [røz] *adj* abundant; fertile; (coll) buxom
plaque [plak] *f* plate; plaque; splotch; **plaque à crêpes** pancake griddle; **plaque croûteuse** scab; **plaque d'immatriculation, plaque minéralogique** (aut) license plate; **plaque tournante** (rr) turntable; (fig) hub (*of a city*)
plaquer [plake] *tr* to plate; to veneer; to plaster down (*one's hair*); to strike (*a chord*); (football) to tackle; (coll) to jilt; **plaquer à l'électricité** to electroplate ‖ *ref* to lie flat; (aer) to pancake
plaquette [plakɛt] *f* plaque; pamphlet; (histology) platelet
plastic [plastik] *m* plastic bomb
plastique [plastik] *adj* plastic ‖ *m* plastics ‖ *f* plastic art
plastron [plastrɔ̃] *m* shirt front; breastplate; hostile contingent (*in war games*)
plastronner [plastrɔne] *intr* (fig) to throw out one's chest
plat [pla] **plate** [plat] *adj* flat; even; smooth (*sea*); dead (*calm*); corny (*joke*); **à plat** run-down; flat ‖ *m* dish; platter; course (*of meal*); flat (*of hand*); blade (*of oar*); face (*of hammer*); **plat cuisiné** platter, short-

order meal; **plat de côtes** sparerib; **plat du jour** today's special, chef's special; **plat principal, plat de résistance** entree; **plats** (bb) boards

platane [platan] *m* plane tree; **faux platane** sycamore

pla·teau [plato] *m* (*pl* **-teaux**) plateau; tray; shelf; platform; plate; pan (*of scale*); (mov, telv) set; (rr) flatcar; (theat) stage; **plateau porte-disque** turntable (*of phonograph*); **plateau tournant** revolving stage

plate-bande [platbɑd] *f* (*pl* **plates-bandes**) flower bed

plate-forme [platfɔrm] *f* (*pl* **plates-formes**) platform; (rr) flatcar

platine [platin] *m* platinum ‖ *f* plate; platen; lock (*of gun*); stage (*of microscope*)

plati·né -née [platine] *adj* platinum-plated; platinum

platitude [platityd] *f* platitude; flatness; obsequiousness

Platon [platɔ̃] *m* Plato

plâtre [platr] *m* plaster; plaster cast; **essuyer les plâtres** to be the first occupant of a new house; **plâtre à mouler** plaster of Paris

plâtrer [platre] *tr* to plaster; to put in a cast; to fertilize ‖ *ref* (coll) to pile on the make-up or face powder

plausible [plozibl] *adj* plausible

plébéien [plebejɛ̃] **plébéienne** [plebejɛn] *adj & mf* plebeian

plein [plɛ̃] **pleine** [plɛn] *adj* full; round, plump; solid (*bar, wheel, wire, etc.*); continuous (*line*); heavy (*heart*); in foal, with calf, etc.; (coll) drunk; **plein aux as** (coll) well-heeled; **plein de** full of; covered with; preoccupied with; **plein de soi** self-centered ‖ (when standing before noun) *adj* full; high (*tide*); **en plein + noun** in the midst of the **+** noun, right in the **+** noun; at the height of the (*season*); in the open (*air*); out at (*sea*), on the high (*seas*); in broad (*daylight*); in the dead of (*winter*) ‖ *m* full (*of the moon*); bull's-eye; downstroke; **battre son plein** to be in full swing; **en plein** plumb, plump, squarely; **faire le plein (de)** to fill up the tank (with) ‖ **plein** *adv* full; **tout plein** very much

plein-emploi [plɛ̃ɑplwa] *m* full employment

pleu·rard [plœrar] **-rarde** [rard] *adj* (coll) whimpering ‖ *mf* (coll) whimperer

pleurer [plœre] *tr* to weep over; **pleurer misère** to complain of being poor ‖ *intr* to cry, weep; **pleurer à chaudes larmes** to weep bitterly

pleurésie [plœrezi] *f* pleurisy

pleu·reur [plœrœr] **-reuse** [røz] *adj* weeping ‖ *f* paid mourner

pleurnicher [plœrniʃe] *intr* to whimper, snivel

pleurs [plœr] *mpl* tears

pleutre [pløtr] *adj* (coll) cowardly ‖ *m* (coll) coward

pleuvasser [pløvase] *intr* (coll) to drizzle

pleuvoir [pløvwar] §53 *intr & impers* to rain; **pleuvoir à verse, à flots,** or **à seaux** to rain buckets

pli [pli] *m* fold; pleat; bend (*of arm or leg*); hollow (*of knee*); letter; envelope; undulation (*of ground*); (cards) trick; **faux pli** crease, wrinkle; **petit pli** tuck; **sous ce pli** enclosed, herewith; **sous pli cacheté** in a sealed envelope; **sous pli distinct** or **séparé** under separate cover

pliage [plijaʒ] *m* folding

pliant [plijɑ̃] **pliante** [plijɑ̃t] *adj* folding; collapsible; pliant ‖ *m* campstool, folding chair

plier [plije] *tr* to fold; to bend; to force ‖ *intr* to fold; to bend; to yield; **ne pas plier, s.v.p.** (formula on envelope) please do not bend ‖ *ref* to fold; to yield; to fall back (*said of army*)

plisser [plise] *tr* to pleat; to crease; to wrinkle; to squint (*the eyes*) ‖ *intr* to fold ‖ *ref* to wrinkle; to pucker up (*said of mouth*)

plomb [plɔ̃] *m* lead; shot; seal; plumb; sinker (*of fishline*); (elec) fuse; **à plomb** plumb, vertical; straight down, directly; **faire sauter un plomb** to burn or blow out a fuse

plombage [plɔ̃baʒ] *m* filling (*of tooth*); sealing (*e.g., at customs*)

plombagine [plɔ̃baʒin] *f* graphite

plom·bé -bée [plɔ̃be] *adj* leaden; in bond, sealed; filled (*tooth*); livid (*hue*)

plomber [plɔ̃be] *tr* to cover with lead; to seal; to plumb; to fill (*a tooth*); to make livid; to roll (*the ground*)

plomberie [plɔ̃bri] *f* plumbing; plumbing-supply store; leadwork

plombeur [plɔ̃bœr] *m* (mach) roller

plombier [plɔ̃bje] *m* plumber; worker in lead

plonge [plɔ̃ʒ] *f* dishwashing

plon·geant [plɔ̃ʒɑ̃] **-geante** [ʒɑ̃t] *adj* plunging; from above

plongée [plɔ̃ʒe] *f* plunge; dive; dip, slope; **en plongée** submerged

plongeoir [plɔ̃ʒwar] *m* diving board

plongeon [plɔ̃ʒɔ̃] *m* plunge; dive; (football) tackle; **plongeon de haut vol** high dive

plonger [plɔ̃ʒe] §38 *tr* to plunge; to thrust, to stick ‖ *intr* to plunge; to dive; (coll) to have a good view; **plonger raide** to crash-dive ‖ *ref—se plonger dans** to immerse oneself in; to give oneself over to

plon·geur [plɔ̃ʒœr] **-geuse** [ʒøz] *adj* diving ‖ *mf* diver; dishwasher (*in restaurant*) ‖ *m* (mach) plunger; (orn) diver

plot [plo] *m* (elec) contact point

ployer [plwaje] §47 *tr & intr* to bend

pluches [plyʃ] *fpl* (mil) K.P.

pluie [plɥi] *f* rain; shower; **pluies radioactives** fallout

plumage [plymaʒ] *m* plumage

plumard [plymar] *m*—**aller au plumard** (slang) to hit the hay
plume [plym] *f* feather; pen; penpoint
plu·meau [plymo] *m* (*pl* -**meaux**) feather duster
plumer [plyme] *tr* to pluck; (coll) to fleece || *intr* to feather one's oar
plumet [plymɛ] *m* plume
plu·meux [plymø] -**meuse** [møz] *adj* feathery
plumier [plymje] *m* pencil box
plupart [plypar] *f*—**la plupart** most; the most; for the most part; **la plupart de** most; the most; most of, the majority of; **la plupart d'entre nous (eux)** most of us (them); **pour la plupart** for the most part
plu·riel -**rielle** [plyrjɛl] *adj* & *m* plural; **au pluriel** in the plural
plus [ply] ([plyz] before vowel; [plys] in final position) *m* plus; **au plus, tout au plus** at the most, at best; at the latest; at the outside; **d'autant plus** all the more so; **de plus** more; moreover, besides; **de plus en plus** more and more; **en plus extra; en plus de** in addition to, besides; **le plus, la plus, les plus** (the) most; **le plus de** the most; **le plus que** as much as, as fast as; **ni . . . non plus** nor . . . either, e.g., **ni moi non plus** nor I either; **ni plus ni moins** neither more nor less; **non plus** neither, not . . . either; **plus de** more, e.g., **plus de chaleur** more heat; no more, e.g., **plus de potage** no more soup; **qui plus est** what is more, moreover || *adv comp* & *super* §91 more; **des plus + adj** most; **des plus + adj**, extremely + *adj*; (**le**) **plus . . .** (the) most . . ., e.g., **ce que j'aime le plus** what I like (the) most; **le** (or **son, etc.**) **plus +** *adj* the (or his, etc.) most; **ne . . . plus** §90 no more, no longer; **ne . . . plus que** §90 now only, e.g., **il n'y a plus que mon oncle** there is now only my uncle; **on ne peut plus +** *adj* or *adv* extremely + *adj* or *adv*; **plus de** (followed by numeral) more than; **plus jamais** never more; **plus . . . plus** (or **moins**) the more . . . the more (or the less); **plus que** more than; **plus tôt** sooner || *prep* plus
plusieurs [plyzjœr] *adj* & *pron indef* several
plus-que-parfait [plyskəparfɛ] *m* pluperfect
plus-value [plyvaly] *f* (*pl* -**values**) appreciation; increase; surplus; extra cost; surplus value (*in Marxian economics*)
Plutarque [plytark] *m* Plutarch
Pluton [plytɔ̃] *m* Pluto
plutonium [plytɔnjɔm] *m* plutonium
plutôt [plyto] *adv* rather; instead; **plutôt . . . que** rather . . . than
pluvier [plyvje] *m* (orn) plover
plu·vieux [plyvjø] -**vieuse** [vjøz] *adj* rainy
pneu [pnø] *m* (*pl* **pneus**) tire; express letter (*by Parisian tube*); **pneu ballon**

or **confort** balloon tire; **pneu de secours** spare tire
pneumatique [pnømatik] *adj* pneumatic || *m* tire; express letter (*by Parisian tube*)
pneumonie [pnømɔni] *f* pneumonia
pochade [pɔʃad] *f* sketch
po·chard [pɔʃar] -**charde** [ʃard] *mf* (coll) boozer, guzzler
poche [pɔʃ] *f* pocket; bag, pouch; crop (*of bird*)
po·ché -**chée** [pɔʃe] *adj* poached; black (*eye*)
pocher [pɔʃe] *tr* to poach; to dash off (*a sketch*)
pochette [pɔʃɛt] *f* folder; book (*of matches*); kit; fancy handkerchief; **pochette à disque** record jacket; **pochette surprise** surprise package
pocheuse [pɔʃøz] *f* egg poacher
pochoir [pɔʃwar] *m* stencil
poêle [pwal] *m* stove; pall; canopy || *f* frying pan
poêlon [pwalɔ̃] *m* saucepan
poème [pɔɛm] *m* poem; **poème symphonique** tone poem
poésie [pɔezi] *f* poetry; poem
poète [pɔɛt] *mf* poet
poétesse [pɔetɛs] *f* poetess
poétique [pɔetik] *adj* poetic(al) || *f* poetics
pogrom [pɔgrɔm] *m* pogrom
poids [pwa], [pwɑ] *m* weight; **poids lourd** truck
poi·gnant [pwaɲɑ̃] -**gnante** [ɲɑ̃t] *adj* poignant
poignard [pwaɲar] *m* dagger
poignarder [pwaɲarde] *tr* to stab
poigne [pwaɲ] *f* grip, grasp; **à poigne** strong, energetic
poignée [pwaɲe] *f* handful; handle; grip; hilt; **poignée de main** handshake
poignet [pwaɲɛ] *m* wrist; cuff; **poignet mousquetaire** French cuff
poil [pwal] *m* hair; bristle; nap, pile; coat (*of animals*); **à long poil** shaggy; **à poil** naked; bareback; **au poil** (slang) peachy; **avoir un poil dans la main** (coll) to be lazy; **de mauvais poil** (coll) in a bad mood; **de tout poil** (coll) of every shade and hue; **poil follet** down; **reprendre du poil de la bête** (coll) to be one's own self again; **se mettre à poil** to strip to the skin
poi·lu -**lue** [pwaly] *adj* hairy || *m* (mil) doughboy
poinçon [pwɛ̃sɔ̃] *m* punch; stamp; hallmark; **poinçon à glace** ice pick
poinçonner [pwɛ̃sɔne] *tr* to punch; to stamp; to prick; to hallmark
poinçonneuse [pwɛ̃sɔnøz] *f* stamping machine; ticket punch
poindre [pwɛ̃dr] §35 *intr* to dawn; to sprout
poing [pwɛ̃] *m* fist; **dormir à poings fermés** to sleep like a log
point [pwɛ̃] *m* point; stitch; period (*used also in French to mark the divisions of whole numbers*); hole (*in a strap*); mark (*on a test*); (aer,

naut) position; (typ) point; **à point** at the right moment; to a turn, medium; **à point nommé** in the nick of time; **à tel point que** to such a degree that; **au dernier point** to the utmost degree; **de point en point** exactly to the letter; **de tout point, en tout point** entirely; **deux points** colon; **faire le point** to take stock, to get one's bearings; **mettre au point** to focus; to adjust, to tune up; to develop, to perfect; **mettre les points sur les i** to dot one's i's; **point d'appui** fulcrum; base of operations; **point de bâti** (sewing) tack; **point de départ** starting point; **point de repère** point of reference, guide; (surv) bench mark; (fig) landmark; **point d'estime** dead reckoning; **point d'exclamation** exclamation point; **point d'interrogation** question mark; **point d'orgue** (mus) pause; **point du jour** break of day; **point et virgule** semicolon; **point mort** dead center; (aut) neutral; **points et traits** dots and dashes || *adv*—**ne . . . point** §90 not; not at all

pointage [pwɛ̃taʒ] *m* checking; check mark; aiming

pointe [pwɛ̃t] *f* point; tip; peak; head (*of arrow*); nose (*e.g., of bullet*); toe (*of shoe*); twinge (*of pain*); dash (*of, e.g., vanilla*); suggestion, touch; witty phrase, quip; (geog) cape, point; (mil) spearhead; **à pointes** spiked (*shoes*); **de pointe** peak (*e.g., hours*); **discuter sur les pointes d'épingle** to split hairs; **en pointe** tapering; **faire des pointes** to toe-dance; **pointe d'aiguille** needlepoint; **pointe de Paris** wire nail; **pointe de vitesse** spurt; **pointe du jour** daybreak; **sur la pointe des pieds** on tiptoe

poin·teau [pwɛ̃to] *m* (*pl* **-teaux**) checker; needle

pointer [pwɛ̃tœr] *m* pointer (*dog*) || [pwɛ̃te] *tr* to check off; to close in; to prick up (*the ears*); to dot || *intr* to rise, to soar skywards; to stand out; to sprout || *ref* to check in, to show up

poin·teur [pwɛ̃tœr] **-teuse** [tøz] *mf* checker; scorer; timekeeper; gunner; (*dog*) pointer

pointillé [pwɛ̃tije] *m* perforated line

pointil·leux [pwɛ̃tijø] **pointil·leuse** [pwɛ̃tijøz] *adj* punctilious; touchy; captious

poin·tu -tue [pwɛ̃ty] *adj* pointed; shrill; (fig) touchy

pointure [pwɛ̃tyr] *f* size

poire [pwar] *f* pear; bulb (*of camera, syringe, horn, etc.*); (slang) mug; (slang) sucker, sap; **couper la poire en deux** to split the difference; **garder une poire pour la soif** to put something aside for a rainy day; **poire à poudre** powder flask; **poire électrique** pear-shaped switch

poi·reau [pwaro] *m* (*pl* **-reaux**) (bot) leek

poirée [pware] *f* (bot) Swiss chard

poirier [pwarje] *m* pear tree

pois [pwa], [pwɑ] *m* pea; polka dot; **petits pois, pois verts** peas; **pois cassés** split peas; **pois chiche** chickpea; **pois de senteur** sweet pea

poison [pwazɔ̃] *m* poison

pois·sard [pwasar] **pois·sarde** [pwasard] *adj* vulgar || *f* fishwife

poisser [pwase] *tr* to coat with wax or pitch || *intr* to be sticky

pois·seux [pwasø] **pois·seuse** [pwasøz] *adj* sticky

poisson [pwasɔ̃] *m* fish; **poisson d'avril** April Fool (*joke, trick*); **poisson rouge** goldfish

poisson-chat [pwasɔ̃ʃa] *m* (*pl* **poissons-chats**) catfish

poissonnerie [pwasɔnri] *f* fish market

poisson·nier [pwasɔnje] **poisson·nière** [pwasɔnjɛr] *mf* dealer in fish || *f* fishwife; fish kettle

poitrail [pwatraj] *m* breast

poitrinaire [pwatrinɛr] *adj & mf* (pathol) consumptive

poitrine [pwatrin] *f* chest; breast; bosom

poivre [pwavr] *m* pepper

poivrer [pwavre] *tr* to pepper

poivrier [pwavrije] *m* pepper plant; pepper shaker

poivrière [pwavrijɛr] *f* pepper shaker; pepper plantation

poivron [pwavrɔ̃] *m* pepper; sweet pepper plant

poix [pwa], [pwɑ] *f* pitch; **poix sèche** resin

poker [pɔkɛr] *m* poker; four of a kind

polaire [pɔlɛr] *adj* pole, polar

polariser [pɔlarize] *tr* to polarize

pôle [pol] *m* pole

po·li -lie [pɔli] *adj* polished; polite || *m* polish, gloss

police [pɔlis] *f* police; policy; **police d'assurance** insurance policy

policer [pɔlise] §51 *tr* to civilize; (obs) to police

Polichinelle [pɔliʃinɛl] *m* Punch; **de polichinelle** open (*secret*)

poli·cier [pɔlisje] **-cière** [sjɛr] *adj* police (*investigation, dog, etc.*); detective (*e.g., story*) || *m* plain-clothes man, detective

polio [pɔljo] *mf* (coll) polio victim || *f* (coll) polio

polir [pɔlir] *tr* to polish

polissoir [pɔliswar] *m* polisher

polis·son [pɔlisɔ̃] **polis·sonne** [pɔlisɔn] *adj* smutty || *mf* scamp, rascal

politesse [pɔlites] *f* politeness; **politesses** civilities, compliments

politicard [pɔlitikar] *m* unscrupulous politician

politi·cien [pɔlitisjɛ̃] **-cienne** [sjɛn] *adj* short-sighted; insincere || *mf* politician

politique [pɔlitik] *adj* political; prudent, wise || *m* politician; statesman || *f* politics; policy; cunning, shrewdness

pollen [pɔllɛn] *m* pollen

polluer [pɔllɥe] *tr* to pollute

polo [pɔlo] *m* polo

Pologne [pɔlɔɲ] *f* Poland; **la Pologne** Poland

polo·nais [pɔlɔnɛ] **-naise** [nɛz] *adj* Polish || *m* Polish (*language*) || (*cap*) *mf* Pole

polonium [pɔlɔnjɔm] *m* polonium

pol·tron [pɔltrɔ̃] **-tronne** [trɔn] *adj* cowardly || *mf* coward

polycopie [pɔlikɔpi] *f* mimeographing; **tiré à la polycopie** mimeographed

polycopié [pɔlikɔpje] *m* mimeographed university lectures

polycopier [pɔlikɔpje] *tr* to mimeograph

polygame [pɔligam] *adj* polygamous || *mf* polygamist

polyglotte [pɔliglɔt] *adj* polyglot || *mf* polyglot, linguist

polygone [pɔligɔn] *m* polygon; shooting range

polynôme [pɔlinom] *m* polynomial

polype [pɔlip] *m* polyp

polythéiste [pɔliteist] *adj* polytheistic || *mf* polytheist

pom [pɔ̃] *interj* bang!

pommade [pɔmad] *f* pomade; **passer de la pommade à** (coll) to soft-soap

pomme [pɔm] *f* apple; ball, knob; head (*of lettuce*); **pomme de discorde** bone of contention; **pomme de pin** pine cone; **pomme de terre** potato; **pommes chips** potato chips; **pommes de terre au four** baked potatoes; scalloped potatoes; **pommes de terre en robe de chambre, en robe des champs,** or **en chemise** potatoes in their jackets; **pommes de terre sautées** fried potatoes; **pommes frites** French fried potatoes; **pommes soufflées** potato puffs; **pommes vapeur** boiled potatoes; steamed potatoes

pom·meau [pɔmo] *m* (*pl* **-meaux**) pommel; butt (*of fishing pole*)

pomme·lé **-lée** [pɔmle] *adj* dappled; fleecy (*clouds*); mackerel (*sky*)

pommette [pɔmɛt] *f* cheekbone

pommier [pɔmje] *m* apple tree

pompe [pɔ̃p] *f* pomp; pump; **à la pompe** on draught; **pompe à incendie** fire engine; **pompe aspirante** suction pump; **pompes funèbres** funeral

pomper [pɔ̃pe] *tr* to pump; to suck in

pompette [pɔ̃pɛt] *adj* (coll) tipsy

pom·peux [pɔ̃pø] **-peuse** [pøz] *adj* pompous; high-flown

pom·pier [pɔ̃pje] **-pière** [pjɛr] *adj* conventional; pretentious || *mf* fitter || *m* fireman

pompiste [pɔ̃pist] *mf* filling-station attendant

pomponner [pɔ̃pɔne] *tr* & *ref* to dress up

ponçage [pɔ̃saʒ] *m* sandpapering; pumicing

ponce [pɔ̃s] *f* pumice stone

pon·ceau [pɔ̃so] (*pl* **-ceaux**) *adj* poppyred || *m* rude bridge; culvert

poncer [pɔ̃se] §51 *tr* to sandpaper; to pumice

poncho [pɔ̃tʃo] *m* poncho

poncif [pɔ̃sif] *m* banality

ponctualité [pɔ̃ktɥalite] *f* punctuality

ponctuation [pɔ̃ktɥasjɔ̃] *f* punctuation

ponc·tuel **-tuelle** [pɔ̃ktɥɛl] *adj* punctual

ponctuer [pɔ̃ktɥe] *tr* to punctuate

pondération [pɔ̃derɑsjɔ̃] *f* balance; weighting

pondé·ré **-rée** [pɔ̃dere] *adj* moderate, well-balanced; weighted

pondérer [pɔ̃dere] §10 *tr* to balance; to weight

pondeuse [pɔ̃døz] *f* layer (*hen*); (coll) prolific woman

pondre [pɔ̃dr] *tr* to lay (*an egg*); (coll) to turn out (*a book*); (slang) to bear (*a child*) || *intr* to lay

poney [pɔnɛ] *m* pony

pont [pɔ̃] *m* bridge; (naut) deck; **faire le pont** (coll) to take the intervening day or days off; **pont aérien** airlift; **pont arrière** (aut) rear-axle assembly; **pont cantilever, pont à consoles** cantilever bridge; **ponts et chaussées** [pɔ̃zeʃose] highway department; **pont suspendu** suspension bridge

ponte [pɔ̃t] *f* egg laying; eggs

pontet [pɔ̃tɛ] *m* trigger guard

pontife [pɔ̃tif] *m* pontiff

pont-levis [pɔ̃lvi] *m* (*pl* **ponts-levis**) drawbridge

ponton [pɔ̃tɔ̃] *m* pontoon; landing stage

pont-promenade [pɔ̃prɔmnad] *m* (*pl* **ponts-promenades**) promenade deck

pool [pul] *m* pool (*combine*)

pope [pɔp] *m* Orthodox priest

popeline [pɔplin] *f* poplin

popote [pɔpɔt] *adj invar* (coll) stay-athome || *f* (mil) mess; (coll) cooking; **faire la popote** (coll) to do the cooking oneself

populace [pɔpylas] *f* populace, rabble

populaire [pɔpylɛr] *adj* popular; vulgar, common

populariser [pɔpylarize] *tr* to popularize

popularité [pɔpylarite] *f* popularity

population [pɔpylasjɔ̃] *f* population

popu·leux [pɔpylø] **-leuse** [løz] *adj* populous; crowded

populo [pɔpylo] *m* (coll) rabble

porc [pɔr] *m* pig, hog; pork

porcelaine [pɔrsəlɛn] *f* porcelain; china

porcelet [pɔrsəle] *m* piglet

porc-épic [pɔrkepik] *m* (*pl* **porcs-épics** [pɔrkepik]) porcupine

porche [pɔrʃ] *m* porch, portico

porcher [pɔrʃe] *m* swineherd

porcherie [pɔrʃəri] *f* pigpen

pore [pɔr] *m* pore

po·reux [pɔrø] **-reuse** [røz] *adj* porous

pornographie [pɔrnɔgrafi] *f* pornography

porphyre [pɔrfir] *m* porphyry

port [pɔr] *m* port; carrying; wearing; bearing; shipping charges; **arriver à bon port** to arrive safe; **port d'attache** home port; **port d'escale** port of call; **port franc** duty-free; free port; **port payé** postpaid

portable [pɔrtabl] *adj* portable; wearable

portail [pɔrtaj] *m* portal, gate

por·tant [pɔrtã] **-tante** [tãt] *adj* bearing; lifting; **être bien portant** to be in good health ‖ *m* handle

porta·tif [pɔrtatif] **-tive** [tiv] *adj* portable

porte [pɔrt] *f* door; doorway; gate; **fausse porte** blind door; **porte à deux battants** double door; **porte à tambour** revolving door; **porte battante** swinging door; **porte cochère** covered carriage entrance

porte-à-faux [pɔrtafo] *m invar*—**en porte-à-faux** out of line; (fig) in an untenable position

porte-aiguilles [pɔrtegчi] *m invar* needle case

porte-allumettes [pɔrtalymɛt] *m invar* matchbox

porte-assiette [pɔrtasjɛt] *m* (*pl* -**assiette** or -**assiettes**) place mat

porte-avions [pɔrtavjɔ̃] *m invar* aircraft carrier

porte-bagages [pɔrtbagaʒ] *m invar* baggage rack

porte-bannière [pɔrtbanjɛr] *mf* (*pl* -**bannière** or -**bannières**) colorbearer

porte-bonheur [pɔrtbɔnœr] *m invar* good-luck charm

porte-carte [pɔrtəkart] *m* (*pl* -**carte** or -**cartes**) card case

porte-chapeaux [pɔrtʃapo] *m invar* hatrack

porte-cigarette [pɔrtsigarɛt] *m: invar* cigarette holder

porte-cigarettes [pɔrtsigarɛt] *m invar* cigarette case

porte-clés or **porte-clefs** [pɔrtəkle] *m invar* key ring

porte-disques [pɔrtdisk] *m invar* record case

porte-documents [pɔrtdɔkymã] *m invar* letter case, portfolio

porte-drapeau [pɔrtdrapo] *m* (*pl* -**drapeau** or -**drapeaux**) standard-bearer

portée [pɔrte] *f* range, reach; import, significance; litter; (mus) staff; **à la portée de** within reach of; **à portée de la voix** within speaking distance; **à portée de l'oreille** within hearing distance; **hors de la portée de** out of reach of

portefaix [pɔrtəfɛ] *m* porter; dock hand

porte-fenêtre [pɔrtfənɛtr], [pɔrtəfnɛtr] *f* (*pl* **portes-fenêtres**) French window, French door

portefeuille [pɔrtəfœj] *m* portfolio; wallet, billfold

porteman·teau [pɔrtmãto] *m* (*pl* -**teaux**) clothes tree; **en portemanteau** square (*shoulders*)

porte-mine [pɔrtəmin] *m* (*pl* -**mine** or **mines**) mechanical pencil

porte-monnaie [pɔrtmɔnɛ] *m invar* change purse

porte-parapluies [pɔrtparaplчi] *m invar* umbrella stand

porte-parole [pɔrtparɔl] *m invar* spokesman, mouthpiece

porte-plume [pɔrtəplym] *m invar* penholder; **porte-plume réservoir** fountain pen

porter [pɔrte] *tr* to carry; to bear; to wear; to propose (*a toast*); **être porté à** to be inclined to; **être porté sur** to have a weakness for; **porter à l'écran** (mov) to put on the screen ‖ *intr* to carry; **porter sur** to bear down on, to emphasize; to be aimed at ‖ *ref* to be worn; to proceed, to go; to be, e.g., **comment vous portez-vous?** how are you?; **se porter à** to indulge in; **se porter candidat** to run as a candidate

porte-savon [pɔrtsavɔ̃] *m* (*pl* -**savon** or -**savons**) soap dish

porte-serviettes [pɔrtsɛrvjɛt] *m invar* towel rack

por·teur [pɔrtœr] **-teuse** [tøz] *mf* porter; bearer; holder

porte-vêtement [pɔrtəvɛtmã] *m invar* clothes hanger

porte-voix [pɔrtəvwa] *m invar* megaphone; **mettre les mains en porte-voix** to cup one's hands

por·tier [pɔrtje] **-tière** [tjɛr] *mf* concierge ‖ *m* doorman ‖ *f* door (*of car*); portiere

portillon [pɔrtijɔ̃] *m* gate; (rr) side gate (*at crossing*); **refouler du portillon** (slang) to have bad breath

portion [pɔrsjɔ̃] *f* portion; share

portique [pɔrtik] *m* portico

porto [pɔrto] *m* port wine

portori·cain [pɔrtorikɛ̃] **-caine** [kɛn] *adj* Puerto Rican ‖ (*cap*) *mf* Puerto Rican

Porto Rico [pɔrtoriko] *f* Puerto Rico

portrait [pɔrtrɛ] *m* portrait; **être tout le portrait de** to be the very image of; **portrait à mi-corps** half-length portrait; **portrait de face** full-faced portrait

portraitiste [pɔrtretist] *mf* portrait painter

portu·gais [pɔrtygɛ] **-gaise** [gɛz] *adj* Portuguese ‖ *m* Portuguese (*language*) ‖ (*cap*) *mf* Portuguese (*person*)

Portugal [pɔrtygal] *m*—**le Portugal** Portugal

pose [poz] *f* pose; laying, setting in place; (phot) exposure

po·sé **-sée** [poze] *adj* poised, steady; trained (*voice*)

posément [pozemã] *adv* calmly, steadily, carefully

posemètre [pozmɛtr] *m* (phot) light meter, exposure meter

poser [poze] *tr* to place; to arrange; to ask (*a question*); to set up (*a principle*) ‖ *intr* to pose ‖ *ref* to pose; to alight; to land; **se poser en** to set oneself up as

po·seur [pozœr] **-seuse** [zøz] *mf* layer; poseur; phony; **poseur d'affiches** billposter

posi·tif [pozitif] **-tive** [tiv] *adj* & *m* positive

position [pozisjɔ̃] *f* position

posséder [pɔsede] §10 *tr* to possess, own; to have a command of, to know perfectly ‖ *ref* to control oneself

possession [pɔsesjɔ̃] *f* possession

possibilité [pɔsibilite] *f* possibility
possible [pɔsibl] *adj & m* possible
postage [pɔstaʒ] *m* mailing
pos•tal -tale [pɔstal] *adj* (*pl* **-taux** [to])
postal
postdate [pɔstdat] *f* postdate
postdater [pɔstdate] *tr* to postdate
poste [pɔst] *m* post; station; set; position, job; **poste de douane** port of entry; **poste d'émetteur** broadcasting station; **poste de radio** radio set; **poste de repérage** tracking station; **poste de secours** first-aid station; **poste des malades** (nav) sick bay; **poste d'essence** gas station; **poste d'incendie** fire station; **poste supplémentaire** (telp) extension || *f* post, mail; **mettre à la poste** to mail; **poste restante** general delivery; **postes** post office department
poster [pɔste] *tr* to post || *ref* to lie in wait
postérité [pɔsterite] *f* posterity
posthume [pɔstym] *adj* posthumous
postiche [pɔstiʃ] *adj* false; detachable || *m* toupee; switch, false hair
pos•tier [pɔstje] **-tière** [tjɛr] *mf* postal clerk
postscolaire [pɔstskɔler] *adj* adult (*education*); extension (*courses*)
post-scriptum [pɔstskriptɔm] *m invar* postscript
postu•lant [pɔstylɑ̃] **-lante** [lɑ̃t] *mf* applicant, candidate; postulant
postuler [pɔstyle] *tr* to apply for || *intr* to apply; **postuler pour** to represent (*a client*)
posture [pɔstyr] *f* posture; situation
pot [po] *m* pot; pitcher, jug; jar; can; **découvrir le pot aux roses** (coll) to discover the secret; **payer les pots cassés** (coll) to pay the piper; **pot à bière** beer mug; **pot à fleurs** flowerpot; **pot d'échappement** (aut) muffler; **pot de noir** cloudy weather; **pot d'étain** pewter tankard; **tourner autour du pot** (coll) to beat about the bush
potable [pɔtabl] *adj* drinkable; (coll) acceptable, passable
potache [pɔtaʃ] *m* (coll) schoolboy
potage [pɔtaʒ] *m* soup; **potage de maïs** hominy; **pour tout potage** (lit) all told
pota•ger [pɔtaʒe] **-gère** [ʒɛr] *adj* vegetable || *m* vegetable garden
potasse [pɔtas] *f* potash
potasser [pɔtase] *tr* (coll) to bone up on || *intr* (coll) to grind away
potas•seur [pɔtasœr] **potas•seuse** [pɔtasøz] *mf* (coll) grind
potassium [pɔtasjɔm] *m* potassium
pot-au-feu [pɔtofø] *adj invar* (coll) home-loving || *m invar* beef stew
pot-de-vin [podvɛ̃] *m* (*pl* **pots-de-vin**) bribe, money under the table
po•teau [pɔto] *m* (*pl* **-teaux**) post, pole; **poteau de but** goal post; **poteau indicateur** signpost
pote•lé -lée [pɔtle] *adj* chubby
potence [pɔtɑ̃s] *f* gallows; bracket
potentat [pɔtɑ̃ta] *m* potentate

poten•tiel -tielle [pɔtɑ̃sjɛl] *adj & m* potential
poterie [pɔtri] *f* pottery; metalware; **poterie mordorée** lusterware
poterne [pɔtern] *f* postern
potiche [pɔtiʃ] *f* large Oriental vase; (fig) figurehead
potin [pɔtɛ̃] *m* piece of gossip; racket; **faire du potin** (coll) to raise a row; **potins** gossip
potiner [pɔtine] *intr* to gossip
potion [posjɔ̃] *f* potion
potiron [pɔtirɔ̃] *m* pumpkin; **potiron lumineux** jack-o'-lantern
pou [pu] *m* (*pl* **poux**) louse
poubelle [pubel] *f* garbage can
pouce [pus] *m* thumb; big toe; inch; **manger sur le pouce** (coll) to eat on the run
poudre [pudr] *f* powder; face powder; **en poudre** powdered; granulated (*sugar*); **il n'a pas inventé la poudre** (coll) he's not so smart; **jeter de la poudre aux yeux de** to deceive; **poudre dentifrice** tooth powder; **se mettre de la poudre** to powder one's nose
poudrer [pudre] *tr* to powder
poudrerie [pudrəri] *f* powder mill
pou•dreux [pudrø] **-dreuse** [drøz] *adj* powdery; dusty || *f* sugar shaker
poudrier [pudrije] *m* compact
poudrière [pudrijɛr] *f* powder magazine; (fig) powder keg
poudroyer [pudrwaje] §47 *intr* to raise the dust; to shine through the dust
pouf [puf] *m* hassock, pouf || *interj* plop!; **faire pouf** (slang) to flop
pouffer [pufe] *intr* to burst out laughing
pouil•leux [pujø] **pouil•leuse** [pujøz] *adj* lousy; sordid || *mf* person covered with lice
pouillot [pujo] *m* (orn) warbler
poulailler [pulaje] *m* henhouse; (theat) peanut gallery
poulain [pulɛ̃] *m* colt, foal
poule [pul] *f* hen; chicken; (*in games*) pool; jackpot; (turf) sweepstakes; (coll) skirt, dame; (slang) tart, mistress; **ma poule** (coll) my pet; **poule au pot** chicken stew; **poule d'Inde** turkey hen; **poule mouillée** (coll) milksop; **tuer la poule aux œufs d'or** to kill the goose that lays the golden eggs
poulet [pulɛ] *m* chicken, (coll) love letter; **mon petit poulet** (coll) my pet; **poulet d'Inde** turkey cock
poulette [pulɛt] *f* pullet; (coll) gal; **ma poulette** (coll) darling
pouliche [puliʃ] *f* filly
poulie [puli] *f* pulley; block
poulpe [pulp] *m* octopus
pouls [pu] *m* pulse; **tâter le pouls à** to feel the pulse of
poumon [pumɔ̃] *m* lung
poupe [pup] *f* (naut) stern, poop
poupée [pupe] *f* doll; dummy; sore finger; (mach) headstock
pou•pon [pupɔ̃] **-ponne** [pɔn] *mf* baby; chubby-faced youngster

pouponnière [pupɔnjɛr] *f* nursery
pour [pur] *m*—le pour et le contre the pros and the cons ‖ *adv*—pour lors then; pour peu que however little; pour que in order that; pour . . . que however, e.g., pour charmante qu'elle soit however charming she may be ‖ *prep* for; in order to; pour ainsi dire so to speak; pour cent per cent
pourboire [purbwar] *m* tip
pour·ceau [purso] *m* (*pl* -ceaux) swine, hog, pig
pourcentage [pursɑ̃taʒ] *m* percentage
pourchasser [purʃase] *tr* to hound
pourlécher [purleʃe] §10 *ref* to smack one's lips
pourparlers [purparle] *mpl* talks, parley, conference
pourpoint [purpwɛ̃] *m* doublet
pourpre [purpr] *adj* purple ‖ *m* purple (*violescent*) ‖ *f* purple (*deep red, crimson*)
pourquoi [purkwa] *m* why; le pourquoi et le comment the why and the wherefore ‖ *adv* & *conj* why; pourquoi pas? why not?
pour·ri -rie [puri] *adj* rotten; spoiled ‖ *m* rotten part
pourrir [purir] *tr, intr, & ref* to rot; to spoil; to corrupt
pourriture [purityr] *f* rot; decay; corruption
poursuite [pursɥit] *f* pursuit; (law) action, suit; (coll) spotlight
poursui·vant [pursɥivɑ̃] -vante [vɑ̃t] *mf* pursuer; (law) plaintiff
poursuivre [pursɥivr] §67 *tr* to pursue, chase; to proceed with; to persecute; to sue ‖ *intr* to continue ‖ *ref* to be continued
pourtant [purtɑ̃] *adv* however, nevertheless, yet
pourtour [purtur] *m* circumference
pourvoi [purvwa] *m* (law) appeal
pourvoir [purvwar] §54 *tr*—pourvoir de to supply with, to provide with; to favor with ‖ *intr*—pourvoir à to provide for, to attend to ‖ *ref* (law) to appeal
pourvoyeur [purvwajœr] **pourvoyeuse** [purvwajøz] *mf* provider, supplier; caterer; pourvoyeurs gun crew
pourvu que [purvykə] *conj* provided that
pousse [pus] *f* shoot, sprout
pous·sé -sée [puse] *adj* elaborate; searching, exhaustive ‖ *f* push, shove; thrust; rise; pressure; (rok) thrust
pousse-café [puskafe] *m invar* liqueur
pousser [puse] *tr* to push, to shove, to egg on, to urge; to utter (*a cry*); to heave (*a sigh*); pousser plus loin to carry further ‖ *intr* to push, shove; to grow; to push on ‖ *ref* to push oneself forward
poussette [puset] *f* baby carriage
poussier [pusje] *m* coal dust
poussière [pusjɛr] *f* dust; powder; poussière d'eau spray; une pous-

sière a trifle; une poussière de a lot of
poussié·reux [pusjɛrø] -reuse [røz] *adj* dusty; powdery
pous·sif [pusif] **pous·sive** [pusiv] *adj* wheezy
poussin [pusɛ̃] *m* chick
poussoir [puswar] *m* push button
poutre [putr] *f* beam; joist; girder
poutrelle [putrɛl] *f* small girder
pouvoir [puvwar] *m* power; **pouvoir d'achat** purchasing power ‖ §55 *tr* to be able to do; je n'y puis rien I can't or cannot help it, I can do nothing about it ‖ *intr* to be able; on ne peut mieux couldn't be better; on ne peut plus I (we, they, etc.) can do no more; I'm (we're, they're, etc.) all in ‖ *aux* used to express 1) ability, e.g., elle peut prédire l'avenir she is able to predict the future, she can predict the future; 2) permission, e.g., vous pouvez partir you may go; e.g., puis-je partir? may I go?; 3) possibility, e.g., il peut pleuvoir it may rain; e.g., il a pu oublier son parapluie he may have forgotten his umbrella; 4) optative, e.g., puisse-t-il venir! may he come! ‖ *impers ref*—il se peut que it is possible that, e.g., il se peut qu'il vienne ce soir it is possible that he may come this evening, he may come this evening; il se pourrait bien que it might well be that, e.g., il se pourrait bien qu'il vînt ce soir it might well be that he will come this evening, he might come this evening ‖ *ref* to be possible; cela ne se peut pas that is not possible
pragmatique [pragmatik] *adj* pragmatic(al)
prairie [prɛri], [preri] *f* meadow; les Prairies the prairie
praticable [pratikabl] *adj* practicable; passable ‖ *m* practicable stage property; (mov, telv) camera platform
prati·cien [pratisjɛ̃] -cienne [sjɛn] *mf* practitioner
prati·quant [pratikɑ̃] -quante [kɑ̃t] *adj* practicing (*e.g., Catholic*); churchy ‖ *mf* churchgoer
pratique [pratik] *adj* practical ‖ *f* practice; contact, company; customer; libre pratique freedom of worship; (naut) freedom from quarantine
pratiquement [pratikmɑ̃] *adv* practically, in practice
pratiquer [pratike] *tr* to practice; to cut, make (*e.g., a hole*); to frequent; to read a great deal of ‖ *intr* to practice (*said, e.g., of doctor*); to practice one's religion ‖ *ref* to be practiced, done; to rule, prevail (*said of prices*)
pré [pre] *m* meadow; sur le pré on the field of honor (*dueling ground*)
préalable [prealabl] *adj* previous; preliminary ‖ *m* prerequisite; au préalable before, in advance
préambule [preɑ̃byl] *m* preamble
préau [preo] *m* (*pl* préaux) yard
préavis [preavi] *m* advance warning;

avec **préavis** person-to-person (*telephone call*)
précaire [prekɛr] *adj* precarious
précaution [prekosjɔ̃] *f* precaution
précautionner [prekosjɔne] *tr* to caution || *intr* to be on one's guard
précaution·neux [prekosjɔnø] **précaution·neuse** [prekosjɔnøz] *adj* precautious
précé·dent [presedɑ̃] **-dente** [dɑ̃t] *adj* preceding || *m* precedent
précéder [presede] §10 *tr* & *intr* to precede
précepte [presɛpt] *m* precept
précep·teur [presɛptœr] **-trice** [tris] *mf* tutor
prêche [prɛʃ] *m* sermon
prêcher [preʃe] *tr* to preach; to preach to || *intr* to preach; **prêcher d'exemple** to practice what one preaches
prê·cheur [prɛʃœr] **-cheuse** [ʃøz] *adj* preaching || *mf* sermonizer
pré·cieux [presjø] **-cieuse** [sjøz] *adj* precious; valuable; affected
préciosité [presjozite] *f* preciosity (*French literary style corresponding to English euphuism*)
précipice [presipis] *m* precipice
précipi·té -tée [presipite] *adj* hurried, precipitous || *m* precipitate
précipiter [presipite] *tr* to hurl || *ref* to hurl oneself; to precipitate; to hurry, rush
pré·cis [presi] **-cise** [siz] *adj* precise; sharp, e.g., **trois heures précises** three o'clock sharp || *m* abstract, summary
préciser [presize] *tr* to specify || *intr* to be precise || *ref* to become clear; to take shape, to jell
précision [presizjɔ̃] *f* precision; **précisions** data
préci·té -tée [presite] *adj* aforementioned
précoce [prekɔs] *adj* precocious; (bot) early
précon·çu -çue [prekɔ̃sy] *adj* preconceived
préconiser [prekɔnize] *tr* to advocate, recommend
précurseur [prekyrsœr] *adj masc* precursory || *m* forerunner, harbinger
prédateur [predatœr] *adj masc* predatory || *m* predatory animal
prédécesseur [predesesœr] *m* predecessor
prédicateur [predikatœr] *m* preacher
prédiction [prediksjɔ̃] *f* prediction
prédire [predir] §40 *tr* to predict
prédisposer [predispoze] *tr* to predispose
prédomi·nant [predɔminɑ̃] **-nante** [nɑ̃t] *adj* predominant
préémi·nent [preeminɑ̃] **-nente** [nɑ̃t] *adj* preeminent
préfabri·qué -quée [prefabrike] *adj* prefabricated
préface [prefas] *f* preface
préfacer [prefase] §51 *tr* to preface
préfecture [prefɛktyr] *f* prefecture; **préfecture de police** police headquarters
préférable [preferabl] *adj* preferable

préférence [preferɑ̃s] *f* preference
préférer [prefere] §10 *tr* to prefer
préfet [prefɛ] *m* prefect; **préfet de police** police commissioner
préfixe [prefiks] *m* prefix
préfixer [prefikse] *tr* to prefix
préhistorique [preistɔrik] *adj* prehistoric
préjudice [preʒydis] *m* prejudice, detriment; **porter préjudice à** to injure, to harm; **sans préjudice de** without affecting
préjudiciable [preʒydisjabl] *adj* detrimental
préjudicier [preʒydisje] *intr* (with *dat*) to harm, damage
préjugé [preʒyʒe] *m* prejudice
préjuger [preʒyʒe] §38 *tr* to foresee || *intr*—**préjuger de** to prejudge
prélart [prelar] *m* tarpaulin
prélasser [prelase] *ref* to lounge
prélat [prela] *m* prelate
prélèvement [prelɛvmɑ̃] *m* deduction; sample; levy
prélever [prelve] §2 *tr* to set aside, deduct; to take (*a sample*); to levy; **prélever à** to take from
préliminaire [preliminɛr] *adj* & *m* preliminary
prélude [prelyd] *m* prelude
préluder [prelyde] *intr* to warm up (*said of singer, musician, etc.*); **préluder à** to prelude
prématu·ré -rée [prematyre] *adj* premature
préméditer [premedite] *tr* to premeditate
prémices [premis] *fpl* first fruits; beginning
pre·mier [prəmje] **-mière** [mjɛr] *adj* first; raw (*materials*); prime (*number*); the First, e.g., **Jean premier** John the First || (when standing before noun) *adj* first; prime (*minister*); maiden (*voyage*); early (*infancy*) || *m* first; **jeune premier** leading man; **premier de cordée** leader || *f* first; first class; (theat) première; **jeune première** leading lady || *pron* (*masc* & *fem*) first
premier-né [prəmjene] **première-née** [prəmjɛrne] (*pl* **premiers-nés**) *adj* & *mf* first-born
prémisse [premis] *f* premise
prémonition [premɔnisjɔ̃] *f* premonition
prémunir [premynir] *tr* to forewarn || *ref*—**se prémunir contre** to protect oneself against
pre·nant [prənɑ̃] **-nante** [nɑ̃t] *adj* sticky; winning, pleasing
prendre [prɑ̃dr] §56 *tr* to take; to take on; to take up; to catch; to get (*to obtain and bring*); to steal (*a kiss*); to buy (*a ticket*); to make (*an appointment*); **à tout prendre** all things considered; **prendre de l'âge** to be getting old; **prendre la mer** to take to sea; **prendre l'eau** to leak; **prendre le large** to take to the open sea; **prendre q.ch. à qn** to take s.th. from s.o.; to charge s.o. s.th. (*i.e., a cer-*

tain sum of money); **prendre son temps** to take one's time ‖ *intr* to catch (*said of fire*); to take root; to form (*said of ice*); to set (*said of mortar*); to stick (*to a pan or dish*); to catch on (*said of a style*); to turn (*right or left*); **prendre à droite** to bear to the right; **qu'est-ce qui lui prend?** what's come over him? ‖ *ref* to get caught, to catch (*e.g., on a nail*); to congeal; to clot; to curdle; to jam; to take from each other; **pour qui se prend-il?** who does he think he is?; **s'en prendre à qn de q.ch.** to blame s.o. for s.th.; **se prendre à** to begin to; **se prendre d'amitié** to strike up a friendship; **se prendre de vin** to get drunk; **s'y prendre** to go about it

pre·neur [prənœr] -**neuse** [nøz] *mf* taker; buyer; payee; lessee

prénom [prenõ] *m* first name

prénommer [prenɔme] *tr* to name ‖ *ref* —**il (elle, etc.) se prénomme** his (her, etc.) first name is

préoccupation [preɔkypɑsjõ] *f* preoccupation

préoccuper [preɔkype] *tr* to preoccupy ‖ *ref*—**se préoccuper de** to pay attention to; to be concerned about

prépara·teur [preparatœr] -**trice** [tris] *mf* laboratory assistant

préparatifs [preparatif] *mpl* preparations

préparation [preparɑsjõ] *f* preparation; notice, warning

préparatoire [preparatwar] *adj* preparatory

préparer [prepare] *tr, intr, & ref* to prepare

prépondé·rant [prepõderã] -**rante** [rãt] *adj* preponderant

prépo·sé -**sée** [prepoze] *mf* employee, clerk; **préposé de la douane** customs officer; **préposée au vestiaire** hatcheck girl

préposer [prepoze] *tr*—**préposer qn à q.ch.** to put s.o. in charge of s.th.

préposition [prepozisjõ] *f* preposition

prérogative [prerɔgativ] *f* prerogative

près [prɛ] *adv* near; **à beaucoup près** by far; **à cela près** except for that; **à peu d'exceptions près** with few exceptions; **à peu près** about, practically; **à . . . près** except for; within, e.g., **je peux vous dire l'heure à cinq minutes près** I can tell you what time it is within five minutes; **au plus près** to the nearest point; **de près** close; closely; **ici près** near here; **près de** near; nearly, about; alongside, at the side of; **près de + inf** about to + *inf*; **tout près** nearby, right here ‖ *prep* near; to, at

présage [prezaʒ] *m* presage, foreboding

présager [prezaʒe] §38 *tr* to presage, forebode; to anticipate

pré·salé [presale] *m* (*pl* **prés-salés**) salt-meadow sheep; salt-meadow mutton

presbyte [prɛsbit] *adj* far-sighted ‖ *mf* far-sighted person

presbytère [prɛsbiter] *m* presbytery

presbyté·rien [prɛsbiterjɛ̃] -**rienne** [rjɛn] *adj & mf* Presbyterian

presbytie [prɛsbisi] *f* far-sightedness

prescription [prɛskripsjõ] *f* prescription

prescrire [prɛskrir] §25 *tr* to prescribe ‖ *ref* to be prescribed

préséance [preseãs] *f* precedence

présence [prezãs] *f* presence; attendance; **en présence** face to face

pré·sent [prezã] -**sente** [zãt] *adj* present ‖ *m* present, gift; (gram) present; **les présents** those present

présentable [prezãtabl] *adj* presentable

présenta·teur [prezãtatœr] -**trice** [tris] *mf* (rad) announcer; **présentateur de disques** disk jockey

présentation [prezãtɑsjõ] *f* presentation; introduction; appearance; look, form (*of a new product*)

présentement [prezãtmã] *adv* right now

présenter [prezãte] *tr* to present; to introduce; to offer; to pay (*one's respects*) ‖ *ref* to present oneself; to present itself; **se présenter à** to be a candidate for

présérie [preseri] *f* (com) trial run, sample run

préservatif [prezɛrvatif] *m* preventive; condom

préserver [prezɛrve] *tr* to preserve

présidence [prezidãs] *f* presidency; chairmanship; presidential mansion

prési·dent [prezidã] -**dente** [dãt] *mf* president; chairman; presiding judge ‖ *f* president's wife; chairwoman; **madame la présidente** madam chairman

présiden·tiel -**tielle** [prezidãsjɛl] *adj* presidential

présider [prezide] *tr* to preside over ‖ *intr* to preside; **présider à** to preside over

présomp·tif [prezõptif] -**tive** [tiv] *adj* presumptive, presumed

présomption [prezõpsjõ] *f* presumption

présomp·tueux [prezõptɥø] -**tueuse** [tɥøz] *adj* presumptuous

presque [prɛsk(ə)] *adv* almost, nearly; **presque jamais** hardly ever; **presque personne** scarcely anybody

presqu'île [prɛskil] *f* peninsula

pres·sant [prɛsã] **pres·sante** [prɛsãt] *adj* pressing, urgent

presse [prɛs] *f* press; hurry, rush; crowd; hand screw, clamp; **mettre sous presse** to go to press

pres·sé -**sée** [prese] *adj* pressed; pressing, urgent; squeezed

presse-bouton [prɛsbutõ] *adj invar* push-button (*warfare*)

presse-citron [prɛssitrõ] *m invar* lemon squeezer

pressentiment [prɛsãtimã] *m* presentiment, foreboding

pressentir [prɛsãtir] §41 *tr* to have a foreboding of; to sound out

presse-papiers [prɛspapje] *m invar* paperweight

presse-purée [prɛspyre] *m invar* potato masher

presser [prese], [prɛse] *tr* to press; to squeeze; to hurry, hasten || *intr* to be urgent || *ref* to hurry; **se presser à** to crowd around

pressing [prɛsiŋ] *m* dry cleaner's, tailor shop

pression [prɛsjɔ̃] *f* pressure; snap fastener; **à la pression** on draught; **pression artérielle** blood pressure

pressoir [prɛswar] *m* press

pressurer [presyre] *tr* to press, squeeze; to bleed white, to wring money out of

pressuriser [presyrize] *tr* to pressurize

prestance [prɛstɑ̃s] *f* commanding appearance, dignified bearing

prestation [prɛstɑsjɔ̃] *f* taking (*of oath*); tax; allotment, allowance, benefit

preste [prɛst] *adj* nimble

prestidigita·teur [prɛstidiʒitatœr] **-trice** [tris] *mf* magician

prestidigitation [prɛstidiʒitɑsjɔ̃] *f* sleight of hand, legerdemain

prestige [prɛstiʒ] *m* prestige; illusion, magic

presti·gieux [prɛstiʒjø] **-gieuse** [ʒjøz] *adj* prestigious, famous; marvelous

présumer [prezyme] *tr* to presume; to presume to be || *intr* to presume; **présumer de** to presume upon

présupposer [presypoze] *tr* to presuppose

présure [prezyr] *f* rennet

prêt [prɛ] **prête** [prɛt] *adj* ready; **prêt à porter** ready-to-wear, ready-made; **prêt à tout** ready for anything || *m* loan

prêt-à-porter [prɛtapɔrte] *m* (*pl* **prêts-à-porter** [prɛtapɔrte]) ready-to-wear, ready-made clothes

prêt-bail [prɛbaj] *m invar* lend-lease

préten·dant [pretɑ̃dɑ̃] **-dante** [dɑ̃t] *mf* pretender || *m* suitor

prétendre [pretɑ̃dr] *tr* to claim; to require || *intr*—**prétendre à** to aspire to; to lay claim to

préten·du -due [pretɑ̃dy] *adj* so-called, alleged || *m* fiancé || *f* fiancée

prête-nom [prɛtnɔ̃] *m* (*pl* **-noms**) dummy, figurehead, straw man

prétentaine [pretɑ̃tɛn] *f*—**courir la prétentaine** (coll) to be on the loose; (coll) to have many love affairs

préten·tieux [pretɑ̃sjø] **-tieuse** [sjøz] *adj* pretentious

prétention [pretɑ̃sjɔ̃] *f* pretention, pretense; claim, pretensions

prêter [prete], [prɛte] *tr* to lend; to give (*e.g., help*); to pay (*attention*); to take (*an oath*); to impart (*e.g., luster*); to attribute, ascribe || *intr* to lend; to stretch; **prêter à** to lend itself to || *ref*—**se prêter à** to lend itself to; to be a party to, to countenance; to indulge in

prê·teur [pretœr] **-teuse** [tøz] *mf* lender; **prêteur sur gages** pawnbroker

prétexte [pretɛkst] *m* pretext

prétexter [pretɛkste] *tr* to give as a pretext

prétonique [pretɔnik] *adj* pretonic

prêtre [prɛtr] *m* priest

prêtresse [prɛtrɛs] *f* priestess

prêtrise [pretriz] *f* priesthood

preuve [prœv] *f* proof, evidence

preux [prø] *adj masc* valiant || *m* doughty knight

prévaloir [prevalwar] §71 (*subj* **prévale**, etc.) *intr* to prevail || *ref*—**se prévaloir de** to avail oneself of; to pride oneself on

prévarication [prevarikɑsjɔ̃] *f* breach of trust

prévariquer [prevarike] *intr* to betray one's trust

prévenance [prevnɑ̃s] *f* kindness, thoughtfulness

préve·nant [prevnɑ̃] **-nante** [nɑ̃t] *adj* attentive, considerate; prepossessing

prévenir [prevnir] §72 *tr* to anticipate; to avert, forestall; to ward off, to prevent; to notify, inform; to bias, to prejudice

préven·tif [prevɑ̃tif] **-tive** [tiv] *adj* preventive; pretrial (*detention*)

prévention [prevɑ̃sjɔ̃] *f* bias, prejudice; custody, imprisonment; prevention (*of accidents*); **prévention routière** traffic police; road safety

préve·nu -nue [prevny] *adj* biased, prejudiced; forewarned; accused || *mf* prisoner, accused, defendant

prévision [previzjɔ̃] *f* anticipation, estimate; **prévision du temps** weather forecast; **prévisions** expectations

prévoir [prevwar] §57 *tr* to foresee, anticipate; to forecast

prévoyance [prevwajɑ̃s] *f* foresight

prévoyant [prevwajɑ̃] **prévoyante** [prevwajɑ̃t] *adj* far-sighted, provident

prie-dieu [pridjø] *m invar* prie-dieu || *f* praying mantis

prier [prije] *tr* to ask, to beg; to pray (*God*); **je vous en prie!** I beg your pardon!; by all means!; you are welcome!; please have some!; **je vous prie!** please!; **prier qn de** + *inf* to ask, to beg s.o. to + *inf* || *intr* to pray

prière [prijɛr] *f* prayer; **prière de . . . please . . . ; **prière d'insérer** publisher's insert for reviewers

primaire [primɛr] *adj* primary; first (*offender*); (coll) narrow-minded || *m* (elec) primary; (coll) primitive

primat [prima] *m* (eccl) primate

primate [primat] *m* (zool) primate

primauté [primote] *f* supremacy

prime [prim] *adj* early (*youth*); (math) prime || *f* premium; bonus; free gift; (eccl) prime; **prime de transport** traveling expenses

primer [prime] *tr* to excel; to take priority over; to award a prize to

primerose [primroz] *f* hollyhock

primesau·tier [primsotje] **-tière** [tjɛr] *adj* impulsive, quick

primeur [primœr] *f* freshness; first fruit; early vegetable; (journ) beat,

scoop; **primeurs** fruits and vegetables out of season
primevère [primvɛr] f primrose
primi·tif [primitif] **-tive** [tiv] adj primitive; original, early; primary (colors; tense) || mf primitive
primo [primo] adv firstly
primor·dial -diale [primɔrdjal] adj (pl **-diaux** [djo]) primordial; fundamental, prime, primary
prince [prɛ̃s] m prince; **prince de Galles** Prince of Wales
princesse [prɛ̃sɛs] f princess
prin·cier [prɛ̃sje] **-cière** [sjɛr] adj princely
princi·pal -pale [prɛ̃sipal] adj & m (pl **-paux** [po]) principal, chief
principauté [prɛ̃sipote] f principality
principe [prɛ̃sip] m principle; beginning; source
printa·nier [prɛ̃tanje] **-nière** [njɛr] adj spring; springlike
printemps [prɛ̃tɑ̃] m spring; springtime; **au printemps** in the spring
priorité [prijɔrite] f priority; right of way; **de priorité** preferred (stock); main (road); **priorité à droite,** **priorité à gauche** (public sign) yield
pris [pri] **prise** [priz] adj set, frozen; **être pris** to be busy; **pris de vin** drunk || f capture, seizure; taking; hold; setting; tap, faucet; (med) dose; (naut) prize; **donner prise à** to lay oneself open to; **être aux prises avec** to be struggling with; **hors de prise** out of gear; **lâcher prise** to let go; **prise d'air** ventilator; **prise d'antenne** (rad) lead-in; **prise d'armes** military parade; **prise d'eau** water faucet; hydrant; **prise de bec** (coll) quarrel; **prise de conscience** awakening, awareness; **prise de courant** (elec) plug; (elec) tap, outlet; **prise de position** statement of opinion; **prise de sang** blood specimen; **prise de son** recording; **prise de tabac** pinch of snuff; **prise de terre** (elec) ground connection; **prise de vue(s)** (phot) shot, picture taking; **prise de vue directe** (telv) live broadcast; **prise directe** high gear
prisée [prize] f appraisal
priser [prize] tr to value; to snuff up || intr to take snuff
pri·seur [prizœr] **-seuse** [zøz] mf snuffer || m appraiser
prisme [prism] m prism
prison [prizɔ̃] f prison
prison·nier [prizɔnje] **prison·nière** [prizɔnjɛr] mf prisoner
privautés [privote] fpl liberties
pri·vé -vée [prive] adj private; tame, pet || m private life
priver [prive] tr to deprive || ref to deprive oneself; **se priver de** to do without, to abstain from
privilège [privilɛʒ] m privilege
privilé·gié -giée [privileʒje] adj privileged; preferred (stock)
prix [pri] m price; prize; value; **à aucun prix** not at any price; by no means; **à tout prix** at all costs; **au**

prix de at the price of; at the rate of; compared with; **dans mes prix** within my means; **grand prix** championship race; **hors de prix** at a prohibitive cost; **prix courant** list price; **prix de départ** upset price; **prix de détail** retail price; **prix de fabrique** factory price; **prix de gros** wholesale price; **prix de la vie** cost of living; **prix de location** rent; **prix de revient** cost price; **prix de vente** selling price; **prix fixe** table d'hôte
probabilité [prɔbabilite] f probability
probable [prɔbabl] adj probable, likely
pro·bant [prɔbɑ̃] **-bante** [bɑ̃t] adj convincing; conclusive (evidence)
probe [prɔb] adj honest, upright
problème [prɔblɛm] m problem
procédé [prɔsede] m process; procedure; tip (of cue); **procédés** proceedings; behavior
procéder [prɔsede] §10 intr to proceed; (with dat) to perform, carry out; **procéder de** to arise from
procédure [prɔsedyr] f procedure; proceedings
procès [prɔsɛ] m lawsuit, case; trial; **intenter un procès à** to sue; to prosecute; **sans autre forme de procès** then and there, without appeal
proces·sif [prɔsesif] **proces·sive** [prɔsesiv] adj litigious
procession [prɔsesjɔ̃] f procession
processus [prɔsesys] m process
procès-verbal [prɔsɛvɛrbal] m (pl **-verbaux** [vɛrbo]) report; minutes; ticket (e.g., for speeding)
pro·chain [prɔʃɛ̃] **-chaine** [ʃɛn] adj next; impending; (lit) nearest, immediate; **la prochaine semaine** next week; **la semaine prochaine** next week || m neighbor, fellow-man || f **à la prochaine!** (coll) so long!
prochainement [prɔʃɛnmɑ̃] adv shortly
proche [prɔʃ] adj near; nearby; close (relative) || **proches** mpl close relatives || adv—**de proche en proche** little by little
proclamer [prɔklame] tr to proclaim
proclitique [prɔklitik] adj & m proclitic
procuration [prɔkyrasjɔ̃] f power of attorney; **par procuration** by proxy
procurer [prɔkyre] tr & ref to procure, to get
procureur [prɔkyrœr] m attorney; **procureur de la république** district attorney; **procureur général** attorney general
prodige [prɔdiʒ] m prodigy; wonder
prodi·gieux [prɔdiʒjø] **-gieuse** [ʒjøz] adj prodigious, wonderful; terrific
prodigue [prɔdig] adj prodigal, lavish || mf prodigal, spendthrift
prodiguer [prɔdige] tr to squander, waste; to lavish || ref to not spare oneself; to show off
prodrome [prɔdrom] m harbinger; introduction
produc·teur [prɔdyktœr] **-trice** [tris] adj productive || mf producer

produc·tif [prɔdyktif] **-tive** [tiv] *adj* productive; producing
production [prɔdyksjɔ̃] *f* production
produire [prɔdɥir] §19 *tr* to produce; to create; to introduce ‖ *ref* to take place; to be produced; to show up
produit [prɔdɥi] *m* product; proceeds; offspring; **produit de luxe** luxury item; **produit pharmaceutique** patent medicine, drug; **produits agricoles** agricultural produce; **produits de beauté** cosmetics
proémi·nent [prɔeminã] **-nente** [nãt] *adj* prominent, protuberant
profane [prɔfan] *adj* profane; lay, uninformed ‖ *mf* profane; layman
profaner [prɔfane] *tr* to profane; (fig) to prostitute
proférer [prɔfere] §10 *tr* to utter
professer [prɔfese] *tr* to profess; to teach ‖ *intr* to teach
professeur [prɔfesœr] *m* teacher; professor
profession [prɔfesjɔ̃] *f* profession; occupation, trade
profession·nel -nelle [prɔfesjɔnɛl] *adj & mf* professional
profil [prɔfil] *m* profile; side face; cross section; skyline (*of city*)
profi·lé -lée [prɔfile] *adj* streamlined, aerodynamic
profiler [prɔfile] *tr* to profile ‖ *ref*— **se profiler sur** to stand out against
profit [prɔfi] *m* profit; **mettre à profit** to take advantage of; **profits et pertes** profit and loss
profitable [prɔfitabl] *adj* profitable
profiter [prɔfite] *intr* to profit; to grow; (with *dat*) to profit; **profiter à, dans,** or **en** to profit from
profi·teur [prɔfitœr] **-teuse** [tøz] *mf* profiteer
pro·fond [prɔfɔ̃] **-fonde** [fɔ̃d] *adj* profound; deep; low (*bow; voice*); **peu profond** shallow ‖ *m* depths ‖ *f* (slang) pocket ‖ **profond** *adv* deep
profondément [prɔfɔ̃demã] *adv* profoundly, deeply; soundly; deep
profondeur [prɔfɔ̃dœr] *f* depth
progéniture [prɔʒenityr] *f* progeny; offspring, child
programma·teur [prɔgramatœr] **-trice** [tris] *mf* (mov, rad, telv) programmer
programmation [prɔgramɑsjɔ̃] *f* programming
programme [prɔgram] *m* program; **programme de prévoyance** retirement program; **programme des études** curriculum
programmer [prɔgrame] *tr* to program
program·meur [prɔgramœr] **program·meuse** [prɔgramøz] *mf* (comp) programmer
progrès [prɔgrɛ] *m* progress; **faire des progrès** to make progress
progresser [prɔgrese] *intr* to progress
progres·sif [prɔgresif] **progres·sive** [prɔgresiv] *adj* progressive
progressiste [prɔgresist] *adj & mf* progressive
prohiber [prɔibe] *tr* to prohibit
prohibition [prɔibisjɔ̃] *f* prohibition

proie [prwa], [prwɑ] *f* prey; **de proie** predatory; **en proie à** a prey to
projecteur [prɔʒɛktœr] *m* projector; searchlight; (mov) projection machine
projectile [prɔʒɛktil] *m* projectile; **projectile téléguidé** guided missile
projection [prɔʒɛksjɔ̃] *f* projection
projet [prɔʒɛ] *m* project; draft; sketch, plan; **faire des projets** to make plans; **projet de loi** bill
projeter [prɔʒte] §34 *tr* to project; to pour forth (*smoke*); to cast (*a shadow*); to plan ‖ *intr* to plan
prolétaire [prɔletɛr] *m* proletarian
prolétariat [prɔletarja] *m* proletariat
proléta·rien [prɔletarjɛ̃] **-rienne** [rjɛn] *adj* proletarian
proliférer [prɔlifere] §10 *intr* to proliferate
prolifique [prɔlifik] *adj* prolific
prolixe [prɔliks] *adj* prolix
prologue [prɔlɔg] *m* prologue; preface
prolonger [prɔlɔ̃ʒe] §38 *tr* to prolong; to extend ‖ *ref* to be prolonged; to continue, extend
promenade [prɔmnad] *f* promenade; walk; ride; drive; sail; **faire une promenade** (en auto, à cheval, à motocyclette, en bateau, etc.) to take a ride
promener [prɔmne] §2 *tr* to take for a walk or drive; to walk (*e.g., a dog*); to take along; **envoyer promener qn** (coll) to send s.o. packing; **promener ... sur** to run (*e.g., one's hand, eyes*) over ‖ *ref* to stroll; to go for a walk, ride, drive, or sail; **allez vous promener!** get out of here!
prome·neur [prɔmnœr] **-neuse** [nøz] *mf* walker, stroller
promenoir [prɔmnwar] *m* ambulatory, cloister; (theat) standing room
promesse [prɔmɛs] *f* promise
promettre [prɔmetr] §42 *tr* to promise; **promettre q.ch. à qn** to promise s.th. to s.o. ‖ *intr* to look promising; **promettre à qn de** + *inf* to promise s.o. to + *inf* ‖ *ref* to promise oneself; (with *dat of reflex pron*) to promise oneself (*e.g., a vacation*); **se promettre de** to resolve to
pro·mis [prɔmi] **-mise** [miz] *adj* promised; **promis à** headed for
promiscuité [prɔmiskɥite] *f* indiscriminate mixture; lack of privacy
promontoire [prɔmɔ̃twar] *m* promontory
promo·teur [prɔmɔtœr] **-trice** [tris] *mf* promoter; originator
promotion [prɔmosjɔ̃] *f* promotion; uplift; class (*in school*)
promouvoir [prɔmuvwar] §45 (*pp* **promu**) *tr* to promote
prompt [prɔ̃] **prompte** [prɔ̃t] *adj* prompt, ready, quick
promptitude [prɔ̃tityd] *f* promptness
promulguer [prɔmylge] *tr* to promulgate
prône [pron] *m* homily
prôner [prone] *tr* to extol
pronom [prɔnɔ̃] *m* pronoun
pronomi·nal -nale [prɔnɔminal] *adj* (*pl*

-naux [no]) pronominal; reflexive (*verb*)

pronon·cé -cée [prɔnɔ̃se] *adj* marked; sharp (*curve*); prominent (*nose*)

prononcer [prɔnɔ̃se] §51 *tr* to pronounce; to utter; to deliver (*a speech*); to pass (*judgment*) || *intr* to decide || *ref* to be pronounced; to express an opinion

prononciation [prɔnɔ̃sjɑsjɔ̃] *f* pronunciation

pronostic [prɔnɔstik] *m* prognosis

pronostiquer [prɔnɔstike] *tr* to prognosticate

propagande [prɔpagãd] *f* propaganda; publicity, advertising

propager [prɔpaʒe] §38 *tr* to propagate; to spread || *ref* to be propagated; to spread

propédeutique [prɔpedøtik] *f* (educ) preliminary study

propension [prɔpãsjɔ̃] *f* propensity

prophète [prɔfɛt] *m* prophet

prophétesse [prɔfetɛs] *f* prophetess

prophétie [prɔfesi] *f* prophecy

prophétiser [prɔfetize] *tr* to prophesy

prophylactique [prɔfilaktik] *adj* prophylactic

propice [prɔpis] *adj* propitious; lucky (*star*)

proportion [prɔpɔrsjɔ̃] *f* proportion; en proportion de in proportion to

proportion·né -née [prɔpɔrsjɔne] *adj* proportionate

proportion·nel -nelle [prɔpɔrsjɔnɛl] *adj* proportional

proportionner [prɔpɔrsjɔne] *tr* to proportion

propos [prɔpo] *m* remark; purpose; à ce propos in this connection; à propos by the way; timely, fitting; at the right moment; à propos de with regard to, concerning; à tout propos at every turn; changer de propos to change the subject; de propos délibéré on purpose; des propos en l'air idle talk; hors de propos out of place; irrelevant

proposer [prɔpoze] *tr* to propose; to nominate; to recommend (*s.o.*) || *ref* to have in mind; to apply (*for a job*); se proposer de to intend to

proposition [prɔpozisjɔ̃] *f* proposition; proposal; clause

propre [prɔpr] *adj* clean, neat; original (*meaning*); proper (*name*); literal (*meaning*); propre à fit for, suited to || (when standing before noun) *adj* own || *m* characteristic; au propre in the literal sense; c'est du propre! (coll) what a dirty trick!; en propre in one's own right

pro·pret [prɔprɛ] -prette [prɛt] *adj* (coll) clean, bright

propreté [prɔprɔte] *f* cleanliness, neatness

propriétaire [prɔprijetɛr] *mf* proprietor, owner; landowner || *m* landlord || *f* proprietress; landlady

propriété [prɔprijete] *f* property; propriety, appropriateness

propulseur [prɔpylsœr] *m* engine, motor; outboard motor; (rok) booster

propulsion [prɔpylsjɔ̃] *f* propulsion; propulsion à réaction jet propulsion

prorata [prɔrata] *m* invar—au prorata de in proportion to

proroger [prɔrɔʒe] §38 *tr* to postpone; to extend; to adjourn || *ref* to be adjourned

prosaïque [prozaik] *adj* prosaic

prosateur [prozatœr] *m* prose writer

proscrire [prɔskrir] §25 *tr* to proscribe; to banish, outlaw

pros·crit [prɔskri] -crite [krit] *adj* banished || *mf* outlaw

prose [proz] *f* prose; (coll) style (*of writing*)

prosélyte [prɔzelit] *mf* proselyte

prosodie [prɔzɔdi] *f* prosody

prospecter [prɔspɛkte] *tr & intr* to prospect

prospec·teur [prɔspɛktœr] -trice [tris] *mf* prospector

prospectus [prɔspɛktys] *m* prospectus; handbill

prospère [prɔspɛr] *adj* prosperous

prospérer [prɔspere] §10 *intr* to prosper, to thrive

prospérité [prɔsperite] *f* prosperity

prosternation [prɔsternasjɔ̃] *f* prostration; groveling

prosterner [prɔsterne] *tr* to bend over || *ref* to prostrate oneself; to grovel

prostituée [prɔstitɥe] *f* prostitute

prostituer [prɔstitɥe] *tr* to prostitute

prostration [prɔstrasjɔ̃] *f* prostration

pros·tré -trée [prɔstre] *adj* prostrate

protagoniste [prɔtagɔnist] *m* protagonist

prote [prɔt] *m* (typ) foreman

protection [prɔtɛksjɔ̃] *f* protection; protection civile civil defense

proté·gé -gée [prɔteʒe] *adj* guarded; arterial (*crossing*) || *mf* protégé, dependent; pet

protège-cahier [prɔteʒkaje] *m* (*pl* -cahiers) notebook cover

protège-livre [prɔteʒlivr] *m* (*pl* -livres) dust jacket

protéger [prɔteʒe] §1 *tr* to protect; to be a patron of

protéine [prɔtein] *f* protein

protes·tant [prɔtestã] -tante [tãt] *adj & mf* Protestant; protestant

protestation [prɔtestasjɔ̃] *f* protest

protester [prɔteste] *tr & intr* to protest; protester de to protest

protêt [prɔtɛ] *m* (com) protest

protocole [prɔtɔkɔl] *m* protocol

proton [prɔtɔ̃] *m* proton

protoplasme [prɔtɔplasm] *m* protoplasm

prototype [prɔtɔtip] *m* prototype

protozoaire [prɔtɔzɔɛr] *m* protozoan

protubérance [prɔtyberãs] *f* protuberance

proue [pru] *f* prow, bow

prouesse [prɥɛs] *f* prowess

prouver [pruve] *tr* to prove

provenance [prɔvnãs] *f* origin; en provenance de from

proven·çal -çale [prɔvãsal] (*pl* -çaux [so]) *adj* Provençal || *m* Provençal (*language*) || (*cap*) *mf* Provençal (*person*)

provenir [prɔvnir] §72 *intr (aux*: ÊTRE) —**provenir de** to come from
proverbe [prɔvɛrb] *m* proverb
providence [prɔvidãs] *f* providence
providen·tiel -tielle [prɔvidãsjɛl] *adj* providential
province [prɔvɛ̃s] *adj invar* (coll) provincial ‖ *f* province; **la province** the provinces (*all of France outside of Paris*)
proviseur [prɔvizœr] *m* headmaster
provision [prɔvizjɔ̃] *f* stock, store; deposit; **aller aux provisions** to go shopping; **faire provision de** to stock up on; **provisions** provisions, foodstuffs; **sans provision** bad (*check*)
provisoire [prɔvizwar] *adj* provisional, temporary; emergency
provo·cant [prɔvɔkã] **-cante** [kãt] *adj* provocative
provoquer [prɔvɔke] *tr* to provoke; to cause, bring about; to arouse
proxénète [prɔksenɛt] *mf* procurer ‖ *m* pimp
proximité [prɔksimite] *f* proximity; **à proximité de** near
prude [pryd] *adj* prudish ‖ *f* prude
prudence [prydãs] *f* prudence
pru·dent [prydã] **-dente** [dãt] *adj* prudent
pruderie [prydri] *f* prudery
prud'homme [prydɔm] *m* arbitrator; (obs) solid citizen
prudhommesque [prydɔmɛsk] *adj* pompous
pruine [prɥin] *f* bloom
prune [pryn] *f* plum; **des prunes!** (slang) nuts!; **pour des prunes** (coll) for nothing
pru·neau [pryno] *m (pl* **-neaux**) prune; (slang) bullet
prunelle [prynɛl] *f* pupil (*of eye*); sloe; sloe gin; **jouer de la prunelle** (coll) to ogle; **prunelle de ses yeux** apple of his (one's, etc.) eye
prunellier [prynelje] *m* sloe, blackthorn
prunier [prynje] *m* plum tree
prus·sien [prysjɛ̃] **prus·sienne** [prysjɛn] *adj* Prussian ‖ (*cap*) *mf* Prussian
P.-S. [peɛs] *m* (letterword) (postscriptum) P.S.
psalmodier [psalmɔdje] *tr & intr* to speak in a singsong
psaume [psom] *m* psalm
psautier [psotje] *m* psalter
pseudonyme [psødɔnim] *adj* pseudonymous ‖ *m* pseudonym; nom de plume
psitt [psit] *interj* (coll) hist!
P.S.V. [peɛsve] *m* (letterword) (**pilotage sans visibilité**) blind flying
psychanalyse [psikanaliz] *f* psychoanalysis
psychanalyser [psikanalize] *tr* to psychoanalyze
psyché [psi/e] *f* psyche; cheval glass
psychiatre [psikjatr] *mf* psychiatrist
psychiatrie [psikjatri] *f* psychiatry
psychique [psi/ik] *adj* psychic
psychologie [psikɔlɔʒi] *f* psychology
psychologique [psikɔlɔʒik] *adj* psychologic(al)

psychologue [psikɔlɔg] *mf* psychologist
psychopathe [psikɔpat] *mf* psychopath
psychose [psikoz] *f* psychosis
psychotique [psikɔtik] *adj & mf* psychotic
ptomaïne [ptɔmain] *f* ptomaine
P.T.T. [petete] *fpl* (letterword) (**Postes, télégraphes, et téléphones**) post office, telephone, and telegraph
puant [pɥã] **puante** [pɥãt] *adj* stinking
puanteur [pɥãtœr] *f* stench, stink
puberté [pybɛrte] *f* puberty
pu·blic -blique [pyblik] *adj* public; notorious ‖ *m* public; audience
publication [pyblikɑsjɔ̃] *f* publication; proclamation
publicitaire [pyblisiter] *adj* advertising ‖ *m* advertising man
publicité [pyblisite] *f* publicity; advertising; **publicité aérienne** skywriting
publier [pyblije] *tr* to publish; to publicize, proclaim
puce [pys] *f* flea; **mettre la puce à l'oreille à qn** (fig) to put a bug in s.o.'s ear
pu·ceau [pyso] **-celle** [sɛl] (*pl* **-ceaux**) *adj & mf* (coll) virgin ‖ *f* maid
puceron [pysrɔ̃] *m* plant louse
pudding [pudiŋ] *m* plum pudding
puddler [pydle] *tr* to puddle
pudeur [pydœr] *f* modesty
pudi·bond [pydibɔ̃] **-bonde** [bɔ̃d] *adj* prudish
pudibonderie [pydibɔ̃dri] *f* false modesty
pudique [pydik] *adj* modest, chaste
puer [pɥe] *tr* to reek of ‖ *intr* to stink
pué·ril -rile [pɥeril] *adj* puerile
puérilité [pɥerilite] *f* puerility
pugilat [pyʒila] *m* fight, brawl
pugiliste [pyʒilist] *m* pugilist
pugnace [pygnas] *adj* pugnacious
puî·né -née [pɥine] *adj* younger ‖ *mf* younger child
puis [pɥi] *adv* then; next; **et puis** besides; **et puis après?** (coll) what next?
puisard [pɥizar] *m* drain, cesspool; sump
puisatier [pɥizatje] *m* well digger
puiser [pɥize] *tr* to draw (*water*); **puiser à** or **dans** to draw (*s.th.*) from ‖ *intr*—**puiser à** or **dans** to draw from or on; to dip or reach into
puisque [pɥisk(ə)] *conj* since, as, seeing that
puissamment [pɥisamã] *adv* powerfully; exceedingly
puissance [pɥisãs] *f* power
puis·sant [pɥisã] **puis·sante** [pɥisãt] *adj* powerful
puits [pɥi] *m* well; pit; (min) shaft; (naut) locker; **puits absorbant, puits perdu** cesspool; **puits de pétrole** oil well; **puits de science** fountain of knowledge
pull-over [pulɔvœr], [pylɔvɛr] *m (pl* **-overs**) sweater, pullover
pulluler [pylyle] *intr* to swarm, to teem
pulmonaire [pylmɔnɛr] *adj* pulmonary ‖ *f* (bot) lungwort

pulpe [pylp] *f* pulp
pulsation [pylsɑsjɔ̃] *f* pulsation, beat; pulse
pulsion [pylsjɔ̃] *f* (psychoanal) impulse
pulvérisateur [pylverizatœr] *m* spray, atomizer
pulvériser [pylverize] *tr* to pulverize; to spray
punaise [pynɛz] *f* bug; bedbug; thumbtack
punch [pɔ̃ʃ] *m* punch (*drink*) ‖ [pœnʃ] *m* (boxing) punch
punching-ball [pœnʃiŋbol] *m* punching bag
punir [pynir] *tr & intr* to punish
punition [pynisjɔ̃] *f* punishment
pupille [pypil], [pypij] *mf* ward ‖ *f* pupil (*of eye*)
pupitre [pypitr] *m* desk; stand, rack; lectern; console, controls; **pupitre à musique** music stand
pur pure [pyr] *adj* pure ‖ *mf* diehard; **les purs** the pure in heart
purée [pyre] *f* purée; mashed potatoes; (coll) wretch; **être dans la purée** (coll) to be broke; **purée de pois** (culin, fig) pea soup ‖ *interj* (slang) how awful!
pureté [pyrte] *f* purity
purga·tif [pyrgatif] **-tive** [tiv] *adj & m* purgative
purgatoire [pyrgatwar] *m* purgatory
purge [pyrʒ] *f* purge
purger [pyrʒe] §38 *tr* to purge; to pay off (*e.g., a mortgage*); to serve (*a sentence*)

purifier [pyrifje] *tr* to purify
puri·tain [pyritɛ̃] **-taine** [tɛn] *adj & mf* puritan; Puritan
pur-sang [pyrsɑ̃] *adj & m invar* thoroughbred
pus [py] *m* pus
pusillanime [pyzilanim] *adj* pusillanimous
pustule [pystyl] *f* pimple
putain [pytɛ̃] *adj invar* (coll) amiable, agreeable ‖ *f* (vulg) whore
putois [pytwa] *m* skunk, polecat
putréfier [pytrefje] *tr & ref* to decompose, to rot
putride [pytrid] *adj* putrid
puy [pɥi] *m* volcanic peak
puzzle [pœzl] *m* jigsaw puzzle
p.-v. [peve] *m* (letterword) (procèsverbal) (coll) ticket, e.g., **attraper un p.-v.** to get a ticket
pygargue [pigarg] *m* osprey, fish hawk
pygmée [pigme] *m* pygmy
pygméen [pigmeɛ̃] **pygméenne** [pigmeen] *adj* pygmy
pyjama [piʒama] *m* pajamas; **un pyjama** a pair of pajamas
pylône [pilon] *m* pylon; tower
pyramide [piramid] *f* pyramid
Pyrénées [pirene] *fpl* Pyrenees
pyrite [pirit] *f* pyrites
pyrotechnie [pirɔtɛkni] *f* pyrotechnics
pyrotechnique [pirɔteknik] *adj* pyrotechnical
python [pitɔ̃] *m* python
pythonisse [pitɔnis] *f* pythoness
pyxide [piksid] *f* pyx

Q

Q, q [ky] *m invar* seventeenth letter of the French alphabet
quadrant [kwadrɑ̃], [kadrɑ̃] *m* (math) quadrant
quadrilatère [kwadrilatɛr] *m* quadrilateral
quadrupède [kwadrypɛd] *m* quadruped
quadruple [kwadrypl] *adj & m* quadruple
quadrupler [kwadryple] *tr & intr* to quadruple
quadru·plés -plées [kwadryple] *mfpl* quadruplets
quai [ke] *m* quay, wharf; platform (*e.g., in a railroad station*); embankment, levee; **amener à quai** to berth; **le Quai d'Orsay** the French foreign office
qua·ker [kwɛkœr], [kwakɛr] **-keresse** [krɛs] *mf* Quaker
qualifiable [kalifjabl] *adj* describable
quali·fié -fiée [kalifje] *adj* qualified; qualifying; aggravated (*crime*)
qualifier [kalifje] *tr & intr* to qualify
qualité [kalite] *f* quality; title, capacity; **avoir qualité pour** to be authorized to; **en qualité de** in the capacity of

quand [kɑ̃] *adv* when; how soon; **n'importe quand** anytime; **quand même** though, just the same ‖ *conj* when; **quand même even if**
quant [kɑ̃] *adv*—**quant à** as for, as to, as far as; **quant à cela** for that matter
quant-à-soi [kɑ̃taswa] *m* dignity, reserve; **rester** or **se tenir sur son quant-à-soi** to keep one's distance
quantique [kwɑ̃tik] *adj* quantum
quantité [kɑ̃tite] *f* quantity
quan·tum [kwɑ̃tɔm] *m* (*pl* -ta [ta]) quantum
quarantaine [karɑ̃tɛn] *f* age of forty, forty mark, forties; quarantine; **une quarantaine de** about forty
quarante [karɑ̃t] *adj, pron, & m* forty; **quarante et un** forty-one; **quarante et unième** forty-first
quarante-deux [karɑ̃tdø] *adj, pron, & m* forty-two
quarante-deuxième [karɑ̃tdøzjɛm] *adj, pron* (*masc, fem*), *& m* forty-second
quarantième [karɑ̃tjɛm] *adj, pron* (*masc, fem*), *& m* fortieth
quart [kar] *m* quarter; fourth (*in fractions*); quarter of a pound; quarter

of a liter; **bon quart!** (naut) all's well!; **passer un mauvais quart d'heure** to have a trying time; **petit quart** (naut) dogwatch; **prendre le quart** (naut) to come on watch; **quart de cercle** quadrant; **quart de soupir** (mus) sixteenth-note rest; **quart d'heure de Rabelais** day of reckoning; **tous les quarts d'heure au quart d'heure juste** every quarter-hour on the quarter-hour; **un petit quart d'heure** a quarter of an hour or so
quarte [kart] adj quartan (fever) ‖ f half-gallon; (escr) quarte; (mus) fourth
quarte·ron [kartərɔ̃] -ronne [rɔn] mf quadroon ‖ m handful (e.g., of people)
quartette [kwartɛt] m combo (foursome)
quartier [kartje] m quarter; neighborhood; section (of orange); portion; **à quartier** aloof; apart; **avoir quartier libre** (mil) to have a pass; to be off duty; **les beaux quartiers** the upper-class residential district; **mettre en quartiers** to dismember; **quartier d'affaires** business district; **quartier général** (mil) headquarters; **quartier réservé** red-light district; **quartiers** quarters, barracks
quartier-maître [kartjemɛtr] m (pl **quartiers-maîtres**) quartermaster
quartz [kwarts] m quartz
quasar [kwazar], [kazar] m quasar
quasi [kazi] m butt (of a loin cut) ‖ adv almost
quasiment [kazimɑ̃] adv (coll) almost
quatorze [katɔrz] adj & pron fourteen; the Fourteenth, e.g., **Jean quatorze** John the Fourteenth ‖ m fourteen; fourteenth (in dates)
quatorzième [katɔrzjɛm] adj, pron (masc, fem), & m fourteenth
quatrain [katrɛ̃] m quatrain
quatre [katr] adj & pron four; the Fourth, e.g., **Jean quatre** John the Fourth; **quatre à quatre** four at a time; **quatre heures** four o'clock ‖ m four; fourth (in dates); **se mettre en quatre pour** to fall all over oneself for; **se tenir à quatre** to keep oneself under control
quatre-épices [katrepis] m & f invar allspice (plant); **des quatre-épices** allspice (spice)
quatre-saisons [katrəsɛzɔ̃], [katsɛzɔ̃] f invar everbearing small strawberry
quatre-temps [katrətɑ̃] mpl Ember days
quatre-vingt-dix [katrəvɛ̃di(s)] adj, pron, & m ninety
quatre-vingt-dixième [katrəvɛ̃dizjɛm] adj, pron (masc, fem), & m ninetieth
quatre-vingtième [katrəvɛ̃tjɛm] adj, pron (masc, fem), & m eightieth
quatre-vingt-onze [katrəvɛ̃ɔ̃z] adj, pron, & m ninety-one
quatre-vingt-onzième [katrəvɛ̃ɔ̃zjɛm] adj, pron (masc, fem), & m ninety-first
quatre-vingts [katrəvɛ̃] adj & pron

eighty; **quatre-vingt** eighty, e.g., **page quatre-vingt** page eighty ‖ m eighty
quatre-vingt-un [katrəvɛ̃œ̃] adj, pron, & m eighty-one
quatre-vingt-unième [katrəvɛ̃ynjɛm] adj, pron (masc, fem), & m eighty-first
quatrième [katrijɛm] adj, pron (masc, fem), & m fourth
quatuor [kwatɥɔr] m (mus) quartet
que [kə] (or **qu'** [k] before a vowel or mute h) pron rel whom; which, that; **ce que** that which, what ‖ pron interr what; **qu'est-ce que . . . ?** what (as direct object) . . . ?; **qu'est-ce qui . . . ?** what (as subject) . . . ? ‖ adv why, e.g., **qu'avez-vous besoin de tant de livres?** why do you need so many books?; how!, e.g., **que cette femme est belle!** how beautiful that woman is!; **que de** what a lot of, e.g., **que de difficultés!** what a lot of difficulties! ‖ conj that; when, e.g., **un jour que je suis allé chez le dentiste** once when I went to the dentist; since, e.g., **il y a trois jours qu'il est arrivé** it is three days since he came; until, e.g., **attendez qu'il vienne** wait until he comes; than, e.g., **plus grand que moi** taller than I; as, e.g., **aussi grand que moi** as tall as I; but, e.g., **personne que vous** no one but you; whether, e.g., **qu'il parte ou qu'il reste** whether he leaves or stays; (in a conditional sentence without **si**, to introduce the conditional in a dependent clause which represents the main clause of the corresponding sentence in English), e.g., **il ferait faillite que cela ne m'étonnerait pas** if he went bankrupt it would not surprise me; (as a repetition of another conjunction), e.g., **si elle chante et que la salle soit comble** if she sings and there is a full house; e.g., **comme il avait soif et que le vin était bon** as he was thirsty and the wine was good; (in a prayer or exhortation), e.g., **que Dieu vous bénisse!** may God bless you!, God bless you!; (in a command), e.g., **qu'il parle (aille, parte, etc.)** let him speak (go, leave, etc.); **ne . . . que** §90 only, but
quel quelle [kɛl] §80
quelconque [kɛlkɔ̃k] adj indef any; any, whatever; any at all, some kind of ‖ (when standing before noun) adj indef some, some sort of ‖ adj ordinary, nondescript, mediocre
quelque [kɛlkə] adj indef some, any; **quelque chose** (always masc) something; **quelque chose de bon** something good; **quelque part** somewhere; **quelque . . . qui** or **quelque . . . que** whatever . . . ; whichever . . . ; **quelques** a few ‖ adv some, about; **quelque peu** somewhat; **quelque + adj** or **adv . . . que** however + adj or adv
quelquefois [kɛlkəfwa] adv sometimes
quel·qu'un [kɛlkœ̃] -qu'une [kyn] §81
quémander [kemɑ̃de] tr to beg for ‖ intr to beg

qu'en-dira-t-on [kɑ̃diratɔ̃] *m invar*
what other people will say, gossip
quenotte [kənɔt] *f* (coll) baby tooth
quenouille [kənuj] *f* distaff; distaff
side
querelle [kərɛl] *f* quarrel; **chercher
querelle à** to pick a quarrel with; **une
querelle d'Allemand, une mauvaise
querelle** a groundless quarrel
quereller [kərɛle] *tr* to nag, scold ‖
ref to quarrel
querel·leur [kərɛlœr] **querel·leuse**
[kərɛløz] *adj* quarrelsome ‖ *mf*
wrangler ‖ *f* shrew
quérir [kerir] (used only in *inf*) *tr* to
go for, to fetch
question [kɛstjɔ̃] *f* question
questionnaire [kɛstjɔnɛr] *m* questionnaire
questionner [kɛstjɔne] *tr* to question
question·neur [kɛstjɔnœr] **question·
neuse** [kɛstjɔnøz] *adj* inquisitive ‖
mf inquisitive person ‖ *m* (rad, telv)
quizmaster
quête [kɛt] *f* quest; **faire la quête to**
take up the collection
quêter [kete] *tr* to beg or fish for
(*votes, praise, etc.*); to hunt for
(*game*); to collect (*contributions*) ‖
intr to take up a collection
quetsche [kwɛtʃ] *f* quetsch
queue [kø] *f* tail; queue; billiard cue;
train (*of dress*); handle (*of pan*); bottom (*of class*); stem, stalk; **à la
queue leu leu** in single file; **faire la
queue** to line up, to queue up; **fausse
queue** miscue; **queue de cheval** (bot)
horsetail; **queue de loup** (bot) purple
foxglove; **queue de poisson** (aut)
fishtail; **queue de vache** cat's-tail
(*cirrus*); **sans queue ni tête** without
head or tail; **venir en queue** to bring
up the rear
queue-d'aronde [kødarɔ̃d] *f* (*pl* **queues-
d'aronde**) dovetail; **assembler à
queue-d'aronde** to dovetail
queue-de-morue [kødmɔry] *f* (*pl*
queues-de-morue) tails, swallow-
tailed coat; (painting) flat brush
queue-de-rat [kødəra] *f* (*pl* **queues-de-
rat**) rat-tail file; taper
qui [ki] *pron rel* who, whom; which,
that; **ce qui** that which, what; **n'importe qui** anyone; **qui que** anyone,
no one; whoever, e.g., **qui que vous
soyez** whoever you are ‖ *pron interr*
who, whom; **qui est-ce que . . . ?**
whom . . . ?; **qui est-ce qui . . . ?**
who . . . ?
quia [kɥija]—**mettre** or **réduire qn à
quia** (obs) to stump or floor s.o.
quiconque [kikɔ̃k] *pron indef* whoever,
whosoever; whomever; anyone
quidam [kɥidam], [kidam] *m* individual, person
quiétude [kɥijetyd], [kjetyd] *f* peace of
mind; quiet, calm
quignon [kiɲɔ̃] *m* hunk (*of bread*)
quille [kij] *f* keel; pin (*for bowling*);
quilles ninepins
quincaillerie [kɛ̃kajri] *f* hardware;
hardware store

quincail·lier [kɛ̃kaje] **quincail·lière**
[kɛ̃kajɛr] *mf* hardware dealer
quinconce [kɛ̃kɔ̃s] *m* quincunx; **en
quinconce** quincuncially
quinine [kinin] *f* quinine
quinquen·nal -nale [kɥɛ̃kɥɛnnal] *adj*
(*pl* -**naux** [no]) five-year
quinquet [kɛ̃kɛ] *m*—**allume tes quin-
quets!** (slang) open your eyes!
quinquina [kɛ̃kina] *m* cinchona
quin·tal [kɛ̃tal] *m* (*pl* -**taux** [to]) hun-
dredweight; one hundred kilograms
quinte [kɛ̃t] *f* whim; (cards) sequence
of five; (mus) fifth; **quinte de toux**
fit of coughing
quintessence [kɛ̃tesɑ̃s] *f* quintessence
quintette [kɥɛ̃tɛt], [kɛ̃tɛt] *m* (mus)
quintet; (coll) five-piece combo;
quintette à cordes string quintet
quin·teux [kɛ̃tø] -**teuse** [tøz] *adj*
crotchety, fitful, restive
quintu·plés -plées [kɛ̃typle] *mfpl* quintuplets
quinzaine [kɛ̃zen] *f* (group of) fifteen;
two weeks, fortnight; **une quinzaine
de** about fifteen
quinze [kɛ̃z] *adj & pron* fifteen; the
Fifteenth, e.g., **Jean quinze** John the
Fifteenth ‖ *m* fifteen; fifteenth (*in
dates*)
quinzième [kɛ̃zjɛm] *adj, pron* (*masc,
fem*), & *m* fifteenth
quiproquo [kiprɔko] *m* mistaken identity, misunderstanding
quiscale [kɥiskal] *m* (orn) purple
grackle
quittance [kitɑ̃s] *f* receipt
quitte [kit] *adj* free (*from obligation*);
clear (*of debts*); (en) **être quitte pour**
to get off with; **être quitte** to be
quits; **tenir qn quitte de** to release
s.o. from ‖ *m*—**jouer (à) quitte ou
double** to play double or nothing ‖
adv—**quitte à** even if one has to, e.g.,
**commençons par en rire, quitte à en
pleurer plus tard** let us begin by
laughing, even if we have to cry later
on
quitter [kite] *tr* to leave; to take off
(*e.g., a coat*) ‖ *intr* to leave, go away;
ne quittez pas! (telp) hold the line! ‖
ref to part, separate
quitus [kɥitys] *m* discharge, acquit-
tance
qui-vive [kiviv] *m invar*—**sur le qui-
vive** on the qui vive ‖ *interj* (mil)
who goes there?
quoi [kwa] *pron indef* what, which; **à
quoi bon?** what's the use?; **de quoi**
enough; **moyennant quoi** in exchange
for which; **n'importe quoi** anything;
quoi que whatever; **quoi qu'il en soit**
be that as it may; **sans quoi** otherwise
quoique [kwakə] *conj* although, though
quolibet [kɔlibɛ] *m* gibe, quip
quorum [kwɔrɔm], [kɔrɔm] *m* quorum
quota [kwɔta], [kɔta] *m* quota
quote-part [kɔtpar] *f invar* quota, share
quoti·dien [kɔtidjɛ̃] -**dienne** [djɛn] *adj*
daily ‖ *m* daily newspaper
quotient [kɔsjɑ̃] *m* quotient
quotité [kɔtite] *f* share, amount

R

R, r [er], *[er] *m* *invar* eighteenth letter of the French alphabet
rabâcher [rabɑ/e] *tr* to harp on ‖ *intr* to harp on the same thing
rabais [rabɛ] *m* reduction, discount
rabaisser [rabese] *tr* to lower; to disparage
rabat [raba] *m* flap (*vestment*)
rabat-joie [raba3wa] *m* *invar* kill-joy
rabattre [rabatr] §7 *tr* to lower; to discount; to turn down; to fold up; to pull down; to cut back; to flush (*game*) ‖ *intr* to turn; **en rabattre** to come down a peg or two; **rabattre de** to reduce (*a price*) ‖ *ref* to fold; to drop down; to turn the other way; **se rabattre sur** to fall back on
rabat·tu -tue [rabaty] *adj* turndown
rabbin [rabɛ̃] *m* rabbi
rabibocher [rabibɔ/e] *tr* (coll) to patch up ‖ *ref* (coll) to make up
rabiot [rabjo] *m* overtime; extra bit; (mil) extra service; (coll) graft
rabioter [rabjɔte] *tr & intr* to graft
râ·blé -blée [rɑble] *adj* husky
rabot [rabo] *m* plane
raboter [rabɔte] *tr* to plane
rabo·teux [rabɔtø] **-teuse** [tøz] *adj* rough, uneven ‖ *f* (mach) planer
rabou·gri -grie [rabugri] *adj* scrub, scrawny
rabrouer [rabrue] *tr* to snub
racaille [rakɑj] *f* riffraff
raccommodage [rakɔmɔdaʒ] *m* mending; darning; patching
raccommodement [rakɔmɔdmɑ̃] *m* (coll) reconciliation
raccommoder [rakɔmɔde] *tr* to mend; to darn; to patch; (coll) to patch up
raccompagner [rakɔ̃paɲe] *tr* to see back, to see home
raccord [rakɔr] *m* connection; coupling; joint; adapter; **faire un raccord à** to touch up
raccordement [rakɔrdəmɑ̃] *m* connecting, linking, joining
raccorder [rakɔrde] *tr & ref* to connect
raccour·ci -cie [rakursi] *adj* shortened; abridged; squat, dumpy; bobbed (*hair*) ‖ *m* abridgment; shortcut, cutoff; foreshortening; **en raccourci** in miniature; in a nutshell
raccourcir [rakursir] *tr* to shorten; to abridge; to foreshorten ‖ *intr* to grow shorter
raccourcissement [rakursismɑ̃] *m* shortening; abridgment; shrinking
raccroc [rakro] *m* fluke
raccrocher [rakrɔ/e] *tr & intr* to hang up ‖ *ref*—**se raccrocher à** to hang on to
race [ras] *f* race; **de race** thoroughbred
ra·cé -cée [rase] *adj* thoroughbred
rachat [ra/a] *m* repurchase; redemption; ransom
racheter [ra/te] §2 *tr* to buy back; to redeem; to ransom
rachitique [ra/itik] *adj* rickety
rachitisme [ra/itism] *m* rickets

ra·cial -ciale [rasjal] *adj* (*pl* **-ciaux** [sjo]) race, racial
racine [rasin] *f* root; **racine carrée** square root; **racine cubique** cube root
racket [rakɛt] *m* (coll) racket
racketter or **racketteur** [rakɛtœr] *m* racketeer
raclée [rakle] *f* beating
racler [rakle] *tr* to scrape
raclette [raklɛt] *f* scraper; hoe; (phot) squeegee
racloir [raklwar] *m* scraper
raclure [raklyr] *f* scrapings
racolage [rakɔlaʒ] *m* soliciting
racoler [rakɔle] *tr* (coll) to solicit; (archaic) to shanghai
raco·leur [rakɔlœr] **-leuse** [løz] *mf* recruiter ‖ *f* (coll) hustler, streetwalker
racontar [rakɔ̃tar] *m* (coll) gossip
raconter [rakɔ̃te] *tr* to tell, narrate; to describe
racon·teur [rakɔ̃tœr] **-teuse** [tøz] *mf* storyteller
racornir [rakɔrnir] *tr & intr* to harden; to shrivel
radar [radar] *m* radar
rade [rad] *f* roadstead; **en rade** (coll) abandoned
ra·deau [rado] *m* (*pl* **-deaux**) raft
ra·diant [radjɑ̃] **-diante** [djɑ̃t] *adj* (astr, phys) radiant
radiateur [radjatœr] *m* radiator
radiation [radjɑsjɔ̃] *f* radiation; striking off
radi·cal -cale [radikal] *adj & mf* (*pl* **-caux** [ko]) radical ‖ *m* (chem, gram, math) radical
radier [radje] *tr* to cross out, to strike out or off
ra·dieux [radjø] **-dieuse** [djøz] *adj* radiant
radin [radɛ̃] *adj* *masc & fem* (slang) stingy
radio [radjo] *m* radiogram; radio operator ‖ *f* radio; radio set; X ray
radioac·tif [radjɔaktif] **-tive** [tiv] *adj* radioactive
radio-crochet [radjɔkrɔ/ɛ] *m* (*pl* **-crochets**) talent show
radiodiffuser [radjɔdifyze] *tr* to broadcast
radiodiffusion [radjɔdifyzjɔ̃] *f* broadcasting
radiofréquence [radjɔfrekɑ̃s] *f* radiofrequency
radiogramme [radjɔgram] *m* radiogram
radiographier [radjɔgrafje] *tr* to X-ray
radio-journal [radjɔʒurnal] *m* (*pl* **-journaux** [ʒurno]) radio newscast
radiologie [radjɔlɔʒi] *f* radiology
radiophare [radjɔfar] *m* radio beacon
radioreportage [radjɔrəpɔrtaʒ] *m* news broadcast; sports broadcast
radioscopie [radjɔskɔpi] *f* radioscopy, fluoroscopy
radiotélévi·sé -sée [radjɔtelevize] *adj* broadcast over radio and television
radis [radi] *m* radish
radium [radjɔm] *m* radium

radius [radjys] *m* (anat) radius
radotage [radɔtaʒ] *m* drivel, twaddle
radoter [radɔte] *intr* to talk nonsense, to ramble
radoub [radu] *m* (naut) graving
radouber [radube] *tr* (naut) to grave
radoucir [radusir] *tr & ref* to calm down
rafale [rafal] *f* squall, gust; burst of gunfire
raffermir [rafɛrmir] *tr & ref* to harden
raffinage [rafinaʒ] *m* refining
raffinement [rafinmɑ̃] *m* refinement
raffiner [rafine] *tr* to refine || *intr* to be subtle; **raffiner sur** to overdo
raffinerie [rafinri] *f* refinery
raffoler [rafɔle] *intr*—**raffoler de** to dote on, to be wild about
raffut [rafy] *m* (coll) uproar
rafistolage [rafistɔlaʒ] *m* (coll) patching up
rafistoler [rafistɔle] *tr* (coll) to patch up
rafle [rɑfl] *f* raid, mass arrest; stalk; corncob
rafler [rɑfle] *tr* (coll) to carry away, to make a clean sweep of
rafraîchir [rafreʃir] *tr* to cool; to refresh; to freshen up; to trim (*the hair*) || *intr* to cool || *ref* to cool off; to refresh oneself
rafraîchissement [rafreʃismɑ̃] *m* refreshment; cooling off
ragaillardir [ragajardir] *tr* to cheer up
rage [raʒ] *f* rage; rabies; **à la rage** madly; **faire rage** to rage
rager [raʒe] §38 *intr* (coll) to be enraged
ra·geur [raʒœr] **-geuse** [ʒøz] *adj* bad-tempered
ragot [rago] *m* (coll) gossip
ragoût [ragu] *m* stew, ragout; (obs) spice, relish
ragoû·tant [ragutɑ̃] **-tante** [tɑ̃t] *adj* tempting, inviting; pleasing; **peu ragoûtant** not very appetizing
rai [rɛ] *m* ray; spoke
raid [rɛd] *m* raid; air raid; endurance test
raide [rɛd] *adj* stiff; tight, taut; steep; (coll) incredible || *adv* suddenly
raideur [rɛdœr] *f* stiffness
raidillon [rɛdijɔ̃] *m* short steep path
raidir [rɛdir] *tr & ref* to stiffen
raie [rɛ] *f* stripe, streak; stroke; line (*of spectrum*); part (*of hair*); (ichth) ray, skate
raifort [rɛfɔr] *m* horseradish
rail [raj] *m* rail; **rail conducteur** third rail; **remettre sur les rails** (fig) to put back on the track; **sortir des rails** to jump the track
railler [raje] *tr* to make fun of || *intr* to joke || *ref*—**se railler de** to make fun of
raillerie [rɑjri] *f* raillery, banter
rail·leur [rɑjœr] **rail·leuse** [rɑjøz] *adj* teasing, bantering || *mf* teaser
rainette [rɛnɛt] *f* tree frog
rainure [renyr] *f* groove
raisin [rɛzɛ̃] *m* grapes; grape; **raisin d'ours** (bot) bearberry; **raisins de Corinthe** currants; **raisins de mer**

cuttlefish eggs; **raisins de Smyrne** seedless raisins; **raisins secs** raisins
raisiné [rezine] *m* grape jelly; (slang) blood
raison [rɛzɔ̃] *f* reason; ratio, rate; **à raison de** at the rate of; **avoir raison** to be right; **avoir raison de** to get the better of; **donner raison à** to back, support; **en raison de** because of; **raison sociale** trade name; **se faire une raison** to resign oneself
raisonnable [rezɔnabl] *adj* reasonable; rational
raison·né -née [rezɔne] *adj* rational; detailed
raisonnement [rezɔnmɑ̃] *m* reasoning; argument
raisonner [rezɔne] *tr* to reason out; to reason with || *intr* to reason; to argue || *ref* to reason with oneself
raison·neur [rezɔnœr] **raison·neuse** [rezɔnøz] *adj* rational; argumentative || *mf* reasoner; arguer
rajeunir [raʒœnir] *tr* to rejuvenate || *intr* to grow young again || *ref* to pretend to be younger than one is
rajeunissement [raʒœnismɑ̃] *m* rejuvenation
rajouter [raʒute] *tr* to add again; (coll) to add more
rajuster [raʒyste] *tr* to readjust; to adjust || *ref* to adjust one's clothes
râle [rɑl] *m* rale; death rattle; (orn) rail
ralen·ti -tie [ralɑ̃ti] *adj* slow || *m* slowdown; **au ralenti** slowdown (*work*); go-slow (*policy*); slow-motion (*moving picture*); idling (*motor*); **tourner au ralenti** (aut) to idle
ralentir [ralɑ̃tir] *tr, intr, & ref* to slow down; **ralentir** (public sign) slow
ralliement [ralimɑ̃] *m* rally
rallier [ralje] *tr & ref* to rally
rallonge [ralɔ̃ʒ] *f* extra piece; leaf (*of table*); (coll) under-the-table payment; **à rallonges** extension (*table*)
rallonger [ralɔ̃ʒe] §38 *tr & intr* to lengthen
rallumer [ralyme] *tr* to relight; (fig) to rekindle || *intr* to put on the lights again || *ref* to be rekindled
rallye [rali] *m* rallye
ramage [ramaʒ] *m* floral design; warbling
ramas [rama] *m* heap; pack (*e.g., of thieves*)
ramassage [ramasaʒ] *m* gathering; **ramassage scolaire** school-bus service
ramas·sé -sée [ramase] *adj* stocky; compact (*style*)
ramasser [ramase] *tr* to gather; to gather together; to pick up; (coll) to catch (*a scolding; a cold*) || *ref* to gather; to gather oneself together
rambarde [rɑ̃bard] *f* handrail
rame [ram] *f* prop, stick; oar, pole; ream (*of paper*); string (*e.g., of barges*); (rr) train, section; **rame de métro** subway train
ra·meau [ramo] *m* (*pl* -meaux) branch; sprig
ramée [rame] *f* boughs

ramener [ramne] §2 *tr* to lead back; to bring back; to reduce; to restore
ramer [rame] *tr* to stake (*a plant*) || *intr* to row
ra·meur [ramœr] -**meuse** [møz] *mf* rower
ramier [ramje] *m* wood pigeon
ramifier [ramifje] *tr* & *ref* to ramify, to branch out
ramol·li -**lie** [ramɔli] *adj* sodden; (coll) half-witted || *mf* (coll) half-wit
ramollir [ramɔlir] *tr* & *ref* to soften
ramoner [ramɔne] *tr* to sweep (*a chimney*)
ramoneur [ramɔnœr] *m* chimney sweep
ram·pant [rɑ̃pɑ̃] -**pante** [pɑ̃t] *adj* crawling, creeping; (hum) ground (*crew*)
rampe [rɑ̃p] *f* ramp; grade, gradient; banister; flight (*of stairs*); (aer) runway lights; (theat) footlights; **rampe de lancement** launching pad
ramper [rɑ̃pe] *intr* to crawl; to grovel; (bot) to creep
ramure [ramyr] *f* branches; antlers
rancart [rɑ̃kar] *m* (slang) rendezvous; **mettre au rancart** (coll) to scrap, to shelve
rance [rɑ̃s] *adj* rancid
ranch [rɑ̃tʃ] *m* ranch
rancir [rɑ̃sir] *intr* & *ref* to turn rancid
rancœur [rɑ̃kœr] *f* rancor
rançon [rɑ̃sɔ̃] *f* ransom
rançonner [rɑ̃sɔne] *tr* to ransom
rancune [rɑ̃kyn] *f* grudge
rancu·nier [rɑ̃kynje] -**nière** [njɛr] *adj* vindictive
randonnée [rɑ̃dɔne] *f* long walk; long ride
rang [rɑ̃] *m* rank; **au premier rang** in the first row; ranking; **en rang d'oignons** in a line
ran·gé -**gée** [rɑ̃ʒe] *adj* orderly; pitched (*battle*); steady (*person*)
ranger [rɑ̃ʒe] §38 *tr* to range; to rank || *ref* to take one's place; to get out of the way; to mend one's ways; se **ranger à** to adopt, take (*e.g., a suggestion*)
ranimer [ranime] *tr* & *ref* to revive
raout [raut] *m* reception
rapace [rapas] *adj* rapacious || *m* bird of prey
rapatriement [rapatrimɑ̃] *m* repatriation
rapatrier [rapatrije] *tr* to repatriate
râpe [rɑp] *f* rasp; grater
râ·pé -**pée** [rɑpe] *adj* grated; threadbare || *m* (coll) grated cheese
râper [rɑpe] *tr* to rasp, to grate
rapetasser [raptase] *tr* (coll) to patch up
rapetisser [raptise] *tr, intr,* & *ref* to shrink, shorten
râ·peux [rɑpø] -**peuse** [pøz] *adj* raspy, grating
ra·piat [rapja] -**piate** [pjat] *adj* (coll) stingy || *mf* (coll) skinflint
rapide [rapid] *adj* rapid; steep || *m* rapids; (rr) express; **rapides** rapids
rapidité [rapidite] *f* rapidity; steepness
rapiéçage [rapjesaʒ] *m* patching
rapiécer [rapjese] §58 *tr* to patch

rapière [rapjɛr] *f* rapier
rapin [rapɛ̃] *m* dauber; (coll) art student
rapine [rapin] *f* rapine, pillage
rappel [rapɛl] *m* recall; reminder; call-up; recurrence; booster (*shot*); (theat) curtain call; **battre le rappel** to call to arms; **rappel au règlement** point of order; **rappel de chariot** backspacer
rappeler [raple] §34 *tr* to recall; to remind; to call back; to call up || *ref* to remember
rapport [rapɔr] *m* yield, return; report; connection, bearing; (math) ratio; **en rapport avec** in touch with; in keeping with; **par rapport à** in comparison with; **rapports** relations; sexual relations; **sous tous les rapports** in all respects
rapporter [rapɔrte] *tr* to bring back; to yield; to report; to relate; to repeal, call off; to attach; to retrieve (*game*); (bk) to post || *intr* to yield; (coll) to squeal || *ref*—**s'en rapporter à** to leave it up to; **se rapporter à** to be related to, to refer to
rappor·teur [rapɔrtœr] -**teuse** [tøz] *mf* tattletale || *m* recorder; (geom) protractor
rapprochement [raprɔʃmɑ̃] *m* bringing together; parallel; rapprochement
rapprocher [raprɔʃe] *tr* to bring closer; to reconcile; to compare || *ref* to draw closer, to approach; se **rapprocher de** to approximate, to resemble
rapt [rapt] *m* kidnapping
raquette [raket] *f* racket; snowshoe; tennis player; (bot) prickly pear
rare [rar] *adj* rare; scarce; sparse, thin (*hair*)
rarement [rarmɑ̃] *adv* rarely, seldom
rareté [rarte] *f* rarity; scarcity; rareness
ras [rɑ] **rase** [raz] *adj* short (*hair, nap, etc.*); level; close-cropped; close-shaven; open (*country*) || *m*—**à ras de, au ras de** flush with; **ras d'eau** water line; **ras du cou** crew neck; **voler au ras du sol** to skim along the ground
rasade [razad] *f* bumper, glassful
rasage [razaʒ] *m* shearing; shaving
ra·sant [razɑ̃] -**sante** [zɑ̃t] *adj* level; grazing; close to the ground; (coll) boring
rase-mottes [razmɔt] *m invar*—**faire du rase-mottes** or **voler en rase-mottes** to hedgehop
raser [raze] *tr* to shave; to raze; to graze || *ref* to shave
ra·seur [razœr] -**seuse** [zøz] *adj* (coll) boring || *mf* (coll) bore
rasoir [raswar] *adj invar* (slang) boring || *m* razor; (slang) bore; **rasoir à manche** straight razor; **rasoir de sûreté** safety razor
rassasiement [rasazimɑ̃] *m* satiation
rassasier [rasazje] *tr* to satisfy; to satiate || *ref* to have one's fill
rassemblement [rasɑ̃bləmɑ̃] *m* assembling; crowd; muster; (*trumpet call*)

assembly; **rassemblement!** (mil) fall in!

rassembler [rasãmble] *tr & ref* to gather together

rasseoir [raswar] §5 *tr* to reseat; to set in place again ‖ *ref* to sit down again

rasséréner [raserene] §10 *tr & ref* to calm down

rassir [rasir] *intr & ref* (coll) to get stale

ras•sis [rasi] **ras•sise** [rasiz] *adj* level-headed; stale (*bread*)

rassortir [rasɔrtir] *tr* to restock ‖ *ref* to lay in a new stock

rassurer [rasyre] *tr* to reassure ‖ *ref* to be reassured

rastaquouère [rastakwɛr] *m* (coll) flashy stranger

rat [ra] *m* rat; (coll) tightwad; **fait comme un rat** caught like a rat in a trap; **mon rat** (coll) my turtledove; **rat à bourse** gopher; **rat de bibliothèque** bookworm; **rat de cale** stowaway; **rat de cave** thin candle; tax collector; **rat d'égout** sewer rat; **rat des champs** field mouse; **rat d'hôtel** hotel thief; **rat d'Opéra** ballet girl; **rat musqué** muskrat

ratatiner [ratatine] *ref* to shrivel up

ratatouille [ratatuj] *f* (coll) stew; (coll) bad cooking; (coll) blows

rate [rat] *f* spleen; female rat

ra•té -tée [rate] *adj* miscarried; bad (*shot, landing, etc.*) ‖ *mf* failure, dropout

râ•teau [rɑto] *m* (*pl* -teaux) rake

râteler [rɑtle] §34 *tr* to rake

râtelier [rɑtəlje] *m* rack; set of false teeth; **manger à deux râteliers** (coll) to play both sides of the street; **râtelier d'armes** gun rack

rater [rate] *tr* to miss ‖ *intr* to miss, to misfire; to fail

ratiboiser [ratibwaze] *tr* (coll) to take to the cleaners; **ratiboiser q.ch. à qn** (coll) to clean s.o. out of s.th.

ratifier [ratifje] *tr* to ratify

ration [rasjɔ̃] *f* ration

ration•nel -nelle [rasjɔnɛl] *adj* rational

rationnement [rasjɔnmã] *m* rationing

rationner [rasjɔne] *tr* to ration

ratisser [ratise] *tr* to rake; to rake in; to search with a fine-tooth comb; (coll) to fleece

ratissoire [ratiswar] *f* hoe

raton [ratɔ̃] *m* little rat; **raton laveur** raccoon

rattacher [rataʃe] *tr* to tie again; to link; to unite ‖ *ref* to be connected

rattrapage [ratrapaʒ] *m* catch-up; (typ) catchword

rattraper [ratrape] *tr* to catch up to; to recover; to recapture ‖ *ref* to catch up; **se rattraper à** to catch hold of; **se rattraper de** to make good, to recoup

rature [ratyr] *f* erasure

raturer [ratyre] *tr* to cross out

rauque [rok] *adj* hoarse, raucous

ravage [ravaʒ] *m* ravage

ravager [ravaʒe] §38 *tr* to ravage

ravalement [ravalmã] *m* trimming down; resurfacing; disparagement

ravaler [ravale] *tr* to choke down; to disparage; to drag down; to resurface; to eat (*one's words*) ‖ *ref* to lower oneself

ravaudage [ravodaʒ] *m* mending; darning; (fig) patchwork

ravauder [ravode] *tr* to mend; to darn

ravier [ravje] *m* hors-d'oeuvre dish

ravigoter [ravigɔte] *tr* (coll) to revive

ravilir [ravilir] *tr* to debase

ravin [ravɛ̃] *m* ravine

ravine [ravin] *f* mountain torrent

raviner [ravine] *tr* to furrow

ravir [ravir] *tr* to ravish; to kidnap, abduct; to delight, entrance; **ravir q.ch. à qn** to snatch or take s.th. from s.o. ‖ *intr*—**à ravir** marvelously

raviser [ravize] *ref* to change one's mind

ravis•sant [ravisã] **ravis•sante** [ravisãt] *adj* ravishing, entrancing

ravis•seur [ravisœr] **ravis•seuse** [ravisøz] *mf* kidnaper

ravitaillement [ravitajmã] *m* supplying; supplies

ravitailler [ravitaje] *tr* to supply; to fill up the gas tank of (*a vehicle*) ‖ *ref* to lay in supplies; to fill up (*to get gas*)

raviver [ravive] *tr* to revive; to brighten up; to reopen (*an old wound*) ‖ *ref* to revive; to break out again

ravoir [ravwar] (used only in *inf*) *tr* to get back again

rayer [reje] §49 *tr* to cross out, to strike out; to rule, to line; to stripe; to rifle (*a gun*)

rayon [rɛjɔ̃] *m* ray; radius; spoke; shelf; honeycomb; department (*in a store*); point (*of star*); **ce n'est pas mon rayon** (coll) that's not in my line; **rayon de lune** moonbeam; **rayons X** X rays; **rayon visuel** line of sight

rayon•nant [rɛjɔnã] **rayon•nante** [rɛjɔnãt] *adj* radiant; radiating; radioactive; (rad) transmitting

rayonne [rɛjɔn] *f* rayon

rayonner [rɛjɔne] *intr* to radiate

rayure [rejyr] *f* stripe; scratch; rifling

raz [rɑ] *m* race (*channel and current of water*); **raz de marée** tidal wave; landslide (*in an election*)

razzia [razja] *f* raid

razzier [razje] *tr* to raid

réacteur [reaktœr] *m* reactor; **réacteur nucléaire** nuclear reactor

réactif [reaktif] *m* (chem) reagent

réaction [reaksjɔ̃] *f* reaction; kick (*of rifle*); **à réaction** jet; **réaction en chaîne** chain reaction

réactionnaire [reaksjɔnɛr] *adj & mf* reactionary

réadaptation [readaptasjɔ̃] *f* rehabilitation; **réadaptation fonctionnelle** occupational therapy

réadapter [readapte] *tr* to rehabilitate ‖ *ref* to be rehabilitated

réaffirmer [reafirme] *tr* to reaffirm

réagir [reaʒir] *intr* to react

réalisable [realizabl] *adj* feasible; (com) saleable

réalisa•teur [realizatœr] **-trice** [tris]

adj producing || *mf* achiever; producer || *m* (mov, rad, telv) director

réalisation [realizɑsjɔ̃] *f* accomplishment; work; (mov, rad, telv) production; (com) liquidation

réaliser [realize] *tr* to realize; to accomplish; to sell out; (mov) to produce || *ref* to come to pass, to be realized

réalisme [realism] *m* realism

réaliste [realist] *adj* realistic || *mf* realist

réalité [realite] *f* reality

réanimer [reanime] *tr* to revive

réapparaître [reaparɛtr] §12 *intr* to reappear

réapparition [reaparisjɔ̃] *f* reappearance

réarmement [rearmǝmɑ̃] *m* rearmament

réassortir [reasɔrtir] *tr* to restock || *ref* to lay in a new stock

réassurer [reasyre] *tr* to reinsure

rébarba·tif [rebarbatif] -**tive** [tiv] *adj* forbidding, repulsive

rebâtir [rǝbɑtir] *tr* to rebuild

rebattre [rǝbatr] §7 *tr* to beat; to reshuffle; to repeat over and over again

rebat·tu -tue [rǝbaty] *adj* hackneyed

rebelle [rǝbɛl] *adj* rebellious || *mf* rebel

rebeller [rǝbele], [rǝbɛlle] *ref* to rebel

rébellion [rebeljɔ̃] *f* rebellion

rebiffer [rǝbife] *ref* to kick over the traces

reboisement [rǝbwazmɑ̃] *m* reforestation

rebond [rǝbɔ̃] *m* rebound

rebon·di -die [rǝbɔ̃di] *adj* plump, buxom; paunchy

rebondir [rǝbɔ̃dir] *intr* to bounce; (fig) to come up again

rebord [rǝbɔr] *m* edge, border; sill, ledge; hem; brim (*of hat*); rim (*of saucer*); lip (*of cup*)

reboucher [rǝbuʃe] *tr* to recork; to stop up || *ref* to be stopped up

rebours [rǝbur] *m*—**à rebours** backwards; against the grain; the wrong way; backhanded (*compliment*); **à** or **au rebours de** contrary to

rebouter [rǝbute] *tr* to set (*a bone*)

rebrousse-poil [rǝbruspwal]—**à rebrousse-poil** against the grain, the wrong way

rebrousser [rǝbruse] *tr* to brush up; **rebrousser chemin** to turn back; **rebrousser qn** (coll) to rub s.o. the wrong way || *ref* to turn up, to bend back

rebuffade [rǝbyfad] *f* rebuff; **essuyer une rebuffade** to be snubbed

rebut [rǝby] *m* castoff; waste; scum (*of society*); rebuff; **de rebut** castoff; waste; unclaimed (*letter*); **mettre au rebut** to discard

rebu·tant -tante [rǝbytɑ̃] *adj* dull, tedious; repugnant

rebuter [rǝbyte] *tr* to rebuff; to bore; to be repulsive to

recaler [rǝkale] *tr* (coll) to flunk

récapitulation [rekapitylɑsjɔ̃] *f* recapitulation

recéder [rǝsede] §10 *tr* to give or sell back

recel [rǝsɛl] *m* concealment (*of stolen goods; of criminals*)

receler [rǝsle] §2 or **recéler** [rǝsele] §10 *tr* to conceal; to receive (*stolen goods*); to harbor (*a criminal*) || *intr* to hide

rece·leur [rǝslœr] -**leuse** [løz] *mf* fence, receiver of stolen goods

récemment [resamɑ̃] *adv* recently, lately

recensement [rǝsɑ̃smɑ̃] *m* census; **recensement du contingent** draft registration

recenser [rǝsɑ̃se] *tr* to take the census of; to take a count of

recenseur [rǝsɑ̃sœr] *m* census taker

ré·cent [resɑ̃] -**cente** [sɑ̃t] *adj* recent

récépissé [resepise] *m* receipt

réceptacle [resɛptakl] *m* receptacle

récep·teur [resɛptœr] -**trice** [tris] *adj* receiving || *m* receiver

récep·tif [resɛptif] -**tive** [tiv] *adj* receptive

réception [resɛpsjɔ̃] *f* reception; receipt; approval; admission (*to a club*); registration desk (*of hotel*); landing (*of, e.g., a parachutist*); (sports) catch; **accuser réception de** to acknowledge receipt of

réceptionnaire [resɛpsjɔner] *mf* consignee; chief receptionist

récession [resesjɔ̃] *f* recession

recette [rǝsɛt] *f* receipt; collection (*of debts, taxes, etc.*); (culin) recipe; **faire recette** to be a box-office attraction; **recettes de métier** tricks of the trade

recevable [rǝsvabl] *adj* acceptable; admissible

rece·veur [rǝsvœr] -**veuse** [vøz] *mf* collector; conductor (*of bus, streetcar, etc.*); blood recipient; **receveur des postes** postmaster; **receveur universel** recipient of blood from a universal donor

recevoir [rǝsvwar] §59 *tr* to receive; to accommodate; to admit (*to a school, club, etc.*); **être reçu** to be admitted; to pass || *intr* to receive

rechange [rǝʃɑ̃ʒ] *m* replacement, change; **de rechange** spare (*e.g., parts*)

rechaper [rǝʃape] *tr* to recap, to retread

réchapper [reʃape] *intr*—**en réchapper** to get away with it; to get well; **réchapper à** or **de** to escape from

recharge [rǝʃarʒ] *f* refill; recharging; reloading

recharger [rǝʃarʒe] §38 *tr* to recharge; to refill; to reload; to ballast (*a roadbed*)

réchaud [reʃo] *m* hot plate

réchauffer [reʃofe] *tr* & *ref* to warm up

rêche [rɛʃ] *adj* rough, harsh

recherche [rǝʃɛrʃ] *f* search; quest; investigation, piece of research; refinement; **recherches** research

recher·ché -chée [rǝʃɛrʃe] *adj* sought-after, in demand; elaborate; studied, affected

rechercher [rəʃɛrʃe] *tr* to seek, to look for
rechigner [rəʃiɲe] *intr*—**rechigner à** to balk at
rechute [rəʃyt] *f* relapse
rechuter [rəʃyte] *intr* to relapse
récidive [residiv] *f* recurrence; second offense
récidiver [residive] *intr* to recur; to relapse
récif [resif] *m* reef
récipiendaire [resipjɑ̃dɛr] *m* new member, inductee; recipient
récipient [resipjɑ̃] *m* recipient, vessel
réciprocité [resiprɔsite] *f* reciprocity
réciproque [resiprɔk] *adj* reciprocal ‖ *f* converse
récit [resi] *m* recital, account
réci·tal -tale [resital] *m* (*pl* -**tals**) recital
récitation [resitɑsjɔ̃] *f* recitation
réciter [resite] *tr* to recite
récla·mant [reklamɑ̃] -**mante** [mɑ̃t] *mf* claimant
réclamation [reklamɑsjɔ̃] *f* complaint; demand
réclame [reklam] *f* advertising; advertisement; (theat) cue; (typ) catchword; **faire de la réclame** to advertise, to ballyhoo; **réclame à éclipse** flashing sign; **réclame lumineuse** illuminated sign
réclamer [reklame] *tr* to claim; to clamor for; to demand ‖ *intr* to lodge a complaint; to intercede ‖ *ref* —**se réclamer de** to appeal to; to claim kinship with; **se réclamer de qn** to use s.o.'s name as a reference
reclassement [rəklɑsmɑ̃] *m* reclassification
reclasser [rəklɑse] *tr* to reclassify
re·clus [rəkly] -**cluse** [klyz] *adj & mf* recluse
recoin [rəkwɛ̃] *m* nook, cranny
récollection [rekɔlɛksjɔ̃] *f* religious meditation
recoller [rəkɔle] *tr* to paste again
récolte [rekɔlt] *f* harvest
récolter [rekɔlte] *tr* to harvest
recommander [rəkɔmɑ̃de] *tr* to recommend; to register (*a letter*) ‖ *ref* —**se recommander à** to seek the protection of; **se recommander de** to ask (*s.o.*) for a reference
recommencer [rəkɔmɑ̃se] §51 *tr & intr* to begin again
récompense [rekɔ̃pɑ̃s] *f* recompense, reward; award
récompenser [rekɔ̃pɑ̃se] *tr* to recompense
réconcilier [rekɔ̃silje] *tr* to reconcile
reconduire [rəkɔ̃dɥir] §19 *tr* to escort; (coll) to kick out, to send packing
réconfort [rekɔ̃fɔr] *m* comfort
réconfor·tant [rekɔ̃fɔrtɑ̃] -**tante** [tɑ̃t] *adj* consoling; stimulating
réconforter [rekɔ̃fɔrte] *tr* to comfort; to revive ‖ *ref* to recuperate; to cheer up
reconnaissance [rəkɔnɛsɑ̃s] *f* recognition; gratitude; (mil) reconnaissance; **aller en reconnaissance** to recon-

noiter; **reconnaissance de** or **pour** gratitude for
reconnais·sant [rəkɔnɛsɑ̃] **reconnais· sante** [rəkɔnɛsɑ̃t] *adj* grateful; **être reconnaissant de** + *inf* to be grateful for + *ger*; **être reconnaissant de** or **pour** to be grateful for
reconnaître [rəkɔnɛtr] §12 *tr* to recognize; (mil) to reconnoiter ‖ *ref* to recognize oneself; to know where one is; to acknowledge oneself (*e.g.*, *guilty*); **s'y reconnaître** to know where one is
reconquérir [rəkɔ̃kerir] §3 *tr* to reconquer
reconquête [rəkɔ̃kɛt] *f* reconquest
reconsidérer [rəkɔ̃sidere] §10 *tr* to reconsider
reconstituant [rəkɔ̃stitɥɑ̃] *m* tonic
reconstituer [rəkɔ̃stitɥe] *tr* to reconstruct; to restore
reconstruire [rəkɔ̃strɥir] §19 *tr* to reconstruct
record [rəkɔr] *adj invar & m* record
recordman [rəkɔrdman] *m* record holder
recoudre [rəkudr] §13 *tr* to sew up
recouper [rəkupe] *tr* to cut again; to blend (*wines*)
recourir [rəkurir] §14 *intr* to run again; **recourir à** to resort to; to appeal to
recours [rəkur] *m* recourse; **recours en grâce** petition for pardon
recouvrement [rəkuvrəmɑ̃] *m* recovery
recouvrer [rəkuvre] *tr* to recover
recouvrir [rəkuvrir] §65 *tr* to cover; to cover up; to mask; to resurface (*e.g.*, *a road*) ‖ *ref* to overlap
récréation [rekreɑsjɔ̃] *f* recreation; recess (*at school*)
recréer [rəkree] *tr* to re-create
récréer [rekree] *tr & ref* to relax
récrier [rekrije] *ref* to cry out
récrire [rekrir] §25 *tr* to rewrite; to write again
recroquevil·lé -lée [rəkrɔkvije] *adj* shriveled up, curled up; huddled up
recroqueviller [rəkrɔkvije] *tr & ref* to shrivel up, to curl up
re·cru -crue [rəkry] *adj* exhausted
recrue [rəkry] *f* recruit
recruter [rəkryte] *tr* to recruit ‖ *ref* to be recruited
rectangle [rɛktɑ̃gl] *m* rectangle
rectificateur [rɛktifikatœr] *m* rectifier
rectifier [rɛktifje] *tr* to rectify; to true up; to grind (*a cylinder*)
rectum [rɛktɔm] *m* rectum
reçu [rəsy] *m* receipt
recueil [rəkœj] *m* collection; compilation
recueillement [rəkœjmɑ̃] *m* meditation
recueillir [rəkœjir] §18 *tr* to collect, to gather; to take in (*a needy person*); to receive (*a legacy*) ‖ *ref* to collect oneself, to meditate
recuire [rəkɥir] §19 *tr* to anneal, to temper; to cook over again ‖ *intr* (fig) to stew
recul [rəkyl] *m* backing, backward movement; kick, recoil; **être en recul** to be losing ground; **prendre du recul** to consider in perspective

reculer [rəkyle] *tr* to move back; to put off (*e.g., a decision*) || *intr* to move back; to back out; to recoil; **reculer devant** to shrink from || *ref* to move back
reculons [rəkylɔ̃]—**à reculons** backwards
récupération [rekyperɑsjɔ̃] *f* recovery
récupérer [rekypere] §10 *tr* to salvage, to recover; to recuperate; to make up (*e.g., lost hours*); to find another job for || *intr* to recuperate
récurer [rekyre] *tr* to scour
récur·rent [rekyrɑ̃] **récur·rente** [rekyrɑ̃t] *adj* recurrent
récuser [rekyze] *tr* to take exception to || *ref* to refuse to give one's opinion
rédac·teur [redaktœr] **-trice** [tris] *mf* editor; **rédacteur en chef** editor in chief; **rédacteur gérant** managing editor; **rédacteur publicitaire** copywriter; **rédacteur sportif** sports editor
rédaction [redaksjɔ̃] *f* editorial staff; editorial office; edition; editing
reddition [redisjɔ̃] *f* surrender
redécouvrir [rədekuvrir] §65 *tr* to rediscover
rédemp·teur [redɑ̃ptœr] **-trice** [tris] *adj* redemptive || *mf* redeemer
rédemption [redɑ̃psjɔ̃] *f* redemption
redevable [rədvabl] *adj* indebted
redevance [rədvɑ̃s] *f* dues, fees; rent; tax (*on radio sets*)
rédiger [rediʒe] §38 *tr* to edit; to draft; to write up
redingote [rədɛ̃gɔt] *f* frock coat
redire [rədir] §22 *tr* to repeat; to give away (*a secret*) || *intr*—**trouver à redire à** to find fault with
redon·dant [rədɔ̃dɑ̃] **-dante** [dɑ̃t] *adj* redundant
redoutable [rədutabl] *adj* frightening
redoute [rədut] *f* redoubt
redouter [rədute] *tr* to dread
redressement [rədrɛsmɑ̃] *m* straightening out; redress; (elec) rectifying
redresser [rədrese] *tr* to straighten; to hold up (*e.g., the head*); to redress; (elec) to rectify || *ref* to straighten up
redresseur [rədrɛsœr] *m* (elec) rectifier; **redresseur de torts** knight-errant; (coll) reformer
réduction [redyksjɔ̃] *f* reduction
réduire [redɥir] §19 *tr* to reduce; to set (*a bone*)
réduit [redɥi] *m* retreat, nook; redoubt
rééditer [reedite] *tr* to reedit
réel réelle [reɛl] *adj & m* real, actual
réélection [reelɛksjɔ̃] *f* reelection
réellement [reɛlmɑ̃] *adv* really
réescompte [reɛskɔ̃t] *m* rediscount
réexamen [reɛgzamɛ̃] *m* reexamination
réexpédier [reɛkspedje] *tr* to reship; to return to sender
réexpédition [reɛkspedisjɔ̃] *f* reshipment; return
refaire [rəfɛr] §29 *tr* to redo || *intr*—**à refaire** to be done over; to be dealt over || *ref* to recover; to make good one's losses
référence [referɑ̃s] *f* reference
référendum or **referendum** [referɛ̃dɔm] *m* referendum

référer [refere] §10 *intr*—**en référer à** to appeal to || *ref*—**s'en référer à** to leave it up to; **se référer à** to refer to
refermer [rəfɛrme] *tr & ref* to close again, to close
refiler [rəfile] *tr*—**refiler à qn** (slang) to palm off on s.o.
réfléchir [refleʃir] *tr & intr* to reflect || *ref* to be reflected
reflet [rəflɛ] *m* reflection; glint, gleam
refléter [rəflete] §10 *tr* to reflect || *ref* to be mirrored
réflexe [reflɛks] *adj & m* reflex
réflexion [reflɛksjɔ̃] *f* reflection
refluer [rəflye] *intr* to ebb
reflux [rəfly] *m* ebb
refonte [rəfɔ̃t] *f* recasting
réforma·teur [reformatœr] **-trice** [tris] *mf* reformer
réformation [reformasjɔ̃] *f* reformation
réforme [refɔrm] *f* reform; **la Réforme** the Reformation
réfor·mé -mée [refɔrme] *adj* (eccl) Reformed; (mil) disabled
reformer [rəfɔrme] *tr & ref* to regroup
réformer [refɔrme] *tr* to reform; (mil) to discharge || *ref* to reform
refou·lé -lée [rəfule] *adj* (coll) inhibited
refoulement [rəfulmɑ̃] *m* driving back; (psychoanal) repression
refouler [rəfule] *tr* to drive back; to choke back (*a sob*); to sail against (*the current*); to compress, stem; (psychoanal) to repress || *intr* to flow back
réfractaire [refraktɛr] *adj* refractory; rebellious || *mf* insubordinate
réfraction [refraksjɔ̃] *f* refraction
refrain [rəfrɛ̃] *m* refrain; hum; **le même refrain** the same old tune
refréner [rəfrene] §10 *tr* to curb
réfrigérateur [refriʒeratœr] *m* refrigerator
réfrigérer [refriʒere] §10 *tr* to refrigerate; (coll) to chill to the bone
refroidir [rəfrwadir] *tr* to cool; (slang) to rub out || *intr* to cool || *ref* to cool; to catch cold
refroidissement [rəfrwadismɑ̃] *m* cooling
refuge [rəfyʒ] *m* refuge; shelter; safety zone
réfu·gié -giée [refyʒje] *mf* refugee
réfugier [refyʒje] *ref* to take refuge
refus [rəfy] *m* refusal; **refus seulement** regrets only (*to invitation*)
refuser [rəfyze] *tr* to refuse; to refuse to recognize; to flunk; to decline || *intr* to refuse; **refuser de** or **à** to refuse to || *ref* to be refused; **se refuser à** to refuse to accept
réfuter [refyte] *tr* to refute
regagner [rəgaɲe] *tr* to regain
regain [rəgɛ̃] *m* second growth; (fig) aftermath; **regain de** new lease on life
ré·gal [regal] *m* (*pl* **-gals**) treat
régaler [regale] *tr* to treat; to level || *intr* to treat
regard [rəgar] *m* look, glance; **couver du regard** to gloat over; to look fondly at; to look greedily at; **en regard** facing, opposite

regar·dant [rəgardã] -dante [dãt] adj (coll) penny-pinching

regarder [rəgarde] tr to look at; to face; to concern || intr to look; regarder à to pay attention to; to watch (one's money); to mind (the price); y regarder à deux fois to watch one's step, think twice || ref to face each other

régate [regat] f regatta

régence [reʒãs] f regency

régénérer [reʒenere] §10 tr & ref to regenerate

ré·gent [reʒã] -gente [ʒãt] mf regent

régenter [reʒãte] tr & intr to boss

régicide [reʒisid] mf regicide (person) || m regicide (act)

régie [reʒi] f commission, administration; excise tax; stage management; en régie state owned or operated

regimber [rəʒẽbe] intr & ref to revolt; to balk

régime [reʒim] m government, form of government; administration; system; diet; performance, working conditions; rate (of speed; of flow; of charge or discharge of a storage battery); bunch, cluster; stem (of bananas); (gram) complement; (gram) government; en régime permanent under steady working conditions

régiment [reʒimã] m regiment

régimentaire [reʒimãter] adj regimental

région [reʒjõ] f region

régir [reʒir] tr to govern

régisseur [reʒisœr] m manager; stage manager

registre [rəʒistr] m register; damper; throttle valve

réglable [reglabl] adj adjustable

réglage [reglaʒ] m setting, adjusting; lines (on paper); (mach, rad, telv) tuning

règle [regl] f rule; ruler; en règle in order; en règle générale as a general rule; règle à calcul slide rule; règles menstrual period

ré·glé -glée [regle] adj regulated; adjusted, tuned; well-behaved, orderly; ruled (paper); finished, decided

règlement [regləmã] m regulation, rule; settlement; règlement intérieur by-laws

réglementaire [regləmãter] adj regular; regulation

réglementer [regləmãte] tr to regulate, to control

régler [regle] §10 tr to regulate, to put in order; to set (a watch); to settle (an account); to rule (paper); (aut, rad, telv) to tune || intr to pay

réglisse [reglis] m & f licorice

règne [reɲ] m reign; (biol) kingdom

régner [reɲe] §10 intr to reign

regorger [rəgorʒe] §38 intr to overflow; regorger de to abound in

regratter [rəgrate] tr to scrape || intr to pinch pennies

regret [rəgre] m regret; à regret regretfully

regrettable [rəgretabl] adj regrettable

regretter [rəgrete] tr to regret; to long for, to miss || intr to be sorry

régulariser [regylarize] tr to regularize; to adjust, regulate

régularité [regylarite] f regularity

régula·teur [regylatœr] -trice [tris] adj regulating || m (mach) governor

régulation [regylasjõ] f regulation

régu·lier [regylje] -lière [ljer] adj regular; (coll) aboveboard, fair || m regular

réhabiliter [reabilite] tr to rehabilitate

rehausser [rəose] tr to heighten; to enhance

Reims [rẽs] m Rheims

rein [rẽ] m kidney

réincarnation [reẽkarnasjõ] f reincarnation

reine [ren] f queen

reine-claude [renklod] f (pl -claudes or reines-claudes) greengage

reine-des-prés [rendepre] f (pl reines-des-prés) meadowsweet

reine-marguerite [renmargərit] f (pl reines-marguerites) aster

réintégrer [reẽtegre] §10 tr to reinstate; to return to

réitérer [reitere] §10 tr reiterate

rejaillir [rəʒajir] intr to spurt out; to bounce; to splash; rejaillir sur to reflect on

rejet [rəʒe] m casting up; rejection; enjambment; (bot) shoot

rejeter [rəʒte] §34 tr to reject; to throw back; to throw up; to shift (responsibility) || ref to fall back

rejeton [rəʒtõ] m shoot; offshoot, offspring; (coll) child

rejoindre [rəʒwẽdr] §35 tr to rejoin; to overtake || ref to meet

réjouir [reʒwir] tr to gladden, cheer || ref to rejoice, to be delighted

réjouissance [reʒwisãs] f rejoicing; réjouissances festivities

réjouis·sant [reʒwisã] réjouis·sante [reʒwisãt] adj cheery; amusing

relâche [rəlaʃ] m & f respite, letup || f (naut) stop; faire relâche (naut) to make a call; (theat) to close (for a day or two); relâche (public sign) no performance today

relâ·ché -chée [rəlaʃe] adj lax; loose

relâchement [rəlaʃmã] m relaxation; letting up

relâcher [rəlaʃe] tr to loosen; to relax; to release || intr (naut) to make a call || ref to loosen; to become lax

relais [rəle] m relay; shift

relance [rəlãs] f raise (e.g., in poker); outbreak

relancer [rəlãse] §51 tr to start up again; to harass, to hound; to return (the ball); to raise (the ante) || intr (cards) to raise

re·laps -lapse [rəlaps] mf backslider

relater [rəlate] tr to relate

rela·tif [rəlatif] -tive [tiv] adj relative

relation [rəlasjõ] f relation; en relation avec, en relations avec in touch with; relations connections

relativité [rəlativite] f relativity

relaxation [rəlaksasjõ] f relaxation

relaxer [rəlakse] *tr* to relax; to free ‖ *ref* to relax

relayer [rəleje] §49 *tr* to relay; to relieve ‖ *ref* to work in relays or shifts

reléguer [rəlege] §10 *tr* to relegate

relent [rəlɑ̃] *m* musty smell

relève [rəlɛv] *f* relief; change (*of the guard*); **prendre la relève** to take over

rele·vé -vée [rəlve] *adj* lofty, elevated; turned up; graded (*curve*); spicy ‖ *m* check list; tuck (*in dress*); (culin) next course; **faire le relevé de** to survey; to check off; **relevé de compte** bank statement; **relevé de compteur** meter reading; **relevé de notes des écoles** transcript of grades

relèvement [rəlɛvmɑ̃] *m* raising; recovery, improvement; picking up (*e.g., of wounded*); (naut) bearing

relever [rəlve] §2 *tr* to raise; to turn up; to restore; to relieve, enhance; to pick out; to take a reading of; to season; (mil) to relieve ‖ *intr—relever de* to recover from; to depend on ‖ *ref* to rise; to recover; to right itself; to take turns

relief [rəljɛf] *m* relief; **en relief** in relief; **reliefs** leavings

relier [rəlje] *tr* to bind; to link

re·lieur [rəljœr] **-lieuse** [ljøz] *mf* bookbinder

reli·gieux [rəliʒjø] **-gieuse** [ʒjøz] *adj* religious ‖ *m* monk ‖ *f* nun; cream puff

religion [rəliʒjɔ̃] *f* religion

reliquat [rəlika] *m* remainder

relique [rəlik] *f* relic

relire [rəlir] §36 *tr* to read again; to read over again

reliure [rəljyr] *f* binding; bookbinding

reloger [rələʒe] §38 *tr* to find a new home for, to relocate

reluire [rəlɥir] §37 *intr* to shine, gleam, sparkle

relui·sant [rəlɥizɑ̃] **-sante** [zɑ̃t] *adj* shiny, gleaming; **peu reluisant** unpromising, not brilliant

reluquer [rəlyke] *tr* to have an eye on

remâcher [rəmɑʃe] *tr* (coll) to stew over

remailler [rəmɑje] *tr* to mend the meshes of

remanier [rəmanje] *tr* to revise, revamp; to reshuffle

remarier [rəmarje] *tr & ref* to remarry

remarquable [rəmarkabl] *adj* remarkable

remarquer [rəmarke] *tr & intr* to remark, to notice; **faire remarquer** to point out ‖ *ref—se faire remarquer* to make oneself conspicuous

remballer [rɑ̃bale] *tr* to repack

rembarquer [rɑ̃barke] *tr, intr, & ref* to reembark

rembarrer [rɑ̃bare] *tr* to snub, rebuff

remblai [rɑ̃blɛ] *m* fill; embankment

remblayer [rɑ̃bleje] §49 *tr* to fill

rembobiner [rɑ̃bɔbine] *tr* to rewind

remboîter [rɑ̃bwate] *tr* to reset (*a bone*); to recase (*a book*)

rembourrer [rɑ̃bure] *tr* to upholster; to stuff; to pad

rembourrure [rɑ̃buryr] *f* stuffing

remboursement [rɑ̃bursəmɑ̃] *m* reimbursement

rembourser [rɑ̃burse] *tr* to reimburse

rembrunir [rɑ̃brynir] *tr* to darken; to sadden ‖ *ref* to cloud over

remède [rəmɛd] *m* remedy

remédier [rəmedje] *intr* (with *dat*) to remedy

remembrement [rəmɑ̃brəmɑ̃] *m* regrouping

remémorer [rəmemɔre] *tr—remémorer q.ch. à qn* to remind s.o. of s.th. ‖ *ref* to remember

remerciement [rəmɛrsimɑ̃] *m* thanking; **remerciements** thanks; **mille remerciements de** or **pour** a thousand thanks for

remercier [rəmɛrsje] *tr* to thank; to dismiss (*an employee*); to refuse with thanks; **remercier qn de** + *inf* to thank s.o. for + *ger*; **remercier qn de** or **pour** to thank s.o. for

remettre [rəmɛtr] §42 *tr* to remit, to deliver; to put back; to put back on; to give back; to put off; to reset ‖ *ref* to resume; to recover; to pull oneself together; (*said of weather*) to clear; **s'en remettre à** to leave it up to, to depend on

remise [rəmiz] *f* remittance; discount; delivery; postponement; surrender, return; garage; cover (*for game*); **de remise** rented (*car*)

remiser [rəmize] *tr* to put away; to park ‖ *ref* to take cover

rémission [remisjɔ̃] *f* remission

remmailler [rɑ̃mɑje] *tr* to darn

remmener [rɑ̃mne] §2 *tr* to take back

remon·tant [rəmɔ̃tɑ̃] **-tante** [tɑ̃t] *adj* fortifying; remontant (*rose*) ‖ *m* tonic

remonte [rəmɔ̃t] *f* ascent

remontée [rəmɔ̃te] *f* climb; surfacing; comeback

remonte-pente [rəmɔ̃tpɑ̃t] *m* (*pl* -pentes) ski lift

remonter [rəmɔ̃te] *tr* to remount; to pull up; to wind (*a clock*); to pep up; (theat) to put on again ‖ *intr* (*aux:* ÊTRE) to go up again; to date back ‖ *ref* to pep up

remontoir [rəmɔ̃twar] *m* knob (*of stem-winder*)

remontrance [rəmɔ̃trɑ̃s] *f* remonstrance

remontrer [rəmɔ̃tre] *tr* to show again; to point out ‖ *intr—en remontrer à* to outdo, to best

remords [rəmɔr] *m* remorse

remorque [rəmɔrk] *f* tow rope; trailer; **à la remorque** in tow

remorquer [rəmɔrke] *tr* to tow; to haul

remorqueur [rəmɔrkœr] *m* tugboat

rémouleur [remulœr] *m* knife grinder, scissors grinder

remous [rəmu] *m* eddy; wash (*of boat*); agitation

rempailler [rɑ̃pɑje] *tr* to cane

rempart [rɑ̃par] *m* rampart

remplaçable [rɑ̃plasabl] *adj* replaceable

rempla·çant [rɑ̃plasɑ̃] **-çante** [sɑ̃t] *mf* replacement, substitute

remplacement [rãplasmã] *m* replacement

remplacer [rãplase] §51 *tr* to replace; to take the place of; remplacer par to replace with

rem·pli -plie [rãpli] *adj* full ‖ *m* tuck

remplir [rãplir] *tr* to fill; to fill up; to fill out or in; to fulfill ‖ *ref* to fill up

remplissage [rãplisaʒ] *m* filling up

remplumer [rãplyme] *ref* (coll) to put on flesh again; (coll) to make a comeback

remporter [rãpɔrte] *tr* to take back; to carry off; to win

remue-ménage [rəmymenaʒ] *m invar* stir, bustle, to-do

remuer [rəmɥe] *tr* to move; to stir; to remove (*e.g., a piece of furniture*) ‖ *intr* to move ‖ *ref* to move; to hustle

rémunération [remynerasjɔ̃] *f* remuneration

renâcler [rənakle] *intr* to snort; renâcler à (coll) to shrink from, to bridle at

renaissance [rənɛsãs] *f* renascence, rebirth; renaissance

renais·sant [rənɛsã] renais·sante [rənɛsãt] *adj* renascent, reviving; Renaissance

renaître [rənɛtr] §46 *tr* to be reborn; to revive; to grow again

re·nard [rənar] -narde [nard] *mf* fox

renché·ri -rie [rãʃeri] *adj* fastidious

renchérir [rãʃerir] *tr* to make more expensive ‖ *intr* to go up in price; renchérir sur to improve on

rencontre [rãkɔ̃tr] *f* meeting, encounter; clash; collision; aller à la rencontre de to go to meet

rencontrer [rãkɔ̃tre] *tr* to meet, encounter ‖ *ref* to meet; to collide; to occur

rendement [rãdmã] *m* yield; (mech) output, efficiency

rendez-vous [rãdevu] *m* appointment, date; rendezvous; sur rendez-vous by appointment

rendre [rãdr] *tr* to render; to yield; to surrender; to make; to translate; to vomit ‖ *intr* to bring in, yield ‖ *ref* to surrender; se rendre à to go to; se rendre compte de to realize

ren·du -due [rãdy] *adj* arrived; translated; all in, exhausted ‖ *m* rendering; returned article

rêne [ren] *f* rein

rené·gat [rənega] -gate [gat] *mf* renegade

renfer·mé -mée [rãferme] *adj* closemouthed, stand-offish ‖ *m* close smell; sentir le renfermé to smell stuffy

renfermer [rãferme] *tr* to contain; to include ‖ *ref*—se renfermer dans to withdraw into; to confine oneself to

renfler [rãfle] *ref* to swell up

renflouer [rãflue] *tr* to keep afloat; to salvage

renfoncement [rãfɔ̃smã] *m* recess; hollow; dent

renfoncer [rãfɔ̃se] §51 *tr* to recess; to dent; to pull down (*e.g., one's hat*) ‖ *ref* to recede; to draw back

renforcement [rãfɔrsəmã] *m* reinforcement

renforcer [rãfɔrse] §51 *tr* to reinforce

renforcir [rãfɔrsir] *tr* (slang) to strengthen ‖ *intr* (slang) to grow stronger

renfort [rãfɔr] *m* reinforcement

renfro·gné -gnée [rãfrɔɲe] *adj* sullen, glum

renfrogner [rãfrɔɲe] *ref* to scowl

rengager [rãgaʒe] §38 *tr* to rehire ‖ *intr & ref* to reenlist

rengaine [rãgɛn] *f*—la même rengaine the same old story; vieille rengaine old refrain

rengorger [rãgɔrʒe] §38 *ref* to strut

reniement [rənimã] *m* denial

renier [rənje] *tr* to deny; to repudiate

renifler [rənifle] *tr & intr* to sniff

renne [ren] *m* reindeer

renom [rənɔ̃] *m* renown, fame

renom·mé -mée [rənɔme] *adj* renowned, well-known ‖ *f* fame; reputation

renommer [rənɔme] *tr* to reelect; to reappoint

renoncement [rənɔ̃smã] *m* renunciation

renoncer [rənɔ̃se] §51 *tr* to renounce, repudiate ‖ *intr* to give up; (cards) to renege; (with *dat*) to renounce; (with *dat*) to give up, to abandon; y renoncer to give it up

renonciation [rənɔ̃sjasjɔ̃] *f* renunciation; waiver

renoncule [rənɔ̃kyl] *f* buttercup; renoncule double bachelor's-button; renoncule langue spearwort

renouer [rənwe] *tr* to tie again; to resume (*e.g., a conversation*) ‖ *intr* to renew a friendship

renou·veau [rənuvo] *m* (*pl* -veaux) springtime; revival

renouvelable [rənuvlabl] *adj* renewable

renouveler [rənuvle] §34 *tr & ref* to renew

renouvellement [rənuvɛlmã] *m* renewal

rénover [renɔve] *tr* to renew; to renovate

renseignement [rãsɛɲmã] *m* piece of information; de renseignements (mil) intelligence; renseignements information

renseigner [rãsɛɲe] *tr* to inform ‖ *ref* to find out; se renseigner auprès de qn to inquire of s.o.

rentable [rãtabl] *adj* profitable

rente [rãt] *f* revenue, income; annuity; dividend, return; rente viagère life annuity

ren·té -tée [rãte] *adj* well-off

renter [rãte] *tr* to endow

ren·tier [rãtje] -tière [tjer] *mf* person of independent means

ren·tré -trée [rãtre] *adj* sunken (*eyes*); suppressed (*feelings*) ‖ *f* return; reopening (*of school*); yield

rentrer [rãtre] *tr* to bring in or back; to put in; to hold back (*e.g., one's tears*); to draw in (*claws*) ‖ *intr* (*aux:* ÊTRE) to return, to reenter; to go or come home; to be paid or collected; rentrer dans to fit into; to come back to; to get back, recover; **rentrer en soi-même** to take stock of oneself

renverse [rɑ̃vɛrs] *f* shift, turn; **à la renverse** backwards

renversement [rɑ̃vɛrsəmɑ̃] *m* reversal, shift; upset, overturn; overthrow

renverser [rɑ̃vɛrse] *tr* to reverse; to overthrow ‖ *intr & ref* to capsize

renvoi [rɑ̃vwa] *m* dismissal; postponement; reference; return; belch

renvoyer [rɑ̃vwaje] §26 *tr* to dismiss; to fire (*an employee*); to postpone; to refer; to send back

réorganiser [reɔrganize] *tr & ref* to reorganize

réouverture [reuvɛrtyr] *f* reopening

repaire [rəpɛr] *m* den

repaître [rəpɛtr] §12 *tr* to graze; **repaître de** to feast (*e.g., one's eyes*) on ‖ *ref* to eat one's fill (*said of only animals*); **se repaître de** to indulge in, to wallow in

répandre [repɑ̃dr] *tr* to spread; to strew, scatter; to spill; to shed ‖ *ref* to spread; **se répandre en** to be profuse in

répan·du -due [repɑ̃dy] *adj* widespread; widely known

reparaître [rəparɛtr] §12 *intr* to reappear

répara·teur [reparatœr] **-trice** [tris] *adj* restorative ‖ *m* repairman

réparation [reparasjɔ̃] *f* repair; reparation; restoration

réparer [repare] *tr* to repair; to mend, patch; to make up (*a loss*); to redress (*a wrong*); to restore (*one's strength*)

repartie [rəparti], [reparti] *f* repartee

repartir [rəpartir] §64 *tr* to retort ‖ *intr* (*aux:* ÊTRE) to start again; to leave again

répartir [repartir] *tr* to distribute

répartiteur [repartitœr] *m* distributor; assessor

répartition [repartisjɔ̃] *f* distribution; apportionment; range (*of words*)

repas [rəpɑ] *m* meal, repast; **dernier repas** (rel) last supper; **repas champêtre** picnic; **repas de noce** wedding breakfast; **repas froid** cold snack; **repas sur le pouce** takeout meal

repassage [rəpɑsaʒ] *m* recrossing; ironing; stropping; whetting

repasser [rəpɑse] *tr* to pass again; to go over, to review; to iron; to strop; to whet ‖ *intr* to pass by again; to drop in again

repêcher [rəpɛʃe] *tr* to fish out; to give another chance to; (coll) to get (*s.o.*) out of a scrape

repentance [rəpɑ̃tɑ̃s] *f* repentance

repen·tant [rəpɑ̃tɑ̃] **-tante** [tɑ̃t] *adj* repentant

repen·ti -tie [rəpɑ̃ti] *adj* repentant

repentir [rəpɑ̃tir] *m* repentance ‖ §41 *ref* to repent; **se repentir de** to be sorry for, to repent

repérage [rəperaʒ] *m* spotting, locating; tracking; marking with a reference mark; (mov) synchronization

répercussion [repɛrkysjɔ̃] *f* repercussion

répercuter [repɛrkyte] *tr* to reflect ‖ *ref* to reverberate; to have repercussions

repère [rəpɛr] *m* mark, reference

repérer [rəpere] §10 *tr* to locate, spot; to mark with a reference mark; (mov) to synchronize

répertoire [repɛrtwar] *m* repertory; index; **répertoire à onglets** thumb index; **répertoire d'adresses** address book; **répertoire vivant** walking encyclopedia

répéter [repete] §10 *tr & ref* to repeat

répéti·teur [repetitœr] **-trice** [tris] *mf* assistant teacher; coach, tutor

répétition [repetisjɔ̃] *f* repetition; private lesson, tutoring; rehearsal; **répétition des couturières** next to last dress rehearsal; **répétition générale** final dress rehearsal

repeupler [rəpœple] *tr* to repeople; to restock

repiquer [rəpike] *tr* to plant out (*seedlings*); to repave; to restitch; to rerecord; (phot) to retouch ‖ *intr—* **repiquer à** (slang) to come back to

répit [repi] *m* respite, letup

replacement [rəplasmɑ̃] *m* replacement; reinvestment

replacer [rəplase] §51 *tr* to replace; to find a new job for; to reinvest ‖ *ref* to find a new job

replâtrage [rəplɑtraʒ] *m* replastering; makeshift; (fig) patchwork

re·plet [rəplɛ] **-plète** [plɛt] *adj* fat, plump

repli [rəpli] *m* crease, fold; dip, depression; (mil) falling back

replier [rəplije] *tr* to refold; to turn up; to close (*e.g., an umbrella*) ‖ *ref* to curl up, to coil up; (mil) to fall back

réplique [replik] *f* reply, retort; replica; **donner la réplique à qn** to answer s.o.; (theat) to give s.o. his cue; (theat) to play the straight man or stooge for s.o.

répliquer [replike] *tr & intr* to reply

replonger [rəplɔ̃ʒe] §38 *tr* to plunge again ‖ *intr* to dive again ‖ *ref—se* **replonger dans** to get back into

répon·dant [repɔ̃dɑ̃] **-dante** [dɑ̃t] *mf* guarantor; (eccl) server; **avoir du répondant** (coll) to have money behind one

répondre [repɔ̃dr] *tr* to answer (*e.g., yes or no*); to assure ‖ *intr* to answer, reply; to answer back, be saucy; to reecho; **répondre à** to answer (*e.g., a question, letter*); to correspond to; **répondre de** to answer for (*a person*); to guarantee (*a thing*) ‖ *ref* to answer each other; to correspond to each other; to be in harmony

réponse [repɔ̃s] *f* answer, response; **réponse normande** evasive answer

report [rəpɔr] *m* carrying forward or over; carry-over

reportage [rəpɔrtaʒ] *m* reporting

reporter [rəpɔrter] *m* reporter ‖ [rəpɔrte] *tr* to carry back; to postpone; (math) to carry forward ‖ *intr*

(com) to carry stock; **à reporter** carried forward || *ref*—**se reporter à** to be carried back to (*e.g., childhood days*); to refer to
reporteur [rəpɔrtœr] *m* broker
repos [rəpo] *m* rest, repose; **au repos** not running, still; **de tout repos** reliable; **en repos** at rest; **repos!** (mil) at ease!
repo·sé -sée [rəpoze] *adj* refreshed, relaxed
reposer [rəpoze] *tr* to rest || *intr* to rest; **ici repose** . . . here lies . . . || *ref* to rest; **s'en reposer sur** to rely on
repous·sant [rəpusɑ̃] **repous·sante** [rəpusɑ̃t] *adj* repulsive
repousser [rəpuse] *tr* to push, shove; to repulse, repel; to reject, refuse; to postpone; to emboss || *intr* to grow again; to be offensive; (arti) to recoil
repoussoir [rəpuswar] *m* foil; contrast; (mach) driving bolt
reprendre [rəprɑ̃dr] §56 *tr* to take back; to resume; to regain (*consciousness*); to find fault with; to take in (*e.g., a dress*); to catch (*one's breath*); (theat) to put on again || *intr* to start again; to pick up, to improve; to criticize || *ref* to pull oneself together; to correct oneself in speaking
représailles [rəprezaj] *fpl* reprisal
représentant [rəprezɑ̃tɑ̃] *m* representative
représenta·tif -tive [rəprezɑ̃tatif] [tiv] *adj* representative
représentation [rəprezɑ̃tasjɔ̃] *f* representation; performance; remonstrance
représenter [rəprezɑ̃te] *tr* to represent; to put on, to perform || *intr* to make a good showing
répression [represjɔ̃] *f* repression
réprimande [reprimɑ̃d] *f* reprimand
réprimander [reprimɑ̃de] *tr* to reprimand
réprimer [reprime] *tr* to repress
re·pris [rəpri] **-prise** [priz] *adj* recaptured; **être repris de** to suffer from a recurrence of || *m*—**repris de justice** hardened criminal, habitual offender || *f* see **reprise**
reprisage [rəprizaʒ] *m* darning
reprise [rəpriz] *f* recapture; resumption; darning; pickup (*acceleration of motor*); (theat) revival; **à plusieurs reprises** several times; **faire une reprise à** to darn; **par reprises** a little at a time
repriser [rəprize] *tr* to darn; to mend
réproba·teur [reprɔbatœr] **-trice** [tris] *adj* reproving
reproche [rəprɔʃ] *m* reproach
reprocher [rəprɔʃe] *tr* to reproach; to begrudge; (law) to take exception to (*a witness*); **reprocher q.ch. à qn** to reproach s.o. for s.th.; to begrudge s.o. s.th.; to remind s.o. reproachfully of s.th.
reproduction [rəprɔdyksjɔ̃] *f* reproduction
reproduire [rəprɔdɥir] §19 *tr & ref* to reproduce

réprou·vé -vée [repruve] *adj & mf* outcast; damned
réprouver [repruve] *tr* to disapprove
reptile [reptil] *m* reptile
re·pu -pue [rəpy] *adj* satiated
républi·cain [repyblikɛ̃] **-caine** [kɛn] *adj & mf* republican
république [repyblik] *f* republic
répudier [repydje] *tr* to repudiate
répu·gnant [repypɑ̃] **-gnante** [pɑ̃t] *adj* repugnant
répugner [repype] *intr* (with *dat*) to disgust; to balk at; **répugner à + inf** to be loath to + *inf*
répul·sif [repylsif] **-sive** [siv] *adj* repulsive
réputation [repytasjɔ̃] *f* reputation
répu·té -tée [repyte] *adj* of high repute; **être réputé** to be reputed to be
requérir [rəkerir] §3 *tr* to demand; to ask; to require; to summon; to requisition
requête [rəkɛt] *f* petition, appeal
requiem [rekɥijɛm] *m* requiem
requin [rəkɛ̃] *m* shark
réquisition [rekizisjɔ̃] *f* requisition
réquisitionner [rekizisjɔne] *tr* to requisition
réquisitoire [rekizitwar] *m* indictment
res·capé -capée [reskape] *adj* rescued || *mf* survivor
rescinder [resɛ̃de] *tr* to rescind
rescousse [reskus] *f* rescue
ré·seau [rezo] *m* (*pl* **-seaux**) net; network, system; **réseau de barbelés** barbed wire entanglement
réséda [rezeda] *m* mignonette
réservation [rezɛrvasjɔ̃] *f* reservation
réserve [rezɛrv] *f* reserve; reservation; **de réserve** emergency, reserve (*rations, fund, etc.*); **sous réserve que** on condition that; **sous toutes réserves** without committing oneself
réserver [rezɛrve] *tr* to reserve; to set aside || *ref* to set aside for oneself; to wait and see, to hold off
réserviste [rezɛrvist] *m* reservist
réservoir [rezɛrvwar] *m* reservoir, tank; **réservoir de bombes** bomb bay
résidence [rezidɑ̃s] *f* residence
rési·dent [rezidɑ̃] **-dente** [dɑ̃t] *mf* alien, foreigner; (dipl) resident
résiden·tiel -tielle [rezidɑ̃sjɛl] *adj* residential
résider [rezide] *intr* to reside
résidu [rezidy] *m* residue; refuse
résignation [rezipasjɔ̃] *f* resignation
résigner [rezipe] *tr* to resign || *ref* to be or become resigned
résilier [rezilje] *tr* to cancel
résille [rezij] *f* hair net
résine [rezin] *f* resin
résistance [rezistɑ̃s] *f* resistance
résis·tant [rezistɑ̃] **-tante** [tɑ̃t] *adj* resistant; strong; fast (*color*)
résister [reziste] *intr* to be fast, not run (*said of colors or dyes*); (with *dat*) to resist, to withstand, to hold out against; (with *dat*) to weather (*e.g., a storm*); **résister à + inf** to resist + *ger*
réso·lu -lue [rezɔly] *adj* resolute, resolved

résolution [rezɔlysjɔ̃] f resolution; canceling
résonance [rezɔnɑ̃s] f resonance
résonner [rezɔne] intr to resound; to re-echo
résorber [rezɔrbe] tr to absorb || ref to become absorbed
résoudre [rezudr] §60 tr to resolve; to decide; to solve; to persuade; to cancel; être résolu à to be resolved to || intr—résoudre de to decide to || ref—se résoudre à to decide to; to reconcile oneself to; se résoudre en to turn into
respect [rɛspɛ] m respect; présenter ses respects (à) to pay one's respects (to); respect de soi or soi-même self-respect; respect humain [rɛspɛkymɛ̃] fear of what people might say; sauf votre (mon, etc.) respect with all due respect; pardon the language
respectable [rɛspɛktabl] adj respectable
respecter [rɛspɛkte] tr to respect || ref to keep one's self-respect
respec•tif [rɛspɛktif] -tive [tiv] adj respective
respec•tueux [rɛspɛktɥø] -tueuse [tɥøz] adj respectful
respirer [rɛspire] tr to breathe || intr to breathe; to catch one's breath
resplendis•sant [rɛsplɑ̃disɑ̃] resplendis•sante [rɛsplɑ̃disɑ̃t] adj resplendent
responsabilité [rɛspɔ̃sabilite] f responsibility
responsable [rɛspɔ̃sabl] adj responsible; responsable de responsible for; responsable envers accountable to || mf person responsible, person in charge
resquiller [rɛskije] tr (coll) to obtain by fraud || intr (coll) to crash the gate
resquil•leur [rɛskijœr] resquil•leuse [rɛskijøz] mf (coll) gate-crasher
ressac [rəsak] m surf; undertow
ressaisir [rəsezir] tr to recapture || ref to regain one's self-control
ressasser [rəsɑse] tr to go over and over again
ressaut [rəso] m projection; sharp rise
ressemblance [rəsɑ̃blɑ̃s] f resemblance
ressembler [rəsɑ̃ble] intr (with dat) to resemble, look like || ref to resemble one another; to be alike, to look alike
ressemeler [rəsəmle] §34 tr to resole
ressentiment [rəsɑ̃timɑ̃] m resentment
ressentir [rəsɑ̃tir] §41 tr to feel keenly, to be hurt by (an insult); to experience (joy, pain, surprise) || ref—se ressentir de to feel the aftereffects of
resserre [rəsɛr] f shed, storeroom
resserrer [rəsere] tr to tighten; to contract; to close; to lock up (e.g., valuables) again || ref to tighten; to contract
ressort [rəsɔr] m spring; springiness; motive; du ressort de within the jurisdiction of; en dernier ressort without appeal; as a last resort; ressort à boudin coil spring; sans ressort slack
ressortir [rəsɔrtir] intr—ressortir à to come under the jurisdiction of; to

fall under the head of || §64 intr (aux: ÊTRE) to go out again; to stand out, to be evident; faire ressortir to set off; il ressort de it follows from; il ressort que it follows that
ressortis•sant [rəsɔrtisɑ̃] ressortis•sante [rəsɔrtisɑ̃t] adj—ressortissant à under the jurisdiction of || mf national
ressource [rəsurs] f resource
ressouvenir [rəsuvnir] §72 ref to reminisce; se ressouvenir de to recall
ressusciter [resysite] tr to resuscitate; to resurrect || intr (aux: ÊTRE) to rise from the dead; to get well
res•tant [rɛstɑ̃] -tante [tɑ̃t] adj remaining || m remainder
restaurant [rɛstɔrɑ̃] m restaurant; restaurant libre-service self-service restaurant
restauration [rɛstɔrasjɔ̃] f restoration; restaurant business
restaurer [rɛstɔre] tr to restore || ref (coll) to take some nourishment
reste [rɛst] m rest, remainder; remnant; relic; au reste, du reste moreover; de reste spare; restes remains; leftovers
rester [rɛste] intr (aux: ÊTRE) to remain, to stay; to be left over; en rester to stop, to leave off; en rester là to stop right there; il me (te, leur, etc.) reste q.ch. I (you, they, etc.) have s.th. left
restituer [rɛstitɥe] tr to restore; to give back
restitution [rɛstitysjɔ̃] f restitution; restoration
restoroute [rɛstɔrut] m drive-in restaurant
restreindre [rɛstrɛ̃dr] §50 tr to restrict; to curtail || ref to become limited; to cut down expenses
res•treint [rɛstrɛ̃] -treinte [trɛ̃t] adj limited
restriction [rɛstriksjɔ̃] f restriction
résultat [rezylta] m result
résulter [rezylte] intr to result; il en résulte que it follows that
résumé [rezyme] m summary, recapitulation; en résumé in short, in a word
résumer [rezyme] tr to summarize || ref to be summed up
résurrection [rezyrɛksjɔ̃] f resurrection
rétablir [retablir] tr to restore || ref to recover
rétablissement [retablismɑ̃] m restoration; recovery
retailler [rətɑje] tr to resharpen
retape [rətap] f (slang) streetwalking
retaper [rətape] tr (coll) to straighten up; (coll) to give a lick and a promise to || ref (coll) to perk up
retard [rətar] m delay; en retard late; slow (clock); en retard sur behind
retardataire [rətardatɛr] adj tardy; retarded || mf latecomer, straggler
retarder [rətarde] tr to delay; to put off; to set back || intr to go slow, to be behind
retenir [rətnir] §72 tr to hold or keep back; to detain; to remember, note; to reserve; to retain (a lawyer); to

carry (a number) || réf—se retenir à to cling to; se retenir de to refrain from
retentir [rətɑ̃tir] intr to resound
rete·nu -nue [rətny] adj reserved; held back || f withholding; reserve; retenue à la source withholding tax
réticence [retisɑ̃s] f evasiveness, concealment; hesitation; reservation, misgiving
réti·cent [retisɑ̃] -cente [sɑ̃t] adj evasive; hesitant; reserved, withdrawn
réticule [retikyl] m handbag
ré·tif [retif] -tive [tiv] adj restive
rétine [retin] f retina
retirement [rətirmɑ̃] m contraction
retirer [rətire] tr to withdraw; to take off; to fire again || intr to fire again || réf to withdraw; to retire
retombée [rətɔ̃be] f fall; hang (of cloth); retombées radioactives fallout
retomber [rətɔ̃be] intr (aux: ÊTRE) to fall again; to fall; to fall back; to hang, hang down; to relapse
retordre [rətɔrdrə] tr to twist; to wring out
rétorquer [retɔrke] tr to retort
re·tors [rətɔr] -torse [tɔrs] adj twisted; wily; curved (beak) || mf rascal
retouche [rətuʃ] f retouch; (phot) retouching; retouches alterations
retoucher [rətuʃe] tr to retouch; to make alterations on
retour [rətur] m return; turn, bend; reversal (e.g., of opinion); en retour d'équerre at right angles; être de retour to be back; par retour du courrier by return mail; retour à la masse (clcc) ground (on chassis of auto, radio, etc.); retour à la terre (elec) ground; retour d'âge change of life; retour de flamme backfire; retour de manivelle kick (of the crank); (fig) backlash; retour en arrière flashback
retourner [rəturne] tr to send back, to return; to upset; to turn over (e.g., the soil); to turn inside out || intr (aux: ÊTRE) to go back, to return || réf to turn around, to look back; to turn over; (fig) to veer, to shift; s'en retourner to go back; se retourner contre to turn against
retracer [rətrase] §51 tr to retrace; to bring to mind, to recall || réf to come to mind again; to recall
rétracter [retrakte] tr & réf to retract
rétraction [retraksjɔ̃] f contraction
retrait [rətrɛ] m withdrawal; shrinkage; running out (of tide); en retrait set back, recessed; (typ) indented; retrait de permis suspension of driver's license
retraite [rətrɛt] f retreat; retirement; pension; battre en retraite to retreat; en retraite retired; prendre sa retraite to retire; toucher sa retraite to draw one's pension
retrai·té -tée [rətrete] adj pensioned, retired || mf pensioner
retranchement [rətrɑ̃ʃmɑ̃] m retrenchment; cutting out
retrancher [rətrɑ̃ʃe] tr to cut off or

out, to retrench || réf to become entrenched
retransmettre [rətrɑ̃smɛtr] §42 tr to retransmit; to rebroadcast
retransmission [rətrɑ̃smisjɔ̃] f retransmission; rebroadcast
rétré·ci -cie [retresi] adj narrow; shrunk
rétrécir [retresir] tr to shrink; to take in (a garment) || intr & réf to shrink; to narrow
retremper [rətrɑ̃pe] tr to soak again; to retemper; to give new strength or life to || réf to take another dip; to get new vigor
rétribuer [retribɥe] tr to remunerate
rétribution [retribysjɔ̃] f retribution; salary, fee
rétroaction [retrɔaksjɔ̃] f feedback; retroaction
rétrofusée [retrɔfyze] f retrorocket
rétrograder [retrɔgrade] intr to retrogress
rétrospection [retrɔspɛksjɔ̃] f retrospection
retrousser [rətruse] tr to roll up, to turn up; to curl up (one's lip) || réf to turn up or pull up one's clothes
retrouver [rətruve] tr to find again; to recover || réf to be back again; to meet again; to get one's bearings
rétroviseur [retrɔvizœr] m rear-view mirror
rets [rɛ] m—prendre dans des rets to snare
réunification [reynifikɑsjɔ̃] f reunification
réunion [reynjɔ̃] f reunion; meeting
réunir [reynir] tr to unite, join; to reunite; to call together, convene || réf to meet; to reunite
réus·si -sie [reysi] adj successful
réussir [reysir] tr to make a success of, to be good at || intr to succeed; réussir à to succeed in; to pass (an exam)
réussite [reysit] f success; faire une réussite (cards) to play solitaire
revaloir [rəvalwar] §71 tr—revaloir q.ch. à qn to pay s.o. back for s.th.
revan·chard [rəvɑ̃ʃar] -charde [ʃard] adj (coll) vengeful || mf (coll) avenger
revanche [rəvɑ̃ʃ] f revenge; return bout or engagement, return match; en revanche on the other hand; prendre sa revanche sur to get even with
revancher [rəvɑ̃ʃe] réf to get even
rêvasser [revase] intr to daydream
rêvasserie [revasri] f fitful dreaming; daydreaming
rêve [rɛv] m dream
revêche [rəvɛʃ] adj sullen, crabbed
réveil [revɛj] m awakening; alarm clock; (mil) reveille
réveille-matin [revɛjmatɛ̃] m invar alarm clock
réveiller [revɛje] tr & réf to wake up
réveillon [revɛjɔ̃] m Christmas Eve supper; New Year's Eve party
réveillonner [revɛjɔne] intr to celebrate Christmas Eve or New Year's Eve
révéla·teur [revelatœr] -trice [tris] adj

revealing; telltale || *mf* informer || *m* (phot) developer

révélation [revelɑsjɔ̃] *f* revelation

révéler [revele] §10 *tr* to reveal; (phot) to develop

revenant [rəvnɑ̃] *m* ghost

reven·deur [rəvɑ̃dœr] **-deuse** [døz] *mf* retailer; secondhand dealer

revendication [rəvɑ̃dikɑsjɔ̃] *f* claim

revendiquer [rəvɑ̃dike] *tr* to claim; to insist upon; to assume (*a responsibility*)

revendre [rəvɑ̃dr] *tr* to resell

revenez-y [rəvnezi] *m invar* (coll) return; **un goût de revenez-y** (coll) a taste like more

revenir [rəvnir] §72 *intr* (*aux:* ÊTRE) to return, come back; (with *dat*) to suit, to please; **en revenir** to have a narrow escape; **faire revenir** (culin) to brown; **n'en pas revenir** to not get over it; **revenir à** to come to, amount to; to come to (*e.g., mind*); **revenir à soi** to come to; **revenir bredouille** to come back empty-handed; **revenir de** to recover from; to realize (*a mistake*); **revenir de loin** to have been at death's door; **revenir sur** to go back on (*e.g., one's word*) || *ref*—**s'en revenir** to come back

revente [rəvɑ̃t] *f* resale

revenu [rəvny] *m* revenue, income

revenue [rəvny] *f* new growth (*of trees*)

rêver [reve] *tr* to dream || *intr* to dream; **rêver à** to dream of (*think about*); **rêver de** to dream of (*in sleep; to long to*)

réverbère [reverbɛr] *m* streetlight

réverbérer [reverbere] §10 *tr* to reflect (*light, heat, etc.*) || *ref* to be reflected

reverdir [rəvɛrdir] *tr* to make green || *intr* to grow green; to become young again

révérence [reverɑ̃s] *f* reverence; curtsy; **révérence parler** (coll) pardon the language; **tirer sa révérence** to bow out

révéren·cieux [reverɑ̃sjø] **-cieuse** [sjøz] *adj* obsequious

révé·rend [reverɑ̃] **-rende** [rɑ̃d] *adj & m* reverend

révérer [revere] §10 *tr* to revere

rêverie [revri] *f* reverie

revers [rəvɛr] *m* reverse; lapel; (tennis) backhand; **à revers** from behind; **revers de main** slap with the back of the hand

reverser [rəvɛrse] *tr* to pour back; to pour out again

réversible [reversibl] *adj* reversible

revêtement [rəvɛtmɑ̃] *m* surfacing; facing; lining; casing

revêtir [rəvɛtir] §73 *tr* to put on; to clothe, to dress up; to invest; to surface; to line; to face; to assume (*a form; an aspect*)

rê·veur [revœr] **-veuse** [vøz] *adj* dreamy || *mf* dreamer; **cela me laisse rêveur** that leaves me puzzled

revirement [rəvirmɑ̃] *m* sudden reversal; (naut) tack

réviser [revize] *tr* to revise; to review; to overhaul; to recondition

réviseur [revizœr] *m* proofreader

révision [revizjɔ̃] *f* revision; review; overhauling; proofreading

révisionniste [revizjɔnist] *adj & mf* revisionist

revivre [rəvivr] §74 *tr* to live again, relive || *intr* to live again

révocation [revɔkɑsjɔ̃] *f* dismissal; revocation

revoici [rəvwasi] *prep*—**me** (**vous, etc.**) **revoici** (coll) here I am (you are, etc.) again

revoilà [rəvwala] *prep*—**le** (**la, etc.**) **voilà** (coll) there it, he (she, etc.) is again

revoir [rəvwar] *m*—**au revoir** good-by || §75 *tr* to see again; to review; to revise || *ref* to meet again

révol·tant [revɔltɑ̃] **-tante** [tɑ̃t] *adj* revolting

révolte [revɔlt] *f* revolt, rebellion

révol·té **-tée** [revɔlte] *adj & mf* rebel

révolter [revɔlte] *tr & ref* to revolt; **se révolter devant** to be revolted by

révo·lu **-lue** [revɔly] *adj* completed; elapsed; bygone

révolution [revɔlysjɔ̃] *f* revolution

révolutionnaire [revɔlysjɔnɛr] *adj & mf* revolutionary

revolver [revɔlvɛr] *m* revolver

révoquer [revɔke] *tr* to revoke; to countermand; to dismiss; to recall

re·vu **-vue** [rəvy] *adj* revised || *f* see revue

revue [rəvy] *f* review; magazine, journal; (theat) revue; **passer en revue** to review (*past events; troops*)

rez-de-chaussée [redʃose] *m invar* first floor, ground floor

R.F. *abbr* (**République Française**) French Republic

rhabiller [rabije] *tr* to repair; to dress again; to refurbish || *ref* to change one's clothes; **va te rhabiller!** (pej) get out!

rhapsodie [rapsɔdi] *f* rhapsody

Rhénanie [renani] *f* Rhineland

rhéostat [reɔsta] *m* rheostat

rhétorique [retɔrik] *adj* rhetorical || *f* rhetoric

Rhin [rɛ̃] *m* Rhine

rhinocéros [rinɔserɔs] *m* rhinoceros

rhubarbe [rybarb] *f* rhubarb

rhum [rɔm] *m* rum

rhumati·sant [rymatizɑ̃] **-sante** [zɑ̃t] *adj & mf* rheumatic

rhumatis·mal **-male** [rymatismal] *adj* (*pl* **-maux** [mo]) rheumatic

rhumatisme [rymatism] *m* rheumatism

rhume [rym] *m* cold; **rhume des foins** hay fever

riant [rjɑ̃] **riante** [rjɑ̃t] *adj* smiling; cheerful, pleasant

ribambelle [ribɑ̃bɛl] *f* (coll) long string, swarm, lot

ri·baud [ribo] **-baude** [bod] *adj* licentious || *mf* camp follower; debauchee

ricanement [rikanmɑ̃] *m* snicker

ricaner [rikane] *intr* to snicker

ri·chard [riʃar] **-charde** [ʃard] *mf* (coll) moneybags

riche [riʃ] *adj* rich || *m* rich man; **nouveaux riches** newly rich

riche·lieu [riʃəljø] *m* (*pl* **-lieu** or **-lieus**) oxford
richesse [riʃɛs] *f* wealth; richness; **richesses** riches; **richesses naturelles** natural resources
ricin [risɛ̃] *m* castor-oil plant; castor bean
ricocher [rikɔʃe] *intr* to ricochet, rebound
ricochet [rikɔʃɛ] *m* ricochet; **faire des ricochets** to play ducks and drakes; **par ricochet** indirectly
rictus [riktys] *m* rictus; grin
ride [rid] *f* wrinkle; ripple
ri·deau [rido] *m* (*pl* **-deaux**) curtain; **rideau d'arbres** line of trees; **rideau de fer** iron curtain; safety blind (*of a store*); (theat) fire curtain; **rideau de feu** (mil) cover of artillery fire; **rideau de fumée** smoke screen
ridelle [ridɛl] *f* rave, side rails (*of wagon*)
rider [ride] *tr* to wrinkle; to ripple
ridicule [ridikyl] *adj* ridiculous ‖ *m* ridicule
ridiculiser [ridikylize] *tr* to ridicule
rien [rjɛ̃] *m* trifle; **comme un rien** with no trouble at all; **un rien de** just a little (bit) of; **un rien de temps** no time at all ‖ *pron indef*—**de rien** don't mention it, you're welcome; of no importance; **il n'en est rien** such is not the case; **rien ne** or **ne . . . rien** §90B nothing, not anything; **rien de moins (que)** nothing less (than); **rien que** nothing but
rieur [rjœr] **rieuse** [rjøz] *adj* laughing ‖ *mf* laugher, mocker ‖ *f* (orn) black-headed gull
riflard [riflar] *m* coarse file; jack plane; paring chisel
rigide [riʒid] *adj* rigid; stiff; strict
rigolade [rigɔlad] *f* (coll) good time, fun; (coll) big joke
rigole [rigɔl] *f* drain; ditch
rigoler [rigɔle] *intr* (slang) to laugh, to joke
rigo·lo [rigɔlo] **-lote** [lɔt] *adj* (coll) comical; (coll) queer, funny ‖ *mf* (coll) card ‖ *m* (slang) rod, gat
rigou·reux [rigurø] **-reuse** [røz] *adj* rigorous; severe
rigueur [rigœr] *f* rigor, strictness; **à la rigueur** to the letter; as a last resort; **de rigueur** compulsory, de rigueur
rillons [rijɔ̃] *mpl* cracklings
rimail·leur [rimɑjœr] **rimail·leuse** [rimɑjøz] *mf* (coll) rhymester
rime [rim] *f* rhyme; **rimes croisées** alternate rhymes; **rimes plates** couplets of alternate masculine and feminine rhymes
rimer [rime] *tr & intr* to rhyme
rinçage [rɛ̃saʒ] *m* rinse
rince-bouche [rɛ̃sbuʃ] *m invar* mouthwash
rince-bouteilles [rɛ̃sbutɛj] *m invar* (mach) bottle-washing machine
rince-doigts [rɛ̃sdwa] *m invar* fingerbowl
rincer [rɛ̃se] §51 *tr* to rinse; (slang) to ruin, to take to the cleaners

rinçure [rɛ̃syr] *f* rinsing water
ring [riŋ] *m* ring (*for, e.g., boxing*)
ringard [rɛ̃gar] *m* poker (*for fire*)
ripaille [ripɑj] *f* (coll) blowout; **faire ripaille** (coll) to carouse
ripe [rip] *f* scraper
riper [ripe] *tr* to scrape; (naut) to slip ‖ *intr* to slip; to skid
riposte [ripɔst] *f* riposte, retort
riposter [ripɔste] *tr* to riposte, to retort
rire [rir] *m* laugh; laughter; laughing ‖ §61 *intr* to laugh; to joke; to smile; **pour rire** for fun, in jest; **rire dans sa barbe, rire sous cape** to laugh up one's sleeve; **rire de** to laugh at or over; **rire du bout des lèvres, rire du bout des dents** to titter; **rire jaune** to force a laugh ‖ *ref*—**se rire de** to laugh at
ris [ri] *m* (naut) reef; (obs) laughter; **ris d'agneau** or **de veau** sweetbread
risée [rize] *f* scorn; laughingstock; light squall
risible [rizibl] *adj* laughable
risque [risk] *m* risk
ris·qué -quée [riske] *adj* risky; risqué
risquer [riske] *tr* to risk; to hasard (*e.g., a remark*) ‖ *intr*—**risquer de** + *inf* to risk + *ger*; to have a good chance of + *ger*
risque-tout [riskətu] *mf invar* daredevil
rissoler [risɔle] *tr & intr* to brown
ristourne [risturn] *f* rebate, refund; dividend
ristourner [risturne] *tr* to refund
ritournelle [riturnɛl] *f*—**c'est toujours la même ritournelle** it's always the same old story; **ritournelle publicitaire** advertising jingle or slogan
ri·tuel -tuelle [ritɥɛl] *adj & m* ritual
rivage [rivaʒ] *m* shore; bank
ri·val -vale [rival] (*pl* **-vaux** [vo] **-vales**) *adj & mf* rival
rivaliser [rivalize] *intr* to compete; **rivaliser avec** to compete with, to rival
rivalité [rivalite] *f* rivalry
rive [riv] *f* shore; bank
river [rive] *tr* to rivet
rive·rain [rivrɛ̃] **-raine** [rɛn] *adj* waterfront; bordering ‖ *mf* riversider; dweller along a street or road
riveraineté [rivrɛnte] *f* riparian rights
rivet [rivɛ] *m* rivet
rivière [rivjɛr] *f* river, stream, tributary; (turf) water jump; **rivière de diamants** diamond necklace
rixe [riks] *f* brawl
riz [ri] *m* rice; **riz au lait** rice pudding; **riz glacé** polished rice
rizière [rizjɛr] *f* rice field
robe [rɔb] *f* dress; gown; robe; wrapper (*of cigar*); skin (*of onion, sausage, etc.*); husk (*of, e.g., bean*); **robe de chambre** dressing gown; **robe d'intérieur** housecoat
rober [rɔbe] *tr* to husk, to skin; to wrap (*a cigar*)
roberts [rɔbɛr] *mpl* (slang) breasts
robin [rɔbɛ̃] *m* (coll) judge; (pej) shyster
robinet [rɔbinɛ] *m* faucet, tap; cock;

robinet d'eau tiède (coll) bore; robinet mélangeur mixing faucet
robinier [rɔbinje] m (bot) locust tree
robot [rɔbo] m robot
robre [rɔbr] m rubber (in bridge)
robuste [rɔbyst] adj robust; firm
roc [rɔk] m rock
rocaille [rɔkɑj] adj rococo || f stones; rocky ground; stonework
rocail·leux [rɔkɑjø] rocail·leuse [rɔkɑjøz] adj rocky, stony; harsh
roche [rɔʃ] f rock; boulder
rocher [rɔʃe] m rock; crag
rochet [rɔʃɛ] m ratchet; bobbin
ro·cheux [rɔʃø] -cheuse [ʃøz] adj rocky
rodage [rɔdaʒ] m grinding; breaking in; en rodage being broken in, new
roder [rɔde] tr to grind (a valve); to break in (a new car); to polish up (a new play)
rôder [rode] intr to prowl
rô·deur [rodœr] -deuse [døz] adj prowling || mf prowler
rogatons [rɔgatɔ̃] mpl (coll) scraps
rogne [rɔɲ] f (coll) anger; mettre qn en rogne (coll) to make s.o. see red
rogner [rɔɲe] tr to pare, to trim
rognon [rɔɲɔ̃] m kidney
rogomme [rɔgɔm] m—de rogomme (coll) husky, beery (voice)
rogue [rɔg] adj arrogant
roi [rwa], [rwɑ] m king; tirer les rois to gather to eat the Twelfth-night cake
roitelet [rwatlɛ] m kinglet; (orn) kinglet
rôle [rol] m role; roll, muster
ro·main [rɔmɛ̃] -maine [mɛn] adj Roman; roman (type); romaine (lettuce) || m (typ) roman || f romaine (lettuce) || (cap) mf Roman (person)
ro·man [rɔmɑ̃] -mane [man] adj Romance (language); (archit) Romanesque || m novel; roman d'anticipation science-fiction novel; roman policier detective story
romance [rɔmɑ̃s] f ballad
romanche [rɔmɑ̃ʃ] m Romansh
roman·cier [rɔmɑ̃sje] -cière [sjɛr] mf novelist; romancier d'anticipation science-fiction writer
ro·mand [rɔmɑ̃] -mande [mɑ̃d] adj French-speaking (Switzerland)
romanesque [rɔmanɛsk] adj romanesque, romantic, fabulous
roman-feuilleton [rɔmɑ̃fœjtɔ̃] m (pl romans-feuilletons) newspaper serial
roman-fleuve [rɔmɑ̃flœv] m (pl romans-fleuves) saga novel
romani·chel -chelle [rɔmaniʃɛl] mf gypsy, vagrant
romantique [rɔmɑ̃tik] adj & mf romantic
romantisme [rɔmɑ̃tism] m romanticism
romarin [rɔmarɛ̃] m (bot) rosemary
Rome [rɔm] f Rome
rompre [rɔ̃pr] (3d sg pres ind rompt [rɔ̃]) tr to break; to burst; to break in, train; to break off || intr & ref to break
romsteck [rɔmstɛk] m rump steak
ronce [rɔ̃s] f bramble; curly grain (of

wood); en ronces artificielles barbed-wire (fence)
ronchonner [rɔ̃ʃɔne] intr (coll) to bellyache, grumble
rond [rɔ̃] ronde [rɔ̃d] adj round; rounded; plump; straightforward; (slang) tight, drunk || m ring, circle; round slice; (coll) dough, money; en rond in a circle; rond de fumée smoke ring; rond de serviette napkin ring || f round; beat, round; round dance; radius; round hand; (mus) whole note; à la ronde around; s'amuser à la ronde, faire la ronde to go ring-around-a-rosy || rond adv —tourner rond to work or go smoothly
rond-de-cuir [rɔ̃dkɥir] m (pl ronds-de-cuir) leather seat; (pej) bureaucrat
ron·deau [rɔ̃do] m (pl -deaux) rondeau; field roller
ronde·let [rɔ̃dlɛ] -lette [lɛt] adj plump; tidy (sum)
rondelle [rɔ̃dɛl] f disk; slice; washer (of faucet, bolt, etc.)
rondement [rɔ̃dmɑ̃] adv briskly; mener rondement to make short work of; parler rondement to be blunt
rondeur [rɔ̃dœr] f roundness; plumpness; frankness
rond-point [rɔ̃pwɛ̃] m (pl ronds-points) intersection, crossroads; traffic circle; circus, roundabout (Brit)
ronéo [rɔneo] f Mimeograph machine
ronéotyper [rɔneɔtipe] tr to mimeograph
ron·flant [rɔ̃flɑ̃] -flante [flɑ̃t] adj snoring; roaring; whirring; humming; (pej) high-sounding, pretentious
ronflement [rɔ̃fləmɑ̃] m snore; roar; whirr, hum
ronfler [rɔ̃fle] intr to snore; to roar; to whirr, to hum
ron·fleur [rɔ̃flœr] -fleuse [fløz] mf snorer || m vibrator (replacing bell)
ronger [rɔ̃ʒe] §38 tr to gnaw, nibble; to eat away; to bite (one's nails); to corrode; to torment || ref to be worn away; to be eaten away; to eat one's heart out, to fret
ron·geur [rɔ̃ʒœr] -geuse [ʒøz] adj gnawing || m rodent
ronron [rɔ̃rɔ̃] m purr; drone
ronronnement [rɔ̃rɔnmɑ̃] m purring
ronronner [rɔ̃rɔne] intr to purr
roquer [rɔke] intr (chess) to castle
roquet [rɔkɛ] m cur, yapper; (breed of dog) pug
roquette [rɔkɛt] f (plant; missile) rocket
rosace [rozas] f rose window; (archit) rosette
rosa·cé -cée [rozase] adj roselike || f skin eruption
rosaire [rozɛr] m rosary
rosâtre [rozɑtr] adj dusty-pink
rosbif [rɔsbif] m roast beef
rose [roz] adj & m rose, pink (color) || f rose; rose window; dire la rose to box the compass; rose des vents compass card; rose d'Inde (Tagetes) marigold
ro·sé -sée [roze] adj rose, rose-colored || m rosé wine || f see rosée

ro·seau [rozo] *m* (*pl* **-seaux**) reed
rosée [roze] *f* dew
roséole [rozeɔl] *f* rash; rose rash
roseraie [rozrɛ] *f* rose garden
rosette [rɔzɛt] *f* bowknot; rosette; red ink; red chalk
rosier [rozje] *m* rosebush; **rosier églantier** sweetbrier
rosse [rɔs] *adj* nasty, mean; strict, stern; cynical ‖ *f* (coll) beast, stinker; (coll) nag; **sale rosse** (coll) dirty bitch
rossée [rɔse] *f* (coll) thrashing
rosser [rɔse] *tr* to beat up, thrash; (coll) to beat, to best
rossignol [rɔsiɲɔl] *m* skeleton key; (orn) nightingale; (coll) piece of junk, drug on the market
rot [ro] *m* (slang) burp, belch
rota·tif [rɔtatif] **-tive** [tiv] *adj* rotary ‖ *f* rotary press
rotation [rɔtɑsjɔ̃] *f* rotation; turnover (*of merchandise*)
rotatoire [rɔtatwar] *adj* rotary
roter [rɔte] *intr* (slang) to burp
rô·ti -tie [roti] *adj* roasted ‖ *m* roast ‖ *f* piece of toast; **rôtie à l'anglaise** Welsh rarebit
rotin [rɔtɛ̃] *m* rattan; **de** or **en rotin** cane (*chair*); **pas un rotin!** not a penny!
rôtir [rotir] *tr, intr,* & *ref* to roast; to toast; to scorch
rôtisserie [rotisri] *f* rotisserie shop (*where roasted fowl is sold*); grillroom (*restaurant*)
rôtissoire [rotiswar] *f* rotisserie
rotonde [rɔtɔ̃d] *f* rotunda; (rr) roundhouse
rotor [rɔtɔr] *m* rotor
rotule [rɔtyl] *f* kneecap
roture· [rɔtyr] *f* common people
rotu·rier [rɔtyrje] **-rière** [rjɛr] *adj* plebeian, of the common people ‖ *mf* commoner
rouage [rwaʒ] *m* cog; **rouages** movement (*of a watch*)
rou·blard [rublar] **-blarde** [blard] *adj* (coll) wily ‖ *mf* (coll) schemer
roublardise [rublardiz] *f* (coll) cunning
roucoulement [rukulmɑ̃] *m* cooing; billing and cooing
roucouler [rukule] *tr* & *intr* to coo
roue [ru] *f* wheel; **faire la roue** to turn cartwheels; to strut; **roue de secours** spare wheel (*with tire*)
roué rouée [rwe] *adj* slick; knocked out ‖ *mf* slicker ‖ *m* rake
rouelle [rwɛl] *f* fillet (*of veal*)
rouer [rwe] *tr* to break upon the wheel; **rouer de coups** to thrash, beat up
rouerie [ruri] *f* trickery; trick
rouet [rwɛ] *m* spinning wheel
rouge [ruʒ] *adj* red ‖ *m* red; rouge; blush; **porter au rouge** to heat redhot; **rouge à lèvres** lipstick ‖ *adv* red
rou·geaud [ruʒo] **-geaude** [ʒod] *adj* ruddy ‖ *mf* ruddy-faced person
rouge-gorge [ruʒgɔrʒ] *m* (*pl* **rougesgorges**) robin (*Erithacus rubecula*)
rougeole [ruʒɔl] *f* measles

rougeur [ruʒœr] *f* redness; blush; **rougeurs** red spots
rougir [ruʒir] *tr* to redden ‖ *intr* to turn red; to blush
rouille [ruj] *f* rust
rouil·lé -lée [ruje] *adj* rusty; (*out of practice; blighted*) rusty
rouiller [ruje] *tr, intr,* & *ref* to rust
roulade [rulad] *f* trill; (mus) run
rou·lant [rulɑ̃] **-lante** [lɑ̃t] *adj* rolling; (coll) funny
rou·leau [rulo] *m* (*pl* **-leaux**) roller; roll; spool; rolling pin; **rouleau compresseur** road roller
roulement [rulmɑ̃] *m* roll; rotation; rattle, clatter; exchange; **par roulement** in rotation; **roulement à billes** ball bearing
rouler [rule] *tr* to roll; (coll) to take in, cheat ‖ *intr* to roll; to roll along; **rouler sur** to roll in (*wealth*); to turn on ‖ *ref* to roll; to roll up; to toss and turn; (with *dat* of *reflex pron*) to twiddle (*one's thumbs*); **se les rouler** (coll) to not turn a hand
roule-ta-bille [rultabij] *m invar* (coll) rolling stone
roulette [rulɛt] *f* small wheel; castor; roulette; **aller comme sur des roulettes** to go well, to work smoothly
rou·leur [rulœr] **-leuse** [løz] *mf* drifter (*from one job to another*) ‖ *m* freight handler ‖ *f* streetwalker
roulis [ruli] *m* (naut) roll
roulotte [rulɔt] *f* trailer; gypsy wagon
rou·main [rumɛ̃] **-maine** [mɛn] *adj* Rumanian ‖ *m* Rumanian (*language*) ‖ (*cap*) *mf* Rumanian (*person*)
roupiller [rupije] *intr* to take a snooze
rou·quin [rukɛ̃] **-quine** [kin] *adj* (coll) red-headed; ‖ *mf* (coll) redhead ‖ *m* (slang) red wine; **Rouquin** Red (*nickname*)
rouspéter [ruspete] §10 *intr* (coll) to bellyache, to kick
rouspé·teur [ruspetœr] **-teuse** [tøz] *mf* (coll) bellyacher, complainer
roussâtre [rusɑtr] *adj* auburn
rousse [rus] *f* redhead, auburn-haired woman; (slang) cops
rousseur [rusœr] *f* reddishness; freckle
roussir [rusir] *tr* to scorch; to singe ‖ *intr* to become brown; **faire roussir** (culin) to brown
route [rut] *f* road; route, itinerary; **bonne route!** happy motoring!; **en route!** let's go!; **faire fausse route** to take the wrong road; (fig) to be on the wrong track; **mettre en route** to start; **route déformée** rough road; **route déviée** detour
rou·tier [rutje] **-tière** [tjɛr] *adj* road (*e.g., map*) ‖ *m* trucker; bicycle racer; Explorer, Rover (*boy scout*); (naut) track chart; **vieux routier** veteran, old hand
routine [rutin] *f* routine
routi·nier [rutinje] **-nière** [njɛr] *adj* routine; one-track (*mind*)
rouvieux [ruvjø] *adj masc* mangy ‖ *m* mange
rouvrir [ruvrir] §65 *tr* & *intr* to reopen
roux [ru] **rousse** [rus] *adj* russet, red-

dish; red, auburn (*hair*); browned (*butter*) ‖ *mf* redhead ‖ *m* russet, reddish brown, auburn (*color*); brown sauce ‖ *f* see **rousse**
royal royale [rwajal] *adj* (*pl* **royaux** [rwajo]) royal ‖ *f* imperial, goatee
royaliste [rwajalist] *adj* & *mf* royalist
royaume [rwajom] *m* kingdom
royauté [rwajote] *f* royalty
R.S.V.P. [ɛresvepe] *m* (letterword) (**répondez, s'il vous plaît**) R.S.V.P.
R.T.F. [ɛrteɛf] *f* (letterword) (**radio-diffusion-télévision française**) French radio and television
ruade [ryad] *f* kick, buck
ruban [rybɑ̃] *m* ribbon; tape; **ruban adhésif** adhesive tape; **ruban adhésif transparent** transparent tape; **ruban de chapeau** hatband; **ruban de frein** brake lining; **ruban encreur** typewriter ribbon; **ruban magnétique** recording tape
rubéole [rybeɔl] *f* German measles
rubis [rybi] *m* ruby; jewel (*of watch*); **payer rubis sur l'ongle** to pay down on the nail
rubrique [rybrik] *f* rubric; caption, heading; label (*in a dictionary*)
ruche [ryʃ] *f* beehive
rude [ryd] *adj* rude, rough; rugged; hard; steep; (coll) amazing
rudement [rydmɑ̃] *adv* roughly; (coll) awfully, mighty
rudesse [rydɛs] *f* rudeness, roughness; harshness
rudiment [rydimɑ̃] *m* rudiment
rudoyer [rydwaje] §47 *tr* to bully, browbeat; to abuse, treat roughly
rue [ry] *f* street; **rue barrée** (public sign) no thoroughfare; (public sign) closed for repairs; **rue sans issue** (public sign) no outlet
ruée [rɥe] *f* rush; **ruée vers l'or** gold rush
ruelle [rɥɛl] *f* alley, lane; space between bed and wall
ruer [rɥe] *intr* to kick, to buck; **ruer dans les brancards** to kick over the traces ‖ *ref*—**se ruer sur** to rush at
rugir [ryʒir] *intr* to roar, bellow

rugissement [ryʒismɑ̃] *m* roar
ru·gueux [rygø] **-gueuse** [gøz] *adj* rough, rugged
ruine [rɥin] *f* ruin
ruiner [rɥine] *tr* to ruin
ruis·seau [rɥiso] *m* (*pl* **-seaux**) stream, brook; (fig) gutter
ruisseler [rɥisle] §34 *intr* to stream; to drip, to trickle
ruisselet [rɥislɛ] *m* little stream
ruissellement [rɥisɛlmɑ̃] *m* streaming; (*e.g., of light*) flood
rumeur [rymœr] *f* rumor; hum (*e.g., of voices*); roar (*of the sea*); **rumeur publique** public opinion
ru·pin [rypɛ̃] **-pine** [pin] *adj* (slang) rich ‖ *mf* (slang) swell
rupiner [rypine] *tr* & *intr* (coll) to do well
rupteur [ryptœr] *m* (elec) contact breaker
rupture [ryptyr] *f* rupture; breach; break; breaking off
ru·ral -rale [ryral] (*pl* **-raux** [ro]) *adj* rural ‖ *mf* farmer; **ruraux** country people
ruse [ryz] *f* ruse
ru·sé -sée [ryze] *adj* cunning, crafty ‖ *mf* sly one
russe [rys] *adj* Russian ‖ *m* Russian (*language*) ‖ (*cap*) *mf* Russian (*person*)
Russie [rysi] *f* Russia; **la Russie** Russia
rus·taud [rysto] **-taude** [tod] *adj* rustic, clumsy ‖ *mf* bumpkin
rustique [rystik] *adj* rustic; hardy
rustre [rystr] *adj* oafish ‖ *m* bumpkin, oaf; (obs) peasant
rut [ryt] *m* (zool) rut
ruti·lant [rytilɑ̃] **-lante** [lɑ̃t] *adj* bright-red; gleaming
rutiler [rytiler] *intr* to gleam, to glow
rythme [ritm] *m* rhythm; rate (*of production*)
ryth·mé -mée [ritme] *adj* rhythmic(al); cadenced
rythmer [ritme] *tr* to cadence; to mark with a rhythm
rythmique [ritmik] *adj* rhythmic(al)

S

S, s [ɛs], *[ɛs] *m invar* nineteenth letter of the French alphabet
S. *abbr* (**saint**) St.
sa [sa] §88
S.A. [ɛsa] *f* (letterword) (**Société anonyme**) Inc.
sabbat [saba] *m* Sabbath; witches' Sabbath; racket, uproarious gaiety; **sabbat des chats** caterwauling
sabir [sabir] *m* pidgin
sable [sabl] *m* sand; sable; **sable mouvant** quicksand
sabler [sable] *tr* to sandblast; to drink

in one gulp; to toss off (*some champagne*)
sa·bleux [sablø] **-bleuse** [bløz] *adj* sandy ‖ *f* sandblast; sandblaster
sablier [sablije] *m* hourglass; (*for drying ink*) sandbox; dealer in sand
sablière [sablijɛr] *f* sandpit; wall plate; (rr) sandbox
sablon·neux [sablɔnø] **sablon·neuse** [sablɔnøz] *adj* sandy
sablonnière [sablɔnjɛr] *f* sandpit
sabord [sabɔr] *m* porthole
saborder [sabɔrde] *tr* to scuttle

sabot [sabo] *m* wooden shoe; hoof; whipping top; bungled work; ferrule; caster cup; **dormir comme un sabot** to sleep like a top; **sabot de frein** brake shoe; **sabot d'enrayage** wedge, block, scotch

sabotage [sabɔtaʒ] *m* sabotage

saboter [sabɔte] *tr* to sabotage; to bungle || *intr* (coll) to make one's wooden shoes clatter

sabo·teur [sabɔtœr] **-teuse** [tøz] *mf* saboteur; bungler

sabo·tier [sabɔtje] **-tière** [tjer] *mf* maker and seller of wooden shoes || *f* clog dance

sabre [sɑbr] *m* saber

sabrer [sɑbre] *tr* to saber; (coll) to botch; (coll) to cut, condense

sac [sak] *m* sack, bag; **être un sac d'os** [dɔs] to be nothing but skin and bones; **sac à main** handbag; **sac à malice** bag of tricks; **sac à provisions** shopping bag; **sac de couchage** sleeping bag

saccade [sakad] *f* jerk

sacca·dé -dée [sakade] *adj* jerky

saccager [sakaʒe] §38 *tr* to sack; (coll) to upset, to turn topsy-turvy

saccha·rin [sakarɛ̃] **-rine** [rin] *adj* saccharine || *f* saccharin

saccharose [sakaroz] *m* sucrose

sacerdoce [saserdɔs] *m* priesthood

sacerdo·tal -tale [saserdɔtal] *adj* (*pl* **-taux** [to]) sacerdotal, priestly

sachet [saʃɛ] *m* sachet; packet (*of needles, medicine, etc.*); powder charge

sacoche [sakɔʃ] *f* satchel

sacramen·tel -telle [sakramɑ̃tɛl] *adj* sacramental

sacre [sakr] *m* crowning, consecration

sa·cré -crée [sakre] *adj* sacred; (anat) sacral || (when standing before noun) *adj* (coll) darned, blasted

sacrement [sakrəmɑ̃] *m* sacrament

sacrer [sakre] *tr* to crown, to consecrate || *intr* to curse

sacrifice [sakrifis] *m* sacrifice

sacrifier [sakrifje] *tr* to sacrifice

sacrilège [sakrilɛʒ] *adj* sacrilegious || *mf* sacrilegious person || *m* sacrilege

sacristain [sakristɛ̃] *m* sexton

sadique [sadik] *adj* sadistic || *mf* sadist

safran [safrɑ̃] *m* saffron

sagace [sagas] *adj* sagacious, shrewd

sage [saʒ] *adj* wise; well-behaved; modest (*woman*); good (*child*); **soyez sage!** be good! || *mf* sage

sage-femme [saʒfam] *f* (*pl* **sages-femmes**) midwife

sagesse [saʒɛs] *f* wisdom; good behavior

sai·gnant [seɲɑ̃] **-gnante** [ɲɑ̃t] *adj* bleeding; (*wound*) fresh; (*meat*) rare

saignée [seɲe] *f* bloodletting; bend of the arm, small of the arm; (fig) drain on the purse

saignement [seɲmɑ̃] *m* bleeding; **saignement de nez** nosebleed

saigner [seɲe], [seɲe] *tr* & *intr* to bleed; **saigner à blanc**, **saigner aux quatre veines** to bleed white

sail·lant [sajɑ̃] **sail·lante** [sajɑ̃t] *adj* prominent, salient; projecting; high (*cheekbones*)

saillie [saji] *f* projection; spurt; sally, outburst; **faire saillie** to jut out, project

saillir [sajir] (used only in *inf, ger,* & 3d *sg* & *pl*) *tr* (agr) to cover || §69 *intr* to protrude, to project; to spurt

sain [sɛ̃] **saine** [sɛn] *adj* healthy; **sain d'esprit** sane; **sain et sauf** safe and sound

saindoux [sɛ̃du] *m* lard

sainement [sɛnmɑ̃] *adv* soundly

saint [sɛ̃] **sainte** [sɛ̃t] *adj* saintly; sacred, holy || *mf* saint

sainteté [sɛ̃təte] *f* holiness

saisie [sezi] *f* seizure; foreclosure

saisie-arrêt [seziarɛ] *f* (*pl* **-arrêts**) attachment, garnishment

saisir [sezir] *tr* to seize; to sear (*meat*); to grasp (*to understand*); to strike, startle; to overcome; **saisir un tribunal de** to lay before a court || *ref* **—se saisir de** to take possession of

saisissement [sezismɑ̃] *m* chill; shock

saison [sezɔ̃] *f* season

salace [salas] *adj* salacious

salade [salad] *f* salad; (fig) mess; **salade russe** mixed vegetable salad with mayonnaise

saladier [saladje] *m* salad bowl

salaire [saler] *m* salary, wage; recompense, punishment

salariat [salarja] *m* salaried workers, employees; salary (*fixed wage*)

sala·rié -riée [salarje] *adj* salaried, hired || *mf* wage earner; employee

sa·laud [salo] **-laude** [lod] *adj* (coll) slovenly || *mf* (slang) skunk, scoundrel

sale [sal] *adj* dirty; dull (*color*) || *mf* dirty person

sa·lé -lée [sale] *adj* salty, salted; dirty (*joke*); padded (*bill*); (slang) exaggerated || *m* salt pork

saler [sale] *tr* to salt

saleté [salte] *f* dirtiness; piece of dirt; (slang) dirty trick; (slang) dirt

salière [saljer] *f* saltcellar

salir [salir] *tr* & *ref* to soil

salive [saliv] *f* saliva

salle [sal] *f* room; hall; auditorium; ward (*in a hospital*); (theat) audience, house; **salle à manger** dining room; **salle d'armes** fencing room; **salle d'attente** waiting room; **salle de bains** bathroom; **salle d'écoute** language laboratory; **salle de police** (mil) guardhouse; **salle des accouchées** maternity ward; **salle de séjour** living room; **salle des machines** engine room; **salle des pas perdus** lobby, waiting room; **salle de rédaction** city room; **salle de spectacle** movie house; **salle des ventes** salesroom, showroom; **salle de travail** delivery room; **salle d'exposition** showroom

salon [salɔ̃] *m* living room, parlor; exposition; saloon (*ship's lounge*); **salon de beauté** beauty parlor; **salon de l'automobile** automobile show; **salon de thé** tearoom

salon·nard [salɔnar] salon·narde [salɔnard] *mf* sycophant
saloperie [salɔpri] *f* (slang) trash
salopette [salɔpɛt] *f* coveralls, overalls; bib; smock
salpêtre [salpɛtr] *m* saltpeter
salsepareille [salsəparɛj] *f* sarsaparilla
saltimbanque [saltɛ̃bɑ̃k] *mf* tumbler; mountebank, charlatan
salubre [salybr] *adj* salubrious, healthful
saluer [salɥe] *tr* to salute; to greet, to bow to, to wave to
salut [saly] *m* health; safety; salvation; salute; greeting, bow; nod; **salut!** (coll) hi!, howdy!; **salut les gars!**, **salut les copains!** hi, fellows!
salutation [salytɑsjɔ̃] *f* greeting; **salutations distinguées**, or **sincères salutations** (complimentary close) yours truly
salve [salv] *f* salvo, salute
samari·tain [samaritɛ̃] -taine [tɛn] *adj* Samaritan || (*cap*) *mf* Samaritan
samedi [samdi] *m* Saturday
sanatorium [sanatɔrjɔm] *m* sanitarium
sanctifier [sɑ̃ktifje] *tr* to sanctify
sanction [sɑ̃ksjɔ̃] *f* sanction; penalty
sanctionner [sɑ̃ksjɔne] *tr* to sanction; to penalize
sanctuaire [sɑ̃ktɥer] *m* sanctuary
sandale [sɑ̃dal] *f* sandal; gym shoe
sandwich [sɑ̃dwitʃ], [sɑ̃dwiʃ] *m* (*pl* sandwiches, sandwichs) sandwich
sang [sɑ̃] *m* blood; **avoir le sang chaud** (coll) to be a go-getter; **bon sang!** (coll) darn it!; **sang et tripes** blood and guts; **se faire du mauvais sang** to get all stewed up
sang-froid [sɑ̃frwa], [sɑ̃frwɑ] *m* self-control
san·glant [sɑ̃glɑ̃] -glante [glɑ̃t] *adj* bloody; cruel
sangle [sɑ̃gl] *f* cinch
sanglier [sɑ̃glije] *m* wild boar
sanglot [sɑ̃glo] *m* sob
sangloter [sɑ̃glɔte] *intr* to sob
sang-mêlé [sɑ̃mele] *m invar* half-breed
sangsue [sɑ̃sy] *f* bloodsucker, leech
san·guin [sɑ̃gɛ̃] -guine [gin] *adj* sanguine || *f* (fa) sanguine
sanitaire [saniter] *adj* sanitary; hospital, e.g., **avion sanitaire** hospital plane
sans [sɑ̃] *adv*—**sans que** without; **sans quoi** or else || *prep* without; **sans cesse** ceaselessly; **sans façon** informally; **sans fil** wireless
sans-abri [sɑ̃zabri] *mf invar* homeless person
sans-cœur [sɑ̃kœr] *mf invar* heartless person
sans-filiste [sɑ̃filist] *mf* (*pl* -filistes) radio operator; radio amateur
sans-gêne [sɑ̃ʒɛn] *adj invar* offhanded || *mf invar* offhanded person || *m* offhandedness
sansonnet [sɑ̃sɔnɛ] *m* starling; blackbird
sans-travail [sɑ̃travaj] *mf invar* unemployed worker
san·tal [sɑ̃tal] *m* (*pl* -taux [to]) (bot) sandalwood

santé [sɑ̃te] *f* health; sanity; **santé publique** public health service
sape [sap] *f* sap (undermining)
saper [sape] *tr* to sap, to undermine
sapeur [sapœr] *m* (mil) sapper; **fumer comme un sapeur** (coll) to smoke like a chimney
sapeur-pompier [sapœrpɔ̃pje] *m* (*pl* sapeurs-pompiers) fireman; **sapeurs-pompiers** fire department
saphir [safir] *m* sapphire; sapphire needle
sapin [sapɛ̃] *m* fir
sapristi [sapristi] *interj* hang it!
saquer [sake] *tr* (slang) to fire, to sack
sarbacane [sarbakan] *f* blowgun
sarcasme [sarkasm] *m* sarcasm
sarcler [sarkle] *tr* to weed, root out
sarcloir [sarklwar] *m* hoe
Sardaigne [sardɛɲ] *f* Sardinia; **la Sardaigne** Sardinia
sarde [sard] *adj* Sardinian || *m* Sardinian (language) || (*cap*) *mf* Sardinian (person)
sardine [sardin] *f* sardine
S.A.R.L. *abbr* (Société à responsabilité limitée) corporation
sarment [sarmɑ̃] *m* vine; vine shoot
sarra·sin [saʁazɛ̃] -sine [zin] *adj* Saracen || *m* buckwheat || *f* portcullis || (*cap*) *mf* Saracen
sar·rau [saro] *m* (*pl* -raus) smock
sarriette [sarjɛt] *f* (bot) savory
sas [sɑ], [sɑs] *m* sieve; lock (of canal, submarine, etc.); air lock (of caisson, spaceship, etc.); **sas d'évacuation** (aer) escape hatch
sasser [sɑse] *tr* to sift, screen; to pass through a lock
satelliser [satelize] *tr* to make a satellite of; (rok) to put into orbit
satellite [satelit] *adj & m* satellite
satin [satɛ̃] *m* satin
satinette [satinɛt] *f* sateen
satire [satir] *f* satire
satirique [satirik] *adj* satiric(al)
satiriser [satirize] *tr* to satirize
satisfaction [satisfaksjɔ̃] *f* satisfaction
satisfaire [satisfer] §29 *tr* to satisfy || *intr* to satisfy; (with *dat*) to fulfill; (with *dat*) to meet (*a need*) || *ref* to be satisfied
satisfai·sant [satisfəzɑ̃] -sante [zɑ̃t] *adj* satisfactory; satisfying
saturer [satyre] *tr* to saturate
Saturne [satyrn] *m* Saturn
saturnisme [satyrnism] *m* lead poisoning
sauce [sos] *f* sauce; gravy; drawing pencil; (tech) solution
saucer [sose] §51 *tr* to dip in sauce or gravy; (coll) to soak to the skin; (coll) to reprimand severely
saucière [sosjɛr] *f* gravy bowl
saucisse [sosis] *f* sausage; frankfurter
saucisson [sosisɔ̃] *m* bologna, sausage
sauf [sof] sauve [sov] *adj* safe || **sauf** *prep* save, except; barring; subject to (*e.g., correction*)
sauf-conduit [sofkɔ̃dɥi] *m* (*pl* -conduits) safe-conduct
sauge [soʒ] *f* (bot) sage, salvia

saugre·nu -nue [sogrəny] *adj* absurd, silly

saule [sol] *m* willow

saumâtre [somɑtr] *adj* brackish

saumon [somɔ̃] *m* salmon; pig (*of crude metal*)

saumure [somyr] *f* brine

sauner [sone] *intr* to make salt

saupoudrer [sopudre] *tr* to sprinkle (*with powder, sugar; citations*)

saurer [sɔre] *tr* to kipper

saut [so] *m* leap, jump; falls, waterfall; **au saut du lit** on getting out of bed; **faire le saut** to take the fatal step; **faire un saut chez** to drop in on; **par sauts et par bonds** by fits and starts; **saut à la perche** pole vault; **saut de carpe** jackknife; **saut de l'ange** swan dive; **saut en chute libre** skydiving; **saut périlleux** somersault

saut-de-lit [sodli] *m invar* wrap

saut-de-mouton [sodmutɔ̃] *m* (*pl* **sauts-de-mouton**) cloverleaf (*intersection*)

saute [sot] *f* change in direction, shift

saute-mouton [sotmutɔ̃] *m* leapfrog

sauter [sote] *tr* to leap over; to skip || *intr* to leap, jump; to blow up; **faire sauter** to sauté; to flip (*a pancake*); to fire (*an employee*); **sauter à cloche-pied** to hop on one foot; **sauter à pieds joints** to do a standing jump; **sauter aux nues** to get mad

sauterelle [sotrɛl] *f* grasshopper

sauterie [sotri] *f* (coll) hop (*dancing party*)

sau·teur [sotœr] **-teuse** [tøz] *adj* jumping || *mf* jumper || *m* jumper, jumping horse || *f* frying pan

sautiller [sotije] *intr* to hop

sautoir [sotwar] *m* St. Andrew's cross; **en sautoir** crossways

sauvage [sovaʒ] *adj* savage; wild; shy || *mf* savage

sauvagerie [sovaʒri] *f* savagery; wildness; shyness

sauvegarde [sovgard] *f* safeguard

sauvegarder [sovgarde] *tr* to safeguard

sauve-qui-peut [sovkipø] *m invar* panic, stampede, rout

sauver [sove] *tr* to save; to rescue || *intr*—**sauve qui peut!** every man for himself! || *ref* to run away; to escape; (theat) to exit; **sauve-toi!** (coll) scram!

sauvetage [sovtaʒ] *m* salvage; lifesaving, rescue

sauveteur [sovtœr] *adj masc* lifesaving || *m* lifesaver

sauveur [sovœr] *adj masc* Saviour || *m* savior; **Le Sauveur** the Saviour

savamment [savamɑ̃] *adv* knowingly; skillfully

savane [savan] *f* prairie, savanna

sa·vant [savɑ̃] **-vante** [vɑ̃t] *adj* scholarly, learned || *mf* scientist, scholar, savant; **savant atomiste** nuclear physicist

savate [savat] *f* old slipper; foot boxing; (coll) butterfingers; **traîner la savate** to be down at the heel

saveur [savœr] *f* savor, taste

savoir [savwar] *m* learning || §62 *tr & intr* to know; to know how to; **à**

savoir namely, to wit; **à savoir que** with the understanding that; **en savoir long** to know all about it; **pas que je sache** not that I know of

savoir-faire [savwarfɛr] *m invar* knowhow

savon [savɔ̃] *m* soap; (slang) sharp reprimand; **savon en paillettes** soap flakes

savonnage [savɔnaʒ] *m* soaping

savonner [savɔne] *tr* to soap

savonnerie [savɔnri] *f* soap factory

savonnette [savɔnɛt] *f* toilet soap

savon·neux [savɔnø] **savon·neuse** [savɔnøz] *adj* soapy

savourer [savure] *tr* to savor

savou·reux [savurø] **-reuse** [røz] *adj* savory, tasty

saxon [saksɔ̃] **saxonne** [saksɔn] *adj* Saxon || *m* Saxon (*language*) || (*cap*) *mf* Saxon (*person*)

saxophone [saksɔfɔn] *m* saxophone

saynète [sɛnɛt] *f* sketch, playlet

sca·bieux [skabjø] **-bieuse** [bjøz] *adj* scabby || *f* scabious

sca·breux [skabrø] **-breuse** [brøz] *adj* rough (*road*); risky (*business*); scabrous (*remark*)

scalpel [skalpɛl] *m* scalpel

scalper [skalpe] *tr* to scalp

scandale [skɑdal] *m* scandal; disturbance

scanda·leux [skɑdalø] **-leuse** [løz] *adj* scandalous

scandaliser [skɑdalize] *tr* to lead astray; **to scandalize** || *ref* to take offense

scander [skɑde] *tr* to scan (*verses*)

scandinave [skɑdinav] *adj* Scandinavian || *m* Scandinavian (*language*) || (*cap*) *mf* Scandinavian (*person*); **Scandinaves** Scandinavian countries

scaphandre [skafɑdr] *m* diving suit; spacesuit; **scaphandre autonome** aqualung

scaphandrier [skafɑdrije] *m* diver

scarlatine [skarlatin] *f* scarlet fever

scarole [skarɔl] *f* escarole

sceau [so] *m* (*pl* **seaux**) seal

scélé·rat [selera] **-rate** [rat] *adj* villainous || *mf* villain

scellé [sɛle] *m* seal

sceller [sɛle] *tr* to seal

scénario [senarjo] *m* scenario

scène [sɛn] *f* scene; stage; theater

scénique [senik] *adj* scenic

scepticisme [sɛptisism] *m* skepticism

sceptique [sɛptik] *adj & mf* skeptic

sceptre [sɛptr] *m* scepter

schah [ʃa] *m* shah

schelem [ʃlɛm] *m* slam (*at bridge*)

schéma [ʃema] *m* diagram

schisme [ʃism] *m* schism

schizophrène [skizɔfrɛn] *adj & mf* schizophrenic

schlague [ʃlag] *f* flogging

schooner [skunœr], [ʃunœr] *m* schooner

sciatique [sjatik] *adj* sciatic || *f* (pathol) sciatica

scie [si] *f* saw; (coll) bore, nuisance; **scie à découper** jig saw

sciemment [sjamɑ̃] *adv* knowingly

science [sjɑ̃s] *f* science; learning, knowledge
science-fiction [sjɑ̃sfiksjɔ̃] *f* science fiction
scientifique [sjɑ̃tifik] *adj* scientific ‖ *mf* scientist
scier [sje] *tr* to saw; (coll) to bore ‖ *intr* (naut) to row backwards
scierie [siri] *f* sawmill
scieur [sjœr] *m* sawyer
scinder [sɛ̃de] *tr* to divide ‖ *ref* to be divided
scintil·lant [sɛ̃tijɑ̃] **scintil·lante** [sɛ̃tijɑ̃t] *adj* scintillating; twinkling
scintillation [sɛ̃tijɑ̃sjɔ̃] *f* twinkling, twinkle; (phys) scintillation
scintillement [sɛ̃tijmɑ̃] *m* twinkling
scintiller [sɛ̃tije] *intr* to scintillate; to twinkle
scion [sjɔ̃] *m* scion; tip (*of fishing rod*)
scission [sisjɔ̃] *f* schism; (biol & phys) fission
sciure [sjyr] *f* sawdust
sclérose [skleroz] *f* sclerosis
scolaire [skɔlɛr] *adj* school
scolastique [skɔlastik] *adj* & *m* scholastic ‖ *f* scholasticism
sconse [skɔ̃s] *m* skunk fur; skunk
scories [skɔri] *fpl* slag, dross
scorpion [skɔrpjɔ̃] *m* scorpion
scout scoute [skut] *adj* & *m* scout
scoutisme [skutism] *m* scouting
scribe [skrib] *m* scribe
script [skript] *m* scrip; (typ) script
scripturaire [skriptyrɛr] *adj* Scriptural ‖ *m* fundamentalist
scrofule [skrɔfyl] *f* scrofula
scrotum [skrɔtɔm] *m* scrotum
scrupule [skrypyl] *m* scruple
scrupu·leux [skrypylø] **-leuse** [løz] *adj* scrupulous
scruter [skryte] *tr* to scrutinize
scrutin [skrytɛ̃] *m* ballot; balloting, voting, poll; **dépouiller le scrutin** to count the votes; **scrutin de ballottage** runoff election
scrutiner [skrytine] *intr* to ballot
sculpter [skylte] *tr* to sculpture; to carve (*wood*)
sculpteur [skyltœr] *m* sculptor
sculpture [skyltyr] *f* sculpture
s.d. *abbr* (**sans date**) n.d.
S.D.N. [ɛsdeen] *f* (letterword) (**Société des Nations**) League of Nations
se [sə] §87
séance [seɑ̃s] *f* session, sitting; seat (*in an assembly*); performance, showing; séance; **séance tenante** on the spot
séant [seɑ̃] **séante** [seɑ̃t] *adj* fitting, decent; sitting (*as a king or a court in session*) ‖ *m* buttocks, bottom; **se mettre sur son séant** to sit up (*in bed*)
seau [so] *m* (*pl* **seaux**) bucket, pail; **il pleut à seaux** it's raining cats and dogs; **seau à charbon** coal scuttle
sébile [sebil] *f* wooden bowl
sec [sɛk] **sèche** [sɛʃ] *adj* dry; sharp; rude; unguarded (*card*); total (*loss*); **en cinq sec** in a jiffy; **sec comme un hareng** (coll) long and thin; **tout sec** and nothing more ‖ *m* dryness; **à sec** dry; (coll) broke ‖ *f see* **sèche** ‖ *sec adv*—**aussi sec** (slang) on the spot;

boire sec to drink one's liquor straight; **frapper sec** to land a hard fast punch; **parler sec** to talk tough
sécession [sesesjɔ̃] *f* secession
sèche [sɛʃ] *f* (slang) fag, cigarette
sèche-cheveux [sɛʃʃəvø] *m invar* hair drier
sécher [seʃe] §10 *tr* to dry; to season; to cut (*a class*) ‖ *intr* to become dry
sécheresse [seʃrɛs] *f* dryness; drought; baldness (*of style*); curtness; (fig) coldness
séchoir [seʃwar] *m* drier; drying room; clotheshorse
se·cond [səgɔ̃] **-conde** [gɔ̃d] *adj* & *pron* second; **en second** next in rank ‖ *m* second ‖ *f see* **seconde**
secondaire [səgɔ̃dɛr] *adj* & *m* secondary
seconde [səgɔ̃d] *f* second (*in time; musical interval; of angle*); second class
seconder [səgɔ̃de] *tr* to help, second
secouer [səkwe] *tr* to shake; to shake off or down ‖ *ref* to pull oneself together
secourable [səkurabl] *adj* helpful
secourir [səkurir] §14 *tr* to help, aid
secourisme [səkurism] *m* first aid
secouriste [səkurist] *mf* first-aider; first-aid worker
secours [səkur] *m* help, aid; **au secours!** help!; **de secours** emergency; spare (*tire*); **des secours** supplies, relief
secousse [səkus] *f* shake, jolt; (elec) shock
se·cret [səkrɛ] **-crète** [krɛt] *adj* secret; secretive ‖ *m* secret; secrecy; **au secret** in solitary confinement ‖ *f see* **secrète**
secrétaire [səkretɛr] *mf* secretary ‖ *m* secretary (*desk*)
secrète [səkrɛt] *f* central intelligence
sécréter [sekrete] §10 *tr* to secrete
sectaire [sɛktɛr] *adj* & *mf* sectarian
secte [sɛkt] *f* sect
secteur [sɛktœr] *m* sector; (elec) house current, local supply circuit; **secteur postal** postal zone; (mil) A.P.O. number
section [sɛksjɔ̃] *f* section; cross section
sectionner [sɛksjɔne] *tr* to section; to cut ‖ *ref* to break apart
séculaire [sekylɛr] *adj* secular
sécu·lier [sekylje] **-lière** [ljɛr] *adj* & *m* secular
sécurité [sekyrite] *f* security
séda·tif [sedatif] **-tive** [tiv] *adj* & *m* sedative
sédation [sedɑsjɔ̃] *f* sedation
sédentaire [sedɑ̃tɛr] *adj* sedentary
sédiment [sedimɑ̃] *m* sediment
sédi·tieux [sedisjø] **-tieuse** [sjøz] *adj* seditious
sédition [sedisjɔ̃] *f* sedition
séduc·teur [sedyktœr] **-trice** [tris] *adj* seducing, bewitching ‖ *mf* seducer ‖ *f* vamp
séduction [sedyksjɔ̃] *f* seduction
séduire [sedɥir] §19 *tr* to seduce; to charm, to bewitch; to bribe
sédui·sant [sedɥizɑ̃] **-sante** [zɑ̃t] *adj* seductive, tempting

segment [sɛgmã] *m* segment; **segment de piston** piston ring

ségrégation [segregɑsjɔ̃] *f* segregation

ségrégationniste [segregɑsjɔnist] *adj* segregationist

seiche [sɛʃ] *f* cuttlefish

séide [seid] *m* henchman

seigle [sɛgl] *m* rye

seigneur [sɛɲœr] *m* lord

sein [sɛ̃] *m* breast; bosom; womb; **au sein de** in the heart of

seine [sɛn] *f* dragnet

seing [sɛ̃] *m* signature; **sous seing privé** privately witnessed

seize [sɛz] *adj & pron* sixteen; the Sixteenth, e.g., **Jean seize** John the Sixteenth ‖ *m* sixteen; sixteenth (*in dates*)

seizième [sɛzjɛm] *adj, pron* (*masc, fem*), *& m* sixteenth

séjour [seʒur] *m* stay, visit

séjourner [seʒurne] *intr* to reside; to stay, to visit

sel [sɛl] *m* salt; **gros sel** coarse salt; (fig) dirty joke; **sel ammoniac** sal ammoniac; **sel gemme** rock salt

sélec·tif [selɛktif] **-tive** [tiv] *adj* selective

sélection [selɛksjɔ̃] *f* selection

sélectionner [selɛksjɔne] *tr* to select

self [sɛlf] *f* (elec) coil, spark coil

self-service [sɛlfsɛrvis] *m* self-service

selle [sɛl] *f* saddle; seat (*of bicycle, motorcycle, etc.*); sculptor's tripod; stool, movement; (culin) saddle; **aller à la selle** to go to the toilet

seller [sɛle] *tr* to saddle

sellier [sɛlje] *m* saddler

selon [səlɔ̃] *adv*—**c'est selon** that depends; **selon que** according as ‖ *prep* according to; after (*e.g., my own heart*)

semailles [səmɑj] *fpl* sowing, seeding

semaine [səmɛn] *f* week; week's wages; set of seven; **à la petite semaine** day-to-day, hand-to-mouth; short-sighted; **de semaine** on duty during the week; **la semaine des quatre jeudis** (coll) never; **semaine anglaise** five-day workweek

semai·nier [səmenje] **-nière** [njɛr] *mf* week worker ‖ *m* highboy; office calendar

sémantique [semɑ̃tik] *adj* semantic ‖ *f* semantics

sémaphore [semafɔr] *m* semaphore

semblable [sɑ̃blabl] *adj* similar, like ‖ *m* fellow-man, equal

semblant [sɑ̃blɑ̃] *m* semblance, appearance; **faire semblant** to pretend

sembler [sɑ̃ble] *intr* to seem; to seem to

semelle [səmɛl] *f* sole; foot (*of stocking*); tread (*of tire*); bed (*of concrete*)

semence [səmɑ̃s] *f* seed; semen; brad; **semence de perles** seed pearls

semer [səme] §2 *tr* to seed, to sow; to scatter, strew; to lay (*mines*); (slang) to outdistance; (slang) to drop (*an acquaintance*)

semestre [səmɛstr] *m* semester; six-month period

semes·triel **-trielle** [səmɛstrijɛl] *adj* six-month; semester

se·meur [səmœr] **-meuse** [møz] *mf* sower; spreader of gossip ‖ *f* seeder, drill

semi-chenillé [səmiʃnije] *m* half-track

semi-conduc·teur [səmikɔ̃dyktœr] **-trice** [tris] *adj* semiconductive ‖ *m* semiconductor

semifi·ni **-nie** [səmifini] *adj* unfinished

sémil·lant [semijɑ̃] **sémil·lante** [semijɑ̃t] *adj* sprightly, lively

séminaire [seminɛr] *m* seminary; seminar; conference

semi-remorque [səmirəmɔrk] *f* (*pl* -remorques) semitrailer

semis [səmi] *m* sowing; seedling; seedbed

sémite [semit] *adj* Semitic ‖ (*cap*) *mf* Semite

sémitique [semitik] *adj* Semitic

semoir [səmwar] *m* seeder, drill

semonce [səmɔ̃s] *f* reprimand; (naut) order to heave to

semoncer [səmɔ̃se] §51 *tr* to reprimand; (naut) to order to heave to

semoule [səmul] *f* (culin) semolina

sénat [sena] *m* senate

sénateur [senatœr] *m* senator

sénile [senil] *adj* senile

sens [sɑ̃s] *m* sense, meaning; opinion; direction; **en sens inverse** in the opposite direction; **sens dessus dessous** [sɑ̃dəsydəsu] upside down; **sens devant derrière** [sɑ̃dəvɑ̃dɛrjɛr] back to front; **sens interdit** (public sign) no entry; **sens obligatoire** (public sign) right way, this way; **sens unique** (public sign) one way

sensation [sɑ̃sɑsjɔ̃] *f* sensation

sensation·nel **-nelle** [sɑ̃sɑsjɔnɛl] *adj* sensational

sen·sé **-sée** [sɑ̃se] *adj* sensible

sensibiliser [sɑ̃sibilize] *tr* to sensitize

sensibilité [sɑ̃sibilite] *f* sensibility; sensitivity

sensible [sɑ̃sibl] *adj* sensitive; sensible, appreciable, perceptible

sensi·tif [sɑ̃sitif] **-tive** [tiv] *adj* sensory; sensitive, touchy

senso·riel **-rielle** [sɑ̃sɔrjɛl] *adj* sensory

sen·suel **-suelle** [sɑ̃sɥel] *adj* sensual

sent-bon [sɑ̃bɔ̃] *m invar* odor, perfume

sentence [sɑ̃tɑ̃s] *f* proverb; (law) sentence

senteur [sɑ̃tœr] *f* odor, perfume

sentier [sɑ̃tje] *m* path; **hors des sentiers battus** off the beaten track

sentiment [sɑ̃timɑ̃] *m* sentiment, feeling

sentimen·tal **-tale** [sɑ̃timɑ̃tal] *adj* (*pl* **-taux** [to]) sentimental

sentine [sɑ̃tin] *f* bilge

sentinelle [sɑ̃tinɛl] *f* sentinel

sentir [sɑ̃tir] §41 *tr* to feel; to smell; to smell like, smell of; to taste of; to have all the earmarks of; to show the effects of; **ne pas pouvoir sentir qn** to be unable to stand s.o. ‖ *intr* to smell; to smell bad ‖ *ref* to feel; to be felt; **se sentir de** to feel the effects of

seoir [swar] §5A (3d *pl pres ind* **siéent;**

used only in 3d *sg* & *pl* of most simple tenses) *intr* (with *dat*) to be suitable to, to become; to be fitting to, to be proper for || (used only in *inf* and 2d *sg* & *pl* and 1st *pl impv*) *ref* (coll & poetic) to sit down, have a seat
séparation [separɑsjɔ̃] *f* separation
séparer [separe] *tr* & *ref* to separate, to divide
sept [sɛt] *adj* & *pron* seven; the Seventh, e.g., **Jean sept** John the Seventh; **sept heures** seven o'clock || *m* seven; seventh (*in dates*)
septembre [sɛptɑ̃br] *m* September
septième [sɛtjɛm] *adj, pron* (*masc, fem*), & *m* seventh
septique [sɛptik] *adj* septic
sépulcre [sepylkr] *m* sepulcher
sépulture [sepyltyr] *f* grave, tomb, burial place; burial
séquelle [sekɛl] *f* gang; (pathol) complications; **séquelles** aftermath
séquence [sekɑ̃s] *f* sequence; (*in poker*) straight
séquestrer [sekɛstre] *tr* to sequester
séraphin [serafɛ̃] *m* seraph; (coll) angel
serbe [sɛrb] *adj* Serb || (*cap*) *mf* Serb
se·rein [sərɛ̃] **-reine** [rɛn] *adj* serene || *m* night dew
sérénade [serenad] *f* serenade
sérénité [serenite] *f* serenity
serf [sɛr], [sɛrf] **serve** [sɛrv] *mf* serf
serge [sɛrʒ] *f* serge
sergent [sɛrʒɑ̃] *m* sergeant
série [seri] *f* series, string, set; (elec) series; **de série** standard; stock (*car*); **en série** in (a) series; mass, e.g., **fabrication en série** mass production; **hors série** outsize (*wearing apparel*); discontinued (*as an item of manufacture*); custom-built; almost unheard of; **série noire** run of bad luck
sé·rieux [serjø] **-rieuse** [rjøz] *adj* serious
serin [sərɛ̃] *m* canary; (coll) simpleton
seringa [sərɛ̃ga] *m* mock orange
seringue [sərɛ̃g] *f* syringe; (hort) spray gun; **seringue à graisse** grease gun; **seringue à injections** hypodermic syringe; **seringue à instillations** nasal spray
serment [sɛrmɑ̃] *m* oath; **prêter serment** to take oath
sermon [sɛrmɔ̃] *m* sermon
sermonner [sɛrmɔne] *tr* to sermonize
serpe [sɛrp] *f* billhook
serpent [sɛrpɑ̃] *m* snake, serpent; **serpent à sonnettes** rattlesnake; **serpent caché sous les fleurs** snake in the grass
serpenter [sɛrpɑ̃te] *intr* to wind
serpen·tin [sɛrpɑ̃tɛ̃] **-tine** [tin] *adj* serpentine || *m* coil; worm (*of still*); paper streamer
serpillière [sɛrpijɛr] *f* floorcloth; sacking, burlap
serpolet [sɛrpɔle] *m* thyme
serre [sɛr] *f* greenhouse; **serres** claws, talons
ser·ré -rée [sɛre] *adj* tight; narrow; compact; close || **serré** *adv*—**jouer serré** to play it close to the vest

serre-fils [sɛrfil] *m invar* (elec) binding post
serre-freins [sɛrfrɛ̃] *m invar* brakeman
serre-livres [sɛrlivr] *m invar* book end
serrement [sɛrmɑ̃] *m* squeezing, pressing; (min) partition (*to keep out water*); (pathol) pang; **serrement de cœur** heaviness of heart; **serrement de main** handshake
serrer [sɛre] *tr* to press; to squeeze; to wring; to tighten; to close up (*ranks*); to clasp, shake, e.g., **serrer la main à** to shake hands with; to grit (*one's teeth*); to put on (*the brakes*) || *intr*—**serrez à droite** (public sign) squeeze to right || *ref* to squeeze together, to be close together
serre-tête [sɛrtɛt] *m invar* headband; kerchief; crash helmet; (telp) headset
serrure [sɛryr] *f* lock; **serrure de sûreté** safety lock
serrurier [sɛryrje] *m* locksmith
sertir [sɛrtir] *tr* to set (*a stone*)
sérum [serɔm] *m* serum
servage [sɛrvaʒ] *m* serfdom
ser·veur [sɛrvœr] **-veuse** [vøz] *mf* (tennis) server || *m* waiter; barman || *f* waitress; barmaid; extra maid; (mach) coffee maker
serviable [sɛrvjabl] *adj* obliging
service [sɛrvis] *m* service; agency; **être de service** to be on duty; **service compris** tip included; **service de garde** twenty-four-hour service; **service des abonnés absents** telephone answering service; **service des renseignements téléphoniques** information; **service sanitaire** ambulance corps
serviette [sɛrvjɛt] *f* napkin; towel; brief case; **serviette de bain** bath towel; **serviette éponge** washcloth; Turkish towel; **serviette hygiénique** sanitary napkin
servile [sɛrvil] *adj* servile
servir [sɛrvir] §63 *tr* to serve; to deal (*cards*) || *intr* to serve; **servir à** to be useful for, to serve as; **servir à qn de** to serve s.o. as; **servir de** to serve as, to function as || *ref* to help oneself; **se servir chez** to patronize; **se servir de** to use
serviteur [sɛrvitœr] *m* servant
servitude [sɛrvityd] *f* servitude; (law) easement
servofrein [sɛrvɔfrɛ̃] *m* power brake
ses [se] §88
sésame [sezam] *m* sesame
session [sesjɔ̃] *f* session
seuil [sœj] *m* threshold
seul seule [sœl] *adj* alone; lonely || (when standing before noun) *adj* sole, single, only || *pron indef* single one, only one; single person, only person || **seul** *adv* alone
seulement [sœlmɑ̃] *adv* only, even || *conj* but
sève [sɛv] *f* sap; vim
sévère [sevɛr] *adj* severe; stern; strict
sévices [sevis] *mpl* cruelty, brutality
sévir [sevir] *intr* to rage
sevrage [səvraʒ] *m* weaning

sevrer [səvre] §2 *tr* to wean
sexe [sɛks] *m* sex; **le beau sexe** the fair sex; **le sexe fort** the sterner sex
sextant [sɛkstɑ̃] *m* sextant
sextuor [sɛkstɥɔr] *m* (mus) sextet
sexuel sexuelle [sɛksɥɛl] *adj* sexual
seyant [sɛjɑ̃] **seyante** [sɛjɑ̃t] *adj* becoming
shampooing [ʃɑ̃pwɛ̃] *m* shampoo
shérif [ʃerif] *m* sheriff
short [ʃɔrt] *m* shorts
si [si] *m invar* if; **des si et des car** ifs and buts || *adv* so; as; (to contradict a negative statement or question) yes, e.g., **Vous ne le saviez pas. Si!** You didn't know. Yes, I did!; **si bien que** so that, with the result that; **si peu que** so little that; **si peu que ce soit** however little it may be; **si** + *adj* or *adv* + **que** + *subj* however + *adj* or *adv* + *ind*, e.g., **si vite qu'il s'en aille** however fast he goes away || *conj* if; whether; **si . . . ne** unless, e.g., **si je ne me trompe** unless I am mistaken; **si ce n'est** unless; **si tant est que** if it is true that
sia·mois [sjamwa] **-moise** [mwaz] *adj* Siamese || (*cap*) *mf* Siamese
sibé·rien [siberjɛ̃] **-rienne** [rjɛn] *adj* Siberian || (*cap*) *mf* Siberian
sibylle [sibil] *f* sibyl
Sicile [sisil] *f* Sicily; **la Sicile** Sicily
sici·lien [sisiljɛ̃] **-lienne** [ljɛn] *adj* Sicilian || (*cap*) *mf* Sicilian
sidé·ral -rale [sideral] *adj* (*pl* **-raux** [ro]) sidereal
sidérer [sidere] §10 *tr* (coll) to flabbergast
sidérurgie [sideryrʒi] *f* iron and steel industry
sidérurgique [sideryrʒik] *adj* iron-and-steel
siècle [sjɛkl] *m* century; age; (eccl) world
siège [sjɛʒ] *m* seat; headquarters; (eccl) see; (mil) siege; **siège à glissière** glider; **siège baquet** (*pl* **sièges baquets**) bucket seat; **siège éjectable** ejection seat
siéger [sjeʒe] §1 *intr* to sit, to be in session; (*said of malady*) to be seated
sien [sjɛ̃] **sienne** [sjɛn] §89
sieste [sjɛst] *f* siesta; **faire la sieste** to take a siesta
sifflement [sifləmɑ̃] *m* whistle; hiss; swish, whiz
siffler [sifle] *tr* to whistle (*e.g., a tune*); to hiss, boo; to whistle to || *intr* to whistle; to hiss; to swish, to whiz
sifflet [sifle] *m* whistle
sif·fleur [siflœr] **sif·fleuse** [sifløz] *mf* whistler
sigle [sigl] *m* abbreviation; word formed by literation; acronym
si·gnal [siɲal] *m* (*pl* **-gnaux** [ɲo]) signal; sign; (telp) busy signal
signa·lé -lée [siɲale] *adj* signal, noteworthy
signalement [siɲalmɑ̃] *m* description
signaler [siɲale] *tr* to signal; to point out || *ref* to distinguish oneself
signalisation [siɲalizasjɔ̃] *f* signs
signataire [siɲatɛr] *adj & mf* signatory

signature [siɲatyr] *f* signature; signing
signe [siɲ] *m* sign; **faire signe à** to motion to, to signal; **signe de ponctuation** punctuation mark; **signe de tête** nod
signer [siɲe] *tr* to sign || *ref* to cross oneself
signet [siɲɛ], [sinɛ] *m* bookmark
significa·tif [siɲifikatif] **-tive** [tiv] *adj* significant
signifier [siɲifje] *tr* to signify; to mean
silence [silɑ̃s] *m* silence
silen·cieux [silɑ̃sjø] **-cieuse** [sjøz] *adj* silent || *m* (aut) muffler
silex [silɛks] *m* flint
silhouette [silwɛt] *f* silhouette
silhouetter [silwete] *tr* to silhouette
silicium [silisjɔm] *m* silicon
silicone [silikon] *f* silicone
sillage [sijaʒ] *m* wake
sillet [sijɛ] *m* (mus) nut
sillon [sijɔ̃] *m* furrow; groove; **sillon sonore** sound track
sillonner [sijɔne] *tr* to furrow; to groove; to cross, to streak
silo [silo] *m* silo
silure [silyr] *m* catfish
simagrée [simagre] *f* pretense
similaire [similɛr] *adj* similar
similigravure [similigravyr] *f* halftone
similitude [similityd] *f* similarity
similor [similɔr] *m* ormolu
simple [sɛ̃pl] *adj* simple; **passer en simple police** to go to police court; **simple particulier** private citizen; **simple soldat** private || *mf* simpleminded person || *m* simple (*herb*); (tennis) singles
sim·plet [sɛ̃plɛ] **-plette** [plɛt] *adj* artless
simplifier [sɛ̃plifje] *tr* to simplify
simpliste [sɛ̃plist] *adj* oversimple
simulacre [simylakr] *m* sham; **simulacre de combat** sham battle
simuler [simyle] *tr* to simulate
simulta·né -née [simyltane] *adj* simultaneous
sinapisme [sinapism] *m* mustard plaster
sincère [sɛ̃sɛr] *adj* sincere
sincérité [sɛ̃serite] *f* sincerity
sinécure [sinekyr] *f* sinecure
singe [sɛ̃ʒ] *m* monkey; (slang) boss; **grimacer comme un vieux singe** to grin like a Cheshire cat
singer [sɛ̃ʒe] §38 *tr* to ape
singerie [sɛ̃ʒri] *f* monkeyshine; grimace; monkey cage
singulariser [sɛ̃gylarize] *tr* to draw attention to || *ref* to stand out
singu·lier [sɛ̃gylje] **-lière** [ljɛr] *adj & m* singular
sinistre [sinistr] *adj* sinister || *m* disaster
sinis·tré -trée [sinistre] *adj* damaged, ruined; homeless; shipwrecked || *mf* victim
sinon [sinɔ̃] *adv* if not; perhaps even; **sinon que** except for the fact that || *prep* except for, except to || *conj* except, unless; or else, else, otherwise
si·nueux [sinɥø] **-nueuse** [nɥøz] *adj* sinuous, winding
sinus [sinys] *m* sinus; (trig) sine

sionisme [sjɔnism] *m* Zionism
siphon [sifɔ̃] *m* siphon; siphon bottle; trap (*double-curved pipe*)
siphonner [sifɔne] *tr* to siphon
sirène [siren] *f* siren; foghorn
sirop [siro] *m* syrup; **sirop pectoral** cough syrup
siroter [sirɔte] *tr & intr* (coll) to sip
sis [si] **sise** [siz] *adj* located
sismographe [sismɔgraf] *m* seismograph
~sismologie [sismɔlɔʒi] *f* seismology
site [sit] *m* site; lay of the land
sitôt [sito] *adv* immediately; **sîtot dit, sitôt fait** no sooner said than done; **sitôt que** as soon as
sittelle [sitɛl] *f* (orn) nuthatch
situation [sitɥasjɔ̃] *f* situation; **situation sans issue** deadlock, impasse
situer [sitɥe] *tr* to situate, to locate
six [si(s)] *adj & pron* six; the Sixth, e.g., **Jean six** John the Sixth; **six heures** six o'clock || *m* six; sixth (*in dates*)
sixième [sizjɛm] *adj, pron* (*masc, fem*), & *m* sixth
six-quatre-deux [siskatdø]—**à la six-quatre-deux** (coll) slapdash
sizain [sizɛ̃] *m* six-line verse; pack (*of cub scouts*)
sizerin [sizrɛ̃] *m* (orn) redpoll
ski [ski] *m* ski; skiing; **faire du ski** to go skiing; **ski nautique** water-skiing
skier [skje] *intr* to ski
skieur [skjœr] **skieuse** [skjøz] *mf* skier
slalom [slalɔm] *m* slalom
slave [slav] *adj* Slav; Slavic || *m* Slavic (*language*) || (*cap*) *mf* Slav (*person*)
slogan [slɔgã] *m* (com) slogan
slovaque [slɔvak] *adj* Slovak || *m* Slovak (*language*) || (*cap*) *mf* Slovak (*person*)
smoking [smɔkiŋ] *m* tuxedo
snack [snak] *m* snack bar
S.N.C.F. [ɛsenseef] *f* (letterword) (**Société nationale des Chemins de fer français**) French railroad
snob [snɔb] *adj invar* snobbish || *mf* (*pl* **snob** or **snobs**) snob
snober [snɔbe] *tr* to snub
snobisme [snɔbism] *m* snobbery
sobre [sɔbr] *adj* sober, moderate; simple (*ornamentation*)
sobriété [sɔbrijete] *f* sobriety; moderation (*in eating, speaking*)
sobriquet [sɔbrikɛ] *m* nickname
soc [sɔk] *m* plowshare
sociable [sɔsjabl] *adj* sociable, neighborly; social (*creature*)
so·cial -ciale [sɔsjal] *adj* (*pl* **-ciaux** [sjo]) social
sociali·sant [sɔsjalizã] **-sante** [zãt] *adj* socialistic || *mf* socialist sympathizer
socialiser [sɔsjalize] *tr* to socialize
socialisme [sɔsjalism] *m* socialism
socialiste [sɔsjalist] *adj & mf* socialist
sociétaire [sɔsjeter] *mf* stockholder; member (*e.g., of an acting company*)
société [sɔsjete] *f* society; company; firm, partnership; **société anonyme** stock company, corporation; **société de prévoyance** benefit society; **Société des Nations** League of Nations

sociologie [sɔsjɔlɔʒi] *f* sociology
socle [sɔkl] *m* pedestal; footing, socle
socque [sɔk] *m* clog, sabot; (theat) comedy
socquette [sɔkɛt] *f* anklet
Socrate [sɔkrat] *m* Socrates
soda [sɔda] *m* soda water
sodium [sɔdjɔm] *m* sodium
sœur [sœr] *f* sister; **et ta sœur!** (slang) knock it off!; **ma sœur** (eccl) sister
sofa [sɔfa] *m* sofa
soi [swa] §85, §85B; **à part soi** to oneself (himself, etc.); **de soi, en soi** in itself
soi-disant [swadizã] *adj invar* so-called, self-styled || *adv* supposedly
soie [swa] *f* silk; bristle
soierie [swari] *f* silk goods; silk factory
soif [swaf] *f* thirst; **avoir soif** to be thirsty
soi·gné -gnée [swaɲe] *adj* well-groomed, trim; polished (*speech*)
soigner [swaɲe] *tr* to nurse, take care of; to groom; to polish (*one's style*)
soigneur [swaɲœr] *m* (sports) trainer
soi·gneux [swaɲø] **-gneuse** [ɲøz] *adj* careful, meticulous
soi-même [swamɛm] §86
soin [swɛ̃] *m* care, attention; treatment; **aux bons soins de** in care of (*c/o*); **être aux petits soins auprès de** to wait on (*s.o.*) hand and foot; **premiers soins** first aid; **soins d'urgence** first aid
soir [swar] *m* evening, night; **hier soir** last night; **le soir** in the evening, at night
soirée [sware] *f* evening; evening party; **en soirée** evening (*performance*); **soirée dansante** dance
soit [swa], [swat] *conj* take for instance, e.g., **soit quatre multiplié par deux** take for instance four multiplied by two; say, e.g., **bien des hommes étaient perdus, soit un million** many men were lost, say a million; **soit . . soit either . . . or, whether . . .** or; **soit que . . . soit que** whether **. . . or** || [swat] *interj* so be it!, all right!
soixante [swasãt] *adj, pron, & m* sixty; **soixante et onze** seventy-one; **soixante et onzième** seventy-first; **soixante et un** sixty-one; **soixante et unième** sixty-first
soixante-dix [swasãtdi(s)] *adj, pron, & m* seventy
soixante-dixième [swasãtdizjɛm] *adj, pron* (*masc, fem*), & *m* seventieth
soixantième [swasãtjɛm] *adj, pron* (*masc, fem*), & *m* sixtieth
soja [sɔʒa] *m* soybean
sol [sɔl] *m* soil; ground; floor
solaire [sɔler] *adj* solar
soldat [sɔlda] *m* soldier
soldatesque [sɔldatɛsk] *adj* barrack-room (*humor; manners*) || *f* rowdies
solde [sɔld] *m* balance (*of an account*); remnant; clearance sale; **en solde** reduced (*in price*) || *f* (mil) pay
solder [sɔlde] *tr* to settle (*an account*); to sell out; (mil) to pay || *intr* to sell out

sol·deur [sɔldœr] **-deuse** [dǿz] *mf* dealer in seconds and remnants

sole [sɔl] *f* sole (*fish*); field (*used for crop rotation*)

soleil [sɔlɛj] *m* sun; sunshine, sunlight; sunflower; pinwheel; **il fait du soleil** or **il fait soleil** it is sunny

solen·nel -nelle [sɔlanɛl] *adj* solemn

solénoïde [sɔlenɔid] *m* solenoid

solfège [sɔlfɛʒ] *m* sol-fa

solidage [sɔlidaʒ] *f* goldenrod

solidaire [sɔlidɛr] *adj* interdependent; jointly binding; **solidaire de** responsible for; answerable to; integral with, in one piece with

solidariser [sɔlidarize] *ref* to join together

solidarité [sɔlidarite] *f* solidarity, interdependence

solide [sɔlid] *adj & m* solid

solidité [sɔlidite] *f* solidity; soundness; strength (*e.g., of a fabric*)

soliloque [sɔlilɔk] *m* soliloquy

soliste [sɔlist] *mf* soloist

solitaire [sɔliter] *adj* solitary; lonely || *m* solitary, anchorite; old wild boar; solitaire

solitude [sɔlityd] *f* solitude

solive [sɔliv] *f* joist

soli·veau [sɔlivo] *m* (*pl* **-veaux**) small joist; (coll) nobody

solliciter [sɔllisite] *tr* to solicit; to apply for; to incite; to attract (*attention; iron*); to induce || *intr* to seek favors

sollici·teur [sɔllisitœr] **-teuse** [tǿz] *mf* solicitor, office seeker, petitioner, lobbyist

solo [sɔlo] *adj invar & m* solo

solstice [sɔlstis] *m* solstice

soluble [sɔlybl] *adj* soluble; solvable

solution [sɔlysjɔ̃] *f* solution

solutionner [sɔlysjɔne] *tr* to solve

solvabilité [sɔlvabilite] *f* solvency

solvable [sɔlvabl] *adj* solvent

solvant [sɔlvɑ̃] *m* solvent

sombre [sɔ̃br] *adj* somber; sullen

sombrer [sɔ̃bre] *intr* to sink; to vanish (*as a fortune*)

sommaire [sɔmer] *adj & m* summary

sommation [sɔmasjɔ̃] *f* summons; (law) summons; sentry challenge; **faire les trois sommations** to read the riot act

somme [sɔm] *m* nap || *f* sum; **en somme, somme toute** in short, when all is said and done

sommeil [sɔmɛj] *m* sleep; **avoir sommeil** to be sleepy

sommeiller [sɔmeje] *intr* to doze; to lie dormant

sommelier [sɔmǝlje] *m* wine steward

sommer [sɔme] *tr* to add up; to summon, to issue a legal writ to

sommet [sɔmɛ] *m* summit, top; apex (*of a triangle*); vertex (*of an angle*); (fig) acme

sommier [sɔmje] *m* bedspring; ledger; crossbeam; (archaic) pack animal; **sommier élastique** spring mattress

sommité [sɔmite] *f* pinnacle, crest; leader, authority

somnambule [sɔmnɑ̃byl] *adj* sleepwalking || *mf* sleepwalker

somnifère [sɔmnifer] *adj & m* soporific

somnolence [sɔmnɔlɑ̃s] *f* drowsiness; indolence, laziness

somno·lent [sɔmnɔlɑ̃] **-lente** [lɑ̃t] *adj* somnolent, drowsy; indolent

somnoler [sɔmnɔle] *intr* to doze

somptuaire [sɔ̃ptɥer] *adj* luxury (*tax*)

somp·tueux [sɔ̃ptɥø] **-tueuse** [tɥǿz] *adj* sumptuous

son [sɔ̃] *adj poss* §88 || *m* sound; bran

sonate [sɔnat] *f* sonata

sondage [sɔ̃daʒ] *m* sounding, probing; **sondage de l'opinion** public-opinion poll; **sondage d'exploration** wildcat (*well*)

sonde [sɔ̃d] *f* lead, probe; borer, drill

sonder [sɔ̃de] *tr* to sound, probe, bore, fathom; to explore, reconnoiter; to poll (*e.g., public opinion*); to sound out (*s.o.*)

son·deur [sɔ̃dœr] **-deuse** [dǿz] *mf* prober, sounder

songe [sɔ̃ʒ] *m* dream

songe-creux [sɔ̃ʒkrǿ] *m invar* visionary, pipe dreamer

songer [sɔ̃ʒe] §38 *tr* to dream up || *intr* to dream; to think; to intend to; **songer à** to think of; to imagine, to dream of; **songez-y!** think it over!

songerie [sɔ̃ʒri] *f* reverie, daydreaming

son·geur [sɔ̃ʒœr] **-geuse** [ʒǿz] *adj* dreamy, preoccupied || *mf* daydreamer

sonique [sɔnik] *adj* sonic, of sound

sonnaille [sɔnaj] *f* cowbell, sheepbell

sonnailler [sɔnaje] *m* bellwether || *intr* to ring often and without cause

son·nant [sɔnɑ̃] **sonnante** [sɔnɑ̃t] *adj* striking (*clock*); metal (*money*); at the stroke of, e.g., **à huit heures sonnantes** at the stroke of eight

son·né -née [sɔne] *adj* past, e.g., **deux heures sonnées** past two o'clock; over, e.g., **il a soixante ans sonnés** he is over sixty; (slang) cuckoo, nuts; (slang) stunned

sonner [sɔne] *tr* to ring; to ring for; to sound || *intr* to ring; to strike; to sound

sonnerie [sɔnri] *f* chimes, chiming; set of bells, carillon; fanfare; ring (*of a telephone, doorbell, etc.*); alarm or striking mechanism (*of clock*)

sonnet [sɔne] *m* sonnet

sonnette [sɔnɛt] *f* doorbell; pile driver

sonneur [sɔnœr] *m* bellringer; trumpeter

sonore [sɔnɔr] *adj* sonorous; sound (*wave, track*); echoing (*hall, cathedral, etc.*); (phonet) voiced || *f* voiced consonant

sonoriser [sɔnɔrize] *tr* to record sound effects on (*a film*); to equip (*an auditorium*) with loudspeakers

sonorité [sɔnɔrite] *f* sonority, resonance

sonotone [sɔnɔtɔn] *m* hearing aid

sophistication [sɔfistikɑsjɔ̃] *f* adulteration

sophisti·qué -quée [sɔfistike] *adj* adulterated; artificial, counterfeit

sophistiquer [sɔfistike] *tr* to adulterate; to subtilize

Sophocle [sɔfɔkl] *m* Sophocles

sopraniste [sɔpranist] *m* male soprano
sopra·no [sɔprano] *mf* (*pl* **-ni** [ni]) or
-nos) soprano ‖ *m* soprano (*voice*)
sorbet [sɔrbɛ] *m* sherbet
sorbetière [sɔrbətjer] *f* ice-cream
freezer
sorbon·nard [sɔrbɔnar] **sorbon·narde**
[sɔrbɔnard] *mf* (coll) Sorbonne student; (coll) Sorbonne professor
sorcellerie [sɔrsɛlri] *f* sorcery
sor·cier [sɔrsje] **-cière** [sjer] *adj* sorcerer's; **cela n'est pas sorcier** there's
no trick to that ‖ *m* sorcerer, wizard
‖ *f* sorceress, witch; **vieille sorcière**
old hag
sordide [sɔrdid] *adj* sordid
sornette [sɔrnɛt] *f* nonsense
sort [sɔr] *m* fate, destiny; fortune, lot;
spell, charm
sortable [sɔrtabl] *adj* suitable, acceptable; presentable
sor·tant [sɔrtã] **-tante** [tãt] *adj* retiring
(*congressman*); winning (*number*) ‖
mf person leaving
sorte [sɔrt] *f* sort, kind; state, condition; way, manner; **de la sorte** this
way, thus; **de sorte que** so that, with
the result that; **en quelque sorte** in
a certain way; **en sorte que** in such
a way that
sortie [sɔrti] *f* exit, way out; outing,
jaunt; quitting time; outburst, tirade;
(mil) sortie; **sortie de bain** bathrobe; **sortie de bal** evening wrap;
sortie de secours emergency exit;
sortie de voiture(s) driveway
sortilège [sɔrtilɛʒ] *m* spell, charm
sortir [sɔrtir] §64 *tr* to take out, to
bring out; to publish ‖ *intr* (*aux*:
ÊTRE) to go out, to come out; to
come forth; to stand out; **au sortir de**
on coming out of; **sortir de** + *inf*
(coll) to have just + *pp*
S.O.S. [ɛsoɛs] *m* (letterword) S.O.S.
sosie [sozi] *m* double
sot [so] **sotte** [sɔt] *adj* stupid, silly ‖
mf fool, simpleton
sottise [sɔtiz] *f* stupidity, silliness,
foolishness
sou [su] *m* sou; (fig) penny, farthing;
sans le sou penniless; **sou à sou** or
sou par sou a penny at a time
soubassement [subɑsmã] *m* subfoundation, infrastructure
soubresaut [subrəso] *m* sudden start,
jerk; palpitation, jump (*of the heart*)
soubrette [subrɛt] *f* (theat) soubrette;
(coll) attractive chambermaid
souche [suʃ] *f* stump; stock; stack (*of
fireplace*); strain (*of virus*); (coll)
dolt
souci [susi] *m* care; marigold; **sans
souci** carefree
soucier [susje] *ref* to care, concern
oneself
soucieusement [susjøzmã] *adv* uneasily, anxiously; with concern
sou·cieux [susjø] **-cieuse** [sjøz] *adj*
solicitous, concerned; uneasy, anxious
soucoupe [sukup] *f* saucer; **soucoupe
volante** flying saucer
soudage [sudaʒ] *m* soldering; welding

sou·dain [sudɛ̃] **-daine** [dɛn] *adj* sudden ‖ **soudain** *adv* suddenly
soudainement [sudɛnmɑ̃] *adv* suddenly
soudaineté [sudɛnte] *f* suddenness
souda·nais [sudane] **-naise** [nez] *adj*
Sudanic ‖ *m* Sudanic (*language*) ‖
(*cap*) *mf* Sudanese (*person*)
soude [sud] *f* (chem) soda
souder [sude] *tr* to solder; to weld ‖
ref to knit (*as bones do*)
soudeur [sudœr] *m* welder
soudoyer [sudwaje] §47 *tr* to bribe; to
hire (*assassins*)
soudure [sudyr] *f* solder; soldering;
soldered joint; knitting (*of bones*);
faire la soudure to bridge the gap;
soudure autogène welding
soue [su] *f* pigsty
soufflage [suflaʒ] *m* blowing; glass
blowing
souffle [sufl] *m* breath; breathing
souf·flé -flée [sufle] *adj* puffed up ‖
m soufflé
souffler [sufle] *tr* to blow; to blow out
(*a candle*); to blow up (*a balloon*);
to prompt (*an actor*); to huff (*a
checker*); to suggest (*an idea*); **ne pas
souffler mot** to not breathe a word;
souffler à l'oreille to whisper; **souffler q.ch. à qn** to take s.th. from s.o.
‖ *intr* to blow; to pant, puff; to take
a breather, to catch one's breath
soufflerie [sufləri] *f* bellows; wind tunnel
soufflet [suflɛ] *m* slap in the face; affront, insult; bellows; gore (*of dress*);
(rr) flexible cover (*between two cars*)
souffleter [suflǝte] §34 *tr* to slap in the
face; to affront
souf·fleur [suflœr] **souf·fleuse** [sufløz]
mf (theat) prompter ‖ *m* glass blower
‖ *f* (mach) blower
soufflure [suflyr] *f* blister, bubble
souffrance [sufrãs] *f* suffering; **en souffrance** unfinished (*business*); outstanding (*bill*); unclaimed (*parcel*);
at a standstill, suspended
souf·frant [sufrã] **souf·frante** [sufrãt]
adj suffering; sick, ailing
souffre-douleur [sufrədulœr] *m invar*
butt (*of a joke*), laughingstock
souffre·teux [sufrətø] **-teuse** [tøz] *adj*
sickly; destitute, half-starved
souffrir [sufrir] §65 *tr* to suffer; to
stand, bear, tolerate; to permit ‖ *intr*
to suffer ‖ *ref* to put up with each
other
soufre [sufr] *m* sulfur
soufrer [sufre] *tr* to sulfurate
souhait [swɛ] *m* wish; **à souhait** to
one's liking, to perfection; **à vos
souhaits!** (salutation) gesundheit!;
souhaits good wishes; **souhaits de
bonne année** New Year's greetings
souhaitable [swɛtabl] *adj* desirable
souhaiter [swɛte] *tr* to wish; to wish
for; to wish to; **je vous la souhaite
bonne et heureuse** I wish you a happy
New Year
souille [suj] *f* wallow
souiller [suje] *tr* to dirty, spot, stain,
soil, sully
souillon [sujɔ̃] *f* (coll) scullery maid

souillure [sujyr] *f* spot, stain
soûl [su] **soûle** [sul] *adj* drunk; sottish ‖ *m* fill, e.g., **manger son soûl** to eat one's fill
soulagement [sulaʒmɑ̃] *m* relief; comfort
soulager [sulaʒe] §38 *tr* to relieve; to comfort
soûler [sule] *tr* (slang) to cram down one's throat; (slang) to get (*s.o.*) drunk ‖ *ref* (fig) to have one's fill; (slang) to get drunk
soulèvement [sulɛvmɑ̃] *m* upheaval; uprising; surge; **soulèvement de cœur** nausea
soulever [sulve] §2 *tr* to raise, heave, lift (up); to stir up ‖ *ref* to rise; to raise oneself; to revolt
soulier [sulje] *m* shoe
soulignement [sulipəmɑ̃] *m* underlining
souligner [sulipe] *tr* to underline; to emphasize
soulte [sult] *f* balance due
soumettre [sumɛtr] §42 *tr* to submit; to subject; to overcome, subdue ‖ *ref* to submit, surrender
sou·mis [sumi] **-mise** [miz] *adj* submissive, subservient; subject; amenable (*to a law*)
soumission [sumisjɔ̃] *f* submission, surrender; bid (*to perform a service*); guarantee
soumissionnaire [sumisjɔnɛr] *mf* bidder
soupape [supap] *f* valve; **soupape à réglage** or **à papillon** damper; **soupape de sûreté** safety valve; **soupape électrique** rectifier
soupçon [supsɔ̃] *m* suspicion; misgiving; dash, touch (*small amount*)
soupçonner [supsɔne] *tr & intr* to suspect
soupçon·neux [supsɔnø] **soupçon·neuse** [supsɔnøz] *adj* suspicious
soupe [sup] *f* vegetable soup; sop (*bread*); (mil) mess; **de soupe** on K.P.; **soupe au lait** (coll) meantempered person; **soupe populaire** soup kitchen; **trempé comme une soupe** soaking wet
soupente [supɑ̃t] *f* attic
souper [supe] *m* supper ‖ *intr* to have supper
soupeser [supəze] §2 *tr* to heft, to weigh (*e.g., a package*) in one's hand
soupière [supjɛr] *f* soup tureen
soupir [supir] *m* sigh; breath; (mus) quarter rest
soupi·rail [supiraj] *m* (*pl* **-raux** [ro]) cellar window
soupirant [supirɑ̃] *m* suitor
soupirer [supire] *intr* to sigh; **soupirer après** or **pour** to long for
souple [supl] *adj* supple; flexible, pliant; versatile, adaptable
souplesse [suplɛs] *f* suppleness, flexibility
souquer [suke] *tr* to haul taut ‖ *intr* to pull hard (*on the oars*)
source [surs] *f* source; spring, fountain; **source de pétrole** oil well; **source jaillissante** gusher
sourcier [sursje] *m* dowser
sourcil [surci] *m* eyebrow

sourciller [sursije] *intr* to knit one's brows; **sans sourciller** without batting an eye
sourcil·leux [sursijø] **sourcil·leuse** [sursijøz] *adj* supercilious
sourd [sur] **sourde** [surd] *adj* deaf; quiet; dull (*sound, color*); deep (*voice*); undeclared (*war*); (phonet) unvoiced; **sourd comme un pot** (coll) stone-deaf ‖ *mf* deaf person ‖ *f* unvoiced consonant
sourdement [surdəmɑ̃] *adv* secretly; heavily; dully
sourdine [surdin] *f* (mus) mute; **à la sourdine** muted; **en sourdine** on the sly
sourd-muet [surmɥe] **sourde-muette** [surdəmɥɛt] (*pl* **sourds-muets**) *adj* deaf and dumb, deaf-mute ‖ *mf* deaf-mute
sourdre [surdr] (used in: *inf*; 3d *sg & pl pres ind* **sourd, sourdent**) *intr* to spring, well up
souricier [surisje] *m* mouser
souricière [surisjɛr] *f* mousetrap; (fig) trap
sourire [surir] *m* smile ‖ §61 *intr* to smile; **sourire à** to smile at; to smile on; to look good to
souris [suri] *m* (obs) smile ‖ *f* mouse
sour·nois [surnwa] **-noise** [nwaz] *adj* sly, cunning, artful
sous [su] *prep* under; on (*a certain day; certain conditions*); **sous caoutchouc** rubber-covered; **sous clef** under lock and key; **sous la main** at hand; **sous les drapeaux** in the army; **sous main** underhandedly; **sous peu** shortly; **sous un certain angle** from a certain point of view
sous-alimentation [suzalimɑ̃tasjɔ̃] *f* undernourishment
sous-bois [subwa] *m* underbrush, undergrowth
sous-chef [suʃɛf] *m* (*pl* **-chefs**) assistant (*to the head man*), deputy, second-in-command
souscripteur [suskriptœr] *m* subscriber (*to a loan or charity*); signer (*of a commercial paper*)
souscription [suskripsjɔ̃] *f* signature; subscription; **souscription de soutien** sustaining membership
souscrire [suskrir] §25 *tr & intr* to subscribe
sous-cuta·né -née [sukytane] *adj* subcutaneous
sous-dévelop·pé -pée [sudɛvlɔpe] *adj* underdeveloped
sous-diacre [sudjakr] *m* subdeacon
sous-direc·teur [sudirɛktœr] **-trice** [tris] *mf* (*pl* **-directeurs**) second-in-command
sous-entendre [suzɑ̃tɑ̃dr] *tr* to understand (*what is not expressed*); to imply
sous-entendu [suzɑ̃tɑ̃dy] *m* inference, implication, innuendo, double meaning, double entendre
sous-entente [suzɑ̃tɑ̃t] *f* mental reservation; hidden, cryptic meaning

sous-entrepreneur [suzɑ̃trəprənœr] *m* (*pl* **-entrepreneurs**) subcontractor
sous-estimer [suzɛstime] *tr* to underestimate
sous-fifre [sufifr] *m* (*pl* **-fifres**) (coll) underling
sous-garde [sugard] *f* trigger guard
sous-lieutenant [suljøtnɑ̃] *m* (*pl* **-lieutenants**) second lieutenant
sous-location [sulɔkasjɔ̃] *f* sublease
sous-louer [sulwe] *tr* to sublet, sublease
sous-main [sumɛ̃] *m invar* desk blotter; **en sous-main** underhandedly
sous-marin [sumarɛ̃] **-marine** [marin] *adj & m* (*pl* **-marins**) submarine
sous-marinier [sumarinje] *m* (*pl* **-mariniers**) submarine crewman
sous-mentonnière [sumɑ̃tɔnjər] *f* (*pl* **-mentonnières**) chin strap
sous-nappe [sunap] *f* (*pl* **-nappes**) table pad
sous-off [suzɔf] *m* (*pl* **-offs**) noncom
sous-officier [suzɔfisje] *m* (*pl* **-officiers**) noncommissioned officer
sous-ordre [suzɔrdr] *m* (*pl* **-ordres**) underling, subordinate; (biol) suborder; **en sous-ordre** subordinate; subordinately
sous-production [suprɔdyksjɔ̃] *f* underproduction
sous-produit [suprɔdɥi] *m* (*pl* **-produits**) by-product
sous-secrétaire [suskretɛr] *m* (*pl* **-secrétaires**) undersecretary
sous-secrétariat [suskretarja] *m* undersecretaryship
sous-seing [susɛ̃] *m invar* privately witnessed document
soussi·gné -gnée [susiɲe] *adj & mf* undersigned
sous-sol [susɔl] *m* (*pl* **-sols**) subsoil; basement
sous-titre [sutitr] *m* (*pl* **-titres**) subtitle
sous-titrer [sutitre] *tr* to subtitle
soustraction [sustraksjɔ̃] *f* subtraction; (law) purloining
soustraire [sustrer] §68 *tr* to remove; take away; to subtract; to deduct; **soustraire de** to subtract from; **soustraire q.ch. à qn** to take s.th. away from s.o.; to steal s.th. from s.o. || *ref* to withdraw; **se soustraire à** to escape from
sous-traitant [sutretɑ̃] *m* (*pl* **-traitants**) subcontractor; sublessee
sous-traité [sutrete] *m* (*pl* **-traités**) subcontract
sous-traiter [sutrete] *tr & intr* to subcontract
sous-ventrière [suvɑ̃trijer] *f* (*pl* **-ventrières**) girth
sous-verre [suver] *m invar* passe-partout; coaster
sous-vêtement [suvɛtmɑ̃] *m* (*pl* **-vêtements**) undergarment
soutache [sutaʃ] *f* braid
soutacher [sutaʃe] *tr* to trim with braid
soutane [sutan] *f* soutane, cassock
soutanelle [sutanɛl] *f* frock coat; choir robe

soute [sut] *f* (naut) storeroom; **soute à charbon** coal bunker
soutenable [sutnabl] *adj* supportable, tenable
soutenance [sutnɑ̃s] *f* defense (*of an academic thesis*)
soutènement [sutɛnmɑ̃] *m* support
souteneur [sutnœr] *m* pimp
soutenir [sutnir] §72 *tr* to support, bear; to sustain; to insist, claim; to defend (*a thesis*) || *ref* to stand up; to keep afloat
soute·nu -nue [sutny] *adj* sustained; elevated (*style*); steady (*market*); true (*colors*)
souter·rain [suterɛ̃] **souter·raine** [suterɛn] *adj* subterranean, underground; underhanded || *m* tunnel, subway (*for pedestrians*)
soutien [sutjɛ̃] *m* support; stand-by
soutien-gorge [sutjɛ̃gɔrʒ] *m* (*pl* **soutiens-gorge**) brassiere
soutirage [sutiraʒ] *m* racking
soutirer [sutire] *tr* to rack (*wine*); **soutirer q.ch. à qn** to get s.th. out of s.o., to sponge on s.o. for s.th.
souvenir [suvnir] *m* memory, remembrance; souvenir || §72 *intr*—**faire souvenir qn de q.ch.** to remind s.o. of s.th. || *ref* to remember; **se souvenir de** to remember
souvent [suvɑ̃] *adv* often
souve·rain [suvrɛ̃] **-raine** [rɛn] *adj & mf* sovereign || *m* sovereign (*coin*)
souveraineté [suvrɛnte] *f* sovereignty
soviet [sɔvjɛt] *m* soviet
soviétique [sɔvjetik] *adj* Soviet || (*cap*) *mf* Soviet Russian
soya [sɔja] *m* soybean
soyeux [swajø] **soyeuse** [swajøz] *adj* silky
S.P. *abbr* (**sapeurs-pompiers**) fire department
spa·cieux [spasjø] **-cieuse** [sjøz] *adj* spacious, roomy
spadassin [spadasɛ̃] *m* hatchet man, hired thug
spaghetti [spagetti] *mpl* spaghetti
sparadrap [sparadra] *m* adhesive tape
spartiate [sparsjat] *adj* Spartan || (*cap*) *mf* Spartan
spasme [spasm] *m* spasm
spasmodique [spasmɔdik] *adj* spasmodic; (pathol) spastic
spath [spat] *m* (mineral) spar
spa·tial -tiale [spasjal] *adj* (*pl* **-tiaux** [sjo]) spatial
spatule [spatyl] *f* spatula; (orn) spoonbill
spea·ker [spikœr] **-kerine** [krin] *mf* (rad, telv) announcer || *m* speaker (*presiding officer*)
spé·cial -ciale [spesjal] *adj* (*pl* **-ciaux** [sjo]) special
spécialiser [spesjalize] *tr & ref* to specialize
spécialiste [spesjalist] *mf* specialist; expert
spécialité [spesjalite] *f* specialty; specialization; patent medicine
spé·cieux [spesjø] **-cieuse** [sjøz] *adj* specious
spécifier [spesifje] *tr* to specify

spécifique [spesifik] adj & m specific
spécimen [spesimɛn] adj & m specimen
spectacle [spɛktakl] m spectacle, sight; show; play; à grand spectacle spectacular (production)
specta·teur [spɛktatœr] -trice [tris] mf spectator
spectre [spɛktr] m ghost; spectrum; (fig) specter
spécula·teur [spekylatœr] -trice [tris] mf speculator
spéculer [spekyle] tr to speculate
spéléologie [speleɔlɔʒi] f speleology
sperme [spɛrm] m sperm
sphère [sfɛr] f sphere
sphérique [sferik] adj spherical
sphinx [sfɛ̃ks] m sphinx
spider [spidɛr] m (aut) rumble seat
spi·nal -nale [spinal] adj (pl -naux [no]) spinal
spi·ral -rale [spiral] (pl -raux [ro]) adj spiral || m hairspring (of watch) || f spiral; en spirale spiral
spire [spir] f turn (in a wire); whorl (of a shell)
spirée [spire] f (bot) spirea
spirite [spirit] adj & mf spiritualist
spiri·tuel -tuelle [spiritɥel] adj spiritual; sacred (music); witty || m ecclesiastical power
spiri·tueux [spiritɥø] -tueuse [tɥøz] adj spirituous || m spirituous liquor
spleen [splin] m boredom, melancholy
splendeur [splɑ̃dœr] f splendor
splendide [splɑ̃did] adj splendid; bright, brilliant
spolia·teur [spɔljatœr] -trice [tris] adj despoiling || mf despoiler
spolier [spɔlje] tr to despoil
spon·gieux [spɔ̃ʒjø] -gieuse [ʒjøz] adj spongy
sponta·né -née [spɔ̃tane] adj spontaneous
sporadique [spɔradik] adj sporadic(al)
sport [spɔr] adj invar sport, sporting; sportsmanlike || m sport
spor·tif [spɔrtif] -tive [tiv] adj sport, sporting || mf athlete, player || m sportsman
spot [spɔt] m spotlight; (radar) blip
spoutnik [sputnik] m sputnik
spu·meux [spymø] -meuse [møz] adj frothy, foamy
squale [skwal] m (ichth) dogfish
squelette [skəlɛt] m skeleton
squelettique [skəletik] adj skeletal
S.R. abbr (Service de renseignements) information desk or bureau
stabiliser [stabilize] tr to stabilize
stabilité [stabilite] f stability
stable [stabl] adj stable
stade [stad] m stadium; (fig) stage (of development)
stage [staʒ] m probationary period, apprenticeship
stagiaire [staʒjɛr] adj & mf apprentice
stag·nant [stagnɑ̃] -nante [nɑ̃t] adj stagnant
stalle [stal] f stall
stance [stɑ̃s] f stanza
stand [stɑ̃d] m stands; shooting gallery; pit (for motor racing)

standard [stɑ̃dar] adj invar standard || m standard; switchboard
standardiser [stɑ̃dardize] tr to standardize
standardiste [stɑ̃dardist] mf switchboard operator, telephone operator
standing [stɑ̃diŋ] m status, standing; standard of living; de grand standing luxury (apartments)
star [star] f (mov, theat) star
starter [starter], [startœr] m (aut) choke; (sports) starter
station [stasjɔ̃] f station; resort; (rr) flag station; station d'écoute monitoring station; station d'émission broadcasting station; station de repérage tracking station; station de taxis taxi stand; station orbitale space station
stationnaire [stasjɔnɛr] adj stationary || m gunboat
stationnement [stasjɔnmɑ̃] m parking; stationnement interdit (public sign) no parking
stationner [stasjɔne] intr to stop; to park
station-service [stasjɔ̃sɛrvis] f (pl stations-service) service station
statique [statik] adj static
statisti·cien [statistisjɛ̃] -cienne [sjɛn] mf statistician
statistique [statistik] adj statistical || f statistics
statuaire [statɥɛr] adj statuary || mf sculptor || f statuary
statue [staty] f statue
statuer [statɥe] tr to hand down (a ruling) || intr to hand down a ruling
statu quo [statykwo], [statuko] m status quo
stature [statyr] f stature
statut [staty] m statute; legal status
statutaire [statytɛr] adj statutory
Ste abbr (Sainte) St. (female saint)
Sté abbr (Société) Inc.
sténo [steno] f stenographer; stenography
sténodactylo [stenɔdaktilo] f shorthand typist; shorthand typing
sténogramme [stenɔgram] m shorthand notes
sténographe [stenɔgraf] mf stenographer
sténographie [stenɔgrafi] f stenography
sténographier [stenɔgrafje] tr to take down in shorthand
stéréo [stereo] adj invar stereo || f—en stéréo (electron) in stereo
stéréophonie [stereɔfɔni] f stereophonic sound system; en stéréophonie stereophonic (e.g., broadcast)
stéréoscopique [stereɔskɔpik] adj stereo, stereoscopic
stéréoty·pé -pée [stereɔtipe] adj stereotyped
stérile [steril] adj sterile
stériliser [sterilize] tr to sterilize
stérilité [sterilite] f sterility
sterling [stɛrliŋ] adj invar sterling
stéthoscope [stetɔskɔp] m stethoscope
stick [stik] m walking stick
stigmate [stigmat] m stigma
stigmatiser [stigmatize] tr to stigmatize

stimu·lant [stimylã] -lante [lãt] adj &
 m stimulant
stimuler [stimyle] tr to stimulate
stimu·lus [stimylys] m (pl -li [li])
 (physiol) stimulus
stipendier [stipãdje] tr to hire (e.g., an
 assassin); to bribe
stipuler [stipyle] tr to stipulate
stock [stɔk] m goods, stock; hoard
stocker [stɔke] tr & intr to stockpile
stockiste [stɔkist] m authorized dealer
 (carrying parts, motors, etc.)
stoï·cien [stɔisjẽ] -cienne [sjɛn] adj &
 mf Stoic
stoïque [stɔik] adj stoical || mf stoic
stop [stɔp] m stop; stoplight; du stop
 (coll) hitchhiking || interj stop!
stoppage [stɔpaʒ] m reweaving, invisible mending
stopper [stɔpe] tr to reweave; to stop ||
 intr to stop
store [stɔr] m blind; window awning;
 outside window shade
strabique [strabik] adj squint-eyed
strabisme [strabism] m squint
strapontin [strapɔ̃tẽ] m jump seat;
 (theat) attached folding seat
strass [stras] m paste (jewelry)
stratagème [strataʒɛm] m stratagem
strate [strat] f (geol) stratum
stratège [strateʒ] m strategist
stratégie [strateʒi] f strategy
stratégique [strateʒik] adj strategic(al)
stratégiste [strateʒist] m strategist
stratifier [stratifje] tr & ref to stratify
stratosphère [stratɔsfɛr] f stratosphere
strict stricte [strikt] adj strict
stri·dent [stridã] -dente [dãt] adj strident
strie [stri] f streak; stripe
strier [strije] tr to streak; to score,
 groove
strontium [strɔ̃sjɔm] m strontium
strophe [strɔf] f verse, stanza; strophe
structu·ral -rale [stryktyral] adj (pl
 -raux [ro]) structural
structure [stryktyr] f structure
strychnine [striknin] f strychnine
stuc [styk] m stucco; enduire de stuc
 to stucco
stu·dieux [stydjø] -dieuse [djøz] adj
 studious
studio [stydjo] m studio
stupé·fait [stypefɛ] -faite [fɛt] adj
 dumfounded, amazed
stupé·fiant [stypefjã] -fiante [fjãt] adj
 astounding || m drug, narcotic
stupéfier [stypefje] tr to astound; to
 stupefy (as with a drug)
stupeur [stypœr] f stupor; amazement
stupide [stypid] adj stupid
stupidité [stypidite] f stupidity
stuquer [styke] tr to stucco
style [stil] m style; stylus
styler [stile] tr to train
stylet [stilɛ] m stiletto
styliser [stilize] tr to stylize
stylo [stilo] m pen, fountain pen; stylo
 à bille ball-point pen
styptique [stiptik] adj & m styptic
suaire [sɥɛr] m shroud, winding sheet

suave [sɥav] adj sweet (perfume, music, etc.); bland (food); suave
subcons·cient [sypkɔ̃sjã] subcons·ciente
 [sypkɔ̃sjãt] adj & m subconscious
subdiviser [sybdivize] tr to subdivide
subir [sybir] tr to submit to; to undergo; to feel, experience; to take (an
 exam); to serve (a sentence)
su·bit [sybi] -bite [bit] adj sudden
subjec·tif [sybʒɛktif] -tive [tiv] adj
 subjective
subjonc·tif [sybʒɔ̃ktif] -tive [tiv] adj
 & m subjunctive
subjuguer [sybʒyge] tr to dominate; to
 spellbind
sublime [syblim] adj sublime
sublimer [syblime] tr to sublimate
submerger [sybmɛrʒe] §38 tr to sub-
 merge
submersible [sybmɛrsibl] adj & m submersible
submersion [sybmɛrsjɔ̃] f submersion
subodorer [sybɔdɔre] tr to scent
 (game); (fig) to scent (a plot)
subordon·né -née [sybɔrdɔne] adj & mf
 subordinate
subordonner [sybɔrdɔne] tr to subordinate
suborner [sybɔrne] tr to bribe
subrécargue [sybrekarg] m supercargo
subreptice [sybrɛptis] adj surreptitious
subsé·quent [sypsekã] -quente [kãt]
 adj subsequent
subside [sypsid], [sybzid] m subsidy
subsidiaire [sypsidjɛr] adj subsidiary
subsistance [sybzistãs], [sypsistãs] f
 subsistence; (mil) rations
subsister [sybziste], [sypsiste] intr to
 subsist
substance [sypstãs] f substance; en
 substance briefly
substan·tiel -tielle [sypstãsjɛl] adj substantial
substan·tif [sypstãtif] -tive [tiv] adj &
 m substantive
substituer [sypstitɥe] tr—substituer qn
 or q.ch. à to substitute s.o. or s.th.
 for, e.g., une biche fut substituée à
 Iphigénie a hind was substituted for
 Iphigenia || ref—se substituer à to
 take the place of
substitut [sypstity] m substitute
substitution [sypstitysjɔ̃] f substitution
substrat [sypstra] m substratum
subterfuge [sypterfyʒ] m subterfuge
sub·til -tile [syptil] adj subtle; fine
 (powder, dust, etc.); quick (poison);
 delicate (scent); clever (crook)
subtiliser [syptilize] tr to pick (a purse)
 || intr to split hairs
subtilité [syptilite] f subtlety
subur·bain [sybyrbẽ] -baine [bɛn] adj
 suburban
subvenir [sybvənir] §72 intr (with dat)
 to supply, provide, satisfy
subvention [sybvãsjɔ̃] f subsidy, subvention
subventionner [sybvãsjɔne] tr to subsidize
subver·sif [sybvɛrsif] -sive [siv] adj
 subversive
subvertir [sybvɛrtir] tr to subvert

suc [syk] *m* juice; sap; (fig) essence
succéda·né -née [syksedane] *adj & m* substitute
succéder [syksede] §10 *intr* to happen; (with *dat*) to succeed, follow; **suc-céder à** to succeed to (*the throne, a fortune*) || *ref* to follow one after the other, to follow one another
succès [syksε] *m* success; outcome; **avoir du succès** to be a success
succes·sif [syksεsif] **succes·sive** [syksεsiv] *adj* successive
succession [syksεsjɔ̃] *f* succession; in-heritance; heirs
suc·cinct [syksε̃] **-cincte** [sε̃t] *adj* suc-cinct; scanty; meager
succion [syksjɔ̃] *f* suction
succomber [sykɔ̃be] *intr* to succumb
succursale [sykyrsal] *f* branch
sucer [syse] §51 *tr* to suck
sucette [sysεt] *f* pacifier; lollipop, sucker
su·ceur [sysœr] **-ceuse** [søz] *adj* suck-ing || *m* nozzle
suçoter [sysɔte] *tr* to suck away at
sucre [sykr] *m* sugar; **sucre brut** brown sugar; **sucre candi** rock candy; **sucre de canne** cane sugar; **sucre glace** con-fectioners' sugar
su·cré -crée [sykre] *adj* sugary; with sugar, e.g., **du café sucré** coffee with sugar || *f*—**faire la sucrée** to be mealy-mouthed
sucrer [sykre] *tr* to sugar; (slang) to take away, to cut out || *ref* (slang) to grab the lion's share
sucrerie [sykrəri] *f* sugar refinery; **su-creries** candy
su·crier [sykrije] **-crière** [krijεr] *adj* sugar || *m* sugar bowl
sud [syd] *adj invar & m* south
sud-améri·cain [sydamerikε̃] **-caine** [kεn] *adj* South American || (*cap*) *mf* (*pl* **Sud-Américains**) South Ameri-can
sudation [sydɑsjɔ̃] *f* sweating
sud-est [sydεst] *adj invar & m* south-east
sudiste [sydist] *mf* Southerner (*in U.S.A.*)
sud-ouest [sydwεst] *adj invar & m* southwest
sud-vietna·mien [sydvjεtnamjε̃] **-mien-ne** [mjεn] *adj* South Vietnamese || (*cap*) *mf* (*pl* **Sud-Vietnamiens**) South Vietnamese
suède [sɥεd] *m* suede || (*cap*) *f* Swe-den; **la Suède** Sweden
sué·dois [sɥedwa] **-doise** [dwaz] *adj* Swedish || *m* Swedish (*language*) || (*cap*) *mf* Swede
suée [sɥe] *f* sweating
suer [sɥe] *tr & intr* to sweat
sueur [sɥœr] *f* sweat
suffire [syfir] §66 *intr* to suffice; (with *dat*) to suffice; **il suffit de** + *inf* it suffices to + *inf*; **suffire à** + *inf* to suffice to + *inf*; **suffit!** enough! || *ref* to be self-sufficient
suffisance [syfizɑ̃s] *f* sufficiency; self-sufficiency, smugness

suffi·sant [syfizɑ̃] **-sante** [zɑ̃t] *adj* suf-ficient; smug, sophomoric; impudent || *mf* prig
suffixe [syfiks] *m* suffix
suffoquer [syfɔke] *tr & intr* to suffo-cate, choke, stifle, smother
suffrage [syfraʒ] *m* suffrage, vote; pub-lic approval; **au suffrage universel** by popular vote; **suffrage capacitaire** suffrage contingent upon literacy tests; **suffrage censitaire** suffrage upon payment of taxes
suggérer [sygʒere] §10 *tr* to suggest
sugges·tif [sygʒεstif] **-tive** [tiv] *adj* suggestive
suggestion [sygʒεstjɔ̃] *f* suggestion
suggestionner [sygʒεstjɔne] *tr* to in-fluence by means of suggestion
suicide [sɥisid] *adj* suicidal || *m* suicide (*act*)
suici·dé -dée [sɥiside] *adj* dead by sui-cide || *mf* suicide (*person*)
suicider [sɥiside] *ref* to commit suicide
suie [sɥi] *f* soot
suif [sɥif] *m* tallow
suint [sɥε̃] *m* wool fat, wool grease
suinter [sɥε̃te] *intr* to seep, to ooze; to sweat (*said of wall*); to run (*said of wound*)
suisse [sɥis] *adj* Swiss; **faire suisse** to eat or drink by oneself; to go Dutch || *m* Swiss guard; uniformed usher; **petit suisse** cream cheese || (*cap*) *f* Switzerland; **la Suisse** Switzerland || **Suisse Suissesse** [sɥisεs] *mf* Swiss (*person*)
suite [sɥit] *f* suite; consequence; con-tinuation, sequel (*of literary work*); sequence, series; **à la suite de** after; **de suite** in succession; in a row; **par la suite** later on; **par suite** conse-quently; **par suite de** because of
sui·vant [sɥivɑ̃] **-vante** [vɑ̃t] *adj* next, following, subsequent || *mf* follower; next (person) || *f* servant, confidante || **suivant** *adv*—**suivant que** accord-ing as || **suivant** *prep* according to
sui·veur [sɥivœr] **-veuse** [vøz] *adj* follow-up (*e.g., car*) || *mf* follower
sui·vi -vie [sɥivi] *adj* connected, coher-ent; popular
suivre [sɥivr] §67 *tr* to follow; to take (*a course in school*); **suivre la mode** (fig) to follow suit || *intr* to follow; **à suivre** to be continued || *ref* to fol-low in succession; to follow one after the other
su·jet [syʒε] **-jette** [ʒεt] *adj* subject; apt, liable; inclined || *mf* subject (*of a government*); **mauvais sujet** ne'er-do-well || *m* subject, topic; (gram) subject; **au sujet de** about, concern-ing
sujétion [syʒesjɔ̃] *f* subjection
sulfamide [sylfamid] *m* sulfa drug
sulfure [sylfyr] *m* sulfide
sulfurique [sylfyrik] *adj* sulfuric
sultan [syltɑ̃] *m* sultan
sumac [symak] *m* sumac; **sumac véné-neux** poison ivy
super [sypεr] *m* (coll) high-test gas

superbe [sypɛrb] *adj* superb; proud || *m* proud person || *f* pride
supercarburant [sypɛrkarbyrɑ̃] *m* high-test gasoline
supercherie [sypɛrʃəri] *f* hoax, swindle
superfétatoire [sypɛrfetatwar] *adj* redundant
superficie [sypɛrfisi] *f* surface, area
superfi·ciel -cielle [sypɛrfisjɛl] *adj* superficial
super·flu -flue [sypɛrfly] *adj* superfluous || *m* superfluity, excess
supé·rieur -rieure [sypɛrjœr] *adj* superior; higher; upper (*e.g., story*); supérieur à above; more than || *mf* superior
supérieurement [sypɛrjœrmɑ̃] *adv* superlatively, exceptionally
supériorité [sypɛrjɔrite] *f* superiority
superla·tif [sypɛrlatif] **-tive** [tiv] *adj* & *m* superlative; au superlatif superlatively; in the superlative
supermarché [sypɛrmarʃe] *m* supermarket
superposer [sypɛrpɔze] *tr* to superimpose || *ref* to intervene
supersonique [sypɛrsɔnik] *adj* supersonic
supersti·tieux [sypɛrstisjø] **-tieuse** [sjøz] *adj* superstitious
superstition [sypɛrstisjɔ̃] *f* superstition
superstrat [sypɛrstra] *m* superstratum
superviser [sypɛrvize] *tr* to inspect; to revise; to correct; to supervise
supplanter [syplɑ̃te] *tr* to supplant
suppléance [sypleɑ̃s] *f* substituting; temporary post
suppléant [sypleɑ̃] **suppléante** [sypleɑ̃t] *adj* substituting || *mf* substitute (*e.g., a teacher, judge*)
suppléer [syplee] *tr* to supply; to take the place of; to make up for (*what is lacking*); to fill in (*the gaps*); to substitute for (*s.o.*); to fill (*a vacancy*) || *intr*—suppléer à to make up for (*s.th.*)
supplément [syplemɑ̃] *m* supplement
supplé·tif [sypletif] **-tive** [tiv] *adj* & *m* (mil) auxiliary
suppliant [syplijɑ̃] **suppliante** [syplijɑ̃t] *adj* & *mf* suppliant, supplicant
supplice [syplis] *m* torture; punishment; être au supplice to be in agony
supplicier [syplisje] *tr* to torture to death; to torment
supplier [syplije] *tr* to beseech, implore, supplicate; je vous en supplie I beg you; supplier qn de to implore s.o. to
supplique [syplik] *f* petition
support [sypɔr] *m* support, prop, pillar, bracket, strut; standard (*e.g., for a lamp*)
support-chaussette [sypɔrʃosɛt] *m* (*pl* supports-chaussette) garter (*for men*)
supporter [sypɔrtœr], [sypɔrter] *m* fan, devotee, supporter, partisan || [sypɔrte] *tr* to support, to prop up; to bear, to endure; to stand, to tolerate, to put up with || *intr*—supporter de + *inf* to tolerate or stand

for + *ger* || *ref* to be tolerated; to put up with each other
suppo·sé -sée [sypoze] *adj* supposed, admitted; spurious, assumed || supposé *prep* supposing, admitting, granting
supposer [sypoze] *tr* to suppose; to imply; à supposer que . . . suppose that . . . ; supposer un testament to palm off a forged will
supposition [sypozisjɔ̃] *f* supposition; forgery, fraudulent substitution or alteration; supposition de part or supposition d'enfant false claim of maternity and maternal rights
suppositoire [sypozitwar] *m* suppository
suppôt [sypo] *m* henchman, tool, agitator, hireling; suppôt de Bacchus drunkard; suppôt du diable imp
suppression [sypresjɔ̃] *f* suppression; elimination (*of a job*); discontinuance (*of a festival*); killing (*of a person*); suppression de part or suppression d'enfant concealment of a child's birth or death
supprimer [syprime] *tr* to suppress, to cancel, to abolish; to cut out, to omit; (slang) to eliminate, liquidate || *ref* to kill oneself
suppurer [sypyre] *intr* to suppurate
supputation [sypytasjɔ̃] *f* calculation, evaluation, reckoning
supputer [sypyte] *tr* to calculate (*e.g., forthcoming profits, expenses*)
suprême [syprɛm] *adj* supreme; last
sur sure [syr] *adj* sour || **sur** *prep* on, over; about, concerning; with (*on the person of*); out of, in, e.g., un jour sur quatre one day out of four, one day in four; after, e.g., page sur page page after page; sur ce, sur quoi whereupon; sur le fait in the act
sûr sûre [syr] *adj* sure; trustworthy; safe; certain; à coup sûr, pour sûr for sure, without fail
surabon·dant [syrabɔ̃dɑ̃] **-dante** [dɑ̃t] *adj* superabundant
surabonder [syrabɔ̃de] *intr* to superabound; surabonder de or en to be glutted with
surajouter [syraʒute] *tr* to add on
suralimentation [syralimɑ̃tasjɔ̃] *f* forced feeding; (aut) supercharging
suran·né -née [syrane] *adj* outmoded, out-of-date, superannuated; expired (*driver's license, passport, etc.*)
surboum [syrbum] *f* (slang) dance, hop
surcharge [syrʃarʒ] *f* surcharge; overwriting; (sports) handicap (*of weight on a horse*)
surcharger [syrʃarʒe] §38 *tr* to surcharge; to write a word over (*another word*); to write a word over a crossed-out word on (*a document*)
surchauffe [syrʃof] *f* superheating; overheating (*of the economy*)
surchauffer [syrʃofe] *tr* to superheat (*steam; an oven*); to overheat (*an oven, iron, etc.*)
surchoix [syrʃwa] *m* finest quality

surclasser [syrklɑse] *tr* to outclass
surcompo·sé -sée [syrkɔ̃poze] *adj* (gram) double-compound
surcompression [syrkɔ̃presjɔ̃] *f* pressurization, high compression
surcompri·mé -mée [syrkɔ̃prime] *adj* high-compression (*engine*)
surcomprimer [syrkɔ̃prime] *tr* to supercharge; to pressurize
surcontrer [syrkɔ̃tre] *tr* (cards) to redouble
surcouper [syrkupe] *tr* (cards) to overtrump
surcroît [syrkrwɑ], [syrkrwa] *m* addition, increase; **de surcroît** or **par surcroît** in addition, extra
surdi-mutité [syrdimчtite] *f* deaf-muteness
surdité [syrdite] *f* deafness
su·reau [syro] *m* (*pl* -**reaux**) elderberry
surélévation [syrelevasjɔ̃] *f* escalation, excessive increase; extra story (*added to a building*)
surélever [syrelve] §2 *tr* to raise, raise up; to drive up; to jack up
surenchère [syrɑ̃ʃɛr] *f* higher bid; **surenchère électorale** campaign promise, political outbidding
surenchérir [syrɑ̃ʃerir] *intr* to make a higher bid; **surenchérir sur qn** to outbid s.o.
surestimer [syrɛstime] *tr* to overestimate
su·ret [syrɛ] -**rette** [rɛt] *adj* tart
sûreté [syrte] *f* safety, security; sureness (*of touch; of taste*); surety; **en sûreté** out of harm's way; in custody, confined (*e.g., in prison*); **sûreté individuelle** legal protection (*e.g., against arbitrary arrest*); **Sûreté nationale** or **la Sûreté** central intelligence; **sûretés** precautions; guarantees, security (*for a loan*)
surévaluer [syrevalчe] *tr* to overvalue
surexciter [syrɛksite] *tr* to overexcite
surexposer [syrɛkspoze] *tr* (phot) to overexpose
surexposition [syrɛkspozisjɔ̃] *f* (phot) overexposure
surface [syrfas] *f* surface; financial backing; **faire surface** to surface (*said of a submarine*)
surfaire [syrfɛr] §29 *tr* & *intr* to overprice; to overrate
sur·fin [syrfɛ̃] -**fine** [fin] *adj* superfine
surge·lé -lée [syrʒəle] *adj* frozen (*foods*)
surgeon [syrʒɔ̃] *m* offshoot, sucker
surgir [syrʒir] *intr* to spring up; arise, appear; to arrive, reach port
surglacer [syrglase] §51 *tr* to glaze; to ice (*cake*)
surhaussement [syrosmɑ̃] *m* heightening, raising; banking (*of road*)
surhausser [syrose] *tr* to heighten, to raise; to force up (*prices*); to force up the price of (*s.th.*); to bank (*a road*)
surhomme [syrɔm] *m* superman
surhu·main [syrymɛ̃] -**maine** [mɛn] *adj* superhuman

surimpression [syrɛ̃presjɔ̃] *f* superimposition; (mov) montage
surintendant [syrɛ̃tɑ̃dɑ̃] *m* superintendent, administrator
surir [syrir] *intr* to turn sour
sur-le-champ [syrlʃɑ̃] *adv* on the spot, immediately
surlendemain [syrlɑ̃dmɛ̃] *m*—**le surlendemain** the second day after, two days later
surlier [syrlje] *tr* to whip (*a rope*)
surmenage [syrmənaʒ] *m* overworking, fatigue
surmener [syrməne] §2 *tr* & *ref* to overwork
sur-moi [syrmwa] *m* superego
surmonter [syrmɔ̃te] *tr* to surmount ‖ *intr* to come to the top (*said of oil in water*)
surmouler [syrmule] *tr* to cast from another mold
surmultiplication [syrmyltiplikɑsjɔ̃] *f* (aut) overdrive
surnager [syrnaʒe] §38 *intr* to float; to survive
surnatu·rel -relle [syrnatyrɛl] *adj* & *m* supernatural
surnom [syrnɔ̃] *m* nickname, sobriquet
surnombre [syrnɔ̃br] *m* excess number; **en surnombre** supernumerary; spare; **rester en surnombre** to be odd man; **surnombre des habitants** overpopulation
surnommer [syrnɔme] *tr* to name, call, nickname
surnuméraire [syrnymerɛr] *adj* supernumerary, extra ‖ *mf* substitute, supernumerary
suroffre [syrɔfr] *f* better or higher offer
suroît [syrwa] *m* southwest wind
surpasser [syrpɑse] *tr* to surpass; to astonish ‖ *ref* to outdo oneself
surpaye [syrpɛj] *f* extra pay
surpayer [syrpɛje] §49 *tr* to pay too much to; to pay too much for
surpeu·plé -plée [syrpœple] *adj* overpopulated
surpeuplement [syrpœpləmɑ̃] *m* overpopulation
surplis [syrpli] *m* surplice
surplomber [syrplɔ̃be] *tr* & *intr* to overhang
surplus [syrply] *m* surplus; **au surplus** moreover
surpopulation [syrpɔpylɑsjɔ̃] *f* overpopulation
surprendre [syrprɑ̃dr] §56 *tr* to surprise; to come upon by chance; to detect; to overtake, catch
surprise [syrpriz] *f* surprise
surprise-party or **surprise-partie** [syrprizparti] *f* (*pl* **surprises-parties**) private dancing party
surproduction [syrprɔdyksjɔ̃] *f* overproduction
surréalisme [syrealism] *m* surrealism
sursaut [syrso] *m* sudden start; **en sursaut** with a start
sursauter [syrsote] *intr* to give a jump, to start, to jerk

surseoir [syrswar] §5B (*fut* surseoirai, etc.) *tr* to postpone, defer, put off || *intr*—surseoir (with *dat*) to stay (*an investigation; an execution*)
sursis [syrsi] *m* suspension (*of penalty*); postponement, deferment, stay; en sursis, avec sursis suspended (*sentence*)
surtaxe [syrtaks] *f* surtax, surcharge; surtaxe postale postage due
surtaxer [syrtakse] *tr* to surtax
surtension [syrtɑ̃sjɔ̃] *f* (elec) surge
surtout [syrtu] *m* topcoat; centerpiece, epergne || *adv* especially, particularly
surveillance [syrvɛjɑ̃s] *f* supervision; (*by the police*) surveillance
surveil·lant [syrvɛjɑ̃] surveil·lante [syrvɛjɑ̃t] *mf* supervisor, superintendent, overseer; surveillant d'études study-hall proctor
surveiller [syrvɛje] *tr* to inspect, to put under surveillance; to supervise, watch over, monitor
survenir [syrvənir] §72 *intr* (*aux*: ÊTRE) to arrive unexpectedly, to happen suddenly, to crop up
survenue [syrvəny] *f* unexpected arrival
survêtement [syrvɛtmɑ̃] *m* track suit, sweat shirt
survie [syrvi] *f* survival; afterlife; (law) survivorship
survivance [syrvivɑ̃s] *f* survival
survi·vant [syrvivɑ̃] -vante [vɑ̃t] *adj* surviving || *mf* survivor
survivre [syrvivr] §74 *intr* to survive; (with *dat*) to survive, outlive
survoler [syrvɔle] *tr* to fly over; to skim over (*e.g., a problem*)
survol·té -tée [syrvɔlte] *adj* electrified, charged with emotion
sus [sys], [sy] *adv*—en sus de in addition to || *interj* up and at it (them)!
susceptible [sysɛptibl] *adj* susceptible; susceptible de capable of
susciter [sysite] *tr* to stir up, evoke, rouse; (lit) to raise up
sus·dit [sysdi] -dite [dit] *adj* aforesaid
susmention·né -née [sysmɑ̃sjɔne] *adj* aforementioned
sus·pect [syspɛ], [syspɛkt] -pecte [pɛkt] *adj* suspect, suspicious || *mf* suspect
suspecter [syspɛkte] *tr* to suspect
suspendre [syspɑ̃dr] *tr* to suspend; to hang, to hang up; être suspendu aux lèvres de qn to hang on s.o.'s every word || *ref* to be hung; to hang on
suspen·du -due [syspɑ̃dy] *adj* suspended; hanging
suspens [syspɑ̃] *m* suspense; en suspens suspended; in abeyance; outstanding
suspension [syspɑ̃sjɔ̃] *f* suspension
suspi·cieux [syspisjø] -cieuse [sjøz] *adj* suspicious
suspicion [syspisjɔ̃] *f* suspicion
sustenter [systɑ̃te] *tr* to sustain || *ref* to sustain oneself
susurrer [sysyre] *tr* & *intr* to murmur, to whisper

susvi·sé -sée [sysvize] *adj* above-mentioned
suture [sytyr] *f* suture
suturer [sytyre] *tr* to suture
suze·rain [syzrɛ̃] -raine [rɛn] *adj* & *mf* suzerain
svastika [svastika] *m* swastika
svelte [svɛlt] *adj* slender, lithe, willowy
S.V.P. [ɛsvepe] *m* (letterword) (s'il vous plaît) if you please, please
sweater [switœr] *m* sweater
sycophante [sikɔfɑ̃t] *m* informer
syllabe [silab] *f* syllable
syllogisme [silɔʒism] *m* syllogism
sylphe [silf] *m* sylph
sylvestre [silvɛstr] *adj* sylvan
symbole [sɛ̃bɔl] *m* symbol; Symbole des apôtres Apostles' Creed
symbolique [sɛ̃bɔlik] *adj* symbolic(al)
symboliser [sɛ̃bɔlize] *tr* to symbolize
symbolisme [sɛ̃bɔlism] *m* symbolism
symétrie [simetri] *f* symmetry
symétrique [simetrik] *adj* symmetric(al)
sympathie [sɛ̃pati] *f* fondness, liking; sympathy
sympathique [sɛ̃patik] *adj* likable, attractive; sympathetic
sympathi·sant [sɛ̃patizɑ̃] -sante [zɑ̃t] *adj* sympathetic || *mf* sympathizer
sympathiser [sɛ̃patize] *intr* to get along well; sympathiser avec to be drawn toward
symphonie [sɛ̃fɔni] *f* symphony
symptôme [sɛ̃ptom] *m* symptom
synagogue [sinagɔg] *f* synagogue
synchrone [sɛ̃krɔn] *adj* synchronous
synchroniser [sɛ̃krɔnize] *tr* to synchronize
syncope [sɛ̃kɔp] *f* faint, swoon, syncope; syncopation
syndicat [sɛ̃dika] *m* labor union; syndicat d'initiative chamber of commerce; syndicat patronal employers' association
syndicats-patrons [sɛ̃dikapatrɔ̃] *adj invar* labor-management
syndiquer [sɛ̃dike] *tr* & *ref* to syndicate
synonyme [sinɔnim] *adj* synonymous || *m* synonym
synopsis [sinɔpsis] *m* & *f* (mov) synopsis
syntaxe [sɛ̃taks] *f* syntax
synthèse [sɛ̃tɛz] *f* synthesis
synthétique [sɛ̃tetik] *adj* synthetic
synthétiser [sɛ̃tetize] *tr* to synthesize
syntonisation [sɛ̃tɔnizasjɔ̃] *f* tuning (*of radio*)
syntoniser [sɛ̃tɔnize] *tr* to tune in
syphilis [sifilis] *f* syphilis
Syrie [siri] *f* Syria; la Syrie Syria
sy·rien [sirjɛ̃] -rienne [rjɛn] *adj* Syrian || (*cap*) *mf* Syrian (*person*)
systématique [sistematik] *adj* systematic
systématiser [sistematize] *tr* to systematize
système [sistɛm] *m* system; courir, porter, or taper sur le système à qn (slang) to get on s.o.'s nerves; système D (coll) resourcefulness
systole [sistɔl] *f* systole

T

T, t [te] *m invar* twentieth letter of the French alphabet
t. *abbr* (**tome**) vol.
ta [ta] §88
tabac [taba] *m* tobacco; tobacco shop; **avoir le gros tabac** (slang) to be a hit; **passer qn à tabac** (coll) to give s.o. the third degree; **tabac à chiquer** chewing tobacco; **tabac à priser** snuff
tabagie [tabaʒi] *f* smoke-filled room
tabasser [tabase] *tr* (slang) to give a licking to, to shellac
tabatière [tabatjɛr] *f* snuffbox; skylight, dormer window
tabernacle [tabɛrnakl] *m* tabernacle
table [tabl] *f* table; **aimer la table** to like good food; **à table!** dinner is served!; **dresser** or **mettre la table** to set the table; **faire table rase** to make a clean sweep; **sainte table** altar rail; **se mettre à table** (slang) to tell all, to confess, to squeal; **table à abattants** gate-leg table; **table à ouvrage** worktable; **table à rallonges** extension table; **table de chevet, table de nuit** bedside table; **table d'écoute** wiretap; **table de jeu** card table; **table des matières** table of contents; **table de toilette** dressing table; **table d'hôte** table d'hôte; chef's special; **table d'opération** operating table; **table gigogne** nest of tables; **table interurbaine** long-distance switchboard; **table roulante** serving cart; **tenir table ouverte** to keep open house
ta·bleau [tablo] *m* (*pl* **-bleaux**) painting, picture; scoreboard; board; table, catalogue; panel (*of jurors*); **tableau d'affichage** bulletin board; **tableau d'avancement** senority list; **tableau de bord** dashboard; instrument panel; **tableau de distribution** switchboard; **tableau d'honneur** honor roll; **tableau noir** blackboard; **tableau vivant** tableau
tabler [table] *intr*—**tabler sur** to count on; to use as a base
tablette [tablɛt] *f* shelf; mantelpiece; bar (*e.g., of chocolate*); **rayez cela de vos tablettes** don't count on it; **tablettes** pocket notebook
table-valise [tabləvaliz] *f* (*pl* **tables-valises**) folding table
tablier [tablije] *m* apron; roadway (*of bridge*); hood (*of chimney*); **tablier de fer** protective shutter (*on store window*)
ta·bou -bou or **boue** [tabu] *adj & m* taboo
tabouret [taburɛ] *m* stool; footstool
tabulaire [tabylɛr] *adj* tabular
tabulateur [tabylatœr] *m* tabulator
tac [tak] *m* click, clack; **du tac au tac** tit for tat; **tac tac tac tac!** rat-a-tat-tat!
tache [taʃ] *f* spot, stain; blemish, flaw; blot, smear; speck; **faire tache** to be out of place; **faire tache d'huile** to spread; **sans tache** spotless, unblemished; **tache de rousseur, tache de son** freckle; **tache de vin** birthmark; **tache originelle** original sin; **tache solaire** sunspot
tâche [taʃ] *f* task, job; **prendre à tâche de** to try to; **travailler à la tâche** to do piecework
tacher [taʃe] *tr & ref* to spot, stain
tâcher [taʃe] *tr*—**tâcher que** to see to it that ‖ *intr*—**tâcher de** to try to; **y tâcher** to try
tâcheron [taʃrɔ̃] *m* small jobber; pieceworker; hard worker; wage slave
tacheter [taʃte] §34 *tr* to spot, to speckle
tacite [tasit] *adj* tacit
taciturne [tasityrn] *adj* taciturn
tacot [tako] *m* (coll) jalopy
tact [takt] *m* tact; sense of touch
tacticien [taktisjɛ̃] *m* tactician
tactique [taktik] *adj* tactical ‖ *f* tactics
taffetas [tafta] *m* taffeta; **taffetas gommé** adhesive tape
Tage [taʒ] *m* Tagus
taïaut [tajo] *interj* tallyho!
taie [te] *f* (pathol) leukoma; **avoir une taie sur l'œil** (fig) to be blinded by prejudice; **taie d'oreiller** pillowcase
taillader [tajade] *tr & ref* to slash, cut
taille [taj] *f* cutting (*e.g., of diamond*); trimming (*e.g., of hedge*); height, stature; waist; waistline; size; cut (*of garment*); **à la taille de, de la taille de** to the measure of, suitable for; **avoir la taille fine** to have a slim waist; **de taille** big enough, strong enough; (coll) big; **être de taille à** to be up to, to be big enough to; **taille de guêpe** wasp waist; **taille en dessous** next size smaller; **taille en dessus** next size larger
tail·lé -lée [taje] *adj* cut; trimmed; **bien taillé** well-built; **taillé pour** cut out for
taille-crayon [tajkrɛjɔ̃] *m* (*pl* **-crayon** or **-crayons**) pencil sharpener
taille-douce [tajdus] *f* (*pl* **tailles-douces**) copperplate
taille-pain [tajpɛ̃] *m invar* bread knife; bread slicer
tailler [taje] *tr* to cut; to sharpen (*a pencil*); to prune, trim (*a tree*); to carve (*stone*); to clip (*hair*) ‖ *intr* (cards) to deal ‖ *ref* to carve out (*a path; a career*); (coll) to beat it
tailleur [tajœr] *m* tailor; woman's suit; (cards) dealer; **en tailleur** squatting (*while tailoring*); **tailleur de diamants** diamond cutter; **tailleur de pierre** stonecutter; **tailleur sur mesure** lady's tailor-made suit
taillis [taji] *m* thicket, copse
tain [tɛ̃] *m* silvering (*of mirror*)
taire [tɛr] §52 (3d *sg pres ind* **tait**) *tr* to hush up, to hide; **la tairas-tu?** (slang) will you shut your trap?; **taire q.ch. à qn** to keep s.th. from s.o. ‖ *intr*—**faire taire** to silence ‖ *ref* to keep

quiet, keep still; **se taire sur** to say nothing about; **tais-toi!** shut up!
talent [talɑ̃] *m* talent
talen·tueux [talɑ̃tɥø̸] **-tueuse** [tɥø̸z] *adj* talented
taloche [talɔʃ] *f* plastering trowel; (coll) clout, smack
talon [talɔ̃] *m* heel; stub
talonner [talɔne] *tr* to tail; to harass; to dig one's spurs into ‖ *intr* to bump
talus [taly] *m* slope; embankment
tambour [tɑ̃bur] *m* drum; drummer; entryway; spool (*of reel*); **tambour battant** (coll) roughly; (coll) quickly; **tambour cylindrique** revolving door; **tambour de basque** tambourine; **tambour de freins** brake drum; **tambour de ville** town crier
tambouriner [tɑ̃burine] *tr* to drum; to broadcast far and wide ‖ *intr* to beat a tattoo; to drum
tambour-major [tɑ̃burmaʒɔr] *m* (*pl* **tambours-majors**) drum major
tamis [tami] *m* sieve; **passer au tamis** to sift; **tamis à farine** flour sifter
Tamise [tamiz] *f* Thames
tamiser [tamize] *tr* & *intr* to sift
tampon [tɑ̃pɔ̃] *m* plug; bung; swab; rubber stamp; buffer; cancellation, postmark; (surg) tampon; **tampon buvard** hand blotter; **tampon encreur** stamp pad
tamponner [tɑ̃pɔne] *tr* to swab, to dab; to bump, to bump into; (surg) to tampon
tan [tɑ̃] *adj invar* tan ‖ *m* tanbark
tancer [tɑ̃se] §51 *tr* to scold
tandem [tɑ̃dɛm] *m* tandem; **en tandem** tandem
tandis que [tɑ̃dikə], [tɑ̃diskə] *conj* while; whereas
tangage [tɑ̃gaʒ] *m* (naut) pitching
Tanger [tɑ̃ʒe] *m* Tangier
tangible [tɑ̃ʒibl] *adj* tangible
tanguer [tɑ̃ge] *intr* to pitch (*said of ship*)
tanière [tanjɛr] *f* den, lair
tanker [tɑ̃kɛr] *m* oil tanker
tan·nant [tanɑ̃] **tan·nante** [tanɑ̃t] *adj* (coll) boring
tanne [tan] *f* spot (*on leather*); blackhead
tanner [tane] *tr* to tan; (coll) to pester
tannerie [tanri] *f* tannery
tanneur [tanœr] *m* tanner
tan-sad [tɑ̃sad] *m* (*pl* **-sads**) rear seat (*of motorcycle*)
tant [tɑ̃] *adv* so, so much; so long; **en tant que** as; in so far as; **si tant est que** if it is true that; **tant bien que mal** somehow or other; **tant de** so many; so much; **tant mieux** so much the better; **tant pis** so much the worse; never mind; **tant qu'à faire** while we're (you've, etc.) at it; **tant que** as well as; as long as; **tant s'en faut** far from it; **tant soit peu** ever so little; **vous m'en direz tant** (coll) you've just said a mouthful
tante [tɑ̃t] *f* aunt; (slang) fairy; **ma tante** (coll) the hockshop
tantième [tɑ̃tjɛm] *m* percentage
tantine [tɑ̃tin] *f* (coll) auntie

tantôt [tɑ̃to] *m* (coll) afternoon ‖ *adv* in a little while; a little while ago; (coll) in the afternoon; **à tantôt** see you soon; **tantôt . . . tantôt** sometimes . . . sometimes
taon [tɑ̃] *m* horsefly
tapage [tapaʒ] *m* uproar
tapa·geur [tapaʒœr] **-geuse** [ʒø̸z] *adj* loud
tape [tap] *f* tap, slap
ta·pé **-pée** [tape] *adj* dried (*fruit*); rotten in spots; (coll) crazy; (slang) worn (*with age or fatigue*); **bien tapé** (coll) well done; (coll) nicely served; (coll) to the point
tape-à-l'œil [tapalœj] *adj* gaudy, showy ‖ *m invar* mere show
taper [tape] *tr* to tap, to slap; to type; (coll) to hit (*s.o. for money*) ‖ *intr* to tap, to slap; to type; (coll) to go to the head (*said of wine*); **ça tape ici** (slang) it hurts here; **taper dans** (coll) to use; **taper dans le mille** (coll) to succeed; **taper dans l'œil de qn** (coll) to make a hit with s.o.; **taper de** to hit (*e.g., 100 m.p.h.*); **taper des pieds** to stamp one's feet; **taper sur** (coll) to get on (*s.o.'s nerves*); **taper sur le ventre de qn** (coll) to give s.o. a poke in the ribs; **taper sur qn** (coll) to run down s.o., to give s.o. a going-over
tapette [tapɛt] *f* carpet beater; fly swatter; handball; (slang) fairy; **avoir une fière tapette** (coll) to be a chatterbox
tapin [tapɛ̃] *m* (coll) drummer boy; (slang) solicitation (*by a prostitute*)
tapinois [tapinwa]—**en tapinois** stealthily
tapir [tapir] *ref* to crouch, to squat; to hide
tapis [tapi] *m* carpet; rug; game of chance; **mettre sur le tapis** to bring up for discussion; **tapis de bain** bath mat; **tapis de sol** ground cloth; **tapis de table** table covering; **tapis roulant** conveyor belt; moving sidewalk
tapis-brosse [tapibrɔs] *m* (*pl* **-brosses**) doormat
tapisser [tapise] *tr* to upholster; to tapestry; to wallpaper
tapisserie [tapisri] *f* upholstery; tapestry; **faire tapisserie** to be a wallflower
tapis·sier [tapisje] **tapis·sière** [tapisjɛr] *mf* upholsterer; tapestry maker; paperhanger
tapoter [tapɔte] *tr* & *intr* to tap
taquet [takɛ] *m* wedge, peg; (mach) tappet; (naut) cleat; **taquet d'arrêt** (rr) scotch, wedge
ta·quin [takɛ̃] **-quine** [kin] *adj* teasing ‖ *mf* tease
taquiner [takine] *tr* to tease
taquinerie [takinri] *f* teasing
taraud [taro] *m* (mach) tap
tarauder [tarode] *tr* (mach) to tap; (coll) to pester
taraudeuse [tarodø̸z] *f* tap wrench
tard [tar] *m*—**sur le tard** late in the day; late in life ‖ *adv* late; **pas plus tard que** no later than; **plus tard** later on

tarder [tarde] *intr* to delay; **tarder à** to be long in ‖ *impers*—**il tarde** (with *dat*) **de** long to, e.g., **il lui tarde de vous voir** he longs to see you

tar·dif [tardif] **-dive** [div] *adj* late; backward; tardy

tardivement [tardivmã] *adv* belatedly

tare [tar] *f* defect, blemish; taint; loss in value; tare (*weight*)

tarer [tare] *tr* to damage; to taint; to tare ‖ *ref* to spoil

targette [tarʒɛt] *f* latch

targuer [targe] *ref*—**se targuer de** to pride oneself on

tarière [tarjɛr] *f* auger, drill

tarif [tarif] *m* price list; rate, tariff; **plein tarif** full fare; **tarifs postaux** postal rates

tarifaire [tarifɛr] *adj* tariff

tarifer [tarife] *tr* to price; to rate

tarir [tarir] *tr* to drain, exhaust, dry up ‖ *intr* to dry up, to run dry; **ne pas tarir** to never run out ‖ *ref* to dry up; to be exhausted

tarse [tars] *m* tarsus; instep

tartare [tartar] *adj* tartar (*sauce*); Tartar ‖ (*cap*) *mf* Tartar

tarte [tart] *adj* (coll) silly, stupid; (coll) ugly ‖ *f* pie, tart; (slang) slap

tartine [tartin] *f* slice of bread and butter or jam; (coll) long-winded speech; (coll) rambling article

tartiner [tartine] *tr* to spread

tartre [tartr] *m* tartar; scale

tartuferie [tartyfri] *f* hypocrisy

tas [tɑ] *m* heap, pile; **mettre en tas** to pile up; **prendre sur le tas** to catch red-handed; **tas de foin** haystack; **un tas de** (coll) a lot of

tasse [tɑs] *f* cup; **tasse à café** coffee cup; **tasse à thé** teacup; **tasse de café** cup of coffee

tas·seau [tɑso] *m* (*pl* **-seaux**) bracket; cleat; lug (*on casting*)

tasser [tɑse] *tr* to cram; to tamp; **bien tassé** (coll) brimful ‖ *intr* to grow thick ‖ *ref* to settle; to huddle; (coll) to go back to normal

taste-vin [tastəvɛ̃] *m invar* wine taster (*cup*); sampling tube

tata [tata] *f* (slang) auntie

tâter [tate] *tr* to feel, to touch; to test, to feel out; **tâter le pouls à qn** to feel s.o.'s pulse ‖ *intr*—**tâter de** to taste; to experience; to try one's hand at ‖ *ref* to stop to think, to ponder

tâte-vin [tatvɛ̃] *m invar* wine taster (*cup*); sampling tube

tatil·lon [tatijɔ̃] **tatil·lonne** [tatijɔn] *adj* fussy, hairsplitting ‖ *mf* hairsplitter

tâtonner [tatone] *intr* to grope

tâtons [tatɔ̃]—**à tâtons** gropingly

tatouage [tatwaʒ] *m* tattoo

tatouer [tatwe] *tr* to tattoo

taudis [todi] *m* hovel; **taudis** *mpl* slums

taule [tol] *f* (slang) fleabag; **faire de la taule** (slang) to do a stretch

taupe [top] *f* mole; moleskin

taupin [topɛ̃] *m* (mil) sapper; (coll) engineering student

taupinière [topinjɛr] *f* molehill

tau·reau [toro] *m* (*pl* **-reaux**) bull

taux [to] *m* rate; **taux d'escompte** discount rate

taveler [tavle] §34 *tr* to spot ‖ *ref* to become spotted

taverne [tavɛrn] *f* inn, tavern

taxation [taksɑsjɔ̃] *f* fixing (*of prices, wages, etc.*); assessment; taxation

taxe [taks] *f* fixed price; rate; tax; **taxe à la valeur ajoutée** value-added tax; **taxe de luxe** luxury tax; **taxe de séjour** nonresident tax; **taxe directe** sales tax; **taxe perçue** postage paid; **taxe supplémentaire** postage due; **taxe sur les spectacles** entertainment tax

taxer [takse] *tr* to fix the price of; to regulate the rate of; to assess; to tax; **taxer qn de** to tax or charge s.o. with ‖ *ref* to set an offering price; **se taxer de** to accuse oneself of

taxi [taksi] *m* taxi; (coll) cabdriving; **hep taxi!** taxi! ‖ *mf* (coll) cabdriver

taxidermie [taksidɛrmi] *f* taxidermy

taxiphone [taksifɔn] *m* pay phone

Tchécoslovaquie [tʃekɔslɔvaki] *f* Czechoslovakia; **la Tchécoslovaquie** Czechoslovakia

tchèque [tʃɛk] *adj* Czech ‖ *m* Czech (*language*) ‖ (*cap*) *mf* Czech (*person*)

te [tə] §87

techni·cien [tɛknisjɛ̃] **-cienne** [sjɛn] *mf* technician; engineer

technique [tɛknik] *adj* technical ‖ *f* technique; engineering

teck [tɛk] *m* teak

teigne [tɛɲ] *f* moth; ringworm; (fig) pest, nuisance

teindre [tɛdr] §50 *tr* to dye; to tint ‖ *ref* to be tinted; to dye or tint one's hair; (with *dat* of *reflex pron*) to dye or tint (*one's hair*)

teint [tɛ̃] **teinte** [tɛ̃t] *adj* dyed; with dyed hair ‖ *m* dye; complexion; **bon teint** fast color ‖ *f* tint, shade; (fig) tinge

teinter [tɛ̃te] *tr* to tint; to tinge

teinture [tɛ̃tyr] *f* dye; dyeing; tincture; (fig) smattering; **teinture d'iode** (pharm) iodine

teinturerie [tɛ̃tyrri] *f* dry cleaner's; dyer's; dyeing

teintu·rier [tɛ̃tyrje] **-rière** [rjɛr] *mf* dry cleaner; dyer

tel telle [tɛl] *adj* such; like, e.g., **tel père tel fils** like father like son; **de telle sorte que** so that; **tel ou tel** such and such a; **tel que** such as, the same as, as; **tel quel** as is ‖ *mf*—**un tel** or **une telle** so-and-so ‖ *pron* such a one, such

télé [tele] *f* (coll) TV; (coll) TV set

télécommander [telekɔmɑ̃de] *tr* to operate by remote control; (fig) to inspire, influence

téléférique [teleferik] *m* skyride, cableway

télégramme [telegram] *m* telegram

télégraphe [telegraf] *m* telegraph

télégraphier [telegrafje] *tr & intr* to telegraph

télégraphiste [telegrafist] *mf* telegrapher

téléguider [telegide] *tr* to guide (*e.g.*, *a missile*); (coll) to influence
téléimprimeur [teleẽprimœr] *m* teletype, teleprinter
télémètre [telemɛtr] *m* telemeter; range finder
téléobjectif [teleɔbʒɛktif] *m* telephoto lens
télépathie [telepati] *f* telepathy
téléphérique [teleferik] *m* skyride, cableway
téléphone [telefɔn] *m* telephone
téléphoner [telefɔne] *tr* & *intr* to telephone
téléphoniste [telefɔnist] *mf* telephone operator || *m* lineman || *f* telephone girl
télescope [telɛskɔp] *m* telescope
télescoper [telɛskɔpe] *tr* & *ref* to telescope
télescopique [telɛskɔpik] *adj* telescopic
téléscripteur [teleskriptœr] *m* teletype, teletypewriter
télésiège [telesjeʒ] *m* chair lift
téléski [teleski] *m* ski lift
téléspecta·teur [telespɛktatœr] -trice [tris] *mf* (television) viewer
télétype [teletip] *m* teletype
téléviser [televize] *tr* to televise
téléviseur [televizœr] *m* television set; téléviseur à servo-réglage remote-control television set
télévision [televizjɔ̃] *f* television; (coll) television set
télévi·suel -suelle [televizɥɛl] *adj* television
tellement [tɛlmã] *adv* so much, so; tellement de so much, so many; tellement que to such an extent that
téméraire [temerɛr] *adj* rash, reckless, foolhardy
témérité [temerite] *f* temerity, rashness
témoignage [temwaɲaʒ] *m* testimony, witness; en témoignage de quoi in witness whereof; rendre témoignage à or pour to testify in favor of
témoigner [temwaɲe] *tr* to show; to testify || *intr* to testify; témoigner de to give evidence of; to bear witness to
témoin [temwɛ̃] *m* (anat) type, model; pilot || *m* witness; control (*in scientific experiment*); second (*in duel*) prendre à témoin to call to witness; témoin à charge witness for the prosecution; témoin à décharge witness for the defense; témoin oculaire eyewitness
tempe [tãp] *f* (anat) temple
tempérament [tãperamã] *m* temperament; amorous nature; à tempérament on the installment plan
tempérance [tãperãs] *f* temperance
tempé·rant [tãperã] -rante [rãt] *adj* temperate
température [tãperatyr] *f* temperature
tempé·ré -rée [tãpere] *adj* temperate; tempered; restrained
tempérer [tãpere] §10 *tr* to temper || *ref* to moderate
tempête [tãpɛt] *f* tempest, storm; affronter la tempête (fig) to face the music; tempête dans un verre d'eau tempest in a teapot; tempête de neige

blizzard; tempête de poussière dust storm; tempête de sable sandstorm
tempêter [tãpɛte] *intr* to storm
tempé·tueux [tãpetɥø] -tueuse [tɥøz] *adj* tempestuous
temple [tãpl] *m* temple; chapel, church
tempo [tɛmpo], [tɛpo] *m* tempo
temporaire [tãpɔrɛr] *adj* temporary
tempo·ral -rale [tãpɔral] *adj* (*pl* -raux [ro]) (anat) temporal
tempo·rel -relle [tãpɔrɛl] *adj* temporal
temporiser [tãpɔrize] *intr* to temporize, to stall
temps [tã] *m* time; times; cycle (*of internal-combustion engine*); position, movement (*in gymnastics, fencing, carrying of arms*); weather, e.g., quel temps fait-il? what is the weather like?; (gram) tense; (mus) beat, measure; à temps in time; avoir fait son temps to have seen better days; dans le temps formerly; temps en temps from time to time; en même temps at the same time; en temps et lieu in due course; en temps utile in due course; faire son temps to do time (*in prison*); gagner du temps to save time; le bon vieux temps the good old days; Le Temps Father Time; temps atomique atomic era; temps d'arrêt pause, halt
tenable [tənabl] *adj*—pas tenable untenable; unbearable
tenace [tənas] *adj* tenacious
ténacité [tenasite] *f* tenacity
tenailler [tənaje] *tr* to torture
tenailles [tənaj] *fpl* pincers
tenan·cier [tənãsje] -cière [sjɛr] *mf* sharecropper; lessee; keeper (*e.g., of a dive*)
te·nant [tənã] -nante [nãt] *adj* attached (*collar*) || *mf* (sports) holder (*of a title*) || *m* champion, supporter; connaître les tenants et les aboutissants to know the ins and outs; d'un seul tenant in one piece
tendance [tãdãs] *f* tendency
tendan·cieux [tãdãsjø] -cieuse [sjøz] *adj* tendentious, slanted
ten·deur [tãdœr] -deuse [døz] *mf* paperhanger; layer (*of traps*) || *m* stretcher
tendoir [tãdwar] *m* clothesline
tendon [tãdɔ̃] *m* tendon
tendre [tãdr] *adj* tender || *tr* to stretch; to hang; to bend (*a bow*); to lay (*a trap*); to strain (*one's ear*); to hold out, to reach out || *intr*—tendre à to aim at; to tend toward || *ref* to become strained
tendresse [tãdrɛs] *f* tenderness, love, affection; (coll) partiality; mille tendresses (*closing of letter*) fondly
tendreté [tãdrəte] *f* tenderness
ten·du -due [tãdy] *adj* tense, taut; strained; stretched out; tendu de hung with
ténèbres [tenɛbr] *fpl* darkness
téné·breux [tenebrø] -breuse [brøz] *adj* dark; somber (*person*); shady (*deal*); obscure (*style*)
te·neur [tənœr] -neuse [nøz] *mf* holder; teneur de livres bookkeeper

|| **teneur** *f* tenor, gist; text; grade (*e.g., of ore*)

ténia [tenja] *m* tapeworm

tenir [tənir] §72 *tr* to hold; to keep; to take up (*space*); **être tenu à** to be obliged to; **être tenu de** to be responsible for || *intr* to hold; **il ne tient qu'à vous** it's up to you; **tenez!** here!; **tenir à** to insist upon; to care for, to value; to be caused by; **tenir de** to take after, to resemble; **tenir debout** (fig) to hold water, to ring true; **tenir q.ch. de qn** to have s.th. from s.o., to learn s.th. from s.o.; **tiens!** well!, hey! || *ref* to stay, remain; to sit up; to stand up; to behave; to contain oneself; **à quoi s'en tenir** what to believe; **s'en tenir à** to limit oneself to; to abide by

tennis [tenis] *m* tennis; tennis court

ténor [tenɔr] *adj masc* tenor || *m* tenor; star performer

tension [tɑ̃sjɔ̃] *f* tension; blood pressure; **avoir de la tension** to have high blood pressure; **haute tension** (elec) high tension; **tension artérielle** blood pressure

tentacule [tɑ̃takyl] *m* tentacle

tenta·teur [tɑ̃tatœr] **-trice** [tris] *mf* tempter

tentation [tɑ̃tasjɔ̃] *f* temptation

tentative [tɑ̃tativ] *f* attempt

tente [tɑ̃t] *f* tent; awning

tente-abri [tɑ̃tabri] *f* (*pl* **tentes-abris** [tɑ̃tabri]) pup tent

tenter [tɑ̃te] *tr* to tempt; to attempt || *intr*—**tenter de** to attempt to

tenture [tɑ̃tyr] *f* drape; hangings; wallpaper

te·nu -nue [təny] *adj* firm (*securities, market, etc.*); **bien tenu** well-kept || *f* see **tenue**

té·nu -nue [teny] *adj* tenuous; thin

tenue [təny] *f* holding; managing; upkeep, maintenance; behavior; bearing; dress, costume; uniform; session; (mus) hold; **avoir de la tenue** to have good manners; **avoir une bonne tenue** (horsemanship) to have a good seat; **en tenue** in uniform; **grande tenue** (mil) full dress; **petite tenue** (mil) undress; **tenue des livres** bookkeeping; **tenue de soirée** evening clothes; **tenue de ville** street clothes

térébenthine [terebɑ̃tin] *f* turpentine

tergiverser [terʒiverse] *intr* to duck, equivocate, vacillate

terme [term] *m* term; end, limit; quarterly payment; **avant terme** prematurely; **terme fatal** last day of grace

terminaison [terminɛzɔ̃] *f* ending, termination

termi·nal -nale [terminal] *adj* (*pl* **-naux** [no]) terminal

terminer [termine] *tr & ref* to terminate

terminus [terminys] *m* terminal || *interj* the end has come!

termite [termit] *m* termite

terne [tern] *adj* dull, drab

ternir [ternir] *tr & ref* to tarnish

terrain [terɛ̃] *m* ground; terrain; playing field; dueling field; **ne pas être**

sur son terrain to be out of one's depth; **tâter le terrain** to find out the lay of the land; **terrain à bâtir** or **à lotir** building plot; **terrain brûlant** (fig) unsafe ground; **terrain d'atterrissage** landing field; **terrain d'aviation** airfield; **terrain de courses** race track; **terrain de jeux** playground; **terrain de manœuvres** parade ground; **terrain vague** vacant lot

terrasse [teras] *f* terrace; sidewalk café; **terrasse en plein air** outdoor café

terrasser [terase] *tr* to embank; to floor, to knock down

terre [ter] *f* earth; land; (elec) ground; **descendre à terre** to go ashore; **la Terre Sainte** the Holy Land; **mettre pied à terre** to dismount; **par terre** on the floor; on the ground; **terre cuite** terra cotta; **Terre de Feu** Tierra del Fuego; **terre ferme** terra firma; **terre franche** loam

ter·reau [tero] *m* (*pl* **-reaux**) compost

terre-neuve [ternœv] *m invar* Newfoundland dog ||—**Terre-Neuve** *f* Newfoundland

terre-plein [terplɛ̃] *m* (*pl* **-pleins**) median, divider (*of road*); fill, embankment; earthwork, rampart; terrace; (rr) roadbed

terrer [tere] *tr* to earth up (*e.g., a tree*); to earth over (*seed*) || *ref* to burrow; to entrench oneself

terrestre [terestr] *adj* land; terrestrial

terreur [terœr] *f* terror; **la Terreur** the Reign of Terror

ter·reux [terø] **ter·reuse** [terøz] *adj* earthy; dirty; sallow (*complexion*)

terrible [teribl] *adj* terrible; terrific

ter·rien [terjɛ̃] **ter·rienne** [terjen] *adj* landed (*gentry*) || *mf* landowner; landlubber || *m* earthman

terrier [terje] *m* hole, burrow; (*dog*) terrier

terrifier [terifje] *tr* to terrify

terrir [terir] *intr* to come close to shore (*said of fish*)

territoire [teritwar] *m* territory

terroir [terwar] *m* soil; homeland

terroriser [terɔrize] *tr* to terrorize

tertiaire [tersjer] *adj* tertiary

tertre [tertr] *m* mound, knoll

tes [te] §88

tesson [tesɔ̃] *m* shard; broken glass

test [test] *m* test; (zool) shell; **test de niveau** placement test

testament [testamɑ̃] *m* testament; will

testa·teur [testatœr] **-trice** [tris] *mf* testator

tester [teste] *tr* to test || *intr* to make one's will

testicule [testikyl] *m* testicle

tétanos [tetanos] *m* tetanus

têtard [tetar] *m* tadpole; (bot) pollard

tête [tet] *f* head; heading (*e.g., of chapter*); **à la tête de** in charge of, at the head of; **à tête reposée** at (one's) leisure; **avoir la tête près du bonnet** (coll) to be quick-tempered; **avoir une bonne tête** to have a pleasant look or expression; **de tête** in one's mind's eye, mentally; capable, e.g., **une femme de tête** a capable woman;

en avoir par-dessus la tête (coll) to be fed up with it; en tête foremost, at the front, leading; en tête à tête avec alone with; faire la tête à to frown at, to give a dirty look to; faire une tête to wear a long face; forte tête strong-minded person; jeter à la tête à qn (fig) to cast in s.o.'s face; la tête en bas head downwards, upside down; la tête la première headfirst, headlong; laver la tête à qn (coll) to give s.o. a dressing down; mauvaise tête troublemaker; monter à la tête de qn to go to s.o.'s head; n'en faire qu'à sa tête to be a law unto oneself; par tête per capita, per head; piquer une tête to take a header, to dive; saluer de la tête to nod; se mettre en tête de to take it into one's head to; se payer la tête de qn (coll) to pull s.o.'s leg; tenir tête à to face up to, to stand up to; tête baissée headlong, heedless; tête brûlée daredevil; tête chercheuse homing head (of missile); tête d'affiche (theat) headliner; tête de bois blockhead; tête de cuvée choice wine; tête de lecture (elec) playback head; tête de ligne truck terminal; tête de linotte scatterbrain; tête de pont (mil) bridgehead, beachhead; tête de Turc butt, scapegoat, fall guy; tête montée excitable person; tête morte et tibias skull and crossbones; tomber sur la tête (coll) to be off one's rocker

tête-à-queue [tɛtakø] m invar about-face, slue

tétée [tete] f sucking; feeding time
téter [tete] §10 tr & intr to suck
tétine [tetin] f nipple; teat
téton [tetɔ̃] m (coll) tit
tétras [tetra] m grouse
tette [tɛt] f (coll) tit
tê·tu -tue [tɛty] adj stubborn
teuf-teuf [tœftœf] m (pl teuf-teuf or teufs-teufs) (coll) jalopy || interj chug!, chug!
tévé [teve] f (acronym) (télévision) TV
texte [tɛkst] m text; apprendre son texte (theat) to learn one's lines
textile [tɛkstil] adj & m textile
tex·tuel -tuelle [tɛkstɥɛl] adj textual; verbatim
texture [tɛkstyr] f texture
thaï [tai] adj invar & m Thai
thaïlan·dais [tajlɑ̃dɛ] -daise [dɛz] adj Thai || (cap) mf Thai
Thaïlande [tajlɑ̃d] f Thailand
thaumaturge [tomatyrʒ] m miracle worker, magician
thé [te] m tea
théâ·tral -trale [teatral] adj (pl -traux [tro]) theatrical
théâtre [teatr] m theater; stage, boards; scene (e.g., of the crime)
théier [teje] théière [tejɛr] adj tea || m tea (shrub) || f see théière
théière [tejɛr] f teapot
thème [tɛm] m theme; translation (into a foreign language)
théologie [teɔlɔʒi] f theology
théorème [teɔrɛm] m theorem

théorie [teɔri] f theory; procession
théorique [teɔrik] adj theoretical
thérapeutique [terapøtik] adj therapeutic || f therapeutics
thérapie [terapi] f therapy
Thérèse [terɛz] f Theresa
ther·mal -male [tɛrmal] adj (pl -maux [mo]) thermal
thermique [tɛrmik] adj thermal
thermocouple [tɛrmɔkupl] m thermocouple
thermodynamique [tɛrmɔdinamik] adj thermodynamic || f thermodynamics
thermomètre [tɛrmɔmɛtr] m thermometer
thermonucléaire [tɛrmɔnykleɛr] adj thermonuclear
Thermopyles [tɛrmɔpil] fpl—les Thermopyles Thermopylae
thermos [tɛrmɔs] f thermos bottle
thermosiphon [tɛrmɔsifɔ̃] m hot-water heater
thermostat [tɛrmɔsta] m thermostat
thésauriser [tezorize] tr & intr to hoard
thésauri·seur [tezorizœr] -seuse [zøz] mf hoarder
thèse [tɛz] f thesis
thon [tɔ̃] m tuna
thorax [tɔraks] m thorax
thrène [trɛn] m threnody
thuriféraire [tyriferɛr] m incense bearer; flatterer
thym [tɛ̃] m thyme
thyroïde [tiroid] adj & f thyroid
tiare [tjar] f tiara (papal miter); papacy
tibia [tibja] m tibia; shin; tibias croisés et tête de mort skull and crossbones
tic [tik] m (pathol) tic; tic tac ticktock
ticket [tikɛ] m ticket (of bus, subway, etc.); check (for article in baggage room); ration stamp; sans tickets unrationed; ticket de quai platform ticket
tic-tac [tiktak] m invar tick
tiède [tjɛd] adj lukewarm; mild
tiédeur [tjedœr] f lukewarmness; mildness
tiédir [tjedir] tr to take the chill off || intr to become lukewarm
tien [tjɛ̃] tienne [tjɛn] §89
tiens [tjɛ̃] interj well!, hey!
tiers [tjɛr] tierce [tjɛrs] adj third; tertian (fever) || m third (in fractions); le tiers a third; the third party; le tiers et le quart (coll) everybody and anybody || f (typ) press proof
tige [tiʒ] f stem; trunk; shaft; shank; piston rod; leg (of boot); stock (of genealogy)
tignasse [tiɲas] f shock, mop (of hair)
tigre [tigr] m tiger
ti·gré -grée [tigre] adj striped; speckled, spotted
tigresse [tigrɛs] f tigress
tillac [tijak] m top deck (of old-time ships)
tilleul [tijœl] m linden
timbale [tɛ̃bal] f metal cup, mug; (culin) mold; (mus) kettledrum; décrocher la timbale (coll) to carry off the prize
timbalier [tɛ̃balje] m kettledrummer

timbrage [tɛ̃braʒ] m stamping; cancellation (of mail)

timbre [tɛ̃br] m bell; doorbell; buzzer; seal, stamp; postage stamp; postmark; snare (of drum); (phonet, phys) timbre

tim•bré -brée [tɛ̃bre] adj stamped; ringing (voice); (coll) cracked, crazy

timbre-poste [tɛ̃brəpɔst] m (pl timbres-poste) postage stamp

timbrer [tɛ̃bre] tr to stamp; to postmark

timbres-prime [tɛ̃mbrəprim] mpl trading stamps

timide [timid] adj timid, shy

timon [timɔ̃] m pole (of carriage); beam (of plow); (naut) helm

timonier [timɔnje] m helmsman; wheel horse

timo•ré -rée [timɔre] adj timorous

tin [tɛ̃] m chock

tinette [tinɛt] f firkin (tub); bucket (for fecal matter)

tintamarre [tɛ̃tamar] m uproar

tintement [tɛ̃tmã] m tolling (of bell); tinkle (of bell); ringing (in ears)

tinter [tɛ̃te] tr to toll ‖ intr to toll; to tinkle; to jingle, to clink; to ring (said of ears)

tintin [tɛ̃tɛ̃] m—faire tintin (slang) to do without ‖ interj (slang) nothing doing!

tintouin [tɛ̃twɛ̃] m (coll) trouble

tique [tik] f (ent) tick

tiquer [tike] intr to twitch; (coll) to wince; sans tiquer (coll) without turning a hair

tir [tir] m shooting; firing; aim; shooting gallery; tir à la cible target practice; tir à l'arc archery; tir au fusil gunnery; tir au pigeon trapshooting

tirade [tirad] f (theat) long speech

tirage [tiraʒ] m drawing; towing; draft (of chimney); printing; circulation (of newspaper); (coll) tension, friction; tirage à part offprint; tirage au sort lottery drawing; tirage de luxe deluxe edition

tiraillement [tirajmã] m pain, cramp; conflict, tension

tirailler [tiraje] tr to pull about, to tug at; to pester ‖ intr to blaze away; tirailler sur to snipe at ‖ ref to have a misunderstanding

tirailleur [tirajœr] m sharpshooter; sniper; (fig) free lance

tirant [tirã] m string; strap; tirant d'eau draft (of ship)

tire [tir] f (heral) row (of vair); (slang) car, auto; (Canad) taffy pull

ti•ré -rée [tire] adj drawn; printed ‖ m shooting preserve; payee; tiré à part offprint

tire-au-flanc [tiroflã] m invar malingerer, shirker

tire-botte [tirbɔt] m (pl -bottes) bootjack

tire-bouchon [tirbuʃɔ̃] m (pl -bouchons) corkscrew; corkscrew curl

tire-bouchonner [tirbuʃɔne] tr to twist in a spiral

tire-bouton [tirbutɔ̃] m (pl -boutons) buttonhook

tire-clou [tirklu] m (pl -clous) nail puller

tire-d'aile [tirdɛl]—à tire-d'aile with wings outspread, swiftly

tire-fond [tirfɔ̃] m invar spike; screw eye

tire-larigot [tirlarigo]—boire à tire-larigot to drink like a fish

tire-ligne [tirliɲ] m (pl -lignes) ruling pen

tirelire [tirlir] f piggy bank; (face) (coll) mug; (head) (coll) noggin; (slang) belly

tire-l'œil [tirlœj] m invar eye catcher

tirer [tire] tr to draw; to pull, to tug; to shoot, to fire; to run off, to print; to take out; to take, to get; to stick out (one's tongue); tirer au clair to bring out into the open; tirer parti de to turn to account ‖ intr to pull; to shoot; to draw (e.g., to a close); to draw (said of chimney); tirer à, vers, or sur to border on ‖ ref to extricate oneself; s'en tirer to manage; se tirer d'affaire to pull through, to get along

tiret [tirɛ] m dash; blank (to be filled in)

tirette [tirɛt] f slide (of desk); damper (of chimney)

tireur [tirœr] m marksman; drawer, payer (of check); printer; tireur de bois flotté log driver; tireur d'élite sharpshooter; tireur d'épée fencer; tireur isolé sniper

tireuse [tirøz] f markswoman; tireuse de cartes fortuneteller

tiroir [tirwar] m drawer; (mach) slide valve; à tiroirs episodic (play, novel, etc.)

tiroir-caisse [tirwarkɛs] m (pl tiroirs-caisses) cash register

tisane [tizan] f tea, infusion; (coll) bad champagne; (slang) slap

tison [tizɔ̃] m ember; (fig) firebrand

tisonner [tizɔne] tr to poke

tisonnier [tizɔnje] m poker

tissage [tisaʒ] m weaving

tisser [tise] tr & intr to weave

tisse•rand [tisrã] -rande [rãd] mf weaver

tis•seur [tisœr] tis•seuse [tisøz] mf weaver

tissu [tisy] m tissue; cloth; fabric, material; pack (of lies)

tissu-éponge [tisyepɔ̃ʒ] m (pl tissus-éponges) toweling, terry cloth

tissure [tisyr] f texture; (fig) framework

titane [titan] m titanium

titi [titi] m (slang) street urchin

Titien [tisjɛ̃] m—le Titien Titian

titre [titr] m title; title page; heading; fineness (of coinage); claim, right; concentration (of a solution); à juste titre rightly so; à titre de in the capacity of; by virtue of; à titre d'emprunt as a loan; à titre d'essai on trial; à titre gratuit or gracieux free of charge; titres qualifications; (com) securities

titrer [titre] tr to title; to subtitle (films)

tituber [titybe] *intr* to stagger
titulaire [tityle̞r] *adj* titular || *mf* incumbent; holder (*of passport, license, degree, post*)
titulariser [titylarize] *tr* to confirm the appointment of
toast [tost] *m* toast; **porter un toast à** to toast
toboggan [tɔbɔgã] *m* toboggan; toboggan run; slide, chute
toc [tɔk] *adj invar* (coll) worthless; (coll) crazy || *m* (mach) chuck; (coll) imitation; **en toc** (coll) worthless; **toc, toc!** knock, knock!
tohu-bohu [tɔybɔy] *m* hubbub
toi [twa] §85, §87
toile [twal] *f* cloth; linen; canvas, painting; (theat) curtain; **toile à coton** calico; **toile à laver** dishrag; **toile à matelas** ticking; **toile à voile** sailcloth; **toile cirée** oilcloth; **toile d'araignée** cobweb; **toile de fond** backdrop
toilette [twale̞t] *f* toilet; dressing table; dress, outfit (*of a woman*); **aimer la toilette** to be fond of clothing; **faire la toilette de** to lay out (*a corpse*)
toi-même [twame̞m] §86
toise [twaz] *f* fathom; **passer à la toise** to measure the height of
toiser [twaze] *tr* to size up
toison [twazɔ̃] *f* fleece; mop (*of hair*); **Toison d'or** Golden Fleece
toit [twa] *m* roof; rooftop; home, house; **crier sur les toits** to shout from the housetops
toiture [twatyr] *f* roofing
tôle [tol] *f* sheet metal; tole (*decorative metalware*); **tôle de blindage** armor plate; **tôle étamée** tin plate; **tôle galvanisée** galvanized iron; **tôle noire** sheet iron; **tôle ondulée** corrugated iron
tolérable [tɔlerabl] *adj* tolerable, bearable
tolérance [tɔlerãs] *f* tolerance
tolérer [tɔlere] §10 *tr* to tolerate
tôlerie [tolri] *f* sheet metal; rolling mill
tolet [tɔle̞] *m* oarlock
tomaison [tɔme̞zɔ̃] *f* volume number
tomate [tɔmat] *f* tomato
tombe [tɔ̃b] *f* tomb; grave; tombstone
tom·beau [tɔ̃bo] *m* (*pl* **-beaux**) tomb; **à tombeau couvert** lickety-split
tombée [tɔ̃be] *f* fall (*of rain, snow, etc.*); **tombée de la nuit** nightfall
tomber [tɔ̃be] *tr* to throw (*a wrestler*); (coll) to remove (*a piece of clothing*); (slang) to seduce (*a woman*) || *intr* (*aux:* ÊTRE) to fall, to drop; **tomber amoureux** to fall in love; **tomber bien** to happen just in time; **tomber en panne** to have a breakdown; **tomber sur** to run into, chance upon; to turn to (*said of conversation*)
tombe·reau [tɔ̃bro] *m* (*pl* **-reaux**) dump truck; dumpcart; load
tombola [tɔ̃bɔla] *m* raffle
tome [tɔm] *m* tome, volume
ton [tɔ̃] *adj poss* §88 || *m* tone; (mus) key

to·nal **-nale** [tɔnal] *adj* (*pl* **-nals**) tonal
ton·deur [tɔ̃dœr] **-deuse** [døz] *mf* shearer || *f* shears; **tondeuse à cheveux** hair clippers; **tondeuse à gazon** lawn mower; **tondeuse (à gazon) à moteur** power mower; **tondeuse électrique** electric clippers; **tondeuse mécanique** cropper; power mower
tondre [tɔ̃dr] *tr* to clip; to shear; to mow
toni·fiant [tɔnifjã] **-fiante** [fjãt] *adj* & *m* tonic
tonifier [tɔnifje] *tr* to tone up
tonique [tɔnik] *adj* & *m* tonic
toni·truant [tɔnitryã] **-truante** [tryãt] *adj* (coll) thunderous
tonne [tɔn] *f* ton; tun
ton·neau [tɔno] *m* (*pl* **-neaux**) barrel; cart; roll (*of automobile, airplane, etc.*); (naut) ton; **au tonneau** on draught; **tonneau de poudre** powder keg
tonnelet [tɔnle̞] *m* keg
tonnelier [tɔnəlje] *m* cooper
tonnelle [tɔne̞l] *f* arbor
tonner [tɔne] *intr* to thunder
tonnerre [tɔne̞r] *m* thunder
tonte [tɔ̃t] *f* clipping; shearing; mowing
tonton [tɔ̃tɔ̃] *m* (slang) uncle
top [tɔp] *m* beep
topaze [tɔpaz] *f* topaz
toper [tɔpe] *intr* to shake hands on it; **tope là!** it's a deal!
topinambour [tɔpinãbur] *m* Jerusalem artichoke
topique [tɔpik] *adj* local, regional
topographie [tɔpɔgrafi] *f* topography
toquade [tɔkad] *f* (coll) infatuation
toquante [tɔkãt] *f* (coll) ticker (*watch*)
toque [tɔk] *f* toque; cap (*of chef; of judge*)
to·qué **-quée** [tɔke] *adj* (coll) crazy, cracked || *mf* (coll) nut
toquer [tɔke] *tr* to infatuate || *intr* (coll) to rap, tap || *ref*—**se toquer de** to be infatuated with
torche [tɔrʃ] *f* torch; **se mettre en torche** to fail to open (*said of parachute*); **torche électrique** flashlight
torcher [tɔrʃe] *tr* to wipe clean; to rush through, to botch; to daub with clay and straw
torchère [tɔrʃe̞r] *f* candelabrum; floor lamp
torchis [tɔrʃi] *m* adobe
torchon [tɔrʃɔ̃] *m* dishcloth; rag; (coll) scribble; **le torchon brûle** they're squabbling
torchonner [tɔrʃɔne] *tr* (coll) to botch
tor·dant [tɔrdã] **-dante** [dãt] *adj* (coll) sidesplitting
tord-boyaux [tɔrbwajo] *m invar* (coll) rotgut
tordeuse [tɔrdøz] *f* moth
tordoir [tɔrdwar] *m* wringer; rope-making machine
tordre [tɔrdr] *tr* to twist; to wring || *ref* to twist; to writhe; **se tordre de rire** to split one's sides laughing
tornade [tɔrnad] *f* tornado
toron [tɔrɔ̃] *m* strand (*of rope*)
torpédo [tɔrpedo] *f* (archaic) open touring car

torpeur [tɔrpœr] f torpor
torpille [tɔrpij] f torpedo; (arti) mine
torpiller [tɔrpije] tr to torpedo
torpilleur [tɔrpijœr] m torpedo boat; torpedoman
torque [tɔrk] f coil of wire; twist (of tobacco)
torréfaction [tɔrefaksjɔ̃] f roasting
torréfier [tɔrefje] tr to roast
torrent [tɔrɑ̃] m torrent
torride [tɔrid] adj torrid
tors [tɔr] torse [tɔrs] adj twisted; crooked || m twist || see torse m
torsade [tɔrsad] f twisted cord; coil (of hair); à torsades fringed
torsader [tɔrsade] tr to twist
torse [tɔrs] m torso, trunk
torsion [tɔrsjɔ̃] f twisting, torsion
tort [tɔr] m wrong; harm; à tort wrongly; à tort et à travers at random, wildly; carelessly, inconsiderately; à tort ou à raison rightly or wrongly; avoir tort to be wrong; donner tort à to lay the blame on; faire tort à to wrong
torticolis [tɔrtikɔli] m stiff neck
tortillard [tɔrtijar] adj masc knotty || m (coll) jerkwater train
tortiller [tɔrtije] tr to twist, to twirl; (slang) to gulp down || intr to wriggle; (coll) to beat about the bush || ref to wriggle, squirm; to writhe, twist
tor•tu -tue [tɔrty] adj crooked || f turtle, tortoise
tor•tueux [tɔrtɥø] -tueuse [tɥøz] adj winding; devious, underhanded
torture [tɔrtyr] f torture
torturer [tɔrtyre] tr to torture
torve [tɔrv] adj menacing
tos•can [tɔskɑ̃] -cane [kan] adj Tuscan || m Tuscan (dialect) || (cap) mf Tuscan (person)
tôt [to] adv soon; early; au plus tôt as soon as possible; at the earliest; le plus tôt possible as soon as possible; pas de si tôt not soon; tôt ou tard sooner or later
to•tal -tale [tɔtal] adj & m (pl -taux [to]) total
totaliser [tɔtalize] tr to total
totalitaire [tɔtaliter] adj totalitarian
totem [tɔtɛm] m totem
toton [tɔtɔ̃] m teetotum
toubib [tubib] m (coll) medical officer; (coll) doctor, physician
tou•chant [tuʃɑ̃] -chante [ʃɑ̃t] adj touching || touchant prep touching, concerning
touche [tuʃ] f touch; key (of piano or typewriter); stop (of organ); fret (of guitar); fingerboard (of violin); hit (in fencing); bite (on fishline); goad (for cattle); tab (of file index); thumb index; (elec) contact; (coll) look, appearance; touche de blocage shift lock; touche de manœuvre shift key
touche-à-tout [tuʃatu] m invar (coll) busybody
toucher [tuʃe] m touch, sense of touch || tr to touch; to concern; to cash (a check); to draw out (money); to goad

(cattle); (mus) to pluck (the strings) || intr to touch; toucher à to touch (one's food, capital, etc.); to touch on; to call at (a port); to be about to achieve (one's aim); toucher de to play (e.g., the piano) || ref to touch
touer [twe] tr to warp, to kedge
touffe [tuf] f tuft; clump (of trees)
touffeur [tufœr] f suffocating heat
touf•fu -fue [tufy] adj bushy; (fig) dense
touille [tuj] m dogfish, shark
touiller [tuje] tr (coll) to stir; (coll) to mix; (coll) to shuffle
toujours [tuʒur] adv always; still; anyhow; M. Toujours (coll) yes man; pour toujours forever
toupet [tupɛ] m tuft (of hair); forelock (of horse); (coll) nerve, brass
toupie [tupi] f top; molding board; silly woman
tour [tur] m turn; tour; trick; lathe; à tour de bras with all one's might; à tour de rôle in turn; en un tour de main in a jiffy; faire le tour de to tour, to visit; to walk or ride around; faire un tour de to take a walk or ride in; tour à tour by turns; tour de bâton (coll) rake-off, killing; tour de main, tour d'adresse sleight of hand; tour de poitrine chest size; tour de taille waist measurement; tour de tête hat size; tours et retours twists and turns || f tower; (chess) castle, rook; (mil) turret; tour de contrôle control tower; tour de guet lookout tower
tourbe [turb] f peat; mob
tourbillon [turbijɔ̃] m whirl; whirlpool; whirlwind
tourbillonner [turbijɔne] intr to whirl, to swirl
tourelle [turɛl] f turret
tourillon [turijɔ̃] m axle; trunnion
touriste [turist] adj & mf tourist
tourment [turmɑ̃] m torment
tourmente [turmɑ̃t] f storm
tourmenter [turmɑ̃te] tr to torment || ref to fret
tour•nant [turnɑ̃] -nante [nɑ̃t] adj turning, revolving || m turn; turning point; water wheel
tourne-à-gauche [turnagoʃ] m invar wrench; saw set; diestock
tournebroche [turnəbrɔʃ] m roasting jack, turnspit
tourne-disque [turnədisk] m (pl -disques) record player
tournedos [turnədo] m filet mignon
tournée [turne] f round; en tournée (theat) on tour; faire une tournée to take a trip; tournée électorale political campaign
tournemain [turnəmɛ̃]—en un tournemain in a split second
tourne-pierre [turnəpjer] m (pl -pierres) (orn) turnstone
tourner [turne] tr to turn; to turn over; to shoot (a moving picture; a scene); to outflank; tourner et retourner to turn over and over || intr to turn; (mov) to shoot a picture; (theat) to tour; la tête me (lui, etc.) tourne my

(his, etc.) head is turning, I feel (he feels, etc.) dizzy; **silence, on tourne!** quiet on the set!; **tourner à** or **en** to turn into; **tourner autour du pot** (coll) to beat about the bush; **tourner bien** to turn out well; **tourner en rond** to go around in circles, to spin; **tourner mal** to go bad ‖ *ref* to turn

tournesol [turnəsɔl] *m* litmus; sunflower

tournevis [turnəvis] *m* screwdriver

tourniquet [turnikɛ] *m* turnstile; revolving door; revolving display stand; (surg) tourniquet; **passer au tourniquet** (slang) to be court-martialed

tournoi [turnwa] *m* tournament

tournoyer [turnwaje] §47 *intr* to turn, to wheel; to twirl; to tourney

tournure [turnyr] *f* turn, course (*of events*); wording, phrasing, turn (*of phrase*); expression; shape, figure

tourte [turt] *adj* (slang) stupid ‖ *f* (coll) dolt; **tourte à la viande** meat pie

tour·teau [turto] *m* (*pl* **-teaux**) oil cake; crab

tourte·reau [turtəro] *m* (*pl* **-reaux**) turtledove, young lover

tourterelle [turtərɛl] *f* turtledove

tourtière [turtjɛr] *f* pie pan

toussailler [tusɑje] *intr* to keep on coughing

Toussaint [tusɛ̃] *f* All Saints' Day; **la Toussaint** All Saints' Day

tousser [tuse] *intr* to cough; to clear one's throat

tousserie [tusri] *f* constant coughing

toussotement [tusɔtmɑ̃] *m* slight coughing

toussoter [tusɔte] *intr* to cough slightly

tout [tu] **toute** [tut] (*pl* **tous toutes**) *adj* any, every, all; **tous les** all, all of, e.g., **tous les hommes** all men, all of the men; whole, entire, e.g., **toute la journeé** the whole day; **à tout coup** every time; **à toute heure** at any time; **tous les deux** both ‖ *m* (*pl* **touts**) whole, all; everything; sum; **du tout** (coll) not at all; **en tout** wholly, in all; **pas du tout** not at all ‖ **tout toute** (*pl* **tous** [tus] **toutes**) *pron* all, everything, anything; **à tout prendre** on the whole; **tout compté** all things considered ‖ **tout** *adv* all, quite, completely; very, e.g., **un des tout premiers** one of the very foremost; **tout à côté de** right next to; **tout à coup** suddenly; **tout à fait** quite; **tout à l'heure** in a little while; a little while ago; **tout au plus** at most; **tout de même** however, all the same; **tout de suite** at once, immediately; **tout en** while, e.g., **tout en parlant** while talking; **tout éveillé** wide awake; **tout fait** ready-made; **tout haut** aloud; **tout neuf** brand-new; **tout nu** stark-naked; **tout près** nearby; **tout . . . que** despite the fact that, e.g., **tout vieux qu'il était** despite the fact that he was old ‖ **toute toutes** *adv* (before a feminine word beginning with a

consonant or an aspirate **h**) all, quite, completely, e.g., **elles sont toutes seules** they are all (or quite or completely) alone

tout-à-l'égout [tutalegu] *m invar* sewerage

toute-épice [tutepis] *f* (*pl* **toutes-épices** [tutepis]) allspice (*berry*)

toutefois [tutfwa] *adv* however

toute-puissance [tutpɥisɑ̃s] *f* omnipotence

toutou [tutu] *m* (coll) doggie

Tout-Paris [tupari] *m invar* high society, smart set (*in Paris*)

tout-petit [tupəti] *m* (*pl* **-petits**) toddler

tout-puissant [tupɥisɑ̃] **toute-puissante** [tutpɥisɑ̃t] (*pl* **tout-puissants toutes-puissantes**) *adj* almighty ‖ **le Tout-Puissant** the Almighty

tout-venant [tuvnɑ̃] *m invar* all comers; run-of-the-mine coal; run-of-the-mill product; ordinary run of people

toux [tu] *f* cough

toxicomane [tɔksikɔman] *adj* addicted ‖ *mf* drug addict

toxicomanie [tɔksikɔmani] *f* drug addiction

toxique [tɔksik] *adj* toxic ‖ *m* poison

trac [trak] *m* (coll) stage fright; **avoir le trac** (coll) to lose one's nerve; **tout à trac** without thinking

tracas [traka] *m* worry, trouble

tracasser [trakase] *tr* & *ref* to worry

tracasserie [trakasri] *f* bother; **tracasseries** interference

tracassin [trakasɛ̃] *m* (coll) worry

trace [tras] *f* trace; track, trail; sketch; footprint; **marcher sur les traces de** to follow in the footsteps of

tracé [trase] *m* tracing; **faire le tracé de** to lay out; (math) to plot

tracer [trase] §51 *tr* to trace, draw

tra·ceur [trasœr] **-ceuse** [søz] *mf* tracer ‖ *m* tracer (*radioactive substance*)

trachée [traʃe] *f* trachea, windpipe

trachée-artère [traʃeartɛr] *f* (*pl* **trachées-artères**) windpipe

tract [trakt] *m* tract

tractation [traktasjɔ̃] *f* underhanded deal

tracteur [traktœr] *m* tractor

traction [traksjɔ̃] *f* traction; **faire des tractions** to do chin-ups; **traction avant** front-wheel drive

tradition [tradisjɔ̃] *f* tradition

tradition·nel **-nelle** [tradisjɔnɛl] *adj* traditional

traduc·teur [tradyktœr] **-trice** [tris] *mf* translator

traduction [tradyksjɔ̃] *f* translation

traduire [tradɥir] §19 *tr* to translate; **traduire en justice** to haul into court

trafic [trafik] *m* traffic, trade; **trafic d'influence** influence peddling; **trafic routier** highway traffic

trafi·quant [trafikɑ̃] **-quante** [kɑ̃t] *mf* racketeer; **trafiquant en stupéfiants** dope peddler

trafiquer [trafike] *tr* to traffic in ‖ *intr* to traffic; **trafiquer de** to traffic in or on

trafi·queur [trafikœr] **-queuse** [køz] *mf* racketeer

tragédie [traʒedi] *f* tragedy
tragé·dien [traʒedjɛ̃] **-dienne** [djɛn] *mf* tragedian
tragique [traʒik] *adj* tragic
trahir [trair] *tr* to betray
trahison [traizɔ̃] *f* betrayal; treason
train [trɛ̃] *m* pace, speed; manner, way; series; raft (*of logs*); (rr) train; (coll) row, racket; **être en train de** + *inf* to be in the act or process of + *ger*; (translated by a progressive form of the verb), e.g., **je suis en train d'écrire** I am writing; **mettre en train** to start; **train arrière** (aut) rear-axle assembly; (rr) rear car; **train avant** (aut) front-axle assembly; **train d'atterrissage** landing gear; **train de banlieue** suburban train; **train de marchandises** freight train; **train de vie** way of life; standard of living; **train direct** through train; **train omnibus** local train; **train sanitaire** military hospital train
trai·nant [trɛnɑ̃] **-nante** [nɑ̃t] *adj* trailing; creeping; drawling; languid
trai·nard [trɛnar] **-narde** [nard] *mf* straggler
traîne [trɛn] *f* train (*of dress*); dragnet; **à la traîne** dragging; straggling; in tow
traî·neau [trɛno] *m* (*pl* **-neaux**) sleigh; sled; sledge; dragnet
traînée [trɛne] *f* trail, train; (coll) streetwalker
traîner [trɛne] *tr* to drag, to lug; to drawl; to shuffle (*the feet*) ‖ *intr* to drag; to straggle; to lie around ‖ *ref* to crawl; to creep; to limp
traî·neur [trɛnœr] **-neuse** [nøz] *mf* straggler; loiterer
train-train [trɛ̃trɛ̃] *m* routine
traire [trɛr] §68 *tr* to milk
trait [trɛ] *m* arrow, dart; dash; stroke; feature (*of face*); trait, characteristic; trace (*of harness*); **avoir trait à** to refer to; **de trait** draft (*horse*); **d'un trait** in one gulp; **partir comme un trait** to be off like a shot; **tracer à grands traits** to trace in broad outlines; **trait d'esprit** witticism; **trait d'héroïsme** heroic deed; **trait d'union** hyphen; **trait pour trait** exactly
traitable [trɛtabl] *adj* tractable
traite [trɛt] *f* trade, traffic; milking; (com) draft; **tout d'une traite at a** single stretch
traité [trɛte] *m* treatise; treaty
traitement [trɛtmɑ̃] *m* treatment; salary; **mauvais traitements** affront, mistreatment
traiter [trɛte] *tr* to treat; to receive; **traiter qn de** to call s.o. (*a name*) ‖ *intr* to negotiate; **traiter de** to deal with
traiteur [trɛtœr] *m* caterer; (obs) restaurateur
traî·tre [trɛtr] **-tresse** [trɛs] *adj* traitorous; treacherous; (coll) single ‖ *mf* traitor; (theat) villain ‖ *f* traitress
traîtrise [trɛtriz] *f* treachery
trajectoire [traʒɛktwar] *f* trajectory
trajet [traʒɛ] *m* distance, trip, passage; (aer) flight

tralala [tralala] *m* (coll) fuss
trame [tram] *f* weft; web (*of life*); conspiracy
tramer [trame] *tr* to weave; to hatch (*a plot*) ‖ *ref* to be plotted
traminot [tramino] *m* traction-company employee
tramontane [tramɔ̃tan] *f* north wind; **perdre la tramontane** to lose one's bearings
tramp [trɑp] *m* tramp steamer
tramway [tramwɛ] *m* streetcar
tran·chant [trɑ̃ʃɑ̃] **-chante** [ʃɑ̃t] *adj* cutting; glaring; trenchant ‖ *m* cutting edge; knife; side (*of hand*); **à double tranchant** or **à deux tranchants** two-edged
tranche [trɑ̃ʃ] *f* slice; section; portion, installment; group (*of figures*); cross section; **doré sur tranches** gilt-edged; (coll) gilded (*e.g., youth*); **une tranche de vie** a slice of life
tranchée [trɑ̃ʃe] *f* trench; **tranchées** colic
trancher [trɑ̃ʃe] *tr* to cut off; to slice; to decide, settle ‖ *intr* to decide once and for all; to stand out; **trancher avec** to contrast with; **trancher dans le vif** to cut to the quick; (fig) to take drastic measures; **trancher de** (lit) to affect the manners of
tranquille [trɑ̃kil] *adj* quiet, tranquil; **laissez-moi tranquille** leave me alone; **soyez tranquille** don't worry
tranquilli·sant [trɑ̃kilizɑ̃] **-sante** [zɑ̃t] *adj* tranquilizing ‖ *m* tranquilizer
tranquilliser [trɑ̃kilize] *tr* to tranquilize; to reassure ‖ *ref* to calm down
tranquillité [trɑ̃kilite] *f* tranquillity
transaction [trɑ̃zaksjɔ̃] *f* transaction; compromise
transat [trɑ̃zat] *m* (coll) transatlantic liner; (coll) deck chair ‖ **la Transat** (coll) the French Line
transatlantique [trɑ̃zatlɑ̃tik] *adj & m* transatlantic
transbordement [trɑ̃sbɔrdəmɑ̃] *m* transshipment, transfer
transborder [trɑ̃sbɔrde] *tr* to transship, to transfer
transbordeur [trɑ̃sbɔrdœr] *m* transporter bridge
transcender [trɑ̃sɑ̃de] *tr & ref* to transcend
transcription [trɑ̃skripsjɔ̃] *f* transcription
transcrire [trɑ̃skrir] §25 *tr* to transcribe; **transcrire en clair** to decode
transe [trɑ̃s] *f* apprehension, anxiety; trance; **être dans des transes** to be quaking in one's boots
transept [trɑ̃sɛpt] *m* transept
transférer [trɑ̃sfere] §10 *tr* to transfer; to convey
transfert [trɑ̃sfɛr] *m* transfer, transference
transfo [trɑ̃sfo] *m* (coll) transformer
transforma·teur [trɑ̃sfɔrmatœr] **-trice** [tris] *adj* (elec) transforming ‖ *m* (elec) transformer; **transformateur abaisseur** (de tension) step-down transformer; **transformateur de sonnerie** doorbell transformer; **transfor-**

mateur élévateur (de tension) step-up transformer

transformer [trãsfɔrme] *tr* & *ref* to transform

transfuge [trãsfyʒ] *m* turncoat

transfuser [trãsfyze] *tr* to transfuse; to instill

transfusion [trãsfyzjɔ̃] *f* transfusion

transgresser [trãsgrese] *tr* to transgress

transgression [trãsgresjɔ̃] *f* transgression

transhumer [trãzyme] *tr* & *intr* to move from winter to summer pasture

tran·si -sie [trãzi], [trãsi] *adj* chilled to the bone; numb, transfixed (*with fright*)

transiger [trãziʒe] §38 *intr* to compromise

transistor [trãzistɔr] *m* transistor

transit [trãzit] *m* transit

transi·tif [trãzitif] -tive [tiv] *adj* transitive

transition [trãzisjɔ̃] *f* transition

transitoire [trãzitwar] *adj* transitory; transitional

translation [trãslɑsjɔ̃] *f* transfer, translation

translitérer [trãslitere] §10 *tr* to transliterate

translucide [trãslysid] *adj* translucent

transmetteur [trãsmɛtœr] *adj masc* transmitting || *m* (telg, telp) transmitter; transmetteur d'ordres (naut) engine-room telegraph

transmettre [trãsmɛtr] §42 *tr* to transmit; to transfer; (sports) to pass

transmission [trãsmisjɔ̃] *f* transmission; broadcast; transmission en différé recorded broadcast; transmission en direct live broadcast; transmissions (mil) signal corps

transmuer [trãsmɥe] *tr* to transmute

transmuter [trãsmyte] *tr* to transmute

transparaître [trãsparɛtr] §12 *intr* to show through

transpa·rent [trãsparã] -rente [rãt] *adj* transparent

transpercer [trãspɛrse] §51 *tr* to transfix

transpiration [trãspirɑsjɔ̃] *f* perspiration

transpirer [trãspire] *tr* to sweat || *intr* to sweat, perspire; to leak out (*said of news*)

transplanter [trãsplãte] *tr* to transplant

transport [trãspɔr] *m* transport; transportation; transport au cerveau cerebral hemorrhage

transpor·té -tée [trãspɔrte] *adj* enraptured, carried away

transporter [trãspɔrte] *tr* to transport

transposer [trãspoze] *tr* to transpose

transver·sal -sale [trãsvɛrsal] *adj* (*pl* -saux [so]) transversal; cross (*street*)

trapèze [trapɛz] *m* trapeze; trapezoid

trappe [trap] *f* trap door; pitfall, trap; Trappist monastery; Trappe Trappist order

trappeur [trapœr] *m* trapper

tra·pu -pue [trapy] *adj* stocky, squat

traque [trak] *f* driving of game

traquenard [traknar] *m* trap, booby trap, pitfall

traquer [trake] *tr* to hem in, to bring to bay

traumatique [tromatik] *adj* traumatic

tra·vail [travaj] *m* (*pl* -vaux [vo]) work; workmanship; en travail in labor; Travail Labor; travail à la pièce, travail à la tâche piecework; travail d'équipe teamwork; travail de Romain herculean task; travaux forcés hard labor; travaux ménagers housework || *m* (*pl* -vails) stocks (*for horses*)

travail·lé -lée [travaje] *adj* finely wrought, elaborate; labored

travailler [travaje] *tr* to work; to worry || *intr* to work; to warp (*said of wood*)

travail·leur [travajœr] travail·leuse [travajøz] *adj* hardworking || *mf* worker, toiler

travailliste [travajist] *adj* & *mf* Labourite (Brit)

travée [trave] *f* span (*of bridge*); row of seats; (archit) bay

traveling [travliŋ] *m* (mov, telv) dolly (*for camera*)

travers [traver] *m* breadth; fault, failing; à travers across, through; de travers awry; en travers de across; par le travers de abreast of

traverse [travers] *f* crossbeam; cross street; setback; rung (*of ladder*); (rr) tie; de traverse cross (*e.g., street*); mettre à la traverse de to oppose

traversée [traverse] *f* crossing

traverser [traverse] *tr* to cross; to cut across

traver·sier [traversje] -sière [sjɛr] *adj* cross, crossing

traversin [traversɛ̃] *m* bolster (*of bed*)

traves·ti -tie [travesti] *adj* disguised; costume (*ball*) || *m* fancy costume, disguise; transvestite; female impersonator

travestir [travestir] *tr* to travesty; to disguise

travestissement [travestismã] *m* travesty; disguise

trébucher [trebyʃe] *intr* to stumble

tréfiler [trefile] *tr* to wiredraw

trèfle [trefl] *m* clover; trefoil; cloverleaf (*intersection*); (cards) club; (cards) clubs

tréfonds [trefɔ̃] *m* secret depths

treillage [trejaʒ] *m* trellis

treillager [trejaʒe] §38 *tr* to trellis

treille [trej] *f* grape arbor

treillis [treji] *m* latticework; iron grating; denim; treillis métallique wire netting

treillisser [trejise] *tr* to trellis

treize [trez] *adj* & *pron* thirteen; the Thirteenth, e.g., Jean treize John the Thirteenth || *m* thirteen; thirteenth (*in dates*); treize à la douzaine baker's dozen

treizième [trezjem] *adj, pron* (*masc, fem*), & *m* thirteenth

tréma [trema] *m* dieresis

tremble [trãbl] *m* aspen (*tree*)

tremblement [trãbləmã] *m* trembling; tremblement de terre earthquake

trembler [trãble] *intr* to tremble

trembleur [trɑ̃blœr] *m* vibrator, buzzer; (rel) Shaker; (rel) Quaker
trembloter [trɑ̃blɔte] *intr* to quiver; to quaver
trémie [tremi] *f* hopper
trémoussement [tremusmɑ̃] *m* fluttering, flutter; jiggling, jiggle
trémousser [tremuse] *ref* to flutter; to jiggle; (coll) to bustle
trempage [trɑ̃paʒ] *m* soaking
trempe [trɑ̃p] *f* temper; soaking; (slang) scolding
trempée [trɑ̃pe] *f* tempering
tremper [trɑ̃pe] *tr* to temper; to dilute; to dunk ‖ *intr* to soak; to become involved (*in, e.g., a crime*)
trempette [trɑ̃pɛt] *f*—**faire la trempette** to dunk; **faire trempette** to take a dip
tremplin [trɑ̃plɛ̃] *m* springboard, diving board; trampoline; ski jump; (fig) springboard
trentaine [trɑ̃tɛn] *f* age of thirty; **une trentaine de** about thirty
trente [trɑ̃t] *adj & pron* thirty; **sur son trente et un** (coll) all spruced up; **trente et un** thirty-one; **trente et unième** thirty-first ‖ *m* thirty; thirtieth (*in dates*); **trente et un** thirty-one; thirty-first (*in dates*); **trente et unième** thirty-first
trente-deux [trɑ̃tdø] *adj, pron, & m* thirty-two
trente-deuxième [trɑ̃tdøzjɛm] *adj, pron* (*masc, fem*), *& m* thirty-second
trente-six [trɑ̃tsi(s)] *adj, pron, & m* thirty-six; **tous les trente-six du mois** (coll) once in a blue moon
trentième [trɑ̃tjɛm] *adj, pron* (*masc, fem*), *& m* thirtieth
trépas [trepɑ] *m* (lit) death; **passer de vie à trépas** (lit) to pass away
trépasser [trepɑse] *intr* (lit) to die
trépied [trepje] *m* tripod
trépigner [trepiɲe] *intr* to stamp one's feet
très [trɛ] *adv* very; **le très honorable** the Right Honorable
trésor [trezɔr] *m* treasure; **Trésor** Treasury
trésorerie [trezɔrri] *f* treasury
tréso·rier [trezɔrje] **-rière** [rjɛr] *mf* treasurer
tressaillement [tresajmɑ̃] *m* start, quiver
tressaillir [tresajir] §69 *intr* to give a start, to quiver
tressauter [tresote] *intr* to start
tresse [trɛs] *f* tress
tresser [trese] *tr* to braid, to plait; to weave (*e.g., a basket*)
tré·teau [treto] *m* (*pl* **-teaux**) trestle; **sur les tréteaux** (theat) on the boards
treuil [trœj] *m* windlass; winch
trêve [trɛv] *f* truce; respite; **trêve de ... that's enough ...**
tri [tri] *m* sorting
triage [triaʒ] *m* sorting, selection; classification; (rr) shifting
triangle [trijɑ̃gl] *m* triangle
tribord [tribɔr] *m* starboard
tribu [triby] *f* tribe
tribu·nal [tribynal] *m* (*pl* **-naux** [no]) tribunal, court; **en plein tribunal** in

open court; **tribunal de police** police court; **tribunaux pour enfants** juvenile courts
tribune [tribyn] *f* rostrum, tribune; gallery; grandstand; **monter à la tribune** to take the floor; **tribune des journalistes** press box; **tribune d'orgue** organ loft; **tribune libre** open forum
tribut [triby] *m* tribute
tributaire [tribytɛr] *adj & m* tributary; **être tributaire de** to be dependent upon
tricher [triʃe] *tr & intr* to cheat
tricherie [triʃri] *f* cheating
tri·cheur [triʃœr] **-cheuse** [ʃøz] *mf* cheater; **tricheur professionnel** card-sharper
tricolore [trikɔlɔr] *adj & m* tricolor
tricot [triko] *m* knitting; knitted garment
tricotage [trikɔtaʒ] *m* knitting
tricoter [trikɔte] *tr & intr* to knit
trier [trije] *tr* to pick out, to screen; **trier sur le volet** to hand-pick
trieur [trijœr] **trieuse** [trijøz] *mf* sorter ‖ *m & f* (mach) sorter
trigonométrie [trigɔnɔmetri] *f* trigonometry
trille [trij] *m* trill
triller [trije] *tr & intr* to trill
trillion [triljɔ̃] *m* quintillion (U.S.A.); trillion (Brit)
trilogie [trilɔʒi] *f* trilogy
trimbaler [trɛ̃bale] *tr* to cart around
trimer [trime] *intr* to slave
trimestre [trimɛstr] *m* quarter (*of a year*); quarter's salary; quarter's rent; (educ) term
tringle [trɛ̃gl] *f* rod; **tringle de rideau** curtain rod
trinité [trinite] *f* trinity
trinquer [trɛ̃ke] *intr* to clink glasses, to toast; (slang) to drink; **trinquer avec** to hobnob with
trio [trijo] *m* trio
triom·phant [trijɔ̃fɑ̃] **-phante** [fɑ̃t] *adj* triumphant
triomphe [trijɔ̃f] *m* triumph; **faire triomphe à** to welcome in triumph
tripar·ti·tie [triparti] *adj* tripartite
tripartite [tripartit] *adj* tripartite
tripatouiller [tripatuje] *tr* (coll) to tamper with
tripette [tripɛt] *f*—**ça ne vaut pas tripette** it's not worth a wooden nickel
triple [tripl] *adj & m* triple
tri·plé -plée [triple] *mf* triplet
tripler [triple] *tr & intr* to triple
triplicata [triplikata] *m invar* triplicate
tripot [tripo] *m* gambling den; house of ill repute
tripoter [tripɔte] *tr* to finger, toy with ‖ *intr* to dabble, to potter around; to rummage
trique [trik] *f* (coll) cudgel
triste [trist] *adj* sad
tristesse [tristɛs] *f* sadness, sorrow
triturer [trityre] *tr* to pulverize, to grind ‖ *ref*—**se triturer la cervelle** to rack one's brains
tri·vial -viale [trivjal] *adj* (*pl* **-viaux** [vjo]) trivial; vulgar, coarse

trivialité [trivjalite] *f* triviality; vulgarity, coarseness

troc [trɔk] *m* barter; swap; **troc pour troc** even up

troglodyte [trɔglɔdit] *m* cave dweller; (orn) wren

trognon [trɔɲɔ̃] *m* core; (slang) darling, pet

Troie [trwɑ], [trwa] *f* Troy

trois [trwɑ] *adj & pron* three; the Third, e.g., **Jean trois** John the Third; **trois heures** three o'clock ‖ *m* three; third (*in dates*)

troisième [trwazjɛm] *adj, pron* (*masc, fem*), *& m* third

trolley [trɔlɛ] *m* trolley

trolleybus [trɔlɛbys] *m* trackless trolley

trombe [trɔ̃b] *f* waterspout; **entrer en trombe** to dash in; **trombe d'eau** deluge

trombone [trɔ̃bɔn] *m* trombone; paper clip

trompe [trɔ̃p] *f* horn; trunk (*of elephant*); beak (*of insect*); **trompe d'Eustache** Eustachian tube

trompe-la-mort [trɔ̃plamɔr] *mf invar* daredevil

trompe-l'œil [trɔ̃plœj] *m invar* dummy effect; (coll) bluff, fake; **en trompe-l'œil** in perspective

tromper [trɔ̃pe] *tr* to deceive, to cheat ‖ *ref* to be wrong; **se tromper de** to be mistaken about

tromperie [trɔ̃pri] *f* deceit; fraud; illusion

trompeter [trɔ̃pte] §34 *tr & intr* to trumpet

trompette [trɔ̃pɛt] *m* trumpeter ‖ *f* trumpet; **en trompette** turned up

trom·peur [trɔ̃pœr] **-peuse** [pøz] *adj* false, lying ‖ *mf* deceiver

tronc [trɔ̃] *m* trunk; (slang) head; **tronc des pauvres** poor box

tronche [trɔ̃ʃ] *f* (slang) noodle

tronçon [trɔ̃sɔ̃] *m* stump; section (*e.g., of track*)

trône [tron] *m* throne

trôner [trone] *intr* to sit in state ‖ *ref* —**se trôner sur** to lord it over

tronquer [trɔ̃ke] *tr* to truncate, to cut off; to mutilate

trop [tro] *m* excess; too much; **de trop** too much; to excess; in the way, e.g., **il est de trop ici** he is in the way here; **par trop** altogether, excessively; **trop de . . .** too much . . . ; too many . . . ‖ *adv* too; too much; **trop lourd** overweight

trophée [trɔfe] *m* trophy

tropi·cal -cale [trɔpikal] *adj* (*pl* -caux [ko]) tropical

trop-plein [trɔplɛ̃] *m* (*pl* -pleins) overflow

troquer [trɔke] *tr* to barter; **troquer contre** to swap for

trot [tro] *m* trot; **au trot** at a trot; (coll) on the double, quickly

trotte [trɔt] *f* (coll) quite a distance to walk

trotter [trɔte] *intr* to trot

trot·teur [trɔtœr] **trot·teuse** [trɔtøz] *mf* (turf) trotter ‖ *f* second hand; **trotteuse centrale** sweep-second

trottin [trɔtɛ̃] *m* errand girl

trottinette [trɔtinet] *f* scooter

trottoir [trɔtwar] *m* sidewalk; **faire le trottoir** to walk the streets (*said of prostitute*)

trou [tru] *m* hole; pothole; eye (*of needle*); gap; jerkwater town; **faire son trou** to feather one's nest; **faire un trou à la lune** to fly the coop; **trou d'air** air pocket; **trou de clef** keyhole (*of clock*); **trou de la serrure** keyhole; **trou d'obus** shell hole; **trou du souffleur** prompter's box; **trou individuel** (mil) foxhole

trouble [trubl] *adj* muddy, cloudy, turbid (*liquid*); murky (*sky*); misty (*glass*); blurred (*image; sight*); dim (*light*); vague, disquieting ‖ *m* disquiet; unrest; trouble (*illness*)

trouble-fête [trubləfɛt] *mf invar* wet blanket, kill-joy

troubler [truble] *tr* to upset, trouble; to make muddy; to disturb; to make cloudy; to blur ‖ *ref* to become muddy or cloudy; to lose one's composure

trouée [true] *f* gap, breach; (mil) breakthrough

trouille [truj] *f*—**avoir la trouille** (slang) to get cold feet

troupe [trup] *f* troop; band, party; (theat) troupe

trou·peau [trupo] *m* (*pl* -peaux) flock; herd; **attention aux troupeaux** (public sign) cattle crossing

troupier [trupje] *m* (coll) soldier; **jurer comme un troupier** to swear like a trooper

trousse [trus] *f* case, kit; **avoir qn à ses trousses** to have s.o. at one's heels; **trousse de première urgence** first-aid kit

trous·seau [truso] *m* (*pl* -seaux) trousseau; outfit; bunch (*of keys*)

troussequin [truskɛ̃] *m* cantle

trousser [truse] *tr* to turn up; to tuck up; to polish off; (culin) to truss ‖ *ref* to lift one's skirts

trouvaille [truvɑj] *f* find

trouver [truve] *tr* to find ‖ *ref* to be found; to find oneself; to be, e.g., **où se trouve-t-il?** where is he?; **il se trouve que . . .** it happens that . . . ; **se trouver mal** to feel ill

troyen [trwajɛ̃] **troyenne** [trwajɛn] *adj* Trojan ‖ (*cap*) *mf* Trojan

truand [tryɑ̃] **truande** [tryɑ̃d] *adj & m* good-for-nothing

truc [tryk] *m* gadget, device; (coll) trick, gimmick; (coll) thing; (coll) what's-his-name

truchement [tryʃmɑ̃] *m* spokesman; interpreter; **par le truchement de** thanks to, through

trucu·lent [trykylɑ̃] **-lente** [lɑ̃t] *adj* truculent

truelle [tryɛl] *f* trowel

truffe [tryf] *f* truffle

truie [tryi] *f* sow

truisme [tryism] *m* truism

truite [tryit] *f* trout

tru·meau [trymo] *m* (*pl* -meaux) trumeau (*mirror with painting above in same frame*)

truquage [tryka3] *m* faking
truquer [tryke] *tr* to fake; to cook (*the accounts*); to stack (*the deck*); to load (*the dice*); to fix (*the outcome of a fight*) ‖ *intr* to resort to fakery
trust [trœst] *m* trust, holding company
T.S.F. [teesεf] *f* (letterword) (**télégraphie sans fil**) wireless; radio
t. s. v. p. *abbr* (**tournez s'il vous plaît**) over (*please turn the page*)
tu [ty] §87; **être à tu et à toi avec** to hobnob with
T.U. [tey] *m* (letterword) (**temps universel**) universal time, Greenwich Mean Time
tube [tyb] *m* tube; pipe; (anat) duct; (slang) hit
tubercule [tybεrkyl] *m* tubercle; tuber
tuberculose [tybεrkyloz] *f* tuberculosis
tue-mouches [tymuʃ] *m invar* flypaper
tuer [tɥe] *tr* to kill ‖ *ref* to be killed; to kill oneself
tuerie [tyri] *f* slaughter
tue-tête [tytεt]—**à tue-tête** at the top of one's voice
tuile [tɥil] *f* tile; (coll) nasty blow
tuilerie [tɥilri] *f* tileworks
tulipe [tylip] *f* tulip
tumeur [tymœr] *f* tumor
tumulte [tymylt] *m* tumult, hubbub
tungstène [tœksten] *m* tungsten
tunique [tynik] *f* tunic
tunnel [tynεl] *m* tunnel; **passer sous un tunnel** to go through a tunnel; **tunnel aérodynamique** wind tunnel
turban [tyrbã] *m* turban
turbine [tyrbin] *f* turbine
turbu·lent [tyrbylã] **-lente** [lãt] *adj* turbulent
turc turque [tyrk] *adj* Turkish ‖ *m* Turkish (*language*) ‖ (*cap*) *mf* Turk (*person*)

turf [tyrf] *m*—**le turf** the turf, the track
turfiste [tyrfist] *m* turfman, racegoer
turlututu [tyrlytyty] *interj* fiddlesticks!, nonsense!
Turquie [tyrki] *f* Turkey; **la Turquie** Turkey
turquoise [tyrkwaz] *m* turquoise (*color*) ‖ *f* turquoise (*stone*)
tutelle [tytεl] *f* guardianship, tutelage; trusteeship
tu·teur [tytœr] **-trice** [tris] *mf* guardian ‖ *m* (hort) stake, prop
tutoyer [tytwaje] §47 *tr* to thou, to address familiarly ‖ *ref* to thou each other, to be on a first-name basis
tuyau [tɥijo], [tyjo] *m* (*pl* **tuyaux**) pipe, tube; fluting; (coll) tip; **tuyau d'arrosage** garden hose; **tuyau d'échappement** exhaust; **tuyau d'incendie** fire hose
tuyauter [tɥijote], [tyjote] *tr* to flute; (coll) to tip off ‖ *intr* (coll) to crib
tuyauterie [tɥijotri] *f* pipe mill; piping; (aut) manifold; **tuyauterie d'admission** intake manifold; **tuyauterie d'échappement** exhaust manifold
tympan [tẽpã] *m* eardrum; (archit, mus) tympanum
type [tip] *m* type; (coll) fellow, character
typer [tipe] *tr* to type
typhoïde [tifɔid] *adj & f* typhoid
typhon [tifɔ̃] *m* typhoon
typique [tipik] *adj* typical; South American (*music*)
typographie [tipɔgrafi] *f* typography
typographique [tipɔgrafik] *adj* typographic(al)
tyran [tirã] *m* tyrant; (orn) kingbird
tyrannie [tirani] *f* tyranny
tyrannique [tiranik] *adj* tyrannic(al)

U

U, u [y], *[y] *m invar* twenty-first letter of the French alphabet
Ukraine [ykren] *f* Ukraine
ukrai·nien [ykrenjẽ] **-nienne** [njεn] *adj* Ukrainian ‖ *m* Ukrainian (*language*) ‖ (*cap*) *mf* Ukrainian (*person*)
ulcère [ylsεr] *m* ulcer, sore
ulcérer [ylsere] §10 *tr* to ulcerate; to embitter ‖ *ref* to ulcerate; to fester
ulté·rieur -rieure [ylterjœr] *adj* ulterior; subsequent
ultimatum [yltimatɔm] *m* ultimatum
ultime [yltim] *adj* ultimate, final
ultra-court [yltrakur] **-courte** [kurt] *adj* (electron) ultrashort
ultravio·let [yltravjɔle] **-lette** [lεt] *adj & m* ultraviolet
ululer [ylyle] *intr* to hoot
un [œ̃] **une** [yn] *adj & pron* one; **l'un à l'autre** to each other, to one another; **l'un et l'autre** both; **l'un l'autre** each other, one another; **ni**

l'un ni l'autre neither, neither one; **un à un** one by one; **une heure** one o'clock ‖ *art indef* a ‖ *m* one ‖ *f*— **la une** the front page
unanime [ynanim] *adj* unanimous
unanimité [ynanimite] *f* unanimity
Unesco [ynεsko] *f* (acronym) (**Organisation des Nations Unies pour l'Éducation, la Science et la Culture**) —**l'Unesco** UNESCO
u·ni -nie [yni] *adj* united; smooth; level; uneventful; plain; solid (*color*); together (*said, e.g., of the hands of a clock*) ‖ *m* plain cloth
unicorne [ynikɔrn] *m* unicorn
unification [ynifikasjɔ̃] *f* unification
unifier [ynifje] *tr* to unify ‖ *ref* to consolidate, merge; to become unified
uniforme [ynifɔrm] *adj & m* uniform
uniformiser [ynifɔrmize] *tr* to make uniform
uniformité [ynifɔrmite] *f* uniformity

unijambiste [yniʒɑ̃bist] *adj* one-legged ‖ *mf* one-legged person
unilaté·ral -rale [ynilateral] *adj* (*pl* -raux [ro]) unilateral
union [ynjɔ̃] *f* union; **union libre** common-law marriage
unique [ynik] *adj* only, single; unique
unir [ynir] *tr & ref* to unite
unisson [ynisɔ̃] *m* unison
unitaire [yniter] *adj* unit
unité [ynite] *f* unity; unit; battleship; (coll) one million old francs
univers [yniver] *m* universe
univer·sel -selle [yniversɛl] *adj & m* universal
universitaire [yniversiter] *adj* university
université [yniversite] *f* university
uranium [yranjɔm] *m* uranium
ur·bain [yrbɛ̃] -baine [bɛn] *adj* urban; urbane
urbaniser [yrbanize] *tr* to urbanize
urbanisme [yrbanism] *m* city planning
urbaniste [yrbanist] *adj* zoning (*ordinance*) ‖ *mf* city planner
urbanité [yrbanite] *f* urbanity
urètre [yrɛtr] *m* urethra
urgence [yrʒɑ̃s] *f* urgency; emergency; emergency case; **d'urgence** emergency (*e.g., hospital ward*); right away, without delay
ur·gent [yrʒɑ̃] -gente [ʒɑ̃t] *adj* urgent; emergency (*case*); (formula on letter or envelope) rush ‖ *m* urgent matter
urinaire [yriner] *adj* urinary
uri·nal [yrinal] *m* (*pl* -naux [no]) urinal (*for use in bed*)
urine [yrin] *f* urine
uriner [yrine] *tr & intr* to urinate
urinoir [yrinwar] *m* urinal (*place*)
urne [yrn] *f* urn; ballot box; **aller aux urnes** to go to the polls
urologie [yrɔlɔʒi] *f* urology
U.R.S.S. [yɛrɛsɛs] *f* (letterword) (Union des Républiques Socialistes Soviétiques) U.S.S.R.
Ursse [yrs] *f* (acronym) (Union des Républiques Socialistes Soviétiques) U.S.S.R.
urticaire [yrtiker] *f* hives
urubu [yryby] *m* turkey vulture

us [ys] *mpl*—**les us et (les) coutumes** the manners and customs
U.S. [yɛs] *adj* (letterword) (United States) U.S., e.g., **l'aviation U.S.** U.S. aviation
U.S.A. [yɛsa] *mpl* (letterword) (United States of America) U.S.A.
usage [yzaʒ] *m* usage; custom; use; **faire de l'usage** to wear well; **hors d'usage** outmoded; (gram) obsolete; **manquer d'usage** to lack good breeding; **usage du monde** good breeding, savoir-vivre
usa·gé -gée [yzaʒe] *adj* secondhand; worn-out, used
usa·ger [yzaʒe] -gère [ʒer] *mf* user
usant [yzɑ̃] usante [yzɑ̃t] *adj* exhausting, wearing
u·sé -sée [yze] *adj* worn-out; trite, commonplace
user [yze] *tr* to wear out; to wear away; to ruin (*e.g., health*) ‖ *intr*—**en user bien avec** to treat well; **user de** to use ‖ *ref* to wear out
usine [yzin] *f* factory, mill, plant; **usine à gaz** gasworks
usiner [yzine] *tr* to machine, to tool
usi·nier [yzinje] -nière [njer] *adj* manufacturing; factory (*town*) ‖ *m* manufacturer
usi·té -tée [yzite] *adj* used, in use; **peu usité** out of use, rare
ustensile [ystɑ̃sil] *m* utensil, implement
u·suel -suelle [yzɥɛl] *adj* usual
usure [yzyr] *f* usury; wear; wear and tear
usurper [yzyrpe] *tr* to usurp
utérus [yterys] *m* uterus, womb
utilisable [ytilizabl] *adj* usable
utilisa·teur [ytilizatœr] -trice [tris] *mf* user
utilitaire [ytiliter] *adj* utilitarian; utility (*vehicle, goods, etc.*)
utilité [ytilite] *f* utility, usefulness, use; (theat) support; (theat) supporting rôle; **jouer les utilités** (fig) to play second fiddle; **utilités** (theat) small parts
utopique [ytɔpik] *adj* utopian
utopiste [ytɔpist] *mf* utopian

V

V, v [ve] *m invar* twenty-second letter of the French alphabet
v. *abbr* (**voir**) see; (**volume**) vol.
vacance [vakɑ̃s] *f* vacancy, opening; **vacances** vacation
vacancier [vakɑ̃sje] *m* vacationist
va·cant [vakɑ̃] -cante [kɑ̃t] *adj* vacant
vacarme [vakarm] *m* din, racket
vacation [vakasjɔ̃] *f* investigation; **vacations** fee; recess
vaccin [vaksɛ̃] *m* vaccine
vaccination [vaksinasjɔ̃] *f* vaccination
vaccine [vaksin] *f* cowpox
vacciner [vaksine] *tr* to vaccinate

vache [vaʃ] *adj* embarrassing (*question*); cantankerous (*person*) ‖ *f* cow; cowhide; (*woman*) (slang) bitch; (*man*) (slang) swine, rat; (*policeman*) (slang) flatfoot, bull; **en vache** leather (*e.g., suitcase*); **manger de la vache enragée** (coll) not to have a red cent to one's name; **oh, la vache!** damn it!; **parler français comme une vache espagnole** (coll) to murder the French language; **vache à eau** canvas bucket (*for camping*); **vache à lait** milch cow; (coll) gull, sucker

vachement [vaʃmɑ̃] *adv* (slang) tremendously
va·cher [vaʃe] -chère [ʃɛr] *mf* cowherd
vacherie [vaʃri] *f* cowshed; dairy farm; (coll) dirty trick
vachette [vaʃɛt] *f* young calf; calf (*leather*)
vaciller [vasije] *intr* to vacillate, waver; to flicker; to totter
vacuité [vakɥite] *f* vacuity, emptiness
vacuum [vakɥɔm] *m* vacuum
vade-mecum [vademekɔm] *m invar* handbook, vade mecum
vadrouille [vadruj] *f* (naut) mop, swab; (slang) bender, spree
vadrouiller [vadruje] *intr* (slang) to ramble around, to gad about
vadrouil·leur [vadrujœr] vadrouil·leuse [vadrujøz] *mf* (slang) rounder
va-et-vient [vaevjɛ̃] *m invar* backward-and-forward motion; hurrying to and fro; comings and goings; ferryboat; (elec) two-way switch
vaga·bond [vagabɔ̃] -bonde [bɔ̃d] *adj* vagabond || *mf* vagabond, tramp
vagabondage [vagabɔ̃daʒ] *m* vagrancy; vagabondage interdit (public sign) no loitering, no begging
vagabonder [vagabɔ̃de] *intr* to wander about, to roam, to tramp
vagir [vaʒir] *intr* to cry, wail
vague [vag] *adj* vague; vacant (*look; lot*); waste (*land*) || *m* vagueness; (fig) space, thin air || *f* wave; la nouvelle vague the wave of the future; vague de fond ground swell
vaguemestre [vagmɛstr] *m* (mil, nav) mail clerk
vaguer [vage] *intr* to wander
vaillance [vajɑ̃s] *f* valor
vail·lant [vajɑ̃] vail·lante [vajɑ̃t] *adj* valiant; up to scratch
vain [vɛ̃] vaine [vɛn] *adj* vein; en vain in vain
vaincre [vɛ̃kr] §70 *tr* to defeat, conquer; to overcome (*fear, instinct, etc.*) || *intr* to conquer || *ref* to control oneself
vain·cu -cue [vɛ̃ky] *adj* defeated, beaten, conquered || *mf* loser
vainqueur [vɛ̃kœr] *adj masc* victorious || *m* victor, winner
vairon [vɛrɔ̃] *adj masc* whitish (*eye*); vairons of different colors (*said of eyes*) || *m* (ichth) minnow
vais·seau [vɛso] *m* (*pl* -seaux) vessel; nave (*of church*); vaisseau amiral flagship; vaisseau sanguin blood vessel; vaisseau spatial spaceship
vaisseau-école [vɛsoekɔl] *m* (*pl* vaisseaux-écoles) (nav) training ship
vaisselier [vɛsəlje] *m* china closet
vaisselle [vɛsɛl] *f* dishes; faire la vaisselle to wash the dishes; vaisselle plate plate (*of gold or silver*)
val [val] *m* (*pl* vaux [vo] or vals) (obs) valley; à val going down the valley; à val de (obs) down from
valable [valabl] *adj* valid; worthwhile (*e.g., experience*)
valence [valɑ̃s] *f* (chem) valence

valen·tin [valɑ̃tɛ̃] -tine [tin] *mf* valentine (*sweetheart*)
valet [valɛ] *m* valet; holdfast, clamp; (cards) jack; valet de chambre valet; valet de ferme hired man; valet de pied footman
valeur [valœr] *f* value, worth, merit; valor; (*person, thing, or quality worth having*) asset; (com) security, stock; de valeur able; valuable; (Canad) too bad, unfortunate; envoyer en valeur déclarée to insure (*a package*); mettre en valeur to develop (*e.g., a region*); to set off, enhance
valeu·reux [valœrø] -reuse [røz] *adj* valorous, brave
validation [validɑsjɔ̃] *f* validation
valide [valid] *adj* valid; fit, able-bodied
valider [valide] *tr* to validate
validité [validite] *f* validity
valise [valiz] *f* suitcase; faire ses valises to pack, to pack one's bags; valise diplomatique diplomatic pouch
vallée [vale] *f* valley
vallon [valɔ̃] *m* vale, dell
valoir [valwar] §71 *tr* to equal; on service en vaut un autre one good turn deserves another; valoir q.ch. à qn to get or bring s.o. s.th., e.g., cela lui a valu une amélioration that got him a raise; e.g., la condamnation lui a valu cinq ans de prison the verdict brought him five years in prison || *intr* to be worth; autant vaut y renoncer might as well give up; cela ne vaut rien it's worth nothing; faire valoir to set off to advantage; to use to advantage; to develop (*one's land*); to invest (*funds, capital*); to put forward (*one's reasons*); faire valoir que . . . to argue that . . . || *impers*—il vaut mieux it would be better to, e.g., il vaut mieux attendre it would be better to wait; mieux vaut tard que jamais better late than never || *ref*—les deux se valent one is as good as the other
valse [vals] *f* waltz
valser [valse] *tr & intr* to waltz
valve [valv] *f* (aut, bot, zool) valve; (elec) vacuum tube
valvule [valvyl] *f* valve
vamp [vãp] *f* vamp
vamper [vãpe] *tr* (coll) to vamp
vampire [vãpir] *m* vampire
van [vã] *m* van (*for moving horses*)
vandale [vãdal] *adj* vandal; Vandal || *m* vandal || (*cap*) *mf* Vandal
vandalisme [vãdalism] *m* vandalism
vanille [vanij] *f* vanilla
vani·teux [vanitø] -teuse [tøz] *adj* vain, conceited
vanne [van] *f* sluice gate, floodgate; butterfly valve; (slang) gibe
van·neau [vano] *m* (*pl* -neaux) (orn) lapwing
vanner [vane] *tr* to winnow; to tire out
vannerie [vanri] *f* basketry
vannier [vanje] *m* basket maker
van·tail [vãtaj] *m* (*pl* -taux [to]) leaf (*of door, shutter, sluice gate, etc.*)

van·tard [vɑ̃tar] **-tarde** [tard] *adj* bragging, boastful ‖ *mf* braggart
vantardise [vɑ̃tardiz] *f* bragging, boasting
vanter [vɑ̃te] *tr* to praise; to boost, to push (*a product on the market*) ‖ *ref* to brag, to boast
va-nu-pieds [vanypje] *mf invar* (coll) tramp
vapeur [vapœr] *m* steamship ‖ *f* steam; vapor, mist; **à la vapeur** steamed (*e.g., potatoes*); under steam; (coll) **at full speed**; **à vapeur** steam (*e.g., engine*); **vapeurs** low spirits
vaporisateur [vapɔrizatœr] *m* atomizer, spray
vaporiser [vapɔrize] *tr & ref* to vaporize; to spray
vaquer [vake] *intr* to take a recess; **vaquer à** to attend to ‖ *impers*—**il vaque** there is vacant
varappe [varap] *f* cliff; rock climbing
varech [varɛk] *m* wrack, seaweed
vareuse [varøz] *f* (mil) blouse; (nav) peacoat
variable [varjabl] *adj & f* variable
va·riant [varjɑ̃] **-riante** [rjɑ̃t] *adj & f* variant
variation [varjɑsjɔ̃] *f* variation
varice [varis] *f* varicose veins
varicelle [varisɛl] *f* chicken pox
va·rié -riée [varje] *adj* varied
varier [varje] *tr & intr* to vary
variété [varjete] *f* variety; **variétés** selections (*from literary works*); vaudeville
variole [varjɔl] *f* smallpox
vari·queux [varikø] **-queuse** [køz] *adj* varicose
Varsovie [varsɔvi] *f* Warsaw
vase [vɑs] *m* vase; vessel; **en vase clos** shut up; in an airtight chamber; **vase de nuit** chamber pot ‖ *f* mud, slime
vaseline [vazlin] *f* vaseline
va·seux [vazø] **-seuse** [zøz] *adj* muddy, slimy; (coll) all in, tired; (coll) fuzzy, obscure
vasistas [vazistɑs] *m* transom
vasouiller [vazuje] *tr* (coll) to make a mess of ‖ *intr* (coll) to go badly
vasque [vask] *f* basin (*of fountain*)
vas·sal -sale [vasal] (*pl* **vas·saux** [vaso] **-sales**) *adj & mf* vassal
vaste [vast] *adj* vast
vastement [vastəmɑ̃] *adv* (coll) very
Vatican [vatikɑ̃] *m* Vatican
vaticane [vatikan] *adj fem* Vatican
va-tout [vatu] *m*—**jouer son va-tout** to stake one's all
vaudeville [vodvil] *m* vaudeville (*light theatrical piece interspersed with songs*); (obs) satirical song
vaudou [vodu] *adj invar & m* voodoo
vau-l'eau [volo]—**à vau-l'eau** downstream; **s'en aller à vau-l'eau** (fig) to go to pot
vau·rien [vorjɛ̃] **-rienne** [rjɛn] *mf* good-for-nothing
vautour [votur] *m* vulture
vautrer [votre] *ref* to wallow
veau [vo] *m* (*pl* **veaux**) calf; veal; calfskin; (coll) lazybones, dope; **pleurer**

comme un veau to cry like a baby; **veau marin** seal
vé·cu -cue [veky] *adj* true to life
vedette [vədɛt] *f* patrol boat; scout; lead, star; **en vedette** in the limelight; **mettre en vedette** to headline, to highlight; **vedette de l'écran** movie star; **vedette du petit écran** television star
végé·tal -tale [veʒetal] (*pl* **-taux** [to]) *adj* vegetable, vegetal ‖ *m* vegetable
végéta·rien [veʒetarjɛ̃] **-rienne** [rjɛn] *adj & mf* vegetarian
végétation [veʒetɑsjɔ̃] *f* vegetation; **végétations** (**adénoïdes**) adenoids
végéter [veʒete] §10 *intr* to vegetate
véhémence [veemɑ̃s] *f* vehemence
véhé·ment [veemɑ̃] **-mente** [mɑ̃t] *adj* vehement
véhicule [veikyl] *m* vehicle
veille [vɛj] *f* watch, vigil; wakefulness; **à la veille de** on the eve of; just before; on the verge or point of; **la veille de** the eve of; the day before; **la Veille de Noël** Christmas Eve; **la Veille du jour de l'An** New Year's Eve; **veilles** sleepless nights, late nights; night work
veillée [veje] *f* evening; social evening; **veillée funèbre, veillée du corps** wake
veiller [veje] *tr* to sit up with, to watch over ‖ *intr* to sit up, to stay up; to keep watch; **veiller à** to look after, to see to
veil·leur [vɛjœr] **veil·leuse** [vɛjøz] *mf* watcher ‖ *m* watchman; **veilleur de nuit** night watchman ‖ *f* see **veilleuse**
veilleuse [vɛjøz] *f* night light; rushlight; pilot light; **mettre en veilleuse** to turn down low; to dim (*the headlights*); to slow down (*production in a factory*)
vei·nard [venar] **-narde** [nard] *adj* (coll) lucky ‖ *mf* (coll) lucky person
veine [vɛn] *f* vein; luck; **veine alors!** (coll) swell!
veiner [vene] *tr* to vein
vei·neux [venø] **-neuse** [nøz] *adj* veined; venous
vélaire [velɛr] *adj & f* velar
vêler [vele] *intr* to calve
vélin [velɛ̃] *m* vellum
velléitaire [veleitɛr] *adj & mf* erratic
velléité [veleite] *f* stray impulse, fancy; **velléité de sourire** slight smile
vélo [velo] *m* bike; **faire du vélo** to go bicycle riding
vélocité [velɔsite] *f* velocity; speed; agility
vélomoteur [velɔmɔtœr] *m* motorbike
velours [vəlur] *m* velvet; **velours côtelé** corduroy
velou·té -tée [vəlute] *adj* velvety ‖ *m* velvetiness
velouter [vəlute] *tr* to make velvety
ve·lu -lue [vəly] *adj* hairy
vélum [velɔm] *m* awning
velvet [vɛlvɛt] *m* velveteen
venaison [vənɛzɔ̃] *f* venison
ve·nant [vənɑ̃] **-nante** [nɑ̃t] *adj* coming; thriving ‖ *mf* comer; **à tout venant** to all comers

vendange [vɑ̃dɑ̃ʒ] f grape harvest; vintage

vendanger [vɑ̃dɑ̃ʒe] §38 tr to pick (the grapes) || intr to harvest grapes

ven·deur [vɑ̃dœr] -deuse [døz] mf seller, vendor; salesclerk; vendeur ambulant peddler || m salesman || f salesgirl, saleslady

vendre [vɑ̃dr] tr to sell; to sell out, to betray; à vendre for sale; vendre au détail to retail; vendre aux enchères to auction off; vendre en gros to wholesale || ref to sell; to sell oneself, to sell out

vendredi [vɑ̃drədi] m Friday; vendredi saint Good Friday

ven·du -due [vɑ̃dy] adj sold; corrupt || mf traitor

véné·neux [venenø] -neuse [nøz] adj poisonous

vénérable [venerabl] adj venerable

vénérer [venere] §10 tr to venerate

véné·rien [venerjɛ̃] -rienne [rjɛn] adj venereal || mf person with venereal disease

vengeance [vɑ̃ʒɑ̃s] f vengeance, revenge

venger [vɑ̃ʒe] §38 tr to avenge || ref to get revenge

ven·geur [vɑ̃ʒœr] -geuse [ʒøz] adj avenging || mf avenger

veni·meux [vənimø] -meuse [møz] adj venomous

venin [vənɛ̃] m venom

venir [vənir] §72 intr (aux: ÊTRE) to come; à venir forthcoming; faire venir to send for; où voulez-vous en venir? what are you getting at?; venez avec (coll) come along; venir de to have just, e.g., il vient de partir he has just left || impers—il me (nous, etc.) vient à l'esprit que it occurs to me (to us, etc.) that

Venise [vəniz] f Venice

véni·tien [venisjɛ̃] -tienne [sjɛn] adj Venetian || (cap) mf Venetian

vent [vɑ̃] m wind; avoir le vent en poupe to be in luck; avoir vent de to get wind of; contre vents et marées through thick and thin; en plein vent in the open air; être dans le vent to be up to date; il fait du vent it is windy; les vents (mus) the woodwinds; vent arrière tailwind; vent coulis draft; vent debout headwind; vent en poupe (naut) tailwind

vente [vɑ̃t] f sale; felling (of timber); en vente on sale; en vente libre (pharm) on sale without a prescription; jeunes ventes new overgrowth; vente amiable private sale; vente à tempérament installment selling; vente à terme sale on time; vente au détail retailing; vente en gros wholesaling

ventilateur [vɑ̃tilatœr] m ventilator; fan; electric fan

ventiler [vɑ̃tile] tr to ventilate; to value separately; (bk) to apportion

ventouse [vɑ̃tuz] f sucker; suction cup; suction grip; nozzle (of vacuum cleaner); vent

ventre [vɑ̃tr] m belly; stomach; womb;

à plat ventre prostrate; à ventre déboutonné (coll) excessively; (coll) with all one's might; avoir q.ch. dans le ventre (coll) to have s.th. on the ball; bas ventre (fig) genitals; ventre à terre (coll) lickety-split

ventricule [vɑ̃trikyl] m ventricle

ventriloque [vɑ̃trilɔk] mf ventriloquist

ventriloquie [vɑ̃trilɔki] f ventriloquism

ventripo·tent [vɑ̃tripɔtɑ̃] -tente [tɑ̃t] adj (coll) potbellied

ven·tru -true [vɑ̃try] adj potbellied

ve·nu -nue [vəny] adj—bien venu successful; welcome || mf—le premier venu the first comer; just anyone; les nouveaux venus the newcomers || f coming, advent

Vénus [venys] f Venus

vénusté [venyste] f charm, grace

vêpres [vɛpr] fpl vespers

ver [vɛr] m worm; tirer les vers du nez à to worm secrets out of, to pump; ver à soie silkworm; ver de terre earthworm; ver luisant glowworm

véracité [verasite] f veracity

véranda [verɑ̃da] f veranda

ver·bal -bale [vɛrbal] adj (pl -baux [bo]) verbal; (gram) verb

verbaliser [vɛrbalize] intr to write out a report or summons; verbaliser contre qn to give s.o. a ticket (e.g., for speeding)

verbe [vɛrb] m verb; avoir le verbe haut to talk loud; Verbe (eccl) Word

ver·beux [vɛrbø] -beuse [bøz] adj verbose, wordy

verbiage [vɛrbjaʒ] m verbiage

verdâtre [vɛrdɑtr] adj greenish

verdeur [vɛrdœr] f greenness; vigor, spryness; crudeness (of speech)

verdict [vɛrdik], [vɛrdikt] m verdict

verdir [vɛrdir] tr & intr to turn green

verdoyer [vɛrdwaje] §47 intr to become green

verdure [vɛrdyr] f verdure; greens

vé·reux [verø] -reuse [røz] adj wormy

verge [vɛrʒ] f rod; shank (of anchor); penis

verger [vɛrʒe] m orchard

verglas [vɛrgla] m glare ice; sleet

vergogne [vɛrgɔɲ] f—sans vergogne immodest, brazen; immodestly, brazenly

véridique [veridik] adj veracious

vérifica·teur [verifikatœr] -trice [tris] mf inspector, examiner; vérificateur comptable auditor

vérification [verifikasjɔ̃] f verification; auditing; ascertainment

vérifier [verifje] tr to verify; to audit; to ascertain

véritable [veritabl] adj veritable; real, genuine

vérité [verite] f truth; à la vérité to tell the truth; dire à qn ses quatre vérités (coll) to give s.o. a piece of one's mind; en vérité truly, in truth

ver·meil -meille [vɛrmɛj] adj rosy

vermillon [vɛrmijɔ̃] adj invar & m vermilion

vermine [vɛrmin] f vermin

vermou·lu -lue [vɛrmuly] *adj* worm-eaten
vermout or **vermouth** [vɛrmut] *m* vermouth
vernaculaire [vɛrnakylɛr] *adj* vernacular
vernir [vɛrnir] *tr* to varnish; **être verni** (coll) to be lucky
vernis [vɛrni] *m* varnish; (fig) veneer
vernissage [vɛrnisaʒ] *m* varnishing; private viewing (*of pictures*)
vernisser [vɛrnise] *tr* to glaze
vérole [vɛrɔl] *f* (slang) syphilis; **petite vérole** smallpox
verre [vɛr] *m* glass; crystal (*of watch*); **verre à vitre** windowpane; **verre consigné** bottle with deposit; **verre de contact** contact lens; **verre de lampe** lamp chimney; **verre dépoli** frosted glass; **verre perdu** disposable bottle (*no deposit)*; **verres** eyeglasses; **verres de soleil** sunglasses; **verres grossissants** magnifying glasses; **verre taillé** cut glass
verrière [vɛrjer] *f* stained-glass window
verrou [vɛru] *m* bolt; **être sous les verrous** to be locked up
verrouiller [vɛruje] *tr* to bolt; to lock up ‖ *ref* to lock oneself in
verrue [vɛry] *f* wart
vers [vɛr] *m* verse; **les vers** verse, poetry ‖ *prep* toward; about, e.g., **vers les cinq heures** about five o'clock
Versailles [vɛrsaj] *f* Versailles
versant [vɛrsɑ̃] *m* slope, side
versatile [vɛrsatil] *adj* fickle
verse [vɛrs] *f*—**pleuvoir à verse** to pour
ver·sé -sée [vɛrse] *adj*—**versé dans** versed in
versement [vɛrsəmɑ̃] *m* deposit; installment; **versement anticipé** payment in advance
verser [vɛrse] *tr* to pour; to upset; to tip over; to deposit ‖ *intr* to overturn
verset [vɛrsɛ] *m* (Bib) verse
versification [vɛrsifikasjɔ̃] *f* versification
versifier [vɛrsifje] *tr & intr* to versify
version [vɛrsjɔ̃] *f* version; translation from a foreign language
verso [vɛrso] *m* verso; **au verso** on the back
vert [vɛr] **verte** [vɛrt] *adj* green; verdant; vigorous (*person*); new (*wine*); raw (*leather*); sharp (*scolding*); spicy (*story*); **ils sont trop verts!** sour grapes! ‖ *m* green; greenery; **mettre au vert** to put out to pasture; **se mettre au vert** to take a rest in the country
vert-de-gris [vɛrdəgri] *m invar* verdigris
vertèbre [vɛrtɛbr] *f* vertebra
verté·bré -brée [vɛrtebre] *adj & m* vertebrate
verti·cal -cale [vɛrtikal] (*pl* -**caux** [ko] -**cales**) *adj* vertical ‖ *m* (astr) vertical circle ‖ *f* vertical
vertige [vɛrtiʒ] *m* vertigo, dizziness
vertigo [vɛrtigo] *m* staggers (*of horse*); caprice
vertu [vɛrty] *f* virtue

ver·tueux [vɛrtɥø] **-tueuse** [tɥøz] *adj* virtuous
verve [vɛrv] *f* verve
ver·veux [vɛrvø] **-veuse** [vøz] *adj* lively, animated ‖ *m* fishnet
vésanie [vezani] *f* madness
vesce [vɛs] *f* vetch
vésicule [vezikyl] *f* vesicle; blister; **vésicule bilaire** gall bladder
vespasienne [vɛspazjɛn] *f* street urinal
vessie [vɛsi] *f* bladder; **vessie à glace** ice bag
veste [vɛst] *f* coat, suit coat; **remporter une veste** (coll) to suffer a setback; **retourner sa veste** (coll) to do an about-face; **veste croisée** double-breasted coat; **veste de pyjama** pajama top; **veste de sport** sport coat; **veste d'intérieur, veste d'appartement** lounging robe; **veste droite** single-breasted coat
vestiaire [vɛstjɛr] *m* checkroom, cloakroom
vestibule [vɛstibyl] *m* vestibule
vestige [vɛstiʒ] *m* vestige; footprint
veston [vɛstɔ̃] *m* coat
Vésuve [vezyv] *m—le Vésuve** Vesuvius
vêtement [vɛtmɑ̃] *m* garment; **vêtements** clothes
vétéran [veterɑ̃] *m* veteran
vétérinaire [veteriner] *adj & mf* veterinary
vétille [vetij] *f* trifle
vétiller [vetije] *intr* to split hairs
vêtir [vɛtir] §73 *tr & ref* to dress
veto [veto] *m* veto; **mettre** or **opposer son veto à** to veto
vétuste [vetyst] *adj* decrepit, rickety
veuf [vœf] **veuve** [vœv] *adj* widowed ‖ *m* widower ‖ *f* see **veuve**
veule [vøl] *adj* (coll) feeble, weak
veuvage [vœvaʒ] *m* widowhood; widowerhood
veuve [vœv] *f* widow
vexation [vɛksasjɔ̃] *f* vexation
vexer [vɛkse] *tr* to vex
via [vja] *prep* via
viaduc [vjadyk] *m* viaduct
via·ger [vjaʒe] **-gère** [ʒer] *adj* life, for life ‖ *m* life annuity
viande [vjɑ̃d] *f* meat; **amène ta viande!** (slang) get over here!
vibration [vibrasjɔ̃] *f* vibration
vibrer [vibre] *intr* to vibrate
vicaire [vikɛr] *m* vicar
vice [vis] *m* vice; defect; **vice de conformation** physical defect; **vice de forme** (law) irregularity, flaw; **vice versa** vice versa
vice-amiral [visamiral] *m* (*pl* -**amiraux** [amiro]) vice-admiral
vice-président [visprezidɑ̃] **-présidente** [prezidɑ̃t] *mf* (*pl* -**présidents**) vice-president
vice-roi [visrwa] *m* (*pl* -**rois**) viceroy
vice-versa [viseversa], [visversa] *adv* vice versa
vi·cié -ciée [visje] *adj* foul, polluted; poor, thin (*blood*)
vicier [visje] *tr* to foul, to pollute; to taint, to spoil
vi·cieux [visjø] **-cieuse** [sjøz] *adj* vicious; wrong (*use*); libertine; balky

vici·nal -nale [visinal] *adj* (*pl* **-naux** [no]) local, side (*road*)
vicissitude [visisityd] *f* vicissitude
vicomte [vikɔ̃t] *m* viscount
victime [viktim] *f* victim
victoire [viktwar] *f* victory
victo·rieux [viktɔrjø] **-rieuse** [rjøz] *adj* victorious
victuailles [viktɥaj] *fpl* victuals, foods
vidange [vidɑ̃ʒ] *f* draining; night soil; drain (*of pipe, sink, etc.*)
vidanger [vidɑ̃ʒe] §38 *tr* to drain
vide [vid] *adj* empty; blank; vacant ‖ *m* emptiness, void; vacuum
vi·dé -dée [vide] *adj* cleaned (*fish, fowl, etc.*); played out, exhausted
vide-bouteille [vidbutɛj] *m* (*pl* **-bouteilles**) siphon
vide-cave [vidkav] *m invar* sump pump
vide-citron [vidsitrɔ̃] *m* (*pl* **-citrons**) lemon squeezer
vide-gousset [vidgusɛ] *m* (*pl* **-goussets**) (hum) thief
vide-ordures [vidɔrdyr] *m invar* garbage shoot
vide-poches [vidpɔʃ] *m invar* dresser; pin tray; (aut) glove compartment
vider [vide] *tr* to empty; to drain; to clean (*fish, fowl, etc.*); to settle (*a question*); **se faire vider de** (coll) to get thrown out of; to be fired from; to be expelled from
vi·deur [vidœr] **-deuse** [døz] *mf* (coll) bouncer (*in a night club*)
viduité [vidɥite] *f* widowhood
vidure [vidyr] *f* guts (*e.g., of cleaned fish*); **vidures de poubelle** garbage
vie [vi] *f* life; livelihood, living; **à vie** for life; **de ma (sa, etc.) vie** in my (his, etc.) life, e.g., **je ne l'ai jamais vu de ma vie** I have never seen it in my life; **jamais de la vie!** not on your life!; **vie de bâton de chaise** disorderly life; **vie de château** life of ease
vieillard [vjejar] *m* old man; **les vieillards** old people
vieille [vjej] *f* old woman
vieilleries [vjejri] *fpl* old things; old ideas
vieillesse [vjɛjɛs] *f* old age
vieil·li -lie [vjeji] *adj* aged; out-of-date, antiquated
vieillir [vjejir] *tr* to age; to make (*s.o.*) look older ‖ *intr* to age, to grow old ‖ *ref* to make oneself look older
vieil·lot [vjejo] **vieil·lotte** [vjejɔt] *adj* (coll) oldish, quaint
vielle [vjɛl] *f* (hist) hurdy-gurdy
Vienne [vjɛn] *f* Vienna; Vienne (*city in France*)
vien·nois [vjɛnwa] **vien·noise** [vjɛnwaz] *adj* Viennese ‖ (*cap*) *mf* Viennese
vierge [vjɛrʒ] *adj* virginal; virgin; blank; unexposed (*film*) ‖ *f* virgin
Vietnam [vjɛtnam] *m*—**le Vietnam** Vietnam
vietna·mien [vjɛtnamjɛ̃] **-mienne** [mjɛn] *adj* Vietnamese ‖ (*cap*) *mf* Vietnamese
vieux [vjø] (or **vieil** [vjɛj] before vowel or mute h) **vieille** [vjɛj] *adj* old (*wine*) ‖ (when standing before

noun) *adj* old; old-fashioned; obsolete (*word, meaning, etc.*) ‖ *mf* old person ‖ *m* old man; **les vieux** old people; **mon vieux** (coll) my boy ‖ *f* see **vieille**
vif [vif] **vive** [viv] *adj* alive, living; lively, quick; bright, intense; hearty, heartfelt; sharp (*criticism*); keen (*pleasure*); spring (*water*) ‖ *m* quick; **couper dans le vif** to take drastic measures; **entrer dans le vif de** to get to the heart of; **peindre au vif** to paint from life; **piqué au vif** stung to the quick
vif-argent [vifarʒɑ̃] *m* quicksilver; (*person*) live wire
vigie [viʒi] *f* lookout
vigilance [viʒilɑ̃s] *f* vigilance
vigi·lant [viʒilɑ̃] **-lante** [lɑ̃t] *adj* vigilant ‖ *m* night watchman
vigile [viʒil] *m* night watchman ‖ *f* (eccl) vigil
vigne [viɲ] *f* vine; vineyard; **vigne blanche** clematis; **vigne de Judas** bittersweet; **vigne vierge** Virginia creeper
vigne·ron [viɲrɔ̃] **-ronne** [rɔn] *mf* vinegrower; vintner
vignette [viɲɛt] *f* vignette; tax stamp; gummed tab
vignoble [viɲɔbl] *m* vineyard
vigou·reux [vigurø] **-reuse** [røz] *adj* vigorous
vigueur [vigœr] *f* vigor; **entrer en vigueur** to go into effect
vil vile [vil] *adj* vile; cheap
vi·lain [vilɛ̃] **-laine** [lɛn] *adj* nasty; ugly; naughty ‖ *mf* nasty person
vilebrequin [vilbrəkɛ̃] *m* brace (*of brace and bit*); crankshaft
vilenie [vilni] *f* villainy; abuse
villa [villa] *f* villa; cottage, small one-story home
village [vilaʒ] *m* village
villa·geois [vilaʒwa] **-geoise** [ʒwaz] *mf* villager
ville [vil] *f* city; town; **aller en ville** to go downtown; **la Ville Lumière** the City of Light (*Paris*); **ville champignon** boom town; **ville satellite** suburban town; **villes jumelées** twin cities; **villes réunies** twin cities
villégiature [vileʒiatyr] *f* vacation
vin [vɛ̃] *m* wine; **avoir le vin gai** to be hilariously drunk; **être entre deux vins** to be tipsy; **vin d'honneur** reception (*at which toasts are offered*); **vin d'orange** sangaree; **vin mousseux** sparkling wine; **vin ordinaire** table wine
vinaigre [vinɛgr] *m* vinegar
vinaigrette [vinɛgrɛt] *f* French dressing, vinaigrette sauce
vindica·tif [vɛ̃dikatif] **-tive** [tiv] *adj* vindictive
vingt [vɛ̃] *adj* & *pron* twenty; the Twentieth, e.g., Jean vingt John the Twentieth; **vingt et un** [vɛ̃teœ̃] twenty-one; twenty-first, e.g., **Jean vingt et un** John the Twenty-first; **vingt et unième** twenty-first ‖ *m* twenty; twentieth (*in dates*); **vingt et**

un twenty-one; twenty-first (*in dates*); **vingt et unième** twenty-first
vingtaine [vɛ̃tɛn] *f* score; **une vingtaine de** about twenty
vingt-deux [vɛ̃tdø] *adj & pron* twenty-two; **the Twenty-second**, e.g., **Jean vingt-deux** John the Twenty-second ‖ *m* twenty-two; twenty-second (*in dates*) ‖ *interj* (slang) beware!; cheese it!
vingt-deuxième [vɛ̃tdøzjɛm] *adj, pron* (*masc, fem*), & *m* twenty-second
vingt-et-un [vɛ̃tecœ̃] *m* (cards) twenty-one
vingtième [vɛ̃tjɛm] *adj, pron* (*masc, fem*), & *m* twentieth
vinyle [vinil] *m* vinyl
viol [vjɔl] *m* rape
violation [vjɔlɑsjɔ̃] *f* violation
violence [vjɔlɑ̃s] *f* violence
vio·lent [vjɔlɑ̃] **-lente** [lɑ̃t] *adj* violent
violenter [vjɔlɑ̃te] *tr* to do violence to
violer [vjɔle] *tr* to violate; to break (*the faith*); to rape, ravish
vio·let [vjɔlɛ] **-lette** [lɛt] *adj & m* violet (*color*) ‖ *f* (bot) violet
violon [vjɔlɔ̃] *m* violin; (slang) calaboose, jug; **payer les violons** (coll) to pay the piper; **violon d'Ingres** hobby
violoncelle [vjɔlɔ̃sɛl] *m* violoncello
violoniste [vjɔlɔnist] *mf* violinist
vipère [vipɛr] *f* viper
virage [viraʒ] *m* turning; turn, e.g., **pas de virage à gauche** no left turn; (aer) bank; (phot) toning; **virage en épingle à cheveux** hairpin curve; **virages** (public sign) winding road; **virage sur place** U-turn
virago [virago] *f* mannish woman
virée [vire] *f* (coll) spin (*in a car*); (coll) round (*of bars*)
virement [virmɑ̃] *m* transfer (*of funds*); (naut) tacking
virer [vire] *tr* to transfer (*funds*); (phot) to tone ‖ *intr* to turn; (aer) to bank; **virer à** to turn (*sour, red, etc.*); **virer de bord** (naut) to tack
virevolte [virvɔlt] *f* turn; about-face
virevolter [virvɔlte] *intr* to make an about-face; to go hither and thither
virginité [virʒinite] *f* virginity, maidenhood
virgule [virgyl] *f* (gram) comma; (*used in French to set off the decimal fraction from the integer*) decimal point
virilité [virilite] *f* virility
virole [virɔl] *f* ferrule
virologie [virɔlɔʒi] *f* virology
vir·tuel **-tuelle** [virtɥɛl] *adj* potential; (mech, opt, phys) virtual
virtuose [virtɥoz] *mf* virtuoso
virtuosité [virtɥozite] *f* virtuosity
virulence [virylɑ̃s] *f* virulence
viru·lent [virylɑ̃] **-lente** [lɑ̃t] *adj* virulent
virus [virys] *m* virus
vis [vis] *f* screw; thread (*of screw*); spiral staircase; **fermer à vis** to screw shut; **serrer la vis à** (fig) to put the screws on; **vis à métaux** machine screw; **vis de blocage** setscrew
visa [viza] *m* visa; (fig) approval

visage [vizaʒ] *m* face; **à deux visages** two-faced; **faire bon visage à** to pretend to be friendly to; **trouver visage de bois** to find the door closed; **visages pâles** palefaces; **voir qn sous son vrai visage** to see s.o. in his true colors
visagiste [vizaʒist] *mf* beautician
vis-à-vis [vizavi] *adv* vis-à-vis; **vis-à-vis de** vis-à-vis; towards; in the presence of ‖ *m* vis-à-vis; **en vis-à-vis** facing
viscère [visɛr] *m* organ; **viscères** viscera
visée [vize] *f* aim
viser [vize] *tr* to aim; to aim at; to concern; to visa ‖ *intr* to aim; **viser à** to aim at; to aim to
viseur [vizœr] *m* viewfinder; sight (*of gun*); **viseur de lancement** bombsight
visibilité [vizibilite] *f* visibility; **sans visibilité** blind (*flying*)
visible [vizibl] *adj* visible; obvious; (coll) at home, free; (coll) open to the public
visière [vizjɛr] *f* visor; sight (*of gun*); **rompre en visière à** to take a stand against
vision [vizjɔ̃] *f* vision
visionnaire [vizjɔnɛr] *adj & mf* visionary
visionner [vizjɔne] *tr* to view, inspect
visionneuse [vizjɔnøz] *f* viewer
visite [vizit] *f* visit; inspection; **en de visite** visiting; **faire, rendre visite à** to visit
visiter [vizite] *tr* to visit; to inspect
visi·teur [vizitœr] **-teuse** [tøz] *adj* visiting (*e.g., nurse*) ‖ *mf* visitor; inspector
vison [vizɔ̃] *m* mink
vis·queux [viskø] **-queuse** [køz] *adj* viscous
visser [vise] *tr* to screw; to screw on; (coll) to put the screws on
visualiser [vizɥalize] *tr* to visualize
vi·suel **-suelle** [vizɥɛl] *adj* visual
vi·tal **-tale** [vital] *adj* (*pl* **-taux** [to]) vital
vitaliser [vitalize] *tr* to vitalize
vitalité [vitalite] *f* vitality
vitamine [vitamin] *f* vitamin
vite [vit] *adj* fast, swift ‖ *adv* fast, quickly; **faites vite!** hurry up!
vitesse [vites] *f* speed, velocity; rate; **à toute vitesse** at full speed; **changer de vitesse** (aut) to shift gears; **en grande vitesse** (rr) by express; **en petite vitesse** (rr) by freight; **en première (seconde, etc.) vitesse** (aut) in first (second, etc.) gear; **vitesse acquise** momentum
viticole [vitikɔl] *adj* wine
vitrage [vitraʒ] *m* glasswork; small window curtain; sash; glazing
vi·trail [vitraj] *m* (*pl* **-traux** [tro]) stained-glass window
vitre [vitr] *f* windowpane, pane; (aut) window; **casser les vitres** (coll) to kick up a fuss
vi·tré **-trée** [vitre] *adj* glazed; vitreous (*humor*); glassed-in

vi·treux [vitrǿ] **-treuse** [trǿz] *adj* glassy; vitreous

vitrier [vitrije] *m* glazier

vitrine [vitrin] *f* show window; showcase; glass cabinet; **lécher les vitrines** (coll) to go window-shopping

vitupérer [vitypere] §10 *tr* to vituperate, abuse ‖ *intr*—**vitupérer contre** (coll) to vituperate

vivace [vivas] *adj* hardy, vigorous; long-lived; (bot) perennial

vivacité [vivasite] *f* vivacity

vivan·dier [vivãdje] **-dière** [djɛr] *mf* sutler ‖ *f* camp follower

vi·vant [vivã] **-vante** [vãt] *adj* living, alive; lively; modern (*language*) ‖ *m*—**bon vivant** high liver, jolly companion; **du vivant de** during the lifetime of; **les vivants et les morts** the quick and the dead

vivat [viva] *m* viva ‖ *interj* viva!

vivement [vivmã] *adv* quickly; warmly; deeply; sharply, briskly

viveur [vivœr] *m* pleasure seeker, rounder

vivier [vivje] *m* fish preserve, fishpond

vivifier [vivifje] *tr* to vivify, vitalize

vivisection [vivisɛksjɔ̃] *f* vivisection

vivoir [vivwar] *m* (Canad) living room

vivoter [vivɔte] *intr* (coll) to live from hand to mouth

vivre [vivr] *m*—**le vivre et le couvert** room and board; **le vivre et le vêtement** food and clothing; **vivres** provisions; (mil) rations, supplies ‖ §74 *tr* to live (*one's life, faith, art*); to live through, to experience ‖ *intr* to live; **être difficile à vivre** to be difficult to live with; **qui vive?** (mil) who is there?; **qui vivra verra** time will tell; **vive!, vivent!** viva!, long live!; **vivre au jour le jour** to live from hand to mouth; **vivre de** to live on

vizir [vizir] *m* vizier

vlan [vlã] *interj* whack!

vocable [vɔkabl] *m* word

vocabulaire [vɔkabylɛr] *m* vocabulary

vo·cal -cale [vɔkal] *adj* (*pl* **-caux** [ko]) vocal

vocaliser [vɔkalize] *tr, intr, & ref* to vocalize

vocatif [vɔkatif] *m* vocative

vocation [vɔkɑsjɔ̃] *f* vocation, calling; **vocation pédagogique** teaching career

vociférer [vɔsifere] §10 *tr* to shout (*e.g., insults*) ‖ *intr* to vociferate

vœu [vǿ] *m* (*pl* **vœux**) vow; wish; resolution; **meilleurs vœux!** best wishes!; **tous mes vœux!** my best wishes!

vogue [vɔg] *f* vogue, fashion; **en vogue** in vogue, in fashion

voguer [vɔge] *intr* to sail; **vogue la galère!** let's chance it, here goes!

voici [vwasi] *prep* here is, here are; for, e.g., **voici quatre jours qu'elle est partie** she has been gone for four days; **le voici** here he is; **nous voici** here we are; **que voici** here, e.g., **mon frère que voici va vous accompagner** my brother here is going to accompany you

voie [vwa] *f* way; road; lane (*of high-*

way); (anat) tract; (rr) track; **en voie de** on the road to, nearing; **être en bonne voie** to be doing well; **voie d'eau** leak; **voie de garage** driveway; **voie d'évitement** siding; **Voie lactée** Milky Way; **voie maritime** seaway; **voie(s) de fait** (law) assault and battery; **voie surface** surface mail

voilà [vwala] *prep* there is, there are; here is, here are; that's, e.g., **voilà pourquoi** that's why; ago, e.g., **voilà quatre jours qu'elle est partie** she left four days ago; **voilà, monsieur** there you are, sir

voile [vwal] *m* veil; (phot) fog (*on negative*); **voile du palais** soft palate; **voile noir** (pathol) blackout ‖ *f* sail; sailboat; **faire voile sur** to set sail for

voi·lé -lée [vwale] *adj* veiled; overcast; muffled; warped; husky (*voice*); (phot) fogged; **peu voilé** thinly veiled, broad (*e.g., hint*)

voiler [vwale] *tr* to veil; (phot) to fog ‖ *ref* to cloud over; to become warped

voi·lier [vwalje] **-lière** [ljɛr] *adj* sailing ‖ *m* sailboat; sailmaker; migratory bird

voilure [vwalyr] *f* sails; warping

voir [vwar] §75 *tr* to see; **faire voir** to show; **voir jouer** to see (*s.o.*) playing, to see (*s.o.*) play; to see (*s.th.*) played; **voir qn qui vient** to see s.o. coming, to see s.o. come; **voir venir qn** to see s.o. coming, to see s.o. come; (fig) to see through s.o. ‖ *intr* to see; **faites voir!** let's see it!, let me see it!; **j'en ai vu bien d'autres** I have seen worse than that; **n'avoir rien à voir avec, à,** or **dans** to have nothing to do with; **voir à** + *inf* to see that + *ind*, e.g., **voir à nous loger** to see that we are housed; **voir au dos** see other side, turn the page; **voyons!** see here!, come now! ‖ *ref* to see oneself; to see one another; to be obvious; to be seen, to be found

voire [vwar] *adv* nay, indeed; **voire même** or even, and even

voirie [vwari] *f* highway department; garbage collection; dump

voi·sé -sé [vwaze] *adj* voiced

voi·sin [vwazɛ̃] **-sine** [zin] *adj* neighboring; adjoining; **voisin de** near ‖ *mf* neighbor

voisinage [vwazinaʒ] *m* neighborhood; neighborliness

voisiner [vwazine] *intr* to visit one's neighbors; **voisiner avec** to be placed next to

voiture [vwatyr] *f* vehicle; carriage; (aut, rr) car; **en voiture!** all aboard!; **petite voiture** (coll) wheelchair; **voiture à bras** handcart; **voiture d'enfant** baby carriage; **voiture de pompier** fire engine; **voiture de remise** rented car; **voiture de série** stock car; **voiture de tourisme** pleasure car; **voiture d'infirme** wheelchair; **voiture d'occasion** used car

voiture-bar [vwatyrbar] *f* (*pl* **voitures-bars**) club car

voiture-lit [vwatyrli] *f* (*pl* **voitures-lits**) sleeping car

voiturer [vwatyre] *tr* to transport, to convey
voiture-restaurant [vwatyrrɛstɔrɑ̃] *f* (*pl* **voitures-restaurants**) dining car
voiture-salon [vwatyrsalɔ̃] *f* (*pl* **voitures-salons**) parlor car
voix [vwa], [vwɑ] *f* voice; vote; **à haute voix** aloud; in a loud voice; **à pleine voix** at the top of one's voice; **à voix basse** in a low voice; **à voix haute** in a loud voice; **de vive voix** by word of mouth; **voix de tête**, **voix de fausset** falsetto
vol [vɔl] *m* theft, robbery; flight; flock; **au vol** in flight; in passing; **à vol d'oiseau** as the crow flies; **de haut vol** high-flying; big-time (*crook*); **vol avec effraction** burglary; **vol cosmique** space flight; **vol plané** volplane; **vol sans visibilité** blind flying
volage [vɔlaʒ] *adj* fickle, changeable
volaille [vɔlɑj] *f* (slang) hens (*women*); (slang) gal
vo·lant [vɔlɑ̃] **-lante** [lɑ̃t] *adj* flying ‖ *m* steering wheel; flywheel; shuttlecock; sail (*of windmill*); flounce (*of dress*); leaf (*attached to stub*); **volant de sécurité** safety margin, reserve
vola·til -tile [vɔlatil] *adj* volatile ‖ *m* bird; fowl
volatiliser [vɔlatilize] *tr & ref* to volatilize
volcan [vɔlkɑ̃] *m* volcano
volcanique [vɔlkanik] *adj* volcanic
vole [vɔl] *f*—**faire la vole** to take all the tricks
volée [vɔle] *f* volley; flight (*of birds; of stairs*); flock; **à la volée** on the wing; at random; **à toute volée** loud and clear; **de haute volée** upperclass; **de la première volée** first-class, crack; **sonner à toute volée** to peal out
voler [vɔle] *tr* to rob; to steal; to fly at; **ne l'avoir pas volé** to deserve all that is coming; **voler à** to steal from ‖ *intr* to rob; to steal; to fly
volet [vɔlɛ] *m* shutter; inside flap; end paper; (aer) flap; **trier sur le volet** to choose with care
voleter [vɔlte] §34 *intr* to flutter
vo·leur [vɔlœr] **-leuse** [løz] *adj* thievish ‖ *mf* thief; **au voleur!** stop thief!; **voleur à la tire** pickpocket; **voleur à l'étalage** shoplifter; **voleur de grand chemin** highwayman
volition [vɔlisjɔ̃] *f* volition
volley-ball [vɔlebol] *m* volleyball
volontaire [vɔlɔ̃tɛr] *adj* voluntary; headstrong, willful; determined (*chin*) ‖ *mf* volunteer
volonté [vɔlɔ̃te] *f* will; wishes; **à volonté** at will; **bonne volonté** good will; **faire ses quatre volontés** (coll) to do just as one pleases; **mauvaise volonté** ill will
volontiers [vɔlɔ̃tje] *adv* gladly, willingly
volt [vɔlt] *m* volt
voltage [vɔltaʒ] *m* voltage
volte-face [vɔltəfas] *f invar* volte-face
voltige [vɔltiʒ] *f* acrobatics
voltiger [vɔltiʒe] §38 *intr* to flit about; to flutter

voltmètre [vɔltmɛtr] *m* voltmeter
volubile [vɔlybil] *adj* voluble
volume [vɔlym] *m* volume; **faire du volume** (coll) to put on airs
volumi·neux [vɔlyminø] **-neuse** [nøz] *adj* voluminous
volupté [vɔlypte] *f* voluptuousness, ecstasy
volup·tueux [vɔlyptɥø] **-tueuse** [tɥøz] *adj* voluptuous ‖ *mf* voluptuary
vomir [vɔmir] *tr & intr* to vomit
vomissure [vɔmisyr] *f* vomit
vorace [vɔras] *adj* voracious
voracité [vɔrasite] *f* voracity
vos [vo] §88
vo·tant [vɔtɑ̃] **-tante** [tɑ̃t] *mf* voter
vote [vɔt] *m* vote; **passer au vote** to vote on; **vote affirmatif** yea; **vote négatif** nay; **vote par correspondance** absentee ballot; **vote par procuration** proxy
voter [vɔte] *tr* to vote; to vote for ‖ *intr* to vote; **voter à mains levées** to vote by show of hands; **voter par assis et levé** to give one's vote by standing or by remaining seated
vo·tif [vɔtif] **-tive** [tiv] *adj* votive
votre [vɔtr] §88
vôtre [votr] §89
vouer [vwe] *tr* to vow, to dedicate; to doom, to condemn; **voué à** headed for; doomed to ‖ *ref*—**se vouer à** to dedicate oneself to
vouloir [vulwar] *m* will ‖ §76 *tr* to want, to wish; to require; **je voudrais** I would like; I would like to; **veuillez** + *inf* please + *inf*; **voulez-vous vous taire?** will you be quiet?; **vouloir bien** to be glad to, to be willing to; **vouloir dire** to mean ‖ *intr*—**en vouloir à** to bear a grudge against; **je veux!** (slang) and how!; **je veux bien** I'm quite willing; **si vous voulez bien** if you don't mind ‖ *ref*—**s'en vouloir** to have it in for each other
vou·lu -lue [vuly] *adj* required; deliberate
vous [vu] §85, §87; **vous autres Américains** you Americans
vous-même [vumɛm] §86
voussoir [vuswar] *m* (archit) arch stone
voussure [vusyr] *f* arch, arching
voûte [vut] *f* vault; **voûte céleste** canopy of heaven
voûter [vute] *tr* to vault; to bend ‖ *ref* to become round-shouldered
vouvoyer [vuvwaje] §47 *tr* to address with the pronoun **vous** (*instead of* **tu**)
voy. *abbr* (**voyez**) see
voyage [vwajaʒ] *m* trip, journey, voyage; ride (*in car, train, plane, etc.*); **voyage à forfait** all-expense tour; **voyage aller et retour** round trip; **voyage de noces** honeymoon
voyager [vwajaʒe] §38 *intr* to travel
voya·geur [vwajaʒœr] **-geuse** [ʒøz] *mf* traveler; passenger
voyance [vwajɑ̃s] *f* clairvoyance
voyant [vwajɑ̃] **voyante** [vwajɑ̃t] *adj* loud, gaudy ‖ *mf* clairvoyant ‖ *m* signal; (aut) gauge ‖ *f* fortuneteller
voyelle [vwajɛl] *f* vowel

voyeur [vwajœr] **voyeuse** [vwajøz] *mf*
voyeur || *m* Peeping Tom
voyou [vwaju] **voyoute** [vwajut] *adj*
gutter (*e.g., language*) || *mf* gutter-
snipe; brat; hoodlum
vrac [vrak]—**en vrac** unpacked, loose;
in bulk; in disorder
vrai vraie [vrɛ], [vre] *adj* true, real,
genuine || *m* truth; **à vrai dire** to tell
the truth; **pour vrai** (coll) for good
vraiment [vrɛmɑ̃] *adv* truly, really
vraisemblable [vrɛsɑ̃blabl] *adj* probable, likely; true to life, realistic
(*play, novel*)
vraisemblance [vrɛsɑ̃blɑ̃s] *f* probability,
likelihood; realism
vrille [vrij] *f* drill; (aer) spin; (bot)
tendril
vriller [vrije] *tr* to bore || *intr* to go
into a tailspin
vrombir [vrɔ̃bir] *intr* to throb; to buzz;
to hum, to purr (*said of motor*)
vu vue [vy] *adj* seen, regarded; **bien
vu de** in favor with; **mal vu de** out of

favor with || *m*—**au vu de** upon pres-
entation of; **au vu et au su de tout le
monde** openly || *f* view; sight; eye-
sight; **avoir à vue** to have in mind; **à
vue** in sight; (com) on demand; **à vue
de nez** at first sight; **à vue d'œil** visi-
bly; quickly; **à vue by sight; en vue
in evidence; in sight; en vue de** in order to; **garder à vue** to keep under
observation, to keep locked up; **perdre qn de vue** to lose sight of s.o.; to
get out of touch with s.o.; **vue à vol
d'oiseau** bird's-eye view; **vues sur**
designs on || **vu** *prep* considering, in
view of; **vu que** whereas
vulcaniser [vylkanize] *tr* to vulcanize
vulgaire [vylger] *adj* common, vulgar;
ordinary, everyday; vernacular || *m*
common herd; vernacular
vulgariser [vylgarize] *tr* to popularize;
to make vulgar
vulgarité [vylgarite] *f* vulgarity
vulnérable [vylnerabl] *adj* vulnerable
Vve *abbr* (**veuve**) widow

W

W, w [dubləve] *m invar* twenty-third
letter of the French alphabet
wagon [vagɔ̃] *m* (rr) car, coach; (coll)
big car; **un wagon** (coll) a lot; **wagon
à bagages** baggage car; **wagon à
bestiaux** cattle car; **wagon couvert**
boxcar; **wagon de marchandises**
freight car; **wagon frigorifique** or
réfrigérant refrigerator car; **wagon
plat** flat car
wagon-bar [vagɔ̃bar] *m* (*pl* **wagons-
bars**) club car
wagon-citerne [vagɔ̃sitɛrn] *m* (*pl* **wa-
gons-citernes**) tank car
wagon-lit [vagɔ̃li] *m* (*pl* **wagons-lits**)
sleeping car
wagon-poste [vagɔ̃pɔst] *m* (*pl* **wagons-
poste**) mail car
wagon-réservoir [vagɔ̃rezɛrvwar] *m*
(*pl* **wagons-réservoirs**) tank car
wagon-restaurant [vagɔ̃rɛstorɑ̃] *m* (*pl*
wagons-restaurants) dining car

wagon-salon [vagɔ̃salɔ̃] *m* (*pl* **wagons-
salons**) parlor car
wagon-tombereau [vagɔ̃tɔ̃bro] *m* (*pl*
wagons-tombereaux) dump truck
wallace [valas] *f* drinking fountain
wal·lon [walɔ̃] **wal·lonne** [walɔn] *adj*
Walloon || *m* Walloon (*dialect*) ||
(*cap*) *mf* Walloon
warrant [warɑ̃], [varɑ̃] *m* receipt
water-polo [watɛrpolo] *m* water polo
waterproof [watɛrpruf] *adj invar* wa-
terproof || *m invar* raincoat
waters [watɛr], [vatɛr] *mpl* toilet
watt [wat] *m* watt
watt-heure [watœr] *m* (*pl* **watts-heures**)
watt-hour
wattman [watman] *m* motorman
wattmètre [watmɛtr] *m* wattmeter
week-end [wikɛnd] *m* (*pl* **-ends**) week-
end
whisky [wiski] *m* whiskey; **whisky
écossais** Scotch
wolfram [vɔlfram] *m* wolfram

X

X, x [iks], *[iks] *m invar* twenty-
fourth letter of the French alphabet
Xavier [gzavje] *m* Xavier
xénon [ksenɔ̃] *m* xenon

xénophobe [ksenofɔb] *adj* xenophobic
|| *mf* xenophobe
Xérès [kerɛs], [gzerɛs] *m* Jerez; sherry
Xerxès [gzɛrsɛs] *m* Xerxes
xylophone [ksilofɔn] *m* xylophone

Y

Y, y [igrɛk], *[igrɛk] *m invar* twenty-fifth letter of the French alphabet
y [i] *pron pers* §87 to it, to them; at it, at them; in it, in them; by it, by them; of it, of them, e.g., **j'y pense** I am thinking of it or them; (untranslated with certain verbs), e.g., **je n'y vois pas** I don't see; e.g., **il s'y connaît** (coll) he's an expert, he knows what he's talking about; him, her, e.g., **je m'y fie** I trust him; **allez-y!** go ahead!, start!; **ça y est!** that's it!; **je n'y suis pour personne** I am not at home for anybody; **je n'y suis pour rien** I have nothing to do with it; **j'y suis!** I've got it! ‖ *adv* there; here, in, e.g., **Monsieur votre père y est-il?** is your father here?, is your father in?
yacht [jɔt], [jak] *m* yacht; **yacht à glace** iceboat
yacht-club [jɔtklœb] *m* yacht club
yankee [jãki] *adj masc* Yankee ‖ (*cap*) *mf* Yankee
yèble [jɛbl] *f* (bot) elder; **l'yèble** the elder
yeoman [jɔman] *m* yeoman
yeuse [jøz] *f* holm oak; **l'yeuse** the holm oak
yeux [jø] *mpl* see **œil**
yé-yé [jeje] (*pl* -yés) *adj & mf* jitterbug
yiddish [jidiʃ] *adj invar & m* Yiddish
yogourt [jɔgur] *m* yogurt
yole [jɔl] *f* yawl
Yonne [jɔn] *f* Yonne; **l'Yonne** the Yonne
yougoslave [jugɔslav] *adj* Yugoslav ‖ (*cap*) *mf* Yugoslav
Yougoslavie [jugɔslavi] *f* Yugoslavia; **la Yougoslavie** Yugoslavia
youyou [juju] *m* dinghy

Z

Z, z [zɛd] *m invar* twenty-sixth letter of the French alphabet
za·zou -zoue [zazu] *adj* (coll) jazzy ‖ *m* (coll) zoot suiter
zèbre [zɛbr] *m* zebra; (slang) guy
zébrer [zebre] §10 *tr* to stripe; **le soleil zèbre** the sun casts streaks of light on
zébrure [zebryr] *f* stripe
zéla·teur [zelatœr] **-trice** [tris] *mf* zealot
zèle [zɛl] *m* zeal
zénith [zenit] *m* zenith
zéphyr [zefir] *m* zephyr
zeppelin [zɛplɛ̃] *m* zeppelin
zéro [zero] *m* zero
zest [zɛst] *m*—**entre le zist et le zest** (coll) betwixt and between ‖ *interj* tush!
zeste [zɛst] *m* peel (*of citrus fruit*); dividing membrane (*of nut*); **pas un zeste** (fig) not a particle of difference
Zeus [zøs] *m* Zeus
zézaiement [zezɛmã] *m* lisp
zézayer [zezeje] §49 *intr* to lisp
zibeline [ziblin] *f* sable
zieuter [zjøte] *tr* (slang) to get a load of
zigzag [zigzag] *m* zigzag; gypsy moth
zigzaguer [zigzage] *intr* to zigzag
zinc [zɛ̃g] *m* zinc; (coll) bar
zizanie [zizani] *f* wild rice; tare; **semer la zizanie** to sow discord
zodiaque [zɔdjak] *m* zodiac
zone [zon] *f* zone; **zone bleue** center city with limited parking
zoo [zɔo] *m* zoo
zoologie [zɔɔlɔʒi] *f* zoology
zoologique [zɔɔlɔʒik] *adj* zoologic(al)
zouave [zwav] *m* Zouave; **faire le zouave** (coll) to play the fool
zut [zyt] *interj* heck!, hang it!

Part Two

ANGLAIS-FRANÇAIS

LA PRONONCIATION DE L'ANGLAIS

Les signes suivants représentent à peu près tous les sons de la langue anglaise.

VOYELLES

SIGNE	SON	EXEMPLE
[æ]	Plus fermé que a dans **patte**.	**hat** [hæt]
[ɑ]	Comme a dans **pâte**.	**father** ['fɑðər] **proper** ['prɑpər]
[ɛ]	Comme e dans **sec**.	**met** [mɛt]
[e]	Comme **e** dans **récit**. Surtout en position finale, [e] se prononce comme s'il était suivi de [ɪ].	**fate** [fet] **they** [ðe]
[ə]	C'est **e** muet, par ex., **e** dans **gouvernement**.	**heaven** ['hɛvən] **pardon** ['pɑrdən]
[i]	Comme **i** dans **mine**.	**she** [ʃi] **machine** [mə'ʃin]
[ɪ]	Moins fermé que **i** dans **mirage**.	**fit** [fɪt] **beer** [bɪr]
[o]	Comme **au** dans **haut**. Surtout en position finale, [o] se prononce comme s'il était suivi de [ʊ].	**nose** [noz] **road** [rod] **row** [ro]
[ɔ]	Un peu plus fermé que o dans **donne**.	**bought** [bɔt] **law** [lɔ]
[ʌ]	Plus ou moins comme **eu** dans **peur**.	**cup** [kʌp] **come** [kʌm] **mother** ['mʌðər]
[ʊ]	Moins fermé que **ou** dans **doublage**.	**pull** [pʊl] **book** [bʊk] **wolf** [wʊlf]
[u]	Comme **ou** dans **doublage**.	**move** [muv] **tomb** [tum]

DIPHTONGUES

SIGNE	SON	EXEMPLE
[aɪ]	Comme **ai** dans **ail**.	**night** [naɪt] **eye** [aɪ]
[aʊ]	Comme **aou** dans **caoutchouc**.	**found** [faʊnd] **cow** [kaʊ]
[ɔɪ]	Comme **oy** dans **boy**.	**voice** [vɔɪs] **oil** [ɔɪl]

CONSONNES

SIGNE	SON	EXEMPLE
[b]	Comme **b** dans **bébé**.	**bed** [bɛd] **robber** ['rɑbər]
[d]	Comme **d** dans **don**.	**dead** [dɛd] **add** [æd]

3

SIGNE	SON	EXEMPLE
[dʒ]	Comme dj dans djinn.	gem [dʒɛm] jail [dʒel]
[ð]	Comme la consonne castillane d intervocalique de moda.	this [ðɪs] father ['faðər]
[f]	Comme f dans fin.	face [fes] phone [fon]
[g]	Comme g dans gallois.	go [go] get [gɛt]
[h]	Comme la consonne allemande h de Haus ou comme la consonne espagnole j de jota mais moins aspiré.	hot [hɑt] alcohol ['ælkə‚hɔl]
[j]	Comme i dans hier ou comme y dans yod.	yes [jɛs] unit ['junɪt]
[k]	Comme k dans kiosque ou comme c dans cote, mais accompagné d'une aspiration.	cat [kæt] chord [kɔrd] kill [kɪl]
[l]	Comme l ou ll dans pulluler.	late [let] allow [ə'lau]
[m]	Comme m dans mère.	more [mor] command [kə'mænd]
[n]	Comme n dans note.	nest [nɛst] manner ['mænər]
[ŋ]	Comme ng dans parking.	king [kɪŋ] conquer ['kaŋkər]
[p]	Comme p dans père, mais accompagné d'une aspiration.	pen [pɛn] cap [kæp]
[r]	Le r le plus commun dans une grande partie de l'Angleterre et dans la plus grande partie des États-Unis et du Canada, c'est le r rétroflexe, une semi-voyelle dont l'articulation se produit par la pointe de la langue élevée vers la voûte du palais. Cette consonne est très faible dans la position intervocalique ou à la fin de la syllabe et, par conséquent, elle y est très peu audible. L'articulation de cette consonne tend à colorier le son des voyelles voisines. Le r, précédé des sons [ʌ] ou [ə], donne sa propre couleur à ces sons et disparaît complètement en tant que son consonant.	run [rʌn] far [far] art [ɑrt] carry ['kæri] burn [bʌrn] learn [lʌrn] weather ['wɛðər]
[s]	Comme ss dans classe.	send [sɛnd] cellar ['sɛlər]
[ʃ]	Comme ch dans chose.	shall [ʃæl] machine [mə'ʃin] nation ['neʃən]
[t]	Comme t dans table, mais accompagné d'une aspiration.	ten [tɛn] dropped [drɑpt]
[tʃ]	Comme tch dans caoutchouc.	child [tʃaɪld] much [mʌtʃ] nature ['netʃər]
[θ]	Comme la consonne castillane c de cinco.	think [θɪŋk] truth [truθ]
[v]	Comme v dans veuve.	vest [vɛst] over ['ovər] of [av]
[w]	Comme w dans watt; comme le [w] produit en prononçant le mot bois.	work [wʌrk] tweed [twid] queen [kwin]
[z]	Comme s dans rose ou comme z dans zèbre.	zeal [zil] busy ['bɪzi] his [hɪz] winds [wɪndz]
[ʒ]	Comme j dans jardin.	azure ['eʒər] measure ['mɛʒər]

L'accent tonique principal, indiqué par le signe graphique ˈ , et l'accent secondaire, indiqué par le signe graphique ˌ , précèdent la syllabe à laquelle ils s'appliquent, par ex., **fascinate** [ˈfæsɪ ˌnet].

La prononciation des mots composés

Dans la partie anglais-français du Dictionnaire la prononciation figurée de tous les mots anglais simples est indiquée selon une nouvelle adaptation de la méthode de l'Association phonétique internationale, et placée entre crochets à la suite du mot-souche.

Il y a trois genres de mots composés en anglais: (1) les mots dont les éléments composants sont soudés en un mot simple, par ex., **steamboat** vapeur, (2) les mots dont les éléments composants sont reliés entre eux par un trait d'union, par ex., **short-circuit** court-circuiter, et (3) les mots dont les éléments composants restent graphiquement indépendants, par ex., **post card** carte postale. La prononciation des mots composés anglais n'est pas indiquée dans ce Dictionnaire lorsque celle des éléments composants a déjà été indiquée à la suite de ces éléments là où ils apparaissent comme mots-souches. Néanmoins, les accents principaux et secondaires sont indiqués dans l'écriture de ces mots composés, ex.: **steamˈboat**, **shortˈ-cirˈcuit**, **postˈ cardˈ**, **eyeˈ of the mornˈing**.

En ce qui concerne les éléments composants qui se terminent par **-ing** [ɪŋ] dans les mots composés, l'accent seul est précisé lorsque ces éléments se présentent également comme mots-souches suivis de la prononciation figurée, par ex., **playˈing cardˈ**.

Dans les noms dans lesquels les éléments composants **-man** et **-men** portent l'accent secondaire, les voyelles de ces éléments se prononcent comme dans les mots simples **man** et **men**, par ex., **mailman** [ˈmel ˌmæn] et **mailmen** [ˈmel ˌmen]. Dans les noms dans lesquels ces éléments composants sont inaccentués, les voyelles se prononcent dans les deux formes comme **e** muet, par ex., **policeman** [pəˈlɪsmən] et **policemen** [pəˈlɪsmən]. Il y a des noms dans lesquels ces éléments composants se prononcent des deux façons, c'est-à-dire, avec l'accent secondaire ou sans accent, par ex., **doorman** [ˈdor ˌmæn] ou [ˈdormən] et **doormen** [ˈdor-ˌmen] ou [ˈdormən]. Dans ce Dictionnaire la transcription phonétique de ces mots est omise si le premier élément composant se présente ailleurs comme mot-souche suivi de la prononciation figurée. Cependant, l'accentuation de ces mots est indiquée dans le mot-souche même:

> **mailˈmanˈ** *s* (*pl* -menˈ)
> **policeˈman** *s* (*pl* -men)
> **doorˈmanˈ** or **doorˈman** *s* (*pl* -menˈ or -men)

La prononciation des participes passés

Lorsqu'un mot a pour désinence **-ed** (ou **-d** après un **e** muet), et une prononciation conforme aux principes énoncés plus bas, celle-ci ne figurera pas dans ce Dictionnaire, si elle est indiquée quand la forme du mot sans cette désinence se présente comme mot-souche.

La désinence **-ed** (ou **-d** après un **e** muet) du prétérit, du participe passé, et de certains adjectifs possède trois prononciations différentes selon le son de la dernière consonne du radical.

5

1) Si le radical se termine par le son d'une consonne sonore (sauf [d]), que voici: [b], [g], [l], [m], [n], [ŋ], [r], [v], [z], [ð], [ʒ], ou [dʒ] ou par le son d'une voyelle, -ed se prononce [d].

SON DU RADICAL	INFINITIF	PRÉTÉRIT ET PARTICIPE PASSÉ
[b]	ebb [ɛb] rob [rɑb] robe [rob]	ebbed [ɛbd] robbed [rɑbd] robed [robd]
[g]	egg [ɛg] sag [sæg]	egged [ɛgd] sagged [sægd]
[l]	mail [mel] scale [skel]	mailed [meld] scaled [skeld]
[m]	storm [stɔrm] bomb [bɑm] name [nem]	stormed [stɔrmd] bombed [bɑmd] named [nemd]
[n]	tan [tæn] sign [saɪn] mine [maɪn]	tanned [tænd] signed [saɪnd] mined [maɪnd]
[ŋ]	hang [hæŋ]	hanged [hæŋd]
[r]	fear [fɪr] care [kɛr]	feared [fɪrd] cared [kɛrd]
[v]	rev [rɛv] save [sev]	revved [rɛvd] saved [sevd]
[z]	buzz [bʌz] fuse [fjuz]	buzzed [bʌzd] fused [fjuzd]
[ð]	smooth [smuð] bathe [beð]	smoothed [smuðd] bathed [beðd]
[ʒ]	massage [məˈsɑʒ]	massaged [məˈsɑʒd]
[dʒ]	page [pedʒ]	paged [pedʒd]
son de voyelle	key [ki] sigh [saɪ] paw [pɔ]	keyed [kid] sighed [saɪd] pawed [pɔd]

2) Si le radical se termine par le son d'une consonne sourde (sauf [t]), que voici: [f], [k], [p], [s], [θ], [ʃ], ou [tʃ], -ed se prononce [t].

SON DU RADICAL	INFINITIF	PRÉTÉRIT ET PARTICIPE PASSÉ
[f]	loaf [lof] knife [naɪf]	loafed [loft] knifed [naɪft]
[k]	back [bæk] bake [bek]	backed [bækt] baked [bekt]
[p]	cap [kæp] wipe [waɪp]	capped [kæpt] wiped [waɪpt]
[s]	hiss [hɪs] mix [mɪks]	hissed [hɪst] mixed [mɪkst]
[θ]	lath [læθ]	lathed [læt]
[ʃ]	mash [mæʃ]	mashed [mæʃt]
[tʃ]	match [mætʃ]	matched [mætʃt]

3) Si le radical se termine par le son d'une dentale, que voici: [t] ou [d], -ed se prononce [ɪd] ou [əd].

SON DU RADICAL	INFINITIF	PRÉTÉRIT ET PARTICIPE PASSÉ
[t]	wait [wet] mate [met]	waited [ˈwetɪd] mated [ˈmetɪd]
[d]	mend [mɛnd] wade [wed]	mended [ˈmɛndɪd] waded [ˈwedɪd]

6

Notez que le redoublement orthographique de la consonne finale après une voyelle simple accentuée n'altère pas la prononciation de la désinence -ed: **batted** ['bætɪd], **dropped** [drɑpt], **robbed** [rɑbd].

Ces règles s'appliquent aussi aux adjectifs composés qui se terminent par **-ed**. On n'indique que l'accent de ces adjectifs lorsque les éléments composants (le dernier, bien entendu, sans la désinence **-ed**) se présentent ailleurs comme mots-souches suivis de la prononciation figurée, par ex., **flat′-nosed′**.

Cependant, le **-ed** de quelques adjectifs formés sur un radical qui se termine par un son consonantique en plus de ceux qui se terminent par [d] et [t], est prononcé [ɪd] et cette irrégularité s'indique en donnant la prononciation figurée complète, par ex., **blessed** ['blɛsɪd], **crabbed** ['kræbɪd].

7

A

A, a [e] *s* Iière lettre de l'alphabet
a *art indef* un
aback [ə'bæk] *adv* avec le vent dessus; **taken aback** déconcerté
abandon [ə'bændən] *s* abandon *m* ‖ *tr* abandonner
abase [ə'bes] *tr* abaisser, humilier
abasement [ə'besmənt] *s* abaissement *m*
abash [ə'bæʃ] *tr* décontenancer
abashed *adj* confus, confondu
abate [ə'bet] *tr* diminuer, réduire; (*part of price*) rabattre ‖ *intr* se calmer; (*said of wind*) tomber
abbess ['æbɪs] *s* abbesse *f*
abbey ['æbi] *s* abbaye *f*
abbot ['æbət] *s* abbé *m*
abbreviate [ə'brivɪ,et] *tr* abréger
abbreviation [ə,brivɪ'eʃən] *s* abréviation *f*
A B C's [,e,bi'siz] *spl* (letterword) a b c *m*
abdicate ['æbdɪ,ket] *tr & intr* abdiquer
abdomen ['æbdəmən], [æb'domən] *s* abdomen *m*
abduct [æb'dʌkt] *tr* enlever, ravir
abeam [ə'bim] *adv* par le travers
abed [ə'bɛd] *adv* au lit
abet [ə'bɛt] *v* (*pret & pp* **abetted;** *ger* **ahetting**) *tr* encourager
abettor [ə'bɛtər] *s* complice *mf*
abeyance [ə'be-əns] *s* suspension *f*; **in abeyance** en suspens
ab·hor [æb'hɔr] *v* (*pret & pp* **-horred;** *ger* **-horring**) *tr* abhorrer, détester
abhorrent [æb'hɑrənt], [æb'hɔrənt] *adj* détestable, répugnant
abide [ə'baɪd] *v* (*pret & pp* **abode** or **abided**) *tr* attendre ‖ *intr* demeurer, continuer, persister; **to abide by** s'en tenir à; rester fidèle à
abili·ty [ə'bɪlɪti] *s* (*pl* **-ties**) capacité *f*, habileté *f*; talent *m*
abject [æb'dʒɛkt] *adj* abject
ablative ['æblətɪv] *adj & s* ablatif *m*
ablaut ['æblaʊt] *s* apophonie *f*
ablaze [ə'blez] *adj* enflammé; (*colorful*) resplendissant ‖ *adv* en feu
able ['ebəl] *adj* capable, habile; **to be able to** pouvoir
a'ble-bod'ied *adj* robuste, vigoureux; (*seaman*) breveté
abloom [ə'blum] *adj & adv* en fleur
abnormal [æb'nɔrməl] *adj* anormal
abnormali·ty [,æbnɔr'mælɪti] *s* (*pl* **-ties**) anomalie *f*, irrégularité *f*; (*of body*) difformité *f*
aboard [ə'bɔrd] *adv* à bord; **all aboard!** en voiture!; **to go aboard** s'embarquer ‖ *prep* à bord de
abode [ə'bod] *s* demeure *f*, résidence *f*

abolish [ə'bɑlɪʃ] *tr* abolir
A-bomb ['e,bɑm] *s* bombe *f* atomique
abomination [ə,bɑmɪ'neʃən] *s* abomination *f*
aborigines [,æbə'rɪdʒɪ,niz] *spl* aborigènes *mpl*
abort [ə'bɔrt] *intr* avorter
abortion [ə'bɔrʃən] *s* avortement *m*
abound [ə'baʊnd] *intr* abonder
about [ə'baʊt] *adv* à la ronde, tout autour; (*almost*) presque; (*here and there*) çà et là; **to be about to** être sur le point de ‖ *prep* autour de, aux environs de; (*approximately*) environ; au sujet de; vers, e.g., **about six o'clock** vers six heures; **it is about . . .** il s'agit de . . .
about'-face' or **about'-face'** *s* volte-face *f*; (mil) demi-tour *m* ‖ **about'-face'** *intr* faire volte-face
above [ə'bʌv] *adv* en haut; au-dessus, ci-dessus ‖ *prep* au-dessus de; plus que, outre; (*another point on the river*) en amont de; **above all** surtout
above'-men'tioned *adj* susmentionné
abrasive [ə'bresɪv], [ə'brezɪv] *adj & s* abrasif *m*
abreast [ə'brɛst] *adj & adv* de front; **three abreast** par rangs de trois; **to be abreast of** or **with** être en ligne avec; **to keep abreast of** se tenir au courant de
abridge [ə'brɪdʒ] *tr* abréger
abridgment [ə'brɪdʒmənt] *s* abrégé *m*, résumé *m*; réduction *f*
abroad [ə'brɔd] *adv* au loin; (*in foreign parts*) à l'étranger
abrogate ['æbrə,get] *tr* abroger
abrupt [ə'brʌpt] *adj* (*steep; impolite*) abrupt; (*hasty*) brusque, précipité
abscess ['æbsɛs] *s* abcès *m*
abscond [æb'skɑnd] *intr* s'enfuir, déguerpir; **to abscond with** lever le pied avec
absence ['æbsəns] *s* absence *f*
absent ['æbsənt] *adj* absent ‖ [æb'sɛnt] *tr*—**to absent oneself** s'absenter
absentee [,æbsən'ti] *s* absent *m*
ab'sent-mind'ed *adj* absent, distrait
absolute ['æbsə,lut] *adj & s* absolu *m*
absolutely ['æbsə,lutli] *adv* absolument ‖ [,æbsə'lutli] *adv* (coll) absolument
absolve [æb'sɑlv] *tr* absoudre
absorb [æb'sɔrb] *tr* absorber; **to be** or **become absorbed in** s'absorber dans
absorbent [æb'sɔrbənt] *adj* absorbant; (*cotton*) hydrophile ‖ *s* absorbant *m*
absorbing [æb'sɔrbɪŋ] *adj* absorbant
abstain [æb'sten] *intr* s'abstenir

abstemious [æb'stimɪ‧əs] *adj* abstinent, sobre

abstinent ['æbstɪnənt] *adj* abstinent

abstract ['æbstrækt] *adj* abstrait ‖ *s* abrégé *m*, résumé *m* ‖ *tr* résumer ‖ [æb'strækt] *tr* abstraire; (*to remove*) soustraire

abstractedly [æb'stræktɪdli] *adv* d'un œil distrait

abstruse [æb'strus] *adj* abstrus

absurd [æb'sʌrd], [æb'zʌrd] *adj* absurde

absurdi‧ty [æb'sʌrdɪti], [æb'zʌrdɪti] *s* (*pl* -**ties**) absurdité *f*

abundance [ə'bʌndəns] *s* abondance *f*

abundant [ə'bʌndənt] *adj* abondant

abuse [ə'bjus] *s* abus *m*; (*mistreatment*) maltraitement *m*; (*insulting words*) insultes *fpl* ‖ [ə'bjuz] *tr* abuser de; maltraiter; insulter

abusive [ə'bjusɪv] *adj* (*insulting*) injurieux; (*wrong*) abusif

abut [ə'bʌt] *v* (*pret & pp* **abutted**; *ger* **abutting**) *intr*—**to abut on** border, confiner

abutment [ə'bʌtmənt] *s* (*of wall*) contrefort *m*; (*of bridge*) culée *f*; (*of arch*) pied-droit *m*

abyss [ə'bɪs] *s* abîme *m*

A.C. ['e'si] *s* (letterword) (**alternating current**) courant *m* alternatif

academic [,ækə'dɛmɪk] *adj* académique; théorique ‖ *s* étudiant *m* or professeur *m* de l'université

academical [,ækə'dɛmɪkəl] *adj* académique; théorique ‖ **academicals** *spl* costume *m* académique

academician [ə,kædə'mɪʃən] *s* académicien *m*

acade‧my [ə'kædəmi] *s* (*pl* -**mies**) académie *f*; (*preparatory school*) collège *m*

accede [æk'sid] *intr* acquiescer; **to accede to** accéder à; (*the throne*) monter sur

accelerate [æk'sɛlə‧ret] *tr & intr* accélérer

accelerator [æk'sɛlə‧retər] *s* accélérateur *m*

accent ['æksɛnt] *s* accent *m* ‖ ['æksɛnt], [æk'sɛnt] *tr* accentuer

accentuate [æk'sɛntʃu‧et] *tr* accentuer

accept [æk'sɛpt] *tr* accepter

acceptable [æk'sɛptəbəl] *adj* acceptable

acceptance [æk'sɛptəns] *s* acceptation *f*; (*approval*) approbation *f*

acceptation [,æksɛp'teʃən] *s* acceptation *f*; (*meaning*) acception *f*

access ['æksɛs] *s* accès *m*

accessible [æk'sɛsɪbəl] *adj* accessible

accession [æk'sɛʃən] *s* accession *f*

accesso‧ry [æk'sɛsəri] *adj* accessoire ‖ *s* (*pl* -**ries**) accessoire *m*; (*to a crime*) complice *mf*

ac'cess route' *s* voie *f* de raccordement, bretelle *f*

accident ['æksɪdənt] *s* accident *m*; **by accident** par accident

accidental [,æksɪ'dɛntəl] *adj* accidentel ‖ *s* (mus) accident *m*

ac'cident-prone' *adj* prédisposé aux accidents

acclaim [ə'klem] *tr* acclamer

acclimate ['æklɪ,met] *tr* acclimater

accommodate [ə'kamə,det] *tr* accommoder; (*to oblige*) rendre service à; (*to lodge*) loger

accommodating [ə'kamə,detɪŋ] *adj* accommodant, serviable

accommodation [ə,kamə'deʃən] *s* accommodation *f*; **accommodations** commodités *fpl*; (*in a train*) place *f*; (*in a hotel*) chambre *f*; (*room and board*) le vivre et le couvert

accompaniment [ə'kʌmpənɪmənt] *s* accompagnement *m*

accompanist [ə'kʌmpənɪst] *s* accompagnateur *m*

accompa‧ny [ə'kʌmpəni] *v* (*pret & pp* -**nied**) *tr* accompagner

accomplice [ə'kamplɪs] *s* complice *mf*

accomplish [ə'kamplɪʃ] *tr* accomplir

accomplishment [ə'kamplɪʃmənt] *s* accomplissement *m*, réalisation *f*; (*thing itself*) œuvre *f* accomplie; **accomplishments** arts *mpl* d'agrément, talents *mpl*

accord [ə'kɔrd] *s* accord *m*; **in accord** d'accord; **of one's own accord** de son plein gré ‖ *tr* accorder ‖ *intr* se mettre d'accord

accordance [ə'kɔrdəns] *s* accord *m*; **in accordance with** conformément à

according [ə'kɔrdɪŋ] *adj*—**according as** selon que; **according to** selon, d'après, suivant; **according to expert advice** au dire d'experts

accordingly [ə'kɔrdɪŋli] *adv* en conséquence

accordion [ə'kɔrdi‧ən] *s* accordéon *m*

accost [ə'kɔst], [ə'kɑst] *tr* accoster

account [ə'kaunt] *s* compte *m*; profit *m*, calcul *m*; (*narration*) récit *m*; (*report*) compte rendu; (*explanation*) explication *f*; **of no account** sans importance; **on account of** à cause de; **on no account** en aucune façon; **to call to account** demander des comptes à ‖ *intr*—**to account for** expliquer; (*money*) rendre compte de

accountable [ə'kauntəbəl] *adj* responsable; (*explainable*) explicable

accountant [ə'kauntənt] *s* comptable *mf*

account' book' *s* registre *m* de comptabilité

accounting [ə'kauntɪŋ] *s* règlement *m* de comptes; (*profession*) comptabilité *f*

accouterments [ə'kutərmənts] *spl* équipement *m*

accredit [ə'krɛdɪt] *tr* accréditer

accretion [ə'kriʃən] *s* accroissement *m*

accrue [ə'kru] *intr* s'accroître; **to accrue from** dériver de; **to accrue to** échoir à

accumulate [ə'kjumjə,let] *tr* accumuler ‖ *intr* s'accumuler

accuracy ['ækjərəsi] *s* exactitude *f*

accurate ['ækjərɪt] *adj* exact; (*aim*) juste; (*translation*) fidèle

accursed [ə'kʌrsɪd], [ə'kʌrst] *adj* maudit

accusation [,ækjə'zeʃən] *s* accusation *f*

accusative [ə'kjuzətɪv] adj & s accusatif m
accuse [ə'kjuz] tr accuser
accused s accusé m, inculpé m
accustom [ə'kʌstəm] tr accoutumer; to become accustomed s'accoutumer
ace [es] s as m; to have an ace up one's sleeve avoir un atout dans la manche
acetate ['æsɪ,tet] s acétate m
ace'tic ac'id [ə'sitɪk] s acide m acétique
acetone ['æsɪ,ton] s acétone f
acet'ylene torch' [ə'sɛtɪ,lin] s chalumeau m oxyacétylénique
ache [ek] s douleur f || intr faire mal; my head aches j'ai mal à la tête; to be aching to (coll) brûler de
achieve [ə'tʃiv] tr accomplir, atteindre; (a victory) remporter
achievement [ə'tʃivmənt] s accomplissement m, réalisation f; (thing itself) œuvre f remarquable, réussite f; (heroic deed) exploit m
Achil'les' heel' [ə'kɪliz] s talon m d'Achille
acid ['æsɪd] adj & s acide m
acidi·ty [ə'sɪdɪti] s (pl -ties) acidité f
ac'id test' s (fig) épreuve f définitive
acknowledge [æk'nɑlɪdʒ] tr reconnaître; to acknowledge receipt of accuser réception de
acknowledgment [æk'nɑlɪdʒmənt] s reconnaissance f; (of a letter) accusé m de réception; (receipt) récépissé m
acme ['ækmi] s comble m, sommet m
acolyte ['ækə,laɪt] s enfant m de chœur; (priest) acolyte m; assistant m
acorn ['ekɔrn], ['ekərn] s gland m
acoustic [ə'kustɪk] adj acoustique || acoustics s & spl acoustique f
acquaint [ə'kwent] tr informer; to be acquainted se connaître; to be acquainted with connaître
acquaintance [ə'kwentəns] s connaissance f
acquiesce [,ækwɪ'ɛs] intr acquiescer
acquiescence [,ækwɪ'ɛsəns] s acquiescement m, consentement m
acquire [ə'kwaɪr] tr acquérir; (friends; a reputation) s'acquérir
acquirement [ə'kwaɪrmənt] s acquisition f
acquisition [,ækwɪ'zɪʃən] s acquisition f
acquisitive [ə'kwɪzɪtɪv] adj âpre au gain, avide
acquit [ə'kwɪt] v (pret & pp acquitted; ger acquitting) tr acquitter; to acquit oneself se comporter
acquittal [ə'kwɪtəl] s acquittement m
acre ['ekər] s acre f
acrid ['ækrɪd] adj âcre
acrimonious [,ækrɪ'monɪ·əs] adj acrimonieux
acrobat ['ækrə,bæt] s acrobate mf
acrobatic [,ækrə'bætɪk] adj acrobatique || acrobatics s (profession) acrobatie f; acrobatics spl (stunts) acrobaties
acronym ['ækrənɪm] s sigle m
acropolis [ə'krɑpəlɪs] s acropole f

across [ə'krɔs], [ə'krɑs] adv en travers, à travers; (sidewise) en largeur || prep en travers de; (e.g., the street) de l'autre côté de; across country à travers champs; to come across rencontrer par hasard; to go across traverser
acrostic [ə'krɔstɪk], [ə'krɑstɪk] s acrostiche m
act [ækt] s action f, acte m; (circus, rad, telv) numéro m; (sport) loi f; (law, theat) acte; (coll) allure f affectée, comédie f; in the act sur le fait, en flagrant délit || tr jouer; to act the fool faire le pitre || intr agir; se conduire; (theat) jouer; to act as servir de; to act on influer sur
acting ['æktɪŋ] adj intérimaire || s (actor's art) jeu m; (profession) théâtre m
action ['ækʃən] s action f; (law) acte m; (mach) jeu m; (theat) intrigue f; out of action hors de service; to go into action (mil) aller au feu; to suit the action to the word joindre le geste à la parole; to take action prendre des mesures
activate ['æktɪ,vet] tr activer
active ['æktɪv] adj actif
activi·ty [æk'tɪvɪti] s (pl -ties) activité f
actor ['æktər] s acteur m
actress ['æktrɪs] s actrice f
actual ['æktʃu·əl] adj véritable, réel, effectif
actually ['æktʃu·əli] adv réellement, en réalité, effectivement
actuar·y ['æktʃu,ɛri] s (pl -ies) actuaire m
actuate ['æktʃu,et] tr actionner; (to motivate) animer
acuity [ə'kju·ɪti] s acuité f
acumen [ə'kjumən] s finesse f
acute [ə'kjut] adj aigu; (fig) avisé
acutely [ə'kjutli] adv profondément
A.D. ['e'di] adj (letterword) (Anno Domini) ap. J.-C.
ad [æd] s (coll) annonce f
adage ['ædɪdʒ] s adage m
Adam ['ædəm] s Adam m; I don't know him from Adam (coll) je ne le connais ni d'Ève ni d'Adam
adamant ['ædəmənt] adj inflexible
Ad'am's ap'ple s pomme f d'Adam
adapt [ə'dæpt] tr adapter
adaptation [,ædæp'teʃən] s adaptation f
adapter [ə'dæptər] s adaptateur m, raccord m; (phot) bague f porte-objectif
add [æd] tr ajouter; to add up additionner || intr additionner; to add up to s'élever à
adder ['ædər] s (zool) vipère f
addict ['ædɪkt] s toxicomane mf; (sports) fanatique mf || [ə'dɪkt] tr atteindre de toxicomanie; to be addicted to (to enjoy) s'adonner à
addiction [ə'dɪkʃən] s toxicomanie f; addiction to penchant m pour
add'ing machine' s machine f à calculer, additionneuse f

addition [ə'dɪʃən] *s* addition *f*; **in addition to** en plus de
additive ['ædɪtɪv] *adj & s* additif *m*
addle ['ædəl] *tr* brouiller
address [ə'drɛs], ['ædrɛs] *s* adresse *f* || [ə'drɛs] *s* discours *m*; **to deliver an address** prononcer un discours || *tr* adresser; s'adresser à; (*an audience*) faire un discours à
address' book' *s* carnet *m* d'adresses
addressee [,ædrɛ'si] *s* destinataire *mf*
adduce [ə'd(j)us] *tr* alléguer; (*proof*) fournir
adenoids ['ædə ,nɔɪdz] *spl* végétations *fpl* adénoïdes
adept [ə'dɛpt] *adj* habile || *s* adepte *mf*
adequate ['ædɪkwɪt] *adj* suffisant, adéquat; **adequate to** à la hauteur de, proportionné à
adhere [æd'hɪr] *intr* adhérer
adherence [æd'hɪrəns] *s* adhérence *f*
adherent [æd'hɪrənt] *adj & s* adhérent *m*
adhesion [æd'hiʒən] *s* adhésion *f*; (pathol) adhérence *f*
adhesive [æd'hisɪv], [æd'hizɪv] *adj & s* adhésif *m*
adhe'sive tape' *s* sparadrap *m*
adieu [ə'd(j)u] *s* (*pl* adieus or adieux) adieu *m* || *interj* adieu!
ad infinitum [æd ,ɪnfɪ'naɪtəm] *adv* sans fin
adjacent [ə'dʒesənt] *adj* adjacent
adjective ['ædʒɪktɪv] *adj & s* adjectif *m*
adjoin [ə'dʒɔɪn] *tr* avoisiner || *intr* être contigus
adjoining [ə'dʒɔɪnɪŋ] *adj* contigu
adjourn [ə'dʒʌrn] *tr* (*to postpone*) remettre, reporter; (*a meeting, a session*) lever; (*sine die; for resumption at another time or place*) ajourner || *intr* s'ajourner; lever la séance
adjournment [ə'dʒʌrnmənt] *s* suspension *f* de séance
adjudge [ə'dʒʌdʒ] *tr* adjuger; (*a criminal*) condamner
adjudicate [ə'dʒudɪ ,ket] *tr & intr* juger
adjunct ['ædʒʌŋkt] *adj & s* adjoint *m*; **adjuncts** accessoires *mpl*
adjust [ə'dʒʌst] *tr* ajuster || *intr* s'adapter
adjustable [ə'dʒʌstəbəl] *adj* réglable
adjustment [ə'dʒʌstmənt] *s* ajustage *m*, réglage *m*; (*arrangement*) ajustement *m*, règlement *m*; (telv) mise *f* au point
adjutant ['ædʒətənt] *s* adjutant *m*
ad-lib [,æd'lɪb] *adj* improvisé || *v* (*pret & pp* -libbed; *ger* -libbing) *tr & intr* improviser (en cascade)
administer [æd'mɪnɪstər] *tr* administrer; **to administer an oath** faire prêter serment || *intr*—**to administer to** pourvoir à, aider, assister
administration [æd ,mɪnɪs'treʃən] *s* administration *f*; gouvernement *m*
administrator [æd'mɪnɪs ,tretər] *s* administrateur *m*
admiral ['ædmɪrəl] *s* amiral *m*
admiral·ty ['ædmɪrəlti] *s* (*pl* -ties) amirauté *f*; ministère *m* de la marine

admiration [,ædmɪ're ʃən] *s* admiration *f*
admire [æd'maɪr] *tr* admirer
admirer [æd'maɪrər] *s* admirateur *m*; (*suitor*) soupirant *m*
admission [æd'mɪʃən] *s* admission *f*; (*price*) entrée *f*; (*confession*) aveu *m*
ad·mit [æd'mɪt] *v* (*pret & pp* -mitted; *ger* -mitting) *tr* admettre; (*e.g., a mistake*) avouer; **admit bearer** laisser passer
admittance [æd'mɪtəns] *s* entrée *f*
admittedly [æd'mɪtɪdli] *adv* manifestement
admonish [æd'monɪʃ] *tr* admonester
ad nauseam [æd'nɔʃɪ·əm], [æd'nɔsɪ·əm] *adv* jusqu'au dégoût
ado [ə'du] *s* agitation *f*; **much ado about nothing** beaucoup de bruit pour rien; **without further ado** sans plus de façons
adolescence [,ædə'lɛsəns] *s* adolescence *f*
adolescent [,ædə'lɛsənt] *adj & s* adolescent *m*
adopt [ə'dopt] *tr* adopter
adoption [ə'dopʃən] *s* adoption *f*
adoptive [ə'doptɪv] *adj* adoptif
adorable [ə'dorəbəl] *adj* adorable
adoration [,ædə'reʃən] *s* adoration *f*
adore [ə'dor] *tr* adorer
adorn [ə'dorn] *tr* orner, parer
adornment [ə'dornmənt] *s* parure *f*
adre'nal glands' [ə'drinəl], [ə'drinəl] *spl* (capsules) surrénales *fpl*
adrenalin [ə'drɛnəlɪn] *s* adrénaline *f*
Adriatic [,edrɪ'ætɪk], [,ædrɪ'ætɪk] *adj & s* Adriatique *f*
adrift [ə'drɪft] *adj & adv* à la dérive
adroit [ə'drɔɪt] *adj* adroit, habile
adulate ['ædʒə ,let] *tr* aduler
adult [ə'dʌlt], ['ædʌlt] *adj & s* adulte *mf*
adulterate [ə'dʌltə ,ret] *tr* frelater
adulteration [ə ,dʌltə'reʃən] *s* frelatage *m*
adulterer [ə'dʌltərər] *s* adultère *m*
adulteress [ə'dʌltərɪs] *s* adultère *f*
adulterous [ə'dʌltərəs] *adj* adultère
adulter·y [ə'dʌltəri] *s* (*pl* -ies) adultère *m*
adumbrate [æd'ʌmbret], ['ædəm ,bret] *tr* ébaucher; (*to foreshadow*) présager
advance [æd'væns], [æd'vɑns] *s* avance *f*; **advances** propositions *fpl*; propositions malhonnêtes; **in advance** d'avance; en avance || *tr* avancer || *intr* avancer, s'avancer; (*said of prices*) augmenter; (*said of stocks*) monter
advancement [æd'vænsmənt], [æd'vɑnsmənt] *s* avancement *m*
advance' pay'ment *s* versement *m* anticipé
advantage [æd'væntɪdʒ], [æd'vɑntɪdʒ] *s* avantage *m*; **to take advantage of** profiter de
advent ['ædvɛnt] *s* venue *f*; **Advent** (eccl) Avent *m*
adventitious [,ædvɛn'tɪʃəs] *adj* adventice

adventure [æd'vɛntʃər] s aventure f
adventurer [æd'vɛntʃərər] s aventurier m
adventuress [æd'vɛntʃərɪs] s aventurière f
adventurous [æd'vɛntʃərəs] adj aventureux
adverb ['ædvʌrb] s adverbe m
adversar•y ['ædvər‚sɛri] s (pl -ies) adversaire mf
adverse [æd'vʌrs], ['ædvʌrs] adj adverse
adversi•ty [æd'vʌrsiti] s (pl -ties) adversité f
advertise ['ædvər‚taɪz], [‚ædvər'taɪz] tr & intr annoncer
advertisement [‚ædvər'taɪzmənt], [æd-'vʌrtɪzmənt] s annonce f
advertiser ['ædvər‚taɪzər], [‚ædvər-'taɪzər] s annonceur m
advertising ['ædvər‚taɪzɪŋ] s réclame f
ad'vertising a'gency s agence f de publicité
ad'vertising man' s entrepreneur m de publicité
advice [æd'vaɪs] s conseil m; conseils; a piece of advice un conseil
advisable [æd'vaɪzəbəl] adj opportun, recommandable
advise [æd'vaɪz] tr conseiller; (to inform) aviser; to advise against déconseiller; to advise s.o. to + inf conseiller à qn de + inf
advisedly [æd'vaɪzɪdli] adv en connaissance de cause
advisement [æd'vaɪzmənt] s conseils mpl; to take under advisement mettre en délibération
adviser [æd'vaɪzər] s conseiller m
advisory [æd'vaɪzəri] adj consultatif
advocacy ['ædvəkəsi] s plaidoyer m
advocate ['ædvə‚ket] s partisan m; (lawyer) avocat m || tr préconiser
Aege'an Sea' [ɪ'dʒi-ən] s mer f Égée, mer de l'Archipel
aegis ['idʒɪs] s égide f
aerate ['ɛret] tr aérer
aerial ['ɛri-əl] adj aérien || s antenne f
aerodynamic [‚ɛrodaɪ'næmɪk] adj aérodynamique || aerodynamics s aérodynamique f
aeronautic [‚ɛro'nɔtɪk] adj aéronautique || aeronautics s aéronautique f
aerosol ['ɛrə‚sol] s aérosol m
aerospace ['ɛrə‚spes] adj aérospatial
Aeschylus ['ɛskɪləs] s Eschyle m
aesthete ['ɛsθit] s esthète mf
aesthetic [ɛs'θɛtɪk] adj esthétique || aesthetics s esthétique f
afar [ə'fɑr] adv au loin
affable ['æfəbəl] adj affable
affair [ə'fɛr] s affaire f; (of lovers) affaire de cœur
affect [ə'fɛkt] tr affecter
affectation [‚æfɛk'teʃən] s affectation f
affected adj affecté, maniéré
affection [ə'fɛkʃən] s affection f
affectionate [ə'fɛkʃənɪt] adj affectueux
affidavit [‚æfɪ'devɪt] s déclaration f sous serment
affiliate [ə'fɪlɪ‚et] s (com) société f affiliée || tr affilier || intr s'affilier

affini•ty [ə'fɪnɪti] s (pl -ties) affinité f; (inlawry) alliance f
affirm [ə'fʌrm] tr & intr affirmer
affirmative [ə'fʌrmətɪv] adj affirmatif .|| s affirmative f
affix ['æfɪks] s affixe m || [ə'fɪks] tr annexer; (a signature) apposer; (guilt) attribuer; (on the wall) afficher
afflict [ə'flɪkt] tr affliger
affliction [ə'flɪkʃən] s (sorrow) affliction f; (disorder) infirmité f
affluence ['æflu-əns] s affluence f de biens, richesse f
afford [ə'ford] tr fournir; se permettre, avoir de quoi payer
affront [ə'frʌnt] s affront m || tr insulter
Afghanistan [æf'gænɪ‚stæn] s l'Afghanistan m
afire [ə'faɪr] adj & adv en feu
aflame [ə'flem] adj & adv en flammes
afloat [ə'flot] adj & adv à flot; (rumor) en circulation; to keep afloat on the water se tenir sur l'eau
afoot [ə'fut] adj & adv à pied; (underway) en œuvre
aforesaid [ə'for‚sɛd] adj susdit; ci-dessus mentionné
afraid [ə'fred] adj effrayé; to be afraid avoir peur
afresh [ə'frɛʃ] adv à nouveau
Africa ['æfrɪkə] s Afrique f; l'Afrique
African ['æfrɪkən] adj africain || s Africain m
after ['æftər], ['ɑftər] adj suivant, postérieur || adv après, plus tard || prep après, à la suite de; (in the manner or style of) d'après; (not translated in expressions of time), e.g., eight minutes after ten dix heures huit || conj après que
af'ter-din'ner adj d'après dîner
af'ter-effect' s contrecoup m; after-effects (pathol) séquelles fpl
af'ter-glow' s lueur f du coucher
af'ter-im'age s image f consécutive
af'ter-life' s survie f
aftermath ['æftər‚mæθ], ['ɑftər‚mæθ] s conséquences fpl sérieuses, suites fpl; (agr) regain m
af'ter-noon' s après-midi m & f; good afternoon! bonjour!
af'ter-shav'ing lo'tion s eau f de Cologne pour la barbe
af'ter-taste' s arrière-goût m
af'ter-thought' s réflexion f après coup
afterward ['æftərwərd], ['ɑftərwərd] adv après, ensuite
again [ə'gɛn] adv encore, de plus; de nouveau, encore une fois; now and again de temps en temps
against [ə'gɛnst] prep contre; against the grain à rebrousse-poil; over against en face de; par contraste avec
age [edʒ] s âge m; (about a hundred years) siècle m; for ages depuis longtemps; of age majeur; to come of age atteindre sa majorité; under age mineur || tr & intr vieillir
aged [edʒd] adj (wine, cheese, etc.)

vieilli; (*of the age of*) âgé de ||
['edʒɪd] *adj* âgé, vieux
agen‧cy ['edʒənsi] *s* (*pl* **-cies**) agence
f; (*means*) action *f*
agenda [ə'dʒɛndə] *s* ordre *m* du jour
agent ['edʒənt] *s* agent *m*; (*means*)
moyen *m*; (com) commissionnaire *m*
agglomeration [ə͵glɑmə'reʃən] *s* agglomération *f*
aggrandizement [ə'grændɪzmənt] *s*
agrandissement *m*
aggravate ['ægrə͵vet] *tr* aggraver;
(coll) exaspérer
aggregate ['ægrɪ͵get] *adj* global || *s*
agrégat *m* || *tr* rassembler; (coll)
s'élever à
aggression [ə'grɛʃən] *s* agression *f*
aggressive [ə'grɛsɪv] *adj* agressif; (*live-
wire*) entreprenant
aggressor [ə'grɛsər] *s* agresseur *m*
aghast [ə'gæst], [ə'gɑst] *adj* abasourdi
agile ['ædʒɪl] *adj* agile
agility [ə'dʒɪlɪti] *s* agilité *f*
agitate ['ædʒɪ͵tet] *tr* agiter
agitator ['ædʒɪ͵tetər] *s* agitateur *m*
aglow [ə'glo] *adj* & *adv* rougeoyant
agnostic [æg'nɑstɪk] *adj* & *s* agnostique *mf*
ago [ə'go] *adv* il y a, e.g., **two days
ago** il y a deux jours
agog [ə'gɑg] *adj* & *adv* en émoi
agonizing ['ægə͵naɪzɪŋ] *adj* angoissant
ago‧ny ['ægəni] *s* (*pl* **-nies**) angoisse *f*;
(*death struggle*) agonie *f*
agrarian [ə'grɛrɪ‧ən] *adj* agraire; (law)
agrairien || *s* agrairien *m*
agree [ə'gri] *intr* être d'accord, s'accorder; **agreed!** d'accord!; **to agree
to** consentir à
agreeable [ə'gri‧əbəl] *adj* agréable,
sympathique; (*consenting*) d'accord
agreement [ə'grimənt] *s* accord *m*;
contrat *m*
agriculture ['ægrɪ͵kʌltʃər] *s* agriculture *f*
aground [ə'graʊnd] *adj* (naut) échoué
|| *adv*—**to run aground** échouer
ague ['egju] *s* fièvre *f* intermittente;
accès *m* de frisson
ahead [ə'hɛd] *adj* & *adv* en avant;
ahead of avant; devant; **straight
ahead** tout droit; **to get ahead of**
devancer
ahem [ə'hɛm] *interj* hum!
ahoy [ə'hɔɪ] *interj*—**ship ahoy!** ohé
du navire!
aid [ed] *s* (*assistance*) aide *f*; (*assist-
ant*) aide *mf* || *tr* aider
aide-de-camp ['eddə'kæmp] *s* (*pl*
aides-de-camp) officier *m* d'ordonnance, aide *m* de camp
ail [el] *tr* affliger; **what ails you?**
qu'avez-vous? || *intr* être souffrant
ailment ['elmənt] *s* indisposition *f*,
maladie *f*
aim [em] *s* but *m*, objectif *m*; (*of gun*)
pointage *m* || *tr* diriger; (*a blow*) al-
longer; (*a telescope, cannon, etc.*)
pointer, viser || *intr* viser
air [ɛr] *s* air *m*; **on the air** à la radio,
à la télévision, à l'antenne; **to put on
airs** prendre des airs; **to put on the**

air radiodiffuser; **to walk on air** ne
pas toucher terre; **up in the air** con-
fondu, sidéré; (*angry*) très monté ||
tr aérer; (*a question*) ventiler; (*feelings*) donner libre cours à
air-borne ['ɛr͵born] *adj* aéroporté
air' brake' *s* frein *m* à air comprimé
air'-condi'tion *tr* climatiser
air' condi'tioner *s* climatiseur *m*
air' condi'tioning *s* climatisation *f*
air'craft' *s* aéronef *m*, appareil *m*
d'aviation
air'craft car'rier *s* porte-avions *m*
air'drop' *s* parachutage *m* || *tr* para-
chuter
air'field' *s* terrain *m* d'aviation, aéro-
drome *m*
air' force' *s* forces *fpl* aériennes
air' gap' *s* (elec) entrefer *m*
air' let'ter *s* aérogramme *m*
air'lift' *s* pont *m* aérien
air'line' *s* ligne *f* aérienne
air'line pi'lot *s* pilote *m* de ligne
air'li'ner *s* avion *m* de transport
air'mail' *adj* aéropostal || *s* poste *f*
aérienne; **by airmail** par avion
air'plane' *s* avion *m*
air' pock'et *s* trou *m* d'air
air' pollu'tion *s* pollution *f* de l'air
air'port' *s* aéroport *m*
air' raid' *s* attaque *f* aérienne
air'-raid drill' *s* exercice *m* d'alerte
aérienne
air'-raid shel'ter *s* abri *m*
air'-raid ward'en *s* chef *m* d'îlot
air'-raid warn'ing *s* alarme *f* aérienne
air'sick' *adj* atteint du mal de l'air
air'sick'ness *s* mal *m* de l'air
air' sleeve' or **sock'** *s* manche *f* à air
air'strip' *s* piste *f*
air' term'inal *s* aérogare *f*
air'tight' *adj* hermétique
air'waves' *spl* ondes *fpl* radiophoniques
air'way' *s* route *f* aérienne
air‧y ['ɛri] *adj* (*comp* **-ier**; *super* **-iest**)
aérien; gracieux; (coll) maniéré
aisle [aɪl] *s* (*through rows of seats*)
passage *m* central, allée *f*; (*in a
train*) couloir *m*; (*long passageway
in a church*) nef *f* latérale
ajar [ə'dʒɑr] *adj* entrebâillé
akimbo [ə'kɪmbo] *adj* & *adv*—**with
arms akimbo** les poings sur les
hanches
akin [ə'kɪn] *adj* apparenté
alabaster ['ælə͵bæstər], ['ælə͵bɑstər]
s albâtre *m*
alacrity [ə'lækrɪti] *s* vivacité *f*, empressement *m*
alarm [ə'lɑrm] *s* alarme *f*; (*of clock*)
sonnerie *f* || *tr* alarmer
alarm' clock' *s* réveille-matin *m*, réveil
m
alarming [ə'lɑrmɪŋ] *adj* alarmant
alas [ə'læs], [ə'lɑs] *interj* hélas!
Albanian [æl'benɪ‧ən] *adj* albanais || *s*
(*language*) albanais *m*; (*person*)
Albanais
albatross ['ælbə͵trɔs], ['ælbə͵trɑs] *s*
albatros *m*
albi‧no [æl'baɪno] *adj* albinos || *s* (*pl*
-nos) albinos *m*

album ['ælbəm] *s* album *m*
albumen [æl'bjumən] *s* albumen *m*
alchemy ['ælkɪmɪ] *s* alchimie *f*
alcohol ['ælkə‚hɔl], ['ælkə‚hɑl] *s* alcool *m*
alcoholic [‚ælkə'hɔlɪk], [‚ælkə'hɑlɪk] *adj & s* alcoolique *mf*
alcove ['ælkov] *s* niche *f*; (*for a bed*) alcôve *f*
alder ['ɔldər] *s* aune *m*
alder‚man ['ɔldərmən] *s* (*pl* -men) conseiller *m* municipal
ale [el] *s* ale *f*
alembic [ə'lɛmbɪk] *s* alambic *m*; (fig) creuset *m*
alert [ə'lʌrt] *adj & s* alerte *f* ‖ *tr* alerter
alfalfa [æl'fælfə] *s* luzerne *f*
algebra ['ældʒɪbrə] *s* algèbre *f*
Algeria [æl'dʒɪrɪ‚ə] *s* Algérie *f*
Algerian [æl'dʒɪrɪ‚ən] *adj* (*of Algeria*) algérien; (*of Algiers, the Barbary state*) algérois ‖ *s* Algérien *m*; Algérois *m*
Algiers [æl'dʒɪrz] *s* Alger *m*
alias ['elɪ‚əs] *s* nom *m* d'emprunt ‖ *adv* alias, autrement dit
ali‚bi ['ælɪ‚baɪ] *s* (*pl* -bis) excuse *f*; (law) alibi *m*
alien ['eljən], ['elɪ‚ən] *adj & s* étranger *m*
alienate ['eljə‚net], ['elɪ‚ə‚net] *tr* s'aliéner; (*to transfer*) aliéner
alight [ə'laɪt] *adj* allumé ‖ *v* (*pret & pp* alighted or alit [ə'lɪt]) *intr* descendre, se poser; (aer) (*on land*) atterrir; (aer) (*on sea*) amerrir
align [ə'laɪn] *tr* aligner ‖ *intr* s'aligner
alike [ə'laɪk] *adj* pareils, e.g., **these books are alike** ces livres sont pareils; **to look alike** se ressembler ‖ *adv* de la même façon
alimony ['ælɪ‚monɪ] *s* pension *f* alimentaire après divorce
alive [ə'laɪv] *adj* vivant; vif; **alive to** sensible à
alka‚li ['ælkə‚laɪ] *s* (*pl* -lis or -lies) alcali *m*
alkaline ['ælkə‚laɪn], ['ælkəlɪn] *adj* alcalin
all [ɔl] *adj indef* tout; tout le ‖ *s* tout *m* ‖ *pron indef* tout; tous; **all of** tout lc; **first of all** tout d'abord; **is that all?** c'est tout?; (*ironically*) ce n'est que ça?; **not at all** pas du tout ‖ *adv* tout; **all at once** tout à coup; **all but** presque; **all in** (coll) éreinté; **all in all** à tout prendre; **all off** (slang) abandonné; **all right** bon, ça va, très bien; **all's well!** (naut) bon quart!; **all the better** tant mieux; **all told** en tout; **fifteen (thirty, etc.) all** (tennis) égalité à quinze (trente, etc.); **to be all for** ne demander mieux que
allay [ə'le] *tr* apaiser
all'-clear' *s* fin *f* d'alerte
allege [ə'lɛdʒ] *tr* alléguer; déclarer sous serment; affirmer sans preuve
alleged *adj* présumé, prétendu, censé
allegedly [ə'lɛdʒɪdlɪ] *adv* prétendument, censément
allegiance [ə'lidʒəns] *s* allégeance *f*

allegoric(al) [‚ælɪ'gɑrɪk(əl)], [‚ælɪ'gɔrɪk(əl)] *adj* allégorique
allego‚ry ['ælɪ‚gorɪ] *s* (*pl* -ries) allégorie *f*
aller‚gy ['ælərdʒɪ] *s* (*pl* -gies) allergie *f*
alleviate [ə'livɪ‚et] *tr* soulager, alléger
alley ['ælɪ] *s* ruelle *f*; **that is up my alley** (slang) cela est dans mes cordes
al'ley cat' *s* chat *m* de gouttière
alliance [ə'laɪ‚əns] *s* alliance *f*
alligator ['ælɪ‚getər] *s* alligator *m*
al'ligator pear' *s* poire *f* d'avocat
al'ligator wrench' *s* clef *f* à machoires dentées
alliteration [ə‚lɪtə're‚fən] *s* allitération *f*
all'-know'ing *adj* omniscient
allocate ['ælə‚ket] *tr* allouer, assigner
allot [ə'lɑt] *v* (*pret & pp* allotted; ger allotting) *tr* répartir
allotment [ə'lɑtmənt] *s* allocation *f*; (*from social security*) prestation *f*
all'-out' *adj* total
allow [ə'lau] *tr* permettre; (*a fact; a privilege*) accorder; (*as an allocation*) allouer ‖ *intr*—**to allow for** tenir compte de
allowance [ə'lau‚əns] *s* allocation *f*, indemnité *f*; concession *f*; tolérance *f*
alloy ['ælɔɪ], [ə'lɔɪ] *s* alliage *m* ‖ [ə'lɔɪ] *tr* allier
all' right' *interj* bon!, très bien!, ça va!; (*agreed!*) c'est entendu!, d'accord!
all'-round' *adj* (*athlete*) complet; (*man*) universel; total, global
All' Saints'' Day' *s* la Toussaint
All' Souls'' Day' *s* la fête des Morts
all'spice' *s* (*plant*) quatre-épices *f*; (*berry*) toute-épice *f*; piment *m*
all'-time' *adj* record
allude [ə'lud] *intr*—**to allude to** faire allusion à
allure [ə'lur] *tr* séduire, tenter
allurement [ə'lurmənt] *s* charme *m*
alluring [ə'lurɪŋ] *adj* séduisant
all' wet' *adj* (coll) fichu, erroné
al‚ly ['ælaɪ], [ə'laɪ] *s* (*pl* -lies) allié *m* ‖ [ə'laɪ] *v* (*pret & pp* -lied) *tr* allier
almanac ['ɔlmə‚næk] *s* almanach *m*
almighty [ɔl'maɪtɪ] *adj* omnipotent
almond ['amənd], ['æmənd] *s* amande *f*
al'mond tree' *s* amandier *m*
almost ['ɔlmost], [ɔl'most] *adv* presque; **I almost fell** j'ai failli tomber
alms [amz] *s & spl* aumône *f*
alms'house' *s* hospice *m*
aloe ['ælo] *s* aloès *m*
aloft [ə'lɔft], [ə'lɑft] *adv* en l'air; (aer) en vol; (naut) en haut
alone [ə'lon] *adj* seul, e.g., **my arm alone suffices** mon bras seul suffit; e.g., **the metropolis alone** la seule métropole; **let alone . . .** sans compter . . . ; **to leave alone** laisser tranquille ‖ *adv* seulement
along [ə'lɔŋ], [ə'lɑŋ] *adv* avec; **all along** tout le temps; **come along!** venez donc!; **to get along** s'en aller; se porter, faire des progrès ‖ *prep* le long de; sur
along'side' *adv* à côté ‖ *prep* à côté de

aloof [ə'luf] *adj* isolé, peu abordable ‖ *adv* à l'écart, à distance
aloud [ə'laud] *adv* à haute voix
alpenstock ['ælpən,stɑk] *s* bâton *m* ferré
alphabet ['ælfə,bɛt] *s* alphabet *m*
alpine ['ælpaɪn] *adj* alpin
Alps [ælps] *spl*—**the Alps** les Alpes *fpl*
already [ɔl'rɛdi] *adv* déjà
Alsatian [æl'seʃən] *adj* alsacien ‖ *s* (*dialect*) alsacien *m*; (*person*) Alsacien *m*
also ['ɔlso] *adv* aussi, également
altar ['ɔltər] *s* autel *m*
al'tar boy' *s* enfant *m* de chœur
al'tar cloth' *s* nappe *f* d'autel
al'tar-piece' *s* rétable *m*
al'tar rail' *s* grille *f* du chœur
alter ['ɔltər] *tr* altérer; (*a suit of clothes*) retoucher, faire des retouches à; (*an animal*) châtrer ‖ *intr* se modifier
alteration [,ɔltə'reʃən] *s* altération *f*; (*in a building*) modification *f*; **alterations** (*in clothing*) retouches *fpl*
alternate ['ɔltərnɪt], ['æltərnɪt] *adj* alternatif; (*angle*) alterne; (*rhyme*) croisé ‖ ['ɔltər,net], ['æltər,net] *tr* faire alternance à ‖ *intr* alterner
al'ternating cur'rent *s* courant *m* alternatif
alternative [ɔl'tʌrnətɪv], [æl'tʌrnətɪv] *adj* alternatif ‖ *s* alternative *f*
although [ɔl'ðo] *conj* bien que, quoique
altitude ['æltɪ,t(j)ud] *s* altitude *f*
al-to ['ælto] *s* (*pl* -tos) alto *m*
altogether [,ɔltə'gɛðər] *adv* ensemble; entièrement; tout compris
altruist ['æltru·ɪst] *adj* & *s* altruiste *mf*
alum ['æləm] *s* alun *m*
aluminum [ə'lumɪnəm] *s* aluminium *m*
alum·nus [ə'lʌmnəs] *s* (*pl* -ni [naɪ]) diplômé *m*, ancien étudiant *m*
alveo·lus [æl'vi·ələs] *s* (*pl* -li [,laɪ]) alvéole *m*
always ['ɔlwɪz], ['ɔlwez] *adv* toujours
A.M. ['e'ɛm] *adv* (letterword) (**ante meridiem**) du matin
amalgam [ə'mælgəm] *s* amalgame *m*
amalgamate [ə'mælgə,met] *tr* amalgamer ‖ *intr* s'amalgamer
amass [ə'mæs] *tr* amasser
amateur ['æmətʃər] *adj* & *s* amateur *m*
amaze [ə'mez] *tr* étonner
amazing [ə'mezɪŋ] *adj* étonnant
amazon ['æmə,zɑn], ['æməzən] *s* amazone *f*; **Amazon** Amazone *f*; (*river*) fleuve *m* des Amazones
ambassador [æm'bæsədər] *s* ambassadeur *m*
ambassadress [æm'bæsədrɪs] *s* ambassadrice *f*, ambassadeur *m*
amber ['æmbər] *adj* ambré ‖ *s* ambre *m* jaune, ambre succin
ambidextrous [,æmbɪ'dɛkstrəs] *adj* ambidextre
ambigui·ty [,æmbɪ'gju·ɪti] *s* (*pl* -ties) ambiguïté *f*
ambition [æm'bɪʃən] *s* ambition *f*
ambitious [æm'bɪʃəs] *adj* ambitieux

amble ['æmbəl] *s* amble *m* ‖ *intr* (*to stroll*) déambuler; (*equit*) ambler
ambulance ['æmbjələns] *s* ambulance *f*
am'bulance corps' *s* service *m* sanitaire
am'bulance driv'er *s* ambulancier *m*
ambulatory ['æmbjələ,tori] *adj* ambulatoire
ambush ['æmbuʃ] *s* embuscade *f* ‖ *tr* embusquer
ameliorate [ə'miljə,ret] *tr* améliorer ‖ *intr* s'améliorer
amen ['e'mɛn], ['ɑ'mɛn] *s* amen *m* ‖ *interj* ainsi soit-il!
amenable [ə'minəbəl], [ə'mɛnəbəl] *adj* docile; **amenable to** (*a court*) justiciable de; (*a fine*) passible de; (*a law*) soumis à; (*persuasion*) disposé à; (*a superior*) responsable envers
amend [ə'mɛnd] *tr* amender ‖ *intr* s'amender
amendment [ə'mɛndmənt] *s* amendement *m*
amends [ə'mɛndz] *spl* dédommagement *m*; **to make amends to** dédommager
ameni·ty [ə'minɪti], [ə'mɛnɪti] *s* (*pl* -ties) aménité *f*; **amenities** agréments *mpl*; civilités *fpl*
America [ə'mɛrɪkə] *s* Amérique *f*; l'Amérique
American [ə'mɛrɪkən] *adj* américain ‖ *s* Américain *m*
Amer'ican Eng'lish *s* anglais *m* d'Amérique, américain *m*
Amer'ican In'dian *s* amérindien *m*
Americanism [ə'mɛrɪkə,nɪzəm] *s* (*word*) américanisme *m*; patriotisme *m* américain
Amer'ican plan' *s* pension *f* complète
Amer'ican way of life' *s* mode *m* de vie américain
amethyst ['æmɪθɪst] *s* améthyste *f*
amiable ['emɪ·əbəl] *adj* aimable
amicable ['æmɪkəbəl] *adj* amical
amid [ə'mɪd] *prep* au milieu de
amid'ships *adv* au milieu du navire
amidst [ə'mɪdst] *prep* au milieu de
amiss [ə'mɪs] *adj* détraqué; **not amiss** pas mal; **something amiss** quelque chose qui manque, quelque chose qui cloche ‖ *adv* de travers; **to take amiss** prendre en mauvaise part
ami·ty ['æmɪti] *s* (*pl* -ties) amitié *f*
ammeter ['æm,mitər] *s* ampèremètre *m*
ammonia [ə'monɪ·ə] *s* (*gas*) ammoniac *m*; (*gas dissolved in water*) ammoniaque *f*
ammunition [,æmjə'nɪʃən] *s* munitions *fpl*
amnesia [æm'niʒɪ·ə], [æm'niʒə] *s* amnésie *f*
amnes·ty ['æmnɪsti] *s* (*pl* -ties) amnistie *f* ‖ *v* (*pret* & *pp* -tied) *tr* amnistier
amoeba [ə'mibə] *s* amibe *f*
among [ə'mʌŋ] *prep* entre, parmi
amorous ['æmərəs] *adj* amoureux
amorphous [ə'mɔrfəs] *adj* amorphe
amortize ['æmər,taɪz] *tr* amortir
amount [ə'maunt] *s* montant *m*, quantité *f* ‖ *intr*—**to amount to** s'élever à
ampere ['æmpɪr] *s* ampère *m*

amphibian [æm'fıbı·ən] *adj* & *s* amphibie *mf*; amphibien *m*

amphibious [æm'fıbı·əs] *adj* amphibie

amphitheater ['æmfı͵θi·ətər] *s* amphithéâtre *m*

ample ['æmpəl] *adj* ample; (*speech*) satisfaisant; (*reward*) suffisant

amplifier ['æmplı͵faı·ər] *s* amplificateur *m*

ampli·fy ['æmplı͵faı] *v* (*pret* & *pp* -fied) *tr* amplifier

amplitude ['æmplı͵t(j)ud] *s* amplitude *f*

am'plitude modula'tion *s* modulation *f* d'amplitude

amputate ['æmpjə͵tet] *tr* amputer

amputee [͵æmpjə'ti] *s* amputé *m*

amuck [ə'mʌk] *adv*—to run amuck s'emballer

amulet ['æmjəlıt] *s* amulette *f*

amuse [ə'mjuz] *tr* amuser

amusement [ə'mjuzmənt] *s* amusement *m*

amusing [ə'mjuzıŋ] *adj* amusant

an [æn], [ən] *art indef* (devant un son vocalique) un

anachronism [ə'nækrə͵nızəm] *s* anachronisme *m*

analogous [ə'næləgəs] *adj* analogue

analo·gy [ə'nælədʒi] *s* (*pl* -gies) analogie *f*

analy·sis [ə'nælısıs] *s* (*pl* -ses [͵siz]) analyse *f*

analyst ['ænəlıst] *s* analyste *mf*

analytic(al) [͵ænə'lıtık(əl)] *adj* analytique

analyze ['ænə͵laız] *tr* analyser

anarchist ['ænərkıst] *s* anarchiste *mf*

anarchy ['ænərki] *s* anarchie *f*

anathema [ə'næθımə] *s* anathème *m*

anatomic(al) [͵ænə'tamık(əl)] *adj* anatomique

anato·my [ə'nætəmi] *s* (*pl* -mies) anatomie *f*

ancestor ['ænsestər] *s* ancêtre *m*

ances·try ['ænsestri] *s* (*pl* -tries) ancêtres *mpl*, aïeux *mpl*; (*line*) ascendance *f*

anchor ['æŋkər] *s* ancre *f*; anchors aweigh! ancres levées!; to cast anchor jeter l'ancre, mouiller l'ancre; to weigh anchor lever l'ancre || *tr* & *intr* ancrer

ancho·vy ['æntʃovi] *s* (*pl* -vies) anchois *m*

ancient ['enʃənt] *adj* ancien

and [ænd] *conj* et; and/or et/ou; and so forth et ainsi de suite

andiron ['ænd͵aı·ərn] *s* chenet *m*

anecdote ['ænık͵dot] *s* anecdote *f*

anemia [ə'nimı·ə] *s* anémie *f*

anesthesia [͵ænıs'θiʒə] *s* anesthésie *f*

anesthetic [͵ænıs'θetık] *adj* & *s* anesthésique *m*

anesthetist [æ'nesθıtıst] *s* anesthésiste *mf*

anesthetize [æ'nesθı͵taız] *tr* anesthésier

aneurysm ['ænjə͵rızəm] *s* anévrisme *m*

anew [ə'n(j)u] *adv* à (or de) nouveau

angel ['endʒəl] *s* ange *m*; (*financial backer*) (coll) bailleur *m* de fonds

angelic(al) [æn'dʒelık(əl)] *adj* angélique

anger ['æŋgər] *s* colère *f* || *tr* mettre en colère, fâcher

angina pectoris [æn'dʒaınə'pektərıs] *s* angine *f* de poitrine

angle ['æŋgəl] *s* angle *m* || *tr* (journ) présenter sous un certain angle || *intr* pêcher à la ligne; to angle for essayer d'attraper; (*a compliment*) quêter

angler ['æŋglər] *s* pêcheur *m* à la ligne; (*schemer*) intrigant *m*

an·gry ['æŋgri] *adj* (*comp* -grier; *super* -griest) fâché; angry at fâché de; angry with fâché contre; to become angry se mettre en colère

anguish ['æŋgwıʃ] *s* angoisse *f*

angular ['æŋgjələr] *adj* angulaire; (*features*) anguleux

animal ['ænıməl] *adj* & *s* animal *m*

animate ['ænımıt] *adj* animé || ['ænı͵met] *tr* animer

an'imated cartoon' *s* dessins *mpl* animés

animation [͵ænı'meʃən] *s* animation *f*

animosi·ty [͵ænı'masıti] *s* (*pl* -ties) animosité *f*

animus ['ænıməs] *s* animosité *f*; intention *f*

anion ['æn͵aı·ən] *s* anion *m*

anise ['ænıs] *s* anis *m*

aniseed ['ænı͵sid] *s* graine *f* d'anis

ankle ['æŋkəl] *s* cheville *f*

anklet ['æŋklıt] *s* socquette *f*; bracelet *m* de cheville

annals ['ænəlz] *spl* annales *fpl*

anneal [ə'nil] *tr* recuire, détremper

annex ['ænɛks] *s* annexe *f* || [ə'nɛks] *tr* annexer, rattacher

annexation [͵ænɛks'eʃən] *s* annexion *f*, rattachement *m*

annihilate [ə'naı·ı͵let] *tr* annihiler

annihilation [ə͵naı·ı'leʃən] *s* anéantissement *m*

anniversa·ry [͵ænı'vʌrsəri] *adj* anniversaire || *s* (*pl* -ries) anniversaire *m*

annotate ['ænə͵tet] *tr* annoter

announce [ə'nauns] *tr* annoncer

announcement [ə'naunsmənt] *s* annonce *f*, avis *m*

announcer [ə'naunsər] *s* annonceur *m*; (rad) présentateur *m*, speaker *m*

annoy [ə'nɔı] *tr* ennuyer, tourmenter

annoyance [ə'nɔı·əns] *s* ennui *m*

annoying [ə'nɔı·ıŋ] *adj* ennuyeux

annual ['ænju·əl] *adj* annuel || *s* annuaire *m*; plante *f* annuelle

annui·ty [ə'n(j)u·ıti] *s* (*pl* -ties) (*annual payment*) annuité *f*; (*of a retired person*) pension *f* de retraite, pension viagère

an·nul [ə'nʌl] *v* (*pret* & *pp* -nulled; *ger* -nulling) *tr* annuler; abolir

anode ['ænod] *s* anode *f*

anodyne ['ænə͵daın] *adj* & *s* anodin *m*

anoint [ə'nɔınt] *tr* oindre

anon [ə'nan] *adv* tout à l'heure

anonymity [͵ænə'nımıti] *s* anonymat *m*

anonymous [ə'nanıməs] *adj* anonyme

another [ə'nʌðər] *adj* & *pron indef* un autre; (*an additional*) encore un; many another beaucoup d'autres

answer ['ænsər], ['ɑnsər] s réponse f; (math) solution f ‖ tr (e.g., yes or no) répondre; (a question, a letter) répondre à ‖ intr répondre; **to answer for** répondre de
an'swer book' s livre m du maître
an'swering ser'vice s (telp) service m des abonnés absents
ant [ænt] s fourmi f
antagonism [æn'tægə‚nɪzəm] s antagonisme m
antagonize [æn'tægə‚naɪz] tr contrarier; (a friend) s'aliéner
Antarctic [ænt'ɑrktɪk] adj & s Antarctique f
Antarctica [ænt'ɑrktɪkə] s l'Antarctique f
Antarc'tic O'cean s Océan m glacial antarctique
ante ['ænti] s mise f ‖ tr miser ‖ intr miser, caver; **ante up!** misez!
anteater ['ænt‚itər] s fourmilier m
antecedent [‚æntɪ'sidənt] adj & s antécédent m
antechamber ['æntɪ‚tʃembər] s antichambre f
antelope ['æntɪ‚lop] s antilope f
anten·na [æn'tenə] s (pl -nae [ni]) (ent) antenne f ‖ s (pl -nas) (rad) antenne f
antepenult [‚æntɪ'pinʌlt] s antépénultième f
anterior [æn'tɪrɪ·ər] adj antérieur
anthem ['ænθəm] s hymne m; (eccl) antienne f, hymne f
ant' hill' s fourmilière f
antholo·gy [æn'θɑlədʒi] s (pl -gies) anthologie f
anthropoid ['ænθro‚pɔɪd] adj & s anthropoïde m
antiaircraft [‚æntɪ'er‚kræft], [‚æntɪ-'er‚krɑft] adj antiaérien, contre-avions
antibiotic [‚æntɪbaɪ'ɑtɪk] adj & s antibiotique m
antibod·y ['æntɪ‚bɑdi] s (pl -ies) anticorps m
anticipate [æn'tɪsɪ‚pet] tr anticiper; (to expect) s'attendre à
anticipation [æn‚tɪsɪ'peʃən] s anticipation f
anticlimax [‚æntɪ'klaɪmæks] s chute f dans le trivial, désillusion f
antics ['æntɪks] spl bouffonnerie f
antidote ['æntɪ‚dot] s antidote m
antifreeze [‚æntɪ'friz] s antigel m
antiglare [‚æntɪ'glɛr] adj antiaveuglant
antiknock [‚æntɪ'nɑk] adj & s antidétonant m
an'timis'sile mis'sile [‚æntɪ'mɪsəl] s missile m antimissile
antimony ['æntɪ‚moni] s antimoine m
antipa·thy [æn'tɪpəθi] s (pl -thies) antipathie f
antiperspirant [‚æntɪ'pʌrspərənt] s antitranspirant m
antiphon ['æntɪ‚fɑn] s antienne f
antiquated ['æntɪ‚kwetɪd] adj vieilli, démodé
antique [æn'tik] adj antique; ancien ‖ s (piece of furniture) original m; **antiques** meubles mpl d'époque

antique' deal'er s antiquaire m
antique' shop' s magasin m d'antiquités, maison f de meubles d'époque
antiqui·ty [æn'tɪkwɪti] s (pl -ties) antiquité f; (oldness) ancienneté f
anti-Semitic [‚æntɪsɪ'mɪtɪk] adj antisémite, antisémitique
antiseptic [‚æntɪ'septɪk] adj & s antiseptique m
an'titank' gun' [‚æntɪ'tæŋk] s canon m antichar
antithe·sis [æn'tɪθɪsɪs] s (pl -ses [‚siz]) antithèse f
antitoxin [‚æntɪ'tɑksɪn] s antitoxine f
antiwar [‚æntɪ'wɔr] adj antimilitariste
antler ['æntlər] s andouiller m
antonym ['æntənɪm] s antonyme m
anvil ['ænvɪl] s enclume f
anxie·ty [æŋ'zaɪ·əti] s (pl -ties) anxiété f, inquiétude f
anxious ['æŋkʃəs] adj inquiet, soucieux; **to be anxious to** avoir envie de, tenir beaucoup à
any ['ɛni] adj indef quelque, du; aucun; **any day** n'importe quel jour; **any place** n'importe où; **any time** n'importe quand, à tout moment; **any way** n'importe comment, de toute façon ‖ pron indef quiconque; quelques-uns §81; **not . . . any** ne . . . aucun §90; ne . . . en . . . pas, e.g., **I will not give him any** je ne lui en donnerai pas ‖ adv un peu
an'y·bod'y pron indef quelqu'un §81; n'importe qui; **not . . . anybody** ne . . . personne
an'y·how' adv en tout cas; cependant
an'y·one' pron indef quelqu'un §81; n'importe qui; quiconque; **not . . . anyone** ne . . . personne, e.g., **I don't see anyone** je ne vois personne
an'y·thing' pron indef quelque chose; n'importe quoi; **anything at all** quoi que ce soit, si peu que ce soit; **anything but** rien moins que; **anything else?** et avec ça?, ensuite?; **not . . . anything** ne . . . rien
an'y·way' adv en tout cas
an'y·where' adv n'importe où; **not . . . anywhere** ne . . . nulle part
aor·ta [e'ɔrtə] s (pl -tas or -tae [ti]) aorte f
apace [ə'pes] adv vite, rapidement
apache [ə'pɑʃ], [ə'pæʃ] s apache m ‖ **Apache** [ə'pætʃi] s apache m
apart [ə'pɑrt] adj séparé ‖ adv à part, à l'écart; **apart from** en dehors de
apartment [ə'pɑrtmənt] s appartement m
apart'ment house' s maison f de rapport, immeuble m d'habitation
apathetic [‚æpə'θɛtɪk] adj apathique
apa·thy ['æpəθi] s (pl -thies) apathie f
ape [ep] s singe m ‖ tr singer
aperture ['æpərtʃər] s ouverture f; (phonet) aperture f
apex ['epɛks] s (pl apexes or apices ['æpɪ‚siz]) sommet m; (astr) apex m
aphid ['efɪd], ['æfɪd] s puceron m
aphorism ['æfə‚rɪzəm] s aphorisme m
aphrodisiac [‚æfrə'dɪzɪ‚æk] adj & s aphrodisiaque m

apiar·y ['epı‚eri] s (pl -ies) rucher m
apiece [ə'pis] adv la pièce, chacun
apish ['epıʃ] adj simiesque; (fig) imitateur
aplomb [ə'plɑm], [ə'plɔm] s aplomb m
apocalyptic(al) [ə‚pɑkə'lıptık(əl)] adj apocalyptique
Apocrypha [ə'pɑkrıfə] s apocryphes mpl
apogee ['æpə‚dʒi] s apogée m
Apollo [ə'pɑlo] s Apollon m
apologetic [ə‚pɑlə'dʒetık] adj prêt à s'excuser, humble, penaud
apologize [ə'pɑlə‚dʒaız] intr faire des excuses, s'excuser
apolo·gy [ə'pɑlədʒi] s (pl -gies) excuse f; (makeshift) semblant m, prétexte m; (apologia) apologie f
A.P.O. number ['e'pi'o‚nʌmbər] s (letterword) (**Army Post Office**) secteur m postal
apoplectic [‚æpə'plektık] adj & s apoplectique mf
apoplexy ['æpə‚pleksi] s apoplexie f
apostle [ə'pɑsəl] s apôtre m
Apos'tles' Creed' s symbole m des apôtres
apos'tle·ship' s apostolat m
apostrophe [ə'pɑstrəfi] s apostrophe f
apothecar·y [ə'pɑθı‚keri] s (pl -ies) apothicaire m
appall [ə'pɔl] tr épouvanter, effrayer, consterner
appalling [ə'pɔlıŋ] adj épouvantable
appara·tus [‚æpə'retəs], [‚æpə'rætəs] s (pl -tus or -tuses) appareil m, dispositif m
appar·el [ə'pærəl] s (equipment; clothes) appareil m; (clothes) habillement m ‖ v (pret & pp -eled or -elled; ger -eling or -elling) tr habiller, vêtir; parer
apparent [ə'pærənt], [ə'perənt] adj apparent; (heir) présomptif
apparition [‚æpə'rıʃən] s apparition f
appeal [ə'pil] s appel m, recours m; charme m, attrait m; (law) pourvoi m ‖ tr (a case) faire appeler ‖ intr séduire, charmer; s'adresser, recourir; (law) appeler, pourvoir en cassation
appealing [ə'pilıŋ] adj séduisant, attrayant, sympathique
appear [ə'pır] intr (to come into view; to be published; to seem) paraître; (to come into view) apparaître
appearance [ə'pırəns] s (look) apparence f, aspect m; (act of showing up) apparition f; (in print) parution f; **to all appearances** selon toute vraisemblance; **to make one's appearance** faire acte de présence
appease [ə'piz] tr apaiser
appeasement [ə'pizmənt] s apaisement m
appeaser [ə'pizər] s conciliateur m, pacificateur m
appel'late court' [ə'pelıt], [ə'pelet] s tribunal m d'appel; **highest appellate court** cour f de cassation
append [ə'pend] tr apposer, ajouter

appendage [ə'pendıdʒ] s dépendance f, accessoire m
appendecto·my [‚æpən'dektəmi] s (pl -mies) appendicectomie f
appendicitis [ə‚pendı'saıtıs] s appendicite f
appen·dix [ə'pendıks] s (pl -dixes or -dices [dı‚siz]) appendice m
appertain [‚æpər'ten] intr se rapporter
appetite ['æpı‚taıt] s appétit m
appetizer ['æpı‚taızər] s apéritif m
appetizing ['æpı‚taızıŋ] adj appétissant
applaud [ə'plɔd] tr applaudir; (to approve) applaudir à; **to applaud s.o. for** applaudir qn de ‖ intr applaudir
applause [ə'plɔz] s applaudissements mpl
apple ['æpəl] s pomme f; (tree) pommier m
ap'ple·jack' s calvados m
ap'ple of the eye' s prunelle f des yeux
ap'ple or'chard s pommeraie f, verger m à pommes
ap'ple pie' s tarte f aux pommes
ap'ple pol'isher s (coll) chien m couchant, flagorneur m
ap'ple·sauce' s compote f de pommes; (slang) balivernes fpl
ap'ple tree' s pommier m
ap'ple turn'over s chausson m (aux pommes)
appliance [ə'plaı·əns] s appareil m; application f; **appliances** accessoires mpl
applicable ['æplıkəbəl] adj applicable
applicant ['æplıkənt] s candidat m, postulant m
application [‚æplı'keʃən] s application f; (for a job) demande f, sollicitation f
applica'tion blank' s formule f
applied' arts' spl arts mpl industriels
ap·ply [ə'plaı] v (pret & pp -plied) tr appliquer ‖ intr s'appliquer; **to apply for** solliciter, postuler; **to apply to** s.o. s'adresser à qn
appoint [ə'pɔınt] tr nommer, désigner; (obs) équiper
appointed adj désigné; (time) convenu, dit
appointment [ə'pɔıntmənt] s (engagement) rendez-vous m; (to a position) désignation f, nomination f; **appointments** (of a room) aménagements mpl; **by appointment** sur rendez-vous
apportion [ə'porʃən] tr répartir; (com) ventiler
appraisal [ə'prezəl] s appréciation f, estimation f, évaluation f; (by an appraiser) expertise f
appraise [ə'prez] tr priser, estimer, évaluer; faire l'expertise de
appraiser [ə'prezər] s priseur m, estimateur m, évaluateur m; expert m, commissaire-priseur m
appreciable [ə'priʃı·əbəl] adj appréciable, sensible
appreciate [ə'priʃı‚et] tr apprécier; (to be grateful for) reconnaître; (to be aware of) être sensible à, s'apercevoir de ‖ intr augmenter, hausser

appreciation [ə͵priʃɪ'eʃən] s appréciation f; reconnaissance f, gratitude f; (rise in value) plus-value f
appreciative [ə'priʃɪ͵etɪv] adj reconnaissant
apprehend [͵æprɪ'hɛnd] tr comprendre; (to seize; to fear) appréhender
apprehension [͵æprɪ'hɛnʃən] s appréhension f
apprehensive [͵æprɪ'hɛnsɪv] adj craintif
apprentice [ə'prɛntɪs] s apprenti m
apprentice-ship' s apprentissage m
apprise [ə'praɪz] tr prévenir, informer, mettre au courant
approach [ə'protʃ] s approche f; to make approaches to faire des avances à || tr approcher, approcher de, s'approcher de || intr approcher, s'approcher
approachable [ə'protʃəbəl] adj abordable, accessible
approbation [͵æprə'beʃən] s approbation f
appropriate [ə'proprɪ·ɪt] adj approprié || [ə'proprɪ͵et] tr (to take for oneself) s'approprier; (to assign) affecter
appropriation [ə͵proprɪ'eʃən] s appropriation f; (assigning) affectation f; (govt) crédit m budgétaire
approval [ə'pruvəl] s approbation f, consentement m; on approval à l'essai, à condition
approve [ə'pruv] tr approuver || intr être d'accord; to approve of approuver
approximate [ə'praksɪmɪt] adj approximatif || [ə'praksɪ͵met] tr se rapprocher de
appurtenance [ə'pʌrtɪnəns] s appartenance f; attirail m; appurtenances dépendances fpl
apricot ['eprɪ͵kat], ['æprɪ͵kat] s abricot m; (tree) abricotier m
April ['eprɪl] s avril m
A'pril fool' s (joke) poisson m d'avril; (victim) dupe f, dindon m
A'pril Fools'' Day' s le jour du poisson d'avril
apron ['eprən] s tablier m; (aer) aire f de manœuvre
apropos [͵æprə'po] adj opportun || adv opportunément; apropos of quant à, à l'égard de
apse [æps] s abside f
apt [æpt] adj apte; bien à propos; apt to enclin à, porté à
aptitude ['æptɪ͵t(j)ud] s aptitude f
aquacade ['ækwə͵ked] s féerie f sur l'eau, spectacle m aquatique
aqualung ['ækwə͵lʌŋ] s scaphandre m autonome
aquamarine [͵ækwəmə'rin] s aigue-marine f
aquaplane ['ækwə͵plen] s aquaplane m
aquari·um [ə'kwɛrɪ·əm] s (pl -ums or -a [ə]) aquarium m
aquatic [ə'kwætɪk], [ə'kwatɪk] adj aquatique || aquatics spl sports mpl nautiques
aqueduct ['ækwə͵dʌkt] s aqueduc m
aquiline ['ækwɪ͵laɪn] adj aquilin

Arab ['ærəb] adj arabe || s (horse) arabe m; (person) Arabe mf
Arabian [ə'rebɪ·ən] adj arabe || s Arabe mf
Arabic ['ærəbɪk] adj arabique || s (language) arabe m
Ar'abic nu'meral s chiffre m arabe
arbiter ['arbɪtər] s arbitre m
arbitrary ['arbɪ͵trɛri] adj arbitraire
arbitrate ['arbɪ͵tret] tr & intr arbitrer
arbitration [͵arbɪ'treʃən] s arbitrage m
arbitrator ['arbɪ͵tretər] s arbitre m; (law) amiable compositeur m
arbor ['arbər] s berceau m, charmille f; (mach) arbre m
arbore·tum [͵arbə'ritəm] s (pl -tums or -ta [tə]) jardin m botanique d'arbres
arbutus [ar'bjutəs] s arbousier m
arc [ark] s (elec, geom) arc m
arcade [ar'ked] s arcade f; galerie f
arcane [ar'ken] adj mystérieux
arch [artʃ] adj insigne; espiègle || s (of a building, cathedral, etc.) arc m; (of bridge) arche f; (of vault) voûte f || tr voûter; (the back) arquer || intr se voûter; s'arquer
archaic [ar'ke·ɪk] adj archaïque
archaism ['arke͵ɪzəm], ['arki͵ɪzəm] s archaïsme m
archangel ['ark͵endʒəl] s archange m
arch'bish'op s archevêque m
arch'duke' s archiduc m
arched [artʃt] adj voûté, courbé, arqué
archeologist [͵arkɪ'alədʒɪst] s archéologue mf
archeology [͵arkɪ'alɪdʒi] s archéologie f
archer ['artʃər] s archer m
archery ['artʃəri] s tir m à l'arc
archetype ['arkɪ͵taɪp] s archétype m
archipela·go [͵arkɪ'pɛləgo] s (pl -gos or -goes) archipel m
architect ['arkɪ͵tɛkt] s architecte m
architecture ['arkɪ͵tɛktʃər] s architecture f
archives ['arkaɪvz] spl archives fpl
arch'priest' s archiprêtre m
arch'way' s voûte f, arcade f
Arctic ['arktɪk] adj & s (ocean) Arctique m; (region) Arctique f
arc' weld'ing s soudure f à l'arc
ardent ['ardənt] adj ardent
ardor ['ardər] s ardeur f
arduous ['ardʒu·əs], ['ardju·əs] adj ardu, difficile
area ['ɛrɪ·ə] s aire f, surface f; territoire m; (mil) secteur m, zone f
arena [ə'rinə] s arène f
Argentina [͵ardʒɛn'tinə] s Argentine f; l'Argentine
argue ['argju] tr (a question) discuter; (a case) plaider; (a point) soutenir; (to imply) arguer; to argue s.o. into + ger persuader à qn de + inf || intr discuter, argumenter; plaider
argument ['argjəmənt] s (proof; reason; theme) argument m; discussion f, argumentation f; dispute f
argumentative [͵argjə'mɛntətɪv] adj disposé à argumenter, raisonneur
aria ['arɪ·ə], ['ɛrɪ·ə] s aria f

arid [ˈærɪd] *adj* aride
aridity [əˈrɪdɪti] *s* aridité *f*
arise [əˈraɪz] *v* (*pret* **arose** [əˈroz]; *pp* **arisen** [əˈrɪzən]) *intr* (*to rise*) se lever; (*to originate*) provenir, prendre naissance; (*to occur*) se produire; (*to be raised, as objections*) s'élever
aristocra·cy [ˌærɪsˈtɑkrəsi] *s* (*pl* -cies) aristocratie *f*
aristocrat [əˈrɪstəˌkræt] *s* aristocrate *mf*
aristocratic [əˌrɪstəˈkrætɪk] *adj* aristocrate
Aristotle [ˈærɪˌstɑtəl] *s* Aristote *m*
arithmetic [əˈrɪθmətɪk] *s* arithmétique *f*
arithmetician [əˌrɪθməˈtɪʃən] *s* arithméticien *m*
ark [ɑrk] *s* arche *f*
arm [ɑrm] *s* bras *m*; (mil) arme *f*; **arm in arm** bras dessus bras dessous; **at arm's length** à bout de bras; **under my (your, etc.) arm** sous mon (ton, etc.) aisselle; **up in arms** en rébellion ouverte ‖ *tr* armer ‖ *intr* s'armer
armada [ɑrˈmɑdə], [ɑrˈmedə] *s* armada *f*, grande flotte *f*
armadil·lo [ˌɑrməˈdɪlo] *s* (*pl* -los) tatou *m*
armament [ˈɑrməmənt] *s* armement *m*
armature [ˈɑrməˌtʃər] *s* (elec) induit *m*
arm'band' *s* brassard *m*
arm'chair' *s* fauteuil *m*
Armenian [ɑrˈminɪ·ən] *adj* arménien ‖ *s* (*language*) arménien *m*; (*person*) Arménien
armful [ˈɑrmˌfʊl] *s* brassée *f*
arm'hole' *s* emmanchure *f*, entournure *f*
armistice [ˈɑrmɪstɪs] *s* armistice *m*
armor [ˈɑrmər] *s* (*personal*) armure *f*; (on ships, tanks, etc.) cuirasse *f*, blindage *m* ‖ *tr* cuirasser, blinder ‖ *intr* se mettre l'armure
ar'mored car' *s* fourgon *m* blindé
ar'mor plate' *s* plaque *f* de blindage
ar'mor-plate' *tr* cuirasser, blinder
armor·y [ˈɑrməri] *s* (*pl* -ies) ateliers *mpl* d'armes, salle *f* d'armes
arm'pit' *s* aisselle *f*
arm'rest' *s* appui-bras *m*, accoudoir *m*
arms' race' *s* course *f* aux armements
ar·my [ˈɑrmi] *adj* militaire ‖ *s* (*pl* -mies) armée *f*
aroma [əˈromə] *s* arôme *m*
aromatic [ˌærəˈmætɪk] *adj* aromatique
around [əˈraʊnd] *adv* autour, alentour; de tous côtés ‖ *prep* autour de; **around 1950** (coll) vers 1950
arouse [əˈraʊz] *tr* éveiller; (*from sleep*) réveiller
arpeg·gio [ɑrˈpɛdʒo] *s* (*pl* -gios) arpège *m*
arraign [əˈren] *tr* accuser; (law) mettre en accusation
arrange [əˈrendʒ] *tr* arranger ‖ *intr* s'arranger
arrangement [əˈrendʒmənt] *s* arrangement *m*
array [əˈre] *s* ordre *m*; (*display*) étalage *m*; (*adornment*) parure *f*; (mil) rangée *f*, rangs *mpl* ‖ *tr* ranger, disposer; (*to adorn*) parer
arrearage [əˈrɪrɪdʒ] *s* arriéré *m*

arrears [əˈrɪrz] *spl* arriéré *m*; **in arrears** arriéré
arrest [əˈrɛst] *s* (*capture*) arrestation *f*; (*halt*) arrêt *m* ‖ *tr* arrêter; fixer; (*attention*) retenir
arrival [əˈraɪvəl] *s* arrivée *f*; (*of goods or ships*) arrivage *m*
arrive [əˈraɪv] *intr* arriver
arrogance [ˈærəgəns] *s* arrogance *f*
arrogant [ˈærəgənt] *adj* arrogant
arrogate [ˈærəˌget] *tr*—**to arrogate to oneself** s'arroger
arrow [ˈæro] *s* flèche *f*
ar'row·head' *s* tête *f* de flèche; (bot) sagittaire *m*
arsenal [ˈɑrsənəl] *s* ateliers *mpl* d'armes; manufacture *f* d'armes
arsenic [ˈɑrsɪnɪk] *s* arsenic *m*
arson [ˈɑrsən] *s* incendie *m* volontaire
arsonist [ˈɑrsənɪst] *s* incendiaire *mf*
art [ɑrt] *s* art *m*
arterial [ɑrˈtɪrɪ·əl] *adj* artériel
arteriosclerotic [ɑrˌtɪrɪ·osklɪˈrɑtɪk] *adj* artérioscléreux
arter·y [ˈɑrtəri] *s* (*pl* -ies) artère *f*
arte'sian well' [ɑrˈtiʒən] *s* puits *m* artésien
artful [ˈɑrtfəl] *adj* ingénieux; (*crafty*) artificieux, sournois; artificiel
arthritis [ɑrˈθraɪtɪs] *s* arthrite *f*
artichoke [ˈɑrtɪˌtʃok] *s* artichaut *m*
article [ˈɑrtɪkəl] *s* article; **article of clothing** objet *m* d'habillement
articulate [ɑrˈtɪkjəlɪt] *adj* articulé; (*expressing oneself clearly*) clair, expressif; (*speech*) intelligible; (*creature*) doué de la parole ‖ [ɑrˈtɪkjəˌlet] *tr* articuler ‖ *intr* s'articuler
artifact [ˈɑrtɪˌfækt] *s* artefact *m*
artifice [ˈɑrtɪfɪs] *s* artifice *m*
artificial [ˌɑrtɪˈfɪʃəl] *adj* artificiel
artificiali·ty [ˌɑrtɪˌfɪʃɪˈælɪti] *s* (*pl* -ties) manque *m* de naturel
artillery [ɑrˈtɪləri] *s* artillerie *f*
artil'lery·man *s* (*pl* -men) artilleur *m*
artisan [ˈɑrtɪzən] *s* artisan *m*
artist [ˈɑrtɪst] *s* artiste *mf*
artistic [ɑrˈtɪstɪk] *adj* artistique, artiste
artistry [ˈɑrtɪstri] *s* art *m*, habileté *f*
artless [ˈɑrtlɪs] *adj* naturel; ingénu, naïf; sans art
arts' and crafts' *spl* arts et métiers *mpl*
Aryan [ˈɛrɪ·ən], [ˈɑrjən] *adj* aryen ‖ *s* (*person*) Aryen *m*
as [æz], [əz] *pron rel* que, e.g., **the same as** le même que ‖ *adv* aussi, e.g., **as . . . as** aussi . . . que; **as for** quant à; **as is** tel quel; **as of** (*a certain date*) en date du; **as regards** en ce qui concerne; **as soon as** aussitôt que; **as though** comme si; **as yet** jusqu'ici ‖ *prep* comme ‖ *conj* puisque; comme; que
asbestos [æsˈbɛstəs] *s* amiante *m*, asbeste *m*
ascend [əˈsɛnd] *tr* (*a ladder*) monter à; (*a mountain*) gravir; (*a river*) remonter ‖ *intr* monter, s'élever
ascendancy [əˈsɛndənsi] *s* supériorité *f*, domination *f*
ascension [əˈsɛnʃən] *s* ascension *f*
Ascen'sion Day' *s* Ascension *f*

ascent [ə'sɛnt] s ascension f
ascertain [,æsər'ten] tr vérifier
ascertainment [,æsər'tenmənt] s constatation f
ascetic [ə'sɛtɪk] adj ascétique ‖ s ascète mf
asceticism [ə'sɛtɪ,sɪzəm] s ascétisme m, ascèse f
ascor'bic ac'id [ə'skɔrbɪk] s acide m ascorbique
ascribe [ə'skraɪb] tr attribuer, imputer
aseptic [ə'sɛptɪk], [e'sɛptɪk] adj aseptique
ash [æʃ] s cendre f; (tree) frêne m
ashamed [ə'ʃemd] adj honteux; to be ashamed avoir honte
ash'can' s poubelle f
ashen ['æʃən] adj cendré
ashore [ə'ʃor] adv à terre; to go ashore débarquer
ash'tray' s cendrier m
Ash' Wednes'day s le mercredi des Cendres
Asia ['eʒə], ['eʃə] s Asie f; l'Asie
A'sia Mi'nor s Asie f Mineure; l'Asie Mineure
aside [ə'saɪd] s aparté m ‖ adv de côté, à part; (aloof, at a distance) à l'écart; aside from en dehors de, à part; to step aside s'écarter; (fig) quitter la partie
asinine ['æsɪ,naɪn] adj stupide
ask [æsk], [ɑsk] tr (a favor; one's way) demander; (a question) poser; to ask s.o. about s.th. interroger qn au sujet de q.ch.; to ask s.o. for s.th. demander q.ch. à qn; to ask s.o. to + inf demander à qn de + inf, prier qn de + inf ‖ intr—to ask about s'enquérir de; to ask for (a package; a porter) demander; (to inquire about) demander après; you asked for it (you're in for it) (coll) c'est bien fait pour vous
askance [ə'skæns] adv de côté; to look askance at regarder de travers
askew [ə'skju] adj & adv de travers, en biais, de biais
asleep [ə'slip] adj endormi; to fall asleep s'endormir
asp [æsp] s aspic m
asparagus [ə'spærəgəs] s asperge f; (stalks and tips used as food) des asperges
aspect ['æspɛkt] s aspect m
aspen ['æspən] s tremble m
aspersion [ə'spʌrʒən], [ə'spʌrʃən] s (sprinkling) aspersion f; (slander) calomnie f
asphalt ['æsfɔlt], ['æsfælt] s asphalte m
asphyxiate [æs'fɪksɪ,et] tr asphyxier
aspirate ['æspɪrɪt] adj & s (phonet) aspiré m ‖ ['æspɪ,ret] tr aspirer
aspire [ə'spaɪr] intr—to aspire to aspirer à
aspirin ['æspɪrɪn] s aspirine f
ass [æs] s âne m
assail [ə'sel] tr assaillir
assailant [ə'selənt] s assaillant m
assassin [ə'sæsɪn] s assassin m
assassinate [ə'sæsɪ,net] tr assassiner

assassination [ə,sæsɪ'neʃən] s assassinat m
assault [ə'sɔlt] s assaut m; (rape) viol m; (law) voie f de fait ‖ tr assaillir
assault' and bat'tery s (law) voies fpl de fait
assay [ə'se], ['æse] s essai m; métal m titré ‖ [ə'se] tr essayer; titrer
assayer [ə'se·ər] s essayeur m
as'say val'ue s teneur f
assemblage [ə'sɛmblɪdʒ] s assemblage m
assemble [ə'sɛmbəl] tr assembler ‖ intr s'assembler, se réunir
assem·bly [ə'sɛmbli] s (pl -blies) (meeting) assemblée f, réunion f; (assembling) assemblage m, montage m
assem'bly hall' s salle f de conférences; (educ) grand amphithéâtre m
assem'bly line' s chaîne f de fabrication, chaîne de montage
assem'bly room' s salle f de réunion; (mach) atelier m de montage
assent [ə'sɛnt] s assentiment m ‖ intr assentir
assert [ə'sʌrt] tr affirmer; (one's rights) revendiquer; to assert oneself imposer le respect, s'imposer
assertion [ə'sʌrʃən] s assertion f
assess [ə'sɛs] tr (damages, taxes, etc.) évaluer; (value of property) coter; (property for tax purposes) grever
assessment [ə'sɛsmənt] s évaluation f; cote f; charge f, taxe f
assessor [ə'sɛsər] s répartiteur m d'impôts
asset ['æsɛt] s avantage m; possession f; assets biens mpl, avoirs mpl, actif m
assiduous [ə'sɪdʒu·əs], [ə'sɪdju·əs] adj assidu
assign [ə'saɪn] tr assigner; (mil) affecter
assignation [,æsɪg'neʃən] s assignation f; rendez-vous m illicite
assignment [ə'saɪnmənt] s attribution f; (schoolwork) devoirs mpl; (law) assignation f, transfer m; (mil) affectation f
assimilate [ə'sɪmɪ,let] tr assimiler ‖ intr s'assimiler
assimilation [ə,sɪmɪ'leʃən] s assimilation f
assist [ə'sɪst] tr assister, aider, secourir ‖ intr être assistant
assistance [ə'sɪstəns] s assistance f, aide f, secours m
assistant [ə'sɪstənt] adj & s assistant m, adjoint m
assizes [ə'saɪzɪz] spl assises fpl
associate [ə'soʃɪ·ɪt], [ə'soʃɪ,et] adj associé ‖ s associé m ‖ [ə'soʃɪ,et] tr associer ‖ intr s'associer
association [ə,soʃɪ'eʃən] s association f
assonance ['æsənəns] s assonance f
assort [ə'sɔrt] tr assortir ‖ intr s'associer
assorted adj assorti
assortment [ə'sɔrtmənt] s assortiment m
assuage [ə'swedʒ] tr assouvir; soulager, apaiser
assume [ə's(j)um] tr supposer; (various

forms) affecter; (*a fact*) présumer; (*a name*) emprunter; (*duties*) assumer, se charger de
assumed *adj* supposé; (*borrowed*) d'emprunt, emprunté; (*feigned*) feint
assumed' name' *s* nom *m* d'emprunt, nom de guerre
assuming [ə's(j)umɪŋ] *adj* prétentieux
assumption [ə'sʌmpʃən] *s* présomption *f*, hypothèse *f*; (*of virtue*) affectation *f*; (*of power*) appropriation *f*; **Assumption** (eccl) Assomption *f*
assurance [ə'ʃurəns] *s* assurance *f*, confiance *f*; promesse *f*
assure [ə'ʃur] *tr* assurer, garantir
astatine ['æstə,tin] *s* astate *m*
aster ['æstər] *s* aster *m*; (*China aster*) reine-marguerite *f*
asterisk ['æstə,rɪsk] *s* astérisque *m*
astern [ə'stʌrn] *adv* à l'arrière
asthma ['æzmə], ['æsmə] *s* asthme *m*
astonish [ə'stanɪʃ] *tr* étonner
astonishing [ə'stanɪʃɪŋ] *adj* étonnant
astonishment [ə'stanɪʃmənt] *s* étonnement *m*
astound [ə'staund] *tr* stupéfier, ahurir, étonner
astounding [ə'staundɪŋ] *adj* étonnant, abasourdissant; (*success*) foudroyant
astraddle [ə'strædəl] *adv* à califourchon
astray [ə'stre] *adv*—**to go astray** s'égarer; **to lead astray** égarer
astride [ə'straɪd] *adv* à califourchon || *prep* à califourchon sur
astrologer [ə'straləʤər] *s* astrologue *m*
astrology [ə'straləʤi] *s* astrologie *f*
astronaut ['æstrə,nɔt] *s* astronaute *mf*
astronautics [,æstrə'nɔtɪks] *s* astronautique *f*
astronomer [ə'stranəmər] *s* astronome *m*
astronomic(al) [,æstrə'namɪk(əl)] *adj* astronomique
as'tronom'ical year' *s* année *f* solaire, année tropique
astronomy [ə'stranəmi] *s* astronomie *f*
astute [ə'st(j)ut] *adj* astucieux, fin
asunder [ə'sʌndər] *adj* séparé || *adv* en deux
asylum [ə'saɪləm] *s* asile *m*
at [æt], [ət] *prep* à, e.g., **at Paris** à Paris; chez, e.g., **at John's** chez Jean; en, e.g., **at the same time** en même temps
atheism ['eθi,ɪzəm] *s* athéisme *m*
atheist ['eθi·ɪst] *s* athée *mf*
atheistic [,eθi'ɪstɪk] *adj* athée
Athens ['æθɪnz] *s* Athènes *f*
athlete ['æθlit] *s* athlète *m*, sportif *m*
ath'lete's foot' *s* pied *m* d'athlète
athletic [æθ'lɛtɪk] *adj* athlétique || **athletics** *s* athlétisme *m*
athwart [ə'θwɔrt] *adv* par le travers
Atlantic [æt'læntɪk] *adj* & *s* Atlantique *m*
atlas ['ætləs] *s* atlas *m*
atmosphere ['ætməs,fɪr] *s* atmosphère *f*
atmospheric [,ætməs'fɛrɪk] *adj* atmosphérique || **atmospherics** *spl* parasites *mpl* atmosphériques
atom ['ætəm] *s* atome *m*

atomic [ə'tamɪk] *adj* atomique
atom'ic bomb' *s* bombe *f* atomique
atom'ic nuc'leus *s* noyau *m* d'atome
atom'ic pile' *s* pile *f* atomique
atom'ic struc'ture *s* édifice *m* atomique
atomize ['ætə,maɪz] *tr* atomiser
atomizer ['ætə,maɪzər] *s* atomiseur *m*, vaporisateur *m*
atone [ə'ton] *intr*—**to atone for** expier
atonement [ə'tonmənt] *s* expiation *f*
atrocious [ə'troʃəs] *adj* atroce
atroci·ty [ə'trasɪti] *s* (*pl* **-ties**) atrocité *f*
atro·phy ['ætrəfi] *s* atrophie *f* || *v* (*pret* & *pp* **-phied**) *tr* atrophier || *intr* s'atrophier
attach [ə'tætʃ] *tr* attacher; (*property*) saisir; (*salary*) mettre opposition sur; **to be attached to** s'attacher à
attachment [ə'tætʃmənt] *s* attache *f*; (*of the sentiments*) attachement *m*; (law) opposition *f*, saisie-arrêt *f*
attack [ə'tæk] *s* attaque *f* || *tr* attaquer; s'attaquer à || *intr* attaquer
attacker [ə'tækər] *s* assaillant *m*
attain [ə'ten] *tr* atteindre
attainment [ə'tenmənt] *s* acquisition *f*, réalisation *f*; **attainments** connaissances *fpl*
attar ['ætər] *s* essence *f*
attempt [ə'tempt] *s* tentative *f*, essai *m*; (*assault*) attentat *m* || *tr* tenter; (*s.o.'s life*) attenter à
attend [ə'tend] *tr* (*a performance*) assister à; (*a sick person*) soigner; (*a person*) servir; **to attend classes** suivre des cours || *intr*—**to attend to** vaquer à, s'occuper de
attendance [ə'tendəns] *s* assistance *f*; présence *f*; (med) soins *mpl*
attendant [ə'tendənt] *adj* concomitant || *s* assistant *m*; (*to royalty*) serviteur *m*; **attendants** suite *f*
attention [ə'tenʃən] *s* attention *f*; **attention: Mr. Doe** à l'attention de M. Dupont; **attentions** égards *mpl* || *interj* attention!; (mil) garde à vous!
attentive [ə'tentɪv] *adj* attentif
attenuate [ə'tenju,et] *tr* amincir; (*words; bacteria*) atténuer
attest [ə'test] *tr* attester || *intr*—**to attest to** attester
Attic ['ætɪk] *adj* attique || (*l.c.*) *s* mansarde *f*, grenier *m*, soupente *f*
attire [ə'taɪr] *s* vêtement *m*, parure *f* || *tr* habiller, vêtir; parer
attitude ['ætɪ,t(j)ud] *s* attitude *f*
attorney [ə'tʌrni] *s* avoué *m*, avocat *m*
attor'ney gen'eral *s* procureur *m* général, ministre *m* de justice
attract [ə'trækt] *tr* attirer
attraction [ə'trækʃən] *s* attraction *f*; attrait *m*, attirance *f*
attractive [ə'træktɪv] *adj* attirant, attrayant; (*said, e.g., of a force*) attractif
attribute ['ætrɪ,bjut] *s* attribut *m* || [ə'trɪbjut] *tr* attribuer
attrition [ə'trɪʃən] *s* attrition *f*, usure *f*
attune [ə't(j)un] *tr* accorder
auburn ['ɔbərn] *adj* auburn, brun rougeâtre

auction ['ɔkʃən] s vente f aux enchères || tr vendre aux enchères
auctioneer [,ɔkʃən'ɪr] s adjudicateur m, commissaire-priseur m || tr & intr vendre aux enchères
audacious [ɔ'deʃəs] adj audacieux
audacity [ɔ'dæsɪti] s audace f
audience ['ɔdɪ·əns] s (hearing; formal interview) audience f; (assembly of hearers or spectators) assistance f, salle f, auditoire m; (those who follow what one says or writes) public m
au'dio fre'quency ['ɔdɪ,o] s audio-fréquence f
audiometer [,ɔdɪ'amɪtər] s audiomètre m
audit ['ɔdɪt] s apurement m || tr apurer; **to audit a class** assister à la classe en auditeur libre
audition [ɔ'dɪʃən] s audition f || tr & intr auditionner
auditor ['ɔdɪtər] s (com) comptable m agréé, expert comptable m; (educ) auditeur m libre
auditorium [,ɔdɪ'torɪ·əm] s auditorium m, salle f, amphithéâtre m
auditory ['ɔdɪ,tori] adj auditif
auger ['ɔgər] s tarière f
aught [ɔt] s zéro m || pron indef—**for aught I know** autant que je sache || adv du tout
augment [ɔg'mɛnt] tr & intr augmenter
augur ['ɔgər] s augure m || tr & intr augurer; **to augur well** être de bon augure
augu·ry ['ɔgjəri] s (pl -ries) augure m
august [ɔ'gʌst] adj auguste || **August** ['ɔgəst] s août m
auk [ɔk] s guillemot m
aunt [ænt], [ɑnt] s tante f
aureomycin [,ɔrɪ·o'maɪsɪn] s (pharm) auréomycine f
auricle ['ɔrɪkəl] s auricule f, oreillette f
aurora [ə'rorə] s aurore f
auscultate ['ɔskəl,tet] tr ausculter
auspices ['ɔspɪsɪz] spl auspices mpl
auspicious [ɔs'pɪʃəs] adj propice, favorable
austere [ɔs'tɪr] adj austère
Australia [ɔ'streljə] s Australie f; l'Australie
Australian [ɔ'streljən] adj australien || s (person) Australien m
Austria ['ɔstrɪ·ə] s Autriche f; l'Autriche
Austrian ['ɔstrɪ·ən] adj autrichien || s (person) Autrichien m
authentic [ɔ'θɛntɪk] adj authentique
authenticate [ɔ'θɛntɪ,ket] tr authentifier, constater l'authenticité de
author ['ɔθər] s auteur m
authoress ['ɔθərɪs] s femme f auteur
authoritarian [ɔ,θɑrɪ'tɛrɪ·ən], [ɔ,θɔrɪ'tɛrɪ·ən] adj autoritaire || s homme m autoritaire
authoritative [ɔ'θɑrɪ,tetɪv], [ɔ'θɔrɪ,tetɪv] adj autorisé; (dictatorial) autoritaire
authori·ty [ɔ'θɑrɪti], [ɔ'θɔrɪti] s (pl -ties) autorité f; **on good authority** de bonne part

authorize ['ɔθə,raɪz] tr autoriser
au'thor·ship' s paternité f
au·to ['ɔto] s (pl -tos) (coll) auto f, voiture f
autobiogra·phy [,ɔtobaɪ'agrəfi], [,ɔtobɪ'agrəfi] s (pl -phies) autobiographie f
autocrat ['ɔtə,kræt] s autocrate mf
autocratic(al) [,ɔtə'krætɪk(əl)] adj autocratique
autograph ['ɔtə,græf], ['ɔtə,grɑf] s autographe m || tr écrire l'autographe sur, dédicacer
au'tographed cop'y s exemplaire m dédicacé
au'to·intox'ica'tion s auto-intoxication f
automat ['ɔtə,mæt] s restaurant m libre service
automate ['ɔtə,met] tr automatiser
automatic [,ɔtə'mætɪk] adj automatique || s revolver m
automat'ic transmis'sion s changement m de vitesse automatique
automation [,ɔtə'meʃən] s automatisation f, automation f
automa·ton [ɔ'tamə,tan] s (pl -tons or -ta [tə]) automate m
automobile [,ɔtəmo'bil], [,ɔtə'mobil] s automobile f
automobile' show' s salon m de l'automobile
automotive [,ɔtə'motɪv] adj automobile; automoteur
autonomous [ɔ'tanəməs] adj autonome
autonomy [ɔ'tanəmi] s autonomie f
autop·sy ['ɔtɑpsi] s (pl -sies) autopsie f
autumn ['ɔtəm] s automne m
autumnal [ɔ'tʌmnəl] adj automnal, d'automne
auxilia·ry [ɔg'zɪljəri] adj auxiliaire || s (pl -ries) auxiliaire mf; **auxiliaries** (mil) troupes fpl auxiliaires
avail [ə'vel] s utilité f || tr profiter à; **to avail oneself of** avoir recours à, profiter de || intr être utile, servir
available [ə'veləbəl] adj disponible; (e.g., train) accessible; **to make available** to mettre à la disposition de
avalanche ['ævə,læntʃ], ['ævə,lɑntʃ] s avalanche f
avarice ['ævərɪs] s avarice f
avaricious [,ævə'rɪʃəs] adj avaricieux
avenge [ə'vɛndʒ] tr venger
avenger [ə'vɛndʒər] s vengeur m
avenue ['ævə,n(j)u] s avenue f
aver [ə'vʌr] v (pret & pp **averred**; ger **averring**) tr avérer, affirmer
average ['ævərɪdʒ] adj moyen || s moyenne f; **on the average** en moyenne || tr prendre la moyenne de || intr atteindre une moyenne
averse [ə'vʌrs] adj—**averse to** hostile à, opposé à, ennemi de
aversion [ə'vʌrʒən] s aversion f
avert [ə'vʌrt] tr détourner, écarter, empêcher, éviter
aviar·y ['evɪ,ɛri] s (pl -ies) volière f
aviation [,evɪ'eʃən] s aviation f
aviator ['evɪ,etər] s aviateur m
avid ['ævɪd] adj avide; **avid for** avide de

avidity [ə'vɪdɪti] s avidité f
avoca·do [ˌævo'kɑdo] s (pl -dos) avocat m
avocation [ˌævə'keʃən] s occupation f, profession f; distraction f
avoid [ə'vɔɪd] tr éviter
avoidable [ə'vɔɪdəbəl] adj évitable
avoidance [ə'vɔɪdəns] s dérobade f
avow [ə'vau] tr avouer
avowal [ə'vau·əl] s aveu m
avowedly [ə'vau·ɪdli] adv ouvertement, franchement
await [ə'wet] tr attendre
awake [ə'wek] adj éveillé || v (pret & pp awoke [ə'wok] or awaked) tr éveiller || intr s'éveiller
awaken [ə'wekən] tr éveiller, réveiller || intr se réveiller
awakening [ə'wekənɪŋ] s réveil m; (disillusionment) désabusement m
award [ə'wɔrd] s prix m; (law) dommages et intérêts mpl || tr décerner; accorder
aware [ə'wer] adj conscient; to become aware of se rendre compte de
awareness [ə'wernɪs] s conscience f
away [ə'we] adj absent || adv au loin, loin; away from éloigné de, loin de; to do away with abolir; to get away s'absenter; (to escape) échapper; to go away s'en aller; to make away with (to steal) dérober; to run away se sauver; to send away renvoyer; to take away enlever || interj hors d'ici!; away with! à bas!
awe [ɔ] s crainte f révérentielle || tr inspirer de la crainte à

awesome ['ɔsəm] adj impressionnant
awful ['ɔfəl] adj terrible; (coll) terrible, affreux
awfully ['ɔfəli] adv terriblement; (coll) joliment, rudement
awhile [ə'hwaɪl] adv quelque temps, un peu, un moment
awkward ['ɔkwərd] adj gauche, maladroit; (moment) embarrassant
awl [ɔl] s alène f
awning ['ɔnɪŋ] s tente f; (in front of store) banne f
A.W.O.L. ['e'dʌbəlˌju'o'ɛl] (letterword ['ewɔl] (acronym) s (absent without leave) absence f illégale; to be A.W.O.L. être absent sans permission
awry [ə'raɪ] adv de travers
ax [æks] s hache f
axiom ['æksɪ·əm] s axiome m
axiomatic [ˌæksɪ·ə'mætɪk] adj axiomatique
axis ['æksɪs] s (pl axes ['æksiz]) axe m
axle ['æksəl] s essieu m
ax'le grease' s cambouis m
ay or aye [aj] s oui m; aye aye, sir! oui, commandant!, sir, capitaine!; the ayes have it les oui l'emportent || [e] adv toujours
azalea [ə'zeljə] s azalée f
azimuth ['æzɪməθ] s azimut m
Azores [ə'zorz], ['ezorz] spl Açores fpl
Aztecs ['æztɛks] spl Aztèques mpl
azure ['æʒər], ['eʒər] adj azuré, d'azur || s azur m || tr azurer

B

B, b [bi] s IIᵉ lettre de l'alphabet
babble ['bæbəl] s babil m || tr (secrets) dire à tort et à travers || intr babiller; (said of birds) jaser; (said of brook) murmurer
babbling ['bæblɪŋ] adj (gossiper) babillard; (brook) murmurant || s babillage m
babe [beb] s bébé m, bambin m; (naive person) (coll) enfant mf; (pretty girl) (coll) pépée f, môme f
babel ['bebəl] s brouhaha m, vacarme m
baboon [bæ'bun] s babouin m
ba·by ['bebi] s (pl -bies) bébé m; (youngest child) cadet m, benjamin m; baby! (honey!) (coll) ma choute! || v (pret & pp -bied) tr traiter en bébé, dorloter; (e.g., a machine) traiter avec soin
ba'by car'riage s voiture f d'enfant, poussette f; (with hood) landau m
ba'by grand' s piano m demi-queue
ba'by-sit'ter s gardienne f d'enfants, garde-bébé mf
ba'by talk' s babil m enfantin

ba'by teeth' spl dents fpl de lait
baccalaureate [ˌbækə'lɔrɪ·ɪt] s baccalauréat m
bacchanal ['bækənəl] adj bachique || s bacchanale f; (person) noceur m
bachelor ['bætʃələr] s célibataire m; (graduate) bachelier m
bach'elor apart'ment s garçonnière f
bach'elor girl' s garçonne f
bach'elor·hood' s célibat m
bach'elor's-but'ton s (bot) bluet m, barbeau m
bach'elor's degree' s baccalauréat m
bacil·lus [bə'sɪləs] s (pl -li [laɪ]) bacille m
back [bæk] adj postérieur || s dos m; (of house; of head or body) derrière m; (of house; of car) arrière m; (of room) fond m; (of fabric) envers m; (of seat) dossier m; (of medal; of hand) revers m; (of page) verso m; (sports) arrière; back to back dos à dos; with one's back to the wall poussé au pied du mur, aux abois || adv en arrière, à l'arrière; as far back as déjà en, dès; back and forth

de long en large; **back of** derrière; **back to front** sens devant derrière; **in back** par derrière; **some weeks back** il y a quelques semaines; **to be back** être de retour; **to come back** revenir; **to go back** retourner; **to go back home** rentrer; **to go back on** (coll) abandonner; **to go back to** (*to hark back to*) remonter à; **to make one's way back** s'en retourner || *tr* faire faire marche arrière à; (*e.g., a car*) faire reculer; (*to support*) appuyer, soutenir; (*to reinforce*) renforcer; (*e.g., a racehorse*) parier pour; **to back s.o. up** soutenir qn; **to back water** nager à culer || *intr* reculer; faire marche arrière; **to back down** (fig) se rétracter, se retirer; **to back out of** (*e.g., an agreement*) se dédire de, se soustraire à; **to back up** reculer

back'ache' *s* mal *m* de dos

back'bite' *v* (*pret* **-bit;** *pp* **-bitten** or **bit**) *tr* médire de || *intr* médire

back'bit'er *s* médisant *m*

back'bone' *s* colonne *f* vertébrale, épine *f* dorsale, échine *f*; (*of a fish*) grande arête *f*; (*of an enterprise*) colonne *f*, appui *m*; (fig) caractère *m*, cran *m*; **to have no backbone** (fig) avoir l'échine souple

back'break'ing *adj* éreintant, dur

back'door' *adj* (fig) secret, clandestin

back' door' *s* porte *f* de derrière; (fig) petite porte

back'down' *s* (coll) palinodie *f*

back'drop' *s* toile *f* de fond

backer ['bækər] *s* (*of team, party, etc.*) supporter *m*; (com) bailleur *m* de fonds, commanditaire *m*

back'fire' *s* retour *m* de flamme, pétarade *f*; (*for firefighting*) contre-feu *m*; (mach) contre-allumage *m* || *intr* donner des retours de flamme; (fig) produire un résultat imprévu

backgammon ['bæk,gæmən], [,bæk-'gæmən] *s* trictrac *m*, jacquet *m*

back'ground' *s* fond *m*; (*of person*) origines *fpl*, éducation *f*; (*music, sound effects, etc.*) fond sonore

back'hand' *s* (tennis) revers *m*

back'hand'ed *adj* de revers; (*compliment*) à rebours, équivoque

backing ['bækɪŋ] *s* (*support*) appui *m*, soutien *m*; (*reinforcement*) renforcement *m*; (*backing up*) recul *m*

back' in'terest *m* arrérage *m*; arrérages *mpl*

back'lash' *s* contrecoup *m*

back'light'ing *s* contre-jour *m*

back'log' *s* arriéré *m*, accumulation *f*

back' num'ber *s* (*of newspaper, magazine*) vieux numéro *m;* (coll) vieux jeu *m*

back' pay' *s* salaire *m* arriéré *m*; (mil) arriéré *m* de solde

back' pay'ment *s* arriéré *m*

back' scratch'er *s* gratte-dos *m*; (slang) lèche-bottes *m*

back' seat' *s* banquette *f* arrière; **to take a back seat** (fig) aller au second plan

back'side' *s* derrière *m*, postérieur *m*

back'slide' *intr* récidiver

back'slid'er *s* récidiviste *mf*, relaps *m*

back'space key' *s* rappel *m* de chariot

back'spac'er *s* rappel *m* de chariot

back'spin' *s* (*of ball*) coup *m* en bas, effet *m*

back'stage' *adv* dans les coulisses

back'stairs' *adj* caché, indirect

back' stairs' *spl* escalier *m* de service

back'stitch' *s* point *m* arrière

back'stop' *s* (baseball) attrapeur *m* || *v* (*pret* & *pp* **-stopped;** *ger* **-stopping**) *tr* (coll) soutenir

back'stroke' *s* (*of piston*) course *f* de retour; (swimming) brasse *f* sur le dos

back'swept wing' *s* aile *f* en flèche

back' talk' *s* réplique *f* impertinente

back' tax'es *spl* impôts *mpl* arriérés

back'track' *intr* rebrousser chemin

back'up' *s* appui *m*, soutien *m*

back'up light' *s* phare *m* de recul

backward ['bækwərd] *adj* (*in direction*) en arrière, rétrograde; (*in time*) en retard; (*in development*) arriéré, attardé || *adv* en arrière; (*opposite to the normal*) à rebours; (*walking*) à reculons; (*flowing*) à contre-courant; (*stroking of the hair*) à contre-poil; **backward and forward** de long en large; **to go backward and forward** aller et venir

back'ward-and-for'ward mo'tion *s* va-et-vient *m*

backwardness ['bækwərdnɪs] *s* retard *m*, lenteur *f*

backwards ['bækwərdz] *adv* var of **backward**

back'wash' *s* remous *m*

back'wa'ter *s* (*of river*) bras *m* mort; (*e.g., of water wheel*) remous *m*; (fig) endroit *m* isolé, trou *m*

back' wheel' *s* roue *f* arrière

back'woods' *spl* forêts *fpl* de l'intérieur; bled *m*, brousse *f*

back'woods'man *s* (*pl* **-men**) défricheur *m* de forêts, coureur *m* des bois

back'yard' *s* derrière *m* (de la maison)

bacon ['bekən] *s* lard *m*, bacon *m*; (slang) butin *m*; **to bring home the bacon** (coll) remporter la timbale

bacteria [bæk'tɪrɪ·ə] *spl* bactéries *fpl*

bacteriology [bæk,tɪrɪ'ɑlədʒi] *s* bactériologie *f*

bacteri·um [bæk'tɪrɪ·əm] *s* (*pl* **-a** [ə])
bactérie *f*

bad [bæd] *adj* mauvais §91; (*wicked*) méchant; (*serious*) grave; **from bad to worse** de mal en pis; **too bad!** c'est dommage!

bad' breath' *s* haleine *f* forte

bad' com'pany *s* mauvaises fréquentations *fpl*

bad' debt' *s* mauvaise créance *f*

bad' egg' *s* (slang) mauvais sujet *m*

bad' exam'ple *s* exemple *m* pernicieux

badge [bædʒ] *s* insigne *m*, plaque *f*

badger ['bædʒər] *s* blaireau *m* || *tr* harceler, ennuyer

bad' lot' *s* voyous *mpl*, racaille *f*

badly ['bædli] *adv* mal §91; (*seriously*) gravement; **to want badly** avoir grande envie de
bad'man' *s* (*pl* **-men'**) bandit *m*
badness ['bædnɪs] *s* mauvaise qualité *f*; (*of character*) méchanceté *f*
bad'-tem'pered *adj* susceptible, méchant; (*e.g., horse*) vicieux, rétif
baffle ['bæfəl] *s* déflecteur *m*, chicane *f* ‖ *tr* déconcerter, confondre
baffling ['bæflɪŋ] *adj* déconcertant
bag [bæg] *s* sac *m*; (*suitcase*) valise *f*; (*of game*) chasse *f* ‖ *v* (*pret* & *pp* **bagged**; *ger* **bagging**) *tr* ensacher, mettre en sac; (*game*) abattre, tuer ‖ *intr* (*said of clothing*) faire poche
bagful ['bæg,fʊl] *s* sachée *f*
baggage ['bægɪdʒ] *s* bagage *m*, bagages
bag'gage car' *s* (rr) fourgon *m* à bagages
bag'gage check' *s* bulletin *m* de bagages
bag'gage room' *s* bureau *m* de gare expéditeur; (*checkroom*) consigne *f*
bag'gage truck' *s* chariot *m* à bagages; (*hand truck*) diable *m*
bag·gy ['bægi] *adj* (*comp* **-gier**; *super* **-giest**) bouffant
bag' of tricks' *s* sac *m* à malice
bag'pipe' *s* cornemuse *f*
bail [bel] *s* caution *f*; **to be out on bail** être libre sous caution; **to put up bail** se porter caution ‖ *tr* cautionner; **to bail out** se porter caution pour; (*a boat*) écoper ‖ *intr*—**to bail out** (aer) sauter en parachute
bailiff ['belɪf] *s* (*of a court*) huissier *m*, bailli *m*; (*on a farm*) régisseur *m*
bailiwick ['belɪwɪk] *s* bailliage *m*, rayon *m*; (fig) domaine *m*
bait [bet] *s* appât *m*, amorce *f* ‖ *tr* appâter, amorcer; (*to harass*) harceler
bake [bek] *tr* faire cuire au four; **to bake bread** boulanger, faire le pain ‖ *intr* cuire au four
baked' pota'toes *spl* pommes *fpl* de terre au four
bakelite ['bekə,laɪt] *s* bakélite *f*
baker ['bekər] *s* boulanger *m*
bak'er's doz'en *s* treize *m* à la douzaine
baker·y ['bekəri] *s* (*pl* **-ies**) boulangerie *f*
baking ['bekɪŋ] *s* cuisson *f* au four
bak'ing pow'der *s* levure *f* anglaise
bak'ing so'da *s* bicarbonate *m* de soude
balance ['bæləns] *s* balance *f*, équilibre *m*; (*scales*) balance *f*; (*what is left*) reste *m*; (com) solde *m*, report *m* ‖ *tr* balancer; (*an account*) solder ‖ *intr* se balancer; se solder
bal'ance of pay'ments *s* balance *f* des comptes
bal'ance of pow'er *s* équilibre *m* politique
bal'ance of trade' *s* balance du commerce
bal'ance sheet' *s* bilan *m*
bal'ance wheel' *s* balancier *m*
balancing ['bælənsɪŋ] *s* balancement

m; équilibrage *m*; ajustement *m*; (com) règlement *m* des comptes
balco·ny ['bælkəni] *s* (*pl* **-nies**) balcon *m*; (*in a theater*) galerie *f*
bald [bɔld] *adj* chauve; (*fact, statement, etc.*) simple, net, carré
balderdash ['bɔldər,dæʃ] *s* galimatias *m*, fatras *m*
baldness ['bɔldnɪs] *s* calvitie *f*
bale [bel] *s* balle *f* ‖ *tr* emballer
Balear'ic Is'lands [,bælɪ'ærɪk] *spl* Baléares *fpl*
baleful ['belfəl] *adj* funeste, fatal; triste
balk [bɔk] *s* déception *f*, contretemps *m*; (*beam*) poutre *f*; (agr) billon *m* ‖ *tr* frustrer ‖ *intr* regimber
Balkan ['bɔlkən] *adj* balkanique
balk·y ['bɔki] *adj* (*comp* **-ier**; *super* **-iest**) regimbé, rétif
ball [bɔl] *s* balle *f*; (*in billiards; in bearings*) bille *f*; (*spherical body*) boule *f*; (*dance*) bal *m*; (sports) ballon *m*; **to be on the ball** (slang) être toujours là pour le coup; **to have s.th. on the ball** (slang) avoir q.ch. dans le ventre; **to play ball** jouer au ballon; (slang) coopérer; (*to be in cahoots*) (slang) être en tandem ‖ *tr*—**to ball up** (slang) bousiller, embrouiller
ballad ['bæləd] *s* (*song*) romance *f*, complainte *f*; (*poem*) ballade *f*
ball' and chain' *s* boulet *m*; (slang) femme *f*, épouse *f*
ball'-and-sock'et joint' *s* joint *m* à rotule
ballast ['bæləst] *s* (aer, naut) lest *m*; (rr) ballast *m* ‖ *tr* lester; ballaster
ball' bear'ing *s* bille *f*, roulement *m* à billes
ball' cock' *s* robinet *m* à flotteur
ballerina [,bælə'rinə] *s* ballerine *f*
ballet ['bæle] *s* ballet *m*
ballistic [bə'lɪstɪk] *adj* balistique ‖ **ballistics** *s* balistique *f*
ballis'tic mis'sile *s* engin *m* balistique
balloon [bə'lun] *s* ballon *m* ‖ *tr* ballonner ‖ *intr* ballonner, se ballonner
ballot ['bælət] *s* scrutin *m*; (*individual ballot*) bulletin *m* ‖ *intr* scrutiner, voter
bal'lot box' *s* urne *f*; **to stuff the ballot boxes** bourrer les urnes
balloting ['bælətɪŋ] *s* scrutin *m*
ball'-point pen' *s* stylo *m* à bille
ball'room' *s* salon *m* de bal, salle *f* de danse
ballyhoo ['bælɪ,hu] *s* publicité *f* tapageuse ‖ *tr* faire de la réclame pour
balm [bam] *s* baume *m* ‖ *tr* parfumer
balm·y ['bami] *adj* (*comp* **-ier**; *super* **-iest**) embaumé; (slang) toqué
baloney [bə'loni] *s* (culin) mortadelle *f*; (slang) fadaises *fpl*
balsam ['bɔlsəm] *s* baume *m*
bal'sam fir' *s* sapin *m* baumier
bal'sam pop'lar *s* peuplier *m* baumier
Balt [bɔlt] *s* Balte *mf*
Bal'timore o'riole ['bɔltɪ,mor] *s* loriot *m* de Baltimore
baluster ['bæləstər] *s* balustre *m*

balustrade [ˌbæləs'tred] *s* balustrade *f*, rampe *f*
bamboo [bæm'bu] *s* bambou *m*
bamboozle [bæm'buzəl] *tr* (slang) mystifier
ban [bæn] *s* ban *m*, interdiction *f*; **bans** bans *mpl* ‖ *v* (*pret & pp* **banned**; *ger* **banning**) *tr* mettre au ban
banal ['benəl], [bə'næl] *adj* banal
banali·ty [bə'nælɪti] *s* (*pl* **-ties**) banalité *f*
banana [bə'nænə] *s* banane *f*
banan′a tree′ *s* bananier *m*
band [bænd] *s* bande *f*, lien *m*; musique *f*, fanfare *f*; (*dance band*) orchestre *m*; (*strip of color*) raie *f*; **to beat the band** (slang) sans pareille; (*hastily*) vivement ‖ *tr* entourer de bandes; (*a bird*) marquer de bandes ‖ *intr*—**to band together** se grouper
bandage ['bændɪdʒ] *s* (*dressing*) pansement *m*; (*holding the dressing in place*) bandage *m* ‖ *tr* panser; bander
band′box′ *s* carton *m* de modiste
bandit ['bændɪt] *s* bandit *m*
band′mas′ter *s* chef *m* de musique
band′ saw′ *s* scie *f* à ruban
band′stand′ *s* kiosque *m*
band′wag′on *s* char *m* de la victoire; **to jump on the bandwagon** suivre la majorité victorieuse
ban·dy ['bændi] *adj* tortu ‖ *v* (*pret & pp* **-died**) *tr* renvoyer, échanger; **to bandy words** se renvoyer des paroles ‖ *intr* se disputer
ban′dy-leg′ged *adj* bancal
bane [ben] *s* poison *m*; ruine *f*
baneful ['benfəl] *adj* funeste, nuisible
bang [bæŋ] *s* coup *m*; (*of a door*) claquement *m*; (*of fireworks; of a gun*)· détonation *f*; **bangs** frange *f*; **to go off with a bang** détoner; (slang) réussir ‖ *tr* frapper; (*a door*) faire claquer; **to bang down** (*e.g., a lid*) abattre violemment; **to bang up** (slang) rosser, cogner ‖ *intr* claquer avec fracas; **to bang against** cogner; **to bang on** frapper à ‖ *interj* pan!; pom!
bang′-up′ *adj* (slang) de premier ordre, à la hauteur
banish ['bænɪʃ] *tr* bannir, exiler
banishment ['bænɪʃmənt] *s* bannissement *m*
banister ['bænɪstər] *s* balustre *m*; **banisters** balustrade *f*, rampe *f*
bank [bæŋk] *s* banque *f*; (*of river*) rive *f*, bord *m*; (*shoal*) banc *m*; (*slope*) talus *m*, terrasse *f*; (*in a gambling game*) cave *f*; (aer) virage *m* incliné; **to break the bank** faire sauter la banque ‖ *tr* terrasser; (*money*) déposer; (*an airplane*) incliner ‖ *intr* (aer) virer, virer sur l'aile, s'incliner; **to bank on** compter sur
bank′ account′ *s* compte *m* en banque
bank′book′ *s* carnet *m* de banque
banked *adj* incliné
banker ['bæŋkər] *s* banquier *m*
banking ['bæŋkɪŋ] *adj* bancaire
bank′ note′ *s* billet *m* de banque

bank′roll′ *s* paquet *m* de billets, liasse *f* de billets
bankrupt ['bæŋkrʌpt] *adj & s* failli *m*; (*with guilt*) banqueroutier *m*; **to go bankrupt** faire banqueroute ‖ *tr* mettre en faillite
bankrupt·cy ['bæŋkrʌptsi] *s* (*pl* **-cies**) banqueroute *f*
bank′ vault′ *s* chambre *f* forte
banner ['bænər] *s* bannière *f*
ban′ner cry′ *s* cri *m* de guerre
ban′ner year′ *s* année *f* record
banquet ['bæŋkwɪt] *s* banquet *m* ‖ *intr* banqueter
bantam ['bæntəm] *adj* nain ‖ *s* poulet *m* nain, poulet de Bantam
ban′tam·weight′ *s* poids *m* bantam
banter ['bæntər] *s* badinage *m* ‖ *tr & intr* badiner
bantering ['bæntərɪŋ] *adj* railleur, goguenard
baptism ['bæptɪzəm] *s* baptême *m*
baptismal [bæp'tizməl] *adj* baptismal
baptis′mal certif′icate *s* extrait *m* baptême, bulletin *m* de naissance
baptis′mal font′ *s* fonts *mpl* baptismaux
Baptist ['bæptɪst] *s* baptiste *mf*
baptister·y ['bæptɪstəri] *s* (*pl* **-ies**) baptistère *m*
baptize [bæp'taɪz], ['bæptaɪz] *tr* baptiser
bar [bɑr] *s* barre *f*, barreau *m*; (*obstacle*) barrière *f*, empêchement *m*; (*barroom; counter*) bar *m*; (*profession of law*) barreau *m*; (*of public opinion*) tribunal *m*; (*of chocolate*) tablette *f*; (*mus*) mesure *f*; (phys) bar; **behind bars** sous les barreaux ‖ *prep* —**bar none** sans exception ‖ *v* (*pret & pp* **barred**; *ger* **barring**) *tr* barrer
barb [bɑrb] *s* barbillon *m*; dent *f* d'une flèche; (*in metalwork*) barbe *f* ‖ *tr* garnir de barbillons
Barbados [bɑr'bedoz] *s* la Barbade
barbarian [bɑr'bɛrɪ·ən] *adj & s* barbare *mf*
barbaric [bɑr'bærɪk] *adj* barbare
barbarism ['bɑrbə͵rɪzəm] *s* barbarie *f*; (*in speech or writing*) barbarisme *m*
barbari·ty [bɑr'bærɪti] *s* (*pl* **-ties**) barbarie *f*
barbarous ['bɑrbərəs] *adj* barbare
barbecue ['bɑrbɪ͵kju] *s* grillade *f* en plein air ‖ *tr* griller à la sauce piquante
bar′becue pit′ *s* rôtisserie *f* en plein air
barbed *adj* barbelé, pointu
barbed′ wire′ *s* fil *m* de fer barbelé
barbed′-wire entan′glement *s* réseau *m* de barbelés
barber ['bɑrbər] *s* coiffeur *m*; (*who shaves*) barbier *m*
bar′ber pole′ *s* enseigne *f* de barbier
bar′ber·shop′ *s* salon *m* de coiffeur
bar′ber·shop quartet′ *s* ensemble *m* harmonique de chanteurs amateurs
barbiturate [bɑr'bɪtʃə͵ret], [͵bɑrbɪ'tjʊret] *adj & s* barbiturique *m*
bard [bɑrd] *s* barde *m*
bare [bɛr] *adj* nu; découvert; simple ‖ *tr* mettre à nu

bare'back' adv à nu
bare'faced' adj éhonté, effronté, sans déguisement
bare'foot' adj nu-pieds
bare'head'ed adj nu-tête
bare'leg'ged adj nu-jambes
barely ['bɛrli] adv à peine
bareness ['bɛrnɪs] s nudité f, dénuement m; (of style) pauvreté f
bar'fly' s (pl -flies) (slang) pilier m de cabaret
bargain ['bɑrgɪn] s (deal) marché m, affaire f; (cheap purchase) solde m, occasion f; into the bargain par-dessus le marché || tr—to bargain away vendre à perte || intr entrer en négociations; she gave him more than he bargained for (fig) elle lui a donné du fil à retordre; to bargain over marchander; to bargain with traiter avec
bar'gain count'er s rayon m des soldes
bar'gain sale' s vente f de soldes
barge [bɑrdʒ] s barge f, chaland m, péniche f || intr—to barge into entrer sans façons
baritone ['bærɪ‚ton] adj de baryton || s baryton m
barium ['bɛrɪ‚əm] s baryum m
bark [bɑrk] s (of tree) écorce f; (of dog) aboiement m; (boat) trois-mâts m; his bark is worse than his bite il fait plus de bruit que de mal || tr—to bark out dire d'un ton sec || intr aboyer; to bark up the wrong tree suivre une mauvaise piste
bar'keep'er s barman m
barker ['bɑrkər] (coll) s bonimenteur m, barnum m
barley ['bɑrli] s orge f
bar'maid' s fille f de comptoir, demoiselle f de comptoir, serveuse f
barn [bɑrn] s (for grain) grange f; (for horses) écurie f; (for livestock) étable f
barnacle ['bɑrnəkəl] s (on a ship) anatife m, patelle f; (goose) bernacle f
barn' owl' s (Tyto alba) effraie f
barn'storm' intr aller en tournée
barn'yard' s basse-cour f
barometer [bə'rɑmɪtər] s baromètre m
barometric [‚bærə'mɛtrɪk] adj barométrique
baron ['bærən] s baron m; (of steel, coal, lumber) (coll) magnat m
baroness ['bærənɪs] s baronne f
baroque [bə'rok] adj & s baroque m
bar'rack-room' adj (humor; manners) soldatesque, de caserne || s chambrée f
barracks ['bærəks] spl caserne f
barrage [bə'rɑʒ] s barrage m
barred adj barré; (excluded) exclu
barrel ['bærəl] s tonneau m, fût m; large barrel barrique f; small barrel baril m, baricaut m, barillet m
bar'rel or'gan s orgue m de Barbarie
barren ['bærən] adj stérile; (bare) nu; (of style) aride, sec
barricade [‚bærɪ'ked] s barricade f || tr barricader

barrier ['bærɪ‚ər] s barrière f
bar'rier reef' s récif-barrière m
barring ['bɑrɪŋ] prep sauf
barrister ['bærɪstər] s (Brit) avocat m
bar'room' s cabaret m, bar m, bistrot m
bar'tend'er s barman m
barter ['bɑrtər] s échange m, troc m || tr échanger
ba'sal metab'olism ['besəl] s métabolisme m basal
basalt [bə'sɔlt], ['bæsɔlt] s basalte m
base [bes] adj bas, vil || s base f; fondement m, ligne f d'appui, principe m; (pedestal) socle m || tr baser; fonder
base'ball' s base-ball m
base'board' s moulure f de base
basement ['besmənt] s sous-sol m, cave f
base'ment win'dow s soupirail m
bash [bæʃ] tr cogner, assommer
bashful ['bæʃfəl] adj timide
basic ['besɪk] adj fondamental, de base, essentiel; (alkaline) basique
basil ['bæzəl] s basilic m
basilica [bə'sɪlɪkə] s basilique f
basin ['besɪn] s bassin m; (washbasin) cuvette f; (bowl) bol m
ba·sis ['besɪs] s (pl -ses [siz]) base f, fondement m; on the basis of sur la base de
bask [bæsk], [bɑsk] intr se chauffer
basket ['bæskɪt], ['bɑskɪt] s panier m; (with a handle) corbeille f; (carried on the back) hotte f
bas'ket-ball' s basket-ball m, basket m
bas'ket lunch' s panier-repas m
bas'ket-mak'er s vannier m
bas'ket-work' s vannerie f
Basque [bæsk] adj basque || s (language) basque m; (person) Basque mf
bass [bes] adj grave, bas || s (mus) basse f || [bæs] s (ichth) bar m
bass' drum' [bes] s grosse caisse f
bassinet [‚bæsɪ'nɛt], ['bæsɪ‚nɛt] s bercelonnette f
bassoon [bə'sun] s basson m
bass viol ['bes'vaɪ‚əl] s basse f de viole
basswood ['bæs‚wʊd] s tilleul m
bastard ['bæstərd] adj & s bâtard m
baste [best] tr (to thrash) rosser; (to scold) éreinter; (culin) arroser; (sewing) faufiler, baguer, bâtir
bastion ['bæstʃən], ['bæstɪ‚ən] s bastion m
bat [bæt] s bâton m; (for cricket) bat m; (sports) batte f; (zool) chauvesouris f; (blow) (coll) coup m; to be at bat tenir la batte; to go to bat for (coll) intervenir au profit de; to have bats in the belfry (coll) avoir une araignée dans le plafond || v (pret & pp batted; ger batting) tr battre
batch [bætʃ] s (of papers) liasse f; (coll) fournée f, lot m
bated adj—with bated breath en baissant la voix, dans un souffle
bath [bæθ], [bɑθ] s bain m; (bathroom) salle f de bains; to take a bath prendre un bain, se baigner
bathe [beð] tr baigner || intr se baigner

bather ['beðər] s baigneur m
bath'house' s établissement m de bains; (at the seashore) cabine f
bath'ing suit' s costume m de bain
bath'ing trunks' s slip m de bain
bath' mat' s tapis m de bain
bath'robe' s peignoir m
bath'room' s salle f de bains
bath'room fix'tures spl appareils mpl sanitaires
bath'room scale' s pèse-personne m
bath' tow'el s serviette f de bain
bath'tub' s baignoire f
baton [bæ'tɑn], ['bætən] s baguette f, bâton m de chef d'orchestre
battalion [bə'tæljən] s bataillon m
batten ['bætən] tr—**to batten down the hatches** condamner les panneaux
batter ['bætər] s (culin) pâte f; (sports) batteur m || tr battre
bat'tering ram' s bélier m
batter·y ['bætəri] s (pl -ies) (elec, mil, mus) batterie f; (primary cell) pile f; (secondary cell or cells) accumulateur m, accu m
battle ['bætəl] s bataille f; **to do battle** livrer combat || tr & intr combattre
bat'tle-ax' s hache f d'armes; (shrew) (slang) harpie f, mégère f
bat'tle cruis'er s croiseur m de bataille
bat'tle cry' s cri m de guerre
bat'tle·field' s champ m de bataille
bat'tle-front' s front m de bataille
bat'tle line' s ligne f de feu
battlement ['bætəlmənt] s créneau m; **battlements** parapet m, rempart m
bat'tle roy'al s mêlée f générale
bat'tle·ship' s cuirassé m, navire m de guerre
bat·ty ['bæti] adj (comp -tier; super -tiest) (slang) dingo, maboul, braque
bauble ['bɔbəl] s babiole f, bagatelle f; (of jester) marotte f
Bavaria [bə'vɛrɪ·ə] s la Bavière
Bavarian [bə'vɛrɪ·ən] adj bavarois || s Bavarois m
bawd·y ['bɔdi] adj (comp -ier; super -iest) obscène, impudique
bawl [bɔl] tr—**to bawl out** (slang) engueuler || intr gueuler; (to cry) sangloter
bawl'ing out' s (slang) engueulade f
bay [be] adj & s baie f; **at bay** aux abois || intr aboyer, hurler
bay'ber'ry s (pl -ries) baie f
bay'berry tree' s laurier m
bayonet ['be·ənɪt] s baïonnette f || tr percer d'un coup de baïonnette
bayou ['baɪ·u], ['baɪ·o] s anse f
bay' rum' s eau f de toilette au laurier
bay' win'dow s fenêtre f en saillie; (slang) bedaine f, gros ventre m
bazaar [bə'zɑr] s bazar m; (social event) kermesse f
B.C. ['bi'si] adv (letterword) (before Christ) av. J.-C.
be [bi] v (pres am [æm], is [ɪz], are [ɑr]; pret was [wɑz] or [wʌz], were [wʌr]; pp been [bɪn]) intr être; avoir, e.g., **to be five years old** avoir cinq ans; e.g., **to be ten feet long**

avoir dix pieds de long; e.g., **what is the matter with you?** qu'avez-vous?; **here is** or **here are** voici; **how are you?** comment allez-vous?, ça va?, comment vous portez-vous?; **how much is that?** combien coûte cela?, c'est combien ça?; **so be it** ainsi soit-il; **there is** or **there are** il y a; (in directing the attention) voilà; (in expressions like **it is warm** il fait chaud or **I am cold** j'ai froid, see the noun || aux (to form the passive voice) être, e.g., **he is loved by everybody** il est aimé de tout le monde; (progressive not expressed in French), e.g., **he is eating** il mange; **to be to** + inf devoir + inf, e.g., **I am to give a speech** je dois prononcer un discours
beach [bitʃ] s plage f, bord m de la mer; grève f, rivage m || tr & intr échouer
beach'comb'er s batteur m de grève
beach'head' s (mil) tête f de pont
beach' umbrel'la s parasol m de plage
beacon ['bikən] s signal m, phare m || tr éclairer || intr briller
bead [bid] s perle f, grain m; (of a gun) guidon m; **beads** collier m; (of sweat) gouttes fpl; (eccl) chapelet m; **to draw a bead on** viser; **to tell one's beads** égrener son chapelet
beadle ['bidəl] s bedeau m, appariteur m
beagle ['bigəl] s beagle m, briquet m
beak [bik] s bec m; (nose) (slang) pif m; (slang) grand nez m crochu
beaker ['bikər] s coupe f, vase m à bec, verre m à expérience
beam [bim] s poutre f; (plank) madrier m; (of roof) solive f; (of ship) bau m, barrot m; (of light; of hope) rayon m; (rad) faisceau m; **on the beam** (slang) sur la bonne piste; **to be off the beam** (slang) faire fausse route || tr (light, waves, etc.) émettre; **to beam a broadcast** faire une émission || intr rayonner
bean [bin] s haricot m; fève f; (slang) caboche f; **to spill the beans** (coll) vendre la mèche
beaner·y ['binəri] s (pl -ies) (slang) gargote f
bean'pole' s perche f à fèves; (person) (slang) asperge f
bean'stalk' s tige f de fève, tige de haricot
bear [bɛr] s ours m; (in the stock market) baissier m || v (pret bore [bor]; pp borne [born]) tr porter; (a child) enfanter; (interest on money) rapporter; (to put up with) souffrir, supporter; **to bear the market** jouer à la baisse || intr porter; **to bear down** appuyer; **to bear up against** résister à; **to bear upon** avoir du rapport à; **to bring to bear** mettre en jeu
bearable ['bɛrəbəl] adj supportable
bear' cub' s ourson m
beard [bɪrd] s barbe f || tr braver, narguer
bearded adj barbu

beardless ['bɪrdlɪs] *adj* imberbe, sans barbe

bearer ['bɛrər] *s* porteur *m*

bearing ['bɛrɪŋ] *s* port *m*, maintien *m*; (mach) roulement *m*, coussinet *m*; (naut) relèvement *m*; **to get one's bearings** se retrouver; **to have a bearing on** s'appliquer à; **to take bearings** (naut) faire le point

bear' mar'ket *s* marché *m* à la baisse

bear'skin' *s* peau *f* d'ours; colback *m*

beast [bist] *s* bête *f*, animal *m*; (*person*) brute *f*, animal *m*

beast·ly ['bistli] *adj* (*comp* **-lier**; *super* **-liest**) brutal, bestial; (coll) abominable, détestable

beast' of bur'den *s* bête *f* de somme, bête de charge

beat [bit] *s* battement *m*; (*of policeman*) ronde *f*; (mus) mesure *f*, temps *m* ‖ *v* (*pret* **beat**; *pp* **beat** or **beaten**) *tr* battre; (*to defeat*) vaincre, battre; **that beats me!** (slang) ça me dépasse!; **to beat back** or **down** rabattre; **to beat in** enfoncer; **to beat it** (slang) filer, décamper; **to beat s.o. hollow** (coll) battre qn à plate couture; **to beat s.o. out of money** (slang) escroquer qn; **to beat time** battre la mesure; **to beat up** (slang) rosser ‖ *intr* battre; **to beat around the bush** (coll) tourner autour du pot

beater ['bitər] *s* batteur *m*; (culin) fouet *m*

beati·fy [bɪ'ætɪ,faɪ] *v* (*pret & pp* **-fied**) *tr* béatifier

beating ['bitɪŋ] *s* battement *m*; (*blows*) bastonnade *f*, rossée *f*; (*defeat*) (coll) raclée *f*

beatitude [bɪ'ætɪ,t(j)ud] *s* béatitude *f*

beau [bo] *s* (*pl* **beaus** or **beaux** [boz]) beau *m*, galant *m*

beautician [bju'tɪʃən] *s* coiffeur *m*, coiffeuse *f*, esthéticienne *f*

beautiful ['bjutɪfəl] *adj* beau

beautifully ['bjutɪfəli] *adv* admirablement

beauti·fy ['bjutɪ,faɪ] *v* (*pret & pp* **-fied**) *tr* embellir

beau·ty ['bjuti] *s* (*pl* **-ties**) beauté *f*

beau'ty con'test *s* concours *m* de beauté

beau'ty par'lor or **beau'ty shop'** *s* salon *m* or institut *m* de beauté

beau'ty queen' *s* reine *f* de beauté

beau'ty sleep' *s* sommeil *m* avant minuit

beau'ty spot' *s* (*place*) coin *m* délicieux; (*on face*) grain *m* de beauté

beaver ['bivər] *s* castor *m*

becalm [bɪ'kɑm] *tr* calmer, apaiser; (naut) abriter

because [bɪ'kɔz] *conj* parce que; **because of** à cause de, par suite de

beck [bɛk] *s*—**to be at s.o.'s beck and call** obéir à qn au doigt et à l'œil

beckon ['bɛkən] *tr* faire signe à, appeler ‖ *intr* appeler

be·come [bɪ'kʌm] *v* (*pret* **-came**; *pp* **-come**) *tr* convenir à, aller à, seoir à ‖ *intr* devenir; se faire, e.g., **to become a doctor** se faire médecin; e.g., **to become known** se faire connaître;

to become accustomed s'accoutumer; **to become old** vieillir; **what has become of him?** qu'est-ce qu'il est devenu?

becoming [bɪ'kʌmɪŋ] *adj* convenable, seyant

bed [bɛd] *s* lit *m*; couche *f*; **to go to bed** se coucher; **to put to bed** coucher

bed' and board' *s* le vivre et le couvert

bed'bug' *s* punaise *f* (des lits)

bed'clothes' *spl* couvertures *fpl* et draps *mpl*

bedding ['bɛdɪŋ] *s* literie *f*

bedeck [bɪ'dɛk] *tr* parer, orner, chamarrer; **to bedeck oneself** s'attifer

bed'fast' *adj* cloué au lit

bed'fel'low *s* camarade *m* de lit

bedizen [bɪ'daɪzən], [bɪ'dɪzən] *tr* attifer, chamarrer

bed'jack'et *s* liseuse *f*

bedlam ['bɛdləm] *s* pétaudière *f*, tumulte *m*

bed'lamp' *s* lampe *f* de chevet

bed' lin'en *s* literie *f*, draps *mpl* en toile de fil

bed'pan' *s* bassin *m* (de lit)

bed'post' *s* pied *m* de lit

bedraggled [bɪ'drægəld] *adj* crotté, échevelé

bedridden ['bɛd,rɪdən] *adj* alité, cloué au lit

bed'rock' *s* roche *f* de fond; tuf *m*; (fig) fondement *m*

bed'room' *s* chambre *f* à coucher

bed'room lamp' *s* lampe *f* de chevet

bed'side' *s* bord *m* du lit, chevet *m*

bed'side book' *s* livre *m* de chevet

bed'sore' *s* escarre *f*

bed'spread' *s* dessus-de-lit *m*

bed'spring' *s* sommier *m*

bed'stead' *s* bois *m* de lit

bed' tick' *s* coutil *m*

bed'time' *s* l'heure *f* du coucher

bed' warm'er *s* chauffe-lit *m*

bed'wet'ting *s* énurésie *f*

bee [bi] *s* abeille *f*; (*get-together*) réunion *f*; (*contest*) concours *m*

beech [bitʃ] *s* hêtre *m*

beech' mar'ten *s* (zool) fouine *f*

beech'nut' *s* faîne *f*

beef [bif] *s* bœuf *m* ‖ *tr*—**to beef up** (coll) renforcer ‖ *intr* (slang) rouspéter

beef' cat'tle *s* bœufs *mpl* de boucherie

beef'steak' *s* bifteck *m*

beef' stew' *s* ragoût *m* de bœuf

bee'hive' *s* ruche *f*

bee'keep'er *s* apiculteur *m*

bee'keep'ing *s* apiculture *f*

bee'line' *s*—**to make a beeline for** aller en droite ligne à

beer [bɪr] *s* bière *f*

beer' bot'tle *s* canette *f* (de bière)

bees'wax' *s* cire *f* d'abeille

beet [bit] *s* betterave *f*

beetle ['bitəl] *s* scarabée *m*, escarbot *m*

bee'tle-browed' *adj* à sourcils épais, à sourcils fournis

be·fall [bɪ'fɔl] *v* (*pret* **-fell**; *pp* **-fallen**) *tr* arriver à ‖ *intr* arriver

befitting [bɪ'fɪtɪŋ] *adj* convenable, seyant
before [bɪ'for] *adv* avant, auparavant || *prep* avant; (*in front of*) devant; **before** + *ger* avant de + *inf* || *conj* avant que
before'hand' *adv* d'avance, préalablement, auparavant
befriend [bɪ'frɛnd] *tr* venir en aide à
befuddle [bɪ'fʌdəl] *tr* embrouiller
beg [bɛg] *v* (*pret & pp* **begged; ger begging**) *tr* mendier; (*to entreat*) prier || *intr* mendier; (*said of dog*) faire le beau; **I beg of you** je vous en prie; **to beg for** solliciter; **to beg off** s'excuser; **to go begging** (fig) rester pour compte
be·get [bɪ'gɛt] *v* (*pret* **-got;** *pp* **-gotten** or **-got;** *ger* **-getting**) *tr* engendrer
beggar ['bɛgər] *s* mendiant *m*
beggarly ['bɛgərli] *adj* chétif, misérable
be·gin [bɪ'gɪn] *v* (*pret* **-gan** ['gæn]; *pp* **-gun** ['gʌn]; *ger* **-ginning**) *tr & intr* commencer; **beginning with** à partir de; **to begin to** commencer à
beginner [bɪ'gɪnər] *s* débutant *m*, commençant *m*; (*tyro*) blanc-bec *m*, novice *m*, béjaune *m*; (mil) bleu *m*
beginning [bɪ'gɪnɪŋ] *s* commencement *m*, début *m*
begrudge [bɪ'grʌdʒ] *tr* donner à contrecœur; **to begrudge s.o. s.th.** envier q.ch. à qn
beguile [bɪ'gaɪl] *tr* charmer, tromper
behalf [bɪ'hæf], [bɪ'haf] *s*—**on behalf of** de la part de, au nom de
behave [bɪ'hev] *intr* se comporter, se conduire; se comporter bien
behavior [bɪ'hevjər] *s* comportement *m*, conduite *f*
behead [bɪ'hɛd] *tr* décapiter
beheading [bɪ'hɛdɪŋ] *s* décapitation *f*
behest [bɪ'hɛst] *s* ordre *m*, demande *f*
behind [bɪ'haɪnd] *s* derrière *m* || *adv* derrière, par derrière; **to be behind** être en retard; **to fall behind** traîner en arrière || *prep* derrière; en arrière de; **behind the back of** dans le dos de; **behind time** en retard
be·hold [bɪ'hold] *v* (*pret & pp* **-held** ['hɛld]) *tr* contempler || *interj* voyez!, voici!
behoove [bɪ'huv] *impers*—**it behooves him to** il lui appartient de; **it does not behoove him to** mal lui sied de
being ['bi·ɪŋ] *adj*—**for the time being** pour le moment || *s* être *m*
belabor [bɪ'lebər] *tr* rosser; (fig) trop insister sur
belated [bɪ'letɪd] *adj* attardé, tardif
belch [bɛltʃ] *s* éructation *f*; rot *m* (slang) || *tr & intr* éructer
bel·fry ['bɛlfri] *s* (*pl* **-fries**) beffroi *m*, clocher *m*
Belgian ['bɛldʒən] *adj* belge || *s* Belge *mf*
Belgium ['bɛldʒəm] *s* Belgique *f*; la Belgique
be·lie [bɪ'laɪ] *v* (*pret & pp* **-lied** ['laɪd]; *ger* **-lying** ['laɪ·ɪŋ]) *tr* démentir
belief [bɪ'lif] *s* croyance *f*

believable [bɪ'livəbəl] *adj* croyable
believe [bɪ'liv] *tr & intr* croire; **to believe in** croire à or en; **to make believe** faire semblant, feindre
believer [bɪ'livər] *s* croyant *m*
belittle [bɪ'lɪtəl] *tr* rabaisser
bell [bɛl] *s* cloche *f*; (*of a clock or gong*) timbre *m*; (*small bell*) sonnette *f*, clochette *f*; (*big bell*) bourdon *m*; (*on animals*) grelot *m*, clarine *f*, sonnaille *f*; (*of a trumpet*) pavillon *m*; **bells** sonnerie *f* || *tr* attacher un grelot à
belladonna [ˌbɛlə'danə] *s* belladone *f*
bell'-bot'tom trou'sers *spl* pantalon *m* à pattes d'éléphant
bell'boy' *s* chasseur *m*, garçon *m* d'hôtel
bell' glass' *s* globe *m*, garde-poussière *m*
bell'hop' *s* chasseur *m*, garçon *m* d'hôtel
bellicose ['bɛlɪˌkos] *adj* belliqueux
belligerent [bə'lɪdʒərənt] *adj & s* belligérant *m*
bell' jar' *s* var of **bell glass**
bellow ['bɛlo] *s* mugissement *m*; **bellows** (*of camera; of fireplace*) soufflet *m*; (*of organ; of forge*) soufflerie *f* || *intr* mugir, beugler
bell'pull' *s* cordon *m* de sonnette
bell' ring'er *s* sonneur *m*; carillonneur *m*
bell'-shaped' *adj* en forme de cloche
bell' tow'er *s* clocher *m*, campanile *m*
bellwether ['bɛlˌwɛðər] *s* sonnailler *m*
bel·ly ['bɛli] *s* (*pl* **-lies**) ventre *m* || *v* (*pret & pp* **-lied**) *intr*—**to belly out** s'enfler
bel'ly·ache' *s* (coll) mal *m* de ventre || *intr* (slang) rouspéter
bel'ly·but'ton *s* (coll) nombril *m*
bel'ly dance' *s* (coll) danse *f* du ventre
bel'ly flop' *s* plat ventre *m* (acrobatique)
bellyful ['bɛliˌful] *s* (slang) ventrée *f*
bel'ly-land' *intr* (aer) aterrir sur le ventre
belong [bɪ'lɔŋ], [bɪ'laŋ] *intr* (*to have the proper qualities*) aller bien; **to belong in** devoir être dans, e.g., **this chair belongs in that corner** cette chaise doit être dans ce coin-là; **to belong to** appartenir à; **to belong together** aller ensemble
belongings [bɪ'lɔŋɪŋz], [bɪ'laŋɪŋz] *spl* biens *mpl*, effets *mpl*
beloved [bɪ'lʌvɪd], [bɪ'lʌvd] *adj & s* bien-aimé *m*
below [bɪ'lo] *adv* dessous, au-dessous, en bas; (*as follows, following*) ci-dessous, ci-après || *prep* sous, au-dessous de; (*another point on the river*) en aval de
belt [bɛlt] *s* ceinture *f*; zone *f*; (*of a machine*) courroie *f*; **to tighten one's belt** se serrer la ceinture || *tr* ceindre; (slang) cogner
belt' buck'le *s* boucle *f* de ceinturon
belt' convey'or *s* tapis *m* roulant
belted *adj* à ceinture
belt'way' *s* route *f* de ceinture, boulevard *m* périphérique

bemoan [bɪ'mon] *tr* déplorer
bemuse [bɪ'mjuz] *tr* stupéfier, hébéter
bench [bɛntʃ] *s* banc *m*; (law) siège *m*
bench' mark' *s* repère *m*
bend [bend] *s* courbure *f*; (*of road*) tournant *m*; (*of river*) sinuosité *f*; **bends** mal *m* des caissons ‖ *v* (*pret & pp* **bent** [bent]) *tr* courber; (*the elbow; a person to one's will*) plier; (*the knee*) fléchir ‖ *intr* courber; plier; **do not bend** (label) ne pas plier; **to bend down** se courber
bender ['bendər] *s*—**to go on a bender** (slang) faire la bombe
beneath [bɪ'niθ] *adv* dessous, au-dessous, en bas ‖ *prep* sous, au-dessous de
benediction [ˌbenɪ'dɪkʃən] *s* bénédiction *f*
benefactor ['benɪˌfæktər], [ˌbenɪ'fæktər] *s* bienfaiteur *m*
beneficence [bɪ'nɛfɪsəns] *s* bienfaisance *f*
beneficent [bɪ'nɛfɪsənt] *adj* bienfaisant
beneficial [ˌbenɪ'fɪʃəl] *adj* profitable, avantageux; (*remedy*) salutaire
beneficiar·y [ˌbenɪ'fɪʃɪˌɛri] *s* (*pl* **-ies**) bénéficiaire *mf*, ayant droit *m*
benefit ['benɪfɪt] *s* profit *m*; (theat) bénéfice *m*; **benefits** bienfaits *mpl*, avantages *mpl*; **for the benefit of** au profit de ‖ *tr* profiter (with *dat*) ‖ *intr* bénéficier
ben'efit soci'ety *s* société *f* de prévoyance
benevolent [bɪ'nɛvələnt] *adj* bienveillant, bienfaisant, bénévole
benign [bɪ'naɪn] *adj* bénin
bent [bent] *adj* courbé, plié; (*person's back*) voûté; (*determined*) résolu; **bent over** (*shoulders*) voûté; (*figure, person*) courbé; **to be bent on** être acharné à ‖ *s* penchant *m*; **to have a bent for** avoir du goût pour
benzene [ben'zin] *s* (chem) benzène *m*
benzine [ben'zin] *s* benzine *f*
bequeath [bɪ'kwið], [bɪ'kwiθ] *tr* léguer
bequest [bɪ'kwɛst] *s* legs *m*
berate [bɪ'ret] *tr* gronder
be·reave [bɪ'riv] *v* (*pret & pp* **-reaved** or **-reft** ['rɛft]) *tr* priver; (*to cause sorrow to*) affliger
bereavement [bɪ'rivmənt] *s* privation *f*; (*sorrow*) deuil *m*, affliction *f*
Berlin [bər'lɪn] *adj* berlinois ‖ *s* Berlin *m*
Berliner [bər'lɪnər] *s* berlinois *m*
Bermuda [bər'mjudə] *s* les Bermudes *fpl*
ber·ry ['bɛri] *s* (*pl* **-ries**) baie *f*; (*seed*) grain *m*
berserk [bər'sʌrk], [bər'zʌrk] *adv* frénétiquement; **to go berserk** frapper à tort et à travers
berth [bʌrθ] *s* couchette *f*; (*at a dock*) emplacement *m*; (*space to move about*) évitage *m*; (fig) poste *m*, situation *f* ‖ *tr* (*a ship*) accoster
beryllium [bə'rɪlɪ·əm] *s* béryllium *m*
be·seech [bɪ'sitʃ] *v* (*pret & pp* **-sought** ['sɔt] or **-seeched**) *tr* supplier

be·set [bɪ'sɛt] *v* (*pret & pp* **-set**; *ger* **-setting**) *tr* assiéger, assaillir
beside [bɪ'saɪd] *prep* à côté de, auprès de; **to be beside oneself** être hors de soi; **to be beside oneself with** (*e.g., joy*) être transporté de
besides [bɪ'saɪdz] *adv* en outre, de plus; (*otherwise*) d'ailleurs ‖ *prep* en sus de, en plus de, outre
besiege [bɪ'sidʒ] *tr* assiéger
besmear [bɪ'smɪr] *tr* barbouiller
besmirch [bɪ'smʌrtʃ] *tr* souiller
best [bɛst] *adj super* (le) meilleur §91 ‖ *s* (le) meilleur *m*; **at best** au mieux; **to do one's best** faire de son mieux; **to get the best of it** avoir le dessus; **to make the best of** s'accommoder de ‖ *adv super* (le) mieux §91 ‖ *tr* l'emporter sur
bestial ['bɛstjəl], ['bɛstʃəl] *adj* bestial, brutal
best' man' *s* garçon *m* d'honneur
bestow [bɪ'sto] *tr* accorder, conférer
bestowal [bɪ'sto·əl] *s* don *m*, dispensation *f*
best' sel'ler *s* livre *m* à succès, succès *m* de librairie
bet [bɛt] *s* pari *m*, gageure *f*; **make your bets!** faites vos jeux! ‖ *v* (*pret & pp* **bet** or **betted**; *ger* **betting**) *tr & intr* parier; **you bet!** (slang) je vous crois!, tu parles!
be·take [bɪ'tek] *v* (*pret* **-took**; *pp* **-taken**) *tr*—**to betake oneself** se rendre
betray [bɪ'tre] *tr* trahir
betrayal [bɪ'tre·əl] *s* trahison *f*
betrayer [bɪ'tre·ər] *s* traître *m*
betroth [bɪ'troð], [bɪ'troθ] *tr*—**to be betrothed** se fiancer
betrothal [bɪ'troðəl], [bɪ'troθəl] *s* fiançailles *fpl*
better ['bɛtər] *adj comp* meilleur §91; **better than** meilleur que ‖ *adv comp* mieux §91; **better than** mieux que; (followed by numeral) plus de; **it is better to** il vaut mieux de; **so much the better** tant mieux; **to be better** (*in better health*) aller mieux; **to be better to** valoir mieux; **to get better** s'améliorer; **to get the better of** l'emporter sur; **to think better** se raviser ‖ *tr* améliorer ‖ *intr* s'améliorer
bet'ter half' *s* (coll) chère moitié *f*
bet'ting odds' *spl* cote *f* (des paris)
bettor ['bɛtər] *s* parieur *m*, gageur *m*
between [bɪ'twin] *adv* au milieu; dans l'intervalle ‖ *prep* entre; **between friends** dans l'intimité
between'-decks' *s* (naut) entrepont *m*
bev·el ['bɛvəl] *adj* biseauté, taillé en biseau ‖ *s* (*instrument*) équerre *f*; (*sloping part*) biseau *m* ‖ *v* (*pret & pp* **-eled** or **-elled**; *ger* **-eling** or **-elling**) *tr* biseauter, chanfreiner, équerrer
beverage ['bɛvərɪdʒ] *s* boisson *f*
bev·y ['bɛvi] *s* (*pl* **-ies**) bande *f*
bewail [bɪ'wel] *tr* lamenter, pleurer
beware [bɪ'wer] *tr* se bien garder de ‖ *intr* prendre garde; **to beware of**

prendre garde à ‖ *interj* gare!, prenez garde!
bewilder [bɪ'wɪldər] *tr* confondre, ahurir
bewilderment [bɪ'wɪldərmənt] *s* confusion *f*, ahurissement *m*
bewitch [bɪ'wɪtʃ] *tr* ensorceler
bewitching [bɪ'wɪtʃɪŋ] *adj* enchanteur
beyond [bɪ'jɑnd] *s*—**the beyond** l'au-delà *m* ‖ *adv* au-delà ‖ *prep* au-delà de; **beyond a doubt** hors de doute; **it's beyond me** (coll) je n'y comprends rien; **to go beyond** dépasser
biannual [baɪ'ænju·əl] *adj* semi-annuel
bias ['baɪ·əs] *adj* biais ‖ *s* biais *m*; (fig) prévention *f*, préjugé *m* ‖ *tr* prédisposer, prévenir, rendre partial
bib [bɪb] *s* bavette *f*
Bible ['baɪbəl] *s* Bible *f*
Biblical ['bɪblɪkəl] *adj* biblique
bibliographer [,bɪblɪ'ɑgrəfər] *s* bibliographe *m*
bibliogra·phy [,bɪblɪ'ɑgrəfi] *s* (*pl* -phies) bibliographie *f*
biceps ['baɪsɛps] *s* biceps *m*
bicker ['bɪkər] *intr* se quereller, se chamailler
bickering ['bɪkərɪŋ] *s* bisbille *f*
bicuspid [baɪ'kʌspɪd] *s* prémolaire *f*
bicycle ['baɪsɪkəl] *s* bicyclette *f*, vélo *m* ‖ *intr* faire de la bicyclette, aller à bicyclette
bi'cycle path' *s* piste *f* cyclable
bicyclist ['baɪsɪklɪst] *s* cycliste *mf*
bid [bɪd] *s* enchère *f*, offre *f*, mise *f*; (e.g., *to build a school*) soumission *f*; (cards) demande *f* ‖ *v* (*pret* **bade** [bæd] or **bid**; *ger* **bidden** ['bɪdən]) *tr* inviter; (*to order*) commander; (cards) demander; **to bid ten thousand on** mettre une enchère de dix mille sur ‖ *intr*—**to bid on** mettre une enchère sur
bidder ['bɪdər] *s* enchérisseur *m*, offrant *m*; (*person who submits an estimate*) soumissionnaire *mf*
bidding ['bɪdɪŋ] *s* enchères *fpl*; **at s.o.'s bidding** aux ordres de qn
bide [baɪd] *tr*—**to bide one's time** attendre l'heure or le bon moment
biennial [baɪ'ɛnɪ·əl] *adj* biennal
bier [bɪr] *s* (*frame or stand*) catafalque *m*; (*coffin*) cercueil *m*
biff [bɪf] *s* (slang) gnon *m*, beigne *f* ‖ *tr* (slang) gifler, cogner
bifocal [baɪ'fokəl] *adj* bifocal ‖ **bifocals** *spl* lunettes *fpl* bifocales
big [bɪg] *adj* (*comp* **bigger**; *super* **biggest**) gros, grand; (*man*) de grande taille ‖ *adv*—**to grow big** grossir, grandir; **to talk big** (slang) se vanter
bigamist ['bɪgəmɪst] *s* bigame *mf*
bigamous ['bɪgəməs] *adj* bigame
bigamy ['bɪgəmi] *s* bigamie *f*
big'-boned' *adj* ossu, à gros os
big' busi'ness *s* (pej) les grosses affaires *fpl*
Big' Dip'per *s* Grande Ourse *f*
big' game' *s* fauves *mpl*, gros gibier *m*
big'-heart'ed *adj* généreux, cordial
big'mouth' *s* (slang) gueulard *m*

bigot ['bɪgət] *s* bigot *m*
bigoted ['bɪgətɪd] *adj* bigot
bigot·ry ['bɪgətri] *s* (*pl* -ries) bigoterie *f*
big' shot' *s* (slang) grand manitou *m*, gros bonnet *m*
big' splash' *s* (slang) sensation *f* à tout casser
big' stiff' *s* (slang) personnage *m* guindé
big' talk' *s* (slang) vantardise *f*
big'-time op'erator *s* (slang) gros trafiquant *m*
big' toe' *s* orteil *m*, gros orteil
big' top' *s* (*circus tent*) chapiteau *m*
big' wheel' *s* (slang) gros bonnet *m*, grand manitou *m*, grosse légume *f*
big'wig' *s* (coll) gros bonnet *m*, grand manitou *m*, grosse légume *f*
bike [baɪk] *s* (coll) bécane *f*, vélo *m*
bile [baɪl] *s* bile *f*
bilge [bɪldʒ] *s* sentine *f*, cale *f*
bilge' wa'ter *s* eau *f* de cale
bilingual [baɪ'lɪŋgwəl] *adj* bilingue
bilious ['bɪljəs] *adj* bilieux
bilk [bɪlk] *s* tromperie *f*, escroquerie *f* ‖ *tr* tromper, escroquer
bill [bɪl] *s* (*invoice*) facture *f*, mémoire *m*; (*in a hotel*) note *f*; (*in a restaurant*) addition *f*; (*currency*) billet *m*; (*of a bird*) bec *m*; (*posted*) affiche *f*, placard *m*, écriteau *m*; (*in a legislature*) projet *m* de loi; **post no bills** (public sign) défense d'afficher; **to head the bill** (theat) avoir la vedette ‖ *tr* facturer
bill'board' *s* tableau *m* d'affichage, panneau *m* d'affichage
billet ['bɪlɪt] *s* (*order*) billet *m* de logement; (*of metal or wood*) billette *f* ‖ *tr* loger, cantonner
bill'fold' *s* portefeuille *m*
bil'liard ball' *s* bille *f*
billiards ['bɪljərdz] *s* & *spl* billard *m*
bil'liard ta'ble *s* billard *m*
billion ['bɪljən] *s* (U.S.A.) milliard *m*; (Brit) billion *m*
billionaire [,bɪljən'ɛr] *s* milliardaire *mf*
bill' of exchange' *s* lettre *f* de change, traite *f*
bill' of fare' *s* carte *f* du jour
bill' of health' *s* patente *f* de santé
bill' of lad'ing *s* connaissement *m*
bill' of rights' *s* déclaration *f* des droits de l'homme
bill' of sale' *s* acte *m* de vente
billow ['bɪlo] *s* flot *m*, grosse vague *f* ‖ *intr* ondoyer
billowy ['bɪlo·i] *adj* onduleux, ondoyant
bill'post'er *s* colleur *m* d'affiches, afficheur *m*
bil·ly ['bɪli] *s* (*pl* -lies) bâton *m*
bil'ly goat' *s* (coll) bouc *m*
bimonthly [baɪ'mʌnθli] *adj* bimestriel
bin [bɪn] *s* huche *f*, coffre *m*
binary ['baɪnəri] *adj* binaire
binaural [baɪ'nɔrəl], [bɪn'ɔrəl] *adj* stéréophonique; à deux oreilles
bind [baɪnd] *v* (*pret* & *pp* **bound** [baʊnd]) *tr* lier, attacher; (*a book*) relier; (*s.o. to an agreement*) obliger

binder ['baɪndər] s (*person*) lieur m; (*of books*) relieur m; (*agreement*) conventions fpl; (mach) lieuse f
binder·y ['baɪndəri] s (pl -ies) atelier m de reliure
binding ['baɪndɪŋ] adj obligatoire; (med) astringent; **binding on all concerned** solidaire ‖ s reliure f
bind'ing post' s (elec) borne f
binge [bɪndʒ] s (coll) noce f, bombe f
bingo ['bɪŋgo] s loto m
binocular [bɪ'nɑkjələr] adj & s binoculaire m; **binoculars** jumelles fpl
binomial [baɪ'nomɪəl] adj & s binôme m
biochemistry [,baɪ·o'kɛmɪstri] s biochimie f
biographer [baɪ'ɑgrəfər] s biographe mf
biographic(al) [,baɪ·ə'græfɪk(əl)] adj biographique
biogra·phy [baɪ'ɑgrəfi] s (pl -phies) biographie f
biologist [baɪ'ɑlədʒɪst] s biologiste mf
biology [baɪ'ɑlədʒi] s biologie f
biophysics [,baɪ·ə'fɪzɪks] s biophysique f
biop·sy ['baɪ·ɑpsi] s (pl -sies) biopsie f
bipartisan [baɪ'pɑrtɪzən] adj bipartite
bipartite [baɪ'pɑrtaɪt] adj biparti
biped ['baɪpɛd] adj & s bipède m
biplane ['baɪ,plen] s biplan m
birch [bʌrtʃ] s bouleau m; (for whipping) verges fpl ‖ tr battre à coups de verges
birch' rod' s verges fpl
bird [bʌrd] s oiseau m; (slang) type m, individu m; **a bird in the hand is worth two in the bush** un "tiens" vaut mieux que deux "tu l'auras"; **to give s.o. the bird** (slang) envoyer qn promener; **to kill two birds with one stone** faire d'une pierre deux coups
bird' bath' s baignoire f pour oiseaux, bain m pour oiseaux
bird'cage' s cage f d'oiseau
bird' call' s appeau m, pipeau m
bird' dog' s chien m pour la plume
bird' fan'cier s oiselier
birdie ['bʌrdi] s oiselet m, oisillon m
bird'lime' s glu f
bird' of pas'sage s oiseau m de passage
bird' of prey' s oiseau m de proie
bird'seed' s alpiste m, chènevis m
bird's'-eye' s (pattern) œil-de-perdrix m
bird's'-eye view' s vue f à vol d'oiseau, tour m d'horizon, vue d'ensemble
biretta [bɪ'rɛtə] s barette f
birth [bʌrθ] s naissance f; **to give birth to** donner naissance à
birth' certif'icate s acte m de naissance, bulletin m de naissance
birth' control' s contrôle m des naissances, procréation f dirigée
birth'day' s anniversaire m; **happy birthday!** heureux anniversaire!
birth'day cake' s gâteau m d'anniversaire
birth'day pres'ent s cadeau m d'anniversaire

birth'mark' s tache f, envie f
birth'place' s lieu m de naissance
birth' rate' s natalité f, taux m de natalité
birth'right' s droit m de naissance; droit d'aînesse
biscuit ['bɪskɪt] s petit pain m, crêpe f au beurre, gâteau m feuilleté
bisect [baɪ'sɛkt] tr couper en deux, diviser en deux
bisexual [baɪ'sɛkʃʊ·əl] adj bissexuel
bishop ['bɪʃəp] s évêque m; (chess) fou m
bishopric ['bɪʃəprɪk] s évêché m
bison ['baɪsən], ['baɪzən] s bison m
bisulfate [baɪ'sʌlfet] s bisulfate m
bisulfite [baɪ'sʌlfaɪt] s bisulfite m
bit [bɪt] s morceau m, bout m, brin m; (of a bridle) mors m; (of a drill) mèche f; **bit by bit** petit à petit
bitch [bɪtʃ] s (dog) chienne f; (fox) renarde f; (wolf) louve f; (vulgar) vache f
bite [baɪt] s (of food) bouchée f; (by an animal) morsure f; (by an insect) piqûre f; (by a fish on a hook) touche f ‖ v (pret bit [bɪt]; pp bit or bitten ['bɪtən]) tr mordre; (said of an insect or snake) piquer
biting ['baɪtɪŋ] adj mordant; (cold) piquant; (wind) coupant
bit' play'er s figurant m
bitter ['bɪtər] adj amer; (cold) âpre; noir; (fight) acharné; (style) mordant ‖ **bitters** spl bitter m
bit'ter end' s—**to the bitter end** jusqu'au bout
bit'ter-end'er s (coll) intransigeant m, jusqu'au-boutiste mf
bitterness ['bɪtərnɪs] s amertume f; (of winter) âpreté f; (fig) aigreur f
bit'ter-sweet' adj aigre-doux ‖ s douce-amère f
bitumen [bɪ't(j)umən] s bitume m
bivou·ac ['bɪvʊ,æk], ['bɪvwæk] s bivouac m, cantonnement m ‖ v (pret & pp -acked; ger -acking) intr bivouaquer
biweekly [baɪ'wikli] adj bimensuel ‖ adv bimensuellement
biyearly [baɪ'jɪrli] adj semestriel ‖ adv semestriellement
bizarre [bɪ'zɑr] adj bizarre
blab [blæb] v (pret & pp **blabbed**; ger **blabbing**) tr ébruiter ‖ intr jaser
blabber ['blæbər] intr jaser
blab'ber-mouth' s (slang) jaseur m
black [blæk] adj & s noir m ‖ tr noircir; **to black out** faire le black-out dans
black'-and-blue' adj meurtri
black'-and-white' adj en blanc et noir
black'ball' tr blackbouler
black'ber'ry s (pl -ries) mûre f, mûre de ronce
black'berry bush' s mûrier m sauvage
black'bird' s (Turdus merula) merle m
black'board' s tableau m noir
black'board eras'er s éponge f, chiffon m
black' cur'rant s cassis m
black' damp' s mofette f

blacken ['blækən] *tr* noircir
black′ eye′ *s* œil *m* poché; **to give s.o. a black eye** pocher l'œil à qn; (fig) ruiner la réputation de qn
black′-eyed Su′san ['suzən] *s* marguerite *f* américaine
blackguard ['blægard] *s* vaurien *m*, salaud *m*
black′head′ *s* comédon *m*, tanne *f*
black′-headed gull′ *s* mouette *f* rieuse
blacking ['blækɪŋ] *s* cirage *m* noir
blackish ['blækɪʃ] *adj* noirâtre
black′jack′ *s* assommoir *m*; (cards) vingt-et-un *m* || *tr* assommer
black′ lead′ [lɛd] *s* mine *f* de plomb
black′ let′ter *s* caractère *m* gothique
black′ list′ *s* liste *f* noire
black′-list′ *tr* mettre à l'index, mettre en quarantaine
black′ lo′cust *s* (bot) faux acacia *m*
black′ mag′ic *s* magie *f* noire
black′mail′ *s* chantage *m* || *tr* faire chanter || *intr* faire du chantage
blackmailer ['blæk‚melər] *s* maître *m* chanteur
black′ mark′ *s* (of censure) tache *f*
black′ mar′ket *s* marché *m* noir
black′ marketeer′ [‚markɪ'tir] *s* trafiquant *m* du marché noir
black′out′ *s* black-out *m*; (of aviator) cécité *f* temporaire
black′ pep′per *s* poivre *m* noir
black′ sheep′ *s* (fig) brebis *f* galeuse
black′smith′ *s* forgeron *m*, maréchalferrant *m*
bladder ['blædər] *s* vessie *f*
bladderwort ['blædər‚wʌrt] *s* utriculaire *f*
blade [bled] *s* lame *f*; (of grass) brin *m*; (of propeller) aile *f*, pale *f*; (of oar) plat *m*; (young man) gaillard *m*; (mach) ailette *f*, palette *f*, aube *f*
blah [bla] *s* (slang) sornettes *fpl*, fadaises *fpl*, bêtises *fpl*
blah-blah ['bla'bla] *s* baratin *m*
blamable ['blemabəl] *adj* blâmable, coupable
blame [blem] *s* blâme *m*; reproches *mpl* || *tr* blâmer; reprocher; s'en prendre à
blameless ['blemlɪs] *adj* sans reproche
blame′wor′thy *adj* blâmable
blanch [blæntʃ], [blantʃ] *tr & intr* blanchir
bland [blænd] *adj* doux, suave; (with dissimulation) narquois
blandish ['blændɪʃ] *tr* flatter, cajoler
blandishment ['blændɪʃmənt] *s* flatterie *f*; attrait *m*, charme *m*
blank [blæŋk] *adj* blanc; (check; form) en blanc; (mind) confondu, déconcerté || *s* blanc *m*; trou *m*, vide *m*, lacune *f*; (metal mold) flan *m*; (form to be filled out) fiche *f*, formule *f*, feuille *f*; (space to be filled in) tiret *m* || *tr*—**to blank out** effacer || *intr*—**to blank out** (coll) s'évanouir
blank′ check′ *s* chèque *m* en blanc; (fig) chèque en blanc
blanket ['blæŋkɪt] *adj* général || *s* couverture *f* || *tr* envelopper; traiter sous une rubrique générale

blank′ verse′ *s* vers *mpl* blancs
blare [blɛr] *s* bruit *m*; (of trumpet) sonnerie *f* || *tr* faire retentir; (like a trumpet) sonner || *intr* retentir
blarney ['blarni] *s* (coll) flagornerie *f* || *tr* (coll) flagorner
blaspheme [blæs'fim] *tr & intr* blasphémer
blasphemous ['blæsfɪməs] *adj* blasphématoire, blasphémateur
blasphe·my ['blæsfɪmi] *s* (pl -mies) blasphème *m*
blast [blæst], [blast] *s* rafale *f*, souffle *m*; explosion *f*; (of dynamite) charge *f*; (of whistle) coup *m*; (of trumpet) sonnerie *f*; **at full blast** à toute allure || *tr* (to blow up) faire sauter; (hopes) ruiner; (a plant) flétrir || *intr* (said of plant) se faner; **to blast off** (said of rocket) se mettre à feu
blast′ fur′nace *s* haut fourneau *m*
blasting ['blæstɪŋ], ['blastɪŋ] *s* abattage *m* à la poudre; (of hopes) anéantissement *m*; (coll) abattage *m*, verte semonce *f*
blast′ing cap′ *s* capsule *f* fulminante
blast′off′ *s* mise *f* à feu
blatant ['bletənt] *adj* criard; (injustice) criant
blaze [blez] *s* flamme *f*, flambée *f*; (e.g., blazing house) incendie *m*; **to run like blazes** (slang) courir furieusement || *tr*—**to blaze the trail** frayer la piste || *intr* flamboyer, s'embraser
blazing ['blezɪŋ] *adj* embrasé, en feu; (sun) flamboyant
blazon ['blezən] *s* (heral) blason *m* || *tr* célébrer; exalter; (heral) blasonner; **to blazon out** proclamer
bleach [blitʃ] *s* décolorant *m*, eau *f* de Javel; (for hair) eau oxygénée || *tr* blanchir, décolorer
bleachers ['blitʃərz] *spl* gradins *mpl*, tribune *f*
bleak [blik] *adj* froid, morne, nu
blear-eyed ['blɪr‚aɪd] *adj* chassieux, larmoyant; (dull) d'un esprit épais
blear·y ['blɪri] *adj* (comp -ier; super -iest) (eyes) chassieux; (prospect) voilé, incertain
bleat [blit] *s* bêlement *m* || *intr* bêler, béguéter
bleed [blid] *v* (pret & pp bled [blɛd]) *tr & intr* saigner; **to bleed white** saigner à blanc
bleeding ['blidɪŋ] *adj* saignant || *s* saignement *m*; (bloodletting) saignée *f*
blemish ['blɛmɪʃ] *s* défaut *m*, tache *f* || *tr* défigurer; (a reputation) tacher
blench [blɛntʃ] *intr* pâlir; (to draw back) broncher
blend [blɛnd] *s* mélange *m* || *v* (pret & pp blended or blent [blɛnt]) *tr* mêler, mélanger; fondre, marier || *intr* se fondre, se marier
bless [blɛs] *tr* bénir
blessed ['blɛsɪd] *adj* béni, saint; (happy) bienheureux
blessing ['blɛsɪŋ] *s* bénédiction *f*; (at meals) bénédicité *m*

blight [blaɪt] s rouille f, nielle f; (of peaches) cloque f; (of potatoes; of vines) brunissure f; (fig) flétrissure f ‖ tr rouiller, nieller; (hopes, aspirations) flétrir, frustrer
blimp [blɪmp] s vedette f (aérienne)
blind [blaɪnd] adj aveugle; blind by birth aveugle-né; blind in one eye borgne; blind person aveugle m ‖ s store m; (for hunting) guet-apens m; (fig) feinte f; (cards) talon m ‖ tr aveugler; (by dazzling) éblouir
blind' al'ley s cul-de-sac m, impasse f
blinder ['blaɪndər] s œillère f
blind' flight' s vol m à l'aveuglette
blind' fly'ing s (aer) pilotage m sans visibilité
blind'fold' adj les yeux bandés ‖ s bandeau m ‖ tr bander les yeux de
blindly ['blaɪndli] adv aveuglément
blind' man' s aveugle m
blind'man's buff' s colin-maillard m
blindness ['blaɪndnɪs] s cécité f; (fig) aveuglement m
blind' spot' s côté m faible
blink [blɪŋk] s clignotement m ‖ tr faire clignoter ‖ intr clignoter
blinker ['blɪŋkər] s feu m clignotant; (for horses) œillère f; (for signals) projecteur m clignotant
blink'er light' s feu m à éclipses
blip [blɪp] s spot m
bliss [blɪs] s félicité f, béatitude f
blissful ['blɪsfəl] adj bienheureux
blister ['blɪstər] s ampoule f, bulle f ‖ tr couvrir d'ampoules; (paint) boursoufler ‖ intr se couvrir d'ampoules; se boursoufler
blithe [blaɪð], [blaɪθ] adj gai, joyeux
blitzkrieg ['blɪts‚krig] s guerre f éclair
blizzard ['blɪzərd] s tempête f de neige
bloat [blot] tr boursoufler, enfler ‖ intr se boursoufler, enfler
blob [blab] s motte f; (of color) tache f; (of ink) pâté m
block [blak] s bloc m; (toy) cube m; (of shares) tranche f; (of houses) pâté m, îlot m ‖ tr (a project) contrecarrer; (a wall) condamner, murer; to block up boucher, bloquer
blockade [bla'ked] s blocus m; to run the blockade forcer le blocus ‖ tr bloquer
block' and tac'kle s palan m
block'head' s sot m, niais m
blond [bland] adj & s blond m
blonde [bland] adj & s blonde f
blood [blʌd] s sang m; parenté f, race f; in cold blood de sang-froid; to put new blood into infuser un sang nouveau à
blood' and guts' spl sang m et tripes
blood' bank' s banque f du sang
blood' count' s numération f globulaire
blood'curd'ling adj horripilant
blood'hound' s limier m
bloodless ['blʌdlɪs] adj exsangue; (revolution) sans effusion de sang
bloodletting ['blʌd‚letɪŋ] s saignée f; (fig) effusion f de sang
blood' or'ange s sanguine f
blood' plas'ma s plasma m sanguin

blood' poi'soning s septicémie f, empoisonnement m du sang
blood' pres'sure s tension f artérielle
blood'shed' s effusion f de sang
blood'shot' adj injecté, éraillé
blood' spec'imen s prise f de sang
blood'stained' adj taché de sang
blood'stream' s circulation f du sang
blood'suck'er s sangsue f
blood' test' s examen m du sang
blood'thirst'y adj sanguinaire
blood' transfu'sion s transfusion f de sang, transfusion sanguine
blood' type' s groupe m de sang
blood' ves'sel s vaisseau m sanguin
blood•y ['blʌdi] adj (comp -ier; super -iest) sanglant
bloom [blum] s fleur f; fraîcheur f; (of a fruit) velouté m, duvet m; in bloom en fleur ‖ intr fleurir
bloomers ['blumərz] spl culotte f de femme
blooper ['blupər] s (coll) gaffe f, bévue f; (rad) poste m brouilleur
blossom ['blasəm] s fleur f; in blossom en fleur ‖ intr fleurir; to blossom out s'épanouir
blot [blat] s tache f; (of ink) pâté m ‖ v (pret & pp blotted; ger blotting) tr tacher, barbouiller; (ink) sécher; to blot out rayer ‖ intr (said of ink) boire
blotch [blatʃ] s tache f; (on face) pustule f ‖ tr couvrir de taches; (the skin) marbrer
blotch•y ['blatʃi] adj (comp -ier; super -iest) brouillé, tacheté
blotter ['blatər] s buvard m
blot'ting pa'per s papier m buvard
blouse [blaus] s corsage m; (children's) chemise f; (mil) vareuse f
blow [blo] s coup m; to come to blows en venir aux coups ‖ v (pret blew [blu]; pp blown) tr souffler; to blow one's nose se moucher; to blow out (a candle) éteindre; to blow up faire sauter; (a photograph) agrandir; (a balloon) gonfler ‖ intr souffler; (slang) décamper en vitesse; to blow out (said of a tire) éclater; to blow over passer; to blow up éclater; (slang) se mettre en colère
blower ['blo•ər] s soufflerie f; (mach) ventilateur m
blow'fly' s (pl -flies) mouche f à viande
blow'gun' s sarbacane f
blow'hard' s (slang) hâbleur m
blow'hole' s (of tunnel) ventilateur m; (of whale) évent m
blowing ['blo•ɪŋ] s soufflage m; (of the wind) soufflement m
blow'out' s (of a tire) éclatement m; (orgy) (slang) gueuleton m
blow'pipe' s chalumeau m
blow'torch' s lampe f à souder
blubber ['blʌbər] s graisse f de baleine ‖ tr bredouiller ‖ intr pleurer comme un veau
bludgeon ['blʌdʒən] s matraque f ‖ tr assommer
blue [blu] adj bleu; to be blue (coll) broyer du noir, avoir le cafard ‖ s

bleu *m;* **from out of the blue** du ciel, à l'improviste; **the blues** le cafard, l'humeur *f* noire || *tr* bleuir

blue'bell' *s* jacinthe *f* des bois

blue'ber'ry *s* (*pl* -**ries**) myrtille *f*

blue'bird' *s* oiseau *m* bleu

blue'-black' *adj* noir tirant sur le bleu

blue' blood' *s* sang *m* royal; aristocrate *mf*

blue'bot'tle *s* bluet *m*, barbeau *m*

blue' cheese' *s* roquefort *m* américain

blue' chip' *s* valeur-vedette *f*, valeur *f* de tout repos

blue'-gray' *adj* gris bleuté, gris-bleu

blue'jay' *s* geai *m* bleu

blue' jeans' *spl* blue-jean *m*

blue' moon' *s*—**once in a blue moon** tous les trente-six du mois

blue'nose' *s* puritain *m*, collet *m* monté

blue'-pen'cil *v* (*pret* & *pp* -**ciled** or -**cilled**; *ger* -**ciling** or -**cilling**) *tr* corriger au crayon bleu; couper, censurer

blue'print' *s* dessin *m* négatif, photocalque *m*; (fig) plan *m*, schéma *m* || *tr* planifier

blue'stock'ing *s* (coll) bas-bleu *m*

bluff [blʌf] *adj* abrupt; (*cliff*) accore, escarpé; (*person*) brusque || *s* (*cliff*) falaise *f*, cap *m* à pic; (*deception*) bluff *m;* **to call s.o.'s bluff** relever un défi || *tr* & *intr* bluffer

bluffer ['blʌfər] *s* bluffeur *m*

bluish ['bluⲻɪʃ] *adj* bleuté, bleuâtre

blunder ['blʌndər] *s* bévue *f*, gaffe *f* || *intr* faire une bévue, gaffer; **to blunder into** se heurter contre; **to blunder upon** découvrir par hasard; tomber sur

blunt [blʌnt] *adj* (*blade*) émoussé; (*point*) épointé; (*person*) brusque || *tr* émousser; épointer

bluntly ['blʌntli] *adv* brusquement, sans façons; carrément, sans ménagements

blur [blʌr] *s* barbouillage *m* || *v* (*pret* & *pp* **blurred**; *ger* **blurring**) *tr* embrouiller, voiler

blurb [blʌrb] *s* annonce *f*; publicité *f* au protège-livre

blurt [blʌrt] *tr*—**to blurt out** laisser échapper, lâcher

blush [blʌʃ] *s* rougeur *f;* **at first blush** au premier abord || *intr* rougir

bluster ['blʌstər] *s* rodomontade *f*, fanfaronnade *f* || *intr* (*of wind*) souffler en rafales; (*of person*) faire du fracas

blustery ['blʌstəri] *adj* (*wind*) orageux; (*person*) bravache, fanfaron

boar [bor] *s* (*male swine*) verrat *m*; (*wild hog*) sanglier *m*

board [bord] *s* planche *f*; (*e.g., of directors*) conseil *m*, commission *f*; (*meals*) le couvert; **above board** cartes sur table; **on board** à bord || *tr* (*a ship*) monter à bord de; (*paying guests*) nourrir || *intr* monter à bord; (*said of paying guest*) prendre pension

board' and room' *s* pension *f* et chambre *f*

boarder ['bordər] *s* pensionnaire *mf*; (*student*) interne *mf*

board'ing-house' *s* pension *f* (de famille)

board' of direc'tors *s* conseil *m* d'administration, gérance *f*

board' of trade' *s* association *f* des industriels et commerçants

board' of trustees' *s* comité *m* administrateur (*e.g., of a university*)

board'walk' *s* promenade *f* planchéiée au bord de la mer; (*over mud*) caillebotis *m*

boast [bost] *s* vanterie *f* || *intr* se vanter

boastful ['bostfəl] *adj* vantard

boasting ['bostɪŋ] *s* jactance *f*

boat [bot] *s* bateau *m*; (*small boat*) embarcation *f;* **to miss the boat** (coll) manquer le coche

boat' hook' *s* gaffe *f*

boat'house' *s* hangar *m* à bateaux or à canots

boating ['botɪŋ] *s* canotage *m;* **to go boating** faire du canotage

boat'load' *s* batelée *f*

boat'man *s* (*pl* -**men**) batelier *m*

boat' race' *s* régate *f*

boatswain ['bosən], ['bot‚swen] *s* maître *m* d'équipage

bob [bɑb] *s* plomb *m*; (*of hair*) chignon *m* || *v* (*pret* & *pp* **bobbed**; *ger* **bobbing**) *intr* s'agiter, danser

bobbin ['bɑbɪn] *s* bobine *f*

bob'by pin' *s* épingle *f* à cheveux

bob'by-socks' *spl* (coll) socquettes *fpl*, chaussettes *fpl* basses

bobbysoxer ['bɑbɪ ‚sɑksər] *s* (coll) zazou *m*, jeune lycéenne *f*

bob'sled' *s* bobsleigh *m*

bob'tail' *adj* à queue écartée || *tr* couper court

bode [bod] *tr* & *intr* présager

bodily ['bɑdɪli] *adj* corporel, physique || *adv* corporellement, en corps

bod·y ['bɑdi] *s* (*pl* -**ies**) corps *m*; (*dead body*) cadavre *m*; (*solidity*) consistance *f*; (*flavor of wine*) sève *f*, générosité *f*; (aer) fuselage *m*; (aut) carrosserie *f;* **to come in a body** venir en corps

bod'y·guard' *s* garde *m* du corps; (*group*) garde *f* du corps

bog [bɑg] *s* marécage *m*, fondrière *f* || *v* (*pret* & *pp* **bogged**; *ger* **bogging**) *intr*—**to bog down** s'enliser

bogey·man ['bogi ‚mæn] *s* (*pl* -**men**) croque-mitaine *m*

bogus ['bogəs] *adj* faux, simulé

Bohemia [bo'himⲻⲻə] *s* (*country*) Bohême *f*, la Bohême; (*of artistic world*) la bohème

Bohemian [bo'himⲻⲻən] *adj* bohémien; (*unconventional, arty*) bohème, de bohème || *s* (*person living in the country of Bohemia*) Bohémien *m*; (*artist*) bohème *mf*

boil [bɔɪl] *s* ébullition *f*; (*on the skin*) furoncle *m*, clou *m* || *tr* faire bouillir || *intr* bouillir

boiled' din'ner *s* pot-au-feu *m*

boiled' ham' *s* jambon *m* d'York

boiled' pota'toes *spl* pommes *fpl* bouillies, pommes vapeur

boiler ['bɔɪlər] *s* chaudière *f*
boi'ler•mak'er chaudronnier *m*
boiling ['bɔɪlɪŋ] *adj* bouillonnant ‖ *s* ébullition *f*, bouillonnement *m*
boisterous ['bɔɪstərəs] *adj* bruyant, débordant
bold [bold] *adj* hardi, osé, téméraire; (*headland*) à pic; (*look*) assuré
bold'face' *s* (typ) caractères *mpl* gras
bold'-faced' *adj* (*forward*) effronté
boldness ['boldnɪs] *s* hardiesse *f*; effronterie *f*
boll' wee'vil [bol] *s* anthonome *m* du coton, charançon *m* du coton
bologna [bə'lonə], [bə'lonjə] *s* mortadelle *f*, gros saucisson *m*
Bolshevik ['bɑl/əvɪk], ['bol/əvɪk] *adj* bolcheviste, bolchevique ‖ *s* Bolcheviste *mf*, Bolchevique *mf*
bolster ['bolstər] *s* traversin *m* ‖ *tr* soutenir
bolt [bolt] *s* verrou *m*; (*with a thread at one end*) boulon *m*; (*of cloth*) rouleau *m* ‖ *tr* verrouiller; (*food*) gober; (*e.g., a political party*) lâcher ‖ *intr* décamper
bomb [bɑm] *s* bombe *f* ‖ *tr* bombarder
bombard [bɑm'bɑrd] *tr* bombarder
bombardier [,bɑmbər'dɪr] *s* bombardier *m*
bombardment [bɑm'bɑrdmənt] *s* bombardement *m*
bombast ['bɑmbæst] *s* boursouflure *f*
bombastic [bɑm'bæstɪk] *adj* boursouflé
bomb' bay' *s* (aer) soute *f* à bombes
bomb' cra'ter *s* entonnoir *m*, trou *m* d'obus
bomber ['bɑmər] *s* avion *m* de bombardement, bombardier *m*
bombing ['bɑmɪŋ] *s* bombardement *m*
bomb'proof' *adj* à l'épreuve des bombes
bomb'shell' *s* obus *m*; **to fall like a bombshell** tomber comme une bombe
bomb' shel'ter *s* abri *m* à l'épreuve des bombes
bomb'sight' *s* viseur *m* de lancement
bona fide ['bonə,faɪdə] *adj & adv* de bonne foi
bonanza [bo'nænzə] *s* aubaine *f*, filon *m*
bonbon ['bɑn,bɑn] *s* bonbon *m*
bond [bɑnd] *s* lien *m*; (com) obligation *f*; **in bond** en entrepôt ‖ *tr* (com) entreposer, mettre en entrepôt
bondage ['bɑndɪdʒ] *s* esclavage *m*
bond'hold'er *s* obligataire *mf*
bone [bon] *s* os *m*; (*of a fish*) arête *f*; **to have a bone to pick** avoir maille à partir ‖ *tr* (*meat or fish*) désosser ‖ *intr*—**to bone up on** (*a subject*) (slang) potasser, piocher
bone'head' *s* (slang) ignorant *m*
boneless ['bonlɪs] *adj* sans os; sans arêtes
bone' of conten'tion *s* pomme *f* de discorde
boner ['bonər] *s* (coll) bourde *f*
bonfire ['bɑn,faɪr] *s* feu *m* de joie; (*for burning trash*) feu de jardin

bonnet ['bɑnɪt] *s* bonnet *m*; chapeau *m* à brides; (fig) chapeau
bonus ['bonəs] *s* boni *m*, prime *f*
bon•y ['boni] *adj* (*comp* -**ier**; *super* -**iest**) osseux; (*thin*) décharné
boo [bu] *s* huée *f*, sifflement *m*; **not to say boo** ne pas souffler mot ‖ *tr & intr* huer, siffler
boob [bub] *s* (coll) emplâtre *m*
boo•by ['bubi] *s* (*pl* -**bies**) (coll) nigaud *m*
boo'by hatch' *s* (slang) asile *m* d'aliénés; (*prison*) (slang) violon *m*
boo'by prize' *s* fiche *f* de consolation
boo'by trap' *s* engin *m* piégé; (fig) attrape-nigaud *m*
boo'by-trap' *v* (*pret & pp* -**trapped**; *ger* -**trapping**) *tr* piéger
book [bʊk] *s* livre *m*; (*of tickets*) carnet *m*; (*libretto*) livret *m*; **by the book** d'après le texte, selon les règles; **to make book** (sports) inscrire les paris ‖ *tr* (*a seat or room*) retenir, réserver
book'bind'er *s* relieur *m*
book'bind'er•y *s* (*pl* -**ies**) atelier *m* de reliure
book'bind'ing *s* reliure *f*
book'case' *s* bibliothèque *f*, étagère *f*
book' end' *s* serre-livres *m*, appui-livres *m*
booking ['bʊkɪŋ] *s* réservation *f*; (theat) location *f*
bookish ['bʊkɪ/] *adj* livresque; (*person*) studieux
book'keep'er *s* comptable *mf*, teneur *m* de livres
book'keep'ing *s* comptabilité *f*
book' learn'ing *s* science *f* livresque
booklet ['bʊklɪt] *s* livret *m*; (*notebook*) cahier *m*; (*pamphlet*) brochure *f*
book'lov'er *s* bibliophile *mf*
book'mark' *s* signet *m*
bookmobile ['bʊkmo,bil] *s* bibliobus *m*
book'plate' *s* ex-libris *m*
book'rack' *s* étagère *f*
book' review' *s* compte *m* rendu
book'sel'ler *s* libraire *mf*
book'shelf' *s* (*pl* -**shelves**) rayon *m*, étagère *f*
book'stand' *s* étalage *m* de livres; (*in a station*) bibliothèque *f*
book'store' *s* librairie *f*
book' val'ue *s* (com) valeur *f* comptable
book'worm' *s* ciron *m*; (fig) rat *m* de bibliothèque
boom [bum] *s* retentissement *m*, grondement *m*; (*rapid rise or growth*) vague *f* de prospérité, boom *m*; (naut) bout-dehors *m* ‖ *intr* retentir; (com) prospérer ‖ *interj* boum!
boomerang ['bumə,ræŋ] *s* boomerang *m*
boom' town' *s* ville *f* champignon
boon [bun] *s* bienfait *m*, avantage *m*; (archaic) don *m*, faveur *f*
boon' compan'ion *s* joyeux compagnon *m*
boor [bʊr] *s* rustre *m*, goujat *m*
boost [bust] *s* relèvement *m*; (*help*)

aide *f* ‖ *tr* soulever par derrière; (*prices*) hausser; (*to praise*) faire la réclame pour

booster ['bustər] *s* (*enthusiastic backer*) réclamiste *mf*; (*go-getter*) homme *m* d'expédition, lanceur *m* d'affaires; (elec) survolteur *m*; (rok) booster *m*, propulseur *m*

boost′er rock′et *s* fusée *f* de lancement

boost′er shot′ *s* piqûre *f* de rappel

boot [but] *s* botte *f*, bottine *f*; **to boot** en sus; **to lick s.o.′s boots** (coll) lécher les bottes à qn ‖ *tr* botter

boot′black′ *s* cireur *m* de bottes

booth [buθ] *s* (*at fair*) baraque *f*; (*e.g., for telephoning*) cabine *f*

boot′leg′ *adj* (slang) clandestin, de contrebande ‖ *v* (*pret & pp* **-legged**; *ger* **-legging**) *tr* (slang) faire la contrebande de ‖ *intr* (slang) faire la contrebande

bootlegger ['but,lɛgər] *s* (slang) contrebandier *m*; (slang) contrebandier *m* d'alcool, bootlegger *m*

boot′leg′ging *s* contrebande *f*

boot′lick′ *tr* (coll) lécher les bottes à

boo·ty ['buti] *s* (*pl* **-ties**) butin *m*

booze [buz] *s* (coll) boisson *f* alcoolique ‖ *intr* (coll) s'adonner à la boisson

border ['bɔrdər] *s* bord *m*, bordure *f*; (*of field and forest; of a piece of cloth*) lisière *f*; (*of a road*) marge *f*; (*of a country*) frontière *f*; (*edging*) galon *m*, bordé *m* ‖ *tr* border; (*a handkerchief*) lisérer ‖ *intr*—**to border on** confiner à, toucher à; (*a color*) tirer sur

bor′der·line′ *adj* indéterminé ‖ *s* ligne *f* de démarcation

bore [bor] *s* trou *m*; (*of gun*) calibre *m*; (*of cannon*) âme *f*; (*of cylinder*) alésage *m*; (*nuisance*) ennui *m*; (*person*) raseur *m* ‖ *tr* percer; (*a cylinder*) aléser; (*to annoy*) ennuyer

boreal ['borɪ·əl] *adj* boréal

boredom ['bordəm] *s* ennui *m*

boring ['borɪŋ] *adj* ennuyeux, rasant, rasoir ‖ *s* perçage *m*, percement *m*

born [bɔrn] *adj* né; **to be born** naître

borough ['bʌro] *s* (*town*) bourg *m*; circonscription *f* électorale

borrow ['bɑro], ['bɔro] *tr* emprunter; **to borrow from** emprunter à

borrower ['bɑro·ər], ['bɔro·ər] *s* emprunteur *m*

bor′rower's card′ *s* bulletin *m* de prêt

borrowing ['bɑro·ɪŋ], ['bɔro·ɪŋ] *s* emprunt *m*

borzoi ['bɔrzɔɪ] *s* lévrier *m* russe

bosom ['buzəm] *s* sein *m*, poitrine *f*; (*of the Church*) giron *m*

boss [bɔs], [bas] *s* patron *m*, chef *m*; (*foreman*) contremaître *m* ‖ *tr* diriger

boss·y ['bɔsi], ['basi] *adj* (*comp* **-ier**; *super* **-iest**) autoritaire; **to be bossy** jordonner

botanical [bə'tænɪkəl] *adj* botanique

botanist ['batənɪst] *s* botaniste *mf*

botany ['batəni] *s* botanique *f*

both [boθ] *adj* deux, e.g., **with both hands** à deux mains; les deux, e.g.,

both books les deux livres ‖ *pron* les deux, tous les deux ‖ *conj* à la fois; **both . . . and** aussi bien . . . que, e.g., **both in England and France** aussi bien en Angleterre qu'en France

bother ['baðər] *s* ennui *m* ‖ *tr* ennuyer, déranger ‖ *intr* se déranger

bothersome ['baðərsəm] *adj* importun

bottle ['batəl] *s* bouteille *f* ‖ *tr* mettre en bouteille, embouteiller

bot′tle cap′ *s* capsule *f*

bot′tled gas′ *s* gaz *m* en cylindre

bot′tle·neck′ *s* goulot *m*; (fig) embouteillage *m*

bot′tle o′pener *s* ouvre-bouteilles *m*

bottler ['batlər] *s* metteur *m* en bouteilles

bottling ['batlɪŋ] *s* mise *f* en bouteilles

bottom ['batəm] *s* fond *m*; **at the bottom of** au fond de; (*the page*) en bas de; **to reach the bottom of the barrel** (coll) être à fond de cale

bot′tom dol′lar *s* dernier sou *m*

bottomless ['batəmlɪs] *adj* sans fond

bough [bau] *s* rameau *m*

boulder ['boldər] *s* bloc *m*, rocher *m*

boulevard ['bulə,vard] *s* boulevard *m*

bounce [bauns] *s* (*elasticity*) bond *m*; (*of a ball*) rebond *m* ‖ *tr* faire rebondir; (slang) flanquer à la porte ‖ *intr* rebondir

bouncer ['baunsər] *s* (*in night club*) (coll) videur *m*, gorille *m*

bound [baund] *adj* (*tied*) lié; (*obliged*) obligé, tenu; **bound for** en partance pour ‖ *s* bond *m*, saut *m*; **bounds** bornes *fpl*, limites *fpl*; **out of bounds** hors jeu; (*prohibited*) défendu ‖ *tr* borner, limiter ‖ *intr* bondir

bounda·ry ['baundəri] *s* (*pl* **-ries**) borne *f*, limite *f*

boun′dary stone′ *s* borne *f*

boundless ['baundlɪs] *adj* sans bornes

boun·ty ['baunti] *s* (*pl* **-ties**) largesse *f*; (*award*) prime *f*

bouquet [bu'ke], [bo'ke] *s* bouquet *m*

bout [baut] *s* rencontre *f*; (*e.g., of fever*) accès *m*; (sports) match *m*

bow [bau] *s* inclination *f*, révérence *f*; (*of ship*) avant *m*, proue *f* ‖ *tr* incliner, courber ‖ *intr* s'incliner, se courber; **to bow down** se prosterner; **to bow out** se retirer; **to bow to** saluer ‖ [bo] *s* (*weapon*) arc *m*; (*bowknot*) nœud *m*; (*of violin*) archet *m* ‖ *intr* (mus) tirer l'archet

bowdlerize ['baudlə,raɪz] *tr* expurger

bowel ['bau·əl] *s* intestin *m*, boyau *m*; **bowels** entrailles *fpl*

bow′el move′ment *s* selle *f*; **to have a bowel movement** aller à la selle

bower ['bau·ər] *s* berceau *m*, tonnelle *f*

bow′ie knife′ ['bo·ɪ], ['bu·i] *s* couteau-poignard *m*

bowknot ['bo,nat] *s* nœud *m* en forme de rose, rosette *f*

bowl [bol] *s* bol *m*, jatte *f*; (*of pipe*) fourneau *m*; (*of spoon*) cuilleron *m*; **bowls** (sports) boules *fpl* ‖ *tr* rouler, lancer; **to bowl over** (*to overturn*) (coll) renverser; (slang) déconcerter

|| *intr*—**to bowl along** rouler rapidement
bowlegged ['bo ‚lɛgd], ['bo ‚lɛgɪd] *adj* aux jambes arquées
bowler ['bolər] *s* (*hat*) chapeau *m* melon; (*in cricket*) lanceur *m*; (*in bowling*) joueur *m* de boules
bowling ['bolɪŋ] *s* jeu *m* de boules, jeu de quilles
bowl'ing al'ley *s* boulodrome *m*
bowl'ing green' *s* boulingrin *m*
bowl'ing pin' *s* quille *f*
bowsprit ['bausprɪt], ['bosprɪt] *s* beaupré *m*
bow' tie' [bo] *s* nœud *m* papillon
box [baks] *s* boîte *f*; (*law*) barre *f*; (theat) loge *f*, baignoire *f*; **box on the ear** claque *f* || *tr* emboîter; (*to hit*) boxer; **to box the compass** réciter la rose des vents || *intr* (sports) boxer
box'car' *s* (rr) wagon *m* couvert
boxer ['baksər] *s* (*person*) boxeur *m*; (*dog*) boxer *m*
boxing ['baksɪŋ] *s* emboîtage *m*; (sports) boxe *f*
box' of'fice *s* bureau *m* de location
box'-office flop' *s* (slang) four *m*
box'-office hit' *s* pièce *f* à succès
box'wood' *s* buis *m*
boy [bɔɪ] *s* garçon *m*; (*little boy*) garçonnet *m*
boycott ['bɔɪkat] *s* boycottage *m* || *tr* boycotter
boy' friend' *s* ami *m*, camarade *m*; (*of a girl*) bon ami *m*
boyhood ['bɔɪhud] *s* enfance *f*, jeunesse *f*, adolescence *f*
boyish ['bɔɪ‧ɪʃ] *adj* de garçon
boy' scout' *s* boy-scout *m*
bra [bra] *s* (coll) soutien-gorge *m*
brace [bres] *s* attache *f*, lien *m*; (*of game birds*) couple *f*; (*of pistols*) paire *f*; (*to impart a rotary movement to a bit*) vilebrequin *m*; (aer, aut) entretoise *f*; (mus, typ) accolade *f* || *tr* ancrer, entretoiser; (*to tone up*) fortifier, remonter || *intr*—**to brace up** prendre courage
brace' and bit' *s* vilebrequin *m*
bracelet ['breslɪt] *s* bracelet *m*
bracer ['bresər] *s* tonique *m*
bracing ['bresɪŋ] *adj* tonique, fortifiant
bracket ['brækɪt] *s* console *f*; (*grouping*) niveau *m*; (mach) chaise *f*; (typ) crochet *m* || *tr* grouper; (typ) mettre entre crochets
brackish ['brækɪʃ] *adj* saumâtre
brad [bræd] *s* semence *f*, clou *m* (sans tête)
brag [bræg] *s* (*pret & pp* **bragged**; *ger* **bragging**) *intr* se vanter
braggadoci‧o [‚brægə'doʃɪ ‚o] *s* (*pl* **-os**) fanfaronnade *f*; (*person*) fanfaron *m*
braggart ['brægərt] *s* vantard *m*
bragging ['brægɪŋ] *s* vanterie *f*
Brah‧man ['bramən] *s* (*pl* **-mans**) brahmane *m*
braid [bred] *s* tresse *f*, passement *m*; (mil) galon *m*; **to trim with braid** soutacher || *tr* passementer; (*the hair*) tresser

braille [brel] *s* braille *m*
brain [bren] *s* cerveau *m*; **brains** cervelle *f*; (fig) intelligence *f*, cerveau; **to rack one's brains** se creuser la cervelle || *tr* casser la tête à
brain' child' *s* idée *f* de génie
brainless ['brenlɪs] *adj* sans cervelle
brain'storm' *s* accès *m* de folie; (coll) confusion *f* mentale; (coll) trouvaille *f*, bonne idée *f*
brain'wash' *tr* (*by use of torture, drugs, etc.*) faire un lavage de cerveau à; (*by means of commercials, sales talk, etc.*) bourrer le crâne de
brain'wash'ing *s* lavage *m* de cerveau; bourrage *m* de crâne
brain'work' *s* travail *m* intellectuel
brain‧y ['breni] *adj* (*comp* **-ier**; *super* **-iest**) (coll) intelligent, à l'esprit vif
braise [brez] *tr* braiser, endauber
brais'ing pan' *s* braisière *f*
brake [brek] *s* frein *m*; **to put on the brakes** serrer les freins || *tr & intr* freiner
brake' drum' *s* tambour *m* de frein
brake' light' *s* (aut) feu *m* de freinage
brake' lin'ing *s* garniture *f* de frein
brake'man *s* (*pl* **-men**) serre-freins *m*
brake' ped'al *s* pédale *f* de frein
brake' shoe' *s* sabot *m* de frein
bramble ['bræmbəl] *s* ronce *f*
bran [bræn] *s* son *m*, bran *m*
branch [bræntʃ] *s* branche *f*; (*of tree*) rameau *m*, branche; (*of a business*) succursale *f*, filiale *f* || *intr*—**to branch off** s'embrancher, se bifurquer; **to branch out** se ramifier
branch' line' *s* embranchement *m*
branch' of'fice *s* succursale *f*; bureau *m* de quartier
branch' road' *s* embranchement *m*
brand [brænd] *s* (*trademark*) marque *f*; (*torch*) brandon *m*; (*coal*) tison *m*; (*on a criminal*) flétrissure *f*; (*on cattle*) marque || *tr* marquer au fer rouge, flétrir
brand'ing i'ron *s* fer *m* à flétrir
brandish ['brændɪʃ] *tr* brandir
brand'-new' *adj* tout neuf, flambant neuf
bran‧dy ['brændi] *s* (*pl* **-dies**) eau-de-vie *f*
brash [bræʃ] *adj* impertinent
brass [bræs], [bras] *s* laiton *m*; (mil) (coll) officiers *mpl* supérieurs, galonnard *m*; (slang) toupet *m*, culot *m*; **big brass** (slang) grosses légumes *fpl*; **the brasses** (mus) les cuivres
brass' band' *s* fanfare *f*, musique *f*
brassiere [brə'zɪr] *s* soutien-gorge *m*
brass' knuck'les *spl* coup-de-poing *m*
brass' tack' *s* semence *f* (de tapissier); **to get down to brass tacks** (coll) en venir aux faits
brat [bræt] *s* (coll) gamin *m*, gosse *mf*
brava‧do [brə'vado] *s* (*pl* **-does** or **-dos**) bravade *f*
brave [brev] *adj* brave || *s* guerrier *m* peau-rouge || *tr* braver
bravery ['brevəri] *s* bravoure *f*
bra‧vo ['bravo] *s* (*pl* **-vos**) bravo *m* || *interj* bravo!

brawl [brɔl] *s* bagarre *f*, querelle *f* ‖ *intr* se bagarrer, se quereller
brawler ['brɔlər] *s* bagarreur *m*
brawn [brɔn] *s* muscle *m*; muscles bien développés; (culin) fromage *m* de cochon
brawn·y ['brɔni] *adj* (*comp* -ier; *super* -iest) bien découplé, musclé
bray [bre] *s* braiment *m* ‖ *intr* braire
braze [brez] *tr* braser
brazen ['brezən] *adj* effronté ‖ *tr*—**to brazen through** mener à bonne fin avec une effronterie audacieuse
Brazil [brə'zɪl] *s* le Brésil
Brazilian [brə'zɪljən] *adj* brésilien ‖ *s* (*person*) Brésilien *m*
Brazil' nut' *s* noix *f* du Brésil
breach [britʃ] *s* (*in a wall*) brèche *f*; (*violation*) infraction *f* ‖ *tr* ouvrir une brèche dans
breach' of con'tract *s* rupture *f* de contrat
breach' of prom'ise *s* rupture *f* de fiançailles
breach' of the peace' *s* attentat *m* contre l'ordre public
breach' of trust' *s* abus *m* de confiance
bread [brɛd] *s* pain *m* ‖ *tr* paner, gratiner
bread' and but'ter *s* (fig) gagne-pain *m*
bread'bas'ket *s* panier *m* à pain, corbeille *f* à pain
bread'board' *s* planche *f* à pain
bread' crumbs' *spl* chapelure *f*
breaded *adj* (culin) au gratin
bread'ed veal' cut'let *s* escalope *f* panée de veau
bread'fruit' *s* fruit *m* à pain; (*tree*) arbre *m* à pain, jacquier *m*
bread' knife' *s* couteau *m* à pain
breadth [brɛdθ] *s* largeur *f*
bread'win'ner *s* soutien *m* de famille
break [brek] *s* rupture *f*; (*of an object*) brisure *f*, cassure *f*; (*in time or space*) trou *m*, pause *f*; (slang) chance *f* ‖ *v* (*pret* **broke** [brok]; *pp* **broken**) *tr* rompre, briser, casser; (*a law*) violer; (*the heart*) fendre; (*one's word*) manquer à; (*a will; a soldier by reducing his rank*) casser; **to break bread** rompre le pain; **to break down** (*for analysis*) analyser; **to break in** (*a door*) enfoncer; (*a new car*) roder ‖ *intr* rompre, briser, se briser; (*said of clouds*) se dissiper; (*said of waves*) déferler; **to break down** avoir une panne
breakable ['brekəbəl] *adj* fragile
breakage ['brekɪdʒ] *s* casse *f*
break'down' *s* (*stoppage*) arrêt *m*; (*disaster*) débâcle *f*; (*of health*) épuisement *m*; (*of negotiations*) rupture *f*; (*for analysis*) analyse *f*, ventilation *f*; (mach) panne *f*
breaker ['brekər] *s* brisant *m*
breakfast ['brɛkfəst] *s* **petit déjeuner** *m* ‖ *intr* prendre le petit déjeuner
break'fast food' *s* céréales *fpl* (pour le petit déjeuner)
break'neck' *adj* vertigineux; **at breakneck speed** à tombeau ouvert
break' of day' *s* point *m* du jour

break'through' *s* (mil) percée *f*; (fig) découverte *f* sensationnelle
break'up' *s* dissolution *f*; écroulement *m*; (*in health*) abattement *m*
break'wa'ter *s* digue *f*, brise-lames *m*
breast [brɛst] *s* sein *m*; (*of cooked chicken*) blanc *m*; **to make a clean breast of it** se déboutonner
breast'bone' *s* sternum *m*; (*of fowl*) bréchet *m*
breast' feed'ing *s* allaitement *m*
breast'plate' *s* (*of high priest*) pectoral *m*; (*of armor*) plastron *m*
breast'stroke' *s* brasse *f*
breast'work' *s* (mil) parapet *m*
breath [brɛθ] *s* haleine *f*, souffle *m*; **last breath** dernier soupir *m*; **out of breath** hors d'haleine
breathe [brið] *tr* & *intr* respirer, souffler; **not to breathe a word** ne pas souffler mot
breathing ['briðɪŋ] *s* souffle *m*
breath'ing space' *s* répit *m*
breathless ['brɛθlɪs] *adj* haletant, hors d'haleine; inanimé
breath'tak'ing *adj* émouvant, sensationnel
breech [britʃ] *s* culasse *f*
breech'es bu'oy *s* (naut) bouée-culotte *f*
breed [brid] *s* race *f* ‖ *v* (*pret* & *pp* **bred** [brɛd]) *tr* engendrer; (*e.g., cattle*) élever ‖ *intr* se reproduire
breeder ['bridər] *s* éleveur *m*
breeding ['bridɪŋ] *s* (*of animals*) élevage *m*; **good breeding** savoir-vivre *m*
breeze [briz] *s* brise *f*
breez·y ['brizi] *adj* (*comp* -ier; *super* -iest) aéré; (coll) désinvolte, dégagé
brethren ['brɛðrɪn] *spl* frères *mpl*
Breton ['brɛtən] *adj* breton ‖ *s* (*language*) breton *m*; (*person*) Breton *m*
breviar·y ['brivɪ‚ɛri], ['brɛvɪ‚ɛri] *s* (*pl* -ies) (eccl) bréviaire *m*
brevi·ty ['brɛvɪti] *s* (*pl* -ties) brièveté *f*
brew [bru] *s* breuvage *m*, infusion *f* ‖ *tr* infuser; (*beer*) brasser ‖ *intr* s'infuser
brewer ['bru·ər] *s* brasseur *m*
brew'er's yeast' *s* levure *f* de bière
brewer·y ['bru·əri] *s* (*pl* -ies) brasserie *f*
brewing ['bru·ɪŋ] *s* brassage *m*
bribe [braɪb] *s* pot-de-vin *m* ‖ *tr* corrompre, suborner, soudoyer
briber·y ['braɪbəri] *s* (*pl* -ies) corruption *f*, subornation *f*
brick [brɪk] *s* brique *f* ‖ *tr* briqueter
brick'bat' *s* brocard *m*; **to hurl brickbats** lancer des brocards
brick'lay'er *s* briqueteur *m*
brick'work' *s* briquetage *m*
brick'yard' *s* briqueterie *f*
bridal ['braɪdəl] *adj* nuptial
bride [braɪd] *s* (nouvelle) mariée *f*
bride'groom' *s* (nouveau) marié *m*
brides'maid' *s* demoiselle *f* d'honneur
bride'-to-be' *s* future femme *f*
bridge [brɪdʒ] *s* pont *m*; (cards, dentistry) bridge *m*; (naut) passerelle *f*; **to burn one's bridges** couper les ponts ‖ *tr* construire un pont sur; **to bridge a gap** combler une lacune

bridge'head' s (mil) tête f de pont
bridle ['braidəl] s bride f; (fig) frein m || tr brider; (fig) freiner || intr se raidir
bri'dle path' s piste f cavalière
brief [brif] adj bref || s résumé m; (law) dossier m; **briefs** slip m; **to hold a brief for** plaider pour || tr mettre au courant
brief' case' s serviette f
briefing ['brifɪŋ] s briefing m, renseignements mpl tactiques
briefly ['brifli] adv bref, brièvement, en substance
brier ['braɪ.ər] s ronce f
brig [brɪg] s prison f navale; (ship) brick m
brigade [brɪ'ged] s brigade f
brigadier [ˌbrɪgə'dɪr] s général m de brigade
brigand ['brɪgənd] s brigand m
brigantine ['brɪgənˌtin], ['brɪgənˌtaɪn] s brigantin m
bright [braɪt] adj brillant; (day) clair; (color) vif; (person) (fig) brillant
brighten ['braɪtən] tr faire briller; égayer, réjouir || intr s'éclaircir
bright' ide'a s (coll) idée f lumineuse
brightness ['braɪtnɪs] s éclat m, clarté f; (of mind) vivacité f
brilliance ['brɪljəns] or **brilliancy** ['brɪljənsi] s brillant m, éclat m
brilliant ['brɪljənt] adj & s brillant m
brim [brɪm] s bord m || v (pret & pp brimmed; ger brimming) intr—**to brim over (with)** déborder (de)
brimful ['brɪmˌfʊl] adj à ras bords
brim'stone' s soufre m
brine [braɪn] s saumure f
bring [brɪŋ] v (pret & pp brought [brɔt]) tr apporter; (a person) amener, conduire; **to bring back** rapporter; (a person) ramener; **to bring down** (baggage) descendre; (with a gun) abattre; **to bring in** entrer, introduire; **to bring out** faire ressortir; (e.g., a book) publier; **to bring together** réunir; **to bring to pass** causer, opérer; **to bring up** éduquer, élever; (baggage) monter
bring'ing-up' s éducation f
brink [brɪŋk] s bord m
brisk [brɪsk] adj vif, actif, animé
brisket ['brɪskɪt] s (culin) poitrine f
bristle ['brɪsəl] s soie f; (of brush) poil m || tr hérisser || intr se hérisser
bristling ['brɪslɪŋ] adj hérissé
Bris'tol board' ['brɪstəl] s bristol m
Britain ['brɪtən] s Grande-Bretagne f; la Grande-Bretagne
British ['brɪtɪʃ] adj britannique || **the British** les Britanniques
Britisher ['brɪtɪʃər] s Britannique mf
Briton ['brɪtən] s Britannique mf
Brittany ['brɪtəni] s Bretagne f; la Bretagne
brittle ['brɪtəl] adj fragile, cassant
broach [brotʃ] s broche f; (for tapping casks) mèche f à percer || tr (e.g., a keg of beer) mettre en perce; (a subject) entamer

broad [brɔd] adj (wide) large; (immense) vaste; (mind, views) libéral, tolérant; (accent) fort, prononcé; (use, sense) répandu, général; (daylight) plein; (joke, story) grossier, salé
broad'-backed' adj d'une belle carrure
broad'brimmed' adj à larges bords
broad'cast' adj diffusé; (rad) radiodiffusé || s (rad) radiodiffusion f, émission f || v (pret & pp -cast) tr diffuser, répandre || (pret & pp -cast or -casted) tr radiodiffuser || intr (rad) émettre
broad'casting sta'tion s station f d'émission
broad'cloth' s popeline f
broaden ['brɔdən] tr élargir || intr s'élargir
broad'-gauge' adj à voie large
broad' jump' s saut m en longueur
broad'-mind'ed adj à l'esprit large
broad'side' s bordée f; (typ) placard m
brocade [bro'ked] s brocart m || tr brocher
broccoli ['brakəli] s brocoli m
brochure [bro'ʃʊr] s brochure f
brogue [brog] s accent m irlandais; (shoe) soulier m grossier
broil [brɔɪl] s grillade f; (quarrel) rixe f || tr & intr griller
broiler ['brɔɪlər] s gril m
broke [brok] adj (slang) fauché
broken ['brokən] adj brisé, cassé; (promise; ranks; beam) rompu
brok'en-down' adj délabré; en panne
bro'ken-heart'ed adj au cœur brisé
broker ['brokər] s courtier m
brokerage ['brokərɪdʒ] s courtage m
bromide ['bromaɪd] s bromure m; (coll) platitude f
bromine ['bromin] s brome m
bronchial ['brɑŋkɪ.əl] adj bronchique
bron'chial tube' s bronche f
bronchitis [brɑŋ'kaɪtɪs] s bronchite f
bron·co ['brɑŋko] s (pl -cos) cheval m sauvage
bronze [brɑnz] adj bronzé || s bronze m || tr bronzer || intr se bronzer
brooch [brotʃ], [brutʃ] s broche f
brood [brud] s couvée f; (of children) nichée f || intr couver; (to sulk) broyer du noir; **to brood over** songer sombrement à
brood' hen' s couveuse f
brood'mare' s poulinière f
brook [brʊk] s ruisseau m || tr—**to brook no** ne pas tolérer
brooklet ['brʊklɪt] s ruisseau m
broom [brum], [brʊm] s balai m; (bot) genêt m
broom'stick' s manche m à balai
broth [brɔθ], [brɑθ] s bouillon m, consommé m
brothel ['brɑθəl], ['brɑðəl] s bordel m
brother ['brʌðər] s frère m
broth'er·hood' s fraternité f
broth'er-in-law' s (pl **brothers-in-law**) beau-frère m
brotherly ['brʌðərli] adj fraternel || adv fraternellement
brow [braʊ] s (forehead) front m;

(*eyebrow*) sourcil *m*; **to knit one's brow** froncer le sourcil
brow'beat' *v* (*pret* **-beat**; *pp* **-beaten**) *tr* rabrouer, brusquer
brown [braʊn] *adj* marron; (*paper*) gris; (*bread*) bis; (*shoes*) jaune; (*butter*) roux, noir; (*hair*) brun, châtain ‖ *tr* brunir; (culin) rissoler, dorer
brownish ['braʊnɪʃ] *adj* brunâtre
brown' stud'y *s*—**in a brown study** absorbé dans des méditations
brown' sug'ar *s* cassonade *f*, sucre *m* brut
browse [braʊz] *intr* (*said of animals*) brouter; (*said of booklovers*) butiner; (*said of customers for secondhand books*) bouquiner
bruise [bruz] *s* (*on body or fruit*) meurtrissure *f*; (*on body*) contusion *f* ‖ *tr* meurtrir, contusionner
bruiser ['bruzər] *s* (coll) costaud *m*
bruit [brut] *tr* ébruiter; **to bruit about** répandre
brunette [bru'nɛt] *adj* & *s* brune *f*, brunette *f*
brunt [brʌnt] *s* choc *m*, assaut *m*; **to bear the brunt of** (fig) faire tous les frais de
brush [brʌʃ] *s* brosse *f*; (*countryside*) brousse *f*; (elec) balai *m* ‖ *tr* brosser; **to brush aside** écarter ‖ *intr*—**to brush against** frôler; **to brush up on** repasser, rafraîchir
brush'-off' *s* (slang) affront *m*; **to give a brush-off to** (slang) expédier avec rudesse
brush'wood' *s* broussailles *fpl*, brindilles *fpl*
brusque [brʌsk] *adj* brusque
Brussels ['brʌsəlz] *s* Bruxelles *f*
Brus'sels sprouts' *mpl* chou *m* de Bruxelles
brutal ['brutəl] *adj* brutal
brutali·ty [bru'tælɪti] *s* (*pl* **-ties**) brutalité *f*
brute [brut] *adj* brutal ‖ *s* bête *f*, animal *m*; (*person*) brute *f*, animal *m*
brutish ['brutɪʃ] *adj* grossier, brut, brutal
bubble ['bʌbəl] *s* bulle *f* ‖ *intr* bouillonner; (*said of drink*) pétiller; **to bubble over** déborder
bub'ble gum' *s* gomme *f* à claquer
bub·bly ['bʌbli] *adj* (*comp* **-blier**; *super* **-bliest**) bouillonnant, gazeux
bubon'ic plague' [bju'banɪk] *s* peste *f* bubonique
buccaneer [ˌbʌkə'nɪr] *s* boucanier *m*
buck [bʌk] *s* (*red deer*) cerf *m*; (*fallow deer*) daim *m*; (*roebuck*) chevreuil *m*; (slang) dollar *m*; the male of many animals such as: (*goat*) bouc *m*; (*rabbit*) lapin *m*; (*hare*) lièvre *m*; **to pass the buck** (coll) renvoyer la balle ‖ *tr*—**to buck off** (*a rider*) désarçonner; **to buck up** (coll) remonter le courage de ‖ *intr*—**to buck up** (coll) reprendre courage
bucket ['bʌkɪt] *s* seau *m*; **to kick the bucket** (slang) casser sa pipe
buck'et seat' *s* siège *m* baquet

buckle ['bʌkəl] *s* boucle *f* ‖ *tr* boucler ‖ *intr* arquer, gauchir; **to buckle down** s'appliquer
buck' pri'vate *s* simple soldat *m*
buckram ['bʌkrəm] *s* bougran *m*
buck'saw' *s* scie *f* à bûches
buck'shot' *s* gros plomb *m*
buck'tooth' *s* (*pl* **-teeth**) dent *f* saillante
buck'wheat' *s* sarrasin *m*
buck'wheat cake' *s* crêpe *f* de sarrasin
bud [bʌd] *s* bouton *m*, bourgeon *m* ‖ *v* (*pret* & *pp* **budded**; *ger* **budding**) *intr* boutonner, bourgeonner
Buddhism ['bʊdɪzəm] *s* bouddhisme *m*
Buddhist ['bʊdɪst] *adj* & *s* bouddhiste *mf*
budding ['bʌdɪŋ] *adj* en bouton; (*beginning*) en germe, naissant
bud·dy ['bʌdi] *s* (*pl* **-dies**) (coll) copain *m*
budge [bʌdʒ] *tr* faire bouger ‖ *intr* bouger
budget ['bʌdʒɪt] *s* budget *m* ‖ *tr* comptabiliser, inscrire au budget
budgetary ['bʌdʒɪˌteri] *adj* budgétaire
buff [bʌf] *adj* (*color*) chamois ‖ *s* (coll) fanatique *mf*, enthousiaste *mf* ‖ *tr* polir, émeuler
buffa·lo ['bʌfəˌlo] *s* (*pl* **-loes** or **-los**) bison *m*; (*water buffalo; Cape buffalo*) buffle *m*
buffer ['bʌfər] *s* (mach) brunissoir *m*; (rr) (*on cars*) tampon *m*; (rr) (*at end of track*) butoir *m*
buff'er state' *s* état *m* tampon
buff'er zone' *s* zone *f* tampon
buffet [bu'fe] *s* buffet *m* ‖ ['bʌfɪt] *tr* frapper (violemment)
buffet' lunch' [bu'fe] *s* lunch *m*
buffoon [bə'fun] *s* bouffon *m*
buffooner·y [bə'funəri] *s* (*pl* **-ies**) bouffonnerie *f*
bug [bʌg] *s* insecte *m*; (*germ*) microbe *m*; (*in a mechanical device*) vice *m*, défaut *m*; (coll) idée *f* fixe, lutin *m*; (Brit) punaise *f*; **he's a bug for . . .** (coll) il est fou de . . . ‖ *v* (*pret* & *pp* **bugged**; *ger* **bugging**) *tr* (slang) installer une table d'écoute dans; installer un microphone dans; (*to annoy*) (slang) embêter, emmerder
bug'bear' *s* épouvantail *m*, croquemitaine *m*; (*pet peeve*) bête *f* noire
bug'-eyed' *adj* (slang) aux yeux saillants
bug·gy ['bʌgi] *adj* (*comp* **-gier**; *super* **-giest**) infesté d'insectes; infesté; (slang) fou ‖ *s* (*pl* **-gies**) buggy *m* à quatre roues; (*two-wheeled*) buggy, boguet *m*
bug'house' *s* (slang) cabanon *m*
bugle ['bjugəl] *s* (bot) bugle *f*; (mus) clairon *m* ‖ *tr* & *intr* claironner
bu'gle call' *s* sonnerie *f* de clairon
bugler ['bjuglər] *s* clairon *m*
build [bɪld] *s* structure *f*; (*of human body*) taille *f*, charpente *f* ‖ *v* (*pret* & *pp* **built** [bɪlt]) *tr* bâtir, construire
builder ['bɪldər] *s* constructeur *m*; (*of bridges, roads, etc.*) entrepreneur *m*

building ['bɪldɪŋ] s immeuble m, bâtiment m, édifice m

build'ing and loan' associa'tion s société f de prêt à la construction

build'ing lot' s terrain m à bâtir

built'-in' adj incorporé

built'-up' adj aggloméré; (heel) renforcé; (land) bâti

bulb [bʌlb] s bulbe m; (of vaporizer) poire f; (bot) oignon m; (elec) ampoule f

bulbous ['bʌlbəs] adj bulbeux

Bulgaria [bʌl'gɛrɪ·ə] s Bulgarie f; la Bulgarie

Bulgarian [bʌl'gɛrɪ·ən] adj bulgare || s (language) bulgare m; (person) Bulgare mf

bulge [bʌldʒ] s bosse f, bombement m; (mil) saillant m || tr bourrer, gonfler || intr faire une bosse, bomber

bulk [bʌlk] s masse f, volume m; **in bulk** en bloc; (com) en vrac || tr entasser (en vrac) || intr tenir de la place; **to bulk large** devenir important

bulk'head' s (naut) cloison f

bulk·y ['bʌlki] adj (comp -ier; super -iest) volumineux

bull [bul] s taureau m; (on the stock exchange) haussier m, spéculateur m à la hausse; (eccl) bulle f; (policeman) (slang) flic m, vache f; (exaggeration) (slang) blague f, boniment m, chiqué m; **like a bull in a china shop** comme un éléphant dans un magasin de porcelaine; **to take the bull by the horns** (fig) prendre le taureau par les cornes || tr—**to bull the market** jouer à la hausse

bull'dog' s bouledogue m

bull'doze' tr passer au bulldozer; (coll) intimider

bulldozer ['bul,dozər] s chasse-terre m, bulldozer m

bullet ['bulɪt] s balle f

bulletin ['bulətɪn] s bulletin m; (e.g., of a university) annuaire m

bul'letin board' s tableau m d'affichage

bul'let-proof' adj à l'épreuve des balles || tr blinder

bul'let-proof vest' s gilet m pare-balles

bull'fight' s course f de taureaux

bull'fight'er s torero m

bull'fight'ing s tauromachie f

bull'finch' s bouvreuil m

bull'frog' s grenouille f d'Amérique

bull'head' s (ichth) chabot m, cabot m; (miller's-thumb) meunier m, cabot

bull'head'ed adj entêté

bullion ['buljən] s (of gold) or m; (of silver) argent m; encaisse f métallique, lingots mpl d'or, lingots d'argent; (on uniform) cordonnet m d'or, cordonnet d'argent

bull' mar'ket s marché m à la hausse

bullock ['bulək] s bœuf m

bull' pen' s toril m; (jail) poste m de détention préventive

bull'ring' s arène f, arène pour les courses de taureaux

bull's'-eye' s mouche f; **to hit the bull's-eye** faire mouche

bull's'-eye win'dow s œil-de-bœuf m

bull'ter'rier s bull-terrier m

bul·ly ['buli] adj (coll) épatant || s (pl -lies) brute f, brutal m; (at school) brimeur m, tyranneau m || v (pret & pp -lied) tr brutaliser, malmener; (at school) brimer, tyranniser

bulrush ['bul,rʌʃ] s jonc m des marais

bulwark ['bulwərk] s rempart m; (naut) pavois m || tr garnir de remparts; (fig) protéger

bum [bʌm] adj (slang) moche, de camelote || s (slang) clochard m || v (pret & pp bummed; ger bumming) tr & intr (slang) écornifler

bumble ['bʌmbəl] tr bâcler || intr (to stumble) trébucher; (in speaking) bafouiller; (said of bee) bourdonner

bum'ble·bee' s bourdon m

bump [bʌmp] s choc m; (protuberance) bosse f; (of car on rough road) cahot m || tr cogner, tamponner, heurter; **to bump off** (to kill) (slang) buter || intr se cogner; **to bump along** (said of car) cahoter; **to bump into** buter contre, choquer

bumper ['bʌmpər] adj exceptionnel || s (aut) pare-chocs m; (rr) tampon m

bumpkin ['bʌmpkɪn] s péquenot m, rustre m

bumptious ['bʌmpʃəs] adj outrecuidant

bump·y ['bʌmpi] adj (comp -ier; super -iest) bosselé; (road) cahoteux

bun [bʌn] s brioche f, petit pain m; (hair) chignon m

bunch [bʌntʃ] s botte f; (of bananas) régime m; (of flowers) bouquet m; (of grapes) grappe f; (of keys) trousseau m; (of people) groupe m, bande f; (of ribbons) flot m; (of twigs) paquet m; (on body) bosse f || tr grouper || intr se serrer

buncombe ['bʌŋkəm] s (coll) balivernes fpl, sornettes fpl

bundle ['bʌndəl] s paquet m; (of banknotes, papers, etc.) liasse f || tr empaqueter, mettre en paquet; **to bundle up** (in warm clothing) emmitoufler || intr—**to bundle up** s'emmitoufler

bung [bʌŋ] s bonde f || tr mettre une bonde à

bungalow ['bʌŋgə,lo] s bungalow m

bung'hole' s bonde f

bungle ['bʌŋgəl] s gâchis m, bousillage m || tr saboter, bousiller || intr saboter

bungler ['bʌŋglər] s gâcheur m, bousilleur m

bungling ['bʌŋglɪŋ] adj gauche, maladroit || s maladresse f

bunion ['bʌnjən] s oignon m (au pied)

bunk [bʌŋk] s couchette f; (slang) balivernes fpl, sornettes fpl || intr (coll) se coucher

bunk' bed' s (naut) cadre m

bunker ['bʌŋkər] s (golf) banquette f; (naut) soute f

bun·ny ['bʌni] s (pl -nies) petit lapin m

bunting ['bʌntɪŋ] s drapeaux mpl; (cloth) étamine f; (orn) bruant m

buoy [bɔɪ], ['bu·i] s bouée f || tr—**to buoy up** faire flotter; (fig) soutenir

buoyancy ['bɔɪ·ənsi], ['bujənsi] *s* flottabilité *f*
buoyant ['bɔɪ·ənt], ['bujənt] *adj* flottant; (*cheerful*) plein d'allant, plein de ressort
bur [bʌr] *s* (*of chestnut*) bogue *f*; (*ragged metal edge*) bavure *f*, barbe *f*
burble ['bʌrbəl] *s* murmure *m* ‖ *intr* murmurer
burden ['bʌrdən] *s* fardeau *m*, charge *f*; (mus) refrain *m* ‖ *tr* charger
burdensome ['bʌrdənsəm] *adj* onéreux
burdock ['bʌrdɑk] *s* bardane *f*
bureau ['bjʊro] *s* commode *f*, chiffonier *m*; (*office*) bureau *m*
bureaucra·cy [bju'rɑkrəsi] *s* (*pl* -**cies**) bureaucratie *f*
bureaucrat ['bjʊrə‚kræt] *s* bureaucrate *mf*
bureaucratic [‚bjʊrə'krætɪk] *adj* bureaucratique
bu'reau of vi'tal statis'tics *s* bureau *m* de l'état civil
burg [bʌrg] *s* (coll) hameau *m*, patelin *m*; (coll) ville *f*
burglar ['bʌrglər] *s* cambrioleur *m*
bur'glar alarm' *s* signalisateur *m* antivol, sonnette *f* d'alarme
burglarize ['bʌrglə‚raɪz] *tr* cambrioler
bur'glar·proof' *adj* incrochetable
burglar·y ['bʌrgləri] *s* (*pl* -**ies**) cambriolage *m*
Burgundian [bər'gʌndɪ·ən] *adj* bourguignon ‖ *s* (*dialect*) bourguignon *m*; (*person*) Bourguignon *m*
Burgundy ['bʌrgəndi] *s* Bourgogne *f*; la Bourgogne ‖ **burgun·dy** *s* (-**dies**) (*wine*) bourgogne *m*
burial ['bɛrɪ·əl] *s* enterrement *m*, inhumation *f*
bur'ial ground' *s* cimetière *m*
burlap ['bʌrlæp] *s* toile *f* d'emballage, serpillière *f*
burlesque [bər'lɛsk] *adj* & *s* burlesque *m* ‖ *tr* parodier
burlesque' show' *s* music-hall *m*
bur·ly ['bʌrli] *adj* (*comp* -**lier**; *super* -**liest**) solide, costaud
Burma ['bʌrmə] *s* Birmanie *f*; la Birmanie
Bur·mese [bər'miz] *adj* birman ‖ *s* (*pl* -**mese**) (*language*) birman *m*; (*person*) Birman *m*
burn [bʌrn] *s* brûlure *f* ‖ *v* (*pret & pp* **burned** or **burnt** [bʌrnt]) *tr* & *intr* brûler; **to burn out** (elec) griller
burner ['bʌrnər] *s* brûleur *m*; (*using gas*) bec *m*; (*of a stove*) feu *m*
burning ['bʌrnɪŋ] *adj* brûlant; (*in flames*) en feu ‖ *s* brûlure *f*; (*fire*) incendie *m*
burnish ['bʌrnɪʃ] *tr* brunir, polir
burrow ['bʌro] *s* terrier *m* ‖ *tr* creuser ‖ *intr* se terrer
bursar ['bʌrsər] *s* économe *m*
burst [bʌrst] *s* éclat *m*, explosion *f* ‖ *v* (*pret & pp* **burst**) *tr* faire éclater; (*a balloon*) crever; (*a boiler; one's buttons*) faire sauter ‖ *intr* éclater, exploser; (*said of tire*) crever; **to burst into tears** fondre en larmes; **to burst out laughing** éclater de rire

bur·y ['bɛri] *v* (*pret & pp* -**ied**) *tr* enterrer, ensevelir; (*e.g., pirate treasure*) enfouir
bus [bʌs] *s* (*pl* **busses** or **buses**) autobus *m*; (*interurban or sightseeing*) car *m*, autocar *m* ‖ *v* (*pret & pp* **bused** or **bussed**; *ger* **busing** or **bussing**) *tr* transporter en autobus
bus'boy' *s* aide-serveur *m*
bush [bʊʃ] *s* buisson *m*; (*shrub*) arbuste *m*; (*in Africa and Australia*) brousse *f*; **to beat around the bush** tourner autour du pot, tortiller
bushed [bʊʃt] *adj* (coll) éreinté
bushel ['bʊʃəl] *s* boisseau *m*
bushing ['bʊʃɪŋ] *s* manchon *m*, douille *f*, bague *f*, coussinet *m*
bush·y ['bʊʃi] *adj* (*comp* -**ier**; *super* -**iest**) (*countryside*) buissonneux; (*hair*) touffu; (*eyebrows*) broussailleux
business ['bɪznɪs] *adj* commercial ‖ *s* affaires *fpl*; (*subject*) sujet *m*; (theat) jeux *mpl* de scène; **it's none of your business** cela ne vous regarde pas; **mind your own business!** occupez-vous de vos affaires!, faites votre métier!; **to mean business** (coll) ne pas plaisanter; **to send about one's business** envoyer paître
busi'ness dis'trict *s* quartier *m* commerçant
busi'ness hours' *s* heures *fpl* d'ouverture
busi'ness house' *s* maison *f* de commerce
busi'ness·like' *adj* pratique; (*manner, transaction*) sérieux
busi'ness·man' *s* (*pl* -**men'**) homme *m* d'affaires; **big businessman** grand industriel *m*, chef *m* d'industrie
busi'ness man'ager *s* directeur *m* commercial
busi'ness reply' card' *s* carte *f* postale avec réponse payée
busi'ness suit' *s* complet *m* veston
busi'ness·wom'an *s* (*pl* -**wom'en**) femme *f* d'affaires
buskin ['bʌskɪn] *s* brodequin *m*
bus' sta'tion *s* gare *f* routière
bus' stop' *s* arrêt *m* d'autobus
bust [bʌst] *s* buste *m*; (*of woman*) gorge *f*, buste; (slang) faillite *f* ‖ *tr* (mil) limoger; (slang) casser ‖ *intr* (slang) échouer
busting ['bʌstɪŋ] *s* (mil) cassation *f*
bustle ['bʌsəl] *s* remue-ménage *m*, affairement *m*, branle-bas *m* ‖ *intr* se remuer, s'affairer
bustling ['bʌslɪŋ] *adj* affairé
bus·y ['bɪzi] *adj* (*comp* -**ier**; *super* -**iest**) occupé ‖ *v* (*pret & pp* -**ied**) *tr* —**to busy oneself with** s'occuper de
bus'y·bod'y *s* (*pl* -**ies**) officieux *m*
bus'y sig'nal *s* (telp) signal *m* de ligne occupée
but [bʌt] *adv* seulement; ne . . . que, e.g., **to have nothing but trouble** n'avoir que des ennuis; **but for** sans; **but for that** à part cela ‖ *prep* sauf, excepté; **all but** presque ‖ *conj* mais
butcher ['bʊtʃər] *s* boucher *m* ‖ *tr* (*an*

animal for meat) abattre, dépecer; (*to massacre; to bungle*) massacrer
butch'er knife' *s* couperet *m*, coutelas *m* (de boucher)
butch'er shop' *s* boucherie *f*
butler ['bʌtlər] *s* maître *m* d'hôtel, intendant *m*
butt [bʌt] *s* bout *m*; (*cask*) futaille *f*; (*of a gun*) crosse *f*; (*of a cigarette*) mégot *m*; (*of a joke*) souffre-douleur *m*, plastron *m*; (*blow*) coup *m* de tête, coup de corne; (slang) postérieur *m*, derrière *m* ‖ *tr* (*like a goat*) donner un coup de corne à ‖ *intr*— **to butt up against** buter contre; **to butt in** (coll) intervenir sans façon
butte [bjut] *s* butte *f*, tertre *m*, puy *m*
butt' end' *s* gros bout *m*
butter ['bʌtər] *s* beurre *m* ‖ *tr* beurrer; **to butter up** (coll) passer de la pommade à, pateliner
but'ter·cup' *s* renoncule *f*, bouton-d'or *m*
but'ter dish' *s* beurrier *m*, beurrière *f*
but'ter·fat' *s* crème *f*
but'ter·fin'gered *adj* maladroit
but'ter·fin'gers *s* brise-tout *mf*
but'ter·fly' *s* (*pl* -**flies**) papillon *m*
but'ter knife' *s* couteau *m* à beurre
but'ter·milk' *s* babeurre *m*
but'ter·scotch' *s* caramel *m* au beurre
buttocks ['bʌtəks] *spl* fesses *fpl*
button ['bʌtən] *s* bouton *m* ‖ *tr* boutonner
but'ton·hole' *s* boutonnière *f* ‖ *tr* (coll) retenir (*qqn*) par le pan de sa veste
but'ton·hook' *s* tire-bouton *m*
buttress ['bʌtrɪs] *s* contrefort *m* ‖ *tr* arc-bouter; (fig) étayer
buxom ['bʌksəm] *adj* plantureuse
buy [baɪ] *s*—**a good buy** (coll) une bonne affaire ‖ *v* (*pret & pp* **bought** [bɔt]) *tr* acheter; (*a ticket*) prendre; **to buy a drink for** payer un verre à; **to buy back** racheter; **to buy from** acheter à or de; **to buy out** (*a part-*

ner) désintéresser; **to buy s.o. off** se débarrasser de qn, racheter qn; **to buy up** accaparer
buyer ['baɪ·ər] *s* acheteur *m*
buzz [bʌz] *s* bourdonnement *m*; **to give s.o. a buzz** (*on the telephone*) (coll) passer un coup de fil à ‖ *tr* (aer) survoler à basse altitude ‖ *intr* bourdonner
buzzard ['bʌzərd] *s* buse *f*
buzz' bomb' *s* bombe *f* volante
buzzer ['bʌzər] *s* trembleur *m*
buzz' saw' *s* scie *f* circulaire
by [baɪ] *adv* près, auprès; (*aside*) de côté; **by and by** tout à l'heure, sous peu; **by and large** généralement parlant ‖ *prep* par; (*near*) près de; **by a head** (*taller*) d'une tête; **by day** pendant la journée; **by far** de beaucoup; **by Monday** d'ici à lundi; **by profession** de profession; **by the way** à propos; **to be followed (loved, etc.)** **by** être suivi (aimé, etc.) de
by-and-by ['baɪ·ən'baɪ] *s* proche avenir *m*; **in the sweet by-and-by** à la Saint-Glinglin
by'gone' *adj* d'autrefois, passé
by'law' *s* ordonnance *f*, règlement *m*
by'-line' *s* signature *f* de journaliste
by'-pass' *s* déviation *f*; (elec) dérivation *f* ‖ *tr* éviter, contourner; (mach) amener or placer en dérivation
by'-play' *s* (theat) jeu *m* en aparté
by'-prod'uct *s* sous-produit *m*
by'-road' *s* chemin *m* détourné
bystander ['baɪ‚stændər] *s* spectateur *m*, assistant *m*
by'way' *s* chemin *m* écarté, voie *f* indirecte
by'word' *s* dicton *m*, proverbe *m*; objet *m* de dérision
Byzantine ['bɪzən‚tin], [bɪ'zæntin] *adj & s* byzantin *m*
Byzantium [bɪ'zænʃɪ·əm], [bɪ'zæntɪ·əm] *s* Byzance *f*

C

C, c [si] *s* IIIᵉ lettre de l'alphabet
cab [kæb] *s* taxi *m*; (*of locomotive or truck*) cabine *f*; (*hansom*) fiacre *m*, cab *m*
cabaret [‚kæbə're] *s* boîte *f* de nuit, cabaret *m*
cabbage ['kæbɪdʒ] *s* chou *m*
cab'driv'er *s* chauffeur *m* de taxi
cabin ['kæbɪn] *s* case *f*, cabane *f*; (*of ship or airplane*) cabine *f*
cab'in boy' *s* (naut) mousse *m*
cabinet ['kæbɪnɪt] *s* cabinet *m*; (*cupboard*; *radio cabinet*) meuble *m*; meuble à tiroirs; (*of professional men*) étude *f*, cabinet; (*of officers*) cabinet, bureau *m* directoire, comité *m*, conseil *m*

cab'inet-mak'er *s* ébéniste *m*, menuisier *m*
cab'inet mem'ber *s* ministre *m*
cable ['kebəl] *s* câble *m* ‖ *tr & intr* câbler
ca'ble car' *s* funiculaire *m*, téléférique *m*
ca'ble·gram' *s* câblogramme *m*
ca'ble ship' *s* câblier *m*
ca'ble's length' *s* encablure *f*
caboose [kə'bus] *s* (naut) coquerie *f*; (rr) fourgon *m* de queue, wagon *m* du personnel
cab'stand' *s* station *f* de taxi
cache [kæʃ] *s* cachette *f*, cache *f* ‖ *tr* mettre dans une cachette, cacher
cachet [kæ'ʃe] *s* cachet *m*

cackle ['kækəl] *s* caquet *m* ‖ *intr* caqueter; (*said of goose*) cacarder
cacopho·ny [kə'kɑfəni] *s* (*pl* -nies) cacophonie *f*
cac·tus ['kæktəs] *s* (*pl* -tuses or -ti [taɪ]) cactus *m*
cad [kæd] *s* malotru *m*
cadaver [kə'dævər] *s* cadavre *m*
cad·dy ['kædi] *s* (*pl* -dies) boîte *f* à thé; (*person*) cadet *m*, caddie *m*
cadence ['kedəns] *s* cadence *f*
cadet [kə'det] *s* cadet *m*
cadmium ['kædmɪ·əm] *s* cadmium *m*
Caesar'ean opera'tion [sɪ'zerɪ·ən] *s* césarienne *f*
café [kæ'fe] *s* cabaret *m*; café-restaurant *m*
ca'fé soci'ety *s* gens *mpl* chic des cabarets à la mode
cafeteria [ˌkæfə'tɪrɪ·ə] *s* cafétéria *f*, restaurant *m* de libre-service
caffeine [kæ'fin], ['kæfin], ['kæfi·ɪn] *s* caféine *f*
cage [kedʒ] *s* cage *f* ‖ *tr* mettre en cage
ca·gey ['kedʒi] *adj* (*comp* -gier; *super* -giest) (coll) rusé, fin
cahoots [kə'huts] *s*—**in cahoots** (slang) de mèche
Cain [ken] *s* Caïn *m*; **to raise Cain** (coll) faire le diable à quatre
Cairo ['kaɪro] *s* Le Caire
caisson ['kesən] *s* caisson *m*
cais'son disease' *s* maladie *f* des caissons
cajole [kə'dʒol] *tr* cajoler, enjôler
cajoler·y [kə'dʒoləri] *s* (*pl* -ies) cajolerie *f*, enjôlement *m*
cake ˈ[kek] *s* gâteau *m*; (*one-layer cake*) galette *f*; (*pastry*) pâtisserie *f*; (*of soap, wax*) pain *m*; (*of ice*) bloc *m*; (*crust*) croûte *f*; **to sell like hot cakes** (coll) se vendre comme des petits pains; **to take the cake** (coll) être la fin des haricots ‖ *tr* couvrir d'une croûte ‖ *intr* s'agglutiner, faire croûte
calabash ['kælə,bæʃ] *s* calebasse *f*; (*tree*) calebassier *m*
calaboose ['kælə,bus] *s* (coll) violon *m*, tôle *f*
calamitous [kə'læmɪtəs] *adj* calamiteux
calami·ty [kə'læmɪti] *s* (*pl* -ties) calamité *f*
calci·fy ['kælsɪ,faɪ] *v* (*pret & pp* -fied) *tr* calcifier ‖ *intr* se calcifier
calcium ['kælsɪ·əm] *s* calcium *m*
calculate ['kælkjə,let] *tr & intr* calculer
calculating ['kælkjə,letɪŋ] *adj* calculateur
calculation [ˌkælkjə'leʃən] *s* calcul *m*
calcu·lus ['kælkjələs] *s* (*pl* -luses or -li [ˌlaɪ]) (math, pathol) calcul *m*
caldron ['kɔldrən] *s* (culin) chaudron *m*; (mach) chaudière *f*
calendar ['kæləndər] *s* calendrier *m*
cal'endar year' *s* année *f* civile
calender ['kæləndər] *s* calandre *f* ‖ *tr* calandrer, cylindrer
calf [kæf], [kɑf] *s* (*pl* calves [kævz], [kɑvz]) veau *m*; (*of leg*) mollet *m*

calf'skin' *s* veau *m*, peau *f* de veau
calf's' **liv'er** *s* foie *m* de veau
caliber ['kælɪbər] *s* calibre *m*
calibrate ['kælɪ,bret] *tr* calibrer
cali·co ['kælɪ,ko] *s* (*pl* -coes or -cos) calicot *m*, indienne *f*
California [ˌkælɪ'fɔrnɪ·ə] *s* Californie *f*; la Californie
calipers ['kælɪpərz] *spl* compas *m* à calibrer
caliph ['kelɪf], ['kælɪf] *s* calife *m*
caliphate ['kælɪ,fet] *s* califat *m*
calisthenic [ˌkælɪs'θenɪk] *adj* callisthénique ‖ **calisthenics** *spl* callisthénie *f*
calk [kɔk] *s* crampon *m* à glace ‖ *tr* calfater
call [kɔl] *s* appel *m*; (*cry*) cri *m*; (*visit*) visite *f*; (*at a port*) escale *f*; **to have no call** to n'avoir aucune raison de ‖ *tr* appeler; (*e.g., the doctor*) faire venir; (*a meeting*) convoquer; **to call aside** prendre à part; **to call back** rappeler; **to call down** (*from upstairs*) faire descendre; (*the wrath of the gods*) invoquer; (*to scold*) (coll) gronder; **to call off** (*a dog*) rappeler; (coll) annuler, décommander; **to call the roll** faire l'appel; **to call to mind** rappeler; **to call to order** rappeler à l'ordre; **to call up** (coll) passer un coup de fil à; (mil) mobiliser ‖ *intr* appeler; crier; (*to visit*) faire une visite; (naut) faire escale; **to call upon** faire appel à; **to call upon s.o. to speak** inviter qn à prendre la parole
call' bell' *s* sonnette *f*
call' box' *s* guérite *f* téléphonique
call' boy' *s* (*in a hotel*) chasseur *m*; (theat) avertisseur *m*
caller ['kɔlər] *s* visiteur *m*
call' girl' *s* call-girl *f*
calling ['kɔlɪŋ] *s* vocation *f*, profession *f*; (*of a meeting*) convocation *f*
cal'ling card' *s* carte *f* de visite
call' let'ter *s* (telg, rad) indicatif *m* d'appel
call' mon'ey *s* prêts *mpl* au jour le jour
callous ['kæləs] *adj* (*foot, hand, etc.*) calleux; (*unfeeling*) endurci, insensible
callow ['kælo] *adj* inexpérimenté, novice
cal'low youth' *s* blanc-bec *m*
callus ['kæləs] *s* (*on skin*) cal *m*, durillon *m*, callosité *f*; (bot) cal *m*
calm [kɑm] *adj & s* calme *m* ‖ *tr* calmer; **to calm down** pacifier ‖ *intr* —**to calm down** se calmer; (*said of wind or sea*) calmir
calorie ['kæləri] *s* calorie *f*
calum·ny ['kæləmni] *s* (*pl* -nies) calomnie *f*
calva·ry ['kælvəri] *s* (*pl* -ries) calvaire *m*; **Calvary** le Calvaire
calve [kæv], [kɑv] *intr* vêler
cam [kæm] *s* came *f*
cambric ['kembrɪk] *s* batiste *f*
camel ['kæməl] *s* chameau *m*
camellia [kə'miljə] *s* camélia *m*
came·o ['kæmi,o] *s* (*pl* -os) camée *m*

camera ['kæmərə] s appareil m (photographique)
cam'era·man' s (pl -men') photographe m
camouflage ['kæmə,flɑʒ] s camouflage m || tr camoufler
camp [kæmp] s camp m || intr camper; to go camping faire du camping
campaign [kæm'pen] s campagne f || intr faire campagne
campaigner [kæm'penər] s propagandiste mf; vétéran m
camp' bed' s lit m de camp, lit de sangle
camp' chair' s chaise f pliante
camper ['kæmpər] s campeur m
camp'fire' s feu m de camp
camp'ground' s camping m
camphor ['kæmfər] s camphre m
camping ['kæmpɪŋ] s camping m
camp'stool' s pliant m
campus ['kæmpəs] s campus m, terrain m universitaire
cam'shaft' s arbre m à cames
can [kæn] s boîte f; (e.g., for gasoline) bidon m || v (pret & pp canned; ger canning) tr mettre en boîte, conserver; (to dismiss) (slang) dégommer || v (pret & cond could [kʊd]) aux—Albert can't do it Albert ne peut (pas) le faire; can he swim? sait-il nager?
Canada ['kænədə] s le Canada
Canadian [kə'nedɪ·ən] adj canadien || s (person) Canadien m
canal [kə'næl] s canal m
canar·y [kə'neri] s (pl -ies) canari m, serin m
can·cel ['kænsəl] v (pret & pp -celed or -celled; ger -celing or -celling) tr annuler; (a word) biffer, rayer; (a contract) résilier; (a postage stamp) oblitérer; to cancel an invitation décommander les invités; to cancel each other out s'annuler, se détruire
cancellation [,kænsə'leʃən] s annulation f; (of postage stamp) oblitération f; (of contract) résiliation f
cancer ['kænsər] s cancer m
cancerous ['kænsərəs] adj cancéreux
candela·brum [,kændə'lebrəm] s (pl -bra [brə] or -brums) candélabre m
candid ['kændɪd] adj franc
candida·cy ['kændɪdəsi] s (pl -cies) candidature f
candidate ['kændɪ,det] s candidat m
candied adj candi
candied' fruit' s fruit m candi
candle ['kændəl] s bougie f; (of tallow) chandelle f; (eccl) cierge m
can'dle·hold'er s bougeoir m
can'dle·light' s lumière f de bougie
can'dle·pow'er s (phys) bougie f
can'dle·stick' s chandelier m, bougeoir m
can'dle ta'ble s guéridon m
candor ['kændər] s franchise f, loyauté f
can·dy ['kændi] s (pl -dies) confiserie f, bonbons mpl; candies douceurs fpl; piece of candy bonbon || v (pret & pp -died) tr glacer, faire candir || intr se candir

can'dy box' s boîte f à bonbons
can'dy corn' s grains mpl de maïs soufflés et sucrés
can'dy dish' s bonbonnière f
can'dy store' s confiserie f
cane [ken] s canne f; (bot) canne || tr canner, rempailler
cane' chair' s chaise f cannée
cane' sug'ar s sucre m de canne
canine ['kenaɪn] adj canin || s (tooth) canine f
canister ['kænɪstər] s boîte f métallique; (mil) boîte à mitraille
canker ['kæŋkər] s chancre m; (in fruit; in society) ver m rongeur || tr ronger; (society) corrompre
canned' goods' spl conserves fpl, aliments mpl conservés
canned' mu'sic s (coll) musique f enregistrée
canner·y ['kænəri] s (pl -ies) conserverie f
cannibal ['kænɪbəl] adj & s cannibale mf
canning ['kænɪŋ] s conservation f
can'ning fac'tory s conserverie f
cannon ['kænən] s canon m
cannonade [,kænə'ned] s canonnade f || tr canonner
can'non·ball' s boulet m (de canon)
can'non fod'der s chair f à canon
can·ny ['kæni] adj (comp -nier; super -niest) prudent, circonspect; rusé, malin
canoe [kə'nu] s canoë m
canoeist [kə'nu·ɪst] s canoéiste mf
canon ['kænən] s canon m
canonical [kə'nɑnɪkəl] adj canonique, canonial || canonicals spl vêtements mpl sacerdotaux
canonize ['kænə,naɪz] tr canoniser
can' o'pener s ouvre-boîtes m
cano·py ['kænəpi] s (pl -pies) dais m; (over an entrance) marquise f
cant [kænt] s cant m, cafardise f; (argot) jargon m || tr (to tip) incliner || intr (to tip) s'incliner; (to be hypocritical) papelarder
cantaloupe ['kæntə,lop] s cantaloup m
cantankerous [kæn'tæŋkərəs] adj revêche, acariâtre
cantata [kən'tɑtə] s cantate f
canteen [kæn'tin] s (shop) cantine f; (water flask) bidon m; (service club) foyer m du soldat, du marin, etc.
canter ['kæntər] s petit galop m || intr aller au petit galop
canticle ['kæntɪkəl] s cantique m, hymne f
cantilever ['kæntɪ,livər] adj & s cantilever m
can'tilever bridge' s pont m cantilever, pont à consoles
canton [kæn'tɑn] s canton m
canvas ['kænvəs] s (cloth) canevas m; (picture) toile f
canvass ['kænvəs] s enquête f, sondage m; (pol) tournée f électorale || tr (a voter) solliciter la voix de; (a district) faire une tournée électorale dans; (com) prospecter || intr (com) faire la place; to canvass for (a can-

didate) faire une campagne électorale en faveur de

canyon ['kænjən] *s* cañon *m*

cap [kæp] *s* (*with visor*) casquette *f*; (*without brim*) bonnet *m*; (*to wear with academic gown*) toque *f*, mortier *m*; (*of bottle*) capsule *f*; (*of cartridge*) amorce *f*, capsule; (*of fountain pen*) capuchon *m*, chapeau *m*; (*of valve; to cover photographic lens*) chapeau; **to set one's cap for** chercher à captiver ‖ *v* (*pret & pp* **capped;** *ger* **capping**) *tr* coiffer; (*a bottle*) capsuler; (*a cartridge*) amorcer; (*a success*) couronner; (*to outdo*) (coll) surpasser

cap. *abbr* (**capital letter**) maj.

capable ['kepəbəl] *adj* capable

capacious [kə'pefəs] *adj* spacieux, vaste, ample

capaci·ty [kə'pæsıti] *s* (*pl* **-ties**) capacité *f*; **filled to capacity** comble; **in the capacity of** en tant que, en qualité de, à titre de

cap' and gown' *s* costume *m* académique, toge *f* et mortier *m*; **in cap and gown** en toque et en toge

cape [kep] *s* (*clothing*) cape *f*, pèlerine *f*; (geog) cap *m*, promontoire *m*

Cape' of Good Hope' *s* Cap *m* de Bonne Espérance

caper ['kepər] *s* cabriole *f*, gambade *f*; (bot) câpre *f* ‖ *tr* cabrioler, gambader

Cape'town' *s* Le Cap

capital ['kæpıtəl] *adj* capital; excellent ‖ *s* (*city*) capitale *f*; (*archit*) chapiteau *m*; (*com*) capital *m*; (*typ*) majuscule *f*, capitale; **small capital** petite capitale

cap'ital and la'bor *spl* le capital et le travail

capitalism ['kæpıtə,lızəm] *s* capitalisme *m*

capitalist ['kæpıtəlıst] *adj & s* capitaliste *mf*

capitalize ['kæpıtə,laız] *tr & intr* capitaliser; (*typ*) écrire avec une majuscule; **to capitalize on** miser sur, tourner à son profit, tirer parti de

cap'ital let'ter *s* majuscule *f*

cap'ital pun'ishment *s* peine *f* capitale

capitol ['kæpıtəl] *s* capitole *m*

capitulate [kə'pıtfə,let] *intr* capituler

capon ['kepαn] *s* chapon *m*

caprice [kə'pris] *s* caprice *m*

capricious [kə'prıfəs] *adj* capricieux

capsize ['kæpsaız] *tr* faire chavirer ‖ *intr* chavirer, capoter

capstan ['kæpstən] *s* cabestan *m*

capsule ['kæpsəl] *s* capsule *f*; (bot, rok) capsule

captain ['kæptən] *s* capitaine *m*; chef *m*; (sports) chef d'équipe ‖ *tr* commander, diriger

captain·cy ['kæptənsi] *s* (*pl* **-cies**) direction *f*, commandement *m*; grade *m* de capitaine

caption ['kæpfən] *s* légende *f*; (mov) sous-titre *m* ‖ *tr* intituler, donner un sous-titre à

captious ['kæpfəs] *adj* pointilleux, chicaneux; (*insidious*) captieux

captivate ['kæptı,vet] *tr* captiver

captive ['kæptıv] *adj & s* captif *m*

captivi·ty [kæp'tıvıti] *s* (*pl* **-ties**) captivité *f*

captor ['kæptər] *s* ravisseur *m*; (naut) auteur *m* d'une prise

capture ['kæptfər] *s* capture *f*, prise *f* ‖ *tr* capturer

car [kαr] *s* auto *f*, voiture *f*; (*of elevator*) cabine *f*; (rr) wagon *m*, voiture; (*for mail, baggage, etc.*) (rr) fourgon *m*

carafe [kə'ræf] *s* carafe *f*

caramel ['kærəməl], ['kαrməl] *s* caramel *m*

carat ['kærət] *s* carat *m*

caravan ['kærə,væn] *s* caravane *f*

caravansa·ry [,kærə'vænsəri] *s* (*pl* **-ries**) caravansérail *m*

caraway ['kærə,we] *s* carvi *m*

car'away seed' *s* graine *f* de carvi

car'barn' *s* dépôt *m* de tramways

carbide ['kαrbaıd] *s* carbure *m*

carbine ['kαrbaın] *s* carabine *f*

carbol'ic ac'id [kαr'bαlık] *s* acide *m* phénique

carbon ['kαrbən] *s* (*chemical element*) carbone *m*; (*part of arc light or battery*) charbon *m*; (*in auto cylinder*) calamine *f*; papier *m* carbone

car'bonated wa'ter ['kαrbə,netıd] *s* eau *f* gazeuse, soda *m*

car'bon cop'y *s* double *m* au carbone; (fig) calque *m*; (*person*) (fig) sosie *m*

car'bon diox'ide *s* gaz *m* carbonique

car'bon monox'ide *s* oxyde *m* de carbone

car'bon pa'per *s* papier *m* carbone

carbuncle ['kαrbʌŋkəl] *s* furoncle *m*

carburetor ['kαrbə,retər] *s* carburateur *m*

carcass ['kαrkəs] *s* (*dead body*) cadavre *m*; (*without offal*) carcasse *f*

card [kαrd] *s* carte *f*; (*for filing*) fiche *f*; (*for carding*) carde *f*; (coll) original *m*, numéro *m*, type *m*; **to put one's cards on the table** jouer cartes sur table ‖ *tr* carder, peigner

card'board' *s* carton *m*

card' case' *s* porte-cartes *m*

card' cat'alogue *s* fichier *m*

cardiac ['kαrdı,æk] *adj* cardiaque ‖ *s* (*patient*) (coll) cardiaque *mf*

cardinal ['kαrdınəl] *adj & s* cardinal *m*

card' in'dex *s* fichier *m*

cardiogram ['kαrdı·o,græm] *s* cardiogramme *m*

card'sharp' *s* tricheur *m*

card' ta'ble *s* table *f* de jeu

card' trick' *s* tour *m* de cartes

care [ker] *s* (*attention*) soin *m*; (*anxiety*) souci *m*; (*responsibility*) charge *f*; (*upkeep*) entretien *m*; **in care of** aux bons soins de, à l'attention de; **take care!** faites attention!; **to take care not to** se garder de; **to take care of** se charger de; (*a sick person*) soigner; **to take care to** avoir soin de ‖ *intr*—**I don't care** ça m'est égal; **to care about** se soucier de, se préoccuper de; **to care for** (*s.o.*) avoir de la sympathie pour; (*s.th.*) trouver plaisir à; (*a sick person*) soigner; **to care to** désirer, vouloir

careen [kə'rin] *tr* faire coucher sur le côté || *intr* donner de la bande, s'incliner

career [kə'rɪr] *s* carrière *f*

care'free' *adj* sans souci, insouciant

careful ['kɛrfəl] *adj* soigneux, attentif; **be careful!** soyez prudent!

careless ['kɛrlɪs] *adj* (*neglectful*) négligent; (*nonchalant*) insouciant

carelessness ['kɛrlɪsnɪs] *s* négligence *f*

caress [kə'rɛs] *s* caresse *f* || *tr* caresser

caret ['kærət] *s* guidon *m* de renvoi

care'tak'er *s* concierge *mf*, gardien *m*

care'taker gov'ernment *s* gouvernement *m* intérimaire

care'worn' *adj* rongé par les soucis

car'fare' *s* prix *m* du trajet, place *f*; **to pay carfare** payer le parcours

car·go ['kargo] *s* (*pl* **-goes** or **-gos**) cargaison *f*

car' heat'er *s* chauffage *m* de voiture

Car'ibbe'an Sea· [ˌkærɪ'bi·ən], [kə-'rɪbi·ən] *s* Mer *f* des Caraïbes, Mer des Antilles

caricature ['kærɪkətʃər] *s* caricature *f* || *tr* caricaturer

caricaturist [ˈkærɪkətʃ/ərɪst] *s* caricaturiste *mf*

caries ['kɛriz], ['kɛrɪˌiz] *s* carie *f*

carillon ['kærɪˌlan], [kə'rɪljən] *s* carillon *m* || *tr & intr* carillonner

car'load' *s* voiturée *f*

carnage ['karnɪdʒ] *s* carnage *m*

carnal ['karnəl] *adj* charnel; sexuel

car'nal sin' *s* péché *m* de la chair

carnation [karˈneʃən] *s* œillet *m*

carnival ['karnɪvəl] *s* carnaval *m*; fête *f*

car·ol ['kærəl] *s* chanson *f*, cantique *m*; (*Christmas carol*) noël *m* || *v* (*pret & pp* **-oled** or **-olled**; *ger* **-oling** or **-olling**) *tr & intr* chanter

carom ['kærəm] *s* carambolage *m* || *intr* caramboler

carouse [kə'rauz] *intr* faire la bombe

carp [karp] *s* carpe *f* || *intr* se plaindre

carpenter ['karpəntər] *s* charpentier *m*; (*joiner*) menuisier *m*

carpentry ['karpəntri] *s* charpenterie *f*

carpet ['karpɪt] *s* tapis *m* || *tr* recouvrir d'un tapis

car'pet sweep'er *s* balai *m* mécanique

car'port' *s* abri *m* pour auto

car'-rent'al serv'ice *s* entreprise *f* de location de voitures

carriage ['kærɪdʒ] *s* voiture *f*; (*used to transport royalty*) carrosse *m*; (*bearing*) port *m*, maintien *m*; (*cost of transport*) frais *mpl* de port; (*of typewriter; of rocket*) chariot *m*; (*of gun*) affût *m*

carrier ['kærɪ·ər] *s* (*person*) porteur *m*; (*e.g., a teamster*) camionneur *m*, voiturier *m*; (*vehicle*) transporteur *m*

car'rier pig'eon *s* pigeon *m* voyageur

car'rier wave' *s* onde *f* porteuse

carrion ['kærɪ·ən] *s* charogne *f*

carrot ['kærət] *s* carotte *f*

carrousel [ˌkærə'zɛl] *s* (*merry-go-round*) manège *m* de chevaux de bois; (*hist*) carrousel *m*

car·ry ['kæri] *v* (*pret & pp* **-ried**) *tr* porter; (*in adding numbers*) retenir; **to be carried** (parl) être voté, être adopté; **to be carried away** (*e.g., with enthusiasm*) être entraîné, s'importer; **to carry away** or **off** emporter, enlever; **to carry back** rapporter; **to carry down** descendre; **to carry forward** avancer; (bk) reporter; **to carry on** continuer; (*e.g., a conversation*) soutenir; **to carry oneself straight** se tenir droit; **to carry out** (*a plan*) exécuter; **to carry over** (bk) reporter; **to carry through** mener à bonne fin; **to carry up** monter; **to carry with one** (*e.g., an audience*) entraîner || *intr* (*said of voice or sound*) porter; **to carry on** continuer; (*in a ridiculous manner*) (coll) faire des espiègleries; (*angrily*) (coll) s'emporter

car' sick'ness *s* mal *m* de la route

cart [kart] *s* charrette *f*; **to put the cart before the horse** mettre la charrue devant les bœufs || *tr* charrier; (*to truck*) camionner

cartel [kar'tɛl] *s* cartel *m*

cartilage ['kartɪlɪdʒ] *s* cartilage *m*

cartographer [kar'tagrəfər] *s* cartographe *m*

carton ['kartən] *s* carton *m*, boîte *f*

cartoon [kar'tun] *s* dessin *m* humoristique; caricature *f*; (*comic strip*) bande *f* dessinée; (mov) dessin animé || *tr* caricaturer

cartoonist [kar'tunɪst] *s* caricaturiste *mf*

cartridge ['kartrɪdʒ] *s* cartouche *f*; capsule *f* enregistreuse de pick-up

car'tridge belt' *s* cartouchière *f*

car'tridge case' *s* cartouchière *f*

cart'wheel' *s* roue *f*; **to turn cartwheels** faire la roue

carve [karv] *tr & intr* sculpter; (culin) découper

carver ['karvər] *s* sculpteur *m*; (culin) découpeur *m*

carv'ing knife' *s* couteau *m* à découper

cascade [kæs'ked] *s* cascade *f* || *intr* cascader

case [kes] *s* (*instance, example*) cas *m*; (*for packing; of clock or piano*) caisse *f*; (*for cigarettes, eyeglasses, cartridges*) étui *m*; (*for jewels, silver, etc.*) écrin *m*; (*for watch*) boîtier *m*; (*for pillow*) taie *f*; (*for surgical instruments*) trousse *f*; (*for sausage*) peau *f*; (*showcase*) vitrine *f*; (*covering*) enveloppe *f*, couverture *f*; (law) cause *f*; (typ) casse *f*; **as the case may be** selon le cas; **in any case** en tout cas; **in case** au cas où; **in case of emergency** en cas d'imprévu; **in no case** en aucun cas; **just in case** à tout hasard; **to win one's case** avoir gain de cause || *tr* (*to put into a case*) encaisser; (*to package*) envelopper; (*to observe*) (slang) observer, épier

case'hard'en *tr* aciérer, cémenter; (fig) endurcir
casein ['kesi·ɪn] *s* caséine *f*
casement ['kesmənt] *s* croisée *f*
cash [kæʃ] *s* espèces *fpl*; **cash down** argent comptant; **cash offer** offre *f* réelle; **cash on delivery** livraison contre remboursement; **cash on hand** fonds *mpl* en caisse; **in cash** en numéraire ‖ *tr* toucher, encaisser ‖ *intr* —**to cash in on** (coll) tirer parti de
cash' and car'ry *s* achat *m* au comptant et à emporter
cash' bal'ance *s* solde *m* de caisse
cash' dis'count *s* escompte *m* au comptant
cashew ['kæʃu] *s* noix *f* d'acajou, anacarde *m*; (*tree*) anacardier *m*
cash'ew nut' *s* noix *f* d'acajou
cashier [kæ'ʃɪr] *s* caissier *m*
cashmere ['kæʃmɪr] *s* cachemire *m*
cash' reg'ister *s* caisse *f* enregistreuse
casing ['kesɪŋ] *s* enveloppe *f*, chemise *f*, coffrage *m*; (*of door or window*) chambranle *m*
cask [kæsk], [kɑsk] *s* tonneau *m*, fût *m*
casket ['kæskɪt], ['kɑskɪt] *s* (*for jewels*) écrin *m*, cassette *f*; (*for interment*) cercueil *m*
casserole ['kæsə‚rol] *s* terrine *f*
cassock ['kæsək] *s* soutane *f*
cast [kæst], [kɑst] *s* (*mold*) moule *m*; (*of metal*) fonte *f*; (*of fish line*) lancer *m*; (*throw*) jet *m*; (*for broken limb*) plâtre *m*; (*squint*) léger strabisme *m*; (theat) distribution *f* ‖ *v* (*pret & pp* **cast**) *tr* fondre, jeter en moule; (*to throw*) lancer; (*a glance*) jeter; (*a play*) distribuer les rôles de; **to be cast in one piece with** venir de fonte avec; **to cast aside** mettre de côté; **to cast lots** tirer au sort; **to cast off** rejeter; **to cast out** mettre à la porte; (*a spell*) exorciser ‖ *intr* (fishing) lancer la canne; **to cast about for** chercher; **to cast off** (naut) larguer les amarres
castanets [‚kæstə'nɛts] *spl* castagnettes *fpl*
cast'away' *adj & s* naufragé *m*
caste [kæst], [kɑst] *s* caste *f*
caster ['kæstər], ['kɑstər] *s* (*wheel*) roulette *f*; (*cruet stand*) huilier *m*; (*shaker*) saupoudreuse *f*
castigate ['kæstɪ‚get] *tr* châtier, corriger
Castile [kæs'til] *s* Castille *f*; la Castille
Castilian [kæs'tɪljən] *adj* castillan ‖ *s* (*language*) castillan *m*; (*person*) Castillan *m*
casting ['kæstɪŋ] *s* fonte *f*; (*thing cast*) pièce *f* fondue; (*act*) lancement *m*; (fishing) pêche *f* au lancer; (theat) distribution *f*
cast'ing rod' *s* canne *f* à lancer
cast' i'ron *s* fonte *f*
cast'-i'ron *adj* en fonte
cast'-iron stom'ach *s* estomac *m* d'autruche
castle ['kæsəl], ['kɑsəl] *s* château *m*; (*fortified castle*) château fort; (chess) tour *f* ‖ *tr & intr* (chess) roquer

cast'off' *adj & s* rejeté *m*
cas'tor oil' ['kæstər], ['kɑstər] *s* huile *f* de ricin
castrate ['kæstret] *tr* castrer
casual ['kæʒu·əl] *adj* casuel; (*indifferent*) insouciant, désinvolte
casually ['kæʒu·əli] *adv* nonchalamment, avec désinvolture; (*by chance*) fortuitement
casual·ty ['kæʒu·əlti] *s* (*pl* **-ties**) accident *m*; (*person*) accidenté *m*; casualties (mil) pertes *fpl*
cas'ualty list' *s* état *m* des pertes
cat [kæt] *s* (*tomcat*) chat *m*; (*female cat*) chatte *f*; (naut) capon *m*; (*shrew*) (coll) cancanière *f*, chipie *f*; **a cat may look at a queen** un chien regarde bien un évêque; **to let the cat out of the bag** (coll) vendre or éventer la mèche; **to rain cats and dogs** (coll) pleuvoir à seaux
cataclysm ['kætə‚klɪzəm] *s* cataclysme *m*
catacombs ['kætə‚komz] *spl* catacombes *fpl*
catalogue ['kætə‚lɔg], ['kætə‚lɑg] *s* catalogue *m*; (*of university*) annuaire *m* ‖ *tr* cataloguer, classer
Catalonia [‚kætə'lonɪ·ə] *s* Catalogne *f*; la Catalogne
catalyst ['kætəlɪst] *s* catalyseur *m*
catapult ['kætə‚pʌlt] *s* catapulte *f* ‖ *tr* catapulter
cataract ['kætə‚rækt] *s* cataracte *f*
catarrh [kə'tɑr] *s* catarrhe *m*
catastrophe [kə'tæstrəfi] *s* catastrophe *f*
cat'call' *s* huée *f*; (theat) coup *m* de sifflet ‖ *tr & intr* (theat) siffler
catch [kætʃ] *s* prise *f*; (*on door*) loquet *m*; (*on buckle*) ardillon *m*; (*caught by fisherman*) pêche *f*; (mach) cliquet *m*, chien *m*; **there's a catch to it** (coll) c'est une attrape ‖ *v* (*pret & pp* **caught** [kɔt]) *tr* attraper; (*a train; a fish; fire*) prendre; (*a word or sound*) saisir; (*e.g., one's coat*) accrocher; **caught like a rat in a trap** fait comme un rat; **to catch hold of** saisir, s'accrocher à; **to catch s.o. in the act** prendre qn sur le fait; **to catch up** (*in a mistake*) surprendre ‖ *intr* prendre; (*said of fire*) s'allumer, s'enflammer, se prendre; **to catch on** (*a nail, thorn, etc.*) s'accrocher à; (*to understand*) (coll) comprendre; (*to become popular*) (coll) devenir célèbre, devenir populaire; **to catch up** se rattraper; **to catch up with** rattraper
catch'all' *s* débarras *m*, fourre-tout *m*
catching ['kætʃɪŋ] *adj* contagieux; (*e.g., smile*) communicatif
catch' ques'tion *s* (coll) colle f
catch'word' *s* mot *m* de ralliement, slogan *m*; (*cliché*) rengaine *f*, scie *f*; (*at the bottom of page*) réclame *f*; (theat) réplique *f*; (typ) mot-souche *m*
catch·y ['kætʃi] *adj* (*comp* **-ier**; *super* **-iest**) (*tune*) facile à retenir, entraînant; (*question*) insidieux, à traquenard
catechism ['kætɪ‚kɪzəm] *s* catéchisme *m*

categorical [ˌkætɪ'gɑrɪkəl], [ˌkætɪ-
'gɔrɪkəl] adj catégorique
catego·ry ['kætɪˌgori] s (pl -ries) catégorie f
cater ['ketər] tr (e.g., a wedding)
fournir le buffet de || intr être four-
nisseur; to cater to pourvoir à; (to
favor) entourer de prévenances
cat'er-cor'nered ['kætər ˌkɔrnərd] adj
diagonal || adv diagonalement
caterer ['ketərər] s fournisseur m,
traiteur m
caterpillar ['kætər ˌpɪlər] s chenille f
cat'erpillar trac'tor s autochenille f
cat'fish' s poisson-chat m
cat'gut' s boyau m de chat; (string)
corde f à boyau, boyau; (surg) catgut m
cathedral [kə'θidrəl] s cathédrale f
catheter ['kæθɪtər] s (med) cathéter m
catheterization [ˌkæθɪtərɪ'zeʃən] s
(surg) cathétérisme m
cathode ['kæθod] s cathode m
catholic ['kæθəlɪk] adj (universal)
catholique; tolérant, large, e.g., he
has a catholic mind il a l'esprit large,
il est fort tolérant || (cap) adj & s
catholique mf
Catholicism [kə'θɑlɪ'sɪzəm] s catholicisme m
catholicity [ˌkæθə'lɪsɪti] s catholicité
f, universalité f; (tolerance) largeur
f d'esprit, tolérance f
catkin ['kætkɪn] s (bot) chaton m
cat'nap' s petit somme m
cat'nip s herbe-aux-chats f, cataire f
cat-o'-nine-tails [ˌkætə'naɪnˌtelz] s
chat m à neuf queues
cat's'-paw' s (naut) risée f; (coll) dupe f
catsup ['kætsəp], ['ketʃəp] s sauce f
tomate
cattle ['kætəl] s bœufs mpl; (including
horses) gros bétail m, bestiaux mpl
cat'tle car' s fourgon m à bestiaux
cat'tle cross'ing s passage m de troupeaux
cat'tle-man s (pl -men) éleveur m de
bétail
cat'tle thief' s voleur m de bétail
cat·ty ['kæti] adj (comp -tier; super
-tiest) (coll) cancanier, méchant
cat'ty-cor'ner adj (coll) diagonal || adv
(coll) diagonalement
cat'walk' s passerelle f
Caucasian [kɔ'keʒən], [kɔ'keʃən] adj
caucasien || s Caucasien m
caucus ['kɔkəs] s comité m électoral ||
intr se grouper en comité électoral
cauliflower ['kɔlɪˌflɑu·ər] s chou-fleur
m
caulk [kɔk] tr calfater
cause [kɔz] s cause f; to have cause to
avoir lieu de || tr causer; to cause to
+ inf faire + inf, e.g., he caused him
to stumble il l'a fait trébucher
cause'way' s chaussée f
caustic ['kɔstɪk] adj caustique
cauterize ['kɔtəˌraɪz] tr cautériser
caution ['kɔʃən] s prudence f, précau-
tion f; (warning) avertissement m ||
tr mettre en garde, avertir

cautious ['kɔʃəs] adj prudent, circonspect
cavalcade [ˌkævəl'ked], ['kævəlˌked]
s cavalcade f
cavalier [ˌkævə'lɪr] adj & s cavalier m
caval·ry ['kævəlri] s (pl -ries) cavalerie f
cav'alry·man' or cav'alry·man s (pl
-men' or -men) cavalier m
cave [kev] s caverne f || intr—to cave
in s'effondrer
cave'-in' s effondrement m
cavern ['kævərn] s caverne f
caviar ['kævɪˌɑr], ['kɑvɪˌɑr] s caviar
m
cav·il ['kævɪl] v (pret & pp -iled or
-illed; ger -iling or -illing) intr ergoter, chicaner
cavi·ty ['kævɪti] s (pl -ties) cavité f
cavort [kə'vɔrt] intr gambader, caracoler
caw [kɔ] s croassement m || intr croas-
ser, crialler
cease [sis] s cessation f; without cease
sans cesse || tr & intr cesser; to cease
fire cesser le feu
cease'-fire' s cessez-le-feu m
ceaseless ['sislɪs] adj incessant, continuel
cedar ['sidər] s cèdre m
cede [sid] tr & intr céder
cedilla [sɪ'dɪlə] s cédille f
ceiling ['silɪŋ] s plafond m; to hit the
ceiling (coll) sortir de ses gonds
ceil'ing lamp' s plafonnier m
ceil'ing price' s prix m maximum
celebrant ['sɛlɪbrənt] s (eccl) célébrant
m
celebrate ['sɛlɪˌbret] tr célébrer
celebrated adj célèbre
celebration [ˌsɛlɪ'breʃən] s célébration
f, fête f
celebri·ty [sɪ'lɛbrɪti] s (pl -ties) célébrité f; (e.g., movie star) vedette f
celery ['sɛləri] s céleri m
celestial [sɪ'lɛstʃəl] adj céleste
celiba·cy ['sɛlɪbəsi] s (pl -cies) célibat m
celibate ['sɛlɪˌbet], ['sɛlɪbɪt] adj & s
célibataire mf
cell [sɛl] s cellule f; (of electric battery) élément m
cellar ['sɛlər] s (basement; wine cellar)
cave f; (often partly above ground)
sous-sol m
cellist or 'cellist ['tʃɛlɪst] s violon-
celliste mf
cel·lo or 'cel·lo ['tʃɛlo] s (pl -los) violoncelle m
cellophane ['sɛləˌfen] s cellophane f
celluloid ['sɛljəˌlɔɪd] s celluloïd m
Celt [sɛlt], [kɛlt] s Celte mf
Celtic ['sɛltɪk], ['kɛltɪk] adj celte, cel-
tique || s celtique m
cement [sɪ'mɛnt] s ciment m || tr
cimenter
cement' mix'er s bétonnière f
cemeter·y ['sɛmɪˌtɛri] s (pl -ies) cimetière m
censer ['sɛnsər] s encensoir m
censor ['sɛnsər] s censeur m || tr cen-
surer

cen'sor·ship' s censure f
censure ['sɛnʃər] s blâme m || tr blâmer
census ['sɛnsəs] s recensement m, dénombrement m; (in Roman Empire) cens m
cen'sus tak'er s recenseur m; (in ancient Rome) censeur m
cent [sɛnt] s cent m; not to have a red cent to one's name n'avoir pas un sou vaillant
centaur ['sɛntɔr] s centaure m
centenarian [ˌsɛntɪ'nɛrɪ·ən] s centenaire mf
centennial [sɛn'tɛnɪ·əl] adj centennal || s centenaire m
center ['sɛntər] adj central || s centre m; (middle) milieu m || tr centrer || intr—to center on concentrer sur
centering ['sɛntərɪŋ] s centrage m; (phot) cadrage m
cen'ter·piece' s surtout m; milieu m de table
centigrade ['sɛntɪˌgred] adj & s centigrade m
centimeter ['sɛntɪˌmitər] s centimètre m
centipede ['sɛntɪˌpid] s mille-pattes m, myriapodes mpl
central ['sɛntrəl] adj & s central m
Cen'tral Amer'ica s l'Amérique f centrale
Cen'tral Intel'ligence s la Sûreté, la Sûreté nationale
centralize ['sɛntrəˌlaɪz] tr centraliser || intr se centraliser
centrifugal [sɛn'trɪfjʊgəl] adj centrifuge
centrifuge ['sɛntrɪˌfjudʒ] s essoreuse f || tr essorer
centu·ry ['sɛntʃəri] s (pl -ries) siècle m
cen'tury-old' adj séculaire
ceramic [sɪ'ræmɪk] adj céramique || ceramics s (art) céramique f; spl (objects) céramiques
cereal ['sɪrɪ·əl] adj céréalier || s (grain) céréale f; (oatmeal) flocons mpl d'avoine; (cornflakes) flocons de maïs; (cooked cereal) bouillie f, gruau m
cerebral ['sɛrɪbrəl] adj cérébral
ceremonial [ˌsɛrɪ'monɪ·əl] adj cérémonial; (e.g., tribal rites) cérémoniel || s cérémonial m
ceremonious [ˌsɛrɪ'monɪ·əs] adj cérémonieux
ceremo·ny ['sɛrɪˌmoni] s (pl -nies) cérémonie f; to stand on ceremony faire des cérémonies
certain ['sʌrtən] adj certain; a certain certain; certain people certains; for certain pour sûr, à coup sûr; to make certain of s'assurer de
certainly ['sʌrtənli] adv certainement
certain·ty ['sʌrtənti] s (pl -ties) certitude f
certificate [sər'tɪfɪkɪt] s certificat m; (of birth, of marriage, etc.) bulletin m, acte m, extrait m; (proof) attestation f
cer'tified cop'y s extrait m; (formula used on documents) pour copie conforme

cer'tified pub'lic account'ant s expert-comptable m, comptable m agréé
certi·fy ['sʌrtɪˌfaɪ] v (pret & pp -fied) tr certifier
cervix ['sʌrvɪks] s (pl cervices [sər'vaɪsiz]) nuque f
cessation [sɛ'seʃən] s cessation f, cesse f
cesspool ['sɛsˌpul] s fosse f d'aisance, cloaque m
Ceylon [sɪ'lɑn] s Ceylan m
Ceylo·nese [ˌsilə'niz] adj cingalais || s (pl -nese) Cingalais m
chafe [tʃef] tr écorcher, irriter || intr s'écorcher, s'irriter
chaff [tʃæf], [tʃɑf] s balle f; (banter) raillerie f || tr railler, persifler
chaf'ing dish' s réchaud m de table, chauffe-plats m
chagrin [ʃə'grɪn] s mortification f, humiliation f || tr mortifier, humilier
chain [tʃen] s chaîne f || tr enchaîner
chain' gang' s forçats mpl à la chaîne
chain' reac'tion s (phys) réaction f en chaîne
chain' smok'er s fumeur m à la file
chain'stitch' s point m de chaînette
chain' store' s magasin m à succursales multiples, économat m
chair [tʃɛr] s chaise f; (held by university professor) chaire f; (of presiding officer; presiding officer himself) fauteuil m; to take a chair prendre un siège, s'asseoir; to take the chair occuper le fauteuil, présider une assemblée || tr présider
chair' lift' s télé-siège m
chair'man s (pl -men) président m
chair'man·ship' s présidence f
chair'wom'an s (pl -wom'en) présidente f
chalice ['tʃælɪs] s calice m
chalk [tʃɔk] s craie f; a piece of chalk une craie, un morceau de craie || tr marquer avec de la craie, écrire à la craie
chalk·y ['tʃɔki] adj (comp -ier; super -iest) crayeux
challenge ['tʃælɪndʒ] s défi m; (objection) contestation f; (mil) qui-vive m; (sports) challenge m || tr défier; (to question) mettre en question, contester; (mil) crier qui-vive à
chamber ['tʃembər] s chambre f
chamberlain ['tʃembərlɪn] s chambellan m
cham'ber·maid' s femme f de chambre
cham'ber mu'sic s musique f de chambre
Cham'ber of Com'merce s syndicat m d'initiative
chameleon [kə'milɪ·ən] s caméléon m
chamfer ['tʃæmfər] s chanfrein m || tr chanfreiner
cham·ois ['ʃæmi] s (pl -ois) chamois m
champ [tʃæmp] s mâchonnement m || tr mâcher bruyamment; to champ the bit ronger le frein
champagne [ʃæm'pen] s champagne m || (cap) adj champenois || (cap) s Champagne f; la Champagne
champion ['tʃæmpɪ·ən] s champion m || tr se faire le champion de, défendre

cham'pion·ship' *s* championnat *m*
chance [t/æns], [t/ɑns] *adj* fortuit, de rencontre ‖ *s* hasard *m*; risque *m*; (*opportunity*) occasion *f*; **by chance** par hasard, fortuitement; **chances** chances *fpl*, sort *m*; **to take a chance** encourir un risque; acheter un billet de loterie; **to take chances** jouer gros jeu ‖ *tr* hasarder, risquer ‖ *intr*—**to chance to** venir à, avoir l'occasion de; **to chance upon** rencontrer par hasard
chancel ['t/ænsəl], ['t/ɑnsəl] *s* chœur *m*, sanctuaire *m*
chanceller·y ['t/ænsələri], ['t/ɑnsələri] *s* (*pl* **-ies**) chancellerie *f*
chancellor ['t/ænsələr], ['t/ɑnsələr] *s* chancelier *m*, ministre *m*
chancre ['/æŋkər] *s* chancre *m*
chandelier [,/ændə'lɪr] *s* lustre *m*
change [t/endʒ] *s* changement *m*; (*coins*) monnaie *f*; **change in the wind** saute *f* de vent; **change of address** changement de domicile; **change of clothes** vêtements *mpl* de rechange; **for a change** comme distraction; pour changer ‖ *tr* changer; changer de, e.g., **to change religions** changer de culte; **to change sides** tourner casaque ‖ *intr* changer; (*said of voice at puberty*) muer; **to change over** (*e.g., from one system to another*) passer
changeable ['t/endʒəbəl] *adj* changeable; (*weather*) variable; (*character*) changeant, mobile
changeless ['t/endʒlɪs] *adj* immuable
change' of life' *s* retour *m* d'âge
change' of voice' *s* mue *f*
change'o'ver *s* changement *m*, renversement *m*, relève *f*
change' purse' *s* porte-monnaie *m*
chan·nel ['t/ænəl] *s* (*body of water joining two others*) canal *m*; (*bed of river*) chenal *m*; (*means of communication*) voie *f*, canal; (*passage*) conduit *m*; (*groove*) cannelure *f*; (*strait*) bras *m* de mer; (*for trade*) débouché *m*; (*rad, telv*) canal; (*rad, telv*) chaîne *f*; (*telv*) canal (*Canad*); **through channels** par la voie hiérarchique ‖ *v* (*pret & pp* **-neled** or **-nelled**; *ger* **-neling** or **-nelling**) *tr* creuser, canneler
Chan'nel Is'lands *spl* îles *fpl* Anglo-Normandes
chant [t/ænt], [t/ɑnt] *s* chant *m*; (*song sung in a monotone*) plain-chant *m*, psalmodie *f* ‖ *tr & intr* psalmodier
chanter ['t/æntər], ['t/ɑntər] *s* chantre *m*
chantey ['/ænti], ['t/ænti] *s* chanson *f* de bord
chaos ['ke·ɑs] *s* chaos *m*
chaotic [ke'ɑtɪk] *adj* chaotique
chap [t/æp] *s* crevasse *f*, gerçure *f*; (*coll*) type *m*, individu *m* ‖ *v* (*pret & pp* **chapped**; *ger* **chapping**) *tr* crevasser, gercer ‖ *intr* se crevasser, se gercer
chapel ['t/æpəl] *s* chapelle *f*; (*in a*

house) oratoire *m*; (*Protestant chapel*) temple *m*
chaperon ['/æpə,rɑn] *s* chaperon *m*, duègne *f* ‖ *tr* chaperonner
chaplain ['t/æplɪn] *s* aumônier *m*
chaplet ['t/æplɪt] *s* chapelet *m*
chapter ['t/æptər] *s* chapitre *m*; (*of an association*) bureau *m* régional
char [t/ɑr] *v* (*pret & pp* **charred**; *ger* **charring**) *tr & intr* charbonner; **to become charred** se charbonner, se carboniser
character ['kærɪktər] *s* caractère *m*; (*theat*) personnage *m*; (*coll*) type *m*, sujet *m*
char'acter ac'tor *s* acteur *m* de genre
characteristic [,kærɪktə'rɪstɪk] *adj & s* caractéristique *f*
characterize ['kærɪktə,raɪz] *tr* caractériser
char'acter ref'erence *s* certificat *m* de moralité
char'coal' *s* charbon *m* de bois
char'coal burn'er *s* charbonnier *m*
char'coal pen'cil *s* charbon *m*, crayon *m* de fusain
charge [t/ɑrdʒ] *s* charge *f*; prix *m*; (*against a defendant*) chef *m* d'accusation; (*made to a jury*) résumé *m*; **on a charge of** sous l'inculpation de; **to reverse the charges** téléphoner en p.c.v.; **to take charge of** se charger de; **without charge** gratis ‖ *tr* charger; **to charge s.o. s.th. for s.th.** prendre or demander q.ch. à qn pour q.ch.; **to charge to s.o.'s account** mettre sur le compte de qn ‖ *intr* (*mil*) charger; **to charge down on** foncer sur
charge' account' *s* compte *m* courant
charger ['t/ɑrdʒər] *s* cheval *m* de bataille; (*elec*) chargeur *m*
chariot ['t/ærɪ·ət] *s* char *m*
charitable ['t/ærɪtəbəl] *adj* charitable
chari·ty ['t/ærɪti] *s* (*pl* **-ties**) charité *f*; (*alms*) bienfaisance *f*, aumônes *fpl*; (*institution*) société *f* or œuvre *f* de bienfaisance; **for charity's sake** par charité
charlatan [/ɑrlətən] *s* charlatan *m*
charm [t/ɑrm] *s* charme *m*; (*e.g., on a bracelet*) breloque *f*, porte-bonheur *m* ‖ *tr* charmer
charming ['t/ɑrmɪŋ] *adj* charmeur, charmant
charnel ['t/ɑrnəl] *adj* de charnier ‖ *s* charnier *m*, ossuaire *m*
chart [t/ɑrt] *s* (*map*) carte *f*; (*graph*) dessin *m* graphique; (*diagram*) diagramme *m*; (*table*) tableau *m* ‖ *tr* inscrire sur un dessin graphique; (*naut*) porter sur une carte, dresser la carte de
charter ['t/ɑrtər] *s* charte *f*; (*of bank*) privilège *m*; (*naut*) affrètement *m* ‖ *tr* accorder une charte à; (*a ship*) affréter, noliser; (*a bus*) louer
char'ter mem'ber *s* membre *m* fondateur
char'wom'an *s* (*pl* **-wom'en**) nettoyeuse *f*

chase [tʃes] s chasse *f*, poursuite *f*; (*for printing*) châssis *m* ‖ *tr* chasser; (*a gem*) enchâsser; (*gold*) ciseler; (*metal*) repousser; **to chase away** chasser ‖ *intr*—**to chase after** pourchasser, poursuivre

chaser [ˈtʃesər] s chasseur *m*; (*of women*) (coll) coureur *m*; (*taken after an alcoholic drink*) (coll) rince-gueule *m*

chasm [ˈkæzəm] s abîme *m*

chas·sis [ˈtʃæsi] s (*pl* **-sis** [siz]) châssis *m*

chaste [tʃest] *adj* chaste

chasten [ˈtʃesən] *tr* châtier

chastise [tʃæsˈtaɪz] *tr* châtier, corriger

chastisement [ˈtʃæstɪzmənt], [tʃæsˈtaɪzmənt] s châtiment *m*

chastity [ˈtʃæstɪti] s chasteté *f*

chat [tʃæt] s causerie *f*, causette *f* ‖ *v* (*pret & pp* **chatted**; *ger* **chatting**) *intr* causer, bavarder

chattel [ˈtʃætəl] s bien *m* meuble, objet *m* mobiliaire

chatter [ˈtʃætər] s bavardage *m*, caquetage *m* ‖ *intr* bavarder, caqueter; (*said of teeth*) claquer

chat'ter·box' s bavard *m*, babillard *m*

chauffeur [ˈʃofər], [ʃoˈfʌr] s chauffeur *m*

chauvinistic [ˌʃovɪˈnɪstɪk] *adj* chauvin

cheap [tʃip] *adj* bon marché; (coll) honteux; **to get off cheap** (coll) en être quitte à bon compte

cheapen [ˈtʃipən] *tr* baisser le prix de; diminuer la valeur de

cheap'skate' s (slang) rat *m*

cheat [tʃit] s tricheur *m*, fraudeur *m* ‖ *tr* tricher, frauder ‖ *intr* (e.g., *at cards*) tricher; (e.g., *in an examination*) frauder

cheating [ˈtʃitɪŋ] s tricherie *f*, fraude *f*

check [tʃɛk] s (*stopping*) arrêt *m*; (*brake*) frein *m*; (*supervision*) contrôle *m*, vérification *f*; (*in a restaurant*) addition *f*; (*drawn on a bank*) chèque *m*; (e.g., *of a chessboard*) carreau *m*; (*of the king in chess*) échec *m*; (*for baggage*) bulletin *m*; (*pass-out check*) contremarque *f*; (*chip, counter*) jeton *m*; **in check** en échec ‖ *tr* arrêter, freiner; contrôler, vérifier; (*baggage*) faire enregistrer; (e.g., *one's coat*) mettre au vestiaire; (*the king in chess*) faire échec à; **to check off** pointer, cocher ‖ *intr* s'arrêter; **to check in** (*at a hotel*) s'inscrire sur le registre; **to check out** (*of a hotel*) régler sa note; **to check up on** contrôler, examiner

check'book' s carnet *m* de chèques, chéquier *m*

checked *adj* (*checkered*) à carreaux; (*syllable*) entravé

checker [ˈtʃɛkər] s (*inspector*) contrôleur *m*; (*piece used in game*) pion *m*; (*square of checkerboard*) carreau *m*; **checkers** jeu *m* de dames ‖ *tr* quadriller; (*to divide in squares*) quadriller; (*to scatter here and there*) diaprer

check'er·board' s damier *m*

checkered *adj* (*divided into squares*) quadrillé, à carreaux; (*varied*) varié, accidenté; (*career, life*) plein de vicissitudes, mouvementé

check' girl' s préposée *f* au vestiaire

check'ing account' s compte *m* en banque

check' list' s liste *f* de contrôle

check' mark' s trait *m* de repère, repère *m*, coche *f*

check'mate' s échec et mat *m*; (fig) échec *m* ‖ *tr* faire échec et mat à, mater ‖ *intr* faire échec et mat, mater ‖ *interj* échec et mat!

check'-out count'er s caisse *f* de supermarché

check'point' s contrôle *m* de police

check'room' s (*cloakroom*) vestiaire *m*; (*baggage room*) consigne *f*

check'up' s vérification *f*, examen *m*

cheek [tʃik] s joue *f*; (coll) aplomb *m*, toupet *m*

cheek'bone' s pommette *f*

cheep [tʃip] *intr* piauler

cheer [tʃɪr] s bonne humeur *f*, gaieté *f*; encouragement *m*, e.g., **word of cheer** parole *f* d'encouragement; **cheers** acclamations *fpl*, bravos *mpl*, vivats *mpl*; **three cheers for . . .!** vive . . .!; **to give three cheers** pousser trois hourras ‖ *tr* (*to cheer up*) encourager, égayer; (*to applaud*) acclamer, applaudir ‖ *intr* pousser des vivats, applaudir; **cheer up!** courage!

cheerful [ˈtʃɪrfəl] *adj* de bonne humeur, gai; (*place*) d'aspect agréable

cheerfully [ˈtʃɪrfəli] *adv* gaiement; (*willingly*) de bon cœur

cheer'lead'er s chef *m* de claque

cheerless [ˈtʃɪrlɪs] *adj* morne, triste

cheese [tʃiz] s fromage *m* ‖ *tr*—**cheese it, the cops!** (slang) vingt-deux, les flics!

cheese'cake' s (slang) les pin up *fpl*

cheese' cake' s soufflé *m* au fromage, tarte *f* au fromage

cheese'cloth' s gaze *f*

chees·y [ˈtʃizi] *adj* (*comp* **-ier**; *super* **-iest**) caséeux; (slang) miteux

cheetah [ˈtʃita] s guépard *m*

chef [ʃɛf] s chef *m* de cuisine, maître queux *m*

chemical [ˈkɛmɪkəl] *adj* chimique ‖ s produit *m* chimique

chemist [ˈkɛmɪst] s chimiste *mf*

chemistry [ˈkɛmɪstri] s chimie *f*

cherish [ˈtʃɛrɪʃ] *tr* chérir; (*an idea*) nourrir; (*a hope*) caresser

cher·ry [ˈtʃɛri] s (*pl* **-ries**) cerise *f*; (*tree*) cerisier *m*

cher'ry tree' s cerisier *m*

cher·ub [ˈtʃɛrəb] s (*pl* **-ubim** [əbɪm]) chérubin *m* ‖ s (*pl* **-ubs**) (fig) chérubin *m*

chess [tʃes] s échecs *mpl*; **to play chess** jouer aux échecs

chess'board' s échiquier *m*

chess'man' s (*pl* **-men'**) pièce *f* du jeu d'échecs

chess' set' s échecs *mpl*

chest [tʃest] s caisse *f*; (*of drawers*)

commode *f*; (anat) poitrine *f*; **to get s.th. off one's chest** (coll) se déboutonner, dire ce qu'on a sur le cœur

chestnut ['tʃɛsnət] *adj* (*color*) châtain ‖ *s* (*color*) châtain *m*; (*nut*) châtaigne *f*; (*tree*) châtaignier *m*

chest' of drawers' *s* commode *f*, chiffonnier *m*

cheval' glass' [ʃə'væl] *s* psyché *f*

chevron ['ʃɛvrən] *s* chevron *m*

chew [tʃu] *tr* mâcher; (*tobacco*) chiquer

chewing ['tʃu·ɪŋ] *s* mastication *f*

chew'ing gum' *s* gomme *f* à mâcher, chewing-gum *m*

chicaner·y [ʃɪ'kɛnəri] *s* (*pl* -ies) truc *m*, ruse *f*, artifice *m*

chick [tʃɪk] *s* poussin *m*; (*girl*) (slang) tendron *m*

chickadee ['tʃɪkə,di] *s* (*Parus atricapillus*) mésange *f* boréale.

chicken ['tʃɪkən] *s* poulet *m*; **to be chicken** (slang) avoir la frousse ‖ *intr*—**to chicken out** (slang) caner

chick'en coop' *s* poulailler *m*

chick'en-heart'ed *adj* froussard, poltron

chick'en pox' *s* varicelle *f*

chick'en stew' *s* poule-au-pot *m*

chick'en wire' *s* treillis *m* métallique

chick'pea' *s* pois *m* chiche

chico·ry ['tʃɪkəri] *s* (*pl* -ries) chicorée *f*

chide [tʃaɪd] *v* (*pret* **chided** or **chid** [tʃɪd]; *pp* **chided, chid,** or **chidden** ['tʃɪdən]) *tr* & *intr* gronder

chief [tʃif] *adj* principal, en chef ‖ *s* chef *m*; (*boss*) (coll) patron *m*

chief' exec'utive *s* chef *m* de l'exécutif

chief' jus'tice *s* président *m* de la Cour suprême

chiefly ['tʃifli] *adv* principalement

chief' of police' *s* préfet *m* de police

chief' of staff' *s* chef *m* d'état-major

chief' of state' *s* chef *m* d'État

chieftain ['tʃiftən] *s* chef *m*

chiffon [ʃɪ'fɑn] *s* mousseline *f* de soie

chiffonier [,ʃɪfə'nɪr] *s* chiffonnier *m*

chilblain ['tʃɪl,blen] *s* engelure *f*

child [tʃaɪld] *s* (*pl* **children** ['tʃɪldrən]) enfant *mf*; **with child** enceinte

child'birth' *s* accouchement *m*

child'hood *s* enfance *f*

childish ['tʃaɪldɪʃ] *adj* enfantin, puéril

child' la'bor *s* travail *m* des enfants

child'like' *adj* enfantin, d'enfant

child's' play' *s* jeu *m* d'enfant; **it's child's play** c'est l'enfance de l'art

child' wel'fare *s* protection *f* de l'enfance

Chile ['tʃili] *s* le Chili

chil'i pep'per ['tʃili] *s* piment *m*

chill [tʃɪl] *adj* & *s* froid *m*; **sudden chill** saisissement *m*, coup *m* de froid; **to take the chill off** faire tiédir ‖ *tr* refroidir; (*a person*) transir, faire frissonner; (*wine*) frapper

chill·y ['tʃili] *adj* (*comp* -ier; *super* -iest) froid; (*sensitive to cold*) frileux; **it is chilly** il fait frisquet

chime [tʃaɪm] *s* coup *m* de son; **chimes** (*at doorway*) sonnerie *f*; (*in bell tower*) carillon *m* ‖ *tr* & *intr* carillonner

chimera [kaɪ'mɪrə], [kɪ'mɪrə] *s* chimère *f*

chiming ['tʃaɪmɪŋ] *s* carillonnement *m*, sonnerie *f*

chimney ['tʃɪmni] *s* cheminée *f*; (*of lamp*) verre *m*

chim'ney pot' *s* abat-vent *m*, mitre *f*

chim'ney sweep' *s* ramoneur *m*

chimpanzee [tʃɪm'pænzi], [,tʃɪmpæn-'zi] *s* chimpanzé *m*

chin [tʃɪn] *s* menton *m*

china ['tʃaɪnə] *s* porcelaine *f* de Chine; **China** Chine *f*; la Chine

chi'na clos'et *s* vitrine *f*

chi'na·ware' *s* porcelaine *f*

Chi·nese [tʃaɪ'niz] *adj* chinois ‖ *s* (*language*) chinois *m* ‖ *s* (*pl* -nese) Chinois *m* (*person*)

Chi'nese lan'tern *s* lanterne *f* vénitienne, lampion *m*

chink [tʃɪŋk] *s* fente *f*, crevasse *f*; **chink in one's armor** (coll) défaut *m* de la cuirasse

chin' strap' *s* sous-mentonnière *f*, jugulaire *f*

chip [tʃɪp] *s* copeau *m*, éclat *m*; (*in gambling*) jeton *m*; **to be a chip off the old block** (coll) chasser de race, être un rejeton de la vieille souche ‖ *v* (*pret* & *pp* **chipped**; *ger* **chipping**) *tr* enlever un copeau à ‖ *intr* s'écailler; **to chip in** contribuer

chipmunk ['tʃɪp,mʌŋk] *s* tamias *m* rayé

chipper ['tʃɪpər] *adj* (coll) en forme, guilleret

chiropodist [kaɪ'rɑpədɪst], [kɪ'rɑpə-dɪst] *s* pédicure *mf*

chiropractor ['kaɪrə,præktər] *s* chiropracteur *m*

chirp [tʃʌrp] *s* gazouillis *m*, pépiement *m* ‖ *intr* gazouiller, pépier

chis·el ['tʃɪzəl] *s* ciseau *m* ‖ *v* (*pret* & *pp* **-eled** or **-elled**; *ger* **-eling** or **-elling**) *tr* ciseler; (*a person*) (slang) escroquer; **to chisel s.o. out of s.th.** (slang) escroquer q.ch. à qn

chiseler ['tʃɪzələr] *s* ciseleur *m*; (slang) escroc *m*

chit [tʃɪt] *s* note *f*, ticket *m*; (coll) gamin *m*

chit'-chat' *s* bavardage *m*

chivalrous ['ʃɪvəlrəs] *adj* honorable, courtois; (lit) chevaleresque

chivalry ['ʃɪvəlri] *s* (*of Middle Ages*) chevalerie *f*; (*politeness*) courtoisie *f*, galanterie *f*

chive [tʃaɪv] *s* ciboulette *f*, civette *f*

chloride ['klɔraɪd] *s* chlorure *m*

chlorinate ['klɔrɪ,net] *tr* (*water*) verduniser

chlorination [,klɔrɪ'neʃən] *s* verdunisation *f*

chlorine ['klɔrin] *s* chlore *m*

chloroform ['klɔrə,fɔrm] *s* chloroforme *m* ‖ *tr* chloroformer

chlorophyll ['klɔrəfɪl] *s* chlorophylle *f*

chock [tʃɑk] *s* cale *f*; (naut) poulie *f* ‖ *tr* caler

chock'-full' *adj* bondé, comble, bourré

chocolate ['tʃɔkəlɪt], ['tʃɑkəlɪt] *adj* & *s* chocolat *m*

choc'olate bar' s tablette f de chocolat
choice [tʃɔɪs] adj de choix, choisi ‖ m choix m; **by choice** par goût, volontairement
choir [kwaɪr] s chœur m
choir'boy' s enfant m de chœur
choir'mas'ter s chef m de chœur; (eccl) maître m de chapelle
choir' robe' s soutanelle f
choke [tʃok] s (aut) starter m ‖ tr étouffer; (to obstruct) obstruer, boucher; **to choke back, down, or off** étouffer; **to choke up** obstruer, engorger ‖ intr étouffer; **to choke up** (e.g., with tears) étouffer
choke' coil' s (elec) bobine f de réactance
choker ['tʃokər] s (scarf) foulard m; (necklace) collier m court
choking ['tʃokɪŋ] s étouffement m
cholera ['kɑlərə] s choléra m
choleric ['kɑlərɪk] adj coléreux
cholesterol [kə'lɛstə,rol], [kə'lɛstə,rɑl] s cholestérol m
choose [tʃuz] v (pret **chose** [tʃoz]; pp **chosen** ['tʃozən]) tr & intr choisir
choos·y ['tʃuzi] adj (comp **-ier**; super **-iest**) (coll) difficile à plaire, chipoteur
chop [tʃɑp] s coup m de hache; (culin) côtelette f; **to lick one's chops** (coll) se lécher or s'essuyer les babines ‖ v (pret & pp **chopped**; ger **chopping**) tr hacher, couper; **to chop down** abattre; **to chop off** trancher, couper; **to chop up** couper en morceaux, hacher ‖ intr (said of waves) clapoter
chopper ['tʃɑpər] s (of butcher) couperet m; (coll) hélicoptère m; **choppers** (slang) les dents fpl
chop'ping block' s billot m, hachoir m
chop·py ['tʃɑpi] adj (comp **-pier**; ger **-piest**) agité; (waves) clapoteux
chop'stick' s baguette f, bâtonnet m
choral ['korəl] adj choral
chorale [ko'rɑl] s choral m
cho'ral soci'ety s chorale f
chord [kɔrd] s accord m; (geom) corde f
chore [tʃor] s devoir m; (burdensome chore) corvée f, besogne f
choreography [,korɪ'ɑgrəfi] s chorégraphie f
chorister ['kɑrɪstər], ['kɔrɪstər] s choriste mf
chortle ['tʃɔrtəl] intr glousser
chorus ['korəs] s chœur m, chorale f; (of song) refrain m; (of protest) concert m ‖ tr répéter en chœur, faire chorus
cho'rus boy' s boy m
cho'rus girl' s girl f
cho'sen few' ['tʃozən] s élite f
chow [tʃau] s (dog) chow-chow m; (mil) boustifaille f, mangeaille f
chow'-chow' s (culin) macédoine f assaisonnée
chowder ['tʃaudər] s soupe f au poisson
Christ [kraɪst] s Christ m; le Christ
christen ['krɪsən] tr baptiser
Christendom ['krɪsəndəm] s chrétienté f

christening ['krɪsənɪŋ] s baptême m
Christian ['krɪstʃən] adj & s chrétien m
Christianity [,krɪstʃɪ'ænɪti] s christianisme m
Christianize ['krɪstʃə,naɪz] tr christianiser
Christ'ian name' s nom m de baptême
Christmas ['krɪsməs] adj de Noël ‖ s Noël m; **Merry Christmas!** Joyeux Noël!
Christ'mas card' s carte f de Noël
Christ'mas car'ol s chanson f de Noël, chant m de Noël; (eccl) cantique m de Noël
Christ'mas Day' s le jour de Noël
Christ'mas Eve' s la veille de Noël
Christ'mas gift' s cadeau m de Noël
Christ'mas tree' s arbre m de Noël
Christ'mas tree lights' spl guirlandes fpl
chromatic [kro'mætɪk] adj chromatique
chrome [krom] adj chromé ‖ s acier m chromé; (color) jaune m; (chem) chrome m ‖ tr chromer
chromium ['kromɪ-əm] s chrome m
chromosome ['kromə,som] s chromosome m
chronic ['krɑnɪk] adj chronique
chronicle ['krɑnɪkəl] s chronique f ‖ tr faire la chronique de
chronicler ['krɑnɪklər] s chroniqueur m
chronologic(al) [,krɑnə'lɑdʒɪk(əl)] adj chronologique
chronolo·gy [krə'nɑlədʒi] s (pl **-gies**) chronologie f
chronometer [krə'nɑmɪtər] s chronomètre m
chrysanthemum [krɪ'sænθɪməm] s chrysanthème m
chub·by ['tʃʌbi] adj (comp **-bier**; super **-biest**) joufflu, potelé, dodu
chuck [tʃʌk] s (tap, blow, etc.) petite tape f; (under the chin) caresse f sous le menton; (of lathe) mandrin m; (bottom chuck and chuck rib) paleron m; (top chuck roast and chuck rib) entrecôte f ‖ tr tapoter; **to chuck away** jeter
chuckle ['tʃʌkəl] s gloussement m, petit rire m ‖ intr glousser, rire tout bas
chum [tʃʌm] s (coll) copain m ‖ v (pret & pp **chummed**; ger **chumming**) intr—**to chum around with** (coll) fraterniser avec
chum·my ['tʃʌmi] adj (comp **-mier**; super **-miest**) intime, familier
chump [tʃʌmp] s (slang) ballot m, lourdaud m
chunk [tʃʌŋk] s gros morceau m; (e.g., of wood) bloc m
church [tʃʌrtʃ] s église f
church'go'er s pratiquant m
church'man s (pl **-men**) (clergyman) ecclésiastique m; (layman) membre m d'une église, fidèle mf, paroissien m
church' mem'ber s fidèle mf
church' ser'vice s office m, culte m
church'yard' s cimetière m
churlish ['tʃʌrlɪʃ] adj rustre, grossier; (out of sorts) grincheux
churn [tʃʌrn] s baratte f ‖ tr (cream)

baratter; (*e.g., water*) agiter; **to churn butter** battre le beurre || *intr* bouillonner
chute [ʃut] *s* glissière *f*; parachute *m*; (*of river*) rapide *m*, chute *f* d'eau
Cicero ['sisə,ro] *s* Cicéron *m*
cider ['saɪdər] *s* cidre *m*
cigar [sɪ'gɑr] *s* cigare *m*
cigarette [,sɪgə'rɛt] *s* cigarette *f*
cigarette' butt' *s* mégot *m*
cigarette' case' *s* étui *m* à cigarettes
cigarette' fiend' *s* fumeur *m* enragé
cigarette' hold'er *s* fume-cigarette *m*
cigarette' light'er *s* briquet *m*
cigar' hold'er *s* fume-cigare *m*
cigar' store' *s* bureau *m* de tabac
cinch [sɪntʃ] *s* (*of saddle*) sangle *f*; **it's a cinch** (coll) c'est couru d'avance || *tr* sangler; (*to make sure of*) (slang) assurer
cinder ['sɪndər] *s* cendre *f* || *tr* cendrer
Cinderella [,sɪndə'rɛlə] *s* la Cendrillon *f*
cin'der track' *s* piste *f* cendrée
cinema ['sɪnəmə] *s* cinéma *m*
cinnamon ['sɪnəmən] *s* cannelle *f*
cipher ['saɪfər] *s* zéro *m*; (*code*) chiffre *m*; **in cipher** en chiffres || *tr* & *intr* chiffrer
circle ['sʌrkəl] *s* cercle *m*; (*coterie*) milieu *m*, monde *m*; **to have circles around the eyes** avoir les yeux cernés || *tr* ceindre, entourer; (*to travel around*) faire le tour de
circuit ['sʌrkɪt] *s* circuit *m*; (*of judge*) tournée *f*
cir'cuit break'er *s* (elec) disjoncteur *m*
cir'cuit court' *s* cour *f* d'assises
circuitous [sər'kju·ɪtəs] *adj* détourné, indirect
circular ['sʌrkjələr] *adj* & *s* circulaire *f*
circulate ['sʌrkjə,let] *tr* faire circuler || *intr* circuler
circulation [,sʌrkjə'leʃən] *s* circulation *f*; (*of newspaper*) tirage *m*
circumcise ['sʌrkəm,saɪz] *tr* circoncire
circumcision [,sʌrkəm'sɪʒən] *s* circoncision *f*
circumference [sər'kʌmfərəns] *s* circonférence *f*
circumflex ['sʌrkəm,flɛks] *adj* & *s* circonflexe *m*
circumlocution [,sʌrkəmlo'kjuʃən] *s* circonlocution *f*
circumscribe [,sʌrkəm'skraɪb] *tr* circonscrire
circumspect ['sʌrkəm,spɛkt] *adv* circonspect
circumstance ['sʌrkəm,stæns] *s* circonstance *f*; (*pomp*) cérémonie *f*; **in easy circumstances** aisé; **under no circumstance** sous aucun prétexte; **under the circumstances** dans ces conditions
circumstantial [,sʌrkəm'stænʃəl] *adj* (*derived from circumstances*) circonstanciel; (*detailed*) circonstancié
cir'cumstan'tial ev'idence *s* preuves *fpl* indirectes
circumvent [,sʌrkəm'vɛnt] *tr* circonvenir
circus ['sʌrkəs] *s* cirque *m*; (Brit) rond-point *m*
cirrhosis [sɪ'rosɪs] *s* cirrhose *f*
cistern ['sɪstərn] *s* citerne *f*
citadel ['sɪtədəl] *s* citadelle *f*
citation [saɪ'teʃən] *s* citation *f*; (*award*) présentation *f*, mention *f*
cite [saɪt] *tr* citer
cither ['sɪθər] *s* cithare *f*
citified ['sɪtɪ,faɪd] *adj* urbain
citizen ['sɪtɪzən] *s* citoyen *m*
citizen·ry ['sɪtɪzənri] *s* (*pl* **-ries**) citoyens *mpl*
cit'izen·ship' *s* citoyenneté *f*
citric ['sɪtrɪk] *adj* citrique
citron ['sɪtrən] *s* cédrat *m*; (*tree*) cédratier *m*
citronella [,sɪtrə'nɛlə] *s* citronnelle *f*
cit'rus fruit' ['sɪtrəs] *s* agrumes *mpl*
cit·y ['sɪti] *s* (*pl* **-ies**) ville *f*; **the City** (*district within ancient boundaries*) la Cité
cit'y coun'cil *s* conseil *m* municipal
cit'y hall' *s* hôtel *m* de ville
cit'y plan'ner *s* urbaniste *mf*
cit'y plan'ning *s* urbanisme *m*
civ'et cat' ['sɪvɪt] *s* civette *f*
civic ['sɪvɪk] *adj* civique; **civics** instruction *f* civique
civies ['sɪviz] *spl* (coll) vêtements *mpl* civils; **in civies** en civil, en bourgeois
civil ['sɪvɪl] *adj* civil; (*courteous*) poli
civ'il defense' *s* protection *f* civile
civ'il engineer'ing *s* génie *m* civil
civilian [sɪ'vɪljən] *adj* & *s* civil *m*
civil'ian life' *s* vie *f* civile
civili·ty [sɪ'vɪlɪti] *s* (*pl* **-ties**) civilité *f*
civilization [,sɪvɪlɪ'zeʃən] *s* civilisation *f*
civilize ['sɪvɪ,laɪz] *tr* civiliser
civ'il rights' *spl* droits *mpl* civiques, droits politiques
civ'il serv'ant *s* fonctionnaire *mf*
civ'il serv'ice *s* fonction *f* publique
civ'il war' *s* guerre *f* civile; **Civil War** (*of the United States*) Guerre de Sécession
clack [klæk] *s* claquement *m* || *intr* claquer
clad [klæd] *adj* vêtu, habillé
claim [klem] *s* demande *f*; (*to a right*) revendication *f*; (*in prospecting*) concession *f* || *tr* (*a right*) réclamer, revendiquer; (*to require*) exiger, demander; **to claim that . . .** prétendre que . . . ; **to claim to** prétendre
claimant ['klemənt] *s* prétendant *m*, ayant droit *m*
clairvoyance [klɛr'vɔɪ·əns] *s* voyance *f*, seconde vue *f*; (*keen insight*) clairvoyance *f*
clairvoyant [klɛr'vɔi·ənt] *adj* clairvoyant || *s* voyante *f*; voyant *m*
clam [klæm] *s* palourde *f* || *v* (*pret* & *pp* **clammed**; *ger* **clamming**) *intr*—**to clam up** (slang) se taire
clam'bake' *s* pique-nique *m* aux palourdes
clamber ['klæmbər] *intr* grimper; **to clamber over** or **up** escalader
clam·my ['klæmi] *adj* (*comp* **-mier**; *super* **-miest**) moite; (*clinging*) collant
clamor ['klæmər] *s* clameur *f* || *intr* vociférer; **to clamor for** réclamer

clamorous ['klæmərəs] *adj* bruyant
clamp [klæmp] *s* crampon *m*, agrafe
f; (med) clamp *m* ‖ *tr* fixer, attacher;
to clamp together cramponner ‖ *intr*
—**to clamp down on** (coll) visser
clan [klæn] *s* clan *m*
clandestine [klæn'dɛstɪn] *adj* clandestin
clang [klæŋ] *s* bruit *m* métallique, choc
m retentissant, cliquetis *m* ‖ *tr* faire
résonner ‖ *intr* résonner
clank [klæŋk] *s* bruit *m* sec, bruit métallique, cliquetis *m* ‖ *tr* faire résonner ‖ *intr* résonner
clannish ['klænɪʃ] *adj* partisan
clap [klæp] *s* coup *m*; (with hand)
tape *f*; (with the hands) battement *m*
‖ *v* (pret & pp **clapped**; ger **clapping**)
tr battre; (into jail) (coll) fourrer;
to clap the hands claquer or battre
les mains ‖ *intr* applaudir, claquer
clapper ['klæpər] *s* applaudisseur *m*;
(of bell) battant *m*
claque [klæk] *s* (paid clappers) claque
f; (crush hat) claque *m*
claret ['klærɪt] *s* bordeaux *m*
clari·fy ['klærɪ,faɪ] *v* (pret & pp **-fied**)
tr clarifier
clarinet [,klærɪ'nɛt] *s* clarinette *f*
clarity ['klærɪti] *s* clarté *f*
clash [klæʃ] *s* choc *m*; (conflict) dispute *f*; (of colors) disparate *f* ‖ *intr*
se heurter, s'entre-choquer; (said of
colors) former une disparate
clasp [klæsp], [klɑsp] *s* agrafe *f*, fermoir *m*; (embrace) étreinte *f* ‖ *tr*
agrafer; (to embrace) étreindre
clasp' knife' *s* couteau *m* pliant
class [klæs], [klɑs] *s* classe *f* ‖ *tr*
classer
classic ['klæsɪk] *adj* & *s* classique *m*
classical ['klæsɪkəl] *adj* classique
classicism ['klæsɪ,sɪzəm] *s* classicisme
m
classicist ['klæsɪsɪst] *s* classique *mf*
classification [,klæsɪfɪ'keʃən] *s* classification *f*, classement *m*
classified *adj* classifié, classé; (documents) secret, confidentiel
clas'sified adver'tise'ments *spl* petites
annonces *fpl*
classi·fy ['klæsɪ,faɪ] *v* (pret & pp **-fied**)
tr classifier
class'mate' *s* camarade *mf* de classe
class'room' *s* salle *f* de classe, classe *f*
class·y ['klæsi] *adj* (comp **-ier**; super
-iest) (slang) chic
clatter ['klætər] *s* fracas *m* ‖ *intr* faire
un fracas
clause [klɔz] *s* clause *f*, article *m*;
(gram) proposition *f*
clavicle ['klævɪkəl] *s* clavicule *f*
claw [klɔ] *s* (of animal) griffe *f*; (of
crab) pince *f*; (of hammer) panne *f*
fendue ‖ *tr* griffer, déchirer
clay [kle] *s* argile *f*, glaise *f*
clay' pig'eon *s* pigeon *m* d'argile
clay' pipe' *s* pipe *f* en terre
clay' pit' *s* argilière *f*, glaisière *f*
clean [klin] *adj* propre; (precise) net ‖
adv net; tout à fait ‖ *tr* nettoyer;
(fish) vider; (streets) balayer; **to
clean out** curer; (a person) (slang)

mettre à sec, décaver; **to clean up**
nettoyer ‖ *intr* faire le nettoyage
clean'-cut' *adj* bien délimité, net; (e.g.,
athlete) bien découplé
cleaner ['klinər] *s* nettoyeur *m*, dégraisseur *m*; **to be taken to the
cleaners** (slang) se faire rincer
cleaning ['klinɪŋ] *s* nettoyage *m*
clean'ing wom'an *s* femme *f* de ménage
cleanliness ['klɛnlɪnɪs] *s* propreté *f*,
netteté *f*
cleanse [klɛnz] *tr* nettoyer, écurer;
(e.g., a wound) assainir; (e.g., one's
thoughts) purifier
cleanser ['klɛnzər] *s* produit *m* de nettoyage; (soap) détersif *m*
clean'-shav'en *adj* rasé de frais
cleans'ing cream' *s* crème *f* de démaquillage
clean'up' *s* nettoiement *m*
clear [klɪr] *adj* clair; (sharp) net;
(free) dégagé, libre; (unmortgaged)
franc d'hypothèque; **to become clear**
s'éclaircir; **to keep clear of** éviter ‖
tr (to brighten) éclaircir; (e.g., a
fence) franchir; (obstacles) dégager;
(land) défricher; (goods in customs)
dédouaner; (an account) solder; **to
clear away** écarter, enlever; **to clear
oneself** se disculper; **to clear out**
(e.g., a garden) jardiner; **to clear the
table** desservir, enlever le couvert,
ôter la nappe; **to clear up** éclaircir ‖
intr (said of weather) s'éclaircir; **to
clear out** (coll) filer, se sauver
clearance ['klɪrəns] *s* permis *m*, laissez-passer *m*, autorisation *f*; (between
two objects) espace *m* libre; (com)
compensation *f*; (mach) espace *m*
mort, jeu *m*
clear'ance sale' *s* vente *f* de soldes
clear'-cut' *adj* net, tranché; (case)
absolu
clear'-head'ed *adj* lucide, perspicace
clearing ['klɪrɪŋ] *s* (in clouds) éclaircie
f; (in forest) clairière *f*, trouée *f*
clear'ing house' *s* (com) comptoir *m* de
règlement, chambre *f* de compensation
clearness ['klɪrnɪs] *s* clarté *f*, netteté *f*
clear'-sight'ed *adj* perspicace, clair-voyant
cleat [klit] *s* taquet *m*
cleavage ['klivɪdʒ] *s* clivage *m*
cleave [kliv] *v* (pret & pp **cleft** [klɛft]
or **cleaved**) *tr* fendre ‖ *intr* se fendre;
to cleave to s'attacher à, adhérer à
cleaver ['klivər] *s* couperet *m*, hachoir
m
clef [klɛf] *s* (mus) clef *f*
cleft [klɛft] *adj* fendu ‖ *s* fente *f*,
crevasse *f*
cleft' pal'ate *s* palais *m* fendu, fissure
f palatine
clemen·cy ['klɛmənsi] *s* (pl **-cies**)
clémence *f*
clement ['klɛmənt] *adj* clément
clench [klɛntʃ] *tr* serrer, crisper
cler·gy ['klʌrdʒi] *s* (pl **-gies**) (members)
clergé *m*; (profession) clergie *f*
cler'gy·man *s* (pl **-men**) ecclésiastique
m, clerc *m*

cleric ['klɛrɪk] *s* clerc *m*, ecclésiastique *m*

clerical ['klɛrɪkəl] *adj* clerical; de bureau || *s* clerical *m*; **clericals** habit *m* ecclésiastique

cler′ical er′ror *s* faute *f* de copiste, faute de sténographe

cler′ical work′ *s* travail *m* de bureau

clerk [klʌrk] *s* (*clerical worker*) employé *m* de bureau, commis *m*; (*in lawyer's office*) clerc *m*; (*in store*) vendeur *m*; (*in bank*) comptable *mf*; (*of court*) greffier *m*; (eccl) clerc

clever ['klɛvər] *adj* habile, adroit

cliché [kli'ʃe] *s* cliché *m*, expression *f* consacrée

click [klɪk] *s* cliquetis *m*, clic *m*; (*of heels*) bruit *m* sec; (*of tongue*) claquement *m*; (*of a machine*) déclic *m* || *intr* cliqueter, faire un déclic; (*to succeed*) (coll) réussir; (*to get along well*) (coll) s'entendre à merveille

client ['klaɪ·ənt] *s* client *m*

clientele [ˌklaɪ·ən'tɛl] *s* clientèle *f*

cliff [klɪf] *s* falaise *f*, talus *m* raide

climate ['klaɪmɪt] *s* climat *m*

climax ['klaɪmæks] *s* point *m* culminant, comble *m*

climb [klaɪm] *s* montée *f*, ascension *f* || *tr & intr* monter, gravir; grimper; **to climb down** descendre

climber ['klaɪmər] *s* grimpeur *m*; (bot) plante *f* grimpante; (*social climber*) parvenu *m*, arriviste *mf*

climbing ['klaɪmɪŋ] *s* montée *f*, escalade *f*

clinch [klɪntʃ] *s* crampon *m*, rivet *m*; (boxing) corps-à-corps *m* || *tr* river; (*a bargain*) boucler || *intr* se prendre corps à corps

clincher ['klɪntʃər] *s* (coll) argument *m* sans réplique

cling [klɪŋ] *v* (*pret & pp* **clung** [klʌŋ]) *intr* s'accrocher, se cramponner; **to cling to** (*a person*) se serrer contre; (*a belief*) adhérer à

cling′stone peach′ *s* alberge *f*

clinic ['klɪnɪk] *s* clinique *f*

clinical ['klɪnɪkəl] *adj* clinique

clinician [klɪ'nɪʃən] *s* clinicien *m*

clink [klɪŋk] *s* cliquetis *m*; (*e.g., of glasses*) tintement *m*, choc *m* || *tr* (*glasses, in a toast*) choquer; **to clink glasses with** trinquer avec || *intr* tinter, cliqueter

clip [klɪp] *s* attache *f*; (*brooch*) agrafe *f*, clip *m*; (*of gun*) chargeur *m*; (*blow*) (coll) taloche *f*; (*fast pace*) (coll) pas *m* rapide || *v* (*pret & pp* **clipped**; *ger* **clipping**) *tr* (*to fasten*) attacher; (*hair*) rafraîchir; (*sheep*) tondre; (*one's words*) avaler

clipper ['klɪpər] *s* (aer) clipper *m*; (naut) voilier *m* de course; **clippers** tondeuse *f*

clipping ['klɪpɪŋ] *s* tondage *m*; (*of sheep*) tonte *f*; (*of one's hair*) taille *f*; (*of newspaper*) coupure *f* (de presse); **clippings** (*cuttings, shavings, etc.*) rognures *fpl*, chutes *fpl*

clip′ping ser′vice *s* argus *m*

clique [klik] *s* coterie *f*, clan *m*, chapelle *f*

cloak [klok] *s* manteau *m* || *tr* masquer

cloak′-and-dag′ger *adj* (*e.g., story*) de cape et d'épée

cloak′room′ *s* vestiaire *m*; (rr) consigne *f*

clock [klɑk] *s* pendule *f*; (*e.g., in a tower*) horloge *f*; **to turn back the clock** retarder l'horloge; (fig) revenir en arrière || *tr* chronométrer

clock′mak′er *s* horloger *m*

clock′ tow′er *s* tour *f* de l'horloge

clock′wise′ *adj & adv* dans le sens des aiguilles d'une montre

clock′work′ *s* mouvement *m* d'horlogerie; **like clockwork** (coll) comme une horloge

clod [klɑd] *s* motte *f*; (*person*) rustre *mf*

clod′hop′per *s* cul-terreux *m*; (*shoe*) godillot *m*

clog [klɑg] *s* (*shoe*) galoche *f*, socque *m*; (*hindrance*) entrave *f* || *v* (*pret & pp* **clogged**; *ger* **clogging**) *tr* (*e.g., a pipe*) boucher; (*e.g., traffic*) entraver || *intr* se boucher

cloister ['klɔɪstər] *s* cloître *m* || *tr* cloîtrer

close [klos] *adj* proche, tout près; (*game; weave; formation, order*) serré; (*friend*) intime; (*friendship*) étroit; (*room*) renfermé, étouffant; (*translation*) fidèle; **close to** près de || *adv* près, de près || [kloz] *s* (*enclosure*) clos *m*; (*end*) fin *f*; (*closing*) fermeture *f* || *tr* fermer; (*to end*) conclure, terminer; (*an account*) régler, clôturer; (*ranks*) serrer, resserrer; (*a meeting*) lever; **close quotes** fermez les guillemets; **to close in** enfermer; **to close out** (com) liquider, solder || *intr* se fermer; finir, se terminer; (*on certain days*) (theat) faire relâche; **close in on** (*the enemy*) aborder

close′ call′ [klos] *s*—**to have a close call** (coll) l'échapper belle

close-cropped ['klos'krɑpt] *adj* coupé ras

closed [klozd] *adj* fermé; (*road*) barré; (*e.g., pipe*) obturé, bouché; (*ranks*) serré; (public sign in front of theater) relâche; **with closed eyes** les yeux clos

closed′ car′ *s* conduite *f* intérieure

closed′-cir′cuit tel′evision *s* télévision *f* en circuit fermé

closed′ sea′son *s* fermeture *f* de la chasse, fermeture de la pêche

closefisted ['klos'fɪstəd] *adj* ladre, avare

close-fitting ['klos'fɪtɪŋ] *adj* collant, ajusté, qui moule le corps

close-grained ['klos'grend] *adj* serré

closely ['klosli] *adv* (*near*) de près, étroitement; (*exactly*) exactement

close-mouthed ['klos'mauðd] *adj* peu communicatif, économe de mots

closeness ['klosnɪs] *s* (*nearness*) proximité *f*; (*accuracy*) exactitude *f*; (*stinginess*) avarice *f*; (*of weather*) lourdeur *f*; (*of air*) manque *m* d'air

close′ shave′ [klos] *s*—**to have a close shave** se faire raser de près; (coll) échapper à un cheveu près

closet ['klɑzɪt] *s* placard *m*

clos′et dra′ma *s* spectacle *m* dans un fauteuil

close-up ['klos‚ʌp] *s* premier plan *m*, gros plan

closing ['klozɪŋ] *adj* dernier, final ‖ *s* fermeture *f*; (*of account; of meeting*) clôture *f*

clos′ing-out′ sale′ *s* soldes *mpl* des fins de séries

clos′ing price′ *s* dernier cours *m*

clot [klɑt] *s* caillot *m* ‖ *v* (*pret & pp* **clotted**; *ger* **clotting**) *tr* cailler ‖ *intr* se cailler

cloth [klɔθ], [klɑθ] *s* étoffe *f*; (*fabric*) tissu *m*; (*of wool*) drap *m*; (*of cotton or linen*) toile *f*; **cloths** (*for cleaning*) chiffons *mpl*, torchons *mpl*, linge *m*; **the cloth** le clergé

clothe [kloð] *v* (*pret & pp* **clothed** or **clad** [klæd]) *tr* habiller, vêtir; (*e.g., with authority*) revêtir, investir

clothes [kloz], [kloθz] *spl* vêtements *mpl*, habits *mpl*; (*underclothes, shirts, etc.; wash*) linge *m*; **in plain clothes** en civil; **to put on one's clothes** s'habiller; **to take off one's clothes** se déshabiller

clothes′bas′ket *s* panier *m* à linge

clothes′brush′ *s* brosse *f* à habits

clothes′ clos′et *s* garde-robe *f*, penderie *f*, placard *m*

clothes′ dry′er *s* séchoir *m* à linge

clothes′ hang′er *s* cintre *m*

clothes′horse′ *s* séchoir-chevalet *m*

clothes′line′ *s* corde *f* à linge, étendoir *m*

clothes′ moth′ *s* gerce *f*

clothes′pin′ *s* pince *f* à linge

clothes′ rack′ *s* patère *f*

clothier ['kloðjər] *s* confectionneur *m*, marchand *m* de confections

clothing ['kloðɪŋ] *s* vêtements *mpl*

cloud [klaud] *s* nuage *m*; (*heavy cloud; multitude*) nuée *f*; **in the clouds** dans les nues ‖ *tr* couvrir de nuages; (*phot*) voiler ‖ *intr* (*phot*) se voiler; **to cloud over** or **up** se couvrir de nuages

cloud′burst′ *s* averse *f*, rafale *f* de pluie

cloud′ cham′ber *s* (phys) chambre *f* d'ionisation

cloudless ['klaudlɪs] *adj* sans nuages

cloud·y ['klaudi] *adj* (*comp* **-ier**; *super* **-iest**) nuageux; (phot) voilé

clout [klaut] *s* (coll) gifle *f* ‖ *tr* (coll) gifler

clove [klov] *s* clou *m* de girofle, girofle *m*; (*of garlic*) gousse *f*; (bot) giroflier *m*

clove′ hitch′ *s* demi-clef *f* à capeler

clo′ven hoof′ ['klovən] *s* pied *m* fourchu; **to show the cloven hoof** (coll) montrer le bout de l'oreille

clover ['klovər] *s* trèfle *m*; **to be in clover** (coll) être sur le velours

clo′ver·leaf′ *s* (*pl* **-leaves**) feuille *f* de trèfle; (*intersection*) croisement *m* en trèfle, saut-de-mouton *m*

clown [klaun] *s* clown *m*, pitre *m*, bouffon *m* ‖ *intr* faire le pitre

clownish ['klaunɪʃ] *adj* bouffon; (*clumsy*) empoté, rustre

cloy [klɔɪ] *tr* rassasier

club [klʌb] *s* massue *f*, gourdin *m*, assommoir *m*; cercle *m*, amicale *f*, club *m*; (*cards*) trèfle *m*; (*golf*) crosse *f*, club *m* ‖ *v* (*pret & pp* **clubbed**; *ger* **clubbing**) *tr* (*to strike*) assommer; (*to pool*) mettre en commun ‖ *intr*—**to club together** s'associer; se cotiser

club′ car′ *s* voiture-salon *f*

club′foot′ *s* (*pl* **-feet**) pied *m* équin, pied bot

club′foot′ed *adj*—**to be clubfooted** avoir le pied bot, être pied-bot

club′house′ *s* club *m*, cercle *m*

club′man *s* (*pl* **-men**) clubman *m*

club′room′ *s* salle *f* de réunion

club′ steak′ *s* aloyau *m* de bœuf

club′wom′an *s* (*pl* **-wom′en**) cercleuse *f*

cluck [klʌk] *s* gloussement *m* ‖ *intr* glousser

clue [klu] *s* indice *m*, indication *f*; **to find the clue** trouver la clef; **to give s.o. a clue** mettre qn sur la piste; **to have the clue** tenir le bout du fil

clump [klʌmp] *s* (*of earth*) bloc *m*, masse *f*; (*of trees*) bouquet *m*; (*of shrubs or flowers*) massif *m*; (*gait*) pas *m* lourd ‖ *intr*—**to clump along** marcher lourdement

clum·sy ['klʌmzi] *adj* (*comp* **-sier**; *super* **-siest**) (*worker*) maladroit, gauche; (*work*) bâclé, grossier

cluster ['klʌstər] *s* bouquet *m*, massif *m*; (*of grapes*) grappe *f*; (*of pears*) glane *f*; (*of bananas*) régime *m*; (*of diamonds*) épi *m*, nœud *m*; (*of stars*) amas *m* ‖ *tr* grouper ‖ *intr*—**to cluster around** se rassembler; **to cluster together** se conglomérer

clutch [klʌtʃ] *s* (*grasp, grip*) griffe *f*, serre *f*; (aut) embrayage *m*; (aut) pédale *f* d'embrayage; **to fall into the clutches of** tomber sous la patte de; **to let in the clutch** embrayer; **to throw out the clutch** débrayer ‖ *tr* saisir, empoigner ‖ *intr*—**to clutch at** se raccrocher à

clutter ['klʌtər] *s* encombrement *m* ‖ *tr*—**to clutter up** encombrer

Co. *abbr* (**Company**) Cⁱᵉ

c/o *abbr* (**in care of**) a/s (aux soins de)

coach [kotʃ] *s* coche *m*, carrosse *f*; (*bus*) autocar *m*, car *m*; (*two-door sedan*) coche *m*; (rr) voiture *f*; (sports) entraîneur *m*, moniteur *m* ‖ *tr* donner des leçons particulières à; entraîner; (*for an exam*) préparer à un examen, chauffer; (*an actor*) faire répéter

coach′-and-four′ *s* carrosse *f* à quatre chevaux

coach′ box′ *s* siège *m* du cocher

coach′ house′ *s* remise *f*

coaching ['kotʃɪŋ] *s* leçons *fpl* particulières, chauffage *m*, répétitions *fpl*; (sport) entraînement *m*

coach′man *s* (*pl* **-men**) cocher *m*

coagulate [ko'ægjə,let] *tr* coaguler ‖ *intr* se coaguler
coal [kol] *adj* charbonnier, houiller ‖ *s* houille *f*, charbon *m*; **coals** (*embers*) tisons *mpl*, charbons ardents; **to carry coals to Newcastle** porter de l'eau à la rivière
coal' bin' *s* coffre *m* à charbon
coal' bunk'er *s* soute *f* à charbon
coal' car' *s* wagon-tombereau *m*
coal'deal'er *s* charbonnier *m*
coalesce [,ko-ə'lɛs] *intr* s'unir, se combiner, fusionner
coal' field' *s* bassin *m* houiller
coalition [,ko-ə'lɪ/ən] *s* coalition *f*; **to form a coalition** se coaliser
coal' mine' *s* houillère *f*
coal' oil' *s* pétrole *m* lampant
coal' scut'tle *s* seau *m* à charbon
coal' tar' *s* goudron *m* de houille
coal'yard' *s* charbonnerie *f*
coarse [kors] *adj* (*in manners*) grossier; (*composed of large particles*) gros; (*hair, skin*) rude
coarse'-grained' *adj* à gros grain; (*wood*) à gros fil
coarseness ['korsnɪs] *s* grossièreté *f*; (*of hair, skin*) rudesse *f*
coast [kost] *s* côte *f*; **the coast is clear** la route est libre ‖ *intr* caboter; (*said of automobile*) aller au débrayé; (*said of bicycle*) aller en roue libre; **to coast along** continuer sur sa lancée
coastal ['kostəl] *adj* côtier
coaster ['kostər] *s* dessous-de-verre *m*, sous-verre *m*; (*naut*) caboteur *m*
coast'er brake' *s* frein *m* à contre-pédalage
coast' guard' *s* service *m* de guet le long des côtes
coast'-guard cut'ter *s* garde-côte *m*
coast'guards'man *s* (*pl* -**men**) soldat *m* chargé de la garde des côtes
coasting ['kostɪŋ] *s* (*e.g., on a cycle*) descente *f* en roue libre
coast'ing trade' *s* cabotage *m*
coast'line' *s* littoral *m*
coast'wise' *adj* côtier ‖ *adv* le long de la côte
coat [kot] *s* (*jacket*) veste *f*; (*suitcoat*) veston *m*; (*topcoat*) manteau *m*; (*of an animal*) robe *f*, pelage *m*, livrée *f*; (*of paint*) couche *f* ‖ *tr* enduire; (*with chocolate*) enrober; (*a pill*) dragéifier
coat' hang'er *s* cintre *m*, portemanteau *m*
coating ['kotɪŋ] *s* enduit *m*, couche *f*
coat' of arms' *s* écu *m* armorial; (*bearings*) blason *m*, armoiries *fpl*
coat' of mail' *s* cotte *f* de mailles
coat'rack' *s* portemanteau *m*
coat'room' *s* vestiaire *m*
coat'tail' *s* basque *f*
coauthor [ko'ɔθər] *s* coauteur *m*
coax [koks] *tr* cajoler, amadouer
cob [kab] *s* (*of corn*) épi *m* de maïs; (*horse*) cob *m*; (*swan*) cygne *m* mâle
cobalt ['kobɔlt] *s* cobalt *m*
cobbler ['kablər] *s* cordonnier *m*; (*cake*) tourte *f* aux fruits; (*drink*) boisson *f* glacée

cobble•stone ['kabəl,ston] *s* pavé *m*
cob'web' *s* toile *f* d'araignée
cocaine [ko'ken] *s* cocaïne *f*
cock [kak] *s* coq *m*; (*faucet*) robinet *m*; (*of gun*) chien *m* ‖ *tr* (*one's ears*) dresser, redresser; (*one's hat*) mettre sur l'oreille, retrousser; (*a rifle*) armer
cockade [ka'ked] *s* cocarde *f*
cock-a-doodle-doo ['kakə,dudəl'du] *interj* cocorico!
cock'-and-bull' sto'ry *s* coq-à-l'âne *m*
cock'crow' *s* cocorico *m*
cocked' hat' *s* chapeau *m* à cornes; **to knock into a cocked hat** (slang) démolir, aplatir
cock'er span'iel ['kakər] *s* cocker *m*
cock'eyed' *adj* (coll) de travers, de biais; (slang) insensé
cock'fight' *s* combat *m* de coqs
cockle ['kakəl] *s* (bot) nielle *f*; (zool) bucarde *f*, clovisse *f*
cock'pit' *s* (aer) cockpit *m*, carlingue *f*
cock'roach' *s* blatte *f*, cafard *m*
cockscomb ['kaks,kom] *s* crête *f* de coq; (bot) crête-de-coq *f*
cock'sure' *adj* (coll) sûr et certain
cock'tail' *s* cocktail *m*
cock'tail dress' *s* robe *f* de cocktail
cock'tail par'ty *s* cocktail *m*
cock'tail shak'er *s* shaker *m*
cock•y ['kaki] *adj* (*comp* -**ier**; *super* -**iest**) (coll) effronté, suffisant
cocoa ['koko] *s* cacao *m*; (*drink*) chocolat *m*
co'coa bean' *s* cacao *m*
coconut ['kokə,nʌt] *s* noix *f* de coco, coco *m*
co'conut palm' *s* cocotier *m*
cocoon [kə'kun] *s* cocon *m*
cod [kad] *s* (ichth) morue *f*
C.O.D. ['si'o'di] *s* (letterword) (**Collect on Delivery**) C.R., contre remboursement, e.g., **send it to me C.O.D.** envoyez-le-moi C.R.
coddle ['kadəl] *tr* dorloter, gâter
code [kod] *s* code *m*; (*secret code*) chiffre *m* ‖ *tr* chiffrer
code' word' *s* mot *m* convenu
codex ['kodɛks] *s* (*pl* **codices** ['kodɪ,siz], ['kadɪ,siz]) manuscrit *m* ancien
cod'fish' *s* morue *f*
codger ['kadʒər] *s*—**old codger** (coll) vieux bonhomme *m*
codicil ['kadɪsɪl] *s* (*of will*) codicille *m*; (*of contract, treaty, etc.*) avenant *m*
codi•fy ['kadɪ,faɪ], ['kodɪ,faɪ] *v* (*pret & pp* -**fied**) *tr* codifier
cod'-liver oil' *s* huile *f* de foie de morue
coed ['ko,ɛd] *s* collégienne *f*, étudiante *f* universitaire
coeducation [,ko-ɛdʒə'ke/ən] *s* coéducation *f*
co'educa'tional school' [,ko-ɛdʒə'ke-/ənəl] *s* école *f* mixte
coefficient [,ko-ɪ'fɪ/ənt] *s* coefficient *m*
coerce [ko'ʌrs] *tr* contraindre, forcer
coercion [ko'ʌr/ən] *s* coercition *f*

coexist [ˌko·ɪgˈzɪst] intr coexister
coexistence [ˌko·ɪgˈzɪstəns] s coexistence f
coffee [ˈkɔfi], [ˈkɑfi] s café m; black coffee café noir, café nature; ground coffee café moulu; roasted coffee café brûlé, café torréfié
cof'fee and rolls' s café m complet
cof'fee bean' s grain m de café
cof'fee break' s pause-café f
cof'fee·cake' s gimblette f (qui se prend avec le café)
cof'fee cup' s tasse f à café
cof'fee grind'er s moulin m à café
cof'fee grounds' spl marc m de café
cof'fee mak'er s percolateur m
cof'fee mill' s moulin m à café
cof'fee planta'tion s caféière f
cof'fee·pot' s cafetière f; (for pouring) verseuse f
cof'fee roast'er s brûloir m
cof'fee shop' s (of hotel) hôtel-restaurant m; (in station) buffet m
cof'fee tree' s caféier m
coffer [ˈkɔfər], [ˈkɑfər] s coffre m, caisse f; (archit) caisson m; coffers trésor m, fonds mpl
cof'fer·dam' s coffre m, bâtardeau m
coffin [ˈkɔfɪn], [ˈkɑfɪn] s cercueil m, bière f
cog [kɑg] s dent f; (cogwheel) roue f dentée; to slip a cog (coll) avoir des absences
cogency [ˈkodʒənsi] s force f (de persuasion)
cogent [ˈkodʒənt] adj puissant, convaincant
cogitate [ˈkɑdʒɪˌtet] tr & intr méditer
cognac [ˈkonjæk], [ˈkɑnjæk] s cognac m
cognate [ˈkɑgnet] adj congénère, apparenté ‖ s congénère mf; (word) mot m apparenté
cognizance [ˈkɑgnɪzəns], [ˈkɑnɪzəns] s connaissance f
cognizant [ˈkɑgnɪzənt], [ˈkɑnɪzənt] adj informé
cog'wheel' s roue f dentée
cohabit [ko·ˈhæbɪt] intr cohabiter
coheir [ko·ˈer] s cohéritier
cohere [ko·ˈhɪr] intr s'agglomérer, adhérer; (said of reasoning or style) se suivre logiquement, correspondre
coherent [ko·ˈhɪrənt] adj cohérent
cohesion [ko·ˈhiʒən] s cohésion f
coiffeur [kwɑˈfʌr] s coiffeur m pour dames
coiffure [kwɑˈfjur] s coiffure f ‖ tr coiffer
coil [kɔɪl] s (something wound in a spiral) rouleau m; (single turn of spiral) tour m; (of a still) serpentin m; (of hair) boucle f; (elec) bobine f; coils (of snake) nœuds mpl ‖ tr enrouler; (naut) lover, gléner ‖ intr s'enrouler; (said of snake or stream) serpenter
coil' spring' s ressort m en spirale, ressort à boudin
coin [kɔɪn] s monnaie f; (single coin) pièce f de monnaie; (wedge) coin m; in coin en espèces, en numéraire; to

pay back s.o. in his own coin rendre à qn la monnaie de sa pièce; to toss a coin jouer à pile ou face ‖ tr (a new word; a story or lie) forger, inventer; to coin money frapper de la monnaie; (coll) faire des affaires d'or, s'enrichir à vue d'œil
coinage [ˈkɔɪnɪdʒ] s monnayage m; (fig) invention f
coincide [ˌko·ɪnˈsaɪd] intr coïncider
coincidence [ko·ˈɪnsɪdəns] s coïncidence f
coition [ko·ˈɪʃən] or coitus [ˈko·ɪtəs] s coït m
coke [kok] s coke m ‖ tr cokéfier ‖ intr se cokéfier
colander [ˈkʌləndər], [ˈkɑləndər] s passoire f
cold [kold] adj froid; it is cold (said of weather) il fait froid; to be cold (said of person) avoir froid ‖ s froid m; (indisposition) rhume m; to be left out in the cold (slang) rester en carafe; to catch a cold attraper un rhume, s'enrhumer
cold' blood' s—in cold blood de sang-froid
cold'-blood'ed adj insensible; (sensitive to cold) frileux; (zool) à sang froid
cold' chis'el s ciseau m à froid
cold' com'fort s maigre consolation f
cold' cream' s cold-cream m
cold' cuts' spl viandes fpl froides, assiette f anglaise
cold' feet' [fit] spl—to have cold feet (coll) avoir froid aux yeux
cold' front' s front m froid
cold'-heart'ed adj au cœur dur, insensible
coldness [ˈkoldnɪs] s froideur f; (in the air) froidure f
cold' should'er s—to give s.o. the cold shoulder (coll) battre froid à qn
cold' snap' s coup m de froid
cold' stor'age s entrepôt m frigorifique; in cold storage en glacière
cold'-stor'age adj frigorifique
cold' war' s guerre f froide
cold' wave' s vague f de froid
coleslaw [ˈkol ˌslɔ] s salade f de chou
colic [ˈkɑlɪk] s colique f
coliseum [ˌkɑlɪˈsi·əm] s colisée m
collaborate [kəˈlæbəˌret] intr collaborer
collaborationist [kəˌlæbəˈreʃənɪst] s collaborationniste mf
collaborator [kəˈlæbəˌretər] s collaborateur m
collapse [kəˈlæps] s écroulement m, effondrement m; (of prices; of government) chute f; (of prices; of a beam) fléchissement m; (pathol) collapsus m ‖ intr s'écrouler, s'effondrer; (said of government) tomber; (said of structure or prices) s'effondrer; (said of balloon) se dégonfler
collapsible [kəˈlæpsɪbəl] adj démontable, rabattable, pliant
collar [ˈkɑlər] s (of dress, shirt) collet m, col m; (worn by dog; on pigeon) collier m; (mach) collier ‖ tr colleter; (coll) empoigner

col′lar·band′ s pied m de col (d'une chemise)

col′lar·bone′ s clavicule f

collate [kə'let], ['kɑlet] tr collationner, conférer

collateral [kə'lætərəl] adj accessoire; correspondant; (kin) collatéral ‖ s (kin) collatéral m; (com) nantissement m

collation [kə'leʃən] s collation f

colleague ['kɑlig] s collègue mf

collect ['kɑlɛkt] s (eccl) collecte f ‖ [kə'lɛkt] tr rassembler; (taxes) percevoir, lever; (stamps, antiques) collectionner; (eggs; classroom papers; tickets) ramasser; (mail) faire la levée de; (debts) recouvrer; (gifts, money) collecter; (one's thoughts; anecdotes) recueillir; **to collect oneself** se reprendre, se remettre ‖ intr (for the poor) quêter; (to gather together) se rassembler, se réunir; (to pile up) s'amasser ‖ adv en p.c.v., e.g., **to telephone collect** téléphoner en p.c.v.

collect′ call′ s (telp) communication f P.C.V.

collected adj recueilli, maître de soi

collection [kə'lɛkʃən] s collection f; (of taxes) perception f, levée f, recouvrement m; (of mail) levée f; (of verses) recueil m

collec′tion plate′ s plateau m de quête

collective [kə'lɛktɪv] adj collectif

collector [kə'lɛktər] s (of stamps, antiques) collectionneur m; (of taxes) percepteur m, receveur m, collecteur m; (of tickets) contrôleur m

college ['kɑlɪdʒ] s (of cardinals, electors, etc.) collège m; (school in a university) faculté f; (U.S.A.) école f des arts et sciences

collegian [kə'lidʒɪ·ən] s étudiant m

collegiate [kə'lidʒɪ·ɪt] adj collégial, de l'université, universitaire

collide [kə'laɪd] intr se heurter, se tamponner; **to collide with** se heurter à or contre, heurter contre

collier ['kɑljər] s houilleur m; (ship) charbonnier m

collier·y ['kɑljəri] s (pl -ies) houillère f

collision [kə'lɪʒən] s collision f

collocate ['kɑlo,ket] tr disposer en rapport; (creditors) colloquer

colloid ['kɑlɔɪd] adj colloïdal ‖ s colloïde m

colloquial [kə'lokwɪ·əl] adj familier

colloquialism [kə'lokwɪ·ə,lɪzəm] s expression f familière

collo·quy ['kɑləkwi] s (pl -quies) colloque m

collusion [kə'luʒən] s collusion f; **to be in collusion with** être d'intelligence avec

cologne [kə'lon] s eau f de Cologne

Colombia [kə'lʌmbɪ·ə] s Colombie f; **la Colombie**

colon ['kolən] s (anat) côlon m; (gram) deux points mpl

colonel ['kʌrnəl] s colonel m

colonial [kə'lonɪ·əl] adj & s colonial m

colonist ['kɑlənɪst] s colon m

colonize ['kɑlə,naɪz] tr & intr coloniser

colonnade [,kɑlə'ned] s colonnade f

colo·ny ['kɑləni] s (pl -nies) colonie f

colophon ['kɑlə,fɑn] s colophon m

color ['kʌlər] s couleur f; **the colors** les couleurs, le drapeau; **to call to the colors** appeler sous les drapeaux; **to give or lend color to** colorer; (fig) rendre vraisemblable; **to show one's true colors** se révéler sous son vrai jour; **under color of** sous couleur de; **with flying colors** enseignes déployées ‖ tr colorer; (e.g., a drawing) colorier; (to exaggerate) donner de l'éclat à, imager; (to dye) teindre ‖ intr se colorer; (to blush) rougir

col′or·bear′er s porte-drapeau m

col′or·blind′ adj daltonien, aveugle des couleurs

colored adj coloré; (person) de couleur; (drawing) colorié

colorful ['kʌlərfəl] adj (striking) coloré; (unusual) pittoresque

col′or guard′ s garde f d'honneur du drapeau

coloring ['kʌlərɪŋ] adj colorant ‖ s colorant m; (of painting, complexion, style) coloris m

colorless ['kʌlərlɪs] adj incolore

col′or photog′raphy s photographie f en couleurs

col′or salute′ s (mil) salut m au drapeau, salut aux couleurs

col′or ser′geant s sergent-chef m, sergent-major m

col′or tel′evision s télévision f en couleurs

colossal [kə'lɑsəl] adj colossal

colossus [kə'lɑsəs] s colosse m

colt [kolt] s poulain m

Columbus [kə'lʌmbəs] s Colomb m

column ['kɑləm] s colonne f; (journ) rubrique f, chronique f, courrier m; (mil) colonne

columnar [kə'lʌmnər] adj en colonne

columnist ['kɑləmɪst] s chroniqueur m, courriériste mf

coma ['komə] s (pathol) coma m

comb [kom] s peigne m; (currycomb) étrille f; (of rooster; of wave) crête f; (filled with honey) rayon m ‖ tr peigner; explorer minutieusement, fouiller; **to comb out** démêler ‖ intr (said of waves) déferler

com·bat ['kɑmbæt] s combat m ‖ ['kɑmbæt], [kəm'bæt] v (pret & pp -bated or -batted; ger -bating or -batting) tr & intr combattre

combatant ['kɑmbətənt] adj & s combattant m

com′bat du′ty s service m de combat, service au front

combination [,kɑmbɪ'neʃən] s combinaison f

combine ['kɑmbaɪn] s trust m, combinaison f financière, entente f industrielle; (agr) moissonneuse-batteuse f ‖ [kəm'baɪn] tr combiner ‖ intr se liguer, fusionner; (chem) se combiner

combin′ing form′ s élément m de composition

combo ['kɑmbo] s (*of four musicians*) quartette *f*
combustible [kəm'bʌstɪbəl] *adj* & *s* combustible *m*
combustion [kəm'bʌstʃən] *s* combustion *f*
come [kʌm] *v* (*pret* **came** [kem]; *pp* **come**) *intr* venir; **come in!** entrez!; **to come after** succéder à, suivre; (*to come to get*) venir chercher; **to come apart** se séparer, se défaire; **to come around** (*to snap back*) se rétablir; (*to give in*) céder; **to come at** (*to attack*) se jeter sur; **to come back** revenir; (coll) revenir en vogue; **to come before** précéder; (*e.g., a legislature*) se mettre devant; **to come between** s'interposer entre; **to come by** (*to get*) obtenir; (*to pass*) passer; **to come down** descendre; **to come downstairs** descendre (en bas); **to come down with** tomber malade avec; **to come for** venir chercher; **to come from** provenir de, dériver de; (*said of wind*) chasser de; **to come in** entrer; entrer dans; (*said of tide*) monter; (*said of style*) entrer en vogue; **to come in for** avoir part à; (*e.g., an inheritance*) succéder à; (*e.g., sympathy*) s'attirer; **to come off** se détacher; (*to take place*) avoir lieu; en sortir, e.g., **to come off victorious** en sortir vainqueur; **to come out** sortir; (*said of sun, stars; said of book*) paraître; (*said of buds*) éclore; (*said of news*) se divulguer; (*said of debutante*) débuter; **to come out for** se prononcer pour; **to come over** se laisser persuader; arriver, e.g., **what's come over him?** qu'est-ce qui lui est arrivé?; **to come through** (*e.g., fields*) passer par, passer à travers; (*e.g., a wall*) pénétrer; (*an illness*) surmonter; se tirer indemne; **to come to** revenir à soi; **to come together** s'assembler, se réunir; **to come true** se réaliser; **to come up** monter; (*to occur*) se présenter; **to come upstairs** monter (en haut); **to come up to** monter jusqu'à, venir à; **to come up with** proposer
come'-and-go' *s* va-et-vient *m*
come'back' *s* (*of style*) (coll) retour *m* en vogue; (*of statesman*) (coll) retour *m* au pouvoir; (slang) réplique *f*, riposte *f*; **to stage a comeback** (coll) se réhabiliter, faire une belle remontée
comedian [kə'midɪ·ən] *s* comique *m*; (*on the legitimate stage*) comédien *m*; auteur *m* comique
comedienne [kə͵midɪ'ɛn] *s* comédienne *f*
come'down' *s* humiliation *f*, déchéance *f*
come•dy ['kɑmədi] *s* (*pl* -dies) comédie *f*
come•ly ['kʌmli] *adj* (*comp* -lier; *super* -liest) (*attractive*) avenant, gracieux; (*decorous*) convenable, bienséant
come'-on' *s* (slang) leurre *m*, attrape *f*
comet ['kɑmɪt] *s* comète *f*
comfort ['kʌmfərt] *s* confort *m*; consolation *f*; (*person*) consolateur *m*;

comforts commodités *fpl*, agréments *mpl* ‖ *tr* consoler, réconforter
comfortable ['kʌmfərtəbəl] *adj* confortable; (*in a state of comfort*) bien; (*well-off*) à l'aise
comforter ['kʌmfərtər] *s* consolateur *m*; (*bedcover*) couvre-pieds *m* piqué; (*of wool*) cache-nez *m*; (*for baby*) tétine *f*, sucette *f*
comforting ['kʌmfərtɪŋ] *adj* consolateur, réconfortant
com'fort sta'tion *s* châlet *m* de nécessité, lieux *mpl* d'aisances, toilette *f*
comic ['kɑmɪk] *adj* & *s* comique *m*; **comics** (*cartoons*) dessins *mpl* humoristiques
com'ic op'era *s* opéra *m* bouffe
com'ic strip' *s* bande *f* humoristique
coming ['kʌmɪŋ] *adj* qui vient; (*future*) d'avenir, de demain ‖ *s* arrivée *f*, venue *f*; **comings and goings** allées et venues
com'ing out' *s* (*of stocks, bonds, etc.*) émission *f*; (*of a book*) parution *f*; (*of a young lady*) début *m*
comma ['kɑmə] *s* virgule *f*; (*in French a period or sometimes a small space is used to mark the divisions of whole numbers*) point *m*
command [kə'mænd], [kə'mɑnd] *s* (*leadership*) gouvernement *m*; (*order, direction*) commandement *m*, ordre *m*; (*e.g., of a foreign language*) maîtrise *f*; **to be at s.o.'s command** être aux ordres de qn; **to have a command of** (*a language*) posséder; **to have at one's command** avoir à sa disposition ‖ *tr* commander, ordonner; (*respect*) inspirer; (*to look out over*) dominer; (*a language*) connaître ‖ *intr* (mil) commander, donner les ordres
commandant [͵kɑmən'dænt], [͵kɑmən'dɑnt] *s* commandant *m*
commandeer [͵kɑmən'dɪr] *tr* réquisitionner
commander [kə'mændər], [kə'mɑndər] *s* commandant *m*
comman'der in chief' *s* commandant *m* en chef
commanding [kə'mændɪŋ], [kə'mɑndɪŋ] *adj* imposant; (*in charge*) d'autorité
commemorate [kə'mɛməret] *tr* commémorer, célébrer
commence [kə'mɛns] *tr* & *intr* commencer
commencement [kə'mɛnsmənt] *s* commencement *m*; (educ) jour *m* de la distribution des prix, jour de la collation des grades
commence'ment ex'ercise *s* cérémonie *f* de remise des diplômes
commend [kə'mɛnd] *tr* (*to praise*) louer; (*to entrust*) confier, recommander
commendable [kə'mɛndəbəl] *adj* louable
commendation [͵kɑmən'deʃən] *s* louange *f*, éloge *m*; (mil) citation *f*
comment ['kɑmənt] *s* remarque *f*, observation *f*, commentaire *m* ‖ *intr*

faire des observations; **to comment on** commenter

commentar•y ['kɑmən,tɛri] s (pl -ies) commentaire m

commentator ['kɑmən,tetər] s commentateur m

commerce ['kɑmərs] s commerce m, négoce m

commercial [kə'mʌrʃəl] adj commercial, commerçant || s annonce f publicitaire

commercialize [kə'mʌrʃə,laɪz] tr commercialiser

commiserate [kə'mɪzə,ret] intr—to **commiserate with** compatir aux malheurs de

commiseration [kə,mɪzə'reʃən] s commisération f

commissar [,kɑmɪ'sɑr] s commissaire m

commissar•y ['kɑmɪ,sɛri] s (pl -ies) (person) commissaire m; (canteen) cantine f

commission [kə'mɪʃən] s commission f; (board, council) conseil m; (com) guelte f; (mil) brevet m; **out of commission** hors de service; (naut) désarmé || tr commissionner; (mil) promouvoir

commis'sioned of'ficer s breveté m

commissioner [kə'mɪʃənər] s commissaire m

com•mit [kə'mɪt] v (pret & pp -mitted; ger -mitting) tr (an error, crime, etc.) commettre; (one's soul, one's money, etc.) confier; (one's word) engager; (to a mental hospital) interner; **to commit to memory** apprendre par cœur; **to commit to prison** envoyer en prison; **to commit to writing** coucher par écrit

commitment [kə'mɪtmənt] s (act of committing) perpétration f; (to a mental institution) internement m; (to prison) emprisonnement m; (to a cause) engagement m

committal [kə'mɪtəl] s (of a crime) perpétration f; (of a task) délégation f; **committal to prison** mise en prison

commit'tal ser'vice s (eccl) prières fpl au bord de la tombe

committee [kə'mɪti] s comité m, commission f

commode [kə'mod] s (toilet) chaise f percée; (dressing table) grande table f de nuit

commodious [kə'modɪ•əs] adj spacieux, confortable

commodi•ty [kə'mɑdɪti] s (pl -ties) denrée f, marchandise f

common ['kɑmən] adj commun || s terrain m communal; **commons** communaux mpl; (of school) réfectoire m; **the Commons** (Brit) les communes fpl

com'mon car'rier s entreprise f de transports

commoner ['kɑmənər] s homme m du peuple, roturier m; (Brit) membre m de la Chambre des communes

com'mon law' s droit m coutumier, coutume f

com'mon-law mar'riage s union f libre, collage m

Com'mon Mar'ket s Marché m Commun

com'mon noun' s nom m commun

com'mon•place' adj banal || s banalité f

com'mon sense' s sens m commun

com'mon-sense' adj sensé

com'mon stock' s action f ordinaire, actions ordinaires

commonweal ['kɑmən,wil] s bien m public

com'mon•wealth' s état m, république f

commotion [kə'moʃən] s commotion f

commune [kə'mjun] intr s'entretenir; (eccl) communier

communicant [kə'mjunɪkənt] s informateur m; (eccl) communiant m

communicate [kə'mjunɪ,ket] tr & intr communiquer

communicating [kə'mjunɪ,ketɪŋ] adj communicant

communication [kə,mjunɪ'keʃən] s communication f

communicative [kə'mjunɪ,ketɪv] adj communicatif

communion [kə'mjunjən] s communion f; **to take communion** communier

communism ['kɑmjə,nɪzəm] s communisme m

communist ['kɑmjənɪst] adj & s communiste mf

communi•ty [kə'mjunɪti] s (pl -ties) (locality) voisinage m; (group of people living together) communauté f

commu'nity chest' s caisse f de secours

commutation [,kɑmjə'teʃən] s commutation f

commuta'tion tick'et s carte f d'abonnement

commutator ['kɑmjə,tetər] s (elec) collecteur m

commute [kə'mjut] tr échanger; (e.g., a prison term) commuer || intr s'abonner au chemin de fer; voyager avec carte d'abonnement

commuter [kə'mjutər] s abonné m au chemin de fer

compact [kəm'pækt] adj compact || ['kɑmpækt] s (agreement) pacte m; (for cosmetics) poudrier m, boîte f à poudre

companion [kəm'pænjən] s compagnon m; (female companion) compagne f

companionable [kəm'pænjənəbəl] adj sociable

compan'ion•ship' s camaraderie f

compan'ion•way' s escalier m des cabines

compa•ny ['kʌmpəni] s (pl -nies) compagnie f; (com) société f, compagnie; (naut) équipage m; (theat) troupe f; **to have company** avoir du monde; **to keep bad company** fréquenter la mauvaise compagnie; **to keep company** sortir ensemble; **to keep s.o. company** tenir compagnie à qn; **to part company** se séparer

comparative [kəm'pærətɪv] adj comparatif; (anatomy, literature, etc.) comparé || s comparatif m compare [kəm'pɛr] s—beyond compare incomparablement, sans égal || tr comparer; compared to en comparaison de; to be compared to se comparer à

comparison [kəm'pærɪsən] s comparaison f

compartment [kəm'pɑrtmənt] s compartiment m

compass ['kʌmpəs] s (for showing direction) boussole f; (range, reach) portée f; (for drawing circles) compas m; to box the compass réciter la rose des vents || tr—to compass about entourer

com'pass card' s rose f des vents

compassion [kəm'pæʃən] s compassion f

compassionate [kəm'pæʃənɪt] adj compatissant

compatibility [kəm,pætɪ'bɪlɪti] s compatibilité f, convenance f

com·pel [kəm'pɛl] v (pret & pp -pelled; ger -pelling) tr contraindre, obliger; (respect, silence) imposer

compelling [kəm'pɛlɪŋ] adj irrésistible; (motive) impérieux

compendious [kəm'pɛndɪ·əs] adj abrégé, succinct

compensate ['kɑmpən,set] tr compenser; to compensate s.o. for dédommager qn de || intr—to compensate for compenser

compensation [,kɑmpən'seʃən] s compensation f

compete [kəm'pit] intr concourir

competence ['kɑmpɪtəns] or competency·['kɑmpɪtənsi] s compétence f

competent ['kɑmpɪtənt] adj compétent

competition [,kɑmpɪ'tɪʃən] s concurrence f, compétition f; (contest) concours m; (sports) compétition, épreuve f

competitive [kəm'pɛtɪtɪv] adj compétitif

compet'itive exam'ination s concours m

competitor [kəm'pɛtɪtər] s concurrent m

compilation [,kɑmpɪ'leʃən] s compilation f

compile [kəm'paɪl] tr compiler

complacency [kəm'plesənsi] s complaisance f; (self-satisfaction) suffisance f

complacent [kəm'plesənt] adj complaisant; content de soi, suffisant

complain [kəm'plen] intr se plaindre

complainant [kəm'plenənt] s plaignant m

complaint [kəm'plent] s plainte f; (grievance) grief m; (illness) maladie f, mal m

complaisant [kəm'plezənt], ['kɑmplɪ,zænt] adj complaisant

complement ['kɑmplɪmənt] s complément m; (mil) effectif m || ['kɑmplɪ,mɛnt] tr compléter

complete [kəm'plit] adj complet || tr compléter

complex [kəm'plɛks], ['kɑmplɛks] adj complexe || ['kɑmplɛks] s complexe m

complexion [kəm'plɛkʃən] s (texture of skin, especially of face) teint m; (general aspect) caractère m; (constitution) complexion f

compliance [kəm'plaɪ·əns] s complaisance f; soumission f, conformité f; in compliance with conformément à

complicate ['kɑmplɪ,ket] tr compliquer

complicated adj compliqué

complication [,kɑmplɪ'keʃən] s complication f

complici·ty [kəm'plɪsɪti] s (pl -ties) complicité f

compliment ['kɑmplɪmənt] s compliment m; compliments (kind regards) civilités fpl; to pay a compliment to faire un compliment à; with the compliments of the author hommage de l'auteur || tr complimenter

com'plimen'tary cop'y [,kɑmplɪ'mɛntəri] s exemplaire m en hommage; to give a complimentary copy of a book faire hommage d'un livre

com'plimen'tary tick'et s billet m de faveur

com·ply [kəm'plaɪ] v (pret & pp -plied) intr—to comply with se conformer à, acquiescer à

component [kəm'ponənt] adj composant || s (chem) composant m; (mech, math) composante f

comportment [kəm'portmənt] s comportement m

compose [kəm'poz] tr composer; to be composed of se composer de; to compose oneself se calmer

composed adj paisible, tranquille

composer [kəm'pozər] s compositeur m

compos'ing stick' s compositeur m

composite [kəm'pɑzɪt] adj & s composé m

composition [,kɑmpə'zɪʃən] s composition f

compositor [kəm'pɑzɪtər] s compositeur m

compost ['kɑmpost] s compost m

composure [kəm'poʒər] s calme m, sang-froid m

compote ['kɑmpot] s (stewed fruits) compote f; (dish) compotier m

compound ['kɑmpaund] adj composé || s composé m; (gram) mot m composé; (math) complexe m; (mil) enceinte f || [kɑm'paund] tr composer, combiner; (interest) capitaliser

comprehend [,kɑmprɪ'hɛnd] tr comprendre

comprehensible [,kɑmprɪ'hɛnsɪbəl] adj compréhensible

comprehension [,kɑmprɪ'hɛnʃən] s compréhension f

comprehensive [,kɑmprɪ'hɛnsɪv] adj compréhensif, étendu; (study, view, measure) d'ensemble

compress ['kɑmprɛs] s (med) compresse f || [kɑm'prɛs] tr comprimer

compression [kɑm'prɛʃən] s compression f

comprise [kəm'praɪz] tr comprendre, renfermer

compromise ['kɑmprə,maɪz] s com-

promis *m*; (*with one's conscience*) transaction *f*; **rough compromise** cote *f* mal taillée ‖ *tr* (*e.g., one's honor*) compromettre ‖ *intr* (*to make concessions*) transiger
comptroller [kən'trolər] *s* vérificateur *m*, contrôleur *m*
compulsive [kəm'pʌlsɪv] *adj* obligatoire; (psychol) compulsif
compulsory [kəm'pʌlsəri] *adj* obligatoire, forcé
compute [kəm'pjut] *tr* computer, calculer, supputer ‖ *intr* calculer
computer [kəm'pjutər] *s* ordinateur *m*
comrade ['kɑmræd], ['kɑmrɪd] *s* camarade *mf*
com'rade in arms' *s* compagnon *m* d'armes
com'rade•ship' *s* camaraderie *f*
con [kɑn] *s* contre *m* ‖ *v* (*pret & pp* **conned**; *ger* **conning**) *tr* étudier; (naut) gouverner; (slang) escroquer
concave ['kɑnkev], [kɑn'kev] *adj* concave
conceal [kən'sil] *tr* dissimuler
concealment [kən'silmənt] *s* dissimulation *f*; (*place*) cachette *f*
concede [kən'sid] *tr & intr* concéder
conceit [kən'sit] *s* (*vanity*) vanité *f*; (*witty expression*) saillie *f*, mot *m*; **conceits** concetti *mpl*
conceited *adj* vaniteux, vain
conceivable [kən'sivəbəl] *adj* concevable
conceive [kən'siv] *tr & intr* concevoir
concentrate ['kɑnsən,tret] *tr* concentrer ‖ *intr* se concentrer
concentra'tion camp' [,kɑnsən'treʃən] *s* camp *m* de concentration
concentric [kən'sɛntrɪk] *adj* concentrique
concept ['kɑnsept] *s* concept *m*
conception [kən'sepʃən] *s* conception *f*
concern [kən'sʌrn] *s* (*business establishment*) maison *f*, compagnie *f*; (*worry*) inquiétude *f*; (*relation, reference*) intérêt *m*; (*matter*) affaire *f* ‖ *tr* concerner; **as concerns** quant à; **persons concerned** intéressés *mpl*; **to be concerned** être inquiet; **to be concerned about** se préoccuper de; **to be concerned with** s'intéresser à; **to whom it may concern** à qui de droit
concerning [kən'sʌrnɪŋ] *prep* concernant, en ce qui concerne, touchant
concert ['kɑnsərt] *s* concert *m*; **in concert** de concert ‖ [kən'sʌrt] *tr* concerter ‖ *intr* se concerter
con'cert•mas'ter *s* premier violon *m* soliste
concer•to [kən'tʃɛrto] *s* (*pl* **-tos** or **-ti** [ti]) concerto *m*
concession [kən'sɛʃən] *s* concession *f*
conciliate [kən'sɪlɪ,et] *tr* concilier
conciliatory [kən'sɪlɪ•ə,tori] *adj* conciliatoire
concise [kən'saɪs] *adj* concis
conclude [kən'klud] *tr & intr* conclure
conclusion [kən'kluʒən] *s* conclusion *f*
conclusive [kən'klusɪv] *adj* concluant

concoct [kən'kɑkt] *tr* confectionner; (*a story*) inventer; (*a plan*) machiner
concoction [kɑn'kɑkʃən] *s* confection *f*; (*mixture*) mélange *m*; (pej) drogue *f*
concomitant [kən'kɑmɪtənt] *adj* concomitant ‖ *s* accompagnement *m*
concord ['kɑŋkɔrd] *s* concorde *f*; (gram) concordance *f*; (mus) accord *m*
concordance [kən'kɔrdəns] *s* concordance *f*
concourse ['kɑŋkors] *s* (*of people*) concours *m*, foule *f*; (*road*) boulevard *m*; (*of railroad station*) hall *m*, salle *f* des pas perdus
concrete ['kɑnkrit], [kɑn'krit] *adj* concret; de béton ‖ *s* concret *m*; (*for construction*) béton *m* ‖ *tr* (*a sidewalk*) bétonner
con'crete block' *s* parpaing *m*
con'crete mix'er *s* bétonnière *f*
con•cur [kən'kʌr] *v* (*pret & pp* **-curred**; *ger* **-curring**) *intr* (*said of events*) concourir; (*said of persons*) s'accorder
concurrence [kən'kʌrəns] *s* concours *m*
concurrent [kən'kʌrənt] *adj* concourant
concussion [kən'kʌʃən] *s* secousse *f*, ébranlement *m*; (pathol) commotion *f*
condemn [kən'dɛm] *tr* condamner
condemnation [,kɑndɛm'neʃən] *s* condamnation *f*
condense [kən'dɛns] *tr* condenser ‖ *intr* se condenser
condenser [kən'dɛnsər] *s* condenseur *m*; (elec) condensateur *m*
condescend [,kɑndɪ'sɛnd] *intr* condescendre
condescending [,kɑndɪ'sɛndɪŋ] *adj* condescendant
condescension [,kɑndɪ'sɛnʃən] *s* condescendance *f*
condiment ['kɑndɪmənt] *s* condiment *m*
condition [kən'dɪʃən] *s* condition *f*; **on condition that** à condition que ‖ *tr* conditionner
conditional [kən'dɪʃənəl] *adj & s* conditionnel *m*
condole [kən'dol] *intr*—**to condole with** offrir ses condoléances à
condolence [kən'doləns] *s* condoléances *fpl*
condone [kən'don] *tr* pardonner, tolérer
conducive [kən'd(j)usɪv] *adj* favorable
conduct ['kɑndʌkt] *s* conduite *f*, comportement *m* ‖ [kən'dʌkt] *tr* conduire
conductor [kən'dʌktər] *s* (*on bus or streetcar*) receveur *m*; (mus) chef *m* d'orchestre; (rr) chef de train; (elec, phys) conducteur *m*; (elec, phys) (in predicate after **to be**, it may be translated by an adjective) conducteur, e.g., **metals are good conductors of electricity** les métaux sont bons conducteurs de l'électricité
conduit ['kɑndɪt], ['kɑndʊ•ɪt] *s* conduit *m*; (elec) caniveau *m*

cone [kon] *s* cône *m*; (*for popcorn, ice cream*) cornet *m*, plaisir *m*
confection [kən'fɛkʃən] *s* confiserie *f*
confectioner [kən'fɛkʃənər] *s* confiseur *m*
confec'tioners' sug'ar *s* sucre *m* glace
confectioner·y [kən'fɛkʃə͵nɛri] *s* (*pl* -ies) confiserie *f*
confedera·cy [kən'fədərəsi] *s* (*pl* -cies) confédération *f*; (*for unlawful purposes*) conspiration *f*, entente *f*
confederate [kən'fɛdərɪt] *adj* confédéré ‖ *s* complice *mf*; **Confederate** (hist) Confédéré *m* ‖ [kən'fɛdə͵ret] *tr* confédérer ‖ *intr* se confédérer
con·fer [kən'fʌr] *v* (*pret & pp* -ferred; *ger* -ferring) *tr & intr* conférer
conference ['kɑnfərəns] *s* conférence *f*; (*interview*) entretien *m*; (sports) groupement *m* (d'équipes)
conferment [kən'fʌrmənt] *s* (*of degrees*) collation *f*
confess [kən'fɛs] *tr* confesser ‖ *intr* se confesser
confession [kən'fɛʃən] *s* confession *f*
confessional [kən'fɛʃənəl] *s* confessional *m*
confessor [kən'fɛsər] *s* confesseur *m*
confidant [͵kɑnfɪ'dænt], ['kɑnfɪ͵dænt] *s* confident *m*
confide [kən'faɪd] *tr* confier ‖ *intr*— **to confide in** se confier à
confidence ['kɑnfɪdəns] *s* confiance *f*; (*secret*) confidence *f*; **in strict confidence** sous toute réserve; **to have confidence in** se confier à
confident ['kɑnfɪdənt] *adj* confiant ‖ *s* confident *m*
confidential [͵kɑnfɪ'dɛnʃəl] *adj* confidentiel
confiden'tial sec'retary *s* secrétaire *m* particulière, secrétaire *f* particulière
confine ['kɑnfaɪn] *s* (obs) confinement *m*; **the confines** les confins *mpl* ‖ [kən'faɪn] *tr* confiner, enfermer; (*to keep within limits*) limiter; **to be confined** (*said of woman*) accoucher; **to be confined to bed** être alité
confinement [kən'faɪnmənt] *s* limitation *f*; (*in prison*) emprisonnement *m*; (*in childbirth*) accouchement *m*
confirm [kən'fʌrm] *tr* confirmer
confirmed *adj* (*reassured*) confirmé; (*bachelor*) endurci; (*drunkard*) fieffé; (*drinker*) invétéré; (*smoker*) émérite
confiscate ['kɑnfɪs͵ket] *tr* confisquer
conflagration [͵kɑnflə'greʃən] *s* conflagration *f*, incendie *m*
conflict ['kɑnflɪkt] *s* conflit *m* ‖ [kən-'flɪkt] *intr* être en contradiction, se heurter
conflicting [kən'flɪktɪŋ] *adj* contradictoire; (*events, class hours, etc.*) incompatible
con'flict of in'terest *s* conflit *m* d'intérêts, conflit des intérêts
conform [kən'fɔrm] *tr* conformer ‖ *intr* se conformer, s'accommoder
conformist [kən'fɔrmɪst] *s* conformiste *mf*
conformi·ty [kən'fɔrmɪti] *s* (*pl* -ties)

conformité *f*; **in conformity with** conformément à
confound [kɑn'faʊnd] *tr* confondre ‖ ['kɑn'faʊnd] *tr* maudire; **confound it!** diable!
confounded *adj* confus; (*damned*) sacré
confrere ['kɑnfrer] *s* confrère *m*
confront [kən'frʌnt] *tr* (*to face boldly*) affronter, faire face à; (*witnesses; documents*) confronter; **to be confronted by** se trouver en face de
confuse [kən'fjuz] *tr* confondre; **to get confused** devenir confus, s'embrouiller
confusing [kən'fjuzɪŋ] *adj* déroutant, embrouillant
confusion [kən'fjuʒən] *s* confusion *f*
confute [kən'fjut] *tr* réfuter
congeal [kən'dʒil] *tr* congeler ‖ *intr* se congeler
congenial [kən'dʒinjəl] *adj* sympathique, agréable; compatible; **congenial to** or **with** apparenté à, conforme au tempérament de
congenital [kən'dʒɛnɪtəl] *adj* congénital
con'ger eel' ['kɑŋgər] *s* congre *m*, anguille *f* de mer
congest [kən'dʒɛst] *tr* congestionner ‖ *intr* se congestionner
congestion [kən'dʒɛstʃən] *s* congestion *f*
conglomeration [kən͵glamə're͵ʃən] *s* conglomération *f*
congratulate [kən'grætʃə͵let] *tr* féliciter, congratuler; **to congratulate s.o. for** féliciter qn de or pour; **to congratulate s.o. for** + *ger* féliciter qn de + *inf*
congratulations [kən͵grætʃə'leʃənz] *spl* félicitations *fpl*
congregate ['kɑŋgrɪ͵get] *tr* rassembler ‖ *intr* se rassembler
congregation [͵kɑŋgrɪ'geʃən] *s* rassemblement *m*; (*parishioners*) fidèles *mfpl*; (*Protestant parishioners; committee of Roman Catholic prelates*) congrégation *f*
congress ['kɑŋgrɪs] *s* congrès *m*
congressional [kən'grɛʃənəl] *adj* parlementaire
con'gress·man *s* (*pl* -men) congressiste *m*, parlementaire *m*
con'gress·wom'an *s* (*pl* -wom'en) congressiste *f*, parlementaire *f*
congruent ['kɑŋgru·ənt] *adj* (math) congru
conical ['kɑnɪkəl] *adj* conique
conjecture [kən'dʒɛktʃər] *s* conjecture *f* ‖ *tr & intr* conjecturer
conjugal ['kɑndʒəgəl] *adj* conjugal
conjugate ['kɑndʒə͵get] *tr* conjuguer
conjugation [͵kɑndʒə'geʃən] *s* conjugaison *f*
conjunction [kən'dʒʌŋkʃən] *s* conjonction *f*
conjuration [͵kɑndʒə'reʃən] *s* conjuration *f*
conjure [kən'dʒur] *tr* (*to appeal to solemnly*) conjurer ‖ ['kɑndʒər], ['kʌndʒər] *tr* (*to exorcise, drive away*) conjurer; **to conjure up** évoquer ‖ *intr* faire de la sorcellerie

connect [kə'nɛkt] *tr* relier, joindre; (e.g., *two parties on the telephone*) mettre en communication; (*a pipe, an electrical device*) brancher, connecter ‖ *intr* se lier, se joindre; **to connect with** (*said of train*) correspondre avec
connected *adj* (*related*) connexe; (*logical*) suivi
connecting [kə'nɛktɪŋ] *adj* de liaison; (*wire*) de connexion; (*pipe*) de raccord; (*street*) communiquant
connect'ing rod' *s* bielle *f*
connection [kə'nɛkʃən] *s* connexion *f*, liaison *f*; (*between two causes*) connexité *f*; (*in families*) parenté *f*, parent *m*; (*by telephone*) communication *f*; (*of trains*) correspondance *f*; (elec) connexion; **connections** (*in the business world*) clientèle *f*, relations *fpl*; (*in families*) alliés *mpl*, consanguins *mpl*; **in connection with** à propos de
con'ning tow'er ['kɑnɪŋ] *s* (e.g., *on battleship*) poste *m* or tourelle *f* de commandement; (*on sub*) kiosque *m*
conniption [kə'nɪpʃən] *s* (coll) rogne *f*
connive [kə'naɪv] *intr* être de connivence, être complice
connote [kə'not] *tr* (*to signify*) signifier, vouloir dire; (*to imply*) suggérer, sous-entendre
connubial [kə'n(j)ubɪ·əl] *adj* conjugal
conquer ['kɑŋkər] *tr* conquérir
conqueror ['kɑŋkərər] *s* conquérant
conquest ['kɑŋkwɛst] *s* conquête *f*
conscience ['kɑnʃəns] *s* conscience *f*; **in all conscience** en conscience; **to have on one's conscience** avoir sur la conscience
conscientious [,kɑnʃɪ'ɛnʃəs] *adj* consciencieux
conscien'tious objec'tor [əb'dʒɛktər] *s* objecteur *m* de conscience
conscious ['kɑnʃəs] *adj* conscient; **to be conscious** (*not unconscious*) avoir connaissance; **to be conscious of** avoir conscience de
consciousness ['kɑnʃəsnɪs] *s* (*not sleep or coma*) connaissance *f*; (*awareness*) conscience *f*
conscript ['kɑnskrɪpt] *s* (mil) conscrit *m*; (nav) inscrit *m* maritime ‖ [kən-'skrɪpt] *tr* (mil) enrôler; (nav) inscrire
conscription [kən'skrɪpʃən] *s* conscription *f*
consecrate ['kɑnsɪ,kret] *tr* consacrer; (e.g., *bread*) bénir; (*a king or bishop*) sacrer
consecration [,kɑnsɪ'kreʃən] *s* consécration *f*; (*to a task*) dévouement *m*; (*of a king or bishop*) sacre *m*
consecutive [kən'sɛkjətɪv] *adj* de suite, consécutif
consensus [kən'sɛnsəs] *s* consensus *m*
consent [kən'sɛnt] *s* consentement *m*; **by common consent** d'un commun accord ‖ *intr* consentir
consequence ['kɑnsɪ,kwɛns] *s* conséquence *f*

consequential [,kɑnsɪ'kwɛnʃəl] *adj* conséquent, logique
consequently ['kɑnsɪ,kwɛntli] *adv* conséquemment, par conséquent '
conservation [,kɑnsər've/ən] *s* conservation *f*
conservatism [kən'sʌrvə,tɪzəm] *s* conservatisme *m*
conservative [kən'sʌrvətɪv] *adj* & *s* conservateur *m*; **at a conservative estimate** au bas mot, au moins
conservato·ry [kən'sʌrvə,tori] *s* (*pl* -ries) (*of music*) conservatoire *m*; (*greenhouse*) serre *f*
conserve [kən'sʌrv] *tr* conserver
consider [kən'sɪdər] *tr* considérer
considerable [kən'sɪdərəbəl] *adj* considérable
considerate [kən'sɪdərɪt] *adj* prévenant, plein d'égards
consideration [kən,sɪdə're/ən] *s* considération *f*; (*remuneration*) rétribution *f*; (*favor*) indulgence *f*; **to take into consideration** tenir compte de; **under consideration** à l'étude
considering [kən'sɪdərɪŋ] *prep* eu égard à; **considering that** vu que
consign [kən'saɪn] *tr* consigner
consignee [,kɑnsaɪ'ni] *s* consignataire *m*
consignment [kən'saɪnmənt] *s* consignation *f*, livraison *f*
consist [kən'sɪst] *intr*—**to consist in** consister dans or en; **to consist in** + *ger* consister à + *inf*; **to consist of** consister dans or en
consisten·cy [kən'sɪstənsi] *s* (*pl* -cies) (*logical connection*) conséquence *f*; (*firmness, amount of firmness*) sistance *f*
consistent [kən'sɪstənt] *adj* (*agreeing with itself or oneself*) conséquent; (*holding firmly together*) consistant; **consistent with** compatible avec
consisto·ry [kən'sɪstəri] *s* (*pl* -ries) consistoire *m*
consolation [,kɑnsə'le/ən] *s* consolation *f*
console ['kɑnsol] *s* console *f* ‖ [kən-'sol] *tr* consoler
con'sole ta'ble *s* console *f*
consolidate [kən'sɑlɪ,det] *tr* consolider
consonant ['kɑnsənənt] *adj* (*in sound*) consonant; **consonant with** d'accord avec ‖ *s* consonne *f*
consort ['kɑnsərt] *s* compagnon *m*; (*husband*) conjoint *m*; (*wife*) conjointe *f*; prince *m* consort; (*convoy*) conserve *f* ‖ [kən'sɔrt] *tr* unir ‖ *intr* s'associer; (*to harmonize*) s'accorder; **to consort with** s'associer à or avec
conspicuous [kən'spɪkju·əs] *adj* apparent, frappant; (*attracting special attention*) voyant; **to make oneself conspicuous** se faire remarquer
conspira·cy [kən'spɪrəsi] *s* (*pl* -cies) conspiration *f*, conjuration *f*
conspirator [kən'spɪrətər] *s* conspirateur *m*, conjuré *m*
conspire [kən'spaɪr] *intr* conspirer
constable ['kɑnstəbəl], ['kʌnstəbəl] *s* garde *m* champêtre; juge *m* de paix

constancy ['kɑnstænsi] s constance f
constant ['kɑnstənt] adj constant ‖ s constante f
constantly ['kɑnstəntli] adv constamment
constellation [,kɑnstə'leʃən] s constellation f
constipate ['kɑnstɪ ,pet] tr constiper
constipation [,kɑnstɪ'peʃən] s constipation f
constituen·cy [kən'stɪtʃʊ·ənsi] s (pl -cies) électeurs mpl, commettants mpl; circonscription f électorale
constituent [kən'stɪtʃʊ·ənt] adj constituant, constitutif ‖ s élément m, constituant m; (voter, client) électeur m, commettant m
constitute ['kɑnstɪ ,t(j)ut] tr constituer
constitution [,kɑnstɪ't(j)uʃən] s constitution f
constrain [kən'stren] tr contraindre
constraint [kən'strent] s contrainte f; (restraint) retenue f; (uneasiness) gêne f
constrict [kən'strɪkt] tr resserrer
construct [kən'strʌkt] tr construire
construction [kən'strʌkʃən] s construction f; interprétation f
constructive [kən'strʌktɪv] adj constructif, constructeur
construe [kən'stru] tr expliquer, interpréter; (gram) construire
consul ['kɑnsəl] s consul m
consular ['kɑns(j)ələr] adj consulaire
consulate ['kɑns(j)əlɪt] s consulat m
consult [kən'sʌlt] tr consulter ‖ intr consulter; se consulter
consultant [kən'sʌltənt] s conseiller m, consultant m
consultation [,kɑnsəl'teʃən] s consultation f; (eccl, law) consulte f
consume [kən's(j)um] tr (to make use of, use up) consommer; (to use up entirely; to destroy) consumer, épuiser
consumer [kən's(j)umər] s consommateur m; (of gas, electricity, etc.) abonné m
consum'er goods' spl denrées fpl de consommation
consummate [kən'sʌmɪt] adj consommé ‖ ['kɑnsə ,met] tr consommer
consumption [kən'sʌmpʃən] s consommation f; (pathol) tuberculose f pulmonaire
consumptive [kən'sʌmptɪv] adj destructeur; (pathol) poitrinaire ‖ s (pathol) poitrinaire mf
contact ['kɑntækt] s contact m; to put in contact mettre en contact ‖ tr (coll) prendre contact avec, contacter ‖ intr prendre contact
con'tact lens' s verre m de contact, lentille f de contact
contagion [kən'tedʒən] s contagion f
contagious [kən'tedʒəs] adj contagieux
contain [kən'ten] tr contenir; (one's sorrow) apprivoiser
container [kən'tenər] s boîte f, contenant m, récipient m
containment [kən'tenmənt] s refoulement m, retenue f

contaminate [kən'tæmɪ ,net] tr contaminer
contamination [kən ,tæmɪ'neʃən] s contamination f
contemplate ['kɑntəm ,plet] tr & intr contempler; (e.g., a trip) projeter; to contemplate + ger penser + inf
contemplation [,kɑntəm'pleʃən] s contemplation f
contemporaneous [kən ,tempə'renɪ·əs] adj contemporain
contemporar·y [kən'tempə ,reri] adj contemporain ‖ s (pl -ies) contemporain m
contempt [kən'tempt] s mépris m, nargue f; (law) contumace f; to hold in contempt mépriser
contemptible [kən'temptɪbəl] adj méprisable
contempt' of court' s outrage m à la justice
contemptuous [kən'temptʃʊ·əs] adj méprisant
contend [kən'tend] tr prétendre ‖ intr combattre; to contend with lutter contre
contender [kən'tendər] s concurrent m, compétiteur m
content [kən'tent] adj & s content m ‖ ['kɑntent] s contenu m; contents contenu; (of table of contents) matières fpl ‖ [kən'tent] tr contenter
contented [kən'tentɪd] adj content, satisfait
contention [kən'tenʃən] s (strife) dispute f, différend m; (point argued for) point m discuté, argument m; (law) contentieux m
contentious [kən'tenʃəs] adj contentieux
contentment [kən'tentmənt] s contentement m
contest ['kɑntest] s (struggle, fight) lutte f, dispute f; (competition) concours m, compétition f ‖ [kən'test] tr & intr contester
contestant [kən'testənt] s concurrent m
context ['kɑntekst] s contexte m
contiguous [kən'tɪgjʊ·əs] adj contigu
continence ['kɑntɪnəns] s continence f
continent ['kɑntɪnənt] adj & s continent m
continental [,kɑntɪ'nentəl] adj continental
contingen·cy [kən'tɪndʒənsi] s (pl -cies) contingence f
contingent [kən'tɪndʒənt] adj & s contingent m
continual [kən'tɪnjʊ·əl] adj continuel
continuation [kən ,tɪnjʊ'eʃən] s continuation f; (e.g., of a story) suite f
continue [kən'tɪnjʊ] tr & intr continuer; continued on page two (three, etc.) suite page deux (trois, etc.); to be continued à suivre
continui·ty [,kɑntɪ'n(j)u·ɪti] s (pl -ties) continuité f; (mov, rad, telv) découpage m, scénario m
continuous [kən'tɪnjʊ·əs] adj continu
contin'uous show'ing s (mov) spectacle m permanent

contin'uous waves' *spl* ondes *fpl* entretenues

contortion [kən'tɔrʃən] *s* contorsion *f*

contour ['kantur] *s* contour *m* || *tr* contourner

con'tour line' *s* courbe *f* de niveau

contraband ['kantrə,bænd] *adj* contrebandier || *s* contrebande *f*

contrabass ['kantrə,bes] *s* contrebasse *f*

contraceptive [,kantrə'sɛptɪv] *adj* & *s* contraceptif *m*

contract ['kantrækt] *s* contrat *m* || ['kantrækt], [kən'trækt] *tr* contracter || *intr* se contracter

contraction [kən'trækʃən] *s* contraction *f*

contractor [kən'træktər] *s* entrepreneur *m*

contradict [,kantrə'dɪkt] *tr* contredire

contradiction [,kantrə'dɪkʃən] *s* contradiction *f*

contradictory [,kantrə'dɪktəri] *adj* contradictoire

contral·to [kən'trælto] *s* (*pl* -tos) contralto *m*

contraption [kən'træpʃən] *s* (coll) machin *m*, truc *m*

contra·ry ['kantreri] *adj* contraire || *adv* contrairement || [kən'treri] *adj* (coll) obstiné, têtu || ['kantreri] *s* (*pl* -ries) contraire *m*; on the contrary au contraire, par contre

contrast ['kantræst] *s* contraste *m* || [kən'træst] *tr* & *intr* contraster

contravene [,kantrə'vin] *tr* contredire; (*a law*) contrevenir (with *dat*)

contribute [kən'trɪbjut] *tr* (e.g., *a sum of money*) contribuer pour || *intr* contribuer; (*to a newspaper, conference, etc.*) collaborer

contribution [,kantrɪ'bjuʃən] *s* contribution *f*, apport *m*; (e.g., *for charity*) souscription *f*; (*to a newspaper, conference, etc.*) collaboration *f*

contributor [kən'trɪbjutər] *s* (*donor*) donneur *m*; (e.g., *to a charitable cause*) souscripteur *m*; (*to a newspaper, conference, etc.*) collaborateur *m*

contrite [kən'traɪt] *adj* contrit

contrition [kən'trɪʃən] *s* contrition *f*

contrivance [kən'traɪvəns] *s* invention *f*, expédient *m*; (*gadget*) dispositif *m*

contrive [kən'traɪv] *tr* inventer || *intr* s'arranger; to contrive to trouver moyen de

con·trol [kən'trol] *s* direction *f*, autorité *f*; (*mastery*) maîtrise *f*; (*surveillance*) contrôle *m*; controls commandes *fpl* || *v* (*pret* & *pp* -trolled; *ger* -trolling) *tr* diriger; maîtriser; (*to give surveillance to*) contrôler; (*to handle the controls of*) commander; to control oneself se contrôler

controller [kən'trolər] *s* contrôleur *m*, appareil *m* de contrôle; (elec) controller *m*

control' pan'el *s* (aer) planche *f* de bord, tableau *m* de bord

control' stick' *s* (aer) manche *m* à balai

control' tow'er *s* poste-vigie *m*, tourelle *f* de commandement

controversial [,kantrə'vʌrʃəl] *adj* controversable

controver·sy ['kantrə,vʌrsi] *s* (*pl* -sies) controverse *f*; dispute *f*, querelle *f*

controvert ['kantrə,vʌrt], [,kantrə'vʌrt] *tr* controverser; contredire

contumacious [,kant(j)u'meʃəs] *adj* rebelle, récalcitrant

contume·ly ['kant(j)umɪli] *s* (*pl* -lies) injure *f*, outrage *m*, mépris *m*

contusion [kən't(j)uʒən] *s* contusion *f*

conundrum [kə'nʌndrəm] *s* devinette *f*, énigme *f*

convalesce [,kanvə'lɛs] *intr* guérir, se remettre, se rétablir

convalescence [,kanvə'lɛsəns] *s* convalescence *f*

convalescent [,kanvə'lɛsənt] *adj* & *s* convalescent *m*

convales'cent home' *s* maison *f* de repos

convene [kən'vin] *tr* assembler, convoquer || *intr* s'assembler

convenience [kən'vinjəns] *s* commodité *f*; (e.g., *in the home*) confort *m*; at your earliest convenience aussitôt que possible

convent ['kanvɛnt] *s* couvent *m* (de religieuses)

convention [kən'vɛnʃən] *s* assemblée *f*, congrès *m*; (*agreement*) convention *f*; (*accepted usage*) convention sociale; conventions convenances *fpl*, bienséances *fpl*

conventional [kən'vɛnʃənəl] *adj* conventionnel; (*in conduct*) respectueux des convenances; (*everyday*) usuel; (*model, type*) traditionnel

converge [kən'vʌrdʒ] *intr* converger

conversant [kən'vʌrsənt] *adj* familier, versé

conversation [,kanvər'seʃən] *s* conversation *f*

conversational [,kanvər'seʃənəl] *adj* de conversation

converse ['kanvʌrs] *adj* & *s* contraire *m*, inverse *m*, réciproque *f* || [kən'vʌrs] *intr* converser

conversion [kən'vʌrʒən] *s* conversion *f*

convert ['kanvʌrt] *s* converti *m* || [kən'vʌrt] *tr* convertir || *intr* se convertir

converter [kən'vʌrtər] *s* convertisseur *m*

convertible [kən'vʌrtɪbəl] *adj* (*person*) convertissable; (*thing; security*) convertible; (aut) décapotable || *s* (aut) décapotable *f*

convex ['kanvɛks], [kan'vɛks] *adj* convexe, bombé

convey [kən've] *tr* transporter; (e.g., *a message*) communiquer; (e.g., *property*) transmettre; (law) céder

conveyance [kən've·əns] *s* transport *m*; (*vehicle*) moyen *m* de transport, voiture *f*; (*of message*) communication *f*; (*transfer*) transmission *f*; (law) transfert *m*, cession *f*

conveyor [kən've·ər] *s* transporteur *m*, convoyeur *m*

convey'or belt' *s* tapis *m* roulant

convict ['kanvɪkt] *s* condamné *m*, for-

çat *m* ‖ [kən'vɪkt] *tr* condamner, convaincre
conviction [kən'vɪkʃən] *s* condamnation *f*; (*certainty*) conviction *f*
convince [kən'vɪns] *tr* convaincre
convincing [kən'vɪnsɪŋ] *adj* convaincant
convivial [kən'vɪvɪ-əl] *adj* jovial, plein d'entrain
convocation [ˌkɑnvə'keʃən] *s* (*calling together*) convocation *f*; (*meeting*) assemblée *f*
convoke [kən'vok] *tr* convoquer
convolution [ˌkɑnvə'luʃən] *s* (*of brain*) circonvolution *f*
convoy ['kɑnvɔɪ] *s* convoi *m*, conserve *f*, e.g., **to sail in convoy** naviguer de conserve ‖ *tr* convoyer
convulse [kən'vʌls] *tr* convulsionner, convulser; **to be convulsed with laughter** se tordre de rire
coo [ku] *intr* roucouler
cooing ['ku-ɪŋ] *s* roucoulement *m*
cook [kʊk] *s* cuisinier *m*, chef *m*; (*female cook*) cuisinière *f* ‖ *tr* cuisiner, faire cuire; **to cook up** (*a plot*) machiner, tramer ‖ *intr* faire la cuisine, cuisiner; (*said of food*) cuire
cook′book′ *s* livre *m* de cuisine
cooker ['kʊkər] *s* réchaud *m*, cuisinière *f*
cookery ['kʊkəri] *s* cuisine *f*
cookie ['kʊki] *s* var of **cooky**
cooking ['kʊkɪŋ] *s* cuisine *f*; (e.g., *of meat*) cuisson *f*
cook′ing uten′sils *spl* batterie *f* de cuisine
cook′stove′ *s* cuisinière *f*
cook·y ['kʊki] *s* (*pl* -ies) biscuit *m*, gâteau *m* sec
cool [kul] *adj* frais; (e.g., *to an idea*) indifférent; **it is cool out** il fait frais; **to keep cool** tenir au frais; se tenir tranquille ‖ *tr* rafraîchir *f* ‖ *tr* rafraîchir, refroidir; **to cool one's heels** (coll) se morfondre ‖ *intr* se refroidir, se rafraîchir; **to cool down** se calmer; **to cool off** se refroidir
cooler ['kulər] *s* frigorifique *m*; (*prison*) (slang) violon *m*, tôle *f*
cool′-head′ed *adj* imperturbable, de sang-froid
coolness ['kulnɪs] *s* fraîcheur *f*; (*of disposition*) sang-froid *m*, calme *m*; (*stand-offishness*) froideur *f*
coon [kun] *s* raton *m* laveur
coop [kup] *s* poulailler *m*; **to fly the coop** (slang) débiner, décamper ‖ *tr* enfermer dans un poulailler; **to coop up** claquemurer
co-op ['ko-ɑp], [ko'ɑp] *s* entreprise *f* coopérative
cooper ['kupər] *s* tonnelier *m*
cooperate [ko'ɑpəˌret] *intr* coopérer; (*to be helpful*) faire preuve de bonne volonté
cooperation [koˌɑpə'reʃən] *s* coopération *f*
cooperative [ko'ɑpəˌretɪv] *adj* coopératif
coordinate [ko'ɔrdɪnɪt] *adj* coordonné

‖ *s* coordonnée *f* ‖ [ko'ɔrdɪˌnet] *tr* coordonner
coot [kut] *s* foulque *f*; **old coot** (coll) vieille baderne *f*
cootie ['kuti] *s* (slang) pou *m*
cop [kɑp] *s* (slang) flic *m* ‖ *v* (*pret & pp* **copped**; *ger* **copping**) *tr* (slang) dérober
copartner [ko'pɑrtnər] *s* coassocié *m*, coparticipant *m*; (*in crime*) complice *mf*
cope [kop] *intr*—**to cope with** faire face à, tenir tête à
cope′stone′ *s* couronnement *m*
copier ['kɑpɪ-ər] *s* (*person who copies*) copiste *mf*, imitateur *m*; (*apparatus*) appareil *m* à copier
copilot ['koˌpaɪlət] *s* copilote *m*
coping ['kopɪŋ] *s* faîte *m*, comble *m*; (*of bridge*) chape *f*
copious ['kopɪ-əs] *adj* copieux
copper ['kɑpər] *adj* de cuivre, en cuivre; (*color*) cuivré ‖ *s* cuivre *m*; (*coin*) petite monnaie *f*; (slang) flic *m*
cop′per·smith′ *s* chaudronnier *m*
coppery ['kɑpəri] *adj* cuivreux
coppice ['kɑpɪs] *s* taillis *m*
copulate ['kɑpjəˌlet] *intr* s'accoupler
copulation [ˌkɑpjə'leʃən] *s* copulation *f*, accouplement *m*
cop·y ['kɑpi] *s* (*pl* -ies) copie *f*; (*of a book*) exemplaire *m*; (*of a magazine*) numéro *m*; (*for printer*) original *m*; **to make copies** exécuter des doubles ‖ *v* (*pret & pp* -ied) *tr & intr* copier
cop′y·book′ *s* cahier *m*
cop′y·cat′ *s* (coll) imitateur *m*, singe *m*
cop′y·right′ *s* propriété *f* artistique or littéraire, droit *m* de l'artiste or de l'auteur, copyright *m*; (formula on printed matter) dépôt *m* légal ‖ *tr* réserver les droits de publication de
cop′y·right′ed *adj* (formula used on printed material) droits de reproduction réservés
cop′y·writ′er *s* rédacteur *m* d'annonces publicitaires
co·quet [ko'ket] *v* (*pret & pp* -quetted; *ger* -quetting) *intr* coqueter
coquet·ry ['kokətri], [ko'ketri] *s* (*pl* -ries) coquetterie *f*
coquette [ko'ket] *s* coquette *f* ‖ *intr* coqueter
coquettish [ko'ketɪʃ] *adj* coquet
coral ['kɑrəl], ['kɔrəl] *adj* de corail, en corail ‖ *s* corail *m*
cor′al reef′ *s* récif *m* de corail
cord [kɔrd] *s* corde *f*; (*string*) ficelle *f*; (*attached to a bell*) cordon *m*; (elec) fil *m* ‖ *tr* corder
cordage ['kɔrdɪdʒ] *s* cordage *m*
cordial ['kɔrdʒəl] *adj & s* cordial *m*
cordiali·ty [kɔr'dʒælɪti] *s* (*pl* -ties) cordialité *f*
corduroy ['kɔrdəˌrɔɪ] *s* velours *m* côtelé; **corduroys** pantalon en velours côtelé
core [kor] *s* cœur *m*; (elec) noyau *m*; **rotten to the core** pourri à la base ‖ *tr* vider
corespondent [ˌkorɪs'pɑndənt] *s* complice *mf* d'adultère

cork [kɔrk] s liège m; (of bottle) bouchon m; **to take the cork out of de**boucher || tr boucher
corking ['kɔrkɪŋ] adj (coll) épatant
cork' oak' s chêne-liège m
cork'screw' s tire-bouchon m
cork'-tipped' adj à bout de liège
cormorant ['kɔrmərənt] s cormoran m
corn [kɔrn] s (in U.S.A.) maïs m; (in England) blé m; (in Scotland) avoine f; (single seed) grain m; (on foot) cor m, durillon m; (whiskey) (coll) eau-de-vie f de grain; (slang) platitude f, banalité f
corn' bread' s pain m de maïs
corn'cob' s épi m de maïs; (without the grain) rafle f
corn'cob pipe' s pipe f en rafle de maïs
corn'crib' s dépôt m de maïs
cornea ['kɔrnɪ·ə] s cornée f
corned' beef' s bœuf m salé
corner ['kɔrnər] adj cornier || s coin m, angle m; (of room) encoignure f; (of lips) commissure f; **around the corner** au tournant; **in a corner** (fig) au pied du mur, à l'accul: **to cut a corner close** prendre un virage à la corde; **to cut corners** (in spending) rogner les dépenses; (in work) bâcler un travail || tr coincer, acculer; (the market) accaparer
cor'ner cup'board s encoignure f
cor'ner room' s pièce f d'angle
cor'ner·stone' s pierre f angulaire
cornet [kɔr'nɛt] s cornet m; (head-dress) cornette f; (mil) cornette m; (mus) cornet à pistons
corn' exchange' s bourse f des céréales
corn'field' s (in U.S.A.) champ m de maïs; (in England) champ de blé; (in Scotland) champ d'avoine
corn'flakes' spl paillettes fpl de maïs
corn' flour' s farine f de maïs
corn'flow'er s bluet m, barbeau m
corn' frit'ter s crêpes fpl de maïs
corn'husk' s enveloppe f de l'épi de maïs
cornice ['kɔrnɪs] s corniche f
corn' meal' s farine f de maïs
corn' on the cob' s maïs m en épi
corn' pad' s bourrelet m coricide
corn' pone' s pain m de maïs
corn' pop'per s appareil m pour faire éclater le maïs
corn' remov'er s coricide m
corn' silk' s barbe f de maïs
corn'stalk' s tige f de maïs
corn'starch' s fécule f de maïs
cornucopia [,kɔrnə'kopɪ·ə] s corne f d'abondance
Cornwall ['kɔrn,wɔl], ['kɔrnwəl] s la Cornouailles
corn·y ['kɔrni] adj (comp -ier; super -iest) (slang) banal, trivial, fade
corollar·y ['kɑrə,lɛri], ['kɔrə,lɛri] s (pl -ies) corollaire m
coronary ['kɑrə,nɛri], ['kɔrə,nɛri] adj coronaire
coronation [,kɑrə'neʃən], [,kɔrə'neʃən] s couronnement m, sacre m
cor'oner's in'quest ['kɑrənərz], ['kɔrənərz] s enquête f judiciaire par-de-

vant jury (en cas de mort violente ou suspecte)
coronet ['kɑrə,nɛt], ['kɔrə,nɛt] s diadème m; (worn by members of nobility) couronne f; (worn by earl or baron) tortil m
corporal ['kɔrpərəl] adj corporel || s (mil) caporal m
corporate ['kɔrpərɪt] adj incorporé
corporation [,kɔrpə'reʃən] s société f anonyme, compagnie f anonyme
corporeal [kɔr'porɪ·əl] adj corporel, matériel
corps [kor] s (pl corps [korz]) corps m; (mil) corps d'armée
corpse [kɔrps] s cadavre m
corps'man s (pl -men) (mil) infirmier m
corpulent ['kɔrpjələnt] adj corpulent
corpuscle ['kɔrpəsəl] s (phys) corpuscule m; (physiol) globule m
corpus delicti ['kɔrpəsdɪ'lɪktaɪ] s (law) corps m du délit
cor·ral [kə'ræl] s corral m, enclos m || v (pret & pp -ralled; ger -ralling) tr enfermer dans un corral; (fig) saisir
correct [kə'rɛkt] adj correct || tr corriger
correction [kə'rɛkʃən] s correction f
corrective [kə'rɛktɪv] adj & s correctif m
correc'tive lens'es spl verres mpl correcteurs
correctness [kə'rɛktnɪs] s correction f
correlate ['kɑrə,let], ['kɔrə,let] tr mettre en corrélation || intr correspondre; **to correlate with** correspondre à
correlation [,kɑrə'leʃən], [,kɔrɪ'leʃən] s corrélation f
correspond [,kɑrɪ'spɑnd], [,kɔrɪ'spɑnd] intr correspondre
correspondence [,kɑrɪ'spɑndəns], [,kɔrɪ'spɑndəns] s correspondance f
correspondent [,kɑrɪ'spɑndənt], [,kɔrɪ'spɑndənt] adj & s correspondant m
corresponding [,kɑrɪ'spɑndɪŋ], [,kɔrɪ'spɑndɪŋ] adj correspondant
corridor ['kɑrɪdər], ['kɔrɪdər] s corridor m, couloir m
corroborate [kə'rɑbə,ret] tr corroborer
corrode [kə'rod] tr corroder || intr se corroder
corrosion [kə'roʒən] s corrosion f
corrosive [kə'rosɪv] adj & s corrosif m
corrugated ['kɑrə,getɪd], ['kɔrə,getɪd] adj ondulé
corrupt [kə'rʌpt] adj corrompu || tr corrompre
corruption [kə'rʌpʃən] s corruption f
corsage [kɔr'sɑʒ] s bouquet m
corsair ['kɔr,sɛr] s corsaire m
corset ['kɔrsɪt] s corset m
Corsica ['kɔrsɪkə] s Corse f; la Corse
Corsican ['kɔrsɪkən] adj corse || s (dialect) corse m; (person) Corse mf
cortege [kɔr'teʒ] s cortège m
cor·tex ['kɔr,tɛks] s (pl -tices [tɪ,siz]) cortex m
cortisone ['kɔrtɪ,son] s cortisone f
coruscate ['kɑrəs,ket], ['kɔrəs,ket] intr scintiller

cosmetic [kɑz'mɛtɪk] *adj & s* cosmétique *m*

cosmic ['kɑzmɪk] *adj* cosmique

cosmonaut ['kɑzmə‚nɔt] *s* cosmonaute *mf*

cosmopolitan [‚kɑzmə'pɑlɪtən] *adj & s* cosmopolite *mf*

cosmos ['kɑzməs] *s* cosmos *m*

Cossack ['kɑ‚sæk] *adj* cosaque ‖ *s* Cosaque *mf*

cost [kɔst], [kɑst] *s* coût *m*; (*price*) prix *m*; **at all costs** à tout prix, coûte que coûte; **at cost** au prix coûtant; **costs** frais *mpl*; (law) dépens *mpl* ‖ *v* (*pret & pp* **cost**) *intr* coûter

cost′ account′ing *s* comptabilité *f* industrielle

costliness ['kɔstlɪnɪs], ['kɑstlɪnɪs] *s* cherté *f*, haut prix *m*

cost‧ly ['kɔstli], ['kɑstli] *adj* (*comp* **-lier**; *super* **-liest**) coûteux, cher

cost′ of liv′ing *s* coût *m* de la vie

cost′ price′ *s* prix *m* coûtant; (*net price*) prix de revient

costume ['kɑst(j)um] *s* costume *m*

cos′tume ball′ *s* bal *m* costumé

cos′tume jew′elry *s* bijoux *mpl* en toc

costumer [kɑs't(j)umər] *s* costumier *m*

cot [kɑt] *s* lit *m* de sangle

coterie ['kotəri] *s* coterie *f*

cottage ['kɑtɪdʒ] *s* chalet *m*, cabanon *m*, villa *f*; (*with a thatched roof*) chaumière *f*

cot′tage cheese′ *s* lait *m* caillé, caillé *m*, jonchée *f*

cot′ter pin′ ['kɑtər] *s* goupille *f* fendue, clavette *f*

cotton ['kɑtən] *adj* cotonnier, de coton ‖ *s* coton *m* ‖ *intr*—**to cotton up to** (coll) éprouver de la sympathie pour

cot′ton bat′ting *s* coton *m* or ouate *f* hydrophile

cot′ton field′ *s* cotonnerie *f*

cot′ton gin′ *s* égreneuse *f*

cot′ton mill′ *s* filature *f* de coton, cotonnerie *f*

cot′ton pick′er *s* cotonnier *m*

cot′ton pick′ing *s* récolte *f* du coton

cot′ton‧seed′ *s* graine *f* de coton

cot′tonseed oil′ *s* huile *f* de coton

cot′ton waste′ *s* déchets *mpl* or bourre *f* de coton

cot′ton‧wood′ *s* peuplier *m* de Virginie

cottony ['kɑtəni] *adj* cotonneux

couch [kautʃ] *s* (*without back*) divan *m*; (*with back*) sofa *m*, canapé *m* ‖ *tr* (*a demand, a letter*) rédiger ‖ *intr* (*to lie in wait*) se tapir

cougar ['kugər] *s* couguar *m*, cougouar *m*

cough [kɔf], [kɑf] *s* toux *f* ‖ *tr*—**to cough up** cracher en toussant; (slang) (*money*) cracher ‖ *intr* tousser

cough′ drop′ *s* pastille *f* pectorale, pastille pour la toux

cough′ syr′up *s* sirop *m* pectoral, sirop contre la toux

could [kud] *aux*—**he could not come** il ne pouvait pas venir; **he couldn't do it** il n'a (pas) pu le faire; **he couldn't do it if he wanted to** il ne pourrait

(pas) le faire s'il le voulait, il ne saurait (pas) le faire s'il le voulait

council ['kaunsəl] *s* conseil *m*; (eccl) concile *m*

coun′cil‧man *s* (*pl* **-men**) conseiller *m* municipal

councilor ['kaunsələr] *s* conseiller *m*

coun‧sel ['kaunsəl] *s* conseil *m*, avis *m*; (*lawyer*) avocat *m* ‖ *v* (*pret & pp* **-seled** or **-selled**; *ger* **-seling** or **-selling**) *tr & intr* conseiller; **to counsel s.o. to** + *inf* conseiller à qn de + *inf*

counselor ['kaunsələr] *s* conseiller *m*, conseil *m*; (*lawyer*) avocat *m*

count [kaunt] *s* compte *m*; (*nobleman*) comte *m* ‖ *tr* compter; **to count the votes** dépouiller le scrutin ‖ *intr* compter; **count off!** (mil) comptez-vous!; **to count for** valoir; **to count on** (*to have confidence in*) compter sur (*s.o. or s.th.*); **to count on** + *ger* compter + *inf*

countable ['kauntəbəl] *adj* comptable

count′down′ *s* compte *m* à rebours

countenance ['kauntɪnəns] *s* mine *f*, contenance *f*; **to give countenance to** appuyer; **to keep one's countenance** garder son sérieux; **to lose countenance** perdre contenance ‖ *tr* soutenir, approuver

counter ['kauntər] *adj* contraire ‖ *s* compteur *m*; (*piece of wood or metal for keeping score*) jeton *m*; (*board in shop over which business is transacted*) comptoir *m*; (*in a bar or café*) zinc *m*; **under the counter** en dessous de table, sous le comptoir, sous cape ‖ *adv* contrairement; en sens inverse; **to run counter to** aller à l'encontre de ‖ *tr* contrarier, contrecarrer; (*a move, e.g., in chess*) contrer; (*an opinion*) prendre le contre-pied de ‖ *intr* parer le coup, parer un coup; **to counter with** riposter par

coun′ter‧act′ *tr* contrebalancer

coun′ter‧attack′ *s* contre-attaque *f* ‖ **coun′ter‧attack′** *tr* contre-attaquer

coun′ter‧bal′ance *s* contrepoids *m* ‖ **coun′ter‧bal′ance** *tr* contrebalancer

coun′ter‧clock′wise′ *adj & adv* en sens inverse des aiguilles d'une montre

coun′ter‧cur′rent *s* contre-courant *m*

coun′ter‧es′pionage *s* contre-espionnage *m*

counterfeit ['kauntərfɪt] *adj* contrefait; (*beauty*) sophistiqué ‖ *s* contrefaction *f*, contrefaçon *f*; (*money*) fausse monnaie *f* ‖ *tr* contrefaire; (*e.g., an illness*) feindre

counterfeiter ['kauntər‚fɪtər] *s* contrefacteur *m*; (*of money*) faux-monnayeur *m*

coun′terfeit mon′ey *s* fausse monnaie *f*, faux billets *mpl*

coun′ter‧ir′ritant *adj & s* révulsif *m*

countermand ['kauntər‚mænd], ['kauntər‚mɑnd] *s* contre-ordre *m* ‖ *tr* contremander

coun′ter‧march′ *s* contremarche *f* ‖ *intr* faire une contremarche

coun′ter‧meas′ure *s* contre-mesure *f*

coun′ter‧offen′sive *s* contre-offensive *f*

coun'ter·pane' s courtepointe f
coun'ter·part' s contrepartie f, homologue m
coun'ter·point' s contrepoint m
coun'ter·poise' s contrepoids m ‖ tr faire équilibre à
coun'ter·rev'olu'tionar·y adj contrerévolutionnaire ‖ s (pl -ies) contrerévolutionnaire mf
coun'ter·sign' s contremarque f; (signature) contreseing m; (mil) mot m d'ordre ‖ tr contresigner
coun'ter·sig'nature s contreseing m
coun'ter·sink' s fraise f ‖ v (pret & pp -sunk) tr fraiser
coun'ter·spy' s (pl -spies) contre-esp:on m
coun'ter·stroke' s contrecoup m
coun'ter·weight' s contrepoids m
countess ['kauntɪs] s comtesse f
countless ['kauntlɪs] adj innombrable
countrified ['kʌntrɪˌfaɪd] adj provincial, compagnard
coun·try ['kʌntri] s (pl -tries) (territory of a nation) pays m; (land of one's birth) patrie f; (region) contrée f; (not the city) campagne f
coun'try club' s club m privé situé hors des agglomérations
coun'try estate' s domaine m
coun'try·folk' s campagnards mpl
coun'try gen'tleman s châtelain m, propriétaire m d'un château
coun'try house' s maison f de campagne
coun'try·man s (pl -men) (of the same country) compatriote mf; (rural) compagnard m
coun'try·side' s paysage m, campagne f
coun'try town' s petite ville f de province
coun'try·wide' adj national
coun'try·wom'an s (pl -wom'en) (of the same country) compatriote f; (rural) campagnarde f
coun·ty ['kaunti] s (pl -ties) comté m
coun'ty seat' s chef-lieu m de comté
coupé [kupe] s coupé m
couple ['kʌpəl] s (man and wife; male and female; friends) couple m, paire f; (of eggs, cakes, etc.) couple f; (elec, mech) couple m ‖ tr coupler, accoupler; (mach) embrayer ‖ intr s'accoupler
coupler ['kʌplər] s (mach) coupleur m
coupling ['kʌplɪŋ] s accouplement m; (mach) couplage m
coupon ['k(j)upɑn] s coupon m, bon m
courage ['kʌrɪdʒ] s courage m
courageous [kə'redʒəs] adj courageux
courier ['kʌrɪ·ər], ['kurɪ·ər] s courrier m; (on horseback) estafette f
course [kors] s cours m; carrière f, voie f, course f; (of a meal) service m, plat m; (of a stream) parcours m, cours m; (direction) route f, chemin m; in due course en temps voulu; in the course of au cours de; in the course of time avec le temps; of course! naturellement!, bien entendu!; to give a course faire un cours; to set a course for (naut) mettre le

cap sur; to take a course suivre un cours ‖ tr & intr courir
court [kort] s cour f; (of law) tribunal m, cour; (sports) terrain m, court m; out of court à l'amiable ‖ tr courtiser, faire la cour à; (favor, votes) briguer, solliciter; (danger) aller audevant de
courteous ['kʌrtɪ·əs] adj poli, courtois
courtesan ['kʌrtɪzən], ['kortɪzən] s courtisane f
courte·sy ['kʌrtɪsi] s (pl -sies) politesse f, courtoisie f; through the courtesy of avec la gracieuse permission de
court'house' s palais m de justice
courtier ['kortɪ·ər] s courtisan m
court' jest'er s bouffon m du roi
court·ly ['kortli] adj (comp -lier; super -liest) courtois, élégant
court'-mar'tial s (pl courts-martial) conseil m de guerre ‖ v (pret & pp -tialed or -tialled; ger -tialing or -tialling) tr traduire en conseil de guerre; to be court-martialed passer en conseil de guerre
court' plas'ter s taffetas m gommé, sparadrap m
court'room' s salle f du tribunal
court'ship s cour f
court'yard' s cour f
cousin ['kʌzɪn] s cousin m
cove [kov] s anse f, crique f
covenant ['kʌvənənt] s contrat m, accord m, pacte m; (Bib) alliance f
cover ['kʌvər] s couverture f; (lid) couvercle m; (for furniture) housse f; (of wild game) remise f, gîte m; (com) couverture f, provision f, marge f; (mach) chape f, (phila) enveloppe f; from cover to cover de la première page à la dernière; to take cover se mettre à l'abri; under cover (e.g., of trees) sous les couverts; (safe from harm) à couvert; under cover of sous le couvert de, dissimulé dans; under separate cover sous pli distinct ‖ tr couvrir; (a certain distance) parcourir; (a newspaper story) faire le reportage de; (one's tracks) brouiller; (with, e.g., chocolate) enrober; to cover up recouvrir ‖ intr se couvrir; (to brood) couver
coverage ['kʌvərɪdʒ] s (amount or space covered) portée f; (of news) reportage m; (insurance) assurance f, couverture f d'assurance
cov'er-alls' spl salopette f, bleus mpl
cov'er charge' s couvert m
cov'ered wag'on s chariot m couvert
cov'er girl' s cover-girl f, pin up f
covering ['kʌvərɪŋ] s couverture f, recouvrement m
covert ['kʌvərt] adj couvert, caché
cov'er-up' s subterfuge m; (reply) réponse f évasive
covet ['kʌvɪt] tr convoiter
covetous ['kʌvɪtəs] adj cupide, avide
covetousness ['kʌvɪtəsnɪs] s convoitise f, cupidité f

covey ['kʌvi] s couvée f; (in flight) volée f
cow [kau] s vache f; (of seal, elephant) femelle f || tr (coll) intimider
coward ['kau·ərd] s lâche mf
cowardice ['kau·ərdɪs] s lâcheté f
cowardly ['kau·ərdli] adj lâche || adv lâchement, peureusement
cow'bell' s grelot m, clarine f
cow'boy' s cow-boy m
cow'catch'er s (rr) chasse-bestiaux m
cower ['kau·ər] intr se tapir
cow'herd' s vacher m, bouvier m
cow'hide' s vache f, peau f de vache; fouet m || tr fouetter
cowl [kaul] s capuchon m, cagoule f; (of chimney) chapeau m; (aer, aut) capot m
cow'lick' s mèche f rebelle
cow'pox' s (pathol) vaccine f
coxcomb ['kaks,kom] s (conceited person) petit-maître m, fat m; (bot) crête-de-coq f
coxswain ['kaksən], ['kak,swen] s patron m de chaloupe; (rowing) barreur m
coy [kɔɪ] adj réservé, modeste
co·zy ['kozi] adj (comp -zier; super -ziest) douillet, intime || s (pl -zies) couvre-théière m
C.P.A. ['si'pi'e] s (letterword) (certified public accountant) expert-comptable m, comptable m agréé
crab [kræb] s crabe m; (grouch) grincheux m || v (pret & pp crabbed; ger crabbing) intr (coll) se plaindre
crab' ap'ple s pomme f sauvage
crabbed ['kræbɪd] adj acariâtre; (handwriting) de chat; (author) hermétique; (style) entortillé
crab·by ['kræbi] adj (comp -bier; super -biest) (coll) revêche, grognon
crack [kræk] adj (troops) d'élite; (coll) expert, de premier ordre || s (noise) bruit m sec, craquement m; (of whip) claquement m; (fissure) fente f; (e.g., in a dish) fêlure f; (e.g., in a wall) lézarde f; (in skin) gerçure f; (joke) bon mot m; **crack of dawn** pointe f du jour || tr (one's fingers; petroleum) faire craquer; (a whip) claquer; (to split) fendre; (e.g., a dish) fêler; (e.g., a wall) lézarder; (the skin) gercer; (nuts) casser; **to crack a joke** (slang) faire or lâcher une plaisanterie; **to crack up** (to praise) (coll) vanter, prôner; (to crash) (coll) écraser || intr (to make a noise) craquer; (said of whip) claquer; (to be split) se fendre; (said of dish) se fêler; (said of wall) se lézarder; (said of skin) se gercer; **to crack up** (to crash) (coll) s'écraser; (to break down) (coll) craquer, s'effondrer
crack'-brained' adj timbré; **to be crack-brained** avoir le cerveau fêlé
crack'down' s (coll) répression f
cracked adj (split) fendu, fêlé; (foolish) (coll) timbré, toqué, cinglé
cracker ['krækər] s biscuit m sec
crack'er-bar'rel adj (coll) en chambre, au petit pied

crack'er·jack' adj (slang) expérimenté, remarquable || s (slang) crack m
cracking ['krækɪŋ] s (of petroleum) cracking m
crackle ['krækəl] s crépitation f || intr crépiter, pétiller
crack'le·ware' s porcelaine f craquelée
crackling ['kræklɪŋ] s crépitement m, pétillement m; (culin) couenne f rissolée; **cracklings** cretons mpl
crack'pot' adj & s (slang) original m, excentrique mf
crack' shot' s (coll) fin tireur m
crack'-up' s (collision) (coll) écrasement m; (breakdown) (coll) effondrement m
cradle ['kredəl] s berceau m || tr bercer
cra'dle·song' s berceuse f
craft [kræft], [krɑft] s métier m; (trickery) artifice m; (naut) embarcation f, barque f
craftiness ['kræftɪnɪs], ['krɑftɪnɪs] s ruse f, astuce f
crafts·man s (pl -men) artisan m
crafts'man·ship' s habileté f technique; exécution f
craft·y ['kræfti], ['krɑfti] adj (comp -ier; super -iest) rusé
crag [kræg] s rocher m escarpé
cram [kræm] v (pret & pp crammed; ger cramming) tr (with food) bourrer, gaver; (with people) bonder; (for an exam) (coll) chauffer || intr se bourrer, se gaver; (for an exam) (coll) potasser
cramp [kræmp] s (metal bar; clamp) crampon m; (in a muscle) crampe f; (carpentry) serre-joint m || tr cramponner, agrafer; presser, serrer; (one's movements, style, or manner of living) gêner
cranberry ['kræn,beri] s (pl -ries) (Vaccinium oxycoccus or V. uliginosum) canneberge f, airelle f canneberge
crane [kren] s (mach, orn) grue f || tr (one's neck) allonger, tendre || intr allonger le cou
crani·um ['kreni·əm] s (pl -a [ə]) crâne m
crank [kræŋk] s manivelle f; (person) (coll) excentrique mf || tr (a motor) faire partir à la manivelle
crank'case' s carter m
crank'shaft' s vilebrequin m
crank·y ['kræŋki] adj (comp -ier; super -iest) revêche, grincheux; (not working well) détraqué; (queer) excentrique
cran·ny ['kræni] s (pl -nies) fente f, crevasse f; (corner) coin m
crape [krep] s crêpe m
crape'hang'er s (slang) rabat-joie m
craps [kræps] s (slang) jeu m de dés; **to shoot craps** (slang) jouer aux dés
crash [kræʃ] s fracas m, écroulement m; (of thunder) coup m; (e.g., of airplane) écrasement m; (e.g., on stock market) krach m || tr briser, fracasser; (e.g., an airplane) écraser || intr retentir; (said of airplane) s'écraser; (to fail) craquer; **to crash into** em-

boutir, tamponner; **to crash through** enfoncer
crash′ dive′ *s* brusque plongée *f*
crash′ hel′met *s* casque *m*
crash′-land′ing *s* crash *m*, atterrissage *m* violent
crass [kræs] *adj* grossier; (*ignorance*) crasse
crate [kret] *s* caisse *f* à claire-voie, cageot *m* ‖ *tr* emballer dans une caisse à claire-voie
crater ['kretər] *s* cratère *m*
cravat [krə'væt] *s* cravate *f*
crave [krev] *tr* désirer ardemment; implorer; requérir, e.g., **the problem craves serious consideration** le problème requiert une considération sérieuse; **to crave s.o.'s pardon** demander pardon à qn ‖ *intr*—**to crave for** désirer ardemment; implorer
craven ['krevən] *adj & s* poltron *m*
craving ['krevɪŋ] *s* désir *m* ardent, désir obsédant
craw [krɔ] *s* jabot *m*
crawl [krɔl] *s* rampement *m*; (swimming) crawl *m* ‖ *intr* ramper; **to be crawling with** fourmiller de, grouiller de; **to crawl along** se traîner; **to crawl on one's hands and knees** aller à quatre pattes; **to crawl over** escalader; **to crawl up** grimper
crayon ['kre·ən] *s* crayon *m* de pastel, pastel *m* ‖ *tr* crayonner
craze [krez] *s* manie *f*, toquade *f* ‖ *tr* rendre fou
cra·zy ['krezi] *adj* (*comp* -zier; *super* -ziest) fou; (*rickety*) délabré; **to be crazy about** (coll) être fou de, être toqué de; **to drive crazy** rendre fou, affoler
cra′zy bone′ *s* nerf *m* du coude
cra′zy quilt′ *s* courtepointe *f* multicolore
creak [krik] *s* cri *m*, grincement *m* ‖ *intr* crier, grincer
creak·y ['kriki] *adj* (*comp* -ier; *super* -iest) criard
cream [krim] *s* crème *f*; **creams** (*with chocolate coating*) chocolats *mpl* fourrés ‖ *tr* écrémer; (*butter and sugar together*) mélanger ‖ *intr* crémer
cream′ cheese′ *s* fromage *m* à la crème, fromage blanc, petit suisse *m*
creamer·y ['kriməri] *s* (*pl* -ies) laiterie *f*; compagnie *f* laitière
cream′ of tar′tar *s* crème *f* de tartre
cream′ pitch′er *s* crémière *f*
cream′ puff′ *s* chou *m* à la crème
cream′ sep′arator ['sɛpə‚retər] *s* écrémeuse *f*
cream·y ['krimi] *adj* (*comp* -ier; *super* -iest) crémeux
crease [kris] *s* pli *m*, faux pli *m* ‖ *tr & intr* plisser
create [kri'et] *tr* créer
creation [kri'eʃən] *s* création *f*
creative [kri'etɪv] *adj* créateur, inventif
creator [kri'etər] *s* créateur *m*
creature ['kritʃər] *s* créature *f*
credence ['kridəns] *s* créance *f*, croyance *f*, foi *f*

credentials [krɪ'dɛnʃəlz] *spl* papiers *mpl*, pièces *fpl* justificatives, lettres *fpl* de créance
credibility [‚krɛdɪ'bɪlɪti] *s* crédibilité *f*
credible ['krɛdɪbəl] *adj* croyable, digne de foi
credit ['krɛdɪt] *s* crédit *m*; (*belief; claim*) créance *f*; **on credit** à crédit; **to be a credit to** faire honneur à; **to take credit for** s'attribuer le mérite de ‖ *tr* croire, ajouter foi à; (com) créditer, porter au crédit
creditable ['krɛdɪtəbəl] *adj* estimable, honorable
cred′it card′ *s* carte *f* de crédit
creditor ['krɛdɪtər] *s* créditeur *m*, créancier *m*
cre·do ['krido], ['kredo] *s* (*pl* -dos) credo *m*
credulous ['krɛdʒələs] *adj* crédule
creed [krid] *s* credo *m*; (*denomination*) foi *f*
creek [krik] *s* ruisseau *m*
creep [krip] *v* (*pret & pp* **crept** [krɛpt]) *intr* ramper; (*stealthily*) se glisser; (*slowly*) se traîner, se couler; (*to climb*) grimper; (*with a sensation of insects*) fourmiller; **to creep up on** s.o. s'approcher de qn à pas lents
creeper ['kripər] *s* plante *f* rampante
creeping ['kripɪŋ] *adj* lent, traînant; (*plant*) rampant ‖ *s* rampement *m*
creep·y ['kripi] *adj* (*comp* -ier; *super* -iest) (coll) mystérieux; **to feel creepy** fourmiller
cremate ['krimet] *tr* incinérer
cremation [krɪ'meʃən] *s* crémation *f*, incinération *f*
cremato·ry ['krimə‚tori] *adj* crématoire ‖ *s* (*pl* -ries) crématoire *m*, four *m* crématoire
Creole ['kri·ol] *adj* créole ‖ *s* (*language*) créole *m*; (*person*) Créole *mf*
crepe [krep] *s* crêpe *m*; (*pancake*) crêpe *f*
crepe′ pa′per *s* papier *m* crêpe
crescent ['krɛsənt] *s* croissant *m*
cress [krɛs] *s* cresson *m*
crest [krɛst] *s* crête *f*
crested ['krɛstɪd] *adj* à crête; (*with feathers*) huppé
crest′fall′en *adj* abattu, découragé
Cretan ['kritən] *adj* crétois ‖ *s* Crétois *m*
Crete [krit] *s* Crète *f*; **la Crète**
cretin ['kritən] *s* crétin *m*
crevice ['krɛvɪs] *s* crevasse *f*, fente *f*
crew [kru] *s* équipe *f*; (*of a ship*) équipage *m*; (*group, especially of armed men*) bande *f*, troupe *f*
crew′ cut′ *s* cheveux *mpl* en brosse
crew′ mem′ber *s* équipier *m*
crib [krɪb] *s* lit *m* d'enfant; crèche *f*, mangeoire *f*; (*for grain*) coffre *m*; (*student's pony*) corrigé *m* employé subrepticement ‖ *v* (*pret & pp* **cribbed**; *ger* **cribbing**) *tr & intr* (coll) copier à la dérobée
cricket ['krɪkɪt] *s* (ent) grillon *m*; (sports) cricket *m*; (coll) franc jeu *m*, jeu loyal; **to be cricket** être de bonne guerre

crier ['kraɪ·ər] s crieur m
crime [kraɪm] s crime m; (misdemeanor) délit m
criminal ['krɪmɪnəl] adj & s criminel m
crim'inal code' s code m pénal
crim'inal court' s cour f d'assises
crim'inal law' s loi f pénale
crimp [krɪmp] s (in cloth) pli m; (in hair) frisure f; (recruiter) racoleur m; to put a crimp in (coll) mettre obstacle à || tr (cloth) plisser; (hair) friser, crêper; (metal) onduler
crimson ['krɪmzən] adj & s cramoisi m
cringe [krɪndʒ] intr s'humilier, s'abaisser
cringing ['krɪndʒɪŋ] adj craintif, servile || s crainte f, servilité f
crinkle ['krɪŋkəl] s pli m, ride f || tr froisser, plisser || intr se froisser
cripple ['krɪpəl] s estropié m; (lame person) boiteux m || tr estropier; (a machine) disloquer; (business or industry) paralyser; (a ship) désemparer
cri·sis ['kraɪsɪs] s (pl -ses [siz]) crise f
crisp [krɪsp] adj croustillant; (tone) tranchant, brusque; (air) vif, frais
crisscross ['krɪs‚krɔs], ['krɪs‚krɑs] adj entrecroisé, treillissé || s entrecroisement m; (e.g., of wires) enchevêtrement m || adv en forme de croix || tr entrecroiser || intr s'entrecroiser
criteri·on [kraɪ'tɪrɪ·ən] s (pl -a [ə] or -ons) critère m
critic ['krɪtɪk] s critique mf; (faultfinder) critiqueur m, désapprobateur m
critical ['krɪtɪkəl] adj critique
critically ['krɪtɪkəli] adv en critique; critically ill gravement malade
criticism ['krɪtɪ‚sɪzəm] s critique f
criticize ['krɪtɪ‚saɪz] tr & intr critiquer
croak [krok] s (of raven) croassement m; (of frog) coassement m || intr (said of raven) croasser; (said of frog) coasser; (to die) (slang) mourir
Croat ['kro·æt] s (language) croate m; (person) Croate mf
Croatian [kro'eʃən] adj croate || s (language) croate m; (person) Croate mf
cro·chet [kro'ʃe] s crochet m || v (pret & pp -cheted ['ʃed]; ger -cheting ['ʃe·ɪŋ]) tr & intr tricoter au crochet
crochet' nee'dle s crochet m
crock [krɑk] s pot m de terre
crockery ['krɑkəri] s faïence f, poterie f
crocodile ['krɑkə‚daɪl] s crocodile m
croc'odile tears' spl larmes fpl de crocodile
crocus ['krokəs] s crocus m
crone [kron] s vieille femme f au visage parcheminé
cro·ny ['kroni] s (pl -nies) copain m
crook [kruk] s (hook) croc m; (of shepherd) houlette f; (of bishop) crosse f; (in road) courbure f; (person) (coll) escroc m || tr courber || intr se courber
crooked ['krukɪd] adj courbé, crochu; (path; conduct) tortueux; (tree; nose; legs) tortu; (person) (coll) malhonnête, fourbe

croon [krun] intr chanter des chansons sentimentales
crooner ['krunər] s chanteur m de charme
crop [krɑp] s récolte f; (head of hair) cheveux mpl ras; (of bird) jabot m; (whip) fouet m; (of whip) manche m; (of appointments, promotions, heroes, discoveries) moisson f || v (pret & pp cropped; ger cropping) tr tondre; (head of hair) couper, tailler; (ears of animal) essoriller || intr—to crop up (coll) surgir, s'élever brusquement
croquet [kro'ke] s croquet m
crosier ['kroʒər] s crosse f
cross [krɔs], [krɑs] adj transversal, oblique; (breed) croisé; (ill-humored) maussade || s croix f; (of races or breeds; of roads) croisement m || tr croiser; (the sea; a street) traverser; (breeds) croiser, métisser; (the threshold) franchir; (said of one road with respect to another) couper; (the letter t) barrer; (e.g., s.o.'s plans) (coll) contrecarrer; to cross oneself (eccl) se signer; to cross out biffer, rayer || intr se croiser, passer; to cross over passer de l'autre côté
cross'bones' spl tibias mpl croisés
cross'bow' s arbalète f
cross'breed' v (pret & pp -bred) tr croiser, métisser
cross'-coun'try adj à travers champs
cross'cur'rent s contre-courant m; tendance f contraire
cross'-examina'tion s contre-interrogatoire m
cross'-exam'ine tr contre-interroger, contre-examiner
cross'-eyed' adj louche
crossing ['krɔsɪŋ], ['krɑsɪŋ] s croisement m; (of ocean) traversée f; (of river, mountain, etc.) passage m; (rr) passage m à niveau
cross'ing gate' s barrière f d'un passage à niveau
cross'patch' s (coll) grincheux m, grognon m
cross'piece' s entretoise f
cross' ref'erence s renvoi m
cross'road' s voie f transversale, chemin m de traverse; crossroads carrefour m, croisement m
cross' sec'tion s coupe f transversale; (e.g., of building) section f; (of opinion) sondage m, groupe m représentatif; tranche f de vie
cross'-sec'tion tr couper transversalement
cross' street' s rue f de traverse, rue transversale
cross'wise' adv en croix, en sautoir
cross'word puz'zle s mots mpl croisés
crotch [krɑtʃ] s (forked piece) fourche f; (between legs) entrejambe f, enfourchure f
crotchet ['krɑtʃɪt] s (mus) noire f; (coll) lubie f
crotchety ['krɑtʃɪti] adj capricieux, fantasque

crouch [kraʊtʃ] *s* accroupissement *m* || *intr* s'accroupir, se blottir

croup [krup] *s* (*of horse*) croupe *f*; (pathol) croup *m*

croupier ['krupɪ·ər] *s* croupier *m*

crouton ['krutɑn] *s* croûton *m*

crow [kro] *s* corbeau *m*; (*rook*) corneille *f*, freux *m*; **as the crow flies** à vol d'oiseau; **to eat crow** (coll) avaler des couleuvres || *intr* (*said of cock*) chanter; (*said of babies*) gazouiller; **to crow over** chanter victoire sur, triompher bruyamment de

crow′bar′ *s* levier *m*; (*for forcing doors*) pince-monseigneur *f*

crowd [kraʊd] *s* foule *f*; (*large flock of people*) affluence *f*, presse *f*; (*mob, common people*) populace *f*, vulgaire *m*; (*clique, set*) bande *f*, monde *m*; **a crowd** (*of people*) du monde, beaucoup de monde || *tr* serrer, entasser; (*to push*) pousser; (*a debtor*) presser; **to crowd out** ne pas laisser de place à || *intr* affluer, s'amasser; **to crowd around** se presser autour de; **to crowd in** s'attrouper

crowded *adj* encombré, bondé

crow′foot′ *s* renoncule *f*, bouton *m* d'or

crowing ['kro·ɪŋ] *s* chant *m* de coq, cocorico *m*; (*of babies*) gazouillement *m*

crown [kraʊn] *s* couronne *f*; (*of hat*) calotte *f* || *tr* couronner, sacrer; (checkers) damer; **to crown s.o.** (slang) flanquer un coup sur la tête à qn

crowning ['kraʊnɪŋ] *s* couronnement *m*

crown′ prince′ *s* prince *m* héritier

crown′ prin′cess *s* princesse *f* héritière

crow's′-foot′ *s* (*pl* -feet) patte-d'oie *f*

crow's′-nest *s* (naut) nid *m* de pie, tonneau *m* de vigie

crucial ['kruʃəl] *adj* crucial

crucible ['krusɪbəl] *s* creuset *m*

crucifix ['krusɪfɪks] *s* crucifix *m*, christ *m*

crucifixion [ˌkrusɪ'fɪkʃən] *s* crucifixion *f*

cruci·fy ['krusɪ ˌfaɪ] *v* (*pret & pp* -fied) *tr* crucifier

crude [krud] *adj* (*raw, unrefined*) cru, brut; (*lacking culture*) fruste, grossier; (*unfinished*) informe, grossier, mal développé; (*oil*) brut

crudi·ty ['krudɪti] *s* (*pl* -ties) crudité *f*; (*of person*) grossièreté *f*

cruel ['kru·əl] *adj* cruel

cruel·ty ['kru·əlti] *s* (*pl* -ties) cruauté *f*

cruet ['kru·ɪt] *s* burette *f*

cru′et stand′ *s* huilier *m*

cruise [kruz] *s* croisière *f* || *intr* croiser

cruiser ['kruzər] *s* croiseur *m*

cruising ['kruzɪŋ] *adj* en croisière; (*taxi*) en maraude

cruis′ing range′ *s* autonomie *f*

cruis′ing speed′ *s* vitesse *f* de route

cruller ['krʌlər] *s* beignet *m*

crumb [krʌm] *s* miette *f*; (*soft part of bread*) mie *f* || *tr* (*cutlets, etc.*) paner

crumble ['krʌmbəl] *tr* émietter, ré-

duire en miettes; (*e.g., stone*) effriter || *intr* s'émietter; s'effriter; (*to fall to pieces*) s'écrouler

crum·my ['krʌmi] *adj* (*comp* -mier; *super* -miest) (slang) sale, minable

crumple ['krʌmpəl] *tr* friper, froisser; (*a fender*) mettre en accordéon || *intr* se friper, se froisser

crunch [krʌntʃ] *tr* croquer, broyer || *intr* (*said of snow*) craquer

crupper ['krʌpər] *s* croupière *f*

crusade [kru'sed] *s* croisade *f* || *intr* se croiser, prendre part à une croisade

crush [krʌʃ] *s* écrasement *m*; (*of people*) presse *f*, foule *f*; **to have a crush on** (slang) avoir un béguin pour || *tr* écraser; (*e.g., stone*) broyer, concasser; (*to oppress, grieve*) accabler, aplatir

crush′ hat′ *s* claque *m*, gibus *m*

crust [krʌst] *s* croûte *f*

crustacean [krʌs'teʃən] *s* crustacé *m*

crust·y ['krʌsti] *adj* (*comp* -ier; *super* -iest) croustillant; (*said of person*) bourru, hargneux

crutch [krʌtʃ] *s* béquille *f*

crux [krʌks] *s* nœud *m*

cry [kraɪ] *s* (*pl* cries) cri *m*; (*of wolf*) hurlement *m*; (*of bull*) mugissement *m*; **to cry one's eyes out** pleurer à chaudes larmes; **to have a good cry** donner libre cours aux larmes || *v* (*pret & pp* cried) *tr* crier; **to cry out** crier || *intr* crier; (*to weep*) pleurer; **to cry for** crier à; **to cry for joy** pleurer de joie; **to cry out** pousser des cris, s'écrier; **to cry out against** crier à

cry′ba′by *s* (*pl* -bies) pleurard *m*

crypt [krɪpt] *s* crypte *f*

cryptic(al) ['krɪptɪk(əl)] *adj* secret, occulte; (*silence*) énigmatique

crystal ['krɪstəl] *s* cristal *m*

crys′tal ball′ *s* boule *f* de cristal

crystalline ['krɪstəlɪn], ['krɪstə ˌlaɪn] *adj* cristallin

crystallize ['krɪstə ˌlaɪz] *tr* cristalliser; (*sugar*) candir || *intr* cristalliser; (*said of sugar*) se candir; (*said of one's thoughts*) (fig) se cristalliser

cub [kʌb] *s* petit *m*; (*of bear*) ourson *m*; (*of fox*) renardeau *m*; (*of lion*) lionceau *m*; (*of wolf*) louveteau *m*

Cuban ['kjubən] *adj* cubain || *s* Cubain *m*

cubbyhole ['kʌbɪ ˌhol] *s* retraite *f*; (*in wall*) placard *m*; (*in furniture*) case *f*

cube [kjub] *adj & s* cube *m*; **in cubes** (*said of sugar*) en morceaux || *tr* cuber

cube′ root′ *s* racine *f* cubique

cubic ['kjubɪk] *adj* cubique, cube

cu′bic me′ter *s* mètre *m* cube

cub′ report′er *s* reporter *m* débutant

cub′ scout′ *s* louveteau *m*

cuckold ['kʌkəld] *adj & s* cocu *m*, cornard *m* || *tr* cocufier

cuckoo ['kuku] *adj* (slang) niais, benêt || *s* coucou *m*

cuck′oo clock′ *s* coucou *m*

cucumber ['kjukəmbər] *s* concombre *m*

cud [kʌd] s bol m alimentaire; **to chew the cud** ruminer

cuddle ['kʌdəl] tr serrer doucement dans les bras || intr (said of lovers) s'étreindre; **to cuddle up** se pelotonner

cudg•el ['kʌdʒəl] s gourdin m, trique f; **to take up the cudgels for** prendre fait et cause pour || v (pret & pp -eled or -elled; ger -eling or -elling) tr bâtonner, rosser

cue [kju] s avis m; (hint) mot m; (rod used in billiards; persons in line) queue f; (mus) indication f de rentrée; (theat) réclame f; **to give s.o. the cue** faire la leçon à qn, donner le mot à qn; **to take one's cue from** se conformer à

cuff [kʌf] s (of shirt) poignet m, manchette f; (of coat or trousers) parement m; (blow) taloche f, manchette f || tr talocher, flanquer une taloche à

cuff' link' s bouton m de manchette

cuirass [kwɪ'ræs] s cuirasse f

cuisine [kwɪ'zin] s cuisine f

culinary ['kjulɪ ˌnɛri] adj culinaire

cull [kʌl] tr choisir; (to gather, pluck) cueillir; **to cull from** recueillir dans

culm [kʌlm] s chaume m; (coal dust) charbonnaille f

culminate ['kʌlmɪˌnet] intr (astr) culminer; **to culminate in** finir par, se terminer en

culmination [ˌkʌlmɪ'neʃən] s point m culminant; (astr) culmination f

culottes [k(j)u'lɑts] spl pantalon m de plage

culpable ['kʌlpəbəl] adj coupable

culprit ['kʌlprɪt] s coupable mf; (accused) accusé m, prévenu m

cult [kʌlt] s culte m

cultivate ['kʌltɪˌvet] tr cultiver

cultivation [ˌkʌltɪ'veʃən] s culture f

cultivator ['kʌltɪˌvetər] s (person) cultivateur m, exploitant m agricole; (mach) cultivateur m, scarificateur m

cultural ['kʌltʃərəl] adj culturel

culture ['kʌltʃər] s culture f || tr cultiver

cultured adj (learned) cultivé, lettré

cul'tured pearl' s perle f de culture

culvert ['kʌlvərt] s ponceau m, cassis m

cumbersome ['kʌmbərsəm] adj incommode, encombrant; (clumsy) lourd, difficile à manier

cummerbund ['kʌmərˌbʌnd] s ceinture f d'étoffe

cumulative ['kjumjəˌletɪv] adj croissant, cumulatif

cunning ['kʌnɪŋ] adj (sly) astucieux, rusé; (clever) habile, fin; (attractive) gentil || s (slyness) astuce f, ruse f; (cleverness) habileté f, finesse f

cup [kʌp] s tasse f; (of metal) gobelet m, timbale f; (bot, eccl) calice m; (mach) godet m graisseur; (sports) coupe f || v (pret & pp cupped; ger cupping) tr (surg) ventouser

cupboard ['kʌbərd] s armoire f; (in wall) placard m

Cupid ['kjupɪd] s Cupidon m

cupidity [kju'pɪdɪti] s cupidité f

cupola ['kjupələ] s coupole f

cur [kʌr] s chien m métis, roquet m; (despicable person) mufle m

curate ['kjurɪt] s vicaire m

curative ['kjurətɪv] adj curatif

curator [kju'retər] s conservateur m

curb [kʌrb] s bordure f de pavés, bord m de trottoir; (of well) margelle f; (of bit) gourmette f; (market) coulisse f; (check, restraint) frein m || tr (a horse) gourmer; (passions, anger, desires) réprimer, refréner; **curb your dog** (public sign) faites faire votre chien dans le ruisseau

curb' serv'ice s restoroute m

curb'stone' s garde-pavé m; **curbstones** bordure f de pavés

curd [kʌrd] s caillé m; **curds** caillebotte f || tr cailler, caillebotter || intr se cailler, se caillebotter

curdle ['kʌrdəl] tr cailler; (the blood) figer || intr se cailler; se figer

curds' and whey' spl lait m caillé sucré

cure [kjur] s guérison f; (treatment) cure f; (remedy) remède m || tr guérir; (meat; leather) saler; (a pipe) culotter

cure'-all' s panacée f

curfew ['kʌrfju] s couvre-feu m

curi•o ['kjurɪˌo] s (pl -os) bibelot m

curiosi•ty [ˌkjurɪ'asɪti] s (pl -ties) curiosité f

curious ['kjurɪ•əs] adj curieux

curl [kʌrl] s boucle f, frisure f; (spiral-shaped) volute f; (of smoke) spirale f || tr boucler, friser; (to coil, to roll up) enrouler, tire-bouchonner; **to curl one's lip** faire la moue || intr boucler, friser; (said of smoke) s'élever en spirales; (said of waves) onduler, déferler; **to curl up** (said of leaves, paper, etc.) se recroqueviller; (in bed) se rouler en boule

curlew ['kʌrl(j)u] s courlis m

curlicue ['kʌrlɪˌkju] s paraphe m

curl'ing i'ron s fer m à friser

curl'pa'per s papillote f

curl•y ['kʌrli] adj (comp -ier; super -iest) bouclé, frisé

curmudgeon [kər'mʌdʒən] s (crosspatch) bourru m, sale bougre m; (miser) ladre mf

currant ['kʌrənt] s groseille f

curren•cy ['kʌrənsi] s (pl -cies) circulation f; (legal tender) monnaie f, devises fpl; **to give currency to** donner cours à

current ['kʌrənt] adj courant; (month) en cours; (accepted) admis, reçu; (present-day) actuel || s courant m; (stream) courant, cours m

cur'rent account' s compte m courant

cur'rent events' spl actualités fpl

cur'rent fail'ure s panne f de secteur

cur'rent is'sue s dernier numéro m

curricu•lum [kə'rɪkjələm] s (pl -lums or -la [lə]) programme m scolaire, plan m d'études

cur•ry ['kʌri] s (pl -ries) cari m || v (pret & pp -ried) tr (a horse) étriller; (culin) apprêter au cari; **to curry favor with** faire la cour à

cur'ry•comb' s étrille f || tr étriller

cur′ry pow′der s cari m
curse [kʌrs] s malédiction f; (oath) juron m ‖ tr maudire ‖ intr jurer, sacrer
cursed ['kʌrsɪd], [kʌrst] adj maudit, exécrable, sacré
cursive ['kʌrsɪv] adj cursif ‖ s cursive f
cursory ['kʌrsəri] adj superficiel, précipité
curt [kʌrt] adj brusque, court
curtail [kər'tel] tr amoindrir, diminuer; (expenses) restreindre; (rights) enlever
curtailment [kʌr'telmənt] s diminution f; (of expenses) restriction f; (of rights) privation f
curtain ['kʌrtən] s rideau m ‖ tr garnir de rideaux; (to hide) cacher sous des rideaux; **to curtain off** séparer par un rideau
cur′tain call′ s rappel m
cur′tain rais′er s (play) lever m de rideau
cur′tain ring′ s anneau m de rideau
cur′tain rod′ s tringle f de rideau
curt·sy ['kʌrtsi] s (pl -sies) révérence f ‖ v (pret & pp -sied) intr faire la révérence
curvature ['kʌrvətʃər] s courbure f; (of spine) déviation f
curve [kʌrv] s courbe f; (of road) virage m; (curvature) courbure f ‖ tr courber ‖ intr se courber
curved adj courbe, courbé
cushion ['kuʃən] s coussin m ‖ tr (a chair) rembourrer; (a shock) amortir
cuspidor ['kʌspɪ,dər] s crachoir m
cuss [kʌs] s (person) (coll) vaurien m, chenapan m ‖ tr (coll) maudire ‖ intr (coll) jurer, sacrer
cuss′word′ s (coll) juron m
custard ['kʌstərd] s flan m, œufs mpl au lait, crème f caramel
custodian [kəs'todɪ·ən] s gardien m; concierge mf
custo·dy ['kʌstədi] s (pl -dies) garde f; emprisonnement m; **in custody** en sûreté; **to take into custody** mettre en état d'arrestation
custom ['kʌstəm] s coutume f; (customers) clientèle f; **customs** douane f; (duties) droits mpl de douane
customary ['kʌstə,mɛri] adj coutumier, ordinaire, habituel
custom-built ['kʌstəm'bɪlt] adj hors série, fait sur commande
customer ['kʌstəmər] s client m, chaland m; (coll) individu m, type m; **customers** clientèle f, achalandage m
cus′tom·house′ adj douanier ‖ s douane f
custom-made ['kʌstəm'med] adj fait sur commande; (clothes) sur mesure
cus′toms clear′ance s expédition f douanière
cus′toms of′ficer s douanier m
cus′toms un′ion s union f douanière
cus′toms tai′lor s tailleur m à façon
cut [kʌt] adj coupé; **cut out** taillé, e.g., **he is not cut out for that** il n'est pas taillé pour cela; e.g., **your work is cut out for you** voilà votre besogne

taillée ‖ s coupe f; (piece cut off) tranche f, morceau m; (slash) coupure f; (with knife, whip, etc.) coup m; (in prices, wages, etc.) réduction f, baisse f; (of a garment) coupe; (typ) gravure f, planche f; (absence from school) (coll) séchage m; (in winnings, earnings, etc.) (slang) part f; **the cheap cuts** les bas morceaux mpl ‖ v (pret & pp cut; ger cutting) tr (meat, bread) trancher; (prices) réduire, baisser; (e.g., a hole) pratiquer; (glass, diamonds) tailler; (fingernails) rogner; (an article, play, speech) sabrer, faire des coupures à; (a phonograph record) enregistrer; (a class) (coll) sécher; **to cut down** faucher, abattre; (expenses) réduire; **to cut off, out,** or **up** découper, couper; **to cut short** couper court à ‖ intr couper; trancher; **to cut in** (a conversation) s'immiscer dans; (coll) enlever la danseuse d'un autre; **to cut off** (debate) clore; **to cut up** (slang) faire le pitre
cut′-and-dried′ adj décidé d'avance, tout fait; monotone, rasoir
cutaneous [kju'tenɪ·əs] adj cutané
cut′away′ s frac m
cut′back′ s réduction f; (mov) retour m en arrière
cute [kjut] adj (coll) mignon; (shrewd) (coll) rusé
cut′ glass′ s cristal m taillé
cuticle ['kjutɪkəl] s cuticule f
cutlass ['kʌtləs] s coutelas m
cutlery ['kʌtləri] s coutellerie f
cutlet ['kʌtlɪt] s côtelette f; (without bone) escalope f
cut′off′ s point m de coupure; (road) raccourci m; (of river) bras m mort; (of cylinder) obturateur m
cut′out′ s (aut) échappement m libre; (elec) coupe-circuit m; (mov) décor m découpé
cut′-rate′ adj à prix réduit
cutter ['kʌtər] s (naut) cotre m
cut′throat′ s coup-jarret m
cutting ['kʌtɪŋ] adj tranchant; (tone, remark) mordant, cinglant ‖ s coupe f; (from a newspaper) coupure f; (e.g., of prices) réduction f; (hort) bouture f; (mov) découpage m
cuttlefish ['kʌtəl,fɪʃ] s seiche f
cut′wa′ter s (naut) étrave f; (of bridge) bec m
cyanamide [saɪ'ænə,maɪd] s cyanamide f
cyanide ['saɪ·ə,naɪd] s cyanure m
cyanosis [ˌsaɪ·ə'nosɪs] s cyanose f
cycle ['saɪkəl] s cycle m; (of internal-combustion engine) temps m; (phys) période f ‖ v intr faire de la bicyclette
cyclic(al) ['saɪklɪk(əl)], ['sɪklɪk(əl)] adj cyclique
cyclist ['saɪklɪst] s cycliste mf
cyclone ['saɪklon] s cyclone m
cyclops ['saɪkləps] s cyclope m
cyclotron ['saɪklo,tran], ['sɪklo,tran] s cyclotron m
cylinder ['sɪlɪndər] s cylindre m; (of revolver) barillet m

cyl'inder block' *s* cylindre *m*
cyl'inder bore' *s* alésage *m*
cyl'inder head' *s* culasse *f*
cylindric(al) [sɪ'lɪndrɪk(əl)] *adj* cylindrique
cymbal ['sɪmbəl] *s* cymbale *f*
cynic ['sɪnɪk] *adj* & *s* cynique *m*
cynical ['sɪnɪkəl] *adj* cynique
cynicism ['sɪnɪ‚sɪzəm] *s* cynisme *m*
cynosure ['saɪnə‚ʃʊr], ['sɪnə‚ʃʊr] *s* guide *m*, exemple *m*, norme *f*; (*center of attention*) clou *m*; (astr) cynosure *f*
cypress ['saɪprəs] *s* cyprès *m*

Cyprus ['saɪprəs] *s* Chypre *f*
Cyrillic [sɪ'rɪlɪk] *adj* cyrillique
cyst [sɪst] *s* kyste *m*; (*on the skin*) vésicule *f*
czar [zɑr] *s* tsar *m*, czar *m*
czarina [zɑ'rinə] *s* tsarine *f*, czarine *f*
Czech [tʃɛk] *adj* tchèque ‖ *s* (*language*) tchèque *m*; (*person*) Tchèque *mf*
Czecho-Slovak ['tʃɛko'slovæk] *adj* tchécoslovaque ‖ *s* Tchécoslovaque *mf*
Czecho-Slovakia [‚tʃɛkoslo'vækɪə] *s* Tchécoslovaquie *f*; la Tchécoslovaquie

D

D, d [di] *s* IVe lettre de l'alphabet
dab [dæb] *s* touche *f*; (*of ink*) tache *f*; (*of butter*) petit morceau *m* ‖ *v* (*pret* & *pp* dabbed; *ger* dabbing) *tr* essuyer légèrement; (*to pat*) tapoter
dabble ['dæbəl] *tr* humecter ‖ *intr* barboter; to dabble in se mêler de; to dabble in the stock market boursicoter
dad [dæd] *s* (coll) papa *m*
dad·dy ['dædi] *s* (*pl* -dies) papa *m*
dad'dy-long'legs' *s* (*pl* -legs) faucheux *m*
daffodil ['dæfədɪl] *s* jonquille *f* des prés, narcisse *m* des bois
daff·y ['dæfi] *adj* (*comp* -ier; *super* -iest) (coll) timbré, toqué
dagger ['dægər] *s* poignard *m*, dague *f*; (typ) croix *f*, obel *m*; to look daggers at foudroyer du regard
dahlia ['dæljə] *s* dahlia *m*
dai·ly ['deli] *adj* quotidien, journalier ‖ *s* (*pl* -lies) quotidien *m* ‖ *adv* journellement
dain·ty ['denti] *adj* (*comp* -tier; *super* -tiest) délicat ‖ *s* (*pl* -ties) friandise *f*
dair·y ['dɛri] *s* (*pl* -ies) laiterie *f*; (*shop*) crémerie *f*; (*farm*) vacherie *f*
dair'y farm' *s* vacherie *f*
dair'y·man *s* (*pl* -men) laitier *m*
dais ['de·ɪs] *s* estrade *f*
dai·sy ['dezi] *s* (*pl* -sies) marguerite *f*
dal·ly ['dæli] *v* (*pret* & *pp* -lied) *intr* badiner; (*to delay*) s'attarder
dam [dæm] *s* barrage *m*; (*female quadruped*) mère *f* ‖ *v* (*pret* & *pp* dammed; *ger* damming) *tr* contenir, endiguer
damage ['dæmɪdʒ] *s* dommage *m*, dégâts *mpl*; (*to engine, ship, etc.*) avaries *fpl*; (*to one's reputation*) tort *m*; damages (law) dommages-intérêts *mpl* ‖ *tr* endommager; (*merchandise; a machine*) avarier; (*a reputation*) faire du tort à
damaging ['dæmɪdʒɪŋ] *adj* dommageable, préjudiciable
damascene ['dæmə‚sin], [‚dæmə'sin]

adj damasquiné ‖ *s* damasquinage *m* ‖ *tr* damasquiner
Damascus [də'mæskəs] *s* Damas *f*
dame [dem] *s* dame *f*; (coll) jupon *m*
damn [dæm] *s* juron *m*, gros mot *m*; I don't give a damn (slang) je m'en fiche; that's not worth a damn (slang) ça ne vaut pas un pet de lapin, ça ne vaut pas chipette ‖ *tr* condamner; (*to criticize harshly*) éreinter; (*to curse*) maudire; damn it! oh, la vache!; to damn with faint praise assommer avec des fleurs ‖ *intr* maudire
damnation [dæm'neʃən] *s* damnation *f*
damned [dæmd] *adj* damné *m* ‖ *s*—the damned les damnés ‖ *adv* (slang) diablement, bigrement
damp [dæmp] *adj* humide, moite ‖ *s* humidité *f*; (*firedamp*) grisou *m* ‖ *tr* (*to dampen*) humecter, mouiller; (*a furnace*) étouffer; (*sound; electromagnetic waves*) amortir
dampen ['dæmpən] *tr* humecter; (*enthusiasm*) refroidir; (*to muffle*) amortir
damper ['dæmpər] *s* (*of chimney*) registre *m*; (*of stovepipe*) soupape *f* de réglage; (*of piano*) étouffoir *m*; to put a damper on (fig) jeter un froid sur
damsel ['dæmzəl] *s* demoiselle *f*
dance [dæns], [dɑns] *s* danse *f*; bal *m*, soirée *f* dansante ‖ *tr* & *intr* danser
dance' band' *s* orchestre *m* de danse
dance' floor' *s* piste *f* de danse
dance' hall' *s* dancing *m*, salle *f* de danse
dance' pro'gram *s* carnet *m* de bal
dancer ['dænsər], ['dɑnsər] *s* danseur *m*
danc'ing part'ner *s* danseur *m*
dandelion ['dændɪ‚laɪ·ən] *s* pissenlit *m*
dandruff ['dændrəf] *s* pellicules *fpl*
dan·dy ['dændi] *adj* (*comp* -dier; *super* -diest) (coll) chic, chouette ‖ *s* (*pl* -dies) dandy *m*, élégant *m*
Dane [den] *s* Danois *m*
danger ['dendʒər] *s* danger *m*

dangerous ['dendʒərəs] *adj* dangereux
dangle ['dæŋgəl] *tr* faire pendiller ‖ *intr* pendiller
Danish ['denɪʃ] *adj & s* danois *m*
dank [dæŋk] *adj* humide, moite
Danube ['dænjub] *s* Danube *m*
dapper ['dæpər] *adj* fringant, élégant
dappled ['dæpəld] *adj* tacheté; (*sky*) pommelé; (*horse*) moucheté, miroité
dare [dɛr] *s* défi *m*; **to take a dare** relever un défi ‖ *tr* défier; oser; **to dare s.o. to** + *inf* défier qn de + *inf* ‖ *intr* oser; **to dare** + *inf* oser + *inf*
dare'dev'il *s* risque-tout *mf*
daring ['dɛrɪŋ] *adj* audacieux, hardi ‖ *s* audace *f*, hardiesse *f*
dark [dɑrk] *adj* sombre, obscur; (*color*) foncé; (*complexion*) basané, brun; **it is dark** il fait noir, il fait nuit ‖ *s* obscurité *f*, ténèbres *fpl*
Dark' Ag'es *spl* âge *m* des ténèbres
darken ['dɑrkən] *tr* assombrir; (*the complexion*) brunir; (*a color*) foncer ‖ *intr* s'assombrir; (*said of forehead*) se rembrunir
dark' horse' *s* (pol) candidat *m* obscur; (sports) outsider *m*
darkly ['dɑrkli] *adv* obscurément; (*mysteriously*) ténébreusement; (*threateningly*) d'un air menaçant
dark' meat' *s* viande *f* brune; (*of game*) viande noire
darkness ['dɑrknɪs] *s* obscurité *f*
dark'room' *s* (phot) chambre *f* noire
darling ['dɑrlɪŋ] *adj & s* chéri *m*, bien-aimé *m*; **my darling** mon chou
darn [dɑrn] *s* reprise *f*, raccommodage *m* ‖ *tr* repriser, raccommoder ‖ *interj* zut!
darn'ing egg' *s* œuf *m* à repriser
darn'ing nee'dle *s* aiguille *f* à repriser
dart [dɑrt] *s* dard *m*; (*small missile used in a game*) fléchette *f* ‖ *intr* se précipiter, aller comme une flèche
dash [dæʃ] *s* trait *m*; (*small amount*) soupçon *m*, petit brin *m*; (*of color*) pointe *f*, touche *f*; (*splash*) choc *m*, floc *m*; (*spirit*) élan *m*, fougue *f*; (*in printing, writing*) tiret *m*; (*in telegraphy*) trait *m*, longue *f* ‖ *tr* (*quickly*) précipiter; (*violently*) heurter; (*hopes*) abattre; **to dash off** écrire d'un trait, esquisser; **to dash to pieces** fracasser ‖ *intr* se précipiter; **to dash against** se heurter contre; **to dash by** filer à grand train; **to dash in** entrer en trombe; **to dash off** or **out** s'élancer, s'élancer dehors
dash'board' *s* tableau *m* de bord
dashing ['dæʃɪŋ] *adj* impétueux, fougueux; (*elegant*) fringant
dastard ['dæstərd] *adj & s* lâche *mf*
data ['detə], ['dætə] *spl* données *fpl*
da'ta proc'essing *s* analyse *f* des renseignements, étude *f* des données
date [det] *s* (*time*) date *f*; (*on books, on coins*) millésime *m*; (*palm*) dattier *m*; (*fruit*) datte *f*; (*of note, of loan*) terme *m*, échéance *f*; (*appointment*) rendez-vous *m*; **out of date** suranné, périmé; **to date** à ce jour; **up to date** à la page, au courant ‖ *tr* dater;

(*e.g., a work of art*) assigner une date à; (coll) fixer un rendez-vous avec ‖ *intr* (*to be outmoded*) dater; **to date from** dater de, remonter à
date' line' *s* ligne *f* de changement de date
date' palm' *s* dattier *m*
dative ['detɪv] *s* datif *m*
daub [dɔb] *s* barbouillage *m* ‖ *tr* barbouiller
daughter ['dɔtər] *s* fille *f*
daugh'ter-in-law' *s* (*pl* **daughters-in-law**) belle-fille *f*, bru *f*
daunt [dɔnt] *tr* intimider, abattre
dauntless ['dɔntlɪs] *adj* intrépide
dauphin ['dɔfɪn] *s* dauphin *m*
davenport ['dævən,port] *s* canapé-lit *m*
daw [dɔ] *s* choucas *m*
dawdle ['dɔdəl] *intr* flâner, muser
dawn [dɔn] *s* aube *f*, aurore *f* ‖ *intr* poindre; **to dawn on** venir à l'esprit à
day [de] *adj* (*work*) diurne; (*worker*) de journée ‖ *s* jour *m*; (*of travel, work, worry*) journée *f*; (*of the month*) quantième *m*; **a day** (*per day*) par jour; **by the day** à la journée; **day by day** au jour le jour, jour par jour; **every day** tous les jours, chaque jour; **every other day** tous les deux jours; **from day to day** de jour en jour; **good old days** bon vieux temps; **in less than a day** du jour au lendemain; **in these days** de nos jours; **in those days** à ce moment-là, à cette époque; **one fine day** un beau jour; **the day after** le lendemain; le lendemain de; **the day after tomorrow** après-demain; l'après-demain *m*; **the day before** la veille; la veille de; **the day before yesterday** avant-hier; l'avant-hier *m*
day' bed' *s* canapé-lit *m*
day'break' *s* pointe *f* du jour, lever *m* du jour; **at daybreak** au jour levant
day' coach' *s* (rr) voiture *f*
day'dream' *s* rêvasserie *f*, rêverie *f* ‖ *intr* rêvasser, rêver creux
day'dream'er *s* songe-creux *m*, songeur *m*
day'dream'ing *s* rêvasserie *f*
day' la'borer *s* journalier *m*
day'light' *s* jour *m*; **in broad daylight** en plein jour; **to see daylight** (coll) comprendre; (coll) voir la fin d'une tâche difficile
day'light-sav'ing time' *s* heure *f* d'été
day' lil'y *s* lis *m* jaune, belle-d'un-jour *f*
day' nurs'ery *s* garderie *f* d'enfants, crèche *f*
day' off' *s* jour *m* de congé, jour chômé
day' of reck'oning *s* jour *m* de règlement; (*last judgment*) jour d'expiation
day' shift' *s* équipe *f* de jour
day' stu'dent *s* externe *mf*
day'time' *s* jour *m*, journée *f*
daze [dez] *s* étourdissement *m*; **in a daze** hébété ‖ *tr* étourdir
dazzle ['dæzəl] *s* éblouissement *m* ‖ *tr* éblouir
dazzling ['dæzlɪŋ] *adj* éblouissant
D.C. ['di'si] *s* (letterword) (**District of**

Columbia) le district de Columbia; **(direct current)** le courant continu
D'-day' *s* le jour J
deacon ['dikən] *s* diacre *m*
deaconess ['dikənis] *s* diaconesse *f*
dead [dɛd] *adj* mort; *(tired)* épuisé; *(color)* terne; *(business)* stagnant; *(sleep)* profond; *(calm)* plat; *(loss)* sec; *(typewriter key)* immobile; **on a dead level** à franc niveau ‖ *s*—**in the dead of night** au milieu de la nuit; **the dead** les morts; **the dead of winter** le cœur de l'hiver ‖ *adv* absolument; **to stop dead** s'arrêter net
dead'beat' *s* (slang) écornifleur *m*
dead' bolt' *s* pêne *m* dormant
dead' calm' *s* calme *m* plat
dead' cen'ter *s* point *m* mort
dead'-drunk' *adj* ivre mort
deaden ['dɛdən] *tr* amortir; *(sound)* assourdir
dead' end' *s* cul-de-sac *m*, impasse *f*
dead'latch' *s* pêne *m* dormant
dead'-let'ter of'fice *s* bureau *m* des rebuts
dead'line' *s* dernier délai *m*, date *f* limite
dead'lock' *s* serrure *f* à pêne dormant; (fig) impasse *f* ‖ *tr* faire aboutir à une impasse
dead•ly ['dɛdli] *adj* *(comp* -**lier;** *super* -**liest)** mortel; *(sin)* capital
dead' pan' *s* (slang) visage *m* sans expression
dead' reck'oning *s* estime *f*; *(position)* point *m* d'estime
dead' ring'er *s* (coll) portrait *m* vivant
dead' sol'dier *s* *(bottle)* (slang) cadavre *m*
dead' weight' *s* poids *m* mort
dead'wood' *s* bois *m* mort; (fig) objet *m* or individu *m* inutile
deaf [dɛf] *adj* sourd; **to turn a deaf ear** faire la sourde oreille
deaf'-and-dumb' *adj* sourd-muet
deafen ['dɛfən] *tr* assourdir
deafening ['dɛfəniŋ] *adj* assourdissant
deaf'-mute' *adj* & *s* sourd-muet *m*
deafness ['dɛfnis] *s* surdité *f*
deal [dil] *s* affaire *f*; *(cards)* main *f*, donne *f*; **a good deal (of)** or **a great deal (of)** beaucoup (de); **to think a great deal of s.o.** estimer qn ‖ *v* *(pret & pp* dealt [dɛlt]) *tr* *(a blow)* donner, porter; *(cards)* donner, distribuer; **to deal out** *(e.g., gifts)* distribuer, répartir; *(alms)* dispenser; *(justice)* rendre ‖ *intr* négocier; *(cards)* faire la donne; **to deal in** faire le commerce de; **to deal with** *(a person)* traiter avec; *(a subject)* traiter de
dealer ['dilər] *s* marchand *m*, négociant *m*; *(of cards)* donneur *m*; *(middleman, e.g., in selling automobiles)* concessionnaire *m*, stockiste *m*
dean [din] *s* doyen *m*
dean'ship *s* doyenné *m*, décanat *m*
dear [dɪr] *adj* cher; **dear me!** mon Dieu!; **Dear Sir** *(salutation in a letter)* Monsieur ‖ *s* chéri *m*, chérie *f*
dearie ['dɪri] *s* (coll) petite, chérie *f*

dearth [dʌrθ] *s* disette *f*, pénurie *f*
death [dɛθ] *s* mort *f*; **at death's door** à deux doigts de la mort; **to bore to death** raser; **to put to death** mettre à mort; **to starve to death** mourir de faim; **faire mourir de faim**
death'bed' *s* lit *m* de mort
death'blow' *s* coup *m* mortel
death' certif'icate *s* constatation *f* de décès, extrait *m* mortuaire
death' house' *s* quartier *m* de la mort
death' knell' *s* glas *m* funèbre
deathless ['dɛθlis] *adj* immortel
deathly ['dɛθli] *adj* mortel ‖ *adv* mortellement, comme la mort
death' mask' *s* masque *m* mortuaire
death' pen'alty *s* peine *f* capitale
death' rate' *s* mortalité *f*, taux *m* de mortalité
death' rat'tle *s* râle *m* de la mort
death' war'rant *s* ordre *m* d'exécution
death'watch' *s* veillée *f* funèbre
deb [dɛb] *s* (slang) débutante *f*
debacle [də'bakəl] *s* débâcle *f*
de•bar [dɪ'bar] *v* *(pret & pp* -**barred;** *ger* -**barring)** *tr* exclure; empêcher
debark [dɪ'bark] *tr* & *intr* débarquer
debarkation [,dɪbar'keʃən] *s* débarquement *m*
debase [dɪ'bes] *tr* avilir, abaisser; *(e.g., money)* altérer
debatable [dɪ'betəbəl] *adj* discutable
debate [dɪ'bet] *s* débat *m*; **under debate** en discussion ‖ *tr* & *intr* discuter
debauch [dɪ'bɔtʃ] *s* débauche *f* ‖ *tr* débaucher, corrompre
debauchee [,dɛbɔ'ʃi], [,dɛbɔ'tʃi] *s* débauché *m*
debaucher•y [dɪ'bɔtʃəri] *s* *(pl* -**ies)** débauche *f*
debenture [dɪ'bɛntʃər] *s* *(bond)* obligation *f*; *(voucher)* reçu *m*
debilitate [dɪ'bɪlɪ,tet] *tr* débiliter
debili•ty [dɪ'bɪlɪti] *s* *(pl* -**ties)** débilité *f*
debit ['dɛbɪt] *s* débit *m*; *(entry on debit side)* article *m* au débit ‖ *tr* débiter, porter au débit
deb'it bal'ance *s* solde *m* débiteur
debonair [,dɛbə'nɛr] *adj* gai, jovial; élégant, charmant
debris [də'bri], ['dɛbri] *s* débris *mpl*, détritus *m*; *(from ruined buildings)* décombres *mpl*
debt [dɛt] *s* dette *f*; **to run into debt** s'endetter
debtor ['dɛtər] *s* débiteur *m*
debut [de'bju], ['dɛbju] *s* début *m* ‖ *intr* débuter
debutante [,dɛbju'tant], ['dɛbjə,tænt] *s* débutante *f*
decade ['dɛked] *s* décennie *f*, décade *f*
decadence [dɪ'kedəns] *s* décadence *f*
decadent [dɪ'kedənt] *adj* & *s* décadent *m*
decal ['dikæl], [dɪ'kæl], ['dɛkəl] *s* décalcomanie *f*
decamp [dɪ'kæmp] *intr* décamper
decanter [dɪ'kæntər] *s* carafe *f*
decapitate [dɪ'kæpɪ,tet] *tr* décapiter
decay [dɪ'ke] *s* *(rotting)* pourriture *f*; *(decline)* décadence *f*; *(falling to pieces)* délabrement *m*; *(of teeth)*

carie *f* || *tr* pourrir; (*teeth*) carier ||
intr pourrir, se gâter; (*said of teeth*)
se carier; tomber en décadence or
ruine; délabrer
decease [dɪ'sis] *s* décès *m* || *intr* dé-
céder
deceit [dɪ'sit] *s* tromperie *f*
deceitful [dɪ'sitfəl] *adj* trompeur
deceive [dɪ'siv] *tr* & *intr* tromper
decelerate [dɪ'sɛlə,ret] *tr* & *intr* ralentir
December [dɪ'sɛmbər] *s* décembre *m*
decen·cy ['disənsi] *s* (*pl* -cies) décence
f; decencies convenances *fpl*
decent ['disənt] *adj* décent
decentralize [dɪ'sɛntrə,laɪz] *tr* décentraliser
deception [dɪ'sɛpʃən] *s* tromperie *f*
deceptive [dɪ'sɛptɪv] *adj* trompeur
decide [dɪ'saɪd] *tr* décider; (*the out-
come*) décider de || *intr* décider, se
décider; **to decide to** + *inf* décider
de + *inf*, se décider à + *inf*; **to de-
cidè upon a day** fixer un jour
deciduous [dɪ'sɪdʒʊ·əs], [dɪ'sɪdjʊ·əs]
adj caduc
decimal ['dɛsɪməl] *adj* décimal || *s*
décimale *f*
dec'imal point' *s* (*in French the comma
is used to separate the decimal fraction from the integer*) virgule *f*
decimate ['dɛsɪ,met] *tr* décimer
decipher [dɪ'saɪfər] *tr* déchiffrer
decision [dɪ'sɪʒən] *s* décision *f*
decisive [dɪ'saɪsɪv] *adj* décisif
deck [dɛk] *s* (*of cards*) jeu *m*, paquet
m; (*of ship*) pont *m*; **between decks**
(naut) dans l'entrepont || *tr*—**to deck
out** parer, orner
deck' chair' *s* transatlantique *m*, transat *m*, chaise *f* longue de bord
deck' hand' *s* matelot *m* de pont
deck'-land' *intr* apponter
deck'-land'ing *s* appontage *m*
deck'le edge' ['dɛkəl] *s* barbes *fpl*,
bords *mpl* baveux
declaim [dɪ'klem] *tr* & *intr* déclamer
declaration [,dɛklə're ʃən] *s* déclaration *f*
declarative [dɪ'klærətɪv] *adj* déclaratif
declare [dɪ'klɛr] *tr* & *intr* déclarer
declension [dɪ'klɛnʃən] *s* (gram) déclinaison *f*
declination [,dɛklɪ'neʃən] *s* (astr, geog)
déclinaison *f*
decline [dɪ'klaɪn] *s* déclin *m*, déca-
dence *f*; (*in prices*) baisse *f* || *tr* &
intr décliner
declivi·ty [dɪ'klɪvɪti] *s* (*pl* -ties) déclivité *f*, pente *f*
decode [dɪ'kod] *tr* décoder, déchiffrer
decompose [,dikəm'poz] *tr* décom-
poser || *intr* se décomposer
decomposition [,dikɑmpə'zɪʃən] *s* décomposition *f*
decompression [,dikəm'prɛʃən] *s* décompression *f*
decontamination [,dikɑn,tæmɪ'neʃən]
s décontamination *f*
decorate ['dɛkə,ret] *tr* décorer
decoration [,dɛkə'reʃən] *s* décoration *f*
decorator ['dɛkə,retər] *s* décorateur *m*

decorous ['dɛkərəs], [dɪ'korəs] *adj*
convenable, correct, bienséant
decorum [dɪ'korəm] *s* décorum *m*
decoy [dɪ'kɔɪ], ['dikɔɪ] *s* leurre *m*, ap-
pât *m*; (*bird*) appeau *m* || *tr* [dɪ'kɔɪ]
tr leurrer
decrease ['dikris], [dɪ'kris] *s* diminu-
tion *f* || [dɪ'kris] *tr* & *intr* diminuer
decree [dɪ'kri] *s* décret *m*, arrêté *m*;
(*of divorce*) ordonnance *f* || *tr* décré-
ter, arrêter, ordonner
decrepit [dɪ'krepɪt] *adj* décrépit
de·cry [dɪ'kraɪ] *v* (*pret* & *pp* -cried)
tr décrier, dénigrer
dedicate ['dɛdɪ,ket] *tr* dédier
dedication [,dɛdɪ'keʃən] *s* consécration
f; (*e.g., in a book*) dédicace *f*
dedicatory ['dɛdɪkə,tori] *adj* dédicatoire
deduce [dɪ'd(j)us] *tr* déduire, inférer
deduct [dɪ'dʌkt] *tr* déduire
deduction [dɪ'dʌkʃən] *s* déduction *f*
deed [did] *s* action *f*, acte *m*; (law)
acte, titre *m*, contrat *m*; **deed of val-
or** haut fait *m*; **good deed** bonne
action; **in deed** dans le fait || *tr* trans-
férer par un acte
deem [dim] *tr* estimer, juger, croire ||
intr penser
deep [dip] *adj* profond; (*sound*) grave;
(*color*) foncé; de profondeur, e.g.,
to be twenty feet deep avoir vingt
pieds de profondeur; **deep in debt**
criblé de dettes; **deep in thought**
plongé dans la méditation || *adv* pro-
fondément; **deep into the night** très
avant dans la nuit
deepen ['dipən] *tr* approfondir || *intr*
s'approfondir
deep'-freeze' *v* (*pret* -froze; *pp* -frozen)
tr congeler à basse température
deep'-laid' *adj* habilement ourdi
deep' mourn'ing *s* grand deuil *m*
deep'-root'ed *adj* profondément enraciné
deep'-sea fish'ing *s* grande pêche *f* au
large, pêche maritime
deer [dɪr] *s* (*red deer*) cerf *m*; (*fallow
deer*) daim *m*; (*roe deer*) chevreuil *m*
deer'skin' *s* peau *f* de daim
deface [dɪ'fes] *tr* défigurer
de facto [di'fækto] *adv* de fait, de facto
defamation [,dɛfə'meʃən], [,difə'me-
ʃən] *s* diffamation *f*, injures *fpl*
defame [dɪ'fem] *tr* diffamer
default [dɪ'fɔlt] *s* manque *m*, défaut
m; (*on an obligation*) carence *f*; **by
default** par défaut; (sports) par for-
fait; **in default of** à défaut de || *tr* (*a
debt*) manquer de s'acquitter de ||
intr ne pas tenir ses engagements;
(sports) perdre par forfait
defeat [dɪ'fit] *s* défaite *f*; **unexpected
defeat** contre-performance *f* || *tr*
vaincre, battre, défaire
defeatism [dɪ'fitɪzəm] *s* défaitisme *m*
defeatist [dɪ'fitɪst] *adj* & *s* défaitiste
mf
defecate ['dɛfɪ,ket] *intr* déféquer
defect [dɪ'fɛkt], ['difɛkt] *s* défaut *m*,
imperfection *f*, vice *m* || [dɪ'fɛkt]
intr faire défection, déserter

defection [dɪ'fɛkʃən] *s* défection *f*
defective [dɪ'fɛktɪv] *adj* défectueux, vicieux; (gram) défectif
defend [dɪ'fɛnd] *tr* défendre
defendant [dɪ'fɛndənt] *s* (law) défendeur *m*, intimé *m*
defense [dɪ'fɛns] *s* défense *f*
defenseless [dɪ'fɛnslɪs] *adj* sans défense
defensive [dɪ'fɛnsɪv] *adj* défensif || *s* défensive *f*
de•fer [dɪ'fʌr] *v* (*pret & pp* **-ferred**; *ger* **-ferring**) *tr* différer; (mil) mettre en sursis || *intr*—**to defer to** déférer à
deference ['dɛfərəns] *s* déférence *f*
deferential [ˌdɛfə'rɛnʃəl] *adj* déférent
deferment [dɪ'fʌrmənt] *s* ajournement *m*, remise *f*; (*extension of time*) délai *m*; (mil) sursis *m* d'appel
defiance [dɪ'faɪ·əns] *s* défi *m*, provocation *f*, nargue *f*; **in defiance of** au mépris de, en dépit de
defiant [dɪ'faɪ·ənt] *adj* provocant, hostile, de défi
deficien•cy [dɪ'fɪʃənsi] *s* (*pl* **-cies**) déficience *f*, insuffisance *f*; (*of vitamins or minerals*) carence *f*; (com) déficit *m*
deficient [dɪ'fɪʃənt] *adj* déficient, insuffisant
deficit ['dɛfɪsɪt] *adj* déficitaire || *s* déficit *m*
defile [dɪ'faɪl], ['difaɪl] *s* défilé *m* || [dɪ'faɪl] *tr* souiller || *intr* défiler
defilement [dɪ'faɪlmənt] *s* souillure *f*
define [dɪ'faɪn] *tr* définir
definite ['dɛfɪnɪt] *adj* défini; (*opinions, viewpoints*) décidé
definitely ['dɛfɪnɪtli] *adv* décidément, nettement
definition [ˌdɛfɪ'nɪʃən] *s* définition *f*
definitive [dɪ'fɪnɪtɪv] *adj* définitif
deflate [dɪ'flet] *tr* dégonfler; (*currency*) amener la déflation de || *intr* se dégonfler
deflation [dɪ'fleʃən] *s* dégonflement *m*; (*of prices*) déflation *f*
deflect [dɪ'flɛkt] *tr & intr* dévier
deflower [di'flaʊ·ər] *tr* déflorer; (*to strip of flowers*) défleurir
deforest [di'fɑrɪst], [di'fɔrɪst] *tr* déboiser
deform [dɪ'fɔrm] *tr* déformer
deformed *adj* contrefait, difforme
deformi•ty [dɪ'fɔrmɪti] *s* (*pl* **-ties**) difformité *f*
defraud [dɪ'frɔd] *tr* frauder
defray [dɪ'fre] *tr* payer, supporter
defrost [di'frɔst], [di'frɑst] *tr* décongeler, dégivrer
defroster [di'frɔstər], [di'frɑstər] *s* déglaceur *m*, dégivreur *m*
defrosting [di'frɔstɪŋ], [di'frɑstɪŋ] *s* dégèlement *m*, dégivrage *m*
deft [dɛft] *adj* adroit, habile; (*hand*) exercé, preste
defunct [dɪ'fʌŋkt] *adj* défunt; (*practice, style, etc.*) tombé en désuétude
de•fy [dɪ'faɪ] *v* (*pret & pp* **-fied**) *tr* défier, braver, porter un défi à
degeneracy [dɪ'dʒɛnərəsi] *s* dégénérescence *f*

degenerate [dɪ'dʒɛnərɪt] *adj & s* dégénéré *m* || [dɪ'dʒɛnəˌret] *intr* dégénérer
degrade [dɪ'gred] *tr* dégrader
degrading [dɪ'gredɪŋ] *adj* dégradant
degree [dɪ'gri] *s* degré *m*; (*from a university*) grade *m*; (*of humidity*) titre *m*; **to take a degree** obtenir ses diplômes, obtenir ses titres universitaires
dehumidi•fy [ˌdihju'mɪdɪˌfaɪ] *v* (*pret & pp* **-fied**) *tr* déshumidifier
dehydrate [di'haɪdret] *tr* déshydrater; (*the body*) dessécher
deice [di'aɪs] *tr* déglacer, dégivrer
deicer [di'aɪsər] *s* dégivreur *m*, antigivrant *m*
dei•fy ['di·ɪˌfaɪ] *v* (*pret & pp* **-fied**) *tr* déifier
deign [den] *intr*—**to deign to** daigner
dei•ty ['di·ɪti] *s* (*pl* **-ties**) divinité *f*; (mythol) déité *f*; **the Deity** Dieu *m*
dejected [dɪ'dʒɛktɪd] *adj* abattu, découragé
dejection [dɪ'dʒɛkʃən] *s* abattement *m*
delay [dɪ'le] *s* retard *m*; (*postponement*) sursis *m*, remise *f*; **without delay** sans délai; **without further delay** sans plus tarder || *tr* retarder; (*to put off*) remettre, différer || *intr* tarder, s'attarder
delayed′-ac′tion *adj* à action différée
delayed′-ac′tion switch′ *s* minuterie *f* d'escalier
delayed′-time′ switch′ *s* coupe-circuit *m* à action différée
dele ['dili] *s* (typ) deleatur *m*
delectable [dɪ'lɛktəbəl] *adj* délectable
delegate ['dɛlɪˌget], ['dɛlɪgɪt] *s* délégué *m*; (*at a convention*) congressiste *mf*, délégué *f* || ['dɛlɪˌget] *tr* déléguer
delegation [ˌdɛlɪ'geʃən] *s* délégation *f*
delete [dɪ'lit] *tr* supprimer
deletion [dɪ'liʃən] *s* suppression *f*; (*the deleted part*) passage *m* supprimé
deliberate [dɪ'lɪbərɪt] *adj* (*premeditated*) délibéré, réfléchi; (*cautious*) circonspect; (*slow*) lent || [dɪ'lɪbəˌret] *tr & intr* délibérer
deliberately [dɪ'lɪbərɪtli] *adv* (*on purpose*) exprès, de propos délibéré; (*without hurrying*) posément, sans hâte
deliberation [dɪˌlɪbə'reʃən] *s* délibération *f*; (*slowness*) lenteur *f*
delica•cy ['dɛlɪkəsi] *s* (*pl* **-cies**) délicatesse *f*; (*choice food*) friandise *f*, gourmandise *f*
delicate ['dɛlɪkɪt] *adj* délicat
delicatessen [ˌdɛlɪkə'tɛsən] *s* charcuterie *f*
delicious [dɪ'lɪʃəs] *adj* délicieux
delight [dɪ'laɪt] *s* délice *m*, délices *fpl*, plaisir *m* || *tr* enchanter, ravir || *intr* —**to delight in** se délecter à
delighted *adj* enchanté, ravi, content
delightful [dɪ'laɪtfəl] *adj* délicieux, ravissant, enchanteur
delineate [dɪ'lɪnɪˌet] *tr* esquisser
delinquen•cy [dɪ'lɪŋkwənsi] *s* (*pl* **-cies**) délit *m*, faute *f*; (*e.g., of juveniles*) délinquance *f*

delinquent [dɪ'lɪŋkwənt] *adj* négligent, coupable; (*in payment*) arriéré; (*in guilt*) délinquant ‖ *s* délinquant *m*; créancier *m* en retard

delirious [dɪ'lɪrɪ·əs] *adj* délirant

deliri·um [dɪ'lɪrɪ·əm] *s* (*pl* -ums or -a [ə]) délire *m*

deliver [dɪ'lɪvər] *tr* délivrer; (*e.g.*, *laundry*) livrer; (*mail*) distribuer; (*a blow*) asséner; (*an opinion*) exprimer; (*a speech*) prononcer; (*energy*) débiter, fournir; **to be delivered of a child** accoucher d'un enfant

deliver·y [dɪ'lɪvəri] *s* (*pl* -ies) *s* remise *f*; (*e.g.*, *of a package*) livraison *f*; (*of mail*) distribution *f*; (*of a speech; of electricity*) débit *m*; (*of a woman in childbirth*) accouchement *m*, délivrance *f*; **free delivery** livraison franco

deliv'ery·man *s* (*pl* -men) livreur *m*

deliv'ery room' *s* salle *f* d'accouchement, salle de travail

deliv'ery truck' *s* fourgon *m* à livraison

dell [dɛl] *s* vallon *m*

delouse [di'laʊs], [di'laʊz] *tr* épouiller

delphinium [dɛl'fɪnɪ·əm] *s* dauphinelle *f*, pied-d'alouette *m*

delta ['dɛltə] *s* delta *m*

delude [dɪ'lud] *tr* duper, tromper

deluge ['dɛljudʒ] *s* déluge *m* ‖ *tr* inonder

delusion [dɪ'luʒən] *s* illusion *f*, tromperie *f*; **delusions** (psychopathol) hallucinations *fpl*; **delusions of grandeur** folie *f* des grandeurs

delusive [dɪ'lusɪv] or delusory [dɪ'lusəri] *adj* trompeur

de luxe [dɪ'lʊks], [dɪ'lʌks] *adj & adv* de luxe

delve [dɛlv] *intr*—**to delve into** fouiller dans, approfondir

demagnetize [di'mægnɪ,taɪz] *tr* démagnétiser, désaimanter

demagogue ['dɛmə,gɑg] *s* démagogue *mf*

demand [dɪ'mænd], [dɪ'mɑnd] *s* exigence *f*; (*of the buying public*) demande *f*; **demands** exigences; **in great demand** très recherché; **on demand** sur demande ‖ *tr* exiger

demanding [dɪ'mændɪŋ], [dɪ'mɑndɪŋ] *adj* exigeant

demarcate [dɪ'mɑrket], ['dimɑr,ket] *tr* délimiter

demean [dɪ'min] *tr* dégrader; **to demean oneself** se conduire

demeanor [dɪ'minər] *s* conduite *f*, tenue *f*

demented [dɪ'mɛntɪd] *adj* aliéné, fou

demerit [di'merɪt] *s* démérite *m*

demigod ['dɛmɪ,gɑd] *s* demi-dieu *m*

demijohn ['dɛmɪ,dʒɑn] *s* dame-jeanne *f*

demilitarize [di'mɪlɪtə,raɪz] *tr* démilitariser

demise [dɪ'maɪz] *s* décès *m*

demitasse ['dɛmɪ,tæs], ['dɛmɪ,tɑs] *s* petite tasse *f* à café; (*contents*) café *m* noir

demobilize [di'mobɪ,laɪz] *tr* démobiliser

democra·cy [dɪ'mɑkrəsi] *s* (*pl* -cies) démocratie *f*

democrat ['dɛmə,kræt] *s* démocrate *mf*

democratic [,dɛmə'krætɪk] *adj* démocratique

demolish [dɪ'mɑlɪʃ] *tr* démolir

demolition [,dɛmə'lɪʃən], [,dimə'lɪʃən] *s* démolition *f*

demon ['dimən] *s* démon *m*

demoniac [dɪ'monɪ,æk] *adj & s* démoniaque *mf*

demonic [dɪ'mɑnɪk] *adj* démoniaque

demonstrate ['dɛmən,stret] *tr* démontrer ‖ *intr* (*to show feelings in public gatherings*) manifester

demonstration [,dɛmən'streʃən] *s* démonstration *f*; (*public show of feeling*) manifestation *f*

demonstrative [dɪ'mɑnstrətɪv] *adj* démonstratif

demonstrator ['dɛmən,stretər] *s* (*salesman*) démonstrateur *m*; (*agitator*) manifestant *m*

demoralize [dɪ'mɑrə,laɪz], [dɪ'mɔrə,laɪz] *tr* démoraliser

demote [dɪ'mot] *tr* rétrograder

demotion [dɪ'moʃən] *s* rétrogradation *f*

de·mur [dɪ'mʌr] *v* (*pret & pp* -murred; *ger* -murring) *intr* faire des objections

demure [dɪ'mjʊr] *adj* modeste, posé

demurrage [dɪ'mʌrɪdʒ] *s* (naut) surestarie *f*

den [dɛn] *s* (*of animals; of thieves*) repaire *m*, retraite *f*; (*of wild beasts*) antre *m*; (*of lions*) tanière *f*; (*room in a house*) cabinet *m* de travail, fumoir *m*; (Cub Scouts) sizaine *f*

denaturalize [di'nætʃərə,laɪz] *tr* dénaturaliser

denial [dɪ'naɪ·əl] *s* (*contradiction*) dénégation *f*, démenti *m*; (*refusal*) refus *m*, déni *m*

denim ['dɛnɪm] *s* coutil *m*

denizen ['dɛnɪzən] *s* habitant *m*

Denmark ['dɛnmɑrk] *s* le Danemark

denomination [dɪ,nɑmɪ'neʃən] *s* dénomination *f*; (*of coin or stamp*) valeur *f*; (eccl) secte *f*, confession *f*, communion *f*

denote [dɪ'not] *tr* dénoter

denounce [dɪ'naʊns] *tr* dénoncer

dense [dɛns] *adj* dense; (*stupid*) bête

densi·ty ['dɛnsɪti] *s* (*pl* -ties) densité *f*

dent [dɛnt] *s* marque *f* de coup, creux *m*; (*in a knife; in a fortune*) brèche *f*; **to make a dent in** faire une brèche à ‖ *tr* ébrécher

dental ['dɛntəl] *adj* dentaire; (phonet) dental ‖ *s* dentale *f*

den'tal floss' *s* fil *m* dentaire

den'tal sur'geon *s* chirurgien-dentiste *m*

dentifrice ['dɛntɪfrɪs] *s* dentifrice *m*

dentist ['dɛntɪst] *s* dentiste *mf*

dentistry ['dɛntɪstri] *s* odontologie *f*

denture ['dɛntʃər] *s* (*set of teeth*) denture *f*; (*set of artificial teeth*) dentier *m*, râtelier *m*

denunciation [dɪ,nʌnsɪ'eʃən], [dɪ,nʌnʃɪ'eʃən] *s* dénonciation *f*

de·ny [dɪ'naɪ] *v* (*pret & pp* -nied) *tr* nier, démentir; **to deny oneself** se refuser, se priver

deodorant [di'odərənt] *adj & s* désodorisant *m*
deodorize [di'odə,raɪz] *tr* désodoriser
depart [dɪ'pɑrt] *intr* partir; **to depart from** se départir de
departed *adj* (*dead*) mort, défunt
department [dɪ'pɑrtmənt] *s* département *m*; (*of hospital*) service *m*; (*of agency*) bureau *m*; (*of store*) rayon *m*, comptoir *m*; (*of university*) section *f*
Depart'ment of State' *s* ministère *m* des affaires étrangères
depart'ment store' *s* grands magasins *mpl*, galerie *f*
departure [dɪ'pɑrtʃər] *s* départ *m*
depend [dɪ'pɛnd] *intr* dépendre; **to depend on** or **upon** dépendre de
dependable [dɪ'pɛndəbəl] *adj* sûr; (*person*) digne de confiance
dependence [dɪ'pɛndəns] *s* dépendance *f*; **dependence on** dépendance de; (*trust in*) confiance en
dependen·cy [dɪ'pɛndənsi] *s* (*pl* -**cies**) dépendance *f*; (*country, territory*) possession *f*, colonie *f*
dependent [dɪ'pɛndənt] *adj* dépendant; **dependent on** dépendant de; (*s.o. for family support*) à la charge de ‖ *s* charge *f* de famille
depend'ent clause' *s* proposition *f* subordonnée
depict [dɪ'pɪkt] *tr* dépeindre, décrire
depiction [dɪ'pɪkʃən] *s* peinture *f*
deplete [dɪ'plit] *tr* épuiser
depletion [dɪ'pliʃən] *s* épuisement *m*
deplorable [dɪ'plorəbəl] *adj* déplorable
deplore [dɪ'plor] *tr* déplorer
deploy [dɪ'plɔɪ] *tr* (mil) déployer ‖ *intr* (mil) se déployer
deployment [dɪ'plɔɪmənt] *s* (mil) déploiement *m*
depolarize [di'polə,raɪz] *tr* dépolariser
depopulate [di'pɑpjə,let] *tr & intr* dépeupler
deport [dɪ'port] *tr* déporter; **to deport oneself** se comporter
deportation [,dipor'teʃən] *s* déportation *f*
deportee [,dipor'ti] *s* déporté *m*
deportment [dɪ'portmənt] *s* comportement *m*, tenue *f*, manières *fpl*
depose [dɪ'poz] *tr & intr* déposer
deposit [dɪ'pɑzɪt] *s* dépôt *m*; (*as pledge*) cautionnement *m*, arrhes *fpl*, gage *m*; **no deposit** (*bottle*) perdu; **to pay a deposit** verser une provision, un acompte, or une caution; **with deposit** (*on a bottle*) consigné ‖ *tr* déposer; laisser comme provision
depos'it account' *s* compte *m* courant
depositor [dɪ'pɑzɪtər] *s* déposant *m*
deposito·ry [dɪ'pɑzɪ,tori] *s* (*pl* -**ries**) dépôt *m*; (*person*) dépositaire *mf*
depot ['dipo], ['depo] *s* dépôt *m*; (rr) gare *f*
depraved [dɪ'prevd] *adj* dépravé
depravi·ty [dɪ'præviti] *s* (*pl* -**ties**) dépravation *f*
deprecate ['dɛprɪ,ket] *tr* désapprouver
depreciate [dɪ'priʃɪ,et] *tr* déprécier ‖ *intr* se déprécier

depreciation [dɪ,priʃɪ'eʃən] *s* dépréciation *f*
depredation [,dɛprɪ'deʃən] *s* déprédation *f*
depress [dɪ'prɛs] *tr* déprimer; (*prices*) abaisser
depressing [dɪ'prɛsɪŋ] *adj* attristant
depression [dɪ'prɛʃən] *s* dépression *f*
deprive [dɪ'praɪv] *tr* priver
depth [dɛpθ] *s* profondeur *f*; (*in sound*) gravité *f*; **depths** abîme *m*; **in the depth of winter** en plein hiver; **to go beyond one's depth** perdre pied; sortir de sa compétence
depth' bomb' *s* bombe *f* sous-marine
depth' charge' *s* grenade *f* sous-marine
deputation [,dɛpjə'teʃən] *s* députation *f*
deputize ['dɛpjə,taɪz] *tr* députer
depu·ty ['dɛpjəti] *s* (*pl* -**ties**) député *m*
derail [dɪ'rel] *tr* faire dérailler ‖ *intr* dérailler
derailment [dɪ'relmənt] *s* déraillement *m*
derange [dɪ'rendʒ] *tr* déranger
derangement [dɪ'rendʒmənt] *s* dérangement *m*; (*of mind*) aliénation *f*
der·by ['dʌrbi] *s* (*pl* -**bies**) (*race*) derby *m*; (*hat*) chapeau *m* melon
derelict ['dɛrɪlɪkt] *adj* abandonné, délaissé; (*in one's duty*) négligent ‖ *s* épave *f*
dereliction [,dɛrɪ'lɪkʃən] *s* abandon *m*, renoncement *m*
deride [dɪ'raɪd] *tr* tourner en dérision, ridiculiser
derision [dɪ'rɪʒən] *s* dérision *f*
derisive [dɪ'raɪsɪv] *adj* dérisoire
derivation [,dɛrɪ'veʃən] *s* dérivation *f*
derivative [dɪ'rɪvətɪv] *adj & s* dérivé *m*
derive [dɪ'raɪv] *tr & intr* dériver
dermatology [,dʌrmə'tɑlədʒi] *s* dermatologie *f*
derogatory [dɪ'rɑgə,tori] *adj* péjoratif
derrick ['dɛrɪk] *s* grue *f*; (*for extracting oil*) derrick *m*
dervish ['dʌrvɪʃ] *s* derviche *m*
desalinization [di,selɪnɪ'zeʃən] *s* dessalement *m*
desalt [di'sɔlt] *tr* dessaler
descend [dɪ'sɛnd] *tr* descendre ‖ *intr* descendre; (*said of rain*) tomber; **to be descended from** descendre de; **to descend on** s'abattre sur
descendant [dɪ'sɛndənt] *adj & s* descendant *m*
descendent [dɪ'sɛndənt] *adj* descendant
descent [dɪ'sɛnt] *s* descente *f*; (*drop in temperature*) chute *f*; (*lineage*) descendance *f*, naissance *f*
describe [dɪ'skraɪb] *tr* décrire
description [dɪ'skrɪpʃən] *s* description *f*
descriptive [dɪ'skrɪptɪv] *adj* descriptif
de·scry [dɪ'skraɪ] *v* (*pret & pp* -**scried**) *tr* découvrir, apercevoir
desecrate ['dɛsɪ,kret] *tr* profaner
desegregate [di'sɛgrɪ,get] *intr* supprimer la ségrégation raciale
desegregation [di,sɛgrɪ'geʃən] *s* déségrégation *f*
desensitize [di'sɛnsɪ,taɪz] *tr* désensibiliser

desert ['dɛzərt] *adj & s* désert *m* ‖ [dɪ'zʌrt] *s* mérite *m*; **to get one's just deserts** recevoir son salaire, recevoir sa juste punition ‖ *tr & intr* déserter
deserted *adj* (*person*) abandonné; (*place*) désert, nu
deserter [dɪ'zʌrtər] *s* déserteur *m*
desertion [dɪ'zʌrʃən] *s* désertion *f*
deserve [dɪ'zʌrv] *tr & intr* mériter
deservedly [dɪ'zʌrvɪdli] *adv* à juste titre, dignement
deserving [dɪ'zʌrvɪŋ] *adj* méritoire, digne
design [dɪ'zaɪn] *s* (*combination of details; art of designing; work of art*) dessin *m*; (*plan, scheme*) dessein *m*, projet *m*, plan *m*; (*model, outline*) modèle *m*, type *m*, grandes lignes *fpl*; **to have designs on** avoir des desseins sur ‖ *tr* inventer, projeter; (*e.g., a dress*) dessiner; (*a secret plan*) combiner; **designed for** destiné à
designate ['dɛzɪg,net] *tr* désigner
designer [dɪ'zaɪnər] *s* dessinateur *m*
designing [dɪ'zaɪnɪŋ] *adj* artificieux, intrigant ‖ *s* dessin *m*
desirable [dɪ'zaɪrəbəl] *adj* désirable
desire [dɪ'zaɪr] *s* désir *m* ‖ *tr* désirer
desirous [dɪ'zaɪrəs] *adj* désireux
desist [dɪ'zɪst] *intr* cesser
desk [dɛsk] *s* bureau *m*; (*in schoolroom*) pupitre *m*; (*of cashier*) caisse *f*
desk' blot'ter *s* sous-main *m*
desk' clerk' *s* réceptionnaire *mf*
desk' set' *s* écritoire *f*
desolate ['dɛsəlɪt] *adj* désert; (*sad*) désolé; (*alone*) abandonné ‖ ['dɛsə,let] *tr* désoler
desolation [,dɛsə'leʃən] *s* désolation *f*
despair [dɪ'spɛr] *s* désespoir *m*, désespérance *f* ‖ *intr* désespérer
despairing [dɪ'spɛrɪŋ] *adj* désespéré
despera·do [,dɛspə'redo], [,dɛspə'rado] *s* (*pl* -**does** or -**dos**) hors-la-loi *m*
desperate ['dɛspərɪt] *adj* capable de tout, poussé à bout; (*bitter, excessive*) acharné, à outrance; (*hopeless*) désespéré; (*remedy*) héroïque
desperation [,dɛspə'reʃən] *s* désespoir *m*; (*recklessness*) témérité *f*
despicable ['dɛspɪkəbəl] *adj* méprisable, mesquin
despise [dɪ'spaɪz] *tr* mépriser, dédaigner
despite [dɪ'spaɪt] *prep* en dépit de, malgré
despoil [dɪ'spɔɪl] *tr* dépouiller
desponden·cy [dɪ'spandənsi] *s* (*pl* -**cies**) abattement *m*, accablement *m*
despondent [dɪ'spandənt] *adj* abattu, accablé, déprimé
despot ['dɛspat] *s* despote *m*, tyran *m*
despotic [dɛs'patɪk] *adj* despotique
despotism ['dɛspə,tɪzəm] *s* despotisme *m*
dessert [dɪ'zʌrt] *s* dessert *m*
dessert' spoon' *s* cuiller *f* à dessert
destination [,dɛstɪ'neʃən] *s* destination *f*
destine ['dɛstɪn] *tr* destiner

desti·ny ['dɛstɪni] *s* (*pl* -**nies**) destin *m*, destinée *f*
destitute ['dɛstɪ,t(j)ut] *adj* indigent; dépourvu
destitution [,dɛstɪ't(j)uʃən] *s* dénuement *m*, indigence *f*
destroy [dɪ'strɔɪ] *tr* détruire
destroyer [dɪ'strɔɪ·ər] *s* destructeur *m*; (*nav*) destroyer *m*
destruction [dɪ'strʌkʃən] *s* destruction *f*
destructive [dɪ'strʌktɪv] *adj* destructeur, destructif
desultory ['dɛsəl,tori] *adj* décousu, sans suite; (*conversation*) à bâtons rompus
detach [dɪ'tætʃ] *tr* détacher
detachable [dɪ'tætʃəbəl] *adj* détachable, démontable; (*collar*) faux
detached *adj* détaché
detachment [dɪ'tætʃmənt] *s* détachement *m*
detail [dɪ'tel], ['ditel] *s* détail *m*; (mil) extrait *m* de l'ordre du jour; (mil) détachement *m* ‖ [dɪ'tel] *tr* détailler
detailed' state'ment *s* bordereau *m*
detain [dɪ'ten] *tr* retenir, retarder; (*in prison*) détenir
detect [dɪ'tɛkt] *tr* déceler, détecter
detection [dɪ'tɛkʃən] *s* détection *f*
detective [dɪ'tɛktɪv] *adj* (*device*) détecteur; (*film, novel*) policier ‖ *s* détective *m*, agent *m* de la sûreté
detec'tive sto'ry *s* roman *m* policier
detector [dɪ'tɛktər] *s* détecteur *m*
detention [dɪ'tɛnʃən] *s* détention *f*
de·ter [dɪ'tʌr] *v* (*pret & pp* -**terred**; *ger* -**terring**) *tr* détourner
detergent [dɪ'tʌrdʒənt] *adj & s* détersif *m*
deteriorate [dɪ'tɪrɪ·ə,ret] *tr* détériorer ‖ *intr* se détériorer
determination [dɪ,tʌrmɪ'neʃən] *s* détermination *f*
determine [dɪ'tʌrmɪn] *tr* déterminer
determined *adj* déterminé, résolu
deterrent [dɪ'tʌrənt] *adj & s* préventif *m*
detest [dɪ'tɛst] *tr* détester
dethrone [dɪ'θron] *tr* détrôner
detonate ['dɛtə,net], ['ditə,net] *tr* faire détoner, faire éclater ‖ *intr* détoner
detour ['ditur], [dɪ'tur] *s* déviation *f*; (*indirect manner*) détour *m* ‖ *tr & intr* dévier
detract [dɪ'trækt] *tr* diminuer ‖ *intr*—**to detract from** amoindrir
detractor [dɪ'træktər] *s* détracteur *m*
detriment ['dɛtrɪmənt] *s* détriment *m*
detrimental [,dɛtrɪ'mɛntəl] *adj* préjudiciable, nuisible
deuce [d(j)us] *s* deux *m*; **what the deuce!** (coll) diantre!, que diable!
devaluate [di'vælju,et] *tr* dévaluer
devaluation [di,vælju'eʃən] *s* dévaluation *f*
devastate ['dɛvəs,tet] *tr* dévaster
devastating ['dɛvəs,tetɪŋ] *adj* dévastateur; (coll) écrasant, accablant
devastation [,dɛvəs'teʃən] *s* dévastation *f*
develop [dɪ'vɛləp] *tr* développer; (*a mine*) exploiter; (*e.g., a fever*) con-

tracter; (phot) révéler, développer ‖ *intr* se développer; (*to become evident*) se produire, se manifester

developer [dɪ'vɛləpər] *s* entrepreneur *m*; (*builder*) maître *m* d'œuvre; (phot) révélateur *m*

development [dɪ'vɛləpmənt] *s* développement *m*; (*event*) événement *m* récent; (*of housing*) cité *f*, grand ensemble *m*

deviate ['divɪˌet] *s* perverti *m* ‖ *tr* faire dévier ‖ *intr* dévier

deviation [ˌdivɪ'eʃən] *s* déviation *f*

device [dɪ'vaɪs] *s* appareil *m*, dispositif *m*; (*trick*) stratagème *m*, ruse *f*; (*motto*) emblème *m*, devise *f*; **to leave s.o. to his own devices** abandonner qn à ses propres moyens

dev·il ['dɛvəl] *s* diable *m*; **speak of the devil!** (coll) je vois un loup!; **to be between the devil and the deep blue sea** (coll) se trouver entre l'enclume et le marteau; **to raise the devil** (slang) faire le diable à quatre ‖ *v* (*pret & pp* -iled *or* -illed; *ger* -iling *or* -illing) *tr* épicer fortement; (coll) tourmenter

devilish ['dɛvəlɪʃ] *adj* diabolique; (*roguish*) coquin

dev'il-may-care' *adj* insouciant, étourdi

devilment ['dɛvəlmənt] *s* (*mischief*) diablerie *f*; (*evil*) méchanceté *f*

devil·try ['dɛvəltri] *s* (*pl* -tries) méchanceté *f*, cruauté *f*; (*mischief*) espièglerie *f*

devious ['divɪ·əs] *adj* (*straying*) détourné, dévié; (*roundabout; shifty*) tortueux

devise [dɪ'vaɪz] *tr* combiner, inventer; (law) léguer

devoid [dɪ'vɔɪd] *adj* dépourvu, vide, dénué

devolve [dɪ'vɑlv] *intr*—**to devolve on, to,** *or* **upon** échoir à

devote [dɪ'vot] *tr* consacrer

devoted *adj* dévoué; **devoted to** voué à, dévoué à, attaché à

devotee [ˌdɛvə'ti] *s* dévot *m*, adepte *mf*; (sports) fervent *m*, fanatique *mf*

devotion [dɪ'voʃən] *s* dévotion *f*; (*to study, work, etc.*) dévouement *m*; **devotions** dévotions, prières *fpl*

devour [dɪ'vaʊr] *tr* dévorer

devout [dɪ'vaʊt] *adj* dévot, pieux

dew [d(j)u] *s* rosée *f*

dew'drop' *s* goutte *f* de rosée

dew'lap' *s* fanon *m*, double menton *m*

dew·y ['d(j)u·i] *adj* (*comp* -ier; *super* -iest) couvert de rosée

dexterity [dɛks'tɛrɪti] *s* dextérité *f*, adresse *f*

diabetes [ˌdaɪ·ə'bitɪs], [ˌdaɪ·ə'bitiz] *s* diabète *m*

diabetic [ˌdaɪ·ə'bɛtɪk], [ˌdaɪ·ə'bitɪk] *adj & s* diabétique *mf*

diabolic(al) [ˌdaɪ·ə'bɑlɪk(əl)] *adj* diabolique

diacritical [ˌdaɪ·ə'krɪtɪkəl] *adj* diacritique

diadem ['daɪ·əˌdɛm] *s* diadème *m*

diaere·sis [daɪ'ɛrɪsɪs] *s* (*pl* -ses [ˌsiz]) diérèse *f*; (*mark*) tréma *m*

diagnose [ˌdaɪ·əg'nos], [ˌdaɪ·əg'noz] *tr* diagnostiquer

diagno·sis [ˌdaɪ·əg'nosɪs] *s* (*pl* -ses [siz]) diagnostic *m*

diagonal [daɪ'ægənəl] *adj* diagonal ‖ *s* diagonale *f*

dia·gram ['daɪ·əˌgræm] *s* diagramme *m*, croquis *m* coté ‖ *v* (*pret & pp* -gramed *or* -grammed; *ger* -graming *or* -gramming) *tr* représenter schématiquement

di·al ['daɪ·əl], [daɪl] *s* cadran *m* ‖ *v* (*pret & pp* -aled *or* -alled; *ger* -aling *or* -alling) *tr* (*a telephone number*) composer ‖ *intr* faire un numéro

dialect ['daɪ·əˌlɛkt] *s* dialecte *m*

dialing ['daɪ·əlɪŋ] *s* (telp) composition *f* du numéro

dialogue ['daɪ·əˌlɔg], ['daɪ·əˌlɑg] *s* dialogue *m*

di'al tel'ephone *s* téléphone *m* automatique, automatique *m*

di'al tone' *s* (telp) tonalité *f*

diameter [daɪ'æmɪtər] *s* diamètre *m*

diametric(al) [ˌdaɪ·ə'mɛtrɪk(əl)] *adj* diamétral

diamond ['daɪmənd] *s* diamant *m*; (*figure of a rhombus*) losange *m*; (baseball) petit champ *m*; (cards) carreau *m*

diaper ['daɪ·əpər] *s* lange *m*, couche *f* ‖ *tr* (*to variegate*) diaprer

diaphanous [daɪ'æfənəs] *adj* diaphane

diaphragm ['daɪ·əˌfræm] *s* diaphragme *m*

diarrhea [ˌdaɪ·ə'ri·ə] *s* diarrhée *f*

dia·ry ['daɪ·əri] *s* (*pl* -ries) journal *m*

diastole [daɪ'æstəli] *s* diastole *f*

diathermy ['daɪ·əˌθɜrmi] *s* diathermie *f*

diatribe ['daɪ·əˌtraɪb] *s* diatribe *f*

dice [daɪs] *spl* dés *mpl*; **no dice!** (slang) pas moyen!; **to load the dice** piper les dés ‖ *tr* couper en cubes

dice'box' *s* cornet *m* à dés

dichoto·my [daɪ'kɑtəmi] *s* (*pl* -mies) dichotomie *f*

dictaphone ['dɪktəˌfon] *s* (trademark) dictaphone *m*

dictate ['dɪktet] *s* précepte *m*, règle *f* ‖ *tr & intr* dicter

dictation [dɪk'teʃən] *s* dictée *f*; **to take dictation from** écrire sous la dictée de

dictator ['dɪktetər], [dɪk'tetər] *s* dictateur *m*

dic'tator·ship' *s* dictature *f*

diction ['dɪkʃən] *s* diction *f*

dictionar·y ['dɪkʃənˌɛri] *s* (*pl* -ies) dictionnaire *m*

dic·tum ['dɪktəm] *s* (*pl* -ta [tə]) dicton *m*; (law) opinion *f*, arrêt *m*

didactic(al) [daɪ'dæktɪk(əl)], [dɪ'dæktɪk(əl)] *adj* didactique

die [daɪ] *s* (*pl* dice [daɪs]) dé *m*; **the die is cast** le dé en est jeté ‖ *s* (*pl* dies) (*for stamping coins, medals, etc.*) coin *m*; (*for cutting threads*) filière *f*; (*key pattern*) jeu *m* ‖ *v* (*pret & pp* died; *ger* dying) *intr* mourir; **to be dying** se mourir; **to be dying to** (coll) mourir d'envie de; **to die away**

s'éteindre; **to die laughing** (coll) mourir de rire
die′hard′ *adj* intransigeant ‖ *s* intransigeant *m*, jusqu'au-boutiste *mf*
die′sel en′gine [′dizəl] *s* diesel *m*, moteur *m* diesel
die′sel oil′ *s* gas-oil *m*
die′stock′ *s* porte-filière *m*
diet [′daɪ·ət] *s* nourriture *f*; (*congress;* abstention from food) diète *f*; (*special menu*) régime *m* ‖ *intr* être or se mettre au régime, suivre un régime
dietetic [,daɪ·ə′tɛtɪk] *adj* diététique ‖ **dietetics** *s* diététique *f*
dietician [,daɪ·ə′tɪʃən] *s* diététicien *m*
differ [′dɪfər] *intr* différer; **to differ with** être en désaccord avec
difference [′dɪfərəns] *s* différence *f*; (*controversy*) différend *m*; **to make no difference** ne rien faire; **to split the difference** partager le différend
different [′dɪfərənt] *adj* différent
differential [,dɪfə′rɛnʃəl] *adj* différentiel ‖ *s* (mach) différentiel *m*; (math) différentielle *f*
differentiate [,dɪfə′rɛnʃɪ,et] *tr* différencier ‖ *intr* se différencier
difficult [′dɪfɪ,kʌlt] *adj* difficile
difficul·ty [′dɪfɪ,kʌlti] *s* (*pl* **-ties**) difficulté *f*
diffident [′dɪfɪdənt] *adj* défiant, timide
diffuse [dɪ′fjus] *adj* diffus ‖ [dɪ′fjuz] *tr* diffuser ‖ *intr* se diffuser
dig [dɪg] *s*—**to give s.o. a dig** (coll) lancer un trait à qn ‖ *v* (*pret & pp* **dug** [dʌg]; *ger* **digging**) *tr* bêcher, creuser; **to dig up** déterrer ‖ *intr* bêcher
digest [′daɪdʒɛst] *s* abrégé *m*, résumé *m*; (*publication*) digest *m*, sélection *f*; (law) digeste *m* ‖ [dɪ′dʒɛst], [daɪ′dʒɛst] *tr & intr* digérer
digestible [dɪ′dʒɛstɪbəl], [daɪ′dʒɛstɪbəl] *adj* digestible
digestion [dɪ′dʒɛstʃən], [daɪ′dʒɛstʃən] *s* digestion *f*
digestive [dɪ′dʒɛstɪv], [daɪ′dʒɛstɪv] *adj* digestif
diges′tive tract′ *s* appareil *m* digestif
digit [′dɪdʒɪt] *s* chiffre *m*; (*finger*) doigt *m*; (*toe*) doigt du pied
digitalis [,dɪgɪ′tælɪs], [,dɪdʒɪ′telɪs] *s* (bot) digitale *f*; (pharm) digitaline *f*
dignified *adj* distingué; (*air*) digne
digni·fy [′dɪgnɪ,faɪ] *v* (*pret & pp* **-fied**) *tr* glorifier, honorer
dignitar·y [′dɪgnɪ,teri] *s* (*pl* **-ies**) dignitaire *mf*
digni·ty [′dɪgnɪti] *s* (*pl* **-ties**) dignité *f*; **to stand on one's dignity** rester sur son quant-à-soi, le prendre de haut
digress [dɪ′grɛs], [daɪ′grɛs] *intr* faire une digression
digression [dɪ′grɛʃən], [daɪ′grɛʃən] *s* digression *f*
dihedral [daɪ′hidrəl] *adj & s* dièdre *m*
dike [daɪk] *s* digue *f*
dilapidated [dɪ′læpɪ,detɪd] *adj* délabré, déglingué
dilate [daɪ′let] *tr* dilater ‖ *intr* se dilater

dilatory [′dɪlə,tori] *adj* lent, tardif; (*strategy, answer*) dilatoire
dilemma [dɪ′lɛmə] *s* dilemme *m*
dilettan·te [,dɪlə′tænti] *adj* dilettante ‖ *s* (*pl* **-tes** or **-ti** [ti]) dilettante *mf*
diligence [′dɪlɪdʒəns] *s* diligence *f*
diligent [′dɪlɪdʒənt] *adj* diligent
dill [dɪl] *s* fenouil *m* bâtard, aneth *m*
dillydal·ly [′dɪlɪ,dæli] *v* (*pret & pp* **-lied**) *intr* traînasser
dilute [dɪ′lut], [daɪ′lut] *adj* dilué ‖ [dɪ′lut] *tr* diluer, délayer
dilution [dɪ′luʃən] *s* dilution *f*
dim [dɪm] *adj* faible, indistinct; (*forebodings*) obscur; (*memory*) effacé; (*color*) terne; (*idea of what is going on*) obtus, confus; **to take a dim view of** envisager sans enthousiasme ‖ *v* (*pret & pp* **dimmed**; *ger* **dimming**) *tr* affaiblir, obscurcir; (*beauty*) ternir; (*the headlights*) baisser, mettre en code ‖ *intr* s'affaiblir, s'obscurcir; (*said of color, beauty, etc.*) se ternir
dime [daɪm] *s* monnaie *f* de dix cents américains
dimension [dɪ′mɛnʃən] *s* dimension *f*
diminish [dɪ′mɪnɪʃ] *tr & intr* diminuer
diminutive [dɪ′mɪnjətɪv] *adj & s* diminutif *m*
dimi·ty [′dɪmɪti] *s* (*pl* **-ties**) basin *m*, brillanté *m*
dimly [′dɪmli] *adv* indistinctement
dimmers [′dɪmərz] *spl* (aut) feux *mpl* code, feux de croisement; **to put on the dimmers** se mettre en code
dimple [′dɪmpəl] *s* fossette *f*
dim′wit′ *s* (slang) sot *m*, niais *m*
din [dɪn] *s* tapage *m*, fracas *m* ‖ *v* (*pret & pp* **dinned**; *ger* **dinning**) *tr* assourdir; répéter sans cesse ‖ *intr* sonner bruyamment
dine [daɪn] *tr* fêter par un dîner ‖ *intr* dîner; **to dine out** dîner en ville
diner [′daɪnər] *s* dîneur *m*; (*shortorder restaurant*) plats-cuisinés *m*; (rr) wagon-restaurant *m*
dinette [daɪ′nɛt] *s* coin-repas *m*
ding-dong [′dɪŋ,dɔŋ], [′dɪŋ,dɑŋ] *s* tintement *m*, digue-din-don *m*
din·ghy [′dɪŋgi] *s* (*pl* **-ghies**) canot *m*, youyou *m*
din·gy [′dɪndʒi] *adj* (*comp* **-gier**; *super* **-giest**) défraîchi, terne
din′ing car′ *s* wagon-restaurant *m*
din′ing hall′ *s* salle *f* à manger; (*of university*) réfectoire *m*
din′ing room′ *s* salle *f* à manger
din′ing-room suite′ *s* salle *f* à manger
dinner [′dɪnər] *s* dîner *m*
din′ner coat′ *s* smoking *m*
din′ner dance′ *s* dîner *m* suivi de bal
din′ner guest′ *s* convive *mf*, invité *m*
din′ner jack′et *s* smoking *m*
din′ner pail′ *s* potager *m*
din′ner set′ *s* service *m* de table
din′ner time′ *s* heure *f* du dîner
dinosaur [′daɪnə,sɔr] *s* dinosaure *m*
dint [dɪnt] *s*—**by dint of** à force de
diocese [′daɪ·ə,sis], [′daɪ·əsɪs] *s* diocèse *m*
diode [′daɪ·od] *s* diode *f*
dioxide [daɪ′aksaɪd] *s* bioxyde *m*

dip [dɪp] *s* (*immersion*) plongeon *m*; (*swim*) baignade *f*; (*slope*) pente *f*; (*of magnetic needle*) inclinaison *f* ‖ *v* (*pret & pp* **dipped**; *ger* **dipping**) *tr* plonger; (*a flag*) marquer ‖ *intr* plonger; (*said of magnetic needle*) incliner; (*said of scale*) pencher; **to dip into** (*a book*) feuilleter; (*one's capital*) prendre dans

diphtheria [dɪf'θɪrɪ·ə] *s* diphtérie *f*

diphthong ['dɪfθɔŋ], ['dɪfθɑŋ] *s* diphtongue *f*

diphthongize ['dɪfθɔŋ ˌgaɪz], ['dɪfθɑŋˌgaɪz] *tr* diphtonguer ‖ *intr* se diphtonguer

diploma [dɪ'plomə] *s* diplôme *m*

diploma·cy [dɪ'ploməsɪ] *s* (*pl* **-cies**) diplomatie *f*

diplomat ['dɪplə ˌmæt] *s* diplomate *mf*

diplomatic [ˌdɪplə'mætɪk] *adj* diplomatique, diplomate

dip'lomat'ic pouch' *s* valise *f* diplomatique

dipper ['dɪpər] *s* louche *f*, cuiller *f* à pot

dip'stick' *s* jauge *f*

dire [daɪr] *adj* affreux, terrible

direct [dɪ'rɛkt], [daɪ'rɛkt] *adj* direct; franc, sincère ‖ *tr* diriger; (*to order*) ordonner; (*a letter, question, etc.*) adresser; (*to point out*) indiquer; (*theat*) mettre en scène

direct' cur'rent *s* courant *m* continu

direct' di'aling *s* (telp) automatique *m* interurbain

direct' hit' *s* coup *m* or tir *m* direct

direction [dɪ'rɛkʃən], [daɪ'rɛkʃən] *s* direction *f*; (*e.g., of a street*) sens *m*; (*theat*) mise *f* en scène; **directions** instructions *fpl*; (*for use*) mode *m* d'emploi

directional [dɪ'rɛkʃənəl], [daɪ'rɛkʃənəl] *adj* directionnel

direc'tional sig'nal *s* clignotant *m*

directive [dɪ'rɛktɪv], [daɪ'rɛktɪv] *s* ordre *m*, avis *m*

direct' ob'ject *s* (gram) complément *m* direct

director [dɪ'rɛktər], [daɪ'rɛktər] *s* directeur *m*, administrateur *m*, chef *m*; (*of a board*) membre *m* du conseil, votant *m*; (theat) metteur *m* en scène

direc'tor·ship' *s* direction *f*, directorat *m*

directo·ry [dɪ'rɛktərɪ], [daɪ'rɛktərɪ] *s* (*pl* **-ries**) (*board of directors*) conseil *m* d'administration; (*e.g., of telephone*) annuaire *m*; (*e.g., of genealogy*) almanach *m*; (eccl) directoire *m*

dirge [dʌrdʒ] *s* hymne *f* or chant *m* funèbre

dirigible ['dɪrɪdʒɪbəl] *adj & s* dirigeable *m*

dirt [dʌrt] *s* saleté *f*, ordure *f*; (*on clothes, skin, etc.*) crasse *f*; (*mire*) crotte *f*, boue *f*; (*earth*) terre *f*

dirt'-cheap' *adj* vendu à vil prix

dirt' road' *s* chemin *m* de terre

dirt·y ['dʌrtɪ] *adj* (*comp* **-ier**; *super* **-iest**) sale, malpropre; (*clothes, skin, etc.*) crasseux; (*muddy*) crotté, boueux; (*mean*) méchant, vilain

dir'ty lin'en *s* linge *m* sale; **don't wash your dirty linen in public** il faut laver son linge sale en famille

dir'ty trick' *s* (slang) sale tour *m*

disabili·ty [ˌdɪsə'bɪlɪtɪ] *s* (*pl* **-ties**) incapacité *f*, invalidité *f*

disabil'ity pen'sion *s* pension *f* d'invalidité

disable [dɪs'ebəl] *tr* rendre incapable, mettre hors de combat; (*to hurt the limbs of*) estropier, mutiler

disabled *adj* (*serviceman*) invalide; (*ship*) désemparé

disa'bled vet'eran *s* invalide *m*, réformé *m*

disabuse [ˌdɪsə'bjuz] *tr* désabuser

disadvantage [ˌdɪsəd'væntɪdʒ], [ˌdɪsəd'vɑntɪdʒ] *s* désavantage *m* ‖ *tr* désavantager

disadvantageous [dɪs ˌædvən'tedʒəs] *adj* désavantageux

disagree [ˌdɪsə'gri] *intr* différer; **to disagree with** (*to cause discomfort to*) ne pas convenir à; (*to dissent from*) donner tort à

disagreeable [ˌdɪsə'gri·əbəl] *adj* désagréable; (*mood, weather, etc.*) maussade

disagreement [ˌdɪsə'grimənt] *s* désaccord *m*, différend *m*

disallow [ˌdɪsə'laʊ] *tr* désapprouver, rejeter

disappear [ˌdɪsə'pɪr] *intr* disparaître; (phonet) s'amuïr

disappearance [ˌdɪsə'pɪrəns] *s* disparition *f*; (phonet) amuïssement *m*

disappoint [ˌdɪsə'pɔɪnt] *tr* décevoir, désappointer

disappointed *adj* déçu

disappointment [ˌdɪsə'pɔɪntmənt] *s* déception *f*, désappointement *m*

disapproval [ˌdɪsə'pruvəl] *s* désapprobation *f*

disapprove [ˌdɪsə'pruv] *tr & intr* désapprouver

disarm [dɪs'ɑrm] *tr & intr* désarmer

disarmament [dɪs'ɑrməmənt] *s* désarmement *m*

disarming [dɪs'ɑrmɪŋ] *adj* désarmant

disarray [ˌdɪsə're] *s* désarroi *m*, désordre *m*; **in disarray** (*said of apparel*) à demi vêtu ‖ *tr* mettre en désarroi

disassemble [ˌdɪsə'sɛmbəl] *tr* démonter, désassembler

disassociate [ˌdɪsə'soʃɪ ˌet] *tr* dissocier

disaster [dɪ'zæstər], [dɪ'zɑstər] *s* désastre *m*

disastrous [dɪ'zæstrəs], [dɪ'zɑstrəs] *adj* désastreux

disavow [ˌdɪsə'vaʊ] *tr* désavouer

disavowal [ˌdɪsə'vaʊ·əl] *s* désaveu *m*

disband [dɪs'bænd] *tr* licencier, congédier ‖ *intr* se débander, se disperser

dis·bar [dɪs'bɑr] *v* (*pret & pp* **-barred**; *ger* **-barring**) *tr* (law) rayer du barreau

disbelief [ˌdɪsbɪ'lif] *s* incroyance *f*

disbelieve [ˌdɪsbɪ'liv] *tr & intr* ne pas croire

disburse [dɪs'bʌrs] *tr* débourser

disbursement [dɪs'bʌrsmənt] *s* déboursement *m*; **disbursements** débours *mpl*

disc [dɪsk] *s* disque *m*

discard [dɪs'kard] *s* rebut *m*; (cards) écart *m*; **discards** marchandises *fpl* de rebut || *tr* mettre de côté, jeter; (cards) écarter || *intr* (cards) se défausser

discern [dɪ'zʌrn], [dɪ'sʌrn] *tr* discerner, percevoir

discernible [dɪ'zʌrnɪbəl], [dɪ'sʌrnɪbəl] *adj* discernable

discerning [dɪ'zʌrnɪŋ], [dɪ'sʌrnɪŋ] *adj* judicieux, pénétrant, éclairé

discernment [dɪ'zʌrnmənt], [dɪ'sʌrnmənt] *s* discernement *m*

discharge [dɪs'tʃardʒ] *s* décharge *f*; (*of a prisoner*) élargissement *m*; (*from a job*) congé *m*, renvoi *m*; (*from the armed forces*) libération *f*; (*from the armed forces for unfitness*) réforme *f*; (*from a wound*) suppuration *f* || *tr* décharger; (*a prisoner*) élargir; (*an employee*) congédier, renvoyer, licencier; (*a soldier*) libérer, réformer || *intr* se décharger; (pathol) suppurer

disciple [dɪ'saɪpəl] *s* disciple *m*

disciplinarian [,dɪsɪplɪ'nɛrɪ·ən] *s* partisan *m* d'une forte discipline; personne *f* qui impose une forte discipline

disciplinary ['dɪsɪplɪ,nɛri] *adj* disciplinaire

discipline ['dɪsɪplɪn] *s* discipline *f* || *tr* discipliner

disclaim [dɪs'klem] *tr* désavouer, renier

disclaimer [dɪs'klemər] *s* désaveu *m*

disclose [dɪs'kloz] *tr* découvrir, révéler

disclosure [dɪs'kloʒər] *s* découverte *f*, révélation *f*

discolor [dɪs'kʌlər] *tr* décolorer || *intr* se décolorer

discoloration [dɪs,kʌlə'reʃən] *s* décoloration *f*

discomfit [dɪs'kʌmfɪt] *tr* décontenancer, bafouer

discomfiture [dɪs'kʌmfɪtʃər] *s* déconfiture *f*, déconvenue *f*

discomfort [dɪs'kʌmfərt] *s* malaise *f*; (*inconvenience*) gêne *f* || *tr* gêner

disconcert [,dɪskən'sʌrt] *tr* déconcerter

disconnect [,dɪskə'nɛkt] *tr* désunir, séparer; (*a mechanism*) débrayer; (*a plug*) débrancher; (*current*) couper

disconsolate [dɪs'kansəlɪt] *adj* désolé, inconsolable

discontent [,dɪskən'tɛnt] *adj* mécontent || *s* mécontentement *m* || *tr* mécontenter

discontented *adj* mécontent

discontinue [,dɪskən'tɪnju] *tr* discontinuer

discontinuous [,dɪskən'tɪnju·əs] *adj* discontinu

discord ['dɪskɔrd] *s* discorde *f*, désaccord *m*; (mus) discordance *f*

discordance [dɪs'kɔrdəns] *s* discordance *f*

discotheque ['dɪskə,tɛk] *s* discothéque *f*

discount ['dɪskaunt] *s* escompte *m*, remise *f*, rabais *m* || ['dɪskaunt], [dɪs'kaunt] *tr* escompter, rabattre

dis/count rate/ *s* taux *m* d'escompte

discourage [dɪs'kʌrɪdʒ] *tr* décourager

discouragement [dɪs'kʌrɪdʒmənt] *s* découragement *m*

discourse ['dɪskors], [dɪs'kors] *s* discours *m* || [dɪs'kors] *intr* discourir

discourteous [dɪs'kʌrtɪ·əs] *adj* impoli, discourtois

discourte·sy [dɪs'kʌrtəsi] *s* (*pl* -sies) impolitesse *f*, discourtoisie *f*

discover [dɪs'kʌvər] *tr* découvrir

discoverer [dɪs'kʌvərər] *s* découvreur *m*

discover·y [dɪs'kʌvəri] *s* (*pl* -ies) découverte *f*

discredit [dɪs'krɛdɪt] *s* discrédit *m* || *tr* discréditer

discreditable [dɪs'krɛdɪtəbəl] *adj* déshonorant, peu honorable

discreet [dɪs'krit] *adj* discret

discrepan·cy [dɪs'krɛpənsi] *s* (*pl* -cies) désaccord *m*, différence *f*

discretion [dɪs'krɛʃən] *s* discrétion *f*

discriminate [dɪs'krɪmɪ,net] *tr* & *intr* discriminer; **to discriminate against** défavoriser

discrimination [dɪs,krɪmɪ'neʃən] *s* discrimination *f*

discriminatory [dɪs'krɪmɪnə,tori] *adj* discriminatoire

discus ['dɪskəs] *s* (sports) disque *m*, palet *m*

discuss [dɪs'kʌs] *tr* & *intr* discuter

discussion [dɪs'kʌʃən] *s* discussion *f*

disdain [dɪs'den] *s* dédain *m* || *tr* dédaigner

disdainful [dɪs'denfəl] *adj* dédaigneux

disease [dɪ'ziz] *s* maladie *f*

diseased *adj* malade

disembark [,dɪsɛm'bark] *tr* & *intr* débarquer

disembarkation [dɪs,ɛmbar'keʃən] *s* débarquement *m*

disembow·el [,dɪsɛm'bau·əl] *v* (*pret* & *pp* -eled *or* -elled; *ger* -eling *or* -elling) *tr* éventrer

disenchant [,dɪsɛn'tʃænt], [,dɪsɛn-'tʃant] *tr* désenchanter

disenchantment [,dɪsɛn'tʃæntmənt], [,dɪsɛn'tʃantmənt] *s* désenchantement *m*

disengage [,dɪsɛn'gedʒ] *tr* dégager; (*toothed wheels*) désengrener; (*a motor*) débrayer || *intr* se dégager

disengagement [,dɪsɛn'gedʒmənt] *s* dégagement *m*, détachement *m*

disentangle [,dɪsɛn'tæŋgəl] *tr* démêler, débrouiller

disentanglement [,dɪsɛn'tæŋgəlmənt] *s* démêlage *m*, débrouillement *m*

disestablish [,dɪsɛs'tæblɪʃ] *tr* (*the Church*) séparer de l'État

disfavor [dɪs'fevər] *s* défaveur *f* || *tr* défavoriser

disfigure [dɪs'fɪgjər] *tr* défigurer, enlaidir

disfigurement [dɪs'fɪgjərmənt] *s* défiguration *f*

disfranchise [dɪs'fræntʃaɪz] *tr* priver de ses droits civiques

disgorge [dɪs'gɔrdʒ] *tr & intr* dégorger

disgrace [dɪs'gres] *s* déshonneur *m* || *tr* déshonorer; (*to deprive of favor*) disgracier; **to disgrace oneself** se déshonorer

disgraceful [dɪs'gresfəl] *adj* déshonorant, honteux

disgruntled [dɪs'grʌntəld] *adj* contrarié, de mauvaise humeur

disguise [dɪs'gaɪz] *s* déguisement *m* || *tr* déguiser

disgust [dɪs'gʌst] *s* dégoût *m* || *tr* dégoûter

disgusting [dɪs'gʌstɪŋ] *adj* dégoûtant

dish [dɪʃ] *s* plat *m*; (*food*) mets *m*, plat; **to wash the dishes** faire la vaisselle || *tr*—**to dish up** servir

dish' clos'et *s* étagère *f* à vaisselle

dish'cloth' *s* lavette *f*

dishearten [dɪs'hɑrtən] *tr* décourager

dishev-el [dɪ'ʃɛvəl] *v* (*pret & pp* **-eled** or **-elled**; *ger* **-eling** or **-elling**) *tr* écheveler

dishonest [dɪs'ɑnɪst] *adj* malhonnête, déloyal

dishones-ty [dɪs'ɑnɪsti] *s* (*pl* **-ties**) malhonnêteté *f*, déloyauté *f*, improbité *f*

dishonor [dɪs'ɑnər] *s* déshonneur *m* || *tr* déshonorer

dishonorable [dɪs'ɑnərəbəl] *adj* déshonorant

dish'pan' *s* bassine *f*

dish' rack' *s* égouttoir *m*

dish'rag' *s* lavette *f*

dish'tow'el *s* torchon *m*

dish'wash'er *s* machine *f* à laver la vaisselle, lave-vaisselles *f*; (*person*) plongeur *m*

dish'wa'ter *s* eau *f* de vaisselle

disillusion [ˌdɪsɪ'luʒən] *s* désillusion *f* || *tr* désillusionner

disillusionment [ˌdɪsɪ'luʒənmənt] *s* désillusionnement *m*

disinclination [dɪsˌɪnklɪ'neʃən] *s* répugnance *f*, aversion *f*

disinclined [ˌdɪsɪn'klaɪnd] *adj* indisposé

disinfect [ˌdɪsɪn'fɛkt] *tr* désinfecter

disinfectant [ˌdɪsɪn'fɛktənt] *adj & s* désinfectant *m*

disingenuous [ˌdɪsɪn'dʒɛnju-əs] *adj* insincère, sans franchise

disinherit [ˌdɪsɪn'hɛrɪt] *tr* déshériter

disintegrate [dɪs'ɪntɪˌgret] *tr* désagréger; (nucl) désintégrer || *intr* se désagréger; (nucl) se désintégrer

disintegration [dɪsˌɪntɪ'greʃən] *s* désagrégation *f*; (nucl) désintégration *f*

disin-ter [ˌdɪsɪn'tʌr] *v* (*pret & pp* **-terred**; *ger* **-terring**) *tr* déterrer

disinterested [dɪs'ɪntəˌrɛstɪd], [dɪs'ɪntrɪstɪd] *adj* désintéressé

disjointed [dɪs'dʒɔɪntɪd] *adj* désarticulé; (*e.g., style*) décousu

disjunctive [dɪs'dʒʌŋktɪv] *adj* disjonctif; (*pronoun*) tonique

disk [dɪsk] *s* disque *m*

disk' jock'ey *s* présentateur *m* de disques

dislike [dɪs'laɪk] *s* aversion *f*; **to take a dislike for** prendre en aversion || *tr* ne pas aimer

dislocate ['dɪslo ˌket] *tr* disloquer; (*a joint*) luxer

dislodge [dɪs'lɑdʒ] *tr* déplacer; (*e.g., the enemy*) déloger

disloyal [dɪs'lɔɪ-əl] *adj* déloyal

disloyal-ty [dɪs'lɔɪ-əlti] *s* (*pl* **-ties**) déloyauté *f*

dismal ['dɪzməl] *adj* sombre, triste

dismantle [dɪs'mæntəl] *tr* démanteler; (*a machine*) démonter; (*a ship*) désarmer

dismay [dɪs'me] *s* consternation *f* || *tr* consterner

dismember [dɪs'mɛmbər] *tr* démembrer

dismiss [dɪs'mɪs] *tr* congédier; (*a servant*) renvoyer; (*an employee*) licencier; (*a government official*) destituer; (*a class in school*) terminer

dismissal [dɪs'mɪsəl] *s* congédiement *m*; (*from a job*) congé *m*, renvoi *m*; (*of an appeal*) (law) rejet *m*

dismount [dɪs'maunt] *tr* démonter || *intr* descendre

disobedience [ˌdɪsə'bidɪ-əns] *s* désobéissance *f*

disobedient [ˌdɪsə'bidɪ-ənt] *adj* désobéissant

disobey [ˌdɪsə'be] *tr* désobéir (with *dat*); **to be disobeyed** être désobéi || *intr* désobéir

disorder [dɪs'ɔrdər] *s* désordre *m* || *tr* désordonner

disorderly [dɪs'ɔrdərli] *adj* désordonné, déréglé; (*crowd*) turbulent, effervescent

disor'derly con'duct *s* conduite *f* désordonnée

disor'derly house' *s* maison *f* de prostitution; maison de jeu

disorganize [dɪs'ɔrgəˌnaɪz] *tr* désorganiser

disoriented [dɪs'ɔrɪˌɛntɪd] *adj* désorienté

disown [dɪs'on] *tr* désavouer, renier

disparage [dɪ'spærɪdʒ] *tr* dénigrer, déprécier

disparagement [dɪ'spærɪdʒmənt] *s* dénigrement *m*, dépréciation *f*

disparate ['dɪspərɪt] *adj* disparate

dispari-ty [dɪ'spærɪti] *s* (*pl* **-ties**) disparité *f*

dispassionate [dɪs'pæʃənɪt] *adj* calme; impartial

dispatch [dɪ'spætʃ] *s* dépêche *f*; (*shipment*) envoi *m*, expédition *f*; (*promptness*) promptitude *f* || *tr* dépêcher; (coll) expédier

dis-pel [dɪ'spɛl] *v* (*pret & pp* **-pelled**; *ger* **-pelling**) *tr* dissiper, disperser

dispensa-ry [dɪ'spɛnsəri] *s* (*pl* **-ries**) dispensaire *m*

dispensation *s* [ˌdɪspɛn'seʃən] (*dispensing*) dispensation *f*; (*exemption*) dispense *f*

dispense [dɪ'spɛns] *tr* dispenser, distribuer || *intr*—**to dispense with** se passer de; se défaire de

dispenser [dɪ'spɛnsər] *s* dispensateur *m*; (*automatic*) distributeur *m*

disperse [dɪ'spʌrs] *tr* disperser ‖ *intr* se disperser
dispersion [dɪ'spʌrʒən], [dɪ'spʌrʃən] *s* dispersion *f*
dispirit [dɪ'spɪrɪt] *tr* décourager
displace [dɪs'ples] *tr* déplacer; (*to take the place of*) remplacer
displaced' per'son *s* personne *f* déplacée
displacement [dɪs'plesmənt] *s* déplacement *m*; (*substitution*) remplacement *m*
display [dɪ'sple] *s* exposition *f*, étalage *m*; (*of emotion*) manifestation *f* ‖ *tr* exposer, étaler; (*anger, courage, etc.*) manifester; (*ignorance*) révéler
display' cab'inet *s* vitrine *f*
display' win'dow *s* vitrine *f*, devanture *f*
displease [dɪs'pliz] *tr* déplaire (with *dat*)
displeasing [dɪs'plizɪŋ] *adj* déplaisant
displeasure [dɪs'plɛʒər] *s* déplaisir *m*, mécontentement *m*
disposable [dɪ'spozəbəl] *adj* (*available*) disponible; (*made to be disposed of*) à jeter; (*container*) perdu, e.g., **disposable bottle** verre perdu
disposal [dɪ'spozəl] *s* disposition *f*; (*of a question*) résolution *f*; (*of trash, garbage, etc.*) destruction *f*
dispose [dɪ'spoz] *tr* disposer ‖ *intr* disposer; **to dispose of** disposer de; (*to get rid of*) se défaire de; (*a question*) résoudre, trancher
disposed *adj*—**to be disposed to** se disposer à, être porté à
disposition [ˌdɪspə'zɪʃən] *s* disposition *f*; (*mental outlook*) naturel *m*; (mil) dispositif *m*
dispossess [ˌdɪspə'zɛs] *tr* déposséder; expulser
disproof [dɪs'pruf] *s* réfutation *f*
disproportionate [ˌdɪsprə'porʃənɪt] *adj* disproportionné
disprove [dɪs'pruv] *tr* réfuter
dispute [dɪs'pjut] *s* dispute *f*; **beyond dispute** incontestable ‖ *tr* disputer ‖ *intr* se disputer
disquali•fy [dɪs'kwɑlɪˌfaɪ] *v* (*pret & pp -fied*) *tr* disqualifier
disquiet [dɪs'kwaɪ•ət] *s* inquiétude *f* ‖ *tr* inquiéter
disquisition [ˌdɪskwɪ'zɪʃən] *s* essai *m*, traité *m* considérable
disregard [ˌdɪsrɪ'gɑrd] *s* indifférence *f*; **disregard for** manque *m* d'égards envers ‖ *tr* ne pas faire cas de, passer sous silence
disrepair [ˌdɪsrɪ'pɛr] *s* délabrement *m*
disreputable [dɪs'rɛpjətəbəl] *adj* déshonorant, suspect; (*shabby*) débraillé, râpé
disrepute [ˌdɪsrɪ'pjut] *s* discrédit *m*
disrespect [ˌdɪsrɪ'spɛkt] *s* irrévérence *f*; manque *m* de respect, irrespect *m*
disrespectful [ˌdɪsrɪ'spɛktfəl] *adj* irrévérencieux, irrespectueux; **to be disrespectful to** manquer de respect à
disrobe [dɪs'rob] *tr* déshabiller ‖ *intr* se déshabiller
disrupt [dɪs'rʌpt] *tr* rompre; (*to throw into disorder*) bouleverser

disruption [dɪs'rʌpʃən] *s* rupture *f*; (*disorganization*) bouleversement *m*
dissatisfaction [ˌdɪssætɪs'fækʃən] *s* mécontentement *m*
dissatisfied *adj* mécontent
dissatis•fy [dɪs'sætɪsˌfaɪ] *v* (*pret & pp -fied*) *tr* mécontenter
dissect [dɪ'sɛkt] *tr* disséquer
dissection [dɪ'sɛkʃən] *s* dissection *f*
dissemble [dɪ'sɛmbəl] *tr & intr* dissimuler
disseminate [dɪ'sɛmɪˌnet] *tr* disséminer
dissension [dɪ'sɛnʃən] *s* dissension *f*
dissent [dɪ'sɛnt] *s* dissentiment *m*; (*nonconformity*) dissidence *f* ‖ *intr* différer
dissenter [dɪ'sɛntər] *s* dissident *m*
dissertation [ˌdɪsər'teʃən] *s* dissertation *f*; (*for a degree*) thèse *f*; (*speech*) discours *m*
disservice [dɪ'sʌrvɪs] *s* mauvais service *m*, tort *m*
dissidence ['dɪsɪdəns] *s* dissidence *f*
dissident ['dɪsɪdənt] *adj & s* dissident *m*
dissimilar [dɪ'sɪmɪlər] *adj* dissemblable
dissimilate [dɪ'sɪmɪˌlet] *tr* (phonet) dissimiler
dissimulate [dɪ'sɪmjəˌlet] *tr & intr* dissimuler
dissipate ['dɪsɪˌpet] *tr* dissiper; (*energy, heat, etc.*) disperser ‖ *intr* se dissiper
dissipated *adj* dissipé; débauché
dissipation [ˌdɪsɪ'peʃən] *s* dissipation *f*; (*of energy, heat, etc.*) dispersion *f*
dissociate [dɪ'soʃɪˌet] *tr* dissocier ‖ *intr* se dissocier
dissolute ['dɪsəˌlut] *adj* dissolu
dissolution [ˌdɪsə'luʃən] *s* dissolution *f*
dissolve [dɪ'zɑlv] *tr* dissoudre ‖ *intr* se dissoudre
dissonance ['dɪsənəns] *s* dissonance *f*
dissuade [dɪ'swed] *tr* dissuader
distaff ['dɪstæf], ['dɪstɑf] *s* quenouille *f*
dis'taff side' *s* côté *m* maternel
distance ['dɪstəns] *s* distance *f*; **at a distance** à distance; **in the distance** au loin, dans le lointain ‖ *tr* distancer
distant ['dɪstənt] *adj* distant; (*uncle, cousin, etc.*) éloigné
distaste [dɪs'test] *s* dégoût *m*, aversion *f*
distasteful [dɪs'testfəl] *adj* dégoûtant, répugnant
distemper [dɪs'tɛmpər] *s* (*of dog*) roupie *f*; (painting) détrempe *f* ‖ *tr* peindre en détrempe
distend [dɪ'stɛnd] *tr* distendre ‖ *intr* se distendre
distension [dɪ'stɛnʃən] *s* distension *f*
distill [dɪ'stɪl] *tr* distiller
distillation [ˌdɪstɪ'leʃən] *s* distillation *f*
distiller•y [dɪs'tɪləri] *s* (*pl -ies*) distillerie *f*
distinct [dɪs'tɪŋkt] *adj* distinct; (*unusual*) insigne
distinction [dɪs'tɪŋkʃən] *s* distinction *f*
distinctive [dɪs'tɪŋktɪv] *adj* distinctif
distinguish [dɪs'tɪŋgwɪʃ] *tr* distinguer; **to distinguish oneself** se distinguer, se faire remarquer
distinguished *adj* distingué

distort [dɪs'tɔrt] *tr* déformer
distortion [dɪs'tɔrʃən] *s* déformation *f*; (*of meaning*) sens *m* forcé; (phot, rad) distorsion *f*
distract [dɪ'strækt] *tr* (*to amuse*) distraire; (*to bewilder*) bouleverser
distracted *adj* bouleversé, éperdu
distraction [dɪ'strækʃən] *s* (*amusement*) distraction *f*; (*madness*) folie *f*
distraught [dɪ'strɔt] *adj* bouleversé
distress [dɪ'strɛs] *s* détresse *f* ‖ *tr* affliger
distress′ call′ *s* signal *m* de détresse
distressing [dɪ'strɛsɪŋ] *adj* affligeant, pénible
distribute [dɪ'strɪbjʊt] *tr* distribuer
distribution [ˌdɪstrə'bjuʃən] *s* distribution *f*
distributor [dɪ'strɪbjətər] *s* distributeur *m*; (*for a product*) concessionnaire *mf*
district ['dɪstrɪkt] *s* contrée *f*, région *f*; (*of a city*) quartier *m*; (*administrative division*) district *m*, circonscription *f* ‖ *tr* diviser en districts
dis′trict attor′ney *s* procureur *m* de la République, procureur général
distrust [dɪs'trʌst] *s* défiance *f*, méfiance *f* ‖ *tr* se défier de, se méfier de
distrustful [dɪs'trʌstfəl] *adj* défiant
disturb [dɪ'stʌrb] *tr* déranger, troubler; (*the peace*) perturber
disturbance [dɪ'stʌrbəns] *s* dérangement *m*, trouble *m*; (*riot*) bagarre *f*, émeute *f*; (*in the atmosphere or magnetic field*) perturbation *f*
disuse [dɪs'jus] *s* désuétude *f*
ditch [dɪtʃ] *s* fossé *m*; **to the last ditch** jusqu'à la dernière extrémité ‖ *tr* fossoyer; (slang) se défaire de ‖ *intr* (aer) faire un amerrissage forcé
ditch′ reed′ *s* (bot) laîche *f*
dither ['dɪðər] *s* agitation *f*; **to be in a dither** (coll) s'agiter sans but
dit·to ['dɪto] *s* (*pl* -tos) le même; (*on a duplicating machine*) copie *f*, duplicata *m* ‖ *adv* dito, de même, idem ‖ *tr* copier, reproduire
dit·ty ['dɪti] *s* (*pl* -ties) chansonnette *f*; **old ditty** (coll) vieux refrain *m*
diva ['divɑ] *s* diva *f*
divan ['daɪvæn], ['daɪvæn] *s* divan *m*
dive [daɪv] *s* plongeon *m*; (*of a submarine*) plongée *f*; (aer) piqué *m*; (coll) gargote *f*, cabaret *m* borgne ‖ *v* (*pret & pp* dived or dove [dov]) *intr* plonger; (*said of submarine*) plonger, effectuer une plongée; (aer) piquer; **to dive for** (e.g., *pearls*) pêcher; **to dive into** (coll) piquer une tête dans
dive′-bomb′ *tr & intr* bombarder en piqué
dive′ bomb′er *s* bombardier *m* à piqué
dive′ bomb′ing *s* bombardement *m* en piqué, piqué *m*
diver ['daɪvər] *s* plongeur *m*; (*person who works under water*) scaphandrier *m*; (orn) plongeon *m*
diverge [dɪ'vʌrdʒ], [daɪ'vʌrdʒ] *intr* diverger

divers ['daɪvərz] *adj* divers
diverse [dɪ'vʌrs], [daɪ'vʌrs], ['daɪvʌrs] *adj* divers
diversi·fy [dɪ'vʌrsɪˌfaɪ], [daɪ'vʌrsɪˌfaɪ] *v* (*pret & pp* -fied) *tr* diversifier ‖ *intr* se diversifier
diversion [dɪ'vʌrʒən], [daɪ'vʌrʒən] *s* diversion *f*
diversi·ty [dɪ'vʌrsɪti], [daɪ'vʌrsɪti] *s* (*pl* -ties) diversité *f*
divert [dɪ'vʌrt], [daɪ'vʌrt] *tr* détourner; (*to entertain*) distraire, divertir
diverting [dɪ'vʌrtɪŋ], [daɪ'vʌrtɪŋ] *adj* divertissant
divest [dɪ'vɛst], [daɪ'vɛst] *tr* dépouiller; **to divest oneself of** se défaire de; (*property, holdings*) se déposséder de
divide [dɪ'vaɪd] *s* (geog) ligne *f* de partage ‖ *tr* diviser ‖ *intr* se diviser
dividend ['dɪvɪˌdɛnd] *s* dividende *m*
dividers [dɪ'vaɪdərz] *spl* compas *m* de mesure
dividing [dɪ'vaɪdɪŋ] *s* division *f*; **dividing up** répartition *f*, partage *m*
divination [ˌdɪvɪ'neʃən] *s* divination *f*
divine [dɪ'vaɪn] *adj* divin ‖ *s* ecclésiastique *mf* ‖ *tr* deviner
diviner [dɪ'vaɪnər] *s* devin *m*
diving ['daɪvɪŋ] *s* plongeon *m*
div′ing bell′ *s* cloche *f* à plongeur
div′ing board′ *s* plongeoir *m*, tremplin *m*
div′ing suit′ *s* scaphandre *m*
divin′ing rod′ [dɪ'vaɪnɪŋ] *s* baguette *f* divinatoire
divini·ty [dɪ'vɪnɪti] *s* (*pl* -ties) divinité *f*; (*subject of study*) théologie *f*; **the Divinity** Dieu *m*
divisible [dɪ'vɪzɪbəl] *adj* divisible
division [dɪ'vɪʒən] *s* division *f*
divisor [dɪ'vaɪzər] *s* diviseur *m*
divorce [dɪ'vors] *s* divorce *m*; **to get a divorce** divorcer; **to get a divorce from** (*husband or wife*) divorcer d'avec ‖ *tr* (*the married couple*) divorcer; (*husband or wife*) divorcer d'avec ‖ *intr* divorcer
divorcee [dɪvor'si] *s* divorcée *f*
divulge [dɪ'vʌldʒ] *tr* divulguer
dizziness ['dɪzɪnɪs] *s* vertige *m*
diz·zy ['dɪzi] *adj* (*comp* -zier; *super* -ziest*) vertigineux; (coll) étourdi, farfelu; **to feel dizzy** avoir le vertige; **to make dizzy** étourdir
do [du] *v* (3d *pers* does [dʌz]; *pret* did [dɪd]; *pp* done [dʌn]; *ger* doing ['du·ɪŋ]) *tr* faire; (*homage; justice; a good turn*) rendre; **to do over** refaire; **to do up** emballer, envelopper ‖ *intr* faire; **how do you do?** enchanté de faire votre connaissance; comment allez-vous?; **that will do** c'est bien; en voilà assez; **that will never do** cela n'ira jamais; **to do away with** supprimer; **to do without** se passer de; **will I do?** suis-je bien comme ça?; **will it do?** ça va-t-il comme ça? ‖ *aux* used in English but not specifically expressed in French: 1) in questions, e.g., **do you speak French?** parlez-vous français?; 2) in negative sentences, e.g., **I do not speak French**

je ne parle pas français; 3) as a substitute for another verb in an elliptical question, e.g., **I saw him. Did you?** je l'ai vu. L'avez-vous vu?; 4) for emphasis, e.g., **I do believe what you told me** je crois bien ce que vous m'avez dit; 5) in inversions after certain adverbs, e.g., **hardly did we finish when . . .** à peine avons-nous fini que . . . ; 6) in an imperative entreaty, e.g., **do come in!** entrez donc!

do. *abbr* (ditto) d°

docile ['dɑsɪl] *adj* docile

dock [dɑk] *s* embarcadère *m*, quai *m*; *(area including piers and waterways)* bassin *m*, dock *m*; (bot) oseille *f*, patience *f*; (law) banc *m* des prévenus ‖ *tr* faire entrer au bassin; *(an animal)* couper la queue à; *(s.o.'s salary)* retrancher ‖ *intr* (naut) s'amarrer au quai

docket ['dɑkɪt] *s* (law) rôle *m*; **on the docket** pendant, non jugé; **to put on the docket** (coll) prendre en main

dock' hand' *s* docker *m*

docking ['dɑkɪŋ] *s* (rok) arrimage *m*

dock' work'er *s* docker *m*

dock'yard' *s* chantier *m*

doctor ['dɑktər] *s* docteur *m*; *(woman)* femme *f* docteur; (med) docteur, médecin *m*; (med) doctoresse *f*; **Doctor Curie** *(professor, Ph.D., etc.)* Monsieur Curie; Madame Curie ‖ *tr* soigner; *(e.g., a chipped vase)* réparer; *(e.g., the facts)* falsifier ‖ *intr* pratiquer la médecine; (coll) être en traitement; (coll) prendre des médicaments

doctorate ['dɑktərɪt] *s* doctorat *m*

Doc'tor of Laws' *s* docteur *m* en droit

doctrine ['dɑktrɪn] *s* doctrine *f*

document ['dɑkjəmənt] *s* document *m* ‖ ['dɑkjə‚ment] *tr* documenter

documenta·ry [‚dɑkjə'mentəri] *adj* documentaire ‖ *s* (*pl* -ries) documentaire *m*

documentation [‚dɑkjəmɛn'teʃən] *s* documentation *f*

doddering ['dɑdərɪŋ] *adj* tremblotant, gâteux

dodge [dɑdʒ] *s* écart *m*, esquive *f*; (coll) ruse *f*, truc *m* ‖ *tr* esquiver; *(a question)* éluder ‖ *intr* s'esquiver

do·do ['dodo] *s* (*pl* -dos *or* -does) (orn) dronte *m*, dodo *m*; (coll) vieux fossile *m*, innocent *m*

doe [do] *s* *(of fallow deer)* daine *f*; *(hind)* biche *f*; *(roe doe)* chevrette *f*; *(of hare)* hase *f*; *(of rabbit)* lapine *f*

doe'skin' *s* peau *f* de daim

doff [dɑf], [dɔf] *tr* ôter

dog [dɔg], [dɑg] *s* chien *m*; **let sleeping dogs lie** il ne faut pas réveiller le chat qui dort; **to go to the dogs** (coll) se débaucher; *(said of business)* (coll) aller à vau-l'eau; **to put on the dog** (coll) faire de l'épate ‖ *v* (*pret & pp* **dogged**; *ger* **dogging**) *tr* poursuivre

dog'catch'er *s* employé *m* de la fourrière

dog' days' *spl* canicule *f*

doge [dodʒ] *s* doge *m*

dog'face' *s* (slang) troufion *m*

dog'fight' *s* (aer) combat *m* aérien tournoyant et violent; (coll) bagarre *f*

dogged ['dɔgɪd], ['dɑgɪd] *adj* tenace, obstiné

doggerel ['dɔgərəl], ['dɑgərəl] *s* vers *mpl* de mirliton

dog·gy ['dɔgi], ['dɑgi] *adj* (*comp* -gier; *super* -giest) canin, de chien ‖ *s* (*pl* -gies) toutou *m*

dog'house' *s* niche *f* à chien; **in the doghouse** (slang) en disgrâce

dog' in the man'ger *s* chien *m* du jardinier

dog' Lat'in *s* latin *m* de cuisine

dogma ['dɔgmə], ['dɑgmə] *s* dogme *m*

dogmatic [dɔg'mætɪk], [dɑg'mætɪk] *adj* dogmatique ‖ **dogmatics** *s* dogmatique *f*

dog' pound' *s* fourrière *f*

dog' rac'ing *s* courses *fpl* de lévriers

dog' rose' *s* rose *f* des haies

dog's'-ear' *s* corne *f* ‖ *tr* corner

dog' show' *s* exposition *f* canine

dog' sled' *or* **dog' sledge'** *s* traîneau *m* à chiens

dog's' life' *s* vie *f* de chien

Dog' Star' *s* Canicule *f*

dog' tag' *s* (mil) plaque *f* d'identité

dog'-tired' *adj* éreinté, fourbu

dog'tooth' *s* (*pl* -teeth) dent *f* de chien, canine *f*; (archit, bot, mach) dent-de-chien *f*

dog'tooth vi'olet *s* dent-de-chien *f*

dog'trot' *s* petit-trot *m*

dog'watch' *s* (naut) petit quart *m*

dog'wood' *s* cornouiller *m*

doi·ly ['dɔɪli] *s* (*pl* -lies) napperon *m*; *(underplate)* garde-nappe *m*

doings ['du·ɪŋz] *spl* actions *fpl*, œuvres *fpl*, faits et gestes *mpl*

do-it-yourself [‚du·ɪtʃər'sɛlf] *adj* de bricolage ‖ *s* bricolage *m*

doldrums ['doldrəmz], ['dɑldrəmz] *spl* marasme *m*; (naut) zone *f* des calmes

dole [dol] *s* aumône *f*; indemnité *f* de chômage ‖ *tr*—**to dole out** distribuer parcimonieusement

doleful ['dolfəl] *adj* dolent

doll [dɑl] *s* poupée *f* ‖ *tr*—**to be dolled up** (coll) être tiré à quatre épingles ‖ *intr*—**to doll up** (coll) se parer, s'endimancher

dollar ['dɑlər] *s* dollar *m*

dol·ly ['dɑli] *s* (*pl* -lies) *(low movable frame)* chariot *m*; *(hand truck)* diable *m*; *(child's doll)* poupée *f*; (mov, telv) travelling *m*

dolphin ['dɑlfɪn] *s* dauphin *m*

dolt [dolt] *s* nigaud *m*, lourdaud *m*

doltish ['doltɪʃ] *adj* nigaud, lourdaud

domain [do'men] *s* domaine *m*; *(private estate)* terres *fpl*, propriété *f*

dome [dom] *s* dôme *m*, coupole *f*

dome' light' *s* (aut) plafonnier *m*

domestic [də'mestɪk] *adj & s* domestique *mf*

domesticate [də'mestɪ‚ket] *tr* domestiquer

domesticity [ˌdɒmes'tɪsɪti] *s* caractère *m* casanier; vie *f* familiale
domicile ['dɒmɪsɪl], ['dɒmɪˌsaɪl] *s* domicile *m* ‖ *tr* domicilier
dominance ['dɒmɪnəns] *s* prédominance *f*; (genetics) dominance *f*
dominant ['dɒmɪnənt] *adj* prédominant, dominant ‖ *s* (mus) dominante *f*
dominate ['dɒmɪˌnet] *tr* & *intr* dominer
dominating ['dɒmɪˌnetɪŋ] *adj* dominateur
domination [ˌdɒmɪ'neʃən] *s* domination *f*
domineer [ˌdɒmɪ'nɪr] *intr* se montrer tyrannique
domineering [ˌdɒmɪ'nɪrɪŋ] *adj* tyrannique, autoritaire
dominion [də'mɪnjən] *s* domination *f*; (*of British Commonwealth*) dominion *m*
domi·no ['dɒmɪˌno] *s* (*pl* -noes or -nos) domino *m*; **dominoes** *sg* (*game*) les dominos
don [dɒn] *s* (*tutor*) précepteur *m* ‖ *v* (*pret* & *pp* **donned**; *ger* **donning**) *tr* mettre, enfiler
donate ['donet] *tr* faire un don de
donation [do'neʃən] *s* don *m*, cadeau *m*
done [dʌn] *adj* fait; **are you done?** en avez-vous fini?; **it is done** (*it is finished*) c'en est fait; **to be done** (*e.g., beefsteak*) être cuit; **to have done with** en finir avec; **well done!** très bien!, bravo!, à la bonne heure!
done' for' *adj* (*tired out*) (coll) fourbu; (*ruined*) (coll) abattu; (*out of the running*) (coll) hors de combat; (*dead*) (coll) estourbi
donkey ['dɒŋki], ['dʌŋki] *s* âne *m*, baudet *m*
donor ['donər] *s* donneur *m*; (law) donateur *m*
doodle ['dudəl] *tr* & *intr* griffonner
doom [dum] *s* condamnation *f*; destin *m* funeste ‖ *tr* condamner
dooms'day' *s* jugement *m* dernier
door [dor] *s* porte *f*; (*of a carriage or automobile*) portière *f*; (*one part of a double door*) battant *m*; **behind closed doors** à huis clos; **to see to the door** conduire à la porte; **to show s.o. the door** éconduire qn, mettre qn à la porte
door'bell' *s* timbre *m*, sonnette *f*
door'bell transform'er *s* transformateur *m* de sonnerie
door' check' *s* arrêt *m* de porte
door'frame' *s* chambranle *m*, huisserie *f*, dormant *m*
door'head' *s* linteau *m*
door'jamb' *s* jambage *m*
door'knob' *s* bouton *m* de porte
door'knock'er *s* heurtoir *m*, marteau *m* de porte
door' latch' *s* loquet *m*
door'man *s* (*pl* -men) portier *m*
door'mat' *s* essuie-pieds *m*, paillasson *m*
door'nail' *s* clou *m* de porte; **dead as a doornail** (coll) bien mort
door'post' *s* montant *m* de porte

door' scrap'er ['skrepər] *s* décrottoir *m*, grattepieds *m*
door'sill' *s* seuil *m*, traverse *f*
door'step' *s* seuil *m*, pas *m*
door'stop' *s* entrebâilleur *m*, butoir *m*
door'-to-door' *adj* porte-à-porte
door'way' *s* porte *f*, portail *m*
dope [dop] *s* enduit *m*; (slang) narcotique *m*, stupéfiant *m*; (*information*) (slang) renseignements *mpl*; (*fool*) (slang) cornichon *m* ‖ *tr* enduire; (slang) doper, stupéfier; **to dope out** (slang) deviner, déchiffrer
dope' fiend' *s* (slang) toxicomane *mf*
dope' ped'dler *s* trafiquant *m* de stupéfiants
dormant ['dɔrmənt] *adj* endormi, assoupi; latent; **to lie dormant** dormir
dor'mer win'dow ['dɔrmər] *s* lucarne *f*
dormito·ry ['dɔrmɪˌtori] *s* (*pl* -ries) (*room*) dortoir *m*; (*building*) pavillon *m* des étudiants, maison *f* de résidence
dor'mitory com'plex *s* cité *f* universitaire
dor·mouse ['dɔrˌmaʊs] *s* (*pl* -mice) loir *m*
dosage ['dosɪdʒ] *s* dosage *m*
dose [dos] *s* dose *f* ‖ *tr* donner en doses; donner un médicament à
dossier ['dɑsɪˌe] *s* dossier *m*
dot [dɑt] *s* point *m*; **on the dot** (coll) à l'heure tapante; pile, e.g., **at noon on the dot** à midi pile ‖ *v* (*pret* & *pp* **dotted**; *ger* **dotting**) *tr* (*to make with dots*) pointiller; **to dot one's i's** mettre les points sur les i
dotage ['dotɪdʒ] *s* radotage *m*
dotard ['dotərd] *s* gâteux *m*, gaga *m*
dote [dot] *intr* radoter; **to dote on** raffoler de
doting ['dotɪŋ] *adj* radoteur; (*loving to excess*) qui aime follement
dots' and dash'es *spl* (telg) points et traits *mpl*
dot'ted line' *s* ligne *f* pointillée, ligne hachée; **to sign on the dotted line** signer aveuglément
double ['dʌbəl] *adj* & *adv* double, en deux, deux fois ‖ *s* double *m*; (cards) contre *m*; (*stunt man*) (mov) cascadeur *m*; **doubles** (tennis) double; **on the double!** (coll) dare-dare!, au trot! ‖ *tr* doubler; (cards) contrer; **to double up** plier en deux ‖ *intr* doubler; (cards) contrer; **to double back** faire un crochet; **to double up** se plier, se tordre
dou'ble-act'ing *adj* à double effet
dou'ble-bar'reled *adj* (*gun*) à deux coups
dou'ble bass' [bes] *s* contrebasse *f*
dou'ble bed' *s* grand lit *m*, lit à deux places
dou'ble boil'er *s* bain-marie *m*
dou'ble-breast'ed *adj* croisé
dou'ble chin' *s* double menton *m*
dou'ble cross' *s* (slang) entourloupette *f*, double jeu *m*
dou'ble-cross' *tr* (coll) doubler, rouler, faire une entourloupette à

dou′ble-cross′er *s* (slang) personne *f* double, faux jeton *m*

dou′ble date′ *s* partie *f* carrée, sortie *f* à quatre

dou′ble-deal′er *s* personne *f* double, homme *m* à deux visages

dou′ble-deal′ing *adj* hypocrite ‖ *s* duplicité *f*

dou′ble-deck′er *s* (*bed*) lits *mpl* superposés, lits gigognes, lit à deux étages; (*bus*) autobus *m* à deux étages; (*sandwich*) double sandwich *m*; (aer, naut) deux-ponts *m*

dou′ble-edged′ *adj* à deux tranchants, à double tranchant

double entendre [′dubəlɑn′tɑndrə] *s* expression *f* à double entente, mot *m* à double sens

dou′ble-en′try *adj* en partie double

dou′ble-faced′ *adj* à double face

dou′ble fea′ture *s* (mov) deux grands films *mpl*, double programme *m*

dou′ble-joint′ed *adj* désarticulé

dou′ble-lock′ *tr* fermer à double tour

dou′ble-park′ *tr* faire stationner en double file ‖ *intr* stationner en double file

dou′ble room′ *s* chambre *f* à deux lits

dou′ble-spaced′ *adj* à l'interligne

dou′ble stand′ard *s* code *m* de morale à deux aspects; **to have a double standard** avoir deux poids et deux mesures

doublet [′dʌblɪt] *s* (*close-fitting jacket*) pourpoint *m*; (*counterfeit stone; each of two words having the same origin*) doublet *m*

dou′ble-talk′ *s* (coll) non-sens *m*; (coll) paroles *fpl* creuses or ambiguës, mots *mpl* couverts

dou′ble time′ *s* (*for work*) salaire *m* double; (mil) pas *m* redoublé

doubleton [′dʌbəltən] *s* deux cartes *fpl* d'une couleur

dou′ble track′ *s* double piste *f*

doubling [′dʌblɪŋ] *s* doublement *m*

doubly [′dʌbli] *adv* doublement

doubt [daut] *s* doute *m*; **beyond a doubt** à n'en pas douter; **no doubt** sans doute ‖ *tr* douter de; **to doubt that** douter que; **to doubt whether** douter si ‖ *intr* douter

doubter [′dautər] *s* douteur *m*

doubtful [′dautfəl] *adj* douteux; indécis, hésitant

doubtless [′dautlɪs] *adv* sans doute

douche [duʃ] *s* douche *f*; (*instrument*) seringue *f* à lavement ‖ *tr* doucher ‖ *intr* se doucher

dough [do] *s* pâte *f*; (slang) fric *m*; **big dough** (slang) grosse galette *f*

dough′boy′ *s* (coll) troufion *m*, biffin *m*; (*in the first World War*) poilu *m*

dough′nut′ *s* beignet *m*

dough·ty [′dauti] *adj* (*comp* -**tier**; *super* -**tiest**) vaillant, preux

dough·y [′do·i] *adj* (*comp* -**ier**; *super* -**iest**) pâteux

dour [daur], [dur] *adj* (*severe*) austère; (*obstinate*) buté; (*gloomy*) mélancolique

douse [daus] *tr* tremper, arroser; (slang) éteindre

dove [dʌv] *s* colombe *f*

dovecote [′dʌv͵kot] *s* pigeonnier *m*, colombier *m*

Dover [′dovər] *s* Douvres

dove′tail′ *s* queue-d'aronde *f*, adent *m* ‖ *tr* assembler à queue-d'aronde, adenter; (fig) raccorder, opérer le raccord entre ‖ *intr* se raccorder

dove′tailed′ *adj* à queue-d'aronde

dowager [′dau·ədʒər] *s* douairière *f*

dow·dy [′daudi] *adj* (*comp* -**dier**; *super* -**diest**) gauche, fagoté, mal habillé

dow·el [′dau·əl] *s* goujon *m* ‖ *v* (*pret & pp* -**eled** or -**elled**; *ger* -**eling** or -**elling**) *tr* goujonner

dower [′dau·ər] *s* (*widow's portion*) douaire *m*; (*marriage portion*) dot *f*; (*natural gift*) don *m* ‖ *tr* assigner un douaire à; doter

down [daun] *adj* bas; (*train*) descendant; (*storage battery*) épuisé; (*tire*) à plat; (*sun*) couché; (*wind, sea, etc.*) calmé; (*blinds; prices*) baissé; (*stocks*) en moins-value; (*sad*) abattu, triste ‖ *s* duvet *m*; (*sand hill*) dune *f* ‖ *adv* en bas, au bas, vers les bas; à terre; (*south*) au sud; **down!** (*in elevator*) on descend!, pour la descente!; **down from** du haut de; **down there** là-bas; **down to** jusqu'à; **down under** aux antipodes; **down with ...!** à bas ...!; for expressions like **to go down** descendre or **to pay down** payer comptant, see the verb ‖ *prep* en bas de; (*along*) le long de; (*a stream*) en descendant ‖ *tr* descendre, abattre; (*to swallow*) (coll) avaler

down′-and-out′ *adj* décavé

down′beat′ *s* (mus) temps *m* fort, frappé *m*, premier accent *m*

down′cast′ *adj* abattu, baissé

down′fall′ *s* chute *f*, ruine *f*

down′grade′ *adj* (coll) descendant ‖ *s* descente *f*; **to be on the downgrade** déchoir ‖ *adv* en déclin ‖ *tr* déclasser

down′heart′ed *adj* abattu, découragé

down′hill′ *adj* descendant ‖ *adv*—**to go downhill** aller en descendant; (fig) décliner

down′ pay′ment *s* acompte *m*

down′pour′ *s* déluge *m*, averse *f*

down′right′ *adj* absolu, véritable ‖ *adv* tout à fait, absolument

down′stairs′ *adj* rez-de-chaussée *m* ‖ *adv* en bas; **to go downstairs** descendre

down′stream′ *adv* en aval

down′stroke′ *s* (*of piston*) course *f* descendante; (*in writing*) jambage *m*

down′town′ *adj* du centre ‖ *s* centre *m* ‖ *adv* en ville

down′trend′ *s* tendance *f* à la baisse

downtrodden [′daun͵trɑdən] *adj* opprimé

downward [′daunwərd] *adj* descendant ‖ *adv* en bas, en descendant

downwards [′daunwərdz] *adv* en bas, en descendant

down′wash′ *s* (aer) air *m* déplacé

down·y [′dauni] *adj* (*comp* -**ier**; *super*

-iest) duveteux; (*velvety*) velouté; (*soft*) mou, moelleux

dow·ry ['dauri] *s* (*pl* **-ries**) dot *f*

dowser ['dauzər] *s* sourcier *m*, hydroscope *m*

doze [doz] *s* petit somme *m* || *intr* sommeiller; **to doze off** s'assoupir

dozen ['dʌzən] *s* douzaine *f*; **a dozen . . .** une douzaine de . . . ; **by the dozen** à la douzaine

D.P. *abbr* (**displaced person**) personne *f* déplacée

Dr. *abbr* (**Doctor**) Dr

drab [dræb] *adj* (*comp* **drabber**; *super* **drabbest**) gris || *s* gris *m*

drach·ma ['drækmə] *s* (*pl* **-mas** or **-mae** [mi]) drachme *f*

draft [dræft], [draft] *s* courant *m* d'air; (*pulling; current of air in chimney*) tirage *m*; (*sketch, outline*) ébauche *f*; (*of a letter, novel, etc.*) brouillon *m*, premier jet *m*; (*of a bill in Congress*) projet *m*; (*of a law*) avant-projet *m*; (*drink*) trait *m*, gorgée *f*; (com) mandat *m*, traite *f*; (mil) conscription *f*; (naut) tirant *m* d'eau; **drafts** (*game*) dames *fpl*; **on draft** à la pression; **to be exempted from the draft** être exempté du service militaire || *tr* (*a document*) rédiger, faire le brouillon de; (*a bill in Congress*) dresser; (*a recruit*) appeler sous les drapeaux; **to be drafted** être appelé sous les drapeaux

draft' beer' *s* bière *f* pression

draft' board' *s* conseil *m* de révision; commission *f* locale des conscriptions

draft' call' *s* appel *m* sous les drapeaux

draft' dodg'er ['dadʒər] *s* embusqué *m*

draftee [,dræf'ti], [,draf'ti] *s* appelé *m* (sous les drapeaux), conscrit *m*

draft' horse' *s* cheval *m* de trait

drafting ['dræftɪŋ], ['draftɪŋ] *s* dessin *m* industriel

draft'ing room' *s* bureau *m* d'études

drafts'man *s* (*pl* **-men**) dessinateur *m*; (*man who draws up documents*) rédacteur *m*

draft·y ['dræfti], ['drafti] *adj* (*comp* **-ier**; *super* **-iest**) plein de courants d'air

drag [dræg] *s* (*net*) drège *f*; (*sledge or sled*) traîneau *m*; (*stone drag*) fardier *m*; (*brake*) enrayure *f*; (*impediment*) entrave *f*; (aer) résistance *f* à l'avancement || *v* (*pret & pp* **dragged**) *ger* **dragging**) *tr* traîner; (*one's feet*) traînasser; (*a net*) draguer; (*a field*) herser; **to drag down** entraîner; **to drag in** introduire de force; **to drag out** faire sortir de force || *intr* traîner à terre; se traîner

drag'net' *s* traîneau *m*, chalut *m*

dragon ['drægən] *s* dragon *m*

drag'on·fly' *s* (*pl* **-flies**) demoiselle *f*, libellule *f*

dragoon [drə'gun] *s* dragon *m* || *tr* tyranniser; forcer, contraindre

drain [dren] *s* (*sewer*) égout *m*; (*pipe*) tuyau *m* d'égout; (*ditch*) tranchée *f* d'écoulement; (*source of continual expense*) saignée *f*; (med) drain *m* ||

tr (*wet ground*) drainer; (*a glass or cup*) vider entièrement; (*a crankcase*) vidanger; (*s.o. of strength*) épuiser; (med) drainer || *intr* s'égoutter, s'écouler

drainage ['drenɪdʒ] *s* drainage *m*

drain'board' *s* égouttoir *m*

drain' cock' *s* purgeur *m*

drain'pipe' *s* tuyau *m* d'écoulement, drain *m*

drain' plug' *s* bouchon *m* de vidange

drake [drek] *s* canard *m* mâle

dram [dræm] *s* (*weight*) drachme *m*; (*drink*) petit verre *f*, goutte *f*

drama ['dramə], ['dræmə] *s* drame *m*

dra'ma crit'ic *s* chroniqueur *m* dramatique

dra'ma review' *s* avant-première *f*

dramatic [drə'mætɪk] *adj* dramatique || **dramatics** *s* dramaturgie *f*, art *m* dramatique

dramatist ['dræmətɪst] *s* auteur *m* dramatique, dramaturge *mf*

dramatize ['dræmə,taɪz] *tr* dramatiser

drape [drep] *s* rideau *m*; (*hang of a curtain, skirt, etc.*) drapement *m* || *tr* draper, tendre; se draper dans

draper·y ['drepəri] *s* (*pl* **-ies**) draperie *f*; **draperies** rideaux *mpl*, tentures *fpl*

drastic ['dræstɪk] *adj* énergique, radical; (*laxative*) drastique

draught [dræft], [draft] *s* (*of fish*) coup *m* de filet; (*drink*) trait *m*, gorgée *f*; (naut) tirant *m* d'eau;

draughts (*game*) dames *fpl*; **on draught** à la pression

draught' beer' *s* bière *f* pression

draught'board' *s* damier *m*

draw [drɔ] *s* tirage *m*; (*in a game or other contest*) partie *f* nulle, match *m* nul || *v* (*pret* **drew** [dru]; *pp* **drawn** [drɔn]) *tr* tirer; (*a crowd*) attirer; (*a design*) dessiner; (*a card*) tirer; (*trumps*) faire tomber; (*a bow*) bander, tendre; (*water*) puiser; **to draw a conclusion** tirer une conséquence; **to draw aside** prendre à l'écart; **to draw blood** faire saigner; **to draw interest** porter intérêt; **to draw lots** tirer au sort; **to draw off** (*e.g., a liquid*) soutirer; **to draw out** (*a person*) faire parler; (*an activity*) prolonger, traîner; **to draw up** (*a list*) dresser; (*a plan*) rédiger; (naut) jauger || *intr* tirer; dessiner; faire partie nulle, faire match nul; **to draw away** s'éloigner; **to draw back** reculer, se retirer; **to draw near** approcher; s'approcher de

draw'back' *s* désavantage *m*, inconvénient *m*

draw'bridge' *s* pont-levis *m*

drawee [,drɔ'i] *s* tiré *m*, accepteur *m*

drawer ['drɔ·ər] *s* dessinateur *m*; (com) tireur *m* || [drɔr] *s* tiroir *m*; **drawers** caleçon *m*

drawing ['drɔ·ɪŋ] *s* dessin *m*; (*in a lottery*) tirage *m*

draw'ing board' *s* planche *f* à dessin

draw'ing card' *s* attrait *m*, attraction *f*

draw'ing room' *s* salon *m*

draw'knife' *s* (*pl* **-knives**) plane *f*

drawl [drɔl] *s* voix *f* traînante ‖ *tr* dire d'une voix traînante ‖ *intr* traîner la voix en parlant

drawn′ but′ter [drɔn] *s* beurre *m* fondu; sauce *f* blanche

drawn′ work′ *s* broderie *f* à fils tirés

dray [dre] *s* haquet *m*, charrette *f*; (*sledge*) fardier *m*, schlitte *f*

drayage ['dre·ɪdʒ] *s* charriage *m*, charroi *m*; frais *mpl* de transport

dray′ horse′ *s* cheval *m* de trait

dray′man *s* (*pl* -men) haquetier *m*

dread [drɛd] *adj* redoutable, terrible ‖ *s* terreur *f*, crainte *f* ‖ *tr* & *intr* redouter, craindre

dreadful ['drɛdfəl] *adj* épouvantable

dream [drim] *s* rêve *m*, songe *m*; (*fancy, illusion*) rêverie *f*, songerie *f* ‖ *v* (*pret* & *pp* **dreamed** or **dreamt** [drɛmt]) *tr*—**to dream up** rêver ‖ *intr* rêver, songer; **to dream of** (*future plans*) rêver à; (*s.o.*) rêver de

dreamer ['drimər] *s* rêveur *m*

dream′land′ *s* pays *m* des songes

dream′ world′ *s* monde *m* des rêves

dream·y ['drimi] *adj* (*comp* -ier; *super* -iest) rêveur; (*slang*) épatant

drear·y ['drɪri] *adj* (*comp* -ier; *super* -iest) triste, morne; monotone

dredge [drɛdʒ] *s* drague *f* ‖ *tr* draguer

dredger ['drɛdʒər] *s* dragueur *m*; (*mach*) drague *f*

dredging ['drɛdʒɪŋ] *s* dragage *m*

dregs [drɛgz] *spl* lie *f*

drench [drɛntʃ] *tr* tremper, inonder

dress [drɛs] *s* habillement *m*, costume *m*; (*woman's attire*) toilette *f*, mise *f*; (*woman's dress*) robe *f* ‖ *tr* habiller, vêtir; (*to apply a dressing to*) panser; (culin) garnir; **to dress down** (coll) passer un savon à, chapitrer; **to dress up** parer; (*ranks*) (mil) aligner; **to get dressed** s'habiller ‖ *intr* s'habiller, se vêtir; (mil) s'aligner; **to dress up** se parer

dress′ ball′ *s* bal *m* paré

dress′ cir′cle *s* corbeille *f*, premier balcon *m*

dress′ coat′ *s* frac *m*

dresser ['drɛsər] *s* coiffeuse *f*; commode *f* à miroir; (*sideboard*) dressoir *m*; **to be a good dresser** être recherché dans sa mise

dress′ form′ *s* mannequin *m*

dress′ goods′ *spl* étoffes *fpl* pour costumes

dressing ['drɛsɪŋ] *s* toilette *f*; (*for food*) assaisonnement *m*, sauce *f*; (*stuffing for fowl*) farce *f*; (*fertilizer*) engrais *m*; (*for a wound*) pansement *m*

dress′ing down′ *s* (coll) savon *m*, verte réprimande *f*, algarade *f*

dress′ing gown′ *s* peignoir *m*, robe *f* de chambre

dress′ing room′ *s* cabinet *m* de toilette; (theat) loge *f*

dress′ing sta′tion *s* poste *m* de secours

dress′ing ta′ble *s* coiffeuse *f*, toilette *f*

dress′mak′er *s* couturière *f*

dress′mak′ing *s* couture *f*

dress′making estab′lishment *s* maison *f* de couture

dress′ rehear′sal *s* répétition *f* en costume; **final dress rehearsal** répétition générale

dress′ shield′ *s* dessous-de-bras *m*

dress′ shirt′ *s* chemise *f* à plastron

dress′ shop′ *s* magasin *m* de modes

dress′ suit′ *s* habit *m* de cérémonie, tenue *f* de soirée

dress′ tie′ *s* cravate *f* de smoking, cravate-plastron *f*

dress′ u′niform *s* (mil) grande tenue *f*

dress·y ['drɛsi] *adj* (*comp* -ier; *super* -iest) (coll) élégant, chic

dribble ['drɪbəl] *s* dégouttement *m*; (*of child*) bave *f*; (sports) dribble *m* ‖ *tr* (sports) dribbler ‖ *intr* dégoutter; (*said of child*) baver; (sports) dribbler

driblet ['drɪblɪt] *s* chiquet *m*; **in driblets** au compte-gouttes

dried′ ap′ple [draɪd] *s* pomme *f* tapée

dried′ beef′ *s* viande *f* boucanée

dried′ fig′ *s* figue *f* sèche

dried′ fruit′ *s* fruit *m* sec

dried′ pear′ *s* poire *f* tapée

drier ['draɪ·ər] *s* (*for clothes*) séchoir *m*, sécheuse *f*; (*for paint*) siccatif *m*; (mach) sécheur *m*

drift [drɪft] *s* dérive *f*; (*of sand, snow*) amoncellement *m*; (*of meaning*) sens *m*, direction *f* ‖ *intr* aller à la dérive; (*said of snow*) s'amonceler; (aer, naut) dériver; (fig) se laisser aller, flotter

drift′ ice′ *s* glaces *fpl* flottantes

drift′wood′ *s* bois *m* flotté

drill [drɪl] *s* foret *m*; (*machine*) perforatrice *f*; (*fabric*) coutil *m*, treillis *m*; (*furrow*) sillon *m*; (*agricultural implement*) semoir *m*; (*in school; on the drill ground*) exercice *m* ‖ *tr* instruire; (*e.g., students*) former, entraîner; (mach) forer; (mil) faire faire l'exercice à; **to drill s.th. into s.o.** seriner q.ch. à qn ‖ *intr* faire l'exercice; former

driller ['drɪlər] *s* foreur *m*

drill′ field′ or **drill′ ground′** *s* terrain *m* d'exercice

drill′mas′ter *s* moniteur *m*; (mil) instructeur *m*

drill′ press′ *s* foreuse *f* à colonnes

drink [drɪŋk] *s* boisson *f*, breuvage *m*; boire *m*, e.g., **food and drink** le boire et le manger ‖ *v* (*pret* **drank** [dræŋk]; *pp* **drunk** [drʌŋk]) *tr* boire; (*e.g., with a meal*) prendre; **to drink down** boire d'un trait ‖ *intr* boire; **to drink out of** (*a glass*) boire dans; (*a bottle*) boire à; **to drink to the health of** boire à la santé de

drinkable ['drɪŋkəbəl] *adj* buvable, potable

drinker ['drɪŋkər] *s* buveur *m*

drink′ing cup′ *s* tasse *f* à boire, gobelet *m*

drink′ing foun′tain *s* fontaine *f* à boire, borne-fontaine *f*

drink′ing song′ *s* chanson *f* à boire

drink′ing trough′ *s* abreuvoir *m*

drink′ing wa′ter s eau f potable
drip [drɪp] s (drop) goutte f; (dripping) égout m, dégouttement m; (person) (slang) cornichon m || v (pret & pp dripped; ger dripping) intr dégoutter, goutter
drip′ cof′fee s café-filtre m
drip′ cof′fee mak′er s cafetière f à filtre
drip′-dry′ adj à séchage rapide; (label on shirt) repassage inutile
dripolator [′drɪpə‚letər] s filtre m à café
drip′ pan′ s égouttoir m
dripping [′drɪpɪŋ] s ruissellement m; **drippings** graisse f de rôti
drive [draɪv] s (in an automobile) promenade f; (road) chaussée f; (vigor) énergie f, initiative f; (fund-raising) campagne f; (push forward) propulsion f; (aut) (point of power application to roadway) traction f; (golf) crossée f; (mach) transmission f; **to go for a drive** faire une promenade en auto || v (pret drove [drov]; pp driven [′drɪvən] tr (an automobile, locomotive, etc.; an animal; a person in an automobile) conduire; (a nail) enfoncer; (a bargain) conclure; (the ball in a game) renvoyer, chasser; (to push, force) pousser, forcer; (to overwork) surmener; **to drive away** chasser; **to drive back** repousser; (e.g., in a car) reconduire; **to drive crazy** rendre fou; **to drive in** enfoncer; **to drive out** chasser; **to drive to despair** conduire au désespoir || intr conduire; **drive slowly** (public sign) marcher au pas; **to drive away** partir, démarrer; **to drive back** rentrer en auto; **to drive on** continuer sa route; **to drive out** sortir
drive′-in′ s (motion-picture theater) cinéma m auto; (restaurant) restoroute m
driv·el [′drɪvəl] s (slobber) bave f; (nonsense) bêtises fpl || v (pret -eled or -elled; ger -eling or -elling) intr baver; (to talk nonsense) radoter
driver [′draɪvər] s chauffeur m, conducteur m; (of a carriage) cocher m; (of a locomotive) mécanicien m; (of pack animals) toucheur m
driv′er's li′cense s permis m de conduire
drive′ shaft′ s arbre m d'entraînement
drive′way′ s voie f de garage, sortie f de voiture
drive′ wheel′ s roue f motrice, roue de transmission
driv′ing school′ s auto-école f
drizzle [′drɪzəl] s pluie f fine, bruine f || intr bruiner, brouillasser
droll [drol] adj drôle, drolatique
dromedar·y [′drɑmə‚dɛri] s (pl -ies) dromadaire m
drone [dron] s bourdonnement m; (of plane or engine) vrombissement m, ronron m; fainéant m; (aer) avion m téléguidé, avion sans pilote; (ent) faux bourdon m || intr bourdonner, ronronner

drool [drul] intr baver
droop [drup] s inclinaison f || intr se baisser; (to lose one's pep) s'alanguir; (bot) languir
drooping [′drupɪŋ] adj languissant
drop [drɑp] s goutte f; (fall) chute f; (slope) précipice m; (depth of drop) hauteur f de chute; (in price; in temperature) baisse f; (lozenge) pastille f; (of supplies from an airplane) droppage m; **a drop in the bucket** une goutte d'eau dans la mer || v (pret & pp dropped; ger dropping) tr laisser tomber; (a curtain; the eyes, voice) baisser; (from an airplane) lâcher; (e.g., a name from a list) omettre, supprimer; (a remark) glisser; (a conversation; relations; negotiations) cesser; (anchor) jeter, mouiller; (an idea, a habit, etc.) renoncer à; **to drop off** déposer || intr tomber; se laisser tomber; baisser; cesser; **to drop in** entrer en passant; **to drop in on** faire un saut chez; **to drop off** se détacher; s'endormir; **to drop out of** (to quit) renoncer à, abandonner
drop′ cur′tain s rideau m d'entracte
drop′ ham′mer s marteau-pilon m
drop′ kick′ s coup m tombé
drop′ leaf′ s abattant m
drop′light′ s lampe f suspendue
drop′out′ s raté m; **to become a drop-out** abandonner les études
dropper [′drɑpər] s compte-gouttes m
dropsy [′drɑpsi] s hydropisie f
drop′ ta′ble s table f à abattants
dross [drɔs], [drɑs] s scories mpl, écume f
drought [draut] s sécheresse f
drove [drov] s troupeau m; (multitude) foule f, flots mpl; **in droves** par bandes
drover [′drovər] s bouvier m
drown [draun] tr noyer; **to drown out** couvrir || intr se noyer
drowse [drauz] intr somnoler, s'assoupir
drow·sy [′drauzi] adj (comp -sier; super -siest) somnolent
drub [drʌb] v (pret & pp drubbed; ger drubbing) tr flanquer une raclée à, rosser
drudge [drʌdʒ] s homme m de peine, piocheur m; **harmless drudge** (e.g., who compiles dictionaries) grattepapier m inoffensif
drudger·y [′drʌdʒəri] s (pl -ies) corvée f, travail m pénible
drug [drʌg] s drogue f, stupéfiant m, produit m pharmaceutique; **drug on the market** rossignol m || v (pret & pp drugged; ger drugging) tr (a person) donner un stupéfiant à, stupéfier; (food or drink) ajouter un stupéfiant à
drug′ ad′dict s toxicomane mf
drug′ addic′tion s toxicomanie f
druggist [′drʌgɪst] s pharmacien m
drug′ hab′it s toxicomanie f, vice m des stupéfiants

drug'store' *s* pharmacie-bazar *f*, pharmacie *f*
drug' traf'fic *s* trafic *m* des stupéfiants
druid ['dru-ɪd] *s* druide *m*
drum [drʌm] *s* (*cylinder; instrument of percussion*) tambour *m*; (*container for oil, gasoline, etc.*) bidon *m*; **to play the drum** battre du tambour || *v* (*pret & pp* **drummed;** *ger* **drumming**) *tr* (*e.g., a march*) tambouriner; rassembler au son du tambour; **to drum into** fourrer dans; **to drum up customers** racoler des clients || *intr* jouer du tambour; (*with the fingers*) tambouriner; (*on the piano*) pianoter
drum' and bu'gle corps' *s* clairons et tambours *mpl*, clique *f*
drum' beat' *s* coup *m* de tambour
drum'fire' *s* (mil) tir *m* nourri, feu *m* roulant
drum'head' *s* peau *f* de tambour; (naut) noix *f*
drum' ma'jor *s* tambour-major *m*
drummer ['drʌmər] *s* tambour *m*; (*salesman*) (coll) commis *m* voyageur
drum'stick' *s* baguette *f* de tambour; (*of chicken*) (coll) cuisse *f*, pilon *m*
drunk [drʌŋk] *adj* ivre, soûl; **to get drunk** s'enivrer; **to get s.o. drunk** enivrer qn || *s* (*person*) (coll) ivrogne *m*; (*state*) ivresse *f*; **to go on a drunk** (coll) se soûler
drunkard ['drʌŋkərd] *s* ivrogne *m*
drunken ['drʌŋkən] *adj* enivré
drunk'en driv'ing *s* conduite *f* en état d'ivresse
drunkenness ['drʌŋkənnɪs] *s* ivresse *f*
dry [draɪ] *adj* (*comp* **drier;** *super* **driest**) sec; (*thirsty*) assoiffé; (*boring*) aride || *s* (*pl* **drys**) (*prohibitionist*) antialcoolique *mf* || *v* (*pret & pp* **dried**) *tr* sécher; (*the dishes*) essuyer || *intr* sécher; **to dry up** se dessécher; (slang) se taire
dry' bat'tery *s* pile *f* sèche; (*number of dry cells*) batterie *f* de piles
dry' cell' *s* pile *f* sèche
dry'-clean' *tr* nettoyer à sec
dry' clean'er *s* nettoyeur *m* à sec, teinturier *m*
dry' clean'er's *s* teinturerie *f*
dry' clean'ing *s* nettoyage *m* à sec
dry' dock' *s* cale *f* sèche, bassin *m* de radoub
dry'-eyed' *adj* d'un œil sec
dry' goods' *spl* tissus *mpl*, étoffes *fpl*
dry' ice' *s* glace *f* sèche
dry' land' *s* terre *f* ferme
dry' meas'ure *s* mesure *f* à grains
dryness ['draɪnɪs] *s* sécheresse *f*; (*e.g., of a speaker*) aridité *f*
dry' nurse' *s* nourrice *f* sèche
dry' rot' *s* carie *f* sèche
dry' run' *s* exercice *m* simulé, répétition *f*, examen *m* blanc
dry' sea'son *s* saison *f* sèche
dry' wash' *s* blanchissage *m* sans repassage
dual ['d(j)u-əl] *adj* double || *s* duel *m*
dub [dʌb] *s* (slang) balourd *m* || *v* (*pret & pp* **dubbed;** *ger* **dubbing**) *tr* (*to nickname*) donner un sobriquet à; (*to*

knight) donner l'accolade à, adouber; (*a tape recording or movie film*) doubler
dubbing ['dʌbɪŋ] *s* (mov) doublage *m*
dubious ['d(j)ubɪ-əs] *adj* (*undecided*) hésitant; (*questionable*) douteux
ducat ['dʌkət] *s* ducat *m*
duchess ['dʌtʃɪs] *s* duchesse *f*
duch·y ['dʌtʃi] *s* (*pl* **-ies**) duché *m*
duck [dʌk] *s* canard *m*; (*female*) cane *f*; (*motion*) esquive *f*; **ducks** (*trousers*) pantalon *m* de coutil || *tr* (*the head*) baisser || *intr* se baisser; **to duck out** (coll) s'esquiver
ducking ['dʌkɪŋ] *s* plongeon *m*, bain *m* forcé
duckling ['dʌklɪŋ] *s* caneton *m*; (*female*) canette *f*
ducks' and drakes' *s*—**to play at ducks and drakes** faire des ricochets sur l'eau; (fig) jeter son argent par les fenêtres
duck'-toed' *adj* qui marche en canard
duct [dʌkt] *s* conduit *m*, canal *m*
duct'less glands' ['dʌktlɪs] *spl* glandes *fpl* closes
duct'work' *s* tuyauterie *f*, canalisation *f*
dud [dʌd] *s* (slang) obus *m* qui a raté; (slang) raté *m*, navet *m*; **duds** (*clothes*) (coll) frusques *fpl*, nippes *fpl*
dude [d(j)ud] *s* poseur *m*, gommeux *m*
dude' ranch' *s* ranch *m* d'opérette
due [d(j)u] *adj* dû; (*note*) échéant; (*bill*) exigible; (*train, bus, person*) attendu; **due to** par suite de; **in due form** en bonne forme, en règle; **to fall due** venir à l'échéance; **when is the train due?** à quelle heure doit arriver le train? || *s* dû *m*; **dues** cotisation *f*; **to pay one's dues** cotiser || *adv* droit vers, e.g., **due north** droit vers le nord
due' date' *s* échéance *f*
duel ['d(j)u-əl] *s* duel *m*; **to fight a duel** se battre en duel || *v* (*pret & pp* **dueled** or **duelled;** *ger* **dueling** or **duelling**) *intr* se battre en duel
duelist or **duellist** ['d(j)u-əlɪst] *s* duelliste *m*
duenna [d(j)u'ɛnə] *s* duègne *f*
dues'-pay'ing *adj* cotisant
duet [d(j)u'ɛt] *s* duo *m*
duke [d(j)uk] *s* duc *m*
dukedom ['d(j)ukdəm] *s* duché *m*
dull [dʌl] *adj* (*not sharp*) émoussé; (*color*) terne; (*sound; pain*) sourd; (*stupid*) lourd; (*business*) lent; (*boring*) ennuyeux; (*flat*) fade, insipide; **to become dull** s'émousser; (*said of senses*) s'engourdir || *tr* (*a knife*) émousser; (*color*) ternir; (*sound; pain*) amortir; (*spirits*) hébéter, engourdir || *intr* s'émousser; se ternir; s'amortir; s'engourdir
dullard ['dʌlərd] *s* lourdaud *m*, hébété *m*
dullness ['dʌlnɪs] *s* (*of knife*) émoussement *m*; (*e.g., of wits*) lenteur *f*
duly ['d(j)uli] *adv* dûment, justement
dumb [dʌm] *adj* (*lacking the power to speak*) muet; (coll) gourde, imbécile;

completely dumb (coll) bouché à l'émeri; **to play dumb** (coll) feindre l'innocence
dumb'bell' *s* (sports) haltère *m*; (slang) gourde *f*, imbécile *mf*
dumb' crea'ture *s* animal *m*, brute *f*
dumb'wait'er *s* monte-plats *m*; (*serving table*) table *f* roulante
dumfound ['dʌm,faund] *tr* abasourdir, ébahir
dum·my ['dʌmi] *adj* faux, factice || *s* (*pl* **-mies**) (*dress form*) mannequin; (*in card games*) mort *m*; (*figurehead, straw man*) prête-nom *m*, homme *m* de paille; (*skeleton copy of a book or magazine*) maquette *f*; (*object put in place of the real thing*) simulacre *m*; (slang) bêta *m*, ballot *m*
dump [dʌmp] *s* (*pile of rubbish*) amas *m*, tas *m*; (*place*) dépotoir *m*; (mil) dépôt *m*; (slang) taudis *m*; **to be down in the dumps** (coll) avoir le cafard || *tr* décharger, déverser; (*on rubbish pile*) jeter au rebut; (com) vendre en faisant du dumping
dumping ['dʌmpɪŋ] *s* (com) dumping *m*
dumpling ['dʌmplɪŋ] *s* dumpling *m*, boulette *f*
dump' truck' *s* tombereau *m*
dump·y ['dʌmpi] *adj* (*comp* **-ier**; *super* **-iest**) (*short and fat*) courtaud, trapu; (*shabby*) râpé, minable
dun [dʌn] *adj* isabelle || *s* créancier *m* importun; (*demand for payment*) demande *f* pressante || *v* (*pret & pp* **dunned**; *ger* **dunning**) *tr* (*for payment*) importuner, poursuivre
dunce [dʌns] *s* âne *m*, cancre *m*
dunce' cap' *s* bonnet *m* d'âne
dune [d(j)un] *s* dune *f*
dung [dʌŋ] *s* fumier *m*
dungarees [,dʌŋgə'riz] *spl* pantalon *m* de treillis, treillis *m*, bleu *m*
dungeon ['dʌndʒən] *s* cachot *m*, cul-de-basse-fosse *m*; (*keep of castle*) donjon *m*
dung'hill' *s* tas *m* de fumier
dunk [dʌŋk] *tr & intr* tremper
du·o ['d(j)u·o] *s* (*pl* **-os**) duo *m*
duode·num [,d(j)u·ə'dinəm] *s* (*pl* **-na** [nə]) duodénum *m*
dupe [d(j)up] *s* dupe *f*, dindon *m* de la farce || *tr* duper
duplex ['d(j)upleks] *adj* double, duplex || *s* maison *f* double
du'plex house' *s* maison *f* double
duplicate ['d(j)uplɪkɪt] *adj* double || *s* duplicata *m*, polycopie *f*; **in duplicate** en double, en duplicata || ['d(j)uplɪ-,ket] *tr* faire le double de, reproduire; (*on a machine*) polycopier, ronéocopier
du'plicating machine' *s* duplicateur *m*
duplici·ty [d(j)u'plɪsɪti] *s* (*pl* **-ties**) duplicité *f*
durable ['d(j)urəbəl] *adj* durable
duration [d(j)u're/ən] *s* durée *f*
duress ['d(j)ures], [d(j)u'res] *s* contrainte *f*; emprisonnement *m*
during ['d(j)urɪŋ] *prep* pendant

dusk [dʌsk] *s* crépuscule *m*; **at dusk** entre chien et loup
dust [dʌst] *s* poussière *f* || *tr* (*to free of dust*) épousseter; (*to sprinkle with dust*) saupoudrer; **to dust off** épousseter
dust' bowl' *s* région *f* dénudée
dust'cloth' *s* chiffon *m* à épousseter
dust' cloud' *s* nuage *m* de poussière
duster ['dʌstər] *s* (*made of feathers*) plumeau *m*; (*made of cloth*) chiffon *m*; (*overgarment*) cache-poussière *m*
dust' jack'et *s* protège-livre *m*, couvre-livre *m*, liseuse *f*
dust'pan' *s* pelle *f* à ordures
dust' rag' *s* chiffon *m* à épousseter
dust·y ['dʌsti] *adj* (*comp* **-ier**; *super* **-iest**) poussiéreux; (*color*) cendré
Dutch [dʌtʃ] *adj* hollandais, néerlandais; (slang) allemand || *s* (*language*) hollandais *m*, néerlandais *m*; (slang) allemand *m*; **in Dutch** (slang) en disgrâce; **the Dutch** les Hollandais *mpl*, les Néerlandais *mpl*; (slang) les Allemands *mpl*; **we will go Dutch** (coll) chacun paiera son écot
Dutch'man *s* (*pl* **-men**) Hollandais *m*, Néerlandais *m*; (slang) Allemand *m*
Dutch' treat' *s*—**to have a Dutch treat** (coll) faire suisse, payer son écot
dutiable ['d(j)utɪ·əbəl] *adj* soumis aux droits de douane
dutiful ['d(j)utɪfəl] *adj* respectueux, soumis, plein d'égards
du·ty ['d(j)uti] *s* (*pl* **-ties**) devoir *m*; **duties** fonctions *fpl*; (*taxes, customs*) droits *mpl*; **to be off duty** ne pas être de service, avoir quartier libre; **to be on duty** être de service, être de garde
du'ty-free' *adj* exempt de droits
dwarf [dwɔrf] *adj & s* nain *m* || *tr & intr* rapetisser
dwell [dwel] *v* (*pret & pp* **dwelled** or **dwelt** [dwelt]) *intr* demeurer; **to dwell on** appuyer sur
dwelling ['dwelɪŋ] *s* demeure *f*, habitation *f*
dwell'ing house' *s* maison *f* d'habitation
dwindle ['dwɪndəl] *intr* diminuer; **to dwindle away** s'affaiblir
dye [daɪ] *s* teinture *f* || *v* (*pret & pp* **dyed**; *ger* **dyeing**) *tr* teindre
dyed'-in-the-wool' *adj* intransigeant
dyeing ['daɪ·ɪŋ] *s* teinture *f*
dyer ['daɪ·ər] *s* teinturier *m*
dying ['daɪ·ɪŋ] *adj* mourant, moribond
dynamic [daɪ'næmɪk], [dɪ'næmɪk] *adj* dynamique || **dynamics** *s* dynamique *f*
dynamite ['daɪnə,maɪt] *s* dynamite *f* || *tr* dynamiter
dyna·mo ['daɪnə,mo] *s* (*pl* **-mos**) dynamo *f*
dynast ['daɪnæst] *s* dynaste *m*
dynas·ty ['daɪnəsti] *s* (*pl* **-ties**) dynastie *f*
dysentery ['dɪsən,teri] *s* dysenterie *f*
dyspepsia [dɪs'pɛpsɪ·ə], [dɪs'pɛpʃə] *s* dyspepsie *f*

E

E, e [i] *s* Vᵉ lettre de l'alphabet
each [itʃ] *adj indef* chaque ‖ *pron
indef* chacun; **each other** nous, se;
l'un l'autre; **to each other** l'un à
l'autre ‖ *adv* chacun; *(apiece)* pièce,
la pièce
eager ['igər] *adj* ardent, empressé;
eager for avide de; **to be eager to**
brûler de, désirer ardemment
ea′ger bea′ver *s* bûcheur *m*, mouche *f*
du coche
eagerness ['igərnıs] *s* ardeur *f*, empressement *m*
eagle ['igəl] *s* aigle *m*
ea′gle-eyed′ *adj* à l'œil d'aigle
ea′gle ray′ *s* (ichth) aigle *m* de mer
eaglet ['iglıt] *s* aiglon *m*
ear [ɪr] *s* oreille *f*; *(of corn or wheat)*
épi *m*; **to box s.o.'s ears** frotter les
oreilles à qn; **to prick up one's ears**
dresser l'oreille; **to turn a deaf ear**
faire la sourde oreille ‖ *intr (said of
grain)* épier
ear′ache′ *s* douleur *m* d'oreille
ear′drop′ *s* pendant *m* d'oreille
ear′drum′ *s* tympan *m*
ear′flap′ *s* lobe *m* de l'oreille; *(on a
cap)* protège-oreilles *m*
earl [ʌrl] *s* comte *m*
earldom ['ʌrldəm] *s* comté *m*
ear·ly ['ʌrli] *(comp* -lier; *super* -liest)
adj primitif; *(first in a series)* premier; *(occurring in the near future)*
prochain; *(in the morning)* matinal;
(ahead of time) en avance; **at an
early age** dès l'enfance ‖ *adv* de
bonne heure, tôt; anciennement; **as
early as** dès
ear′ly bird′ *s* matinal *m*
car′ly mass′ *s* première messe *f*
ear′ly-morn′ing *adj* matinal
ear′ly ris′er *s* matinal *m*
ear′ly-ris′ing *adj* matineux, matinal
ear′mark′ *s* marque *f*, cachet *m* ‖ *tr*
(animals) marquer à l'oreille; *(e.g.,
money)* spécialiser; **to earmark for**
affecter à, assigner à
ear′muff′ *s* couvre-oreille *m*
earn [ʌrn] *tr* gagner; *(to get as one's
due)* mériter; *(interest)* rapporter
earnest ['ʌrnıst] *adj* sérieux; **in earnest**
sérieusement ‖ *s* gage *m*; (com)
arrhes *fpl*
earnings ['ʌrnɪŋz] *spl (wages)* gages
mpl; *(profits)* profit *m*, bénéfices
mpl
ear′phone′ *s* écouteur *m*; **earphones**
casque *m*, écouteurs
ear′ring′ *s* boucle *f* d'oreille
ear′split′ting *adj* assourdissant
earth [ʌrθ] *s* terre *f*; **to come down to
earth** retomber des nues; **where on
earth . . . ?** où diable . . . ?
earthen ['ʌrθən] *adj* de terre, en terre
ear′then·ware′ *s* faïence *f*
earthly ['ʌrθli] *adj* terrestre
earth′man′ or **earth′·man** *s (pl* **men′** or
men) terrien *m*

earth′quake′ *s* tremblement *m* de terre
earth′work′ *s* terrassement *m*
earth′worm′ *s* lombric *m*, ver *m* de
terre
earth·y ['ʌrθi] *adj (comp* -ier; *super*
-iest) terreux; *(worldly)* mondain;
(unrefined) grossier, terre à terre
ear′ trum′pet *s* cornet *m* acoustique
ease [iz] *s* aise *f*; *(readiness, naturalness)* désinvolture *f*; *(comfort, well-
being)* bien-être *m*, tranquillité *f*; **at
ease** tranquille; (mil) au repos; **to
take one's ease** prendre ses aises;
with ease facilement ‖ *tr* faciliter; *(a
burden)* alléger; *(e.g., one's mind)*
calmer, apaiser; *(to let up on)* ralentir ‖ *intr* se calmer, s'apaiser
easel ['izəl] *s* chevalet *m*
easement ['izmənt] *s* (law) servitude *f*
easily ['izıli] *adv* facilement, aisément;
(certainly) sans doute
easiness ['izınıs] *s* facilité *f*; *(of manner)* désinvolture *f*, insouciance *f*
east [ist] *adj* & *s* est *m* ‖ *adv* à l'est,
vers l'est
Easter ['istər] *s* Pâques *m*; **Happy
Easter!** Joyeuses Pâques!
East′er egg′ *s* œuf *m* de Pâques
East′er Mon′day *s* lundi *m* de Pâques
eastern ['istərn] *adj* oriental, de l'est
East′ern Stand′ard Time′ *s* l'heure *f* de
l'Est
East′ern Town′ships *spl (in Canada)*
Cantons *mpl* de l'Est
eastward ['istwərd] *adv* vers l'est
eas·y ['izi] *adj (comp* -ier; *super* -iest)
facile; *(easygoing)* aisé, désinvolte ‖
adv (coll) facilement; (coll) lentement; **to take it easy** (coll) en prendre à son aise
eas′y chair′ *s* fauteuil *m*, bergère *f*
eas′y·go′ing *adj* insouciant, nonchalant, commode à vivre
eas′y mark′ *s* jobard *m*
eas′y pay′ments *spl* facilités *fpl* de
paiement
eat [it] *v (pret* **ate** [et]; *pp* **eaten**
['itən]) *tr* manger; **to eat away** ronger ‖ *intr* manger
eatable ['itəbəl] *adj* comestible
eaves [ivz] *spl* avant-toits *mpl*
eaves′drop′ *v (pret* & *pp* **-dropped**; *ger*
-dropping) *intr* écouter à la porte
ebb [eb] *s* reflux *m*, baisse *f* ‖ *intr*
refluer, baisser; **to ebb and flow**
monter et baisser, fluer et refluer
ebb′ and flow′ *s* flux et reflux *m*
ebb′ tide′ *s* marée *f* descendante, jusant
m
ebon·y ['ɛbəni] *s (pl* -ies) ébène *f*;
(tree) ébénier *m*
ebullient [ɪ'bʌljənt] *adj* bouillonnant;
(fig) enthousiaste, exubérant
eccentric [ɛk'sentrık] *adj* excentrique
‖ *s (odd person)* excentrique *mf*; *(device)* excentrique *m*

eccentrici·ty [ˌɛksɛn'trɪsɪti] *s* (*pl* -ties) excentricité *f*
ecclesiastic [ɪˌklizɪ'æstɪk] *adj* & *s* ecclésiastique *m*
echelon ['ɛʃəˌlɑn] *s* échelon *m* ‖ *tr* (mil) échelonner
ech·o ['ɛko] *s* (*pl* -oes) écho *m* ‖ *tr* répéter ‖ *intr* faire écho
eclectic [ɛk'lɛktɪk] *adj* & *s* éclectique *mf*
eclipse [ɪ'klɪps] *s* éclipse *f* ‖ *tr* éclipser
eclogue ['ɛklɔg], ['ɛklɑg] *s* églogue *f*
ecology [ɪ'kɑlədʒi] *s* écologie *f*
economic [ˌikə'nɑmɪk], [ˌɛkə'nɑmɪk] *adj* économique ‖ **economics** *s* économique *f*
economical [ˌikə'nɑmɪkəl], [ˌɛkə'nɑmɪkəl] *adj* économe
economize [ɪ'kɑnəˌmaɪz] *tr* & *intr* économiser
econo·my [ɪ'kɑnəmi] *s* (*pl* -mies) économie *f*
ecsta·sy ['ɛkstəsi] *s* (*pl* -sies) extase *f*
ecstatic [ɛk'stætɪk] *adj* & *s* extatique *mf*
Ecuador ['ɛkwəˌdɔr] *s* l'Équateur *m*
ecumenic(al) [ˌɛkjə'mɛnɪk(əl)] *adj* œcuménique
eczema ['ɛksɪmə], [ɛg'zimə] *s* eczéma *m*
ed·dy ['ɛdi] *s* (*pl* -dies) tourbillon *m* ‖ *v* (*pret* & *pp* -died) *intr* tourbillonner
edelweiss ['ɛdəlˌvaɪs] *s* edelweiss *m*, fleur *f* de neige
Eden ['idən] *s* (fig) éden *m*
edge [ɛdʒ] *s* bord *m*; (*of a knife, sword, etc.*) fil *m*, tranchant *m*; (*of a field, forest, etc.*; *of a strip of cloth*) lisière *f*; · (slang) avantage *m*; **on edge** de chant; (*nervous*) énervé, crispé; **to be on edge** avoir les nerfs à fleur de peau; **to have the edge on** (coll) enfoncer; **to set the teeth on edge** agacer les dents ‖ *tr* border; (*to sharpen*) affiler, aiguiser ‖ *intr* s'avancer de biais; **to edge away** s'écarter peu à peu; **to edge in** se glisser parmi or dans
edge'ways' *adv* de côté, de biais
edging ['ɛdʒɪŋ] *s* bordure *f*
edg·y ['ɛdʒi] *adj* (*comp* -ier; *super* -iest) (*nervous*) crispé, irritable
edible ['ɛdɪbəl] *adj* comestible
edict ['idɪkt] *s* édit *m*
edification [ˌɛdɪfɪ'keʃən] *s* édification *f*
edifice ['ɛdɪfɪs] *s* édifice *m*
edi·fy ['ɛdɪˌfaɪ] *v* (*pret* & *pp* -fied) *tr* édifier
edifying ['ɛdɪˌfaɪ·ɪŋ] *adj* édifiant
edit ['ɛdɪt] *tr* préparer la publication de; (*e.g., a newspaper*) diriger, rédiger; (*a text*) éditer
edition [ɪ'dɪʃən] *s* édition *f*
editor ['ɛdɪtər] *s* (*of newspaper or magazine*) rédacteur *m*; (*of manuscript*) éditeur *m*; (*of feature or column*) chroniqueur *m*, courriériste *mf*
editorial [ˌɛdɪ'torɪ·əl] *adj* & *s* éditorial *m*
edito'rial of'fice *s* rédaction *f*

edito'rial pol'icy *s* ligne *f* politique
edito'rial staff' *s* rédaction *f*
ed'itor in chief' *s* rédacteur *m* en chef
educate ['ɛdʒuˌket] *tr* instruire, éduquer
educated *adj* cultivé, instruit
education [ˌɛdʒu'keʃən] *s* éducation *f*, instruction *f*
educational [ˌɛdʒu'keʃənəl] *adj* éducatif, éducateur
educator ['ɛdʒuˌketər] *s* éducateur *m*
eel [il] *s* anguille *f*
ee·rie or **ee·ry** ['ɪri] *adj* (*comp* -rier; *super* -riest) mystérieux, spectral
efface [ɪ'fes] *tr* effacer
effect [ɪ'fɛkt] *s* effet *m*; **in effect** en fait, effectivement; **to be in effect** être en vigueur; **to feel the effects of** se ressentir de; **to go into effect, to take effect** prendre effet; (*said of law*) entrer en vigueur ‖ *tr* effectuer, mettre à exécution
effective [ɪ'fɛktɪv] *adj* efficace; (*actually in effect*) en vigueur; (*striking*) impressionnant; **to become effective** produire son effet; (*to go into effect*) entrer en vigueur
effectual [ɪ'fɛktʃu·əl] *adj* efficace
effectuate [ɪ'fɛktʃu ˌet] *tr* effectuer
effeminacy [ɪ'fɛmɪnəsi] *s* effémination *f*
effeminate [ɪ'fɛmɪnɪt] *adj* efféminé; **to become effeminate** s'efféminer
effervesce [ˌɛfər'vɛs] *intr* être en effervescence
effervescent [ˌɛfər'vɛsənt] *adj* effervescent
effete [ɪ'fit] *adj* stérile, épuisé
efficacious [ˌɛfɪ'keʃəs] *adj* efficace
efficacy ['ɛfɪkəsi] *s* efficacité *f*
efficien·cy [ɪ'fɪʃənsi] *s* (*pl* -cies) efficacité *f*; (*of business*) efficience *f*; (*of machine*) rendement *m*; (*of person*) compétence *f*
effi'ciency ex'pert *s* ingénieur *m* en organisation
efficient [ɪ'fɪʃənt] *adj* efficace; (*of machine*) efficient, de bon rendement; (*of person*) efficient, compétent
effi·gy ['ɛfɪdʒi] *s* (*pl* -gies) effigie *f*
effort ['ɛfərt] *s* effort *m*
effronter·y [ɪ'frʌntəri] *s* (*pl* -ies) effronterie *f*
effusion [ɪ'fjuʒən] *s* effusion *f*
effusive [ɪ'fjusɪv] *adj* démonstratif; **to be effusive** in se répandre en
e.g. *abbr* (Lat: *exempli gratia* for example) par ex., ex.
egg [ɛg] *s* œuf *m* ‖ *tr*—**to egg on** pousser, inciter
egg'beat'er *s* fouet *m*, batteur *m* à œufs
egg'cup' *s* coquetier *m*
egg'head' *s* (slang) intellectuel *m*
eggnog ['ɛgˌnɑg] *s* lait *m* de poule
egg'plant' *s* aubergine *f*
egg' poach'er *s* pocheuse *f*
egg'shell' *s* coquille *f* d'œuf
egg' white' *s* blanc *m* d'œuf
egoism ['ɛgoˌɪzəm], ['igoˌɪzəm] *s* égoïsme *m*

egoist ['ego·ɪst], ['igo·ɪst] s égoïste m/
egotism ['ɛgo‚tɪzəm], ['igo‚tɪzəm] s
égotisme m
egotist ['ɛgotɪst], ['igotɪst] s égotiste
m/
egregious [ɪ'gridʒəs] adj insigne, notoire
egress ['igrɛs] s sortie f, issue f
egret ['igrɛt] s aigrette f
Egypt ['idʒɪpt] s Égypte f; l'Égypte
Egyptian [ɪ'dʒɪpʃən] adj égyptien || s
Égyptien m
ei'der down' ['aɪdər] s édredon m
ei'der duck' s eider m
eight [et] adj & pron huit || s huit m;
(group of eight) huitaine f; about
eight une huitaine de; eight o'clock
huit heures
eight'ball' s—behind the eightball
(coll) dans le pétrin
eighteen ['et'tin] adj, pron, & s dix-
huit m
eighteenth ['et'tinθ] adj & pron dix-
huitième (masc, fem); the Eighteenth
dix-huit, e.g., John the Eighteenth
Jean dix-huit || s dix-huitième m; the
eighteenth (in dates) le dix-huit
eighth [etθ] adj & pron huitième (masc,
fem); the Eighth huit, e.g., John the
Eighth Jean huit || s huitième m; the
eighth (in dates) le huit
eightieth ['etɪ·ɪθ] adj & pron quatre-
vingtième (masc, fem) || s quatre-
vingtième m
eigh·ty ['eti] adj & pron quatre-vingts
|| s (pl -ties) quatre-vingts m
eight'y-first' adj & pron quatre-vingt-
unième (masc, fem) || s quatre-vingt-
unième m
eight'y-one' adj, pron, & s quatre-vingt-
un m
either ['iðər], ['aɪðər] adj & pron
indef l'un ou l'autre; l'un et l'autre;
on either side de chaque côté || adv—
not either non plus || conj—either
. . . or ou . . . ou, soit . . . soit, ou
bien . . . ou bien
ejaculate [ɪ'dʒækjə‚let] tr & intr crier;
(physiol) éjaculer
eject [ɪ'dʒɛkt] tr éjecter; (to evict) expulser, chasser
ejection [ɪ'dʒɛkʃən] s éjection f; (eviction) expulsion f
ejec'tion seat' s (aer) siège m éjectable
eke [ik] tr—to eke out gagner avec
difficulté
elaborate [ɪ'læbərɪt] adj élaboré,
soigné; (ornate) orné, travaillé; (in-
volved) compliqué, recherché ||
[ɪ'læbə‚ret] tr élaborer || intr—to
elaborate on or upon donner des détails sur
elapse [ɪ'læps] intr s'écouler
elastic [ɪ'læstɪk] adj & s élastique m
elasticity [ɪ‚læs'tɪsɪti], [‚ɪlæs'tɪsɪti] s
élasticité f
elated [ɪ'letɪd] adj transporté, exalté
elation [ɪ'leʃən] s transport m, exulta-
tion f
elbow ['ɛlbo] s coude m; at one's
elbow à portée de la main; to rub

elbows with coudoyer || tr coudoyer;
to elbow one's way se frayer un
chemin à coups de coude || intr jouer
des coudes
el'bow grease' s (coll) huile f de coude
el'bow·room' s espace m; to have elbowroom avoir ses coudées franches
elder ['ɛldər] adj aîné, plus âgé || s
aîné m; (senior) doyen m; (bot) sureau m; (eccl) ancien m
el'der·ber'ry s (pl -ries) sureau m;
(berry) baie f de sureau
elderly ['ɛldərli] adj vieux, âgé
eld'er states'man s vétéran m de la politique
eldest ['ɛldɪst] adj (l')aîné, (le) plus âgé
elect [ɪ'lɛkt] adj élu || s—the elect les
élus mpl || tr élire
election [ɪ'lɛkʃən] s élection f
electioneer [ɪ‚lɛkʃə'nɪr] intr faire la
campagne électorale, solliciter des
voix
elective [ɪ'lɛktɪv] adj électif; (optional)
facultatif || s matière f à option
elec'toral col'lege [ɪ'lɛktərəl] s collège
m électoral
electorate [ɪ'lɛktərɪt] s corps m électoral, électeurs mpl, votants mpl
electric(al) [ɪ'lɛktrɪk(əl)] adj électrique
elec'trical engineer' s ingénieur m électricien
elec'trical engineer'ing s technique f
électrique
elec'tric blan'ket s couverture f chauffante
elec'tric chair' s chaise f électrique
elec'tric clothes' dri'er s séchoir m
électrique
elec'tric eel' s gymnote m
elec'tric eye' s cellule f photo-électri-
que
elec'tric fan' s ventilateur m électrique
elec'tric heat'er s radiateur m électrique
electrician [ɪ‚lɛk'trɪʃən], [‚ɪlɛk'trɪʃən]
s électricien m
electricity [ɪ‚lɛk'trɪsɪti], [‚ɪlɛk'trɪsɪti]
s électricité f
elec'tric light' s lampe f électrique
elec'tric me'ter s compteur m de courant
elec'tric mix'er s batteur m électrique
elec'tric per'colator s cafetière f électrique
elec'tric range' s cuisinière f électrique
elec'tric shav'er s rasoir m électrique
elec'tric shock' treat'ment s (med) électrochoc m
electri·fy [ɪ'lɛktrɪ‚faɪ] v (pret & pp
-fied) tr (to provide with electric
power) électrifier; (to communicate
electricity to; to thrill) électriser
elec·tro [ɪ'lɛktro] s (pl -tros) électrotype m
electrocute [ɪ'lɛktrə‚kjut] tr électrocuter
electrode [ɪ'lɛktrod] s électrode f
electrolysis [ɪ‚lɛk'trɑlɪsɪs], [‚ɛlɛk-
'trɑlɪsɪs] s électrolyse f
electrolyte [ɪ'lɛktrə‚laɪt] s électrolyte m
electromagnet [ɪ‚lɛktrə'mægnɪt] s électro-aimant m

electromagnetic [ɪˌlɛktrəmæg'nɛtɪk] *adj* électromagnétique
electron [ɪ'lɛktrɑn] *s* électron *m*
elec'tron gun' *s* canon *m* à électrons
electronic [ɪˌlɛk'trɑnɪk], [ˌɛlɛk'trɑnɪk] *adj* électronique ‖ **electronics** *s* électronique *f*
elec'tron mi'croscope *s* microscope *m* électronique
electroplate [ɪ'lɛktrəˌplet] *tr* galvaniser
electrotype [ɪ'lɛktrəˌtaɪp] *s* électrotype *m* ‖ *tr* électrotyper
elegance ['ɛlɪgəns] *s* élégance *f*
elegant ['ɛlɪgənt] *adj* élégant
elegiac [ˌɛlɪ'dʒaɪ·æk] [ɪ'lidʒɪˌæk] *adj* élégiaque
ele·gy ['ɛlɪdʒɪ] *s* (*pl* **-gies**) élégie *f*
element ['ɛlɪmənt] *s* élément *m*
elementary [ˌɛlɪ'mɛntərɪ] *adj* élémentaire
elephant ['ɛlɪfənt] *s* éléphant *m*
elevate ['ɛlɪˌvet] *tr* élever
elevated *adj* élevé; (*style*) soutenu; (*train, railway, etc*) aérien
el'evated rail'way *s* métro *m* aérien
elevation [ˌɛlɪ've/ən] *s* élévation *f*
elevator ['ɛlɪˌvetər] *s* ascenseur *m*; (*for freight*) monte-charge *m*; (*for hoisting grain*) élévateur *m*; (*warehouse for storing grain*) silo *m* à céréales; (aer) gouvernail *m* d'altitude, gouvernail de profondeur
eleven [ɪ'lɛvən] *adj & pron* onze ‖ *s* onze *m*; **eleven o'clock** onze heures
eleventh [ɪ'lɛvənθ] *adj & pron* onzième (*masc, fem*); **the Eleventh** onze, e.g., **John the Eleventh** Jean onze ‖ *s* onzième *m*; **the eleventh** (*in dates*) le onze
elev'enth hour' *s* dernier moment *m*
elf [ɛlf] *s* (*pl* **elves** [ɛlvz]) elfe *m*
elicit [ɪ'lɪsɪt] *tr* (*e.g., a smile*) provoquer, faire sortir; (*e.g., help*) obtenir
elide [ɪ'laɪd] *tr* élider
eligible ['ɛlɪdʒɪbəl] *adj* éligible; (*e.g., bachelor*) sortable
eliminate [ɪ'lɪmɪˌnet] *tr* éliminer
elision [ɪ'lɪʒən] *s* élision *f*
elite [e'lit] *s* élite *f*
elk [ɛlk] *s* élan *m*
ellipse [ɪ'lɪps] *s* (geom) ellipse *f*
ellip·sis [ɪ'lɪpsɪs] *s* (*pl* **-ses** [siz]) ellipse *f*; (*punctuation*) points *mpl* de suspension
elliptic(al) [ɪ'lɪptɪk(əl)] *adj* elliptique
elm [ɛlm] *s* orme *m*
elongate [ɪ'lɔŋget], [ɪ'lɑŋget] *tr* allonger, prolonger
elope [ɪ'lop] *intr* s'enfuir avec un amant
elopement [ɪ'lopmənt] *s* enlèvement *m* consenti
eloquence ['ɛləkwəns] *s* éloquence *f*
eloquent ['ɛləkwənt] *adj* éloquent
else [ɛls] *adj*—**nobody else** personne d'autre; **nothing else** rien d'autre; **somebody else** quelqu'un d'autre, un autre; **something else** autre chose; **what else** quoi encore; **who else** qui encore; **who's else** de qui d'autre ‖ *adv* d'une autre façon, autrement; **how(ever) else** de toute autre façon;

nowhere else nulle part ailleurs; **or else** sinon, ou bien, sans quoi; **somewhere else** ailleurs, autre part; **when else** quand encore; **where else** où encore
else'where' *adv* ailleurs, autre part
elucidate [ɪ'lusɪˌdet] *tr* élucider
elude [ɪ'lud] *tr* éluder, se soustraire à; (*a pursuer*) échapper à
elusive [ɪ'lusɪv] *adj* évasif, fuyant; (*baffling*) insaisissable, déconcertant
emaciated [ɪ'me/ɪˌetɪd] *adj* émacié; **to become emaciated** s'émacier
emanate ['ɛməˌnet] *intr* émaner
emancipate [ɪ'mænsɪˌpet] *tr* émanciper
embalm [ɛm'bɑm] *tr* embaumer
embalming [ɛm'bɑmɪŋ] *s* embaumement *m*
embankment [ɛm'bæŋkmənt] *s* (*of river*) digue *f*; (*of road*) remblai *m*
embar·go [ɛm'bɑrgo] *s* (*pl* **-goes**) embargo *m* ‖ *tr* mettre un embargo sur
embark [ɛm'bɑrk] *intr* s'embarquer
embarkation [ˌɛmbɑr'keʃən] *s* embarquement *m*
embarrass [ɛm'bærəs] *tr* faire honte à; (*to make difficult*) embarrasser
embarrassment [ɛm'bærəsmənt] *s* honte *f*; (*difficulty*) embarras *m*
embas·sy ['ɛmbəsɪ] *s* (*pl* **-sies**) ambassade *f*
em·bed [ɛm'bɛd] *v* (*pret & pp* **-bedded**; *ger* **-bedding**) *tr* encastrer
embellish [ɛm'bɛlɪ/] *tr* embellir
embellishment [ɛm'bɛlɪ/mənt] *s* embellissement *m*
ember ['ɛmbər] *s* tison *m*; **embers** braise *f*
Em'ber days' *spl* quatre-temps *mpl*
embezzle [ɛm'bɛzəl] *tr* détourner, s'approprier ‖ *intr* commettre des détournements
embezzler [ɛm'bɛzlər] *s* détourneur *m* de fonds
embitter [ɛm'bɪtər] *tr* aigrir
emblazon [ɛm'blezən] *tr* embellir; exalter, célébrer
emblem ['ɛmbləm] *s* emblème *m*
emblematic(al) [ˌɛmblə'mætɪk(əl)] *adj* emblématique
embodiment [ɛm'bɑdɪmənt] *s* personnification *f*, incarnation *f*
embod·y [ɛm'bɑdɪ] *v* (*pret & pp* **-ied**) *tr* personnifier, incarner; (*to include*) incorporer
embolden [ɛm'boldən] *tr* enhardir
embolism ['ɛmbəˌlɪzəm] *s* embolie *f*
emboss [ɛm'bɔs], [ɛm'bɑs] *tr* (*to raise in relief*) graver en relief; (*metal*) bosseler; (*e.g., leather*) gaufrer, repousser
embouchure [ˌɑmbu'/ʊr] *s* embouchure *f*; (mus) position *f* des lèvres
embrace [ɛm'bres] *s* étreinte *f*, embrassement *m* ‖ *tr* étreindre, embrasser ‖ *intr* s'étreindre, s'embrasser
embroider [ɛm'brɔɪdər] *tr* broder
embroider·y [ɛm'brɔɪdərɪ] *s* (*pl* **-ies**) broderie *f*
embroil [ɛm'brɔɪl] *tr* (*to throw into confusion*) embrouiller; (*to involve in contention*) brouiller

embroilment [ɛmˈbrɔɪlmənt] s embrouillage m, brouillamini m, imbroglio m

embry•o [ˈɛmbrɪ ˌo] s (pl -os) embryon m

embryology [ˌɛmbrɪˈalədʒi] s embryologie f

embryonic [ˌɛmbrɪˈanɪk] adj embryonnaire

emend [ɪˈmɛnd] tr corriger

emendation [ˌimɛnˈdeʃən] s correction f

emerald [ˈɛmərəld] s émeraude f

emerge [ɪˈmʌrdʒ] intr émerger

emergence [ɪˈmʌrdʒəns] s émergence f

emergen•cy [ɪˈmʌrdʒənsi] adj urgent, d'urgence; (exit) de secours ‖ s (pl -cies) cas m urgent

emer′gency brake′ s frein m de secours

emer′gency ex′it s sortie f de secours

emer′gency land′ing s atterrissage m forcé

emer′gency opera′tion s (med) opération f à chaud

emer′gency ra′tions spl vivres mpl de réserve

emer′gency ward′ s salle f d'urgence

emeritus [ɪˈmɛrɪtəs] adj honoraire, d'honneur

emersion [ɪˈmʌrʒən], [ɪˈmʌrʃən] s émersion f

emery [ˈɛməri] s émeri m

em′ery cloth′ s toile f d'émeri

em′ery wheel′ s meule f en émeri

emetic [ɪˈmɛtɪk] adj & s émétique m

emigrant [ˈɛmɪgrənt] adj & s émigrant m

emigrate [ˈɛmɪ ˌgret] intr émigrer

eminence [ˈɛmɪnəns] s éminence f

eminent [ˈɛmɪnənt] adj éminent; most eminent (eccl) éminentissime

emissar•y [ˈɛmɪ ˌsɛri] s (pl -ies) émissaire m

emit [ɪˈmɪt] v (pret & pp emitted; ger emitting) tr émettre; (a gas, an odor, etc.) exhaler

emolument [ɪˈmaljəmənt] s émoluments mpl

emotion [ɪˈmoʃən] s émotion f

emotional [ɪˈmoʃənəl] adj émotif, émotionnable

emperor [ˈɛmpərər] s empereur m

empha•sis [ˈɛmfəsɪs] s (pl -ses [ˌsiz]) accentuation f, mise f en relief; énergie f, force f; (on word or phrase) accent m d'insistance; to place emphasis on insister vivement sur; with emphasis on en insistant particulièrement sur

emphasize [ˈɛmfə ˌsaɪz] tr accentuer, mettre en relief; appuyer sur, souligner

emphatic [ɛmˈfætɪk] adj accentué, énergique

emphysema [ˌɛmfɪˈsimə] s emphysème m

empire [ˈɛmpaɪr] s empire m

empiric(al) [ɛmˈpɪrɪk(əl)] adj empirique

empiricist [ɛmˈpɪrɪsɪst] s empirique m

emplacement [ɛmˈplesmənt] s emplacement m

employ [ɛmˈplɔɪ] s service m ‖ tr employer

employee [ɛmˈplɔɪ•i], [ˌɛmplɔɪˈi] s employé m

employer [ɛmˈplɔɪ•ər] s employeur m, patron m, chef m

employment [ɛmˈplɔɪmənt] s emploi m

employ′ment a′gency s bureau m de placement

empower [ɛmˈpau•ər] tr autoriser

empress [ˈɛmprɪs] s impératrice f

emptiness [ˈɛmptɪnɪs] s vide m

emp•ty [ˈɛmpti] adj (comp -tier; super -tiest) vide; (hollow) creux, vain; (coll) affamé ‖ v (pret & pp -tied) tr vider ‖ intr se vider; (said of river) se jeter; (said of auditorium) se dégarnir

emp′ty-hand′ed adj & adv les mains vides

emp′ty-head′ed adj écervelé

empye•ma [ˌɛmpɪˈimə] s (pl -mata [mətə]) empyème m

empyrean [ˌɛmpɪˈri•ən] s empyrée m

emu [ˈimju] s (zool) émeu m

emulate [ˈɛmjə ˌlet] tr chercher à égaler, imiter ‖ intr rivaliser

emulator [ˈɛmjə ˌletər] s émule mf

emulsi•fy [ɪˈmʌlsɪ ˌfaɪ] v (pret & pp -fied) tr émulsionner

emulsion [ɪˈmʌlʃən] s émulsion f

enable [ɛnˈebəl] tr—to enable to rendre capable de, mettre à même de

enact [ɛnˈækt] tr (to decree) décréter, arrêter; (theat) représenter

enactment [ɛnˈæktmənt] s loi f; (establishing) établissement m; (govt) promulgation f; (law) décret m; (theat) représentation f

enam•el [ɪˈnæməl] s émail m ‖ v (pret & pp -eled or -elled; ger -eling or -elling) tr émailler

enameling [ɪˈnæməlɪŋ] s émaillage m

enam′el•ware′ s ustensiles mpl en fer émaillé

enamor [ɛnˈæmər] tr rendre amoureux; to become enamored with s'énamourer de

encamp [ɛnˈkæmp] tr & intr camper

encampment [ɛnˈkæmpmənt] s campement m

encase [ɛnˈkes] tr mettre en caisse; enfermer, envelopper

encephalitis [ɛn ˌsɛfəˈlaɪtɪs] s encéphalite f

enchain [ɛnˈtʃen] tr enchaîner

enchant [ɛnˈtʃænt], [ɛnˈtʃant] tr enchanter

enchanting [ɛnˈtʃæntɪŋ], [ɛnˈtʃantɪŋ] adj charmant, ravissant; (casting a spell) enchanteur

enchantment [ɛnˈtʃæntmənt], [ɛnˈtʃantmənt] s enchantement m

enchantress [ɛnˈtʃæntrɪs], [ɛnˈtʃantrɪs] s enchanteresse f

encircle [ɛnˈsʌrkəl] tr encercler, cerner; (a word) entourer d'un cercle

enclitic [ɛnˈklɪtɪk] adj & s enclitique m

enclose [ɛnˈkloz] tr enclore, entourer; (in a letter) inclure, joindre

enclosed adj (in a letter) ci-joint, ci-inclus

enclosure [ɛn'kloʒər] *s* clôture *f*, enceinte *f*, enclos *m*; (*e.g., in a letter*) pièce *f* jointe, pièce annexée

encomi·um [ɛn'komɪ·əm] *s* (*pl* -ums or -a [ə]) panégyrique *m*, éloge *m*

encompass [ɛn'kʌmpəs] *tr* entourer, renfermer

encore ['ɑnkor] *s* rappel *m*, bis *m* ‖ *tr* bisser ‖ *interj* bis!

encounter [ɛn'kauntər] *s* rencontre *f* ‖ *tr* rencontrer ‖ *intr* se rencontrer, combattre

encourage [ɛn'kʌrɪdʒ] *tr* encourager

encouragement [ɛn'kʌrɪdʒmənt] *s* encouragement *m*

encroach [ɛn'krotʃ] *intr*—**to encroach on** or **upon** empiéter sur; abuser de

encumber [ɛn'kʌmbər] *tr* encombrer, embarrasser; (*with debts*) grever

encumbrance [ɛn'kʌmbrəns] *s* encombrement *m*, embarras *m*; (law) charge *f*

encyclical [ɛn'sɪklɪkəl], [ɛn'saɪklɪkəl] *adj & s* encyclique *f*

encyclopedia [ɛn͵saɪklə'pidɪ·ə] *s* encyclopédie *f*

encyclopedic [ɛn͵saɪklə'pidɪk] *adj* encyclopédique

end [ɛnd] *s* (*in time*) fin *f*; (*in space; small piece*) bout *m*; (*purpose*) but *m*; (*end of set period of time*) terme *m*; **at loose ends** en pagaille; **at the end, in the end** à la fin; **to be at the end of one's rope** être au bout de son rouleau; **to bring to an end** mettre fin à; **to come to an end** prendre fin; **to make both ends meet** joindre les deux bouts; **to stand on end** (*said of hair*) se dresser; **to this end** à cet effet ‖ *tr* achever, terminer ‖ *intr* s'achever, se terminer; **to end up by** finir par

endanger [ɛn'dendʒər] *tr* mettre en danger

endear [ɛn'dɪr] *tr* faire aimer; **to endear oneself to** se faire aimer de

endeavor [ɛn'dɛvər] *s* effort *m*, tentative *f* ‖ *intr*—**to endeavor to** s'efforcer de, tâcher de

endemic [ɛn'dɛmɪk] *adj* endémique

ending ['ɛndɪŋ] *s* fin *f*, terminaison *f*; (gram) désinence *f*

endive ['ɛndaɪv] *s* (*blanched type*) endive *f*; (*Cichorium endivia*) chicorée *f* frisée

endless ['ɛndlɪs] *adj* sans fin

end'most' *adj* extrême

endocrine ['ɛndo͵kraɪn], ['ɛndokrɪn] *adj* endocrine

endorse [ɛn'dɔrs] *tr* endosser; (*a candidate*) appuyer; (*a plan*) souscrire à

endorsement [ɛn'dɔrsmənt] *s* endos *m*, endossement *m*; (*approval*) appui *m*, approbation *f*

endorser [ɛn'dɔrsər] *s* endosseur *m*

endow [ɛn'dau] *tr* doter, fonder

endowment [ɛn'daumənt] *s* dotation *f*, fondation *f*; (*talent*) don *m*

endow'ment fund' *s* caisse *f* de dotation

end' pa'per *s* pages *fpl* de garde

endurance [ɛn'd(j)urəns] *s* endurance *f*

endur'ance test' *s* épreuve *f* d'endurance

endure [ɛn'd(j)ur] *tr* endurer ‖ *intr* durer

enduring [ɛn'd(j)urɪŋ] *adj* durable

enema ['ɛnəmə] *s* lavement *m*

ene·my ['ɛnəmi] *adj* ennemi ‖ *s* (*pl* -mies) ennemi *m*

en'emy al'ien *s* étranger *m* ennemi

energetic [͵ɛnər'dʒɛtɪk] *adj* énergique

ener·gy ['ɛnərdʒi] *s* (*pl* -gies) énergie *f*

en'ergy bal'ance *s* (nucl) bilan *m* énergétique

enervate ['ɛnər͵vet] *tr* énerver

enfeeble [ɛn'fibəl] *tr* affaiblir

enfold [ɛn'fold] *tr* envelopper, enrouler; (*to embrace*) embrasser

enforce [ɛn'fors] *tr* (*a law*) faire exécuter, mettre en vigueur; (*one's rights, one's point of view*) faire valoir, appuyer; (*e.g., obedience*) imposer

enforcement [ɛn'forsmənt] *s* contrainte *f*; (*of a law*) exécution *f*, mise *f* en vigueur

enfranchise [ɛn'fræntʃaɪz] *tr* affranchir; donner le droit de vote à

engage [ɛn'gedʒ] *tr* engager; (*to hire*) engager, embaucher; (*to reserve*) retenir, réserver, louer; (*s.o.'s attention*) fixer, attirer; (*the clutch*) embrayer; (*toothed wheels*) engrener; **to be engaged in** s'occuper de; **to be engaged to be married** être fiancé; **to engage s.o. in conversation** entamer une conversation avec qn ‖ *intr* s'engager; (mach) engrener; **to engage in** s'embarquer dans, entrer en or dans

engaged *adj* (*to be married*) fiancé; (*busy*) occupé, pris; (mach) en prise; (mil) aux prises, aux mains

engagement [ɛn'gedʒmənt] *s* engagement *m*; (*betrothal*) fiançailles *fpl*; (*appointment*) rendez-vous *m*; (mach) embrayage *m*, engrenage *m*; (mil) engagement, combat *m*

engage'ment ring' *s* bague *f* or anneau *m* de fiançailles

engaging [ɛn'gedʒɪŋ] *adj* engageant, attirant

engender [ɛn'dʒɛndər] *tr* engendrer

engine ['ɛndʒɪn] *s* machine *f*; (*of automobile*) moteur *m*

engineer [͵ɛndʒə'nɪr] *s* ingénieur *m*; (*engine driver*) mécanicien *m* ‖ *tr* diriger or construire en qualité d'ingénieur; (coll) manigancer, machiner

engineering [͵ɛndʒə'nɪrɪŋ] *s* génie *m*

en'gine house' *s* dépôt *m* de pompes à incendie

en'gine·man' or **en'gine·man** *s* (*pl* -men' or -men) mécanicien *m*

en'gine room' *s* chambre *f* des machines

en'gine-room tel'egraph *s* (naut) transmetteur *m* d'ordres

en'gine trou'ble *s* panne *f* de moteur

England ['ɪŋglənd] *s* Angleterre *f*; l'Angleterre

English ['ɪŋglɪʃ] *adj* anglais ‖ *s* (*language*) anglais *m*; (billiards) effet *m*; **the English** les Anglais

Eng'lish Chan'nel *s* Manche *f*

Eng'lish dai'sy s marguerite *f* des champs
Eng'lish horn' s cor *m* anglais
Eng'lish·man s (*pl* -men) Anglais *m*
Eng'lish-speak'ing *adj* anglophone, d'expression anglaise; (*country*) de langue anglaise
Eng'lish·wom'an s (*pl* -wom'en) Anglaise *f*
engraft [ɛn'græft], [ɛn'grɑft] *tr* greffer; (fig) implanter
engrave [ɛn'grev] *tr* graver
engraver [ɛn'grevər] s graveur *m*
engraving [ɛn'grevɪŋ] s gravure *f*
engross [ɛn'gros] *tr* absorber, occuper; (*a document*) grossoyer
engrossing [ɛn'grosɪŋ] *adj* absorbant
engulf [ɛn'gʌlf] *tr* engouffrer, engloutir
enhance [ɛn'hæns], [ɛn'hɑns] *tr* rehausser, relever
enhancement [ɛn'hænsmənt], [ɛn'hɑnsmənt] s rehaussement *m*
enigma [ɪ'nɪgmə] s énigme *f*
enigmatic(al) [ˌɪnɪg'mætɪk(əl)] *adj* énigmatique
enjoin [ɛn'dʒɔɪn] *tr* enjoindre; (*to forbid*) interdire
enjoy [ɛn'dʒɔɪ] *tr* jouir de; **to enjoy +** *ger* prendre plaisir à + *inf*; **to enjoy oneself** s'amuser, se divertir
enjoyable [ɛn'dʒɔɪ·əbəl] *adj* agréable, plaisant; (*show, party, etc.*) divertissant
enjoyment [ɛn'dʒɔɪmənt] s (*pleasure*) plaisir *m*; (*pleasurable use*) jouissance *f*
enkindle [ɛn'kɪndəl] *tr* allumer
enlarge [ɛn'lɑrdʒ] *tr* agrandir, élargir; (phot) agrandir ‖ *intr* s'agrandir, s'élargir; **to enlarge on** or **upon** discourir longuement sur, amplifier
enlargement [ɛn'lɑrdʒmənt] s agrandissement *m*
enlighten [ɛn'laɪtən] *tr* éclairer
enlightenment [ɛn'laɪtənmənt] s éclaircissements *mpl*; **the Enlightenment** le siècle des lumières
enlist [ɛn'lɪst] *tr* enrôler ‖ *intr* s'enrôler, s'engager
enlist'ed man' s homme *m* de troupe
enlistment [ɛn'lɪstmənt] s enrôlement *m*, engagement *m*
enliven [ɛn'laɪvən] *tr* animer, égayer
enmesh [ɛn'mɛʃ] *tr* prendre dans les rets; (*e.g., in an evil design*) empêtrer; (mach) engrener
enmi·ty ['ɛnmɪti] s (*pl* -ties) inimitié *f*
ennoble [ɛn'nobəl] *tr* ennoblir; (*to confer a title of nobility upon*) anoblir
ennui ['ɑnwi] s ennui *m*
enormous [ɪ'nɔrməs] *adj* énorme
enormously [ɪ'nɔrməsli] *adv* énormément
enough [ɪ'nʌf] *adj, s, & adv* assez; **more than enough** plus qu'il n'en faut; **that's enough!** en voilà assez!; **to be intelligent enough** être assez intelligent; **to have enough to live on** avoir de quoi vivre ‖ *interj* assez!, ça suffit!
enounce [ɪ'naʊns] *tr* énoncer

enrage [ɛn'redʒ] *tr* faire enrager, rendre furieux; **to be enraged** enrager
enrapture [ɛn'ræptʃər] *tr* ravir, transporter
enrich [ɛn'rɪtʃ] *tr* enrichir
enrichment [ɛn'rɪtʃmənt] s enrichissement *m*
enroll [ɛn'rol] *tr* enrôler; (*a student*) inscrire; (*to wrap up*) enrouler ‖ *intr* s'enrôler; (*said of student*) prendre ses inscriptions, se faire inscrire
enrollment [ɛn'rolmənt] s enrôlement *m*; (*of a student*) inscription *f*; (*wrapping up*) enroulement *m*
ensconce [ɛn'skɑns] *tr* cacher; **to ensconce oneself** s'installer
ensemble [ɑn'sɑmbəl] s ensemble *m*
ensign ['ɛnsaɪn] s enseigne *f* ‖ ['ɛnsən], ['ɛnsaɪn] s (nav) enseigne *m* de deuxième classe
ensilage ['ɛnsɪlɪdʒ] s fourrage *m* d'un silo américain ‖ *tr* ensiler
enslave [ɛn'slev] *tr* asservir, réduire en esclavage
enslavement [ɛn'slevmənt] s asservissement *m*
ensnare [ɛn'snɛr] *tr* prendre au piège, attraper
ensue [ɛn's(j)u] *intr* s'ensuivre, résulter
ensuing [ɛn's(j)u·ɪŋ] *adj* suivant
ensure [ɛn'ʃʊr] *tr* assurer, garantir
entail [ɛn'tel] *tr* occasionner, entraîner
entangle [ɛn'tæŋgəl] *tr* embrouiller
entanglement [ɛn'tæŋgəlmənt] s embrouillement *m*, embarras *m*
enter ['ɛntər] *tr* (*a room, a house, etc.*) entrer dans; (*a school, the army, etc.*) entrer à; (*e.g., a period of convalescence*) entrer en; (*a highway, a public square, etc.*) déboucher sur; (*e.g., a club*) devenir membre de; (*a request*) enregistrer, consigner par écrit; (*a student, a contestant, etc.*) admettre, faire inscrire; (*in the customhouse*) déclarer; (*to make a record of*) inscrire, porter; **to enter one's name for** se faire inscrire à or pour ‖ *intr* entrer; (theat) entrer en scène; **to enter into** entrer à, dans, or en; (*to be an ingredient of*) entrer pour; **to enter on** or **upon** entreprendre, débuter dans
enterprise ['ɛntər‚praɪz] s (*undertaking*) entreprise *f*; (*spirit, push*) esprit *m* d'entreprise, allant *m*, entrain *m*
enterprising ['ɛntər‚praɪzɪŋ] *adj* entreprenant
entertain [‚ɛntər'ten] *tr* (*to distract*) amuser, divertir; (*to show hospitality to*) recevoir; (*at a meal*) régaler; (*a hope*) entretenir, nourrir; (*an idea*) concevoir ‖ *intr* recevoir
entertainer [‚ɛntər'tenər] s (*host*) hôte *m*, amphitryon *m*; amuseur *m*; (*comedian*) comique *mf*
entertaining [‚ɛntər'tenɪŋ] *adj* amusant, divertissant
entertainment [‚ɛntər'tenmənt] s (*distraction*) amusement *m*, divertissement *m*; (*show*) spectacle *m*; (*as a guest*) accueil *m*, hospitalité *f*

en'tertain'ment tax' *s* taxe *f* sur les spectacles
enthrall [ɛn'θrɔl] *tr* (*to charm*) captiver, charmer; (*to enslave*) asservir, rendre esclave
enthrone [ɛn'θron] *tr* introniser
enthuse [ɛn'θ(j)uz] *tr* (coll) enthousiasmer ‖ *intr* (coll) s'enthousiasmer
enthusiasm [ɛn'θ(j)uzɪ,æzəm] *s* enthousiasme *m*
enthusiast [ɛn'θ(j)uzɪ,æst] *s* enthousiaste *mf*; (*camera fiend, sports fan, etc.*) fanatique *mf*, enragé *m*
enthusiastic [ɛn,θ(j)uzɪ'æstɪk] *adj* enthousiaste; (*for sports, music, a hobby*) fanatique, enragé
entice [ɛn'taɪs] *tr* attirer, séduire; (*to evil*) tenter, chercher à séduire
enticement [ɛn'taɪsmənt] *s* attrait *m*, appât *m*; tentation *f*, séduction *f*
entire [ɛn'taɪr] *adj* entier
entirely [ɛn'taɪrli] *adv* entièrement, en entier; (*absolutely*) tout à fait, absolument
entire·ty [ɛn'taɪrti] *s* (*pl* -ties) totalité *f*, entier *m*; **in its entirety** dans sa totalité
entitle [ɛn'taɪtəl] *tr* (*to name*) intituler; (*to qualify*) donner le droit à; **to be entitled to** avoir droit à
enti·ty ['ɛntɪti] *s* (*pl* -ties) entité *f*
entomb [ɛn'tum] *tr* ensevelir
entombment [ɛn'tummənt] *s* ensevelissement *m*
entomology [,ɛntə'malədʒi] *s* entomologie *f*
entourage [,antu'raʒ] *s* entourage *m*
entrails ['ɛntrelz], ['ɛntrəlz] *spl* entrailles *fpl*
entrain [ɛn'tren] *tr* faire prendre le train, embarquer; (*to carry along*) entraîner ‖ *intr* embarquer, s'embarquer
entrance ['ɛntrəns] *s* entrée *f*; (theat) entrée en scène; **entrance to . . .** (public sign) accès à . . . ‖ [ɛn-'træns], [ɛn'trans] *tr* enchanter, ensorceler; **to be entranced** s'extasier
en'trance examina'tion *s* examen *m* d'entrée
en'trance fee' *s* droits *mpl* d'entrée
entrancing [ɛn'trænsɪŋ], [ɛn'transɪŋ] *adj* enchanteur, ensorceleur
entrant ['ɛntrənt] *s* inscrit *m*; (*in a competition*) concurrent *m*, participant *m*
en·trap [ɛn'træp] *v* (*pret & pp* -trapped; *ger* -trapping) *tr* attraper
entreat [ɛn'trit] *tr* supplier, prier, conjurer
entreat·y [ɛn'triti] *s* (*pl* -ies) supplication *f*, prière *f*
entree ['antre] *s* (*entrance; course preceding the roast*) entrée *f*; (*main dish*) plat *m* de résistance
entrench [ɛn'trɛntʃ] *tr* retrancher; **to be entrenched** se retrancher ‖ *intr*— **to entrench on** or **upon** empiéter sur
entrust [ɛn'trʌst] *tr*—**to entrust s.o. with s.th., to entrust s.th. to s.o.** confier q.ch. à qn
en·try ['ɛntri] *s* (*pl* -tries) entrée *f*; (*in*

a dictionary) article *m*, entrée; (*on a register*) inscription *f*; (*in a competition*) concurrent *m*, participant *m*; (*thing entered for judging in a competition*) objet *m* exposé
en'try blank' *s* feuille *f* d'inscription
entwine [ɛn'twaɪn] *tr* entrelacer, enlacer ‖ *intr* s'entrelacer, s'enlacer
enumerate [ɪ'n(j)umə,ret] *tr* énumérer
enunciate [ɪ'nʌnsɪ,et], [ɪ'nʌnʃɪ,et] *tr* énoncer, déclarer; (*to articulate*) articuler, prononcer
envelop [ɛn'vɛləp] *tr* envelopper
envelope ['ɛnvə,lop], ['anvə,lop] *s* enveloppe *f*; **in an envelope** sous enveloppe, sous pli
envenom [ɛn'vɛnəm] *tr* envenimer, empoisonner
enviable ['ɛnvɪ·əbəl] *adj* enviable, digne d'envie
envious ['ɛnvɪ·əs] *adj* envieux
environment [ɛn'vaɪrənmənt] *s* environnement *m*, milieu *m*
environs [ɛn'vaɪrənz] *spl* environs *mpl*
envisage [ɛn'vɪzɪdʒ] *tr* envisager
envoi ['ɛnvɔɪ] *s* envoi *m*
envoy ['ɛnvɔɪ] *s* envoyé *m*, émissaire *m*; (*of poem*) envoi *m*
en·vy ['ɛnvi] *s* (*pl* -vies) envie *f* ‖ *v* (*pret & pp* -vied) *tr* envier
enzyme ['ɛnzaɪm], ['ɛnzɪm] *s* enzyme *m & f*
epaulet ['ɛpə,lɛt] *s* épaulette *f*
epergne [ɪ'pʌrn], [e'pɛrn] *s* surtout *m*
ephemeral [ɪ'fɛmərəl] *adj* éphémère
epic ['ɛpɪk] *adj* épique ‖ *s* épopée *f*
epicure ['ɛpɪ,kjʊr] *s* gourmet *m*, gastronome *m*
epidemic [,ɛpɪ'dɛmɪk] *adj* épidémique ‖ *s* épidémie *f*
epidemiology [,ɛpɪ,dimɪ'alədʒi] *s* épidémiologie *f*
epidermis [,ɛpɪ'dʌrmɪs] *s* épiderme *m*
epiglottis [,ɛpɪ'glatɪs] *s* épiglotte *f*
epigram ['ɛpɪ,græm] *s* épigramme *f*
epilepsy ['ɛpɪ,lɛpsi] *s* épilepsie *f*
epileptic [,ɛpɪ'lɛptɪk] *adj & s* épileptique *mf*
epilogue ['ɛpɪ,lɔg], ['ɛpɪ,lag] *s* épilogue *m*
episcopal [ɪ'pɪskəpəl] *adj* épiscopal
Episcopalian [ɪ,pɪskə'peli·ən] *adj* épiscopal ‖ *s* épiscopal *m*
episode ['ɛpɪ,sod] *s* épisode *m*
episodic [,ɛpɪ'sadɪk] *adj* épisodique
epistle [ɪ'pɪsəl] *s* épître *f*
epitaph ['ɛpɪ,tæf] *s* épitaphe *f*
epithet ['ɛpɪ,θɛt] *s* épithète *f*
epitome [ɪ'pɪtəmi] *s* (*abridgment*) épitomé *m*; (*representative of a class*) modèle *m*, personnification *f*
epitomize [ɪ'pɪtə,maɪz] *tr* abréger; personnifier
epoch ['ɛpək], ['ipak] *s* époque *f*
epochal ['ɛpəkəl] *adj* mémorable
ep'och-mak'ing *adj* qui fait époque
Ep'som salts' ['ɛpsəm] *spl* epsomite *f*, sels *mpl* d'Epsom
equable ['ɛkwəbəl], ['ikwəbəl] *adj* uniforme, égal; tranquille
equal ['ikwəl] *adj* égal; **to be equal to** égaler, valoir; (*e.g., the occasion*)

être à la hauteur de; **to be equal to** +
ger être de force à + *inf*, être à même
de + *inf*; **to get equal with** (coll) se
venger de ‖ *s* égal *m*, pareil *m* ‖ *v*
(*pret* & *pp* **equaled** or **equalled;** *ger*
equaling or **equalling**) *tr* égaler
equali•ty [ɪ'kwɑlɪti] *s* (*pl* **-ties**) égalité *f*
equalize ['ikwə,laɪz] *tr* égaliser
equally ['ikwəli] *adv* également
equanimity [,ikwə'nɪmɪti] *s* équanimité *f*, égalité *f* d'âme
equate [i'kwet] *tr* égaliser, mettre en
équation
equation [i'kweʒən], [i'kweʃən] *s*
équation *f*
equator [i'kwetər] *s* équateur *m*
equatorial [,ikwə'torɪ•əl] *adj* équato-
rial
equestrian [ɪ'kwɛstrɪ•ən] *adj* équestre
‖ *s* cavalier *m*, écuyer *m*
equilateral [,ikwɪ'lætərəl] *adj* équi-
latéral
equilibrium [,ikwɪ'lɪbrɪ•əm] *s* équilibre *m*
equinoctial [,ikwɪ'nɑkʃəl] *adj* équi-
noxial
equinox ['ikwɪ,nɑks] *s* équinoxe *m*
equip [ɪ'kwɪp] *v* (*pret* & *pp* **equipped;**
ger **equipping**) *tr* équiper, outiller; **to
equip with** munir de
equipment [ɪ'kwɪpmənt] *s* équipement
m, matériel *m*
equipoise ['ikwɪ,pɔɪz], ['ɛkwɪ,pɔɪz] *s*
équilibre *m* ‖ *tr* équilibrer
equitable ['ɛkwɪtəbəl] *adj* équitable
equi•ty ['ɛkwɪti] *s* (*pl* **-ties**) équité *f*;
(com) part *f* résiduaire
equivalent [ɪ'kwɪvələnt] *adj* & *s* équivalent *m*
equivocal [ɪ'kwɪvəkəl] *adj* équivoque
equivocate [ɪ'kwɪvə,ket] *intr* équivoquer
equivocation [ɪ,kwɪvə'keʃən] *s* ter-
giversation *f*, équivoque *f*
era ['ɪrə], ['irə] *s* ère *f*, époque *f*
eradicate [ɪ'rædɪ,ket] *tr* déraciner,
extirper
erase [ɪ'res] *tr* effacer, biffer
eraser [ɪ'resər] *s* gomme *f* à effacer;
brosse *f*
erasure [ɪ'reʃər] *s* effacement *m*, rature *f*
ere [ɛr] *prep* (poetic) avant ‖ *conj*
(poetic) avant que
erect [ɪ'rɛkt] *adj* droit, debout ‖ *tr* (*to
set in an upright position*) dresser,
élever; (*a building*) ériger, édifier;
(*a machine*) monter
erection [ɪ'rɛkʃən] *s* érection *f*
erg [ʌrg] *s* erg *m*
ermine ['ʌrmɪn] *s* hermine *f*
erode [ɪ'rod] *tr* éroder
erosion [ɪ'roʒən] *s* érosion *f*
erotic [ɪ'rɑtɪk] *adj* érotique
err [ʌr] *intr* se tromper, faire erreur,
errer; (*to do wrong*) s'égarer, pécher
errand ['ɛrənd] *s* commission *f*, course
f; **to go on** or **to run an errand** faire
une course
er′rand boy′ *s* coursier *m*, garçon de
courses

erratic [ɪ'rætɪk] *adj* variable; capricieux, excentrique
erroneous [ɪ'ronɪ•əs] *adj* erroné
error ['ɛrər] *s* erreur *f*
erudite ['ɛr(j)u,daɪt] *adj* érudit
erudition [,ɛr(j)u'dɪʃən] *s* érudition *f*
erupt [ɪ'rʌpt] *intr* faire éruption
eruption [ɪ'rʌpʃən] *s* éruption *f*
escalate ['ɛskə,let] *tr* escalader
escalation [,ɛskə'leʃən] *s* escalade *f*
escalator ['ɛskə,letər] *s* escalator *m*,
escalier *m* mécanique or roulant
escallop [ɛs'kæləp] *s* coquille *f* Saint-
Jacques, peigne *m*, pétoncle *m*;
(culin) coquille au gratin ‖ *tr* (*the
edges*) denteler, découper; (culin)
gratiner et cuire au four et à la crème
escapade [,ɛskə'ped] *s* fredaine *f*,
frasque *f*; (*getting away*) escapade *f*
escape [ɛs'kep] *s* (*getaway*) évasion *f*,
fuite *f*; (*from responsibilities, duties,
etc.*) évasion, escapade *f*; (*of gas,
liquid, etc.*) échappement *m*, fuite;
(*of a clock*) échappement; **to have a
narrow escape** l'échapper belle; **to
make one's escape** se sauver, s'échapper ‖ *tr* échapper à, éviter ‖ *intr*
échapper, s'échapper, s'évader; **to
escape from** échapper à
escape′ clause′ *s* échappatoire *f*
escapee [,ɛskə'pi] *s* évadé *m*, échappé
m
escape′ hatch′ *s* (aer) sas *m* d'évacuation
escape′ lit′erature *s* littérature *f* d'évasion
escapement [ɛs'kepmənt] *s* issue *f*, débouché *m*; (mach) échappement *m*
escape′ wheel′ *s* roue *f* de rencontre
escarole ['ɛskə,rol] *s* scarole *f*
escarpment [ɛs'kɑrpmənt] *s* escarpement *m*
eschew [ɛs't/u] *tr* éviter, s'abstenir de
escort ['ɛskɔrt] *s* escorte *f*; (*gentleman
escort*) cavalier *m* ‖ [ɛs'kɔrt] *tr*
escorter
escutcheon [ɛs'kʌtʃən] *s* écusson *m*
Eski•mo ['ɛskɪ,mo] *adj* eskimo, esquimau ‖ *s* (*pl* **-mos** or **-mo**) (*language;
dog*) esquimau *m*; (*person*) Eskimo
m, Esquimau *m*
Es′kimo wom′an *s* Esquimaude *f*,
femme *f* esquimau
esopha•gus [i'sɑfəgəs] *s* (*pl* **-gi** [,'dʒaɪ])
œsophage *m*
esoteric [,ɛso'tɛrɪk] *adj* ésotérique
especial [ɛs'pɛʃəl] *adj* spécial
especially [ɛs'pɛʃəli] *adv* surtout, particulièrement
espionage ['ɛspɪ,anɪdʒ], [,ɛspɪ•ə'naʒ]
s espionnage *m*
espousal [ɛs'pauzəl] *s* épousailles *f*;
espousal of (*a cause*) adoption de,
adhésion à
espouse [ɛs'pauz] *tr* épouser; (*to advocate, adopt*) adopter, embrasser
Esq. *abbr* (**Esquire**)—**John Smith, Esq.**
Monsieur Jean Smith
esquire [ɛs'kwaɪr], ['ɛskwaɪr] *s* (hist)
écuyer *m*
essay ['ɛse] *s* essai *m* ‖ *tr* essayer
essayist ['ɛse•ɪst] *s* essayiste *mf*

essence ['ɛsəns] s essence f
essential [ɛ'sɛnʃəl] adj & s essentiel m
establish [ɛs'tæblɪʃ] tr établir
establishment [ɛs'tæblɪʃmənt] s établissement m
estate [ɛs'tet] s (landed property) domaine m, propriété f, terres fpl; (a person's possessions) biens mpl, possessions fpl; (left by a decedent) héritage m, succession f; (social status) rang m, condition f; (hist) état m
esteem [ɛs'tim] s estime f ‖ tr estimer
esthete ['ɛsθit] s esthète mf
esthetic [ɛs'θɛtɪk] adj esthétique ‖ esthetics s esthétique f
estimable ['ɛstɪməbəl] adj estimable
estimate ['ɛstɪˌmet], ['ɛstɪmɪt] s évaluation f, appréciation f; (appraisal) estimation f ‖ ['ɛstɪˌmet] tr (to judge, deem) apprécier, estimer; (the cost) estimer, évaluer
estimation [ˌɛstɪ'meʃən] s (opinion) jugement m; (esteem) estime f; (appraisal) estimation f; **in my estimation** à mon avis
Estonia [ɛs'tonɪˌə] s Estonie f; l'Estonie
estrangement [ɛs'trendʒmənt] s éloignement m; (a becoming unfriendly) désaffection f
estuar·y ['ɛstʃuˌɛri] s (pl -ies) estuaire m
etch [ɛtʃ] tr & intr graver à l'eau-forte
etcher ['ɛtʃər] s aquafortiste m
etching ['ɛtʃɪŋ] s eau-forte f
eternal [ɪ'tʌrnəl] adj éternel
eterni·ty [ɪ'tʌrnɪti] s (pl -ties) éternité f
ether ['iθər] s éther m
ethereal [ɪ'θɪrɪ·əl] adj éthéré
ethical ['ɛθɪkəl] adj éthique
ethics ['ɛθɪks] s (branch of philosophy) étique f, morale f; spl (one's conduct, one's moral principles) morale
Ethiopia [ˌiθɪ'opɪ·ə] s Éthiopie f; l'Éthiopie
Ethiopian [ˌiθɪ'opɪ·ən] adj éthiopien ‖ s (language) éthiopien m; (person) Éthiopien m
ethnic(al) ['ɛθnɪk(əl)] adj ethnique
ethnography [ɛθ'nɑgrəfi] s ethnographie f
ethnology [ɛθ'nɑlədʒi] s ethnologie f
ethyl ['ɛθɪl] s éthyle m
ethylene ['ɛθɪˌlin] s éthylène m
etiquette ['ɛtɪˌkɛt] s étiquette f
etymolo·gy [ˌɛtɪ'mɑlədʒi] s (pl -gies) étymologie f
ety·mon ['ɛtɪˌmɑn] s (pl -mons or -ma [mə]) étymon m
eucalyp·tus [ˌjukə'lɪptəs] s (pl -tuses or -ti [taɪ]) eucalyptus m
Eucharist ['jukərɪst] s Eucharistie f
euchre ['jukər] s euchre m ‖ tr (coll) l'emporter sur
eulogize ['julə,dʒaɪz] tr faire l'éloge de
eulo·gy ['julədʒi] s (pl -gies) éloge m
eunuch ['junək] s eunuque m
euphemism ['jufɪˌmɪzəm] s euphémisme m
euphemistic [ˌjufɪ'mɪstɪk] adj euphémique

euphonic [ju'fɑnɪk] adj euphonique
eupho·ny ['jufəni] s (pl -nies) euphonie f
euphoria [ju'forɪ·ə] s euphorie f
euphuism ['jufju,ɪzəm] s euphuisme m; préciosité f
Europe ['jurəp] s Europe f; l'Europe
European [ˌjurə'pi·ən] adj européen ‖ s Européen m
euthanasia [ˌjuθə'neʒə] s euthanasie f
evacuate [ɪ'vækjuˌet] tr évacuer ‖ intr s'évacuer
evade [ɪ'ved] tr échapper à, éviter, esquiver ‖ intr s'évader
evaluate [ɪ'væljuˌet] tr évaluer
Evangel [ɪ'vændʒəl] s évangile m
evangelic(al) [ˌivæn'dʒɛlɪk(əl)], [ˌɛvən'dʒɛlɪk(əl)] adj évangélique
evangelist [ɪ'vændʒəlɪst] s évangéliste m
evaporate [ɪ'væpəˌret] tr évaporer ‖ intr s'évaporer
evasion [ɪ'veʒən] s évasion f; subterfuge m, détour m
evasive [ɪ'vesɪv] adj évasif
eve [iv] s veille f; (poetic) soir m; **on the eve of** à la veille de; **Eve** Ève f
even ['ivən] adj (smooth) uni; (number) pair; (equal, uniform) égal; (temperament) calme, rassis, égal; **even with** à fleur de; **to be even** être quitte; (cards, sports) être manche à manche ou point à point; **to get even with** (coll) rendre la pareille à ‖ adv même; **even** + comp encore + comp, e.g., **even better** encore mieux; **even so** quand même ‖ tr aplanir, égaliser
evening ['ivnɪŋ] adj du soir ‖ s soir m; **all evening** toute la soirée; **every evening** tous les soirs; **in the evening** le soir; **the evening before** la veille au soir
eve′ning clothes′ s tenue f de soirée; (for women) toilette f de soirée; (for men) habit m de soirée
eve′ning damp′ s serein m
eve′ning prim′rose s onagraire f
eve′ning star′ s étoile f du soir, étoile du berger
eve′ning wrap′ s sortie f de bal
e′ven·song′ s (eccl) vêpres fpl
event [ɪ'vɛnt] s événement m; **at all events** or **in any event** en tout cas; **in the event that** dans le cas où
eventful [ɪ'vɛntfəl] adj mouvementé; mémorable
eventual [ɪ'vɛntʃu·əl] adj final
eventuali·ty [ɪˌvɛntʃu'ælɪti] s (pl -ties) éventualité f
eventually [ɪ'vɛntʃu·əli] adv finalement, à la longue
eventuate [ɪ'vɛntʃuˌet] intr—**to eventuate in** se terminer par, aboutir à
ever ['ɛvər] adv (at all times) toujours; (at any time) jamais; **ever since** dès lors, depuis; **for ever and ever** à tout jamais; **hardly ever** presque jamais
ev′er·glade′ s région f marécageuse
ev′er·green′ adj toujours vert ‖ s arbre m vert; **evergreens** plantes fpl vertes, verdure f décorative

ev'er·last'ing *adj* éternel; (*continual*) sempiternel, perpétuel
ev'er·more' *adv* toujours; for evermore à jamais
every ['ɛvri] *adj* tous les; (*each*) chaque, tout; (coll) tout, e.g., every bit as good as tout aussi bon que; every man for himself sauve qui peut; every now and then de temps en temps; every once in a while de temps à autre; every other day tous les deux jours; every other one un sur deux; every which way (coll) de tous côtés; (coll) en désordre
ev'ery·bod'y *pron indef* tout le monde
ev'ery·day' *adj* de tous les jours
ev'ery·man' *s* Monsieur Tout-le-monde
ev'ery·one' or ev'ery one' *pron indef* chacun, tous, tout le monde
ev'ery·thing' *pron indef* tout
ev'ery·where' *adv* partout, de toutes parts; partout où; everywhere else partout ailleurs
evict [ɪ'vɪkt] *tr* évincer, expulser
eviction [ɪ'vɪkʃən] *s* éviction *f*
evidence ['ɛvɪdəns] *s* évidence *f*; (*proof*) preuve *f*, témoignage *m* ‖ *tr* manifester, démontrer
evident ['ɛvɪdənt] *adj* évident
evidently ['ɛvɪdəntli], [ˌɛvɪ'dɛntli] *adv* évidemment
evil ['ivəl] *adj* mauvais, méchant ‖ *s* mal *m*, méchanceté *f*
evildoer ['ivəl ˌdu·ər] *s* malfaisant *m*, méchant *m*
e'vil·do'ing *s* malfaisance *f*
e'vil eye' *s* mauvais œil *m*
e'vil-mind'ed *adj* malintentionné, malin
E'vil One' *s* Esprit *m* malin
evince [ɪ'vɪns] *tr* montrer, manifester
evocative [ɪ'vɑkətɪv] *adj* évocateur
evoke [ɪ'vok] *tr* évoquer
evolution [ˌɛvə'luʃən] *s* évolution *f*
evolve [ɪ'vɑlv] *tr* développer, élaborer ‖ *intr* évoluer
ewe [ju] *s* brebis *f*
ewer ['ju·ər] *s* aiguière *f*
exact [ɛg'zækt] *adj* exact ‖ *tr* exiger
exacting [ɛg'zæktɪŋ] *adj* exigeant
exactly [ɛg'zæktli] *adv* exactement; (*sharp, on the dot*) précisément, justement
exactness [ɛg'zæktnɪs] *s* exactitude *f*
exaggerate [ɛg'zædʒəˌret] *tr* exagérer
exalt [ɛg'zɔlt] *tr* exalter
exam [ɛg'zæm] *s* (coll) examen *m*
examination [ɛgˌzæmɪ'neʃən] *s* examen *m*; to take an examination se présenter à, passer, or subir un examen
examine [ɛg'zæmɪn] *tr* examiner
examiner [ɛg'zæmɪnər] *s* inspecteur *m*, vérificateur *m*; (*in a school*) examinateur *m*
example [ɛg'zæmpəl], [ɛg'zɑmpəl] *s* exemple *m*; for example par exemple
exasperate [ɛg'zæspəˌret] *tr* exaspérer
exasperation [ɛgˌzæspə're ʃən] *s* exaspération *f*
excavate ['ɛkskəˌvet] *tr* excaver
exceed [ɛk'sid] *tr* excéder
exceedingly [ɛk'sidɪŋli] *adv* extrêmement

ex·cel [ɛk'sɛl] *v* (*pret & pp* -celled; *ger* -celling) *tr* surpasser ‖ *intr* exceller; to excel in exceller dans; to excel in + *ger* exceller à + *inf*
excellence ['ɛksələns] *s* excellence *f*
excellen·cy ['ɛksələnsi] *s* (*pl* -cies) excellence *f*; Your Excellency Votre Excellence
excelsior [ɛk'sɛlsɪ·ər] *s* copeaux *mpl* d'emballage
except [ɛk'sɛpt] *adv*—except for excepté; except that excepté que ‖ *prep* excepté ‖ *tr* excepter
exception [ɛk'sɛpʃən] *s* exception *f*; to take exception to trouver à redire à; with the exception of à l'exception de
exceptional [ɛk'sɛpʃənəl] *adj* exceptionnel
excerpt ['ɛksʌrpt], [ɛk'sʌrpt] *s* extrait *m*, citation *f* ‖ [ɛk'sʌrpt] *tr* extraire
excess ['ɛksɛs], [ɛk'sɛs] *adj* excédentaire ‖ [ɛk'sɛs] *s* (*amount or degree*) excédent *m*, excès *m*; (*excessive amount; immoderate indulgence*) excès *m*; in excess of en plus de
ex'cess bag'gage *s* excédent *m* de bagages
ex'cess fare' *s* supplément *m*
excessive [ɛk'sɛsɪv] *adj* excessif
ex'cess-prof'its tax' *s* contribution *f* sur les bénéfices extraordinaires
ex'cess weight' *s* excédent *m* de poids
exchange [ɛks't ʃendʒ] *s* échange *m*; (*barter*) troc *m*; (com) bourse *f*; (tele) central *m* ‖ *tr* échanger; (*to barter*) troquer; to exchange compliments échanger des politesses; to exchange for échanger contre, échanger pour
exchequer [ɛks't ʃɛkər], ['ɛkst ʃɛkər] *s* trésor *m* public; ministère *m* des finances; (hist) échiquier *m*
excise [ɛk'saɪz], ['ɛksaɪz] *s* contributions *fpl* indirectes ‖ *tr* effacer, rayer; (surg) exciser
excitable [ɛk'saɪtəbəl] *adj* excitable
excite [ɛk'saɪt] *tr* exciter
excitement [ɛk'saɪtmənt] *m* agitation *f*, excitation *f*
exciting [ɛk'saɪtɪŋ] *adj* émotionnant, entraînant, passionnant
exclaim [ɛks'klem] *tr* s'écrier, e.g., "All is lost!" he exclaimed "Tout est perdu!" s'écria-t-il ‖ *intr* s'exclamer, se récrier
exclamation [ˌɛksklə'meʃən] *s* exclamation *f*
exclama'tion mark' *s* point *m* d'exclamation
exclude [ɛks'klud] *tr* exclure
excluding [ɛks'kludɪŋ] *prep* à l'exclusion de, sans compter
exclusion [ɛks'kluʒən] *s* exclusion *f*
exclusive [ɛks'klusɪv] *adj* exclusif; (*expensive; fashionable*) (coll) choisi, select; exclusive of à l'exclusion de
exclu'sive rights' *spl* exclusivité *f*
exclu'sive show'ing *s* (public sign in front of a theater) en exclusivité
excommunicate [ˌɛkskə'mjunɪˌket] *tr* excommunier

excommunication [,εkskə,mjunı'keʃən] s excommunication f
excoriate [εks'korı ,et] tr (fig) vitupérer
excrement ['εkskrəmənt] s excrément m
excruciating [εks'kruʃı ,etıŋ] adj affreux, atroce
exculpate ['εkskʌl ,pet], [εks'kʌlpet] tr disculper
excursion [εks'kʌrʒən], [εks'kʌrʃən] s excursion f
excusable [εks'kjuzəbəl] adj excusable
excuse [εks'kjus] s excuse f || [εks-'kjuz] tr excuser; **excuse me!** pardon!, je m'excuse!, **to excuse oneself** s'excuser
execrate ['εksı ,kret] tr exécrer; (to curse) maudire
execute ['εksı ,kjut] tr exécuter
execution [,εksı'kjuʃən] s exécution f
executioner [,εksı'kjuʃənər] s bourreau m
executive [εg'zεkjətıv] adj (powers) exécutif; (position) administratif || s exécutif m; (of school, business, etc.) directeur m, administrateur m
Exec′utive Man′sion s (U.S.A.) demeure f du Président
executor [εg'zεkjətər] s exécuteur m testamentaire
executrix [εg'zεkjətrıks] s exécutrice f testamentaire
exemplary [εg'zεmpləri], ['εgzəm-,plεri] adj exemplaire
exempli·fy [εg'zεmplı ,faı] v (pret & pp -fied) tr démontrer par des exemples; (to be a model of) servir d'exemple à
exempt [εg'zεmpt] adj exempt || tr exempter
exemption [εg'zεmpʃən] s exemption f; **exemptions** (from taxes) déductions fpl
exercise ['εksər ,saız] s exercice m; **exercises** cérémonies fpl || tr exercer || intr s'exercer, s'entraîner
exert [εg'zʌrt] tr exercer; **to exert oneself** faire des efforts
exertion [εg'zʌrʃən] s effort m; (e.g., of power) exercice m
exhalation [,εks ,hə'leʃən] s (of air) expiration f; (of gas, vapors, etc.) exhalaison f
exhale [εks'hel], [εg'zel] tr (air from lungs) expirer; (gas, vapor) exhaler || intr expirer; s'exhaler
exhaust [εg'zɔst] s échappement m; gaz mpl d'échappement || tr épuiser; faire le vide dans
exhaust′ fan′ s ventilateur m aspirant
exhaustion [εg'zɔstʃən] s épuisement m
exhaustive [εg'zɔstıv] adj exhaustif
exhaust′ man′ifold s tuyauterie f or collecteur m d'échappement
exhaust′ pipe′ s tuyau m d'échappement
exhaust′ valve′ s soupape f d'échappement
exhibit [εg'zıbıt] s exhibition f; (of art) exposition f; (law) document m à l'appui, pièce f à conviction || tr

exhiber; (e.g., pictures) exposer || intr faire une exposition
exhibition [,εksı'bıʃən] s exhibition f
exhibitor [εg'zıbıtər] s exposant m
exhilarate [εg'zılə ,ret] tr égayer, animer
exhort [εg'zɔrt] tr exhorter
exhume [εks'hjum], [εg'zjum] tr exhumer
exigen·cy ['εksıdʒənsi] s (pl -cies) exigence f
exigent ['εksıdʒənt] adj exigeant
exile ['εgzaıl], ['εksaıl] s exil m; (person) exilé m || tr exiler
exist [εg'zıst] intr exister
existence [εg'zıstəns] s existence f
exit ['εgzıt], ['εksıt] s sortie f || intr sortir
exodus ['εksədəs] s exode m
exonerate [εg'zɑnə ,ret] tr (to free from blame) disculper; (to free from an obligation) exonérer, dispenser
exorbitant [εg'zɔrbıtənt] adj exorbitant
exorcize ['εksɔr ,saız] tr exorciser
exotic [εg'zɑtık] adj exotique
expand [εks'pænd] tr (a gas, metal, etc.) dilater; (to enlarge, develop) élargir, développer; (to unfold, stretch out) étendre, déployer; (the chest) gonfler; (math) développer || intr se dilater; s'élargir, se développer; s'étendre, se déployer; se gonfler
expanse [εks'pæns] s étendue f
expansion [εks'pænʃən] s expansion f
expan′sion joint′ s joint m de dilatation thermique
expansive [εks'pænsıv] adj expansif; (broad) large, étendu
expatiate [εks'peʃı ,et] intr discourir, s'étendre
expatriate [εks'petrı ,ıt] adj & s expatrié m || [εks'petrı ,et] tr expatrier
expect [εks'pεkt] tr (to await the coming of) attendre; (to look for as likely) s'attendre à; **to expect it** s'y attendre; **to expect s.o. to** + inf s'attendre à ce que qn + subj; **to expect** + inf s'attendre à + inf
expectan·cy [εks'pεktənsi] s (pl -cies) attente f, expectative f
expect′ant moth′er [εks'pεktənt] s future mère f
expectation [,εkspεk'teʃən] s expectative f, espérance f
expectorate [εks'pεktə ,ret] tr & intr expectorer
expedien·cy [εks'pidı·ənsi] s (pl -cies) convenance f, opportunité f; opportunisme m, débrouillage m
expedient [εks'pidı·ənt] adj expédient; (looking out for oneself) débrouillard || s expédient m
expedite ['εkspı ,daıt] tr expédier
expedition [,εkspı'dıʃən] s expédition f; célérité f, promptitude f
expeditionary [,εkspı'dıʃən ,εri] adj expéditionnaire
expeditious [,εkspı'dıʃəs] adj expéditif
ex·pel [εks'pεl] v (pret & pp -pelled; ger -pelling) tr expulser; (from school) renvoyer

expend [εks'pεnd] *tr* (*to pay out*) dépenser; (*to use up*) consommer
expendable [εks'pεndəbəl] *adj* non récupérable; (*soldier*) sacrifiable
expenditure [εks'pεndɪt∫ər] *s* dépense *f*; consommation *f*
expense [εks'pεns] *s* dépense *f*; **at the expense of** aux dépens de; **expenses** frais *mpl*; (*for which a person will be reimbursed*) indemnité *f*; **to meet expenses** faire face aux dépenses
expense′ account′ *s* état *m* de frais, note *f* de frais
expensive [εks'pεnsɪv] *adj* cher, couteux; (*tastes*) dispendieux
experience [εks'pɪrɪ·əns] *s* expérience *f* || *tr* éprouver
experienced *adj* expérimenté
experiment [εks'pεrɪmənt] *s* expérience *f* || [εks'pεrɪ‚ment] *intr* faire des expériences, expérimenter
expert ['εkspərt] *adj* & *s* expert *m*
expertise [‚εkspər'tiz] *s* maîtrise *f*
expiate ['εkspɪ‚et] *tr* expier
expire [εks'paɪr] *tr* & *intr* expirer
expired *adj* (*lease; passport*) expiré; (*note; permit*) périmé; (*e.g., driver's license*) suranné; (*insurance policy*) déchu
explain [εks'plen] *tr* expliquer; **to explain oneself** s'expliquer || *intr* expliquer
explainable [εks'plenəbəl] *adj* explicable
explanation [‚εksplə'ne∫ən] *s* explication *f*
explanatory [εks'plænə‚tori] *adj* explicatif
explicit [εks'plɪsɪt] *adj* explicite
explode [εks'plod] *tr* faire sauter; (*a theory, opinion, etc.*) discréditer || *intr* exploser, éclater, sauter
exploit [εks'plɔɪt], ['εksplɔɪt] *s* exploit *m* || [εks'plɔɪt] *tr* exploiter
exploitation [‚εksplɔɪ'te∫ən] *s* exploitation *f*
exploration [‚εksplə're∫ən] *s* exploration *f*
explore [εks'plor] *tr* explorer
explorer [εks'plorər] *s* explorateur *m*; (*boy scout*) routier *m*
explosion [εks'ploʒən] *s* explosion *f*
explosive [εks'plosɪv] *adj* explosif; (*mixture*) explosible || *s* explosif *m*
exponent [εks'ponənt] *s* interprète *mf*; (math) exposant *m*
export ['εksport] *s* exportation *f* || [εks'port], ['εksport] *tr* & *intr* exporter
exportation [‚εkspor'te∫ən] *s* exportation *f*
exporter ['εksportər], [εks'portər] *s* exportateur *m*
expose [εks'poz] *tr* exposer; (*to unmask*) démasquer, dévoiler; (phot) impressionner
exposé [‚εkspo'ze] *s* dévoilement *m*, révélation *f*, mise *f* en lumière
exposition [‚εkspə'zɪ∫ən] *s* exposition *f*
expostulate [εks'pɑst∫ə‚let] *intr* faire des remontrances; **to expostulate with** faire des remontrances à

exposure [εks'poʒər] *s* exposition *f*; (*unmasking*) dévoilement *m*; (phot) exposition *f*; (phot) durée *f* d'exposition
expound [εks'paund] *tr* exposer
express [εks'prεs] *adj* exprès, formel; (*train; gun*) express || *s* (*merchandise*) messagerie *f*; (*train*) express *m*, rapide *m*; **by express** (rr) en grande vitesse || *adv* (rr) en grande vitesse || *tr* exprimer; (*merchandise*) envoyer en grande vitesse; (*through the express company*) expédier par les messageries; **to express oneself** s'exprimer
express′ com′pany *s* messageries *fpl*
express′ high′way *s* autoroute *f*
expression [εks'prε∫ən] *s* expression *f*
expressive [εks'prεsɪv] *adj* expressif
expressly [εks'prεsli] *adv* exprès
express′man *s* (*pl* -men) entrepreneur *m* de messageries; facteur *m*, agent *m* d'un service de messageries
express′ train′ *s* train *m* express
express′way′ *s* autoroute *f*
expropriate [εks'propri‚et] *tr* exproprier
expulsion [εks'pʌl∫ən] *s* expulsion *f*; (*from schools*) renvoi *m*
expunge [εks'pʌndʒ] *tr* effacer, supprimer, rayer
expurgate ['εkspər‚get] *tr* expurger
exquisite ['εkskwɪzɪt], [εks'kwɪzɪt] *adj* exquis
ex-service·man [‚εks'sʌrvɪs‚mæn] *s* (*pl* -men′) ancien combattant *m*
extant ['εkstənt], [εks'tænt] *adj* existant, subsistant
extemporaneous [εks‚tεmpə'renɪ·əs] *adj* improvisé, impromptu
extemporaneously [εks‚tεmpə'renɪ·əsli] *adv* à l'impromptu, d'abondance
extempore [εks'tεmpəri] *adj* improvisé || *adv* d'abondance, à l'impromptu
extemporize [εks'tεmpə‚raɪz] *tr* & *intr* improviser
extend [εks'tεnd] *tr* étendre; (*a period of time; a street; a line*) prolonger; (*a treaty; a session; a right; a due date*) proroger; (*a helping hand*) tendre || *intr* s'étendre
extended *adj* étendu, prolongé
extension [εks'tεn∫ən] *s* extension *f*; prolongation *f*; (*board for a table*) rallonge *f*; (*to building*) annexe *f*; (telp) poste *m*
exten′sion cord′ *s* cordon *m* prolongateur, prolongateur *m*
exten′sion lad′der *s* échelle *f* à coulisse
exten′sion ta′ble *s* table *f* à rallonges
extensive [εks'tεnsɪv] *adj* vaste, étendu
extent [εks'tεnt] *s* étendue *f*; **to a certain extent** dans une certaine mesure; **to a great extent** en grande partie, considérablement; **to the full extent** dans toute la mesure
extenuate [εks'tεnju‚et] *tr* atténuer; minimiser
exterior [εks'tɪrɪ·ər] *adj* & *s* extérieur *m*
exterminate [εks'tʌrmɪ‚net] *tr* exterminer

external [εks'tʌrnəl] *adj* extérieur; (pharm, med) externe || **externals** *spl* dehors *mpl*, apparences *fpl*; (*superficialities*) choses *fpl* secondaires
extinct [εks'tɪŋkt] *adj* (*volcano*) éteint; disparu; tombé en désuétude
extinction [εks'tɪŋkʃən] *s* extinction *f*
extinguish [εks'tɪŋgwɪʃ] *tr* éteindre
extinguisher [εks'tɪŋgwɪʃər] *s* (*for candles*) éteignoir *m*; (*for fires*) extincteur *m*
extirpate ['εkstər,pet], [εks'tʌrpet] *tr* extirper
ex·tol [εks'tol], [εks'tɑl] *v* (*pret & pp* -tolled; *ger* -tolling) *tr* exalter, vanter
extort [εks'tɔrt] *tr* extorquer
extortion [εks'tɔrʃən] *s* extorsion *f*
extortionist [εks'tɔrʃənɪst] *s* extorqueur *m*
extra ['εkstrə] *adj* supplémentaire; (*of high quality*) extra, extra-fin; (*spare*) de rechange || *s* extra *m*; (*of a newspaper*) édition *f* spéciale; (mov, theat) figurant *m* || *adv* en plus, en sus; (*not on the bill*) non compris
ex'tra board' *s* (*for extension table*) rallonge *f*
ex'tra charge' *s* supplément *m*
extract ['εkstrækt] *s* extrait *m* || [εks-'trækt] *tr* extraire
extraction [εks'trækʃən] *s* extraction *f*
extracurricular [,εkstrəkə'rɪkjələr] *adj* extra-scolaire
extradite ['εkstrə,daɪt] *tr* extrader
extradition [,εkstrə'dɪʃən] *s* extradition *f*
ex'tra-dry' *adj* (*champagne*) très sec
ex'tra fare' *s* supplément *m* de billet
extramural [,εkstrə'mjʊrəl] *adj* à l'extérieur de la ville; à l'exterieur de l'université
extraneous [εks'trenɪ·əs] *adj* étranger
extraordinary [εks'trɔrdɪ,nεri], [,εkstrə'ɔrdɪ,nεri] *adj* extraordinaire
extrapolate [εks'træpə,let] *tr & intr* extrapoler
extrasensory [,εkstrə'sεnsəri] *adj* extra-sensoriel
ex'tra-spe'cial *adj* extra
extravagance [εks'trævəgəns] *s* (*lavishness*) prodigalité *f*, gaspillage *m*; (*folly*) extravagance *f*
extravagant [εks'trævəgənt] *adj* (*person*) dépensier, prodigue; (*price*) exorbitant; (*e.g., praise*) outré; (*e.g., claims*) exagéré, extravagant
extreme [εks'trim] *adj & s* extrême *m*; **in the extreme, to extremes** à l'extrême
extremely [εks'trimli] *adv* extrêmement
extreme' unc'tion *s* extrême-onction *f*
extremist [εks'trimɪst] *adj & s* extrémiste *mf*
extremi·ty [εks'trεmɪti] *s* (*pl* -ties) extrémité *f*; **extremities** extrémités
extricate ['εkstrɪ,ket] *tr* dégager; (*a*

gas) libérer; **to extricate oneself from** se tirer de, se dépêtrer de
extrinsic [εks'trɪnsɪk] *adj* extrinsèque
extrovert ['εkstrə,vʌrt] *adj & s* extraverti *m*
extrude [εks'trud] *intr* faire saillie, dépasser
exuberant [εg'z(j)ubərənt] *adj* exubérant
exude [εg'zud], [εk'sud] *tr & intr* exsuder
exult [εg'zʌlt] *intr* exulter
exultant [εg'zʌltənt] *adj* triomphant
eye [aɪ] *s* œil *m*; (*of needle*) chas *m*, trou *m*; (*of hook and eye*) porte *f*; **to catch s.o.'s eye** tirer l'œil à qn; **to lay eyes on** jeter les yeux sur; **to make eyes at** (coll) faire les yeux doux à; **to see eye to eye with s.o.** voir les choses du même œil que qn; **with an eye to** en vue de; **without batting an eye** (coll) sans sourciller || *v* (*pret & pp* eyed; *ger* eying or eyeing) *tr* toiser, reluquer
eye'ball' *s* globe *m* oculaire
eye' bank' *s* banque *f* des yeux
eye'bolt' *s* boulon *m* à œil
eye'brow' *s* sourcil *m*
eye'cup' *s* œillère *f*
eye' drops' *spl* collyre *m*
eyeful ['aɪful] *s* vue *f*, coup *m* d'œil; **to get an eyeful** (coll) s'en mettre plein la vue, se rincer l'œil
eye'glass' *s* (*of optical instrument*) oculaire *m*; (*eyecup*) œillère *f*; **eyeglasses** lunettes *fpl*
eye'lash' *s* cil *m*; (*fringe of hair*) cils *mpl*
eyelet ['aɪlɪt] *s* œillet *m*; (*of sail*) œil *m* de pie
eye'lid' *s* paupière *f*
eye' of the morn'ing *s* astre *m* du jour
eye' o'pener ['opənər] *s* révélation *f*; (coll) goutte *f* de bonne heure
eye'piece' *s* oculaire *m*
eye'shade' *s* visière *f*, abat-jour *m*
eye' shad'ow *s* fard *m* à paupière
eye'shot' *s* portée *f* de la vue
eye'sight' *s* vue *f*; (*eyeshot*) portée *f* de la vue
eye' sock'et *s* orbite *f* de l'œil
eye'sore' *s* objet *m* déplaisant
eye'strain' *s* fatigue *f* des yeux; **to suffer from eyestrain** avoir les yeux fatigués
eye'-test chart' *s* tableau *m* de lecture pour la vision
eye'tooth' *s* (*pl* -teeth) dent *f* œillère or canine; **to cut one's eyeteeth** (coll) ne pas être un blanc-bec; **to give one's eyeteeth for** (coll) donner la prunelle de ses yeux pour
eye'wash' *s* collyre *m*; (slang) de l'eau bénite de cour, de la poudre aux yeux
eye'wit'ness *s* témoin *m* oculaire
ey·rie or **ey·ry** ['εri] *s* (*pl* -ries) aire *f* (de l'aigle); (fig) nid *m* d'aigle

F

F, f [ɛf] *s* VIᵉ lettre de l'alphabet
fable ['febəl] *s* fable *f*
fabric ['fæbrɪk] *s* tissu *m*, étoffe *f*
fabricate ['fæbrɪ‚ket] *tr* fabriquer
fabrication [‚fæbrɪ'keʃən] *s* fabrication *f*; (*lie*) mensonge *m*
fabulous ['fæbjələs] *adj* fabuleux
façade [fə'sɑd] *s* façade *f*
face [fes] *s* visage *m*, figure *f*; (*side*) face *f*; (*of the earth*) surface *f*; (*appearance, expression*) mine *f*, physionomie *f*; **about face!** (mil) demitour! **to keep a straight face** montrer un front sérieux; **to lose face** perdre la face; **to make a face** faire une grimace; **to set one's face against** faire front à ‖ *tr* faire face à; (*a wall*) revêtir; (*a garment*) mettre un revers à ‖ *intr*—**to face about** faire demi-tour; **to face up** faire face à, affronter
face′ card′ *s* figure *f*
face′ lift′ing *s* ridectomie *f*
face′ pow′der *s* poudre *f* de riz
facet ['fæsɪt] *s* facette *f*
facetious [fə'siʃəs] *adj* plaisant
face′ tow′el *s* serviette *f* de toilette
face′ val′ue *s* valeur *f* faciale, valeur nominale
facial ['feʃəl] *adj* facial ‖ *s* massage *m* esthétique
fa′cial tis′sue *s* serviette *f* à démaquiller
facilitate [fə'sɪlɪ‚tet] *tr* faciliter
facili-ty [fə'sɪlɪti] *s* (*pl* **-ties**) facilité *f*; **facilities** installations *fpl*
facing ['fesɪŋ] *s* revêtement *m*; (*of garment*) revers *m*
facsimile [fæk'sɪmɪli] *s* fac-similé *m*
fact [fækt] *s* fait *m*; **in fact** en fait, de fait; **the fact is that** c'est que
faction ['fækʃən] *s* faction *f*
factor ['fæktər] *s* facteur *m* ‖ *tr* résoudre or décomposer en facteurs
facto-ry ['fæktəri] *s* (*pl* **-ries**) usine *f*, fabrique *f*
fac′tory price′ *s* prix *m* de facture
factual ['fæktʃu‚əl] *adj* vrai, réel
facul-ty ['fækəlti] *s* (*pl* **-ties**) faculté *f*; (*teaching staff*) corps *m* enseignant
fad [fæd] *s* mode *f*, marotte *f*; **latest fad** dernier cri *m*
fade [fed] *tr* déteindre, décolorer ‖ *intr* déteindre, se décolorer; (*to lose vigor, freshness*) se faner; **to fade in** apparaître graduellement; **to fade out** disparaître graduellement
fade′-in′ *s* (mov) apparition *f* en fondu
fade′-out′ *s* (mov) fondu *m*
fag [fæg] *s* (slang) cibiche *f* ‖ *v* (*pret & pp* **fagged**; *ger* **fagging**) *tr*—**to fag out** éreinter
fagot ['fægət] *s* fagot *m*; (*for filling up trenches*) fascine *f* ‖ *tr* fagoter
fail [fel] *s*—**without fail** sans faute ‖ *tr* manquer à; (*a student*) refuser; (*an examination*) échouer à or dans

‖ *intr* manquer, faire défaut; (*to not succeed*) échouer, rater; (*said of motor*) tomber en panne; (*to weaken*) baisser, faiblir; **to fail in** faillir à; **to fail to** manquer de, faillir à; **to fail to do** or **to keep** faillir à
failing ['felɪŋ] *adj* défaillant ‖ *s* défaut *m* ‖ *prep* à défaut de
failure ['feljər] *s* insuccès *m*, échec *m*; (*lack*) manque *m*, défaut *m*; (*person*) raté *m*; (com) faillite *f*
faint [fent] *adj* faible; **to feel faint** se sentir mal ‖ *s* évanouissement *m* ‖ *intr* s'évanouir
faint′-heart′ed *adj* timide, peureux
fair [fɛr] *adj* juste, équitable; (*honest*) loyal, honnête; (*average*) moyen, passable; (*clear*) clair; (*beautiful*) beau; (*pleasing*) agréable, plaisant; (*of hair*) blond; (*complexion*) blanc; **to be fair** (*to be just*) être de bonne guerre ‖ *s* foire *f*, fête *f*; (*bazaar*) kermesse *f* ‖ *adv* impartialement; **to bid fair to** avoir des chances de; **to play fair** jouer franc jeu
fair′ cop′y *s* copie *f* au net
fair′ground′ *s* champ *m* de foire
fairly ['fɛrli] *adv* impartialement, loyalement; assez
fair′-mind′ed *adj* impartial
fairness ['fɛrnɪs] *s* impartialité *f*, justice *f*; (*of complexion*) clarté *f*
fair′ play′ *s* franc jeu *m*
fair′ sex′ *s* beau sexe *m*
fair′way′ *s* (golf) parcours *m* normal; (naut) chenal *m*
fair′-weath′er *adj* (e.g., *friend*) des beaux jours
fair-y ['fɛri] *adj* féerique ‖ *s* (*pl* **-ies**) fée *f*; (*homosexual*) (coll) tante *f*
fair′y-land′ *s* royaume *m* des fées
fair′y tale′ *s* conte *m* de fées
fair′y god′mother *s* marraine *f* fée; (coll) marraine gâteau
faith [feθ] *s* foi *f*; **to break faith with** manquer de foi à; **to keep faith with** tenir ses engagements envers; **to pin one's faith on** mettre tout son espoir en
faithful ['feθfəl] *adj* fidèle ‖ *s*—**the faithful** les fidèles *mpl*
faithless ['feθlɪs] *adj* infidèle
fake [fek] *adj* (coll) faux ‖ *s* faux *m*, article *m* truqué ‖ *tr* truquer
faker ['fekər] *s* truqueur *m*
falcon ['fɔkən], ['fɔlkən] *s* faucon *m*
falconer ['fɔkənər], ['fɔlkənər] *s* fauconnier *m*
fall [fɔl] *adj* automnal ‖ *s* chute *f*; (*of prices*) baisse *f*; (*season*) automne *m* & *f*; **falls** chute d'eau ‖ *v* (*pret* **fell** [fɛl]; *pp* **fallen** ['fɔlən]) *intr* tomber; (*said of prices*) baisser; **fall in!** (mil) rassemblement!; **fall out!** (mil) rompez les rangs!; **to fall down** (*said of person*) tomber par terre; (*said of building*) s'écrouler; **to fall for** (coll)

se laisser prendre à; (*to fall in love with*) (coll) tomber amoureux de; **to fall in** s'effondrer; (mil) former des rangs; **to fall into the trap** donner dans le piège; **to fall off** tomber de; (*to decline*) baisser, diminuer; **to fall out** (*to disagree*) se brouiller; **to fall over oneself to** (coll) se mettre en quatre pour

fallacious [fə'leʃəs] *adj* fallacieux
falla·cy ['fæləsi] *s* (*pl* -cies) erreur *f*, fausseté *f*
fall' guy' *s* (slang) tête *f* de Turc
fallible ['fælɪbəl] *adj* faillible
fall'ing star' *s* étoile *f* filante
fall'out' *s* pluies *fpl* radioactives, retombées *fpl* radioactives
fall'out shel'ter *s* abri *m* antiatomique
fallow ['fælo] *adj* en friche, en jachère || *s* friche *f*, jachère *f* || *tr* laisser en friche or en jachère
false [fɔls] *adj* faux; artificiel, simulé; (*hair*) postiche || *adv* faussement; **to play false** tromper
false' alarm' *s* fausse alerte *f*
false' bot'tom *s* double fond *m*
false' cog'nate *s* faux ami *m*
false' eye'lashes *spl* cils *mpl* postiches
false' face' *s* masque *m*
false'-heart'ed *adj* perfide, traître
false'hood *s* mensonge *m*
false' pretens'es *spl* faux-semblants *mpl*
false' return' *s* fausse déclaration *f* d'impôts
false' step' *s* faux-pas *m*
false' teeth' ['tiθ] *spl* fausses dents *fpl*
falset·to [fɔl'sɛto] *s* (*pl* -tos) fausset *m*, voix *f* de tête; (*person*) fausset *m*
falsi·fy ['fɔlsɪ‚faɪ] *v* (*pret & pp* -fied) *tr* falsifier, fausser
falsi·ty ['fɔlsɪti] *s* (*pl* -ties) fausseté *f*
falter ['fɔltər] *s* vacillation *f*, hésitation *f*; (*of speech*) balbutiement *m* || *intr* vaciller, hésiter; balbutier
fame [fem] *s* renom *m*, renommée *f*
famed *adj* renommé, célèbre
familiar [fə'mɪljər] *adj & s* familier *m*; **to become familiar with** se familiariser avec
familiari·ty [fə‚mɪlɪ'ærɪti] *s* (*pl* -ties) familiarité *f*
familiarize [fə'mɪljə‚raɪz] *tr* familiariser
fami·ly ['fæmɪli] *adj* familial; **in a** or **the family way** (coll) dans une position intéressante; (coll) en famille (Canad) || *s* (*pl* -lies) famille *f*
fam'ily man' *s* (*pl* **men'**) père *m* de famille; (*stay-at-home*) homme *m* casanier, pantouflard *m*
fam'ily name' *s* nom *m* de famille
fam'ily physi'cian *s* médecin *m* de famille
fam'ily tree' *s* arbre *m* généalogique
famine ['fæmɪn] *s* famine *f*
famish ['fæmɪʃ] *tr* affamer, priver de vivres || *intr* souffrir de la faim
famished *adj* affamé, famélique; **to be famished** (coll) mourir de faim
famous ['feməs] *adj* renommé, célèbre
fan [fæn] *s* éventail *m*; (mach) ventilateur *m*; (coll) fanatique *mf*, enragé

m || *v* (*pret & pp* **fanned**; *ger* **fanning**) *tr* éventer; (*to winnow*) vanner; (*e.g., passions*) exciter || *intr*—**to fan out** se déployer en éventail
fanatic [fə'nætɪk] *adj & s* fanatique *mf*
fanatical [fə'nætɪkəl] *adj* fanatique
fanaticism [fə'nætɪ‚sɪzəm] *s* fanatisme *m*
fan' belt' *s* (aut) courroie *f* de ventilateur
fancied *adj* imaginaire, supposé
fanciful ['fænsɪfəl] *adj* fantaisiste, capricieux
fan·cy ['fænsi] *adj* (*comp* -cier; *super* -ciest) ornemental; (*goods, clothes, bread*) de fantaisie; (*high-quaity*) fin, extra, de luxe || *s* (*pl* -cies) fantaisie *f*, caprice *m*; **to take a fancy to** prendre du goût pour; (*a loved one*) prendre en affection || *v* (*pret & pp* -cied) *tr* s'imaginer, se figurer; **to fancy oneself** s'imaginer; **to fancy that** imaginer que
fan'cy dress' *s* costume *m* de fantaisie, travesti *m*
fan'cy dress' ball' *s* bal *m* costumé, bal travesti
fan'cy foods' *spl* comestibles *mpl* de fantaisie
fan'cy-free' *adj* libre, gai, sans amour
fan'cy jew'elry *s* bijouterie *f* de fantaisie
fan'cy skat'ing *s* patinage *m* de fantaisie
fan'cy·work' *s* broderie *f*, ouvrage *m* d'agrément
fanfare ['fænfɛr] *s* fanfare *f*
fang [fæŋ] *s* croc *m*; (*of snake*) crochet *m*
fantastic(al) [fæn'tæstɪk(əl)] *adj* fantastique
fanta·sy ['fæntəzi], ['fæntəsi] *s* (*pl* -sies) fantaisie *f*
far [far] *adj* lointain; **on the far side of** à l'autre côté de || *adv* loin; **as far as** autant que; (*up to*) jusqu'à; **as far as I am concerned** quant à moi; **as far as I know** pour autant que je sache; **by far** de beaucoup; **far and wide** partout; **far away** au loin; **far from** loin de; **far from it** tant s'en faut; **far into the night** fort avant dans la nuit; **far into the woods** avant dans le bois; **far off** au loin; **how far?** jusqu'où?; **how far is it from . . . ?** combien y a-t-il de . . . ?; **in so far as** dans la mesure où; **so far** or **thus far** jusqu'ici; **to go far to** contribuer pour beaucoup à
far'away' *adj* éloigné, distant
farce [fars] *s* farce *f*
farcical ['farsɪkəl] *adj* grotesque, ridicule
fare [fer] *s* prix *m*, tarif *m*; (*cost of taxi*) course *f*; (*passenger in taxi*) client *m*; (*passenger in bus*) voyageur *m*; (culin) chère *f*, ordinaire *m*; **fares, please!** vos places, s'il vous plaît! || *intr* se porter; **how did you fare?** comment ça s'est-il passé?
Far' East' *s* Extrême-Orient *m*

fare'well' s adieu m; to bid s.o. farewell dire adieu à qn
far'-fetched' adj tiré par les cheveux
far-flung ['fɑr'flʌŋ] adj étendu, vaste, d'une grande envergure
farm [fɑrm] s ferme f; (sharecropper's farm) métairie f || tr cultiver, exploiter; to farm out donner à ferme; (work) donner en exploitation à l'extérieur || intr faire de la culture
farmer ['fɑrmər] s fermier m
farm' hand' s valet m de ferme
farm'house' s ferme f, maison f de ferme
farming ['fɑrmɪŋ] s agriculture f, exploitation f agricole
farm'yard' s cour f de ferme
Far' North' s Grand Nord m
far'-off' adj lointain, éloigné
far'-reach'ing adj à longue portée
far'sight'ed adj prévoyant; (physiol) presbyte
farther ['fɑrðər] adj plus éloigné || adv plus loin
farthest ['fɑrðɪst] adj (le) plus éloigné || adv le plus loin; au plus
farthing ['fɑrðɪŋ] s liard m
fascinate ['fæsɪ‚net] tr fasciner
fascinating ['fæsɪ‚netɪŋ] adj fascinateur, fascinant
fascism ['fæʃɪzəm] s fascisme m
fascist ['fæʃɪst] adj & s fasciste mf
fashion ['fæʃən] s mode f, vogue f; (manner) façon f, manière f; after a fashion tant bien que mal; in fashion à la mode, en vogue; out of fashion démodé || tr façonner
fashionable ['fæʃənəbəl] adj à la mode, élégant, chic
fash'ion design'ing s haute couture f
fash'ion plate' s gravure f de mode; (person) (coll) élégant m
fash'ion show' s présentation f de collection
fast [fæst], [fɑst] adj rapide; (fixed) solide, fixe; (clock) en avance; (friend) fidèle; (color) grand, bon, e.g., fast color grand teint, bon teint; (person) (slang) dévergondé; to make fast fixer, fermer || s jeûne m; to break one's fast rompre le jeûne || adv vite, rapidement; (firmly) solidement, ferme; (asleep) profondément; to hold fast tenir bon; to live fast (coll) faire la noce, mener la vie à grandes guides; to stand fast against tenir tête à || intr jeûner
fast' day' s jour m de jeûne, jour maigre
fasten ['fæsən], ['fɑsən] tr attacher, fixer; (e.g., a belt) ajuster || intr s'attacher, se fixer
fastener ['fæsənər], ['fɑsənər] s attache f, agrafe f
fastidious [fæs'tɪdɪ‚əs] adj délicat, dégoûté, difficile
fasting ['fæstɪŋ], ['fɑstɪŋ] s jeûne m
fat [fæt] adj (comp fatter; super fattest) (plump; greasy) gras; (large) gros; (soil) riche; (spark) nourri; to get fat engraisser || s graisse f; (of meat) gras m

fatal ['fetəl] adj fatal
fatalism ['fetə‚lɪzəm] s fatalisme m
fatalist ['fetəlɪst] s fataliste mf
fatali·ty [fə'tælɪti] s (pl -ties) fatalité f; (in accidents, war, etc.) mort f, accident m mortel
fate [fet] s sort m, destin m; the Fates les Parques fpl
fated adj destiné, voué
fateful ['fetfəl] adj fatal; (prophetic) fatidique
fat'head' s (coll) crétin m, sot m
father ['fɑðər] s père m; Father (salutation given a priest) Monsieur l'abbé || tr servir de père à; (to beget) engendrer; (an idea, project) inventer
fa'ther-hood' s paternité f
fa'ther-in-law' s (pl fathers-in-law) beau-père m
fa'ther-land' s patrie f
fatherless ['fɑðərlɪs] adj sans père, orphelin de père
fatherly ['fɑðərli] adj paternel
Fa'ther Time' s le Temps
fathom ['fæðəm] s brasse f || tr sonder
fathomless ['fæðəmlɪs] adj insondable
fatigue [fə'tig] s fatigue f; fatigues (mil) bleus mpl
fatigue' clothes' spl tenue f de corvée
fatigue' du'ty s (mil) corvée f
fatten ['fætən] tr & intr engraisser
fat·ty ['fæti] adj (comp -tier; super -tiest) gras, grassieux; (tissue) adipeux; (chubby) (coll) potelé, dodu || s (pl -ties) (coll) bon gros m
fatuous ['fætʃu‚əs] adj sot, idiot
faucet ['fɔsɪt] s robinet m
fault [fɔlt] s faute f; (geol) faille f; to a fault à l'excès; to find fault with trouver à redire à
fault'find'er s critiqueur m, éplucheur m
fault'find'ing adj chicaneur || s chicanerie f, critique f
faultless ['fɔltlɪs] adj sans défaut
fault·y ['fɔlti] adj (comp -ier; super -iest) fautif, défectueux
faun [fɔn] s faune m
fauna ['fɔnə] s faune f
favor ['fevər] s faveur f; do me the favor to faites-moi le plaisir de; to be in favor of être partisan de; to be in favor with jouir de la faveur de; to decide in s.o.'s favor donner gain de cause à qn || tr favoriser; (to look like) (coll) tenir de; (e.g., a sore leg) (coll) ménager
favorable ['fevərəbəl] adj favorable
favorite ['fevərɪt] adj & s favori m
fawn [fɔn] adj (color) fauve || s faon m || intr—to fawn upon (said of dog) faire des caresses à; (said of person) faire le chien couchant auprès de
faze [fez] tr (coll) affecter, troubler
FBI [‚ɛf‚bi'ɑɪ] s (letterword) (Federal Bureau of Investigation) Sûreté f nationale, Sûreté (the French equivalent)
fear [fɪr] s crainte f, peur f || tr craindre, avoir peur de || intr craindre, avoir peur
fearful ['fɪrfəl] adj (frightened) peu-

reux, effrayé; (*frightful*) effrayant; (coll) énorme, effrayant

fearless ['fɪrlɪs] *adj* sans peur

feasible ['fizɪbəl] *adj* faisable

feast [fist] *s* festin *m*, régal *m* ‖ *tr* régaler ‖ *intr* faire bonne chère; **to feast on** se régaler de

feast' day' *s* fête *f*, jour *m* de fête

feat [fit] *s* exploit *m*, haut fait *m*

feather ['fɛðər] *s* plume *f*; **feather in one's cap** (coll) fleuron *m* à sa couronne; **in fine feather** (coll) plein d'entrain ‖ *tr* emplumer; (*an oar*) ramener à plat; **to feather one's nest** (coll) faire son beurre

feath'er bed' *s* lit *m* de plumes, couette *f*

feath'er-bed'ding *s* emploi *m* de plus d'ouvriers qu'il n'en faut

feath'er-brained' *adj* braque, étourdi

feath'er dust'er *s* plumeau *m*

feath'er-edge' *s* (*of board*) biseau *m*; (*of tool*) morfil *m*

feath'er-weight' *s* poids-plume *m*

feathery ['fɛðəri] *adj* plumeux

feature ['fitʃər] *s* trait *m*, caractéristique *f*; (mov) long métrage *m*, grand film *m* ‖ *tr* caractériser; offrir comme attraction principale

fea'ture writ'er *s* rédacteur *m*

February ['fɛbru ˌɛri] *s* février *m*

feces ['fisiz] *spl* fèces *fpl*

feckless ['fɛklɪs] *adj* veule, faible

federal ['fɛdərəl] *adj & s* fédéral *m*

federate ['fɛdə ˌret] *adj* fédéré ‖ *tr* fédérer ‖ *intr* se fédérer

federation [ˌfɛdə'reʃən] *s* fédération *f*

fedora [fɪ'dorə] *s* chapeau *m* mou

fed' up' [fɛd] *adj*—**to be fed up** (coll) en avoir marre; **to be fed up with** (coll) avoir plein le dos de

fee [fi] *s* honoraires *mpl*, cachet *m*; **for a nominal fee** pour une somme symbolique

feeble ['fibəl] *adj* faible

fee'ble-mind'ed *adj* imbécile; obtus, à l'esprit lourd

feed [fid] *s* nourriture *f*, pâture *f*; (mach) alimentation *f*; (slang) grand repas *m* ‖ *v* (*pret & pp* fed [fɛd]) *tr* nourrir, donner à manger à; (*a machine*) alimenter ‖ *intr* manger; **to feed upon** se nourrir de

feed'back' *s* réalimentation *f*, régénération *f*, contre-réaction *f*

feed' bag' *s* musette-mangeoire *f*; **to put on the feed bag** (slang) casser la croûte

feeder ['fidər] *s* alimenteur *m*; (elec) canal *m* d'amenée

feed' pump' *s* pompe *f* d'alimentation

feed' trough' *s* mangeoire *f*, auge *f*

feed' wire' *s* (elec) fil *m* d'amenée

feel [fil] *s* sensation *f* ‖ *v* (*pret & pp* felt* [fɛlt]) *tr* sentir, éprouver; (*the pulse*) tâter; (*to examine*) palper; **to feel one's way** avancer à tâtons ‖ *intr* (*sick, tired, etc.*) se sentir; **to feel for** tâtonner, chercher à tâtons; (*to sympathize with*) (coll) être plein de pitié pour; **to feel like** avoir envie de

feeler ['filər] *s* (ent) antenne *f*; **to put out a feeler** (coll) tâter le terrain

feeling ['filɪŋ] *s* (*with senses*) toucher *m*, tact *m*; (*with hands*) tâtage *m*; (*impression, emotion*) sentiment *m*; **feelings** sensibilité *f*

feign [fen] *tr & intr* feindre

feint [fent] *s* feinte *f* ‖ *intr* feinter

feldspar ['fɛld ˌspar] *s* feldspath *m*

felicitate [fə'lɪsɪ ˌtet] *tr* féliciter

felicitous [fə'lɪsɪtəs] *adj* heureux, à propos

fell [fɛl] *adj* cruel, féroce ‖ *tr* abattre

felloe ['fɛlo] *s* jante *f*

fellow ['fɛlo] *s* (*of a society*) membre *m*; (*holder of a fellowship*) boursier *m*; (*friend, neighbor, etc.*) homme *m*, compagnon *m*; (coll) type *m*, bonhomme *m*, gars *m*; **poor fellow!** (coll) pauvre garçon!

fel'low cit'izen *s* concitoyen *m*

fel'low coun'tryman *s* compatriote *mf*

fel'low crea'ture *s* semblable *mf*

fel'low-man' *s* (*pl* -men') semblable *m*, prochain *m*

fel'low mem'ber *s* confrère *m*

fel'low-ship' *s* camaraderie *f*; (*scholarship*) bourse *f*; (*organization*) association *f*

fel'low stu'dent *s* condisciple *m*

fel'low trav'eler *s* compagnon *m* de voyage; (pol) compagnon de route

felon ['fɛlən] *s* criminel *m*; (pathol) panaris *m*

felo-ny ['fɛləni] *s* (*pl* -nies) crime *m*

felt [fɛlt] *s* feutre *m* ‖ *tr* feutrer

female ['fimel] *adj* (*sex*) féminin; (*animal, plant, piece of a device*) femelle ‖ *s* (*person*) femme *f*; (*plant, animal*) femelle *f*

feminine ['fɛmɪnɪn] *adj & s* féminin *m*

feminism ['fɛmɪ ˌnɪzəm] *s* féminisme *m*

fen [fɛn] *s* marécage *m*

fence [fɛns] *s* barrière *f*, clôture *f*; palissade *f*; (*for stolen goods*) receleur *m*; **on the fence** (coll) indécis, en balance ‖ *tr* clôturer ‖ *intr* faire de l'escrime

fencing ['fɛnsɪŋ] *s* (*enclosure*) clôture *f*; (sports) escrime *f*

fenc'ing acad'emy *s* salle *f* d'armes

fenc'ing mas'ter *s* maître *m* d'armes

fenc'ing match' *s* assaut *m* d'armes

fend [fɛnd] *tr*—**to fend off** parer ‖ *intr* —**to fend for oneself** (coll) se débrouiller, se tirer d'affaire

fender ['fɛndər] *s* (*mudguard*) aile *f*, garde-boue *m*; (*of locomotive*) chasse-pierres *m*; (*of fireplace*) garde-feu *m*

fennel ['fɛnəl] *s* fenouil *m*

ferment ['fʌrmɛnt] *s* ferment *m* ‖ [fər-'mɛnt] *tr* faire fermenter; (*wine*) cuver ‖ *intr* fermenter

fern [fʌrn] *s* fougère *f*

ferocious [fə'roʃəs] *adj* féroce

feroci-ty [fə'rasɪti] *s* (*pl* -ties) férocité *f*

ferret ['fɛrɪt] *s* furet *m* ‖ *tr*—**to ferret out** dénicher ‖ *intr* fureter

Fer'ris wheel' ['fɛrɪs] *s* grande roue *f*

fer-ry ['fɛri] *s* (*pl* -ries) bac *m*; (*to transport trains*) ferry-boat *m* ‖ *v* (*pret* & *pp* **-ried**) *tr* & *intr* passer en bac

fer'ry·boat' *s* bac *m*; (*to transport trains*) ferry-boat *m*

fer'ry·man *s* (*pl* **-men**) passeur *m*

fertile ['fʌrtɪl] *adj* fertile, fécond

fertilize ['fʌrtɪ,laɪz] *tr* fertiliser; (*to impregnate*) féconder

fertilizer ['fʌrtɪ,laɪzər] *s* engrais *m*, amendement *m*; (bot) fécondateur *m*

fervent ['fʌrvənt] *adj* fervent

fervid ['fʌrvɪd] *adj* fervent

fervor ['fʌrvər] *s* ferveur *f*

fester ['fɛstər] *s* ulcère *m* ‖ *tr* ulcérer ‖ *intr* s'ulcérer

festival ['fɛstɪvəl] *adj* de fête ‖ *s* fête *f*; (mov, mus) festival *m*

festive ['fɛstɪv] *adj* de fête, gai

festivi·ty [fɛs'tɪvɪti] *s* (*pl* **-ties**) festivité *f*

festoon [fɛs'tun] *s* feston *m* ‖ *tr* festonner

fetch [fɛtʃ] *tr* aller chercher; (*a certain price*) se vendre à

fetching ['fɛtʃɪŋ] *adj* (coll) séduisant

fete [fɛt] *s* fête *f* ‖ *tr* fêter

fetish ['fɛtɪʃ], ['fitɪʃ] *s* fétiche *m*

fetlock ['fɛtlɑk] *s* boulet *m*; (*tuft of hair*) fanon *m*

fetter ['fɛtər] *s* lien *m*; **fetters** fers *mpl*, chaînes *fpl* ‖ *tr* enchaîner, entraver

fettle ['fɛtəl] *s* condition *f*, état *m*; **in fine fettle** en pleine forme

fetus ['fitəs] *s* fœtus *m*

feud [fjud] *s* querelle *f*, vendetta *f* ‖ *intr* se quereller, être à couteaux tirés

feudal ['fjudəl] *adj* féodal

feudalism ['fjudə,lɪzəm] *s* féodalisme *m*

fever ['fivər] *s* fièvre *f*

fe'ver blis'ter *s* bouton *m* de fièvre

feverish ['fivərɪʃ] *adj* fiévreux

few [fju] *adj* peu de; **a few** . . . quelques . . . ; **quite a few** pas mal de; **the few** . . . les rares . . . ‖ *pron indef* peu; **a few** quelques-uns §81; **quite a few** beaucoup

fiancé [,fi·ɑn'se] *s* fiancé *m*

fiancée [,fi·ɑn'se] *s* fiancée *f*

fias·co [fɪ'æsko] *s* (*pl* **-cos** or **-coes**) fiasco *m*, échec *m*

fiat ['faɪ·ət], ['faɪ·æt] *s* ordonnance *f*, autorisation *f*

fib [fɪb] *s* (coll) petit mensonge *m*, blague *f* ‖ *v* (*pret* & *pp* **fibbed**; *ger* **fibbing**) *intr* (coll) blaguer

fiber ['faɪbər] *s* fibre *f*

fibrous ['faɪbrəs] *adj* fibreux

fickle ['fɪkəl] *adj* inconstant, volage

fiction ['fɪkʃən] *s* fiction *f*; (*branch of literature*) ouvrages *mpl* d'imagination, romans *mpl*

fictional ['fɪkʃənəl] *adj* romanesque, d'imagination

fictionalize ['fɪkʃənə,laɪz] *tr* romancer

fictitious [fɪk'tɪʃəs] *adj* fictif

fiddle ['fɪdəl] *s* violon *m* ‖ *tr*—**to fiddle away** (coll) gaspiller ‖ *intr* jouer du violon; **to fiddle around or with** (coll) tripoter

fiddler ['fɪdlər] *s* (coll) violoneux *m*

fid'dle·stick' *s* (coll) archet *m*; **fiddlesticks!** (coll) quelle blague!

fiddling ['fɪdlɪŋ] *adj* (coll) musard

fideli·ty [faɪ'dɛlɪti], [fɪ'dɛlɪti] *s* (*pl* **-ties**) fidélité *f*

fidget ['fɪdʒɪt] *intr* se trémousser; **to fidget with** tripoter

fidgety ['fɪdʒɪti] *adj* nerveux

fiduciar·y [fɪ'd(j)uʃɪ,ɛri] *adj* fiduciaire ‖ *s* (*pl* **-ies**) fiduciaire *m*

fie [faɪ] *interj* fi!; **fie on** . . . ! nargue de . . . !

field [fild] *s* champ *m*; (*area, activity*) domaine *m*, aire *f*; (aer, sports) terrain *m*; (elec) champ; (*of motor or dynamo*) (elec) inducteur *m*; (mil) aire *f*, théâtre *m*

field' day' *s* (*cleanup*) (mil) manœuvres *fpl* de garnison; (sports) manifestation *f* sportive

fielder ['fildər] *s* (baseball) chasseur *m*, homme *m* de champ

field' glass'es *spl* jumelles *fpl*

field' hock'ey *s* hockey *m* sur gazon

field' hos'pital *s* ambulance *f*, formation *f* sanitaire

field' mag'net *s* aimant *m* inducteur

field' mar'shal *s* maréchal *m*

field' mouse' *s* mulot *m*

field'piece' *s* pièce *f* de campagne

fiend [find] *s* démon *m*; (*mischiefmaker*) (coll) espiègle *mf*; (*enthusiast*) (coll) mordu *m*; (*addict*) (coll) toxicomane *mf*

fiendish ['findɪʃ] *adj* diabolique

fierce [fɪrs] *adj* féroce, farouche; (*wind*) furieux; (coll) très mauvais

fierceness ['fɪrsnɪs] *s* férocité *f*

fier·y ['faɪri], ['faɪ·əri] *adj* (*comp* **-ier**; *super* **-iest**) ardent; (*speech*) enflammé; (*horse, person, etc.*) fougueux

fife [faɪf] *s* fifre *m*

fifteen ['fɪf'tin] *adj, pron,* & *s* quinze *m*; **about fifteen** une quinzaine de

fifteenth ['fɪf'tinθ] *adj* & *pron* quinzième (*masc, fem*); **the Fifteenth** quinze, e.g., **John the Fifteenth** Jean quinze ‖ *s* quinzième *m*; **the fifteenth** (*in dates*) le quinze

fifth [fɪfθ] *adj* & *pron* cinquième (*masc, fem*); **the Fifth** cinq, e.g., **John the Fifth** Jean cinq ‖ *s* cinquième *m*; (mus) quinte *f*; **the fifth** (*in dates*) le cinq

fifth' col'umn *s* cinquième colonne *f*

fiftieth ['fɪftɪ·ɪθ] *adj* & *pron* cinquantième (*masc, fem*) ‖ *s* cinquantième *m*

fif·ty ['fɪfti] *adj* & *pron* cinquante ‖ *s* (*pl* **-ties**) cinquante *m*; **about fifty** une cinquantaine *f*; **fifties** (*years of the decade*) années *fpl* cinquante

fif'ty-fif'ty *adv*—**to go fifty-fifty** (coll) être de moitié, être en compte à demi

fig [fɪg] *s* figue *f*; (*tree*) figuier *m*; **a fig for** . . . ! (coll) nargue de . . . !

fight [faɪt] *s* combat *m*, bataille *f*; (*spirit*) cœur *m*; **to pick a fight with** chercher querelle à ‖ *v* (*pret* & *pp* **fought** [fɔt]) *tr* combattre, se battre contre; **to fight off** repousser ‖ *intr*

combattre, se battre; **to fight shy of** se défier de
fighter ['faɪtər] *s* combattant *m*; *(game person)* batailleur *m*; (aer) chasseur *m*, avion *m* de chasse
fight'er pi'lot *s* chasseur *m*
fig' leaf' *s* feuille *f* de figuier; *(on statues)* feuille de vigne
figment ['fɪgmənt] *s* fiction *f*, invention *f*
figurative ['fɪgjərətɪv] *adj* figuratif; *(meaning)* figuré
figure ['fɪgjər] *s* figure *f*; *(bodily form)* taille *f*; (math) chiffre *m*; **to be good at figures** être bon en calcul; **to have a good figure** avoir de la ligne; **to keep one's figure** garder sa ligne || *tr* figurer; *(to embellish)* orner de motifs; *(to imagine)* se figurer, s'imaginer; **to figure out** calculer; (coll) déchiffrer || *intr* figurer; **to figure on** compter sur
fig'ured bass' [bes] *s* (mus) basse *f* chiffrée
fig'ured silk' *s* soie *f* à dessin
fig'ure‐head' *s* prête-nom *m*, homme *m* de paille; (naut) figure *f* de proue
fig'ure of speech' *s* figure *f* de rhétorique
fig'ure skat'ing *s* patinage *m* de fantaisie
filament ['fɪləmənt] *s* filament *m*
filbert ['fɪlbərt] *s* noisette *f*, aveline *f*; *(tree)* noisetier *m*, avelinier *m*
filch [fɪltʃ] *tr* chaparder, chiper
file [faɪl] *s* *(tool)* lime *f*; *(for papers)* classeur *m*; *(for cards)* fichier *m*; *(personal record)* dossier *m*; *(line)* file *f*; **in single file** en file indienne, à la queue leu leu; **to form single file** dédoubler les rangs || *tr* limer; classer, ranger; *(a petition)* déposer; **to file down** enlever à la lime || *intr*—**to file off** défiler; **to file out** sortir un à un
file' case' *s* fichier *m*
file' clerk' *s* employé *m*, commis *m*
file' num'ber *s* *(e.g., used in answering a letter)* référence *f*
filial ['fɪlɪ‐əl], ['fɪljəl] *adj* filial
filiation [,fɪlɪ'eʃən] *s* filiation *f*
filibuster ['fɪlɪ,bʌstər] *s* *(use of delaying tactics)* obstruction *f*; *(legislator)* obstructionniste *mf*; *(pirate)* flibustier *m* || *tr* *(legislation)* obstruer || *intr* faire de l'obstruction
filigree ['fɪlɪ,gri] *adj* filigrané || *s* filigrane *m* || *tr* filigraner
filing ['faɪlɪŋ] *s* *(of documents)* classement *m*; *(with a tool)* limage *m*; **filings** limaille *f*, grains *mpl* de limaille
fil'ing cab'inet *s* classeur *m*
fil'ing card' *s* fiche *f*
Filipi·no [,fɪlɪ'pino] *adj* philippin || *s* *(pl* -nos) Philippin *m*
fill [fɪl] *s* suffisance *f*; *(earth, stones, etc.)* remblai *m*; **to have one's fill of** avoir tout son soûl de || *tr* remplir; *(a prescription)* exécuter; *(a tooth)* plomber; *(a cylinder with gas)* charger; *(a hollow or gap)* combler; *(a job)* occuper; **to fill in** remblayer,

combler; **to fill out** *(a questionnaire)* remplir || *intr* se remplir; **to fill out** se gonfler; *(said of sail)* s'enfler; **to fill up** se combler; *(to fill the tank full)* faire le plein
filler ['fɪlər] *s* remplissage *m*; *(of cigar)* tripe *f*; *(sizing)* apprêt *m*, mastic *m*; *(in notebook)* papier *m*; (journ) pesée *f*
fillet ['fɪlɪt] *s* bande *f*; *(for hair)* bandeau *m*; (archit) moulure *f* || ['fɪle], ['fɪlɪt] *s* (culin) filet *m* || *tr* couper en filets
filling ['fɪlɪŋ] *adj* *(food)* rassasiant || *s* *(of job)* occupation *f*; *(of tooth)* plombage *m*; *(e.g., of turkey)* farce *f*; *(of cigar)* tripe *f*
fill'ing sta'tion *s* poste *m* d'essence
fill'ing-station attend'ant *s* pompiste *mf*
fillip ['fɪlɪp] *s* tonique *m*, stimulant *m*; *(with finger)* chiquenaude *f* || *tr* donner une chiquenaude à
fil·ly ['fɪli] *s* *(pl* -lies) pouliche *f*; (coll) fillette *f*
film [fɪlm] *s* film *m*; *(in a roll)* pellicule *f*, film || *tr* filmer
filming ['fɪlmɪŋ] *s* filmage *m*
film' li'brary *s* cinémathèque *f*
film' mak'er *s* cinéaste *mf*
film' star' *s* vedette *f* du cinéma
film'strip' *s* film *m* fixe
film·y ['fɪlmi] *adj* *(comp* -ier; *super* -iest) diaphane, voilé
filter ['fɪltər] *s* filtre *m* || *tr* & *intr* filtrer
filtering ['fɪltərɪŋ] *s* filtrage *m*; *(of water)* filtration *f*
fil'ter pa'per *s* papier-filtre *m*
fil'ter tip' *adj* à bout-filtre || *s* bout-filtre *m*, bout-filtrant *m*
filth [fɪlθ] *s* saleté *f*, ordure *f*; (fig) obscénité *f*
filth·y ['fɪlθi] *adj* *(comp* -ier; *super* -iest) sale, immonde
filth'y lu'cre ['lukər] *s* (coll) lucre *m*
fin [fɪn] *s* nageoire *f*
final ['faɪnəl] *adj* final; *(last in a series)* ultime, définitif || *s* examen *m* final; (sports) finale *f*
finale [fɪ'nɑli] *s* (mus) final *m*
finalist ['faɪnəlɪst] *s* finaliste *mf*
finally ['faɪnəli] *adv* finalement, enfin
finance [fɪ'næns], ['faɪnæns] *s* finance *f* || *tr* financer
financial [fɪ'nænʃəl], [faɪ'nænʃəl] *adj* financier; *(interest; distress)* pécuniaire
financier [,fɪnən'sɪr], [,faɪnən'sɪr] *s* financier *m*
financing [fɪ'nænsɪŋ], ['faɪnænsɪŋ] *s* financement *m*
finch [fɪntʃ] *s* pinson *m*
find [faɪnd] *s* trouvaille *f* || *v* *(pret* & *pp* **found** [faund]) *tr* trouver; **to find out** apprendre || *intr* (law) déclarer; **to find out (about)** se renseigner (sur), se mettre au courant (de); **find out!** vous devez le trouver!
finder ['faɪndər] *s* *(of camera)* viseur *m*; *(of optical instrument)* chercheur *m*

finding ['faɪndɪŋ] s découverte f; (law) décision f; **findings** conclusions fpl
fine [faɪn] adj fin; (weather) beau; (person, manners, etc.) distingué, excellent; **that's fine!** bien!, parfait! || s amende f || tr mettre à l'amende
fine' arts' spl beaux-arts mpl
fineness ['faɪnɪs] s finesse f; (of metal) titre m
fine' print' s petits caractères mpl
finer·y ['faɪnəri] s (pl -ies) parure f
finespun ['faɪn͵spʌn] adj ténu; (fig) subtil
finesse [fɪ'nɛs] s finesse f; (in bridge) impasse f; **to use finesse** finasser || tr faire l'impasse à
fine'-toothed comb' s peigne m aux dents fines, peigne fin
finger ['fɪŋgər] s doigt m; (slang) mouchard m, indicateur m; **not to lift a finger** (fig) ne pas remuer le petit doigt; **to burn one's fingers** (fig) se faire échauder; **to put one's finger on the spot** (fig) mettre le doigt dessus; **to slip between the fingers** glisser entre les doigts; **to snap one's fingers at** (fig) faire la figue à, narguer; **to twist around one's little finger** (coll) mener par le bout du nez, faire tourner comme un toton || tr toucher du doigt, manier; (mus) doigter; (slang) espionner; (slang) identifier
fin'ger board' s (of guitar) touche f; (of piano) clavier m
fin'ger bowl' s rince-doigts m
fin'ger dexter'ity s (mus) doigté m
fingering ['fɪŋgərɪŋ] s maniement m; (mus) doigté m
fin'ger·nail' s ongle m
fin'gernail pol'ish s brillant m
fin'ger·print' s empreinte f digitale || tr prendre les empreintes digitales de
fin'ger·tip' s bout m du doigt; **to have at one's fingertips** tenir sur le bout du doigt
finicky ['fɪnɪki] adj méticuleux
finish ['fɪnɪʃ] s (perfection) achevé m, fini m; (elegance) finesse f; (conclusion) fin f; (gloss, coating, etc.) fini m || tr & intr finir; **to finish** + ger finir de + inf; **to finish by** + ger finir par + inf
fin'ishing touch' s dernière main f
finite ['faɪnaɪt] adj & s fini m
Finland ['fɪnlənd] s Finlande f; **la Finlande**
Finlander ['fɪnləndər] s Finlandais m
Finn [fɪn] s (member of a Finnish-speaking group of people) Finnois m; (native or inhabitant of Finland) Finlandais m
Finnish ['fɪnɪʃ] adj & s finnois m
fir [fʌr] s sapin m
fire [faɪr] s feu m; (destructive burning) incendie m; **to catch fire** prendre feu; **to set on fire** mettre le feu à || tr mettre le feu à; (e.g., passions) enflammer; (a weapon) tirer; (a rocket) lancer; (an employee) (coll) renvoyer || interj (warning) au feu!; (command to fire) feu!

fire' alarm' s avertisseur m d'incendie; (box) poste m avertisseur d'incendie
fire'arm' s arme f à feu
fire'ball' s globe m de feu; (mil) grenade f incendiaire
fire'bird' s loriot m d'Amérique
fire'boat' s bateau-pompe m
fire'box' s boîte f à feu; (rr) foyer m
fire'brand' s tison m; (coll) brandon m de discorde
fire'break' s tranchée f garde-feu, pare-feu m
fire'brick' s brique f réfractaire
fire' brigade' s corps m de sapeurs-pompiers
fire'bug' s (coll) incendiaire mf
fire' chief' s capitaine m des pompiers
fire' com'pany s corps m de sapeurs-pompiers; (insurance company) compagnie f d'assurance contre l'incendie
fire'crack'er s pétard m
fire'damp' s grisou m
fire' depart'ment s service m des incendies, sapeurs-pompiers mpl
fire'dog' s chenet m, landier m
fire' drill' s exercices mpl de sauvetage en cas d'incendie
fire' en'gine s pompe f à incendie
fire' escape' s échelle f de sauvetage, escalier m de secours
fire' extin'guisher s extincteur m
fire'fly' s (pl -flies) luciole f
fire'guard' s (before hearth) pare-étincelles m; (in forest) pare-feu m
fire' hose' s manche f d'incendie
fire'house' s caserne f de pompiers, poste m de pompiers
fire' hy'drant s bouche f d'incendie
fire' insur'ance s assurance f contre l'incendie
fire' i'rons spl garniture f de foyer
fire'less cook'er ['faɪrlɪs] s marmite f norvégienne
fire'man s (pl -men) (man who stokes fires) chauffeur m; (man who extinguishes fires) sapeur-pompier m, pompier m
fire'place' s cheminée f, foyer m
fire'plug' s bouche f d'incendie
fire' pow'er s puissance f de feu
fire'proof' adj ignifuge; (dish) apyre || tr ignifuger
fire' sale' s vente f après incendie
fire' screen' s écran m de cheminée, garde-feu m
fire' ship' s brûlot m
fire' shov'el s pelle f à feu
fire'side' s coin m du feu
fire'trap' s édifice m qui invite l'incendie
fire' wall' s coupe-feu m
fire'ward'en s garde m forestier, vigie f
fire'wa'ter s (slang) gnole f, whisky m
fire'wood' s bois m de chauffage
fire'works' spl feu m d'artifice
firing ['faɪrɪŋ] s (of furnace) chauffe f; (of bricks, ceramics, etc.) cuite f; (of gun) tir m, feu m; (by a group of soldiers) fusillade f; (of an internal-combustion engine) allumage m; (of an employee) (coll) renvoi m

fir'ing line' s ligne f de feu, chaîne f de combat
fir'ing or'der s rythme m d'allumage
fir'ing pin' s percuteur m, aiguille f
fir'ing squad' s peloton m d'exécution; (for ceremonies) piquet m d'honneurs funèbres
firm [fʌrm] adj & adv ferme; **to stand firm** tenir bon ‖ s maison f de commerce, firme f
firmament ['fʌrməmənt] s firmament m
firm' name' s nom m commercial
firmness ['fʌrmnɪs] s fermeté f
first [fʌrst] adj, pron, & s premier m; **at first** au commencement, au début; **first come first served** les premiers vont devant; **from the first** depuis le premier jour; **John the First** Jean premier ‖ adv premièrement, d'abord; **first and last** en tout et pour tout; **first of all, first off** tout d'abord, de prime abord
first' aid' s premiers soins mpl, premiers secours mpl
first'-aid' kit' s boîte f à pansements, trousse f de première urgence
first'-aid' sta'tion s poste m de secours
first'-born' adj & s premier-né m
first'-class' adj de première classe, de premier ordre ‖ adv en première classe
first' cous'in s cousin m germain
first' draft' s brouillon m, premier jet m
first' fin'ger s index m
first' floor' s rez-de-chaussée m
first' fruits' spl prémices fpl
first'hand' adj & adv de première main
first' lieuten'ant s lieutenant m en premier
firstly ['fʌrstli] adv en premier lieu, d'abord
first' mate' s (naut) second m
first' name' s prénom m, petit nom m
first' night' s (theat) première f
first-nighter [,fʌrst'naɪtər] s (theat) habitué m des premières
first' offend'er s délinquant m primaire
first' of'ficer s (naut) officier m en second
first' prize' s (in a lottery) gros lot m; **to win first prize** remporter le prix
first' quar'ter s (of the moon) premier quartier m
first'-rate' adj de premier ordre, de première qualité; (coll) excellent ‖ adv (coll) très bien, à merveille
first'-run mov'ie s film m en exclusivité
fiscal ['fɪskəl] adj fiscal
fis'cal year' s exercice m budgétaire
fish [fɪʃ] s poisson m; **to be like a fish out of water** être comme un poisson sur la paille; **to be neither fish nor fowl** être ni chair ni poisson; **to drink like a fish** boire comme un trou; **to have other fish to fry** avoir d'autres chiens à fouetter ‖ tr pêcher; (rr) éclisser; **to fish out** or **up** repêcher ‖ intr pêcher; **to fish for compliments** quêter des compliments; **to go fishing** aller à la pêche; **to take fishing** emmener à la pêche
fish'bone' s arête f

fish'bowl' s bocal m
fisher ['fɪʃər] s pêcheur m; (zool) martre f
fish'er·man s (pl -men) pêcheur m
fisher·y ['fɪʃəri] s (pl -ies) (activity; business) pêche f; (grounds) pêcherie f
fish' hawk' s aigle m pêcheur
fish'hook' s hameçon m
fishing ['fɪʃɪŋ] adj pêcheur, de pêche ‖ s pêche f
fish'ing ground' s pêcherie f
fish'ing reel' s moulinet m
fish'ing rod' s canne f à pêche
fish'ing tack'le s attirail m de pêche
fish'line' s ligne f de pêche
fish' mar'ket s poissonnerie f
fish'plate' s (rr) éclisse f
fish'pool' s vivier m
fish' spear' s foëne f, fouëne f
fish' sto'ry s hâblerie f, blague f
fish'tail' s queue f de poisson; (aer) embardée f ‖ intr (aer) embarder
fish'wife' s (pl -wives') poissonnière f; (foul-mouthed woman) poissarde f
fish'worm' s asticot m
fish·y ['fɪʃi] adj (comp -ier; super -iest) (eyes) (coll) vitreux; (coll) véreux, louche
fission ['fɪʃən] s (biol) scission f; (nucl) fission f
fissionable ['fɪʃənəbəl] adj fissible, fissile
fissure ['fɪʃər] s fissure f, fente f ‖ tr fissurer ‖ intr se fissurer
fist [fɪst] s poing m; (typ) petite main f; **to shake one's fist at** menacer du poing
fist'fight' s combat m à coup de poings
fistful ['fɪstful] s poignée f
fisticuffs ['fɪstɪ ,kʌfs] spl empoignade f or rixe f à coups de poing; (sports) boxe f
fit [fɪt] adj (comp fitter; super fittest) bon, convenable; capable, digne; (in good health) en forme, sain; **fit to be tied** (coll) en colère; **fit to drink** buvable; **fit to eat** mangeable; **to feel fit** être frais et dispos ‖ s ajustement m; (of clothes) coupe f, façon f; (of fever, rage, coughing) accès m; **by fits and starts** par accès; **fit of coughing** quinte f de toux ‖ v (pret & pp fitted; ger fitting) tr ajuster; (s.th. in s.th) emboîter; **to fit for** (e.g., a task) préparer à; **to fit out** or up aménager; **to fit out with** garnir de ‖ intr s'emboîter; **to fit in with** s'accorder avec, convenir à
fitful ['fɪtfəl] adj intermittent
fitness ['fɪtnɪs] s convenance f; (for a task) aptitude f; (good shape) bonne forme f
fitter ['fɪtər] s ajusteur m; (of machinery) monteur m; (of clothing) essayeur m
fitting ['fɪtɪŋ] adj convenable, approprié, à propos ‖ s ajustage m; (of a garment) essayage m; **fittings** aménagements mpl; (of metal) ferrures fpl

five [faɪv] *adj & pron* cinq ‖ *s* cinq *m*;
  five o'clock cinq heures
five′-year plan′ *s* plan *m* quinquennal
fix [fɪks] *s* (coll) mauvais pas *m*; **to be
  in a fix** (coll) être dans le pétrin ‖ *tr*
  réparer; (*e.g., a date; a photographic
  image; prices; one's eyes*) fixer;
  (slang) donner son compte à
fixedly [ˈfɪksɪdli] *adv* fixement
fixing [ˈfɪksɪŋ] *s* fixation *f*; (phot)
  fixage *m*; **fixings** (slang) collation *f*,
  des mets *mpl*
fix′ing bath′ *s* bain *m* de fixage, fixa-
  teur *m*
fixture [ˈfɪkstʃər] *s* accessoire *m*, garniture *f*; **fixtures** meubles *mpl* à demeure
fizz [fɪz] *s* pétillement *m* ‖ *intr* pétiller
fizzle [ˈfɪzəl] *s* (coll) avortement *m* ‖
  intr (coll) avorter; **to fizzle out** (coll)
  tomber à l'eau, échouer
flabbergasted   [ˈflæbərˌgæstɪd] *adj*
  (coll) éberlué, épaté
flab·by [ˈflæbi] *adj* (*comp* -**bier**; *super*
  -**biest**) mou, flasque
flag [flæg] *s* drapeau *m* ‖ *v* (*pret & pp*
  flagged; *ger* **flagging**) *tr*—**to flag s.o.**
  transmettre des signaux à qn en agi-
  tant un fanion ‖ *intr* faiblir, se relâcher
flag′ cap′tain *s* (nav) capitaine *m* de
  pavillon
flag′man *s* (*pl* -**men**) signaleur *m*; (rr)
  garde-voie *m*
flag′ of truce′ *s* drapeau *m* parlementaire
flag′pole′ *s* hampe *f* de drapeau;
  (naut) mât *m* de pavillon; (surv)
  jalon *m*
flagrant [ˈflegrənt] *adj* scandaleux;
  (*e.g., injustice*) flagrant
flag′ship′ *s* (nav) vaisseau *m* amiral
flag′staff′ *s* hampe *f* de drapeau
flag′stone′ *s* dalle *f*
flag′ stop′ *s* (rr) halte *f*, arrêt *m* facultatif
flag′-wav′ing *adj* cocardier ‖ *s* patriotisme *m* de façade
flail [flel] *s* fléau *m* ‖ *tr* (agr) battre au
  fléau; (fig) éreinter
flair [fler] *s* flair *m*; aptitude *f*
flak [flæk] *s* tir *m* contre-avions
flake [flek] *s* (*of snow; of cereal*) flocon *m*; (*of soap; of mica*) paillette *f*;
  (*of paint*) écaille *f* ‖ *intr* tomber en
  flocons; **to flake off** s'écailler
flak·y [ˈfleki] *adj* (*comp* -**ier**; *super*
  -**iest**) floconneux, lamelleux
flamboyant [flæmˈbɔɪ·ənt] *adj* fleuri,
  orné, coloré; (archit) flamboyant
flame [flem] *s* flamme *f*; (coll) amant
  m, amante *f* ‖ *tr* flamber ‖ *intr*
  flamber, flamboyer
flamethrower [ˈflemˌθro·ər] *s* lance-
  flammes *m*
flaming [ˈflemɪŋ] *adj* flambant
flamin·go [fləˈmɪŋgo] *s* (*pl* -**gos** or
  -**goes**) flamant *m*
flammable [ˈflæməbəl] *adj* inflammable
Flanders [ˈflændərz] *s* Flandre *f*; la
  Flandre

flange [flændʒ] *s* rebord *m*, saillie *f*;
  (*of wheel*) jante *f*; (*of rail*) patin *m*
flank [flæŋk] *s* flanc *m* ‖ *tr* flanquer
flannel [ˈflænəl] *s* flanelle *f*
flap [flæp] *s* (*part that can be folded
  under*) rabat *m*; (*fold in clothing*)
  pan *m*; (*of a cap*) couvre-nuque *m*;
  (*of a pocket; of an envelope*) patte
  f; (*of wings*) coup *m*, battement *m*;
  (*of a table*) battant *m*; (*of a sail,
  flag, etc.*) claquement *m*; (*slap*) tape
  f; (aer) volet *m* ‖ *v* (*pret & pp*
  flapped; *ger* **flapping**) *tr* (*wings,
  arms, etc.*) battre; (*to slap*) taper ‖
  intr battre; (*said of sail, flag, etc.*)
  claquer; (*said of curtain*) voltiger;
  (*to hang down*) pendre
flap′jack′ *s* (coll) crêpe *f*
flare [fler] *s* éclat *m* vif; (*e.g., of skirt;
  of pipe or funnel*) évasement *m*; (*for
  signaling*) fusée *f* éclairante ‖ *tr* évaser ‖ *intr* flamboyer; (*to spread outward*) s'évaser; **to flare up** s'enflammer; (*to reappear*) se produire
  de nouveau; (*to become angry*) s'emporter
flare′-up′ *s* flambée *f* soudaine; (*of illness*) recrudescence *f*; (*of anger*)
  accès *m* de colère
flash [flæʃ] *s* éclair *m*; (*of hope*) lueur
  f, rayon *m*; (*of wit*) trait *m*; (*of
  genius*) éclair; (*brief moment*) instant
  m; (*ostentation*) (coll) tape-à-l'œil *m*;
  (*last-minute news*) (coll) nouvelle *f*
  éclair; **flash in the pan** (coll) feu *m*
  de paille; **in a flash** en un clin d'œil ‖
  tr projeter; (*a gem*) faire étinceler;
  (*to show off*) faire parade de; (*a message*) répandre, transmettre ‖ *intr*
  jeter des éclairs; (*said of gem, eyes,
  etc.*) étinceler; **to flash by** passer
  comme un éclair
flash′back′ *s* (mov) retour *m* en arrière,
  rappel *m*
flash′ bulb′ *s* ampoule *f* flash, flash *m*
flash′ flood′ *s* crue *f* subite
flashing [ˈflæʃɪŋ] *adj* éclatant; (*light*)
  à éclats; (*signal*) clignotant ‖ *s* bande
  f de solin
flash′light′ *s* lampe *f* torche, lampe de
  poche; (phot) lampe éclair
flash′light bat′tery *s* pile *f* torche
flash·y [ˈflæʃi] *adj* (*comp* -**ier**; *super*
  -**iest**) (coll) tapageur, criard
flask [flæsk], [flɑsk] *s* flacon *m*,
  gourde *f*; (*in lab*) ballon *m*, flacon
flat [flæt] *adj* (*comp* **flatter**; *super*
  flattest) plat, uni; (*nose*) aplati; (*refusal*) net; (*beer*) éventé; (*tire*) dégonflé; (*dull, tasteless*) fade, terne;
  (mus) bémol ‖ *s* appartement *m*;
  (*flat tire*) crevaison *f*; (*of sword*)
  plat *m*; (mus) bémol *m*; (theat) châssis *m* ‖ *adv* (*outright*) (coll) nettement, carrément; **to fall flat** tomber à
  plat; (fig) manquer son effet; **to sing
  flat** chanter faux
flat′boat′ *s* plate *f*
flat-broke [ˈflætˈbrok] *adj* (coll) complètement fauché, à la côte
flat′car′ *s* plate-forme *f*

flat′foot′ s (slang) flic m
flat′-foot′ed adj aux pieds plats; (coll) franc, brutal
flat′i′ron s fer m à repasser
flatly [′flætli] adv net, platement
flat′-nosed′ adj camard, camus
flatten [′flætən] tr aplatir, aplanir; (metallurgy) laminer || intr s'aplatir, s'aplanir; **to flatten out** (aer) se redresser
flatter [′flætər] tr & intr flatter
flatterer [′flætərər] s flatteur m
flattering [′flætərɪŋ] adj flatteur
flatter·y [′flætəri] s (pl -ies) flatterie f
flat′ tire′ s pneu m dégonflé, à plat, or crevé, crevaison f
flat′top′ s (nav) porte-avions m
flatulence [′flætʃələns] s boursouflure f; (pathol) flatulence f
flat′ware′ s couverts mpl; (plates) assiettes fpl
flaunt [flɔnt], [flɑnt] tr faire étalage de
flautist [′flɔtɪst] s flûtiste mf
flavor [′flevər] s saveur f, goût m; (of ice cream) parfum m || tr assaisonner, parfumer
flavoring [′flevərɪŋ] s assaisonnement m; (lemon, rum, etc.) parfum m
flaw [flɔ] s défaut m, tache f; (crack) fêlure f; (in metal) paille f; (in diamond) crapaud m
flawless [′flɔlɪs] adj sans défaut, sans tache
flax [flæks] s lin m
flaxen [′flæksən] adj de lin, blond
flax′seed′ s graine f de lin
flay [fle] tr écorcher; (to criticize) rosser, fustiger
flea [fli] s puce f
flea′bite′ s piqûre f de puce; (trifle) vétille f
fleck [flɛk] s tache f; (particle) particule f || tr tacheter
fledgling [′flɛdʒlɪŋ] adj (lawyer, teacher) en herbe, débutant || s oisillon m; (novice) débutant m, béjaune m
flee [fli] v (pret & pp **fled** [flɛd]) tr & intr fuir
fleece [flis] s toison f || tr tondre; (to strip of money) (coll) écorcher, plumer
fleec·y [′flisi] adj (comp -ier; super -iest) laineux; (snow, wool) floconneux; (hair) moutonneux; (clouds) moutonné
fleet [flit] adj rapide || s flotte f
fleet′-foot′ed adj au pied léger
fleeting [′flitɪŋ] adj passager, fugitif
Fleming [′flɛmɪŋ] s Flamand m
Flemish [′flɛmɪʃ] adj & s flamand m
flesh [flɛʃ] s chair f; **in the flesh** en chair et en os; **to lose flesh** perdre de l'embonpoint; **to put on flesh** prendre de l'embonpoint, s'empâter
flesh′ and blood′ s nature f humaine; (relatives) famille f, parenté f
flesh′-col′ored adj couleur f de chair, carné
flesh′pot′ s (pot for cooking meat) pot-au-feu m; **fleshpots** (high living) luxe m, grande chère f; (evil places) mai-

sons fpl de débauche, mauvais lieux mpl
flesh′ wound′ [wund] s blessure f en séton, blessure superficielle
flesh·y [′flɛʃi] adj (comp -ier; super -iest) charnu
flex [flɛks] tr & intr fléchir
flexible [′flɛksɪbəl] adj flexible
flick [flɪk] s (with finger) chiquenaude f; (with whip) petit coup m; **flicks** (coll) ciné m || tr faire une chiquenaude à; (a whip) faire claquer
flicker [′flɪkər] s petite lueur f vacillante; (of eyelids) battement m; (of emotion) frisson m || intr trembloter, vaciller; (said of eyelids) ciller
flier [′flaɪ·ər] s aviateur m; (coll) spéculation f au hasard; (rr) rapide m; (handbill) (coll) prospectus m
flight [flaɪt] s fuite f; (of airplane) vol m; (of birds) volée f; (of stairs) volée; (of fancy) élan m; **to put to flight** mettre en fuite; **to take flight** prendre la fuite
flight′ deck′ s (nav) pont m d'envol
flight′ record′er s enregistreur m en vol
flight·y [′flaɪti] adj (comp -ier; super -iest) volage, léger; braque, écervelé
flim-flam [′flɪm‚flæm] s (coll) baliverne f; (fraud) (coll) escroquerie f || v (pret & pp **-flammed**; ger **-flamming**) tr (coll) escroquer
flim·sy [′flɪmzi] adj (comp -sier; super -siest) léger; (e.g., cloth) fragile; (e.g., excuse) frivole
flinch [flɪntʃ] intr reculer, fléchir; **without flinching** sans broncher, sans hésiter
fling [flɪŋ] s jet m; **to go on a fling** faire la noce; **to have a fling at** tenter; **to have one's fling** jeter sa gourme || v (pret & pp **flung** [flʌŋ]) tr lancer; (on the floor, out the window; in jail) jeter; **to fling open** ouvrir brusquement
flint [flɪnt] s silex m; (of lighter) pierre f
flint′lock′ s fusil m à pierre
flint·y [′flɪnti] adj (comp -ier; super -iest) siliceux; (heart) de pierre, insensible
flip [flɪp] adj (comp **flipper**; super **flippest**) (coll) mutin, moqueur || s chiquenaude f; (somersault) culbute f; (aer) petit tour m de vol || v (pret & pp **flipped**; ger **flipping**) tr donner une chiquenaude à; (a page) tourner rapidement; **to flip a coin** jouer à pile ou face; **to flip over** (a phonograph record) retourner
flippancy [′flɪpənsi] s désinvolture f
flippant [′flɪpənt] adj désinvolte
flipper [′flɪpər] s nageoire f
flirt [flʌrt] s flirteur m, flirt m || intr flirter; (said only of a man) conter fleurette
flit [flɪt] v (pret & pp **flitted**; ger **flitting**) intr voleter; **to flit away** passer rapidement; **to flit here and there** voltiger
float [flot] s (raft) radeau m; (on fish line; in carburetor; on seaplane) flot-

teur *m*; (*on fish line or net*) flotte *f*; (*of mason*) aplanissoire *f*; (*in parade*) char *m* de cavalcade, char de Carnaval ‖ *tr* faire flotter; (*a loan*) émettre, contracter ‖ *intr* flotter, nager; (*on one's back*) faire la planche

floater ['flotər] *s* vagabond *m*; (*illegal voter*) faux électeur *m*

floating ['flotɪŋ] *adj* flottant; (*free*) libre ‖ *s* flottement *m*; (*of loan*) émission *f*

float'ing is'land *s* (culin) œufs *mpl* à la neige

flock [flɑk] *s* (*of birds*) volée *f*; (*of sheep*) troupeau *m*; (*of people*) foule *f*, bande *f*; (*of nonsense*) tas *m*; (*of faithful*) ouailles *fpl* ‖ *intr* s'assembler; **to flock in** entrer en foule; **to flock together** s'attrouper

floe [flo] *s* banquise *f*; (*floating piece of ice*) glaçon *m* flottant

flog [flɑg] *v* (*pret & pp* **flogged**; *ger* **flogging**) *tr* fouetter, flageller

flogging ['flɑgɪŋ] *s* fouet *m*

flood [flʌd] *s* inondation *f*; (*caused by heavy rain*) déluge *m*; (*sudden rise of river*) crue *f*; (*of tide*) flot *m*; (*of words, tears, light*) flots *mpl*, déluge ‖ *tr* inonder; (*to overwhelm*) submerger, inonder; (*a carburetor*) noyer ‖ *intr* (*said of river*) déborder; (aut) se noyer

flood'gate' *s* (*of a dam*) vanne *f*; (*of a canal*) porte *f* d'écluse

flood'light' *s* phare *m* d'éclairage, projecteur *m* de lumière ‖ *tr* illuminer par projecteurs

flood' tide' *s* marée *f* montante, flux *m*

floor [flor] *s* (*inside bottom surface of room*) plancher *m*, parquet *m*; (*story of building*) étage *m*; (*of swimming pool, the sea, etc.*) fond *m*; (*of assembly hall*) enceinte *f*, parquet; (*of the court*) prétoire *m*, parquet; (naut) varangue *f*; **to ask for the floor** réclamer la parole; **to give s.o. the floor** donner la parole à qn; **to have the floor** avoir la parole; **to take the floor** prendre la parole ‖ *tr* parqueter; (*an opponent*) terrasser; (*to disconcert*) (coll) désarçonner

flooring ['florɪŋ] *s* planchéiage *m*, parquetage *m*

floor' lamp' *s* lampe *f* à pied, lampadaire *m*

floor' mop' *s* brosse *f* à parquet

floor' show' *s* spectacle *m* de cabaret

floor' tim'ber *s* (naut) varangue *f*

floor'walk'er *s* chef *m* de rayon

floor' wax' *s* cire *f* à parquet, encaustique *f*

flop [flɑp] *s* (coll) insuccès *m*, échec *m*; (*literary work or painting*) (coll) navet *m*; (*play*) (coll) four *m*; **to take a flop** (coll) faire patapouf ‖ *v* (*pret & pp* **flopped**; *ger* **flopping**) *intr* tomber lourdement; (*to fail*) (coll) échouer, rater

flora ['florə] *s* flore *f*

floral ['florəl] *adj* floral

florescence [flo'rɛsəns] *s* floraison *f*

florid ['flɑrɪd], ['flɔrɪd] *adj* fleuri, flamboyant; (*complexion*) rubicond

Florida ['flɑrɪdə], ['flɔrɪdə] *s* Floride *f*; la Floride

Flor'ida Keys' *spl* Cayes *fpl* de la Floride

floss [flɔs], [flɑs] *s* bourre *f*; (*of corn*) barbe *f*

floss' silk' *s* bourre *f* de soie, filoselle *f*

floss·y ['flɔsi], ['flɑsi] *adj* (*comp* **-ier**; *super* **-iest**) soyeux; (slang) pimpant, tapageur

flotsam ['flɑtsəm] *s* épave *f*

flot'sam and jet'sam *s* choses *fpl* de flot et de mer, épaves *fpl*

flounce [flauns] *s* volant *m* ‖ *tr* garnir de volants ‖ *intr* s'élancer avec emportement

flounder ['flaundər] *s* flet *m*; (*plaice*) carrelet *m*, plie *f* ‖ *intr* patauger

flour [flaur] *s* farine *f* ‖ *tr* fariner

flourish ['flʌrɪʃ] *s* fioriture *f*; (*on a signature*) paraphe *m*; (*of trumpets*) fanfare *m*; (*brandishing*) brandissement *m* ‖ *tr* brandir; (*to wave*) agiter ‖ *intr* fleurir, prospérer

flourishing ['flʌrɪʃɪŋ] *adj* florissant

flour' mill' *s* moulin *m*, minoterie *f*

floury ['flauri] *adj* farineux

flout [flaut] *tr* se moquer de, narguer ‖ *intr* se moquer

flow [flo] *s* écoulement *m*; (*of tide, blood, words*) flot *m*, flux *m*; (*of blood to the head*) afflux *m*; (*rate of flow*) débit *m*; (*current*) courant *m* ‖ *intr* écouler; (*said of tide*) monter; (*said of blood in the body*) circuler; (fig) couler; **to flow into** déboucher dans, se verser dans; **to flow over** déborder

flower ['flau·ər] *s* fleur *f* ‖ *tr & intr* fleurir

flow'er bed' *s* plate-bande *f*, parterre *m*; (*round flower bed*) corbeille *f*

flow'er gar'den *s* jardin *m* de fleurs, jardin d'agrément

flow'er girl' *s* bouquetière *f*; (*at a wedding*) fille *f* d'honneur

flow'er·pot' *s* pot *m* à fleurs

flow'er shop' *s* boutique *f* de fleuriste

flow'er show' *s* exposition *f* horticole, floralies *fpl*

flow'er stand' *s* jardinière *f*

flowery ['flau·əri] *adj* fleuri

flu [flu] *s* (coll) grippe *f*

fluctuate ['flʌktʃu,et] *intr* fluctuer

flue [flu] *s* tuyau *m*

fluency ['flu·ənsi] *s* facilité *f*

fluent ['flu·ənt] *adj* disert, facile; (*flowing*) coulant

fluently ['flu·əntli] *adv* couramment

fluff [flʌf] *s* (*velvety cloth*) peluche *f*; (*tuft of fur, dust, etc.*) duvet *m*; (*boner made by actor*) (coll) loup *m* ‖ *tr* lainer, rendre pelucheux; (*one's entrance*) (coll) louper; (*one's lines*) (coll) bouler ‖ *intr* pelucher

fluff·y ['flʌfi] *adj* (*comp* **-ier**; *super* **-iest**) duveteux; (*hair*) flou

fluid ['flu·ɪd] *adj & s* fluide *m*

fluke [fluk] *s* (*of anchor*) patte *f*; (billiards) raccroc *m*, coup *m* de veine

flume [flum] s canalisation *f*, ravin *m*
flunk [flʌŋk] *tr* (*a student*) (coll) recaler, coller; (*an exam*) rater || *intr* être recalé, se faire coller
flunk·y ['flʌŋki] s (*pl* -ies) laquais *m*
fluorescent [,flu·ə'rɛsənt] *adj* fluorescent
fluoridate ['florɪ,det], ['flurɪ,det] *tr* & *intr* fluorider
fluoridation [,florɪ'deʃən], [,flurɪ'deʃən] s fluoridation *f*
fluoride ['flu·ə,raɪd] s fluorure *m*
fluorine ['flu·ə,rin] s fluor *m*
fluoroscopy [,flu·ə'rɑskəpi] s radioscopie *f*
fluorspar ['flu·ər,spɑr] s spath *m* fluor
flur·ry ['flʌri] s (*pl* -ries) agitation *f*; (*of wind, snow, etc.*) rafale *f* || *v* (*pret* & *pp* -ried) *tr* agiter
flush [flʌʃ] *adj* (*level*) à ras; (*well-provided*) bien pourvu; (*healthy*) vigoureux; **flush with** au ras de, au niveau de || s (*of light*) éclat *m*; (*in the cheeks*) rougeur *f*; (*of joy*) transport *m*; (*of toilet*) chasse *f* d'eau; (*in poker*) flush *m*; **in the first flush of** dans l'ivresse or le premier éclat de || *adv* à ras, de niveau; (*directly*) droit || *tr* (*a bird*) lever; **to flush a toilet** tirer la chasse d'eau; **to flush out** (*e.g., a drain*) laver à grande eau || *intr* (*to blush*) rougir
flush' switch' s interrupteur *m* encastré
flush' tank' s réservoir *m* de chasse
flush' toi'let s water-closet *m* à chasse d'eau
fluster ['flʌstər] s agitation *f*; **in a fluster** en émoi || *tr* agiter
flute [flut] s flûte *f* || *tr* (*a column*) canneler; (*a dress*) tuyauter
flutist ['flutɪst] s flûtiste *mf*
flutter ['flʌtər] s battement *m*; **all of a flutter** (coll) tout agité || *intr* voleter; (*said of pulse*) battre fébrilement; (*said of heart*) palpiter
flux [flʌks] s flux *m*; (*for fusing metals*) acide *m* à souder; **to be in flux** être dans un état indécis
fly [flaɪ] s (*pl* **flies**) mouche *f*; (*for fishing*) mouche artificielle; (*of trousers*) braguette *f*; (*of tent*) auvent *m*; **flies** (theat) cintres *mpl*; **fly in the ointment** (fig) ombre *f* au tableau; **on the fly** au vol || *v* (*pret* **flew** [flu]; *pp* **flown** [flon]) *tr* (*a kite*) faire voler; (*an airplane*) piloter; (*freight or passengers*) transporter en avion; (*e.g. the Atlantic*) survoler; (*to flee from*) fuir || *intr* voler; (*to flee*) fuir; (*said of flag*) flotter; **to fly blind** voler à l'aveuglette; **to fly by** voler; **to fly in the face of** porter un défi à; **to fly off** s'envoler; **to fly off the handle** (coll) sortir de ses gonds; **to fly open** s'ouvrir brusquement; **to fly over** survoler
fly'blow' s œufs *mpl* de mouche
fly'-by-night' *adj* mal financé, indigne de confiance || s financier *m* qui lève le pied
fly' cast'ing s pêche *f* à la mouche noyée

fly'catch'er s attrape-mouches *m*; (bot) dionée *f*, attrape-mouches; (orn) gobe-mouches *m*
fly'-fish' *intr* pêcher à la mouche
flying ['flaɪ·ɪŋ] *adj* volant; rapide; court, passager || s aviation *f*; vol *m*
fly'ing but'tress s arc-boutant *m*
fly'ing col'ors—with flying colors drapeau *m* déployé; brillamment
fly'ing field' s champ *m* d'aviation
fly'ing-fish' s poisson *m* volant
fly'ing sau'cer s soucoupe *f* volante
fly'ing start' s départ *m* lancé
fly'ing time' s heures *fpl* de vol
fly'leaf' s (*pl* -leaves) feuille *f* de garde, garde *f*
fly' net' s (*for a bed*) moustiquaire *f*; (*for a horse*) chasse-mouches *m*
fly'pa'per s papier *m* tue-mouches
fly' rod' s canne *f* à pêche
fly'speck' s chiure *f*, chiasse *f*
fly' swat'ter [,swɑtər] s chasse-mouches *m*, émouchoir *m*
fly'trap' s attrape-mouches *m*
fly'wheel' s volant *m*
foal [fol] s poulain *m* || *intr* mettre bas
foam [fom] s écume *f*; (*on beer*) mousse *f* || *intr* écumer, mousser
foam' rub'ber s caoutchouc *m* mousse
foam·y ['fomi] *adj* (*comp* -ier; *super* -iest) écumeux, mousseux
fob [fɑb] s (*pocket*) gousset *m*; (*ornament*) breloque *f* || *v* (*pret* & *pp* **fobbed**; *ger* **fobbing**) *tr*—**to fob off s.th. on** s.o. refiler q.ch. à qn
f.o.b. or **F.O.B.** [,ɛf,o'bi] *adv* (letter-word) (**free on board**) franco de bord, départ usine
focal ['fokəl] *adj* focal
fo·cus ['fokəs] s (*pl* -cuses or -ci [saɪ]) foyer *m*; **in focus** au point; **out of focus** non réglé, hors du point focal || *v* (*pret* & *pp* -cused or -cussed; *ger* -cusing or -cussing) *tr* mettre au point, faire converger; (*a beam of electrons*) focaliser; (*e.g., attention*) concentrer || *intr* converger; **to focus on** se concentrer sur
fodder ['fɑdər] s fourrage *m*
foe [fo] s ennemi *m*, adversaire *mf*
fog [fɑg], [fɔg] s brouillard *m*; (naut) brume *f*; (phot) voile *m* || *v* (*pret* & *pp* **fogged**; *ger* **fogging**) *tr* embrumer; (phot) voiler || *intr* s'embrumer; (phot) se voiler
fog' bank' s banc *m* de brume
fog' bell' s cloche *f* de brume
fog'bound' *adj* arrêté par le brouillard, pris dans le brouillard
fog·gy ['fɑgi], ['fɔgi] *adj* (*comp* -gier; *super* -giest) brumeux; (phot) voilé; (fig) confus, flou; **it is foggy** il fait du brouillard
fog'horn' s sirène *f*, corne *f*, or trompe *f* de brume
foible ['fɔɪbəl] s faible *m*, marotte *f*
foil [fɔɪl] s (*thin sheet of metal*) feuille *f*, lame *f*; (*of mirror*) tain *m*; (*sword*) fleuret *m*; (*person whose personality sets off another's*) repoussoir *m* || *tr* déjouer, frustrer

foil'-wrapped' *adj* ceint de papier d'argent

foist [fɔist] *tr*—**to foist oneself upon** s'imposer chez; **to foist s.th. on s.o.** imposer q.ch. à qn

fold [fold] *s* pli *m*, repli *m*; (*for sheep*) parc *m*, bergerie *f*; (*of fat*) bourrelet *m*; (*of the faithful*) bercail *m* ‖ *tr* plier, replier; (*one's arms*) se croiser; **to fold in** (culin) incorporer; **to fold up** replier ‖ *intr* se replier; **to fold up** (theat) faire four; (coll) s'effondrer

folder ['foldər] *s* (*covers for holding papers*) chemise *f*; (*pamphlet*) dépliant *m*; (*person folding newspapers*) plieur *m*

folderol ['faldə,ral] *s* sottise *f*; (*piece of foolishness*) bagatelle *f*

folding ['foldɪŋ] *adj* pliant, repliant, rabattable

fold'ing cam'era *s* appareil *m* pliant

fold'ing chair' *s* chaise *f* pliante, chaise brisée

fold'ing cot' *s* lit *m* pliant or escamotable

fold'ing door' *s* porte *f* à deux battants

fold'ing rule' *s* mètre *m* pliant

fold'ing screen' *s* paravent *m*

fold'ing seat' *s* strapontin *m*

foliage ['folɪ·ɪdʒ] *s* feuillage *m*, feuillu *m*

foli·o ['folɪ,o] *adj* in-folio ‖ *s* (*pl* -os) (*sheet*) folio *m*; (*book*) in-folio *m* ‖ *tr* folioter, paginer

folk [fok] *adj* populaire, traditionnel, du peuple ‖ *s* (*pl* folk or folks) peuple *m*, race *f*; **folks** (coll) gens *mpl*, personnes *fpl*; **my folks** (coll) les miens *mpl*, ma famille

folk' dance' *s* danse *f* folklorique

folk'lore' *s* folklore *m*

folk' mu'sic *s* musique *f* populaire

folk' song' *s* chanson *f* du terroir

folk·sy ['foksi] *adj* (*comp* -sier; *super* -siest) (coll) sociable, liant; (*like common people*) (coll) du terroir

folk'ways' *spl* coutumes *fpl* traditionnelles

follicle ['falɪkəl] *s* follicule *m*

follow ['falo] *tr* suivre; (*to come after*) succéder (with *dat*); (*to understand*) comprendre; (*a profession*) embrasser; **to follow up** poursuivre; (*e.g., a success*) exploiter ‖ *intr* suivre; (*one after the other*) se suivre; **as follows** comme suit; **it follows that** il s'ensuit que

follower ['falo·ər] *s* suivant *m*; partisan *m*, disciple *m*

following ['falo·ɪŋ] *adj* suivant ‖ *s* (*of a prince*) suite *f*; (*followers*) partisans *mpl*, disciples *mpl*

fol'low the lead'er *s* jeu *m* de la queue leu leu

fol'low-up' *adj* de continuation, complémentaire; (*car*) suiveur ‖ *s* soins *mpl* post-hospitaliers

fol·ly ['fali] *s* (*pl* -lies) sottise *f*; (*madness*) folie *f*; **follies** spectacle *m* de music-hall, folies *fpl*

foment [fo'mɛnt] *tr* fomenter

fond [fand] *adj* affectueux, tendre; **to become fond of** s'attacher à

fondle ['fandəl] *tr* caresser

fondness ['fandnɪs] *s* affection *f*, tendresse *f*; (*appetite*) goût *m*, penchant *m*

font [fant] *s* source *f*; (*for holy water*) bénitier *m*; (*for baptism*) fonts *mpl*; (typ) fonte *f*

food [fud] *adj* alimentaire ‖ *s* nourriture *f*, aliments *mpl*; **food for thought** matière *f* à réflexion; **good food** bonne cuisine *f*

food' and cloth'ing *s* le vivre et le vêtement

food' and drink' *s* le boire et le manger

food'stuffs' *spl* denrées *fpl* alimentaires, vivres *mpl*

fool [ful] *s* sot *m*; (*jester*) fou *m*; (*person imposed on*) innocent *m*, niais *m*; **to make a fool of** se moquer de; **to play the fool** faire le pitre ‖ *tr* mystifier, abuser; **to fool away** gaspiller sottement ‖ *intr* faire la bête; **to fool around** (coll) gâcher son temps; **to fool with** (coll) tripoter

fooler·y ['fuləri] *s* (*pl* -ies) sottise *f*, ânerie *f*

fool'har'dy *adj* (*comp* -dier; *super* -diest) téméraire

fooling ['fulɪŋ] *s* tromperie *f*; **no fooling!** sans blague!

foolish ['fulɪʃ] *adj* sot, niais; ridicule, absurde

fool'proof' *adj* à toute épreuve; infaillible

fools'cap' *s* papier *m* ministre

fool's' er'rand *s*—**to go on a fool's errand** y aller pour des prunes

foot [fut] *s* (*pl* feet [fit]) pied *m*; (*of cat, dog, bird*) patte *f*; **on foot** à pied; **to drag one's feet** aller à pas de tortue; **to have one foot in the grave** avoir un pied dans la tombe; **to put one's best foot forward** (coll) partir du bon pied; **to put one's foot down** faire acte d'autorité; **to put one's foot in it** (coll) mettre les pieds dans le plat; **to stand on one's own feet** voler de ses propres ailes; **to tread under foot** fouler aux pieds ‖ *tr* (*the bill*) payer; **to foot it** aller à pied

footage ['futɪdʒ] *s* (mov, telv) (*in French* métrage *m*, *i.e., length of film in meters*) longueur *f* d'un film en pieds

foot'-and-mouth' disease' *s* (vet) fièvre *f* aphteuse

foot'ball' *s* football *m* américain; (*ball*) ballon *m*

foot' brake' *s* frein *m* à pédale

foot'bridge' *s* passerelle *f*

foot'fall' *s* pas *m* léger, bruit *m* de pas

foot'hills' *spl* contreforts *mpl*, collines *fpl* basses

foot'hold' *s*—**to gain a foothold** prendre pied

footing ['futɪŋ] *s* équilibre *m*; (archit) empattement *m*, base *f*, socle *m*; **to be on a friendly footing** être en bons termes; **to be on an equal footing**

être sur un pied d'égalité; **to lose one's footing** perdre pied
foot'lights' *spl* (theat) rampe *f*
foot'lock'er *s* (mil) cantine *f*
foot'loose' *adj* libre, sans entraves
foot'man *s* (*pl* **-men**) valet *m* de pied
foot'mark' *s* empreinte *f* de pied
foot'note' *s* note *f* au bas de la page
foot'pad' *s* voleur *m* de grand chemin
foot'path' *s* sentier *m* pour piétons
foot'print' *s* empreinte *f* de pas, trace *f*
foot' race' *s* course *f* à pied
foot'rest' *s* cale-pied *m*, repose-pied *m*
foot' sol'dier *s* fantassin *m*
foot'sore' *adj* aux pieds endoloris, éclopé
foot'step' *s* pas *m*; **to follow in s.o.'s footsteps** suivre les traces de qn
foot'stone' *s* pierre *f* tumulaire (au pied d'une tombe); (archit) première pierre
foot'stool' *s* tabouret *m*
foot' warm'er *s* chauffe-pieds *m*
foot'wear' *s* chaussures *fpl*
foot'work' *s* jeu *m* de jambes
foot'worn' *adj* usé; (*person*) aux pieds endoloris
fop [fɑp] *s* petit-maître *m*, bellâtre *m*
for [fɔr], [fər] *prep* pour; de, e.g., **to thank s.o. for** remercier qn de; e.g., **time for dinner** l'heure du dîner; e.g., **to cry for joy** pleurer de joie; e.g., **request for money** demande d'argent; à, e.g., **for sale** à vendre; e.g., **to sell for a high price** vendre à un prix élevé; e.g., **it is for you to decide** c'est à vous de décider; par, e.g., **famous for** célèbre par; e.g., **for example** par exemple; e.g., **for pity's sake** par pitié; contre, e.g., **a remedy for** un remède contre; as **for** quant à; **for** + *ger* pour + *perf inf*, e.g., **he was punished for stealing** il fut puni pour avoir volé; **for all that** malgré tout cela; **for short** en abrégé; **he has been in Paris for a week** il est à Paris depuis une semaine, il y a une semaine qu'il est à Paris; **he was in Paris for a week** il était à Paris pendant une semaine; **to be for** (*to be in favor of*) être en faveur de, être partisan de or pour; **to use s.th. for s.th.** employer q.ch. comme q.ch.; e.g., **to use coal for fuel** employer le charbon comme combustible || *conj* car, parce que
forage ['fɑrɪdʒ], ['fɔrɪdʒ] *s* fourrage *m* || *tr & intr* fourrager
foray ['fɑre], ['fɔre] *s* incursion *f* || *tr* saccager, fourrager || *intr* faire une incursion
for·bear [fɔr'bɛr] *v* (*pret* **-bore**; *pp* **-borne**) *tr* s'abstenir de || *intr* se montrer patient
forbearance [fɔr'bɛrəns] *s* abstention *f*; patience *f*
for·bid [fɔr'bɪd] *v* (*pret* **-bade** or **-bad** ['bæd]; *pp* **-bidden**; *ger* **-bidding**) *tr* défendre, interdire; **God forbid!** qu'à Dieu ne plaise!; **to forbid s.o. s.th.** défendre q.ch. à qn; **to forbid s.o. to** défendre à qn de

forbidden [fɔr'bɪdən] *adj* défendu
forbidding [fɔr'bɪdɪŋ] *adj* rebutant, rébarbatif, sinistre
force [fors] *s* force *f*; (*of a word*) signification *f*, valeur *f*; **in force** en vigueur; **in full force** en force; **the allied forces** les puissances alliées || *tr* forcer; **to force back** repousser; (*air; water*) refouler; **to force in** (e.g., *a door*) enfoncer; **to force one's way into** (e.g., *a house*) pénétrer de force dans; **to force s.o.'s hand** forcer la main à qn; **to force s.o. to** + *inf* forcer qn à or de + *inf*; **to force s.th. into s.th.** faire entrer q.ch. dans q.ch.; **to force up** (e.g., *prices*) faire monter
forced' draft' *s* tirage *m* forcé
forced' land'ing *s* atterrissage *m* forcé
forced' march' *s* marche *f* forcée
force'-feed' *tr* (*pret & pp* **-fed**) gaver, suralimenter
force'-feed'ing *s* suralimentation *f*
forceful ['forsfəl] *adj* énergique
for·ceps ['fɔrsɛps] *s* (*pl* **-ceps** or **-cipes** [sɪ ˌpiz]) (dent, surg) pince *f*; (obstet) forceps *m*
force' pump' *s* pompe *f* foulante
forcible ['fɔrsɪbəl] *adj* énergique, vigoureux; (*convincing*) convaincant; (*imposed*) forcé
ford [ford] *s* gué *m* || *tr* franchir à gué
fore [for] *adj* antérieur; (naut) de l'avant || *s* (naut) avant *m*; **to the fore** en vue, en vedette || *adv* à l'avant || *interj* (golf) gare devant!
fore' and aft' *adv* de l'avant à l'arrière
fore'arm' *s* avant-bras *m* || **fore·arm'** *tr* prémunir; (*to warn*) avertir
fore'bear' *s* ancêtre *m*
foreboding [for'bodɪŋ] *s* (*sign*) présage *m*; (*feeling*) pressentiment *m*
fore'cast' *s* prévision *f* || *v* (*pret & pp* **-cast** or **-casted**) *tr* pronostiquer
forecastle ['foksəl], ['for ˌkæsəl], ['for-ˌkɑsəl] *s* gaillard *m* d'avant
fore·close' *tr* exclure; (law) forclore; **to foreclose the mortgage** saisir l'immeuble hypothéqué
foreclosure [for'kloʒər] *s* saisie *f*, forclusion *f*
fore·doom' *tr* condamner par. avance
fore' edge' *s* (bb) tranche *f*
fore'fa'ther *s* aïeul *m*, ancêtre *m*
fore'fin'ger *s* index *m*
fore'foot' *s* (*pl* **-feet**) patte *f* de devant
fore'front' *s* premier rang *m*; **in the forefront** en première ligne
fore·go' *v* (*pret* **-went**; *pp* **-gone**) *tr* (*to give up*) renoncer à
foregoing ['for ˌgo·ɪŋ], [for'go·ɪŋ] *adj* précédent, antérieur; (*facts, text, etc. already cited*) déjà cité, ci-dessus
fore'gone' *adj* inévitable; (*anticipated*) décidé d'avance, prévu
fore'ground' *s* premier plan *m*
fore'hand'ed *adj* prévoyant; (*thrifty*) ménager
forehead ['fɑrɪd], ['fɔrɪd] *s* front *m*
foreign ['fɑrɪn], ['fɔrɪn] *adj* étranger
for'eign affairs' *spl* affaires *fpl* étrangères

foreigner ['furɪnər], ['fɔrɪnər] s étranger m
for'eign exchange' s change m étranger; (currency) devises fpl
for'eign min'ister s ministre m des affaires étrangères
for'eign of'fice s ministère m des affaires étrangères
for'eign serv'ice s (dipl) service m diplomatique; (mil) service m à l'étranger
for'eign trade' s commerce m extérieur
fore'leg' s jambe f de devant
fore'lock' s mèche f sur le front; (of horse) toupet m; to take time by the forelock saisir l'occasion par les cheveux
fore'man s (pl -men) chef m d'équipe; (in machine shop, factory) contremaître m; (of jury) premier juré m
foremast ['formǝst], ['fɔr‚mæst], ['fɔr‚mɑst] s mât m de misaine
fore'most' adj premier, principal || adv au premier rang
fore'noon' s matinée f
fore'part' s avant m, devant m, partie f avant
fore'paw' s patte f de devant
fore'quar'ter s quartier m de devant
fore'run'ner s précurseur m, avant-coureur m; (sign) signe m avant-coureur
foresail ['forsǝl], ['fɔr‚sel], s misaine f, voile f de misaine
fore·see' v (pret -saw; pp -seen) tr prévoir
foreseeable [fɔr'si·ǝbǝl] adj prévisible
fore·shad'ow tr présager, préfigurer
fore·short'en tr dessiner en raccourci
fore·short'ening s raccourci m
fore'sight' s prévision f, prévoyance f
fore'sight'ed adj prévoyant
fore'skin' s prépuce m
forest ['fɑrɪst], ['fɔrɪst] adj forestier || s forêt f
fore'stage' s (theat) avant-scène f
fore·stall' tr anticiper, devancer
for'est rang'er s garde m forestier
forestry ['fɑrɪstri], ['fɔrɪstri] s sylviculture f
fore'taste' s avant-goût m
fore·tell' v (pret & pp -told) tr prédire
fore'thought' s prévoyance f; (law) préméditation f
for·ev'er adv pour toujours, à jamais
fore·warn' tr avertir, prévenir
fore'word' s avant-propos m, avis m au lecteur
forfeit ['fɔrfɪt] adj perdu || s (pledge) dédit m, gage m; (fine) amende f; to play at forfeits jouer aux gages || tr être déchu de, être privé de
forfeiture ['fɔrfɪt/ǝr] s perte f; (fine) amende f, confiscation f
forge [fordʒ] s forge f || tr forger; (e.g., documents) contrefaire, falsifier
forger ['fordʒǝr] s forgeur m; (e.g., of documents) faussaire mf
forger·y ['fordʒǝri] s (pl -ies) contrefaçon f; (of a document, a painting, etc.) faux m
for·get [fɔr'gɛt] v (pret -got; pp -got or

-gotten; ger -getting) tr & intr oublier; forget it! n'y pensez plus!; to forget to + inf oublier de + inf
forgetful [fɔr'gɛtfǝl] adj oublieux
forget'-me-not' s myosotis m, ne-m'oubliez-pas m
forgivable [fɔr'gɪvǝbǝl] adj pardonnable
for·give [fɔr'gɪv] v (pret -gave; pp -given) tr & intr pardonner
forgiveness [fɔr'gɪvnɪs] s pardon m
forgiving [fɔr'gɪvɪŋ] adj indulgent, miséricordieux
for·go [fɔr'go] v (pret -went; pp -gone) tr renoncer à, s'abstenir de
fork [fɔrk] s fourche f; (of road, tree, stem) fourche f, bifurcation f; (at table) fourchette f || tr & intr fourcher, bifurquer
forked adj fourchu
forked' light'ning s éclairs mpl en zigzag
fork'lift truck' s chariot m élévateur
forlorn [fɔr'lɔrn] adj (destitute) abandonné; (hopeless) désespéré; (wretched) misérable
forlorn' hope' s tentative f désespérée
form [fɔrm] s forme f; (paper to be filled out) formule f, fiche f, feuille f; (construction to give shape to cement) coffrage m || tr former || intr se former
formal ['fɔrmǝl] adj cérémonieux, officiel; (formalistic) formaliste; (superficial) formel, de pure forme
for'mal attire' s tenue f de cérémonie
for'mal call' s visite f de politesse
for'mal din'ner s dîner m de cérémonie, dîner prié
formali·ty [fɔr'mælɪti] s (pl -ties) formalité f; (stiffness) raideur f; (polite conventions) cérémonie f, étiquette f
for'mal par'ty s soirée f de gala
for'mal speech' s discours m d'apparat
format ['fɔrmæt] s format m
formation [fɔr'me/ǝn] s formation f
former ['fɔrmǝr] adj antérieur, précédent; (long past) ancien; (first of two things mentioned) premier || pron—the former celui-là §84; le premier
formerly ['fɔrmǝrli] adv autrefois, anciennement, jadis
form'fit'ting adj ajusté, moulant
formidable ['fɔrmɪdǝbǝl] adj formidable
formless ['fɔrmlɪs] adj informe
form' let'ter s lettre f circulaire
formu·la ['fɔrmjǝlǝ] s (pl -las or -lae [‚li]) formule f
formulate ['fɔrmjǝ‚let] tr formuler
for·sake [fɔr'sek] v (pret -sook ['sʊk]; pp -saken [‚sekǝn]) tr abandonner, délaisser
fort [fort] s fort m, forteresse f; hold the fort! (coll) je vous confie la maison!
forte [fort] s fort m
forth [forθ] adv en avant; and so forth et ainsi de suite; from this day forth à partir de ce jour; to go forth sortir, se mettre en route
forth'com'ing adj à venir, à paraître

forth'right' *adj* net, direct ‖ *adv* droit, carrément; (*immediately*) tout de suite

forth'with' *adv* sur-le-champ

fortieth ['fɔrtɪ·ɪθ] *adj & pron* quarantième (*masc, fem*) ‖ *s* quarantième *m*

fortification [,fɔrtɪfɪ'keʃən] *s* fortification *f*

forti·fy ['fɔrtɪ,faɪ] *v* (*pret & pp* -fied) *tr* fortifier; (*wine*) viner

fortitude ['fɔrtɪ,t(j)ud] *s* force *f* d'âme

fortnight ['fɔrt,naɪt], ['fɔrtnɪt] *s* quinze jours *mpl*, quinzaine *f*

fortress ['fɔrtrɪs] *s* forteresse *f*

fortuitous [fɔr't(j)u·ɪtəs] *adj* (*accidental*) fortuit; (*lucky*) fortuné

fortunate ['fɔrtʃənɪt] *adj* heureux

fortune ['fɔrtʃən] *s* fortune *f*; **to make a fortune** faire fortune; **to tell s.o. his fortune** dire la bonne aventure à qn

for'tune hunt'er *s* coureur *m* de dots

for'tune-tel'ler *s* diseuse *f* de bonne aventure

for·ty ['fɔrti] *adj & pron* quarante ‖ *s* (*pl* -ties) quarante *m*; **about forty** une quarantaine

fo·rum ['forəm] *s* (*pl* -rums or -ra [rə]) forum *m*; (*e.g., of public opinion*) tribune *m*; **open forum** tribune *f* libre

forward ['fɔrwərd] *adj* de devant; (*precocious*) avancé, précoce; (*bold*) audacieux, effronté ‖ *s* (*sports*) avant *m* ‖ *adv* en avant; **to bring forward** (bk) reporter; **to come forward** s'avancer; **to look forward to** compter sur, se faire une fête de ‖ *tr* envoyer, expédier; (*a letter*) faire suivre; (*a project*) avancer, favoriser

for'warding address' *s* adresse *f* d'expédition, adresse d'envoi

fossil ['fɑsɪl] *adj & s* fossile *m*

foster ['fɑstər], ['fɔstər] *adj* de lait, nourricier ‖ *tr* encourager, entretenir

fos'ter broth'er *s* frère *m* de lait

fos'ter fa'ther *s* père *m* nourricier

foul [faʊl] *adj* immonde; (*air*) vicié; (*wind*) contraire; (*weather*) gros, sale; (*breath*) fétide; (*language*) ordurier; (*water*) bourbeux; (*ball*) hors jeu ‖ *s* (baseball) faute *f*; (boxing) coup *m* bas ‖ *adv* déloyalement ‖ *tr* (sports) commettre une faute contre ‖ *intr* (*said of anchor, propeller, rope, etc.*) s'engager

foul-mouthed ['faʊl'maʊðd], ['faʊl'maʊθt] *adj* mal embouché

foul' play' *s* malveillance *f*; (sports) jeu *m* déloyal

found [faʊnd] *tr* fonder, établir; (*metal*) fondre

foundation [faʊn'deʃən] *s* (*basis; masonry support*) fondement *m*; (*act of endowing*) dotation *f*; (*endowment*) fondation *f*

founder ['faʊndər] *s* fondateur *m*; (*in foundry*) fondeur *m* ‖ *intr* (*said of horse*) boiter bas; (*said of building*) s'effondrer; (naut) sombrer

foundling ['faʊndlɪŋ] *s* enfant *m* trouvé

found'ling hos'pital *s* hospice *m* des enfants trouvés

found·ry ['faʊndri] *s* (*pl* -ries) fonderie *f*

found'ry·man *s* (*pl* -men) fondeur *m*

fount [faʊnt] *s* source *f*

fountain ['faʊntən] *s* fontaine *f*

foun'tain-head' *s* source *f*, origine *f*

Foun'tain of Youth' *s* fontaine *f* de Jouvence

foun'tain pen' *s* stylo *m*

four [for] *adj & pron* quatre ‖ *s* quatre *m*; **four o'clock** quatre heures; **on all fours** à quatre pattes

four'-cy'cle *adj* (mach) à quatre temps

four'-cyl'inder *adj* (mach) à quatre cylindres

four'-flush' *intr* (coll) bluffer, faire le fanfaron

fourflusher ['for,flʌʃər] *s* (coll) bluffeur *m*

four'-foot'ed *adj* quadrupède

four' hun'dred *adj & pron* quatre cents ‖ *s* quatre cents *m*; **the Four Hundred** la haute société; le Tout Paris

four'-in-hand' *s* (*tie*) cravate-plastron *f*; (*team*) attelage *m* à quatre

four'-lane' *adj* à quatre voies

four'-leaf clo'ver *s* trèfle *m* à quatre feuilles

four'-motor plane' *s* quadrimoteur *m*

four'-o'clock' *s* (*Mirabilis jalapa*) belle-de-nuit *f*

four' of a kind' *s* (cards) un carré

four'-post'er *s* lit *m* à colonnes

four'score' *adj* quatre-vingts

foursome ['forsəm] *s* partie *f* double

fourteen ['for'tin] *adj, pron, & s* quatorze *m*

fourteenth ['for'tinθ] *adj & pron* quatorzième (*masc, fem*); **the Fourteenth** quatorze, e.g., **John the Fourteenth** Jean quatorze ‖ *s* quatorze *m*; **the fourteenth** (*in dates*) le quatorze

fourth [forθ] *adj & pron* quatrième (*masc, fem*); **the Fourth** quatre, e.g., **John the Fourth** Jean quatre ‖ *s* quatrième *m*; (*in fractions*) quart *m*; **the fourth** (*in dates*) le quatre

fourth' estate' *s* quatrième pouvoir *m*

fowl [faʊl] *s* volaille *f*

fox [fɑks] *s* renard *m* ‖ *tr* (coll) mystifier

fox'glove' *s* digitale *f*

fox'hole' *s* renardière *f*; (mil) gourbi *m*, abri *m* de tranchée

fox'hound' *s* fox-hound *m*

fox' hunt' *s* chasse *f* au renard

fox' ter'rier *s* fox-terrier *m*

fox' trot' *s* (*of animal*) petit trot *m*; (*dance*) fox-trot *m*

fox·y ['fɑksi] *adj* (*comp* -ier; *super* -iest) rusé, madré

foyer ['fɔɪ·ər] *s* (*lobby*) foyer *m*; (*entrance hall*) vestibule *m*

fracas ['frekəs] *s* bagarre *f*, rixe *f*

fraction ['frækʃən] *s* fraction *f*

fractional ['frækʃənəl] *adj* fractionnaire

frac'tional cur'rency *s* monnaie *f* divisionnaire

fracture ['fræktʃər] *s* fracture *f*; **to set**

a fracture réduire une fracture ‖ *tr* fracturer

fragile ['frædʒɪl] *adj* fragile

fragment ['frægmənt] *s* fragment *m* ‖ *tr* fragmenter

fragrance ['fregrəns] *s* parfum *m*

fragrant ['fregrənt] *adj* parfumé

frail [frel] *adj* frêle; (*e.g., virtue*) fragile, faible ‖ *s* (*basket*) couffe *f*

frail·ty ['frelti] *s* (*pl* -ties) fragilité *f*; (*weakness*) faiblesse *f*

frame [frem] *s* (*of picture, mirror*) cadre *m*; (*of glasses*) monture *f*; (*of window, car*) châssis *m*; (*of window, motor*) bâti *m*; (*support, stand*) armature *f*; (*structure*) charpente *f*; (*for embroidering*) métier *m*; (*of comic strip*) cadre, dessin *m*; (*mov, telv*) image *f* ‖ *tr* former, charpenter; (*a picture*) encadrer; (*film*) cadrer; (*an answer*) formuler; (*slang*) monter une accusation contre

frame' house' *s* maison *f* en bois

frame' of mind' *s* disposition *f* d'esprit

frame'-up' *s* (slang) coup *m* monté

frame'work' *s* charpente *f*, squelette *m*

framing ['fremɪŋ] *s* (mov, phot) cadrage *m*

France [fræns], [frɑns] *s* France *f*; la France

franchise ['fræntʃaɪz] *s* concession *f*, privilège *m*; droit *m* de vote

frank [fræŋk] *adj* franc ‖ *s* franchise *f* postale; **Frank** (*medieval German person*) Franc *m*; (*masculine name*) François *m* ‖ *tr* affranchir

frankfurter ['fræŋkfərtər] *s* saucisse *f* de Francfort

frankincense ['fræŋkɪn‚sɛns] *s* oliban *m*

Frankish ['fræŋkɪʃ] *adj* franc ‖ *s* francique *m*

frankness ['fræŋknɪs] *s* franchise *f*

frantic ['fræntɪk] *adj* frénétique

fraternal [frə'tʌrnəl] *adj* fraternel

fraterni·ty [frə'tʌrnɪti] *s* (*pl* -ties) fraternité *f*; (*association*) confrérie *f*; (*at a university*) club *m* d'étudiants, amicale *f* estudiantine

fraternize ['frætər‚naɪz] *intr* fraterniser

fraud [frɔd] *s* fraude *f*; (*person*) imposteur *m*, fourbe *mf*

fraudulent ['frɔdjələnt] *adj* frauduleux, en fraude

fraught [frɔt] *adj*—**fraught with** chargé de

fray [fre] *s* bagarre *f* ‖ *tr* érailler ‖ *intr* s'érailler

freak [frik] *s* (*sudden fancy*) caprice *m*; (*anomaly*) curiosité *f*; (*person, animal*) monstre *m*

freakish ['frikɪʃ] *adj* capricieux; bizarre; (*grotesque*) monstrueux

freckle ['frɛkəl] *s* tache *f* de rousseur, éphélide *f*

freckly ['frɛkli] *adj* couvert de taches de rousseur

free [fri] *adj* (*comp* **freer** ['fri·ər]; *super* **freest** ['fri·ɪst]) libre; (*without charge*) gratuit; (*without extra charge*) franc, exempt; (*e.g., end of a*

rope) dégagé; (*with money, advice, etc.*) libéral, généreux; (*manner, speech, etc.*) franc, ouvert; **to set free** libérer, affranchir ‖ *adv* franco, gratis, gratuitement; (naut) largue, e.g., **running free** courant largue ‖ *v* (*pret & pp* **freed** [frid]; *ger* **freeing** ['fri·ɪŋ]) *tr* libérer; (*a prisoner*) affranchir, élargir; (*to disengage*) dégager; (*from an obligation*) exempter

free' and eas'ly *adj* désinvolte, dégagé

freebooter ['fri‚butər] *s* flibustier *m*, maraudeur *m*

free' com'peti'tion *s* libre concurrence *f*

freedom ['fridəm] *s* liberté *f*

free'dom of speech' *s* liberté *f* de la parole

free'dom of the press' *s* liberté *f* de la presse

free'dom of the seas' *s* liberté *f* des mers

free'dom of thought' *s* liberté *f* de la pensée

free'dom of wor'ship *s* liberté *f* du culte, libre pratique *f*

free'-for-all' *s* foire *f* d'empoigne, mêlée *f*

free' hand' *s* carte *f* blanche

free'-hand draw'ing *s* dessin *m* à main levée

free'hand'ed *adj* libéral, généreux

free'hold' *s* (law) propriété *f* foncière perpétuelle; (hist) franc-alleu *m*

free' lance' *s* franc-tireur *m*

free'man *s* (*pl* -men) homme *m* libre; (*citizen*) citoyen *m*

Free'ma'son *s* franc-maçon *m*

Free'ma'sonry *s* franc-maçonnerie *f*

free' of charge' *adj & adv* gratis, exempt de frais

free' on board' *adv* franco de bord, départ usine

free' port' *s* port *m* franc

free' speech' *s* liberté *f* de la parole

free'-spo'ken *adj* franc; **to be freespoken** avoir son franc-parler

free'think'er *s* libre penseur *m*

free' thought' *s* libre pensée *f*

free' tick'et *s* billet *m* de faveur

free' trade' *s* libre-échange *m*

free' trad'er *s* libre-échangiste *mf*

free'way' *s* autoroute *f*

free' will' *adj* volontaire, de plein gré

free' will' *s* libre arbitre *m*; **of one's own free will** de son propre gré

freeze [friz] *s* congélation *f* ‖ *v* (*pret* **froze** [froz]; *pp* **frozen**) *tr* geler, congeler; (*assets, credits, etc.*) geler, bloquer; (*e.g., meat*) congeler ‖ *intr* geler; **it is freezing** il gèle

freezer ['frizər] *s* (*for making ice cream*) sorbetière *f*; (*for foods*) congélateur *m*

freight [fret] *s* fret *m*, chargement *m*; (*cost*) fret, prix *m* du transport; **by freight** (rr) en petite vitesse ‖ *tr* transporter; (*a ship, truck, etc.*) charger

freight' car' *s* wagon *m* de marchandises, wagon à caisse

freighter ['fretər] *s* cargo *m*

freight' plat'form *s* quai *m* de déchargement

freight' sta'tion *s* gare *f* de marchandises

freight' train' *s* train *m* de marchandises

freight' yard' *s* (rr) cour *f* de marchandises

French [frɛntʃ] *adj* français ‖ *s* (*language*) français *m*; **the French** les Français

French'' Cana'dian *s* Franco-Canadien *m*

French'-Cana'dian *adj* franco-canadien

French' chalk' *s* craie *f* de tailleur, stéatite *f*

French' cuff' *s* poignet *m* mousquetaire

French' door' *s* porte-fenêtre *f*

French' dress'ing *s* vinaigrette *f*

French' fries' *spl* frites *fpl*

French' horn' *s* (mus) cor *m* d'harmonie

French' horse'power *s* (735 watts) cheval-vapeur *m*, cheval *m*

French' leave' *s*—**to take French leave** filer à l'anglaise

French'man *s* (*pl* -**men**) Français *m*

French' roll' *s* petit pain *m*

French'-speak'ing *adj* francophone; (*country*) de langue française

French' tel'ephone *s* combiné *m*

French' toast' *s* pain *m* perdu

French' win'dow *s* porte-fenêtre *f*

French'wom'an *s* (*pl* -**wom'en**) Française *f*

frenzied ['frɛnzid] *adj* frénétique

fren·zy ['frɛnzi] *s* (*pl* -**zies**) frénésie *f*

frequen·cy ['frikwənsi] *s* (*pl* -**cies**) fréquence *f*

fre'quency modula'tion *s* modulation *f* de fréquence

frequent ['frikwənt] *adj* fréquent ‖ [frɪ'kwɛnt], ['frikwənt] *tr* fréquenter

frequently ['frikwəntli] *adv* fréquemment

fres·co ['frɛsko] *s* (*pl* -**coes** or -**cos**) fresque *f* ‖ *tr* peindre à fresque

fresh [frɛʃ] *adj* frais; (*water*) doux; (*e.g., idea*) nouveau; (*wound*) saignant; (*cheeky*) (coll) osé, impertinent; **fresh paint!** (public sign) attention, peinture fraîche! ‖ *adv* nouvellement; **fresh in** (coll) récemment arrivé; **fresh out** (coll) récemment épuisé

freshen ['frɛʃən] *tr* rafraîchir ‖ *intr* se rafraîchir; (*said of wind*) fraîchir

freshet ['frɛʃɪt] *s* crue *f*

fresh'man *s* (*pl* -**men**) étudiant *m* de première année, bizut *m*

freshness ['frɛʃnɪs] *s* fraîcheur *f*; (*sauciness*) impudence *f*, impertinence *f*

fresh'-wa'ter *adj* d'eau douce

fret [frɛt] *s* (*interlaced design*) frette *f*; (*uneasiness*) inquiétude *f*; (mus) touchette *f* ‖ *v* (*pret & pp* **fretted**; *ger* **fretting**) *tr* ajourer ‖ *intr* s'inquiéter, geindre

fretful ['frɛtfəl] *adj* irritable, boudeur

fret'work' *s* ajour *m*, ornementation *f* ajourée

Freudianism ['frɔɪdɪ·ə‚nɪzəm] *s* freudisme *m*

friar ['fraɪ·ər] *s* moine *m*

fricassee [‚frɪkə'si] *s* fricassée *f*

friction ['frɪkʃən] *s* friction *f*

fric'tion tape' *s* chatterton *m*, ruban *m* isolant

Friday ['fraɪdi] *s* vendredi *m*

fried [fraɪd] *adj* frit

fried' egg' *s* œuf *m* sur le plat

friend [frɛnd] *s* ami *m*; **to make friends with** se lier d'amitié avec

friend·ly ['frɛndli] *adj* (*comp* -**lier**; *super* -**liest**) amical, sympathique

friendship ['frɛndʃɪp] *s* amitié *f*

frieze [friz] *s* (archit) frise *f*

frigate ['frɪgɪt] *s* frégate *f*

fright [fraɪt] *s* frayeur *f*, effroi *m*; (*grotesque or ridiculous person*) (coll) épouvantail *m*; **to take fright at** s'effrayer de

frighten ['fraɪtən] *tr* effrayer; **to frighten away** effaroucher, faire fuir

frightful ['fraɪtfəl] *adj* effroyable; (coll) affreux; (*huge*) (coll) énorme

frigid ['frɪdʒɪd] *adj* frigide; (*zone*) glacial

frigidity [frɪ'dʒɪdɪti] *s* frigidité *f*

frill [frɪl] *s* (*on shirt front*) jabot *m*; (*frippery*) falbala *m*

fringe [frɪndʒ] *s* frange *f*; (*border*) bordure *f*; (opt) frange; **on the fringe of** en marge de ‖ *tr* franger

fringe' ben'efits *spl* supplément *m* de solde, bénéfices *mpl* marginaux

fripper·y ['frɪpəri] *s* (*pl* -**ies**) (*flashiness*) clinquant *m*; (*inferior goods*) camelote *f*

frisk [frɪsk] *tr* (slang) fouiller, palper ‖ *intr*—**to frisk about** gambader, folâtrer

frisk·y ['frɪski] *adj* (*comp* -**ier**; *super* -**iest**) vif, folâtre; (*horse*) fringant

fritter ['frɪtər] *s* beignet *m* ‖ *tr*—**fritter away** gaspiller

frivolous ['frɪvələs] *adj* frivole

frizzle ['frɪzəl] *s* frisure *f* ‖ *tr* frisotter; (culin) faire frire ‖ *intr* frisotter; (culin) grésiller

friz·zly ['frɪzli] *adj* (*comp* -**zlier**; *super* -**zliest**) crépu, crépelu

fro [fro] *adv*—**to and fro** de long en large; **to go to and fro** aller et venir

frock [frɑk] *s* robe *f*; (*overalls, smock*) blouse *f*; (eccl) froc *m*

frock' coat' *s* redingote *f*

frog [frɑg], [frɔg] *s* grenouille *f*; (*in throat*) chat *m*

frog'man' *s* (*pl* -**men'**) homme-grenouille *m*

frogs'' legs' *spl* cuisses *fpl* de grenouille

frol·ic ['frɑlɪk] *s* gaieté *f*, ébats *mpl* ‖ *v* (*pret & pp* -**icked**; *ger* -**icking**) *intr* s'ébattre, folâtrer

frolicsome ['frɑlɪksəm] *adj* folâtre

from [frʌm], [frɑm], [frəm] *prep* de; de la part de, e.g., **greetings from your friend** compliments de la part de votre ami; contre, e.g., **a shelter from the rain** un abri contre la pluie; **from a certain angle** sous un certain angle; **from . . . to** depuis . . .

jusqu'à; **from what I hear** d'après ce que j'apprends; **the flight from** le vol en provenance de; **to drink from** (*a glass*) boire dans; (*a bottle*) boire à; **to learn from a book** apprendre dans un livre; **to steal from** voler à
front [frʌnt] *adj* antérieur, de devant ‖ *s* devant *m*; (*first place*) premier rang *m*; (aut) avant *m*; (geog, mil, pol) front *m*; (*figurehead*) (coll) prête-nom *m*; **in front** par devant; **in front of** en face de, devant; **to put up a bold front** (coll) faire bonne contenance ‖ *tr* (*to face*) donner sur; (*to confront*) affronter ‖ *intr*—**to front on** donner sur
frontage ['frʌntɪdʒ] *s* façade *f*; (*along a street, lake, etc.*) largeur *f*
front' door' *s* porte *f* d'entrée
front' drive' *s* (aut) traction *f* avant
frontier [frʌn'tɪr] *adj* frontalier ‖ *s* frontière *f*; (hist) front *m* de colonisation, front pionnier
frontiers'man *s* (*pl* **-men**) frontalier *m*, broussard *m*
frontispiece ['frʌntɪs‚pis] *s* frontispice *m*; (archit) façade *f* principale
front' lines' *spl* avant-postes *mpl*
front' mat'ter *s* (*of book*) feuilles *fpl* liminaires
front' of'fice *s* direction *f*
front' porch' *s* porche *m*
front' room' *s* chambre *f* sur la rue
front' row' *s* premier rang *m*
front' seat' *s* siège *m* avant; (aut) banquette *f* avant
front' steps' *spl* perron *m*
front' view' *s* vue *f* de face
front' yard' *s* devant *m* de la maison
frost [frɔst], [frɑst] *s* (*freezing*) gelée *f*; (*frozen dew*) givre *m* ‖ *tr* (*to freeze*) geler; (*to cover with frost*) givrer; (culin) glacer
frost'bite' *s* engelure *f*
frost'ed glass' *s* verre *m* dépoli
frosting ['frɔstɪŋ], ['frɑstɪŋ] *s* (*on glass*) dépolissage *m*; (culin) fondant *m*
frost·y ['frɔsti], ['frɑsti] *adj* (*comp* **-ier**; *super* **-iest**) couvert de givre; (*reception, welcome*) glacé, glacial
froth [frɔθ], [frɑθ] *s* écume *f*; (*on soap, beer, chocolate*) mousse *f*; (*frivolity*) futilité *f* ‖ *intr* mousser; (*at the mouth*) écumer
froth·y ['frɔθi], ['frɑθi] *adj* (*comp* **-ier**; *super* **-iest**) écumeux; (*soap, beer, chocolate*) mousseux; (*frivolous*) creux, futile
froward ['frowərd] *adj* obstiné, revêche
frown [fraun] *s* froncement *m* de sourcils ‖ *intr* froncer les sourcils; **to frown at** or **on** être contraire à, désapprouver
frows·y or **frowz·y** ['frauzi] *adj* (*comp* **-ier**; *super* **-iest**) malpropre, négligé, peu soigné; (*smelling bad*) malodorant
fro'zen as'sets ['frozən] *spl* fonds *mpl* gelés
fro'zen foods' *spl* aliments *mpl* surgelés

frugal ['frugəl] *adj* sobre, modéré; (*meal*) frugal
fruit [frut] *adj* fruitier ‖ *s* fruit *m*; les fruits, e.g., **I like fruit** j'aime les fruits
fruit' cake' *s* cake *m*
fruit' cup' *s* coupe *f* de fruits
fruit' fly' *s* mouche *f* du vinaigre
fruitful ['frutfəl] *adj* fructueux, fécond
fruition [fru'ɪ/ən] *s* réalisation *f*; **to come to fruition** fructifier
fruit' juice' *s* jus *m* de fruits
fruitless ['frutlɪs] *adj* stérile, vain
fruit' sal'ad *s* macédoine *f* de fruits, salade *f* de fruits
fruit' stand' *s* étalage *m* de fruits
fruit' store' *s* fruiterie *f*
frumpish ['frʌmpɪ/] *adj* fagoté, négligé
frustrate ['frʌstret] *tr* frustrer
fry [fraɪ] *s* (*pl* **fries**) (culin) friture *f*; (ichth) fretin *m* ‖ *v* (*pret* & *pp* **fried**) *tr* faire frire; (*to sauté*) faire sauter ‖ *intr* frire
fry'ing pan' *s* poêle *f* à frire; **to jump from the frying pan into the fire** sauter de la poêle dans le feu
fudge [fʌdʒ] *s* fondant *m* de chocolat; (*humbug*) blague *f*
fuel ['fju·əl] *s* combustible *m*; (aut) carburant *m*; (fig) aliment *m* ‖ *v* (*pret* & *pp* **fueled** or **fuelled**; *ger* **fueling** or **fuelling**) *tr* pourvoir en combustible
fu'el gauge' *s* jauge *f* de combustible
fu'el line' *s* conduite *f* de combustible
fu'el oil' *s* mazout *m*, fuel-oil *m*, fuel *m*
fu'el tank' *s* réservoir *m* de carburant; (aut) réservoir à essence
fugitive ['fjudʒɪtɪv] *adj* & *s* fugitif *m*
ful·crum ['fʌlkrəm] *s* (*pl* **-crums** or **-cra** [krə]) point *m* d'appui
fulfill [ful'fɪl] *tr* accomplir; (*an obligation*) s'acquitter de, remplir
fulfillment [ful'fɪlmənt] *s* accomplissement *m*
full [ful] *adj* plein; (*dress, garment*) ample, bouffant; (*schedule*) chargé; (*lips*) gros, fort; (*brother, sister*) germain; (*having no more room*) complet; **full to overflowing** plein à déborder ‖ *s* plein *m*; **in full** intégralement, entièrement; (*to spell in full*) en toutes lettres; **to the full** complètement ‖ *adv* complètement; **full in the face** en pleine figure; **full many a** bien des; **full well** parfaitement ‖ *tr* (*cloth*) fouler
full' blast' *adv* (coll) en pleine activité
full'-blood'ed *adj* robuste; (*thoroughbred*) pur sang
full-blown ['ful'blon] *adj* achevé, développé; en pleine fleur
full'-bod'ied *adj* (e.g., *wine*) corsé
full' dress' *s* grande tenue *f*
full'-dress coat' *s* frac *m*
full'-faced' *adj* (*portrait*) de face
full-fledged ['ful'fledʒd] *adj* véritable, rien moins que
full-grown ['ful'gron] *adj* (*plant*) mûr; (*tree*) de haute futaie; (*person*) adulte

full′ house′ *s* (poker) main *f* pleine; (theat) salle *f* comble
full′-length′ *adj* (*portrait*) en pied
full′-length mir′ror *s* psyché *f*
full′-length mov′ie *s* long métrage *m*
full′ load′ *s* plein chargement *m*
full′ meas′ure *s* mesure *f* comble
full′ moon′ *s* pleine lune *f*
full′ name′ *s* nom *m* et prénoms *mpl*
full′ pow′ers *spl* pleins pouvoirs *mpl*
full′ rest′ *s* (mus) pause *f*
full′ sail′ *adv* toutes voiles dehors
full′ ses′sion *s* assemblée *f* plénière
full′-sized′ *adj* de grandeur nature
full′ speed′ *s* toute vitesse *f*
full′ stop′ *s* (gram) point *m* final; **to come to a full stop** s'arrêter net
full′ swing′ *s*—**in full swing** en pleine activité, en train
full′ tilt′ *adv* à toute vitesse
full′ time′ *adv* à pleines journées
full′-time′ *adj* à temps plein
full′ view′ *s*—**in full view** à la vue de tous
full′ weight′ *s* poids *m* juste
fully [′fʊli], [′fʊlli] *adv* entièrement, pleinement
fulsome [′fʊlsəm], [′fʌlsəm] *adj* écœurant, bas, servile
fumble [′fʌmbəl] *tr* manier maladroitement; (*the ball*) ne pas attraper, laisser tomber ‖ *intr* tâtonner
fume [fjum] *s* (*bad humor*) rage *f*; **fumes** fumées *fpl*, vapeurs *fpl* ‖ *tr & intr* fumer
fumigate [′fjumɪ‚get] *tr* fumiger
fun [fʌn] *s* amusement *m*, gaieté *f*; (*badinage*) plaisanterie *f*; **in fun** pour rire; **to have fun** s'amuser; **to make fun of** se moquer de
function [′fʌŋkʃən] *s* fonction *f*; (*meeting*) cérémonie *f* ‖ *intr* fonctionner; **to function as** faire fonction de
functional [′fʌŋkʃənəl] *adj* fonctionnel
functionar·y [′fʌŋkʃə‚nɛri] *s* (*pl* -ies) fonctionnaire *mf*
fund [fʌnd] *s* fonds *m*; **funds** fonds *mpl* ‖ *tr* (*a debt*) consolider
fundamental [‚fʌndə′mɛntəl] *adj* fondamental ‖ *s* principe *m*, base *f*
fundamentalist [‚fʊndə′mɛntəlɪst] *s* (rel) scripturaire *m*
funeral [′fjunərəl] *adj* (*march, procession, ceremony*) funèbre; (*expenses*) funéraire ‖ *s* funérailles *fpl*
fu′neral direc′tor *s* entrepreneur *m* de pompes funèbres
fu′neral home′ or **par′lor** *s* chapelle *f* mortuaire; salon *m* mortuaire (Canad); (*business*) entreprise *f* de pompes funèbres
fu′neral proces′sion *s* convoi *m* funèbre, enterrement *m*, deuil *m*
fu′neral serv′ice *s* office *m* des morts
funereal [fju′nɪrɪ·əl] *adj* funèbre
fungus [′fʌŋgəs] *s* (*pl* **funguses** or **fungi** [′fʌndʒaɪ]) (bot) champignon *m*; (pathol) fongus *m*
funicular [fju′nɪkjələr] *adj* & *s* funiculaire *m*
funk [fʌŋk] *s* (coll) frousse *f*

fun·nel [′fʌnəl] *s* entonnoir *m*; (*smokestack*) cheminée *f*; (*tube for ventilation*) tuyau *m* ‖ *v* (*pret & pp* -neled or -nelled; *ger* -neling or -nelling) *tr* verser avec un entonnoir; (*to channel*) concentrer
funnies [′fʌniz] *spl* pages *fpl* comiques
fun·ny [′fʌni] *adj* (*comp* -nier; *super* -niest) comique; amusant, drôle; (coll) bizarre, curieux; **to strike s.o. as funny** paraître drôle à qn
fun′ny pa′per *s* pages *fpl* comiques
fur [fʌr] *s* fourrure *f*; (*on tongue*) empâtement *m*; **furs** pelleteries *fpl*
furbish [′fʌrbɪʃ] *tr* fourbir; **to furbish up** remettre à neuf
furious [′fjʊrɪ·əs] *adj* furieux
furl [fʌrl] *tr* (naut) ferler
fur′-lined′ *adj* doublé de fourrure
furlough [′fʌrlo] *s* permission *f*; **on furlough** en permission ‖ *tr* donner une permission à
furnace [′fʌrnɪs] *s* (*to heat a house*) calorifère *m*; (*to produce steam*) chaudière *f*; (*e.g., to smelt ores*) fourneau *m*; (rr) foyer *m*; (fig) fournaise *f*
furnish [′fʌrnɪʃ] *tr* fournir; (*a house*) meubler
fur′nished apart′ment *s* garni *m*, appartement *m* meublé
furnishings [′fʌrnɪʃɪŋz] *spl* ameublement *m*; (*things to wear*) articles *mpl* d'habillement
furniture [′fʌrnɪtʃər] *s* meubles *mpl*; **a piece of furniture** un meuble; **a suite of furniture** un mobilier
fur′niture deal′er *s* marchand *m* de meubles
fur′niture pol′ish *s* encaustique *f*
fur′niture store′ *s* maison *f* d'ameublement
fur′niture ware′house *s* garde-meuble *m*
furor [′fjʊrɔr] *s* fureur *f*
furrier [′fʌrɪ·ər] *s* fourreur *m*, pelletier *m*
furrow [′fʌro] *s* sillon *m* ‖ *tr* sillonner
fur·ry [′fʌri] *adj* (*comp* -rier; *super* -riest) fourré, à fourrure
further [′fʌrðər] *adj* additionnel, supplémentaire ‖ *adv* plus loin; (*besides*) en outre, de plus ‖ *tr* avancer, favoriser
furtherance [′fʌrðərəns] *s* avancement *m*
fur′ther·more′ *adv* de plus, d'ailleurs
furthest [′fʌrðɪst] *adj* (le) plus éloigné ‖ *adv* le plus loin
furtive [′fʌrtɪv] *adj* furtif
fu·ry [′fjʊri] *s* (*pl* -ries) furie *f*
furze [fʌrz] *s* genêt *m* épineux, ajonc *m* d'Europe
fuse [fjuz] *s* (*tube or wick filled with explosive material*) étoupille *f*, mèche *f*; (*device for exploding a bomb or projectile*) fusée *f*; (elec) fusible *m*, plomb *m* de sûreté, plomb fusible; **to burn** or **blow out a fuse** faire sauter un plomb ‖ *tr* fondre; étoupiller ‖ *intr* se fondre
fuse′ box′ *s* boîte *f* à fusibles

fuselage ['fjuzəlɪdʒ], [ˌfjuzə'lɑʒ] s
fuselage m
fusible ['fjuzɪbəl] adj fusible
fusillade [ˌfjuzɪ'led] s fusillade f
fusion ['fjuʒən] s fusion f
fuss [fʌs] s fracas m; (dispute) bagarre
f; **to kick up a fuss** (coll) faire un tas
d'histoires; **to make a fuss over** faire
grand cas de || intr faire des embar-
ras, simagrées, or chichis; **to fuss
over** être aux petits soins auprès de
fuss·y ['fʌsi] adj (comp -ier; super
-iest) tracassier, tatillon; (in dress)
pomponné

fustian ['fʌstʃən] s (cloth) futaine f;
(bombast) grandiloquence f
futile ['fjutɪl] adj futile
future ['fjutʃər] adj futur, d'avenir || s
avenir m; (gram) futur m; **futures**
(com) valeurs fpl négociées à terme;
in the future à l'avenir; **in the near
future** à brève échéance
fuzz [fʌz] s (on a peach) duvet m; (on
a blanket) peluche f; (in pockets and
corners) bourre f
fuzz·y ['fʌzi] adj (comp -ier; super
-iest) pelucheux; (hair) crêpelu; (indistinct) flou

G

G, g [dʒi] s VIIe lettre de l'alphabet
gab [gæb] s (coll) bavardage m, langue
f || v (pret & pp gabbed; ger gabbing)
intr (coll) bavarder
gabardine ['gæbər ˌdin] s gabardine f
gabble ['gæbəl] s jacasserie f || intr
jacasser
gable ['gebəl] s (of roof) pignon m;
(over a door or window) gable m
ga′ble end′ s pignon m
ga′ble roof′ s comble m sur pignon, toit
m à deux pentes
gad [gæd] v (pret & pp gadded; ger
gadding) intr—**to gad about** courir
la prétantaine, vadrouiller
gad′·about′ s vadrouilleur m
gad′fly′ s (pl -flies) taon m
gadget ['gædʒɪt] s dispositif m; (un-
named article) machin m, truc m
Gaelic ['gelɪk] adj & s gaélique m
gaff [gæf] s gaffe f; **to stand the gaff**
(slang) ne pas broncher
gaffer ['gæfər] s (coll) vieux bonhomme m
gag [gæg] s bâillon m; (interpolation
by an actor) gag m; (joke) blague f
|| v (pret & pp gagged; ger gagging)
tr bâillonner || intr avoir des haut-le-
cœur
gage [gedʒ] s (pledge) gage m; (challenge) défi m
gaie·ty ['ge·ɪti] s (pl -ties) gaieté f
gaily ['geli] adv gaiement
gain [gen] s gain m; (increase) accrois-
sement m || tr gagner; (to reach) at-
teindre, gagner || intr gagner du ter-
rain; (said of invalid) s'améliorer;
(said of watch) avancer; **to gain on**
prendre de l'avance sur
gainful ['genfəl] adj profitable
gain′say′ v (pret & pp -said [ˌsed],
[ˌsed]) tr (to deny) nier; (to contradict) contredire; **not to gainsay** ne
pas disconvenir de
gait [get] s démarche f, allure f
gaiter ['getər] s guêtre f
gala ['gælə], ['gelə] adj de gala || s
gala m
galax·y ['gæləksi] s (pl -ies) galaxie f

gale [gel] s gros vent m; **gales of
laughter** éclats mpl de rire; **to
weather a gale** étaler un coup de vent
gall [gɔl] s bile f, fiel m; (something
bitter) (fig) fiel m, amertume f; (au-
dacity) (coll) toupet m || tr écorcher
par le frottement; (fig) irriter
gallant ['gælənt] adj (spirited, daring)
vaillant, brave; (stately, grand) fier,
noble; (showy, gay) élégant, superbe,
de fête || ['gælənt], [gə'lænt] adj
galant || s galant m; vaillant m ||
[gə'lænt] intr faire le galant
gallant·ry ['gæləntri] s (pl -ries) galanterie f; (bravery) vaillance f
gall′ blad′der s vésicule f biliaire
gall′ duct′ s conduit m biliaire
galleon ['gælɪən] s (naut) galion m
galler·y ['gæləri] s (pl -ies) galerie f;
(cheapest seats in theater) poulailler
m; **to play to the gallery** poser pour
la galerie
galley ['gæli] s (ship) galère f; (ship's
kitchen) coquerie f; (typ) galée f
gal′ley proof′ s placard m; épreuve f
en placard
gal′ley slave′ s galérien m
Gallic ['gælɪk] adj gaulois
Gal′lic wit′ s esprit m gaulois
galling ['gɔlɪŋ] adj irritant, blessant
gallivant ['gælɪ ˌvænt] intr courailler
gall′nut′ s noix f de galle
gallon ['gælən] s gallon m américain
galloon [gə'lun] s galon m
gallop ['gæləp] s galop m || tr faire
galoper || intr galoper
gal·lows ['gæloz] s (pl -lows or -lowses)
gibet m, potence f
gal′lows bird′ s (coll) gibier m de potence
gall′stone′ s calcul m biliaire
galore [gə'lor] adv à foison, à gogo
galoshes [gə'lɑʃɪz] spl caoutchoucs
mpl
galvanize ['gælvə ˌnaɪz] tr galvaniser
gal′vanized i′ron s tôle f galvanisée
gambit ['gæmbɪt] s gambit m
gamble ['gæmbəl] s risque m, affaire f
de chance || tr jouer; **to gamble away**

perdre au jeu || *intr* jouer; jouer à la Bourse; (fig) prendre des risques
gambler ['gæmblər] *s* joueur *m*
gambling ['gæmblɪŋ] *s* jeu *m*
gam'bling den' *s* tripot *m*
gam'bling house' *s* maison *f* de jeu
gam'bling ta'ble *s* table *f* de jeu
gam·bol ['gæmbəl] *s* gambade *f* || *v* (*pret & pp* **-boled** or **-bolled;** *ger* **-boling** or **-bolling**) *intr* gambader
gambrel ['gæmbrəl] *s* (*hock*) jarret *m*; (*in butcher shop*) jambier *m*
gam'brel roof' *s* toit *m* en croupe
game [gem] *adj* crâne, résolu; (*leg*) boiteux || *s* jeu *m*; (*contest*) match *m*; (*score necessary to win*) partie *f*; (*animal or bird*) gibier *m*; **to make game of** tourner en dérision
game'bag' *s* carnassière *f*, gibecière *f*
game' bird' *s* oiseau *m* que l'on chasse
game'cock' *s* coq *m* de combat
game'keep'er *s* garde-chasse *m*
game' of chance' *s* jeu *m* de hasard
game' preserve' *s* chasse *f* gardée
game' war'den *s* garde-chasse *m*
gamut ['gæmət] *s* gamme *f*
gam·y ['gemi] *adj* (*comp* **-ier;** *super* **-iest**) (*having flavor of uncooked game*) faisandé; (*plucky*) crâne
gander ['gændər] *s* jars *m*
gang [gæŋ] *adj* multiple || *s* (*of workmen*) équipe *f*, brigade *f*; (*of thugs*) bande *f*; (*of wrongdoers*) séquelle *f*, clique *f* || *intr*—**to gang up** se concerter; **to gang up on** se liguer contre
gangling ['gæŋglɪŋ] *adj* dégingandé
gangli·on ['gæŋglɪ·ən] *s* (*pl* **-ons** or **-a** [ə]) ganglion *m*
gang'plank' *s* passerelle *f*, planche *f* de débarquement
gangrene ['gæŋgrin] *s* gangrène *f* || *tr* gangrener || *intr* se gangrener
gangster ['gæŋstər] *s* bandit *m*, gangster *m*
gang'way' *s* (*passageway*) passage *m*, coursive *f*; (*gangplank*) planche *f* de débarquement; (*in ship's side*) coupée *f* || *interj* rangez-vous!, dégagez!
gan·try ['gæntri] *s* (*pl* **-tries**) (*for barrels*) chantier *m*; (*for crane*) portique *m*; (rr) pont *m* à signaux
gan'try crane' *s* grue *f* à portique
gap [gæp] *s* lacune *f*; (*in wall*) brèche *f*; (*between mountains*) col *m*, gorge *f*; (*between two points of view*) abîme *m*, gouffre *m*
gape [gep], [gæp] *s* ouverture *f*, brèche *f*; (*yawn*) bâillement *m*; (*look of astonishment*) badauderie *f* || *intr* (*to yawn*) bâiller; (*to look with astonishment*) badauder; **to gape at** regarder bouche bée
garage [gə'raʒ] *s* garage *m*
garb [garb] *s* costume *m* || *tr* vêtir
garbage ['garbɪdʒ] *s* ordures *fpl*
gar'bage can' *s* poubelle *f*
gar'bage collec'tor *s* boueur *m*
gar'bage dispos'al *s* destruction *f* des ordures ménagères
gar'bage truck' *s* benne *f* à ordures
garble ['garbəl] *tr* mutiler, tronquer
garden ['gardən] *s* jardin *m*; (*of vege-*

tables) potager *m*; (*of flowers*) parterre *m* || *intr* jardiner
gar'den cit'y *s* cité-jardin *f*
gardener ['gardnər] *s* jardinier *m*
gardening ['gardnɪŋ] *s* jardinage *m*
gar'den par'ty *s* garden-party *f*
gargle ['gargəl] *s* gargarisme *m* || *intr* se gargariser
gargoyle ['gargɔɪl] *s* gargouille *f*
garish ['gerɪʃ], ['gærɪʃ] *adj* cru, rutilant, criard
garland ['garlənd] *s* guirlande *f* || *tr* guirlander
garlic ['garlɪk] *s* ail *m*
garment ['garmənt] *s* vêtement *m*
gar'ment bag' *s* housse *f* à vêtements
garner ['garnər] *tr* (*to gather, collect*) amasser; (*cereals*) engranger
garnet ['garnɪt] *adj & s* grenat *m*
garnish ['garnɪʃ] *s* garniture *f* || *tr* garnir; (law) effectuer une saisie-arrêt sur
garret ['gærɪt] *s* grenier *m*; (*dormer room*) mansarde *f*
garrison ['gærɪsən] *s* garnison *f* || *tr* (*troops*) mettre en garnison; (*a city*) mettre des troupes en garnison dans
garrote [gə'rat], [gə'rot] *s* (*method of execution*) garrotte *f*; (*iron collar used for such an execution*) garrot *m* || *tr* garrotter
garrulous ['gær(j)ələs] *adj* bavard
garter ['gartər] *s* jarretelle *f*, jarretière *f*; (*for men's socks*) support-chaussette *m*, fixe-chaussette *m*
garth [garθ] *s* cour *f* intérieure d'un cloître
gas [gæs] *s* gaz *m*; (coll) essence *f*; (*empty talk*) (coll) bavardage *m*; **out of gas** en panne sèche || *v* (*pret & pp* **gassed;** *ger* **gassing**) *tr* gazer, asphyxier || *intr* dégager des gaz; (*to talk nonsense*) (coll) bavarder
gas'bag' *s* enveloppe *f* à gaz; (coll) blagueur *m*, baratineur *m*
gas' burn'er *s* bec *m* de gaz
gas' cham'ber *s* chambre *f* à gaz
Gascony ['gæskəni] *s* Gascogne *f*; la Gascogne
gas' en'gine *s* moteur *m* à gaz
gaseous ['gæsɪ·əs] *adj* gazeux
gas' gen'erator *s* gazogène *m*
gash [gæʃ] *s* entaille *f*; (*on face*) balafre *f* || *tr* entailler; balafrer
gas' heat' *s* chauffage *m* au gaz
gas' heat'er *s* (*for hot water*) chauffe-eau *m* à gaz; (*for house heat*) calorifère *m* à gaz
gas'hold'er *s* gazomètre *m*
gasi·fy ['gæsɪ‚faɪ] *v* (*pret & pp* **-fied**) *tr* gazéifier || *intr* se gazéifier
gas' jet' *s* bec *m* de gaz
gasket ['gæskɪt] *s* joint *m*
gas'light' *s* éclairage *m* au gaz
gas' main' *s* conduite *f* de gaz
gas' mask' *s* masque *m* à gaz
gas' me'ter *s* compteur *m* à gaz
gasoline ['gæsə‚lin], [‚gæsə'lin] *s* essence *f*
gas'oline can' *s* bidon *m* d'essence
gas'oline gauge' *s* voyant *m* d'essence
gas'oline pump' *s* pompe *f* à essence

gasp [gæsp], [gɑsp] s halètement m; (of surprise; of death) hoquet m || tr —to gasp out (a word) dire dans un souffle || intr haleter

gas' pipe' s conduite f de gaz

gas' produc'er s gazogène m

gas' range' s fourneau m à gaz, cuisinière f à gaz

gas' sta'tion s poste m d'essence

gas' stove' s cuisinière f à gaz, réchaud m à gaz

gas' tank' s gazomètre m; (aut) réservoir m d'essence

gastric ['gæstrɪk] adj gastrique

gastronomy [gæs'trɑnəmi] s gastronomie f

gas'works' spl usine f à gaz

gate [get] s porte f; (in fence or wall) grille f; (main gate) portail f; (of sluice) vanne f; (number paying admission; amount paid) entrée f; (rr) barrière f; to crash the gate resquiller

gate-crasher ['get‚kræʃər] s (coll) resquilleur m

gate'keep'er s portier m; (rr) gardebarrière mf

gate'-leg ta'ble s table f à abattants

gate'post' s montant m

gate'way' s passage m, entrée f; (main entrance) portail m

gather ['gæðər] tr amasser, rassembler; (the harvest) rentrer; (fruits, flowers, etc.) cueillir, ramasser; (one's thoughts) recueillir; (bb) rassembler; (sewing) froncer; (to deduce) (fig) conclure; to gather dust s'encrasser; to gather oneself together se ramasser || intr se réunir, s'assembler; (said of clouds) s'amonceler

gathering ['gæðərɪŋ] s réunion m, rassemblement m; (of harvest) récolte f; (of fruits, flowers, etc.) cueillette f; (bb) assemblage m; (sewing) froncis m

gaud·y ['gɔdi] adj (comp -ier; super -iest) criard, voyant

gauge [gedʒ] s jauge f, calibre m; (of liquid in a container) niveau m; (of gasoline, oil, etc.) indicateur m; (of carpenter) trusquin m; (rr) écartement m || tr jauger, calibrer; (a person; s.o.'s capacities; a distance) juger de, jauger

gauge' glass' s indicateur m de niveau

Gaul [gɔl] s Gaule f; la Gaule

Gaulish ['gɔlɪʃ] adj & s gaulois m

gaunt [gɔnt], [gɑnt] adj décharné, étique, efflanqué

gauntlet ['gɔntlɪt], ['gɑntlɪt] s gantelet m; to run the gauntlet passer par les baguettes; to take up the gauntlet relever le gant; to throw down the gauntlet jeter le gant

gauze [gɔz] s gaze f

gavel ['gævəl] s marteau m

gawk [gɔk] s (coll) godiche mf || intr (coll) bayer aux corneilles; to gawk at (coll) regarder bouche bée

gawk·y ['gɔki] adj (comp -ier; super -iest) godiche

gay [ge] adj gai

gay' blade' s (coll) joyeux drille m

gaze [gez] s regard m fixe || intr regarder fixement

gazelle [gə'zɛl] s gazelle f

gazette [gə'zɛt] s gazette f; journal m officiel

gazetteer [‚gæzə'tɪr] s dictionnaire m géographique

gear [gɪr] s attirail m, appareil m; (of transmission, steering, etc.) mécanisme m; (adjustment of automobile transmission) marche f, vitesse f; (two or more toothed wheels meshed together) engrenage m; out of gear débrayé; to throw into gear embrayer; to throw out of gear débrayer; (fig) disloquer || tr & intr engrener

gear'box' s (aut) boîte f de vitesses

gear'shift' s changement m de vitesse

gear'shift lev'er s levier m de changement de vitesse

gear'wheel' s roue f d'engrenage

gee [dʒi] interj sapristi!; (to the right) hue!; gee up! hue!

Gei'ger count'er ['gaɪgər] s compteur m de Geiger

gel [dʒɛl] s (chem) gel m

gelatine ['dʒɛlətɪn] s gélatine f

geld [gɛld] v (pret & pp gelded or gelt [gɛlt]) tr châtrer

gelding ['gɛldɪŋ] s hongre m

gem [dʒɛm] s gemme f; (fig) bijou m

gender ['dʒɛndər] s (gram) genre m; (coll) sexe m

gene [dʒin] s (biol) gène m

genealo·gy [‚dʒɛnɪ'ælədʒi], [‚dʒini-'ælədʒi] s (pl -gies) généalogie f

general ['dʒɛnərəl] adj & s général m; in general en général

gen'eral deliv'ery s poste f restante

generalissi·mo [‚dʒɛnərə'lɪsɪmo] s (pl -mos) généralissime m

generali·ty [‚dʒɛnə'rælɪti] s (pl -ties) généralité f

generalize ['dʒɛnərə‚laɪz] tr & intr généraliser

generally ['dʒɛnərəli] adv généralement

gen'eral practi'tioner s médecin m de médecine générale

gen'eral·ship' s tactique f; (office) généralat m

gen'eral staff' s état-major m

generate ['dʒɛnə‚ret] tr générer; (to beget) engendrer; (geom) engendrer

gen'erating sta'tion s usine f génératrice, centrale f

generation [‚dʒɛnə'reʃən] s génération f

generator ['dʒɛnə‚retər] s (chem) gazogène m; (elec) génératrice f

generic [dʒɪ'nɛrɪk] adj générique

generosi·ty [‚dʒɛnə'rɑsɪti] s (pl -ties) générosité f

generous ['dʒɛnərəs] adj généreux; abondant

gene·sis ['dʒɛnɪsɪs] s (pl -ses [‚siz]) genèse f; Genesis (Bib) La Genèse

genetic [dʒɪ'nɛtɪk] adj génétique || genetics s génétique f

Geneva [dʒɪ'nivə] s Genève f

genial ['dʒinɪ‚əl] adj affable

genie ['dʒini] s génie m

genital ['dʒenɪtəl] *adj* génital || **genitals** *spl* organes *mpl* génitaux
genitive ['dʒenɪtɪv] *s* génitif *m*
genius ['dʒinjəs], ['dʒinɪ·əs] *s* (*pl* **geniuses**) génie *m* || *s* (*pl* **genii** ['dʒinɪ,aɪ]) génie *m*
Genoa ['dʒeno·ə] *s* Gênes *f*
genocide ['dʒenə,saɪd] *s* génocide *m*
genteel [dʒen'til] *adj* distingué, de bon ton; élégant, chic
gentian ['dʒenʃən] *s* gentiane *f*
gentile ['dʒentaɪl] *s* non-juif *m*, chrétien *m*
gentili·ty [dʒen'tɪlɪti] *s* (*pl* -ties) (*birth*) naissance *f* distinguée; (*breeding*) politesse *f*
gentle ['dʒentəl] *adj* doux; (*in birth*) noble, bien né; (*e.g.*, *tap on the shoulder*) léger
gen'tle·folk' *s* gens *mpl* de bonne naissance
gen'tle·man *s* (*pl* -men) monsieur *m*; (*man of independent means*) rentier *m*; (hist) gentilhomme *m*
gentlemanly ['dʒentəlmənli] *adj* bien élevé, de bon ton
gen'tleman's agree'ment *s* engagement *m* sur parole, contrat *m* verbal
gen'tle sex' *s* sexe *m* faible
gentry ['dʒentri] *s* gens *mpl* de bonne naissance; (Brit) petite noblesse *f*
genuine ['dʒenju·ɪn] *adj* véritable, authentique; (*person*) sincère, franc
genus ['dʒinəs] *s* (*pl* **genera** ['dʒenərə] or **genuses**) genre *m*
geogra·phy [dʒɪ'ɑgrəfi] *s* (*pl* -phies) géographie *f*
geologic(al) [,dʒi·ə'lɑdʒɪk(əl)] *adj* géologique
geolo·gy [dʒɪ'ɑlədʒi] *s* (*pl* -gies) géologie *f*
geometric(al) [,dʒi·ə'metrɪk(əl)] *adj* géométrique
geome·try [dʒɪ'ɑmɪtri] *s* (*pl* -tries) géométrie *f*
geophysics [,dʒi·ə'fɪzɪks] *s* géophysique *f*
geopolitics [,dʒi·ə'pɑlɪtɪks] *s* géopolitique *f*
George [dʒɔrdʒ] *s* Georges *m*
geranium [dʒɪ'renɪ·əm] *s* géranium *m*
geriatrics [,dʒerɪ'ætrɪks] *s* gériatrie *f*
germ [dʒʌrm] *s* germe *m*
German ['dʒʌrmən] *adj* allemand || *s* (*language*) allemand *m*; (*person*) Allemand *m*
germane [dʒer'men] *adj* à propos, pertinent; **germane to** se rapportant à
Ger'man mea'sles *s* rubéole *f*
Ger'man sil'ver *s* maillechort *m*, argentan *m*
Germa·ny ['dʒʌrməni] *s* (*pl* -nies) Allemagne *f*; l'Allemagne
germicidal [,dʒʌrmɪ'saɪdəl] *adj* germicide
germicide ['dʒʌrmɪ,saɪd] *s* germicide *m*
germinate ['dʒʌrmɪ,net] *intr* germer
germ' war'fare *s* guerre *f* bactériologique
gerontology [,dʒerɑn'tɑlədʒi] *s* gérontologie *f*
gerund ['dʒerənd] *s* gérondif *m*

gestation [dʒes'teʃən] *s* gestation *f*
gesticulate [dʒes'tɪkjə,let] *intr* gesticuler
gesture ['dʒestʃər] *s* geste *m* || *intr* faire des gestes; **to gesture to** faire signe à
get [get] *v* (*pret* got [gɑt]; *pp* got or gotten ['gɑtən]; *ger* getting) *tr* obtenir, procurer; (*to receive*) avoir, recevoir; (*to catch*) attraper; (*to seek*) chercher, aller chercher; (*to reach*) atteindre; (*to find*) trouver, rencontrer; (*to obtain and bring*) prendre; (*e.g.*, *dinner*) faire; (*rad*) avoir, prendre, accrocher; (*to understand*) (coll) comprendre; **to get across** faire accepter; faire comprendre; **to get a kick out of** (coll) prendre plaisir à; **to get back** ravoir, se faire rendre; **to get down** descendre; (*to swallow*) avaler; **to get in** rentrer; **to get s.o. to** + *inf* persuader à qn de + *inf*; **to get s.th. done** faire faire q.ch. || *intr* (*to become*) devenir, se faire; (*to arrive*) arriver, parvenir; **get up!** (*said to an animal*) hue!; **to get about** (*said of news*) se répandre; (*said of convalescent*) être de nouveau sur pied; **to get accustomed** to se faire à; **to get across** traverser; **to get along** circuler; (*to succeed*) se tirer d'affaire; **to get along without** se passer de; **to get angry** se fâcher; **to get away** s'évader; **to get away with** s'en aller avec; (coll) s'en tirer avec; **to get back** reculer; (*to return*) rentrer; **to get back at** (coll) rendre la pareille à, se venger sur; **to get by** passer; (*to manage*, *to shift*) (coll) s'en tirer sans peine; **to get dark** tomber nuit; **to get down** descendre; **to get going** se mettre en marche; **to get in** or **into** entrer dans; **to get off** with en être quitte pour; **to get on** monter sur; (*a car*) monter dans; continuer; (*to succeed*) faire des progrès; **to get out** sortir; **to get rid of** se défaire de; **to get to** arriver à; (*to have an opportunity to*) avoir l'occasion de; **to get up** se lever; **to not get over it** (coll) ne pas en revenir
get'away' *s* démarrage *m*; (*flight*) fuite *f*
get'-togeth'er *s* réunion *f*
get'up' *s* (*style*) (coll) présentation *f*; (*outfit*) (coll) affublement *m*
geyser ['gaɪzər] *s* geyser *m* || ['gizər] *s* (Brit) chauffe-eau *m* à gaz
ghast·ly ['gæstli], ['gɑstli] *adj* (*comp* -lier; *super* -liest) livide, blême; horrible, affreux
Ghent [gent] *s* Gand *m*
gherkin ['gʌrkɪn] *s* cornichon *m*
ghet·to ['geto] *s* (*pl* -tos) ghetto *m*
ghost [gost] *s* revenant *m*; (*shade*, *semblance*) ombre *f*; **not the ghost of a chance** pas la moindre chance; **to give up the ghost** rendre l'âme, rendre l'esprit
ghost·ly ['gostli] *adj* (*comp* -lier; *super* -liest) spectral, fantomatique
ghost' sto'ry *s* histoire *f* de revenants

ghost' town' *s* ville *f* morte
ghost' writ'er *s* nègre *m*
ghoul [gul] *s* goule *f*; (*body snatcher*) déterreur *m* de cadavres
ghoulish ['gulɪʃ] *adj* vampirique
GI ['dʒi'aɪ] (letterword) (**General Issue**) *adj* fourni par l'armée ‖ *s* (*pl* **GI's**) soldat *m* américain, simple soldat
giant ['dʒaɪ-ənt] *adj & s* géant *m*
giantess ['dʒaɪ-əntɪs] *s* géante *f*
gibberish ['dʒɪbərɪʃ], ['gɪbərɪʃ] *s* baragouin *m*
gibbet ['dʒɪbɪt] *s* gibet *m*, potence *f*
gibe [dʒaɪb] *s* raillerie *f*, moquerie *f* ‖ *tr & intr* railler; **to gibe at** se moquer de, railler
giblets ['dʒɪblɪts] *spl* abattis *m*, abats *mpl*
gid·dy ['gɪdi] *adj* (*comp* **-dier**; *super* **-diest**) étourdi; (*height*) vertigineux; (*foolish*) léger, frivole
Gideon ['gɪdɪ-ən] *s* (Bib) Gédéon *m*
gift [gɪft] *s* cadeau *m*; (*natural ability*) don *m*, talent *m* ‖ *tr* douer
gifted *adj* doué
gift' horse' *s*—**never look a gift horse in the mouth** à cheval donné on ne regarde pas à la bride
gift' of gab' *s* (coll) bagou *m*, faconde *f*
gift' shop' *s* boutique *f* de souvenirs, magasin *m* de nouveautés
gift'-wrap' *v* (*pret & pp* **-wrapped**; *ger* **-wrapping**) *tr* faire un paquet cadeau de
gigantic [dʒaɪ'gæntɪk] *adj* gigantesque
giggle ['gɪgəl] *s* petit rire *m* ‖ *intr* pousser des petits rires, glousser
gigo·lo ['dʒɪgə‚lo] *s* (*pl* **-los**) gigolo *m*
GI Joe [‚dʒi‚aɪ'dʒo] *s* le troufion
gild [gɪld] *v* (*pret & pp* **gilded** or **gilt** [gɪlt]) *tr* dorer
gilding ['gɪldɪŋ] *s* dorure *f*
gill [gɪl] *s* (*of cock*) fanon *m*; **gills** (*of fish*) ouïes *fpl*, branchies *fpl*
gilt [gɪlt] *adj & s* doré *m*
gilt'-edged' *adj* (e.g., *book*) doré sur tranche; (*securities*) de premier ordre, de tout repos
gimcrack ['dʒɪm‚kræk] *adj* de pacotille, de camelote ‖ *s* babiole *f*
gimlet ['gɪmlɪt] *s* vrille *f*, perçoir *m*
gimmick ['gɪmɪk] *s* (coll) truc *m*, machin *m*; (*trick*) tour *m*
gin [dʒɪn] *s* (*alcoholic liquor*) gin *m*, genièvre *m*; (*for cotton, corn, etc.*) égreneuse *f*; (*snare*) trébuchet *m* ‖ *v* (*pret & pp* **ginned**; *ger* **ginning**) *tr* égrener
ginger ['dʒɪndʒər] *s* gingembre *m*; (fig) entrain *m*, allant *m*
gin'ger ale' *s* boisson *f* gazeuse au gingembre
gin'ger·bread' *s* pain *m* d'épice; ornement *m* de mauvais goût
gingerly ['dʒɪndʒərli] *adj* précautionneux ‖ *adv* tout doux, avec précaution
gin'ger·snap' *s* gâteau *m* sec au gingembre
gingham ['gɪŋəm] *s* guingan *m*
giraffe [dʒɪ'ræf], [dʒɪ'rɑf] *s* girafe *f*

gird [gʌrd] *v* (*pret & pp* **girt** [gʌrt] or **girded**) *tr* ceindre; **to gird on** se ceindre de; **to gird oneself for** se préparer à
girder ['gʌrdər] *s* poutre *f*
girdle ['gʌrdəl] *s* ceinture *f* ‖ *tr* ceindre, entourer
girl [gʌrl] *s* jeune fille *f*; (*little girl*) petite fille; (*servant*) bonne *f*
girl' friend' *s* (*sweetheart*) petite amie *f*, bonne amie *f*; (*female friend*) amie *f*, camarade *f*
girl'hood *s* enfance *f*, jeunesse *f* d'une femme
girlish ['gʌrlɪʃ] *adj* de jeune fille, de petite fille
girl' scout' *s* éclaireuse *f*, guide *f*
girls'' school' *s* école *f* de filles
girth [gʌrθ] *s* (*band*) sangle *f*; (*measure around*) circonférence *f*; (*of person*) tour *m* de taille
gist [dʒɪst] *s* fond *m*, essence *f*
give [gɪv] *s* élasticité *f* ‖ *v* (*pret* **gave** [gev]; *pp* **given** ['gɪvən]) *tr* donner; (*a speech, a lecture, a class; a smile*) faire; **to give away** donner, distribuer; révéler; **to give back** rendre, remettre; **to give forth** or **off** émettre; **to give oneself up** se rendre; **to give up** renoncer à, abandonner ‖ *intr* donner; **to give in** se rendre; **to give out** manquer; (*to become exhausted*) s'épuiser; **to give way** faire place, reculer
give'-and-take' *s* compromis *m*; échange *m* de propos plaisants
give'away' *s* (coll) révélation *f* involontaire; (coll) trahison *f*; **to play giveaway** jouer à qui perd gagne
given ['gɪvən] *adj* donné; **given that** vu que, étant donné que
giv'en name' *s* prénom *m*
giver ['gɪvər] *s* donneur *m*, donateur *m*
gizzard ['gɪzərd] *s* gésier *m*
glacial ['gleʃəl] *adj* glacial; (chem) en cristaux; (geol) glaciaire
glacier ['gleʃər] *s* glacier *m*
glad [glæd] *adj* (*comp* **gladder**; *super* **gladdest**) content, heureux; **to be glad to** être content or heureux de
gladden ['glædən] *tr* réjouir
glade [gled] *s* clairière *f*, éclaircie *f*
glad' hand' *s* (coll) accueil *m* chaleureux
gladiator ['glædɪ‚etər] *s* gladiateur *m*
gladiola [‚glædɪ'olə], [glə'daɪ-ələ] *s* glaïeul *m*
gladly ['glædli] *adv* volontiers, avec plaisir
gladness ['glædnɪs] *s* joie *f*, plaisir *m*
glad' rags' *spl* (slang) frusques *fpl* des grands jours
glamorous ['glæmərəs] *adj* ravissant, éclatant
glamour ['glæmər] *s* charme *m*, éclat *m*
glam'our girl' *s* ensorceleuse *f*
glance [glæns], [glɑns] *s* coup *m* d'œil; **at a glance** d'un seul coup d'œil; **at first glance** à première vue ‖ *intr* jeter un regard; **to glance at** jeter un coup d'œil sur; **to glance off** ricocher, dévier; **to glance through a book**

feuilleter un livre; **to glance up** lever les yeux

gland [glænd] *s* glande *f*

glanders ['glændərz] *spl* (vet) morve *f*

glare [glɛr] *s* lumière *f* éblouissante; *(look)* regard *m* irrité || *intr* éblouir, briller; **to glare at** lancer un regard méchant à, foudroyer du regard

glare' ice' *s* verglas *m*

glaring ['glɛrɪŋ] *adj* éblouissant; *(mistake, fact)* évident, qui saute aux yeux; *(blunder, abuse)* grossier, scandaleux

glass [glæs], [glɑs] *s* verre *m*; *(mirror)* glace *f*; **glasses** lunettes *fpl*

glass' blow'er ['blo·ər] *s* verrier-souffleur *m*

glass' case' *s* vitrine *f*

glass' cut'ter *s* *(tool)* diamant *m*; *(workman)* vitrier *m*

glass' door' *s* porte *f* vitrée

glassful ['glæsfʊl], ['glɑsfʊl] *s* verre *m*

glass' house' *s* serre *f*; (fig) maison *f* de verre

glass' ware' *s* verrerie *f*

glass' wool' *s* laine *f* de verre

glass' works' *s* verrerie *f*, glacerie *f*

glass·y ['glæsi], ['glɑsi] *adj* *(comp* **-ier;** *super* **-iest)** vitreux; *(smooth)* lisse

glaze [glez] *s* *(ceramics)* vernis *m*; *(culin)* glace *f*; *(tex)* lustre *m* || *tr* *(to cover with a glossy coating)* glacer; *(to fit with glass)* vitrer

glazier ['gleʒər] *s* vitrier *m*

gleam [glim] *s* rayon *m*; *(of hope)* lueur *f* || *intr* rayonner, reluire

glean [glin] *tr* glaner

glee [gli] *s* allégresse *f*, joie *f*

glee' club' *s* orphéon *m*, société *f* chorale

glen [glɛn] *s* vallon *m*, ravin *m*

glib [glɪb] *adj* *(comp* **glibber;** *super* **glibbest)** facile; *(tongue)* délié

glide [glaɪd] *s* glissement *m*; (aer) vol *m* plané; (mus) port *m* de voix; (phonet) son *m* transitoire || *intr* glisser, se glisser; (aer) planer

glider ['glaɪdər] *s* *(porch seat)* siège *m* à glissière; (aer) planeur *m*

glimmer ['glɪmər] *s* faible lueur *f* || *intr* jeter une faible lueur

glimmering ['glɪmərɪŋ] *adj* faible, vacillant || *s* faible lueur *f*, miroitement *m*; soupçon *m*, indice *m*

glimpse [glɪmps] *s* aperçu *m*; **to catch a glimpse of** entrevoir, aviser || *tr* entrevoir

glint [glɪnt] *s* reflet *m*, éclair *m* || *intr* jeter un reflet, étinceler

glisten ['glɪsən] *s* scintillement *m* || *intr* scintiller

glitter ['glɪtər] *s* éclat *m*, étincellement *m* || *intr* étinceler

gloaming ['glomɪŋ] *s* crépuscule *m*, jour *m* crépusculaire

gloat [glot] *intr* éprouver un malin plaisir; **to gloat over** faire des gorges chaudes de; *(e.g., one's victim)* couver du regard

global ['globəl] *adj* sphérique; mondial

globe [glob] *s* globe *m*

globe'-trot'ter *s* globe-trotter *m*

globule ['glabjʊl] *s* globule *m*

gloom [glum] *s* obscurité *f*, ténèbres *fpl*; tristesse *f*

gloom·y ['glumi] *adj* *(comp* **-ier;** *super* **-iest)** sombre, lugubre; *(ideas)* noir

glori·fy ['glorɪ͵faɪ] *v* *(pret & pp* **-fied)** *tr* glorifier

glorious ['glorɪ·əs] *adj* glorieux

glo·ry ['glori] *s* *(pl* **-ries)** gloire *f*; **to be in one's glory** être aux anges; **to go to glory** (slang) aller à la ruine || *v* *(pret & pp* **-ried)** *intr*—**to glory in** se glorifier de

gloss [glɔs], [glɑs] *s* lustre *m*; *(on cloth)* cati *m*; *(on floor)* brillant *m*; *(note, commentary)* glose *f*; **to take off the gloss from** décatir || *tr* lustrer; **to gloss over** maquiller, farder

glossa·ry ['glɑsəri] *s* *(pl* **-ries)** glossaire *m*

gloss·y ['glɔsi], ['glɑsi] *adj* *(comp* **-ier;** *super* **-iest)** lustré, brillant

glot'tal stop' ['glɑtəl] *s* coup *m* de glotte

glottis ['glɑtɪs] *s* glotte *f*

glove [glʌv] *s* gant *m* || *tr* ganter

glove' compart'ment *s* boîte *f* à gants

glow [glo] *s* rougeoiement *m* || *intr* rougeoyer

glower ['glaʊ·ər] *s* grise mine *f* || *intr* avoir l'air renfrogné

glowing ['glo·ɪŋ] *adj* rougeoyant, incandescent; *(healthy)* rayonnant; *(cheeks)* vermeil; *(reports)* enthousiaste, élogieux

glow'worm' *s* ver *m* luisant

glucose ['glukos] *s* glucose *m*

glue [glu] *s* colle *f* || *tr* coller

glue'pot' *s* pot *m* à colle

gluey ['glu·i] *adj* *(comp* **gluier;** *super* **gluiest)** gluant

glum [glʌm] *adj* *(comp* **glummer;** *super* **glummest)** maussade, renfrogné

glut [glʌt] *s* surabondance *f*; *(on the market)* engorgement *m* || *v* *(pret & pp* **glutted;** *ger* **glutting)** *tr* *(with food)* rassasier; *(the market)* inonder, engorger

glutton ['glʌtən] *s* glouton *m*

gluttonous ['glʌtənəs] *adj* glouton

glutton·y ['glʌtəni] *s* *(pl* **-ies)** gloutonnerie *f*

glycerine ['glɪsərɪn] *s* glycérine *f*

G.M.T. *abbr* **(Greenwich mean time** *temps moyen de Greenwich)* T.U., temps *m* universel

gnarl [nɑrl] *s* (bot) nœud *m* || *tr* tordre || *intr* grogner

gnarled [nɑrld] *adj* noueux

gnash [næʃ] *tr*—**to gnash the teeth** grincer des dents or les dents

gnat [næt] *s* moucheron *m*, moustique *m*

gnaw [nɔ] *tr* ronger

gnome [nom] *s* gnome *m*

go [go] *s* *(pl* **goes)** aller *m*; **a lot of go** (slang) beaucoup d'allant; **it's no go** (coll) ça ne marche pas, pas mèche; **to have a go at** (coll) essayer; **to make a go of** (coll) réussir à || *v* (*pret* went [wɛnt]; *pp* gone [gɔn], [gɑn]) *tr*—to go it alone le faire tout seul ‖ *intr* aller; (*to work, operate*) marcher; y aller, e.g., did you go? y êtes-vous allé?; devenir, e.g., to go crazy devenir fou; faire, e.g., to go quack-quack faire couin-couin; going, going, gone! une fois, deux fois, adjugé!; go to it! allez-y!; to be going to or to go to + *inf* aller + *inf*, e.g., I am going to the store to buy some shoes je vais au magasin acheter des souliers; (to express futurity from the point of view of the present or past) aller + *inf*, e.g., he is going to get married il va se marier; e.g., he was going to get married il allait se marier; to go (*to take out*) à emporter; to go against contrarier; to go ahead of dépasser; to go away s'en aller; to go back retourner; (*to return home*) rentrer; (*to back up*) reculer; (*to date back*) remonter; to go by passer; (*a rule, model, etc.*) agir selon; to go down descendre; (*said of sun*) se coucher; (*said of ship*) sombrer; to go fishing aller à la pêche; to go for or to go get aller chercher; to go in entrer; entrer dans; (*to fit into*) tenir dans; to go in for se consacrer à; to go in with s'associer à or avec, se joindre à; to go off (*said of bomb, gun, etc.*) partir; to go on + *ger* continuer à + *inf*; to go out sortir; (*said of light, fire, etc.*) s'éteindre; to go over (*to examine*) parcourir, repasser; to go through (*e.g., a door*) passer par; (*e.g., a city*) traverser; (*a fortune*) dissiper, dilapider, to go together (*said, e.g., of colors*) s'assortir; (*said of lovers*) être très liés; to go under succomber; (*said, e.g., of submarine*) plonger; (*a false name*) être connu sous; to go up monter; to go with accompagner; (*a color, dress, etc.*) s'assortir avec; to go without se passer de; to let go of lâcher

goad [god] *s* aiguillon *m* ‖ *tr* aiguillonner

go'-ahead' *adj* (coll) entreprenant ‖ *s* (coll) signal *m* d'aller en avant

goal [gol] *s* but *m*

goal'keep'er *s* goal *m*, gardien *m* de but

goal' line' *s* ligne *f* de but

goal' post' *s* montant *m*, poteau *m* de but

goat [got] *s* chèvre *f*; (*male goat*) bouc *m*; (coll) dindon *m*; to get the goat of (slang) exaspérer, irriter

goatee [go'ti] *s* barbiche *f*

goat'herd' *s* chevrier *m*

goat'skin' *s* peau *f* de chèvre

goat'suck'er *s* (orn) engoulevent *m*

gob [gɑb] *s* (coll) grumeau *m*; (coll) marin *m*

gobble ['gɑbəl] *s* glouglou *m* ‖ *tr* engloutir, bâfrer ‖ *intr* bâfrer; (*said of turkey*) glouglouter

gobbledegook ['gɑbəldɪ,gʊk] *s* (coll) palabre *m & f*, charabia *m*

go'-between' *s* intermédiaire *mf*; (*in shady love affairs*) entremetteur *m*

goblet ['gɑblɪt] *s* verre *m* à pied

goblin ['gɑblɪn] *s* lutin *m*

go'-by' *s* (coll) affront *m*; to give s.o. the go-by (coll) brûler la politesse à qn

go'cart' *s* chariot *m*; (*baby carriage*) poussette *f*; (*handcart*) charrette *f* à bras

god [gɑd] *s* dieu *m*; God forbid qu'à Dieu ne plaise; God grant plût à Dieu; God willing s'il plaît à Dieu

god'child' *s* (*pl* -chil'dren) filleul *m*

god'daugh'ter *s* filleule *f*

goddess ['gɑdɪs] *s* déesse *f*

god'fa'ther *s* parrain *m*

God'-fear'ing *adj* dévot, pieux

God'forsak'en *adj* abandonné de Dieu; (coll) perdu, misérable

god'head' *s* divinité *f*; Godhead Dieu *m*

godless ['gɑdlɪs] *adj* athée, impie

god·ly ['gɑdli] *adj* (*comp* -lier; *super* -liest) dévot, pieux

god'moth'er *s* marraine *f*

God's' a'cre *s* le champ de repos

god'send' *s* aubaine *f*

god'son' *s* filleul *m*

God'speed' *s* bonne chance *f*, bon voyage *m*

go-getter ['go,gɛtər] *s* (coll) homme *m* d'expédition, lanceur *m* d'affaires

goggle ['gɑgəl] *intr* rouler de gros yeux; (*to open the eyes wide*) écarquiller les yeux

gog'gle-eyed' *adj* aux yeux saillants

goggles ['gɑgəlz] *spl* lunettes *fpl* protectrices

going ['go·ɪŋ] *adj* en marche; going on two o'clock presque deux heures ‖ *s* départ *m*; good going! bien joué!

go'ing concern' *s* maison *f* en pleine activité

go'ings on' *spl* (coll) chahut *m*, tapage *m*; (coll) événements *mpl*

goiter ['gɔɪtər] *s* goitre *m*

gold [gold] *adj* d'or, en or ‖ *s* or *m*

gold'beat'er *s* batteur *m* d'or

gold'beater's skin' *s* baudruche *f*

gold'crest' *s* roitelet *m* à tête dorée

golden ['goldən] *adj* d'or; (*gilt*) doré; (*hair*) d'or, d'un blond doré; (*opportunity*) favorable, magnifique

gold'en age' *s* âge *m* d'or

gold'en calf' *s* veau *m* d'or

Gold'en Fleece' *s* Toison *f* d'or

gold'en mean' *s* juste-milieu *m*

gold'en plov'er *s* pluvier *m* doré

gold'en·rod' *s* solidage *f*, gerbe *f* d'or

gold'en rule' *s* règle *f* de la charité chrétienne

gold'en wed'ding *s* noces *fpl* d'or, jubilé *m*

gold'-filled' *adj* (*tooth*) aurifié

gold'finch' *s* chardonneret *m*

gold'fish' *s* poisson *m* rouge

goldilocks ['goldɪ,lɑks] *s* jeune fille *f* aux cheveux d'or

gold' leaf' *s* feuille *f* d'or

gold' mine' *s* mine *f* d'or; to strike a gold mine (fig) dénicher le bon filon, faire des affaires d'or

gold' plate' s vaisselle f d'or
gold'-plate' tr plaquer d'or
gold' rush' s ruée f vers l'or
gold'smith' s orfèvre m
gold' stan'dard s étalon-or m
golf [gɑlf] s golf m ‖ intr jouer au golf
golf' club' s crosse f de golf, club m; (association) club m de golf
golfer ['gɑlfər] s joueur m de golf
golf' links' spl terrain m de golf
gondola ['gɑndələ] s gondole f
gondolier [,gɑndə'lɪr] s gondolier m
gone [gɔn], [gɑn] adj parti, disparu; (used up) épuisé; (ruined) ruiné, fichu; (dead) mort; **far gone** avancé; **gone on** (in love with) (coll) entiché de, épris de
gong [gɔŋ], [gɑŋ] s gong m
gonorrhea [,gɑnə'ri·ə] s blennorragie f
goo [gu] s (slang) matière f collante
good [gʊd] adj (comp **better;** super **best**) bon §91; (child) sage; (meals) soigné; **good for you!** bien joué!; **to be good at** être fort en, être expert à; **to make good** prospérer; (a loss) compenser; (a promise) tenir; **will you be good enough to** voulez-vous être assez aimable de ‖ s bien m; **for good** pour de bon, définitivement; **goods** biens mpl; (com) marchandises fpl; **to catch with the goods** (slang) prendre la main dans le sac; **to the good** de gagné, e.g., **all or so much to the good** autant de gagné ‖ interj bon!, bien!, à la bonne heure!; **very good!** parfait!
good' afternoon' s bonjour m
good'-by' or **good'-bye'** s adieu m ‖ interj au revoir!; (before a long journey) adieu!
good' cit'izenship s civisme m
good' day' s bonjour m
good' deed' s bonne action f
good' egg' s (slang) chic type m
good' eve'ning s bonsoir m
good' fel'low s brave garçon m, brave type m
good' fel'lowship s camaraderie f
good'-for-noth'ing adj inutile m ‖ s bon m à rien
Good' Fri'day s le Vendredi saint
good' grac'es spl bonnes grâces fpl
good'-heart'ed adj au cœur généreux
good'-hu'mored adj de bonne humeur
good'-look'ing adj beau, joli
good' looks' spl belle mine f
good' luck' s bonne chance f
good·ly ['gʊdli] adj (comp **-lier;** super **-liest**) considérable, important; (quality) bon; (appearance) beau
good' morn'ing s bonjour m
good'-na'tured adj aimable, accommodant
goodness ['gʊdnɪs] s bonté f; **for goodness' sake!** pour l'amour de Dieu!; **goodness knows** Dieu seul sait ‖ interj mon Dieu!
good' night' s bonne nuit f
good' sense' s bon sens m
good'-sized' adj de grandeur moyenne, assez grand

good' speed' s succès m, bonne chance f
good'-tem'pered adj de caractère facile, d'humeur égale
good' time' s bon temps m; **to have a good time** prendre du bon temps, bien s'amuser; **to make good time** arriver en peu de temps
good' turn' s bienfait m, service m
good' will' s bonne volonté f; (com) achalandage m
good' works' spl bonnes œuvres fpl
good·y ['gʊdi] adj (coll) d'une piété affectée ‖ s (pl **-ies**) (coll) petit saint m; **goodies** friandises fpl ‖ interj chouette!; chic!
gooey ['gu·i] adj (comp **gooier;** super **gooiest**) (slang) gluant; (sentimental) (slang) à l'eau de rose
goof [guf] s (slang) toqué m ‖ intr— **to goof off** (slang) tirer au flanc
goof·y ['gufi] adj (comp **-ier;** super **-iest**) (slang) toqué, maboul
goon [gun] s (roughneck) (coll) dur m; (coll) terroriste m professionnel; (slang) niais m
goose [gus] s (pl **geese** [gis]) oie f; **to kill the goose that lays the golden eggs** tuer la poule aux œufs d'or ‖ s (pl **gooses**) (of tailor) carreau m
goose'ber'ry s (pl **-ries**) groseille f verte
goose' egg' s œuf m d'oie; (slang) zéro m
goose' flesh' s chair f de poule
goose'neck' s col m de cygne
goose' pim'ples spl chair f de poule
goose' step' s (mil) pas m de l'oie
goose'-step' v (pret & pp **-stepped**; ger **-stepping**) intr marcher au pas de l'oie
gopher ['gofər] s citelle m
gore [gor] s (blood) sang m caillé; (sewing) soufflet m ‖ tr percer d'un coup de corne; (sewing) tailler en pointe
gorge [gɔrdʒ] s gorge f ‖ tr gorger ‖ intr se gorger
gorgeous ['gɔrdʒəs] adj magnifique
gorilla [gə'rɪlə] s gorille m
gorse [gɔrs] s (bot) genêt m épineux
gor·y ['gori] adj (comp **-ier;** super **-iest**) ensanglanté, sanglant
gosh [gɑʃ] interj (coll) sapristi!, mon Dieu!
goshawk ['gɑs,hɔk] s autour m
gospel ['gɑspəl] s évangile m; **Gospel** Évangile m
gos'pel truth' s parole f d'Évangile
gossamer ['gɑsəmər] adj ténu ‖ s toile f d'araignée, fils mpl de la Vierge; (gauze) gaze f
gossip ['gɑsɪp] s commérage m, cancan m; (person) commère f; **piece of gossip** potin m, racontar m ‖ intr cancaner
gos'sip col'umnist s échotier m
Gothic ['gɑθɪk] adj & s gothique m
gouge [gaʊdʒ] s gouge f ‖ tr gouger; (to swindle) empiler
goulash ['gulɑʃ] s goulasch m & f
gourd [gord], [gʊrd] s gourde f

gourmand ['gurmənd] *s* gourmand *m*; (*glutton*) glouton *m*

gourmet ['gurme] *s* gourmet *m*

gout [gaut] *s* goutte *f*

govern ['gʌvərn] *tr* gouverner; (gram) régir ‖ *intr* gouverner

governess ['gʌvərnɪs] *s* institutrice *f*, gouvernante *f*

government ['gʌvərnmənt] *s* gouvernement *m*

governmental [,gʌvərn'mɛntəl] *adj* gouvernemental

governor ['gʌvərnər] *s* gouverneur *m*; (mach) régulateur *m*

gown [gaun] *s* robe *f*

grab [græb] *s* prise *f*; (coll) vol *m*, coup *m* ‖ *v* (*pret & pp* grabbed; *ger* grabbing) *tr* empoigner, saisir ‖ *intr* —to grab at s'agripper à

grab′ bag′ *s* sac *m* à surprises

grace [gres] *s* grâce *f*; (*prayer at table before meals*) bénédicité *m*; (*prayer at table after meals*) grâces; (*extension of time*) délai *m* de grâce ‖ *tr* orner; honorer

graceful ['gresfəl] *adj* gracieux

grace′ note′ *s* note *f* d'agrément, appoggiature *f*

gracious ['greʃəs] *adj* gracieux; (*compassionate*) miséricordieux

grackle ['grækəl] *s* (myna) mainate *m*; (*purple grackle*) quiscale *m*

gradation [gre'deʃən] *s* gradation *f*

grade [gred] *s* (rank) grade *m*; (of oil) grade; qualité *f*; (school class) classe *f*, année *f*; (mark in school) note *f*; (slope) pente *f*; **to make the grade** réussir ‖ *tr* classer; (a school paper) noter; (land) niveler

grade′ cross′ing *s* (rr) passage *m* à niveau

grade′ school′ *s* école *f* primaire

gradient ['gredɪ·ənt] *adj* montant ‖ *s* pente *f*; (phys) gradient *m*

gradual ['grædʒu·əl] *adj & s* graduel *m*

gradually ['grædʒu·əli] *adv* graduellement, peu à peu

graduate ['grædʒu·ɪt] *s* diplômé *m* ‖ ['grædʒu,et] *tr* conférer un diplôme à, décerner des diplômes à; (to mark with degrees) graduer ‖ *intr* recevoir son diplôme

grad′uate school′ *s* faculté *f* des hautes études

grad′uate stu′dent *s* étudiant *m* avancé, étudiant de maîtrise, de doctorat

grad′uate work′ *s* études *fpl* avancées

grad′uat′ing class′ *s* classe *f* sortante

graduation [,grædʒu'eʃən] *s* collation *f* des grades; (e.g., marking on beaker) graduation *f*

graft [græft], [grɑft] *s* (hort, surg) greffe *f*; (coll) gratte *f*, grattage *m* ‖ *tr & intr* (hort, surg) greffer; (coll) gratter

grafter ['græftər], ['grɑftər] *s* (hort) greffeur *m*; (coll) homme *m* véreux, concussionnaire *mf*

gra′ham bread′ ['gre·əm] *s* pain *m* entier

gra′ham flour′ *s* farine *f* entière

grain [gren] *s* (small seed; tiny particle of sand, etc.; small unit of weight; small amount) grain *m*; (cereal seeds) grains *mpl*, céréales *fpl*; (in stone) fil *m*; (in wood) fibres *fpl*; **against the grain** à contre-fil, à rebrousse-poil ‖ *tr* grener; (wood, etc.) veiner

grain′ el′evator *s* dépôt *m* et élévateur *m* à grains

grain′field′ *s* champ *m* de blé

graining ['grenɪŋ] *s* grenage *m*; (of painting) veinage *m*

gram [græm] *s* gramme *m*

grammar ['græmər] *s* grammaire *f*

grammarian [grə'mɛrɪ·ən] *s* grammairien *m*

gram′mar school′ *s* école *f* primaire

grammatical [grə'mætɪkəl] *adj* grammatical

grana·ry ['grænəri] *s* (pl -ries) grenier *m*

grand [grænd] *adj* magnifique; (person) grand; (coll) formidable

grand′aunt′ *s* grand-tante *f*

grand′child′ *s* (pl -chil′dren) petit-fils *m*; petite-fille *f*; **grandchildren** petits-enfants *mpl*

grand′daugh′ter *s* petite-fille *f*

grand′ duch′ess *s* grande-duchesse *f*

grand′ duch′y *s* grand-duché *m*

grand′ duke′ *s* grand-duc *m*

grandee [græn'di] *s* grand *m* d'Espagne

grand′fa′ther *s* grand-père *m*

grand′father's clock′ *s* pendule *f* à gaine, horloge *f* comtoise

grandiose ['grændɪ,os] *adj* grandiose; pompeux

grand′ ju′ry *s* jury *m* d'accusation

grand′ lar′ceny *s* grand larcin *m*

grand′ lodge′ *s* grand orient *m*

grandma ['grænd,mɑ], ['græm,mɑ], ['græmə] *s* (coll) grand-maman *f*

grand′moth′er *s* grand-mère *f*

grand′neph′ew *s* petit-neveu *m*

grand′niece′ *s* petite-nièce *f*

grand′ op′era *s* grand opéra *m*

grandpa ['grænd,pɑ], ['græn,pɑ], ['græmpə] *s* (coll) grand-papa *m*

grand′par′ent *s* grand-père *m*; grand-mère *f*; **grandparents** grands-parents *mpl*

grand′ pian′o *s* piano *m* à queue

grand′ slam′ *s* grand chelem *m*

grand′son′ *s* petit-fils *m*

grand′stand′ *s* tribune *f*, gradins *mpl*

grand′ to′tal *s* total *m* global

grand′un′cle *s* grand-oncle *m*

grand′ vizier′ *s* grand vizir *m*

grange [grendʒ] *s* ferme *f*; syndicat *m* d'agriculteurs

granite ['grænɪt] *s* granite *m*, granit *m*

gran·ny ['græni] *s* (pl -nies) (coll) grand-mère *f*

gran′ny knot′ *s* nœud *m* de vache

grant [grænt], [grɑnt] *s* concession *f*; (subsidy) subvention *f*; (scholarship) bourse *f* ‖ *tr* concéder, accorder; (a wish) exaucer; (e.g., a charter) octroyer; (a degree) décerner; **to take for granted** escompter, tenir pour évident; traiter avec indifférence

grantee [græn'ti], [grɑn'ti] *s* donataire *mf*

grantor [græn'tɔr], [grɑn'tɔr] *s* donateur *m*

granular ['grænjələr] *adj* granulaire

granulate ['grænjə‚let] *tr* granuler ‖ *intr* se granuler

gran'ulated sug'ar *s* sucre *m* cristallisé

granule ['grænjʊl] *s* granule *m*, granulé *m*

grape [grep] *s* (*fruit*) raisin *m*; (*vine*) vigne *f*; (*single grape*) grain *m* de raisin

grape' ar'bor *s* treille *f*

grape'fruit' *s* (*fruit*) pamplemousse *m* & *f*; (*tree*) pamplemoussier *m*

grape' juice' *s* jus *m* de raisin

grape'shot' *s* mitraille *f*

grape'vine' *s* vigne *f*; (*chain of gossip*) source *f* de canards

graph [græf], [grɑf] *s* graphique *m*; (*gram*) graphie *f*

graphic(al) ['græfɪk(əl)] *adj* graphique; (*fig*) vivant, net

graphite ['græfaɪt] *s* graphite *m*

graph' pa'per *s* papier *m* quadrillé

grapnel ['græpnəl] *s* grappin *m*

grapple ['græpəl] *s* grappin *m*; (*fight*) corps à corps *m* ‖ *tr* saisir au grappin; (*a person*) empoigner à bras le corps ‖ *intr* (*to fight*) lutter corps à corps; **to grapple with** en venir aux prises avec, s'attaquer à

grap'pling i'ron *s* grappin *m*

grasp [græsp], [grɑsp] *s* prise *f*; **to have a good grasp of** avoir une profonde connaissance de; **within one's grasp** à sa portée ‖ *tr* saisir ‖ *intr*— **to grasp at** tâcher de saisir; saisir avidement

grasping ['græspɪŋ], ['grɑspɪŋ] *adj* avide, rapace

grass [græs], [grɑs] *s* herbe *f*; (*pasture*) herbage *m*; (*lawn*) gazon *m*; **keep off the grass** (public sign) ne marchez pas sur le gazon; **to go to grass** (fig) s'étaler par terre

grass'hop'per *s* sauterelle *f*

grass'-roots' *adj* populaire, du peuple

grass' seed' *s* graine *f* fourragère; (*for lawns*) graine *f* pour gazon

grass' snake' *s* (*Tropidonotus natrix*) couleuvre *f* à collier

grass' wid'ow *s* demi-veuve *f*

grass·y ['græsi], ['grɑsi] *adj* (*comp* -ier; *super* -iest) herbeux

grate [gret] *s* grille *f*, grillage *m* ‖ *tr* (*to put a grate on*) griller; (*e.g., cheese*) râper; **to grate the teeth** grincer des dents ‖ *intr* grincer; **to grate on** écorcher

grateful ['gretfəl] *adj* reconnaissant; agréable; **to be grateful for** être reconnaissant de or pour

grater ['gretər] *s* râpe *f*

grati·fy ['grætɪ‚faɪ] *v* (*pret & pp* -fied) *tr* faire plaisir à, satisfaire

gratifying ['grætɪ‚faɪ·ɪŋ] *adj* agréable, satisfaisant

grating ['gretɪŋ] *adj* grinçant ‖ *s* grillage *m*, grille *f*

gratis ['gretɪs], ['grætɪs] *adj* gratuit, gracieux ‖ *adv* gratis, gratuitement

gratitude ['grætɪ‚t(j)ud] *s* gratitude *f*,

reconnaissance *f*; **gratitude for** reconnaissance de or pour

gratuitous [grə't(j)u·ɪtəs] *adj* gratuit

gratui·ty [grə't(j)u·ɪti] *s* (*pl* -ties) gratification *f*, pourboire *m*

grave [grev] *adj* grave ‖ *s* fosse *f*, tombe *f*

gravedigger ['grev‚dɪgər] *s* fossoyeur *m*

gravel ['grævəl] *s* gravier *m*; (*pathol*) gravelle *f*

grav'en im'age ['grevən] *s* image *f* taillée

grave'stone' *s* pierre *f* tombale

grave'yard' *s* cimetière *m*

gravitate ['grævɪ‚tet] *intr* graviter

gravitation [‚grævɪ'teʃən] *s* gravitation *f*

gravi·ty ['grævɪti] *s* (*pl* -ties) gravité *f*; (*phys*) pesanteur *f*, gravité

gra·vy ['grevi] *s* (*pl* -vies) (*juice from cooking meat*) jus *m*; (*sauce made with this juice*) sauce *f*; (*slang*) profit *m* facile, profit supplémentaire

gra'vy boat' *s* saucière *f*

gra'vy train' *s* (slang) assiette *f* au beurre

gray [gre] *adj* gris; (*gray-haired*) gris, chenu; **to turn gray** grisonner ‖ *s* gris *m* ‖ *intr* grisonner

gray'beard' *s* barbon *m*, ancien *m*

gray'-haired' *adj* gris, chenu

gray'hound' *s* lévrier *m*; (*female*) levrette *f*

grayish ['gre·ɪʃ] *adj* grisâtre

gray' mat'ter *s* substance *f* grise

graze [grez] *tr* (*to touch lightly*) frôler, effleurer; (*to scratch lightly in passing*) érafler; (*to pasture*) faire paître ‖ *intr* paître

grease [gris] *s* graisse *f* ‖ [gris], [griz] *tr* graisser

grease' cup' [gris] *s* godet *m* graisseur

grease' gun' [gris] *s* graisseur *m*, seringue *f* à graisse

grease' paint' [gris] *s* fard *m*, grimage *m*

greas·y ['grisi], ['grizi] *adj* (*comp* -ier; *super* -iest) graisseux, gras

great [gret] *adj* grand; (coll) excellent, formidable; **a great deal, a great many** beaucoup

great'-aunt' *s* grand-tante *f*

Great' Bear' *s* Grande Ourse *f*

Great' Brit'ain *s* Grande Bretagne *f*; la Grande Bretagne

great'coat' *s* capote *f*

Great' Dane' *s* danois *m*

Great'er Lon'don *s* le Grand Londres

Great'er New' York' *s* le Grand New York

great'-grand'child' *s* (*pl* -chil'dren) arrière-petit-fils *m*; arrière-petite-fille *f*; **great-grandchildren** arrière-petits-enfants *mpl*

great'-grand'daugh'ter *s* arrière-petite-fille *f*

great'-grand'fa'ther *s* arrière-grand-père *m*, bisaïeul *m*

great'-grand'moth'er *s* arrière-grand-mère *f*, bisaïeule *f*

great'-grand'par'ents *spl* arrière-grands-parents *mpl*
great'-grand'son *s* arrière-petit-fils *m*
greatly ['gretli] *adv* grandement, fort, beaucoup
great'-neph'ew *s* petit-neveu *m*
greatness ['gretnɪs] *s* grandeur *f*
great'-niece' *s* petite-nièce *f*
great'-un'cle *s* grand-oncle *m*
Great' War' *s* Grande Guerre *f*
Grecian ['griʃən] *adj* grec ‖ *s* (*person*) Grec *m*
Greece [gris] *s* Grèce *f*; la Grèce
greed [grid] *s* avidité *f*
greed·y ['gridi] *adj* (*comp* -ier; *super* -iest) avide
Greek [grik] *adj* grec ‖ *s* (*language*) grec *m*; (*unintelligible language*) (coll) hébreu *m*, e.g., it's Greek to me (coll) c'est de l'hébreu pour moi; (*person*) Grec *m*
Greek' fire' *s* feu *m* grégeois
green [grin] *adj* vert; inexpérimenté, novice ‖ *s* vert *m*; (*lawn*) gazon *m*; (golf) pelouse *f* d'arrivée; **greens** légumes *mpl* verts
green'back' *s* (U.S.A.) billet *m* de banque
greener·y ['grinəri] *s* (*pl* -ies) verdure *f*
green'-eyed' *adj* aux yeux verts; (*envious*) jaloux
green'gage' *s* (bot) reine-claude *f*
green'gro'cer·y *s* (*pl* -ies) fruiterie *f*
green'horn' *s* blanc-bec *m*, bleu *m*
green'house' *s* serre *f*
greenish ['grinɪʃ] *adj* verdâtre
Greenland ['grinlənd] *s* le Groënland
green' light' *s* feu *m* vert, voie *f* libre
greenness ['grinnɪs] *s* verdure *f*; (*unripeness*) verdeur *f*; inexpérience *f*, naïveté *f*
green' pep'per *s* poivron *m* vert
green'room' *s* (theat) foyer *m*
greensward ['grin‚swɔrd] *s* pelouse *f*
green' thumb' *s*—**to have a green thumb** avoir la main verte
greet [grit] *tr* saluer; (*to welcome*) accueillir
greeting ['gritɪŋ] *s* salutation *f*; (*welcome*) accueil *m*; **greetings** (*on greeting card*) vœux *mpl* ‖ **greetings** *interj* salut!
greet'ing card' *s* carte *f* de vœux
gregarious [grɪ'gɛrɪ·əs] *adj* grégaire
Gregorian [grɪ'gorɪ·ən] *adj* grégorien
grenade [grɪ'ned] *s* grenade *f*
grey [gre] *adj*, *s*, & *intr* var of **gray**
grey'hound' *s* var of **grayhound**
grid [grɪd] *s* (*of storage battery and vacuum tube*) grille *f*; (*on map*) quadrillage *m*; (culin) gril *m*
griddle ['grɪdəl] *s* plaque *f* chauffante
grid'dle·cake' *s* crêpe *f*
grid'i'ron *s* gril *m*; (sports) terrain *m* de football
grid' leak' *s* résistance *f* de fuite de la grille
grid' line' *s* ligne *f* de quadrillage
grief [grif] *s* chagrin *m*, affliction *f*; **to come to grief** finir mal
grief'-strick'en *adj* affligé, navré
grievance ['grivəns] *s* grief *m*

grieve [griv] *tr* chagriner, affliger ‖ *intr* se chagriner, s'affliger
grievous ['grivəs] *adj* grave, douloureux
griffin ['grɪfɪn] *s* griffon *m*
grill [grɪl] *s* gril *m*; (*grating*) grille *f* ‖ *tr* griller; (*an accused person*) (coll) cuisiner
grille [grɪl] *s* grille *f*; (aut) calandre *f*
grilled' beef'steak *s* châteaubriand *m*
grill'room' *s* grill-room *m*
grim [grɪm] *adj* (*comp* **grimmer**; *super* **grimmest**) (*fierce*) menaçant; (*repellent*) macabre; (*unyielding*) implacable; (*stern-looking*) lugubre
grimace ['grɪməs], [grɪ'mes] *s* grimace *f* ‖ *intr* grimacer
grime [graɪm] *s* crasse *f*, saleté *f*
grim·y ['graɪmi] *adj* (*comp* -ier; *super* -iest) crasseux, sale
grin [grɪn] *s* grimace *f*; (*smile*) large sourire *m* ‖ *v* (*pret* & *pp* **grinned**; *ger* **grinning**) *intr* avoir un large sourire, rire à belles dents
grind [graɪnd] *s* (*of coffee*) moulure *f*; (*job*) (coll) boulot *m*, collier *m*; (*student*) (coll) bûcheur *m*; **daily grind** (coll) train-train *m* quotidien ‖ *v* (*pret* & *pp* **ground** [graʊnd]) *tr* (*coffee*, *flour*) moudre; (*food*) broyer; (*meat*) hacher; (*a knife*) aiguiser; (*the teeth*) grincer; (*valves*) roder ‖ *intr* grincer; **to grind away at** (coll) bûcher
grinder ['graɪndər] *s* (*for coffee*, *pepper*, *etc.*) moulin *m*, broyeur *m*; (*for meat*) hachoir *m*; (*for tools*) repasseur *m*; (*back tooth*) molaire *f*
grind'stone' *s* meule *f*, pierre *f* à aiguiser
grip [grɪp] *s* prise *f*; (*with hand*) poigne *f*; (*handle*) poignée *f*; (*handbag*) sac *m* de voyage; (*understanding*) compréhension *f*; **to come to grips** en venir aux prises; **to lose one's grip** lâcher prise ‖ *v* (*pret* & *pp* **gripped**; *ger* **gripping**) *tr* serrer, saisir fortement; (*e.g., a theater audience*) empoigner
gripe [graɪp] *s* (coll) rouspétance *f* ‖ *intr* (coll) rouspéter, ronchonner
grippe [grɪp] *s* grippe *f*
gripping ['grɪpɪŋ] *adj* passionnant
gris·ly ['grɪzli] *adj* (*comp* -lier; *super* -liest) horrible, macabre
grist [grɪst] *s* blé *m* à moudre
gristle ['grɪsəl] *s* cartilage *m*
gris·tly ['grɪsli] *adj* (*comp* -tlier; *super* -tliest) cartilagineux
grist'mill' *s* moulin *m* à blé
grit [grɪt] *s* grès *m*, sable *m*; (*courage*) cran *m*; **grits** gruau *m* ‖ *v* (*pret* & *pp* **gritted**; *ger* **gritting**) *tr* (*one's teeth*) grincer
grit·ty ['grɪti] *adj* (*comp* -tier; *super* -tiest) sablonneux; (fig) plein de cran
griz·zly ['grɪzli] *adj* (*comp* -zlier; *super* -zliest) grisonnant ‖ *s* (*pl* -zlies) ours *m* gris
griz'zly bear' *s* ours *m* gris
groan [gron] *s* gémissement *m* ‖ *intr* gémir

grocer ['grosər] *s* épicier *m*
grocer·y ['grosəri] *s* (*pl* -ies) épicerie *f*;
groceries denrées *fpl*
gro'cery store' *s* épicerie *f*
grog [grɑg] *s* grog *m*
grog·gy ['grɑgi] *adj* (*comp* -gier; *super*
-giest) (coll) vacillant; (*shaky, e.g.,
from a blow*) (coll) étourdi; (*drunk*)
(coll) gris, ivre
groin [grɔɪn] *s* (anat) aine *f*; (archit)
arête *f*
groom [grum] *s* (*bridegroom*) marié *m*;
(*stableboy*) palefrenier *m* ‖ *tr*
soigner, astiquer; (*horses*) panser; (*a
politician, a starlet, etc.*) dresser, préparer
grooms'man *s* (*pl* -men) garçon *m*
d'honneur
groove [gruv] *s* rainure *f*; (*of pulley*)
gorge *f*; (*of phonograph record*) sillon *m*; (*mark left by wheel*) ornière
f; (*of window, door, etc.*) feuillure *f*;
in the groove (coll) comme sur des
roulettes; **to get into a groove** (coll)
devenir routinier ‖ *tr* rainer, canneler
grope [grop] *intr* tâtonner; **to grope
for** chercher à tâtons
gropingly ['gropɪŋli] *adv* à tâtons
grosbeak ['gros,bik] *s* gros-bec *m*
gross [gros] *adj* gros; (*fat, burly*) gras,
épais; (*crass, vulgar*) grossier;
(*weight; receipts*) brut; (*displacement*) global ‖ *s invar* recette *f* brute;
(*twelve dozen*) grosse *f* ‖ *tr* produire
en recette brute, produire brut, e.g.,
the business grossed a million dollars
l'entreprise a produit un million de
dollars, brut
gross' na'tional prod'uct *s* produit *m*
national brut
grotesque [gro'tɛsk] *adj* grotesque ‖ *s*
grotesque *m*; (*ornament*) grotesque *f*
grot·to ['grɑto] *s* (*pl* -toes or -tos)
grotte *f*
grouch [grautʃ] *s* (coll) humeur *f*
grognon; (*person*) (coll) grognon *m* ‖
intr (coll) grogner
grouch·y ['grautʃi] *adj* (*comp* -ier; *super* -iest) (coll) grognon, maussade
ground [graund] *s* terre *f*; (*piece of
land*) terrain *m*; (*basis, foundation*)
fondement *m*, base *f*; (*reason*) motif
m, cause *f*; (elec) terre *f*; (*body of
automobile corresponding to ground*)
(elec) masse *f*; **ground for complaint**
grief *m*; **grounds** parc *m*, terrain;
fondement, cause; (*of coffee*) marc
m; **on the ground of** pour raison de,
sous prétexte de; **to be losing ground**
être en recul; **to break ground** donner le premier coup de pioche; **to
have grounds for** avoir matière à; **to
stand one's ground** tenir bon or
ferme; **to yield ground** lâcher pied ‖
tr fonder, baser; (elec) mettre à terre;
grounded (aer) interdit de vol, gardé
au sol; **to ground s.o. in s.th.** enseigner à fond q.ch. à qn
ground' connec'tion *s* prise *f* de terre
ground' crew' *s* équipe *f* au sol, personnel *m* rampant
ground' floor' *s* rez-de-chaussée *m*

ground' glass' *s* verre *m* dépoli
ground' hog' *s* marmotte *f* d'Amérique
grounding ['graundɪŋ] *s* (aer) interdiction *f* de vol; (elec) mise *f* à la masse
ground' installa'tions *spl* (aer) infrastructure *f*
ground' lead' [lid] *s* (elec) conduite *f*
à terre
groundless ['graundlɪs] *adj* sans fondement
ground' meat' *s* viande *f* hachée
ground' plan' *s* plan *m* de base; (archit)
plan horizontal
ground' speed' *s* (aer) vitesse *f* par
rapport au sol
ground' swell' *s* lame *f* de fond
ground' troops' *spl* (mil) effectifs *mpl*
terrestres
ground' wire' *s* (elec) fil *m* de terre, fil
de masse
ground'work' *s* fondement *m*, fond *m*
group [grup] *s* groupe *m* ‖ *tr* grouper
‖ *intr* se grouper
grouse [graus] *s* coq *m* de bruyère ‖
intr (slang) grogner
grove [grov] *s* bocage *m*, bosquet *m*
grov·el ['grʌvəl], ['grɑvəl] *v* (*pret &
pp* -eled or -elled; *ger* -eling or -el-
ling) *intr* se vautrer; (*before s.o.*)
ramper
grow [gro] *v* (*pret* grew [gru]; *pp*
grown [gron]) *tr* cultiver, faire pousser; (*a beard*) laisser pousser ‖ *intr*
croître; (*said of plants*) pousser; (*said
of seeds*) germer; (*to become*) deve-
·nir; **to grow angry** se mettre en colère; **to grow old** vieillir; **to grow out
of** se développer de; (*e.g., a suit of
clothes*) devenir trop grand pour; **to
grow up** grandir, profiter
growl [graul] *s* grondement *m*, grognement *m* ‖ *tr & intr* gronder, grogner
grown'-up' *adj* adulte ‖ *s* (*pl* grown-
ups) adulte *mf*; **grown-ups** grandes
personnes *fpl*
growth [groθ] *s* croissance *f*, développement *m*; (*increase*) accroissement
m; (*of trees, grass, etc.*) pousse *f*;
(pathol) excroissance *f*, grosseur *f*
grub [grʌb] *s* asticot *m*; (*person*)
homme *m* de peine; (*food*) (coll)
boustifaille *f* ‖ *v* (*pret & pp* grubbed;
ger grubbing) *tr* défricher ‖ *intr*
fouiller
grub·by ['grʌbi] *adj* (*comp* -bier; *super*
-biest) sale, malpropre
grudge [grʌdʒ] *s* rancune *f*; **to have a
grudge against** garder rancune à ‖ *tr*
donner à contre-cœur
grudgingly ['grʌdʒɪŋli] *adv* à contrecœur
gruel ['gru·əl] *s* gruau *m*, bouillie *f*
grueling ['gru·əlɪŋ] *adj* éreintant
gruesome ['grusəm] *adj* macabre
gruff [grʌf] *adj* bourru, brusque;
(*voice*) rauque, gros
grumble ['grʌmbəl] *s* grognement *m* ‖
intr grogner, grommeler
grump·y ['grʌmpi] *adj* (*comp* -ier; *super* -iest) maussade, grognon
grunt [grʌnt] *s* grognement *m* ‖ *intr*
grogner

G/-string/ *s* (*loincloth*) pagne *m*; (*worn by women entertainers*) cache-sexe *m*; (mus) corde *f* de sol

guarantee [ˌgærən'ti] *s* garantie *f*; (*guarantor*) garant *m*, répondant *m*; (*security*) caution *f* ‖ *tr* garantir

guarantor ['gærən ˌtɔr] *s* garant *m*

guaran·ty ['gærənti] *s* (*pl* -**ties**) garantie *f* ‖ *v* (*pret & pp* -**tied**) *tr* garantir

guard [gɑrd] *s* garde *f*; (*person*) garde *m*; **on guard** en garde; (*on duty*) de garde; (mil) en faction, de faction; **on one's guard** sur ses gardes; **to mount guard** monter la garde; **under guard** gardé à vue ‖ *tr* garder ‖ *intr* être de faction; **to guard against** se garder de

guard/ du/ty *s* service *m* de garde

guarded *adj* (*remark*) prudent

guard/house/ *s* guérite *f*, corps-de-garde *m*; prison *f* militaire

guardian ['gɑrdɪ·ən] *adj* gardien ‖ *s* gardien *m*; (*of a ward*) tuteur *m*

guard/ian an/gel *s* ange *m* gardien, ange tutélaire

guard/ian·ship/ *s* garde *f*; (law) tutelle *f*

guard/rail/ *s* garde-fou *m*, parapet *m*

guard/room/ *s* corps-de-garde *m*, salle *f* de police; (*prison*) bloc *m*, tôle *f*

guards/man *s* (*pl* -**men**) garde *m*

Guatemalan [ˌgwɑtɪ'mɑlən] *adj* guatémaltèque ‖ *s* Guatémaltèque *mf*

guava ['gwɑvə] *s* goyave *f*; (*tree*) goyavier *m*

guerrilla [gə'rɪlə] *s* guérillero *m*; **guerrillas** (*band*) guérilla *f*

guerril/la war/fare *s* guérilla *f*

guess [gɛs] *s* conjecture *f* ‖ *tr & intr* conjecturer; (*a secret, riddle, etc.*) deviner; (coll) supposer, penser; **I guess so** je crois que oui; **to guess right** bien deviner

guess/work/ *s* supposition *f*; **by guesswork** au jugé

guest [gɛst] *s* invité *m*, hôte *mf*; (*in a hotel*) client *m*, hôte

guest/ room/ *s* chambre *f* d'ami

guest/ speak/er *s* orateur *m* de circonstance

guffaw [gə'fɔ] *s* gros rire *m* ‖ *tr* dire avec un gros rire ‖ *intr* rire bruyamment

Guiana [gɪ'ɑnə], [gɪ'ænə] *s* Guyane *f*; la Guyane

guidance ['gaɪdəns] *s* gouverne *f*; (*guiding*) conduite *f*; (*in choosing a career*) orientation *f*; (*of rocket*) guidage *m*; **for your guidance** pour votre gouverne

guid/ance coun/selor *s* orienteur *m*

guide [gaɪd] *s* guide *m* ‖ *tr* guider

guide/book/ *s* guide *m*

guid/ed mis/sile *s* engin *m* téléguidé

guide/ dog/ *s* chien *m* d'aveugle

guide/ line/ *s* (fig) norme *f*, règle *f*; **guide lines** (*for writing straight lines*) transparent *m*, guide-âne *m*

guide/post/ *s* poteau *m* indicateur

guide/ word/ *s* lettrine *f*

guild [gɪld] *s* association *f*, corporation *f*; (eccl) confrérie *f*; (hist) guilde *f*

guild/hall/ *s* hôtel *m* de ville

guile [gaɪl] *s* astuce *f*, artifice *m*

guileful ['gaɪlfəl] *adj* astucieux, artificieux

guileless ['gaɪllɪs] *adj* candide, innocent

guillotine ['gɪlə ˌtin] *s* guillotine *f* ‖ *tr* guillotiner

guilt [gɪlt] *s* culpabilité *f*

guiltless ['gɪltlɪs] *adj* innocent

guilt·y ['gɪlti] *adj* (*comp* -**ier**; *super* -**iest**) coupable; **found guilty** reconnu coupable

guimpe [gɪmp], [gæmp] *s* empiècement *m*

guinea ['gɪni] *s* guinée *f*; **Guinea** Guinée; **la Guinée**

guin/ea fowl/ or **hen/** *s* poule *f* de Guinée, pintade *f*

guin/ea pig/ *s* cobaye *m*

guise [gaɪz] *s* apparences *fpl*, déguisement *m*; **under the guise of** sous un semblant de, sous le masque de

guitar [gɪ'tɑr] *s* guitare *f*

guitarist [gɪ'tɑrɪst] *s* guitariste *mf*

gulch [gʌltʃ] *s* ravin *m*

gulf [gʌlf] *s* golfe *m*; (fig) gouffre *m*

Gulf/ of Mex/ico *s* Golfe *m* du Mexique

Gulf/ Stream/ *s* Courant *m* du Golfe

gull [gʌl] *s* mouette *f*, goéland *m*; (coll) gogo *m*, jobard *m* ‖ *tr* escroquer, duper

gullet ['gʌlɪt] *s* gosier *m*

gullible ['gʌlɪbəl] *adj* crédule, naïf

gul·ly ['gʌli] *s* (*pl* -**lies**) ravin *m*; (*channel*) rigole *f*

gulp [gʌlp] *s* gorgée *f*, lampée *f*; **at one gulp** d'un trait ‖ *tr*—**to gulp down** avaler à grandes bouchées, lamper; (*e.g., tears*) ravaler, refouler ‖ *intr* avoir la gorge serrée

gum [gʌm] *s* gomme *f*; (*on eyelids*) chassie *f*; (anat) gencive *f* ‖ *v* (*pret & pp* **gummed**; *ger* **gumming**) *tr* gommer; **to gum up** encrasser; (coll) bousiller

gum/ ar/abic *s* gomme *f* arabique

gum/boil/ *s* phlegmon *m*, fluxion *f*

gum/ boot/ *s* botte *f* de caoutchouc

gum/drop/ *s* boule *f* de gomme, pâte *f* de fruits

gum·my ['gʌmi] *adj* (*comp* -**mier**; *super* -**miest**) gommeux; (*eyelids*) chassieux

gumption ['gʌmpʃən] *s* (coll) initiative *f*, cran *m*

gum/shoe/ *s* caoutchouc *m*; (coll) détective *m* ‖ *intr* rôder en tapinois, marcher furtivement

gun [gʌn] *s* fusil *m*; (*for spraying*) pistolet *m*; **to stick to one's guns** (coll) ne pas en démordre ‖ *v* (*pret & pp* **gunned**; *ger* **gunning**) *tr*—**to gun down** tuer d'un coup de fusil, **to gun the engine** (slang) appuyer sur le champignon ‖ *intr*—**to gun for** (*game*) chasser; (*an enemy*) pourchasser

gun/ bar/rel *s* canon *m*

gun/boat/ *s* cannonière *f*

gun/ car/riage *s* affût *m* de canon

gun/cot/ton *s* fulmicoton *m*

gun' crew' *s* peloton *m* de pièce, servants *mpl* de canon
gun'fire' *s* canonnade *f*, coups *mpl* de feu
gun'man *s* (*pl* -men) *s* bandit *m*
gun' met'al *s* métal *m* bleui
gunner ['gʌnər] *s* canonnier *m*, artilleur *m*; (aer) mitrailleur *m*
gunnery ['gʌnəri] *s* tir *m*, canonnage *m*
gunnysack ['gʌni,sæk] *s* sac *m* de serpillière
gun'pow'der *s* poudre *f* à canon
gun'run'ning *s* contrebande *f* d'armes
gun'shot' *s* coup *m* de feu, coup de fusil
gun'smith' *s* armurier *m*
gun'stock' *s* fût *m*
gunwale ['gʌnəl] *s* (naut) plat-bord *m*
gup·py ['gʌpi] *s* (*pl* -pies) guppy *m*
gurgle ['gʌrgəl] *s* glouglou *m*, gargouillement *m* ‖ *intr* glouglouter, gargouiller
gush [gʌʃ] *s* jaillissement *m* ‖ *intr* jaillir; to gush over (coll) s'attendrir sur
gusher ['gʌʃər] *s* puits *m* jaillissant
gush·y ['gʌʃi] *adj* (*comp* -ier; *super* -iest) (coll) démonstratif, expansif
gusset ['gʌsɪt] *s* (*in garment*) soufflet *m*; (mach) gousset *m*
gust [gʌst] *s* bouffée *f*, coup *m*
gusto ['gʌsto] *s* goût *m*, entrain *m*
gust·y ['gʌsti] *adj* (*comp* -ier; *super* -iest) venteux; (*wind*) à rafales
gut [gʌt] *s* boyau *m*; guts (coll) cran *m* ‖ *v* (*pret* & *pp* gutted; *ger* gutting) *tr* raser à l'intérieur; (*to take out the guts of*) vider

gutter ['gʌtər] *s* (*on side of road*) caniveau *m*; (*in street*) ruisseau *m*; (*of roof*) gouttière *f*; (*ditch formed by rain water*) rigole *f*
gut'ter·snipe' *s* (coll) voyou *m*
guttural ['gʌtərəl] *adj* guttural ‖ *s* gutturale *f*
guy [gaɪ] *s* câble *m* tenseur; (naut) hauban *m*; (coll) type *m*, gars *m* ‖ *tr* haubaner; (coll) se moquer de
guy' wire' *s* câble *m* tenseur; (naut) hauban *m*
guzzle ['gʌzəl] *tr* & *intr* boire avidement
guzzler ['gʌzlər] *s* soiffard *m*
gym [dʒɪm] *s* (coll) gymnase *m*
gymnasi·um [dʒɪm'nezɪ·əm] *s* (*pl* -ums or -a [ə]) gymnase *m*
gymnast ['dʒɪmnæst] *s* gymnaste *mf*
gynecology [,gaɪnə'kalədʒi], [,dʒaɪnə-'kalədʒi] *s* gynécologie *f*
gyp [dʒɪp] *s* (slang) escroquerie *f*; (*person*) (slang) aigrefin *m* ‖ *v* (*pret* & *pp* gypped; *ger* gypping) *tr* (slang) tirer une carotte à, refaire, gruger
gypsum ['dʒɪpsəm] *s* gypse *m*
gyp·sy ['dʒɪpsi] *adj* bohémien ‖ *s* (*pl* -sies) bohémien *m*; Gypsy (*language*) tsigane *m*, romanichel *m*; (*person*) gitan *m*, tsigane *mf*, romanichel *m*
gyp'sy moth' *s* zigzag *m*
gyrate ['dʒaɪret] *intr* tournoyer
gyrocompass ['dʒaɪro,kʌmpəs] *s* gyrocompas *m*
gyroscope ['dʒaɪrə,skop] *s* gyroscope *m*

H

H, h [etʃ] *s* VIIIe lettre de l'alphabet
haberdasher ['hæbər,dæʃər] *s* chemisier *m*
haberdasher·y ['hæbər,dæʃəri] *s* (*pl* -ies) chemiserie *f*, confection *f* pour hommes
habit ['hæbɪt] *s* habitude *f*; (*dress*) habit *m*, costume *m*; to get into the habit of s'habituer à
habitual [hə'bɪtʃʊ·əl] *adj* habituel
habituate [hə'bɪtʃʊ,et] *tr* habituer
hack [hæk] *s* (*notch*) entaille *f*; (*cough*) toux *f* sèche; (*hackney*) voiture *f* de louage; (*old nag*) rosse *f*; (*writer*) écrivassier *m* ‖ *tr* hacher
hackney ['hækni] *s* voiture *f* de louage
hackneyed ['hæknid] *adj* banal, battu
hack'saw' *s* scie *f* à métaux
haddock ['hædək] *s* églefin *m*
hag [hæg] *s* (*ugly woman*) guenon *f*; (*witch*) sorcière *f*; old hag vieille fée *f*
haggard ['hægərd] *adj* décharné, hâve; (*wild-looking*) hagard, farouche
haggle ['hægəl] *intr* marchander; to haggle over marchander

Hague [heg] *s*—The Hague La Haye
hail [hel] *s* (*frozen rain*) grêle *f*; within hail à portée de la voix ‖ *tr* saluer; (*a ship, taxi, etc.*) héler ‖ *intr* grêler; to hail from venir de ‖ *interj* salut!
Hail' Mar'y *s* Ave Maria *m*
hail'stone' *s* grêlon *m*
hail'storm' *s* tempête *f* de grêle
hair [hɛr] *s* poil *m*; (*of person*) cheveu *m*; (*head of human hair*) cheveux *mpl*; against the hair à rebroussepoil, à contre-poil; hairs cheveux; to a hair à un cheveu près; to get in s.o.'s hair (slang) porter sur les nerfs à qn; to let one's hair down (slang) en prendre à son aise; to make s.o.'s hair stand on end faire dresser les cheveux à qn; to not turn a hair ne pas tiquer; to split hairs fendre or couper les cheveux en quatre
hair'breadth' *s* épaisseur *f* d'un cheveu; to escape by a hairbreadth l'échapper belle
hair'brush' *s* brosse *f* à cheveux
hair'cloth' *s* thibaude *f*; (*for furniture*) tissu-crin *m*

hair' curl'er [ˌkʌrlər] s frisoir *m*; (*pin*) bigoudi *m*
hair'cut' s coupe *f* de cheveux; to get a haircut se faire couper les cheveux
hair'do' s (*pl* -dos) coiffure *f*
hair'dress'er s coiffeur *m* pour dames; coiffeuse *f*
hair'dress'ing s cosmétique *m*
hair' dri'er s sèche-cheveux *m*, séchoir *m* à cheveux
hair' dye' s teinture *f* des cheveux
hair'line' s (*on face of type*) délié *m*; (*along the upper forehead*) naissance *f* des cheveux, plantation *f* des cheveux
hair' net' s résille *f*
hair'pin' s épingle *f* à cheveux
hair'pin turn' s lacet *m*
hair'-rais'ing adj (coll) horripilant
hair' rib'bon s ruban *m* à cheveux
hair' set' s mise *f* en plis
hair' shirt' s haire *f*, cilice *m*
hair'split'ting adj vétilleux, trop subtil || s ergotage *m*
hair' spray' s (*for setting hair*) laque *f*, fixatif *m*
hair'spring' s spiral *m*
hair' style' s coiffure *f*
hair' ton'ic s lotion *f* capillaire
hair' trig'ger s détente *f* douce
hair·y ['hɛri] adj (*comp* -ier; *super* -iest) poilu, velu; (*on head*) chevelu
Haiti ['heti] s Haïti *f*
Haitian ['hetɪ·ən], ['heʃən] adj haïtien || s Haïtien *m*
halberd ['hælbərd] s hallebarde *f*
hal'cyon days' ['hælsɪ·ən] spl jours *mpl* alcyoniens, jours sereins
hale [hel] adj vigoureux, sain; hale and hearty frais et gaillard || tr haler
half [hæf], [hɑf] adj demi || s (*pl* halves [hævz], [hɑvz]) moitié *f*, la moitié; (*of the hour*) demi *m*; by half de moitié, à demi; half an hour une demi-heure; in half en deux; to go halves être de moitié || adv moitié, à moitié; half . . . half moitié . . . moitié; half past et demie, e.g., half past three trois heures et demie
half'-and-half' adj & adv moitié l'un moitié l'autre, en parties égales || s (*for coffee*) mélange *m* de lait et de crème; (*beer*) mélange de bière et de porter
half'back' s (football) demi-arrière *m*, demi *m*
half'-baked' adj à moitié cuit; (*person*) inexpérimenté; (*plan*) prématuré, incomplet
half' bind'ing s (bb) demi-reliure *f* à petits coins
half'-blood' s métis *m*; demi-frère *m*
half' boot' s demi-botte *f*
half'-bound' adj (bb) en demi-reliure à coins
half'-breed' s métis *m*, sang-mêlé *m*; (*e.g., horse*) demi-sang *m*
half' broth'er s demi-frère *m*
half'-cocked' adv (coll) avec trop de hâte
half'-day' s demi-journée *f*
half'-doz'en s demi-douzaine *f*

half' fare' s demi-tarif *m*, demi-place *f*
half'-full' adj à moitié plein
half'-heart'ed adj sans entrain, hésitant
half'-hol'iday s demi-congé *m*
half' hose' s chaussettes *fpl*
half'-hour' s demi-heure *f*; every half-hour on the half-hour toutes les demi-heures à la demi-heure juste; on the half-hour à la demie
half' leath'er s (bb) demi-reliure *f* à petits coins
half'-length' s demi-longueur *f*
half'-length por'trait s portrait *m* en buste
half'-light' s demi-jour *m*
half'-mast' s—at half-mast en berne, à mi-mât
half'-moon' s demi-lune *f*
half' mourn'ing s demi-deuil *m*
half' note' s (mus) blanche *f*
half' pay' s demi-solde *f*
halfpen·ny ['hepəni], ['hepni] s (*pl* -nies) demi-penny *m*; (fig) sou *m*
half' pint' s demi-pinte *f*; (*little runt*) (slang) petit culot *m*
half'-seas o'ver adj—to be half-seas over avoir du vent dans les voiles
half' shell' s (*either half of a bivalve*) écaille *f*; on the half shell dans sa coquille
half' sis'ter s demi-sœur *f*
half' sole' s demi-semelle *f*
half'-staff' s—at half-staff à mi-mât
half'-tim'bered adj à demi-boisage
half' time' s (sports) mi-temps *m*
half'-time' adj à demi-journée
half' ti'tle s faux titre *m*, avant-titre *m*
half'tone' s (painting, phot) demi-teinte *f*; (typ) similigravure *f*
half' tone' s (mus) demi-ton *m*
half'-track' s semi-chenillé *m*
half'-truth' s demi-vérité *f*
half'turn' s demi-tour *m*; (*of wheel*) demi-révolution *f*
half'way' adj & adv à mi-chemin; halfway through à moitié de; halfway up à mi-côte; to meet s.o. halfway couper la poire en deux avec qn
half'-wit'ted adj à moitié idiot
halibut ['hælɪbət] s flétan *m*
halitosis [ˌhælɪ'tosɪs] s mauvaise haleine *f*
hall [hɔl] s (*passageway*) corridor *m*, couloir *m*; (*entranceway*) entrée *f*, vestibule *m*; (*large meeting room*) salle *f*, hall *m*; (*assembly room of a university*) amphithéâtre *m*; (*building of a university*) bâtiment *m*
halleluiah or hallelujah [ˌhælɪ'lujə] s alléluia *m* || interj alléluia!
hall'mark' s estampile *f*, poinçon *m*; (fig) cachet *m*, marque *f*
hal·lo [hə'lo] s (*pl* -los) holà *m* || intr huer || interj holà!, ohé!; (hunting) taïaut!
hallow ['hælo] tr sanctifier
hallowed adj sanctifié, saint
Halloween or Hallowe'en [ˌhælo'in] s la veille de la Toussaint
hallucination [həˌlusɪ'neʃən] s hallucination *f*

hall'way' s corridor m, couloir m
ha·lo ['helo] s (pl -los or -loes) (meteo) auréole f, halo m; (around a head) auréole
halogen ['hælədʒən] s halogène m
halt [hɔlt] adj boiteux, estropié || s halte f, arrêt m; **to come to a halt** faire halte || tr faire faire halte à || intr faire halte || interj halte!; (mil) halte-là!
halter ['hɔltər] s licou m; (noose) corde f
halting ['hɔltɪŋ] adj boiteux; hésitant
halve [hæv], [hɑv] tr diviser or partager en deux; réduire de moitié
halyard ['hæljərd] s (naut) drisse f
ham [hæm] s (part of leg behind knee) jarret m; (thigh and buttock) fesse f; (culin) cuisse f; (cured) (culin) jambon m; (rad) radio amateur m; (theat) cabotin m; **hams** fesses
hamburger ['hæm,bʌrgər] s sandwich m à la hambourgeoise, hamburger m; (Hamburg steak) biftek m haché
hamlet ['hæmlɪt] s hameau m
hammer ['hæmər] s marteau m; (of gun) chien m, percuteur m || tr marteler; **to hammer out** étendre au marteau; (to resolve) résoudre || intr—to **hammer away at** (e.g., a job) travailler d'arrache-pied à
hammock ['hæmək] s hamac m
hamper ['hæmpər] s manne f || tr embarrasser, gêner, empêcher
hamster ['hæmstər] s hamster m
ham'string' v (pret & pp -strung) tr couper le jarret à; (fig) couper les moyens à
hand [hænd] adj à main, à la main, manuel || s main f; (workman) manœuvre m, ouvrier m; (way of writing) écriture f; (clapping of hands) applaudissements mpl; (of clock or watch) aiguille f; (a round of play) coup m, partie f, main; (of God) doigt m; (measure) palme m; (cards) jeu m; **at hand** sous la main; (said of approaching event) proche, prochain; **by hand** à la main; **hands off!** n'y touchez pas!; **hands up!** haut les mains!; **hand to hand** corps à corps; **on every hand** de toutes parts, de tous côtés; **on the one hand . . . on the other hand** d'une part . . . d'autre part; **to live from hand to mouth** vivre au jour le jour; **to shake hands with** serrer la main à; **to wait on hand and foot** être aux petits soins pour; **to win hands down** gagner dans un fauteuil; **under the hand and seal of** signé et scellé de || tr donner, présenter; (e.g., food at table) passer; **to hand down** (e.g., property) léguer; (a verdict) prononcer; **to hand in** remettre; **to hand on** transmettre; **to hand out** distribuer; **to hand over** céder, livrer
hand'bag' s sac m à main
hand' bag'gage s menus bagages mpl
hand'ball' s pelote f; (game) handball m
hand'bill' s prospectus m

hand'book' s manuel m
hand' brake' s frein m à main
hand'car' s (rr) draisine f
hand'cart' s voiture f à bras
hand'clasp' s poignée f de main
hand' control' s commande f à la main
hand'cuff' s menotte f || tr mettre les menottes à
handful ['hænd,ful] s poignée f
hand' glass' s miroir m à main; (magnifying glass) loupe f à main
hand' grenade' s grenade f à main
handi·cap ['hændɪ,kæp] s handicap m || v (pret & pp -capped; ger -capping) tr handicaper
handicraft ['hændɪ,kræft], ['hændɪ,krɑft] s habileté f manuelle; métier m; **handicrafts** produits mpl d'artisanat
handiwork ['hændɪ,wʌrk] s ouvrage m, travail m manuel; (fig) œuvre f
handkerchief ['hæŋkərtʃɪf], ['hæŋkər,tʃif] s mouchoir m
handle ['hændəl] s (of basket, crock, pitcher) anse f; (of shovel, broom, knife) manche m; (of umbrella, sword, door) poignée f; (of frying pan) queue f; (of pump) brimbale f; (of handcart) brancard m; (of wheelbarrow) bras m; (opportunity, pretext) prétexte m; (mach) manivelle f, manette f; **to fly off the handle** (coll) sortir de ses gonds || tr manier; (with one's hands) palper, tâter; **handle with care** (shipping label) fragile; **to handle roughly** malmener || intr—to **handle well** (mach) avoir de bonnes réactions
han'dle·bars' spl guidon m
handler ['hændlər] s (sports) entraîneur m
handling ['hændlɪŋ] s (e.g., of tool) maniement m; (e.g., of person) traitement m; (of merchandise) manutention f
hand'made' adj fait à la main
hand'maid' or **hand'maid'en** s servante f; (fig) auxiliaire mf
hand'-me-down' s (coll) vêtement m de seconde main
hand' or'gan s orgue m de Barbarie
hand'out' s (notes) (coll) documentation f; (slang) aumône f
hand'-picked' adj trié sur le volet
hand'rail' s main f courante, rampe f
hand'saw' s égoïne f, scie f à main
hand'set' s combiné m
hand'shake' s poignée f de main
handsome ['hænsəm] adj beau; (e.g., fortune) considérable
hand'spring' s—to do a **handspring** prendre appui sur les mains pour faire la culbute
hand'-to-hand' adj corps-à-corps
hand'-to-mouth' adj—to lead a hand-to-mouth existence vivre au jour le jour
hand' truck' s bard m, diable m
hand'work' s travail m à la main
hand'writ'ing s écriture f
handwritten ['hænd,rɪtən] adj manuscrit, autographe

hand·y ['hændi] *adj* (*comp* -ier; *super* -iest) (*easy to handle*) maniable; (*within easy reach*) accessible, sous la main; (*skillful*) adroit, habile; **to come in handy** être très à propos
hand'y·man' *s* (*pl* -men') homme *m* à tout faire, bricoleur *m*
hang [hæŋ] *s* (*of dress, curtain, etc.*) retombée *f*, drapé *m*; (*skill; insight*) adresse *f*, sens *m*; **I don't give a hang!** (coll) je m'en moque pas mal!; **to get the hang** (coll) saisir le truc, attraper le chic ‖ *v* (*pret* & *pp* **hung** [hʌŋ]) *tr* pendre; (*laundry*) étendre; (*wallpaper*) coller; (*one's head*) baisser; **hang it all!** zut alors!; **to hang up** suspendre, accrocher; (telp) raccrocher ‖ *intr* pendre, être accroché; **to hang around** flâner, rôder; **to hang on** se cramponner à, s'accrocher à; (*to depend on*) dépendre de; (*to stay put*) tenir bon; **to hang out** pendre dehors; (slang) percher, loger; **to hang over** (*to threaten*) peser sur, menacer; **to hang together** rester unis; **to hang up** (telp) raccrocher ‖ *v* (*pret* & *pp* **hung** or **hanged**) *tr* (*to execute by hanging*) pendre ‖ *intr* se pendre
hangar ['hæŋər], ['hæŋgɑr] *s* hangar *m*
hang'dog' *adj* (*look*) patibulaire
hanger ['hæŋər] *s* crochet *m*; (*coat-hanger*) cintre *m*, portemanteau *m*
hang'er-on' *s* (*pl* **hangers-on**) parasite *m*, pique-assiette *m*
hanging ['hæŋɪŋ] *adj* pendant, suspendu ‖ *s* pendaison *f*; **hangings** tentures *fpl*
hang'man *s* (*pl* -men) bourreau *m*
hang'nail' *s* envie *f*
hang'out' *s* (coll) repaire *m*
hang'o'ver *s* (coll) gueule *f* de bois
hank [hæŋk] *s* écheveau *m*
hanker ['hæŋkər] *intr*—**to hanker after** or **for** désirer vivement, être affamé de
Hannibal ['hænɪbəl] *s* Annibal *m*
haphazard [,hæp'hæzərd] *adj* fortuit, imprévu; au petit bonheur ‖ *adv* à l'aventure, au hasard
hapless ['hæplɪs] *adj* malheureux, malchanceux
happen ['hæpən] *intr* arriver, se passer; (*to be the case by chance*) survenir; **happen what may** advienne que pourra; **how does it happen that . . . ?** comment se fait-il que . . . ?, d'où vient-il que . . . ?; **to happen on** tomber sur; **to happen to** + *inf* se trouver + *inf*, venir à + *inf*
happening ['hæpənɪŋ] *s* événement *m*
happily ['hæpɪli] *adv* heureusement
happiness ['hæpɪnɪs] *s* bonheur *m*
hap·py ['hæpi] *adj* (*comp* -pier; *super* -piest) heureux; (*pleased*) content; (*hour*) propice; **to be happy to** être heureux or content de
hap'py-go-luck'y *adj* sans souci, insouciant ‖ *adv* (archaic) à l'aventure
hap'py me'dium *s* juste-milieu *m*
Hap'py New' Year' *interj* bonne année!

harangue [hə'ræŋ] *s* harangue *f* ‖ *tr* & *intr* haranguer
harass ['hærəs], [hə'ræs] *tr* harceler; tourmenter
harbinger ['hɑrbɪndʒər] *s* avant-coureur *m*, précurseur *m*
harbor ['hɑrbər] *s* port *m*; ‖ *tr* héberger, donner asile à; (*a criminal, stolen goods, etc.*) receler; (*suspicions; a hope*) entretenir, nourrir; (*a grudge*) garder
har'bor mas'ter *s* capitaine *m* de port
hard [hɑrd] *adj* dur; (*difficult*) difficile; (*water*) cru, calcaire; (*work*) assidu, dur; **to be hard on** (*to treat severely*) être dur or sévère envers; (*to wear out fast*) user ‖ *adv* dur, fort; (*firmly*) ferme; **hard upon** de près, tout contre; **to rain hard** pleuvoir fort; **to try hard** essayer
hard'-and-fast' *adj* strict, inflexible, établi
hard-bitten ['hɑrd'bɪtən] *adj* tenace, dur à cuire
hard'-boiled' *adj* (*egg*) dur; (coll) dur, inflexible
hard' can'dy *s* bonbons *mpl*; **piece of hard candy** bonbon *m*
hard' cash' *s* espèces *fpl* sonnantes
hard' ci'der *s* cidre *m*
hard' coal' *s* houille *f* éclatante, anthracite *m*
hard' drink' *s* boissons *fpl* alcooliques, liqueurs *fpl* fortes
hard' drink'er *s* grand buveur *m*
hard'-earned' *adj* péniblement gagné
harden ['hɑrdən] *tr* durcir, endurcir ‖ *intr* se durcir, s'endurcir
hardening ['hɑrdənɪŋ] *s* durcissement *m*; (fig) endurcissement *m*
hard' fact' *s* fait *m* brutal; **hard facts** réalités *fpl*
hard-fought ['hɑrd'fɔt] *adj* acharné, chaudement disputé
hard'-head'ed *adj* positif, à la tête froide
hard'-heart'ed *adj* dur, sans compassion
hardihood ['hɑrdɪ,hʊd] *s* endurance *f*; courage *m*; audace *f*
hardiness ['hɑrdɪnɪs] *s* vigueur *f*
hard' la'bor *s* travaux *mpl* forcés
hard' luck' *s* guigne *f*, malchance *f*
hardly ['hɑrdli] *adv* guère; à peine, ne . . . guère, e.g., **he hardly thinks of anything else** à peine pense-t-il à autre chose, il ne pense guère à autre chose; **hardly ever** presque jamais
hardness ['hɑrdnɪs] *s* dureté *f*
hard' of hear'ing *adj* dur d'oreille
hard'-pressed' *adj* aux abois, gêné
hard' rub'ber *s* caoutchouc *m* durci, ébonite *f*
hard'-shell' *adj* (*clam*) à carapace dure; (coll) opiniâtre
hard'ship' *s* peine *f*; **hardships** privations *fpl*; fatigues *fpl*
hard'tack' *s* biscuit *m*, biscotin *m*
hard' times' *spl* difficultés *fpl*, temps *mpl* difficiles
hard' to please' *adj* difficile à contenter, exigeant

hard' up' *adj* (coll) à court d'argent; **to be hard up for** (coll) être à court de

hard'ware' *s* quincaillerie *f*; *(trimmings)* ferrure *f*

hard'ware'man *s* (*pl* **-men**) quincaillier *m*

hard'ware store' *s* quincaillerie *f*

hard-won ['hard,wʌn] *adj* chèrement disputé, conquis de haute lutte

hard'wood' *s* bois *m* dur; arbre *m* de bois dur

hard'wood floor' *s* parquet *m*

har·dy ['hardi] *adj* (*comp* **-dier**; *super* **-diest**) vigoureux, robuste; *(rash)* hardi; (hort) résistant

hare [her] *s* lièvre *m*

hare'brained' *adj* écervelé, farfelu

hare'lip' *s* bec-de-lièvre *m*

harem ['herəm] *s* harem *m*

hark [hark] *intr* écouter; **to hark back to** en revenir à || *interj* écoutez!

harken ['harkən] *intr*—**to harken to** écouter

harlequin ['harləkwɪn] *s* arlequin *m*

harlot ['harlət] *s* prostituée *f*, fille *f* publique

harm [harm] *s* mal *m*, dommage *m* || *tr* nuire (with *dat*), faire du mal (with *dat*)

harmful ['harmfəl] *adj* nuisible

harmless ['harmlɪs] *adj* inoffensif

harmonic [har'manɪk] *adj* harmonique

harmonica [har'manɪkə] *s* harmonica *m*

harmonious [har'monɪ·əs] *adj* harmonieux

harmonize ['harmə,naɪz] *tr* harmoniser || *intr* s'harmoniser

harmo·ny ['harməni] *s* (*pl* **-nies**) harmonie *f*

harness ['harnɪs] *s* harnais *m*, harnachement *m*; **to die in the harness** (coll) mourir sous le harnais, mourir debout; **to get back in the harness** (coll) reprendre le collier || *tr* harnacher; (*e.g., a river*) aménager, capter

har'ness ma'ker *s* bourrelier *m*, harnacheur *m*

har'ness race' *s* course *f* attelée

harp [harp] *s* harpe *f* || *intr*—**to harp on** rabâcher

harpist ['harpɪst] *s* harpiste *mf*

harpoon [har'pun] *s* harpon *m* || *tr* harponner

harpsichord ['harpsɪ,kɔrd] *s* clavecin *m*

har·py ['harpi] *s* (*pl* **-pies**) harpie *f*

harrow ['hæro] *s* (agr) herse *f* || *tr* tourmenter; (agr) herser

harrowing ['hæro·ɪŋ] *adj* horripilant

har·ry ['hæri] *v* (*pret & pp* **-ried**) *tr* harceler; (*to devastate*) ravager

harsh [harʃ] *adj* (*life, treatment, etc.*) sévère, dur; (*to the touch*) rude; (*to the taste*) âpre; (*to the ear*) discordant

harshness ['harʃnɪs] *s* dureté *f*, rudesse *f*; âpreté *f*

hart [hart] *s* cerf *m*

harum-scarum ['herəm'skerəm] *adj & s* écervelé || *adv* en casse-cou

harvest ['harvɪst] *s* récolte *f*; (*of grain*) moisson *f* || *tr* récolter, moissonner || *intr* faire la récolte or moisson

harvester ['harvɪstər] *s* moissonneur *m*; (mach) moissonneuse *f*

har'vest home' *s* fin *f* de la moisson; fête *f* de la moisson

har'vest moon' *s* lune *f* des moissons

has-been ['hæz,bɪn] *s* (coll) vieille croûte *f*

hash [hæʃ] *s* hachis *m* || *tr* hacher

hash' house' *s* (slang) gargote *f*

hashish ['hæʃiʃ] *s* hachisch *m*

hasp [hæsp], [hasp] *s* moraillon *m*

hassle ['hæsəl] *s* (coll) querelle *f*, accrochage *m*

hassock ['hæsək] *s* pouf *m*

haste [hest] *s* hâte *f*; **in haste** à la hâte; **to make haste** se hâter

hasten ['hesən] *tr* hâter || *intr* se hâter

hast·y ['hesti] *adj* (*comp* **-ier**; *super* **-iest**) hâtif, précipité; (*rash*) inconsidéré, emporté

hat [hæt] *s* chapeau *m*; **hat in hand** chapeau bas; **hats off to . . . !** chapeau bas devant . . . !; **to keep under one's hat** (coll) garder strictement pour soi; **to talk through one's hat** (coll) parler à tort et à travers; **to throw one's hat in the ring** (coll) descendre dans l'arène

hat'band' *s* ruban *m* de chapeau

hat' block' *s* forme *f* à chapeaux

hat'box' *s* carton *m* à chapeaux

hatch [hætʃ] *s* (*brood*) éclosion *f*; (*trap door*) trappe *f*; (*lower half of door*) demi-porte *f*; (*opening in ship's deck*) écoutille *f*; (*hood over hatchway*) capot *m*; (*lid for opening in ship's deck*) panneau *m* de descente || *tr* (*eggs*) couver, faire éclore; (*a plot*) ourdir, manigancer; (*to hachure*) hachurer || *intr* éclore; (*said of chicks*) sortir de la coquille

hat'check girl' *s* préposée *f* au vestiaire

hatchet ['hætʃɪt] *s* hachette *f*; **to bury the hatchet** faire la paix

hatch'way' *s* écoutille *f*

hate [het] *s* haine *f* || *tr* haïr, détester; **to hate to** haïr de

hateful ['hetfəl] *adj* haïssable

hat'pin' *s* épingle *f* à chapeau

hat'rack' *s* porte-chapeaux *m*

hatred ['hetrɪd] *s* haine *f*

hat' shop' *s* chapellerie *f*

hatter ['hætər] *s* chapelier *m*

haughtiness ['hɔtɪnɪs] *s* hauteur *f*

haugh·ty ['hɔti] *adj* (*comp* **-tier**; *super* **-tiest**) hautain, altier

haul [hɔl] *s* (*pull, tug*) effort *m*; (*amount caught*) coup *m* de filet, prise *f*; (*distance covered*) parcours *m*, distance *f* de transport || *tr* (*to tug*) tirer; (com) transporter

haulage ['hɔlɪdʒ] *s* transport *m*; (*cost*) frais *m* de transport

haunch [hɔntʃ], [hantʃ] *s* (*hip*) hanche *f*; (*hind quarter of an animal*) quartier *m*; (*leg of animal used for food*) cuissot *m*

haunt [hɔnt], [hant] *s* lieu *m* fréquenté, rendez-vous *m*; (*e.g., of criminals*)

repaire *m* ‖ *tr* (*to obsess*) hanter; (*to frequent*) fréquenter
haunt'ed house' *s* maison *f* hantée par les fantômes
Havana [hə'vænə] *s* La Havane
have [hæv] *s*—**the haves and the have-nots** les riches et les pauvres ‖ *v* (3d *pers* **has** [hæz]; *pret* & *pp* **had** [hæd]) *tr* avoir; **to have** + *inf* faire + *inf*, e.g., **I shall have him** go je le ferai aller; **to have** + *pp* faire + *inf*, e.g., **I am going to have a suit made** je vais faire faire un complet; **to have nothing to do with** n'avoir rien à voir avec; **to have on** (*clothing*) porter; **to have s.th. to** + *inf* avoir q.ch. à + *inf*, e.g., **I have a lot of work to do** j'ai beaucoup de travail à faire ‖ *intr*—**to have to** avoir à; devoir; falloir, e.g., **I have to go** il me faut aller; falloir que, e.g., **I have to read him the letter** il faut que je lui lise la lettre ‖ *aux* (to form compound past tenses) avoir, e.g., **I have run too fast** j'ai couru trop vite; (to form compound past tenses with some intransitive verbs and all reflexive verbs) être, e.g., **they have arrived** elles sont arrivées; **to have just** + *pp* venir de + *inf*, e.g., **they have just returned** ils viennent de rentrer; e.g., **they had just returned** ils venaient de rentrer
have'lock *s* couvre-nuque *m*
haven ['hevən] *s* havre *m*, asile *m*
haversack ['hævər‚sæk] *s* havresac *m*
havoc ['hævək] *s* ravage *m*; **to play havoc with** causer des dégâts à
haw [hɔ] *s* (bot) cenelle *f* ‖ *tr* & *intr* tourner à gauche ‖ *interj* dia!, à gauche!
Hawaiian [hə'waɪjən] *adj* hawaïen ‖ *s* Hawaïen *m*
Hawai'ian Is'lands *spl* îles *fpl* Hawaii
haw'-haw' *s* rire *m* bête ‖ *intr* rire bêtement ‖ *interj* heu!
hawk [hɔk] *s* faucon *m*; (*mortarboard*) taloche *f*; (*sharper*) (coll) vautour *m* ‖ *tr* colporter; **to hawk up** expectorer ‖ *intr* chasser au faucon; (*to hawk up phlegm*) graillonner
hawker ['hɔkər] *s* colporteur *m*
hawk' owl' *s* chouette *f* épervière
hawks'bill tur'tle *s* caret *m*, caouane *f*
hawse [hɔz] *s* (*hole*) écubier *m*; (*prow*) nez *m*; (*distance*) évitage *m*
hawse'hole' *s* écubier *m*
hawser ['hɔzər] *s* haussière *f*
haw'thorn' *s* aubépine *f*
hay [he] *s* foin *m*; **to hit the hay** (slang) aller au plumard; **to make hay** faire les foins
hay' fe'ver *s* rhume *m* des foins
hay'field' *s* pré *m* à foin
hay'fork' *s* fourche *f* à foin
hay'loft' *s* fenil *m*, grenier *m* à foin
hay'mak'er *s* (boxing) coup *m* de poing en assommoir
haymow ['he‚mau] *s* fenil *m*; approvisionnement *m* de foin
hay'rack' *s* râtelier *m*

hay'ride' *s* promenade *f* en charrette de foin
hay'seed' *s* graine *f* de foin; (coll) culterreux *m*
hay'stack' *s* meule *f* de foin
hay'wire' *adj* (slang) en pagaille; **to go haywire** (slang) perdre la boussole ‖ *s* fil *m* de fer à lier le foin
hazard ['hæzərd] *s* risque *m*, danger *m*; (golf) obstacle *m*; **at all hazards** à tout hasard ‖ *tr* hasarder, risquer
hazardous ['hæzərdəs] *adj* hasardé
haze [hez] *s* brume *f*; (fig) obscurité *f* ‖ *tr* brimer
hazel ['hezəl] *adj* couleur de noisette, brun clair ‖ *s* (*tree*) noisetier *m*, avelinier *m*
ha'zel·nut' *s* noisette *f*, aveline *f*
hazing ['hezɪŋ] *s* brimade *f*; (*at university*) bizutage *m*
ha·zy ['hezi] *adj* (*comp* **-zier**; *super* **-ziest**) brumeux; (*notion*) nébuleux, vague
H'-bomb' *s* bombe *f* H
he [hi] *pron pers* il §87; lui §85; ce §82B; **he who** celui qui §83
head [hed] *s* tête *f*; (*of bed*) chevet *m*; (*of boil*) tête; (*on glass of beer*) mousse *f*; (*of drum*) peau *f*; (*of cane*) pomme *f*; (*of coin*) face *f*; (*of barrel, cylinder, etc.*) fond *m*; (*of cylinder of automobile engine*) culasse *f*; (*of celery*) pied *m*; (*of ship*) avant *m*; (*of spear, ax, etc.*) fer *m*; (*of arrow*) pointe *f*; (*of business, department, etc.*) chef *m*, directeur *m*; (*of school*) directeur, principal *m*; (*of stream*) source *f*; (*of lake; of the table*) bout *m*, haut bout; (*caption*) titre *m*; (*decisive point*) point *m* culminant, crise *f*; **at the head of** à la tête de; **from head to foot** des pieds à la tête; **head downwards** la tête en bas; **head of cattle** bœuf *m*; **head over heels in love (with)** éperdument amoureux (de); **heads or tails** pile ou face; **over one's head** (*beyond reach*) hors de la portée de qn; (*going to a higher authority*) sans tenir compte de qn; **to be out of one's head** (coll) être timbré ou fou; **to go to one's head** monter à la tête de qn; **to keep one's head** garder son sang-froid; **to keep one's head above water** se tenir à flot; **to not make head or tail of it** n'y comprendre rien; **to put heads together** prendre conseil; **to take it into one's head to** avoir l'idée de, se mettre en tête de; **to win by a head** gagner d'une tête ‖ *tr* (*to direct*) diriger; (*a procession*) conduire, mener; (*an organization; a class in school*) être en tête de; (*a list*) venir en tête de; **to head off** détourner ‖ *intr* (*said of grain*) épier; **to head for** or **towards** se diriger vers
head'ache' *s* mal *m* de tête
head'band' *s* bandeau *m*
head'board' *s* panneau *m* de tête
head'cheese' *s* fromage *m* de tête
head' cold' *s* rhume *m* de cerveau
head'dress' *s* coiffure *f*

head'first' *adv* la tête la première; (*impetuously*) précipitamment

head'frame' *s* (min) chevalement *m*

head'gear' *s* garniture *f* de tête, couvre-chef *m*; (*for protection*) casque *m*

head'hunt'er *s* chasseur *m* de têtes

heading ['hɛdɪŋ] *s* titre *m*; (*of letter*) en-tête *m*; (*of chapter*) tête *f*

headland ['hɛdlənd] *s* promontoire *m*

headless ['hɛdlɪs] *adj* sans tête; (*leaderless*) sans chef

head'light' *s* (aut) phare *m*; (naut) fanal *m*; (rr) feu *m* d'avant

head'line' *s* (*of newspaper*) manchette *f*; (*of article*) titre *m*; **to make the headlines** apparaître aux premières pages des journaux || *tr* mettre en vedette

head'lin'er *s* (slang) tête *f* d'affiche

head'long' *adj* précipité || *adv* précipitamment

head'man' *s* (*pl* -men') chef *m*

head'mas'ter *s* principal *m*, directeur *m*

head'most' *adj* de tête, premier

head' of'fice *s* bureau *m* central; (*director's office*) direction *f*; (*of a corporation*) siège *m* social

head' of hair' *s* chevelure *f*

head'-on' *adj* & *adv* de front, face à face

head'phones' *spl* écouteurs *mpl*, casque *m*

head'piece' *s* (*any covering for head*) casque *m*; (*headset*) écouteur *m*; (*brains, judgment*) tête *f*, caboche *f*; (typ) vignette *f*, en-tête *m*

head'quar'ters *s* bureau *m* central; commissariat *m* de police; (mil) quartier *m* général; (*staff headquarters*) (mil) état-major *m*

head'rest' *s* appui-tête *m*

head'set' *s* casque *m*, écouteurs *mpl*

heads'man *s* (*pl* -men) bourreau *m*

head'stone' *s* pierre *f* tumulaire (à la tête d'une tombe); (*cornerstone*) pierre angulaire

head'strong' *adj* têtu, entêté

head'wait'er *s* maître *m* d'hôtel, steward *m*

head'wa'ters *spl* cours *m* supérieur d'une rivière

head'way' *s* progrès *m*, marche *f* avant; (*between buses*) intervalle *m*; (naut) erre *f*; **to make headway** progresser, aller de l'avant

head'wear' *s* garniture *f* de tête

headwind ['hɛd,wɪnd] *s* vent *m* contraire, vent debout

head'work' *s* travail *m* mental, travail de tête

head·y ['hɛdi] *adj* (*comp* -ier; *super* -iest) (*wine*) capiteux; (*conduct*) emporté; (*news*) excitant; (*perfume*) entêtant

heal [hil] *tr* guérir; (*a wound*) cicatriser || *intr* guérir

healer ['hilər] *s* guérisseur *m*

healing ['hilɪŋ] *s* guérison *f*

health [hɛlθ] *s* santé *f*; **to be in good health** se porter bien, être en bonne santé; **to be in poor health** se porter mal, être en mauvaise santé; **to drink to the health of** boire à la santé de; **to enjoy radiant health** avoir une santé florissante; **to your health!** à votre santé!

healthful ['hɛlθfəl] *adj* sain; (*air, climate, etc.*) salubre; (*recreation, work, etc.*) salutaire

health·y ['hɛlθi] *adj* (*comp* -ier; *super* -iest) sain; (*air, climate, etc.*) salubre; (*person*) bien portant; (*appetite*) robuste

heap [hip] *s* tas *m*, amas *m* || *tr* entasser, amasser; **to heap** (*honors, praise, etc.*) **on s.o.** combler qn de; **to heap** (*insults*) **on s.o.** accabler qn de

hear [hɪr] *v* (*pret* & *pp* **heard** [hʌrd]) *tr* entendre, ouïr; **to hear it said** l'entendre dire; **to hear s.o. sing, to hear s.o. singing** entendre chanter qn, entendre qn qui chante; **to hear s.th. sung** entendre chanter q.ch. || *intr* entendre; **hear! hear!** très bien!, bravo!; **hear ye!** oyez!; **to hear about** entendre parler de; **to hear from** avoir des nouvelles de; **to hear of** entendre parler de; **to hear tell of** (coll) entendre parler de; **to hear that** entendre dire que

hearer ['hɪrər] *s* auditeur *m*; **hearers** auditoire *m*

hearing ['hɪrɪŋ] *s* (*sense*) l'ouïe *f*; (*act; opportunity to be heard*) audition *f*; (law) audience *f*; **in the hearing of** en la présence de, devant; **within hearing** à portée de la voix

hear'ing aid' *s* sonotone *m*, microvibrateur *m*, appareil *m* de correction auditive

hear'say' *s* ouï-dire *m*

hear'say ev'idence *s* simples ouï-dire *mpl*

hearse [hʌrs] *s* corbillard *m*, char *m* funèbre

heart [hɑrt] *s* cœur *m*; (cards) cœur; **after one's heart** selon son cœur; **at heart** au fond; **by heart** par cœur; **heart and soul** corps et âme; **lift up your hearts!** haut les cœurs!; **to break the heart of** fendre le cœur à; **to die of a broken heart** mourir de chagrin; **to eat one's heart out** se ronger le cœur; **to eat to one's heart's content** manger tout son soûl; **to get to the heart of the matter** entrer dans le vif de la question; **to have one's heart in one's work** avoir le cœur à l'ouvrage; **to have one's heart in the right place** avoir le cœur bien placé; **to lose heart** perdre courage; **to open one's heart to** épancher son cœur à; **to take heart** prendre courage; **to take to heart** prendre à cœur; **to wear one's heart on one's sleeve** avoir le cœur sur les lèvres; **with a heavy heart** le cœur gros; **with all one's heart** de tout son cœur; **with one's heart in one's mouth** le gosier serré

heart'ache' *s* peine *f* de cœur

heart' attack' *s* crise *f* cardiaque

heart'beat' *s* battement *m* du cœur

heart'break' *s* crève-cœur *m*

heartbroken ['hɑrt,brokən] *adj* navré, chagriné
heart'burn' *s* pyrosis *m*
heart' cher'ry *s* guigne *f*
heart' disease' *s* maladie *f* de cœur
hearten ['hɑrtən] *tr* encourager
heart' fail'ure *s* arrêt *m* du cœur
heartfelt ['hɑrt,fɛlt] *adj* sincère, cordial, bien senti
hearth [hɑrθ] *s* foyer *m*, âtre *m*
hearth'stone' *s* pierre *f* de cheminée
heartily ['hɑrtɪli] *adv* de bon cœur, sincèrement
heartless ['hɑrtlɪs] *adj* sans cœur
heart' of stone' *s* (fig) cœur *m* de bronze
heart'-rend'ing *adj* désolant, navrant
heart'sick' *adj* désolé, chagrin
heart'strings' *spl* fibres *fpl*, replis *mpl* du cœur
heart'-to-heart' *adj* franc, ouvert; sérieux ‖ *adv* à cœur ouvert
heart' trans'plant *s* greffe *f* du cœur, transplantation *f* cardiaque
heart' trou'ble *s* maladie *f* de cœur
heart'wood' *s* bois *m* de cœur
heart·y ['hɑrti] *adj* (*comp* -ier; *super* -iest) cordial, sincère; (*meal*) copieux; (*laugh*) sonore; (*eater*) gros
heat [hit] *s* chaleur *f*; (*heating*) chauffage *m*; (*rut of animals*) rut *m*; (*in horse racing*) éliminatoire *f*; **in heat** en rut ‖ *tr* échauffer; (*e.g., a house*) chauffer ‖ *intr* s'échauffer; **to heat up** chauffer
heated *adj* chauffé; (fig) chaud, échauffé
heater ['hitər] *s* (*for food*) réchaud *m*; (*for heating house*) calorifère *m*
heath [hiθ] *s* bruyère *f*
hea·then ['hiðən] *adj* païen ‖ *s* (*pl* -then *or* -thens) païen *m*
heathendom ['hiðəndəm] *s* paganisme *m*
heather ['hɛðər] *s* bruyère *f*
heating ['hitɪŋ] *adj* échauffant ‖ *s* chauffage *m*
heat' light'ning *s* éclairs *mpl* de chaleur
heat' shield' *s* (rok) bouclier *m* contre la chaleur, bouclier antithermique
heat'stroke' *s* insolation *f*, coup *m* de chaleur
heat' wave' *s* vague *f* de chaleur; (phys) onde *f* calorifique
heave [hiv] *s* soulèvement *m*; **heaves** (vet) pousse *f* ‖ *v* (*pret & pp* heaved *or* hove [hov]) *tr* soulever; (*to throw*) lancer; (*a sigh*) pousser; (*the anchor*) lever ‖ *intr* se soulever; faire des efforts pour vomir; (*said of bosom*) palpiter
heaven ['hɛvən] *s* ciel *m*; **for heaven's sake** pour l'amour de Dieu; **Heaven** le ciel; **heavens** cieux *mpl*, ciel
heavenly ['hɛvənli] *adj* céleste
heav'enly bod'y *s* corps *m* céleste
heav·y ['hɛvi] *adj* (*comp* -ier; *super* -iest) lourd, pesant; (*heart; crop; eater; baggage; rain, sea, weather*) gros; (*meal*) copieux; (*sleep*) profond; (*work*) pénible; (*book, reading, etc.*) indigeste; (*parts*) (theat) tra-

gique, sombre ‖ *adv* lourd, lourdement; **to hang heavy on** peser sur
heav'y drink'er *s* fort buveur *m*
heav'y·du'ty *adj* extra-fort
heav'y-heart'ed *adj* au cœur lourd
heav'y·set' *adj* de forte carrure, costaud
heav'y·weight' *s* (boxing) poids *m* lourd
Hebraist ['hibre·ɪst] *s* hébraïsant *m*
Hebrew ['hibru] *adj* hébreu, hébraïque ‖ *s* (*language*) hébreu *m*, langue *f* hébraïque; (*man*) Hébreu *m*; (*woman*) Juive *f*
hecatomb ['hɛkə,tom] *s* hécatombe *f*
heckle ['hɛkəl] *tr* interrompre bruyamment, chahuter; (*on account of trifles*) asticoter, harceler
heckler ['hɛklər] *s* interrupteur *m* impertinent, interpellateur *m*
hectic ['hɛktɪk] *adj* fou, bouleversant
hedge [hɛdʒ] *s* haie *f* ‖ *tr* entourer d'une haie; **to hedge in** entourer de tous côtés ‖ *intr* chercher des échappatoires, hésiter; (com) faire la contrepartie
hedge'hog' *s* hérisson *m*; (*porcupine*) porc-épic *m*
hedge'hop' *v* (*pret & pp* -hopped; *ger* -hopping) *intr* (aer) voler en rasemottes
hedgerow ['hɛdʒ,ro] *s* bordure *f* de haies, haie *f* vive
heed [hid] *s* attention *f*, soin *m*; **to take heed** prendre garde ‖ *tr* faire attention à, prendre garde à ‖ *intr* faire attention, prendre garde
heedful ['hidfəl] *adj* attentif
heedless ['hidlɪs] *adj* inattentif
heehaw ['hi,hɔ] *s* hi-han *m* ‖ *intr* pousser des hi-hans
heel [hil] *s* talon *m*; (slang) goujat *m*; **to be down at the heel** traîner la savate; **to cool one's heels** (coll) croquer le marmot, faire le pied de grue
heft·y ['hɛfti] *adj* (*comp* -ier; *super* -iest) costaud; (*heavy*) pesant
heifer ['hɛfər] *s* génisse *f*
height [haɪt] *s* hauteur *f*; (*e.g., of folly*) comble *m*
heighten ['haɪtən] *tr* rehausser; (*to increase the amount of*) augmenter; (*to set off, bring out*) relever ‖ *intr* se rehausser; augmenter
heinous ['henəs] *adj* odieux, atroce
heir [ɛr] *s* héritier *m*; **to become the heir of** hériter de
heir' appar'ent *s* (*pl* **heirs apparent**) héritier *m* présomptif
heiress ['ɛrɪs] *s* héritière *f*
heir'loom' *s* meuble *m*, bijou *m*, or souvenir *m* de famille
Helen ['hɛlən] *s* Hélène *f*
helicopter ['hɛlɪ,kɑptər] *s* hélicoptère *m*
heliport ['hɛlɪ,port] *s* héliport *m*
helium ['hilɪ·əm] *s* hélium *m*
helix ['hilɪks] *s* (*pl* **helixes** *or* **helices** ['hɛlɪ,siz]) hélice *f*; (anat) hélix *m*
hell [hɛl] *s* enfer *m*
hell'bent' *adj* (slang) hardi; **hellbent on** (slang) acharné en diable à

hell'cat' s (*bad-tempered woman*) harpie f; (*witch*) sorcière f
Hellene ['hɛlin] s Hellène mf
Hellenic [hɛ'lɛnɪk], [hɛ'linɪk] adj hellène
hell'fire' s feu m de l'enfer
hellish ['hɛlɪʃ] adj infernal
hel·lo [hɛ'lo] s (pl -los) bonjour m || interj bonjour!; (*on telephone*) allô!
helm [hɛlm] s gouvernail m
helmet ['hɛlmɪt] s casque m
helms'man s (pl -men) homme m de barre
help [hɛlp] s aide f, secours m; (*workers*) main-d'œuvre f; (*office workers*) employés mpl; (*domestic servants*) domestiques mfpl; **help wanted** (*public sign*) offres d'emploi, on embauche; **there's no help for it** il n'y a pas de remède || tr aider, secourir; **so help me God!** que Dieu me juge!; **to help down** aider à descendre; **to help oneself** se défendre; (*to food*) se servir; **to not be able to help ne** pouvoir s'empêcher de || intr aider || interj au secours!
helper ['hɛlpər] s aide mf, assistant m
helpful ['hɛlpfəl] adj utile; (*person*) serviable, secourable
helping ['hɛlpɪŋ] s (*of food*) portion f
helpless ['hɛlplɪs] adj (*weak*) faible; (*powerless*) impuissant; (*penniless*) sans ressource; (*confused*) désemparé; (*situation*) sans recours
helter-skelter ['hɛltər'skɛltər] adj désordonné || s débandade f || adv pêle-mêle
hem [hɛm] s ourlet m, bord m || v (pret & pp hemmed; ger hemming) tr ourler, border; **to hem in** entourer, cerner || intr faire un ourlet; **to hem and haw** ânonner; (fig) tourner autour du pot || interj hum!
hemisphere ['hɛmɪ,sfɪr] s hémisphère m
hemistich ['hɛmɪ,stɪk] s hémistiche m
hem'line' s ourlet m de la jupe
hem'lock' s (*Tsuga canadensis*) sapin m du Canada, pruche f; (*herb and poison*) ciguë f
hemoglobin [,hɛmə'globɪn], [,himə-'globɪn] s hémoglobine f
hemophilia [,hɛmə'fɪlɪ·ə], [,himə-'fɪlɪ·ə] s hémophilie f
hemorrhage ['hɛmərɪdʒ] s hémorragie f
hemorrhoids ['hɛmə,rɔɪdz] spl hémorroïdes fpl
hemostat ['hɛmə,stæt], ['himə,stæt] s hémostatique m
hemp [hɛmp] s chanvre m
hem'stitch' s ourlet m à jour || tr ourler à jour || intr faire un ourlet à jour
hen [hɛn] s poule f
hence [hɛns] adv d'ici; (*therefore*) d'où, donc
hence'forth' adv désormais, dorénavant
hench·man ['hɛntʃmən] s (pl -men) partisan m, acolyte m, complice mf
hen'coop' s cage f à poules, épinette f
hen'house' s poulailler m

henna ['hɛnə] s henné m || tr teindre au henné
hen'peck' tr mener par le bout du nez
Henry ['hɛnri] s Henri m
hep [hɛp] adj (slang) à la page, dans le train; **to be hep to** (slang) être au courant de
her [hʌr] adj poss son §88 || pron pers elle §85; la §87; lui §87
herald ['hɛrəld] s héraut m; (fig) avant-coureur m || tr annoncer; **to herald in** introduire
herald·ry ['hɛrəldri] s (pl -ries) héraldique f, blason m
herb [ʌrb], [hʌrb] s herbe f; (pharm) herbe médicinale or officinale; **herbs for seasoning** fines herbes
herculean [hʌr'kjulɪ·ən], [,hʌrkju'li-ən] adj herculéen
herd [hʌrd] s troupeau m || tr rassembler en troupeau || intr—**to herd together** s'attrouper
herds'man s (pl -men) pâtre m; (*of sheep*) berger m; (*of cattle*) bouvier m
here [hɪr] adv ici; **from here to there** d'ici là; **here and there** çà et là, parci par-là; **here below** ici-bas; **here is** or **here are** voici; **here lies** ci-gît; **that's neither here nor there** ça n'a rien à y voir || interj tenez!; (*answering roll call*) présent!
hereabouts ['hɪrə,bauts] adv près d'ici
here·af'ter s—**the hereafter** l'autre monde || adv désormais, à l'avenir; (*farther along*) ci-après
here·by' adv par ce moyen, par ceci; (*in legal language*) par les présentes
hereditary [hɪ'rɛdɪ,tɛri] adj héréditaire
heredi·ty [hɪ'rɛdɪti] s (pl -ties) hérédité f
here·in' adv ici; (*on this point*) en ceci; (*in this writing*) ci-inclus
here·of' adv de ceci, à ce sujet
here·on' adv là-dessus
here·sy ['hɛrəsi] s (pl -sies) hérésie f
heretic ['hɛrətɪk] adj & s hérétique mf
heretical [hɪ'rɛtɪkəl] adj hérétique
heretofore [,hɪrtu'for] adv jusqu'ici
here'upon' adv là-dessus
here·with' adv ci-joint, avec ceci
heritage ['hɛrɪtɪdʒ] s héritage m
hermetic(al) [hʌr'mɛtɪk(əl)] adj hermétique
hermit ['hʌrmɪt] s ermite m
hermitage ['hʌrmɪtɪdʒ] s ermitage m
herni·a ['hʌrnɪ·ə] s (pl -as or -ae [,i]) hernie f
he·ro ['hɪro] s (pl -roes) héros m
heroic [hɪ'ro·ɪk] adj héroïque || **heroics** spl (*verse*) vers m héroïque; (*language*) grandiloquence f
heroin ['hɛro·ɪn] s héroïne f
heroine ['hɛro·ɪn] s héroïne f
heroism ['hɛro,ɪzəm] s héroïsme m
heron ['hɛrən] s héron m
herring ['hɛrɪŋ] s hareng m
her'ring·bone' s (*in fabrics*) point m de chausson; (*in hardwood floors*) parquet m à batons rompus; (*in design*) arête f de hareng
hers [hʌrz] pron poss le sien §89

her·self' *pron pers* elle §85; soi §85; elle-même §86; se §87

hesitan·cy ['hɛzɪtənsi] *s* (*pl* -cies) hésitation *f*

hesitant ['hɛzɪtənt] *adj* hésitant

hesitate ['hɛzɪ‚tet] *intr* hésiter

hesitation [‚hɛzɪ'teʃən] *s* hésitation *f*

heterodox ['hɛtərə‚daks] *adj* hétérodoxe

heterodyne ['hɛtərə‚daɪn] *adj* hétérodyne

heterogeneous [‚hɛtərə'dʒɪnɪ·əs] *adj* hétérogène

hew [hju] *v* (*pret* hewed; *pp* hewed or hewn) *tr* tailler, couper; to hew down abattre || *intr*—to hew close to the line (coll) agir dans les règles, être très méticuleux

hex [hɛks] *s* porte-guigne *m* || *tr* porter la guigne à

hey [he] *interj* hé!; attention!

hey'day' *s* meilleure période *f*, fleur *f*

hi [haɪ] *interj* salut!

hia·tus [haɪ'etəs] *s* (*pl* -tuses or -tus) (*gap*) lacune *f*; (*in a text; in verse*) hiatus *m*

hibernate ['haɪbər‚net] *intr* hiberner

hibiscus [hɪ'bɪskəs], [haɪ'bɪskəs] *s* hibiscus *m*, ketmie *f*

hiccough or hiccup ['hɪkəp] *s* hoquet *m* || *intr* hoqueter

hick [hɪk] (coll) *adj & s* rustaud *m*

hicko·ry ['hɪkəri] *s* (*pl* -ries) hickory *m*

hidden ['hɪdən] *adj* caché, dérobée; (*mysterious*) occulte

hide [haɪd] *s* peau *f*, cuir *m* || *v* (*pret* hid [hɪd]; *pp* hid or hidden ['hɪdən]) *tr* cacher; to hide s.th. from cacher q.ch. à || *intr* se cacher; to hide from se cacher à

hide'-and-seek' *s* cache-cache *m*

hide'bound' *adj* à l'esprit étroit

hideous ['hɪdɪ·əs] *adj* hideux

hide'-out' *s* (coll) repaire *m*, planque *f*

hiding ['haɪdɪŋ] *s* dissimulation *f*; (*punishment*) (coll) raclée *f*, rossée *f*; in hiding caché

hid'ing place' *s* cachette *f*

hierar·chy ['haɪ·ə‚rarki] *s* (*pl* -chies) hiérarchie *f*

hieroglyphic [‚haɪ·ərə'glɪfɪk] *adj* hiéroglyphique || *s* hiéroglyphe *m*

hi-fi ['haɪ'faɪ] *adj* (coll) de haute fidélité || *s* (coll) haute fidélité *f*

hi'-fi' fan' *s* (coll) fanatique *mf* de la haute fidélité

high [haɪ] *adj* haut; (*river, price, rate, temperature, opinion*) élevé; (*fever, wind*) fort; (*sea, wind*) gros; (*cheekbones*) saillant; (*sound*) aigu; (coll) gris; (culin) avancé; high and dry à sec; high and mighty prétentieux; to be high (coll) avoir son pompon || *s* (aut) prise *f* directe; on high en haut, dans le ciel || *adv* haut; à un prix élevé; high and low partout; to aim high viser haut; to come high se vendre cher

high' al'tar *s* maître-autel *m*

high'ball' *s* whisky *m* à l'eau

high' blood' pres'sure *s* hypertension *f*

high'born' *adj* de haute naissance

high'boy' *s* chiffonnier *m* semainier

high'brow' *adj & s* (slang) intellectuel *m*

high' chair' *s* chaise *f* d'enfant

high' command' *s* haut commandement *m*

high' cost of liv'ing *s* cherté *f* de la vie

high'er educa'tion ['haɪ·ər] *s* enseignement *m* supérieur

high'er-up' *s* (coll) supérieur *m* hiérarchique

high'est bid'der ['haɪ·ɪst] *s* dernier enchérisseur *m*

high' explo'sive *s* haut explosif *m*, explosif puissant

highfalutin [‚haɪfə'lutən] *adj* (coll) pompeux, ampoulé

high' fidel'ity *s* haute fidélité *f*

high' fre'quency *s* haute fréquence *f*

high' gear' *s* (aut) prise *f* directe

high'-grade' *adj* de qualité supérieure

high'-hand'ed *adj* autoritaire, arbitraire

high' hat' *s* chapeau *m* haut de forme

high'-hat' *adj* (coll) snob, poseur || high'-hat' *v* (*pret* & *pp* -hatted; *ger* -hatting) *tr* (coll) traiter de haut en bas

high'-heeled' *adj* à talons hauts

high' horse' *s* raideur *f* hautaine; to get up on one's high horse monter sur ses grands chevaux

high' jinks' [‚dʒɪŋks] *s* (slang) clownerie *f*, drôlerie *f*

high' jump' *s* saut *m* en hauteur

high'-key' *adj* (phot) lumineux

highland ['haɪlənd] *s* pays *m* de montagne; highlands hautes terres *fpl*

high' life' *s* grand monde *m*

high'light' *s* (*big moment*) clou *m*; highlights (*in a picture*) clairs *mpl* || *tr* mettre en vedette

highly ['haɪli] *adv* hautement; (*very*) extrêmement, fort; haut, e.g., highly colored haut en couleur; to think highly of avoir une bonne opinion de

High' Mass' *s* grand-messe *f*

high'-mind'ed *adj* magnanime, noble

highness ['haɪnɪs] *s* hauteur *f*; Highness Altesse *f*

high' noon' *s* plein midi *m*

high'-oc'tane *adj* à indice d'octane élevé

high'-pitched' *adj* aigu; (*roof*) à forte pente

high'-powered' *adj* de haute puissance

high'-pres'sure *adj* à haute pression; (fig) dynamique, persuasif || *tr* (coll) gonfler à bloc

high'-priced' *adj* de prix élevé

high' priest' *s* grand prêtre *m*; (fig) pontife *m*

high'road' *s* grand-route *f*; (fig) bonne voie *f*

high' school' *s* école *f* secondaire publique; (*in France*) lycée *m*

high'-school stu'dent *s* lycéen *m*; collégien *m*

high' sea' *s* houle *f*, grosse mer *f*; high seas haute mer

high' soci'ety *s* la haute société, le beau monde

high'-sound'ing *adj* pompeux, prétentieux
high'-speed' *adj* à grande vitesse
high'-spir'ited *adj* fougueux, plein d'entrain
high' spir'its *spl* gaieté *f*, entrain *m*
high' stakes' *spl*—**to play for high stakes** jouer gros jeu
high-strung ['haɪ'strʌŋ] *adj* tendu, nerveux
high'-test' gas'oline *s* supercarburant *m*
high' tide' *s* marée *f* haute, haute marée
high' time' *s* heure *f*, e.g., **it is high time for you to go** c'est certainement l'heure de votre départ; (slang) bombance *f*, bombe *f*
high' trea'son *s* haute trahison *f*
high' volt'age *s* haute tension *f*
high wa'ter *s* marée *f* haute, hautes eaux *fpl*
high'way' *s* grand-route *f*
high'way commis'sion *s* administration *f* des ponts et chaussées
high'way'man *s* (*pl* -men) voleur *m* de grand chemin
high'way map' *s* carte *f* routière
hijack ['haɪ,dʒæk] *tr* (coll) arrêter et voler sur la route; (coll) saisir de force; (*an airplane*) (coll) détourner
hijacker ['haɪ,dʒækər] *s* (coll) bandit *m*, bandit de grand chemin; (coll) pirate *m* de l'air, pirate aérien
hijacking ['haɪ,dʒækɪŋ] *s* (coll) piraterie *f* aérienne, détournement *m*
hike [haɪk] *s* excursion *f* à pied, voyage *m* pédestre; (*e.g., in rent*) hausse *f* || *tr* hausser, faire monter || *intr* faire de longues promenades à pied
hiker ['haɪkər] *s* excursionniste *mf* à pied, touriste *mf* pédestre
hilarious [hɪ'lɛrɪ·əs], [haɪ'lɛrɪ·əs] *adj* hilare, gai; (*joke*) hilarant
hill [hɪl] *s* colline *f*, coteau *m*; (*incline*) côte *f*; (mil) cote *f*; **over hill and dale** par monts et par vaux || *tr* (*a plant*) butter, chausser
hill'bil'ly *s* (*pl* -lies) montagnard *m* rustique
hillock ['hɪlək] *s* tertre *m*, butte *f*
hill'side' *s* versant *m*, coteau *m*
hill·y ['hɪli] *adj* (*comp* -ier; *super* -iest) montueux, accidenté; (*steep*) en pente, à fortes pentes
hilt [hɪlt] *s* poignée *f*; **up to the hilt** jusqu'à la garde
him [hɪm] *pron pers* lui §85, §87; le §87
him·self' *pron* lui §85; soi §85; lui-même §86; se §87
hind [haɪnd] *adj* postérieur, de derrière || *s* biche *f*
hinder ['hɪndər] *tr* empêcher
hind'most' *adj* dernier, ultime
hind'quar'ter *s* arrière-train *m*, train *m* de derrière; (*of horse*) arrière-main *m*
hindrance ['hɪndrəns] *s* empêchement *m*
hind'sight' *s* (*of firearm*) hausse *f*; compréhension *f* tardive

Hindu ['hɪndu] *adj* hindou || *s* Hindou *m*
hinge [hɪndʒ] *s* charnière *f*, gond *m*; (*of mollusk*) charnière; (bb) onglet *m* || *intr*—**to hinge on** axer sur, dépendre de
hin·ny ['hɪni] *s* (*pl* -nies) bardot *m*
hint [hɪnt] *s* insinuation *f*; (*small quantity*) soupçon *m*; **to take the hint** comprendre à demi-mot, accepter le conseil || *tr* insinuer || *intr* procéder par insinuation; **to hint at** laisser entendre
hinterland ['hɪntər,lænd] *s* arrière-pays *m*
hip [hɪp] *adj* (slang) à la page, dans le train; **to be hip to** (slang) être au courant de || *s* hanche *f*; (*of roof*) arête *f*
hip'bone' *s* os *m* coxal, os de la hanche
hipped *adj*—**to be hipped on** (coll) avoir la manie de
hippety-hop ['hɪpɪtɪ'hɑp] *adv* (coll) en sautillant
hip·po ['hɪpo] *s* (*pl* -pos) (coll) hippopotame *m*
hippopota·mus [,hɪpə'pɑtəməs] *s* (*pl* -muses or -mi [,maɪ]) hippopotame *m*
hip' roof' *s* toit *m* en croupe
hire [haɪr] *s* (*salary*) gages *mpl*; (*renting*) louage *m*; **for hire** à louer; **in the hire of** aux gages de || *tr* (*a person*) engager, embaucher; (*to rent*) louer, prendre en location || *intr*—**to hire out** (*said of person*) se louer, entrer en service
hired' girl' *s* servante *f*, servante de ferme
hired' man' *s* (*pl* men') (coll) valet *m* de ferme, garçon *m* de ferme
hireling ['haɪrlɪŋ] *adj* & *s* mercenaire *m*
hiring ['haɪrɪŋ] *s* embauchage *m*
his [hɪz] *adj poss* son §88 || *pron poss* le sien §89
Hispanic [hɪs'pænɪk] *adj* hispanique
Hispanist ['hɪspənɪst], [hɪs'pænɪst] *s* hispanisant *m*
hiss [hɪs] *s* sifflement *m* || *tr* & *intr* siffler
hist [hɪst] *interj* psitt!, pst!
histology [hɪs'talədʒi] *s* histologie *f*
historian [hɪs'tɔrɪ·ən] *s* historien *m*
historic(al) [hɪs'tarɪk(əl)], [hɪs'tɔrɪk(əl)] *adj* historique
histo·ry ['hɪstəri] *s* (*pl* -ries) histoire *f*
histrionic [,hɪstrɪ'anɪk] *adj* théâtral || **histrionics** *s* art *m* du théâtre; (fig) attitude *f* spectaculaire
hit [hɪt] *s* coup *m*; (*blow that hits its mark*) coup au but, coup heureux; (*sarcastic remark*) coup de patte, trait *m* satirique; (*on the hit parade*) tube *m*; (baseball) coup de batte; (theat) succès *m*, spectacle *m* très couru; (coll) réussite *f*; **to make a hit** (coll) faire sensation || *v* (*pret* & *pp* hit; *ger* hitting) *tr* frapper; (*the mark*) atteindre; (*e.g., a car*) heurter, heurter contre; (*to move the emotions of*) toucher; **to hit it off** (coll)

s'entendre, se trouver d'accord ‖ *intr* frapper; **to hit on** tomber sur, trouver
hit′-and-run′ driv′er *s* chauffard *m* qui abandonne la scène d'un accident, qui prend la fuite
hitch [hɪtʃ] *s* saccade *f*, secousse *f*; obstacle *m*, difficulté *f*; (*knot*) nœud *m*, e.g., **timber hitch** nœud de bois; **without a hitch** sans accroc ‖ *tr* accrocher; (*naut*) nouer; **to hitch up** (*e.g., a horse*) atteler
hitch′hike′ *intr* (coll) faire de l'autostop
hitch′hik′er *s* auto-stoppeur *m*
hitch′hik′ing *s* auto-stop *m*
hitch′ing post′ *s* poteau *m* d'attache
hither [ˈhɪðər] *adv* ici; **hither and thither** çà et là
hith′er·to′ *adv* jusqu'ici, jusqu'à présent
hit′-or-miss′ *adj* capricieux, éventuel
hit′ parade′ *s* (coll) chansons *fpl* populaires du moment
hit′ rec′ord *s* (coll) disque *m* à succès
hive [haɪv] *s* ruche *f*; **hives** (pathol) urticaire *f*
hoard [hord] *s* entassement *m*, trésor *m* ‖ *tr* accumuler secrètement, thésauriser ‖ *intr* accumuler, entasser, thésauriser
hoarding [ˈhordɪŋ] *s* accumulation *f* secrète, thésaurisation *f*
hoarfrost [ˈhorˌfrɔst] *s* givre *m*, gelée *f* blanche
hoarse [hors] *adj* enroué, rauque
hoarseness [ˈhorsnɪs] *s* enrouement *m*
hoar·y [ˈhori] *adj* (*comp* **-ier**; *super* **-iest**) chenu, blanchi
hoax [hoks] *s* mystification *f*, canard *m* ‖ *tr* mystifier
hob [hɑb] *s* (*of fireplace*) plaque *f*; **to play hob** (coll) causer des ennuis; **to play hob with** (coll) bouleverser
hobble [ˈhɑbəl] *s* (*limp*) boitillement *m*; (*rope used to tie legs of animal*) entrave *f* ‖ *tr* faire boiter; (*e.g., a horse*) entraver ‖ *intr* boiter, clocher
hob·by [ˈhɑbi] *s* (*pl* **-bies**) distraction *f*, violon *m* d'Ingres; (orn) hobereau *m*; **to ride one's hobby** enfourcher son dada
hob′by·horse′ *s* cheval *m* de bois
hob′gob′lin *s* lutin *m*; (*bogy*) épouvantail *m*
hob′nail′ *s* caboche *f*
hob·nob [ˈhɑbˌnɑb] *v* (*pret & pp* **-nobbed**; *ger* **-nobbing**) *intr* trinquer ensemble; **to hobnob with** être à tu et à toi avec
ho·bo [ˈhobo] *s* (*pl* **-bos** or **-boes**) chemineau *m*, vagabond *m*
hock [hɑk] *s* (*of horse*) jarret *m*; (*wine*) vin *m* du Rhin; (*pawn*) (coll) gage *m*; **in hock** (coll) au clou; (*in prison*) (coll) au bloc ‖ *tr* couper le jarret à; (*to pawn*) (coll) mettre en gage, mettre au clou
hockey [ˈhɑki] *s* hockey *m*
hock′shop′ *s* (slang) mont-de-piété *m*, clou *m*
hocus-pocus [ˈhokəsˈpokəs] *s* tour *m* de passe-passe; (*meaningless formula*) abracadabra *m*

hod [hɑd] *s* oiseau *m*, auge *f*
hod′ car′rier *s* aide-maçon *m*
hodgepodge [ˈhɑdʒˌpɑdʒ] *s* salmigondis *m*, méli-mélo *m*
hoe [ho] *s* houe *f*, binette *f* ‖ *tr* houer, biner
hog [hɑg], [hɔg] *s* pourceau *m*, porc *m*; (*pig*) cochon ‖ *v* (*pret & pp* **hogged**; *ger* **hogging**) *tr* (slang) s'emparer de, saisir avidement
hog′back′ *s* dos *m* d'âne
hoggish [ˈhɑgɪʃ], [ˈhɔgɪʃ] *adj* glouton
hogs′head′ *s* barrique *f*
hog′wash′ *s* eaux *fpl* grasses; vinasse *f*; (fig) boniments *mpl* à la noix de coco
hoist [hɔɪst] *s* monte-charge *m*, grue *f*; (*shove*) poussée *f* vers le haut ‖ *tr* lever, guinder; (*a flag, sail, boat, etc.*) hisser
hoity-toity [ˈhɔɪtiˈtɔɪti] *adj* hautain; **to be hoity-toity** le prendre de haut
hokum [ˈhokəm] *s* (coll) boniments *mpl*, fumisterie *f*
hold [hold] *s* prise *f*; (*handle*) poignée *f*, manche *m*; (*domination*) pouvoir *m*, autorité *f*; (mus) point *m* d'orgue; (naut) cale *f*; **hold for arrival** (formula on envelope) garder jusqu'à l'arrivée; **to take hold of** empoigner, saisir ‖ *v* (*pret & pp* **held** [held]) *tr* tenir; (*one's breath; s.o.'s attention*) retenir; (*to contain*) contenir; (*a job; a title*) avoir, posséder; (*e.g., a university chair*) occuper; (*a fort*) défendre; (*a note*) (mus) tenir, prolonger; **to be held to be . . .** passer pour . . . ; **to hold back** or **in** retenir; **to hold one's own** rivaliser, se défendre; **to hold out** tendre, offrir; **to hold over** continuer, remettre; **to hold s.o. to be . . .** tenir qn pour . . . ; **to hold s.o. to his word** obliger qn à tenir sa promesse; **to hold up** (*to delay*) retarder; (*to keep from falling*) retenir, soutenir; (*to rob*) (coll) voler à main armée ‖ *intr* (*to hold good*) rester valable, rester en vigueur; **hold on!** (telp) restez en ligne!; **to hold back** se retenir, hésiter; **to hold forth** disserter; **to hold off** se tenir à distance; **to hold on** or **out** tenir bon; **to hold on to** s'accrocher à, se cramponner à; **to hold out for** insister pour
holder [ˈholdər] *s* possesseur *m*; (*of stock*) porteur *m*; (*of stock; of a record*) détenteur *m*; (*of degree, fellowship, etc.*) impétrant *m*; (*for a cigarette*) porte-cigarettes *m*; (*of a post, a right, etc.*) titulaire *mf*; (*for holding, e.g., a hot dish*) poignée *f*
holding [ˈholdɪŋ] *s* possession *f*; **holdings** valeurs *fpl*; (*of an investor*) portefeuille *m*; (*of a landlord*) propriétés *fpl*
hold′ing com′pany *s* holding trust *m*, holding *m*
hold′up′ *s* (*stop, delay*) arrêt *m*; (coll) attaque *f* à main armée, hold-up *m*; **what's the holdup?** (coll) qu'est-ce qu'on attend?
hole [hol] *s* trou *m*; **in the hole** (coll)

dans l'embarras; **to burn a hole in s.o.'s pocket** (coll) brûler la poche à qn; **to get s.o. out of a hole** (coll) tirer qn d'un mauvais pas; **to pick holes in** (coll) trouver à redire à, démolir; **to wear holes in** (*e.g., a garment*) trouer || *intr*—**to hole up** se terrer

holiday ['hɑlɪ‚de] *s* jour *m* de fête, jour férié; (*vacation*) vacances *fpl*

holiness ['holɪnɪs] *s* sainteté *f*; **His Holiness** Sa Sainteté

holla ['hɑlə], [hə'lɑ] *interj* holà!

Holland ['hɑlənd] *s* Hollande *f*; la Hollande

Hollander ['hɑləndər] *s* Hollandais *m*

hollow ['hɑlo] *adj & s* creux *m* || *adv* —**to beat all hollow** (coll) battre à plate couture || *tr* creuser

hol·ly ['hɑli] *s* (*pl* **-lies**) houx *m*

hol′ly·hock′ *s* primerose *f*, rose *f* trémière

holm′ oak′ [hom] *s* yeuse *f*

holocaust ['hɑlə‚kɔst] *s* (*sacrifice*) holocauste *m*; (*disaster*) sinistre *m*

holster ['holstər] *s* étui *m*; (*on saddle*) fonte *f*

ho·ly ['holi] *adj* (*comp* **-lier**; *super* **-liest**) saint; (*e.g., water*) bénit

Ho′ly Ghost′ *s* Saint-Esprit *m*

ho′ly or′ders *spl* ordres *mpl* sacrés

Ho′ly Scrip′ture *s* l'Écriture *f* Sainte

Ho′ly See′ *s* Saint-Siège *m*

ho′ly wa′ter *s* eau *f* bénite

Ho′ly Writ′ *s* l'Écriture *f* Sainte

homage ['hɑmɪdʒ], ['ɑmɪdʒ] *s* hommage *m*

home [hom] *adj* domestique; national, natal || *s* foyer *m*, chez-soi *m*, domicile *m*; (*house*) maison *f*; (*of the arts; native land*) patrie *f*; (*for the sick, poor, etc.*) asile *m*, foyer, hospice *m*; **at home** à la maison; (*at ease*) à l'aise; **make yourself at home** faites comme chez vous || *adv* à la maison; **to see s.o. home** raccompagner qn jusqu'à chez lui; **to strike home** frapper juste, toucher au vif

home′ address′ *s* adresse *f* personnelle

home′bod′y *s* (*pl* **-ies**) casanier *m*, pantouflard *m*

homebred ['hom‚brɛd] *adj* élevé à la maison; du pays, indigène

home′-brew′ *s* boisson *f* faite à la maison

home′com′ing *s* retour *m* au foyer; (*at university, church, etc.*) journée *f* or semaine *f* des anciens

home′ coun′try *s* pays *m* natal

home′ deliv′ery *s* livraison *f* à domicile

home′ econom′ics *s* économie *f* domestique; (*instruction*) enseignement *m* ménager

home′ front′ *s* théâtre *m* d'opérations à l'intérieur du pays

home′land′ *s* patrie *f*, pays *m* natal

homeless ['homlɪs] *adj* sans foyer

home′ life′ *s* vie *f* familiale

home′like′ *adj* familial, comme chez soi

home′-lov′ing *adj* casanier

home·ly ['homli] *adj* (*comp* **-lier**; *super* **-liest**) (*not good-looking*) laid, vilain; (*not elegant*) sans façons

home′made′ *adj* fait à la maison, de ménage

home′mak′er *s* maîtresse *f* de maison, ménagère *f*

home′ of′fice *s* siège *m* social

homeopathy [‚homɪ'ɑpəθi], [‚hɑmɪ'ɑpəθi] *s* homéopathie *f*

home′own′er *s* propriétaire *mf*

home′ plate′ *s* (baseball) marbre *m* (Canad)

home′ port′ *s* port *m* d'attache

home′ rule′ *s* autonomie *f*, gouvernement *m* autonome

home′sick′ *adj* nostalgique; **to be homesick** avoir le mal du pays

home′sick′ness *s* mal *m* du pays, nostalgie *f*

homespun ['hom‚spʌn] *adj* filé à la maison; (fig) simple, sans apprêt

home′stead *s* bien *m* de famille, ferme *f*

home′stretch′ *s* fin *f* de course, dernière étape *f*

home′ team′ *s* locaux *mpl*, équipe *f* qui reçoit

home′town′ *s* ville *f* natale

homeward ['homwərd] *adj* de retour || *adv* vers la maison; vers son pays

home′work′ *s* travail *m* à la maison; devoirs *mpl*

homey ['homi] *adj* (*comp* **homier**; *super* **homiest**) (coll) familial, intime

homicidal [‚hɑmɪ'saɪdəl] *adj* homicide

homicide ['hɑmɪ‚saɪd] *s* (*act*) homicide *m*; (*person*) homicide *mf*

homi·ly ['hɑmɪli] *s* (*pl* **-lies**) homélie *f*

hom′ing head′ *s* (*of missile*) tête *f* chercheuse

hom′ing pi′geon *s* pigeon *m* voyageur

hominy ['hɑmɪni] *s* semoule *f* de maïs

homogeneous [‚homə'dʒɪnɪ·əs], [‚hɑmə'dʒɪnɪ·əs] *adj* homogène

homogenize [hɑ'mɑdʒə‚naɪz] *tr* homogénéiser

homonym ['hɑmənɪm] *s* homonyme *m*

homonymous [hə'mɑnɪməs] *adj* homonyme

homosexual [‚homə'sɛkʃu·əl] *adj & s* homosexuel *m*

hone [hon] *s* pierre *f* à aiguiser || *tr* aiguiser, affiler

honest ['ɑnɪst] *adj* honnête; (*money*) honnêtement acquis

honesty ['ɑnɪsti] *s* honnêteté *f*; (bot) monnaie *f* du pape

hon·ey ['hʌni] *s* miel *m* || *v* (*pret & pp* **-eyed** or **-ied**) *tr* emmieller

hon′ey·bee′ *s* abeille *f* à miel

hon′ey·comb′ *s* rayon *m*, gâteau *m* de cire; (*anything like a honeycomb*) nid *m* d'abeilles || *tr* cribler

honeyed *adj* emmiellé

hon′ey·moon′ *s* lune *f* de miel; voyage *m* de noces || *intr* passer la lune de miel

hon′ey·suck′le *s* chèvrefeuille *m*

honk [hɑŋk], [hɔŋk] *s* (aut) klaxon *m* || *tr* (*the horn*) sonner || *intr* klaxonner

honkytonk ['haŋki‚taŋk], ['hɔŋki-‚tɔŋk] *s* (slang) boui-boui *m*
honor ['anər] *s* honneur *m*; (*award*) distinction *f*; **honors** honneurs ǁ *tr* honorer
honorable ['anərəbəl] *adj* honorable
hon'orable dis'charge *s* (mil) démobilisation *f* honorable
honorari·um [‚anə'rɛrɪ·əm] *s* (*pl* -ums or -a [ə]) *s* honoraires *mpl*
honorary ['anə‚rɛri] *adj* honoraire
honorific [‚anə'rɪfɪk] *adj* honorifique ǁ *s* formule *f* de politesse
hood [hʊd] *s* capuchon *m*, chaperon *m*; (*of chimney*) hotte *f*; (*academic hood*) capuce *m*; (aut) capot *m*; (slang) gangster *m* ǁ *tr* capoter
hoodlum ['hudləm] *s* (coll) chenapan *m*
hoodoo ['hudu] *s* (*bad luck*) guigne *f*; (*rites*) vaudou *m* ǁ *tr* porter la guigne à
hood'wink' *tr* tromper, abuser
hooey ['hu·i] *s* (slang) blague *f*
hoof [huf], [hʊf] *s* sabot *m*; **on the hoof** sur pied ǁ *tr*—**to hoof it** (coll) aller à pied
hoof'beat' *s* pas *m* de cheval
hook [hʊk] *s* crochet *m*; (*for fishing*) hameçon *m*; (*to join two things*) croc *m*; (*boxing*) crochet *m*; **by hook or by crook** (coll) de bric ou de broc, coûte que coûte; **hook line and sinker** (coll) tout à fait, avec tout le bataclan; **to get one's hooks on to** (coll) mettre le grappin sur ǁ *tr* accrocher; (*e.g., a dress*) agrafer; (*e.g., a boat*) crocher, gaffer; (slang) amorcer, attraper; **to hook up** agrater; (*e.g., a loudspeaking system*) monter ǁ *intr* s'accrocher
hookah ['hʊkə] *s* narguilé *m*
hook' and eye' *s* agrafe *f* et porte *f*
hook' and lad'der *s* camion *m* équipé d'une échelle d'incendie
hooked' rug' *s* tapis *m* à points noués
hook'up' *s* (*diagram*) (rad, telv) montage *m*; (*network*) (rad, telv) chaîne *f*
hook'worm' *s* ankylostome *m*
hooky ['hʊki] *s*—**to play hooky** (coll) faire l'école buissonnière
hooligan ['hulɪgən] *s* voyou *m*
hooliganism ['hulɪgən‚ɪzəm] *s* voyouterie *f*
hoop [hup], [hʊp] *s* cerceau *m*; (*of cask*) cercle *m* ǁ *tr* cercler, entourer
hoop' skirt' *s* crinoline *f*
hoot [hut] *s* huée *f*; (*of owl*) ululement *m* ǁ *tr* huer ǁ *intr* huer; (*said of owl*) ululer; **to hoot at** huer
hoot' owl' *s* chat-huant *m*, hulotte *f*
hop [hap] *s* saut *m*; (*dance*) (coll) sauterie *f*, surboum *m*; (coll) vol *m* en avion, étape *f*; **hops** (bot) houblon *m* ǁ *v* (*pret & pp* **hopped**; *ger* **hopping**) *tr* sauter, franchir; (*e.g., a taxi*) (coll) prendre ǁ *intr* sauter, sautiller; **to hop on one foot** sauter a clochepied; **to hop over** sauter
hope [hop] *s* (*feeling of hope*) espérance *f*; (*instance of hope*) espoir *m*; (*person or thing one puts one's hope in*) espérance, espoir ǁ *tr & intr*

espérer; **to hope for** espérer; **to hope to** + *inf* espérer + *inf*
hope' chest' *s* trousseau *m*
hopeful ['hopfəl] *adj* (*feeling hope*) plein d'espoir; (*giving hope*) prometteur
hopeless ['hoplɪs] *adj* sans espoir
hopper ['hapər] *s* (*funnel-shaped container*) trémie *f*; (*of blast furnace*) gueulard *m*
hop'per car' *s* wagon-trémie *m*
hop'scotch' *s* marelle *f*
horde [hord] *s* horde *f*
horehound ['hor‚haʊnd] *s* (bot) marrube *m*
horizon [hə'raɪzən] *s* horizon *m*
horizontal [‚harɪ'zantəl], [‚hɔrɪ'zantəl] *adj* horizontal ǁ *s* horizontale *f*
hor'izon'tal hold' *s* (telv) commande *f* de stabilité horizontale
hormone ['hɔrmon] *s* hormone *f*
horn [hɔrn] *s* (*bony projection on head of certain animals*) corne *f*; (*of anvil*) bigorne *f*; (*of auto*) klaxon *m*; (*of snail; of insect*) antenne *f*; (mus) cor *m*; (*French horn*) (mus) cor d'harmonie; **horns** (*of deer*) bois *m*; **to blow one's own horn** (coll) se vanter, exalter son propre mérite; **to draw in one's horns** (fig) rentrer les cornes; **to toot the horn** corner ǁ *intr*—**to horn in** (slang) intervenir sans façon
horn'beam' *s* (bot) charme *m*
horned' owl' *s* duc *m*
hornet ['hɔrnɪt] *s* frelon *m*
hor'net's nest' *s* guêpier *m*
horn' of plen'ty *s* corne *f* d'abondance
horn'pipe' *s* chalumeau *m*; (*dance*) matelote *f*
horn'rimmed' glas'ses *spl* lunettes *fpl* à monture en corne
horn·y ['hɔrni] *adj* (*comp* -ier; *super* -iest) corné, en corne; (*callous*) calleux; (*horned*) cornu
horoscope ['harə‚skop], ['hɔrə‚skop] *s* horoscope *m*; **to cast s.o.'s horoscope** tirer l'horoscope de qn
horrible ['harɪbəl], ['hɔrɪbəl] *adj* horrible; (coll) horrible, détestable
horrid ['harɪd], ['hɔrɪd] *adj* affreux; (coll) affreux, très désagréable
horri·fy ['harɪ‚faɪ], ['hɔrɪ‚faɪ] *v* (*pret & pp* -fied) *tr* horrifier
horror ['harər], ['hɔrər] *s* horreur *f*; **to have a horror of** avoir horreur de
hors d'oeuvre [ɔr'dʌrv] *s* (*pl* **hors d'oeuvres** [ɔr'dʌrvz]) hors-d'œuvre *m*
horse [hɔrs] *s* cheval *m*; (*of carpenter*) chevalet *m*; **hold your horses!** (coll) arrêtez un moment!; **to back the wrong horse** (coll) miser sur le mauvais cheval; **to be a horse of another color** (coll) être une autre paire de manches; **to eat like a horse** (coll) manger comme un ogre; **to ride a horse** monter à cheval ǁ *intr*—**to horse around** (slang) muser, se baguenauder
horse'back' *s*—**on horseback** à cheval ǁ *adv*—**to ride horseback** monter à cheval

horse'back rid'ing s équitation f, exercice m à cheval
horse' blan'ket s couverture f de cheval
horse' break'er s dompteur m de chevaux
horse'car' s tramway m à chevaux
horse' chest'nut s (tree) marronnier m d'Inde; (nut) marron m d'Inde
horse'cloth' s housse f
horse' coll'ar s collier m de cheval
horse' deal'er s marchand m de chevaux
horse' doc'tor s (coll) vétérinaire m
horse' fly' s (pl flies) taon m
horse'hair' s crin m
horse'hide' s peau f or cuir m de cheval
horse'laugh' s gros rire m bruyant
horse'less car'riage ['hɔrslɪs] s voiture f sans chevaux
horse'man s (pl -men) cavalier m; (at race track) turfiste m
horsemanship ['hɔrsmənˌʃɪp] s équitation f
horse' meat' s viande f de cheval
horse' op'era s (coll) western m
horse' pis'tol s pistolet m d'arçon
horse'play' s jeu m de mains, clownerie f
horse'pow'er s (746 watts) cheval-vapeur anglais
horse' race' s course f de chevaux
horse'rad'ish s raifort m
horse' sense' s (coll) gros bon sens m
horse'shoe' s fer m à cheval
horse'shoe'ing s ferrure f, ferrage m
horse'shoe mag'net s aimant m en fer à cheval
horse' show' s exposition f de chevaux, concours m hippique
horse'tail' s queue f de cheval; (bot) prêle f
horse' thief' s voleur m de chevaux
horse' trad'er s maquignon m
horse' trad'ing s maquignonnage m
horse'whip' s cravache f ‖ v (pret & pp -whipped; ger -whipping) tr cravacher
horse'wom'an s (pl -wom'en) s cavalière f, amazone f
hors•y ['hɔrsi] adj (comp -ier; super -iest) chevalin; (coll) hippomane; (awkward in appearance) (coll) maladroit
horticultural [ˌhɔrtɪ'kʌltərəl] adj horticole
horticulture ['hɔrtɪˌkʌltʃər] s horticulture f
hose [hoz] s (flexible tube) tuyau m ‖ s (pl hose) (stocking) bas m; (sock) chaussette f
hosier ['hoʒər] s bonnetier m
hosiery ['hoʒəri] s la bonneterie; (stockings) les bas mpl
hospice ['haspɪs] s hospice m
hospitable ['haspɪtəbəl], [has'pɪtəbəl] adj hospitalier
hospital ['haspɪtəl] s hôpital m, clinique f, maison f de santé
hospitali•ty [ˌhaspɪ'tælɪti] s (pl -ties) hospitalité f

hospitalize ['haspɪtəˌlaɪz] tr hospitaliser
hos'pital plane' s avion m sanitaire
hos'pital ship' s navire-hôpital m
hos'pital train' s train m sanitaire
host [host] s hôte m; (who entertains dinner guests) amphitryon m; (multitude) foule f, légion f; (army) armée f; **Host** (eccl) hostie f
hostage ['hastɪdʒ] s otage m
hostel ['hastəl] s hôtellerie f; (youth hostel) auberge f de la jeunesse
hostel•ry ['hastəlri] s (pl -ries) hôtellerie f
hostess ['hostɪs] s hôtesse f; (taxi dancer) entraîneuse f
hostile ['hastɪl] adj hostile
hostili•ty [has'tɪlɪti] s (pl -ties) hostilité f
hostler ['haslər], ['aslər] s palefrenier m, valet m d'écurie
hot [hat] adj (comp hotter; super hottest) chaud; (spicy) piquant; (fight, pursuit, etc.) acharné; (in rut) en chaleur; (radioactive) (coll) fortement radioactif; **hot off** (e.g., the press) (coll) sortant tout droit de; **to be hot** (said of person) avoir chaud; (said of weather) faire chaud; **to get hot under the collar** (coll) s'emporter; **to make it hot for** (coll) rendre la vie intenable à, harceler
hot' air' s (slang) hâblerie f, discours mpl vides
hot'-air' fur'nace s calorifère m à air chaud
hot' and cold' run'ning wa'ter s eau f courante chaude et froide
hot'bed' s (hort) couche f, couche de fumier; (e.g., of vice) foyer m; (e.g., of intrigue) officine f
hot'-blood'ed adj au sang fougueux
hot'box' s (rr) coussinet m échauffé
hot' cake' s crêpe f; **to sell like hot cakes** (coll) se vendre comme des petits pains
hot' dog' s saucisse f de Francfort, saucisse chaude
hotel [ho'tɛl] adj hôtelier ‖ s hôtel m
hotel'keep'er s hôtelier m
hot'foot' adv (coll) à toute vitesse ‖ tr —**to hotfoot it after** (coll) s'élancer à la poursuite de
hot'head'ed adj exalté, fougueux
hot'house' s serre f chaude
hot' pad' s (for plates at table) garde-nappe m, dessous-de-plat m
hot' pep'per s piment m rouge
hot' plate' s réchaud m
hot' rod' s (slang) bolide m
hot' rod'der [ˌradər] s (slang) bolide m, casse-cou m
hot' springs' spl sources fpl thermales
hot'-temp'ered adj coléreux, irascible
hot' wa'ter s (coll) mauvaise passe f; **to be in hot water** (coll) être dans le pétrin
hot'-wa'ter boil'er s chaudière f à eau chaude
hot'-wa'ter bot'tle s bouillotte f
hot'-wa'ter heat'er s calorifère m à eau

chaude; (*with instantaneous delivery of hot water*) chauffe-eau *m*

hot′-wa′ter heat′ing *s* chauffage *m* par eau chaude

hot′-wa′ter tank′ *s* réservoir *m* d'eau chaude, bâche *f*

hound [haund] *s* chien *m* de chasse, chien courant; **to follow the hounds** or **to ride to hounds** chasser à courre ‖ *tr* poursuivre avec ardeur, pourchasser

hour [aur] *s* heure *f*; **by the hour** à l'heure; **on the hour** à l'heure sonnante; **to keep late hours** se coucher tard

hour′glass′ *s* sablier *m*

hour′-glass fig′ure *s* taille *f* de guêpe

hour′ hand′ *s* petite aiguille *f*, aiguille des heures

hourly ['aurli] *adj* à l'heure, horaire ‖ *adv* toutes les heures; (*hour by hour*) d'heure en heure

house [haus] *s* (*pl* **houses** ['hauzɪz]) maison *f*; (*legislative body*) chambre *f*; (*theat*) salle *f*, e.g., **full house** salle comble; **to be on the house** (coll) être au frais du patron; **to bring down the house** (theat) faire crouler la salle sous les applaudissements; **to keep house for** tenir la maison de; **to put one's house in order** (fig) mettre de l'ordre dans ses affaires ‖ [hauz] *tr* loger, abriter

house′ arrest′ *s*—**under house arrest** en résidence surveillée

house′boat′ *s* bateau-maison *m*

house′boy′ *s* boy *m*

house′break′er *s* cambrioleur *m*

house′break′ing *s* effraction *f*, cambriolage *m*

housebroken ['haus,brokən] *adj* (*dog or cat*) dressé à la propreté

house′ clean′ing *s* grand nettoyage *m* de la maison

house′coat′ *s* peignoir *m*

house′ cur′rent *s* courant *m* de secteur, secteur *m*

house′fly′ *s* (*pl* -**flies**) mouche *f* domestique

houseful ['haus,ful] *s* pleine maison *f*

house′ fur′nishings *spl* ménage *m*

house′hold′ *adj* domestique, du ménage ‖ *s* ménage *m*, maisonnée *f*

house′hold′er *s* chef *m* de famille, maître *m* de maison

house′ hunt′ing *s* chasse *f* aux appartements

house′keep′er *s* ménagère *f*; (*employee*) femme *f* de charge; (*for a bachelor*) gouvernante *f*

house′keep′ing *s* le ménage, l'économie *f* domestique; **to set up housekeeping** se mettre en ménage

house′maid′ *s* bonne *f*

house′moth′er *s* maîtresse *f* d'internat

house′ of cards′ *s* château *m* de cartes

House′ of Com′mons *s* Chambre *f* des communes

house′ of ill′ repute′ *s* maison *f* mal famée, maison borgne

House′ of Represen′tatives *s* Chambre *f* des Représentants

house′ paint′er *s* peintre *m* en bâtiments

house′ physi′cian *s* (*in hospital*) interne *m*; (e.g., *in hotel*) médecin *m*

house′top′ *s* toit *m*; **to shout from the housetops** (coll) crier sur les toits

house′ trail′er *s* caravane *f*

house′warm′ing *s*—**to have a housewarming** pendre la crémaillère

house′wife′ *s* (*pl* -**wives′**) maîtresse *f* de maison, ménagère *f*

house′work′ *s* travaux *mpl* ménagers; **to do the housework** faire le ménage

housing ['hauzɪŋ] *s* logement *m*, habitation *f*; (*horsecloth*) housse *f*; (mach) enchâssure *f*, carter *m*

hous′ing devel′opment *s* (*houses*) grand ensemble *m*, habitations *fpl* neuves; (*apartments*) cité *f*

hous′ing short′age *s* crise *f* du logement

hovel ['hʌvəl], ['havəl] *s* bicoque *f*, masure *f*; (*shed for cattle, tools, etc.*) appentis *m*

hover ['hʌvər], ['havər] *intr* planer, voltiger; (*to move to and fro near a person*) papillonner; (*to hang around threateningly*) rôder; (*said of smile on lips*) errer; hésiter

how [hau] *s* comment *m*; **the how, the when, and the wherefore** (coll) tous les détails ‖ *adv* comment; **how** + *adj* quel + *adj*, e.g., **how beautiful a morning!** quelle belle matinée!; comme + c'est + *adj*, e.g., **how beautiful it is!** comme c'est beau!; que + c'est + *adj*, e.g., **how beautiful it is!** que c'est beau!; **how are you?** comment allez-vous?, ça va?; **how early** quand, à quelle heure; **how else** de quelle autre manière; **how far** jusqu'où; à quelle distance, e.g., **how far is it?** à quelle distance est-ce?; **how long** (*in time*) jusqu'à quand, combien de temps; **how long is the stick?** quelle est la longueur du bâton?; **how many** combien; **how much** combien; (*at what price*) à combien; **how often** combien de fois; **how old are you?** quel âge avez-vous?; **how soon** quand, à quelle heure; **to know how to** savoir

how-do-you-do ['haudəjə'du] *s*—**that's a fine how-do-you-do!** (coll) en voilà une affaire!

how·ev′er *adv* cependant, pourtant, toutefois; **however little it may be** si peu que ce soit; **however much** or **many it may be** autant que ce soit; **however pretty she may be** quelque jolie qu'elle soit; **however that may be** quoi qu'il en soit ‖ *conj* comme, e.g., **do it however you want** faites-le comme vous voudrez

howitzer ['hau·ɪtsər] *s* obusier *m*

howl [haul] *s* hurlement *m* ‖ *tr* hurler; **to howl down** faire taire en poussant des huées ‖ *intr* hurler; (*said of wind*) mugir

howler ['haulər] *s* hurleur *m*; (coll) grosse gaffe *f*, bourde *f*, bévue *f*

hoyden ['hɔɪdən] *s* petite coquine *f*

H.P. or **hp** *abbr* (**horsepower**) CV
hub [hʌb] *s* moyeu *m*; (fig) centre *m*
hubbub ['hʌbəb] *s* vacarme *m*, tumulte *m*
hub'cap' *s* enjoliveur *m*, chapeau *m* de roue
huckster ['hʌkstər] *s* (*peddler*) camelot *m*; (*adman*) publicitaire *mf*
huddle ['hʌdəl] *s* (coll) conférence *f* secrète; **to go into a huddle** (coll) entrer en conclave ‖ *intr* s'entasser, se presser
hue [hju] *s* teinte *f*, nuance *f*
hue' and cry' *s* clameur *f* de haro; **with hue and cry** à cor et à cri
huff [hʌf] *s* accès *m* de colère; **in a huff** vexé, offensé
hug [hʌg] *s* étreinte *f* ‖ *v* (*pret & pp* **hugged**; *ger* **hugging**) *tr* étreindre; (*e.g., the coast*) serrer; (*e.g., the wall*) raser ‖ *intr* s'étreindre
huge [hjudʒ] *adj* énorme, immense
huh [hʌ] *interj* hein!, hé!
hulk [hʌlk] *s* (*body of an old ship*) carcasse *f*; (*old ship used as warehouse, prison, etc.*) ponton *m*; (*heavy, unwieldy person*) mastodonte *m*
hull [hʌl] *s* (*of certain vegetables*) cosse *f*; (*of nuts*) écale *f*; (*of ship or hydroplane*) coque *f* ‖ *tr* (*e.g., peas*) écosser; (*e.g., almonds*) écaler
hullabaloo ['hʌləbə‚lu], [‚hʌləbə'lu] *s* (coll) boucan *m*, brouhaha *m*
hum [hʌm] *s* (*e.g., of bee*) bourdonnement *m*; (*e.g., of motor*) vrombissement *m*; (*of singer*) fredonnement *m* ‖ *v* (*pret & pp* **hummed**; *ger* **humming**) *tr* (*a melody*) fredonner, chantonner ‖ *intr* (*said of bee*) bourdonner; (*said of machine*) vrombir; (*said of singer*) fredonner, chantonner; (*to be active*) (coll) aller rondement ‖ *interj* hum!
human ['hjumən] *adj* humain
hu'man be'ing *s* être *m* humain
humane [hju'men] *adj* humain, compatissant
humanist ['hjumənɪst] *adj & s* humaniste *m*
humanitarian [hju‚mænɪ'tɛrɪ‚ən] *adj & s* humanitaire *mf*
humani•ty [hju'mænɪti] *s* (*pl* -ties) humanité *f*; **humanities** (*Greek and Latin classics*) humanités classiques; (*belles-lettres*) humanités modernes
hu'man•kind' *s* genre *m* humain
humble ['hʌmbəl], ['ʌmbəl] *adj* humble ‖ *tr* humilier; **to humble oneself** s'humilier
hum'ble pie' *s*—**to eat humble pie** faire amende honorable, s'humilier
hum'bug' *s* blague *f*; (*person*) imposteur *m* ‖ *v* (*pret & pp* -**bugged**; *ger* -**bugging**) *tr* mystifier
hum'drum' *adj* monotone, banal
humer•us ['hjumərəs] *s* (*pl* -i [‚aɪ]) humérus *m*
humid ['hjumɪd] *adj* humide, moite
humidifier [hju'mɪdɪ‚faɪ•ər] *s* humidificateur *m*
humidi•fy [hju'mɪdɪ‚faɪ] *v* (*pret & pp* -**fied**) *tr* humidifier

humidity [hju'mɪdɪti] *s* humidité *f*
humiliate [hju'mɪlɪ‚et] *tr* humilier
humiliating [hju'mɪlɪ‚etɪŋ] *adj* humiliant
humili•ty [hju'mɪlɪti] *s* (*pl* -ties) humilité *f*
hum'ming•bird' *s* oiseau-mouche *m*, colibri *m*
humor ['hjumər], ['jumər] *s* (*comic quality*) humour *m*; (*frame of mind; fluid*) humeur *f*; **out of humor** maussade, grognon; **to be in the humor to** être d'humeur à ‖ *tr* ménager, satisfaire; (*s.o.'s fancies*) se plier à, accéder à
humorist ['hjumərɪst], ['jumərɪst] *s* humoriste *mf*, comique *mf*
humorous ['hjumərəs], ['jumərəs] *adj* humoristique; (*writer*) humoriste
hump [hʌmp] *s* bosse *f*
hump'back' *s* bossu *m*; (*whale*) mégaptère *m*
humus ['hjuməs] *s* humus *m*
hunch [hʌntʃ] *s* bosse *f*; (*premonition*) (coll) pressentiment *m* ‖ *tr* arrondir, voûter ‖ *intr* s'accroupir
hunch'back' *s* bossu *m*
hundred ['hʌndrəd] *adj* cent ‖ *s* cent *m*, centaine *f*; **about a hundred** une centaine; **a hundred** or **one hundred** cent; une centaine; **by the hundreds** par centaines
hun'dred•fold' *adj & s* centuple *m*; **to increase a hundredfold** centupler ‖ *adv* au centuple
hundredth ['hʌndrədθ] *adj, pron, & s* centième *m*
hun'dred•weight' *s* quintal *m*
Hungarian [hʌŋ'gɛrɪ•ən] *adj* hongrois ‖ *s* (*language*) hongrois *m*; (*person*) Hongrois *m*
Hungary ['hʌŋgəri] *s* Hongrie *f*; la Hongrie
hunger ['hʌŋgər] *s* faim *f* ‖ *intr* avoir faim; **to hunger for** être affamé de
hun'ger march' *s* marche *f* de la faim
hun'ger strike' *s* grève *f* de la faim
hun•gry ['hʌŋgri] *adj* (*comp* -**grier**; *super* -**griest**) affamé; **to be hungry** avoir faim
hunk [hʌŋk] *s* gros morceau *m*
hunt [hʌnt] *s* (*act of hunting*) chasse *f*; (*hunting party*) équipage *m* de chasse; **on the hunt for** à la recherche de ‖ *tr* chasser; (*to seek, look for*) chercher; **to hunt down** donner la chasse à, traquer; **to hunt out** faire la chasse à ‖ *intr* chasser; (*with dogs*) chasser à courre; **to go hunting** aller à la chasse; **to hunt for** chercher; **to take hunting** emmener à la chasse
hunter ['hʌntər] *s* chasseur *m*
hunting ['hʌntɪŋ] *adj* de chasse ‖ *s* chasse *f*
hunt'ing dog' *s* chien *m* de chasse
hunt'ing ground' *s* terrain *m* de chasse, chasse *f*
hunt'ing horn' *s* cor *m* de chasse
hunt'ing jack'et *s* paletot *m* de chasse
hunt'ing knife' *s* couteau *m* de chasse

hunt'ing li'cense *s* permis *m* de chasse
hunt'ing lodge' *s* pavillon *m* de chasse
hunt'ing sea'son *s* saison *f* de la chasse
huntress ['hʌntrɪs] *s* chasseuse *f*
hunts'man *s* (*pl* -men) chasseur *m*
hurdle ['hʌrdəl] *s* (*hedge over which horses jump*) haie *f*; (*wooden frame over which runners jump*) barrière *f*; (fig) obstacle *m*; **hurdles course** *f* d'obstacles || *tr* sauter
hur'dle race' *s* course *f* d'obstacles; (turf) course de haies
hurdy-gur-dy ['hʌrdi'gʌrdi] *s* (*pl* -dies) orgue *m* de Barbarie
hurl [hʌrl] *s* lancée *f* || *tr* lancer; **to hurl back** repousser, refouler
hurrah [hʌ'rɑ] *or* **hurray** [hu're] *s* hourra *m* || *interj* hourra!; **hurrah for . . .!** vive . . .!
hurricane ['hʌrɪ͵ken] *s* ouragan *m*, hurricane *m*
hurried ['hʌrid] *adj* pressé, précipité; (*hasty*) hâtif, fait à la hâte
hur-ry ['hʌri] *s* (*pl* -ries) hâte *f*; **to be in a hurry** être pressé || *v* (*pret & pp* -ried) *tr* hâter, presser || *intr* se hâter, se presser; **to hurry after** courir après; **to hurry away** s'en aller bien vite; **to hurry back** revenir vite; **to hurry over** venir vite; **to hurry up** se dépêcher
hurt [hʌrt] *adj* blessé || *s* blessure *f*; (*pain*) douleur *f* || *v* (*pret & pp* hurt) *tr* faire mal à || *intr* faire mal, e.g., **does that hurt?** ça fait mal?; avoir mal, e.g., **my head hurts** j'ai mal à la tête
hurtful ['hʌrtfəl] *adj* nuisible
hurtle ['hʌrtəl] *intr* se précipiter
husband ['hʌzbənd] *s* mari *m*, époux *m* || *tr* ménager, économiser
hus'band·man *s* (*pl* -men) cultivateur *m*
husbandry ['hʌzbəndri] *s* agriculture *f*; (*raising of livestock*) élevage *m*
hush [hʌʃ] *s* silence *m*, calme *m* || *tr* faire taire; **to hush up** (*e.g., a scandal*) étouffer || *intr* se taire || *interj* chut!
hushaby ['hʌʃə͵baɪ] *interj* fais dodo!
hush'-hush' *adj* très secret
hush' mon'ey *s* prix *m* du silence
husk [hʌsk] *s* peau *f*; (*of certain vegetables*) cosse *f*, gousse *f*; (*of nuts*) écale *f*; (*of corn*) enveloppe *f*; (*of oats*) balle *f*; (*of onion*) pelure *f* || *tr* (*grain*) vanner; (*vegetables*) éplucher; (*peas*) écosser; (*nuts*) écaler
husk'ing bee' *s* réunion *f* pour l'épluchage du maïs
husk·y ['hʌski] *adj* (*comp* -ier; *super* -iest) costaud; (*voice*) enroué || *s* (*pl* -ies) (*dog*) chien *m* esquimau
hus·sy ['hʌzi], ['hʌsi] *s* (*pl* -sies) (coll) garce *f*; (coll) coquine *f*
hustle ['hʌsəl] *s* (coll) bousculade *f*, énergie *f*, allant *m* || *tr* pousser, bousculer || *intr* se dépêcher, se presser; (*to work hard*) (coll) se démener, s'activer
hustler ['hʌslər] *s* (*go-getter*) homme *m* d'action; (*swindler*) (slang) filou

m; (*streetwalker*) (slang) traînée *f*, grue *f*
hut [hʌt] *s* hutte *f*, cabane *f*; (mil) baraque *f*
hutch [hʌtʃ] *s* (*for rabbits*) clapier *m*; (*used by baker*) huche *f*, pétrin *m*
hyacinth ['haɪ·əsɪnθ] *s* (*stone*) hyacinthe *f*; (*flower*) jacinthe *f*
hybrid ['haɪbrɪd] *adj & s* hybride *m*
hy·dra ['haɪdrə] *s* (*pl* -dras *or* -drae [dri]) hydre *f*
hydrant ['haɪdrənt] *s* prise *f* d'eau; (*faucet*) robinet *m*; (*fire hydrant*) bouche *f* d'incendie
hydrate ['haɪdret] *s* hydrate *m* || *tr* hydrater || *intr* s'hydrater
hydraulic [haɪ'drɔlɪk] *adj* hydraulique || **hydraulics** *s* hydraulique *f*
hydrau'lic ram' *s* bélier *m* hydraulique
hydrocarbon [͵haɪdrə'kɑrbən] *s* hydrocarbure *m*
hy'drochlo'ric ac'id [͵haɪdrə'klɔrɪk] *s* acide *m* chlorhydrique
hydroelectric [͵haɪdro·ɪ'lɛktrɪk] *adj* hydro-électrique
hydrofoil ['haɪdrə͵fɔɪl] *s* hydrofoil *m*
hydrogen ['haɪdrədʒən] *s* hydrogène *m*
hy'drogen bomb' *s* bombe *f* à hydrogène
hy'drogen perox'ide *s* eau *f* oxygénée
hy'drogen sul'fide *s* hydrogène *m* sulfuré
hydrometer [haɪ'drɑmɪtər] *s* aréomètre *m*, hydromètre *m*
hydrophobia [͵haɪdrə'fobɪ·ə] *s* hydrophobie *f*
hydroplane ['haɪdrə͵plen] *s* hydravion *m*
hydroxide [haɪ'drɑksaɪd] *s* hydroxyde *m*
hyena [haɪ'inə] *s* hyène *f*
hygiene ['haɪdʒin], ['haɪdʒɪ͵in] *s* hygiène *f*
hygienic [͵haɪdʒɪ'ɛnɪk], [haɪ'dʒinɪk] *adj* hygiénique
hymn [hɪm] *s* hymne *m*; (eccl) hymne *f*, cantique *m*
hymnal ['hɪmnəl] *s* livre *m* d'hymnes
hyperacidity [͵haɪpərə'sɪdɪti] *s* hyperacidité *f*
hyperbola [haɪ'pʌrbələ] *s* hyperbole *f*
hyperbole [haɪ'pʌrbəli] *s* hyperbole *f*
hypersensitive [͵haɪpər'sɛnsɪtɪv] *adj* hypersensible, hypersensitif
hypertension [͵haɪpər'tɛnʃən] *s* hypertension *f*
hyphen ['haɪfən] *s* trait *m* d'union
hyphenate ['haɪfə͵net] *tr* joindre avec un trait d'union
hypno·sis [hɪp'nosɪs] *s* (*pl* -ses [siz]) hypnose *f*
hypnotic [hɪp'nɑtɪk] *adj & s* hypnotique *m*
hypnotism ['hɪpnə͵tɪzəm] *s* hypnotisme *m*
hypnotist ['hɪpnətɪst] *s* hypnotiseur *m*
hypnotize ['hɪpnə͵taɪz] *tr* hypnotiser
hypochondriac [͵haɪpə'kɑndrɪ͵æk], [͵hɪpə'kɑndrɪ͵æk] *adj & s* hypocondriaque *mf*

hypocri·sy [hɪ'pɑkrəsi] s (pl -sies) hypocrisie f
hypocrite ['hɪpəkrɪt] s hypocrite mf
hypocritical [,hɪpə'krɪtɪkəl] adj hypocrite
hypodermic [,haɪpə'dʌrmɪk] adj hypodermique
hyposulfite [,haɪpə'sʌlfaɪt] s hyposulfite m
hypotenuse [haɪ'pɑtɪ,n(j)us] s hypoténuse f

hypothe·sis [haɪ'pɑθɪsɪs] s (pl -ses [,siz]) hypothèse f
hypothetic(al) [,haɪpə'θetɪk(əl)] adj hypothétique
hysteria [hɪs'tɪrɪ·ə] s agitation f, frénésie f; (pathol) hystérie f
hysteric [hɪs'terɪk] adj hystérique ‖ hysterics spl crise f de nerfs, crise de larmes, fou rire m
hysterical [hɪs'terɪkəl] adj hystérique

I

I, i [aɪ] s IXᵉ lettre de l'alphabet
I pron je §87; moi §85
iambic [aɪ'æmbɪk] adj ïambique
Iberian [aɪ'bɪrɪ·ən] adj ibérien, ibérique ‖ s Ibérien m
ibex ['aɪbɛks] s (pl ibexes or ibices ['ɪbɪ,siz]) bouquetin m
ice [aɪs] s glace f; to break the ice (fig) rompre la glace; to cut no ice (coll) ne rien casser, ne pas prendre; to skate on thin ice (coll) s'engager sur un terrain dangereux ‖ tr glacer; (e.g., champagne) frapper; (e.g., melon) rafraîchir ‖ intr geler; to ice up (said of windshield, airplane wings, etc.) se givrer
ice′ age′ s époque f glaciaire
ice′ bag′ s sac m à glace
ice′ bank′ s banquise f
iceberg ['aɪs,bʌrg] s banquise f, iceberg m; (person) (coll) glaçon m
ice′boat′ s (icebreaker) brise-glace m; (for sport) bateau m à patins
icebound ['aɪs,baʊnd] adj pris dans les glaces
ice′box′ s glacière f
ice′break′er s brise-glace m
ice′cap′ s calotte f glaciaire
ice′ cream′ s glace f
ice′-cream′ cone′ s cornet m de glace, glace f en cornet
ice′-cream′ freez′er s sorbetière f
ice′ cube′ s glaçon m
ice′-cube′ tray′ s bac m à glaçons
iced′ tea′ s thé m glacé
ice′ floe′ s banquise f
ice′ hock′ey s hockey m sur glace
ice′ jam′ s embâcle m
Iceland ['aɪslənd] s Islande f; l'Islande
Icelander ['aɪs,lændər], ['aɪsləndər] s Islandais m
Icelandic [aɪs'lændɪk] adj & s islandais m
ice′man′ s (pl -men′) glacier m
ice′ pack′ s (pack ice) embâcle m; (med) vessie f de glace
ice′ pail′ s seau m à glace
ice′ pick′ s poinçon m à glace; (of mountain climber) piolet m
ice′ skate′ s patin m à glace
ice′ wa′ter s eau f glacée f

ichthyology [,ɪkθɪ'ɑlədʒi] s ichtyologie f
icicle ['aɪsɪkəl] s glaçon m, chandelle f de glace
icing ['aɪsɪŋ] s (on cake) glaçage m; (aer) givrage m
icon ['aɪkɑn] s icône f
iconoclast [aɪ'kɑnə,klæst] s iconoclaste mf
iconoclastic [aɪ,kɑnə'klæstɪk] adj iconoclaste
iconoscope [aɪ'kɑnə,skop] s (trademark) iconoscope m
icy ['aɪsi] adj (comp icier; super iciest) glacé; (slippery) glissant; (fig) froid, glacial ·
idea [aɪ'di·ə] s idée f; the very idea! par exemple!
ideal [aɪ'di·əl] adj & s idéal m
idealist [aɪ'di·ə·lɪst] adj & s idéaliste mf
idealistic [aɪ,di·əl'ɪstɪk] adj idéaliste
idealize [aɪ'di·ə,laɪz] tr idéaliser
identic(al) [aɪ'dentɪk(əl)] adj identique
identification [aɪ,dentɪfɪ'kefən] s identification f
identifica′tion card′ s carte f d'identité
identifica′tion tag′ s plaque f d'identité
identi·fy [aɪ'dentɪ,faɪ] v (pret & pp -fied) tr identifier
identi·ty [aɪ'dentɪti] s (pl -ties) identité f
ideolo·gy [,aɪdɪ'ɑlədʒi], [,ɪdɪ'ɑlədʒi] s (pl -gies) idéologie f
ides [aɪdz] spl ides fpl
idio·cy ['ɪdɪ·əsi] s (pl -cies) idiotie f
idiom ['ɪdɪ·əm] s (phrase, expression) idiotisme m; (language, style) idiome m
idiomatic [,ɪdɪ·ə'mætɪk] adj idiomatique
idiosyncra·sy [,ɪdɪ·ə'sɪnkrəsi] s (pl -sies) idiosyncrasie f
idiot ['ɪdɪ·ət] s idiot m
idiotic [,ɪdɪ'ɑtɪk] adj idiot
idle ['aɪdəl] adj oisif, désœuvré; (futile) oiseux; to run idle marcher au ralenti ‖ tr—to idle away (time) passer à ne rien faire ‖ intr fainéanter; (mach) tourner au ralenti
idleness ['aɪdəlnɪs] s oisiveté f
idler ['aɪdlər] s oisif m
idling ['aɪdlɪŋ] s (of motor) ralenti m

idol ['aɪdəl] *s* idole *f*
idola·try [aɪ'dɑlətri] *s* (*pl* -**tries**) idolâtrie *f*
idolize ['aɪdə͵laɪz] *tr* idolâtrer
idyll ['aɪdəl] *s* idylle *f*
idyllic [aɪ'dɪlɪk] *adj* idyllique
if [ɪf] *s*—**ifs and buts** des si et des mais || *conj* si; **even if** quand même; **if it is true that** si tant est que; **if not** sinon; **if so** dans ce cas, s'il en est ainsi
ignis fatuus ['ɪgnɪs'fæt/ʊ‑əs] *s* (*pl* **ignes fatui** ['ɪgniz'fæt/ʊ͵aɪ]) feu *m* follet
ignite [ɪg'naɪt] *tr* allumer || *intr* prendre feu
ignition [ɪg'nɪʃən] *s* ignition *f*; (aut) allumage *m*
igni′tion coil′ *s* (aut) bobine *f* d'allumage
igni′tion switch′ *s* (*key*) (aut) clé *f* de contact; (*button*) (aut) bouton *m* de contact
ignoble [ɪg'nobəl] *adj* ignoble
ignominious [͵ɪgnə'mɪnɪ‑əs] *adj* ignominieux
ignoramus [͵ɪgnə'reməs] *s* ignorant *m*
ignorance ['ɪgnərəns] *s* ignorance *f*
ignorant ['ɪgnərənt] *adj* ignorant; **to be ignorant of** ignorer
ignore [ɪg'nor] *tr* ne pas tenir compte de, ne pas faire attention à; (*a suggestion*) passer outre à; (*to snub*) faire semblant de ne pas voir, ignorer à dessein
ilk [ɪlk] *s* espèce *f*; **of that ilk** de cet acabit
ill [ɪl] *adj* (*comp* **worse** [wʌrs]; *super* **worst** [wʌrst]) malade, souffrant || *adv* mal; **to take ill** prendre en mauvaise part; (*to get sick*) tomber malade
ill′-advised′ *adj* (*person*) malavisé; (*action*) peu judicieux
ill′ at ease′ *adj* mal à l'aise
ill-bred ['ɪl'brɛd] *adj* mal élevé
ill′-consid′ered *adj* peu réfléchi, hâtif
ill′-disposed′ *adj* mal disposé, malintentionné
illegal [ɪ'ligəl] *adj* illégal
illegible [ɪ'lɛdʒɪbəl] *adj* illisible
illegitimate [͵ɪlɪ'dʒɪtɪmɪt] *adj* illégitime
ill′-famed′ *adj* mal famé
ill′-fat′ed *adj* malheureux, infortuné
ill-gotten ['ɪl'gɑtən] *adj* mal acquis
ill′ health′ *s* mauvaise santé *f*
ill′-hu′mored *adj* de mauvaise humeur, maussade
illicit [ɪ'lɪsɪt] *adj* illicite
illitera·cy [ɪ'lɪtərəsi] *s* (*pl* -**cies**) ignorance *f*; analphabétisme *m*
illiterate [ɪ'lɪtərɪt] *adj* (*uneducated*) ignorant, illettré; (*unable to read or write*) analphabète || *s* analphabète *mf*
ill′-man′nered *adj* malappris, mal élevé
ill′-na′tured *adj* désagréable, méchant
illness ['ɪlnɪs] *s* maladie *f*
illogical [ɪ'lɑdʒɪkəl] *adj* illogique
ill-spent ['ɪl'spɛnt] *adj* gaspillé
ill′-starred′ *adj* néfaste, de mauvais augure

ill′-tem′pered *adj* désagréable, de mauvais caractère
ill′-timed′ *adj* intempestif, mal à propos
ill′-treat′ *tr* maltraiter, rudoyer
illuminate [ɪ'lumɪ͵net] *tr* illuminer; (*a manuscript*) enluminer
illu′minating gas′ *s* gaz *m* d'éclairage
illumination [ɪ'lumɪ'neʃən] *s* illumination *f*; (*in manuscript*) enluminure *f*
illusion [ɪ'luʒən] *s* illusion *f*
illusive [ɪ'lusɪv] *adj* illusoire, trompeur
illusory [ɪ'lusəri] *adj* illusoire
illustrate ['ɪləs͵tret], [ɪ'lʌstret] *tr* illustrer
illustration *s* [͵ɪləs'treʃən] *s* illustration *f*; (*explanation*) explication *f*, éclaircissement *m*
illustrative [ɪ'lʌstrətɪv] *adj* explicatif, éclairant
illustrator ['ɪləs͵tretər] *s* illustrateur *m*, dessinateur *m*
illustrious [ɪ'lʌstrɪ‑əs] *adj* illustre
ill′ will′ *s* rancune *f*
image ['ɪmɪdʒ] *s* image *f*
image·ry ['ɪmɪdʒri], ['ɪmɪdʒəri] *s* (*pl* -**ries**) images *fpl*
imaginary [ɪ'mædʒɪ͵nɛri] *adj* imaginaire
imagination [ɪ͵mædʒɪ'neʃən] *s* imagination *f*
imagine [ɪ'mædʒɪn] *tr* imaginer, s'imaginer || *intr* imaginer; **imagine!** figurez-vous!
imbecile ['ɪmbɪsɪl] *adj & s* imbécile *mf*
imbecili·ty [͵ɪmbɪ'sɪlɪti] *s* (*pl* -**ties**) imbécillité *f*
imbibe [ɪm'baɪb] *tr* absorber || *intr* boire, lever le coude
imbue [ɪm'bju] *tr* imprégner, pénétrer; **imbued with** imbu de
imitate ['ɪmɪ͵tet] *tr* imiter
imitation [͵ɪmɪ'teʃən] *adj* d'imitation || *s* imitation *f*
imitator ['ɪmɪ͵tetər] *s* imitateur *m*
immaculate [ɪ'mækjəlɪt] *adj* immaculé
immaterial [͵ɪmə'tɪrɪ‑əl] *adj* immatériel; (*pointless*) sans conséquence; **it's immaterial to me** cela m'est égal
immature [͵ɪmə'tjur] *adj* pas mûr, peu mûr; pas adulte
immeasurable [ɪ'mɛʒərəbəl] *adj* immensurable
immediacy [ɪ'midɪ‑əsi] *s* caractère *m* immédiat, imminence *f*
immediate [ɪ'midɪ‑ɪt] *adj* immédiat
immediately [ɪ'midɪ‑ɪtli] *adv* immédiatement
immemorial [͵ɪmɪ'morɪ‑əl] *adj* immémorial
immense [ɪ'mɛns] *adj* immense
immerse [ɪ'mʌrs] *tr* immerger, plonger
immersion [ɪ'mʌrʃən], [ɪ'mʌrʒən] *s* immersion *f*
immigrant ['ɪmɪgrənt] *adj & s* immigrant *m*
immigrate ['ɪmɪ͵gret] *intr* immigrer
immigration [͵ɪmɪ'greʃən] *s* immigration *f*
imminent ['ɪmɪnənt] *adj* imminent, très prochain

immobile [ɪ'mobɪl], [ɪ'mobil] *adj* immobile
immobilize [ɪ'mobɪ ˌlaɪz] *tr* immobiliser
immoderate [ɪ'madərɪt] *adj* immodéré
immodest [ɪ'madɪst] *adj* impudique
immoral [ɪ'marəl], [ɪ'mɔrəl] *adj* immoral
immortal [ɪ'mɔrtəl] *adj & s* immortel *m*
immortalize [ɪ'mɔrtə ˌlaɪz] *tr* immortaliser
immune [ɪ'mjun] *adj* dispensé, exempt; (med) immunisé
immunize ['ɪmjə ˌnaɪz], [ɪ'mjunaɪz] *tr* immuniser
imp [ɪmp] *s* suppôt *m* du diable; (*child*) diablotin *m*, polisson *m*
impact ['ɪmpækt] *s* impact *m*
impair [ɪm'pɛr] *tr* endommager, affaiblir; (*health, digestion*) délabrer
impan•el [ɪm'pænəl] *v* (*pret & pp* -eled or -elled; *ger* -eling or -elling) *tr* appeler à faire partie de; (*a jury*) dresser la liste de
impart [ɪm'part] *tr* imprimer, communiquer; (*to make known*) communiquer
impartial [ɪm'parʃəl] *adj* impartial
impassable [ɪm'pæsəbəl], [ɪm'pasəbəl] *adj* (*road*) impraticable; (*mountain*) infranchissable
impassible [ɪm'pæsɪbəl] *adj* impassible
impassioned [ɪm'pæʃənd] *adj* passionné
impassive [ɪm'pæsɪv] *adj* insensible; (*look, face*) impassible, composé
impatience [ɪm'peʃəns] *s* impatience *f*
impatient [ɪm'peʃənt] *adj* impatient
impeach [ɪm'pitʃ] *tr* accuser; (*s.o.'s honor, veracity*) attaquer
impeachment [ɪm'pitʃmənt] *s* accusation *f*; (*of honor, veracity*) attaque *f*
impeccable [ɪm'pɛkəbəl] *adj* impeccable
impecunious [ˌɪmpɪ'kjunɪ•əs] *adj* besogneux, impécunieux
impede [ɪm'pid] *tr* entraver, empêcher
impediment [ɪm'pɛdɪmənt] *s* obstacle *m*, empêchement *m*
im•pel [ɪm'pɛl] *v* (*pret & pp* -pelled; *ger* -pelling) *tr* pousser, forcer
impending [ɪm'pɛndɪŋ] *adj* imminent
impenetrable [ɪm'pɛnətrəbəl] *adj* impénétrable
impenitent [ɪm'pɛnɪtənt] *adj* impénitent *m*
imperative [ɪm'pɛrɪtɪv] *adj & s* impératif *m*
imperceptible [ˌɪmpər'sɛptɪbəl] *adj* imperceptible
imperfect [ɪm'pʌrfɪkt] *adj & s* imparfait *m*
imperfection [ˌɪmpər'fɛkʃən] *s* imperfection *f*
imperial [ɪm'pɪrɪ•əl] *adj* impérial
imperialist [ɪm'pɪrɪ•əlɪst] *adj & s* impérialiste *mf*
imper•il [ɪm'pɛrɪl] *v* (*pret & pp* -iled or -illed; *ger* -iling or -illing) *tr* mettre en péril, exposer au danger
imperious [ɪm'pɪrɪ•əs] *adj* impérieux

imperishable [ɪm'pɛrɪʃəbəl] *adj* impérissable
impersonal [ɪm'pʌrsənəl] *adj* impersonnel
impersonate [ɪm'pʌrsə ˌnet] *tr* contrefaire, singer; jouer le rôle de
impertinent [ɪm'pʌrtɪnənt] *adj* impertinent
impetuous [ɪm'pɛtʃʊ•əs] *adj* impétueux
impetus ['ɪmpɪtəs] *s* impulsion *f*; (mech) force *f* impulsive; (fig) élan *m*
impie•ty [ɪm'paɪ•əti] *s* (*pl* -ties) impiété *f*
impinge [ɪm'pɪndʒ] *intr*—to impinge on or upon empiéter sur; (*to violate*) enfreindre
impious ['ɪmpɪ•əs] *adj* impie
impish ['ɪmpɪʃ] *adj* espiègle
implant [ɪm'plænt] *tr* implanter
implement ['ɪmplɪmənt] *s* outil *m*, ustensile *m* ‖ *tr* mettre en œuvre, réaliser; (*to provide with implements*) outiller
implicate ['ɪmplɪ ˌket] *tr* impliquer
implicit [ɪm'plɪsɪt] *adj* implicite
implied [ɪm'plaɪd] *adj* implicite, sousentendu
implore [ɪm'plor] *tr* implorer, supplier, solliciter
im•ply [ɪm'plaɪ] *v* (*pret & pp* -plied) *tr* impliquer
impolite [ˌɪmpə'laɪt] *adj* impoli
import ['ɪmport] *s* importance *f*; (*meaning*) sens *m*, signification *f*; (*extent*) portée *f*; (com) article *m* d'importation; **imports** importations *fpl* ‖ [ɪm'port], ['ɪmport] *tr* importer; (*to mean*) signifier, vouloir dire
importance [ɪm'portəns] *s* importance *f*
important [ɪm'portənt] *adj* important
importer [ɪm'portər] *s* importateur *m*
importune [ˌɪmpər't(j)un] *tr* importuner, harceler
impose [ɪm'poz] *tr* imposer ‖ *intr*—to impose on or upon en imposer à, abuser de
imposing [ɪm'pozɪŋ] *adj* imposant
imposition [ˌɪmpə'zɪʃən] *s* (*laying on of a burden or obligation*) imposition *f*; (*rudeness, taking unfair advantage*) abus *m*
impossible [ɪm'pasɪbəl] *adj* impossible
impostor [ɪm'pastər] *s* imposteur *m*
imposture [ɪm'pastʃər] *s* imposture *f*
impotence ['ɪmpətəns] *s* impuissance *f*
impotent ['ɪmpətənt] *adj* impuissant
impound [ɪm'paʊnd] *tr* confisquer, saisir; (*a dog, an auto, etc.*) mettre en fourrière
impoverish [ɪm'pavərɪʃ] *tr* appauvrir
impracticable [ɪm'præktɪkəbəl] *adj* impraticable, inexécutable
impractical [ɪm'præktɪkəl] *adj* peu pratique; (*plan*) impraticable
impregnable [ɪm'prɛgnəbəl] *adj* imprenable, inexpugnable
impregnate [ɪm'prɛgnet] *tr* imprégner; (*to make pregnant*) féconder
impresari•o [ˌɪmprɪ'sarɪ ˌo] *s* (*pl* -os) imprésario *m*
impress [ɪm'prɛs] *tr* (*to have an effect*

on the mind or emotions of) impressionner; *(to mark by using pressure)* imprimer; *(on the memory)* graver; (mil) enrôler de force; **to impress s.o.** **with** pénétrer qn de
impression [ɪm'prɛʃən] *s* impression *f*
impressive [ɪm'prɛsɪv] *adj* impressionnant
imprint ['ɪmprɪnt] *s* empreinte *f*; (typ) rubrique *f*, griffe *f* || [ɪm'prɪnt] *tr* imprimer
imprison [ɪm'prɪzən] *tr* emprisonner
imprisonment [ɪm'prɪzənmənt] *s* emprisonnement *m*
improbable [ɪm'prɑbəbəl] *adj* improbable
impromptu [ɪm'prɑmpt(j)u] *adj & adv* impromptu || *s* (mus) impromptu *m*
impromp'tu speech' *s* improvisation *f*, discours *m* improvisé
improper [ɪm'prɑpər] *adj (not the right)* impropre; *(contrary to good taste or decency)* inconvenant
improve [ɪm'pruv] *tr* améliorer, perfectionner || *intr* s'améliorer, se perfectionner
improvement [ɪm'pruvmənt] *s* amélioration *f*, perfectionnement *m*
improvident [ɪm'prɑvɪdənt] *adj* imprévoyant
improvise ['ɪmprə‚vaɪz] *tr & intr* improviser
imprudent [ɪm'prudənt] *adj* imprudent
impudent ['ɪmpjədənt] *adj* impudent, effronté
impugn [ɪm'pjun] *tr* contester, mettre en doute
impulse ['ɪmpʌls] *s* impulsion *f*
impulsive [ɪm'pʌlsɪv] *adj* impulsif
impunity [ɪm'pjunɪti] *s* impunité *f*
impure [ɪm'pjʊr] *adj* impur
impuri•ty [ɪm'pjʊrɪti] *s (pl -ties)* impureté *f*
impute [ɪm'pjut] *tr* imputer
in [ɪn] *adv* en dedans, à l'intérieur; *(at home)* à la maison, chez soi; (pol) au pouvoir; **all in** *(tired)* (coll) éreinté; **in here** ici, par ici; **in there** là-dedans, là || *prep* dans; en; *(inside)* en dedans de, à l'intérieur de; *(in ratios)* sur, e.g., **one in a hundred** un sur cent; **in that** du fait que || *s* (coll) entrée *f*, e.g., **to have an in with** avoir ses entrées chez
inability [‚ɪnə'bɪlɪti] *s* incapacité *f*, impuissance *f*
inaccessible [‚ɪnæk'sɛsɪbəl] *adj* inaccessible
inaccura•cy [ɪn'ækjərəsi] *s (pl -cies)* inexactitude *f*, infidélité *f*
inaccurate [ɪn'ækjərɪt] *adj* inexact, infidèle
inaction [ɪn'ækʃən] *s* inaction *f*
inactive [ɪn'æktɪv] *adj* inactif
inactivity [‚ɪnæk'tɪvɪti] *s* inactivité *f*
inadequate [ɪn'ædɪkwɪt] *adj* insuffisant
inadvertent [‚ɪnəd'vʌrtənt] *adj* distrait, étourdi; commis par inadvertance
inadvisable [‚ɪnəd'vaɪzəbəl] *adj* imprudent, peu sage
inane [ɪn'en] *adj* inepte, absurde
inanimate [ɪn'ænɪmɪt] *adj* inanimé

inappropriate [‚ɪnə'proprɪ‑ɪt] *adj* inapproprié; *(word)* impropre
inarticulate [‚ɪnɑr'tɪkjəlɪt] *adj* inarticulé; *(person)* muet, incapable de s'exprimer
inartistic [‚ɪnɑr'tɪstɪk] *adj* peu artistique; *(person)* peu artiste
inasmuch as [‚ɪnəz'mʌtʃ ‚æz] *conj* attendu que, vu que
inattentive [‚ɪnə'tɛntɪv] *adj* inattentif
inaudible [ɪn'ɔdɪbəl] *adj* inaudible
inaugural [ɪn'ɔgjərəl] *adj* inaugural || *s* discours *m* d'inauguration
inaugurate [ɪn'ɔgjə‚ret] *tr* inaugurer
inauguration [ɪn‚ɔgjə'reʃən] *s* inauguration *f*; *(investiture)* installation *f*
inborn ['ɪn‚bɔrn] *adj* inné, infus
in'breed'ing *s* croisement *m* consanguin
Inc. *abbr* **(Incorporated)** S.A.
incandescent [‚ɪnkən'dɛsənt] *adj* incandescent
incapable [ɪn'kepəbəl] *adj* incapable
incapacitate [‚ɪnkə'pæsɪ‚tet] *tr* rendre incapable
incarcerate [ɪn'kɑrsə‚ret] *tr* incarcérer
incarnate [ɪn'kɑrnɪt], [ɪn'kɑrnet] *adj* incarné || [ɪn'kɑrnet] *tr* incarner
incarnation [‚ɪnkɑr'neʃən] *s* incarnation *f*
incendiar•y [ɪn'sɛndɪ‚ɛri] *adj* incendiaire || *s (pl -ies)* incendiaire *mf*
incense ['ɪnsɛns] *s* encens *m* || *tr (to burn incense before)* encenser || [ɪn'sɛns] *tr* exaspérer, irriter
in'cense burn'er *s* brûle-parfum *m*
incentive [ɪn'sɛntɪv] *adj & s* stimulant *m*
inception [ɪn'sɛpʃən] *s* début *m*
incessant [ɪn'sɛsənt] *adj* incessant
incest ['ɪnsɛst] *s* inceste *m*
incestuous [ɪn'sɛstʃʊ‑əs] *adj* incestueux
inch [ɪntʃ] *s* pouce *m*; **by inches** peu à peu, petit à petit; **not to give way an inch** ne pas reculer d'une semelle; **within an inch of** à deux doigts de || *intr*—**to inch along** se déplacer imperceptiblement; **to inch forward** avancer peu à peu
incidence ['ɪnsɪdəns] *s* incidence *f*; *(range of occurrence)* portée *f*
incident ['ɪnsɪdənt] *adj & s* incident *m*
incidental [‚ɪnsɪ'dɛntəl] *adj* accidentel, fortuit; *(expenses)* accessoire || **incidentals** *spl* faux frais *mpl*
incidentally [‚ɪnsɪ'dɛntəli] *adv* incidemment, à propos
incinerate [ɪn'sɪnə‚ret] *tr* incinérer
incipient [ɪn'sɪpɪ‑ənt] *adj* naissant
incision [ɪn'sɪʒən] *s* incision *f*
incisive [ɪn'saɪsɪv] *adj* incisif
incisor [ɪn'saɪzər] *s* incisive *f*
incite [ɪn'saɪt] *tr* inciter
inclement [ɪn'klɛmənt] *adj* inclément
inclination [‚ɪnklɪ'neʃən] *s* inclination *f*; *(slope)* inclinaison *f*
incline ['ɪnklaɪn], [ɪn'klaɪn] *s* inclinaison *f*, pente *f* || [ɪn'klaɪn] *tr* incliner || *intr* s'incliner
include [ɪn'klud] *tr* comprendre, comporter; *(to contain)* renfermer; *(e.g., in a letter)* inclure
including [ɪn'kludɪŋ] *prep* y compris;

up to and including page ten jusqu'à la page dix incluse
inclusive [ɪnˈkluːsɪv] *adj* global; *(including everything)* tout compris; **from Wednesday to Saturday inclusive** de mercredi à samedi inclus; **inclusive of** . . . qui comprend . . . || *adv* inclusivement
incogni·to [ɪnˈkɑgnɪˌto] *adj* & *adv* incognito || *s* (*pl* **-tos**) incognito *m*
incoherent [ˌɪnkoˈhɪrənt] *adj* incohérent
incombustible [ˌɪnkəmˈbʌstɪbəl] *adj* incombustible
income [ˈɪnkʌm] *s* revenu *m*, revenus; *(annual income)* rentes *fpl*
in'come tax' *s* impôt *m* sur le revenu
in'come-tax return' *s* déclaration *f* de revenus
in'com'ing *adj* entrant, rentrant; *(tide)* montant || *s* arrivée *f*
incomparable [ɪnˈkɑmpərəbəl] *adj* incomparable
incompatible [ˌɪnkəmˈpætɪbəl] *adj* incompatible
incompetent [ɪnˈkɑmpɪtənt] *adj* & *s* incompétent *m*, incapable *mf*
incomplete [ˌɪnkəmˈplit] *adj* incomplet
incomprehensible [ˌɪnkɑmprɪˈhensɪbəl] *adj* incompréhensible
inconceivable [ˌɪnkənˈsivəbəl] *adj* inconcevable
inconclusive [ˌɪnkənˈklusɪv] *adj* peu concluant, non concluant
incongruous [ɪnˈkɑŋgruˌəs] *adj* incongru, impropre; disparate
inconsequential [ɪnˌkɑnsɪˈkwenʃəl] *adj* sans importance
inconsiderate [ˌɪnkənˈsɪdərɪt] *adj* inconsidéré
inconsisten·cy [ˌɪnkənˈsɪstənsi] *s* (*pl* **-cies**) *(lack of coherence; instability)* inconsistance *f*; *(lack of logical connection or uniformity)* inconséquence *f*
inconsistent [ˌɪnkənˈsɪstənt] *adj* *(lacking coherence of parts; unstable)* inconsistant; *(not agreeing with itself or oneself)* inconséquent
inconspicuous [ˌɪnkənˈspɪkjuˌəs] *adj* peu apparent; peu impressionnant
inconstant [ɪnˈkɑnstənt] *adj* inconstant
incontinent [ɪnˈkɑntɪnənt] *adj* incontinent
incontrovertible [ˌɪnkɑntrəˈvʌrtɪbəl] *adj* incontestable
inconvenience [ˌɪnkənˈvinɪˌəns] *s* incommodité || *tr* incommoder, gêner
inconvenient [ˌɪnkənˈvinɪˌənt] *adj* incommode, gênant; *(time)* inopportun
incorporate [ɪnˈkɔrpəˌret] *tr* incorporer; *(com)* constituer en société anonyme || *intr* s'incorporer; *(com)* se constituer en société anonyme
incorporation [ɪnˌkɔrpəˈreʃən] *s* incorporation *f*; *(of company)* constitution *f* en société anonyme; *(of town)* érection *f* en municipalité
incorrect [ˌɪnkəˈrekt] *adj* incorrect
increase [ˈɪnkris] *s* augmentation *f*; **on the increase** en voie d'accroissement || [ɪnˈkris] *tr* & *intr* augmenter

increasingly [ɪnˈkrisɪŋli] *adv* de plus en plus
incredible [ɪnˈkredɪbəl] *adj* incroyable
incredulous [ɪnˈkredʒələs] *adj* incrédule
increment [ˈɪnkrɪmənt] *s* augmentation *f*
incriminate [ɪnˈkrɪmɪˌnet] *tr* incriminer
incrust [ɪnˈkrʌst] *tr* incruster
incubate [ˈɪnkjəˌbet] *tr* incuber, couver || *intr* couver
incubator [ˈɪnkjəˌbetər] *s* incubateur *m*
inculcate [ɪnˈkʌlket], [ˈɪnkʌlˌket] *tr* inculquer
incumben·cy [ɪnˈkʌmbənsi] *s* (*pl* **-cies**) charge *f*; période *f* d'exercice
incumbent [ɪnˈkʌmbənt] *adj*—**to be incumbent on** incomber (with *dat*) || *m* titulaire *mf*
incunabula [ˌɪnkjuˈnæbjələ] *spl* origines *fpl*; *(books)* incunables *mpl*
in·cur [ɪnˈkʌr] *v* (*pret* & *pp* **-curred;** *ger* **-curring**) *tr* encourir, s'attirer; *(a debt)* contracter
incurable [ɪnˈkjurəbəl] *adj* & *s* incurable *mf*, inguérissable *mf*
incursion [ɪnˈkʌrʒən], [ɪnˈkʌrʃən] *s* incursion *f*
indebted [ɪnˈdetɪd] *adj* endetté; **indebted to s.o. for** redevable à qn de
indecen·cy [ɪnˈdisənsi] *s* (*pl* **-cies**) indécence *f*, impudeur *f*
indecent [ɪnˈdisənt] *adj* indécent, impudique
inde'cent expo'sure *s* attentat *m* à la pudeur
indecisive [ˌɪndɪˈsaɪsɪv] *adj* indécis
indeclinable [ˌɪndɪˈklaɪnəbəl] *adj* *(gram)* indéclinable
indeed [ɪnˈdid] *adv* en effet; *(truly)* en vérité || *interj* vraiment!
indefatigable [ˌɪndɪˈfætɪgəbəl] *adj* infatigable
indefensible [ˌɪndɪˈfensɪbəl] *adj* indéfendable
indefinable [ˌɪndɪˈfaɪnəbəl] *adj* indéfinissable
indefinite [ɪnˈdefɪnɪt] *adj* indéfini
indelible [ɪnˈdelɪbəl] *adj* indélébile
indelicate [ɪnˈdelɪkɪt] *adj* indélicat
indemnification [ɪnˌdemnɪfɪˈkeʃən] *s* indemnisation *f*
indemni·fy [ɪnˈdemnɪˌfaɪ] *v* (*pret* & *pp* **-fied**) *tr* indemniser
indemni·ty [ɪnˈdemnɪti] *s* (*pl* **-ties**) indemnité *f*
indent [ɪnˈdent] *tr* denteler; *(to recess)* renfoncer; *(typ)* mettre en alinéa, rentrer || *intr* *(typ)* faire un alinéa
indentation [ˌɪndenˈteʃən] *s* dentelure *f*; *(notch)* entaille *f*; *(recess)* renfoncement *m*; *(typ)* alinéa *m*
indented *adj* *(typ)* en alinéa
indenture [ɪnˈdentʃər] *s* contrat *m* d'apprentissage || *tr* mettre en apprentissage
independence [ˌɪndɪˈpendəns] *s* indépendance *f*
independen·cy [ˌɪndɪˈpendənsi] *s* (*pl* **-cies**) indépendance *f*; nation *f* indépendante

independent [ˌɪndɪˈpɛndənt] *adj & s* indépendant *m*

indescribable [ˌɪndɪˈskraɪbəbəl] *adj* indescriptible, indicible

indestructible [ˌɪndɪˈstrʌktɪbəl] *adj* indestructible

index [ˈɪndɛks] *s (pl* **indexes** or **indices** [ˈɪndɪˌsiz]) index *m*; *(of prices)* indice *m*; (typ) main *f*; **Index** Index ‖ *tr* répertorier; *(a book)* faire un index à

in'dex card' *s* fiche *f*

in'dex fin'ger *s* index *m*

in'dex tab' *s* onglet *m*

India [ˈɪndɪ·ə] *s* Inde *f*; l'Inde

In'dia ink' *s* encre *f* de Chine

Indian [ˈɪndɪ·ən] *adj* indien ‖ *s* Indien *m*

In'dian club' *s* mil *m*, massue *f*

In'dian corn' *s* maïs *m*

In'dian file' *s* file *f* indienne ‖ *adv* en file indienne, à la queue leu leu

In'dian O'cean *s* mer *f* des Indes, océan *m* Indien

In'dian sum'mer *s* été *m* de la Saint-Martin

In'dia rub'ber *s* caoutchouc *m*, gomme *f*

indicate [ˈɪndɪˌket] *tr* indiquer

indication [ˌɪndɪˈkeʃən] *s* indication *f*

indicative [ɪnˈdɪkətɪv] *adj & s* indicatif *m*

indicator [ˈɪndɪˌketər] *s* indicateur *m*

indict [ɪnˈdaɪt] *tr* (law) inculper

indictment [ɪnˈdaɪtmənt] *s* inculpation *f*, mise *f* en accusation

indifferent [ɪnˈdɪfərənt] *adj* indifférent; *(poor)* médiocre

indigenous [ɪnˈdɪdʒɪnəs] *adj* indigène

indigent [ˈɪndɪdʒənt] *adj* indigent

indigestible [ˌɪndɪˈdʒɛstɪbəl] *adj* indigeste

indigestion [ˌɪndɪˈdʒɛstʃən] *s* indigestion *f*

indignant [ɪnˈdɪgnənt] *adj* indigné

indignation [ˌɪndɪgˈneʃən] *s* indignation *f*

indigni•ty [ɪnˈdɪgnɪti] *s (pl* **-ties**) indignité *f*

indi•go [ˈɪndɪˌgo] *adj* indigo ‖ *s (pl* **-gos** or **-goes**) indigo *m*

indirect [ˌɪndɪˈrɛkt], [ˌɪndaɪˈrɛkt] *adj* indirect

in'direct dis'course *s* discours *m* indirect, style *m* indirect

indiscreet [ˌɪndɪsˈkrit] *adj* indiscret

indispensable [ˌɪndɪsˈpɛnsəbəl] *adj* indispensable

indispose [ˌɪndɪsˈpoz] *tr* indisposer

indisposed *adj* indisposé; *(disinclined)* peu enclin, peu disposé

indissoluble [ˌɪndɪˈsɑljəbəl] *adj* indissoluble

indistinct [ˌɪndɪˈstɪŋkt] *adj* indistinct

individual [ˌɪndɪˈvɪdʒu·əl] *adj* individuel ‖ *s* individu *m*

individuali•ty [ˌɪndɪˌvɪdʒuˈælɪti] *s (pl* **-ties**) individualité *f*

indivisible [ˌɪndɪˈvɪzɪbəl] *adj* indivisible

Indochina [ˈɪndoˈtʃaɪnə] *s* Indochine *f*; l'Indochine

indoctrinate [ɪnˈdɑktrɪˌnet] *tr* endoctriner, catéchiser

Indo-European [ˈɪndoˌjurəˈpi·ən] *adj* indo-européen ‖ *s (language)* indo-européen *m*; *(person)* Indo-Européen *m*

indolent [ˈɪndələnt] *adj* indolent

Indonesia [ˌɪndoˈniʃə], [ˌɪndoˈniʒə] *s* Indonésie *f*; l'Indonésie

Indonesian [ˌɪndoˈniʃən], [ˌɪndoˈniʒən] *adj* indonésien ‖ *s (language)* indonésien *m*; *(person)* Indonésien *m*

indoor [ˈɪnˌdor] *adj* d'intérieur; *(homeloving)* casanier; *(tennis)* couvert; *(swimming pool)* fermé

indoors [ˈɪnˈdorz] *adv* à l'intérieur

induce [ɪnˈd(j)us] *tr* induire; *(to bring about)* provoquer; **to induce s.o. to** porter qn à

induced *adj* provoqué; (elec) induit

inducement [ɪnˈd(j)usmənt] *s* encouragement *m*, mobile *m*, invite *f*

induct [ɪnˈdʌkt] *tr* installer; (mil) incorporer

inductee [ˌɪnˈdʌkti] *s* appelé *m*

induction [ɪnˈdʌkʃən] *s* installation *f*; (elec, logic) induction *f*; (mil) incorporation *f*

induc'tion coil' *s* bobine *f* d'induction

indulge [ɪnˈdʌldʒ] *tr* favoriser; *(s.o.'s desires)* donner libre cours à; *(a child)* tout passer à ‖ *intr* (coll) boire; (coll) fumer; **to indulge in** se livrer à

indulgence [ɪnˈdʌldʒəns] *s* indulgence *f*; **indulgence** in jouissance de

indulgent [ɪnˈdʌldʒənt] *adj* indulgent

industrial [ɪnˈdʌstrɪ·əl] *adj* industriel

industrialist [ɪnˈdʌstrɪ·əlɪst] *s* industriel *m*

industrialize [ɪnˈdʌstrɪ·əˌlaɪz] *tr* industrialiser

industrious [ɪnˈdʌstrɪ·əs] *adj* industrieux, appliqué, assidu

indus•try [ˈɪndəstri] *s (pl* **-tries**) industrie *f*; *(zeal)* assiduité *f*

inebriation [ɪnˌibrɪˈeʃən] *s* ébriété *f*

inedible [ɪnˈɛdɪbəl] *adj* incomestible

ineffable [ɪnˈɛfəbəl] *adj* ineffable

ineffective [ˌɪnɪˈfɛktɪv] *adj* inefficace; *(person)* incapable

ineffectual [ˌɪnɪˈfɛktʃu·əl] *adj* inefficace

inefficient [ˌɪnɪˈfɪʃənt] *adj* inefficace; *(person)* incapable

ineligible [ɪnˈɛlɪdʒɪbəl] *adj* inéligible

inept [ɪnˈɛpt] *adj* inepte

inequali•ty [ˌɪnɪˈkwɑlɪti] *s (pl* **-ties**) inégalité *f*

inequi•ty [ɪnˈɛkwɪti] *s (pl* **-ties**) injustice *f*

inertia [ɪnˈʌrʃə] *s* inertie *f*

inescapable [ˌɪnɛsˈkepəbəl] *adj* inéluctable

inevitable [ɪnˈɛvɪtəbəl] *adj* inévitable

inexact [ˌɪnɛgˈzækt] *adj* inexact

inexcusable [ˌɪnɛksˈkjuzəbəl] *adj* inexcusable

inexhaustible [ˌɪnɛgˈzɔstɪbəl] *adj* inexhaustible, inépuisable

inexorable [ɪnˈɛksərəbəl] *adj* inexorable

inexpedient [ˌɪnɛkˈspidɪ·ənt] *adj* inopportun, peu expédient

inexpensive [ˌɪnɛkˈspɛnsɪv] *adj* pas cher, bon marché

inexperience [ˌɪnɛkˈspɪrɪ·əns] *s* inexpérience *f*

inexperienced *adj* inexpérimenté

inexplicable [ɪnˈɛksplɪkəbəl] *adj* inexplicable

inexpressible [ˌɪnɛkˈsprɛsɪbəl] *adj* inexprimable, indicible

infallible [ɪnˈfælɪbəl] *adj* infaillible

infamous [ˈɪnfəməs] *adj* infâme

infa·my [ˈɪnfəmi] *s* (*pl* -mies) infamie *f*

infan·cy [ˈɪnfənsi] *s* (*pl* -cies) première enfance *f*; (fig) enfance

infant [ˈɪnfənt] *adj* infantile; (*in the earliest stage*) (fig) débutant ‖ *s* nourrisson *m*, bébé *m*; enfant *mf* en bas âge

infantile [ˈɪnfənˌtaɪl], [ˈɪnfəntɪl] *adj* infantile; (*childish*) enfantin

in'fantile paral'ysis *s* paralysie *f* infantile

infan·try [ˈɪnfəntri] *s* (*pl* -tries) infanterie *f*

in'fantry·man *s* (*pl* -men) militaire *m* de l'infanterie, fantassin *m*

infatuated [ɪnˈfætʃuˌetɪd] *adj* entiché, épris; **infatuated with oneself** infatué; **to be infatuated** s'engouer

infect [ɪnˈfɛkt] *tr* infecter

infection [ɪnˈfɛkʃən] *s* infection *f*

infectious [ɪnˈfɛkʃəs] *adj* infectieux; (*laughter*) communicatif, contagieux

in·fer [ɪnˈfʌr] *v* (*pret* & *pp* -ferred; *ger* -ferring) *tr* inférer

inferior [ɪnˈfɪrɪ·ər] *adj* & *s* inférieur *m*

inferiority [ɪnˌfɪrɪˈarɪti] *s* infériorité *f*

inferior'ity com'plex *s* complexe *m* d'infériorité

infernal [ɪnˈfʌrnəl] *adj* infernal

infest [ɪnˈfɛst] *tr* infester

infidel [ˈɪnfɪdəl] *adj* & *s* infidèle *mf*

infideli·ty [ˌɪnfɪˈdɛlɪti] *s* (*pl* -ties) infidélité *f*

in'field' *s* (baseball) petit champ *m*

infiltrate [ɪnˈfɪltret], [ˈɪnfɪlˌtret] *tr* s'infiltrer dans, pénétrer; (*with conspirators*) noyauter ‖ *intr* s'infiltrer

infinite [ˈɪnfɪnɪt] *adj* & *s* infini *m*

infinitely [ˈɪnfɪnɪtli] *adv* infiniment

infinitive [ɪnˈfɪnɪtɪv] *adj* & *s* infinitif *m*

infini·ty [ɪnˈfɪnɪti] *s* (*pl* -ties) infinité *f*; (math) infini *m*

infirm [ɪnˈfʌrm] *adj* infirme, maladif

infirma·ry [ɪnˈfʌrməri] *s* (*pl* -ries) infirmerie *f*

infirmi·ty [ɪnˈfʌrmɪti] *s* (*pl* -ties) infirmité *f*

in'fix *s* infixe *m*

inflame [ɪnˈflem] *tr* enflammer ‖ *intr* s'enflammer

inflammable [ɪnˈflæməbəl] *adj* inflammable

inflammation [ˌɪnfləˈmeʃən] *s* inflammation *f*

inflammatory [ɪnˈflæməˌtori] *adj* incendiaire, provocateur; (pathol) inflammatoire

inflate [ɪnˈflet] *tr* gonfler ‖ *intr* se gonfler

inflation [ɪnˈfleʃən] *s* gonflement *m*; (com) inflation *f*

inflationary [ɪnˈfleʃənˌɛri] *adj* inflationniste

inflect [ɪnˈflɛkt] *tr* infléchir; (*e.g., a noun*) décliner; (*a verb*) conjuguer; (*the voice*) moduler

inflection [ɪnˈflɛkʃən] *s* inflexion *f*

inflexible [ɪnˈflɛksɪbəl] *adj* inflexible

inflict [ɪnˈflɪkt] *tr* infliger

influence [ˈɪnfluˌəns] *s* influence *f* ‖ *tr* influencer, influer sur

in'fluence ped'dling *s* trafic *m* d'influence

influential [ˌɪnfluˈɛnʃəl] *adj* influent

influenza [ˌɪnfluˈɛnzə] *s* influenza *f*

in'flux' *s* afflux *m*

inform [ɪnˈfɔrm] *tr* informer, renseigner; **keep me informed** tenez-moi au courant ‖ *intr*—**to inform on** informer contre, dénoncer

informal [ɪnˈfɔrməl] *adj* sans cérémonie; (*person; manners*) familier; (*unofficial*) officieux

infor'mal dance' *s* sauterie *f*

informant [ɪnˈfɔrmənt] *s* informateur *m*; (*in, e.g., language study*) source *f* d'informations

information [ˌɪnfərˈmeʃən] *s* information *f*, renseignements *mpl*; (telp) service *m* des renseignements téléphoniques; **piece of information** information, renseignement

informational [ˌɪnfərˈmeʃənəl] *adj* instructif, documentaire; (comp) informatique

informa'tion bu'reau *s* bureau *m* de renseignements

informative [ɪnˈfɔrmətɪv] *adj* instructif, édifiant

informed' sour'ces *spl* sources *fpl* bien informées

informer [ɪnˈfɔrmər] *s* délateur *m*, dénonciateur *m*; (*police spy*) indicateur *m*, mouchard *m*

infraction [ɪnˈfrækʃən] *s* infraction *f*

infrared [ˌɪnfrəˈrɛd] *adj* & *s* infrarouge *m*

infrequent [ɪnˈfrikwənt] *adj* peu fréquent, rare

infringe [ɪnˈfrɪndʒ] *tr* enfreindre; (*a patent*) contrefaire ‖ *intr*—**to infringe on** empiéter sur, enfreindre

infringement [ɪnˈfrɪndʒmənt] *s* infraction *f*; (*on patent rights*) contrefaçon *f*

infuriate [ɪnˈfjʊrɪˌet] *tr* rendre furieux

infuse [ɪnˈfjuz] *tr* infuser

infusion [ɪnˈfjuʒən] *s* infusion *f*

ingenious [ɪnˈdʒinjəs] *adj* ingénieux

ingenui·ty [ˌɪndʒɪˈn(j)u·ɪti] *s* (*pl* -ties) ingéniosité *f*

ingenuous [ɪnˈdʒɛnju·əs] *adj* ingénu, naïf

ingenuousness [ɪnˈdʒɛnju·əsnɪs] *s* ingénuité *f*, naïveté *f*

ingest [ɪnˈdʒɛst] *tr* ingérer

ingot [ˈɪŋgət] *s* lingot *m*

in·grained' *adj* imprégné; (*habit*) invétéré; (*prejudice*) enraciné

ingrate [ˈɪngret] *adj* & *s* ingrat *m*

ingratiate [ɪn'greʃɪ͵et] *tr*—**to ingratiate oneself (with)** se faire bien voir (de)
ingratiating [ɪn'greʃɪ͵etɪŋ] *adj* insinuant, persuasif
ingratitude [ɪn'grætɪ͵t(j)ud] *s* ingratitude *f*
ingredient [ɪn'gridɪ-ənt] *s* ingrédient *m*
in'growing nail' *s* ongle *m* incarné
ingulf [ɪn'gʌlf] *tr* engouffrer
inhabit [ɪn'hæbɪt] *tr* habiter
inhabitant [ɪn'hæbɪtənt] *s* habitant *m*
inhale [ɪn'hel] *tr* inhaler, aspirer; (*smoke*) avaler ‖ *intr* (*while smoking*) avaler
inherent [ɪn'hɪrənt] *adj* inhérent
inherit [ɪn'hɛrɪt] *tr* (*e.g., money*) hériter; (*e.g., money to become the heir or successor of*) hériter de; **to inherit s.th. from s.o.** hériter q.ch. de qn
inheritance [ɪn'hɛrɪtəns] *s* héritage *m*
inher'itance tax' *s* droits *mpl* de succession
inheritor [ɪn'hɛrɪtər] *s* héritier *m*
inhibit [ɪn'hɪbɪt] *tr* inhiber
inhibition [͵ɪnɪ'bɪʃən] *s* inhibition *f*
inhospitable [ɪn'hɑspɪtəbəl], [͵ɪnhɑs-'pɪtəbəl] *adj* inhospitalier
inhuman [ɪn'hjumən] *adj* inhumain
inhumane [͵ɪnhju'men] *adj* inhumain, insensible
inhumani·ty [͵ɪnhju'mænɪti] *s* (*pl* -ties) inhumanité *f*
inimical [ɪ'nɪmɪkəl] *adj* inamical
iniqui·ty [ɪ'nɪkwɪti] *s* (*pl* -ties) iniquité *f*
ini·tial [ɪ'nɪʃəl] *adj* initial ‖ *s* initiale *f*; **initials** parafe *m*, initiales ‖ *v* (*pret* -tialed or -tialled; *ger* -tialing or -tialling) *tr* signer de ses initiales, parafer
initiate [ɪ'nɪʃɪ͵et] *s* initié *m* ‖ *tr* initier; (*a project*) commencer
initiation [ɪ͵nɪʃɪ'eʃən] *s* initiation *f*
initiative [ɪ'nɪʃɪ-ətɪv], [ɪ'nɪʃətɪv] *s* initiative *f*
inject [ɪn'dʒɛkt] *tr* injecter; (*a remark or suggestion*) introduire
injection [ɪn'dʒɛkʃən] *s* injection *f*
injudicious [͵ɪndʒu'dɪʃəs] *adj* peu judicieux
injunction [ɪn'dʒʌŋkʃən] *s* injonction *f*; (*law*) mise *f* en demeure
injure ['ɪndʒər] *tr* (*to harm*) nuire (with *dat*); (*to wound*) blesser; (*to offend*) faire tort à, léser
injurious [ɪn'dʒurɪ-əs] *adj* nuisible, préjudiciable; (*offensive*) blessant, injurieux
inju·ry ['ɪndʒəri] *s* (*pl* -ries) blessure *f*, lésion *f*; (*harm*) tort *m*; injure *f*, offense *f*
injustice [ɪn'dʒʌstɪs] *s* injustice *f*
ink [ɪŋk] *s* encre *f* ‖ *tr* encrer
ink' blot' *s* pâté *m*, macule *f*
inkling ['ɪŋklɪŋ] *s* soupçon *m*, pressentiment *m*
ink' pad' *s* tampon *m* encreur
ink'stand' *s* encrier *m*
ink'well' *s* encrier *m* de bureau

ink·y ['ɪŋki] *adj* (*comp* -ier; *super* -iest) noir foncé; taché d'encre
inlaid ['ɪn͵led], [͵ɪn'led] *adj* incrusté
inland ['ɪnlənd] *adj* & *s* intérieur *m* ‖ *adv* à l'intérieur, vers l'intérieur
in'-law' *s* (coll) parent *m* par alliance; **the in-laws** (coll) la belle-famille, les beaux-parents *mpl*
in·lay ['ɪn͵le] *s* incrustation *f* ‖ [ɪn-'le], ['ɪn͵le] *v* (*pret* & *pp* -laid) *tr* incruster
in'let *s* bras *m* de mer, crique *f*; (*e.g., of air*) arrivée *f*
in'mate *s* habitant *m*; (*of an institution*) pensionnaire *mf*
inn [ɪn] *s* auberge *f*
innate [ɪ'net], ['ɪnet] *adj* inné, infus
inner ['ɪnər] *adj* intérieur; (*e.g., ear*) interne; intime, secret
in'ner·spring mat'tress *s* sommier *m* à ressorts internes
in'ner tube' *s* chambre *f* à air
inning ['ɪnɪŋ] *s* manche *f*, tour *m*
inn'keep'er *s* aubergiste *mf*
innocence ['ɪnəsəns] *s* innocence *f*
innocent ['ɪnəsənt] *adj* & *s* innocent *m*
innocuous [ɪ'nɑkju-əs] *adj* inoffensif
innovate ['ɪnə͵vet] *tr* & *intr* innover
innovation [͵ɪnə've ʃən] *s* innovation *f*
innuen·do [͵ɪnju'ɛndo] *s* (*pl* -does) allusion *f*, sous-entendu *m*
innumerable [ɪ'n(j)umərəbəl] *adj* innombrable
inoculate [ɪn'ɑkjə͵let] *tr* inoculer
inoculation [ɪn͵ɑkjə'leʃən] *s* inoculation *f*
inoffensive [͵ɪnə'fɛnsɪv] *adj* inoffensif
inopportune [ɪn͵ɑpər't(i)un] *adj* inopportun, mal choisi
inordinate [ɪn'ɔrdɪnɪt] *adj* désordonné, déréglé; (*unrestrained*) démesuré
inorganic [͵ɪnɔr'gænɪk] *adj* inorganique
in'put' *s* consommation *f*; (elec) prise *f*, entrée *f*
inquest ['ɪnkwɛst] *s* enquête *f*
inquire [ɪn'kwaɪr] *tr* s'informer de, e.g., **to inquire the price of** s'informer du prix de ‖ *intr* s'enquérir; **to inquire about** s'enquérir de, se renseigner sur; **to inquire into** faire des recherches sur
inquir·y [ɪn'kwaɪri], ['ɪnkwɪri] *s* (*pl* -ies) investigation *f*, enquête *f*; (*question*) demande *f*; **to make inquiries** s'informer
inquisition [͵ɪnkwɪ'zɪʃən] *s* inquisition *f*
inquisitive [ɪn'kwɪzɪtɪv] *adj* curieux, questionneur
in'road' *s* incursion *f*, empiètement *m*
ins' and outs' *spl* tours et détours *mpl*
insane [ɪn'sen] *adj* dément, fou; (*unreasonable*) insensé, insane
insane' asy'lum *s* asile *m* d'aliénés
insani·ty [ɪn'sænɪti] *s* (*pl* -ties) démence *f*, aliénation *f*
insatiable [ɪn'seʃəbəl] *adj* insatiable
inscribe [ɪn'skraɪb] *tr* inscrire; (*a book*) dédier
inscription [ɪn'skrɪpʃən] *s* inscription *f*; (*of a book*) dédicace *f*

inscrutable [ɪn'skrutəbəl] *adj* impénétrable, fermé
insect ['ɪnsɛkt] *s* insecte *m*
insecticide [ɪn'sɛktɪ‚saɪd] *adj & s* insecticide *m*
insecure [‚ɪnsɪ'kjʊr] *adj* peu sûr; (*nervous*) inquiet
insensitive [ɪn'sɛnsɪtɪv] *adj* insensible
inseparable [ɪn'sɛpərəbəl] *adj* inséparable
insert ['ɪnsʌrt] *s* (sewing) incrustation *f*; (typ) hors-texte *m*, encart *m* ‖ [ɪn'sʌrt] *tr* insérer, introduire; (typ) encarter
insertion [ɪn'sʌrʃən] *s* insertion *f*; (sewing) incrustation *f*
in·set ['ɪn‚sɛt] *s* (*map, picture, etc.*) médaillon *m*; (sewing) incrustation *f*; (typ) hors-texte *m*, encart *m* ‖ [ɪn'sɛt], ['ɪn‚sɛt] *v* (*pret & pp* -set; *ger* -setting) *tr* insérer; (*a page or pages*) encarter
in'shore' *adj* côtier ‖ *adv* près de la côte
in'side' *adj* d'intérieur, interne; secret ‖ *s* intérieur *m*, dedans *m*; **insides** (coll) entrailles *fpl* ‖ *adv* à l'intérieur; **inside and out** au-dedans et au-dehors; **inside of** à l'intérieur de; **inside out** à l'envers; **to turn inside out** (*e.g., a coat*) retourner ‖ *prep* à l'intérieur de, dans
in'side informa'tion *s* tuyau *m*, tuyaux *m*
insider [‚ɪn'saɪdər] *s* initié *m*
in'side track' *s*—**to have the inside track** prendre à la corde; (fig) avoir un avantage
insidious [ɪn'sɪdɪ·əs] *adj* insidieux
in'sight' *s* pénétration *f*; (psychol) défoulement *m*
insigni·a [ɪn'sɪgnɪ·ə] *s* (*pl* -a or -as) insigne *m*
insignificant [‚ɪnsɪg'nɪfɪkənt] *adj* insignifiant
insincere [‚ɪnsɪn'sɪr] *adj* insincère, peu sincère
insinuate [ɪn'sɪnjʊ‚et] *tr* insinuer
insipid [ɪn'sɪpɪd] *adj* insipide
insist [ɪn'sɪst] *intr* insister; **to insist on** insister sur; **to insist on** + *ger* insister pour + *inf*
insofar as [‚ɪnso'fɑrəz] *conj* pour autant que, dans la mesure où
insolence ['ɪnsələns] *s* insolence *f*
insolent ['ɪnsələnt] *adj* insolent
insoluble [ɪn'saljəbəl] *adj* insoluble
insolven·cy [ɪn'salvənsi] *s* (*pl* -cies) insolvabilité *f*
insolvent [ɪn'salvənt] *adj* insolvable
insomnia [ɪn'samnɪ·ə] *s* insomnie *f*
insomuch [‚ɪnso'mʌtʃ] *adv*—**insomuch as** vu que; **insomuch that** à tel point que
inspect [ɪn'spɛkt] *tr* inspecter
inspection [ɪn'spɛkʃən] *s* inspection *f*
inspector [ɪn'spɛktər] *s* inspecteur *m*
inspiration [‚ɪnspɪ're ʃən] *s* inspiration *f*
inspire [ɪn'spaɪr] *tr* inspirer
inspiring [ɪn'spaɪrɪŋ] *adj* inspirant
install [ɪn'stɔl] *tr* installer
installment [ɪn'stɔlmənt] *s* installation *f*; (*delivery*) livraison *f*; (*serial story*)

feuilleton *m*; (*partial payment*) acompte *m*, versement *m*; **in installments** par acomptes, par tranches
install'ment plan' *s* vente *f* à tempérament or à crédit; **on the installment plan** avec facilités de paiement
instance ['ɪnstəns] *s* cas *m*, exemple *m*; **for instance** par exemple
instant ['ɪnstənt] *adj* imminent, immédiat; **on the fifth instant** le cinq courant ‖ *s* instant *m*, moment *m*
instantaneous [‚ɪnstən'tenɪ·əs] *adj* instantané
instantly ['ɪnstəntli] *adv* à l'instant
instead [ɪn'stɛd] *adv* plutôt, au contraire; à ma (votre, sa, etc.) place; **instead of** au lieu de
in'step' *s* cou-de-pied *m*
instigate ['ɪnstɪ‚get] *tr* inciter
instigation [‚ɪnstɪ'geʃən] *s* instigation *f*
instill [ɪn'stɪl] *tr* instiller
instinct ['ɪnstɪŋkt] *s* instinct *m*
instinctive [ɪn'stɪŋktɪv] *adj* instinctif
institute ['ɪnstɪ‚t(j)ut] *s* institut *m* ‖ *tr* instituer
institution [‚ɪnstɪ't(j)uʃən] *s* institution *f*
instruct [ɪn'strʌkt] *tr* instruire
instruction [ɪn'strʌkʃən] *s* instruction *f*
instructive [ɪn'strʌktɪv] *adj* instructif
instructor [ɪn'strʌktər] *s* instructeur *m*
instrument ['ɪnstrəmənt] *s* instrument *m* ‖ ['ɪnstrə‚ment] *tr* instrumenter
instrumental [‚ɪnstrə'mentəl] *adj* instrumental; **to be instrumental in** contribuer à
instrumentalist [‚ɪnstrə'mentəlɪst] *s* instrumentiste *mf*
instrumentali·ty [‚ɪnstrəmən'tælɪti] *s* (*pl* -ties) intermédiaire *m*, intervention *f*
in'strument board' *s* tableau *m* de bord
in'strument fly'ing *s* radio-navigation *f*, vol *m* aux instruments
in'strument land'ing *s* atterrissage *m* aux instruments
in'strument pan'el *s* tableau *m* de bord
insubordinate [‚ɪnsə'bɔrdɪnɪt] *adj* insubordonné
insufferable [ɪn'sʌfərəbəl] *adj* insupportable, intolérable
insufficient [‚ɪnsə'fɪʃənt] *adj* insuffisant
insular ['ɪnsələr], ['ɪnsjʊlər] *adj* insulaire
insulate ['ɪnsə‚let] *tr* insoler
in'sulating tape' *s* ruban *m* isolant, chatterton *m*
insulation [‚ɪnsə'leʃən] *s* isolation *f*
insulator ['ɪnsə‚letər] *s* isolant *m*
insulin ['ɪnsəlɪn] *s* insuline *f*
insult ['ɪnsʌlt] *s* insulte *f* ‖ [ɪn'sʌlt] *tr* insulter
insulting [ɪn'sʌltɪŋ] *adj* insultant, injurieux
insurance [ɪn'ʃʊrəns] *s* assurance *f*
insure [ɪn'ʃʊr] *tr* assurer
insurer [ɪn'ʃʊrər] *s* assureur *m*
insurgent [ɪn'sʌrdʒənt] *adj & s* insurgé *m*

insurmountable [,ɪnsər'mauntəbəl] *adj* insurmountable
insurrection [,ɪnsə'rɛkʃən] *s* insurrection *f*
intact [ɪn'tækt] *adj* intact
in'take' *s* (*place*) entrée *f*; (*act or amount*) prise *f*; (mach) admission *f*
in'take man'ifold *s* tubulure *f* d'admission, collecteur *m* d'admission
in'take valve' *s* soupape *f* d'admission
intangible [ɪn'tændʒɪbəl] *adj* intangible
integer ['ɪntɪdʒər] *s* nombre *m* entier
integral ['ɪntɪgrəl] *adj* intégral; (*part*) intégrant; **integral with** solidaire de ‖ *s* intégrale *f*
integrate ['ɪntɪ,gret] *tr* intégrer
integration [,ɪntɪ'greʃən] *s* intégration *f*
integrity [ɪn'tɛgrɪti] *s* intégrité *f*
intellect ['ɪntə,lɛkt] *s* intellect *m*; (*person*) intelligence *f*
intellectual [,ɪntə'lɛktʃu·əl] *adj* & *s* intellectuel *m*
intelligence [ɪn'tɛlɪdʒəns] *s* intelligence *f*
intel'ligence bu'reau *s* deuxième bureau *m*, service *m* de renseignements
intel'ligence quo'tient *s* quotient *m* intellectuel
intel'ligence test' *s* test *m* d'habileté mentale
intelligent [ɪn'tɛlɪdʒənt] *adj* intelligent
intelligible [ɪn'tɛlɪdʒɪbəl] *adj* intelligible
intemperate [ɪn'tɛmpərɪt] *adj* intempérant
intend [ɪn'tɛnd] *tr* destiner; signifier, vouloir dire; **to intend to** avoir l'intention de, penser; **to intend to become** se destiner à
intended *adj* & *s* (coll) futur *m*
intense [ɪn'tɛns] *adj* intense
intensi•fy [ɪn'tɛnsɪ,faɪ] *v* (*pret* & *pp* **-fied**) *tr* intensifier ‖ *intr* s'intensifier
intensi•ty [ɪn'tɛnsɪti] *s* (*pl* **-ties**) intensité *f*
intensive [ɪn'tɛnsɪv] *adj* intensif
intent [ɪn'tɛnt] *adj* attentif; (*look, gaze*) fixe, intense; **intent on** résolu à ‖ *s* intention *f*; **to all intents and purposes** en fait, pratiquement
intention [ɪn'tɛnʃən] *s* intention *f*
intentional [ɪn'tɛnʃənəl] *adj* intentionnel, délibéré
intentionally [ɪn'tɛnʃənəli] *adv* exprès, à dessein
in•ter [ɪn'tʌr] *v* (*pret* & *pp* **-terred**; *ger* **-terring**) *tr* enterrer
interact [,ɪntər'ækt] *intr* agir réciproquement
interaction [,ɪntər'ækʃən] *s* interaction *f*
inter•breed [,ɪntər'brid] *v* (*pret* & *pp* **-bred**) *tr* croiser ‖ *intr* se croiser
intercalate [ɪn'tʌrkə,let] *tr* intercaler
intercede [,ɪntər'sid] *intr* intercéder
intercept [,ɪntər'sɛpt] *tr* intercepter
interceptor [,ɪntər'sɛptər] *s* intercepteur *m*
interchange ['ɪntər,tʃendʒ] *s* échange *m*, permutation *f*; (*transfer point*) correspondance *f*; (*on highway*)

échangeur *m* ‖ [,ɪntər'tʃendʒ] *tr* échanger, permuter ‖ *intr* permuter
intercollegiate [,ɪntərkə'lidʒɪ·ɪt] *adj* interuniversitaire, entre universités
intercom ['ɪntər,kɑm] *s* (coll) interphone *m*
intercourse ['ɪntər,kors] *s* relations *fpl*, rapports *mpl*; (*copulation*) copulation *f*, coït *m*
intercross [,ɪntər'krɔs], [,ɪntər'krɑs] *tr* entrecroiser ‖ *intr* s'entrecroiser
interdict ['ɪntər,dɪkt] *s* interdit *m* ‖ [,ɪntər'dɪkt] *tr* interdire; **to interdict s.o. from** + *ger* interdire à qn de + *inf*
interest ['ɪntərɪst], ['ɪntrɪst] *s* intérêt *m*; **the interests** les gens influents; **to pay back with interest** rendre avec usure ‖ ['ɪntərɪst], ['ɪntrɪst], ['ɪntə,rɛst] *tr* intéresser
interested *adj* intéressé; **to be interested in** s'intéresser à or dans
interesting ['ɪntrɪstɪŋ], ['ɪntə,rɛstɪŋ] *adj* intéressant
interfere [,ɪntər'fɪr] *intr* (*to meddle*) s'ingérer; (phys) interférer; **to interfere with** intervenir dans, se mêler de; (*to come into opposition with*) gêner, entraver; **to interfere with each other** interférer (entre eux)
interference [,ɪntər'fɪrəns] *s* interférence *f*, intervention *f*; (phys) interférence *m*; (*jamming*) (rad) brouillage *m*
interim ['ɪntərɪm] *adj* provisoire, par intérim ‖ *s* intérim *m*
interior [ɪn'tɪrɪ·ər] *adj* & *s* intérieur *m*
inte'rior dec'orator *s* décorateur *m* d'intérieurs
interject [,ɪntər'dʒɛkt] *tr* interposer; (*questions*) lancer
interjection [,ɪntər'dʒɛkʃən] *s* intervention *f*; (gram) interjection *f*
interlard [,ɪntər'lɑrd] *tr* entrelarder
interline [,ɪntər'laɪn] *tr* interligner
interlining ['ɪntər,laɪnɪŋ] *s* doublure *f* intermédiaire
interlock [,ɪntər'lɑk] *tr* emboîter, engager ‖ *intr* s'emboîter, s'engager
interloper [,ɪntər'lopər] *s* intrus *m*
interlude ['ɪntər,lud] *s* (mov, mus, telv) interlude *m*; (theat, fig) intermède *m*
intermediar•y [,ɪntər'midɪ,ɛri] *adj* intermédiaire ‖ *s* (*pl* **-ies**) intermédiaire *mf*
intermediate [,ɪntər'midɪ·ɪt] *adj* intermédiaire
interment [ɪn'tʌrmənt] *s* enterrement *m*, sépulture *f*
interminable [ɪn'tʌrmɪnəbəl] *adj* interminable
intermingle [,ɪntər'mɪŋgəl] *tr* entremêler ‖ *intr* s'entremêler
intermission [,ɪntər'mɪʃən] *s* relâche *m*, pause *f*; (theat) entracte *m*
intermittent [,ɪntər'mɪtənt] *adj* intermittent
intermix [,ɪntər'mɪks] *tr* entremêler ‖ *intr* s'entremêler
intern ['ɪntʌrn] *s* interne *mf* ‖ [ɪn'tʌrn] *tr* interner

internal [ɪn'tʌrnəl] *adj* interne
inter'nal-combus'tion en'gine *s* moteur *m* à explosion
inter'nal rev'enue *s* recettes *fpl* fiscales
international [ˌɪntər'næʃənəl] *adj* international; (*exposition*) universel
in'terna'tional date' line' *s* ligne *f* de changement de date
in'terna'tional time' zone' *s* fuseau *m* horaire international
internecine [ˌɪntər'nisɪn] *adj* domestique, intestin; (*war*) sanguinaire, d'extermination
internee [ˌɪntʌr'ni] *s* interné *m*
internment [ɪn'tʌrnmənt] *s* internement *m*
in'tern·ship' *s* internat *m*
interpellate [ˌɪntər'pɛlet], [ɪn'tʌrpɪˌlet] *tr* interpeller
interplanetary [ˌɪntər'plænəˌtɛri] *adj* interplanétaire
interplan'etary trav'el *s* voyages *mpl* interplanétaires
interplay ['ɪntərˌple] *s* interaction *f*
interpolate [ɪn'tʌrpəˌlet] *tr* interpoler
interpose [ˌɪntər'poz] *tr* interposer
interpret [ɪn'tʌrprɪt] *tr* interpréter
interpretation [ɪnˌtʌrprɪ'teʃən] *s* interprétation *f*
interpreter [ɪn'tʌrprɪtər] *s* interprète *mf*
interrogate [ɪn'tɛrəˌget] *tr* interroger
interrogation [ɪnˌtɛrə'geʃən] *s* interrogation *f*
interroga'tion mark' *s* point *m* d'interrogation
interrupt [ˌɪntə'rʌpt] *tr* interrompre
interruption [ˌɪntə'rʌpʃən] *s* interruption *f*
intersect [ˌɪntər'sɛkt] *tr* entrecouper || *intr* s'entrecouper
intersection [ˌɪntər'sɛkʃən] *s* intersection *f*
intersperse [ˌɪntər'spʌrs] *tr* entremêler
interstellar [ˌɪntər'stɛlər] *adj* interstellaire
interstice [ɪn'tʌrstɪs] *s* interstice *m*
intertwine [ˌɪntər'twaɪn] *tr* entrelacer || *intr* s'entrelacer
interval ['ɪntərvəl] *s* intervalle *m*
intervene [ˌɪntər'vin] *intr* intervenir
intervening [ˌɪntər'vinɪŋ] *adj* (*period*) intermédiaire; (*party*) intervenant
intervention [ˌɪntər'vɛnʃən] *s* intervention *f*
interview ['ɪntərˌvju] *s* entrevue *f*; (journ) interview *f* || *tr* avoir une entrevue avec; (journ) interviewer
inter·weave [ˌɪntər'wiv] *v* (*pret* -wove or -weaved; *pp* -wove, woven or weaved) *tr* entrelacer; (*to intermingle*) entremêler
intestate [ɪn'tɛstet], [ɪn'tɛstɪt] *adj & s* intestat *m*
intestine [ɪn'tɛstɪn] *adj & s* intestin *m*
intima·cy ['ɪntɪməsi] *s* (*pl* -cies) intimité *f*; rapports *mpl* sexuels
intimate ['ɪntɪmɪt] *adj & s* intime *mf* || ['ɪntɪˌmet] *tr* donner à entendre
intimation [ˌɪntɪ'meʃən] *s* suggestion *f*, insinuation *f*
intimidate [ɪn'tɪmɪˌdet] *tr* intimider

into ['ɪntu], ['ɪntʊ] *prep* dans, en
intolerant [ɪn'tɑlərənt] *adj* intolérant
intonation [ˌɪnto'neʃən] *s* intonation *f*
intone [ɪn'ton] *tr* (*to begin to sing*) entonner; (*to sing or recite in a monotone*) psalmodier || *intr* psalmodier
intoxicant [ɪn'tɑksɪkənt] *s* boisson *f* alcoolique
intoxicate [ɪn'tɑksɪˌket] *tr* enivrer; (*to poison*) intoxiquer
intoxication [ɪnˌtɑksɪ'keʃən] *s* ivresse *f*; (*poisoning*) intoxication *f*; (fig) enivrement *m*
intractable [ɪn'træktəbəl] *adj* intraitable
intransigent [ɪn'trænsɪdʒənt] *adj* intransigeant
intransitive [ɪn'trænsɪtɪv] *adj* intransitif
intravenous [ˌɪntrə'vinəs] *adj* intraveineux
intrepid [ɪn'trɛpɪd] *adj* intrépide
intricate ['ɪntrɪkɪt] *adj* compliqué
intrigue [ɪn'trig], ['ɪntrig] *s* intrigue *f* || [ɪn'trig] *tr & intr* intriguer
intrinsic(al) [ɪn'trɪnsɪk(əl)] *adj* intrinsèque
introduce [ˌɪntrə'd(j)us] *tr* introduire; (*to make acquainted*) présenter
introduction [ˌɪntrə'dʌkʃən] *s* introduction *f*; (*of one person to another or others*) présentation *f*
introductory [ˌɪntrə'dʌktəri] *adj* préliminaire; (*text*) liminaire; (*speech, letter, etc.*) de présentation
introduc'tory of'fer *s* offre *f* de présentation
introspective · [ˌɪntrə'spɛktɪv] *adj* introspectif; (*person*) méditatif
introvert ['ɪntrəˌvʌrt] *adj & s* introverti *m*
intrude [ɪn'trud] *intr* s'ingérer, s'immiscer; **to intrude on s.o.** déranger qn
intruder [ɪn'trudər] *s* intrus *m*
intrusion [ɪn'truʒən] *s* intrusion *f*
intrusive [ɪn'trusɪv] *adj* importun
intuition [ˌɪnt(j)u'ɪʃən] *s* intuition *f*
inundate ['ɪnənˌdet] *tr* inonder
inundation [ˌɪnən'deʃən] *s* inondation *f*
inure [ɪn'jʊr] *tr* aguerrir, endurcir || *intr* entrer en vigueur; **to inure to** rejaillir sur
invade [ɪn'ved] *tr* envahir
invader [ɪn'vedər] *s* envahisseur *m*
invalid [ɪn'vælɪd] *adj* invalide, nul || ['ɪnvəlɪd] *adj & s* malade *mf*, invalide *mf*
invalidate [ɪn'vælɪˌdet] *tr* invalider
invalidity [ˌɪnvə'lɪdɪti] *s* invalidité *f*
invaluable [ɪn'vælju·əbəl] *adj* inappréciable, inestimable
invariable [ɪn'vɛrɪ·əbəl] *adj* invariable
invasion [ɪn've3ən] *s* invasion *f*
invective [ɪn'vɛktɪv] *s* invective *f*
inveigh [ɪn've] *intr*—**to inveigh against** invectiver contre
inveigle [ɪn'vegəl], [ɪn'vigəl] *tr* séduire, enjôler; **to inveigle s.o.** + *ger* entraîner qn à + *inf*
invent [ɪn'vɛnt] *tr* inventer
invention [ɪn'vɛnʃən] *s* invention *f*

inventive [ɪnˈvɛntɪv] *adj* inventif
inventiveness [ɪnˈvɛntɪvnɪs] *s* esprit *m* inventif
inventor [ɪnˈvɛntər] *s* inventeur *m*
invento·ry [ˈɪnvənˌtori] *s* (*pl* **-ries**) inventaire *m* ‖ *v* (*pret & pp* **-ried**) *tr* inventorier
inverse [ɪnˈvʌrs] *adj & s* inverse *m*
inversion [ɪnˈvʌrʒən], [ɪnˈvʌrʃən] *s* interversion *f*, inversion *f*
invert [ˈɪnvʌrt] *adj & s* inverti *m* ‖ [ɪnˈvʌrt] *tr* inverser; (*an image*) invertir
invertebrate [ɪnˈvʌrtɪˌbret], [ɪnˈvʌrtɪbrɪt] *adj & s* invertébré *m*
invest [ɪnˈvɛst] *tr* investir; (*money*) investir, placer; **to invest with** investir de ‖ *intr* investir or placer de l'argent
investigate [ɪnˈvɛstɪˌget] *tr* examiner, rechercher
investigation [ɪnˌvɛstɪˈgeʃən] *s* investigation *f*
investigator [ɪnˈvɛstɪˌgetər] *s* investigateur *m*, chercheur *m*
investment [ɪnˈvɛstmənt] *s* investissement *m*, placement *m*; (*with an office or dignity*) investiture *f*; (*siege*) investissement
investor [ɪnˈvɛstər] *s* capitaliste *mf*
inveterate [ɪnˈvɛtərɪt] *adj* invétéré
invidious [ɪnˈvɪdɪ·əs] *adj* odieux
invigorate [ɪnˈvɪgəˌret] *tr* vivifier, fortifier
invigorating [ɪnˈvɪgəˌretɪŋ] *adj* vivifiant, fortifiant
invincible [ɪnˈvɪnsɪbəl] *adj* invincible
invisible [ɪnˈvɪzɪbəl] *adj* invisible
invis'ible ink' *s* encre *f* sympathique
invitation [ˌɪnvɪˈteʃən] *s* invitation *f*
invite [ɪnˈvaɪt] *tr* inviter
inviting [ɪnˈvaɪtɪŋ] *adj* invitant
invoice [ˈɪnvɔɪs] *s* facture *f*; **as per invoice** suivant facture ‖ *tr* facturer
invoke [ɪnˈvok] *tr* invoquer
involuntary [ɪnˈvalənˌteri] *adj* involontaire
involve [ɪnˈvalv] *tr* impliquer, entraîner, engager
invulnerable [ɪnˈvʌlnərəbəl] *adj* invulnérable
inward [ˈɪnwərd] *adj* intérieur ‖ *adv* intérieurement, en dedans
iodide [ˈaɪ·əˌdaɪd] *s* iodure *m*
iodine [ˈaɪ·əˌdin] *s* (chem) iode *m* ‖ [ˈaɪ·əˌdaɪn] *s* (pharm) teinture *f* d'iode
ion [ˈaɪ·ən], [ˈaɪ·an] *s* ion *m*
ionize [ˈaɪ·əˌnaɪz] *tr* ioniser
I.O.U. [ˈaɪˌoˈju] *s* (letterword) **(I owe you)** reconnaissance *f* de dette
I.Q. [ˈaɪˈkju] *s* (letterword) **(intelligence quotient)** quotient *m* intellectuel
Iran [ɪˈran], [aɪˈræn] *s* l'Iran *m*
Iranian [aɪˈrenɪ·ən] *adj* iranien ‖ *s* (*language*) iranien *m*; (*person*) Iranien *m*
Iraq [ɪˈrak] *s* l'Irak *m*
Ira·qi [ɪˈraki] *adj* irakien ‖ *s* (*pl* **-qis**) Irakien *m*
irate [ˈaɪret], [aɪˈret] *adj* irrité
ire [aɪr] *s* courroux *m*, colère *f*

Ireland [ˈaɪrlənd] *s* Irlande *f*; l'Irlande *f*
iris [ˈaɪrɪs] *s* iris *m*
Irish [ˈaɪrɪʃ] *adj* irlandais ‖ *s* (*language*) irlandais *m*; **the Irish** les Irlandais
I'rish·man *s* (*pl* **-men**) Irlandais *m*
I'rish stew' *s* ragoût *m* irlandais
I'rish·wom'an *s* (*pl* **-wom'en**) Irlandaise *f*
irk [ʌrk] *tr* ennuyer, fâcher
irksome [ˈʌrksəm] *adj* ennuyeux
iron [ˈaɪ·ərn] *s* fer *m*; (*for pressing clothes*) fer à repasser; **irons** (*fetters*) fers; **to have too many irons in the fire** courir deux lièvres à la fois; **to strike while the iron is hot** battre le fer tant qu'il est chaud ‖ *tr* (*clothes*) repasser; **to iron out** (*a difficulty*) aplanir
i'ron and steel' in'dustry *s* sidérurgie *f*
i'ron-bound' *adj* cerclé; (*unyielding*) inflexible; (*rock-bound*) plein de récifs
ironclad [ˈaɪ·ərnˌklæd] *adj* blindé, cuirassé; (*e.g., contract*) infrangible
i'ron cur'tain *s* rideau *m* de fer
i'ron diges'tion *s* estomac *m* d'autruche
i'ron horse' *s* coursier *m* de fer
ironic(al) [aɪˈranɪk(əl)] *adj* ironique
ironing [ˈaɪ·ərnɪŋ] *s* repassage *m*
i'roning board' *s* planche *f* à repasser
i'ron lung' *s* poumon *m* d'acier
i'ron ore' *s* minerai *m* de fer
i'ron·ware' *s* quincaillerie *f*, ferblanterie *f*
i'ron will' *s* volonté *f* inflexible
i'ron·work' *s* ferrure *f*, ferronnerie *f*
i'ron·work'er *s* ferronnier *m*
iro·ny [ˈaɪrəni] *s* (*pl* **-nies**) ironie *f*
irradiate [ɪˈrediˌet] *tr & intr* irradier
irrational [ɪˈræʃənəl] *adj* irrationnel
irredeemable [ˌɪriˈdiməbəl] *adj* irrémédiable; (*bonds*) non remboursable
irrefutable [ˌɪriˈfjutəbəl], [ɪˈrɛfjutəbəl] *adj* irréfutable
irregular [ɪˈrɛgjələr] *adj & s* irrégulier *m*
irrelevant [ɪˈrɛləvənt] *adj* non pertinent, hors de propos
irreligious [ˌɪriˈlɪdʒəs] *adj* irréligieux
irremediable [ˌɪriˈmidɪ·əbəl] *adj* irrémédiable
irreparable [ɪˈrɛpərəbəl] *adj* irréparable
irreplaceable [ˌɪriˈplesəbəl] *adj* irremplaçable
irrepressible [ˌɪriˈprɛsɪbəl] *adj* irrépressible, irrésistible
irreproachable [ˌɪriˈprotʃəbəl] *adj* irréprochable
irresistible [ˌɪriˈzɪstɪbəl] *adj* irrésistible
irrespective [ˌɪriˈspɛktɪv] *adj*—**irrespective of** indépendant de
irresponsible [ˌɪriˈspansɪbəl] *adj* irresponsable
irretrievable [ˌɪriˈtrivəbəl] *adj* irréparable; (*lost*) irrécupérable
irreverent [ɪˈrɛvərənt] *adj* irrévérencieux
irrevocable [ɪˈrɛvəkəbəl] *adj* irrévocable
irrigate [ˈɪrɪˌget] *tr* irriguer

irrigation [‚ırı'geʃən] *s* irrigation *f*
irritant ['ırıtənt] *adj* & *s* irritant *m*
irritate ['ırı‚tet] *tr* irriter
irritation [‚ırı'teʃən] *s* irritation *f*
irruption [ı'rʌpʃən] *s* irruption *f*
Isaiah [aı'ze·ə] *s* Isaïe *m*
isinglass ['aızıŋ‚glæs], ['aızıŋ‚glɑs]
s gélatine *f*, colle *f* de poisson; (mineral) mica *m*
Islam ['ısləm], [ıs'lɑm] *s* l'Islam *m*
island ['aılənd] *adj* insulaire ‖ *s* île *f*
islander ['aıləndər] *s* insulaire *mf*
isle [aıl] *s* îlot *m*; (poetic) île *f*
isolate ['aısə‚let], ['ısə‚let] *tr* isoler
isolation [‚aısə'leʃən], [‚ısə'leʃən] *s*
isolement *m*
isolationist [‚aısə'leʃənıst], [‚ısə'le-
ʃənıst] *adj* & *s* isolationniste *mf*
isosceles [aı'sɑsə‚liz] *adj* isocèle *m*
isotope ['aısə‚top] *s* isotope *m*
Israel ['ızrı·əl] *s* Israël *m*
Israe·li [ız'reli] *adj* israélien ‖ *s* (*pl*
-lis [liz]) Israélien *m*
Israelite ['ızrı·ə‚laıt] *adj* israélite ‖ *s*
Israélite *mf*
issuance ['ıʃu·əns] *s* émission *f*
issue ['ıʃu] *s* (*way out*) sortie *f*, issue
f; (*outcome*) issue; (*of a magazine*)
numéro *m*; (*offspring*) descendance
f; (*of banknotes, stamps, etc.*) émission *f*; (*under discussion*) point *m* à
discuter; (pathol) écoulement *m*; **at
issue** en jeu, en litige; **to take issue
with** être en désaccord avec; **without issue** sans enfants ‖ *tr* (*a book,
a magazine*) publier; (*banknotes,
stamps, etc.*) émettre; (*a summons*)
lancer; (*an order*) donner; (*a procla-*

mation) faire; (*a verdict*) rendre ‖
intr sortir, déboucher
isthmus ['ısməs] *s* isthme *m*
it [ıt] *pron pers* ce §82B, §85; lui §85;
il §87; le §87; y §87; en §87
Italian [ı'tæljən] *adj* italien ‖ *s* (*language*) italien *m*; (*person*) Italien *m*
italic [ı'tælık] *adj* (typ) italique; **Italic**
italique ‖ **italics** *spl* italique *m*
italicize [ı'tælı‚saız] *tr* mettre en italique
Italy ['ıtəli] *s* Italie *f*; l'Italie
itch [ıtʃ] *s* démangeaison *f*; (pathol)
gale *f* ‖ *tr* démanger (with *dat*) ‖ *intr*
(*said of part of body*) démanger;
(*said of person*) avoir une démangeaison; **to itch to** (fig) avoir une
démangeaison de
itch·y ['ıtʃi] *adj* (*comp* -ier; *super*
-iest) piquant; (pathol) galeux
item ['aıtəm] *s* article *m*; (*in a list*)
point *m*; (*piece of news*) nouvelle *f*
itemize ['aıtə‚maız] *tr* spécifier, énumérer
itinerant [aı'tınərənt], [ı'tınərənt] *adj*
& *s* itinérant *m*
itinerar·y [aı'tınə‚reri], [ı'tınə‚reri]
adj itinéraire ‖ *s* (*pl* -ies) itinéraire *m*
its [ıts] *adj poss* son §88 ‖ *pron poss*
le sien §89
it·self *pron pers* soi §85; lui-même §86;
se §87
ivied ['aıvid] *adj* couvert de lierre
ivo·ry ['aıvəri] *adj* d'ivoire, en ivoire ‖
s (*pl* -ries) ivoire *m*; **to tickle the
ivories** (slang) taquiner l'ivoire
i·vory tow·er *s* (fig) tour *f* d'ivoire
ivy ['aıvi] *s* (*pl* ivies) lierre *m*

J

J, j [dʒe] *s* Xe lettre de l'alphabet
jab [dʒæb] *s* (*with a sharp point; with
a penknife; with the elbow*) coup *m*;
(*with a needle*) piqûre *f*; (*with the
fist*) coup sec ‖ *v* (*pret* & *pp* jabbed;
ger jabbing) *tr* donner un coup de
coude à; piquer; donner un coup sec
à; (*a knife*) enfoncer
jabber ['dʒæbər] *tr* & *intr* jaboter
jack [dʒæk] *s* (aut) cric *m*; (cards)
valet *m*; (elec) jack *m*, prise *f*; (coll)
fric *m*; **Jack** Jeannot *m* ‖ *tr*—**to
jack up** soulever au cric; (*prices*)
faire monter
jackal ['dʒækɔl] *s* chacal *m*
jack·ass· *s* baudet *m*
jack·daw· *s* choucas *m*
jacket ['dʒækıt] *s* (*of a woman; of a
book*) jaquette *f*; (*of a man's suit*)
veston *m*; (*metal casing*) chemise *f*
Jack· Frost· *s* le Bonhomme Hiver
jack·-in-the-box· *s* diable *m* à ressort,
boîte *f* à surprise
jack·knife· *s* (*pl* -knives) couteau *m* de
poche, couteau pliant; (*fancy dive*)
saut *m* de carpe
jack·-of-all·-trades· *s* bricoleur *m*

jack-o'-lantern ['dʒækə‚læntərn] *s* potiron *m* lumineux
jack· pot· *s* gros lot *m*, poule *f*; **to hit
the jackpot** décrocher la timbale
jack· rab·bit *s* lièvre *m* des prairies
Jacob ['dʒekəb] *s* Jacques *m*
jade [dʒed] *s* (*stone; color*) jade *m*;
(*horse*) haridelle *f*; (*woman*) coquine
f, friponne *f*
jaded *adj* éreinté, excédé; blasé
jag [dʒæg] *s* dentelure *f*; **to have a
jag on** (slang) être paf
jagged ['dʒægıd] *adj* dentelé
jaguar ['dʒægwɑr] *s* jaguar *m*
jail [dʒel] *s* prison *f* ‖ *tr* emprisonner
jail·bird· *s* cheval *m* de retour
jailer ['dʒelər] *s* geôlier *m*
jalop·y [dʒə'lɑpi] *s* (*pl* -ies) bagnole *f*,
tacot *m*, guimbarde *f*, clou *m*
jam [dʒæm] *s* confiture *f*; **to be in a
jam** (coll) être dans le pétrin ‖ *v* (*pret*
& *pp* jammed; *ger* jamming) *tr* coincer ‖ *intr* se coincer
jamboree [‚dʒæmbə'ri] *s* (*of boy
scouts*) jamboree *m*; (slang) bombance *f*
James [dʒemz] *s* Jacques *m*

jamming ['dʒæmɪŋ] s (rad) brouillage m

Jane [dʒen] s Jeanne f

jangle ['dʒæŋgəl] s cliquetis m || tr faire cliqueter; (nerves) mettre en boule || intr cliqueter

janitor ['dʒænɪtər] s concierge m

janitress ['dʒænɪtrɪs] s concierge f

January ['dʒænjʊ ˌɛri] s janvier m

ja·pan [dʒə'pæn] s laque m du Japon; Japan le Japon || v (pret & pp -panned; ger -panning) tr laquer

Japa·nese [ˌdʒæpə'niz] adj japonais || s (language) japonais m || s (pl -nese) (person) Japonais m

Jap'anese bee'tle s cétoine f

Jap'anese lan'tern s lanterne f vénitienne

jar [dʒar] s pot m, bocal m; secousse f || v (pret & pp jarred; ger jarring) tr ébranler, secouer § intr trembler, vibrer; (said of sounds, colors, opinions) discorder; to jar on the nerves taper sur les nerfs

jargon ['dʒargən] s jargon m

jasmine ['dʒæsmɪn], ['dʒæzmɪn] s jasmin m

jasper ['dʒæspər] s jaspe m

jaundice ['dʒɔndɪs], ['dʒɑndɪs] s jaunisse f, ictère m

jaundiced adj ictérique; (fig) amer

jaunt [dʒɔnt], [dʒɑnt] s excursion f

jaun·ty ['dʒɔnti], ['dʒɑnti] adj (comp -tier; super -tiest) vif, dégagé; (smart) chic

javelin ['dʒævlɪn], ['dʒævəlɪn] s javelot m

jaw [dʒɔ] s mâchoire f; (of animal) gueule f; jaws (e.g., of death) griffes fpl || tr (slang) engueuler || intr (to gossip) (slang) bavarder

jaw'bone' s mâchoire f, maxillaire m

jay [dʒe] s geai m

jay'walk' intr traverser la rue en dehors des clous

jay'walk'er s piéton m distrait

jazz [dʒæz] s jazz m || tr—to jazz up (coll) animer, égayer

jazz' band' s orchestre m de jazz

jazz' sing'er s chanteur m de rythme

jealous ['dʒɛləs] adj jaloux

jealous·y ['dʒɛləsi] s (pl -ies) jalousie f

jean [dʒin] s treillis m; Jean Jeanne f; jeans pantalon m de treillis

jeep [dʒip] s jeep f

jeer [dʒɪr] s raillerie f || intr railler; to jeer at se moquer de

Jehovah [dʒɪ'hovə] s Jéhovah m

jell [dʒɛl] s gelée f || intr se convertir en gelée; (to take hold) prendre forme, se préciser

jel·ly ['dʒɛli] s (pl -lies) gelée f || v (pret & pp -lied) tr convertir en gelée || intr se convertir en gelée

jel'ly-fish' s méduse f; (person) chiffe f

jeopardize ['dʒɛpərˌdaɪz] tr mettre en danger, compromettre

jeopardy ['dʒɛpərdi] s danger m

jerk [dʒʌrk] s saccade f, secousse f;

(slang) mufle m || tr tirer brusquement, secouer || intr se mouvoir brusquement

jerk'water town' s trou m, petite ville f de province

jerk'water train' s tortillard m

jerk·y ['dʒʌrki] adj (comp -ier; super -iest) saccadé

Jerome [dʒə'rom] s Jérôme m

jersey ['dʒʌrzi] s jersey m

Jerusalem [dʒɪ'rusələm] s Jérusalem f

jest [dʒɛst] s plaisanterie f; in jest en plaisantant || intr plaisanter

jester ['dʒɛstər] s plaisantin m; (medieval clown) bouffon m

Jesuit ['dʒɛʒʊ·ɪt], ['dʒɛzjʊ·ɪt] adj jésuite, jésuitique || s Jésuite m

Jesus ['dʒizəs] s Jésus m

Je'sus Christ' s Jésus-Christ m

jet [dʒɛt] s (color; mineral) jais m; (of water, gas, etc.) jet m; avion m à réaction || v (pret & pp jetted; ger jetting) intr gicler, jaillir; voyager en jet

jet'-black' adj noir de jais

jet' en'gine s moteur m à réaction

jet' fight'er s chasseur m à réaction

jet' fu'el s carburéacteur m

jet'lin'er s avion m de ligne à réaction

jet' plane' s avion m à réaction

jet' propul'sion s propulsion f par réaction

jetsam ['dʒɛtsəm] s marchandise f jetée à la mer

jettison ['dʒɛtɪsən] s jet m à la mer || tr jeter à la mer; (fig) mettre au rebut, rejeter

jet·ty ['dʒɛti] s (pl -ties) (wharf) appontement m; (breakwater) jetée f

Jew [dʒu] s Juif m; (rel) juif m

jewel ['dʒu·əl] s joyau m, bijou m; (of a watch) rubis m; (person) bijou

jew'el case' s écrin m

jeweler or jeweller ['dʒu·ələr] s horloger-bijoutier m, bijoutier m

jewelry ['dʒu·əlri] s joaillerie f

jew'elry store' s bijouterie f; (for watches) horlogerie f

Jewess ['dʒu·ɪs] s Juive f; (rel) juive f

Jewish ['dʒu·ɪʃ] adj juif, judaïque

jews'-harp or jew's-harp ['dʒuz ˌharp] s guimbarde f

jib [dʒɪb] s (mach) flèche f; (naut) foc m

jibe [dʒaɪb] s moquerie f || intr (coll) concorder; to jibe at se moquer de

jif·fy ['dʒɪfi] s (pl -fies)—in a jiffy (coll) en un clin d'œil

jig [dʒɪg] s (dance) gigue f; the jig is up (slang) il n'y a pas mèche, tout est dans le lac

jigger ['dʒɪgər] s mesure f qui contient une once et demie; (for fishing) leurre m; (tackle) palan m; (flea) puce f; (for separating ore) crible m; (naut) tapecul m; (gadget) (coll) machin m

jiggle ['dʒɪgəl] s petite secousse f || tr agiter, secouer || intr se trémousser

jig'saw' tr chantourner

jig' saw' s scie f à chantourner

jig'saw puz'zle *s* casse-tête *m* chinois, puzzle *m*

jilt [dʒɪlt] *tr* lâcher, repousser

jim·my ['dʒɪmi] *s* (*pl* -mies) pince-monseigneur *f* ǁ *v* (*pret* & *pp* -mied) *tr* forcer à l'aide d'une pince-monseigneur

jingle ['dʒɪŋgəl] *s* (*small bell*) grelot *m*; (*sound*) grelottement *m*; (*poem*) rimes *fpl* enfantines; slogan *m* à rimes; (*rad*) réclame *f* chantée ǁ *tr* faire grelotter ǁ *intr* grelotter

jin·go ['dʒɪŋgo] *adj* chauvin ǁ *s* (*pl* -goes) chauvin *m*; by jingo! (coll) sapristi!

jingoism ['dʒɪŋgo,ɪzəm] *s* chauvinisme *m*

jinx [dʒɪŋks] *s* guigne *f* ǁ *tr* (coll) porter la guigne à

jitters ['dʒɪtərz] *spl* (coll) frousse *f*, trouille *f*; to give the jitters to (coll) flanquer la trouille à

jittery ['dʒɪtəri] *adj* froussard

Joan [dʒon] *s* Jeanne *f*

job [dʒɑb] *s* (*piece of work*) travail *m*; (*chore*) besogne *f*, tâche *f*; (*employment*) emploi *m*; (*work done by contract*) travail à forfait; (slang) vol *m*; bad job (fig) mauvaise affaire *f*; by the job à la pièce; on the job faisant un stage; (slang) attentif; soft job (coll) filon *m*, fromage *m*; to be out of a job être en chômage; to lie down on the job (slang) tirer au flanc

jobber ['dʒɑbər] *s* (*pieceworker*) ouvrier *m* à la tâche; (*dishonest official*) agioteur *m*

job'hold'er *s* employé *m*; (*in the government*) fonctionnaire *m*

job' lot' *s* solde *m* de marchandises

job' print'ing *s* bilboquet *m*

jockey ['dʒɑki] *s* jockey *m* ǁ *tr* (coll) manœuvrer

jockstrap ['dʒɑk,stræp] *s* suspensoir *m*

jocose [dʒo'kos] *adj* jovial, joyeux

jocular ['dʒɑkjələr] *adj* facétieux

jog [dʒɑg] *s* saccade *f* ǁ *v* (*pret* & *pp* jogged; *ger* jogging) *tr* secouer; (*the memory*) rafraîchir ǁ *intr*—to jog along aller au petit trot

John [dʒɑn] *s* Jean *m*; john (slang) toilettes *fpl*

John' Bull' *s* l'Anglais *m* typique

John' Doe' *s* M. Dupont, M. Durand

Johnny ['dʒɑni] *s* (coll) Jeannot *m*

john'ny·cake' *s* galette *f* de farine de maïs

John'ny-come'-late'ly *s* (coll) nouveau venu *m*

join [dʒɔɪn] *tr* joindre; (*to meet*) rejoindre; (*a club, a church*) se joindre à, entrer dans; (*a political party*) s'affilier à; (*the army*) s'engager dans; to join s.o. in + *ger* se joindre à qn pour + *inf* ǁ *intr* se joindre

joiner ['dʒɔɪnər] *s* menuisier *m*; (coll) clubiste *mf*

joint [dʒɔɪnt] *adj* joint, combiné ǁ *s* joint *m*; (culin) rôti *m*; (slang) boîte *f*; out of joint disloqué; (fig) de travers

joint' account' *s* compte *m* indivis

joint' commit'tee *s* commission *f* mixte

joint' own'er *s* copropriétaire *mf*

joint'-stock' com'pany *s* société *f* par actions

joist [dʒɔɪst] *s* solive *f*, poutre *f*

joke [dʒok] *s* plaisanterie *f*; to play a joke on faire une attrape à ǁ *intr* plaisanter

joker ['dʒokər] *s* farceur *m*, blagueur *m*; (cards) joker *m*, fou *m*; (coll) clause *f* ambiguë

jol·ly ['dʒɑli] *adj* (*comp* -lier; *super* -liest) joyeux, enjoué ǁ *adv* (coll) rudement

jolt [dʒolt] *s* cahot *m*, secousse *f* ǁ *tr* cahoter, secouer ǁ *intr* cahoter

Jonah ['dʒonə] *s* Jonas *m*

jonquil ['dʒɑŋkwɪl] *s* jonquille *f*

Jordan ['dʒɔrdən] *s* (*country*) Jordanie *f*; la Jordanie; (*river*) Jourdain *m*

josh [dʒɑʃ] *tr* & *intr* (coll) blaguer

jostle ['dʒɑsəl] *tr* bousculer ǁ *intr* se bousculer

jot [dʒɑt] *s*—not a jot pas un iota ǁ *v* (*pret* & *pp* jotted; *ger* jotting) *tr*—to jot down prendre note de

journal ['dʒʌrnəl] *s* journal *m*; (*magazine*) revue *f*; (mach) tourillon *m*; (naut) journal de bord

jour'nal box' *s* boîte *f* d'essieu

journalism ['dʒʌrnə,lɪzəm] *s* journalisme *m*

journalist ['dʒʌrnəlɪst] *s* journaliste *mf*

journey ['dʒʌrni] *s* voyage *m*; trajet *m*, parcours *m* ǁ *intr* voyager

jour'ney·man *s* (*pl* -men) compagnon *m*

joust [dʒʌst], [dʒust], [dʒaust] *s* joute *f* ǁ *intr* jouter

Jove [dʒov] *s* Jupiter *m*; by Jove! parbleu!

jovial ['dʒovɪ·əl] *adj* jovial

jowl [dʒaul] *s* bajoue *f*

joy [dʒɔɪ] *s* joie *f*

joyful ['dʒɔɪfəl] *adj* joyeux

joyless ['dʒɔɪlɪs] *adj* sans joie

joyous ['dʒɔɪ·əs] *adj* joyeux

joy' ride' *s* (coll) balade *f* en auto

joy' stick' *s* manche *m* à balai

Jr. *abbr* (*junior*) fils, e.g., Mr. Martin, Jr. M. Martin fils

jubilant ['dʒubɪlənt] *adj* jubilant

jubilee ['dʒubɪ,li] *s* jubilé *m*

Judaism ['dʒude,ɪzəm] *s* judaïsme *m*

judge [dʒʌdʒ] *s* juge *m* ǁ *tr* & *intr* juger; judging by à en juger par

judge' ad'vocate *s* commissaire *m* du gouvernement

judgment ['dʒʌdʒmənt] *s* jugement *m*

judg'ment day' *s* jour *m* du jugement dernier

judicial [dʒu'dɪʃəl] *adj* judiciaire; (*legal*) juridique

judiciar·y [dʒu'dɪʃɪ,ɛri] *adj* judiciaire ǁ *s* (*pl* -ies) pouvoir *m* judiciaire; (*judges*) judicature *f*

judicious [dʒu'dɪʃəs] *adj* judicieux

jug [dʒʌg] *s* (*of earthenware*) cruche *f*; (*of metal*) broc *m*; (*jail*) (slang) bloc *m*

juggle ['dʒʌgəl] *tr* jongler avec; **to juggle away** escamoter || *intr* jongler
juggler ['dʒʌglər] *s* jongleur *m*; imposteur *m*, mystificateur *m*
jugglery ['dʒʌgləri] *or* **juggling** ['dʒʌglɪŋ] *s* jonglerie *f*; (*trickery*) passe-passe *m*
Jugoslavia ['jugo'slɑvɪ·ə] *s* Yougoslavie *f*; la Yougoslavie
jugular ['dʒʌgjələr], ['dʒugjələr] *adj & s* jugulaire *f*
juice [dʒus] *s* jus *m*; (coll) courant *m* électrique
juic·y ['dʒusi] *adj* (*comp* **-ier;** *super* **-iest**) juteux; (fig) savoureux
jukebox ['dʒuk,bɑks] *s* pick-up *m* électrique à sous, distributeur *m* de musique
July [dʒu'laɪ] *s* juillet *m*
jumble ['dʒʌmbəl] *s* fouilliś *m*, enchevêtrement *m* || *tr* brouiller
jumbo ['dʒʌmbo] *adj* (coll) géant
jump [dʒʌmp] *s* saut *m*, bond *m*; (*nervous start*) sursaut *m*; (sports) saut *m*; (sports) obstacle *m* || *tr* sauter; **to jump ship** tirer une bordée; **to jump the gun** démarrer trop tôt; **to jump the track** dérailler || *intr* sauter, bondir; **to jump at the chance** sauter sur l'occasion
jump' ball' *s* (sports) entre-deux *m*
jump'ing jack' *s* pantin *m*
jump' rope' *s* corde *f* à sauter
jump' seat' *s* strapontin *m*
jump·y ['dʒʌmpi] *adj* (*comp* **-ier;** *super* **-iest**) nerveux
junction ['dʒʌŋkʃən] *s* jonction *f*; (*of railroads, roads*) embranchement *m*
juncture ['dʒʌŋktʃər] *s* jointure *f*; (*occasion*) conjoncture *f*; **at this juncture** en cette occasion
June [dʒun] *s* juin *m*
jungle ['dʒʌŋgəl] *s* jungle *f*
jun'gle war'fare *s* guerre *f* de la brousse
junior ['dʒunjər] *adj* cadet; **Bobby Watson, Junior** le jeune Bobby Watson; **Martin, Junior** Martin fils || *s*

cadet *m*; (educ) étudiant *m* de troisième année
jun'ior of'ficer *s* officier *m* subalterne
juniper ['dʒunɪpər] *s* genévrier *m*
ju'niper ber'ry *s* genièvre *m*
junk [dʒʌŋk] *s* (*old metal*) ferraille *f*; (*worthless objects*) bric-à-brac *m*; (*cheap merchandise*) camelote *f*, pacotille *f*; (coll) gnognote *f*; (naut) jonque *f* || *tr* mettre au rebut
junk' deal'er *s* fripier *m*; marchand *m* de ferraille
junket ['dʒʌŋkɪt] *s* excursion *f*; voyage *m* officiel aux frais de la princesse
junk'man' *s* (*pl* **-men'**) ferrailleur *m*; chiffonnier *m*
junk' shop' *s* boutique *f* de bric-à-brac et friperie; bric-à-brac *m*
junk'yard' *s* cimetière *m* de ferraille
jurisdiction [,dʒurɪs'dɪkʃən] *s* juridiction *f*; **within the jurisdiction of** du ressort de
jurist ['dʒurɪst] *s* légiste *m*
juror ['dʒurər] *s* juré *m*
ju·ry ['dʒuri] *s* (*pl* **-ries**) jury *m*
just [dʒʌst] *adj* juste || *adv* seulement; justement; **just as** à l'instant où; (*in the same way that*) de même que; **just as it is** tel quel; **just out** vient de paraître; **to have just** venir de
justice ['dʒʌstɪs] *s* justice *f*; (*judge*) juge *m*
jus'tice of the peace' *s* juge *m* de paix
justi·fy ['dʒʌstɪ,faɪ] *v* (*pret & pp* **-fied**) *tr* justifier
justly ['dʒʌstli] *adv* justement
jut [dʒʌt] *v* (*pret & pp* **jutted;** *ger* **jutting**) *intr*—**to jut out** faire saillie
jute [dʒut] *s* jute *m*
juvenile ['dʒuvənɪl], ['dʒuve,naɪl] *adj* juvénile, adolescent; (*e.g., books*) pour la jeunesse || *s* adolescent *m*
ju'venile delin'quency *s* délinquance *f* juvénile
ju'venile delin'quent *s* délinquant *m* juvénile; **juvenile delinquents** jeunes délinquants *mpl*
juxtapose [,dʒʌkstə'poz] *tr* juxtaposer

K

K, k [ke] *s* XIe lettre de l'alphabet
kale [kel] *s* chou *m* frisé
kaleidoscope [kə'laɪdə,skop] *s* kaléidoscope *m*
kangaroo [,kæŋgə'ru] *s* kangourou *m*
kan'garoo court' *s* tribunal *m* bidon
Kashmir ['kæʃmɪr] *s* le Cachemire
kash'mir shawl' *s* châle *m* de cachemire
keel [kil] *s* quille *f* || *intr*—**to keel over** (naut) chavirer; (coll) tomber dans les pommes
keen [kin] *adj* (*having a sharp edge*) aiguisé, affilé; (*sharp, cutting*) mordant, pénétrant; (*sharp-witted*) perçant, perspicace; (*eager, much inter-*

ested) enthousiaste, vif; (slang) formidable; **keen on** engoué de, passionné de
keep [kip] *s* entretien *m*; (*of medieval castle*) donjon *m*; **for keeps** (*for good*) (coll) pour de bon; (*forever*) (coll) à tout jamais; **to earn one's keep** (coll) gagner sa nourriture, gagner sa vie; **to play for keeps** (coll) jouer le tout pour le tout || *v* (*pret & pp* **kept** [kɛpt]) *tr* garder, conserver; (*one's word or promise; accounts, a diary*) tenir; (*animals*) élever; (*a garden*) cultiver; (*a hotel, a school, etc.*) diriger; (*an appointment*) ne pas

manquer à; (*a holiday*) observer; (*a person*) avoir à sa charge, entretenir; **keep it up!** ne flanchez pas!, continuez!; **to keep away** éloigner; **to keep back** retenir; **to keep down** baisser; (*prices*) maintenir bas; (*a revolt*) réprimer; **to keep in** retenir; (*a student after school*) garder en retenue; (*dust, fire, etc.*) entretenir; **to keep off** éloigner; **to keep out** tenir éloigné, empêcher d'entrer; **to keep quiet** faire taire; **to keep running** laisser marcher; **to keep score** marquer les points; **to keep servants** avoir des domestiques; **to keep s.o. busy** occuper qn; **to keep s.o. clean** (**cool, warm, etc.**) tenir qn propre (au frais, au chaud, etc.); **to keep s.o. or s.th. from** + *ger* empêcher qn or q.ch. de + *inf*; **to keep s.o. informed about** mettre or tenir qn au courant de; **to keep s.o. waiting** faire attendre qn; **to keep up** maintenir; (*e.g., all night*) faire veiller || *intr* rester, se tenir; (*in good shape*) demeurer, se conserver; (*e.g., from rotting*) se garder; **keep out** (public sign) entrée interdite; **that can keep** (coll) ça peut attendre; **to keep** + *ger* continuer à + *inf*; **to keep away** s'éloigner, se tenir à l'écart; **to keep from** + *ger* s'abstenir de + *inf*; **to keep in with** rester en bons termes avec; **to keep on** + *ger* continuer à + *inf*; **to keep out** rester dehors; **to keep out of** ne pas se mêler de; **to keep quiet** rester tranquille, se taire; **to ̦keep to** (*e.g., the right*) garder (*e.g., la droite*); **to keep up** tenir bon, tenir ferme; **to keep up with** aller de pair avec

keeper ['kipər] *s* gardien *m*, garde *m*; (*of a game preserve*) garde forestier; (*of a horseshoe magnet*) armature *f*

keeping ['kipiŋ] *s* garde *f*, surveillance *f*; (*of a holiday*) observance *f*; **in keeping with** en accord avec; **in safe keeping** sous bonne garde; **out of keeping with** en désaccord avec

keep'sake' *s* souvenir *m*, gage *m* d'amitié

keg [kɛg] *s* tonnelet *m*; (*of herring*) caque *f*

ken [kɛn] *s*—**beyond the ken of** hors de la portée de

kennel ['kɛnəl] *s* chenil *m*

kep·i ['kepi], ['kɛpi] *s* (*pl* -**is**) képi *m*

kept' wom'an [kɛpt] *s* (*pl* **wom'en**) femme *f* entretenue

kerchief ['kʌrtʃif] *s* fichu *m*

kernel ['kʌrnəl] *s* (*inner part of a nut or fruit stone*) amande *f*; (*of wheat or - corn*) grain *m*; (fig) noyau *m*, cœur *m*

kerosene ['kɛrə‚sin], [‚kɛrə'sin] *s* kérosène *m*, pétrole *m* lampant

ker'osene lamp' *s* lampe *f* à pétrole

kerplunk [‚kʌr'pluŋk] *interj* patatras!

ketchup ['kɛtʃəp] *s* sauce *f* tomate, ketchup *m*

kettle ['kɛtəl] *s* chaudron *m*, marmite *f*; (*teakettle*) bouilloire *f*

ket'tle·drum' *s* timbale *f*

key [ki] *adj* clef, clé || *s* clef *f*, clé *f*; (*of piano, typewriter, etc.*) touche *f*; (*wedge or cotter used to lock parts together*) cheville *f*, clavette *f*; (*reef or low island*) caye *f*; (*answer book*) livre *m* du maître; (*tone of voice*) ton *m*; (*to a map*) légende *f*; (bot) samare *f*; (mus) tonalité *f*; (telg) manipulateur *m*; **key to the city** droit *m* de cité; **off key** faux; **on key** juste || *tr* claveter, coincer; **to be keyed up** être surexcité, être tendu

key'board' *s* clavier *m*

key'hole' *s* trou *m* de la serrure; (*of clock*) trou de clef

key'man' *s* (*pl* -**men'**) pivot *m*, homme *m* indispensable

key'note' *s* (mus) tonique *f*; (fig) dominante *f*

key'note speech' *s* discours *m* d'ouverture

key'punch' *s* (mach) perforatrice *f*

key' ring' *s* porte-clefs *m*

key' sig'nature *s* (mus) armature *f* de la clé

key'stone' *s* clef *f* de voûte

key' word' *s* mot-clé *m*

kha·ki ['kɑki], ['kæki] *adj* kaki || *s* (*pl* -**kis**) kaki *m*

khan [kɑn] *s* khan *m*

kibitz ['kibits] *intr* (coll) faire la mouche du coche

kibitzer ['kibitsər] *s* (coll) casse-pieds *mf*, curieux *m*

kick [kik] *s* coup *m* de pied; (*e.g., of a horse*) ruade *f*; (*of a gun*) recul *m*; (*complaint*) (slang) plainte *f*; (*thrill*) (slang) effet *m*, frisson *m*; **to get a kick out of** (slang) s'en payer une tranche de || *tr* donner un coup de pied à; (*a ball*) botter; **to kick out** (coll) chasser à coups de pied; **to kick s.o. in the pants** (coll) botter le derrière à qn; **to kick the bucket** (coll) casser sa pipe, passer l'arme à gauche; **to kick up a row** (slang) déclencher un chahut || *intr* donner un coup de pied; (*said of gun*) reculer; (*said of horse*) ruer; (sports) botter; **to kick against** regimber contre; **to kick off** (football) donner le coup d'envoi

kick'back' *s* contrecoup *m*; (slang) ristourne *f*

kick'off' *s* (sports) coup *m* d'envoi

kid [kid] *s* chevreau *m*; (coll) gosse *mf*, mioche *mf* || *v* (*pret & pp* **kidded**; *ger* **kidding**) *tr & intr* (slang) blaguer; **to kid oneself** (slang) se faire des illusions

kidder ['kidər] *s* (slang) blagueur *m*

kidding ['kidiŋ] *s* (slang) blague *f*; **no kidding!** (slang) sans blague!

kid' gloves' *spl* gants *mpl* de chevreau; **to handle with kid gloves** traiter avec douceur, ménager

kid'nap *v* (*pret & pp* -**naped** or -**napped**; *ger* -**naping** or -**napping**) *tr* kidnapper

kidnaper or **kidnapper** ['kidnæpər] *s* kidnappeur *m*

kidnaping or kidnapping ['kɪdnæpɪŋ] s kidnappage m
kidney ['kɪdni] s rein m; (culin) rognon m
kid'ney bean' s haricot m de Soissons
kid'ney-shaped' adj réniforme
kid'ney stone' s calcul m rénal
kill [kɪl] s mise f à mort; (bag of game) gibier m tué || tr tuer; (an animal) abattre; (a bill, amendment, etc.) mettre son veto à, faire échouer
killer ['kɪlər] s assassin m
kill'er whale' s épaulard m, orque f
killing ['kɪlɪŋ] adj meurtrier; (exhausting; ridiculous) crevant || s tuerie f; to make a killing (coll) réussir un beau coup
kill'-joy' s rabat-joie m, trouble-fête mf
kiln [kɪl], [kɪln] s four m
kil·o ['kɪlo], ['kilo] s (pl -os) kilo m, kilogramme m; kilomètre m
kilocycle ['kɪlə,saɪkəl] s kilocycle m
kilogram ['kɪlə,græm] s kilogramme m
kilometer ['kɪlə,mitər], [kɪ'lamɪtər] s kilomètre m
kilowatt ['kɪlə,wat] s kilowatt m
kilowatt-hour ['kɪlə,wat'aur] s (pl -hours) kilowatt-heure m
kilt [kɪlt] s kilt m
kilter ['kɪltər] s—to be out of kilter (coll) être détraqué
kimo·no [kɪ'monə], [kɪ'mono] s (pl -nos) kimono m
kin [kɪn] s (family relationship) parenté f; (relatives) les parents mpl; of kin apparenté; the next of kin le plus proche parent, les plus proches parents
kind [kaɪnd] adj bon, bienveillant; kind to bon pour; to be so kind as to être assez aimable pour || s espèce f, genre m, sorte f, classe f; all kinds of (coll) quantité de; kind of (coll) plutôt, en quelque sorte; of a kind semblable, de même nature; to pay in kind payer en nature
kindergarten ['kɪndər,gartən] s jardin m d'enfants
kindergartner ['kɪndər,gartnər] s élève mf de jardin d'enfants; (teacher) jardinière f
kind'-heart'ed adj bon, bienveillant
kindle ['kɪndəl] tr allumer || intr s'allumer
kindling ['kɪndlɪŋ] s allumage m; (wood) bois m d'allumage
kin'dling wood' s bois m d'allumage
kind·ly ['kaɪndli] adj (comp -lier; super -liest) (kind-hearted) bon, bienveillant; (e.g., climate) doux; (e.g., terrain) favorable || adv avec bonté, avec bienveillance; to take kindly prendre en bonne part; to take kindly to prendre en amitié
kindness ['kaɪndnɪs] s bonté f, obligeance f
kindred ['kɪndrɪd] adj apparenté, de même nature || s parenté f, famille f; parenté, ressemblance f
kinescope ['kɪnɪ,skop] s (trademark) kinescope m

kinetic [kɪ'nɛtɪk], [kaɪ'nɛtɪk] adj cinétique || kinetics s cinétique f
kinet'ic en'ergy s énergie f cinétique
king [kɪŋ] s roi m; (cards, chess, & fig) roi; (checkers) pion m doublé, dame f || tr (checkers) damer
king'bolt' s cheville f maîtresse
kingdom ['kɪŋdəm] s royaume m; (one of three divisions of nature) règne m
king'fish'er s martin-pêcheur m
king·ly ['kɪŋli] adj (comp -lier; super -liest) royal, de roi, digne d'un roi || adv en roi, de roi, comme un roi
king'pin' s cheville f ouvrière; (bowling) quille f du milieu; (coll) ponte m, pontife m
king' post' s poinçon m
kingship ['kɪŋʃɪp] s royauté f
king'-size' adj grand format, géant
king's' ran'som s rançon f de roi
kink [kɪŋk] s (twist, e.g., in a rope) nœud m; (in a wire) faux pli m; (in hair) frisette f, bouclette f; (soreness in neck) torticolis m; (flaw, difficulty) point m faible; (mental twist) lubie f; (naut) coque f || tr nouer, entortiller || intr se nouer, s'entortiller
kink·y ['kɪŋki] adj (comp -ier; super -iest) crépu, bouclé
kinsfolk ['kɪnz,fok] spl parents mpl
kin'ship s parenté f
kins·man ['kɪnzmən] s (pl -men) parent m
kins·woman ['kɪnz,wumən] s (pl -wom'en) parente f
kipper ['kɪpər] s kipper m || tr saurer
kiss [kɪs] s baiser m || tr embrasser, donner un baiser à || intr s'embrasser
kit [kɪt] s nécessaire m; (tub) tonnelet m; (of traveler) trousse f de voyage; (mil) équipement m, sac m; the whole kit and caboodle (coll) tout le saint-frusquin
kitchen ['kɪtʃən] s cuisine f
kitch'en cup'board s vaisselier m
kitchenette [,kɪtʃə'nɛt] s petite cuisine f
kitch'en gar'den s jardin m potager
kitch'en-maid' s fille f de cuisine
kitch'en police' s (mil) corvée f de cuisine
kitch'en range' s cuisinière f
kitch'en sink' s évier m
kitch'en·ware' s ustensiles mpl de cuisine
kite [kaɪt] s cerf-volant m; (orn) milan m; to fly a kite lancer or enlever un cerf-volant
kith' and kin' [kɪθ] spl amis et parents mpl, cousinage m
kitten ['kɪtən] s chaton m, petit chat m
kittenish ['kɪtənɪʃ] adj enjoué, folâtre; (woman) coquette, chatte
kit·ty ['kɪti] s (pl -ties) minet m, minou m; (in card games) cagnotte f, poule f; kitty, kitty, kitty! minet, minet!
kleptomaniac [,klɛptə'meni,æk] adj & s kleptomane mf
knack [næk] s adresse f, chic m

knapsack ['næp‚sæk] s sac m à dos, havresac m

knave [nev] s fripon m; (cards) valet m

knaver·y ['nevəri] s (pl -ies) friponnerie f

knead [nid] tr pétrir; (to massage) masser

knee [ni] s genou m; to bring s.o. to his knees mettre qn à genoux; to go down on one's knees se mettre à genoux

knee' breech'es spl culotte f courte

knee'cap' s rotule f; (protective covering) genouillère f

knee'-deep' adj jusqu'aux genoux

knee'-high' adj à la hauteur du genou

knee'hole' s trou m, évidement m pour l'entrée des genoux

knee' jerk' s réflexe m rotulien

kneel [nil] v (pret & pp knelt [nɛlt] or kneeled) intr s'agenouiller, se mettre à genoux

knee'pad' s genouillère f

knee'pan' s rotule f

knee' swell' s (of organ) genouillère f

knell [nɛl] s glas m; to toll the knell of sonner le glas de || intr sonner le glas

knickers ['nɪkərz] spl pantalons mpl de golf, knickerbockers mpl

knickknack ['nɪk‚næk] s colifichet m

knife [naɪf] s (pl knives [naɪvz]) couteau m; (of paper cutter or other instrument) couperet m, lame f; to go under the knife (coll) monter or passer sur le billard || tr poignarder

knife' sharp'ener s fusil m, affiloir m

knife' switch' s (elec) interrupteur m à couteau

knight [naɪt] s chevalier m; (chess) cavalier m || tr créer or faire chevalier

knight-errant ['naɪt'ɛrənt] s (pl knights-errant) chevalier m errant

knighthood ['naɪthʊd] s chevalerie f

knightly ['naɪtli] adj chevaleresque

knit [nɪt] v (pret & pp knitted or knit; ger knitting) tr tricoter; (one's brows) froncer; to knit together lier, unir || intr tricoter; (said of bones) se souder

knit' goods' spl tricot m, bonneterie f

knitting ['nɪtɪŋ] s (action) tricotage m; (product) tricot m

knit'ting machine' s tricoteuse f

knit'ting nee'dle s aiguille f à tricoter

knit'wear' s tricot m

knob [nɑb] s (lump) bosse f; (of a door, drawer, etc.) bouton m, poignée f; (of a radio) bouton m

knock [nɑk] s coup m, heurt m; (of an internal-combustion engine) cognement m; (slang) éreintement m, dénigrement m || tr frapper; (repeatedly) cogner à, contre, or sur; (slang) éreinter, dénigrer; to knock about bousculer; to knock against heurter contre; to knock down (with a blow, punch, etc.) renverser; (to the highest bidder) adjuger; to knock in enfoncer; to knock off faire tomber; to knock out faire sortir en cognant; (boxing) mettre knock-out; (to fatigue) (coll) claquer, fatiguer || intr

frapper; (said of internal-combustion engine) cogner; to knock about vagabonder, se balader; to knock against se heurter contre; to knock at or on (e.g., a door) heurter à, frapper à; to knock off (to stop working) (coll) débrayer

knock'down' adj (dismountable) démontable || s (blow) coup m d'assommoir; (discount) escompte m

knocked' out' adj éreinté; (boxing) knock-out

knocker ['nɑkər] s (on a door) heurtoir m, marteau m; (critic) (coll) éreinteur m

knock-kneed ['nɑk‚nid] adj cagneux

knock'out' s (boxing) knock-out m; (person) (coll) type m renversant; (thing) (coll) chose f sensationnelle

knock'out drops' spl (slang) narcotique m

knoll [nol] s mamelon m, tertre m

knot [nɑt] s nœud m; (e.g., of people) groupe m; (naut) nœud m, mille m marin à l'heure; (loosely) (naut) mille marin; to tie a knot faire un nœud; to tie the knot (coll) prononcer le conjungo || v (pret & pp knotted; ger knotting) tr nouer; to knot one's brow froncer le sourcil || intr se nouer

knot'hole' s trou m de nœud

knot·ty ['nɑti] adj (comp -tier; super -tiest) noueux; (e.g., question) épineux

know [no] s—to be in the know (coll) être au courant, être à la page || v (pret knew [n(j)u]; pp known) tr & intr (by reasoning or learning) savoir; (by the senses or by perception; through acquaintance or recognition) connaître; as far as I know autant que je sache; to know about être informé de, savoir; to know best être le meilleur juge; to know how to + inf savoir + inf; to let s.o. know about faire part à qn de; you ought to know better vous devriez avoir honte; you ought to know better than to . . . vous devriez vous bien garder de . . . ; you wouldn't know s.o. from . . . on prendrait qn pour . . .

knowable ['no·əbəl] adj connaissable

know'-how' s technique f, savoir-faire m

knowing ['no·ɪŋ] adj avisé; (look, smile) entendu

knowingly ['no·ɪŋli] adv sciemment, en connaissance de cause; (on purpose) exprès

know'-it-all' adj (coll) omniscient || s (coll) Monsieur Je-sais-tout m

knowledge ['nɑlɪdʒ] s (faculty) science f, connaissances fpl, savoir m; (awareness, familiarity) connaissance f; not to my knowledge pas que je sache; to have a thorough knowledge of posséder une connaissance approfondie de; to my knowledge, to the best of my knowledge à ma connaissance, autant que je sache; without my knowledge à mon insu

knowledgeable ['nɑlɪdʒəbəl] *adj* (coll) intelligent, bien informé
know'-noth'ing *s* ignorant *m*
knuckle ['nʌkəl] *s* jointure *f* or articulation *f* du doigt; (*of a quadruped*) jarret *m*; (mach) joint *m* en charnière; **knuckle of ham** jambonneau *m*; **to rap s.o. over the knuckles** donner sur les doigts or ongles à qn ‖ *intr*—**to knuckle down** se soumettre; (*to work hard*) s'y mettre sérieusement
knurl [nʌrl] *s* molette *f* ‖ *tr* moleter
k.o. ['ke'o] (letterword) (knockout) *s* k.o. *m* ‖ *tr* mettre k.o.

Koran [ko'rɑn], [ko'ræn] *s* Coran *m*
Korea [ko'ri·ə] *s* Corée *f*; la Corée
Korean [ko'ri·ən] *adj* coréen ‖ *s* (*language*) coréen; (*person*) Coréen *m*
kosher ['koʃər] *adj* casher, cawcher; (coll) convenable
kowtow ['kau'tau], ['ko'tau] *intr* se prosterner à la chinoise; **to kowtow to** faire des courbettes à or devant
K.P. ['ke'pi] *s* (letterword) (**kitchen police**) (mil) corvée *f* de cuisine; **to be on K.P. duty** (mil) être de soupe
kudos ['k(j)udɑs] *s* (coll) gloire *f*, éloges *mpl*, flatteries *fpl*

L

L, l [εl] *s* XIIᵉ lettre de l'alphabet
la·bel ['lebəl] *s* étiquette *f*; (*brand*) marque *f*; (*in a dictionary*) rubrique *f*, référence *f* ‖ *v* (*pret & pp* **-beled** or **-belled**; *ger* **-beling** or **-belling**) *tr* étiqueter
labial ['lebɪ·əl] *adj* labial ‖ *s* labiale *f*
labor ['lebər] *adj* ouvrier ‖ *s* travail *m*; (*toil*) labeur *m*, peine *f*; (*job, task*) tâche *f*, besogne *f*; (*manual work involved in an undertaking*; *the wages for such work*) main-d'œuvre *f*; (*wage-earning worker as contrasted with capital and management*) le salariat, le travail; (*childbirth*) couches *fpl*, travail; **to be in labor** être en couches ‖ *tr* (*a point, subject, etc.*) insister sur; (*one's style*) travailler, élaborer ‖ *intr* travailler; (*to toil*) travailler dur, peiner; (*to exert oneself*) s'efforcer; (*said of ship*) fatiguer, bourlinguer; **to labor under** être victime de; **to labor up** (*a hill, slope, etc.*) gravir; **to labor uphill** peiner en côte; **to labor with child** être en travail d'enfant
la'bor and man'agement *spl* la classe ouvrière et le patronat
laborato·ry ['læbərə,tori] *s* (*pl* **-ries**) laboratoire *m*
lab'oratory class' *s* classe *f* de travaux pratiques
labored ['lebərd] *adj* travaillé, trop élaboré; (*e.g., breathing*) pénible
laborer ['lebərər] *s* travailleur *m*, ouvrier *m*; (*unskilled worker*) journalier *m*, manœuvre *m*
laborious [lə'borɪ·əs] *adj* laborieux
la'bor move'ment *s* mouvement *m* syndicaliste
la'bor un'ion *s* syndicat *m*, syndicat ouvrier
Labourite ['lebə,raɪt] *adj & s* (Brit) travailliste *mf*
La'bour Par'ty ['lebər] *adj* (Brit) travailliste ‖ *s* parti *m* travailliste
Labrador ['læbrə,dɔr] *s* le Labrador
laburnum [lə'bʌrnəm] *s* cytise *m*

labyrinth ['læbɪrɪnθ] *s* labyrinthe *m*
lace [les] *s* dentelle *f*; (*string to tie shoe, corset, etc.*) lacet *m*, cordon *m*; (*braid*) broderies *fpl* ‖ *tr* garnir or border de dentelles; (*shoes, corset, etc.*) lacer; (*to braid*) entrelacer; (coll) flanquer une rossée à, rosser
lace' trim'ming *s* passementerie *f*
lace'work' *s* dentelles *fpl*, passementerie *f*
lachrymose ['lækrɪ,mos] *adj* larmoyant
lacing ['lesɪŋ] *s* lacet *m*, cordon *m*; (*trimming*) galon *m*, passement *m*; (coll) rossée *f*
luck [læk] *s* manque *m*, défaut *m*; (*lack of necessities*) pénurie *f*; **for lack of** faute de ‖ *tr* manquer de, être dépourvu de ‖ *intr* (*to be lacking*) manquer
lackadaisical [,lækə'dezɪkəl] *adj* languissant, apathique
lackey ['læki] *s* laquais *m*
lacking ['lækɪŋ] *prep* dépourvu de, dénué de
lack'lus'ter *adj* terne, fade
laconic [lə'kɑnɪk] *adj* laconique
lacquer ['lækər] *s* laque *m* & *f* ‖ *tr* laquer
lac'quer ware' *s* laques *mpl*, objets *mpl* d'art en laque
lacrosse [lə'krɔs], [lə'krɑs] *s* crosse *f*, jeu *m* de crosse; **to play lacrosse** jouer à la crosse
lacu·na [lə'kjunə] *s* (*pl* **-nas** or **-nae** [ni]) lacune *f*
lac·y ['lesi] *adj* (*comp* **-ier**; *super* **-iest**) de dentelle; (fig) fin, léger
lad [læd] *s* garçon *m*, gars *m*
ladder ['lædər] *s* échelle *f*; (*stepping stone*) (fig) marchepied *m*, échelon *m*; (*stepladder*) marchepied, escabeau *m*; (*run in stocking*) (Brit) démaillage *m*; (*stairway*) (naut) escalier *m*
lad'der truck' *s* fourgon-pompe *m* à échelle
la'dies' room' *s* toilettes *fpl* pour dames, lavabos *mpl* pour dames

ladle ['ledəl] *s* louche *f* ‖ *tr* servir à la louche
la·dy ['ledi] *s* (*pl* -dies) dame *f*; **ladies** (public sign) dames; **ladies and gentlemen!** (formula used in addressing an audience) mesdames, mesdemoiselles, messieurs!; messieurs dames! (coll)
la'dy·bird' or **la'dy·bug'** *s* coccinelle *f*, bête *f* à bon Dieu
la'dy·fin'ger *s* biscuit *m* à la cuiller
la'dy-in-wait'ing *s* (*pl* ladies-in-waiting) demoiselle *f* d'honneur
la'dy-kil'ler *s* bourreau *m* des cœurs, tombeur *m* de femmes
la'dy·like' *adj* de bon ton, de dame
la'dy·love' *s* bien-aimée *f*, dulcinée *f*
la'dy of the house' *s* maîtresse *f* de maison
la'dy's maid' *s* camériste *f*
la'dy's man' *s* homme *m* à succès
lag [læg] *s* retard *m* ‖ *v* (*pret & pp* lagged; *ger* lagging) *tr* traîner; **to lag behind** rester en arrière
la'ger beer' ['lɑgər] *s* bière *f* de fermentation basse, lager *m*
laggard ['lægərd] *adj* tardif ‖ *s* traînard *m*
lagoon [lə'gun] *s* lagune *f*
laid' pa'per [led] *s* papier *m* vergé
laid' up' *adj* mis en réserve; (naut) mis en rade; (coll) alité, au lit
lair [lɛr] *s* tanière *f*; (fig) repaire *m*
laity ['le·ɪti] *s* profanes *mfpl*; (eccl) laïques *mfpl*
lake [lek] *adj* lacustre ‖ *s* lac *m*
lamb [læm] *s* agneau *m*
lambaste [læm'best] *tr* (*to thrash*) (coll) flanquer une rossée à; (*to reprimand harshly*) (coll) passer un savon à
lamb' chop' *s* côtelette *f* d'agneau
lambkin ['læmkɪn] *s* agnelet *m*
lamb'skin' *s* peau *f* d'agneau; (*dressed with its wool*) mouton *m*, agnelin *m*
lame [lem] *adj* boiteux; (*sore*) endolori; (*e.g., excuse*) faible, piètre ‖ *tr* estropier, rendre boiteux
lament [lə'mɛnt] *s* lamentation *f*; (*dirge*) complainte *f* ‖ *tr* déplorer ‖ *intr* lamenter, se lamenter
lamentable ['læməntəbəl] *adj* lamentable
lamentation [,læmən'teʃən] *s* lamentation *f*
laminate ['læmɪ,net] *tr* laminer
lamp [læmp] *s* lampe *f*
lamp'black' *s* noir *m* de fumée
lamp' chim'ney *s* verre *m* de lampe
lamp'light' *s* lumière *f* de lampe
lamp'light'er *s* allumeur *m* de réverbères
lampoon [læm'pun] *s* libelle *m*, pasquinade *f* ‖ *tr* faire des libelles contre
lamp'post' *s* réverbère *m*, poteau *m* de réverbère
lamprey ['læmpri] *s* lamproie *f*
lamp'shade' *s* abat-jour *m*
lamp'wick' *s* mèche *f* de lampe
lance [læns], [lɑns] *s* lance *f*; (surg) lancette *f*, bistouri *m* ‖ *tr* percer d'un

coup de lance; (surg) donner un coup de lancette or bistouri à
lancet ['lænsɪt], ['lɑnsɪt] *s* (surg) lancette *f*, bistouri *m*
land [lænd] *adj* terrestre, de terre ‖ *s* terre *f*; **land of milk and honey** pays de cocagne; **to make land** toucher terre; **to see how the land lies** sonder or tâter le terrain ‖ *tr* débarquer, mettre à terre; (*an airplane*) atterrir; (*a fish*) amener à terre; (*e.g., a job*) (coll) décrocher; (*a blow*) (coll) flanquer ‖ *intr* débarquer, descendre à terre; (*said of airplane*) atterrir; **to land on one's feet** retomber sur ses pieds; **to land on the moon** alunir; **to land on the water** amerrir
land' breeze' *s* brise *f* de terre
landed *adj* (*owning land*) terrien; (*real-estate*) immobilier
land'ed prop'erty *s* propriété *f* foncière
land'fall' *s* (*sighting land*) abordage *m*; (*landing of ship or plane*) atterrissage *m*; (*landslide*) glissement *m* de terrain
landing ['lændɪŋ] *s* (*of plane*) atterrissage *m*; (*of ship*) mise *f* à terre, débarquement *m*; (*place where passengers and goods are landed*) débarcadère *m*; (*of stairway*) palier *m*; (*on the moon*) alunissage *m*
land'ing bea'con *s* (aer) radiophare *m* d'atterrissage
land'ing craft' *s* (nav) péniche *f* de débarquement
land'ing field' *s* (aer) terrain *m* d'atterrissage
land'ing force' *s* (nav) détachement *m* de débarquement
land'ing gear' *s* (aer) train *m* d'atterrissage
land'ing par'ty *s* (nav) détachement *m* de débarquement
land'ing stage' *s* débarcadère *m*
land'ing strip' *s* (aer) piste *f* d'atterrissage
land'la'dy *s* (*pl* -dies) (*e.g., of an apartment*) logeuse *f*, propriétaire *f*; (*of a lodging house*) patronne *f*; (*of an inn*) aubergiste *f*
land'locked' *adj* entouré de terre
land'lord' *s* (*e.g., of an apartment*) logeur *m*, propriétaire *m*; (*of a lodging house*) patron *m*; (*of an inn*) aubergiste *m*
landlubber ['lænd,lʌbər] *s* marin *m* d'eau douce
land'mark' *s* point *m* de repère, borne *f*; (*important event*) étape *f* importante; (naut) amer *m*
land' of'fice *s* bureau *m* du cadastre
land'own'er *s* propriétaire *m* foncier
landscape ['lænd,skep] *s* paysage *m* ‖ *tr* aménager en jardins
land'scape ar'chitect *s* architecte *m* paysagiste
land'scape gar'dener *s* jardinier *m* paysagiste
land'scape paint'er *s* paysagiste *mf*
landscapist ['lænd,skepɪst] *s* paysagiste *mf*

land'slide' s glissement m de terrain, éboulement m; (in an election) raz m de marée
landward ['lændwərd] adv du côté de la terre, vers la terre
land' wind' [wɪnd] s vent m de terre
lane [len] s (narrow street or passage) ruelle f; (in the country) sentier m; (of an automobile highway) voie f; (line of cars) file f; (of an air or ocean route) route f de navigation
langsyne ['læŋ'saɪn] s (Scotch) le temps jadis ‖ adv (Scotch) au temps jadis
language ['læŋgwɪdʒ] s langage m; (e.g., of a nation) langue f
languid ['læŋgwɪd] adj languissant
languish ['læŋgwɪʃ] intr languir
languor ['læŋgər] s langueur f
languorous ['læŋgərəs] adj langoureux
lank [læŋk] adj efflanqué, maigre; (hair) plat, e.g., lank hair cheveux plats
lank·y ['læŋki] adj (comp -ier; super -iest) grand et maigre
lanolin ['lænəlɪn] s lanoline f
lantern ['læntərn] s lanterne f
lan'tern slide' s diapositive f
lanyard ['lænjərd] s (around the neck) cordon m; (arti) tire-feu m; (naut) ride f
lap [læp] s (of human body or clothing) genoux mpl, giron m; (of garment) genoux, pan m; (with the tongue) coup m de langue; (of the waves) clapotis m; (in a race) (sports) tour m; last lap dernière étape f ‖ v (pret & pp lapped; ger lapping) tr (with the tongue) laper; to lap up laper; (coll) gober ‖ intr laper; (said of waves) clapoter; to lap over déborder
lap' dog' s bichon m, chien m de manchon
lapel [lə'pɛl] s revers m
Lap'land' s Laponie f; la Laponie
Laplander ['læp,lændər] s Lapon m
Lapp [læp] s (language) lapon m; (person) Lapon m
lap' robe' s couverture f de voyage
lapse [læps] s (passing of time) laps m; (slipping into guilt or error) faute f, écart m; (fall, decline) chute f; (e.g., of an insurance policy) expiration f, échéance f; (of memory) absence f, défaillance f ‖ intr (to elapse) s'écouler, passer; (to err) manquer à ses devoirs; (to decline) déchoir; (said, e.g., of a right) périmer, tomber en désuétude; (said, e.g., of a legacy) devenir caduc; (said, e.g., of an insurance policy) cesser d'être en vigueur
lap'wing' s (orn) vanneau m huppé
larce·ny ['lɑrsəni] s (pl -nies) larcin m, vol m
larch [lɑrtʃ] s (bot) mélèze m
lard [lɑrd] s saindoux m ‖ tr larder
larder ['lɑrdər] s garde-manger m
large [lɑrdʒ] adj grand; at large en liberté
large' intes'tine s gros intestin m

largely ['lɑrdʒli] adv principalement
largeness ['lɑrdʒnɪs] s grandeur f
large'-scale' adj sur une large échelle, de grande envergure
lariat ['læri·ət] s (for catching animals) lasso m; (for tying grazing animals) longe f
lark [lɑrk] s alouette f; (prank) espièglerie f; to go on a lark (coll) faire la bombe
lark'spur' s (rocket larkspur) pied-d'alouette m; (field larkspur) consoude f royale
lar·va ['lɑrvə] s (pl -vae [vi]) larve f
laryngeal [lə'rɪndʒɪ·əl], [,lærɪn'dʒɪ·əl] adj laryngé, laryngien
laryngitis [,lærɪn'dʒaɪtɪs] s laryngite f
laryngoscope [lə'rɪŋgə,skop] s laryngoscope m
larynx ['lærɪŋks] s (pl larynxes or larynges [lə'rɪndʒiz]) larynx m
lascivious [lə'sɪvɪ·əs] adj lascif
lasciviousness [lə'sɪvɪ·əsnɪs] s lasciveté f
laser ['lezər] s (acronym) (light amplification by stimulated emission of radiation) laser m
lash [læʃ] s (cord on end of whip) mèche f; coup m; (splatter of rain on window) fouettement m; (eyelash) cil m ‖ tr fouetter, cingler; (to bind, tie) lier; (naut) amarrer ‖ intr fouetter; to lash out at cingler
lashing ['læʃɪŋ] s fouettée f; (rope) amarre f; (naut) amarrage m
lass [læs] s jeune fille f, jeunesse f; bonne amie f
lassitude ['læsɪ,t(j)ud] s lassitude f
las·so ['læso], [læ'su] s (pl -sos or -soes) lasso m
last [læst], [lɑst] adj (in a series) dernier (before noun), e.g., the last week of the war la dernière semaine de la guerre; (just elapsed) dernier (after noun), e.g., last week la semaine dernière; before last avant-dernier, e.g., the time before last l'avant-dernière fois; the last two les deux derniers ‖ s dernier m; (the end) fin f, bout m; (for holding shoe) forme f; at last enfin, à la fin; at long last à la fin des fins; the last of the month la fin du mois; to the last jusqu'à la fin, jusqu'au bout ‖ intr durer; (to hold out) tenir
last' eve'ning adv hier soir
lasting ['læstɪŋ], ['lɑstɪŋ] adj durable
lastly ['læstli], ['lɑstli] adv pour finir, en dernier lieu, enfin
last'-minute news' s nouvelles fpl de dernière heure
last' name' s nom m, nom de famille
last' night' adv hier soir; cette nuit
last' quar'ter s dernier quartier m
last' sleep' s sommeil m de la mort
last' straw' s—that's the last straw! c'est le comble!
Last' Sup'per s (eccl) Cène f
last will' and test'ament s testament m, acte m de dernière volonté
last' word' s dernier mot m; (latest style) (coll) dernier cri m

latch [lætʃ] *s* loquet *m* ‖ *tr* fermer au loquet
latch'key' *s* clef *f* de porte d'entrée
latch'string' *s* cordon *m* de loquet
late [let] *adj* (*happening after the usual time*) tardif; (*person; train, bus, etc.*) en retard; (*e.g., art*) de la dernière époque; (*events*) dernier, récent; (*news*) de la dernière heure; (*incumbent of an office*) ancien; (*deceased*) défunt, feu; **at a late hour in** (*the night, the day*) bien avant dans, à une heure avancée de; **in the late seventeenth century (eighteenth century, etc.)** vers la fin du dix-septième siècle (dix-huitième siècle, etc.); **it is late** il est tard; **of late** dernièrement, récemment, depuis peu; **to be late** être en retard; **to be late in** + *ger* tarder à + *inf* ‖ *adv* tard, tardivement; (*after the appointed time*) en retard; **late in** (*the afternoon, the season, the week, the month*) vers la fin de; **late in life** sur le tard; **very late in** (*the night, the day*) bien avant dans, à une heure avancée de
late-comer ['let͵kʌmər] *s* (*newcomer*) nouveau venu *m*; (*one who arrives late*) retardataire *mf*
lateen' sail' [læ'tin] *s* voile *f* latine
lateen' yard' *s* antenne *f*
lately ['letli] *adv* dernièrement, récemment, depuis peu
latency ['letənsi] *s* latence *f*
latent ['letənt] *adj* latent
later ['letər] *adj comp* plus tard, plus tardif; (*event*) subséquent, plus récent; (*kings, luminaries, etc.*) derniers en date; **later than** postérieur à ‖ *adv comp* plus tard; **later on** plus tard, par la suite; **see you later** (coll) à tout à l'heure
lateral ['lætərəl] *adj* latéral
lath [læθ], [lɑθ] *s* latte *f* ‖ *tr* latter
lathe [leð] *s* (mach) tour *m*; **to turn on a lathe** façonner au tour
lather ['læðər] *s* (*of soap*) mousse *f*; (*of horse*) écume *f* ‖ *tr* savonner ‖ *intr* (*said of soap*) mousser; (*said of horse*) être couvert d'écume
lathing ['læθɪŋ], ['lɑθɪŋ] *s* lattage *m*
Latin ['lætɪn], ['lætən] *adj* latin ‖ *s* (*language*) latin *m*; (*person*) Latin *m*
Lat'in Amer'ica *s* l'Amérique *f* latine
Lat'in-Amer'ican *adj* latino-américain ‖ *s* Latino-américain *m*
latitude ['lætɪ͵t(j)ud] *s* latitude *f*
latrine [lə'trin] *s* latrines *fpl*
latter ['lætər] *adj* dernier; **the latter part of** (*e.g., a century*) la fin de ‖ *pron*—**the latter** celui-ci §84; le dernier
lattice ['lætɪs] *adj* treillissé ‖ *s* treillis *m* ‖ *tr* treillisser
lat'tice gird'er *s* poutre *f* à croisillons
lat'tice-work' *s* treillis *m*, grillage *m*
laud [lɔd] *tr* louer
laudable ['lɔdəbəl] *adj* louable
laudanum ['lɔdənəm], ['lɔdnəm] *s* laudanum *m*
laudatory ['lɔdə͵tori] *adj* laudatif, élogieux

laugh [læf], [lɑf] *s* rire *m* ‖ *tr*—**to laugh away** chasser en riant; **to laugh off** tourner en plaisanterie ‖ *intr* rire; **to laugh at** rire de
laughable ['læfəbəl], ['lɑfəbəl] *adj* risible
laughing ['læfɪŋ], ['lɑfɪŋ] *adj* riant, rieur; **it's no laughing matter** il n'y a pas de quoi rire ‖ *s* rire *m*
laugh'ing gas' *s* gaz *m* hilarant
laugh'ing-stock' *s* risée *f*, fable *f*
laughter ['læftər], ['lɑftər] *s* rire *m*
launch [lɔntʃ], [lɑntʃ] *s* (*open motorboat*) canot *m* automobile, vedette *f*; (naut) chaloupe *f* ‖ *tr* lancer; (*an attack*) déclencher ‖ *intr*—**to launch into, to launch out on** se lancer dans
launching ['lɔntʃɪŋ], ['lɑntʃɪŋ] *s* lancement *m*
launch'ing pad' *s* rampe *f* de lancement, aire *f* de lancement
launder ['lɔndər], ['lɑndər] *tr* blanchir
launderer ['lɔndərər], ['lɑndərər] *s* blanchisseur *m*, buandier *m*
laundering ['lɔndərɪŋ], ['lɑndərɪŋ] *s* blanchissage *m*
laundress ['lɔndrɪs], ['lɑndrɪs] *s* blanchisseuse *f*, buandière *f*
laun-dry ['lɔndri], ['lɑndri] *s* (*pl* -dries) linge *m* à blanchir, lessive *f*; (*room*) buanderie *f*; (*business*) blanchisserie *f*
laun'dry-man *s* (*pl* -men) blanchisseur *m*, buandier *m*
laun'dry room' *s* buanderie *f*
laun'dry-wom'an *s* (*pl* -wom'en) blanchisseuse *f*, buandière *f*
laureate ['lɔri-ɪt] *adj* & *s* lauréat *m*
lau-rel ['lɔrəl], ['lɑrəl] *s* laurier *m*; **to rest on one's laurels** s'endormir sur ses lauriers ‖ *v* (*pret & pp* -reled or -relled) *ger* -reling or -relling) *tr* couronner de lauriers
lava ['lɑvə], ['lævə] *s* lave *f*
lavaliere [͵lævə'lɪr] *s* pendentif *m*
lavato-ry ['lævə͵tori] *s* (*pl* -ries) (*room equipped for washing hands and face; bowl with running water*) lavabo *m*; (*toilet*) lavabos
lavender ['lævəndər] *s* lavande *f*
lav'ender wa'ter *s* eau *f* de lavande
lavish ['lævɪʃ] *adj* prodigue; (*reception, dinner, etc.*) somptueux, magnifique ‖ *tr* prodiguer
law [lɔ] *s* (*of man, of nature, of science*) loi *f*; (*branch of knowledge concerned with law; body of laws; study of law, profession of law*) droit *m*; **to go to law** recourir à la justice; **to go to law with s.o.** citer qn en justice; **to lay down the law** faire la loi; **to practice law** exercer le droit; **to read law** étudier le droit, faire son droit
law'-abid'ing *adj* soumis aux lois, respectueux des lois
law' and or'der *s* ordre *m* public; **to maintain law and order** maintenir or faire régner l'ordre
law'break'er *s* transgresseur *m* de la loi
law' court' *s* cour *f* de justice, tribunal *m*

lawful ['lɔfəl] *adj* légal, légitime

lawless ['lɔlɪs] *adj* sans loi; (*unbridled*) sans frein, déréglé

law'mak'er *s* législateur *m*

lawn [lɔn] *s* pelouse *f*, gazon *m*; (*fabric*) batiste *f*, linon *m*

lawn' mow'er *s* tondeuse *f* de gazon

law' of'fice *s* étude *f* (d'avocat)

law' of na'tions *s* loi *f* des nations

law' of the jun'gle *s* loi *f* de la jungle

law' stu'dent *s* étudiant *m* en droit

law'suit' *s* procès *m*

lawyer ['lɔjər] *s* avocat *m*

lax [læks] *adj* (*in morals, discipline, etc.*) relâché, négligent; (*loose, not tense*) lâche; (*vague*) vague, flou

laxative ['læksətɪv] *adj & s* laxatif *m*

lay [le] *adj* (*not belonging to clergy*) laïc or laïque; (*not having special training*) profane ‖ *s* situation *f*; (*poem*) lai *m* ‖ *v* (*pret & pp* **laid** [led]) *tr* poser, mettre; (*a trap*) tendre; (*eggs*) pondre; (*e.g., bricks*) ranger; (*a foundation*) jeter, établir; (*a cable*) poser; (*a mine*) (naut) mouiller; **to be laid in Rome (in France, etc.)** (*said, e.g., of scene*) se passer à Rome (en France, etc.); **to lay aside, away,** or **by** mettre de côté; **to lay down** (*one's life*) sacrifier; (*one's weapons*) déposer; (*conditions*) imposer; **to lay down the law to s.o.** (coll) rappeler qn à l'ordre; **to lay in** (*supplies*) faire provision de; **to lay into s.o.** (coll) sauter dessus qn; **to lay it on thick** (coll) y aller fort; **to lay low** (*to overwhelm*) abattre, terrasser; **to lay off** (*an employee*) congédier; (*to mark the boundaries of*) tracer; (*to stop bothering*) (coll) laisser tranquille; **to lay on** (*paint*) appliquer; (*hands; taxes*) imposer; **to lay open** mettre à nu; **to lay out** arranger; (*to display*) étaler; (*to outline*) tracer; (*money*) débourser; (*a corpse*) faire la toilette de; (*a garden*) aménager; **to lay up** (*to stock up on*) amasser; (*to injure*) aliter; (*a boat*) mettre en rade ‖ *intr* (*said of hen*) pondre; **to lay about** frapper de tous côtés; **to lay for** être à l'affût de, guetter; **to lay into** (slang) rosser, battre; **to lay off** (coll) cesser; **to lay off smoking** (coll) renoncer au tabac; **to lay over** faire escale; **to lay to** (naut) se mettre à la cape

lay' broth'er *s* frère *m* lai, frère convers

layer ['le·ər] *s* couche *f*; (*hen*) pondeuse *f* ‖ *tr* (hort) marcotter

lay'er cake' *s* gâteau *m* sandwich

layette [le'ɛt] *s* layette *f*

lay' fig'ure *s* mannequin *m*

laying ['le·ɪŋ] *s* pose *f*; (*of foundation*) assise *f*; (*of eggs*) ponte *f*

lay'man *s* (*pl* **-men**) (*person who is not a clergyman*) laïc *m* or laïque *mf*; (*person who has no special training*) profane *mf*

lay'off' *s* (*discharge*) renvoi *m*; (*unemployment*) chômage *m*

lay' of the land' *s* configuration *f* du terrain; (fig) aspect *m* de l'affaire

lay'out' *s* plan *m*, dessin *m*, tracé *m*; (*of tools*) montage *m*; (*organization*) disposition *f*; (*banquet*) (coll) festin *m*

lay'o'ver *s* arrêt *m* en cours de route

lay' sis'ter *s* sœur *f* laie, sœur converse

laziness ['lezɪnɪs] *s* paresse *f*

la·zy ['lezi] *adj* (*comp* **-zier**; *super* **-ziest**) paresseux

la'zy·bones' *s* (coll) flemmard *m*, fainéant *m*

lb. *abbr* (**pound**) livre *f*

lea [li] *s* (*meadow*) pâturage *m*, prairie *f*

lead [lɛd] *adj* en plomb, de plomb ‖ [lɛd] *s* plomb *m*; (*of lead pencil*) mine *f* (de plombagine); (*for sounding depth*) (naut) sonde *f*; (typ) interligne *f* ‖ [lɛd] *v* (*pret & pp* **leaded**) *tr* plomber; (typ) interligner ‖ [lid] *s* (*foremost place*) avance *f*; (*guidance*) direction *f*, conduite *f*; (*leash*) laisse *f*; (*of a newspaper article*) article *m* de fond; (*leading role*) premier rôle *m*; (*leading man*) jeune premier *m*; (elec) câble *m* de canalisation, conducteur *m*; (elec, mach) avance; (min) filon *m*; **to follow s.o.'s lead** suivre l'exemple de qn; **to have the lead** (cards) avoir la main; **to return the lead** (cards) rejouer la couleur; **to take the lead** prendre le pas ‖ [lid] *v* (*pret & pp* **led** [lɛd]) *tr* conduire, mener; (*to command*) commander, diriger; (*to be foremost in*) être à la tête de; (*e.g., an orchestra*) diriger; (*a good or bad life*) mener; (*a certain card*) attaquer de; (*a certain card suit*) attaquer; (elec, mach) canaliser; **to lead away** or **off** emmener; **to lead off** (*to start*) commencer; **to lead on** encourager; **to lead s.o. to believe** mener qn à croire ‖ *intr* aller devant, tenir la tête; (cards) avoir la main; **to lead to** conduire à, mener à; (*another street, a certain result, etc.*) aboutir à; **to lead up to** (*a great work*) préluder à (*un grand ouvrage*); (*a subject*) amener (*un sujet*)

leaden ['lɛdən] *adj* (*of lead; like lead*) de plomb, en plomb; (*heavy as lead*) pesant; (*sluggish*) alangui; (*complexion*) plombé

leader ['lidər] *s* chef *m*, guide *mf*; (*ringleader*) tête *f*; chef d'orchestre; (*in a dance; among animals*) meneur *m*; (*in a newspaper*) article *m* de fond; (*of a reel of tape or film*) amorce *f*; (*bargain*) article réclame; (*vein of ore*) filon *m*

leadership ['lidər,ʃɪp] *s* direction *f*; don *m* de commandement

leading ['lidɪŋ] *adj* principal, premier

lead'ing edge' *s* (aer) bord *m* d'attaque

lead'ing la'dy *s* vedette *f*, étoile *f*, jeune première *f*

lead'ing man' *s* (*pl* **men'**) jeune premier *m*

lead'ing ques'tion *s* question *f* tendancieuse

lead'-in wire' ['lid,ɪn] *s* (rad, telv) fil *m* d'amenée

lead′ pen′cil [lɛd] *s* crayon *m* (à mine de graphite)

lead′ poi′soning [lɛd] *s* saturnisme *m*

leaf [lif] *s* (*pl* **leaves** [livz]) feuille *f*; (*inserted leaf of table*) rallonge *f*; (*hinged leaf of door or table top*) battant *m*; **to shake like a leaf** trembler comme une feuille; **to turn over a new leaf** tourner la page, faire peau neuve ‖ *intr*—**to leaf through** feuilleter

leafless ['liflɪs] *adj* sans feuilles, dénudé

leaflet ['liflɪt] *s* dépliant *m*, papillon *m*, feuillet *m*; (bot) foliole *f*

leaf′stalk′ *s* (bot) pétiole *m*

leaf·y ['lifi] *adj* (*comp* **-ier**; *super* **-iest**) feuillu, touffu

league [lig] *s* (*unit of distance*) lieue *f*; (*association, alliance*) ligue *f* ‖ *tr* liguer ‖ *intr* se liguer

League′ of Na′tions *s* Société *f* des Nations

leak [lik] *s* fuite *f*; (*in a ship*) voie *f* d'eau; (*of electricity, heat, etc.*) perte *f*, fuite; (*of news, secrets, money, etc.*) fuite; **to spring a leak** avoir une fuite; (naut) faire une voie d'eau ‖ *tr* faire couler; (*gas, steam; secrets, news*) laisser échapper ‖ *intr* fuire, s'écouler; (naut) faire eau; **to leak away** se perdre; **to leak out** (*said of news, secrets, etc.*) transpirer, s'ébruiter

leakage ['likɪdʒ] *s* fuite *f*; (elec) perte *f*

leak·y ['liki] *adj* (*comp* **-ier**; *super* **-iest**) percé, troué; qui a des fuites; (*shoes*) qui prennent l'eau; (coll) indiscret

lean [lin] *adj* maigre; (*gasoline mixture*) pauvre ‖ *s* inclinaison *f*; (*of meat*) maigre *m* ‖ *v* (*pret & pp* **leaned** or **leant** [lɛnt]) *tr* incliner; **to lean s.th. against s.th.** appuyer q.ch. contre q.ch. ‖ *intr* s'incliner, pencher; **to lean against** s'appuyer contre; **to lean forward** s'incliner or se pencher en avant; **to lean out of** (*e.g., a window*) se pencher par; **to lean over** se pencher; (*e.g., s.o.'s shoulder*) se pencher sur; **to lean toward** (fig) incliner à or vers, pencher pour or vers

leaning ['linɪŋ] *adj* penché ‖ *s* inclinaison *f*; (fig) inclination *f*, penchant *m*

lean′-to′ *s* (*pl* **-tos**) appentis *m*

lean′ years′ *spl* années *fpl* maigres

leap [lip] *s* saut *m*, bond *m*; **by leaps and bounds** par sauts et par bonds; **leap in the dark** saut *m* à l'aveuglette ‖ *v* (*pret & pp* **leaped** or **leapt** [lɛpt]) *tr* sauter, franchir ‖ *intr* sauter, bondir; **to leap across** or **over** sauter; **to leap up** sursauter; (*said, e.g., of flame*) jaillir

leap′ day′ *s* jour *m* intercalaire

leap′frog′ *s* saute-mouton *m*

leap′ year′ *s* année *f* bissextile

learn [lʌrn] *v* (*pret & pp* **learned** or **learnt** [lʌrnt]) *tr* apprendre ‖ *intr* apprendre; **to learn to** apprendre à

learned ['lʌrnɪd] *adj* savant, érudit

learn′ed jour′nal *s* revue *f* d'une société savante

learn′ed profes′sion *s* profession *f* libérale

learn′ed soci′ety *s* société *f* savante

learn′ed word′ *s* mot *m* savant

learner ['lʌrnər] *s* élève *mf*; (*beginner*) débutant *m*, apprenti *m*

learn′er's per′mit *s* (aut) permis *m* de conduire (*d'un élève chauffeur*)

learning ['lʌrnɪŋ] *s* (*act and time devoted*) étude *f*; (*scholarship*) savoir *m*, érudition *f*, science *f*

lease [lis] *s* bail *m*; **to give a new lease on life** donner un regain de vie ‖ *tr* (*in the role of landlord*) donner or louer à bail; (*in the role of tenant*) prendre à bail

lease′hold′ *adj* tenu à bail ‖ *s* tenure *f* à bail

leash [liʃ] *s* laisse *f*; **on the leash** en laisse, à l'attache; **to strain at the leash** (fig) ruer dans les brancards ‖ *tr* tenir en laisse

least [list] *adj super* (le) moindre §91 ‖ *s* (le) moins *m*; **at least** du moins; **at the very least** tout au moins; **not in the least** pas le moins du monde, nullement ‖ *adv super* (le) moins §91

leather ['lɛðər] *s* cuir *m*

leath′er·back tur′tle *s* luth *m*

leath′er·neck′ *s* (slang) fusilier *m* marin

leathery ['lɛðəri] *adj* (*e.g., steak*) (coll) coriace

leave [liv] *s* permission *f*; **by your leave** ne vous en déplaise; **on leave** en congé; (mil) en permission; **to give leave to s.o.** permettre or accorder à qn de; **to take leave** (**of**) prendre congé (de), faire ses adieux (à) ‖ *v* (*pret & pp* **left** [lɛft]) *tr* (*to let stay; to stop, give up; to disregard*) laisser; (*to go away from*) partir de, quitter; (*to bequeath*) léguer, laisser; (*a wife*) quitter, abandonner; **to be left** rester, e.g., **the letter was left unanswered** la lettre est restée sans réponse; e.g., **there are three dollars left** il reste trois dollars; **to be left for s.o. to** être à qn de; **to be left over** rester; **to leave about** (*without putting away*) laisser traîner; **to leave alone** laisser tranquille; **to leave it up to** s'en remettre à, s'en rapporter à; **to leave no stone unturned** faire flèche de tout bois, mettre tout en œuvre; **to leave off** (*a piece of clothing*) ne pas mettre; (*a passenger*) déposer; **to leave off** + *ger* cesser de + *inf*, renoncer à + *inf*; **to leave out** omettre ‖ *intr* partir, s'en aller; **where did we leave off?** où en sommes-nous restés?

leaven ['lɛvən] *s* levain *m* ‖ *tr* faire lever; (fig) transformer, modifier

leavening ['lɛvənɪŋ] *adj* transformateur ‖ *s* levain *m*

leave′ of ab′sence *s* congé *m*

leave′-tak′ing *s* congé *m*, adieux *mpl*

leavings ['livɪŋz] *spl* restes *mpl*, reliefs *mpl*

Leba·nese [ˌlɛbə'niz] *adj* libanais ‖ *s* (*pl* **-nese**) Libanais *m*

Lebanon ˌ'lɛbənən] *s* le Liban
lecher ['lɛtʃər] *s* débauché *m*, libertin *m* ‖ *intr* vivre dans la débauche
lecherous ['lɛtʃərəs] *adj* lubrique, lascif
lechery ['lɛtʃəri] *s* lubricité *f*, lasciveté *f*
lectern ['lɛktərn] *s* lutrin *m*
lecture ['lɛktʃər] *s* conférence *f*; (*tedious reprimand*) sermon *m* ‖ *tr* faire une conférence à; (*to rebuke*) sermonner ‖ *intr* faire une conférence or des conférences
lecturer ['lɛktʃərər] *s* conférencier *m*
ledge [lɛdʒ] *s* saillie *f*, corniche *f*; (*projection in a wall*) corniche *f*
ledger ['lɛdʒər] *s* (*slab*) pierre *f* tombale; (com) grand livre *m*
ledg'er line' *s* (mus) ligne *f* supplémentaire
lee [li] *s* (*shelter*) (naut) abri *m*; (*quarter toward which wind blows*) côté *m* sous le vent; **lees** lie *f*
leech [litʃ] *s* sangsue *f*; **to stick like a leech** to s.o. s'accrocher à qn
leek [lik] *s* poireau *m*
leer [lɪr] *s* regard *m* lubrique, œillade *f* ‖ *intr* lancer or jeter une œillade; **to leer at** lorgner
leer•y ['lɪri] *adj* (*comp* -ier; *super* -iest) (coll) soupçonneux, méfiant
leeward ['liwərd], ['lu·ərd] *adj & adv* sous le vent ‖ *s* côté *m* sous le vent; **to pass to leeward of** passer sous le vent de
Lee'ward Is'lands ['liwərd] *spl* îles *fpl* Sous-le-Vent
lee'way' *s* (aer, naut) dérive *f*; (*of time, money*) (coll) marge *f*; (*for action*) (coll) champ *m*, liberté *f*
left [lɛft] *adj* gauche; (*left over*) de surplus ‖ *s* (*left hand*) gauche *f*; (boxing) gauche *m*; **on the left, to the left** à gauche; **the Left** (pol) la gauche; **to make a left** tourner à gauche ‖ *adv* à gauche
left' field' *s* (baseball) gauche *f* du grand champ
left'-hand' drive' *s* conduite *f* à gauche
left'-hand'ed *adj* gaucher; (*clumsy*) gauche; (*counterclockwise*) à gauche, en sens inverse des aiguilles d'une montre; (*e.g., compliment*) douteux, ambigu
leftish ['lɛftɪʃ] *adj* gauchisant
leftism ['lɛftɪzəm] *s* gauchisme *m*
leftist ['lɛftɪst] *adj & s* gauchiste *mf*
left'o'ver *adj* de surplus, restant ‖ **leftovers** *spl* restes *mpl*
left'-wing' *adj* gauchiste, gauchisant
left-winger ['lɛft'wɪŋər] *s* (coll) gauchiste *mf*
left•y [lɛfti] *adj* (coll) gaucher ‖ *s* (*pl* -ies) (coll) gaucher *m*
leg [lɛg] *s* jambe *f*; (*of boot or stocking*) tige *f*; (*of fowl; of frogs*) cuisse *f*; (*of journey*) étape *f*; **to be on one's last legs** n'avoir plus de jambes; **to pull the leg of** (coll) se payer la tête de, faire marcher
lega•cy ['lɛgəsi] *s* (*pl* -cies) legs *m*
legal ['ligəl] *adj* légal; (*practice*) juridique
le'gal hol'iday *s* jour *m* férié

legali•ty [lɪ'gælɪti] *s* (*pl* -ties) légalité *f*
legalize ['ligə‚laɪz] *tr* légaliser
le'gal ten'der *s* cours *m* légal, monnaie *f* libératoire
legate ['lɛgɪt] *s* ambassadeur *m*, envoyé *m*; (eccl) légat *m*
legatee [‚lɛgə'ti] *s* légataire *mf*
legation [lɪ'geʃən] *s* légation *f*
legend ['lɛdʒənd] *s* légende *f*
legendary ['lɛdʒən‚dɛri] *adj* légendaire
legerdemain [‚lɛdʒərdɪ'men] *s* escamotage *m*, passe-passe *m*
leggings ['lɛgɪŋz] *spl* jambières *fpl*, guêtres *fpl*, leggings *fpl*
leg•gy ['lɛgi] *adj* (*comp* -gier; *super* -giest) (*awkward*) dégingandé; (*attractive*) aux longues jambes élégantes
leg'horn' *s* (*hat*) chapeau *m* de paille d'Italie; (*chicken*) leghorn *f*; **Leghorn** Livourne *f*
legibility [‚lɛdʒɪ'bɪlɪti] *s* lisibilité *f*
legible ['lɛdʒɪbəl] *adj* lisible
legion ['lidʒən] *s* légion *f*
legislate ['lɛdʒɪs‚let] *tr* imposer à force de loi ‖ *intr* faire des lois, légiférer
legislation [‚lɛdʒɪs'leʃən] *s* législation *f*
legislative ['lɛdʒɪs‚letɪv] *adj* législatif
legislator ['lɛdʒɪs‚letər] *s* législateur *m*
legislature ['lɛdʒɪs‚letʃər] *s* assemblée *f* législative, législature *f*
legitimacy [lɪ'dʒɪtɪməsi] *s* légitimité *f*
legitimate [lɪ'dʒɪtɪmɪt] *adj* légitime ‖ [lɪ'dʒɪtɪ‚met] *tr* légitimer
legit'imate dra'ma *s* théâtre *m* régulier
legitimize [lɪ'dʒɪtɪ‚maɪz] *tr* légitimer
leg' of lamb' *s* gigot *m* d'agneau
leg' of mut'ton *s* gigot *m*
leg'-of-mut'ton sleeve' *s* manche *f* gigot
legume ['lɛgjum], [lɪ'gjum] *s* (*pod*) légume *m*; (bot) légumineuse *f*
leisure ['liʒər], ['lɛʒər] *s* loisir *m*; **at leisure** à loisir; **in leisure moments** à temps perdu
lei'sure class' *s* désœuvrés *mpl*, rentiers *mpl*
lei'sure hours' *spl* heures *fpl* de loisir
leisurely ['liʒərli], ['lɛʒərli] *adj* tranquille, posé ‖ *adv* posément, sans hâte
lemon ['lɛmən] *s* citron *m*; (*e.g., worthless car*) (coll) clou *m*
lemonade [‚lɛmə'ned] *s* citronnade *f*
lem'on squeez'er *s* presse-citron *m*
lem'on tree' *s* citronnier *m*
lem'on verbe'na [vər'binə] *s* verveine *f* citronnelle
lend [lɛnd] *v* (*pret & pp* lent [lɛnt]) *tr* prêter
lender ['lɛndər] *s* prêteur *m*
lend'ing li'brary *s* bibliothèque *f* de prêt
length [lɛŋθ] *s* longueur *f*; (*e.g., of string*) bout *m*, morceau *m*; (*of time*) durée *f*; **at length** longuement, en détail; (*finally*) enfin, à la fin; **in length** de longueur; **to go to any length to** ne reculer devant rien pour; **to keep at arm's length** tenir à distance

lengthen ['lɛŋθən] *tr* allonger, rallonger || *intr* s'allonger
length'wise' *adj* longitudinal || *adv* en longueur, dans le sens de la longueur
length·y ['lɛŋθi] *adj* (*comp* -ier; *super* -iest) prolongé, assez long
leniency ['linɪ·ənsi] *s* douceur *f*, clémence *f*
lenient ['linɪ·ənt] *adj* doux, clément
lens [lɛnz] *s* lentille *f*; (anat) cristallin *m*
Lent [lɛnt] *s* le Carême
Lenten ['lɛntən] *adj* de carême
lentil ['lɛntəl] *s* lentille *f*
leopard ['lɛpərd] *s* léopard *m*
leper ['lɛpər] *s* lépreux *m*
lep'er house' *s* léproserie *f*
leprosy ['lɛprəsi] *s* lèpre *f*
leprous ['lɛprəs] *adj* lépreux
lesbian ['lɛzbɪ·ən] *adj* érotique; **Lesbian** lesbien || *s* (*female homosexual*) lesbienne *f*; **Lesbian** Lesbien *m*
lesbianism ['lɛzbɪ·ə ,nɪzəm] *s* saphisme *m*
lese majesty ['liz'mædʒɪsti] *s* crime *m* de lèse-majesté
lesion ['liʒən] *s* lésion *f*
less [lɛs] *adj comp* moindre §91 || *s* moins *m* || *adv comp* moins §91; **less and less** de moins en moins; **less than** moins que; (*followed by numeral*) moins de; **the less . . . the less** (or **the more**) moins . . . moins (or plus)
lessee [lɛs'i] *s* preneur *m*; (*e.g., of house*) locataire *mf*; (*e.g., of gasoline station*) concessionnaire *mf*
lessen ['lɛsən] *tr* diminuer, amoindrir || *intr* se diminuer, s'amoindrir
lesser ['lɛsər] *adj comp* moindre §91
lesson ['lɛsən] *s* leçon *f*
lessor ['lɛsər] *s* bailleur *m*
lest [lɛst] *conj* de peur que, de crainte que
let [lɛt] *v* (*pret & pp* let; *ger* letting) *tr* laisser; (*to rent*) louer; **let** + *inf* que + *subj*, e.g., **let him come in** qu'il entre; **let alone** sans parler de, sans compter; **let well enough alone** le mieux est souvent l'ennemi du bien; **let us eat, work, etc.** mangeons, travaillons, etc.; **to be well off with en** être quitte pour; **to let** à louer, e.g., **house to let** maison à louer; **to let alone, to let be** laisser tranquille; **to let by** laisser passer; **to let down** baisser, descendre; (*one's hair*) dénouer, défaire; (*e.g., a garment*) allonger; (*to leave in the lurch*) laisser en panne, faire faux bond à; **to let fly** décocher; **to let go** laisser partir; **to let have** laisser, e.g., **he let Robert have it for three dollars** il l'a laissé à Robert pour trois dollars; **to let in** laisser entrer; **to let in the clutch** (aut) embrayer; **to let into** admettre dans; **to let loose** lâcher; **to let off** laisser partir; (*e.g., steam from a boiler*) laisser échapper, lâcher; (*e.g., a culprit*) pardonner à; **to let oneself go** se laisser aller; **to let on that** (coll) faire croire que; **to let out** faire or laisser sortir; (*e.g., a*

dress) élargir; (*a cry; a secret; a prisoner*) laisser échapper; (*to reveal*) révéler, divulguer; **to let out on bail** relâcher sous caution; **to let out the clutch** débrayer; **to let slip** laisser tomber; **to let s.o.** + *inf* permettre à qn de + *inf*; laisser qn + *inf*, e.g., **he let Mary go to the theater** il a laissé Marie aller au théâtre; **to let s.o. in on** (*a secret*) (coll) confier à qn; (*e.g., a racing tip*) (coll) tuyauter qn sur; **to let s.o. know s.th.** faire savoir q.ch. à qn, mettre qn au courant de q.ch.; **to let s.o. off** faire grâce à qn de; **to let stand** laisser, e.g., **he let the errors stand** il a laissé les fautes; **to let s.th. go for** (*a low price*) laisser q.ch. pour; **to let through** laisser passer; **to let up** laisser monter || *intr* (*said of house, apartment, etc.*) se louer; **to let down** (coll) ralentir; **to let go of** lâcher prise de; **to let out** (*said of class, school, etc.*) finir, se terminer; **to let up** (*coll*) ralentir, diminuer; (*on discipline; on a person*) devenir moins sévère
let'down' *s* diminution *f*; (*disappointment*) déception *f*
lethal ['liθəl] *adj* mortel; (*weapon*) meurtrier
lethargic [lɪ'θɑrdʒɪk] *adj* léthargique
lethar·gy ['lɛθərdʒi] *s* (*pl* -gies) léthargie *f*
Lett [lɛt] *s* Letton *m*
letter ['lɛtər] *s* lettre *f*; **to the letter** à la lettre, au pied de la lettre || *tr* marquer avec des lettres
let'ter box' *s* boîte *f* aux lettres
let'ter car'rier *s* facteur *m*
let'ter drop' *s* passe-lettres *m*, fente *f* (dans la porte pour le courrier)
lettered *adj* (*person*) lettré
let'ter file' *s* classeur *m* de lettres
let'ter·head' *s* en-tête *m*
lettering ['lɛtərɪŋ] *s* (*action*) lettrage *m*; (*title*) inscription *f*
let'ter of cred'it *s* lettre *f* de crédit
let'ter o'pener *s* coupe-papier *m*
let'ter pa'per *s* papier *m* à lettres
let'ter·per'fect *adj* correct; sûr
let'ter press' *s* presse *f* à copier
let'ter-press' *s* impression *f* typographique; (*in distinction to illustrations*) texte *m*
let'ter scales' *spl* pèse-lettre *m*
let'ter·word' *s* sigle *m*
Lettish ['lɛtɪʃ] *adj & s* letton *m*
lettuce ['lɛtɪs] *s* laitue *f*
let'up' *s* accalmie *f*, pause *f*; **without letup** sans relâche
leucorrhea [,lukə'ri·ə] *s* leucorrhée *f*
leukemia [lu'kimɪ·ə] *s* leucémie *f*
Levant [lɪ'vænt] *s* Levant *m*
Levantine ['lɛvən,tin], [lɪ'væntɪn] *adj* levantin || *s* Levantin *m*
levee ['lɛvi] *s* (*embankment*) levée *f*, digue *f*; réception *f* royale
lev·el ['lɛvəl] *adj* de niveau; (*flat*) égal, uni; (*spoonful*) arasé; **level with** de niveau avec, à fleur de || *s* niveau *m*; **on a level with** au niveau de; **to be**

on the level (coll) être de bonne foi; to find one's level trouver son niveau ‖ v (pret & pp -eled or -elled; ger -eling or -elling) tr niveler; (to smooth, flatten out) aplanir, araser; (to bring down) raser; (a gun) braquer; (accusations, sarcasm) lancer, diriger; to level out égaliser; to level up (aer) redresser ‖ intr (aer) redresser; to level with (coll) parler franchement à

lev'el·head'ed adj équilibré, pondéré

lev'eling rod' s (surv) jalon-mire m, jalon m d'arpentage

lever ['livər], ['lɛvər] s levier m ‖ tr soulever or ouvrir au moyen d'un levier

leverage ['livərɪdʒ], ['lɛvərɪdʒ] s puissance f or force f de levier; (fig) influence f, avantage m

leviathan [lɪ'vaɪ-əθən] s léviathan m

levitation [,lɛvɪ'teʃən] s lévitation f

levi·ty ['lɛvɪti] s (pl -ties) légèreté f

lev·y ['lɛvi] s (pl -ies) levée f ‖ v (pret & pp -ied) tr lever; (a fine) imposer

lewd [lud] adj luxurieux, lubrique

lewdness ['ludnɪs] s luxure f, lubricité f

lexical ['lɛksɪkəl] adj lexical

lexicographer [,lɛksɪ'kɑgrəfər] s lexicographe mf

lexicographic(al) [,lɛksɪkə'græfɪk(əl)] adj lexicographique

lexicography [,lɛksɪ'kɑgrəfi] s lexicographie f

lexicology [,lɛksɪ'kɑlədʒi] s lexicologie f

lexicon ['lɛksɪkən] s lexique m

liabili·ty [,laɪ-ə'bɪlɪti] s (pl -ties) responsabilité f; (e g., to disease) prédisposition f; liabilities obligations fpl, dettes fpl

liabil'ity insur'ance s assurance f tous risques

liable ['laɪ-əbəl] adj sujet; liable for (a debt, fine, etc.) passible de, responsable de; we (you, etc.) are liable to + inf (coll) il se peut que nous (vous, etc.) + pres subj; (coll) il est probable que nous (vous, etc.) + pres ind

liaison ['li·ə,zɑn], [li'ezən] s liaison f

liar ['laɪ-ər] s menteur m

libation [laɪ'beʃən] s libation f

li·bel ['laɪbəl] s diffamation f, calomnie f; (in writing) écrit m diffamatoire ‖ v (pret & pp -beled or -belled; ger -beling or -belling) tr diffamer, calomnier

libelous ['laɪbələs] adj diffamatoire, calomnieux

liberal ['lɪbərəl] adj libéral; (share, supply, etc.) libéral, généreux, copieux; (ideas) large ‖ s libéral m

liberali·ty [,lɪbə'rælɪti] s (pl -ties) libéralité f; (breadth of mind) largeur f de vues

lib'eral·mind'ed adj tolérant

liberate ['lɪbə,ret] tr libérer

liberation [,lɪbə'reʃən] s libération f

liberator ['lɪbə,retər] s libérateur m

libertine ['lɪbər,tin] adj & s libertin m

liber·ty ['lɪbərti] s (pl -ties) liberté f; at liberty en liberté; at liberty to libre de; to take the liberty to se permettre de, prendre la liberté de

libidinous [lɪ'bɪdɪnəs] adj libidineux

libido [lɪ'bido], [lɪ'baɪdo] s libido f

librarian [laɪ'brɛrɪ-ən] s bibliothécaire mf

librar·y ['laɪ,brɛri], ['laɪbrəri] s (pl -ies) bibliothèque f

li'brary num'ber s cote f

libret·to [lɪ'brɛto] s (pl -tos) livret m, libretto m

license ['laɪsəns] s permis m, licence f; (to drive) permis de conduire ‖ tr accorder un permis à, autoriser

li'cense num'ber s numéro m d'immatriculation; (aut) numéro minéralogique

li'cense plate' or **tag'** s plaque f d'immatriculation, plaque minéralogique

licentious [laɪ'sɛnʃəs] adj licencieux

lichen ['laɪkən] s lichen m

lick [lɪk] s coup m de langue; (salt lick) terrain m salifère; (blow) (coll) coup m; at full lick (coll) à plein gaz; to give a lick and a promise to (coll) nettoyer à la six-quatre-deux; (coll) faire un brin de toilette à ‖ tr lécher; (e.g., the fingers) se lécher; (to beat, thrash) (coll) enfoncer les côtes à, rosser; (to beat, surpass, e.g., in a sporting event) (coll) battre, enfoncer; (e.g., a problem) (coll) venir à bout de; to lick into shape (coll) dégrossir; to lick up lécher

licking ['lɪkɪŋ] s léchage m; (drubbing) (coll) raclée f

licorice ['lɪkərɪs] s réglisse f

lid [lɪd] s couvercle m; (eyelid) paupière f; (hat) (slang) couvre-chef m

lie [laɪ] s mensonge m; to give the lie to donner le démenti à ‖ v (pret & pp lied; ger lying) tr—to lie one's way out se tirer d'affaire par des mensonges ‖ intr mentir ‖ v (pret lay; pp lain [lɛn]; ger lying) intr être couché; (to be located) se trouver; (e.g., in the grave) gésir, e.g., here lies ci-gît; to lie down se coucher

lie' detec'tor s détecteur m de mensonges

lien [lin], ['li·ən] s privilège m, droit m de rétention

lieu [lu] s—in lieu of au lieu de

lieutenant [lu'tɛnənt] s lieutenant m; (nav) lieutenant m de vaisseau

lieuten'ant colo'nel s lieutenant-colonel m

lieuten'ant comman'der s (nav) capitaine m de corvette

lieuten'ant gov'ernor s (U.S.A.) vice-gouverneur m; (Brit) lieutenant-gouverneur m

lieuten'ant jun'ior grade' s (nav) enseigne m de première classe

life [laɪf] s (pl lives [laɪvz]) vie f; (of light bulb, lease, insurance policy) durée f; bigger than life plus grand que nature; for dear life de toutes ses forces; for life à vie, pour la vie, à perpétuité; **for the life of me!** (coll) de ma vie!; **lives lost** morts *mpl*; **long life** longévité *f*; **never in my life!**, **not on your life!** jamais de la vie!; **run for your life!** sauve qui peut!; **such is life!** c'est la vie!; **taken from life** pris sur le vif; **to come to life** revenir à la vie; **to depart this life** quitter ce monde; **to risk life and limb** risquer sa peau

life′ annu′ity *s* rente *f* viagère
life′ belt′ *s* ceinture *f* de sauvetage
life′blood′ *s* sang *m*; (fig) vie *f*
life′boat′ *s* chaloupe *f* de sauvetage; (*for shore-based rescue services*) canot *m* de sauvetage
life′ buoy′ *s* bouée *f* de sauvetage
life′ float′ *s* radeau *m* de sauvetage
life′ guard′ *s* (mil) garde *f* du corps
life′guard′ *s* sauveteur *m*, maître nageur *m*
life′ impris′onment *s* emprisonnement *m* à vie
life′ insur′ance *s* assurance *f* sur la vie, assurance-vie *f*
life′ jack′et *s* gilet *m* de sauvetage
lifeless ['laɪflɪs] *adj* sans vie, inanimé; (*colors*) embu, terne
life′like′ *adj* vivant, ressemblant
life′ line′ *s* ligne *f* or corde *f* de sauvetage
life′long′ *adj* de toute la vie, perpétuel
life′ mem′ber *s* membre *m* à vie
life′ of lei′sure *s* vie *f* de château
life′ of Ri′ley ['raɪli] *s* (slang) joyeuse vie *f*, vie oisive
life′ of the par′ty *s* (coll) boute-en-train *m*
life′ preserv′er [prɪ'zʌrvər] *s* appareil *m* de sauvetage
lifer ['laɪfər] *s* (slang) condamné *m* à perpétuité
life′ raft′ *s* radeau *m* de sauvetage
lifesaver ['laɪf,sevər] *s* sauveteur *m*; (fig) planche *f* de salut
life′sav′ing *s* sauvetage *m*
life′ sen′tence *s* condamnation *f* à perpétuité
life′-size′ *adj* de grandeur nature
life′time′ *adj* à vie ‖ *s* vie *f*, toute une vie; **in his lifetime** de son vivant
life′work′ *s* travail *m* de toute une vie
lift [lɪft] *s* haussement *m*, levée *f*; aide *f*; (aer) poussée *f*; (Brit) ascenseur *m*; (*of dumbbell or weight*) (sports) arraché *m*; **to give a lift to** (*by offering a ride*) conduire d'un coup de voiture, faire monter dans la voiture; (*to aid*) donner un coup de main à; ranimer ‖ *tr* lever, soulever; (*heart, mind, etc.*) élever, ranimer; (*a sail*) soulager; (*an embargo*) lever; (e.g., *passages from a book*) démarquer, plagier; (*to rob*) (slang) dérober; **to lift up** (*the hands*) lever; (*the head*) relever; (*the voice*) élever ‖ *intr* se lever, se soulever; (*said of clouds, fog, etc.*) se lever, se dissiper
lift′ bridge′ *s* pont *m* levant, pont-levis *m*
lift′off′ *s* (rok) montée verticale, chandelle *f*

lift′ truck′ *s* chariot *m* élévateur
ligament ['lɪgəmənt] *s* ligament *m*
ligature ['lɪgətʃər] *s* ligature *f*
light [laɪt] *adj* léger; (*having illumination*) éclairé; (*color, complexion, hair*) clair; (*beer*) blond; (*wine*) léger; **to make light of** faire peu de cas de ‖ *s* lumière *f*; (*to control traffic*) feu *m*; (*window or other opening in a wall*) jour *m*; (*example, shining figure*) lumière; (*headlight of automobile*) phare *m*; du feu, e.g., **do you have a light?** (e.g., *to light a cigarette*) avez-vous du feu?; **according to one's lights** selon ses lumières, dans la mesure de son intelligence; **against the light** à contre-jour; **in a false light** sous un faux jour; **in a new light** sous un jour nouveau; **in the same light** sous le même aspect; **it is light (out)** il fait jour; **lights** (*navigation lights; parking lights*) feux *mpl*; (*of sheep, calf, etc.*) mou *m*; **lights out** (mil) l'extinction *f* des feux; **to bring to light** mettre au jour; **to come to light** se révéler; **to shed** or **throw light on** éclairer; **to strike a light** allumer ‖ *adv* à vide; **to run light** (*said of engine*) aller haut le pied ‖ *v* (pret & pp **lighted** or **lit** [lɪt]) *tr* (*to furnish with illumination*) éclairer, illuminer; (*to set afire, ignite*) allumer; **to light the way for** éclairer; **to light up** illuminer ‖ *intr* s'éclairer, s'illuminer; allumer; (*to perch*) se poser; **to light from** or **off** (*an auto, carriage, etc.*) descendre de; **to light into** (*to attack; to berate*) (slang) tomber sur; **to light out** (*to skedaddle*) (slang) décamper; **to light up** s'éclairer, s'illuminer; **to light upon** (*by happenstance*) tomber sur, trouver par hasard
light′ bulb′ *s* ampoule *f* électrique, lampe *f* électrique
light′ complex′ion *s* teint *m* clair
lighten ['laɪtən] *tr* (*to make lighter in weight*) alléger, soulager; (*to provide more light*) éclairer, illuminer; (*to give a lighter or brighter hue to*) éclaircir; (*grief, punishment, etc.*) adoucir ‖ *intr* (*to become less dark or sorrowful*) s'éclairer; (*to give off flashes of lightning*) faire des éclairs; (*to becomes less weighty*) s'alléger
lighter ['laɪtər] *s* (*to light cigarette*) briquet *m*; (*flat-bottomed barge*) chaland *m*, péniche *f*
light′-fin′gered *adj* à doigts agiles
light′-foot′ed *adj* au pied léger
light′-head′ed *adj* étourdi
light′-heart′ed *adj* joyeux, allègre, au cœur léger
light′house′ *s* phare *m*
lighting ['laɪtɪŋ] *s* allumage *m*, éclairage *m*
light′ing fix′tures *spl* appareils *mpl* d'éclairage
light′ me′ter *s* posemètre *m*
lightness ['laɪtnɪs] *s* (*in weight*) légèreté *f*; (*in illumination; of complexion*) clarté *f*

light·ning ['laɪtnɪŋ] *s (electric discharge)* foudre *f; (light produced by this discharge)* éclairs *mpl* ‖ *v (ger -ning) intr* faire des éclairs

light'ning arrest'er [ə ˌrɛstər] *s* parafoudre *m*

light'ning bug' *s* luciole *f*

light'ning rod' *s* paratonnerre *m*

light' op'era *s* opérette *f*

light' read'ing *s* livres *mpl* d'agrément; lecture *f* légère or amusante

light'ship' *s* bateau-feu *m*

light-struck ['laɪt ˌstrʌk] *adj* (phot) voilé

light' wave' *s* onde *f* lumineuse

light'weight' *adj* léger ‖ *s* (sports) poids *m* léger

light'weight coat' *s* surtout *m* de demi-saison

light'-year' *s* année-lumière *f*

likable ['laɪkəbəl] *adj* sympathique

like [laɪk] *adj (alike)* pareils, semblables; pareil à, semblable à; *(typical of)* caractéristique de; *(poles of a magnet)* (elec) de même nom; **like father like son** tel père tel fils; **that is like him** il n'en fait pas d'autres ‖ *s* pareil *m*, semblable *m*; **likes** *(desires)* goût *m*, inclinations *fpl*; **the likes of him** son pareil ‖ *adv*—**like enough** probablement; **like mad** comme un fou ‖ *prep* comme; **like that** de la sorte ‖ *conj* (coll) de la même manière que, comme ‖ *tr* aimer, aimer bien, trouver bon; plaire (with *dat*), e.g., **I like milk** le lait me plaît; se plaire, e.g., **I like it in the country** je me plais à la campagne ‖ *intr* vouloir; **as you like** comme vous voudrez; **if you like so** si vous voulez

likelihood ['laɪklɪ ˌhʊd] *s* probabilité *f*, vraisemblance *f*

like·ly ['laɪkli] *adj (comp -lier; super -liest)* probable, vraisemblable; **to be likely to** + *inf* être probable que + *ind*, e.g., **Mary is likely to come to see us tomorrow** il est probable que Marie viendra nous voir demain ‖ *adv* probablement, vraisemblablement

like'-mind'ed *adj* du même avis

liken ['laɪkən] *tr* comparer, assimiler

likeness ['laɪknɪs] *s' (picture or image)* portrait *m*; *(similarity)* ressemblance *f*

like'wise' *adv* également, de même; **to do likewise** en faire autant

liking ['laɪkɪŋ] *s* sympathie *f*, penchant *m*; **to one's liking** à souhait; **to take a liking to** *(a thing)* accueillir avec sympathie; *(a person)* montrer de la sympathie à, se prendre d'amitié pour

lilac ['laɪlək] *adj & s* lilas *m*

Lilliputian [ˌlɪlɪ'pjuʃən] *adj & s* lilliputien *m*

lilt [lɪlt] *s* cadence *f*

lil·y ['lɪli] *s (pl -ies)* lis *m*, lis blanc; *(royal arms of France)* fleur *f* de lis; **to gild the lily** orner la beauté même

lil'y of the val'ley *s* muguet *m*

lil'y pad' *s* feuille *f* de nénuphar

lil'y-white' *adj* blanc comme le lis, lilial

Li'ma bean' ['laɪmə] *s (Phaseolus limensis)* haricot *m* de Lima

limb [lɪm] *s (arm or leg)* membre *m*; *(of a tree)* branche *f*; *(of a cross; of the sea)* bras *m*; (astr, bot) limbe *m*; **to be out on a limb** (coll) être sur la corde raide

limber ['lɪmbər] *adj* souple, flexible ‖ *intr*—**to limber up** se dégourdir

lim·bo ['lɪmbo] *s (pl -bos)* limbes *mpl*

lime [laɪm] *s (calcium oxide)* chaux *f; (linden tree)* tilleul *m*; *(Citrus aurantifolia)* citron *m*; **sweet lime** *(Citrus limetta)* lime *f*

lime'kiln' *s* four *m* à chaux

lime'light' *s*—**to be in the limelight** être sous les feux de la rampe

limerick ['lɪmərɪk] *s* poème *m* humoristique en cinq vers

lime'stone' *adj* calcaire ‖ *s* calcaire *m*, pierre *f* à chaux

limit ['lɪmɪt] *s* limite *f*, borne *f*; **to be the limit** *(to be exasperating)* (coll) être le comble; *(to be bizarre)* (coll) être impayable; **to go the limit** aller jusqu'au bout ‖ *tr* limiter, borner

limitation [ˌlɪmɪ'teʃən] *s* limitation *f*

lim'ited-ac'cess high'way *s* autoroute *f*

lim'ited mon'archy *s* monarchie *f* constitutionnelle

limitless ['lɪmɪtlɪs] *adj* sans bornes, illimité

limousine ['lɪmə ˌzin], [ˌlɪmə'zin] *s* (aut) limousine *f*

limp [lɪmp] *adj* mou, flasque, souple ‖ *s* boiterie *f* ‖ *intr* boiter

limpid ['lɪmpɪd] *adj* limpide

linchpin ['lɪntʃ ˌpɪn] *s* cheville *f* d'essieu, esse *f*

linden ['lɪndən] *s* tilleul *m*

line [laɪn] *s* ligne *f; (of poetry)* vers *m*; *(rope, string)* cordage *m*, corde *f; (wrinkle)* ride *f; (dash)* trait *m; (bar)* barre *f; (lineage)* lignée *f; (trade)* métier *m; (of merchandise)* article *m; (of traffic)* file *f; (mil)* rang *m; (of the spectrum)* (phys) raie *f;* **hold the line!** (telp) ne quittez pas!; **in line** aligné, en rang; **in line with** conforme à, d'accord avec; **on the line** (telp) au bout du fil; **out of line** désaligné; en désaccord; **to bring into line with** mettre d'accord avec; **to drop s.o. a line** envoyer un mot à qn; **to fall into line** se mettre en ligne, s'aligner; **to hand s.o. a line** (slang) faire du baratin à qn, bourrer le crâne de qn; **to have a line on** (coll) se tuyauter sur; **to learn one's lines** apprendre son texte or rôle; **to read between the lines** lire entre les lignes; **to stand or wait in line** faire la queue; **to toe the line** se mettre au pas ‖ *tr* aligner; *(a face)* rider; *(a suit, coat, etc.)* doubler; *(brakes)* fourrer; **to be lined with** *(e.g., trees)* être bordé de ‖ *intr*—**to line up** s'aligner, se mettre en ligne; faire la queue

lineage ['lɪnɪ ɪdʒ] *s* lignée *f*, race *f*

lineal ['lɪnɪ·əl] *adj* linéal; (*succession*) en ligne directe
lineaments ['lɪnɪ·əmənts] *spl* linéaments *mpl*
linear ['lɪnɪ·ər] *adj* linéaire
lined' pa'per *s* papier *m* rayé
line'man *s* (*pl* -**men**) (elec) poseur *m* de lignes; (rr) garde-ligne *m*
linen ['lɪnən] *adj* de lin ‖ *s* (*fabric*) toile *f* de lin; (*yarn*) fil *m* de lin; (*sheets, tablecloths, underclothes, etc.*) linge *m*, lingerie *f*; **pure linen** pur fil
lin'en clos'et *s* lingerie *f*
line' of fire' *s* (mil) ligne *f* de tir
line' of sight' *s* ligne *f* de mire
liner ['laɪnər] *s* (naut) paquebot *m*
line'-up' *s* mise *f* en rang; personnel *m*; (*arrangement*) disposition *f*; (*of prisoners*) défilé *m* de détenus, alignement *m* de suspects; (sports) composition *f*
linger ['lɪŋgər] *intr* s'attarder; (*said of hope, doubt, etc.*) persister; **to linger on** traîner; **to linger over** s'attarder sur
lingerie [,læn·ʒə'ri] *s* lingerie *f* fine pour dames, lingerie de dame
lingering ['lɪŋgərɪŋ] *adj* prolongé, lent
lingual ['lɪŋgwəl] *adj* lingual ‖ *s* (*consonant*) linguale *f*
linguist ['lɪŋgwɪst] *s* (*person skilled in several languages*) polyglotte *mf*; (*specialist in linguistics*) linguiste *mf*
linguistic [lɪŋ'gwɪstɪk] *adj* linguistique ‖ **linguistics** *s* linguistique *f*
liniment ['lɪnɪmənt] *s* liniment *m*
lining ['laɪnɪŋ] *s* (*of a coat*) doublure *f*; (*of a hat*) coiffe *f*; (*of auto brake*) garniture *f*; (*of furnace, wall, etc.*) revêtement *m*
link [lɪŋk] *s* maillon *m*, chaînon *m*; (fig) lien *m*; **links** terrain *m* de golf ‖ *tr* enchaîner; lier ‖ *intr*—**to link in, on,** or **up** se lier
linnet ['lɪnɪt] *s* (orn) linotte *f*
linoleum [lɪ'nolɪ·əm] *s* linoléum *m*
linotype ['laɪnə,taɪp] (trademark) *s* linotype *f* ‖ *tr & intr* composer à la lino
lin'otype op'erator *s* linotypiste *mf*
linseed ['lɪn,sid] *s* linette *f*, graine *f* de lin
lin'seed oil' *s* huile *f* de lin
lint [lɪnt] *s* bourre *f*, filasse *f*; (*used to dress wounds*) charpie *f*
lintel ['lɪntəl] *s* linteau *m*
lion ['laɪ·ən] *s* lion *m*; (fig) lion; **to put one's head in the lion's mouth** se fourrer dans la gueule du loup or du lion
lioness ['laɪ·ənɪs] *s* lionne *f*
li'on-heart'ed *adj* au cœur de lion
lionize ['laɪ·ə,naɪz] *tr* faire une célébrité de, traiter en vedette
li'ons' den' *s* (Bib) fosse *f* aux lions
li'on's share' *s* part *f* du lion
lip [lɪp] *s* lèvre *f*; (*edge*) bord *m*; (slang) impertinence *f*; **to hang on the lips of** être suspendu aux lèvres de; **to smack one's lips** se lécher les babines

lip'read' *v* (*pret & pp* -**read** [,rɛd]) *tr & intr* lire sur les lèvres
lip' read'ing *s* lecture *f* sur les lèvres
lip' serv'ice *s* dévotion *f* des lèvres
lip'stick' *s* bâton *m* de rouge à lèvres
lique-fy ['lɪkwɪ,faɪ] *v* (*pret & pp* -**fied**) *tr* liquéfier
liqueur [lɪ'kʌr] *s* liqueur *f*
liquid ['lɪkwɪd] *adj* liquide ‖ *s* liquide *m*; (*consonant*) liquide *f*
liq'uid as'sets *spl* valeurs *fpl* disponibles
liquidate ['lɪkwɪ,det] *tr & intr* liquider
liquidity [lɪ'kwɪdɪti] *s* liquidité *f*
liquor ['lɪkər] *s* boisson *f* alcoolique, spiritueux *m*; (culin) jus *m*, bouillon *m*
Lisbon ['lɪzbən] *s* Lisbonne *f*
lisle [laɪl] *s* fil *m* d'Écosse, fil retors de coton
lisp [lɪsp] *s* zézayement *m*, blésement *m* ‖ *intr* zézayer, bléser
lissome ['lɪsəm] *adj* souple, flexible; (*nimble*) agile, leste
list [lɪst] *s* liste *f*; (*selvage*) lisière *f*; (naut) bande *f*; **to enter the lists** entrer en lice; **to have a list** (naut) donner de la bande ‖ *tr* cataloguer, enregistrer ‖ *intr* (naut) donner de la bande
listen ['lɪsən] *intr* écouter; **to listen in** rester à l'écoute; **to listen to** écouter; **to listen to reason** entendre raison
listener ['lɪsənər] *s* auditeur *m*; (educ) auditeur libre
listening ['lɪsənɪŋ] *s* écoute *f*
lis'tening post' *s* poste *m* d'écoute
listless ['lɪstlɪs] *adj* apathique, inattentif
list' price' *s* prix *m* courant, cote *f*
lita·ny ['lɪtəni] *s* (*pl* -**nies**) litanie *f*
liter ['litər] *s* litre *m*
literal ['lɪtərəl] *adj* littéral; (*person*) prosaïque
literary ['lɪtə,rɛri] *adj* littéraire
literate ['lɪtərɪt] *adj* qui sait lire et écrire; (*well-read*) lettré ‖ *s* personne *f* qui sait lire et écrire; lettré *m*, érudit *m*
literati [,lɪtə'rati] *spl* littérateurs *mpl*
literature ['lɪtərətʃər] *s* littérature *f*; (com) documentation *f*
lithe [laɪð] *adj* souple, flexible
lithia ['lɪθɪ·ə] *s* (chem) lithine *f*
lithium ['lɪθɪ·əm] *s* (chem) lithium *m*
lithograph ['lɪθə,græf], ['lɪθə,graf] *s* lithographie *f* ‖ *tr* lithographier
lithographer [lɪ'θɑgrəfər] *s* lithographe *mf*
lithography [lɪ'θɑgrəfi] *s* lithographie *f*
Lithuania [,lɪθu'enɪ·ə] *s* Lituanie *f*; la Lituanie
Lithuanian [,lɪθu'enɪ·ən] *adj* lituanien ‖ *s* (*language*) lituanien *m*; (*person*) Lituanien *m*
litigant ['lɪtɪgənt] *adj* plaidant ‖ *s* plaideur *m*
litigate ['lɪtɪ,get] *tr* mettre en litige ‖ *intr* plaider
litigation [,lɪtɪ'geʃən] *s* litige *m*

lit′mus pa′per ['lɪtməs] *s* papier *m* de tournesol

litter ['lɪtər] *s* fouillis *m*; (*things strewn about*) jonchée *f*; (*scattered rubbish*) ordures *fpl*; (*young brought forth at one birth*) portée *f*; (*bedding for animals*) litière *f*; (*vehicle carried by men or animals*) palanquin *m*; (*stretcher*) civière *f* ‖ *tr* joncher ‖ *intr* (*to bring forth young*) mettre bas

lit′ter·bug′ *s* souillon *m*, malpropre *m*, personne *f* qui dépose des ordures et des papiers dans la rue

littering ['lɪtərɪŋ] *s*—**no littering** (public sign) défense de déposer des ordures

little ['lɪtəl] *adj* petit; (*in amount*) peu de, e.g., **little money** peu d'argent; **a little** un peu de, e.g., **a little money** un peu d'argent ‖ *s* peu *m*; **a little** un peu; **to make little of, to think little of** faire peu de cas de; **wait a little** attendez un petit moment, attendez quelques instants ‖ *adv* peu §91; ne . . . guère §90, e.g., **she little thinks that** elle ne se doute guère que; **little by little** peu à peu, petit à petit

Lit′tle Bear′ *s* Petite Ourse *f*

Lit′tle Dip′per *s* Petit Chariot *m*

lit′tle fin′ger *s* petit doigt *m*, auriculaire *m*; **to twist around one's little finger** mener par le bout du nez

lit′tle·neck′ *s* coque *f* de Vénus

littleness ['lɪtəlnɪs] *s* petitesse *f*

lit′tle owl′ *s* (*Athene noctua*) chouette *f* chevêche, chevêche *f*

lit′tle peo′ple *spl* (*fairies*) fées *fpl*; (*common people*) menu peuple *m*

Lit′tle Red Rid′ing·hood′ *s* le Petit Chaperon rouge

lit′tle slam′ *s* (bridge) petit chelem *m*

liturgic(al) [lɪ'tʌrdʒɪk(əl)] *adj* liturgique

litur·gy ['lɪtərdʒi] *s* (*pl* -gies) liturgie *f*

livable ['lɪvəbəl] *adj* (*house*) habitable; (*life, person*) supportable

live [laɪv] *adj* vivant, vif; (*coals; flame*) ardent; (elec) sous tension; (telv) en direct ‖ [lɪv] *tr* vivre; **to live down** faire oublier ‖ *intr* vivre; (*in a certain locality*) demeurer, habiter; **live and learn** qui vivra verra; **to live high** mener grand train; **to live in** (e.g., *a city*) habiter; **to live on** continuer à vivre; (e.g., *meat*) vivre de; (*a benefactor*) vivre aux crochets de; (*one's capital*) manger; **to live up to** (e.g., *one's reputation*) faire honneur à

live′ coal′ [laɪv] *s* charbon *m* ardent

livelihood ['laɪvlɪ ˌhʊd] *s* vie *f*; **to earn one's livelihood** gagner sa vie

livelong ['lɪv ˌlɔŋ], ['lɪv ˌlɑŋ] *adj*—**all the livelong day** toute la sainte journée

live·ly ['laɪvli] *adj* (*comp* -lier; *super* -liest) animé, vivant, plein d'entrain; (*merry*) enjoué, gai; (*active, keen*) vif; (*resilient*) élastique

liven ['laɪvən] *tr* animer ‖ *intr* s'animer

liver ['lɪvər] *s* vivant *m*; (e.g., *in cities*) habitant *m*; (anat) foie *m*

liver·y ['lɪvəri] *s* (*pl* -ies) livrée *f*

liv′ery·man *s* (*pl* -men) loueur *m* de chevaux

liv′ery sta′ble *s* écurie *f* de louage

live′ show′ [laɪv] *s* (telv) prise *f* de vues en direct

live′stock′ [laɪv] *s* bétail *m*, bestiaux *mpl*, cheptel *m*

live′ tel′evision broad′cast [laɪv] *s* prise *f* de vues en direct

live′ wire′ [laɪv] *s* fil *m* sous tension; (slang) type *m* dynamique

livid ['lɪvɪd] *adj* livide

living ['lɪvɪŋ] *adj* vivant, en vie ‖ *s* vie *f*; **to earn** or **to make a living** gagner sa vie

liv′ing quar′ters *spl* appartements *mpl*, habitations *fpl*

liv′ing room′ *s* salle *f* de séjour, salon *m*

liv′ing space′ *s* espace *m* vital

liv′ing wage′ *s* salaire *m* suffisant pour vivre, salaire de base

lizard ['lɪzərd] *s* lézard *m*

load [lod] *s* charge *f*; **loads (of)** (coll) énormément (de); **to get a load of** (slang) observer, écouter; **to have a load on** (slang) avoir son compte ‖ *tr* charger ‖ *intr* charger; se charger

loaded *adj* chargé; (*very drunk*) (slang) soûl; (*very rich*) (slang) huppé

load′ed dice′ *spl* dés *mpl* pipés

load′stone′ *s* pierre *f* d'aimant; (fig) aimant *m*

loaf [lof] *s* (*pl* **loaves** [lovz]) pain *m* ‖ *intr* flâner

loafer ['lofər] *s* flâneur *m*

loam [lom] *s* terre *f* franche, glaise *f*; (*mixture used in making molds*) potée *f*

loamy ['lomi] *adj* franc, glaiseux

loan [lon] *s* prêt *m*, emprunt *m* ‖ *tr* prêter

loan′ shark′ *s* usurier *m*

loan′ word′ *s* mot *m* d'emprunt

loath [loθ] *adj*—**loath to** peu enclin à

loathe [loð] *tr* détester

loathing ['loðɪŋ] *s* dégoût *m*

loathsome ['loðsəm] *adj* dégoûtant

lob [lab] *s* (tennis) lob *m* ‖ *v* (*pret & pp* lobbed; *ger* lobbing) *tr* frapper en hauteur, lober

lob·by ['labi] *s* (*pl* -bies) vestibule *m*; (e.g., *in a theater*) foyer *m*; (*pressure group*) groupe *m* de pression, lobby *m* ‖ *v* (*pret & pp* -bied) *intr* faire les couloirs

lobbying ['labɪ·ɪŋ] *s* intrigues *fpl* de couloir

lobbyist ['labɪ·ɪst] *s* intrigant *m* de couloir

lobe [lob] *s* lobe *m*

lobster ['labstər] *s* (*spiny lobster*) langouste *f*; (*Homarus*) homard *m*

lob′ster pot′ *s* casier *m* à homards

local ['lokəl] *adj* local ‖ *s* (*of labor union*) succursale *f*; (journ) informations *fpl* régionales; (rr) train *m* omnibus

locale [lo'kæl] *s* lieu *m*, milieu *m*; scène *f*

locali·ty [lo'kælɪti] s (pl -ties) localité f
localize ['lokə‚laɪz] tr localiser
lo'cal supply' cir'cuit s secteur m
locate [lo'ket], ['loket] tr (to discover the location of) localiser; (to place, to settle) placer, installer; (to ascribe a particular location to) situer; **to be located** se trouver ‖ intr se fixer, s'établir
location [lo'keʃən] s (place, position) situation f, emplacement m; (act of placing) établissement m; (act of finding) localisation f, détermination f; (of a railroad line) tracé m; **on location** (mov) en extérieur
loca'tion shot' s (mov) extérieur m
lock [lak] s serrure f; (of a canal) écluse f; (of hair) mèche f, boucle f; (of a firearm) platine f; (wrestling) clef f; **lock, stock, and barrel** tout le bataclan, tout le fourbi; **under lock and key** sous clé ‖ tr fermer à clef; (to key) caler, bloquer; (a boat) écluser, sasser; (a switch) (rr) verrouiller; **to be locked in each other's arms** être enlacés; **to lock in** enfermer à clef; **to lock out** fermer la porte à sur; (workers) fermer les ateliers contre; **to lock up** fermer à clef, mettre sous clé; (e.g., a prisoner) boucler, enfermer; (a form) (typ) serrer ‖ intr (said of door) fermer à clef; (said of brake, wheel, etc.) se bloquer; **to lock into** s'engrener dans
locker ['lakər] s armoire f, coffre m de sûreté; (in a station or airport) casier m; (in a gym) vestiaire m
lock'er room' s vestiaire m à cases individuelles
locket ['lakɪt] s médaillon m
lock' jaw' s trisme m
lock' nut' s contre-écrou m
lock'out' s lock-out m
lock'smith' s serrurier m
lock' step' s—**to march in lock step** emboîter le pas
lock' stitch' s point m indécousable
lock'ten'der s éclusier m
lock'up' s (prison) (coll) bloc m, violon m
lock' wash'er s rondelle f Grower, rondelle à ressort
locomotive [‚lokə'motɪv] s locomotive f
lo·cus ['lokəs] s (pl -ci [saɪ]) lieu m; (math) lieu géométrique
locust ['lokəst] s (Pachytylus) (ent) criquet m migrateur, locuste f; (Cicada) (ent) cigale f; (bot) faux acacia m
lode [lod] s filon m, veine f
lode'star' s (astr) étoile f polaire; (fig) pôle m d'attraction
lodge [ladʒ] s (of gatekeeper; of animal; of Mason) loge f; (residence, e.g., for hunting) pavillon m; (hotel) relais m, hostellerie f ‖ tr loger; **to lodge a complaint with** porter plainte auprès de ‖ intr loger; (said of arrow, bullet) se loger

lodger ['ladʒər] s locataire mf, pensionnaire mf
lodging ['ladʒɪŋ] s logement m; (of a complaint) déposition f
loft [lɔft], [laft] s (attic) grenier m, soupente f; (hayloft) fenil m; (in theater or church) tribune f; (in store or office building) atelier m
loft·y ['lɔfti], ['lafti] adj (comp -ier; super -iest) (towering; sublime) élevé, exalté; (haughty) hautain
log [lɔg], [lag] s bûche f, rondin m; (record book) registre m de travail; (aer) livre m de vol; (record book) (naut) journal m de bord; (chip log) (naut) loch m; (rad) carnet m d'écoute; **to sleep like a log** dormir comme une souche ‖ v (pret & pp logged; ger logging) tr (wood) tronçonner; (an event) porter au journal; (a certain distance) (naut) filer ‖ intr (to cut wood) couper des rondins
logarithm ['lɔgə‚rɪðəm], ['lagə‚rɪðəm] s logarithme m
log'book' s (aer) livre m de vol; (naut) journal m de bord, livre de loch
log' cab'in s cabane f en rondins
log' chip' s (naut) flotteur m de loch
log' driv'er s flotteur m
log' driv'ing s flottage m
logger ['lɔgər], ['lagər] s bûcheron m; (loader) (mach) grue f de chargement; (mach) tracteur m
log'ger-head' s tête f de bois; **at loggerheads** en bisbille, aux prises
logic ['ladʒɪk] s logique f
logical ['ladʒɪkəl] adj logique
logician [lo'dʒɪʃən] s logicien m
logistic(al) [lo'dʒɪstɪk(əl)] adj logistique
logistics [lo'dʒɪstɪks] s logistique f
log'jam' s embâcle m de bûches; (fig) bouchon m, embouteillage m
log' line' s (naut) ligne f de loch
log'roll' intr faire trafic de faveurs politiques
log'wood' s bois m de campêche; (tree) campêche m
loin [lɔɪn] s (of beef) aloyau m; (of veal) longe f; (of pork) échine f; **to gird up one's loins** se ceindre les reins
loin'cloth' s pagne m
loiter ['lɔɪtər] tr—**to loiter away** perdre en flânant ‖ intr flâner
loiterer ['lɔɪtərər] s flâneur m
loll [lall] intr se prélasser, s'allonger, s'affaler
lollipop ['lali‚pap] s sucette f
Lom'bardy pop'lar ['lambərdi] s peuplier m noir
London ['lʌndən] adj londonien ‖ s Londres m
Londoner ['lʌndənər] s Londonien m
lone [lon] adj solitaire, seul; (sole, single) unique
loneliness ['lonlɪnɪs] s solitude f
lone·ly ['lonli] adj (comp -lier; super -liest) solitaire, isolé
lonesome ['lonsəm] adj solitaire, seul
lone' wolf' s (fig) solitaire mf, ours m
long [lɔŋ], [laŋ] (comp **longer** ['lɔŋ-

gər], ['laŋgər); *super* **longest** ['lɔŋgɪst], ['laŋgɪst]) *adj* long; de long, de longueur, e.g., **two meters long** deux mètres de long or de longueur ‖ *adv* longtemps; **as long as** aussi longtemps que; (*provided that*) tant que; **before long** sous peu; **how long?** combien de temps?, depuis combien de temps?, depuis quand?; **long ago** il y a longtemps; **long before** longtemps avant; **longer** plus long; **long since** depuis longtemps; **no longer** ne . . . plus longtemps; **ne** . . . plus, e.g., **I could no longer see him** je ne pouvais plus le voir; **so long!** (coll) à bientôt!; **so long as** tant que; **to be long in** tarder à ‖ *intr*—**to long for** soupirer pour or après
long'boat' *s* chaloupe *f*
long' dis'tance *s* (telp) l'interurbain *m*; **to call s.o. long distance** appeler qn par l'interurbain
long'-dis'tance call' *s* (telp) appel *m* interurbain
long'-dis'tance flight' *s* (aer) vol *m* au long cours, raid *m* aérien
long'-drawn'-out' *adj* prolongé; (*story*) délayé
longevity [lɑn'dʒɛvɪti] *s* longévité *f*
long' face' *s* (coll) triste figure *f*
long'hair' *adj* & *s* intellectuel *m*; fanatique *mf* de la musique classique
long'hand' *s* écriture *f* ordinaire; **in longhand** à la main
longing ['lɔŋɪŋ], ['laŋɪŋ] *adj* ardent ‖ *s* désir *m* ardent
longitude ['lɑndʒɪ,t(j)ud] *s* longitude *f*
long' jump' *s* saut *m* en longueur
long-lived ['lɔŋ'laɪvd], ['laŋ'lɪvd], ['laŋ'laɪvd], ['laŋ'lɪvd]) *adj* à longue vie; persistant
long'-play'ing rec'ord *s* disque *m* de longue durée
long' prim'er ['prɪmər] *s* (typ) philosophie *f*
long'-range' *adj* à longue portée; (*e.g., plan*) à long terme
long'shore'man *s* (*pl* -men) arrimeur *m*, débardeur *m*
long'-stand'ing *adj* de longue date
long'-suf'fering *adj* patient, endurant
long' suit' *s* (cards) couleur *f* longue, longue *f*; (fig) fort *m*
long'-term' *adj* à longue échéance
long'-wind'ed ['wɪndɪd] *adj* interminable; (*person*) intarissable
look [lʊk] *s* (*appearance*) aspect *m*; (*glance*) regard *m*; **looks** apparence *f*, mine *f*; **to take a look at** jeter un coup d'œil sur or à ‖ *tr* regarder; (*e.g., one's age*) paraître; **to look daggers at** lancer un regard furieux à; **to look the part** avoir le physique de l'emploi; **to look up** (*e.g., in a dictionary*) chercher, rechercher; (*to visit*) aller voir, venir voir ‖ *intr* regarder; (*to seek*) chercher; **it looks like rain** le temps est à la pluie; **look here!** dites donc!; **look out!** gare!, attention!; **to look after** s'occuper de; (*e.g., an invalid*) soigner; **to look at** regarder; **to look away** détourner

les yeux; **to look back** regarder en arrière; **to look down on** mépriser; **to look for** chercher; (*to expect*) s'attendre à; **to look forward to** s'attendre à, attendre avec impatience; **to look ill** avoir mauvaise mine; **to look in on** passer voir; **to look into** examiner, vérifier; **to look like** (*s.o. or s.th.*) ressembler à; (*to give promise of*) avoir l'air de; **to look out** faire attention; (*e.g., the window*) regarder par; **to look out on** donner sur; **to look through** (*a window*) regarder par; (*a telescope*) regarder dans; (*a book*) feuilleter; **to look toward** regarder du côté de; **to look up** lever les yeux; **to look up to** respecter; **to look well** avoir bonne mine
looker-on [,lʊkər'ɑn], [,lʊkər'ɔn] *s* (*pl* lookers-on) spectateur *m*, assistant *m*
look'ing glass' *s* miroir *m*
look'out' *s* guet *m*; (*person*) guetteur *m*; (*place*) poste *m* d'observation; (*person or place*) (naut) vigie *f*; **that's his lookout** (coll) ça, c'est son affaire; **to be on the lookout for** être à l'affût de
loom [lum] *s* métier *m* ‖ *intr* apparaître indistinctement; s'élever; menacer, paraître imminent
loon [lun] *s* lourdaud *m*, sot *m*; (orn) plongeon *m*
loon·y ['luni] *adj* (*comp* -ier; *super* -iest) (slang) toqué ‖ *s* (*pl* -ies) (slang) toqué *m*
loop [lup] *s* boucle *f*; (*for fastening a button*) bride *f*; (*circular route*) boulevard *m* périphérique; (*in skating*) croisé *m*; **to loop the loop** (aer) boucler la boucle ‖ *tr* & *intr* boucler
loop'hole' *s* meurtrière *f*; (fig) échappatoire *f*
loop'-the-loop' *s* looping *m*
loose [lus] *adj* lâche; (*stone, tooth*) branlant; (*screw*) desserré; (*pulley, wheel*) fou; (*rope*) mou, détendu; (*coat, dress*) vague, ample; (*earth, soil*) meuble, friable; (*bowels*) relâché; (*style*) décousu; (*translation*) libre, peu exact; (*life, morals*) relâché, dissolu; (*woman*) facile; (*unpackaged*) en vrac; (*unbound, e.g., pages*) détaché; **to become loose** se détacher; **to break loose** (*from captivity*) s'évader; (fig) se déchaîner; **to let loose** lâcher, lâcher la bride à ‖ *s*—**to be on the loose** (*to debauch*) (coll) courir la prétentaine; (*to be out of work*) (coll) être sans occupation ‖ *tr* lâcher; (*to untie*) détacher
loose' end' *s* (fig) affaire *f* pendante; **at loose ends** s'œuvré, indécis
loose'-leaf note'book *s* cahier *m* à feuilles mobiles
loosen ['lusən] *tr* lâcher, relâcher; (*a screw*) desserrer ‖ *intr* se relâcher
looseness ['lusnɪs] *s* relâchement *m*; (*of garment*) ampleur *f*; (*play of screw*) jeu *m*, desserrage *m*
loose'strife' *s* (*common yellow type*)

chasse-bosse *f*, grande lysimaque *f*; (*spiked-purple type*) salicaire *f*
loose'-tongued' *adj*—**to be loose-tongued** avoir la langue déliée
loot [lut] *s* butin *m*, pillage *m* || *tr* piller, saccager
lop [lɑp] *v* (*pret* & *pp* **lopped**; *ger* **lopping**) *tr*—**to lop off** abattre, trancher; (*a tree, a branch*) élaguer || *intr* pendre
lope [lop] *s* galop *m* lent || *intr*—**to lope along** aller doucement
lop'sid'ed *adj* déjeté, bancal
loquacious [loˈkweʃəs] *adj* loquace
lord [lɔrd] *s* seigneur *m*; (hum & poetic) époux *m*; (Brit) lord *m* || *tr*—**to lord it over** dominer despotiquement
lord·ly [ˈlɔrdli] *adj* (*comp* **-lier**; *super* **-liest**) de grand seigneur, majestueux; (*arrogant*) hautain, altier
Lord's' Day' *s* jour *m* du Seigneur
lordship [ˈlɔrdʃɪp] *s* seigneurie *f*
Lord's' Prayer' *s* oraison *f* dominicale
Lord's' Sup'per *s* communion *f*, cène *f*; Cène
lore [lor] *s* savoir *m*, science *f*; tradition *f* populaire
lorgnette [lɔrnˈjɛt] *s* (*eyeglasses*) face-à-main *m*; (*opera glasses*) lorgnette *f*
lor·ry [ˈlɑri], [ˈlɔri] *s* (*pl* **-ries**) lorry *m*, wagonnet *m*; (*truck*) (Brit) camion *m*; (*wagon*) (Brit) fardier *m*
lose [luz] *v* (*pret* & *pp* **lost** [lɔst], [lɑst]) *tr* perdre; (*a patient who dies*) ne pas réussir à sauver; (*several minutes, as a timepiece does*) retarder de; **to lose oneself in** s'absorber dans; **to lose one's way** s'égarer || *intr* perdre; (*said of timepiece*) retarder
loser [ˈluzər] *s* perdant *m*
losing [ˈluzɪŋ] *adj* perdant || **losings** *spl* pertes *fpl*
loss [lɔs], [lɑs] *s* perte *f*; **to be at a loss** ne savoir que faire; **to be at a loss to** avoir de la peine à, être bien embarrassé pour; **to sell at a loss** vendre à perte
loss' of face' *s* perte *f* de prestige
lost [lɔst], [lɑst] *adj* perdu; **lost in thought** perdu or absorbé dans ses pensées; **lost to** perdu pour
lost'-and-found' depart'ment *s* bureau *m* des objets trouvés
lost' sheep' *s* brebis *f* perdue, brebis égarée
lot [lɑt] *s* lot *m*; (*for building*) lotissement *m*, lot; (*fate*) sort *m*, lot; **a bad lot** (coll) un mauvais sujet, de la mauvaise graine; **a lot of** or **lots of** (coll) un tas de; **a queer lot** (coll) un drôle de numéro; **in a lot** en bloc; **to cast** or **to throw in one's lot with** tenter la fortune avec; **to draw** or **to cast lots** tirer au sort; **such a lot of** tellement de; **what a lot of . . . !** que de . . . !
lotion [ˈloʃən] *s* lotion *f*
lotter·y [ˈlɑtəri] *s* (*pl* **-ies**) loterie *f*
lotto [ˈlɑto] *s* loto *m*
lotus [ˈlotəs] *s* lotus *m*

loud [laud] *adj* haut, fort; (*noisy*) bruyant; (*voice*) fort; (*showy*) voyant || *adv* fort; (*noisily*) bruyamment; **out loud** à haute voix
loud·mouthed [ˈlaud͵mauθt], [ˈlaud͵mauðd] *adj* au verbe haut
loud'speak'er *s* haut-parleur *m*
Louisiana [lu͵izɪˈænə] *s* Louisiane *f*; la Louisiane
lounge [laundʒ] *s* divan *m*, sofa *m*; (*room*) petit salon *m*, salle *f* de repos; (*in a hotel*) hall *m* || *intr* flâner; (*e.g., in a chair*) se vautrer
lounge' liz'ard *s* (slang) gigolo *m*
louse [laus] *s* (*pl* **lice** [lais]) pou *m*; (slang) salaud *m* || *tr*—**to louse up** (slang) bâcler
lous·y [ˈlauzi] *adj* (*comp* **-ier**; *super* **-iest**) pouilleux; (*mean; ugly*) (coll) moche; (*bungling*) (coll) maladroit, gauche; **lousy with** (slang) chargé de
lout [laut] *s* lourdaud *m*, balourd *m*
louver [ˈluvər] *s* abat-vent *m*; (aut) auvent *m*
lovable [ˈlʌvəbəl] *adj* aimable, sympathique
love [lʌv] *s* amour *m*; affection *f*; (tennis) zéro *m*; **in love with** amoureux de; **love at first sight** le coup de foudre; **love to all!** vives amitiés à tous!; **not for love or money** pour rien au monde; **to make love to** faire la cour à; **with much love!** avec mes affectueuses pensées! || *tr* & *intr* aimer
love' affair' *s* affaire *f* de cœur
love'birds' *spl* inséparables *mpl*; nouveaux mariés *mpl*
love' child' *s* enfant *mf* de l'amour
love' feast' *s* (eccl) agape *f*
love' game' *s* (tennis) jeu *m* blanc
love' knot' *s* lacs *m* d'amour
loveless [ˈlʌvlɪs] *adj* sans amour; (*feeling no love*) insensible à l'amour
love' let'ter *s* billet *m* doux
lovelorn [ˈlʌv͵lɔrn] *adj* délaissé d'amour; éperdu d'amour
love·ly [ˈlʌvli] *adj* (*comp* **-lier**; *super* **-liest**) beau; (*adorable*) charmant, gracieux; (*enjoyable*) (coll) agréable, aimable
love' match' *s* mariage *m* d'amour
love' po'tion *s* philtre *m* d'amour
lover [ˈlʌvər] *s* amoureux *m*, amant *m*; (*of hunting, sports, music, etc.*) amateur *m*, fanatique *mf*
love' seat' *s* causeuse *f*
love'sick' *adj* féru d'amour
love'sick'ness *s* mal *m* d'amour
love' song' *s* romance *f*, chanson *f* d'amour
loving [ˈlʌvɪŋ] *adj* aimant, affectueux; affectionné, e.g., **your loving daughter** votre fille affectionnée
lov'ing cup' *s* coupe *f* de l'amitié; trophée *m*
lov'ing-kind'ness *s* bonté *f* d'âme
low [lo] *adj* bas; (*speed; price*) bas; (*speed; price; number; light*) faible; (*opinion*) défavorable; (*dress*) décolleté; (*sound, note*) bas, grave; (*fever*) lent; (*bow*) profond; **to lay low** éten-

dre, terrasser; **to lie low** se tenir coi
|| *s* bas *m*; (*moo of cow*) meuglement
m; (aut) première vitesse *f*; (meteo)
dépression *f* || *adv* bas; **to speak low**
parler à voix basse || *intr* (*said of
cow*) meugler
low'born' *adj* de basse naissance
low'boy' *s* commode *f* basse
low'brow' *adj* (coll) peu intellectuel ||
s (coll) ignorant *m*
low'-cost' hous'ing *s* habitations *fpl* à
loyer modéré or à bon marché
Low' Coun'tries *spl* Pays-Bas *mpl*
low'-down' *adj* (coll) bas, vil || **low'-
down'** *s* (slang) faits *mpl* véritables;
to give s.o. the low-down on (slang)
tuyauter qn sur
lower ['lo·ər] *adj* inférieur, bas || *tr* &
intr baisser || ['lau·ər] *intr* se ren-
frogner, regarder de travers
low'er berth' ['lo·ər] *s* couchette *f* in-
férieure
low'er case' ['lo·ər] *s* (typ) bas *m* de
casse
low'er mid'dle class' ['lo·ər] *s* petite
bourgeoisie *f*
lowermost ['lo·ər,most] *adj* (le) plus
bas
low'-fre'quency *adj* à basse fréquence
low' gear' *s* première vitesse *f*
lowland ['loland] *s* plaine *f* basse;
Lowlands (*in Scotland*) Basse-Écosse *f*
low·ly ['loli] *adj* (*comp* **-lier**; *super*
-liest) humble, modeste; (*in growth
or position*) bas, infime
Low' Mass' *s* messe basse *f*, petite
messe
low'-mind'ed *adj* d'esprit vulgaire
low' neck' *s* décolleté *m*
low'-necked' *adj* décolleté
low'-pitched' *adj* (*sound*) grave; (*roof*)
à faible inclinaison
low'-pres'sure *adj* à basse pression
low'-priced' *adj* à bas prix
low' shoe' *s* soulier *m* bas
low'-speed' *adj* à petite vitesse
low'-spir'ited *adj* abattu
low' spir'its *spl* abattement *m*, accablement *m*
low' tide' *s* marée *f* basse
low' vis'ibil'ity *s* (aer) mauvaise visibilité *f*
low'-warp' *adj* (tex) de basse lice
low' wa'ter *s* (*of river*) étiage *m*; (*of
sea*) niveau *m* des basses eaux; marée
f basse
loyal ['lɔɪ·əl] *adj* loyal
loyalist ['lɔɪ·əlɪst] *s* loyaliste *mf*
loyal·ty ['lɔɪ·əlti] *s* (*pl* **-ties**) loyauté *f*
lozenge ['lazɪndʒ] *s* (*candy cough
drop*) pastille *f*; (geom) losange *m*
LP ['el'pi] *s* (letterword) (trademark)
(**long-playing**) disque *m* de longue
durée
lubricant ['lubrɪkənt] *adj* & *s* lubrifiant
m
lubricate ['lubrɪ,ket] *tr* lubrifier
lubricous ['lubrɪkəs] *adj* (*slippery*)
glissant; (*lewd*) lubrique; inconstant
lucerne [lu'sʌrn] *s* luzerne *f*
lucid ['lusɪd] *adj* lucide
luck [lʌk] *s* (*good or bad*) chance *f*;

(*good*) chance, bonne chance; **to be
down on one's luck, to be out of luck**
avoir de la malchance, être dans la
déveine; **to be in luck** avoir de la
chance, avoir de la veine; **to bring
luck** porter bonheur; **to try one's
luck** tenter la fortune, tenter l'aventure; **worse luck!** tant pis!, pas de
chance!
luckily ['lʌkɪli] *adv* heureusement, par
bonheur
luckless ['lʌklɪs] *adj* malheureux, malchanceux
luck·y ['lʌki] *adj* (*comp* **-ier**; *super*
-iest) heureux, fortuné; (*supposed to
bring luck*) porte-bonheur; **how
lucky!** quelle chance!; **to be lucky**
avoir de la chance
luck'y charm' *s* porte-bonheur *m*
luck'y find' *s* (coll) trouvaille *f*
luck'y hit' *s* (coll) coup *m* de bonheur
lucrative ['lukrətɪv] *adj* lucratif
ludicrous ['ludɪkrəs] *adj* ridicule,
risible
lug [lʌg] *s* oreille *f*; (*pull, tug*) saccade
f || *v* (*pret* & *pp* **lugged**; *ger* **lugging**)
tr traîner, tirer; (*to bring up irrele-
vantly*) (coll) ressortir, amener de
force
luggage ['lʌgɪdʒ] *s* bagages *mpl*
lug'gage car'rier *s* porte-bagages *m*
lugubrious [lu'g(j)ubrɪ·əs] *adj* lugubre
lukewarm ['luk,wɔrm] *adj* tiède
lull [lʌl] *s* accalmie *f* || *tr* bercer, en-
dormir, calmer
lulla·by ['lʌlə,baɪ] *s* (*pl* **-bies**) berceuse *f*
lumbago [lʌm'bego] *s* lumbago *m*
lumber ['lʌmbər] *s* bois *m* de char-
pente, bois de construction || *intr* se
traîner lourdement
lum'ber·jack' *s* bûcheron *m*
lum'ber jack'et *s* canadienne *f*
lum'ber·man *s* (*pl* **-men**) (*dealer*) exploitant *m* forestier, propriétaire *m*
forestier; (*man who cuts down lumber*) bûcheron *m*
lum'ber raft' *s* train *m* de flottage
lum'ber room' *s* fourre-tout *m*, débarras *m*
lum'ber·yard' *s* chantier *m* de bois, dépôt *m* de bois de charpente
luminar·y ['lumɪ ,nɛri] *s* (*pl* **-ies**) corps
m lumineux; (astr) luminaire *m*; (*person*) (fig) lumière *f*
luminescent [,lumɪ'nɛsənt] *adj* luminescent
luminous ['lumɪnəs] *adj* lumineux
lummox ['lʌməks] *s* (coll) lourdaud *m*
lump [lʌmp] *s* masse *f*; (*of earth*) motte
f; (*of sugar*) morceau *m*; (*of salt,
flour, porridge, etc.*) grumeau *m*;
(*swelling*) bosse *f*; (*of ice, stone, etc.*)
bloc *m*; **in the lump** en bloc; **to get a
lump in one's throat** avoir un serre-
ment de gorge || *tr* réunir; **to lump
together** prendre en bloc, englober ||
intr—**to lump along** marcher d'un
pas lourd
lumpish ['lʌmpɪʃ] *adj* balourd
lump' sug'ar *s* sucre *m* en morceaux
lump' sum' *s* somme *f* globale

lump·y ['lʌmpi] *adj* (*comp* **-ier**; *super* **-iest**) grumeleux; (*covered with lumps*) couvert de bosses; (*sea*) clapoteux

luna·cy ['lunəsi] *s* (*pl* **-cies**) folie *f*

lu'nar land'ing *s* alunissage *m*

lu'nar mod'ule *s* (rok) module *m* lunaire

lunatic ['lunətɪk] *adj & s* fou *m*

lu'natic asy'lum *s* maison *f* de fous

lu'natic fringe' *s* minorité *f* fanatique

lunch [lʌntʃ] *s* (*midday meal*) déjeuner *m*; (*light meal*) collation *f*, petit repas *m* ‖ *intr* déjeuner; (*to snack*) casser la croûte, manger sur le pouce

lunch' bas'ket *s* panier *m* à provisions

lunch' cloth' *s* nappe *f* à thé

lunch' coun'ter *s* snack *m*, buffet *m*

luncheon ['lʌntʃən] *s* déjeuner *m*

luncheonette [ˌlʌntʃə'nɛt] *s* brasserie *f*, café-restaurant *m*

lunch'room' *s* brasserie *f*, café-restaurant *m*

lunch'time' *s* heure *f* du déjeuner

lung [lʌŋ] *s* poumon *m*

lunge [lʌndʒ] *s* mouvement *m* en avant; (*with a sword*) botte *f* ‖ *intr* se précipiter en avant; (*with a sword*) se fendre; **to lunge at** porter une botte à

lurch [lʌrtʃ] *s* embardée *f*; (*of person*) secousse *f*; **to leave in the lurch** laisser en plan ‖ *intr* faire une embardée; (*said of person*) vaciller

lure [lʊr] *s* (*decoy*) leurre *m*, amorce *f*; (fig) attrait *m* ‖ *tr* leurrer; **to lure away** détourner

lurid ['lʊrɪd] *adj* sensationnel; (*gruesome*) terrible, macabre; (*fiery*) rougeoyant; (*livid*) blafard

lurk [lʌrk] *intr* se cacher; (*to prowl*) rôder

luscious ['lʌʃəs] *adj* délicieux, succulent; luxueux, somptueux

lush [lʌʃ] *adj* plein de sève; (*abundant*) luxuriant; opulent, luxueux

lust [lʌst] *s* désir *m* ardent; (*greed*)

convoitise *f*, soif *f*; (*strong sexual appetite*) luxure *f*

luster ['lʌstər] *s* lustre *m*

lus'ter·ware' *s* poterie *f* lustrée, poterie à reflets métalliques

lustful ['lʌstfəl] *adj* luxurieux, lascif

lustrous ['lʌstrəs] *adj* lustré, chatoyant

lust·y ['lʌsti] *adj* (*comp* **-ier**; *super* **-iest**) robuste, vigoureux

lute [lut] *s* (mus) luth *m*; (*substance used to close or seal a joint*) (chem) lut *m*

Lutheran ['luθərən] *adj* luthérien ‖ *s* Luthérien *m*

Luxemburg ['lʌksəmˌbʌrg] *s* le Luxembourg

luxuriant [lʌg'ʒʊrɪ·ənt], [lʌk'ʃʊrɪ·ənt] *adj* luxuriant; (*overornamented*) surchargé

luxurious [lʌg'ʒʊrɪ·əs], [lʌk'ʃʊrɪ·əs] *adj* luxueux, somptueux

luxu·ry ['lʌkʃəri], ['lʌgʒəri] *s* (*pl* **-ries**) luxe *m*

lux'ury i'tem *s* produit *m* de luxe

lux'ury tax' *s* impôt *m* somptuaire

lyceum [laɪ'si·əm] *s* lycée *m*

lye [laɪ] *s* lessive *f*

lying ['laɪ·ɪŋ] *adj* menteur ‖ *s* le mensonge

ly'ing-in' hos'pital *s* maternité *f*, clinique *f* d'accouchement

lymph [lɪmf] *s* lymphe *f*

lymphatic [lɪm'fætɪk] *adj* lymphatique

lynch [lɪntʃ] *tr* lyncher

lynching ['lɪntʃɪŋ] *s* lynchage *m*

lynx [lɪŋks] *s* lynx *m*

Lyons ['laɪ·ənz] *s* Lyon *m*

lyre [laɪr] *s* (mus) lyre *f*

lyric ['lɪrɪk] *adj* lyrique ‖ *s* poème *m* lyrique; **lyrics** (*of song*) paroles *fpl*; (theat) chansons *fpl* du livret

lyrical ['lɪrɪkəl] *adj* lyrique

lyricism ['lɪrɪ ˌsɪzəm] *s* lyrisme *m*

lyricist ['lɪrɪsɪst] *s* poète *m* lyrique; (*writer of words for songs*) parolier *m*

M

M, m [ɛm] XIIIᵉ lettre de l'alphabet

ma'am [mæm], [mɑm] *s* (coll) madame *f*

macadam [mə'kædəm] *s* macadam *m*

macadamize [mə'kædəˌmaɪz] *tr* macadamiser

macaroon [ˌmækə'run] *s* macaron *m*

macaw [mə'kɔ] *s* (orn) ara *m*

mace [mes] *s* masse *f*

mace'bear'er *s* massier *m*

machination [ˌmækɪ'neʃən] *s* machination *f*

machine [mə'ʃin] *s* machine *f*; (*of a political party*) noyau *m* directeur, leviers *mpl* de commande ‖ *tr* usiner, façonner

machine' gun' *s* mitrailleuse *f*

ma·chine'-gun' *v* (*pret & pp* **-gunned**; *ger* **-gunning**) *tr* mitrailler

ma·chine'-made' *adj* fait à la machine

machiner·y [mə'ʃinəri] *s* (*pl* **-ies**) machinerie *f*, machines *fpl*; (*of a watch*; *of government*) mécanisme *m*; (*in literature*) merveilleux *m*

machine' screw' *s* vis *f* à métaux

machine' shop' *s* atelier *m* d'usinage

machine' tool' *s* machine-outil *f*

machine' transla'tion *s* traduction *f* automatique

machinist [mə'ʃinɪst] *s* mécanicien *m*

mackerel ['mækərəl] *s* maquereau *m*

mack'erel sky' *s* ciel *m* pommelé or moutonné

mad [mæd] *adj* (*comp* **madder**; *super*

maddest) fou; (dog) enragé; (coll) fâché, irrité; as mad as a hatter fou à lier; like mad (coll) comme un fou, éperdument; to be mad about (coll) être fou or passionné de; to drive mad rendre fou

madam ['mædəm] s madame f; (of a brothel) (slang) tenancière f

mad'cap' adj & s écervelé m, étourdi m

madden ['mædən] tr rendre fou ‖ intr devenir fou

made-to-order ['medtə'ərdər] adj fait sur demande; (clothing) fait sur mesure

made'-up' adj inventé; (artificial) postiche; (face) maquillé

mad'house' s maison f de fous

mad'man' s (pl -men') fou m

madness ['mædnɪs] s folie f; (of dog) rage f

Madonna [mə'danə] s madone f; (eccl) Madone

maelstrom ['melstrəm] s maelstrom m, tourbillon m

magazine ['mægə,zin], [,mægə'zin] s (periodical) revue f, magazine m; (warehouse; for cartridges of gun or camera; for munitions or powder) magasin m; (naut) soute f

mag'azine' rack' s casier m à revues

Magdalen ['mægdələn] s Madeleine f

Maggie ['mægi] s (coll) Margot f

maggot ['mægət] s asticot m

Magi ['medʒaɪ] spl mages mpl

magic ['mædʒɪk] adj magique ‖ s magie f; as if by magic comme par enchantement

magician [mə'dʒɪʃən] s magicien m

magisterial [,mædʒɪs'tɪrɪ-əl] adj magistral

magistrate ['mædʒɪs,tret] s magistrat m

Magna Charta ['mægnə'kɑrtə] s la Grande Charte f

magnanimous [mæg'nænɪməs] adj magnanime

magnate ['mægnet] s magnat m

magnesium [mæg'niʃɪ-əm], [mæg'niʒɪ-əm] s magnésium m

magnet ['mægnɪt] s aimant m

magnetic [mæg'netɪk] adj magnétique; (fig) attrayant, séduisant

magnetism ['mægnɪ,tɪzəm] s magnétisme m

magnetize ['mægnɪ,taɪz] tr aimanter

magne•to [mæg'nito] s (pl -tos) magnéto f

magnificent [mæg'nɪfɪsənt] adj magnifique

magni•fy ['mægnɪ,faɪ] v (pret & pp -fied) tr grossir; (opt) grossir

mag'nifying glass' s loupe f

magnitude ['mægnɪ,t(j)ud] s grandeur f; (astr) magnitude f

magpie ['mæg,paɪ] s (orn, fig) pie f

mahlstick ['mɑl,stɪk], ['mɔl,stɪk] s appui-main m

mahoga•ny [mə'hagəni] s (pl -nies) acajou m

Mahomet [mə'hamɪt] s Mahomet m

mahout [mə'haʊt] s cornac m

maid [med] s (servant) bonne f; (young girl) jeune fille f, demoiselle f

maiden ['medən] s jeune fille f, demoiselle f

maid'en•hair' s (bot) capillaire m

maid'en•head' s hymen m

maid'en•hood' s virginité f

maid'en la'dy s demoiselle f, célibataire f

maidenly ['medənli] adj virginal, de jeune fille

maid'en name' s nom m de jeune fille

maid'en voy'age s premier voyage m

maid'-in-wait'ing s (pl maids-in-waiting) fille f d'honneur, dame f d'honneur

maid' of hon'or s demoiselle f d'honneur

maid'serv'ant s fille f de service, servante f

mail [mel] adj postal ‖ s courrier m; (system) poste f; (armor) mailles fpl, cotte f de mailles; by return mail par retour du courrier; mails poste ‖ tr mettre à la poste, envoyer par la poste

mail'bag' s sac m postal

mail'boat' s paquebot m, bateau-poste m

mail'box' s boîte f aux lettres

mail' car' s fourgon m postal, bureau m ambulant, wagon-poste m

mail' car'rier s facteur m

mail' clerk' s postier m; (mil, nav) vaguemestre m; (rr) convoyeur m des postes

mailing ['melɪŋ] s envoi m

mail'ing list' s liste f d'adresses, (of subscribers) liste d'abonnés

mail'ing per'mit s (label on envelopes) dispensé du timbrage

mail'man' s (pl -men') facteur m

mail' or'der s commande f par la poste

mail'-order house' s établissement m de vente par correspondance or de vente sur catalogue; comptoir m postal (Canad)

mail'-order sell'ing s vente f par correspondance

mail'plane' s avion m postal

mail' train' s train-poste m

maim [mem] tr mutiler, estropier

main [men] adj principal ‖ s égout m collecteur, canalisation f or conduite f principale; in the main en général, pour la plupart

main' clause' s proposition f principale

main' course' s (culin) plat m principal, pièce f de résistance

main' deck' s pont m principal

main' floor' s rez-de-chaussée m

mainland ['men,lænd], ['menlənd] s terre f ferme, continent m

main' line' s (rr) grande ligne f

mainly ['menli] adv principalement

mainstay ['menmæst], ['men,mæst], ['men,mast] s grand mât m

mainsail ['mensəl], ['men,sel] s grand-voile f

main'spring' s (of watch) ressort m moteur, grand ressort; (fig) mobile m essentiel, principe m

main'stay' s (naut) étai m de grand mât; (fig) point m d'appui

main' street' s rue f principale
maintain [men'ten] tr maintenir; (e.g., a family) entretenir, faire subsister
maintenance ['mentınəns] s entretien m, maintien m; (department entrusted with upkeep) services mpl d'entretien, maintenance f
maître d'hôtel [,metərdo'tel] s maître m d'hôtel
maize [mez] s maïs m
majestic [mə'dʒɛstık] adj majestueux
majes•ty ['mædʒısti] s (pl -ties) majesté f
major ['medʒər] adj majeur ‖ s (person of full legal age) majeur m; (educ) spécialisation f; (mil) commandant m ‖ intr (educ) se spécialiser
Majorca [mə'dʒɔrkə] s Majorque f; île f de Majorque
Majorcan [mə'dʒɔrkən] adj majorquin ‖ s Majorquin m
ma'jor gen'eral s général m de division
majori•ty [mə'dʒɑrıti], [mə'dʒɔrıti] adj majoritaire ‖ s (pl -ties) majorité f; (mil) grade m de commandant; the majority of la plupart de
major'ity vote' s scrutin m majoritaire
make [mek] s fabrication f; (brand name) marque f; modèle m ‖ v (pret & pp made [med]) tr faire; rendre, e.g., to make sick rendre malade; (money) gagner; (the cards) battre; (a train) attraper; to make into transformer en; to make known faire savoir; to make out déchiffrer, distinguer; (a bill, receipt, check) écrire; (a list) dresser; to make s.o. + inf faire + inf + inf, e.g., I will make my uncle talk je ferai parler mon oncle ‖ intr être, e.g., to make sure être sûr; to make believe feindre; to make good réussir; to make off filer, décamper
make'-believe' adj simulé ‖ s faux-semblant m, feinte f
maker ['mekər] s fabricant m
make'shift' adj de fortune, de circonstance ‖ s expédient m; (person) bouche-trou m
make'-up' s arrangement m, composition f; (cosmetic) maquillage m; (typ) mise f en pages, imposition f
make'-up man' s (theat) maquilleur m; (typ) metteur m en pages, imposeur m
make'weight' s complément m de poids
making ['mekıŋ] s fabrication f; (of a dress; of a cooked dish) confection f; makings éléments mpl constitutifs; (money) recettes fpl; to have the makings of avoir l'étoffe de
maladjusted [,mælə'dʒʌstıd] adj inadapté
maladjustment [,mælə'dʒʌstmənt] s inadaptation f
mala•dy ['mælədi] s (pl -dies) maladie f
malaise [mæ'lez] s malaise m
malaria [mə'lɛrı•ə] s malaria f, paludisme m
Malay ['mele], [mə'le] adj malais ‖ s (language) malais m; (person) Malais m

Malaya [mə'le•ə] s Malaisie f; la Malaisie
malcontent ['mælkən,tent] adj & s mécontent m
male [mel] adj & s mâle m
malediction [,mælı'dık/ən] s malédiction f
malefactor ['mælı,fæktər] s malfaiteur m
male' nurse' s infirmier m
malevolent [mə'lɛvələnt] adj malveillant
malfeasance [,mæl'fizəns] s prévarication f, trafic m
malice ['mælıs] s méchanceté f
malicious [mə'lı/əs] adj méchant
malign [mə'laın] adj pernicieux; malveillant ‖ tr calomnier
malignan•cy [mə'lıgnənsi] s (pl -cies) malignité f
malignant [mə'lıgnənt] adj méchant, malin
malinger [mə'lıŋgər] intr faire le malade
malingerer [mə'lıŋgərər] s simulateur m
mall [mɔl], [mæl] s mail m
mallard ['mælərd] s (orn) col-vert m
malleable ['mælı•əbəl] adj malléable
mallet ['mælıt] s maillet m
mallow ['mælo] s (bot) mauve f
malnutrition [,mæln(j)u'trı/ən] s sous-alimentation f, malnutrition f
malodorous [mæl'odərəs] adj malodorant
malpractice [mæl'præktıs] s incurie f; méfait m
malt [mɔlt] s malt m
maltreat [mæl'trit] tr maltraiter
mamma ['mɑmə], [mə'mɑ] s maman f
mammal ['mæməl] s mammifère m
mammalian [mæ'melı•ən] adj & s mammifère m
mammoth ['mæmə θ] adj énorme, colossal ‖ s mammouth m
man [mæn] s (pl men [mɛn]) s homme m; (servant) domestique m; (worker) ouvrier m, employé m; (checkers) pion m; (chess) pièce f; a man on, e.g., what can a man do? qu'est-ce qu'on peut faire?; every man for himself! sauve qui peut!; man alive! (coll) tiens!; fichtre!; man and wife mari et femme; men at work (public sign) travaux en cours ‖ v (pret & pp manned; ger manning) tr (a ship) équiper; (a fort) garnir; (a cannon, the pumps, etc.) armer; (a battery) servir
man' about town' s boulevardier m, coureur m de cabarets
manacle ['mænəkəl] s manilla f; manacles menottes fpl ‖ tr mettre les menottes à
manage ['mænıdʒ] tr gérer, diriger; (to handle) manier ‖ intr se débrouiller; how did you manage to . . . ? comment avez-vous fait pour . . . ?; to manage to s'arranger pour
manageable ['mænıdʒəbəl] adj maniable

management ['mænɪdʒmənt] s direction f, gérance f; (group who manage) direction, administration f; (in contrast to labor) patronat m; under new management (public sign) changement de propriétaire
manager ['mænədʒər] s directeur m, gérant m; (e.g., of a department) chef m; (impresario) manager m
managerial [ˌmænə'dʒɪrɪ-əl] adj patronal
man'aging ed'itor s rédacteur m gérant
Manchuria [mæn'tʃurɪ-ə] s Mandchourie f; la Mandchourie
man'darin or'ange ['mændərɪn] s mandarine f
mandate ['mændet] s mandat m || tr placer sous le mandat de
mandatory ['mændəˌtori] adj obligatoire
mandolin ['mændəlɪn] s mandoline f
mandrake ['mændrek] s mandragore f
mane [men] s crinière f
maneuver [mə'nuvər] s manœuvre m || tr & intr manœuvrer
manful ['mænfəl] adj viril, hardi
manganese ['mæŋɡəˌnis], ['mæŋɡə-ˌniz] s manganèse m
mange [mendʒ] s gale f
manger ['mendʒər] s mangeoire f, crèche f
mangle ['mæŋɡəl] s calandre f || tr lacérer, mutiler; (to press) calandrer
man•gy ['mendʒi] adj (comp -gier; super -giest) galeux; (dirty, squalid) miteux
man'han'dle tr malmener
man'hole' s trou m d'homme, regard m
manhood ['mænhud] s virilité f; humanité f
man'hunt' s chasse f à l'homme; chasse au mari
mania ['menɪ-ə] s manie f
maniac ['menɪˌæk] adj & s maniaque mf
maniacal [mə'naɪ-əkəl] adj maniaque
manicure ['mænɪˌkjur] s soins mpl esthétiques des mains et des ongles; (person) manucure mf || tr manucurer
manicurist ['mænɪˌkjurɪst] s manucure mf
manifest ['mænɪˌfɛst] adj manifeste || s (naut) manifeste m || tr & intr manifester
manifestation [ˌmænɪfɛs'teʃən] s manifestation f
manifes•to [ˌmænɪ'fɛsto] s (pl -toes) manifeste m
manifold ['mænɪˌfold] adj multiple, nombreux || s (aut) tuyauterie f, collecteur m
manikin ['mænɪkɪn] s mannequin m; (dwarf) nabot m
man' in the moon' s homme m dans la lune
man' in the street' s homme m de la rue
manipulate [mə'nɪpjəˌlet] tr manipuler
man'kind' s le genre humain, l'humanité f || **man'kind'** s le sexe fort, les hommes mpl
manliness ['mænlɪnɪs] s virilité f

man•ly ['mænli] adj (comp -lier; super -liest) viril, masculin
manna ['mænə] s manne f
manned' space'craft s vaisseau m spatial habité
mannequin ['mænɪkɪn] s mannequin m
manner ['mænər] s manière f; by all manner of means certainement; by no manner of means en aucune manière; in a manner of speaking pour ainsi dire; in the manner of à la, e.g., in the manner of the French, in the French manner à la manière française, à la française; manners manières; manners of the time mœurs fpl de l'époque; to the manner born créé et mis au monde pour ça
mannerism ['mænəˌrɪzm] s maniérisme m
mannish ['mænɪʃ] adj hommasse
man' of let'ters s homme m de lettres, bel esprit m
man' of parts' s homme m de talent
man' of straw' s homme m de paille
man' of the world' s homme m du monde
man-of-war [ˌmænəv'wɔr] s (pl men-of-war) navire m de guerre
manor ['mænər] s seigneurie f
man'or house' s château m, manoir m
man' o'verboard' interj un homme à la mer!
man'pow'er s main-d'œuvre f; (mil) effectifs mpl
manse [mæns] s maison f du pasteur
man'serv'ant s (pl men'serv'ants) valet m
mansion ['mænʃən] s hôtel m particulier; château m, manoir m
man'slaugh'ter s (law) homicide m involontaire
mantel ['mæntəl] s manteau m de cheminée
man'tel•piece' s manteau m de cheminée; dessus m de cheminée
mantilla [mæn'tɪlə] s mantille f
mantle ['mæntəl] s manteau m, mante f; (of gaslight) manchon m || tr envelopper d'une mante; couvrir, revêtir; (to hide) voiler || intr (said of face) rougir
manual ['mænju-əl] adj manuel || s (book) manuel m; (of arms) (mil) maniement m; (mus) clavier m d'orgue
man'ual dexter'ity s habileté f manuelle
man'ual train'ing s apprentissage m manuel
manufacture [ˌmænjə'fæktʃər] s fabrication f; (thing manufactured) produit m fabriqué || tr fabriquer
manufacturer [ˌmænjə'fæktʃərər] s fabricant m
manure [mə'n(j)ur] s fumier m || tr fumer
manuscript ['mænjəˌskrɪpt] adj & s manuscrit m
many ['meni] adj beaucoup de; a good many bien des, maintes; how many combien de; many another bien d'autres; many more beaucoup d'autres;

so many tant de; **too many** trop de; **twice as many** deux fois autant de || *pron* beaucoup; **as many as** autant de; jusqu'à, e.g., **as many as twenty** jusqu'à vingt; **how many** combien; **many a** maint; **many another** bien d'autres; **many more** beaucoup d'autres; **so many** tant; **too many** trop; **twice as many** deux fois autant

man′y-sid′ed *adj* polygonal; (*having many interests or capabilities*) complexe

map [mæp] *s* carte *f*; (*of a city*) plan *m* || *v* (*pret & pp* **mapped**; *ger* **mapping**) *tr* faire la carte de; **to map out** tracer le plan de; **to put on the map** (coll) faire connaître, mettre en vedette

maple ['mepəl] *s* érable *m*

ma′ple sug′ar *s* sucre *m* d'érable

mar [mɑr] *v* (*pret & pp* **marred**; *ger* **marring**) *tr* défigurer, gâcher

marathon ['mærə ,θɑn] *s* marathon *m*

maraud [mə'rɔd] *tr* piller || *intr* marauder

marauder [mə'rɔdər] *s* maraudeur *m*

marauding [mə'rɔdɪŋ] *adj* maraudeur || *s* maraude *f*

marble ['mɑrbəl] *s* marbre *m*; (*little ball of glass*) bille *f*; **marbles** (game) jeu *m* de billes || *tr* marbrer; (*the edge of a book*) jasper

march [mɑrtʃ] *s* marche *f*; **March** mars *m*; **to steal a march on** prendre de l'avance sur || *tr* faire marcher || *intr* marcher

marchioness ['mɑrʃənɪs] *s* marquise *f*

mare [mɛr] *s* (*female horse*) jument *m*; (*female donkey*) ânesse *f*

Margaret ['mɑrgərɪt] *s* Marguerite *f*

margarine ['mɑrdʒərɪn] *s* margarine *f*

margin ['mɑrdʒɪn] *s* marge *f*; (*border*) bord *m*; (com) acompte *m*

marginal ['mɑrdʒɪnəl] *adj* marginal

mar′gin release′ *s* déclenche-marge *f*

mar′gin stop′ *s* margeur *m*

marigold ['mærɪ ,gold] *s* (*Calendula*) souci *m*; (*Tagetes*) œillet *m* d'Inde

marihuana or **marijuana** [,mærɪ-'hwɑnə] *s* marihuana *f* or marijuana *f*

marinate ['mærɪ ,net] *tr* mariner

marine [mə'rin] *adj* marin, maritime || *s* flotte *f*; (nav) fusilier *m* marin; **tell it to the marines!** (coll) à d'autres!

Marine′ Corps′ *s* infanterie *f* de marine

mariner ['mærɪnər] *s* marin *m*

marionette [,mærɪ·ə'nɛt] *s* marionnette *f*

marital ['mærɪtəl] *adj* matrimonial

mar′ital sta′tus *s* état *m* civil

maritime ['mærɪ ,taɪm] *adj* maritime

marjoram ['mɑrdʒərəm] *s* marjolaine *f*; origan *m*

mark [mɑrk] *s* marque *f*, signe *m*; (*of punctuation*) point *m*; (*in an examination*) note *f*; (*spot, stain*) tache *f*, marque; (*monetary unit*) mark *m*; (*starting point in a race*) ligne *f* de départ; **as a mark of** en témoignage de; **Mark** Marc *m*; **on your mark!** à vos marques!; **to hit the mark** mettre dans le mille, atteindre le but; **to**

leave one's mark laisser son empreinte; **to make one's mark** se faire un nom, marquer; **to miss the mark** manquer le but; **to toe the mark** se conformer au mot d'ordre || *tr* marquer; (*a student; an exam*) donner une note à; (*e.g., one's approval*) témoigner; **to mark down** noter; (com) démarquer; **to mark off** distinguer; **to mark up** (com) majorer

mark′down′ *s* rabais *m*

marker ['mɑrkər] *s* marqueur *m*; (*of boundary*) borne *f*; (*landmark*) repère *m*

market ['mɑrkɪt] *s* marché *m*; **to bear the market** jouer à la baisse; **to bull the market** jouer à la hausse; **to play the market** jouer à la bourse; **to put on the market** lancer, vendre, or mettre sur le marché || *tr* commercialiser

marketable ['mɑrkɪtəbəl] *adj* vendable

mar′ket bas′ket *s* panier *m* à provisions

marketing ['mɑrkɪtɪŋ] *s* marché *m*; (*of a product*) commercialisation *f*, exploitation *f*

mar′ket·place′ *s* place *f* du marché

mar′ket price′ *s* cours *m* du marché, prix *m* courant

mark′ing gauge′ *s* trusquin *m*

marks·man ['mɑrksmən] *s* (*pl* **-men**) tireur *m*

marks′man·ship′ *s* habileté *f* au tir, adresse *f* au tir

mark′up′ *s* (*profit*) marge *f* bénéficiaire; (*price increase*) majoration *f* de prix

marl [mɑrl] *s* marne *f* || *tr* marner

marmalade ['mɑrmə ,led] *s* marmelade *f*

maroon [mə'run] *adj & s* (*color*) lie *f* de vin, rouge *m* violacé || *tr* abandonner, isoler

marquee [mɑr'ki] *s* marquise *f*

marquis ['mɑrkwɪs] *s* marquis *m*

marquise [mɑr'kiz] *s* marquise *f*

marriage ['mærɪdʒ] *s* mariage *m*

marriageable ['mærɪdʒəbəl] *adj* mariable

mar′riage certif′icate *s* acte *m* de mariage

mar′riage por′tion *s* dot *f*

mar′riage rate′ *s* taux *m* de nuptialité

mar′ried life′ ['mærɪd] *s* vie *f* conjugale

marrow ['mæro] *s* moelle *f*

mar·ry ['mæri] *v* (*pret & pp* **-ried**) *tr* (*to join in wedlock*) marier; (*to take in marriage*) se marier avec; **to get married to** se marier avec; **to marry off** marier || *intr* se marier

Mars [mɑrz] *s* Mars *m*

Marseilles [mɑr'selz] *s* Marseille *f*

marsh [mɑrʃ] *s* marais *m*, marécage *m*

mar·shal ['mɑrʃəl] *s* maître *m* des cérémonies; (*policeman*) shérif *m*; (mil) maréchal *m* || *v* (*pret & pp* **-shaled** or **-shalled**; *ger* **-shaling** or **-shalling**) *tr* conduire; (*one's reasons, arguments, etc.*) ranger, rassembler

marsh′ mal′low *s* (bot) guimauve *f*

marsh′mal′low *s* (*candy*) pâte *f* de guimauve; bonbon *m* à la guimauve

marsh·y ['marʃi] *adj* (*comp* **-ier;** *super* **-iest**) marécageux

mart [mart] *s* marché *m*, foire *f*

marten ['martən] *s* (*pine marten*) martre *f*; (*beech marten*) fouine *f*

Martha ['marθə] *s* Marthe *f*

martial ['marʃəl] *adj* martial

mar'tial law' *s* loi *f* martiale

martin ['martɪn] *s* (orn) martinet *m*

martinet [ˌmartɪ'nɛt], ['martɪˌnɛt] *s* pètesec *m*

martyr ['martər] *s* martyr *m* ‖ *tr* martyriser

martyrdom ['martərdəm] *s* martyre *m*

mar·vel ['marvəl] *s* merveille *f* ‖ *v* (*pret & pp* **-veled** or **-velled;** *ger* **-veling** or **-velling**) *intr* s'émerveiller; **to marvel at** s'émerveiller de

marvelous ['marvələs] *adj* merveilleux

Marxist ['marksɪst] *adj & s* marxiste *mf*

Maryland ['mɛrələnd] *s* le Maryland

marzipan ['marzɪˌpæn] *s* massepain *m*

mascara [mæs'kærə] *s* rimmel *m*

mascot ['mæskat] *s* mascotte *f*

masculine ['mæskjəlɪn] *adj & s* masculin *m*

mash [mæʃ] *s* (*crushed mass*) bouillie *f*; (*to form wort*) fardeau *m* ‖ *tr* écraser; (*malt, in brewing*) brasser

mashed' pota'toes *spl* purée *f* de pommes de terre

masher ['mæʃər] *s* (*device*) broyeur *m*; (slang) tombeur *m*

mask [mæsk], [mask] *s* masque *m*; (phot) cache *m* ‖ *tr* masquer; (phot) poser un cache à ‖ *intr* se masquer

masked' ball' *s* bal *m* masqué

mason ['mesən] *s* maçon *m*; **Mason** Maçon

mason·ry ['mesənri] *s* (*pl* **-ries**) maçonnerie *f*; **Masonry** Maçonnerie

masquerade [ˌmæskə'red], [ˌmaskə-'red] *s* mascarade *f* ‖ *intr* se déguiser; **to masquerade as** se faire passer pour

mass [mæs] *s* masse *f*; (eccl) messe *f* ‖ *tr* masser ‖ *intr* se masser

massacre ['mæsəkər] *s* massacre *m* ‖ *tr* massacrer

massage [mə'saʒ] *s* massage *m* ‖ *tr* masser

mass' arrest' *s* rafle *f*

masseur [mə'sʌr] *s* masseur *m*

masseuse [mə'suz] *s* masseuse *f*

massive ['mæsɪv] *adj* massif

mass' me'dia ['midɪ·ə] *spl* communication *f* de masse

mass' meet'ing *s* meeting *m* monstre, rassemblement *m*

mass' produc'tion *s* fabrication *f* en série

mast [mæst], [mast] *s* mât *m*; (*food for swine*) gland *m*, faîne *f*; **before the mast** comme simple matelot

master ['mæstər], ['mastər] *s* maître *m*; (*employer*) chef *m*, patron *m*; (*male head of household*) maître de maison; (*title of respect*) Monsieur *m*; (naut) commandant *m* ‖ *tr* maîtriser; (*a subject*) connaître à fond, posséder

mas'ter bed'room *s* chambre *f* du maître

mas'ter build'er *s* entrepreneur *m* de bâtiments

masterful ['mæstərfəl], ['mastərfəl] *adj* magistral, expert; impérieux, en maître

mas'ter key' *s* passe-partout *m*

masterly ['mæstərli], ['mastərli] *adj* magistral, de maître ‖ *adv* magistralement

mas'ter mechan'ic *s* maître *m* mécanicien

mas'ter·mind' *s* organisateur *m*, cerveau *m* ‖ *tr* organiser, diriger

mas'ter of cer'emonies *s* maître *m* des cérémonies; (*in a night club, on television, etc.*) animateur *m*

mas'ter·piece' *s* chef-d'œuvre *m*

mas'ter stroke' *s* coup *m* de maître

mas'ter·work' *s* chef-d'œuvre *m*

master·y ['mæstəri], ['mastəri] *s* (*pl* **-ies**) maîtrise *f*

mast'head' *s* (*of a newspaper*) en-tête *m*; (naut) tête *f* de mât

masticate ['mæstɪˌket] *tr* mastiquer

mastiff ['mæstɪf], ['mastɪf] *s* mâtin *m*

masturbate ['mæstərˌbet] *tr* masturber ‖ *intr* se masturber

mat [mæt] *s* (*for floor*) natte *f*; (*for a cup, vase, etc.*) dessous *m* de plat; (*before a door*) paillasson *m* ‖ *v* (*pret & pp* **matted;** *ger* **matting**) *tr* (*to cover with matting*) couvrir de nattes; (*hair*) emmêler; (*with blood*) coller ‖ *intr* s'emmêler

match [mætʃ] *s* allumette *f*; (*wick*) mèche *f*; (*counterpart*) égal *m*, pair *m*; (*suitable partner in marriage*) parti *m*; (*suitably associated pair*) assortiment *m*; (*game, contest*) match *m*, partie *f*; **to be a match for** être de la force de, être à la hauteur de; **to meet one's match** trouver son pareil ‖ *tr* égaler; (*objects*) faire pendant à, assortir ‖ *intr* s'assortir

match'box' *s* boîte *f* d'allumettes, porte-allumettes *m*

matchless ['mætʃlɪs] *adj* incomparable, sans pareil

match'mak'er *s* marieur *m*

mate [met] *s* compagnon *m*; (*husband*) conjoint *m*; (*wife*) conjointe *f*; (*to a female*) mâle *m*; (*to a male*) femelle *f*; (*checkmate*) mat *m*; (naut) officier *m* en second, second maître *m* ‖ *tr* marier; (zool) accoupler ‖ *intr* se marier; s'accoupler

material [mə'tɪrɪ·əl] *adj* matériel; important ‖ *s* matériel *m*; (*what a thing is made of*) matière *f*; (*cloth, fabric*) étoffe *f*; (archit) matériau *m*; **materials** matériaux *mpl*

materialist [mə'tɪrɪ·əlɪst] *s* matérialiste *mf*

materialistic [məˌtɪrɪ·ə'lɪstɪk] *adj* matérialiste, matériel

materialize [mə'tɪrɪ·əˌlaɪz] *intr* se matérialiser; (*to be realized*) se réaliser

matériel [məˌtɪrɪ'ɛl] *s* matériel *m*

maternal [mə'tʌrnəl] *adj* maternel

maternity [mə'tʌrnɪti] s maternité f
mater'nity hos'pital s maternité f
mater'nity room' s salle f d'accouchement
mater'nity ward' s salle f des accouchées
math [mæθ] s (coll) math fpl
mathematical [,mæθɪ'mætɪkəl] adj mathématique
mathematician [,mæθɪmə'tɪʃən] s mathématicien m
mathematics [,mæθɪ'mætɪks] s mathématiques fpl
matinée [,mætɪ'ne] s matinée f
mat'ing sea'son s saison f des amours
matins ['mætɪnz] spl matines fpl
matriarch ['metrɪ,ɑrk] s matrone f
matriar·chy ['metrɪ,ɑrki] s (pl -chies) matriarcat m
matricide ['metrɪ,saɪd], ['mætrɪ,saɪd] s (person) matricide mf; (action) matricide m
matriculate [mə'trɪkjə,let] tr immatriculer || intr s'inscrire à l'université, prendre ses inscriptions
matriculation [mə,trɪkjə'leʃən] s inscription f, immatriculation f
matrimonial [,mætrɪ'monɪ-əl] adj matrimonial
matrimo·ny ['mætrɪ,moni] s (pl -nies) mariage m, vie f conjugale
ma·trix ['metrɪks], ['mætrɪks] s (pl -trices [trɪ,siz] or -trixes) matrice f
matron ['metrən] s (woman no longer young, and of good standing) matrone f; intendante f, surveillante f
matronly ['metrənli] adj de matrone, digne, respectable
matter ['mætər] s matière f; (pathol) pus m; **a matter of** affaire de, une question de; **for that matter** à vrai dire; **it doesn't matter** cela ne fait rien; **no matter** n'importe, pas d'importance; **no matter when** n'importe quand; **no matter where** n'importe où; **no matter who** n'importe qui; **what is the matter?** qu'y a-t-il?; **what is the matter with you?** qu'avez-vous? || intr importer
mat'ter of course' s chose f qui va de soi
mat'ter of fact' s—**as a matter of fact** en réalité, effectivement, de fait
matter-of-fact ['mætərəv,fækt] adj prosaïque, terre à terre
mattock ['mætək] s pioche f
mattress ['mætrɪs] s matelas m
mature [mə'tʃur], [mə'tur] adj mûr; (due) échu || tr faire mûrir || intr mûrir; (to become due) échoir
maturity [mə'tʃurɪti], [mə'turɪti] s maturité f; (com) échéance f
maudlin ['mɔdlɪn] adj larmoyant
maul [mɔl] tr malmener; (to split) fendre au coin
maulstick ['mɔl,stɪk] s appui-main m
Maun'dy Thurs'day [mɔndi] s jeudi m saint
mausole·um [,mɔsə'li-əm] s (pl -ums or -a [ə]) mausolée m
maw [mɔ] s (of birds) jabot m; (of fish) poche f d'air

mawkish ['mɔkɪʃ] adj à l'eau de rose; (sickening) écœurant
maxim ['mæksɪm] s maxime f
maximum ['mæksɪməm] adj & s maximum m
May [me] s mai m || (l.c.) v (pret & cond might [maɪt]) aux—**it may be** il ne peut; **may I?** vous permettez?; **may I** + inf puis-je + inf, est-ce que je peux + inf; **may I** (may we, etc.) + inf peut-on + inf; **may you be happy!** puissiez-vous être heureux!
maybe ['mebi] adv peut-être
May' Day' s le premier mai m
mayhem ['mehɛm], ['me·ɛm] s mutilation f
mayonnaise [,me·ə'nez] s mayonnaise f
mayor ['me·ər], [mer] s maire m
May'pole s mai m
May' queen' s reine f du premier mai
maze [mez] s labyrinthe m, dédale m
me [mi] pron moi §85, §87; **me** §87
meadow ['medo] s prairie f, pré m
mead'ow·land' s herbage m, prairie f
meager ['migər] adj maigre
meal [mil] s repas m; (grain) farine f; **to miss a meal** serrer la ceinture d'un cran
meal' tick'et s ticket-repas m; (job) gagne-pain m
meal'time' s heure f du repas
meal·y ['mili] adj (comp -ier; super -iest) farineux
mean [min] adj (intermediate) moyen; (low in station or rank) bas, humble; (shabby) vil, misérable; (stingy) mesquin; (small-minded) bas, vilain, méprisable; (vicious) sauvage, mal intentionné; **no mean** fameux, excellent || s milieu m, moyen terme m; (math) moyenne f; **by all means** de toute façon, je vous en prie; **by means of** au moyen de; **by no means** en aucune façon; **means** ressources fpl, fortune f; (agency) moyen m; **means to an end** moyens d'arriver à ses fins; **not by any means!** jamais de la vie! || v (pret & pp meant [ment]) tr vouloir dire, signifier; (to intend) entendre; (to entail) entraîner; **to mean s.th. for s.o.** destiner q.ch. à qn; **to mean to** avoir l'intention de, compter || intr —**to mean well** avoir de bonnes intentions
meander [mɪ'ændər] s méandre m || intr faire des méandres
meaning ['minɪŋ] s signification f, sens m; intention f
meaningful ['minɪŋfəl] adj significatif
meaningless ['minɪŋlɪs] adj sans signification, dénué de sens
meanness ['minnɪs] s bassesse f, vilenie f; (stinginess) mesquinerie f
mean'time' s—**in the meantime** dans l'intervalle, sur ces entrefaites || adv entre-temps, en attendant
mean'while' s & adv var of **meantime**
measles ['mizəlz] s rougeole f; (German measles) rubéole f
mea·sly ['mizli] adj (comp -slier; super -sliest) rougeoleux; (slang) piètre, insignifiant

measurable ['mɛʒərəbəl] adj mesurable
measure ['mɛʒər] s mesure f; (step, procedure) mesure, démarche f; (legislative bill) projet m de loi; (mus, poetic) mesure; **in a large measure** en grande partie; **in a measure** dans une certaine mesure; **to take measures** to prendre des mesures pour; **to take s.o.'s measure** (fig) prendre la mesure de qn || tr mesurer; **to measure out** mesurer, distribuer || intr mesurer
measurement ['mɛʒərmənt] s mesure f; **to take s.o.'s measurements** prendre les mesures de qn
meas'uring cup' s verre m gradué
meat [mit] s viande f; (food in general) nourriture f; (gist) moelle f, substance f
meat'ball' s boulette f de viande
meat'hook' s croc m, allonge f
meat' mar'ket s boucherie f
meat' pie' s tourte f à la viande, pâté m en croûte
meat·y ['miti] adj (comp -ier; super -iest) charnu; (fig) plein de substance, étoffé
Mecca ['mɛkə] s La Mecque
mechanic [mə'kænɪk] s mécanicien m; **mechanics** mécanique f
mechanical [mə'kænɪkəl] adj mécanique; (fig) mécanique, machinal
mechan'ical draw'ing s dessin m industriel
mechan'ical engineer' s ingénieur m mécanicien
mechan'ical toy' s jouet m mécanique
mechanics [mɪ'kænɪks] s mécanique f
mechanism ['mɛkə,nɪzəm] s mécanisme m
mechanize ['mɛkə,naɪz] tr mécaniser
medal ['mɛdəl] s médaille f
medallion [mɪ'dæljən] s médaillon m
meddle ['mɛdəl] intr s'ingérer; **to meddle in** or **with** se mêler de, s'immiscer dans
meddler ['mɛdlər] s intrigant m, touche-à-tout m
meddlesome ['mɛdəlsəm] adj intrigant
median ['midɪ·ən] adj médian || s médiane f
me'dian strip' s bande f médiane
mediate ['midɪ,et] tr procurer par médiation, négocier || intr s'entremettre, s'interposer
mediation [,midɪ'eʃən] s médiation f
mediator ['midɪ,etər] s médiateur m
medical ['mɛdɪkəl] adj médical
med'ical stu'dent s étudiant m en médecine
medicinal [mə'dɪsɪnəl] adj médicinal
medicine ['mɛdɪsɪn] s (science and art) médecine f; (pharm) médicament m
med'icine cab'inet s armoire f à pharmacie
med'icine kit' s pharmacie f portative
med'icine man' s (pl men') sorcier m indien; (mountebank) charlatan m
medi·co ['mɛdɪ,ko] s (pl -cos) (slang) carabin m, morticole m
medieval [,midɪ'ivəl], [,mɛdɪ'ivəl] adj médiéval

medievalist [,midɪ'ivəlɪst], [,mɛdɪ'ivəlɪst] s médiéviste mf
mediocre ['midɪ,okər], [,midɪ'okər] adj médiocre
mediocri·ty [,midɪ'ɑkrɪti] s (pl -ties) médiocrité f
meditate ['mɛdɪ,tet] tr & intr méditer
meditation [,mɛdɪ'teʃən] s méditation f
Mediterranean [,mɛdɪtə'renɪ·ən] adj méditerranéen || s Méditerranée f
medi·um ['midɪ·əm] adj moyen; (culin) à point || s (pl -ums or -a [ə]) milieu m; (means) moyen m; (in spiritualism) médium m; (journ) organe m; **through the medium of** par l'intermédiaire de
me'dium of exchange' s agent m monétaire
me'dium-range' adi à portée moyenne
me'dium-sized' adj de grandeur moyenne
medlar ['mɛdlər] s (fruit) nèfle f; (tree) néflier m
medley ['mɛdli] s mélange m; (mus) pot-pourri m
medul·la [mɪ'dʌlə] s (pl -lae [li]) moelle f
Medusa [mə'duzə] s Méduse f
meek [mik] adj doux, humble
meekness ['miknɪs] s douceur f, humilité f
meerschaum ['mɪrʃəm], ['mɪrʃəm] s écume f de mer; pipe f d'écume de mer
meet [mit] adj—**it is meet that** il convient que || s (sports) meeting m || v (pret & pp met [mɛt]) tr rencontrer; (to make the acquaintance of) faire la connaissance de; (to go to meet) aller au-devant de; (a car in the street; a person on the sidewalk) croiser; (by appointment) retrouver, rejoindre; (difficulties; expenses) faire face à; (one's debts) honorer; (one's death) trouver; (a need) satisfaire à; (an objection) réfuter; (the ear) frapper; **meet my wife** (my friend, etc.) je vous présente ma femme (mon ami, etc.) || intr se rencontrer; se retrouver, se rejoindre; (to assemble) se réunir; (to join, touch) se joindre, se toucher; (said of rivers) confluer; (said of roads; said of cars, persons, etc.) se croiser; **till we meet again** au revoir; **to meet with** se rencontrer avec, rencontrer; (difficulties, an affront, etc.) subir
meeting ['mitɪŋ] s rencontre f; (session) séance f; (assemblage) réunion f, assemblée f; (of two rivers) confluent m; (of two cars; of two roads) croisement m
meet'ing of the minds' s bonne entente f
meet'ing place' s rendez-vous m
megacycle ['mɛgə,saɪkəl] s mégacycle m
megaphone ['mɛgə,fon] s mégaphone m, porte-voix m
megohm ['mɛg,om] s mégohm m

melancholia [ˌmɛlən'koli·ə] s mélancolie f

melanchol·y ['mɛlən·kɑli] adj mélancolique ‖ s (pl -ies) mélancolie f

melee ['mele], ['mɛle] s mêlée f

mellow ['mɛlo] adj moelleux; enjoué, débonnaire; (ripe) mûr ‖ tr rendre moelleux, mûrir

melodic [mɪ'lɑdɪk] adj mélodique

melodious [mɪ'lodɪ·əs] adj mélodieux

melodramatic [ˌmɛlədrə'mætɪk] adj mélodramatique

melo·dy ['mɛlədi] s (pl -dies) mélodie f

melon ['mɛlən] s melon m

melt [mɛlt] tr & intr fondre; **to melt into** (e.g., tears) fondre en

melt′ing pot′ s creuset m

member ['mɛmbər] s membre m

mem′ber·ship′ s membres mpl; (in a club, etc.) association f

membrane ['mɛmbren] s membrane f

memen·to [mɪ'mɛnto] s (pl -tos or -toes) mémento m

mem·o ['mɛmo] s (pl -os) (coll) note f, rappel m

mem′o book′ s calepin m, mémento m

memoir ['mɛmwɑr] s biographie f; memoirs mémoires mpl

mem′o pad′ s bloc-notes m, bloc m

memoran·dum [ˌmɛmə'rændəm] s (pl -dums or -da [də]) memorandum m; note f, rappel m

memorial [mɪ'morɪ·əl] adj commémoratif ‖ s mémorial m; pétition f, mémoire m

memo′rial arch′ s arc m de triomphe

Memo′rial Day′ s la journée du Souvenir

memorialize [mɪ'morɪ·ə ˌlaɪz] tr commémorer

memorize ['mɛmə ˌraɪz] tr apprendre par cœur

memo·ry ['mɛməri] s (pl -ries) mémoire f; **from memory** de mémoire; **in memory of** en souvenir de, à la mémoire de

menace ['mɛnɪs] s menace f ‖ tr & intr menacer

menagerie [mə'næʒəri], [mə'nædʒəri] s ménagerie f

mend [mɛnd] s raccommodage m, reprise f ‖ tr réparer; (to patch) raccommoder; (stockings) repriser; (to reform) améliorer ‖ intr s'améliorer, s'amender

mendacious [mɛn'deʃəs] adj mensonger

mendicant ['mɛndɪkənt] adj & s mendiant m

mending ['mɛndɪŋ] s raccommodage m; (of stockings) reprisage m

menfolk ['mɛn ˌfok] spl hommes mpl

menial ['minɪ·əl] adj servile ‖ s domestique mf

menses ['mɛnsiz] spl menstrues fpl

men′s′ fur′nishings spl confection f pour hommes

men′s′ room′ s toilettes fpl pour hommes, lavabos mpl pour messieurs

menstruate ['mɛnstru ˌet] intr avoir ses règles

mental ['mɛntəl] adj mental

men′tal arith′metic s calcul m mental

men′tal defec′tive s débile mf

men′tal ill′ness s maladie f mentale

mentali·ty [mɛn'tælɪti] s (pl -ties) mentalité f

men′tal reserva′tion s arrière-pensée f

men′tal test′ s test m psychologique

mention ['mɛnʃən] s mention f ‖ tr mentionner; **don′t mention it** il n'y a pas de quoi, je vous en prie

menu ['mɛnju], ['menju] s menu m, carte f

meow [mɪ'au] s miaou m ‖ intr miauler

Mephistophelian [ˌmɛfɪstə'fili·ən] adj méphistophélique

mercantile ['mʌrkən ˌtil], ['mʌrkən ˌtaɪl] adj commercial, commerçant

mercenar·y ['mʌrsə ˌnɛri] adj mercenaire ‖ s (pl -ies) mercenaire mf

merchandise ['mʌrtʃən ˌdaɪz] s marchandise f

merchant ['mʌrtʃənt] adj & s marchand m

mer′chant·man s (pl -men) navire m marchand

mer′chant marine′ s marine f marchande

mer′chant ves′sel s navire m marchand

merciful ['mʌrsɪfəl] adj miséricordieux

merciless ['mʌrsɪlɪs] adj impitoyable

mercurial [mer'kjurɪ·əl] adj inconstant, versatile; (lively) vif

mercu·ry ['mʌrkjəri] s (pl -ries) mercure m

mer·cy ['mʌrsi] s (pl -cies) miséricorde f, pitié f; **at the mercy of** à la merci de

mere [mɪr] adj simple, pur; seul, e.g., **at the mere thought of it** à la seule pensée de cela; rien que, e.g., **to shudder at the mere thought of it** frissonner rien que d'y penser

meretricious [ˌmɛrɪ'trɪʃəs] adj factice, postiche; de courtisane

merge [mʌrdʒ] tr fusionner ‖ intr fusionner; (said of two roads) converger; **to merge into** se fondre dans

merger ['mʌrdʒər] s fusion f

meridian [mə'rɪdɪ·ən] adj & s méridien m

meringue [mə'ræŋ] s meringue f

merit ['mɛrɪt] s mérite m ‖ tr mériter

meritorious [ˌmɛrə'torɪ·əs] adj méritoire; (person) méritant

merlin ['mʌrlɪn] s (orn) émerillon m

mermaid ['mʌr ˌmed] s sirène f

merriment ['mɛrɪmənt] s gaieté f, réjouissance f

mer·ry ['mɛri] adj (comp -rier; super -riest) gai, joyeux; **to make merry** se divertir

Mer′ry Christ′mas s Joyeux Noël m

mer′ry-go-round′ s chevaux mpl de bois, manège m forain

mer′ry·mak′er s noceur m, fêtard m

mesh [mɛʃ] s (network) réseau m; (each open space of net) maille f; (net) filet m; (engagement of gears) engrenage m; **meshes** rets m, filets

mpl || *tr* (mach) engrener || *intr* s'engrener
mesmerize ['mɛsmə,raɪz] *tr* magnétiser
mess [mɛs] *s* gâchis *m*; (*refuse*) saleté *f*; (*meal*) (mil) ordinaire *m*; (*for officers*) (mil) mess *m*; **to get into a mess** se mettre dans le pétrin; **to make a mess of** gâcher || *tr*—**to mess up** (*to botch*) gâcher; (*to dirty*) salir || *intr*—**to mess around** (*to putter*) (coll) bricoler; (*to waste time*) (coll) lambiner
message ['mɛsɪdʒ] *s* message *m*
messenger ['mɛsəndʒər] *s* messager *m*; (*one who goes on errands*) commissionnaire *m*
mess′ hall′ *s* cantine *f*; (*for officers*) mess *m*
Messiah [mə'saɪ·ə] *s* Messie *m*
mess′ kit′ *s* gamelle *f*
mess′mate′ *s* camarade *mf* de table; (nav) camarade de plat
mess′ of pot′tage ['pɑtɪdʒ] *s* (Bib) plat *m* de·lentilles
Messrs. ['mɛsərz] *pl* of **Mr.**
mess·y ['mɛsi] *adj* (*comp* -ier; *super* -iest) en désordre; (*dirty*) sale, poisseux
metal ['mɛtəl] *s* métal *m*
metallic [mɪ'tælɪk] *adj* métallique
metallurgy ['mɛtə,lʌrdʒi] *s* métallurgie *f*
met′al pol′ish *s* brillant *m* à métaux
met′al·work′ *s* serrurerie *f*, travail *m* des métaux
metamorpho·sis [,mɛtə'mɔrfəsɪs] *s* (*pl* -ses [,siz]) métamorphose *f*
metaphony [mə'tæfəni] *s* métaphonie *f*, inflexion *f*
metaphor ['mɛtəfər], ['mɛtə,fɔr] *s* métaphore *f*
metaphorical [,mɛtə'fɑrɪkəl], [,mɛtə-'fɔrɪkəl] *adj* métaphorique
metathe·sis [mɪ'tæθɪsɪs] *s* (*pl* -ses [,siz]) métathèse *f*
mete [mit] *tr*—**to mete out** distribuer
meteor ['mitɪ·ər] *s* étoile *f* filante; (*atmospheric phenomenon*) météore *m*
meteoric [,mitɪ'ɑrɪk], [,mitɪ'ɔrɪk] *adj* météorique; (fig) fulgurant
meteorite ['mitɪ·ə,raɪt] *s* météorite *m* & *f*
meteorology [,mitɪ·ə'rɑlədʒi] *s* météorologie *f*
meter ['mitər] *s* (*unit of measurement; verse*) mètre *m*; (*instrument for measuring gas, electricity, water*) compteur *m*; (mus) mesure *f*
me′ter read′er *s* releveur *m* de compteurs
methane ['mɛθen] *s* méthane *m*
method ['mɛθəd] *s* méthode *f*
methodic(al) [mɪ'θɑdɪk(əl)] *adj* méthodique
Methodist ['mɛθədɪst] *adj* & *s* méthodiste *mf*
Methuselah [mɪ'θuzələ] *s* Mathusalem *m*
meticulous [mɪ'tɪkjələs] *adj* méticuleux
metric(al) ['mɛtrɪk(əl)] *adj* métrique
metrics ['mɛtrɪks] *s* métrique *f*

metronome ['mɛtrə,nom] *s* métronome *m*
metropolis [mɪ'trɑpəlɪs] *s* métropole *f*
metropolitan [,mɛtrə'pɑlɪtən] *adj* & *s* métropolitain *m*
mettle ['mɛtəl] *s* ardeur *f*, fougue *f*; **to be on one's mettle** se piquer au jeu
mettlesome ['mɛtəlsəm] *adj* ardent, vif, fougueux
mew [mju] *s* miaulement *m* || *intr* miauler
Mexican ['mɛksɪkən] *adj* mexicain || *s* Mexicain *m*
Mexico ['mɛksɪ,ko] *s* le Mexique
Mex′ico Cit′y *s* Mexico
mezzanine ['mɛzə,nin] *s* entresol *m*; (theat) mezzanine *m* & *f*, corbeille *f*
mica ['maɪkə] *s* mica *m*
microbe ['maɪkrob] *s* microbe *m*
microbiology [,maɪkrəbaɪ'ɑlədʒi] *s* microbiologie *f*
microfilm ['maɪkrə,fɪlm] *s* microfilm *m* || *tr* microfilmer
microgroove ['maɪkrə,gruv] *adj* & *s* microsillon *m*
mi′crogroove rec′ord *s* disque *m* à microsillons
microphone ['maɪkrə,fon] *s* microphone *m*
microscope ['maɪkrə,skop] *s* microscope *m*
microscopic [,maɪkrə'skɑpɪk] *adj* microscopique
microwave ['maɪkrə,wev] *s* micro-onde *f*
mid [mɪd] *adj*—**in mid course** à mi-chemin
mid′day′ *s* midi *m*
middle ['mɪdəl] *adj* moyen, du milieu || *s* milieu *m*; **in the middle of** au milieu de
mid′dle age′ *s* âge *m* moyen; **Middle Ages** moyen-âge *m*
middle-aged ['mɪdəl,edʒd] *adj* d'un âge moyen
mid′dle class′ *s* classe *f* moyenne, bourgeoisie *f*
mid′dle-class′ *adj* bourgeois
Mid′dle East′ *s* Moyen-Orient *m*
Mid′dle Eng′lish *s* moyen anglais *m*
mid′dle fin′ger *s* majeur *m*, doigt *m* du milieu
mid′dle·man′ *s* (*pl* -men′) intermédiaire *mf*
middling ['mɪdlɪŋ] *adj* moyen, assez bien, passable || *adv* (coll) assez bien, passablement
mid·dy ['mɪdi] *s* (*pl* -dies) (coll) aspirant *m*
mid′dy blouse′ *s* marinière *f*
midget ['mɪdʒɪt] *s* nain *m*, nabot *m*
midland ['mɪdlənd] *adj* de l'intérieur || *s* centre *m* du pays
mid′night′ *adj* de minuit; **to burn the midnight oil** pâlir sur les livres, se crever les livres || *s* minuit *m*
midriff ['mɪdrɪf] *s* diaphragme *m*
mid′ship′man *s* (*pl* -men) aspirant *m*
midst [mɪdst] *s* centre *m*; **in our (your, etc.) midst** parmi nous (vous, etc.); **in the midst of** au milieu de

mid'stream' s—in midstream au milieu du courant
mid'sum'mer s milieu m de l'été
mid'way' adj & adv à mi-chemin ||
mid'way' s fête f foraine
mid'week' s milieu m de la semaine
mid'wife' s (pl -wives') sage-femme f
mid'win'ter s milieu m de l'hiver
mid'year' s mi-année f
mien [min] s mine f, aspect m
miff [mɪf] s (coll) fâcherie f || tr (coll) fâcher
might [maɪt] s puissance f, force f; with might and main, with all one's might de toute sa force || aux used to form the potential mood, e.g., she might not be able to come il se pourrait qu'elle ne puisse pas venir
mightily ['maɪtɪli] adv puissamment; (coll) énormément
might·y ['maɪti] adj (comp -ier; super -iest) puissant; (of great size) grand, vaste || adv (coll) rudement, diablement
mignonette [,mɪnjə'nɛt] s réséda m
migraine ['maɪgren] s migraine f
migrate ['maɪgret] intr émigrer
migratory ['maɪgrə ,tori] adj migratoire
milch [mɪltʃ] adj laitier
mild [maɪld] adj doux
mildew ['mɪl ,d(j)u] s moisissure f; (on vine) mildiou m, blanc m
mildness ['maɪldnɪs] s douceur f
mile [maɪl] s mille m
mileage ['maɪlɪdʒ] s distance f en milles; (charge) tarif m au mille
mile'post' s borne f milliaire
mile'stone' s borne f milliaire; (fig) jalon m
militancy ['mɪlɪtənsi] s esprit m militant
militant ['mɪlɪtənt] adj & s militant m
militarism ['mɪlɪtə ,rɪzəm] s militarisme m
militarize ['mɪlɪtə ,raɪz] tr militariser
military ['mɪlɪ ,teri] adj & s militaire m
mil'itary police'man s (pl -men) agent m de la police militaire
militate ['mɪlɪ ,tet] intr militer
militia [mɪ'lɪʃə] s milice f
mili'tia·man s (pl -men) milicien m
milk [mɪlk] adj laitier || s lait m || tr traire; abuser de, exploiter; to milk s.th. from s.o. soutirer q.ch. à qn
milk' can' s pot m à lait, berthe f
milk' car'ton s boîte f de lait, berlingot m
milk' di'et s régime m lacté
milk'maid' s laitière f
milk'man' s (pl -men') laitier m, crémier m
milk' pail' s seau m à lait
milk'sop' s poule f mouillée
milk' tooth' s dent f de lait
milk'weed' s laiteron m
milk·y ['mɪlki] adj (comp -ier; super -iest) laiteux
Milk'y Way' s Voie f Lactée
mill [mɪl] s moulin m; (factory) fabrique f, usine f; millième m de dollar; to put through the mill (coll)

faire passer au laminoir || tr moudre, broyer; (a coin) créneler; (gears) fraiser; (steel) laminer; (ore) bocarder; (chocolate) faire mousser || intr —to mill around circuler
millennial [mɪ'lɛnɪ-əl] adj millénaire
millenni·um [mɪ'lɛnɪ-əm] s (pl -ums or -a [ə]) millénaire m
miller ['mɪlər] s meunier m
millet ['mɪlɪt] s millet m
milligram ['mɪlɪ ,græm] s milligramme m
millimeter ['mɪlɪ ,mitər] s millimètre m
milliner ['mɪlɪnər] s modiste f
mil'linery shop' ['mɪlɪ ,neri], ['mɪlɪnəri] s boutique f de modiste
milling ['mɪlɪŋ] s (of grain) mouture f
mill'ing machine' s fraiseuse f
million ['mɪljən] adj million de || s million m
millionaire [,mɪljən'ɛr] s millionnaire mf
millionth ['mɪljənθ] adj & pron millionième (masc, fem) || s millionième m
mill'pond' s retenue f, réservoir m
mill'race' s bief m
mill'stone' s meule f; (fig) boulet m
mill' wheel' s roue f de moulin
mill'work' s ouvrage m de menuiserie
mime [maɪm] s mime mf || tr & intr mimer
mimeograph ['mɪmɪ-ə ,græf], ['mɪmɪ-ə ,grɑf] s ronéo f || tr ronéocopier, ronéotyper
mim·ic ['mɪmɪk] s mime mf, imitateur m || v (pret & pp -icked; ger -icking) tr mimer, imiter
mimic·ry ['mɪmɪkri] s (pl -ries) mimique f, imitation f
minaret [,mɪnə'rɛt], ['mɪnə ,rɛt] s minaret m
mince [mɪns] tr (meat) hacher menu || intr minauder
mince'meat' s hachis m de viande et de fruits aromatisés; to make mincemeat of (coll) mettre en marmelade
mind [maɪnd] s esprit m; to be of one mind être d'accord; to change one's mind changer d'avis; to have a mind to avoir envie de; to have in mind avoir en vue; to lose one's mind perdre la raison; to make up one's mind to prendre le parti de; to slip one's mind échapper à qn; to speak one's mind donner son avis || tr (to take care of) garder; (to obey) obéir (with dat); (to be troubled by) s'inquiéter de; (e.g., one's manners) faire attention à; (e.g., a dangerous step) prendre garde à; mind your own business! occupez-vous de vos affaires! || intr —do you mind? cela ne vous gêne pas?, cela ne vous gêne pas?; if you don't mind si cela ne vous fait rien, si cela vous est égal; never mind! n'importe!
mindful ['maɪndfəl] adj attentif; mindful of attentif à, soigneux de
mind' read'er s liseur m de la pensée
mind' read'ing s lecture f de la pensée
mine [maɪn] s mine f || pron poss le mien §89; à moi §85 A, 10 || tr (coal,

minerals, etc.) extraire; (*to under-mine; to lay mines in*) miner
mine'field' *s* champ *m* de mines
mine'lay'er *s* poseur *m* de mines
miner ['maɪnər] *s* mineur *m*
mineral ['mɪnərəl] *adj & s* minéral *m*
mineralogy [ˌmɪnə'rɑlədʒi] *s* minéralogie *f*
min'eral wool' *s* laine *f* minérale, laine de scories
mine'sweep'er *s* dragueur *m* de mines
mingle ['mɪŋgəl] *tr* mêler, mélanger ‖ *intr* se mêler, se mélanger
miniature ['mɪnɪ·ətʃər], ['mɪnɪtʃər] *s* miniature *f*
miniaturization [ˌmɪnɪ·ətʃərɪ'zeʃən], [ˌmɪnɪtʃərɪ'zeʃən] *s* miniaturisation *f*
miniaturize ['mɪnɪ·ətʃəˌraɪz], ['mɪnɪtʃəˌraɪz] *tr* miniaturiser
minimal ['mɪnɪməl] *adj* minimum
minimize ['mɪnəˌmaɪz] *tr* minimiser
minimum ['mɪnɪməm] *adj* minimum; (*temperature*) minimal ‖ *s* minimum
min'imum wage' *s* salaire *m* minimum, minimum *m* vital
mining ['maɪnɪŋ] *adj* minier ‖ *s* exploitation *f* des mines; (nav) pose *f* de mines
minion ['mɪnjən] *s* favori *m*; (*henchman*) séide *m*
miniskirt ['mɪnɪˌskʌrt] *s* minijupe *f*
minister ['mɪnɪstər] *s* ministre *m*; (eccl) pasteur *m* ‖ *intr*—**to minister to** (*the needs of*) subvenir à; (*a person*) soigner; (*a parish*) desservir
ministerial [ˌmɪnɪs'tɪrɪ·əl] *adj* ministériel
minis·try ['mɪnɪstri] *s* (*pl* -**tries**) ministère *m*; (eccl) clergé *m*; (eccl) pastorat *m*
mink [mɪŋk] *s* vison *m*
minnow ['mɪno] *s* vairon *m*
minor ['maɪnər] *adj & s* mineur *m*
Minorca [mɪ'nɔrkə] *s* Minorque *f*; île *f* de Minorque
minori·ty [mɪ'nɑriti], [mɪ'nɔriti] *adj* minoritaire ‖ *s* (*pl* -**ties**) minorité *f*
minstrel ['mɪnstrəl] *s* (*in a minstrel show*) interprète *m* de chants nègres; (hist) ménestrel *m*
mint [mɪnt] *s* hôtel *m* des Monnaies, Monnaie *f*; (bot) menthe *f*; (fig) mine *f* ‖ *tr* frapper, monnayer; (fig) forger
minuet [ˌmɪnju'et] *s* menuet *m*
minus ['maɪnəs] *adj* négatif ‖ *s* moins *m* ‖ *prep* moins; (coll) sans, dépourvu de
minute [maɪ'n(j)ut] *adj* (*tiny*) minime; (*meticulous*) minutieux ‖ ['mɪnɪt] *s* minute *f*; **minutes** compte *m* rendu, procès-verbal *m* de séance; (often omitted in expressions of time), e.g., **ten after two, ten minutes after two** deux heures dix; **up to the minute de** la dernière heure; à la dernière mode; au courant
min'ute hand' ['mɪnɪt] *s* grande aiguille *f*
min'ute steak' ['mɪnɪt] *s* entrecôte *f* minute

minutiae [mɪ'n(j)uʃɪˌi] *spl* minuties *fpl*
minx [mɪŋks] *s* effrontée *f*
miracle ['mɪrəkəl] *s* miracle *m*
mir'acle play' *s* miracle *m*
miraculous [mɪ'rækjələs] *adj* miraculeux
mirage [mɪ'rɑʒ] *s* mirage *m*
mire [maɪr] *s* fange *f*
mirror ['mɪrər] *s* miroir *m*, glace *f* ‖ *tr* refléter
mirth [mʌrθ] *s* joie *f*, gaieté *f*
mir·y ['maɪri] *adj* (*comp* -**ier**; *super* -**iest**) fangeux
misadventure [ˌmɪsəd'vɛntʃər] *s* mésaventure *f*
misanthrope ['mɪsənˌθrop] *s* misanthrope *mf*
misapprehension [ˌmɪsæprɪ'hɛnʃən] *s* fausse idée *f*, malentendu *m*
misappropriation [ˌmɪsə ˌproprɪ'eʃən] *s* détournement *m* de fonds
misbehave [ˌmɪsbɪ'hev] *intr* se conduire mal
misbehavior [ˌmɪsbɪ'hevɪ·ər] *s* mauvaise conduite *f*
miscalculation [ˌmɪskælkjə'leʃən] *s* mécompte *m*
miscarriage [mɪs'kærɪdʒ] *s* fausse couche *f*; (*of letter*) perte *f*; (*of justice*) déni *m*, mal-jugé *m*; (fig) avortement *m*, insuccès *m*
miscar·ry [mɪs'kæri] *v* (*pret & pp* -**ried**) *intr* faire une fausse couche; (*said, e.g., of letter*) s'égarer; (fig) avorter, échouer
miscellaneous [ˌmɪsə'lenɪ·əs] *adj* divers, mélangé
miscella·ny ['mɪsəˌleni] *s* (*pl* -**nies**) miscellanées *fpl*
mischief ['mɪstʃɪf] *s* (*harm*) tort *m*; (*disposition to annoy*) méchanceté *f*; (*prankishness*) espièglerie *f*
mis'chief-mak'er *s* brandon *m* de discorde
mischievous ['mɪstʃɪvəs] *adj* (*harmful*) nuisible; (*mean*) méchant; (*prankish*) espiègle
misconception [ˌmɪskən'sɛpʃən] *s* conception *f* erronée
misconduct [mɪs'kɑndʌkt] *s* inconduite *f*; (*e.g., of a business*) mauvaise administration *f* ‖ [ˌmɪskən'dʌkt] *tr* mal administrer; **to misconduct one-self** se conduire mal
misconstrue [ˌmɪskən'stru], [mɪs'kɑnstru] *tr* mal interpréter
miscount [mɪs'kaʊnt] *s* erreur *f* de calcul ‖ *tr & intr* mal compter
miscue [mɪs'kju] *s* fausse queue *f*; (*blunder*) bévue *f* ‖ *intr* faire fausse queue; (theat) se tromper de réplique
mis·deal ['mɪsˌdil] *s* maldonne *f*, mauvaise donne *f* ‖ [mɪs'dil] *v* (*pret & pp* -**dealt**) *tr* mal distribuer ‖ *intr* faire maldonne
misdeed [mɪs'did], ['mɪsˌdid] *s* méfait *m*
misdemeanor [ˌmɪsdɪ'minər] *s* mauvaise conduite *f*; (law) délit *m* correctionnel

misdirect [‚mɪsdɪ'rɛkt], [‚mɪsdaɪ-'rɛkt] *tr* mal diriger
misdoing [mɪs'du·ɪŋ] *s* méfait *m*
miser ['maɪzər] *s* avare *mf*
miserable ['mɪzərəbəl] *adj* misérable
miserly ['maɪzərli] *adj* avare
miser·y ['mɪzəri] *s* (*pl* -ies) misère *f*, détresse *f*
misfeasance [mɪs'fizəns] *s* (law) abus *m* de pouvoir
misfire [mɪs'faɪr] *s* raté *m* ‖ *intr* rater
mis·fit ['mɪs ‚fɪt] *s* (*clothing*) vêtement *m* manqué; (*thing*) laissé-pour-compte *m*; (fig) inadapté *m* ‖ [mɪs-'fɪt] *v* (*pret & pp* -fitted; *ger* -fitting) *tr* mal aller (with *dat*) ‖ *intr* mal aller
misfortune [mɪs'fɔrtʃən] *s* infortune *f*, malheur *m*
misgiving [mɪs'gɪvɪŋ] *s* pressentiment *m*, appréhension *f*, soupçon *m*
misgovern [mɪs'gʌvərn] *tr* mal gouverner
misguidance [mɪs'gaɪdəns] *s* mauvais conseils *mpl*
misguided [mɪs'gaɪdɪd] *adj* mal placé, hors de propos; (*e.g., youth*) dévoyé
mishap ['mɪshæp], [mɪs'hæp] *s* contretemps *m*, mésaventure *f*
misinform [‚mɪsɪn'fɔrm] *tr* mal renseigner
misinterpret [‚mɪsɪn'tʌrprɪt] *tr* mal interpréter
misjudge [mɪs'dʒʌdʒ] *tr & intr* mal juger
mis·lay [mɪs'le] *v* (*pret & pp* -laid) *tr* égarer, perdre
mis·lead [mɪs'lid] *v* (*pret & pp* -led) *tr* égarer; corrompre
misleading [mɪs'lidɪŋ] *adj* trompeur
mismanagement [mɪs'mænɪdʒmənt] *s* mauvaise administration *f*
misnomer [mɪs'nomər] *s* faux nom *m*
misplace [mɪs'ples] *tr* mal placer; (*to mislay*) (coll) égarer, perdre
misprint ['mɪs ‚prɪnt] *s* erreur *f* typographique, coquille *f* ‖ [mɪs'prɪnt] *tr* imprimer incorrectement
mispronounce [‚mɪsprə'nauns] *tr* mal prononcer
misquote [mɪs'kwot] *tr* citer à faux, citer inexactement
misrepresent [‚mɪsrɛprɪ'zɛnt] *tr* représenter sous un faux jour; (*e.g., facts*) dénaturer, travestir
miss [mɪs] *s* coup *m* manqué; Miss Mademoiselle *f*, Mlle; (*winner of beauty contest*) Miss *f* ‖ *tr* manquer; (*to feel the absence of*) regretter; (*not to run into*) ne pas voir, ne pas rencontrer; (*e.g., one's way*) se tromper de; **he misses you very much** vous lui manquez beaucoup ‖ *intr* manquer
missal ['mɪsəl] *s* missel *m*
misshapen [mɪs'ʃepən] *adj* difforme, contrefait
missile ['mɪsɪl] *s* projectile *m*; (*guided missile*) missile *m*
mis'sile launch'er *s* lance-fusées *m*
missing [mɪsɪŋ] *adj* manquant, absent;

perdu; **missing in action** (mil) porté disparu; **to be missing** manquer, e.g., **three are missing** il en manque trois
miss'ing per'sons *spl* disparus *mpl*
mission ['mɪʃən] *s* mission *f*
missionar·y ['mɪʃən ‚ɛri] *adj* missionnaire ‖ *s* (*pl* -ies) missionnaire *m*
missis ['mɪsɪz] *s*—**the missis** (coll) votre femme *f*
missive ['mɪsɪv] *adj & s* missive *f*
mis·spell [mɪs'spɛl] *v* (*pret & pp* -spelled or -spelt) *tr & intr* écrire incorrectement
misspelling [mɪs'spɛlɪŋ] *s* faute *f* d'orthographe
misspent [mɪs'spɛnt] *adj* gaspillé; dissipé
misstatement [mɪs'stetmənt] *s* rapport *m* inexact, erreur *f* de fait
misstep [mɪs'stɛp] *s* faux pas *m*
miss·y ['mɪsi] *s* (*pl* -ies) (coll) mademoiselle *f*
mist [mɪst] *s* brume *f*, buée *f*; (*fine spray*) vapeur *f*; (*of tears*) voile *m*
mis·take [mɪs'tek] *s* faute *f*; **by mistake** par erreur, par méprise; **to make a mistake** se tromper ‖ *v* (*pret* -took; *pp* -taken) *tr* (*to misunderstand*) mal comprendre; (*to be wrong about*) se tromper de; **to mistake s.o. for s.e. else** prendre qn pour qn d'autre
mistaken [mɪs'tekən] *adj* erroné, faux; (*person*) dans l'erreur
mistak'en iden'tity *s* erreur *f* d'identité, erreur sur la personne
mistakenly [mɪs'tekənli] *adv* par erreur
mister ['mɪstər] *s*—**the mister** (coll) votre mari *m* ‖ *interj* (slang & pej) Jules!, mon petit bonhomme!
mistletoe ['mɪsəl ‚to] *s* gui *m*
mistreat [mɪs'trit] *tr* maltraiter
mistreatment [mɪs'tritmənt] *s* mauvais traitement *m*
mistress ['mɪstrɪs] *s* maîtresse *f*
mistrial [mɪs'traɪ·əl] *s* (law) procès *m* entaché de nullité
mistrust [mɪs'trʌst] *s* méfiance *f* ‖ *tr* se méfier de ‖ *intr* se méfier
mistrustful [mɪs'trʌstfəl] *adj* méfiant
mist·y ['mɪsti] *adj* (*comp* -ier; *super* -iest) brumeux; vague, indistinct
misunder·stand [‚mɪsʌndər'stænd] *v* (*pret & pp* -stood) *tr* mal comprendre
misunderstanding [‚mɪsʌndər'stændɪŋ] *s* malentendu *m*
misuse [mɪs'jus] *s* mauvais usage *m*, abus *m*; (*of words*) emploi *m* abusif ‖ [mɪs'juz] *tr* faire mauvais usage de, abuser de; (*a person*) maltraiter
misword [mɪs'wʌrd] *tr* mal rédiger, mal exprimer
mite [maɪt] *s* (*small contribution*) obole *f*; (*small amount*) brin *m*, bagatelle *f*; (ent) mite *f*
miter ['maɪtər] *s* (*carpentry*) onglet *m*; (eccl) mitre *f* ‖ *tr* tailler à onglet
mi'ter box' *s* boîte *f* à onglets
mitigate ['mɪtɪ ‚get] *tr* adoucir, atténuer
mitt [mɪt] *s* (*fingerless glove*) mitaine *f*; (*mitten*) moufle *f*; (baseball) gant *m* de prise; (*hand*) (slang) main *f*

mitten ['mɪtən] s moufle f
mix [mɪks] tr mélanger, mêler; (cement; a cake) malaxer; (the cards; the salad) touiller; **to mix up** (to confuse) confondre ‖ intr se mélanger, se mêler; **to mix with** s'associer à or avec
mixed adj mélangé; (races; style; colors) mêlé; (feelings; marriage; school; doubles) mixte; (candy) assorti; (salad, vegetables, etc.) panaché; (number) fractionnaire
mixed' drink' s boisson f mélangée
mixer ['mɪksər] s (device) mélangeur m; (for, e.g., concrete) malaxeur m; **to be a good mixer** (coll) avoir le don de plaire
mix'ing fau'cet s robinet m mélangeur
mixture ['mɪkstʃər] s mélange m
mix'-up' s embrouillage m
mizzen ['mɪzən] s artimon m
moan [mon] s gémissement m ‖ intr gémir
moat [mot] s fossé m
mob [mɑb] s populace f; (crush of people) cohue f grouillante; (crowd bent on violence) foule f en colère, ameutement m ‖ v (pret & pp mobbed; ger mobbing) tr s'attrouper autour de; fondre sur, assaillir
mobile ['mobɪl], ['mobil] adj & s mobile m
mobility [mo'bɪlɪti] s mobilité f
mobilization [ˌmobɪlɪ'zeʃən] s mobilisation f
mobilize ['mobɪˌlaɪz] tr & intr mobiliser
mob' rule' s loi f de la populace
mobster ['mɑbstər] s (slang) gangster m
moccasin ['mɑkəsɪn] s mocassin m
Mo'cha cof'fee ['mokə] s moka m
mock [mɑk] adj simulé, contrefait ‖ s moquerie f ‖ tr se moquer de, moquer; (to imitate) contrefaire, singer; (to deceive) tromper ‖ intr se moquer; **to mock at** se moquer de; **to mock up** construire une maquette de
mock' elec'tion s élection f blanche
mocker·y ['mɑkəri] s (pl -ies) moquerie f; (subject of derision) objet m de risée; (poor imitation) parodie f; (e.g., of justice) simulacre m
mockingbird ['mɑkɪŋˌbɑrd] s moqueur m, oiseau m moqueur
mock' or'ange s seringa m
mock' tur'tle soup' s potage m à la tête de veau
mock'-up' s maquette f
mode [mod] s (kind) mode m; (fashion) mode f; (gram, mus) mode m
mod·el ['mɑdəl] adj modèle ‖ s modèle m; (for dressmaker or artist; at a fashion show) mannequin m; (of a statue) maquette f ‖ v (pret & pp -eled or -elled; ger -eling or -elling) tr modeler ‖ intr dessiner des modèles; servir de modèle, poser
mod'el air'plane s aéromodèle m
mod'el-air'plane build'er s aéromodéliste mf
mod'el-air'plane build'ing s aéromodélisme m

moderate ['mɑdərɪt] adj modéré ‖ ['mɑdəˌret] tr modérer; (a meeting) présider ‖ intr se modérer; présider
moderator ['mɑdəˌretər] s (over an assembly) président m; (mediator; substance used for slowing down neutrons) modérateur m
modern ['mɑdərn] adj moderne
modernize ['mɑdərˌnaɪz] tr moderniser
mod'ern lan'guages spl langues fpl vivantes
modest ['mɑdɪst] adj modeste
modes·ty ['mɑdɪsti] s (pl -ties) modestie f
modicum ['mɑdɪkəm] s petite quantité f
modifier ['mɑdɪˌfaɪ-ər] s (gram) modificateur m
modi·fy ['mɑdɪˌfaɪ] v (pret & pp -fied) tr modifier
modish ['modɪʃ] adj à la mode, élégant
modulate ['mɑdʒəˌlet] tr & intr moduler
modulation [ˌmɑdʒə'leʃən] s modulation f
mohair ['moˌhɛr] s mohair m
Mohammedan [mo'hæmɪdən] adj mahométan ‖ s mahométan m
Mohammedanism [mo'hæmɪdəˌnɪzəm] s mahométisme m
moist [mɔɪst] adj humide; (e.g., skin) moite
moisten ['mɔɪsən] tr humecter ‖ intr s'humecter
moisture ['mɔɪstʃər] s humidité f
molar ['molər] adj & s molaire f
molasses [mə'læsɪz] s mélasse f
mold [mold] s moule m; (fungus) moisi m, moisissure f; (agr) humus m, terreau m; (fig) trempe f ‖ tr mouler; (to make moldy) moisir ‖ intr moisir, se moisir
molder ['moldər] s mouleur m ‖ intr tomber en poussière
molding ['moldɪŋ] s moulage m; (cornice, shaped strip of wood, etc.) moulure f
mold·y ['moldi] adj (comp -ier; super -iest) moisi
mole [mol] s (breakwater) môle m; (inner harbor) bassin m; (spot on skin) grain m de beauté; (small mammal) taupe f
molecule ['mɑlɪˌkjul] s molécule f
mole'hill' s taupinière f
mole'skin' s (fur) taupe f; (fabric) moleskine f
molest [mə'lɛst] tr déranger, inquiéter; molester, rudoyer
moll [mɑl] s (slang) femme f du Milieu
molli·fy ['mɑlɪˌfaɪ] v (pret & pp -fied) tr apaiser, adoucir
mollusk ['mɑləsk] s mollusque m
mollycoddle ['mɑlɪˌkɑdəl] s poule f mouillée ‖ tr dorloter
molt [molt] s mue f ‖ intr muer
molten ['moltən] adj fondu
molybdenum [mə'lɪbdɪnəm], [ˌmɑlɪb-'dinəm] s molybdène m
moment ['momənt] s moment m; **at**

any **moment** d'un moment à l'autre;
at that **moment** à ce moment-là; at
this **moment** en ce moment; in a **moment** dans un instant; of great **moment** d'une grande importance; one
moment please! (telp) ne quittez pas!
momentary ['momən‚teri] adj momen-
tané
momentous [mo'mɛntəs] adj important, d'importance
momen·tum [mo'mɛntəm] s (pl -tums
or -ta [tə]) élan m; (mech) force f
d'impulsion, quantité f de mouvement
monarch ['manərk] s monarque m
monarchic(al) [mə'narkɪk(əl)] adj monarchique
monar·chy ['manərki] s (pl -chies) monarchie f
monaster·y ['manɛs‚teri] s (pl -ies)
monastère m
monastic [mə'næstɪk] adj monastique
monasticism [mə'næstɪ‚sɪzəm] s monachisme m
Monday ['mʌndi] s lundi m
monetary ['manɪ‚teri] adj (pertaining
to coinage) monétaire; (pertaining to
money) pécuniaire
money ['mʌni] s argent m; (legal tender of a country) monnaie f; to get
one's **money's worth** en avoir pour
son argent; to make **money** gagner
de l'argent
mon'ey·bag' s sacoche f; **moneybags**
(wealth) (coll) sac m; (wealthy person) (coll) richard m
mon'ey belt' s ceinture f porte-monnaie
moneychanger ['mʌni‚tʃendʒər] s
changeur m, cambiste m
moneyed ['mʌnid] adj possédant
mon'ey·lend'er s bailleur m de fonds
mon'ey·mak'er s amasseur m d'argent;
(fig) source f de gain
mon'ey or'der s mandat m postal
Mongol ['maŋgəl], ['maŋgal] adj
mongol ‖ s (language) mongol m;
(person) Mongol m
mon·goose ['maŋgus] s (pl -gooses)
mangouste f
mongrel ['mʌŋgrəl], ['maŋgrəl] adj &
s métis m
monitor ["manɪtər] s contrôleur m; (at
school) pion m, moniteur m ‖ tr contrôler; (rad) écouter
monk [mʌŋk] s moine m
monkey ['mʌŋki] s singe m; (female)
guenon f; to make a **monkey of** tourner en ridicule ‖ intr—to **monkey
around** tripoter; to **monkey around
with** tripoter; to **monkey with** (to
tamper with) tripatouiller
mon'key·shine' s (slang) singerie f
mon'key wrench' s clé f anglaise
monks'hood s (bot) napel m
monocle ['manəkəl] s monocle m
monogamy [mə'nagəmi] s monogamie f
monogram ['manə‚græm] s monogramme m
monograph ['manə‚græf], ['manə-
‚graf] s monographie f
monolithic [‚manə'lɪθɪk] adj monolithique

monologue ['manə‚lɔg], ['manə‚lag] s
monologue m
monomania [‚manə'menɪ·ə] s monomanie f
monomial [mə'nomɪ·əl] s monôme m
monoplane ['manə‚plen] s monoplan m
monopolize [mə'napə‚laɪz] tr monopoliser
monopo·ly [mə'napəli] s (pl -lies) monopole m
monorail ['manə‚rel] s monorail m
monosyllable ['manə‚sɪləbəl] s monosyllabe m
monotheist ['manə‚θi·ɪst] adj & s monothéiste mf
monotonous [mə'natənəs] adj monotone
monotony [mə'natəni] s monotonie f
monotype ['manə‚taɪp] s monotype m;
(machine to set type) monotype f
monoxide [mə'naksaɪd] s oxyde m,
e.g., **carbon monoxide** oxyde m de
carbone
monsignor [man'sinjər] s (pl **mon-
signors** or **monsignori** [‚mansi'njo-
ri]) (eccl) monseigneur m
monsoon [man'sun] s mousson f
monster ['manstər] adj & s monstre m
monstrance ['manstrəns] s ostensoir m
monstrous ['manstrəs] adj monstrueux
month [mʌnθ] s mois m
month·ly ['mʌnθli] adj mensuel ‖ s (pl
-lies) revue f mensuelle; **monthlies**
(coll) règles fpl ‖ adv mensuellement
monument ['manjəmənt] s monument m
moo [mu] s meuglement m ‖ intr meugler
mood [mud] s humeur f, disposition f;
(gram) mode m; **moods** accès mpl
de mauvaise humeur
mood·y ['mudi] adj (comp -ier; super
-iest) d'humeur changeante; (melancholy) maussade
moon [mun] s lune f ‖ intr—to **moon
about** musarder; (to daydream about)
rêver à
moon'beam' s rayon m de lune
moon'light' s clair m de lune
moon'light'ing s deuxième emploi m
moon'shine' s clair m de lune; (idle
talk) baliverne f; (coll) alcool m de
contrebande
moon' shot' s tir m à la lune
moor [mʊr] s lande f, bruyère f; **Moor**
Maure m ‖ tr amarrer ‖ intr s'amarrer
Moorish ['mʊrɪʃ] adj mauresque
moose [mus] s (pl **moose**) élan m du
Canada, orignal m; (European elk)
élan m
moot [mut] adj discutable
mop [map] s balai m à franges; (of
hair) tignasse f ‖ v (pret & pp
mopped; ger mopping) tr nettoyer
avec un balai à franges; (e.g., one's
brow) s'essuyer; to **mop up** (mil)
nettoyer
mope [mop] intr avoir le cafard
moral ['marəl], ['mɔrəl] adj moral ‖
s (of a fable) morale f; **morals** mœurs
fpl

morale [məˈræl], [məˈrɑl] *s* moral *m*
morali·ty [məˈrælɪti] *s* (*pl* -ties) moralité *f*
morass [məˈræs] *s* marais *m*
moratori·um [ˌmɔrəˈtɔrɪ·əm], [ˌmɑrə-
ˈtɔrɪ·əm] *s* (*pl* -ums or -a [ə]) moratoire *m*, moratorium *m*
morbid [ˈmɔrbɪd] *adj* morbide
mordacious [mɔrˈdeʃəs] *adj* mordant
mordant [ˈmɔrdənt] *adj & s* mordant *m*
more [mor] *adj comp* plus de §91; plus
nombreux; de plus, e.g., **one minute
more** une minute de plus; **more than**
plus que; (followed by numeral) plus
de ‖ *s* plus *m*; **all the more so** d'autant plus; **what is more** qui plus est;
what more do you need? que vous
faut-il de plus? ‖ *pron indef* plus, davantage ‖ *adv comp* plus §91; davantage; **more and more** de plus en plus;
more or less plus ou moins; **more
than** plus que, davantage que; (followed by numeral) plus de; **neither
more nor less** ni plus ni moins; **never
more** jamais plus, plus jamais; **no
more** ne . . . plus §90; **once more** une
fois de plus; **the more** . . . **the more**
(or **the less**) plus . . . plus (or moins)
more·o′ver *adv* de plus, du reste
Moresque [moˈrɛsk] *adj* mauresque
morgue [mɔrg] *s* institut *m* médico-
légal, morgue *f*; (journ) archives *fpl*
Mormon [ˈmɔrmən] *adj & s* mormon *m*
morning [ˈmɔrnɪŋ] *adj* matinal, du
matin ‖ *s* matin *m*; (*time between
sunrise and noon*) matinée *f*, matin;
in the morning le matin; **the morning
after** le lendemain matin; (coll) le
lendemain de bombe
morn′ing coat′ *s* jaquette *f*
morn′ing-glo′ry *s* (*pl* -ries) belle-de-
jour *f*
morn′ing sick′ness *s* des nausées *fpl*
morn′ing star′ *s* étoile *f* du matin
Moroccan [məˈrakən] *adj* marocain ‖
s Marocain *m*
morocco [məˈrako] *s* (*leather*) maroquin *m*; **Morocco** le Maroc
moron [ˈmoran] *s* arriéré *m*; (coll)
minus *mf*, minus habens *mf*
morose [məˈros] *adj* morose
morphine [ˈmɔrfin] *s* morphine *f*
morphology [mɔrˈfalədʒi] *s* morphologie *f*
morrow [ˈmaro], [ˈmɔro] *s*—**on the
morrow (of)** le lendemain (de)
Morse′ code′ [mɔrs] *s* alphabet *m*
morse
morsel [ˈmɔrsəl] *s* morceau *m*
mortal [ˈmɔrtəl] *adj & s* mortel *m*
mortality [mɔrˈtælɪti] *s* mortalité *f*
mortar [ˈmɔrtər] *s* mortier *m*
mor′tar·board′ *s* bonnet *m* carré; (*of
mason*) taloche *f*
mortgage [ˈmɔrgɪdʒ] *s* hypothèque *f*
‖ *tr* hypothéquer
mortgagee [ˌmɔrgɪˈdʒi] *s* créancier *m*
hypothécaire
mortgagor [ˈmɔrgɪdʒər] *s* débiteur *m*
hypothécaire
mortician [mɔrˈtɪʃən] *s* entrepreneur *m*
de pompes funèbres

morti·fy [ˈmɔrtɪˌfaɪ] *v* (*pret & pp*
-fied) *tr* mortifier
mortise [ˈmɔrtɪs] *s* mortaise *f* ‖ *tr* mortaiser
mortuar·y [ˈmɔrtʃʊˌɛri] *adj* mortuaire
‖ *s* (*pl* -ies) morgue *f*; chapelle *f* mortuaire
mosaic [moˈze·ɪk] *adj & s* mosaïque *f*
Moscow [ˈmaskau], [ˈmasko] *s* Moscou *m*
Moses [ˈmozɪz], [ˈmozɪs] *s* Moïse *m*
Mos·lem [ˈmazləm], [ˈmasləm] *adj*
musulman ‖ *s* (*pl* -lems or -lem) musulman *m*
mosque [mask] *s* mosquée *f*
mosqui·to [məsˈkito] *s* (*pl* -toes or -tos)
moustique *m*
mosqui′to net′ *s* moustiquaire *f*
moss [mɔs], [mas] *s* mousse *f*
moss·y [ˈmɔsi], [ˈmasi] *adj* (*comp* -ier;
super -iest) moussu
most [most] *adj super* (le) plus de §91,
(la) plupart de; **for the most part**
pour la plupart ‖ *s* (le) plus, (la)
plupart; **at the most** au plus, tout au
plus; **most of** la plupart de; **to make
the most of** tirer le meilleur parti
possible de ‖ *pron indef* la plupart ‖
adv super (le) plus §91, e.g., **what I
like** (the) **most** ce que j'aime le plus;
the (or **his**, etc.) **most** + *adj* le (or
son, etc.) plus + *adj* ‖ *adv* très,
bien, fort, des plus
mostly [ˈmostli] *adv* pour la plupart,
principalement
motel [moˈtɛl] *s* motel *m*
moth [mɔθ], [maθ] *s* teigne *f*, papillon
m nocturne; (*clothes moth*) mite *f*
moth′ball′ *s* boule *f* antimite, boule de
naphtaline
moth-eaten [ˈmɔθˌitən], [ˈmaθˌitən]
adj mité
mother [ˈmʌðər] *s* mère *f* ‖ *tr* servir de
mère à; (*to coddle*) dorloter
moth′er coun′try *s* mère patrie *f*
Moth′er Goos′e's Nurs′ery Rhymes′
spl les Contes de ma mère l'oie
moth′er·hood′ *s* maternité *f*
moth′er-in-law′ *s* (*pl* mothers-in-law)
belle-mère *f*
motherless [ˈmʌðərlɪs] *adj* orphelin de
mère
motherly [ˈmʌðərli] *adj* maternel
mother-of-pearl [ˈmʌðərəvˈpʌrl] *adj* de
nacre, en nacre ‖ *s* nacre *f*
Moth′er's Day′ *s* fête *f* des mères
moth′er supe′rior *s* mère *f* supérieure
moth′er tongue′ *s* langue *f* maternelle
moth′er wit′ *s* bon sens *m*, esprit *m*
moth′ hole′ *s* trou *m* de mite
moth′proof′ *adj* antimite ‖ *tr* rendre
antimite
moth·y [ˈmɔθi], [ˈmaθi] *adj* (*comp
-ier*; *super* -iest) mité, plein de mites
motif [moˈtif] *s* motif *m*
motion [ˈmoʃən] *s* mouvement *m*; (*ges-
ture*) geste *m*; (*in a deliberating assembly*) motion *f*, proposition *f* ‖ *intr*
—**to motion to** faire signe à
motionless [ˈmoʃənlɪs] *adj* immobile
mo′tion pic′ture *s* film *m*; **motion pictures** cinéma *m*

mo′tion-pic′ture *adj* cinématographique

mo′tion-pic′ture the′ater *s* cinéma *m*

motivate ['motɪ ,vet] *tr* motiver

motive ['motɪv] *adj* moteur ‖ *s* mobile *m*, motif *m*

mo′tive pow′er *s* force *f* motrice

motley ['mɑtlɪ] *adj* bigarré; (*mixed*) mélangé

motor ['motər] *adj* & *s* moteur *m* ‖ *intr* aller en voiture

mo′tor-bike′ *s* vélomoteur *m*

mo′tor-boat′ *s* canot *m* automobile

mo′tor-bus′ *s* autocar *m*

motorcade ['motər,ked] *s* défilé *m* de voitures

mo′tor-car′ *s* automobile *f*

mo′tor-cy′cle *s* moto *f*

motorist ['motərɪst] *s* automobiliste *mf*

motorize ['motə ,raɪz] *tr* motoriser

mo′tor launch′ *s* chaloupe *f* à moteur

mo′tor-man *s* (*pl* -men) conducteur *m*, wattman *m*

mo′tor pool′ *s* parc *m* automobile

mo′tor scoot′er *s* scooter *m*

mo′tor ship′ *s* navire *m* à moteurs

mo′tor truck′ *s* camion *m* automobile

mo′tor ve′hicle *s* véhicule *m* automobile

mottle ['mɑtəl] *tr* marbrer, tacheter

mot·to ['mɑto] *s* (*pl* -toes or -tos) devise *f*

mound [maund] *s* monticule *m*

mount [maunt] *s* montage *m*; (*hill, mountain*) mont *m*; (*horse for riding*) monture *f* ‖ *tr* & *intr* monter

mountain ['mauntən] *s* montagne *f*

moun′tain climb′ing *s* alpinisme *m*

mountaineer [,mauntə'nɪr] *s* montagnard *m*; (*climber*) alpiniste *mf*

mountainous ['mauntənəs] *adj* montagneux

moun′tain range′ *s* chaîne *f* de montagnes

mountebank ['mauntɪ ,bæŋk] *s* saltimbanque *mf*

mounting ['mauntɪŋ] *s* montage *m*

mourn [morn] *tr* & *intr* pleurer

mourner ['mornər] *s* affligé *m*; (*woman hired as mourner*) pleureuse *f*; pénitent *m*; **mourners** deuil *m*

mourn′er's bench′ *s* banc *m* des pénitents

mournful ['mornfəl] *adj* lugubre

mourning ['mornɪŋ] *s* deuil *m*

mouse [maus] *s* (*pl* mice [maɪs]) souris *f*

mouse′hole′ *s* trou *m* de souris

mouser ['mauzər] *s* souricier *m*

mouse′trap′ *s* souricière *f*

moustache [məs'tæʃ], [məs'tɑʃ] *s* moustache *f*

mouth [mauθ] *s* (*pl* mouths [mauðz]) bouche *f*; (*of gun; of, e.g., wolf*) gueule *f*; (*of river*) embouchure *f*; **by mouth** par voie buccale; **to make s.o.'s mouth water** faire venir l'eau à la bouche à qn

mouthful ['mauθ ,fʊl] *s* bouchée *f*

mouth′ or′gan *s* harmonica *m*

mouth′piece′ *s* embouchure *f*; (*person*) porte-parole *m*

mouth′wash′ *s* rince-bouche *m*, eau *f* dentifrice

movable ['muvəbəl] *adj* mobile

move [muv] *s* mouvement *m*; (*from one house to another*) déménagement *m*; **on the move** en mouvement ‖ *tr* remuer; (*to excite the feelings of*) émouvoir; **to move that** (parl) proposer que; **to move up** (*a date*) avancer ‖ *intr* remuer; (*to stir*) se remuer; (*said of traffic, crowd, etc.*) circuler; (*e.g., to another city*) déménager; **don't move!** ne bougez pas!; **to move away** or **off** s'éloigner; **to move back** reculer; **to move in** emménage

movement ['muvmənt] *s* mouvement *m*

movie ['muvi] *s* (coll) film *m*; **movies** (coll) cinéma *m*

mov′ie cam′era *s* caméra *f*

movie-goer ['muvi ,go·ər] *s* (coll) amateur *m* de cinéma

mov′ie house′ *s* (coll) cinéma *m*, salle *f* de spectacles

moving ['muvɪŋ] *adj* mouvant, en marche; (*touching*) émouvant; (*force*) moteur ‖ *s* mouvement *m*; (*from one house to another*) déménagement *m*

mov′ing pic′ture *s* film *m*; **moving pictures** cinéma *m*

mov′ing-pic′ture the′ater *s* cinéma *m*

mov′ing spir′it *s* âme *f*

mov′ing stair′way *s* escalier *m* mécanique, escalier roulant

mov′ing van′ *s* voiture *f* de déménagement

mow [mo] *v* (*pret* mowed; *pp* mowed or mown) *tr* faucher; (*a lawn*) tondre; **to mow down** faucher

mower ['mo·ər] *s* faucheur *m*; (mach) faucheuse *f*; (*for lawns*) (mach) tondeuse *f*

m.p.h. ['ɛm'pi'etʃ] *spl* (letterword) (miles per hour—six tenths of a mile equaling approximately one kilometer) km/h

Mr. ['mɪstər] *s* Monsieur *m*, M.

Mrs. ['mɪsɪz] *s* Madame *f*, Mme

much [mʌtʃ] *adj* beaucoup de, e.g., **much time** beaucoup de temps; bien de + *art*, e.g., **much trouble** bien du mal ‖ *pron indef* beaucoup; **too much** trop ‖ *adv* beaucoup, bien §91; **however much** pour autant que; **how much** combien; **much less** encore moins; **too much** trop; **very much** beaucoup

mucilage ['mjusɪlɪdʒ] *s* colle *f* de bureau; (*gummy secretion in plants*) mucilage *m*

muck [mʌk] *s* fange *f*

muck′rake′ *intr* (coll) dévoiler des scandales

mucous ['mjukəs] *adj* muqueux

mu′cous lin′ing *s* (anat) muqueuse *f*

mucus ['mjukəs] *s* mucus *m*, mucosité *f*

mud [mʌd] *s* boue *f*; **to sling mud at** couvrir de boue

muddle ['mʌdəl] *s* confusion *f*, fouillis *m* ‖ *tr* embrouiller ‖ *intr*—**to muddle through** se débrouiller

mud′dle·head′ *s* brouillon *m*
mud·dy ['mʌdi] *adj* (*comp* **-dier;** *super* **-diest**) boueux; (*clothes*) crotté ‖ *v* (*pret & pp* **-died**) *tr* salir; (*clothes*) crotter; (*a liquid*) troubler; (fig) embrouiller
mud′guard′ *s* garde-boue *m*
mud′hole′ *s* bourbier *m*
mudslinger ['mʌd͵slɪŋər] *s* (fig) calomniateur *m*
muff [mʌf] *s* manchon *m*; (*failure*) coup *m* raté ‖ *tr* rater, louper
muffin ['mʌfɪn] *s* petit pain *m* rond, muffin *m*
muffle ['mʌfəl] *tr* (*a sound*) assourdir; (*the face*) emmitoufler
muffler ['mʌflər] *s* (*scarf*) cache-nez *m*; (aut) pot *m* d'échappement, silencieux *m*
mufti ['mʌfti] *s* vêtement *m* civil; **in mufti** en civil, en pékin, en bourgeois
mug [mʌg] *s* timbale *f*, gobelet *m*; (*tankard*) chope *f*; (slang) gueule *f*, museau *m* ‖ *v* (*pret & pp* **mugged;** *ger* **mugging**) *tr* (e.g., *a suspect*) (slang) photographier; (*a victim*) (slang) saisir à la gorge ‖ *intr* (slang) faire des grimaces
mug·gy ['mʌgi] *adj* (*comp* **-gier;** *super* **-giest**) lourd, étouffant
mulat·to [mju'læto], [mə'læto] *s* (*pl* **-toes**) mulâtre *m*
mulber·ry ['mʌl͵bɛri] *s* (*pl* **-ries**) mûre *f*; (*tree*) mûrier *m*
mulct [mʌlkt] *tr* (*a person*) priver, dépouiller; (*money*) carotter, extorquer
mule [mjul] *s* (*female mule; slipper*) mule *f*; (*male mule*) mulet *m*
muleteer [͵mjulə'tɪr] *s* muletier *m*
mulish ['mjulɪʃ] *adj* têtu, entêté
mull [mʌl] *tr* chauffer avec des épices; (*to muddle*) embrouiller ‖ *intr*—**to mull over** réfléchir sur, remâcher
mullion ['mʌljən] *s* meneau *m*
multigraph ['mʌltɪ͵græf], ['mʌltɪ͵graf] *s* (trademark) ronéo *f* ‖ *tr* ronéotyper, polycopier
multilateral [͵mʌltɪ'lætərəl] *adj* multilatéral
multiple ['mʌltɪpəl] *adj & s* multiple *m*
multiplici·ty [͵mʌltɪ'plɪsɪti] *s* (*pl* **-ties**) multiplicité *f*
multi·ply ['mʌltɪ͵plaɪ] *v* (*pret & pp* **-plied**) *tr* multiplier ‖ *intr* se multiplier
multitude ['mʌltɪ͵t(j)ud] *s* multitude *f*
mum [mʌm] *adj* silencieux; **mum's the word!** motus!, bouche cousue!; **to keep mum about** ne souffler mot de
mumble ['mʌmbəl] *tr & intr* marmotter
mummer·y ['mʌməri] *s* (*pl* **-ies**) momerie *f*
mum·my ['mʌmi] *s* (*pl* **-mies**) momie *f*; (slang) maman *f*
mumps [mʌmps] *s* oreillons *mpl*
munch [mʌntʃ] *tr* mâchonner
mundane ['mʌnden] *adj* mondain
municipal [mju'nɪsɪpəl] *adj* municipal
municipali·ty [mju͵nɪsɪ'pælɪti] *s* (*pl* **-ties**) municipalité *f*
munificent [mju'nɪfɪsənt] *adj* munificent

munition [mju'nɪʃən] *s* munition *f* ‖ *tr* approvisionner de munitions
muni′tion dump′ *s* dépôt *m* de munitions
mural ['mjʊrəl] *adj* mural ‖ *s* peinture *f* murale
murder ['mʌrdər] *s* assassinat *m*, meurtre *m* ‖ *tr* assassiner; (*a language, proper names, etc.*) (coll) estropier, écorcher
murderer ['mʌrdərər] *s* meurtrier *m*, assassin *m*
murderess ['mʌrdərɪs] *s* meurtrière *f*
murderous ['mʌrdərəs] *adj* meurtrier
murk·y ['mʌrki] *adj* (*comp* **-ier;** *super* **-iest**) ténébreux, nébuleux
murmur ['mʌrmər] *s* murmure *m* ‖ *tr & intr* murmurer
muscle ['mʌsəl] *s* muscle *m*
muscular ['mʌskjələr] *adj* musclé, musculeux; (*system, tissue, etc.*) musculaire
muse [mjuz] *s* muse *f*; **the Muses** les Muses ‖ *intr* méditer; **to muse on** méditer
museum [mju'zi·əm] *s* musée *m*
muse′um piece′ *s* pièce *f* de musée
mush [mʌʃ] *s* bouillie *f*; (coll) sentimentalité *f* de guimauve
mush′room′ *s* champignon *m* ‖ *intr* pousser comme un champignon
mush′room cloud′ *s* champignon *m* atomique
mush·y ['mʌʃi] *adj* (*comp* **-ier;** *super* **-iest**) mou; (*ground*) détrempé; (coll) à la guimauve, sentimental
music ['mjuzɪk] *s* musique *f*; **to face the music** (coll) affronter les opposants; **to set to music** mettre en musique
musical ['mjuzɪkəl] *adj* musical
mu′sical com′edy *s* comédie *f* musicale
musicale [͵mjuzɪ'kæl] *s* soirée *f* musicale; matinée *f* musicale
mu′sic box′ *s* boîte *f* à musique
mu′sic cab′inet *s* casier *m* à musique
mu′sic hall′ *s* salle *f* de musique; (Brit) music-hall *m*
musician [mju'zɪʃən] *s* musicien *m*
mu′sic lov′er *s* mélomane *mf*
musicology [͵mjuzɪ'kɑlədʒi] *s* musicologie *f*
mu′sic rack′ or **mu′sic stand′** *s* pupitre *m* à musique
musk [mʌsk] *s* musc *m*
musk′ deer′ *s* porte-musc *m*
musketeer [͵mʌskɪ'tɪr] *s* mousquetaire *m*
musk′mel′on *s* melon *m*; cantaloup *m*
musk′rat′ *s* rat *m* musqué, ondatra *m*
Mus·lim ['mʌzlɪm] *adj* musulman ‖ *s* (*pl* **-lims** or **-lim**) musulman *m*
muslin ['mʌzlɪn] *s* mousseline *f*
muss [mʌs] *tr* (*the hair*) ébouriffer; (*the clothing*) froisser
Mussulman ['mʌsəlmən] *adj & s* musulman *m*
muss·y ['mʌsi] *adj* (*comp* **-ier;** *super* **-iest**) en désordre, froissé
must [mʌst] *s* moût *m*; nécessité *f* absolue ‖ *aux* used to express 1)

necessity, e.g., **he must go away** il
doit s'en aller; 2) conjecture, e.g., **he
must be ill** il doit être malade; **he
must have been ill** il a dû être malade
mustache [məs'tæʃ], [məs'taʃ], ['mʌs-
tæʃ] *s* moustache *f*
mustard ['mʌstərd] *s* moutarde *f*
mus'tard plas'ter *s* sinapisme *m*
muster ['mʌstər] *s* rassemblement *m*;
(mil) revue *f*; **to pass muster** être
porté à l'appel; (fig) être acceptable
‖ *tr* rassembler; **to muster in** enrôler;
to muster out démobiliser; **to muster
up courage** prendre son courage à
deux mains
mus'ter roll' *s* feuille *f* d'appel
mus•ty ['mʌsti] *adj* (*comp* **-tier**; *super*
-tiest) (*moldy*) moisi; (*stale*) renfermé; (*antiquated*) désuet
mutation [mju'teʃən] *s* mutation *f*
mute [mjut] *adj* muet ‖ *s* muet *m*;
(mus) sourdine *f* ‖ *tr* amortir; (mus)
mettre une sourdine à
mutilate ['mjutɪˌlet] *tr* mutiler
mutineer [ˌmjutɪ'nɪr] *s* mutin *m*
mutinous ['mjutɪnəs] *adj* mutiné
muti•ny ['mjutɪni] *s* (*pl* **-nies**) mutine-
rie *f* ‖ *v* (*pret* & *pp* **-nied**) *intr* se
mutiner
mutt [mʌt] *s* (*dog*) (slang) cabot *m*;
(*person*) (slang) nigaud *m*
mutter ['mʌtər] *tr* & *intr* marmonner
mutton ['mʌtən] *s* mouton *m*

mut'ton•chop' *s* côtelette *f* de mouton;
muttonchops favoris *mpl* en côtelette
mutual ['mjutʃu•əl] *adj* mutuel
mu'tual aid' *s* entraide *f*
mu'tual fund' *s* mutuelle *f*
muzzle ['mʌzəl] *s* (*projecting part of
head of animal*) museau *m*; (*device
to keep animal from biting*) muselière
f; (*of firearm*) gueule *f* ‖ *tr* museler
my [maɪ] *adj poss* mon §88
myriad ['mɪrɪ•əd] *adj* innombrable ‖
s myriade *f*
myrrh [mɪr] *s* myrrhe *f*
myrtle ['mʌrtəl] *s* myrte *m*; (*periwinkle*) pervenche *f*
my•self' *pron pers* moi §85; moi-même
§86; me §87
mysterious [mɪs'tɪrɪ•əs] *adj* mystérieux
myster•y ['mɪstəri] *s* (*pl* **-ies**) mystère *m*
mystic ['mɪstɪk] *adj* & *s* mystique *mf*
mystical ['mɪstɪkəl] *adj* mystique
mysticism ['mɪstɪˌsɪzəm] *s* mysticisme *m*
mystification [ˌmɪstɪfɪ'keʃən] *s* mystification *f*
mysti•fy ['mɪstɪˌfaɪ] *v* (*pret* & *pp*
-fied) *tr* mystifier
myth [mɪθ] *s* mythe *m*
mythical ['mɪθɪkəl] *adj* mythique
mythological [ˌmɪθə'ladʒɪkəl] *adj*
mythologique
mytholo•gy [mɪ'θalədʒi] *s* (*pl* **-gies**)
mythologie *f*

N

N, n [ɛn] *s* XIVᵉ lettre de l'alphabet
nab [næb] *v* (*pret* & *pp* **nabbed**; *ger*
nabbing) *tr* (slang) happer; (*to arrest*) (slang) pincer, harponner
nag [næg] *s* bidet *m* ‖ *v* (*pret* & *pp*
nagged; *ger* **nagging**) *tr* & *intr* gronder constamment; **to nag at** gronder
constamment
nail [nel] *s* (*of finger*) ongle *m*; (*to be
hammered*) clou *m*; **to bite one's
nails** se ronger les ongles; **to hit the
nail on the head** mettre le doigt dessus, frapper juste ‖ *tr* clouer; (*a lie*)
mettre à découvert; (coll) saisir, attraper
nail'brush' *s* brosse *f* à ongles
nail' clip'pers *spl* coupe-ongles *m*
nail' file' *s* lime *f* à ongles
nail' pol'ish *s* vernis *m* à ongles
nail' scis'sors *s* & *spl* ciseaux *mpl* à
ongles
nail' set' *s* chasse-clou *m*
naïve [na'iv] *adj* naïf
naked ['nekɪd] *adj* nu; **to strip naked**
se mettre tout nu; mettre tout nu;
with the naked eye à l'œil nu
namby-pamby ['næmbi'pæmbi] *adj*
minaudier
name [nem] *s* nom *m*; (*reputation*)
renom *m*; **by name** de nom; **by the**

name of sous le nom de; **to call
names** traiter de tous les noms; **what
is your name?** comment vous appe-
lez-vous? ‖ *tr* nommer; (*a price*)
fixer, indiquer
name' day' *s* fête *f*
nameless ['nemlɪs] *adj* sans nom,
anonyme; (*horrid*) odieux
namely ['nemli] *adv* à savoir, nommément
name'sake' *s* homonyme *m*
nan•ny ['næni] *s* (*pl* **-nies**) nounou *f*
nan'ny goat' *s* (coll) chèvre *f*, bique *f*
nap [næp] *s* (*short sleep*) somme *m*,
sieste *f*; (*of cloth*) poil *m*, duvet *m*;
to take a nap faire un petit somme ‖
v (*pret* & *pp* **napped**; *ger* **napping**)
intr faire un somme; manquer de
vigilance; **to catch napping** prendre
au dépourvu
napalm ['nepam] *s* (mil) napalm *m*
nape [nep] *s* nuque *f*
naphtha ['næfθə] *s* naphte *m*
napkin ['næpkɪn] *s* serviette *f*
nap'kin ring' *s* rond *m* de serviette
Napoleonic [nəˌpolɪ'anɪk] *adj* napo-
léonien
narcissus [nar'sɪsəs] *s* narcisse *m*; **Narcissus** Narcisse

narcotic [nɑr'kɑtɪk] adj & s narcotique m

narrate [næ'ret] tr narrer, raconter

narration [næ're∫ən] s narration f

narrative ['nærətɪv] adj narratif ‖ s narration f, récit m

narrator [næ'retər] s narrateur m

narrow ['næro] adj étroit; (e.g., margin of votes) faible ‖ narrows spl détroit m, goulet m ‖ tr rétrécir ‖ intr se rétrécir

nar'row escape' s—to have a narrow escape l'échapper belle

nar'row gauge' s voie f étroite

nar'row-mind'ed adj à l'esprit étroit, intolérant

nasal ['nezəl] adj nasal; (sound, voice) nasillard ‖ s (phonet) nasale f

nasalize ['nezə‚laɪz] tr & intr nasaliser

nasturtium [nə'stʌr∫əm] s capucine f

nas·ty ['næsti], ['nɑsti] adj (comp -tier; super -tiest) mauvais, sale, dégoûtant; féroce, farouche; désagréable

nation ['ne∫ən] s nation f

national ['næ∫ənəl] adj & s national m

na'tional an'them s hymne m national

nationalism ['næ∫ənə‚lɪzəm] s nationalisme m

nationali·ty [‚næ∫ən'ælɪti] s (pl -ties) nationalité f

nationalize ['næ∫ənə‚laɪz] tr nationaliser, étatiser

na'tion·wide' adj de toute la nation

native ['netɪv] adj natif; (land, language) natal; native of originaire de ‖ s natif m; (original inhabitant) naturel m, indigène mf, autochtone mf

na'tive land' s pays m natal

nativi·ty [nə'tɪvɪti] s (pl -ties) naissance f; (astrol) nativité f; Nativity Nativité f

NATO ['neto] s (acronym) (North Atlantic Treaty Organization) l'O.T.A.N. f, l'OTAN f

nat·ty ['næti] adj (comp -tier; super -tiest) coquet, élégant, soigné

natural ['næt∫ərəl] adj naturel ‖ s (mus) bécarre m; (mus) touche f blanche; a natural (coll) juste ce qu'il faut

naturalism ['næt∫ərə‚lɪzəm] s naturalisme m

naturalist ['næt∫ərəlɪst] s naturaliste mf

naturalization [‚næt∫ərəlɪ'ze∫ən] s naturalisation f

naturaliza'tion pa'pers spl déclaration f de naturalisation

naturalize ['næt∫ərə‚laɪz] tr naturaliser

nature ['net∫ər] s nature f

naught [nɔt] s zéro m; rien m; to come to naught n'aboutir à rien

naugh·ty ['nɔti] adj (comp -tier; super -tiest) méchant, vilain; (story) risqué

nausea ['nɔ∫i·ə], ['nɔsi·ə] s nausée f

nauseate ['nɔ∫i‚et], ['nɔsi‚et] tr donner la nausée à ‖ intr avoir des nausées

nauseating ['nɔ∫i‚etɪŋ], ['nɔsi‚etɪŋ] adj nauséabond

nauseous ['nɔ∫i·əs], ['nɔsi·əs] adj nauséeux

nautical ['nɔtɪkəl] adj nautique; naval, marin

naval ['nevəl] adj naval

na'val acad'emy s école f navale

na'val of'ficer s officier m de marine

na'val sta'tion s station f navale

nave [nev] s (of a church) nef f, vaisseau m; (of a wheel) moyeu m

navel ['nevəl] s nombril m

na'vel or'ange s orange f navel

navigable ['nævɪgəbəl] adj (river) navigable; (aircraft) dirigeable; (ship) bon marcheur

navigate ['nævɪ‚get] tr gouverner, conduire; (the sea) naviguer sur ‖ intr naviguer

navigation [‚nævɪ'ge∫ən] s navigation f

navigator ['nævɪ‚getər] s navigateur m

na·vy ['nevi] adj bleu marine ‖ s (pl -vies) marine f militaire, marine de guerre; (color) bleu m marine

na'vy bean' s haricot m blanc

na'vy blue' s bleu m marine

na'vy yard' s chantier m naval

nay [ne] adv non; voire, même ‖ s non m; (parl) vote m négatif

Nazarene [‚næzə'rin] adj nazaréen ‖ s (person) Nazaréen m

Nazi ['nɑtsi], ['nætsi] adj & s nazi m

n.d. abbr (no date) s.d.

Ne'apol'itan ice' cream' [‚ni·ə'pɑlɪtən] s glace f panachée

neap' tide' [nip] s morte-eau f

near [nɪr] adj proche, prochain; d'imitation; near at hand tout près; near side (of horse) côté m de montoir ‖ adv près, de près; presque; to come near s'approcher ‖ prep près de; auprès de ‖ tr s'approcher de

near'by' adj proche ‖ adv tout près

Near' East' s—the Near East le Proche Orient

nearly ['nɪrli] adv presque, de près; faillir, manquer de, e.g., I nearly fell j'ai failli tomber

near'-sight'ed adj myope

near'-sight'edness s myopie f

neat [nit] adj soigné, rangé; concis; (clever) adroit; (liquor) nature; (slang) chouette

neat's'-foot oil' s huile f de pied de bœuf

nebu·la ['nɛbjələ] s (pl -lae [‚li] or -las) nébuleuse f

nebulous ['nɛbjələs] adj nébuleux

necessarily [‚nɛsɪ'sɛrɪli] adv nécessairement, forcément

necessary ['nɛsɪ‚sɛri] adj nécessaire

necessitate [nɪ'sɛsɪ‚tet] tr nécessiter, exiger

necessi·ty [nɪ'sɛsɪti] s (pl -ties) nécessité f

neck [nɛk] s cou m; (of bottle) col m, goulot m; (of land) cap m; (of tooth) collet m; (of violin) manche m, collet; (strait) étroit m; neck and neck manche à manche; to break one's neck (coll) se rompre le cou; to stick one's neck out prêter le flanc; to win

by a neck gagner par une encolure ‖ *intr* (slang) se peloter
neck'band' *s* tour *m* de cou
neckerchief ['nɛkərtʃɪf] *s* foulard *m*
necking ['nɛkɪŋ] *s* (slang) pelotage *m*
necklace ['nɛklɪs] *s* collier *m*
neck'piece' *s* col *m* de fourrure
neck'tie' *s* cravate *f*
neck'tie pin' *s* épingle *f* de cravate
necrolo·gy [nɛ'krɑlədʒi] *s* (*pl* -gies) nécrologie *f*
nectar ['nɛktər] *s* nectar *m*
nectarine [,nɛktə'rin] *s* brugnon *m*
nee [ne] *adj* née
need [nid] *s* besoin *m*; (*want, poverty*) besoin, indigence *f*, nécessité *f*; **if need be** au besoin, s'il le faut ‖ *tr* avoir besoin de, falloir, e.g., **he needs money** il a besoin d'argent, il lui faut de l'argent; demander, e.g., **the motor needs oil** le moteur demande de l'huile ‖ *aux* devoir
needful ['nidfəl] *adj* nécessaire
needle ['nidəl] *s* aiguille *f* ‖ *tr* (*to prod*) aiguillonner; (coll) taquiner; (*a drink*) (coll) corser
nee'dle·point' *s* broderie *f* sur canevas; (*lace*) dentelle *f* à l'aiguille
needless ['nidlɪs] *adj* inutile
nee'dle·work' *s* ouvrage *m* à l'aiguille
need·y ['nidi] *adj* (*comp* -ier; *super* -iest) nécessiteux ‖ *s*—**the needy** les nécessiteux
ne'er-do-well ['nɛrdu,wɛl] *adj* propre à rien ‖ *s* vaurien *m*
nefarious [nɪ'fɛrɪ·əs] *adj* scélérat
negate ['nɛget], [nɪ'get] *tr* invalider; nier
negation [nɪ'geʃən] *s* négation *f*
negative ['nɛgətɪv] *adj* négatif ‖ *s* (*opinion*) négative *f*; (gram) négation *f*; (phot) négatif *m*
neglect [nɪ'glɛkt] *s* négligence *f* ‖ *tr* négliger; **to neglect to** négliger de
négligée or **negligee** [,nɛglɪ'ʒe] *s* négligé *m*, robe *f* de chambre
negligence ['nɛglɪdʒəns] *s* négligence *f*
negligent ['nɛglɪdʒənt] *adj* négligent
negligible ['nɛglɪdʒɪbəl] *adj* négligeable
negotiable [nɪ'goʃɪ·əbəl] *adj* négociable
negotiate [nɪ'goʃɪ·et] *tr & intr* négocier
negotiation [nɪ,goʃɪ'eʃən] *s* négociation *f*
negotiator [nɪ'goʃɪ,etər] *s* négociateur *m*
Ne·gro ['nigro] *adj* noir, nègre ‖ *s* (*pl* -groes) noir *m*, nègre *m*
neigh [ne] *s* hennissement *m* ‖ *intr* hennir
neighbor ['nebər] *adj* voisin ‖ *s* voisin *m*; (fig) prochain *m* ‖ *tr* avoisiner ‖ *intr* être voisin
neigh'bor·hood' *s* voisinage *m*; **in the neighborhood of** aux environs de; (*approximately, about*) (coll) environ
neighborliness ['nebərlɪnɪs] *s* bon voisinage *m*
neighborly ['nebərli] *adj* bon voisin
neither ['niðər], ['naɪðər] *adj indef* ni, e.g., **neither one of us** ni l'un ni

l'autre ‖ *pron indef* ni, e.g., **neither** ni l'un ni l'autre ‖ *conj* ni; ni . . . non plus, e.g., **neither do I** ni moi non plus; **neither . . . nor** ni . . . ni
neme·sis ['nɛmɪsɪs] *s* (*pl* -ses [,siz]) juste châtiment *m*; **Nemesis** Némésis *f*
neologism [ni'ɑlə,dʒɪzəm] *s* néologisme *m*
neon ['ni·ɑn] *s* néon *m*
ne'on lamp' *s* lampe *f* au néon
ne'on sign' *s* réclame *f* lumineuse
neophyte ['ni·ə,faɪt] *s* néophyte *mf*
nephew ['nɛfju], ['nɛvju] *s* neveu *m*
neptunium [nɛp't(j)unɪ·əm] *s* neptunium *m*
Nero ['nɪro] *s* Néron *m*
nerve [nʌrv] *adj* nerveux ‖ *s* nerf *m*; audace *f*; **to get on s.o.'s nerves** porter sur les nerfs à qn; **to have a lot of nerve** avoir du toupet; **to have nerves of steel** avoir du nerf; **to lose one's nerve** avoir le trac
nerve' cen'ter *s* nœud *m* vital; (anat) centre *m* nerveux
nerve'-rack'ing *adj* énervant, agaçant
nervous ['nʌrvəs] *adj* nerveux
ner'vous break'down *s* épuisement *m* nerveux, dépression *f* nerveuse
nerv·y ['nʌrvi] *adj* (*comp* -ier; *super* -iest) nerveux, musclé; (coll) audacieux, culotté; (slang) dévergondé
nest [nɛst] *s* nid *m*; (*set of things fitting together*) jeu *m* ‖ *intr* se nicher
nest' egg' *s* nichet *m*; (fig) boursicot *m*, bas *m* de laine
nestle ['nɛsəl] *intr* se blottir, se nicher
nest' of ta'bles *s* table *f* gigogne
net [nɛt] *adj* net ‖ *s* filet *m*; (*for fishing; for catching birds*) nappe *f*; (tex) tulle *m* ‖ *v* (*pret & pp* **netted**; *ger* **netting**) *tr* (*a profit*) réaliser
Netherlander ['nɛðər,lændər], ['nɛðərləndər] *s* Néerlandais *m*
Netherlands ['nɛðərləndz] *s*—**The Netherlands** les Pays-Bas *mpl*
nettle ['nɛtəl] *s* ortie *f* ‖ *tr* piquer au vif
net'work' *s* réseau *m*; (rad, telv) chaîne *f*, réseau
neuralgia [n(j)u'rældʒə] *s* névralgie *f*
neuro·sis [n(j)u'rosɪs] *s* (*pl* -ses [siz]) névrose *f*
neurotic [n(j)u'rɑtɪk] *adj & s* névrosé *m*
neuter ['n(j)utər] *adj & s* neutre *m*
neutral ['n(j)utrəl] *adj* neutre ‖ *s* neutre *m*; (*gear*) point *m* mort
neutrality [n(j)u'trælɪti] *s* neutralité *f*
neutralize ['n(j)utrə,laɪz] *tr* neutraliser
neutron ['n(j)utrɑn] *s* neutron *m*
neu'tron bomb' *s* bombe *f* à neutrons
never ['nɛvər] *adv* jamais §90B; ne . . . jamais §90, e.g., **he never talks** il ne parle jamais
nev'er·more' *adv* ne . . . plus jamais ‖ *interj* jamais plus!, plus jamais!
nev'er·the·less' *adv* néanmoins
new [n(j)u] *adj* (*unused*) neuf; (*other, additional, different*) nouveau (before noun); (*recent*) nouveau (after noun); (*inexperienced*) novice; (*wine*)

jeune; **what's new?** quoi de nouveau?, quoi de neuf?

new'born' *adj* nouveau-né

new'born child' *s* nouveau-né *m*

New'cas'tle *s*—**to carry coals to Newcastle** porter de l'eau à la rivière

newcomer ['n(j)u‚kʌmər] *s* nouveau venu *m*

New' Cov'enant *s* (Bib) nouvelle alliance *f*

newel ['n(j)u‧əl] *s* (*of winding stairs*) noyau *m*; (*post at end of stair rail*) pilastre *m*

New' Eng'land *s* Nouvelle-Angleterre *f*; la Nouvelle-Angleterre

newfangled ['n(j)u‚fæŋɡəld] *adj* à la dernière mode, du dernier cri

Newfoundland ['n(j)ufənd‚lænd] *s* Terre-Neuve *f*; **in** or **to Newfoundland** à Terre-Neuve ‖ [n(j)u'faʊndlənd] *s* (*dog*) terre-neuve *m*

newly ['n(j)uli] *adv* nouvellement

new'ly‧wed' *s* nouveau marié *m*

new' moon' *s* nouvelle lune *f*

newness ['n(j)unɪs] *s* nouveauté *f*

New' Or'leans ['ɔrlɪ‧ənz] *s* la Nouvelle-Orléans

news [n(j)uz] *s* nouvelles *fpl*; **a news item** un fait-divers; **a piece of news** une nouvelle

news' a'gency *s* agence *f* d'information, agence de presse; agence à journaux

news'beat' *s* exclusivité *f*

news'boy' *s* vendeur *m* de journaux

news' bul'letin *s* bulletin *m* d'actualités

news'cast' *s* journal *m* parlé; journal télévisé

news'cast'er *s* reporter *m* de la radio

news' con'ference *s* conférence *f* de presse

news' cov'erage *s* reportage *m*

news'deal'er *s* marchand *m* de journaux

news' ed'itor *s* rédacteur *m* publicitaire

news'let'ter *s* circulaire *f* publicitaire

news'man' *s* (*pl* **-men'**) journaliste *m*; (*dealer*) marchand *m* de journaux

New' South' Wales' *s* la Nouvelle-Galles du Sud

news'pa'per *adj* journalistique ‖ *s* journal *m*

news'paper clip'ping *s* coupure *f* de presse

news'paper‧man' *s* (*pl* **-men'**) journaliste *m*; (*dealer*) marchand *m* de journaux

news'paper rack' *s* casier *m* à journaux

news'paper se'rial *s* feuilleton *m*

news'print' *s* papier *m* journal

news'reel' *s* actualités *fpl*

news'room' *s* salle *f* de rédaction

news'stand' *s* kiosque *m*

news'week'ly *s* (*pl* **-lies**) hebdomadaire *m*

news'wor'thy *adj* d'actualité

New' Tes'tament *s* Nouveau Testament *m*

New' Year's' Day' *s* le jour de l'an

New' Year's' Eve' *s* la Saint-Sylvestre

New' Year's' greet'ings *spl* souhaits *mpl* de nouvel An

New' Year's' resolu'tion *s* résolution *f* de nouvel An

New' York' [jɔrk] *adj* newyorkais ‖ *s* New York *m*

New' York'er ['jɔrkər] *s* newyorkais *m*

next [nɛkst] *adj* (*in time*) prochain, suivant; (*in place*) voisin; (*first in the period which follows*) prochain (before noun), e.g., **the next time** la prochaine fois; (*following the present time*) prochain (after noun), e.g., **next week** la semaine prochaine; **next to** à côté de ‖ *adv* après, ensuite; la prochaine fois; **who comes next?** à qui le tour? ‖ *interj* au premier de ces messieurs!, au suivant!

next'-door' *adj* d'à côté, voisin ‖ **next'-door'** *adv* à côté; **next-door to** à côté de; à côté de chez

next' of kin' *s* (*pl* **next of kin**) proche parent *m*

Niag'ara Falls' [naɪ'æɡərə] *s* les chutes *fpl* du Niagara

nib [nɪb] *s* pointe *f*; (*of pen*) bec *m*

nibble ['nɪbəl] *s* grignotement *m*; (*on fish line*) touche *f*; (fig) morceau *m* ‖ *tr & intr* grignoter

nice [naɪs] *adj* agréable, gentil, aimable; (*distinction*) subtil, fin; (*weather*) beau; **nice and . . .** (coll) très; **not nice** (coll) vilain

nicely ['naɪsli] *adv* bien; avec délicatesse

nice‧ty ['naɪsəti] *s* (*pl* **-ties**) précision *f*; (*subtlety*) finesse *f*

niche [nɪtʃ] *s* niche *f*; (*job, position*) place *f*, poste *m*

nick [nɪk] *s* (*e.g., on china*) brèche *f*; **in the nick of time** à point nommé, à pic ‖ *tr* ébrécher; (*for money, favors*) (slang) cramponner

nickel ['nɪkəl] *s* (*metal*) nickel *m*; (*coin*) pièce *f* de cinq sous ‖ *tr* nickeler

nick'el plate' *s* nickelure *f*

nick'el-plate' *tr* nickeler

nicknack ['nɪk‚næk] *s* colifichet *m*

nick'name' *s* sobriquet *m*, surnom *m* ‖ *tr* donner un sobriquet à, surnommer

nicotine ['nɪkə‚tin] *s* nicotine *f*

niece [nis] *s* nièce *f*

nif‧ty ['nɪfti] *adj* (*comp* **-tier;** *super* **-tiest**) (slang) coquet, pimpant

niggard ['nɪɡərd] *adj & s* avare *mf*

night [naɪt] *s* nuit *f*; (*evening*) soir *m*; **last night** (*night that has just passed*) cette nuit; (*last evening*) hier soir; **night before last** avant-hier soir

night'cap' *s* bonnet *m* de nuit, casque *m* à mèche; (*drink*) posset *m*

night' club' *s* boîte *f* de nuit

night'fall' *s* tombée *f* de la nuit

night'gown' *s* chemise *f* de nuit

night'hawk' *s* noctambule *mf*; (orn) engoulevent *m*

nightingale ['naɪtən‚ɡel] *s* rossignol *m*

night'latch' *s* serrure *f* à ressort

night' light' *s* veilleuse *f*

night'long' *adj* de toute la nuit ‖ *adv* pendant toute la nuit

nightly ['naɪtli] *adj* nocturne; de chaque nuit || *adv* nocturnement; chaque nuit

night'mare' *s* cauchemar *m*

nightmarish ['naɪt,merɪʃ] *adj* (coll) cauchemardeux

night' owl' *s* (coll) noctambule *mf*

night' school' *s* cours *mpl* du soir

night'shade' *s* morelle *f*

night' shift' *s* équipe *f* de nuit

night' watch'man *s* (*pl* -men) veilleur *m* de nuit

nihilism ['naɪ·ɪ,lɪzəm] *s* nihilisme *m*

nil [nɪl] *s* rien *m*

Nile [naɪl] *s* Nil *m*

nimble ['nɪmbəl] *adj* agile, leste; (*mind*) délié

nim·bus ['nɪmbəs] *s* (*pl* -buses or -bi [baɪ]) nimbe *m*, auréole *f*; (meteo) nimbus *m*

nincompoop ['nɪnkəm,pup] *s* nigaud *m*

nine [naɪn] *adj* & *pron* neuf || *s* neuf *m*; **nine o'clock** neuf heures

nine'pins' *s* quilles *fpl*

nineteen ['naɪn'tin] *adj, pron,* & *s* dix-neuf *m*

nineteenth ['naɪn'tinθ] *adj* & *pron* dix-neuvième (*masc, fem*); **the Nineteenth** dix-neuf, e.g., **John the Nineteenth** Jean dix-neuf || *s* dix-neuvième *m*; **the nineteenth** (*in dates*) le dix-neuf

ninetieth ['naɪntɪ·ɪθ] *adj* & *pron* quatre-vingt-dixième (*masc, fem*) || *s* quatre-vingt-dixième *m*

nine·ty ['naɪntɪ] *adj* & *pron* quatre-vingt-dix || *s* (*pl* -ties) quatre-vingt-dix *m*

nine'ty-first' *adj* & *pron* quatre-vingt-onzième (*masc, fem*) || *s* quatre-vingt-onzième *m*

nine'ty-one' *adj, pron,* & *s* quatre-vingt-onze *m*

ninth [naɪnθ] *adj* & *pron* neuvième (*masc, fem*); **the Ninth** neuf, e.g., **John the Ninth** Jean neuf || *s* neuvième *m*; **the ninth** (*in dates*) le neuf

nip [nɪp] *s* pincement *m*, petite morsure *f*; (*of cold weather*) morsure; (*of liquor*) goutte *f* || *v* (*pret* & *pp* **nipped;** *ger* **nipping**) *tr* pincer, donner une petite morsure à; **to nip in the bud** tuer dans l'œuf || *intr* (coll) biberonner, picoler

nipple ['nɪpəl] *s* mamelon *m*; (*of nursing bottle*) tétine *f*; (mach) raccord *m*

nip·py ['nɪpi] *adj* (*comp* -pier; *super* -piest) piquant; (*cold*) vif; (Brit) leste, rapide

nirvana [nɪr'vɑnə] *s* le nirvâna

nit [nɪt] *s* pou *m*; (*egg*) lente *f*

niter ['naɪtər] *s* nitrate *m* de potasse; nitrate de soude

nitrate ['naɪtret] *s* azotate *m*, nitrate *m*; (*fertilizer*) engrais *m* nitraté || *tr* nitrater

nitric ['naɪtrɪk] *adj* azotique, nitrique

nitrogen ['naɪtrədʒən] *s* azote *m*

nitroglycerin [,naɪtrə'glɪsərɪn] *s* nitroglycérine *f*

nitrous ['naɪtrəs] *adj* azoteux

ni'trous ox'ide *s* oxyde *m* azoteux, protoxyde *m* d'azote

nit'wit' *s* (coll) imbécile *mf*

no [no] *adj indef* aucun, nul, pas de §90B; **no admittance** entrée *f* interdite; **no answer** pas de réponse; **no comment!** rien à dire!; **no go** or **no soap** (coll) pas mèche *f*; **no kidding** (coll) blague *f* à part; **no littering** défense *f* de déposer des ordures; **no loitering** vagabondage *m* interdit; **no parking** stationnement *m* interdit; **no place** nulle part; **no place else** nulle part ailleurs; **no shooting** chasse *f* réservée; **no smoking** défense de fumer; **no thoroughfare** circulation *f* interdite, passage *m* interdit; **no use** inutile; **with no** sans || *s* non *m* || *adv* non; **no good** vil; **no longer** ne . . . plus §90, e.g., **he no longer works here** il ne travaille plus ici; **no more** ne . . . plus §90, e.g., **he has no more** il n'en a plus; **no more** . . . (or *comp* in -er) **than** ne . . . pas plus . . . que, e.g., **she is no happier than he** elle n'est pas plus heureuse que lui

No'ah's Ark' ['no·əz] *s* l'arche *f* de Noé

nobili·ty [no'bɪlɪti] *s* (*pl* -ties) noblesse *f*

noble ['nobəl] *adj* & *s* noble *mf*

no'ble·man *s* (*pl* -men) noble *m*

nobleness ['nobəlnɪs] *s* noblesse *f*

nobod·y ['no,bɑdi], ['nobədi] *s* (*pl* -ies) nullité *f* || *pron indef* personne; ne . . . personne §90, e.g., **I see nobody there** je n'y vois personne; personne ne, nul ne §90, e.g., **nobody knows it** personne ne le sait, nul ne le sait

nocturnal [nɑk'tʌrnəl] *adj* nocturne

nocturne ['nɑktʌrn] *s* nocturne *m*

nod [nɑd] *s* signe *m* de tête; (*greeting*) inclination *f* de tête || *v* (*pret* & *pp* **nodded;** *ger* **nodding**) *tr* (*the head*) incliner; **to nod assent** faire un signe d'assentiment || *intr* (*with sleep*) dodeliner de la tête; (*to greet*) incliner la tête

node [nod] *s* nœud *m*

noise [nɔɪz] *s* bruit *m* || *tr* (*a rumor*) ébruiter

noiseless ['nɔɪzlɪs] *adj* silencieux

nois·y ['nɔɪzi] *adj* (*comp* -ier; *super* -iest) bruyant

nomad ['nomæd] *adj* & *s* nomade *mf*

no' man's' land' *s* région *f* désolée; (mil) zone *f* neutre

nominal ['nɑmɪnəl] *adj* nominal

nominate ['nɑmɪ,net] *tr* désigner; (*to appoint*) nommer

nomination [,nɑmɪ'neʃən] *s* désignation *f*, investiture *f*

nominative ['nɑmɪnətɪv] *adj* & *s* nominatif *m*

nominee [,nɑmɪ'ni] *s* désigné *m*, candidat *m*

nonbelligerent [,nɑnbə'lɪdʒərənt] *adj* & *s* non-belligérant *m*

nonbreakable [nɑn'brekəbəl] *adj* incassable

nonchalant ['nɑnʃələnt], (,nɑnʃə'lɑnt] *adj* nonchalant
noncom ['nɑn,kɑm] *s* (coll) sous-off *m*
noncombatant [nɑn'kɑmbətənt] *adj* & *s* non-combattant *m*
noncommissioned [,nɑnkə'mɪʃənd] *adj* non breveté
non'commis'sioned of'ficer *s* sous-officier *m*
noncommittal [,nɑnkə'mɪtəl] *adj* évasif, réticent
nonconductor [,nɑnkən'dʌktər] *s* nonconducteur *m*, mauvais conducteur *m*
nonconformist [,nɑnkən'fɔrmɪst] *adj* & *s* non-conformiste *mf*
nondenominational [,nɑndɪ,nɑmɪ'neʃənəl] *adj* indépendant, qui ne fait partie d'aucune secte religieuse; (*school*) laïque
nondescript ['nɑndɪ,skrɪpt] *adj* indéfinissable, inclassable
none [nʌn] *pron indef* aucun §90B; (*nobody*) personne, nul §90B; ne . . . aucun, ne . . . nul §90; n'en . . . pas, e.g., **I have none** je n'en ai pas; (*as a response on the blank of an official form*) néant ‖ *adv*—**to be none the wiser** ne pas en être plus sage
nonenti·ty [nɑn'entɪti] *s* (*pl* -ties) nullité *f*
none'such' *s* nonpareil *m*; (*apple*) nonpareille *f*; (bot) lupuline *f*, minette *f*
nonfiction [nɑn'fɪkʃən] *s* littérature *f* autre que le roman
nonfulfillment [,nɑnfʊl'fɪlmənt] *s* inaccomplissement *m*
nonintervention [,nɑnɪntər'venʃən] *s* non-intervention *f*
nonmetal ['nɑn,metəl] *s* métalloïde *m*
nonpartisan [nɑn'pɑrtɪzən] *adj* neutre, indépendant
nonpayment [nɑn'pemənt] *s* non-paiement *m*
non·plus ['nɑnplʌs], [nɑn'plʌs] *s* perplexité *f* ‖ *v* (*pret* & *pp* -plused or -plussed; *ger* -plusing or -plussing) *tr* déconcerter, dérouter
nonresident [nɑn'rezɪdənt] *adj* & *s* non-résident *m*
nonresidential [nɑn,rezɪ'denʃəl] *adj* commercial
nonreturnable [,nɑnrɪ'tʌrnəbəl] *adj* (*bottle*) perdu
nonscientific [nɑn,saɪ·ən'tɪfɪk] *adj* anti-scientifique
nonsectarian [,nɑnsək'terɪ·ən] *adj* non-sectaire; qui ne fait partie d'aucune secte religieuse; (*education*) laïque
nonsense ['nɑnsens] *s* bêtise *f*, non-sens *m*
nonskid ['nɑn'skɪd] *adj* antidérapant
nonstop ['nɑn'stɑp] *adj* & *adv* sans arrêt; sans escale
nonviolence [nɑn'vaɪ·ələns] *s* non-violence *f*
noodle ['nudəl] *s* nouille *f*; (*fool*) (slang) niais *m*; (*head*) (slang) tronche *f*
nook [nʊk] *s* coin *m*, recoin *m*
noon [nun] *s* midi *m*

no' one' or **no'-one'** *pron indef* personne §90B; ne . . personne §90, e.g., **I see no one there** je n'y vois personne; personne ne, nul ne §90B, e.g., **no one knows it** personne ne le sait, nul ne le sait; **no one else** personne d'autre
noon'time' *s* midi *m*
noose [nus] *s* nœud *m* coulant; (*for hanging*) corde *f*, hart *f*
nor [nɔr] *conj* ni
norm [nɔrm] *s* norme *f*
normal ['nɔrməl] *adj* normal
Norman ['nɔrmən] *adj* normand ‖ *s* (*dialect*) normand *m*; (*person*) Normand *m*
Normandy ['nɔrməndi] *s* Normandie *f*; la Normandie
Norse [nɔrs] *adj* & *s* norrois *m*
Norse'man *s* (*pl* -men) Norrois *m*
north [nɔrθ] *adj* & *s* nord *m* ‖ *adv* au nord, vers le nord
North' Af'rican *adj* nord-africain ‖ *s* Nord-Africain *m*
north'east' *adj* & *s* nord-est *m*
north'east'er *s* vent *m* du nord-est
northern ['nɔrðərn] *adj* septentrional, du nord
North' Kore'a *s* Corée *f* du Nord; la Corée du Nord
North' Kore'an *adj* nord-coréen ‖ *s* (*person*) Nord-Coréen *m*
North' Pole' *s* pôle *m* Nord
northward ['nɔrθwərd] *adv* vers le nord
north'west' *adj* & *s* nord-ouest *m*
north' wind' *s* bise *f*
Norway ['nɔrwe] *s* Norvège *f*; la Norvège
Norwegian [nɔr'widʒən] *adj* norvégien ‖ *s* (*language*) norvégien *m*; (*person*) Norvégien *m*
nose [noz] *s* nez *m*; (*of certain animals*) museau *m*; **to blow one's nose** se moucher; **to have a nose for** avoir le flair de; **to keep one's nose to the grindstone** travailler sans relâche, buriner; **to lead by the nose** mener par le bout du nez; **to look down one's nose at** faire un nez à; **to thumb one's nose at** faire un pied de nez à; **to turn up one's nose at** faire la nique à; **under the nose of** à la barbe de ‖ *tr* flairer, sentir; **to nose out** flairer, dépister ‖ *intr*—**to nose about** fouiner; **to nose over** capoter
nose' bag' *s* musette *f*
nose'bleed' *s* saignement *m* de nez
nose' cone' *s* ogive *f*
nose' dive' *s* piqué *m*
nose'-dive' *intr* descendre en piqué
nose' drops' *spl* instillations *fpl* nasales
nose'gay' *s* bouquet *m*
nose' glass'es *spl* pince-nez *m*
nostalgia [nɑ'stældʒə] *s* nostalgie *f*
nostalgic [nɑ'stældʒɪk] *adj* nostalgique
nostril ['nɑstrɪl] *s* narine *f*; (*of horse, cow, etc.*) naseau *m*
nostrum ['nɑstrəm] *s* (*quack and his medicine*) orviétan *m*; panacée *f*
nos·y ['nozi] *adj* (*comp* -ier; *super* -iest) fureteur, indiscret

not [nɑt] *adv* ne §87, §90C; ne ... pas §90, e.g., **he is not here** il n'est pas ici; non, non pas; **not at all** pas du tout; **not much** peu de chose; **not one** pas un; **not that** non pas que; **not yet** pas encore; **to think not** croire que non

notable ['notəbəl] *adj* & *s* notable *m*

notarize ['notə,raɪz] *tr* authentiquer

notarized *adj* authentique

nota·ry ['notəri] *s* (*pl* **-ries**) notaire *m*

notation [no'teʃən] *s* notation *f*

notch [nɑtʃ] *s* coche *f*, entaille *f*; (*of a belt*) cran *m*; (*of a wheel*) dent *f*; (*gap in a mountain*) brèche *f* ‖ *tr* encocher, entailler

note [not] *s* note *f*; (*short letter*) billet *m*; **notes** commentaires *mpl*; (*of a speech*) feuillets *mpl*; **note to the reader** avis *m* au lecteur ‖ *tr* noter; **to note down** prendre note de

note'book' *s* cahier *m*; (*bill book, memo pad, etc.*) carnet *m*, calepin *m*

note'book cov'er *s* protège-cahier *m*

noted ['notɪd] *adj* éminent, distingué, connu

note' pad' *s* bloc-notes *m*

note'wor'thy *adj* notable, remarquable

nothing ['nʌθɪŋ] *s* rien *m* ‖ *pron indef* rien §90B; ne ... rien §90, e.g., **I have nothing** je n'ai rien; **nothing at all** rien du tout; **nothing doing!** (slang) pas mèche! ‖ *adv*—**nothing less than** rien moins que

nothingness ['nʌθɪŋnɪs] *s* néant *m*

notice ['notɪs] *s* (*warning; advertisement*) avis *m*; (*in a newspaper*) annonce *f*; (*observation*) attention *f*; (*of dismissal*) congé *m*; **at short notice** à bref délai; **to take notice of** faire attention à; **until further notice** jusqu'à nouvel ordre ‖ *tr* s'apercevoir de, remarquer

noticeable ['notɪsəbəl] *adj* apparent, perceptible

notification [,notɪfɪ'keʃən] *s* notification *f*, avertissement *m*

noti·fy ['notɪ,faɪ] *v* (*pret* & *pp* **-fied**) *tr* aviser, avertir

notion ['noʃən] *s* notion *f*; intention *f*; **notions** mercerie *f*; **to have a notion to** avoir dans l'idée, avoir envie de

notorie·ty [,notə'raɪ·ɪti] *s* (*pl* **-ties**) renom *m* déshonorant, triste notoriété *f*

notorious [no'torɪ·əs] *adj* insigne, mal famé; (*person*) d'une triste notoriété

no'-trump' *adj* & *s* sans-atout *m*

notwithstanding [,nɑtwɪð'stændɪŋ], [,nɑtwɪθ'stændɪŋ] *adv* nonobstant, néanmoins ‖ *prep* malgré ‖ *conj* quoique

nought [nɔt] *s* var of **naught**

noun [naʊn] *s* nom *m*

nourish ['nʌrɪʃ] *tr* nourrir

nourishment ['nʌrɪʃmənt] *s* nourriture *f*, alimentation *f*

Nova Scotia [,novə'skoʃə] *s* Nouvelle-Écosse *f*; la Nouvelle-Écosse

novel ['nɑvəl] *adj* nouveau; original, bizarre ‖ *s* roman *m*

novelette [,nɑvəl'ɛt] *s* nouvelle *f*, bluette *f*

novelist ['nɑvəlɪst] *s* romancier *m*

novel·ty ['nɑvəlti] *s* (*pl* **-ties**) nouveauté *f*; **novelties** bibelots *mpl*, souvenirs *mpl*

November [no'vɛmbər] *s* novembre *m*

novice ['nɑvɪs] *s* novice *mf*

novitiate [no'vɪʃɪ·ɪt] *s* noviciat *m*

novocaine ['novə,ken] *s* novocaïne *f*

now [naʊ] *adv* maintenant; just **now** tout à l'heure, naguère; **now and again** de temps en temps ‖ *interj* allez-y!

nowadays ['naʊ·ə,dez] *adv* de nos jours

no'way' or **no'ways'** *adv* en aucune façon

no'where' *adv* nulle part; ne ... nulle part; **nowhere else** nulle autre part, nulle part ailleurs

noxious ['nɑkʃəs] *adj* nocif

nozzle ['nɑzəl] *s* (*of hose*) ajutage *m*; (*of fire hose*) lance *f*; (*of sprinkling can*) pomme *f*; (*of candlestick*) douille *f*; (*of pitcher; of gas burner*) bec *m*; (*of carburetor*) buse *f*; (*of vacuum cleaner*) suceur *m*; (*nose*) (slang) museau *m*

nth [ɛnθ] *adj* énième, nième; **for the nth time** pour la énième fois; **the nth power** la énième puissance

nuance [nju'ɑns], ['nju·ɑns] *s* nuance *f*

nub [nʌb] *s* protubérance *f*; (*piece*) petit morceau *m*; (slang) nœud *m*

nuclear ['n(j)uklɪ·ər] *adj* nucléaire

nu'clear pow'er plant' *s* centrale *f* nucléaire

nu'clear test' ban' *s* interdiction *f* des essais nucléaires

nucleolus [n(j)u'kli·ələs] *s* nucléole *m*

nucleon ['n(j)ukli·ɑn] *s* nucléon *m*

nucle·us ['n(j)ukli·əs] *s* (*pl* **-i** [,aɪ] or **-uses**) noyau *m*

nude [n(j)ud] *adj* nu ‖ *s* nu *m*; **in the nude** nu, sans vêtements

nudge [nʌdʒ] *s* coup *m* de coude ‖ *tr* pousser du coude

nudist ['n(j)udɪst] *adj* & *s* nudiste *mf*

nudity ['n(j)udɪti] *s* nudité *f*

nugget ['nʌgɪt] *s* pépite *f*

nuisance ['n(j)usəns] *s* ennui *m*; (*person*) peste *f*

null [nʌl] *adj* indef nul

null' and void' *adj* nul et non avenu

nulli·fy ['nʌlɪ,faɪ] *v* (*pret* & *pp* **-fied**) *tr* annuler

numb [nʌm] *adj* engourdi; **to grow numb** s'engourdir ‖ *tr* engourdir

number ['nʌmbər] *s* numéro *m*, chiffre *m*; (*quantity*) nombre *m*; **wrong number** faux numéro ‖ *tr* numéroter; nombrer; (*to amount to*) s'élever à, compter; **to number among** compter parmi

numberless ['nʌmbərlɪs] *adj* innombrable

numbness ['nʌmnɪs] *s* engourdissement *m*

numeral ['n(j)umərəl] *adj* numéral ‖ *s* numéro *m*, chiffre *m*

numeration [ˌn(j)umə'reʃən] *s* numération *f*
numerical [n(j)u'mɛrɪkəl] *adj* numérique
numerous ['n(j)umərəs] *adj* nombreux
numismatic [ˌn(j)umɪz'mætɪk] *adj* numismatique ‖ **numismatics** *s* numismatique *f*
numskull ['nʌmˌskʌl] *s* (coll) sot *m*
nun [nʌn] *s* religieuse *f*, nonne *f*
nunci·o ['nʌnʃɪˌo] *s* (*pl* -os) nonce *m*
nuptial ['nʌpʃəl] *adj* nuptial ‖ **nuptials** *spl* noces *fpl*
nurse [nʌrs] *s* infirmière *f*; (*male nurse*) infirmier *m*; (*wet nurse*) nourrice *f*; (*practical nurse*) garde-malade *mf*; (*children's nurse*) bonne *f* d'enfant, nurse *f* ‖ *tr* soigner; (*hopes; plants; a baby*) nourrir
nurse'maid' *s* bonne *f* d'enfant
nurser·y ['nʌrsəri] *s* (*pl* -ies) chambre *f* des enfants; (*for day care*) crèche *f*, pouponnière *f*; (*hort*) pépinière *f*
nurs'ery·man *s* (*pl* -men) pépiniériste *m*
nurs'ery school' *s* maternelle *f*
nursing ['nʌrsɪŋ] *s* soins *mpl*; (*profession*) métier *m* d'infirmière; (*by mother*) nourriture *f*
nurs'ing bot'tle *s* biberon *m*
nurs'ing home' *s* maison *f* de repos, maison de santé
nursling ['nʌrslɪŋ] *s* nourrisson *m*

nurture ['nʌrtʃər] *s* éducation *f*; nourriture *f* ‖ *tr* élever; (*to nurse*) nourrir
nut [nʌt] *s* noix *f*, e.g., **Brazil nut** noix du Brésil; (*of walnut tree*) noix; (*of filbert*) noisette *f*; (*to screw on a bolt*) écrou *m*; (slang) extravagant *m*; **to be nuts about** (slang) être follement épris de
nut'crack'er *s* casse-noisettes *m*, casse-noix *m*; (orn) casse-noix
nut'hatch' *s* sittelle *f*
nut'meat' *s* graine *f* de fruit sec, graine de noix
nutmeg ['nʌtˌmɛg] *s* (*seed or spice*) noix *f* muscade, muscade *f*; (*tree*) muscadier *m*
nutriment ['n(j)utrɪmənt] *s* nourriture *f*
nutrition [n(j)u'trɪʃən] *s* nutrition *f*
nutritious [n(j)u'trɪʃəs] *adj* nutritif
nut'shell' *s* coquille *f* de noix; **in a nutshell** en un mot
nut·ty ['nʌti] *adj* (*comp* -tier; *super* -tiest) à goût de noisette, à goût de noix; (slang) cinglé
nuzzle ['nʌzəl] *tr* fouiller du groin ‖ *intr* fouiller du groin; s'envelopper chaudement; **to nuzzle up to** se pelotonner contre
nylon ['naɪlɑn] *s* nylon *m*; **nylons** bas *mpl* de nylon, bas nylon
nymph [nɪmf] *s* nymphe *f*

O

O, o [o] *s* XVᵉ lettre de l'alphabet
oaf [of] *s* lourdaud *m*, rustre *m*
oak [ok] *s* chêne *m*
oaken ['okən] *adj* de chêne, en chêne
oakum ['okəm] *s* étoupe *f*
oar [or], [ɔr] *s* rame *f*, aviron *m*
oar'lock' *s* tolet *m*
oars'man' *s* (*pl* -men') rameur *m*
oa·sis [o'esɪs] *s* (*pl* -ses [siz]) oasis *f*
oat [ot] *s* avoine *f*; **oats** (*edible grain*) avoine; **to feel one's oats** être imbu de sa personne; **to sow one's wild oats** (coll) jeter sa gourme
oat'meal' *s* farine *f* d'avoine; (*breakfast food*) flocons *mpl* d'avoine
obbligato [ˌɑblɪ'gɑto] *s* accompagnement *m* à volonté
obdurate ['ɑbdjərɪt] *adj* obstiné, endurci
obedience [o'bidɪ·əns] *s* obéissance *f*
obedient [o'bidɪ·ənt] *adj* obéissant
obeisance [o'besəns], [o'bisəns] *s* hommage *m*; (*greeting*) révérence *f*
obelisk ['ɑbəlɪsk] *s* obélisque *m*
obese [o'bis] *adj* obèse
obesity [o'bisɪti] *s* obésité *f*

obey [ə'be] *tr* obéir (with *dat*); **to be obeyed** être obéi ‖ *intr* obéir
obfuscate [ɑb'fʌsket], ['ɑbfəsˌket] *tr* offusquer
obituar·y [o'bɪtʃu·ˌɛri] *adj* nécrologique ‖ *s* (*pl* -ies) nécrologie *f*
object ['ɑbdʒɪkt] *s* objet *m* ‖ [ɑb'dʒɛkt] *tr* objecter, rétorquer ‖ *intr* faire des objections; **to object to** s'opposer à, avoir des objections contre
objection [ɑb'dʒɛkʃən] *s* objection *f*
objectionable [ɑb'dʒɛkʃənəbəl] *adj* répréhensible; répugnant, désagréable
objective [ɑb'dʒɛktɪv] *adj* & *s* objectif *m*
obligate ['ɑblɪˌget] *tr* obliger
obligation [ˌɑblɪ'geʃən] *s* obligation *f*
obligatory ['ɑblɪgəˌtori], [ə'blɪgəˌtori] *adj* obligatoire
oblige [ə'blaɪdʒ] *tr* obliger; **much obliged** bien obligé, très reconnaissant; **to be obliged to** être obligé de
obliging [ə'blaɪdʒɪŋ] *adj* accommodant, obligeant
oblique [ə'blik], [ə'blaɪk] *adj* oblique
obliterate [ə'blɪtəˌret] *tr* effacer, oblitérer
oblivion [ə'blɪvɪ·ən] *s* oubli *m*
oblivious [ə'blɪvɪ·əs] *adj* oublieux
oblong ['ɑblɔŋ], ['ɑblɑŋ] *adj* oblong

obnoxious [əb'nɑkʃəs] *adj* odieux, désagréable
oboe ['obo] *s* hautbois *m*
oboist ['obo·ɪst] *s* hautboïste *mf*
obscene [ɑb'sin] *adj* obscène
obsceni·ty [ɑb'sɛnɪti], [ɑb'sinɪti] *s (pl -ties)* obscénité *f*
obscure [əb'skjʊr] *adj* obscur; *(vowel)* relâché, neutre
obscuri·ty [əb'skjʊrɪti] *s (pl -ties)* obscurité *f*
obsequies ['ɑbsɪkwiz] *spl* obsèques *fpl*
obsequious [əb'sikwɪ·əs] *adj* obséquieux
observance [əb'zʌrvəns] *s* observance *f*
observant [əb'zʌrvənt] *adj* observateur
observation [,ɑbzər've ʃən] *s* observation *f*
observato·ry [əb'zʌrvə,tori] *s (pl -ries)* observatoire *m*
observe [əb'zʌrv] *tr* observer; *(silence)* garder; *(a holiday)* célébrer; dire, remarquer
observer [əb'zʌrvər] *s* observateur *m*
obsess [əb'sɛs] *tr* obséder
obsession [əb'sɛʃən] *s* obsession *f*
obsolescent [,ɑbsə'lɛsənt] *adj* vieillissant
obsolete ['ɑbsəlit] *adj* désuet, vieilli; (gram) obsolète
obstacle ['ɑbstəkəl] *s* obstacle *m*
ob'stacle course' *s* champ *m* d'obstacles, piste *f* d'obstacles
obstetrical [ɑb'stɛtrɪkəl] *adj* obstétrique
obstetrics [ɑb'stɛtrɪks] *spl* obstétrique *f*
obstina·cy ['ɑbstɪnəsi] *s (pl -cies)* obstination *f*, entêtement *m*
obstinate ['ɑbstɪnɪt] *adj* obstiné
obstreperous [əb'strɛpərəs] *adj* turbulent
obstruct [əb'strʌkt] *tr* obstruer; *(movements)* empêcher, entraver
obstruction [əb'strʌkʃən] *s* obstruction *f*; *(on railroad tracks)* obstacle *m*; *(to movement)* empêchement *m*, entrave *f*
obtain [əb'ten] *tr* obtenir, se procurer || *intr* prévaloir
obtrusive [əb'trusɪv] *adj* importun, intrus
obtuse [əb't(j)us] *adj* obtus
obviate ['ɑbvɪ,et] *tr* obvier (with *dat*)
obvious ['ɑbvɪ·əs] *adj* évident
occasion [ə'keʒən] *s* occasion *f*; **on occasion** en de différentes occasions || *tr* occasionner
occasional [ə'keʒənəl] *adj* fortuit, occasionnel; *(verses)* de circonstance; *(showers)* épars; *(chair)* volant
occasionally [ə'keʒənəli] *adv* de temps en temps, occasionnellement
occident ['ɑksɪdənt] *s* occident *m*
occidental [,ɑksə'dɛntəl] *adj & s* occidental *m*
occlusion [ə'kluʒən] *s* occlusion *f*
occlusive [ə'klusɪv] *adj* occlusif || *s* occlusive *f*
occult [ə'kʌlt], ['ɑkʌlt] *adj* occulte
occupancy ['ɑkjəpənsi] *s* occupation *f*, habitation *f*
occupant ['ɑkjəpənt] *s* occupant *m*

occupation [,ɑkjə'pe ʃən] *s* occupation *f*
occupational [,ɑkjə'pe ʃənəl] *adj* professionnel; de métier
oc'cupa'tional ther'apy *s* thérapie *f* rééducative, réadaptation *f* fonctionnelle
occu·py ['ɑkjə,paɪ] *v (pret & pp -pied)* *tr* occuper; **to be occupied with** s'occuper de
oc·cur [ə'kʌr] *v (pret & pp -curred; ger -curring) intr* arriver, avoir lieu; *(to be found; to come to mind)* se présenter; **it occurs to me that** il me vient à l'esprit que
occurrence [ə'kʌrəns] *s* événement *m*; cas *m*, exemple *m*; **everyday occurrence** fait *m* journalier
ocean ['o ʃən] *s* océan *m*
oceanic [,o ʃɪ'ænɪk] *adj* océanique
o'cean lin'er *s* paquebot *m* transocéanique
ocher ['okər] *s* ocre *f*
o'clock [ə'klɑk] *adv*—**it is one o'clock** il est une heure; **it is two o'clock** est deux heures
octane ['ɑkten] *s* octane *m*
oc'tane num'ber *s* indice *m* d'octane
octave ['ɑktɪv], ['ɑktev] *s* octave *f*
October [ɑk'tobər] *s* octobre *m*
octo·pus ['ɑktəpəs] *s (pl -puses or -pi* [,paɪ]*)* pieuvre *f*, poulpe *m*
octoroon [,ɑktə'run] *s* octavon *m*
ocular ['ɑkjələr] *adj & s* oculaire *m*
oculist ['ɑkjəlɪst] *s* oculiste *mf*
odd [ɑd] *adj (number)* impair; *(that doesn't match)* dépareillé, déparié; *(queer)* bizarre, étrange; *(occasional)* divers; quelque, e.g., **three hundred odd horses** quelque trois cents chevaux; et quelques || **odds** *spl* chances *fpl*; *(disparity)* inégalité *f*; *(on a horse)* cote *f*; **at odds** en désaccord, en bisbille; **by all odds** sans aucun doute; **to be at odds with** être mal avec; **to give odds to** donner de l'avance à; **to set at odds** brouiller
oddi·ty ['ɑdɪti] *s (pl -ties)* bizarrerie *f*
odd' jobs' *spl* bricolage *m*, petits travaux *mpl*
odd' man' out' *s*—**to be odd man out** être en trop
odds' and ends' *spl* petits bouts *mpl*, bribes *fpl*; *(trinkets)* bibelots *mpl*; *(food)* restes *mpl*
ode [od] *s* ode *f*
odious ['odɪ·əs] *adj* odieux
odor ['odər] *s* odeur *f*; **to be in bad odor** être mal vu
odorless ['odərlɪs] *adj* inodore
Odyssey ['ɑdɪsi] *s* Odyssée *f*
Oedipus ['ɛdɪpəs], ['idəpəs] *s* Œdipe *m*
of [ɑv], [ʌv], [əʌ] *prep* de; à, e.g., **to think of** penser à; e.g., **to ask s.th. of s.o.** demander q.ch. à qn; en, e.g., **a doctor of medicine** un docteur en médecine; moins, e.g., **a quarter of two** deux heures moins le quart; entre, e.g., **he of all people** lui entre tous; d'entre, e.g., **five of them** cinq d'entre eux; par, e.g., **of necessity** par nécessité; en de, e.g., **made of**

wood en bois, de bois; (not translated), e.g., **the fifth of March** le cinq mars; e.g., **we often see her of a morning** nous la voyons souvent le matin

off [ɔf], [ɑf] *adj* mauvais, e.g., **off day** (*bad day*) mauvaise journée; libre, e.g., **off day** journée libre; de congé, e.g., **off day** jour de congé; (*account, sum*) inexact; (*meat*) avancé; (*electric current*) coupé; (*light*) éteint; (*radio; faucet*) fermé; (*street*) secondaire, transversal; (*distant*) éloigné, écarté || *adv* loin; à . . . de distance, e.g., **three kilometers off** à trois kilomètres de distance; parti, e.g., **they're off!** les voilà partis!; bas, e.g., **hats off!** chapeaux bas!; (*naut*) au large; (*theat*) à la cantonade || *prep* de; (*at a distance from*) éloigné de, écarté de; (*naut*) au large de, à la hauteur de; **from off** de dessous de

offal ['ɑfəl], ['ɔfəl] *s* (*of butchered meat*) abats *mpl*; (*refuse*) ordures *fpl*

off' and on' *adv* de temps en temps, par intervalles

off'beat' *adj* (slang) insolite, rare

off' chance' *s* chance *f* improbable

off'-col'or *adj* décoloré; (*e.g., story*) grivois, vert

offend [əˈfɛnd] *tr* offenser; **to be offended** s'offenser || *intr*—**to offend against** enfreindre

offender [əˈfɛndər] *s* offenseur *m*; (*criminal*) délinquant *m*, coupable *mf*

offense [əˈfɛns] *s* offense *f*; (law) délit *m*; **to take offense (at)** s'offenser (de)

offensive [əˈfɛnsɪv] *adj* offensant, blessant; (mil) offensif || *s* offensive *f*

offer ['ɔfər], ['ɑfər] *s* offre *f* || *tr* offrir; (*excuses; best wishes*) présenter; (*prayers*) adresser || *intr*—**to offer to** faire l'offre de; faire mine de, e.g., **he offered to fight** il a fait mine de se battre

offering ['ɔfərɪŋ], ['ɑfərɪŋ] *s* offre *f*; (eccl) offrande *f*

off'hand' *adj* improvisé; brusque || *adv* au pied levé; brusquement

office ['ɔfɪs], ['ɑfɪs] *s* fonction *f*, office *m*; (*in business, school, government*) bureau *m*; (*national agency*) office *m*; (*of lawyer*) étude *f*; (*of doctor*) cabinet *m*; **elective office** poste *m* électif; **good offices** bons offices; **to run for office** se présenter aux élections

of'fice boy' *s* coursier *m*, commissionnaire *m* de bureau

of'fice desk' *s* bureau *m* ministre

of'fice-hold'er *s* fonctionnaire *mf*

of'fice hours' *spl* heures *fpl* de bureau; (*of doctor, counselor, etc.*) heures de consultation

officer ['ɔfɪsər], ['ɑfɪsər] *s* (*of a company*) administrateur *m*, dirigeant *m*; (*of army, an order, a society, etc.*) officier *m*; (*police officer*) agent *m* de police, officier de police; **officer of the day** (mil) officier de service

of'ficer can'didate *s* élève-officier *m*

of'fice seek'er *s* solliciteur *m*

of'fice supplies' *spl* fournitures *fpl* de bureau, articles *mpl* de bureau

of'fice-supply' store' *s* papeterie *f*

of'fice work' *s* travail *m* de bureau

official [əˈfɪʃəl] *adj* officiel; (*e.g., stationery*) réglementaire || *s* fonctionnaire *mf*, officiel *m*; **officials** cadres *mpl*; (*executives*) dirigeants *mpl*

offi'cial board' *s* comité *m* directeur

officialese [ə,fɪʃəˈliz] *s* jargon *m* administratif

officiate [əˈfɪʃi,et] *intr* (eccl) officier; **to officiate as** exercer les fonctions de

officious [əˈfɪʃəs] *adj* trop empressé; **to be officious** faire l'officieux

offing ['ɔfɪŋ], ['ɑfɪŋ] *s*—**in the offing** au large; (fig) en perspective

off'-lim'its *adj* défendu; (public sign) défense d'entrer, entrée interdite; (mil) interdit aux troupes

off'-peak' heat'er *s* thermosiphon *m* à accumulation

off'print' *s* tiré *m* à part

off'-seas'on *s* morte-saison *f*

off'set' *s* compensation *f*; (typ) offset *m* || **off'set'** *v* (*pret & pp* -set; *ger* -setting) *tr* compenser

off'shoot' *s* rejeton *m*

off'shore' *adj* éloigné de la côte, du côté de la terre; (*wind*) de terre || *adv* au large, vers la haute mer

off'side' *adv* (sports) hors jeu

off'spring' *s* descendance *f*; (*descendant*) rejeton *m*, enfant *mf*; (*result*) conséquence *f*

off'stage' *adj* dans les coulisses || *adv* à la cantonade

off'-the-cuff' *adj* (coll) impromptu

off'-the-rec'ord *adj* confidentiel

often ['ɔfən], ['ɑfən] *adv* souvent; **how often?** combien de fois?; **tous les combien?; not often** rarement; **once too often** une fois de trop

ogive ['odʒaɪv], [oˈdʒaɪv] *s* ogive *f*

ogle ['ogəl] *tr* lancer une œillade à; (*to stare at*) dévisager

ogre ['ogər] *s* ogre *m*

ohm [om] *s* ohm *m*

oil [ɔɪl] *s* huile *f*; (*painting*) huile, peinture *f* à l'huile; **holy oil** huile sainte, saintes huiles; **to pour oil on troubled waters** calmer la tempête, verser de l'huile sur les plaies de qn; **to smell of midnight oil** sentir l'huile; **to strike oil** atteindre une nappe pétrolifère; (fig) trouver le filon || *tr* huiler; (*to bribe*) graisser la patte à || *intr* (naut) faire le plein de mazout

oil' burn'er *s* réchaud *m* à pétrole

oil'can' *s* bidon *m* d'huile, burette *f* d'huile

oil'cloth' *s* toile *f* cirée

oil' com'pany *s* société *f* pétrolière

oil'cup' *s* (mach) godet *m* graisseur

oil' drum' *s* bidon *m* d'huile

oil' field' *s* gisement *m* pétrolifère

oil' gauge' *s* jauge *f* de niveau d'huile

oil′ lamp′ s lampe f à huile, lampe à pétrole
oil′man′ s (pl **-men′**) (retailer) huilier m; (operator) pétrolier m
oil′ pump′ s pompe f à huile
oil′ stove′ s poêle m à mazout, fourneau m à pétrole
oil′ tank′er s pétrolier m, tanker m
oil′ well′ s puits m à pétrole
oil-y ['ɔɪli] adj (comp **-ier**; super **-iest**) huileux, oléagineux; (fig) onctueux
ointment ['ɔɪntmənt] s onguent m, pommade f
O.K. ['o'ke] (letterword) adj (coll) très bien, parfait ‖ s (coll) approbation f ‖ adv (coll) très bien ‖ v (pret & pp **O.K.'d**; ger **O.K.'ing**) tr (coll) approuver ‖ interj O.K.!, ça colle!
okra ['okrə] s gombo m, ketmie f comestible
old [old] adj vieux; (of former times) ancien; (wine) vieux; **any old** n'importe, e.g., **any old time** n'importe quand; quelconque, e.g., **any old book** un livre quelconque; **at . . . years old** à l'âge de . . . ans; **how old is . . .?** quel âge a . . .?; **of old** d'autrefois, de jadis; **to be . . . years old** avoir . . . ans
old′ age′ s vieillesse f, âge m avancé
old′-clothes′man′ s (pl **-men′**) fripier m
old′ coun′try s mère patrie f
Old′ Cov′enant s (Bib) ancienne alliance f
old′-fash′ioned adj démodé, suranné; (literary style) vieillot
old′ fo′gey or **old′ fo′gy** ['fogi] s (pl **-gies**) vieux bonhomme m, grime m
Old′ French′ s ancien français m
Old′ Glo′ry s le drapeau des États-Unis
old′ hag′ s vieille fée f
old′ hand′ s vieux routier m
old′ lad′y s vieille dame f; (coll) grand-mère f
old′ maid′ s vieille fille f
old′ mas′ter s grand maître m; œuvre f d'un grand maître
old′ moon′ s Lune f à son décours
old′ peo′ple's home′ s hospice m de vieillards
old′ salt′ s loup m de mer
old′ school′ s vieille école f, vieille roche f
oldster ['oldstər] s vieillard m, vieux m
Old′ Tes′tament s Ancien Testament m
old′-time′ adj du temps jadis, d'autrefois
old′-tim′er s (coll) vieux m de la vieille, vieux routier m
old′ wives′′ tale′ s conte m de bonne femme
Old Wom′an who lived′ in a shoe′ s mère f Gigogne
Old′ World′ s vieux monde m
old′-world′ adj de l'ancien monde; du vieux monde
oleander [ˌolɪ'ændər] s laurier-rose m
olfactory [al'fæktəri] adj olfactif
oligar·chy ['alɪˌgarki] s (pl **-chies**) oligarchie f

olive ['alɪv] adj olive; (complexion) olivâtre ‖ s olive f; (tree) olivier m
ol′ive branch′ s rameau m d'olivier
ol′ive grove′ s olivaie f
ol′ive oil′ s huile f d'olive
Oliver ['alɪvər] s Olivier m
ol′ive tree′ s olivier m
olympiad [o'lɪmpɪˌæd] s olympiade f
Olympian [o'lɪmpɪ·ən] adj olympien
Olympic [o'lɪmpɪk] adj olympique ‖ **Olympics** spl jeux mpl olympiques
omelet ['aməˌlet], ['amlɪt] s omelette f
omen ['omən] s augure m, présage m
ominous ['amɪnəs] adj de mauvais augure
omission [o'mɪʃən] s omission f
omit [o'mɪt] v (pret & pp **omitted**; ger **omitting**) tr omettre
omnibus ['amnɪˌbʌs], ['amnɪbəs] adj & s omnibus m
omnipotent [am'nɪpətənt] adj omnipotent
omniscient [am'nɪʃənt] adj omniscient
omnivorous [am'nɪvərəs] adj omnivore
on [an], [ɔn] adj (light, radio) allumé; (faucet) ouvert; (machine, motor) en marche; (electrical appliance) branché; (brake) serré; (steak, chops, etc.) dans la poêle; (game, program, etc.) commencé ‖ adv—and so on et ainsi de suite; **come on!** (coll) allons donc!; **farther on** plus loin; **from this day on** à dater de ce jour; **later on** plus tard; **move on!** circulez!; **to be on** (theat) être en scène; **to be on to s.o.** (coll) voir clair dans le jeu de qn; **to have on** être vêtu de, porter; **to . . . on** continuer à + inf, e.g., **to sing on** continuer à chanter; **well on** avancé, e.g., **well on in years** d'un âge avancé ‖ prep sur; (at the time of) lors de; à, e.g., **on foot** à pied; e.g., **on my arrival** à mon arrivée; e.g., **on page three** à la page trois; e.g., **on the first floor** au rez-de-chaussée; e.g., **on the right** à droite; en, e.g., **on a journey** en voyage; e.g., **on arriving** en arrivant; e.g., **on fire** en feu; e.g., **on sale** en vente; e.g., **on the or an average** en moyenne; e.g., **on the top of** en dessus de; dans, e.g., **on a farm** dans une ferme; e.g., **on the jury** dans le jury; e.g., **on the street** dans la rue; e.g., **on the train** dans le train; e.g., **he came on the train** il est venu par le train; e.g., **on a fine day** par un beau jour; de, e.g., **on good authority** de source certaine, de bonne part; e.g., **on the north** du côté du nord; e.g., **on the one hand . . .** on the other hand d'une part . . . d'autre part; e.g., **on this side de** ce côté-ci; e.g., **to have pity on** avoir pitié de; e.g., **to live on bread and water** vivre de pain et d'eau; sous, e.g., **on a charge of** sous l'inculpation de; e.g., **on pain of death** sous peine de mort; (not translated), e.g., **on Tuesday** mardi; e.g., **on Tuesdays** le mardi, tous les mardis; e.g., **on July fourteenth** le qua-

torze juillet; contre, e.g., **an attack on** une attaque contre; **it's on me** (*it's my turn to pay*) (coll) c'est ma tournée; **it's on the house** (coll) c'est la tournée du patron; **on examination** après examen; **on it** y, e.g., **there is the shelf; put the book on it** voilà l'étagère; mettez-y le livre; **on or about** (*a certain date*) aux environs de; **on or after** (*a certain date*) à partir de; **on tap** en perce, à la pression; **on the spot** (*immediately*) sur-le-champ; (*there*) sur place; (slang) en danger imminent; **to be on the committee** faire partie du comité; **to march on a city** marcher sur une ville **on′ and on′** *adv* continuellement, sans fin

once [wʌns] *s*—**this once** pour cette fois-ci ‖ *adv* une fois; (*formerly*) autrefois; **all at once** (*all together*) tous à la fois; (*suddenly*) tout à coup; **at once** tout de suite, sur-le-champ; (*at the same time*) à la fois, en même temps; **for once** pour une fois; **once and for all** une bonne fois, une fois pour toutes; **once in a while** de temps en temps; **once more** encore une fois; **once or twice** une ou deux fois; **once upon a time there was** il était une fois ‖ *conj* une fois que, dès que

once′-o′ver *s* (slang) examen *m* rapide; travail *m* hâtif; **to give the once-over to** (slang) jeter un coup d'œil à

one [wʌn] *adj & pron* un; un certain, e.g., **one** Dupont un certain Dupont; un seul, e.g., **with one voice** d'une seule voix; unique, e.g., **one price** prix unique; (not translated when preceded by an adjective), e.g., **the red pencil and the blue one** le crayon rouge et le bleu; **not one** pas un; **one and all** tous; **one and only** unique, e.g., **the one and only closet in the house** l'armoire unique de la maison; seul et unique, e.g., **my one and only umbrella** mon seul et unique parapluie; **one another** l'un l'autre; les uns les autres; **one by one** un à un; **that one** celui-là; **the one that** celui qui; **this one** celui-ci; **to become one** s'unir, se marier ‖ *s* un *m*; **one o'clock** une heure ‖ *pron indef* on §87, e.g., **one cannot go there alone** on ne peut pas y aller seul; **one's** son, e.g., **one's son** son fils

one′-horse′ *adj* à un cheval; (coll) provincial, insignifiant

one′-horse town′ *s* (coll) trou *m*

onerous [ˈɑnərəs] *adj* onéreux

one·self′ *pron* soi §85; soi-même §86; se §87, e.g., **to cut oneself** se couper; **to be oneself** se conduire sans affectation

one′-sid′ed *adj* à un côté, à une face; (*e.g., decision*) unilatéral; (*unfair*) partial, injuste

one′-track′ *adj* à une voie; (coll) routinier

one′-way′ *adj* à sens unique

one′-way tick′et *s* billet *m* d'aller, billet simple

onion [ˈʌnjən] *s* oignon *m*; **to know one's onions** (coll) connaître son affaire

on′ion-skin′ *s* papier *m* pelure

on′look′er *s* assistant *m*, spectateur *m*

only [ˈonli] *adj* seul, unique; (*child*) unique ‖ *adv* seulement; ne . . . que, e.g., **I have only two** je n'en ai que deux; réservé, e.g., **staff only** (public sign) réservé au personnel ‖ *conj* mais, si ce n'était que

on′rush′ *s* ruée *f*

on′set′ *s* attaque *f*; **at the onset** de prime abord, au premier abord

onslaught [ˈɑn͵slɔt], [ˈɔn͵slɔt] *s* assaut *m*

on′-the-job′ *adj* (*training*) en stage; (coll) alerte

onus [ˈonəs] *s* charge *f*, fardeau *m*

onward [ˈɑnwərd] or **onwards** [ˈɑnwərdz] *adv* en avant

onyx [ˈɑnɪks] *s* onyx *m*

ooze [uz] *s* suintement *m*; (*mud*) vase *f*, limon *m* ‖ *tr* filtrer ‖ *intr* suinter, filtrer; **to ooze out** s'écouler

opal [ˈopəl] *s* opale *f*

opaque [oˈpek] *adj* opaque; (*style*) obscur

open [ˈopən] *adj* ouvert; (*personality*) franc, sincère; (*job, position*) vacant; (*hour*) libre; (*automobile*) découvert; (*market; trial*) public; (*question*) pendant, indécis; (*wound*) béant; (*to attack, to criticism, etc.*) exposé; (sports) international; **to break** or **crack open** éventrer; **to throw open the door** ouvrir la porte toute grande ‖ *s* ouverture *f*; (*in the woods*) clairière *f*; **in the open** au grand air, à ciel ouvert; (*in the open country*) en rase campagne; (*in the open sea*) en pleine mer; (*without being hidden*) découvert; (*openly*) ouvertement ‖ *tr* ouvrir; (*a canal lock*) lâcher; **to open fire** déclencher le feu ‖ *intr* ouvrir, s'ouvrir; (*said, e.g., of a play*) commencer, débuter; **to open into** aboutir à, déboucher sur; **to open on** donner sur; **to open up** s'épanouir, s'ouvrir

o′pen-air′ *adj* en plein air, au grand air

o′pen-eyed′ *adj* les yeux écarquillés

o′pen-hand′ed *adj* libéral, la main ouverte

o′pen-heart′ed *adj* ouvert, franc

o′pen-heart′ sur′gery *s* chirurgie *f* à cœur ouvert

o′pen house′ *s* journée *f* d'accueil; **to keep open house** tenir table ouverte

opening [ˈopənɪŋ] *s* ouverture *f*; (*in the woods*) clairière *f*; (*vacancy*) vacance *f*, poste *m* vacant; (*chance to say something*) occasion *f* favorable

o′pening night′ *s* première *f*

o′pening num′ber *s* ouverture *f*

o′pening price′ *s* cours *m* de début

o′pen-mind′ed *adj* à l'esprit ouvert, sans parti pris

o′pen se′cret *s* secret *m* de Polichinelle

o′pen shop′ *s* atelier *m* ouvert aux non-syndiqués

o'pen·work' s ouvrage m à jour, ajours mpl
opera ['apərə] s opéra m
op'era glass'es spl jumelles fpl de spectacle
op'era hat' s claque m, gibus m
op'era house' s opéra m
operate ['apə ,ret] tr actionner, faire marcher; exploiter || intr fonctionner; s'opérer; (surg) opérer; to operate on (surg) opérer
operatic [,apə'rætɪk] adj d'opéra
opera'ting expen'ses spl (overhead) frais mpl généraux, frais d'exploitation
op'erating room' s salle f d'opération
op'erating ta'ble s table f d'opération, billard m
operation [,apə're ʃən] s opération f; (of a business, of a machine, etc.) fonctionnement m; (med) intervention f chirurgicale, opération
operative ['apə ,retɪv], ['apərətɪv] adj opératif; (surg) opératoire || s (workman) ouvrier m; (spy) agent m, espion m
operator ['apə ,retər] s opérateur m; (e.g., of a mine) propriétaire m exploitant; (of an automobile) conducteur m; téléphoniste mf, standardiste mf; (slang) chevalier m d'industrie, aigrefin m
operetta [,apə'retə] s opérette f
opiate ['opɪ·ɪt], ['opɪ·et] adj opiacé || s médicament m opiacé; (coll) narcotique m
opinion [ə'pɪnjən] s opinion f; in my opinion à mon avis
opinionated [ə'pɪnjə ,netɪd] adj fier de ses opinions, dogmatique
opium ['opɪ·əm] s opium m
o'pium den' s fumerie f
o'pium pop'py s œillette f
opossum [ə'pasəm] s opossum m, sarigue f
opponent [ə'ponənt] s adversaire mf, opposant m
opportune [,apər't(j)un] adj opportun, convenable
opportunist [,apər't(j)unɪst] s opportuniste mf
opportuni·ty [,apər't(j)unɪtɪ] s (pl -ties) occasion f; chance f
oppose [ə'poz] tr s'opposer à
opposite ['apəsɪt] adj opposé, contraire; d'en face, e.g., the house opposite la maison d'en face || s opposé m, contraire m || adv en face, vis-à-vis || prep en face de, à l'opposite de
op'posite num'ber s (fig) homologue mf
opposition [,apə'zɪ ʃən] s opposition f
oppress [ə'pres] tr opprimer; (to weigh heavily upon) oppresser
oppression [ə'pre ʃən] s oppression f
oppressive [ə'presɪv] adj oppressif; (stifling) étouffant, accablant
oppressor [ə'presər] s oppresseur m
opprobrious [ə'probrɪ·əs] adj infamant, injurieux, honteux
opprobrium [ə'probrɪ·əm] s opprobre m

optic ['aptɪk] adj optique || optics s optique f
optical ['aptɪkəl] adj optique
op'tical illu'sion s illusion f d'optique
optician [ap'tɪ ʃən] s opticien m
optimism ['aptɪ ,mɪzəm] s optimisme m
optimist ['aptɪmɪst] s optimiste mf
optimistic [,aptɪ'mɪstɪk] adj optimiste
option ['ap ʃən] s option f
optional ['ap ʃənəl] adj facultatif
optometrist [ap'tamɪtrɪst] s opticien m; optométriste mf (Canad)
opulent ['apjələnt] adj opulent
or [ɔr] conj ou
oracle ['arəkəl], ['ɔrəkəl] s oracle m
oracular [o'rækjələr] adj d'oracle; dogmatique, sentencieux; (ambiguous) équivoque
oral ['orəl] adj oral
orange ['arɪndʒ], ['ɔrɪndʒ] adj orangé, orange || s (color) orangé m, orange m; (fruit) orange f
orangeade [,arɪndʒ'ed], [,ɔrɪndʒ'ed] s orangeade f
or'ange blos'som s fleur f d'oranger
or'ange grove' s orangeraie f
or'ange juice' s jus m d'orange
or'ange squeez'er s presse-fruits m
or'ange tree' s oranger m
orang-outang [o'ræŋu ,tæŋ] s orangoutan m
oration [o're ʃən] s discours m
orator ['arətər], ['ɔrətər] s orateur m
oratorical [,arə'tarɪkəl], [,ɔrə'tɔrɪkəl] adj oratoire
oratori·o [,arə'tori ,o], [,ɔrə'tɔri ,o] s (pl -os) oratorio m
orato·ry ['arə ,tori], ['ɔrə ,tori] s (pl -ries) art m oratoire; (eccl) oratoire m
orb [ɔrb] s orbe m
orbit ['ɔrbɪt] s orbite f; in orbit sur orbite || tr (e.g., the sun) tourner autour de; (e.g., a rocket) mettre en orbite, satelliser || intr se mettre en orbite
orchard ['ɔrtʃərd] s verger m
orchestra ['ɔrkɪstrə] s orchestre m
orchestrate ['ɔrkɪ ,stret] tr orchestrer
orchid ['ɔrkɪd] s orchidée f
ordain [ɔr'den] tr destiner; (eccl) ordonner; to be ordained (eccl) recevoir les ordres
ordeal [ɔr'dil], [ɔr'di·əl] s épreuve f; (hist) ordalie f
order ['ɔrdər] s ordre m; (of words) ordonnance f; (for merchandise, a meal, etc.) commande f; (military formation) ordre m; (law) arrêt m, arrêté m; in order en ordre; in order of appearance (theat) dans l'ordre d'entrée en scène; in order that pour que, afin que; in order to + inf pour + inf, afin de + inf; on order en commande, commandé; order! à l'ordre!; orders (eccl) les ordres; (mil) la consigne; pay to the order of (com) payez à l'ordre de; to get s.th. out of order détraquer q.ch.; to put in order mettre en règle || tr ordonner; (com) commander; to order around

faire aller et venir; **to order s.o. to** +
inf ordonner à qn de + *inf*

or'der blank' *s* bon *m* de commande,
bulletin *m* de commande

order·ly ['ɔrdərli] *adj* ordonné; (*life*)
réglé; **to be orderly** avoir de l'ordre ‖
s (*pl* **-lies**) (med) ambulancier *m*, infirmier *m*; (mil) planton *m*

ordinal ['ɔrdɪnəl] *adj & s* ordinal *m*

ordinance ['ɔrdɪnəns] *s* ordonnance *f*

ordinary ['ɔrdɪn,ɛri] *adj* ordinaire; **out
of the ordinary** exceptionnel

ordination [,ɔrdɪn'eʃən] *s* ordination *f*

ordnance ['ɔrdnəns] *s* artillerie *f*;
(*branch of an army*) service *m* du
matériel

ore [or] *s* minerai *m*

oregano [ə'rɛgə,no] *s* origan *m*

organ ['ɔrgən] *s* (anat, journ) organe
m; (mus) orgue *m*

organdy ['ɔrgəndi] *s* organdi *m*

or'gan grind'er *s* joueur *m* d'orgue

organic [ɔr'gænɪk] *adj* organique

organism ['ɔrgə,nɪzəm] *s* organisme *m*

organist ['ɔrgənɪst] *s* organiste *mf*

organization [,ɔrgənɪ'zeʃən] *s* organisation *f*

organize ['ɔrgə,naɪz] *tr* organiser

organizer ['ɔrgə,naɪzər] *s* organisateur
m

or'gan loft' *s* tribune *f* d'orgue

orgasm ['ɔrgæzəm] *s* orgasme *m*

or·gy ['ɔrdʒi] *s* (*pl* **-gies**) orgie *f*

orient ['ori·ənt] *s* orient *m*; **Orient**
Orient ‖ ['ori,ɛnt] *tr* orienter

oriental [,ori'ɛntəl] *adj* oriental ‖
(*cap*) *s* Oriental *m*

orientate ['ori·ɛn,tet] *tr* orienter

orientation [,ori·ɛn'teʃən] *s* orientation *f*

orifice ['arɪfɪs], ['ɔrɪfɪs] *s* orifice *m*

origin ['arədʒɪn], ['ɔrədʒɪn] *s* origine *f*

original [ə'rɪdʒɪnəl] *adj* (*new, not
copied; inventive*) original; (*earliest*)
originel, primitif; (*first*) originaire,
premier ‖ *s* original *m*

originality [ə,rɪdʒɪ'nælɪti] *s* originalité *f*

originate [ə'rɪdʒə,net] *tr* faire naître,
créer ‖ *intr* prendre naissance; **to
originate from** provenir de

oriole ['ori,ol], ['ɔri,ol] *s* loriot *m*

ormolu ['ɔrmə,lu] *s* bronze *m* doré;
(*powdered gold for gilding*) or *m*
moulu; (*alloy of zinc and copper*)
similor *m*

ornament ['ɔrnəmənt] *s* ornement *m* ‖
['ɔrnə,mɛnt] *tr* ornementer, orner

ornamental [,ɔrnə'mɛntəl] *adj* orne-
mental

ornate [ɔr'net], ['ɔrnet] *adj* orné, fleuri

ornery ['ɔrnəri] *adj* (coll) acariâtre,
intraitable

ornithology [,ɔrnɪ'θalədʒi] *f* ornithologie *f*

orphan ['ɔrfən] *adj & s* orphelin *m*

orphanage ['ɔrfənɪdʒ] *s* (*asylum*) orphelinat *m*; (*orphanhood*) orpheli-
nage *m*

Orpheus ['ɔrfjus], ['ɔrfi·əs] *s* Orphée
m

orthodox ['ɔrθə,daks] *adj* orthodoxe

orthogra·phy [ɔr'θagrəfi] *s* (*pl* **-phies**)
orthographe *f*

oscillate ['asɪ,let] *intr* osciller

osier ['oʒər] *s* osier *m*

osmosis [az'mosɪs], [as'mosɪs] *s* osmose *f*

osprey ['aspri] *s* aigle *m* pêcheur

ossi·fy ['asɪ,faɪ] *v* (*pret & pp* **-fied**) *tr*
ossifier ‖ *intr* s'ossifier

ostensible [as'tɛnsɪbəl] *adj* prétendu,
apparent, soi-disant

ostentatious [,astɛn'teʃəs] *adj* ostentatoire, fastueux

osteopathy [,astɪ'apəθi] *s* ostéopathie *f*

ostracism ['astrə,sɪzəm] *s* ostracisme *m*

ostracize ['astrə,saɪz] *tr* frapper d'ostracisme

ostrich ['astrɪtʃ] *s* autruche *f*

other ['ʌðər] *adj* autre; **every other
day** tous les deux jours; **every other
one** un sur deux ‖ *pron indef* autre
‖ *adv*—**other than** autrement que

otherwise ['ʌðər,waɪz] *adv* autrement,
à part cela ‖ *conj* sinon, e.g., **come
at once, otherwise it will be too late**
venez tout de suite, sinon il sera trop
tard; sans cela, e.g., **thanks, otherwise I'd have forgotten** merci, sans
cela j'aurais oublié

otter ['atər] *s* loutre *f*

Ottoman ['atəmən] *adj* ottoman ‖
(*l.c.*) *s* (*corded fabric*) ottoman *m*;
(*divan*) ottomane *f*; (*footstool*) pouf
m; **Ottoman** (*person*) Ottoman *m*

ouch [autʃ] *interj* aïe!

ought [ɔt] *s* zéro *m*; **for ought I know**
pour autant que je sache ‖ *aux* used
to express obligation, e.g., **he ought
to go away** il devrait s'en aller; e.g.,
he ought to have gone away il aurait
dû s'en aller

ounce [auns] *s* once *f*

our [aur] *adj poss* notre §88

ours [aurz] *pron poss* le nôtre §89

our·selves' *pron pers* nous-mêmes §86;
nous §85, §87

oust [aust] *tr* évincer, chasser

out [aut] *adj* extérieur; absent; (*fire*)
éteint; (*secret*) divulgé; (*tide*) bas;
(*flower*) épanoui; (*rope*) filé; (*lease*)
expiré; (*gear*) débrayé; (*unconscious
person*) évanoui; (*boxer*) knockouté;
(*book, magazine, etc.*) paru, publié;
(*out of print, out of stock*) épuisé;
(*a ball*) (sports) hors jeu; (*a player*)
(sports) éliminé ‖ *s* (*pretext*) échappatoire *f*; **to be on the outs with** être
brouillé avec ‖ *adv* dehors, au dehors; (*outdoors*) en plein air; **out and
out** complètement; **out for** en quête
de; **out for lunch** parti déjeuner; **out
of** (*cash*) démuni de; (*a glass, cup,
etc.*) dans; (*a bottle*) à; (*the window;
curiosity, friendship, respect, etc.*)
par; (*range, sight*) hors de; de, e.g.,
to cry out of joy pleurer de joie; e.g.,
made out of fait de, sur, e.g., **nine
times out of ten** neuf fois sur dix; **out
with it!** allez, dites-le!; **to be out** (*to
be absent*) être sorti; faire, e.g., **the
sun is out** il fait du soleil; **to be out**

of bounds (sports) être hors jeu ‖ *prep* par ‖ *interj* hors d'ici!, ouste!
out′ and away′ *adv* de beaucoup, de loin
out′-and-out′ *adj* vrai; (*fanatic*) intransigeant; (*liar*) achevé
out′-and-out′er *s* (coll) intransigeant *m*
out′bid′ *v* (*pret* **-bid**; *pp* **-bid** or **-bidden**; *ger* **-bidding**) *tr* enchérir sur; (fig) renchérir sur ‖ *intr* surenchérir
out′board mo′tor *s* moteur *m* hors-bord
out′break′ *s* déchaînement *m*; (*of hives; of anger; etc.*) éruption *f*; (*of epidemic*) manifestation *f*; (*insurrection*) révolte *f*
out′build′ing *s* annexe *f*, dépendance *f*
out′burst′ *s* explosion *f*; (*of anger*) accès *m*; (*of laughter*) éclat *m*; (*e.g., of generosity*) élan *m*
out′cast′ *adj* & *s* banni *m*, proscrit *m*
out′caste′ *adj* hors caste ‖ *s* hors-caste *mf*
out′come′ *s* résultat *m*, dénouement *m*
out′cry′ *s* (*pl* **-cries**) clameur *f*; (*of indignation*) levée *f* de boucliers
out·dat′ed *adj* démodé, suranné
out′dis′tance *tr* dépasser; (sports) distancer
out′do′ *v* (*pret* **-did**; *pp* **-done**) *tr* surpasser, l'emporter sur; **to outdo oneself** se surpasser
out′door′ *adj* au grand air; (sports) de plein air
out′door grill′ *s* rôtisserie *f* en plein air
out′doors′ *s* rase campagne *f*, plein air *m* ‖ *adv* au grand air, en plein air; en plein air; ‹(*outside of the house*) hors de la maison; (*at night*) à la belle étoile
out′door swim′ming pool′ *s* piscine *f* à ciel ouvert
outer [′aʊtər] *adj* extérieur, externe
out′er space′ *s* cosmos *m*, espace *m* cosmique
out′field′ *s* (*baseball*) grand champ *m*
out′fit′ *s* équipement *m*, attirail *m*; (*caseful of implements*) trousse *f*, nécessaire *m*; (*ensemble*) costume et accessoires *mpl*; (*of a bride*) trousseau *m*; (*team*) équipe *f*; (*group of soldiers*) unité *f*; (com) compagnie *f* ‖ *v* (*pret* & *pp* **-fitted**; *ger* **-fitting**) *tr* équiper
out′go′ing *adj* en partance, partant; (*officeholder*) sortant; (*friendly*) communicatif, sympathique
out′grow′ *v* (*pret* **-grew**; *pp* **-grown**) *tr* devenir plus grand que; (*e.g., childhood clothes, activities, etc.*) devenir trop grand pour; abandonner, se défaire de
out′growth′ *s* excroissance *f*; (fig) résultat *m*, conséquence *f*
outing [′aʊtɪŋ] *s* excursion *f*, sortie *f*
outlandish [aʊt′lændɪʃ] *adj* bizarre, baroque
out′last′ *tr* durer plus longtemps que; survivre (with *dat*)
out′law′ *s* hors-la-loi *m*, proscrit *m* ‖ *tr* mettre hors la loi, proscrire

out′lay′ *s* débours *mpl*, dépenses *fpl* ‖
out′lay′ *v* (*pret* & *pp* **-laid**) *tr* débourser, dépenser
out′let′ *s* sortie *f*, issue *f*; (*escape valve*) déversoir *m*; (*for, e.g., pent-up emotions*) exutoire *m*; (com) débouché *m*; (elec) prise *f* de courant; **no outlet** (public sign) rue sans issue
out′line′ *s* (*profile*) contour *m*; (*sketch*) esquisse *f*; (*summary*) aperçu *m*; (*of a work in preparation*) plan *m*; (*main points*) grandes lignes *fpl* ‖ *tr* esquisser; (*a work in preparation*) ébaucher
out′live′ *tr* survivre (with *dat*)
out′lived′ *adj* caduc, désuet
out′look′ *s* perspective *f*, point *m* de vue
out′ly′ing *adj* éloigné, écarté, isolé
outmoded [,aʊt′modɪd] *adj* démodé
out′num′ber *tr* surpasser en nombre
out′-of-date′ *adj* démodé, suranné
out′-of-door′ *adj* au grand air
out′-of-doors′ *adj* au grand air ‖ *s* rase campagne *f*, plein air *m* ‖ *adv* au grand air, hors de la maison
out′ of or′der *adj* en panne; **to be out of order** (*to be out of sequence*) ne pas être dans l'ordre
out′ of print′ *adj* épuisé
out′ of tune′ *adj* désaccordé ‖ *adv* faux, e.g., **to sing out of tune** chanter faux
out′ of work′ *adj* en chômage
out′pa′tient *s* malade *mf* de consultation externe
out′patient clin′ic *s* consultation *f* externe
out′post′ *s* avant-poste *m*, antenne *f*
out′put′ *s* rendement *m*, débit *m*; (*of a mine; of a worker*) production *f*
out′rage *s* outrage *m*; (*wanton violence*) atrocité *f*, attentat *m* honteux ‖ *tr* faire outrage à, outrager; (*a woman*) violer
outrageous [aʊt′redʒəs] *adj* outrageux; (*intolerable*) insupportable
out′rank′ *tr* dépasser en grade, dépasser en rang
out′rid′er *s* explorateur *m*; cow-boy *m*; (*mounted attendant*) piqueur *m*
outrigger [′aʊt,rɪgər] *s* (*outboard framework*) balancier *m*; (*oar support*) porte-en-dehors *m*
out′right′ *adj* pur, absolu; (*e.g., manner*) franc, direct ‖ **out′right′** *adv* complètement; (*frankly*) franchement; (*at once*) sur le coup
out′set′ *s* début *m*, commencement *m*
out′side′ *adj* du dehors, d'extérieur ‖ **out′side′** *s* dehors *m*, extérieur *m*; surface *f*; **at the outside** tout au plus, au maximum ‖ **out′side′** *adv* dehors, à l'extérieur; (*outdoors*) en plein air; **outside of** en dehors de, à l'extérieur de; (*except for*) sauf ‖ **out′side′** or **out′side′** *prep* en dehors de, à l'extérieur de
outsider [,aʊt′saɪdər] *s* étranger *m*; (*intruder*) intrus *m*; (*uninitiated*) profane *mf*; (*dark horse*) outsider *m*
out′size′ *adj* hors série

out'skirts' spl approches fpl, périphérie f

out'spo'ken adj franc; **to be outspoken** avoir son franc-parler

out'stand'ing adj saillant; (eminent) hors pair, hors ligne; (debts) à recouvrer, impayé

outward ['aʊtwərd] adj extérieur; (apparent) superficiel; (direction) en dehors ‖ adv au dehors, vers le dehors

out'weigh' tr peser plus que; (in value) l'emporter en valeur sur

out'wit' v (pret & pp -witted; ger -witting) tr duper, déjouer; (a pursuer) dépister

oval ['ovəl] adj & s ovale m

ova·ry ['ovəri] s (pl -ries) ovaire m

ovation [o'veʃən] s ovation f

oven ['ʌvən] s four m; (fig) fournaise f

over ['ovər] adj fini, passé; (additional) en plus; (excessive) en excès; plus, e.g., **eight and over** huit et plus ‖ adv au-dessus, dessus; (on the other side) de l'autre côté; (again) de nouveau; (on the reverse side of sheet of paper) au verso; (finished) passé, achevé; **all over** (everywhere) partout; (finished) fini; (completely) jusqu'au bout des ongles; **I'll be right over** (coll) j'arrive tout de suite; **over!** (turn the page!) voir au verso!, tournez!; (rad) à vous!; **over again** de nouveau, encore une fois; **over against** en face de; (compared to) auprès de; **over and above** en plus de; **over and out!** (rad) terminé!; **over and over** à coups répétés, à plusieurs reprises; **over here** ici, de ce côté; **over there** là-bas; **to be over** (an illness) s'être remis de; **to hand over** remettre ‖ prep au-dessus de; (on top of) sur, par-dessus; (with motion) par-dessus, e.g., **to jump over a fence** sauter par-dessus une barrière; (a period of time) pendant, au cours de; (near) près de; (a certain number or amount) plus de, au-dessus de; (concerning) à propos de, au sujet de; (on the other side of) au delà de, de l'autre côté de; à, e.g., **over the telephone** au téléphone; (while doing s.th.) tout en prenant, e.g., **over a cup of coffee** tout en prenant une tasse de café; **all over** répandu sur; **over and above** en sus de, en plus de; **to fall over** (e.g., a cliff) tomber du haut de; **to reign over** régner sur

o'ver·all' adj hors tout, complet; général, total ‖ **overalls** spl combinaison f d'homme, cotte f, salopette f

o'ver·awe' tr impressionner, intimider

o'ver·bear'ing adj impérieux, tranchant, autoritaire

o'ver·board' adv par-dessus bord; **man overboard!** un homme à la mer!; **to throw overboard** jeter par-dessus le bord; (fig) abandonner

o'ver·cast' adj obscurci, nuageux ‖ s ciel m couvert ‖ v (pret & pp -cast) tr obscurcir, couvrir

o'ver·charge' s prix m excessif, majoration f excessive; (elec) surcharge f ‖ **o'ver·charge'** tr (e.g., an account) majorer; (elec) surcharger; **to overcharge s.o. for s.th.** faire payer trop cher q.ch. à qn

o'ver·coat' s pardessus m

o'ver·come' v (pret -came; pp -come) tr vaincre; (difficulties) surmonter

o'ver·con'fidence s témérité f, confiance f exagérée

o'ver·con'fident adj téméraire, excessivement confiant

o'ver·cooked' adj trop cuit

o'ver·crowd' tr bonder; (a town, region, etc.) surpeupler

o'ver·do' v (pret -did; pp -done) tr exagérer; **overdone** (culin) trop cuit ‖ intr se surmener

o'ver·dose' s dose f excessive

o'ver·draft' s découvert m, solde m débiteur

o'ver·draw' v (pret -drew; pp -drawn) tr tirer à découvert ‖ intr excéder son crédit

o'ver·drive' s (aut) surmultiplication f

o'ver·due' adj en retard; (com) échu, arriéré

o'ver·eat' v (pret -ate; pp -eaten) tr & intr trop manger

o'ver·exer'tion s surmenage m

o'ver·expose' tr surexposer

o'ver·expo'sure s surexposition f

o'ver·flow' s débordement m; (pipe) trop-plein m ‖ **o'ver·flow'** tr & intr déborder

o'ver·fly' v (pret -flew; pp -flown) tr survoler

o'ver·grown' adj démesuré; (e.g., child) trop grand pour son âge; **overgrown with** (e.g., weeds) envahi par, recouvert de

o'ver·hang' v (pret & pp -hung) tr surplomber, faire saillie au-dessus de; (to threaten) menacer ‖ intr (to jut out) faire saillie

o'ver·haul' s remise f en état ‖ **o'ver·haul'** tr remettre en état; (to catch up to) rattraper

o'ver·head' adj élevé; aérien, surélevé ‖ s (overpass) pont-route m; (com) frais mpl généraux ‖ **o'ver·head'** adv au-dessus de la tête, en haut

o'ver·head valve' s soupape f en tête

o'ver·hear' v (pret & pp -heard) tr entendre par hasard; (a conversation) surprendre

o'ver·heat' tr surchauffer

overjoyed [ˌovər'dʒɔɪd] adj ravi, transporté de joie

overland ['ovər ˌlænd], ['ovərlənd] adj & adv par terre, par voie de terre

o'ver·lap' v (pret & pp -lapped; ger -lapping) tr enchevaucher ‖ intr chevaucher

o'ver·lap'ping s recouvrement m, chevauchement m; (of functions, offices, etc.) double emploi m

o'ver·load' s surcharge f; **sudden overload** (elec) coup m de collier ‖ **o'ver·load'** tr surcharger

o'ver·look' *tr* donner sur, avoir vue sur; (*to ignore*) fermer les yeux sur, passer sous silence; (*to neglect*) oublier, négliger

o'ver·lord' *s* suzerain *m* || o'ver·lord' *tr* dominer, tyranniser

overly ['ovərli] *adv* (coll) trop, à l'excès

o'ver·night' *adv* toute la nuit; du jour au lendemain; **to stay overnight** passer la nuit

o'ver·night' bag' *s* sac *m* de nuit

o'ver·pass' *s* passage *m* supérieur, pont-route *m*

o'ver·pay'ment *s* surpaye *f*, rétribution *f* excessive

o'ver·pop·u·la'tion *s* surpeuplement *m*, surpopulation *f*

o'ver·pow'er *tr* maîtriser; **overpowered with grief** accablé de douleur

o'ver·pow'ering *adj* accablant, irrésistible

o'ver·produc'tion *s* surproduction *f*

o'ver·rate' *tr* surestimer

o'ver·reach' *tr* dépasser

o'ver·ripe' *adj* blet, trop mûr

o'ver·rule' *tr* décider contre; (*to set aside*) annuler, casser

o'ver·run' *v* (*pret* -ran; *pp* -run; *ger* -running) *tr* envahir; (*to flood*) inonder; (*limits, boundaries, etc.*) dépasser || *intr* déborder

o'ver·sea' or o'ver·seas' *adj* d'outre-mer || o'ver·sea' or o'ver·seas' *adv* outre-mer

o'ver·see' *v* (*pret* -saw; *pp* -seen) *tr* surveiller

o'ver·se'er *s* surveillant *m*, inspecteur *m*

o'ver·shad'ow *tr* ombrager; (fig) éclipser

o'ver·shoes' *spl* caoutchoucs *mpl*

o'ver·sight' *s* inadvertance *f*, étourderie *f*

o'ver·sleep' *v* (*pret* & *pp* -slept) *intr* dormir trop longtemps

o'ver·step' *v* (*pret* & *pp* -stepped; *ger* -stepping) *tr* dépasser, outrepasser

o'ver·stock' *tr* surapprovisionner

o'ver·stuffed' *adj* rembourré

o'ver·sup·ply' *s* (*pl* -plies) excédent *m*, abondance *f* || o'ver·sup·ply' *v* (*pret* & *pp* -plied) *tr* approvisionner avec excès

overt ['ovərt], [o'vʌrt] *adj* ouvert, manifeste; (*intentional*) prémédité

o'ver·take' *v* (*pret* -took; *pp* -taken) *tr* rattraper; (*a runner*) dépasser; (*an automobile*) doubler; (*to surprise*) surprendre

o'ver·tax' *tr* surtaxer; (*to tire*) surmener, excéder

o'ver-the-coun'ter *adj* vendu directement à l'acheteur

o'ver·throw' *s* renversement *m* || o'ver·throw' *v* (*pret* -threw; *pp* -thrown) *tr* renverser

o'ver·time' *adj* & *adv* en heures supplémentaires || *s* heures *fpl* supplémentaires

o'ver·tone' *s* (mus) harmonique *m*; (fig) signification *f*, sous-entendu *m*

o'ver·trump' *tr* surcouper

overture ['ovərtʃər] *s* ouverture *f*

o'ver·turn' *tr* renverser, chavirer || *intr* chavirer; (aer, aut) capoter

overweening [,ovər'winɪŋ] *adj* arrogant, outrecuidant

o'ver·weight' *adj* au-dessus du poids normal; (*fat*) obèse || *s* excédent *m* de poids

overwhelm [,ovər'hwɛlm] *tr* accabler, écraser; (*with favors, gifts, etc.*) combler

o'ver·work' *s* surmenage *m*, excès *m* de travail || o'ver·work' *tr* surmener, surcharger; abuser de, trop employer || *intr* se surmener

Ovid ['ɑvɪd] *s* Ovide *m*

ow [au] *interj* aïe!

owe [o] *tr* devoir || *intr* avoir des dettes; **to owe for** avoir à payer, devoir

owing ['o·ɪŋ] *adj* dû, redû; **owing to** à cause de, en raison de

owl [aul] *s* (*Asio*) hibou *m*; (*Strix*) chouette *f*, hulotte *f*; (*Tyto alba*) effraie *f*

own [on] *adj* propre, e.g., **my own brother** mon propre frère || *s*—**all its own** spécial, authentique, e.g., **an aroma all its own** un parfum spécial, un parfum authentique; **my own (your own, etc.)** le mien (le vôtre, etc.) §89; **of my own (of their own, etc.)** bien à moi (bien à eux, etc.); **on one's own** à son propre compte, .de son propre chef; **to come into one's own** entrer en possession de son bien; (*to win out*) obtenir des succès; (*to receive due praise*) recevoir les honneurs qu'on mérite; **to hold one's own** se maintenir, se défendre || *tr* posséder; être propriétaire de; (*to acknowledge*) reconnaître || *intr*—**to own to** convenir de, reconnaître; **to own up** (coll) faire des aveux; **to own up to** (coll) faire l'aveu de, avouer

owner ['onər] *s* propriétaire *mf*, possesseur *m*

ownership ['onər,ʃɪp] *s* propriété *f*, possession *f*

own'er's li'cense *s* carte *f* grise

ox [ɑks] *s* (*pl* oxen ['ɑksən]) bœuf *m*

ox'cart' *s* char *m* à bœufs

oxfords ['ɑksfərdz] *spl* richelieus *mpl*

oxide ['ɑksaɪd] *s* oxyde *m*

oxidize ['ɑksɪ,daɪz] *tr* oxyder || *intr* s'oxyder

oxygen ['ɑksɪdʒən] *s* oxygène *m*

oxygenate ['ɑksɪdʒə,net] *tr* oxygéner

ox'ygen tent' *s* tente *f* à oxygène

oxytone ['ɑksɪ,ton] *adj* & *s* oxyton *m*

oyster ['ɔɪstər] *adj* huîtrier || *s* huître *f*

oys'ter bed' *s* huîtrière *f*, banc *m* d'huîtres

oys'ter cock'tail *s* huîtres *fpl* écaillées aux condiments

oys'ter farm' *s* parc *m* à huîtres, clayère *f*

oys'ter fork' *s* fourchette *f* à huîtres

oys'ter knife' *s* couteau *m* à huîtres

oys′ter·man *s* (*pl* **-men**) écailler *m*
oys′ter op′ener *s* (*person*) écailler *m*;
(*implement*) ouvre-huîtres *m*
oys′ter plant′ *s* salsifis *m*

oys′ter shell′ *s* coquille *f* d'huître
oys′ter stew′ *s* soupe *f* à huîtres
ozone ['ozon] *s* ozone *m*; (coll) air *m*
frais

P

P, p [pi] *s* XVIᵉ lettre de l'alphabet
pace [pes] *s* pas *m*; **to keep pace with**
marcher de pair avec; **to put through
one's paces** mettre à l'épreuve; **to set
the pace** mener le train ‖ *tr* arpenter;
to pace off mesurer au pas ‖ *intr*
aller au pas
pace′mak′er *s* meneur *m* de train
pacific [pə'sɪfɪk] *adj* pacifique ‖ **Pacific** *adj* & *s* Pacifique *m*
pacifier ['pæsɪ,faɪ·ər] *s* pacificateur
m; (*teething ring*) sucette *f*
pacifism ['pæsɪ,fɪzəm] *s* pacifisme *m*
pacifist ['pæsɪfɪst] *adj* & *s* pacifiste *mf*
paci·fy ['pæsɪ,faɪ] *v* (*pret* & *pp* **-fied**)
tr pacifier
pack [pæk] *s* paquet *m*; (*of peddler*)
ballot *m*; (*of soldier*) paquetage *m*,
sac *m*; (*of beast of burden*) bât *m*;
(*of hounds*) meute *f*; (*of evildoers; of
wolves*) bande *f*; (*of lies*) tissu *m*; (*of
playing cards*) jeu *m*; (*of cigarettes*)
paquet; (*of floating ice*) banquise *f*;
(*of troubles*) foule *f*; (*of fools*) tas *m*;
(med) enveloppement *m* ‖ *tr* emballer, empaqueter; mettre en boîte;
(*e.g., earth*) tasser; (*to stuff*) bourrer;
to send packing (coll) envoyer promener ‖ *intr* faire ses bagages
package ['pækɪdʒ] *s* paquet *m* ‖ *tr* empaqueter
pack′age plan′ *s* voyage *m* à forfait
pack′ an′imal *s* bête *f* de somme
packet ['pækɪt] *s* paquet *m*; (naut)
paquebot *m*; (pharm) sachet *m*
pack′ing box′ or **case′** *s* caisse *f* d'emballage
pack′ing house′ *s* conserverie *f*
pack′sad′dle *s* bât *m*
pack′thread′ *s* ficelle *f*
pack′train′ *s* convoi *m* de bêtes de
somme
pact [pækt] *s* pacte *m*
pad [pæd] *s* bourrelet *m*; (*of writing
paper*) bloc *m*; (*for inking*) tampon
m; (*of an aquatic plant*) feuille *f*;
(*for launching a rocket*) rampe *f*;
(*sound of footsteps*) pas *m* ‖ *v* (*pret
& pp* **padded**; *ger* **padding**) *tr* rembourrer; (*to expand unnecessarily*)
délayer ‖ *intr* aller à pied
pad′ded cell′ *s* cellule *f* matelassée, cabanon *m*
paddle ['pædəl] *s* (*of a canoe*) pagaie
f; (*for table tennis*) raquette *f*; (*of a
wheel*) aube *f*; (*for beating*) palette *f*
‖ *tr* pagayer; (*to spank*) fesser ‖ *intr*
pagayer; (*to splash*) barboter
pad′dle wheel′ *s* roue *f* à aubes

paddock ['pædək] *s* enclos *m*; (*at race
track*) paddock *m*
pad′dy wag′on ['pædi] *s* (slang) panier
m à salade
pad′lock′ *s* cadenas *m* ‖ *tr* cadenasser
pagan ['pegən] *adj* & *s* païen *m*
paganism ['pegə,nɪzəm] *s* paganisme *m*
page [pedʒ] *s* (*of a book*) page *f*; (*boy
attendant*) page *m*; (*in a hotel or
club*) chasseur *m* ‖ *tr* (*a book*) paginer; appeler, demander, e.g., **you
are being paged** on vous demande
pageant ['pædʒənt] *s* parade *f* à grand
spectacle
pageant·ry ['pædʒəntri] *s* (*pl* **-ries**)
grand apparat *m*; vaines pompes *fpl*
page′ proof′ *s* seconde épreuve *f*;
(journ) morasse *f*
paginate ['pædʒɪ,net] *tr* paginer
paging ['pedʒɪŋ] *s* mise *f* en pages
paid′ in full′ [ped] *adj* (formula
stamped on bill) pour acquit
paid′ vaca′tion *s* congé *m* payé
pail [pel] *s* seau *m*
pain [pen] *s* douleur *f*; **on pain of** sous
peine de; **to take pains** se donner de
la peine ‖ *tr* faire mal (with *dat*); **it
pains me to** il me coûte de ‖ *intr*
faire mal
painful ['penfəl] *adj* douloureux
pain′kil′ler *s* (coll) calmant *m*
painless ['penlɪs] *adj* sans douleur
pains′tak′ing *adj* soigneux; (*work*)
soigné
paint [pent] *s* peinture *f*; **wet paint**
peinture fraîche; (public sign) attention à la peinture! ‖ *tr* & *intr* peindre
paint′box′ *s* boîte *f* de couleurs
paint′brush′ *s* pinceau *m*
paint′ buck′et *s* camion *m*
painter ['pentər] *s* peintre *mf*
painting ['pentɪŋ] *s* peinture *f*
paint′ remov′er *s* décapant *m*
pair [pɛr] *s* paire *f*; (*of people*) couple
m ‖ *tr* accoupler ‖ *intr* s'accoupler
pair′ of scis′sors *s* ciseaux *mpl*
pair′ of trou′sers *s* pantalon *m*
pajamas [pə'dʒɑməz], [pə'dʒæməz]
spl pyjama *m*, pyjamas
Pakistan [,pɑkɪ'stɑn] *s* le Pakistan
Pakista·ni [,pɑkɪ'stɑni] *adj* pakistanais
‖ *s* (*pl* **-nis**) Pakistanais *m*
pal [pæl] *s* copain *m* ‖ *v* (*pret & pp*
palled; *ger* **palling**) *intr* (coll) être de
bons copains; **to pal with** être copain
de
palace ['pælɪs] *s* palais *m*
palatable ['pælətəbəl] *adj* savoureux;
(*acceptable*) agréable

palatal ['pælətəl] *adj* palatal ‖ *s* palatale *f*

palate ['pælɪt] *s* palais *m*

pale [pel] *adj* pâle ‖ *s* pieux *m*; limites *fpl* ‖ *intr* pâlir

pale'face' *s* visage *m* pâle

palette ['pælɪt] *s* palette *f*

palfrey ['pɔlfri] *s* palefroi *m*

palisade [,pælɪ'sed] *s* palissade *f*; (*line of cliffs*) falaise *f*

pall [pɔl] *s* poêle *m*, drap *m* mortuaire; (*to cover chalice*) pale *f*; (*vestment*) pallium *m* ‖ *intr* devenir fade; **to pall on** rassasier

pall'bear'er *s* porteur *m* d'un cordon du poêle

pallet ['pælɪt] *s* grabat *m*

palliate ['pælɪ,et] *tr* pallier

pallid ['pælɪd] *adj* pâle, blême

pallor ['pælər] *s* pâleur *f*

palm [pɑm] *s* (*of the hand*) paume *f*; (*measure*) palme *m*; (*leaf*) palme *f*; (*tree*) palmier *m*; **to carry off the palm** remporter la palme; **to grease the palm of** (slang) graisser la patte à ‖ *tr* (*a card*) escamoter; **to palm off s.th. on s.o.** refiler q.ch. à qn

palmet•to [pæl'meto] *s* (*pl* -tos or -toes) palmier *m* nain

palmist ['pɑmɪst] *s* chiromancien *m*

palmistry ['pɑmɪstri] *s* chiromancie *f*

palm' leaf' *s* palme *f*

palm' oil' *s* huile *f* de palme

Palm' Sun'day *s* le dimanche des Rameaux

palm' tree' *s* palmier *m*

palpable ['pælpəbəl] *adj* palpable

palpitate ['pælpɪ,tet] *intr* palpiter

pal•sy ['pɔlzi] *s* (*pl* -sies) paralysie *f* ‖ *v* (*pret & pp* -sied) *tr* paralyser

pal•try ['pɔltri] *adj* (*comp* -trier; *super* -triest) misérable

pamper ['pæmpər] *tr* choyer, gâter

pamphlet ['pæmflɪt] *s* brochure *f*

pan [pæn] *s* casserole *f*; (*basin; scale of a balance*) bassin *m*; (slang) binette *f*; **Pan** Pan *m* ‖ *v* (*pret & pp* **panned**; *ger* **panning**) *tr* (*gold*) laver à la batée; (coll) débiner, éreinter ‖ *intr* laver à la batée; (mov) panoramiquer; **to pan out well** (coll) réussir

panacea [,pænə'si•ə] *s* panacée *f*

Panama ['pænə,mɑ], [,pænə'mɑ] *s* le Panama

Pan'ama Canal' *s* canal *m* de Panama

Pan'ama Canal' Zone' *s* zone *f* canal du Panama

Pan'ama hat' *s* panama *m*

Pan-American [,pænə'merɪkən] *adj* panaméricain

pan'cake' *s* crêpe *f* ‖ *intr* (aer) descendre à plat, se plaquer

pan'cake land'ing *s* atterrissage *m* plaque, sur le ventre, or à plat

panchromatic [,pænkro'mætɪk] *adj* panchromatique

pancreas ['pænkrɪ•əs] *s* pancréas *m*

pander ['pændər] *s* entremetteur *m* ‖ *intr* servir d'entremetteur; **to pander to** se prêter à; encourager

pane [pen] *s* carreau *m*, vitre *f*

pan•el ['pænəl] *s* panneau *m*; (*on wall*) lambris *m*; liste *f*, tableau *m*; groupe *m* de discussion ‖ *v* (*pret & pp* -eled or -elled; *ger* -eling or -elling) *tr* (*a room*) garnir de boiseries; (*a wall*) lambrisser

pan'el discus'sion *s* colloque *m*

panelist ['pænəlɪst] *s* membre *m* d'un groupe de discussion

pang [pæŋ] *s* élancement *m*, angoisse *f*

pan'han'dle *s* queue *f* de la poêle; (geog) projection *f* d'un territoire dans un autre ‖ *intr* (slang) mendigoter

pan'han'dler *s* (slang) mendigot *m*

pan•ic ['pænɪk] *adj & s* panique *f* ‖ *v* (*pret & pp* -icked; *ger* -icking) *tr* semer la panique dans ‖ *intr* être pris de panique

pan'ic-strick'en *adj* pris de panique

pano•ply ['pænəpli] *s* (*pl* -plies) panoplie *f*

panorama [,pænə'ræmə], [,pænə'rɑmə] *s* panorama *m*

pan•sy ['pænzi] *s* (*pl* -sies) pensée *f*; (slang) tapette *f*

pant [pænt] *s* halètement *m*; **pants** pantalon *m*; **to wear the pants** (coll) porter la culotte ‖ *intr* haleter, panteler

pantheism ['pænθi,ɪzəm] *s* panthéisme *m*

pantheon ['pænθi,ɑn], ['pænθi•ən] *s* panthéon *m*

panther ['pænθər] *s* panthère *f*

panties ['pæntiz] *spl* culotte *f*

pantomime ['pæntə,maɪm] *s* pantomime *f*

pan•try ['pæntri] *s* (*pl* -tries) office *m & f*, dépense *f*

pap [pæp] *s* bouillie *f*

papa ['pɑpə], [pə'pɑ] *s* papa *m*

papa•cy ['pepəsi] *s* (*pl* -cies) papauté *f*

paper ['pepər] *s* papier *m*; (*newspaper*) journal *m*; (*of needles*) carte *f* ‖ *tr* tapisser

pa'per•back' *s* livre *m* broché; (*pocketbook*) livre de poche

pa'per•boy' *s* vendeur *m* de journaux

pa'per clip' *s* attache *f*, trombone *m*

pa'per cone' *s* cornet *m* de papier

pa'per cup' *s* verre *m* en carton, gobelet *m* de papier

pa'per cut'ter *s* coupe-papier *m*

pa'per hand'kerchief *s* mouchoir *m* à jeter, mouchoir en papier

pa'per•hang'er *s* tapissier *m*

pa'per knife' *s* coupe-papier *m*

pa'per mill' *s* papeterie *f*

pa'per mon'ey *s* papier-monnaie *m*

pa'per nap'kin *s* serviette *f* en papier

pa'per plate' *s* assiette *f* en carton, assiette de papier

pa'per tape' *s* bande *f* de papier

pa'per tow'el *s* serviette *f* de toilette en papier

pa'per•weight' *s* presse-papiers *m*

pa'per work' *s* travail *m* de bureau

papier-mâché [,pepərmə'ʃe] *s* papier-pierre *m*, papier *m* mâché

paprika [pæ'prikə], ['pæprɪkə] *s* paprika *m*

papy·rus [pə'paɪrəs] *s* (*pl* **ri** [raɪ])
papyrus *m*
par [pɑr] *s* pair *m*; (golf) normale *f* du
parcours; **at par** au pair; **to be on a
par with** aller de pair avec
parable ['pærəbəl] *s* parabole *f*
parabola [pə'ræbələ] *s* parabole *f*
parachute ['pærə‚ʃut] *s* parachute *m*
|| *tr & intr* parachuter
par'achute jump' *s* saut *m* en parachute
parachutist ['pærə‚ʃutɪst] *s* parachutiste *mf*
parade [pə'red] *s* défilé *m*; (*ostenta-
tion*) parade *f*; (mil) parade || *tr*
faire parade de || *intr* défiler; para-
der
paradise ['pærə‚daɪs] *s* paradis *m*
paradox ['pærə‚dɑks] *s* paradoxe *m*
paradoxical [‚pærə'dɑksɪkəl] *adj* paradoxal
paraffin ['pærəfɪn] *s* paraffine *f* || *tr*
paraffiner
paragon ['pærə‚gɑn] *s* parangon *m*
paragraph ['pærə‚græf], ['pærə‚grɑf]
s paragraphe *m*
Paraguay ['pærə‚gwe], ['pærə‚gwaɪ] *s*
le Paraguay
Paraguayan [‚pærə'gwe·ən], [‚pærə-
'gwaɪ·ən] *adj* paraguayen || *s* Para-
guayen *m*
parakeet ['pærə‚kit] *s* perruche *f*
paral·lel ['pærə‚lɛl] *adj* parallèle || *s*
(*line*) parallèle *f*; (*latitude; declination; comparison*) parallèle *m*; **parallels** (typ) barres *fpl*; **without parallel**
sans pareil || *v* (*pret & pp* **-leled** or
-lelled; *ger* **-leling** or **-lelling**) *tr* mettre en parallèle; entrer en parallèle
avec, égaler
par'allel bars' *spl* barres *fpl* parallèles
paraly·sis [pə'rælɪsɪs] *s* (*pl* **-ses** [‚siz])
paralysie *f*
paralytic [‚pærə'lɪtɪk] *adj & s* paralytique *mf*
paralyze ['pærə‚laɪz] *tr* paralyser
paramount ['pærə‚maunt] *adj* suprême, capital
paranoiac [‚pærə'nɔɪ·æk] *adj & s*
paranoïaque *mf*
parapet ['pærə‚pɛt] *s* parapet *m*
paraphernalia [‚pærəfər'nelɪ·ə] *spl* effets *mpl* personnels; attirail *m*
paraphrase ['pærə‚frez] *s* remaniement
m || *tr* remanier
parasite ['pærə‚saɪt] *s* parasite *m*
parasitic(al) [‚pærə'sɪtɪk(əl)] *adj* parasite
parasol ['pærə‚sɔl], ['pærə‚sɑl] *s* parasol *m*, ombrelle *f*
paratrooper ['pærə‚trupər] *s* parachutiste *m*
parboil ['pɑr‚bɔɪl] *tr* faire cuire légèrement; (*vegetables*) blanchir
par·cel ['pɑrsəl] *s* colis *m*, paquet *m* ||
v (*pret & pp* **-celed** or **-celled**; *ger*
-celing or **-celling**) *tr* morceler; **to
parcel out** répartir
par'cel post' *s* colis *mpl* postaux
parch [pɑrtʃ] *tr* dessécher; (*beans,
grain, etc.*) griller
parchment ['pɑrtʃmənt] *s* parchemin *m*
pardon ['pɑrdən] *s* pardon *m*; (*remis-

sion of penalty by the state*) grâce *f*;
I beg your pardon je vous demande
pardon || *tr* pardonner; pardonner
(with *dat*); (*a criminal*) grâcier; **to
pardon** s.o. **for** s.th. pardonner q.ch.
à qn
pardonable ['pɑrdənəbəl] *adj* pardonnable
pare [pɛr] *tr* (*potatoes, fruit, etc.*)
éplucher; (*the nails*) rogner; (*costs*)
réduire
parent ['pɛrənt] *s* père *m* or mère *f*;
origine *f*, base *f*; **parents** parents *mpl*,
père et mère
parentage ['pɛrəntɪdʒ] *s* paternité *f* or
maternité *f*; naissance *f*, origine *f*
parenthe·sis [pə'rɛnθɪsɪs] *s* (*pl* **-ses**
[‚siz]) parenthèse *f*; **in parentheses**
entre parenthèses
parenthood ['pɛrənt‚hud] *s* paternité *f*
or maternité *f*
pariah [pə'raɪ·ə], ['pɑrɪ·ə] *s* paria *m*
par'ing knife' *s* couteau *m* à éplucher
Paris ['pærɪs] *s* Paris *m*
parish ['pærɪʃ] *adj* paroissien || *s* pa-
roisse *f*
parishioner [pə'rɪʃənər] *s* paroissien *m*
Parisian [pə'rɪʒən], [pə'riʒən] *adj & s*
parisien *m*
parity ['pærɪti] *s* parité *f*
park [pɑrk] *s* parc *m* || *tr* garer, par-
quer || *intr* stationner
parked *adj* en stationnement
parking ['pɑrkɪŋ] *s* parcage *m*; (*e.g.,
in a city street*) stationnement *m*; **no
parking** (public sign) stationnement
interdit
park'ing lights' *spl* (aut) feux *mpl* de
stationnement, feux de position
park'ing lot' *s* parking *m*, parc *m* à
autos
park'ing me'ter *s* parcomètre *m*
park'ing tick'et *s* contravention *f*, papillon *m*
park'way' *s* route *f* panoramique;
(*turnpike*) autoroute *f*
parley ['pɑrli] *s* pourparlers *mpl* || *intr*
parlementer
parliament ['pɑrlɪmənt] *s* parlement *m*
parliamentarian [‚pɑrlɪmen'tɛrɪ·ən] *s*
expert *m* en usages parlementaires
parlor ['pɑrlər] *s* salon *m*; (*in an institution*) parloir *m*
par'lor car' *s* (rr) wagon-salon *m*
par'lor game' *s* jeu *m* de société
Parnassus [pɑr'næsəs] *s* le Parnasse
parochial [pə'rokɪ·əl] *adj* paroissial;
(*attitude*) provincial
paro'chial school' *s* école *f* confession-
nelle, école libre
paro·dy ['pærədi] *s* (*pl* **-dies**) parodie *f*
|| *v* (*pret & pp* **-died**) *tr* parodier
parole [pə'rol] *s* parole *f* d'honneur;
liberté *f* sur parole || *tr* libérer sur
parole
par·quet [pɑr'ke], [pɑr'kɛt] *s* parquet
m; (theat) premiers rangs *mpl* du
parterre || *v* (*pret & pp* **-queted**
['ked], ['kɛtɪd]; *ger* **-queting** ['ke·
ɪŋ], ['kɛtɪŋ]) *tr* parqueter
parricide ['pærɪ‚saɪd] *s* (*act*) parricide
m; (*person*) parricide *mf*

parrot ['pærət] *s* perroquet *m* ‖ *tr* répéter or imiter comme un perroquet

par·ry ['pæri] *s* (*pl* **-ries**) parade *f* ‖ *v* (*pret* & *pp* **-ried**) *tr* parer; (*a question*) éluder

parse [pars] *tr* faire l'analyse grammaticale de

parsimonious [ˌparsɪ'monɪ·əs] *adj* parcimonieux, regardant

parsley ['parsli] *s* persil *m*

parsnip ['parsnɪp] *s* panais *m*

parson ['parsən] *s* curé *m*; pasteur *m* protestant

parsonage ['parsənɪdʒ] *s* presbytère *m*

part [part] *s* partie *f*; (*share*) part *f*; (*of a machine*) organe *m*, pièce *f*; (*of the hair*) raie *f*; (*theat*) rôle *m*; **for my part** pour ma part; **for the most part** pour la plupart; **in part** en partie; **in these parts** dans ces parages; **on the part of** de la part de; **parts** qualités *fpl*; parties (génitales); **to be or form part of** faire partie de; **to be part and parcel of** faire partie intégrante de; **to do one's part** faire son devoir; **to live a part** (theat) entrer dans la peau d'un personnage; **to look the part** avoir le physique de l'emploi; **to take part in** prendre part à; **to take the part of** prendre parti pour; jouer le rôle de ‖ *adv* partiellement, en partie; **part . . . part** moitié . . . moitié ‖ *tr* séparer; **to part the hair** se faire une raie ‖ *intr* se séparer; (*said, e.g., of road*) diverger; (*to break*) rompre; **to part with** se défaire de; se dessaisir de

par·take [par'tek] *v* (*pret* **-took**; *pp* **-taken**) *intr*—**to partake in** participer à; **to partake of** (*e.g., a meal*) prendre; (*e.g., joy*) participer de

partial ['parʃəl] *adj* partiel; (*prejudiced*) partial

participant [par'tɪsɪpənt] *adj* & *s* participant *m*

participate [par'tɪsɪˌpet] *intr* participer

participation [parˌtɪsɪ'peʃən] *s* participation *f*

participle ['partɪˌsɪpəl] *s* participe *m*

particle ['partɪkəl] *s* particule *f*

particular [pər'tɪkjələr] *adj* particulier; difficile, exigeant; méticuleux; **a particular . . .** un certain . . . ‖ *s* détail *m*

particularize [pər'tɪkjələˌraɪz] *tr* & *intr* individualiser, particulariser

parting ['partɪŋ] *s* séparation *f*

partisan ['partɪzən] *adj* & *s* partisan *m*

partition [par'tɪʃən] *s* partage *m*; (*wall*) paroi *f*, cloison *f* ‖ *tr* partager; **to partition off** séparer par des cloisons

partner ['partnər] *s* partenaire *mf*; (*husband*) conjoint *m*; (*wife*) conjointe *f*; (*in a dance*) cavalier *m*; (*in business*) associé *m*

part′ner·ship′ *s* association *f*; (com) société *f*

part′ of speech′ *s* partie *f* du discours

part′ own′er *s* copropriétaire *mf*

partridge ['partrɪdʒ] *s* perdrix *m*

part′-time′ *adj* & *adv* à mi-temps

par·ty ['parti] *adj* de gala ‖ *s* (*pl* **-ties**) fête *f*, soirée *f*; (*diversion of a group of persons; individual named in contract or lawsuit*) partie *f*; (*with whom one is conversing*) interlocuteur *m*; (mil) détachement *m*, peloton *m*; (pol) parti *m*; (telp) correspondant *m*; (coll) individu *m*; **to be a party to** être complice de

party-goer ['parti ˌgo·ər] *s* invité *m*; (*nightlifer*) noceur *m*

par′ty line′ *s* (*between two properties*) limite *f*; (telp) ligne *f* à postes groupés ‖ **par′ty line′** *s* ligne du parti; (*of communist party*) directives *fpl* du parti

par′ty pol′itics *s* politique *f* de parti

par′ty wall′ *s* mur *m* mitoyen

pass [pæs], [pas] *s* (*navigable channel; movement of hands of magician; in sports*) passe *f*; (*straits*) pas *m*; (*in mountains*) col *m*, passage *m*; (*document*) laissez-passer *m*; difficulté *f*; (mil) permission *f*; (rr) permis *m* de circulation; (theat) billet *m* de faveur ‖ *tr* passer; (*an exam*) réussir à; (*e.g., a student*) recevoir; (*a law*) adopter, voter; (*a red light*) brûler; (*to get ahead of*) dépasser; (*a car going in the same direction*) doubler; (*s.o. or s.th. coming toward one*) croiser; (*a certain place*) passer devant; **to pass around** faire circuler; **to pass oneself off as** se faire passer pour; **to pass out** distribuer; **to pass over** passer sous silence; (*to hand over*) transmettre; **to pass s.th. off on s.o.** repasser or refiler q.ch. à qn ‖ *intr* passer; (educ) être reçu; **bring to pass** réaliser; **to come to pass** se passer; **to pass as or for** passer pour; **to pass away** disparaître; (*to die out*) s'éteindre; (*to die*) mourir; **to pass by** passer devant; **to pass out** sortir; (slang) s'évanouir; **to pass over** passer sur; (*an obstacle*) franchir; (*said of storm*) s'éloigner; (*to pass through*) traverser; **to pass over to** (*e.g., the enemy*) passer à

passable ['pæsəbəl], ['pasəbəl] *adj* passable; (*road, river, etc.*) franchissable

passage ['pæsɪdʒ] *s* passage *m*; (*of time*) cours *m*; (*of a law*) adoption *f*

pass′book′ *s* carnet *m* de banque

passenger ['pæsəndʒər] *adj* (*e.g., train*) de voyageurs; (*e.g., pigeon*) de passage ‖ *s* voyageur *m*, passager *m*

passer-by ['pæsər'baɪ], ['pasər'baɪ] *s* (*pl* **passers-by**) passant *m*

passing ['pæsɪŋ], ['pasɪŋ] *adj* passager *s* (*act of passing*) dépassement *m*; (*death*) trépas *m*; (*of time*) écoulement *m*; (*of a law*) adoption *f*; (*in an examination*) la moyenne; une mention passable

passion ['pæʃən] *s* passion *f*

passionate ['pæʃənɪt] *adj* passionné

passive ['pæsɪv] *adj* & *s* passif *m*

pass′key′ *s* passe-partout *m*

pass′-out′ check′ *s* contremarque *f*

Pass′o′ver *s* Pâque *f*
pass′port′ *s* passeport *m*
pass′word′ *s* mot *m* de passe
past [pæst], [pɑst] *adj* passé, dernier; (*e.g., president*) ancien ‖ *s* passé *m* ‖ *prep* au-delà de, passé; plus de; hors de, e.g., **past all understanding** hors de toute compréhension; **it's twenty past five** il est cinq heures vingt; **it's past three o'clock** il est trois heures passées
paste [pest] *s* (*glue*) colle *f* de pâte; (*jewelry*) strass *m*; (culin) pâte *f* ‖ *tr* coller
paste′board′ *s* carton *m*
pastel [pæs′tɛl] *adj & s* pastel *m*
pasteurize [′pæstə‚raɪz] *tr* pasteuriser
pastime [′pæs‚taɪm], [′pɑs‚taɪm] *s* passe-temps *m*
past′ mas′ter *s* expert *m* en la matière, passé maître
pastor [′pæstər], [′pɑstər] *s* pasteur *m*
pastoral [′pæstərəl], [′pɑstərəl] *adj* pastoral ‖ *s* pastorale *f*
pastorate [′pæstərɪt], [′pɑstərɪt] *s* pastorat *m*
pas·try [′pestri] *s* (*pl* **-tries**) pâtisserie *f*
pas′try cook′ *s* pâtissier *m*
pas′try shop′ *s* pâtisserie *f*
pasture [′pæstʃər], [′pɑstʃər] *s* pâturage *m*, pâture *f* ‖ *tr* faire paître ‖ *intr* paître
past·y [′pesti] *adj* (*comp* **-ier**; *super* **-iest**) pâteux; (*face*) terreux
pat [pæt] *adj* à propos; (*e.g., excuse*) tout prêt ‖ *s* petite tape *f*; caresse *f*; (*of butter*) coquille *f* ‖ *v* (*pret & pp* **patted**; *ger* **patting**) *tr* tapoter; caresser; **to pat on the back** encourager, complimenter
patch [pætʃ] *s* (*e.g., of cloth*) pièce *f*, raccommodage *m*; (*of land*) parcelle *f*; (*of ice*) plaque *f*; (*of inner tube*) rustine *f*; (*e.g., of color*) tache *f*; (*beauty spot*) mouche *f* ‖ *tr* rapiécer; **to patch up** rapetasser; (*e.g., a quarrel*) arranger, raccommoder
patent [′petənt] *adj* patent ‖ [′pætənt] *adj* breveté ‖ *s* brevet *m* d'invention; **patent applied for** une demande de brevet a été déposée ‖ *tr* breveter
pat′ent leath′er [′pætənt] *s* cuir *m* verni
pat′ent med′icine [′pætənt] *s* specialité *f* pharmaceutique
pat′ent rights′ [′pætənt] *spl* propriété *f* industrielle
paternal [pə′tʌrnəl] *adj* paternel
paternity [pə′tʌrnɪti] *s* paternité *f*
path [pæθ], [pɑθ] *s* sentier *m*; (*in garden*) allée *f*; (*of bullet, heavenly body, etc.*) trajectoire *f*; (*for, e.g., riding horses*) piste *f*; **to beat a path** frayer un chemin
pathetic [pə′θɛtɪk] *adj* pathétique
path′find′er *s* pionnier *m*
pathology [pə′θɑlədʒi] *s* pathologie *f*
pathos [′peθɑs] *s* pathétique *m*
path′way′ *s* sentier *m*; (fig) voie *f*
patience [′peʃəns] *s* patience *f*
patient [′peʃənt] *adj* patient ‖ *s* malade *mf*; (*undergoing surgery*) patient *m*

pati·o [′pɑtɪ‚o] *s* (*pl* **-os**) patio *m*
patriarch [′petrɪ‚ɑrk] *s* patriarche *m*
patrician [pə′trɪʃən] *adj & s* patricien *m*
patricide [′pætrɪ‚saɪd] *s* (*act*) parricide *m*; (*person*) parricide *mf*
Patrick [′pætrɪk] *s* Patrice *m*
patrimo·ny [′pætrɪ‚moni] *s* (*pl* **-nies**) patrimoine *m*
patriot [′petrɪ‚ət], [′pætrɪ‚ət] *s* patriote *mf*
patriotic [‚petrɪ′ɑtɪk], [‚pætrɪ′ɑtɪk] *adj* patriotique, patriote
patriotism [′petrɪ‚ə‚tɪzəm], [′pætrɪ‚ə‚tɪzəm] *s* patriotisme *m*
pa·trol [pə′trol] *s* patrouille *f* ‖ *v* (*pret & pp* **-trolled**; *ger* **-trolling**) *tr* faire la patrouille dans ‖ *intr* patrouiller
patrol′man *s* (*pl* **-men**) *s* agent *m* de police
patrol′ wag′on *s* voiture *f* cellulaire
patron [′petrən], [′pætrən] *adj* patron ‖ *s* protecteur *m*; (com) client *m*
patronage [′petrənɪdʒ], [′pætrənɪdʒ] *s* patronage *m*, clientèle *f*
patronize [′petrə‚naɪz], [′pætrə‚naɪz] *tr* patronner, protéger; traiter avec condescendance; (com) acheter chez
pa′tron saint′ *s* patron *m*
patter [′pætər] *s* petit bruit *m*; (*of rain*) fouettement *m*; (*of magician, peddler, etc.*) boniment *m* ‖ *intr* (*said of rain*) fouetter; (*said of little feet*) trottiner
pattern [′pætərn] *s* patron *m*; modèle *m*
pat·ty [′pæti] *s* (*pl* **-ties**) petit pâté *m*
paucity [′pɔsɪti] *s* rareté *f*; manque *m*, disette *f*
paunch [pɔntʃ] *s* panse *f*
paunch·y [′pɔntʃi] *adj* (*comp* **-ier**; *super* **-iest**) ventru
pauper [′pɔpər] *s* indigent *m*
pause [pɔz] *s* pause *f*; (mus) point *m* d'orgue; **to give pause** to faire hésiter ‖ *intr* faire une pause; hésiter
pave [pev] *tr* paver
pavement [′pevmənt] *s* pavé *m*; (*surface*) chaussée *f*
pavilion [pə′vɪljən] *s* pavillon *m*
paw [pɔ] *s* patte *f*; (coll) main *f* ‖ *tr* donner un coup de patte à ‖ *intr* (*said of horse*) piaffer
pawl [pɔl] *s* cliquet *m* d'arrêt
pawn [pɔn] *s* (*in chess*) pion *m*; (*security, pledge*) gage *m*; (*tool of another person*) jouet *m* ‖ *tr* mettre en gage; **to pawn s.th. off on s.o.** (coll) refiler q.ch. à qn
pawn′bro′ker *s* prêteur *m* sur gages
pawn′shop′ *s* mont-de-piété *m*, crédit *m* municipal
pawn′ tick′et *s* reconnaissance *f* du mont-de-piété
pay [pe] *s* paye *f*; (mil) solde *f* ‖ *v* (*pret & pp* **paid** [ped]) *tr* payer; (mil) solder; (*a compliment; a visit; attention*) faire; **to pay back** payer de retour; **to pay down** payer comptant; **to pay off** (*a debt*) acquitter; (*a mortgage*) purger; (*a creditor*) rembourser; **to pay s.o. for s.th.**

payer qn de q.ch., payer q.ch. à qn ||
intr payer, rapporter; **to pay for**
payer; **to pay off** (coll) avoir du succès; **to pay up** se libérer par un
paiement
payable ['pe·əbəl] *adj* payable
pay' boost' *s* augmentation *f*
pay'check' *s* paye *f*
pay'day' *s* jour *m* de paye
pay'dirt' *s* alluvion *f* exploitable; (coll)
source *f* d'argent
payee [pe'i] *s* bénéficiaire *mf*
pay' en've·lope *s* sachet *m* de paye;
paye *f*
payer ['pe·ər] *s* payeur *m*
pay'load' *s* charge *f* payante; (aer)
poids *m* utile
pay'mas'ter *s* payeur *m*
payment ['pemənt] *m* paiement *m*; (*installment, deposit, etc.*) versement *m*
pay' phone' *s* taxiphone *m*
pay'roll' *s* bulletin *m* de paye; (*for officers*) état *m* de solde; (*for enlisted
men*) feuille *f* de prêt
pay' sta'tion *s* téléphone *m* public
pea [pi] *s* pois *m*; **green peas** petits
pois
peace [pis] *s* paix *f*
peaceable ['pisəbəl] *adj* pacifique
peaceful ['pisfəl] *adj* paisible, pacifique
peace'mak'er *s* pacificateur *m*
peace' of mind' *s* tranquillité *f* d'esprit
peace' pipe' *s* calumet *m* de paix
peach [pitʃ] *s* pêche *f*; (slang) bijou *m*
peach' tree' *s* pêcher *m*
peach·y ['pitʃi] *adj* (*comp* **-ier**; *super*
-iest) (slang) chouette
pea'coat' *s* (naut) caban *m*
pea'cock' *s* paon *m*
pea'hen' *s* paonne *f*
peak [pik] *s* cime *f*, sommet *m*; (*mountain; mountain top*) pic *m*; (*of beard*)
pointe *f*; (*of a cap*) visière *f*; (elec)
pointe
peak' hour' *s* heure *f* de pointe
peak' load' *s* (elec) charge *f* maximum
peak' vol'tage *s* tension *f* de crête
peal [pil] *s* retentissement *m*; (*of bells*)
carillon *m* || *intr* carillonner
peal' of laugh'ter *s* éclat *m* de rire
peal' of thun'der *s* coup *m* de tonnerre
pea'nut' *s* cacahuète *f*; (bot) arachide *f*
pea'nut but'ter *s* beurre *m* de caca-
huètes or d'arachide
pear [per] *s* poire *f*
pearl [pʌrl] *s* perle *f*
pearl' oys'ter *s* huître *f* perlière
pear' tree' *s* poirier *m*
peasant ['pɛzənt] *adj & s* paysan *m*
pea'shoot'er *s* sarbacane *f*
pea' soup' *s* (culin, fig) purée *f* de pois
peat [pit] *s* tourbe *f*
pebble ['pɛbəl] *s* caillou *m*; (*on seashore*) galet *m*
pebbled *adj* (*leather*) grenu
peck [pɛk] *s* coup *m* de bec; (*eight
quarts*) picotin *m*; (*kiss*) (coll) baiser
m d'oiseau, bécot *m*; (coll) tas *m*
|| *tr* becqueter || *intr* picorer; **to peck
at** picorer; (*food*) pignocher
peculation [ˌpɛkjə'leʃən] *s* péculat *m*,
détournement *m* de fonds

peculiar [pɪ'kjuljər] *adj* particulier;
(*strange*) bizarre
pedagogue ['pɛdəˌgɑg] *s* pédagogue *mf*
pedagogy ['pɛdəˌgodʒi], ['pɛdəˌgɑdʒi]
s pédagogie *f*
ped·al ['pɛdəl] *s* pédale *f* || *v* (*pret &
pp* **-aled** or **-alled**; *ger* **-aling** or
-alling) *tr* actionner les pédales de ||
intr pédaler
pedant ['pɛdənt] *s* pédant *m*
pedantic [pɪ'dæntɪk] *adj* pédant
pedant·ry ['pɛdəntri] *s* (*pl* **-ries**) pédanterie *f*
peddle ['pɛdəl] *tr & intr* colporter
peddler ['pɛdlər] *s* colporteur *m*
pedestal ['pɛdɪstəl] *s* piédestal *m*
pedestrian [pɪ'dɛstri·ən] *adj* (*style*)
prosaïque || *s* piéton *m*
pediatrics [ˌpidɪ'ætrɪks], [ˌpɛdɪ'æ-
trɪks] *s* pédiatrie *f*
pedigree ['pɛdɪˌgri] *s* généalogie *f*;
(*table*) arbre *m* généalogique; (*of
animal*) pedigree *m*
pediment ['pɛdɪmənt] *s* fronton *m*
peek [pik] *s* coup *m* d'œil furtif || *intr*
—**to peek at** regarder furtivement
peel [pil] *s* pelure *f*; (*of lemon*) zeste
m || *tr* peler; **to peel off** enlever ||
intr se peler; (*said of paint*) s'écailler
peep [pip] *s* regard *m* furtif; (*of, e.g.,
chickens*) piaulement *m* || *intr* piau-
ler; **to peep at** regarder furtivement
peep'hole' *s* judas *m*
peer [pɪr] *s* pair *m* || *intr* regarder avec
attention; **to peer at** or **into** scruter
peerless ['pɪrlɪs] *adj* sans pareil
peeve [piv] *s* (coll) embêtement *m* || *tr*
(coll) irriter, embêter, fâcher
peevish ['pivɪʃ] *adj* maussade
peg [pɛg] *s* cheville *f*; (*for tent*) piquet
m; **to take down a peg** (coll) rabattre
le caquet de || *v* (*pret & pp* **pegged**;
ger **pegging**) *tr* cheviller; (*e.g., prices*)
indexer, fixer; (*points*) marquer ||
intr piocher; **to peg away at** travailler
ferme à
Pegasus ['pɛgəsəs] *s* Pégase *m*
peg' leg' *s* jambe *f* de bois
peg' top' *s* toupie *f*; **peg tops** pantalon
m fuseau
Pekin·ese [ˌpikɪ'niz] *adj* pékinois || *s*
(*pl* **-ese**) Pékinois *m*
Peking ['pi'kɪŋ] *s* Pékin *m*
pelf [pɛlf] *s* (pej) lucre *m*
pelican ['pɛlɪkən] *s* pélican *m*
pellet ['pɛlɪt] *s* boulette *f*; (*bullet*)
grain *m* de plomb; (pharm) pilule *f*
pell-mell ['pɛl'mɛl] *adj* confus || *adv*
pêle-mêle
pelt [pɛlt] *s* peau *m*; coup *m* violent;
(*of stones, insults, etc.*) grêle *f* || *tr*
cribler; (*e.g., stones*) lancer || *intr*
tomber à verse
pen [pɛn] *s* plume *f*; (*fountain pen*)
stylo *m*; (*corral*) enclos *m*; (fig)
plume; (*prison*) (slang) bloc *m* || *v*
(*pret & pp* **penned**; *ger* **penning**) *tr*
écrire || *v* (*pret & pp* **penned** or **pent**
[pɛnt]; *ger* **penning**) *tr* parquer
penalize ['pinəˌlaɪz] *tr* (*an action*)
sanctionner; (*a person*) punir;
(sports) pénaliser

penal·ty ['pɛnəlti] s (pl -ties) peine f; (for late payment; in a game) pénalité f; **under penalty of** sous peine de
penance ['pɛnəns] s pénitence f
penchant ['pɛnʃənt] s penchant m
pen·cil ['pɛnsəl] s crayon m; (of light) faisceau m || v (pret & pp -ciled or -cilled; ger -ciling or -cilling) tr crayonner
pen'cil sharp'ener s taille-crayon m
pendent ['pɛndent] adj pendant || s pendant m, pendentif m; (of chandelier) pendeloque f
pending ['pɛndɪŋ] adj pendant || prep en attendant
pendulum ['pɛndʒələm] s pendule m
pen'dulum bob' s lentille f
penetrate ['pɛnɪˌtret] tr & intr pénétrer
penguin ['pɛŋgwɪn] s manchot m
pen'hold'er s porte-plume m; (rack) pose-plumes m
penicillin [ˌpɛnɪ'sɪlɪn] s pénicilline f
peninsula [pə'nɪnsələ] s presqu'île f; (large peninsula like Spain or Italy) péninsule f
peninsular [pə'nɪnsələr] adj péninsulaire
penitence ['pɛnɪtəns] s pénitence f
penitent ['pɛnɪtənt] adj & s pénitent m
pen'knife' s (pl -knives) canif m
penmanship ['pɛnmənˌʃɪp] s calligraphie f; (person's handwriting) écriture f
pen' name' s pseudonyme m
pennant ['pɛnənt] s flamme f; (sports) banderole f du championnat
penniless ['pɛnɪlɪs] adj sans le sou
pen·ny ['pɛni] s (pl -nies) (U.S.A.) centime m; **not a penny** pas un sou || s (pl pence [pɛns]) (Brit) penny m
pen'ny-pinch'ing adj regardant
pen'ny·weight' s poids m de 24 grains
pen' pal' s (coll) correspondant m
pen'point' s bec m de plume
pension ['pɛnʃən] s pension f || tr pensionner
pensioner ['pɛnʃənər] s pensionné m
pensive ['pɛnsɪv] adj pensif
Pentagon ['pɛntəˌgɑn] s Pentagone m
Pentecost ['pɛntɪˌkɔst], ['pɛntɪˌkɑst] s la Pentecôte
penthouse ['pɛntˌhaʊs] s toit m en auvent, appentis m; appartement m sur toit, maison f à terrasse
pent-up ['pɛntˌʌp] adj renfermé, refoulé
penult ['pinʌlt] s pénultième f
penum·bra [pɪ'nʌmbrə] s (pl -brae [bri] or -bras) pénombre f
penurious [pɪ'nʊrɪˌəs] adj (stingy) mesquin, parcimonieux; (poor) pauvre
penury ['pɛnjəri] s indigence f, misère f
pen'wip'er s essuie-plume f
peo·ny ['pi·əni] s (pl -nies) pivoine f
people ['pipəl] spl gens mpl, personnes fpl; **many people** beaucoup de monde; **my people** ma famille, mes parents; **people say on** dit || s (pl peoples) peuple m, nation f || tr peupler

pep [pɛp] s (coll) allant m || v (pret & pp pepped; ger pepping) tr—**to pep up** (coll) animer
pepper ['pɛpər] s (spice) poivre m; (fruit) grain m de poivre; (plant) poivrier m; (plant or fruit of the hot or red pepper) piment m rouge; (plant or fruit of the sweet or green pepper) piment doux, poivron m vert || tr poivrer; (e.g., with bullets) cribler
pep'per·box' s poivrière f
pep'per mill' s moulin m à poivre
pep'per·mint' s menthe f poivrée; (lozenge) pastille f de menthe
per [pʌr] prep par; **as per** suivant
perambulator [pər'æmbjəˌletər] s voiture f d'enfant
per capita [pər'kæpɪtə] par tête, par personne
perceive [pər'siv] tr (by the senses) apercevoir; (by understanding) percevoir
per cent or **percent** [pər'sɛnt] pour cent
percentage [pər'sɛntɪdʒ] s pourcentage m; **to get a percentage** (slang) avoir part au gâteau
perceptible [pər'sɛptəbəl] adj perceptible, sensible, appréciable
perception [pər'sɛpʃən] s perception f; compréhension f, pénétration f
perch [pʌrtʃ] s perchoir m; (ichth) perche f || tr percher || intr percher, se percher
percolate ['pʌrkəˌlet] tr & intr filtrer
percolator ['pʌrkəˌletər] s cafetière f à filtre
percussion [pər'kʌʃən] s percussion f
percus'sion cap' s capsule f fulminante
per diem [pər'daɪ·əm] par jour
perdition [pər'dɪʃən] s perdition f
perennial [pə'rɛnɪ·əl] adj perpétuel; (bot) vivace || s plante f vivace
perfect ['pʌrfɪkt] adj & s parfait m || [pər'fɛkt] tr perfectionner
perfidious [pər'fɪdɪ·əs] adj perfide
perfi·dy ['pʌrfɪdi] s (pl -dies) perfidie f
perforate ['pʌrfəˌret] tr perforer
per'forated line' s pointillé m
perforation [ˌpʌrfə're ʃən] s perforation f; (of postage stamp) dentelure f
perforce [pər'fɔrs] adv forcément
perform [pər'fɔrm] tr exécuter; (surg) faire; (theat) représenter || intr jouer; (said of machine) fonctionner
performance [pər'fɔrməns] s exécution f; (production) rendement m; (of a machine) fonctionnement m; (sports) performance f; (theat) représentation f
performer [pər'fɔrmər] s artiste mf
perform'ing arts' spl arts mpl du spectacle
perfume ['pʌrfjum] s parfum m || [pər'fjum] tr parfumer
perfunctory [pər'fʌŋktəri] adj superficiel; négligent
perhaps [pər'hæps] adv peut-être; **perhaps not** peut-être que non
per hour' à l'heure

peril ['pɛrəl] *s* péril *m*
perilous ['pɛrɪləs] *adj* périlleux
period ['pɪrɪ·əd] *s* période *f*; (*in school*) heure *f* de cours; (gram) point *m*; (sports) division *f*
pe'riod cos'tume *s* costume *m* d'époque
pe'riod fur'niture *s* meubles d'époque
periodic [,pɪrɪ'adɪk] *adj* périodique
periodical [,pɪrɪ'adɪkəl] *adj* périodique || *s* publication *f* périodique
peripheral [pə'rɪfərəl] *adj* périphérique
peripher•y [pə'rɪfəri] *s* (*pl* -ies) périphérie *f*
periscope ['pɛrɪ ,skop] *s* périscope *m*
perish ['pɛrɪʃ] *intr* périr
perishable ['pɛrɪʃəbəl] *adj* périssable
perjure ['pʌrdʒər] *tr*—to perjure oneself se parjurer
perju•ry ['pʌrdʒəri] *s* (*pl* -ries) parjure *m*
perk [pʌrk] *tr*—to perk up (*the head*) redresser; (*the ears*) dresser; (*the appetite*) ravigoter || *intr*—to perk up se ranimer
permanence ['pʌrmənəns] *s* permanence *f*
permanent ['pʌrmənənt] *adj* permanent || *s* permanente *f*
per'manent address' *s* domicile *m* fixe
per'manent ten'ure *s* inamovibilité *f*
per'manent wave' *s* ondulation *f* permanente
per'manent way' *s* (rr) matériel *m* fixe
permeate ['pʌrmɪ ,et] *tr & intr* pénétrer
permissible [pər'mɪsɪbəl] *adj* permis
permission [pər'mɪʃən] *s* permission *f*
per•mit ['pʌrmɪt] *s* permis *m*; (com) passavant *m* || [pər'mɪt] *v* (*pret & pp* -mitted; *ger* -mitting) *tr* permettre; to permit s.o. to permettre à qn de
permute [pər'mjut] *tr* permuter
pernicious [pər'nɪʃəs] *adj* pernicieux
pernickety [pər'nɪkɪti] *adj* (coll) pointilleux
perox'ide blonde' [pər'aksaɪd] *s* blonde *f* décolorée
perpendicular [,pʌrpən'dɪkjələr] *adj & s* perpendiculaire *f*
perpetrate ['pʌrpɪ ,tret] *tr* perpétrer
perpetual [pər'pɛtʃu·əl] *adj* perpétuel
perpetuate [pər'pɛtʃu ,et] *tr* perpétuer
perplex [pər'plɛks] *tr* rendre perplexe
perplexed [pər'plɛkst] *adj* perplexe
perplexi•ty [pər'plɛksɪti] *s* (*pl* -ties) perplexité *f*
persecute ['pʌrsɪ ,kjut] *tr* persécuter
persecution [,pʌrsɪ'kjuʃən] *s* persécution *f*
persevere [,pʌrsɪ'vɪr] *intr* persévérer
Persian ['pʌrʒən] *adj* persan || *s* (*language*) persan *m*; (*person*) Persan *m*
Per'sian blind' *s* persienne *f*
Per'sian Gulf' *s* Golfe *m* Persique
Per'sian rug' *s* tapis *m* de Perse
persimmon [pər'sɪmən] *s* plaquemine *f*; (*tree*) plaqueminier *m*
persist [pər'sɪst], [pər'zɪst] *intr* persister; to persist in persister dans; + *ger* persister à + *inf*
persistent [pər'sɪstənt], [pər'zɪstənt] *adj* persistant

person ['pʌrsən] *s* personne *f*; no person personne; per person par personne, chacun
personage ['pʌrsənɪdʒ] *s* personnage *m*
personal ['pʌrsənəl] *adj* personnel || *s* (journ) note *f* dans la chronique mondaine
personali•ty [,pʌrsə'nælɪti] *s* (*pl* -ties) personnalité *f*
per'sonal prop'erty *s* biens *mpl* mobiliers
personi•fy [pər'sanɪ ,faɪ] *v* (*pret & pp* -fied) *tr* personnifier
personnel [,pʌrsə'nɛl] *s* personnel *m*
per'son-to-per'son tel'ephone call' *s* communication *f* avec préavis
perspective [pər'spɛktɪv] *s* perspective *f*
perspicacious [,pʌrspɪ'keʃəs] *adj* perspicace
perspiration [,pʌrspɪ'reʃən] *s* transpiration *f*
perspire [pər'spaɪr] *intr* transpirer
persuade [pər'swed] *tr* persuader; to persuade s.o. of s.th. persuader q.ch. à qn, persuader qn de q.ch.; to persuade s.o. to persuader à qn de
persuasion [pər'sweʒən] *s* persuasion *f*; (*faith*) (coll) croyance *f*
pert [pʌrt] *adj* effronté; (*sprightly*) animé
pertain [pər'ten] *intr*—to pertain to avoir rapport à
pertinacious [,pʌrtɪ'neʃəs] *adj* obstiné, persévérant
pertinent ['pʌrtɪnənt] *adj* pertinent
perturb [pər'tʌrb] *tr* perturber
Peru [pə'ru] *s* le Pérou
peruse [pə'ruz] *tr* lire; lire attentivement
Peruvian [pə'ruvɪ·ən] *adj* péruvien || *s* Péruvien *m*
pervade [pər'ved] *tr* pénétrer, s'infiltrer dans
perverse [pər'vʌrs] *adj* pervers; obstiné; capricieux
perversion [pər'vʌrʒən] *s* perversion *f*
perversi•ty [pər'vʌrsɪti] *s* (*pl* -ties) perversité *f*; obstination *f*
pervert ['pʌrvərt] *s* pervers *m*, perverti *m* || [pər'vʌrt] *tr* pervertir
pes•ky ['pɛski] *adj* (*comp* -kier; *super* -kiest) (coll) importun
pessimism ['pɛsɪ ,mɪzəm] *s* pessimisme *m*
pessimist ['pɛsɪmɪst] *s* pessimiste *mf*
pessimistic [,pɛsɪ'mɪstɪk] *adj* pessimiste
pest [pɛst] *s* insecte *m* nuisible; (*pestilence*) peste *f*; (*annoying person*) raseur *m*
pester ['pɛstər] *tr* casser la tête à, importuner
pest'house' *s* lazaret *m*
pesticide ['pɛstɪ ,saɪd] *s* pesticide *m*
pestiferous [pɛs'tɪfərəs] *adj* pestiféré; (coll) ennuyeux
pestilence ['pɛstɪləns] *s* pestilence *f*
pestle ['pɛsəl] *s* pilon *m*
pet [pɛt] *s* animal *m* favori; familial *m*; (*child*) enfant *m* gâté; (*anger*) accès *m* de mauvaise humeur || *v* (*pret &*

pp petted; *ger* petting) *tr* choyer; (e.g., *an animal's fur*) caresser ‖ *intr* (slang) se bécoter
petal ['pɛtəl] *s* pétale *m*
pet'cock' *s* robinet *m* de purge
Peter ['pitər] *s* Pierre *m*; to rob Peter to pay Paul découvrir saint Pierre pour habiller saint Paul ‖ (*l.c.*) *intr* —to peter out (coll) s'épuiser, s'en aller en fumée
petition [pɪ'tɪʃən] *s* pétition *f* ‖ *tr* adresser or présenter une pétition à
pet' name' *s* mot *m* doux, nom *m* d'amitié
Petrarch ['pitrɑrk] *s* Pétrarque *m*
petri·fy ['pɛtrɪ‚faɪ] *v* (*pret & pp* -fied) *tr* pétrifier ‖ *intr* se pétrifier
petrol ['pɛtrəl] *s* (Brit) essence *f*
petroleum [pɪ'troli·əm] *s* pétrole *m*
pet' shop' *s* boutique *f* aux petites bêtes; (*for birds*) oisellerie *f*
petticoat ['pɛtɪ‚kot] *s* jupon *m*
pet·ty ['pɛti] *adj* (*comp* -tier; *super* -tiest) insignifiant, petit; (*narrow*) mesquin; intolérant
pet'ty cash' *s* petite caisse *f*
pet'ty expen'ses *s* menus frais *mpl*
pet'ty lar'ceny *s* vol *m* simple
pet'ty of'ficer *s* (naut) officier *m* marinier
petulant ['pɛtjələnt] *adj* irritable, boudeur
pew [pju] *s* banc *m* d'église
pewter ['pjutər] *s* étain *m*
Pfc. ['pi'ɛf'si] *s* (letterword) (private first class) soldat *m* de première classe
phalanx ['felæŋks], ['fælæŋks] *s* phalange *f*
phantasm ['fæntæzəm] *s* fantasme *m*
phantom ['fæntəm] *s* fantôme *m*
Pharaoh ['fɛro] *s* Pharaon *m*
pharisee ['færɪ‚si] *s* pharisien *m*; Pharisee Pharisien *m*
pharmaceutical [‚fɑrmə'sutɪkəl] *adj* pharmaceutique
pharmacist ['fɑrməsɪst] *s* pharmacien *m*
pharma·cy ['fɑrməsi] *s* (*pl* -cies) pharmacie *f*
pharynx ['færɪŋks] *s* pharynx *m*
phase [fez] *s* phase *f*; out of phase (*said of motor*) décalé ‖ *tr* mettre en phase; développer en phases successives; (coll) inquiéter; to phase out faire disparaître peu à peu
pheasant ['fɛzənt] *s* faisan *m*
phenobarbital [‚fino'bɑrbɪ‚tæl] *s* phénobarbital *m*
phenomenal [fɪ'nɑmɪ‚nəl] *adj* phénoménal
phenome·non [fɪ'nɑmɪ‚nɑn] *s* (*pl* -na [nə]) phénomène *m*
phial ['faɪ·əl] *s* fiole *f*
philanderer [fɪ'lændərər] *s* coureur *m*, galant *m*
philanthropist [fɪ'lænθrəpɪst] *s* philanthrope *mf*
philanthro·py [fɪ'lænθrəpi] *s* (*pl* -pies) philanthropie *f*
philatelist [fɪ'lætəlɪst] *s* philatéliste *mf*
philately [fɪ'lætəli] *s* philatélie *f*
Philippine ['fɪlɪ‚pin] *adj* philippin ‖ Philippines *spl* Philippines *fpl*

Philistine [fɪ'lɪstin], ['fɪlɪ‚stin], ['fɪlɪ‚staɪn] *adj & s* philistin *m*
philologist [fɪ'lɑlədʒɪst] *s* philologue *mf*
philology [fɪ'lɑlədʒi] *s* philologie *f*
philosopher [fɪ'lɑsəfər] *s* philosophe *mf*
philosophic(al) [‚fɪlə'sɑfɪk(əl)] *adj* philosophique
philoso·phy [fɪ'lɑsəfi] *s* (*pl* -phies) philosophie *f*
philter ['fɪltər] *s* philtre *m*
phlebitis [flɪ'baɪtɪs] *s* phlébite *f*
phlegm [flɛm] *s* flegme *m*; to cough up phlegm cracher des glaires, tousser gras
phlegmatic(al) [flɛg'mætɪk(əl)] *adj* flegmatique
phobia ['fobɪ·ə] *s* phobie *f*
Phoebe ['fibi] *s* Phébé *f*
Phoenicia [fɪ'nɪʃə], [fɪ'niʃə] *s* Phénicie *f*; la Phénicie
Phoenician [fɪ'nɪʃən], [fɪ'niʃən] *adj* phénicien ‖ *s* Phénicien *m*
phoenix ['finɪks] *s* phénix *m*
phone [fon] *s* (coll) téléphone *m* ‖ *tr & intr* (coll) téléphoner
phone' call' *s* coup *m* de téléphone, coup de fil
phonetic [fo'nɛtɪk] *adj* phonétique ‖ phonetics *s* phonétique *f*
phonograph ['fonə‚græf], ['fonə‚grɑf] *s* phonographe *m*
phonology [fə'nɑlədʒi] *s* phonologie *f*
pho·ny ['foni] *adj* (*comp* -nier; *super* -niest) faux, truqué ‖ *s* (*pl* -nies) charlatan *m*
pho'ny war' *s* drôle *f* de guerre
phosphate ['fɑsfet] *s* phosphate *m*
phosphorescent [‚fɑsfə'rɛsənt] *adj* phosphorescent
phospho·rus ['fɑsfərəs] *s* (*pl* -ri [‚raɪ]) phosphore *m*
pho·to ['foto] *s* (*pl* -tos) (coll) photo *f*
photoengraving [‚foto·ɛn'grevɪŋ] *s* photogravure *f*
pho'to fin'ish *s* photo-finish *f*
photogenic [‚foto'dʒɛnɪk] *adj* photogénique
photograph ['fotə‚græf], ['fotə‚grɑf] *s* photographie *f* ‖ *tr* photographier ‖ *intr*—to photograph well être photogénique
photographer [fə'tɑgrəfər] *s* photographe *mf*
photography [fə'tɑgrəfi] *s* photographie *f*
photostat ['fotə‚stæt] *s* (trademark) photostat *m* ‖ *tr & intr* photocopier
phrase [frez] *s* locution *f*, expression *f*; (mus) phrase *f* ‖ *tr* exprimer, rédiger; (mus) phraser
phrenology [frɪ'nɑlədʒi] *s* phrénologie *f*
phys·ic ['fɪzɪk] *s* médicament *m*; (*laxative*) purgatif *m* ‖ *v* (*pret & pp* -icked; *ger* -icking) *tr* purger
physical ['fɪzɪkəl] *adj* physique
phys'ical de'fect *s* vice *m* de conformation
physician [fɪ'zɪʃən] *s* médecin *m*
physicist ['fɪzɪsɪst] *s* physicien *m*

physics ['fɪzɪks] s physique f
physiogno•my [,fɪzɪ'ɑgnəmi], [,fɪzɪ-
'ɑnəmi] s (pl -mies) physionomie f
physiological [,fɪzɪ-ə'lɑdʒɪkəl] adj
physiologique
physiology [,fɪzɪ'ɑlədʒi] s physiologie f
physique [fɪ'zik] s physique m
pi [paɪ] s (math) pi m; (typ) pâté m ||
v (pret & pp pied; ger piing) tr (typ)
mettre en pâte
pianist [pɪ'ænɪst], ['pi·ənɪst] s pianiste
mf
pian•o [pɪ'æno] s (pl -os) piano m
pian'o stool' s tabouret m de piano
picayune [,pɪkə'jun] adj mesquin
picco•lo ['pɪkəlo] s (pl -los) piccolo m
pick [pɪk] s (tool) pic m, pioche f;
(choice) choix m; (choicest) élite f,
fleur f || tr choisir; (flowers) cueillir;
(fibers) effiler; (one's teeth, nose,
etc.) se curer; (a scab) gratter; (a
fowl) plumer; (a bone) ronger; (a
lock) crocheter; (the ground) piocher; (e.g., guitar strings) toucher;
(a quarrel; flaws) chercher; to pick
off enlever; (to shoot) descendre; to
pick out trier; to pick pockets voler
à la tire; to pick to pieces (coll)
éplucher; to pick up ramasser; (one's
strength) reprendre; (speed) accroître; (a passenger) prendre; (a
man overboard) recueillir; (an anchor; a stitch; a fallen child) relever;
(information; a language) apprendre;
(the scent) retrouver; (rad) capter ||
intr (said of birds) picorer; to pick at
(to scold) (coll) gronder; to pick at
one's food manger du bout des dents;
to pick on choisir; (coll) gronder; to
pick up (coll) se rétablir
pick'ax' s pioche f
picket ['pɪkɪt] s (stake, pale) pieu m;
(of strikers; of soldiers) piquet m ||
tr entourer de piquets de grève || intr
faire le piquet
pick'et fence' s palis m
pick'et line' s piquet m de grève
pickle ['pɪkəl] s cornichon m; (brine)
marinade f, saumure f; (coll) gâchis
m || tr conserver dans du vinaigre
pick'lock' s crochet m; (person) crocheteur m
pick'-me-up' s (coll) remontant m
pick'pock'et s voleur m à la tire
pick'up' s chargement m; passager m;
(of a motor) reprise f; (truck; phonograph cartridge) pick-up m; (woman)
(coll) racoleuse f
pick'up arm' s bras m de pick-up
pick'up truck' s camionnette f
pic•nic ['pɪknɪk] s pique-nique m || v
(pret & pp -nicked; ger -nicking) intr
pique-niquer
pictorial [pɪk'torɪ-əl] adj & s illustré m
picture ['pɪktʃər] s tableau m; image
f; photographie f; (painting) peinture
f; (engraving) gravure f; (mov) film
m; (screen) (mov, telv) écran m; the
very picture of le portrait de, l'image
de; to receive the picture (telv) cap-
ter l'image || tr dépeindre, représen-
ter; to picture to oneself s'imaginer

pic'ture gal'lery s musée m de peinture
pic'ture post' card' s carte f postale
illustrée
pic'ture show' s exhibition f de peinture; (mov) cinéma m
pic'ture sig'nal s signal m vidéo
picturesque [,pɪktʃə'resk] adj pittoresque
pic'ture tube' s tube m de l'image
pic'ture win'dow s fenêtre f panoramique
piddling ['pɪdlɪŋ] adj insignifiant
pie [paɪ] s pâté m; (dessert) tarte f;
(bird) pie f
piece [pis] s (of music; of bread) morceau m; (cannon, coin, chessman,
pastry, clothing) pièce f; (of land)
parcelle f; (e.g., of glass) éclat m; a
piece of advice un conseil; a piece
of furniture un meuble; to break into
pieces mettre en pièces, mettre en
morceaux; to give s.o. a piece of
one's mind (coll) dire son fait à qn;
to go to pieces se désagréger; (to be
hysterical) avoir ses nerfs; to pick to
pieces (coll) éplucher || tr rapiécer;
to piece together rassembler, coordonner
piece'meal' adv pièce à pièce
piece'work' s travail m à la tâche
piece'work'er s ouvrier m à la tâche
pied [paɪd] adj bigarré, panaché; (typ)
tombé en pâté
pier [pɪr] s quai m; (of a bridge) pile
f; (of a harbor) jetée f; (wall between
two openings) (archit) trumeau m
pierce [pɪrs] tr & intr percer
piercing ['pɪrsɪŋ] adj perçant; (sharp)
aigu
pier' glass' s grand miroir m
pie•ty ['paɪ·əti] s (pl -ties) piété f
piffle ['pɪfəl] s (coll) futilités fpl, sot-
tises fpl
pig [pɪg] s cochon m, porc m
pigeon ['pɪdʒən] s pigeon m
pi'geon•hole' s boulin m; (in desk) case
f || tr caser; mettre au rancart
pi'geon house' s pigeonnier m
piggish ['pɪgɪʃ] adj goinfre
piggyback ['pɪgi,bæk] adv sur le dos,
sur les epaules; en auto-couchette
pig'gy bank' ['pɪgi] s tirelire f, grenouille f
pig'-head'ed adj cabochard, têtu
pig' i'ron s gueuse f
piglet ['pɪglɪt] s cochonnet m
pigment ['pɪgmənt] s pigment m
pig'pen' s porcherie f
pig'skin' s peau f de porc; (coll) ballon
m du football
pig'sty' s (pl -sties) porcherie f
pig'tail' s queue f, natte f; (of tobacco)
carotte f
pike [paɪk] s pique f; autoroute f à
péage; (fish) brochet m
piker ['paɪkər] s (slang) rat m
pile [paɪl] s tas m; (stake) pieu m; (of
rug) poil m; (of building) masse f;
(elec, phys) pile f; (coll) fortune f;
piles (pathol) hémorroïdes fpl || tr
empiler || intr s'empiler
pile' dri'ver s sonnette f

pilfer ['pɪlfər] *tr & intr* chaparder
pilgrim ['pɪlgrɪm] *s* pèlerin *m*
pilgrimage ['pɪlgrɪmɪdʒ] *s* pèlerinage *m*
pill [pɪl] *s* pilule *f*; (*something unpleasant*) pilule; (coll) casse-pieds *m*
pillage ['pɪlɪdʒ] *s* pillage *m* || *tr & intr* piller
pillar ['pɪlər] *s* pilier *m*
pillo·ry ['pɪləri] *s* (*pl* **-ries**) pilori *m* || *v* (*pret & pp* **-ried**) *tr* clouer au pilori
pillow ['pɪlo] *s* oreiller *m*
pil′low·case′ or **pil′low·slip′** *s* taie *f* d'oreiller
pilot ['paɪlət] *s* pilote *m*; (*of gas range*) veilleuse *f* || *tr* piloter
pi′lot en′gine *s* locomotive-pilote *f*
pi′lot light′ *s* veilleuse *f*
pimp [pɪmp] *s* entremetteur *m*
pimple ['pɪmpəl] *s* bouton *m*
pim·ply ['pɪmpli] *adj* (*comp* **-plier**; *super* **-pliest**) boutonneux
pin [pɪn] *s* épingle *f*; (*of wearing apparel*) agrafe *f*; (*bowling*) quille *f*; (mach) clavette *f*, cheville *f*, goupille *f*; **to be on pins and needles** être sur les chardons ardents || *v* (*pret & pp* **pinned**; *ger* **pinning**) *tr* épingler; (mach) cheviller, goupiller; **to pin down** fixer, clouer
pinafore ['pɪnə,for] *s* tablier *m* d'enfant
pin′ball′ *s* billard *m* américain
pincers ['pɪnsərz] *s & spl* pinces *fpl*
pinch [pɪntʃ] *s* pinçade *f*; (*of salt*) pincée *f*; (*of tobacco*) prise *f*; (*of hunger*) morsure *f*; (*trying time*) moment *m* critique; (slang) arrestation *f*; **in a pinch** au besoin || *tr* pincer; (*to press tightly on*) serrer; (e.g., *one's finger in a door*) se prendre; (*to arrest*) (slang) pincer; (*to steal*) (slang) chiper || *intr* (*said, e.g., of shoe*) gêner; (*to save*) lésiner
pinchers ['pɪntʃərz] *s & spl* pinces *fpl*
pin′cush′ion *s* pelote *f* d'épingles
pine [paɪn] *s* pin *m* || *intr* languir; **to pine for** soupirer après
pine′ap′ple *s* ananas *m*
pine′ cone′ *s* pomme *f* de pin
pine′ nee′dle *s* aiguille *f* de pin
ping [pɪŋ] *s* sifflement *m*; (*in a motor*) cognement *m* || *intr* siffler; cogner
pin′head′ *s* tête *f* d'épingle; (coll) crétin *m*
pink [pɪŋk] *adj* rose || *s* rose *m*; (bot) œillet *m*; **to be in the pink** se porter à merveille
pin′ mon′ey *s* argent *m* de poche
pinnacle ['pɪnəkəl] *s* pinacle *m*
pin′point′ *adj* exact || *s* (fig) point *m* critique || *tr* situer avec précision
pin′prick′ *s* piqûre *f* d'épingle
pint [paɪnt] *s* chopine *f*
pin′up girl′ *s* pin up *f*
pin′wheel′ *s* (*fireworks*) soleil *m*; (*child's toy*) moulinet *m*
pioneer [,paɪə'nɪr] *s* pionnier *m* || *tr* défricher || *intr* faire œuvre de pionnier
pious ['paɪəs] *adj* pieux, dévot
pip [pɪp] *s* (*in fruit*) pépin *m*; (*on

cards, dice, etc.*) point *m*; (rad) top *m*; (vet) pépie *f*
pipe [paɪp] *s* tuyau *m*, tube *m*, conduit *m*; (*to smoke tobacco*) pipe *f*; (*of an organ*) tuyau; (mus) chalumeau *m* || *tr* canaliser || *intr* jouer du chalumeau; **pipe down!** (slang) boucle-la!
pipe′ clean′er *s* cure-pipe *m*
pipe′ dream′ *s* rêve *m*, projet *m* illusoire
pipe′ line′ *s* pipe-line *m*; (*of information*) tuyau *m*
pipe′ or′gan *s* grandes orgues *fpl*
piper ['paɪpər] *s* joueur *m* de chalumeau; (*bagpipe*) cornemuseur *m*; **to pay the piper** payer les violons
pipe′ wrench′ *s* clef *f* à tubes
piping ['paɪpɪŋ] *s* tuyauterie *f*; (sewing) passepoil *m*
pippin ['pɪpɪn] *s* (*apple*) reinette *f*; (*highly admired person or thing*) bijou *m*
piquancy ['pikənsi] *s* piquant *m*
piquant ['pikənt] *adj* piquant
pique [pik] *s* pique *f* || *tr* piquer; **to pique oneself on** se piquer de
pira·cy ['paɪrəsi] *s* (*pl* **-cies**) piraterie *f*
Piraeus [paɪ'ri·əs] *s* Le Pirée
pirate ['paɪrɪt] *s* pirate *m* || *tr* piller || *intr* pirater
pirouette [,pɪru'ɛt] *s* pirouette *f* || *intr* pirouetter
pistol ['pɪstəl] *s* pistolet *m*
piston ['pɪstən] *s* piston *m*
pis′ton ring′ *s* segment *m* de piston
pis′ton rod′ *s* tige *f* de piston
pis′ton stroke′ *s* course *f* de piston
pit [pɪt] *s* fosse *f*, trou *m*; (*in the skin*) marque *f*; (*of certain fruit*) noyau *m*; (*for cockfights, etc.*) arène *f*; (*of the stomach*) creux *m*; (min) puits *m*; (theat) fauteuils *mpl* d'orchestre derrière les musiciens || *v* (*pret & pp* **pitted**; *ger* **pitting**) *tr* trouer; (*the face*) grêler; (*fruit*) dénoyauter; **to pit oneself against** se mesurer contre
pitch [pɪtʃ] *s* (*black sticky substance*) poix *f*; (*throw*) lancement *m*, jet *m*; (*of a boat*) tangage *m*; (*of a roof*) degré *m* de pente; (*of, e.g., a screw*) pas *m*; (*of a tone, of the voice, etc.*) hauteur *f*; (coll) boniment *m*, tamtam *m*; **to such a pitch that** à tel point que || *tr* lancer, jeter; (*hay*) fourcher; (*a tent*) dresser; enduire de poix; (mus) donner le ton de || *intr* (*said of boat*) tanguer; **to pitch in** (coll) se mettre à la besogne; (coll) commencer à manger; **to pitch into** s'attaquer à
pitch′ ac′cent *s* accent *m* de hauteur
pitcher ['pɪtʃər] *s* broc *m*, cruche *f*; (baseball) lanceur *m*
pitch′fork′ *s* fourche *f*; **to rain pitchforks** pleuvoir à torrents
pitch′ pipe′ *s* diapason *m* de bouche
pit′fall′ *s* trappe *f*; (fig) écueil *m*, pierre *f* d'écueil
pith [pɪθ] *s* moelle *f*; (fig) suc *m*
pith·y ['pɪθi] *adj* (*comp* **-ier**; *super* **-iest**) moelleux; (fig) plein de suc
pitiful ['pɪtɪfəl] *adj* pitoyable

pitiless ['pɪtɪlɪs] *adj* impitoyable
pit·y ['pɪti] *s* (*pl* -ies) pitié *f*; **for pity's sake!** par pitié!; **what a pity!** quel dommage! || *v* (*pret & pp* -ied) *tr* avoir pitié de, plaindre
pivot ['pɪvət] *s* pivot *m* || *tr* faire pivoter || *intr* pivoter
placard ['plækɑrd] *s* placard *m*, affiche *f* || *tr* placarder
placate ['pleket] *tr* apaiser
place [ples] *s* endroit *m*; (*job*) poste *m*, emploi *m*; (*seat*) place *f*; (*rank*) rang *m*; **everything in its place** chaque chose à sa place; **in no place** nulle part; **in place of** au lieu de; **in your place** à votre place; **out of place** déplacé; **to change places** changer de place; **to keep one's place** (fig) tenir ses distances; **to take place** avoir lieu || *tr* mettre, placer; (*to find a job for; to invest*) placer; (*to recall*) remettre, se rappeler; (*to set down*) poser || *intr* (turf) finir placé
place·bo [plə'sibo] *s* (*pl* -bos or -boes) remède *m* factice
place' card' *s* marque-place *f*, carton *m* marque-place
place' mat' *s* garde-nappe *m*
placement ['plesmənt] *s* placement *m*; (*location*) emplacement *m*
place'ment exam' *s* examen *m* probatoire
place'-name' *s* nom *m* de lieu, toponyme *m*
placid ['plæsɪd] *adj* placide
plagiarism ['pledʒə‚rɪzəm] *s* plagiat *m*
plagiarize ['pledʒə‚raɪz] *tr* plagier
plague [pleg] *s* peste *f*; (*great public calamity*) fléau *m* || *tr* tourmenter
plaid [plæd] *s* plaid *m*
plain [plen] *adj* clair; simple; (*e.g., answer*) franc; (*color*) uni; (*ugly*) sans attraits || *s* plaine *f*
plain' clothes' *spl*—**in plain clothes** en civil, en bourgeois
plain'clothes'man *s* (*pl* -men') agent *m* en civil
plain' cook'ing *s* cuisine *f* bourgeoise
plain' om'elet *s* omelette *f* nature
plain' speech' *s* franc-parler *m*
plaintiff ['plentɪf] *s* (law) demandeur *m*, plaignant *m*
plaintive ['plentɪv] *adj* plaintif
plan [plæn] *s* plan *m*, projet *m*; (*drawing, diagram*) plan, dessein *m* || *v* (*pret & pp* planned; *ger* planning) *tr* projeter; **to plan to** se proposer de || *intr* faire des projets
plane [plen] *adj* plan, plat || *s* (aer) avion *m*; (bot) platane *m*; (carpentry) rabot *m*; (geom) plan *m* || *tr* raboter
plane' sick'ness *s* mal *m* de l'air
planet ['plænɪt] *s* planète *f*
plane' tree' *s* platane *m*
plan'ing mill' *s* atelier *m* de rabotage
plank [plæŋk] *s* planche *f*; (pol) article *m* d'une plate-forme électorale
plant [plænt], [plɑnt] *s* (*factory*) usine *f*; (*building and equipment*) installation *f*; (bot) plante *f* || *tr* planter

plantation [plæn'teʃən] *s* plantation *f*
planter ['plæntər] *s* planteur *m*
plant' louse' *s* puceron *m*
plasma ['plæzmə] *s* plasma *m*
plaster ['plæstər], ['plɑstər] *s* plâtre *m*; (*poultice*) emplâtre *m* || *tr* plâtrer; (*a bill, poster*) coller; (slang) griser
plas'ter cast' *s* plâtre *m*
plas'ter of Par'is *s* plâtre *m* à mouler
plastic ['plæstɪk] *adj* plastique || *s* (*substance*) plastique *m*; (*art*) plastique *f*
plas'tic bomb' *s* plastic *m*
plas'tic sur'gery *s* chirurgie *f* esthétique, chirurgie plastique
plate [plet] *s* (*dish*) assiette *f*; (*platter*) plateau *m*; (*sheet of metal*) tôle *f*, plaque *f*; vaisselle *f* d'or or d'argent; (anat, elec, phot, rad, zool) plaque; (typ) planche *f* || *tr* plaquer; (elec) galvaniser; (typ) clicher
plateau [plæ'to] *s* plateau *m*, massif *m*
plate' glass' *s* verre *m* cylindré
platen ['plætən] *s* rouleau *m*
platform ['plæt‚fɔrm] *s* plate-forme *f*; (*for arrivals and departures*) quai *m*; (*of a speaker*) estrade *f*; (*political program*) plate-forme
plat'form car' *s* (rr) plate-forme *f*
platinum ['plætɪnəm] *s* platine *m*
plat'inum blonde' *s* blonde *f* platinée
platitude ['plætɪ‚t(j)ud] *s* platitude *f*
Plato ['pleto] *s* Platon *m*
platoon [plə'tun] *s* section *f*
platter ['plætər] *s* plat *m*; (slang) disque *m*
plausible ['plɔzɪbəl] *adj* plausible
play [ple] *s* jeu *m*; (*drama*) pièce *f*; (mach) jeu; **to give full play to** donner libre cours à || *tr* jouer; (*e.g., the fool*) faire; (*cards; e.g., football*) jouer à; (*an instrument*) jouer de; **to play back** (*a tape*) faire repasser; **to play down** diminuer; **to play hooky** faire l'école buissonnière; **to play off** (sports) rejouer; **to play up** accentuer || *intr* jouer; **to play out** s'épuiser; **to play safe** prendre des précautions; **to play sick** faire semblant d'être malade; **to play up to** passer de la pommade à
play'back' *s* (*device*) lecteur *m*; (*reproduction*) lecture *f*
play'back head' *s* tête *f* de lecture
play'bill' *s* programme *m*; (*poster*) affiche *f*
play'er pian'o ['ple·ər] *s* piano *m* mécanique
playful ['plefəl] *adj* enjoué, badin
playgoer ['ple‚go·ər] *s* amateur *m* de théâtre
play'ground' *s* terrain *m* de jeu
play'house' *s* théâtre *m*; (*dollhouse*) maison *f* de poupée
play'ing card' *s* carte *f* à jouer
play'ing field' *s* terrain *m* de sports
play'mate' *s* compagnon *m* de jeu
play'-off' *s* finale *f*, match *m* d'appui
play' on words' *s* jeu *m* de mots
play'pen' *s* parc *m* d'enfants
play'room' *s* salle *f* de jeux
play'thing' *s* jouet *m*

play′time′ s recréation f
playwright [′ple‚raıt] s auteur m dramatique, dramaturge mf
play′writ′ing s dramaturgie f
plea [pli] s requête f, appel m; prétexte m; (law) défense f
plead [plid] v (pret & pp **pleaded** or **pled** [plɛd]) tr & intr plaider; **to plead not guilty** plaider non coupable
pleasant [′plɛzənt] adj agréable
pleasant·ry [′plɛzəntri] s (pl -ries) plaisanterie f
please [pliz] tr plaire (with dat); **it pleases him to** il lui plaît de; **please** + inf veuillez + inf; **to be pleased with** être content or satisfait de ‖ intr plaire; **as you please** comme vous voulez; **if you please** s'il vous plaît
pleasing [′plizıŋ] adj agréable
pleasure [′plɛʒər] s plaisir m; **at the pleasure of** au gré de; **what is your pleasure?** qu'y a-t-il pour votre service?, que puis-je faire pour vous?
pleas′ure car′ s voiture f de tourisme
pleas′ure trip′ s voyage m d'agrément
pleat [plit] s pli m ‖ tr plisser
plebe [plib] s élève m de première année
plebeian [plı′bi·ən] adj & s plébéien m
plebiscite [′plɛbı‚saıt] s plébiscite m
pledge [plɛdʒ] s gage m; engagement m d'honneur, promesse f ‖ tr mettre en gage; (one's word) engager
plentiful [′plɛntıfəl] adj abondant
plenty [′plɛnti] s abondance f; **plenty of** beaucoup de ‖ adv (coll) largement
pleurisy [′plurısi] s pleurésie f
pliable [′plaı·əbəl] adj pliable; docile, maniable
pliers [′plaı·ərz] s & spl pinces fpl, tenailles fpl
plight [plaıt] s embarras m; (promise) engagement m ‖ tr engager; **to plight one's troth** promettre fidélité
plod [plad] v (pret & pp **plodded**; ger **plodding**) tr parcourir lourdement et péniblement ‖ intr cheminer; travailler laborieusement
plot [plat] s complot m; (of a play or novel) intrigue f; (of ground) lopin m, parcelle f; (map) tracé m, plan m; (of vegetables) carré m ‖ v (pret & pp **plotted**; ger **plotting**) tr comploter, tramer; (a tract of land) faire le plan de; (a point) relever; (lines) tracer ‖ intr comploter; **to plot to** + inf comploter de + inf
plough [plau] s, tr & intr var of **plow**
plover [′plʌvər], [′plovər] s pluvier m
plow [plau] s charrue f; (for snow) chasse-neige m ‖ tr labourer; (the sea; the forehead) sillonner; (snow) déblayer; **to plow back** (com) affecter aux investissements ‖ intr labourer; **to plow through** avancer péniblement dans
plow′man s (pl -men) laboureur m
plow′share′ s soc m de charrue
pluck [plʌk] s cran m; (tug) saccade f ‖ tr arracher; (flowers) cueillir; (a fowl) plumer; (one's eyebrows)

épiler; (e.g., the strings of a guitar) pincer ‖ intr—**to pluck at** arracher d'un coup sec; **to pluck up** reprendre courage
pluck·y [′plʌki] adj (comp -ier; super -iest) courageux, crâne
plug [plʌg] s tampon m, bouchon m; (of sink, bathtub, etc.) bonde f; (of tobacco) chique f; (aut) bougie f; (on wall) (elec) prise f; (prongs) (elec) fiche f, prise; (old horse) (coll) rosse f; (hat) (slang) haut-de-forme m; (slang) annonce f publicitaire ‖ v (pret & pp **plugged**; ger **plugging**) tr boucher; (a melon) entamer; **to plug in** (elec) brancher ‖ intr—**to plug away** (coll) persévérer
plum [plʌm] s prune f; (tree) prunier m; (slang) fromage m
plumage [′plumıdʒ] s plumage m
plumb [plʌm] adj d'aplomb; (coll) pur ‖ s plomb m; **out of plumb** hors d'aplomb ‖ adv d'aplomb; (coll) en plein; (coll) complètement ‖ tr sonder
plumb′ bob′ s plomb m
plumber [′plʌmər] s plombier m
plumbing [′plʌmıŋ] s plomberie f
plumb′ line′ s fil m à plomb
plume [plum] s aigrette f; (of a hat, of smoke, etc.) panache m ‖ tr orner de plumes; (feathers) lisser; **to plume oneself on** se piquer de
plummet [′plʌmıt] s plomb m ‖ intr tomber d'aplomb, se précipiter
plump [plʌmp] adj grassouillet, potelé, dodu; brusque ‖ s (coll) chute f lourde; (coll) bruit m sourd ‖ adv en plein; brusquement ‖ tr jeter brusquement; **to plump oneself down** s'affaler ‖ intr tomber lourdement
plunder [′plʌndər] s pillage m; (booty) butin m ‖ tr piller
plunge [plʌndʒ] s plongeon m; (pitching movement) tangage m ‖ tr plonger ‖ intr plonger; se précipiter; (fig) se plonger; (naut) tanguer; (slang) risquer de grosses sommes
plunger [′plʌndʒər] s plongeur m; (slang) risque-tout m
plunk [plʌŋk] adv d'un coup sec; (squarely) carrément ‖ tr jeter bruyamment ‖ intr tomber raide
plural [′plurəl] adj & s pluriel m
plus [plʌs] adj positif ‖ s (sign) plus m; quantité f positive ‖ prep plus
plush [plʌʃ] adj en peluche; (coll) rupin ‖ s peluche f
plush·y [′plʌʃi] adj (comp -ier; super -iest) pelucheux; (coll) rupin
plus′ sign′ s signe m plus
Plutarch [′plutark] s Plutarque m
Pluto [′pluto] s Pluton m
plutonium [plu′toni·əm] s plutonium m
ply [plaı] s (pl **plies**) (e.g., of a cloth) pli m; (of rope, wool, etc.) brin m ‖ v (pret & pp **plied**) tr manier; (a trade) exercer; **to ply s.o. with** presser qn de ‖ intr faire la navette
ply′wood′ s bois m de placage, contreplaqué m

P.M. ['pi'εm] *adv* (letterword) (**post meridiem**) de l'après-midi, du soir
pneumatic [n(j)u'mætɪk] *adj* pneumatique
pneumat'ic drill' *s* foreuse *f* à air comprimé
pneumonia [n(j)u'monɪ'ə] *s* pneumonie *f*
P.O. ['pi'o] *s* (letterword) (**post office**) poste *f*
poach [potʃ] *tr* (*eggs*) pocher ‖ *intr* (hunting) braconner
poached' egg' *s* œuf *m* poché
poacher ['potʃər] *s* braconnier *m*
pock [pɑk] *s* pustule *f*
pocket ['pɑkɪt] *s* poche *f*; (billiards) blouse *f*; (aer) trou *m* d'air ‖ *tr* empocher; (*a billiard ball*) blouser; (*insults*) avaler
pock'et·book' *s* portefeuille *m*; (*small book*) livre *m* de poche
pock'et hand'kerchief *s* mouchoir *m* de poche
pock'et·knife' *s* (*pl* **-knives**) couteau *m* de poche, canif *m*
pock'et mon'ey *s* argent *m* de poche
pock'mark' *s* marque *f* de la petite vérole
pock'marked' *adj* grêlé
pod [pɑd] *s* cosse *f*, gousse *f*
poem ['po·ɪm] *s* poème *m*
poet ['po·ɪt] *s* poète *m*
poetess ['po·ɪtɪs] *s* poétesse *f*
poetic [po'εtɪk] *adj* poétique ‖ **poetics** *s* poétique *f*
poetry ['po·ɪtri] *s* poésie *f*
pogrom ['pogrəm] *s* pogrom *m*
poignancy ['pɔɪnənsi] *s* piquant *m*
poignant ['pɔɪnənt] *adj* poignant
point [pɔɪnt] *s* (*spot, dot, score, etc.*) point *m*; (*tip*) pointe *f*; (*of pen*) bec *m*; (*of conscience*) cas *m*; (*of a star*) rayon *m*; (*of a joke*) piquant *m*; (*of, e.g., grammar*) question *f*; (geog, naut) pointe; (typ) point; **beside the point, off the point** hors de propos; **on the point of** sur le point de; (*death*) à l'article de; **on this point** à cet égard, à ce propos; **point of a compass** aire *f* de vent; **point of order** rappel *m* au règlement; (aut) vis *f* platinées; **to carry one's point** avoir gain de cause; **to come to the point** venir au fait; **to have one's good points** avoir ses qualités; **to make a point of** se faire un devoir de ‖ *tr* (*a gun, telescope, etc.*) braquer, pointer; (*a finger*) tendre; (*the way*) indiquer; (*a wall*) jointoyer; (*to sharpen*) tailler en point; **to point out** signaler, faire remarquer ‖ *intr* pointer; (*said of hunting dog*) tomber en arrêt; **to point at** montrer du doigt
point'-blank' *adj* & *adv* (*fired straight at the mark*) à bout portant; (*straightforward*) à brûle-pourpoint
pointed *adj* pointu; (*remark*) mordant
pointer ['pɔɪntər] *s* (*stick*) baguette *f*; (*of a dial*) aiguille *f*; (*dog*) chien *m* d'arrêt, pointeur *m*
poise [pɔɪz] *s* équilibre *m*; (*assurance*)

aplomb *m* ‖ *tr* tenir en équilibre ‖ *intr* être en équilibre; (*in the air*) planer
poison ['pɔɪzən] *s* poison *m* ‖ *tr* empoisonner
poi'son gas' *s* gaz *m* asphyxiant
poi'son i'vy *s* sumac *m* vénéneux
poisonous ['pɔɪzənəs] *adj* toxique; (*plant*) vénéneux; (*snake*) venimeux
poke [pok] *s* poussée *f*; (*with elbow*) coup *m* de coude; (coll) traînard *m* ‖ *tr* pousser; (*the fire*) tisonner; **to poke fun at** se moquer de; **to poke one's nose into** (coll) fourrer son nez dans; **to poke s.th. into** fourrer q.ch. dans ‖ *intr* aller sans se presser; **poke about** fureter
poker ['pokər] *s* tisonnier *m*; (cards) poker *m*
pok'er face' *s* visage *m* impassible
pok·y ['poki] *adj* (*comp* **-ier**; *super* **-iest**) (coll) lambin, lent
Poland ['polənd] *s* Pologne *f*; la Pologne
polar ['polər] *adj* polaire
po'lar bear' *s* ours *m* blanc
polarize ['polə,raɪz] *tr* polariser
pole [pol] *s* (*long rod or staff*) perche *f*; (*of flag*) hampe *f*; (*upright support*) poteau *m*; (astr, biol, elec, geog, math) pôle *m*; **Pole** (*person*) Polonais *m* ‖ *tr* pousser à la perche
pole'cat' *s* putois *m*
pole'star' *s* étoile *f* polaire
pole' vault' *s* saut *m* à la perche
police [pə'lis] *s* police *f* ‖ *tr* maintenir l'ordre dans
police' brutal'ity *s* brutalité *f* policière
police' commis'sioner *s* préfet *m* de police
police'man *s* (*pl* **-men**) agent *m* de police
police' pre'cinct *s* commissariat *m* de police
police' state' *s* régime *m* policier
police' sta'tion *s* poste *m* de police, commissariat *m*
police'wom'an *s* (*pl* **-wom'en**) femme *f* agent
poli·cy ['pɑlɪsi] *s* (*pl* **-cies**) politique *f*; (ins) police *f*
polio ['polɪ,o] *s* (coll) polio *f*
polish ['pɑlɪʃ] *s* poli *m*; (*for household uses*) cire *f*; (*for shoes*) cirage *m*; (fig) politesse *f*, vernis *m* ‖ *tr* polir; (*shoes, floor, etc.*) cirer; (*one's nails*) vernir; **to polish off** (coll) expédier; (*e.g., a meal*) (slang) engloutir ‖ **Polish** ['polɪʃ] *adj* & *s* polonais *m*
polite [pə'laɪt] *adj* poli
politeness [pə'laɪtnɪs] *s* politesse *f*
politic ['pɑlɪtɪk] *adj* (*prudent*) diplomatique, politique; (*shrewd*) rusé
political [pə'lɪtɪkəl] *adj* politique
politician [,pɑlɪ'tɪʃən] *s* politicien *m*
politics ['pɑlɪtɪks] *s* & *spl* politique *f*
poll [pol] *s* liste *f* électorale; (*vote*) scrutin *m*; (*head*) tête *f*; sondage *m* d'opinion; **to go to the polls** aller aux urnes; **to take a poll** faire une enquête par sondage ‖ *tr* (*e.g., a dele-*

gation) dépouiller le scrutin de; (*a certain number of votes*) recevoir

pollen ['pɑlən] *s* pollen *m*

poll'ing booth' ['polɪŋ] *s* isoloir *m*

polliwog ['pɑlɪ ˌwɑg] *s* têtard *m*

pol'liwog initia'tion *s* baptême *m* de la ligne

poll' tax' *s* taxe *f* par tête

pollute [pə'lut] *tr* polluer

pollution [pə'luʃən] *s* pollution *f*

polo ['polo] *s* polo *m*

polonium [pə'lonɪ·əm] *s* polonium *m*

polygamist [pə'lɪgəmɪst] *s* polygame *mf*

polygamous [pə'lɪgəməs] *adj* polygame

polyglot ['pɑlɪ ˌglɑt] *adj* & *s* polyglotte *mf*

polygon ['pɑlɪ ˌgɑn] *s* polygone *m*

polynomial [ˌpɑlɪ'nomɪ·əl] *s* polynôme *m*

polyp ['pɑlɪp] *s* polype *m*

polytheist ['pɑlɪ ˌθi·ɪst] *s* polythéiste *mf*

polytheistic [ˌpɑlɪθi'ɪstɪk] *adj* polythéiste

pomade [pə'med], [pə'mɑd] *s* pommade *f*

pomegranate ['pɑm ˌgrænɪt] *s* (*shrub*) grenadier *m*; (*fruit*) grenade *f*

pom·mel ['pʌməl], ['pɑməl] *s* pommeau *m* ‖ *v* (*pret* & *pp* -meled or -melled; *ger* -meling or -melling) *tr* rosser

pomp [pɑmp] *s* pompe *f*

pompous ['pɑmpəs] *adj* pompeux

pon·cho ['pɑntʃo] *s* (*pl* -chos) poncho *m*

pond [pɑnd] *s* étang *m*, mare *f*

ponder ['pɑndər] *tr* peser ‖ *intr* méditer; **to ponder over** réfléchir sur

ponderous ['pɑndərəs] *adj* pesant

poniard ['pɑnjərd] *s* poignard *m* ‖ *tr* poignarder

pontiff ['pɑntɪf] *s* pontife *m*

pontifical [pɑn'tɪfɪkəl] *adj* (*e.g.*, *air*) de pontife

pontoon [pɑn'tun] *s* ponton *m*

po·ny ['poni] *s* (*pl* -nies) poney *m*; (*for drinking liquor*) petit verre *m*; (*coll*) aide-mémoire *m* illicite

poodle ['pudəl] *s* caniche *m*

pool [pul] *s* (*small puddle*) mare *f*; (*for swimming*) piscine *f*; (*game*) billard *m*; (*in certain games*) poule *f*; (*of workers*) équipe *f*; (*combine*) pool *m*; (*com*) fonds *m* commun ‖ *tr* mettre en commun

pool'room' *s* salle *f* de billard

pool' ta'ble *s* table *f* de billard

poop [pup] *s* poupe *f*; (*deck*) dunette *f* ‖ *tr* (slang) casser la tête à

poor [pur] *adj* pauvre; (*mediocre*) piètre; (*unfortunate*) pauvre (before noun); (*without money*) pauvre (after noun)

poor' box' *s* tronc *m* des pauvres

poor'house' *s* asile *m* des indigents

poorly ['purli] *adj* souffrant ‖ *adv* mal

pop [pɑp] *s* bruit *m* sec; (*soda*) boisson *f* gazeuse ‖ *v* (*pret* & *pp* **popped**; *ger* **popping**) *tr* (*corn*) faire éclater ‖ *intr*

(*said*, *e.g.*, *of balloon*) crever; (*said of cork*) sauter

pop'corn' *s* maïs *m* éclaté, grains *mpl* de maïs soufflés, pop-corn *m*

pope [pop] *s* pape *m*

pop'eyed' *adj* aux yeux saillants

pop'gun' *s* canonnière *f*

poplar ['pɑplər] *s* peuplier *m*

pop·py ['pɑpi] *s* (*pl* -pies) pavot *m*; (*corn poppy*) coquelicot *m*

pop'py·cock' *s* (coll) fadaises *fpl*

populace ['pɑpjəlɪs] *s* peuple *m*, populace *f*

popular ['pɑpjələr] *adj* populaire

popularize ['pɑpjələ ˌraɪz] *tr* populariser, vulgariser

populate ['pɑpjə ˌlet] *tr* peupler

population [ˌpɑpjə'leʃən] *s* population *f*

populous ['pɑpjələs] *adj* populeux

porcelain ['pɔrsəlɪn], ['pɔrslɪn] *s* porcelaine *f*

porch [pɔrtʃ] *s* (*portico*) porche *m*; (*enclosed*) véranda *f*

porcupine ['pɔrkjə ˌpaɪn] *s* porc-épic *m*

pore [por] *s* pore *m* ‖ *intr*—**to pore over** examiner avec attention, s'absorber dans

pork [pork] *s* porc *m*

pork' and beans' *spl* fèves *fpl* au lard

pork'chop' *s* côtelette *f* de porc

pornography [pɔr'nɑgrəfi] *s* pornographie *f*

porous ['porəs] *adj* poreux

porphy·ry ['pɔrfɪri] *s* (*pl* -ries) porphyre *m*

porpoise ['pɔrpəs] *s* marsouin *m*

porridge ['pɑrɪdʒ], ['pɔrɪdʒ] *s* bouillie *f*, porridge *m*

port [port] *s* port *m*; (*opening in ship's side*) hublot *m*, sabord *m*; (*left side of ship or airplane*) bâbord *m*; (*wine*) porto *m*; (*mach*) orifice *m*

portable ['portəbəl] *adj* portatif

portage ['portɪdʒ] *s* transport *m*; portage *m*

portal ['portəl] *s* portail *m*

portcullis [port'kʌlɪs] *s* herse *f*

portend [por'tend] *tr* présager

portent ['portent] *s* présage *m*

portentous [por'tentəs] *adj* extraordinaire; de mauvais augure

porter ['portər] *s* (*doorkeeper*) portier *m*, concierge *m*; (*in hotels and trains*) porteur *m*

portfoli·o [port'folɪ ˌo] *s* (*pl* -os) portefeuille *m*

port'hole' *s* hublot *m*

porti·co ['portɪ ˌko] *s* (*pl* -coes or -cos) portique *m*

portion ['porʃən] *s* portion *f*; (*dowry*) dot *f* ‖ *tr*—**to portion out** partager, répartir

port·ly ['portli] *adj* (*comp* -lier; *super* -liest) corpulent

port' of call' *s* port *m* d'escale

portrait ['portret], ['portrɪt] *s* portrait *m*; **to sit for one's portrait** se faire faire son portrait

portray [por'tre] *tr* faire le portrait de; dépeindre, décrire; (theat) jouer le rôle de

portrayal [por'tre·əl] *s* représentation *f*; description *f*

Portugal ['pɔrtʃəgəl] *s* le Portugal

Portu·guese ['pɔrtʃə,giz] *adj* portugais ‖ *s* (*language*) portugais *m* ‖ *s* (*pl* -guese) (*person*) Portugais *m*

port' wine' *s* porto *m*

pose [poz] *s* pose *f* ‖ *tr & intr* poser; **to pose as** se poser comme

posh [paʃ] *adj* (slang) chic, élégant

position [pə'zɪʃən] *s* position *f*; (*job*) poste *m*; **in position** en place; **in your position** à votre place

positive ['pazɪtɪv] *adj & s* positif *m*

possess [pə'zɛs] *tr* posséder

possession [pə'zeʃən] *s* possession *f*; **to take possession of** s'emparer de

possible ['pasɪbəl] *adj* possible

possum ['pasəm] *s* opossum *m*; **to play possum** (coll) faire le mort

post [post] *s* (*upright*) poteau *m*; (*job, position*) poste *m*; (*post office*) poste *f*; (mil) poste *m* ‖ *tr* (*a notice, placard, etc.*) afficher, placarder; (*a letter*) poster, mettre à la poste; (*a sentinel*) poster; (*with news*) tenir au courant; **post no bills** (public sign) défense d'afficher

postage ['postɪdʒ] *s* port *m*, affranchissement *m*

post'age due' *s* port *m* dû, affranchissement *m* insuffisant

post'age me'ter *s* affranchisseuse *f* à compteur

post'age stamp' *s* timbre-poste *m*

postal ['postəl] *adj* postal

post'al card' *s* carte *f* postale

post'al clerk' *s* postier *m*

post'al mon'ey or'der *s* mandat-poste *m*

post'al per'mit *s* franchise *f* postale, dispensé *m* du timbrage

post'al sav'ings bank' *s* caisse *f* d'épargne postale

post' card' *s* carte *f* postale

post'date' *s* postdate *f* ‖ **post'date'** *tr* postdater

poster ['postər] *s* affiche *f*

posterity [pas'tɛrɪti] *s* postérité *f*

postern ['postərn] *s* poterne *f*

post'haste' *adv* en toute hâte

posthumous ['pastʃuməs] *adj* posthume

post'man *s* (*pl* -men) facteur *m*

post'mark' *s* cachet *m* d'oblitération, timbre *m* ‖ *tr* timbrer

post'mas'ter *s* receveur *m* des postes, administrateur *m* du bureau de postes

post'master gen'eral *s* ministre *m* des Postes et Télécommunications

post-mortem [,post'mɔrtəm] *adj* après décès; (fig) après le fait ‖ *s* autopsie *f*; discussion *f* après le fait

post' of'fice *s* bureau *m* de poste

post'-office box' *s* case *f* postale, boîte *f* postale

post'paid' *adv* port payé, franc de port, franco de port

postpone [post'pon] *tr* remettre, différer; (*a meeting*) ajourner

postponement [post'ponmənt] *s* remise *f*, ajournement *m*

postscript ['post,skrɪpt] *s* post-scriptum *m*

posture ['pastʃər] *s* posture *f* ‖ *intr* prendre une posture

post'war' *adj* d'après-guerre

po·sy ['pozi] *s* (*pl* -sies) fleur *f*; bouquet *m*

pot [pat] *s* pot *m*; (*in gambling*) mise *f*; **to go to pot** (slang) s'en aller à vau-l'eau

potash ['pat,æʃ] *s* potasse *f*

potassium [pə'tæsɪəm] *s* potassium *m*

pota·to [pə'teto] *s* (*pl* -toes) pomme *f* de terre; (*sweet potato*) patate *f*

pota'to chips' *spl* pommes *fpl* chips; croustelle *f* (Canad)

potbellied ['pat,belid] *adj* ventru

poten·cy ['potənsi] *s* (*pl* -cies) puissance *f*; virilité *f*

potent ['potənt] *adj* puissant, fort; (*effective*) efficace

potentate ['potən,tet] *s* potentat *m*

potential [pə'tenʃəl] *adj & s* potentiel *m*

pot'hang'er *s* crémaillère *f*

pot'herb' *s* herbe *f* potagère

pot'hold'er *s* poignée *f*

pot'hole' *s* nid *m* de poule

pot'hook' *s* croc *m*

potion ['poʃən] *s* potion *f*

pot'luck' *s*—**to take potluck** manger à la fortune du pot

pot' shot' *s* coup *m* tiré à courte distance

potter ['patər] *s* potier *m* ‖ *intr*—**to potter around** s'occuper de bagatelles, bricoler

pot'ter's clay' *s* terre *f* à potier

pot'ter's field' *s* fosse *f* commune

pot'ter's wheel' *s* roue *f* or tour *m* de potier

potter·y ['patəri] *s* (*pl* -ies) poterie *f*

pouch [pautʃ] *s* poche *f*, petit sac *m*; (*of kangaroo*) poche *f* ventrale; (*for tobacco*) blague *f*

poultice ['poltɪs] *s* cataplasme *m*

poultry ['poltri] *s* volaille *f*

poul'try·man *s* (*pl* -men) éleveur *m* de volailles; (*dealer*) volailleur *m*

pounce [pauns] *intr*—**to pounce on** fondre sur, s'abattre sur

pound [paund] *s* (*weight*) livre *f*; (*for automobiles, stray animals, etc.*) fourrière *f* ‖ *tr* battre; (*to pulverize*) piler, broyer; (*to bombard*) pilonner; (*e.g., an animal*) mettre en fourrière; (*e.g., the sidewalk*) (fig) battre ‖ *intr* battre

pound' ster'ling *s* livre *f* sterling

pour [por] *tr* verser; (*tea*) servir; **to pour off** décanter ‖ *intr* écouler; (*said of rain*) tomber à verse; **to pour out of** sortir à flots

pout [paut] *s* moue *f* ‖ *intr* faire la moue

poverty ['pavərti] *s* pauvreté *f*

POW ['pi'o'dʌbl,ju] *s* (letterword) (**prisoner of war**) P.G.

powder ['paudər] *s* poudre *f* ‖ *tr* réduire en poudre; (*to sprinkle with powder*) poudrer ‖ *intr* se poudrer

pow'dered sug'ar *s* sucre *m* de confiseur

pow'der puff' *s* houppe *f*

pow'der room' s toilettes fpl pour dames
powdery ['pavdəri] adj (like powder) poudreux; (sprinkled with powder) poussiéreux; (crumbly) friable
power ['pav·ər] s pouvoir m; (influential nation; energy, force, strength; of a machine, microscope, number) puissance f; (talent, capacity, etc.) faculté f; the powers that be les autorités fpl; to seize power saisir le pouvoir || tr actionner
pow'er brake' s (aut) servo-frein m
pow'er dive' s piqué m à plein gaz
pow'er-dive' intr piquer à plein gaz
powerful ['pav·ərfəl] adj puissant
pow'er·house' s usine f centrale; (coll) foyer m d'énergie
pow'er lawn'mower s tondeuse f à gazon à moteur
powerless ['pav·ərlıs] adj impuissant
pow'er line' s secteur m de distribution
pow'er mow'er s tondeuse f à gazon à moteur; motofaucheuse f
pow'er of attorn'ey s procuration f, mandat m
pow'er pack' s (rad) unité f d'alimentation
pow'er plant' s (powerhouse) centrale f électrique; (aer, aut) groupe m motopropulseur
pow'er steer'ing s (aut) servo-direction f
practicable ['præktıkəbəl] adj praticable
practical ['præktıkəl] adj pratique
prac'tical joke' s farce f, attrape f
prac'tical jok'er s fumiste m
practically ['præktıkəli] adv pratiquement; (more or less) à peu près
prac'tical nurse' s garde-malade mf
practice ['præktıs] s pratique f; (of a profession) exercice m; (of a doctor) clientèle f; in practice en pratique, pratiquement; (well-trained) en forme; out of practice rouillé || tr pratiquer; (a profession) exercer, pratiquer; (e.g., the violin) s'exercer à; to practice what one preaches prêcher d'exemple || intr faire des exercices, s'exercer; (said of doctor, lawyer, etc.) exercer
practiced adj expert
practitioner [præk'tı/ənər] s praticien m
prairie ['preri] s steppes fpl; the prairie les Prairies fpl
praise [prez] s louange f || tr louer
praise'wor'thy adj louable
pram [præm] s voiture f d'enfant
prance [præns], [prɑns] intr caracoler, cabrioler
prank [præŋk] s espièglerie f
prate [pret] intr bavarder, papoter
prattle ['prætəl] s bavardage m, papotage m || intr bavarder, papoter; (said of children) babiller
prawn [prɔn] s crevette f rose, bouquet m
pray [pre] tr & intr prier
prayer [prer] s prière f
prayer' book' s livre m de prières

pray'ing man'tis ['mæntıs] s mante f religieuse
preach [prit/] tr & intr prêcher
preacher ['prit/ər] s prédicateur m
preamble ['pri,æmbəl] s préambule m
precarious [prı'kerı·əs] adj précaire
precaution [prı'kɔ/ən] s précaution f
precede [prı'sid] tr & intr précéder
precedent ['presıdənt] s précédent m
precept ['prisept] s précepte m
precinct ['prisıŋkt] s enceinte f; circonscription f électorale
precious ['pre/əs] adj précieux || adv—precious little (coll) très peu
precipice ['presıpıs] s précipice m
precipitate [prı'sıpı,tet] adj & s précipité m || tr précipiter || intr se précipiter
precipitous [prı'sıpıtəs] adj escarpé; (hurried) précipité
precise [prı'sais] adj précis
precision [prı'sıʒən] s précision f
preclude [prı'klud] tr empêcher
precocious [prı'ko/əs] adj précoce
preconceived [,prikən'sivd] adj préconçu
predatory ['predə,tori] adj rapace; (zool) prédateur
predicament [prı'dıkəmənt] s situation f difficile
predict [prı'dıkt] tr prédire
prediction [prı'dık/ən] s prédiction f
predispose [,pridıs'poz] tr prédisposer
predominant [prı'dɑmınənt] adj prédominant
preeminent [prı'emınənt] adj prééminent
preempt [prı'empt] tr s'approprier
preen [prin] tr lisser; to preen oneself se bichonner; être fier, se piquer
prefabricated [pri'fæbrı,ketıd] adj préfabriqué
preface ['prefıs] s préface f || tr préfacer
pre·fer [prı'fʌr] v (pret & pp -ferred; ger -ferring) tr préférer
preferable ['prefərəbəl] adj préférable
preference ['prefərəns] s préférence f
preferred' stock' s actions f privilégiées
prefix ['prifıks] s préfixe m || tr préfixer
pregnan·cy ['pregnənsi] s (pl -cies) grossesse f
pregnant ['pregnənt] adj enceinte, grosse; (fig) gros
prehistoric [,prihıs'tɑrık], [,prihıs'tɔrık] adj préhistorique
prejudice ['pred͡ʒədıs] s préjugé m; (detriment) préjudice m || tr prévenir, prédisposer; (to harm) porter préjudice à
prejudicial [,pred͡ʒə'dı/əl] adj préjudiciable
prelate ['prelıt] s prélat m
preliminar·y [prı'lımı,neri] adj préliminaire s (pl -ies) préliminaire m
prelude ['preljud], ['prilud] s prélude m || tr introduire; préluder à; (a piece of music) préluder par
premature [,primə't(j)ur] adj prématuré; (plant) hâtif
premeditate [prı'medı,tet] tr préméditer

premier [prɪ'mɪr], ['primɪ·ər] *s* premier ministre *m*
première [prə'mjɛr], [prɪ'mɪr] *s* première *f*; (*actress*) vedette *f*
premise ['premɪs] *s* prémisse *f*; **on the premises** sur les lieux; **premises** local *m*, locaux *mpl*
premium ['primɪ·əm] *s* prime *f*
premonition [,primə'nɪʃən] *s* prémonition *f*
preoccupation [pri,akjə'peʃən] *s* préoccupation *f*
preoccu·py [pri'akjə,paɪ] *v* (*pret & pp* -**pied**) *tr* préoccuper
prepaid [pri'ped] *adj* payé d'avance; (*letter*) affranchi
preparation [,prepə'reʃən] *s* préparation *f*; **preparations** (*for a trip; for war*) préparatifs *mpl*
preparatory [prɪ'pærə,tori] *adj* préparatoire
prepare [prɪ'pɛr] *tr* préparer ‖ *intr* se préparer
preparedness [prɪ'perɪdnɪs], [prɪ'perdnɪs] *s* préparation *f*; armement *m* préventif
pre·pay [pri'pe] *v* (*pret & pp* -**paid**) *tr* payer d'avance
preponderant [prɪ'pandərənt] *adj* prépondérant
preposition [,prepə'zɪʃən] *s* préposition *f*
prepossessing [,pripə'zɛsɪŋ] *adj* avenant, agréable
preposterous [prɪ'pastərəs] *adj* absurde, extravagant
prep' school' [prep] *s* école *f* préparatoire
prerecorded [,prirɪ'kɔrdɪd] *adj* (rad, telv) différé
prerequisite [pri'rɛkwɪzɪt] *s* préalable *m*; (educ) cours *m* préalable
prerogative [prɪ'ragətɪv] *s* prérogative *f*
presage ['presɪdʒ] *s* présage *m*; (*foreboding*) pressentiment *m* ‖ [prɪ'sedʒ] *tr* présager; pressentir
Presbyterian [,prɛzbɪ'tɪrɪ·ən] *adj & s* presbytérien *m*
prescribe [prɪ'skraɪb] *tr* prescrire ‖ *intr* faire une ordonnance
prescription [prɪ'skrɪpʃən] *s* prescription *f*; (*pharm*) ordonnance *f*
presence ['prezəns] *s* présence *f*
present ['prezənt] *adj* (*at this time*) actuel; (*at this place or time*) présent; **to be present at** assister à ‖ *s* cadeau *m*, présent *m*; (*present time or tense*) présent; **at present** à présent ‖ [prɪ'zɛnt] *tr* présenter
presentable [prɪ'zɛntəbəl] *adj* présentable, sortable
presentation [,prezən'teʃən], [,prizən-'teʃən] *s* présentation *f*
presenta'tion cop'y *s* exemplaire *m* offert à titre d'hommage
presentiment [prɪ'zɛntɪmənt] *s* pressentiment *m*
presently ['prezəntli] *adv* tout à l'heure; (*now*) à présent
preservé [prɪ'zʌrv] *s* confiture *f*; (*for game*) chasse *f* gardée ‖ *tr* préserver, conserver; (*to can*) conserver

pre-shrunk [pri'ʃrʌŋk] *adj* irrétrécissable
preside [prɪ'zaɪd] *intr* présider; **to preside over** présider
presiden·cy ['prezɪdənsi] *s* (*pl* -**cies**) présidence *f*
president ['prezɪdənt] *s* président *m*; (*of a university*) recteur *m*
presidential [,prezɪ'dɛnʃəl] *adj* présidentiel
press [pres] *s* presse *f*; (*e.g., for wine*) pressoir *m*; (*pressure*) pression *f*; (*for clothes*) armoire *f*; (*in weight lifting*) développé *m*; **in press** (*said of clothes*) lisse et net; (*said of book being published*) sous presse; **to go to press** être mis sous presse ‖ *tr* presser; (*e.g., a button*) appuyer sur, presser; (*clothes*) donner un coup de fer à, repasser ‖ *intr* presser; **to press against** se serrer contre; **to press forward, to press on** presser le pas
press' a'gent *s* agent *m* de publicité
press' box' *s* tribune *f* des journalistes
press' card' *s* coupe-file *m* d'un journaliste
press' con'ference *s* conférence *f* de presse
press' gal'lery *s* tribune *f* de la presse
pressing ['presɪŋ] *adj* pressé, pressant
press' release' *s* communiqué *m* de presse
pressure ['preʃər] *s* pression *f*
pres'sure cook'er *s* autocuiseur *m*, cocotte *f* minute
pressurize ['preʃə,raɪz] *tr* pressuriser
prestige [pres'tiʒ], ['prestɪdʒ] *s* prestige *m*
presumably [prɪ'z(j)uməbli] *adv* probablement
presume [prɪ'z(j)um] *tr* présumer; **to presume to** présumer ‖ *intr* présumer; **to presume on** or **upon** abuser de
presumption [prɪ'zʌmpʃən] *s* présomption *f*
presumptuous [prɪ'zʌmptʃʊ·əs] *adj* présomptueux
presuppose [,prisə'poz] *tr* présupposer
pretend [prɪ'tend] *tr* feindre; **to pretend to** + *inf* feindre de + *inf* ‖ *intr* feindre; **to pretend to** (*e.g., the throne*) prétendre à
pretender [prɪ'tendər] *s* prétendant *m*; (*imposter*) simulateur *m*
pretense [prɪ'tens], ['pritens] *s* prétention *f*; feinte *f*; **under false pretenses** par des moyens frauduleux; **under pretense of** sous prétexte de
pretension [prɪ'tenʃən] *s* prétention *f*
pretentious [prɪ'tenʃəs] *adj* prétentieux
pretext ['pritekst] *s* prétexte *m*
pretonic [prɪ'tanɪk] *adj* prétonique
pret·ty ['prɪti] *adj* (*comp* -**tier**; *super* -**tiest**) joli; (coll) considérable ‖ *adv* assez; très
prevail [prɪ'vel] *intr* prévaloir, régner; **to prevail on** or **upon** persuader
prevailing [prɪ'velɪŋ] *adj* prédominant; (*wind*) dominant; (*fashion*) en vogue
prevalent ['prevələnt] *adj* commun, courant

prevaricate [prɪ'værɪˌket] *intr* mentir
prevent [prɪ'vɛnt] *tr* empêcher
prevention [prɪ'vɛnʃən] *s* empêchement *m*; (e.g., *of accidents*) prévention *f*
preventive [prɪ'vɛntɪv] *adj* & *s* préventif *m*
preview ['priˌvju] *s* (*of something to come*) amorce *f*; (*private showing*) (mov) avant-première *f*; (*show of brief scenes for advertising*) film *m* annonce
previous ['privɪ·əs] *adj* précédent, antérieur; (*notice*) préalable; (coll) pressé ‖ *adv*—**previous to** antérieurement à
prewar ['pri·ˌwɔr] *adj* d'avant-guerre
prey [pre] *s* proie *f*; **to be a prey to** être en proie à ‖ *intr*—**to prey on** or **upon** faire sa proie de; (e.g., *a seacoast*) piller; (e.g., *the mind*) ronger, miner
price [praɪs] *s* prix *m* ‖ *tr* mettre un prix à, tarifer; s'informer du prix de
price' control' *s* contrôle *m* des prix
price' cut'ting *s* rabais *m*, remise *f*
price' fix'ing *s* stabilisation *f* des prix
price' freez'ing *s* blocage *m* des prix
priceless ['praɪslɪs] *adj* sans prix; (coll) impayable, absurde
price' list' *s* liste *f* de prix, tarif *m*
price' war' *s* guerre *f* des prix
prick [prɪk] *s* piqûre *f*; (*spur; sting of conscience*) aiguillon *m* ‖ *tr* piquer; **to prick up** (*the ears*) dresser
prick·ly ['prɪkli] *adj* (*comp* **-lier**; *super* **-liest**) épineux
prick'ly heat' *s* lichen *m* vésiculaire, miliaire *f*
prick'ly pear' *s* figue *f* de Barbarie; (*plant*) figuier *m* de Barbarie
pride [praɪd] *s* orgueil *m*; (*satisfaction*) fierté *f*; **to take pride in** être fier de ‖ *tr*—**to pride oneself on** or **upon** s'enorgueillir de
priest [prist] *s* prêtre *m*
priestess ['pristɪs] *s* prêtresse *f*
priesthood ['prist·hʊd] *s* sacerdoce *m*
priest·ly ['pristli] *adj* (*comp* **-lier**; *super* **-liest**) sacerdotal
prig [prɪg] *s* poseur *m*, pédant *m*
prim [prɪm] *adj* (*comp* **primmer**; *super* **primmest**) compassé, guindé
prima·ry ['praɪˌmeri], ['praɪməri] *adj* primaire ‖ *s* (*pl* **-ries**) élection *f* primaire; (elec) primaire *m*
primate ['praɪmet] *s* (eccl) primat *m*; (zool) primate *m*
prime [praɪm] *adj* premier, principal; (*of the best quality*) de première qualité, (le) meilleur; (math) prime ‖ *s* fleur *f*, perfection *f*; commencement *m*, premiers jours *mpl*; **prime of life** fleur or force de l'âge ‖ *tr* amorcer; (*a surface to be painted*) appliquer une couche de fond à; (*to supply with information*) mettre au courant
prime' min'ister *s* premier ministre *m*
primer ['praɪmər] *s* premier livre *m* de lecture; manuel *m* élémentaire ‖ ['praɪmər] *s* (*for paint*) couche *f* de fond, impression *f*; (mach) amorce *f*

primeval [praɪ'mivəl] *adj* primitif
primitive ['prɪmɪtɪv] *adj* & *s* primitif *m*
primordial [praɪ'mɔrdɪ·əl] *adj* primordial
primp [prɪmp] *tr* bichonner, pomponner ‖ *intr* se bichonner, se pomponner
prim'rose' *s* primevère *f*
prim'rose path' *s* chemin *m* de velours
prince [prɪns] *s* prince *m*
prince·ly ['prɪnsli] *adj* (*comp* **-lier**; *super* **-liest**) princier
Prince' of Wales' *s* prince *m* de Galles
princess ['prɪnsɪs] *s* princesse *f*
principal ['prɪnsɪpəl] *adj* & *s* principal *m*
principali·ty [ˌprɪnsɪ'pælɪti] *s* (*pl* **-ties**) principauté *f*
principle ['prɪnsɪpəl] *s* principe *m*
print [prɪnt] *s* empreinte *f*; (*printed cloth*) imprimé *m*; (*design in printed cloth*) estampe *f*; (*lettering*) lettres *fpl* moulées; (*act of printing*) impression *f*; (phot) épreuve *f*; **out of print** épuisé; **small print** petits caractères *mpl* ‖ *tr* imprimer; écrire en lettres moulées; publier; (*an edition; a photographic negative*) tirer
print'ed mat'ter *s* imprimés *mpl*
printer ['prɪntər] *s* imprimeur *m*
prin'ter's dev'il *s* apprenti *m* imprimeur
prin'ter's er'ror *s* faute *f* d'impression, coquille *f*
prin'ter's ink' *s* encre *f* d'imprimerie
prin'ter's mark' *s* nom *m* de l'imprimeur
printing ['prɪntɪŋ] *s* imprimerie *f*; (*act*) impression *f*; (*by hand*) écriture *f* en caractères d'imprimerie; édition *f*; tirage *m*; (phot) tirage
print'ing frame' *s* (phot) châssis-presse *m*
print'ing of'fice *s* imprimerie *f*
prior ['praɪ·ər] *adj* antérieur ‖ *s* prieur *m* ‖ *adv* antérieurement; **prior to** avant; avant de
priori·ty [praɪ'arɪti], [praɪ'ɔrɪti] *s* (*pl* **-ties**) priorité *f*
prism ['prɪzəm] *s* prisme *m*
prison ['prɪzən] *s* prison *f* ‖ *tr* emprisonner
prisoner ['prɪzənər], ['prɪznər] *s* prisonnier *m*
pris'on van' *s* voiture *f* cellulaire
pris·sy ['prɪsi] *adj* (*comp* **-sier**; *super* **-siest**) (coll) bégueule
priva·cy ['praɪvəsi] *s* (*pl* **-cies**) intimité *f*; secret *m*
private ['praɪvɪt] *adj* privé, particulier; confidentiel, secret; (*public sign*) défense d'entrer ‖ *s* simple soldat *m*; **in private** dans l'intimité, en particulier; **privates** parties *fpl*
pri'vate cit'izen *s* simple particulier *m*, simple citoyen *m*
pri'vate first' class' *s* soldat *m* de première
pri'vate hos'pital *s* clinique *f*
pri'vate sec'retary *s* secrétaire *m* particulier
privet ['prɪvɪt] *s* troène *m*

privilege ['prɪvɪlɪdʒ] *s* privilège *m*
priv·y ['prɪvi] *adj* privé; **privy to** averti de ‖ *s* (*pl* -ies) cabinets *mpl* au fond du jardin
prize [praɪz] *s* prix *m*; (*something captured*) prise *f* ‖ *tr* faire cas de, estimer
prize′ fight′ *s* match *m* de boxe
prize′ fight′er *s* boxeur *m* professionnel
prize′ ring′ *s* ring *m*
prize′win′ner *s* lauréat *m*; **prizewinners** (*list*) palmarès *m*
pro [pro] *s* (*pl* **pros**) vote *m* affirmatif; (*professional*) (coll) pro *m*; **the pros and the cons** le pour et le contre ‖ *prep* en faveur de
probabili·ty [ˌprɑbə'bɪlɪti] *s* (*pl* -ties) probabilité *f*
probable ['prɑbəbəl] *adj* probable
probably ['prɑbəbli] *adv* probablement
probate ['probet] *s* homologation *f* ‖ *tr* homologuer
probation [pro'beʃən] *s* liberté *f* surveillée; (*on a job*) stage *m*
probe [prob] *s* sondage *m*; (*instrument*) sonde *f*; (*rok*) échos *mpl*; (*rok*) engin *m* exploratoire ‖ *tr* sonder
problem ['prɑbləm] *s* problème *m*
prob′lem child′ *s* enfant *mf* terrible
procedure [pro'sidʒər] *s* procédé *m*
proceed ['prosid] *s*—**proceeds** produit *m*, bénéfices *mpl* ‖ [pro'sid] *intr* avancer, continuer; continuer à parler; **to proceed from** procéder de; **to proceed to** se mettre à; (*to go to*) se diriger à
proceeding [pro'sidɪŋ] *s* procédé *m*; **proceedings** actes *mpl*
process ['prɑses] *s* (*technique*) procédé *m*; (*development*) processus *m*; **in the process of** en train de ‖ *tr* soumettre à un procédé, traiter
procession [pro'sɛʃən] *s* cortège *m*, défilé *m*, procession *f*
pro′cess serv′er *s* huissier *m* exploitant
proclaim [pro'klem] *tr* proclamer
proclitic [pro'klɪtɪk] *adj* & *s* proclitique *m*
procommunist [pro'kɑmjənɪst] *adj* & *s* procommuniste *mf*
procrastinate [pro'kræstɪˌnet] *tr* différer ‖ *intr* remettre les affaires à plus tard
proctor ['prɑktər] *s* surveillant *m*
procure [pro'kjʊr] *tr* obtenir, se procurer; (*a woman*) entraîner à la prostitution ‖ *intr* faire du proxénétisme
procurement [pro'kjʊrmənt] *s* obtention *f*, acquisition *f*
procurer [pro'kjʊrər] *s* proxénète *mf*
prod [prɑd] *s* poussée *f*; (*stick*) aiguillon *m* ‖ *v* (*pret* & *pp* **prodded**; *ger* **prodding**) *tr* aiguillonner
prodigal ['prɑdɪgəl] *adj* & *s* prodigue *mf*
prodigious [pro'dɪdʒəs] *adj* prodigieux
prodi·gy ['prɑdɪdʒi] *s* (*pl* -gies) prodige *m*
produce ['prod(j)us] *s* produit *m*; (*eatables*) denrées *fpl* ‖ [pro'd(j)us] *tr* produire; (*a play*) mettre en scène; (*geom*) prolonger

producer [pro'd(j)usər] *s* producteur *m*
product ['prɑdəkt] *s* produit *m*
production [pro'dʌkʃən] *s* production *f*
profane [pro'fen] *adj* profane; (*language*) impie, blasphématoire ‖ *s* profane *mf*; impie *mf* ‖ *tr* profaner
profani·ty [pro'fænɪti] *s* (*pl* -ties) blasphème *m*
profess [pro'fes] *tr* professer
profession [pro'fɛʃən] *s* profession *f*
professor [pro'fesər] *s* professeur *m*
proffer ['prɑfər] *s* offre *f* ‖ *tr* offrir, tendre
proficient [pro'fɪʃənt] *adj* compétent, expert
profile ['profaɪl] *s* profil *m*; courte biographie *f* ‖ *tr* profiler; **to be profiled against** se profiler sur
profit ['prɑfɪt] *s* bénéfice *m*, profit *m* ‖ *tr* profiter (with *dat*) ‖ *intr* profiter; **to profit from** profiter à, de, or en
profitable ['prɑfɪtəbəl] *adj* profitable
prof′it-and-loss′ account′ *s* compte *m* de profits et pertes
profiteer [ˌprɑfɪ'tɪr] *s* profiteur *m* ‖ *intr* faire des bénéfices excessifs
prof′it tak′ing *s* prise *f* de bénéfices
profligate ['prɑflɪgɪt] *adj* & *s* débauché *m*
pro′ for′ma in′voice [ˌpro'fɔrmə] *s* facture *f* simulée
profound [pro'faʊnd] *adj* profond
pro-French′ *adj* francophile
profuse [prə'fjuz] *adj* abondant; (*extravagant*) prodigue
proge·ny ['prɑdʒəni] *s* (*pl* -nies) progéniture *f*
progno·sis [prɑg'nosɪs] *s* (*pl* -ses [siz]) pronostic *m*
prognosticate [prɑg'nɑstɪˌket] *tr* pronostiquer
pro·gram ['progræm] *s* programme *m* ‖ *v* (*pret* & *pp* -**gramed** or -**grammed**; *ger* -**graming** or -**gramming**) *tr* programmer
programmer ['progræmər] *s* (comp) programmeur *m*; (mov, rad, telv) programmateur *m*
programming ['progræmɪŋ] *s* programmation *f*
progress ['prɑgres] *s* progrès *m*; cours *m*, e.g., **work in progress** travaux en cours; **to make progress** faire des progrès ‖ [prə'gres] *intr* progresser
progressive [prə'gresɪv] *adj* progressif; (pol) progressiste ‖ *s* (pol) progressiste *mf*
prohibit [pro'hɪbɪt] *tr* prohiber, interdire
prohibition [ˌpro·ə'bɪʃən] *s* prohibition *f*
project ['prɑdʒekt] *s* projet *m* ‖ [prə'dʒekt] *tr* projeter ‖ *intr* (*to jut out*) saillir; (theat) passer la rampe
projectile [prə'dʒektɪl] *s* projectile *m*
projection [prə'dʒekʃən] *s* projection *f*; (*something jutting out*) saillie *f*
projec′tion booth′ *s* (mov) cabine *f* de projection
projector [prə'dʒektər] *s* projecteur *m*

proletarian [ˌprolɪˈtɛrɪ·ən] *adj* prolétarien ‖ *s* prolétaire *m*
proletariat [ˌprolɪˈtɛrɪ·ət] *s* prolétariat *m*
proliferate [prəˈlɪfəˌret] *intr* proliférer
prolific [prəˈlɪfɪk] *adj* prolifique
prolix [ˈprolɪks], [proˈlɪks] *adj* prolixe
prologue [ˈprolɔg], [ˈprolag] *s* prologue *m*
prolong [proˈlɔŋ], [proˈlaŋ] *tr* prolonger
promenade [ˌpramɪˈned], [ˌpramɪˈnad] *s* promenade *f*; bal *m* d'apparat; (theat) promenoir *m* ‖ *intr* se promener
prom'enade' deck' *s* (naut) pont-promenade *m*
prominent [ˈpramɪnənt] *adj* proéminent; (*well-known*) éminent
promiscuity [ˌpramɪsˈkju·əti] *s* promiscuité *f*
promise [ˈpramɪs] *s* promesse *f* ‖ *tr* & *intr* promettre; **to promise s.o. to** promettre à qn de; **to promise s.th. to s.o.** promettre q.ch. à qn
prom'issory note' [ˈpramɪˌsori] *m* billet *m* à ordre
promonto·ry [ˈpramənˌtori] *s* (*pl* -ries) promontoire *m*
promote [prəˈmot] *tr* promouvoir
promoter [prəˈmotər] *s* promoteur *m*
promotion [prəˈmoʃən] *s* promotion *f*
prompt [prampt] *adj* prompt; ponctuel ‖ *tr* inciter; (theat) souffler son rôle à
prompter [ˈpramptər] *s* (theat) souffleur *m*
promp'ter's box' *s* (theat) trou *m* du souffleur
promptness [ˈpramptnɪs] *s* promptitude *f*
promulgate [ˈpraməlˌget], [proˈmʌlget] *tr* promulguer
prone [pron] *adj* à plat ventre, prostré; **prone to** enclin à
prong [prɔŋ], [praŋ] *s* dent *f*
pronoun [ˈpronaun] *s* pronom *m*
pronounce [prəˈnauns] *tr* prononcer
pronouncement [prəˈnaunsmənt] *s* déclaration *f*
pronunciation [prəˌnʌnsɪˈeʃən], [prəˌnʌnʃɪˈeʃən] *s* prononciation *f*
proof [pruf] *adj*—**proof against** à l'épreuve de, résistant à ‖ *s* preuve *f*; (phot, typ) épreuve *f*; **to read proof** corriger les épreuves
proof'read'er *s* correcteur *m*
prop [prap] *s* appui *m*; (*to hold up a plant*) tuteur *m*; **props** (theat) accessoires *mpl* ‖ *v* (*pret* & *pp* **propped**; *ger* **propping**) *tr* appuyer; (hort) tuteurer
propaganda [ˌprapəˈgændə] *s* propagande *f*
propagate [ˈprapəˌget] *tr* propager
pro·pel [prəˈpɛl] *v* (*pret* & *pp* -**pelled**; *ger* -**pelling**) *tr* propulser
propeller [prəˈpɛlər] *s* hélice *f*
propensi·ty [prəˈpɛnsɪti] *s* (*pl* -ties) propension *f*
proper [ˈprapər] *adj* propre; (*fitting, correct*) convenable, comme il faut

proper·ty [ˈprapərti] *s* (*pl* -ties) propriété *f*; **properties** (theat) accessoires *mpl*
prop'erty own'er *s* propriétaire *mf*
prop'erty tax' *s* impôt *m* foncier
prophe·cy [ˈprafɪsi] *s* (*pl* -cies) prophétie *f*
prophe·sy [ˈprafɪˌsaɪ] *v* (*pret* & *pp* -sied) *tr* prophétiser
prophet [ˈprafɪt] *s* prophète *m*
prophetess [ˈprafɪtɪs] *s* prophétesse *f*
prophylactic [ˌprofɪˈlæktɪk] *adj* prophylactique ‖ *s* médicament *m* prophylactique
propitiate [prəˈpɪʃɪˌet] *tr* apaiser
propitious [prəˈpɪʃəs] *adj* propice
prop'jet' *s* turbopropulseur *m*
proportion [prəˈporʃən] *s* proportion *f*; **in proportion as** à mesure que; **in proportion to** en proportion de, en raison de; **out of proportion** hors de proportion ‖ *tr* proportionner
proportionate [prəˈporʃənɪt] *adj* proportionné
proposal [prəˈpozəl] *s* proposition *f*; demande *f* en mariage
propose [prəˈpoz] *tr* proposer ‖ *intr* faire sa déclaration; **to propose to** demander sa main à; (*to decide to*) se proposer de
proposition [ˌprapəˈzɪʃən] *s* proposition *f* ‖ *tr* faire des propositions malhonnêtes à
propound [prəˈpaund] *tr* proposer
proprietor [prəˈpraɪ·ətər] *s* propriétaire *mf*
proprietress [prəˈpraɪ·ətrɪs] *s* propriétaire *f*
proprie·ty [prəˈpraɪ·əti] *s* (*pl* -ties) propriété *f*; (*of conduct*) bienséance *f*; **proprieties** convenances *fpl*
propulsion [prəˈpʌlʃən] *s* propulsion *f*
prorate [proˈret] *tr* partager au prorata
prosaic [proˈze·ɪk] *adj* prosaïque
proscenium [proˈsɪnɪ·əm] *s* avant-scène *f*
proscribe [proˈskraɪb] *tr* proscrire
prose [proz] *adj* en prose ‖ *s* prose *f*
prosecute [ˈprasɪˌkjut] *tr* poursuivre
prosecutor [ˈprasɪˌkjutər] *s* (*lawyer*) procureur *m*; (*plaintiff*) plaignant *m*
proselyte [ˈprasɪˌlaɪt] *s* prosélyte *mf*
prose' writ'er *s* prosateur *m*
prosody [ˈprasədi] *s* prosodie *f*
prospect [ˈpraspɛkt] *s* perspective *f*; (*future*) avenir *m*; (com) client *m* éventuel ‖ *tr* & *intr* prospecter; **to prospect for** (*e.g., gold*) chercher
prospector [ˈpraspɛktər] *s* prospecteur *m*
prospectus [prəˈspɛktəs] *s* prospectus *m*
prosper [ˈpraspər] *intr* prospérer
prosperity [prasˈpɛrɪti] *s* prospérité *f*
prosperous [ˈpraspərəs] *adj* prospère
prostitute [ˈprastɪˌt(j)ut] *s* prostituée *f* ‖ *tr* prostituer
prostrate [ˈprastret] *adj* prosterné; (*exhausted*) prostré ‖ *tr* abattre; **to prostrate oneself** se prosterner
prostration [prasˈtreʃən] *s* prostration *f*; (*abasement*) prosternation *f*

protagonist [pro'tægənɪst] s protagoniste m

protect [prə'tɛkt] tr protéger

protection [prə'tɛkʃən] s protection f

protein ['proti·ɪn], ['protin] s protéine f

pro-tempore [pro'tɛmpə,ri] adj intérimaire, par intérim

protest ['protɛst] s protestation f || [pro'tɛst] tr protester de; protester || intr protester

Protestant ['prɑtɪstənt] adj & s protestant m

protocol ['protə,kɑl] s protocole m

proton ['protɑn] s proton m

protoplasm ['protə,plæzəm] s protoplasme m

prototype ['protə,taɪp] s prototype m

protozoan [,protə'zo·ən] s protozoaire m

protract [pro'trækt] tr prolonger

protrude [pro'trud] intr saillir

protuberance [pro't(j)ubərəns] s protubérance f

proud [praʊd] adj fier; (vain) orgueilleux

proud' flesh' s chair f fongueuse

prove [pruv] v (pret proved; pp proved or proven ['pruvən]) tr prouver; (to put to the test) éprouver || intr se montrer, se trouver; to prove to be se révéler, s'avérer

proverb ['prɑvərb] s proverbe m

provide [prə'vaɪd] tr pourvoir, fournir; to provide s.th. for s.o. fournir q.ch. à qn || intr—to provide for pourvoir à; (e.g., future needs) prévoir

provided conj pourvu que, à condition que

providence ['prɑvɪdəns] s providence f; (prudence) prévoyance f

providential [,prɑvɪ'dɛnʃəl] adj providentiel

providing [prə'vaɪdɪŋ] conj pourvu que, à condition que

province ['prɑvɪns] s province f; (sphere) compétence f

prov'ing ground' s terrain m d'essai

provision [prə'vɪʒən] s (supplying) fourniture f; clause f; provisions provisions fpl

provi·so [prə'vaɪzo] s (pl -sos or -soes) condition f, stipulation f

provocative [prə'vɑkətɪv] adj provocant

provoke [prə'vok] tr provoquer; fâcher, contrarier

provoking [prə'vokɪŋ] adj contrariant

prow [praʊ] s proue f

prowess ['praʊ·ɪs] s prouesse f

prowl [praʊl] intr rôder

prowler ['praʊlər] s rôdeur m

proximity [prɑk'sɪmɪti] s proximité f

prox·y ['prɑksi] s (pl -ies) mandat m; (agent) mandataire mf; by proxy par procuration

prude [prud] s prude mf

prudence ['prudəns] s prudence f

prudent ['prudənt] adj prudent

pruder·y ['prudəri] s (pl -ies) pruderie f

prudish ['prudɪʃ] adj prude

prune [prun] s pruneau m || tr élaguer

Prussian ['prʌʃən] adj prussien || s Prussien m

pry [praɪ] v (pret & pp pried) tr—to pry open forcer avec un levier; to pry s.th. out of s.o. extorquer, soutirer q.ch. à qn || intr fureter; to pry into fourrer son nez dans

P.S. ['pi'ɛs] s (letterword) (postscript) P.-S.

psalm [sɑm] s psaume m

Psalter ['sɔltər] s psautier m

pseudo ['s(j)udo] adj faux, supposé, feint, factice

pseudonym ['s(j)udənɪm] s pseudonyme m

psyche ['saɪki] s psyché f

psychiatrist [saɪ'kaɪ·ətrɪst] s psychiatre mf

psychiatry [saɪ'kaɪ·ətri] s psychiatrie f

psychic ['saɪkɪk] adj psychique; médiumnique || s médium m

psychoanalysis [,saɪko·ə'nælɪsɪs] s psychanalyse f

psychoanalyze [,saɪko'ænə,laɪz] tr psychanalyser

psychologic(al) [,saɪko'lɑdʒɪk(əl)] adj psychologique

psychologist [saɪ'kɑlədʒɪst] s psychologue mf

psychology [saɪ'kɑlədʒi] s psychologie f

psychopath ['saɪkə,pæθ] s psychopathe mf

psycho·sis [saɪ'kosɪs] s (pl -ses [siz]) psychose f

psychotic [saɪ'kɑtɪk] adj & s psychotique mf

ptomaine ['tomen] s ptomaïne f

pub [pʌb] s (Brit) bistrot m, café m

puberty ['pjubərti] s puberté f

public ['pʌblɪk] adj & s public m

publication [,pʌblɪ'keʃən] s publication f

publicity [pʌb'lɪsɪti] s publicité f

public'ity stunt' s canard m publicitaire

publicize ['pʌblɪ,saɪz] tr publier

pub'lic li'brary s bibliothèque f municipale

pub'lic-opin'ion poll' s sondage m de l'opinion, enquête f par sondage

pub'lic school' s (U.S.A.) école f primaire; (Brit) école privée

pub'lic serv'ant s fonctionnaire mf

pub'lic speak'ing s art m oratoire, éloquence f

pub'lic toi'let s chalet m de nécessité

pub'lic util'ity s entreprise f de service public; public utilities actions fpl émises par les entreprises de service public

publish ['pʌblɪʃ] tr publier

publisher ['pʌblɪʃər] s éditeur m

pub'lishing house' s maison f d'édition

puck [pʌk] s palet m

pucker ['pʌkər] s fronce m, faux pli m || tr froncer || intr se froncer

pudding ['pʊdɪŋ] s entremets m sucré au lait, crème f

puddle ['pʌdəl] s flaque f || tr puddler

pudg·y ['pʌdʒi] adj (comp -ier; super -iest) bouffi, rondouillard

puerile ['pju·ərɪl] adj puéril

puerili·ty [ˌpjuˈə'rɪlɪti] s (pl -ties) puérilité f

Puerto Rican ['pwɛrto'rikən] adj portoricain ‖ s Portoricain m

puff [pʌf] s souffle m; (of smoke) bouffée f; (in clothing) bouillon m; (in sleeve) bouffant m; (for powder) houppette f; (swelling) bouffissure f; (praise) battage m; (culin) moule m de pâte feuilletée fourré à la crème, à la confiture, etc. ‖ tr lancer des bouffées de; **to puff oneself up** se rengorger; **to puff out** souffler; **to puff up** gonfler ‖ intr souffler; (to swell) gonfler, se gonfler; **to puff at** or **on** (a pipe) tirer sur

puff' paste' s pâte f feuilletée

pugilism ['pjudʒɪˌlɪzəm] s science f pugilistique, boxe f

pugilist ['pjudʒɪlɪst] s pugiliste m

pugnacious [pʌg'neʃəs] adj pugnace

pug'-nosed' adj camus

puke [pjuk] s (slang) dégobillage m ‖ tr & intr (slang) dégobiller

pull [pʊl] s secousse f, coup m; (handle of door) poignée f; (slang) piston m, appuis mpl ‖ tr tirer; (a muscle) tordre; (the trigger) appuyer sur; (a proof) (typ) tirer; **to pull about** tirailler; **to pull away** arracher; **to pull down** baisser; (e.g., a house) abattre; (to degrade) abaisser; **to pull in** rentrer; **to pull off** enlever; (fig) réussir; **to pull on** (a garment) mettre; **to pull oneself together** se ressaisir; **to pull out** sortir; (a tooth) arracher ‖ intr tirer; bouger lentement, bouger avec effort; **to pull at** tirer sur; **to pull for** (slang) plaider en faveur de; **to pull in** rentrer; (said of train) entrer en gare; **to pull out** partir; (said of train) sortir de la gare; **to pull through** se tirer d'affaire; (to get well) se remettre

pull' chain' s chasse f d'eau

pullet ['pʊlɪt] s poulette f

pulley ['pʊli] s poulie f

pulmonary ['pʌlməˌnɛri] adj pulmonaire

pulp [pʌlp] s pulpe f; (to make paper) pâte f; (of tooth) bulbe m; **to beat to a pulp** (coll) mettre en bouillie

pulp' fic'tion s romans mpl à sensation; le roman de la concierge

pulpit ['pʊlpɪt] s chaire f

pulsate ['pʌlset] intr palpiter; vibrer

pulsation [pʌl'seʃən] s pulsation f

pulse [pʌls] s pouls m; **to feel** or **take the pulse of** tâter le pouls à

pulverize ['pʌlvəˌraɪz] tr pulvériser

pu'mice stone' ['pʌmɪs] s pierre f ponce

pum·mel ['pʌməl] v (pret & pp -meled or -melled; ger -meling or -melling) tr bourrer de coups

pump [pʌmp] s pompe f; (slipperlike shoe) escarpin m ‖ tr pomper; (coll) tirer les vers du nez à; **to pump up** pomper; (a tire) gonfler ‖ intr pomper

pump'han'dle s bras m de pompe

pumpkin ['pʌmpkɪn], ['pʌŋkɪn] s citrouille f, potiron m

pun [pʌn] s calembour m, jeu m de mots ‖ v (pret & pp **punned**; ger **punning**) intr faire des jeux de mots

punch [pʌntʃ] s coup m de poing; (to pierce metal) mandrin m; (to drive a nail or bolt) poinçon m; (for tickets) pince f, emporte-pièce m; (drink; blow) punch m; (mach) poinçonneuse f; (energy) (coll) allant m, punch; **to pull no punches** parler carrément ‖ tr donner un coup de poing à; poinçonner

punch' bowl' s bol m à punch

punch' card' s carte f perforée

punch' clock' s horloge f de pointage

punch'-drunk' adj abruti de coups; (coll) abruti, étourdi

punched' tape' s bande f enregistreuse perforée

punch'ing bag' s punching-ball m; (fig) tête f de Turc

punch' line' s point m final, phrase f clé

punctilious [pʌŋk'tɪlɪ·əs] adj pointilleux, minutieux

punctual ['pʌŋktʃu·əl] adj ponctuel

punctuate ['pʌŋktʃu·ˌet] tr & intr ponctuer

punctuation [ˌpʌŋktʃu'eʃən] s ponctuation f

punctua'tion mark' s signe m de ponctuation

puncture ['pʌŋktʃər] s perforation f; (of a tire) crevaison f; (med) ponction f ‖ tr perforer; (a tire) crever; (med) ponctionner

punc'ture-proof' adj increvable

pundit ['pʌndɪt] s pandit m; (savant) mandarin m; (pej) pontife m

pungent ['pʌndʒənt] adj piquant

punish ['pʌnɪʃ] tr & intr punir

punishment ['pʌnɪʃmənt] s punition f; (for a crime) peine f; (severe handling) mauvais traitements mpl

punk [pʌŋk] adj (slang) moche, fichu; **to feel punk** (slang) être mal fichu ‖ s amadou m; mèche f d'amadou; (decayed wood) bois m pourri; (slang) voyou m, mauvais sujet m

punster ['pʌnstər] s faiseur m de calembours

pu·ny ['pjuni] adj (comp -nier; super -niest) chétif, malingre

pup [pʌp] s chiot m

pupil ['pjupəl] s élève mf; (of the eye) pupille f, prunelle f

puppet ['pʌpɪt] s marionnette f; (person controlled by another) fantoche m, pantin m

pup'pet gov'ernment s gouvernement m fantoche

pup'pet show' s spectacle m de marionnettes, marionnettes fpl

pup·py ['pʌpi] s (pl -pies) petit chien m

pup'py love' s premières amours fpl

pup' tent' s tente-abri f

purchase ['pʌrtʃəs] s achat m; (leverage) point m d'appui, prise f ‖ tr acheter

pur'chasing pow'er s pouvoir m d'achat

pure [pjʊr] *adj* pur
purgative ['pʌrgətɪv] *adj & s* purgatif *m*
purgato·ry ['pʌrgə,tori] *s* (*pl* -ries) purgatoire *m*
purge [pʌrdʒ] *s* purge *f* ‖ *tr* purger
puri·fy ['pjʊrɪ,faɪ] *v* (*pret & pp* -fied) *tr* purifier
puritan ['pjʊrɪtən] *adj & s* puritain *m*; **Puritan** puritain
purity ['pjʊrɪti] *s* pureté *f*
purloin [pər'lɔɪn] *tr & intr* voler
purple ['pʌrpəl] *adj* pourpre ‖ *s* (*violescent*) pourpre *m*; (*deep red, crimson*) pourpre *f*; **born to the purple** né dans la pourpre
purport ['pʌrport] *s* sens *m*, teneur *f*; (*intention*) but *m*, objet *m* ‖ [pər-'port] *tr* signifier, vouloir dire
purpose ['pʌrpəs] *s* intention *f*, dessein *m*; (*goal*) but *m*, objet *m*, fin *f*; **for all purposes** à tous usages; pratiquement; **for the purpose of, with the purpose of** dans le dessein de, dans le but de; **for this purpose** à cet effet; **for what purpose?** à quoi bon?, à quelle fin?; **on purpose** exprès, à dessein; **to good purpose, to some purpose** utilement; **to no purpose** vainement; **to serve the purpose** faire l'affaire
purposely ['pʌrpəsli] *adv* exprès, à dessein, de propos délibéré
purr [pʌr] *s* ronron *m* ‖ *intr* ronronner
purse [pʌrs] *s* bourse *f*, porte-monnaie *m*; (*handbag*) sac *m* à main ‖ *tr* (*one's lips*) pincer
purser ['pʌrsər] *s* commissaire *m*
purse' snatch'er ['snætʃər] *s* voleur *m* à la tire
purse' strings' *spl* cordons *mpl* de bourse
pursue [pər's(j)u] *tr* poursuivre; (*a profession*) suivre
pursuit [pər's(j)ut] *s* poursuite *f*; profession *f*
pursuit' plane' *s* chasseur *m*, avion *m* de chasse
purvey [pər've] *tr* fournir
pus [pʌs] *s* pus *m*
push [pʊʃ] *s* poussée *f* ‖ *tr* pousser; (*a button*) appuyer sur, presser; **to push around** (coll) rudoyer; **to push aside** écarter; **to push away** or **back** repousser; **to push in** enfoncer; **to push over** faire tomber; **to push through** amener à bonne fin; (*a resolution, bill, etc.*) faire adopter ‖ *intr* pousser; **to push forward** or **on** avancer; **to push off** se mettre en route; (naut) pousser au large
push' but'ton *s* bouton *m* électrique, poussoir *m*
push'-but'ton war'fare *s* guerre *f* presse-bouton
push'cart' *s* voiture *f* à bras
pushing ['pʊʃɪŋ] *adj* entreprenant; indiscret; agressif
pusillanimous [,pjusɪ'lænɪməs] *adj* pusillanime

puss [pʊs] *s* minet *m*; (slang) gueule *f*; **sly puss** (*girl*) (coll) futée *f* ‖ *interj* minet!
Puss' in Boots' *s* Chat *m* botté
puss' in the cor'ner *s* les quatre coins *mpl*
puss·y ['pʊsi] *s* (*pl* -ies) *s* minet *m* ‖ *interj* minet!
puss'y wil'low *s* saule *m* nord-américain aux chatons très soyeux
put [pʊt] *v* (*pret & pp* put; *ger* putting) *tr* mettre, placer; (*to throw*) lancer; (*a question*) poser; **to put across** passer; faire accepter; **to put aside** mettre de côté; **to put away** ranger; (*to jail*) mettre en prison; **to put back** remettre; retarder; **to put down** poser; (*e.g., a name*) noter; (*a revolution*) réprimer; (*to lower*) baisser; **to put off** renvoyer; (*to mislead*) dérouter; **to put on** (*clothes*) mettre; (*a play*) mettre en scène, monter; (*a brake*) serrer; (*a light, radio, etc.*) allumer; (*to feign*) feindre, simuler; **to put oneself out** se déranger; **to put on sale** mettre en vente; mettre en solde; **to put out** (*the hand*) étendre; (*the fire, light, etc.*) éteindre; (*s.o.'s eyes*) crever; (*e.g., a book*) publier; (*to show to the door*) mettre dehors; (*to vex*) contrarier; **to put over** (coll) faire accepter; **to put s.o. through** s.th. faire subir q.ch. à qn; **to put through** passer; (*a resolution, bill, etc.*) faire adopter; **to put up** lever; (*a house*) construire, faire relever; (*one's collar, hair, etc.*) relever; (*a picture*) accrocher; (*a notice*) afficher; (*a tent*) dresser; (*an umbrella*) ouvrir; (*the price*) augmenter; (*money as an investment*) fournir; (*resistance*) offrir; (*an overnight guest*) loger; (*fruit, vegetables, etc.*) conserver; (coll) pousser, inciter ‖ *intr* se diriger; **to put on** feindre; **to put up** loger; **to put up with** tolérer
put'-out' *adj* ennuyeux, fâcheux
putrid ['pjutrɪd] *adj* putride
putter ['pʌtər] *intr*—**to putter around** s'occuper de bagatelles
put·ty ['pʌti] *s* (*pl* -ties) mastic *m* ‖ *v* (*pret & pp* -tied) *tr* mastiquer
put'ty knife' *s* (*pl* knives) couteau *m* à mastiquer
put'-up' *adj* (coll) machiné à l'avance, monté
puzzle ['pʌzəl] *s* énigme *f* ‖ *tr* intriguer; **to puzzle out** déchiffrer ‖ *intr* —**to puzzle over** se creuser la tête pour comprendre
puzzler ['pʌzlər] *s* énigme *f*, colle *f*
puzzling ['pʌzlɪŋ] *adj* énigmatique
PW ['pi'dʌbəl,ju] *s* (letterword) (**prisoner of war**) P.G.
pyg·my ['pɪgmi] *adj* pygméen ‖ *s* (*pl* -mies) pygmée *m*
pylon ['paɪlɑn] *s* pylône *m*

pyramid ['pɪrəmɪd] *s* pyramide *f* ‖ *tr* augmenter graduellement ‖ *intr* pyramider
pyre [paɪr] *s* bûcher *m* funéraire
Pyrenees ['pɪrɪ‚niz] *spl* Pyrénées *fpl*
pyrites [paɪ'raɪtiz], ['paɪraɪts] *s* pyrite *f*
pyrotechnical [‚paɪrə'tɛknɪkəl] *adj* pyrotechnique

pyrotechnics [‚paɪrə'tɛknɪks] *spl* pyro-technie *f*
python ['paɪθɑn], ['paɪθən] *s* python *m*
pythoness ['paɪθənɪs] *s* pythonisse *f*
pyx [pɪks] *s* (eccl) ciboire *m*; (*for carrying Eucharist to sick*) (eccl) pyxide *f*; (*at a mint*) boîte *f* des mon-naies

Q

Q, q [kju] *s* XVIIᵉ lettre de l'alphabet
quack [kwæk] *adj* frauduleux, de charlatan ‖ *s* charlatan *m* ‖ *intr* cancaner, faire couin-couin
quacker·y ['kwækəri] *s* (*pl* -ies) char-latanisme *m*
quadrangle ['kwɑd‚ræŋgəl] *s* plan *m* quadrangulaire; cour *f* carrée
quadrant ['kwɑdrənt] *s* (*instrument*) quart *m* de cercle, secteur *m*; (math) quadrant *m*
quadroon [kwɑd'run] *s* quarteron *m*
quadruped ['kwɑdrə‚pɛd] *adj* & *s* qua-drupède *m*
quadruple ['kwɑdrupəl] or [kwɑd-'rupəl] *adj* & *s* quadruple *m* ‖ *tr* & *intr* quadrupler
quadruplets ['kwɑdru‚plɛts], [kwɑd-'ruplɛts] *spl* quadruplés *mpl*
quaff [kwɑf], [kwæf] *s* lampée *f* ‖ *tr* & *intr* boire à longs traits
quagmire ['kwæg‚maɪr] *s* bourbier *m*, fondrière *f*
quail [kwel] *s* caille *f* ‖ *intr* fléchir
quaint [kwent] *adj* pittoresque, bizarre
quake [kwek] *s* tremblement *m*; (*earth-quake*) tremblement de terre ‖ *intr* trembler
Quaker ['kwekər] *adj* & *s* quaker *m*
Quak′er meet′ing *s* réunion *f* de qua-kers; (coll) réunion où il y a très peu de conversation
quali·fy ['kwɑlɪ‚faɪ] *v* (*pret & pp* -fied*) *tr* qualifier; (*e.g., a recommen-dation*) apporter des réserves à, mo-difier; **to qualify oneself for** se pré-parer à, se rendre apte à ‖ *intr* se qualifier
quali·ty ['kwɑlɪti] *s* (*pl* -ties) qualité *f*; (*of a sound*) timbre *m*
qualm [kwɑm] *s* scrupule *m*; (*remorse*) remords *m*; (*nausea*) soulèvement *m* de cœur
quanda·ry ['kwɑndəri] *s* (*pl* -ries) in-certitude *f*, impasse *f*
quanti·ty ['kwɑntɪti] *s* (*pl* -ties) quan-tité *f*
quan·tum ['kwɑntəm] *adj* quantique ‖ *s* (*pl* -ta [tə]) quantum *m*
quan′tum the′ory *s* théorie *f* des quanta
quarantine ['kwɑrən‚tin], ['kwɔrən-‚tin] *s* quarantaine *f* ‖ *tr* mettre en quarantaine
quar·rel ['kwɑrəl], ['kwɔrəl] *s* querelle

f, dispute *f*; **to have no quarrel with** n'avoir rien à redire à; **to pick a quarrel with** chercher querelle à ‖ *v* (*pret & pp* -reled or -relled; *ger* -reling or -relling*) *intr* se quereller, se disputer; **to quarrel over** contester sur, se disputer
quarrelsome ['kwɑrəlsəm], ['kwɔrəl-səm] *adj* querelleur
quar·ry ['kwɑri], ['kwɔri] *s* (*pl* -ries) carrière *f*; (*hunted animal*) proie *f* ‖ *v* (*pret & pp* -ried*) *tr* extraire ‖ *intr* exploiter une carrière
quart [kwɔrt] *s* quart *m* de gallon, pinte *f*
quarter ['kwɔrtər] *s* quart *m*; (*Ameri-can coin*) vingt-cinq cents *mpl*; (*of a year*) trimestre *m*; (*of town; of beef; of moon; of shield*) quartier *m*; **a quarter after one** une heure et quart; **a quarter of an hour** un quart d'heure; **a quarter to one** une heure moins le quart; **at close quarters** corps à corps; **quarters** (mil) quar-tiers *mpl*, cantonnement *m* ‖ *tr* & *intr* (mil) loger, cantonner
quar′ter-deck′ *s* gaillard *m* d'arrière
quar′ter-hour′ *s* quart *m* d'heure; **every quarter-hour on the quarter-hour** tous les quarts d'heure au quart d'heure juste
quarter·ly ['kwɔrtərli] *adj* trimestriel ‖ *s* (*pl* -lies) publication *f* or revue *f* trimestrielle ‖ *adv* trimestriellement, par trimestre
quar′ter·mas′ter *s* (mil) quartier-maître *m*, intendant *m* militaire
Quar′ter·master Corps′ *s* Intendance *f*, service *m* de l'Intendance
quar′ter note′ *s* (mus) noire *f*
quar′ter rest′ *s* (mus) soupir *m*
quar′ter tone′ *s* (mus) quart *m* de ton
quartet [kwɔr'tɛt] *s* quatuor *m*
quartz [kwɔrts] *s* quartz *m*
quasar ['kwesɑr] *s* (astr) quasar *m*
quash [kwɑʃ] *tr* étouffer; (*to set aside*) annuler, invalider
quatrain ['kwɑtren] *s* quatrain *m*
quaver ['kwevər] *s* tremblement *m*; (*in the singing voice*) trémolo *m*; (mus) croche *f* ‖ *intr* trembloter
quay [ki] *s* quai *m*, débarcadère *m*
queen [kwin] *s* reine *f*; (cards, chess) reine

queen' bee' *s* reine *f* des abeilles
queen' dow'ager *s* reine *f* douairière
queen·ly ['kwinli] *adj* (*comp* **-lier**; *super* **-liest**) de reine, digne d'une reine
queen' moth'er *s* reine *f* mère
queen' post' *s* faux poinçon *m*
queer [kwɪr] *adj* bizarre, drôle; (*suspicious*) (coll) suspect; (*homosexual*) (coll) pervers, inverti; **to feel queer** (coll) se sentir indisposé ‖ *s* excentrique *mf*; (*homosexual*) (coll) tapette *f*, inverti *m* ‖ *tr* (slang) faire échouer, déranger
quell [kwɛl] *tr* étouffer, réprimer; (*pain, sorrow, etc.*) calmer
quench [kwɛntʃ] *tr* (*the thirst*) étancher; (*a rebellion*) étouffer; (*a fire*) éteindre
que·ry ['kwɪri] *s* (*pl* **-ries**) question *f*; doute *m*; (*question mark*) point *m* d'interrogation ‖ *v* (*pret* & *pp* **-ried**) *tr* questionner; mettre en doute; (*to affix a question mark*) marquer d'un point d'interrogation
quest [kwɛst] *s* quête *f*; **in quest of** en quête de
question ['kwɛstʃən] *s* question *f*; doute *m*; **beyond question** indiscutable, incontestable; **it is a question of** il s'agit de; **out of the question** impossible, impensable; **to ask s.o. a question** poser une question à qn; **to beg the question** faire une pétition de principe; **to call into question** mettre en question; **to move the previous question** (parl) demander la question préalable; **without question** sans aucun doute ‖ *tr* interroger, questionner; (*to cast doubt upon*) douter de, contester
questionable ['kwɛstʃənəbəl] *adj* discutable, douteux
ques'tion mark' *s* point *m* d'interrogation
questionnaire [,kwɛstʃən'ɛr] *s* questionnaire *m*
queue [kju] *s* queue *f* ‖ *intr*—**to queue up** faire la queue
quibble ['kwɪbəl] *intr* chicaner, ergoter
quibbling ['kwɪblɪŋ] *s* chicane *f*
quick [kwɪk] *adj* rapide, vif ‖ *s*—**the quick and the dead** les vivants et les morts; **to cut to the quick** piquer au vif
quicken ['kwɪkən] *tr* accélérer; (*e.g., the imagination*) animer ‖ *intr* s'accélérer; s'animer
quick'lime' *s* chaux *f* vive
quick' lunch' *s* casse-croûte *m*, repas *m* léger
quickly ['kwɪkli] *adv* vite, rapidement
quick'sand' *s* sable *m* mouvant
quick'sil'ver *s* vif-argent *m*, mercure *m*
quick'-tem'pered *adj* coléreux
quiet ['kwaɪ-ət] *adj* (*still*) tranquille, silencieux; (*person*) modeste, discret; (*market*) (com) calme; **be quiet!** taisez-vous!; **to keep quiet** rester tranquille; (*to not speak*) se taire ‖ *s* tranquillité *f*; (*rest*) repos *m*; **on the quiet** en douce, à la dérobée ‖

tr calmer, tranquilliser; (*a child*) faire taire ‖ *intr*—**to quiet down** se calmer
quill [kwɪl] *s* plume *f* d'oie; (*hollow part*) tuyau *m* (de plume); (*of hedgehog, porcupine*) piquant *m*
quilt [kwɪlt] *s* courtepointe *f* ‖ *tr* piquer
quince [kwɪns] *s* coing *m*; (*tree*) cognassier *m*
quinine ['kwaɪnaɪn] *s* quinine *f*
quinsy ['kwɪnzi] *s* angine *f*
quintessence [kwɪn'tɛsəns] *s* quintessence *f*
quintet [kwɪn'tɛt] *s* quintette *m*
quintuplets ['kwɪntʊ,plɛts], [kwɪn-'tʌplɛts], [kwɪn't(j)uplɛts] *spl* quintuplés *mpl*
quip [kwɪp] *s* raillerie *f*, quolibet *m* ‖ *v* (*pret* & *pp* **quipped**; *ger* **quipping**) *tr* dire sur un ton railleur ‖ *intr* railler
quire [kwaɪr] *s* main *f*
quirk [kwʌrk] *s* excentricité *f*; (*subterfuge*) faux-fuyant *m*; **quirk of fate** caprice *m* du sort
quit [kwɪt] *adj* quitte; **to be quits** être quitte; **to call it quits** cesser, s'y renoncer; **we are quits** nous voilà quittes ‖ *v* (*pret* & *pp* **quit** ou **quitted**; *ger* **quitting**) *tr* (*e.g., a city*) quitter; (*one's work, a pursuit, etc.*) cesser; **to quit** + *ger* s'arrêter de + *inf* ‖ *intr* partir; (coll) lâcher la partie
quite [kwaɪt] *adv* tout à fait; **quite a story** (coll) toute une histoire
quitter ['kwɪtər] *s* défaitiste *m*, lâcheur *m*
quiver ['kwɪvər] *s* tremblement *m*; (*to hold arrows*) carquois *m* ‖ *intr* trembler
quixotic [kwɪks'ɑtɪk] *adj* de don Quichotte; visionnaire, exalté
quiz [kwɪz] *s* (*pl* **quizzes**) interrogation *f*, colle *f* ‖ *v* (*pret* & *pp* **quizzed**; *ger* **quizzing**) *tr* examiner, interroger
quiz' sec'tion *s* classe *f* d'exercices
quiz' show' *s* émission-questionnaire *f*
quizzical ['kwɪzɪkəl] *adj* curieux; (*laughable*) risible; (*mocking*) railleur
quoin [kɔɪn], [kwɔɪn] *s* angle *m*; (*cornerstone*) pierre *f* d'angle; (*wedge*) coin *m*, cale *f* ‖ *tr* coincer, caler
quoit [kwɔɪt], [kɔɪt] *s* palet *m*; **to play quoits** jouer au palet
quondam ['kwɑndæm] *adj* ci-devant, d'autrefois
quorum ['kworəm] *s* quorum *m*
quota ['kwotə] *s* quote-part *f*; (*e.g., of immigration*) quota *m*, contingent *m*
quotation [kwo'teʃən] *s* (*from a book*) citation *f*; (*of prices*) cours *m*, cote *f*
quota'tion marks' *spl* guillemets *mpl*
quote [kwot] *s* (*from a book*) citation *f*; (*of prices*) cours *m*, cote *f*; **in quotes** (coll) entre guillemets ‖ *tr* (*from a book*) citer; (*values*) coter ‖ *intr* tirer des citations; **to quote out of context** citer hors contexte ‖ *interj* je cite
quotient ['kwoʃənt] *s* quotient *m*

R

R, r [ɑr] *s* XVIIIᵉ lettre de l'alphabet
rabbet ['ræbɪt] *s* feuillure *f* ‖ *tr* feuiller
rab·bi ['ræbaɪ] *s* (*pl* -**bis** or -**bies**) rabbin *m*
rabbit ['ræbɪt] *s* lapin *m*
rab′bit stew′ *s* lapin *m* en civet
rabble ['ræbəl] *s* canaille *f*
rab′ble-rous′er *s* fomentateur *m*, agitateur *m*
rabies ['rebiz], ['rebɪ‚iz] *s* rage *f*
raccoon [ræ'kun] *s* raton *m* laveur
race [res] *s* race *f*; (*contest*) course *f*;
(*channel to lead water*) bief *m*;
(*rapid current*) raz *m* ‖ *tr* lutter de
vitesse avec; (*e.g., a horse*) faire
courir; (*a motor*) emballer ‖ *intr*
faire une course, courir; (*said of motor*) s'emballer
race′ horse′ *s* cheval *m* de course
race′ ri′ot *s* émeute *f* raciale
race′ track′ *s* champ *m* de courses, hippodrome *m*
racial ['reʃəl] *adj* racial
rac′ing car′ *s* automobile *f* de course
rac′ing odds′ *spl* cote *f*
rack [ræk] *s* (*shelf*) étagère *f*; (*to hang
clothes*) portemanteau *m*; (*for baggage*) porte-bagages *m*; (*for guns;
for fodder*) râtelier *m*; (*for torture*)
chevalet *m*; (*bar made to gear with a
pinion*) crémaillère *f*; **to go to rack
and ruin** aller à vau-l'eau ‖ *tr* (*with
hunger, remorse, etc.*) tenailler; (*one's
brains*) se creuser
racket ['rækɪt] *s* raquette *f*; (*noise*)
vacarme *m*; (*slang*) racket *m*; **to
make a racket** faire du tapage
racketeer [‚rækɪ'tɪr] *s* racketter *m* ‖
intr pratiquer l'escroquerie
rack′ rail′way *s* chemin *m* de fer à
crémaillère
rac·y ['resi] *adj* (*comp* -**ier**; *super* -**iest**)
plein de verve, vigoureux; parfumé;
(*off-color*) sale, grivois
radar ['redɑr] *s* (acronym) (**radio de-
tecting and ranging**) radar *m*
ra′dar sta′tion *s* poste *m* radar
radiant ['redɪ‚ənt] *adj* radieux, rayonnant; (astr & phys) radiant
radiate ['redɪ‚et] *tr* rayonner; (*e.g.,
happiness*) répandre ‖ *intr* rayonner
radiation [‚redɪ'eʃən] *s* rayonnement
m, radiation *f*
radia′tion sick′ness *s* mal *m* des rayons
radiator ['redɪ‚etər] *s* radiateur *m*
ra′diator cap′ *s* bouchon *m* de radiateur
radical ['rædɪkəl] *adj* & *s* radical *m*
radi·o ['redɪ‚o] *s* (*pl* -**os**) radio *f* ‖ *tr*
radiodiffuser
radioactive [‚redɪ·o'æktɪv] *adj* radioactif
ra′dioac′tive fall′out *s* retombées *fpl*
radioactives
ra′dio am′ateur *s* sans-filiste *mf*
ra′dio announ′cer *s* speaker *m*
ra′dio·broad′cast′ing *s* radiodiffusion *f*
ra′dio·fre′quency *s* radiofréquence *f*

radiogram ['redɪ·o‚græm] *s* radiogramme *m*
ra′dio lis′tener *s* auditeur *m* de la radio
radiology [‚redɪ'ɑlədʒi] *s* radiologie *f*
ra′dio net′work *s* chaîne *f* de radiodiffusion
ra′dio news′cast *s* journal *m* parlé,
radio-journal *m*
ra′dio receiv′er *s* récepteur *m* de radio
radioscopy [‚redɪ'ɑskəpi] *s* radioscopie *f*
ra′dio set′ *s* poste *m* de radio
ra′dio sta′tion *s* poste *m* émetteur
ra′dio tube′ *s* lampe *f* de radio
radish ['rædɪʃ] *s* radis *m*
radium ['redɪ·əm] *s* radium *m*
radi·us ['redɪ·əs] *s* (*pl* -**i** [‚aɪ] or -**uses**)
rayon *m*; (anat) radius *m*; **within a
radius of** dans un rayon de, à . . . à
la ronde
raffish ['ræfɪʃ] *adj* bravache; (*flashy*)
criard
raffle ['ræfəl] *s* tombola *f* ‖ *tr* mettre
en tombola
raft [ræft], [rɑft] *s* radeau *m*; **a raft of**
(coll) un tas de
rafter ['ræftər], ['rɑftər] *s* chevron *m*
rag [ræg] *s* chiffon *m*; **in rags** en haillons; **to chew the rag** (slang) tailler
une bavette
ragamuffin ['rægə‚mʌfɪn] *s* gueux *m*,
va-nu-pieds *m*; (*urchin*) gamin *m*
rag′ doll′ *s* poupée *f* de chiffon
rage [redʒ] *s* rage *f*; **to be all the rage**
faire fureur; **to fly into a rage** entrer
en fureur ‖ *intr* faire rage
rag′ fair′ *s* marché *m* aux puces
ragged ['rægɪd] *adj* en haillons; (*edge*)
hérissé
ragpicker ['ræg‚pɪkər] *s* chiffonnier *m*
rag′time′ *s* rythme *m* syncopé du jazz;
musique *f* syncopée du jazz
rag′weed′ *s* ambrosie *f*
ragwort ['ræg‚wʌrt] *s* (*Senecio vulga-
ris*) séneçon *m*; (*S. jacobaea*) jaco-
bée *f*
raid [red] *s* incursion *f*, razzia *f*; (*by
police*) descente *f*; (mil) raid *m* ‖ *tr*
razzier; faire une descente dans
rail [rel] *s* rail *m*; (*railing*) balustrade
f; (*of stairway*) rampe *f*; (*of, e.g., a
bridge*) garde-fou *m*; (orn) râle *m*; **by
rail** par chemin de fer ‖ *intr* invectiver; **to rail at** invectiver
rail′ fence′ *s* palissade *f* à claire-voie
rail′head′ *s* tête *f* de ligne
railing ['relɪŋ] *s* balustrade *f*
rail′road′ *adj* ferroviaire ‖ *s* chemin *m*
de fer ‖ *tr* (*a bill*) faire voter en vitesse; (coll) emprisonner à tort
rail′road cros′sing *s* passage *m* à niveau
railroader ['rel‚rodər] *s* cheminot *m*
rail′road sta′tion *s* gare *f*
rail′way′ *adj* ferroviaire ‖ *s* chemin *m*
de fer
raiment ['remənt] *s* habillement *m*
rain [ren] *s* pluie *f*; **in the rain** sous la
pluie ‖ *tr* faire pleuvoir ‖ *intr* pleu-

voir; **it is raining cats and dogs** il pleut à seaux

rainbow ['ren ,bo] *s* arc-en-ciel *m*

rain'coat' *s* imperméable *m*

rain'fall' *s* chute *f* de pluie

rain'proof' *adj* imperméable

rain' wa'ter *s* eau *f* de pluie

rain·y ['reni] *adj* (*comp* **-ier**; *super* **-iest**) pluvieux

raise [rez] *s* augmentation *f*; (*in poker*) relance *f* ‖ *tr* augmenter; (*plants, animals, children; one's voice; a number to a certain power*) élever; (*an army, a camp, a siege; anchor; game*) lever; (*an objection, questions, etc.*) soulever; (*doubts; a hope; a storm*) faire naître; (*a window*) relever; (*one's head, one's voice; prices; the land*) hausser; (*a flag*) arborer; (*the dead*) ressusciter; (*money*) se procurer; (*the ante*) relancer; **to raise up** soulever, dresser

raisin ['rezən] *s* raisin *m* sec, grain *m* de raisin sec

rake [rek] *s* râteau *m*; (*person*) débauché *m* ‖ *tr* ratisser; **to rake together** râteler

rake'-off' *s* (coll) gratte *f*

rakish ['rekɪʃ] *adj* gaillard; dissolu

ral·ly ['ræli] *s* (*pl* **-lies**) ralliement *m*; réunion *f* politique; (*in a game*) reprise *f*; (*auto race*) rallye *m* ‖ *v* (*pret & pp* **-lied**) *tr* rallier ‖ *intr* se rallier; (*from illness*) se remettre; (sports) se reprendre; **to rally to the side of** se rallier à

ram [ræm] *s* bélier *m* ‖ *v* (*pret & pp* **rammed**; *ger* **ramming**) *tr* tamponner; **to ram down or in** enfoncer ‖ *intr* se tamponner; **to ram into** tamponner

ramble ['ræmbəl] *s* flânerie *f* ‖ *intr* flâner, errer à l'aventure; (*to talk aimlessly*) divaguer

rami·fy ['ræmɪ ,faɪ] *v* (*pret & pp* **-fied**) *tr* ramifier ‖ *intr* se ramifier

ramp [ræmp] *s* rampe *f*

rampage ['ræmpedʒ] *s* tempête *f*; **to go on a rampage** se déchaîner

rampart ['ræmpɑrt] *s* rempart *m*

ram'rod' *s* écouvillon *m*

ram'shack'le *adj* délabré

ranch [ræntʃ] *s* ranch *m*, rancho *m*

rancid ['rænsɪd] *adj* rance

rancor ['rænkər] *s* rancœur *f*

random ['rændəm] *adj* fortuit; **at random** au hasard

range [rendʒ] *s* (*row*) rangée *f*; (*scope*) portée *f*; (*mountains*) chaîne *f*; (*stove*) cuisinière *f*; (*for rifle practice*) champ *m* de tir; (*of colors, musical notes, prices, speeds, etc.*) gamme *f*; (*of words*) répartition *f*; (*of voice*) tessiture *f*; (*of vision, of activity, etc.*) champ *m*; (*for pasture*) grand pâturage *m*; **within range of** à portée de ‖ *tr* ranger ‖ *intr* se ranger; **to range from** s'échelonner entre, varier entre; **to range over** parcourir

range' find'er *s* télémètre *m*

rank [ræŋk] *adj* fétide, rance; (*injustice*) criant; (*vegetation*) luxuriant ‖

s rang *m* ‖ *tr* ranger ‖ *intr* occuper le premier rang; **to rank above** être supérieur à; **to rank with** aller de pair avec

rank' **and file'** *s* hommes *mpl* de troupe; commun *m* des mortels; (*of the party, union, etc.*) commun *m*

rankle ['ræŋkəl] *tr* ulcérer; irriter ‖ *intr* s'ulcérer

ransack ['rænsæk] *tr* fouiller, fouiller dans; mettre à sac

ransom ['rænsəm] *s* rançon *f* ‖ *tr* rançonner

rant [rænt] *intr* tempêter

rap [ræp] *s* tape *f*; (*noise*) petit coup *m* sec; (slang) éreintement *m*; **to not care a rap** (slang) s'en ficher; **to take the rap** (slang) se laisser châtier ‖ *v* (*pret & pp* **rapped**; *ger* **rapping**) *tr & intr* frapper d'un coup sec

rapacious [rə'peʃəs] *adj* rapace

rape [rep] *s* viol *m* ‖ *tr* violer

rapid ['ræpɪd] *adj* rapide ‖ **rapids** *spl* rapides *mpl*

rap'id-fire' *adj* à tir rapide

rapidity [rə'pɪdəti] *s* rapidité *f*

rapier ['repɪ·ər] *s* rapière *f*

rapt [ræpt] *adj* ravi; absorbé

rapture ['ræptʃər] *s* ravissement *m*

rare [rɛr] *adj* rare; (*meat*) saignant; (*amusing*) (coll) impayable

rare' bird' *s* merle *m* blanc

rarely ['rɛrli] *adv* rarement

rascal ['ræskəl] *s* coquin *m*

rash [ræʃ] *adj* téméraire ‖ *s* éruption *f*

rasp [ræsp], [rɑsp] *s* crissement *m*; (*tool*) râpe *f* ‖ *tr* râper ‖ *intr* crisser

raspber·ry ['ræz ,beri], ['rɑz,bɛri] *s* (*pl* **-ries**) framboise *f*

rasp'berry bush' *s* framboisier *m*

rat [ræt] *s* rat *m*; (*false hair*) (coll) postiche *m*; (*deserter*) (slang) lâcheur *m*; (*informer*) (slang) mouchard *m*; (*scoundrel*) (slang) cochon *m*; **rats!** zut!; **to smell a rat** (coll) soupçonner anguille sous roche

ratchet ['rætʃɪt] *s* encliquetage *m*

rate [ret] *s* taux *m*; (*for freight, mail, a subscription*) tarif *m*; **at any rate** en tout cas; **at the rate of** à raison de ‖ *tr* évaluer; mériter ‖ *intr* (coll) être favori

rate' of exchange' *s* cours *m*

rather ['ræðər], ['rɑðər] *adv* plutôt; (*fairly*) assez; **rather than** plutôt que ‖ *interj* je vous crois!

rathskeller ['ræts ,kɛlər] *s* caveau *m*

rati·fy ['rætɪ ,faɪ] *v* (*pret & pp* **-fied**) *tr* ratifier

rating ['retɪŋ] *s* classement *m*, cote *f*

ra·tio ['reʃo], ['reʃɪ ,o] *s* (*pl* **-tios**) raison *f*, rapport *m*

ration ['reʃən], ['ræʃən] *s* ration *f* ‖ *tr* rationner

rational ['ræʃənəl] *adj* rationnel

ra'tion book' *s* tickets *mpl* de rationnement

ra'tion card' *s* carte *f* de ravitaillement

rat' poi'son *s* mort *m* aux rats

rat'-tail file' *s* queue-de-rat *f*

rattan [ræ'tæn] *s* rotin *m*

rattle ['rætəl] s (*number of short, sharp sounds*) bruit *m* de ferraille, cliquetis *m*; (*noisemaking device*) crécelle *f*; (*child's toy*) hochet *m*; (*in the throat*) râle *m* ‖ *tr* agiter; (*to confuse*) (coll) affoler; **to rattle off** débiter comme un moulin ‖ *intr* cliqueter; (*said of windows*) trembler

rat′tle·snake′ s serpent *m* à sonnettes

rat′trap′ s ratière *f*

raucous ['rɔkəs] adj rauque

ravage ['rævɪdʒ] s ravage *m*; **ravages** (*of time*) injure *f* ‖ *tr* ravager

rave [rev] s (coll) éloge *m* enthousiaste ‖ *intr* délirer; **to rave about** or **over** s'extasier devant or sur

raven ['revən] s corbeau *m*

ravenous ['rævənəs] adj vorace

rave′ review′ s article *m* dithyrambique

ravine [rə'vin] s ravin *m*

ravish ['rævɪʃ] *tr* ravir

ravishing ['rævɪʃɪŋ] adj ravissant

raw [rɔ] adj cru; (*sugar, metal*) brut; (*silk*) grège; (*wound*) vif; (*wind*) aigre; (*weather*) humide et froid; novice, inexpérimenté

raw′boned′ adj décharné

raw′ deal′ s (slang) mauvais tour *m*

raw′hide′ s cuir *m* vert

raw′ mate′rial s matière *f* première, matières premières, matière brute

ray [re] s (*of light*) rayon *m*; (*fish*) raie *f*

rayon ['re·ɑn] s rayonne *f*

raze [rez] *tr* raser

razor ['rezər] s rasoir *m*

ra′zor blade′ s lame *f* de rasoir

ra′zor strop′ s cuir *m* à rasoir

razz [ræz] *tr* (slang) mettre en boîte

reach [ritʃ] s portée *f*; **out of reach (of)** hors d'atteinte (de), hors de portée (de); **within reach of** à portée de ‖ *tr* atteindre; arriver à; **to reach out** (*a hand*) tendre; (*an arm*) allonger ‖ *intr* s'étendre

react [rɪ'ækt] *intr* réagir

reaction [rɪ'ækʃən] s réaction *f*

reactionar·y [rɪ'ækʃən‚ɛri] adj réactionnaire ‖ s (*pl* -ies) réactionnaire *mf*

reactor [rɪ'æktər] s réacteur *m*

read [rid] v (*pret & pp* **read** [rɛd]) *tr* lire; **to read over** parcourir ‖ *intr* lire; (*said of passage, description, etc.*) se lire; (*said, e.g., of thermometer*) marquer; **to read on** continuer à lire; **to read up on** étudier ‖

reader ['ridər] s lecteur *m*; livre *m* de lecture

readily ['rɛdɪli] adv (*willingly*) volontiers; (*easily*) facilement

reading ['ridɪŋ] s lecture *f*

read′ing desk′ s pupitre *m*

read′ing glass′ s loupe *f*; **reading glasses** lunettes *fpl* pour lire

read′ing lamp′ s lampe *f* de bureau

read′ing room′ s salle *f* de lecture

read·y ['rɛdi] adj (*comp* -ier; *super* -iest) prêt; (*quick*) vif; (*money*) comptant ‖ v (*pret & pp* -ied) *tr* préparer ‖ *intr* se préparer

read′y cash′ s argent *m* comptant

read′y-made′ suit′ s (*for men*) complet *m* de confection; (*for women*) costume *m* de confection

ready-to-eat ['rɛdɪə'it] adj prêt à servir

ready-to-wear ['rɛdɪə'wɛr] adj prêt à porter ‖ s prêt-à-porter *m*

reaffirm [‚ri·ə'fʌrm] *tr* réaffirmer

reagent [rɪ'edʒənt] s (chem) réactif *m*

real ['ri·əl] adj vrai, réel

re′al estate′ s biens *mpl* immobiliers

re′al-estate′ adj immobilier

realism ['ri·ə‚lɪzəm] s réalisme *m*

realist ['ri·əlɪst] s réaliste *mf*

realistic [‚ri·ə'lɪstɪk] adj réaliste

reali·ty [ri'ælɪti] s (*pl* -ties) réalité *f*

realize ['ri·ə‚laɪz] *tr* se rendre compte de, s'apercevoir de; (*hopes, profits, etc.*) réaliser

really ['ri·əli] adv vraiment

realm [rɛlm] s royaume *m*; (*field*) domaine *m*

realtor ['ri·əl‚tɔr], ['ri·əltər] s agent *m* immobilier

ream [rim] s rame *f*; **reams** (coll) masses *fpl* ‖ *tr* aléser

reap [rip] *tr* moissonner; (*to gather*) recueillir

reaper ['ripər] s moissonneur *m*; (mach) moissonneuse *f*

reappear [‚ri·ə'pɪr] *intr* réapparaître

reappearance [‚ri·ə'pɪrəns] s réapparition *f*

reapportionment [‚ri·ə'pɔrʃənmənt] s nouvelle répartition *f*

rear [rɪr] adj arrière, d'arrière, de derrière ‖ s derrière *m*; (*of a car, ship, etc.; of an army*) arrière *m*; (*of a row*) queue *f*; **to the rear!** (mil) demi-tour à droite! ‖ *tr* élever ‖ *intr* (*said of animal*) se cabrer

rear′ ad′miral s contre-amiral *m*

rear′-axle assem′bly s (*pl* -blies) pont *m* arrière

rear′ drive′ s traction *f* arrière

rearmament [ri'arməmənt] s réarmement *m*

rearrange [‚ri·ə'rendʒ] *tr* arranger de nouveau

rear′-view mir′ror s rétroviseur *m*

rear′ win′dow s (aut) lunette *f* arrière

reason ['rizən] s raison *f*; **by reason of** à cause de; **for good reason** pour cause; **to listen to reason** entendre raison; **to stand to reason** être de toute évidence ‖ *tr & intr* raisonner

reasonable ['rizənəbəl] adj raisonnable

reassessment [‚ri·ə'sɛsmənt] s réévaluation *f*

reassure [‚ri·ə'ʃur] *tr* rassurer

reawaken [‚ri·ə'wekən] *tr* réveiller ‖ *intr* se réveiller

rebate ['ribet], [rɪ'bet] s rabais *m*, escompte *m*; ristourne *f*, bonification *f* ‖ *tr* faire un rabais sur

rebel ['rɛbəl] adj & s rebelle *mf* ‖ **re·bel** [rɪ'bɛl] v (*pret & pp* -belled; *ger* -belling) *intr* se rebeller

rebellion [rɪ'bɛljən] s rébellion *f*

rebellious [rɪ'bɛljəs] adj rebelle

re·bind [ri'baɪnd] v (*pret & pp* -bound) *tr* (bb) relier à neuf

rebirth ['ribʌrθ] s renaissance f
rebore [ri'bor] tr rectifier
rebound ['ri,baʊnd], [ri'baʊnd] s rebondissement m ‖ [ri'baʊnd] intr rebondir
rebroad·cast [ri'brɔd,kæst], [ri'brɔd,kɑst] s retransmission f ‖ v (pret & pp -cast or -casted) tr retransmettre
rebuff [ri'bʌf] s rebuffade f ‖ tr mal accueillir
re·build [ri'bɪld] v (pret & pp -built) tr reconstruire
rebuke [ri'bjuk] s réprimande f ‖ tr réprimander
re·but [ri'bʌt] v (pret & pp -butted; ger -butting) tr réfuter, repousser
rebuttal [ri'bʌtəl] s réfutation f
recall [ri'kɔl], ['rikəl] s rappel m ‖ [ri'kɔl] tr rappeler; se rappeler de
recant [ri'kænt] tr rétracter ‖ intr se rétracter
re·cap ['ri,kæp], [ri'kæp] v (pret & pp -capped; ger -capping) tr rechaper
recapitulation [,rikə,pɪtʃə'leʃən] s récapitulation f
re·cast ['ri,kæst], ['ri,kɑst] s refonte f ‖ [ri'kæst], [ri'kɑst] v (pret & pp -cast) tr (metal; a play, novel, etc.) refondre; (the actors of a play) redistribuer
recede [ri'sid] intr reculer; (said of forehead, chin, etc.) fuir; (said of sea) se retirer
receipt [ri'sit] s (for goods) récépissé m; (for money) récépissé, reçu m; (recipe) recette f; **receipts** recettes; **to acknowledge receipt of** accuser réception de ‖ tr acquitter
receive [ri'siv] tr recevoir; (stolen goods) recéler; (a station) (rad) capter; **received payment** pour acquit ‖ intr recevoir
receiver [ri'sivər] s (of letter) destinataire mf; (in bankruptcy) syndic m, liquidateur m; (telp) récepteur m
receiv'ing set' s poste m récepteur
recent ['risənt] adj récent
recently ['risəntli] adv récemment
receptacle [ri'septəkəl] s récipient m; (elec) prise f femelle
reception [ri'sepʃən] s réception f; (welcome) accueil m
recep'tion desk' s réception f
receptionist [ri'sepʃənɪst] s préposé m à la réception
receptive [ri'septɪv] adj réceptif
recess [ri'ses], ['rises] s (of court, legislature, etc.) ajournement m; (at school) récréation f; (in a wall) niche f ‖ [ri'ses] tr ajourner; (s.th., e.g., in a wall) encastrer ‖ intr s'ajourner
recession [ri'seʃən] s récession f
recipe ['resi,pi] s recette f
recipient [ri'sɪpɪ-ənt] s (person) bénéficiaire mf; (of a degree, honor, etc.) récipiendaire m; (of blood) receveur m
reciprocal [ri'sɪprəkəl] adj réciproque
reciprocity [,resi'prɑsɪti] s réciprocité f
recital [ri'saɪtəl] s récit m; (of music or poetry) récital m

recite [ri'saɪt] tr réciter; narrer
reckless ['rɛklɪs] adj téméraire, imprudent, insouciant
reckon ['rɛkən] tr calculer; considérer; (coll) supposer, imaginer ‖ intr calculer; **to reckon on** compter sur; **to reckon with** tenir compte de
reclaim [ri'klem] tr récupérer; (e.g., waste land) mettre en valeur; (a person) réformer
reclamation [,rɛklə'meʃən] s récupération f; (e.g., of waste land) mise f en valeur; (of a person) réforme f
recline [ri'klaɪn] tr appuyer, reposer ‖ intr s'appuyer, se reposer
recluse [ri'klus], ['rɛklus] adj & s reclus m
recognition [,rɛkəg'nɪʃən] s reconnaissance f
recognize ['rɛkəg,naɪz] tr reconnaître; (parl) donner la parole à
recoil [ri'kɔɪl] s répugnance f; (of, e.g., firearm) recul m ‖ intr reculer
recollect [,rɛkə'lɛkt] tr se rappeler
recollection [,rɛkə'lɛkʃən] s souvenir m
recommend [,rɛkə'mɛnd] tr recommander
recompense ['rɛkəm,pɛns] s récompense f ‖ tr récompenser
reconcile ['rɛkən,saɪl] tr réconcilier; **to reconcile oneself to** se résigner à
reconnaissance [ri'kɑnɪsəns] s reconnaissance f
reconnoiter [,rɛkə'nɔɪtər], [,rikə'nɔɪtər] tr & intr reconnaître
reconquer [ri'kɑŋkər] tr reconquérir
reconquest [ri'kɑŋkwɛst] s reconquête f
reconsider [,rikən'sɪdər] tr reconsidérer
reconstruct [,rikən'strʌkt] tr reconstruire; (a crime) reconstituer
reconversion [,rikən'vʌrʒən], [,rikən-'vʌrʃən] s reconversion f
record ['rɛkərd] s enregistrement m, registre m; (to play on the phonograph) disque m; (mil) état m de service; (sports) record m; **off the record** en confidence; **records** archives fpl; **to break the record** battre le record; **to have a good record** être bien noté; (at school) avoir de bonnes notes ‖ [ri'kɔrd] tr enregistrer
rec'ord chang'er s tourne-disque m automatique
recorder [ri'kɔrdər] s appareil m enregistreur; (law) greffier m; (mus) flûte f à bec
rec'ord hold'er s recordman m
recording [ri'kɔrdɪŋ] adj enregistreur ‖ s enregistrement m
record'ing tape' s ruban m magnétique
rec'ord li'brary s discothèque m
rec'ord play'er s électrophone m
recount ['ri,kaʊnt] s nouveau dépouillement m du scrutin ‖ [ri'kaʊnt] tr (to count again) recompter ‖ [ri-'kaʊnt] tr (to tell) raconter
recoup [ri'kup] tr recouvrer; **to recoup s.o. for** dédommager qn de
recourse [ri'kors], ['rikors] s recours m; **to have recourse to** recourir à
recover [ri'kʌvər] tr (to get back) re-

couvrer; (*to cover again*) recouvrir || *intr* (*to get well*) se rétablir

recover·y [rɪ'kʌvəri] *s* (*pl* -ies) récupération *f*, recouvrement *m*; (*e.g., of health*) rétablissement *m*

recreant ['rɛkrɪ·ənt] *adj & s* lâche *mf*; traître *m*; apostat *m*

recreation [ˌrɛkrɪ'eʃən] *s* récréation *f*

recruit [rɪ'krut] *s* recrue *f* || *tr* recruter; **to be recruited** se recruter

rectangle ['rɛkˌtæŋgəl] *s* rectangle *m*

rectifier ['rɛktəˌfaɪ·ər] *s* rectificateur *m*; (elec) redresseur *m*

recti·fy ['rɛktɪˌfaɪ] *v* (*pret & pp* -**fied**) *tr* rectifier; (elec) redresser

rec·tum ['rɛktəm] *s* (*pl* -**ta** [tə]) rectum *m*

recumbent [rɪ'kʌmbənt] *adj* couché

recuperate [rɪ'kjupəˌret] *tr & intr* récupérer

re·cur [rɪ'kʌr] *v* (*pret & pp* -**curred**; *ger* -**curring**) *intr* revenir, se reproduire; revenir à la mémoire de

recurrent [rɪ'kʌrənt] *adj* récurrent

red [rɛd] *adj* (*comp* **redder**; *super* **reddest**) rouge || *s* (*color*) rouge *m*; **in the red** en déficit; **Red** (*communist*) rouge *mf*; (*nickname*) Rouquin *m*

red'bait' *tr* taxer de communiste

red'bird' *s* cardinal *m* d'Amérique, tangara *m*

red'-blood'ed *adj* vigoureux

red'breast' *s* rouge-gorge *m*

red'cap' *s* porteur *m*; (Brit) soldat *m* de la police militaire

red' cell' *s* globule *m* rouge

Red' Cross' *s* Croix-Rouge *f*

redden ['rɛdən] *tr & intr* rougir

redeem [rɪ'dim] *tr* racheter; (*a pawned article*) dégager; (*a promise*) remplir; (*a debt*) s'acquitter de, acquitter

redeemer [rɪ'dimər] *s* rédempteur *m*

redemption [rɪ'dɛmpʃən] *s* rachat *m*; (rel) rédemption *f*

red'-haired' *adj* roux

red'hand'ed *adj & adv* sur le fait, en flagrant délit

red'head' *s* (*woman*) rousse *f*

red' her'ring *s* hareng *m* saur; (fig) faux-fuyant *m*

red'-hot' *adj* chauffé au rouge; ardent; (*news*) tout frais

rediscount [ri'dɪskaʊnt] *s* réescompte *m* || *tr* réescompter

rediscover [ˌridɪs'kʌvər] *tr* redécouvrir

red'-let'ter day' *s* jour *m* mémorable

red' light' *s* feu *m* rouge; **to go through a red light** brûler un feu rouge

red'-light' dis'trict *s* quartier *m* réservé

red' man' *s* (*pl* **men'**) Peau-Rouge *m*

re·do ['ri'du] *v* (*pret* -**did**; *pp* -**done**) *tr* refaire

redolent ['rɛdələnt] *adj* parfumé; **redolent of** exhalant une senteur de; qui fait penser à

redoubt [rɪ'daʊt] *s* redoute *f*

redound [rɪ'daʊnd] *intr* contribuer; **to redound to** tourner à

red' pep'per *s* piment *m* rouge

redress [rɪ'drɛs], ['ridrəs] *s* redressement *m* || [rɪ'drɛs] *tr* redresser

Red' Rid'ing·hood' *s* Chaperon rouge *m*

red'skin' *s* Peau-Rouge *mf*

red' tape' *s* paperasserie *f*, chinoiseries *fpl* administratives

reduce [rɪ'd(j)us] *tr* réduire || *intr* maigrir

reduc'ing ex'ercises *spl* exercices *mpl* amaigrissants

reduction [rɪ'dʌkʃən] *s* réduction *f*

redundant [rɪ'dʌndənt] *adj* redondant

red' wine' *s* vin *m* rouge

red'wing' *s* (orn) mauvis *m*

red'wood' *s* séquoia *m*

reed [rid] *s* (*of instrument*) anche *f*; (bot) roseau *m*; **reeds** (mus) instruments *mpl* à anche

reedit [ri'ɛdɪt] *tr* rééditer

reef [rif] *s* récif *m*; (*of sail*) ris *m* || *tr* (naut) prendre un ris dans

reefer ['rifər] *s* caban *m*; (slang) cigarette *f* à marijuana

reek [rik] *intr* fumer; **to reek of** or **with** empester, puer

reel [ril] *s* bobine *f*; (*of film*) rouleau *m*, bobine; (*of fishing rod*) moulinet *m*; (*sway*) balancement *m*; **off the reel** (coll) d'affilée || *tr* bobiner; **to reel off** dévider; (coll) réciter d'un trait || *intr* chanceler

reelection [ˌri·ɪ'lɛkʃən] *s* réélection *f*

reenlist [ˌri·ɛn'lɪst] *tr* rengager || *intr* rengager, se rengager

reenlistment [ˌri·ɛn'lɪstmənt] *s* rengagement *m*; (*person*) rengagé *m*

reen·try [ri'ɛntri] *s* (*pl* -**tries**) rentrée *f*; (rok) retour *m* à la Terre

reexamination [ˌri·ɛgˌzæmɪ'neʃən] *s* réexamen *m*

re·fer [rɪ'fʌr] *v* (*pret & pp* -**ferred**; *ger* -**ferring**) *tr* renvoyer || *intr*—**to refer to** se référer à

referee [ˌrɛfə'ri] *s* arbitre *m* || *tr & intr* arbitrer

reference ['rɛfərəns] *s* référence *f*

ref'erence room' *s* bibliothèque *f* de consultation

referen·dum [ˌrɛfə'rɛndəm] *s* (*pl* -**da** [də]) référendum *m*

refill ['rifɪl] *s* recharge *f* || [ri'fɪl] *tr* remplir à nouveau

refine [rɪ'faɪn] *tr* raffiner

refinement [rɪ'faɪnmənt] *s* raffinage *m*; (*e.g., of manners*) raffinement *m*

refiner·y [rɪ'faɪnəri] *s* (*pl* -ies) raffinerie *f*

reflect [rɪ'flɛkt] *tr* réfléchir || *intr* (*to meditate*) réfléchir; **to reflect on** or **upon** réfléchir à or sur; nuire à la réputation de

reflection [rɪ'flɛkʃən] *s* (*e.g., of light; thought*) réflexion *f*; (*reflected light; image*) reflet *m*; **to cast reflections on** faire des réflexions à

reflex ['riflɛks] *adj & s* réflexe *m*

reforestation [ˌrifɑrɪs'teʃən], [ˌrifɔrɪs'teʃən] *s* reboisement *m*

reform [rɪ'fɔrm] *s* reforme *f* || *tr* réformer || *intr* se réformer

reformation [ˌrɛfər'meʃən] *s* réformation *f*; **the Reformation** la Réforme

reformato·ry [rɪ'fɔrmə,tori] s (pl -ries) maison f de correction
reformer [rɪ'fɔrmər] s réformateur m
reform' school' s maison f de correction
refraction [rɪ'fræk∫ən] s réfraction f
refrain [rɪ'fren] s refrain m || intr s'abstenir
refresh [rɪ'frɛ∫] tr rafraîchir || intr se rafraîchir
refreshing [rɪ'frɛ∫ɪŋ] adj rafraîchissant
refreshment [rɪ'frɛ∫mənt] s rafraîchissement m
refresh'ment bar' s buvette f
refrigerate [rɪ'frɪdʒə,ret] tr réfrigérer
refrigerator [rɪ'frɪdʒə,retər] s (icebox) glacière; réfrigérateur m; (condenser) congélateur m
refrig'erator car' s (rr) wagon m frigorifique
re·fuel [ri'fjul] v (pret & pp -fueled or -fuelled; ger -fueling or -fuelling) tr ravitailler en carburant || intr se ravitailler en carburant
refuge ['rɛfjudʒ] s refuge m; **to take refuge (in)** se réfugier (dans)
refugee [,rɛfju'dʒi] s réfugié m
refund ['rifʌnd] s remboursement m || [rɪ'fʌnd] tr (to pay back) rembourser || [ri'fʌnd] tr (to fund again) consolider
refurnish [ri'fʌrnɪ∫] tr remeubler
refusal [rɪ'fjuzəl] s refus m
refuse ['rɛfjus] s ordures fpl, détritus mpl || [rɪ'fjuz] tr & intr refuser
refute [rɪ'fjut] tr réfuter
regain [rɪ'gen] tr regagner; (consciousness) reprendre
regal ['rigəl] adj royal
regale [rɪ'gel] tr régaler
regalia [rɪ'gelɪ·ə] spl atours mpl, ornements mpl; (of an office) insignes mpl
regard [rɪ'gard] s considération f; (esteem) respect m; (look) regard m; **in** or **with regard to** à l'égard de; **regards** sincères amitiés fpl || tr considérer, estimer; **as regards** quant à
regarding [rɪ'gardɪŋ] prep au sujet de, touchant
regardless [rɪ'gardlɪs] adj inattentif || adv (coll) coûte que coûte; **regardless of** sans tenir compte de
regatta [rɪ'gætə] s régates fpl
regen·cy ['ridʒənsi] s (pl -cies) régence f
regenerate [rɪ'dʒɛnə,ret] tr régénérer || intr se régénérer
regent ['ridʒənt] s régent m
regicide ['rɛdʒɪ,saɪd] s (act) régicide m; (person) régicide mf
regime [re'ʒim] s régime m
regiment ['rɛdʒɪmənt] s régiment m || ['rɛdʒɪ,mɛnt] tr enrégimenter, régenter
regimental [,rɛdʒɪ'mɛntəl] adj régimentaire || **regimentals** spl tenue f militaire
region ['ridʒən] s région f
register ['rɛdʒɪstər] s registre m || tr enregistrer; (a student; an automobile) immatriculer; (a letter) recommander || intr s'inscrire

reg'istered let'ter s lettre f recommandée
reg'istered mail' s envoi m en recommandé
reg'istered nurse' s infirmière f diplômée
registrar ['rɛdʒɪs,trar] s archiviste mf, secrétaire mf
registration [,rɛdʒɪs'tre∫ən] s enregistrement m; immatriculation f, inscription f; (of mail) recommandation f
registra'tion blank' s fiche f d'inscription
registra'tion fee' s frais mpl d'inscription
registra'tion num'ber s (of soldier or student) numéro m matricule
re·gret [rɪ'grɛt] s regret m; **regrets** excuses fpl || v (pret & pp -gretted; ger -gretting) tr regretter
regrettable [rɪ'grɛtəbəl] adj regrettable
regular ['rɛgjələr] adj & s régulier m
reg'ular fel'low s (coll) chic type m
regularity [,rɛgjə'lærɪti] s régularité f
regularize ['rɛgjələ,raɪz] tr régulariser
regulate ['rɛgjə,let] tr régler; (to control) réglementer
regulation [,rɛgjə'le∫ən] s régulation f; (rule) règlement m
rehabilitate [,rihə'bɪlɪ,tet] tr réadapter; (in reputation, standing, etc.) réhabiliter
rehearsal [rɪ'hʌrsəl] s répétition f
rehearse [rɪ'hʌrs] tr & intr répéter
reign [ren] s règne m || intr régner
reimburse [,ri·ɪm'bʌrs] tr rembourser
rein [ren] s rêne f; **to give free rein to** donner libre cours à || tr contenir, freiner
reincarnation [,ri·ɪnkar'ne∫ən] s réincarnation f
rein'deer' s renne m
reinforce [,ri·ɪn'fors] tr renforcer; (concrete) armer
reinforcement [,ri·ɪn'forsmənt] s renforcement m
reinstate [,ri·ɪn'stet] tr rétablir
reiterate [ri'ɪtə,ret] tr réitérer
reject ['ridʒɛkt] s pièce f or article m de rebut; **rejects** rebuts mpl || [rɪ'dʒɛkt] tr rejeter
rejection [rɪ'dʒɛk∫ən] s rejet m, refus m
rejoice [rɪ'dʒɔɪs] intr se réjouir
rejoin [ri'dʒɔɪn] tr rejoindre
rejoinder [rɪ'dʒɔɪndər] s réplique f; (law) réponse f à une réplique
rejuvenation [rɪ,dʒuvɪ'ne∫ən] s rajeunissement m
rekindle [ri'kɪndəl] tr rallumer
relapse [rɪ'læps] s rechute f || intr rechuter
relate [rɪ'let] tr (to narrate) relater; (e.g., two events) établir un rapport entre; **to be related** être apparenté
relation [rɪ'le∫ən] s relation f; récit m, relation; (relative) parent m; (kinship) parenté f; **in relation to** or **with** par rapport à; **relations** (of a sexual nature) rapports mpl
relationship [rɪ'le∫ən,∫ɪp] s (connection) rapport m; (kinship) parenté f

relative ['rɛlətɪv] *adj* relatif || *s* parent *m*

relativity [ˌrelə'tɪvəti] *s* relativité *f*

relax [rɪ'læks] *tr* détendre; **to be relaxed** être décontracté or détendu || *intr* se détendre

relaxation [ˌrɪlæks'eʃən] *s* détente *f*, délassement *m*

relaxing [rɪ'læksɪŋ] *adj* tranquillisant, apaisant; (*diverting*) délassant

relay ['rile], [rɪ'le] *s* relais *m* || *v* (*pret & pp* **-layed**) *tr* relayer; (rad, telg, telp, telv) retransmettre || [ri'le] *v* (*pret & pp* **-laid**) *tr* tendre de nouveau

re′lay race′ *s* course *f* de relais

release [rɪ'lis] *s* délivrance *f*; (*from jail*) mise *f* en liberté; (*permission*) autorisation *f*; (aer) lâchage *m*; (mach) déclenchement *m* || *tr* délivrer; (*from jail*) mettre en liberté; autoriser; (*a bomb*) lâcher

relegate ['rɛlɪˌget] *tr* reléguer

relent [rɪ'lɛnt] *intr* se laisser attendrir, s'adoucir

relentless [rɪ'lɛntlɪs] *adj* implacable

relevant ['rɛlɪvənt] *adj* pertinent

reliable [rɪ'laɪ·əbəl] *adj* digne de confiance, digne de foi

reliance [rɪ'laɪ·əns] *s* confiance *f*

relic ['rɛlɪk] *s* (rel) relique *f*; (fig) vestige *m*

relief [rɪ'lif] *s* soulagement *m*; (*projection of figures; elevation*) relief *m*; (*aid*) secours *m*; (*welfare program*) aide *f* sociale; (mil) relève *f*; **in relief** en relief

relieve [rɪ'liv] *tr* soulager; (*to aid*) secourir; (*to release from a post; to give variety to*) relevei, (mil) relever

religion [rɪ'lɪdʒən] *s* religion *f*

religious [rɪ'lɪdʒəs] *adj* religieux

relinquish [rɪ'lɪŋkwɪʃ] *tr* abandonner

relish ['rɛlɪʃ] *s* goût *m*; (*condiment*) assaisonnement *m*; **relish for** penchant pour || *tr* goûter, apprécier

reluctance [rɪ'lʌktəns] *s* répugnance *f*; **with reluctance** à contrecœur

reluctant [rɪ'lʌktənt] *adj* hésitant, peu disposé

re·ly [rɪ'laɪ] *v* (*pret & pp* **-lied**) *intr*— **to rely on** compter sur, se fier à

remain [rɪ'men] *s*—**remains** restes *mpl*; œuvres *fpl* posthumes || *intr* rester

remainder [rɪ'mendər] *s* reste *m*; **remainders** bouillons *mpl* || *tr* solder

re·make [ri'mek] *v* (*pret & pp* **-made**) *tr* refaire

remark [rɪ'mɑrk] *s* remarque *f*, observation *f* || *tr & intr* remarquer, observer; **to remark on** faire des remarques sur

remarkable [rɪ'mɑrkəbəl] *adj* remarquable

remar·ry [rɪ'mæri] *v* (*pret & pp* **-ried**) *tr* remarier; se remarier avec || *intr* se remarier

reme·dy ['rɛmɪdi] *s* (*pl* **-dies**) remède *m* || *v* (*pret & pp* **-died**) *tr* remédier (with *dat*)

remember [rɪ'mɛmbər] *tr* se souvenir de, se rappeler; **remember me to** rap-

pelez-moi au bon souvenir de || *intr* se souvenir, se rappeler

remembrance [rɪ'mɛmbrəns] *s* souvenir *m*

remind [rɪ'maɪnd] *tr* rappeler

reminder [rɪ'maɪndər] *s* note *f* de rappel, mémento *m*

reminisce [ˌrɛmɪ'nɪs] *intr* se livrer au souvenirs, raconter ses souvenirs

remiss [rɪ'mɪs] *adj* négligent

remission [rɪ'mɪʃən] *s* rémission *f*

re·mit [rɪ'mɪt] *v* (*pret & pp* **-mitted**; *ger* **-mitting**) *tr* remettre || *intr* se calmer

remittance [rɪ'mɪtəns] *s* remise *f*, envoi *m*

remnant ['rɛmnənt] *s* reste *m*; (*of cloth*) coupon *m*; (*at reduced price*) solde *m*

remod·el [ri'mɑdəl] *v* (*pret & pp* **-eled** or **-elled**; *ger* **-eling** or **-elling**) *tr* modeler de nouveau, remanier; (*a house*) transformer

remonstrance [rɪ'mɑnstrəns] *s* remontrance *f*

remonstrate [rɪ'mɑnstret] *intr* protester; **to remonstrate with** faire des remontrances à

remorse [rɪ'mɔrs] *s* remords *m*

remorseful [rɪ'mɔrsfəl] *adj* contrit, repentant, plein de remords

remote [rɪ'mot] *adj* éloigné

remote′ control′ *s* commande *f* à distance, télécommande *f*

removable [rɪ'muvəbəl] *adj* amovible

removal [rɪ'muvəl] *s* enlèvement *m*; (*from house*) déménagement *m*; (*dismissal*) révocation *f*

remove [rɪ'muv] *tr* enlever, ôter; éloigner; (*furniture*) déménager; (*to dismiss*) révoquer || *intr* se déplacer; déménager

remuneration [rɪˌmjunə'reʃən] *s* rémunération *f*

renaissance [ˌrenə'sɑns], [rɪ'nesəns] *s* renaissance *f*

rend [rɛnd] *v* (*pret & pp* **rent** [rɛnt]) *tr* déchirer; (*to split*) fendre; (*the air; the heart*) fendre

render ['rɛndər] *tr* rendre; (*a piece of music*) interpréter; (*lard*) fondre

rendez·vous ['rɑndəˌvu] *s* (*pl* **-vous** [ˌvuz]) rendez-vous *m* || *v* (*pret & pp* **-voused** [ˌvud]; *ger* **-vousing** [ˌvu·ɪŋ]) *intr* se rencontrer

rendition [rɛn'dɪʃən] *s* (*translation*) traduction *f*; (mus) interprétation *f*

renegade ['rɛnɪˌged] *s* renégat *m*

renege [rɪ'nɪg] *s* renonce *f* || *intr* renoncer; (coll) se dédire, ne pas tenir sa parole

renew [rɪ'n(j)u] *tr* renouveler || *intr* se renouveler

renewable [rɪ'n(j)u·əbəl] *adj* renouvelable

renewal [rɪ'n(j)u·əl] *s* renouvellement *m*

renounce [rɪ'naʊns] *s* renonce *f* || *tr* renoncer (with *dat*) || *intr* renoncer

renovate ['rɛnəˌvet] *tr* renouveler; (*a room, a house, etc.*) mettre à neuf, rénover, transformer

renown [rɪ'naʊn] *s* renom *m*
renowned [rɪ'naʊnd] *adj* renommé
rent [rɛnt] *adj* déchiré ‖ *s* loyer *m*, location *f*; (*tear, slit*) déchirure *f*; **for rent** à louer ‖ *tr* louer ‖ *intr* se louer
rental ['rɛntəl] *s* loyer *m*, location *f*
rent′al a′gen‧cy *s* (*pl* **-cies**) agence *f* de location
rent′ed car′ *s* voiture *f* de louage, voiture de location; (*chauffeur-driven limousine*) voiture de grande remise
renter ['rɛntər] *s* locataire *mf*
renunciation [rɪ‚nʌnsɪ'eʃən] *s* renonciation *f*
reopen [ri'opən] *tr* & *intr* rouvrir
reopening [ri'opənɪŋ] *s* réouverture *f*; (*of school*) rentrée *f*
reorganize [ri'ɔrgə‚naɪz] *tr* réorganiser ‖ *intr* se réorganiser
repair [rɪ'pɛr] *s* réparation *f*; **in good repair** en bon état ‖ *tr* réparer ‖ *intr* se rendre
repaper [ri'pepər] *tr* retapisser
reparation [‚rɛpə'reʃən] *s* réparation *f*
repartee [‚rɛpɑr'ti] *s* repartie *f*
repast [rɪ'pæst], [rɪ'pɑst] *s* repas *m*
repatriate [ri'petrɪ‚et] *tr* rapatrier
re‧pay [rɪ'pe] *v* (*pret* & *pp* **-paid**) *tr* rembourser; récompenser
repayment [rɪ'pemənt] *s* remboursement *m*; récompense *f*
repeal [rɪ'pil] *s* révocation *f*, abrogation *f* ‖ *tr* révoquer, abroger
repeat [rɪ'pit] *s* répétition *f* ‖ *tr* & *intr* répéter
re‧pel [rɪ'pɛl] *v* (*pret* & *pp* **-pelled**; *ger* **-pelling**) *tr* repousser; dégoûter
repent [rɪ'pɛnt] *tr* se repentir de ‖ *intr* se repentir
repentance [rɪ'pɛntəns] *s* repentir *m*
repentant [rɪ'pɛntənt] *adj* repentant
repercussion [‚ripər'kʌʃən] *s* répercussion *f*, contrecoup *m*
reperto‧ry ['rɛpər‚tori] *s* (*pl* **-ries**) répertoire *m*
repetition [‚rɛpɪ'tɪʃən] *s* répétition *f*
replace [rɪ'ples] *tr* (*to put back*) remettre en place; (*to take the place of*) remplacer
replaceable [rɪ'plesəbəl] *adj* remplaçable, amovible
replacement [rɪ'plesmənt] *s* replacement *m*; (*substitution*) remplacement *m*; (*substitute part*) pièce *f* de rechange; (*person*) remplaçant *m*
replenish [rɪ'plɛnɪʃ] *tr* réapprovisionner; remplir
replete [rɪ'plit] *adj* rempli, plein
replica ['rɛplɪkə] *s* reproduction *f*, réplique *f*
re‧ply [rɪ'plaɪ] *s* (*pl* **-plies**) réponse *f*, réplique *f* ‖ *v* (*pret* & *pp* **-plied**) *tr* & *intr* répondre, répliquer
reply′ cou′pon *s* coupon-réponse *m*
report [rɪ'port] *s* rapport *m*; (*rumor*) bruit *m*; (*e.g., of firearm*) détonation *f* ‖ *tr* rapporter; dénoncer; **it is reported that** le bruit court que; **reported missing** porté manquant ‖ *intr* faire un rapport; (*to show up*) se présenter

report′ card′ *s* bulletin *m* scolaire
reportedly [rɪ'portɪdli] *adv* au dire de tout le monde
reporter [rɪ'portər] *s* reporter *m*
reporting [rɪ'portɪŋ] *s* reportage *m*
repose [rɪ'poz] *s* repos *m* ‖ *tr* reposer; (*confidence*) placer ‖ *intr* reposer
reprehend [‚rɛprɪ'hɛnd] *tr* reprendre
represent [‚rɛprɪ'zɛnt] *tr* représenter
representation [‚rɛprɪzɛn'teʃən] *s* représentation *f*
representative [‚rɛprɪ'zɛntətɪv] *adj* représentatif ‖ *s* représentant *m*
repress [rɪ'prɛs] *tr* réprimer; (*psychoanal*) refouler
repression [rɪ'prɛʃən] *s* répression *f*; (*psychoanal*) refoulement *m*
reprieve [rɪ'priv] *s* sursis *m* ‖ *tr* surseoir à l'exécution de
reprimand ['rɛprɪ‚mænd], ['rɛprɪ‚mɑnd] *s* réprimande *f* ‖ *tr* réprimander
reprint ['ri‚prɪnt] *s* (*book*) réimpression *f*; (*offprint*) tiré *m* à part ‖ [ri'prɪnt] *tr* réimprimer
reprisal [rɪ'praɪzəl] *s* représailles *fpl*
reproach [rɪ'protʃ] *s* reproche *m*; opprobre *m* ‖ *tr* reprocher; couvrir d'opprobre; **to reproach s.o. for s.th.** reprocher q.ch. à qn
reproduce [‚riprə'd(j)us] *tr* reproduire ‖ *intr* se reproduire
reproduction [‚riprə'dʌkʃən] *s* reproduction *f*
reproof [rɪ'pruf] *s* reproche *m*
reprove [rɪ'pruv] *tr* réprimander
reptile ['rɛptɪl] *s* reptile *m*
republic [rɪ'pʌblɪk] *s* république *f*
republican [rɪ'pʌblɪkən] *adj* & *s* républicain *m*
repudiate [rɪ'pjudɪ‚et] *tr* répudier
repugnant [rɪ'pʌgnənt] *adj* répugnant
repulse [rɪ'pʌls] *s* refus *m*; (*setback*) échec *m* ‖ *tr* repousser
repulsive [rɪ'pʌlsɪv] *adj* répulsif
reputation [‚rɛpjə'teʃən] *s* réputation *f*
repute [rɪ'pjut] *s* réputation *f*; **of ill repute** mal famé ‖ *tr*—**to be reputed to be** être réputé
reputedly [rɪ'pjutɪdli] *adv* suivant l'opinion commune
request [rɪ'kwɛst] *s* demande *f*; **on request** sur demande ‖ *tr* demander
Requiem ['rikwɪ‚ɛm], ['rɛkwɪ‚ɛm] *s* Requiem *m*
require [rɪ'kwaɪr] *tr* exiger
requirement [rɪ'kwaɪrmənt] *s* exigence *f*; besoin *m*
requisite ['rɛkwɪzɪt] *adj* requis ‖ *s* chose *f* nécessaire; condition *f* nécessaire
requisition [‚rɛkwɪ'zɪʃən] *s* réquisition *f* ‖ *tr* réquisitionner
requital [rɪ'kwaɪtəl] *s* récompense *f*; (*retaliation*) revanche *f*
requite [rɪ'kwaɪt] *tr* récompenser; (*to avenge*) venger
re‧read [ri'rid] *v* (*pret* & *pp* **-read** ['rɛd]) *tr* relire
resale ['ri‚sel], [ri'sel] *s* revente *f*
rescind [rɪ'sɪnd] *tr* abroger
rescue ['rɛskju] *s* sauvetage *m*; **to the**

rescue au secours, à la rescousse ‖ *tr* sauver, secourir

res'cue par'ty *s* équipe *f* de secours

research [rɪ'sʌrtʃ], ['risʌrtʃ] *s* recherche *f* ‖ *intr* faire des recherches

re·sell [ri'sɛl] *v* (*pret* & *pp* -**sold**) *tr* revendre

resemblance [rɪ'zɛmbləns] *s* ressemblance *f*

resemble [rɪ'zɛmbəl] *tr* ressembler (**with** *dat*); **to resemble one another** se ressembler

resent [rɪ'zɛnt] *tr* s'offenser de

resentful [rɪ'zɛntfəl] *adj* offensé

resentment [rɪ'zɛntmənt] *s* ressentiment *m*

reservation [,rɛzər've∫ən] *s* location *f*, réservation *f*; (*Indian land*) réserve *f*; **without reservation** sans réserve

reserve [rɪ'zʌrv] *s* réserve *f* ‖ *tr* réserver

reservist [rɪ'zʌrvɪst] *s* réserviste *m*

reser'voir ['rɛzər,vwɑr] *s* réservoir *m*

re·set [ri'sɛt] *v* (*pret* & *pp* -**set**; *ger* -**setting**) *tr* remettre; (*a gem*) remonter

re·ship [ri'∫ɪp] *v* (*pret* & *pp* -**shipped**; *ger* -**shipping**) *tr* réexpédier; (*on a ship*) rembarquer ‖ *intr* se rembarquer

reshipment [ri'∫ɪpmənt] *s* réexpédition *f*; (*on a ship*) rembarquement *m*

reside [rɪ'zaɪd] *intr* résider, demeurer

residence ['rɛzɪdəns] *s* résidence *f*, domicile *m*

resident ['rɛzɪdənt] *adj* & *s* habitant *m*

residential [,rɛzɪ'dɛn∫əl] *adj* résidentiel

residue ['rɛzɪ,d(j)u] *s* résidu *m*

resign [rɪ'zaɪn] *tr* démissionner de, résigner; **to resign oneself to** se résigner à ‖ *intr* démissioner; se résigner; **to resign from** démissionner de

resignation [,rɛzɪg'ne∫ən] *s* (*from a job, etc.*) démission *f*; (*submissive state*) résignation *f*

resin ['rɛzɪn] *s* résine *f*

resist [rɪ'zɪst] *tr* résister (**with** *dat*); **to resist** + *ger* s'empêcher de + *inf* ‖ *intr* résister

resistance [rɪ'zɪstəns] *s* résistance *f*

resole [ri'sol] *tr* ressemeler

resolute ['rɛzə,lut] *adj* résolu

resolution [rɛzə'lu∫ən] *s* résolution *f*

resolve [rɪ'zɔlv] *s* résolution *f* ‖ *tr* résoudre ‖ *intr* résoudre, se résoudre

resonance ['rɛzənəns] *s* résonance *f*

resort [rɪ'zɔrt] *s* station *f*, e.g., **health resort** station climatique; (*for help or support*) recours *m*; **as a last resort** en dernier ressort ‖ *intr*—**to resort to** recourir à

resound [rɪ'zaund] *intr* résonner

resource [rɪ'sors], ['risors] *s* ressource *f*

resourceful [rɪ'sorsfəl] *adj* débrouillard

respect [rɪ'spɛkt] *s* respect *m*; **in many respects** à bien des égards; **in this respect** sous ce rapport; **to pay one's respects (to)** présenter ses respects (à); **with respect to** par rapport à ‖ *tr* respecter

respectable [rɪ'spɛktəbəl] *adj* respectable; considérable

respectful [rɪ'spɛktfəl] *adj* respectueux

respectfully [rɪ'spɛktfəli] *adv* respectueusement; **respectfully yours** (complimentary close) veuillez agreer l'assurance de mes sentiments très respectueux

respective [rɪ'spɛktɪv] *adj* respectif

res'piratory tract' ['rɛspɪrə,tori], [rɪ'spaɪrə,tori] *s* appareil *m* respiratoire

respite ['rɛspɪt] *s* répit *m*; **without respite** sans relâche

resplendent [rɪ'splɛndənt] *adj* resplendissant

respond [rɪ'spand] *intr* répondre

response [rɪ'spans] *s* réponse *f*

responsibili·ty [rɪ,spansɪ'bɪlɪti] *s* (*pl* -**ties**) responsabilité *f*

responsible [rɪ'spansɪbəl] *adj* responsable; (*person*) digne de confiance; (*job, position*) de confiance; **responsible for** responsable de; **responsible to** responsable envers

responsive [rɪ'spansɪv] *adj* sensible, réceptif; prompt à sympathiser

rest [rɛst] *s* repos *m*; (*lack of motion*) pause *f*; (*what remains*) reste *m*; (*mus*) silence *m*; **at rest** en repos; (*dead*) mort; **the rest** les autres; (*the remainder*) le restant; **the rest of us** nous autres; **to come to rest** s'immobiliser; **to lay to rest** enterrer ‖ *tr* reposer ‖ *intr* reposer, se reposer; **to rest on** reposer sur, s'appuyer sur

restaurant ['rɛstərənt], ['rɛstə,rant] *s* restaurant *m*

rest' cure' *s* cure *f* de repos

restful ['rɛstfəl] *adj* reposant; (*calm*) tranquille, paisible

rest'ing place' *s* lieu *m* de repos, gîte *m*; (*of the dead*) dernière demeure *f*

restitution [,rɛstɪ't(j)u∫ən] *s* restitution *f*

restive ['rɛstɪv] *adj* rétif

restless ['rɛstlɪs] *adj* agité, inquiet; sans repos

restock [ri'stak] *tr* réapprovisionner; (*with fish or game*) repeupler

restoration [,rɛstə're∫ən] *s* restauration *f*

restore [rɪ'stor] *tr* restaurer; (*health*) rétablir; (*to give back*) restituer

restrain [rɪ'stren] *tr* retenir, contenir

restraint [rɪ'strent] *s* restriction *f*, contrainte *f*

restrict [rɪ'strɪkt] *tr* restreindre

restriction [rɪ'strɪk∫ən] *s* restriction *f*

rest' room' *s* cabinet *m* d'aisance

result [rɪ'zʌlt] *s* résultat *m*; **as a result of** par suite de ‖ *intr* résulter; **to result in** aboutir à

resume [rɪ'z(j)um] *tr* & *intr* reprendre

résumé [,rɛz(j)u'me] *s* résumé *m*

resumption [rɪ'zʌmp∫ən] *s* reprise *f*

resurface [ri'sʌrfɪs] *tr* refaire le revêtement de ‖ *intr* (*said of submarine*) faire surface

resurrect [,rɛzə'rɛkt] *tr* & *intr* ressusciter

resurrection [ˌrɛzə'rɛkʃən] *s* résurrection *f*
resuscitate [rɪ'sʌsɪˌtet] *tr* & *intr* ressusciter
retail ['ritel] *adj* & *adv* au détail || *s* vente *f* au détail || *tr* vendre au détail, détailler || *intr* se vendre au détail
retailer ['ritelər] *s* détaillant *m*
retain [rɪ'ten] *tr* retenir; engager
retaliate [rɪ'tælɪˌet] *intr* prendre sa revanche, user de représailles
retaliation [rɪˌtælɪ'eʃən] *s* représailles *fpl*
retard [rɪ'tɑrd] *s* retard *m* || *tr* retarder
retch [rɛtʃ] *tr* vomir || *intr* avoir un haut-le-cœur
retching ['rɛtʃɪŋ] *s* haut-le-cœur *m*
reticence ['rɛtɪsəns] *s* réserve *f*
reticent ['rɛtɪsənt] *adj* réservé
retina ['rɛtɪnə] *s* rétine *f*
retinue ['rɛtɪˌn(j)u] *s* suite *f*, cortège *m*
retire [rɪ'taɪr] *tr* mettre à la retraite || *intr* se retirer
retired *adj* en retraite
retirement [rɪ'taɪrmənt] *s* retraite *f*
retire'ment pro'gram *s* programme *m* de prévoyance
retiring [rɪ'taɪrɪŋ] *adj* (*shy*) effacé; (*e.g.*, *congressman*) sortant
retort [rɪ'tɔrt] *s* riposte *f*, réplique *f*; (chem) cornue *f* || *tr* & *intr* riposter
retouch [ri'tʌtʃ] *tr* retoucher
retrace [ri'tres] *tr* retracer; (*one's steps*) revenir sur
retract [rɪ'trækt] *tr* rétracter || *intr* se rétracter
retractable [rɪ'træktəbəl] *adj* (aer) escamotable
re·tread ['riˌtrɛd] *s* pneu *m* rechapé || [ri'trɛd] *v* (*pret* & *pp* **-treaded**) *tr* rechaper || *v* (*pret* **-trod**; *pp* **-trod** or **-trodden**) *tr* & *intr* repasser
retreat [rɪ'trit] *s* retraite *f*; **to beat a retreat** battre en retraite || *intr* se retirer
retrench [rɪ'trɛntʃ] *tr* restreindre || *intr* faire des économies
retribution [ˌrɛtrɪ'bjuʃən] *s* rétribution *f*
retrieve [rɪ'triv] *tr* retrouver, recouvrer; (*a fortune, a reputation, etc.*) rétablir; (*game*) rapporter || *intr* (*said of hunting dog*) rapporter
retriever [rɪ'trivər] *s* retriever *m*
retroactive [ˌrɛtro'æktɪv] *adj* rétroactif
retrogress ['rɛtrəˌgrɛs] *intr* rétrograder
retrorocket ['rɛtroˌrɑkɪt] *s* rétrofusée *f*
retrospect ['rɛtrəˌspɛkt] *s*—**to consider in retrospect** jeter un coup d'œil rétrospectif à
retrospective [ˌrɛtrə'spɛktɪv] *adj* rétrospectif
re·try [ri'traɪ] *v* (*pret* & *pp* **-tried**) *tr* essayer de nouveau; (law) juger à nouveau
return [rɪ'tʌrn] *adj* de retour; **by return mail** par retour du courrier || *s* retour *m*; (*profit*) bénéfice *m*; (*yield*) rendement *m*; (*unwanted merchandise*) rendu *m*; (*of ball*) renvoi *m*; (*of income tax*) déclaration *f*; **in return**

(**for**) en retour (de); **returns** (*profits*) recettes *fpl*; (*of an election*) résultats *mpl* || *tr* rendre; (*to put back*) remettre; (*to bring back*) rapporter; (*e.g.*, *a letter*) retourner || *intr* (*to go back*) retourner; (*to come back*) revenir; (*to get back home*) rentrer; **to return empty-handed** revenir bredouille
return' address' *s* adresse *f* de l'expéditeur
return' bout' *s* revanche *f*
return' game' or **match'** *s* match *m* retour
return' tick'et *s* aller et retour *m*
return' trip' *s* voyage *m* de retour
reunification [riˌjunɪfɪ'keʃən] *s* réunification *f*
reunion [ri'junjən] *s* réunion *f*
reunite [ˌriju'naɪt] *tr* réunir || *intr* se réunir
rev [rɛv] *s* (coll) tour *m* || *v* (*pret* & *pp* **revved**; *ger* **revving**) *tr* (coll) accélérer; (*to race*) (coll) emballer || *intr* (coll) s'accélérer
revamp [ri'væmp] *tr* refaire
reveal [rɪ'vil] *tr* révéler
reveille ['rɛvəli] *s* réveil *m*
rev·el ['rɛvəl] *s* fête *f*; **revels** ébats *mpl*, orgie *f* || *v* (*pret* & *pp* **-eled** or **-elled**; *ger* **-eling** or **-elling**) *intr* faire la fête, faire la bombe; **to revel in** se délecter à
revelation [ˌrɛvə'leʃən] *s* révélation *f*; **Revelation** (Bib) Apocalypse *f*
revel·ry ['rɛvəlri] *s* (*pl* **-ries**) réjouissances *fpl*, orgie *f*
revenge [rɪ'vɛndʒ] *s* vengeance *f*; **to take revenge on s.o. for s.th.** se venger de q.ch. sur qn || *tr* venger
revengeful [rɪ'vɛndʒfəl] *adj* vindicatif
revenue ['rɛvəˌn(j)u] *s* revenu *m*
rev'enue cut'ter *s* garde-côte *m*, vedette *f*
rev'enue stamp' *s* timbre *m* fiscal
reverberate [rɪ'vʌrbəˌret] *intr* résonner
revere [rɪ'vɪr] *tr* révérer
reverence ['rɛvərəns] *s* révérence *f* || *tr* révérer
reverend ['rɛvərənd] *adj* & *s* révérend *m*
reverent ['rɛvərənt] *adj* révérenciel
reverie ['rɛvəri] *s* rêverie *f*
reversal [rɪ'vʌrsəl] *s* renversement *m*
reverse [rɪ'vʌrs] *adj* contraire || *s* contraire *m*; (*of medal; of fortune*) revers *m*; (*of page*) verso *m*; (aut) marche *f* arrière || *tr* renverser; (*a sentence*) (law) révoquer || *intr* renverser; (*said of motor*) faire machine arrière; (aut) faire marche arrière
reverse' lev'er *s* levier *m* de renvoi
reverse' side' *s* revers *m*, dos *m*
reversible [rɪ'vʌrsɪbəl] *adj* réversible
revert [rɪ'vʌrt] *intr* revenir, faire retour
review [rɪ'vju] *s* revue *f*; (*of a book*) compte *m* rendu; (*of a lesson*) révision *f* || *tr* revoir; (*a book*) faire la critique de; (*a lesson*) réviser, revoir; (*past events; troops*) passer en revue || *intr* faire des révisions
revile [rɪ'vaɪl] *tr* injurier, outrager
revise [rɪ'vaɪz] *s* révision *f*; (typ)

épreuve *f* de révision ‖ *tr* réviser; (*a book*) revoir
revised′ edi′tion *s* édition *f* revue et corrigée
revision [rɪ'vɪʒən] *s* révision *f*
revisionist [rɪ'vɪʒənɪst] *adj & s* révisionniste *mf*
revival [rɪ'vaɪvəl] *s* retour *m* à la vie; (*of learning*) renaissance *f*; (rel) réveil *m*; (theat) reprise *f*
reviv′al meet′ings *spl* (rel) réveils *mpl*
revive [rɪ'vaɪv] *tr* ranimer; (*a victim*) ressusciter; (*a memory*) réveiller; (*a play*) reprendre ‖ *intr* reprendre; se ranimer
revoke [rɪ'vok] *tr* révoquer
revolt [rɪ'volt] *s* révolte *f* ‖ *tr* révolter ‖ *intr* se révolter
revolting [rɪ'voltɪŋ] *adj* dégoûtant, repoussant; rebelle, révolté
revolution [‚revə'luʃən] *s* révolution *f*
revolutionar‧y [‚revə'luʃə‚neri] *adj* révolutionnaire ‖ *s* (*pl* -ies) révolutionnaire *mf*
revolve [rɪ'vɑlv] *tr* faire tourner; (*in one's mind*) retourner ‖ *intr* tourner
revolver [rɪ'vɑlvər] *s* revolver *m*
revolv′ing book′case *s* bibliothèque *f* tournante
revolv′ing door′ *s* porte *f* à tambour, tambour *m* cylindrique
revolv′ing fund′ *s* fonds *m* de roulement
revolv′ing stage′ *s* scène *f* tournante
revue [rɪ'vju] *s* (theat) revue *f*
revulsion [rɪ'vʌlʃən] *s* aversion *f*, répugnance *f*; (*change of feeling*) revirement *m*
reward [rɪ'wɔrd] *s* récompense *f* ‖ *tr* récompenser
rewarding [rɪ'wɔrdɪŋ] *adj* rémunérateur; (*experience*) enrichissant
re‧wind [ri'waɪnd] *v* (*pret & pp* -wound*) tr* (*film, tape, etc.*) renverser la marche de; (*a typewriter ribbon*) embobiner de nouveau; (*a clock*) remonter
rewire [ri'waɪr] *tr* (*a building*) refaire l'installation électrique dans
re‧write [ri'raɪt] *v* (*pret* -wrote; *pp* -written) *tr* récrire
rhapso‧dy ['ræpsədi] *s* (*pl* -dies) *s* rhapsodie *f*
rheostat ['ri‧ə ‚stæt] *s* rhéostat *m*
rhetoric ['retərɪk] *s* rhétorique *f*
rhetorical [rɪ'tɑrɪkəl], [rɪ'tɔrɪkəl] *adj* rhétorique
rheumatic [ru'mætɪk] *adj* rhumatismal; (*person*) rhumatisant ‖ *s* rhumatisant *m*
rheumatism ['rumə‚tɪzəm] *s* rhumatisme *m*
Rhine [raɪn] *s* Rhin *m*
Rhineland ['raɪn‚lænd] *s* Rhénanie *f*
rhine′stone′ *s* faux diamant *m*
rhinoceros [raɪ'nɑsərəs] *s* rhinocéros *m*
rhubarb ['rubarb] *s* rhubarbe *f*
rhyme [raɪm] *s* rime *f*; **in rhyme** en vers ‖ *tr & intr* rimer
rhythm ['rɪðəm] *s* rythme *m*
rhythmic(al) ['rɪðmɪk(əl)] *adj* rythmique

rib [rɪb] *s* côte *f*; (*of umbrella*) baleine *f*; (archit, biol, mach) nervure *f* ‖ *v* (*pret & pp* ribbed; *ger* ribbing) *tr* garnir de nervures; (slang) taquiner
ribald ['rɪbəld] *adj* grivois
ribbon ['rɪbən] *s* ruban *m*
rice [raɪs] *s* riz *m*
rice′ field′ *s* rizière *f*
rice′ pud′ding *s* riz *m* au lait
rich [rɪtʃ] *adj* riche; (*voice*) sonore; (*wine*) généreux; (*funny*) (coll) impayable; (coll) ridicule; **to get rich** s'enrichir; **to strike it rich** trouver le bon filon ‖ **riches** *spl* richesses *fpl*
rickets ['rɪkɪts] *s* rachitisme *m*
rickety ['rɪkɪti] *adj* (*object*) boiteux, délabré; (*person*) chancelant; (*suffering from rickets*) rachitique
rickshaw ['rɪk ‚ʃɔ] *s* pousse-pousse *m*
rid [rɪd] *v* (*pret & pp* rid; *ger* ridding) *tr* débarrasser; **to get rid of** se débarrasser de
riddance ['rɪdəns] *s* débarras *m*; **good riddance!** bon débarras!
riddle ['rɪdəl] *s* devinette *f*, énigme *f* ‖ *tr*—**to riddle with** cribler de
ride [raɪd] *s* promenade *f*; **to take a ride** faire une promenade (en auto, à cheval, à motocyclette, etc.); **to take s.o. for a ride** (*to dupe s.o.*) (slang) faire marcher qn; (*to murder s.o.*) (slang) descendre qn ‖ *v* (*pret* rode [rod]; *pp* ridden ['rɪdən]) *tr* monter à; (coll) se moquer de; **ridden** dominé; **to ride out** (*e.g., a storm*) étaler ‖ *intr* monter à cheval (à bicyclette, etc.); **to let ride** (coll) laisser courir
rider ['raɪdər] *s* (*on horseback*) cavalier *m*; (*on a bicycle*) cycliste *mf*; (*in a vehicle*) voyageur *m*; (*to a document*) annexe *f*
ridge [rɪdʒ] *s* arête *f*, crête *f*; (*of a fabric*) grain *m*
ridge′pole′ *s* faîtage *m*
ridicule ['rɪdɪ ‚kjul] *s* ridicule *m* ‖ *tr* ridiculiser
ridiculous [rɪ'dɪkjələs] *adj* ridicule
rid′ing acad′emy *s* école *f* d'équitation
rid′ing boot′ *s* botte *f* de cheval, botte à l'écuyère
rid′ing hab′it *s* habit *m* d'amazone
rife [raɪf] *adj* répandu; **rife with** abondant en
riffraff ['rɪf ‚ræf] *s* racaille *f*
rifle ['raɪfəl] *s* fusil *m*; (*spiral groove*) rayure *f* ‖ *tr* piller; (*a gun barrel*) rayer
rift [rɪft] *s* fente *f*, crevasse *f*; (*disagreement*) désaccord *m*
rig [rɪg] *s* équipement *m*; (*carriage*) équipage *m*; (naut) gréement *m*; (*getup*) (coll) accoutrement *m* ‖ *v* (*pret & pp* rigged; *ger* rigging) *tr* équiper; (*to falsify*) truquer; (naut) gréer; **to rig out with** (coll) accoutrer de
rigging ['rɪgɪŋ] *s* gréement *m*; (*fraud*) truquage *m*
right [raɪt] *adj* droit; (*change, time, etc.*) exact; (*statement, answer, etc.*) correct; (*conclusion, word, etc.*)

juste; (*name*) vrai; (*moment, house, road, etc.*) bon, e.g., **it's not the right road** ce n'est pas la bonne route; qu'il faut, e.g., **it's not the right village** (**spot, boy, etc.**) ce n'est pas le village (endroit, garçon, etc.) qu'il faut; **to be all right** aller très bien; **to be right** avoir raison ‖ *s* (*justice*) droit *m*; (*reason*) raison *f*; (*right hand*) droite *f*; (*fist or blow in boxing*) droit; **all rights reserved** tous droits réservés; **by right of** à titre de; **by rights** de plein droit; **by the right!** (mil) guide à droite!; **on the right** à droite; **right and wrong** le bien et le mal; **rights** droits; **to be in the right** avoir raison ‖ *adv* directement; correctement; complètement; bien, en bon état; (*to the right*) à droite; (coll) très; même, e.g., **right here** ici même; **all right!** d'accord!; **right and left** à droite et à gauche; **right away** tout de suite; **to put right** mettre bon ordre à, mettre en état ‖ *tr* faire droit à; (*to correct*) corriger; (*to set upright*) redresser ‖ *intr* se redresser ‖ *interj* parfait!

right′ about′ face′ *s* volte-face *f* ‖ *interj* (mil) demi-tour à droite!

righteous ['raɪtʃəs] *adj* juste; vertueux

right′ field′ *s* (baseball) champ *m* droit

rightful ['raɪtfəl] *adj* légitime

right′-hand drive′ *s* conduite *f* à droite

right-hander ['raɪt'hændər] *s* droitier *m*

right′-hand man′ *s* bras *m* droit

rightist ['raɪtɪst] *adj & s* droitier *m*

rightly ['raɪtli] *adv* à bon droit, à juste titre; correctement, avec sagesse; **rightly or wrongly** à tort ou à raison

right′ of assem′bly *s* liberté *f* de réunion

right′ of way′ *s* droit *m* de passage; **to yield the right of way** céder le pas

rights′ of man′ *spl* droits *mpl* de l'homme

right to work ['raɪttə'wʌrk] *s* liberté *f* du travail des ouvriers non syndiqués

right′-wing′ *adj* de droite

right-winger ['raɪt'wɪŋər] *s* (coll) droitier *m*

rigid ['rɪdʒɪd] *adj* rigide

rigmarole ['rɪgmə,rol] *s* galimatias *m*

rigor ['rɪgər] *s* rigueur *f*; (pathol) rigidité *f*

rigorous ['rɪgərəs] *adj* rigoureux

rile [raɪl] *tr* (coll) exaspérer

rill [rɪl] *s* ruisselet *m*

rim [rɪm] *s* bord *m*, rebord *m*; (*of spectacles*) monture *f*; (*of wheel*) jante *f*

rind [raɪnd] *s* écorce *f*; (*of cheese*) croûte *f*; (*of bacon*) couenne *f*

ring [rɪŋ] *s* anneau *m*; (*for the finger*) bague *f*, anneau; (*for some sport or exhibition*) piste *f*; (*for boxing*) ring *m*; (*for bullfight*) arène *f*; (*of a group of people*) cercle *m*; (*of evildoers*) gang *m*; (*under the eyes*) cerne *m*; (*sound*) son *m*; (*of bell, clock, telephone, etc.*) sonnerie *f*; (*of a small bell; in the ears; of the glass of glassware*) tintement *m*; (*to summon a*

person) coup *m* de sonnette; (*quality*) timbre *m*; (telp) coup de téléphone ‖ *v* (*pret & pp* ringed) *tr* cerner ‖ *intr* décrire des cercles ‖ *v* (*pret* rang [ræŋ]; *pp* rung [rʌŋ]) *tr* sonner; **to ring up** (telp) donner un coup de téléphone à ‖ *intr* sonner; (*said, e.g., of ears*) tinter; **to ring out** résonner

ring′bolt′ *s* piton *m*

ring′dove′ *s* (orn) ramier *m*

ring′ fin′ger *s* annulaire *m*

ringing ['rɪŋɪŋ] *adj* résonnant, retentissant ‖ *s* sonnerie *f*; (*in the ears*) tintement *m*

ring′lead′er *s* meneur *m*

ringlet ['rɪŋlɪt] *s* bouclette *f*

ring′mas′ter *s* maître *m* de manège, chef *m* de piste

ring′side′ *s* premier rang *m*

ring′snake′ *s* (*Tropidonotus natrix*) couleuvre *f* à collier

ring′worm′ *s* teigne *f*

rink [rɪŋk] *s* patinoire *f*

rinse [rɪns] *s* rinçage *m* ‖ *tr* rincer

riot ['raɪ·ət] *s* émeute *f*; (*of colors*) orgie *f*; **to run riot** se déchaîner; (*said of plants or vines*) pulluler ‖ *intr* émeuter

rioter ['raɪ·ətər] *s* émeutier *m*

rip [rɪp] *s* déchirure *f* ‖ *v* (*pret & pp* ripped; *ger* ripping) *tr* déchirer; **to rip away** or **off** arracher; **to rip open** or **up** découdre; (*a letter, package, etc.*) ouvrir en le déchirant ‖ *intr* se déchirer

rip′ cord′ *s* (*of parachute*) cordelette *f* de déclenchement

ripe [raɪp] *adj* mûr; (*cheese*) fait; (*olive*) noir

ripen ['raɪpən] *tr & intr* mûrir

ripple ['rɪpəl] *s* ride *f*; (*sound*) murmure *m* ‖ *tr* rider ‖ *intr* se rider; murmurer

rise [raɪz] *s* hausse *f*, augmentation *f*; (*of ground; of the voice*) élévation *f*; (*of a heavenly body; of the curtain*) lever *m*; (*in one's employment, in one's fortunes*) ascension *f*; (*of water*) montée *f*; (*of a source of water*) naissance *f*; **to get a rise out of** (slang) se payer la tête de; **to give rise to** donner naissance à ‖ *v* (*pret* rose [roz]; *pp* risen ['rɪzən]) *intr* s'élever, monter; (*to get out of bed; to stand up; to ascend in the heavens*) se lever; (*to revolt*) se soulever; (*said, e.g., of a danger*) se montrer; (*said of a fluid*) jaillir; (*in someone's esteem*) grandir; (*said of river*) prendre sa source; **to rise above** dépasser; (*unfortunate events, insults, etc.*) se montrer supérieur à; **to rise to** (*e.g., the occasion*) se montrer à la hauteur de

riser ['raɪzər] *s* (*of staircase*) contremarche *f*; (*of gas or water*) colonne *f* montante; **to be a late riser** faire la grasse matinée; **to be an early riser** être matinal

risk [rɪsk] *s* risque *m* ‖ *tr* risquer

risk·y ['rɪski] *adj* (*comp* -ier; *super* -iest) dangereux, hasardeux, risqué

risqué [rɪs'ke] *adj* risqué, osé
rite [raɪt] *s* rite *m*; **last rites** derniers
sacrements *mpl*
ritual ['rɪtʃʊ·əl] *adj & s* rituel *m*
ri·val ['raɪvəl] *adj & s* rival *m* ‖ *v*
(*pret & pp* -valed or -valled; *ger*
-valing or -valling) *tr* rivaliser avec
rival·ry ['raɪvəlri] *s* (*pl* -ries) rivalité *f*
river ['rɪvər] *adj* fluvial ‖ *s* fleuve *m*;
(*tributary*) rivière *f*; (*stream*) cours
m d'eau; **down the river** en aval; **up
the river** en amont
riv'er bas'in *s* bassin *m* fluvial
riv'er·bed' *s* lit *m* de rivière
riv'er·front' *s* rive *f* d'un fleuve
riv'er·side' *adj* riverain ‖ *s* rive *f*
rivet ['rɪvɪt] *s* rivet *m* ‖ *tr* river
riv'et gun' *s* riveuse *f* pneumatique
rivulet ['rɪvjəlɪt] *s* ruisselet *m*
R.N. ['ɑr'en] *s* (letterword) (**registered nurse**) infirmière *f* diplômée
roach [rotʃ] *s* (ent) blatte *f*, cafard *m*;
(ichth) gardon *m*
road [rod] *s* route *f*, chemin *m*; (naut)
rade *f*; **road under construction** (public sign) travaux
road'bed' *s* assiette *f*; (rr) infrastructure *f*
road'block' *s* barrage *m*
road' hog' *s* écraseur *m*, chauffard *m*
road'house' *s* guinguette *f* au bord de
la route
road' map' *s* carte *f* routière
road' ser'vice *s* secours *m* routier
road'side' *s* bord *m* de la route
road' sign' *s* poteau *m* indicateur
road'stead' *s* rade *f*
road'way' *s* chaussée *f*
roam [rom] *tr* parcourir; (*the seas*)
sillonner ‖ *intr* errer, rôder
roar [ror] *s* rugissement *m*; (*of cannon,
engine, etc.*) grondement *m*; (*of
crowd*) hurlement *m*; (*of laughter*)
éclat *m* ‖ *intr* rugir; gronder; hurler
roast [rost] *s* rôti *m*; (*of coffee*) torréfaction *f* ‖ *tr* rôtir; (*coffee*) torréfier;
(*chestnuts*) griller ‖ *intr* se rôtir; se
torréfier
roast' beef' *s* rosbif *m*, rôti *m* de bœuf
roaster ['rostər] *s* (*appliance*) rôtissoire
f; (*for coffee*) brûloir *m*; (*fowl*) volaille *f* à rôtir
roast' pork' *s* porc *m* rôti
rob [rɑb] *v* (*pret & pp* robbed; *ger*
robbing) *tr & intr* voler;˙**to rob s.o.
of s.th.** voler q.ch. à qn
robber ['rɑbər] *s* voleur *m*
robber·y ['rɑbəri] *s* (*pl* -ies) vol *m*
robe [rob] *s* robe *f*; (*of a professor,
judge, etc.*) toge *f*; (*dressing gown*)
robe *f* de chambre; (*for lap in a carriage*) couverture *f* ‖ *tr* revêtir d'une
robe ‖ *intr* revêtir sa robe
robin ['rɑbɪn] *s* (*Erithacus rubecula*)
rouge-gorge *m*; (*Turdus migratorius*)
grive *f* migratoire
robot ['robɑt] *s* robot *m*
robust [ro'bʌst] *adj* robuste
rock [rɑk] *s* roche *f*; (*eminence*) roc
m, rocher *m*; (*sticking out of water*)
rocher; (*one that is thrown*) pierre *f*;
(slang) diamant *m*; **on the rocks**

(coll) fauché, à sec; (*said of liquor*)
(coll) sur glace ‖ *tr* balancer; (*to
rock to sleep*) bercer ‖ *intr* se balancer; se bercer
rock'-bot'tom *adj* (le) plus bas ‖ *s* (le)
fin fond *m*
rock' can'dy *s* candi *m*
rock' crys'tal *s* cristal *m* de roche
rocker ['rɑkər] *s* bascule *f*; (*chair*)
chaise *f* à bascule; **to go off one's
rocker** (slang) perdre la boussole
rock'er arm' *s* culbuteur *m*
rocket ['rɑkɪt] *s* fusée *f*; (arti, bot) roquette *f* ‖ *intr* monter en chandelle;
(*said of prices*) monter en flèche
rock'et bomb' *s* bombe *f* volante, fusée *f*
rock'et launch'er *s* lance-fusées *m*;
(arti) lance-roquettes *m*
rock'et ship' *s* fusée *f* interplanétaire,
fusée interstellaire
rock' gar'den *s* jardin *m* de rocaille
rock'ing chair' *s* fauteuil *m* à bascule
rock'ing horse' *s* cheval *m* à bascule
Rock' of Gibral'tar [dʒɪ'brɔltər] *s*
rocher *m* de Gibraltar
rock' salt' *s* sel *m* gemme
rock' wool' *s* laine *f* minérale, laine de
verre
rock·y ['rɑki] *adj* (*comp* -ier; *super*
-iest) rocheux, rocailleux
Rock'y Moun'tains *spl* Montagnes *fpl*
Rocheuses
rod [rɑd] *s* baguette *f*; (*for punishment*) verge *f*; (*of the retina; elon-
gated microorganism*) bâtonnet *m*;
(*of authority*) main *f*; (*of curtain*)
tringle *f*; (*for fishing*) canne *f*; (Bib)
lignée *f*, race *f*; (mach) bielle *f*;
(surv) jalon *m*; (*revolver*) (slang) pétard *m*; **rod and gun** la chasse et la
pêche
rodent ['rodənt] *adj & s* rongeur *m*
roe [ro] *s* (*deer*) chevreuil *m*; (*of fish*)
œufs *mpl*
roger ['rɑdʒər] *interj* O.K.!; (rad) message reçu!
rogue [rog] *s* coquin *m*
rogues' gal'lery *s* fichier *m* de la police
de portraits de criminels
roguish ['rogɪʃ] *adj* espiègle, coquin
roister ['rɔɪstər] *intr* faire du tapage
role or **rôle** [rol] *s* rôle *m*
roll [rol] *s* rouleau *m*; (*of thunder,
drums, etc.*) roulement *m*; (*roll call*)
appel *m*; (*list*) rôle *m*; (*of film*) rouleau; (*of paper money*) liasse *f*; (*of
dice*) coup *m*; (*of a boat*) roulis *m*;
(*of fat*) bourrelet *m*; (culin) petit
pain *m*; **to call the roll** faire l'appel
‖ *tr* rouler; **to roll over** retourner; **to
roll up** enrouler ‖ *intr* rouler; (*said
of thunder*) gronder; (*to sway*) se
balancer; (*to overturn*) faire panache; (*said of ship*) rouler; **to roll
over** se retourner; **to roll up** se rouler
roll'back' *s* repoussement *m*; (com)
baisse *f* de prix
roll' call' *s* appel *m*; (*vote*) appel nominal
roller ['rolər] *s* rouleau *m*; (*of a skate*)
roulette *f*; (*wave*) lame *f* de houle

roll'er bear'ing *s* coussinet *m* à rouleaux
roll'er coast'er *s* montagnes *fpl* russes
roll'er skate' *s* patin *m* à roulettes
roll'er-skate' *intr* patiner sur des roulettes
roll'er-skating rink' *s* skating *m*
roll'er tow'el *s* essuie-mains *m* à rouleau, serviette *f* sans fin
roll'ing mill' *s* usine *f* de laminage; (*set of rollers*) laminoir *m*
roll'ing pin' *s* rouleau *m*
roll'ing stock' *s* (rr) matériel *m* roulant
roll'-top desk' *s* bureau *m* à cylindre
roly-poly ['roli'poli] *adj* rondelet
romaine [ro'men] *s* romaine *f*
roman ['romən] *adj* & *s* (typ) romain *m*; **Roman** Romain *m*
Ro'man can'dle *s* chandelle *f* romaine
Ro'man Cath'olic *adj* & *s* catholique *mf*
Romance ['romæns], [ro'mæns] *adj* roman || (*l.c.*) [ro'mæns], ['romæns] *s* roman *m* de chevalerie; (*made-up story*) conte *m* bleu; (*love affair*) idylle *f*; (mus) romance *f* || (*l.c.*) [ro'mæns] *intr* exagérer, broder
Romanesque [,romən'esk] *adj* & *s* roman *m*
Ro'man nose' *s* nez *m* aquilin
Ro'man nu'meral *s* chiffre *m* romain
romantic [ro'mæntɪk] *adj* (*genre; literature; scenery*) romantique; (*imagination*) romanesque
romanticism [ro'mæntɪ,sɪzəm] *s* romantisme *m*
romanticist [ro'mæntɪsɪst] *s* romantique *mf*
romp [ramp] *intr* s'ébattre
rompers ['rampərz] *spl* barboteuse *f*
roof [ruf], [rʊf] *s* toit *m*; (*of the mouth*) palais *m*; **to raise the roof** (slang) faire un boucan de tous les diables
roofer ['rufər], ['rʊfər] *s* couvreur *m*
roof' gar'den *s* terrasse *f* avec jardin, pergola *f*
rook [rʊk] *s* (chess) tour *f*; (orn) freux *m*, corneille *f* || *tr* (coll) rouler; **to rook s.o. out of s.th.** (coll) filouter q.ch. à qn
rookie ['rʊki] *s* (slang) bleu *m*
room [rum], [rʊm] *s* pièce *f*; (*especially bedroom*) chambre *f*; (*where people congregate*) salle *f*; (*space*) place *f*; **to make room for** faire place à || *intr* vivre en garni; **to room with** partager une chambre avec
room' and board' *s* le vivre et le couvert
room' clerk' *s* employé *m* à la réception
roomer ['rumər], ['rʊmər] *s* locataire *mf*
roomette [ru'mɛt] *s* chambrette *f* de sleeping
room'ing house' *s* maison *f* meublée, maison garnie
room'mate' *s* camarade *mf* de chambre
room·y ['rumi], ['rʊmi] *adj* (*comp* -ier; *super* -iest) spacieux, ample
roost [rust] *s* perchoir *m*; (coll) logis *m*, demeure *f*; **to rule the roost** (coll) faire la loi || *intr* se percher, percher
rooster ['rustər] *s* coq *m*
root [rut], [rʊt] *s* racine *f*; **to get to the root of** approfondir; **to take root** prendre racine || *tr* fouiller; **to root out** déraciner || *intr* s'enraciner; **to root around in** fouiller dans; **to root for** (coll) applaudir, encourager
rooter ['rutər], ['rʊtər] *s* (coll) fanatique *mf*, fana *mf*
rope [rop] *s* corde *f*; (*lasso*) corde à nœud coulant; **to jump rope** sauter à la corde; **to know the ropes** (slang) connaître les ficelles || *tr* corder; (*cattle*) prendre au lasso; **to rope in** (slang) entraîner
rope' lad'der *s* échelle *f* de corde
rope' walk'er *s* funambule *mf*, danseur *m* de corde
rosa·ry ['rozəri] *s* (*pl* -ries) rosaire *m*
rose [roz] *adj* rose || *s* (*color*) rose *m*; (bot) rose *f*
rose' bee'tle *s* cétoine *f* dorée
rose'bud' *s* bouton *m* de rose
rose'bush' *s* rosier *m*
rose'-col'ored *adj* rosé, couleur de rose; **to see everything through rose-colored glasses** voir tout en rose
rose' gar'den *s* roseraie *f*
rosemar·y ['roz,mɛri] *s* (*pl* -ies) romarin *m*
rose' of Shar'on ['ʃɛrən] *s* rose *f* de Saron
rosette [ro'zɛt] *s* rosette *f*; (archit, elec) rosace *f*
rose' win'dow *s* rosace *f*, rose *f*
rose'wood' *s* bois *m* de rose, palissandre *m*
rosin ['razɪn] *s* colophane *f*
roster ['rastər] *s* liste *f*, appel *m*; (educ) heures *fpl* de classe; (mil) tableau *m* de service; (naut) rôle *m*
rostrum ['rastrəm] *s* tribune *f*
ros·y ['rozi] *adj* (*comp* -ier; *super* -iest) rosé; (*complexion*) vermeil; (fig) riant
rot [rat] *s* pourriture *f*; (slang) sottise *f* || *v* (*pret* & *pp* rotted; *ger* rotting) *tr* & *intr* pourrir
ro'tary press' ['rotəri] *s* rotative *f*
rotate ['rotet], [ro'tet] *tr* & *intr* tourner; (agr) alterner
rotation [ro'teʃən] *s* rotation *f*; **in rotation** à tour de rôle
rote [rot] *s* routine *f*; **by rote** par cœur, machinalement
rot'gut' *s* (slang) tord-boyaux *m*
rotisserie [ro'tɪsəri] *s* rôtissoire *f*
rotogravure [,rotəgrə'vjʊr], [,rotə'grevjʊr] *s* rotogravure *f*
rotten ['ratən] *adj* pourri
rotund [ro'tʌnd] *adj* rond, arrondi; (*e.g., language*) ampoulé
rotunda [ro'tʌndə] *s* rotonde *f*
rouge [ruʒ] *s* fard *m*, rouge *m* || *tr* farder || *intr* se farder, se mettre du rouge
rough [rʌf] *adj* rude; (*uneven*) inégal; (*coarse*) grossier; (*unfinished*) brut; (*road*) raboteux; (*game*) brutal; (*sea*) agité; (*guess*) approximatif || *tr*—**to**

rough it faire du camping, coucher sur la dure; **to rough up** malmener
rough' draft' s ébauche f, avant-projet m, brouillon m
rough'house' s boucan m, chahut m ‖ intr faire du boucan, chahuter
rough' ide'a s aperçu m
roughly ['rʌfli] adv grossièrement; brutalement; approximativement
rough'neck' s (coll) canaille f
roulette [ru'lɛt] s roulette f
round [raʊnd] adj rond; (rounded) arrondi, rond; (e.g., shoulders) voûté; **three (four, etc.) feet round** trois (quatre, etc.) pieds de tour ‖ s rond m; (inspection) ronde f; (of golf; of drinks; of postman, doctor, etc.) tournée f; (of applause) salve f; (of ammunition) cartouche f; (of veal) noix f; (boxing) round m; **to go the rounds** faire le tour ‖ adv à la ronde; **round about** aux alentours; **the year round** pendant toute l'année; **to pass round** faire circuler, passer à la ronde ‖ prep autour de ‖ tr (to make round) arrondir; (e.g., a corner) tourner, prendre; (a cape) doubler; **to round off** or **out** arrondir; (to finish) achever; **to round up** rassembler; (suspects) cueillir ‖ intr s'arrondir
roundabout ['raʊndə,baʊt] adj indirect ‖ s détour m; (carrousel) (Brit) manège m; (traffic circle) (Brit) rond-point m
rounder ['raʊndər] s (coll) fêtard m
round'house' s (rr) rotonde f
round'-shoul'dered adj voûté
round' steak' s gîte m à la noix
round' ta'ble s table f ronde; **Round Table** Table ronde
round'-trip' tick'et s billet m d'aller et retour
round'up' s (of cattle) rassemblement m; (of suspects) rafle f
rouse [raʊz] tr réveiller ‖ intr se réveiller
rout [raʊt] s déroute f ‖ tr mettre en déroute
route [rut], [raʊt] s route f; (of, e.g., bus) ligne f, parcours m ‖ tr acheminer
routine [ru'tin] adj routinier ‖ s routine f
rove [rov] intr errer, vagabonder
rover ['rovər] s vagabond m
row [raʊ] s (coll) altercation f, prise f de bec; **to raise a row** (coll) faire du boucan ‖ [ro] s rang m; (of, e.g., houses) rangée f; (boat ride) promenade f en barque; **in a row** à la file; (without interruption) de suite; **in rows** par rangs ‖ intr ramer
rowboat ['ro,bot] s bateau m à rames, canot m
row·dy ['raʊdi] adj (comp -dier; super -diest) tapageur ‖ s (pl -dies) tapageur m
rower ['ro·ər] s rameur m
rowing ['ro·ɪŋ] s nage f, canotage m, sport m de l'aviron
royal ['rɔɪ·əl] adj royal
royalist ['rɔɪ·əlɪst] adj & s royaliste mf

royal·ty ['rɔɪ·əlti] s (pl -ties) royauté f; droit m d'auteur; redevance f, droit d'inventeur
r.p.m. ['ɑr'pi'ɛm] spl (letterword) (revolutions per minute) tours mpl à la minute
rub [rʌb] s frottement m; **there's the rub** (coll) voilà le hic ‖ v (pret & pp rubbed; ger rubbing) tr frotter; **to rub elbows with** coudoyer; **to rub out** effacer; (slang) descendre, liquider ‖ intr se frotter; (said, e.g., of moving parts) frotter; **to rub off** s'enlever, disparaître
rubber ['rʌbər] s caoutchouc m; (eraser) gomme f à effacer; (in bridge) robre m; **rubbers** (overshoes) caoutchoucs
rub'ber band' s élastique m
rubberize ['rʌbə,raɪz] tr caoutchouter
rub'ber·neck' s (coll) badaud m ‖ intr (coll) badauder
rub'ber plant' s figuier m élastique, caoutchoutier m; (tree) arbre m à caoutchouc, hévéa m
rub'ber stamp' s tampon m; (coll) béni-oui-oui m
rub'ber-stamp' tr apposer le tampon sur; (with a person's signature) estampiller; (coll) approuver à tort et à travers
rub'bing al'cohol s alcool m pour les frictions
rubbish ['rʌbɪʃ] s détritus m, rebut m; (coll) imbécillités fpl
rubble ['rʌbəl] s (broken stone) décombres mpl; (used in masonry) moellons mpl
rub'down' s friction f
rubric ['rubrɪk] s rubrique f
ru·by ['rubi] adj (lips) vermeil ‖ s (pl -bies) rubis m
rucksack ['rʌk,sæk] s sac-à-dos m
rudder ['rʌdər] s gouvernail m
rud·dy ['rʌdi] adj (comp -dier; super -diest) rougeaud, coloré
rude [rud] adj (rough, rugged) rude; (discourteous) impoli, grossier
rudeness ['rudnɪs] s rudesse f; impolitesse f
rudiment ['rudɪmənt] s rudiment m
rue [ru] tr regretter amèrement
rueful ['rufəl] adj lamentable; triste
ruffian ['rʌfɪ·ən] s brute f
ruffle ['rʌfəl] s (in water) rides fpl; (of drum) roulement m; (sewing) jabot m plissé ‖ tr (to crease; to vex) froisser; (the water) rider; (its feathers) hérisser; (one's hair) ébouriffer
rug [rʌg] s tapis m, carpette f
rugged ['rʌgɪd] adj rude, sévère; (road, country, etc.) raboteux; (person) robuste; (e.g., machine) résistant à toute épreuve
ruin ['ru·ɪn] s ruine f ‖ tr ruiner
rule [rul] s règle f; autorité f; (reign) règne m; (law) décision f; **as a rule** en général; **by rule of thumb** empiriquement, à vue de nez ‖ tr gouverner; (to lead) diriger, guider; (one's passions) contenir; (with lines) ré-

gler; (law) décider; **to rule out** écarter, éliminer || *intr* gouverner; (*to be the rule*) prévaloir; **to rule over** régner sur

ruler ['rulər] *s* dirigeant *m*; souverain *m*; (*for ruling lines*) règle *f*

ruling ['rulɪŋ] *adj* actuel; (*e.g., classes*) dirigeant; (*quality, trait, etc.*) dominant || *s* (*of paper*) réglage *m*; (*law*) décision *f*

rum [rʌm] *s* rhum *m*

Rumanian [ru'menɪ·ən] *adj* roumain || *s* (*language*) roumain *m*; (*person*) Roumain *m*

rumble ['rʌmbəl] *s* (*of thunder*) grondement *m*; (*of a cart*) roulement *m*; (*of intestines*) gargouillement *m*; (slang) rixe *f* entre gangs || *intr* gronder, rouler

ruminate ['rumɪ‚net] *tr & intr* ruminer

rummage ['rʌmɪdʒ] *intr* fouiller

rum′mage sale′ *s* vente *f* d'objets usagés

rumor ['rumər] *s* rumeur *f* || *tr*—**it is rumored that** le bruit court que

rump [rʌmp] *s* (*of animal*) croupe *f*; (*of bird*) croupion *m*; (*cut of meat*) culotte *f*; (*buttocks*) postérieur *m*

rumple ['rʌmpəl] *s* faux pli *m* || *tr* (*paper, cloth, etc.*) froisser, chiffonner; (*one's hair*) ébouriffer

rump′ steak′ *s* romsteck *m*

rumpus ['rʌmpəs] *s* (coll) chahut *m*; (*argument*) (coll) prise *f* de bec; **to raise a rumpus** (coll) déclencher un chahut; faire une scène violente

rum′pus room′ *s* salle *f* de jeux

run [rʌn] *s* course *f*; (*e.g., of good or bad luck*) suite *f*; (*on a bank by depositors*) descente *f*; (*of salmon*) remonte *f*; (*of, e.g., a bus*) parcours *m*; (*in a stocking*) échelle *f*, démaillage *m*; (cards) séquence *f*; (mus) roulade *f*; **in the long run** à la longue; **on the run** à la débandade, en fuite; **run of bad luck** série *f* noire; **the general run** la généralité; **to give free run to** donner libre carrière à; **to give s.o. a run for his money** en donner à qn pour son argent; **to have a long run** (theat) tenir longtemps l'affiche; **to have the run of** avoir libre accès à or dans; **to keep s.o. on the run** ne laisser aucun répit à qn; **to make a run in** (*a stocking*) démailler || *v* (*pret* **ran** [ræn]; *pp* **run**; *ger* **running**) *tr* (*the streets; a race; a risk*) courir; (*a motor, machine, etc.*) faire marcher; (*an organization, project, etc.*) diriger; (*a business, factory, etc.*) exploiter; (*a blockade*) forcer; (*a line*) tracer; (turf) faire courir; **to run aground** échouer; **to run down** (*to knock down*) renverser; (*to find*) dépister; (*game*) mettre aux abois; (*to disparage*) (coll) dénigrer; **to run in** (*a motor*) roder; **to run off** (*a liquid*) faire écouler; (*copies, pages, etc.*) tirer; **to run through** (*e.g., with a sword*) transpercer; **to run up** (*a flag*) hisser; (*a debt*) (coll) laisser accumuler || *intr* courir; (*said, e.g., of water*;

said of fountain pen, nose, etc.) couler; (*said of stockings*) se démailler; (*said of salmon*) faire la montaison; (*said of colors*) s'étaler, se déteindre; (*said of sore*) suppurer; (*said of rumor, news, etc.*) circuler, courir; (*for office*) se présenter; (mach) fonctionner, marcher; (theat) rester à l'affiche, se jouer; **run along!** filez!; **to run across** (*to meet by chance*) rencontrer par hasard; **to run along** border, longer; (*to go*) s'en aller; **to run at** se jeter sur; **to run away** se sauver, s'enfuir; (*said of horse*) s'emballer, s'emporter; **to run away with** enlever; **to run down** (*e.g., a hill*) descendre en courant; (*said of spring*) se détendre; (*said of watch*) s'arrêter (faute d'être remonté); (*said of storage battery*) se décharger, s'épuiser; **to run for** (*an office*) poser sa candidature pour; **to run in the family** tenir de famille; **to run into** heurter; (*to meet*) (coll) rencontrer; **to run off** se sauver, s'enfuir; (*said of liquid*) s'écouler; **to run out** (*said of passport, lease, etc.*) expirer; **to run out of** être à court de; **to run over** (*said of a liquid*) déborder; (*an article, a text, etc.*) parcourir; (*s.th. in the road*) passer sur; (*e.g., a pedestrian*) écraser; **to run through** (*an article, text, etc.*) parcourir; (*a fortune*) gaspiller

run′away′ *adj* fugitif; (*horse*) emballé || *s* fugitif *m*; cheval *m* emballé

run′down′ *s* compte rendu *m*, récit *m*

run′-down′ *adj* délabré; (*person; battery*) épuisé, à plat; (*clock spring*) détendu

rung [rʌŋ] *s* (*of ladder or chair*) barreau *m*; (*of wheel*) rayon *m*

runner ['rʌnər] *s* (*person*) coureur *m*; (*messenger*) courrier *m*; (*of ice skate or sleigh*) patin *m*; (*narrow rug*) rampe *f* d'escalier; (*strip of cloth for table top*) chemin *m* de table; (*in stockings*) démaillage *m*; (bot) coulant *m*

run′ner-up′ *s* (*pl* **runners-up**) bon second *m*, premier accessit *m*

running ['rʌnɪŋ] *adj* (*person; water; expenses*) courant; (*stream; knot; style*) coulant; (*sore*) suppurant; (*e.g., motor*) en marche || *s* (*of man or animal*) course *f*; (*of water*) écoulement *m*; (*of machine*) fonctionnement *m*, marche *f*; (*of business*) direction *f*

run′ning board′ *s* marchepied *m*

run′ning com′mentar′y *s* (*pl* **-ies**) (rad, telv) reportage *m* en direct

run′ning head′ *s* titre *m* courant

run′ning start′ *s* départ *m* lancé

run′off′ elec′tion *s* scrutin *m* de ballottage

run′proof′ *adj* indémaillable

runt [rʌnt] *s* avorton *m*

run′way′ *s* piste *f*, rampe *f*

rupture ['rʌptʃər] *s* rupture *f*; (pathol) hernie *f* || *tr* rompre; (*a ligament,*

blood vessel, etc.) se rompre ‖ *intr* se
rompre
rural ['rʊrəl] *adj* rural
ru'ral free' deliv'ery *s* distribution *f*
gratuite par le facteur rural
ru'ral police'man *s* garde *m* champêtre
ruse [ruz] *s* ruse *f*
rush [rʌʃ] *adj* urgent ‖ *s* course *f* précipitée, ruée *f*; précipitation *f*; (bot)
jonc *m*; (formula on envelope or letterhead) urgent; **to be in a rush to**
être pressé de ‖ *tr* pousser vivement;
(*e.g., to the hospital*) transporter
d'urgence; (*a piece of work*) exécuter
d'urgence; (*e.g., a girl*) (slang) insister auprès de; **to rush through** (*e.g.,
a law*) faire passer à la hâte ‖ *intr* se
précipiter, se ruer; **to rush about** courir ça et là; **to rush headlong** foncer
tête baissée; **to rush into** (*e.g., a
room*) faire irruption dans; (*an affair*) se jeter dans; **to rush out** sortir
précipitamment; **to rush through**
(*one's lessons, prayers, etc.*) expédier;
(*e.g., a town*) traverser à toute vitesse; (*a tourist attraction*) visiter au
pas de course; (*a book*) lire à la hâte;
to rush to s'empresser de; **to rush to**
one's face (*said of blood*) monter au
visage à qn
rush'-bot'tomed chair' *s* chaise *f* à
fond de paille
rush' hours' *spl* heures *fpl* d'affluence
or de pointe
rush' or'der *s* commande *f* urgente
russet ['rʌsɪt] *adj* roussâtre, roux
Russia ['rʌʃə] *s* Russie *f*; la Russie
Russian ['rʌʃən] *adj* russe ‖ *s* (*language*) russe *m*; (*person*) Russe *mf*
rust [rʌst] *s* rouille *f* ‖ *tr* rouiller ‖ *intr*
se rouiller
rustic ['rʌstɪk] *adj* rustique; simple,
net; (pej) rustaud ‖ *s* paysan *m*, villageois *m*
rustle ['rʌsəl] *s* bruissement *m*; (*of,
e.g., a dress*) froufrou *m* ‖ *tr* faire
bruire; (*cattle*) (coll) voler ‖ *intr*
bruire; (*said, e.g., of a dress*) froufrouter; **to rustle around** (coll) se
démener
rust'proof' *adj* inoxydable
rust·y ['rʌsti] *adj* (*comp* -ier; *super*
-iest) rouillé
rut [rʌt] *s* ornière *f*; (zool) rut *m*
ruthless ['ruθlɪs] *adj* impitoyable
rye [raɪ] *s* seigle *m*; whisky *m* de seigle

S

S, s [ɛs] *s* XIXᵉ lettre de l'alphabet
Sabbath ['sæbəθ] *s* sabbat *m*; dimanche *m*
sabbat'ical year' [sə'bætɪkəl] *s* année
f de congé
saber ['sebər] *s* sabre *m* ‖ *tr* sabrer
sable ['sebəl] *adj* noir ‖ *s* (*animal, fur*)
zibeline *f*; noir *m*; **sables** vêtements
mpl de deuil
sabotage ['sæbə,tɑʒ] *s* sabotage *m* ‖ *tr*
& *intr* saboter
saccharin ['sækərɪn] *s* saccharine *f*
sachet [sæ'ʃe] *s* sachet *m* (à parfums)
sack [sæk] *s* sac *m*; (*wine*) xérès *m* ‖
tr mettre en sac; (mil) saccager;
(coll) saquer, congédier
sack'cloth' *s* grosse toile *f* d'emballage,
serpillière *f*; (*worn for penitence*)
cilice *m*; **in sackcloth and ashes** sous
le sac et la cendre
sacrament ['sækrəmənt] *s* sacrement *m*
sacramental [,sækrə'mɛntəl] *adj* sacra-
mentel
sacred ['sekrəd] *adj* sacré
sa'cred cow' *s* (fig) monstre *m* sacré
sacrifice ['sækrɪ,faɪs] *s* sacrifice *m*; **at
a sacrifice** à perte ‖ *tr* & *intr* sacrifier
sacrilege ['sækrəlɪdʒ] *s* sacrilège *m*
sacrilegious [,sækrɪ'lɪdʒəs], [,sækrɪ-
'lidʒəs] *adj* sacrilège
sacristan ['sækrɪstən] *s* sacristain *m*
sad [sæd] *adj* (*comp* **sadder**; *super*
saddest) triste
sadden ['sædən] *tr* attrister ‖ *intr* s'attrister
saddle ['sædəl] *s* selle *f* ‖ *tr* seller; **to
saddle with** charger de, encombrer de
sad'dle·bag' *s* sacoche *f* (de selle)
saddlebow ['sædəl,bo] *s* arçon *m* de
devant
saddler ['sædlər] *s* sellier *m*
sad'dle·tree' *s* arçon *m*
sadist ['sædɪst], ['sedɪst] *s* sadique *mf*
sadistic [sæ'dɪstɪk], [se'dɪstɪk] *adj* sadique
sadness ['sædnɪs] *s* tristesse *f*
sad' sack' *s* (slang) bidasse *mf*
safe [sef] *adj* (*from danger*) sûr; (*unhurt*) sauf; (*margin*) certain; **safe and
sound** sain et sauf; **safe from** à l'abri
de ‖ *s* coffre-fort *m*, caisse *f*
safe'-con'duct *s* sauf-conduit *m*
safe'-depos'it box' *s* coffre *m* à la
banque; coffret de sûreté (Canad)
safe'guard' *s* sauvegarde *f* ‖ *tr* sauvegarder
safe'keep'ing *s* bonne garde *f*
safe·ty ['sefti] *adj* de sûreté ‖ *s* (*pl*
-ties) (*state of being safe*) sécurité *f*,
sûreté *f*; (*avoidance of danger*) salut
m
safe'ty belt' *s* ceinture *f* de sécurité
safe'ty match' *s* allumette *f* de sûreté
safe'ty pin' *s* épingle *f* de sûreté
safe'ty ra'zor *s* rasoir *m* de sûreté
safe'ty valve' *s* soupape *f* de sûreté
saffron ['sæfrən] *adj* safrané ‖ *s* safran *m*
sag [sæg] *s* affaissement *m* ‖ *v* (*pret &*

pp sagged; *ger* **sagging)** *intr* s'affaisser
sagacious [sə'geʃəs] *adj* sagace
sage [sedʒ] *adj* sage ‖ *s* sage *m/*; *(plant)* sauge *f*
sage'brush' *s* armoise *f*
sail [sel] *s* voile *f*; *(sails)* voilure *f*; *(of windmill)* aile *f*; **full sail** toutes voiles dehors; **to set sail** mettre les voiles; **to take a sail** faire une promenade à la voile; **to take in sail** baisser pavillon ‖ *tr (a ship)* gouverner, commander; *(to travel over)* naviguer sur ‖ *intr* naviguer; **to sail along the coast** côtoyer; **to sail into** (coll) assaillir
sail'boat' *s* bateau *m* à voiles
sail'cloth' *s* toile *f* à voile
sailing ['selɪŋ] *s* navigation *f*; *(working of ship)* manœuvre *f*; *(of pleasure craft)* voile *f*
sail'ing ves'sel *s* voilier *m*
sail'mak'er *s* voilier *m*
sailor ['selər] *s* marin *m*; *(simple crewman)* matelot *m*
saint [sent] *adj & s* saint *m*
saint'hood *s* sainteté *f*
saintliness ['sentlɪnɪs] *s* sainteté *f*
Saint' Vi'tus's dance' ['vaɪtəsəz] *s* (pathol) danse *f* de Saint-Guy
sake [sek] *s*—**for the sake of** pour l'amour de, dans l'intérêt de; **for your sake** pour vous
salable ['seləbəl] *adj* vendable
salacious [sə'leʃəs] *adj* lubrique
salad ['sæləd] *s* salade *f*
sal'ad bowl' *s* saladier *m*
sala·ry ['sæləri] *s (pl* **-ries)** salaire *m*
sale [sel] *s* vente *f*; **for sale** en vente; **on sale** en solde, en réclame
sales' clerk' *s* vendeur *m*
sales'girl' *s* vendeuse *f*, demoiselle *f* de magasin
sales'la'dy *s (pl* **-dies)** vendeuse *f*
sales'man *s (pl* **-men)** vendeur *m*, commis *m*
sales'man·ship' *s* l'art *m* de vendre
sales' promo'tion *s* stimulation *f* de la vente
sales'room' *s* salle *f* de vente
sales' talk' *s* raisonnements *mpl* destinés à convaincre le client
sales' tax' *s* taxe *f* sur les ventes, impôt *m* indirect
saliva [sə'laɪvə] *s* salive *f*
sallow ['sælo] *adj* olivâtre
sal·ly ['sæli] *s (pl* **-lies)** saillie *f*; (mil) sortie *f* ‖ *v (pret & pp* **-lied)** *intr* faire une sortie
salmon ['sæmən] *adj & s* saumon *m*
saloon [sə'lun] *s* cabaret *m*, estaminet *m*, bistrot *m*; (naut) salon *m*
salt [sɔlt] *s* sel *m* ‖ *tr* saler; **to salt away** (coll) économiser, mettre de côté
salt'cel'lar *s* salière *f*
salt' lick' *s* terrain *m* salifère
salt'pe'ter *s (potassium nitrate)* salpêtre *m*; *(sodium nitrate)* nitrate *m* du Chili
salt' pork' *s* salé *m*
salt'sha'ker *s* salière *f*

salt·y ['sɔlti] *adj (comp* **-ier;** *super* **-iest)** salé
salute [sə'lut] *s* salut *m* ‖ *tr* saluer
salvage ['sælvɪdʒ] *s* sauvetage *m*; biens *mpl* sauvés ‖ *tr* sauver; récupérer
salvation [sæl'veʃən] *s* salut *m*
Salva'tion Ar'my *s* Armée *f* du Salut
salve [sæv], [sɑv] *s* onguent *m*, pommade *f*; baume *m* ‖ *tr* appliquer un onguent sur; (fig) apaiser
sal·vo ['sælvo] *s (pl* **-vos** or **-voes)** salve *f*
Samaritan [sə'mærɪtən] *adj* samaritain ‖ *s* Samaritain *m*
same [sem] *adj & pron indef* même (before noun); **at the same time** en même temps, au même moment, à la fois; **it's all the same to me** ça m'est égal; **just the same, all the same** malgré tout, quand même; **the same . . . as** le même . . . que
sameness ['semnɪs] *s* monotonie *f*
sample ['sæmpəl] *s* échantillon *m* ‖ *tr* échantillonner; essayer
sam'ple cop'y *s (pl* **-ies)** numéro *m* spécimen
sancti·fy ['sæŋktɪ‚faɪ] *v (pret & pp* **-fied)** *tr* sanctifier
sanctimonious [‚sæŋktɪ'monɪ·əs] *adj* papelard, bigot
sanction ['sæŋkʃən] *s* sanction *f* ‖ *tr* sanctionner
sanctuar·y ['sæŋktʃʊ‚eri] *s (pl* **-ies)** sanctuaire *m*; refuge *m*, asile *m*
sand [sænd] *s* sable *m* ‖ *tr* sablonner
sandal ['sændəl] *s* sandale *f*
san'dal·wood' *s* santal *m*
sand'bag' *s* sac *m* de sable
sand' bar' *s* banc *m* de sable
sand'blast' *s* jet *m* de sable; *(apparatus)* sableuse *f* ‖ *tr* sabler
sand'box' *s* (rr) sablière *f*
sand'glass' *s* sablier *m*
sand'pa'per *s* papier *m* de verre ‖ *tr* polir au papier de verre
sand'pi'per *s* bécasseau *m*
sand'stone' *s* grès *m*
sand'storm' *s* tempête *f* de sable
sandwich ['sændwɪtʃ] *s* sandwich *m* ‖ *tr* intercaler
sand'wich man' *s* homme-affiche *m*
sand·y ['sændi] *adj (comp* **-ier;** *super* **-iest)** sablonneux; *(hair)* blond roux
sane [sen] *adj* sain, équilibré; *(principles)* raisonnable
sanguine ['sæŋgwɪn] *adj* confiant, optimiste; *(countenance)* sanguin
sanitary ['sænɪ‚teri] *adj* sanitaire
san'itary nap'kin *s* serviette *f* hygiénique
sanitation [‚sænɪ'teʃən] *s* hygiène *f*, salubrité *f*; *(drainage)* assainissement *m*
sanity ['sænɪti] *s* santé *f* mentale; bon sens *m*
Santa Claus ['sæntə‚klɔz] *s* le père Noël
sap [sæp] *s* sève *f*; (mil) sape *f*; (coll) poire *f*, nigaud *m* ‖ *v (pret & pp* **sapped;** *ger* **sapping)** *tr* tirer la sève de; *(to weaken)* affaiblir; (mil) saper

sapling ['sæplɪŋ] *s* jeune arbre *m*; jeune homme *m*
sapphire ['sæfaɪr] *s* saphir *m*
Saracen ['særəsən] *adj* sarrasin ‖ *s* Sarrasin *m*
sarcasm ['sɑrkæzəm] *s* sarcasme *m*
sardine [sɑr'din] *s* sardine *f*; **packed in like sardines** serrés comme des harengs
Sardinia [sɑr'dɪnɪ·ə] *s* Sardaigne; la Sardaigne
Sardinian [sɑr'dɪnɪ·ən] *adj* sarde ‖ *s* (*language*) sarde *m*; (*person*) Sarde *mf*
sarsaparilla [ˌsɑrsəpə'rɪlə] *s* salsepareille *f*
sash [sæʃ] *s* ceinture *f*; (*of window*) châssis *m*
sash' win'dow *s* fenêtre *f* à guillotine
sas·sy ['sæsi] *adj* (*comp* **-sier**; *super* **-siest**) (coll) impudent, effronté
satchel ['sætʃəl] *s* sacoche *f*; (*of schoolboy*) carton *m*
sate [set] *tr* soûler
sateen [sæ'tin] *s* satinette *f*
satellite ['sætə‿laɪt] *adj* & *s* satellite *m*
sat'ellite coun'try *s* pays *m* satellite
satiate ['seʃɪ‿et] *adj* rassasié ‖ *tr* rassasier
satin ['sætɪn] *s* satin *m*
satire ['sætaɪr] *s* satire *f*
satiric(al) [sə'tɪrɪk(əl)] *adj* satirique
satirize ['sætɪ‿raɪz] *tr* satiriser
satisfaction [ˌsætɪs'fækʃən] *s* satisfaction *f*
satisfactory [ˌsætɪs'fæktəri] *adj* satisfaisant
satis·fy ['sætɪs‿faɪ] *v* (*pret* & *pp* **-fied**) *tr* satisfaire; (*a requirement, need, etc.*) satisfaire (with *dat*) ‖ *intr* satisfaire
saturate ['sætʃə‿ret] *tr* saturer
Saturday ['sætərdi] *s* samedi *m*
Saturn ['sætərn] *s* Saturne *m*
sauce [sɔs] *s* sauce *f*; (coll) insolence *f*, toupet *m* ‖ *tr* assaisonner ‖ [sɔs], [sæs] *tr* (coll) parler avec impudence à
sauce'pan' *s* casserole *f*
saucer ['sɔsər] *s* soucoupe *f*
sau·cy ['sɔsi] *adj* (*comp* **-cier**; *super* **-ciest**) impudent, effronté
sauerkraut ['saur‿kraut] *s* choucroute *f*
saunter ['sɔntər] *s* flânerie *f* ‖ *intr* flâner
sausage ['sɔsɪdʒ] *s* saucisse *f*, saucisson *m*
sauté [so'te] *tr* sauter, faire sauter
savage ['sævɪdʒ] *adj* & *s* sauvage *mf*
savant ['sævənt] *s* savant *m*, érudit *m*
save [sev] *prep* sauf, excepté ‖ *tr* sauver; (*money*) épargner; (*time*) gagner ‖ *intr* économiser
saving ['sevɪŋ] *adj* économe ‖ **savings** *spl* épargne *f*, économies *fpl*
sav'ings account' *s* dépôt *m* d'épargne
sav'ings and loan' associa'tion *s* caisse *f* d'épargne et de prêt
sav'ings bank' *s* caisse *f* d'épargne
sav'ings book' *s* livret *m* de caisse d'épargne
savior ['sevjər] *s* sauveur *m*

Saviour ['sevjər] *s* Sauveur *m*
savor ['sevər] *s* saveur *f* ‖ *tr* savourer ‖ *intr*—**to savor of** avoir un goût de
savor·y ['sevəri] *adj* (*comp* **-ier**; *super* **-iest**) (*taste*) savoureux; (*smell*) odorant ‖ *s* (*pl* **-ies**) (bot) sariette *f*
saw [sɔ] *s* scie *f*; (*proverb*) dicton *m* ‖ *tr* scier
saw'dust' *s* sciure *f* de bois
saw'horse' *s* chevalet *m*
saw'mill' *s* scierie *f*
Saxon ['sæksən] *adj* saxon ‖ *s* (*language*) saxon *m*; (*person*) Saxon *m*
saxophone ['sæksə‿fon] *s* saxophone *m*
say [se] *s* mot *m*; **to have one's say** avoir son mot à dire ‖ *v* (*pret* & *pp* **said** [sed]) *tr* dire; **I should say not!** absolument pas!; **I should say so!** je crois bien!; **it is said on dit**; **no sooner said than done** sitôt dit, sitôt fait; **that is to say** c'est-à-dire; **to go without saying** aller sans dire; **you said it!** (coll) et comment!, tu parles!
saying ['se·ɪŋ] *s* proverbe *m*
scab [skæb] *s* croûte *f*; (*strikebreaker*) jaune *m*; canaille *f*
scabbard ['skæbərd] *s* fourreau *m*
scab·by ['skæbi] *adj* (*comp* **-bier**; *super* **-biest**) croûteux; (coll) vil
scabrous ['skæbrəs] *adj* scabreux; (*uneven*) rugueux
scads [skædz] *spl* (slang) des tas *mpl*
scaffold ['skæfəld] *s* échafaud *m*; (*used in construction*) échafaudage *m*
scaffolding ['skæfəldɪŋ] *s* échafaudage *m*
scald [skɔld] *tr* échauder
scale [skel] *s* (*of thermometer, map, salaries, etc.*) échelle *f*; (*for weighing*) plateau *m*; (*incrustation*) tartre *m*; (bot, zool) écaille *f*; (mus) échelle *f*; **on a large scale** sur une grande échelle; **scales** balance *f*; **to tip the scales** faire pencher la balance ‖ *tr* escalader; **to scale down** réduire l'échelle de
scallop ['skɑləp], ['skæləp] *s* coquille *f* Saint-Jacques, peigne *m*, pétoncle *m*; (*thin slice of meat*) escalope *f*; (*on edge of cloth*) feston *m* ‖ *tr* (*the edges*) denteler, découper; (culin) gratiner et cuire au four et à la crème
scalp [skælp] *s* cuir *m* chevelu; (*Indian trophy*) scalp *m* ‖ *tr* scalper; (*tickets*) (coll) faire le trafic de; (*to hoodwink*) (slang) abuser de
scalpel ['skælpəl] *s* scalpel *m*
scal·y ['skeli] *adj* (*comp* **-ier**; *super* **-iest**) écailleux
scamp [skæmp] *s* garnement *m*
scamper ['skæmpər] *intr* courir allégrement; **to scamper away** or **off** détaler
scan [skæn] *v* (*pret* & *pp* **scanned**; *ger* **scanning**) *tr* scruter; (*e.g., a page*) jeter un coup d'œil sur; (*verses*) scander; (telv) balayer
scandal ['skændəl] *s* scandale *m*
scandalize ['skændə‿laɪz] *tr* scandaliser
scandalous ['skændələs] *adj* scandaleux
Scandinavian [ˌskændɪ'nevɪ·ən] *adj*

scandinave ‖ s (language) scandinave m; (person) Scandinave mf
scanning ['skænɪŋ] s (telv) balayage m
scant [skænt] adj maigre; (attire) léger, sommaire ‖ tr réduire; lésiner sur
scant·y ['skænti] adj (comp -ier; super -iest) rare, maigre; léger
scapegoat ['skep‚got] s bouc m émissaire
scar [skɑr] s cicatrice f; (on face) balafre f ‖ v (pret & pp scarred; ger scarring) tr balafrer
scarce [skɛrs] adj rare, peu abondant
scarcely ['skɛrsli] adv à peine, presque pas; ne . . . guère §90; scarcely ever rarement
scarci·ty ['skɛrsɪti] s (pl -ties) manque m, pénurie f
scare [skɛr] s panique f, effroi m ‖ tr épouvanter, effrayer; to scare away or off effaroucher; to scare up (coll) procurer ‖ intr s'effaroucher
scare'crow' s épouvantail m
scarf [skɑrf] s (pl scarfs or scarves [skɑrvz]) foulard m, écharpe f
scarlet ['skɑrlɪt] adj & s écarlate f
scar'let fe'ver s scarlatine f
scar·y ['skɛri] adj (comp -ier; super -iest) (easily frightened) (coll) peureux, ombrageux; (causing fright) (coll) effrayant
scathing ['skeðɪŋ] adj cinglant
scatter ['skætər] tr éparpiller; (a mob) disperser ‖ intr se disperser
scat'ter·brained' adj (coll) étourdi
scenari·o [sɪ'nɛri‚o], [sɪ'nɑri‚o] s (pl -os) scénario m
scene [sin] s scène f; (landscape) paysage m; behind the scenes dans les coulisses; to make a scene faire une scène
scener·y ['sinəri] s (pl -ies) paysage m; (theat) décor m, décors
sceneshifter ['sin‚ʃɪftər] s (theat) machiniste m
scenic ['sinɪk], ['senɪk] adj pittoresque; spectaculaire; (theat) scénique
sce'nic rail'way s chemin m de fer en miniature des parcs d'attraction
scent [sent] s odeur f; parfum m; (trail) piste f ‖ tr parfumer; (an odor) renifler; (game as a dog does; a trap) flairer
scepter ['septər] s sceptre m
sceptic ['skeptɪk] adj & s sceptique mf
sceptical ['skeptɪkəl] adj sceptique
scepticism ['skeptɪ‚sɪzəm] s scepticisme m
schedule ['skɛdjʊl] s (of work) plan m; (of things to do) emploi m du temps; (of prices) barème m; (rr) horaire m; on schedule selon l'horaire; selon les prévisions ‖ tr classer; inscrire au programme, à l'horaire, etc.; scheduled to speak prévu comme orateur
scheme [skim] s projet m; machination f, truc m ‖ tr projeter ‖ intr ruser
schemer ['skimər] s faiseur m de projets; intrigant m
schism ['sɪzəm] s schisme m, scission f
scholar ['skɑlər] s (pupil) écolier m;

(learned person) érudit m, savant m; (holder of scholarship) boursier m
scholarly ['skɑlərli] adj érudit, savant ‖ adv savamment
schol'ar·ship' s érudition f; (award) bourse f
scholasticism [skə'læstɪ‚sɪzəm] s scolastique f
school [skul] adj scolaire; school zone (public sign) ralentir école ‖ s école f; (of a university) faculté f; (of fish) banc m ‖ tr instruire, discipliner
school' board' s conseil m de l'instruction publique
school'book' s livre m de classe, livre scolaire
school'boy' s écolier m
school'girl' s écolière f
school'house' s maison f d'école
schooling ['skulɪŋ] s instruction f, enseignement m; discipline f; frais mpl de l'éducation
schoolmarm ['skul‚mɑrm] s maîtresse f d'école, institutrice f
school'mas'ter s maître m d'école, instituteur m
school'mate' s camarade mf d'école, condisciple m
school'room' s classe f, salle f de classe
school'teach'er s enseignant m, instituteur m
school'yard' s cour f de récréation
school' year' s année f scolaire
schooner ['skunər] s schooner m, goélette f
sciatica [saɪ'ætɪkə] s (pathol) sciatique f
science ['saɪ·əns] s science f
sci'ence fic'tion s science-fiction f
scientific [‚saɪ·ən'tɪfɪk] adj scientifique
scientist ['saɪ·əntɪst] s homme m de science, savant m
scimitar ['sɪmɪtər] s cimeterre m
scintillate ['sɪntɪ‚let] intr scintiller, étinceler
scion ['saɪ·ən] s héritier m; (hort) scion m
scissors ['sɪzərz] s & spl ciseaux mpl
scis'sors-grind'er s rémouleur m; (orn) engoulevent m
scoff [skɔf], [skɑf] s raillerie f ‖ intr —to scoff at se moquer de
scold [skold] s harpie f ‖ tr & intr gronder
scolding ['skoldɪŋ] s gronderie f
scoop [skup] s pelle f à main; (for coal) seau m; (kitchen utensil) louche f; (of dredge) godet m; (journ) nouvelle f sensationnelle; (naut) écope f ‖ tr creuser; to scoop out excaver à la pelle; (water) écoper
scoot [skut] intr (coll) détaler
scooter ['skutər] s trottinette f, patinette f
scope [skop] s (field) domaine m, étendue f; (reach) portée f, envergure f; to give free scope to donner libre carrière à
scorch [skɔrtʃ] tr roussir; flétrir, dessécher

scorched'-earth' pol'icy s politique f de la terre brûlée

scorching ['skɔrtʃɪŋ] adj brûlant; caustique, mordant

score [skor] s compte m, total m; (twenty) vingtaine f; (notch) entaille f; (on metal) rayure f, éraflure f; (mus) partition f; (sports) score m, marque f; **on that score** à cet égard; **to keep score** compter les points ‖ tr (to notch) entailler; (to criticize) blâmer; (metal) rayer, érafler; (a success) remporter; (e.g., a goal) marquer; (mus) orchestrer

score'board' s tableau m

score'keep'er s marqueur m

scorn [skɔrn] s mépris m, dédain m ‖ tr mépriser, dédaigner ‖ intr—**to scorn to** dédaigner de

scorpion ['skɔrpɪ·ən] s scorpion m

Scot [skɑt] s Écossais m

Scotch [skɑtʃ] adj écossais; (slang) avare, chiche ‖ s (dialect) écossais m; whisky m écossais; **the Scotch** les Écossais ‖ (l.c.) s (wedge) cale f; (notch) entaille f ‖ tr caler; entailler; (a rumor) étouffer

Scotch'man s (pl -men) Écossais m

Scotch' pine' s pin m sylvestre

Scotch' tape' s (trademark) ruban m cellulosique, adhésif m scotch

Scotland ['skɑtlənd] s Écosse f; l'Écosse

Scottish ['skɑtɪʃ] adj écossais ‖ s (dialect) écossais m; **the Scottish** les Écossais

scoundrel ['skaʊndrəl] s coquin m, fripon m, canaille f

scour [skaʊr] tr récurer; (e.g., the countryside) parcourir

scourge [skʌrdʒ] s nerf m de bœuf, discipline f; (fig) fléau m ‖ tr fouetter, flageller

scout [skaʊt] adj scout ‖ s éclaireur m; (boy scout) scout m, éclaireur; **a good scout** (coll) un brave gars ‖ tr reconnaître; (to scoff at) repousser avec dédain ‖ intr aller en reconnaissance

scouting ['skaʊtɪŋ] s scoutisme m

scout'ing par'ty s (pl -ties) (mil) détachement m de reconnaissance

scout'mas'ter s chef m de troupe

scowl [skaʊl] s renfrognement m ‖ intr se renfrogner

scram [skræm] v (pret & pp scrammed; ger scramming) intr (coll) ficher le camp; **scram!** (coll) fiche-moi le camp!

scramble ['skræmbəl] s bousculade f ‖ tr brouiller ‖ intr se disputer; grimper à quatre pattes

scram'bled eggs' spl œufs mpl brouillés

scrap [skræp] s ferraille f; (little bit) petit morceau m; (fight) (coll) chamaillerie f ‖ v (pret & pp scrapped; ger scrapping) tr mettre au rebut ‖ intr (coll) se chamailler

scrap'book' s album m de découpures

scrape [skrep] s grincement m; (coll) mauvaise affaire f ‖ tr gratter, râcler

scrap' heap' s tas m de rebut

scrap' i'ron s ferraille f

scrap' pa'per s bloc-notes m; (refuse) papier m de rebut

scratch [skrætʃ] s égratignure f; **to start from scratch** partir de rien ‖ tr gratter, égratigner

scratch' pad' s bloc-notes m, brouillon m

scratch' pa'per s bloc-notes m

scrawl [skrɔl] s griffonnage m ‖ tr & intr griffonner

scraw·ny ['skrɔni] adj (comp -nier; super -niest) décharné, mince

scream [skrim] s cri m perçant; (slang) personne f ridicule; (slang) chose f ridicule ‖ tr & intr pousser des cris, crier

screech [skritʃ] s cri m perçant ‖ intr jeter des cris perçants

screech' owl' s chat-huant m; (barn owl) effraie f

screen [skrin] s écran m; grillage m en fil de fer, treillis m métallique; (for sifting) crible m ‖ tr abriter; (candidates) trier; (mov) porter à l'écran

screen' grid' s (electron) grille f blindée

screen'play' s scénario m; drame m filmé

screen' test' s bout m d'essai

screw [skru] s vis f; (naut) hélice f; **to have a screw loose** (coll) être toqué ‖ tr visser; **to screw off** dévisser; **to screw tight** visser à bloc; **to screw up** (one's courage) rassembler ‖ intr se visser

screw'ball' adj & s (slang) extravagant m, loufoque m

screw'driv'er s tournevis m

screw' eye' s vis f à œil

screw' press' s cric m à vis

screw' propel'ler s hélice f

screw·y ['skru·i] adj (comp -ier; super -iest) (slang) loufoque

scrib'al er'ror ['skraɪbəl] s faute f de copiste

scribble ['skrɪbəl] s griffonnage m ‖ tr & intr griffonner

scribe [skraɪb] s scribe m

scrimmage ['skrɪmɪdʒ] s mêlée f

scrimp [skrɪmp] tr lésiner sur ‖ intr lésiner

scrip [skrɪp] s monnaie f scriptural, script m

script [skrɪpt] s manuscrit m, original m; (handwriting) écriture f; (mov) scénario m; (typ) script m

scriptural ['skrɪptʃərəl] adj biblique

scripture ['skrɪptʃər] s citation f tirée de l'Écriture; **Scripture** l'Écriture f; **the Scriptures** les Écritures

script'writ'er s scénariste mf

scrofula ['skrɑfjələ] s scrofule f

scroll [skrol] s rouleau m; (archit) volute f

scroll'work' s ornementation f en volute

scro·tum ['skrotəm] s (pl -ta [tə] or -tums) scrotum m, bourses fpl

scrub [skrʌb] adj rabougri ‖ s arbuste m rabougri; personne f malingre; (sports) joueur m novice ‖ v (pret &

pp **scrubbed;** *ger* **scrubbing)** *tr* frotter, nettoyer, récurer
scrub′bing brush′ *s* brosse *f* de chiendent
scrub′wom′an *s* (*pl* -**wom′en**) nettoyeuse *f*
scruff [skrʌf] *s* nuque *f*
scruple [ˈskrupəl] *s* scrupule *f*
scrupulous [ˈskrupjələs] *adj* scrupuleux
scrutinize [ˈskrutɪˌnaɪz] *tr* scruter
scruti·ny [ˈskrutɪni] *s* (*pl* -**nies**) examen *m* minutieux
scuff [skʌf] *s* usure *f* ‖ *tr* érafler
scuffle [ˈskʌfəl] *s* bagarre *f* ‖ *intr* se bagarrer
scull [skʌl] *s* (*stern oar*) godille *f*; aviron *m* de couple ‖ *tr* godiller ‖ *intr* ramer en couple
sculler·y [ˈskʌləri] *s* (*pl* -**ies**) arrière-cuisine *f*
scul′lery maid′ *s* laveuse *f* de vaisselle
scullion [ˈskʌljən] *s* marmiton *m*
sculptor [ˈskʌlptər] *s* sculpteur *m*
sculptress [ˈskʌlptrɪs] *s* femme *f* sculpteur
sculpture [ˈskʌlptʃər] *s* sculpture *f* ‖ *tr & intr* sculpter
scum [skʌm] *s* écume *f*; (*of society*) canaille *f* ‖ *v* (*pret & pp* **scummed;** *ger* **scumming**) *tr & intr* écumer
scum·my [ˈskʌmi] *adj* (*comp* -**mier;** *super* -**miest**) écumeux; (fig) vil
scurrilous [ˈskʌrɪləs] *adj* injurieux, grossier, outrageant
scur·ry [ˈskʌri] *v* (*pret & pp* -**ried**) *intr* —**to scurry around** galoper; **to scurry away** or **off** déguerpir
scur·vy [ˈskʌrvi] *adj* (*comp* -**vier;** *super* -**viest**) méprisable, vil ‖ *s* scorbut *m*
scuttle [ˈskʌtəl] *s* (*bucket for coal*) seau *m* à charbon; (*trap door*) trappe *f*; (*run*) course *f* précipitée; (naut) écoutillon *m* ‖ *tr* saborder ‖ *intr* filer, déguerpir
scut′tle·butt′ *s* (coll) on-dit *m*
scythe [saɪð] *s* faux *f*
sea [si] *s* mer *f*; **at sea** en mer; (fig) désorienté; **by the sea** au bord de la mer; **to put to sea** prendre le large
sea′board′ *s* littoral *m*
sea′ breeze′ *s* brise *f* de mer
sea′coast′ *s* côte *f*, littoral *m*
seafarer [ˈsiˌferər] *s* marin *m*; voyageur *m* par mer
sea′food′ *s* fruits *mpl* de mer, marée *f*
seagoing [ˈsiˌgo·ɪŋ] *adj* de haute mer, au long cours
sea′ gull′ *s* mouette *f*, goéland *m*
seal [sil] *s* sceau *m*; (zool) phoque *m* ‖ *tr* sceller
sea′ legs′ *spl* pied *m* marin
sea′ lev′el *s* niveau *m* de la mer
seal′ing wax′ *s* cire *f* à cacheter
seal′skin′ *s* peau *f* de phoque
seam [sim] *s* couture *f*; (*of metal*) joint *m*; (geol) fissure *f*; (min) couche *f*
sea′man *s* (*pl* -**men**) marin *m*
sea′ mile′ *s* mille *m* marin
seamless [ˈsimlɪs] *adj* sans couture; (mach) sans soudure
seamstress [ˈsimstrɪs] *s* couturière *f*

seam·y [ˈsimi] *adj* (*comp* -**ier;** *super* -**iest**) plein de coutures; vil, vilain
séance [ˈse·ɑns] *s* séance *f* de spiritisme
sea′plane′ *s* hydravion *m*
sea′port′ *s* port *m* de mer
sea′ pow′er *s* puissance *f* maritime
sear [sɪr] *adj* desséché ‖ *s* cicatrice *f* de brûlure ‖ *tr* dessécher; marquer au fer rouge
search [sʌrtʃ] *s* recherche *f*; **in search of** à la recherche de ‖ *tr & intr* fouiller; **to search for** chercher
searching [ˈsʌrtʃɪŋ] *adj* pénétrant, scrutateur
search′light′ *s* projecteur *m*
search′ war′rant *s* mandat *m* de perquisition
seascape [ˈsiˌskep] *s* panorama *m* marin; (*painting*) marine *f*
sea′ shell′ *s* coquille *f* de mer
sea′shore′ *s* bord *m* de la mer
sea′sick′ *adj*—**to be seasick** avoir le mal de mer
sea′sick′ness *s* mal *m* de mer
season [ˈsizən] *s* saison *f* ‖ *tr* assaisonner; (*troops*) aguerrir; (*wood*) sécher
seasonal [ˈsizənəl] *adj* saisonnier
seasoning [ˈsizənɪŋ] *s* assaisonnement *m*
sea′son's greet′ings *spl* meilleurs souhaits *mpl*, tous mes vœux *mpl*
sea′son tick′et *s* carte *f* d'abonnement
seat [sit] *s* place *f*, siège *m*; (*of trousers*) fond *m*; **have a seat** asseyez-vous donc; **keep your seat** restez assis ‖ *tr* asseoir; (*a number of persons*) contenir; **to be seated** (*to sit down*) s'asseoir; (*to be in sitting posture*) être assis
seat′ belt′ *s* ceinture *f* de sécurité
seat′ cov′er *s* (aut) housse *f*
SEATO [ˈsito] *s* (acronym) (**Southeast Asia Treaty Organization**) OTASE *f*
sea′ wall′ *s* digue *f*
sea′way′ *s* voie *f* maritime; (*of ship*) sillage *m*; (*rough sea*) mer *f* dure
sea′weed′ *s* algue *f* marine; plante *f* marine
sea′wor′thy *adj* en état de naviguer
secede [sɪˈsid] *intr* se séparer, faire sécession
secession [sɪˈsɛʃən] *s* sécession *f*
seclude [sɪˈklud] *tr* tenir éloigné; (*to shut up*) enfermer
secluded *adj* retiré, écarté
seclusion [sɪˈkluʒən] *s* retraite *f*
second [ˈsɛkənd] *adj & pron* deuxième (*masc, fem*), second; **the Second** deux, e.g., **John the Second** Jean deux; **to be second in command** commander en second; **to be second to none** ne le céder à personne ‖ *s* deuxième *m*, second *m*; (*in time;* *musical interval; of angle*) seconde *f*; (*in a duel*) témoin *m*, second *m*; (com) article *m* de deuxième qualité; **the second** (*in dates*) le deux ‖ *adv* en second lieu ‖ *tr* affirmer; (*to back up*) seconder
secondar·y [ˈsɛkənˌderi] *adj* secondaire ‖ *s* (*pl* -**ies**) (elec) secondaire *m*

sec'ond best' *s* pis-aller *m*
sec'ond-best' *adj* (*everyday*) de tous les jours; **to come off second-best** être battu
sec'ond-class' *adj* de second ordre; (rr) de seconde classe
sec'ond hand' *s* trotteuse *f*
sec'ond·hand' *adj* d'occasion, de seconde main
sec'ond·hand book'dealer *s* bouquiniste *mf*
sec'ond lieuten'ant *s* sous-lieutenant *m*
sec'ond mate' *s* (naut) second maître *m*
sec'ond-rate' *adj* de second ordre
sec'ond sight' *s* seconde vue *f*
sec'ond wind' *s*—**to get one's second wind** reprendre haleine
secre·cy ['sikrəsi] *s* (*pl* -cies) secret *m*; **in secrecy** en secret
secret ['sikrɪt] *adj* & *s* secret *m*; **in secret** en secret
secretar·y ['sɛkrɪ‚teri] *s* (*pl* -ies) secrétaire *mf*; (*desk*) secrétaire *m*
se'cret bal'lot *s* scrutin *m* secret
secrete [sɪ'krit] *tr* cacher; (physiol) sécréter
secretive [sɪ'kritɪv] *adj* cachottier
se'cret serv'ice *s* deuxième bureau *m*
sect [sɛkt] *s* secte *f*
sectarian [sɛk'tɛrɪ·ən] *adj* sectaire; (*school*) confessionnel ‖ sectaire *mf*
section ['sɛkʃən] *s* section *f*
sectionalism ['sɛkʃənə‚lɪzəm] *s* régionalisme *m*
sec'tion hand' *s* cantonnier *m*
sector ['sɛktər] *s* secteur *m*; (*instrument*) compas *m* de proportion
secular ['sɛkjələr] *adj* (*worldly, of this world*) séculier; (*century-old*) séculaire ‖ *s* séculier *m*
secularism ['sɛkjələ‚rɪzəm] *s* laïcisme *m*, mondanité *f*
secure [sɪ'kjʊr] *adj* sûr ‖ *tr* obtenir; (*to make fast*) fixer
securi·ty [sɪ'kjʊrɪti] *s* (*pl* -ties) sécurité *f*; (*pledge*) garantie *f*; (*person*) garant *m*; **securities** valeurs *fpl*
sedan [sɪ'dæn] *s* (aut) conduite *f* intérieure
sedan' chair' *s* chaise *f* à porteurs
sedate [sɪ'det] *adj* calme, discret
sedation [sɪ'deʃən] *s* sédation *f*
sedative ['sɛdətɪv] *adj* & *s* sédatif *m*
sedentary ['sɛdən‚teri] *adj* sédentaire
sedge [sɛdʒ] *s* (*Carex*) laîche *f*
sediment ['sɛdɪmənt] *s* sédiment *m*
sedition [sɪ'dɪʃən] *s* sédition *f*
seditious [sɪ'dɪʃəs] *adj* séditieux
seduce [sɪ'd(j)us] *tr* séduire
seducer [sɪ'd(j)usər] *s* séducteur *m*
seduction [sɪ'dʌkʃən] *s* séduction *f*
seductive [sɪ'dʌktɪv] *adj* séduisant
sedulous ['sɛdʒələs] *adj* assidu
see [si] *s* (eccl) siège *m* ‖ *v* (*pret* saw [sɔ]; *pp* seen [sin]) *tr* voir; **see other side** (*turn the page*) voir au dos; **to see s.o. play, to see s.o. playing** voir jouer qn, voir qn qui joue; **to see s.th. played** voir jouer q.ch. ‖ *intr* voir; **to see through s.o.** (fig) voir venir qn
seed [sid] *s* graine *f*, semence *f*; sperme

m; (*in fruit*) pépin *m*; (fig) germe *m*; **to go to seed** monter en graine ‖ *tr* semer, ensemencer
seed'bed' *s* semis *m*
seeder ['sidər] *s* (mach) semeuse *f*
seedling ['sidlɪŋ] *s* semis *m*
seed·y ['sidi] *adj* (*comp* -ier; *super* -iest) (coll) râpé, miteux
seeing ['si·ɪŋ] *adj* voyant ‖ *s* vue *f* ‖ *conj* vu que
See'ing Eye' dog' *s* chien *m* d'aveugle
seek [sik] *v* (*pret* & *pp* sought [sɔt]) *tr* chercher ‖ *intr* chercher; **to seek after** rechercher; **to seek to** chercher à
seem [sim] *intr* sembler
seemingly ['simɪŋli] *adv* en apparence
seem·ly ['simli] *adj* (*comp* -lier; *super* -liest) gracieux; (*correct*) bienséant
seep [sip] *intr* suinter
seer [sɪr] *s* prophète *m*, voyant *m*
see'saw' *s* balançoire *f*, bascule *f*; (*motion*) va-et-vient *m* ‖ *intr* basculer, balancer
seethe [sið] *intr* bouillonner
segment ['sɛgmənt] *s* segment *m*
segregate ['sɛgrɪ‚get] *tr* mettre à part, isoler
segregation [‚sɛgrɪ'geʃən] *s* ségrégation *f*
segregationist [‚sɛgrɪ'geʃənɪst] *s* ségrégationniste *mf*
seismograph ['saɪzmə‚græf], ['saɪzmə‚grɑf] *s* sismographe *m*
seismology [saɪz'mɑlədʒi] *s* sismologie *f*
seize [siz] *tr* saisir
seizure ['siʒər] *s* prise *f*; (law) saisie *f*; (pathol) attaque *f*
seldom ['sɛldəm] *adv* rarement
select [sɪ'lɛkt] *adj* choisi ‖ *tr* choisir, sélectionner
selection [sɪ'lɛkʃən] *s* sélection *f*
selective [sɪ'lɛktɪv] *adj* sélectif
self [sɛlf] *adj* de même ‖ *s* (*pl* selves [sɛlvz]) moi *m*, être *m*; **all by one's self** tout seul; **one's better self** notre meilleur côté ‖ *pron*—**payable to self** payable à moi-même
self'-addressed en'velope *s* enveloppe *f* adressée à l'envoyeur
self'-cen'tered *adj* égocentrique
self'-con'fidence *s* confiance *f* en soi
self'-con'fident *adj* sûr de soi
self'-con'scious *adj* gêné, embarrassé
self'-control' *s* sang-froid *m*, maîtrise *f* de soi
self'-defense' *s* autodéfense *f*; **in self-defense** en légitime défense
self'-deni'al *s* abnégation *f*
self'-deter'mina'tion *s* autodétermination *f*
self'-dis'cipline *s* discipline *f* personnelle
self'-ed'ucated *adj* autodidacte
self'-employed' *adj* indépendant
self'-esteem' *s* amour-propre *m*
self'-ev'ident *adj* évident aux yeux de tout le monde
self'-explan'ator'y *adj* qui s'explique de soi-même
self'-gov'ernment *s* autonomie *f*; maîtrise *f* de soi

self'-impor'tant *adj* suffisant, présomptueux
self'-indul'gence *s* faiblesse *f* envers soi-même, intempérance *f*
self'-in'terest *s* intérêt *m* personnel
selfish ['sɛlfɪʃ] *adj* égoïste
selfishness ['sɛlfɪʃnɪs] *s* égoïsme *m*
selfless ['sɛlflɪs] *adj* désintéressé
self'-love' *s* égoïsme *m*
self'-made man' *s* (*pl* **men'**) fils *m* de ses œuvres
self'-por'trait *s* autoportrait *m*
self'-possessed' *adj* maître de soi
self'-pres'erva'tion *s* conservation *f* de soi-même
self'-reli'ant *adj* sûr de soi, assuré
self'-respect'ing *adj* correct, honorable
self'-right'eous *adj* pharisaïque
self'-sac'rifice' *s* abnégation *f*
self'same' *adj* identique
self'-sat'isfied' *adj* content de soi
self'-seek'ing *adj* égoïste, intéressé
self'-serv'ice *s* libre-service *m*
self'-serv'ice laun'dry *s* (*pl* -**dries**) laverie *f* libre-service, laverie automatique
self'-start'er *s* démarreur *m* automatique
self'-styled' *adj* soi-disant
self'-taught' *adj* autodidacte
self'-tim'er *s* (phot) retardateur *m*
self'-willed' *adj* obstiné, entêté
self'-wind'ing *adj* à remontage automatique
sell [sɛl] *v* (*pret & pp* **sold** [sold]) *tr* vendre; **to sell out** solder; (*to betray*) vendre ‖ *intr* vendre; **to sell for** (*e.g., ten dollars*) se vendre à
seller ['sɛlər] *s* vendeur *m*
Selt'zer wa'ter ['sɛltsər] *s* eau *f* de Seltz
selvage ['sɛlvɪdʒ] *s* (*of fabric*) lisière *f*; (*of lock*) gâche *f*
semantic [sɪ'mæntɪk] *adj* sémantique ‖ **semantics** *s* sémantique *f*
semaphore ['sɛmə‚for] *s* sémaphore *m*
semblance ['sɛmbləns] *s* semblant *m*
semen ['simɛn] *s* sperme *m*, semence *f*
semester [sɪ'mɛstər] *adj* semestriel ‖ *s* semestre *m*
semicircle ['sɛmɪ‚sʌrkəl] *s* demi-cercle *m*
semicolon ['sɛmɪ‚kolən] *s* point-virgule *m*
semiconductor [‚sɛmɪkən'dʌktər] *s* semi-conducteur *m*
semiconscious [‚sɛmɪ'kɑnʃəs] *adj* à demi conscient
semifinal [‚sɛmɪ'faɪnəl] *adj* avant-dernière ‖ *s* demi-finale *f*
semilearned [‚sɛmɪ'lʌrnɪd] *adj* à moitié savant
seminar ['sɛmɪ‚nɑr] *s* séminaire *m*
seminar·y ['sɛmɪ‚nɛri] *s* (*pl* -**ies**) séminaire *m*
semiprecious [‚sɛmɪ'prɛʃəs] *adj* fin, semi-précieux
Semite ['sɛmaɪt], ['simaɪt] *s* Sémite *mf*
Semitic [sɪ'mɪtɪk] *adj* (*e.g., language*) sémitique; (*person*) sémite

semitrailer ['sɛmɪ‚trelər] *s* semi-remorque *f*
senate ['sɛnɪt] *s* sénat *m*
senator ['sɛnətər] *s* sénateur *m*
send [sɛnd] *v* (*pret & pp* **sent** [sɛnt]) *tr* envoyer; (rad, telv) émettre; **to send back** renvoyer; **to send out** envoyer; **to send s.o. for s.th. or s.o.** envoyer qn chercher q.ch. or qn; **to send s.o. to** + *inf* envoyer qn + *inf* ‖ *intr* (rad, telv) émettre; **to send for** envoyer chercher
sender ['sɛndər] *s* expéditeur *m*; (telg) transmetteur *m*
send'-off' *s* manifestation *f* d'adieu
senile ['sinaɪl], ['sinɪl] *adj* sénile
senility [sɪ'nɪlɪti] *s* sénilité *f*
senior ['sinjər] *adj* aîné; (*clerk, partner, etc.*) principal; (*rank*) supérieur; père, e.g., **Maurice Laporte, Senior** Maurice Laporte père ‖ *s* aîné *m*, doyen *m*; (*U.S. upperclassman*) étudiant *m* de dernière année
sen'ior cit'izens *spl* les vieilles gens *fpl*
seniority [sin'jɑrɪti], [sin'jɔrɪti] *s* ancienneté *f*, doyenneté *f*
sen'ior staff' *s* personnel *m* hors classe
sensation [sɛn'seʃən] *s* sensation *f*
sensational [sɛn'seʃənəl] *adj* sensationnel
sense [sɛns] *s* sens *m*; (*wisdom*) bon sens; (*e.g., of pain*) sensation *f*; **to make sense out of** arriver à comprendre ‖ *tr* percevoir, sentir
senseless ['sɛnslɪs] *adj* (*lacking perception*) insensible; (*unconscious*) sans connaissance; (*unreasonable*) insensé
sense' of guilt' *s* remords *m*
sense' or'gans *spl* organes *mpl* des sens
sensibili·ty [‚sɛnsɪ'bɪlɪti] *s* (*pl* -**ties**) sensibilité *f*; susceptibilité *f*
sensible ['sɛnsɪbəl] *adj* sensible; (*endowed with good sense*) sensé, raisonnable
sensitive ['sɛnsɪtɪv] *adj* sensible; (*touchy*) susceptible, sensitif
sensitize ['sɛnsɪ‚taɪz] *tr* sensibiliser
sensory ['sɛnsəri] *adj* sensoriel
sensual ['sɛnʃʊ·əl] *adj* sensuel
sensuous ['sɛnʃʊ·əs] *adj* sensuel
sentence ['sɛntəns] *s* (gram) phrase *f*; (law) sentence *f* ‖ *tr* condamner
sentiment ['sɛntɪmənt] *s* sentiment *m*
sentimental [‚sɛntɪ'mɛntəl] *adj* sentimental
sentinel ['sɛntɪnəl] *s* sentinelle *f*; **to stand sentinel** être en sentinelle
sen·try ['sɛntri] *s* (*pl* -**tries**) sentinelle *f*
sen'try box' *s* guérite *f*
separate ['sɛpərɪt] *adj* séparé ‖ ['sɛpə‚ret] *tr* séparer ‖ *intr* se séparer
separation [‚sɛpə'reʃən] *s* séparation *f*
September [sɛp'tɛmbər] *s* septembre *m*
septic ['sɛptɪk] *adj* septique
sepulcher ['sɛpəlkər] *s* sépulcre *m*
sequel ['sikwəl] *s* conséquence *f*; (*something following*) suite *f*
sequence ['sikwəns] *s* succession *f*, ordre *m*; (cards, mov) séquence *f*; (*of tenses*) (gram) concordance *f*
sequester [sɪ'kwɛstər] *tr* séquestrer

sequin ['sikwɪn] s paillette f
ser·aph ['sɛrəf] s (pl -aphs or -aphim
[əfɪm]) séraphin m
Serb [sʌrb] adj serbe || s Serbe mf
sere [sɪr] adj sec, desséché
serenade [ˌsɛrə'ned] s sérénade f || tr
donner une sérénade à || intr donner
des sérénades
serene [sɪ'rin] adj serein
serenity [sɪ'rɛnɪti] s sérénité f
serf [sʌrf] s serf m
serfdom ['sʌrfdəm] s servage m
serge [sʌrdʒ] s serge f
sergeant ['sɑrdʒənt] s sergent m
ser'geant-at-arms' s (pl sergeants-at-
arms) huissier m, sergent m d'armes
ser'geant ma'jor s (pl sergeant majors)
sergent-major m
serial ['sɪrɪ·əl] adj de série || s roman-
feuilleton m
serially ['sɪrɪ·əli] adv en série; (in installments) en feuilleton
se'rial num'ber s numéro m d'ordre;
(mil) numéro m matricule
se·ries ['sɪriz] s (pl -ries) série f; in
series en série
serious ['sɪrɪ·əs] adj sérieux
seriousness ['sɪrɪ·əsnɪs] s sérieux m,
gravité f
sermon ['sʌrmən] s sermon m
sermonize ['sʌrməˌnaɪz] tr & intr
sermonner
serpent ['sʌrpənt] s serpent m
se·rum ['sɪrəm] s (pl -rums or -ra [rə])
sérum m
servant ['sʌrvənt] s domestique mf;
(civil servant) fonctionnaire mf;
(housemaid) bonne f; (humble servant) (fig) serviteur m
serv'ant girl' s servante f
serv'ant prob'lem s crise f domestique
serve [sʌrv] tr servir; to serve s.o. as
servir à qn de; to serve time purger
une peine || intr servir; to serve as
(to function as) servir de; (to be useful for) servir à
service ['sʌrvɪs] s service m; (eccl)
office m; the services (mil) les forces
fpl armées || tr entretenir, réparer
serviceable ['sʌrvɪsəbəl] adj utile, pratique; résistant
serv'ice club' s foyer m du soldat
serv'ice·man' s (pl -men') réparateur
m; (mil) militaire m
serv'ice rec'ord s état m de service
serv'ice sta'tion s station-service f
serv'ice stripe' s chevron m, galon m
servile ['sʌrvɪl] adj servile
servitude ['sʌrvɪˌt(j)ud] s servitude f
sesame ['sɛsəmi] s sésame m; open
sesame! sésame, ouvre-toi!
session ['sɛʃən] s session f; to be in
session siéger
set [sɛt] adj (rule) établi; (price) fixe;
(time) fixé; (smile; locution) figé
|| s ensemble m; (of dishes, linen,
etc.) assortiment m; (of dishes) service m; (of kitchen utensils) batterie
f; (of pans; of weights; of tickets)
série f; (of tools, chessmen, oars,
etc.) jeu m; (of books) collection f;
(of diamonds) parure f; (of tennis)

set m; (of cement) prise f; (of a garment) tournure f; (group of persons)
coterie f; (mov) plateau m; (rad)
poste m; (theat) mise f en scène; set
of false teeth dentier m; set of teeth
denture f || v (pret & pp set; ger
setting) tr mettre, placer, poser; (a
date, price, etc.) fixer; (a gem) monter; (a trap) tendre; (a timepiece)
mettre à l'heure, régler; (the hair)
mettre en plis; (a bone) remettre; to
set aside mettre de côté; annuler; to
set going mettre en marche; to set off
mettre en valeur; (e.g., a rocket)
lancer, tirer || intr se figer; (said of
sun, moon, etc.) se coucher; (said of
hen) couver; (said of garment) tomber; to set about, to set out to se
mettre à; to set upon attaquer
set'back' s revers m, échec m
set'screw' s vis f de pression
settee [se'ti] s canapé m; (for two)
canapé à deux places, causeuse f
setting ['sɛtɪŋ] s cadre m; (of a gem)
monture f; (of cement) prise f; (of
sun) coucher m; (of a bone) recolle-
ment m; (of a watch) réglage m; (adjustment) ajustage m; (theat) mise f
en scène
set'ting-up' ex'ercises spl gymnastique
f rythmique, gymnastique suédoise
settle ['sɛtəl] tr établir; (a region) coloniser; (a dispute, account, debt,
etc.) régler; (a problem) résoudre;
(doubts, fears, etc.) calmer || intr se
coloniser; se calmer; (said of weather) se mettre au beau; (said of building) se tasser; (said of sediment, dust,
etc.) se déposer; (said of liquid) se
clarifier; to settle down s'établir; (to
be less wild) se ranger; to settle down
to (a task) s'appliquer à; to settle on
se décider pour
settlement ['sɛtəlmənt] s établissement
m, colonie f; (of an account, dispute,
etc.) règlement m; (of a debt) liquidation f; (settlement house) œuvre f
sociale
settler ['sɛtlər] s colon m
set'up' s port m, maintien m; (of the
parts of a machine) installation f;
(coll) organisation f
seven ['sɛvən] adj & pron sept || s sept
m; seven o'clock sept heures
seventeen [ˌsɛvən'tin] adj, pron, & s
dix-sept m
seventeenth [ˌsɛvən'tinθ] adj & pron
dix-septième (masc, fem); the Seventeenth dix-sept, e.g., John the Seven-
teenth Jean dix-sept || s dix-septième
m; the seventeenth (in dates) le dix-
sept
seventh ['sɛvənθ] adj & pron septième
(masc, fem); the Seventh sept, e.g.,
John the Seventh Jean sept || s sep-
tième m; the seventh (in dates) le
sept
seventieth ['sɛvəntɪ·θ] adj & pron
soixante-dixième (masc, fem) || s
soixante-dixième m
seven·ty ['sɛvənti] adj & pron soixante-
dix || s (pl -ties) soixante-dix m

sev′enty-first′ adj & pron soixante et onzième (masc, fem) ‖ s soixante et onzième m

sev′enty-one′ adj, pron, & s soixante et onze m

sever ['sɛvər] tr séparer; (relations) rompre ‖ intr se séparer

several ['sɛvərəl] adj & pron indef plusieurs

severance ['sɛvərəns] s séparation f; (of relations) rupture f; (of communications) interruption f

sev′erance pay′ s indemnité f pour cause de renvoi

severe [sɪ'vɪr] adj sévère; (weather) rigoureux; (pain) aigu; (illness) grave

sew [so] v (pret sewed; pp sewed or sewn) tr & intr coudre

sewage ['s(j)u·ɪdʒ] s eaux fpl d'égouts

sewer ['s(j)u·ər] s égout m ‖ ['so·ər] s (one who sews) couseur m

sewerage ['s(j)u·ərɪdʒ] s (removal) vidange f; (system) système m d'égouts; (sewage) eaux fpl d'égouts

sew′ing bas′ket s nécessaire m de couture

sew′ing machine′ s machine f à coudre

sex [sɛks] s sexe m; the fair sex le beau sexe; the sterner sex le sexe fort; to have sex with (coll) avoir des rapports avec

sex′ appeal′ s sex-appeal m

sextant ['sɛkstənt] s sextant m

sextet [sɛks'tɛt] s sextuor m

sexton ['sɛkstən] s sacristain m

sexual ['sɛkʃu·əl] adj sexuel

sex·y ['sɛksi] adj (comp -ier; super -iest) (slang) aguichant, grivois; (story) érotique

sh [ʃ] interj chut!

shab·by ['ʃæbi] adj (comp -bier; super -biest) râpé, usé; (mean) mesquin; (house) délabré

shack [ʃæk] s cabane f, case f

shackle ['ʃækəl] s boucle f; shackles entraves fpl ‖ tr entraver

shad [ʃæd] s alose f

shade [ʃed] s ombre f; (of lamp) abat-jour m; (of window) store m; (hue; slight difference) nuance f; (little bit) soupçon m ‖ tr ombrager; (to make gradual changes in) nuancer

shadow ['ʃædo] s ombre f ‖ tr ombrager; (to spy on) filer, pister

shad′ow gov′ernment s gouvernement m fantôme

shadowy ['ʃædo·i] adj ombreux, sombre; (fig) vague, obscur

shad·y ['ʃedi] adj (comp -ier; super -iest) ombreux, ombragé; (coll) louche

shaft [ʃæft], [ʃɑft] s (of mine; of elevator) puits m; (of feather) tige f; (of arrow) bois m; (of column) fût m, tige; (of flag) mât m; (of wagon) brancard m, limon m; (of motor) arbre m; (of light) rayon m; (to make fun of s.o.) trait m

shag·gy ['ʃægi] adj (comp -gier; super -giest) poilu, à longs poils

shag′gy dog′ sto′ry s (pl -ries) histoire f sans queue ni tête

shake [ʃek] s secousse f ‖ v (pret shook [ʃuk]; pp shaken) tr secouer; (the head) hocher, secouer; (one's hand) serrer; to shake down faire tomber; (a thermometer) secouer; (slang) escroquer; to shake off secouer; (to get rid of) se débarrasser de; to shake up (a liquid) agiter; (fig) ébranler ‖ intr trembler

shake′down′ s (slang) exaction f, concussion f

shaker ['ʃekər] s (for salt) salière f; (for cocktails) shaker m

shake′up′ s bouleversement m; (reorganization) remaniement m

shak·y ['ʃeki] adj (comp -ier; super -iest) tremblant, chancelant; (hand; writing) tremblé; (voice) tremblotant

shall [ʃæl] v (cond should [ʃud]) aux used to express 1) the future indicative, e.g., I shall arrive j'arriverai; 2) the future perfect indicative, e.g., I shall have arrived je serai arrivé; 3) the potential mood, e.g., what shall he do? que doit-il faire?

shallow ['ʃælo] adj peu profond; (dish) plat; (fig) creux, superficiel ‖ shallows spl haut-fond m

sham [ʃæm] adj feint, simulé ‖ s feinte f, simulacre m; (person) imposteur m ‖ v (pret & pp shammed; ger shamming) tr & intr feindre, simuler

sham′ bat′tle s combat m simulé

shambles ['ʃæmbəlz] spl boucherie f; ravage m, ruine f; (disorder) pagaille f

shame [ʃem] s honte f; shame on you!, for shame! quelle honte!; what a shame! quel dommage! ‖ tr faire honte à

shame′faced′ adj penaud

shameful ['ʃemfəl] adj honteux

shameless ['ʃemlɪs] adj éhonté

shampoo [ʃæm'pu] s shampooing m ‖ tr (the hair) laver; (a person) faire un shampooing à

shamrock ['ʃæmrɑk] s trèfle m d'Irlande

Shanghai ['ʃæŋhaɪ], [ʃæŋ'haɪ] s Changhaï ‖ (l.c.) tr (coll) racoler

Shangri-la [,ʃæŋgrɪ'lɑ] s le pays de Cocagne

shank [ʃæŋk] s jambe f, tibia m; (of horse) canon m; (of anchor) verge f; (culin) manche m; (of a column) fût m

shan·ty ['ʃænti] s (pl -ties) masure f, bicoque f

shan′ty·town′ s bidonville m

shape [ʃep] s forme f; in bad shape (coll) mal en point; out of shape déformé ‖ tr former ‖ intr se former; to shape up prendre forme; avancer

shapeless ['ʃeplɪs] adj informe

shape·ly ['ʃepli] adj (comp -lier; super -liest) bien proportionné, bien fait, svelte

share [ʃɛr] s part f; (of stock in a company) action f ‖ tr partager ‖ intr— to share in prendre part à, participer à

sharecropper ['ʃɛr ,krɑpər] s métayer m

share′hold′er s actionnaire mf

shark [ʃɑrk] *s* requin *m*; (*swindler*) escroc *m*; (slang) as *m*, expert *m*

sharp [ʃɑrp] *adj* aigu; (*wind, cold, pain, fight, criticism, edge, trot, mind*) vif; (*knife*) tranchant; (*point; tongue*) acéré; (*slope*) raide; (*curve*) prononcé; (*turn*) brusque; (*photograph*) net; (*hearing*) fin; (*step, gait*) rapide; (*taste*) piquant; (*reprimand*) vert; (*keen*) éveillé; (*cunning*) rusé, fin; (mus) dièse; (*stylish*) (coll) chic; **sharp features** traits *mpl* accentués ‖ *adv* vivement; brusquement; précis, sonnant, tapant, e.g., **at four o'clock sharp** à quatre heures précises, sonnantes, or tapantes; **to stop short** s'arrêter net or pile ‖ *s* (mus) dièse *m* ‖ *tr* (mus) diéser

sharpen [ˈʃɑrpən] *tr* aiguiser; (*a pencil*) tailler ‖ *intr* s'aiguiser

sharpener [ˈʃɑrpənər] *s* aiguisoir *m*

sharper [ˈʃɑrpər] *s* filou *m*, tricheur *m*

sharp′shoot′er *s* tireur *m* d'élite

shatter [ˈʃætər] *tr* fracasser, briser ‖ *intr* se fracasser, se briser

shat′ter-proof′ *adj* de sécurité

shave [ʃev] *s*—**to get a shave** se faire raser, se faire faire la barbe; **to have a close shave** (coll) l'échapper belle ‖ *tr* (*hair, beard, etc.*) raser; (*a person*) faire la barbe à, raser; (e.g., *wood*) doler; (e.g., *expenses*) rogner ‖ *intr* se raser, se faire la barbe

shaving [ˈʃeviŋ] *s* rasage *m*; **shavings** rognures *fpl*, copeaux *mpl*

shav′ing brush′ *s* blaireau *m*

shav′ing soap′ *s* savon *m* à barbe

shawl [ʃɔl] *s* châle *m*, fichu *m*

she [ʃi] *s* femelle *f* ‖ *pron pers* elle §85, §87; ce §82B; **she who** celle qui §83

sheaf [ʃif] *s* (*pl* **sheaves** [ʃivz]) gerbe *f*; (*of papers*) liasse *f*

shear [ʃɪr] *s* lame *f* de ciseau; **shears** ciseaux *mpl*; (*to cut metal*) cisaille *f* ‖ *v* (*pret* **sheared**; *pp* **sheared** or **shorn** [ʃorn]) *tr* (*sheep*) tondre; (*velvet*) ciseler; (*metal*) cisailler; **to shear off** couper

sheath [ʃiθ] *s* (*pl* **sheaths** [ʃiðz]) gaine *f*, fourreau *m*

sheathe [ʃið] *tr* envelopper; (*a sword*) rengainer

shed [ʃɛd] *s* hangar *m*; (*for, e.g., tools*) remise *f*; (*line from which water flows in two directions*) ligne *f* de faîte ‖ *v* (*pret* & *pp* **shed**; *ger* **shedding**) *tr* répandre, verser; (e.g., *leaves*) perdre; (e.g., *light; skin*) jeter

sheen [ʃin] *s* lustre *m*, brillant *m*

sheep [ʃip] *s* (*pl* **sheep**) mouton *m*; (*ewe*) brebis *f*

sheep′dog′ *s* chien *m* de berger

sheep′fold′ *s* bergerie *f*

sheepish [ˈʃipɪʃ] *adj* penaud; timide

sheep′skin′ *s* (*undressed*) peau *f* de mouton; (*dressed*) basane *f*; (*diploma*) (coll) peau d'âne

sheep′skin jack′et *s* canadienne *f*

sheer [ʃɪr] *adj* transparent; léger; (*stocking*) extra-fin; (*steep*) à pic; (fig) pur; (fig) vif, e.g., **by sheer force** de vive force ‖ *intr* faire une embardée

sheet [ʃit] *s* (e.g., *for the bed*) drap *m*; (*of paper*) feuille *f*; (*of metal*) tôle *f*, lame *f*; (*of water*) nappe *f*; (*of ice*) couche *f*; (naut) écoute *f*; **white as a sheet** blanc comme un linge

sheet′ light′ning *s* fulguration *f*, éclairs *mpl* en nappe

sheet′ met′al *s* tôle *f*

sheet′ mu′sic *s* morceaux *mpl* de musique

sheik [ʃik] *s* cheik *m*; (coll) tombeur *m* de femmes

shelf [ʃɛlf] *s* (*pl* **shelves** [ʃɛlvz]) tablette *f*, planche *f*; (*of cupboard; of library*) rayon *m*; (geog) plateau *m*; **on the shelf** au rancart, laissé à l'écart

shell [ʃɛl] *s* coque *f*, coquille *f*; (*of nut*) écale *f*, coque; (*of pea*) cosse *f*; (*of oyster, clam, etc.*) écaille *f*; (*of building, ship, etc.*) carcasse *f*; (*projectile*) obus *m*; (*long, narrow racing boat*) yole *f* ‖ *tr* écaler, écosser; (mil) bombarder, pilonner; **to shell out** (coll) débourser ‖ *intr*—**to shell out** (coll) casquer

shel·lac [ʃəˈlæk] *s* laque *f*, gomme *f* laque ‖ *v* (*pret* & *pp* **-lacked**; *ger* **-lacking**) *tr* laquer; (slang) tabasser

shell′fish′ *s* fruits *mpl* de mer, coquillages *mpl*

shell′ hole′ *s* entonnoir *m*, trou *m* d'obus

shell′ shock′ *s* commotion *f* cérébrale

shelter [ˈʃɛltər] *s* abri *m* ‖ *tr* abriter

shelve [ʃɛlv] *tr* (*a book*) ranger; (*merchandise*) entreposer; (*a project, a question, etc., by putting it aside*) enterrer, classer; (*to provide with shelves*) garnir de tablettes, rayons, or planches

shepherd [ˈʃɛpərd] *s* berger *m*; (fig) pasteur *m* ‖ *tr* veiller sur, guider

shep′herd dog′ *s* berger *m*, chien *m* de berger

shepherdess [ˈʃɛpərdɪs] *s* bergère *f*

sherbet [ˈʃʌrbət] *s* sorbet *m*

sheriff [ˈʃɛrɪf] *s* shérif *m*

sher·ry [ˈʃɛri] *s* (*pl* **-ries**) xérès *m*

shield [ʃild] *s* bouclier *m*; (elec) blindage *m*; (heral, hist) écu *m*, écusson *m* ‖ *tr* protéger; (elec) blinder

shift [ʃɪft] *s* changement *m*; (*in wind, temperature, etc.*) saute *f*; (*group of workmen*) équipe *f* de relais; (fig) expédient *m* ‖ *tr* changer; (*the blame, the guilt, etc.*) rejeter; **to shift gears** changer de vitesse ‖ *intr* changer; changer de place; changer de direction; **to shift for oneself** se débrouiller tout seul

shift′ key′ *s* touche *f* majuscules

shiftless [ˈʃɪftlɪs] *adj* mollasse, peu débrouillard

shift·y [ˈʃɪfti] *adj* (*comp* **-ier**; *super* **-iest**) roublard; (*look*) chafouin; (*eye*) fuyant

shimmer [ˈʃɪmər] *s* chatoiement *m*, miroitement *m* ‖ *intr* chatoyer, miroiter

shin [ʃɪn] *s* tibia *m*; (culin) jarret *m* ‖ *v* (*pret* & *pp* **shinned**; *ger* **shinning**) *intr*—**to shin up** grimper

shin′bone′ *s* tibia *m*

shine [ʃaɪn] *s* brillant *m*; (*of cloth, clothing, etc.*) luisant *m*; (*on shoes*) coup *m* de cirage; **to take a shine to** (slang) s'enticher de ‖ *v* (*pret* & *pp* **shined**) *tr* faire briller, faire reluire; (*shoes*) cirer ‖ *v* (*pret* & *pp* **shone** [ʃon]) *intr* briller, reluire

shiner [′ʃaɪnər] *s* (slang) œil *m* poché

shingle [′ʃɪŋɡəl] *s* bardeau *m*; (*of doctor, lawyer, etc.*) (coll) enseigne *f*; **shingles** (pathol) zona *m*

shining [′ʃaɪnɪŋ] *adj* brillant, luisant

shin·y [′ʃaɪni] *adj* (*comp* **-ier**; *super* **-iest**) brillant, reluisant; (*from much wear*) lustré

ship [ʃɪp] *s* navire *m*; (*steamer, liner*) paquebot *m*; (aer) appareil *m*; (nav) bâtiment *m* ‖ *v* (*pret* & *pp* **shipped**; *ger* **shipping**) *tr* expédier; (*a cargo; water*) embarquer; (*oars*) armer, rentrer ‖ *intr* s'embarquer

ship′board′ *s* bord *m*; **on shipboard** à bord

ship′build′er *s* constructeur *m* de navires

ship′build′ing *s* construction *f* navale

ship′mate′ *s* compagnon *m* de bord

shipment [′ʃɪpmənt] *s* expédition *f*; (*goods shipped*) chargement *m*

ship′own′er *s* armateur *m*

shipper [′ʃɪpər] *s* expéditeur *m*

shipping [′ʃɪpɪŋ] *s* embarquement *m*, expédition *f*; (naut) transport *m* maritime

ship′ping clerk′ *s* expéditionnaire *mf*

ship′ping mem′o *s* connaissement *m*

ship′ping room′ *s* salle *f* d'expédition

ship′shape′ *adj* & *adv* en bon ordre

ship′s′ pa′pers *spl* papiers *mpl* de bord

ship′s′ time′ *s* heure *f* locale du navire

ship′-to-shore′ ra′di·o [′ʃɪptə′ʃor] *s* (*pl* **-os**) liaison *f* radio maritime

ship′wreck′ *s* naufrage *m* ‖ *tr* faire naufrager ‖ *intr* faire naufrage

ship′yard′ *s* chantier *m* de construction navale ou maritime

shirk [ʃʌrk] *tr* manquer à, esquiver ‖ *intr* négliger son devoir

shirred′ eggs′ [ʃʌrd] *spl* œufs *mpl* pochés à la crème

shirt [ʃʌrt] *s* chemise *f*; **keep your shirt on!** (slang) ne vous emballez pas!; **to lose one's shirt** perdre jusqu'à son dernier sou

shirt′band′ *s* encolure *f*

shirt′ front′ *s* plastron *m* de chemise

shirt′ sleeve′ *s* manche *f* de chemise; **in shirt sleeves** en bras de chemise

shirt′tails′ *spl* pans *mpl* de chemise

shirt′waist′ *s* chemisier *m*

shiver [′ʃɪvər] *s* frisson *m* ‖ *intr* frissonner

shoal [ʃol] *s* banc *m*, bas-fond *m*

shock [ʃɑk] *s* (*bump, clash*) choc *m*, heurt *m*; (*upset, misfortune; earthquake tremor*) secousse *f*; (*of grain*) gerbe *f*, moyette *f*; (*of hair*) tignasse *f*; (elec) commotion *f*, choc; **to die of**

shock mourir de saisissement ‖ *tr* choquer; (elec) commotionner, choquer

shock′ absorb′er [æb‚sɔrbər] *s* amortisseur *m*

shocking [′ʃɑkɪŋ] *adj* choquant, scandaleux

shock′ troops′ *spl* troupes *fpl* de choc

shod·dy [′ʃɑdi] *adj* (*comp* **-dier**; *super* **-diest**) inférieur, de pacotille

shoe [ʃu] *s* soulier *m*; **to be in the shoes of** être dans la peau de; **to put one's shoes on** se chausser; **to take one's shoes off** se déchausser ‖ *v* (*pret* & *pp* **shod** [ʃɑd]) *tr* chausser; (*a horse*) ferrer

shoe′black′ *s* cireur *m* de bottes

shoe′horn′ *s* chausse-pied *m*

shoe′lace′ *s* lacet *m*, cordon *m* de soulier

shoe′mak′er *s* cordonnier *m*

shoe′ pol′ish *s* cirage *m* de chaussures

shoe′shine′ *s* cirage *m*

shoe′ store′ *s* magasin *m* de chaussures

shoe′string′ *s* lacet *m*, cordon *m* de soulier; **on a shoestring** avec de minces capitaux

shoe′tree′ *s* embauchoir *m*, forme *f*

shoo [ʃu] *tr* chasser ‖ *interj* ch!, filez!

shoot [ʃut] *s* (*sprout, twig*) rejeton *m*, pousse *f*; (*for grain, sand, etc.*) goulotte *f*; (*contest*) concours *m* de tir; (*hunting party*) partie *f* de chasse ‖ *v* (*pret* & *pp* **shot** [ʃɑt]) *tr* tirer; (*a person*) tuer d'un coup de fusil; (*to execute with a discharge of rifles*) fusiller; (*with a camera*) photographier; (*a scene; a motion picture*) tourner, roder; (*the sun*) prendre la hauteur de; (*dice*) jeter; **to shoot down** abattre; **to shoot up** (slang) cribler de balles ‖ *intr* tirer; s'élancer, se précipiter; (*said of pain*) lanciner; (*said of star*) filer; **to shoot at** faire feu sur; (*to strive for*) viser; **to shoot up** (*said of plant*) pousser; (*said of plant*) pousser; (*said of flame*) jaillir; (*said of prices*) augmenter

shooting [′ʃutɪŋ] *s* tir *m*; (phot) prise *f* de vues

shoot′ing gal′ler·y *s* (*pl* **-ies**) stand *m* de tir, tir *m*

shoot′ing match′ *s* concours *m* de tir

shoot′ing script′ *s* découpage *m*

shoot′ing star′ *s* étoile *f* filante

shop [ʃɑp] *s* (*store*) boutique *f*; (*workshop*) atelier *m*; **to talk shop** parler boutique, parler affaires ‖ *v* (*pret* & *pp* **shopped**; *ger* **shopping**) *intr* faire des emplettes, faire des courses; magasiner (Canad); **to go shopping** faire des emplettes, faire des courses; **to shop around** être à l'affût de bonnes occasions; **to shop for** chercher à acheter

shop′girl′ *s* vendeuse *f*

shop′keep′er *s* boutiquier *m*

shoplifter [′ʃɑp‚lɪftər] *s* voleur *m* à l'étalage

shopper [′ʃɑpər] *s* acheteur *m*

shopping [′ʃɑpɪŋ] *s* achat *m*; (*purchases*) achats *mpl*, emplettes *fpl*

shop'ping bag' s sac m à provisions
shop'ping cen'ter s centre m commercial
shop'ping dis'trict s quartier m commerçant
shop' stew'ard s délégué m d'atelier
shop'win'dow s vitrine f, devanture f
shop'worn' adj défraîchi
shore [ʃor] s rivage m, rive f, bord m; (sandy beach) plage f; shores (poetic) pays m ‖ tr—to shore up étayer
shore' din'ner s dîner m de marée
shore' leave' s (nav) descente f à terre
shore'line' s ligne f de côte
shore' patrol' s patrouille f de garde-côte; (police) (nav) police f militaire de la marine
short [ʃɔrt] adj court; (person) petit; (temper) brusque; (phonet) bref; in short en somme; short of breath poussif; to be short for (coll) être le diminutif de; to be short of être à court de ‖ s (elec) court-circuit m; (mov) court-métrage m; shorts culotte f courte, culotte de sport ‖ adv court, de court; to run short of être à court de, manquer de; to sell short (com) vendre à découvert; to stop short s'arrêter net ‖ tr (elec) court-circuiter ‖ intr (elec) se mettre en court-circuit
shortage ['ʃɔrtɪdʒ] s manque m, pénurie f; crise f, e.g., housing shortage crise du logement; (com) déficit m; shortages manquants mpl
short'cake' s gâteau m recouvert de fruits frais m
short'-change' tr ne pas rendre assez de monnaie à; (to cheat) (coll) rouler
short' cir'cuit s court-circuit m
short'-cir'cuit tr court-circuiter
short'com'ing s défaut m
short'cut' s raccourci m
shorten ['ʃɔrtən] tr raccourcir ‖ intr se raccourcir
shortening ['ʃɔrtənɪŋ] s raccourcissement m; (culin) saindoux m
short'hand' adj sténographique ‖ s sténographie f; to take down in shorthand sténographier
short'hand notes' spl sténogramme m
short'hand typ'ist s sténodactylo mf
short-lived ['ʃɔrt'laɪvd], ['ʃɔrt'lɪvd] adj de courte durée, bref
shortly ['ʃɔrtli] adv tantôt, sous peu; brièvement; (curtly) sèchement; shortly after peu après
short'-range' adj à courte portée
short' sale' s vente f à découvert
short'-sight'ed adj myope; to be short-sighted (fig) avoir la vue courte
short' sto'ry s nouvelle f, conte m
short'-tem'pered adj vif, emporté
short'-term' adj à court terme
short'wave' adj aux petites ondes, aux ondes courtes ‖ s petite onde f, onde courte
short' weight' s poids m insuffisant
shot [ʃɑt] adj (silk) changeant; (e.g., chances) (coll) réduit à zéro; (drunk) (slang) paf ‖ s coup m de feu, décharge f; (marksman) tireur m; (pel-

lets) petits plombs mpl; (of a rocket into space) lancement m, tir m; (in certain games) shoot m; (snapshot) instantané m; (mov) plan m; (hypodermic injection) (coll) piqûre f; (drink of liquor) (slang) verre m d'alcool; a long shot un gros risque, une chance sur mille; to fire a shot at tirer sur; to start like a shot partir comme un trait
shot'gun' s fusil m de chasse
shot'-put' s (sports) lancement m du poids
should [ʃʊd] aux used to express 1) the present conditional, e.g., if I waited for him, I should miss the train si je l'attendais, je manquerais le train; 2) the past conditional, e.g., if I had waited for him, I should have missed the train si je l'avais attendu, j'aurais manqué le train; 3) the potential mood, e.g., he should go at once il devrait aller aussitôt; e.g., he should have gone at once il aurait dû aller aussitôt; 4) a softened affirmation, e.g., I should like a drink je prendrais bien quelque chose à boire; e.g., I should have thought that you would have known better j'aurais cru que vous auriez été plus avisé
shoulder ['ʃoldər] s épaule f; (of a road) accotement m; across the shoulder en bandoulière, en écharpe; shoulders (of a garment) carrure f ‖ tr (a gun) mettre sur l'épaule; to shoulder aside pousser de l'épaule
shoul'der blade' s omoplate f
shoul'der strap' s (of underwear) épaulette f; (mil) bandoulière f
shout [ʃaut] s cri m ‖ tr crier; to shout down huer ‖ intr crier
shove [ʃʌv] s poussée f, bourrade f ‖ tr pousser, bousculer ‖ intr pousser; to shove off pousser au large; (slang) filer, décamper
shov•el ['ʃʌvəl] s pelle f ‖ v (pret & pp -eled or -elled; ger -eling or -elling) tr pelleter; (e.g., snow) balayer
show [ʃo] s exposition f; apparence f; (display) étalage m; (of hands) levée f; (each performance) séance f; (mov) film m; (theat) spectacle m; to make a show of faire parade de ‖ v (pret showed; pp shown [ʃon] or showed) tr montrer; (one's passport) présenter; (a film) projeter; (e.g., to the door) conduire; to show off faire étalage de; to show up (coll) démasquer ‖ intr se montrer; to show through transparaître; to show up (against a background) ressortir; (coll) faire son apparition
show' bill' s affiche f
show'boat' s bateau-théâtre m
show' busi'ness s l'industrie f du spectacle
show'case' s vitrine f
show'down' s cartes fpl sur table, moment m critique; to come to a showdown en venir au fait
shower ['ʃau•ər] s averse f, ondée f; (of blows, bullets, kisses, etc.) pluie

f; (*bath*) douche *f* ‖ *tr* faire pleuvoir; **to shower with** combler de ‖ *intr* pleuvoir à verse
show′er bath′ *s* douche *f*
show′ girl′ *s* girl *f*
show′man *s* (*pl* -**men**) impresario *m*; **he's a great showman** c'est un as pour la mise en scène
show′-off′ *s* (coll) m'as-tu-vu *m*
show′piece′ *s* pièce *f* maîtresse
show′place′ *s* lieu *m* célèbre
show′room′ *s* salon *m* d'exposition
show′ win′dow *s* vitrine *f*
show•y [′ʃo·i] *adj* (*comp* -**ier**; *super* -**iest**) fastueux; (*gaudy*) voyant
shrapnel [′ʃræpnəl] *s* shrapnel *m*, obus *m* à mitraille; éclat *m* d'obus
shred [ʃrɛd] *s* morceau *m*, lambeau *m*; **not a shred of** pas l'ombre de; **to tear to shreds** mettre en lambeaux ‖ *v* (*pret & pp* **shredded** or **shred**; *ger* **shredding**) *tr* mettre en lambeaux, déchiqueter
shrew [ʃru] *s* (*nagging woman*) mégère *f*; (zool) musaraigne *f*
shrewd [ʃrud] *adj* sagace, fin
shriek [ʃrik] *s* cri *m* perçant ‖ *intr* pousser un cri perçant
shrike [ʃraɪk] *s* pie-grièche *f*
shrill [ʃrɪl] *adj* aigu, perçant
shrimp [ʃrɪmp] *s* crevette *f*; (*insignificant person*) gringalet *m*
shrine [ʃraɪn] *s* tombeau *m* de saint; (*reliquary*) châsse *f*; (*holy place*) lieu *m* saint, sanctuaire *m*
shrink [ʃrɪŋk] *v* (*pret* **shrank** [ʃræŋk] or **shrunk** [ʃrʌŋk]; *pp* **shrunk** or **shrunken**) *tr* rétrécir ‖ *intr* se rétrécir; **to shrink away** or **back from** reculer devant
shrinkage [′ʃrɪŋkɪdʒ] *s* rétrécissement *m*
shriv•el [′ʃrɪvəl] *v* (*pret & pp* -**eled** or -**elled**; *ger* -**eling** or -**elling**) *tr* ratatiner, recroqueviller ‖ *intr* se ratatiner, se recroqueviller
shroud [ʃraud] *s* linceul *m*; (*veil*) voile *m*; **shrouds** (naut) haubans *mpl* ‖ *tr* ensevelir; voiler
Shrove′ Tues′day [ʃrov] *s* mardi *m* gras
shrub [ʃrʌb] *s* arbuste *m*
shrubber•y [′ʃrʌbəri] *s* (*pl* -**ies**) bosquet *m*
shrug [ʃrʌg] *s* haussement *m* d'épaules ‖ *v* (*pret & pp* **shrugged**; *ger* **shrugging**) *tr* (*one's shoulders*) hausser; **to shrug off** minimiser; ne tenir aucun compte de ‖ *intr* hausser les épaules
shudder [′ʃʌdər] *s* frisson *m*, frémissement *m* ‖ *intr* frissonner, frémir
shuffle [′ʃʌfəl] *s* (*of cards*) battement *m*, mélange *m*; (*of feet*) frottement *m*; (*change of place*) déplacement *m* ‖ *tr* (*cards*) battre; (*the feet*) traîner; (*to mix up*) mêler, brouiller ‖ *intr* battre les cartes; traîner les pieds
shuf′fle•board′ *s* jeu *m* de palets
shun [ʃʌn] *v* (*pret & pp* **shunned**; *ger* **shunning**) *tr* éviter, fuir
shunt [ʃʌnt] *tr* garer, manœuvrer; (elec) shunter, dériver

shut [ʃʌt] *adj* fermé ‖ *v* (*pret & pp* **shut**; *ger* **shutting**) *tr* fermer; **to shut in** enfermer; **to shut off** couper; **to shut up** enfermer; (coll) faire taire ‖ *intr* se fermer; **shut up!** (slang) taistoi!, ferme-la!
shut′down′ *s* fermeture *f*
shutter [′ʃʌtər] *s* volet *m*, contrevent *m*; (*over store window*) rideau *m*; (phot) obturateur *m*
shuttle [′ʃʌtəl] *s* navette *f* ‖ *intr* faire la navette
shut′tle train′ *s* navette *f*
shy [ʃaɪ] *adj* (*comp* **shyer** or **shier**; *super* **shyest** or **shiest**) timide, sauvage; (*said of horse*) ombrageux; **I am shy a dollar** il me faut un dollar; **to be shy of** se méfier de ‖ *v* (*pret & pp* **shied**) *intr* (*said of horse*) faire un écart; **to shy away from** éviter
shyster [′ʃaɪstər] *s* (coll) avocat *m* marron
Sia•mese [ˌsaɪ·əˈmiz] *adj* siamois ‖ *s* (*pl* -**mese**) Siamois *m*
Si′amese twins′ *spl* frères *mpl* siamois
Siberian [saɪˈbɪrɪ·ən] *adj* sibérien ‖ *s* Sibérien *m*
sibyl [′sɪbɪl] *s* sibylle *f*
sic [sik], [sɪk] *adv* sic ‖ [sɪk] *v* (*pret & pp* **sicked**; *ger* **sicking**) *tr*—**sic 'em!** (coll) pille!; **to sic on** lancer après
Sicilian [sɪˈsɪljən] *adj* sicilien ‖ *s* Sicilien *m*
Sicily [′sɪsɪli] *s* Sicile *f*; **la Sicile**
sick [sɪk] *adj* malade; **to be sick and tired of** (coll) en avoir plein le dos de, en avoir marre de; **to be sick at** or **to one's stomach** avoir mal au cœur, avoir des nausées; **to take sick** tomber malade
sick′bed′ *s* lit *m* de malade
sicken [′sɪkən] *tr* rendre malade ‖ *intr* tomber malade; (*to be disgusted*) être écœuré
sickening [′sɪkənɪŋ] *adj* écœurant, dégoûtant
sick′ head′ache *s* migraine *f* avec nausées
sickle [′sɪkəl] *s* faucille *f*
sick′ leave′ *s* congé *m* de maladie
sick•ly [′sɪkli] *adj* (*comp* -**lier**; *super* -**liest**) maladif, débile
sickness [′sɪknɪs] *s* maladie *f*; nausée *f*
side [saɪd] *adj* latéral, de côté ‖ *s* côté *m*; (*of phonograph*) face *f*; (*of team, government, etc.*) camp *m*, parti *m*, côté *m*; **this side up** (*on package*) haut ‖ *intr*—**to side with** prendre le parti de
side′ arms′ *spl* armes *fpl* de ceinturon
side′board′ *s* buffet *m*, desserte *f*
side′burns′ *spl* favoris *mpl*
side′ dish′ *s* plat *m* d'accompagnement
side′ door′ *s* porte *f* latérale, porte *f* de service
side′ effect′ *s* effet *m* secondaire
side′ en′trance *s* entrée *f* latérale
side′ glance′ *s* regard *m* de côté
side′ is′sue *s* question *f* d'intérêt secondaire
side′line′ *s* occupation *f* secondaire; **on the sidelines** sans y prendre part

sidereal [saɪ'dɪrɪ·əl] adj sidéral
side' road' s chemin m de traverse
side'sad'dle adv en amazone
side' show' s spectacle m forain; (fig) événement m secondaire
side'slip' s glissade f sur l'aile
side'split'ting adj désopilant
side' step' s écart m
side'-step' v (pret & pp -stepped; ger -stepping) tr éviter ‖ intr faire un pas de côté
side'stroke' s nage f sur le côté
side'track' s voie f de garage ‖ tr écarter, dévier; (rr) aiguiller sur une voie de garage
side' view' s vue f de profil
side'walk' s trottoir m
side'walk café' s terrasse f de café
sideward ['saɪdwərd] adj latéral ‖ adv latéralement, de côté
side'ways' adj latéral ‖ adv latéralement, de côté
side' whisk'ers spl favoris mpl
side'wise' adj latéral ‖ adv latéralement, de côté
siding ['saɪdɪŋ] s (rr) voie f d'évitement, voie de garage
sidle ['saɪdəl] intr avancer de biais; to sidle up to se couler auprès de
siege [sidʒ] s siège m; to lay siege to mettre le siège devant
siesta [si'ɛstə] s sieste f; to take a siesta faire la sieste
sieve [sɪv] s crible m, tamis m ‖ tr passer au crible, au tamis
sift [sɪft] tr passer au crible, passer au tamis; (flour) tamiser; (fig) examiner soigneusement
sigh [saɪ] s soupir m ‖ intr soupirer
sight [saɪt] s vue f; (of firearm) mire f; (of telescope, camera, etc.) viseur m; chose f digne d'être vue; a sight of (coll) énormément de; at sight à vue; à livre ouvert; by sight de vue; in sight of à la vue de; sad sight spectacle m navrant; sights curiosités fpl; to catch sight of apercevoir; what a sight you are! comme vous voilà fait! ‖ tr & intr viser
sight' draft' s (com) effet m à vue
sight'-read' v (pret & pp -read [ˌrɛd]) tr & intr lire à livre ouvert; (mus) déchiffrer
sight' read'er s déchiffreur m
sight'see'ing s tourisme m; to go sightseeing visiter les curiosités
sightseer ['saɪtˌsi·ər] s touriste mf, excursionniste mf
sign [saɪn] s signe m; (on a store) enseigne f ‖ tr signer; to sign up engager, embaucher ‖ intr signer; to sign off (rad) terminer l'émission; to sign up for (coll) s'inscrire à
sig·nal ['saɪnəl] adj signalé, insigne ‖ s signal m ‖ v (pret & pp -naled or -nalled; ger -naling or -nalling) tr faire signe à, signaler ‖ intr faire des signaux
sig'nal tow'er s tour f de signalisation
signature ['saɪnətʃər] s signature f; (mus) armature f; (rad) indicatif m
sign'board' s panneau m d'affichage

signer ['saɪnər] s signataire mf
sig'net ring' ['saɪgnɪt] s chevalière f
significance [sɪg'nɪfɪkəns] s importance f; (meaning) signification f
significant [sɪg'nɪfəkənt] adj important; significatif
signi·fy ['saɪgnɪˌfaɪ] v (pret & pp -fied) tr signifier
sign'post' s poteau m indicateur
silence ['saɪləns] s silence m ‖ tr faire taire, réduire au silence
silent ['saɪlənt] adj silencieux
si'lent mov'ie s film m muet
silhouette [ˌsɪlu'ɛt] s silhouette f ‖ tr silhouetter
silicon ['sɪlɪkən] s silicium m
silicone ['sɪlɪˌkon] s silicone f
silk [sɪlk] s soie f
silk'-cotton tree' s fromager m
silken ['sɪlkən] adj soyeux
silk' hat' s haut-de-forme m
silk'-stock'ing adj aristocratique ‖ s aristocrate mf
silk'worm' s ver m à soie
silk·y ['sɪlki] adj (comp -ier; super -iest) soyeux
sill [sɪl] s (of window) rebord m; (of door) seuil m; (of walls) sablière f
sil·ly ['sɪli] adj (comp -lier; super -liest) sot, niais
si·lo ['saɪlo] s (pl -los) silo m ‖ tr ensiler
silt [sɪlt] s vase f
silver ['sɪlvər] s argent m ‖ tr argenter; (a mirror) étamer
sil'ver·fish' s (ent) poisson m d'argent
sil'ver foil' s feuille f d'argent
sil'ver lin'ing s beau côté m, côté brillant
sil'ver plate' s argenterie f
sil'ver screen' s écran m
sil'ver·smith' s orfèvre m
sil'ver spoon' s—born with a silver spoon in one's mouth né coiffé
sil'ver-tongued' adj à la langue dorée, éloquent
sil'ver·ware' s argenterie f
similar ['sɪmɪlər] adj semblable
similari·ty [ˌsɪmɪ'lærɪti] s (pl -ties) ressemblance f, similitude f
simile ['sɪmɪli] s comparaison f
simmer ['sɪmər] tr mijoter ‖ intr mijoter; to simmer down s'apaiser
Simon ['saɪmən] s Simon m; Simon says . . . (game) Caporal a dit . . .
simper ['sɪmpər] s sourire m niais ‖ intr sourire bêtement
simple ['sɪmpəl] adj & s simple m
sim'ple-mind'ed adj simple, naïf; niais
simpleton ['sɪmpəltən] s niais m
simpli·fy ['sɪmplɪˌfaɪ] v (pret & pp -fied) tr simplifier
simulate ['sɪmjəˌlet] tr simuler
simultaneous [ˌsaɪməl'tenɪ·əs], [ˌsɪməl'tenɪ·əs] adj simultané
sin [sɪn] s péché m ‖ v (pret & pp sinned; ger sinning) intr pécher
since [sɪns] adv & prep depuis ‖ conj depuis que; (inasmuch as) puisque
sincere [sɪn'sɪr] adj sincère
sincerity [sɪn'sɛrɪti] s sincérité f
sine [saɪn] s (trig) sinus m

sinecure ['saɪnɪ͵kjʊr], ['sɪnɪ͵kjʊr] *s* sinécure *f*
sinew ['sɪnju] *s* tendon *m*; (fig) nerf *m*, force *f*
sinful ['sɪnfəl] *adj* (*person*) pécheur; (*act, intention*) coupable
sing [sɪŋ] *v* (*pret* **sang** [sæŋ] or **sung** [sʌŋ]; *pp* **sung**) *tr & intr* chanter
singe [sɪndʒ] *v* (*ger* **singeing**) *tr* roussir; (*poultry*) flamber
singer ['sɪŋər] *s* chanteur *m*
single ['sɪŋgəl] *adj* seul, unique; (*unmarried*) célibataire; (*e.g., room in a hotel*) à un lit; (*bed*) à une place; (*e.g., devotion*) simple, honnête ‖ *tr* —**to single out** distinguer, choisir
sin'gle bless'edness ['blɛsɪdnɪs] *s* le bonheur *m* du célibat
sin'gle·breast'ed *adj* droit
sin'gle-en'try *adj* (bk) en partie simple
sin'gle-en'try book'keeping *s* comptabilité *f* simple
sin'gle file' *s*—**in single file** en file indienne, à la file
sin'gle-hand'ed *adj* sans aide, tout seul
sin'gle life' *s* vie *f* de célibataire
sin'gle room' *s* chambre *f* à un lit
sin'gle-track' *adj* (rr) à voie unique; (coll) d'une portée limitée
sing'song' *adj* monotone ‖ *s* mélopée *f*
singular ['sɪŋgjələr] *adj & s* singulier *m*
sinister ['sɪnɪstər] *adj* sinistre
sink [sɪŋk] *s* évier *m*; (*drain*) égout *m* ‖ *v* (*pret* **sank** [sæŋk] or **sunk** [sʌŋk]; *pp* **sunk**) *tr* enfoncer; (*a ship*) couler, faire sombrer; (*a well*) creuser; (*money*) immobiliser ‖ *intr* s'enfoncer, s'affaisser; (*under the water*) couler, sombrer; (*said of heart*) se serrer; (*said of health, prices, sun, etc.*) baisser; **to sink into** plonger dans; (*an armchair*) s'effondrer dans
sink'ing fund' *s* caisse *f* d'amortissement
sinless ['sɪnlɪs] *adj* sans péché
sinner ['sɪnər] *s* pécheur *m*
sintering ['sɪntərɪŋ] *s* (metallurgy) frittage *m*
sinuous ['sɪnju·əs] *adj* sinueux
sinus ['saɪnəs] *s* sinus *m*
sip [sɪp] *s* petite gorgée *f*, petit coup *m* ‖ *v* (*pret & pp* **sipped**; *ger* **sipping**) *tr* boire à petit coups, siroter
siphon ['saɪfən] *s* siphon *m* ‖ *tr* siphonner
si'phon bot'tle *s* siphon *m*
sir [sʌr] *s* monsieur *m*; (*British title*) Sir *m*; **Dear Sir** Monsieur
sire [saɪr] *s* sire *m*; (*of a quadruped*) père *m* ‖ *tr* engendrer
siren ['saɪrən] *s* sirène *f*
sirloin ['sʌrlɔɪn] *s* aloyau *m*
sirup ['sɪrəp], ['sʌrəp] *s* sirop *m*
sis·sy ['sɪsi] *s* (*pl* **-sies**) efféminé *m*; fillette *f*; (*cowardly fellow*) poule *f* mouillée
sister ['sɪstər] *adj* (fig) jumeau ‖ *s* sœur *f*
sis'ter-in-law' *s* (*pl* **sisters-in-law**) belle-sœur *f*
sit [sɪt] *v* (*pret & pp* **sat** [sæt]; *ger* **sitting**) *intr* s'asseoir; être assis; (*said of hen on eggs*) couver; (*for a portrait*) poser; (*said of legislature, court, etc.*) siéger; **to sit down** s'asseoir; **to sit still** ne pas bouger; (*to sit up* se redresser; se tenir droit; **to sit up and beg** (*said of dog*) faire le beau
sit'-down strike' *s* grève *f* sur le tas
site [saɪt] *s* site *m*
sitting ['sɪtɪŋ] *s* séance *f*
sit'ting duck' *s* (coll) cible *f* facile
sit'ting room' *s* salon *m*
situate ['sɪtʃu͵et] *tr* situer
situation [͵sɪtʃu'eʃən] *s* situation *f*; poste *m*, emploi *m*
sitz' bath' [sɪts] *s* bain *m* de siège
six [sɪks] *adj & pron* six ‖ *s* six *m*; **at sixes and sevens** de travers, en désaccord; **six o'clock** six heures
sixteen ['sɪks'tin] *adj, pron, & s* seize *m*
sixteenth ['sɪks'tinθ] *adj & pron* seizième (*masc, fem*); **the Sixteenth** seize, e.g., **John the Sixteenth** Jean seize ‖ *s* seizième *m*; **the sixteenth** (*in dates*) le seize
sixth [sɪksθ] *adj & pron* sixième (*masc, fem*); **the Sixth** six, e.g., **John the Sixth** Jean six ‖ *s* sixième *m*; **the sixth** (*in dates*) le six
sixtieth ['sɪkstɪ·ɪθ] *adj & pron* soixantième (*masc, fem*) ‖ *s* soixantième *m*
six·ty ['sɪksti] *adj & pron* soixante; **about sixty** une soixantaine de ‖ *s* (*pl* **-ties**) soixante *m*; (*age of*) soixantaine *f*
sizable ['saɪzəbəl] *adj* assez grand, considérable
size [saɪz] *s* grandeur *f*; dimensions *fpl*; (*of a person or garment*) taille *f*; (*of a shoe, glove, or hat*) pointure *f*; (*of a shirt collar*) encolure *f*; (*of a book or box*) format *m*; (*to fill a porous surface*) apprêt *m*; **what size hat do you wear?** du combien coiffez-vous?; **what size shoes do you wear?** du combien chaussez-vous? ‖ *tr* classer; (*wood to be painted*) coller; **to size up** juger
sizzle ['sɪzəl] *s* grésillement *m* ‖ *intr* grésiller
skate [sket] *s* patin *m*; (ichth) raie *f*; **good skate** (slang) brave homme *m* ‖ *intr* patiner; **to go skating** faire du patin
skat'ing rink' *s* patinoire *f*
skein [sken] *s* écheveau *m*
skeleton ['skɛlɪtən] *s* squelette *m*
skel'eton key' *s* crochet *m*
skeptic ['skɛptɪk] *adj & s* sceptique *mf*
skeptical ['skɛptɪkəl] *adj* sceptique
skepticism ['skɛptɪ͵sɪzəm] *s* scepticisme *m*
sketch [skɛtʃ] *s* esquisse *f*; (*pen or pencil drawing*) croquis *m*, esquisse; (lit) aperçu *m*; (theat) sketch *m* ‖ *tr* esquisser ‖ *intr* croquer
sketch'book' *s* album *m* de croquis
skew [skju] *adj & s* biais *m* ‖ *intr* biaiser
skewer ['skju·ər] *s* brochette *f* ‖ *tr* embrocher
ski [ski] *s* ski *m* ‖ *intr* skier; **to go skiing** faire du ski

ski′ boots′ *spl* chaussures *fpl* de ski
skid [skɪd] *s* (*sidewise*) dérapage *m*; (*forward*) patinage *m*; (*of wheel*) sabot *m*, patin *m* ‖ *v* (*pret & pp* **skidded;** *ger* **skidding**) *tr* enrayer, bloquer ‖ *intr* (*sidewise*) déraper; (*forward*) patiner
skid′ row′ [ro] *s* quartier *m* mal famé
skier [′ski·ər] *s* skieur *m*
skiff [skɪf] *s* skiff *m*, esquif *m*
skiing [′ski·ɪŋ] *s* ski *m*
ski′ jack′et *s* anorak *m*
ski′ jump′ *s* (*place to jump*) tremplin *m*; (*act of jumping*) saut *m* en skis
ski′ lift′ *s* remonte-pente *m*, téléski *m*
skill [skɪl] *s* habilité *f*, adresse *f*; (*job*) métier *m*
skilled *adj* habile, adroit
skillet [′skɪlɪt] *s* casserole *f*; (*frying pan*) poêle *f*
skillful [′skɪlfəl] *adj* habile, expert
skim [skɪm] *v* (*pret & pp* **skimmed;** *ger* **skimming**) *tr* (*milk*) écrémer; (*molten metal*) écumer; (*to graze*) raser ‖ *intr* —to skim over passer légèrement sur
ski′ mask′ *s* passe-montagne *m*
skimmer [′skɪmər] *s* écumoire *f*; (*straw hat*) canotier *m*
skim′ milk′ *s* lait *m* écrémé
skimp [skɪmp] *tr* bâcler ‖ *intr* lésiner; **to skimp on** lésiner sur
skimp·y [′skɪmpi] *adj* (*comp* -**ier;** *super* -**iest**) maigre; (*garment*) étriqué; avare, mesquin
skin [skɪn] *s* peau *f*; **by the skin of one's teeth** de justesse, par un cheveu; **soaked to the skin** trempé jusqu'aux os; **to strip to the skin** se mettre à poil ‖ *v* (*pret & pp* **skinned;** *ger* **skinning**) *tr* écorcher, dépouiller; (*e.g., an elbow*) s'écorcher; **to skin alive** (coll) écorcher vif
skin′-deep′ *adj* superficiel; (*beauty*) à fleur de peau
skin′ div′er *s* plongeur *m* autonome
skin′flint′ *s* grippe-sou *m*
skin′ game′ *s* (slang) escroquerie *f*
skin′ graft′ing *s* greffe *f* cutanée, autoplastie *f*
skin·ny [′skɪni] *adj* (*comp* -**nier;** *super* -**niest**) maigre, décharné
skip [skɪp] *s* saut *m* ‖ *v* (*pret & pp* **skipped;** *ger* **skipping**) *tr* sauter; **skip it!** ça suffit!, laisse tomber!; **to skip rope** sauter à la corde ‖ *intr* sauter; **to skip out** or **off** filer
ski′ pole′ *s* bâton *m* de skis
skipper [′skɪpər] *s* patron *m* ‖ *tr* commander, conduire
skirmish [′skʌrmɪʃ] *s* escarmouche *f* ‖ *intr* escarmoucher
skirt [skʌrt] *s* jupe *f*; (*woman*) (slang) jupe ‖ *tr* côtoyer, longer; éviter
ski′ run′ *s* descente *f* en skis
ski′ stick′ *s* bâton *m* de skis
skit [skɪt] *s* sketch *m*
skittish [′skɪtɪʃ] *adj* capricieux; timide; (*e.g., horse*) ombrageux
skulduggery [skʌl′dʌgəri] *s* (coll) fourberie *f*, ruse *f*, cuisine *f*
skull [skʌl] *s* crâne *m*

skull′ and cross′bones *s* tibias *mpl* croisés et tête *f* de mort
skull′cap′ *s* calotte *f*
skunk [skʌŋk] *s* mouffette *f*; (*person*) (coll) salaud *m*
sky [skaɪ] *s* (*pl* **skies**) ciel *m*; **to praise to the skies** porter aux nues
sky′div′er *s* parachutiste *mf*
sky′div′ing *s* parachutisme *m*, saut *m* en chute libre
sky′lark′ *s* (*Alauda arvensis*) alouette *f*, alouette des champs ‖ *intr* (coll) batifoler
sky′light′ *s* lucarne *f*
sky′line′ *s* ligne *m* d'horizon; (*of city*) profil *m*
sky′rock′et *s* fusée *f* volante ‖ *intr* monter en flèche
sky′scrap′er *s* gratte-ciel *m*
slab [slæb] *s* (*of stone*) dalle *f*; (*slice*) tranche *f*
slack [slæk] *adj* lâche, mou; négligent ‖ *s* mou *m*; (*slowdown*) ralentissement *m*; **slacks** pantalon *m* ‖ *tr* relâcher; (*lime*) éteindre; **to slack off** larguer ‖ *intr*—**to slack off** or **up** se relâcher
slacken [′slækən] *tr* relâcher; (*to slow down*) ralentir ‖ *intr* se relâcher; se ralentir
slacker [′slækər] *s* flemmard *m*; (mil) tire-au-flanc *m*, embusqué *m*
slack′ hours′ *spl* heures *fpl* creuses
slag [slæg] *s* scorie *f*
slake [slek] *tr* apaiser, étancher; (*lime*) éteindre
slalom [′slɑləm] *s* slalom *m*
slam [slæm] *s* claquement *m*; (cards) chelem *m*; (coll) critique *f* sévère ‖ *v* (*pret & pp* **slammed;** *ger* **slamming**) *tr* claquer; (coll) éreinter; **to slam down** on flanquer sur ‖ *intr* claquer
slander [′slændər] *s* calomnie *f* ‖ *tr* calomnier
slanderous [′slændərəs] *adj* calomnieux
slang [slæŋ] *s* argot *m*
slant [slænt] *s* pente *f*; (*bias*) point *m* de vue ‖ *tr* mettre en pente, incliner; donner un biais spécial à ‖ *intr* être en pente, s'incliner
slap [slæp] *s* tape *f*, claque *f*; (*in the face*) soufflet *m*, gifle *f* ‖ *v* (*pret & pp* **slapped;** *ger* **slapping**) *tr* taper, gifler
slap′dash′ *adj*—**in a slapdash manner** à la va-comme-je-te-pousse ‖ *adv* à la six-quatre-deux
slap′stick′ *adj* bouffon ‖ *s* bouffonnerie *f*
slash [slæʃ] *s* entaille *f* ‖ *tr* taillader; (*e.g., prices*) réduire beaucoup
slat [slæt] *s* latte *f*
slate [slet] *s* ardoise *f*; (*of candidates*) liste *f* ‖ *tr* couvrir d'ardoises; inscrire sur la liste, désigner
slate′ pen′cil *s* crayon *m* d'ardoise
slate′ roof′ *s* toit *m* d'ardoises
slattern [′slætərn] *s* (*slovenly woman*) marie-salope *f*; (*slut*) voyoute *f*, gueuse *f*
slaughter [′slɔtər] *s* boucherie *f* ‖ *tr* abattre; massacrer

slaught′er·house′ *s* abattoir *m*
Slav [slɑv], [slæv] *adj* slave ‖ *s* (*language*) slave *m*; (*person*) Slave *mf*
slave [slev] *adj* & *s* esclave *mf* ‖ *intr* besogner, trimer
slave′ driv′er *s* (hist, fig) négrier *m*
slavery [′slevəri] *s* esclavage *m*; (*institution of keeping slaves*) esclavagisme *m*
slave′ ship′ *s* négrier *m*
slave′ trade′ *s* traite *f* des noirs
Slavic [′slɑvɪk], [′slævɪk] *adj* & *s* slave *m*
slavish [′slevɪʃ] *adj* servile
slay [sle] *v* (*pret* **slew** [slu]; *pp* **slain** [slen]) *tr* tuer, massacrer
slayer [′sle·ər] *s* meurtrier *m*
sled [slɛd] *s* luge *f* ‖ *v* (*pret* & *pp* **sledded**; *ger* **sledding**) *intr* faire de la luge, luger
sledge′ ham′mer [slɛdʒ] *s* massette *f*, masse *f*
sleek [slik] *adj* lisse, luisant ‖ *tr* lisser
sleep [slip] *s* sommeil *m*; **to go to sleep** s'endormir; **to put to sleep** endormir ‖ *v* (*pret* & *pp* **slept** [slɛpt]) *tr*—**to sleep it over, to sleep on it** prendre conseil de son oreiller; **to sleep off** (*a hangover, headache, etc.*) faire passer en dormant ‖ *intr* dormir; (*e.g., with a woman*) coucher; **to sleep late** faire la grasse matinée; **to sleep like a log** dormir comme un loir
sleeper [′slipər] *s* dormeur *m*; (*girder*) poutre *f* horizontale; (*tie*) (rr) traverse *f*
sleep′ing bag′ *s* sac *m* de couchage
sleep′ing car′ *s* wagon-lit *m*
sleep′ing pill′ *s* somnifère *m*
sleepless [′sliplɪs] *adj* sans sommeil
sleep′less night′ *s* nuit *f* blanche
sleep′walk′er *s* somnambule *mf*
sleep·y [′slipi] *adj* (*comp* -ier; *super* -iest) endormi, somnolent; **to be sleepy** avoir sommeil
sleep′y·head′ *s* endormi *m*, grand dormeur *m*
sleet [slit] *s* grésil *m* ‖ *intr* grésiller
sleeve [sliv] *s* manche *f*; (mach) manchon *m*, douille *f*; **to laugh in** or **up one's sleeve** rire sous cape
sleigh [sle] *s* traîneau *m* ‖ *intr* aller en traîneau
sleigh′ bell′ *s* grelot *m*
sleigh′ ride′ *s* promenade *f* en traîneau
sleight′ of hand′ [slaɪt] *s* prestidigitation *f*, tours *mpl* de passe-passe
slender [′slɛndər] *adj* svelte, mince, élancé; (*resources*) maigre
sleuth [sluθ] *s* limier *m*, détective *m*
slew [slu] *s* (coll) tas *m*, floppée *f*
slice [slaɪs] *s* tranche *f* ‖ *tr* trancher
slick [slɪk] *adj* lisse; (*appearance*) élégant; (coll) rusé ‖ *s* tache *f*, e.g., **oil slick** tache d'huile ‖ *tr* lisser; **to slick up** (coll) mettre en ordre
slicker [′slɪkər] *s* ciré *m*, imper *m*; (coll) enjôleur
slide [slaɪd] *s* (*sliding*) glissade *f*, glissement *m*; (*sliding place*) glissoire *m*; (*of microscope*) plaque *f*; (*of trombone*) coulisse *f*; (*on a slide rule*)

curseur *m*; (*piece that slides*) glissière *f*; (*phot*) diapositive *f* ‖ *v* (*pret* & *pp* **slid** [slɪd]) *tr* glisser ‖ *intr* glisser; **to let slide** ne faire aucun cas de, laisser aller
slide′ fas′tener *s* fermeture *f* éclair
slide′ rule′ *s* règle *f* à calcul
slide′ valve′ *s* soupape *f* à tiroir
slid′ing con′tact *s* curseur *m*
slid′ing door′ *s* porte *f* à coulisse
slid′ing scale′ *s* échelle *f* mobile
slight [slaɪt] *adj* léger; (*slender; insignificant*) mince; (*e.g., effort*) faible ‖ *s* affront *m* ‖ *tr* faire peu de cas de, dédaigner; (*a person*) méconnaître
slim [slɪm] *adj* (*comp* **slimmer**; *super* **slimmest**) mince, svelte; (*chance, excuse*) mauvais; (*resources*) maigre
slime [slaɪm] *s* limon *m*, vase *f*; (*of snakes, fish, etc.*) bave *f*
slim·y [′slaɪmi] *adj* (*comp* -ier; *super* -iest) limoneux, vaseux
sling [slɪŋ] *s* (*to shoot stones*) fronde *f*; (*to hold up a broken arm*) écharpe *f*; (*shoulder strap*) bretelle *f*, bandoulière *f* ‖ *v* (*pret* & *pp* **slung** [slʌŋ]) *tr* lancer; passer en bandoulière
sling′shot′ *s* fronde *f*
slink [slɪŋk] *v* (*pret* & *pp* **slunk** [slʌŋk]) *intr*—**to slink away** s'esquiver
slip [slɪp] *s* glissade *f*, glissement *m*; bout *m* de papier; (*for indexing, filing, etc.*) fiche *f*; (*cutting from plant*) bouture *f*; (*piece of underclothing*) combinaison *f*; (*blunder*) faux pas *m*, bévue *f*; (naut) cale *f*; **to give the slip to** échapper à ‖ *v* (*pret* & *pp* **slipped**; *ger* **slipping**) *tr* glisser; **to slip off** (*a garment*) enlever, ôter; **to slip on** (*a garment, shoes, etc.*) enfiler; **to slip one's mind** sortir de l'esprit, échapper à qn ‖ *intr* glisser; (*to blunder*) faire un faux pas; **to let slip** laisser échapper; **to slip away** or **off** s'échapper, se dérober; **to slip by** s'échapper; (*said of time*) s'écouler; **to slip up** se tromper
slip′cov′er *s* housse *f*
slipper [′slɪpər] *s* pantoufle *f*
slippery [′slɪpəri] *adj* glissant; (*deceitful*) rusé
slip′-up′ *s* (coll) erreur *f*, bévue *f*
slit [slɪt] *s* fente *f*, fissure *f* ‖ *v* (*pret* & *pp* **slit**; *ger* **slitting**) *tr* fendre; (*e.g., pages*) couper; **to slit the throat of** égorger
slob [slɑb] *s* (slang) rustaud *m*
slobber [′slɑbər] *s* bave *f*; (fig) sentimentalité *f* ‖ *intr* baver
sloe [slo] *s* (*shrub*) prunellier *m*; (*fruit*) prunelle *f*
slogan [′slogən] *s* mot *m* d'ordre, devise *f*; (com) slogan *m*
sloop [slup] *s* sloop *m*
slop [slɑp] *s* lavure *f*, rinçure *f* ‖ *v* (*pret* & *pp* **slopped**; *ger* **slopping**) *tr* répandre ‖ *intr* se répandre; **to slop over** déborder
slope [slop] *s* pente *f*; (*of a roof*) inclinaison *f*; (*of a region, mountain,*

etc.) versant *m* ‖ *tr* pencher, incliner ‖ *intr* se pencher, s'incliner

slop·py ['slɑpi] *adj* (*comp* **-pier**; *super* **-piest**) mouillé; (*dress*) négligé, mal ajusté; (*work*) bâclé

slot [slɑt] *s* entaille *f*, rainure *f*; (*e.g., in a coin telephone*) fente *f*

sloth [sloθ], [slɔθ] *s* paresse *f*; (zool) paresseux *m*

slot' machine' *s* (*for gambling*) appareil *m* à sous; (*for vending*) distributeur *m* automatique

slouch [slautʃ] *s* démarche *f* lourde; (*person*) lourdaud *m* ‖ *intr* ne pas se tenir droit; (*e.g., in a chair*) se vautrer; **to slouch along** traîner le pas

slouch' hat' *s* chapeau *m* mou

slough [slau] *s* bourbier *m* ‖ [slʌf] *s* (*of snake*) dépouille *f*; (pathol) escarre *f* ‖ *tr*—**to slough off** se débarrasser de ‖ *intr* muer, se dépouiller

Slovak ['slovæk], [slo'væk] *adj* slovaque ‖ *s* (*language*) slovaque *m*; (*person*) Slovaque *mf*

sloven·ly ['slʌvənli] *adj* (*comp* **-lier**; *super* **-liest**) négligé, malpropre

slow [slo] *adj* lent; (*sluggish*) traînard; (*clock, watch*) en retard; (*in understanding*) lourdaud ‖ *adv* lentement ‖ *tr & intr* ralentir; **SLOW** (public sign) ralentir; **to slow down** ralentir

slow'down' *s* grève *f* perlée

slow' mo'tion *s* ralenti *m*; **in slow motion** au ralenti, en ralenti

slow'poke' *s* (coll) lambin *m*, traînard *m*

slug [slʌg] *s* (*used as coin*) jeton *m*; (*of linotype*) ligne-bloc *f*; (zool) limace *f*; (*blow*) (coll) bon coup *m*; (*drink*) (coll) gorgée *f* ‖ *v* (*pret & pp* **slugged**; *ger* **slugging**) *tr* (coll) flanquer un coup à

sluggard ['slʌgərd] *s* paresseux *m*

sluggish ['slʌgiʃ] *adj* traînard

sluice [slus] *s* canal *m*; (*floodgate*) écluse *f*; (*dam; flume*) bief *m*

sluice' gate' *s* vanne *f*

slum [slʌm] *s* bas quartiers *mpl* ‖ *v* (*pret & pp* **slummed**; *ger* **slumming**) *intr*—**to go slumming** aller visiter les taudis

slumber ['slʌmbər] *s* sommeil *m*, assoupissement *m* ‖ *intr* sommeiller

slum' dwell'ing *s* taudis *m*

slump [slʌmp] *s* affaissement *m*; (com) crise *f*, baisse *f* ‖ *intr* s'affaisser; (*said of prices, stocks, etc.*) dégringoler, s'effondrer

slur [slʌr] *s* (*in pronunciation*) mauvaise articulation *f*; (*insult*) affront *m*; (mus) liaison *f*; **to cast a slur on** porter atteinte à ‖ *v* (*pret & pp* **slurred**; *ger* **slurring**) *tr* (*a sound, a syllable*) mal articuler; (*a person*) déprécier; (mus) lier; **to slur over** glisser sur

slush [slʌʃ] *s* fange *f*, boue *f* liquide; (*gush*) sensiblerie *f*

slut [slʌt] *s* chienne *f*; (*slovenly woman*) marie-salope *f*

sly [slai] *adj* (*comp* **slyer** or **slier**; *super* **slyest** or **sliest**) rusé, sournois; (*mischievous*) espiègle, futé; **on the sly** furtivement, en cachette

smack [smæk] *s* claquement *m*; (*with the hand*) gifle *f*, claque *f*; (*trace, touch*) soupçon *m*; (*kiss*) (coll) gros baiser *m* ‖ *adv* en plein ‖ *tr* claquer ‖ *intr*—**to smack of** sentir; avoir un goût de

small [smɔl] *adj* petit §91; (*income*) modique; (*short in stature*) court; (*petty*) mesquin; (typ) minuscule

small' arms' *spl* armes *fpl* portatives

small' beer' *s* petite bière *f*; (slang) petite bière

small' busi'ness *s* petite industrie *f*

small' cap'ital *s* (typ) petite capitale *f*

small' change' *s* petite monnaie *f*, menue monnaie

small' fry' *s* menu fretin *m*

small' intes'tine *s* intestin *m* grêle

small'-mind'ed *adj* mesquin, étriqué, étroit

small' of the back' *s* chute *f* des reins, bas *m* du dos

smallpox ['smɔl,pɑks] *s* variole *f*

small' print' *s* petits caractères *mpl*

small' talk' *s* ragots *mpl*, papotage *m*

small'-time' *adj* de troisième ordre, insignifiant, petit

small'-town' *adj* provincial

smart [smɑrt] *adj* intelligent, éveillé; (*pace*) vif; (*person, clothes*) élégant, chic; (*pain*) cuisant; (*saucy*) impertinent ‖ *s* douleur *f* cuisante ‖ *intr* brûler, cuire; (*said of person with hurt feelings*) être cinglé

smart' al'eck [,ælik] *s* (coll) fat *m*, présomptueux *m*

smart' set' *s* monde *m* élégant, gens *mpl* chic

smash [smæʃ] *s* fracassement *m*, fracas *m*; (coll) succès *m* ‖ *tr* fracasser ‖ *intr* se fracasser; **to smash into** emboutir, écraser

smash' hit' *s* (coll) succès *m*, (coll) pièce *f* à succès

smash'-up' *s* collision *f*; débâcle *f*, culbute *f*

smattering ['smætəriŋ] *s* légère connaissance *f*, teinture *f*

smear [smir] *s* tache *f*; (*vilification*) calomnie *f*; (med) frottis *m* ‖ *tr* tacher; calomnier; (*to coat*) enduire

smear' campaign' *s* campagne *f* de calomnies

smell [smel] *s* odeur *f*; (*aroma*) parfum *m*, senteur *f*; (*sense*) odorat *m* ‖ *v* (*pret & pp* **smelled** or **smelt** [smelt]) *tr & intr* sentir; **to smell of** sentir

smell'ing salts' *spl* sels *mpl* volatils

smell·y ['smeli] *adj* (*comp* **-ier**; *super* **-iest**) malodorant, puant

smelt [smelt] *s* (*fish*) éperlan *m* ‖ *tr & intr* fondre

smile [smail] *s* sourire *m* ‖ *intr* sourire; **to smile at** sourire à

smirk [smʌrk] *s* minauderie *f* ‖ *intr* minauder

smite [smait] *v* (*pret* **smote** [smot]; *pp* **smitten** ['smitən] or **smit** [smit]) *tr* frapper; **to smite down** abattre

smith [smıθ] *s* forgeron *m*
smith·y ['smıθi] *s* (*pl* -ies) forge *f*
smitten ['smıtən] *adj* frappé, affligé;
(coll) épris, amoureux
smock [smɑk] *s* blouse *f*; (*of artists*)
sarrau *m*; (*buttoned in back*) tablier
m
smock' frock' *s* sarrau *m*
smog [smɑg] *s* (coll) brouillard *m*
fumeux
smoke [smok] *s* fumée *f*; (coll) cigarette *f*; to go up in smoke s'en aller
en fumée || *tr & intr* fumer
smoked' glass'es *spl* verres *mpl* fumés
smoke'-filled room' *s* tabagie *f*
smoke'less pow'der ['smoklıs] *s* poudre *f* sans fumée
smoker ['smokər] *s* fumeur *m*; (*room*)
fumoir *m*; (*meeting*) réunion *f* de
fumeurs; (rr) compartiment *m* pour
fumeurs
smoke' rings' *spl* ronds *mpl* de fumée
smoke' screen' *s* rideau *m* de fumée
smoke'stack' *s* cheminée *f*
smoking ['smokıŋ] *s* le fumer *m*; no
smoking (public sign) défense de
fumer
smok'ing car' *s* voiture *f* de fumeurs
smok'ing jack'et *s* veston *m* d'intérieur
smok'ing room' *s* fumoir *m*
smok·y ['smoki] *adj* (*comp* -ier; *super*
-iest) fumeux, enfumé
smolder ['smoldər] *s* fumée *f* épaisse;
feu *m* qui couve || *intr* brûler sans
flamme; (*said of fire, anger, rebellion, etc.*) couver
smooch [smutʃ] *intr* (coll) se bécoter
smooth [smuð] *adj* uni, lisse; (*gentle,
mellow*) doux, moelleux; (*operation*)
doux, régulier; (*style*) facile || *tr* unir,
lisser; to smooth away (*e.g., obstacles*) aplanir, enlever; to smooth
down (*to calm*) apaiser, calmer; to
smooth out défroisser
smooth'-faced' *adj* imberbe
smooth-shaven ['smuð'ʃevən] *adj* rasé
de près
smooth·y ['smuði] *s* (*pl* -ies) (coll)
chattemite *f*, flagorneur *m*
smother ['smʌðər] *tr* suffoquer, étouffer; (culin) recouvrir
smudge [smʌdʒ] *s* tache *f*; (*smoke*)
fumée *f* épaisse || *tr* tacher; (agr)
fumiger
smudge' pot' *s* fumigène *m*
smug [smʌg] *adj* (*comp* smugger; *super*
smuggest) fat, suffisant
smuggle ['smʌgəl] *tr* introduire en con-
trebande, faire la contrebande de ||
intr faire la contrebande
smuggler ['smʌglər] *s* contrebandier *m*
smuggling ['smʌglıŋ] *s* contrebande *f*
smut [smʌt] *s* tache *f* de suie; (*obscenity*) ordure *f*; (agr) nielle *f*
smut·ty ['smʌti] *adj* (*comp* -tier; *super*
-tiest) taché de suie, noirci; (*obscene*)
ordurier; (agr) niellé
snack [snæk] *s* casse-croûte *m*; to
have a snack casser la croûte
snack' bar' *s* snack-bar *m*, snack *m*
snag [snæg] *s* (*of tree; of tooth*) chicot
m; to hit a snag se heurter à un obs-

tacle || *v* (*pret & pp* snagged; *ger*
snagging) *tr* (*a stocking*) faire un accroc à
snail [snel] *s* escargot *m*; at a snail's
pace à pas de tortue, comme un escargot
snake [snek] *s* serpent *m* || *intr* ser-
penter
snake' in the grass' *s* serpent *m* caché
sous les fleurs; ami *m* perfide, traître
m, individu *m* louche
snap [snæp] *s* (*breaking*) cassure *f*;
(*crackling sound*) bruit *m* sec; (*of the
fingers*) chiquenaude *f*; (*bite*) coup *m*
de dents; (*cookie*) biscuit *m* cro-
quant; (*catch or fastener*) bouton-
pression *m*, fermoir *m*; (phot) instantané *m*; (slang) jeu *m* d'enfant,
coup facile; cold snap coup *m* de
froid; it's a snap! (slang) c'est du
tout cuit! || *v* (*pret & pp* snapped; *ger*
snapping) *tr* casser net; (*one's fingers, a whip, etc.*) faire claquer; (*a
picture, a scene*) prendre un instan-
tané de; to snap up happer, saisir ||
intr casser net; faire un bruit sec;
(*from fatigue*) s'effondrer; to snap
at donner un coup de dents à; (*to
speak sharply to*) rembarrer; (*an opportunity*) saisir; to snap out of it
(slang) se secouer; to snap shut se
fermer avec un bruit sec
snap' course' *s* (slang) cours *m* tout
mâché
snap'drag'on *s* (bot) gueule-de-loup *f*
snap' fas'tener *s* bouton-pression *m*
snap' judg'ment *s* décision *f* prise sans
réflexion
snap·py ['snæpi] *adj* (*comp* -pier;
super -piest) mordant, acariâtre;
(*quick, sudden*) vif; make it snappy!
(slang) grouillez-vous!
snap'shot' *s* instantané *m*
snare [snɛr] *s* collet *m*; (*trap*) piège *m*;
(*of a drum*) timbre *m*, corde *f* de tim-
bre || *tr* prendre au collet, prendre au
piège
snare' drum' *s* caisse *f* claire
snarl [snɑrl] *s* (*sound*) grognement *m*;
(*intertwining*) enchevêtrement *m* || *tr*
dire en grognant; enchevêtrer || *intr*
grogner; s'enchevêtrer
snatch [snætʃ] *s* arrachement *m*; petit
moment *m*; (*bit, scrap*) bribe *f*, fragment *m*; (*in weight lifting*) arraché *m*
|| *tr* saisir brusquement, arracher; to
snatch from arracher à; to snatch up
ramasser vivement || *intr*—to snatch
at saisir au vol
sneak [snik] *adj* furtif || *s* chipeur *m*,
mauvais type *m* || *tr* (*e.g., a drink*)
prendre à la dérobée; glisser furtive-
ment; (coll) chiper || *intr* se glisser
furtivement; to sneak into se faufiler
dans; to sneak out s'esquiver
sneaker ['snikər] *s* espadrille *f*
sneak' thief' *s* chipeur *m*, voleur *m* à
la tire
sneak·y ['sniki] *adj* (*comp* -ier; *super*
-iest) furtif, sournois
sneer [snır] *s* ricanement *m* || *intr*
ricaner; to sneer at se moquer de

sneeze [sniz] *s* éternuement *m* || *intr* éternuer; **it's not to be sneezed at** (coll) il ne faut pas cracher dessus

snicker ['snɪkər] *s* rire *m* bête; (*sneer*) rire narquois; (*in response to smut*) petit rire grivois || *intr* rire bêtement; **to snicker at** se moquer de

sniff [snɪf] *s* reniflement *m*; (*odor*) parfum *m*; (*e.g.*, *of air*) bouffée *f* || *tr* renifler; (*e.g.*, *fresh air*) humer; (*e.g.*, *a scandal*) flairer; **to sniff up** renifler || *intr* renifler; **to sniff at** flairer; (*to disdain*) cracher sur

sniffle ['snɪfəl] *s* reniflement *m*; **to have the sniffles** être enchifrené || *intr* renifler

snip [snɪp] *s* (*e.g.*, *of cloth*) petit bout *m*; (*cut*) coup *m* de ciseaux; (coll) personne *f* insignifiante || *v* (*pret & pp* snipped; *ger* snipping) *tr* couper; **to snip off** enlever, détacher

snipe [snaɪp] *s* (orn) bécassine *f* || *intr* —**to snipe at** canarder

sniper ['snaɪpər] *s* tireur *m* embusqué

snippet ['snɪpɪt] *s* petit bout *m*, bribe *f*; personne *f* insignifiante

snip•py ['snɪpi] *adj* (*comp* -pier; *super* -piest) hautain, brusque

snitch [snɪtʃ] *tr* (coll) chaparder || *intr* (coll) moucharder; **to snitch on** (coll) moucharder

sniv•el ['snɪvəl] *s* pleurnicherie *f*; (*mucus*) morve *f* || *v* (*pret & pp* -eled or -elled; *ger* -eling or -elling) *intr* pleurnicher; (*to have a runny nose*) être morveux

snob [snɑb] *s* snob *m*

snobbery ['snɑbəri] *s* snobisme *m*

snobbish ['snɑbɪʃ] *adj* snob

snoop [snup] *s* (coll) curieux *m* || *intr* (coll) fouiner, fureter

snoop•y ['snupi] *adj* (*comp* -ier; *super* -iest) (coll) curieux

snoot [snut] *s* (slang) nez *m*

snoot•y ['snuti] *adj* (*comp* -ier; *super* -iest) (slang) snob, hautain

snooze [snuz] *s* (coll) petit somme *m* || *intr* (coll) sommeiller

snore [snor] *s* ronflement *m* || *intr* ronfler

snort [snɔrt] *s* ébrouement *m*; (*of person, horse, etc.*) reniflement *m* || *tr* dire en reniflant, grogner || *intr* s'ébrouer, renifler bruyamment

snot [snɑt] *s* (slang) morve *f*

snot•ty ['snɑti] *adj* (*comp* -tier; *super* -tiest) (coll) morveux; (slang) snob, hautain

snout [snaut] *s* museau *m*; (*of pig*) groin *m*; (*of bull*) mufle *m*; (*something shaped like the snout of an animal*) bec *m*, tuyère *f*

snow [sno] *s* neige *f* || *intr* neiger; **it is snowing** il neige; **to shovel snow** balayer la neige

snow'ball' *s* boule *f* de neige || *tr* lancer des boules de neige à || *intr* faire boule de neige

snow' blind'ness *s* cécité *f* des neiges

snow'-capped' *adj* couronné de neige

snow'-clad' *adj* enneigé

snow'drift' *s* congère *f*

snow'fall' *s* chute *f* de neige; (*amount*) enneigement *m*

snow'flake' *s* flocon *m* de neige

snow' flur'ry *s* (*pl* -ries) bouffée *f* de neige

snow' line' *s* limite *f* des neiges éternelles

snow'man' *s* (*pl* -men') bonhomme *m* de neige

snow'plow' *s* chasse-neige *m*

snow'shoe' *s* raquette *f*

snow'slide' *s* avalanche *f*

snow'storm' *s* tempête *f* de neige

snow' tire' *s* pneu *m* à neige

snow'white' *adj* blanc comme la neige || **Snowwhite** *s* Blanche-Neige *f*

snow•y ['sno·i] *adj* (*comp* -ier; *super* -iest) neigeux

snow'y owl' *s* chouette *f* blanche

snub [snʌb] *s* affront *m*, rebuffade *f* || *v* (*pret & pp* snubbed; *ger* snubbing) *tr* traiter avec froideur, rabrouer

snub•by ['snʌbi] *adj* (*comp* -bier; *super* -biest) trapu; (*nose*) camus

snub'-nosed' *adj* camard

snuff [snʌf] *s* tabac *m* à priser; (*of a candlewick*) mouchure *f*; **to be up to snuff** (*to be shrewd*) (slang) être dessalé; (*to be up to par*) (slang) être dégourdi || *tr* priser; (*a candle*) moucher; **to snuff out** éteindre

snuff'box' *s* tabatière *f*

snuffers ['snʌfərz] *spl* mouchettes *fpl*

snug [snʌg] *adj* (*comp* snugger; *super* snuggest) confortable; (*garment*) bien ajusté; (*bed*) douillet; (*sheltered*) abrité; (*hidden*) caché; **snug and warm** bien au chaud; **snug as a bug in a rug** comme un poisson dans l'eau

snuggle ['snʌgəl] *tr* serrer dans ses bras || *intr* se pelotonner; **to snuggle up to** se serrer tout près de

so [so] *adv* si, tellement; ainsi; donc; par conséquent, aussi; **or so** plus ou moins; **so as to** afin de, pour; **so far** jusqu'ici; **so long!** (coll) à bientôt!; **so many** tant; tant de; **so much** tant; tant de; **so that** pour que, afin que; de sorte que; **so to speak** pour ainsi dire; **so what?** (slang) et alors?; **to hope so** espérer bien; **to think so** croire que oui || *conj* (coll) de sorte que

soak [sok] *s* trempage *m*; (slang) sac *m* à vin, soûlard *m* || *tr* tremper; (*to swindle*) (slang) estamper; **to soak the skin** tremper jusqu'aux os || *intr* tremper

so'-and-so' *s* (*pl* -sos) (pej) triste individu *m*, mauvais sujet *m*; **Mr. So-and-so** Monsieur un tel

soap [sop] *s* savon *m* || *tr* savonner

soap'box' *s* caisse *f* à savon; (fig) plateforme *f*

soap'box or'ator *s* orateur *m* de carrefour

soap' bub'ble *s* bulle *f* de savon

soap' dish' *s* plateau *m* à savon

soap' fac'to·ry *s* (*pl* -ries) savonnerie *f*

soap' flakes' *spl* savon *m* en paillettes

soap' op'era *s* mélo *m*

soap' pow'der *s* savon *m* en poudre

soap'stone' *s* pierre *f* de savon; craie *f* de tailleur

soap'suds' *spl* mousse *f* de savon, eau *f* de savon

soap·y ['sopi] *adj* (*comp* **-ier**; *super* **-iest**) savonneux

soar [sor] *intr* planer dans les airs; prendre l'essor, monter subitement

sob [sɑb] *s* sanglot *m* ‖ *v* (*pret & pp* **sobbed**; *ger* **sobbing**) *intr* sangloter

sober ['sobər] *adj* sobre; (*expression*) grave; (*truth*) simple; (*not drunk*) pas ivre; (*no longer drunk*) dégrisé ‖ *tr* calmer; **to sober up** dégriser ‖ *intr*— **to sober up** se dégriser

sobriety [so'braɪ·əti] *s* sobriété *f*

sob' sis'ter *s* (slang) journaliste *f* larmoyante

sob' sto'ry *s* (*pl* **-ries**) (slang) lamentation *f*, jérémiade *f*

so'-called' *adj* dit; soi-disant, prétendu; ainsi nommé

soccer ['sɑkər] *s* football *m*

sociable ['soʃəbəl] *adj* sociable

social ['soʃəl] *adj* social ‖ *s* réunion *f* sans cérémonie

so'cial climb'er *s* parvenu *m*, arriviste *mf*

so'cial events' *spl* mondanités *fpl*

socialism ['soʃə‚lɪzəm] *s* socialisme *m*

socialist ['soʃəlɪst] *s* socialiste *mf*

socialite ['soʃə‚laɪt] *s* (coll) membre *m* de la haute société

so'cial reg'ister *s* annuaire *m* de la haute société

so'cial secu'rity *s* sécurité *f* sociale, assistance *f* familiale

so'cial serv'ice *s* assistance *f* sociale, aide *f* sociale, aide familiale

so'cial stra'ta [‚streta], [‚strætə] *spl* couches *fpl* sociales

so'cial work'er *s* assistant *m* social, travailleuse *f* familiale

socie·ty [sə'saɪ·əti] *s* (*pl* **-ties**) société *f*

soci'ety col'umn *s* carnet *m* mondain

soci'ety ed'itor *s* chroniqueur *m* mondain

sociology [‚sosɪ'alədʒi], [‚soʃɪ'alədʒi] *s* sociologie *f*

sock [sɑk] *s* chaussette *f*; (slang) coup *m* de poing ‖ *tr* (slang) donner un coup de poing à

socket ['sɑkɪt] *s* (*of bone*) cavité *f*, glène *f*; (*of candlestick*) tube *m*; (*of caster*) sabot *m*; (*of eye*) orbite *f*; (*of tooth*) alvéole *m*; (elec) douille *f*

sock'et joint' *s* joint *m* à rotule

sock'et wrench' *s* clé *f* à tube

sod [sɑd] *s* gazon *m*; motte *f* de gazon ‖ *v* (*pret & pp* **sodded**; *ger* **sodding**) *tr* gazonner

soda ['sodə] *s* (*soda water*) soda *m*; (chem) soude *f*

so'da crack'er *s* biscuit *m* soda

so'da wa'ter *s* soda *m*

sodium ['sodɪ·əm] *s* sodium *m*

sofa ['sofə] *s* canapé *m*, sofa *m*

soft [sɔft], [sɑft] *adj* (*yielding*) mou; (*mild*) doux; (*weak in character*) faible; **to go soft** (coll) perdre la boule

soft'-boiled egg' *s* œuf *m* à la coque

soft' coal' *s* houille *f* grasse

soft' drink' *s* boisson *f* non-alcoolisée

soften ['sɔfən], ['sɑfən] *tr* amollir; (*e.g., noise*) atténuer; (*one's voice*) adoucir; (*one's moral fiber*) affaiblir; **to soften up** amollir ‖ *intr* s'amollir; s'adoucir; s'affaiblir

soft' land'ing *s* (rok) arrivée *f* en douceur

soft' ped'al *s* (mus) pédale *f* sourde

soft'-ped'al *v* (*pret & pp* **-aled** or **-alled**; *ger* **-aling** or **-alling**) *tr* (coll) atténuer, modérer

soft' soap' *s* savon *m* mou, savon noir; (coll) pommade *f*

soft'-soap' *tr* (coll) passer de la pommade à

sog·gy ['sagi] *adj* (*comp* **-gier**; *super* **-giest**) saturé, détrempé

soil [sɔɪl] *s* sol *m*, terroir *m* ‖ *tr* salir, souiller ‖ *intr* se salir

soil' pipe' *s* tuyau *m* de descente

sojourn ['sodʒʌrn] *s* séjour *m* ‖ ['so-dʒʌrn], [so'dʒʌrn] *intr* séjourner

solace ['salɪs] *s* consolation *f* ‖ *tr* consoler

solar ['solər] *adj* solaire

so'lar bat'tery *s* photopile *f*

sold [sold] *adj*—**sold out** (*no more room*) complet; (*no more merchandise*) épuisé; **to be sold on** (coll) raffoler de ‖ *interj* (*to the highest bidder*) adjugé!

solder ['sadər] *s* soudure *f* ‖ *tr* souder

sol'dering i'ron *s* fer *m* à souder

soldier ['soldʒər] *s* soldat *m*

sole [sol] *adj* seul, unique ‖ *s* (*of shoe*) semelle *f*; (*of foot*) plante *f*; (*fish*) sole *f* ‖ *tr* ressemeler

solemn ['saləm] *adj* sérieux, grave; (*ceremony*) solennel

solicit [sə'lɪsɪt] *tr* solliciter ‖ *intr* quêter; (*with immoral intentions*) racoler

solicitor [sə'lɪsɪtər] *s* solliciteur *m*; agent *m*, représentant *m*; (com) démarcheur *m*; (law) procureur *m*; (Brit) avoué *m*

solicitous [sə'lɪsɪtəs] *adj* soucieux

solid ['salɪd] *adj* solide; (*clouds*) dense; (*gold*) massif; (*opinion*) unanime; (*color*) uni; (*hour, day, week*) entier; (*e.g., three days*) d'affilée ‖ *s* solide *m*

sol'id geom'etry *s* géométrie *f* dans l'espace

solidity [sə'lɪdɪti] *s* solidité *f*, consistance *f*

solilo·quy [sə'lɪləkwi] *s* (*pl* **-quies**) soliloque *m*

solitaire ['salɪ‚ter] *s* solitaire *m*; (cards) patience *f*, réussite *f*; **to play solitaire** faire une réussite

solitar·y ['salɪ‚teri] *adj* solitaire ‖ *s* (*pl* **-ies**) solitaire *m*

solitude ['salɪ‚t(j)ud] *s* solitude *f*

so·lo ['solo] *adj* solo ‖ *s* (*pl* **-los**) solo *m*

soloist ['solo·ɪst] *s* soliste *mf*

solstice ['salstɪs] *s* solstice *m*

soluble ['saljəbəl] *adj* soluble

solution [sə'luʃən] s solution f
solvable ['salvəbəl] adj soluble
solve [salv] tr résoudre
solvency ['salvənsi] s solvabilité f
solvent ['salvənt] adj (substance) solubilisant; (person or business) solvable || s (of a substance) solvant m
somber ['sambər] adj sombre
some [sʌm] adj indef quelque, du; **some way or other** d'une manière ou d'une autre || pron indef certains, quelques-uns §81; en §87 || adv un peu, passablement, assez; environ; quelque, e.g., **some two hundred soldiers** quelque deux cents soldats
some'bod'y pron indef quelqu'un §81; **somebody else** quelqu'un d'autre || s (pl -ies) (coll) quelqu'un m
some'day' adv un jour
some'how' adv dans un sens, je ne sais comment; **somehow or other** d'une manière ou d'une autre
some'one' pron indef quelqu'un §81
somersault ['sʌmər,sɔlt] s saut m périlleux
some'thing s (coll) quelque chose m || pron indef quelque chose (masc) || adv quelque peu, un peu
some'time' adj ancien, ci-devant || adv un jour; un de ces jours
some'times' adv quelquefois, de temps en temps; **sometimes . . . sometimes** tantôt . . . tantôt
some'way' adv d'une manière ou d'une autre
some'what' adv un peu, assez
some'where' adv quelque part; **somewhere else** ailleurs, autre part
somnambulist [sam'næmbjəlɪst] s somnambule mf
somnolent ['samnələnt] adj somnolent
son [sʌn] s fils m
sonata [sə'natə] s sonate f
song [sɔŋ], [saŋ] s chanson f; (of praise) hymne m; **to buy for a song** (coll) acheter pour une bouchée de pain
song'bird' s oiseau m chanteur
song' book' s recueil m de chansons
Song' of Songs' s (Bib) Cantique m des Cantiques
song' thrush' s grive f musicienne
song'writ'er s chansonnier m
sonic ['sanɪk] adj sonique
son'ic boom' s double bang m
son'-in-law' s (pl sons-in-law) gendre m, beau fils m
sonnet ['sanɪt] s sonnet m
son-ny ['sʌni] s (pl -nies) fiston m
soon [sun] adv bientôt; (early) tôt; **as soon as** aussitôt que, dès que, sitôt que; **as soon as possible** le plus tôt possible; **how soon** quand; **no sooner said than done** sitôt dit sitôt fait; **soon after** tôt après; **sooner** plus tôt; (rather) (coll) plutôt; **sooner or later** tôt ou tard; **so soon** si tôt; **too soon** trop tôt
soot [sʊt], [sut] s suie f || tr—**to soot up** encrasser de suie || intr s'encrasser
soothe [suð] tr calmer, apaiser; flatter

soothsayer ['suθ,se·ər] s devin m
soot·y ['sʊti], ['suti] adj (comp -ier; super -iest) (color; flame) fuligineux; couvert de suie
sop [sap] s morceaux m trempé; (fig) os m à ronger, cadeau m || v (pret & pp sopped; ger sopping) tr tremper, faire tremper; **to sop up** absorber
sophisticated [sə'fɪstɪ,ketɪd] adj mondain, sceptique; complexe
sophistication [sə,fɪstɪ'keʃən] s mondanité f
sophomore ['safə,mor] s étudiant m de deuxième année
sophomoric [,safə'mɔrɪk] adj naïf, suffisant, présomptueux
sopping ['sapɪŋ] adj détrempé, trempé || adv—**sopping wet** trempé comme une soupe
sopran·o [sə'præno], [sə'prano] adj de soprano || s (pl -os) soprano f; (boy) soprano m
sorcerer ['sɔrsərər] s sorcier m
sorceress ['sɔrsərɪs] s sorcière f
sorcer·y ['sɔrsəri] s (pl -ies) sorcellerie f
sordid ['sɔrdɪd] adj sordide
sore [sor] adj douloureux, enflammé; (coll) fâché || s plaie f, ulcère m
sore'head' s (coll) rouspéteur m, grincheux m
sorely ['sorli] adv gravement, grièvement; cruellement
soreness ['sornɪs] s douleur f, sensibilité f
sore' throat' s—**to have a sore throat** avoir mal à la gorge
sorori·ty [sə'rarɪti], [sə'rɔrɪti] s (pl -ties) club m d'étudiantes universitaires
sorrow ['saro], ['sɔro] s chagrin m, peine f, affliction f, tristesse f || intr s'affliger, avoir du chagrin; être en deuil; **to sorrow for** s'affliger de
sorrowful ['sarəfəl], ['sɔrəfəl] adj (person) affligé, attristé; (news) affligeant
sor·ry ['sari], ['sɔri] adj (comp -rier; super -riest) désolé, navré, fâché; (appearance) piteux, misérable; (situation) triste; **to be or feel sorry** regretter; **to be or feel sorry for** regretter; **to be sorry** to + inf regretter de + inf || interj pardon!
sort [sɔrt] s sorte f, espèce f, genre m; **a sort of** une espèce de; **out of sorts** de mauvaise humeur || tr classer; **to sort out** trier
so'-so' adj (coll) assez bon, passable, supportable || adv assez bien, comme ci comme ça
sot [sat] s ivrogne mf
soul [sol] s âme f; **not a soul** (coll) pas un chat; **upon my soul!** par ma foi!
sound [saund] adj sain; solide, en bon état; (sleep) profond || s son m; (probe) sonde f; (geog) goulet m, détroit m, bras m de mer || adv (asleep) profondément || tr sonner; (to take a sounding of) sonder; **to sound out** sonder; **to sound the horn** klaxonner, corner || intr sonner; son-

der; **to sound off** parler haut; **to sound strange** sembler bizarre
sound′ bar′rier *s* mur *m* du son
sound′ film′ *s* film *m* sonore
sound′ hole′ *s* (*of a violin*) ouïe *f*
soundly ['saʊndli] *adj* sainement; profondément; (*hard*) bien
sound′ post′ *s* (*of a violin*) âme *f*
sound′proof′ *adj* insonorisé, insonore ‖ *tr* insonoriser
sound′ track′ *s* piste *f* sonore
sound′ wave′ *s* onde *f* sonore
soup [sup] *s* potage *m*, bouillon *m*; (*with vegetables*) soupe *f*; **in the soup** (coll) dans le pétrin or la mélasse
soup′ kitch′en *s* soupe *f* populaire
soup′ spoon′ *s* cuiller *f* à soupe
soup′ tureen′ *s* soupière *f*
sour [saʊr] *adj* aigre; (*grapes*) vert; (*apples*) sur; (*milk*) tourné ‖ *tr* rendre aigre ‖ *intr* tourner, s'aigrir
source [sors] *s* source *f*
source′ lan′guage *s* langue *f* source
source′ mate′rial *s* sources *fpl* originales
sour′ cher′ry *s* (*pl* -ries) griotte *f*; (*tree*) griottier *m*
sour′ grapes′ *interj* ils sont trop verts!
sour′puss′ *s* (slang) grincheux *m*
south [saʊθ] *adj* & *s* sud *m*; **the South** (*of France, Italy, etc.*) le Midi; (*of U.S.A.*) le Sud ‖ *adv* au sud, vers le sud
South′ Af′rica *s* la République sud-africaine
South′ Amer′ica *s* Amérique *f* du Sud; l'Amérique du Sud
South′ Amer′ican *adj* sud-américain ‖ *s* (*person*) Sud-Américain *m*
south′east′ *adj* & *s* sud-est *m*
southern ['sʌðərn] *adj* du sud, méridional
southerner ['sʌðərnər] *s* Méridional *m*; (U.S.A.) sudiste *mf*
South′ Kore′a *s* Corée *f* du Sud; la Corée du Sud
South′ Kore′an *adj* sud-coréen ‖ *s* (*person*) Sud-Coréen *m*
south′paw′ *adj* & *s* (coll) gaucher *m*
South′ Pole′ *s* pôle *m* Sud
South′ Vietnam·ese′ [vɪˌɛtnə'miz] *adj* sud-vietnamien ‖ *s* (*pl* -ese) Sud-Vietnamien *m*
southward ['saʊθwərd] *adv* vers le sud
south′west′ *adj* & *s* sud-ouest *m*
souvenir [ˌsuvə'nɪr] *s* souvenir *m*
sovereign ['savrɪn], ['sʌvrɪn] *adj* souverain ‖ *s* (*king; coin*) souverain *m*; (*queen*) souveraine *f*
sovereign·ty ['savrɪnti], ['sʌvrɪnti] *s* (*pl* -ties) souveraineté *f*
soviet ['sovɪˌɛt], [ˌsovɪ'ɛt] *adj* soviétique ‖ *s* soviet *m*; **Soviet** (*person*) Soviétique *mf*
So′viet Rus′sia *s* la Russie *f* soviétique
So′viet Un′ion *s* Union *f* soviétique
sow [saʊ] *s* truie *f* ‖ [so] *v* (*pret* sowed; *pp* sown or sowed) *tr* (*seed*; *a field*) semer; (*a field*) ensemencer
soybean ['sɔɪˌbin] *s* soya *m*, soja *m*
spa [spɑ] *s* ville *f* d'eau, station *f* thermale, bains *mpl*

space [spes] *s* espace *m*; (typ) espace *f* ‖ *tr* espacer
space′ age′ *s* âge *m* de l'exploration spatiale
space′ bar′ *s* barre *f* d'espacement
space′craft′ *s* astronef *m*
space′ flight′ *s* voyage *m* spatial, vol *m* spatial
space′ heat′er *s* chaufferette *f*
space′ hel′met *s* casque *m* de cosmonaute
space′man′ or **space′man** *s* (*pl* -men′ or -men) homme *m* de l'espace, astronaute *m*, cosmonaute *m*
space′ probe′ *s* coup *m* de sonde dans l'espace; (*rocket*) fusée *f* sonde
spacer ['spesər] *s* (*of typewriter*) barre *f* d'espacement
space′ship′ *s* vaisseau *m* spatial, astronef *m*
space′ sta′tion *s* station *f* orbitale
space′ suit′ *s* (rok) scaphandre *m* des cosmonautes
space′ walk′ *s* promenade *f* dans l'espace
spacious ['speʃəs] *adj* spacieux
spade [sped] *s* bêche *f*; (cards) pique *m*; **to call a spade a spade** (coll) appeler un chat un chat
spade′work′ *s* gros travail *m*, défrichnage *m*
spaghetti [spə'gɛti] *s* spaghetti *mpl*
Spain [spen] *s* Espagne *f*; l'Espagne
span [spæn] *s* portée *f*; (*of time*) durée *f*; (*of hand*) empan *m*; (*of wing*) envergure *f*; (*of bridge*) travée *f* ‖ *v* (*pret* & *pp* spanned; *ger* spanning) *tr* couvrir, traverser
spangle ['spæŋgəl] *s* paillette *f* ‖ *tr* orner de paillettes
Spaniard ['spænjərd] *s* Espagnol *m*
spaniel ['spænjəl] *s* épagneul *m*
Spanish ['spænɪʃ] *adj* espagnol ‖ *s* (*language*) espagnol *m*; **the Spanish** (*persons*) les Espagnols *mpl*
Span′ish-Amer′ican *adj* hispano-américain ‖ *s* Hispano-Américain *m*
Span′ish broom′ *s* genêt *m* d'Espagne
Span′ish fly′ *s* cantharide *f*
Span′ish Main′ *s* Terre *f* ferme; mer *f* des Antilles
Span′ish moss′ *s* tillandsie *f*
spank [spæŋk] *tr* fesser
spanking ['spæŋkɪŋ] *adj* (Brit) de premier ordre; **at a spanking pace** à toute vitesse ‖ *s* fessée *f*
spar [spar] *s* (mineral) spath *m*; (naut) espar *m* ‖ *v* (*pret* & *pp* sparred; *ger* sparring) *intr* s'entraîner à la boxe; se battre
spare [spɛr] *adj* (*thin*) maigre; (*available*) disponible; (*interchangeable*) de rechange; (*left over*) en surnombre ‖ *tr* (*to save*) épargner, économiser; (*one's efforts*) ménager; (*a person*) faire grâce à, traiter avec indulgence; (*time, money, etc.*) disposer de; (*something*) se passer de
spare′ parts′ *spl* pièces *fpl* détachées, pièces de rechange
spare′rib′ *s* côte *f* découverte de porc, plat *m* de côtes

spare' room' s chambre f d'ami
spare' tire' s pneu m de rechange
spare' wheel' s roue f de secours
sparing ['spɛrɪŋ] adj économe, frugal
spark [spɑrk] s étincelle f
spark' coil' s bobine f d'allumage
spark' gap' s (of induction coil) éclateur m; (of spark plug) entrefer m
sparkle ['spɑrkəl] s étincellement m, éclat m ‖ intr étinceler
sparkling ['spɑrklɪŋ] adj étincelant; (wine) mousseux; (soft drink) gazeux
spark' plug' s bougie f
sparrow ['spæro] s moineau m
spar'row hawk' s épervier m
sparse [spɑrs] adj clairsemé, rare; peu nombreux
Spartan ['spɑrtən] adj spartiate ‖ s Spartiate mf
spasm ['spæzəm] s spasme m
spasmodic [spæz'mɑdɪk] adj intermittent, irrégulier; (pathol) spasmodique
spastic ['spæstɪk] adj spasmodique
spat [spæt] s (coll) dispute f, prise f de bec; spats demi-guêtres fpl ‖ v (pret & pp spatted; ger spatting) intr se disputer
spatial ['speʃəl] adj spatial, de l'espace
spatter ['spætər] s éclaboussure f ‖ tr éclabousser
spatula ['spætʃələ] s spatule f
spawn [spɔn] s frai m ‖ tr engendrer ‖ intr frayer
spay [spe] tr châtrer
speak [spik] v (pret spoke [spok]; pp spoken) tr (a word, one's mind, the truth) dire; (a language) parler ‖ intr parler; so to speak pour ainsi dire; speaking! à l'appareil!; to speak out or up parler plus haut, élever la voix; (fig) parler franc
speak'-eas'y s (pl -ies) bar m clandestin
speaker ['spikər] s parleur m; (person addressing a group) conférencier m; (presiding officer) speaker m, président m; (rad) haut-parleur m
spear [spɪr] s lance f ‖ tr percer d'un coup de lance
spear'head' s fer m de lance; (mil) pointe f, avancée f ‖ tr (e.g., a campaign) diriger
spear'mint' s menthe f verte
special ['spɛʃəl] adj spécial, particulier ‖ s train m spécial
spe'cial-deliv'ery let'ter s lettre f exprès
specialist ['spɛʃəlɪst] s spécialiste mf
specialize ['spɛʃə,laɪz] tr spécialiser ‖ intr se spécialiser
special·ty ['spɛʃəlti] s (pl -ties) spécialité f
specie ['spisi] s—in specie en espèces
spe·cies ['spisiz] s (pl -cies) espèce f
specific [spɪ'sɪfɪk] adj & s spécifique m
specif'ic grav'ity s poids m spécifique
speci·fy ['spɛsɪ,faɪ] v (pret & pp -fied) tr spécifier
specimen ['spɛsɪmən] s spécimen m; (coll) drôle m de type
specious ['spiʃəs] adj spécieux
speck [spɛk] s (on fruit, face, etc.) tache f; (in the distance) point m;

(small quantity) brin m, grain m, atome m ‖ tr tacheter
speckle ['spɛkəl] s petite tache f ‖ tr tacheter, moucheter
spectacle ['spɛktəkəl] s spectacle m; spectacles lunettes fpl
spec'tacle case' s étui m à lunettes
spectator ['spɛktetər], [spɛk'tetər] s spectateur m
specter ['spɛktər] s spectre m
spec·trum ['spɛktrəm] s (pl -tra [trə] or -trums) spectre m
speculate ['spɛkjə,let] intr spéculer
speculator ['spɛkjə,letər] s spéculateur m, boursicotier m
speech [spitʃ] s discours m; (language) langage m; (of a people or region) parler m; (power of speech) parole f; (theat) tirade f; to make a speech prononcer un discours
speech' clin'ic s centre m de rééducation de la parole
speech' correc'tion s rééducation f de la parole
speechless ['spitʃlɪs] adj sans parole, muet; (fig) sidéré, stupéfié
speed [spid] s vitesse f; at full speed à toute vitesse ‖ v (pret & pp speeded or sped [spɛd]) tr dépêcher, hâter ‖ intr se dépêcher; to speed up aller plus vite
speeding ['spidɪŋ] s excès m de vitesse
speed' king' s as m du volant
speed' lim'it s vitesse f maximum
speedometer [spi'dɑmɪtər] s indicateur m de vitesse
speed' rec'ord s record m de vitesse
speed'-up' s accélération f
speed'way' s (racetrack) piste f d'autos; (highway) autoroute f
speed·y ['spidi] adj (comp -ier; super -iest) rapide, vite, prompt
speed' zone' s zone f de vitesse surveillée
spell [spɛl] s sortilège m; intervalle m; (attack) accès m ‖ v (pret & pp spelled or spelt [spɛlt]) tr (orally) épeler; (in writing) orthographier, écrire; to spell out (coll) expliquer en détail ‖ v (pret & pp spelled) tr (to relieve) remplacer, relever, relayer
spell'bind'er s orateur m fascinant, orateur entraînant
spell'bound' adj fasciné
spelling ['spɛlɪŋ] s orthographe f
spell'ing bee' s concours m d'orthographe
spelunker [spɪ'lʌŋkər] s spéléo m
spend [spɛnd] v (pret & pp spent [spɛnt]) tr dépenser; (a period of time) passer
spender ['spɛndər] s dépensier m
spend'ing mon'ey s argent m de poche pour les menues dépenses
spend'thrift' s prodigue mf, grand dépensier m
sperm [spɑrm] s sperme m
sperm' whale' s cachalot m
spew [spju] tr & intr vomir
sphere [sfɪr] s sphère f; corps m céleste
spherical ['sfɛrɪkəl] adj sphérique

sphinx [sfɪŋks] *s* (*pl* **sphinxes** or **sphinges** ['sfɪndʒiz]) sphinx *m*
spice [spaɪs] *s* épice *f*; (fig) sel *m*, piquant *m* ‖ *tr* épicer
spick-and-span ['spɪkənd'spæn] *adj* brillant comme un sou neuf; tiré à quatre épingles
spic·y ['spaɪsi] *adj* (*comp* **-ier**; *super* **-iest**) épicé, aromatique; (*e.g.*, *gravy*) relevé; (*conversation*, *story*, *etc.*) épicé, salé, piquant, grivois
spider ['spaɪdər] *s* araignée *f*
spi'der·web' *s* toile *f* d'araignée
spiff·y ['spɪfi] *adj* (*comp* **-ier**; *super* **-iest**) (slang) épatant, élégant
spigot ['spɪgət] *s* robinet *m*
spike [spaɪk] *s* pointe *f*; (*nail*) clou *m* à large tête; (bot) épi *m*; (rr) crampon *m* ‖ *tr* clouer; ruiner, supprimer; (*a drink*) (coll) corser à l'alcool ‖ *intr* (bot) former des épis
spill [spɪl] *s* chute *f*, culbute *f* ‖ *v* (*pret* & *pp* **spilled** or **spilt** [spɪlt]) *tr* renverser; (*a liquid*) répandre; (*a rider*) désarçonner; (*passengers*) verser ‖ *intr* se répandre, s'écouler
spill'way' *s* déversoir *m*
spin [spɪn] *s* tournoiement *m*, rotation *f*; (*on a ball*) effet *m*; (aer) vrille *f*; **to go for a spin** (coll) se balader en voiture; **to go into a spin** (aer) descendre en vrille ‖ *v* (*pret* & *pp* **spun** [spʌn]; *ger* **spinning**) *tr* filer; faire tournoyer ‖ *intr* filer; tournoyer
spinach ['spɪnɪtʃ], ['spɪnɪdʒ] *s* épinard *m*; (*leaves used as food*) des épinards
spinal ['spaɪnəl] *adj* spinal
spi'nal col'umn *s* colonne *f* vertébrale
spi'nal cord' *s* moelle *f* épinière
spindle ['spɪndəl] *s* fuseau *m*
spin'-dri'er *s* essoreuse *f*
spin'-dry' *v* (*pret* & *pp* **-dried**) *tr* essorer
spine [spaɪn] *s* épine *f* dorsale, échine *f*; (*quill*, *fin*) épine; (*ridge*) arête *f*; (*of book*) dos *m*; (fig) courage *m*
spineless ['spaɪnlɪs] *adj* sans épines; (*weak*) mou; **to be spineless** (fig) avoir l'échine souple
spinet ['spɪnɪt] *s* épinette *f*
spinner ['spɪnər] *s* fileur *m*; machine *f* à filer
spinning ['spɪnɪŋ] *adj* tournoyant ‖ *s* (*act*) filage *m*; (*art*) filature *f*
spin'ning wheel' *s* rouet *m*
spinster ['spɪnstər] *s* célibataire *f*, vieille fille *f*
spiraea [spaɪ'ri·ə] *s* spirée *f*
spi·ral ['spaɪrəl] *adj* spiral, en spirale ‖ *s* spirale *f* ‖ *v* (*pret* & *pp* **-raled** or **-ralled**; *ger* **-raling** or **-ralling**) *intr* tourner en spirale; (aer) vriller
spi'ral stair'case *s* escalier *m* en colimaçon
spire [spaɪr] *s* aiguille *f*; (*of clock tower*) flèche *f*
spirit ['spɪrɪt] *s* esprit *m*; (*enthusiasm*) feu *m*; (*temper*, *genius*) génie *m*; (*ghost*) esprit, revenant *m*; **high spirits** joie *f*, abandon *m*; **spirits** (*alcoholic liquor*) esprit *m*, spiritueux *m*; **to raise the spirits of** remonter le

courage de ‖ *tr*—**to spirit away** enlever, faire disparaître mystérieusement
spirited *adj* animé, vigoureux
spiritless ['spɪrɪtlɪs] *adj* sans force, abattu, déprimé
spir'it lev'el *s* niveau *m* à bulle
spiritual ['spɪrɪtʃu·əl] *adj* spirituel ‖ *s* chant *m* religieux populaire
spiritualism ['spɪrɪtʃu·ə,lɪzəm] *s* spiritisme *m*
spiritualist ['spɪrɪtʃu·əlɪst] *s* spirite *mf*; (philos) spiritualiste *mf*
spir'ituous bev'erages ['spɪrɪtʃu·əs] *spl* boissons *fpl* spiritueuses
spit [spɪt] *s* salive *f*; (culin) broche *f* ‖ *v* (*pret* & *pp* **spat** [spæt] or **spit**; *ger* **spitting**) *tr* & *intr* cracher
spite [spaɪt] *s* dépit *m*, rancune *f*; **in spite of** en dépit de, malgré ‖ *tr* dépiter, contrarier
spiteful ['spaɪtfəl] *adj* rancunier
spit'fire' *s* mégère *f*
spit'ting im'age *s* (coll) portrait *m* craché
spittoon [spɪ'tun] *s* crachoir *m*
splash [splæʃ] *s* éclaboussure *f*; (*of waves*) clapotis *m*; **to make a splash** (coll) faire sensation ‖ *tr* & *intr* éclabousser
splash'down' *s* (rok) amerrissage *m*
spleen [splin] *s* rate *f*; (fig) maussaderie *f*, mauvaise humeur *f*; **to vent one's spleen on** décharger sa bile sur
splendid ['splendɪd] *adj* splendide; (coll) admirable, superbe
splendor ['splendər] *s* splendeur *f*
splice [splaɪs] *s* (*in rope*) épissure *f*; (*in wood*) enture *f* ‖ *tr* (*rope*) épisser; (*wood*) enter; (*film*) réparer, coller; (slang) marier
splint [splɪnt] *s* éclisse *f* ‖ *tr* éclisser
splinter ['splɪntər] *s* éclat *m*, éclisse *f*; (*lodged under the skin*) écharde *f* ‖ *tr* briser en éclats ‖ *intr* voler en éclats
splin'ter group' *s* minorité *f* dissidente, groupe *m* fragmentaire
split [splɪt] *adj* fendu; (*pea*) cassé; (*skirt*) déchiré ‖ *s* fente *f*, fissure *f*; (*quarrel*) rupture *f*; (*one's share*) part *f*; (*bottle*) quart *m*, demi *m*; (gymnastics) grand écart *m* ‖ *v* (*pret* & *pp* **split**; *ger* **splitting**) *tr* fendre; (*money*, *work*, *ticket*) partager; (*in two*) couper; (*a hide*) dédoubler; **to split hairs** couper les cheveux en quatre; **to split one's sides laughing** se tenir les côtes de rire; **to split the difference** couper la poire en deux ‖ *intr* se fendre; **to split away (from)** se séparer (de)
split' fee' *s* (*between doctors*) dichotomie *f*
split' personal'ity *s* personnalité *f* dédoublée
split' tick'et *s* (pol) panachage *m*
splitting ['splɪtɪŋ] *adj* violent; (*headache*) atroce ‖ *s* fendage *m*; (*of the atom*) désintégration *f*; (*of the personality*) dédoublement *m*
splotch [splɑtʃ] *s* tache *f* ‖ *tr* tacher, barbouiller

splurge [splʌrdʒ] s (coll) épate f || intr (coll) se payer une fête; (to show off) (coll) faire de l'épate

splutter ['splʌtər] s crachement m || tr —**to splutter out** bredouiller || intr crachoter; (said of candle, grease, etc.) grésiller

spoil [spɔil] s (object of plunder) prise f, proie f; **spoils** (booty) butin m, dépouilles fpl; (emoluments, especially of public office) assiette f au beurre, part f du gâteau || v (pret & pp **spoiled** or **spoilt** [spɔilt]) tr gâter, abîmer || intr se gâter, s'abîmer; **to be spoiling for** (coll) brûler du désir de

spoilage ['spɔilidʒ] s déchet m

spoiled adj gâté

spoil'sport' s rabat-joie m

spoils' sys'tem s système m des postes aux petits copains

spoke [spok] s rai m, rayon m; (of a ladder) échelon m

spokes'man s (pl -men) porte-parole m

sponge [spʌndʒ] s éponge f || tr éponger; (a meal) (coll) écornifler || intr (coll) écornifler; **to sponge on** (coll) vivre aux crochets de

sponge' cake' s gâteau m de Savoie, gâteau mousseline

sponger ['spʌndʒər] s écornifleur m, pique-assiette mf

sponge' rub'ber s caoutchouc m mousse

spon·gy ['spʌndʒi] adj (comp -gier; super -giest) spongieux

sponsor ['spɑnsər] s patron m; (godfather) parrain m; (godmother) marraine f; (law) garant m; (rad, telv) commanditaire m || tr patronner; (law) se porter garant de; (rad, telv) commanditer

spon'sor·ship' s patronnage m

spontaneous [spɑn'teniˌəs] adj spontané

spoof [spuf] s (slang) mystification f; (slang) parodie f || tr (slang) mystifier; (slang) blaguer || intr (slang) blaguer

spook [spuk] s (coll) revenant m, spectre m

spool [spul] s bobine f

spoon [spun] s cuiller f; **to be born with a silver spoon in one's mouth** (coll) être né coiffé || tr prendre dans une cuiller; **to spoon off** enlever avec la cuiller || intr (coll) se faire des mamours

spooner ['spunər] s (coll) peloteur m

spoonerism ['spunəˌrizəm] s contrepèterie f

spoon'-feed' v (pret & pp -fed) tr nourrir à la cuiller; (an industry) subventionner; (coll) mâcher la besogne à

spoonful ['spunˌful] s cuillerée f

spoon·y ['spuni] adj (comp -ier; super -iest) (coll) peloteur

sporadic(al) [spə'rædik(əl)] adj sporadique

spore [spor] s spore f

sport [sport] adj sportif, de sport || s sport m; amusement m, jeu m; (biol) mutation f; (coll) chic type m; **a good**

sport un bon copain; (a good loser) un beau joueur; **in sport** par plaisanterie; **to make sport of** tourner en ridicule || tr faire parade de, arborer || intr s'amuser, jouer

sport' clothes' spl vêtements mpl de sport

sport'ing goods' spl articles mpl de sport

sports'cast'er s radioreporter m sportif

sports' ed'itor s rédacteur m sportif

sports' fan' s fanatique mf, enragé m des sports

sports'man s (pl -men) sportif m

sports'man·like' adj sportif

sports'man·ship' s sportivité f

sports'wear' s vêtements mpl sport

sports'writ'er s reporter m sportif

sport·y ['sporti] adj (comp -ier; super -iest) (coll) sportif; (smart in dress) (coll) chic; (flashy) (coll) criard, voyant; (coll) dissolu, libertin

spot [spɑt] s tache f; (place) endroit m, lieu m; **on the spot** sur place; (slang) dans le pétrin; **spots** (before eyes) mouches fpl || v (pret & pp **spotted**; ger **spotting**) tr tacher; (coll) repérer, détecter || intr se tacher

spot' cash' s argent m comptant

spot' check' s échantillonnage m

spot'-check' tr échantillonner

spotless ['spɑtlis] adj sans tache

spot'light' s spot m; (aut) projecteur m auxiliaire orientable; **to hold the spotlight** (fig) être en vedette || tr diriger les projecteurs sur; (fig) mettre en vedette

spot' remov'er [rɪ ˌmuvər] s détachant m

spot' weld'ing s soudage m par points

spouse [spauz], [spaus] s (man) époux m, conjoint m; (woman) épouse f, conjointe f

spout [spaut] s tuyau m de décharge; (e.g., of teapot) bec m; (of sprinkling can) col m, queue f; (of water) jet m || tr faire jaillir; (e.g., insults) (coll) déclamer || intr jaillir; **to spout off** (coll) déclamer

sprain [spren] s foulure f, entorse f || tr fouler, se fouler

sprawl [sprɔl] intr s'étaler, se carrer

spray [spre] s (of ocean) embruns mpl; (branch) rameau m; (for insects) liquide m insecticide; (for weeds) produit m herbicide; (for spraying insects or weeds) pulvérisateur m; (for spraying perfume) vaporisateur m || tr pulvériser; (with a vaporizer) vaporiser; (hort) désinfecter par pulvérisation d'insecticide; **to spray paint on** peindre au pistolet || intr— **to spray out** gicler

sprayer ['spreˌər] s vaporisateur m, pulvérisateur m

spray' gun' s pulvérisateur m; (for paint) pistolet m; (hort) seringue f

spread [spred] adj étendu, écarté, ouvert || s étendue f, rayonnement m; (on bed) dessus-de-lit m, couvre-lit m; (on sandwich) pâte f; (buffet lunch) collation f || v (pret & pp spread) *tr* étendre, étaler; (*news*) répandre; (*disease*) propager; (*the wings*) déployer; (*a piece of bread*) tartiner || *intr* s'étendre, s'étaler; se répandre, rayonner

spree [spri] *s* bombance *f*, orgie *f*; to go on a spree (coll) faire la bombe

sprig [sprɪg] *s* brin *m*, brindille *f*

spright·ly ['spraɪtli] *adj* (*comp* -lier; *super* -liest) vif, enjoué

spring [sprɪŋ] *adj* printanier || *s* (*of water*) source *f*; (*season*) printemps *m*; (*jump*) saut *m*, bond *m*; (*elastic device*) ressort *m*; (*quality*) élasticité *f* || *v* (*pret* sprang [spræŋ] *or* sprung [sprʌŋ]; *pp* sprung) *tr* (*the frame of a car*) faire déjeter; (*a lock*) faire jouer; (*a leak*) contracter; (*a question*) proposer à l'improviste; (*a prisoner*) (coll) faire sortir de prison || *intr* sauter, bondir; (*said of oil, water, etc.*) jaillir; to spring up se lever; naître

spring'-and-fall' *adj* (*coat*) de demi-saison

spring'board' *s* tremplin *m*

spring' fe'ver *s* (hum) malaise *m* des premières chaleurs, flemme *f*

spring'like' *adj* printanier

spring'time' *s* printemps *m*

sprinkle ['sprɪŋkəl] *s* pluie *f* fine; (culin) pincée *f* || *tr* (*with water*) asperger, arroser; (*with powder*) saupoudrer; (*to strew*) parsemer || *intr* tomber en pluie fine

sprinkler ['sprɪŋklər] *s* arrosoir *m*

sprinkling ['sprɪŋklɪŋ] *s* aspersion *f*, arrosage *m*; (*with holy water*) aspersion; (*with powder*) saupoudrage *m*; (*of knowledge*) bribes *fpl*, notions *fpl*; (*of persons*) petit nombre *m*

sprin'kling can' *s* arrosoir *m*

sprint [sprɪnt] *s* course *f* de vitesse, sprint *m* || *intr* faire une course de vitesse, courir à toute vitesse

sprite [spraɪt] *s* lutin *m*

sprocket ['sprɑkɪt] *s* dent *f* de pignon; (*wheel*) pignon *m* de chaîne

sprock'et wheel' *s* pignon *m* de chaîne

sprout [spraʊt] *s* pousse *f*, rejeton *m*; (*of seed*) germe *m* || *intr* (*said of plant*) pousser, pointer; (*said of seed*) germer

spruce [sprus] *adj* pimpant, tiré à quatre épingles || *s* sapin *m*; (*Norway spruce*) épicéa *m* commun || *intr* —to spruce up se faire beau, se pomponner

spry [spraɪ] *adj* (*comp* spryer *or* sprier; *super* spryest *or* spriest) vif, alerte

spud [spʌd] *s* (*chisel*) bédane *f*; (agr) arrache-racines *m*; (coll) pomme *f* de terre, patate *f*

spun' glass' [spʌn] *s* coton *m* de verre

spunk [spʌŋk] *s* (coll) cran *m*, courage *m*

spur [spʌr] *s* éperon *m*; (*of rooster*) ergot *m*; (*stimulant*) aiguillon *m*, stimulant *m*; (rr) embranchement *m*; on the spur of the moment sous l'impulsion du moment || *v* (*pret & pp*

spurred; *ger* spurring) *tr* éperonner; to spur on aiguillonner, stimuler

spurious ['spjʊrɪ·əs] *adj* faux; (*sentiments*) simulé, feint; (*document*) apocryphe

spurn [spʌrn] *tr* repousser avec mépris, faire fi de

spurt [spʌrt] *s* jaillissement *m*, giclée *f*, jet *m*; (*of enthusiasm*) élan *m*; effort *m* soudain || *intr* jaillir; to spurt out gicler

sputnik ['spʊtnɪk], ['spʌtnɪk] *s* spoutnik *m*

sputter ['spʌtər] *s* (*manner of speaking*) bredouillement *m*; (*of candle*) grésillement *m*; (*of fire*) crachement *m* || *tr* (*words*) débiter en lançant des postillons || *intr* postillonner; (*said of candle*) grésiller; (*said of fire*) cracher, pétiller

spu·tum ['spjutəm] *s* (*pl* -ta [tə]) crachat *m*

spy [spaɪ] *s* (*pl* spies) espion *m* || *v* (*pret & pp* spied) *tr* (*to catch sight of*) entrevoir; to spy out découvrir par ruse || *intr* espionner; to spy on épier, guetter

spy'glass' *s* longue-vue *f*

spying ['spaɪ·ɪŋ] *s* espionnage *m*

spy' ring' *s* réseau *m* d'espionnage

squabble ['skwɑbəl] *s* chamaillerie *f* || *intr* se chamailler

squad [skwɑd] *s* escouade *f*, peloton *m*; (*of detectives*) brigade *f*

squadron ['skwɑdrən] *s* (aer) escadrille *f*; (mil) escadron *m*; (nav) escadre *f*

squalid ['skwɑlɪd] *adj* sordide

squall [skwɔl] *s* bourrasque *f*, rafale *f*; (*cry*) braillement *m*; (coll) grabuge *m* || *intr* souffler en bourrasque; brailler

squalor ['skwɑlər] *s* saleté *f*; misère *f*

squander ['skwɑndər] *tr* gaspiller

square [skwɛr] *adj* carré; (*honest*) loyal, franc; (*real*) véritable; (*conventional*) (slang) formaliste; nine (ten, etc.) inches square de neuf (dix, etc.) pouces en carré; nine (ten, etc.) square inches neuf (dix, etc.) pouces carrés; to get square with (coll) régler ses comptes avec; we'll call it square (coll) nous sommes quittes || *s* carré *m*; (*of checkerboard or chessboard*) case *f*; (*city block*) pâté *m* de maisons; (*open area in town or city*) place *f*; (*of carpenter*) équerre *f*; to be on the square (coll) jouer franc jeu || *adv* carrément || *tr* carrer; (*a number*) élever au carré; (*wood, marble, etc.*) équarrir; (*a debt*) régler; (bk) balancer || *intr*— to square off (coll) se mettre en posture de combat; to square with (*to tally with*) s'accorder avec; régler ses comptes avec

square' dance' *s* quadrille *m* américain

square' deal' *s* (coll) procédé *m* loyal

square' meal' *s* repas *m* copieux

square' root' *s* racine *f* carrée

squash [skwɑʃ] *s* écrasement *m*; (bot) courge *f*; (sports) squash *m* || *tr* écraser || *intr* s'écraser

squash·y ['skwɑʃi] *adj* (*comp* **-ier;** *super* **-iest)** mou et humide; (*fruit*) à pulpe molle
squat [skwɑt] *adj* accroupi; (*heavyset*) trapu, ramassé ‖ *s* position *f* accroupie ‖ *v* (*pret* & *pp* **squatted;** *ger* **squatting)** *intr* s'accroupir; (*to settle*) s'installer sans titre légal
squatter ['skwɑtər] *s* squatter *m*
squaw [skwɔ] *s* femme *f* peau-rouge
squawk [skwɔk] *s* cri *m* rauque; (slang) protestation *f*, piaillerie *f* ‖ *intr* pousser un cri rauque; (slang) protester, piailler
squeak [skwik] *s* grincement *m*; (*of living being*) couic *m*, petit cri *m* ‖ *intr* grincer; pousser des petits cris, couiner
squeal [skwil] *s* cri *m* aigu ‖ *intr* piailler; (slang) manger le morceau; **to squeal on** (slang) moucharder
squealer ['skwilər] *s* (coll) cafard *m*
squeamish ['skwimɪʃ] *adj* trop scrupuleux; prude; sujet aux nausées
squeeze [skwiz] *s* pression *f*; (coll) extorsion *f*; **it's a tight squeeze** (coll) ça tient tout juste ‖ *tr* serrer; (*fruit*) presser; **to squeeze from** (coll) extorquer à; **to squeeze into** faire entrer de force dans ‖ *intr* se blottir; **to squeeze through** se frayer un passage à travers
squeezer ['skwizər] *s* presse *f*, pressefruits *m*
squelch [skwɛltʃ] *s* (coll) remarque *f* écrasante ‖ *tr* écraser, réprimer
squid [skwɪd] *s* calmar *m*
squill [skwɪl] *s* (bot) scille *f*; (zool) squille *f*
squint [skwɪnt] *s* coup *m* d'œil furtif; (pathol) strabisme *m* ‖ *tr* fermer à moitié ‖ *intr* loucher; **to squint at** regarder furtivement
squint'-eyed' *adj* bigle, strabique; malveillant
squire [skwaɪr] *s* écuyer *m*; (*lady's escort*) cavalier *m* servant; (*property owner*) propriétaire *m* terrien; juge *m* de paix ‖ *tr* escorter
squirm [skwʌrm] *s* tortillement *m* ‖ *intr* se tortiller; **to squirm out of** se tirer de
squirrel ['skwʌrəl] *s* écureuil *m*
squirt [skwʌrt] *s* giclée *f*, jet *m*; (*syringe*) seringue *f*; (coll) morveux *m* ‖ *tr* faire gicler ‖ *intr* gicler, jaillir
stab [stæb] *s* coup *m* de poignard, de couteau; (*wound*) estafilade *f*; (coll) coup d'essai; **to make a stab at** (coll) s'essayer à ‖ *v* (*pret* & *pp* **stabbed;** *ger* **stabbing)** *tr* poignarder
stabilize ['stebəl‚aɪz] *tr* stabiliser
stab' in the back' *s* coup *m* de Jarnac, coup de traître
stable ['stebəl] *adj* stable ‖ *s* (*for cows*) étable *f*; (*for horses*) écurie *f*
stack [stæk] *s* tas *m*, pile *f*; (*of hay, straw, etc.*) meule *f*; (*of sheaves*) gerbier *m*; (*e.g., of rifles*) faisceau *m*; (*of ship or locomotive*) cheminée *f*; (*of fireplace*) souche *f*; **stacks** (*in library*) rayons *mpl* ‖ *tr* entasser, em-

piler; mettre en meule, en gerbier, or en faisceau; (*a deck of cards*) truquer, donner un coup de pouce à; **to stack arms** former les faisceaux
stadi·um ['stedɪ‚əm] *s* (*pl* **-ums** or **-a** [ə]) stade *m*
staff [stæf], [stɑf] *s* bâton *m*; (*of pilgrim*) bourdon *m*; (*of flag*) hampe *f*; (*of newspaper*) rédaction *f*; (*employees*) personnel *m*; (*servants*) domestiques *mfpl*; (*support*) soutien *m*; (mil) état-major *m*; (mus) portée *f* ‖ *tr* fournir, pourvoir de personnel; nommer le personnel pour
staff' head'quarters *spl* (mil) état-major *m*
staff' of'ficer *s* officier *m* d'état-major
stag [stæg] *adj* exclusivement masculin; **to go stag** aller sans compagne ‖ *s* homme *m*; (*male deer*) cerf *m*
stage [stedʒ] *s* stade *m*, étape *f*, phase *f*; (*of rocket*) étage *m*; (*stagecoach*) diligence *f*; (*scene*) champ *m* d'action, scène *f*; (*staging*) échafaudage *m*; (*platform*) estrade *f*; (*of microscope*) platine *f*; (theat) scène; **by easy stages** par petites étapes; **by successive stages** par échelons; **to go on the stage** monter sur les planches ‖ *tr* (*a play, demonstration, riot, etc.*) monter; (*a play*) mettre en scène
stage' coach' *s* diligence *f*, coche *m*
stage' craft' *s* technique *f* de la scène
stage' door' *s* entrée *f* des artistes
stage'-door John'ny *s* (*pl* **-nies**) coureur *m* de girls
stage' effect' *s* effet *m* scénique
stage' fright' *s* trac *m*
stage' hand' *s* machiniste *m*
stage' left' *s* côté *m* jardin
stage' man'ager *s* régisseur *m*
stage' name' *s* nom *m* de théâtre
stage' prop'erties *spl* accessoires *mpl*
stage' right' *s* côté *m* cour
stage'-struck' [strʌk] *adj* entiché de théâtre
stage' whis'per *s* aparté *m*
stagger ['stægər] *tr* ébranler; (*to surprise*) étonner; (*to arrange*) disposer en chicane, en zigzag; (*hours of work, train schedules, etc.*) échelonner ‖ *intr* chanceler, tituber
staggering ['stægərɪŋ] *adj* chancelant; (*amazing*) étonnant
staging ['stedʒɪŋ] *s* échafaudage *m*; (theat) mise *f* en scène
stagnant ['stægnənt] *adj* stagnant
stag' par'ty *s* (*pl* **-ties**) (coll) réunion *f* entre hommes, réunion d'hommes seuls
staid [sted] *adj* posé, sérieux
stain [sten] *s* tache *f*, souillure *f* ‖ *tr* tacher, souiller; (*to tint*) teindre ‖ *intr* se tacher
stained' glass' *s* vitre *f* de couleur
stained'-glass win'dow *s* vitrail *m*
stain'less steel' ['stenlɪs] *s* acier *m* inoxydable
stair [stɛr] *s* escalier *m*; (*step of a series*) marche *f*, degré *m*; **stairs** escalier *m*
stair'case' *s* escalier *m*

stair'way' s escalier m
stair'well' s cage f d'escalier
stake [stek] s pieu m, poteau m; (*of tent*) piquet m; (*marker*) jalon m; (*for burning condemned persons*) bûcher m; (*in a game of chance*) mise f, enjeu m; **at stake** en jeu; **to pull up stakes** (coll) déménager ‖ tr (*a road*) bornoyer; (*plants*) échalasser, ramer; (*money*) risquer; (*to back financially*) (slang) fournir aux besoins de; **to stake all** mettre tout en jeu; **to stake off** or **out** jalonner, piqueter
stale [stel] adj (*bread*) rassis; (*wine or beer*) éventé; (*air*) confiné; (*joke*) vieux; (*check*) proscrit; (*subject*) rabattu; (*news*) défloré, défraîchi; **to smell stale** (*said of room*) sentir le renfermé
stale'mate' s (chess) pat m; (fig) impasse f; **in stalemate** pat ‖ tr (chess) faire pat; (fig) paralyser
stalk [stɔk] s tige f; (*of flower or leaf*) queue f ‖ tr traquer, suivre à la piste ‖ intr marcher fièrement, marcher à grandes enjambées
stall [stɔl] s stalle f; (*at a market*) étal m, échoppe f; (slang) prétexte m ‖ tr mettre dans une stalle; (*a car*) caler; (*an airplane*) mettre en perte de vitesse; **to stall off** (coll) différer sous prétexte ‖ intr (*said of motor*) se bloquer; **to stall for time** (slang) temporiser
stallion ['stæljən] s étalon m
stalwart ['stɔlwərt] adj robuste; vaillant ‖ s partisan m loyal
stamen ['stemən] s étamine f
stamina ['stæmɪnə] s vigueur f, résistance f
stammer ['stæmər] s bégaiement m, balbutiement m ‖ tr & intr bégayer, balbutier
stammerer ['stæmərər] s bègue mf
stamp [stæmp] s empreinte f; (*for postage*) timbre m; (*for stamping*) poinçon m ‖ tr (*mail*) affranchir; (*money; leather; a medal*) frapper, estamper; (*a document*) timbrer; (*a passport*) viser; **to stamp one's feet** trépigner; **to stamp one's foot** frapper du pied; **to stamp out** (e.g., a rebellion) écraser, étouffer
stampede [stæm'pid] s débandade f; (*rush*) ruée f; (*of people*) sauve-qui-peut m ‖ tr provoquer la ruée de ‖ intr se débander
stamped' self'-addressed' en'velope s enveloppe f timbrée par l'expéditeur
stamp'ing grounds' spl—**to be on one's stamping grounds** (slang) être sur son terrain, être dans son domaine
stamp' pad' s tampon m encreur
stamp'-vend'ing machine' s distributeur m automatique de timbres-poste
stance [stæns] s attitude f, posture f
stanch [stɑntʃ] adj ferme, solide; vrai, loyal; (*watertight*) étanche ‖ tr étancher
stand [stænd] s résistance f; position f; (*of a merchant*) étal m, éventaire m;

(*of a speaker*) tribune f, estrade f; (*of a horse*) aplombs mpl; (*piece of furniture*) guéridon m, console f; (*to hold music, papers*) pupitre m; **stands** tribune f, stand m ‖ v (*pret & pp* stood [stud]) tr mettre, placer, poser; (*the cold*) supporter; (*a shock; an attack*) soutenir; (*a round of drinks*) (coll) payer; **to stand off** repousser; **to stand up** (*to keep waiting*) (coll) poser un lapin à ‖ intr se lever, se mettre debout; se tenir debout, être debout; en être, e.g., **how does it stand?** où en est-il?; **to stand aloof** or **aside** se tenir à l'écart; **to stand by** se tenir prêt; (*e.g., a friend*) rester fidèle à; **to stand fast** tenir bon; **to stand for** (*to mean*) signifier; (*to affirm*) soutenir; (*to allow*) tolérer; **to stand in for** doubler, remplacer; **to stand in line** faire la queue; **to stand out** sortir, saillir; **to stand up** se lever, se mettre debout; se tenir debout, être debout; **to stand up against** or **to** tenir tête à; **to stand up for** prendre fait et cause pour
standard ['stændərd] adj (*product, part, unit*) standard, de série, normal; (*current*) courant; (*author, book, work*) classique; (*edition*) définitif; (*keyboard of typewriter*) universel; (*coinage*) au titre ‖ s norme f, mesure f, règle f, pratique f; (*of quantity, weight, value*) standard m; (*banner*) étendard m; (*of lamp*) support m; (*of wires*) pylône m; (*of coinage*) titre m; (*for a monetary system*) étalon m; (fig) degré m, niveau m; **standards** critères mpl; **up to standard** suivant la norme
stand'ard·bear'er s porte-drapeau m
stand'ard gauge' s voie f normale
standardize ['stændər͵daɪz] tr standardiser
stand'ard of liv'ing s niveau m de vie
stand'ard time' s heure f légale
standee [stæn'di] s voyageur m debout; (theat) spectateur m debout
stand'-in' s (mov, theat) doublure f, remplaçant m; (coll) appuis mpl, piston m
standing ['stændɪŋ] adj (*upright*) debout; (*statue*) en pied; (*water*) stagnant; (*army; committee*) permanent; (*price; rule; rope*) fixe; (*custom*) établi, courant; (*jump*) à pieds joints ‖ s standing m, position f, importance f; **in good standing** estimé, accrédité; **of long standing** de longue date
stand'ing ar'my s armée f permanente
stand'ing room' s places fpl debout
stand'ing vote' s vote m par assis et levé
stand'pat' adj & s (coll) immobiliste mf
stand'pat'ter s (coll) immobiliste mf
stand'point' s point m de vue
stand'still' s arrêt m, immobilisation f; **to come to a standstill** s'arrêter court
stanza ['stænzə] s strophe f
staple ['stepəl] adj principal ‖ s (*product*) produit m principal; (*for hold-*

ing papers together) agrafe *f*; (bb) broche *f*; **staples** denrées *fpl* principales ‖ *tr* agrafer; (*books*) brocher
stapler ['steplər] *s* agrafeuse *f*; (bb) brocheuse *f*
star [stɑr] *s* astre *m*; (*heavenly body except sun and moon; figure that represents a star*) étoile *f*; (*of stage or screen*) vedette *f* ‖ *v* (*pret & pp* **starred**; *ger* **starring**) *tr* étoiler, consteller; (mov, rad, telv, theat) mettre en vedette; (typ) marquer d'un astérisque ‖ *intr* apparaître comme vedette
starboard ['stɑrbərd], ['stɑr‚bord] *adj* de tribord ‖ *s* tribord *m* ‖ *adv* à tribord
star′ board′er *s* (coll) pensionnaire *mf* de prédilection
starch [stɑrtʃ] *s* amidon *m*; (*for fabrics*) empois *m*; (*formality*) raideur *f*; (bot, culin) fécule *f*; (coll) force *f*, vigueur *f* ‖ *tr* empeser
starch•y ['stɑrtʃi] *adj* (*comp* **-ier**; *super* **-iest**) empesé; (*foods*) féculent; (*manner*) raide, guindé
stare [stɛr] *s* regard *m* fixe ‖ *tr*—**to stare s.o. in the face** dévisager qn; (*to be obvious to s.o.*) sauter aux yeux de qn ‖ *intr* regarder fixement; **to stare at** regarder fixement, dévisager
star′fish′ *s* étoile *f* de mer
star′gaze′ *intr* regarder les étoiles; rêvasser, être dans la lune
stark [stɑrk] *adj* pur; rigide; désert, solitaire ‖ *adv* entièrement
stark′-na′ked *adj* tout nu
star′light′ *s* lumière *f* des étoiles
starling ['stɑrlɪŋ] *s* étourneau *m*
star•ry ['stɑrɪ] *adj* (*comp* **-rier**; *super* **-riest**) étoilé
Stars′ and Stripes′ *spl* bannière *f* étoilée
Star′-Spangled Ban′ner *s* bannière *f* étoilée
start [stɑrt] *s* commencement *m*, début *m*; (*sudden start*) sursaut *m*, haut-le-corps *m* ‖ *tr* commencer; (*a car, a motor, etc.*) mettre en marche, démarrer; (*a conversation*) entamer; (*a hare*) lever; (*a deer*) lancer; **to start + ger** se mettre à + *inf* ‖ *intr* commencer, débuter; démarrer; (*to be startled*) sursauter; **starting from** or **with** à partir de; **to start after** sortir à la recherche de; **to start out** se mettre en route
starter ['stɑrtər] *s* initiateur *m*; (aut) démarreur *m*; (sports) starter *m*
start′ing point′ *s* point *m* de départ
startle ['stɑrtəl] *tr* faire tressaillir ‖ *intr* tressaillir
startling ['stɑrtlɪŋ] *adj* effrayant; (*event*) sensationnel; (*resemblance*) saisissant
starvation [stɑr've ʃən] *s* inanition *f*, famine *f*
starva′tion di′et *s* diète *f* absolue
starva′tion wag′es *spl* salaire *m* de famine
starve [stɑrv] *tr* affamer; faire mourir

de faim; **to starve out** réduire par la faim ‖ *intr* être affamé; être dans la misère; mourir de faim; (coll) mourir de faim
state [stet] *s* état *m*; (*pomp*) apparat *m*; **to lie in state** être exposé solennellement ‖ *tr* affirmer, déclarer; (*an hour or date*) régler, fixer; (*a problem*) poser
stateless ['stetlɪs] *adj* apatride
state•ly ['stetli] *adj* (*comp* **-lier**; *super* **-liest**) majestueux, imposant
statement ['stetmənt] *s* énoncé *m*, exposé *m*; (*account, report*) compte rendu *m*, rapport *m*; (*of an account*) (com) relevé *m*
state′ of mind′ *s* état *m* d'esprit, état d'âme
state′room′ *s* (naut) cabine *f*; (rr) compartiment *m*
states′man *s* (*pl* **-men**) homme *m* d'État
static ['stætɪk] *adj* statique; (rad) parasite ‖ *s* (rad) parasites *mpl*
station ['steʃən] *s* station *f*; (*for police; for selling gasoline; for broadcasting*) poste *m*; (*of bus, subway, rail line, taxi; for observation*) station; (rr) gare *f* ‖ *tr* poster, placer
sta′tion a′gent *s* chef *m* de gare
stationary ['steʃən‚ɛri] *adj* stationnaire
sta′tion break′ *s* (rad) pause *f*
stationer ['steʃənər] *s* papetier *m*
stationery ['steʃən‚ɛri] *s* papeterie *f*, fournitures *fpl* de bureau
sta′tionery store′ *s* papeterie *f*
sta′tion house′ *s* commissariat *m* de police
sta′tion identifica′tion *s* (rad) indicatif *m*
sta′tion-mas′ter *s* chef *m* de gare
sta′tion wag′on *s* familiale *f*, break *m*
statistical [stə'tɪstɪkəl] *adj* statistique
statistician [‚stætɪs'tɪʃən] *s* statisticien *m*
statistics [stə'tɪstɪks] *s* (*science*) statistique *f* ‖ *spl* (*data*) statistique, statistiques
statue ['stætʃu] *s* statue *f*
Stat′ue of Lib′erty *s* Liberté *f* éclairant le monde
statuesque [‚stætʃu'ɛsk] *adj* sculptural
stature ['stætʃər] *s* stature *f*, taille *f*; caractère *m*, stature
status ['stetəs] *s* condition *f*; rang *m*, standing *m*
sta′tus quo′ [kwo] *s* statu quo *m*
sta′tus seek′er *s* obsédé *m* du standing
sta′tus sym′bol *s* symbole *m* du rang social
statute ['stætʃut] *s* statut *m*
statutory ['stætʃu‚tori] *adj* statutaire
staunch [stɔntʃ], [stɑntʃ] *adj & tr* var of **stanch**
stave [stev] *s* bâton *m*; (*of barrel*) douve *f*; (*of ladder*) échelon *m*; (mus) portée *f* ‖ *v* (*pret & pp* **staved** or **stove** [stov]) *tr*—**to stave in** défoncer, crever; **to stave off** détourner, éloigner
stay [ste] *s* (*visit*) séjour *m*; (*prop*) étai *m*; (*of a corset*) baleine *f*; (*of execution*) sursis *m*; (fig) soutien *m* ‖

tr arrêter ‖ *intr* rester; séjourner; (*at a hotel*) descendre; **to stay put** ne pas bouger; **to stay up** veiller

stay′-at-home′ *adj & s* casanier *m*

stead [stɛd] *s*—**in s.o.'s stead** à la place de qn; **to stand s.o. in good stead** être fort utile à qn

stead′fast′ *adj* ferme; constant

stead·y ['stɛdi] *adj* (*comp* **-ier;** *super* **-iest**) ferme, solide; régulier; (*market*) soutenu ‖ *v* (*pret & pp* **-ied**) *tr* raffermir ‖ *intr* se raffermir

steak [stek] *s* (*slice*) tranche *f*; bifteck *m*

steal [stil] *s* (coll) vol *m*; (*bargain*) (coll) occasion *f* ‖ *v* (*pret* **stole** [stol]; *pp* **stolen**) *tr* voler; **to steal s.th. from s.o.** voler q.ch. à qn ‖ *intr* voler; **to steal away** se dérober; **to steal into** se glisser dans; **to steal upon** s'approcher en tapinois de

stealth [stɛlθ] *s*—**by stealth** en tapinois, à la dérobée

steam [stim] *s* vapeur *f*; (*e.g., on a window*) buée *f*; **full steam ahead!** en avant à toute vapeur!; **to get up steam** faire monter la pression; **to let off steam** lâcher la vapeur; (fig) s'épancher ‖ *tr* passer à la vapeur; (culin) cuire à la vapeur; **to steam up** (*e.g., a window*) embuer ‖ *intr* dégager de la vapeur, fumer; s'évaporer; **to steam ahead** avancer à la vapeur; (fig) faire des progrès rapides; **to steam up** s'embuer

steam′boat′ *s* vapeur *m*

steam′ chest′ *s* boîte *f* à vapeur

steam′ en′gine *s* machine *f* à vapeur

steamer ['stimər] *s* vapeur *m*

steam′ heat′ *s* chauffage *m* à la vapeur

steam′ roll′er *s* rouleau *m* compresseur; (fig) force *f* irrésistible

steam′ship′ *s* vapeur *m*

steam′ shov′el *s* pelle *f* à vapeur

steam′ ta′ble *s* table *f* à compartiments chauffés à la vapeur

steed [stid] *s* coursier *m*

steel [stil] *adj* (*industry*) sidérurgique ‖ *s* acier *m*; (*for striking fire from flint*) briquet *m*; (*for sharpening knives*) fusil *m* ‖ *tr* aciérer; **to steel oneself against** se cuirasser contre

steel′ wool′ *s* laine *f* d'acier, paille *f* de fer

steel′works′ *spl* aciérie *f*

steelyard ['stil‚jɑrd], ['stiljərd] *s* romaine *f*

steep [stip] *adj* raide, abrupt; (*cliff*) escarpé; (*price*) (coll) exorbitant ‖ *tr* tremper; (*e.g., tea*) infuser; **steeped in** saturé de; (*ignorance*) pétri de; (*the classics*) nourri de

steeple ['stipəl] *s* clocher *m*; (*spire*) flèche *f*

stee′ple·chase′ *s* course *f* d'obstacles

steer [stir] *s* bouvillon *m* ‖ *tr* diriger, conduire; (naut) gouverner ‖ *intr* se diriger; (naut) se gouverner; **to steer clear of** (coll) éviter

steerage ['stɪrɪdʒ] *s* entrepont *m*

steer′age pas′senger *s* passager *m* d'entrepont

steer′ing wheel′ *s* volant *m*; (naut) roue *f* de gouvernail

stellar ['stɛlər] *adj* stellaire; (*rôle*) de vedette

stem [stɛm] *s* (*of plant; of key*) tige *f*; (*of column; of tree*) fût *m*, tige; (*of fruit*) queue *f*; (*of pipe; of feather*) tuyau *m*; (*of goblet*) pied *m*; (*of watch*) remontoir *m*; (*of word*) radical *m*, thème *m*; (naut) étrave *f*; **from stem to stern** de l'étrave à l'étambot, d'un bout à l'autre ‖ *v* (*pret & pp* **stemmed**; *ger* **stemming**) *tr* (*e.g., grapes*) égrapper; (*e.g., the flow of blood*) étancher; (*the tide*) lutter contre, refouler; (*to check*) arrêter, endiguer ‖ *intr*—**to stem from** provenir de

stem′-wind′er *s* montre *f* à remontoir

stench [stɛntʃ] *s* puanteur *f*

sten·cil ['stɛnsəl] *s* pochoir *m*; (*work produced by it*) travail *m* au pochoir; (*for reproducing typewriting*) stencil *m* ‖ *v* (*pret & pp* **-ciled** or **-cilled**; *ger* **-ciling** or **-cilling**) *tr* passer au pochoir; tirer au stencil

stenographer [stə'nɑgrəfər] *s* sténo *f*, sténographe *mf*

stenography [stə'nɑgrəfi] *s* sténographie *f*

step [stɛp] *s* pas *m*; (*of staircase*) marche *f*, degré *m*; (*footprint*) trace *f*; (*of carriage*) marchepied *m*; (*of ladder*) échelon *m*; (*procedure*) démarche *f*; **in step with** au pas avec; **step by step** pas à pas; **watch your step!** prenez garde de tomber!; (fig) évitez tout faux pas! ‖ *v* (*pret & pp* **stepped**; *ger* **stepping**) *tr* échelonner; **to step off** mesurer au pas ‖ *intr* faire un pas; marcher; (coll) aller en toute hâte; **to step aside** s'écarter; **to step back** reculer; **to step in** entrer; **to step on it** (coll) mettre tous les gaz; **to step on the starter** appuyer sur le démarreur

step′broth′er *s* demi-frère *m*

step′child′ *s* (*pl* **-child′ren**) beau-fils *m*; belle-fille *f*

step′daugh′ter *s* belle-fille *f*

step′fa′ther *s* beau-père *m*

step′lad′der *s* échelle *f* double, marchepied *m*, escabeau *m*

step′moth′er *s* belle-mère *f*

steppe [stɛp] *s* steppe *f*

step′ping stone′ *s* pierre *f* de passage; (fig) marchepied *m*

step′sis′ter *s* demi-sœur *f*

step′son′ *s* beau-fils *m*

stere·o ['stɛri‚o], ['stɪrɪ‚o] *adj* (coll) stéréo, stéréophonique; (coll) stéréoscopique ‖ *s* (*pl* **-os**) (coll) disque *m* stéréo; (coll) émission *f* en stéréophonique; (coll) photographie *f* stéréoscopique

stereotyped ['stɛri‚ə‚taɪpt], ['stɪrɪ·ə‚taɪpt] *adj* stéréotypé

sterile ['stɛrɪl] *adj* stérile

sterilize ['stɛri‚laɪz] *tr* stériliser

sterling ['stʌrlɪŋ] *adj* de bon aloi ‖ *s* livres *fpl* sterling; argent *m* au titre; vaisselle *f* d'argent

stern [stʌrn] *adj* sévère, austère; (*look*) rébarbatif ‖ *s* poupe *f*

stethoscope ['stɛθə,skop] *s* stéthoscope *m*

stevedore ['stivə,dor] *s* arrimeur *m*

stew [st(j)u] *s* ragoût *m* ‖ *tr* mettre en ragoût ‖ *intr* (coll) être dans tous ses états

steward ['st(j)u·ərd] *s* régisseur *m*, intendant *m*; maître *m* d'hôtel; (aer, naut) steward *m*

stewardess ['st(j)u·ərdɪs] *s* (aer) hôtesse *f* de l'air; (naut) stewardesse *f*

stewed′ fruit′ *s* compote *f*

stewed′ toma′toes *spl* purée *f* de tomates

stick [stɪk] *s* bâtonnet *m*, bâton *m*; (*rod*) verge *f*; (*wand*; *drumstick*) baguette *f*; (*of chewing gum*; *of dynamite*) bâton; (*firewood*) bois *m* sec; (*walking stick*) canne *f*; (naut) mât *m*; (typ) composteur *m* ‖ *v* (*pret & pp* **stuck** [stʌk]) *tr* piquer, enfoncer; (*to fasten in position*) clouer, ficher, planter; (*to glue*) coller; (*a pig*) saigner; (coll) confondre; **stick 'em up!** (slang) haut les mains!; **to be stuck** être pris; (*e.g., in the mud*) s'enliser; (*to be unable to continue*) (coll) être en panne; **to stick it out** (coll) tenir jusqu'au bout; **to stick out** (*one's tongue*) tirer; (*one's head*) passer; (*one's chest*) bomber; **to stick up** (*in order to rob*) (slang) voler à main armée ‖ *intr* se piquer, s'enfoncer; se ficher, se planter; (*to be jammed*) être pris, se coincer; (*to adhere*) coller; (*to remain*) continuer, rester; **to stick out** saillir, dépasser; (*to be evident*) sauter aux yeux; **to stick up for** (coll) prendre la défense de

sticker ['stɪkər] *s* étiquette *f* gommée; (*difficult question*) (coll) colle *f*

stick′pin′ *s* épingle *f* de cravate

stick′-up′ *s* (slang) attaque *f* à main armée, hold-up *m*

stick·y ['stɪki] *adj* (*comp* **-ier**; *super* **-iest**) gluant, collant; (*hands*) poisseux; (*weather*) étouffant; (*question*) épineux; (*unaccommodating*) tatillon

stiff [stɪf] *adj* raide, difficile, ardu; (*joint*) ankylosé; (*brush*; *batter*) dur; (*style*, *manner*) guindé, empesé; (*drink*) fort; (*price*) (coll) salé, exagéré ‖ *s* (*corpse*) (slang) macchabée *m*

stiff′ col′lar *s* col *m* empesé

stiffen ['stɪfən] *tr* raidir, tendre; (culin) épaissir ‖ *intr* se raidir

stiff′ neck′ *s* torticolis *m*

stiff′-necked′ *adj* obstiné, entêté

stiff′ shirt′ *s* chemise *f* empesée, chemise à plastron

stifle ['staɪfəl] *tr & intr* étouffer

stig·ma ['stɪgmə] *s* (*pl* **-mas** or **-mata** [mətə]) stigmate *m*

stigmatize ['stɪgmə,taɪz] *tr* stigmatiser

stilet·to [stɪ'lɛto] *s* (*pl* **-tos**) stylet *m*

still [stɪl] *adj* tranquille, calme; immobile; silencieux; (*wine*) non mousseux ‖ *s* alambic *m*; (phot) image *f*; (mov)

photogramme *m*; (poetic) silence *m* ‖ *adv* (*yet*) encore, toujours ‖ *conj* cependant, pourtant ‖ *tr* calmer, apaiser; (*to silence*) faire taire ‖ *intr* se calmer, s'apaiser; se taire

still′born′ *adj* mort-né

still′ life′ *s* (*pl* **still lifes** or **still lives**) nature *f* morte

stilt [stɪlt] *s* échasse *f*; (*in the water*) pilotis *m*

stilted *adj* guindé; (archit) surhaussé

stimulant ['stɪmjələnt] *adj & s* stimulant *m*

stimulate ['stɪmjə,let] *tr* stimuler

stimu·lus ['stɪmjələs] *s* (*pl* **-li** [,laɪ]) stimulant *m*, aiguillon *m*; (physiol) stimulus *m*

sting [stɪŋ] *s* piqûre *f*; (*stinging organ*) aiguillon *m*, dard *m* ‖ *v* (*pret & pp* **stung** [stʌŋ]) *tr & intr* piquer

stin·gy ['stɪndʒi] *adj* (*comp* **-gier**; *super* **-giest**) avare, pingre

stink [stɪŋk] *s* puanteur *f* ‖ *v* (*pret* **stank** [stæŋk]; *pp* **stunk** [stʌŋk]) *tr* **—to stink up** empester, empuantir ‖ *intr* puer, empester; **to stink of** puer, empester

stinker ['stɪŋkər] *s* (slang) peau *f* de vache, chameau *m*

stint [stɪnt] *s* tâche *f*, besogne *f*; **without stint** sans réserve, sans limite ‖ *tr* limiter, réduire; **to stint oneself** se priver ‖ *intr* lésiner, être chiche

stipend ['staɪpənd] *s* traitement *m*, honoraires *mpl*

stipulate ['stɪpjə,let] *tr* stipuler

stir [stʌr] *s* remuement *m*, agitation *f*; (*prison*) (slang) bloc *m*; **to create a stir** faire sensation ‖ *v* (*pret & pp* **stirred**; *ger* **stirring**) *tr* remuer, agiter; **to stir up** (*trouble*) fomenter ‖ *intr* remuer, s'agiter, bouger

stirring ['stʌrɪŋ] *adj* entraînant

stirrup ['stʌrəp], ['stɪrəp] *s* étrier *m*

stitch [stɪtʃ] *s* point *m*; (*in knitting*) maille *f*; (surg) point de suture; **not a stitch of** (coll) pas un brin de; **stitch in the side** point de côté; **to be in stitches** (coll) se tenir les côtes ‖ *tr* coudre; (bb) brocher; (surg) suturer ‖ *intr* coudre

stock [stɑk] *s* approvisionnement *m*, stock *m*; (*assortment*) assortiment *m*; capital *m*, fonds *m*; (*shares*) valeurs *fpl*, actions *fpl*; (*of meat*) bouillon *m*; (*of a tree*) tronc *m*; (*of an anvil*) billot *m*; (*of a rifle*) crosse *f*; (*of a tree*; *of a family*) souche *f*; (*livestock*) bétail *m*, bestiaux *mpl*; (*handle*) poignée *f*; (*for dies*) tourne-à-gauche *m*; (hort) ente *f*; **in stock** en magasin; **on the stocks** (fig) sur le métier; **out of stock** épuisé; **stocks** (*for punishment*) pilori *m*; (naut) chantier *m*; **to take stock** faire le point; **to take stock in** (coll) faire grand cas de; **to take stock of** faire l'inventaire de ‖ *tr* approvisionner; garder en magasin; (*a forest or lake*) peupler; (*a farm*) monter en bétail; (*a pool*) empoissonner

stockade [stɑˈked] *s* palanque *f*, palissade *f* ‖ *tr* palissader
stock'breed'er *s* éleveur *m* de bestiaux
stock'breed'ing *s* élevage *m*
stock'bro'ker *s* agent *m* de change, courtier *m* de bourse
stock' car' *s* (aut) voiture *f* de série; (rr) wagon *m* à bestiaux
stock' com'pany *s* (com) société *f* anonyme; (theat) troupe *f* à demeure
stock' div'idend *s* action *f* gratuite
stock' exchange' *s* bourse *f*
stock'hold'er *s* actionnaire *mf*
stocking [ˈstɑkɪŋ] *s* bas *m*
stock' mar'ket *s* bourse *f*, marché *m* des valeurs; **to play the stock market** jouer à la bourse
stock'pile' *s* stocks *mpl* de réserve ‖ *tr* & *intr* stocker
stock' rais'ing *s* élevage *m*
stock'room' *s* magasin *m*
stock•y [ˈstɑki] *adj* (*comp* **-ier;** *super* **-iest**) trapu, costaud
stock'yard' *s* parc *m* à bétail
stoic [ˈsto·ɪk] *adj* & *s* stoïque; **Stoic** stoïcien *m*
stoke [stok] *tr* (*a fire*) attiser; (*a furnace*) alimenter, charger
stoker [ˈstokər] *s* chauffeur *m*; (mach) stoker *m*
stolid [ˈstɑlɪd] *adj* flegmatique, impassible, lourd
stomach [ˈstʌmək] *s* estomac *m* ‖ *tr* digérer; (coll) digérer, avaler
stom'ach ache' *s* mal *m* d'estomac
stone [ston] *s* pierre *f*; (*of fruit*) noyau *m*; (pathol) calcul *m*; (typ) marbre *m* ‖ *tr* lapider; (*fruit*) dénoyauter
stone'-broke' *adj* (coll) complètement fauché, raide
stone'-deaf' *adj* sourd comme un pot
stone'ma'son *s* maçon *m*
stone' quar'ry *s* (*pl* **-ries**) carrière *f*
stone's' throw' *s*—**within a stone's throw** à un jet de pierre
ston•y [ˈstoni] *adj* (*comp* **-ier;** *super* **-iest**) pierreux; (fig) dur, endurci
stooge [studʒ] *s* (theat) compère *m*; (slang) homme *f* de paille, acolyte *m*
stool [stul] *s* tabouret *m*, escabeau *m*; (*bowel movement*) selles *fpl*
stool' pi'geon *s* appeau *m*; (slang) mouchard *m*, mouton *m*
stoop [stup] *s* courbure *f*, inclinaison *f*; (*porch*) véranda *f* ‖ *intr* se pencher; se tenir voûté; (*to debase oneself*) s'abaisser
stoop'-shoul'dered *adj* voûté
stop [stɑp] *s* arrêt *m*; (*in telegrams*) stop *m*; (*full stop*) point *m*; (*of a guitar*) touche *f*; (mus) jeu *m* d'orgue; (public sign) stop; **to put a stop to** mettre fin à ‖ *v* (*pret* & *pp* **stopped;** *ger* **stopping**) *tr* arrêter; (*a check*) faire opposition à; **to stop up** boucher ‖ *intr* s'arrêter, arrêter; **to stop + ger** cesser de + *inf*, s'arrêter de + *inf*; **to stop off** descendre en passant; **to stop off at** s'arrêter un moment à; **to stop over** (aer, naut) faire escale
stop'cock' *s* robinet *m* d'arrêt

stop'gap' *adj* provisoire ‖ *s* bouche-trou *m*
stop'light' *s* signal *m* lumineux; (aut) feu *m* stop, stop *m*
stop'o'ver *s* arrêt *m* en cours de route, étape *f*
stoppage [ˈstɑpɪdʒ] *s* arrêt *m*; (*of payments*) suspension *f*; (*of wages*) retenue *f*; obstruction *f*; (pathol) occlusion *f*
stopper [ˈstɑpər] *s* bouchon *m*, tampon *m*
stop' sign' *s* signal *m* d'arrêt
stop' thief' *interj* au voleur!
stop'watch' *s* chronomètre *m* à déclic, compte-secondes *m*
storage [ˈstorɪdʒ] *s* emmagasinage *m*, entreposage *m*; **to put in storage** entreposer
stor'age bat'ter•y *s* (*pl* **-ies**) (elec) accumulateur *m*, accu *m*
store [stor] *s* magasin *m*, boutique *f*; approvisionnement *m*; (*warehouse*) (Brit) entrepôt *m*; **stores** matériel *m*; vivres *mpl*; **to set great store by** faire grand cas de ‖ *tr* emmagasiner; (*to warehouse*) entreposer; (*to supply or stock*) approvisionner; **to store away** or **up** accumuler
store'house' *s* magasin *m*, entrepôt *m*; (*of information*) mine *f*
store'keep'er *s* boutiquier *m*
store'room' *s* dépense *f*, office *f*; (*for furniture*) garde-meuble *m*; (naut) soute *f*
stork [stɔrk] *s* cigogne *f*
storm [stɔrm] *s* orage *m*; (mil) assaut *m*; (fig) tempête *f*; **to take by storm** prendre d'assaut ‖ *tr* livrer l'assaut à ‖ *intr* faire de l'orage; (fig) tempêter
storm' cloud' *s* nuage *m* orageux; (fig) nuage noir
storm' door' *s* contre-porte *f*
storm' pet'rel [ˈpɛtrəl] *s* oiseau *m* des tempêtes
storm' sash' *s* contre-fenêtre *f*
storm' troops' *spl* troupes *fpl* d'assaut
storm' win'dow *s* contre-fenêtre *f*
storm•y [ˈstɔrmi] *adj* (*comp* **-ier;** *super* **-iest**) orageux
sto•ry [ˈstori] *s* (*pl* **-ries**) histoire *f*; (*tale*) conte *m*; (*plot*) intrigue *f*; (*floor*) étage *m*; (coll) mensonge *m*, histoire
sto'ry•tel'ler *s* conteur *m*; (*fibber*) menteur *m*
stout [staut] *adj* corpulent, gros; vaillant; ferme, résolu; (*strong*) fort ‖ *s* stout *m*
stout'-heart'ed *adj* au cœur vaillant
stove [stov] *s* (*for heating a house or room*) poêle *m*; (*for cooking*) fourneau *m* de cuisine, cuisinière *f*
stove'pipe' *s* tuyau *m* de poêle; (*hat*) (coll) huit-reflets *m*, tuyau de poêle
stow [sto] *tr* mettre en place, ranger; (naut) arrimer; **to stow with** remplir de ‖ *intr*—**to stow away** s'embarquer clandestinement
stowage [ˈsto·ɪdʒ] *s* arrimage *m*; (*costs*) frais *mpl* d'arrimage
stow'away' *s* passager *m* clandestin

straddle ['strædǝl] *tr* enfourcher, chevaucher ‖ *intr* se mettre à califourchon; (coll) répondre en normand
strafe [strɑf], [stref] *s* (slang) bombardement *m*, marmitage *m* ‖ *tr* (slang) bombarder, marmiter
straggle ['strægǝl] *intr* traîner; (*to be scattered*) s'éparpiller; **to straggle along** marcher sans ordre
straggler ['stræglǝr] *s* traînard *m*
straight [stret] *adj* droit; direct; loyal, honnête; correct, en ordre; (*hair*) raide; (*whiskey*) sec; (*candid*) franc; (*hanging straight*) d'aplomb; **to set s.o. straight** faire la leçon à qn ‖ *s* (poker) séquence *f* ‖ *adv* droit; directement; loyalement, honnêtement; (*without interruption*) de suite; **straight ahead** tout droit; **straight out** franchement, sans detours; **straight through** de part en part; d'un bout à l'autre; **to go straight** (coll) vivre honnêtement
straighten ['stretǝn] *tr* redresser; mettre en ordre ‖ *intr* se redresser
straight′ face′ *s*—**to keep a straight face** montrer un front sérieux
straight′for′ward *adj* franc, direct; loyal
straight′ off′ *adv* sur-le-champ, d'emblée
straight′ ra′zor *s* rasoir *m* à main
straight′way′ *adv* sur-le-champ, d'emblée
strain [stren] *s* tension *f*; (*of a muscle*) foulure *f*; (*descendants*) lignée *f*; (*ancestry; type of virus*) souche *f*; (*trait*) héritage *m*, tendance *f*; (*vein*) ton *m*, sens *m*; (*bit*) trace *f*; (coll) grand effort *m*; **mental strain** surmenage *m* intellectuel; **strains** (*of, e.g., the Marseillaise*) accents *mpl*; **sweet strains** doux accords *mpl* ‖ *tr* forcer; (*e.g., a wrist*) se fouler; (*e.g., one's eyes*) se fatiguer; (*e.g., part of a machine*) déformer; (*e.g., a liquid*) filtrer, tamiser; **to strain oneself** surmener ‖ *intr* s'efforcer; filtrer, tamiser; (*to trickle*) suinter; (*said of beam, ship, motor, etc.*) fatiguer; **to strain at** (*a leash, rope, etc.*) tirer sur; (*to balk at*) reculer devant
strained *adj* (*smile*) forcé; (*friendship*) tendu
strainer ['strenǝr] *s* passoire *f*, filtre *m*
strait [stret] *s* détroit *m*; **straits** détroit; **to be in dire straits** être dans la plus grande gêne
strait′ jack′et *s* camisole *f* de force
strait′-laced′ *adj* prude, collet monté, puritain
Straits′ of Do′ver *spl* Pas *m* de Calais
strand [strænd] *s* (*beach*) plage *f*, grève *f*; (*of rope or cable*) toron *m*; (*of thread*) brin *m*; (*of pearls*) collier *m*; (*of hair*) cheveu *m* ‖ *tr* toronner; (*to undo strands of*) décorder; (*a ship*) échouer
stranded *adj* abandonné; (*lost*) égaré; (*ship*) échoué; (*rope or cable*) à torons; **to leave s.o. stranded** laisser qn en plan
strange [strendʒ] *adj* étrange; (*unfa-*

miliar) inconnu, étranger; (*unaccustomed*) inhabituel
stranger ['strendʒǝr] *s* étranger *m*; visiteur *m*
strangle ['stræŋgǝl] *tr* étrangler, étouffer ‖ *intr* s'étrangler
strap [stræp] *s* (*of leather, rubber, etc.*) courroie *f*; (*of cloth, metal, leather, etc.*) bande *f*; (*to sharpen a razor*) cuir *m* à rasoir; (*of, e.g., a harness*) sangle *f* ‖ *v* (*pret & pp* **strapped**; *ger* **strapping**) *tr* attacher avec une courroie, sangler; (*a razor*) repasser sur le cuir
strap′hang′er *s* (coll) voyageur *m* debout
strapping ['stræpɪŋ] *adj* bien découplé, robuste; (coll) énorme, gros
stratagem ['strætǝdʒǝm] *s* stratagème *m*
strategic(al) [strǝ'tidʒɪk(ǝl)] *adj* stratégique
strategist ['strætɪdʒɪst] *s* stratège *m*
strate·gy ['strætɪdʒi] *s* (*pl* **-gies**) stratégie *f*
strati·fy ['strætɪˌfaɪ] *v* (*pret & pp* **-fied**) *tr* stratifier ‖ *intr* se stratifier
stratosphere ['strætǝˌsfɪr], ['stretǝˌsfɪr] *s* stratosphère *f*
stra·tum ['stretǝm], ['strætǝm] *s* (*pl* **-ta** [tǝ] *or* **-tums**) couche *f*; (*e.g., of society*) classe *f*, couche
straw [strɔ] *s* paille *f*; (*for drinking*) chalumeau *m*, paille; **it's the last straw!** c'est le bouquet!
straw′ber′ry *s* (*pl* **-ries**) fraise *f*; (*plant*) fraisier *m*
straw′hat′ *s* chapeau *m* de paille; (*skimmer*) canotier *m*
straw′ man′ *s* (*pl* **men′**) (*figurehead*) homme *m* de paille; (*scarecrow*) épouvantail *m*; (*red herring*) canard *m*, diversion *f*
straw′ mat′tress *s* paillasse *f*
straw′ vote′ *s* vote *m* d'essai
stray [stre] *adj* égaré; (*bullet*) perdu; (*scattered*) épars ‖ *s* animal *m* égaré ‖ *intr* s'égarer
streak [strik] *s* raie *f*, rayure *f*, bande *f*; (*of light*) trait *m*, filet *m*; (*of lightning*) éclair *m*; (*layer*) veine *f*; (*bit*) trace *f*; **like a streak** comme un éclair; **streak of luck** filon *m* ‖ *tr* rayer, strier, zébrer ‖ *intr* faire des raies; passer comme un éclair
stream [strim] *s* ruisseau *m*; (*steady flow of current*) courant *m*; (*of people, abuse, light, etc.*) flot *m*; (*of, e.g., automobiles*) défilé *m* ‖ *intr* couler; (*said of blood*) ruisseler; (*said of light*) jaillir; (*said of flag*) flotter; **to stream out** sortir à flots
streamer ['strimǝr] *s* banderole *f*
stream′lined′ *adj* aérodynamique, caréné; (fig) abrégé, concis
stream′lin′er *s* train *m* caréné de luxe
street [strit] *s* rue *f*; (*surface of the street*) chaussée *f*
street′ Ar′ab *s* gamin *m* des rues
street′car′ *s* tramway *m*
street′ clean′er *s* balayeur *m*; (mach) balayeuse *f*

street′ clothes′ *spl* vêtements *mpl* de ville
street′ floor′ *s* rez-de-chaussée *m*
street′light′ *s* réverbère *m*
street′ sprink′ler *s* arroseuse *f*
street′ u′rinal *s* vespasienne *f*, édicule *m*, urinoir *m*
street′walk′er *s* racoleuse *f*, fille *f* des rues
strength [strɛŋθ] *s* force *f*; intensité *f*; (*of a fabric*) solidité *f*; (*of spirituous liquors*) degré *m*, titre *m*; (com) tendance *f* à la hausse; (mil) effectif *m*; **on the strength of** sur la foi de
strengthen ['strɛŋθən] *tr* fortifier, renforcer; consolider ‖ *intr* se fortifier, se renforcer
strenuous ['strɛnjʊ·əs] *adj* actif, énergique; (*work*) ardu; (*effort*) acharné; (*objection*) vigoureux
stress [strɛs] *s* tension *f*, force *f*; (mach) stress *m*, tension; (phonet) accent *m* d'intensité; **to lay stress on** insister sur ‖ *tr* (e.g., *a beam*) charger; (*a syllable*) accentuer; insister sur, appuyer sur
stress′ ac′cent *s* accent *m* d'intensité
stretch [strɛtʃ] *s* allongement *m*; (*of the arm; of the meaning*) extension *f*; (*of the imagination*) effort *m*; (*distance in time or space*) intervalle *m*; (*section of road*) section *f*; (*section of country, water, etc.*) étendue *f*; **at a stretch** d'un trait; **in one stretch** d'une seule traite; **to do a stretch** (slang) faire de la taule ‖ *tr* tendre; (*the sense of a word*) forcer; (*a sauce*) allonger; **to stretch oneself** s'étirer; **to stretch out** allonger, étendre; (*the hand*) tendre ‖ *intr* s'étirer; (*said of shoes, gloves, etc.*) s'élargir; **to stretch out** s'allonger, s'étendre
stretcher ['strɛtʃər] *s* (*for gloves, trousers, etc.*) tendeur *m*; (*for a painting*) châssis *m*; (*to carry sick or wounded*) civière *f*, brancard *m*
stretch′er·bear′er *s* brancardier *m*
strew [stru] *v* (*pret* strewed; *pp* strewed or strewn) *tr* semer, éparpiller; (e.g., *with flowers*) joncher, parsemer
stricken ['strɪkən] *adj* frappé; (e.g., *with grief*) affligé; (*crossed out*) rayé; **stricken with** atteint de
strict [strɪkt] *adj* strict; (*exacting*) sévère
stricture ['strɪktʃər] *s* critique *f* sévère; (pathol) rétrécissement *m*
stride [straɪd] *s* enjambée *f*; **to hit one's stride** attraper la cadence; **to make great (or rapid) strides** avancer à grands pas; **to take in one's stride** faire sans le moindre effort ‖ *v* (*pret* strode [strod]; *pp* stridden ['strɪdən]) *tr* parcourir à grandes enjambées; (*to straddle*) enfourcher ‖ *intr* —**to stride across** or **over** enjamber; **to stride along** marcher à grandes enjambées
strident ['straɪdənt] *adj* strident
strife [straɪf] *s* lutte *f*
strike [straɪk] *s* (*blow*) coup *m*; (*stopping of work*) grève *f*; (*discovery of*

ore, oil, etc.) rencontre *f*; (baseball) coup du batteur; **to go on strike** se mettre en grève ‖ *v* (*pret & pp* struck [strʌk]) *tr* frapper; (*coins*) frapper; (*a match*) frotter; (*a bargain*) conclure; (*camp*) lever; (*the sails; the colors*) amener; (*the hour*) sonner; (*root; a pose*) prendre; **how does he strike you?** quelle impression vous fait-il?; **to strike it rich** trouver le filon; **to strike out** rayer; **to strike up** (*a song, piece of music, etc.*) attaquer, entonner; (*an acquaintance, conversation, etc.*) lier ‖ *intr* frapper; (*said of clock*) sonner; (*said of workers*) faire la grève; (mil) donner l'assaut; **to strike out** se mettre en route
strike′break′er *s* briseur *m* de grève, jaune *m*
striker ['straɪkər] *s* frappeur *m*; (*on door*) marteau *m*; (*worker on strike*) gréviste *mf*
striking ['straɪkɪŋ] *adj* frappant, saisissant; (*workers*) en grève
strik′ing pow′er *s* force *f* de frappe
string [strɪŋ] *s* ficelle *f*; (*of onions or garlic; of islands; of pearls; of abuse*) chapelet *m*; (*of words, insults*) enfilade *f*, kyrielle *f*; (e.g., *of cars*) file *f*; (*of beans*) fil *m*; (*for shoes*) lacet *m*; (mus) corde *f*; **strings** instruments *mpl* à cordes; **to pull strings** (fig) tirer les ficelles; **with no strings attached** (coll) sans restriction ‖ *v* (*pret & pp* strung [strʌŋ]) *tr* mettre une ficelle à, garnir de cordes; (e.g., *a violin*) mettre les cordes à; (*a bow*) bander; (*a tennis racket*) corder; (*beads, sentences, etc.*) enfiler; (*a cord, a thread, a wire, etc.*) tendre; (*to tune*) monter; **to string along** (slang) lanterner, faire marcher; **to string up** (coll) pendre ‖ *intr*—**to string along with** (slang) collaborer avec, suivre
string′ bean′ *s* haricot *m* vert
stringed′ in′strument *s* instrument *m* à cordes
stringent ['strɪndʒənt] *adj* rigoureux; (*tight*) tendu; (*convincing*) convaincant
string′ quartet′ *s* quatuor *m* à cordes
string·y ['strɪŋi] *adj* (*comp* -ier; *super* -iest) fibreux, filandreux
strip [strɪp] *s* (*of paper, cloth, land*) bande *f*; (*of metal*) lame *f*, ruban *m* ‖ *v* (*pret & pp* stripped; *ger* stripping) *tr* dépouiller; (*to strip bare*) mettre à nu; (*the bed*) défaire; (*a screw*) arracher le filet de, faire foirer; (*tobacco*) écoter; **to strip down** (e.g., *a motor*) démonter; **to strip off** enlever; (e.g., *bark*) écorcer ‖ *intr* se déshabiller
stripe [straɪp] *s* raie *f*, bande *f*; (*on cloth*) rayure *f*; (*flesh wound*) marque *f*; (mil, nav) chevron *m*, galon *m*; **to win one's stripes** gagner ses galons ‖ *tr* rayer
strip′ min′ing *s* exploitation *f* minière à ciel ouvert

strip'tease' *s* strip-tease *m*, déshabillage *m* suggestif
stripteaser ['strɪp͵tizər] *s* effeuilleuse *f*, strip-teaseuse *f*
strive [straɪv] *v* (*pret* strove [strov]; *pp* striven ['strɪvən]) *intr* s'efforcer; to strive after rechercher; to strive against lutter contre; to strive to s'efforcer à, s'évertuer à
stroke [strok] *s* coup *m*; (*of pen; of wit*) trait *m*; (*of arms in swimming*) brassée *f*; (*caress with hand*) caresse *f* de la main; (*of a piston*) course *f*; (*of lightning*) foudre *f*; (pathol) attaque *f* d'apoplexie; at the stroke of sonnant, e.g., at the stroke of five à cinq heures sonnantes; to not do a stroke of work ne pas en ficher une ramée || *tr* caresser de la main
stroll [strol] *s* promenade *f*; to take a stroll aller faire un tour || *intr* se promener
stroller ['strolər] *s* promeneur *m*; (*for babies*) poussette *f*
strong [strɔŋ], [straŋ] *adj* (*comp* stronger ['strɔŋgər], ['straŋgər]; *super* strongest ['strɔŋgɪst], ['straŋgɪst]) fort; (*stock market*) ferme; (*musical beat*) marqué; (*spicy*) piquant; (*rancid*) rance
strong'box' *s* coffre-fort *m*
strong' drink' *s* boissons *fpl* spiritueuses
strong'hold' *s* place *f* forte
strong' man' *s* (*pl* men') (e.g., *in a circus*) hercule *m* forain; (*leader, good planner*) animateur *m*; (*dictator*) chef *m* autoritaire
strong'-mind'ed *adj* résolu, décidé; (*woman*) hommasse
strontium ['strɑnʃɪ·əm] *s* strontium *m*
strop [strɑp] *s* cuir *m* à rasoir || *v* (*pret & pp* stropped; *ger* stropping) *tr* repasser sur le cuir
strophe ['strofi] *s* strophe *f*
structure ['strʌktʃər] *s* structure *f*; (*building*) édifice *m*
struggle ['strʌgəl] *s* lutte *f* || *intr* lutter; to struggle along avancer péniblement
strug'gle for exist'ence *s* lutte *f* pour la vie
strum [strʌm] *v* (*pret & pp* strummed; *ger* strumming) *tr* (*an instrument*) gratter de; (*a tune*) tapoter || *intr* jouailler; to strum on plaquer des arpèges sur
strumpet ['strʌmpɪt] *s* putain *f*
strut [strʌt] *s* (*brace, prop*) étai *m*, support *m*, entretoise *f*; démarche *f* orgueilleuse || *v* (*pret & pp* strutted; *ger* strutting) *intr* se pavaner
strychnine ['strɪknaɪn], ['strɪknɪn] *s* strychnine *f*
stub [stʌb] *s* (*fragment*) tronçon *m*; (*of a tree*) souche *f*; (*of a pencil; of a cigar, cigarette*) bout *m*; (*of a check*) talon *m*, souche || *v* (*pret & pp* stubbed; *ger* stubbing) *tr*—to stub one's toe se cogner le bout du pied
stubble ['stʌbəl] *s* éteule *f*, chaume *m*; (*of beard*) poil *m* court et raide
stubborn ['stʌbərn] *adj* obstiné; (*head-

strong*) têtu; (*resolute*) acharné; (*fever*) rebelle; (*soil*) ingrat
stuc·co ['stʌko] *s* (*pl* -coes or -cos) stuc *m* || *tr* stuquer
stuck [stʌk] *adj* coincé, pris; (*glued*) collé; (*unable to continue*) en panne; stuck on (coll) entiché de
stuck'-up' *adj* (coll) hautain, prétentieux
stud [stʌd] *s* clou *m* à grosse tête; (*ornament*) clou doré; (*on shirt*) bouton *m*; (*studhorse*) étalon *m*; (*horse farm*) haras *m*; (*bolt*) goujon *m*; (archit) montant *m* || *v* (*pret & pp* studded; *ger* studding) *tr* clouter; studded with jonché de, parsemé de
stud' bolt' *s* goujon *m*
student ['st(j)udənt] *adj* estudiantin || *s* étudiant *m*; (*researcher*) chercheur *m*
stu'dent bod'y *s* étudiants *mpl*
stu'dent cen'ter *s* foyer *m* d'étudiants, centre *m* social des étudiants
stu'dent nurse' *s* élève *f* infirmière
stud' farm' *s* haras *m*
stud'horse' *s* étalon *m*
studied ['stʌdid] *adj* prémédité; recherché
studi·o ['st(j)udɪ͵o] *s* (*pl* -os) studio *m*, atelier *m*
studious ['st(j)udɪ·əs] *adj* studieux, appliqué
stud·y ['stʌdi] *s* (*pl* -ies) étude *f*; rêverie *f*; cabinet *m* || *v* (*pret & pp* -ied) *tr & intr* étudier
stuff [stʌf] *s* matière *f*; chose *f*; to know one's stuff (coll) s'y connaître || *tr* bourrer; (*with food*) gaver; (*furniture*) rembourrer; (*an animal*) empailler; (culin) farcir; to stuff up boucher || *intr* se gaver
stuffed' shirt' *s* collet *m* monté
stuffing ['stʌfɪŋ] *s* rembourrage *m*; (culin) farce *f*
stuff·y ['stʌfi] *adj* (*comp* -ier; *super* -iest) mal ventilé; (*tedious*) ennuyeux; (*pompous*) collet monté; to smell stuffy sentir le renfermé
stumble ['stʌmbəl] *intr* trébucher; (*in speaking*) hésiter
stum'bling block' *s* pierre *f* d'achoppement
stump [stʌmp] *s* (*of tree*) souche *f*; (e.g., *of arm*) moignon *m*; (*of tooth*) chicot *m* || *tr* (*a design*) estomper; (coll) embarrasser, coller; (*a state, district, region*) (coll) faire une tournée électorale en, dans, or à || *intr* clopiner
stump' speak'er *s* orateur *m* de carrefour
stump' speech' *s* harangue *f* électorale improvisée
stun [stʌn] *v* (*pret & pp* stunned; *ger* stunning) *tr* étourdir
stunning ['stʌnɪŋ] *adj* (coll) étourdissant, épatant
stunt [stʌnt] *s* atrophie *f*; (*underdeveloped creature*) avorton *m*; (coll) tour *m* de force, acrobatie *f* || *tr* atrophier || *intr* (coll) faire des acrobaties

stunted adj rabougri
stunt' fly'ing s vol m de virtuosité, acrobatie f aérienne
stunt' man' s (pl **men'**) cascadeur m, doublure f
stupe·fy ['st(j)upɪˌfaɪ] v (pret & pp **-fied**) tr stupéfier
stupendous [st(j)u'pɛndəs] adj prodigieux, formidable
stupid ['st(j)upɪd] adj stupide
stupor ['st(j)upər] s stupeur f
stur·dy ['stʌrdi] adj (comp **-dier**; super **-diest**) robuste, vigoureux; (resolute) ferme, hardi
sturgeon ['stʌrdʒən] s esturgeon m
stutter ['stʌtər] s bégaiement m || tr & intr bégayer
sty [staɪ] s (pl **sties**) porcherie f; (pathol) orgelet m
style [staɪl] s style m; (fashion) mode f; (elegance) ton m, chic m; **to live in great style** mener grand train || tr appeler, dénommer; **to style oneself** s'intituler
stylish ['staɪlɪʃ] adj à la mode, élégant, chic
sty·mie ['staɪmi] v (pret & pp **-mied**; ger **-mieing**) tr contrecarrer
styp'tic pen'cil ['stɪptɪk] s crayon m styptique
suave [swɑv], [swev] adj suave; (person) affable; (manners) doucereux
sub [sʌb] s (coll) sous-marin m
subconscious [səb'kɑnʃəs] adj & s subconscient m
sub'divide' or **sub'divide'** tr subdiviser || intr se subdiviser
subdue [səb'd(j)u] tr subjuguer, vaincre, asservir; (color, light, sound) adoucir, amortir; (passions, feelings) dompter
sub'head' s sous-titre m
subject ['sʌbdʒɪkt] adj sujet, assujetti, soumis || s sujet m; (e.g., in school) matière f || [səb'dʒɛkt] tr assujettir, soumettre
subjection [səb'dʒɛkʃən] s sujétion f, soumission f
subjective [səb'dʒɛktɪv] adj subjectif
sub'ject mat'ter s matière f
subjugate ['sʌbdʒəˌget] tr subjuguer
subjunctive [səb'dʒʌŋktɪv] adj & s subjonctif m
sub'lease' s sous-location f || **sub'lease'** tr sous-louer
sub·let [səb'lɛt], ['sʌbˌlɛt] v (pret & pp **-let**; ger **-letting**) tr sous-louer
sub'machine' gun' s mitraillette f
sub'marine' adj & s sous-marin m
sub'marine chas'er s chasseur m de sous-marins
submerge [səb'mʌrdʒ] tr submerger || intr (said of submarine) plonger
submersion [səb'mʌrʒən], [səb'mʌrʃən] s submersion f
submission [səb'mɪʃən] s soumission f; (delivery) présentation f
submissive [səb'mɪsɪv] adj soumis
sub·mit [səb'mɪt] v (pret & pp **-mitted**; ger **-mitting**) tr soumettre || intr se soumettre
subordinate [səb'ɔrdɪnɪt] adj & s

subordonné m || [səb'ɔrdɪˌnet] tr subordonner
subpoena [sʌb'pinə], [sə'pinə] s assignation f, citation f || tr citer
subscribe [səb'skraɪb] tr souscrire || intr—**to subscribe to** (an opinion; a charity; a loan; a newspaper) souscrire à; (a newspaper) s'abonner à
subscriber [səb'skraɪbər] s abonné m
subscription [səb'skrɪpʃən] s souscription f; (to newspaper or magazine) abonnement m; (to club) cotisation f; **to take out a subscription for s.o.** abonner qn; **to take out a subscription to** s'abonner à
subsequent ['sʌbsɪkwənt] adj subséquent, suivant
subservient [səb'sʌrvɪ·ənt] adj asservi, subordonné
subside [səb'saɪd] intr (said of water, ground, etc.) s'abaisser; (said of storm, excitement, etc.) s'apaiser
subsidiar·y [səb'sɪdɪˌɛri] adj subsidiaire || s (pl **-ies**) filiale f
subsidize ['sʌbsɪˌdaɪz] tr subventionner; suborner
subsi·dy ['sʌbsɪdi] s (pl **-dies**) subside m, subvention f
subsist [səb'sɪst] intr subsister
subsistence [səb'sɪstəns] s (supplies) subsistance f; existence f
sub'soil' s sous-sol m
substance ['sʌbstəns] s substance f
sub·stand'ard adj inférieur au niveau normal
substantial [səb'stænʃəl] adj substantiel; (wealthy) aisé, cossu
substantiate [səb'stænʃɪˌet] tr établir, vérifier
substantive ['sʌbstəntɪv] adj & s substantif m
sub'sta'tion s (of post office) bureau m auxiliaire; (elec) sous-station f
substitute ['sʌbstɪˌt(j)ut] s (person) remplaçant m, suppléant m, substitut m; (e.g., for coffee) succédané m || tr remplacer, e.g., **they substituted copper for silver** ils ont remplacé l'argent par le cuivre; substituer, e.g., **a hind was substituted for Iphigenia** une biche fut substituée à Iphigénie || intr servir de remplaçant; **to substitute for** remplacer, suppléer
substitution [ˌsʌbstɪ't(j)uʃən] s substitution f
sub'stra'tum s (pl **-ta** [tə] or **-tums**) substrat m
subterfuge ['sʌbtərˌfjudʒ] s subterfuge m, faux-fuyant m
subterranean [ˌsʌbtə'renɪ·ən] adj souterrain
sub'ti'tle s sous-titre m
subtle ['sʌtəl] adj subtil
subtle·ty ['sʌtəlti] s (pl **-ties**) subtilité f
subtract [səb'trækt] tr soustraire
subtraction [səb'trækʃən] s soustraction f
suburb ['sʌbʌrb] s ville f de la banlieue; **the suburbs** la banlieue
suburban [sə'bʌrbən] adj suburbain
suburbanite [sə'bʌrbəˌnaɪt] s banlieusard m

subvention [səb'vɛnʃən] *s* subvention *f* || *tr* subventionner
subversive [səb'vʌrsɪv] *adj* subversif || *s* factieux *m*
subvert [səb'vʌrt] *tr* corrompre; renverser
sub'way' *s* métro *m*; (*tunnel for pedestrians*) souterrain *m*
sub'way car' *s* voiture *f* de métro
sub'way sta'tion *s* station *f* de métro
succeed [sək'sid] *tr* succéder (with *dat*); **to succeed one another** se succéder || *intr* réussir; **to succed in** + *ger* réussir à + *inf*; **to succeed to** (*the throne; a fortune*) succéder à
success [sək'sɛs] *s* succès *m*, réussite *f*; **to be a success** avoir du succès
successful [sək'sɛsfəl] *adj* réussi; heureux, prospère
succession [sək'sɛʃən] *s* succession *f*; **in succession** de suite
successive [sək'sɛsɪv] *adj* successif
succor ['sʌkər] *s* secours *m* || *tr* secourir
succotash ['sʌkə‚tæʃ] *s* plat *m* de fèves et de maïs
succumb [sə'kʌm] *intr* succomber
such [sʌtʃ] *adj & pron indef* tel, pareil, semblable; **such a** un tel; **such and such** tel et tel; **such as** tel que
suck [sʌk] *s*—**to give suck to** allaiter || *tr* sucer; (*a nipple*) téter; **to suck in** aspirer; (*to absorb*) sucer || *intr* sucer; téter
sucker ['sʌkər] *s* suceur *m*; (*sucking organ*) suçoir *m*, ventouse *f*; (bot) drageon *m*; (ichth) rémora *m*; (*gullible person*) (coll) gogo *m*; (*lollipop*) (coll) sucette *f*
suckle ['sʌkəl] *tr* allaiter
suck'ling pig' *s* cochon *m* de lait
suction ['sʌkʃən] *s* succion *f*
suc'tion cup' *s* ventouse *f*
suc'tion pump' *s* pompe *f* aspirante
sudden ['sʌdən] *adj* brusque, soudain; **all of a sudden** tout à coup
suddenly ['sʌdənli] *adv* tout à coup
suds [sʌdz] *spl* eau *f* savonneuse; mousse *f* de savon
sue [s(j)u] *tr* poursuivre en justice || *intr* intenter un procès
suede [swed] *s* suède *m*; (*for shoes*) daim *m*
suet ['s(j)u‧ɪt] *s* graisse *f* de rognon
suffer ['sʌfər] *tr* souffrir; (*to allow*) permettre; (*a defeat*) essuyer, subir || *intr* souffrir
sufferance ['sʌfərəns] *s* tolérance *f*
suffering ['sʌfərɪŋ] *adj* souffrant || *s* souffrance *f*
suffice [sə'faɪs] *tr* suffire (with *dat*) || *intr* suffire; **it suffices to** + *inf* il suffit de + *inf*
sufficient [sə'fɪʃənt] *adj* suffisant
suffix ['sʌfɪks] *s* suffixe *m*
suffocate ['sʌfə‚ket] *tr & intr* suffoquer, étouffer
suffrage ['sʌfrɪdʒ] *s* suffrage *m*
suffragist ['sʌfrədʒɪst] *s* partisan *m* du droit de vote des femmes
suffuse [sə'fjuz] *tr* baigner, saturer
sugar ['ʃugər] *s* sucre *m* || *tr* sucrer;

(*a cake*) saupoudrer de sucre; (*a pill*) recouvrir de sucre || *intr* former du sucre
sug'ar beet' *s* betterave *f* sucrière, betterave à sucre
sug'ar bowl' *s* sucrier *m*
sug'ar cane' *s* canne *f* à sucre
sug'ar-coat' *tr* dragéifier; (fig) dorer
sug'ar dad'dy *s* (*pl* -**dies**) papa *m* gâteau
sug'ar ma'ple *s* érable *m* à sucre
sug'ar pea' *s* mange-tout *m*
sug'ar tongs' *spl* pince *f* à sucre
sugary ['ʃugəri] *adj* sucré; (fig) doucereux
suggest [səg'dʒɛst] *tr* suggérer
suggestion [səg'dʒɛstʃən] *s* suggestion *f*; nuance *f*, pointe *f*, soupçon *m*
suggestive [səg'dʒɛstɪv] *adj* suggestif
suicidal [‚s(j)u‧ɪ'saɪdəl] *adj* suicidaire
suicide ['s(j)u‧ɪ‚saɪd] *s* (*act*) suicide *m*; (*person*) suicidé *m*; **to commit suicide** se suicider
suit [s(j)ut] *s* costume *m*; (*men's*) complet *m*, costume; (*women's*) costume tailleur, tailleur *m*; (*lawsuit*) procès *m*; (*plea*) requête *f*; (cards) couleur *f*; **to follow suit** jouer la couleur; (fig) en faire autant || *tr* adapter; convenir (with *dat*), e.g., **does that suit him?** cela lui convient?; aller (with *dat*), seoir (with *dat*), e.g., **the dress suits her well** la robe lui va bien, la robe lui sied bien || *intr* convenir, aller
suitable ['s(j)utəbəl] *adj* convenable, à propos; compétent
suit'case' *s* valise *f*
suite [swit] *s* suite *f* || [s(j)ut] *s* (*of furniture*) ameublement *m*, mobilier *m*
suiting ['s(j)utɪŋ] *s* étoffe *f* pour complets
suit' of clothes' *s* complet-veston *m*
suitor ['s(j)utər] *s* prétendant *m*, soupirant *m*
sul'fa drugs' ['sʌlfə] *spl* sulfamides *mpl*
sulfide ['sʌlfaɪd] *s* sulfure *m*
sulfur ['sʌlfər] *adj* soufré || *s* soufre *m* || *tr* soufrer
sulfuric [sʌl'fjurɪk] *adj* sulfurique
sul'fur mine' *s* soufrière *f*
sulk [sʌlk] *s* bouderie *f* || *intr* bouder
sulk·y ['sʌlki] *adj* (*comp* -**ier**; *super* -**iest**) boudeur, maussade
sullen ['sʌlən] *adj* maussade, rébarbatif
sul·ly ['sʌli] *v* (*pret & pp* -**lied**) *tr* souiller
sulphur ['sʌlfər] *adj*, *s & tr* var of **sulfur**
sultan ['sʌltən] *s* sultan *m*
sul·try ['sʌltri] *adj* (*comp* -**trier**; *super* -**triest**) étouffant, suffocant
sum [sʌm] *s* somme *f*; tout *m*, total *m*; **in sum** somme toute || *v* (*pret & pp* summed; *ger* summing) *tr*—**to sum up** résumer
sumac or **sumach** ['ʃumæk], ['sumæk] *s* sumac *m*
summarize ['sʌmə‚raɪz] *tr* résumer
summa·ry ['sʌməri] *adj* sommaire || *s* (*pl* -**ries**) sommaire *m*

summer ['sʌmər] *adj* estival || *s* été *m* || *intr* passer l'été
sum'mer resort' *s* station *f* estivale
sum'mer school' *s* cours *m* d'été, cours de vacances
summery ['sʌməri] *adj* estival, d'été
summit ['sʌmɪt] *s* sommet *m*
sum'mit con'ference *s* conférence *f* au sommet
summon ['sʌmən] *tr* appeler, convoquer; (law) sommer, citer, assigner
summons ['sʌmənz] *s* appel *m*; (law) citation *f*, assignation *f*, exploit *m*
sumptuous ['sʌmptʃu·əs] *adj* somptueux
sun [sʌn] *s* soleil *m* || *v* (*pret & pp* sunned; *ger* sunning) *tr* exposer au soleil || *intr* prendre le soleil
sun' bath' *s* bain *m* de soleil
sun'beam' *s* rayon *m* de soleil
sun'bon'net *s* capeline *f*
sun'burn' *s* coup *m* de soleil || *v* (*pret & pp* -burned or -burnt) *tr* hâler, basaner || *intr* se basaner
sun'burned' *adj* brûlé par le soleil
sundae ['sʌndi] *s* coupe *f* de glace garnie de fruits
Sunday ['sʌndi] *adj* dominical || *s* dimanche *m*
Sun'day best' *s* (coll) habits *mpl* du dimanche
Sun'day driv'er *s* chauffeur *m* du dimanche
Sun'day school' *s* école *f* du dimanche
sunder ['sʌndər] *tr* séparer, rompre
sun'di'al *s* cadran *m* solaire, gnomon *m*
sun'down' *s* coucher *m* du soleil
sundries ['sʌndriz] *spl* articles *mpl* divers
sundry ['sʌndri] *adj* divers
sun'fish' *s* poisson-lune *m*
sun'flow'er *s* soleil *m*, tournesol *m*
sun'glass'es *spl* lunettes *fpl* de soleil, verres *mpl* fumés
sunken ['sʌŋkən] *adj* creux, enfoncé; (*rock*) noyé; (*ship*) sous-marin
sun' lamp' *s* lampe *f* à rayons ultraviolets
sun'light' *s* lumière *f* du soleil
sun·ny ['sʌni] *adj* (*comp* -nier; *super* -niest) ensoleillé; (*happy*) enjoué; **it is sunny** il fait du soleil
sun'ny side' *s* côté *m* exposé au soleil; (fig) bon côté
sun' par'lor *s* véranda *f*
sun'rise' *s* lever *m* du soleil
sun'set' *s* coucher *m* du soleil
sun'shade' *s* (*over door*) banne *f*; parasol *m*; abat-jour *m*, visière *f*
sun'shine' *s* clarté *f* du soleil, soleil *m*; (fig) gaieté *f* rayonnante; **in the sunshine** en plein soleil
sun'spot' *s* tache *f* solaire
sun'stroke' *s* insolation *f*
sun' tan' *s* hâle *m*
sun'-tan oil' *s* huile *f* solaire
sun'up' *s* lever *m* du soleil
sun' vi'sor *s* abat-jour *m*
sup [sʌp] *v* (*pret & pp* supped; *ger* supping) *intr* souper
super ['supər] *adj* (slang) superbe, for-

midable || *s* (theat) figurant *m*; (slang) concierge *mf*
su'per·abun'dant *adj* surabondant
superannuated [ˌsupər'ænju·ˌetɪd] *adj* (*person*) retraité; (*thing*) suranné
superb [su'pʌrb], [sə'pʌrb] *adj* superbe
su'per·car'go *s* (*pl* -goes or -gos) subrécargue *m*
su'per·charge' *s* surcompression *f* || *tr* surcomprimer
supercilious [ˌsupər'sɪlɪ·əs] *adj* sourcilleux, hautain, arrogant
superficial [ˌsupər'fɪʃəl] *adj* superficiel
superfluous [su'pʌrflu·əs] *adj* superflu
su'per·high'way' *s* autoroute *f*
su'per·hu'man *adj* surhumain
su'per·impose' *tr* superposer
su'per·intend' *tr* surveiller; diriger
superintendent [ˌsupərɪn'tendənt] *s* directeur *m*, directeur en chef; (*of a building*) concierge *mf*
superior [sə'pɪrɪ·ər], [su'pɪrɪ·ər] *adj & s* supérieur *m*
superiority [sə,pɪrɪ'arɪti], [su,pɪrɪ·'arɪti] *s* supériorité *f*
superlative [sə'pʌrlətɪv], [su'pʌrlətɪv] *adj & s* superlatif *m*
su'per·man' *s* (*pl* -men') surhomme *m*
su'per·mar'ket *s* supermarché *m*
su'per·nat'ural *adj & s* surnaturel *m*
supersede [ˌsupər'sid] *tr* remplacer
su'per·sen'sitive *adj* hypersensible
su'per·son'ic *adj* supersonique
superstition [ˌsupər'stɪʃən] *s* superstition *f*
superstitious [ˌsupər'stɪʃəs] *adj* superstitieux
supervene [ˌsupər'vin] *intr* survenir
supervise ['supər,vaɪz] *tr* surveiller; diriger
supervision [ˌsupər'vɪʒən] *s* surveillance *f*; direction *f*
supervisor ['supər,vaɪzər] *s* surveillant *m*, inspecteur *m*; directeur *m*
supper ['sʌpər] *s* souper *m*
sup'per·time' *s* heure *f* du souper
supplant [sə'plænt] *tr* supplanter
supple ['sʌpəl] *adj* souple, flexible
supplement ['sʌplɪmənt] *s* supplément *m* || ['sʌplɪ,ment] *tr* ajouter à
suppliant ['sʌplɪ·ənt] *adj & s* suppliant *m*
supplicant ['sʌplɪkənt] *s* suppliant *m*
supplicate ['sʌplɪ,ket] *tr* supplier
supplier [sə'plaɪ·ər] *s* fournisseur *m*, pourvoyeur *m*
sup·ply [sə'plaɪ] *s* (*pl* -plies) fourniture *f*, provision *f*; (mil) approvisionnement *m*; **supplies** fournitures; (*of food*) vivres *mpl* || *v* (*pret & pp* -plied) *tr* fournir; (*a person, a city, a fort*) pourvoir, munir; (*a need*) répondre à; (*what is lacking*) suppléer; (mil) approvisionner
supply' and demand' *spl* l'offre *f* et la demande
support [sə'port] *s* soutien *m*, appui *m*; ressources *fpl*, de quoi vivre *m*; (*pillar*) support *m* || *tr* soutenir, appuyer; (*e.g., a wife*) entretenir, soutenir; (*to*

hold up; to corroborate; to tolerate) supporter; **to support oneself** gagner sa vie

supporter [sə'pɔrtər] *s* partisan *m*, supporter *m*; (*for part of body*) suspensoir *m*

suppose [sə'poz] *tr* supposer; s'imaginer; **I suppose so** probablement; **suppose that . . .** à supposer que . . .; **suppose we take a walk?** si nous faisions une promenade?; **to be supposed to** + *inf* devoir + *inf*; (*to be considered to be*) être censé + *inf*

supposedly [sə'pozɪdli] *adv* censément

supposition [ˌsʌpə'zɪʃən] *s* supposition *f*

supposito•ry [sə'pʌzɪˌtori] *s* (*pl* -ries) suppositoire *m*

suppress [sə'prɛs] *tr* supprimer; (*rebellion; anger*) réprimer, contenir; (*a yawn*) étouffer, empêcher

suppression [sə'prɛʃən] *s* suppression *f*; (*of a rebellion*) subjugation *f*, répression *f*; (*of a yawn*) empêchement *m*

suppurate ['sʌpjəˌret] *intr* suppurer

supreme [sə'prim], [su'prim] *adj* suprême

supreme′ court′ *s* cour *f* de cassation

surcharge ['sʌrˌtʃɑrdʒ] *s* surcharge *f* || [ˌsʌr'tʃɑrdʒ], ['sʌrˌtʃɑrdʒ] *tr* surcharger

sure [ʃur] *adj* sûr, certain; (*e.g., hand*) ferme; **for sure** à coup sûr, pour sûr; **to be sure to** + *inf* ne pas manquer de + *inf*; **to make sure** s'assurer || *adv* (coll) certainement; **sure enough** (coll) effectivement, assurément || *interj* (slang) mais oui!, bien sûr!, entendu!

sure′-foot′ed *adj* au pied sûr

sure•ty ['ʃurti], ['ʃurɪti] *s* (*pl* -ties) sûreté *f*

surf [sʌrf] *s* barre *f*, ressac *m*, brisants *mpl*

surface ['sʌrfɪs] *adj* superficiel || *s* surface *f*; (area) superficie *f*; **on the surface** à la surface, en apparence; **to float under the surface** nager entre deux eaux || *tr* polir la surface de; (*a road*) recouvrir, revêtir || *intr* (*said of submarine*) faire surface

sur′face mail′ *s* courrier *m* par voie ordinaire

surf′board′ *s* planche *f* pour le surf, surfboard *m*

surfeit ['sʌrfɪt] *s* satiété *f* || *tr* rassasier || *intr* se rassasier

surf′rid′ing *s* surfing *m*, planking *m*

surge [sʌrdʒ] *s* houle *f*; (elec) surtension *f* || *intr* être houleux; se répandre; **to surge up** s'enfler, s'élever

surgeon ['sʌrdʒən] *s* chirurgien *m*

surger•y ['sʌrdʒəri] *s* (*pl* -ies) chirurgie *f*; salle *f* d'opération

surgical ['sʌrdʒɪkəl] *adj* chirurgical

sur•ly ['sʌrli] *adj* (*comp* -lier; *super* -liest) hargneux, maussade, bourru

surmise [sər'maɪz], ['sʌrmaɪz] *s* conjecture *f* || [sər'maɪz] *tr & intr* conjecturer

surmount [sər'maunt] *tr* surmonter

surname ['sʌrˌnem] *s* nom *m* de famil-

le; surnom *m* || *tr* donner un nom de famille à; surnommer

surpass [sər'pæs], [sər'pɑs] *tr* surpasser

surplice ['sʌrplɪs] *s* surplis *m*

surplus ['sʌrplʌs] *adj* excédent, excédentaire, en excédent || *s* surplus *m*, excédent *m*

sur′plus bag′gage *s* excédent *m* de bagages

surprise [sər'praɪz] *adj* à l'improviste, brusqué, inopiné || *s* surprise *f*, étonnement *m*; **to take by surprise** prendre à l'improviste, prendre au dépourvu || *tr* surprendre; **to be surprised at** être surpris de

surprise′ attack′ *s* attaque *f* brusquée

surprise′ pack′age *s* surprise *f*, pochette *f* surprise

surprise′ par′ty *s* (*pl* -ties) réunion *f* à l'improviste

surprising [sər'praɪzɪŋ] *adj* surprenant

surrealism [sə'ri-əˌlɪzəm] *s* surréalisme *m*

surrender [sə'rɛndər] *s* reddition *f*, soumission *f*; (*e.g., of prisoners, goods*) remise *f*; (*e.g., of rights, property*) cession *f* || *tr* rendre, céder || *intr* se rendre

surren′der val′ue *s* valeur *f* de rachat

surreptitious [ˌsʌrɛp'tɪʃəs] *adj* subreptice

surround [sə'raund] *tr* entourer

surrounding [sə'raundɪŋ] *adj* entourant, environnant || **surroundings** *spl* environs *mpl*, alentours *mpl*; entourage *m*, milieu *m*

surtax ['sʌrˌtæks] *s* surtaxe *f* || *tr* surtaxer

surveillance [sər'vel(j)əns] *s* surveillance *f*

survey ['sʌrve] *s* (*for verification*) contrôle *m*; (*for evaluation*) appréciation *f*, évaluation *f*; (*report*) expertise *f*, aperçu *m*; (*of a whole*) vue *f* d'ensemble, tour *m* d'horizon; (*measured plan or drawing*) levé *m*, plan *m*; (surv) lever *m* or levé des plans; **to make a survey** (*to map out*) lever un plan; (*to poll*) effectuer un contrôle par sondage || [sʌr've], ['sʌrve] *tr* contrôler; apprécier, évaluer, faire l'expertise de; (*as a whole*) jeter un coup d'œil sur; (*to poll*) sonder; (*e.g., a farm*) arpenter, faire l'arpentage de; (*e.g., a city*) faire le levé de

sur′vey course′ *s* cours *m* général

surveying [sʌr've-ɪŋ] *s* arpentage *m*, géodésie *f*, levé *m* des plans

surveyor [sər've-ər] *s* arpenteur *m*

survival [sər'vaɪvəl] *s* survivance *f*; (*after death*) survie *f*

survive [sər'vaɪv] *tr* survivre (with *dat*) || *intr* survivre

surviving [sər'vaɪvɪŋ] *adj* survivant

survivor [sər'vaɪvər] *s* survivant *m*

survivorship [sər'vaɪvərˌʃɪp] *s* (law) survie *f*

susceptible [sə'sɛptɪbəl] *adj* (*capable*) susceptible; (*liable, subject*) sensible; (*to love*) facilement amoureux

suspect ['sʌspɛkt], [səs'pɛkt] *adj & s*

suspect *m* || [səs'pɛkt] *tr* soupçonner || *intr* s'en douter

suspend [səs'pɛnd] *tr* suspendre

suspenders [səs'pɛndərz] *spl* bretelles *fpl*

suspense [səs'pɛns] *s* suspens *m*

suspension [səs'pɛnʃən] *s* suspension *f*; suspension of driver's license retrait *m* de permis

suspen'sion bridge' *s* pont *m* suspendu

suspicion [səs'pɪʃən] *s* soupçon *m*

suspicious [səs'pɪʃəs] *adj* (*inclined to suspect*) soupçonneux; (*subject to suspicion*) suspect

sustain [səs'ten] *tr* soutenir; (*a loss, injury, etc.*) éprouver

sustenance ['sʌstɪnəns] *s* subsistance *f*; (*food*) nourriture *f*

swab [swɑb] *s* écouvillon *m*; (naut) faubert *m*; (surg) tampon *m* || *v* (*pret & pp* swabbed; *ger* swabbing) *tr* écouvillonner

swaddle [ˈswɑdəl] *tr* emmailloter

swad'dling clothes' *spl* maillot *m*

swagger [ˈswægər] *s* fanfaronnade *f* || *intr* faire des fanfaronnades

swain [swen] *s* garçon *m*; jeune berger *m*; soupirant *m*

swallow [ˈswɑlo] *s* gorgée *f*; (orn) hirondelle *f* || *tr & intr* avaler

swal'low-tailed coat' *s* frac *m*

swamp [swɑmp] *s* marécage *m* || *tr* submerger, inonder

swamp·y [ˈswɑmpi] *adj* (*comp* -ier; *super* -iest) marécageux

swan [swɑn] *s* cygne *m*

swan' dive' *s* saut *m* de l'ange

swank [swæŋk] *adj* (slang) élégant, chic

swan' knight' *s* chevalier *m* au cygne

swan's'-down' *s* cygne *m*, duvet *m* de cygne

swan' song' *s* chant *m* du cygne

swap [swɑp] *s* (coll) troc *m* || *v* (*pret & pp* swapped; *ger* swapping) *tr & intr* troquer

swarm [swɔrm] *s* essaim *m* || *intr* essaimer; (fig) fourmiller

swarth·y [ˈswɔrði], [ˈswɔrθi] *adj* (*comp* -ier; *super* -iest) basané, brun, noiraud

swashbuckler [ˈswɑʃ‚bʌklər] *s* rodomont *m*, bretteur *m*

swat [swɑt] *s* (coll) coup *m* violent || *v* (*pret & pp* swatted; *ger* swatting) *tr* (coll) frapper; (*a fly*) (coll) écraser

sway [swe] *s* balancement *m*; (*domination*) empire *m* || *tr* balancer || *intr* se balancer; (*to hesitate*) balancer

swear [swɛr] *v* (*pret* swore [swor]; *pp* sworn [sworn]) *tr* jurer; to swear in faire prêter serment à; to swear off jurer de renoncer à || *intr* jurer; to swear at injurier; to swear by (*e.g., a remedy*) préconiser; to swear to déclarer sous serment; jurer de + *inf*

swear' words' *spl* gros mots *mpl*

sweat [swɛt] *s* sueur *f* || *v* (*pret & pp* sweat or sweated) *tr* (*e.g., blood*) suer; (slang) faire suer; to sweat it out (slang) en baver jusqu'à la fin || *intr* suer

sweater [ˈswɛtər] *s* chandail *m*

sweat' shirt' *s* maillot *m* de sport

sweat·y [ˈswɛti] *adj* (*comp* -ier; *super* -iest) suant

Swede [swid] *s* Suédois *m*

Sweden [ˈswidən] *s* Suède *f*; la Suède

Swedish [ˈswidɪʃ] *adj & s* suédois *m*

sweep [swip] *s* balayage *m*; étendue *f*; (*curve*) courbe *f*; (*of wind*) souffle *m*; (*of well*) chadouf *m*; at one sweep d'un seul coup; to make a clean sweep of faire table rase de; (*to win all of*) rafler || *v* (*pret & pp* swept [swɛpt]) *tr* balayer; (*the chimney*) ramoner; (*for mines*) draguer || *intr* balayer; s'étendre

sweeper [ˈswipər] *s* balayeur *m*; (mach) balai *m* mécanique

sweeping [ˈswipɪŋ] *adj* (*movement*) vigoureux; (*statement*) catégorique || *s* balayage *m*; sweepings balayures *fpl*

sweep'-sec'ond *s* trotteuse *f* centrale

sweep'stakes' *s* or *spl* loterie *f*; (turf) sweepstake *m*

sweet [swit] *adj* doux; sucré; (*perfume, music, etc.*) suave; (*sound*) mélodieux; (*milk*) frais; (*person*) charmant, gentil; (*dear*) cher; to be sweet on (coll) avoir un béguin pour; to smell sweet sentir bon || sweets *spl* sucreries *fpl*

sweet'bread' *s* ris *m* de veau

sweet'bri'er *s* églantier *m*

sweeten [ˈswitən] *tr* sucrer; purifier; (fig) adoucir || *intr* s'adoucir

sweet'heart' *s* petite amie *f*, chérie *f*; sweethearts amoureux *mpl*

sweet' mar'joram *s* marjolaine *f*

sweet'meats' *spl* sucreries *fpl*

sweet' pea' *s* gesse *f* odorante, pois *m* de senteur

sweet' pep'per *s* piment *m* doux, poivron *m*

sweet' pota'to *s* patate *f* douce

sweet'-scent'ed *adj* parfumé

sweet'-toothed' *adj* friand de sucreries

sweet' wil'liam *s* œillet *m* de poète

swell [swɛl] *adj* (coll) élégant; (slang) épatant || *s* gonflement *m*; (*of sea*) houle *f*; (mus) crescendo *m*; (pathol) enflure *f*; (coll) rupin *m* || *v* (*pret* swelled; *pp* swelled or swollen [ˈswolən]) *tr* gonfler, enfler || *intr* se gonfler, s'enfler; (*said of sea*) se soulever; (fig) augmenter

swell'head'ed *adj* suffisant, vaniteux

swelter [ˈswɛltər] *intr* étouffer de chaleur

swept'back wing' *s* aile *f* en flèche

swerve [swʌrv] *s* écart *m*, déviation *f*; (aut) embardée *f* || *tr* faire dévier || *intr* écarter, dévier; (aut) faire une embardée

swift [swɪft] *adj* rapide || *adv* vite || *s* (orn) martinet *m*

swig [swɪg] *s* (coll) lampée *f*, trait *m* || *v* (*pret & pp* swigged; *ger* swigging) *tr & intr* lamper

swill [swɪl] *s* eaux *fpl* grasses, ordures *fpl*; (*drink*) lampée *f* || *tr & intr* lamper

swim [swɪm] *s* nage *f*; **to be in the swim** (coll) être dans le train ‖ *v* (*pret* **swam** [swæm]; *pp* **swum** [swʌm]; *ger* **swimming**) *tr* nager ‖ *intr* nager; (*said of head*) tourner; **to swim across** traverser à la nage; **to swim under water** nager entre deux eaux

swimmer ['swɪmər] *s* nageur *m*

swimming ['swɪmɪŋ] *s* natation *f*, nage *f*

swim'ming pool' *s* piscine *f*

swim'ming suit' *s* maillot *m* de bain

swim'ming trunks' *spl* slip *m* de bain

swindle ['swɪndəl] *s* escroquerie *f* ‖ *tr* escroquer

swine [swaɪn] *s* (*pl* **swine**) cochon *m*, pourceau *m*, porc *m*

swing [swɪŋ] *s* balancement *m*, oscillation *f*; (*device used for recreation*) escarpolette *f*; (*trip*) tournée *f*; (*boxing*, *mus*) swing *m*; **in full swing** en pleine marche ‖ *v* (*pret* & *pp* **swung** [swʌŋ]) *tr* balancer, faire osciller; (*the arms*) agiter; (*a sword*) brandir; (*e.g.*, *an election*) mener à bien ‖ *intr* se balancer; (*said of pendulum*) osciller; (*said of door*) pivoter; (*said of bell*) branler; **to swing open** s'ouvrir tout d'un coup

swing'ing door' *s* porte *f* va-et-vient

swinish ['swaɪnɪʃ] *adj* cochon

swipe [swaɪp] *s* (coll) coup *m* à toute volée ‖ *tr* (coll) frapper à toute volée; (*to steal*) (slang) chiper

swirl [swʌrl] *s* remous *m*, tourbillon *m* ‖ *tr* faire tourbillonner ‖ *intr* tourbillonner

swish [swɪʃ] *s* (*e.g.*, *of a whip*) sifflement *m*; (*of a dress*) froufrou *m*; (*e.g.*, *of water*) susurrement *m* ‖ *tr* (*a whip*) faire siffler; (*its tail*) battre ‖ *intr* siffler; froufrouter; susurrer

Swiss [swɪs] *adj* suisse ‖ *s* Suisse *m*; **the Swiss** les Suisses *mpl*

Swiss' chard' [tʃɑrd] *s* bette *f*, poirée *f*

Swiss' cheese' *s* emmenthal *m*, gruyère *m*

Swiss' Guard' *s* suisse *m*

switch [swɪtʃ] *s* (*stick*) badine *f*; (*exchange*) échange *m*; (*hairpiece*) postiche *m*; (elec) interrupteur *m*; (rr) aiguille *f* ‖ *tr* cingler; (*places*) échanger; (rr) aiguiller; **to switch off** couper; (*a light*) éteindre; **to switch on** mettre en circuit; (*a light*) allumer ‖ *intr* changer de place

switch'back' *s* chemin *m* en lacet

switch'board' *s* tableau *m* de distribution; standard *m* téléphonique

switch'board op'erator *s* standardiste *mf*

switch'ing en'gine *s* locomotive *f* de manœuvre

switch'man *s* (*pl* -**men**) aiguilleur *m*

switch' tow'er *s* poste *m* d'aiguillage

switch'yard' *s* gare *f* de triage

Switzerland ['swɪtsərlənd] *s* Suisse *f*; la Suisse

swiv·el ['swɪvəl] *s* pivot *m*; (*link*) émerillon *m* ‖ *v* (*pret* & *pp* -**eled** or -**elled**; *ger* -**eling** or -**elling**) *tr* faire pivoter ‖ *intr* pivoter

swiv'el chair' *s* fauteuil *m* tournant

swoon [swun] *s* évanouissement *m* ‖ *intr* s'évanouir

swoop [swup] *s* attaque *f* brusque; **at one fell swoop** d'un seul coup ‖ *intr* foncer, fondre; **to swoop down on** s'abattre sur

sword [sord] *s* épée *f*; **to cross swords with** croiser le fer avec; **to put to the sword** passer au fil de l'épée

sword' belt' *s* ceinturon *m*

sword'fish' *s* espadon *m*

swords'man *s* (*pl* -**men**) épéiste *m*

sword' swal'lower ['swɑlo·ər] *s* avaleur *m* de sabres

sword' thrust' *s* coup *m* de pointe, coup d'épée

sworn [sworn] *adj* (*enemy*) juré; **sworn in** assermenté

sycophant ['sɪkəfənt] *s* flagorneur *m*

syllable ['sɪləbəl] *s* syllabe *f*

sylla·bus ['sɪləbəs] *s* (*pl* -**bi** [ˌbaɪ] or -**buses**) programme *m*

syllogism ['sɪləˌdʒɪzəm] *s* syllogisme *m*

sylph [sɪlf] *s* sylphe *m*

sylvan ['sɪlvən] *adj* sylvestre

symbol ['sɪmbəl] *s* symbole *m*

symbolic(al) [sɪm'bɑlɪk(əl)] *adj* symbolique

symbolism ['sɪmbəˌlɪzm] *s* symbolisme *m*

symbolize ['sɪmbəˌlaɪz] *tr* symboliser

symmetric(al) [sɪ'mɛtrɪk(əl)] *adj* symétrique

symme·try ['sɪmɪtri] *s* (*pl* -**tries**) symétrie *f*

sympathetic [ˌsɪmpə'θɛtɪk] *adj* compatissant; bien disposé; (anat, physiol) sympathique

sympathize ['sɪmpəˌθaɪz] *intr*—**to sympathize with** compatir à; comprendre

sympa·thy ['sɪmpəθi] *s* (*pl* -**thies**) sympathie *f*; (*shared sorrow*) compassion *f*; **to be in sympathy with** être en sympathie avec; **to extend one's sympathy** to offrir ses condoléances à

sym'pathy strike' *s* grève *f* de solidarité

sympho·ny ['sɪmfəni] *s* (*pl* -**nies**) symphonie *f*

symposi·um [sɪm'pozɪ·əm] *s* (*pl* -**a** [ə]) colloque *m*, symposium *m*

symptom ['sɪmptəm] *s* symptôme *m*

synagogue ['sɪnəˌgɔg], ['sɪnəˌgɑg] *s* synagogue *f*

synchronize ['sɪŋkrəˌnaɪz] *tr* synchroniser

synchronous ['sɪŋkrənəs] *adj* synchrone

syncopation [ˌsɪŋkə'peʃən] *s* syncope *f*

syncope ['sɪŋkəˌpi] *s* syncope *f*

syndicate ['sɪndɪkɪt] *s* syndicat *m* ‖ ['sɪndɪˌket] *tr* syndiquer ‖ *intr* se syndiquer

synonym ['sɪnənɪm] *s* synonyme *m*

synonymous [sɪ'nɑnɪməs] *adj* synonyme

synop·sis [sɪ'nɑpsɪs] *s* (*pl* -**ses** [siz]) abrégé *m*, résumé *m*; (mov) synopsis *m* & *f*

syntax ['sɪntæks] *s* syntaxe *f*

synthe·sis ['sɪnθɪsɪs] *s* (*pl* -**ses** [ˌsiz]) synthèse *f*

synthesize ['sɪnθɪˌsaɪz] *tr* synthétiser

synthetic(al) [sɪn'θetɪk(əl)] adj synthétique

syphilis ['sɪfɪlɪs] s syphilis f

Syria ['sɪrɪ·ə] s Syrie f; la Syrie

Syrian ['sɪrɪ·ən] adj syrien ‖ s (language) syrien m; (person) Syrien m

syringe [sɪ'rɪndʒ], ['sɪrɪndʒ] s seringue f ‖ tr seringuer

syrup ['sɪrəp], ['sʌrəp] s sirop m

system ['sɪstəm] s système m; (of lines, wires, pipes, roads) réseau m

systematic(al) [,sɪstə'mætɪk(əl)] adj systématique

systematize ['sɪstəmə,taɪz] tr systématiser

systole ['sɪstəli] s systole f

T

ʹ, t [ti] s XXᵉ lettre de l'alphabet

tab [tæb] s patte f; (label) étiquette f; to keep tab on (coll) garder à l'œil; to pick up the tab (coll) payer l'addition

tab·by ['tæbi] s (pl -bies) chat m moucheté; (female cat) chatte f; (old maid) vieille fille f; (spiteful female) vieille chipie f

tabernacle ['tæbər,nækəl] s tabernacle m

table ['tebəl] s table f; (tableland) plateau m; (list, chart) tableau m, table; to clear the table ôter le couvert; to set the table mettre le couvert ‖ tr ajourner la discussion de

tab·leau ['tæblo] s (pl -leaus or -leaux [loz]) tableau m vivant

ta'ble·cloth' s nappe f

table d'hôte ['tɑbəl'dot] s repas m à prix fixe

ta'ble·land' s plateau m

ta'ble lin'en s nappage m, linge m de table

ta'ble man'ners spl—to have good table manners bien se tenir à table

tab'le·mate' s commensal m

ta'ble of con'tents s table f des matières

ta'ble·spoon' s cuiller f à soupe

tablespoonful ['tebəl,spun,fʊl] s cuillerée f à soupe or à bouche

tablet ['tæblɪt] s (writing pad) bloc-notes m, bloc m; (lozenge) pastille f, comprimé m; plaque f commémorative

ta'ble talk' s propos mpl de table

ta'ble ten'nis s tennis m de table

ta'ble·top' s dessus m de table

ta'ble·ware' s ustensiles mpl de table

ta'ble wine' s vin m ordinaire

tabloid ['tæblɔɪd] adj (press, article, etc.) à sensation ‖ s journal m de petit format à l'affût du sensationnel

taboo [tə'bu] adj & s tabou m ‖ tr déclarer tabou

tabular ['tæbjələr] adj tabulaire

tabulate ['tæbjə,let] tr disposer en forme de table or en tableaux, dresser un tableau de, aligner en colonnes

tabulator ['tæbjə,letər] s tabulateur m

tacit ['tæsɪt] adj tacite

taciturn ['tæsɪtərn] adj taciturne

tack [tæk] s (nail) semence f; (plan) voie f, tactique f; (of sail) amure f; (naut) bordée f; (sewing) point m de

bâti ‖ tr clouer; (sewing) bâtir ‖ intr louvoyer

tackle ['tækəl] s attirail m; (for lifting) treuil m; (football) plaquage m; (naut) palan m ‖ tr empoigner, saisir; (a problem, job, etc.) chercher à résoudre, attaquer; (football) plaquer

tack·y ['tæki] adj (comp -ier; super -iest) collant; (coll) râpé, minable

tact [tækt] s tact m

tactful ['tæktfəl] adj plein de tact; to be tactful avoir du tact

tactical ['tæktɪkəl] adj tactique

tactician [tæk'tɪʃən] s tacticien m

tactics ['tæktɪks] spl tactique f

tactless ['tæktlɪs] adj sans tact

tadpole ['tæd,pol] s têtard m

taffeta ['tæfɪtə] s taffetas m

taffy ['tæfi] s pâte f à berlingots; (coll) flagornerie f

tag [tæg] s (label) étiquette f; (of shoelace) ferret m; (game) chat m perché ‖ v (pret & pp tagged; ger tagging) tr étiqueter; (in the game of tag) attraper ‖ intr (coll) suivre de près; to tag along behind s.o. (coll) traîner derrière qn

tag' day' s jour m de collecte publique

tag' end' s queue f; (remnant) coupon m

Tagus ['tegəs] s Tage m

tail [tel] s queue f; (of shirt) pan m; tails (of a coin) pile f; (coll) frac m; to turn tail tourner les talons ‖ tr (coll) suivre de tout près ‖ intr—to tail after marcher sur les talons de; to tail off s'éteindre, disparaître

tail' assem'bly s (pl -blies) (aer) empennage m

tail' end' s queue f, fin f

tail'light' s feu m arrière

tailor ['telər] s tailleur m ‖ tr (a suit) faire ‖ intr être tailleur

tailoring ['telərɪŋ] s métier m de tailleur

tai'lor-made suit' s (men's) costume m sur mesure, complet m sur mesure; (women's) costume m tailleur, tailleur m

tai'lor shop' s boutique f de tailleur

tail'piece' s queue f; (of stringed instrument) cordier m

tail'race' s canal m de fuite

tail'spin' s chute f en vrille

tail'wind' s (aer) vent m arrière; (naut) vent en poupe

taint [tent] *s* tache *f* ‖ *tr* tacher; (*food*) gâter

take [tek] *s* prise *f*; (mov) prise de vues; (slang) recette *f* ‖ *v* (*pret* took [tʊk]; *pp* taken) *tr* prendre; (*a walk; a trip*) faire; (*a course; advice*) suivre; (*an examination*) passer; (*a person on a trip*) emmener; (*the occasion*) profiter de; (*a photograph*) prendre; (*a newspaper*) être abonné à; (*a purchase*) garder; (*a certain amount of time*) falloir, e.g., **it takes an hour to walk there** il faut une heure pour y aller à pied; (*to lead*) conduire, mener; (*to tolerate, stand*) supporter; (*a seat*) prendre, occuper, e.g., **this seat is taken** cette place est prise or occupée; **do you take that to be important?** tenez-vous cela pour important?; **I take it that** je suppose que; **take it easy!** (coll) allez-y doucement!; **to be taken ill** tomber malade; **to take amiss** prendre mal; **to take away** enlever; emmener; (*to subtract*) soustraire, retrancher; **to take down** descendre; (*a building*) démolir; (*in writing*) noter; **to take in** (*a roomer*) recevoir; (*laundry*) prendre à faire à la maison; (*the harvest*) rentrer; (*a seam*) reprendre; (*to include*) embrasser; (*to deceive*) (coll) duper; **to take off** ôter, enlever; (*from the price*) rabattre; (*to imitate*) (coll) singer; **to take on** (*passengers*) prendre; (*a responsibility*) prendre sur soi; (*workers*) embaucher, prendre; **to take out** sortir; (*a bullet from a wound; a passage from a text; an element from a compound*) extraire; (*public sign*) à emporter; **to take place** avoir lieu; **to take s.th. from s.o.** enlever, ôter, or prendre q.ch. à qn; **to take up** (*to carry up*) monter; (*to remove*) enlever; (*a dress*) raccourcir; (*an idea, method, etc.*) adopter; (*a profession*) embrasser, prendre; (*a question, a study, etc.*) aborder ‖ *intr* prendre; **to not take to** (*a person*) prendre en grippe; **to take after** ressembler à; (*to chase*) poursuivre; **to take off** s'en aller; (aer) décoller; **to take to** (*flight; the woods*) prendre; (*a bad habit*) se livrer à; (*a person*) se prendre d'amitié avec; (*to like*) s'adonner à; **to take to** + *ger* se mettre à + *inf*; **to take up with s.o.** (coll) se lier avec qn

take′-off′ *s* (aer) décollage *m*; (coll) caricature *f*

tal′cum pow′der [ˈtælkəm] *s* poudre *f* de talc

tale [tel] *s* conte *m*; mensonge *m*; (gossip) racontar *m*, histoire *f*

tale′bear′er *s* rapporteur *m*

talent [ˈtælənt] *s* talent *m*; gens *mpl* de talent

talented [ˈtæləntɪd] *adj* doué, talentueux

tal′ent scout′ *s* dénicheur *m* de vedettes

tal′ent show′ *s* crochet *m* radiophonique, radio-crochet *m*

talk [tɔk] *s* paroles *fpl*; (gossip) racon-

tars *mpl*, dires *mpl*; (lecture) conférence *f*, causerie *f*; **to cause talk** défrayer la chronique; **to have a talk with** s'entretenir avec ‖ *tr* parler; **to talk over** discuter; **to talk up** vanter ‖ *intr* parler; (*to chatter, gossip, etc.*) bavarder, jaser; **to talk back** répliquer; **to talk on** continuer à parler

talkative [ˈtɔkətɪv] *adj* bavard

talker [ˈtɔkər] *s* parleur *m*; **a great talker** (coll) un causeur, un hâbleur

talkie [ˈtɔki] *s* (coll) film *m* parlant

talk′ing doll′ [ˈtɔkɪŋ] *s* poupée *f* parlante

talk′ing pic′ture *s* film *m* parlant

tall [tɔl] *adj* haut, élevé; (person) grand; (coll) exagéré

tallow [ˈtælo] *s* suif *m*

tal·ly [ˈtæli] *s* (pl -lies) compte *m*, pointage *m* ‖ *v* (*pret & pp* -lied) *tr* pointer, contrôler ‖ *intr* s'accorder

tallyho [ˈtælɪ ˌho] *interj* taïaut!

tal′ly sheet′ *s* feuille *f* de pointage, bordereau *m*

talon [ˈtælən] *s* serre *f*

tamarack [ˈtæmə ˌræk] *s* mélèze *m* d'Amérique

tambourine [ˌtæmbəˈrin] *s* tambour *m* de basque

tame [tem] *adj* apprivoisé; (*e.g., lion*) dompté; (*e.g., style*) fade, terne ‖ *tr* apprivoiser; (*e.g., a lion*) dompter

tamp [tæmp] *tr* bourrer; (*e.g., a hole in the ground*) damer

tamper [ˈtæmpər] *intr*—**to tamper with** se mêler de; (*a lock*) fausser; (*a document*) falsifier; (*a witness*) suborner

tampon [ˈtæmpɑn] *s* (surg) tampon *m* ‖ *tr* (surg) tamponner

tan [tæn] *adj* jaune, (*e.g., skin*) bronzé, hâlé ‖ *v* (*pret & pp* tanned; *ger* tanning) *tr* tanner; (*e.g., the skin*) bronzer, hâler ‖ *intr* se hâler

tandem [ˈtændəm] *adj & adv* en tandem, en flèche ‖ *s* tandem *m*

tang [tæŋ] *s* goût *m* vif, saveur *f*; (ringing sound) tintement *m*

tangent [ˈtændʒənt] *adj* tangent ‖ *s* tangente *f*; **to fly off at** or **on a tangent** changer brusquement de sujet

tangerine [ˌtændʒəˈrin] *s* mandarine *f*

tangible [ˈtændʒɪbəl] *adj* tangible

Tangier [tænˈdʒɪr] *s* Tanger *m*

tangle [ˈtæŋgəl] *s* enchevêtrement *m* ‖ *tr* enchevêtrer ‖ *intr* s'enchevêtrer

tank [tæŋk] *s* réservoir *m*; (mil) char *m*

tank′ car′ *s* (rr) wagon-citerne *m*

tanker [ˈtæŋkər] *s* (ship) bateau-citerne *m*; (truck) camion-citerne *m*; (plane) ravitailleur *m*

tank′ truck′ *s* camion-citerne *m*

tanner [ˈtænər] *s* tanneur *m*

tanner·y [ˈtænəri] *s* (pl -ies) tannerie *f*

tantalize [ˈtæntə ˌlaɪz] *tr* tenter, allécher

tantamount [ˈtæntə ˌmaunt] *adj* équivalent

tantrum [ˈtæntrəm] *s* accès *m* de colère; **in a tantrum** en rogne

tap [tæp] *s* petit coup *m*; (faucet) robinet *m*; (elec) prise *f*; (mach) taraud *m*; **on tap** au tonneau, en perce;

(*available*) (coll) disponible; **taps** (mil) l'extinction *f* des feux ‖ *v* (*pret & pp* **tapped**; *ger* **tapping**) *tr* taper; (*a cask*) mettre en perce; (*a tree*) entailler; (*a telephone*) passer à la table d'écoute; (*a nut*) tarauder; (*resources, talent, etc.*) drainer; (elec) brancher sur ‖ *intr* taper

tap′ dance′ *s* danse *f* à claquettes

tap′-dance′ *intr* danser les claquettes, faire les claquettes

tap′ dan′cer *s* danseur *m* à claquettes

tape [tep] *s* ruban *m* ‖ *tr* (*an electric wire*) guiper; (*land*) mesurer au cordeau; (*to tape-record*) enregistrer sur ruban

tape′ meas′ure *s* mètre-ruban *m*, centimètre *m*

taper ['tepər] *s* (*for lighting candles*) allumette-bougie *f*; (eccl) cierge *m* ‖ *tr* intr s'effiler

tape′-record′ *tr* enregistrer sur ruban magnétique or au magnétophone

tape′ record′er *s* magnétophone *m*

tapes·try ['tæpɪstri] *s* (*pl* **-tries**) tapisserie *f* ‖ *v* (*pret & pp* **-tried**) *tr* tapisser

tape′worm′ *s* ver *m* solitaire

tappet ['tæpɪt] *s* (mach) taquet *m*

tap′room′ *s* débit *m* de boissons, buvette *f*

tap′ wa′ter *s* eau *f* du robinet

tap′ wrench′ *s* taraudeuse *f*

tar [tɑr] *s* goudron *m*; (coll) marin *m* ‖ *v* (*pret & pp* **tarred**; *ger* **tarring**) *tr* goudronner; **to tar and feather** enduire de goudron et de plumes

tar·dy ['tɑrdi] *adj* (*comp* **-dier**; *super* **-diest**) lent; retardataire, en retard

tare [ter] *s* (*weight*) tare *f*; (Bib) ivraie *f* ‖ *tr* tarer

target ['tɑrgɪt] *s* cible *f*; (*goal*) but *m*; (mil) objectif *m*; (*butt*) (fig) cible

tar′get ar′ea *s* zone *f* de tir

tar′get lan′guage *s* langue *f* cible

tar′get prac′tice *s* tir *m* à la cible

tariff ['tærɪf] *s* (*duties*) droits *mpl* de douane; (*rates in general*) tarif *m*

tarnish ['tɑrnɪʃ] *s* ternissure *f* ‖ *tr* ternir ‖ *intr* se ternir

tar′ pa′per *s* papier *m* goudronné

tarpaulin [tɑr'pɔlɪn] *s* bâche *f*, prélart *m*

tarragon ['tærəgən] *s* estragon *m*

tar·ry ['tɑri] *adj* (*comp* **-rier**; *super* **-riest**) goudronneux ‖ ['tæri] *v* (*pret & pp* **-ried**) *intr* tarder; (*to stay*) rester, demeurer

tart [tɑrt] *adj* aigrelet; (*reply*) mordant ‖ *s* tarte *f*; (slang) grue *f*, poule *f*

tartar ['tɑrtər] *adj* (*sauce*) tartare; **Tartar** tartare ‖ *s* (*on teeth*) tartre *m*; **Tartar** Tartare *mf*

task [tæsk], [tɑsk] *s* tâche *f*; **to bring** or **take to task** prendre à partie

task′ force′ *s* (mil) groupement *m* stratégique mixte

task′mas′ter *s* chef *m* de corvée; (fig) tyran *m*

tassel ['tæsəl] *s* gland *m*; (*on corn*) barbe *f*; (*on nightcap*) mèche *f*; (bot) aigrette *f*

taste [test] *s* goût *m*, saveur *f*; (*sense of what is fitting*) goût, bon goût ‖ *tr* goûter; (*to sample*) goûter à; (*to try out*) goûter de ‖ *intr* goûter; **to taste like** avoir le goût de; **to taste of** avoir un goût de

taste′ bud′ *s* papille *f* gustative

tasteless ['testlɪs] *adj* sans saveur, fade; (*in bad taste*) de mauvais goût

tast·y ['testi] *adj* (*comp* **-ier**; *super* **-iest**) (coll) savoureux; (coll) de bon goût

tatter ['tætər] *s* lambeau *m* ‖ *tr* mettre en lambeaux

tatterdemalion [ˌtætərdɪ'meljen], [ˌtætərdɪ'mæljən] *s* loqueteux *m*

tattered *adj* en lambeaux, en loques

tattle ['tætəl] *s* bavardage *m*; (*gossip*) cancan *m* ‖ *intr* bavarder; cancaner

tat′tle·tale′ *adj* révélateur ‖ *s* rapporteur *m*, cancanier *m*

tattoo [tæ'tu] *s* tatouage *m*; (mil) retraite *f* ‖ *tr* tatouer

taunt [tɔnt], [tɑnt] *s* sarcasme *m* ‖ *tr* bafouer

taut [tɔt] *adj* tendu

tavern ['tævərn] *s* café *m*, bar *m*, bistrot *m*; (*inn*) taverne *f*

taw·dry ['tɔdri] *adj* (*comp* **-drier**; *super* **-driest**) criard, voyant

taw·ny ['tɔni] *adj* (*comp* **-nier**; *super* **-niest**) fauve; (*skin*) basané

tax [tæks] *s* impôt *m*; **to reduce the tax on** dégrever ‖ *tr* imposer; (*e.g., one's patience*) mettre à l'épreuve; **to tax s.o. with** (*e.g., laziness*) taxer qn de

taxable ['tæksəbəl] *adj* imposable

taxation [tæk'seʃən] *s* imposition *f*; charges *fpl* fiscales, impôts *mpl*

tax′ collec′tor *s* percepteur *m*

tax′ cut′ *s* dégrèvement *m* d'impôt

tax′ eva′sion *s* fraude *f* fiscale

tax′-exempt′ *adj* net d'impôt, exempt d'impôts

tax·i ['tæksi] *s* (*pl* **-is**) taxi *m* ‖ *v* (*pret & pp* **-ied**; *ger* **-iing** or **-ying**) *tr* (aer) rouler au sol ‖ *intr* aller en taxi; (aer) rouler au sol ‖ *interj* hep taxi!

tax′i·cab′ *s* taxi *m*

tax′i danc′er *s* taxi-girl *f*

taxidermy ['tæksɪˌdʌrmi] *s* taxidermie *f*

tax′i driv′er *s* chauffeur *m* de taxi

tax′i·plane′ *s* avion-taxi *m*

tax′i stand′ *s* station *f* de taxis

tax′pay′er *s* contribuable *mf*

tax′ rate′ *s* taux *m* de l'impôt

tea [ti] *s* thé *m*; (*medicinal infusion*) tisane *f*

tea′ bag′ *s* sachet *m* de thé

tea′ ball′ *s* boule *f* à thé

tea′cart′ *s* table *f* roulante

teach [titʃ] *v* (*pret & pp* **taught** [tɔt]) *tr* enseigner; **to teach s.o. s.th.** enseigner q.ch. à qn; **to teach s.o. to +** *inf* enseigner à qn à + *inf* ‖ *intr* enseigner

teacher ['titʃər] *s* instituteur *m*, enseignant *m*; (*such as adversity*) (fig) maître *m*

teach′er's pet′ *s* élève *m* gâté

teaching ['titʃɪŋ] *s* enseignement *m*

teach′ing aids′ *spl* matériel *m* auxiliaire d'enseignement
teach′ing staff′ *s* corps *m* enseignant
tea′cup′ *s* tasse *f* à thé
tea′ dance′ *s* thé *m* dansant
teak [tik] *s* teck *m*
tea′ket′tle *s* bouilloire *f*
team [tim] *s* (*of horses, oxen, etc.*) attelage *m*; (sports) équipe *f* ‖ *tr* atteler ‖ *intr*—**to team up with** faire équipe avec
team′mate′ *s* équipier *m*
teamster ['timstər] *s* (*of horses*) charretier *m*; (*of a truck*) camionneur *m*
team′work′ *s* travail *m* en équipe; (*spirit*) esprit *m* d'équipe
tea′pot′ *s* théière *f*
tear [tɪr] *s* larme *f*; **to burst into tears** fondre en larmes ‖ [tɛr] *s* déchirure *f* ‖ [tɛr] *v* (*pret* **tore** [tor]; *pp* **torn** [torn]) *tr* déchirer; **to tear away, down, off,** or **out** arracher; **to tear up** (*e.g., a letter*) déchirer ‖ *intr* se déchirer; **to tear along** filer précipitamment, aller à fond de train
tear′ bomb′ [tɪr] *s* bombe *f* lacrymogène
tear′ duct′ [tɪr] *s* conduit *m* lacrymal
tearful ['tɪrfəl] *adj* larmoyant, éploré
tear′ gas′ [tɪr] *s* gaz *m* lacrymogène
tear-jerker ['tɪr,dʒʌrkər] *s* (slang) comédie *f* larmoyante
tea′room′ *s* salon *m* de thé
tease [tiz] *tr* taquiner
tea′spoon′ *s* cuiller *f* à café
teaspoonful ['ti,spun,ful] *s* cuillerée *f* à café
teat [tit] *s* tétine *f*
tea′time′ *s* l'heure *f* du thé
technical ['tɛknɪkəl] *adj* technique
technicali‧ty [,tɛknɪ'kælɪti] *s* (*pl* **-ties**) technicité *f*; (*fine point*) subtilité *f*
technician [tɛk'nɪʃən] *s* technicien *m*
technique [tɛk'nik] *s* technique *f*
ted′dy bear′ ['tɛdi] *s* ours *m* en peluche
tedious ['tidɪ‧əs], ['tidʒəs] *adj* ennuyeux, fatigant
teem [tim] *intr* fourmiller; **to teem with** abonder en, fourmiller de
teeming ['timɪŋ] *adj* fourmillant; (*rain*) torrentiel
teen-ager ['tin,edʒər] *s* adolescent *m* de 13 à 19 ans
teens [tinz] *spl* numéros anglais qui se terminent en **-teen** (de 13 à 19); adolescence *f* de 13 à 19 ans; **to be in one's teens** être adolescent
tee‧ny ['tini] *adj* (*comp* **-nier;** *super* **-niest**) (coll) minuscule, tout petit
teeter ['titər] *s* branlement *m*; balançoire *f* ‖ *intr* se balancer, chanceler
teethe [tið] *intr* faire ses dents
teething ['tiðɪŋ] *s* dentition *f*
teeth′ing ring′ *s* sucette *f*
teetotaler [ti'totələr] *s* antialcoolique *mf* (*qui s'abstient totalement de boissons alcooliques*)
tele‧cast ['tɛlɪ,kæst], ['tɛlɪ,kɑst] *s* émission *f* télévisée ‖ *v* (*pret & pp* **-cast** or **-casted**) *tr & intr* téléviser
telegram ['tɛlɪ,græm] *s* télégramme *m*

telegraph ['tɛlɪ,græf], ['tɛlɪ,grɑf] *s* télégraphe *m* ‖ *tr & intr* télégraphier
telegrapher [tɪ'lɛgrəfər] *s* télégraphiste *mf*
tel′egraph pole′ *s* poteau *m* télégraphique
telemeter [tɪ'lɛmɪtər] *s* télémètre *m*
telepathy [tɪ'lɛpəθi] *s* télépathie *f*
telephone ['tɛlɪ,fon] *s* téléphone *m* ‖ *tr & intr* téléphoner
tel′ephone booth′ *s* cabine *f* téléphonique
tel′ephone call′ *s* appel *m* téléphonique
tel′ephone direc′tory *s* annuaire *m* du téléphone
tel′ephone exchange′ *s* central *m* téléphonique
tel′ephone op′erator *s* standardiste *mf*, téléphoniste *mf*
tel′ephone receiv′er *s* récepteur *m* de téléphone
tel′ephoto lens′ ['tɛlɪ,foto] *s* téléobjectif *m*
teleprinter ['tɛlɪ,prɪntər] *s* téléimprimeur *m*
telescope ['tɛlɪ,skop] *s* télescope *m* ‖ *tr* télescoper ‖ *intr* se télescoper
telescopic [,tɛlɪ'skɑpɪk] *adj* télescopique
teletype ['tɛlɪ,taɪp] *s* (trademark) télétype *m*
tel′etype′writ′er *s* téléscripteur *m*
teleview ['tɛlɪ,vju] *tr & intr* voir à la télévision
televiewer ['tɛlɪ,vju‧ər] *s* téléspectateur *m*
televise ['tɛlɪ,vaɪz] *tr* téléviser
television ['tɛlɪ,vɪʒən] *adj* télévisuel ‖ *s* télévision *f*
tel′evision screen′ *s* écran *m* de télévision, petit écran
tel′evision set′ *s* téléviseur *m*
tell [tɛl] *v* (*pret & pp* **told** [told]) *tr* dire; (*a story*) raconter; (*to count*) compter; (*to recognize as distinct*) distinguer; **tell me another!** (coll) à d'autres!; **to tell off** compter; (coll) dire son fait à; **to tell s.o. to** + *inf* dire à qn de + *inf* ‖ *intr* produire un effet; **do tell!** (coll) vraiment!; **to tell on** influer sur; (coll) dénoncer; **who can tell?** qui sait?
teller ['tɛlər] *s* narrateur *m*; (*of a bank*) caissier *m*; (*of votes*) scrutateur *m*
temper ['tɛmpər] *s* humeur *f*, caractère *m*; (*of steel, glass, etc.*) trempe *f*; **to keep one's temper** retenir sa colère; **to lose one's temper** se mettre en colère ‖ *tr* tremper ‖ *intr* se tremper
temperament ['tɛmpərəmənt] *s* tempérament *m*
temperamental [,tɛmpərə'mɛntəl] *adj* constitutionnel; capricieux, instable
temperance ['tɛmpərəns] *s* tempérance *f*
temperate ['tɛmpərɪt] *adj* tempéré; (*in food or drink*) tempérant
temperature ['tɛmpərətʃər] *s* température *f*
tempest ['tɛmpɪst] *s* tempête *f*; **tempest in a teapot** tempête dans un verre d'eau

tempestuous [tɛm'pɛstʃu·əs] *adj* tempétueux

temple ['tɛmpəl] *s* temple *m*; (*side of forehead*) tempe *f*; (*of spectacles*) branche *f*

templet ['tɛmplɪt] *s* gabarit *m*

tem·po ['tɛmpo] *s* (*pl* -pos or -pi [pi]) tempo *m*

temporal ['tɛmpərəl] *adj* temporel; (anat) temporal

temporary ['tɛmpə‚rɛri] *adj* temporaire

temporize ['tɛmpə‚raɪz] *intr* temporiser

tempt [tɛmpt] *tr* tenter

temptation [tɛmp'teʃən] *s* tentation *f*

tempter ['tɛmptər] *s* tentateur *m*

tempting ['tɛmptɪŋ] *adj* tentant

ten [tɛn] *adj* & *pron* dix; **about ten** une dizaine de ‖ *s* dix *m*; **ten o'clock** dix heures

tenable ['tɛnəbəl] *adj* soutenable

tenacious [tɪ'neʃəs] *adj* tenace

tenacity [tɪ'næsɪti] *s* ténacité *f*

tenant ['tɛnənt] *s* locataire *mf*

ten'ant farm'er *s* métayer *m*

tend [tɛnd] *tr* soigner; (*sheep*) garder; (*a machine*) surveiller ‖ *intr*—**to tend to** (*to be disposed to*) tendre à; (*to attend to*) vaquer à; **to tend towards** tendre vers or à

tenden·cy ['tɛndənsi] *s* (*pl* -cies) tendance *f*

tender ['tɛndər] *adj* tendre ‖ *s* offre *f*; (aer, naut) ravitailleur *m*; (rr) tender *m* ‖ *tr* offrir

ten'der-heart'ed *adj* au cœur tendre

ten'der-loin' *s* filet *m*

tenderness ['tɛndərnɪs] *s* tendresse *f*; (*of, e.g., the skin*) sensibilité *f*; (*of, e.g., meat*) tendreté *f*

tendon ['tɛndən] *s* tendon *m*

tendril ['tɛndrɪl] *s* vrille *f*

tenement ['tɛnɪmənt] *s* maison *f* d'habitation

ten'ement house' *s* maison *f* de rapport; (*in the slums*) taudis *m*

tenet ['tɛnɪt] *s* doctrine *f*, principe *m*

tennis ['tɛnɪs] *s* tennis *m*

ten'nis court' *s* court *m* de tennis

tenor ['tɛnər] *s* teneur *f*, cours *m*; (mus) ténor *m*

tense [tɛns] *adj* tendu ‖ *s* (gram) temps *m*

tension ['tɛnʃən] *s* tension *f*

tent [tɛnt] *s* tente *f*

tentacle ['tɛntəkəl] *s* tentacule *m*

tentative ['tɛntətɪv] *adj* provisoire; (*hesitant*) timide

tenth [tɛnθ] *adj* & *pron* dixième (*masc, fem*); **the Tenth** dix, e.g., **John the Tenth** Jean dix ‖ *s* dixième *m*; **the tenth** (*in dates*) le dix

tent' pole' *s* montant *m* de tente

tenuous ['tɛnju·əs] *adj* ténu

tenure ['tɛnjər] *s* (*possession*) tenure *f*; (*of an office*) occupation *f*; (*protection from dismissal*) inamovibilité *f*

tepid ['tɛpɪd] *adj* tiède

term [tʌrm] *s* terme *m*; (*of imprisonment*) temps *m*; (*of office*) mandat *m*; (*of the school year*) semestre *m*; **terms** conditions *fpl* ‖ *tr* appeler, qualifier

termagant ['tʌrməgənt] *s* mégère *f*

terminal ['tʌrmɪnəl] *adj* terminal ‖ *s* (elec) borne *f*; (rr) terminus *m*

terminate ['tʌrmɪ‚net] *tr* terminer ‖ *intr* se terminer

termination [‚tʌrmɪ'neʃən] *s* conclusion *f*; (*extremity*) bout *m*; (*of word*) désinence *f*

terminus ['tʌrmɪnəs] *s* bout *m*, extrémité *f*; (*boundary*) borne *f*; (rr) terminus *m*

termite ['tʌrmaɪt] *s* termite *m*

term' pa'per *s* dissertation *f*

terrace ['tɛrəs] *s* terrasse *f* ‖ *tr* disposer en terrasse

terra firma ['tɛrə'fʌrmə] *s* terre *f* ferme

terrain [tɛ'ren] *s* terrain *m*

terrestrial [tə'rɛstrɪ·əl] *adj* terrestre

terrible ['tɛrɪbəl] *adj* terrible; (*extremely bad*) atroce

terrific [tə'rɪfɪk] *adj* terrible, terrifiant; (coll) formidable

terri·fy ['tɛrɪ‚faɪ] *v* (*pret* & *pp* -fied) *tr* terrifier

territo·ry ['tɛrɪ‚tori] *s* (*pl* -ries) territoire *m*

terror ['tɛrər] *s* terreur *f*

terrorize ['tɛrə‚raɪz] *tr* terroriser

ter'ry cloth' ['tɛri] *s* tissu-éponge *m*

terse [tʌrs] *adj* concis, succinct

tertiary ['tʌrʃɪ‚ɛri], ['tʌrʃəri] *adj* tertiaire

test [tɛst] *s* épreuve *f*; (*exam*) examen *m*; (*trial*) essai *m*; (*e.g., of intelligence*) test *m* ‖ *tr* éprouver, mettre à l'épreuve; examiner, tester

testament ['tɛstəmənt] *s* testament *m*

test' ban' *s* interdiction *f* des essais nucléaires

test' flight' *s* vol *m* d'essai

testicle ['tɛstɪkəl] *s* testicule *m*

testi·fy ['tɛstɪ‚faɪ] *v* (*pret* & *pp* -fied) *tr* déclarer ‖ *intr* déposer; **to testify to** témoigner de

testimonial [‚tɛstɪ'monɪ·əl] *s* attestation *m*

testimo·ny ['tɛstɪ‚moni] *s* (*pl* -nies) témoignage *m*

test' pat'tern *s* (telv) mire *f*

test' pi'lot *s* pilote *m* d'essai

test' tube' *s* éprouvette *f*

tes·ty ['tɛsti] *adj* (*comp* -tier; *super* -tiest) susceptible

tetanus ['tɛtənəs] *s* tétanos *m*

tether ['tɛðər] *s* attache *f*; **at the end of one's tether** à bout de ressources ‖ *tr* mettre à l'attache

tetter ['tɛtər] *s* (pathol) dartre *f*

text [tɛkst] *s* texte *m*

text'book' *s* manuel *m* scolaire, livre *m* de classe

textile ['tɛkstɪl], ['tɛkstaɪl] *adj* & *s* textile *m*

textual ['tɛkstʃu·əl] *adj* textuel

texture ['tɛkstʃər] *s* texture *f*; (*woven fabric*) tissu *m*

Thai ['tɑ·i], [taɪ] *adj* thaï, thaïlandais ‖ *s* (*language*) thaï *m*; (*person*)

Thaïlandais *m*; **the Thai** les Thaïlandais
Thailand ['taɪlənd] *s* Thaïlande *f*; la Thaïlande
Thames [temz] *s* Tamise *f*
than [ðæn] *conj* que; (*before a numeral*) de, e.g., **more than three** plus de trois
thank [θæŋk] *adj* (*e.g., offering*) de reconnaissance ‖ **thanks** *spl* remerciements *mpl*; **thanks to** grâce à ‖ **thanks** *interj* merci!; **no thanks!** merci! ‖ **thank** *tr* remercier; **thank you** je vous remercie; **thank you for** merci de or pour; **thank you for** + *ger* merci de + *inf*; **to thank s.o. for** remercier qn de or pour; **to thank s.o. for** + *ger* remercier qn de + *inf*
thankful ['θæŋkfəl] *adj* reconnaissant
thankless ['θæŋklɪs] *adj* ingrat
Thanksgiv'ing Day' *s* le jour d'action de grâces
that [ðæt] *adj dem* (*pl* those) ce §82; **that one** celui-là §84 ‖ *pron dem* (*pl* those) celui §83; celui-là §84 ‖ *pron rel* qui; que ‖ *pron neut* cela, ça; **that is** c'est-à-dire; **that's all** voilà tout; **that will do** cela suffit ‖ *adv* tellement, si, aussi; **that far** si loin, aussi loin; **that much, that many** tant ‖ *conj* que; (*in order that*) pour que, afin que; **in that** en ce que
thatch [θætʃ] *s* chaume *m* ‖ *tr* couvrir de chaume
thatched' cot'tage *s* chaumière *f*
thaw [θɔ] *s* dégel *m* ‖ *tr & intr* dégeler
the [ðə], [ðɪ], [ði] *art def* le §77 ‖ *adv* d'autant plus, e.g., **she will be the happier for it** elle en sera d'autant plus heureuse; **the more . . . the more** plus . . . plus
theater ['θi·ətər] *s* théâtre *m*
the'ater club' *s* association *f* des spectateurs
the'ater-go'er *s* habitué *m* du théâtre
the'ater page' *s* chronique *f* théâtrale
theatrical [θi'ætrɪkəl] *adj* théâtral
thee [ði] *pron pers* (archaic, poetic, Bib) toi §85; te §87
theft [θeft] *s* vol *m*
their [ðer] *adj poss* leur §88
theirs [ðerz] *pron poss* le leur §89
them [ðem] *pron pers* eux §85; les §87; leur §87; **of them** en §87; **to them** leur §87; y §87
theme [θim] *s* thème *m*; (*essay*) composition *f*; (mus) thème
theme' song' *s* leitmotiv *m*; (rad) indicatif *m*
them·selves' *pron pers* soi §85; eux-mêmes §86; se §87; eux §85
then [ðen] *adv* alors; (*next*) ensuite, puis; (*therefore*) donc; **by then** d'ici là; **from then on, since then** depuis lors, dès lors; **then and there** séance tenante; **till then** jusque-là; **what then?** et après?
thence [ðens] *adv* de là; (*from that fact*) pour cette raison
thence'forth' *adv* dès lors
theolo·gy [θi'alədʒi] *s* (*pl* -gies) théologie *f*

theorem ['θi·ərəm] *s* théorème *m*
theoretical [,θi·ə'retɪkəl] *adj* théorique
theo·ry ['θi·əri] *s* (*pl* -ries) théorie *f*
therapeutic [,θerə'pjutɪk] *adj* thérapeutique ‖ **therapeutics** *spl* thérapeutique *f*
thera·py ['θerəpi] *s* (*pl* -pies) thérapie *f*
there [ðer] *adv* là; y §87; **down there, over there** là-bas; **from there** de là; en §87; **in there** là-dedans; **on there** là-dessus; **there is** or **there are** il y a; (*pointing out*) voilà; **under there** là-dessous; **up there** là-haut
there'abouts' *adv* aux environs, près de là; (*approximately*) à peu près
there'af'ter *adv* par la suite
there'by' *adv* par là; de cette manière
therefore ['ðer,for] *adv* par conséquent, donc
there'in' *adv* dedans, là-dedans
there'of' *adv* de cela; en §87
there'upon' *adv* là-dessus §85A; sur ce
there'with' *adv* avec cela
thermal ['θɑrməl] *adj* (*waters*) thermal; (*capacity*) thermique
thermocouple ['θɑrmo,kʌpəl] *s* thermocouple *m*
thermodynamic [,θɑrmodaɪ'næmɪk] *adj* thermodynamique ‖ **thermodynamics** *spl* thermodynamique *f*
thermometer [θər'mamɪtər] *s* thermomètre *m*
thermonuclear [,θɑrmo'n(j)ukli·ər] *adj* thermonucléaire
Thermopylae [θər'mapɪ,li] *s* les Thermopyles *fpl*
ther'mos bot'tle ['θɑrməs] *s* thermos *m & f*, bouteille *f* thermos
thermostat ['θɑrmə,stæt] *s* thermostat *m*
thesau·rus [θi'sɔrəs] *s* (*pl* -ri [raɪ]) trésor *m*; dictionnaire *m* analogique
these [ðiz] *adj dem pl* ces §82 ‖ *pron dem pl* ceux §83; ceux-ci §84
the·sis ['θisɪs] *s* (*pl* -ses [siz]) thèse *f*
they [ðe] *pron pers* ils §87; eux §85; on §87, e.g., **they say** on dit; ce §82B
thick [θɪk] *adj* épais; (*pipe, rod, etc.*) gros; (*forest, eyebrows, etc.*) touffu; (*grass, grain, etc.*) dru; (*voice*) pâteux; (*gravy*) court; (coll) stupide, obtus; (coll) intime ‖ *s* (*of thumb, leg, etc.*) gras *m*; **the thick of** (*e.g., a crowd*) le milieu de; (*e.g., a battle*) le fort de; **through thick and thin** contre vents et marées
thicken ['θɪkən] *tr* épaissir ‖ *intr* s'épaissir; (*said, e.g., of plot*) se corser
thicket ['θɪkɪt] *s* fourré *m*, maquis *m*
thick'-head'ed *adj* à la tête dure
thick'-lipped' *adj* lippu
thick'-set' *adj* trapu
thief [θif] *s* (*pl* thieves [θivz]) voleur *m*
thieve [θiv] *intr* voler
thiever·y ['θivəri] *s* (*pl* -ies) volerie *f*
thigh [θaɪ] *s* cuisse *f*
thigh'bone' *s* fémur *m*
thimble ['θɪmbəl] *s* dé *m*
thin [θɪn] *adj* (*comp* thinner; *super* thinnest) mince; (*person*) élancé, maigre; (*hair*) rare; (*soup*) clair;

(*gravy*) long; (*voice*) grêle; (*excuse*) faible || *v* (*pret* & *pp* **thinned**; *ger* **thinning**) *tr* amincir; (*colors*) délayer; **to thin out** éclaircir || *intr* s'amincir; **to thin out** s'éclaircir

thine [ðaɪn] *adj poss* (archaic, poetic, Bib) ton §88 || *pron poss* (archaic, poetic, Bib) le tien §89

thing [θɪŋ] *s* chose *f*; **for another thing** d'autre part; **for one thing** en premier lieu; **of all things!** par exemple!; **to be the thing** être le dernier cri; **to see things** avoir des hallucinations

thingumbob [ˈθɪŋəmˌbab] *s* (coll) truc *m*, machin *m*

think [θɪŋk] *v* (*pret* & *pp* **thought** [θɔt]) *tr* penser; (*to deem, consider*) estimer; **to think of** (*to have as an opinion of*) penser de || *intr* penser, songer; **to think fast** avoir l'esprit alerte; **to think of** (*to direct one's thoughts toward*) penser à, songer à; **to think of it** or **them** y penser, y songer; **to think so** croire que oui

thinker [ˈθɪŋkər] *s* penseur *m*

third [θʌrd] *adj* & *pron* troisième (*masc, fem*), e.g., **John the Third** Jean trois || *s* troisième *m*; (*in fractions*) tiers *m*; **the third** (*in dates*) le trois

third' degree' *s* (coll) passage *m* à tabac, cuisinage *m*

third' fin'ger *s* annulaire *m*

third' rail' *s* (rr) rail *m* de contact; rail conducteur

third'-rate' *adj* de troisième ordre

thirst [θʌrst] *s* soif *f* || *intr* avoir soif; **to thirst for** avoir soif de

thirst'-quench'ing *adj* désaltérant

thirst·y [ˈθʌrsti] *adj* (*comp* **-ier**; *super* **-iest**) altéré, assoiffé; **to be thirsty** avoir soif

thirteen [ˈθʌrˈtin] *adj, pron,* & *s* treize *m*

thirteenth [ˈθʌrˈtinθ] *adj* & *pron* treizième (*masc, fem*); **the Thirteenth** treize, e.g., **John the Thirteenth** Jean treize || *s* treizième *m*; **the thirteenth** (*in dates*) le treize

thirtieth [ˈθʌrtɪ·əθ] *adj* & *pron* trentième (*masc, fem*) || *s* trentième *m*; **the thirtieth** (*in dates*) trente

thir·ty [ˈθʌrti] *adj* & *pron* trente; **about thirty** une trentaine de || *s* (*pl* **-ties**) trente *m*; **the thirties** les années *fpl* trente

this [ðɪs] *adj dem* (*pl* **these**) ce §82; **this one** celui-ci §84 || *pron dem* (*pl* **these**) celui §83; celui-ci §84 || *pron neut* ceci || *adv* tellement, si, aussi; **this far** si loin, aussi loin; **this much, this many** tant

thistle [ˈθɪsəl] *s* chardon *m*

thither [ˈθɪðər], [ˈðɪðər] *adv* là, de ce côté *m*

thong [θɔŋ], [θɑŋ] *s* courroie *f*

tho·rax [ˈθoræks] *s* (*pl* **-raxes** or **-races** [rəˌsiz]) thorax *m*

thorn [θɔrn] *s* épine *f*

thorn·y [ˈθɔrni] *adj* (*comp* **-ier**; *super* **-iest**) épineux

thorough [ˈθʌro] *adj* approfondi, complet; consciencieux, minutieux

thor'ough·bred' *adj* de race, racé; (*horse*) pur sang || *s* personne *f* racée; (*horse*) pur-sang *m*

thor'ough·fare' *s* voie *f* de communication; **no thoroughfare** (public sign) rue barrée

thor'ough·go'ing *adj* parfait; consciencieux

thoroughly [ˈθʌroli] *adv* à fond

those [ðoz] *adj dem pl* ces §82 || *pron dem pl* ceux §83; ceux-là §84

thou [ðau] *pron pers* (archaic, poetic, Bib) tu §87 || *tr* & *intr* tutoyer

though [ðo] *adv* cependant || *conj* (*although*) bien que, quoique; (*even if*) même si; **as though** comme si

thought [θɔt] *s* pensée *f*

thought' control' *s* asservissement *m* des consciences

thoughtful [ˈθɔtfəl] *adj* pensif; (*considerate*) prévenant, attentif; (*serious*) profond

thoughtless [ˈθɔtlɪs] *adj* étourdi, négligent; inconsidéré

thousand [ˈθauzənd] *adj* & *pron* mille; mil, e.g., **the year one thousand nineteen hundred and eighty-one** l'an mil neuf cent quatre-vingt-un || *s* mille *m*; **a thousand** un millier de, mille

thousandth [ˈθauzəndθ] *adj* & *pron* millième (*masc, fem*) || *s* millième *m*

thrash [θræʃ] *tr* rosser; (agr) battre; **to thrash out** débattre || *intr* s'agiter; (agr) battre le blé

thread [θrɛd] *s* fil *m*; (bot) filament *m*; (mach) filet *m*; **to hang by a thread** ne tenir qu'à un fil; **to lose the thread of** perdre le fil de || *tr* enfiler; (mach) fileter

thread'bare' *adj* élimé, râpé; (*tire*) usé jusqu'à la corde

threat [θrɛt] *s* menace *f*

threaten [ˈθrɛtən] *tr* & *intr* menacer

threatening [ˈθrɛtənɪŋ] *adj* menaçant

three [θri] *adj* & *pron* trois || *s* trois *m*; **three o'clock** trois heures; **three of a kind** (cards) un fredon

three'-cor'nered *adj* triangulaire; (*hat*) tricorne

three'-ply' *adj* à trois épaisseurs; (e.g., *wool*) à trois fils

three' R's' [ɑrz] *spl* la lecture, l'écriture et l'arithmétique, premières notions *fpl*

three'score' *adj* soixante

threno·dy [ˈθrɛnədi] *s* (*pl* **-dies**) thrène *m*

thresh [θrɛʃ] *tr* (agr) battre; **to thresh out** (*a problem*) débattre || *intr* s'agiter; (agr) battre le blé

thresh'ing floor' *s* aire *f*

thresh'ing machine' *s* batteuse *f*

threshold [ˈθrɛʃold] *s* seuil *m*; **to cross the threshold** franchir le seuil

thrice [θraɪs] *adv* trois fois

thrift [θrɪft] *s* économie *f*, épargne *f*

thrift·y [ˈθrɪfti] *adj* (*comp* **-ier**; *super* **-iest**) économe, ménager, frugal; prospère

thrill [θrɪl] *s* frisson *m* ‖ *tr* faire frémir ‖ *intr* frémir

thriller ['θrɪlər] *s* roman *m*, film *m*, or pièce *f* à sensation

thrilling ['θrɪlɪŋ] *adj* émouvant, passionnant

thrive [θraɪv] *v* (*pret* **thrived** or **throve** [θrov]; *pp* **thrived** or **thriven** ['θrɪvən]) *intr* prospérer; (*said of child, plant, etc.*) croître, se développer

throat [θrot] *s* gorge *f*; **to clear one's throat** s'éclaircir le gosier; **to have a sore throat** avoir mal à la gorge

throb [θrɑb] *s* palpitation *f*, battement *m*; (*of motor*) vrombissement *m* ‖ *v* (*pret & pp* **throbbed**; *ger* **throbbing**) *intr* palpiter, battre fort; (*said of motor*) vrombir

throes [θroz] *spl* (*of childbirth*) douleurs *fpl*; (*of death*) affres *fpl*; **in the throes of** luttant avec

throne [θron] *s* trône *m*

throng [θrɔŋ], [θrɑŋ] *s* foule *f*, affluence *f* ‖ *intr* affluer

throttle ['θrɑtəl] *s* (*of steam engine*) régulateur *m*; (aut) étrangleur *m* ‖ *tr* régler; étrangler

through [θru] *adj* direct; (*finished*) fini; (*traffic*) prioritaire ‖ *adv* à travers; complètement ‖ *prep* au travers de, par; grâce à, par le canal de

through·out' *adv* d'un bout à l'autre ‖ *prep* d'un bout à l'autre de; (*during*) pendant tout

through' street' *s* rue *f* à circulation prioritaire

through'way' *s* autoroute *f*

throw [θro] *s* jet *m*, lancement *m*; (*scarf*) châle *m* ‖ *v* (*pret* **threw** [θru]; *pp* **thrown**) *tr* jeter, lancer; (*a glance; the dice*) jeter; (*e.g., a baseball*) lancer; (*e.g., a shadow*) projeter; (*blame; responsibility*) rejeter; (*a rider*) désarçonner; (*a game, career, etc.*) perdre à dessein; **to throw away** jeter; **to throw back** renvoyer; **to throw in** ajouter; **to throw out** expulser, chasser; (*e.g., an odor*) répandre; (*one's chest*) bomber; **throw over** abandonner; **to throw up** jeter en l'air; vomir; (*one's hands*) lever; (*e.g., one's claims*) renoncer à ‖ *intr* jeter, lancer; jeter des dés; **to throw up** vomir

throw'back' *s* recul *m*; (*setback*) échec *m*; (*reversion*) retour *m* atavique

thrum [θrʌm] *v* (*pret & pp* **thrummed**; *ger* **thrumming**) *intr* pianoter

thrush [θrʌʃ] *s* grive *f*

thrust [θrʌst] *s* poussée *f*; (*with a weapon*) coup *m* de pointe; (*with a sword*) coup d'estoc; (*jibe*) trait *m*; (rok) poussée *f*; **thrust and parry** la botte et la parade ‖ *v* (*pret & pp* **thrust**) *tr* pousser; (*e.g., a dagger*) enfoncer; **to thrust oneself on** s'imposer à

thud [θʌd] *s* bruit *m* sourd ‖ *v* (*pret & pp* **thudded**; *ger* **thudding**) *tr & intr* frapper avec un son mat

thug [θʌg] *s* bandit *m*, assassin *m*

thumb [θʌm] *s* pouce *m*; **all thumbs** (coll) maladroit; **to twiddle one's thumbs** se tourner les pouces; **under the thumb of** sous la coupe de ‖ *tr* tripoter; (*a book*) feuilleter; **to thumb a ride** faire de l'auto-stop; **to thumb one's nose at** (coll) faire un pied de nez à

thumb' in'dex *s* onglet *m*, encoche *f*

thumb'print' *s* marque *f* de pouce

thumb'screw' *s* papillon *m*, vis *f* à ailettes

thumb'tack' *s* punaise *f*

thump [θʌmp] *s* coup *m* violent ‖ *tr* cogner ‖ *intr* tomber avec un bruit sourd; (*said, e.g., of marching feet*) sonner lourdement; (*said of heart*) battre fort

thumping ['θʌmpɪŋ] *adj* (coll) énorme

thunder ['θʌndər] *s* tonnerre *m* ‖ *tr* fulminer ‖ *intr* tonner; **to thunder at** tonner contre, tempêter contre

thun'der·bolt' *s* foudre *f*; (*disaster*) coup *m* de foudre

thun'der·clap' *s* coup *m* de tonnerre

thunderous ['θʌndərəs] *adj* orageux; (*voice; applause*) tonnant

thun'der·show'er *s* pluie *f* d'orage

thun'der·storm' *s* orage *m*

thunderstruck ['θʌndər ˌstrʌk] *adj* foudroyé

Thursday ['θʌrzdi] *s* jeudi *m*

thus [ðʌs] *adv* ainsi; (*therefore*) donc; **thus far** jusqu'ici

thwack [θwæk] *s* coup *m* ‖ *tr* flanquer un coup à

thwart [θwɔrt] *adj* transversal ‖ *adv* en travers ‖ *tr* déjouer, frustrer

thy [ðaɪ] *adj* poss (archaic, poetic, Bib) ton §88

thyme [taɪm] *s* thym *m*

thyroid ['θaɪrɔɪd] *s* thyroïde *f*; (pharm) extrait *m* thyroïde

thyself [ðaɪ'sɛlf] *pron* (archaic, poetic, Bib) toi-même §86; te §87

tiara [taɪ'ɑrə], [taɪ'ɛrə] *s* tiare *f*; (*woman's headdress*) diadème *m*

tic [tɪk] *s* (pathol) tic *m*

tick [tɪk] *s* tic-tac *m*; (*e.g., of pillow*) taie *f*; (*e.g., of mattress*) housse *f* de coutil; (ent) tique *f*; **on tick** à crédit ‖ *tr*—**to tick off** (*to check off*) pointer ‖ *intr* tictaquer; (*said of heart*) battre

ticker ['tɪkər] *s* téléimprimeur *m*; (*watch*) (slang) toquante *f*; (*heart*) (slang) cœur *m*

tick'er tape' *s* bande *f* de téléimprimeur

ticket ['tɪkɪt] *s* billet *m*; (*of bus, subway, etc.*) ticket *m*; (*of baggage checkroom*) bulletin *m*; (*of cloakroom*) numéro *m*; (*for boat trip*) passage *m*; (*of a political party*) liste *f* électorale; (*for violation*) (coll) papillon *m* de procès-verbal, contravention *f*; **that's the ticket** (coll) c'est bien ça, à la bonne heure; **tickets, please!** vos places, s'il vous plaît!

tick'et a'gent *s* guichetier *m*

tick'et collec'tor *s* contrôleur *m*

tick'et of'fice *s* guichet *m*; (theat) bureau *m* de location

tick′et scalp′er [‚skælpər] s trafiquant m de billets de théâtre
tick′et win′dow s guichet m
ticking [′tɪkɪŋ] s coutil m
tickle [′tɪkəl] s chatouillement m ‖ tr chatouiller; amuser; plaire (with dat) ‖ intr chatouiller
ticklish [′tɪklɪʃ] adj chatouilleux; (touchy) susceptible; (subject, question) épineux, délicat
tick′-tack-toe′ s morpion m
ticktock [′tɪk‚tɑk] s tic-tac m ‖ intr faire tic-tac
tid′al wave′ [′taɪdəl] s raz m de marée; (e.g., of popular indignation) vague f
tidbit [′tɪd‚bɪt] s bon morceau m
tiddlywinks [′tɪdli‚wɪŋks] s jeu m de puce
tide [taɪd] s marée f; **against the tide** à contre-marée; **to go with the tide** suivre le courant ‖ tr—**to tide over** dépanner, remettre à flot; (a difficulty) venir à bout de
tide′land′ s terres fpl inondées aux grandes marées
tide′wa′ter s eaux fpl de marée; bord m de la mer
tide′water pow′er plant′ s usine f marémotrice
tidings [′taɪdɪŋz] spl nouvelles fpl
ti·dy [′taɪdi] adj (comp -dier; super -diest) propre, net, bien tenu; (considerable) (coll) joli, fameux ‖ s (pl -dies) voile m de fauteuil ‖ v (pret & pp -died) tr mettre en ordre, nettoyer ‖ intr—**to tidy up** faire un brin de toilette
tie [taɪ] s lien m, attache f; (knot) nœud m; (necktie) cravate f; (in games) match m nul; (mus) liaison f; (rr) traverse f ‖ v (pret & pp tied; ger tying) tr lier; (a knot, a necktie, etc.) nouer; (shoelaces; a knot; one′s apron) attacher; (an artery) ligaturer; (a competitor) être à égalité avec; (mus) lier; **tied up** (busy) occupé; **to tie down** assujettir; **to tie up** attacher; (a package) ficeler; (a person) ligoter; (a wound) bander; (funds) immobiliser; (traffic, a telephone line) embouteiller ‖ intr (sports) faire match nul, égaliser
tie′back′ s embrasse f
tie′pin′ s épingle f de cravate
tier [tɪr] s étage m; (of stadium) gradin m
tiger [′taɪgər] s tigre m
ti′ger lil′y s lis m tigré
tight [taɪt] adj serré, juste; (e.g., rope) tendu; (clothes) ajusté; (container) étanche; (game) serré; (money) rare; (miserly) (coll) chiche; (drunk) (coll) rond, noir ‖ **tights** spl collant m, maillot m ‖ adv fermement, bien; **to hold tight** tenir serré; se tenir, se cramponner; **to sit tight** (coll) tenir bon
tighten [′taɪtən] tr (a knot, a bolt) serrer, resserrer; (e.g., a rope) tendre ‖ intr se serrer; se tendre
tight-fisted [′taɪt′fɪstɪd] adj dur à la détente, serré

tight′-fit′ting adj collant, ajusté
tight′rope′ s corde f raide
tight′rope walk′er s funambule mf
tight′ squeeze′ s (coll) situation f difficile, embarras m
tight′wad′ s (coll) grippe-sou m
tigress [′taɪgrɪs] s tigresse f
tile [taɪl] s (for roof) tuile f; (for floor) carreau m ‖ tr (e.g., a house) couvrir de tuiles; (a floor) carreler
tile′ roof′ s toit m de tuiles
till [tɪl] s tiroir-caisse m ‖ prep jusqu'à ‖ conj jusqu'à ce que ‖ tr labourer
tilt [tɪlt] s pente f, inclinaison f; (contest) joute f; **full tilt** à fond de train ‖ tr pencher, incliner; **to tilt back** renverser en arrière; **to tilt up** redresser ‖ intr se pencher, s'incliner; (with lance) jouter; (naut) donner de la bande; **to tilt at** attaquer, critiquer; **to tilt back** se renverser en arrière
timber [′tɪmbər] s bois m de construction; (trees) bois de haute futaie; (rafter) poutre f
tim′ber-land′ s bois m pour exploitation forestière
tim′ber line′ s limite f de la végétation forestière
timbre [′tɪmbər] s (phonet, phys) timbre m
time [taɪm] s temps m; heure f, e.g., **what time is it?** quelle heure est-il?; fois, e.g., **five times** cinq fois; e.g., **five times two is ten** cinq fois deux font dix; (period of payment) délai m; (phot) temps d'exposition; **at that time** à ce moment-là; à cette époque; **at the present time** à l'heure actuelle; **at the same time** en même temps; **at times** parfois; **behind the times** en retard sur son époque; **between times** entre-temps; **full time** plein temps; **in due time** en temps et lieu; **in no time** en moins de rien; **on time** à l'heure, à temps; **several times** à plusieurs reprises; **time and time again** maintes fois; **to beat time** (mus) battre la mesure; **to do time** (coll) faire son temps; **to have a good time** s'amuser bien, se divertir; **to lose time** (said of timepiece) retarder; **to mark time** marquer le pas; **to play for time** (coll) chercher à gagner du temps ‖ tr mesurer la durée de; (sports) chronométrer
time′ bomb′ s bombe f à retardement
time′card′ s registre m de présence
time′ clock′ s horloge f enregistreuse
time′ expo′sure s (phot) pose f
time′ fuse′ s fusée f fusante
time′-hon′ored adj consacré par l'usage
time′keep′er s pointeur m, chronométreur m; pendule f; montre f
timeless [′taɪmlɪs] adj sans fin, éternel
time·ly [′taɪmli] adj (comp -lier; super -liest) opportun, à propos
time′piece′ s pendule f; montre f
timer [′taɪmər] s (person) chronométreur m; (of an electrical appliance) minuterie f
time′ sheet′ s feuille f de présence
time′ sig′nal s signal m horaire

time′ta′ble *s* horaire *m*; (rr) indicateur *m*

time′work′ *s* travail *m* à l'heure

time′worn′ *adj* usé par le temps; (*venerable*) séculaire

time′ zone′ *s* fuseau *m* horaire

timid ['tɪmɪd] *adj* timide

timing ['taɪmɪŋ] *s* chronométrage *m*; choix *m* du moment propice; (*of an electrical appliance*) minuterie *f*; (aut, mach) réglage *m*; (sports) chronométrage; (theat) tempo *m*

tim′ing gears′ *spl* engrenage *m* de distribution

timorous ['tɪmərəs] *adj* timoré, peureux

tin [tɪn] *s* (*element*) étain *m*; (*tin plate*) fer-blanc *m*; (*cup, box, etc.*) boîte *f* ‖ *v* (*pret & pp* **tinned**; *ger* **tinning**) *tr* étamer; (*to can*) (Brit) mettre en boîte

tin′ can′ *s* boîte *f* en fer-blanc, boîte de conserve

tincture ['tɪŋktʃər] *s* teinture *f*

tin′ cup′ *s* timbale *f*

tinder ['tɪndər] *s* amadou *m*

tin′der-box′ *s* briquet *m* à amadou; (fig) foyer *m* de l'effervescence

tin′ foil′ *s* feuille *f* d'étain, papier *m* d'argent

ting-a-ling ['tɪŋə,lɪŋ] *s* drelin *m*

tinge [tɪndʒ] *s* teinte *f*, nuance *f* ‖ *v* (*ger* **tingeing** or **tinging**) *tr* teinter, nuancer

tingle ['tɪŋgəl] *s* picotement *m*, fourmillement *m* ‖ *intr* picoter, fourmiller; (*e.g., with enthusiasm*) tressaillir

tin′ hat′ *s* (coll) casque *m* en acier

tinker ['tɪŋkər] *s* chaudronnier *m* ambulant; (*bungler*) housilleur *m* ‖ *intr* bricoler; **to tinker with** tripatouiller

tinkle ['tɪŋkəl] *s* tintement *m* ‖ *tr* faire tinter ‖ *intr* tinter

tin′ plate′ *s* fer-blanc *m*

tin′-plate′ *tr* étamer

tin′ roof′ *s* toit *m* de fer-blanc

tinsel ['tɪnsəl] *s* clinquant *m*; (*for a Christmas tree*) paillettes *fpl*, guirlandes *fpl* clinquantes

tin′smith′ *s* ferblantier *m*

tin′ sol′dier *s* soldat *m* de plomb

tint [tɪnt] *s* teinte *f* ‖ *tr* teinter

tin′type′ *s* ferrotypie *f*

tin′ware′ *s* ferblanterie *f*

ti·ny ['taɪni] *adj* (*comp* **-nier**; *super* **-niest**) minuscule

tip [tɪp] *s* bout *m*, pointe *f*; (*slant*) inclinaison *f*; (*fee to a waiter*) pourboire *m*; (*secret information*) (slang) tuyau *m* ‖ *v* (*pret & pp* **tipped**; *ger* **tipping**) *tr* incliner; (*the scales*) faire pencher; (*a waiter*) donner un pourboire à, donner la pièce à; **to tip off** (slang) tuyauter; **to tip over** renverser ‖ *intr* se renverser; donner un pourboire

tip′cart′ *s* tombereau *m*

tip′-in′ *s* (bb) hors-texte *m*

tip′-off′ *s* (coll) tuyau *m*

tipped′-in′ *adj* (bb) hors texte

tipple ['tɪpəl] *intr* biberonner

tip′staff′ *s* verge *f* d'huissier; huissier *m* à verge

tip·sy ['tɪpsi] *adj* (*comp* **-sier**; *super* **-siest**) gris, grisé

tip′toe′ *s* pointe *f* des pieds ‖ *v* (*pret & pp* **-toed**; *ger* **-toeing**) *intr* marcher sur la pointe des pieds

tirade ['taɪred] *s* diatribe *f*

tire [taɪr] *s* pneu *m* ‖ *tr* fatiguer ‖ *intr* se fatiguer

tire′ chain′ *s* chaîne *f* antidérapante

tired [taɪrd] *adj* fatigué, las

tire′ gauge′ *s* manomètre *m*

tire′ i′ron *s* démonte-pneu *m*

tireless ['taɪrlɪs] *adj* infatigable

tire′ pres′sure *s* pression *f* des pneus

tire′ pump′ *s* gonfleur *m* pour pneus

tiresome ['taɪrsəm] *adj* fatigant, ennuyeux

tissue ['tɪsju] *s* tissu *m*; (*thin paper*) papier *m* de soie; (*toilet tissue*) papier hygiénique; (*paper handkerchief*) mouchoir *m* à jeter

tis′sue pa′per *s* papier *m* de soie

tit [tɪt] *s* téton *m*; (orn) mésange *f*; **tit for tat** à bon chat bon rat

titanium [taɪ'tenɪ·əm], [tɪ'tenɪ·əm] *s* titane *m*

tithe [taɪð] *s* dixième *m*; (rel) dîme *f* ‖ *tr* soumettre à la dîme; payer la dîme sur

Titian ['tɪʃən] *s* le Titien *m*

Ti′tian red′ *s* blond *m* vénitien

title ['taɪtəl] *s* titre *m* ‖ *tr* intituler

ti′tle deed′ *s* titre *m* de propriété

ti′tle·hold′er *s* tenant *m* du titre

ti′tle page′ *s* page *f* de titre

ti′tle role′ *s* rôle *m* principal

tit′mouse′ *s* (*pl* **-mice**) (orn) mésange *f*

titter ['tɪtər] *s* rire *m* étouffé ‖ *intr* rire en catimini

titular ['tɪtʃələr] *adj* titulaire

to [tu], [tʊ], [tə] *adv*—**to and fro** de long en large ‖ *prep* à; (*towards*) vers; (*in order to*) afin de, pour; envers, pour, e.g., **good to her** bon envers elle, bon pour elle; jusqu'à, e.g., **to this day** jusqu'à ce jour; e.g., **to count to a hundred** compter jusqu'à cent; moins, e.g., **a quarter to eight** huit heures moins le quart; contre, e.g., **seven to one** sept contre un; dans, e.g., **to a certain extent** dans une certaine mesure; en, e.g., **from door to door** de porte en porte; e.g., **I am going to France** je vais en France; de, e.g., **to try to** + *inf* essayer de + *inf*; **to him** lui §87

toad [tod] *s* crapaud *m*

toad′stool′ *s* agaric *m*; champignon *m* vénéneux

to-and-fro ['tu·ənd'fro] *adj* de va-et-vient

toast [tost] *s* pain *m* grillé; (*with a drink*) toast *m* ‖ *tr* griller; porter un toast à, boire à la santé de

toaster ['tostər] *s* grille-pain *m*

toast′mas′ter *s* préposé *m* aux toasts

tobac·co [tə'bæko] *s* (*pl* **-cos**) tabac *m*

tobac′co pouch′ *s* blague *f*

toboggan [tə'bagən] *s* toboggan *m*

tocsin ['tɑksɪn] *s* tocsin *m*; (*bell*) cloche *f* qui sonne le tocsin
today [tʊ'de] *s & adv* aujourd'hui *m*
toddle ['tɑdəl] *s* allure *f* chancelante ‖ *intr* marcher à petits pas chancelants
toddler ['tɑdlər] *s* tout-petit *m*
tod·dy ['tɑdi] *s* (*pl* **-dies**) grog *m*
to-do [tə'du] *s* (*pl* **-dos**) embarras *mpl*, chichis *mpl*, façons *fpl*
toe [to] *s* doigt *m* du pied, orteil *m*; (*of shoe, of stocking*) bout *m* ‖ *v* (*pret & pp* **toed**; *ger* **toeing**) *tr*—**to toe the line** or **the mark** s'aligner, se mettre au pas
toe'nail' *s* ongle *m* du pied
tog [tɑg] *v* (*pret & pp* **togged**; *ger* **togging**) *tr*—**to tog out** or **up** attifer, fringuer ‖ **togs** *spl* fringues *fpl*
together [tʊ'gɛðər] *adv* ensemble; (*at the same time*) en même temps, à la fois
tog'gle switch' ['tɑgəl] *s* (elec) interrupteur *m* à culbuteur or à bascule
toil [tɔɪl] *s* travail *m* dur; **toils** filet *m*, piège *m* ‖ *intr* travailler dur
toilet ['tɔɪlɪt] *s* toilette *f*; (*rest room*) cabinet *m* de toilette
toi'let ar'ticles *spl* objets *mpl* de toilette
toi'let bowl' *s* cuvette *f*
toi'let pa'per *s* papier *m* hygiénique
toi'let seat' *s* siège *m* des toilettes
toi'let set' *s* nécessaire *m* de toilette
toi'let soap' *s* savonnette *f*
toi'let wa'ter *s* eaux *fpl* de toilette
token ['tokən] *adj* symbolique ‖ *s* signe *m*, marque *f*; (*keepsake*) souvenir *m*; (*used as money*) jeton *m*; **by the same token** de plus; **in token of** en témoignage de
tolerance ['tɑlərəns] *s* tolérance *f*
tolerate ['tɑlə,ret] *tr* tolérer
toll [tol] *s* (*of bells*) glas *m*; (*payment*) droit *m* de passage, péage *m*; (*number of victims*) mortalité *f*; (telp) tarif *m* ‖ *tr* tinter; (*to ring the knell for*) sonner le glas de ‖ *intr* sonner le glas
toll' bridge' *s* pont *m* à péage
toll' call' *s* appel *m* interurbain
toll'gate' *s* barrière *f* à péage
toll' road' *s* autoroute *f* à péage
toma·to [tə'meto], [tə'mɑto] *s* (*pl* **-toes**) tomate *f*
tomb [tum] *s* tombeau *m*
tomboy ['tɑm,bɔɪ] *s* garçon *m* manqué
tomb'stone' *s* pierre *f* tombale
tomcat ['tɑm,kæt] *s* matou *m*
tome [tom] *s* tome *m*
tomorrow [tʊ'mɑro], [tʊ'mɔro] *adj, s, & adv* demain *m*; **tomorrow morning** demain matin; **until tomorrow** à demain
tom-tom ['tɑm,tɑm] *s* tam-tam *m*
ton [tʌn] *s* tonne *f*
tone [ton] *s* ton *m* ‖ *tr* accorder; **to tone down** atténuer; **to tone up** renforcer; (*e.g., the muscles*) tonifier ‖ *intr*—**to tone down** se modérer
tone' po'em *s* poème *m* symphonique
tongs [tɔŋz], [tɑŋz] *spl* pincettes *fpl*; (*e.g., for sugar*) pince *f*; (*of blacksmith*) tenailles *fpl*

tongue [tʌŋ] *s* (*language; part of body*) langue *f*; (*of wagon*) timon *m*; (*of buckle*) ardillon *m*; (*of shoe*) languette *f*; **to hold one's tongue** se mordre la langue
tongue-tied ['tʌŋ,taɪd] *adj* bouche cousue
tongue' twist'er *s* phrase *f* à décrocher la mâchoire
tonic ['tɑnɪk] *adj & s* tonique *m*
tonight [tʊ'naɪt] *adj & s* ce soir
tonsil ['tɑnsəl] *s* amygdale *f*
tonsillitis [,tɑnsɪ'laɪtɪs] *s* amygdalite *f*
ton·y ['toni] *adj* (*comp* **-ier**; *super* **-iest**) (slang) élégant, chic
too [tu] *adv* (*also*) aussi; (*more than enough*) trop; (*moreover*) d'ailleurs; **I did too!** mais si!; **too bad!** c'est dommage!; **too many, too much** trop, trop de
tool [tul] *s* outil ‖ *tr* (*a piece of metal*) usiner; (*leather*) repousser; (bb) dorer ‖ *intr*—**to tool along** rouler; **to tool up** s'outiller
tool'box' *s* trousse *f* à outils
tool'mak'er *s* taillandier *m*
toot [tut] *s* son *m* du cor; (*of auto*) coup *m* de klaxon; (*of locomotive*) coup de sifflet ‖ *tr* sonner ‖ *intr* corner; (aut) klaxonner
tooth [tuθ] *s* (*pl* **teeth** [tiθ]) dent *f*; **to grit, grind,** or **gnash the teeth** grincer des dents, crisser des dents
tooth'ache' *s* mal *m* de dents
tooth'brush' *s* brosse *f* à dents
toothless ['tuθlɪs] *adj* édenté
tooth'paste' *s* pâte *f* dentifrice
tooth'pick' *s* cure-dent *m*
tooth' pow'der *s* poudre *f* dentifrice
top [tɑp] *adj* premier, de tête ‖ *s* sommet *m*, cime *f*, faîte *m*; (*of a barrel, table, etc.*) dessus *m*; (*of a page*) haut *m*; (*of a box*) couvercle *m*; (*of a carriage* or *auto*) capote *f*; (*toy*) toupie *f*; (naut) hune *f*; **at the top of** en haut de; (*e.g., one's class*) à la tête de; **at the top of one's voice** à tue-tête; **from top to bottom** de haut en bas, de fond en comble; **on top of** sur; (*in addition to*) en plus de; **tops** (*e.g., of carrots*) fanes *fpl*; **to sleep like a top** dormir comme un sabot ‖ *v* (*pret & pp* **topped**; *ger* **topping**) *tr* couronner, surmonter; (*to surpass*) dépasser; (*a tree, plant, etc.*) écimer
topaz ['topæz] *s* topaze *f*
top' bill'ing *s* tête *f* d'affiche
top'coat' *s* surtout *m* de demi-saison
toper ['topər] *s* soiffard *m*
top' hat' *s* haut-de-forme *m*
top'-heav'y *adj* trop lourd du haut
topic ['tɑpɪk] *s* sujet *m*
top'knot' *s* chignon *m*
top'mast' *s* mât *m* de hune
top'most' *adj* (le) plus haut
top'notch' *adj* (coll) d'élite
topogra·phy [tə'pɑgrəfi] *s* (*pl* **-phies**) topographie *f*
topple ['tɑpəl] *tr & intr* culbuter
topsail ['tɑpsəl], ['tɑp,sel] *s* (naut) hunier *m*
top'soil' *s* couche *f* arable

topsy-turvy ['tɑpsi'tʌrvi] *adj* & *adv* sens dessus dessous
torch [tɔrtʃ] *s* torche *f*, flambeau *m*; (Brit) lampe *f* torche; **to carry the torch for** (slang) avoir un amour sans retour pour
torch'bear'er *s* porte-flambeau *m*; (fig) défenseur *m*
torch'light' *s* lueur *f* des flambeaux
torch'light proces'sion *s* défilé *m* aux flambeaux
torch' song' *s* chanson *f* de l'amour non partagé
torment ['tɔrment] *s* tourment *m* || [tɔr'ment] *tr* tourmenter
torna·do [tɔr'nedo] *s* (*pl* **-does** or **-dos**) tornade *f*
torpe·do [tɔr'pido] *s* (*pl* **-does**) torpille *f* || *tr* torpiller
torpe'do-boat destroy'er *s* contre-torpilleur *m*
torpid ['tɔrpɪd] *adj* engourdi
torque [tɔrk] *s* effort *m* de torsion, couple *m* de torsion
torrent ['tɑrənt], ['tɔrənt] *s* torrent *m*
torrid ['tɑrɪd], ['tɔrɪd] *adj* torride
tor·so ['tɔrso] *s* (*pl* **-sos**) torse *m*
tort [tɔrt] *s* (law) acte *m* dommageable sauf rupture de contrat ou abus de confiance
tortoise ['tɔrtəs] *s* tortue *f*
tor'toise shell' *s* écaille *f*
torture ['tɔrtʃər] *s* torture *f* || *tr* torturer
toss [tɔs], [tɑs] *s* lancement *m*; (*of the head*) mouvement *m* dédaigneux || *tr* lancer; (*one's head*) relever dédaigneusement; (*a rider*) démonter; (*a coin*) jouer à pile et face avec; **to toss about** agiter, ballotter; **to toss off** (*e.g., work*) expédier; (*in one gulp*) lamper; **to toss up** jeter en l'air || *intr* s'agiter; **to toss and turn** se tourner et retourner
toss'up' *s* (coll) coup *m* de pile ou face; chances *fpl* égales
tot [tɑt] *s* bambin *m*, tout petit *m* || *v* (*pret* & *pp* **totted**; *ger* **totting**) *tr*—**to tot up** additionner
to·tal ['totəl] *adj* & *s* total *m*; **as a total** au total || *v* (*pret* & *pp* **-taled** or **-talled**; *ger* **-taling** or **-talling**) *tr* additionner, totaliser; (*to amount to*) s'élever à
totalitarian [to ˌtælɪ'terɪ·ən] *adj* & *mf* totalitaire
totem ['totəm] *s* totem *m*
totter ['tɑtər] *intr* chanceler
touch [tʌtʃ] *s* (*act*) attouchement *m*; (*e.g., of color; with a brush*) touche *f*; (*sense; of pianist*) toucher *m*; (*of typist*) frappe *f*; (*little bit*) pointe *f*, brin *m*; **in touch** en communication; **to get in touch with** prendre contact avec || *tr* toucher; (*for a loan*) (slang) taper; **to touch off** déclencher; **to touch up** retoucher || *intr* se toucher; **to touch on** toucher à
touched *adj* touché; (*crazy*) timbré
touching ['tʌtʃɪŋ] *adj* touchant, émouvant || *prep* touchant, concernant

touch·y ['tʌtʃi] *adj* (*comp* **-ier**; *super* **-iest**) susceptible, irritable
tough [tʌf] *adj* dur, coriace; (*tenacious*) résistant; (*task*) difficile || *s* voyou *m*
toughen ['tʌfən] *tr* endurcir || *intr* s'endurcir
tough' luck' *s* déveine *f*
tour [tur] *s* tour *m*; (*e.g., of inspection*) tournée *f*; **on tour** en tournée || *tr* faire le tour de; (*e.g., a country*) voyager en; (theat) faire une tournée de, en, or dans || *intr* voyager
tour'ing car' *s* voiture *f* de tourisme
tourist ['turɪst] *adj* & *s* touriste *mf*
tournament ['turnəmənt], ['tʌrnəmənt] *s* tournoi *m*
tourney ['turni], ['tʌrni] *s* tournoi *m* || *intr* tournoyer
tourniquet ['turnɪˌket], ['tʌrnɪˌke] *s* (surg) garrot *m*, tourniquet *m*
tousle ['tauzəl] *tr* ébouriffer; tirailler, maltraiter
tow [to] *s* remorque *f*; (*e.g., of hemp*) filasse *f*; **to take in tow** prendre en remorque; (fig) se charger de || *tr* remorquer
towage ['to·ɪdʒ] *s* remorquage *m*; droits *mpl* de remorquage
toward(s) [tord(z)], [tə'word(z)] *prep* vers; (*in regard to*) envers
tow'boat' *s* remorqueur *m*
tow·el ['tau·əl] *s* serviette *f*, essuie-main *m* || *v* (*pret* & *pp* **-eled** or **-elled**; *ger* **-eling** or **-elling**) *tr* essuyer avec une serviette
tow'el rack' *s* porte-serviettes *m*
tower ['tau·ər] *s* tour *f* || *intr* s'élever
towering ['tau·ərɪŋ] *adj* élevé, géant; (*e.g., ambition*) sans bornes
tow'er·man *s* (*pl* **-men**) (aer, rr) aiguilleur *m*
tow'ing serv'ice ['to·ɪŋ] *s* service *m* de dépannage
tow'line' *s* câble *m* de remorque
town [taun] *s* ville *f*; **in town** en ville
town' clerk' *s* secrétaire *m* de mairie
town' coun'cil *s* conseil *m* municipal
town' cri'er *s* crieur *m* public
town' hall' *s* hôtel *m* de ville
town' plan'ning *s* urbanisme *m*
towns'folk' *spl* citadins *mpl*
town'ship *s* commune *f*; (U.S.A.) circonscription *f* administrative de six milles carrés
towns'man ['taunzmən] *s* (*pl* **-men**) citadin *m*
towns'peo'ple *spl* citadins *mpl*
town' talk' *s* sujet *m* du jour
tow'path' *s* chemin *m* de halage
tow'rope' *s* corde *f* de remorque
tow' truck' *s* dépanneuse *f*, voiture *f* de dépannage
toxic ['tɑksɪk] *adj* & *s* toxique *m*
toy [tɔɪ] *adj* petit; d'enfant || *s* jouet *m*, joujou *m*; (*trifle*) bagatelle *f* || *intr* jouer, s'amuser; **to toy with** (*a person*) badiner avec; (*an idea*) caresser
toy' dog' *s* chien *m* de manchon
toy' sol'dier *s* soldat *m* de plomb
trace [tres] *s* trace *f*; (*of harness*) trait *m* || *tr* tracer; (*the whereabouts of*

s.o. or s.th.) pister; (*e.g., an influence*) retrouver les traces de; (*a design seen through thin paper*) calquer; **to trace back** remonter jusqu'à l'origine de
tracer ['tresər] *s* traceur *m*
trac'er bul'let *s* balle *f* traçante
trache·a ['treki·ə] *s* (*pl* -ae [,i]) trachée *f*
tracing ['tresɪŋ] *s* tracé *m*
trac'ing tape' *s* cordeau *m*
track [træk] *s* (*of foot or vehicle*) trace *f*; (*of an animal; in a stadium*) piste *f*; (*of a boat*) sillage *m*; (*of a railroad*) voie *f*; (*of an airplane, of a hurricane*) trajet *m*; (*of a tractor*) chenille *f*; (*course followed*) chemin *m* tracé; (sports) la course et le saut de barrières; (sports) athlétisme *m*; **off the beaten track** hors des sentiers battus; **on the right track** sur la bonne voie; **to be on the wrong track** faire fausse route; **to have an inside track** tenir la corde; **to keep track of** ne pas perdre de vue; **to make tracks** (coll) filer ‖ *tr* traquer; laisser des traces de pas dans; **to track down** dépister
tracking ['trækɪŋ] *s* (*of spaceship*) repérage *m*
track'ing sta'tion *s* poste *m* de repérage
track'less trol'ley *s* trolleybus *m*
track' meet' *s* concours *m* de courses et de sauts, épreuve *f* d'athlétisme
track'walk'er *s* garde-voie *m*
tract [trækt] *s* (*of land*) étendue *f*; (*leaflet*) tract *m*; (anat) voie *f*
traction ['trækʃən] *s* traction *f*
trac'tion com'pany *s* entreprise *f* de transports urbains
tractor ['træktər] *s* tracteur *m*
trade [tred] *s* commerce *m*, négoce *m*; clientèle *f*; (*calling, job*) métier *m*; (*exchange*) échange *m*; (*in slaves*) traite *f*; **to take in trade** reprendre en compte ‖ *tr* échanger; **to trade in** (*e.g., a used car*) donner en reprise ‖ *intr* commercer; **to trade in** faire le commerce de; **to trade on** exploiter
trade'-in' *s* reprise *f*
trade'mark' *s* marque *f* déposée
trade' name' *s* raison *f* sociale
trader ['tredər] *s* commerçant *m*
trade' school' *s* école *f* des arts et métiers
trades'man *s* (*pl* -men) commerçant *m*; (*shopkeeper*) boutiquier *m*; (Brit) artisan *m*
trades' un'ion or **trade' un'ion** *s* syndicat *m* ouvrier
trade' winds' *spl* vents *mpl* alizés
trad'ing post' ['tredɪŋ] *s* factorerie *f*
trad'ing stamp' *s* timbre-prime *m*
tradition [trə'dɪʃən] *s* tradition *f*
traditional [trə'dɪʃənəl] *adj* traditionnel
traf·fic ['træfɪk] *s* (*commerce*) négoce *m*; (*in the street*) circulation *f*; (*illegal*) trafic *m*; (*in, e.g., slaves*) traite *f*; (naut, rr) trafic ‖ *v* (*pret & pp* -ficked; *ger* -ficking) *intr* trafiquer
traf'fic cir'cle *s* rond-point *m*

traf'fic cop' *s* agent *m* de la circulation
traf'fic court' *s* tribunal *m* de simple police (pour les contraventions au code de la route)
traf'fic jam' *s* embouteillage *m*
traf'fic light' *s* feu *m* de circulation
traf'fic sign' *s* panneau *m* de signalisation, poteau *m* indicateur
traf'fic sig'nal *s* signal *m* routier
traf'fic tick'et *s* contravention *f*
traf'fic vi'olator *s* contrevenant *m*
tragedian [trə'dʒidɪ·ən] *s* tragédien *m*
trage·dy ['trædʒɪdi] *s* (*pl* -dies) tragédie *f*
tragic ['trædʒɪk] *adj* tragique
trail [trel] *s* trace *f*, piste *f*; (*e.g., of smoke*) traînée *f* ‖ *tr* traîner; (*to look for*) pister ‖ *intr* traîner; (*said of a plant*) grimper; **to trail off** se perdre
trailer ['trelər] *s* remorque *f*; (*for vacationing*) remorque de plaisance, caravane *f*; (mov) film-annonce *m*
trail'er court' *s* camp *m* pour caravanes
trail'er home' *s* caravane *f*
train [tren] *s* (*of railway cars*) train *m*; (*of dress*) traîne *f*; (*of thought*) enchaînement *m*; (*streak*) traînée *f* ‖ *tr* entraîner, former; (*plants*) palisser; (*a gun; a telescope*) pointer ‖ *intr* s'entraîner
trained' an'imals *spl* animaux *mpl* savants
trained' nurse' *s* infirmière *f* diplômée
trainer ['trenər] *s* (*of animals*) dresseur *m*; (sports) entraîneur *m*
training ['trenɪŋ] *s* entraînement *m*; instruction *f*; (*of animals*) dressage *m*
train'ing school' *s* école *f* technique; (*reformatory*) maison *f* de correction
train'ing ship' *s* navire-école *m*
trait [tret] *s* trait *m*
traitor ['tretər] *s* traître *m*
traitress ['tretrɪs] *s* traîtresse *f*
trajecto·ry [trə'dʒɛktəri] *s* (*pl* -ries) trajectoire *f*
tramp [træmp] *s* vagabond *m*; bruit *m* de pas lourds ‖ *tr* parcourir à pied; (*the street*) battre ‖ *intr* vagabonder; marcher lourdement; **to tramp on** marcher sur
trample ['træmpəl] *tr* fouler, piétiner ‖ *intr*—**to trample on** or **upon** fouler, piétiner
trampoline ['træmpə‚lin] *s* tremplin *m* de gymnase
tramp' steam'er *s* tramp *m*
trance [træns], [trɑns] *s* transe *f*; **in a trance** en transe
tranquil ['træŋkwɪl] *adj* tranquille
tranquilize ['træŋkwɪ‚laɪz] *tr* tranquilliser
tranquilizer ['træŋkwɪ‚laɪzər] *s* tranquillisant *m*
tranquillity [træn'kwɪlɪti] *s* tranquillité *f*
transact [træn'zækt], [træns'ækt] *tr* traiter, négocier ‖ *intr* faire des affaires
transaction [træn'zækʃən], [træns'ækʃən] *s* transaction *f*; (*of business*)

conduite *f*; **transactions** (*of a society*) actes *mpl*

transatlantic [‚trænsət'læntɪk] *adj* & *s* transatlantique *m*

transcend [træn'sɛnd] *tr* transcender ‖ *intr* se transcender

transcribe [træn'skraɪb] *tr* transcrire

transcript ['trænskrɪpt] *s* copie *f*; (*of a meeting*) procès-verbal *m*; (*educ*) livret *m* scolaire

transcription [træn'skrɪpʃən] *s* transcription *f*

transept ['trænsept] *s* transept *m*

trans•fer ['trænsfər] *s* (*e.g.*, *of stock, property, etc.*) transfert *m*; (*from one place to the other*) translation *f*; (*from one job to the other*) mutation *f*; (*of a design*) décalque *m*; (*for bus or subway*) billet *m* de correspondance; (*public sign*) correspondance ‖ [træns'fʌr], ['trænsfər] *v* (*pret & pp* **-ferred**; *ger* **-ferring**) *tr* transférer; transporter; (*e.g.*, *a civil servant*) déplacer; (*a design*) décalquer ‖ *intr* se déplacer; changer de train (de l'autobus, etc.)

transfix [træns'fɪks] *tr* transpercer

transform [træns'fɔrm] *tr* transformer ‖ *intr* se transformer

transformer [træns'fɔrmər] *s* transformateur *m*

transfusion [træns'fjuʒən] *s* transfusion *f*

transgress [træns'grɛs] *tr* & *intr* transgresser

transgression [træns'grɛʃən] *s* transgression *f*

transient ['trænʃənt] *adj* transitoire, passager; (*e.g.*, *guest*) de passage ‖ *s* hôte *mf* de passage

transistor [træn'sɪstər] *s* transistor *m*

transit ['trænsɪt], ['trænzɪt] *s* transit *m*

transition [træn'zɪʃən] *s* transition *f*

transitional [træn'zɪʃənəl] *adj* transitoire, de transition

transitive ['trænsɪtɪv] *adj* transitif ‖ *s* verbe *m* transitif

transitory ['trænsɪ‚tori] *adj* transitoire

translate [træns'let], ['trænslet] *tr* traduire

translation [træns'leʃən] *s* traduction *f*; (*transfer*) translation *f*

translator [træns'letər] *s* traducteur *m*

transliterate [træns'lɪtə‚ret] *tr* translitérer

translucent [træns'lusənt] *adj* translucide, diaphane

transmission [træns'mɪʃən] *s* transmission *f*; (*gear change*) changement *m* de vitesse; (*housing for gears*) boîte *f* de vitesses

transmis/sion-gear/ box/ *s* boîte *f* de vitesses

trans•mit [træns'mɪt] *v* (*pret & pp* **-mitted**; *ger* **-mitting**) *tr* & *intr* transmettre; (*rad*) émettre

transmitter [træns'mɪtər] *s* (telg, telp) transmetteur *m*; (*rad*) émetteur *m*

transmit/ting sta/tion *s* poste *m* émetteur

transmute [træns'mjut] *tr* transmuer

transom ['trænsəm] *s* (*crosspiece*) lin-

teau *m*; (*window over door*) imposte *f*, vasistas *m*; (*of ship*) barre *f* d'arcasse

transparen•cy [træns'pɛrənsi] *s* (*pl* **-cies**) transparence *f*; (phot) diapositive *f*

transparent [træns'pɛrənt] *adj* transparent

transpire [træns'paɪr] *intr* se passer; (*to leak out*) transpirer

transplant ['træns‚plænt], ['træns‚plɑnt] *s* (*organ or tissue*) greffon *m*; (*operation*) greffe *f* ‖ [træns'plænt], [træns'plɑnt] *tr* transplanter; (*e.g.*, *a heart*) greffer

transport ['trænsport] *s* transport *m* ‖ [træns'port] *tr* transporter

transportation [‚trænspor'teʃən] *s* transport *m*; billet *m* de train, de bateau, or d'avion; (*deportation*) transportation *f*

transport/er bridge/ [træns'portər] *s* transbordeur *m*

trans/port work/er *s* employé *m* des entreprises de transport

transpose [træns'poz] *tr* transposer

trans•ship [træns'/ʃɪp] *v* (*pret & pp* **-shipped**; *ger* **-shipping**) *tr* transborder

transshipment [træns'ʃɪpmənt] *s* transbordement *m*

trap [træp] *s* piège *m*; (*pitfall*) trappe *f*; (*double-curved pipe*) siphon *m*; **traps** (mus) batterie *f* de jazz ‖ *v* (*pret & pp* **trapped**; *ger* **trapping**) *tr* prendre au piège, attraper

trap/ door/ *s* trappe *f*

trapeze [trə'piz] *s* trapèze *m*

trapezoid ['træpɪ‚zɔɪd] *s* trapèze *m*

trapper ['træpər] *s* trappeur *m*

trappings ['træpɪŋz] *spl* (*adornments*) atours *mpl*; (*of horse's harness*) harnachement *m*

trap/shoot/ing *s* tir *m* au pigeon

trash [træʃ] *s* déchets *mpl*, rebuts *mpl*; (*junk*) camelote *f*; (*nonsense*) ineptie *f*; (*worthless people*) racaille *f*

trash/ can/ *s* poubelle *f*

travail [trə'vel] *s* labeur *m*; douleur *f* de l'enfantement

trav•el ['trævəl] *s* voyages *mpl*; (mach) course *f* ‖ *v* (*pret & pp* **-eled** or **-elled**; *ger* **-eling** or **-elling**) *tr* parcourir ‖ *intr* voyager; (mach) se déplacer

trav/el bu/reau *s* agence *f* de voyages

traveler ['trævələr] *s* voyageur *m*

trav/eler's check/ *s* chèque *m* de voyage

trav/eling expen/ses *spl* frais *mpl* de voyage

trav/eling sales/man *s* (*pl* **-men**) commis *m* voyageur

traverse [trə'vʌrs] *tr* parcourir, traverser

traves•ty ['trævɪsti] *s* (*pl* **-ties**) *s* travestissement *m* ‖ *v* (*pret & pp* **-tied**) *tr* travestir

trawl [trɔl] *s* chalut *m* ‖ *tr* traîner ‖ *intr* pêcher au chalut

trawler ['trɔlər] *s* chalutier *m*

tray [tre] *s* plateau *m*; (*of refrigerator*) bac *f*; (chem, phot) cuvette *f*

treacherous ['tretʃərəs] *adj* traître
treacher·y ['tretʃəri] *s* (*pl* -ies) trahison *f*
tread [tred] *s* (*step; sound of steps*) pas *m*; (*gait*) allure *f*; (*of stairs*) giron *m*; (*of tire*) chape *f*; (*of shoe*) semelle *f*; (*of egg*) cicatricule *f* ‖ *v* (*pret* **trod** [trad]; *pp* **trodden** ['tradən] or **trod**) *tr* marcher sur, piétiner ‖ *intr* marcher
treadle ['tredəl] *s* pédale *f*
tread/mill/ *s* trépigneuse *f*; (*futile drudgery*) besogne *f* ingrate
treason ['trizən] *s* trahison *f*
treasonable ['trizənəbəl] *adj* traître
treasure ['treʒər] *s* trésor *m* ‖ *tr* garder soigneusement; (*to prize*) tenir beaucoup à
treasurer ['treʒərər] *s* trésorier *m*
treasur·y ['treʒəri] *s* (*pl* -ies) trésorerie *f*; trésor *m*
treat [trit] *s* régal *m*, plaisir *m* ‖ *tr* traiter; régaler; (*to a drink*) payer à boire à ‖ *intr* traiter
treatise ['tritɪs] *s* traité *m*
treatment ['tritmənt] *s* traitement *m*
trea·ty ['triti] *s* (*pl* -ties) traité *m*
treble ['trebəl] *adj* (*threefold*) triple; (*mus*) de soprano ‖ *s* soprano *mf*; (*voice*) soprano *m* ‖ *tr & intr* tripler
tre/ble clef/ [klef] *s* clef *f* de sol
tree [tri] *s* arbre *m*
tree/ farm/ *s* taillis *m*
treeless ['trilɪs] *adj* sans arbres
tree/top/ *s* cime *f* d'un arbre
trellis ['trelɪs] *s* treillis *m*, treillage *m*; (*summerhouse*) tonnelle *f* ‖ *tr* treillager
tremble ['trembəl] *s* tremblement *m* ‖ *intr* trembler
tremendous [trɪ'mendəs] *adj* terrible; (coll) formidable
tremor ['tremər], ['trimər] *s* tremblement *m*
trench [trentʃ] *s* tranchée *f*
trenchant ['trentʃənt] *adj* tranchant
trench/ mor/tar *s* lance-bombes *m*
trend [trend] *s* tendance *f*, cours *m*
trespass ['trespəs] *s* entrée *f* sans permission; délit *m*, offense *f* ‖ *intr* entrer sans permission; **no trespassing** (public sign) défense d'entrer; **to trespass against** offenser; **to trespass on** empiéter sur; (*s.o.'s patience*) abuser de
trespasser ['trespəsər] *s* intrus *m*
tress [tres] *s* tresse *f*; **tresses** chevelure *f*
trestle ['tresəl] *s* tréteau *m*; (*bridge*) pont *m* en treillis
trial ['traɪ·əl] *s* essai *m*; (*difficulty*) épreuve *f*; (law) procès *m*; **on trial à** titre d'essai; (law) en jugement; **to bring to trial** faire passer en jugement
tri/al and er/ror *s*—**by trial and error** par tâtonnements
tri/al balloon/ *s* ballon *m* d'essai
tri/al by ju/ry *s* jugement *m* par jury
tri/al ju/ry *s* jury *m* de jugement
tri/al or/der *s* commande *f* d'essai
tri/al run/ *s* course *f* d'essai
triangle ['traɪ ˌæŋgəl] *s* triangle *m*

tribe [traɪb] *s* tribu *f*
tribunal [trɪ'bjunəl], [traɪ'bjunəl] *s* tribunal *m*
tribune ['trɪbjun] *s* tribune *f*
tributar·y ['trɪbjəˌteri] *adj* tributaire ‖ *s* (*pl* -ies) tributaire *m*
tribute ['trɪbjut] *s* tribut *m*; éloge *m*, compliment *m*; **to pay tribute to** (*e.g., merit*) rendre hommage à
trice [traɪs] *s*—**in a trice** en un clin d'œil
trick [trɪk] *s* tour *m*; (*prank*) farce *f*; (*artifice*) ruse *f*; (*cards in one round*) levée *f*; (*habit*) manie *f*; (*girl*) (coll) belle *f*; **to be up to one's old tricks again** faire encore des siennes; **to play a dirty trick on** faire un vilain tour à; **tricks of the trade** trucs *mpl* du métier ‖ *tr* duper
tricker·y ['trɪkəri] *s* (*pl* -ies) tromperie *f*
trickle ['trɪkəl] *s* filet *m* ‖ *intr* dégoutter
trickster ['trɪkstər] *s* fourbe *mf*
trick·y ['trɪki] *adj* (*comp* -ier; *super* -iest) rusé; (*difficult*) compliqué, délicat
tricolor ['traɪ ˌkʌlər] *adj & s* tricolore *m*
tried [traɪd] *adj* loyal, éprouvé
trifle ['traɪfəl] *s* bagatelle *f* ‖ *tr*—**to trifle away** gaspiller ‖ *intr* badiner
trifling ['traɪflɪŋ] *adj* frivole; insignifiant
trifocals [traɪ'fokəlz] *spl* lunettes *fpl* à trois foyers
trigger ['trɪgər] *s* (*of gun*) détente *f*; (*of any device*) déclencheur *m*; **to pull the trigger** appuyer sur la détente ‖ *tr* déclencher
trig/ger-hap/py *adj*—**to be trigger-happy** (coll) avoir la gâchette facile
trigonometry [ˌtrɪgə'namɪtri] *s* trigonométrie *f*
trill [trɪl] *s* trille *m* ‖ *tr & intr* triller
trillion ['trɪljən] *s* (U.S.A.) billion *m*; (Brit) trillion *m*
trilo·gy ['trɪlodʒi] *s* (*pl* -gies) trilogie *f*
trim [trɪm] *adj* (*comp* **trimmer**; *super* **trimmest**) ordonné, coquet ‖ *s* état *m*; ornement *m*; (*of sails*) orientation *f* ‖ *v* (*pret & pp* **trimmed**; *ger* **trimming**) *tr* enguirlander; (*a Christmas tree*) orner; (*hat, dress, etc.*) garnir; (*the hair*) rafraîchir; (*a candle or lamp*) moucher; (*trees, plants*) tailler; (*the edges of a book*) rogner; (*the sails*) orienter; (coll) battre
trimming ['trɪmɪŋ] *s* (*of clothes, hat, etc.*) garniture *f*; (*of hedges*) taille *f*; (*of sails*) orientation *f*; **to get a trimming** (coll) essuyer une défaite
trini·ty ['trɪnɪti] *s* (*pl* -ties) trinité *f*; **Trinity** Trinité
trinket ['trɪŋkɪt] *s* colifichet *m*; (*trifle*) babiole *f*
tri·o ['tri·o] *s* (*pl* -os) trio *m*
trip [trɪp] *s* voyage *m*; trajet *m*, parcours *m*; (*stumble; blunder*) faux pas *m*; (*act of causing a person to stumble*) croc-en-jambe *m* ‖ *v* (*pret & pp* **tripped**; *ger* **tripping**) *tr* faire tré-

bucher; **to trip up** donner un croc-en-jambe à; prendre en défaut || *intr* trébucher

tripartite [traɪˈpɑrtaɪt] *adj* tripartite

tripe [traɪp] *s* tripe *f*; (slang) fatras *m*

trip/ham/mer *s* marteau *m* à bascule

triple [ˈtrɪpəl] *adj & s* triple *m* || *tr &* *intr* tripler

triplet [ˈtrɪplɪt] *s* (*offspring*) triplet *m*; (*stanza*) tercet *m*; (mus) triolet *m*; **triplets** (*offspring*) triplés *mpl*

triplicate [ˈtrɪplɪkɪt] *adj* triple || *s* triplicata *m*; **in triplicate** en trois exemplaires

tripod [ˈtraɪpɑd] *s* trépied *m*

triptych [ˈtrɪptɪk] *s* triptyque *m*

trite [traɪt] *adj* banal, rebattu

triumph [ˈtraɪ·əmf] *s* triomphe *m* || *intr* triompher; **to triumph over** triompher de

trium/phal arch/ [traɪˈʌmfəl] *s* arc *m* de triomphe

triumphant [traɪˈʌmfənt] *adj* triomphant

trivia [ˈtrɪvɪ·ə] *spl* vétilles *fpl*

trivial [ˈtrɪvɪ·əl] *adj* trivial, insignifiant

triviali·ty [ˌtrɪvɪˈælɪti] *s* (*pl* -ties) trivialité *f*, insignifiance *f*

Trojan [ˈtrodʒən] *adj* troyen || *s* Troyen *m*

Tro/jan Horse/ *s* cheval *m* de Troie

Tro/jan war/ *s* guerre *f* de Troie

troll [trol] *tr & intr* pêcher à la cuiller

trolley [ˈtrɑli] *s* trolley *m*; (*streetcar*) tramway *m*

trol/ley car/ *s* tramway *m*

trol/ley pole/ *s* perche *f*

trolling [ˈtrolɪŋ] *s* pêche *f* à la cuiller

trollop [ˈtrɑləp] *s* souillon *f*; (*prostitute*) traînée *f*

trombone [ˈtrɑmbon] *s* trombone *m*

troop [trup] *s* troupe *f*; **troops** (mil) troupes *fpl* || *tr* (*the colors*) présenter || *intr* s'attrouper

trooper [ˈtrupər] *s* cavalier *m*; membre *m* de la police montée; **to swear like a trooper** jurer comme un charretier

tro·phy [ˈtrofi] *s* (*pl* -phies) trophée *m*; (sports) coupe *f*

tropic [ˈtrɑpɪk] *adj & s* tropique *m*; **tropics** tropiques, zone *f* tropicale

tropical [ˈtrɑpɪkəl] *adj* tropical

trot [trɑt] *s* trot *m* || *v* (*pret & pp* **trotted**; *ger* **trotting**) *tr* faire trotter; **to trot out** (slang) exhiber || *intr* trotter

troth [troθ], [troθ] *s* foi *f*; **in troth** en vérité; **to plight one's troth** promettre fidélité; donner sa promesse de mariage

trouble [ˈtrʌbəl] *s* dérangement *m*; (*illness*) trouble *m*; **that's not worth the trouble** cela ne vaut pas la peine; **that's the trouble** voilà le hic; **the trouble is that . . .** la difficulté c'est que . . . ; **to be in trouble** avoir des ennuis; (*said of a woman*) (coll) faire Pâques avant les Rameaux; **to be looking for trouble** chercher querelle; **to get into trouble** se créer des ennuis, s'attirer une mauvaise affaire;

to take the trouble to se donner la peine de; **with very little trouble** à peu de frais || *tr* déranger; affliger; **to be troubled about** se tourmenter au sujet de; **to trouble oneself** s'inquiéter || *intr* se déranger; **to trouble** to se donner la peine de

trou/ble light/ *s* lampe *f* de secours

trou/ble·mak/er *s* fomentateur *m*, perturbateur *m*

troubleshooter [ˈtrʌbəlˌʃutər] *s* dépanneur *m*; (*in disputes*) arbitre *m*

trou/ble·shoot/ing *s* dépannage *m*; (*of disputes*) composition *f*, arbitrage *m*

troublesome [ˈtrʌbəlsəm] *adj* ennuyeux

trou/ble spot/ *s* foyer *m* de conflit

trough [trɔf], [traf] *s* (e.g., *to knead bread*) pétrin *m*; (*for water for animals*) abreuvoir *m*; (*for feeding animals*) auge *f*; (*under the eaves*) chéneau *m*; (*between two waves*) creux *m*

troupe [trup] *s* troupe *f*

trouper [ˈtrupər] *s* membre *m* de la troupe; vieil acteur *m*; vieux routier *m*

trousers [ˈtrauzərz] *spl* pantalon *m*

trous·seau [truˈso], [ˈtruso] *s* (*pl* -seaux or -seaus) trousseau *m*

trout [traut] *s* truite *f*

trowel [ˈtrau·əl] *s* truelle *f*; (*for gardening*) déplantoir *m*

Troy [trɔɪ] *s* Troie *f*

truant [ˈtru·ənt] *s*—**to play truant** faire l'école buissonnière

truce [trus] *s* trêve *f*

truck [trʌk] *s* camion *m*, poids *m* lourd; (*for baggage*) diable *m*; légumes *mpl*; (coll) rapports *mpl* || *tr* camionner

truck/driv/er *s* camionneur *m*

truck/ farm/ing *s* culture *f* maraîchère

truck/ gar/den *s* jardin *m* maraîcher

trucking [ˈtrʌkɪŋ] *s* camionnage *m*

truculent [ˈtrʌkjələnt], [ˈtrukjələnt] *adj* truculent

trudge [trʌdʒ] *intr* cheminer

true [tru] *adj* vrai; loyal; (*exact*) juste; (*copy*) conforme; **to come true** se réaliser || *tr* rectifier, dégauchir

true/ cop/y *s* (*pl* -ies) copie *f* conforme

true/-heart/ed *adj* au cœur sincère

true/love/ *s* bien-aimé *m*

truffle [ˈtrʌfəl], [ˈtrufəl] *s* truffe *f*

truism [ˈtru·ɪzm] *s* truisme *m*

truly [ˈtruli] *adv* vraiment; sincèrement; **yours truly** (complimentary close) veuillez agréer, Monsieur (Madame, etc.), l'assurance de mes sentiments distingués

trump [trʌmp] *s* atout *m*; brave garçon *m*, brave fille *f*; **no trump** sans atout || *tr* couper; **to trump up** inventer || *intr* couper

trumpet [ˈtrʌmpɪt] *s* trompette *f* || *tr & intr* trompeter

trumpeter [ˈtrʌmpətər] *s* trompette *m*

truncheon [ˈtrʌntʃən] *s* matraque *f*; (*of policeman*) bâton *m*

trunk [trʌŋk] *s* tronc *m*; (*chest for clothes*) malle *f*; (*of elephant*) trompe *f*; (aut) coffre *m*; **trunks** slip *m*

truss [trʌs] *s* (*framework*) armature *f*; (med) bandage *m* herniaire || *tr* armer; (culin) trousser

trust [trʌst] *s* confiance *f*; (*hope*) espoir *m*; (*duty*) charge *f*; (*safekeeping*) dépôt *m*; (com) trust *m*, cartel *m* ‖ *tr* se fier à; (*to entrust*) confier; (com) faire crédit à ‖ *intr* espérer; **to trust in** avoir confiance en
trust' com'pany *s* crédit *m*, société *f* de banque
trustee [trʌs'ti] *s* administrateur *m*; (*of a university*) régent *m*; (*of an estate*) fidéicommissaire *mf*
trusteeship [trʌs'tiʃɪp] *s* tutelle *f*
trustful ['trʌstfəl] *adj* confiant
trust'wor'thy *adj* digne de confiance
trust·y ['trʌsti] *adj* (*comp* -ier; *super* -iest) sûr, loyal ‖ *s* (*pl* -ies) forçat *m* bien noté
truth [truθ] *s* vérité *f*; **in truth** en vérité
truthful ['truθfəl] *adj* véridique
try [traɪ] *s* (*pl* tries) essai *m* ‖ *v* (*pret* & *pp* tried) *tr* mettre à l'épreuve; (law) juger; **to try on** or **out** essayer ‖ *intr* essayer; **to try to** essayer de
trying ['traɪ·ɪŋ] *adj* pénible
tryst [trɪst], [traɪst] *s* rendez-vous *m*
T'-shirt' *s* gilet *m* de peau avec manches
tub [tʌb] *s* cuvier *m*, baquet *m*; (*clumsy boat*) (coll) rafiot *m*
tube [t(j)ub] *s* tube *m*; tunnel *m*; (aut) chambre *f* à air; (*subway*) (Brit) métro *m*
tuber ['t(j)ubər] *s* tubercule *m*
tubercle ['t(j)ubərkəl] *s* tubercule *m*
tuberculosis [t(j)u,bʌrkjə'losɪs] *s* tuberculose *f*
tuck [tʌk] *s* pli *m*, rempli *m* ‖ *tr* plisser, remplier; **to tuck away** reléguer; **to tuck in** rentrer; **to tuck in bed** border; **to tuck up** retrousser
tucker ['tʌkər] *tr*—**to tucker out** (coll) fatiguer
Tuesday ['t(j)uzdi] *s* mardi *m*
tuft [tʌft] *s* touffe *f* ‖ *tr* garnir de touffes ‖ *intr* former une touffe
tug [tʌg] *s* tiraillement *m*, effort *m*; (*boat*) remorqueur *m* ‖ *v* (*pret* & *pp* tugged; *ger* tugging) *tr* tirer fort; (*a boat*) remorquer ‖ *intr* tirer fort
tug'boat' *s* remorqueur *m*
tug' of war' *s* lutte *f* à la corde (de traction)
tuition [t(j)u'ɪʃən] *s* enseignement *m*; (*fees*) frais *mpl* de scolarité
tulip ['t(j)ulɪp] *s* tulipe *f*
tumble ['tʌmbəl] *s* chute *f*; (sports) culbute *f* ‖ *tr* culbuter ‖ *intr* tomber, culbuter; (sports) faire des culbutes; (*to catch on*) (slang) comprendre; **to tumble down** dégringoler
tum'ble·down' *adj* croulant, délabré
tumbler ['tʌmblər] *s* gobelet *m*, verre *m*; acrobate *m*; (*self-righting toy*) poussah *m*, ramponneau *m*
tumor ['t(j)umər] *s* tumeur *f*
tumult ['t(j)umʌlt] *s* tumulte *m*
tun [tʌn] *s* tonne *f*
tuna ['tunə] *s* thon *m*
tune [t(j)un] *s* air *m*; (*manner of acting or speaking*) ton *m*; **in tune** (mus) accordé; (rad) en syntonie; **out of tune** (mus) désaccordé; **to change**

one's **tune** (coll) changer de disque ‖ *tr* accorder; (*a radio or television set*) régler; **to tune in** (rad) syntoniser; **to tune up** régler
tungsten ['tʌŋstən] *s* tungstène *m*
tunic ['t(j)unɪk] *s* tunique *f*
tuning ['t(j)unɪŋ] *s* réglage *m*; (rad) syntonisation *f*
tun'ing coil' *s* bobine *f* de syntonisation
tun'ing fork' *s* diapason *m*
tun·nel ['tʌnəl] *s* tunnel *m*; (min) galerie *f* ‖ *v* (*pret* & *pp* -neled or -nelled; *ger* -neling or -nelling) *tr* percer un tunnel dans or sous
turban ['tʌrbən] *s* turban *m*
turbid ['tʌrbɪd] *adj* trouble
turbine ['tʌrbɪn], ['tʌrbaɪn] *s* turbine *f*
turbojet ['tʌrbo,dʒɛt] *s* turboréacteur *m*; avion *m* à turboréacteur
turboprop ['tʌrbo,prɑp] *s* turbopropulseur *m*; avion *m* à turbopropulseur
turbulent ['tʌrbjələnt] *adj* turbulent
tureen [t(j)u'rin] *s* soupière *f*
turf [tʌrf] *s* gazon *m*; (*sod*) motte *f* de gazon; (*peat*) tourbe *f*; **the turf** le turf
turf'man *s* (*pl* -men) turfiste *mf*
Turk [tʌrk] *s* Turc *m*
turkey ['tʌrki] *s* dindon *m*; (culin) dinde *f*; (*flop*) (slang) four *m*; **Turkey** Turquie *f*; la Turquie
tur'key vul'ture *s* urubu *m*
Turkish ['tʌrkɪʃ] *adj* & *s* turc *m*
Turk'ish delight' *s* loukoum *m*
Turk'ish tow'el *s* serviette *f* éponge
turmoil ['tʌrmɔɪl] *s* agitation *f*
turn [tʌrn] *s* tour *m*; (*change of direction*) virage *m*; (*bend*) tournant *m*; (*of events; of an expression*) tournure *f*; (*in a wire*) spire *f*; (coll) coup *m*, choc *m*; **at every turn** à tout propos; **by turns** tour à tour; **in turn** à tour de rôle; **to a turn** (culin) à point; **to do a good turn** rendre un service; **to take turns** alterner; **to wait one's turn** prendre son tour; **whose turn is it?** à qui le tour? ‖ *tr* tourner; **to turn about** or **around** retourner; **to turn aside** or **away** détourner; **to turn back** renvoyer; (*an attack*) repousser; (*a clock*) retarder; **to turn down** (*a collar*) rabattre; (*e.g., the gas*) baisser; (*an offer*) refuser; **to turn from** détourner de; **to turn in** replier; (*a wrongdoer*) dénoncer; **to turn into** changer en; **to turn off** (*the water, the gas, etc.*) fermer; (*the light, the radio, etc.*) éteindre; (*a road*) quitter; **to turn on** (*the water, the gas, etc.*) ouvrir; (*the light, the radio, the gas, etc.*) allumer; **to turn out** mettre dehors; (*to manufacture*) produire; (*e.g., the light*) éteindre; **to turn over and over** tourner et retourner; **to turn up** (*a collar*) relever; (*one's sleeves*) retrousser; (*to unearth*) déterrer ‖ *intr* tourner; se tourner; (*said of milk*) tourner; (*to toss and turn*) se retourner; (*to be dizzy*) tourner, e.g., **his head is turning** la tête lui tourne; **to turn about** or **around** se retourner, se tourner; **to turn aside** or **away** se détourner; **to turn back** rebrousser

chemin; **to turn down** se rabattre; **to turn in** (coll) aller se coucher; **to turn into** tourner à or en; **to turn on** se jeter sur; (*to depend on*) dépendre de; **to turn out to be** se trouver être; **to turn out well** tourner bien; **to turn over** se retourner; (*said of auto*) capoter; **to turn up** se relever; se présenter, arriver

turn′coat′ *s* transfuge *m*

turn′down′ *adj* rabattu ‖ *s* refus *m*

turn′ing point′ *s* moment *m* décisif

turnip ['tʌrnɪp] *s* navet *m*; (*big watch*) (slang) bassinoire *f*; (slang) tête *f* de bois

turn′key′ *s* geôlier *m*

turn′ of life′ *s* retour *m* d'âge

turn′ of mind′ *s* inclination *f* naturelle

turn′out′ *s* (*gathering*) assistance *f*; (*output*) rendement *m*; (*equipment*) attelage *m*

turn′o′ver *s* renversement *m*; (com) chiffre *m* d'affaires

turn′pike′ *s* autoroute *f* à péage

turn′spit′ *s* tournebroche *m*

turnstile ['tʌrn ˌstaɪl] *s* tourniquet *m*

turn′stone′ *s* (orn) tourne-pierre *m*

turn′ta′ble *s* (*of phonograph*) plateau *m* porte-disque; (rr) plaque *f* tournante

turpentine ['tʌrpən ˌtaɪn] *s* térébenthine *f*

turpitude ['tʌrpɪ ˌt(j)ud] *s* turpitude *f*

turquoise ['tʌrkɔɪz], ['tʌrkwɔɪz] *s* turquoise *f*

turret ['tʌrɪt] *s* tourelle *f*

turtle ['tʌrtəl] *s* tortue *f*

tur′tle-dove′ *s* tourterelle *f*

tur′tle-neck′ *s* col *m* roulé; chandail *m* à col roulé

Tuscan ['tʌskən] *adj & s* toscan *m*

Tuscany ['tʌskəni] *s* Toscane *f*; la Toscane

tusk [tʌsk] *s* défense *f*

tussle ['tʌsəl] *s* bagarre *f* ‖ *intr* se bagarrer

tutor ['t(j)utər] *s* précepteur *m*, répétiteur *m* ‖ *tr* donner des leçons particulières à ‖ *intr* donner des leçons particulières

tuxe·do [tʌk'sido] *s* (*pl* -**dos**) smoking *m*

TV ['ti'vi] *s* (letterword) (**television**) tévé *f*, télé *f*

twaddle ['twɑdəl] *s* fadaises *fpl* ‖ *intr* dire des fadaises

twang [twæŋ] *s* (*of musical instrument*) son *m* vibrant; (*of voice*) ton *m* nasillard ‖ *tr* faire résonner; dire en nasillant ‖ *intr* nasiller

twang·y ['twæŋi] *adj* (*comp* -**ier**; *super* -**iest**) (*nasal*) nasillard; (*resonant*) vibrant

tweed [twid] *s* tweed *m*

tweet [twit] *s* pépiement *m* ‖ *intr* pépier

tweeter ['twitər] *s* (rad) tweeter *m*

tweezers ['twizərz] *spl* brucelles *fpl*; pince *f* à épiler

twelfth [twelfθ] *adj & pron* douzième (*masc, fem*); **the Twelfth** douze, e.g., **John the Twelfth** Jean douze ‖ *s*

douzième *m*; **the twelfth** (*in dates*) le douze

twelve [twelv] *adj & pron* douze; **about twelve** une douzaine de ‖ *s* douze *m*; **twelve o'clock** (*noon*) midi *m*; (*midnight*) minuit *m*

twentieth ['twentɪ·ɪθ] *adj & pron* vingtième (*masc, fem*); **the Twentieth** vingt, e.g., **John the Twentieth** Jean vingt ‖ *s* vingt *m*; **the twentieth** (*in dates*) le vingt

twen·ty ['twenti] *adj & pron* vingt; **about twenty** une vingtaine de ‖ *s* (*pl* -**ties**) vingt *m*; **the twenties** les années *fpl* vingt

twen′ty-first′ *adj & pron* vingt et unième (*masc, fem*); **the Twenty-first** vingt et un, e.g., **John the Twenty-first** Jean vingt et un ‖ *s* vingt et unième *m*; **the twenty-first** (*in dates*) le vingt et un

twen′ty-one′ *adj & pron* vingt et un ‖ *s* vingt et un *m*; (cards) vingt-et-un

twen′ty-sec′ond *adj & pron* vingt-deuxième (*masc, fem*); **the Twenty-second** vingt-deux, e.g., **John the Twenty-second** Jean vingt-deux ‖ *s* vingt-deuxième *m*; **the twenty-second** (*in dates*) le vingt-deux

twen′ty-two′ *adj, pron, & s* vingt-deux *m*

twice [twaɪs] *adv* deux fois; **twice over** à deux reprises

twiddle ['twɪdəl] *tr* tourner, jouer avec; (*e.g., one's moustache*) tortiller

twig [twɪg] *s* brindille *f*

twilight ['twaɪ ˌlaɪt] *adj* crépusculaire ‖ *s* crépuscule *m*

twill [twɪl] *s* croisé *m* ‖ *tr* croiser

twin [twɪn] *adj & s* jumeau *m* ‖ *v* (*pret & pp* **twinned**; *ger* **twinning**) *tr* jumeler

twin′ beds′ *spl* lits *mpl* jumeaux

twine [twaɪn] *s* ficelle *f* ‖ *tr* enrouler ‖ *intr* s'enrouler

twinge [twɪndʒ] *s* élancement *m* ‖ *intr* élancer

twin′jet′ plane′ *s* biréacteur *m*

twinkle ['twɪŋkəl] *s* scintillement *m*; (*of the eye*) clignotement *m* ‖ *intr* scintiller; clignoter

twin′-screw′ *adj* à hélices jumelles

twirl [twʌrl] *s* tournoiement *m* ‖ *tr* faire tournoyer; (*e.g., a cane*) faire des moulinets avec ‖ *intr* tournoyer

twist [twɪst] *s* torsion *f*; (*strand*) cordon *m*; (*of the wrist, of rope, etc.*) tour *m*; (*of the road, river, etc.*) coude *m*; (*of tobacco*) rouleau *m*; (*of the ankle*) entorse *f*; (*of mind or disposition*) prédisposition *f* ‖ *tr* tordre, tortiller ‖ *intr* se tordre, se tortiller; **to twist and turn** (*said, e.g., of road*) serpenter; (*said of sleeper*) se tourner et se retourner

twister ['twɪstər] *s* (coll) tornade *f*

twit [twɪt] *v* (*pret & pp* **twitted**; *ger* **twitting**) *tr* taquiner

twitch [twɪtʃ] *s* crispation *f* ‖ *intr* se crisper

twitter ['twɪtər] *s* gazouillement *m* ‖ *intr* gazouiller

two [tu] *adj & pron* deux ‖ *s* deux *m*; **to put two and two together** raisonner juste; **two o'clock** deux heures

two'-cy'cle *adj* (mach) à deux temps

two'-cyl'inder *adj* (mach) à deux cylindres

two'-edged' *adj* à deux tranchants

two' hun'dred *adj, pron, & s* deux cents *m*

twosome ['tusəm] *s* paire *f*; jeu *m* à deux joueurs

two'-time' *tr* (slang) tromper

tycoon [taɪ'kun] *s* (coll) magnat *m*

type [taɪp] *s* type *m* ‖ *tr* typer; (*to typewrite*) taper; (*a sample of blood*) chercher le groupe sanguin sur ‖ *intr* taper

type'face' *s* œil *m*

type'script' *s* manuscrit *m* dactylographié

typesetter ['taɪp ˌsɛtər] *s* compositeur *m*, typographe *mf*; machine *f* à composer

type'write' *v* (*pret* **-wrote**; *pp* **-written**) *tr & intr* taper à la machine

type'writ'er *s* machine *f* à écrire

type'writer rib'bon *s* ruban *m* encreur

type'writ'ing *s* dactylographie *f*

ty'phoid fe'ver ['taɪfɔɪd] *s* fièvre *f* typhoïde

typhoon [taɪ'fun] *s* typhon *m*

typical ['tɪpɪkəl] *adj* typique

typi-fy ['tɪpɪˌfaɪ] *v* (*pret & pp* **-fied**) *tr* symboliser; être le type de

typ'ing er'ror *s* faute *f* de frappe

typist ['taɪpɪst] *s* dactylo *f*

typographic(al) [ˌtaɪpə'græfɪk(əl)] *adj* typographique

typograph'ical er'ror *s* erreur *f* typographique

typography [taɪ'pɑgrəfi] *s* typographie *f*

tyrannic(al) [tɪ'rænɪk(əl)], [taɪ'rænɪk(əl)] *adj* tyrannique

tyran-ny ['tɪrəni] *s* (*pl* **-nies**) tyrannie *f*

tyrant ['taɪrənt] *s* tyran *m*

ty-ro ['taɪro] *s* (*pl* **-ros**) novice *mf*

U

U, u [ju] *s* XXIe lettre de l'alphabet

ubiquitous [ju'bɪkwɪtəs] *adj* ubiquiste, omniprésent

udder ['ʌdər] *s* pis *m*

ugliness ['ʌglɪnɪs] *s* laideur *f*

ug-ly ['ʌgli] *adj* (*comp* **-lier**; *super* **-liest**) laid; (*disagreeable; mean*) vilain

Ukraine ['jukren], [ju'kren] *s* Ukraine *f*; l'Ukraine

Ukrainian [ju'krenɪ-ən] *adj* ukrainien ‖ *s* (*language*) ukrainien *m*; (*person*) Ukrainien *m*

ulcer ['ʌlsər] *s* ulcère *m*

ulcerate ['ʌlsə ˌret] *tr* ulcérer ‖ *intr* s'ulcérer

ulterior [ʌl'tɪrɪ-ər] *adj* ultérieur; secret, inavoué

ultimate ['ʌltɪmɪt] *adj* ultime, final, définitif

ultima-tum [ˌʌltɪ'metəm] *s* (*pl* **-tums** or **-ta** [tə]) ultimatum *m*

ultrashort [ˌʌltrə'ʃɔrt] *adj* (electron) ultra-court

ultraviolet [ˌʌltrə'vaɪ-əlɪt] *adj & s* ultraviolet *m*

umbil'ical cord' [ʌm'bɪlɪkəl] *s* cordon *m* ombilical

umbrage ['ʌmbrɪdʒ] *s*—**to take umbrage at** prendre ombrage de

umbrella [ʌm'brɛlə] *s* parapluie *m*; (mil) ombrelle *f* de protection

umbrel'la stand' *s* porte-parapluies *m*

umlaut ['umlaut] *s* métaphonie *f*, inflexion *f* vocalique; (*mark*) tréma *m* ‖ *tr* changer le timbre de; écrire avec un tréma

umpire ['ʌmpaɪr] *s* arbitre *m* ‖ *tr & intr* arbitrer

UN ['ju'ɛn] *s* (letterword) (**United Nations**) ONU *f*

unable [ʌn'ebəl] *adj* incapable; **to be unable to** être incapable de

unabridged [ˌʌnə'brɪdʒd] *adj* intégral

unaccented [ʌn'æksɛntɪd], [ˌʌnæk-'sɛntɪd] *adj* inaccentué

unacceptable [ˌʌnək'sɛptəbəl] *adj* inacceptable

unaccountable [ˌʌnə'kauntəbəl] *adj* inexplicable; irresponsable

unaccounted-for [ˌʌnə'kauntɪd ˌfɔr] *adj* inexpliqué, pas retrouvé

unaccustomed [ˌʌnə'kʌstəmd] *adj* inaccoutumé

unafraid [ˌʌnə'fred] *adj* sans peur

unaligned [ˌʌnə'laɪnd] *adj* non-engagé

unanimity [ˌjunə'nɪmɪti] *s* unanimité *f*

unanimous [ju'nænɪməs] *adj* unanime

unanswerable [ʌn'ænsərəbəl] *adj* incontestable, sans réplique; (*argument*) irréfutable

unappreciative [ˌʌnə'priʃɪˌetɪv] *adj* ingrat, peu reconnaissant

unapproachable [ˌʌnə'protʃəbəl] *adj* inabordable; (fig) incomparable

unarmed [ʌn'ɑrmd] *adj* sans armes

unascertainable [ʌn ˌæsər'tenəbəl] *adj* non vérifiable

unasked [ʌn'æskt], [ʌn'ɑskt] *adj* non invité; **to do s.th. unasked** faire q.ch. spontanément

unassembled [ˌʌnə'sɛmbəld] *adj* démonté

unassuming [ˌʌnə's(j)umɪŋ] *adj* modeste, sans prétentions

unattached [ˌʌnə'tætʃt] *adj* indépendant; (*loose*) détaché; (*not engaged to be married*) seul; (mil, nav) en disponibilité

unattainable [,ʌnə'tenəbəl] *adj* inaccessible

unattractive [,ʌnə'træktɪv] *adj* peu attrayant, peu séduisant

unavailable [,ʌnə'veləbəl] *adj* non disponible

unavailing [,ʌnə'velɪŋ] *adj* inutile

unavoidable [,ʌnə'vɔɪdəbəl] *adj* inévitable

unaware [,ʌnə'wɛr] *adj* ignorant; **to be unaware of** ignorer || *adv* à l'improviste; à mon (son, etc.) insu

unawares [,ʌnə'wɛrz] *adv* (*unexpectedly*) à l'improviste; (*unknowingly*) à mon (son, etc.) insu

unbalanced [ʌn'bælənst] *adj* non équilibré; (*mind*) déséquilibré; (*bank account*) non soldé

unbandage [ʌn'bændɪdʒ] *tr* débander

un•bar [ʌn'bɑr] *v* (*pret & pp* **-barred;** *ger* **-barring**) *tr* débarrer

unbearable [ʌn'bɛrəbəl] *adj* insupportable

unbeatable [ʌn'bitəbəl] *adj* imbattable

unbecoming [,ʌnbɪ'kʌmɪŋ] *adj* déplacé, inconvenant; (*dress*) peu seyant

unbelievable [,ʌnbɪ'livəbəl] *adj* incroyable

unbeliever [,ʌnbɪ'livər] *s* incroyant *m*

unbending [ʌn'bɛndɪŋ] *adj* inflexible

unbiased [ʌn'baɪ•əst] *adj* impartial

un•bind [ʌn'baɪnd] *v* (*pret & pp* **-bound**) *tr* délier

unbleached [ʌn'blitʃt] *adj* écru

unbolt [ʌn'bolt] *tr* (*a gun; a door*) déverrouiller; (*a machine*) déboulonner

unborn [ʌn'bɔrn] *adj* à naître, futur

unbosom [ʌn'buzəm] *tr* découvrir; **to unbosom oneself** ouvrir son cœur

unbound [ʌn'baʊnd] *adj* non relié

unbreakable [ʌn'brekəbəl] *adj* incassable

unbroken [ʌn'brokən] *adj* intact; ininterrompu; (*spirit*) indompté; (*horse*) non rompu

unbuckle [ʌn'bʌkəl] *tr* déboucler

unburden [ʌn'bʌrdən] *tr* alléger; **to unburden oneself of** se soulager de

unburied [ʌn'bɛrid] *adj* non enseveli

unbutton [ʌn'bʌtən] *tr* déboutonner

uncalled-for [ʌn'kɔld,fɔr] *adj* déplacé; (*e.g., insult*) gratuit

uncanny [ʌn'kæni] *adj* inquiétant, mystérieux; rare, remarquable

uncared-for [ʌn'kɛrd,fɔr] *adj* négligé; peu soignée

unceasing [ʌn'sisɪŋ] *adj* incessant

unceremonious [,ʌnsɛrɪ'moni•əs] *adj* sans façon

uncertain [ʌn'sʌrtən] *adj* incertain

uncertain•ty [ʌn'sʌrtənti] *s* (*pl* **-ties**) incertitude *f*

unchain [ʌn'tʃen] *tr* désenchaîner

unchangeable [ʌn'tʃendʒəbəl] *adj* immuable

uncharted [ʌn'tʃɑrtɪd] *adj* inexploré

unchecked [ʌn'tʃɛkt] *adj* sans frein, non contenu; non vérifié

uncivilized [ʌn'sɪvɪ,laɪzd] *adj* incivilisé

unclad [ʌn'klæd] *adj* déshabillé

unclaimed [ʌn'klemd] *adj* non réclamé; (*mail*) au rebut

unclasp [ʌn'klæsp], [ʌn'klɑsp] *tr* dégrafer; (*one's hands*) desserrer

unclassified [ʌn'klæsɪ,faɪd] *adj* non classé; (*documents, information, etc.*) pas secret

uncle ['ʌŋkəl] *s* oncle *m*

unclean [ʌn'klin] *adj* sale, immonde

un•clog [ʌn'klɑg] *v* (*pret & pp* **-clogged;** *ger* **-clogging**) *tr* dégager, désobstruer

unclouded [ʌn'klaʊdɪd] *adj* clair, dégagé

uncollectible [,ʌnkə'lɛktɪbəl] *adj* irrécouvrable

uncomfortable [ʌn'kʌmfərtəbəl] *adj* (*causing discomfort*) inconfortable; (*feeling discomfort*) mal à l'aise

uncommitted [,ʌnkə'mɪtɪd] *adj* nonengagé

uncommon [ʌn'kɑmən] *adj* peu commun

uncompromising [ʌn'kɑmprə,maɪzɪŋ] *adj* intransigeant

unconcerned [,ʌnkən'sʌrnd] *adj* indifférent

unconditional [,ʌnkən'dɪʃənəl] *adj* inconditionnel

uncongenial [,ʌnkən'dʒini•əl] *adj* peu sympathique; incompatible; désagréable

unconquerable [ʌn'kɑŋkərəbəl] *adj* invincible

unconquered [ʌn'kɑŋkərd] *adj* invaincu, indompté

unconscious [ʌn'kɑnʃəs] *adj* inconscient; (*temporarily deprived of consciousness*) sans connaissance || *s—* **the unconscious** l'inconscient *m*

unconsciousness [ʌn'kɑnʃəsnɪs] *s* inconscience *f*; perte *f* de connaissance, évanouissement *m*

unconstitutional [,ʌnkɑnstɪ't(j)uʃənəl] *adj* inconstitutionnel

uncontrollable [,ʌnkən'troləbəl] *adj* ingouvernable; (*e.g., desires*) irrésistible; (*e.g., laughter*) inextinguible

unconventional [,ʌnkən'vɛnʃənəl] *adj* original, peu conventionnel; (*person*) non-conformiste

uncork [ʌn'kɔrk] *tr* déboucher

uncouple [ʌn'kʌpəl] *tr* désaccoupler

uncouth [ʌn'kuθ] *adj* gauche, sauvage; (*language*) grossier

uncover [ʌn'kʌvər] *tr* découvrir

unction ['ʌŋkʃən] *s* onction *f*

unctuous ['ʌŋkt/u•əs] *adj* onctueux

uncultivated [ʌn'kʌltɪ,vetɪd] *adj* inculte

uncultured [ʌn'kʌltʃərd] *adj* inculte, sans culture

uncut [ʌn'kʌt] *adj* non coupé; (*stone, diamond*) brut; (*crops*) sur pied; (*book*) non rogné

undamaged [ʌn'dæmɪdʒd] *adj* indemne

undaunted [ʌn'dɔntɪd] *adj* pas découragé; sans peur

undecided [,ʌndɪ'saɪdɪd] *adj* indécis

undefeated [,ʌndɪ'fitɪd] *adj* invaincu

undefended [,ʌndɪ'fɛndɪd] *adj* sans défense

undefiled [,ʌndɪ'faɪld] *adj* sans tache

undeniable [ˌʌndɪ'naɪ·əbəl] *adj* indéniable

under ['ʌndər] *adj* (*lower*) inférieur; (*underneath*) de dessous || *adv* dessous; **to go under** sombrer; **to keep under** tenir dans la soumission || *prep* sous, au-dessous de, dessous; moins de, e.g., **under forty** moins de quarante ans; dans, e.g., **under the circumstances** dans les circonstances; en, e.g., **under treatment** en traitement; e.g., **under repair** en voie de réparation; à, e.g., **under the microscope** au microscope; e.g., **under examination** à l'examen; e.g., **under the terms of** aux termes de; e.g., **under the word** (*in dictionary*) au mot; **to serve under** servir sous les ordres de

un'der·age' *adj* mineur

un'der·arm pad' *s* dessous-de-bras *m*

un'der·bid' *v* (*pret & pp* -bid; *ger* -bidding) *tr* offrir moins que

un'der·brush' *s* broussailles *fpl*

un'der·car'riage *s* (aer) train *m* d'atterrissage; (aut) dessous *m*

un'der·clothes' *spl* sous-vêtements *mpl*

un'der·consump'tion *s* sous-consommation *f*

un'der·cov'er *adj* secret

un'der·cur'rent *s* courant *m* de fond; (fig) vague *f* de fond

un'der·devel'oped *adj* sous-développé

un'der·dog' *s* opprimé *m*; (sports) parti *m* non favori, outsider *m*

underdone ['ʌndər ˌdʌn] *adj* pas assez cuit

un'der·es'timate *tr* sous-estimer

un'der·gar'ment *s* sous-vêtement *m*

un'der·go' *v* (*pret* -went; *pp* -gone) *tr* subir, éprouver, souffrir

un'der·grad'uate *adj & s* non diplômé *m*

un'der·ground' *adj* souterrain; (fig) clandestin || *s* (*subway*) métro *m*; résistance *f*, maquis *m* || *adv* sous terre; **to go underground** (fig) entrer dans la clandestinité, prendre le maquis

un'der·growth' *s* sous-bois *m*; (*underbrush*) broussailles *fpl*

un'der·hand'ed *adj* sournois, dissimulé

un'der·line' or **un'der·line'** *tr* souligner

underling ['ʌndərlɪŋ] *s* sous-ordre *m*, sous-fifre *m*

un'der·mine' *tr* miner, saper

underneath [ˌʌndər'niθ] *adj* de dessous; (*lower*) inférieur || *s* dessous *m* || *adv* dessous, en dessous || *prep* sous, au-dessous de

un'der·nour'ished *adj* sous-alimenté

un'der·nour'ishment *s* sous-alimentation *f*

underpaid [ˌʌndər'ped] *adj* mal rétribué

un'der·pass' *s* passage *m* souterrain

un'der·pin' *v* (*pret & pp* -pinned; *ger* -pinning) *tr* étayer

un'der·priv'ileged *adj* déshérité

un'der·rate' *tr* sous-estimer

un'der·score' *tr* souligner

un'der·sea' *adj* sous-marin || **un'der·sea'** *adv* sous la surface de la mer

un'der·sec'retar'y *s* (*pl* -ies) sous-secrétaire *m*

un'der·sell' *v* (*pret & pp* -sold) *tr* vendre à meilleur marché que; (*for less than the actual value*) solder

un'der·shirt' *s* gilet *m*, maillot *m* de corps

un'der·signed' *adj* soussigné

un'der·skirt' *s* jupon *m*

un'der·stand' *v* (*pret & pp* -stood) *tr & intr* comprendre, entendre

understandable [ˌʌndər'stændəbəl] *adj* compréhensible; **that's understandable** cela se comprend

un'der·stand'ing *adj* compréhensif || *s* compréhension *f*; (*intellectual faculty, mind*) entendement *m*; (*agreement*) accord *m*, entente *f*; **on the understanding that** à condition que; **to come to an understanding** arriver à un accord

un'der·stud'y *s* (*pl* -ies) doublure *f* || *v* (*pret & pp* -ied) *tr* (*an actor*) doubler

un'der·take' *v* (*pret* -took; *pp* -taken) *tr* entreprendre; (*to agree to perform*) s'engager à faire; **to undertake to** s'engager à

undertaker ['ʌndərˌtekər] *s* (*mortician*) entrepreneur *m* de pompes funèbres

undertaking [ˌʌndər'tekɪŋ] *s* entreprise *f*; (*commitment*) engagement *m* || ['ʌndərˌtekɪŋ] *s* service *m* des pompes funèbres

un'der·tone' *s* ton *m* atténué; (*background sound*) fond *m* obscur; **in an undertone** à voix basse

un'der·tow' *s* (*countercurrent below surface*) courant *m* de fond; (*on beach*) ressac *m*

un'der·wear' *s* sous-vêtements *mpl*

un'der·world' *s* (*criminal world*) bas-fonds *mpl*, pègre *f*; (*pagan world of the dead*) enfers *mpl*

un'der·write' or **un'der·write'** *v* (*pret* -wrote; *pp* -written) *tr* souscrire; (ins) assurer

un'der·writ'er *s* souscripteur *m*; (ins) assureur *m*

undeserved [ˌʌndɪ'zʌrvd] *adj* immérité

undesirable [ˌʌndɪ'zaɪrəbəl] *adj* peu désirable; (*e.g., alien*) indésirable || *s* indésirable *mf*

undetachable [ˌʌndɪ'tætʃəbəl] *adj* inséparable

undeveloped [ˌʌndɪ'vɛləpt] *adj* (*land*) inexploité; (*country*) sous-développé

undigested [ˌʌndɪ'dʒɛstɪd] *adj* indigeste

undignified [ʌn'dɪgnɪˌfaɪd] *adj* sans dignité, peu digne

undiscernible [ˌʌndɪ'zʌrnɪbəl], [ˌʌndɪ'sʌrnəbəl] *adj* imperceptible

undisputed [ˌʌndɪs'pjutɪd] *adj* incontesté

undo [ʌn'du] *v* (*pret* -did; *pp* -done) *tr* défaire; (fig) ruiner

undoing [ʌn'du·ɪŋ] *s* perte *f*, ruine *f*

undone [ʌn'dʌn] *adj* défait; (*omitted*) inaccompli; **to come undone** se défaire; **to leave nothing undone** ne rien négliger

undoubtedly [ʌn'dautɪdli] *adv* sans aucun doute, incontestablement
undramatic [ˌʌndrə'mætɪk] *adj* peu dramatique
undress ['ʌn ˌdrɛs], [ʌn'drɛs] *s* déshabillé *m*; *(scanty dress)* petite tenue *f* || [ʌn'drɛs] *tr* déshabiller || *intr* se déshabiller
undrinkable [ʌn'drɪŋkəbəl] *adj* imbuvable
undue [ʌn'd(j)u] *adj* indu
undulate ['ʌndjə ˌlet] *intr* onduler
unduly [ʌn'd(j)uli] *adv* indûment
undying [ʌn'daɪ·ɪŋ] *adj* impérissable
un'earned in'come ['ʌnʌrnd] *s* rente *f*, revenu *m* d'un bien
un'earned in'crement *s* plus-value *f*
unearth [ʌn'ʌrθ] *tr* déterrer
unearthly [ʌn'ʌrθli] *adj* surnaturel, spectral; bizarre; *(hour)* indu
uneasy [ʌn'izi] *adj* inquiet; contraint, gêné
uneatable [ʌn'itəbəl] *adj* immangeable
uneconomic(al) [ˌʌnikə'namɪk(əl)], [ˌʌnɛkə'namɪk(əl)] *adj* peu économique; *(person)* peu économe
uneducated [ʌn'ɛdjə ˌketɪd] *adj* ignorant, sans instruction
unemployed [ˌʌnɛm'plɔɪd] *adj* en chômage, sans travail || *spl* chômeurs *mpl*, sans-travail *mfpl*
unemployment [ˌʌnɛm'plɔɪmənt] *s* chômage *m*
un'employ'ment insur'ance *s* assurance-chômage *f*
unending [ʌn'ɛndɪŋ] *adj* interminable
unequal [ʌn'ikwəl] *adj* inégal; **to be unequal to** *(a task)* ne pas être à la hauteur de
unequaled or **unequalled** [ʌn'ikwəld] *adj* sans égal, sans pareil
unerring [ʌn'ʌrɪŋ], [ʌn'ɛrɪŋ] *adj* infaillible
UNESCO [ju'nɛsko] *s* (acronym) **(United Nations Educational, Scientific, and Cultural Organization)** l'Unesco *f*
unessential [ˌʌnɛ'sɛnʃəl] *adj* non essentiel
uneven [ʌn'ivən] *adj* inégal; *(number)* impair
uneventful [ˌʌnɪ'vɛntfəl] *adj* sans incident, peu mouvementé
unexceptionable [ˌʌnɛk'sɛpʃənəbəl] *adj* irréprochable
unexpected [ˌʌnɛk'spɛktɪd] *adj* inattendu, imprévu
unexplained [ˌʌnɛk'splend] *adj* inexpliqué
unexplored [ˌʌnɛk'splord] *adj* inexploré
unexposed [ˌʌnɛk'spozd] *adj* (phot) vierge
unfading [ʌn'fedɪŋ] *adj* immarcescible
unfailing [ʌn'felɪŋ] *adj* infaillible; *(inexhaustible)* intarissable
unfair [ʌn'fɛr] *adj* injuste, déloyal
unfaithful [ʌn'feθfəl] *adj* infidèle
unfamiliar [ˌʌnfə'mɪljər] *adj* étranger, peu familier
unfasten [ʌn'fæsən], [ʌn'fasən] *tr* défaire, détacher

unfathomable [ʌn'fæðəməbəl] *adj* insondable
unfavorable [ʌn'fevərəbəl] *adj* défavorable
unfeeling [ʌn'filɪŋ] *adj* insensible
unfilled [ʌn'fɪld] *adj* vide; *(post)* vacant
unfinished [ʌn'fɪnɪʃt] *adj* inachevé
unfit [ʌn'fɪt] *adj* impropre, inapte
unfold [ʌn'fold] *tr* déplier || *intr* se déplier
unforeseeable [ˌʌnfor'si·əbəl] *adj* imprévisible
unforeseen [ˌʌnfor'sin] *adj* imprévu
unforgettable [ˌʌnfər'gɛtəbəl] *adj* inoubliable
unforgivable [ˌʌnfər'gɪvəbəl] *adj* impardonnable
unfortunate [ʌn'fɔrtjənɪt] *adj & s* malheureux *m*
un-freeze [ʌn'friz] *v* *(pret* -**froze**; *pp* -**frozen** *tr* dégeler
unfriend·ly [ʌn'frɛndli] *adj* *(comp* -**lier**; *super* -**liest**) inamical
unfruitful [ʌn'frutfəl] *adj* infructueux
unfulfilled [ˌʌnfəl'fɪld] *adj* inaccompli
unfurl [ʌn'fʌrl] *tr* déployer
unfurnished [ʌn'fʌrnɪʃt] *adj* non meublé
ungain·ly [ʌn'genli] *adj* gauche, disgracieux
ungentlemanly [ʌn'dʒɛntəlmənli] *adj* mal élevé, impoli
ungird [ʌn'gʌrd] *tr* déceindre
ungodly [ʌn'gadli] *adj* impie; *(dreadful)* (coll) atroce
ungracious [ʌn'greʃəs] *adj* malgracieux
ungrammatical [ˌʌngrə'mætɪkəl] *adj* peu grammatical
ungrateful [ʌn'gretfəl] *adj* ingrat
ungrudgingly [ʌn'grʌdʒɪŋli] *adj* de bon cœur, libéralement
unguarded [ʌn'gardɪd] *adj* sans défense; *(moment)* d'inattention; *(card)* sec
unguent ['ʌŋgwənt] *s* onguent *m*
unhandy [ʌn'hændi] *adj* maladroit; *(e.g., tool)* incommode, pas maniable
unhap·py [ʌn'hæpi] *adj* *(comp* -**pier**; *super* -**piest**) malheureux, triste; *(unlucky)* malheureux, malencontreux; *(fateful)* funeste
unharmed [ʌn'harmd] *adj* indemne
unharness [ʌn'harnɪs] *tr* dételer
unheal·thy [ʌn'hɛlθi] *adj* *(comp* -**thier**, *super* -**thiest**) malsain; *(person)* maladif
unheard-of [ʌn'hʌrd ˌav] *adj* inouï
unhinge [ʌn'hɪndʒ] *tr* (fig) détraquer
unhitch [ʌn'hɪtʃ] *tr* décrocher; *(e.g., a horse)* dételer
unho·ly [ʌn'holi] *adj* *(comp* -**lier**; *super* -**liest**) profane; (coll) affreux
unhook [ʌn'hʊk] *tr* décrocher; *(e.g., a dress)* dégrafer
unhoped-for [ʌn'hopt ˌfor] *adj* inespéré
unhorse [ʌn'hɔrs] *tr* désarçonner
unhurt [ʌn'hʌrt] *adj* indemne
unicorn ['juni ˌkɔrn] *s* unicorne *m*
unification [ˌjunɪfɪ'keʃən] *s* unification *f*
uniform ['juni ˌfɔrm] *adj & s* uniforme

m ‖ *tr* uniformiser; vêtir d'un uniforme
uniformi•ty [ˌjunɪ'fɔrmɪti] *s* (*pl* -ties) uniformité *f*
uni•fy ['junɪˌfaɪ] *v* (*pret & pp* -fied) unifier
unilateral [ˌjunɪ'lætərəl] *adj* unilatéral
unimpeachable [ˌʌnɪm'pitʃəbəl] *adj* irrécusable
unimportant [ˌʌnɪm'pɔrtənt] *adj* peu important, sans importance
uninhabited [ˌʌnɪn'hæbɪtɪd] *adj* inhabité
uninspired [ˌʌnɪn'spaɪrd] *adj* sans inspiration, sans vigueur
unintelligent [ˌʌnɪn'telɪdʒənt] *adj* inintelligent
unintelligible [ˌʌnɪn'telɪdʒɪbəl] *adj* inintelligible
uninterested [ʌn'ɪntrɪstɪd], [ʌn'ɪntəˌrestɪd] *adj* indifférent
uninteresting [ʌn'ɪntrɪstɪŋ], [ʌn'ɪntəˌrestɪŋ] *adj* peu intéressant
uninterrupted [ˌʌnɪntə'rʌptɪd] *adj* ininterrompu
union ['junjən] *adj* (*leader, scale, card, etc.*) syndical ‖ *s* union *f*; (*of workmen*) syndicat *m*
unionize ['junjəˌnaɪz] *tr* syndiquer ‖ *intr* se syndiquer
un'ion shop' *s* atelier *m* syndical
un'ion suit' *s* sous-vêtement *m* d'une seule pièce
unique [ju'nik] *adj* unique
unison ['junɪsən], ['junɪzən] *s* unisson *m*; **in unison (with)** à l'unisson (de)
unit ['junɪt] *adj* unitaire ‖ *s* unité *f*; (*elec, mach*) groupe *m*
unite [ju'naɪt] *tr* unir ‖ *intr* s'unir
united [ju'naɪtɪd] *adj* uni
Unit'ed King'dom *s* Royaume-Uni *m*
Unit'ed Na'tions *spl* Nations *fpl* Unies
Unit'ed States' *adj* des États-Unis, américain ‖ *s*—**the United States** les États-Unis *mpl*
uni•ty ['junɪti] *s* (*pl* -ties) unité *f*
universal [ˌjunɪ'vʌrsəl] *adj & s* universel *m*
u'niversal joint' *s* joint *m* articulé, cardan *m*
universe ['junɪˌvʌrs] *s* univers *m*
universi•ty [ˌjunɪ'vʌrsɪti] *adj* universitaire ‖ *s* (*pl* -ties) université *f*
unjust [ʌn'dʒʌst] *adj* injuste
unjustified [ʌn'dʒʌstɪˌfaɪd] *adj* injustifié
unkempt [ʌn'kempt] *adj* dépeigné; mal tenu, négligé
unkind [ʌn'kaɪnd] *adj* désobligeant; (*pitiless*) impitoyable, dur
unknowable [ʌn'noˑəbəl] *adj* inconnaissable
unknowingly [ʌn'noˑɪŋli] *adv* inconsciemment
unknown [ʌn'non] *adj* inconnu; (*not yet revealed*) inédit; **unknown to** à l'insu de ‖ *s* inconnu *m*; (*math*) inconnue *f*
un'known quan'tity *s* (math, fig) inconnue *f*
Un'known Sol'dier *s* Soldat *m* inconnu
unlace [ʌn'les] *tr* délacer

unlatch [ʌn'lætʃ] *tr* lever le loquet de
unlawful [ʌn'lɔfəl] *adj* illégal, illicite
unleash [ʌn'liʃ] *tr* lâcher
unleavened [ʌn'levənd] *adj* azyme
unless [ʌn'les] *prep* sauf ‖ *conj* à moins que
unlettered [ʌn'letərd] *adj* illettré
unlike [ʌn'laɪk] *adj* (*not alike*) dissemblables; différent de; (*not typical of*) pas caractéristique de; (*poles of a magnet*) (elec) de noms contraires ‖ *prep* (*contrary to*) à la différence de
unlikely [ʌn'laɪkli] *adj* peu probable
unlimited [ʌn'lɪmɪtɪd] *adj* illimité
unlined [ʌn'laɪnd] *adj* (*coat*) non fourré; (*paper*) non rayé; (*face*) sans rides
unload [ʌn'lod] *tr* décharger; (*a gun*) désarmer; (coll) se décharger de ‖ *intr* décharger
unloading [ʌn'lodɪŋ] *s* déchargement *m*
unlock [ʌn'lɑk] *tr* ouvrir; (*a bolted door*) déverrouiller; (*the jaws*) desserrer
unloose [ʌn'lus] *tr* lâcher; (*to undo*) délier; (*a mighty force*) déchaîner
unloved [ʌn'lʌvd] *adj* peu aimé, haï
unlovely [ʌn'lʌvli] *adj* disgracieux
unluck•y [ʌn'lʌki] *adj* (*comp* -ier; *super* -iest) malchanceux, malheureux
un•make [ʌn'mek] *v* (*pret & pp* -made) *tr* défaire
unmanageable [ʌn'mænɪdʒəbəl] *adj* difficile à manier, ingouvernable
unmanly [ʌn'mænli] *adj* indigne d'un homme, poltron; efféminé
unmannerly [ʌn'mænərli] *adj* impoli, mal élevé
unmarketable [ʌn'mɑrkɪtəbəl] *adj* invendable
unmarriageable [ʌn'mærɪdʒəbəl] *adj* non mariable
unmarried [ʌn'mærɪd] *adj* célibataire
unmask [ʌn'mæsk], [ʌn'mɑsk] *tr* démasquer ‖ *intr* se démasquer
unmatched [ʌn'mætʃt] *adj* sans égal, incomparable; (*unpaired*) désassorti, dépareillé
unmerciful [ʌn'mʌrsɪfəl] *adj* impitoyable
unmesh [ʌn'meʃ] *tr* (mach) désengrener ‖ *intr* (mach) se désengrener
unmindful [ʌn'maɪndfəl] *adj* oublieux
unmistakable [ˌʌnmɪs'tekəbəl] *adj* évident, facilement reconnaissable
unmitigated [ʌn'mɪtɪˌgetɪd] *adj* parfait, fieffé
unmixed [ʌn'mɪkst] *adj* sans mélange
unmoor [ʌn'mur] *tr* désamarrer
unmoved [ʌn'muvd] *adj* impassible
unmuzzle [ʌn'mʌzəl] *tr* démuseler
unnatural [ʌn'nætʃərəl] *adj* anormal, dénaturé; maniéré; artificiel
unnecessary [ʌn'nesəˌseri] *adj* inutile
unnerve [ʌn'nʌrv] *tr* démonter, décontenancer, bouleverser
unnoticeable [ʌn'notɪsəbəl] *adj* imperceptible
unnoticed [ʌn'notɪst] *adj* inaperçu
unobserved [ˌʌnəb'zʌrvd] *adj* inobservé, inaperçu

unobtainable [,ʌnəb'tenəbəl] *adj* introuvable

unobtrusive [,ʌnəb'trusɪv] *adj* discret, effacé

unoccupied [ʌn'akjə,paɪd] *adj* libre, inoccupé

unofficial [,ʌnə'fɪʃəl] *adj* officieux, non officiel

unopened [ʌn'opənd] *adj* fermé; (*letter*) non décacheté

unopposed [,ʌnə'pozd] *adj* sans opposition; (*candidate*) unique

unorthodox [ʌn'ɔrθə,daks] *adj* peu orthodox

unpack [ʌn'pæk] *tr* déballer

unpalatable [ʌn'pælətəbəl] *adj* fade, insipide

unparalleled [ʌn'pærə,lɛld] *adj* sans précédent, sans pareil

unpardonable [ʌn'pardənəbəl] *adj* impardonnable

unpatriotic [,ʌnpetri'atɪk], [,ʌnpætri-'atɪk] *adj* antipatriotique

unperceived [,ʌnpər'sivd] *adj* inaperçu

unperturbable [,ʌnpər'tʌrbəbəl] *adj* imperturbable

unpleasant [ʌn'plɛzənt] *adj* désagréable, déplaisant

unpopular [ʌn'papjələr] *adj* impopulaire

unpopularity [ʌn,papjə'lærɪti] *s* impopularité *f*

unprecedented [ʌn'prɛsɪ,dɛntɪd] *adj* sans précédent, inédit

unprejudiced [ʌn'prɛdʒədɪst] *adj* sans préjugés, impartial

unpremeditated [,ʌnpri'mɛdɪ,tetɪd] *adj* non prémédité

unprepared [,ʌnpri'pɛrd] *adj* sans préparation; (*e.g., speech*) improvisé

unprepossessing [,ʌnpripə'zɛsɪŋ] *adj* peu engageant

unpresentable [,ʌnpri'zɛntəbəl] *adj* peu présentable

unpretentious [,ʌnpri'tɛnʃəs] *adj* sans prétentions, modeste

unprincipled [ʌn'prɪnsɪpəld] *adj* sans principes, sans scrupules

unproductive [,ʌnprə'dʌktɪv] *adj* improductif

unprofitable [ʌn'prafɪtəbəl] *adj* peu profitable, inutile

unpronounceable [,ʌnprə'naunsəbəl] *adj* imprononçable

unpropitious [,ʌnprə'pɪʃəs] *adj* défavorable

unpublished [ʌn'pʌblɪʃt] *adj* inédit

unpunished [ʌn'pʌnɪʃt] *adj* impuni

unqualified [ʌn'kwalə,faɪd] *adj* incompétent; parfait, fieffé

unquenchable [ʌn'kwɛntʃəbəl] *adj* inextinguible

unquestionable [ʌn'kwɛstʃənəbəl] *adj* indiscutable

unravel [ʌn'rævəl] *v* (*pret & pp* **-eled** or **-elled**; *ger* **-eling** or **-elling**) *tr* effiler; (fig) débrouiller ‖ *intr* s'effiler; (fig) se débrouiller

unreachable [ʌn'ritʃəbəl] *adj* inaccessible

unreal [ʌn'ri·əl] *adj* irréel

unreali·ty [,ʌnri'ælɪti] *s* (*pl* **-ties**) irréalité *f*

unreasonable [ʌn'rizənəbəl] *adj* déraisonnable

unrecognizable [ʌn'rɛkəg,naɪzəbəl] *adj* méconnaissable

unreel [ʌn'ril] *tr* dérouler ‖ *intr* se dérouler

unrelenting [,ʌnri'lɛntɪŋ] *adj* implacable

unreliable [,ʌnri'laɪ·əbəl] *adj* peu fidèle, instable, sujet à caution

unremitting [,ʌnri'mɪtɪŋ] *adj* incessant, infatigable

unrented [ʌn'rɛntɪd] *adj* libre, sans locataires

unrepentant [,ʌnri'pɛntənt] *adj* impénitent

un'requit'ed love' [,ʌnri'kwaɪtɪd] *s* amour *m* non partagé

unresponsive [,ʌnri'spansɪv] *adj* peu sensible, froid, détaché

unrest [ʌn'rɛst] *s* agitation *f*, trouble *m*; inquiétude *f*

un·rig [ʌn'rɪg] *v* (*pret & pp* **-rigged**; *ger* **-rigging**) *tr* (naut) dégréer

unrighteous [ʌn'raɪtʃəs] *adj* inique, injuste

unripe [ʌn'raɪp] *adj* vert, pas mûr; précoce

unrivaled or **unrivalled** [ʌn'raɪvəld] *adj* sans rival

unroll [ʌn'rol] *tr* dérouler ‖ *intr* se dérouler

unromantic [,ʌnro'mæntɪk] *adj* peu romanesque, terre à terre

unruffled [ʌn'rʌfəld] *adj* calme, serein

unruly [ʌn'ruli] *adj* indiscipliné, ingouvernable

unsaddle [ʌn'ærdəl] *tr* (*a horse*) desseller; (*a horseman*) désarçonner

unsafe [ʌn'sef] *adj* dangereux

unsaid [ʌn'sɛd] *adj*—**to leave unsaid** passer sous silence

unsalable [ʌn'seləbəl] *adj* invendable

unsanitary [ʌn'sænɪ,tɛri] *adj* peu hygiénique

unsatisfactory [ʌn,sætɪs'fæktəri] *adj* peu satisfaisant

unsatisfied [ʌn'sætɪs,faɪd] *adj* insatisfait, inassouvi

unsavory [ʌn'severi] *adj* désagréable; (fig) équivoque, louche

unscathed [ʌn'skeðd] *adj* indemne

unscientific [,ʌnsaɪ·ən'tɪfɪk] *adj* antiscientifique

unscrew [ʌn'skru] *tr* dévisser

unscrupulous [ʌn'skrupjələs] *adj* sans scrupules

unseal [ʌn'sil] *tr* desceller

unsealed *adj* (*mail*) non clos

unseasonable [ʌn'sizənəbəl] *adj* hors de saison; (*untimely*) inopportun

unseemly [ʌn'simli] *adj* inconvenant

unseen [ʌn'sin] *adj* invisible

unselfish [ʌn'sɛlfɪʃ] *adj* désintéressé

unsettled [ʌn'sɛtəld] *adj* instable; (*region*) non colonisé; (*question*) en suspens; (*weather*) variable; (*bills*) non réglé

unshackle [ʌn'ʃækəl] *tr* désentraver

unshaken [ʌn'ʃekən] *adj* inébranlé

unshapely [ʌn'ʃepli] *adj* difforme, informe
unshaven [ʌn'ʃevən] *adj* non rasé
unsheathe [ʌn'ʃið] *tr* dégainer
unshod [ʌn'ʃɑd] *adj* déchaussé; (*horse*) déferré
unshrinkable [ʌn'ʃrɪŋkəbəl] *adj* irrétrécissable
unsightly [ʌn'saɪtli] *adj* laid, hideux
unsinkable [ʌn'sɪŋkəbəl] *adj* insubmersible
unskilled [ʌn'skɪld] *adj* inexpérimenté; de manœuvre
un'skilled la'borer *s* manœuvre *m*
unskillful [ʌn'skɪlfəl] *adj* maladroit
unsnarl [ʌn'snɑrl] *tr* débrouiller
unsociable [ʌn'soʃəbəl] *adj* insociable
unsold [ʌn'sold] *adj* invendu
unsolder [ʌn'sɑdər] *tr* dessouder
unsophisticated [,ʌnsə'fɪstɪ,ketɪd] *adj* ingénu, naïf, simple
unsound [ʌn'saʊnd] *adj* peu solide; (*false*) faux; (*decayed*) gâté; (*mind*) dérangé; (*sleep*) léger
unspeakable [ʌn'spikəbəl] *adj* indicible; (*disgusting*) sans nom
unsportsmanlike [ʌn'sportsmən,laɪk] *adj* antisportif
unstable [ʌn'stebəl] *adj* instable
unsteady [ʌn'stedi] *adj* chancelant, tremblant, vacillant
unstinted [ʌn'stɪntɪd] *adj* abondant, sans bornes
unstitch [ʌn'stɪtʃ] *tr* découdre
un·stop [ʌn'stɑp] *v* (*pret & pp* -stopped; *ger* -stopping) *tr* déboucher
unstressed [ʌn'strest] *adj* inaccentué
unstrung [ʌn'strʌŋ] *adj* détraqué; (*necklace*) défilé; (*mus*) sans cordes
unsuccessful [,ʌnsək'sesfəl] *adj* non réussi; **to be unsuccessful** ne pas réussir
unsuitable [ʌn's(j)utəbəl] *adj* impropre; (*time*) inopportun; **unsuitable for** peu fait pour, inapte à
unsuspected [,ʌnsəs'pɛktɪd] *adj* insoupçonné
unswerving [ʌn'swʌrvɪŋ] *adj* ferme, inébranlable
unsympathetic [,ʌnsɪmpə'θɛtɪk] *adj* peu compatissant
unsystematic(al) [,ʌnsɪstə'mætɪk(əl)] *adj* non systématique, sans méthode
untactful [ʌn'tæktfəl] *adj* indiscret, indélicat
untamed [ʌn'temd] *adj* indompte
untangle [ʌn'tæŋgəl] *tr* démêler, débrouiller
untenable [ʌn'tenəbəl] *adj* insoutenable
unthankful [ʌn'θæŋkfəl] *adj* ingrat
unthinkable [ʌn'θɪŋkəbəl] *adj* impensable
unthinking [ʌn'θɪŋkɪŋ] *adj* irréfléchi
untidy [ʌn'taɪdi] *adj* désordonné, débraillé
un·tie [ʌn'taɪ] *v* (*pret & pp* -tied; *ger* -tying) *tr* délier, dénouer
until [ʌn'tɪl] *prep* jusqu'à || *conj* jusqu'à ce que, en attendant que
untimely [ʌn'taɪmli] *adj* inopportun; (*premature*) prématuré
untiring [ʌn'taɪrɪŋ] *adj* infatigable

untold [ʌn'told] *adj* incalculable; (*suffering*) inouï; (*joy*) indicible; (*tale*) non raconté
untouchable [ʌn'tʌtʃəbəl] *adj & s* intouchable *mf*
untouched [ʌn'tʌtʃt] *adj* intact; indifférent; non mentionné
untoward [ʌn'tord] *adj* malencontreux
untrained [ʌn'trend] *adj* inexpérimenté; (*animal*) non dressé
untrammeled or **untrammelled** [ʌn'træməld] *adj* sans entraves
untried [ʌn'traɪd] *adj* inéprouvé
untroubled [ʌn'trʌbəld] *adj* calme, insoucieux
untrue [ʌn'tru] *adj* faux; infidèle
untrustworthy [ʌn'trʌst,wʌrði] *adj* indigne de confiance
untruth [ʌn'truθ] *s* mensonge *m*
untruthful [ʌn'truθfəl] *adj* mensonger
untwist [ʌn'twɪst] *tr* détordre || *intr* se détordre
unused [ʌn'juzd] *adj* inutilisé, inemployé; **unused to** [ʌn'juzdtʊ], [ʌn-'justʊ] peu accoutumé à
unusual [ʌn'juʒʊ-əl] *adj* insolite, inusité, inhabituel
unutterable [ʌn'ʌtərəbəl] *adj* indicible, inexprimable
unvanquished [ʌn'væŋkwɪʃt] *adj* invaincu
unvarnished [ʌn'vɑrnɪʃt] *adj* non verni; (fig) sans fard, simple
unveil [ʌn'vel] *tr* dévoiler; (*e.g., a statue*) inaugurer || *intr* se dévoiler
unveiling [ʌn'velɪŋ] *s* dévoilement *m*
unventilated [ʌn'vɛntɪ,letɪd] *adj* sans aération
unvoice [ʌn'vɔɪs] *tr* dévoiser, assourdir
unwanted [ʌn'wɑntɪd] *adj* non voulu
unwarranted [ʌn'wɑrəntɪd] *adj* injustifié; sans garantie
unwary [ʌn'weri] *adj* imprudent
unwavering [ʌn'wevərɪŋ] *adj* constant, ferme, résolu
unwelcome [ʌn'wɛlkəm] *adj* (*e.g., visitor*) importun; (*e.g., news*) fâcheux
unwell [ʌn'wɛl] *adj* indisposé, souffrant; (*menstruating*) indisposée
unwholesome [ʌn'holsəm] *adj* malsain, insalubre
unwieldy [ʌn'wildi] *adj* peu maniable
unwilling [ʌn'wɪlɪŋ] *adj* peu disposé
unwillingly [ʌn'wɪlɪŋli] *adv* à contrecœur
un·wind [ʌn'waɪnd] *v* (*pret & pp* -wound) *tr* dérouler || *intr* se dérouler
unwise [ʌn'waɪz] *adj* peu judicieux, malavisé
unwished-for [ʌn'wɪʃt,fɔr] *adj* non souhaité
unwittingly [ʌn'wɪtɪŋli] *adv* inconsciemment, sans le savoir
unwonted [ʌn'wʌntɪd] *adj* inaccoutumé, peu commun
unworldly [ʌn'wʌrldli] *adj* peu mondain; simple, naïf
unworthy [ʌn'wʌrði] *adj* indigne
un·wrap [ʌn'ræp] *v* (*pret & pp* -wrapped; *ger* -wrapping) *tr* dépaqueter, désenvelopper

unwrinkled [ʌn'rɪŋkəld] *adj* uni, lisse, sans rides

unwritten [ʌn'rɪtən] *adj* non écrit; oral; (*blank*) vierge, blanc

unwrit'ten law' *s* droit *m* coutumier

unyielding [ʌn'jildɪŋ] *adj* ferme, solide; inébranlable

unyoke [ʌn'jok] *tr* dételer

up [ʌp] *adj* montant, ascendant; (*raised*) levé; (*standing*) debout; (*time*) expiré; (*blinds*) relevé; **up in arms** soulevé, indigné || *adv* haut, en haut; **to be up against** se heurter à; **to be up against it** avoir la déveine; **to be up to** être capable de, être à la hauteur de; être à, e.g., **to be up to you (me, etc.)** être à vous (moi, etc.); **up and down** de haut en bas; (*back and forth*) de long en large; **up there** là-haut; **up to** jusqu'à; (*at the level of*) au niveau de, à la hauteur de; **up to and including** jusques et y compris; **what's up?** qu'est-ce qui se passe?; for expressions like **to go up** monter and **to get up** se lever, see the verb || *prep* en haut de, vers le haut de; (*a stream*) en montant || *v* (*pret & pp* upped; *ger* upping) *tr* (coll) faire monter; (*prices, wages*) (coll) élever || *interj* debout!

up-and-coming ['ʌpən'kʌmɪŋ] *adj* (coll) entreprenant

up-and-doing ['ʌpən'du·ɪŋ] *adj* (coll) entreprenant, alerte, énergique

up-and-up ['ʌpən'ʌp] *s*—**to be on the up-and-up** (coll) être en bonne voie; (coll) être honnête

up·braid' *tr* réprimander, reprendre

upbringing ['ʌp‚brɪŋɪŋ] *s* éducation *f*

up'coun'try *adv* (coll) à l'intérieur du pays || *s* (coll) Intérieur *m* du pays

up·date' *tr* mettre à jour

upheaval [ʌp'hivəl] *s* soulèvement *m*

up'hill' *adj* montant; difficile, pénible || **up'hill'** *adv* en montant

up·hold' *v* (*pret & pp* -held) *tr* soutenir, maintenir

upholster [ʌp'holstər] *tr* tapisser

upholsterer [ʌp'holstərər] *s* tapissier *m*

upholster·y [ʌp'holstəri] *s* (*pl* -ies) tapisserie *f*

up'keep' *s* entretien *m*; (*expenses*) frais *mpl* d'entretien

upland ['ʌplənd], ['ʌp‚lænd] *adj* élevé || *s* région *f* montagneuse; **uplands** hautes terres *fpl*

up'lift' *s* élévation *f*; (*moral improvement*) édification *f* || **up·lift'** *tr* soulever, élever

upon [ə'pɑn] *prep* sur; à, e.g., **upon my arrival** à mon arrivée; **upon** + *ger* en + *ger*, e.g., **upon arriving** en arrivant

upper ['ʌpər] *adj* supérieur; haut; (*first*) premier || *s* (*of shoe*) empeigne *f*

up'per berth' *s* couchette *f* du haut, couchette supérieure

up'per-case' *adj* (typ) du haut de casse

up'per clas'ses *spl* hautes classes *fpl*

up'per hand' *s* dessus *m*, haute main *f*

up'per mid'dle class' *s* haute bourgeoisie *f*

up'per·most' *adj* (le) plus haut, (le) plus élevé; (le) premier || *adv* en dessus

uppish ['ʌpɪʃ] *adj* (coll) suffisant, arrogant

up·raise' *tr* lever

up'right' *adj & adv* droit || *s* montant *m*

uprising [ʌp'raɪzɪŋ], ['ʌp‚raɪzɪŋ] *s* soulèvement *m*, insurrection *f*

up'roar' *s* tumulte *m*, vacarme *m*

uproarious [ʌp'rorɪ·əs] *adj* tumultueux; (*funny*) comique, impayable

up·root' *tr* déraciner

ups' **and downs'** *spl* vicissitudes *fpl*

up·set' or **up'set'** *adj* (*overturned*) renversé; (*disturbed*) bouleversé; (*stomach*) dérangé || **up'set'** *s* (*overturn*) renversement *m*; (*of emotions*) bouleversement *m* || **up·set'** *v* (*pret & pp* -set; *ger* -setting) *tr* renverser; bouleverser || *intr* se renverser

up'set price' *s* prix *m* de départ

upsetting [ʌp'setɪŋ] *adj* bouleversant, inquiétant

up'shot' *s* résultat *m*; point *m* essentiel

up'side down' *adv* sens dessus dessous; **to turn upside down** renverser; se renverser; (*said of carriage*) verser

up'stage' *adj & adv* au second plan, à l'arrière-plan; **to go upstage** remonter || *s* arrière-plan *m* || **up'stage'** *tr* (coll) prendre un air dédaigneux envers

up'stairs' *adj* d'en haut || *s* l'étage *m* supérieur || *adv* en haut; **to go upstairs** monter, monter en haut

up·stand'ing *adj* droit; (*vigorous*) gaillard; (*sincere*) honnête, probe

up'start' *adj & s* parvenu *m*

up'stream' *adj* d'amont || *adv* en amont

up'stroke' *s* (*in writing*) délié *m*; (mach) course *f* ascendante

up'surge' *s* poussée *f*

up'swing' *s* mouvement *m* de montée; (com) amélioration *f*

up-to-date ['ʌptə'det] *adj* à la page; (*e.g., account books*) mis à jour

up-to-the-minute ['ʌptəðə'mɪnɪt] *adj* de la dernière heure

up'trend' *s* tendance *f* à la hausse

up'turn' *s* hausse *f*, amélioration *f*

up·turned' *adj* (*e.g., eyes*) levé; (*part of clothing*) relevé; (*nose*) retroussé

upward ['ʌpwərd] *adj* ascendant || *adv* vers le haut; **upward of** plus de

Ural ['jurəl] *adj* Ouralien || *s* Oural *m*; **Urals** Oural

uranium [ju'renɪ·əm] *s* uranium *m*

urban ['ʌrbən] *adj* urbain

urbane [ʌr'ben] *adj* urbain, courtois

urbanite ['ʌrbə‚naɪt] *s* citadin *m*, habitant *m* d'une ville

urbanity [ʌr'bænɪti] *s* urbanité *f*

urbanize ['ʌrbə‚naɪz] *tr* urbaniser

ur'ban renew'al *s* renouveau *m* urbain

urchin ['ʌrtʃɪn] *s* gamin *m*, galopin *m*

ure·thra [ju'riθrə] *s* (*pl* -thras *or* -thrae [θri]) urètre *m*

urge [ʌrdʒ] *s* impulsion *f* || *tr & intr* presser

urgen·cy ['ʌrdʒənsi] *s* (*pl* -cies) urgence *f*; insistance *f*, sollicitation *f*

urgent [ˈʌrdʒənt] *adj* urgent, pressant; (*insistent*) pressant, importun
urinal [ˈjurinəl] *s* (*small building or convenience for men*) urinoir *m*, vespasienne *f*; (*for bed*) urinal *m*
urinary [ˈjurɪˌnɛri] *adj* urinaire
urinate [ˈjurɪˌnet] *tr* & *intr* uriner; pisser (coll)
urine [ˈjurɪn] *s* urine *f*
urn [ʌrn] *s* urne *f*; (*for tea, coffee, etc.*) fontaine *f*
urology [juˈrɑlədʒi] *s* urologie *f*
us [ʌs] *pron pers* nous §85, §87
U.S.A. [ˈjuˈɛsˈe] *s* (letterword) (**United States of America**) E.-U.A. *mpl* or U.S.A. *mpl*
usable [ˈjuzəbəl] *adj* utilisable
usage [ˈjusɪdʒ], [ˈjuzɪdʒ] *s* usage *m*
use [jus] *s* emploi *m*, usage *m*; (*usefulness*) utilité *f*; **in use** occupé; **of what use is it?** à quoi cela sert-il?; **out of use** hors de service; **to be of no use** ne servir à rien; **to have no use for s.o.** tenir qn en mauvaise estime; **to make use of** se servir de; **what's the use?** à quoi bon? ‖ [juz] *tr* employer, se servir de, user de; **to use up** épuiser, user ‖ *intr*—**I used to visit my friend every evening** je visitais mon ami tous les soirs
used [juzd] *adj* usagé, usé; d'occasion, e.g., **used car** voiture *f* d'occasion; **to be used** (*to be put into use*) être usité, être employé; **to be used as** servir de; **to be used to** (*to be useful for*) servir à; **used to** [ˈjustu] accoutumé à; **used up** épuisé
useful [ˈjusfəl] *adj* utile
usefulness [ˈjusfəlnɪs] *s* utilité *f*

useless [ˈjuslɪs] *adj* inutile
user [ˈjuzər] *s* usager *m*; (*of a machine, of gas, etc.*) utilisateur *m*
usher [ˈʌʃər] *s* placeur *m*; ouvreuse *f*; (*doorkeeper*) huissier *m* ‖ *tr*—**to usher in** inaugurer; (*a person*) introduire
U.S.S.R. [ˈjuˈɛsˈɛsˈɑr] *s* (letterword) (**Union of Soviet Socialist Republics**) U.R.S.S. *f*
usual [ˈjuʒu̇ˌəl] *adj* usuel; **as usual** comme d'habitude
usually [ˈjuʒu̇ˌəli] *adv* usuellement, d'habitude, d'ordinaire
usurp [juˈzʌrp] *tr* usurper
usu·ry [ˈjuʒəri] *s* (*pl* -ries) usure *f*
utensil [juˈtɛnsɪl] *s* ustensile *m*
uter·us [ˈjutərəs] *s* (*pl* -i [ˌaɪ]) utérus *m*
utilitarian [ˌjutɪlɪˈtɛrɪ·ən] *adj* utilitaire
utili·ty [juˈtɪlɪti] *s* (*pl* -ties) utilité *f*; service *m* public; **utilities** services en commun (*gaz, transports, etc.*)
utilize [ˈjutɪˌlaɪz] *tr* utiliser
utmost [ˈʌtˌmost] *adj* extrême; plus grand; plus éloigné ‖ *s*—**the utmost** l'extrême *m*, le comble *m*; **to do one's utmost** faire tout son possible; **to the utmost** jusqu'au dernier point
utopia [juˈtopɪ·ə] *s* utopie *f*
utopian [juˈtopɪ·ən] *adj* utopique ‖ *s* utopiste *mf*
utter [ˈʌtər] *adj* complet, total, absolu ‖ *tr* proférer, émettre; (*a cry*) pousser
utterance [ˈʌtərəns] *s* expression *f*, émission *f*; (gram) énoncé *m*; **to give utterance to** exprimer
utterly [ˈʌtərli] *adv* complètement, tout à fait, totalement

V

V, v [vi] *s* XXIIᵉ lettre de l'alphabet
vacan·cy [ˈvekənsi] *s* (*pl* -cies) (*emptiness; gap, opening*) vide *m*; (*unfilled position or job*) vacance *f*; (*in a building*) appartement *m* disponible; (*in a hotel*) chambre *f* de libre; **no vacancy** (public sign) complet
vacant [ˈvekənt] *adj* (*empty*) vide; (*having no occupant; untenanted*) vacant, libre, disponible; (*expression, look*) distrait, vague
va'cant lot' *s* terrain *m* vague
vacate [ˈveket] *tr* quitter, évacuer ‖ *intr* (*to move out*) déménager
vacation [veˈkeʃən] *s* vacances *fpl*; **on vacation** en vacances ‖ *intr* prendre ses vacances, passer les vacances
vacationist [veˈkeʃənɪst] *s* vacancier *m*
vaca'tion with pay' *s* congé *m* payé
vaccinate [ˈvæksɪˌnet] *tr* vacciner
vaccination [ˌvæksɪˈneʃən] *s* vaccination *f*
vaccine [vækˈsin] *s* vaccin *m*
vacillate [ˈvæsɪˌlet] *intr* vaciller

vacui·ty [væˈkjuˌɪti] *s* (*pl* -ties) vacuité *f*
vacu·um [ˈvækjuˌəm] *s* (*pl* -ums or -a [ə]) vacuum *m*, vide *m* ‖ *tr* passer à l'aspirateur, dépoussiérer
vac'uum clean'er *s* aspirateur *m*
vac'uum pump' *s* pompe *f* à vide
vac'uum tube' *s* tube *m* à vide
vagabond [ˈvægəˌbɑnd] *adj* & *s* vagabond *m*
vagar·y [vəˈgɛri] *s* (*pl* -ies) caprice *m*
vagran·cy [ˈvegrənsi] *s* (*pl* -cies) vagabondage *m*
vague [veg] *adj* vague
vain [ven] *adj* vain; **in vain** en vain
vainglorious [venˈglorɪ·əs] *adj* vaniteux
valance [ˈvæləns] *s* cantonnière *f*, lambrequin *m*
vale [vel] *s* vallon *m*
valedicto·ry [ˌvælɪˈdɪktəri] *s* (*pl* -ries) discours *m* d'adieu
valence [ˈveləns] *s* (chem) valence *f*
valentine [ˈvælənˌtaɪn] *s* (*sweetheart*)

valentin *m*; (*card*) carte *f* de la Saint-Valentin

Val'entine Day' *s* la Saint-Valentin

vale' of tears' *s* vallée *f* de larmes

valet ['vælıt], ['væle] *s* valet *m*

valiant ['væljənt] *adj* vaillant

valid ['vælıd] *adj* valable, valide

validate ['vælı̩det] *tr* valider; (sports) homologuer

validation [‚vælı'deʃən] *s* validation *f*; (sports) homologation *f*

validi•ty [və'lıdıtı] *s* (*pl* -ties) validité *f*

valise [və'lis] *s* mallette *f*

valley ['vælı] *s* vallée *f*, vallon *m*; (*of roof*) cornière *f*

valor ['vælər] *s* valeur *f*, vaillance *f*

valorous ['vælərəs] *adj* valeureux

valuable ['vælju•əbəl], ['væljəbəl] *adj* précieux, de valeur || **valuables** *spl* objets *mpl* de valeur

value ['vælju] *s* valeur *f*; (*bargain*) affaire *f*, occasion *f*; **to set a value on** estimer, évaluer || *tr* (*to think highly of*) priser, estimer; (*to set a price for*) estimer, évaluer; **if you value your life** si vous tenez à la vie

val'ue-added tax' *s* taxe *f* à la valeur ajoutée, T.V.A.

valueless ['væljulıs] *adj* sans valeur

valve [vælv] *s* soupape *f*; (*of mollusk; of fruit; of tire*) valve *f*; (*of heart*) valvule *f*; (mus) clé *f*

valve' cap' *s* chapeau *m*, bouchon *m*

valve' gears' *spl* (*of gas engine*) engrenages *mpl* de distribution; (*of steam engine*) mécanisme *m* de distribution

valve'-in-head' en'gine *s* moteur *m* à soupapes en tête, moteur à culbuteurs

valve' seat' *s* siège *m* de soupape

valve' spring' *s* ressort *m* de soupape

valve' stem' *s* tige *f* de soupape

vamp [væmp] *s* (*of shoe*) empeigne *f*; (*patchwork*) rapiéçage *m*; (*woman who preys on man*) (coll) femme *f* fatale, vamp *f* || *tr* (*a shoe*) mettre une empeigne à; (*to piece together*) rapiécer; (*a susceptible man*) (coll) vamper; (*an accompaniment*) (coll) improviser

vampire ['væmpair] *s* vampire *m*; femme *f* fatale, vamp *f*

van [væn] *s* camion *m*, voiture *f* de déménagement; (mil, fig) avant-garde *f*; (*railway car*) (Brit) fourgon *m*

vandal ['vændəl] *adj & s* vandale *m* || (*cap*) *adj* vandale || (*cap*) *s* Vandale *mf*

vandalism ['vændə‚lızəm] *s* vandalisme *m*

vane [ven] *s* (*weathervane*) girouette *f*; (*of windmill*) aile *f*; (*of propeller or turbine*) ailette *f*; (*of feather*) lame *f*

vanguard ['væn‚gɑrd] *s* (mil, fig) avant-garde *f*; **in the vanguard** à l'avant-garde

vanilla [və'nılə] *s* vanille *f*

vanish ['vænıʃ] *intr* s'évanouir, disparaître

van'ishing cream' *s* crème *f* de jour

vani•ty ['vænıtı] *s* (*pl* -ties) vanité *f*; (*dressing table*) table *f* de toilette, coiffeuse *f*; (*vanity case*) poudrier *m*

van'ity case' *s* poudrier *m*, nécessaire *m* de toilette

vanquish ['væŋkwıʃ] *tr* vaincre

van'tage point' ['væntıdʒ] *s* position *f* avantageuse

vapid ['væpıd] *adj* insipide

vapor ['vepər] *s* vapeur *f*

vaporize ['vepə‚raız] *tr* vaporiser || *intr* se vaporiser

va'por trail' *s* (aer) sillage *m* de fumée

variable ['verı‚əbl] *adj & s* variable *f*

variance ['verı‚əns] *s* différence *f*, variation *f*; **at variance with** en désaccord avec

variant ['verı‚ənt] *adj* variant || *s* variante *f*

variation [‚verı'eʃən] *s* variation *f*

varicose ['verı‚kos] *adj* variqueux

var'icose veins' *spl* (pathol) varice *f*

varied ['verid] *adj* varié

variegated ['verı‚ə‚getıd], ['verı‚getıd] *adj* varié; (*spotted*) bigarré, bariolé

varie•ty [və'raı‚ıtı] *s* (*pl* -ties) variété *f*

vari'ety show' *s* spectacle *m* de variétés

various ['verı‚əs] *adj* divers, différent; (*several*) plusieurs; (*variegated*) bigarré

varnish ['vɑrnıʃ] *s* vernis *m* || *tr* vernir; (*e.g., the truth*) farder, embellir

varsi•ty ['vɑrsıtı] *adj* (sports) universitaire || *s* (*pl* -ties) (sports) équipe *f* universitaire principale

var•y ['veri] *v* (*pret & pp* -ied) *tr & intr* varier

vase [ves], [vez] *s* vase *m*

vaseline ['væsə‚lin] *s* (trademark) vaseline *f*

vassal ['væsəl] *adj & s* vassal *m*

vast [væst], [vɑst] *adj* vaste

vastness ['væstnıs], ['vɑstnıs] *s* vaste étendue *f*, immensité *f*

vat [væt] *s* cuve *f*, bac *m*

Vatican ['vætıkən] *adj* vaticane || *s* Vatican *m*

vaudeville ['vodvıl], ['vodəvıl] *s* spectacle *m* de variétés, music-hall *m*; (*light theatrical piece interspersed with songs*) vaudeville *m*

vault [vɔlt] *s* (*underground chamber*) souterrain *m*; (*of a bank*) chambre *f* forte; (*burial chamber*) caveau *m*; (*leap*) saut *m*; (anat, archit) voûte *f* || *tr & intr* sauter

vaunt [vɔnt], [vɑnt] *s* vantardise *f* || *tr* vanter || *intr* se vanter

veal [vil] *s* veau *m*

veal' chop' *s* côtelette *f* de veau

veal' cut'let *s* escalope *f* de veau

veer [vır] *s* virage *m* || *tr* faire virer || *intr* virer

vegetable ['vɛdʒıtəbəl] *adj* végétal || *s* (*plant*) végétal *m*; (*edible part of plant*) légume *m*

veg'etable gar'den *s* potager *m*

veg'etable soup' *s* potage *m* aux légumes

vegetarian [‚vɛdʒı'terı‚ən] *adj & s* végétarien *m*

vegetate ['vɛdʒı‚tet] *intr* végéter

vehemence ['vi•ıməns] *s* véhémence *f*

vehement ['vi•ımənt] *adj* véhément

vehicle ['vi·ıkəl] *s* véhicule *m*
veil [vel] *s* voile *m*; **to take the veil** prendre le voile || *tr* voiler || *intr* se voiler
vein [ven] *s* veine *f* || *tr* veiner
velar ['vilər] *adj* & *s* vélaire *f*
vellum ['veləm] *s* vélin *m*; papier *m* vélin
veloci·ty [vı'lasıti] *s* (*pl* -ties) vitesse *f*
velvet ['velvıt] *s* velours *m*
velveteen [,velvı'tin] *s* velvet *m*
velvety ['velvıti] *adj* velouté
vend [vend] *tr* vendre, colporter
vend′ing machine′ *s* distributeur *m* automatique
vendor ['vendər] *s* vendeur *m*
veneer [və'nır] *s* placage *m*; (fig) vernis *m* || *tr* plaquer
venerable ['venərəbəl] *adj* vénérable
venerate ['venə,ret] *tr* vénérer
venereal [vı'nırı·əl] *adj* vénérien
Venetian [vı'niʃən] *adj* vénitien || *s* Vénitien *m*
Vene′tian blind′ *s* jalousie *f*, store *m* vénitien
vengeance ['vendʒəns] *s* vengeance *f*; **with a vengeance** furieusement, à outrance; (*to the utmost limit*) tant que ça peut
vengeful ['vendʒfəl] *adj* vengeur
Venice ['venıs] *s* Venise *f*
venison ['venısən], ['venızən] *s* venaison *f*
venom ['venəm] *s* venin *m*
venomous ['venəməs] *adj* venimeux
vent [vent] *s* orifice *m*; (*for air*) ventouse *f*; **to give vent to** donner libre cours à || *tr* décharger
ventilate ['ventı,let] *tr* ventiler
ventilator ['ventı,letər] *s* ventilateur *m*
ventricle ['ventrıkəl] *s* ventricule *m*
ventriloquism [ven'trılə,kwızəm] *s* ventriloquie *f*
ventriloquist [ven'trıləkwıst] *s* ventriloque *mf*
venture ['ventʃər] *s* entreprise *f* risquée; **at a venture** à l'aventure || *tr* aventurer || *intr* s'aventurer; **to venture on** hasarder
venturesome ['ventʃərsəm] *adj* aventureux
venturous ['ventʃərəs] *adj* aventureux
venue ['venju] *s* (law) lieu *m* du jugement; **change of venue** (law) renvoi *m*
Venus ['vinəs] *s* Vénus *f*
veracious [vı're ʃəs] *adj* véridique
veraci·ty [vı'ræsıti] *s* (*pl* -ties) véracité *f*
veranda or **verandah** [və'rændə] *s* véranda *f*
verb [vʌrb] *adj* verbal || *s* verbe *m*
verbalize ['vʌrbə,laız] *tr* exprimer par des mots; (gram) changer en verbe || *intr* être verbeux
verbatim [vər'betım] *adj* textuel || *adv* textuellement
verbiage ['vʌrbı·ıdʒ] *s* verbiage *m*
verbose [vər'bos] *adj* verbeux
verdant ['vʌrdənt] *adj* vert; naïf, candide
verdict ['vʌrdıkt] *s* verdict *m*
verdigris ['vʌrdı,gris] *s* vert-de-gris *m*

verdure [vʌrdʒər] *s* verdure *f*
verge [vʌrdʒ] *s* bord *m*, limite *f*; **on the verge of** sur le point de || *intr*—**to verge on** or **upon** toucher à; (*bad faith; the age of forty; etc.*) friser
verification [,verıfı'keʃən] *s* vérification *f*
veri·fy ['verı,faı] *v* (*pret* & *pp* -fied) *tr* vérifier
verily ['verıli] *adv* en vérité
veritable ['verıtəbəl] *adj* véritable
vermilion [vər'mıljən] *adj* & *s* vermillon *m*
vermin ['vʌrmın] *s* (*objectionable person*) vermine *f* || *spl* (*objectionable animals or persons*) vermine
vermouth [vər'muθ], ['vʌrmuθ] *s* vermout *m*
vernacular [vər'nækjələr] *adj* vernaculaire || *s* langue *f* vernaculaire; (*everyday language*) langage *m* vulgaire; (*language peculiar to a class or profession*) jargon *m*
versatile ['vʌrsətıl] *adj* aux talents variés; (*e.g., mind*) universel, souple
verse [vʌrs] *s* vers *mpl*; (*stanza*) strophe *f*; (Bib) verset *m*
versed [vʌrst] *adj*—**versed in** versé dans; spécialiste de
versification [,vʌrsıfı'keʃən] *s* versification *f*
versi·fy ['vʌrsı,faı] *v* (*pret* & *pp* -fied) *tr* & *intr* versifier
version ['vʌrʒən] *s* version *f*
ver·so ['vʌrso] *s* (*pl* -sos) (*e.g., of a coin*) revers *m*; (typ) verso *m*
versus ['vʌrsəs] *prep* contre
verte·bra ['vʌrtıbrə] *s* (*pl* -brae [,bri] or -bras) vertèbre *f*
vertebrate ['vʌrtı,bret] *adj* & *s* vertébré *m*
ver·tex ['vʌrteks] *s* (*pl* -texes or -tices [tı,siz]) sommet *m*
vertical ['vʌrtıkəl] *adj* vertical || *s* verticale *f*
ver′tical hold′ *s* (telv) commande *f* de stabilité verticale
ver′tical rud′der *s* gouvernail *m* de direction
verti·go ['vʌrtı,go] *s* (*pl* -gos or -goes) vertige *m*
very ['veri] *adj* véritable; même, e.g., **at this very moment** à cet instant même || *adv* très, e.g., **I am very hungry** j'ai très faim; bien, e.g., **you are very nice** vous êtes bien gentil; tout, e.g., **the very first** le tout premier; e.g., **my very best** tout mon possible; **for my very own** pour moi tout seul; **very much** beaucoup
vesicle ['vesıkəl] *s* vésicule *f*
vespers ['vespərz] *spl* vêpres *fpl*
vessel ['vesəl] *s* bâtiment *m*, navire *m*; (*container*) vase *m*; (anat, bot, zool) vaisseau *m*
vest [vest] *s* gilet *m*; **to play it close to the vest** (coll) jouer serré || *tr* revêtir; **to vest with** investir de, revêtir de
vest′ed in′terests *spl* classes *fpl* dirigeantes
vestibule ['vestı,bjul] *s* vestibule *m*

ves'tibule car' s (rr) wagon m à soufflets
vestige ['vɛstɪdʒ] s vestige m
vestment ['vɛstmənt] s vêtement m sacerdotal
vest'-pock'et adj de poche, de petit format
ves·try ['vɛstri] s (pl -tries) sacristie f; (committee) conseil m paroissial
ves'try·man s (pl -men) marguillier m
Vesuvius [vɪ's(j)uvɪ·əs] s le Vésuve
vetch [vɛtʃ] s vesce f; (Lathyrus sativus) gesse f
veteran ['vɛtərən] s vétéran m
veterinarian [ˌvɛtərɪ'nɛrɪ·ən] s vétérinaire mf
veterinar·y ['vɛtərɪ ˌnɛri] adj vétérinaire ‖ s (pl -ies) vétérinaire mf
ve·to ['vito] s (pl -toes) veto m ‖ tr mettre son veto à
vex [vɛks] tr vexer, contrarier
vexation [vɛk'seʃən] s vexation f
via ['vaɪ·ə] prep via
viaduct ['vaɪ·əˌdʌkt] s viaduc m
vial ['vaɪ·əl] s fiole f
viand ['vaɪ·ənd] s mets m
vibrate ['vaɪbret] intr vibrer
vibration [vaɪ'breʃən] s vibration f
vicar ['vɪkər] s vicaire m; (in Church of England) curé m
vicarage ['vɪkərɪdʒ] s presbytère m; (duties of vicar) cure f
vicarious [vaɪ'kɛrɪ·əs], [vɪ'kɛrɪ·əs] adj substitut; (punishment) souffert pour autrui; (power, authority) délégué; (enjoyment) partagé
vice [vaɪs] s vice m; (device) étau m
vice'-ad'miral s vice-amiral m
vice'-pres'ident s vice-président m
vice·roy ['vaɪsrɔɪ] s vice-roi m
vice' squad' s brigade f des mœurs
vice versa ['vaɪsə'vʌrsə], ['vaɪs'vʌrsə] adv vice versa
vicini·ty [vɪ'sɪnɪti] s (pl -ties) voisinage m; environs mpl, e.g., New York and vicinity New York et ses environs
vicious ['vɪʃəs] adj vicieux; (mean) méchant; (ferocious) féroce
vicissitude [vɪ'sɪsɪˌt(j)ud] s vicissitude f
victim ['vɪktɪm] s victime f; (e.g., of a collision, fire) accidenté m
victimize ['vɪktɪˌmaɪz] tr prendre pour victime; (to swindle) duper
victor ['vɪktər] s vainqueur m
victorious [vɪk'torɪ·əs] adj victorieux
victo·ry ['vɪktəri] s (pl -ries) victoire f
victuals ['vɪtəlz] spl victuailles fpl
vid'eo sig'nal ['vɪdɪˌo] s signal m d'image
vid'eo tape' s bande f magnétique vidéo
vid'eo tape' record'er s magnétoscope m
vid'eo tape' record'ing s magnétoscope m
vie [vaɪ] v (pret & pp vied; ger vying) intr rivaliser, lutter
Vienna [vɪ'ɛnə] s Vienne f
Vien·nese [ˌvi·ə'niz] adj viennois ‖ s (pl -nese) Viennois m
Vietnam [ˌvɪ·ɛt'nɑm] s le Vietnam

Vietnam·ese [vɪˌɛtnə'miz] adj vietnamien ‖ s (pl -ese) Vietnamien m
view [vju] s vue f; in my view à mon avis, selon mon opinion; in view en vue; in view of étant donné, vu; on view exposé; with a view to en vue de ‖ tr voir, regarder; considérer, examiner
viewer ['vju·ər] s spectateur m; (for film, slides, etc.) visionneuse f; (telv) téléspectateur m
view'find'er s viseur m
view'point' s point m de vue
vigil ['vɪdʒɪl] s veille f; (eccl) vigile f; to keep a vigil veiller
vigilance ['vɪdʒɪləns] s vigilance f
vigilant ['vɪdʒɪlənt] adj vigilant
vignette [vɪn'jɛt] s vignette f
vigor ['vɪgər] s vigueur f
vigorous ['vɪgərəs] adj vigoureux
vile [vaɪl] adj vil; (smell) infect; (weather) sale; (disgusting) détestable
vili·fy ['vɪlɪˌfaɪ] v (pret & pp -fied) tr diffamer, dénigrer
villa ['vɪlə] s villa f
village ['vɪlɪdʒ] s village m
villager ['vɪlɪdʒər] s villageois m
villain ['vɪlən] s scélérat m; (of a play) traître m
villainous ['vɪlənəs] adj vil, infame
villain·y ['vɪləni] s (pl -ies) vilenie f, infamie f
vim [vɪm] s énergie f, vigueur f
vinaigrette' sauce' [ˌvɪnə'grɛt] s vinaigrette f
vindicate ['vɪndɪˌket] tr justifier, défendre
vindictive [vɪn'dɪktɪv] adj vindicatif
vine [vaɪn] s plante f grimpante; (grape plant) vigne f
vinegar ['vɪnɪgər] s vinaigre m
vinegary ['vɪnɪgəri] adj aigre; acariâtre
vine' grow'er [ˌgro·ər] s viticulteur m
vine' stock' s cep m
vineyard ['vɪnjərd] s vignoble m, vigne f
vintage ['vɪntɪdʒ] s vendange f; (year) année f, cru m; (coll) classe f, catégorie f
vin'tage wine' s bon cru m
vin'tage year' s grande année f
vintner ['vɪntnər] s négociant m en vins; (person who makes wine) vigneron m
vinyl ['vaɪnɪl], ['vɪnɪl] s vinyle m
viola [vaɪ'olə], [vɪ'olə] s alto m
violate ['vaɪ·əˌlet] tr violer
violation [ˌvaɪ·ə'leʃən] s violation f
violence ['vaɪ·ələns] s violence f
violent ['vaɪ·ələnt] adj violent
violet ['vaɪ·əlɪt] adj violet ‖ s (color) violet m; (bot) violette f
violin [ˌvaɪ·ə'lɪn] s violon m
violinist [ˌvaɪ·ə'lɪnɪst] s violoniste mf
violoncel·lo [ˌvaɪ·ələn'tʃɛlo], [ˌvi·ələn'tʃɛlo] s (pl -los) violoncelle m
viper ['vaɪpər] s vipère f
vira·go [vɪ'rego] s (pl -goes or -gos) mégère f
virgin ['vɜrdʒɪn] adj vierge ‖ s vierge f; (male virgin) puceau m
Virgin'ia creep'er [vər'dʒɪnɪ·ə] s vigne f vierge

virginity [vər'dʒɪnɪti] *s* virginité *f*
virility [vɪ'rɪlɪti] *s* virilité *f*
virology [vaɪ'rɑlədʒi] *s* virologie *f*
virtual ['vʌrtʃu·əl] *adj* véritable, effectif; (mech, opt, phys) virtuel
virtue ['vʌrtʃu] *s* vertu *f*; mérite *m*, avantage *m*
virtuosi·ty [ˌvʌrtʃu'ɑsɪti] *s* (*pl* -ties) virtuosité *f*
virtuo·so [ˌvʌrtʃu'oso] *s* (*pl* -sos or -si [si]) virtuose *mf*
virtuous ['vʌrtʃu·əs] *adj* vertueux
virulence ['vɪrjələns] *s* virulence *f*
virulent ['vɪrjələnt] *adj* virulent
virus ['vaɪrəs] *s* virus *m*
visa ['vizə] *s* visa *m* || *tr* viser
visage ['vɪzɪdʒ] *s* visage *m*
vis-à-vis [ˌvizə'vi] *adj* face à face || *s* & *adv* vis-à-vis *m* || *prep* vis-à-vis de, vis-à-vis
viscera ['vɪsərə] *spl* viscères *mpl*
viscount ['vaɪkaunt] *s* vicomte *m*
viscountess ['vaɪkauntɪs] *s* vicomtesse *f*
viscous ['vɪskəs] *adj* visqueux
vise [vaɪs] *s* étau *m*
visible ['vɪzɪbəl] *adj* visible
vision ['vɪʒən] *s* vision *f*
visionar·y ['vɪʒəˌneri] *adj* visionnaire || *s* (*pl* -ies) visionnaire *mf*
visit ['vɪzɪt] *s* visite *f* || *tr* visiter; (*e.g., a person*) rendre visite à || *intr* faire des visites
visitation [ˌvɪzɪ'teʃən] *s* visite *f*; justice *f* du ciel; clémence *f* du ciel; (*e.g., in a séance*) apparition *f*; **Visitation** (eccl) Visitation *f*
vis'iting card' *s* carte *f* de visite
vis'iting hours' *spl* heures *fpl* de visite
vis'iting nurse' *s* infirmière *f* visiteuse
vis'iting profes'sor *s* visiting *m*
visitor ['vɪzɪtər] *s* visiteur *m*
visor ['vaɪzər] *s* visière *f*
vista ['vɪstə] *s* perspective *f*
visual ['vɪʒu·əl] *adj* visuel
visualize ['vɪʒu·əˌlaɪz] *tr* (*in one's mind*) se faire une image mentale de, se représenter; (*to make visible*) visualiser
vital ['vaɪtəl] *adj* vital || **vitals** *spl* organes *mpl* vitaux
vitality [vaɪ'tælɪti] *s* vitalité *f*
vitalize ['vaɪtəˌlaɪz] *tr* vitaliser
vitamin ['vaɪtəmɪn] *s* vitamine *f*
vitiate ['vɪʃiˌet] *tr* vicier
vitreous ['vɪtri·əs] *adj* vitreux
vitriolic [ˌvɪtri'ɑlɪk] *adj* (chem) vitriolique; (fig) trempé dans du vitriol
vituperate [vaɪ't(j)upəˌret] *tr* vitupérer
viva ['vivə] *s* vivat *m* || *interj* vive!
vivacious [vɪ'veʃəs], [vaɪ'veʃəs] *adj* vif, animé
vivaci·ty [vɪ'væsɪti], [vaɪ'væsɪti] *s* (*pl* -ties) vivacité *f*
viva voce ['vaɪvə'vosi] *adv* de vive voix
vivid ['vɪvɪd] *adj* vif; (*description*) vivant; (*recollection*) vivace
vivi·fy ['vɪvɪˌfaɪ] *v* (*pret* & *pp* -fied) *tr* vivifier
vivisection [ˌvɪvɪ'sɛkʃən] *s* vivisection *f*

vixen ['vɪksən] *s* mégère *f*; (zool) renarde *f*
viz. *abbr* (Lat: **videlicet** namely, to wit) c.-à-d., à savoir
vizier [vɪ'zɪr], ['vɪzjər] *s* vizir *m*
vocabular·y [vo'kæbjəˌlɛri] *s* (*pl* -ies) vocabulaire *m*
vocal ['vokəl] *adj* vocal; (*inclined to express oneself freely*) communicatif, démonstratif
vocalist ['vokəlɪst] *s* chanteur *m*
vocalize ['vokəˌlaɪz] *tr* vocaliser || *intr* vocaliser; (phonet) se vocaliser
vocation [vo'keʃən] *s* vocation *f*; profession *f*, métier *m*
voca'tional guid'ance [vo'keʃənəl] *s* orientation *f* professionnelle
voca'tional school' *s* école *f* professionnelle
vocative ['vɑkətɪv] *s* vocatif *m*
vociferate [vo'sɪfəˌret] *intr* vociférer
vociferous [vo'sɪfərəs] *adj* vociférant, criard
vogue [vog] *s* vogue *f*; **in vogue** en vogue
voice [vɔɪs] *s* voix *f*; **in a loud voice** à voix haute; **in a low voice** à voix basse; **with one voice** unanimement || *tr* exprimer; (*a consonant*) voiser, sonoriser || *intr* se voiser
voiced *adj* (phonet) voisé, sonore
voiceless ['vɔɪslɪs] *adj* sans voix; (*consonant*) sourd
void [vɔɪd] *adj* vide; (law) nul; **void of** dénué de || *s* vide *m* || *tr* vider; (*the bowels*) évacuer; (law) rendre nul || *intr* évacuer, excréter
voile [vɔɪl] *s* voile *m*
volatile ['vɑlətɪl] *adj* (*solvent*) volatil; (*disposition*) volage; (*temper*) vif
volatilize ['vɑlətəˌlaɪz] *tr* volatiliser || *intr* se volatiliser
volcanic [vɑl'kænɪk] *adj* volcanique
volca·no [vɑl'keno] *s* (*pl* -noes or -nos) volcan *m*
volition [və'lɪʃən] *s* volition *f*, volonté *f*; **of one's own volition** de son propre gré
volley ['vɑli] *s* volée *f* || *tr* lancer à la volée; (sports) reprendre de volée || *intr* lancer une volée
vol'ley·ball' *s* volley-ball *m*
volplane ['vɑlˌplen] *s* vol *m* plané || *intr* descendre en vol plané
volt [volt] *s* volt *m*
voltage ['voltɪdʒ] *s* voltage *m*; **high voltage** haute tension *f*
volt'age drop' *s* perte *f* de charge
volte-face [vɔlt'fɑs] *s* volte-face *f*
volt'me'ter *s* voltmètre *m*
voluble ['vɑljəbəl] *adj* volubile
volume ['vɑljəm] *s* volume *m*; **to speak volumes** en dire long
vol'ume num'ber *s* tomaison *f*
voluminous [və'lumɪnəs] *adj* volumineux
voluntar·y ['vɑlənˌtɛri] *adj* volontaire || *s* (*pl* -ies) (mus) morceau *m* d'orgue improvisé
volunteer [ˌvɑlən'tɪr] *adj* & *s* volontaire *mf* || *tr* offrir volontairement ||

intr (mil) s'engager; **to volunteer to** + *inf* s'offrir à + *inf*
voluptuar•y [və'lʌptʃu‚eri] *adj* voluptuaire ‖ *s* (*pl* -ies) voluptueux *m*
voluptuous [və'lʌptʃu‧əs] *adj* voluptueux
vomit ['vɑmɪt] *s* vomissure *f* ‖ *tr* & *intr* vomir
voodoo ['vudu] *adj* & *s* vaudou *m*
voracious [və'reʃəs] *adj* vorace
voraci•ty [və'ræsɪti] *s* (*pl* -ties) voracité *f*
vor•tex ['vɔrteks] *s* (*pl* -texes or -tices [tɪ‚siz]) vortex *m*, tourbillon *m*
vota•ry ['votəri] *s* (*pl* -ries) fidèle *mf*
vote [vot] *s* vote *m*; **by popular vote** au suffrage universel; **to put to the vote** mettre aux voix; **to tally the votes** dépouiller le scrutin; **vote by show of hands** vote à main levée ‖ *tr* voter; **to vote down** repousser; **to vote in** élire ‖ *intr* voter; **to vote for** voter; **to vote on** passer au vote
voter ['votər] *s* votant *m*, électeur *m*
vot'ing booth' *s* isoloir *m*
vot'ing machine' *s* machine *f* électorale

votive ['votɪv] *adj* votif
vouch [vautʃ] *tr* affirmer, garantir ‖ *intr*—**to vouch for** répondre de
voucher ['vautʃər] *s* garant *m*; (*certificate*) récépissé *m*, pièce *f* comptable
vouch•safe' *tr* octroyer ‖ *intr*—**to vouchsafe to** + *inf* daigner + *inf*
vow [vau] *s* vœu *m*; **to take vows** entrer en religion ‖ *tr* (*e.g., revenge*) jurer ‖ *intr* faire un vœu; **to vow to** faire vœu de
vowel ['vau‧əl] *s* voyelle *f*
voyage ['vɔɪ‧ɪdʒ] *s* (*by air or sea*) traversée *f*; (*any journey*) voyage *m* ‖ *tr* traverser ‖ *intr* voyager
voyager ['vɔɪ‧ɪdʒər] *s* voyageur *m*
vs. *abbr* (*versus*) contre
vulcanize ['vʌlkə‚naɪz] *tr* vulcaniser
vulgar ['vʌlgər] *adj* grossier; (*popular, common; vernacular*) vulgaire
vulgari•ty [vʌl'gærɪti] *s* (*pl* -ties) grossièreté *f*, vulgarité *f*
Vul'gar Lat'in *s* latin *m* vulgaire
vulnerable ['vʌlnərəbəl] *adj* vulnérable
vulture ['vʌltʃər] *s* vautour *m*

W

W, w ['dʌbəl‚ju] *s* XXIIIᵉ lettre de l'alphabet
wad [wɑd] *s* (*of cotton*) tampon *m*; (*of papers*) liasse *f*; (*in a gun*) bourre *f* ‖ *v* (*pret* & *pp* **wadded**; *ger* **wadding**) *tr* bourrer
waddle ['wɑdəl] *s* dandinement *m* ‖ *intr* se dandiner
wade [wed] *tr* traverser à gué ‖ *intr* marcher dans l'eau, patauger; **to wade into** (coll) s'attaquer à; **to wade through** (coll) avancer péniblement dans
wad'ing bird' *s* (orn) échassier *m*
wafer ['wefər] *s* (*thin, crisp cake*) gaufrette *f*; (*pill*) cachet *m*; (*for sealing letters*) pain *m* à cacheter; (eccl) hostie *f*
waffle ['wɑfəl] *s* gaufre *f*
waf'fle i'ron *s* gaufrier *m*
waft [wæft], [wɑft] *tr* porter; (*a kiss*) envoyer ‖ *intr* flotter
wag [wæg] *s* (*of head*) hochement *m*; (*of tail*) frétillement *m*; (*jester*) farceur *m* ‖ *v* (*pret* & *pp* **wagged**; *ger* **wagging**) *tr* (*the head*) hocher; (*the tail*) remuer ‖ *intr* frétiller
wage [wedʒ] *s* salaire *m*; **wages** gages *mpl*, salaire *m*; (fig) salaire, récompense *f* ‖ *tr*—**to wage war** faire la guerre
wage' earn'er [‚ʌrnər] *s* salarié *m*
wage'-price' freeze' *s* blocage *m* des prix et des salaires
wager ['wedʒər] *s* pari *m*; **to lay a wager** faire un pari ‖ *tr* & *intr* parier
wage'work'er *s* salarié *m*
waggish ['wægɪʃ] *adj* plaisant, facétieux

wagon ['wægən] *s* charrette *f*; (*Conestoga wagon; plaything*) chariot *m*; (mil) fourgon *m*; **to be on the wagon** (slang) s'abstenir de boissons alcooliques
wag'tail' *s* hochequeue *m*, bergeronnette *f*
waif [wef] *s* (*foundling*) enfant *m* trouvé; animal *m* égaré or abandonné; (*stray child*) voyou *m*
wail [wel] *s* lamentation *f*, plainte *f* ‖ *intr* se lamenter, gémir
wain•scot ['wenskət], ['wenskɑt] *s* lambris *m* ‖ *v* (*pret* & *pp* -scoted or -scotted; *ger* -scoting or -scotting) *tr* lambrisser
waist [west] *s* (*of human body; corresponding part of garment*) taille *f*, ceinture *f*; (*garment*) corsage *m*, blouse *f*
waist'band' *s* ceinture *f*
waist'cloth' *s* pagne *m*
waistcoat ['west‚kot], ['weskət] *s* gilet *m*
waist'-deep' *adj* jusqu'à la ceinture
waist'line' *s* taille *f*, ceinture *f*; **to keep** or **watch one's waistline** garder or soigner sa ligne
wait [wet] *s* attente *f*; **to lie in wait for** guetter ‖ *tr*—**to wait one's turn** attendre son tour ‖ *intr* attendre; **to wait for** attendre; **to wait on** (*customers; dinner guests*) servir
wait'-and-see' pol'icy *s* attentisme *m*
waiter ['wetər] *s* garçon *m*; (*tray*) plateau *m*
wait'ing list' *s* liste *f* d'attente

wait'ing room' *s* salle *f* d'attente; (*of a doctor*) antichambre *f*
waitress ['wetrɪs] *s* serveuse *f*; **waitress!** mademoiselle!
waive [wev] *tr* renoncer (with *dat*); (*to defer*) différer
waiver ['wevər] *s* renonciation *f*, abandon *m*
wake [wek] *s* (*watch by the body of a dead person*) veillée *f* mortuaire; (*of a boat or other moving object*) sillage *m*; **in the wake of** dans le sillage de, à la suite de || *v* (*pret* **waked** or **woke** [wok]; *pp* **waked**) *tr* réveiller || *intr* —**to wake to** se rendre compte de; **to wake up** se réveiller
wakeful ['wekfəl] *adj* éveillé
wakefulness ['wekfəlnɪs] *s* veille *f*
waken ['wekən] *tr* éveiller, réveiller || *intr* s'éveiller, se réveiller
wale [wel] *s* zébrure *f* || *tr* zébrer
Wales [welz] *s* le pays de Galles
walk [wɔk] *s* (*act*) promenade *f*; (*distance*) marche *f*; (*way of walking, bearing*) démarche *f*; (*of a garden*) allée *f*; (*calling*) métier *m*; **to fall into a walk** (*said of horse*) se mettre au pas; **to go for a walk** faire une promenade || *tr* promener; (*a horse*) promener au pas || *intr* aller à pied, marcher; (*to stroll*) se promener; **to walk away** s'en aller à pied; **to walk off with** (*a prize*) gagner; (*a stolen object*) décamper avec; **to walk out** sortir, partir subitement; (*to go on strike*) se mettre en grève; **to walk out on** abandonner; quitter en colère
walk'away' *s* (coll) victoire *f* facile
walker ['wɔkər] *s* marcheur *m*, promeneur *m*; (*pedestrian*) piéton *m*; (*go-cart*) chariot *m* d'enfant
walkie-talkie ['wɔki'tɔki] *s* (rad) émetteur-récepteur *m* portatif, parle-en-marche *m*
walk'ing pa'pers *spl*—**to give s.o. his walking papers** (coll) congédier qn
walk'ing stick' *s* canne *f*
walk'-on' *s* (*actor*) figurant *m*, comparse *mf*; (*role*) figuration *f*
walk'out' *s* (coll) grève *f* improvisée
walk'o'ver *s* (coll) victoire *f* dans un fauteuil
walk'-up' *s* appartement *m* sans ascenseur
wall [wɔl] *s* mur *m*; (*between rooms; of a pipe, boiler, etc.*) paroi *f*; (*of a fortification*) muraille *f*; **to go to the wall** succomber; perdre la partie || *tr* entourer de murs; **to wall up** murer
wall'board' *s* panneau *m* or carreau *m* de revêtement
wall' clock' *s* pendule *f* murale
wallet ['wɑlɪt] *s* portefeuille *m*
wall'flow'er *s* (bot) ravenelle *f*, giroflée *f*; **to be a wallflower** (coll) faire tapisserie
wall' lamp' *s* applique *f*
wall' map' *s* carte *f* murale
Walloon [wɑ'lun] *adj* wallon || *s* (*dialect*) wallon *m*; (*person*) Wallon *m*
wallop ['wɑləp] *s* (coll) coup *m*, gnon *m*; **with a wallop** (fig) à grand fracas

|| *tr* (coll) tanner le cuir à, rosser; (*a ball*) (coll) frapper raide; (*to defeat*) (coll) battre
wallow ['wɑlo] *s* souille *f* || *intr* se vautrer; (*e.g., in wealth*) nager
wall'pa'per *s* papier *m* peint || *tr* tapisser
walnut ['wɔlnət] *s* noix *f*; (*tree and wood*) noyer *m*
walrus ['wɔlrəs], ['wɑlrəs] *s* morse *m*
Walter ['wɔltər] *s* Gautier *m*
waltz [wɔlts] *s* valse *f* || *tr* & *intr* valser
wan [wɑn] *adj* (*comp* **wanner**; *super* **wannest**) pâle, blême; (*weak*) faible
wand [wɑnd] *s* baguette *f*; (*emblem of authority*) bâton *m*, verge *f*
wander ['wɑndər] *tr* vagabonder sur, parcourir || *intr* errer, vaguer; (*said of one's mind*) vagabonder
wanderer ['wɑndərər] *s* vagabond *m*
wan'der-lust' *s* manie *f* des voyages, bougeotte *f*
wane [wen] *s* déclin *m*; (*of moon*) décours *m* || *intr* décliner; (*said of moon*) décroître
wangle ['wæŋgəl] *tr* (*to obtain by scheming*) (coll) resquiller; (*accounts*) (coll) cuisiner; (*e.g., a leave of absence*) (coll) carotter; **to wangle one's way out of** (coll) se débrouiller de || *intr* (coll) pratiquer le système D
want [wɑnt], [wɔnt] *s* (*need; misery*) besoin *m*; (*lack*) manque *m*; **for want of** faute de, à défaut de; **to be in want** être dans la gêne || *tr* vouloir; (*to need*) avoir besoin de; **to want s.o. to** + *inf* vouloir que qn + *subj*; **to want to** + *inf* avoir envie de + *inf*, vouloir + *inf* || *intr* être dans le besoin; **to be wanting** manquer
want' ads' *spl* petites annonces *fpl*
wanton ['wɑntən] *adj* déréglé; (*e.g., cruelty*) gratuit; (*e.g., child*) espiègle; (*e.g., woman*) impudique
war [wɔr] *s* guerre *f*; **to go to war** se mettre en guerre; (*as a soldier*) aller à la guerre; **to wage war** faire la guerre || *v* (*pret* & *pp* **warred**; *ger* **warring**) *intr* faire la guerre; **to war on** faire la guerre contre
warble ['wɔrbəl] *s* gazouillement *m* || *intr* gazouiller
warbler ['wɔrblər] *s* (orn) fauvette *f*
war' cloud' *s* menace *f* de guerre
war' correspon'dent *s* correspondant *m* de guerre
war' cry' *s* (*pl* **cries**) cri *m* de guerre
ward [wɔrd] *s* (*person, usually a minor under protection of another*) pupille *mf*; (*guardianship*) tutelle *f*; (*of a city*) circonscription *f* électorale, quartier *m*; (*of a hospital*) salle *f*; (*of a lock*) gardes *fpl* || *tr*—**to ward off** parer
war' dance' *s* danse *f* guerrière
warden ['wɔrdən] *s* gardien *m*; (*of a jail*) directeur *m*; (*of a church*) marguillier *m*; (*gamekeeper*) garde-chasse *m*
ward' heel'er *s* politicailleur *m* servile
ward'robe' *s* garde-robe *f*

ward'robe trunk' *s* malle-armoire *f*
ward'room' *s* (nav) carré *m* des officiers
ware [wɛr] *s* faïence *f*; **wares** articles *mpl* de vente, marchandises *fpl*
ware'house' *s* entrepôt *m*
ware'house'man *s* (*pl* **-men**) garde-magasin *m*, magasinier *m*
war'fare' *s* guerre *f*
war'head' *s* charge *f* creuse
war'-horse' *s* cheval *m* de bataille; (coll) vétéran *m*
warily ['wɛrɪli] *adv* prudemment
war'like' *adj* guerrier
war' loan' *s* emprunt *m* de guerre
war' lord' *s* seigneur *m* de la guerre
warm [wɔrm] *adj* chaud; (*welcome, thanks, friend, etc.*) chaleureux; (*heart*) généreux; **it is warm** (*said of weather*) il fait chaud; **to be warm** (*said of person*) avoir chaud; **to keep s.th. warm** tenir q.ch. au chaud; **you're getting warm!** (*you've almost found it!*) vous brûlez! || *tr* chauffer, faire chauffer; **to warm up** réchauffer || *intr* se réchauffer; **to warm up** se réchauffer, chauffer, se chauffer; (*said of speaker, discussion, etc.*) s'animer, s'échauffer
warm'-blood'ed *adj* passionné, ardent; (*animals*) à sang chaud
war' memor'ial *s* monument *m* aux morts de la guerre
warmer ['wɔrmər] *s* (culin) réchaud *m*
warm'-heart'ed *adj* au cœur généreux
warm'ing pan' *s* bassinoire *f*
warmonger ['wɔr‚mʌŋgər] *s* belliciste *mf*
war' moth'er *s* marraine *f* de guerre
warmth [wɔrmθ] *s* chaleur *f*
warm'-up' *s* exercices *mpl* d'assouplissement; mise *f* en condition
warn [wɔrn] *tr* prévenir; **to warn s.o. to** avertir qn de
warning ['wɔrnɪŋ] *s* avertissement *m*; **without warning** par surprise
warn'ing shot' *s* coup *m* de semence
war' of attri'tion *s* guerre *f* d'usure
warp [wɔrp] *s* (*of a fabric*) chaîne *f*; (*of a board*) gauchissement *m*; (naut) touée *f* || *tr* gauchir; (*the mind, judgment, etc.*) fausser; (naut) touer || *intr* se gauchir; (naut) se touer
war'path' *s*—**to be on the warpath** être sur le sentier de la guerre; (*to be out of sorts*) (coll) être d'une humeur de dogue
war'plane' *s* avion *m* de guerre
warrant ['wɔrənt], ['wɑrənt] *s* garantie *f*; certificat *m*; (*for arrest*) mandat *m* d'arrêt || *tr* garantir; certifier; justifier
war'rant of'ficer *s* (mil) sous-officier *m* breveté; (nav) premier maître *m*
warran·ty ['wɔrənti], ['wɑrənti] *s* (*pl* **-ties**) garantie *f*; autorisation *f*
warren ['wɔrən], ['wɑrən] *s* garenne *f*
warrior ['wɔrjər], ['wɑrjər] *s* guerrier *m*
Warsaw ['wɔrsɔ] *s* Varsovie *f*
war'ship' *s* navire *m* de guerre

wart [wɔrt] *s* verrue *f*
war'time' *s* temps *m* de guerre
war'-torn' *adj* dévasté par la guerre
war·y ['wɛri] *adj* (*comp* **-ier**; *super* **-iest**) prudent, avisé
wash [wɑʃ], [wɔʃ] *s* lavage *m*; (*clothes washed or to be washed*) lessive *f*; (*dirty water*) lavure *f*; (*place where the surf breaks; broken water behind a moving ship*) remous *m*; (aer) souffle *m* || *tr* laver; (*one's hands, face, etc.*) se laver; (*dishes, laundry, etc.*) faire; (*e.g., a seacoast*) baigner; **to wash away** enlever; (*e.g., a bank*) affouiller, ronger || *intr* se laver; faire la lessive
washable ['wɑʃəbəl], ['wɔʃəbəl] *adj* lavable
wash'-and-wear' *adj* de repassage superflu de séchage rapide
wash'ba'sin *s* (*basin*) cuvette *f*; (*fixture*) lavabo *m*
wash'bas'ket *s* corbeille *f* à linge
wash'board' *s* planche *f* à laver
wash'bowl' *s* (*basin*) cuvette *f*; (*fixture*) lavabo *m*
wash'cloth' *s* gant *m* de toilette
wash'day' *s* jour *m* de lessive
washed'-out' *adj* délavé, déteint; (coll) flapi, vanné
washed'-up' *adj* (coll) hors de combat, ruiné
washer ['wɑʃər], ['wɔʃər] *s* laveur *m*; (*machine*) laveuse *f*, lessiveuse *f*; (*ring of metal*) rondelle *f*; (*ring of rubber*) rondelle de robinet
wash'er·wom'an *s* (*pl* **-wom'en**) blanchisseuse *f*
wash' goods' *spl* tissus *mpl* grand teint
washing ['wɑʃɪŋ], ['wɔʃɪŋ] *s* lavage *m*; (*act of washing clothes*) blanchissage *m*; (*clothes washed or to be washed*) lessive *f*; **washings** lavures *fpl*
wash'ing machine' *s* machine *f* à laver, laveuse *f* automatique
wash'ing so'da *s* cristaux *mpl* de soude
wash'out' *s* affouillement *m*; (*person*) (coll) raté *m*; **to be a washout** (coll) faire fiasco, faire four
wash'rag' *s* gant *m* de toilette, torchon *m*
wash'room' *s* cabinet *m* de toilette, lavabo *m*
wash' sale' *s* (com) lavage *m* des titres
wash'stand' *s* lavabo *m*
wash'tub' *s* baquet *m*, cuvier *m*
wash' wa'ter *s* lavure *f*
wasp [wɑsp] *s* guêpe *f*
wasp' waist' *s* taille *f* de guêpe
waste [west] *adj* (*land*) inculte; (*material*) de rebut || *s* gaspillage *m*; (*garbage*) déchets *mpl*; (*wild region*) région *f* inculte; (*of time*) perte *f*; (*for wiping machinery*) chiffons *mpl* de nettoyage, effiloche *f* de coton; **to lay waste** dévaster; **wastes** déchets *mpl*; excrément *m* || *tr* gaspiller, perdre || *intr*—**to waste away** dépérir, maigrir
waste'bas'ket *s* corbeille *f* à papier
wasteful ['westfəl] *adj* gaspilleur
waste'pa'per *s* papier *m* de rebut

waste/ pipe/ s tuyau m d'écoulement, vidange f

waste/ prod/ucts spl déchets mpl

wastrel ['westrəl] s gaspilleur m, prodigue mf

watch [wɑtʃ] s montre f; (lookout) garde f, guet m; (naut) quart m; to be on the watch for guetter; to be on watch (naut) être de quart; to keep watch over surveiller || tr (to look at) observer; (to oversee) surveiller || intr être aux aguets; (to keep awake) veiller; to watch for guetter; to watch out faire attention; to watch out for faire attention à; to watch over surveiller; watch out! attention!, gare!

watch/case/ s boîtier m de montre

watch/ chain/ s chaîne f de montre

watch/ charm/ s breloque f

watch/ crys/tal s verre m de montre

watch/dog/ s chien m de garde; gardien m vigilant

watch/dog/ commit/tee s comité m de surveillance

watchful ['wɑtʃfəl] adj vigilant

watchfulness ['wɑtʃfəlnɪs] s vigilance f

watch/mak/er s horloger m

watch/man s (pl -men) gardien m

watch/ night/ s réveillon m du jour de l'an

watch/ pock/et s gousset m

watch/ strap/ s bracelet m d'une montre

watch/tow/er s tour f de guet

watch/word/ s mot m d'ordre, mot de passe; devise f

water ['wɔtər], ['wɑtər] s eau f; of the first water de premier ordre; (diamond) de première eau; to back water (naut) culer; reculer; to be in hot water (coll) être dans le pétrin; to fish in troubled waters pêcher en eau trouble; to hold water (coll) tenir debout, être bien fondé; to make water (to urinate) uriner; (naut) faire eau; to pour or throw cold water on (fig) jeter une douche froide sur, refroidir; to swim under water nager entre deux eaux; to tread water nager debout || tr (e.g., plants) arroser; (horses, cattle, etc.) abreuver; (wine) couper; to water down atténuer || intr (said of horses, cattle, etc.) s'abreuver; (said of locomotive, ship, etc.) faire de l'eau; (said of eyes) se mouiller, larmoyer

wa/ter buf/fa·lo s (pl -loes or -los) buffle m

wa/ter car/rier s porteur m d'eau

wa/ter clos/et s water-closet m, waters mpl

wa/ter·col/or s aquarelle f

wa/ter-cooled/ adj à refroidissement d'eau

wa/ter·course/ s cours m d'eau; (of a stream) lit m

wa/ter·cress/ s cresson m de fontaine

wa/ter cure/ s cure f des eaux

wa/ter·fall/ s chute f d'eau

wa/ter·front/ s terrain m sur la rive

wa/ter gap/ s percée f, trouée f, gorge f

wa/ter ham/mer s (in pipe) coup m de bélier

wa/ter heat/er s chauffe-eau m, chauffe-bain m

wa/ter ice/ s boisson f à demi glacée

wa/tering can/ s arrosoir m

wa/tering place/ s (for cattle) abreuvoir m; (for tourists) ville f d'eau

wa/tering pot/ s arrosoir m

wa/tering trough/ s abreuvoir m

wa/ter jack/et s chemise f d'eau

wa/ter lil/y s nénuphar m

wa/ter line/ s ligne f de flottaison; niveau m d'eau

wa/ter·logged/ adj détrempé

wa/ter main/ s conduite f principale

wa/ter·mark/ s (in paper) filigrane m; (naut) laisse f

wa/ter·mel/on s pastèque f, melon m d'eau

wa/ter me/ter s compteur m à eau

wa/ter pipe/ s conduite f d'eau

wa/ter po/lo s water-polo m

wa/ter pow/er s force f hydraulique, houille f blanche

wa/ter·proof/ adj & s imperméable m

wa/ter rights/ spl droits mpl de captation d'eau, droits d'irrigation

wa/ter·shed/ s ligne f de partage des eaux

wa/ter ski/ing s ski m nautique

wa/ter span/iel s (zool) barbet m

wa/ter·spout/ s descente f d'eau, gouttière f; (funnel of wet air) trombe f

wa/ter-supply sys/tem s service m des eaux; réseau m de conduites d'eau

wa/ter ta/ble s (geol) nappe f phréatique

wa/ter·tight/ adj étanche; (argument) inattaquable; (law) sans clause échappatoire

wa/ter tow/er s château m d'eau

wa/ter wag/on s—to be on the water wagon (coll) s'abstenir de boissons alcooliques

wa/ter·way/ s voie f navigable

wa/ter wheel/ s roue f hydraulique; roue à aubes or à palettes; roue-turbine f

wa/ter wings/ spl flotteur m de natation

wa/ter·works/ s (system) canalisations fpl d'eau; (pumping station) usine f de distribution des eaux

watery ['wɔtəri], ['wɑtəri] adj aqueux; (eyes) larmoyant; (food) insipide, fade

watt [wɑt] s watt m

wattage ['wɑtɪdʒ] s puissance f en watts

watt/-hour/ s (pl watt-hours) watt-heure m

wattle ['wɑtəl] s (of bird) caroncule f; (of fish) barbillon m

watt/me/ter s wattmètre m

wave [wev] s onde f, vague f; (in hair) ondulation f; geste m de la main; (of heat or cold; of people; of the future) vague f; (phys) onde || tr (a handkerchief) agiter; (the hair) onduler; (a hat, newspaper, cane) brandir; to wave aside écarter d'un geste;

to **wave good-bye** faire un signe d'adieu; **to wave one's hand** faire un geste de la main ‖ *intr* s'agiter; (*said of a flag*) ondoyer; **to wave to** faire signe à

wave'length' *s* longueur *f* d'onde

wave' mo'tion *s* mouvement *m* ondulatoire

waver ['wevər] *intr* vaciller

wav·y ['wevi] *adj* (*comp* **-ier**; *super* **-iest**) onduleux, ondoyant; (*hair; road surface*) ondulé; (*line*) tremblé, onduleux

wax [wæks] *s* cire *f* ‖ *tr* cirer ‖ *intr*— **to wax and wane** croître et décroître; **to wax indignant** s'indigner

wax' bean' *s* haricot *m* beurre

wax' pa'per *s* papier *m* paraffiné

wax' ta'per *s* allumette-bougie *f*

wax'wing' *s* (orn) jaseur *m*

wax'works' *s* musée *m* de cire

way [we] *s* voie *f*; (*road*) chemin *m*; (*direction*) côté *m*, sens *m*; (*manner*) façon *f*, manière *f*; (*means*) moyen *m*; (*habit, custom*) manière, habitude *f*, usage *m*; **across the way** en face; **all the way** jusqu'au bout; **by the way** à propos; **by way of** par; comme; **get out of the way!** ôter-vous de là!; **in a way** en un certain sens; **in every way** à tous les égards; **in my** (**his, etc.**) **own way** à ma (sa, etc.) façon or manière; **in no way** en aucune façon; **in some ways** par certains côtés; **in such a way that** de sorte que; **in that way** de la sorte; **in this way** de cette façon; **on the way** chemin faisant; **on the way to** en route pour; **out of the way** écarté; **that way** par là; **the wrong way** le mauvais sens, la mauvaise route; (*the wrong manner*) la mauvaise façon; (*when brushing hair*) à contrepoil; **this way** par ici; **to be in the way** être encombrant; **to feel one's way** avancer à tâtons; **to get out of the way** s'écarter; **to get** (*s.th. or s.o.*) **out of the way** se débarrasser de (*q.ch. or qn*); **to give way** céder; **to go one's own way** faire bande à part; **to go one's way** passer son chemin; **to go out of one's way** faire un détour; (fig) se déranger; **to have one's way** avoir le dernier mot, l'emporter; **to keep out of s.o.'s way** se tenir à l'écart de qn; **to know one's way around** connaître son affaire, être à la coule; **to lead the way** montrer le chemin; **to make one's way** se frayer un chemin; **to make way for** faire place à; **to mend one's ways** s'amender; **to see one's way to** trouver moyen de; **to stand in the way of** barrer le chemin à; **under way** en marche, en cours; **way down** descente *f*; **way in** entrée *f*; **way out** sortie *f*; **ways** (*for launching a ship*) couette *f*, anguilles *fpl*; **way through** passage *m*; **way up** montée *f*; **which way?** par où?

way'bill' *s* feuille *f* de route, lettre *f* de voiture

wayfarer ['we,fɛrər] *s* voyageur *m*, vagabond *m*

way'lay' *v* (*pret & pp* **-laid**) *tr* embusquer; (*to buttonhole*) arrêter au passage

way' of life' *s* manière *f* de vivre, genre *m* de vie, train *m* de vie

way'side' *s* bord *m* de la route; **to fall by the wayside** rester en chemin

wayward ['wewərd] *adj* capricieux; rebelle

we [wi] *pron pers* nous §85, §87; **nous autres**, e.g., **we Americans** nous autres américains

weak [wik] *adj* faible

weaken ['wikən] *tr* affaiblir ‖ *intr* faiblir, s'affaiblir

weakling ['wiklɪŋ] *s* chétif *m*, malingre *mf*; (*in character*) mou *m*

weak'-mind'ed *adj* irrésolu, d'esprit faible; (*feeble-minded*) débile

weakness ['wiknɪs] *s* faiblesse *f*

weal [wil] *s* papule *f*; (archaic) bien *m*

wealth [wɛlθ] *s* richesse *f*

wealth·y ['wɛlθi] *adj* (*comp* **-ier**; *super* **-iest**) riche, opulent

wean [win] *tr* sevrer; **to wean away from** détacher de

weapon ['wɛpən] *s* arme *f*

weaponry ['wɛpənri] *s* armement *m*

wear [wɛr] *s* (*use*) usage *m*; (*wasting away from use*) usure *f*; (*clothing*) vêtements *mpl*, articles *mpl* d'habillement; **for evening wear** pour le soir; **for everyday wear** pour tous les jours ‖ *v* (*pret* **wore** [wor]; *pp* **worn** [worn]) *tr* porter; (*to put on*) mettre; **to wear down** or **out** user; (*e.g., one's patience*) épuiser ‖ *intr* s'user; **to wear off** s'effacer; **to wear on** s'écouler, s'avancer; **to wear out** s'user; **to wear well** durer

wearable ['wɛrəbəl] *adj* mettable

wear' and tear' [tɛr] *s* usure *f*

weariness ['wɪrɪnɪs] *s* lassitude *f*, fatigue *f*; ennui *m*

wear'ing appar'el ['wɛrɪŋ] *s* vêtements *mpl*, habits *mpl*

wearisome ['wɪrɪsəm] *adj* lassant, ennuyeux

wea·ry ['wɪri] *adj* (*comp* **-rier**; *super* **-riest**) las ‖ *v* (*pret & pp* **-ried**) *tr* lasser ‖ *intr* se lasser

weasel ['wizəl] *s* (zool) belette *f*; (slang) mouchard *m*

wea'sel words' *spl* mots *mpl* ambigus

weather ['wɛðər] *s* temps *m*; **to be under the weather** (coll) se sentir patraque; (*from drinking*) (coll) avoir mal aux cheveux; **what's the weather like?** quel temps fait-il? ‖ *tr* altérer; (*e.g., difficulties*) survivre à, étaler ‖ *intr* s'altérer

weath'er balloon' *s* ballon *m* atmosphérique

weath'er-beat'en *adj* usé par les intempéries

weath'er bu'reau *s* bureau *m* météorologique, météo *f*

weath'er·cock' *s* girouette *f*; (fig) girouette, caméléon *m*

weath′er fore′cast s bulletin m météorologique
weath′er fore′casting s prévision f du temps
weath′er·man′ s (pl -men′) météorologue mf, météorologiste mf
weath′er report′ s bulletin m de la météo
weath′er strip′ping s bourrelet m
weath′er vane′ s girouette f
weave [wiv] s armure f || v (pret wove [wov] or weaved; pp wove or woven ['wovən]) tr tisser; **to weave one's way through** se faufiler à travers, se faufiler entre || intr tisser; serpenter, zigzaguer
weaver ['wivər] s tisserand m
web [wɛb] s (piece of cloth) tissu m; (roll of newsprint) rouleau m; (of spider) toile f; (between toes of birds and other animals) palmure f; (of an iron rail) âme f; (fig) trame f
web′-foot′ed adj palmé, palmipède
wed [wɛd] v (pret & pp wed or wedded; ger wedding) tr (to join in wedlock) marier; (to take in marriage) épouser || intr épouser, se marier
wedding ['wɛdɪŋ] adj nuptial || s mariage m, noces fpl
wed′ding ban′quet s repas m de noce
wed′ding cake′ s gâteau m de mariage
wed′ding cer′emo·ny s (pl -nies) cérémonie f nuptiale
wed′ding day′ s jour m des noces; anniversaire m du mariage
wed′ding dress′ s robe f nuptiale, robe de noce
wed′ding march′ s marche f nuptiale
wed′ding night′ s nuit f de noces
wed′ding pres′ent s cadeau m de mariage; **wedding presents** corbeille f de mariage
wed′ding ring′ s anneau m nuptial, alliance f
wedge [wɛdʒ] s coin m || tr coincer
wedlock ['wɛdlɑk] s mariage m
Wednesday ['wɛnzdi] s mercredi m
wee [wi] adj tout petit
weed [wid] s mauvaise herbe f; **the weed** (coll) le tabac; **weeds** vêtements mpl de deuil || tr & intr désherber, sarcler; **to weed out** éliminer, extirper
weed′ing hoe′ s sarcloir m
weed′ kill′er s herbicide m
week [wik] s semaine f; **a week from today** d'aujourd'hui en huit; **week in week out** d'un bout de la semaine à l'autre
week′day′ s jour m de semaine, jour ouvrable
week′end′ s fin f de semaine, week-end m || intr passer le week-end
week·ly ['wikli] adj hebdomadaire || s (pl -lies) hebdomadaire m || adv tous les huit jours
weep [wip] v (pret & pp wept [wɛpt]) tr pleurer || intr pleurer; (to drip) suinter; **to weep for** pleurer; (joy) pleurer de
weep′ing wil′low s saule m pleureur

weep·y ['wipi] adj (comp -ier; super -iest) (coll) pleurnicheur
weevil ['wivəl] s charançon m
weft [wɛft] s (yarns running across warp) trame f; (fabric) tissu m
weigh [we] tr peser; (anchor) lever; **to weigh down** faire pencher; **to weigh in one's hand** soupeser || intr peser; **to weigh heavily with** avoir du poids auprès de; **to weigh in** (sports) se faire peser
weight [wet] s poids m; **to gain weight** prendre du poids; **to lift weights** faire des haltères; **to lose weight** perdre du poids; **to throw one's weight around** (coll) s'imposer || tr charger; (statistically) pondérer; **to weight down** alourdir
weightless ['wetlɪs] adj sans pesanteur
weightlessness ['wetlɪsnɪs] s apesanteur f
weight′ lift′er [,lɪftər] s (sports) haltérophile m
weight′ lift′ing s poids et haltères mpl
weight·y ['weti] adj (comp -ier; super -iest) pesant, lourd; (troublesome) grave; important, puissant
weir [wɪr] s (dam) barrage m; (trap) filet m à poissons
weird [wɪrd] adj surnaturel; étrange
welcome ['wɛlkəm] adj bienvenu; (change, news, etc.) agréable; **to be welcome to** + inf être libre de + inf; **you are welcome!** (i.e., gladly received) soyez le bienvenu!; (in response to thanks) de rien!, je vous en prie!, il n'y a pas de quoi!; **you are welcome to it** c'est à votre disposition; (ironically) je ne vous envie pas || s bienvenue f, bon accueil m || tr souhaiter la bienvenue à, faire bon accueil à, accueillir; **to welcome coldly** faire mauvais accueil à, accueillir froidement
weld [wɛld] s soudure f autogène; (bot) gaude f, réséda m || tr souder à l'autogène
welder ['wɛldər] s soudeur m; (mach) soudeuse f
welding ['wɛldɪŋ] s soudure f autogène
welfare ['wɛl,fɛr] s bien-être m; (for underprivileged) aide f sociale
wel′fare state′ s état-providence m
wel′fare work′ s assistance f sociale
well [wɛl] adj bien (enjoying good health) bien, bien portant; **all's well** tout est bien; **it would be just as well to** il serait bon de; **to be well** aller bien || s puits m; (natural source of water) source f, fontaine f; (of stairway) cage f || adv bien; **as well** aussi; **as well as** aussi bien que; **well and good!** à la bonne heure! || intr—**to well up** jaillir || interj alors!, tiens!
well′-behaved′ adj de bonne conduite; (child) sage
well′-be′ing s bien-être m
well′born′ adj bien né
well-bred ['wɛl'brɛd] adj bien élevé
well′-disposed′ adj bien disposé
well-done ['wɛl'dʌn] adj bien fait; (culin) bien cuit

well′-dressed′ *adj* bien vêtu
well′-fixed′ *adj* (coll) bien renté, riche
well′-formed′ *adj* bien conformé
well′-found′ed *adj* bien fondé
well′-groomed′ *adj* paré, soigné
well′-heeled′ *adj* (coll) huppé, riche
well′-informed′ *adj* bien informé
well′-inten′tioned *adj* bien intentionné
well-kept ['wɛl'kɛpt] *adj* bien tenu; (*secret*) bien gardé
well-known ['wɛl'non] *adj* bien connu, notoire
well′-matched′ *adj* bien assortis
well′-mean′ing *adj* bien intentionné
well′-nigh′ *adv* presque
well′-off′ *adj* fortuné, prospère
well′-preserved′ *adj* bien conservé
well-read ['wɛl'rɛd] *adj* qui a beaucoup de lecture
well-spent ['wɛl'spɛnt] *adj* bien employé
well′spring′ *s* source *f*, source intarissable
well′ sweep′ *s* chadouf *m*
well′-thought′-of′ *adj* de bonne réputation
well′-timed′ *adj* opportun
well-to-do ['wɛltə'du] *adj* aisé, cossu
well-wisher ['wɛl'wɪʃər] *s* partisan *m*, ami *m* fidèle
well′-worn′ *adj* usé; (*subject*) rebattu
Welsh [wɛlʃ] *adj* gallois ‖ *s* (*language*) gallois *m*; **the Welsh** les Gallois *mpl* ‖ (*l.c.*) *intr* (slang) manquer à sa parole, manquer à ses obligations; **to welsh on s.o.** (slang) manquer à qn
Welsh′man *s* (*pl* **-men**) Gallois *m*
Welsh′ rab′bit or **rare′bit** ['rɛrbɪt] *s* fondue *f* au fromage et à la hière sur canapé
welt [wɛlt] *s* zébrure *f*; (*border*) bordure *f*; (*of shoe*) trépointe *f*
welter ['wɛltər] *s* confusion *f*, fouillis *m* ‖ *intr* se vautrer
wel′ter·weight′ *s* (*boxing*) poids *m* mimoyen
wen [wɛn] *s* kyste *m* sébacé, loupe *f*
wench [wɛntʃ] *s* jeune fille *f*, jeune femme *f*
wend [wɛnd] *tr*—**to wend one's way** (**to**) diriger ses pas (vers)
west [wɛst] *adj* & *s* ouest *m* ‖ *adv* à l'ouest, vers l'ouest
western ['wɛstərn] *adj* occidental, de l'ouest ‖ *s* (mov) western *m*
westerner ['wɛstərnər] *s* habitant *m* de l'ouest, Occidental *m*
West′ Ger′many *s* Allemagne *f* de l'Ouest; l'Allemagne de l'Ouest
West′ In′dies ['ɪndɪz] *spl* Indes *fpl* occidentales, Antilles *fpl*
westward ['wɛstwərd] *adv* vers l'ouest
wet [wɛt] *adj* (*comp* **wetter**; *super* **wettest**) mouillé; (*damp*) humide; (*rainy*) pleuvieux; (*paint*) frais; (coll) antiprohibitionniste; **all wet** (slang) fichu, erroné ‖ *s* antiprohibitionniste *mf* ‖ *v* (*pret* & *pp* **wet** or **wetted**; *ger* **wetting**) *tr* mouiller ‖ *intr* se mouiller
wet′ bat′ter·y *s* (*pl* **-ies**) pile *f* à liquide

wet′ blan′ket *s* trouble-fête *mf*, rabat-joie *m*
wet′ nurse′ *s* nourrice *f*
wet′ paint′ *s* peinture *f* fraîche; (public sign) attention à la peinture
whack [hwæk] *s* (coll) coup *m*, gnon *m*; (*try*) (coll) tentative *f*; **to have a whack at** (coll) s'attaquer à ‖ *tr* (coll) cogner
whale [hwel] *s* baleine *f*; (*sperm whale*) cachalot *m*; **to have a whale of a time** (coll) s'amuser follement ‖ *tr* (coll) rosser
whale′bone′ *s* baleine *f*, fanon *m* de baleine
whaler ['hwelər] *s* baleinier *m*
wharf [hwɔrf] *s* (*pl* **wharves** [hwɔrvz] or **wharfs**) quai *m*, débarcadère *m*
what [hwɑt] *adj* *interr* quel §80, e.g., **what time is it?** quelle heure est-il?; e.g., **what is his occupation?** quel est son métier? ‖ *adj* *rel* ce qui, e.g., **I'll give you what water I have left** je vous donnerai ce qui me reste d'eau; ce que, e.g., **I know what drink you want** je sais ce que vous voulez comme boisson ‖ *pron* *interr* qu'est-ce qui, e.g., **what happened?** qu'est-ce qui s'est passé?; que, e.g., **what are you doing?** que faites-vous?; qu'est-ce que, e.g., **what are you doing?** qu'est-ce que vous faites?; comment, e.g., **what is he like?** comment est-il?; combien, e.g., **what is two and two?** combien font deux et deux?; **what** (*did you say*)? comment?; **what else?** quoi d'autre?, quoi encore?; **what for?** pourquoi donc?; **what if** si, e.g., **what if I were to die?** si je venais à mourir?; **what if I did?**, **what of it?**, **so what?** qu'importe?; **what is it?** qu'est-ce que c'est?, qu'est-ce qu'il y a?; **what now?** alors?; **what's that?** qu'est-ce que c'est que cela?; **what then?** et après? ‖ *pron* *rel* ce qui, ce que; ce dont §79, e.g., **I have what you need** j'ai ce dont vous avez besoin; ce à quoi, e.g., **I know what you are thinking of** je sais ce à quoi vous pensez; (sometimes untranslated), e.g., **he asked them what time it was** il leur a demandé l'heure; **to know what's what** (coll) s'y connaître, être au courant ‖ *interj* comment!; **what a** que de, e.g., **what a lot of people!** que de monde!; quel §80, e.g., **what a pity!** quel dommage!
what·ev′er *adj* quel que §80; moindre or quelconque, e.g., **is there any hope whatever?** y a-t-il le moindre espoir?, y a-t-il un espoir quelconque? ‖ *pron* tout ce qui; tout ce que, e.g., **tell him whatever you like** dites-lui tout ce que vous voudrez; quoi que, e.g., **whatever you do** quoi que vous fassiez; **whatever comes** à tout hasard
what′not′ *s* étagère *f*
what's′-his-name′ *s* (coll) Monsieur un tel
wheal [wil] *s* papule *f*

wheat [hwit] *s* blé *m*

wheedle ['hwidəl] *tr* enjôler

wheel [hwil] *s* roue *f*; **at the wheel** au volant || *tr* (*to turn*) faire pivoter; (*a wheelbarrow, table, etc.*) rouler || *intr* pivoter; (*said, e.g., of birds in the sky*) tournoyer; **to wheel about** or **around** faire demi-tour

wheelbarrow ['hwil,bæro] *s* brouette *f*

wheel′base′ *s* (aut) empattement *m*

wheel′chair′ *s* fauteuil *m* roulant pour malade, voiture *f* d'infirme

wheel′ horse′ *s* (*horse*) timonier *m*; (*person*) bûcheur *m*

wheelwright ['hwil,rait] *s* charron *m*

wheeze [hwiz] *s* respiration *f* sifflante; (pathol) cornage *m* || *intr* respirer avec peine, souffler

whelp [hwɛlp] *s* petit *m* || *tr* & *intr* mettre bas

when [hwɛn] *adv* quand || *conj* quand, lorsque; (*on which, in which*) où; (*whereas*) alors que

whence [hwɛns] *adv* & *conj* d'où

when•ev′er *conj* chaque fois que, quand

where [hwɛr] *adv* & *conj* où; **from where** d'où

whereabouts ['hwɛrə,bauts] *s*—**the whereabouts of** l'endroit où se trouve || *adv* & *conj* où donc

whereas [hwɛr'æz] *conj* tandis que, attendu que || *s* considérant *m*

where•by′ *conj* par lequel

wherefore ['hwɛrfor] *s* & *adv* pourquoi *m* || *conj* à cause de quoi

where•from′ *adv* d'où

where•in′ *adv* d'où; en quoi || *conj* où

where•of′ *adv* de quoi || *conj* dont §79

where′up•on′ *adv* sur quoi, sur ce

wherever [hwɛr'evər] *conj* partout où; où que, n'importe où

wherewithal ['hwɛrwið,ɔl] *s* ressources *fpl*, moyens *mpl*

whet [hwɛt] *v* (*pret* & *pp* **whetted;** *ger* **whetting**) *tr* aiguiser

whether ['wɛðər] *conj* si; que, e.g., **it is doubtful whether you can finish** il est douteux que vous puissiez finir; e.g., **whether he is rich or poor** qu'il soit riche ou qu'il soit pauvre; **whether or no** de toute façon; **whether or not** qu'il en soit ainsi ou non

whet′stone′ *s* pierre *f* à aiguiser

whew [hwju] *interj* ouf!

whey [hwe] *s* petit lait *m*

which [hwit∫] *adj interr* quel §80, e.g., **which university do you prefer?** quelle université préférez-vous?; **which one?** lequel? || *adj rel* le . . . que, e.g., **choose which road you prefer** choisissez le chemin que vous préférez || *pron interr* lequel §78; **which is which?** lequel des deux est-ce?; **which of them?** lequel d'entre eux? || *pron rel* qui; que; dont §79

which•ev′er *adj rel* n'importe quel || *pron rel* n'importe lequel

whiff [hwif] *s* bouffé *f*; **to get a whiff of** flairer

while [hwail] *s* temps *m*, moment *m*; **a**

long while longtemps; **a (little) while ago** tout à l'heure; **in a little while** sous peu, tout à l'heure || *conj* pendant que; (*as long as*) tant que; (*although*) quoique || *tr*—**to while away** tuer, faire passer

whim [hwim] *s* caprice *m*, lubie *f*

whimper ['hwimpər] *s* pleurnicherie *f* || *tr* dire en pleurnichant || *intr* pleurnicher

whimsical ['hwimzikəl] *adj* capricieux, lunatique

whine [hwain] *s* geignement *m*; (*of siren*) hurlement *m* || *intr* geindre; (*said of siren*) hurler

whin•ny ['hwini] *s* (*pl* -**nies**) hennissement *m* || *v* (*pret* & *pp* -**nied**) *intr* hennir

whip [hwip] *s* fouet *m* || *v* (*pret* & *pp* **whipped** or **whipt;** *ger* **whipping**) *tr* fouetter; (*to defeat*) battre; (*the end of a rope*) surlier; **to whip out** (*e.g., a gun*) sortir brusquement; **to whip up** (*e.g., a supper*) (coll) préparer à l'improviste; (*e.g., enthusiasm*) (coll) stimuler

whip′cord′ *s* corde *f* à fouet

whip′ hand′ *s* main *f* du fouet; (*upper hand*) avantage *m*, dessus *m*

whip′lash′ *s* mèche *f* de fouet

whipped′ cream′ *s* crème *f* fouettée, chantilly *m*

whipper-snapper ['hwipər,snæpər] *s* freluquet *m*, paltoquet *m*

whip′ping boy′ *s* tête *f* de Turc

whip′ping post′ *s* poteau *m* des condamnés au fouet

whippoorwill [,hwipər'wil] *s* (*Caprimulgus vociferus*) engoulevent *m* américain

whir [hwʌr] *s* ronflement *m* || *v* (*pret* & *pp* **whirred;** *ger* **whirring**) *intr* ronfler

whirl [hwʌrl] *s* tourbillon *m*; (*of events, parties, etc.*) succession *f* ininterrompue || *tr* faire tourbillonner || *intr* tourbillonner; **his head whirls** la tête lui tourne

whirligig ['hwʌrli,gig] *s* tourniquet *m*; (ent) gyrin *m*, tourniquet

whirl′pool′ *s* tourbillon *m*, remous *m*

whirl′wind′ *s* tourbillon *m*

whirlybird ['hwʌrli,bʌrd] *s* (coll) hélicoptère *m*

whisk [hwisk] *s* coup *m* léger; (*broom*) époussette *f*; (culin) fouet *m* || *tr* balayer; (culin) fouetter; **to whisk out of sight** escamoter || *intr* aller comme un trait

whisk′ broom′ *s* époussette *f*

whiskers ['hwiskərz] *spl* barbe *f*, poils *mpl* de barbe; (*on side of face*) favoris *mpl*; (*of cat*) moustaches *fpl*

whiskey ['hwiski] *s* whisky *m*

whisper ['hwispər] *s* chuchotement *m* || *tr* chuchoter, dire à l'oreille || *intr* chuchoter

whispering ['hwispəriŋ] *s* chuchotement *m*

whist [hwist] *s* whist *m*

whistle ['hwisəl] *s* (*sound*) sifflement

m; (*device*) sifflet *m*; **to wet one's whistle** (coll) s'humecter le gosier || *tr* siffler, siffloter || *intr* siffler; **to whistle for** siffler; attendre en vain, se voir obligé de se passer de

whis′tle stop′ *s* arrêt *m* facultatif

whit [hwɪt] *s*—**not a whit** pas un brin; **to not care a whit** s'en moquer

white [hwaɪt] *adj* blanc || *s* blanc *m*; blanc d'œuf; **whites** (pathol) pertes *fpl* blanches

white′caps′ *spl* moutons *mpl*

white′ coal′ *s* houille *f* blanche

white′-col′lar *adj* de bureau

white′ feath′er *s*—**to show the white feather** lâcher pied, flancher, caner

white′fish′ *s* poisson *m* blanc, merlan *m*

white′ goods′ *spl* vêtements *mpl* blancs; tissus *mpl* de coton, cotonnade *f*; (*appliances*) appareils *mpl* électroménagers

white′-haired′ *adj* aux cheveux blancs, chenu; (coll) favori

white′-hot′ *adj* chauffé à blanc

white′ lead′ [lɛd] *s* céruse *f*, blanc *m* de céruse

white′ lie′ *s* mensonge *m* pieux

white′ meat′ *s* blanc *m*

whiten ['hwaɪtən] *tr* & *intr* blanchir

whiteness ['hwaɪtnɪs] *s* blancheur *f*

white′ slav′ery *s* traite *f* des blanches

white′ tie′ *s* cravate *f* blanche; tenue *f* de soirée

white′wash′ *s* blanc *m* de chaux, badigeon *m*; (*cover-up*) couverture *f* || *tr* blanchir à la chaux; (*e.g., a guilty person, a scandal*) blanchir

whither ['hwɪðər] *adv* & *conj* où, là où

whitish ['hwaɪtɪʃ] *adj* blanchâtre

whitlow ['hwɪtlo] *s* panaris *m*

Whitsuntide ['hwɪtsən͵taɪd] *s* saison *f* de la Pentecôte

whittle ['hwɪtəl] *tr* tailler au couteau; **to whittle away** or **down** amenuiser

whiz or **whizz** [hwɪz] *s* sifflement *m*; (slang) prodige *m* || *v* (*pret* & *pp* **whizzed**; *ger* **whizzing**) *intr*—**to whiz by** passer en sifflant, passer comme le vent

who [hu] *pron interr* qui; quel §80; **who else?** qui d'autre?; qui encore?; **who is there?** (mil) qui vive? || *pron rel* qui; celui qui §83

whoa [hwo] *interj* holà!, doucement!

who·ev′er *pron rel* quiconque; celui qui §83; qui que, e.g., **whoever you are** qui que vous soyez

whole [hol] *adj* entier || *s* tout *m*, totalité *f*, ensemble *m*; **on the whole** somme toute, à tout prendre

whole′heart′ed *adj* sincère, de bon cœur

whole′ note′ *s* (mus) ronde *f*

whole′ rest′ *s* (mus) pause *f*

whole′sale′ *adj* & *adv* en gros; (*e.g., slaughter*) en masse || *s* gros *m*, vente *f* en gros || *tr* & *intr* vendre en gros

whole′sale price′ *s* prix *m* de gros

wholesaler ['hol͵selər] *s* commerçant *m* en gros, grossiste *mf*

whole′sale trade′ *s* commerce *m* de gros

wholesome ['holsəm] *adj* sain

wholly ['holi] *adv* entièrement

whom [hum] *pron interr* qui || *pron rel* que; lequel §78; celui que §83; **of whom** dont, de qui §79

whom·ev′er *pron rel* celui que §83; tous ceux que; (with a preposition) quiconque

whoop [hup], [hwup] *s* huée *f*; (*cough*) quinte *f* || *tr*—**to whoop it up** (slang) pousser des cris || *intr* huer

whoop′ing cough′ ['hupɪŋ], ['hʊpɪŋ] *s* coqueluche *f*

whopper ['hwapər] *s* (coll) chose *f* énorme; (*lie*) (coll) gros mensonge *m*

whopping ['hwapɪŋ] *adj* (coll) énorme

whore [hor] *s* putain *f* || *intr*—**to whore around** courir la gueuse

whortleber·ry ['hwʌrtəl͵bɛri] *s* (*pl* -ries) myrtille *f*

whose [huz] *pron interr* à qui, e.g., **whose pen is that?** à qui est ce stylo? || *pron rel* dont, de qui §79; duquel §78

why [hwaɪ] *s* (*pl* **whys** [hwaɪz]) pourquoi *m*; **the why and the wherefore** le pourquoi et le comment || *adv* pourquoi; **why not?** pourquoi pas? || *interj* tiens!; **why, certainly!** mais bien sûr!; **why, yes!** mais oui!

wick [wɪk] *s* mèche *f*

wicked ['wɪkɪd] *adj* méchant, mauvais

wicker ['wɪkər] *adj* en osier || *s* osier *m*

wicket ['wɪkɪt] *s* guichet *m*; (croquet) arceau *m*

wide [waɪd] *adj* large; (*range*) vaste, étendu; (*spread, angle, etc.*) grand; **large de**, c.g., **eight feet wide** large de huit pieds || *adv* loin, partout; **open wide!** ouvrez bien!

wide′-an′gle *adj* grand-angulaire

wide′-awake′ *adj* bien éveillé

widen ['waɪdən] *tr* élargir || *intr* s'élargir

wide′-o′pen *adj* grand ouvert

wide′spread′ *adj* (*arms, wings*) étendu; répandu, universel

widow ['wɪdo] *s* veuve *f* || *tr*—**to be widowed** devenir veuf

widower ['wɪdo·ər] *s* veuf *m*

widowhood ['wɪdo͵hud] *s* veuvage *m*

wid′ow's mite′ *s* obole *f*

wid′ow's weeds′ *spl* deuil *m* de veuve

width [wɪdθ] *s* largeur *f*; (*of cloth*) lé *m*

wield [wild] *tr* (*sword, pen*) manier; (*power*) exercer

wife [waɪf] *s* (*pl* **wives** [waɪvz]) femme *f*, épouse *f*

wig [wɪg] *s* perruque *f*

wiggle ['wɪgəl] *s* tortillement *m* || *tr* agiter || *intr* tortiller, se tortiller

wig′wag′ *s* télégraphie *f* optique || *v* (*pret* & *pp* **-wagged**; *ger* **-wagging**) *tr* transmettre à bras avec fanions || *intr* signaler à bras avec fanions

wigwam ['wɪgwam] *s* wigwam *m*

wild [waɪld] *adj* sauvage; (*untamed*) sauvage, fauve; (*frantic, mad*) frénétique; (*hair; dance; dream*) échevelé; (*passion; torrent; night*) tumultueux;

(*idea*, *plan*) insensé, extravagant; (*life*) déréglé; (*blows*, *bullet*, *shot*) perdu; **wild about** or **for** fou de ‖ **wilds** *spl* régions *fpl* sauvages ‖ *adv* —**to run wild** dépasser toutes les bornes; (*said of plants*) pousser librement
wild' boar' *s* sanglier *m*
wild' card' *s* mistigri *m*
wild'cat' *s* chat *m* sauvage; lynx *m*, (*well*) sondage *m* d'exploration
wild'cat strike' *s* grève *f* sauvage, grève spontanée
wild' cher'ry *s* (*pl* -ries) merise *f*; (*tree*) merisier *m*
wilderness ['wɪldərnɪs] *s* désert *m*
wild'fire' *s* feu *m* grégeois; feu *m* follet; éclairs *mpl* en nappe; **like wild-fire** comme une traînée de poudre
wild' flow'er *s* fleur *f* des champs
wild' goose' *s* oie *f* sauvage
wild'-goose' chase' *s*—**to go on a wild-goose chase** faire buisson creux
wild'life' *s* animaux *mpl* sauvages
wild' oats' *spl*—**to sow one's wild oats** jeter sa gourme
wile [waɪl] *s* ruse *f* ‖ *tr*—**to wile away** tuer, faire passer
will [wɪl] *s* volonté *f*; (law) testament *m*; **against one's will** à contre-cœur; **at will** à volonté; **with a will** de bon cœur ‖ *tr* vouloir; (*to bequeath*) léguer ‖ *intr* vouloir; **do as you will** faites comme vous voudrez ‖ (*pret* & *cond* **would** [wʊd]) *aux* used to express 1) the future indicative, e.g., **he will arrive early** il arrivera de bonne heure; 2) the future perfect indicative, e.g., **he will have arrived before I leave** il sera arrivé avant que je parte; 3) the present indicative denoting habit or custom, e.g., **after breakfast he will go out for a walk every morning** après le petit déjeuner il fait une promenade tous les matins
willful ['wɪlfəl] *adj* volontaire; (*stubborn*) obstiné
willfulness ['wɪlfəlnɪs] *s* entêtement *m*
William ['wɪljəm] *s* Guillaume *m*
willing ['wɪlɪŋ] *adj* disposé, prêt; **to be willing to** vouloir bien; **willing or un-willing** bon gré mal gré
willingly ['wɪlɪŋli] *adv* volontiers
willingness ['wɪlɪŋnɪs] *s* bonne volonté *f*, consentement *m*
will-o'-the-wisp ['wɪləðə'wɪsp] *s* feu *m* follet; (fig) chimère *f*
willow ['wɪlo] *s* saule *m*
willowy ['wɪlo·i] *adj* souple, agile; svelte, élancé; couvert de saules
will' pow'er *s* force *f* de volonté
willy-nilly ['wɪli'nɪli] *adv* bon gré mal gré
wilt [wɪlt] *tr* flétrir ‖ *intr* se flétrir
wil·y ['waɪli] *adj* (*comp* -ier; *super* -iest) rusé, astucieux
wimple ['wɪmpəl] *s* guimpe *f*
win [wɪn] *s* (coll) victoire *f* ‖ *v* (*pret* & *pp* **won** [wʌn]; *ger* **winning**) *tr* gagner; (*a victory*, *a prize*) remporter; **to win back** regagner; **to win over** gagner, convaincre ‖ *intr* ga-

gner; convaincre; **to win out** (coll) réussir
wince [wɪns] *s*—**without a wince** sans sourciller ‖ *intr* tressaillir
winch [wɪntʃ] *s* treuil *m*; (*handle*, *crank*) manivelle *f*
wind [wɪnd] *s* vent *m*; (*breath*) haleine *f*, souffle *m*; **to break wind** lâcher un vent, faire un pet; **to get wind of** avoir vent de; **to sail close to the wind** courir au plus près; **to sail into the wind** aller au lof, venir au lof ‖ *tr* faire perdre le souffle à ‖ *intr* flairer le gibier ‖ [waɪnd] *v* (*pret* & *pp* **wound** [waʊnd]) *tr* enrouler; (*a timepiece*) remonter; (*yarn*, *thread*, *etc.*) pelotonner; **to wind up** enrouler; remonter; (*to finish*) (coll) terminer, régler ‖ *intr* serpenter
windbag ['wɪnd,bæg] *s* (*of bagpipe*) outre *f*; (coll) moulin *m* à paroles
windbreak ['wɪnd,brek] *s* abrivent *m*
wind' cone' [wɪnd] *s* (aer) manche *f* à air
winded ['wɪndɪd] *adj* essoufflé
windfall ['wɪnd,fɔl] *s* (fig) aubaine *f*
wind'ing road' ['waɪndɪŋ] *s* route *f* en lacet
wind'ing sheet' *s* linceul *m*
wind'ing stairs' *spl* escalier *m* en colimaçon
wind' in'strument [wɪnd] *s* (mus) instrument *m* à vent
windlass ['wɪndləs] *s* treuil *m*
windmill ['wɪnd,mɪl] *s* moulin *m* à vent; (*on a modern farm*) aéromoteur *m*; **to tilt at windmills** se battre contre des moulins à vent
window ['wɪndo] *s* fenêtre *f*; (*of ticket office*) guichet *m*; (*of store*) vitrine *f*; (aut) glace *f*
win'dow dress'er *s* étalagiste *mf*
win'dow dress'ing *s* art *m* de l'étalage; (coll) façade *f*
win'dow en'velope *s* enveloppe *f* à fenêtre
win'dow frame' *s* châssis *m*, dormant *m*
win'dow·pane' *s* vitre *f*, carreau *m*
win'dow screen' *s* grillage *m*
win'dow shade' *s* store *m*
win'dow-shop' *v* (*pret* & *pp* -**shopped**; *ger* -**shopping**) *intr* faire du lèche-vitrines, lécher les vitrines
win'dow shut'ter *s* volet *m*
win'dow sill' *s* rebord *m* de fenêtre
windpipe ['wɪnd,paɪp] *s* trachée-artère *f*
windshield ['wɪnd,ʃild] *s* pare-brise *m*
wind'shield wash'er *s* lave-glace *m*
wind'shield wip'er *s* essuie-glace *m*
windsock ['wɪnd,sɑk] *s* manche *f* à air
windstorm ['wɪnd,stɔrm] *s* tempête *f* de vent
wind' tun'nel [wɪnd] *s* tunnel *m* aérodynamique
wind-up ['waɪnd,ʌp] *s* conclusion *f*, fin *f*
windward ['wɪndwərd] *adj* & *adv* au vent ‖ *s* côté *m* du vent; **to turn to windward** louvoyer

wind·y ['wɪndi] *adj* (*comp* **-ier;** *super* **-iest**) venteux; (*verbose*) verbeux; **it is windy** il fait du vent

wine [waɪn] *s* vin *m* ‖ *tr*—**to wine and dine s.o.** fêter qn

wine′ cel′lar *s* cave *f*

wine′glass′ *s* verre *m* à vin

winegrower ['waɪn͵groʊˌər] *s* viticulteur *m*

winegrowing ['waɪn͵groʊ·ɪŋ] *s* viticulture *f*

wine′ list′ *s* carte *f* des vins

wine′ press′ *s* pressoir *m*

winer·y ['waɪnəri] *s* (*pl* **-ies**) pressoir *m*

wine′skin′ *s* outre *f* à vin

wine′ stew′ard *s* sommelier *m*; (*of prince, king*) bouteiller *m*

winetaster ['waɪn͵testər] *s* (*person*) dégustateur *m*; (*pipette*) taste-vin *m*

wing [wɪŋ] *s* aile *f*; (*e.g., of hospital*) pavillon *m*; (pol) parti *m*, faction *f*; **in the wings** (theat) dans la coulisse; **on the wing** au vol; **to take wing** prendre son essor ‖ *tr* (*to wound*) blesser; **to wing one's way** voler

wing′ chair′ *s* fauteuil *m* à oreilles

wing′ col′lar *s* col *m* rabattu

wing′ load′ *s* (aer) charge *f* alaire

wing′ nut′ *s* écrou *m* ailé

wing′spread′ *s* envergure *f*

wink [wɪŋk] *s* clin *m* d'œil; **to not sleep a wink** ne pas fermer l'œil; **to take forty winks** (coll) piquer un roupillon ‖ *tr* cligner ‖ *intr* cligner des yeux; **to wink at** cligner de l'œil à; (*e.g., an abuse*) fermer les yeux sur

winner ['wɪnər] *s* gagnant *m*, vainqueur *m*

winning ['wɪnɪŋ] *adj* gagnant; (*attractive*) séduisant ‖ **winnings** *spl* gains *mpl*

winnow ['wɪno] *tr* vanner, sasser; (*e.g., the evidence*) passer au crible

winsome ['wɪnsəm] *adj* séduisant

winter ['wɪntər] *s* hiver *m* ‖ *intr* passer l'hiver; (*said of animals, troops, etc.*) hiverner

win′ter·green′ *s* (*oil*) wintergreen *m*; (bot) gaulthérie *f*

win·try ['wɪntri] *adj* (*comp* **-trier;** *super* **-triest**) hivernal, froid

wipe [waɪp] *tr* essuyer; **to wipe away** essuyer; **to wipe off** or **out** effacer; (*to annihilate*) anéantir; **to wipe up** nettoyer

wiper ['waɪpər] *s* torchon *m*; (elec) contact *m* glissant; (mach) came *f*

wire [waɪr] *s* fil *m*; télégramme *m*; **hold the wire!** (telp) restez à l'écoute!; **on the wire** (telp) au bout du fil; **reply by wire** réponse *f* télégraphique; **to get in under the wire** arriver juste à temps; terminer juste à temps; **to pull wires** (coll) tirer les ficelles ‖ *tr* attacher avec du fil de fer; (*a message*) télégraphier; (*a house*) canaliser ‖ *intr* télégraphier

wire′ cut′ter *s* coupe-fil *m*

wire′draw′ *v* (*pret* **-drew;** *pp* **-drawn**) *tr* tréfiler

wire′ entan′glement *s* réseau *m* de barbelés

wire′ gauge′ *s* calibre *m* or jauge *f* pour fils métalliques

wire′-haired′ *adj* à poil dur

wireless ['waɪrlɪs] *adj* sans fil

wire′ nail′ *s* clou *m* de Paris

wire′pho′to *s* (*pl* **-tos**) (trademark) (*device*) bélinographe *m*; (*photo*) bélinogramme *m*

wire′pull′ing *s* (coll) influences *fpl* secrètes, piston *m*

wire′ record′er *s* magnétophone *m* à fil d'acier

wire′tap′ *s* (*device*) table *f* d'écoute ‖ *v* (*pret* & *pp* **-tapped;** *ger* **-tapping**) *tr* passer à la table d'écoute

wiring ['waɪrɪŋ] ، (*e.g., of house*) canalisation *f*; (*e.g., of radio*) montage *m*

wir·y ['waɪri] *adj* (*comp* **-ier;** *super* **-iest**) nerveux; (*hair*) raide

wisdom ['wɪzdəm] *s* sagesse *f*

wis′dom tooth′ *s* dent *f* de sagesse

wise [waɪz] *adj* sage; (*step, decision*) judicieux, prudent; **to be wise to** (slang) voir clair dans le jeu de, percer le jeu de; **to get wise** (coll) se mettre au courant ‖ *s*—**in no wise** en aucune manière ‖ *tr*—**to wise up** (slang) avertir, désabuser

wiseacre ['waɪz͵ekər] *s* fat *m*, fierot *m*

wise′crack′ *s* (coll) blague *f*, plaisanterie *f* ‖ *intr* (coll) blaguer, plaisanter

wise′ guy′ *s* (slang) type *m* goguenard

wish [wɪʃ] *s* souhait *m*, désir *m*; **best wishes** meilleurs vœux *mpl*; (formula used to close a letter) amitiés; **last wishes** dernières volontés *fpl*; **to make a wish** faire un vœu ‖ *tr* souhaiter, désirer; **to wish s.o. s.th.** souhaiter q.ch. à qn; **to wish s.o. to** + *inf* souhaiter que qn + *subj*; **to wish to** + *inf* vouloir + *inf*

wish′bone′ *s* fourchette *f*

wishful ['wɪʃfəl] *adj* désireux

wish′ful think′ing *s* optimisme *m* à outrance; **to indulge in wishful thinking** se forger des chimères

wish′ing well′ *s* puits *m* aux souhaits

wistful ['wɪstfəl] *adj* pensif, rêveur

wit [wɪt] *s* esprit *m*; (*person*) homme *m* d'esprit; **to be at one's wits' end** ne plus savoir que faire; **to keep one's wits about one** conserver toute sa présence d'esprit; **to live by one's wits** vivre d'expédients

witch [wɪtʃ] *s* sorcière *f*

witch′craft′ *s* sorcellerie *f*

witch′ doc′tor *s* sorcier *m* guérisseur

witch′es′ Sab′bath *s* sabbat *m*

witch′ ha′zel *s* teinture *f* d'hamamélis; (bot) hamamélis *m*

witch′ hunt′ *s* chasse *f* aux sorcières

with [wɪð], [wɪθ] *prep* avec; (*at the home of*) chez; (*in the case of*) chez; (*in spite of*) malgré; à, e.g., **the girl with the blue eyes** la jeune fille aux yeux bleus; e.g., **coffee with milk** café au lait; e.g., **with open arms** à bras ouverts; e.g., **with these words . . .** à ces mots . . . ; de, e.g., **with a loud**

voice d'une voix forte; e.g., **with all his strength** de toutes ses forces; e.g., **to be satisfied with** être satisfait de; e.g., **to fill with** remplir de
with·draw/ v (pret **-drew;** pp **-drawn**) tr retirer ‖ intr se retirer
withdrawal [wɪð'drɔ·əl], [wɪθ'drɔ·əl] s retrait m
wither ['wɪðər] tr faner ‖ intr se faner
with·hold/ v (pret & pp **-held**) tr (money, taxes, etc.) retenir; (permission) refuser; (the truth) cacher
with·hold/ing tax/ s impôt m retenu à la source
with·in/ adv à l'intérieur; là-dedans §85A ‖ prep à l'intérieur de; (in less than) en moins de; (within the limits of) dans; (in the bosom of) au sein de; (not exceeding a margin of error of) à . . . près, e.g., **I can tell you what time it is within five minutes** je peux vous dire l'heure à cinq minutes près; à portée de, e.g., **within reach** à portée de la main
with·out/ adv au-dehors, dehors ‖ prep au dehors de; (lacking, not with) sans; **to do without** se passer de; **without** + ger sans + inf, e.g., **he left without seeing me** il est parti sans me voir; sans que + subj, e.g., **he left without anyone seeing him** il est parti sans que personne ne le voie
with·stand/ v (pret & pp **-stood**) tr résister à
witness ['wɪtnɪs] s témoin m; **in witness whereof** en foi de quoi; **to bear witness** rendre témoignage ‖ tr (to be present at) être témoin de, assister à; (to attest) témoigner; (e.g., a contract) signer
wit/ness stand/ s barre f des témoins
witticism ['wɪtɪˌsɪzəm] s trait m d'esprit
wittingly ['wɪtɪŋli] adv sciemment
wit·ty ['wɪti] adj (comp **-tier;** super **-tiest**) spirituel
wizard ['wɪzərd] s sorcier m
wizardry ['wɪzərdri] s sorcellerie f
wizened ['wɪzənd] adj desséché
woad [wod] s guède f
wobble ['wɑbəl] intr chanceler; (said of table) branler; (said of voice) chevroter; vaciller
wob·bly ['wɑbli] adj (comp **-blier;** super **-bliest**) vacillant
woe [wo] s malheur m, affliction f; **woe is me!** pauvre de moi!
woebegone ['wobɪˌgɔn], ['wobɪˌgɑn] adj navré, abattu, désolé
woeful ['wofəl] adj triste, désolé; très mauvais
wolf [wʊlf] s (pl **wolves** [wʊlvz]) loup m; galant m, tombeur m de femmes; **to cry wolf** crier au loup; **to keep the wolf from the door** se mettre à l'abri du besoin, joindre les deux bouts ‖ tr & intr engloutir
wolf/ cub/ s louveteau m
wolf/hound/ s chien-loup m
wolf/ pack/ s bande f de loups
wolfram ['wʊlfrəm] s (element) tungstène m; (mineral) wolfram m

wolf's/-bane/ or **wolfs/bane/** s tue-loup m, aconit m, napel m
woman ['wʊmən] s (pl **women** ['wɪmɪn]) femme f
wom/an doc/tor s femme f médecin, doctoresse f
womanhood ['wʊmənˌhʊd] s le sexe féminin; les femmes fpl
womanish ['wʊmənɪʃ] adj féminin; (effeminate) efféminé
wom/an·kind/ s le sexe féminin
wom/an la/borer s femme f manœuvre
woman·ly ['wʊmənli] adj (comp **-lier;** super **-liest**) féminin, femme
wom/an preach/er s femme f pasteur
womb [wum] s utérus m, matrice f; (fig) sein m
wonder ['wʌndər] s merveille f; (feeling of surprise) émerveillement m; (something strange) miracle m; **for a wonder** chose étonnante; **no wonder that . . .** rien d'étonnant que . . . ; **to work wonders** faire des merveilles ‖ tr—**to wonder that** s'étonner que; **to wonder why, if, whether** se demander pourquoi, si ‖ intr—**to wonder at** s'émerveiller de, s'étonner de
won/der drug/ s remède m miracle
wonderful ['wʌndərfəl] adj merveilleux, étonnant
won/der·land/ s pays m des merveilles
wonderment ['wʌndərmənt] s étonnement m
wont [wʌnt], [wɔnt] adj—**to be wont to** avoir l'habitude de ‖ s—**his wont** son habitude
wonted adj habituel, accoutumé
woo [wu] tr courtiser
wood [wʊd] s bois m; (for wine) fût m; **out of the woods** (coll) hors de danger, hors d'affaire; **to take to the woods** se sauver dans la nature; **woods** bois m or mpl
woodbine ['wʊdˌbaɪn] s (honeysuckle) chèvrefeuille m; (Virginia creeper) vigne f vierge
wood/ carv/ing s sculpture f sur bois
wood/chuck/ s marmotte f d'Amérique
wood/cock/ s bécasse f
wood/cut/ s (typ) gravure f sur bois
wood/cut/ter s bûcheron m
wooded ['wʊdɪd] adj boisé
wooden ['wʊdən] adj en bois; (style, manners) guindé, raide
wood/ engrav/ing s (typ) gravure f sur bois
wood/en-head/ed adj (coll) stupide, obtus
wood/en leg/ s jambe f en bois
wood/en shoe/ s sabot m
wood/ grouse/ s grand tétras m, grand coq m de bruyère
woodland ['wʊdlənd] adj sylvestre ‖ s pays m boisé
wood/land scene/ s (painting) paysage m boisé
wood/man s (pl **-men**) bûcheron m
woodpecker ['wʊdˌpɛkər] s pic m; (green woodpecker) pivert m, picvert m
wood/ pig/eon s (orn) ramier m
wood/pile/ s tas m de bois

wood′ screw′ *s* vis *f* à bois
wood′shed′ *s* bûcher *m*
woods′man *s* (*pl* -men) bûcheron *m*; (*trapper*) trappeur *m*, chasseur *m*
wood′ tick′ *s* vrillette *f*
wood′winds′ *spl* (mus) bois *mpl*
wood′work′ *s* (*working in wood*) menuiserie *f*; (*things made of wood*) boiseries *fpl*
wood′work′er *s* menuisier *m*
wood′worm′ *s* (ent) artison *m*
wood·y [ˈwʊdi] *adj* (*comp* -ier; *super* -iest) boisé; (*like wood*) ligneux
wooer [ˈwu·ər] *s* prétendant *m*
woof [wʊf] *s* trame *f*; (*fabric*) tissu *m*
woofer [ˈwʊfər] *s* (rad) boomer *m*, woofer *m*
wool [wʊl] *s* laine *f*
woolen [ˈwʊlən] *adj* de laine ‖ *s* tissu *m* de laine; **woolens** lainage *m*
wool′gath′ering *s* rêvasserie *f*
woolgrower [ˈwʊlˌgro·ər] *s* éleveur *m* des bêtes à laine
wool·ly [ˈwʊli] *adj* (*comp* -lier; *super* -liest) laineux
word [wʌrd] *s* mot *m*; (*promise, assurance*) parole *f*; **in other words** autrement dit; **in your own words** en vous propres termes; **my word!** ça alors!; **not a word!** motus!; **the Word** (eccl) le Verbe; **to break one's word** manquer à sa parole; **to have words with** échanger des propos désagréables avec; **to make s.o. eat his words** faire ravaler ses paroles à qn; **to put in a word** placer un mot; **to take s.o. at his word** prendre qn au mot, croire qn sur parole; **upon my word!** ma foi!; **without a word** sans mot dire; **words** (*e.g., of song*) paroles ‖ *tr* formuler, rédiger
word′-forma′tion *s* formation *f* des mots
wording [ˈwʌrdɪŋ] *s* langage *m*
word′ or′der *s* ordre *m* des mots
word′-stock′ *s* vocabulaire *m*
word·y [ˈwʌrdi] *adj* (*comp* -ier; *super* -iest) verbeux
work [wʌrk] *s* travail *m*, ouvrage *m*; (*production, book*) œuvre *f*, ouvrage; **at work** en œuvre; (*not at home*) au travail, au bureau, à l'usine; **out of work** sans travail, en chômage; **to shoot the works** (slang) mettre le paquet; **works** œuvres; mécanisme *m*; (*of clock*) mouvement *m* ‖ *tr* faire travailler; (*to operate*) faire fonctionner, faire marcher; (*wood, iron*) travailler; (*mine*) exploiter; **to work out** élaborer, résoudre; **to work up** préparer; stimuler ‖ *intr* travailler; (*said of motor, machine, etc.*) fonctionner, marcher; (*said of remedy*) faire de l'effet; (*said of wine, beer*) fermenter; **how will things work out?** à quoi tout cela aboutira-t-il?; **to work hard** travailler dur; **to work loose** se desserrer; **to work out** (sports) s'entraîner; **to work too hard** se surmener
workable [ˈwʌrkəbəl] *adj* (*feasible*)

réalisable; (*that can be worked*) ouvrable
work′bas′ket *s* corbeille *f* à ouvrage
work′bench′ *s* établi *m*
work′book′ *s* manuel *m*; (*notebook*) carnet *m*; (*for student*) cahier *m* de devoirs
work′box′ *s* boîte *f* à ouvrage; (*for needlework*) coffret *m* de travail
work′day′ *adj* de tous les jours; prosaïque, ordinaire ‖ *s* jour *m* ouvrable; (*part of day devoted to work*) journée *f*
worked′-up′ *adj* préparé, ouvré; (*excited*) agité, emballé
worker [ˈwʌrkər] *s* travailleur *m*, ouvrier *m*, employé *m*
work′ force′ *s* main-d'œuvre *f*; personnel *m*
work′horse′ *s* cheval *m* de charge; (*tireless worker*) vrai cheval *m* de labour
work′house′ *s* maison *f* de correction; (Brit) asile *m* des pauvres
work′ing class′ *s* classe *f* ouvrière
work′ing day′ *s* jour *m* ouvrable; (*daily hours for work*) journée *f*
work′ing·girl′ *s* jeune ouvrière *f*
work′ing hours′ *spl* heures *fpl* de travail
work′ing·man′ *s* (*pl* -men′) travailleur *m*
work′ing·wom′an *s* (*pl* -wom′en) ouvrière *f*
work′man *s* (*pl* -men) ouvrier *m*
workmanship [ˈwʌrkmənˌʃɪp] *s* habileté *f* professionnelle, facture *f*; (*work executed*) travail *m*
work′ of art′ *s* œuvre *f* d'art
work′out′ *s* essai *m*, épreuve *f*; (*physical exercise*) séance *f* d'entraînement
work′room′ *s* atelier *m*; (*for study*) cabinet *m* de travail, cabinet d'études
work′shop′ *s* atelier *m*
work′ stop′page *s* arrêt *m* du travail
world [wʌrld] *adj* mondial ‖ *s* monde *m*; **a world of** énormément de; **for all the world** à tous les égards, exactement; **not for all the world** pour rien au monde; **since the world began** depuis que le monde est monde; **the other world** l'autre monde; **to bring into the world** mettre au monde; **to go around the world** faire le tour du monde; **to see the world** voir du pays; **to think the world of** estimer énormément, avoir une très haute opinion de
world′ affairs′ *spl* affaires *fpl* internationales
world′-fa′mous *adj* de renommée mondiale
world′ his′tory ⸖ histoire *f* universelle
world·ly [ˈwʌrldli] *adj* (*comp* -lier; *super* -liest) mondain
world′ly-wise′ *adj*—**to be worldly-wise** savoir ce que c'est que la vie
world′ map′ *s* mappemonde *f*
World′ Se′ries *s* championnat *m* mondial
world′s′ fair′ *s* exposition *f* universelle
world′ war′ *s* guerre *f* mondiale

world'-wide' *adj* mondial, universel
worm [wʌrm] *s* ver *m* ‖ *tr* enlever les vers de; (*a secret, money, etc.*) soutirer; **to worm it out of him** lui tirer les vers du nez ‖ *intr* se faufiler
worm-eaten ['wʌrm ‚itən] *adj* vermoulu
worm' gear' *s* engrenage *m* à vis sans fin
worm'wood' *s* (*Artemisia*) armoise *f*; (*Artemisia absinthium*) armoise absinthe; (*something grievous*) (fig) absinthe *f*
worm·y ['wʌrmi] *adj* (*comp* -ier; *super* -iest) véreux
worn [worn] *adj* usé, fatigué
worn'-out' *adj* épuisé, usé; éreinté
worrisome ['wʌrisəm] *adj* inquiétant; inquiet, anxieux
wor·ry ['wʌri] *s* (*pl* -ries) souci *m*, inquiétude *f*; (*cause of anxiety*) ennui *m*, tracas *m* ‖ *v* (*pret & pp* -ried) *tr* inquiéter; (*to harass, pester*) ennuyer, tracasser; **to be worried** s'inquiéter ‖ *intr* s'inquiéter; **don't worry!** ne vous en faites pas!
worse [wʌrs] *adj comp* pire, plus mauvais §91; **and to make matters worse** et par surcroît de malheur; **so much the worse** tant pis; **to make or get worse** empirer; **what's worse** qui pis est; **worse and worse** de pis en pis ‖ *adv comp* pis, plus mal §91
worsen ['wʌrsən] *tr & intr* empirer
wor·ship ['wʌrʃɪp] *s* culte *m*, adoration *f* ‖ *v* (*pret & pp* -shiped or -shipped; *ger* -shiping or -shipping) *tr* adorer ‖ *intr* prier; (*to go to church*) aller au culte
worshiper or **worshipper** ['wʌrʃɪpər] *s* adorateur *m*, fidèle *mf*
worst [wʌrst] *adj super* pire §91; pis ‖ *s* (le) pire, (le) pis; **to be hurt the worst** être le plus gravement atteint (blessé, etc.); **to get the worst of it** avoir le dessous ‖ *adv super* pis §91
worsted ['wʊstɪd] *adj* de laine peignée ‖ *s* peigné *m*, tissu *m* de laine peignée
wort [wʌrt] *s* (*of beer*) moût *m*
worth [wʌrθ] *adj* digne de; valant, e.g., **book worth three dollars** livre valant trois dollars; **to be worth** valoir; avoir une fortune de; **to be worth +** *ger* valoir la peine de + *inf*; **to be worth while** valoir la peine ‖ *s* valeur *f*; **a dollar's worth of** pour un dollar de
worthless ['wʌrθlɪs] *adj* sans valeur; (*person*) bon à rien, indigne
worth'while' *adj* utile, de valeur
wor·thy ['wʌrði] *adj* (*comp* -thier; *super* -thiest) digne ‖ *s* (*pl* -thies) notable *mf*; (hum, ironical) personnage *m*
would [wʊd] *aux* used to express 1) the past future, e.g., **he said he would come** il a dit qu'il viendrait; 2) the present conditional, e.g., **he would come if he could** il viendrait s'il pouvait; 3) the past conditional, e.g., **he would have come if he had been able (to)** il serait venu s'il avait pu; 4) the

potential mood, e.g., **would that I knew it!** plût à Dieu que je le sache!, je voudrais le savoir!; 5) the past indicative denoting habit or custom in the past, e.g., **he would visit us every day** il nous visitait tous les jours
would'-be' *adj* prétendu
wound [wund] *s* blessure *f* ‖ *tr* blesser
wounded ['wundɪd] *adj* blessé ‖ *s*— **the wounded** les blessés *mpl*
wow [waʊ] *s* (e.g., *of phonograph record*) distorsion *f*; (slang) succès *m* formidable ‖ *tr* (slang) enthousiasmer ‖ *interj* (slang) formidable!
wrack [ræk] *s* vestige *m*; (*ruin*) naufrage *m*; (bot) varech *m*
wraith [reθ] *s* apparition *f*
wrangle ['ræŋgəl] *s* querelle *f* ‖ *intr* se quereller
wrap [ræp] *s* couverture *f*; (*coat*) manteau *m* ‖ *v* (*pret & pp* wrapped; *ger* wrapping) *tr* envelopper, emballer
wrap'around' wind'shield *s* pare-brise *m* panoramique
wrapper ['ræpər] *s* saut-de-lit *m*; (*of newspaper or magazine*) bande *f*; (*of tobacco*) robe *f*
wrap'ping pa'per *s* papier *m* d'emballage
wrath [ræθ], [rɑθ] *s* colère *f*
wrathful ['ræθfəl], ['rɑθfəl] *adj* courroucé, en colère
wreak [rik] *tr* assouvir
wreath [riθ] *s* (*pl* **wreaths** [riðz]) couronne *f*; (*of smoke*) volute *f*, panache *m*
wreathe [rið] *tr* enguirlander; (e.g., *flowers*) entrelacer ‖ *intr* (*said of smoke*) s'élever en volutes
wreck [rɛk] *s* (*shipwreck*) naufrage *m*; (*debris at sea or elsewhere*) épave *f*; (*of train*) déraillement *m*; (*of airplane*) écrasement *m*; (*of auto*) accident *m*; (*of one's hopes*) naufrage; **to be a wreck** être une ruine ‖ *tr* (a *ship, one's hopes*) faire échouer; (a *train*) faire dérailler; (*one's health*) ruiner
wreckage ['rɛkɪdʒ] *s* débris *mpl*, décombres *mpl*, ruines *fpl*
wrecker ['rɛkər] *s* (*tow truck*) dépanneuse *f*; (*person*) dépanneur *m*
wreck'ing car' *s* voiture *f* de dépannage
wreck'ing crane' *s* grue *f* de dépannage
wren [rɛn] *s* (orn) troglodyte *m*; (*kinglet*) (orn) roitelet *m*
wrench [rɛntʃ] *s* clef *f*; (*pull*) secousse *f*; (*twist of a joint*) foulure *f* ‖ *tr* (e.g., *one's ankle*) se fouler; (*to twist*) tordre
wrest [rɛst] *tr* arracher violemment
wrestle ['rɛsəl] *s* lutte *f* ‖ *intr* lutter
wrestling ['rɛslɪŋ] *s* (sports) lutte *f*, catch *m*
wres'tling match' *s* rencontre *f* de catch
wretch [rɛtʃ] *s* misérable *mf*
wretched ['rɛtʃɪd] *adj* misérable
wriggle ['rɪgəl] *s* tortillement *m* ‖ *tr* tortiller ‖ *intr* se tortiller; **to wriggle out of** esquiver adroitement

wrig·gly ['rɪgli] *adj* (*comp* **-glier;** *super* **-gliest**) frétillant; évasif
wring [rɪŋ] *v* (*pret* & *pp* **wrung** [rʌŋ]) *tr* tordre; (*one's hands*) se tordre; (*s.o.'s hand*) serrer fortement; **to wring out** (*clothes*) essorer; (*money, a secret, etc.*) arracher
wringer ['rɪŋər] *s* essoreuse *f*
wrinkle ['rɪŋkəl] *s* (*in skin*) ride *f*; (*in clothes*) pli *m*, faux pli; (*clever idea or trick*) (coll) truc *m* ‖ *tr* plisser ‖ *intr* se plisser
wrin·kly ['rɪŋkli] *adj* (*comp* **-klier;** *super* **-kliest**) ridé, chiffonné
wrist [rɪst] *s* poignet *m*
wrist'band' *s* poignet *m*
wrist' watch' *s* montre-bracelet *f*
writ [rɪt] *s* (eccl) écriture *f*; (law) acte *m* judiciaire
write [raɪt] *v* (*pret* **wrote** [rot]; *pp* **written** ['rɪtən]) *tr* écrire; **to write down** consigner par écrit; baisser le prix de; **to write in** insérer; **to write off** (*a debt*) passer aux profits et pertes; **to write up** rédiger un compte rendu de; (*to ballyhoo*) faire l'éloge de ‖ *intr* écrire; **to write back** répondre par écrit
writer ['raɪtər] *s* écrivain *m*
writ'er's cramp' *s* crampe *f* des écrivains
write'-up' *s* compte *m* rendu; (*ballyhoo*) battage *m*; (com) surestimation *f*
writhe [raɪð] *intr* se tordre
writing ['raɪtɪŋ] *s* l'écriture *f*; (*something written*) écrit *m*, œuvre *f*; (*profession*) métier *m* d'écrivain; **at this writing** au moment où j'écris; **to put in writing** mettre par écrit
writ'ing desk' *s* bureau *m*, écritoire *f*; (*in schoolroom*) pupitre *m*
writ'ing pa'per *s* papier *m* à lettres

wrong [rɔŋ], [rɑŋ] *adj* (*unjust*) injuste; (*incorrect*) erroné; (*road, address, side, place, etc.*) mauvais; **ne pas . . . qu'il faut**, e.g., **I arrived at the wrong city** je ne suis pas arrivé à la ville qu'il fallait; (*word*) impropre; qui ne marche pas, e.g., **something is wrong with the motor** il y a quelque chose qui ne marche pas dans le moteur; **to be wrong** (*i.e., in error*) avoir tort; (*i.e., to blame*) être le coupable ‖ *s* mal *m*; injustice *f*; **to be in the wrong** être dans son tort, avoir tort; **to do wrong** faire du mal, faire du tort ‖ *adv* mal; **to go wrong** faire fausse route; (*said, e.g., of a plan*) ne pas marcher; (*said of one falling into evil ways*) se dévoyer; **to guess wrong** se tromper ‖ *tr* faire du tort à, être injuste envers
wrongdoer ['rɔŋ,du·ər], ['rɑŋ,du·ər] *s* malfaiteur *m*
wrong'do'ing *s* mal *m*, tort *m*; (*misdeeds*) méfaits *mpl*
wrong' num'ber *s* (telp) mauvais numéro *m*; **you have the wrong number** vous vous trompez de numéro
wrong' side' *s* (*e.g., of material*) revers *m*, envers *m*; (*of the street*) mauvais côté *m*; **to drive on the wrong side** circuler à contre-voie; **to get out of bed on the wrong side** se lever du pied gauche; **wrong side out** à l'envers; **wrong side up** sens dessus dessous
wrought' i'ron [rɔt] *s* fer *m* forgé
wrought'-up' *adj* excité, agité
wry [raɪ] *adj* (*comp* **wrier;** *super* **wriest**) tordu, de travers; forcé, ironique
wry'neck' *s* (orn) torcol *m*; (pathol) torticolis *m*

X

X, x [ɛks] *s* XXIVᵉ lettre de l'alphabet
Xavier ['zævɪ·ər], ['zevɪ·ər] *s* Xavier *m*
xenophobe ['zɛnə,fob] *s* xénophobe *mf*
Xerxes ['zʌrksiz] *s* Xerxès *m*
Xmas ['krɪsməs] *adj* de Noël ‖ *s* Noël *m*

X' ray' *s* (*photograph*) radiographie *f*; **to have an X ray** passer à la radio; **X rays** rayons *mpl* X
X'-ray' *adj* radiographique ‖ **X'-ray'** *tr* radiographier
X'-ray treat'ment *s* radiothérapie *f*
xylophone ['zaɪlə,fon] *s* xylophone *m*

Y

Y, y [waɪ] *s* XXVᵉ lettre de l'alphabet
yacht [jɑt] *s* yacht *m*
yacht' club' *s* yacht-club *m*
yah [jɑ] *interj* (*in disgust*) pouah!; (*in derision*) oh là là!

yam [jæm] *s* igname *f*; (*sweet potato*) patate *f* douce
yank [jæŋk] *s* (coll) secousse *f* ‖ *tr* (coll) tirer d'un coup sec
Yankee ['jænki] *adj* & *s* yankee *mf*

yap [jæp] *s* jappement *m*; (slang) criaillerie *f* ‖ *v* (*pret* & *pp* **yapped**; *ger* **yapping**) *intr* japper; (slang) criailler; (slang) dégoiser

yard [jɑrd] *s* cour *f*; (*for lumber, for repairs, etc.*) chantier *m*; (*measure*) yard *m*; (naut) vergue *f*; (rr) gare *f* de triage

yard'arm' *s* (naut) bout *m* de vergue

yard'mas'ter *s* (rr) chef *m* de dépôt

yard'stick' *s* yard *m* en bois (en métal, etc.); (fig) unité *f* de comparaison

yarn [jɑrn] *s* fil *m*, filé *m*; (coll) histoire *f*

yarrow ['jæro] *s* mille-feuille *f*

yaw [jɔ] *s* (naut) embardée *f*; **yaws** (pathol) pian *m* ‖ *intr* faire des embardées

yawl [jɔl] *s* yole *f*

yawn [jɔn] *s* bâillement *m* ‖ *intr* bâiller; être béant

ye (old spelling of **the** [ðə]) *art* le, e.g., **ye olde shoppe** la vieille boutique ‖ [ji] *pron* (obs) vous

yea [je] *s* oui *m*; vote *m* affirmatif ‖ *adv* oui, voire

yeah [jɛ] *adv* (coll) oui; **oh yeah?** (coll) de quoi?; **oh yeah!** (coll) ouais!

yean [jin] *intr* (*said of ewe*) agneler; (*said of goat*) chevreter

year [jɪr] *s* an *m*, année *f*; **to be ... years old** avoir ... ans; **year in year out** bon an mal an

year'book' *s* annuaire *m*

yearling ['jɪrlɪŋ] *s* animal *m* d'un an; (*horse*) yearling *m*

yearly ['jɪrli] *adj* annuel ‖ *adv* annuellement

yearn [jʌrn] *intr*—**to yearn for** soupirer après; **to yearn to** brûler de

yearning ['jʌrnɪŋ] *s* désir *m* ardent

yeast [jist] *s* levure *f*

yell [jɛl] *s* hurlement *m*; (*school yell*) cri *m* de ralliement ‖ *tr* & *intr* hurler

yellow ['jɛlo] *adj* jaune; (*cowardly*) (coll) froussard; (*e.g., press*) à sensation; **to turn yellow** jaunir; (coll) avoir la frousse ‖ *s* jaune *m* ‖ *tr* & *intr* jaunir

yel'low·ham'mer *s* (orn) bruant *m* jaune

yellowish ['jɛlo·ɪʃ] *adj* jaunâtre

yel'low·jack'et *s* (ent) frelon *m*

yel'low streak' *s* (coll) trait *m* de lâcheté

yelp [jɛlp] *s* glapissement *m*, jappement *m* ‖ *intr* glapir, japper

yen [jɛn] *s*—**to have a yen to** or **for** (coll) avoir envie de

yeo·man ['jomən] *s* (*pl* -**men**) yeoman *m*; (*clerical worker*) (nav) commis *m* aux écritures

yeo'man of the guard' *s* (Brit) hallebardier *m* de la garde du corps

yeo'man's serv'ice *s* effort *m* précieux

yes [jɛs] *s* oui *m* ‖ *adv* oui; (to contradict a negative statement or question) si or pardon, e.g., **"You didn't know." "Yes, I did!"** "Vous ne le saviez pas." "Si!" ‖ *v* (*pret* & *pp*

yessed; *ger* **yessing**) *tr* dire oui à ‖ *intr* dire oui

yes' man' *s* (*pl* **men'**) (coll) M. Toujours; **to be a yes man** opiner du bonnet; **yes men** (coll) béni-oui-oui *mpl*

yesterday ['jɛstərdi], ['jɛstər‚de] *adj, s,* & *adv* hier *m*; **yesterday morning** hier matin

yet [jɛt] *adv* encore; **as yet** jusqu'à présent; **not yet** pas encore ‖ *conj* cependant

yew' tree' [ju] *s* if *m*

Yiddish ['jɪdɪʃ] *adj* & *s* yiddish *m*

yield [jild] *s* rendement *m*; (*crop*) produit *m*; (*income produced*) rapport *m*, revenu *m* ‖ *tr* rendre, produire; (*a profit; a crop*) rapporter; (*to surrender*) céder ‖ *intr* produire, rapporter; céder, se rendre; (*public sign*) priorité (à droite; à gauche)

YMCA ['waɪ'ɛm'si'e] *s* (letterword) (**Young Men's Christian Association**) Association *f* des jeunesses chrétiennes

yo·del ['jodəl] *s* tyrolienne *f* ‖ *v* (*pret* & *pp* **-deled** or **-delled**; *ger* **-deling** or **-delling**) *tr* & *intr* jodler

yogurt ['jogʊrt] *s* yogourt *m*

yoke [jok] *s* (*pair of draft animals*) paire *f*; (*device to join a pair of draft animals*) joug *m*; (*of a shirt*) empiècement *m*; (elec) culasse *f*; (fig) joug; **to throw off the yoke** secouer le joug ‖ *tr* accoupler

yokel ['jokəl] *s* rustaud *m*, manant *m*

yolk [jok] *s* jaune *m* d'œuf

yonder ['jɑndər] *adj* ce ... -là là-bas ‖ *adv* là-bas

yore [jor] *s*—**of yore** d'antan

you [ju] *pron pers* vous, toi §85; vous, tu §87; vous, te §87 ‖ *pron indef* (coll) on §87, e.g., **you go in this way** on entre par ici

young [jʌŋ] *adj* (*comp* **younger** ['jʌŋgər]; *super* **youngest** ['jʌŋgɪst]) jeune ‖ **the young** les jeunes; (*of animal*) les petits *mpl*; **to be with young** (*said of animal*) être pleine; **young and old** les grands et les petits

young' la'dy *s* (*pl* -**dies**) jeune fille *f*; (*married*) jeune femme *f*; **young ladies** jeunes personnes *fpl*

young' man' *s* (*pl* **men'**) jeune homme *m*; **young men** jeunes gens *mpl*

young' peo'ple *spl* jeunes gens *mpl*

youngster ['jʌŋstər] *s* gosse *mf*

your [jʊr] *adj poss* votre, ton §88

yours [jʊrz] *pron poss* le vôtre, le tien §89; **a friend of yours** un de vos amis; **cordially yours** (complimentary close) amitiés; **yours truly** or **sincerely yours** (complimentary close) veuillez agréer, Monsieur, l'expression de mes sentiments distingués

your·self [jʊr'sɛlf] *pron pers* (*pl* -**selves** ['sɛlvz]) vous-même, toi-même §86; vous, te §87; vous, toi §85

youth [juθ] *s* (*pl* **youths** [juθs], [juðz]) jeunesse *f*; (*person*) jeune homme *m*; **youths** jeunes *mpl*

youthful ['juθfəl] *adj* jeune, juvénile
yowl [jaʊl] *s* hurlement *m* || *intr* hurler
Yugoslav ['jugo'slɑv] *adj* yougoslave
|| *s* Yougoslave *mf*

Yugoslavia ['jugo'slɑvɪ·ə] *s* Yougo-
slavie *f*; la Yougoslavie
Yule' log' [jul] *s* bûche *f* de Noël
Yule'tide' *s* les fêtes *fpl* de Noël

Z

Z, z [zi] or [zɛd] (Brit) *s* XXVIe lettre
de l'alphabet
za·ny ['zeni] *adj* (*comp* -**nier**; *super*
-**niest**) bouffon, toqué || *s* (*pl* -**nies**)
bouffon *m*
zeal [zil] *s* zèle *m*
zealot ['zɛlət] *s* zélateur *m*, adepte *mf*
zealotry ['zɛlətri] *s* fanatisme *m*
zealous ['zɛləs] *adj* zélé
zebra ['zibrə] *s* zèbre *m*
zenith ['zinɪθ] *s* zénith *m*
zephyr ['zɛfər] *s* zéphyr *m*
zeppelin ['zɛpəlɪn] *s* zeppelin *m*
ze·ro ['zɪro] *s* (*pl* -**ros** or -**roes**) zéro
m || *intr*—**to zero in** (mil) régler la
ligne de mire
ze'ro hour' *s* heure *f* H
zest [zest] *s* enthousiasme *m*; (*agreeable and piquant flavor*) saveur *f*,
piquant *m*
Zeus [zus] *s* Zeus *m*
zig·zag ['zig‚zæg] *adj* & *adv* en zigzag
|| *s* zigzag *m* || *v* (*pret* & *pp* -**zagged**;
ger -**zagging**) *intr* zigzaguer

zinc [zɪŋk] *s* zinc *m*
Zionism ['zaɪ·ə‚nɪzəm] *s* sionisme *m*
zip [zɪp] *s* (coll) sifflement *m*; (coll)
énergie *f* || *v* (*pret* & *pp* **zipped**; *ger*
zipping) *tr* fermer à fermeture éclair
|| *intr* siffler; **to zip by** (coll) passer
comme un éclair
zipper ['zɪpər] *s* fermeture *f* éclair
zither ['zɪθər] *s* cithare *f*
zodiac ['zodɪ‚æk] *s* zodiaque *m*
zone [zon] *s* zone *f*
zon'ing or'dinance *s* réglementation *f*
urbaine
zoo [zu] *s* zoo *m*
zoologic(al) [‚zo·ə'lɑdʒɪk(əl)] *adj* zoologique
zoology [zo'ɑlədʒi] *s* zoologie *f*
zoom [zum] *s* vrombissement *m*; (aer)
montée *f* en chandelle || *intr* vrom-
bir; **to zoom up** monter en chandelle
zoot' suit' [zut] *s* costume *m* zazou
Zu·lu ['zulu] *adj* zoulou || *s* (*pl* -**lus**)
Zoulou *m*

Conversion Tables

American Measurements and the Metric System*

	AMERICAN UNIT	METRIC EQUIVA- LENT	METRIC UNIT	AMERICAN EQUIVA- LENT
Length	one mile (mi.)	1.6 kilometers	un kilomètre (km)	.6 mile
	one yard (yd.)	.9 meter	un mètre (m)	39.34 inches
	one foot (ft.)	30 centimeters	un centimètre (cm)	or 3.28 feet .39 inch
	one inch (in.)	25.4 millime- ters	un millimètre (mm)	.039 inch
Surface	one acre (a.)	.4 hectare	un hectare (ha)	2.5 acres
	one square mile (sq. mi.)	259 hectares	un kilomètre carré (km²)	.39 square mile
Volume	one cubic foot (cu. ft.)	.028 cubic meter	un mètre cube (m³)	35.314 cubic feet
Capacity	one liquid quart (qt.)	.95 liter	un litre (l)	1.057 quarts or .26 gal-
	one gallon (gal.)	3.8 liters		lon
Weight	one pound (lb.)	.45 kilogram	un kilogram (kg) (un kilo)	2.2 pounds
	one ounce (oz.)	28.35 grams	100 grammes	3.5 ounces
	one ton (2,000 pounds)	907.2 kilo- grams	un gramme (g)	15.432 grains

* International System of Units—Le système international d'unités (SI)

Approximate Comparison of Fahrenheit and Centigrade (Celsius) Temperatures

FAHRENHEIT			CENTIGRADE
Boiling point ►	212	100 ◄	Point d'ébullition
	140	60	
	104	40	
	100	38	
Normal body temperature ► (physiol)	98.6	37 ◄	Température normale (physiol)
	97	36	
	88	31	
	77	25	
	68	20	
	59	15	
	50	10	
	41	5	
Freezing point ►	32	0 ◄	Point de congélation
	23	−5	
	14	−10	
	5	−15	
	0	−18	
	−13	−25	
	−22	−30	
	−40	−40	

For exact conversion, use the following:
(a) To convert Fahrenheit into centigrade, subtract 32, multiply by 5, and divide by 9.
(b) To convert centigrade into Fahrenheit, multiply by 9, divide by 5, and add 32.

Tire Pressure

Pounds per square inch *Livres par pouce carré*	Kilograms per square centimeter *Kilogrammes par centimètre carré*	Pounds per square inch *Livres par pouce carré*	Kilograms per square centimeter *Kilogrammes par centimètre carré*
16	1,12	30	2,10
18	1,26	32	2,24
20	1,40	36	2,52
22	1,54	40	2,80
24	1,68	50	3,50
26	1,82	60	4,20
28	1,96	70	4,90

Sizes of Clothing in the United States and France

LADIES—*DAMES*

Size of coats, dresses—*Taille de manteaux, de robes*

American	8	10	12	14	16	18	20
French	38	40	42	44	46	48	50

Size of blouses, sweaters, and slips—*Taille de chemisiers (corsages), de chandails et de combinaisons*

American	32	34	36	38	40	42
French	38	40	42	44	46	48

Size of shoes, slippers—*Pointure de chaussures, de pantoufles*

American	4	5	6	7	8	9
French	36	37	38	39	40	41

MEN—*MESSIEURS*

Size of topcoats, suits—*Taille de pardessus, de costumes*

American	30	32	34	36	38	40	42	44	46
French	40	42	44	46	48	50	52	54	56

Size (neck size) of shirts—*Taille (encolure) de chemises*

American	14	14½	15	15½	16	16½
French	37	38	39	40	41	42

Size of shoes, slippers—*Pointure de chaussures, de pantoufles*

American	8	8½	9	9½	10	10½	11
French	41	42	43	44	45	46	47

Size of hats—*Pointure (tours de la tête en centimètres) de chapeaux*

American	6⅝	6¾	6⅞	7	7⅛	7¼	7⅜	7½	7⅝
French	53	54	55	56	57	58	59	60	61